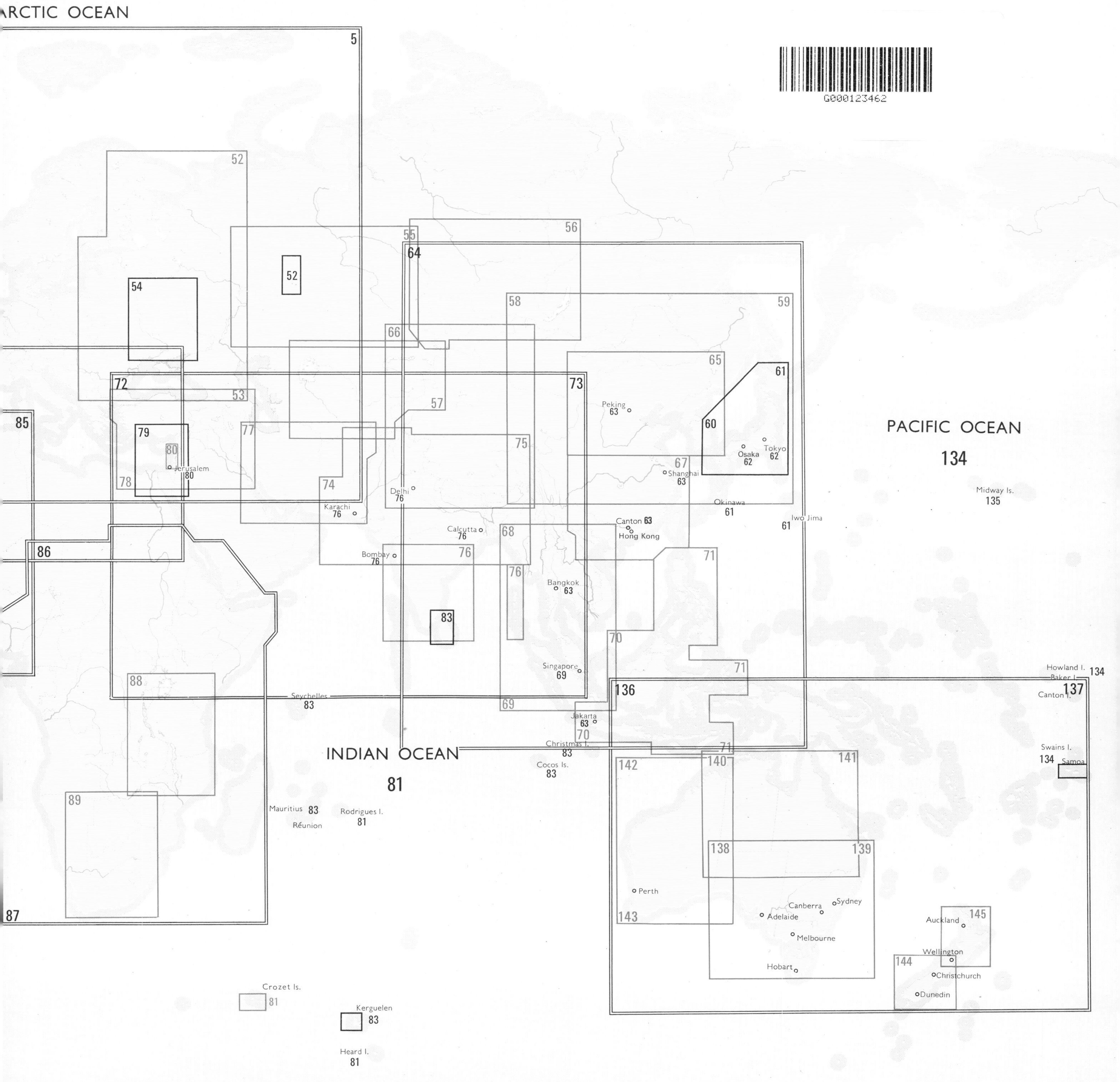

ARCTIC OCEAN

5

52

52

54

55

56

64

58

59

66

65

61

72

73

60

53

57

Peking
63

85

75

Osaka Tokyo
62 62

79

80

67

Shanghai
63

PACIFIC OCEAN

134

78

Jerusalem
180

Okinawa
61

Midway Is.
135

74

Delhi
76

Iwo Jima
61

Karachi
76

Canton 63
Hong Kong

86

Calcutta
76

68

71

Bombay
76

76

Bangkok
63

76

70

83

Singapore
69

71

88

70

Howland I.
Baker I.
134

Seychelles
83

136

Canton I.
137

69

Jakarta
63

Swains I.
134

89

Christmas I.
70

Cocos Is.
83

142

140

141

Samoa

INDIAN OCEAN

81

138

139

Mauritius 83

Rodrigues I.
81

Réunion

143

Perth

Canberra Sydney
Adelaide

Auckland 145

Melbourne

144 Wellington

Crozet Is.
81

Hobart

Christchurch

Kerguelen
83

Dunedin

Heard I.
81

KEY TO MAP PLATES excluding larger scales in North America and Europe *(see other end-paper)*

114 1:12 000 000 and smaller	83 1:3 000 000
116 1:6 000 000	80 1:1 000 000 and larger

Inset maps of islands, cities, etc. are named

General Maps

2/3	World—Political
50/51	U.S.S.R.
82	Africa
91	The Americas
146	Antarctica
147	Arctic Ocean

World Topics (Introductory Section)

8/9	The Earth's Crust	22/23	Settlement
10/11	Land and Sea Forms	24/25	Energy
12/13	Climate	26/27	Industry
14/15	Vegetation	28/29	Trade
16/17	Minerals	30/31	Tourism
18/19	Food	32/33	Environment
20/21	Population	34/35	Navigation

G000123462

THE TIMES

CONCISE
ATLAS
OF THE WORLD

Times Books

Contributors

John C Bartholomew
Editorial Director
John Bartholomew & Son Limited

Hugh Clayton
Agricultural Correspondent
The Times London

Charles Cotter
Late of the Department of Maritime
Studies, Uwist, Cardiff

F W Dunning
Curator
The Geological Museum, London

John Gribbin
Science Policy Research Unit
University of Sussex

H A G Lewis OBE
Geographical Consultant to *The Times*

Kenneth Mellanby
Monks Wood Experimental Station
Institute of Terrestrial Ecology

Eric Rawstron
Professor of Geography
Queen Mary College
University of London

Ian Ridpath
Editor
Encyclopedia of Astronomy and Space

Alan Smith
Department of Geology
University of Cambridge

Peter J Smith
Department of Earth Sciences
The Open University

David Tennant
Travel Correspondent
Thomson Regional Newspapers, London

Roger Vielvoye
Formerly Energy Correspondent
The Times, London

Editorial direction
Barry Winkleman
Paul Middleton

Maps prepared and printed
in Great Britain by
John Bartholomew & Son Limited, Edinburgh

Conurbation maps compiled and drawn by
Fairey Surveys Limited, Maidenhead;
A W Gatrell; and Hunting Surveys Limited

Artwork by Ivan and Robin Dodd, Key Graphics
and Donald Shewan

Preliminary section cartography by
Fairey Surveys Limited, Maidenhead
and filmset by
Crawley Composition Ltd, Crawley, Sussex

Index prepared by
Geographical Research Associates, Maidenhead

Index data processing by
Computer Data Processing Ltd, Haywards Heath

Index set by Computaprint, London

Index printed by The Anchor Press Limited, England

Books bound by Bookbinders Brandt, Holland

Published in 1985 by
Times Books Limited, 16 Golden Square, London W1.

First Edition 1972
Reprinted with revisions 1973, 1974
Revised edition 1975
Reprinted 1976, 1978
Revised edition 1978
Reprinted with revisions 1979
Revised edition 1980
Reprinted with revisions 1982
Reprinted with revisions 1985

Copyright © Times Books Limited and
John Bartholomew & Son Limited
1972, 1973, 1974, 1975, 1976, 1978, 1979, 1980,
1982, 1985

British Library Cataloguing in Publication Data:
'The times' concise atlas of the world
—3rd ed.
1.Atlases, British
912   G1019
ISBN 0 7230 0238 X

All rights reserved including the right to reproduce
this book or parts thereof in any form.

Contents

Acknowledgements

Academy of Sciences of the USSR and the National
Atlas Committee, Moscow

Aeronautical Chart and Information Center, United
States Air Force, St Louis, Missouri

American Geographical Society, New York

The British Petroleum Company Ltd, London

British Tourist Authority, London

Ceskoslovenské Akademie Ved, Prague

Department of Lands and Survey, Wellington,
New Zealand

The Department of the Environment, London

Food & Agriculture Organization of the
United Nations, Rome

French Railways, London

Freytag-Berndt und Artaria, Vienna

Mr P. J. M. Geelan

General Drafting Company Inc, Convent Station,
New Jersey

Dr R. Habel, VEB Hermann Haack,
Geographisch-Kartographische Anstalt, Gotha,
East Germany

The Controller, H.M. Stationery Office, London

Institut Géographique Militaire, Brussels

Le Directeur de l'Institut Géographique National, Paris

Instituto Brasiliero de Geografia e Estatistica,
Rio de Janeiro

International Hydrographic Bureau, Monaco

International Road Federation, London

International Union of Official Travel Organizations,
Geneva

Professor P. E. James, Syracuse University, New York

Mr P. Laffitte, Ecole des Mines, Paris

Dr E. Meynen, Bad Godesberg, West Germany

National Aeronautical and Space Administration,
Washington DC

National Geographic Society, Washington DC

National Library of Scotland, Edinburgh

Director of National Mapping, Department of National
Development, Canberra

Director-General, Ordnance Survey, Southampton

Palomar Observatory, California Institute of Technology

Petroleum Information Bureau, London

Dr B. B. Roberts, Antarctic Place-Names Committee,
London

Mr P. Rouveyrol, Bureau de Recherches Géologiques et
Minières, Paris

Royal Geographical Society, London

Royal Observatory, Edinburgh

Royal Scottish Geographical Society, Edinburgh

The Scientific American, San Francisco

Dr John Paxton, The Editor, The Statesman's Year
Book, London

Dr H. J. Störig, Lexikon-Redaktion, Munich

The Trigonometrical Survey Office, Pretoria

Touring Club Italiano, Milan

Under-Secretary of State, Foreign and Commonwealth
Office, London

Surveys and Mapping Branch, Department of Energy,
Mines, and Resources, Ottawa

United States Army Topographic Command,
Washington DC

United States Board on Geographic Names,
Washington DC

United States Department of State, Washington DC

United States Embassy Press Office, London

Introduction

In presenting a further revision of an atlas which has proved to be extremely popular, we draw attention to an important change in this edition. Place-names in China are given in their Pinyin spellings, a step likewise taken in our larger atlas, the Comprehensive Edition. More is said on the subject below.

The preliminary section of the atlas is concerned with geography in its widest sense: as a science that has much to contribute to the understanding of the contemporary world. In these pages we first describe the origin and geology of the Earth and its physical nature, its resources of climate, vegetation and minerals. Then we examine major features of the geography of man, particularly his settlements and population patterns, his trade and industry, his use of energy, the development of tourism, and the effect of all these activities on the balance of his natural environment. The complex techniques of navigation, which have been central to the development of human history, are described, and the Earth as a whole is placed into its context in the expanding Universe. The present state of our knowledge of the Universe is described; two pages are devoted to maps of the Moon and one to star charts.

In the main body of the atlas the maps, with the exception of those covering the conurbation areas, have been compiled by John Bartholomew & Son Limited of Edinburgh, who have been associated with *The Times* in atlas-publishing since 1922. Several map projections are used, each for its own special properties. Without some adaptation the surface of the spherical earth cannot be transferred to a flat sheet of paper, any more than an orange can be wrapped in a sheet of paper without cutting and folding. Map projections are the means of adapting the round globe to the flat map.

How best to spell place-names, a matter of great complexity, has always been considered carefully in the preparation of atlases published by *The Times*. Difficulties arise from the diversity of writing systems in use in the world and the great number of languages, hundreds of which are inadequately written or have no writing system. In the absence of a uniform and internationally accepted method of recording and writing geographical names, conventional spellings established by long usage furnish us with Athens (English), Athènes (French), Azine (Spanish), etc. *The Times Concise Atlas* gives transliterations in English, e.g. Athinai, with the English conventional name, where appropriate, in parentheses: Athinai (Athens). In general, *The Times Concise Atlas* follows the rules recommended by the United States Board on Geographical Names and the Permanent Committee on Geographical Names for British Official Use.

In all previous editions names in China have been transcribed in terms of the Wade-Giles readings of Chinese characters. With increasing use of Pinyin within China as a roman alphabet equivalent of the Han characters and the recent availability of sufficient sources for names, the publishers decided to replace Wade-Giles by Pinyin in mainland China. In Taiwan, Wade-Giles is still in use and so is retained in this atlas. Neither is Pinyin applicable in Hong Kong where a local system is in use. A special section on the Transcription of Chinese Place-Names has been added to this edition (p.88).

With regard to the sensitive political implications of maps, *The Times Atlas* has always considered its task to be to show facts as they are and not to pass judgements. When delineating a frontier this atlas shows which authority is administering the area at the time the map goes to press. Our wish is to help the traveller, businessman, student or teacher who we hope will buy it. It also follows that place-names are, as far as possible, spelt according to the usage of those administering the region concerned. An atlas can show where a frontier is disputed, but it strays beyond its proper sphere if it tries to adjudicate between the rights and wrongs of the dispute rather than to set down the facts as they are.

The index section contains over 90,000 entries. Not every name on the maps appears in that index, but all towns and physical features other than the smallest are indexed. Place-names and their descriptions (such as Lake or River) are listed in strict alphabetical order, so that Haig L. (Lake) does not immediately follow the town of Haig, but is interrupted by Haiger. Each name is accompanied by its country or location and by the page number and grid reference by letter and numeral.

The information on states and territories which precedes the index section has been revised to accord with the latest information available.

It is with pleasure that we issue this, our latest edition, and we hope the reader will find equal interest and pleasure from its use.

The Earth

The origin of the Earth

The Earth originated as part of the solar system about 4,700 million years ago, probably by the accretion of particles from a cloud of gas and dust (see *The origin of the planets*). Certainly it must have formed in a fairly cold state, for otherwise many of the more volatile elements still present in the Earth would never have been able to condense. On the other hand, the Earth must have warmed up quickly as it increased in size, heat being produced in three ways – by conversion of kinetic energy of the particles coming to rest on the surface of the new planet as the result of great compression in the body's interior, and from decay of radioactive elements.

This heat, which was produced more rapidly than it could escape, had a profound effect on the new Earth's structure. Without it, the Earth would have become a homogeneous globe of silicon compounds, iron and magnesium oxides and smaller quantities of all naturally-occurring elements. As it was, the planet very soon warmed up sufficiently to allow the separation of elements and compounds, to begin. The heavier materials such as iron sank towards the Earth's centre whereas the lighter ones, chiefly silicon compounds, rose towards the surface.

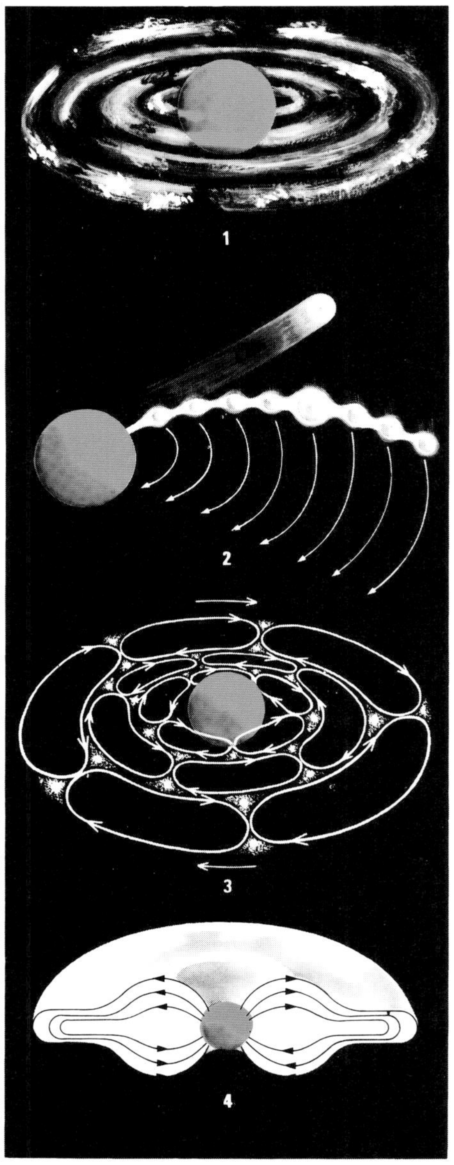

The origin of the planets

Most of the theories about the origin of the planets in the solar system may be divided into two broad types – those which attribute the creation of a solar system to gradual evolutionary processes and those which see it as the result of a catastrophic action.

Kant and Laplace *Nebular Theory*

The earliest theory of the first type was put forward in 1755 by Kant, who suggested that the solar system originated as a spinning disc of material which later separated out into the Sun and the planets. In 1796 this basic idea was developed by Laplace into the nebular theory. Laplace proposed that the Sun was originally a rotating gaseous nebula (1) which gradually contracted under gravitational forces and rotated more and more rapidly until gaseous material was thrown off at the edges to form a series of rings. Each ring then condensed into a separate planet.

Moulton, Chamberlin and Jeans *Tidal Theory*

By 1900 Laplace's theory in its original form had been abandoned, partly because it had proved to be inconsistent with the Sun's observed period of rotation and partly because scientists had shown that Laplace's rings would be too stable to coalesce into planets. So in 1905 Moulton and Chamberlin suggested a return to Buffon's idea of about 200 years before, namely, that the solar system resulted from the collision of the Sun with another body. Thirteen years later this proposal was modified by Jeans, who envisaged not a collision but a close encounter between the Sun and a star (2). As the star passed by the Sun its gravitational attraction drew out from the Sun's surface a long filament of gaseous matter which, being unstable, broke into separate zones. Each zone cooled and contracted into a planet.

Von Weizsäcker's Theory

By the 1930s, however, it had become clear that the sort of filament suggested by Jeans would be so unstable that it would be dispersed into space within a few hours. Moreover, planets such as the Earth are so different from the Sun in composition that they are unlikely to have formed directly from it. So in 1944 von Weizsäcker returned to, and modified, the nebular theory. He suggested that the Sun passed through a vast dense cloud of interstellar dust and gas which it attracted to itself in the form of a disc. The particles in the disc then gradually aggregated into larger and larger lumps which became the planets (3).

Hoyle's Theory

Although the broad outlines of von Weizsäcker's theory are now quite widely accepted, the theory is not entirely satisfactory in detail and so other scientists have proposed variations or even completely different theories. One of the most interesting of modern suggestions was put forward by Hoyle, who drew attention to the role of magnetism. Hoyle proposed that magnetic forces between the Sun and the dust-gas disc gradually move the disc outwards (4). As the disc spread away from the Sun it was capable of carrying smaller and smaller particles and so the larger particles gradually get left behind. This segregation into sizes also implies segregation into different compositions, which quite neatly explains why, when the particles aggregate into planets, the compositions of the planets vary considerably right across the solar system.

The position of the Earth in the Universe

The Earth is the third planet from the Sun and the largest of the group of inner, or terrestrial, planets, the other members of which are Mercury, Venus and Mars. The Sun, the inner planets and the group of outer planets (Jupiter, Saturn, Uranus, Neptune and Pluto – all of which, with the exception of Pluto, are much larger than the Earth) together make up most of the solar system. The solar system is completed by over 400,000 or so asteroids, or minor planets, most of whose orbits lie between Mars and Jupiter and the largest of which is Ceres with a diameter of 730 km. All the planets revolve around the Sun in the same direction and, with the exception of Pluto, their elliptical orbits lie almost in one plane.

Pluto, the outermost planet, is about 5,900 million kilometres, or about 5 light hours, away from the Sun. Yet vast as this distance is, the Sun and planets are but a speck in the universe. For a start, the solar system is but a very small part of the Milky Way, a lens-shaped galaxy which contains some 100,000 million stars like the Sun and vast clouds of hydrogen, helium and dust. The diameter of the Milky Way is about 100,000 light years and the Sun lies about two-thirds of the way from the centre.

The Milky Way, in turn, is only one of many thousands of millions of galaxies scattered throughout the universe. Galaxies tend to cluster; the Milky Way, for example, is but one galaxy in a local group of about 20 and is only about half the size of the largest galaxy in the group. The group itself has a spread of about 5 million light years.

Outside the local group, the furthest known ordinary galaxy is more than 8,000 million light years away, but beyond that are radio galaxies and quasars. Radio galaxies emit vast quantities of radio energy (more than a million times than that emitted by the Milky Way) and are believed to be the sites of gigantic explosions, possibly representing an early stage of galaxy formation. Quasars are very brilliant, but much smaller objects (less than 1 light year across), which are powerful emitters of radio waves and may be the nuclei of distant galaxies. The furthest known object, quasar OQ 172, lies 18,000 million light years away, at the very edge of the detectable universe.

The position of the Earth in the Universe

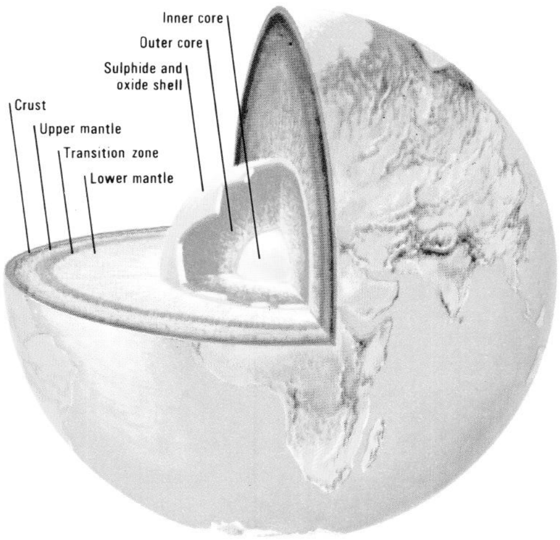

Structure of the solid Earth

The solid Earth consists of three shells: crust, mantle and core. The thin outer shell, the crust, is made up of different types of rock. Under continents it is about 40 km thick and is mostly granitic in composition. Under mountain ranges it may be thicker than 70 km. The oceanic crust is about 8 km thick and is basaltic. The mean crustal density is 2·8 (water = 1·0), and it is about 0·4% of the total mass of the Earth.

The base of the crust is marked by the Mohorovicic discontinuity (Moho or M−). At this level the velocity of the fastest seismic waves sent out by earthquakes rises rapidly from 6 km/sec to ·8 km/sec. Below the Moho lies the mantle. Solid rocks brought up from the mantle by lava flows suggest that it is much less varied than the crust and consists mostly of the rock peridotite. The mantle has a thickness of 2,900 km, density of 4·5, and makes up 67·2% of the Earth's mass. The increase in pressure with depth causes the minerals in peridotite (mainly olivine and pyroxene) to change through a transition zone to new dense minerals unknown at the surface.

The innermost Earth shell is the core. The outer core, 2,200 km thick, is fluid. Motions in the fluid generate the Earth's magnetic field. The inner core, radius 1,270 km, is solid. The core density is 11·0 and contains 32·4% of the Earth's mass. Both cores are probably made of nickel-iron.

Physical characteristics of the Earth
The Earth is not perfectly spherical but has the shape of a spheroid, a sphere flattened at the poles. The average polar radius of 6,357 km is thus smaller than the average equatorial radius of 6,378 km. The overall average radius is 6,371 km, which is the radius of the sphere that has the same volume as the Earth.

The mass of the Earth is 6×10^{24} kg and its average density is about 5·5 grams/cm³. But the average density of the surface rocks is only about 2·8 grams/cm³. There must therefore be an increase in density towards the Earth's centre where the pressure exceeds that of $3\frac{1}{2}$ million atmospheres. The temperature at the centre is uncertain; but is probably no more than about 5,000°C.

More than 70 per cent of the Earth's surface is covered by ocean. Indeed, the Pacific Ocean alone, which with its adjacent seas accounts for more than 35 per cent of the Earth's surface, covers a larger area than that of all the continents combined. More than 65 per cent of the continental area lies in the northern hemisphere, although at the poles themselves this imbalance is reversed.

Metal-bearing rocks deep inside the Earth, contain crystals of ferro-magnetic materials revealed by production of local anomalous magnetism. As the rocks cooled and solidified, the magnetised molecules were aligned like small magnets in the direction of the magnetic poles, thus preserving as 'frozen magnetism' a permanent record of the magnetism at the place and time of their solidification.

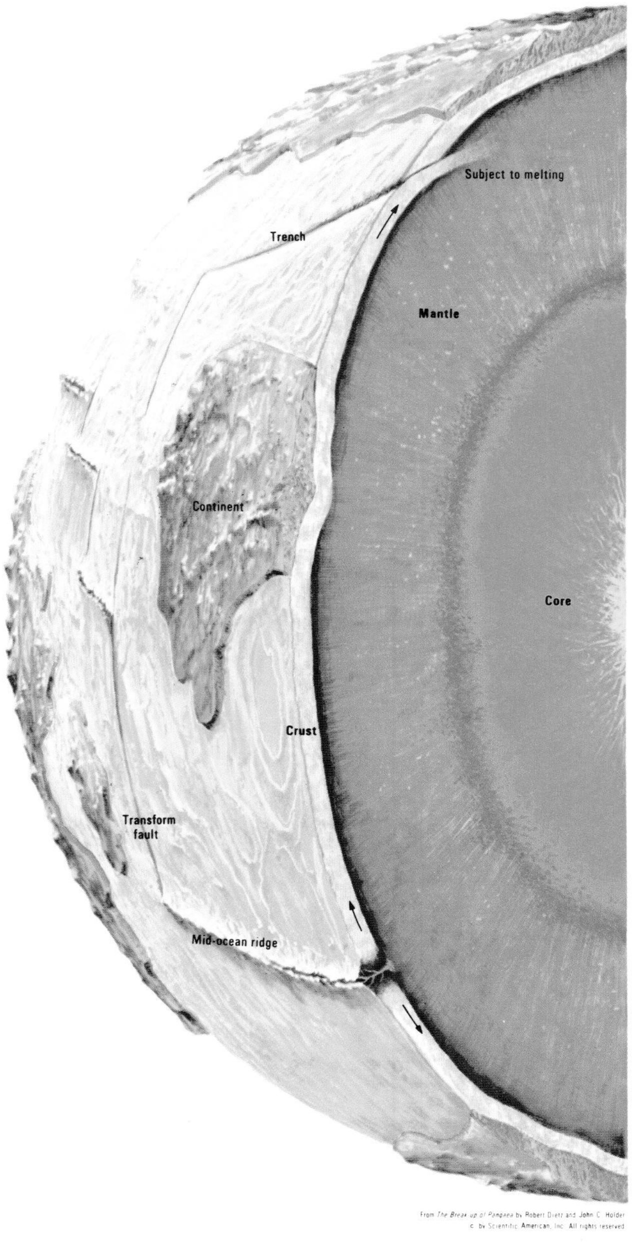

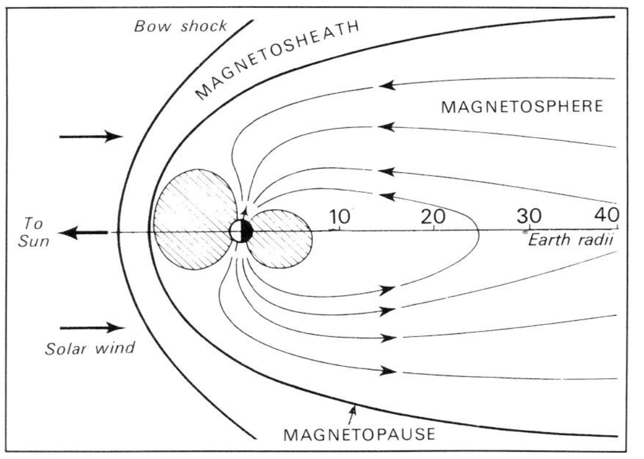

The magnetosphere

Ionized gas, or plasma, streams from the Sun in all directions, and is known as the 'solar wind'. The Earth's fluid iron-nickel core produces a magnetic field which extends beyond the Earth's surface into space. Where the solar wind comes into contact with this magnetic field there is a mutual interaction.

On the side of the Earth facing the Sun the solar wind compresses the Earth's magnetic field, whereas on the side of the Earth away from the Sun the field is greatly elongated. The field is thus confined to a zone known as the magnetosphere, the boundary of which is called the magnetopause. The position of the magnetopause changes a little as the intensity of the solar wind varies, but in the solar direction it lies at an average distance of about 10 Earth radii from the centre of the Earth, whilst in the anti-solar direction, it extends out to very large distances of at least 60 Earth radii.

The solar wind is travelling at almost

1000 km per second when it encounters the Earth's magnetic field. A shock wave is formed several Earth radii from the magnetopause in the direction of the Sun.

The region between the magnetopause and the shock wave front is known as the magnetosheath, or transition region of the magnetosphere.

Earthquakes

An earthquake is a sudden release of strain energy at a point – or, more accurately, within a small zone – in the Earth's crust or upper mantle. Because many shallow earthquakes are obviously related to sudden fault movements, it was once thought that they were responsible for all earthquakes. But it seems likely that at depths greater than a few tens of kilometres the pressure would be too great to allow any fault slippage, whereas earthquakes are known to occur down to depths of about 700 km. The cause of the deeper shocks remains unknown.

Whatever their basic cause, however, most earthquakes are clearly related to plate tectonic processes and occur along plate boundaries – oceanic ridges, oceanic trenches and transform faults. The most intense belt of seismic activity lies around the margin of the Pacific Ocean where 75 per cent of all shallow earthquakes (0–70 km depth), 90 per cent of all intermediate earthquakes (70–300 km) and almost all deep earthquakes (greater than 300 km) occur. Most of the remaining large earthquakes take place along the Alpine-Himalayan chain. Earthquakes are also concentrated along the oceanic ridge system, but most of these are shallow and comparatively small.

There are two ways of specifying the size of an earthquake – by magnitude and intensity. Magnitude is denoted by a number on a logarithmic scale ranging up to about 9·0. It is an absolute measure of the energy released by the earthquake, and so each earthquake is specified by a single magnitude number. Intensity, on the other hand, is denoted by numbered grades on the Modified Mercalli Scale and is based on the damage caused by the earthquake at the Earth's surface as well as on people's reaction to the shock. As these effects decrease with distance from the focus, an earthquake is described by a series of decreasing intensity grades with the highest grade corresponding to the area immediately above the focus.

Earthquake waves

When an earthquake occurs, the shock gives rise to vibrations, or seismic waves, which radiate outwards in all directions from the earthquake's focus. Some of the waves, known as body waves, pass through the Earth's interior; but others, surface waves, travel close to the Earth's surface.

There are two distinct types of body wave. In P, or longitudinal waves the particles of the Earth vibrate backwards and forwards along the direction in which the wave is travelling. In S, or transverse waves the Earth particles move up and down at right angles to the direction of wave travel. Both P and S waves travel along the same paths, except that S waves do not pass through fluids. S waves therefore do not enter the Earth's fluid outer core. In solid materials, however, P waves travel about twice as fast as S waves; so where both P and S waves arrive at a distant measuring station, the P waves arrive first.

The velocities of body waves depend on the physical and chemical state of the material through which they are passing and they generally increase with depth in the Earth. Within any given zone (the mantle, for example), waves are refracted along curved paths which ultimately bring them to the surface. But where the physical properties in the Earth suddenly change, the waves change velocity and are refracted equally abruptly. This occurs chiefly at the crust-mantle and mantle-core boundaries at which there are sharp chemical changes; indeed, these discontinuities were first recognized from the study of seismic waves. The combined effect of refraction and the inability of S waves to travel through the outer core is to prevent most P and S waves reaching the Earth's surface at angles of 105°–142° from the earthquake, a region known as the "shadow zone"

Surface waves are slower than body waves, but they are responsible for most of the ground motion and hence most of the earthquake damage to buildings.

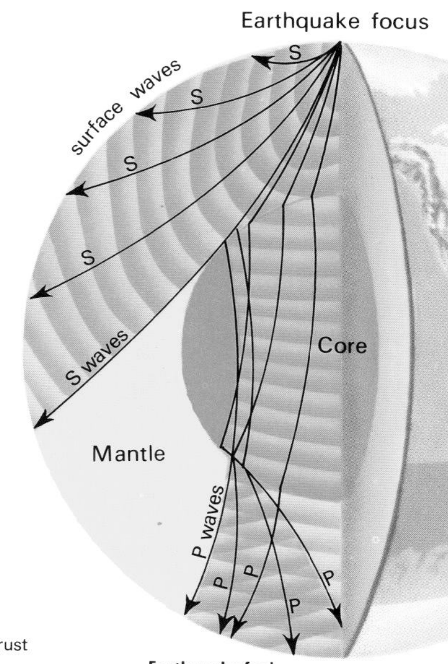

Seismic waves
Body waves, both Primary (P) and Secondary (S), pass through the interior of the Earth. Long waves are the slowest and the most damaging of waves, passing along the surface of the crust. The amplitude or strength of the waves is used to determine the magnitude of the earthquake. Magnitude is graded according to the Richter Scale which is logarithmic: a magnitude of 5 emits waves with a strength ten times that of 4 and one hundred times that of 3 etc.

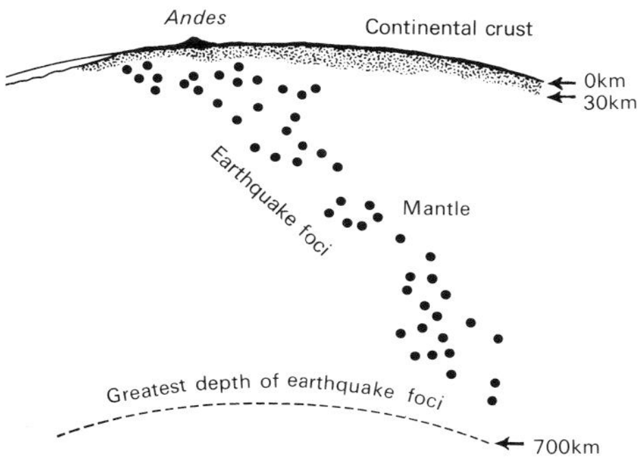

Earthquake foci
The focus of an earthquake is the small zone from which the seismic waves and energy are released. More than 70 per cent of all foci lie within the Earth's upper 70 km, but some earthquakes occur down to depths of about 700 km. Along deep ocean trenches, where the ocean plate descends into the mantle, the downward path of the plate may be traced by plotting the positions of the associated earthquake foci. Along other types of plate boundary the foci are usually much shallower; along the San Andreas fault, for example, they all lie in the upper 20 km or so.

Modified Mercalli Earthquake Intensity Scale
The 12-point scale designed in 1935 grades shocks according to the degree of disturbance felt by ordinary citizens. The numerals I to XII define the categories.

- I Shock not felt except by a few people under special circumstances.
- II Shock felt by few people at rest. Delicately suspended objects swing.
- III Shock felt noticeably indoors. Stationary cars may rock.
- IV Shock felt generally indoors. People awakened, cars rock and windows rattle.
- V Shock felt generally. Some plaster falls, dishes and windows break and pendulum clocks stop.
- VI Shock felt by all. Many frightened, chimneys and plaster damaged, furniture moves and objects upset.
- VII Shock felt in moving cars. People run outdoors. Moderate damage to buildings.
- VIII General alarm, shock very destructive. Damage to weak structures, but little to well-built structures. Furniture overturned.
- IX Panic. Total destruction of weak structures and considerable damage to well-built structures, foundations damaged, underground pipes break and ground fissures and cracks.
- X Panic. All but the very strongest buildings destroyed, foundations ruined, rails bend and water slops over river banks.
- XI Panic. Few buildings survive, broad fissures form and underground pipes out of service.
- XII Panic. Total destruction, waves seen in ground and objects thrown in air.

Volcanoes

There are about 500 active volcanoes situated on tectonic plate margins (see page 8 Plate tectonics). Volcanic belts are of two major types; those at the crest of mid-ocean ridges and those at the convergence of plate boundaries. The most recent eruptions include an eruption at Tristan Da Cunha (1956), the birth of a volcanic island at Surtsey near Iceland (1963), and eruption at Eldfjell, Heimaey in Iceland (1973). Other volcanoes are continuously active but with less dramatic results. They include Cotopaxi and Chimborazo in Ecuador, Popocatepetl in Mexico, and Lassen Peak and Katmai in the USA.

Cinder cone

This is the simplest form of volcano. Material is ejected through the central pipe and each eruption produces new deposits to overlay preceding layers. Gradually the cone is built up with larger fragments remaining near the summit at the steepest angle, around 30 degrees, and the smaller deposits moving to the base of the cone where the angle of rest may be as low as 10 degrees. Cinder cones rarely develop more than a kilometre in diameter.

Shield volcano

If much liquid or viscous lava is produced then deposits slowly build up a shallow-sloped volcano which may stretch up to 20 kilometres across. The gentle slopes are rarely steeper than 10 degrees.

Composite cone

This is the most common type of volcano formed by the vent emitting both rocks and lava at different times. The deposits therefore alternate to form a strong bonded structure resistant to erosion. Examples are Etna in Sicily, Vesuvius by Naples and Fujiyama in Japan.

Caldera

Calderas are formed either as the result of eruptions when the upper part of the cone is destroyed, or else by the collapse of the unsupported rim following the ejection of large quantities of lava. The cone is reduced in height but increased in circumference. Collapse occurs when the reservoir of molten magma issues through a side fissure instead of the central vent. The unsupported floor collapses with the crater rim, considerably enlarging the crater. Crater Lake, Oregon, 6–10 km in diameter, is an example of a caldera.

Flood basalt

Long narrow fissures in the Earth's crust may leak lava and heated rocks spreading them over a vast area. Fissure eruptions have produced the Deccan in India which covers half a million square kilometres.

Gas emission

In periods between eruptions, volcanoes release steam and various gases. As volcanic extinction approaches, lava and ashes are no longer ejected, the leaking gases are not under sufficient pressure to cause a fracture of the lava crust. This is called the solfatara stage after the large crater near Naples in Italy. The gases include sulphuretted hydrogen, sulphur dioxide, carbon dioxide, hydrochloric acid and ammonium chloride.

Explosive volcanoes sometimes eject material mixed with hot gas and this is known as *nuée ardente* or glowing cloud emission.

Volcanoes which emit chiefly steam are called fumaroles. The best example is the Valley of Ten Thousand Smokes near Katmai Volcano in Alaska. Carbon dioxide emitting volcanoes are termed mofettes.

Geysers and mud volcanoes

In certain parts of the world volcanic eruption expresses itself by the ejection of water at a high temperature. Geysers consist of clear water emission, but are called mud volcanoes if the water has a high content of solid matter. Both these mark the terminal phase of volcanic activity. The Waimangu geyser in New Zealand, active until 1904, had a jet fountain 500 feet high.

Volcanic prediction

The monitoring and prediction of volcanic activity is linked to earthquake detection on the site of recently active volcanoes. Most of those close to populated areas have permanently staffed observatories, such as at Mt Etna in Sicily and Mauna Loa in Hawaii. Transportable seismometers at selected locations record the small movements of the magma within the volcano which precede an eruption. The probable point of eruption can then be calculated. Tiltmeters and distance measuring equipment are used to map the changes to the landscape during and after an eruption. On many volcanoes, the slopes tilt downwards after an eruption and then build up slowly towards the next peak of activity. Volcanic movement sometimes produces a change in the local magnetic field caused by a rise in temperature of the underlying magma.

Cross-section through composite volcano

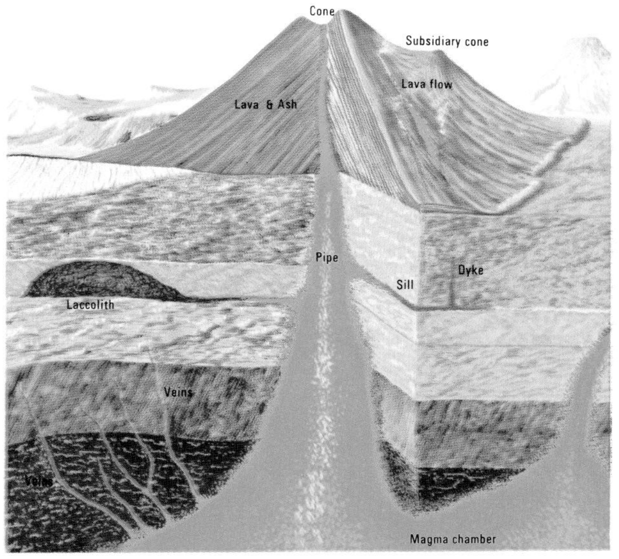

Volcanic activity
Volcanoes are formed when magma or molten material from the mantle or atmosphere, is extruded through weak or fractured points in the Earth's crust. Magma reaches the surface from the magma chamber through a volcanic pipe, but in some instances side vents leak magma through horizontal sills and vertical dykes. When magma reaches the surface it may be in liquid, solid or gaseous form. A lacolith is sometimes formed where molten rock is unable to reach the surface but is under enough pressure before solidifying to distort the overlying strata into a dome.

Caldera

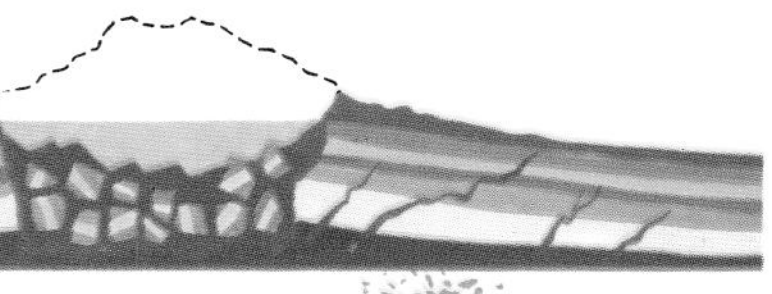

Calderas are large, basin-shaped depressions bounded by steep cliffs, like Crater Lake, Oregon, USA. They are usually formed when the magma chamber cannot support the cone above.

Shield volcano

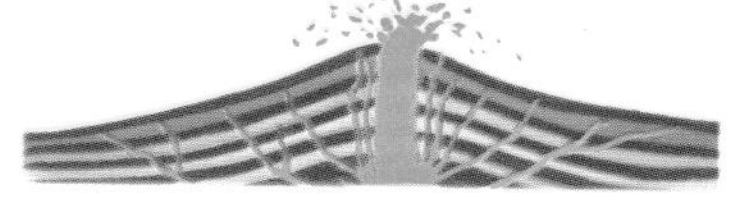

Shield volcanoes, like Kilauea, Hawaii, repeatedly erupt highly fluid basalt lava that spreads out sometimes tens of kilometres.

Flood basalt

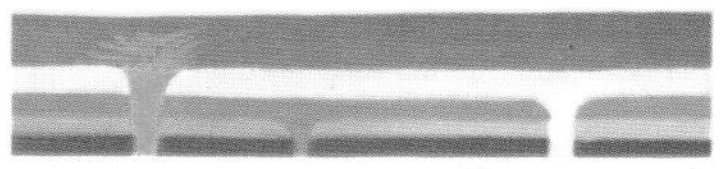

Flood basalt is an outflow of fluid lava from long and narrow fissures. The lava may spread out over vast areas to form extensive plateaux, like the Deccan in central India.

Nuée ardente

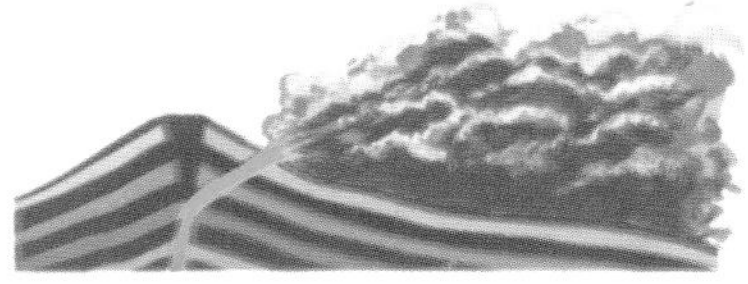

Nuée ardente (glowing cloud) eruptions are violent explosions of gas mixed with rock fragments which are ejected, sometimes to a considerable height, as at Mont Pelée in Martinique in 1902.

Plate tectonics

Earthquakes originate in well-defined zones of the Earth where rocks are actively being deformed. Earthquake zones separate large rigid areas free from active deformation known as tectonic plates. There are at least twelve such plates composing the Earth's outer shell, the lithosphere, and seven of them occupy a very large area, over 40 million square kilometres (see below Relative motions of tectonic plates). The lithosphere averages about 100 km in thickness and rests upon the asthenosphere, the semi-molten upper layer of the mantle. The detailed mechanism of plate movement is unknown but it is probably related to the transfer of heat energy deep within the Earth.

The idea of continual creation and destruction of the crust is seen in the movement of the ocean-floor plates forming mid-ocean ridges and deep trenches at the plate margins. Molten material from below the crust rises to the surface at the oceanic ridge where it forms new crust. To compensate for this additional material the leading edge of the moving plate is deflected downwards back into the mantle.

The theory of ocean-floor plate movement has been substantiated by dating of rock-core samples and comparison between magnetised rocks from either side of median ocean ridges. Deep ocean drilling has revealed that the oldest rock samples are in fact furthest away from the ocean ridge. Similarly, magnetised rock samples taken at an identical distance either side of a ridge show the same pattern of magnetic reversals. The oldest age of the rock samples appear to be about 200 million years, consistent with the estimate of the time when the Pangaea started to break up (see Continental drift).

There are three basic types of plate boundary identified by the differing movements of the plates in relation to one another.

Extensional plate boundary

At an extensional plate boundary new ocean floor is continuously created by the welling up of an oceanic ridge of hot basaltic crustal material from the underlying mantle. This material adheres to the plate edges as they move outwards from the median ridge. This process is known as ocean-floor spreading. The 40,000 km world-wide submarine mountain chain formed by ocean-floor spreading is the longest chain on Earth, but is visible only where exceptionally intense vulcanism, as in Iceland and Tristan da Cunha, raises it above sea-level. The usual ridge height is up to 5 km but widths may extend as far as 4,000 km. The forces of tension between the two diverging plates, cause rifts and transform faults where the fractured margins break up.

As the new ocean floor cools it acquires a weak magnetism. The older ocean floor moves away from the ridge at rates of between one and ten centimetres per year (see map below). The polarity of the Earth's magnetic field changes with time. Thus older ocean floors may be weakly magnetised in a differing direction to the present. The successive polarity changes or reversals, which occur at irregular intervals of a few hundred thousand years, give rise to a magnetic striping on the ocean floor by which older floors may be dated and the history of the oceans interpreted.

Translational plate boundaries

Crust is neither created nor destroyed at translational plate boundaries. The plates slide past each other along vertical faults or fractures known as transform or transcurrent faults. Best known as the San Andreas Fault in California (see diagram) and the Alpine Fault of New Zealand. Seismic activity is considerable along the numerous fracture zones which traverse the ocean ridge transform faults.

Compressional plate boundary

At compressional plate boundaries the older

San Andreas fault

The fault is situated at the western margin of the North American plate which is sliding past the Pacific plate at an average speed of about 6 cms per year and setting up considerable stresses. In 1906, this vertical transform fault on a Translational plate boundary released its accumulated stress energy by a sudden sideways movement resulting in the San Francisco earthquake. Since 1906 the stresses have again been building up. Serious movement may again occur when the strength of the bonding of the two plates is exceeded by the stress.

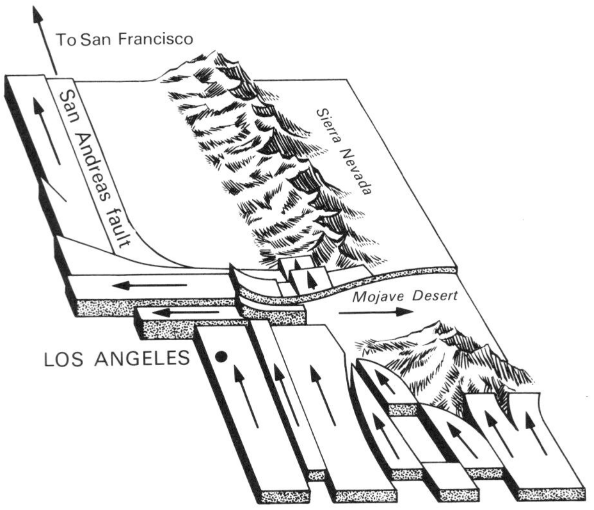

ocean floor sinks into the mantle at a subduction zone or steep zone of underthrust. This type of boundary is marked by ocean trenches where the edges of the crustal plates drop steeply into the mantle and become re-absorbed into the asthenosphere at depths of up to 600 or 700 km. Either plate could be pushed or subducted under the other, but usually, the less rigid and more flexible ocean-floor plate is deflected downwards by the continental plate. The descending plate carries crust material back into the under-lying mantle where it melts and breaks up. As it is less dense than the mantle it rises either towards the oceanic ridge and island arc or towards the continental lithosphere where it causes lava eruptions in a chain of volcanoes. The Aleutian, Japanese and Marianas islands are examples of such island arcs, and the South America Andes is an example of a subduction zone beneath a continental land-mass. The sinking rate of one plate beneath its neighbour appears to be between 2 and 10 cm per year, resulting in intense seismic activity. The Earthquake foci in the subduction zone may be as deep as 700 km but they follow the subducted plate margin and give rise to severe disturbance.

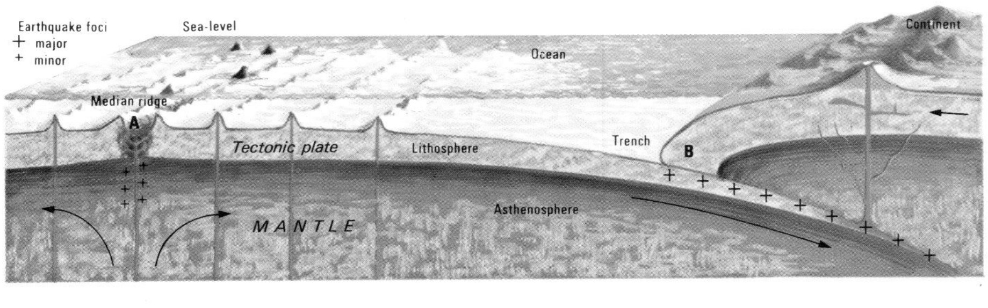

Volcanic activity and earthquakes are associated with plate tectonics. At A, an extensional boundary, magma from the upper mantle forms two parallel ridges. The rift between them broadens and new ridges are formed. At a compressional plate boundary, B, the ocean crust descends to perhaps 700 km, at which depth melting takes place.

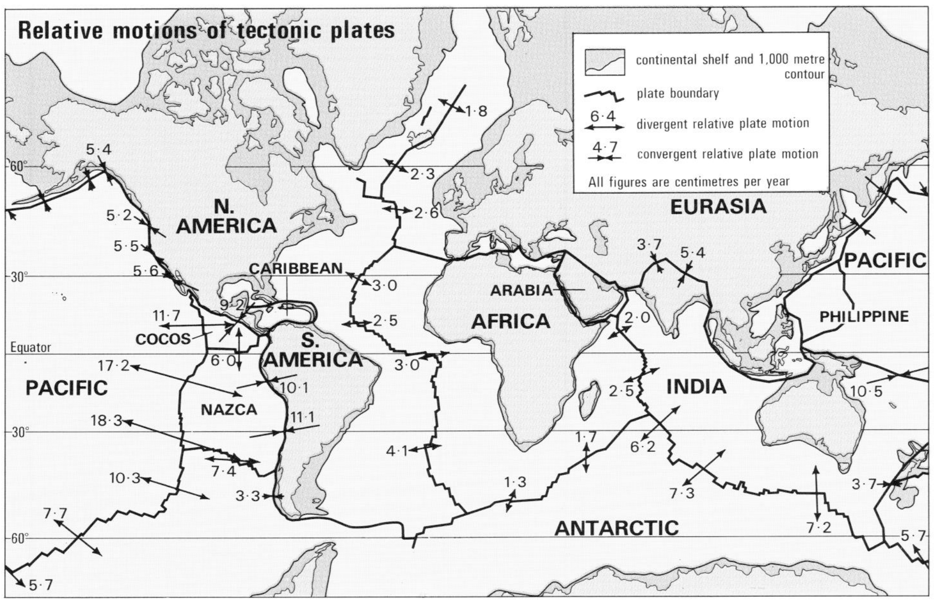

Relative motions of tectonic plates

At mid-ocean ridges, plates are diverging at up to 18 centimetres per year. Where a continental plate meets an ocean plate the less dense continental material "floats" over the descending ocean plate and is pushed up to form a mountain range. Where two continental plates converge the continental material of both plates is forced upwards.

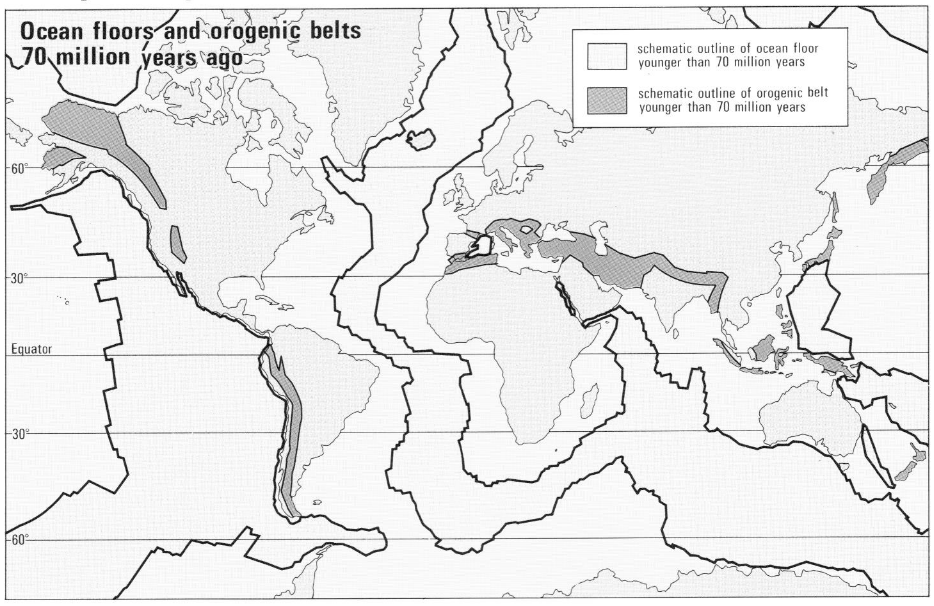

Ocean floors and orogenic belts 70 million years ago

Ocean-floor spreading during the last 70 million years has been particularly apparent in the eastern Pacific and in the mid-Atlantic ridge which extends east of Africa across the south Indian Ocean. In the Americas the active orogenic belts are close up against the spreading plate boundaries. The mid-Atlantic ridge is passive in comparison.

Plate movement

Crustal plate movement occurs continuously in all parts of the globe but varies in type and rate of movement. This movement is generated by the complex interaction of a number of elements; the continental lithosphere plates themselves; the

Present-day plates		
Plate	Area	Continental area
	(millions of sq.km)	
Pacific	108	1·9
Eurasia	68	59·4
N. America	58·8	35·0
S. America	42·7	25·6
India	61	21·7
Africa	78·4	35·4
Antarctic	59·9	17·9
Nazca	16·4	
Cocos	3·1	
Philippine	5·7	
Caribbean	3·5	1·4
Arabia	4·9	4·2

mid-ocean plate boundary ridges; micro-continental plates; island arcs; small enclosed ocean basins; and inland seas.

A variety of movements are therefore possible. The fastest rate of movement is the divergence of the Pacific plate from the Cocos, Nazca and Antarctic plates with a figure of 18·3 cms per year at latitude 30° South (see map above). The Mid-Atlantic Ridge marks the boundary between the American, African and Eurasian plates. This divergence remains fairly constant at between 2 and 4 cms per year. The African, Indian and Antarctic plates are diverging from each other at a rate between 2 and 7 cms per year.

The above map shows that convergent plate motion involves an ocean plate and a continental plate or two continental plates, but rarely two ocean plates. The fastest rate of convergence is between the Cocos and the Caribbean plate in Central America where the Guatemala Trench marks the edge where the Cocos plate is sliding downwards at over 9 cms per year. The Himalayas mark a collision zone between the Eurasian and the Indian plates; the rate of crustal compression here is over 5 cms per year.

Mountain building

Orogeny is the geological process of mountain-building. The two most important agents of orogeny are deformation of Earth's crust (diastrophism), which includes faulting and folding; and vulcanism. Orogeny usually occurs along narrow belts of the Earth's surface and can involve the uplift and deformation of great thicknesses of sedimentary and volcanic rocks. This process is called the orogenic cycle and is associated with the movement of an oceanic plate against a continental land-mass (see Compressional plate boundary above). At this margin many layers of sedimentary and volcanic rock deposited over millions of years become uplifted and deformed. Until recently mountain-building was thought to be more associated with ascending and descending currents within crustal rocks.

The Earth's orogenic belts lie between the stable continental plates and an ocean or inland sea (see map of orogenic belts above). The Andes and Rocky Mountains lie between the American plates and the Pacific Ocean; the Himalayas lie between the stable Eurasian plate and the Indian sub-continent.

The uplifted and deformed rocks formed as a result of plate collision may be mixed with molten igneous rock rising from the mantle as a result of the melting subducted crust. Youngerfold mountains less than 500 million years old consist of these rocks thrust upward and over-folded as in the Alps, or simply uplifted as the central Andes. The rate of uplift may be as much as one centimetre a year. Over-fold mountain ranges are the remnants of earlier folding cycles which have been stranded away from active plate collision margins.

The map above was computed from the relative positions of dated sedimentary and metamorphic rocks plotted with reference to the trapped magnetism fields within them. Latest research reveals over one hundred and fifty magnetic field reversals during the last 70 million years. It is clear that the Earth's major orogenic belts have changed little during that time but the ocean floor areas have spread considerably.

Folding and faulting

When the Earth's crust bends under compression, folds develop. The simplest of these is the monocline, a one-sided fold, although downfolds (synclines) and upfolds (anticlines) are more usual. Increasing pressure steepens the side facing the pressure until one side is pushed under the other, forming a recumbent fold. Finally the fold may break along its axis, one limb being thrust over the other. Mountain chains often demonstrate intense folding, when sediments are crushed between converging plates.

Faults occur when the Earth's crust breaks, often causing earthquakes. When tension stretches the crust normal faulting occurs and the rocks on one side of the fault-plane override those on the other.

A horst is a block of the crust thrust up between faults; the reverse is called a graben or rift valley. Repeated horst and graben forms give basin and range topography as in Nevada, USA.

The upward movement of a roughly circular plug of salt, some thousands of feet in depth, may force up strata and the surface layers to form a salt dome. These are often associated with oil and gas.

Deformations of the Earth's crust

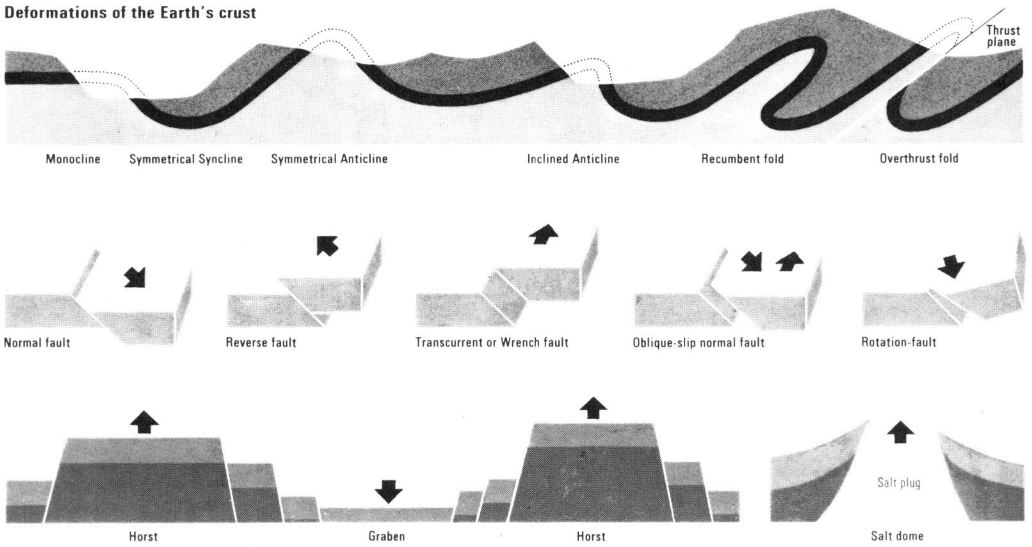

Monocline | Symmetrical Syncline | Symmetrical Anticline | Inclined Anticline | Recumbent fold | Overthrust fold | Thrust plane

Normal fault | Reverse fault | Transcurrent or Wrench fault | Oblique-slip normal fault | Rotation-fault

Horst | Graben | Horst | Salt plug | Salt dome

Folding and faulting

In unstable regions of the Earth's crust stresses may cause folding, fracturing and distortion of sedimentary and volcanic rocks. This is termed crust deformation and is most apparent in the European Alps, South American Andes and the Himalayas. The causes of instability are multiple. Orogenesis or mountain-building deforms the crust, but larger more gentle movements may be caused by isostasy or natural adjustment of crustal levels. A basin accumulating sedimentary deposits may slowly sink under their weight, and weathering may lighten a mountain chain causing it to rise.

The processes and extent of folding and faulting depend on the type and magnitude of the stress; fast or slow, regular or irregular application of stress; the period of time of the stress; the constituency and type of rock or rocks; and relationship with adjacent rock strata. The interrelationships of these factors are so complex that the deformation may range from micro-scopic waves to vast folds tens of kilometres across, and from displacement of single crystals to giant faults.

Folding

Folds are of many types, classified according to the severity and shape of the fold. Basically a fold consists of two limbs or sides with a bisecting axis. If the limbs dip in opposite directions and are divided into two equal halves, the fold is symmetrical; if the axis does not bisect the fold it is asymmetric. An overturned fold has one limb lying partly under the other, and a fold is termed recumbent where one limb is wholly under the other. Folds are usually formed well below the surface and are only exposed by erosion. Anticlinal or synclinal stumps are typical of eroded folds – the ridges of the Appalachian Mountains in the eastern USA are the exposed limbs of folds.

Faulting

A fault is a fracture of the Earth's crust in which the rock on one side of the fracture moves in a different direction to the rock on the opposing side. The fracture and movement along the plane of the fault may be vertical, inclined or horizontal. A normal fault has the inclined plane of fracture exposed as one part of the crust slips downwards and away from another. A reverse fault occurs when compression causes a slab of the crust to slide under an adjacent block. Faults with horizontal rock movement are termed transcurrent or wrench faults, the best-known example of which is the San Andreas fault (see page 8). A combination of movements can produce a highly complex fault structure which creates problems of interpretation for the geologist. The block on one side of a normal fault may slip sideways as well as downwards, it may rotate about a fixed point, or both blocks may move in the same direction but one faster than the other.

Rift valleys or grabens, are caused by the subsidence of elongated blocks of crust sometimes on such a scale that they are marked by chains of volcanoes. The East African Rift Valley System stretches from the coast of Africa opposite Madagascar northwards to the Red Sea and the Mediterranean. Crustal movements upwards produce horst scenery of uplifted blocks; typical examples are the Tien Shan mountains of central Asia, now heavily eroded, and the ranges of Nevada, USA.

Continental crust

A cross-section through the continental crust typically shows the following features: continental margins, younger and older-fold mountain chains, platforms and shields. The continental margin will either be passive as are most Atlantic margins, or active, as are the Pacific margins. Younger-fold mountains formed during the last 500 million years, such as the Rockies and Andes of America, and the Himalayas of Asia, mark the younger subduction zones and occur along most of the active continental margins. Older-fold mountains, like the Appalachians of eastern America and the Caledonian system of Britain and Scandinavia, are nearer to the older subduction zones across which two continents have been joined together. Platforms are areas on which flat-lying sediments have been laid down as in the central United States, Saharan Africa and the Arabian peninsula. Underneath the platforms are highly deformed pre-Cambrian rocks that emerge at the surface as shields. Most of north Canada, central Africa, South America east of the Andes, and Antarctica are shield areas.

The internal structure of the continental crust is known from monitoring seismic activity and from echo-sounding experiments. In most places the crust consists of an upper layer of less dense material over-lying a lower, more dense layer. The boundary between the two is termed the Conrad Discontinuity. The upper layer is 92 per cent igneous and metamorphic and 8 per cent sedimentary in composition. The lower layer is probably basaltic in character or a product of metamorphism called amphibolite, and is derived from partial melting of the mantle. The zone of transition between the continental crust and the underlying magma is called the Mohorovicić Discontinuity.

In comparison with the oceanic crust, the continental crust is less dense with a value of 2·7 as against 3·0; thicker reaching down to a depth of 70 km below mountain belts as opposed to 6 km; and older with some parts aged 3,500 million years and much over 1,500 million years compared with a maximum of 200 million years for the most ancient regions of the submerged oceanic crust.

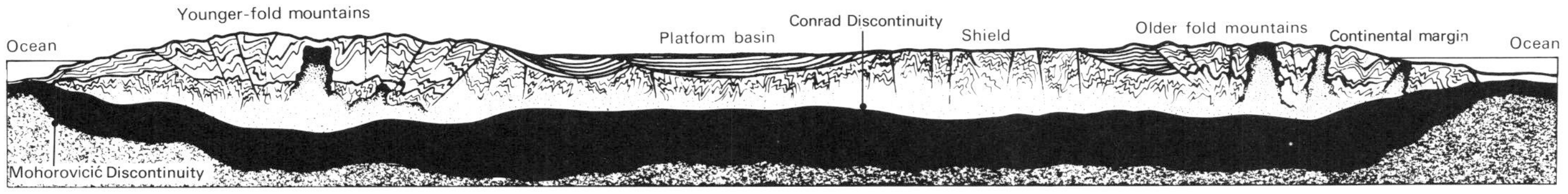

Younger-fold mountains | Conrad Discontinuity | Shield | Older fold mountains | Continental margin | Ocean
Ocean | Platform basin
Mohorovicić Discontinuity

Continental crust
The chemical composition of the crust down to 16 kilometres is: oxygen 46 per cent, silicon 28 per cent, aluminium 8 per cent, iron 5 per cent, calcium 4 per cent, sodium 3 per cent, potassium 2 per cent and magnesium 2 per cent.

Continental drift

Continental drift is a term used to describe the relative motions of the continents.

The relative positions of the continents as far back as 200 million years may be found from the magnetic anomaly maps of the Atlantic and Indian Oceans. The position of the geographic pole of past time may be found from studies of ancient magnetism on continents. From a knowledge of the relative positions and the geographic pole a map of the former positions of continents may be drawn.

Four such maps, drawn by computer, are shown opposite; the Earth 50, 100, 150 and 200 million years ago. By comparing the maps against each other one can see how the Atlantic and Indian Oceans shrank in size as the continents came closer together. As they shrank, a space opened between Eurasia on the one hand and Africa, Arabia, Iran and India on the other. This space is assumed to represent an old ocean, known as the Tethys, that has been completely subducted in the region east of the Mediterranean. The Alpine-Himalayan mountain chain is assumed to represent the final phases of a plate tectonic cycle involving the collision of continents that once bordered the Tethyan Ocean.

About 80 million years ago, Eurasia, Greenland and North America formed a single continent known as Laurasia. One hundred and forty million years ago the southern continents were joined together to form a single continent known as Gondwanaland. About 180 million years ago all the major continents formed a single supercontinent known as Pangaea, first postulated by Wegener over half-a-century ago. Pangaea was itself formed some 250–300 million years ago by the collision of Gondwanaland with Laurasia west of the Urals and of Asia east of the Urals. It is not yet possible to draw maps of the continents prior to about 350 million years ago because the distance between the fragments that collided to form Pangaea prior to their collision cannot be estimated.

Continental drift
Early evidence of break-up and drift of the continents away from the single Pangaea landmass, has been confirmed by recent studies of ancient magnetism. The evidence consisted of matching continental shapes, for example the 'bulge' of Brazil fits closely to the coast of West Africa; and the joining of geological strata across the fit, for example the coal deposits of Uruguay and South Africa. The distribution of certain species of flora and fauna worldwide in the Palaeozoic and Mesozoic eras can only be satisfactorily explained by supporting the theory of continental drift. Animal fossils from Antarctica match those discovered in Argentina and South Africa, and climatic changes to the British Isles during the last 200 million years can be explained by continental movement.

Map 1
50 million years

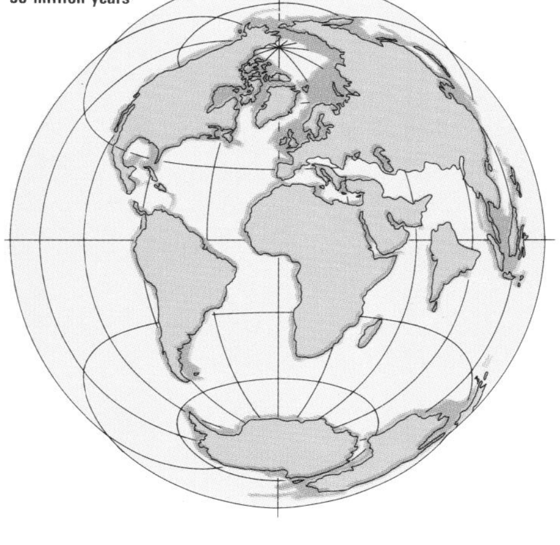

Map 2
100 million years

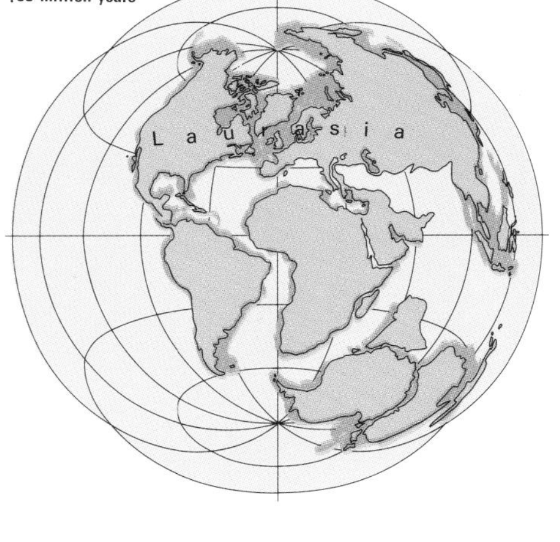

Map 3
150 million years

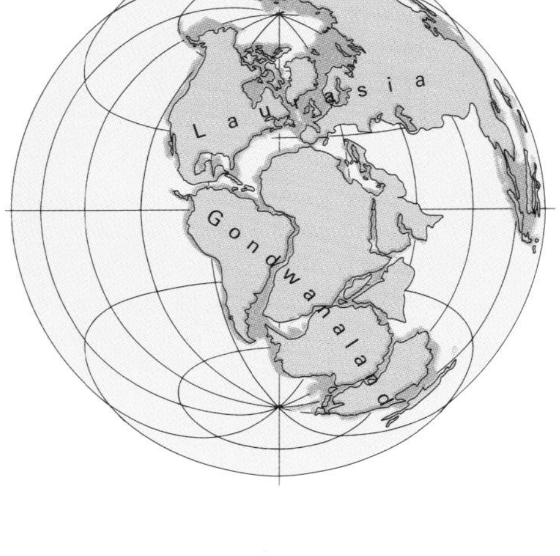

Map 4
200 million years

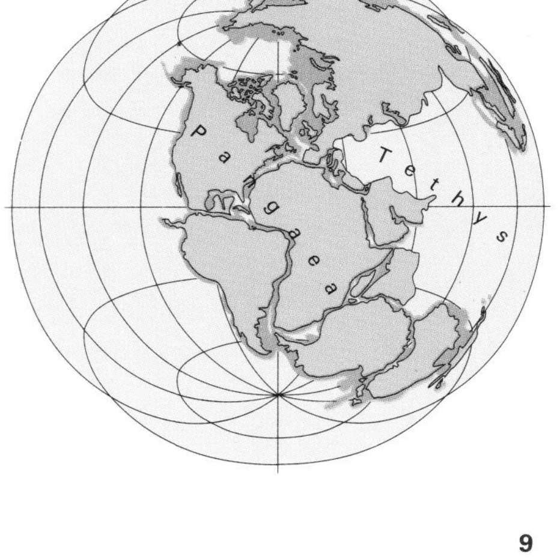

Land and sea forms

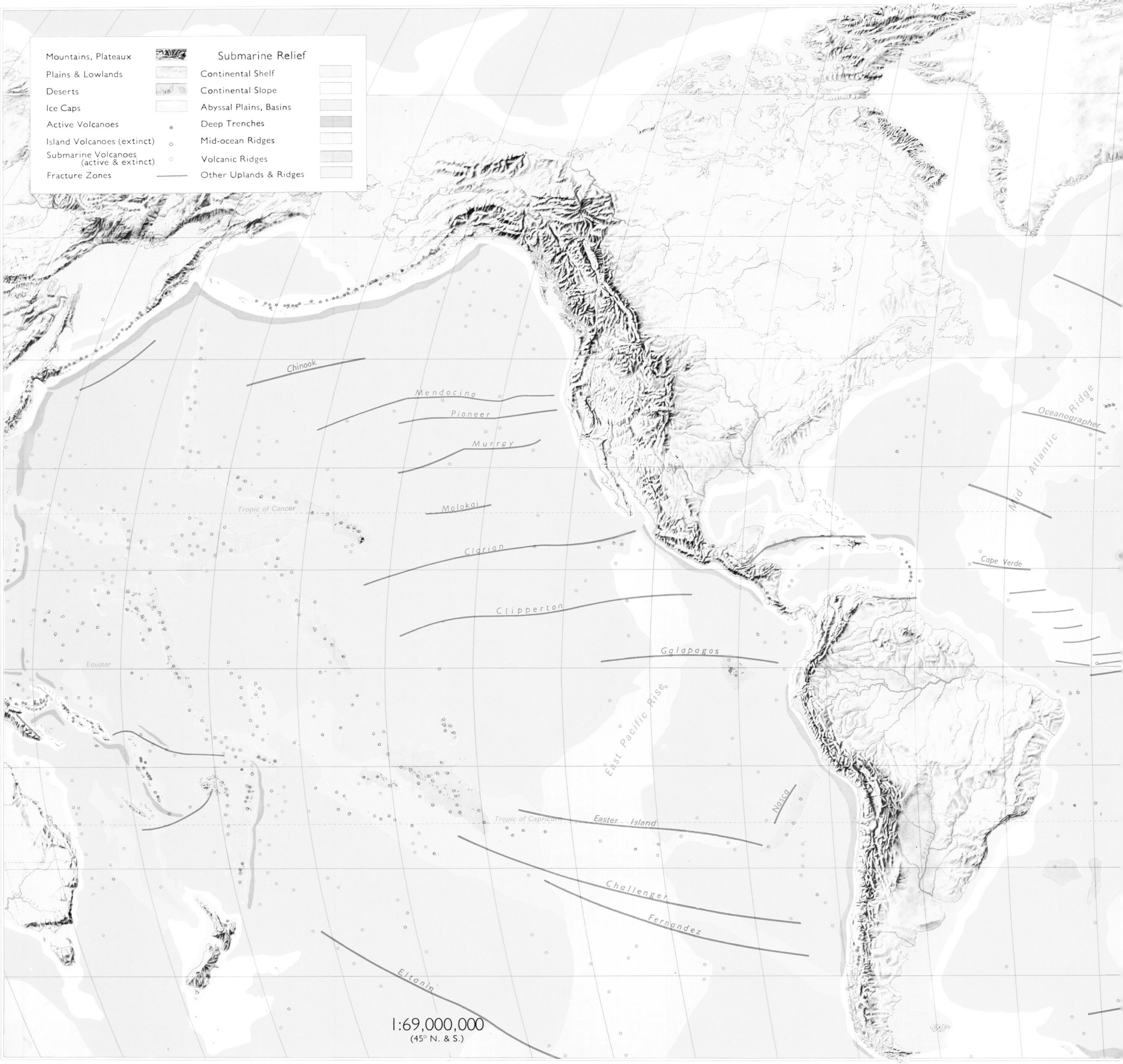

The simplest division of the surface of the Earth is into continents and oceans. All the evidence confirms that the ocean basins were never part of the continental areas and the oldest continental blocks were never part of the true ocean floor.

The rocks of the old continental blocks are markedly different from the young folded mountains. The former are the original blocks, granitic and among the oldest rocks formed in Pre-Cambrian times. The margins of the continents have been repeatedly covered by the sea and the true limit of the continents is the edge of the continental shelf, the physiography of the continents therefore consists basically of the old stable mountain masses, young folded mountain ranges and the coastal plains and continental shelf.

The fundamental difference between the physiography of the oceans and that of the continents arises from distinct geological processes involved in their formation. The granite rocks of the continental masses are lighter than the silica and magnesia (sima) rocks on which they rest, and thus 'float' on them. The floor of the ocean is therefore composed of material denser than that of the surface rocks of the continents.

Different chemical processes operate in the continental and ocean rocks because of their different composition and also because of the atmospheric as opposed to the aqueous environment. The continents are subjected to the severe erosional forces of the weather and to more rapid chemical processes resulting from direct contact with the atmosphere. A wide temperature fluctuation ranging from intense heat to extreme cold has transformed the land forms; but of all the meteorological factors rain is the most destructive.

The Earth's surface features are produced by the interaction of internal and external forces. The former include mountain building, faulting, uplift, vulcanicity, and resistance, of the rocks. The external forces include the physical and chemical reactions that weather the surface rocks, and the main agents of erosion: running water, ice, sea and wind. Each of these gives rise to distinctive land forms, so that we can, for example, identify glaciated landscapes or desert landscapes, but always reflects the interaction of structure and the erosional process.

Running water is the most important sculptor of land forms, and the results of its work can be seen even in desert areas. Valleys are the work of the rivers that flow, or have flowed, through them. Most river systems flow into the sea but some empty into interior lakes, such as the Dead Sea, where water is lost by evaporation.

Glacier ice produced very distinctive land forms, such as trough-shaped valleys, pyramidal peaks and moraines; in the Pleistocene period glaciers were much more widespread than now.

The wind is most effective in areas of sparse or absent vegetation. Only about 25 per cent of the area of the world's deserts are dune-covered. The rest is rocky or gravelly.

The oceans are not subject to the violent effects of heat and frost, wind and rain, only to the quiet forces of sedimentation and gravity. Near the continents the sediments are at their thickest; over the rest of the ocean floor they are seldom more than a few hundred metres thick.

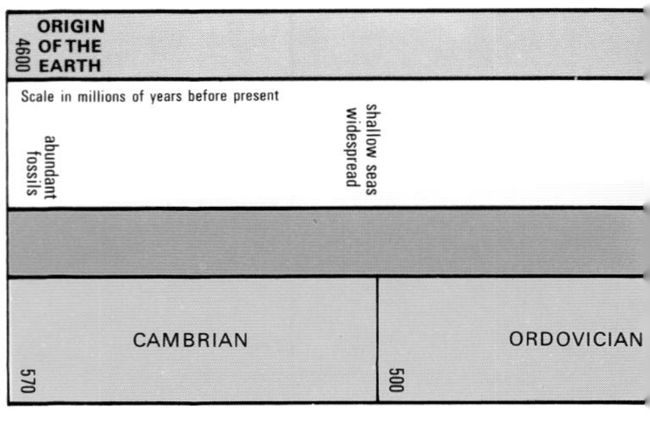

Like the continents, the oceans can be divided into main physiographic categories: continental shelf and slope, continental rises, abyssal plains, ocean ridges and rises and trenches. If we exclude the continental shelf and part of the continental slopes the area of the oceans at 2,000 metres below sea level is about 320 million sq km.

The abyssal plains extend over almost half this area and are below 2,500 metres. At this depth, temperature is never higher than 4°C (39°F).

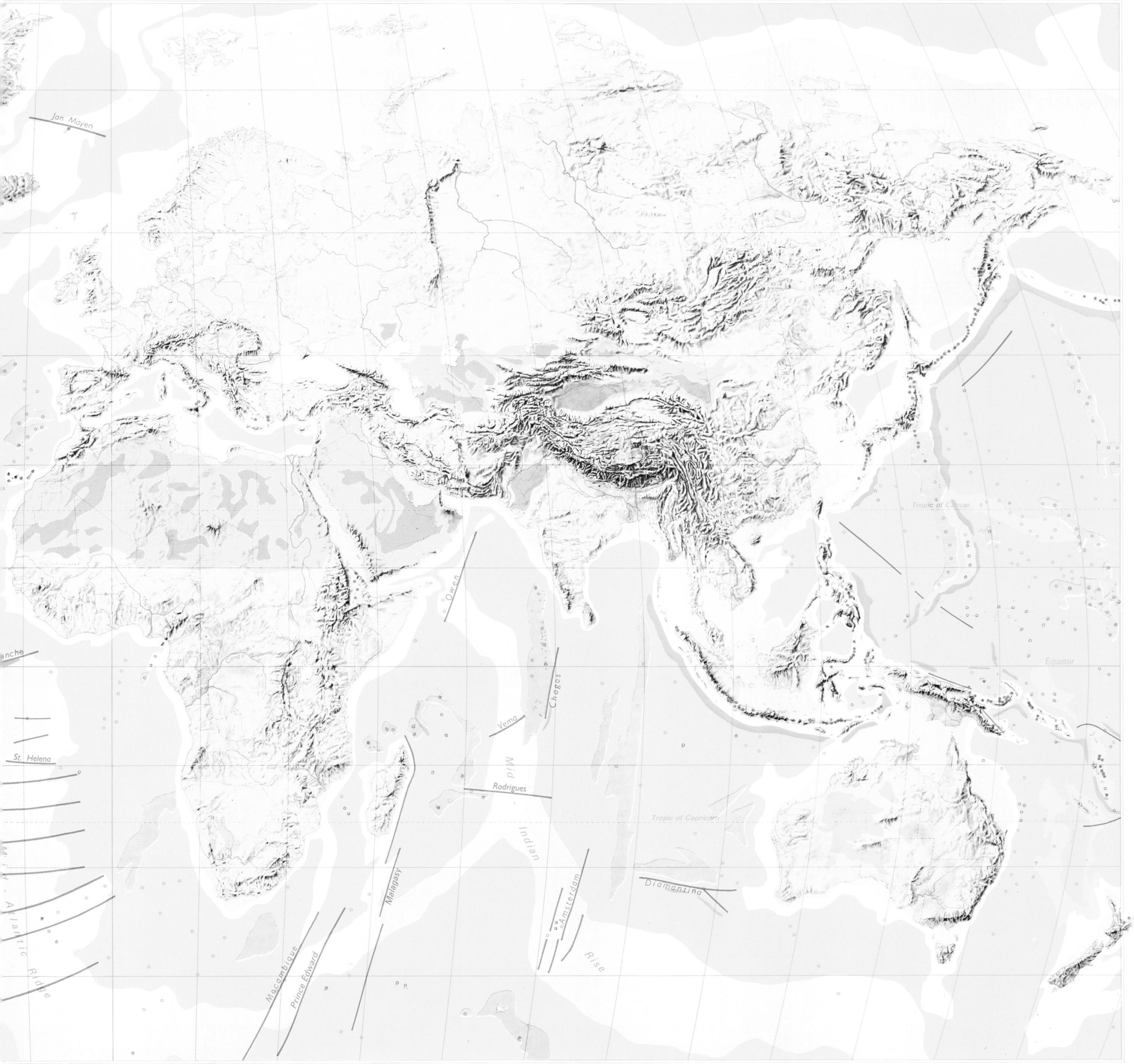

					PRE-CAMBRIAN								PHANEROZOIC
early forms of life	3300		3000				2000			1000		570 abundant fossils	

life comes		rise of fishes	amphibians and trees	ancestral Atlantic closed	Caledonian Mountains	coal forests	Appalachian Mountains	conifers	rise of reptiles	Pangaea formed	opening of present Atlantic disruption of Pangaea	dinosaurs	birds and mammals	plants	dinosaurs extinct	

MARY (PALAEOZOIC)				SECONDARY (MESOZOIC)			TERTIARY & QUATERNARY (CAINOZOIC)					PLEISTOCENE

SILURIAN	DEVONIAN	CARBONIFEROUS	PERMIAN	TRIASSIC	JURASSIC	CRETACEOUS	EOCENE	OLIGOCENE	MIOCENE	PLIOCENE
435	395	345	280	225	193	136	65	38	26	7

Geological periods and the emergence of Man

Modern man has inhabited the Earth for less than one millionth of the total period of its existence, now known to approach some 5,000 million years. Much of this enormous span of time (see top column) was the almost barren and relatively unknown Pre-Cambrian period. For only one eighth of its history has the Earth borne abundant life: the second column shows this Phanerozoic divided into stratigraphic periods, based originally on fossil evidence. The third column details the last two and a half million years, marked by at least seven ice ages and the period when many of the Earth's land forms were shaped. *Homo sapiens* appears only recently, and though he became a cultivator and developed urban living quite early in this final period covering the last 10,000 years, only in the last 250 years has he harnessed the world's power and mineral resources.

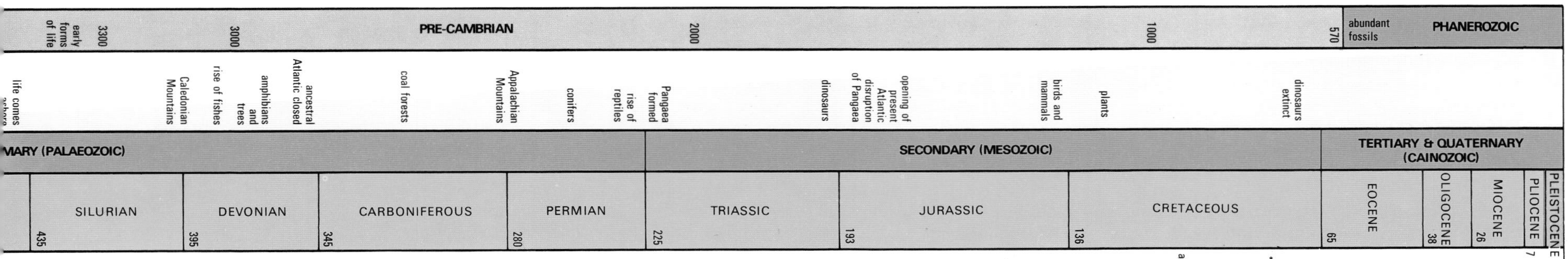

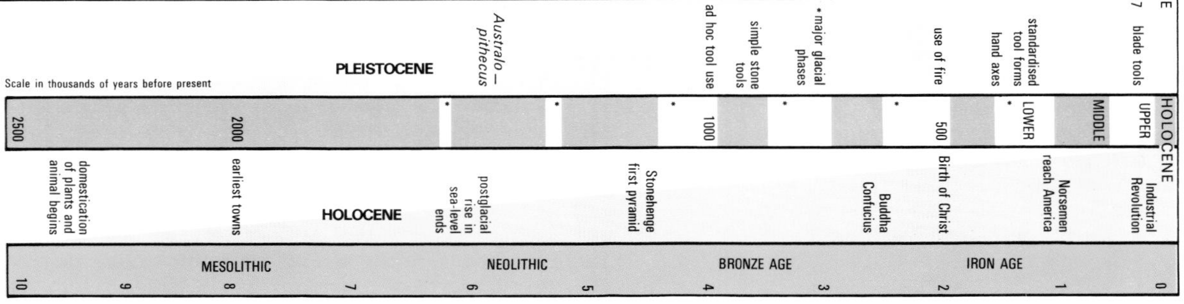

Scale in thousands of years before present

															PLEISTOCENE				HOLOCENE

					Australo-pithecus		ad hoc tool use	simple stone tools	major glacial phases	use of fire	standardised tool forms hand axes	blade tools	Industrial Revolution

2500		2000				1000				500				UPPER	HOLOCENE
											LOWER	MIDDLE			

domestication of plants and animal begins	earliest towns	postglacial rise in sea-level ends	Stonehenge first pyramid	Buddha Confucius	Birth of Christ	Norsemen reach America

MESOLITHIC	NEOLITHIC	BRONZE AGE	IRON AGE
10 9 8	7 6 5	4 3 2	1 0

Atmosphere and climate

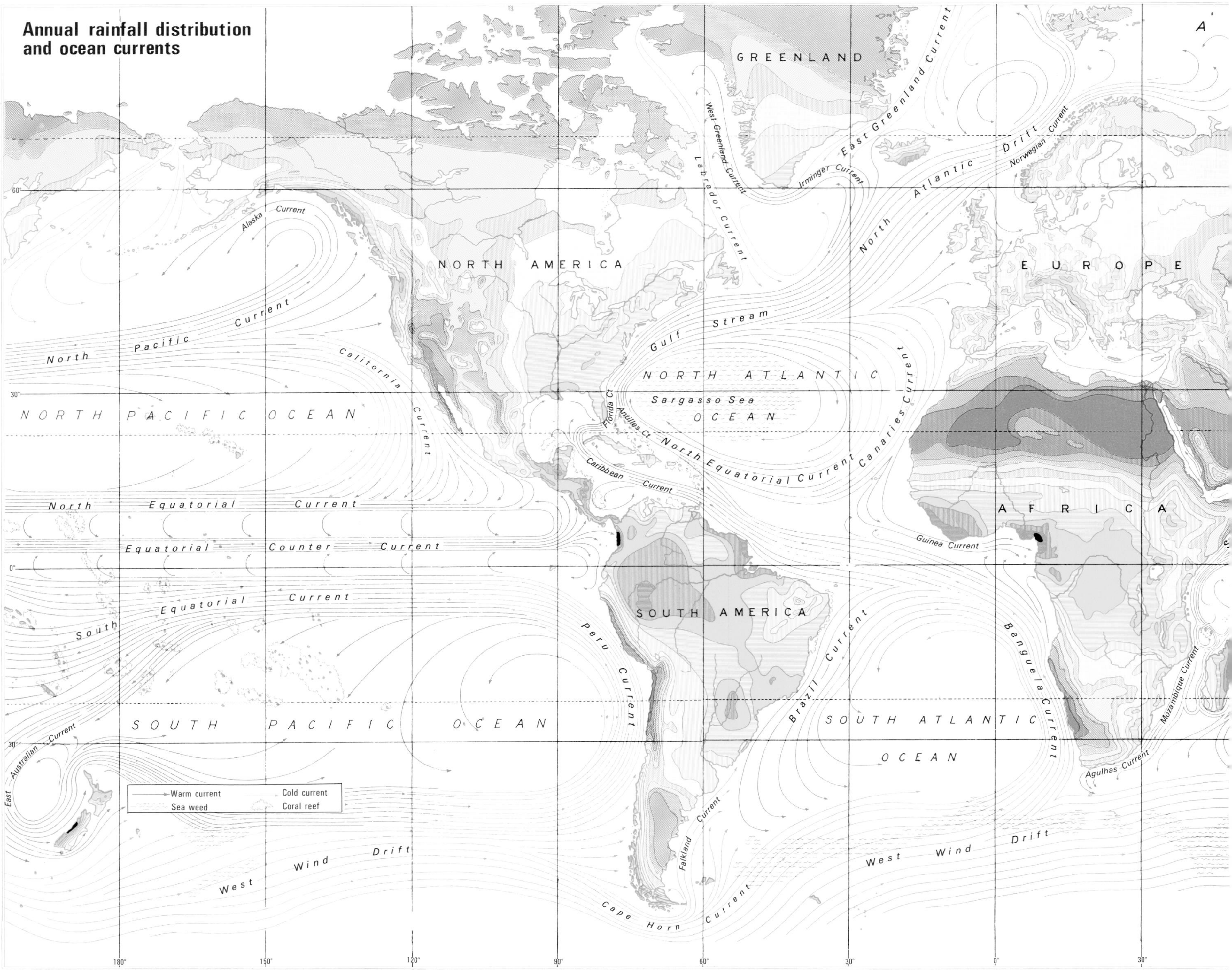

Annual rainfall distribution and ocean currents

Evolution of the atmosphere

The Earth has an atmosphere because it is large enough for its gravitational pull to retain the gases surrounding it. Our present atmosphere is not the first. Most of the gases and probably all of the water in the oceans are the result of volcanic activity.

As the atmosphere lacks certain of the heavy gases it has been suggested that the Earth's original atmosphere was boiled away by a tremendous increase in the Sun's heat. At the same time the water and water vapour then present would also have evaporated. Studies of Mars from the Mariner and Viking spacecraft suggest that the same process happened there too, confirming the validity of this theory.

The Earth's atmosphere once largely consisted of hydrogen, combined with methane and ammonia. The hydrogen was gradually lost and free oxygen was slowly added.

In Cambrian times, between 570 and 500 million years ago, a much greater proportion of carbon dioxide was present in the atmosphere. Since life first appeared, the plants and rocks both on land and in the seas have competed for the carbon dioxide and the free oxygen. There is now a greater quantity of oxygen and carbon dioxide locked up in the rocks of the Earth than is to be found in the whole atmosphere. The balance of the atmosphere today is maintained by the constant erosion of limestone rocks and the decay of vegetable matter.

The composition by volume of the atmosphere is: nitrogen 78·09%, oxygen 20·95%, argon 0·93%, carbon dioxide, 0·03%, and smaller quantities of

helium, krypton and hydrogen, 0·2% water vapour, traces of other gases and atmospheric dust.

Exactly what composition is necessary to support life and how far terrestial species can adapt by evolution to great changes in the composition of the atmosphere is not known. The basic essentials are oxygen, nitrogen, carbon dioxide and water.

The protective atmosphere

Apart from the atmosphere's role as the source of the gases necessary to life, it acts as a great shield against a perpetual bombardment of meteors and deadly rays and particles. Friction with the atmosphere causes all except the largest meteorites to burn themselves out before reaching the surface. Ultra-violet rays are absorbed in a layer of ozone present in the Stratosphere. Charged particles are prevented from reaching the Earth. Their contact with the atmosphere produces the aurora borealis and the aurora australis. Cosmic rays originating either from the Sun or from the outer reaches of space are likewise kept out.

Divisions of the atmosphere

For the first 80 kilometres above the Earth's surface the composition of the atmosphere is constant. Density decreases with height: at 16 kilometres it is only one-tenth of the density at sea level; at 32 kilometres it is one-tenth as dense as at 16 kilometres, and so on.

The terms Troposphere, Stratosphere, Mesosphere, Thermosphere and Exosphere have been used to describe the divisions of the atmosphere.

The Troposphere is the lowest division. Within it takes place nearly all the processes that produce weather and climate; evaporation, precipitation, movement of winds and air currents and the formation of the many types of storm etc.

Above 80 kilometres, oxygen and nitrogen molecules cannot remain associated and tend first to separate into atoms and then to be ionised into charged particles (ions) by the strong solar radiation. At the outermost limits of the atmosphere ionised helium and hydrogen dominate the very tenuous plasma (ionised gas), which, because of its electric charge, is controlled more by the Earth's magnetic field than by gravity.

The Ionosphere is the region of electrification which extends from the upper limit of the Stratosphere as far as the Thermosphere. It consists of a number of belts of radiation designated D, E, F_1 and F_2 which reflect radio waves back to Earth.

The outermost regions are now more commonly termed the Magnetosphere, the region dominated by magnetic fields. Beyond the Magnetosphere interplanetary space is dominated by the Sun's magnetic field and charged particles from the Sun – the solar wind.

Ultra-violet radiation produces concentrations of charged particles which are at their maximum in the upper part of the F_1 layer and the lower part of the F_2 layer.

The electrification belts are not fixed at particular altitudes: light and darkness and other physical factors cause them to move up or down. At night the F layers combine to form a single layer.

Atmosphere and the weather

Climate of the Troposphere close to the Earth's surface may be affected by changing influences high in the atmosphere. The amount of energy that penetrates the Stratosphere appears to follow the Sun's 11 year cycle of activity by altering the percentage of ozone in the Stratosphere. It is probable that energy in the form of ultra-violet waves from the Sun produces a swing in the ozone balance changing the effectiveness of heat absorption by the atmosphere.

At 3,000 and 15,000 kilometres, the two Van Allen radiation belts consist of electrically charged particles which occasionally migrate into the atmosphere. These particles react with atmospheric gases to produce the auroras. There is a strong likelihood that weather patterns are thus affected in the polar latitudes.

Changes in climate have been observed to coincide with changes in the Earth's magnetic field. The nature of the relationship is not known, but the extinction of species of fauna and changes in flora appear to have coincided with abrupt magnetic changes. These are identified by analysis of the direction of the magnetic field trapped within rocks on their formation.

Mean temperature January

Mean temperature July

World's Hottest 58°C/136.4°F

World's Coldest −90°C/−130°F

Prevailing surface wind

| °F | −40 | −30 | −20 | −10 | 0 | 10 | 20 | 30 | 40 | 50 | 60 | 70 | 80 | 90 | °F |
| °C | | −40 | | −30 | | −20 | | −10 | | 0 | | 10 | | 20 | | 30 | °C |

Mean Annual Precipitation

| | 0 | 25 | 100 | 200 | 300 | 400 | 500 | 750 | 1000 | 1500 | 2000 | 3000 | 5000 | Millimetres |
| | 0 | 1 | 3.9 | 7.8 | 11.8 | 15.7 | 19.6 | 29.5 | 39.3 | 59 | 78.7 | 118 | 196.8 | Inches |

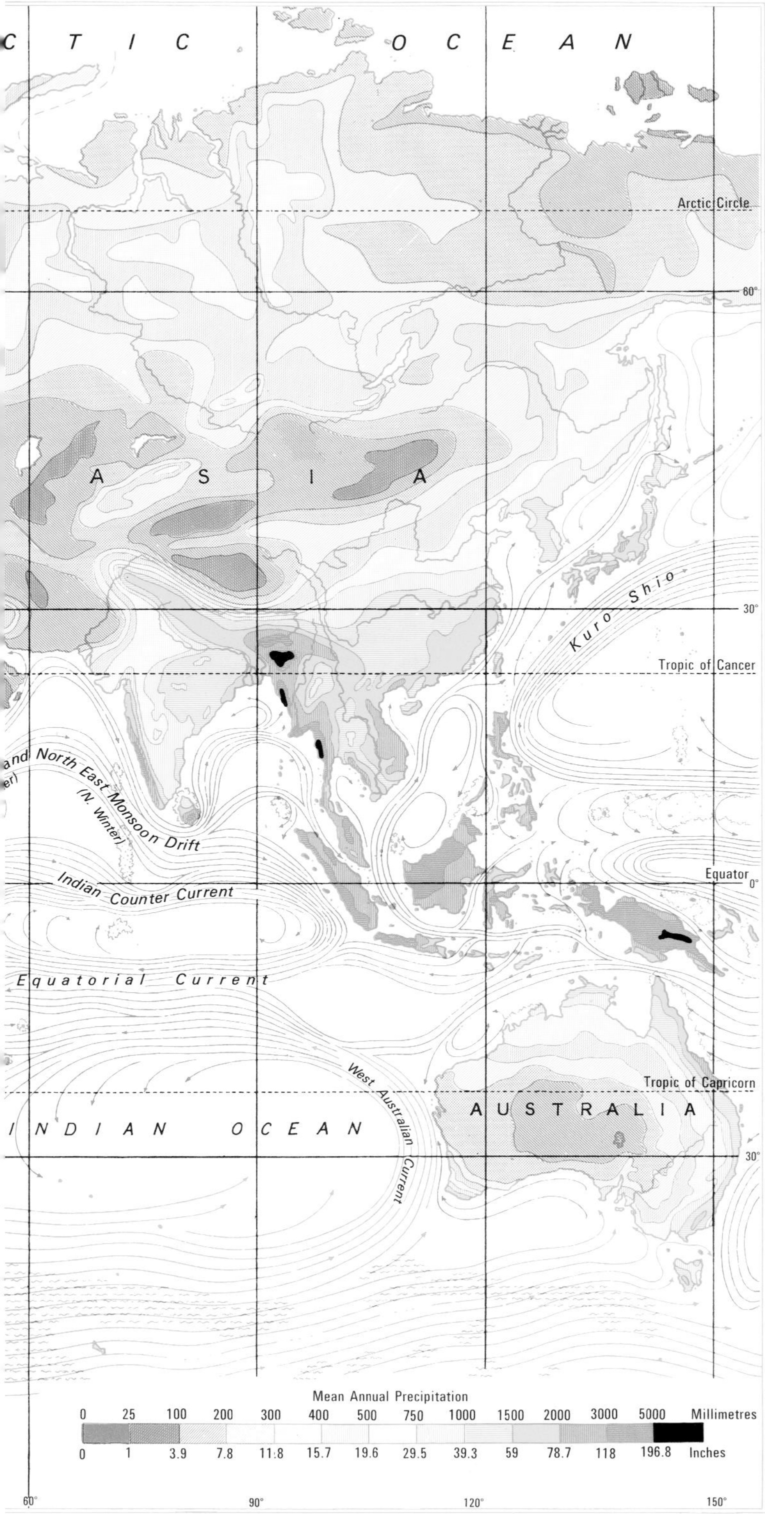

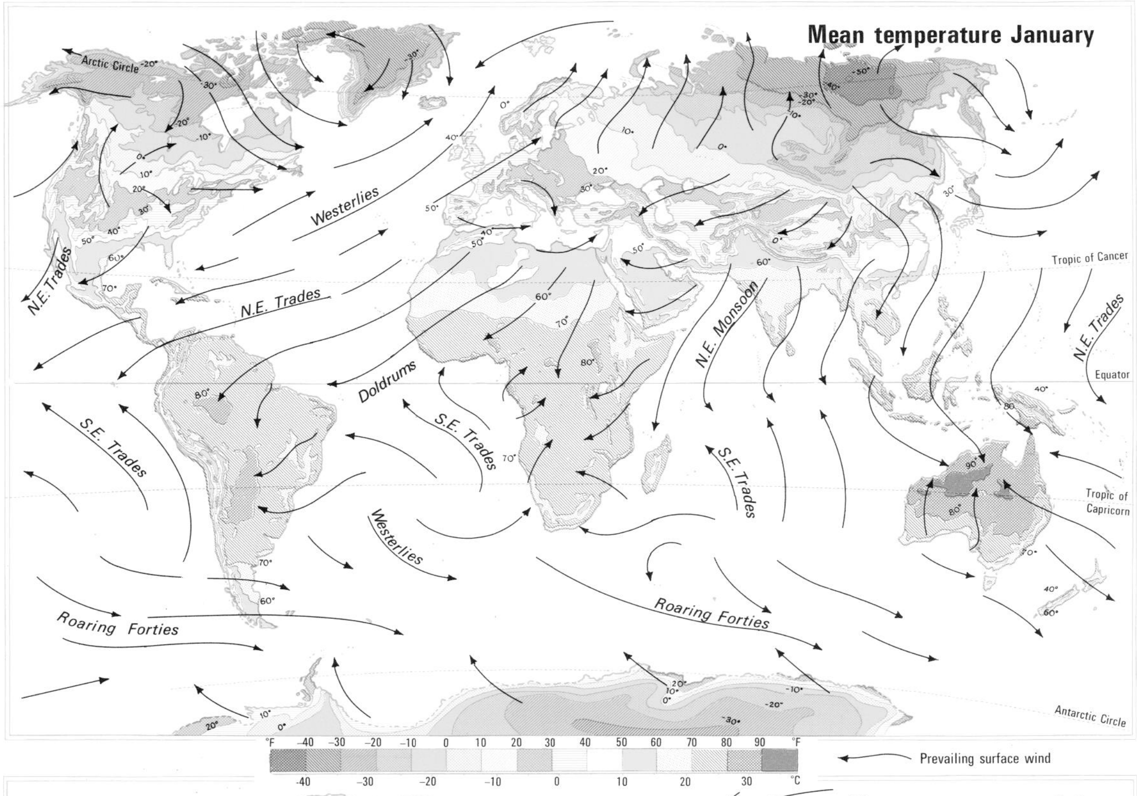

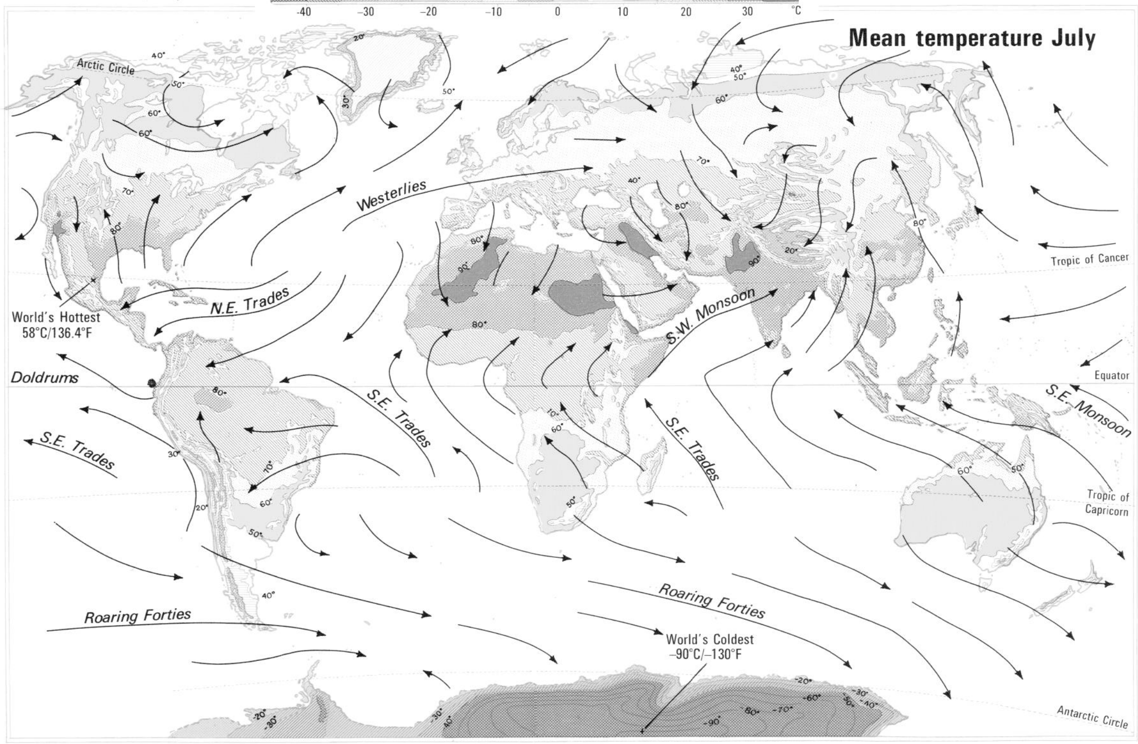

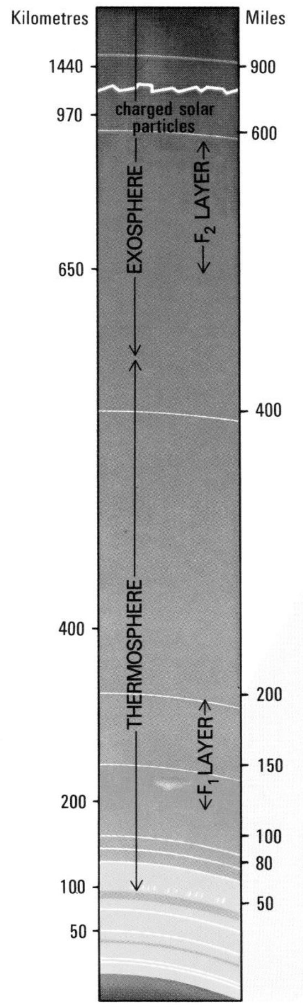

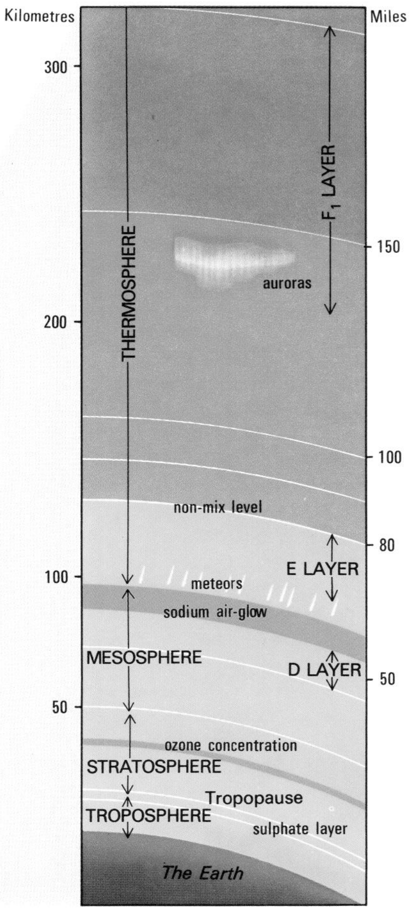

Monitoring the World's weather

International meteorology has made great advances in the last twenty-five years profiting from technological enterprise, notably artificial satellites, high-speed computers and methods of statistical analysis.

In 1961 the United Nations recommended that the World Meteorological Organisation (WMO), undertake a study of two measures. To advance the state of atmospheric science and technology so as to provide greater knowledge of basic physical forces affecting climate and the possibility of large-scale weather modification; and to develop existing weather-forecasting capabilities and to help Member States make effective use of such capabilities through regional meteorological centres. The WMO quickly produced a report on the advance of the atmospheric sciences and application in view of space developments. After four years of discussion and study this report was accepted in the form of the World Weather Watch plan.

The idea of monitoring a global weather system requires world-wide data collection on the condition of the atmosphere and associated geophysical phenomena, its processing to establish likely future weather activity, and a telecommunications network for collection and distribution of processed information. The WMO therefore set up the Global Observing System (GOS), the Global Data-processing System (GDPS), and the Global Telecommunications System (GTS) to carry out these functions.

Details of the activities of these organisations are impressive. In 24 hours the GOS makes about 110,000 observations from 9,000 land stations, 3,000 aircraft and 7,000 merchant ships throughout the world. In remote areas automatic weather stations are being built, and special-purpose ships are being constructed to traverse data-sparse areas. The GDPS has developed its System to manage this huge amount of input information. Giant computers are installed at Melbourne, Moscow and Washington DC, and a model of global weather for the following 24 hours is produced twice a day. These analyses and forecasts are distributed visually and digitally to the 23 Regional Meteorological Centres and 100 National Met. Centres. The GTS uses telegraph, telephone, radio, cable and landlines to distribute the material at speeds of up to 7,200 words per second.

The WMO has also instigated a Global Atmospheric Research Programme (GARP), to extend the scope and accuracy of weather forecasts, and to better understand the physical basis of climate and climatic fluctuations. To do this GARP has set up a series of regional experiments, such as the Atlantic Tropical, Air-Mass Transformation, Monsoon and Polar Experiments. In late 1978 the largest experimental programme will start. Named the First GARP Global Experiment (FGGE), it will monitor the atmospheric condition of the entire globe for one year, and apply world-wide tests of existing climatic models.

Polar-orbiting and geostationary satellites will be used to collect the extensive data for this global experiment.

Water resources and vegetation

Water is essential not only to practically all forms of life but is required in enormous quantities to support our modern industrial society. The average daily consumption for each individual in the UK is about 1 cubic metre, and in the USA the figure approaches ten times this quantity. Domestic use accounts for 20 per cent of this total in the UK and 10 per cent in the US. The need to husband water supplies is obvious in arid climates, but it is only in recent years that the need to conserve water resources in areas of more abundant rainfall, has been appreciated.

Hydrological cycle
Fresh water forms only 2 per cent of the water available on the Earth's surface. Even so, this amount would be more than adequate were not the greatest reserves locked, inaccessibly, in the polar ice caps. The problem therefore, is to provide water where and when it is needed and to ensure that it is not used faster than it can be replaced. The oceans are nature's reservoirs. From them water is evaporated to fall as rain or snow over the land. From the land it returns, mostly through rivers, to the sea. This process is known as the 'hydrological' cycle (see diagram). The maximum water potentially available is therefore dependent on the amount precipitated on the land. Water conservation aims to preserve for subsequent use as much of this water as possible.

Water conservation
When rain falls over land a proportion is quickly evaporated back into the atmosphere. Apart from limited and local measures, not a great deal can be done to conserve this water, nor that which is taken up by plants and returned to the atmosphere by transpiration. Some water 'runs off' and finds its way into rivers. Here control can be exercised, by adopting agricultural methods that will prevent too rapid run-off of surface water, retaining it in the soil for the benefit of crops, or alternatively by constructing drainage channels, dams and reservoirs in which water can be stored for later use. The remainder of the rainfall will sink deep into the earth, where a proportion will be held in rock strata. Rocks with a capacity to hold water are known as 'aquifers'; water is recovered by sinking wells to them.

Elementary though these measures are, they provide the foundation of proper control of water resources. Modern treatments increase the water supply still further by providing for water to be re-used. Water taken for industry can be cleansed and returned to the river from which it came. Further downstream it may be taken into the public water supply, and so into a sewage system from which it is discharged clean for further use.

Simple water conservation techniques can assure adequate supplies for large cities situated on rivers or lakes. Thus London, Washington and Chicago rarely suffer from water shortage. For other cities, not so fortunately situated, methods must be found to bring water from elsewhere. Birmingham in the UK, for example, is supplied with water from central Wales. New York City cannot use the brackish water of the Hudson estuary, but relies on supplies from catchment areas in New York State, some of which are over 160 km (100 miles) away. This water is brought to the metropolis from 27 reservoirs through 640 km (400 miles) of aqueducts and tunnels.

Techniques similar to those used to reclaim land allow arms of the sea to be isolated for conversion into freshwater lakes.

Further possibilities of increasing the water supply bring some hope for the arid regions of the world. For many decades rain has been induced by 'seeding' clouds with silver iodide crystals. This technique has achieved success, but it is extremely costly and uncertain. It cannot succeed unless there are clouds (i.e. water vapour) in the air. More promising are schemes to obtain fresh water from the sea by desalination and this is most commonly done by distillation and freezing. Distillation plants are currently in commercial use, particularly in the Middle East, but the cost is high and the quantity of water produced is small. The use of solar energy to support distillation processes is attractive in that fuel costs are abolished. However, while solar stills have proved successful on a small scale, larger versions have not worked efficiently. Experimental desalination plants based on freezing processes are in operation in the United States, and in Britain a pilot plant of this type is to be constructed in East Anglia.

Oil-rich but arid states have also considered seriously the possibility of towing icebergs from Antarctica to serve as a water supply. Recent estimates show this operation to be comparable in cost with desalination processes.

Types of natural vegetation

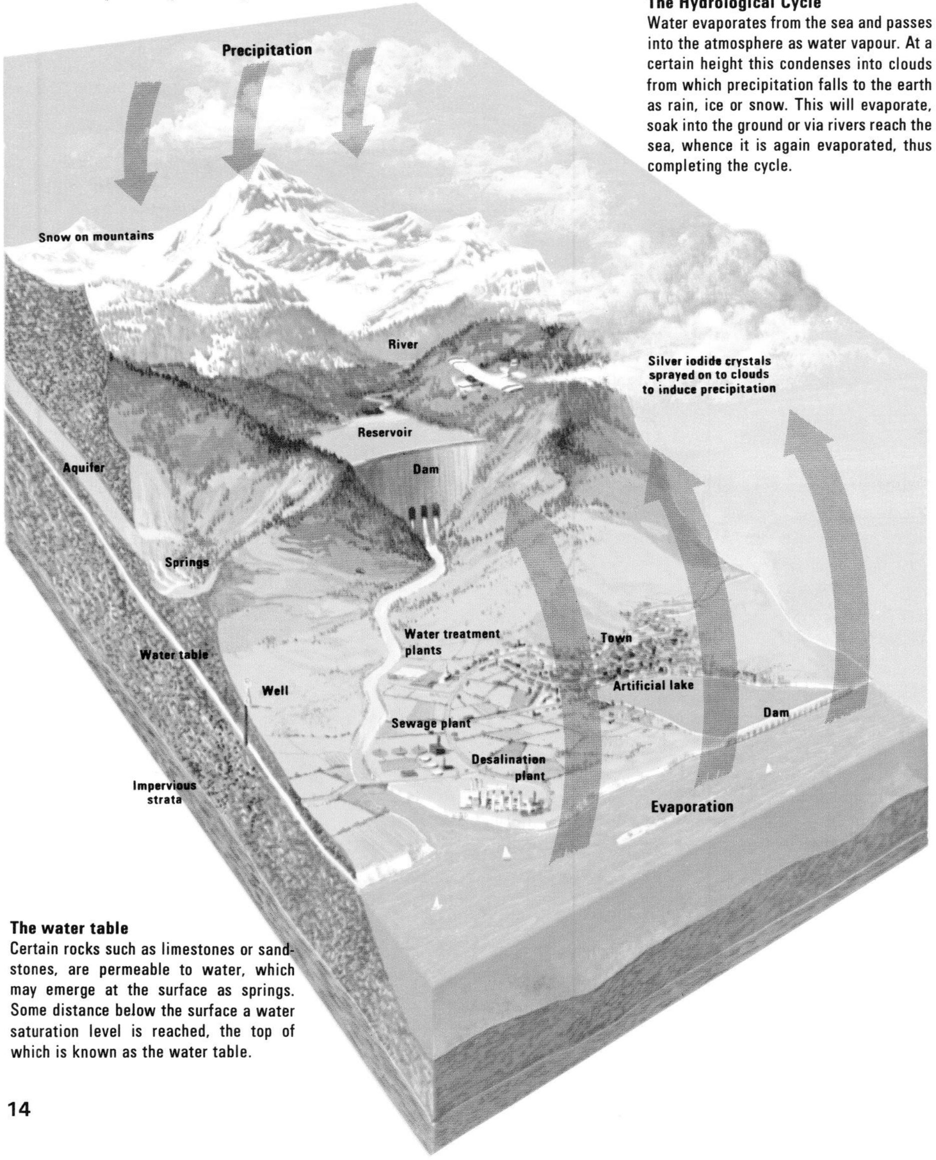

NORTHERN LIMIT OF PALMS

The Hydrological Cycle

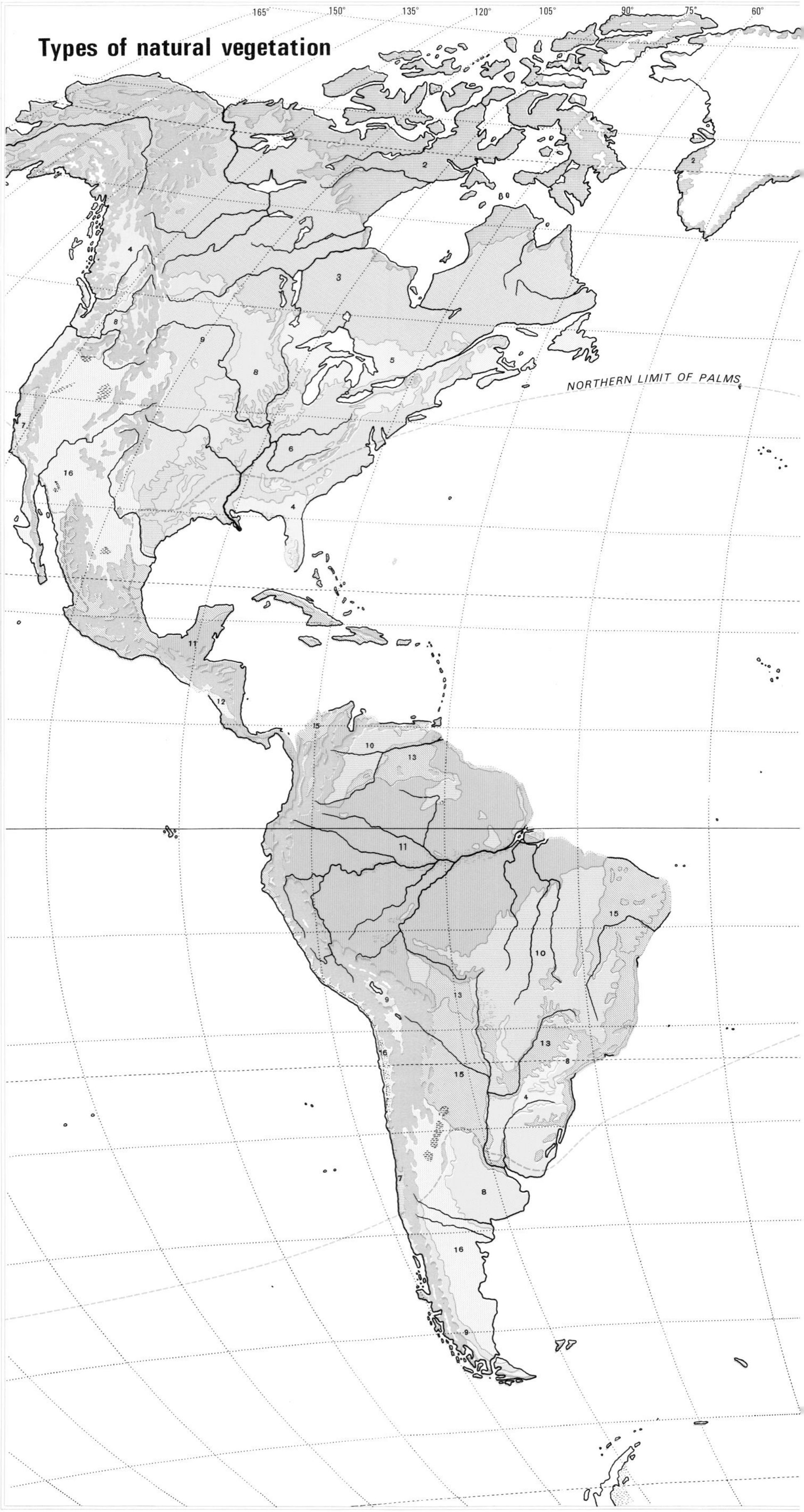

The Hydrological Cycle
Water evaporates from the sea and passes into the atmosphere as water vapour. At a certain height this condenses into clouds from which precipitation falls to the earth as rain, ice or snow. This will evaporate, soak into the ground or via rivers reach the sea, whence it is again evaporated, thus completing the cycle.

The water table
Certain rocks such as limestones or sandstones, are permeable to water, which may emerge at the surface as springs. Some distance below the surface a water saturation level is reached, the top of which is known as the water table.

Natural vegetation
A remarkable feature of the earth's land surface is the extent to which it is covered with plant life. Though there are inhospitable areas – such as the peaks of great mountain ranges and polar ice caps – where plant life all but disappears, for the most part vegetation exists in great abundance. Natural vegetation means the type of plant cover that would occur naturally without man's interference. In western Europe, man's activities have over the centuries so altered the natural plant cover that practically nowhere does it exist in its original form. Yet there is no difficulty in defining the broad categories of plants that flourish in the conditions that prevail locally.

The map on this page displays the major categories of natural vegetation, each characterized by important features which transcend differences between individual species. These vegetation zones are in essence a response to climatic conditions, for although local conditions of soil, relief and micro-climate are all important in determining local particulars of plant cover, the temperature and rainfall conditions of climatic regions exercise substantial control over the nature of plant cover. Thus, since latitude largely determines climate, the vegetation regions north and south of the Equator tend to be a mirror image one of the other. The close relationship between climate and vegetation has provided geographers with a convenient division of the world into major regions, since the particular features of plant life of each region are distinctive.

Vegetation regions
Near the Equator climate varies little throughout the year with rainfall and temperature consistently high. The absence of seasons means that plants do not undergo a resting period, while the abundance of warmth and moisture ensures a particularly luxuriant growth. Thus the characteristic vegetation of areas such as the Amazon and Zaire basins and the islands of Indonesia is dense, almost impenetrable forest, with trees competing for light attaining great heights.

Further away from the Equator lie the tropical

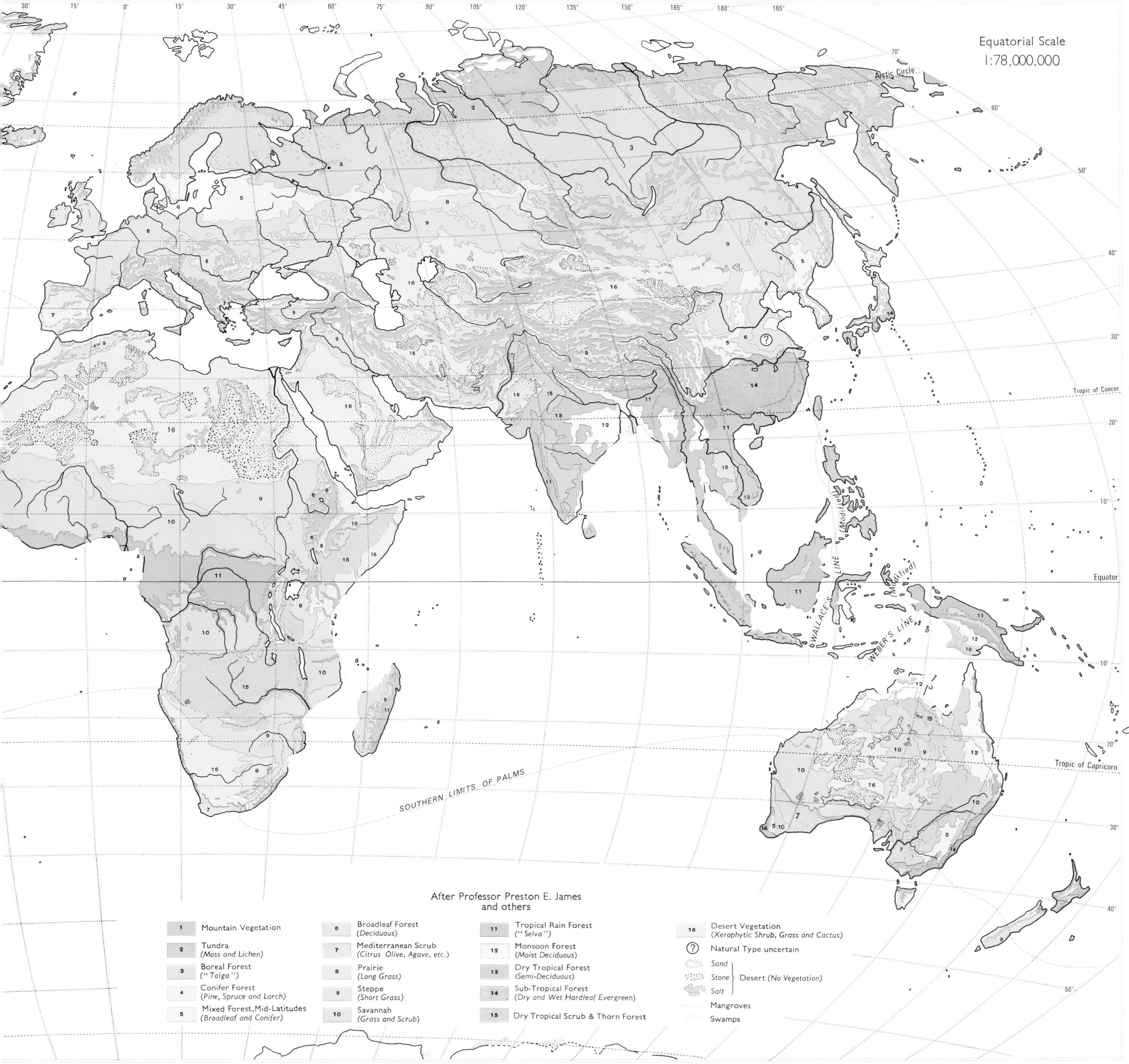

Equatorial Scale
1:78,000,000

After Professor Preston E. James
and others

1	Mountain Vegetation	6	Broadleaf Forest *(Deciduous)*	11	Tropical Rain Forest *(" Selva ")*	16	Desert Vegetation *(Xerophytic Shrub, Grass and Cactus)*
2	Tundra *(Moss and Lichen)*	7	Mediterranean Scrub *(Citrus Olive, Agave, etc.)*	12	Monsoon Forest *(Moist Deciduous)*	?	Natural Type uncertain
3	Boreal Forest *(" Taiga ")*	8	Prairie *(Long Grass)*	13	Dry Tropical Forest *(Semi-Deciduous)*	Sand
4	Conifer Forest *(Pine, Spruce and Larch)*	9	Steppe *(Short Grass)*	14	Sub-Tropical Forest *(Dry and Wet Hardleaf Evergreen)*	Stone } Desert (No Vegetation)
5	Mixed Forest, Mid-Latitudes *(Broadleaf and Conifer)*	10	Savannah *(Grass and Scrub)*	15	Dry Tropical Scrub & Thorn Forest	Salt
						Mangroves
						Swamps

grasslands. Here grass grows in abundance during the rainy season only to be withered by the sun in the ensuing drought. The sparse plant life of the world's deserts shows particular adaptations to drought conditions. Some species develop seeds which lie dormant for long periods and then, when rainfall comes, grow and complete their life cycle in the brief period in which moisture is retained in the soil. Many, including the cactus species' so typical of the arid regions of the western United States, are able to store water efficiently with little loss through transpiration.

The characteristic vegetation of much of Europe, including the British Isles, and the eastern half of the United States, is broad-leaved deciduous forest. In response to the clear climatic differences between summer and winter, trees have adapted to take fullest advantage of the favour-able growing season. The broad leaf structure which allows maximum exposure to light and air means that the tree is an efficient starch-producing organ. This same adaptation renders the plant extremely sensitive to low temperatures and high

winds, and thus these plants lie dormant during winter months. So precise is their adaptation that their activity is not dependent on average climatic conditions but on the likely variations from this average. In Britain the oak and ash are not tempted to unfold their leaves early in a mild spring yet imported species like the horse chestnut will do so. Most cultivated plants are imported or are 'artificial' cross-breeds and lack precise adaptation to prevailing climatic conditions. They need protection by shelter or irrigation or removal of other competitive plants if they are to flourish.

North of the regions of the broad-leaved deciduous forest flourish the conifer forests. In the United States they are developed particularly well in the north-western states. The trees that form these forests are much better adapted to withstanding unfavourable conditions and in-clude the world's most magnificent specimens, in particular the giant redwood trees, which grow to greater heights than any other tree except the eucalyptus. These forests are of substantial econ-omic importance and provide over 30 per cent

of timber needed by the USA.

Climatic variations
We are now in an interglacial period within which minor climatic variations have occurred. Some 3,000 to 4,000 years ago climate in the British Isles was drier, with greater temperature variations between summer and winter so that hazel and birch flourished more than they do now. There is considerable evidence that land bordering the Sahara desert is drier now than it was 2,000 or so years ago, for plants grew more abundantly then, and in north Africa wheat was grown for the Roman Empire in regions which are now semi-desert. Some of this decline is un-doubtably due to unwise farming methods, which have resulted in the loss of topsoil, or to clearance of the natural plant cover to grow crops. A wealth of evidence now shows that both Sahara and Gobi deserts spread towards the Equator when the climate cools slightly – as it has since the 1950s. This, plus overgrazing, is the cause of recent droughts in the Sahel (the region bordering the Sahara to the south), in Ethiopia, and in

Somalia and north-east Kenya.

Although we are concerned mainly with the broad characteristics of the plant life of the major vegetation zones, we should not ignore the strange variations that occur, as species adapt to local conditions. The vegetation of the Everglades in Florida displays a remarkable adaption to the swampy conditions that prevail there, while along tropical coasts mangroves grow and with their preponderance of stilt-like roots keep a firm hold on the shifting ground beneath. These roots, the upper parts of which are exposed at low tide, have pores through which the plant can take oxygen, since there is little oxygen in the muddy water below, where organic matter is decom-posing.

Precise adaptation of particular species to local conditions has been turned to economic advantage. A few species flourish abnormally well where certain minerals are present, and by study of these 'indicator plants', deposits of copper and other ores have been traced in many parts of the world.

Minerals and their uses

Gold

Precious metal and principal international reserve asset underwriting the means of exchange. Used in manufacture, medicine and fabrication for its special corrosive resistant properties. It does not tarnish and is unaffected by most acids. It weighs about two and a half times as much as steel and is very malleable and ductile. Thus it can be hammered to an extremely thin sheet or drawn into the finest of metal wires. Gold is an excellent conductor of electricity. Applications vary from jewellery and coinage to dentistry and electronic circuitry. Over 70 per cent of free world production comes from South Africa. Other producers include North America, USSR, Australia and central Africa. Non-communist output totals over 1,027,000 kilograms annually. For every million parts of ore about 13 parts of gold are extracted.

Silver

Precious metal of wide industrial usage and re-usage. Mine production is around 9,230 tonnes of new silver, to serve both speculative and industrial markets, which include photography and the decorative arts as well as coinage. Main producers include North America, Mexico, Peru and Australia.

Platinum

Often a by-product of copper-nickel mining, a precious metal of catalytic properties in, e.g., making nitric acid. Provides long-lasting protective coatings which are used in chemical, electrical, petroleum, glass and electronic industries. Main producer is South Africa, with 70 per cent of output, in meeting world demand of 1·4m troy oz. USSR and Canada also substantial producers. Platinum metals include Iridium, Rhodium, Palladium, Osmium, Ruthenium. Future demand may be affected by anti-pollution use in reforming petroleum.

Diamond

Precious stone of pure carbon formed at depth under pressure and temperature and then extruded in Kimberlitic rock pipes and dykes – coveted for rarity and qualities such as hardness, cutting and abrasive properties. World output of diamonds for industrial purposes 32,400 metric carats. Gemstone production is just over 13,500 metric carats. Over twenty countries produce diamonds with the bulk of output coming from Zaire, South Africa and the USSR. World synthetic diamond output is over 45 million metric carats.

Copper

One of the oldest known and most exploited metals, the mineral in refined form is used widely through the whole spectrum of industry, half going to electrical and telecommunication sectors. Other big areas of consumption are in general engineering and building components. Its main properties are its capacity as a conductor of heat or electricity, its ductile nature which allows it to be drawn into fine wire, and its value in alloys with zinc and tin. Bronzes are largely copper-tin alloys. Brasses are alloys of copper, zinc and tin. Copper deposits occur in the oceans and promise to extend the life of copper when continental deposits are nearing exhaustion. Total refined output varies because of volatile market conditions, but is now nearly 8 million tonnes. Top producers are USA, USSR, Chile, Zambia, Canada, Zaire, Peru and Australia, with about 20 other significant sources.

Tin

Soft silver-white corrosion-resistant metal used primarily as a coating for steel sheets used in food canning; has strong resistance to atmospheric tarnishing. Widely used in alloys, notably the brasses and bronzes, brazing materials and solder. World consumption is 197 million tonnes, mainly by USA, Japan, UK, Germany and France. Main sources are Malaysia, Bolivia, Thailand and Indonesia. Also mined in Australia, Nigeria, Zaire and Brazil. Total mined output is 181 million tonnes. Prices are subject to international marketing agreements because of importance of material (8 industrial countries account for 80 per cent of consumption).

Lead and Zinc

Major metals smelted from mines to meet consumption of more than 5·5 million tonnes of zinc and over 3·4 million tonnes of lead. Large stocks are kept in Europe, North America and USSR. Zinc is used in die castings for cars, and for brass and galvanizing iron and steel. Also used as a pigment in paints, chemical manufacture and metallurgical processes. Non-ferrous lead goes into production of batteries, and as additive for gasoline; main producers of refined lead are in North America and Europe, while mine production is led by the Americas, Oceania, USSR and Africa. Zinc production is dominated by North America, Europe and socialist countries.

Steel Metals

These include nickel, manganese, chromium, cobalt, molybdenum, tungsten, vanadium, columbium and tantalum, all offering specific qualities and properties for making special steels. Nickel, for example, is essential for making high quality stainless steel, which takes 40 per cent of consumption. Chromium is also necessary for the production of stainless steel. Tungsten is added to steel to produce high grade steels which can be hardened in air instead of water. Manganese is added to iron to produce castings which are not brittle. Base material of steel is iron ore, production of which rises steadily and in 1974 reached 507 million tonnes. The world's biggest producer of iron ore is USSR with around 123 million tonnes. Other big suppliers are Australia, Brazil, China, France, India, Liberia, Sweden and North America (90m tonnes). Ore is sold in lump, sinter and pellet forms for transportation to blast furnaces.

Aluminium

Primary aluminium (which, with titanium and magnesium, is a principal light weight metal) depends on production of bauxite amounting to 78 million tonnes annually. Nearly a fifth of bauxite comes from Jamaica. Other major sources are Australia, USSR, Surinam, Guyana, France, Guinea and Hungary. The USA accounts for about half of the Free World consumption; most primary aluminium goes into fabrication of industrial products made from plate, strip and wire. Alloyed with manganese or titanium, it offers tensile properties combined with lightness. World primary aluminium output is over 13 million tonnes led by North America, USSR, Japan and Norway.

Nuclear Metals

The most important of these is uranium. They include thorium, beryllium, zirconium and hafnium, caesium and ribidium, and rare earths. Development of nuclear power and related industries has expanded the search for and production of the various metals. Uranium production is around 18,500 tonnes a year.

Mercury

Liquid metal with volatile properties, known as quicksilver, derived from cinnabar. Mercury is used in scientific instruments and in chemicals, particularly in the production of chlorine and caustic soda. World mine output is 92 million tonnes. Leading sources are Spain, North America, Italy, Mexico, China, USSR and Yugoslavia.

Cadmium

A soft silvery-white metal occurs together with zinc. Mainly used in plating processes, as a pigment for plastics, for television phosphors and for nickel-cadmium batteries. It is also used for control rods in atomic nuclear reactors. The largest commercial producer is the USA. Total output is well over 10m lbs a year.

Rhenium

Derived from copper ores with molybdenite, this metal has a melting point exceeded only by tungsten. Its outstanding ductility, high temperature strength and corrosion resistance makes it an alternative for platinum as a petrochemical catalyst. Used for camera flash bulb filaments and for alloys. Main sources are Chile. USA, USSR and Sweden. Other electronic metals and minerals are indium, selenium, tellurium and mica.

Phosphate Rock

Universally mined phosphoric material with widespread usage in chemical processes. Output is in excess of 117 million tonnes.

Potash

An alkaline substance used for fertilizers and other chemical synthesis. World production is 24·2 million tonnes, with North America, USSR, Germany and France the leading sources.

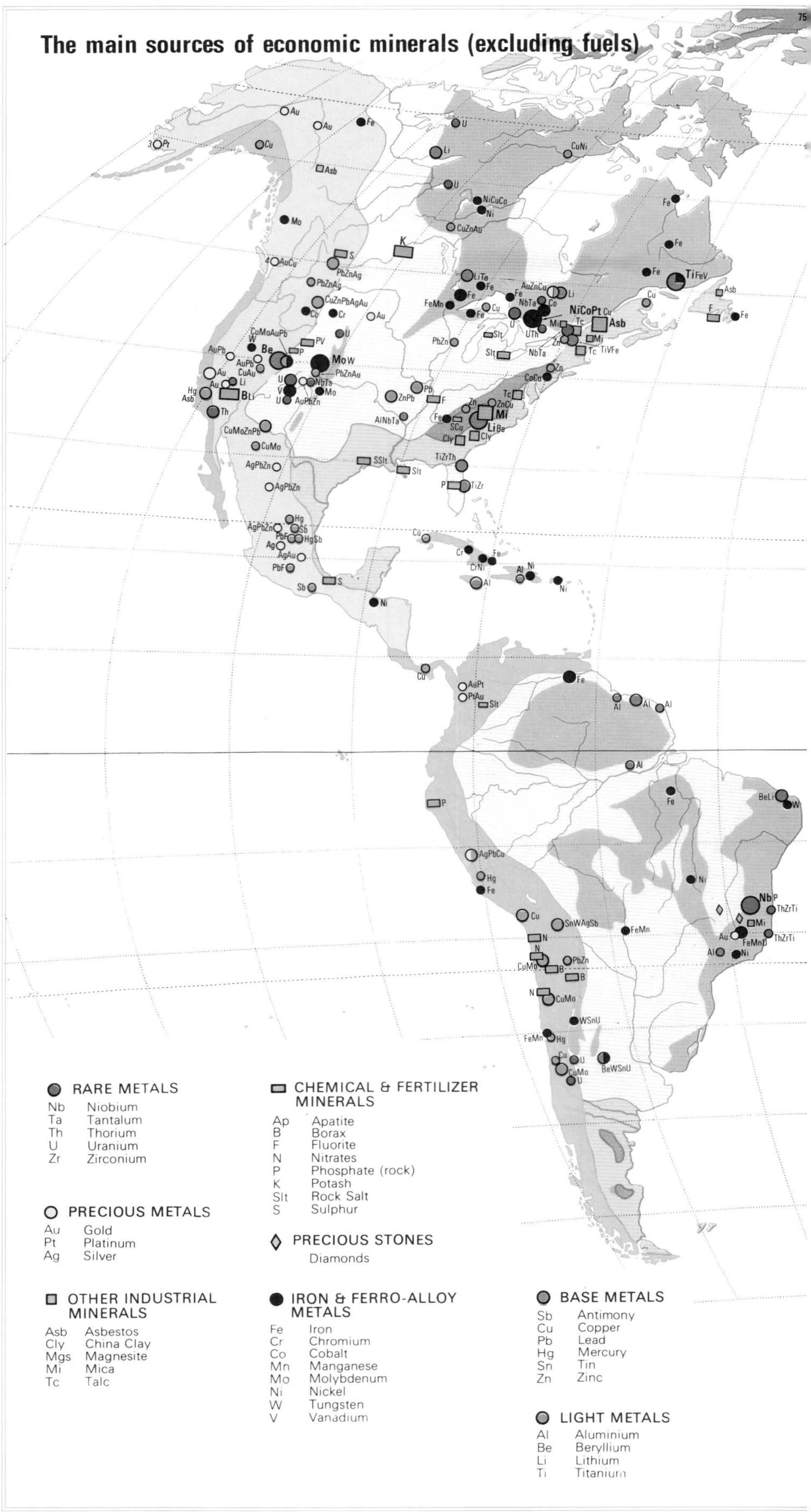

The main sources of economic minerals (excluding fuels)

RARE METALS
Nb Niobium
Ta Tantalum
Th Thorium
U Uranium
Zr Zirconium

PRECIOUS METALS
Au Gold
Pt Platinum
Ag Silver

OTHER INDUSTRIAL MINERALS
Asb Asbestos
Cly China Clay
Mgs Magnesite
Mi Mica
Tc Talc

CHEMICAL & FERTILIZER MINERALS
Ap Apatite
B Borax
F Fluorite
N Nitrates
P Phosphate (rock)
K Potash
Slt Rock Salt
S Sulphur

PRECIOUS STONES
Diamonds

IRON & FERRO-ALLOY METALS
Fe Iron
Cr Chromium
Co Cobalt
Mn Manganese
Mo Molybdenum
Ni Nickel
W Tungsten
V Vanadium

BASE METALS
Sb Antimony
Cu Copper
Pb Lead
Hg Mercury
Sn Tin
Zn Zinc

LIGHT METALS
Al Aluminium
Be Beryllium
Li Lithium
Ti Titanium

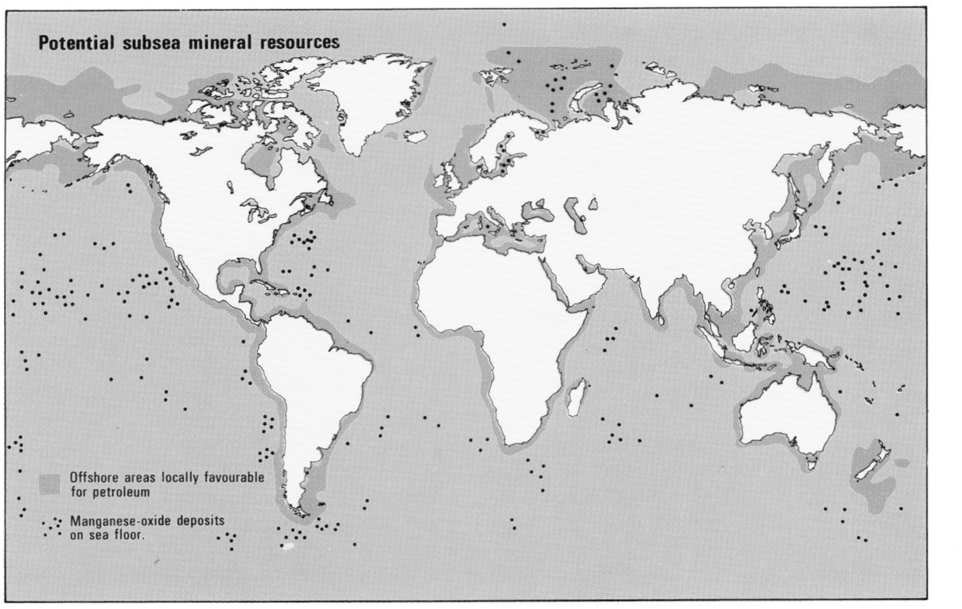

Potential subsea mineral resources

Offshore areas locally favourable for petroleum

Manganese-oxide deposits on sea floor.

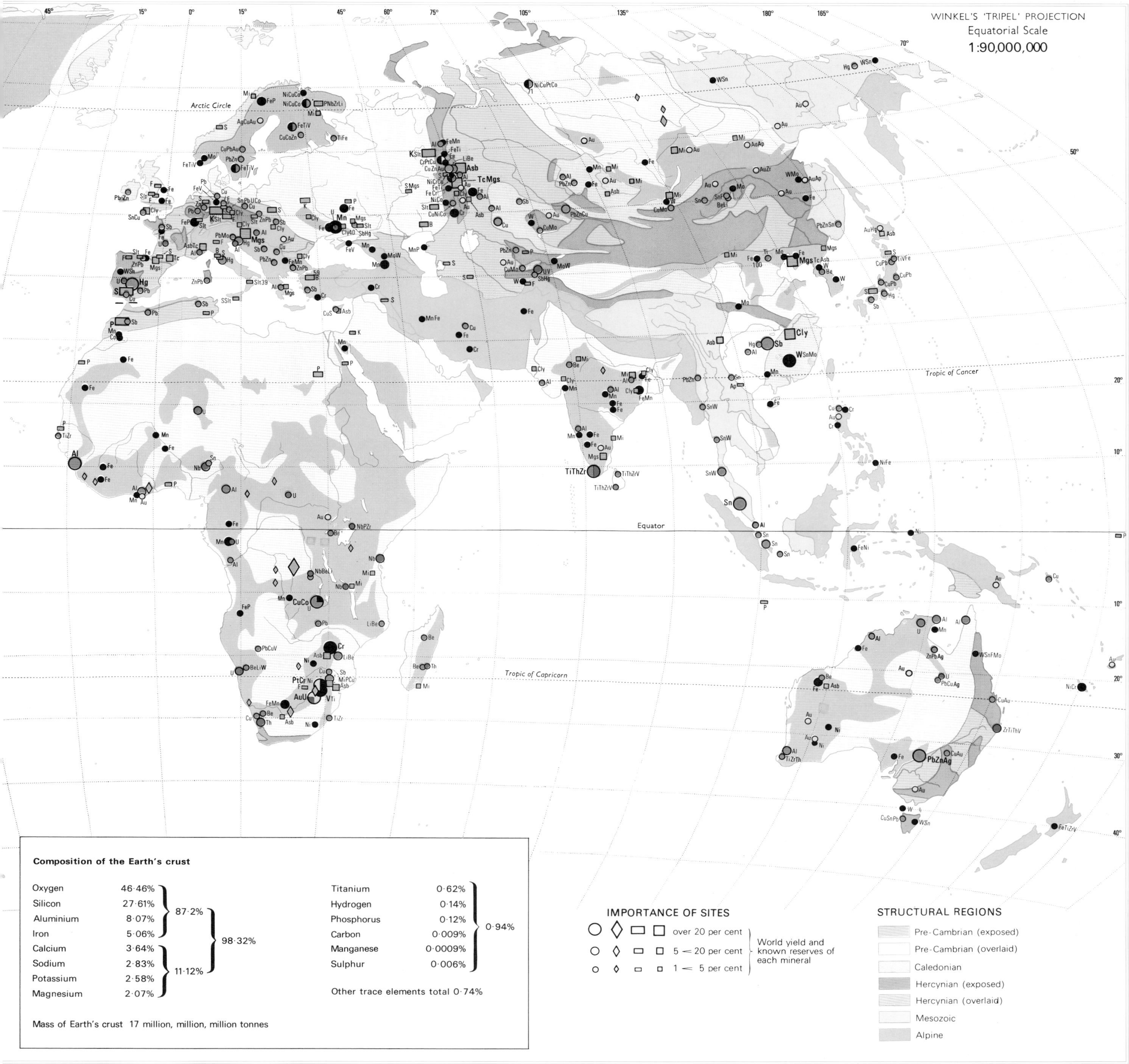

WINKEL'S 'TRIPEL' PROJECTION
Equatorial Scale
1:90,000,000

Composition of the Earth's crust

Oxygen	46·46%		Titanium	0·62%	
Silicon	27·61%	} 87·2%	Hydrogen	0·14%	
Aluminium	8·07%		Phosphorus	0·12%	} 0·94%
Iron	5·06%	} 98·32%	Carbon	0·009%	
Calcium	3·64%		Manganese	0·0009%	
Sodium	2·83%	} 11·12%	Sulphur	0·006%	
Potassium	2·58%				
Magnesium	2·07%		Other trace elements total 0·74%		

Mass of Earth's crust 17 million, million, million tonnes

IMPORTANCE OF SITES

◯ ◇ ▭ ▢ over 20 per cent

◦ ◇ ▭ ▢ 5 — 20 per cent   } World yield and known reserves of each mineral

∘ ◇ ▫ ▫ 1 — 5 per cent

STRUCTURAL REGIONS

Pre-Cambrian (exposed)
Pre-Cambrian (overlaid)
Caledonian
Hercynian (exposed)
Hercynian (overlaid)
Mesozoic
Alpine

Sulphur
Pale yellow non-metallic element used for making sulphuric acid, gunpowder, matches and vulcanite. Also known as brimstone, the primary rock from which various sulphurs are recovered. World brimstone output is around 25 million tonnes. Derived also from natural gas, oil refining and iron pyrites. Chemicals industries are major consumers.

Lithium
Lightest metallic element produced from ore or natural brine in USA, USSR and Brazil for use in chemicals production.

Bismuth
Greyish-white metal mainly supplied by Peru, Bolivia, Mexico, USA, USSR and China. Important catalyst and is often recovered for secondary usage from other mining or smelting operations.

Barytes
The sulphate of barium; produced in 40 countries with output totalling 4 million tonnes. Usually used as weighting agent in drilling through mud for oil and gas. Also goes into making barium chemicals. USA is the largest producer.

Antimony
World output totals over 71,000 tonnes of this brittle metal substance derived from ores and concentrates. Leading suppliers are South Africa, Bolivia, China, Mexico, USSR and Yugoslavia, Thailand and Turkey. Used in battery, paint and oxide manufacture.

Boron
Dark brown non-metallic substance used to make fibreglass, vitreous enamel, heat-resistant glass, detergents and ceramics. Main source is USA borate mines; other supplies from Turkey, Argentina, France and Spain.

Fluorspar
Fusible gem-like mineral of varying quality needed for steel-making, aluminium, and fluorine based chemicals. World output is over 4 million tonnes. Leading producer is Mexico, but major sources also include USA, Argentina, Brazil, Chile, Europe, USSR, South Africa, Far and Middle East (Thailand dominant with China and North Korea).

Asbestos
A mined fibre which is best known of insulant and refractory materials, which also include perlite, sillimanite, vermiculite, graphite and magnesite. Over 5·2 million tonnes are produced annually mainly from Canada, Zimbabwe, USSR, South Africa, China, Italy and USA.

Abrasives
A range of natural materials, apart from diamonds, used for abrasive and polishing purposes. Most common are emery (main sources Turkey, USA, Greece, USSR), corundum (USSR and Zimbabwe), garnet (USA), tripoli (USA), pumice (USA, Germany and Italy). Finely ground and calcined clays are also used with lime, talc, feldspar and whiting. World usage of abrasives is beyond estimate.

Nickel
Element used for steel and other alloys. World consumption 750,500 tonnes, led by main steel producing countries. Main sources: Canada, New Caledonia, Australia, Zimbabwe, USA, USSR, S. Africa and Japan. Latin America is a growing supplier. Biggest single use is in stainless steel.

Cobalt
Much used, like nickel, in special steels and alloys. World output is well over 22,000 tonnes of ore bodies, often associated with copper deposits. Leading sources are Congo, Zambia, Canada, Finland and Germany.

Chromium
Chromium is derived from the ore chromite. Its main usages are in metallurgical (particularly stainless steel), refractory and chemicals industries. Output is 3·3 million tonnes. Largest producers are Zimbabwe, South Africa, USSR, Turkey, Iran, Philippines, Albania and India.

Food and nutrition

Food sources

HIGH YIELD ZONES
- Wheat
- Maize
- Barley, Oats, Rye
- Rice
- Millets
- Sea fishing

LIVESTOCK
- Dairy farming
- Cattle
- Sheep
- Pigs

MAJOR SPECIALISED CROPS
- ▽ Sugar beet/cane
- ● Apples
- ● Bananas
- ● Citrus fruit
- ▼ Vine growing
- ● Coffee
- ● Cocoa
- ↓ Tea
- 1 2 Soybeans/Groundnuts
- 3 4 Cottonseed/Sunflower

LOW YIELD ZONES
- Tundra, Ice-cap
- Forest
- Mountain
- Extensive grassland
- Desert, semi-desert

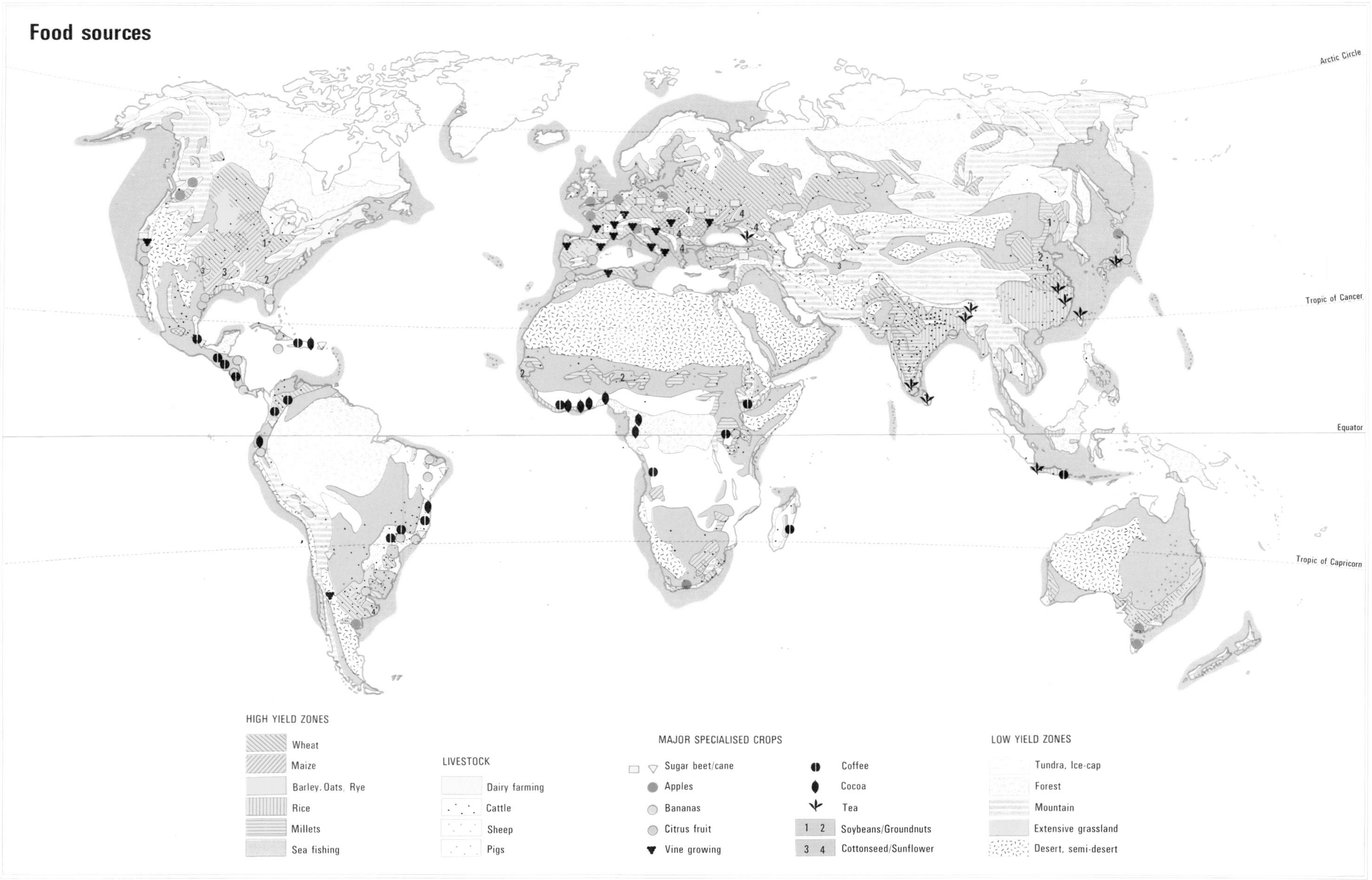

The provision of food from farms and factories depends on the most complex of all economic chains of supply. Basic foodstuffs pass from continent to continent, from temperate to tropical zones and vice versa. Foods are frozen, chilled, dehydrated, cooked and canned, pulped, or distributed fresh. Yet, in spite of better methods of preservation, storage and distribution, there is still not enough to go round. The greatest challenge to mankind is to cultivate and to process enough food to keep pace with the growth of world population, and to contrive efficient means of distribution world wide.

Poor harvests, natural disasters and civil disturbances complicate the task of agricultural scientists and economic planners who try to ease the worst problems. Their job, involving international collaboration, is formidable. In 1975 the world consumed 15,200 billion (i.e. thousand million) calories each day, but by the year 2050 the need will be 73,500 billion, with virtually all the increase concentrated on the regions of the world less well developed economically.

While the demand for food in less prosperous areas is based on grain, the raising of standards of living brings a demand for a higher consumption of animal foods. This implies great pressure to improve land crops, for only about 40 per cent of the world's crops are eaten directly by humans. The rest is fed to animals or represents waste. According to calculations, this means that six out of every seven calories are used to keep animals alive. As over half the Earth's fertile soil available for agriculture is devoted to the raising of animals, the supply of foodstuff to a world population of

possibly 16 billion people by 2050 will require new sources for food if a diet comparable to that of the richer nations is to be attained.

World consumption and production patterns
Roughly 98 per cent of all human food is produced by agriculture, including horticulture; the remaining 2 per cent comes from the oceans. To avoid excessive price increases and rationing, agricultural output must continually be expanded, demanding suitable land, capital, labour and scientific knowledge. The factors of production vary according to region; plant production (i.e. crops) representing the basis of agriculture. The raw materials for raising animals come from plant production, for livestock transforms plants into finished or semi-finished products in a way similar to that of other processing industries.
Food consumption
All supply depends upon the world-wide production of basic foodstuffs, essential for either direct consumption or processing. Among the most important primary agricultural products are grains, used for both human and animal consumption, the animals being reared both for human food (meat and drink) and for their by-products such as wool or hides. Present diets, inadequate in large parts of the world, annually require up to 350 million tonnes of wheat, 176 million tonnes of barley, over 300 million tonnes of maize, and about 265 million tonnes of rice.
Food production
In tonnage terms, the world produces 424 million tonnes of milk, 84 million tonnes of meat (including poultry) and something like 23 million

tonnes of eggs per year. Coffee output fluctuates around 5 million tonnes and wine near 32 million tonnes, while tea and cocoa production total about 3 million tonnes. To these must be added 38 million tonnes of vegetable oils and oil-seeds, and over 100 million tonnes of fresh fruit.

The United States slaughters around 39 million head of cattle annually to feed herself and others. Another 7 million sheep and lambs add to this huge supply of meat. Argentina, producing about 60 million head of cattle in 1976, is a major meat exporter, selling to Europe great quantities of chilled and frozen beef and various canned meats. Australian slaughterings of sheep amount to about 35 million head annually, some 5 million ahead of New Zealand which sells large quantities of lamb to Europe, beef to the USA and mutton to Japan. Nearly 8 million pigs form the stock for the famous Danish bacon industry.

The great dairy industry of Western Europe, is based on an average herd ranging from 5 head per herd in Italy to 22 in the Netherlands and 37 in the UK. With the trend to bigger farms the average herd size is growing each year.

Over the period 1967–77 the trend of food production per capita in the developing countries of the Far East (the world's most concentrated food deficit zone) and the Near East did not keep pace with the rise in population. There was a barely perceptible rise in Latin America, and a slight fall for the developing areas of Africa.

The introduction of new varieties of wheat has made Mexico virtually self-sufficient in this food commodity. Cereal yields have also advanced markedly in the Far East and India. The rising

volume of world agricultural exports, up about 10 per cent annually, reflects the growing interdependence of all nations in exchanging surplus food or co-operating to ease the impact of crop failures. The operation of various international commodity agreements and markets is intended to assist marketing of food.
Changes in food supply
Fishing is a vital industry. The economies of Peru and the Philippines have benefited greatly from substantial landings. In Japan, fish still provides two-thirds of animal protein and in south-east Asia fish is more commonly eaten than meat. About one-third of fish landings round the world go to the production of fish meal to feed poultry and cattle. Over the last three decades many new fishing grounds have been intensively developed, including the Bering Sea (exploited by Japan and the Soviet Union), the north-east Pacific, the north-west Atlantic, many areas around South America, and south-east Asia.

Drought, cyclone and civil disturbance are not the only factors to alter the geographical patterns of food supply year by year; political and economic difficulties sometimes arise as well. National farm policies and subsidies to food industries, have become important elements in the world economy. A decision taken in Europe to restrict imports of a certain food in order to expand indigenous production may have a profound effect on the populations of other continents. The European Community's common agricultural policy and the United States' farm support programmes are of constant importance to the distribution of world food production.

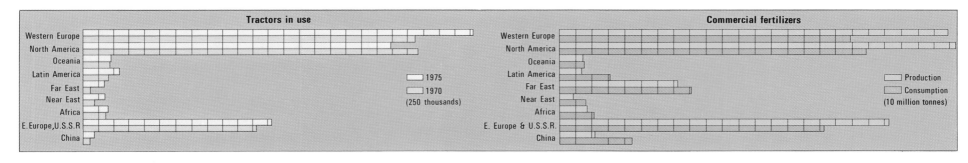

Tractors in use
- Western Europe
- North America
- Oceania
- Latin America
- Far East
- Near East
- Africa
- E. Europe, U.S.S.R.
- China

□ 1975
□ 1970
(250 thousands)

Commercial fertilizers
- Western Europe
- North America
- Oceania
- Latin America
- Far East
- Near East
- Africa
- E. Europe & U.S.S.R.
- China

□ Production
□ Consumption
(10 million tonnes)

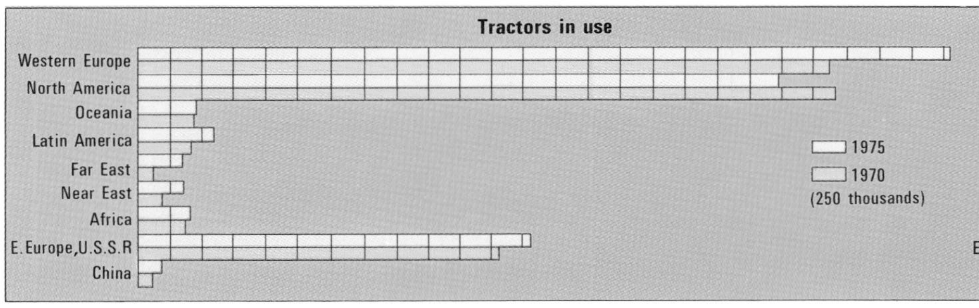

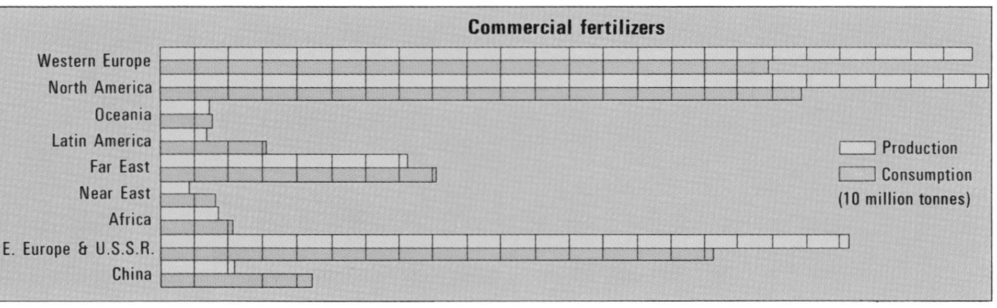

Calorie and protein consumption

Differences in calories and protein intake by different national populations need to be treated with caution. The average per capita difference in calorie intake between Canada and Brazil, for example, is around 550 calories and 35 grams of protein, yet the difference between income groups in urban areas within Brazil itself can be as high as 1,500 calories and 70 gms of protein. Some examples of calories per head per day are United States 3,330; Netherlands 3,320; West Germany 3,220; France 3,210; Italy 3,180; United Kingdom 3,180; Canada 3,180; and Japan 2,460.

To sustain their nutritional standards, nations vary greatly in their levels of consumption. Germany needs 92 kg per head per year of potatoes, compared with 36 kg for the United States. Japan consumes per head annually 90 kg of husked rice; in the UK the rice consumption is 2 kg. France and Italy drink between 100 and 105 litres of wine per head annually, whereas the consumption in the Netherlands is only 10 litres.

The importance of fish and rice in Japanese diets is demonstrated by the consumption of 25 kg per head per year of meat (measured by carcase weight) compared with 70 kg for the United Kingdom and 105 kg for the United States. The latter two nations are leading consumers of eggs in shell at 14 to 17 kg per head per year. Per capita, Finland consumes 258 kg of liquid milk annually, against 118 kg for the USA and 25 kg for Japan. Consumption of fats per head per year is 25 kg in Western Europe and North America, but in Japan the intake is 11 kg – half the level of consumption in Italy.

Innovations in food production

In recent years agricultural technologists have achieved profound changes to increase land yields by biological engineering in one form or another. Developed countries have contributed scientific skills to developing varieties of higher-yielding seed, precision fertilizers, and chemicals for pest control. As well as the 'Green Revolution', as this has become known, progress takes many other forms, such as conditioning the plants and animals of temperate zones to tropical agriculture. Desalination of sea water holds great promise for irrigation, while products unpalatable for human consumption are now being used for the enrichment of foodstuffs or for animal feeds.

There are twelve main categories of innovation in food production:
- high-yielding varieties of certain grains
- developing protein rich plants
- developing animal husbandry in less developed regions
- breeding plants and animals with high inbuilt resistance to pests and diseases
- providing more water
- providing more land
- new methods of getting food from the sea
- cultivation of algae
- producing single-cell protein
- getting food or feed from leaves
- extracting food or feed from wood
- synthetic industrial food production

Innovation in food production is taking an exciting new path in non-agricultural sectors. Fish and other sea foods offer valuable proteins. Their potential contribution to solving the world's food problems is beyond estimate. Fish protein concentrates can be used for either human or animal consumption. Mariculture in shallow waters of certain sea foods represents a major area of new research. The cultivation of algae, rich in proteins, in artificial surroundings to supplement the supply of animal feeding stuffs holds considerable promise.

One of the most dramatic recent developments has been the production of proteins by feeding single-cell organisms either bacteria or yeast on a petroleum base. The waste from various other materials or plants is being used to feed organisms. In the future, the greatest radical innovation is to produce food or feed, without the use of plants. The use of solar or other energy sources will allow amino-acids to be produced on an industrial scale, to be used to fortify foodstuffs. The consequence of the development of food without the use of plants could be enormous, reducing the world's total dependence on agriculture by a factor depending on the degree of scientific progress and scale of commercial exploitation.

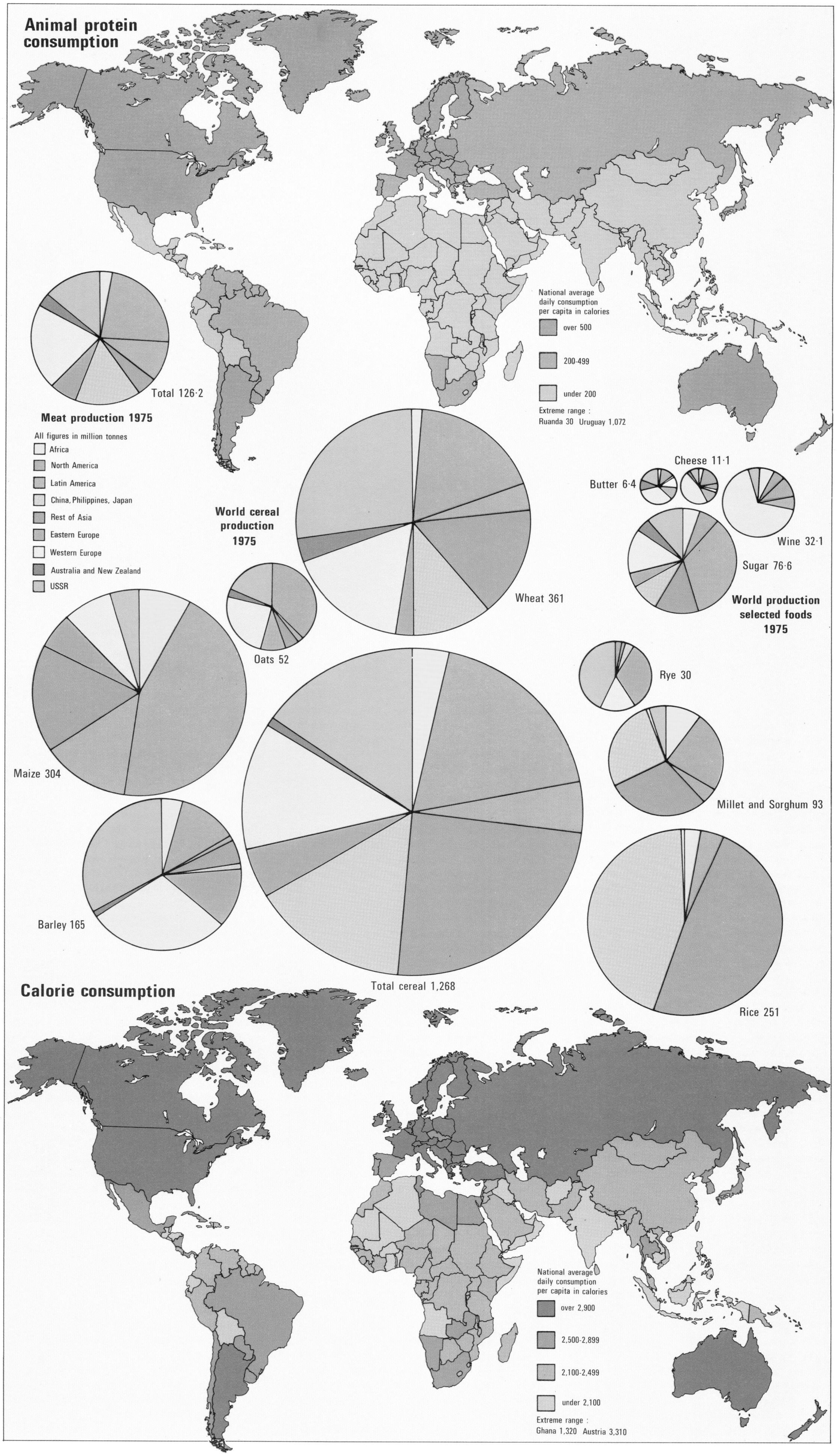

Animal protein consumption

National average daily consumption per capita in calories
- over 500
- 200-499
- under 200

Extreme range : Ruanda 30 Uruguay 1,072

Total 126·2

Meat production 1975

All figures in million tonnes
- Africa
- North America
- Latin America
- China, Philippines, Japan
- Rest of Asia
- Eastern Europe
- Western Europe
- Australia and New Zealand
- USSR

World cereal production 1975

Wheat 361

Oats 52

Maize 304

Barley 165

Total cereal 1,268

Cheese 11·1

Butter 6·4

Wine 32·1

Sugar 76·6

World production selected foods 1975

Rye 30

Millet and Sorghum 93

Rice 251

Calorie consumption

National average daily consumption per capita in calories
- over 2,900
- 2,500-2,899
- 2,100-2,499
- under 2,100

Extreme range : Ghana 1,320 Austria 3,310

Population variations

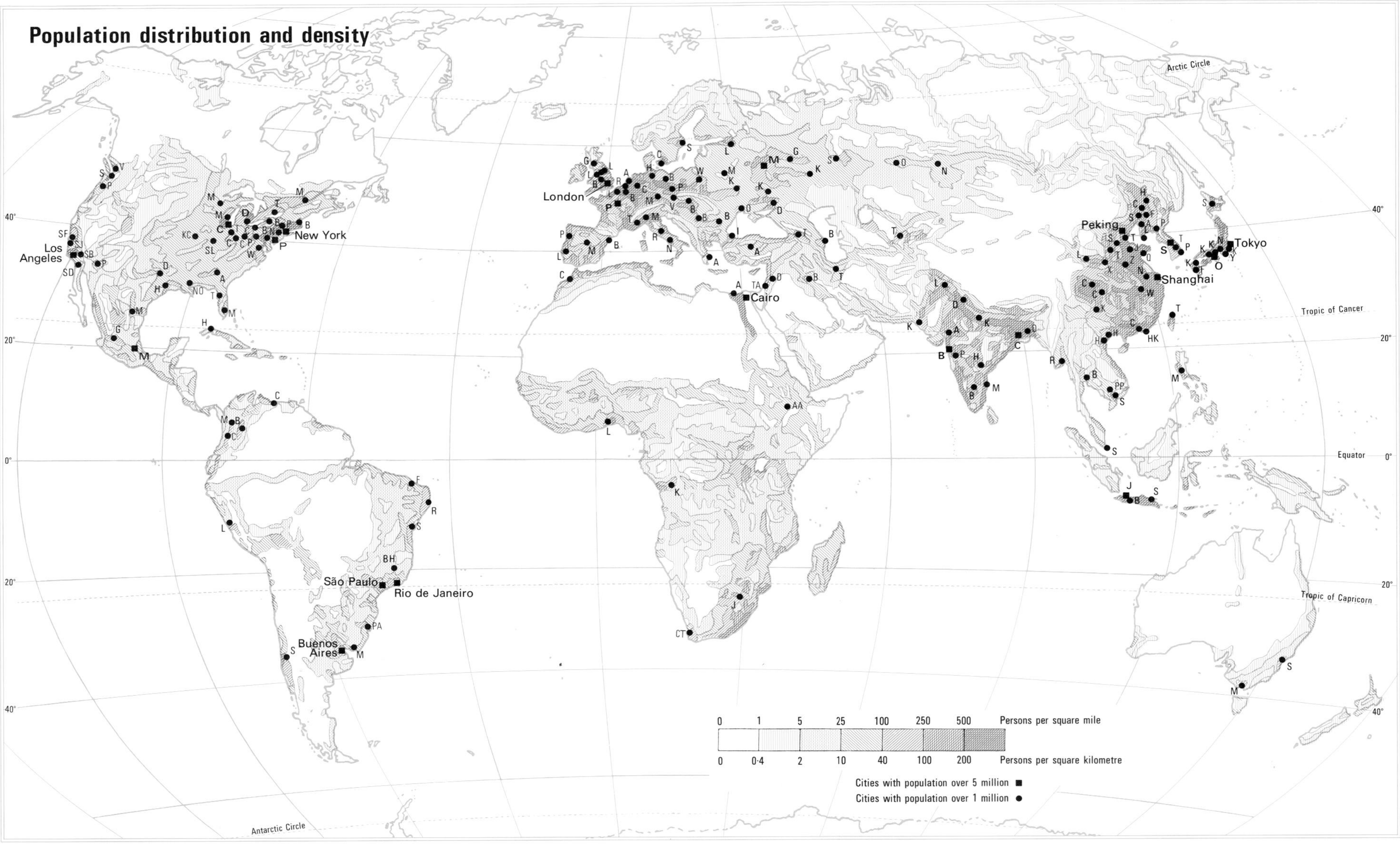

Population distribution and density

In the first 17 centuries AD world population increased by a mere 500 million. Then, largely through reduction in the death-rate rather than increase in fertility, the rate of growth accelerated so that by 1850 a further 500 million had been added, the population then being 1,300 million. A further 400 million was added to this figure in the next 50 years bringing the population in 1900 to 1,700 million.

Between 1930 and the beginning of 1975 the population of the world virtually doubled to about 3,900 million. If the growth rate of the last few decades (1·9%) were to continue there would be over 7,500 million people by AD 2010 representing an increase of 1,100 million in the decade following the end of the century. By 2050 this figure would have risen to 16,000 million and would attain 25,500 million by 2075. At this rate of growth the population doubles every 37 years.

Density and distribution

The mean density of population in 1975 was some 28 per square kilometre (about 73 per square mile). In other words each human being could have 9½ acres (or very nearly 4 hectares) to live on if the population were evenly distributed over all the land surface of the globe. But about 70 per cent of the land is either too cold or too high, too aird or too wet or else infertile and so presents mankind with conditions unfavourable for settlement by more than a very small proportion of even the world's present population. It is no wonder then, that the population is not evenly distributed over the Earth.

To this uneven distribution of population; imposed largely by nature, must be added maldistribution in relation to resources. Much of the land area (one third of the total) that could possibly be cultivated fairly intensively remains virtually unused. Economic efficiency in the actual areas under production varies greatly from one place to another. Less than 10 per cent (13,500,000 square km or 5,200,000 square miles) of the non-polar land surface is occupied by more than 95 per cent of the world's population. Within this proportionately small area, the patterns of distribution and density of population vary very greatly in response to many factors, none of which remains constant in its effect upon mankind save over areas where the pattern of

human culture itself is the same. Thus the map on this page shows a pattern which cannot be interpreted in global terms simply with reference either to the density of population or to the distribution of cities.

Asia

The greatest concentration of people is to be found in monsoon Asia, especially in China, India, Japan and Java. Here, apart from Japan and small localities such as Hong Kong, Singapore, and Shanghai, people are dependent for their livelihood mainly upon agriculture. When the scarcity of cultivable land in monsoon Asia and its huge agricultural population (certainly more than 1,000 million) are taken jointly into account, the distinctive feature of the population distribution over the area is seen to be the prevalence of high rural, agrarian, densities. Farms become small holdings, often of no more than one hectare (two and a half acres) in size; farms larger than ten hectares are very rare indeed, and rural densities of population of 500 per square km (1,300 per square mile) are commonplace. Such densities as these are to be found in, for example, the Ganges plain; the valleys of southern China; much of the Great Plain of China; the Yangtse basin; the rice lands of Honshu, and in Java. Similar rural densities could have developed in the Mississippi lowlands following the discovery of the New World had the Chinese settled there and not the Europeans. Instead it can be seen that neither in North nor South America are extensive Asian-type rural densities to be found. Likewise in Europe agrarian densities are far lower than in monsoon Asia because farms are larger. It should be noted, on the other hand, that agrarian densities in the fertile parts of Europe generally exceed those of similar areas in North America because farm sizes in the mainland of western Europe are small in comparison with those of North America, and are smaller even than those of the United Kingdom.

Europe

The second great concentration of population is to be found in Europe, as is seen from a comparison of maps C and D opposite. Agriculture first led to the dense settlement of population in many areas in Europe but the growth of manufacturing, mining and service industries augmented those densities and led to further concentrations of

people in areas not previously densely settled, e.g. the Ruhr and Lancashire. Unlike monsoon Asia, therefore, western Europe has become densely populated through urban growth and is now predominantly a land of town-dwellers, or town-workers. Nowhere is this fact more plainly visible than in Britain.

N.E. United States

The third great concentration comprises the north-eastern quarter of the USA and the adjacent strip of Canada. The total population of this highly urbanized area slightly exceeds that of Japan and is about equal to that of Indonesia. It is, therefore, much smaller than that of western Europe and is minute in comparison with the concentration in monsoon Asia. Yet this third concentration produces at least as much wealth as Western Europe and considerably more wealth than the whole of monsoon Asia (map E opposite).

In the rest of the world, population density is generally low but there are local pockets of high density in, for example, the Nile Valley of Egypt; California; some coastal areas of South America; central Mexico; parts of western and southern Africa, and in metropolitan Australia. The paramount fact of human geography is, therefore, the emptiness of the Earth. Very little of it is densely populated. Very little of it is overpopulated. Most of it is underpopulated.

Expectation of life

Lack of space may prove less of a problem than how to ensure a more uniform life-expectancy throughout the world. As map B on the opposite page shows, there is a large area including most of Africa, Arabia, Afghanistan, India, Bangladesh, Indo-China and Indonesia where the expectation of life at birth is less than 50 years, whereas in the United States, Canada, Cuba, Jamaica, most of Europe, Japan, and Australasia it is over 70 years. Latin America contrasts sharply with North America, but worst of all is the expectation of less than 40 years indicated for Bangladesh, Madagascar and several other African countries.

These and the other wide variations in life-expectancy illustrated on the map merit more immediate international concern than mere numbers of people or the numerical increase. Although effective measures to reduce the birth rate will contribute to the lowering of the death rate, some

nations with high rate of birth oppose reduction in national birth-rate. As with density of population, problems arising from life-expectancy are not the same the world over; nor can they be solved solely by global strategies; they are regional and local in occurrence and for the most part demand regional and local treatment.

Increase of population

Increase of population is a matter of world concern because of its impact on life-expectancy, the quality of life and local living conditions. The rate of increase (shown on map A above) is highest in parts of Africa and Latin America, and almost tropical and sub-tropical countries have rates greater than the mean (1·9 per cent) for the world as a whole. It should be noted, however, that whereas rates of increase generally diminished a little in a large part of South America during the decade to 1975 the converse is probably true for Africa. Temperate lands of the northern hemisphere show low increases in the period up to 1975 while several, including England and Wales, have more recently recorded small decreases. The trend is towards a numerically static population, the birth rate equating to the death rate.

Rates of change, whether up or down, are less crucial to human well-being and political action than absolute changes represented by the differences between birth-rate and death-rate. China and, even more so, the Indian subcontinent, face the greatest problems of population increase. Their natural resources including availability of land are modest in relation to the total number of people added annually. In India alone, the increase exceeds that in the whole of the Americas. China's population growth is greater than that of Europe and the USSR combined. Mexico's annual increase now exceeds that of the United States and by AD 2000 the population will approach half that of the USA in a land only one-fifth of the area. Indonesia's absolute increase exceeds those of all countries except China and India.

Absolute increase in the population of a given area is caused either by the birth rate exceeding the death rate or by immigration. Large-scale migration occurs where there is disparity between two areas. In the past it was towards areas where agriculture offered better prospects. Today it is towards countries of high technology

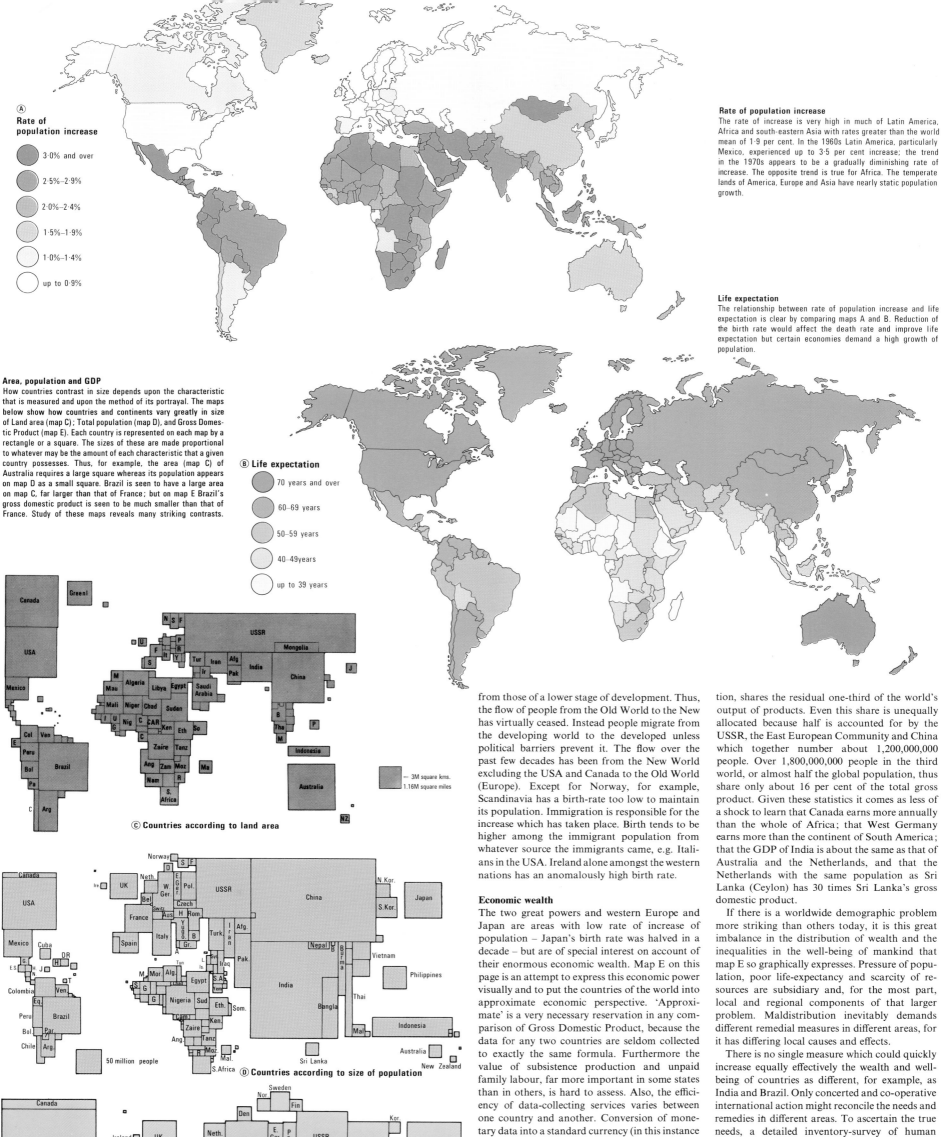

A
Rate of population increase

- 3·0% and over
- 2·5%–2·9%
- 2·0%–2·4%
- 1·5%–1·9%
- 1·0%–1·4%
- up to 0·9%

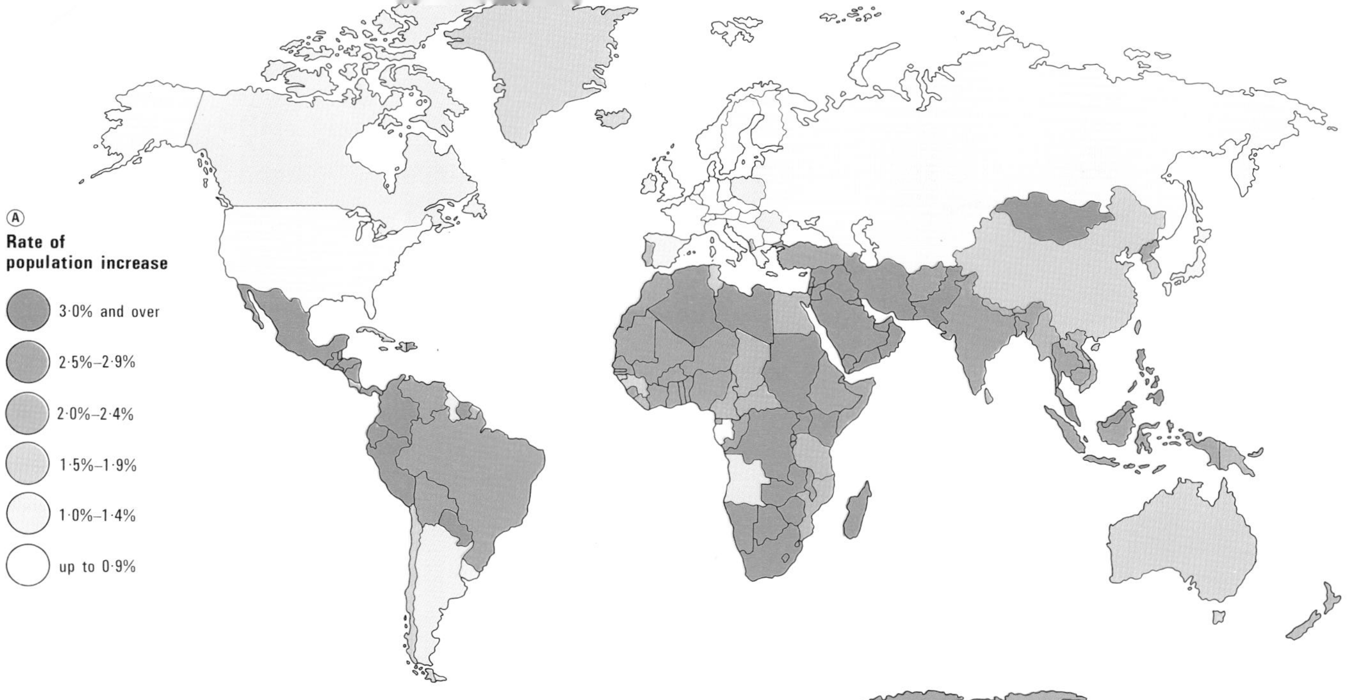

Rate of population increase
The rate of increase is very high in much of Latin America, Africa and south-eastern Asia with rates greater than the world mean of 1·9 per cent. In the 1960s Latin America, particularly Mexico, experienced up to 3·5 per cent increase; the trend in the 1970s appears to be a gradually diminishing rate of increase. The opposite trend is true for Africa. The temperate lands of America, Europe and Asia have nearly static population growth.

Life expectation
The relationship between rate of population increase and life expectation is clear by comparing maps A and B. Reduction of the birth rate would affect the death rate and improve life expectation but certain economies demand a high growth of population.

Area, population and GDP
How countries contrast in size depends upon the characteristic that is measured and upon the method of its portrayal. The maps below show how countries and continents vary greatly in size of Land area (map C); Total population (map D), and Gross Domestic Product (map E). Each country is represented on each map by a rectangle or a square. The sizes of these are made proportional to whatever may be the amount of each characteristic that a given country possesses. Thus, for example, the area (map C) of Australia requires a large square whereas its population appears on map D as a small square. Brazil is seen to have a large area on map C, far larger than that of France; but on map E Brazil's gross domestic product is seen to be much smaller than that of France. Study of these maps reveals many striking contrasts.

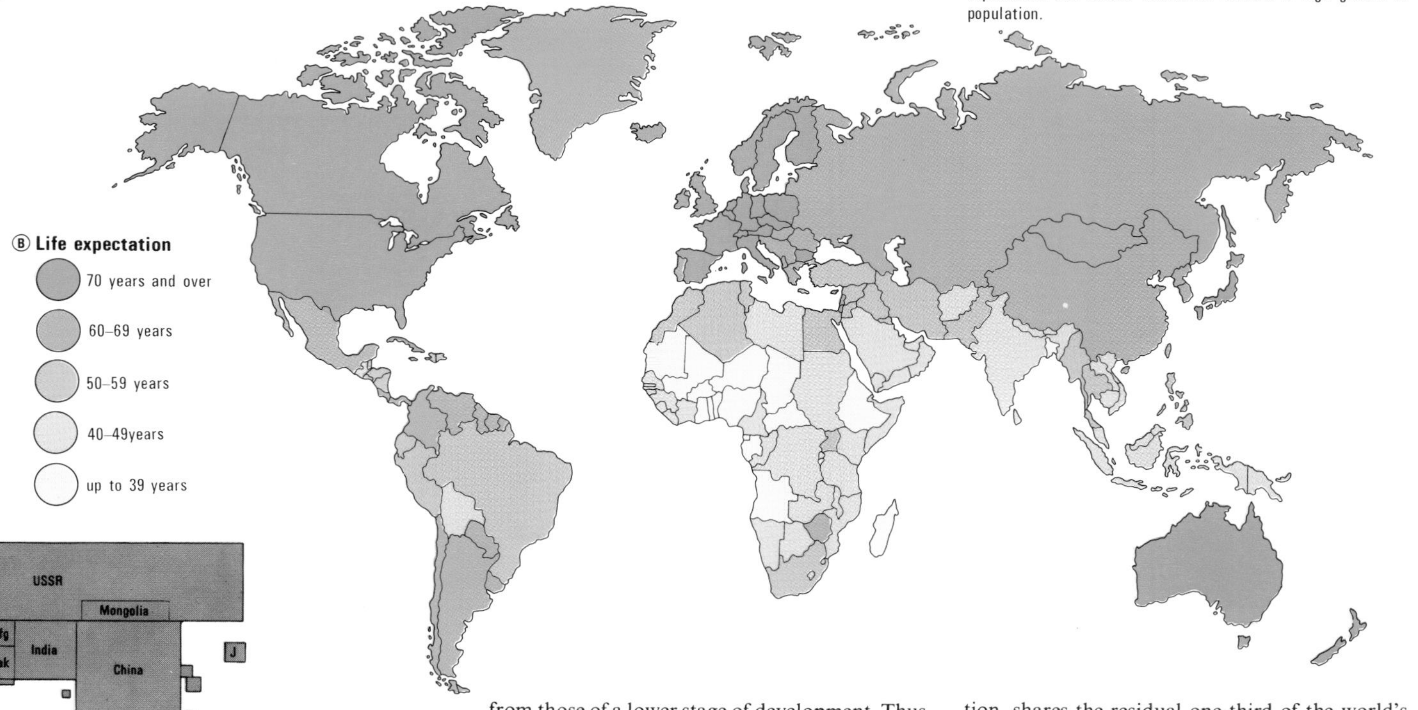

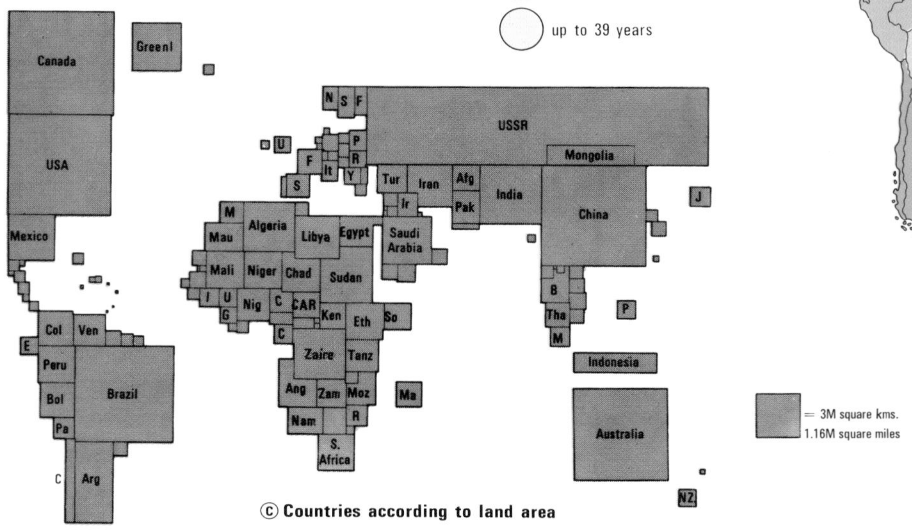

B ● Life expectation
- 70 years and over
- 60–69 years
- 50–59 years
- 40–49 years
- up to 39 years

= 3M square kms.
1.16M square miles

C Countries according to land area

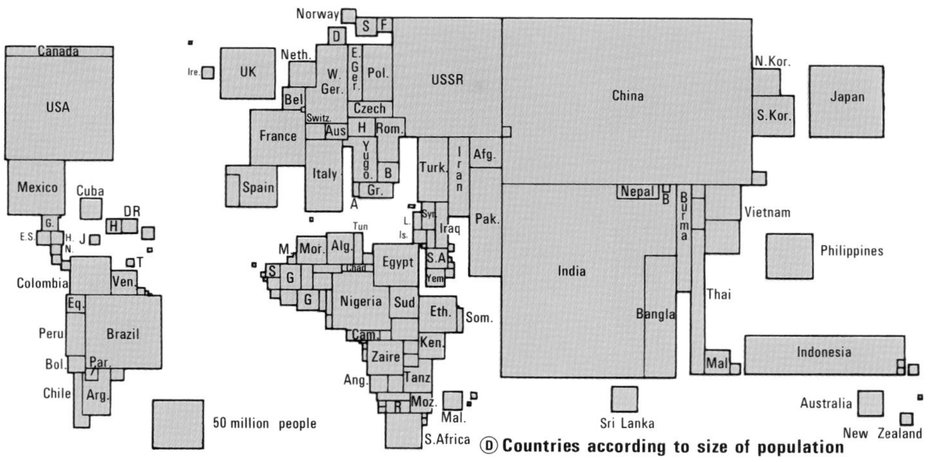

50 million people

D Countries according to size of population

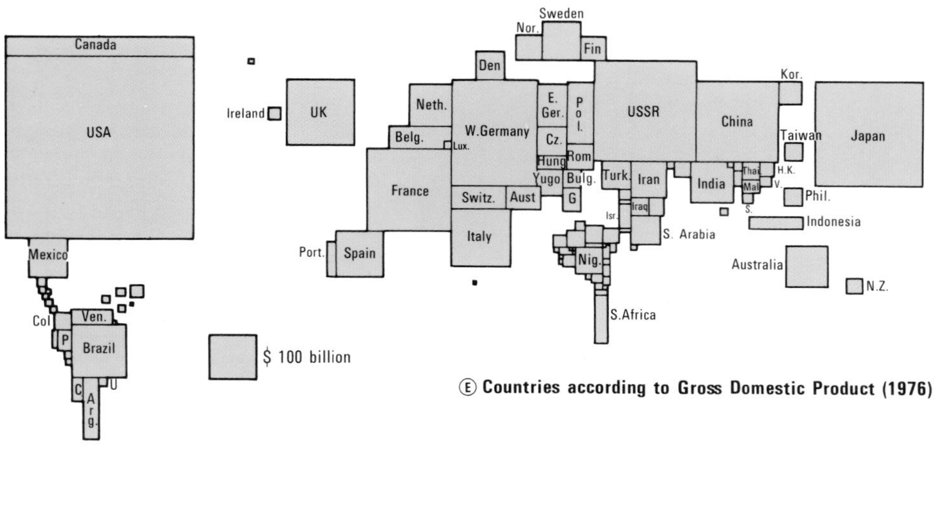

$ 100 billion

E Countries according to Gross Domestic Product (1976)

from those of a lower stage of development. Thus, the flow of people from the Old World to the New has virtually ceased. Instead people migrate from the developing world to the developed unless political barriers prevent it. The flow over the past few decades has been from the New World excluding the USA and Canada to the Old World (Europe). Except for Norway, for example, Scandinavia has a birth-rate too low to maintain its population. Immigration is responsible for the increase which has taken place. Birth tends to be higher among the immigrant population from whatever source the immigrants came, e.g. Italians in the USA. Ireland alone amongst the western nations has an anomalously high birth rate.

Economic wealth
The two great powers and western Europe and Japan are areas with low rate of increase of population – Japan's birth rate was halved in a decade – but are of special interest on account of their enormous economic wealth. Map E on this page is an attempt to express this economic power visually and to put the countries of the world into approximate economic perspective. 'Approximate' is a very necessary reservation in any comparison of Gross Domestic Product, because the data for any two countries are seldom collected to exactly the same formula. Furthermore the value of subsistence production and unpaid family labour, far more important in some states than in others, is hard to assess. Also, the efficiency of data-collecting services varies between one country and another. Conversion of monetary data into a standard currency (in this instance into US dollars) adds a further source of inaccuracy. Nevertheless, map E probably shows the right order of wealth and is so different from normal atlas maps in the size it ascribes to particular countries and continents that it invites examination in some detail.

The outstanding feature is the pre-eminence of North America, with about 40 per cent of the gross global product. Next comes Western Europe with about 25 per cent. These two areas, together with Japan, produces annually at least two-thirds of the world's wealth. The rest of the world, comprising about five-sixths of the total popula-

tion, shares the residual one-third of the world's output of products. Even this share is unequally allocated because half is accounted for by the USSR, the East European Community and China which together number about 1,200,000,000 people. Over 1,800,000,000 people in the third world, or almost half the global population, thus share only about 16 per cent of the total gross product. Given these statistics it comes as less of a shock to learn that Canada earns more annually than the whole of Africa; that West Germany earns more than the continent of South America; that the GDP of India is about the same as that of Australia and the Netherlands, and that the Netherlands with the same population as Sri Lanka (Ceylon) has 30 times Sri Lanka's gross domestic product.

If there is a worldwide demographic problem more striking than others today, it is this great imbalance in the distribution of wealth and the inequalities in the well-being of mankind that map E so graphically expresses. Pressure of population, poor life-expectancy and scarcity of resources are subsidiary and, for the most part, local and regional components of that larger problem. Maldistribution inevitably demands different remedial measures in different areas, for it has differing local causes and effects.

There is no single measure which could quickly increase equally effectively the wealth and well-being of countries as different, for example, as India and Brazil. Only concerted and co-operative international action might reconcile the needs and remedies in different areas. To ascertain the true needs, a detailed inventory-survey of human geography would be necessary, for detailed, objective knowledge of much of the world is still lacking.

Brazil is sparsely peopled, undeveloped and quite capable of absorbing a large number of immigrants provided they were used to develop and exploit the resources of the interior. India is, in contrast, densely populated, intensely but inefficiently developed and quite unsuited to receiving large numbers of immigrants. In Brazil, the key problem is how to organize development; in India, how to undertake redevelopment. Immigration could help Brazil. Emigration would help India.

Patterns of human settlement

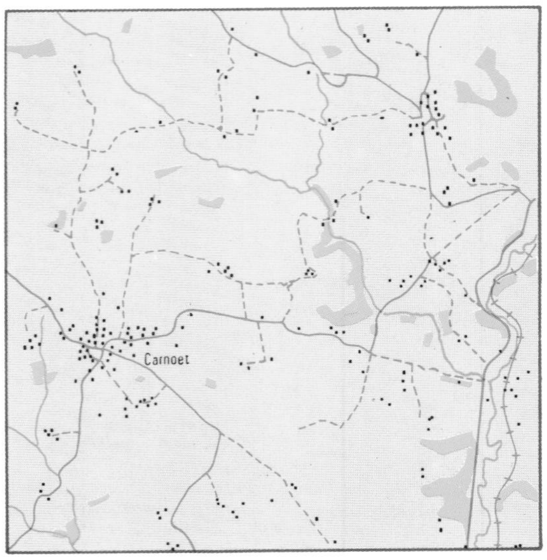

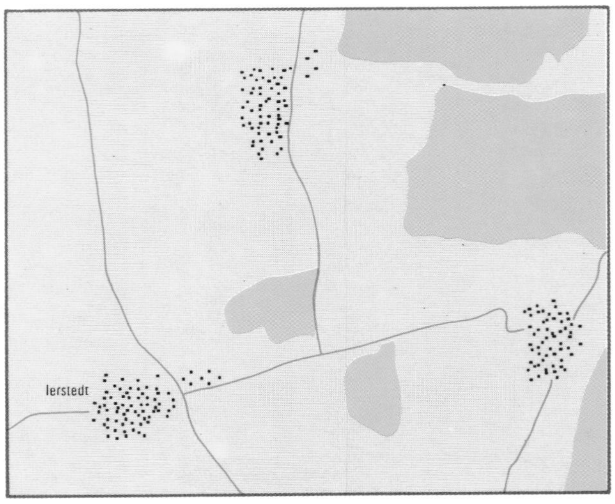

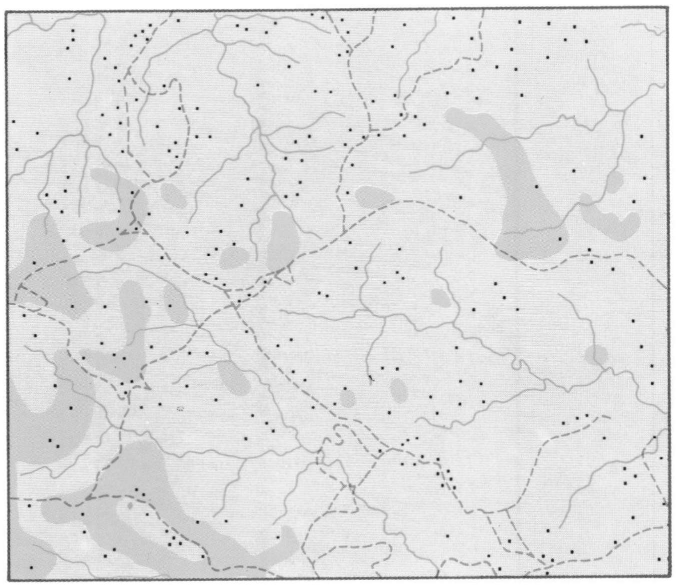

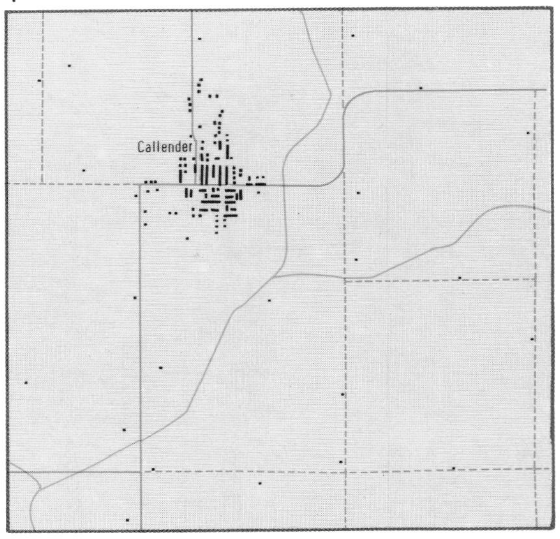

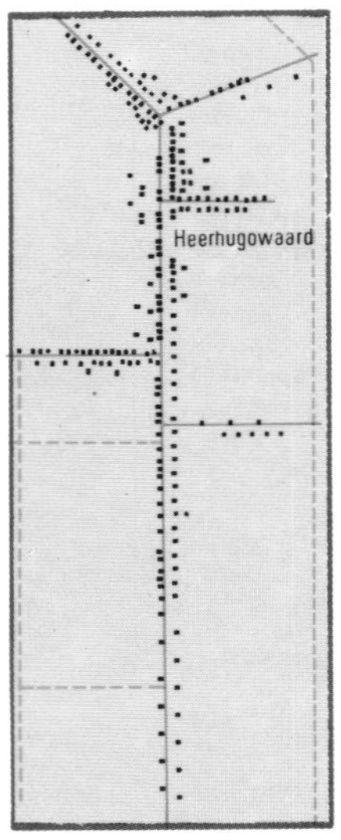

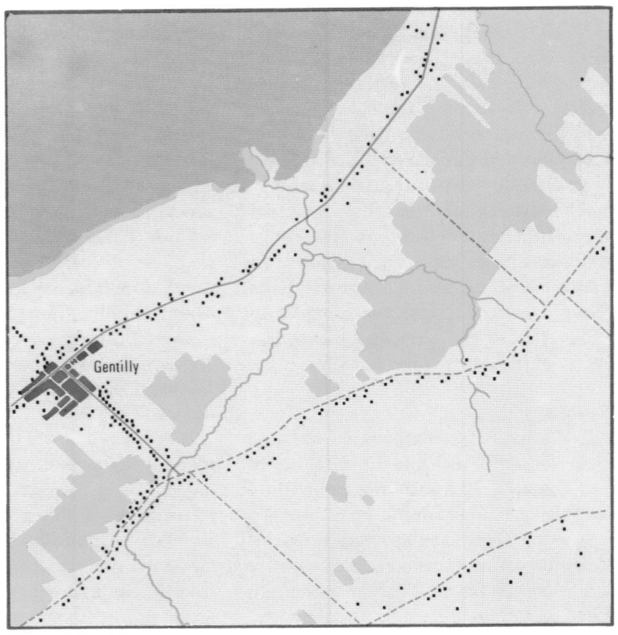

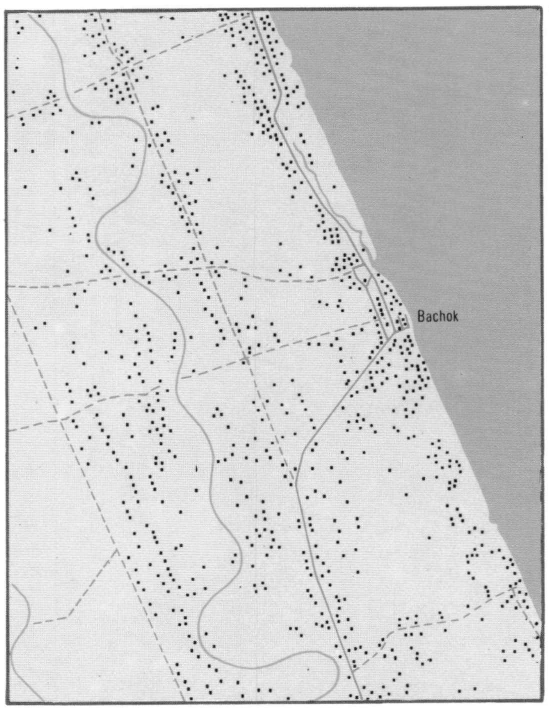

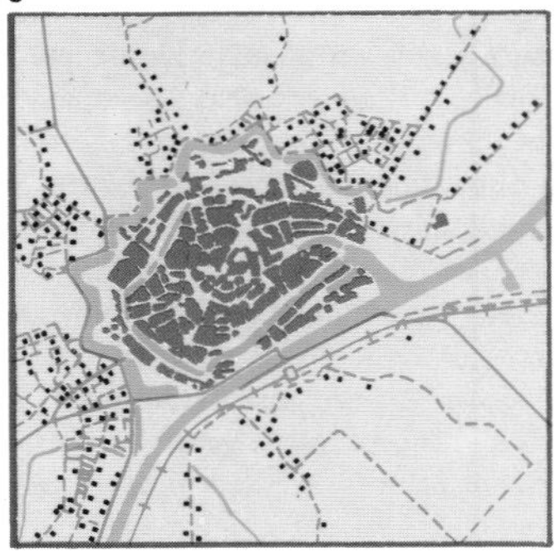

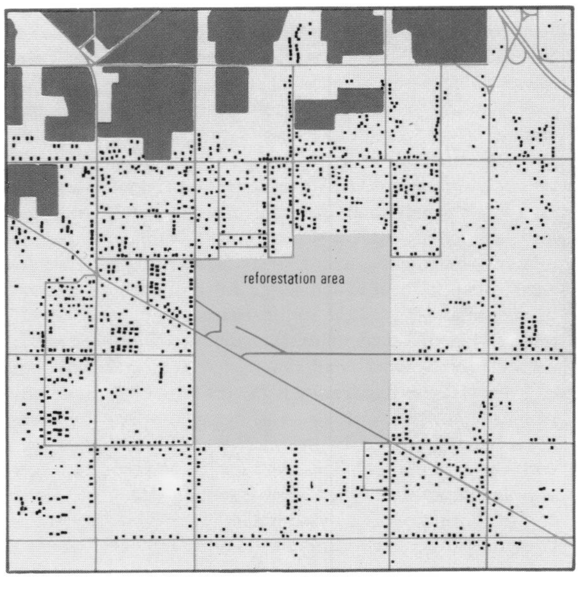

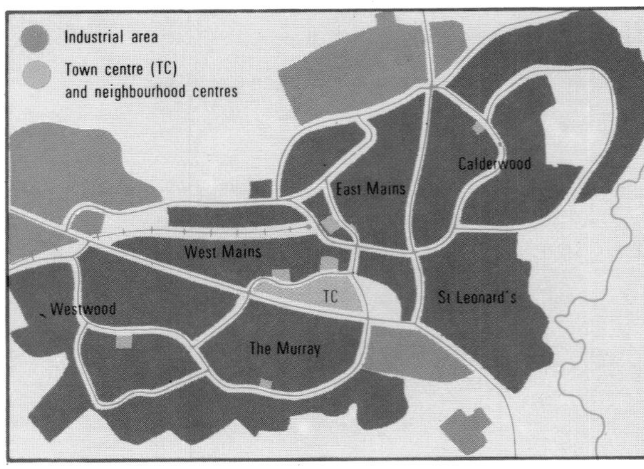

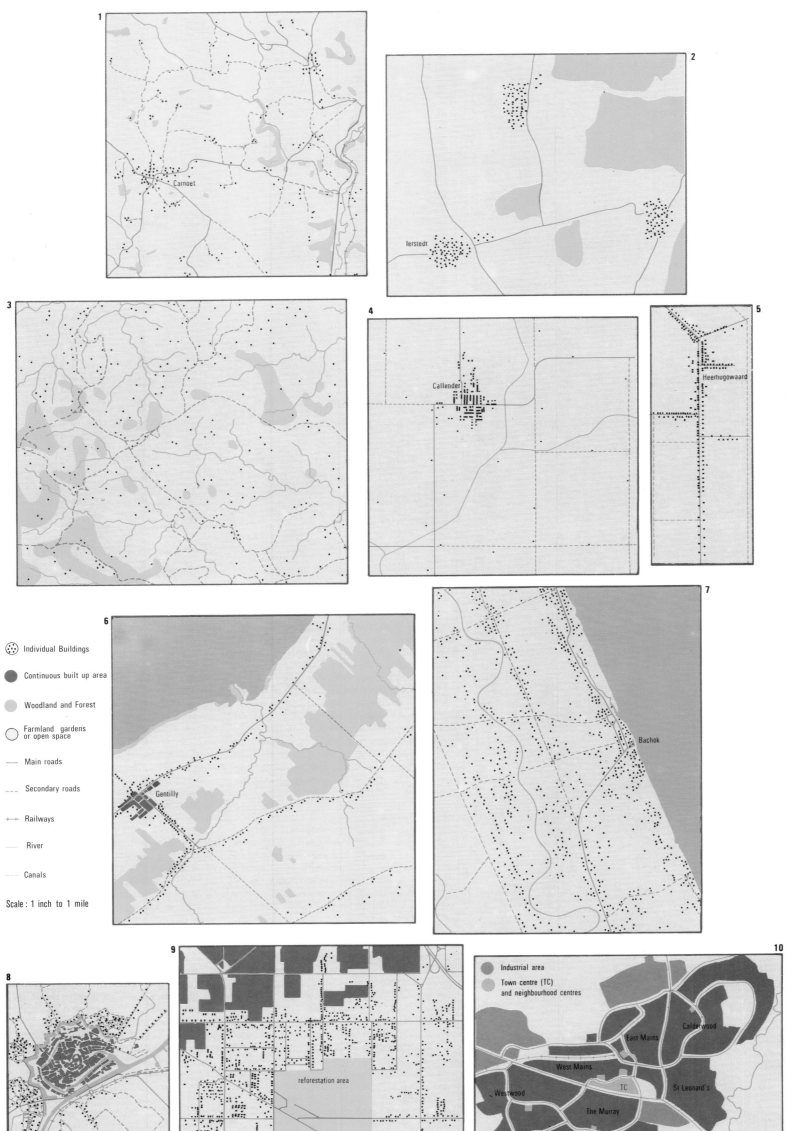

1

Carnoet, France Farmsteads are widely dispersed on compact holdings, with scattered hamlets and small villages containing community facilities like churches, schools and shops. In western Europe such a pattern occurs especially in regions where Celtic traditions survive.

2

Ierstedt, Germany Highly nucleated rural settlement, associated historically with regions of post-Roman Europe settled by Germanic tribes. Even today few farmsteads occur outside the large, rather formless villages, because traditionally farms are composed of separate scattered strips, although land consolidation is now widespread.

3

Kangundo, Kenya Moderately dense pattern of dispersed settlement in a tribal farming economy. Community facilities like markets and schools stand on isolated sites, not having formed, here at least, nuclei around which villages have evolved.

4

Callender, Iowa, USA To dispose of public land to settlers, US government surveys after 1785 created 1-mile square farm units ('sections'), though many have since been subdivided. Dispersed rural settlement thus appeared from the outset, with small nucleated villages at intervals throughout the area. Roads were built along most section boundaries, giving a characteristic checkerboard pattern.

5

Heerhugowaard, Holland Strongly linear rural settlement at high density in a region of intensive farming. Land reclamation confines building to the elevated dikes that line major drainage canals. Villages are large, extending considerable distances along roadsides, but with little opportunity for compact growth.

6

Gentilly, Québec French colonists in North America divided land into narrow plots, initially running back from rivers, with farms close together for safety, and along the river banks for access to water transport. This 'long lot' system later developed to incorporate other rows (ranqs) of farms along roads, often parallel to the rivers. Villages grew up especially around churches.

7

Bachok, Malaya This linear arrangement of houses and villages has been strongly influenced by the existence of parallel sandy beach ridges. These are elevated slightly above the flat intervening tracts that are seasonally flooded for padi (rice) cultivation.

8

Middelburg, Holland Medieval towns in western Europe were small by modern standards and compact. Winding, narrow streets led to a central market square, around which were the town's chief public buildings (town hall, guildhall, the main church – in Middelburg, a 12th century abbey). Walls usually protected the town, but when later demolished, their line is often shown by roughly circular streets. In Middelburg, typical post-medieval fortifications were also constructed with moats and geometrical bastions. Many present-day large cities have such medieval towns as a historic core, but Middelburg has not expanded greatly due to a restricted economic basis.

9

Fort Mann, BC, Canada The characteristic sprawl of the North American 'rural-urban fringe'. Without tight control on development, and often with intense land speculation, sporadic growth of this kind occurs commonly around American cities. Housing appears in small clusters, or along roads, or on scattered individual lots. Non-residential uses develop, especially those needing ample space, e.g. shopping centres, modern factories, motels, drive-in cinemas or schools. Set among all these are recreational open spaces such as golf courses and country clubs. What is left of earlier farmsteads (often in a rundown condition) forms another component in this highly diversified area.

10

East Kilbride, Scotland The British New Towns, all established since 1946, are planned urban communities drawing population chiefly from conurbations (London and Clydeside especially), for which by intention they relieve housing pressures. Local employment is simultaneously created to make each New Town as independent as possible economically and socially. Earlier New Towns are composed of several neighbourhood units around the town centre, each neighbourhood containing facilities for the everyday needs of its residents (primary schools, shops, churches, doctors, meeting halls, etc.). East Kilbride (designated 1947) is an excellent example. Since 1952 somewhat more flexible plans are utilized, but all New Towns have segregated industrial areas and also sophisticated internal circulation systems, emphasising the separation of pedestrians from vehicular traffic.

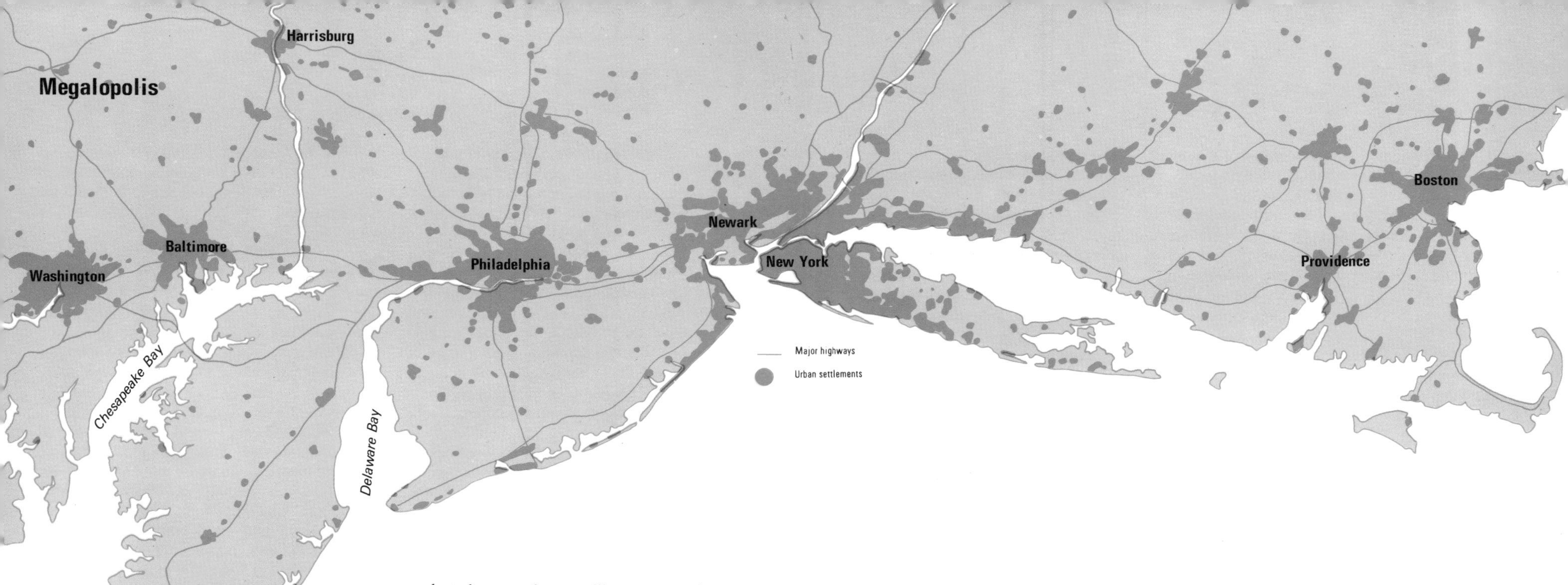

Megalopolis

Harrisburg · Boston · Baltimore · Newark · New York · Providence · Washington · Philadelphia

Chesapeake Bay · Delaware Bay

● ● ● Major highways

● Urban settlements

The distribution of homes and other buildings, constituting the settlement pattern of a region, is affected by a complex interplay of factors.

Rural settlement

Considering rural regions first, there are great differences in the *density* of settlement depending largely upon the carrying capacity of the land in terms of the particular types of agriculture practised, and upon the length of time the region has been settled. The disposition of buildings over the area, or the *form* of settlement, can vary from almost total dispersion to virtually complete clustering, though more often there will be a mixture of scattered farms and small nucleations (i.e. groupings of buildings). Such differences in form stem from variations in, for example, cultural tradition, land ownership systems, types of farming, the technological status of the society or the need for protection from external dangers, either human or environmental. Where an area has been occupied for very considerable periods, there are likely to be changes through time in some or all of these influences and thus the rural settlement pattern itself changes in response: for example, the enclosure movements that led to the consolidation of the earlier strip-field holdings into compact farm units over much of lowland Britain between the 16th and 18th centuries permitted farmers to move their homes from the highly nucleated pre-enclosure villages on to the new compact units, thereby creating the present mixed form of rural settlement that characterizes this region. Thus a *primary*, or original, settlement pattern changes into a *secondary* one.

The rural nucleations, villages and hamlets exhibit a morphology, or layout, which also varies considerably throughout the world. Linear types, e.g. along roadsides or riversides, are extremely common, but so too are compact but irregular groupings, of which the French and German examples are but two types. More regular shapes occur in many regions, e.g. rectangular and roughly circular villages are found in several parts of central and eastern Europe, and a grid plan is normal in Anglo-America.

Urban settlement

The regional or national economy develops and elaborates itself by the expansion of trade and the growth of industry. Both activities require, and create, more sophisticated types of settlement than the village, and towns and cities evolve, supported by an intensifying network of routes. The *degree of urbanisation* in a country is measured by the proportion of its population that live in towns and cities, and this is high (generally well over 60%) in advanced countries.

Urban settlements act as service centres where increasingly specialised activities locate themselves as the towns become larger, and people from usually extensive areas nearby will depend on them to provide goods and services that are unobtainable in smaller settlements, especially the villages. Towns and cities, too, will exhibit their distinctive morphologies, influenced in their case by factors such as the age of the town (for different historical periods tend to have their own characteristic standards and forms of street and building patterns) and by the cultural context in which the town has developed: compare, for example, the medieval and modern sections of European cities, or cities in Europe and India.

Conurbations

During the 19th century in advanced industrial nations, and especially on coalfields with their close grouping of thriving mining and manufacturing towns, continued growth produced the *conurbation*. Economic expansion was accompanied by increase in both population and the built-up areas of the towns, the latter outpacing the former very markedly by the late 1800s. Many urban activities came to require more spacious sites than their earlier counterparts (a trend that has become even more intense during the present century), housing in particular: the increasingly affluent populations in these countries demanded better standards in housing, and the drop in average family size generated an additional component since more homes were now required for a given size of population than when larger families were the rule.

Thus where these expansionist trends occurred in closely neighbouring towns, frequently the built-up areas of each merged with one another, obliterating most of the open spaces which had once separated them. This, then, was the conurbation, dominated by one main city, but composed of many towns, some at least quite sizeable entities in their own right. Generally, however, civic identity is retained for local administration and, especially, for local loyalties among the populace. In Britain, the West Midlands and South Lancashire (see page 11) are examples, and in Germany the Ruhr (see page 35), but all advanced nations contain conurbations.

London

London represents a rather different kind of conurbation, the 'super-city' (other examples being New York, Paris, Tokyo). This results from the surge of growth in one pre-eminent city, overwhelming in its expansion a very large number of villages and small towns which had always been completely overshadowed in size by comparison with the main urban centre.

Up to 1850, as the map shows, London was still reasonably compact, with its chief development on the north bank of the Thames: the paucity of crossing places had hampered development south of the river, away from London's Roman and medieval nucleus (which coincided approximately with the present City of London). Beyond the built-up area in 1850 were small communities which in some cases had already become the homes of wealthy commuters. During the next sixty years, however, growth was extensive.

London's rôle as capital of nation and empire added several millions to its population in this period. But the physical expansion which this necessitated was no longer compact. An intensifying network of railways attracted growth around suburban stations, and the beginnings of the Underground system towards the turn of the century added to these trends. Other forms of surface public transport were also improving, and larger segments of the city's population were becoming able to afford not inconsiderable daily journeys to their work. After 1918 motor buses and cars made travel even easier, many industrial and commercial activities moved to the suburbs from congested inner city locations (generating residential development around their new sites), slum clearance and re-housing programmes created vast new low-density municipal estates at increasing distances from central London, and private housing developments also added great increments to the total built-up area. Meanwhile, dormitory communities were attaching themselves to many outlying towns and villages, before they too became absorbed by the constant progress of urban sprawl. Checks were introduced by the creation of the Green Belt in 1935, by the effects of the Town and Country Planning Acts after the Second World War, and by the establishment of New Towns after 1946, but the conurbation still possesses remarkable economic and social vitality, largely frustrating attempts to constrain it.

Megalopolis

The north-eastern seaboard of the USA, first landfall of most European colonists, became the country's chief centre of economic activity and urbanisation from the outset. Despite subsequent developments elsewhere, this seaboard region between Boston and Washington DC has retained its dominance, to such an extent that though it comprises less than one-twentieth of the area of the USA it contains approximately 42 million people, one in five of the nation's population.

In terms of settlements, it is characterised first by a series of great conurbations, but there is also a dense scatter of other cities of all sizes, as the map shows. What the scale of the map does not allow, however, is to show the smaller communities, quasi-rural in nature, that act essentially as dormitories for the urban centres due to the ease of communication conferred by a complex, highly developed network of roads and, in places, commuter railway services. But the map does indicate that within the boundaries of this region vast tracts of non-urban land occur. Some of these are agricultural, with intensive and prosperous farming, for the most part geared to serving the needs of the region's urban dwellers (especially in milk and fresh vegetables and fruit); but much of the rest of the open land in Megalopolis is devoted to the recreational needs of the region's population, particularly the extensive forested areas of the central and northern Appalachians.

It is the extremely large territorial extent that exhibits such intimate and complicated integration between town and country that led Professor J. Gottmann to identify the whole region as a new and special phenomenon of urbanisation, and to use the word *Megalopolis* to denote it. Yet similar characteristics have by now emerged elsewhere: Chicago – Detroit – Buffalo – Toronto; south-east England – the Midlands – South Lancashire – West Riding of Yorkshire; and Tokyo – Nagoya – Osaka are but three other examples where megalopolitan features are clearly recognisable. The phenomenon cannot fail to multiply, because its essential bases continue to emerge; even planned decentralisation policies will not halt the process, as the dispersion of population and economic activities from major cities and conurbations only relocates them at no great distance away, promoting growth in the smaller urban constituents of a proto-megalopolis or, by creating New Towns, introducing new urban settlements into the open spaces of the region.

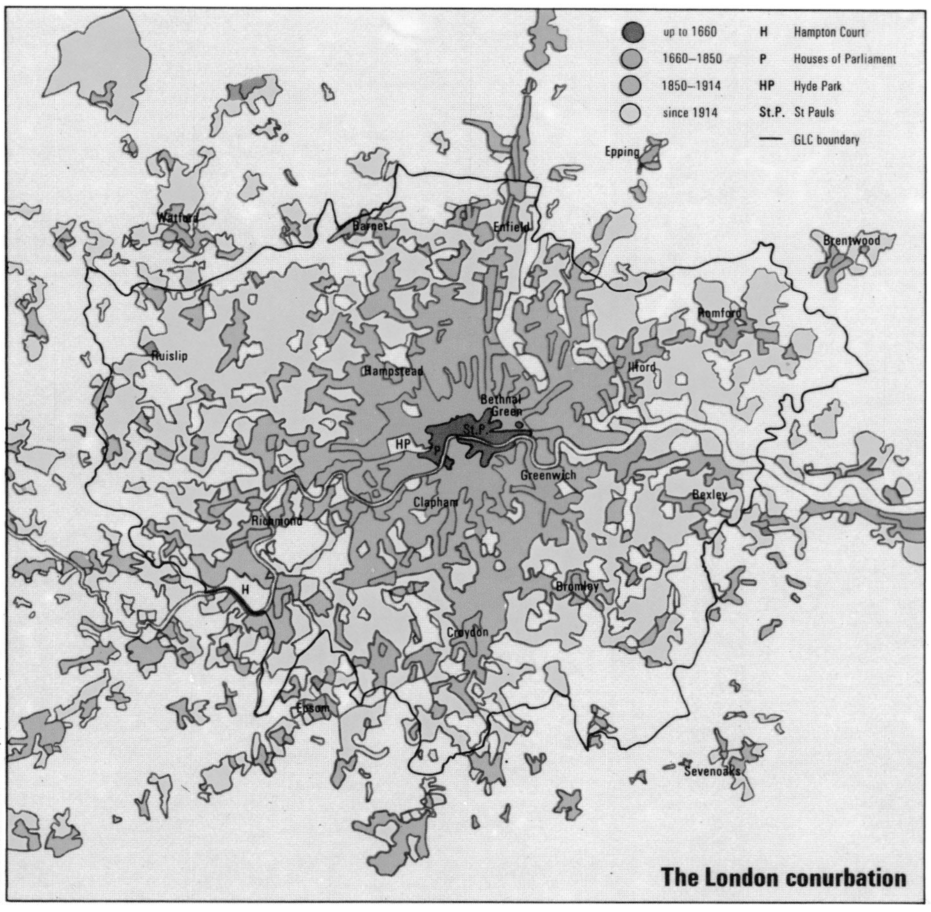

● up to 1660	H Hampton Court
● 1660–1850	P Houses of Parliament
● 1850–1914	HP Hyde Park
● since 1914	St.P. St Pauls
	— GLC boundary

Epping · Watford · Barnet · Enfield · Brentwood · Ruislip · Hampstead · Romford · Ilford · Bethnal Green · St.P · HP · Greenwich · Bexley · Clapham · Richmond · H · Bromley · Croydon · Sevenoaks

based on a map compiled by the Department of the Environment and used with the sanction of the Controller of Her Majesty's Stationery Office

The London conurbation

Fuel and Energy

The relentless increase in the demand of all nations for fuel and power raises important questions about the future security of world energy supplies. Energy consumption accelerates from decade to decade, driven onwards by the world's rising population, the industrialisation of more economies and improvements in living standards.

In the 30 years from 1970 the energy-producing industries will, on conservative estimates, be required to raise their output to four times the total world consumption from the start of the industrial era to the present day. Extra energy resources are almost as vital to world populations as the requirements for food. Indeed, increase in food production calls for increase in energy resources. Maintenance of present rates of economic growth necessitate increased supply of energy.

Energy output

Over the past two decades the increase in world output of energy has reflected both the dominant economic progress of the great industrialised countries and greater utilisation of mineral fuels and electrical power by developing nations.

Using the standard measure of million metric tons of coal equivalent (mtce), total world energy output in 1950 was a little over 2,600 mtce. Coal was the major primary energy source ahead of crude oil and natural gas. All three, supplemented by hydroelectric power, were used to make electricity. By the mid 1970s production had reached over 8,000 mtce and crude oil had taken over from coal as the most important energy source. Nuclear power and tiny amounts of geothermal power had

been introduced into the electricity generating systems. Most expert forecasters now project a global requirement of around 11,000 mtce by 1980 rising to over 20,000 mtce by the year 2000.

Energy consumption

The United States with her massive economic machine, is the largest single consumer of energy, aided by large resources of indigenous fossil fuels and the application of advanced technology to power production. By far the greater part of world energy resources is consumed by North America, the Soviet Union and Western Europe. In more recent years Japan has emerged as a leading consumer, multiplying her requirements six times since 1950 (see map).

Together, these areas account for over 80 per cent of world energy consumption but contain only 25 per cent of world population (see map on page 20). This imbalance, due to the concentration of manufacturing industry has occured over a long period during which the supply of fuel for energy has been relatively abundant.

Energy consumption per capita varies widely from country to country. Increasing industrialisation and application of new techniques to agriculture in the developing countries was, before 1974, beginning to disturb traditional patterns of energy use. However, the rapid increase in oil costs in the mid 1970s had made it difficult for the poorer nations to sustain the use of these new techniques.

Coal, oil, natural gas and water power are not always available in the areas where they are most needed. The result has been that fossil fuels

have had to be transported both within and between continents. This availability of fuel as an export commodity depends on those with indigenous resources – particularly crude oil – selling their surpluses.

Except for short periods of political crisis in the Middle East, supplies of crude oil have always matched or exceeded demand. By the mid-1980s, oil supply from the Middle East and Africa will have reached its peak. Unless the energy-importing nations develop alternative sources of power, an energy crisis with soaring prices could drastically reduce world economic growth.

Nearly all the large industrial countries are dependent on imported oil. The United States which was self-sufficient in the 1950s, imports half of its oil requirements. Higher energy costs make it economically feasible to explore for oil in the deep oceans and the polar regions and to develop the more expensive alternatives such as solar power, tidal and wind power and to consider the extraction of the oil locked in shale rocks and tar sands. The discovery of new sources of oil and the development of alternative forms of energy will not alone be enough to meet energy requirements. Nuclear power and coal are the only sources of energy which can serve as an alternative to oil in the 1980s should supply fall short of world demand.

Oil

The organic remains of the earliest plant, marine and animal life that existed between 400 million and 40 million years ago are the sources of the crude oil deposits now tapped by man to meet

over 40 per cent of the world's total energy requirements. Early civilisations made use of bitumen and lubricants, but it was not until the middle of the 19th century that the first oil wells were drilled.

Total world production of crude oil and natural gas liquids in 1976 amounted to 2,936 million tonnes, the equivalent of 59,555,000 barrels a day. The map of oil supply shows that the western hemisphere accounts for 26·3 per cent of total output compared with 73·7 per cent for the eastern hemisphere (including the 21 per cent share accounted for by the Soviet Union, Eastern Europe and China).

The Middle East, North America, Africa and the Soviet Union are the major producing regions. In recent years, a succession of discoveries has begun to widen the basis of supply. The newer sources of oil include Arctic Alaska, the polar regions, the northern part of the North Sea, the Spanish sector of the Mediterranean, Ecuador, Mexico, Australia, Indonesia, Turkey and parts of South America.

The present estimate of proven reserves is 90,066 million tonnes. The ratio between these reserves and annual production is falling as the rate of discovery of new oil reservoirs around the world slows down. Of the proven quantity, 56 per cent is in the Middle East, nearly 9 per cent in Africa, over 16 per cent in the USSR, Eastern Europe and China, and 6 per cent in North America. Western Europe, because of the oil discoveries in the North Sea, now has nearly 4 per cent of the total. The geographic balance of the proven reserves is 12 per cent for the western hemisphere and 88 per cent for the eastern.

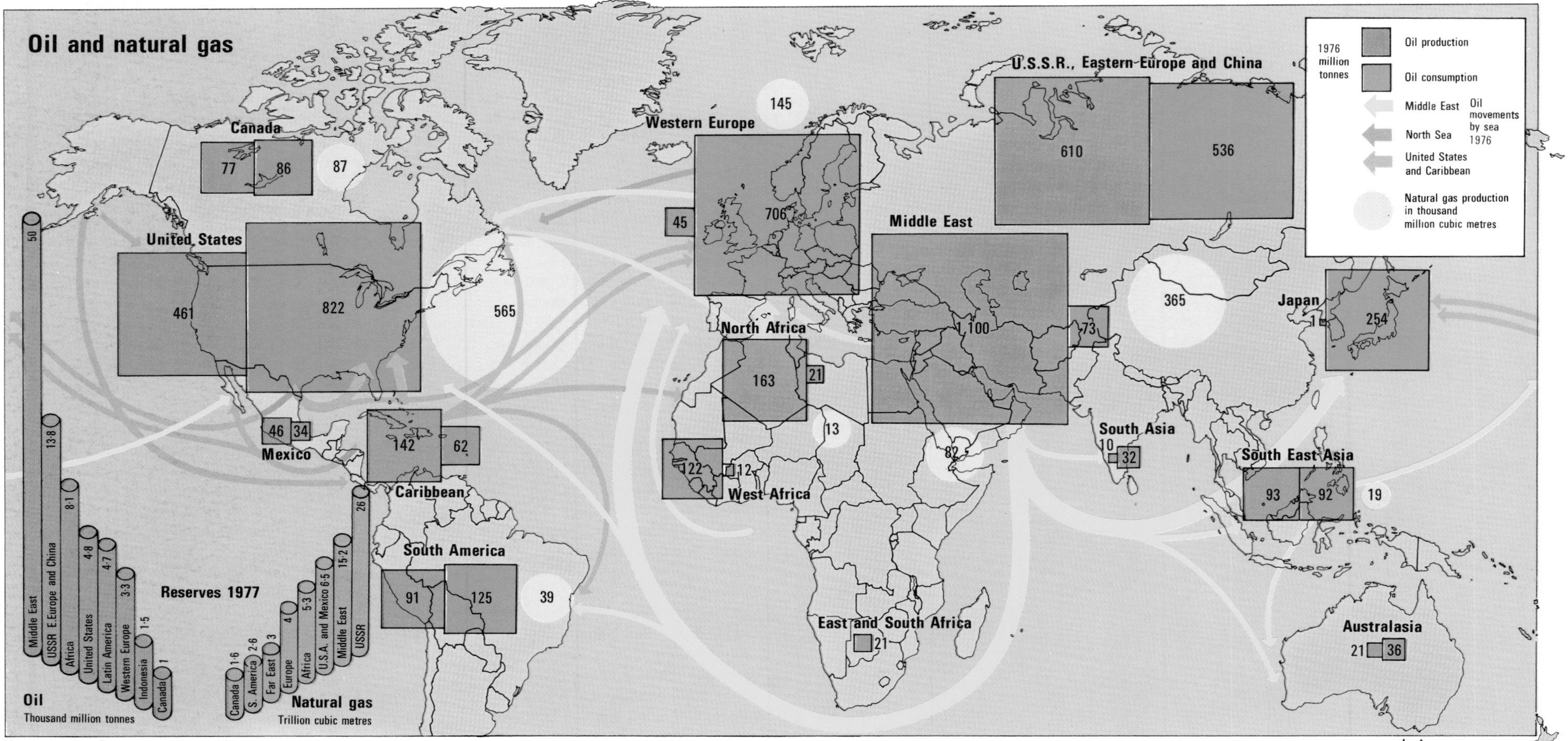

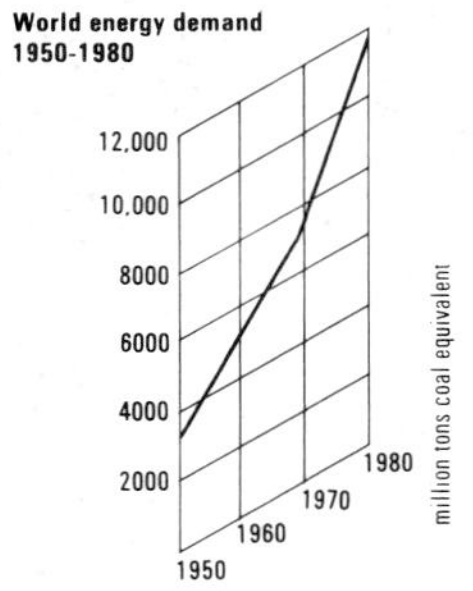

World energy demand 1950-1980

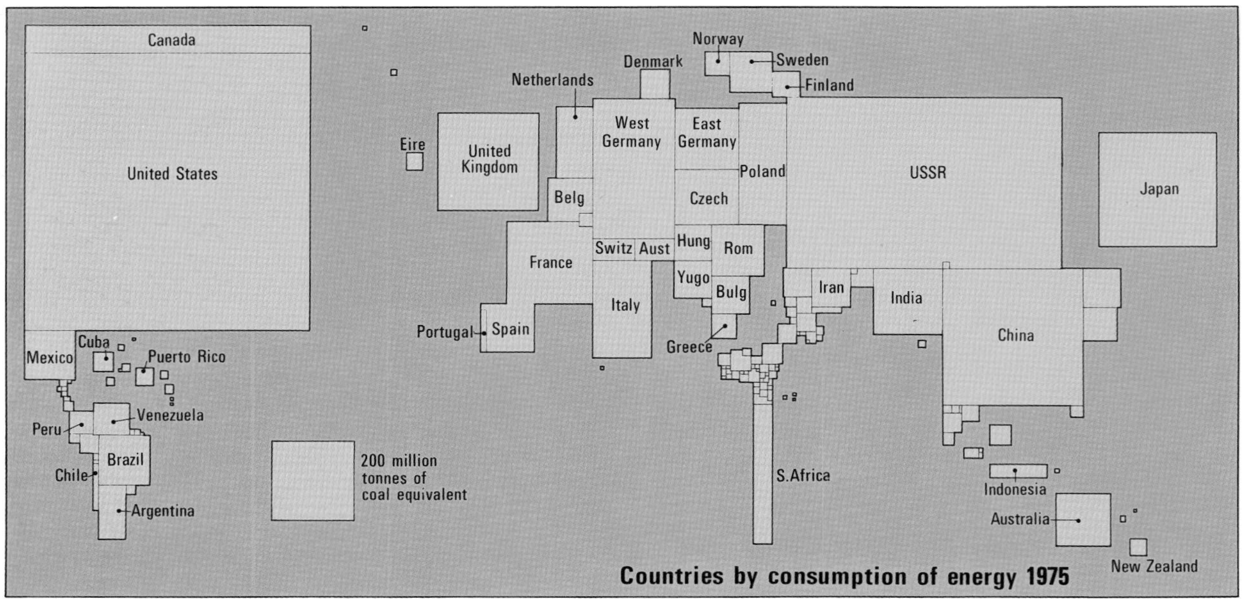

Countries by consumption of energy 1975

Energy consumption

Expressed in the standard measure of tonnes of coal equivalent, the world's demand for primary energy has attained a level of at least 7,000 million tce.

On current trends, projected future growth indicates a need for 11,000 million tce by the end of the present decade. All forms of energy will be required to make a high contribution, though oil is expected to remain the leading source. As the map illustrating the importance of oil to the world economy shows, annual consumption has reached over 2,936 million tonnes, and output more than 2,994 million tonnes; the balance represents stocks. This requires large-scale movements of crude oil and oil products between continents by sea and by pipeline.

More than $550,000 million will be required by the world oil industry in the coming decade to pay for exploration and development. The search for new sources ranges from the Arctic to the Yellow Sea, South China Sea and from north Africa to offshore south America. The emergence of economic nationalism in the Middle East, and the use of the price of oil as a political weapon that has disturbed traditional marketing, has coincided with the transformation of the United States from the status of oil exporter to oil importer. As unlimited oil imports into the 1980s cannot be assured, the United States is trying to reduce its imports from 9 million barrels a day in 1977 to 6 million a day in 1985, by stimulating domestic production and converting from oil to coal in many power stations. Without these measures imports of over 12 million barrels a day would be required in the 1980s to meet a demand of about 20 million barrels a day. In Western Europe demand could also double over the same period to a similar amount and Japanese oil requirements could increase from under 4 million barrels a day to over 10 million barrels a day.

Coal

World output of coal amounts to over 2,200 million tonnes a year. The leading industrialised countries of Western Europe produce over 300 million tonnes a year - equivalent to the total power station requirements of the United States where coal production totals about 550 million tonnes a year. Production of lignite, is nearly 867,000 tonnes a year. The main producers are

East and West Germany and the USSR.

Coal is the fuel on which the industrial base of Europe and America was built. Cheap oil supplies in the 1950s and 1960s brought a sharp decline in production particularly in the older mining areas of Europe and North America. The prospect of a shortfall in oil supplies, coupled with difficulties in the development of nuclear power has brought new life to the coal industry. Fresh reserves are being developed in the United States and Europe. There are massive reserves of coal in the Soviet Union, North America and China.

These coal reserves are extremely large and sufficient to sustain international needs for at least 250 years on present projections of productive activity. Known economic reserves amount to one million million tonnes of which about 430,000 million tonnes could be mined under the prices and technology that are likely to exist in the 1970s and 1980s. Rates of extraction could be stepped up by improvements in mining techniques.

Only deposits that have been drilled and sampled are included in known reserves. Estimates do not include coal possibly existing in areas geologically favourable for the presence of coal. Ultimate global coal reserves probably exceed eight million million tonnes.

Natural gas

Natural gas, of which methane is the main constituent, is a highly efficient fuel now making an increasing contribution to energy resources. It produces twice the heat of town gas, is generally free of sulphur, and offers clean combustion.

Natural gas was first used in the United States

in centres of population close to the gas fields. In Europe most gas was manufactured from coal. The change-over to natural gas came in the 1950s and 1960s with the discovery of reserves in France, Italy and in Holland. Britain is supplied from fields off the coast of East Anglia and from reserves in the northern part of the North Sea.

For decades large quantities of gas produced in association with oil was burned off because there was no way of moving it to the industrial centres. Development of long distance pipelining techniques and the movement of gas in liquefied form has opened up a small world trade in gas.

At the end of 1976 it was estimated that natural gas reserves round the world amounted to 2,325 million million cubic feet, with heavy concentrations in North America, the USSR and Asia.

Nuclear power

High hopes have been placed in the development of nuclear energy to provide the world with a new source of cheap and abundant power. Problems associated with the initial heavy costs of proving the first nuclear power stations against stiff competition from coal and oil have been overcome. Development is now being checked by opposition from environmentalists concerned at the safety aspects of reactors and the possibility that wider sales of nuclear power stations and their associated fuel enrichment and reprocessing facilities could lead to the proliferation of nuclear weapons.

Opposition is strongest in the United States and is reflected in the long delays in obtaining the necessary Government permits for new reactors. In 1977 there were 66 reactors operating in

the USA with a capacity of 41,544 megawatts (9·4 per cent of total capacity). There are a further 142 reactors either under construction or planned.

France has one of the most ambitious nuclear power programmes. It plans to augment its network of 11 reactors producing 9 per cent of the nation's electricity, with 26 new reactors to produce over 70 per cent by 1985.

Development of nuclear power requires new techniques of production and control and fresh supplies of uranium. In non-Communist bloc countries, annual demand for uranium could reach 53,500 tonnes by 1980, roughly in line with production facilities. Reserves are two million tonnes reasonably capable of being recovered on present estimates of prices and demand.

Hydro-Electricity

The building of great dams, tidal barriers and other forms of man-made controls over sea and fresh waters have assisted in the slow but steady development of hydro-electrical generation. Areas well endowed with water resources have already benefited from one of the cheapest sources of power but opportunities for new hydro-electrical projects are limited.

The world's hydro-electricity represents one quarter of total electrical energy supplied - nearly twice as much as output from nuclear power stations. The big producers are North America and the Soviet Union, but within Europe hydro-electric stations are a major source of electricity. Scandinavia and Switzerland have the most highly developed water-power resources, followed by Italy and France.

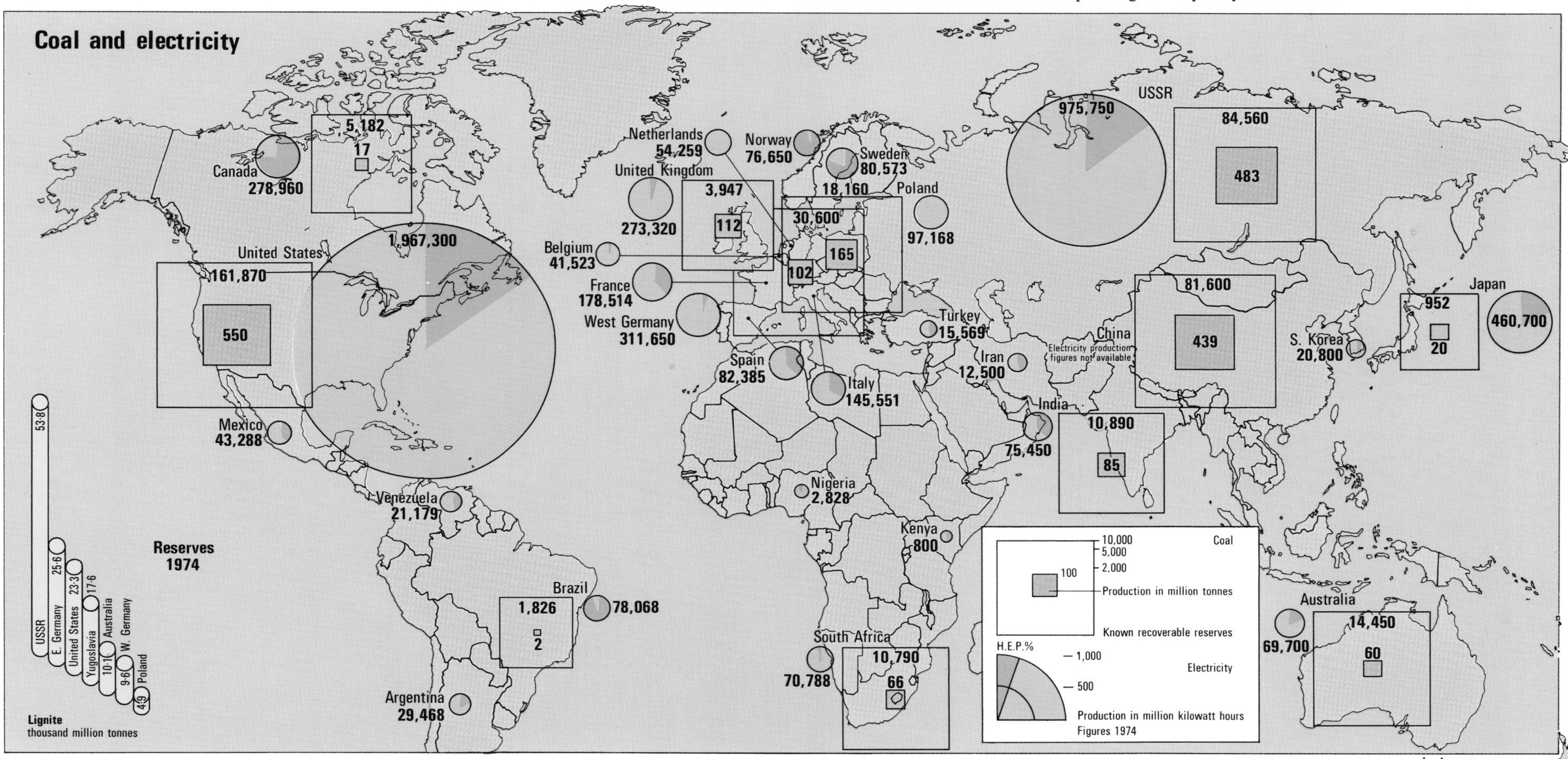

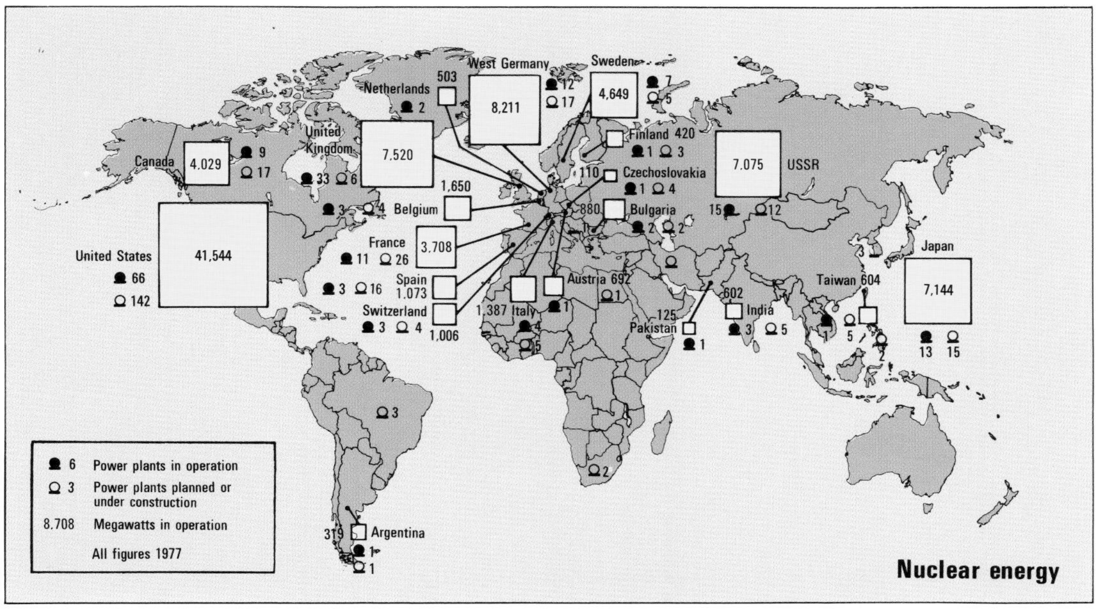

Nuclear energy

Nuclear energy

In 1977 there were 192 nuclear reactors in operation in 21 countries throughout the world with a capacity of 93,261 megawatts. A further seven countries have plans to become nuclear power producers. A total of 306 new reactors are either under construction or planned.

The quest for new forms of energy has also re-awakened interest in using geothermal power – hot steam from great depths below the earth's surface – to produce electricity. Italy leads the world in this field and has geothermal power stations with a capacity of 2,503 megawatts. There are also geothermal developments in the United States, Mexico, Japan and Iceland.

New needs, new sources

Great emphasis is now being placed on development of alternative sources of energy such as solar power, wind power and harnessing the energy contained in the tides. Although cheap to operate, the cost of developing efficient renewable energy systems is high and these sources are unlikely to make a significant contribution until the beginning of the next century.

Scientists are also working on prototype nuclear reactors that 'breed' more nuclear fuel than they consume, which would extend the life of world uranium reserves. Research is under way into the production of oil from coal, shale rocks and heavy tar sands, and into more effective and cleaner ways of burning coal in industry and in power stations. Even further into the future, scientists are working on ways to release energy from the hydrogen in sea water by the process of nuclear fusion. There is also a method of collecting solar energy by artificial satellite and transmitting it to Earth in the form of micro-waves.

Manufacturing industry

The wealth and economic influence of the world's richest nation, the United States of America, is derived from her factories and process plant. Although Europe has been the cradle of the industrial revolution, the New World has produced fresh concepts of manufacturing and the organisation of labour, establishing a chain of production and supply to which all advancing nations aspire, to raise their standards of material well-being. Whole new technologies have resulted from the constant application of the sciences to manufacturing. The consequence has been a worldwide urge to extract more materials to feed by mining or cultivation the industrial machines of all nations seeking to generate the economic wealth required to sustain their populations.

In the 20th century the determinants of economic power have been transformed. This transformation has been greatly affected by two world wars and periodic economic recessions. In the past few decades the rapid expansion in demand for material welfare and economic prosperity have brought an increase in world output of primary and secondary products to levels that have changed the living standards of whole populations. Wherever and however far back the roots of manufacturing, the fastest growth of production has taken place since the mid-fifties as nations embraced more productive concepts, selling their goods to each other and often specialising according to their indigenous skills or resources.

Manufacturing areas
The geographic concentration of world manufacturing power is well illustrated by the selected maps, which include crude steel production and motor vehicle engineering. The most striking development has been a significant shift of manufacturing power towards the Far East, related to the growth of industry in Japan and south-east Asia as well as the industrialisation of mainland China. However, this trend towards a wider distribution of industry has yet to show itself in Africa, the Middle East and to most of South America, areas which largely remain, in industrial terms, that of suppliers of raw materials and food.

Other important features reflected by the maps and in the closely related sections on world trade and energy supply are the re-emergence of Western Europe in the second half of this century, challenging the dominance of North America in global industry, and the establishment of the Soviet Union as a major industrialised nation. In steel manufacture, the Soviet Union and Japan have become main producers, though the former has yet to develop a substantial motor industry.

Textiles, electrical assembly, steel manufacturing, shipbuilding, and car production are now firmly established in the Far East, where output of certain goods has assumed dimensions of world importance in terms both of volume and commercial competitiveness.

Manufacturing growth
The most spectacular growth of production has taken place since the start of the 1960s, for by 1970 manufacturing output on a world basis had expanded by over 50 per cent, that for extractive industries by over 40 per cent, and these are to be compared with around 20 per cent for agricultural production.

Powering this industrial advance have been the factories and plant of North America, Western Europe and Japan. The installations grouped within the western trading nations have consequently lifted the gross domestic product by an average of nearly 5 per cent a year between 1960 and 1970.

The Western Nations, along with the Soviet Union, have made the major contribution to the world's increasing manufacturing capacity. That capacity, as reflected by actual output between 1960 and 1970, shows the following percentage rises in volume terms: light manufacturing 43 per cent; heavy manufacturing 58 per cent; food and drink 48 per cent; textiles 44 per cent; clothing and footwear 27 per cent; furniture and timber products 30 per cent; paper and printing 30 per cent; chemicals and fuel 95 per cent; basic metals 70 per cent; metal products 81 per cent.

Material possessions are greatest in the most industrialised nations. Using the measure of 1,000 inhabitants (taking no account of family groupings), there are over 523 telephones for this unit of population in the United States, 408 in Canada, and well over 200 in Japan and the United Kingdom, whereas Portugal has around 70 and Turkey only 12. With the same unit, there are around 400 television sets for the United States, over 260 for the United Kingdom, 200 in Japan and about 300 in Sweden, which enjoys one of the highest material standards of living.

The motor industry
The desire to own cars and replace them with new models has created one of the greatest and most economically important industries in the world, consuming vast quantities of steel and other materials and providing the backbone to satellite engineering industries. World car output is now over 25 million units with North America's huge assembly lines producing nearly a quarter and Western Europe and Japan much of the remainder. Assembly plants using imported vehicle components have sprung up in the developing world where demand has yet to be matched by the personal affluence needed to attain widespread ownership.

The significance of the motor manufacturing industry is reflected in the fact that many of the production companies have become the biggest corporations in the world. The second largest, General Motors of America, commands sales of over 35 billion dollars per year and has assets worth $21 billion. The largest of all is an oil and petroleum refining group, the Exxon Corporation whose supplies of oil to manufacturing industry are as important as the petrol needed to power car engines. United States motorists buy over 8 million new cars each year attracting imports from Western Europe and Japan, which has now built itself into the second largest manufacturer in the world, and the largest exporter. Overseas sales by Japanese manufacturers in 1974 totalled 1·8 million vehicles worth $3·5 billion. Japan now dominates the market for the small and medium car in most developing countries and has begun to make similar inroads into the European markets. Japanese dominance of the motor cycle industry is even more pronounced and in some European countries domestic producers have gone out of business in the face of Japanese imports.

In addition to passenger cars, commercial vehicles of all kinds from giant railer trucks and earth-moving equipment to farm tractors and delivery vans are produced in growing quantities. Annually the United States alone makes over 6,700,000 passenger cars and over two million vehicles other than cars. In Western Europe, France was the largest producer of passenger cars in 1975 with 2,951,000 units.

Steel
Like motor manufacturing, steel is an industry that is largely confined to the developed countries of the world. Three countries, the USA, the USSR and Japan, account for over half world production which in 1976 topped 661 million tonnes. Most European countries have steel industries. In Japan the growth of the steel industry

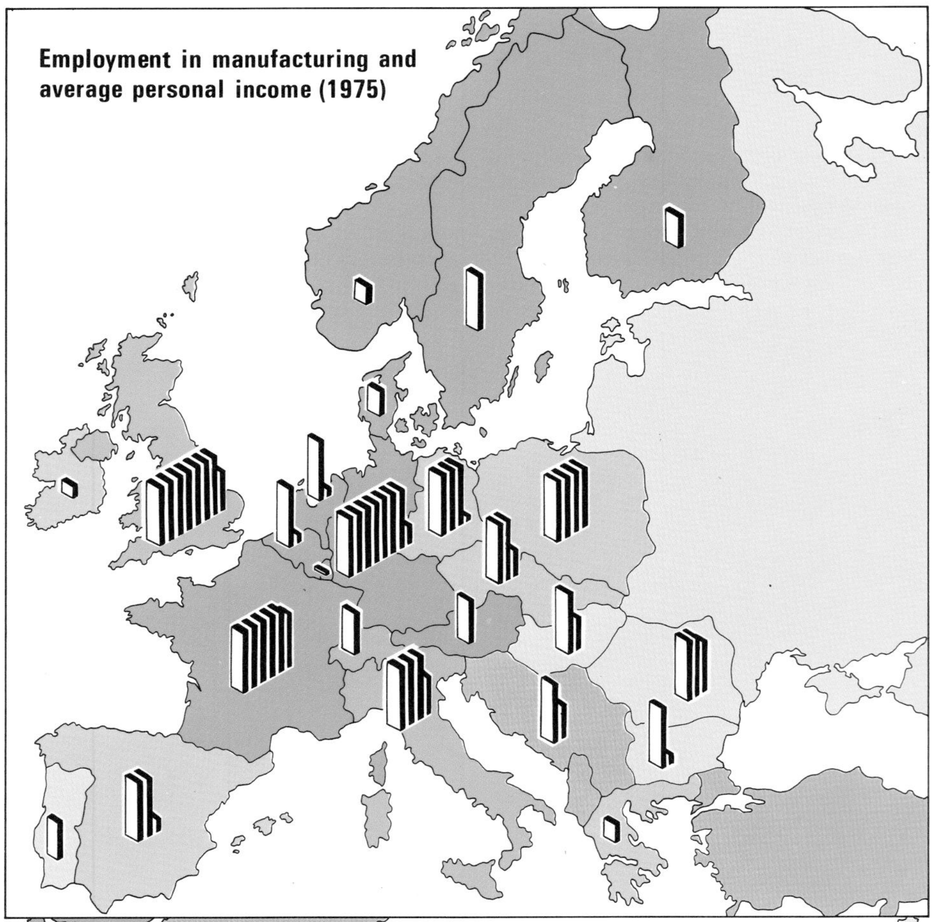

Employment in manufacturing and average personal income (1975)

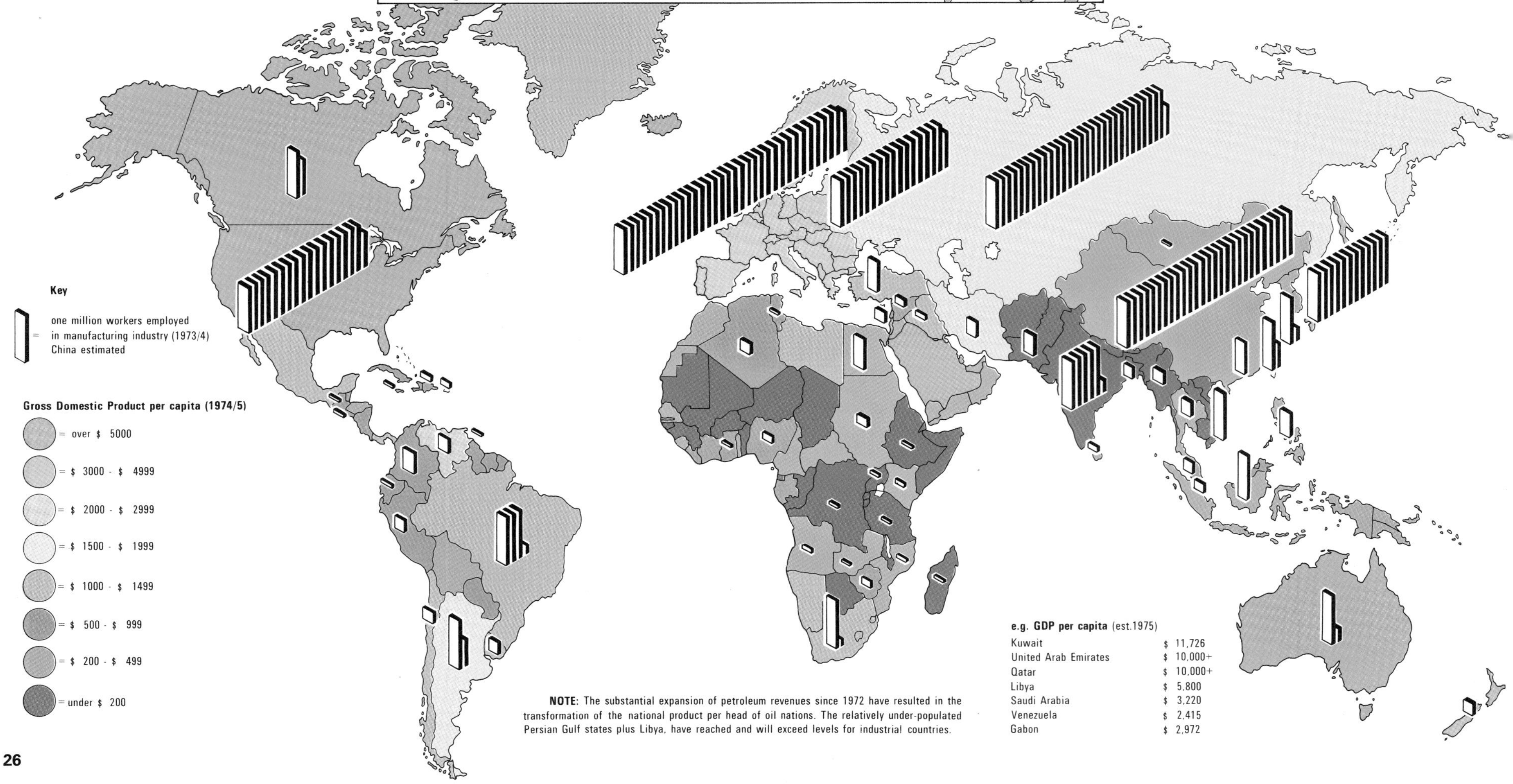

Key

= one million workers employed in manufacturing industry (1973/4) China estimated

Gross Domestic Product per capita (1974/5)

- = over $ 5000
- = $ 3000 - $ 4999
- = $ 2000 - $ 2999
- = $ 1500 - $ 1999
- = $ 1000 - $ 1499
- = $ 500 - $ 999
- = $ 200 - $ 499
- = under $ 200

NOTE: The substantial expansion of petroleum revenues since 1972 have resulted in the transformation of the national product per head of oil nations. The relatively under-populated Persian Gulf states plus Libya, have reached and will exceed levels for industrial countries.

e.g. GDP per capita (est.1975)

Kuwait	$ 11,726
United Arab Emirates	$ 10,000+
Qatar	$ 10,000+
Libya	$ 5,800
Saudi Arabia	$ 3,220
Venezuela	$ 2,415
Gabon	$ 2,972

has paralleled that of its motor manufacturers. Since 1960 Japan has more than trebled its steel output using the very latest giant, continuous process mills and modern furnaces to make products so cheaply that they can be sold across oceans at prices keenly competitive with locally produced steel.

During the period 1970 to 1975 the regional share of world production changed significantly. North America's share decreased by 3½%, and that of Western Europe by 4%. Despite Japanese growth, Asia's share of world production increased by only 2½% during the five years. The greatest increase was that of the USSR and Eastern Europe with over 7% growth.

World trade in steel products of all kinds has risen more than five-fold since the beginning of the 1950s with the pattern of supply shifting according to competitive conditions as well as to such factors as deep water ports to take the largest bulk ore carriers. These are now being constructed in many parts of the world.

Shipbuilding

Japanese shipbuilders have also benefitted from the availability of cheap steel just as a well organised steel industry led to the building of a thriving motor industry. Launchings from Japanese yards in 1973 totalled well over 16·5 million tonnes of shipping compared with about three million tonnes by each of the other main shipbuilding nations, Germany, Sweden and Norway. The fortunes of the world's shipbuilders were based on an apparently unending demand for more and larger oil tankers. But after oil prices quadrupled in 1973 and 1974 the world demand for oil declined sharply. Millions of tonnes of tankers left without cargoes were laid up indefinitely. The flow of orders for new tonnage practically ceased. As a response to these changing forces shipbuilders have drastically pruned their work forces and production facilities and are looking carefully at a variety of new uses for the shipyards such as building oil platforms or even prefabricated houses.

The world steel industry

The world car industry

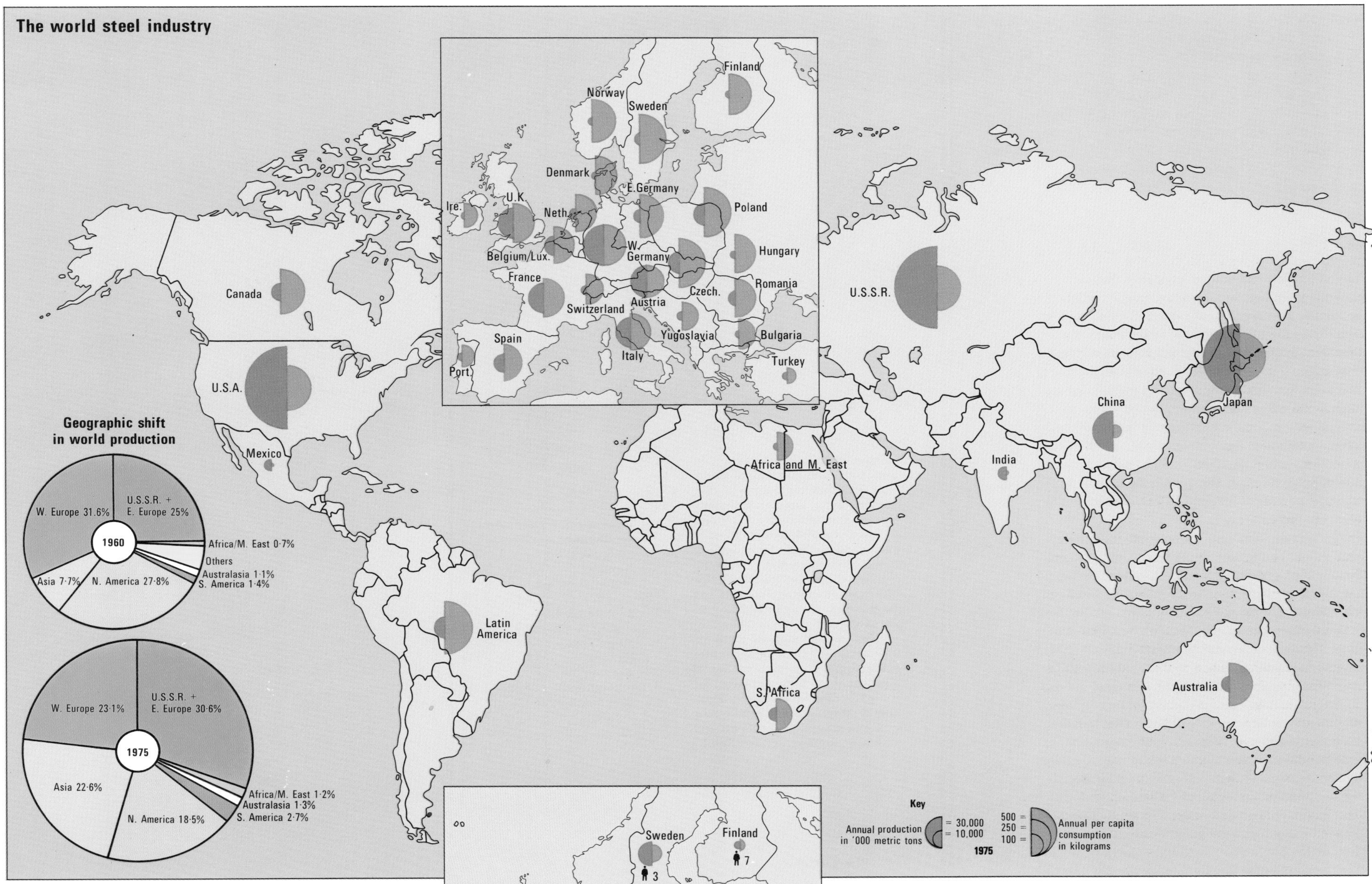

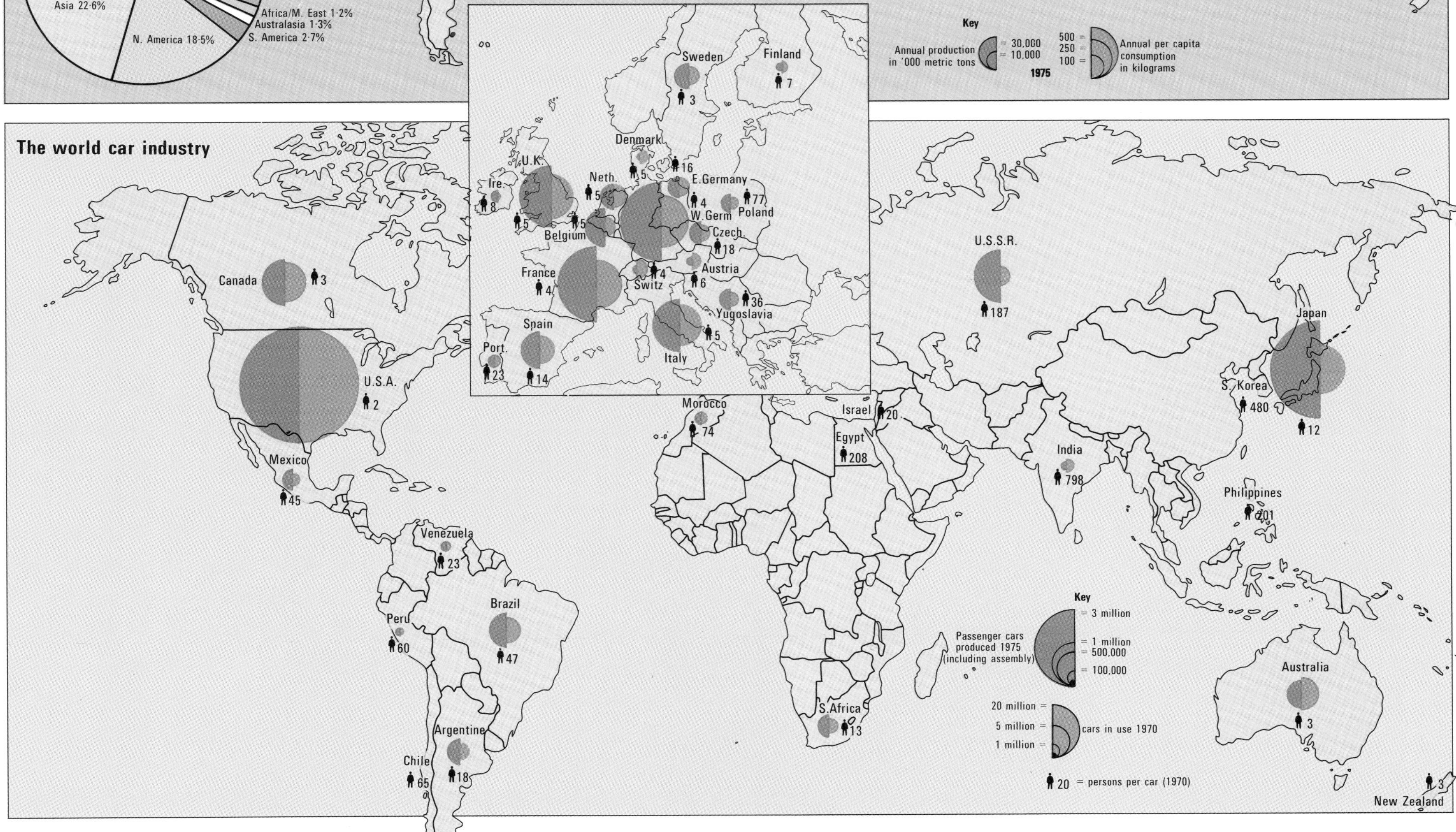

Patterns of world trade

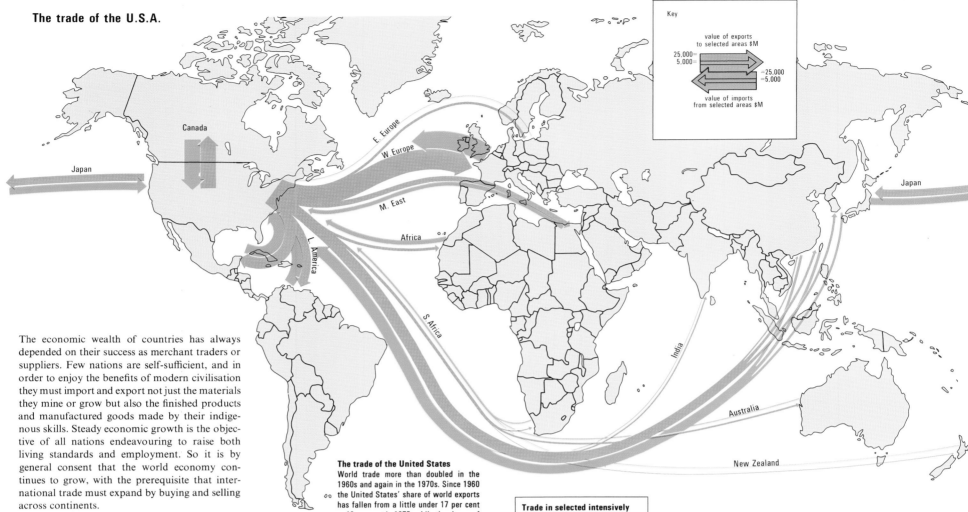

The economic wealth of countries has always depended on their success as merchant traders or suppliers. Few nations are self-sufficient, and in order to enjoy the benefits of modern civilisation they must import and export not just the materials they mine or grow but also the finished products and manufactured goods made by their indigenous skills. Steady economic growth is the objective of all nations endeavouring to raise both living standards and employment. So it is by general consent that the world economy continues to grow, with the prerequisite that international trade must expand by buying and selling across continents.

The mechanisms that move goods and materials farther, faster and in greater quantities year by year are highly complex. Vast sums of currency can be transmitted in seconds by a telephone call from one end of the world to the other, facilitating the shipment of iron ore from Western Australia to Rotterdam or ensuring that an oil or grain cargo on the high seas can be diverted to meet the emergency need of a customer. News of a crop failure in the Far East can send commodity markets into a turmoil of price changes that radically alter the pattern of demand. An expansion of mass production capacity in a major manufacture can transform sources of supply of materials.

Co-operation between governments and their merchant traders and manufacturers has not reduced the competitive spirit necessary for trade to flourish. The rapid rise in the volume of world trade in recent decades, the greater scale of capital movements from nation to nation and also the emergence of multinational companies and agencies have, nevertheless, made national economies more interdependent. Political sovereignty often masks the dependence of countries one on another as traders or suppliers. Technology, worldwide standardisation of man's material needs, a growing demand for the Earth's natural resources and the application of new agricultural and industrial methods have served to promote the expansion in world trade.

The capacity of nations to import to meet the requirements of their citizens, rises as living standards – measured in material possessions and services – improve. But nations that buy must have means to pay: an acceptable form of payment may be goods for barter or money that is convertible according to the importer's economic strength. All international trading nations need to balance their books, and the task of central bankers in keeping international trade flowing is crucial. The financial systems are as vital as communications. Their effectiveness is the preoccupation of economists and bankers round the world.

Industrialisation

The rebuilding of economies after the second world war has been characterised by rapid industrialisation, much under United States leadership, and the wider spread of economic nationalism created with the birth of many new nations once heavily dependent on American, British or French mercantile power and political rule. Efficiency in mass production and technological competence have a profound effect on the nature and routing of world trade. The rebuilding of

The trade of the United States
World trade more than doubled in the 1960s and again in the 1970s. Since 1960 the United States' share of world exports has fallen from a little under 17 per cent to 12 per cent in 1975, while the shares of Western Europe and Japan virtually doubled in the same period. Those of the developing countries declined heavily (their trade depends on foodstuffs and raw materials, for which demand rises only slowly).

Nearly one third of United States exports, as indicated by the maps, is shipped to Western Europe, another 20 per cent is moved across the border to Canada, and nearly 9 per cent goes to Japan. In return, some 20 per cent of United States imports come from Western Europe, 11 per cent from Japan, and 26 per cent from Canada.

Trade in selected intensively manufactured products 1975
(all figures in $M)

Product	Export	Import
Food beverages and tobacco	16,800	9,130
Crude materials excluding fuels	10,730	5,750
Mineral fuels	4,470	27,670
Chemicals	8,710	3,570
Machinery and transport	45,710	24,290
Other manufactured goods	16,610	22,750

The trade of Western Europe

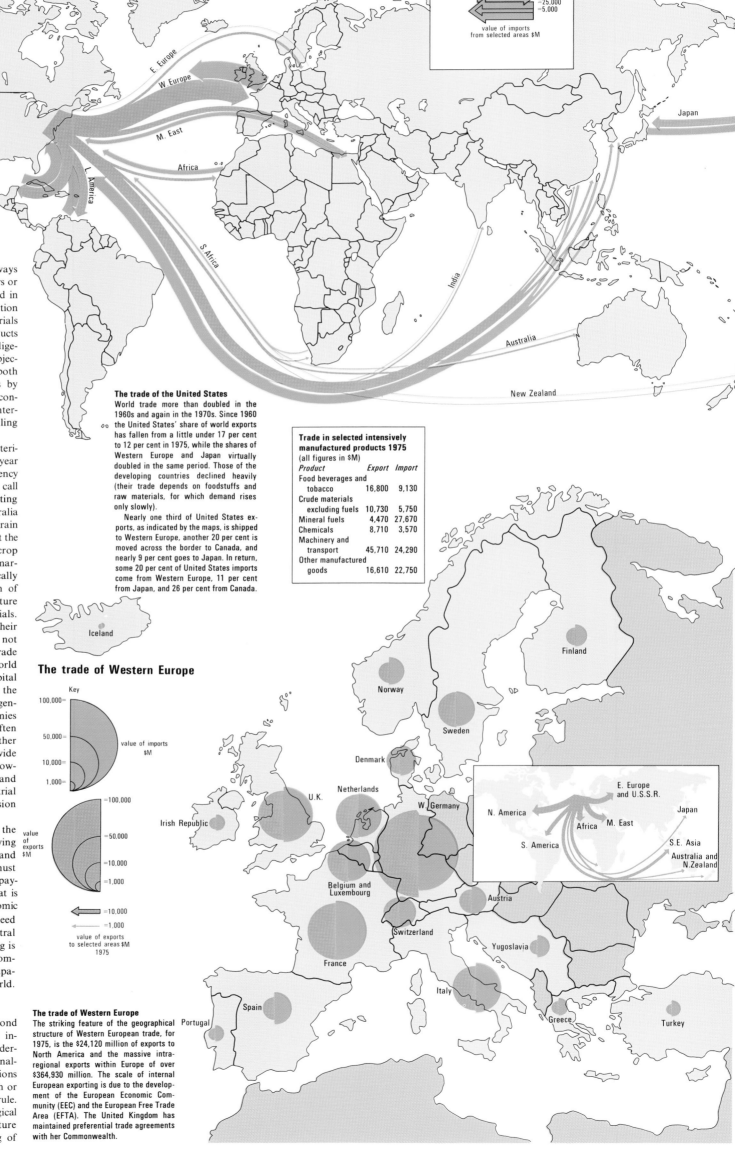

The trade of Western Europe
The striking feature of the geographical structure of Western European trade, for 1975, is the $24,120 million of exports to North America and the massive intra-regional exports within Europe of over $364,930 million. The scale of internal European exporting is due to the development of the European Economic Community (EEC) and the European Free Trade Area (EFTA). The United Kingdom has maintained preferential trade agreements with her Commonwealth.

the Japanese and German economies has been accomplished by each country devoting a high proportion of its national efforts to selling their goods in world markets.

While the United States still accounts for 40 per cent of the non-communist world's production, the European Economic Community and Japan have become major centres of economic power and pace-setters for competition in international markets. Half the world's seaborne tanker and dry cargo shipments are now unloaded in Western Europe, and more than a quarter discharges in the Far East, with Japan at the centre of activity.

Japan

If present patterns of growth stay as they are, the Japanese may surpass the Soviet Union's output in the next 25 years and draw close to that of the United States. In the 15 years from 1960 she has doubled her share of world exports to reach over 7 per cent. Her rate of growth in world trade is about twice as fast as the international average. A substantial competitive endeavour in world markets – she is a leading exporter of ships, electrical goods, fish and motor vehicles – is vital to pay for heavy imports. Japan has to buy half her raw materials abroad to fuel her growth.

United States

With the largest economy in the world and a currency essential for the effective financing of continent-to-continent trade, the USA contributed a vast sum of her national wealth to rebuilding the war-torn countries of the western world. This has required running a balance of payments deficit in virtually every year since the end of the forties. These deficits are now growing to unmanageable proportions. Unlike the industrial countries of Europe and Japan, the United States until the late 1960s, had been self-sufficient in crude oil. The entry of the USA into the world oil markets has helped to trigger the huge increases in oil prices. With over 40 per cent of US oil requirements met from foreign sources in 1977, the true deficit suddenly rose to $40 billion from only $5 billion in the previous year.

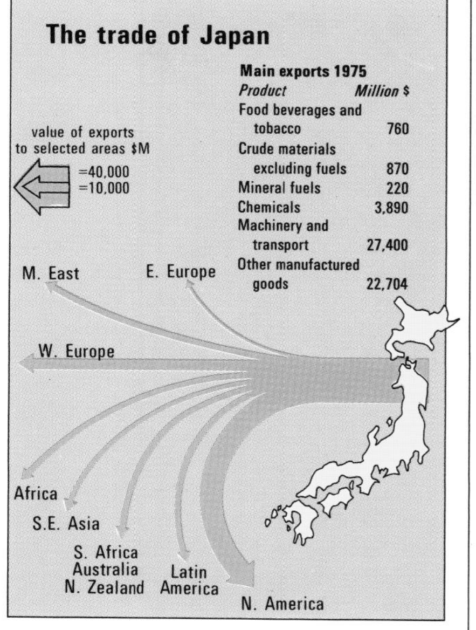

The trade of Japan

Main exports 1975

Product	Million $
Food beverages and tobacco	760
Crude materials excluding fuels	870
Mineral fuels	220
Chemicals	3,890
Machinery and transport	27,400
Other manufactured goods	22,704

value of exports to selected areas $M
=40,000
=10,000

M. East
E. Europe
W. Europe
Africa
S.E. Asia
S. Africa
Australia
N. Zealand
Latin America
N. America

The geographical distribution of Japan's exports is an interesting feature of contemporary world trade. She maintains a firm relationship with industrialised markets and developing regions.

About 22 per cent of Japanese exports by value were sent to the USA and Canada in 1975. A further 14·5 per cent went to the markets of South East Asia and the Middle East, 8 per cent to Africa and 8·5 per cent to Latin America. Western Europe took 14·5 per cent of her exports, while Australasia received 1·5 per cent, and Eastern Europe 4 per cent.

Japan's exports in 1975 were $55,844 million compared with $19,318 million in 1970 and $4,050 million in 1960.

In the 15 years from 1960 to 1975 United States imports from Japan surged from just over one billion dollars to over 11 billion dollars. Initially Japanese imports of US goods lagged well behind but now US exports in 1975 totalled $9·35 billion – halving the deficit of a few years previously.

For 35 years the USA has sought to reduce artificial barriers to international trade, culminating in the famous Kennedy Round of tariff reductions of the sixties. Her gross domestic product is now annually exceeding $1,000 billion, making the nation the richest in the world. Exports in 1976 totalled over $107 billion. Huge sums are transferred every year to developing countries in aid and investment along with human skills and technology. Additionally, the world's most powerful single economy carries a disproportionate share of western defence costs. The attainment of American accord with China and further development of trade with the USSR are seen as the most encouraging factors for the future of international economic co-operation.

Western Europe

The nations of Western Europe are the most potent force in world mercantile trade. Their exports have risen from $52 billion in 1960 to $295 billion by 1976, led during this period by the EEC founder members and the nations of the former European Free Trade Area.

Enlargement of the EEC to 9 nations has provided an economic grouping with a GDP of around $1,000 billion, fast approaching that of the United States ($1,295 billion in 1973). EEC exports in 1973, including intra-area trade, were valued as $210 billion, $149 billion going to countries outside the Community. Her merchant fleet is four times the size of the USA's, and vehicle output is nearly 10 million units annually.

The growth of European exporting power has been equally spectacular, assisted greatly by American-inspired reductions in import tariffs, direct financial aid for industrial reconstruction, and the transfer of technological know-how.

The result has been a transformation of monetary power as well as industrial strength. This has reduced the role of the American dollar and the British pound sterling in supplying the foreign exchange for the finance of world trade. The dollar, of course, remains the standard common currency for the convertibility of money. But this has required new alignments of exchange values to ensure that national monies reflect the strength of nations as international traders as well as the size of their gross national product and stocks of gold.

World trade

An International Monetary Fund helps central bankers to keep money working as hard as the aircraft and ships that ply between markets. United Nations agencies, organisations set up for economic co-operation, and a network of commodity arrangements framed for orderly marketing of essential materials have all been the means for averting chaos and correcting the economic disruption that market forces may create. Whatever the periodic difficulties, such as monetary and materials crises or unfair trade practices, the overall achievement has been the expansion of the volume of world trade by 10 per cent every year to the end of the sixties.

This growth, the aid to international economic development, has not corrected the imbalance between rich and poor countries. In the sixties, the export trade of industrialised countries grew by about 164 per cent, that of developing nations by only 99 per cent. This disparity reflects the rapid growth of trade between developed countries due to the creation of special groups of countries with mutually advantageous arrangements for economic expansion. The EEC and EFTA have been prime examples where intra-group exports have risen sharply.

Prior to enlargement, the EEC was assessed as supplying 29 per cent of world exports, but in fact, half the trade was conducted between the member nations. The disparity can be illustrated by the fact that trade among the main industrial countries of the world grew from $54 billion in 1960 to $161 billion in 1970, while that between developing countries and the industrial countries went up from $19 billion to $40 billion.

Record rates of inflation, higher oil payments and the demise of fixed exchange rates cast their shadow over world trade midway through the seventies. The total value of world exports in 1975 was $567 billion compared with $312 billion in 1970 and $128 billion in 1960. This impressive figure must be treated with caution, for it reflects a sustained world-wide rise in prices, in particular the huge increase in oil bills.

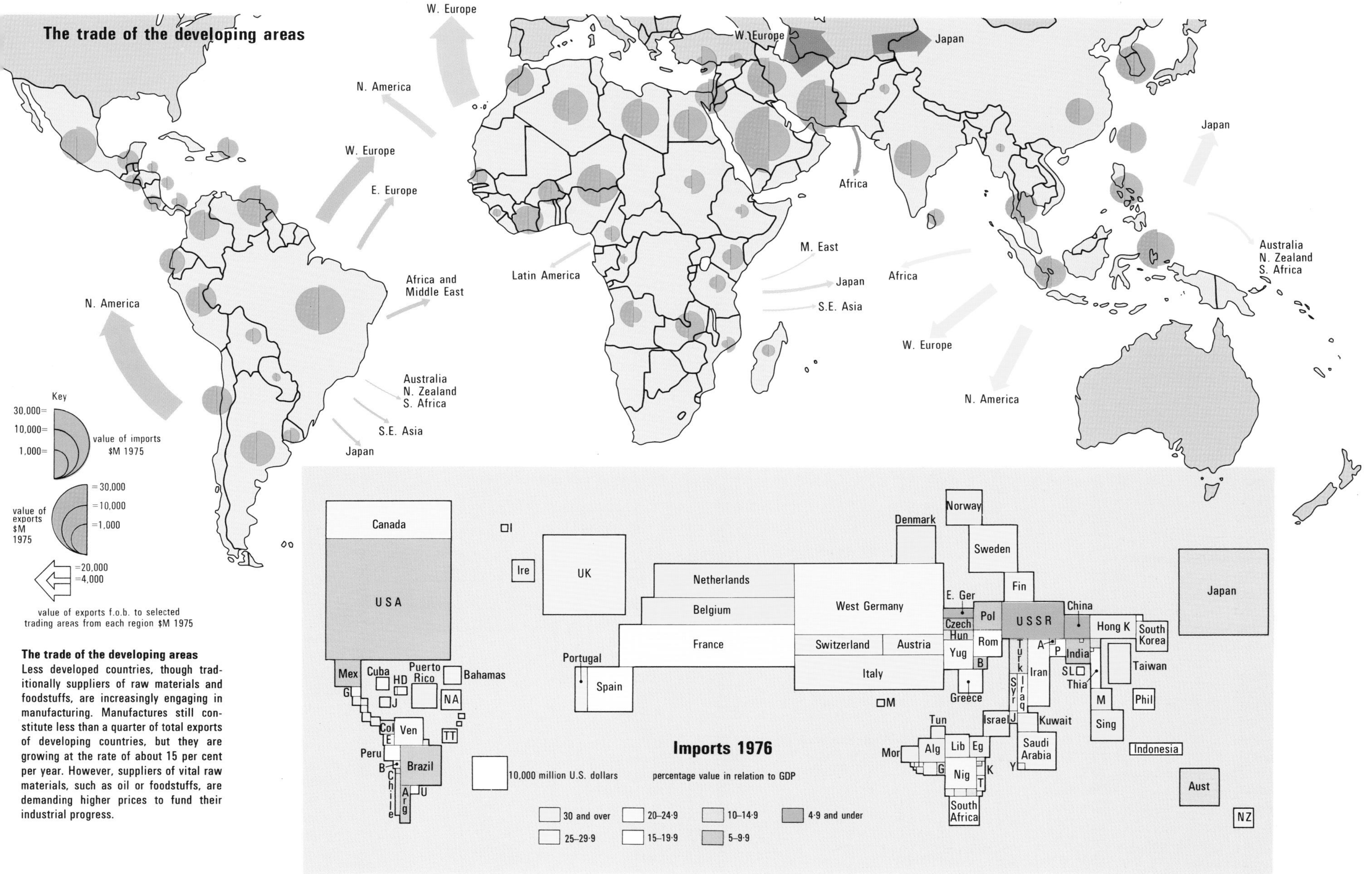

The trade of the developing areas

Less developed countries, though traditionally suppliers of raw materials and foodstuffs, are increasingly engaging in manufacturing. Manufactures still constitute less than a quarter of total exports of developing countries, but they are growing at the rate of about 15 per cent per year. However, suppliers of vital raw materials, such as oil or foodstuffs, are demanding higher prices to fund their industrial progress.

Key
30,000=
10,000=
1,000=
value of imports $M 1975

=30,000
=10,000
=1,000
value of exports $M 1975

=20,000
=4,000
value of exports f.o.b. to selected trading areas from each region $M 1975

Imports 1976

10,000 million U.S. dollars   percentage value in relation to GDP

30 and over   20–24·9   10–14·9   4·9 and under
25–29·9   15–19·9   5–9·9

World tourism

Travelling for pleasure provides the vast majority of people with their only experience of other countries. The number of such travellers is increasing so much that the tourist trade – which transports, accommodates, feeds and entertains them – is now one of the world's largest industries and is growing internationally at a very fast rate. By 1985, it is calculated that 320 million people will be travelling abroad for pleasure, spending approximately $60,000 million in the process.

Already, income from tourism is vital to the national economies of scores of countries. Spain, the most visited land, earned $3,083 million from her foreign visitors in 1976. Tourism has become the leading foreign currency earner for Kenya, bringing in more funds ($68·50 million) than the export of coffee. Canada earns more ($1,930 million) from tourism than from wheat exports.

The growth of tourism

For most of the last thirty years world tourism has grown steadily, other than where wars or major civil commotion has intervened. In 1973 some 200 million tourists grossed around $30,000 million. This fell in 1974 but by 1976 the recovery world-wide was complete and the numbers had risen to 222 million, grossing $45,000 million. That recovery has been maintained, and in many countries accelerated. Portugal is a good example of a country whose tourism was very badly affected by the political events of 1974 (and 1975) but by 1977 it had substantially recovered.

The maps which accompany these notes show clearly which countries receive most holiday visitors and, to a certain extent, who goes where. They cannot show why such pleasure journeys are made – why Spain stands well above all others, for example. One can appreciate that France and Italy are popular, but it takes more than guesswork to establish how Britain has managed to build up its tourist industry to such an extent that it now exceeds that of Switzerland, which has a much longer tradition in tourism.

Contemporary tourism

To some extent the present situation is a reflection of the past – those days of the Grand Tour when no man of substance could consider himself educated without the experience of that journey round selected European cities. It is reflected, too, from those times when travellers discovered the medicinal benefits of certain spas, or the climatic benefits of wintering on the French Riviera. There are small traces, in today's pattern, of those first organized holidays from Britain to the continent which bore the stamp of Mr Thomas Cook well over a century ago.

The current map of world tourist movement has, however, mainly been drafted by the post-war development of the travel industry, particularly within and from Europe. It is an industry which in the main sets out to sell a low cost 'package' of holiday pleasures, and the huge attraction of Spain is the most obvious symbol of its success. This overall success has continued in spite of the slump from the record breaking total of 30 million tourists of 1973 which resulted from the fuel and economic crises and of the political changes, which were followed by steep inflation. The upward curve was once more noticeable in 1976–77.

Spain's success as Europe's main tourist country stemmed from its low cost of living in the 1960s and early 1970s, its high sunshine record, its cheapness of land and subsequent building costs, an availability of inexpensive labour and the active encouragement of tourist investment by the government. The French provide the largest number of visitors to Spain, most coming on camping or caravan holidays, with the West Germans in second place, having overtaken the British in third place. However, holidaymakers from the UK constitute the largest number of foreigners visiting the country by air and indeed it was the British who 'invented' the air package holiday in the 1950s. Even with the rapidly increased costs in Spain which started in 1976 and accelerated in 1977, it remains the most popular country if for no other reason than that it is the only nation in Europe which can cope with the millions who seek the sun mostly on modest budgets.

Canadian tourism

The reasons behind Canada's high position in tourism tables are rather different. In 1976 some 32·2 million visitors (including a high proportion of day visitors) came from the USA. Although this was a drop from the previous year of about 2·4 million they actually brought in more money, largely because of rising costs, the total being $1,346 million. The proximity of the USA, the minimal border formalities and the lack of a language problem (even with the strong French-Canadian movement) 'sold' Canada to the leisure traveller from south of the 49th parallel.

Why do other nationals visit Canada? The next largest number (408,176) crossed the Atlantic from the UK, and clearly demonstrates the importance of historic ties as well as 'family' tourism. Travelling for a holiday with relatives, visiting sons or daughters who have married and moved away, usually means that one remains, in effect, within one's own country. In the case of the UK and countries such as Canada, Australia or New Zealand – and to a lesser extent the USA – such journeys show up on the international statistical tables.

United States tourism

Apart from its 'cross border' neighbours Canada and Mexico, which in 1976 accounted for over 12 million visitors to the country, the USA has only moved into the big international tourism league in the last ten years or so, largely due to two things – the development of cheap air travel and the active promotion of both government and private enterprise (the airlines in particular) to encourage foreigners to visit there. But the air fares motivation has been the greater, coupled with the increased affluence of Europe – and Japan. The USA is still well 'in the red' on her tourism account as her citizens in 1976 spent $1,076 million more on holidays and travel outside the country than incoming tourists earned for her.

A small example of how patterns can change is to be seen in the Caribbean, where for some time the tourist scene has been dominated by visitors from the USA and Canada. In Barbados for instance, nearly 130,000 of the island's 224,314 visitors in 1976 came from those two countries. However, the increasing availability of moderately-priced package holidays based on charter flights, from Britain and West Germany, are bringing more of a European influence to bear and changing the established tourist situation.

European tourism

The popularity of France and Italy lies in the history and cultural tradition of those countries and their great cities. Art treasures, architectural masterpieces and religious buildings are tremendous attractions, as are the gastronomic and wine-growing traditions. Italy and France have also sought to attract the mass market tourists, with such developments as the resorts of the Italian Adriatic coast and the grander projects in the south-west of France.

The UK has only comparatively recently achieved a high place in the list of 'Most visited countries' but in 1976 earned about $3,600 million from foreign visitors. This figure is over $500 million more than the total tourist income for Spain in the same year in spite of the fact that the number of visitors to that country was nearly 26 million while to the UK it was just over 10 million. In tourism, numbers alone do not by any means indicate the true economic effect.

One must keep in mind the fact that international tourism includes travel within the same region. A breakdown of statistics supplied by various European countries shows how large a part their immediate neighbours play in the flow of visitors. Such regional movements account for 88 per cent of the total international tourist traffic in Europe. The detailed 'Who goes where' statistics illustrate this vividly: the British travelling to Spain, France, Ireland, Italy and Germany; the French and the Germans preferring similar European destinations.

Motivation and fulfilment

Overall, the simple desire to take a holiday in totally different surroundings, preferably at low cost and quite often to some large resort on the sea coast, lies behind most tourist journeys. This is the basic reason why people go where they do. Although large functional and to some extent 'artificial' resorts will continue to be very popular and account for the majority of holiday destinations, there is a definite trend away from this by the more discriminating (and often the more frequently travelled) holidaymaker to seek his or her vacation in more genuine surroundings. And the younger generation are much less inclined to be 'packaged' than were the holidaymakers of the expansionist 1960s. Mass travel will undoubtedly continue to grow but along with it will be an increasing desire for independence and less regimentation.

It is clear that tourist travel will do more to shape the way we explore our world than anything else. It will also do more to shape the world we explore. Its future can be predicted, for the forces that control it are known. First, an increase in available leisure time will be matched by an increase of per capita income as well as improvements in transportation systems. Increased leisure time is already having an effect on the lives of the workers in the developed industrial societies. Throughout Europe, as well as North America, the growth of second holidays has been very rapid. As automation of the productive processes becomes more widespread one must pay great heed to predictions such as those of Herman Kahn of the Hudson Institute, who sees the post-industrial society requiring its citizens to work on just 147 days in a year – with a four-day working week and 13 weeks of annual holidays. Leisure in the form of earlier retirement is another inevitability.

Transport developments

Improvements in transport systems are already having an effect on tourism. The importance of the motoring holidaymaker is clearly appreciated by those responsible for the long-term planning of tourist facilities. In Europe one can point to the enormous growth in car ferry services between the UK and the continent as evidence of the importance of motoring, and to the highway construction programmes designed to speed holiday motorists to the pleasure areas.

Railway and road systems carry the largest amount of traffic on short and medium distances, and are being re-organized and expanded to cope with the demands of the next 20 years.

The next 20 years

The development and expansion of air transport will continue to be the most important influencing factor. The increasing use of larger aircraft purely for leisure travel will continue in spite of greatly increased fuel costs. The blurring of the lines between 'scheduled' and 'charter' services will accelerate and it could well be that by the mid-1980s the difference between the two, other than on certain business routes, will be academic.

The last 25 years have seen the industry of tourism grow in size and strength and, at the same time, a greater involvement by governments in the regulation of tourism. The day of 'laissez faire' in tourism is past. The World Tourism Organisation with its HQ in Madrid will increase its influence particularly with the developing nations. Without proper planning and safeguards for the environment in its widest sense, tourism can be a blight. But with the full co-operation on both governmental and private enterprise levels tourism can be of immense benefit financially, commercially, psychologically and also to understanding better the ways and nature of people the world over.

Where the British go		
1	Spain	2,170,000
2	France	2,036,000
3	Italy	690,000
4	West Germany	673,000
5	Netherlands	531,000
6	Belgium	472,000[1]
7	Greece	356,000
8	United States	346,000
9	Switzerland	252,000
10	Canada	200,000
11	Austria	197,000
12	Yugoslavia	196,000
13	Sweden	160,000
14	Norway	150,000
15	Malta	125,000
16	Denmark	109,000
17	Kenya	105,000
18	Morocco	95,000
19	Portugal	85,000
20	South Africa	55,000[2]
21	Cyprus	34,000

Where the Americans go		
1	Canada	11,641,000
2	Mexico	2,715,000
3	Italy	1,845,000
4	United Kingdom	1,490,000
5	West Germany	1,232,000
6	France	1,055,000
7	Switzerland	845,000
8	Spain	793,000
9	The Bahamas	667,000
10	Greece	493,000
11	Netherlands	424,000
12	Bermuda	391,000
13	Japan	277,000
14	Venezuela	266,000
15	Hong Kong	238,000
16	Ireland	231,000
17	Jamaica	229,000
18	Israel	214,000

19	Yugoslavia	189,000
20	Taiwan	125,000[3]
21	Singapore	122,000
22	Thailand	116,000
23	Turkey	114,000
24	Colombia	103,000
25	Korea	102,000
26	Morocco	97,000
27	Philippines	93,000
28	Malaysia	68,000
29	India	62,000
30	Portugal	56,000

Where the French go		
1	Spain	9,476,000
2	Italy	1,678,000
3	United Kingdom	1,171,000
4	Switzerland	644,000
5	West Germany	579,000
6	Austria	385,000
7	Yugoslavia	380,000
8	Tunisia	371,000
9	Greece	311,000
10	Netherlands	251,000
11	Morocco	225,000
12	United States	217,000
13	Portugal	114,000
14	Denmark	107,000
15	Algeria	83,000
16	USSR	71,000
17	Sweden	59,000

Where the West Germans go		
1	Denmark	13,307,000[4]
2	Austria	7,369,000
3	Spain	3,885,000
4	Italy	3,595,000
5	France	2,890,000
6	Switzerland	1,589,000
7	Yugoslavia	1,546,000

8	United Kingdom	1,104,000
9	Netherlands	683,000
10	Greece	519,000
11	United States	365,000
12	Czechoslovakia	325,000
13	Sweden	324,000
14	Norway	320,000
15	Hungary	275,000
16	Turkey	197,000
17	Bulgaria	162,000
18	Romania	149,000
19	Tunisia	139,000
20	USSR	129,000
21	Portugal	105,000

1976 figures in millions rounded to nearest thousand

[1] also includes Luxembourg
[2] provisional
[3] rough estimate
[4] includes all frontier crossings

Income from international tourism

1976 figures expressed in $US millions

United States	5,755
France	3,613
United Kingdom	3,600
West Germany	3,211
Austria	3,131
Spain	3,083
Italy	2,525
Switzerland	1,643
Canada	1,641
Netherlands	1,061
Belgium/Luxembourg	959
Greece	824
Portugal	317
Japan	312

The most visited countries

All figures are 1976

All figures are 1976

- over 20 million
- over 10 million
- over 5 million
- over 2 million
- over 1 million
- over 500 000
- over 300 000
- over 100 000
- over 50 000
- below 50 000

Canada

USA

Mexico

Bermuda

Bahamas

Jamaica

Costa Rica
Panama

Trinidad & Tobago

Venezuela

Colombia

Brazil

Argentina

Denmark

Sweden

Germany E.
Germany W.
Netherlands

Norway

Finland

Poland
Austria
Czechoslovakia
Hungary

USSR

Belgium
Luxembourg

Eire

UK

Yugoslavia
Romania
Bulgaria
Greece

Switzerland

San Marino
Monaco

France

Italy

Spain

Syria
Lebanon
Israel
Jordan

Japan

Korea

Portugal
Malta
Cyprus

Turkey

Iraq

Iran

Afghanistan

China

Morocco

Tunisia

Algeria

Libya

Egypt

Kuwait

Pakistan

India

Hong Kong

Thailand

Vietnam

Philippines

Malaysia

Singapore

Indonesia

Ethiopia

Uganda
Kenya

Tanzania

Fiji

South Africa

Australia

New Zealand

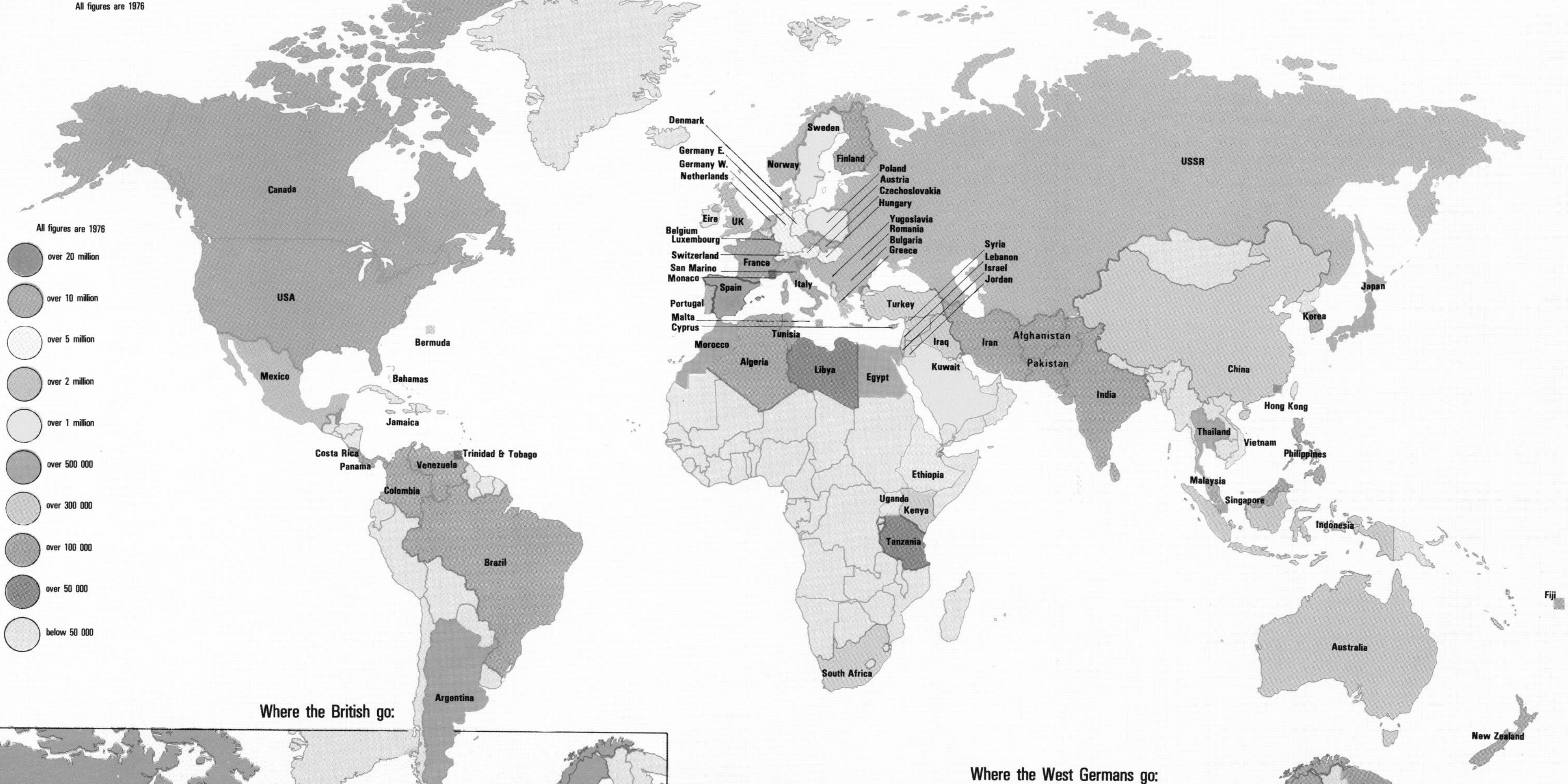

Where the British go:

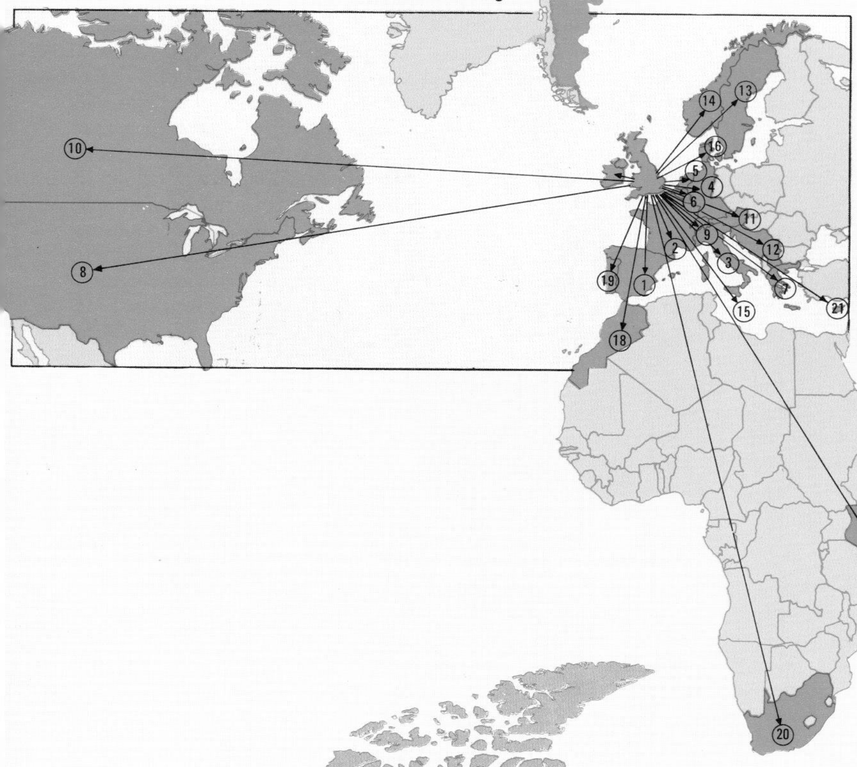

Where the West Germans go:

Where the French go:

Where the Americans go:

31

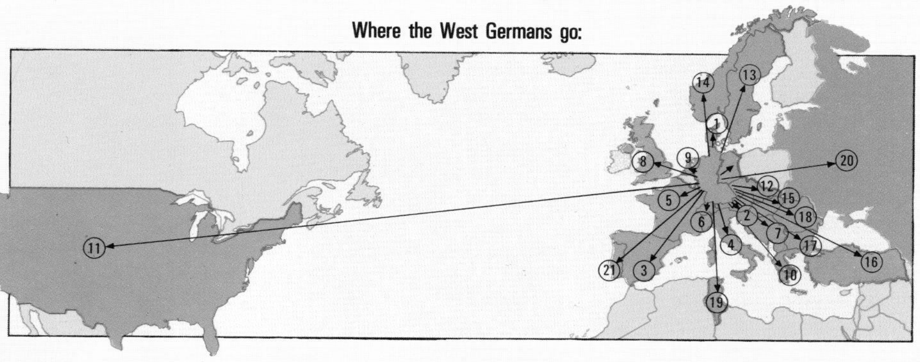

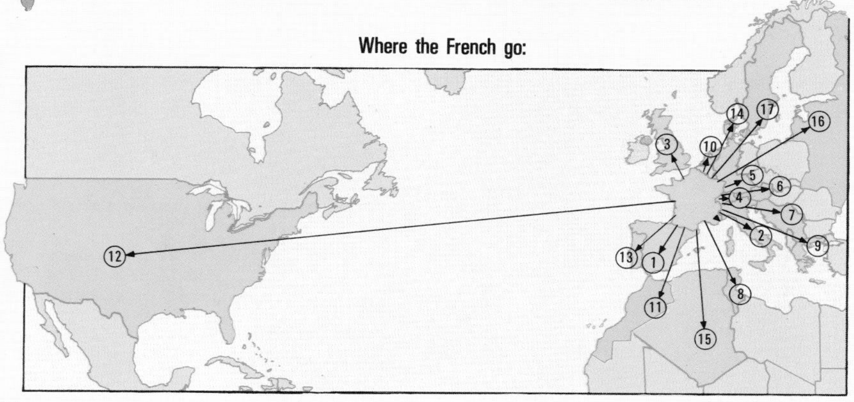

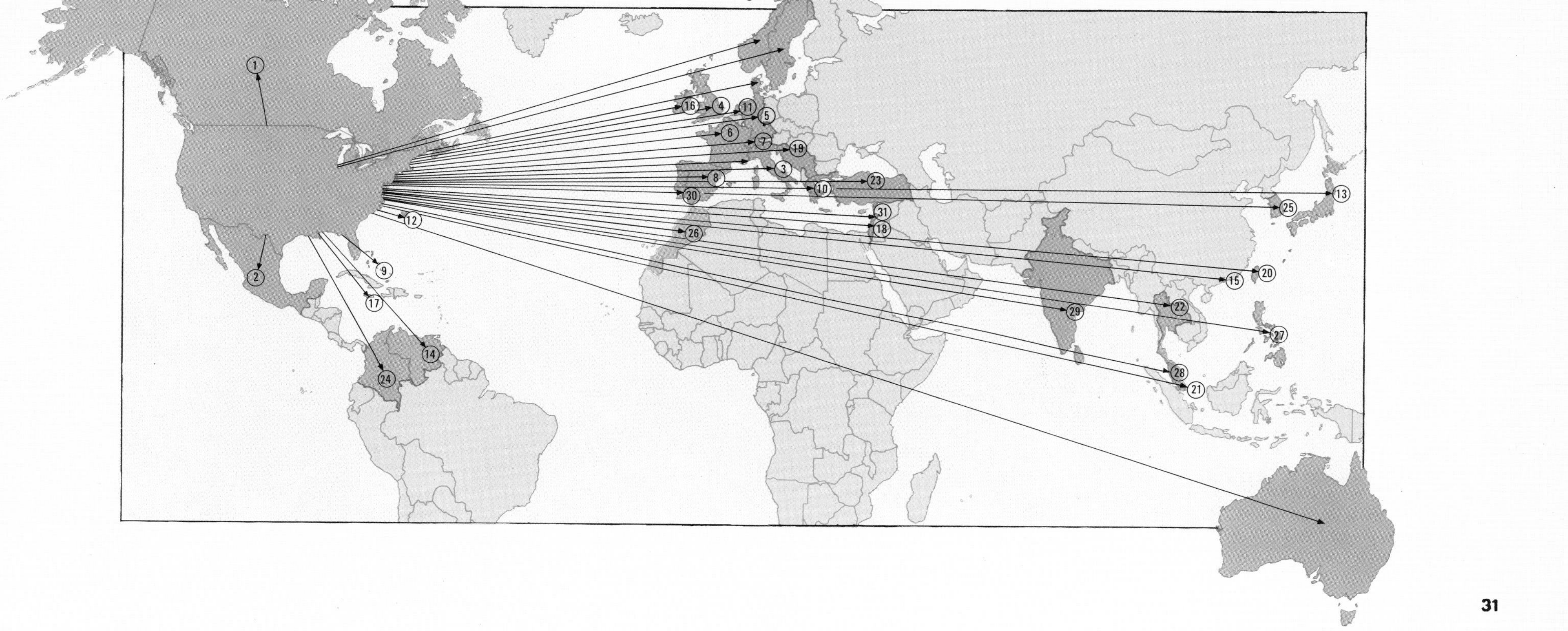

The balance of man's environment

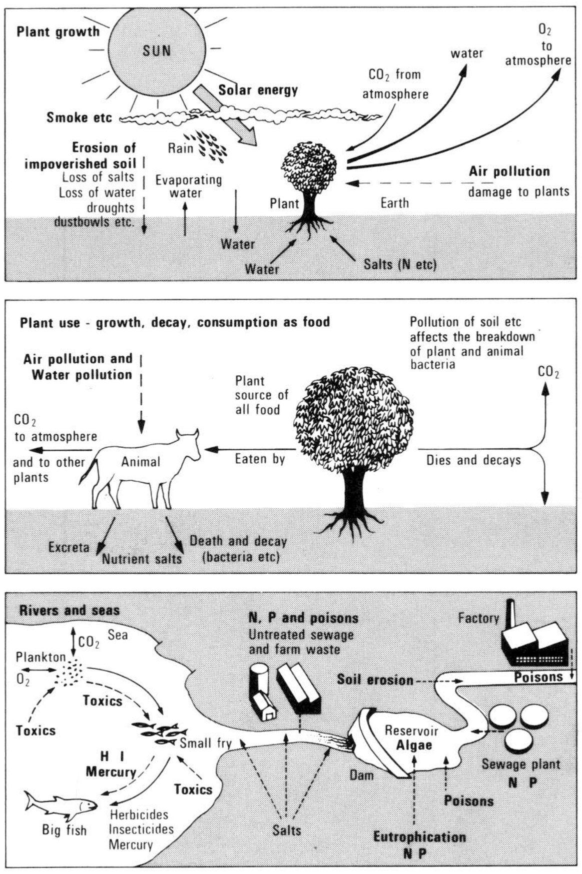

The essential cycles
All life on Earth depends on the essential cycle of energy, water and chemicals depicted here. The source of energy is radiation from the Sun. This radiation covers a wide range of wavelengths, some of which are essential for life, others harmful. The atmosphere filters out the most harmful rays, and admits those which are beneficial. Any atmospheric change alters the proportions of the various types of solar radiation which reach the Earth and the amounts which are lost. Any pollutant affects this balance.

Water, carbon dioxide and oxygen all go through these cycles. The rain falls on the land and sea alike. On land some is taken up by the soil, and is then absorbed by plant roots. A little of this water is used and retained by the plants, more is evaporated ('transpired') into the air. Water is also evaporated from the soil, and from the surface of streams, lakes and, most important, the sea. Solar energy is again involved in this evaporation. The water vapour eventually forms clouds and is deposited again as rain – and so the cycle continues.

The cycle in water is similar to that on land, except that aquatic animals are particularly susceptible to pollution. Pollutants are discharged into rivers, some of which run into lakes where excessive amounts of nutrient salts cause eutrophication. Poisons accumulate in the sea, are taken up by fish and other organisms and passed on (and concentrated) as predators eat their prey.

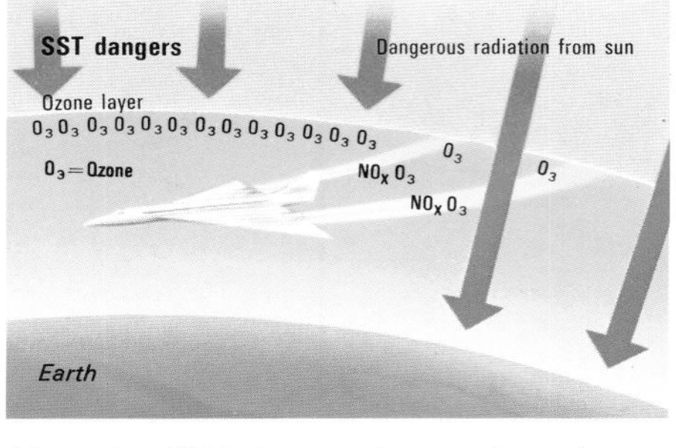

Exhausts from SST in the stratosphere may destroy the ozone layer which shields the earth from dangerous ultraviolet radiation.

The natural balance – gradual change
During the thousands of millions of years of its existence the Earth has undergone many changes. At first it had no atmosphere, then some gases were released from the interior. These were mainly carbon dioxide and water vapour, with a small amount of nitrogen and no free oxygen. The atmosphere's composition changed as the water vapour condensed to form the ocean, and as the carbon dioxide was taken up into carbonate rocks and as a constituent of growing plants. Ultimately some of the carbon was locked up in the fossil fuels produced from this vegetation, and it has remained so stored for millions of years until today, when it is being widely exploited by man. The oxygen in the atmosphere arose mainly as a result of the photosynthesis which reduced the carbon dioxide levels.

Thus throughout geological time the proportions of these gases have varied from epoch to epoch. Our present atmosphere is one stage in this process. Today the Earth is surrounded by a mixture of gases, consisting mainly of some four-fifths of nitrogen and one-fifth of oxygen, with other substances at much lower levels. These include the surprisingly small amount of carbon dioxide – only 0·03 to 0·04 per cent – on which all green plants depend, a varying amount of water vapour, small quantities of helium and other inert gases, and various additions and pollutants arising from man's activities as well as from natural processes. The balance of the atmosphere is maintained mainly by Earth's 'green mantle'. The vast areas of natural forest sustain the level of oxygen required by animal life. Any profound changes in vegetation would ultimately affect the atmosphere, and so affect all animal life also.

The scale of problems arising from interference by man with large natural regimes or ecosystems is perhaps well illustrated by the dilemma over the Brazilian rain forests. For some time there have been investigations and proposals to clear vast tracts of forest for agricultural development or the exploitation of potential mineral reserves. Latin America could certainly benefit socio-economically by some such successful development. Yet there is no clear understanding of what would happen to the climate and the fertility of the soil if a drastic change was attempted. Indeed, there is reason to believe that the decimation of the forests could easily lead to the creation of sterile deserts.

Effects of agriculture
The food for all animals is made by plants, which build up large molecules from the carbon dioxide in the air and water absorbed from the soil, using solar energy in the process. This process of photosynthesis is clearly vulnerable to direct and drastic alterations in the composition of the atmosphere, which in turn could interfere with the hydrological part of the natural cycle. Air pollution can screen radiation from the Sun, thus damaging plant life by reducing or inhibiting photosynthesis.

The changing oceans
Today land covers only about a third of the surface of the Earth; the rest is covered by the oceans. This enormous mass of water, weighing 1,428,000,000,000,000,000 tonnes, plays a big part in stabilizing the conditions of man's environment. Water temperatures fluctuate much less than those of air, and the oceans form a reservoir not only of water but also of carbon dioxide and oxygen, the gases on which life depends. The plant life in the oceans – the phytoplankton – makes an essential contribution to the balance of these gases, producing vast quantities of oxygen by its photosynthesis. The area and the composition of the seas have changed slowly over the whole period of the world's existence.

We tend to accept the world as it is now, or rather as it was before man had noticeably affected it, as the ideal environment both for man and for all animal and plant life. We forget that change has always occurred, and is likely to continue to occur whether or not man dominates the globe. If such changes are gradual, life will survive, and man may even be able to adapt. Man is now so powerful, however, that he could himself suddenly upset the whole balance, changing the climate and the composition of the atmosphere. If there were drastic changes, life in some form, would almost certainly survive. New forms suited to the new conditions would evolve, but man, ingenious as he is, might not be the species most able to adapt.

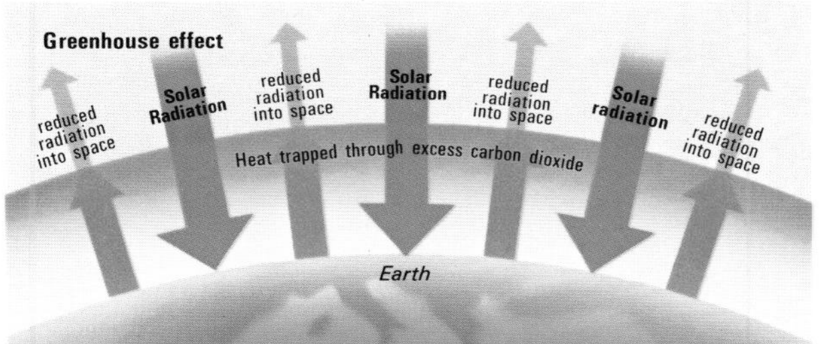

The Greenhouse Effect
Radiation from the Sun passes through space until it reaches the outer atmosphere of the Earth. Much of it is absorbed by the Earth's surface, causing the temperature to rise. The heat is then re-radiated. If the amount of CO_2 in the atmosphere increases, a larger amount of this radiation is trapped as in a glasshouse, instead of being lost into outer space. In the last fifty years the increase in the level of CO_2 in the Earth's atmosphere caused by the burning of fossil fuels has not been enough to raise the Earth's temperature.

Man made changes
Man is the only animal to modify not only his immediate environment but also the appearance and the economy of the whole globe. He can cut down vast areas of natural forest and replace them with arable crops and, sometimes, by man-made desert. He drains the wet places, and irrigates the dry. His industry could alter the whole balance of the atmosphere and the climate of the Earth. He also consumes the Earth's resources, and moves substances from one place to another. The misuse of his powers, and the subsequent release of harmful substances, we call pollution. We must discover which forms of pollution are a danger to man's environment, and control them before they upset the natural balance irreversibly.

Air pollution
Natural catastrophes, as well as human actions, can upset the balance. In 1883 Krakatoa blew up, and put so much dust into the atmosphere that the heat from the Sun was excluded and the average temperature of the Earth was significantly lowered for many months. Today man is polluting the air with dust and smoke, notwithstanding striking local improvements in Pittsburgh and other American cities and in Britain in places where the Clean Air Acts are operative. Air pollution, uncontrolled, could reduce sunlight at ground level and affect the world's climate, making it colder. An opposite effect, a warming of the Earth, could result from the increase in the level of carbon dioxide in the atmosphere. Carbon stored in fossil fuels (coal, oil, natural gas) is released as carbon dioxide gas when the fuels are burned; the levels of CO_2 in the atmosphere are rising slightly each year. This may produce the so-called 'greenhouse effect' (see diagram), and make the world warmer.

Such changes in climate would affect all forms of life. They would also affect the levels of the oceans. In former (natural) ice ages, so much water was immobilised as ice that the levels of the seas fell, to rise again and flood low-lying areas in the next warm epoch. A further rise in the temperature of the Earth could drown many of our cities and much of our most productive agricultural land. Scientists are not agreed on the probabilities of these changes, or on the magnitude of the likely effects, but they do agree that thorough monitoring of the atmosphere and climate is needed to detect the dangers at an early stage. The more optimistic scientists do also suggest that man-made changes in climate are likely to be less significant than the natural and inevitable fluctuations of temperature.

Green plants renew the supply of atmospheric oxygen. The destruction of forests may reduce the speed of renewal; the pollution of the oceans may affect the phytoplankton, which is equally important. This reduction in renewal is, at least in the short term, unlikely to endanger our oxygen supplies, which are probably sufficient for several hundred years, but the long-term composition of the atmosphere probably is being significantly affected, and will need to be safeguarded.

The atmosphere contains toxic gases, perhaps the most important being sulphur dioxide. Two thirds of the output of this gas is from natural sources, particularly the decay of vegetation in swamps, and from volcanoes. This natural SO_2 is just as toxic as that produced by man. It is harmful locally, but global levels are too low to have much effect. Man also raises the level of SO_2 in cities and where he is most numerous, often damaging trees and other plants which are particularly susceptible. These include lichens, mosses and liverworts, which are often absent from cities and from rural areas on the leeward side of cities. SO_2 pollution is at present seldom serious enough to harm man, except when its effects are combined with those of smoke. Among other damaging gases produced by industry is fluorine, which harms vegetation and is particularly dangerous to cattle.

Automobiles and aircraft also pollute the atmosphere. Exhausts from internal combustion engines contain many potentially dangerous substances, including carbon dioxide (CO_2), carbon monoxide (CO), oxides of nitrogen (NO), unburned hydrocarbons and lead. All these pollute the air of cities, often to a dangerous extent. In some areas where this pollution is already serious its effects are exacerbated by climatic factors. A temperature inversion traps the concentrated pollution near to the ground, and if combined with bright sunlight a photochemical reaction produces a toxic smog as seen in California and Tokyo.

Aircraft cause ground level pollution similar to that of automobiles. Supersonic planes (SST) flying in the thin atmosphere of the stratosphere may impose a greater threat. The amount of water vapour and of substances like oxides of nitrogen is likely to exceed, at least locally, the mass of the natural atmosphere, and some scientists are concerned that this may upset the existing conditions. One risk is that levels of ozone (O_3) may be reduced. The ozone in these high levels acts as a filter to the dangerous radiation from the Sun; if the ozone layer is reduced, too much radiation could reach the surface of the Earth. If too much ultraviolet radiation did penetrate to Earth living things would die. Calculations from measurements from rockets fired into the atmosphere indicate the amount of ozone that has to be present. Removal of ozone would come through jet exhausts: nitrous and hydrocarbon substances would modify the rate at which the chemical reaction takes place encouraging the separated two- and one-atom molecules to recombine to reform ozone. These substances would also steal some of the oxygen to form other compounds. The risk of this is probably small, but is one reason why environmentalists have opposed the operation of SST until the whole subject has been thoroughly studied.

In fact the possible changes of flying too many aircraft too high in the stratosphere is open to endless speculation, and will continue to be so until very much more knowledge of the upper atmosphere is obtained from scientific satellite exploration and allied investigations. Influences from the conditions 15 to 30 kilometres high have little direct bearing on the short-term weather forecast. Hence the amount of investigation of atmospheric conditions at these rarified heights has been small.

A potentially greater threat to the ozone layer would be widespread use throughout the world of fluoro-carbide aerosol sprays. The effect of these sprays can be studied directly and there are ample grounds for concern.

Energy and the environment
Human civilisation depends on an increasing supply of energy. At present most of this comes from burning fossil fuels: man is using at a fast rate the stored energy produced over millions of years by photosynthesis. Even with economies, oil reserves will be used up in a hundred years and

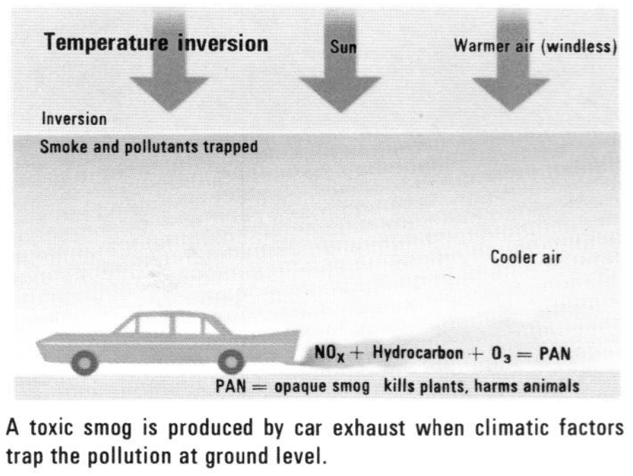

A toxic smog is produced by car exhaust when climatic factors trap the pollution at ground level.

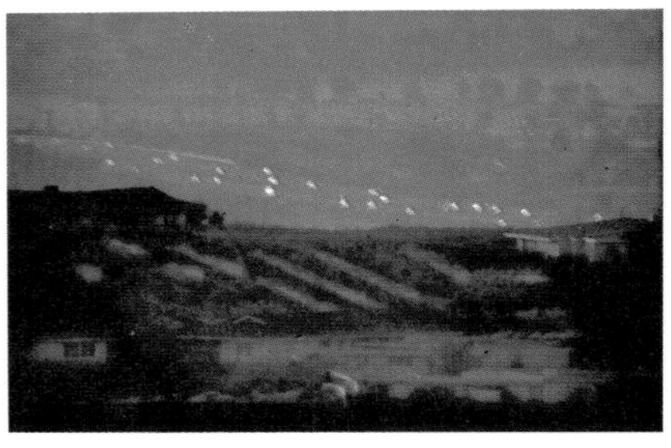

Traffic in Los Angeles

coal in two hundred. This will at least remove certain types of atmospheric pollution. Hydroelectric power is clean, but the amount attainable is limited. The energy of the Sun (solar energy) may be trapped directly and may make some contribution, but most future plans assume that nuclear power will play a greater, and ultimately a predominating, part in supplying man's needs. There are fears, however, concerning radiation hazards in spite of safeguards. Nuclear power stations are today very carefully controlled so that little radiation escapes to pollute the air or the sea, but as they increase in numbers the risk must grow. The greatest danger, however, is from the increasing amounts of radioactive waste, which are difficult to dispose of safely. Atmospheric testing of nuclear weapons imposes a further radiation risk whilst nuclear warfare of a global kind could lead to radiation levels so high as to threaten the existence of mankind.

Much of the energy man produces is lost as wasted heat. This too could eventually upset the climatic balance of the Earth. Already our large cities have a local climate measurably warmer than that of the surrounding country, though global effects are at present negligible. More serious 'thermal pollution' can occur locally when water from rivers and lakes is used for cooling purposes in industry as in large electrical generators, whether using fossil fuels or nuclear fuel. Water effluents from such power stations may be so hot that fish and invertebrates are killed; and even when heat pollution is less serious the water may be de-oxygenated so that aquatic life is asphyxiated. However, most electrical generating authorities are aware of the problem and try to guard against such damage to life.

Fresh water pollution

Rivers, lakes and the sea are all polluted by man. Limited amounts of sewage and other substances are disposed of by the process of self-purification in which nutrient salts are removed and used by living organisms – the normal process of biological cycling. Overloading prevents this from happening, and encourages organisms suited to living under polluted conditions. Man can reverse these processes by proper treatment of urban and industrial effluents but even in these, nutrient salts can cause damage by 'eutrophication', or excessive fertilisation of the water. Fortunately technology has developed methods – the tertiary treatment of effluents – which can obviate this danger, but only at a high cost. In Lake Tahoe in the USA, once very badly polluted, the problem has been overcome in this way.

In modern agriculture, with 'factory farming' where livestock is kept indoors in vast numbers, the animals' excreta, when not used as manure on the land, is often a source of pollution. Inorganic chemical fertilisers may also cause pollution when leached from the land into rivers and lakes.

Pesticides

Modern agriculture depends on chemical pesticides, particularly herbicides (weed-killers) and insecticides. These substances have contributed enormously to solving the problem of world starvation. Unfortunately some pesticides have also become contaminants, not usually at dangerous levels but sometimes in sufficient amounts to have harmful ecological effects locally. The organochlorine insecticides, including DDT and dieldrin, are of special concern. Although the dangers have often been exaggerated, there are many cases of contamination by those substances.

DDT and dieldrin are very stable, long-lasting substances, which is a great advantage in, for example, protecting a house from disease-bearing mosquitoes. However, this very property makes them dangerous because they become concentrated in a particular food chain: a predator like a hawk can eat a number of pigeons or voles containing small amounts of DDT, and retain the DDT until a dangerous level is reached. Fish and other aquatic animals can also cause the concentration of pesticides in rivers, by a factor of as much as 10,000 times. Scientists are trying

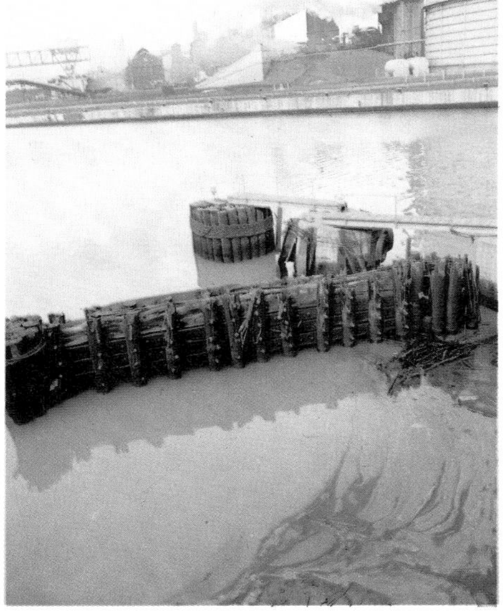

A river in Detroit, showing the effects of pollution.

to replace the more dangerous pesticides with other substances and to develop non-chemical methods of control. This will take time but, although chemical pesticides will be used for many years, with care global pollution will be avoided.

Some quantities of pesticides ultimately end up in the sea. Levels in estuaries and coastal areas can be high enough to damage fish and marine arthropods and even to affect plant life. In the open ocean, however, levels are very low, and there is at present no evidence that the phytoplankton is in danger of being damaged. Some scientists have suggested that levels are likely to increase in the future to danger point, but this does not seem to be happening yet. In fact levels in many marine fish and in the sea birds which eat them are decreasing and not increasing because better controls have been introduced in many countries.

Salt water pollution

The importance of the oceans in sustaining the natural balance cannot be over-stated; pollution of the oceans is therefore a very serious matter. The most obvious pollutant is oil including waste oil discharged by ships, or spilled when oil tankers ships are damaged or wrecked. Some oil is also spilled at terminals where it is pumped ashore from tankers. Leaks from underwater oil wells are difficult to control and can cause pollution more serious than that from the sinking of the largest tanker. Oil is dangerous because it floats on the surface of the ocean and most life, particularly plant life, is found near the surface. Fortunately the most toxic substances in oil are relatively volatile, and evaporate from the ocean's surface, but the tarry residues can damage fish and interfere with the life and photosynthesis of the phytoplankton.

1
Aerial spraying of pesticides, including DDT, is cheap and efficient, but may contaminate rivers, lakes and surrounding land.

2
Radiation escaping from nuclear power stations, and as fallout after testing atom bombs, is all harmful to life.

3
Chemical fertilizers have greatly increased crop production, but they may be washed off or leached out of the soil. They then cause eutrophication, which stimulates the production of harmful algal growth.

4
Rivers are particularly susceptible to pollution. Sewage, untreated or insufficiently treated, is one danger. Even properly treated sewage still contains nutrient salts – nitrogen and phosphorus – the latter coming increasingly from detergents used in domestic washing machines. Some detergents pass unchanged through sewage works, and cause massive amounts of foam on rivers.

5
Estuaries and coastal waters are particularly at risk from pollution, especially from oil.

6
Mining, both deep mining with its associated slag heaps and open cast mining, can destroy vast areas of the countryside. Many industries produce large areas of dereliction, particularly when they become obsolete.

7
Marine pollution from oil results from spillage from tankers and other ships, but underwater oil wells are now an even greater hazard.

8
Automobiles need vast motorways which deface countryside and town alike. They can also cause serious air pollution.

9
An increasing number of farm animals now live indoors ('factory farming') where their excreta, instead of being used as manure on the land, may pollute rivers.

10
Industrial factories and power stations pollute the air with sulphur, fluorine and smoke; they may also pass poisonous effluents and too much waste heat into the rivers.

11
Urban development is at the expense of living forests and agricultural land. Most cities pollute the air with smoke and toxic gases.

12
Large as the oceans are, they cannot absorb unharmed the increasing burden of waste.

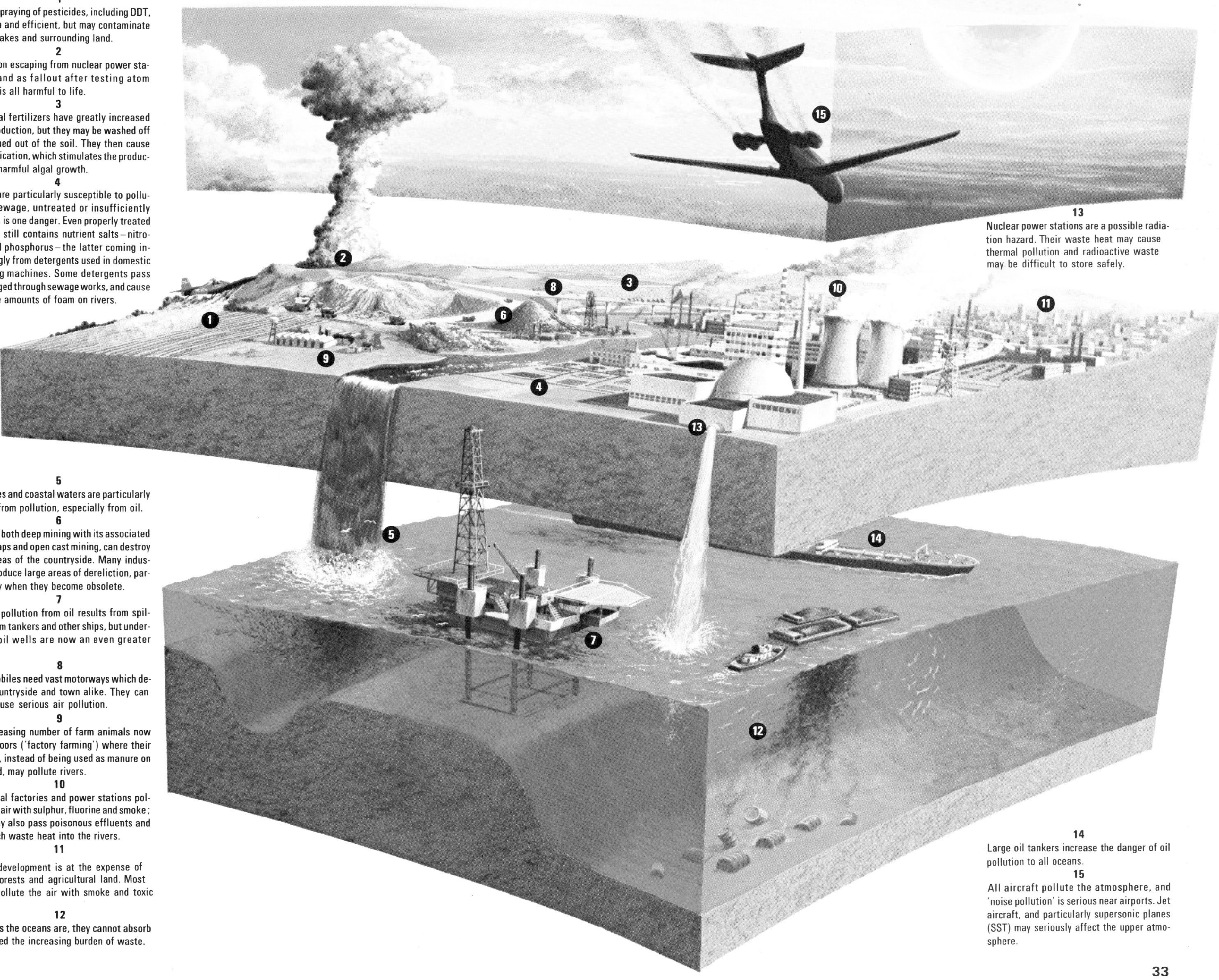

13
Nuclear power stations are a possible radiation hazard. Their waste heat may cause thermal pollution and radioactive waste may be difficult to store safely.

14
Large oil tankers increase the danger of oil pollution to all oceans.

15
All aircraft pollute the atmosphere, and 'noise pollution' is serious near airports. Jet aircraft, and particularly supersonic planes (SST) may seriously affect the upper atmosphere.

Techniques of navigation

Early maps were designed to show the spatial relationship between local geographical features, territorial boundaries, and routes. The early use of maps for finding the way (the essence of navigation) has persisted, first for travellers on land, later for mariners, and more recently for airmen and space travellers. Among the necessary instruments of marine navigation the chart – the seaman's name for a map – is important. In addition to the chart, the other basic navigational tools are 'sailing directions' which, in early times were passed down orally from master to apprentice, but which are now in printed form; the log, or device for measuring the speed of a ship; and, the most important instrument of all, the compass.

The Greeks

Anaximander of Miletus (6th century BC) is credited with having drawn the first map. Anaximander's map, which must have been crude and highly conjectural, marked an important epoch in the history of geography and navigation in particular, and in human progress in general. The first rectangular map was constructed by Democritus (5th century BC) who claimed that the habitable world was one and a half times as long in the east–west direction as it was broad in the north–south direction. It was this concept that led to the use of the terms 'latitude' and 'longitude', meaning respectively breadth and length, for defining terrestrial positions. Dicaearchus (4th century BC) constructed a map on which the first parallel of latitude was drawn through the Pillars of Hercules at the entrance to the Mediterranean Sea and the Island of Rhodes. Eratosthenes (3rd century BC), who made the first scientific attempt at measuring the Earth's size, constructed a map (according to the geographer Strabo) on which seven parallels of latitude and seven meridians or lines passing through the poles and any given place, irregularly spaced, were drawn; but the principles of Eratosthenes' division are not known. Hipparchus (2nd century BC) demanded that the positions of places to be mapped should be verified using astronomical observations. He suggested that parallels of latitude and meridians drawn on maps should be equidistantly spaced, and that to determine relative longitudes meridians should be regulated from eclipse observations.

Ptolemy of Alexandria (c AD 90–168), the 'Prince of Ancient Geographers', was the founder of scientific cartography. His monumental *Geographia* contains detailed explanations of mathematical geography and map projections. Ptolemy suggested that the Earth should be divided on the basis of climatic zones and that longitudes should be measured eastwards from a prime meridian through the 'Fortunate Isles' which he believed to be the westernmost part of the habitable globe. Ptolemy referred to Marinus, a Tyrian cartographer who employed a simple cylindrical projection for his maps.

Medieval navigation

The earliest charts extant are medieval maps of the Mediterranean world: the first record of a chart being used on a ship dating from 1270. By that time the Genoese, Venetians and Pisans had gained control of the maritime trade of the Mediterranean, and significant improvements in nautical science took place during the ascendancy of the Italian City States.

Portolan chart

The renaissance of scientific map-making began with the portolan charts of the thirteenth century to meet the needs of seamen. These charts were hand-drawn, each on a complete skin. The earlier examples are of the Mediterranean and Black Sea regions, but by the seventeenth century they embraced the whole of the known world, A characteristic feature of the portolan chart is the maze of intersecting straight lines which cover the sea area. These are systems of rhumb lines, each radiating from the centre of one of a series of compass roses. It is argued that each system of rhumb lines on a portolan chart denotes a magnetic compass, and that such charts, therefore, were based on compass bearings. If this be so, they must have made their first appearance after the invention of the magnetic compass.

There is no contemporary explanation of how the rhumb lines on a portolan chart were used; but it seems obvious that they were employed for finding the magnetic course to steer from one place to another. To find the course the navigator would place a straight-edge joining the plotted positions of departure and destination; and then, by means of dividers, he would seek the rhumb line most nearly parallel to the straight-edge. By tracing this line to the centre of the appropriate compass rose, he would readily ascertain the compass course to steer.

Magnetic compass

There is no strong evidence to suggest that the magnetic compass was not invented independently in the Mediterranean region; it is likely that it was invented in China perhaps before it made its first appearance, in the 12th century, in the Mediterranean. The 'natural' compass is the horizon of an observer, and in very early times, the horizon was divided into four quadrants by two rectangular diameters to indicate the four principal directions, North, East, South and West. The horizontal angle between the direction of North (or South) and that in which the ship is heading is the 'Course' of the ship. It is easy to see that when a ship is heading in a fixed direction on any given course, the line she traces out on the sea is one that cuts all meridians at the same angle. Such a line is a rhumb line, and because of the convenience of not having to change the ship's course when sailing from one given place to another, the normal navigational practice, especially for short distances, is to sail along a rhumb line.

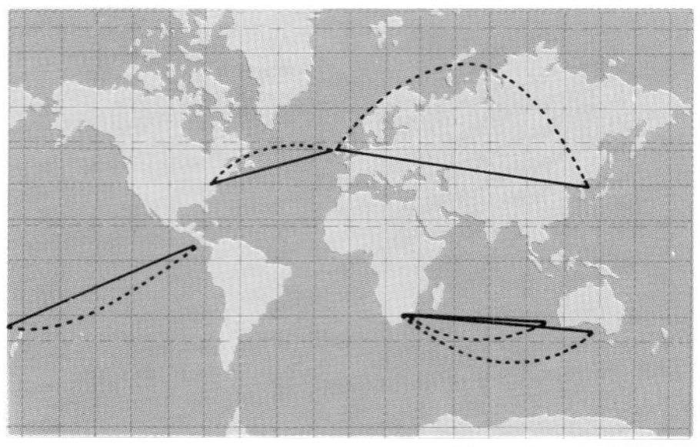

Mercator projection

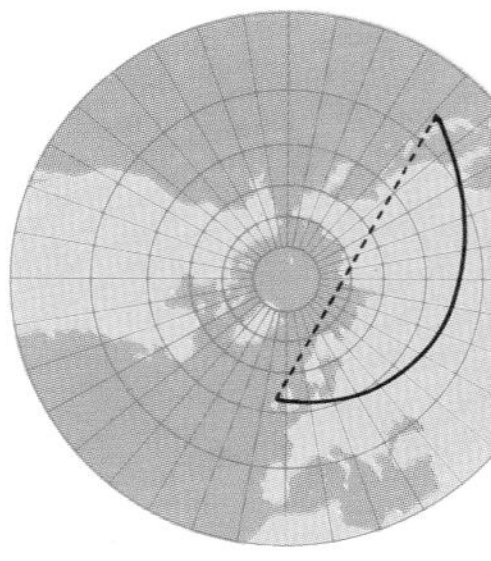

Gnomonic projection

Mercator's projection shows all parallels of latitude as if equal in length to the Equator, although on the globe they are obviously progressively shorter towards the poles. Mercator increased his North–South scale on the meridians to match the increase in East–West scale, so that at any one point scale is equal in both directions and away from that point increases or decreases in equal proportions. Angles from the North–South meridians (i.e. bearings) can therefore be measured with a protractor without distortion. A straight line (rhumb line) thus has a constant bearing, but is not the shortest distance between its two end points. The Gnomonic chart has scale distortion outwards from its centre point, but the shortest distance between two points is the straight line joining them. The route required is therefore first plotted as a straight line on the Gnomonic chart and is then transferred to the Mercator chart as a series of straight lines, the bearing of each being measured with a protractor. A ship or aircraft does not follow the true Great Circle route, which would require continuous slow alteration of bearing, but steers on a constant bearing for a period of time and then changes to the new bearing at the next junction point along the series of straight lines drawn on the chart.

The Mercator map shows Great Circle routes and rhumb lines for three shipping routes and one air route. The latter is also shown on the Gnomonic map. The Great Circle route always lies on the poleward side of the rhumb line between the same points.

The Mercator chart need not be based on the Equator, but can be drawn at right-angles in the Transverse form, based on any meridian. This allows the polar areas to be charted, which is important for air routes although not for shipping. Likewise, the Gnomonic chart need not be centred on a pole but can be drawn centred on any point.

The navigator is, of course, constrained by many factors in laying out his route: the sailor may have to plan his voyage as a series of different Great Circle segments in order to avoid land, shallow water or ice hazards; sailing ships require routes planned with consideration of prevailing and seasonal winds and of ocean currents.

The Golden Age of Discovery

When western Europeans first embarked on Atlantic voyages during the early phase of the Golden Age of Discovery, the need for scientifically constructed charts was pressing. Within the confines of the enclosed Mediterranean, where sailing distances between ports were relatively short, the portolan charts sufficed. But for ocean navigation, in which east–west distances of thousands of miles were common, something better was vitally necessary.

Although seamen must always have known that the Earth is spherical, the charts used by the Portuguese and Spanish mariners during the Age of Discoveries were based on the assumption that the Earth's surface was plane. The graticules or network of grid-lines drawn on the charts were simple rectangular networks in which equidistant parallels of latitude and meridians on the Earth were each projected as equidistant parallel lines forming a 'plane' projection. On such a map of the world every parallel of latitude is projected as a straight line of constant length. On the globe, however, the length of the parallels of latitude diminish from a maximum at the equator in latitude 0° to zero at either pole in latitude 90°.

Mercator chart

The most important step forward on the development of the navigational chart coincided with the publication of a world map in 1569 by the Flemish cartographer Gerhard Kremer, better known as Mercator. This map is the prototype of the modern chart.

On Mercator's world map equidistantly spaced meridians on the Earth are projected as equidistant parallel straight lines, and equidistantly spaced parallels of latitude are projected as parallel straight lines which cut the meridians at right angles. The graticule therefore, is rectangular like that of the 'plane' chart. The important difference is that the spacing of the parallels on a Mercator chart increases polewards in exactly the same proportion as the distortion of the east–west spacing of the meridians. In technical terms the Mercator projection is such that every line on the chart is distorted proportionally and therefore the projection is orthomorphic. In a cartographic sense, this means that angles are not distorted so that lines of constant course, or rhumb lines, are projected as straight lines. A mariner wishing to find the rhumb line course to steer from one place to another simply measures on a Mercator chart the angle which the rhumb line makes with any of the projected meridians.

Gnomonic chart

It was soon realised by early ocean navigators that long voyages could be substantially shortened, when wind and currents allowed, by practising what became known as 'Great Circle Sailing' instead of 'Rhumb Line Sailing'.

A great circle is a circle on a sphere on whose plane the centre of the sphere lies. The shortest route along the surface of a sphere between two points is along the shorter arc of the great circle on which the two points lie. In practising rhumb line sailing, although the navigator benefits in that a constant course is steered, his ship travels a greater distance than would be the case by practising great circle sailing. A major disadvantage of the latter however, is that the course along a great circle route constantly changes. Nevertheless, in the interests of economy of fuel and time, great circle sailing is commonly practised.

On a Mercator chart a great circle is projected as a relatively complex curve. To plot a great circle route on a chart, a navigator employs a chart constructed on the gnomonic projection as an auxiliary to the Mercator chart. Unlike the conventional Mercator projection, the mathematical principles of which were first given by the eminent Elizabethan mathematician Edward Wright, the gnomonic projection is a geometrical or perspective projection in which points on a spherical surface are projected onto a plane touching the surface, by straight lines of projection which emanate from the centre of the sphere. It is clear that on a gnomonic projection great circle arcs are projected as straight lines. To plot a great circle route on a gnomonic chart the navigator simply joins the plotted positions of the points of departure and destination with a straight line. To transfer the great circle route onto a Mercator chart merely involves lifting positions of a series of points on the route as projected on the gnomonic chart and transferring them to the Mercator chart. A fair curve through these points delineates the great circle route on the Mercator chart. The navigator practising great circle sailing sails along a series of short rhumb lines which collectively approximate to the great circle arc described above.

Nautical Astronomy

A system of navigation in which the navigator relies wholly on compass and log to determine direction and distance travelled is known as 'Dead Reckoning' or 'DR Navigation'. Because compass and log are not without errors, and because their errors are cumulative, DR Navigation is unreliable and imperfect. It becomes necessary, in the interests of safety, for a navigator to be able to check his progress by some means other than by DR Navigation.

The defects of DR Navigation led to the development of 'Nautical Astronomy' by which a navigator may find his latitude and longitude from astronomical observations. The basic tools of a nautical astronomer are a *Nautical Almanac*, a sextant and a chronometer. The *Nautical Almanac* gives the celestial positions of the sun, moon, planets and stars used in nautical astronomy, against Greenwich Mean Time or GMT. The sextant is the instrument by which the navigator measures the elevations above his horizon of the sun, moon, planet or star he observes. The chronometer is merely an accurate timekeeper from which the GMT of an astronomical observation on 'sight' is obtained.

In the open sea a navigator may find his latitude from a sight of a celestial body on the celestial sphere bearing due north or south at which time the body reaches its greatest altitude during the day. Such an observation is known as a 'meridian altitude' sight. The celestial sphere is an imaginary sphere surrounding the Earth, on which celestial bodies are assumed to lie. The astronomical navigator constructs a network of guidelines on the celestial sphere like lines of latitude and longitude on the Earth. The equivalent of latitude is declination and that of longitude is called right ascension.

A mariner may find his ship's longitude from an observation of a celestial body provided that the observer knows his latitude. To find longitude it is necessary to solve a spherical triangle at the apexes of which are located, respectively, the celestial pole, the observer's zenith, and the observed body.

Radio and electronic navigation

The application of radio and electronic principles during the 20th century has revolutionised navigation. In the early decades of the century 'radio time signals' were made available for checking chronometers. Later, medium frequency radio direction finding (MF/DF) enabled a navigator to find his ship's position, even in fog when visual observations of the land or the celestial bodies rendered the traditional methods of navigation useless. This method of 'fixing' a position is exactly analogous to the method of taking bearings of lighthouses or other visible landmarks. Later still, the introduction of radar techniques facilitated coastal navigation in low visibility as well as providing efficient means for avoiding collision in fog. Radar, a contraction of 'radio detection and ranging' was developed between 1935 and 1940 independently in a number of countries. Range, direction and velocity are all displayed visually by means of a cathode-ray tube. After the Second World War refinements to radar techniques led in the direction of hyperbolic navigation.

Hyperbolic navigation

During the Second World War the need for sophisticated navigational systems for fast-flying military aircraft led to the introduction of hyper-

bolic navigation.

Hyperbolic navigation is based on the accurate measurement of the difference in times taken by simultaneous signals, transmitted from each of two fixed transmitting stations, to reach an observer.

If an observer receives radio signals transmitted simultaneously from each of two stations then he is able to measure the intervals of time taken for the radio energy to travel from the two stations to his position. Knowing the speed at which radio energy travels he can translate the difference of the two time intervals into a corresponding distance-difference. The position of constant distance-difference relative to the two stations is a hyperbola, which has the stations at its focal points. Such a hyperbola plotted on a chart gives the navigator a line somewhere on which his position is located. By plotting the second hyperbola from observations of a second pair of stations, the observer then locates his position at the point of intersection of the two hyperbolae. Systems of this nature, include the Decca Navigator, Loran and Omega, all of which are extensively used on aircraft and ships (see opposite for description of Decca Navigator System).

To facilitate hyperbolic navigation specially prepared charts, overprinted with families of hyperbolae, are used. Such a chart is called a 'lattice chart'. An example of a Decca Lattice Chart is illustrated.

The sophisticated technology of the Space Age has had a significant impact on navigation of ships and aeroplanes.

Inertial navigation

The system known as 'Inertial Navigation' is essentially, a sophisticated DR system in which the motion of an aircraft or ship is sensed, without compass or log, so that the position of the craft relative to its starting position is at all times known. It is a self-contained system that functions independently of weather conditions that can hamper the nautical astronomer, and of radio signals which may suffer natural or man-made interference. For this latter reason inertial navigation is of particular importance to naval vessels, especially nuclear submarines which attempt to avoid detection.

Satellite, VOR and DME navigation

Another advanced navigational technique of the Space Age is that which employs Earth satellites. By this system position finding to an accuracy of 0·1 miles is possible.

If a satellite is placed in polar orbit and can be tracked and plotted accurately, at a given instant of time its exact latitude, longitude and height is known. The distance of the satellite from a ship is obtained by utilising the Doppler principle that electromagnetic waves are modified by the motion of the source. As the satellite approaches the ship, its rapid motion shortens the wavelength of the signals. More waves therefore reach the ship per second than would be received from a stationary source. The wavelength leng-

thens as the satellite moves away from the ship and fewer waves per second are received. From the change in the number of signals received during transit of the satellite, range can be calculated.

A ship in motion fixes its position from more than one pass of a satellite; if stationary a greater number of fixes can be taken – these are called geodetic fixes and are often used by oil rigs and other off-shore installations such as large navigation beacons and lightships.

The navigation of aircraft is facilitated by VOR (VHF Omnidirectional Range) and DME (Distance Measuring Equipment). VOR allows an airman to navigate from any position directly towards or away from a fixed radio beacon, and DME enables him to measure the distance between his aircraft and the beacon using radio techniques.

Other electronic aids include the radio altimeter to measure the distance above ground, and the ground-speed indicator which uses the Doppler shift in reflected radio waves. Computers convert data to information capable of being instantly read by the pilot, and they are also capable of carrying out position-determining (dead-reckoning) by monitoring all speed and course changes of the aircraft. The automatic pilot can therefore carry out all the tasks necessary for piloting the aircraft.

Navigation, as has been stated, is essentially concerned with finding the way, but in certain instances, of more importance is the avoidance of collision. This becomes crucial in the vicinity of busy airports and seaways. The application of the concept of modern traffic control, in which aircraft are segregated and ships are routed, has marked an important epoch in the recent history of navigation. As far as the airman is concerned the role of the land-based traffic controller is vitally important in the navigation process. The Air Traffic Controller ensures that all the aircraft in his area follow carefully planned and pre-arranged routes. For certain defined points on these routes the controller identifies the height of each aircraft approaching it and the aircraft's arrival time at the point. By radio communication the controller is able to give directions to the pilots to ensure safe landings. The data for each aircraft is given on a 'flight strip', and it is the computerising of these data that will ultimately relieve controllers of much of their present onerous workload. (See Approach and Landing Chart for Heathrow Airport, and en route chart below).

The air and sea navigator is no longer limited to a small number of charts for use during a flight or voyage. He now has a wide variety at differing scales to back up his electronic aids. Coastal and land areas in particular are well mapped, and high-speed and multi-colour printing and symbol standardisation has now ensured that the navigator has information more readily available and more accurate than ever before.

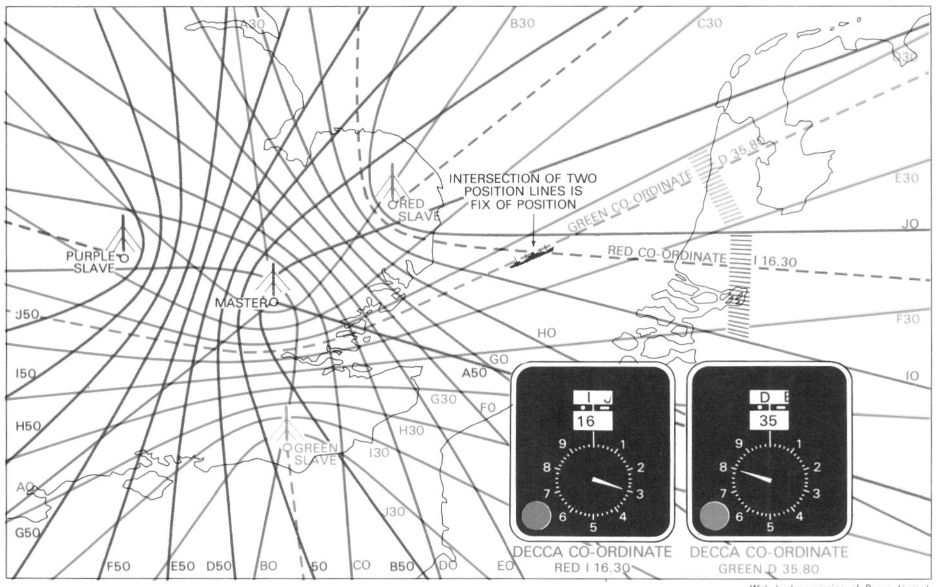

The Decca Navigator Sysytem fixes position using continuous radio waves from two transmitters. In the south-east of England the master transmitter is augmented by purple, red and green slave transmitters. The fix is given by the intersection of two hyperbolic position lines, and is obtained from the readings of two Decometer Indicators.

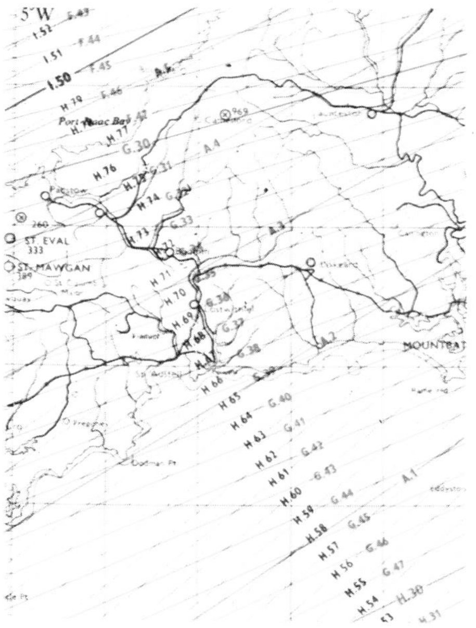

A Decca Lattice Chart used for location of aircraft position. The map shows only coast and rivers, railways, beacons and airfields (with their heights above sea level). The important part of the chart is the system of coloured lines, in purple, red and green, each colour representing directional signals from a fixed transmitter. It is possible to determine the aircraft's position on a line from each transmitter and so fix it on the map by the intersection of the corresponding coloured lines. For example, in the Bristol Channel a good fix can be obtained using the green transmitter with either the red or the purple; using only the latter two colours would give an uncertain fix.

Part of an aeronautical topographical chart. The relief of the land is shown by generalised contours at a 500-foot Vertical Interval, with layer-tinting to assist a quick appreciation of land form. Spot heights are given for the highest summits, which must obviously be avoided. Railways, main roads, towns and major settlements are shown, as these are easily identified from an aircraft. The pattern of runways on the airfield is shown diagrammatically to avoid confusion; note the second airport to the south of Edinburgh (Turnhouse) which has a distinctly different pattern of runways. Direction beacons and flashing lights are marked for night flights. More detailed charts than this one are used for approach and take-off, and for restricted areas or directed flight paths.

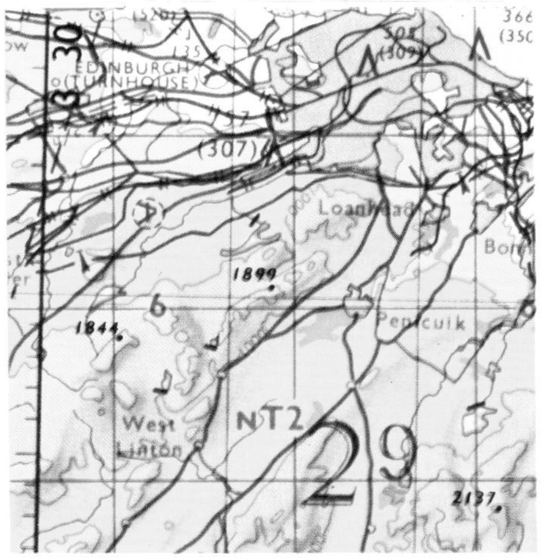

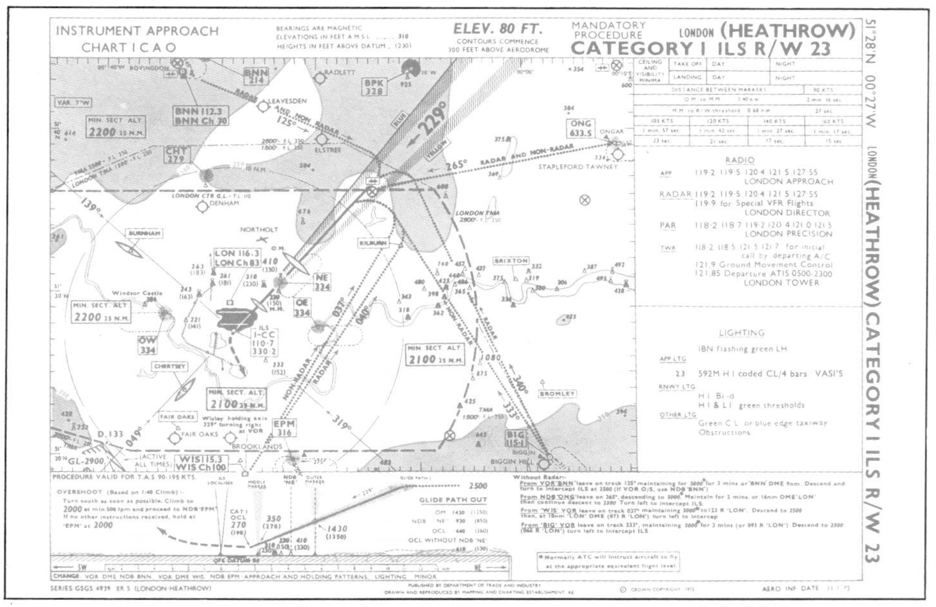

The Approach and Landing Chart for London (Heathrow) Airport illustrates the complexity of operation at a busy international centre. The higher land in the area is colour-tinted, and spot heights of topographical features and of towers, pylons and other obstructions are given not only above sea level but also above airfield altitude as aircraft altimeters can be set to read height above the runway. Beacons, lights, radar information, etc., is given in detail, with routes for visual and instrumental approaches.

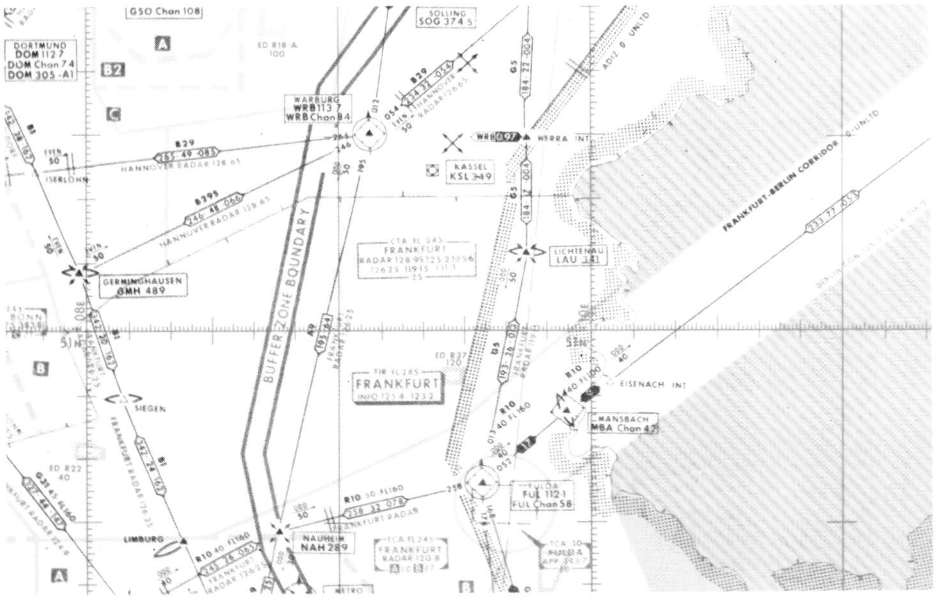

An en route chart gives the pilot the bearings and distances along his route from beacon to beacon, which allows a dead reckoning passage by compass and airspeed indicator, suitably corrected for wind strength and direction. The chart also indicates information such as the aircraft control zones, radar transmitters, and lines of latitude and longitude. This is a specialised chart intended solely for aerial navigation purposes, and needs constant revision.

The Universe

No one knows how large the Universe is, or if indeed it has any limits. It stretches as far as our largest telescopes can see. Even a beam of light, which travels at the fastest known speed in the Universe, 186,000 miles per second, (i.e. the speed of light), takes 10,000 million years to reach the Earth from the remotest visible objects. Space is so vast that ordinary units of distance become insignificant. Distances in astronomy are usually described in light years, the distance that a beam of light covers in one year. This is equivalent to about six million million miles. The nearest star to our Sun, called Alpha Centauri, is 4·3 light years away, which means that we see it as it appeared 4·3 years ago. The remotest visible objects in the Universe are over 10,000 million light years away, which means that we see them as they appeared before the Earth was born.

Star magnitudes

The stars we see at night are relatively close to us in space. They are among the nearest of the estimated 100,000 million stars that make up our whirling star system called the Galaxy, the densest part of which is visible as the faint hazy band called the Milky Way. Stars appear different in brightness because some are genuinely bigger and hotter than others and also because they are all at different distances from the Earth. Astronomers grade star brightness in steps called magnitudes. The brightest-appearing stars are termed first magnitude, and the faintest visible to the naked eye are sixth magnitude. Still fainter stars, visible only through telescopes, are given progressively larger magnitude numbers. Each magnitude step corresponds to a change in brightness of approximately 2½ times.

The beginnings of the Universe

Astronomers speculate that originally the Universe was compressed into a single point from which it began to expand. The event which set off this expansion, and therefore marked the origin of the Universe as we know it, is termed the Big Bang. In this Big Bang, all the matter in the Universe was flung outwards in the form of a dense gas, which has since condensed into giant globules to form galaxies of stars, all of which continue to rush rapidly outwards as space expands.

When did the Big Bang occur? According to current measurements of the rate of expansion of the Universe, all the matter that we now see in space must have been compressed together into a superdense globule between 10,000 million and 20,000 million years ago – about two to four times the age of the Earth. Therefore, modern astronomy allows us to date the Creation with a fair degree of accuracy.

If this view is correct, we should be able to see the Universe as it appeared shortly after it was born by looking deep into space. This is equivalent to looking back in time, because we see objects whose light has taken thousands of millions of years to reach us. Certainly, as we look ever further into space, the Universe begins to change in appearance. Instead of normal-looking galaxies like our own or the Andromeda spiral, astronomers find strange galaxies with brilliant cores known as Seyfert galaxies. Most remote of all are the mysterious quasars, intense sources of light and radio waves which are believed to represent the violent birth of a galaxy. Seyfert galaxies mark a more recent stage than quasars in the evolution of galaxies.

Further confirmation of the Big Bang origin of the Universe has come in recent years with the discovery by radio astronomers of a weak background warmth pervading the Universe. This background radiation is believed to be heat left over from the intense fireball of the Big Bang, and it means that space is not entirely cold, but has a temperature 2·7° above absolute zero on the Centigrade scale.

What will happen to the Universe in the future? One possibility is that the expansion will slow down and the Universe will start to contract again until a further Big Bang. According to one theory, the Universe might continue with endless cycles of expansion and contraction. Astronomers can find no sign that the expansion of the Universe is markedly slowing down. They now think that the Universe will continue to expand forever, slowly thinning out, until all the stars are extinguished and the Universe runs down into eternal darkness.

Composition and structure of the Sun and planets

The **Sun** is a giant gaseous ball of hydrogen and helium with traces of heavier elements such as iron, carbon, calcium and sodium. There is uncertainty about the nature of its internal structure, but there is probably a large core in which thermonuclear reactions produce vast quantities of heat which is transmitted upwards by radiation and convection to the photosphere, the Sun's visible surface. Hydrogen is converted into helium and in the process 4,000,000 tons of matter are lost to the Sun every second. In spite of this staggering loss the supply of hydrogen at the core is sufficient for another 1,500 million years.

Mercury, Venus, Earth and **Mars,** the so-called terrestrial planets, consist largely of silicates (compounds of silicon and oxygen with various metals) and iron. They also include simpler compounds, such as oxides, some of which contain heat-producing radioactive elements. All four planets have undergone differentiation at some stage, with the heavier elements and compounds falling towards the centre. Thus each has a metallic core surrounded by a silicate mantle and topped with a crust of lighter silicates, although the relative sizes of these zones vary from planet to planet. The atmosphere of the Earth consists largely of oxygen and nitrogen, but those of Venus and Mars are predominantly carbon dioxide. Mercury has no atmosphere. The Moon has a composition similar to that of the terrestrial planets but with smaller concentrations of the more volatile elements.

The **Asteroids**, the thousands of small bodies revolving around the Sun mostly between Mars and Jupiter, vary in composition. About 80 per cent of them consist of silicates, 6–10 per cent are made of metal (chiefly iron with some nickel), and the rest are silicate-metal mixtures. Ceres, 429 miles in diameter, is the largest and Pallas (281

miles), is the second largest.

Jupiter is the largest of the planets, having a mass of about two and a half times greater than that of all the other planets combined. Because of its low density it must consist largely of light elements such as hydrogen and helium, although it probably also has a very small rocky core of silicates and iron. Surrounding this hypothetical core is a shell comprising mainly liquid atomic hydrogen, and above that is a surface layer of liquid molecular hydrogen. The atmosphere of Jupiter consists chiefly of hydrogen, helium, ammonia, methane and water. Apart from its great size, Jupiter is remarkable for the Red Spot and bands of clouds which sweep across its face.

Saturn, Uranus and **Neptune** are smaller than Jupiter but also have low densities and are similar in general composition and structure. Their rocky iron-silicate cores are proportionately larger, however, especially in the cases of Uranus and Neptune. All three planets have atmospheres in which the most abundant gas is hydrogen but in which there is little or no ammonia. Methane, on the other hand, is much more abundant than in the atmosphere of Jupiter. Titan, one of the 10 satellites of Saturn, is the largest satellite in the solar system (being larger even than the planet Mercury) and the only one known to have an atmosphere (mainly methane and hydrogen). It also appears to have a unique composition, for it comprises a rocky core surrounded by a wet rocky mantle, a layer of ammonia-water solution, and finally a surface layer of ice and methane. The rings of Saturn probably consist of small ice particles.

Pluto is an anomoly among the outer planets, although very little is really known about it. It is definitely very small, but its precise mass and density are uncertain. It would appear to have no atmosphere.

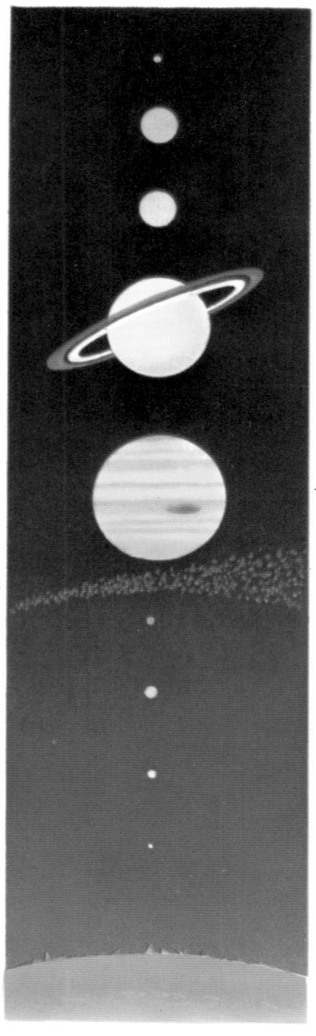

Pluto

Neptune

Uranus

Saturn

Jupiter

The asteroids

Mars

Earth

Venus

Mercury

The Sun

Planetary data	Mercury	Venus	Earth	Mars	Jupiter	Saturn	Uranus	Neptune	Pluto
Orbital revolution	87 days 23 hours	224 days 17 hours	365 days 6 hours	1 year 322 days	10 years 318 days	29 years 168 days	84 years 4 days	164 years 292 days	249 years 330 days
Distance from Sun in miles	36M	67M	92M	141M	465M	886M	1,783M	2,791M	3,671M
Orbital inclination	7°	3° 24′	0°	1° 48′	1° 18′	2° 30′	0° 48′	1° 48′	17° 12′
Equatorial diameter in miles	3,025	3,526	7,926·4	4,200	88,700	75,000	29,300	31,200	3,700
Rotation	59 days	243 days	23 hours 56 mins	24 hours 10 mins	9 hours 50 mins	10 hours 14 mins	10 hours 48 mins	14 hours	153 hours
Satellites	0	0	1	2	17	17	5	2	0
Orbital velocity in miles per second	29·8	21·8	18·5	15	8·1	6	4·2	3·4	3

Big Bang theory
Following initial explosion of exceedingly dense matter dispersal outward continues with simultaneous formation of galaxies. This event is estimated to have taken place between 10 and 20,000 million years ago.

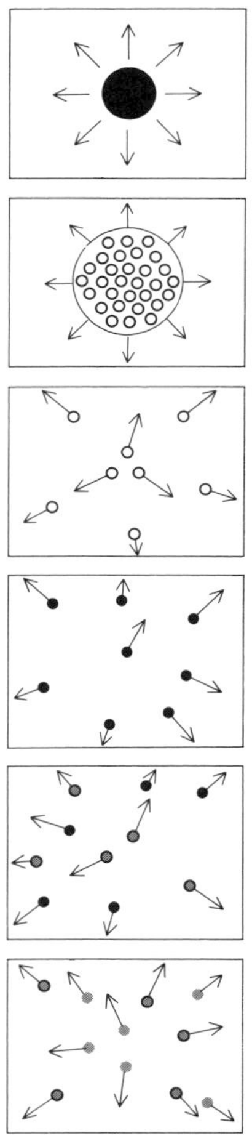

Steady State theory
The Universe did not originate at any one instant in time but all galaxies appear to be continually receding from each other. New matter is created to fill the spaces left and this forms new galaxies. There is strong evidence, particularly observational, against the theory.

○→ galaxies
●→ oldest galaxies
→ youngest galaxies
→ subsequent galaxies

Bode's Law
If 4 is added to the sequence 0, 3, 6, 12, etc., the resulting numbers give the relative distances of the seven nearest planets to the Sun. The Law, first published in 1772 does not appear valid for Neptune and Pluto at the outer reaches of the solar system.

Mercury	Venus	Earth	Mars	Ceres (Asteroid)	Jupiter	Saturn	Uranus
0	3	6	12	24	48	96	192
4	4	4	4	4	4	4	4
4	7	10	16	28	52	100	196

Stars and galaxies

Stars are born from giant clouds of gas and dust in a galaxy. A typical cloud is the famous nebula in the constellation of Orion. The Orion nebula is lit up by stars that have formed within it during the past few million years. Such a cloud can eventually give rise to a whole cluster of perhaps a hundred stars or more, like the Pleiades cluster in Taurus (see photograph).

As the cloud collapses under the inward pull of its own gravity, it breaks up into smaller clumps from which individual stars will form. Each clump continues to get smaller and denser until the pressure and temperature at its centre becomes so extreme that nuclear reactions start to make the gas ball a true, self-luminous star. Sometimes two, three, or more stars come into being close to each other, and remain linked by gravity throughout their lives as a double or multiple star. In some cases, a star may be surrounded by a disc of material left over from its formation, from which a planetary system may grow. Planets are cold and non-luminous and shine only by reflecting the light of their parent stars.

Stars differ in size and temperature depending on how much matter they contain. The Sun,

865,000 miles in diameter, is an average star in its size and temperature. Some stars are smaller and cooler than the Sun; these are known as red dwarfs, and they are so faint that even the nearest is invisible without a telescope. Other stars are larger and hotter than the Sun, so they appear white like Sirius or even blue like Rigel. A star is powered throughout most of its active life by nuclear reactions that turn hydrogen into helium, as the process in a hydrogen bomb. Stars consist mostly of hydrogen, which is by far the most abundant element in the Universe, and of which gas clouds such as the Orion nebula are mostly made.

As a star ages, it begins to run out of hydrogen at its centre. The nuclear fires then move outwards into the layers surrounding the core, generating more energy as they do so. In response to this the star begins to swell up into a red giant, perhaps 100 times its former size. Stars several times heavier than the Sun then undergo a runaway series of nuclear reactions at their core, leading to their eventual eruption in a nuclear holocaust called a supernova. When a star erupts as a supernova, its brightness increases by millions of times for a few days or weeks before it fades away into obscurity.

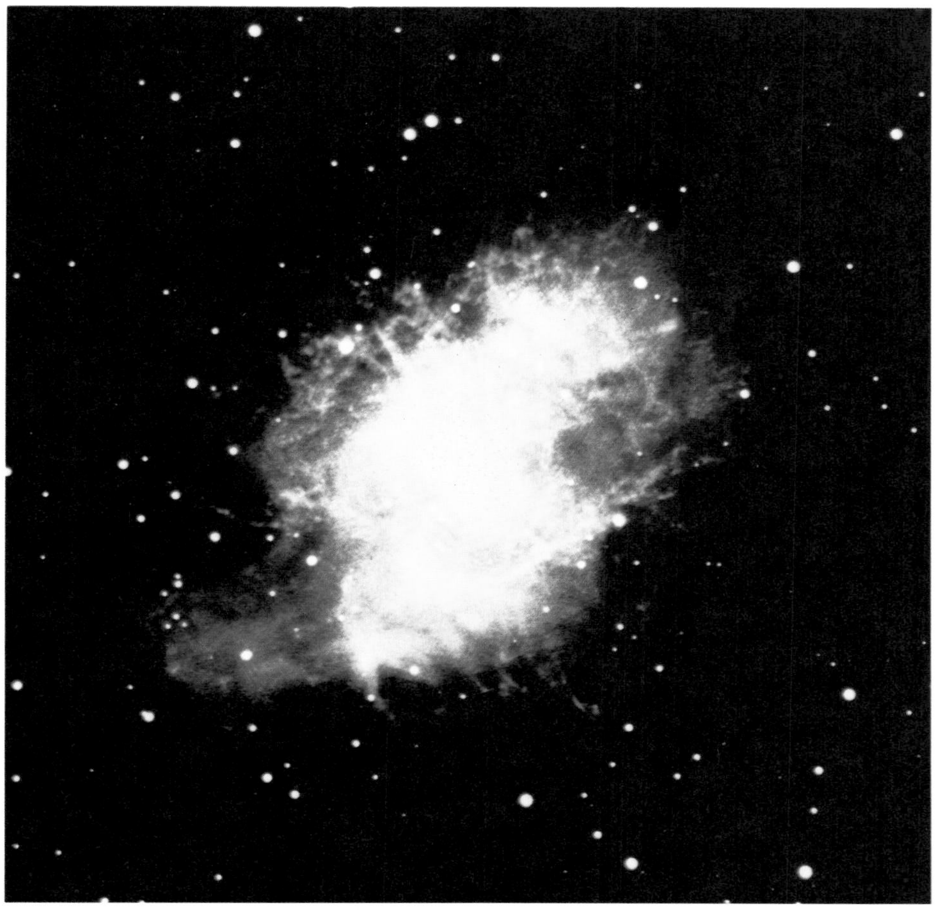

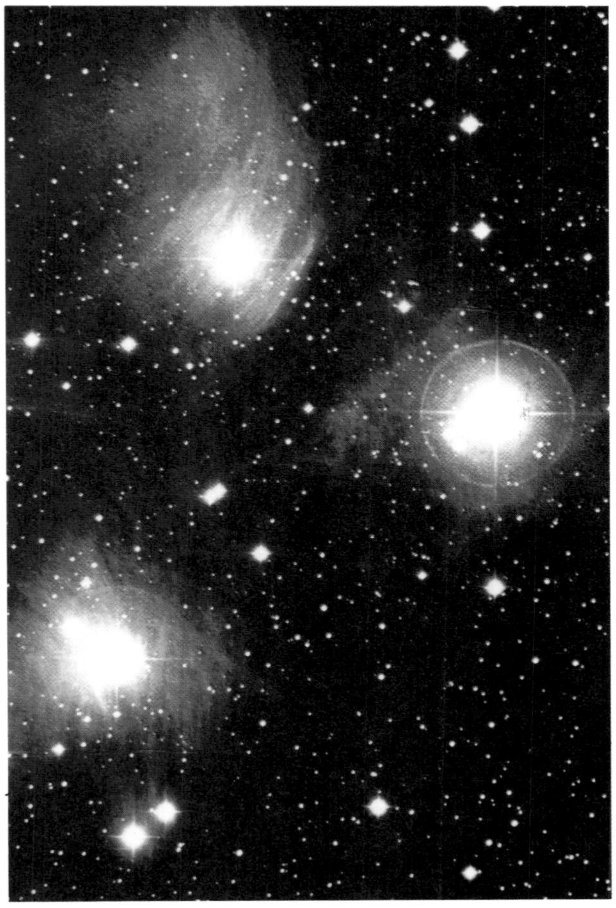

Crab Nebula
The supernova which was expanded to give the Crab Nebula occurred about 4,000 years ago. What we see today is the stage of development after only 920 years. A supernova explosion follows the collapse of a star at very high temperatures, and the rate of ejection of material is very rapid indeed; for about two weeks the radiation may be 200 times that of the Sun. The Nebula is 6,000 light years away in the constellation Taurus.

Pleiades
This cluster of 200 stars is about 130 parsecs distant from the Earth or 425 light years. The cluster is less than 100 million years old and is visible to the naked eye.

Andromeda Galaxy (below)
Sometimes called the Great Galaxy of Andromeda it is a flat, spiral galaxy containing about 100,000,000,000 stars, with two smaller satellite galaxies. Andromeda is 2·2 million light years from Earth.

A supernova explosion throws the star's outer layers off into space, producing an object like the Crab nebula in Taurus (see photograph) which is the remains of a supernova observed by Oriental astronomers in AD1054. During a supernova explosion the erupting star's central core is compressed into a small, dense object known as a neutron star, about 10 miles in diameter. Neutron stars were first detected by radio astronomers in 1967 as the rapidly flashing radio sources known as pulsars. Pulsars are actually fast-spinning neutron stars which emit a flash of energy every time they revolve.

Black holes
If the remnant core of a star weighs more than about three times the Sun, then the inward pull of its own gravity is so strong that it cannot remain as a neutron star. It continues to shrink ever smaller and denser until it vanishes from sight in a black hole. A black hole is formed once the object has reached a certain small size and high density and its gravitational pull is so great that nothing can escape, not even light. The centre of the black hole, the point where all matter is compressed to infinite density and zero volume is termed a 'singularity'. The hole therefore becomes truly black, and cannot be seen from outside. However, matter can fall into a black hole, and this gives a clue to the object's existence. Gas falling into the intense gravitational field around a black hole heats up to many millions of degrees, emitting X-rays which can be detected by satellites orbiting Earth. In this way, astronomers believe they have detected at least one black hole, known as the X-ray source Cygnus X-I, orbiting a visible star catalogued HDE 226868 in the constellation Cygnus about 6,500 light years distant.

Death of the Sun
An ordinary star such as the Sun dies much more quietly. The Sun is nearly 5,000 million years old, which means that it is halfway through its expected life. In about another 5,000 million years it will run out of hydrogen at the core and start to burn helium. It will then swell to 250 times its present size into a red giant star like Arcturus. As it does so it will engulf the planets Mercury, Venus, and perhaps also the Earth. Long before then, life on our planet will have become extinct. At its death, the Earth will be consumed by fire.

The nebulous outer layers of the red giant Sun will then slowly disperse into space, forming a giant smoke ring. This stage will last some fifty thousand years. The Sun's hot core will be left behind as a white dwarf star, about the size of the Earth. Over millions upon millions of years this white dwarf will slowly cool into invisibility by slowly releasing energy from its outer layers. Any

charred remains of the Earth will be engulfed by ice as the white dwarf Sun fades away like a dying ember, leaving only memories of the human civilisation that once flourished around it.

Galaxies and the Universe
The Milky Way Galaxy in which the Solar System is situated probably started to form about 15,000 million years ago; the age of the oldest stars. This Galaxy is about 100,000 light years in diameter; the Sun and its system of nine planets lie about two-thirds of the way from the centre to the limit of the arm of the spiral. Large telescopes reveal countless other galaxies dotted throughout space. One of the nearest of these galaxies is the giant spiral in the constellation Andromeda (see photo) which lies over two million light years from the Earth. If we could see our own Galaxy from the outside, it would probably look much like Andromeda. All the Milky Way stars are orbiting around the centre of the Galaxy; the Sun takes 225 million years to complete the circuit.

Our own Galaxy and the Andromeda spiral are the two largest members of a cluster of about 30 galaxies called the Local Group. Many other galaxies are also bunched into groups like this, although there are plenty of individual galaxies dotted through space.

Two small galaxies, 160,000 light years away, are visible in the Southern Hemisphere. These are known as the Magellanic Clouds and are linked to our own Galaxy through a common envelope of hydrogen gas. Most galaxies are spiral in shape, but some are elliptical. The largest galaxies of all are giant ellipticals, containing a hundred times as many stars as our Milky Way.

As astronomers probed deep into the Universe with large telescopes half a century ago, they found an amazing fact: all galaxies, either individually or in groups, seemed to be rushing away from each other, as though the space between them was expanding. This fact was deduced from the red shift, or lengthening of the wavelength of light received from the galaxies, which would be caused by such a recession. The light waves are stretched out by the Doppler effect and at a given wavelength move towards the red end of the spectrum. The amount of the red shift is measured by the movement of the dark absorption line. This reveals the speed of recession of the galaxy and therefore its distance can be computed. Astronomers therefore began to compare the Universe to a continually inflating balloon. This provided a vital clue to the possible origin of the Universe, (see Big Bang theory).

Future scientific exploration of the centre of our Galaxy will rely on infra-red and radio observations which can penetrate the interstellar dust.

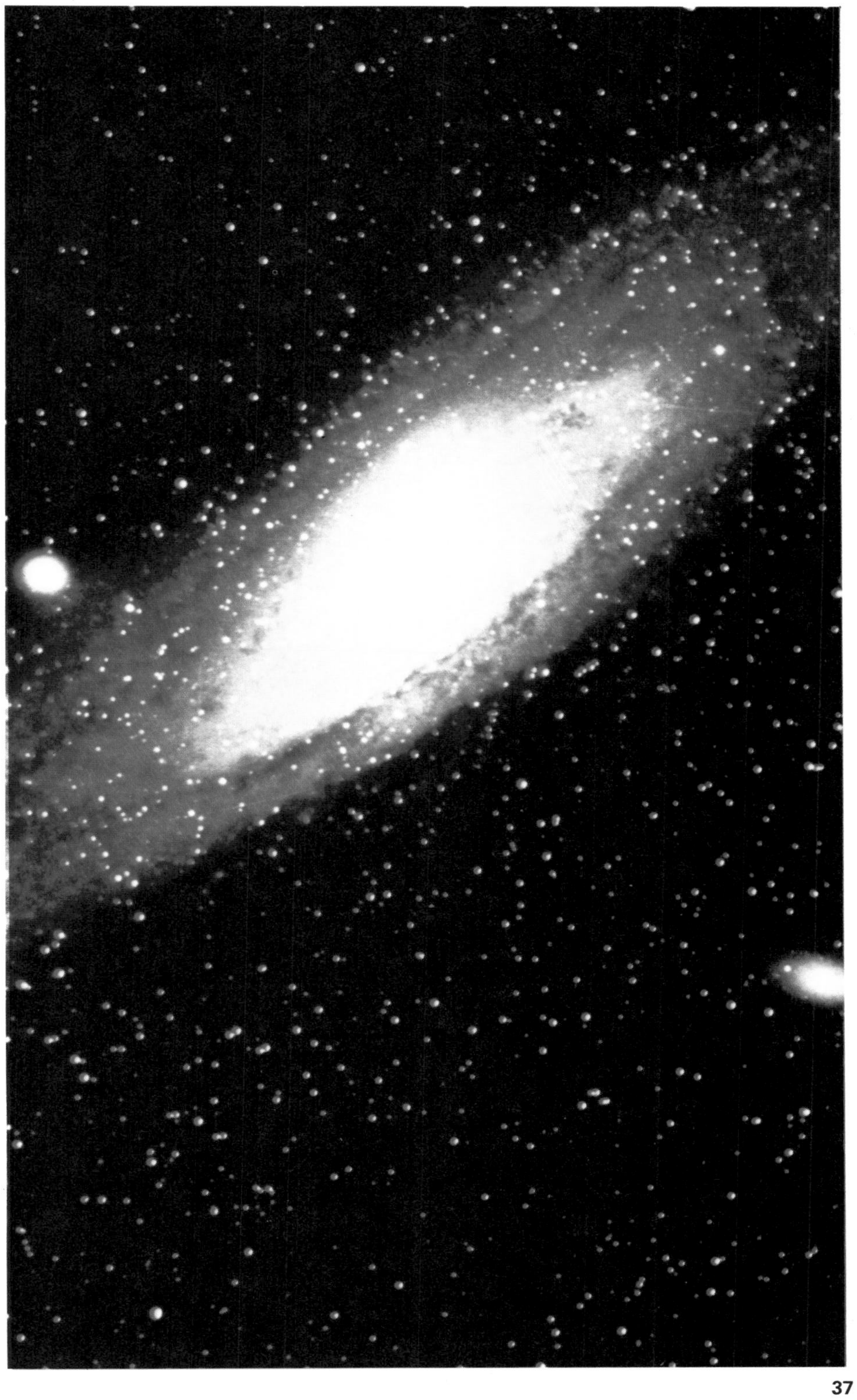

The Moon

The Moon is by far our nearest natural neighbour in space. It orbits the Earth every month at an average distance of 240,000 miles. The Moon is 2,160 miles in diameter, or roughly one-quarter the size of the Earth. No other natural satellite in the solar system is so close in size to its parent body, so astronomers often regard the Earth–Moon pairing as a double planet.

Rocks returned by American astronauts and Soviet automatic landers have confirmed that the Moon was born at the same time as the Earth, approximately 4,700 million years ago. Probably the two objects formed side by side, although it is possible that the Moon formed elsewhere in the solar system and was later captured. Most astronomers now think it unlikely that the Moon split away from the Earth.

The Moon's surface is pitted with craters of varying sizes, from vast basins more than 100 miles in diameter to microscopic pits. Astronomers argued over the origin of these for centuries, but it is now generally agreed that the majority of them were formed by the impact of meteorites long ago in the history of the solar system. This theory has been strengthened by the discovery that similar craters pockmark the surface of other bodies in the solar system, notably the planets Mercury and Mars.

Early in its history the Moon partially melted so that a rocky crust solidified at its surface. This crust has since been buffeted by meteorites which have produced the jumbled highlands. Several particularly large bodies have gouged out lowland basins which have since been flooded with dark lava. These dark lowlands are called the *maria*, or seas.

Unmanned space probes orbiting the Moon have made a complete photographic map of its front and back surface. As the Moon spins on its own axis in the same time as it takes to orbit the Earth (termed a *captured* rotation) no man had seen the far side of the Moon until the first space probes were sent to investigate. It has been found that there are no large *mare* regions on the far side of the Moon, evidently because the Moon's crust is about 25 miles thicker on the far side than on the Earth-turned hemisphere.

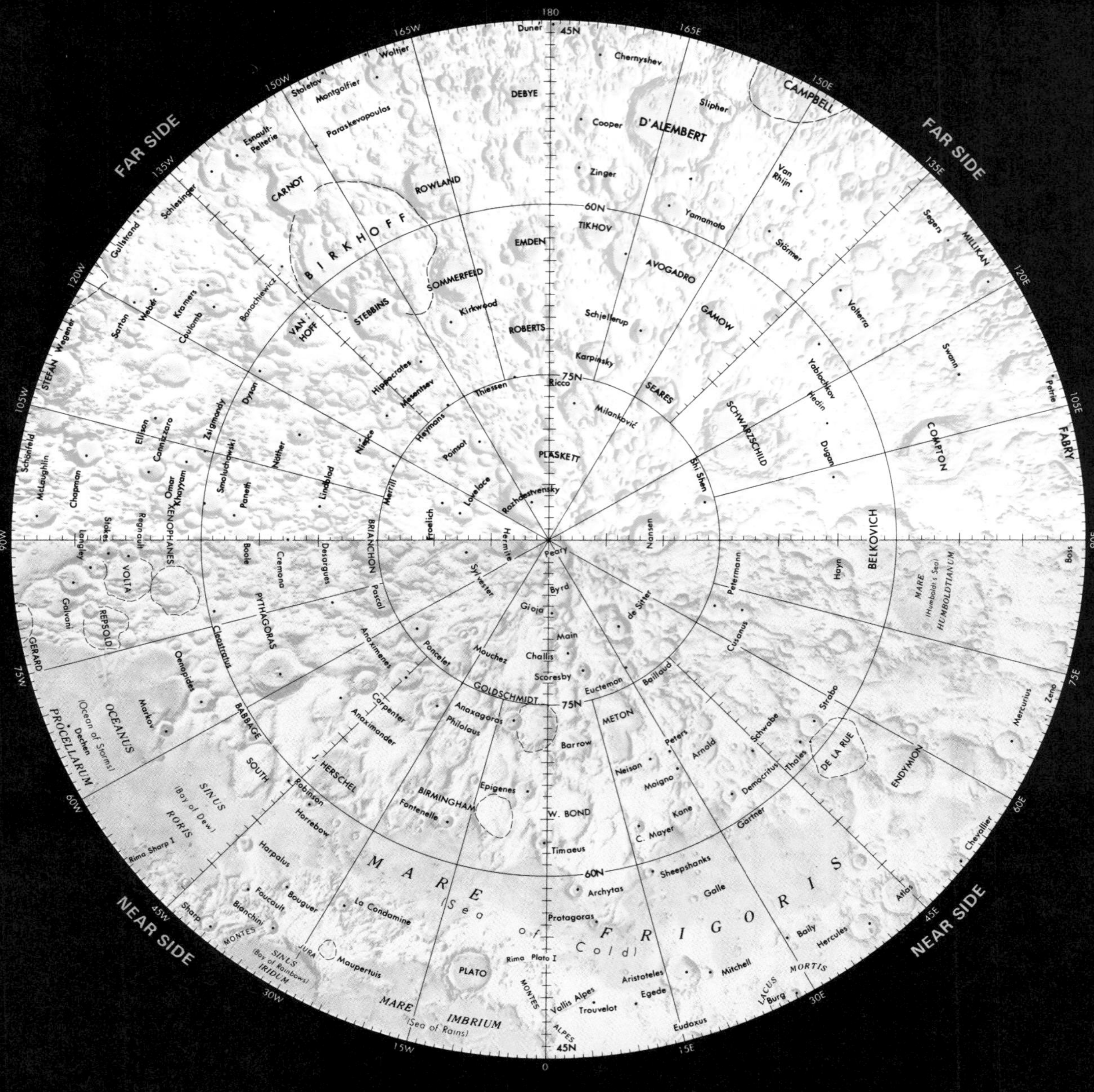

NORTH POLAR REGION

◄ FAR SIDE │ NEAR SIDE ►

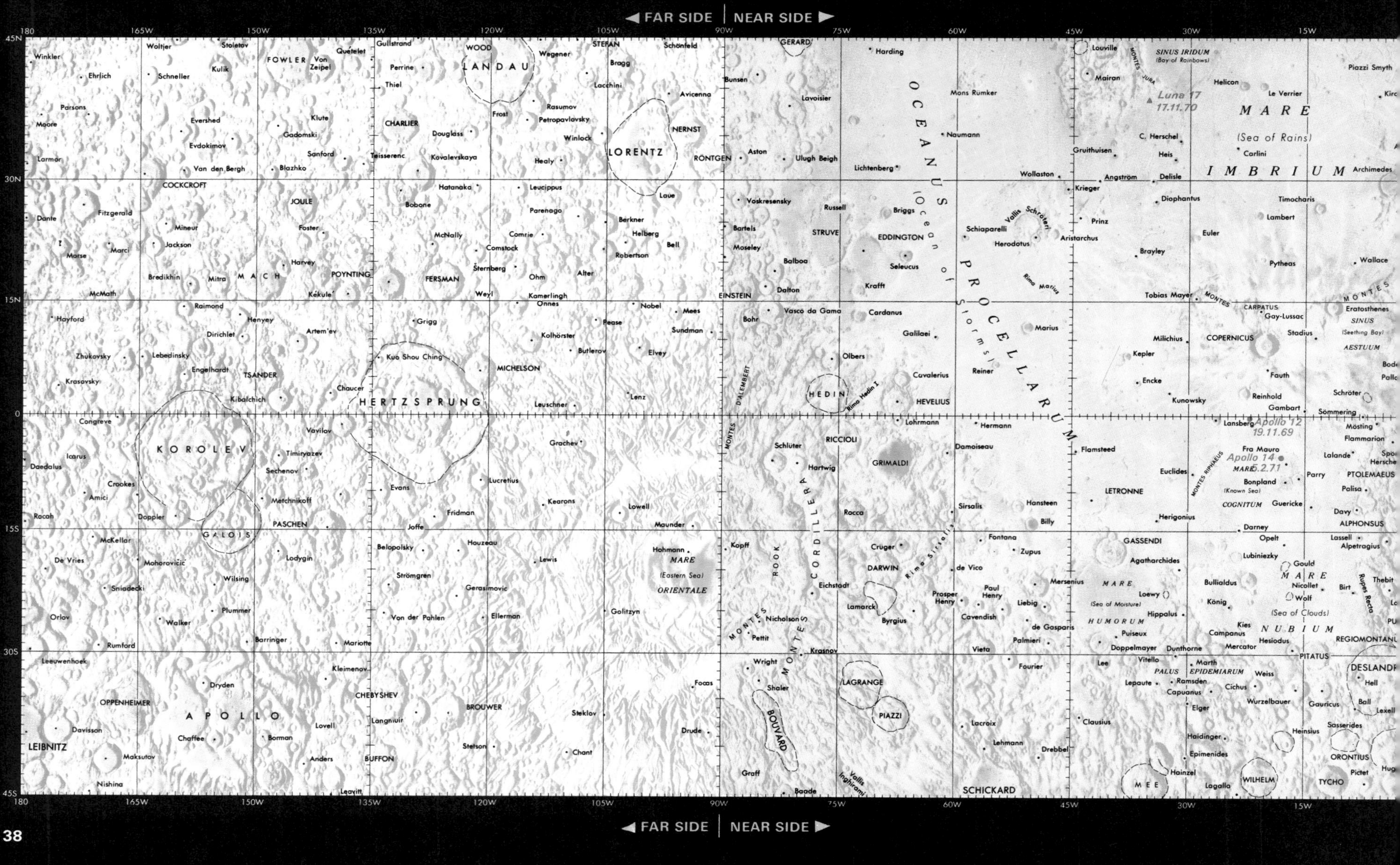

◄ FAR SIDE │ NEAR SIDE ►

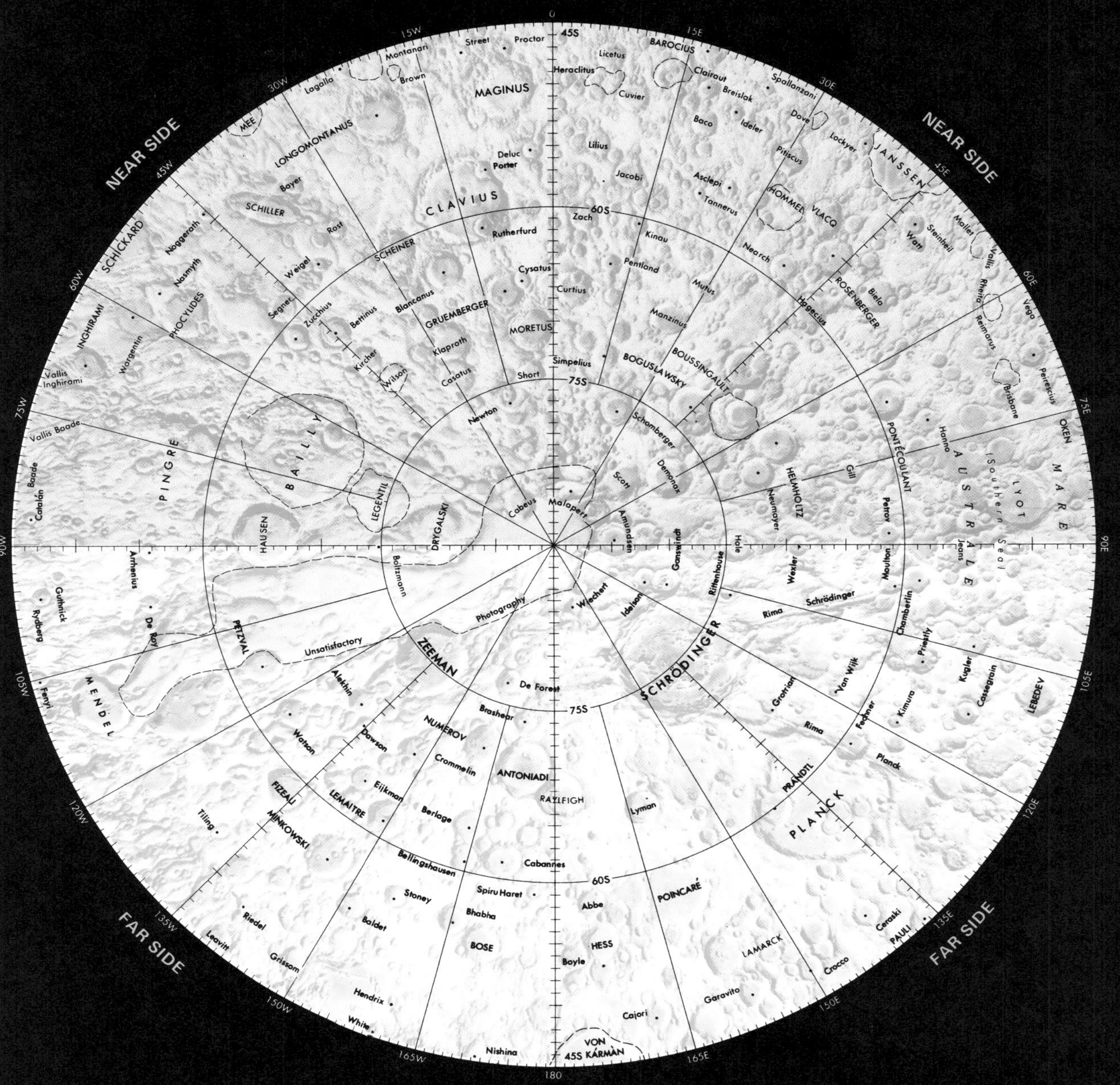

LUNAR DATA

Earth/Moon Mass Ratio	M_e/M_m 81·3015
Density (mean)	3·34g/(cm)^3
Synodic Month (new Moon to new Moon)	29·530, 588d
Sidereal Month (fixed star to fixed star)	27·321, 661d
Inclination of Lunar orbit to eclipse	5°8'43"
Inclination of equator to eclipse	1°40'32"
Inclination of Lunar orbit to Earth's equator	18°·5 to 28°·5
Distance from Moon to Earth (mean)	238·328M (384,400km)
Optical libration in longitude	±7°·6
Optical libration in latitude	±6°·7
Magnitude (mean of full Moon)	−12·7
Temperature	−244°F to +273°F (120°K to 407°K)
Escape velocity	1·48mi/sec (2·38km/sec)
Diameter of Moon	2,160mi (3,476km)
Surface gravity	162·2 cm/sec^2
Orbital velocity	0·64mi/sec (Moon) 1·024km/sec 18·5mi/sec (Earth) 29·6km/sec

SOUTH POLAR REGION

◄ NEAR SIDE | FAR SIDE ►

▲ Landing site of Soviet Moon vehicle "Lunokhod"
● Manned Spacecraft landing site

◄ NEAR SIDE | FAR SIDE ►

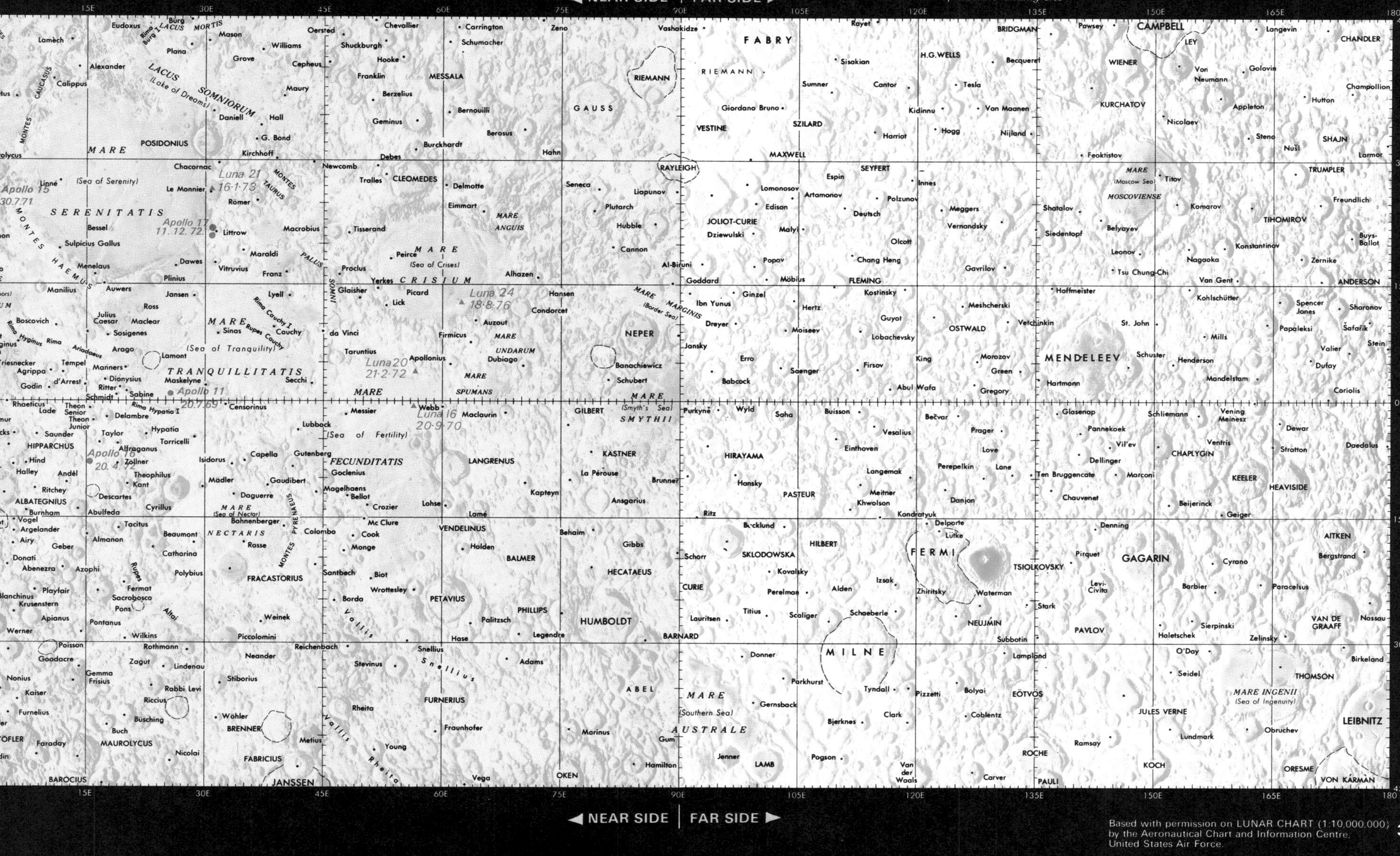

Based with permission on LUNAR CHART (1:10,000,000) by the Aeronautical Chart and Information Centre, United States Air Force.

39

The Stars

STAR MAGNITUDE

0
1
2
3
4
5

Each unit of magnitude indicates
a difference in brightness of 2.512 times.
The brightest star is Sirius (mag-1.47).

**STAR COLOURS
SPECTRAL TYPES**

* Temp. in 000° C

50.0—25.0	O-B
11.0	A
7.5	F
6.0	G
5.0	K
3.5	M

* The surface temperature of a star
is indicated both by its colour
and its spectrum.

Southern Sky

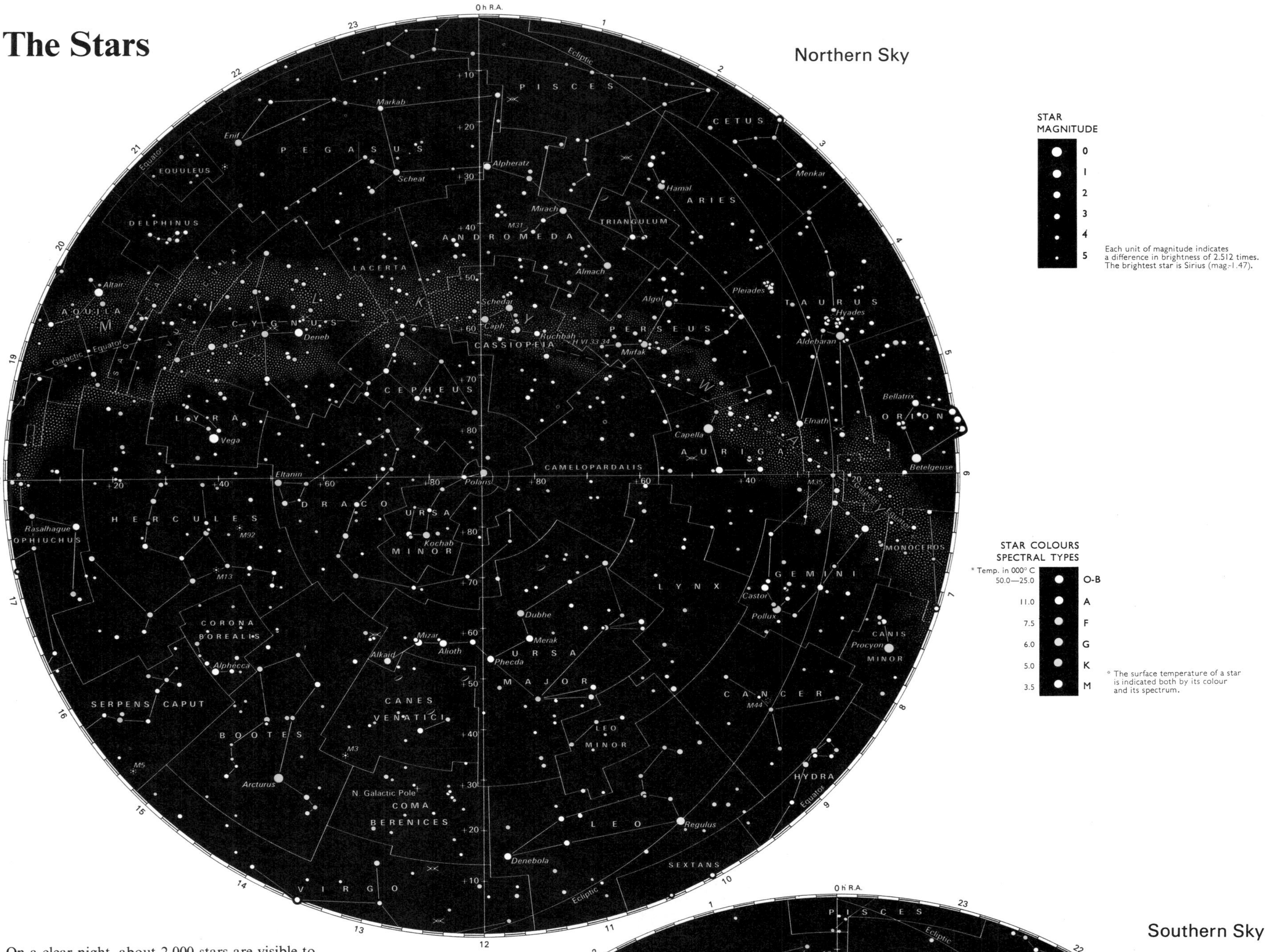

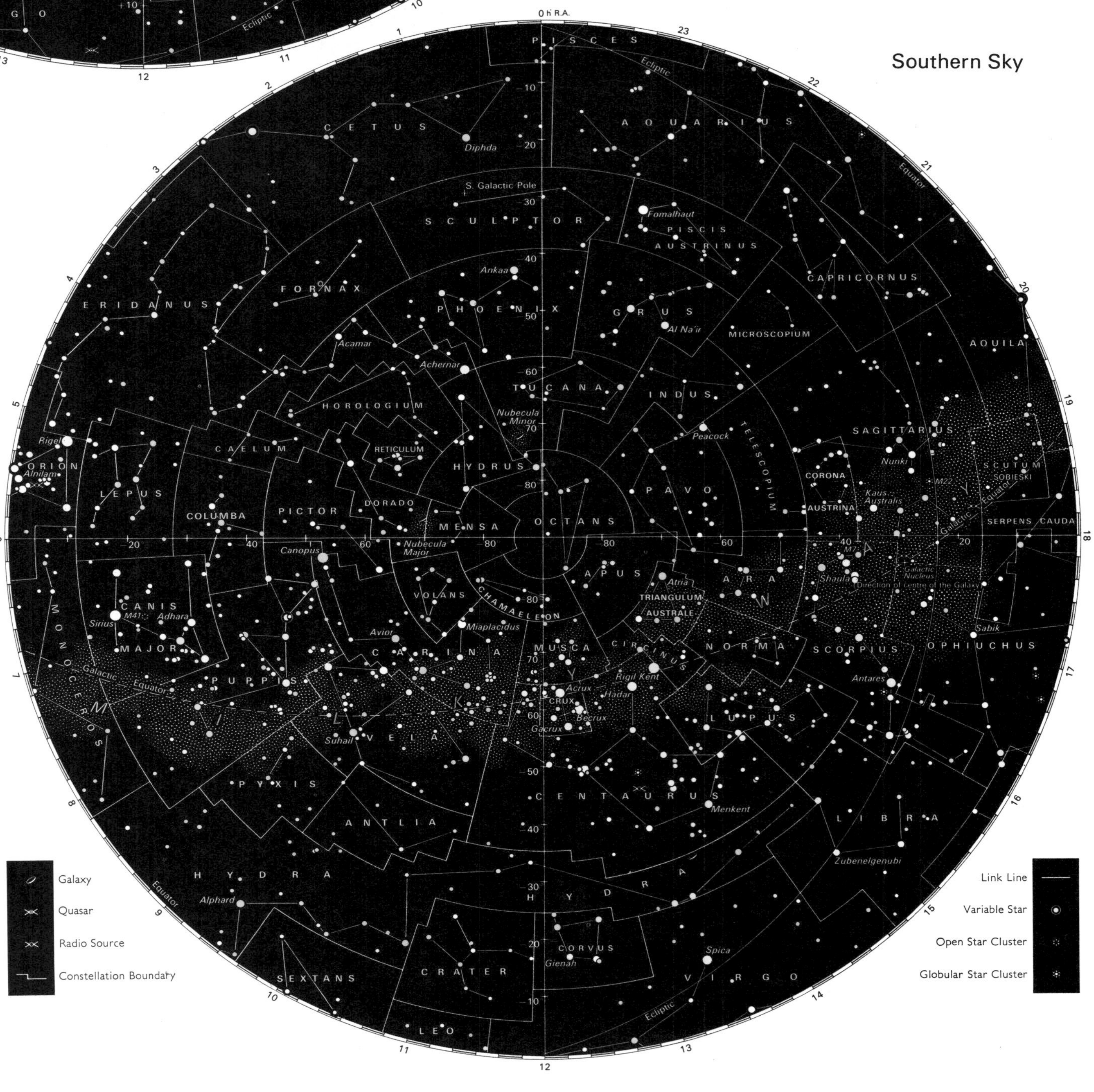

On a clear night, about 2,000 stars are visible to the naked eye at any one time. Countless thousands of others become visible with modest optical aid such as a pair of binoculars or a small telescope. The charts on this page show the main stars of the northern and southern hemisphere of the sky, along with the constellations into which they are grouped. Unless an observer is situated at the north or south pole, he will see some stars in both hemispheres. How far he sees into the opposite hemisphere depends on how close he is to the equator. The number of stars visible depends on the time and the season.

Some constellation figures go back thousands of years to ancient Mediterranean peoples, who placed their mythical beasts and heroes among the stars. Since then, more constellations have been added, particularly in the southern hemisphere which was invisible from the Mediterranean, so that a total of 88 constellations now cover the entire sky. They are useful for indicating the approximate locations of celestial objects. Precise locations are given by the celestial equivalents of longitude and latitude – Right Ascension (R.A., measured in hours, minutes, and seconds) and Declination (measured in degrees).

The size of the star images on the maps represents the perceived brightness of each star. Star brightnesses are measured in magnitudes, with the brightest stars first magnitude, and the faintest stars visible to the naked eye the sixth magnitude. A first magnitude star is 100 times brighter than a sixth magnitude star. Objects brighter than first magnitude are given increasingly large negative magnitudes, such as Sirius −1·47, the planet Venus at its brightest −4·4, the full Moon −12·7, and the Sun −26·8. Objects fainter than sixth magnitude are given progressively larger positive magnitudes. The faintest objects so far detected are around magnitude 24.

Although all stars appear white they are different colours, depending on their temperatures. The stars with coolest surface temperatures appear red, like the red giant Arcturus, while the hottest stars such as Sirius appears white or blue. The temperature of a star can be deduced from an examination of its spectrum; this classification is known as a star's spectral type.

⌇ Galaxy

✳ Quasar

✕ Radio Source

⌐ Constellation Boundary

― Link Line

◉ Variable Star

⊙ Open Star Cluster

✳ Globular Star Cluster

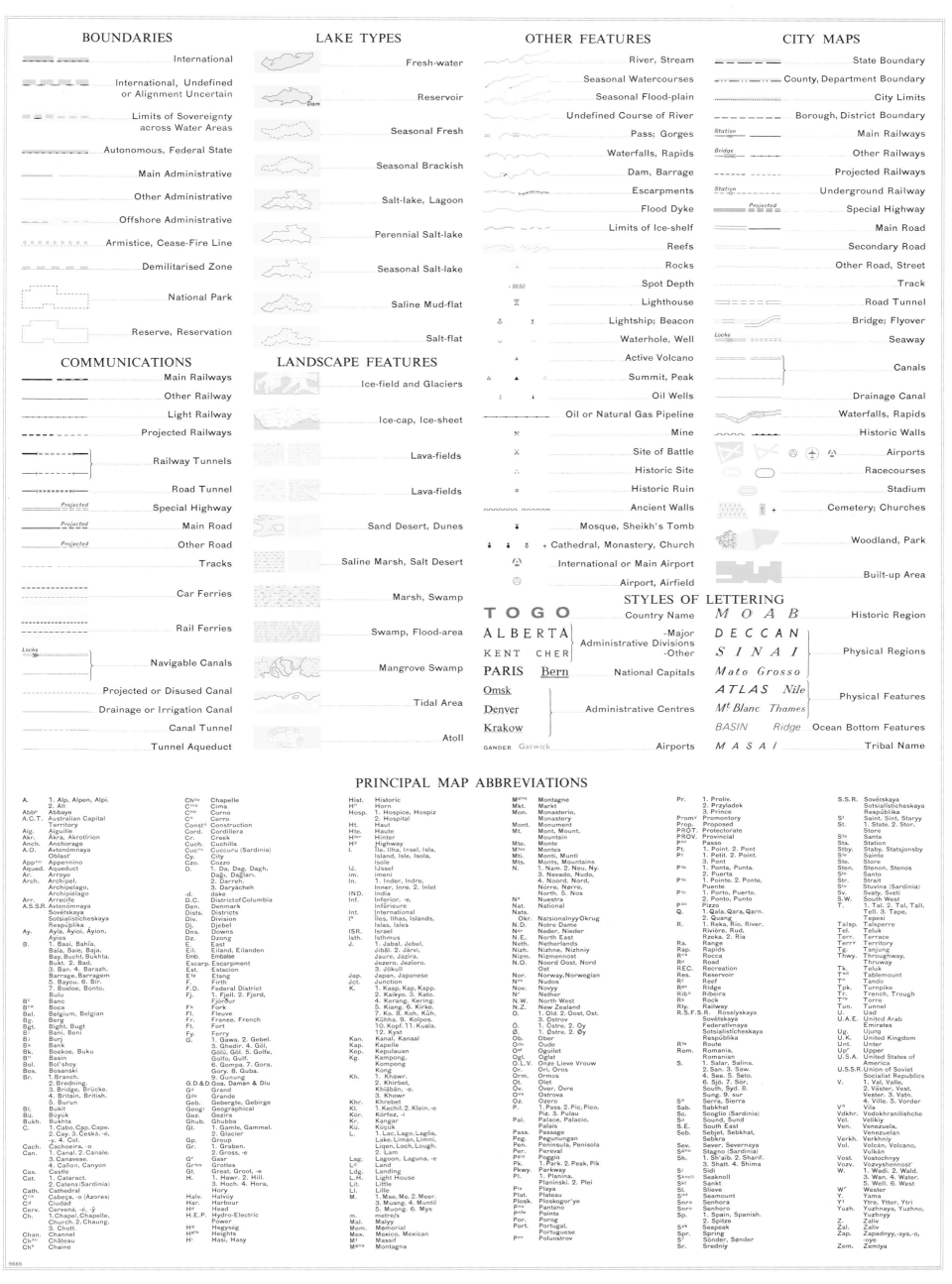

BOUNDARIES

International
International, Undefined or Alignment Uncertain
Limits of Sovereignty across Water Areas
Autonomous, Federal State
Main Administrative
Other Administrative
Offshore Administrative
Armistice, Cease-Fire Line
Demilitarised Zone
National Park
Reserve, Reservation

COMMUNICATIONS

Main Railways
Other Railway
Light Railway
Projected Railways
Railway Tunnels
Road Tunnel
Special Highway — *Projected*
Main Road — *Projected*
Other Road — *Projected*
Tracks
Car Ferries
Rail Ferries
Navigable Canals — *Locks*
Projected or Disused Canal
Drainage or Irrigation Canal
Canal Tunnel
Tunnel Aqueduct

LAKE TYPES

Fresh-water
Reservoir — *Dam*
Seasonal Fresh
Seasonal Brackish
Salt-lake, Lagoon
Perennial Salt-lake
Seasonal Salt-lake
Saline Mud-flat
Salt-flat

LANDSCAPE FEATURES

Ice-field and Glaciers
Ice-cap, Ice-sheet
Lava-fields
Lava-fields
Sand Desert, Dunes
Saline Marsh, Salt Desert
Marsh, Swamp
Swamp, Flood-area
Mangrove Swamp
Tidal Area
Atoll

OTHER FEATURES

River, Stream
Seasonal Watercourses
Seasonal Flood-plain
Undefined Course of River
Pass; Gorges
Waterfalls, Rapids
Dam, Barrage
Escarpments
Flood Dyke
Limits of Ice-shelf
Reefs
Rocks
Spot Depth
Lighthouse
Lightship; Beacon
Waterhole, Well
Active Volcano
Summit, Peak
Oil Wells
Oil or Natural Gas Pipeline
Mine
Site of Battle
Historic Site
Historic Ruin
Ancient Walls
Mosque, Sheikh's Tomb
Cathedral, Monastery, Church
International or Main Airport
Airport, Airfield

· 9650

STYLES OF LETTERING

TOGO — Country Name
ALBERTA — Administrative Divisions -Major
KENT CHER — -Other
PARIS Bern — National Capitals
Omsk
Denver — Administrative Centres
Krakow
GANDER Gatwick — Airports

M O A B — Historic Region
D E C C A N
S I N A I — Physical Regions
Mato Grosso
ATLAS Nile — Physical Features
Mt Blanc Thames
BASIN Ridge — Ocean Bottom Features
M A S A I — Tribal Name

CITY MAPS

State Boundary
County, Department Boundary
City Limits
Borough, District Boundary
Main Railways — *Station*
Other Railways — *Bridge*
Projected Railways
Underground Railway — *Station*
Special Highway — *Projected*
Main Road
Secondary Road
Other Road, Street
Track
Road Tunnel
Bridge; Flyover
Seaway — *Locks*
Canals
Drainage Canal
Waterfalls, Rapids
Historic Walls
Airports
Racecourses
Stadium
Cemetery; Churches
Woodland, Park
Built-up Area

PRINCIPAL MAP ABBREVIATIONS

A.	1. Alp, Alpen, Alpi. 2. Alt
Abbᵉ	Abbaye
A.C.T.	Australian Capital Territory
Aig.	Aiguille
Akr.	Akra, Akrotírion
Anch.	Anchorage
A.O.	Avtonómnaya Oblast'
Appᵑᵒ	Appennino
Aqued.	Aqueduct
Ar.	Arroyo
Arch.	Archipel. Archipelago, Archipiélago
Arr.	Arrecife
A.S.S.R.	Avtonómnaya Sovétskaya Sotsialistícheskaya Respúblika
Ay.	Ayía, Áyioi, Áyion, Ayios
B.	1. Baai, Bahía, Baía, Baie, Baja. Bay, Bukht, Bukhta. Bukt. 2. Bad. 3. Ban. 4. Barazh, Barrage, Barragem 5. Bayou. 6. Bir. 7. Boeloe, Bonto, Bulu
Bᶜ	Banc
Bᶜᵃ	Boca
Bel.	Belgium, Belgian
Bg.	Berg
Bgt.	Bight, Bugt
Bi	Bani, Beni
Bj	Burj
Bk	Bank
Bk.	Boekoe, Buku
Bⁿ	Basin
Bol.	Bol'shoy
Bos.	Bosanski
Br.	1.Branch. 2.Bredning. 3. Bridge, Brücke. 4. Britain, British. 5. Burun
Bt.	Bukit
Bü.	Büyük
Bukh.	Bukhta
C.	1. Cabo, Cap, Cape. 2. Cay. 3. Česká, -é, -ý. 4. Col.
Cach.	Čachoeira, -o
Can.	1. Canal. 2. Canale. 3. Canavese. 4. Cañon, Canyon
Cas.	Castle
Cat.	1. Cataract. 2. Catena (Sardinia)
Cath.	Cathedral
Cᶜᵃ	Cabeça, -o (Azores)
Cᵈ	Ciudad
Cerv.	Cervená, -é, -ý
Ch.	1.Chapel, Chapelle. 2. Chaung. 3. Chott.
Chan.	Channel
Chᵃᵘ	Château
Chⁿ	Chaine

Chˡˡᵉ	Chapelle
Cᵐᵃ	Cima
Cᵐᵒ	Corno
Cᵒ	Cerro
Constⁿ	Construction
Cord.	Cordillera
Cr.	Creek
Cuch.	Cuchilla
Cucᶜᵘ	Cuccuru (Sardinia)
Cy.	City
Czo.	Cozzo
D.	1. Da, Dag, Dagh, Daği, Dağları. 2. Darreh. 3. Daryächeh
-d.	dake
D.C.	District of Columbia
Den.	Denmark
Dists.	Districts
Div.	Division
Dj.	Djebel
Dns.	Downs
Dz.	Dzong
E.	East
Eil.	Eiland, Eilanden
Emb.	Embalse
Escarp.	Escarpment
Est.	Estacion
Eᵗᵉ	Etang
F.	Firth
F.D.	Federal District
Fj.	1. Fjell. 2. Fjord, Fjördur
Fᵏ	Fork
Fl.	Fleuve
Fr.	France, French
Ft.	Fort
Fy.	Ferry
G.	1. Gawa. 2. Gebel. 3. Ghedir. 4. Göl, Gölü, Gôl. 5. Golfe, Golfo, Gulf. 6. Gompa. 7. Gora, Gory. 8. Guba. 9. Gunung
G.D.&D	Goa, Daman & Diu
Gᵈ	Grand
Gᵈᵉ	Grande
Geb.	Gebergte, Gebirge
Geogᶦ	Geographical
Gez.	Gezira
Ghub.	Ghubba
Gl.	1. Gamle, Gammel. 2. Glacier
Gp.	Group
Gr.	1. Graben. 2. Gross, -e
Gⁱ	Gasr
Grᵗᵉˢ	Grottes
Gt.	Great, Groot, -e
H.	1. Hawr. 2. Hill. 3. Hoch. 4. Hora, Hory
Halv.	Halvöy
Har.	Harbour
Hᵈ	Head
H.E.P.	Hydro-Electric Power
Hᵍ	Hegység
Hᵉᵗˢ	Heights
Hⁱ	Hasi, Hasy

Hist.	Historic
Hⁿ	Horn
Hosp.	1. Hospice, Hospiz. 2. Hospital
Ht.	Haut
Hte.	Haute
Hᵗᵉʳ	Hinter
Hʸ	Highway
I.	Ile, Ilha, Insel, Isla, Island, Isle, Isola, Isole
IJ.	IJssel
im.	imeni
In.	1. Inder, Indre, Inner, Inre. 2. Inlet
IND.	India
Inf.	Inferior, -e, Inférieure
Int.	International
Iˢ	Iles, Ilhas, Islands, Islas, Isles
ISR.	Israel
Isth.	Isthmus
J.	1. Jabal, Jebel, Jibâl. 2. Järvi, Jaure, Jazira, Jezero, Jezióro. 3. Jökull
Jap.	Japan, Japanese
Jct.	Junction
K.	1. Kaap, Kap, Kapp. 2. Kaikyo. 3. Kato. 4. Kerang, Kering. 5. Kiang. 6. Kirke. 7. Ko. 8. Koh, Kûh, Kûhha. 9. Kolpos. 10. Kopf. 11. Kuala. 12. Kyst
Kan.	Kanal, Kanaal
Kap.	Kapelle
Kep.	Kepulauan
Kg.	Kampong, Kompong, Kong
Kh.	1. Khawr. 2. Khirbet, Khiâbân, -e. 3. Khowr
Khr.	Khrebet
Kl.	1. Kechil. 2. Klein, -e
Kör.	Körfez, -i
Kr.	Kangar
Kü.	Küçük
L.	1. Lac, Lago, Lagôa, Lake, Liman, Limni, Liqen, Loch, Lough. 2. Lam
Lag.	Lagoon, Laguna, -o
Lᵈ	Land
Ldg.	Landing
L.H.	Light House
Lit.	Little
Ll.	Lille
M.	1. Mae, Me. 2. Meer. 3. Muang. 4. Muntii 5. Muong. 6. Mys
m.	metre/s
Mal.	Malyy
Mem.	Memorial
Mex.	Mexico, Mexican
Mᶠ	Massif
Mᵍⁿᵃ	Montagna

Mᵍⁿᵉ	Montagne
Mkt.	Markt
Mon.	Monasterio, Monastery
Mont.	Monument
Mt.	Mont, Mount, Mountain
Mte.	Monte
Mᵗᵉˢ	Montes
Mti.	Monti, Munti
Mts.	Monts, Mountains
N.	1. Nam. 2. Neu, Ny. 3. Nevado, Nudo, 4. Noord, Nord, Nörre, Nørre, North. 5. Nos
Nᵃ	Nuestra
Nat.	National
Nats.	Nations
Okr.	Natsionalnyy Okrug
N.D.	Notre Dame
Nᵈʳ	Neder, Nieder
N.E.	North East
Neth.	Netherlands
Nizh.	Nizhne, Nizhniy
Nizm.	Nizmennost
N.O.	Noord Oost, Nord Ost
Nor.	Norway, Norwegian
Nᵒˢ	Nudos
Nov.	Novyy
Nʳ	Nether
N.W.	North West
N.Z.	New Zealand
O.	1. Old. 2. Oost, Ost. 3. Ostrov
Ö.	1. Östre. 2. Öy
Ø.	1. Østre. 2. Øy
Ob.	Ober
Oᵈᵉ	Oude
Ogᶠ	Oguilet
O.L.V.	Onze Lieve Vrouw
Or.	Ori, Oros
Ot.	Olet
Öv.	Over, Övre
Oᵛᵃ	Ostrova
Oz.	Ozero
P.	1. Pass. 2. Pic, Pico, Piz. 3. Pulau
Pal.	Palace, Palacio, Palais
Pass.	Passage
Peg.	Pegunungan
Pen.	Peninsula, Penisola
Per.	Pereval
Pᵉⁱᵒ	Poggio
Pk.	1. Park 2. Peak, Pik
Pkwy.	Parkway
Pl.	1. Planina, Planinski. 2. Plei
Pᶦᵃ	Playa
Plat.	Plateau
Plosk.	Ploskogor'ye
Pⁿᵒ	Piano
Pⁿᵗᵉ	Pointe
Por.	Porog
Port.	Portugal, Portuguese
Pᵒᵛ	Poluostrov

Pr.	1. Proliv. 2. Przyladek 3. Prince
Promʸ	Promontory
Prop.	Proposed
PRÔT.	Protectorate
PROV.	Provincial
Pˢᵒ	Passo
Pt.	1. Point. 2. Pont
Pᵗ	1. Petit. 2. Point. 3. Pont
Pᵗᵃ	1. Ponta, Punta. 2. Puerta
Pᵗᵉ	1. Pointe. 2. Ponte, Puente
Pᵗᵒ	1. Porto, Puerto. 2. Ponto, Punto
Pᶻᵒ	Pizzo
Q.	1. Qala, Qara, Qarn. 2. Quang
R.	1. Reka, Rio, River, Rivière, Rud, Rzeka. 2. Ria
Ra.	Range
Rap.	Rapids
Rᶜᵃ	Rocca
Rᵈ	Road
REC.	Recreation
Res.	Reservoir
Rᶠ	Reef
Rᵍᵉ	Ridge
Ribᵃ	Ribeira
Rᵏ	Rock
Rly.	Railway
R.S.F.S.R.	Rossíyskaya Sovétskaya Federatívnaya Sotsialistícheskaya Respúblika
Rᵗᵉ	Route
Rom.	Romania, Romanian
S.	1. Salar, Salina. 2. San. 3. Saw. 4. See. 5. Seto. 6. Sjö. 7. Sör. South, Syd. 8. Sung. 9. sur
Sᵃ	Serra, Sierra
Sab.	Sabkhat
Sc.	Scoglio (Sardinia)
Sᵈ	Sound, Sund
S.E.	South East
Seb.	Sebjet, Sebkhat, Sebkra
Sev.	Sever, Severnaya
Sᵉⁿᵒ	Stagno (Sardinia)
Sh.	1. Sh'aib. 2. Sharif. 3. Shatt. 4. Shima
Sⁱ	Sidi
Sᵏⁿᵒˡˡ	Seaknoll
Sᵏᵗ	Sankt
Sl.	Slieve
Sᵐᵗ	Seamount
Snra	Senhora
Snᵗⁱᵒ	Senhorio
Sp.	1. Spain, Spanish. 2. Spitze
Sᵖᵏ	Seapeak
Spr.	Spring
Sʳ	Sönder, Sønder
Sr.	Sredniy

S.S.R.	Sovétskaya Sotsialistícheskaya Respúblika
Sᵗ	Saint, Sint, Staryy
St.	1. State. 2. Stor. Store
Sᵗᵃ	Santa
Sta.	Station
Stby.	Staby, Statsjonsby
Sᵗᵉ	Sainte
Ste.	Store
Sten.	Stenon, Stenos
Sᵗᵒ	Santo
Str.	Strait
Sᵗᵘ	Stuvina (Sardinia)
Sv.	Svaty, Sveti
S.W.	South West
T.	1. Tal. 2. Tal, Tall, Tell. 3. Tepe, Tepesi
Talsp.	Talsperre
Tel.	Teluk
Terr.	Terrace
Terrʸ	Territory
Tg.	Tanjung
Thwy.	Throughway, Thruway
Tk.	Teluk
Tᵐᵗ	Tablemount
Tᵒ	Tando
Tpk.	Turnpike
Tr.	Trench, Trough
Tᵗᵉ	Torre
Tun.	Tunnel
U.	Uad
U.A.E.	United Arab Emirates
Ug.	Ujung
U.K.	United Kingdom
Unt.	Unter
Upᵖ	Upper
U.S.A.	United States of America
U.S.S.R.	Union of Soviet Socialist Republics
V.	1. Val, Valle, 2. Väster, Vest, Vester. 3. Vatn. 4. Ville. 5. Vorder
Vᵈᵏʰʳ	Vodokhranilishche
Vel.	Velikiy
Ven.	Venezuela, Venezuelan
Verkh.	Verkhniy
Vol.	Volcán, Volcano, Vulkán
Vost.	Vostochnyy
Vozv.	Vozvyshennost'
W.	1. Wadi. 2. Wald. 3. Wan. 4. Water. 5. Well. 6. West
Wᵗ	Wester
Y.	Yama
Yᵗ	Ytre, Ytter, Ytri
Yuzh.	Yuzhnaya, Yuzhno, Yuzhnyy
Z.	Zaliv
Zal.	Zaliv
Zap.	Zapadnyy, -aya, -o, -oye
Zem.	Zemlya

9666

© John Bartholomew & Son Ltd Edinburgh

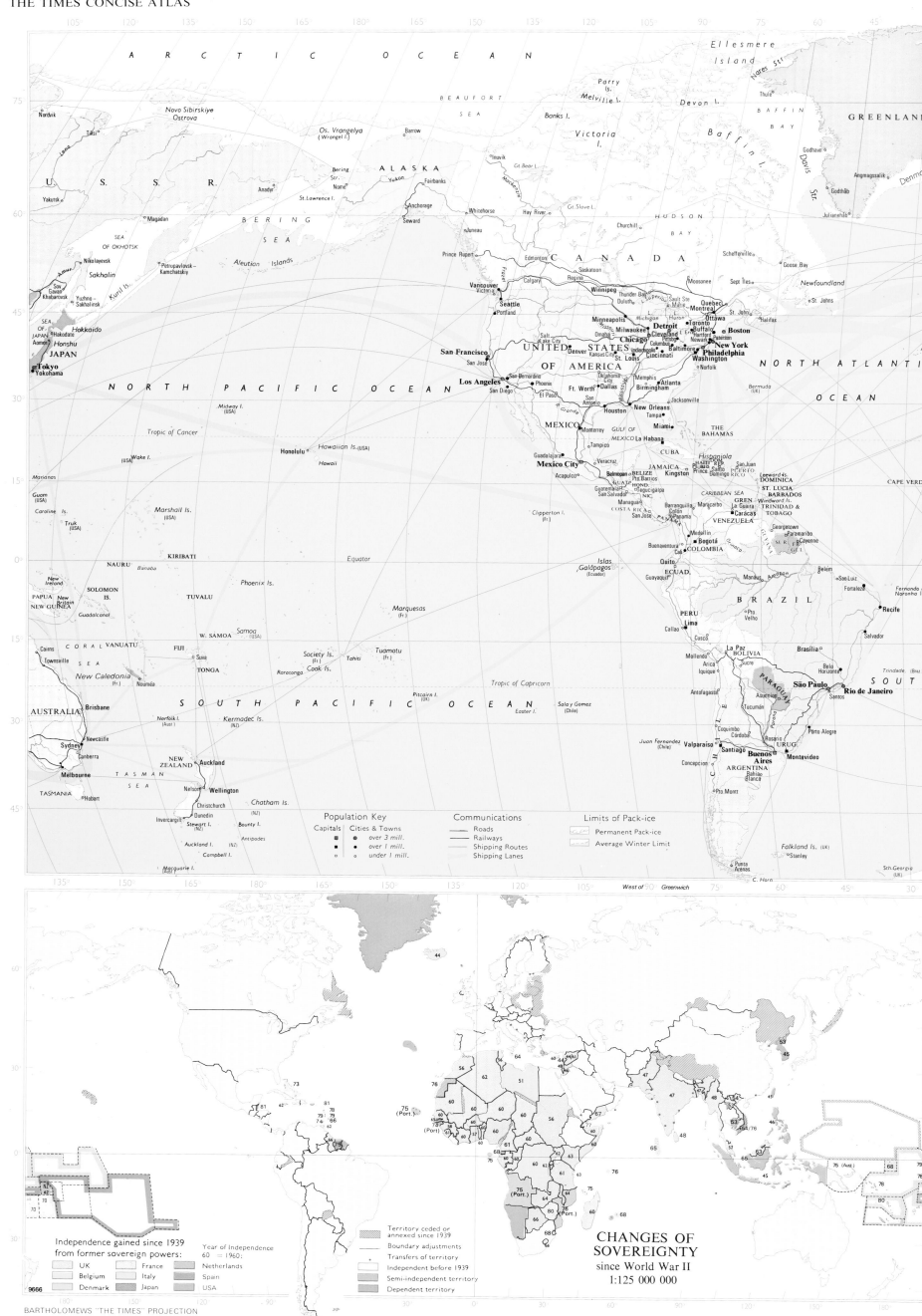

CHANGES OF
SOVEREIGNTY
since World War II
1:125 000 000

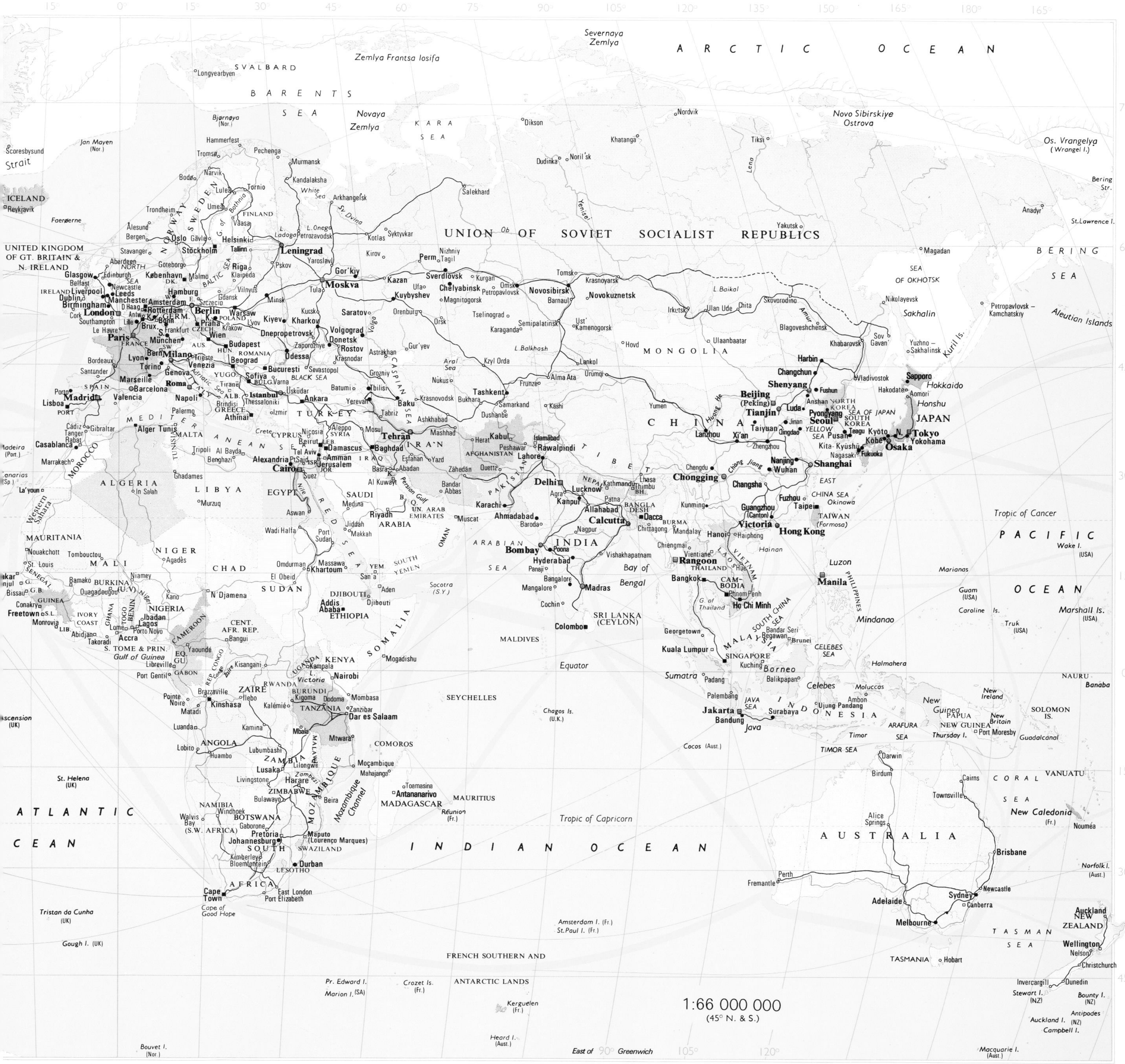

ARCTIC OCEAN
Severnaya Zemlya
Zemlya Frantsa Iosifa
SVALBARD
BARENTS SEA
Novaya Zemlya
KARA SEA
Novo Sibirskiye Ostrova
Os. Vrangelya (Wrangel I.)
Jan Mayen (Nor.)
ICELAND
Reykjavik
Faeroerne
UNITED KINGDOM OF GT. BRITAIN & N. IRELAND
IRELAND
London
Paris
FRANCE
SPAIN
Madrid
Lisboa
PORT.
NORWAY
SWEDEN
FINLAND
Oslo
Stockholm
Helsinki
København
Berlin
Warsaw
Praha
Wien
Budapest
Bucuresti
Beograd
Sofiya
Roma
Athinai
Istanbul
Ankara
TURKEY
Leningrad
Moskva
Kiyev
Odessa
UNION OF SOVIET SOCIALIST REPUBLICS
Sverdlovsk
Chelyabinsk
Novosibirsk
Novokuznetsk
Tashkent
Alma Ata
Baku
Tbilisi
Tehran
IRAN
Baghdad
IRAQ
SYRIA
Damascus
Beirut
Jerusalem
Amman
Cairo
EGYPT
LIBYA
ALGERIA
MOROCCO
Casablanca
Alger
Tunis
MEDITERRANEAN SEA
BLACK SEA
CASPIAN SEA
Aral Sea
Western Sahara
MAURITANIA
MALI
NIGER
CHAD
SUDAN
Khartoum
ETHIOPIA
Addis Ababa
DJIBOUTI
SOMALIA
Mogadishu
KENYA
Nairobi
UGANDA
TANZANIA
Dar es Salaam
ZAIRE
Kinshasa
ANGOLA
ZAMBIA
Lusaka
ZIMBABWE
Harare
MOZAMBIQUE
Maputo
NAMIBIA
BOTSWANA
SOUTH AFRICA
Pretoria
Johannesburg
Durban
Cape Town
Cape of Good Hope
LESOTHO
SWAZILAND
MADAGASCAR
Antananarivo
MAURITIUS
Réunion (Fr.)
COMOROS
SEYCHELLES
NIGERIA
Lagos
Ibadan
GHANA
Accra
IVORY COAST
GUINEA
Freetown
Monrovia
CAMEROON
CENT. AFR. REP.
GABON
Gulf of Guinea
S. TOME & PRIN.
SAUDI ARABIA
Riyadh
Jiddah
Makkah
UN. ARAB EMIRATES
OMAN
Muscat
YEMEN
Aden
Socotra
ARABIAN SEA
AFGHANISTAN
Kabul
PAKISTAN
Karachi
Lahore
Rawalpindi
Islamabad
INDIA
Delhi
Bombay
Calcutta
Madras
Bangalore
Hyderabad
NEPAL
Kathmandu
BANGLADESH
Dacca
BHUTAN
Thimbu
SRI LANKA (CEYLON)
Colombo
MALDIVES
Bay of Bengal
BURMA
Rangoon
THAILAND
Bangkok
CAMBODIA
Phnom Penh
VIETNAM
Hanoi
Ho Chi Minh
LAOS
Vientiane
MALAYSIA
Kuala Lumpur
SINGAPORE
Brunei
INDONESIA
Jakarta
Sumatra
Java
Borneo
Celebes
Moluccas
New Guinea
PAPUA NEW GUINEA
Port Moresby
PHILIPPINES
Manila
Luzon
Mindanao
CHINA
Beijing (Peking)
Tianjin
Shanghai
Chongqing
Wuhan
Guangzhou (Canton)
Victoria
Hong Kong
TAIWAN (Formosa)
Taipei
TIBET
Lhasa
MONGOLIA
Ulaanbaatar
NORTH KOREA
Pyongyang
SOUTH KOREA
Seoul
Pusan
JAPAN
Tokyo
Osaka
Sapporo
Hokkaido
Honshu
SEA OF JAPAN
YELLOW SEA
EAST CHINA SEA
SOUTH CHINA SEA
SEA OF OKHOTSK
Sakhalin
Kuril Is.
BERING SEA
Aleutian Islands
Tropic of Cancer
PACIFIC OCEAN
Marianas
Guam (USA)
Caroline Is.
Marshall Is. (USA)
Wake I. (USA)
NAURU
SOLOMON IS.
VANUATU
New Caledonia (Fr.)
Equator
INDIAN OCEAN
Tropic of Capricorn
ATLANTIC OCEAN
St. Helena (UK)
Tristan da Cunha (UK)
Gough I. (UK)
Bouvet I. (Nor.)
AUSTRALIA
Perth
Adelaide
Melbourne
Sydney
Canberra
Brisbane
Darwin
Alice Springs
TASMANIA
Hobart
ARAFURA SEA
TIMOR SEA
CORAL SEA
TASMAN SEA
NEW ZEALAND
Auckland
Wellington
Christchurch
Chagos Is. (U.K.)
Cocos (Aust.)
Amsterdam I. (Fr.)
St. Paul I. (Fr.)
FRENCH SOUTHERN AND ANTARCTIC LANDS
Kerguelen (Fr.)
Heard I. (Aust.)
Crozet Is. (Fr.)
Pr. Edward I.
Marion I. (SA)
Macquarie I. (Aust.)
1:66 000 000
(45° N. & S.)
East of 90° Greenwich

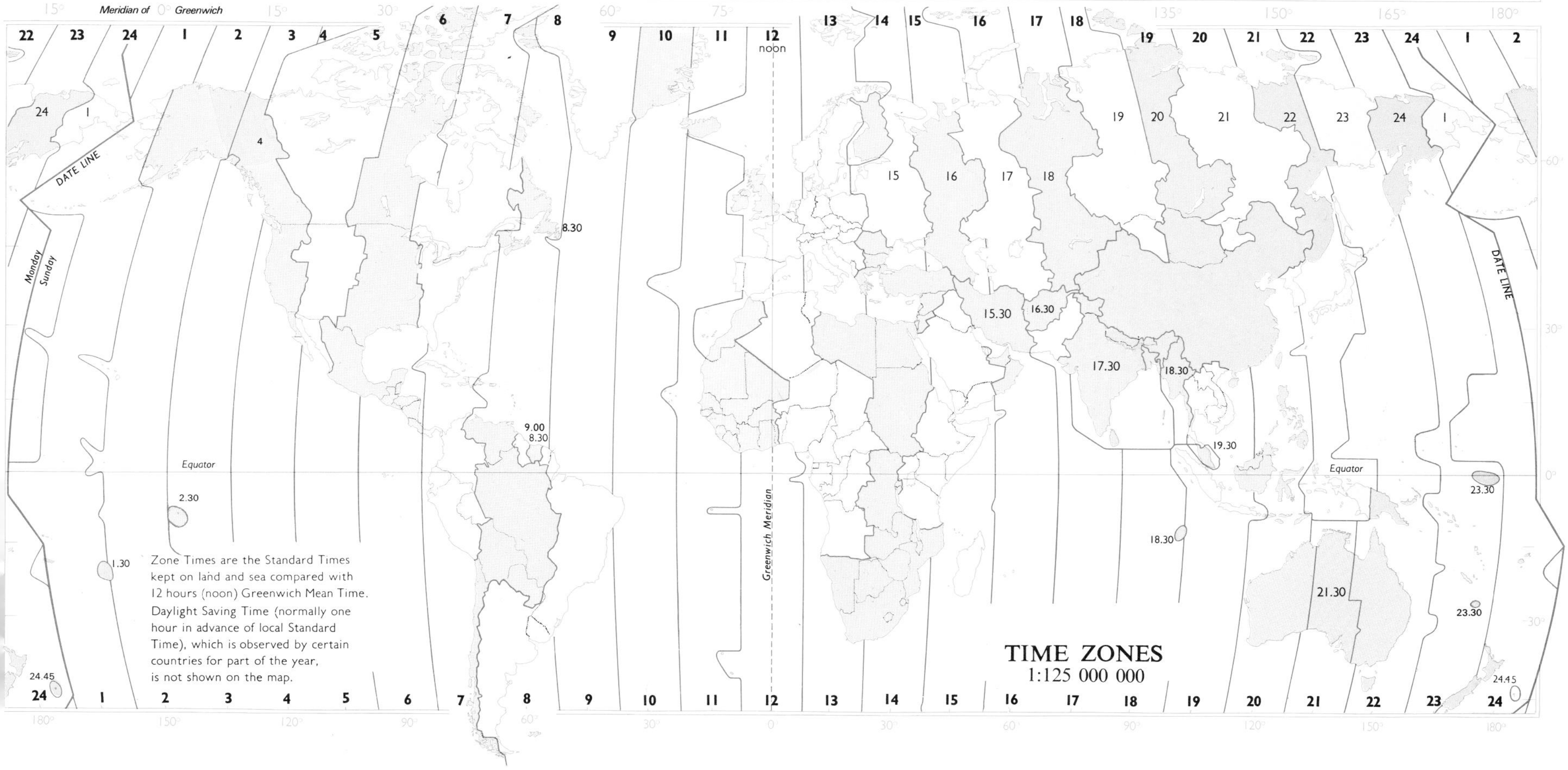

Meridian of 0° Greenwich
22 23 24 1 2 3 4 5 6 7 8 9 10 11 12 13 14 15 16 17 18 19 20 21 22 23 24 1 2
noon
DATE LINE
Monday
Sunday
Equator
Greenwich Meridian
8.30
9.00
15.30
16.30
17.30
18.30
19.30
21.30
23.30
2.30
1.30
24.45
Zone Times are the Standard Times kept on land and sea compared with 12 hours (noon) Greenwich Mean Time. Daylight Saving Time (normally one hour in advance of local Standard Time), which is observed by certain countries for part of the year, is not shown on the map.
TIME ZONES
1:125 000 000

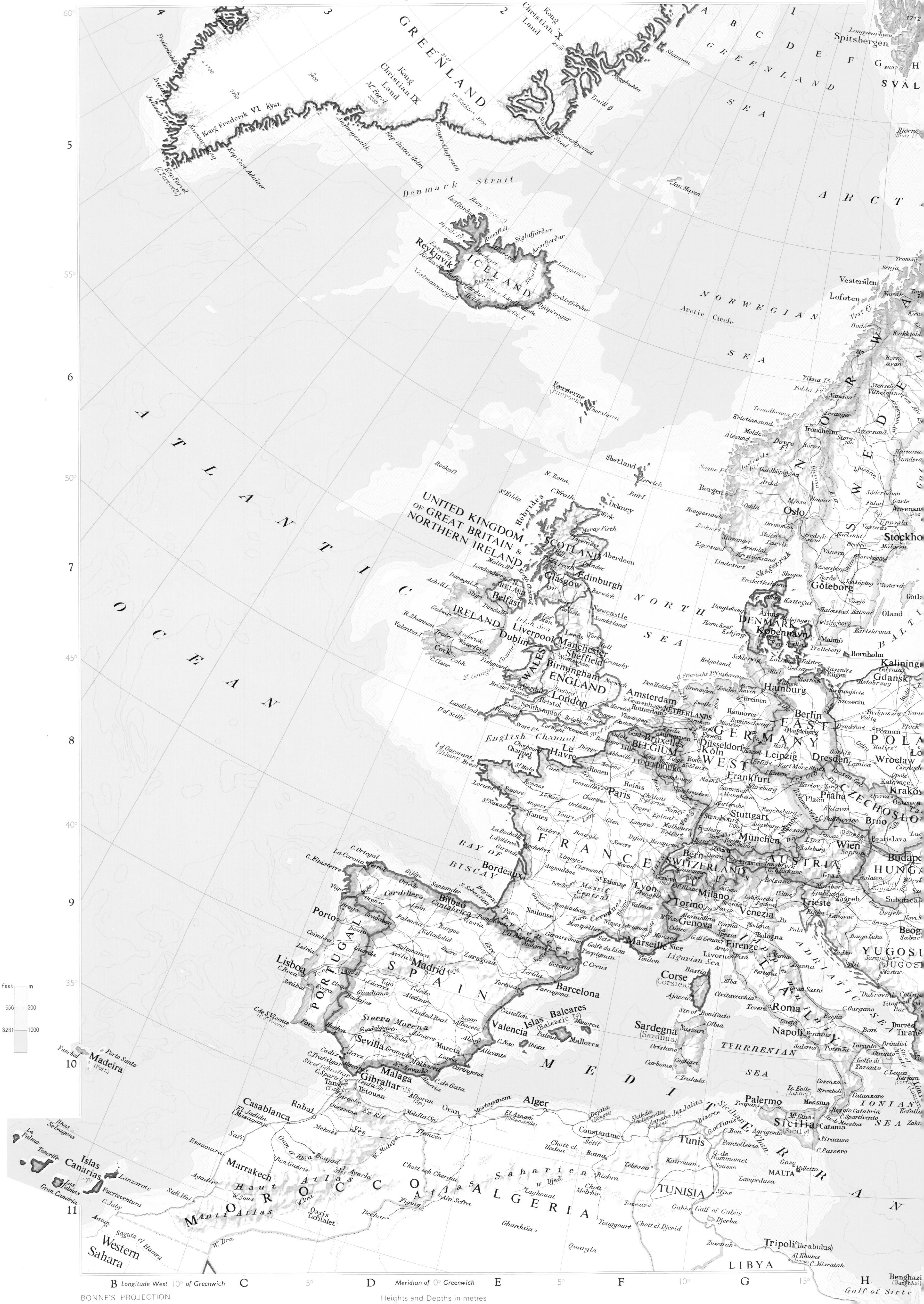

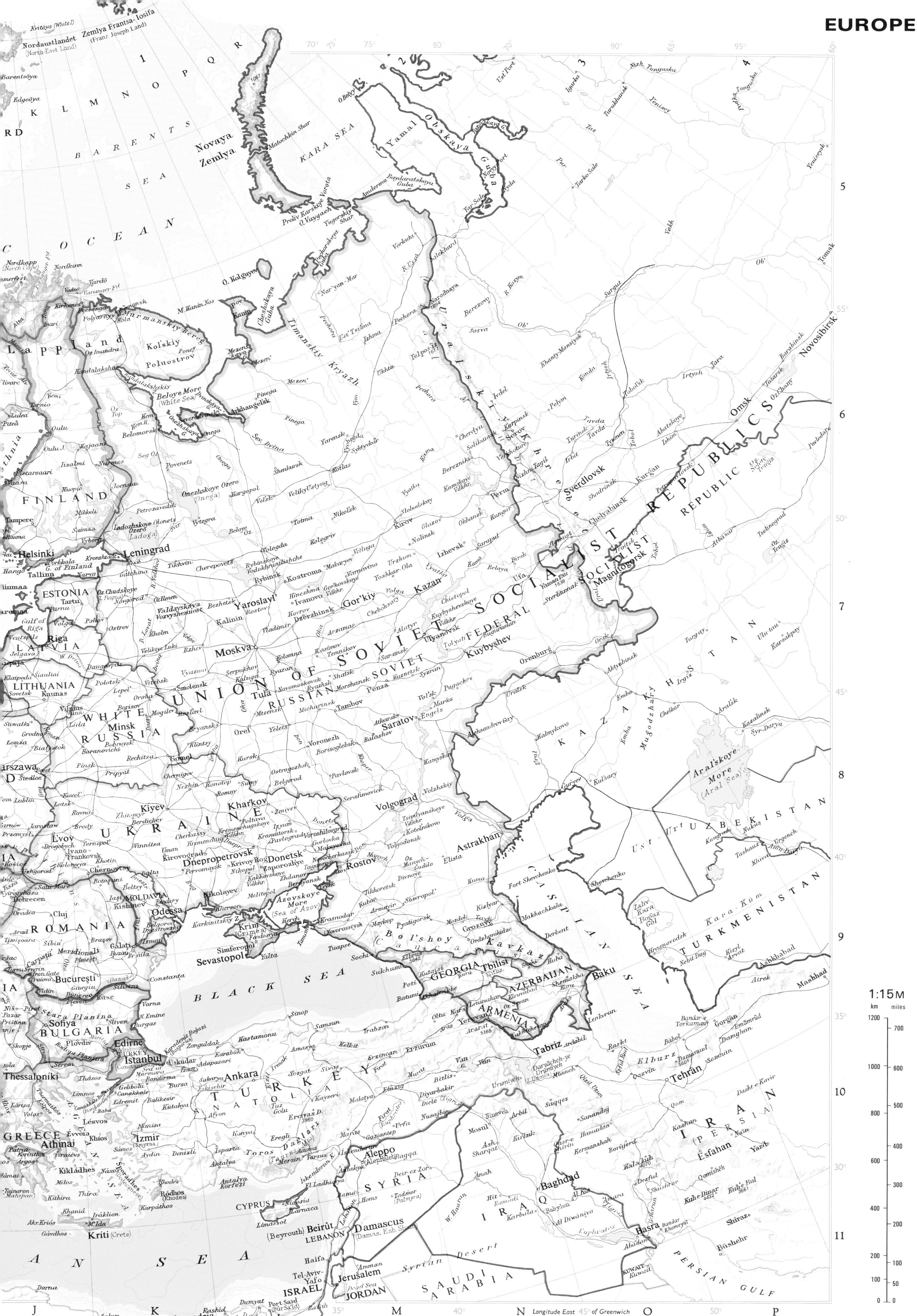
Nordaustlandet
(North-East Land)
Zemlya Frantsa-Iosifa
(Franz Joseph Land)
BARENTS SEA
OCEAN
Novaya Zemlya
KARA SEA
Yamal
Obskaya Guba
Nordkapp
(North Cape)
Kol'skiy Poluostrov
Lappland
Beloye More
(White Sea)
Arkhangel'sk
Timanskiy Kryazh
Ural'skiy Khrebet
FINLAND
Helsinki
Leningrad
Onezhskoye Ozero
(Onega)
Ladozhskoye Ozero
(Ladoga)
ESTONIA
Tallinn
Riga
LATVIA
LITHUANIA
Kaunas
Vilnius
WHITE RUSSIA
Minsk
Warszawa
Moskva
Yaroslavl'
Gor'kiy
Kazan
Kuybyshev
Perm
Sverdlovsk
Chelyabinsk
Magnitogorsk
Omsk
Novosibirsk
Tomsk
Orenburg
UNION OF SOVIET SOCIALIST REPUBLICS
RUSSIAN SOVIET FEDERAL SOCIALIST REPUBLIC
KAZAKHSTAN
Aral'skoye More
(Aral Sea)
UZBEKISTAN
TURKMENISTAN
Kara-Kum
Ust-Urt
Tula
Saratov
Volgograd
Astrakhan
UKRAINE
Kiyev
Kharkov
L'vov
Dnepropetrovsk
Donetsk
Rostov
Odessa
Kishinev
MOLDAVIA
Azovskoye More
(Sea of Azov)
Krim
(Crimea)
Sevastopol
ROMANIA
București
Cluj
BULGARIA
Sofiya
BLACK SEA
Bol'shoy Kavkaz
GEORGIA
Tbilisi
AZERBAIJAN
Baku
ARMENIA
Yerevan
CASPIAN SEA
Krasnovodsk
Ashkhabad
TURKEY
Istanbul
Ankara
Izmir
Edirne
GREECE
Athinai
Thessaloníki
Kriti
(Crete)
Ródhos
(Rhodes)
CYPRUS
SYRIA
Aleppo
Damascus
LEBANON
Beirût
ISRAEL
Jerusalem
JORDAN
IRAQ
Baghdad
Basra
KUWAIT
SAUDI ARABIA
Syrian Desert
IRAN
(PERSIA)
Tehran
Tabriz
Esfahan
Elburz
PERSIAN GULF
Alexandria
Port Said
Longitude East 45° of Greenwich
1:15M
km
miles

© John Bartholomew & Son Ltd Edinburgh

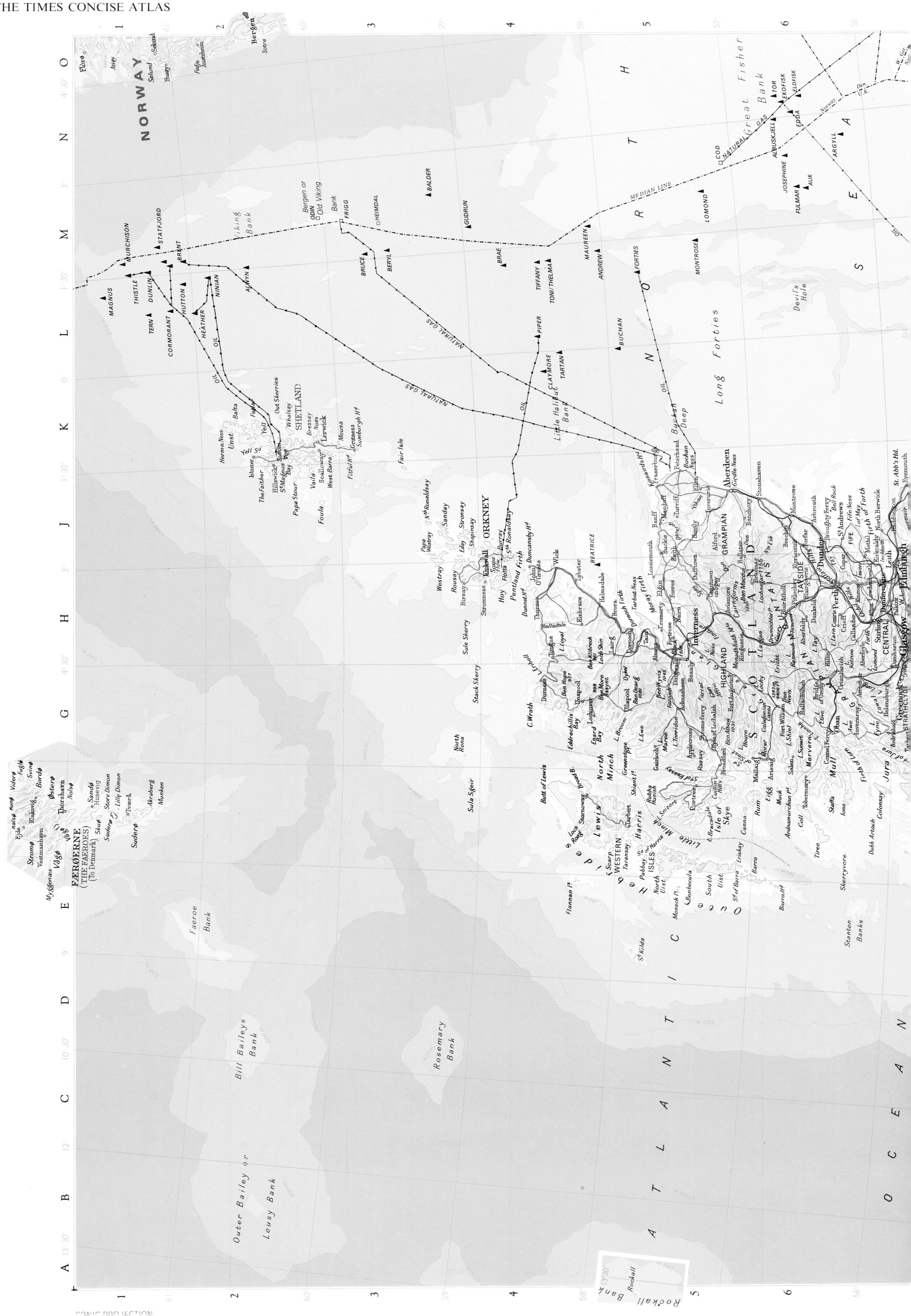

NORWAY

Bergen
Sogne

NORTH

Viking Bank
Bergen or ODIN
Old Viking
FRIGG
HEIMDAL
BALDER
GUDRUN
BRAE
BRUCE
BERYL
ALWYN
TIFFANY
TONI/THELMA
MAUREEN
ANDREW
FORTIES
MONTROSE
LOMOND
COD
NATURAL GAS
MEDIAN LINE
JOSEPHINE
FULMAR AUK
ARGYLL
ABUSKJELL
TOR
EKOFISK
ELDFISK
EPPA

MAGNUS
MURCHISON
STATFJORD
THISTLE DUNLIN
BRENT
TERN
CORMORANT
HUTTON
HEATHER
NINIAN
OIL

PIPER
CLAYMORE
TARTAN
BUCHAN
Little Halibut Bank
NATURAL GAS
OIL

Long Forties
Devil's Hole
Buchan Deep

SHETLAND
Herma Ness
Unst
Yell Sd
Yell
Balta
Fetlar
Out Skerries
Whalsay
Bressay
Noss
Lerwick
Mousa
Sumburgh Hd
Fitful Hd
Isbister
Hillswick
The Faither
St Magnus Bay
Papa Stour
Vaila
Foula
West Burra
Fair Isle

ORKNEY
Kirkwall
Westray
Papa Westray
Rousay
Sanday
Stronsay
Eday
Shapinsay
Birsay
Stromness
Hoy
Flotta
Burray
S⁰ Ronaldsay
Nth Ronaldsay
Pentland Firth
Dunnet Hd
John o'Groats
Duncansby Hd

BEATRICE
Wick

Sule Skerry
Stack Skerry
North Rona
Sula Sgeir

SCOTLAND
HIGHLAND
GRAMPIAN
TAYSIDE
CENTRAL
STRATHCLYDE
Aberdeen
Inverness
Dundee
Perth
Glasgow
Edinburgh
Peterhead
Fraserburgh
Stonehaven
Montrose
Arbroath
Firth of Forth
Moray Firth
Dornoch Firth
Thurso
Halladale
Bonar Br
Brora
Helmsdale

WESTERN ISLES
Lewis
Harris
North Uist
South Uist
Benbecula
Barra
Butt of Lewis
Stornoway
Tarbert
St Kilda
Flannan Is
Monach Is

Skye
Rum
Eigg
Muck
Canna
Coll
Tiree
Mull
Iona
Staffa
Colonsay
Jura
Islay
Oban
Fort William

North Minch
Little Minch
The Minch

FÆRØERNE
(THE FAEROES)
(To Denmark)
Thorshavn
Suderø
Store Dimon
Lille Dimon
Vestmanhavn

Faeroe Bank

Bill Baileys Bank
Outer Bailey or Lousy Bank

Rosemary Bank

Rockall Bank
Rockall

A T L A N T I C   O C E A N

CONIC PROJECTION

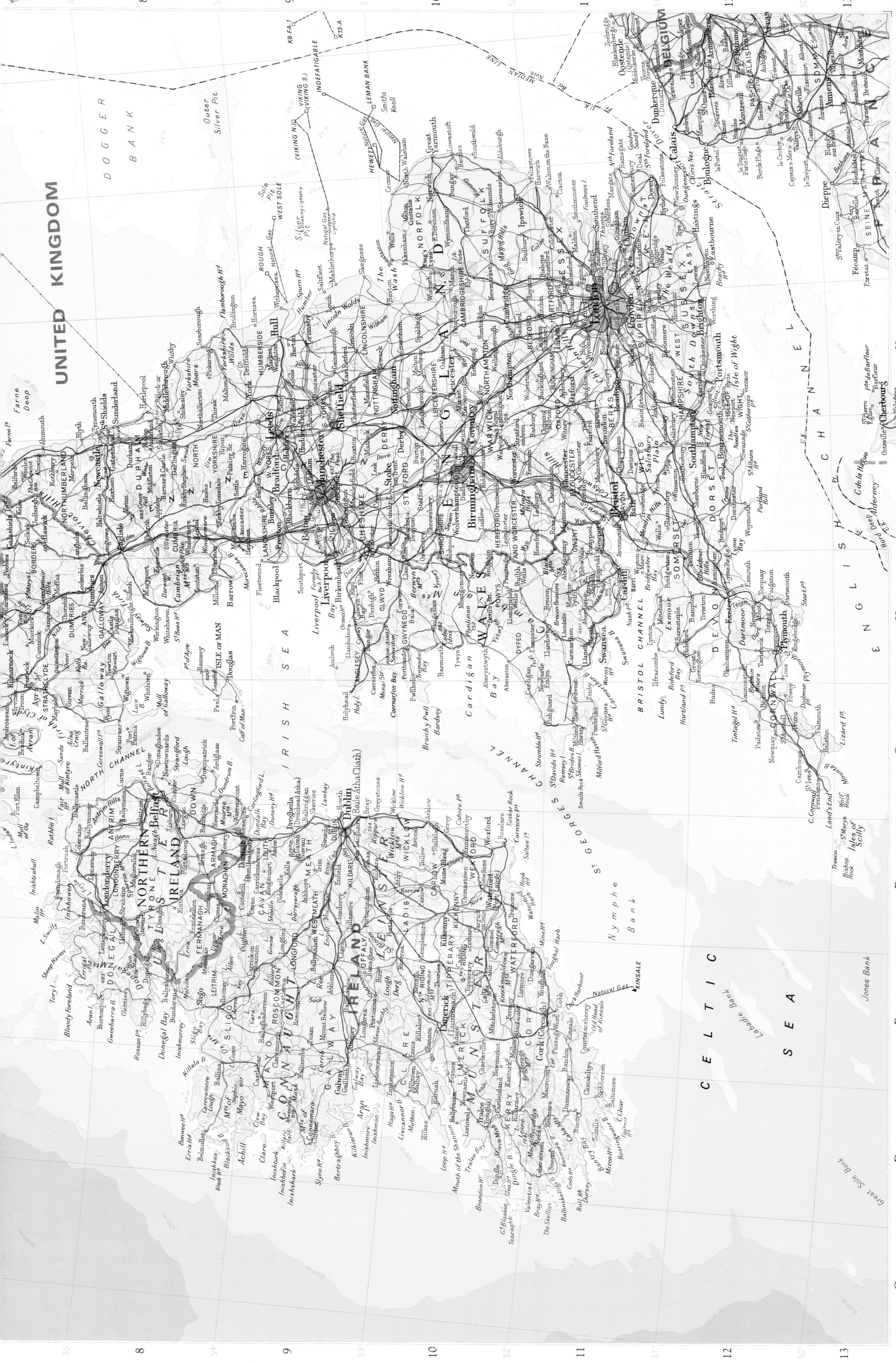

UNITED KINGDOM

DOGGER BANK

ENGLAND

WALES

IRELAND

NORTHERN IRELAND

ULSTER

CONNAUGHT

LEINSTER

MUNSTER

SCOTLAND

IRISH SEA

NORTH CHANNEL

ST GEORGE'S CHANNEL

CELTIC SEA

ENGLISH CHANNEL

BRISTOL CHANNEL

FRANCE

BELGIUM

CHANNEL ISLANDS (U.K.)

London

Dublin (Baile Átha Cliath)

Belfast

Liverpool

Manchester

Leeds

Bradford

Sheffield

Birmingham

Bristol

Cardiff

Swansea

Newcastle

Sunderland

Middlesbrough

Hull

York

Nottingham

Leicester

Coventry

Derby

Stoke

Plymouth

Southampton

Portsmouth

Calais

Boulogne

Dunkerque (Dunkirk)

Ostende (Ostend)

Dieppe

Cherbourg

Guernsey

Jersey

Sark

Alderney

Isle of Man

Douglas

Cork (Corcaigh)

Limerick (Luimneach)

Galway (Gaillimh)

Waterford

Wexford

1:3 M

Heights and Depths in metres

Meridian of 0° Greenwich

© John Bartholomew & Son Ltd Edinburgh

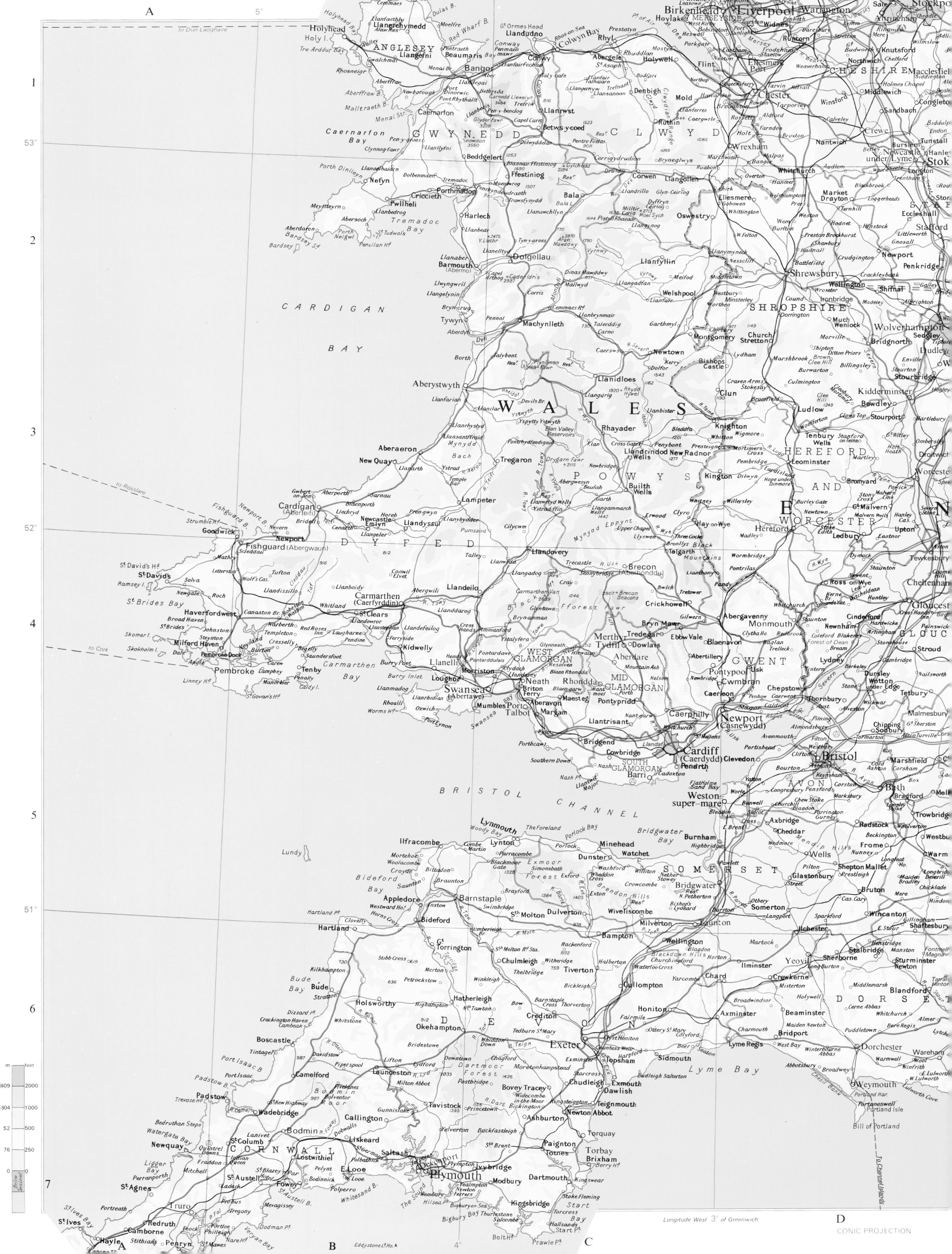
A
B
C
D
1
2
3
4
5
6
7
53°
52°
51°
5°
4°
to Dun Laoghaire
to Rosslare
to Cork
Holyhead
Holy I.
ANGLESEY
Llangefni
Amlwch
Beaumaris
Bangor
Caernarfon
Caernarfon Bay
GWYNEDD
Snowdon 3560
Llandudno
Conwy
Colwyn Bay
Rhyl
Prestatyn
Llanrwst
Betws-y-coed
Beddgelert
Ffestiniog
Porthmadog
Criccieth
Pwllheli
Nefyn
Tremadoc Bay
Bardsey I.
Harlech
Bala
Barmouth
Dolgellau
CLWYD
Denbigh
Ruthin
Mold
Flint
Holywell
Wrexham
Llangollen
Corwen
Oswestry
Chester
Birkenhead
Liverpool
MERSEYSIDE
Wallasey
Hoylake
St. Helens
Widnes
Runcorn
Warrington
Ellesmere Port
Northwich
Knutsford
CHESHIRE
Winsford
Middlewich
Crewe
Nantwich
Whitchurch
Macclesfield
Congleton
Sandbach
Newcastle under Lyme
Stoke
Shrewsbury
SHROPSHIRE
Welshpool
Newtown
Montgomery
Machynlleth
Tywyn
CARDIGAN BAY
Aberystwyth
Llanidloes
WALES
Rhayader
Tregaron
Aberaeron
New Quay
Cardigan
Lampeter
Llandrindod Wells
Builth Wells
POWYS
Knighton
Ludlow
Leominster
Kington
HEREFORD AND WORCESTER
Hereford
Hay-on-Wye
Brecon
Llandovery
Llandeilo
DYFED
Fishguard (Abergwaun)
Goodwick
St. David's
St. Brides Bay
Haverfordwest
Milford Haven
Pembroke
Pembroke Dock
Tenby
Carmarthen
Carmarthen Bay
Kidwelly
Llanelli
Swansea (Abertawe)
Neath
Port Talbot
WEST GLAMORGAN
MID GLAMORGAN
SOUTH GLAMORGAN
Bridgend
Pontypridd
Merthyr Tydfil
Caerphilly
Cardiff (Caerdydd)
Barri
Newport (Casnewydd)
GWENT
Abergavenny
Monmouth
Pontypool
Chepstow
BRISTOL CHANNEL
Bristol
AVON
Bath
Weston-super-Mare
Lundy
Ilfracombe
Lynmouth
Minehead
SOMERSET
Bridgwater
Taunton
Wells
Glastonbury
Yeovil
Barnstaple
Bideford
Bideford Bay
DEVON
Okehampton
Exeter
Tiverton
Crediton
Exmouth
Torquay
Paignton
Plymouth
Tavistock
Dartmoor Forest
Exmoor Forest
CORNWALL
Bude
Launceston
Bodmin
Newquay
Truro
St. Austell
Falmouth
Penryn
Redruth
Camborne
Hayle
St. Ives
Lyme Bay
Lyme Regis
DORSET
Dorchester
Weymouth
Bridport
Sherborne
Bill of Portland
Gloucester
Cheltenham
Stroud
Worcester
Kidderminster
Wolverhampton
Longitude West 3° of Greenwich
CONIC PROJECTION
m feet
609 2000
304 1000
152 500
76 250
0 0
Below Sea Level

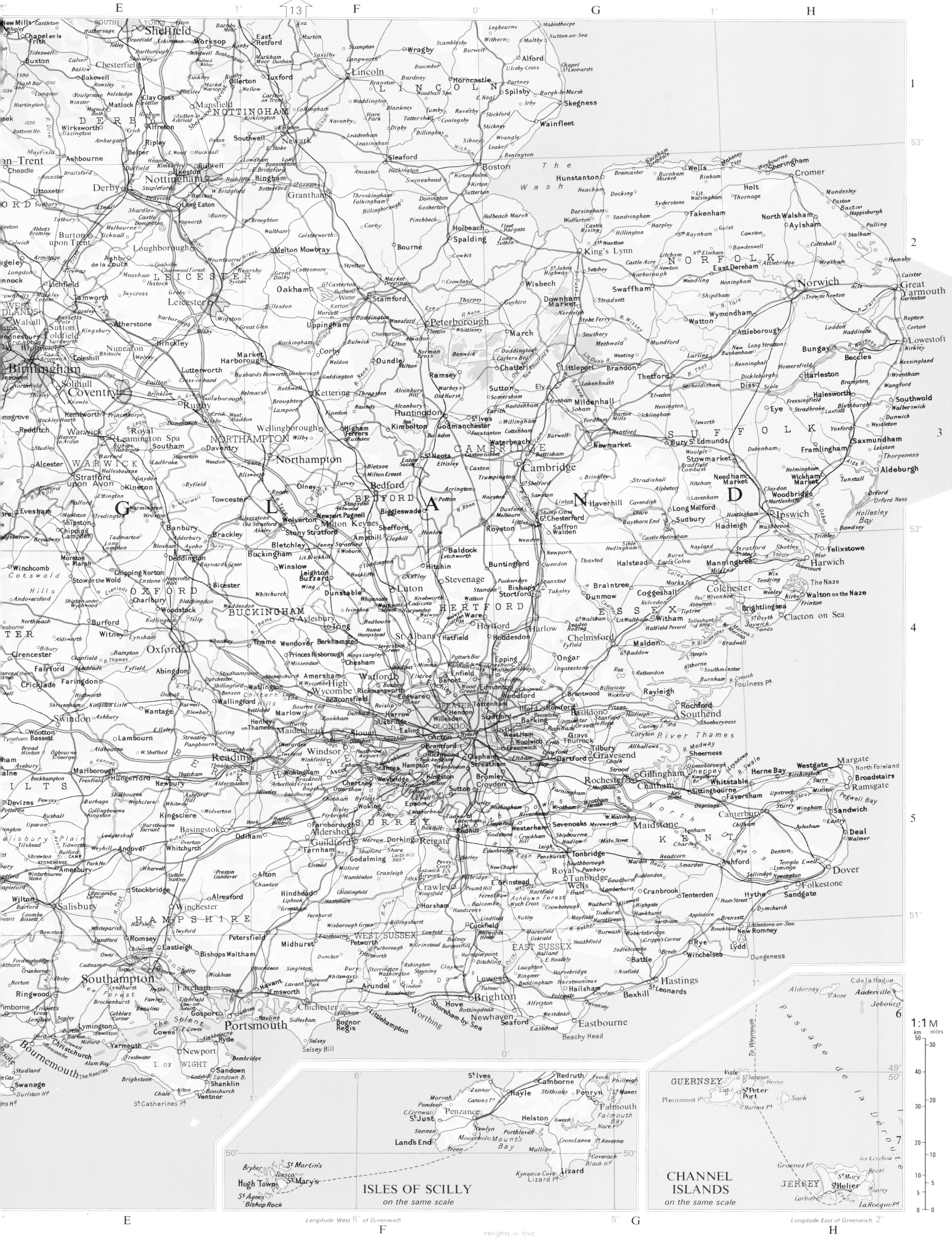

ENGLAND

Major cities and regions shown on the map include:

Sheffield, Chesterfield, Buxton, Nottingham, Derby, Lincoln, Boston, Leicester, Peterborough, Stamford, Northampton, Bedford, Cambridge, Huntingdon, Norwich, Great Yarmouth, King's Lynn, NORFOLK, SUFFOLK, Ipswich, Lowestoft, Bury St Edmunds, Newmarket, Birmingham, Coventry, Warwick, Rugby, Stratford upon Avon, Banbury, Oxford, Buckingham, Milton Keynes, Luton, Hertford, St Albans, Chelmsford, ESSEX, Colchester, Harwich, Clacton on Sea, Southend, London (GREATER LONDON), Reading, Windsor, Guildford, SURREY, Maidstone, KENT, Canterbury, Dover, Folkestone, Margate, Ramsgate, Rochester, Chatham, Gravesend, Tonbridge, Tunbridge Wells, Crawley, WEST SUSSEX, EAST SUSSEX, Brighton, Eastbourne, Hastings, Worthing, Chichester, Portsmouth, Southampton, HAMPSHIRE, Winchester, Salisbury, Bournemouth, I. of WIGHT, Newport, Ryde

ISLES OF SCILLY
on the same scale

St Ives, Camborne, Redruth, Penzance, Helston, Land's End, Penryn, Falmouth, Falmouth Bay, Lizard, Lizard Pt, St Just, Newlyn, Mount's Bay, St Mary's, Hugh Town, St Martin's, Bishop Rock

CHANNEL ISLANDS
on the same scale

GUERNSEY, St Peter Port, Herm, Sark, Alderney, St Anne, Auderville, Jobourg, JERSEY, St Helier, La Rocque Pt, Corbière, Gorey

1:1 M
km miles
50   30
40
30   20
20
10   10
0   0

Longitude West 6° of Greenwich

Longitude East of Greenwich 2°

Heights in feet

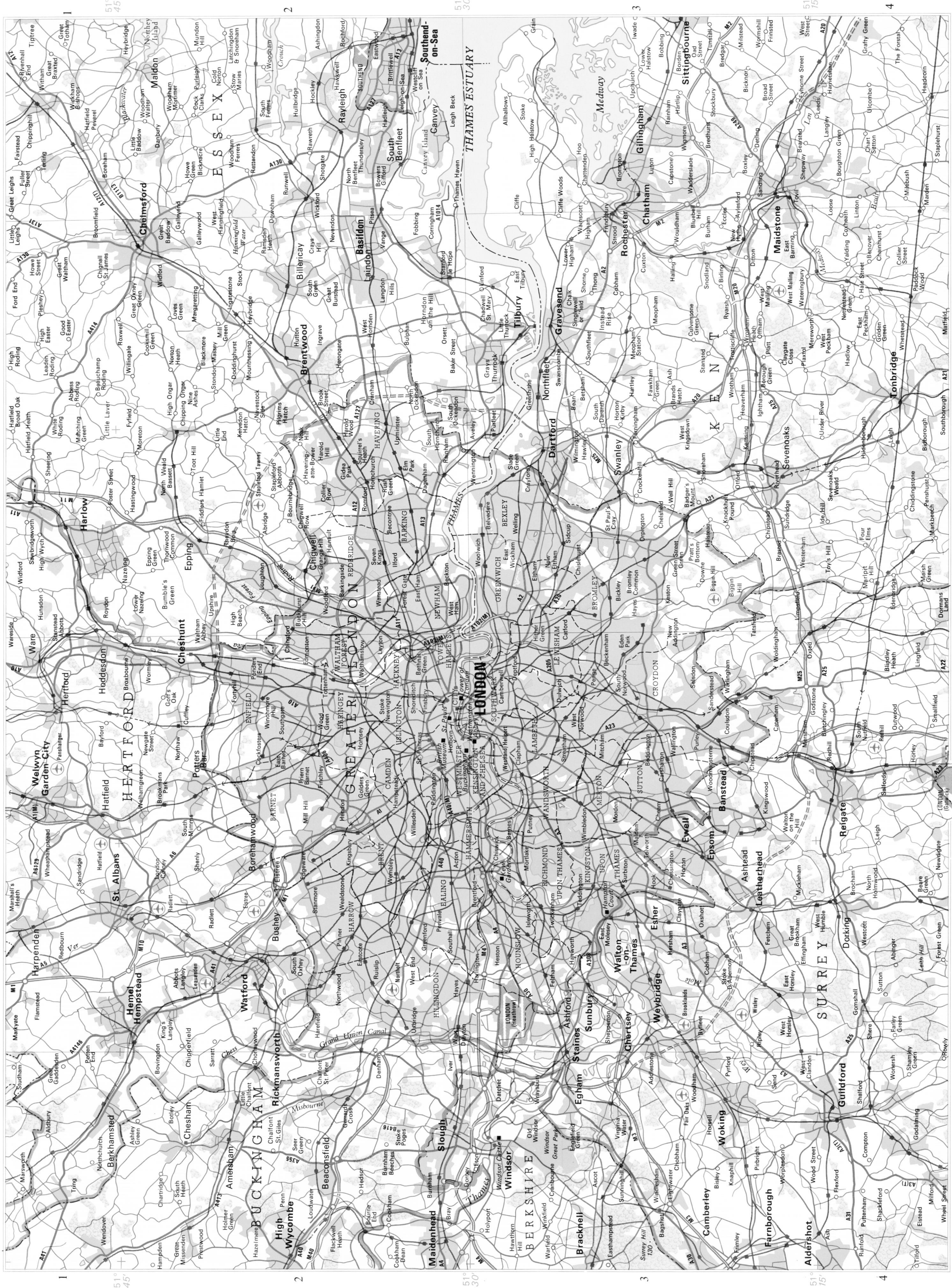

ESSEX

KENT

SURREY

BERKSHIRE

BUCKINGHAM

HERTFORD

GREATER LONDON

LONDON

THAMES ESTUARY

Southend-on-Sea

Chelmsford

Brentwood

Basildon

Harlow

Epping

Gravesend

Dartford

Tilbury

Northfleet

Rochester

Chatham

Gillingham

Sittingbourne

Maidstone

Tonbridge

Sevenoaks

Reigate

Guildford

Woking

Aldershot

Farnborough

Camberley

Bracknell

Maidenhead

Windsor

Slough

High Wycombe

Beaconsfield

Amersham

Chesham

Berkhamsted

Hemel Hempstead

Harpenden

St. Albans

Welwyn Garden City

Hatfield

Hertford

Hoddesdon

Ware

Cheshunt

Potters Bar

Borehamwood

Watford

Bushey

Rickmansworth

Rayleigh

South Benfleet

Canvey Island

Billericay

Staines

Egham

Chertsey

Weybridge

Walton-on-Thames

Esher

Sunbury

Ashford

Leatherhead

Epsom

Ewell

Banstead

Dorking

Swanley

1:300 000

0 5 10 15 km

0 5 10 miles

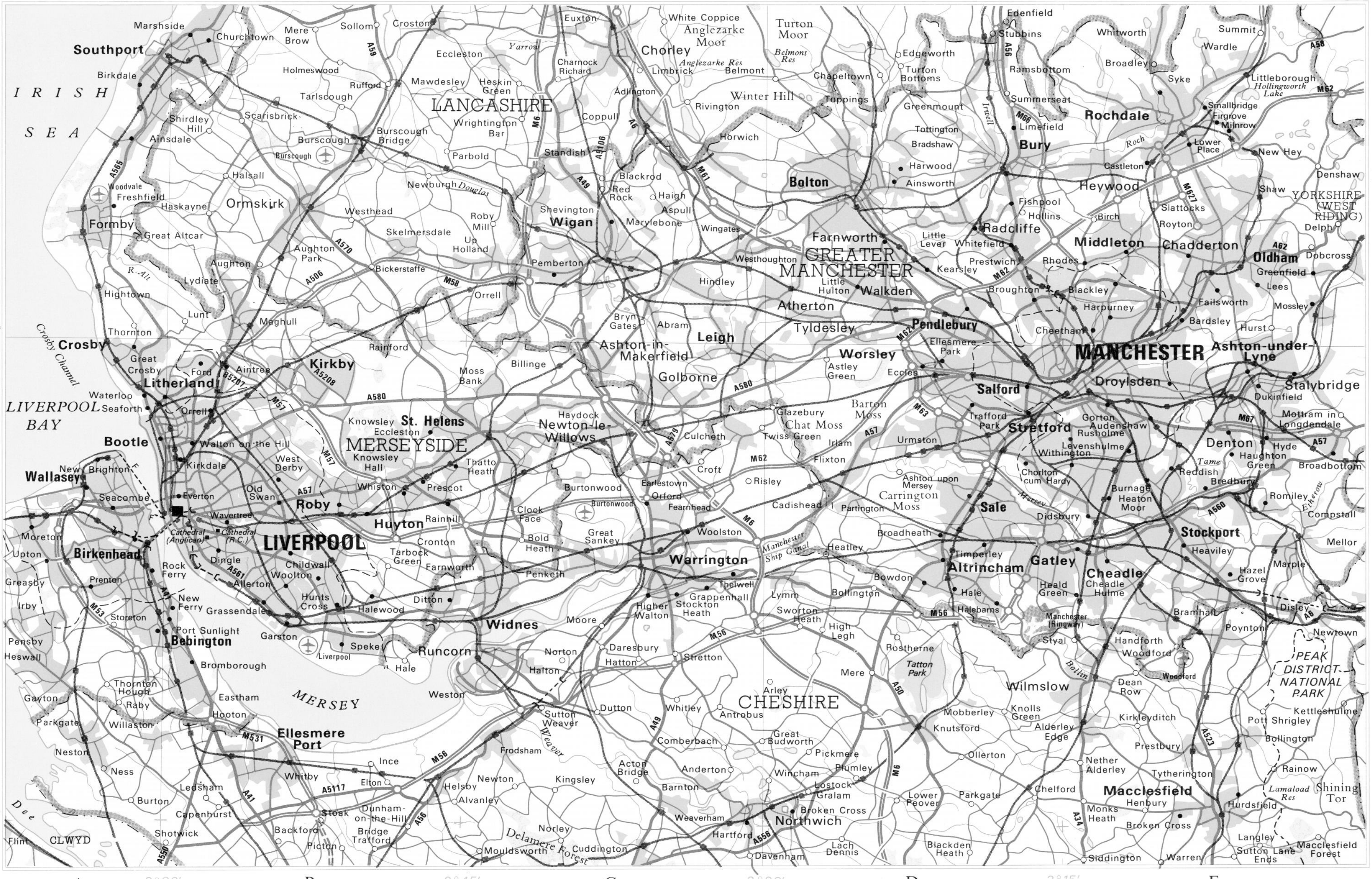

SOUTH LANCASHIRE

IRISH SEA

Southport
Marshside
Churchtown
Birkdale
Mere Brow
Sollom
Croston
Euxton
White Coppice
Anglezarke Moor
Turton Moor
Edenfield
Stubbins
Whitworth
Broadley
Summit
Wardle
Shirldey Hill
Ainsdale
Holmeswood
Eccleston
Charnock Richard
Chorley
Anglezarke Res
Belmont
Chapeltown
Edgworth
Ramsbottom
Syke
Hollingworth Lake
Formby
Freshfield
Woodvale
Rufford
Tarlscough
Mawdesley
Heskin Green
Wrightington Bar
Adlington
Limbrick
Winter Hill
Rivington
Greenmount
Tottington
Summerseat
Rochdale
Smallbridge
Firgrove
Milnrow
Denshaw
YORKSHIRE (WEST RIDING)
Delph

LANCASHIRE

Ormskirk
Great Altcar
Haskayne
Halsall
Scarisbrick
Burscough
Burscough Bridge
Parbold
Newburgh
Douglas
Standish
Blackrod
Red Rock
Haigh
Aspull
Marylebone
Wingates
Bolton
Bradshaw
Harwood
Ainsworth
Bury
Limefield
Castleton
Lower Place
New Hey
Shaw
Mottram in Longdendale

Aughton
Aughton Park
Westhead
Skelmersdale
Up Holland
Orrell
Shevington
Wigan
Pemberton
Hindley
Westhoughton
Little Hulton
Kearsley
Farnworth
Whitefield
Prestwich
Radcliffe
Rhodes
Blackley
Harpurhey
Middleton
Chadderton
Oldham
Greenfield
Lees
Failsworth
Mossley
Hurst

Maghull
Lydiate
Lunt
Thornton
Bickerstaffe
Rainford
Billinge
Bryn Gates
Abram
Leigh
Astley Green
Tyldesley
Walkden
Pendlebury
Cheetham
GREATER MANCHESTER
MANCHESTER
Ashton-under-Lyne
Stalybridge
Dukinfield
Denton
Hyde

Crosby
Great Crosby
Ford
Aintree
Kirkby
Knowsley
St. Helens
Eccleston
Newton-le-Willows
Ashton-in-Makerfield
Golborne
Worsley
Ellesmere Park
Eccles
Salford
Droylsden
Gorton
Audenshaw
Rusholme

MERSEYSIDE
Waterloo
Seaforth
Bootle
Walton on the Hill
West Derby
Knowsley Hall
Whiston
Prescot
Haydock
Thatto Heath
Chat Moss
Barton Moss
Glazebury
Twiss Green
Irlam
Partington
Carrington Moss
Trafford Park
Stretford
Levenshulme
Withington
Chorlton cum Hardy
Reddish
Bredbury
Broadbottom

Litherland
LIVERPOOL BAY
New Brighton
Wallasey
Seacombe
Everton
Kirkdale
Old Swan
Roby
Huyton
Rainhill
Burtonwood
Orford
Fearnhead
Croft
Risley
Flixton
Urmston
Ashton upon Mersey
Sale
Burnage
Heaton Moor
Stockport
Heaviley
Romiley
Compstall

Birkenhead
Rock Ferry
New Ferry
Wavertree
Dingle
Allerton
LIVERPOOL
Cathedral (Anglican)
Cathedral (R.C.)
Childwall
Woolton
Hunts Cross
Grassendale
Garston
Halewood
Ditton
Widnes
Moore
Higher Walton
Stockton Heath
Grappenhall
Warrington
Penketh
Cuerdley
Woolston
Manchester Ship Canal
Heatley
Lymm
Broadheath
Bowdon
Altrincham
Timperley
Gatley
Cheadle
Cheadle Hulme
Hale
Halebarns
Handforth
Woodford
Styal
Bramhall
Poynton
Disley
Newtown

Bebington
Port Sunlight
Bromborough
Eastham
Hooton
Ince
Whitby
Ellesmere Port
Frodsham
Helsby
Newton
Alvanley
Kingsley
Acton Bridge
Anderton
Pickmere
Plumley
Knutsford
Mobberley
Alderley Edge
Nether Alderley
Prestbury
Dean Row
Wilmslow
Knolls Green
Kirkleyditch
Bollington
PEAK DISTRICT NATIONAL PARK
Kettleshulme
Pott Shrigley
Rainow
Shining Tor
Lamaload Res

Prenton
Greasby
Irby
Storeton
Thornton Hough
Raby
Gayton
Parkgate
Neston
Ness
Burton
Ledsham
Capenhurst
Backford
Stoak
Dunham-on-the-Hill
Bridge Trafford
Mouldsworth
Norley
Delamere Forest
Cuddington
Weaverham
Northwich
Hartford
Davenham
Lach Dennis
Rudheath
Gralam
Lostock Gralam
Wincham
Great Budworth
Comberbach
Barnton
Winnington
Barton
Antrobus
Whitley
Dutton
Stretton
Hatton
Daresbury
Norton
Halton
Sutton Weaver
Weston
Hale
Speke

CHESHIRE
CLWYD
Flint

WEST MIDLANDS

WEST MIDLANDS

Bishop's Wood
Brewood
Hatherton
Heath Hayes
Chase Terrace
Burntwood
Streethay
Elford
No Man's Heath
Appleby Parva
Snarestone
Ibstock
Markfield
Newtown Linford
STAFFORD
Kiddemore Green
Coven
Standeford
Cheslyn Hay
A5190
Chasetown
Lichfield
Whittington
Hademore
Seckington
Newton Regis
Austrey
Bilstone
Twycross
Odstone
Nailstone
Bagworth
Thornton
Thornton Resr.
Groby
Ratby

Codsall Wood
Albrighton
Boningale
Codsall
Shareshill
Featherstone
Essington
Landywood
Pelsall
Great Wyrley
Brownhills
Shire Oak
Walsall Wood
Shenstone
Hopwas
Tamworth
Fazeley
Wiggington
Little Hay
Hints
Kettlebrook
Polesworth
Wilnecote
Alvecote
Warton
Orton on the Hill
Sheepy Magna
Wellsborough
Sibson
Market Bosworth
Carlton
Cadeby
Sutton Cheney
Kirkby Mallory
Peckleton
Kirby Muxloe
LEICESTER

Wergs
Pattingham
Tettenhall
Wolverhampton
Wednesfield
Bloxwich
Walsall
Aldridge
Streetly
Mere Green
Little Aston
Drayton Bassett
Dosthill
Middleton
Roughley
Baddesley Ensor
Baxterley
Mancetter
Hartshill
Atherstone
Ratcliffe Culey
Fenny Drayton
Witherley
Higham on the Hill
Burton Hastings
Stoke Golding
Dadlington
Earl Shilton
Elmesthorpe
Thurlaston

SALOP
Hilton
Shipley
Seisdon
Claverley
Heathton
Trysull
Wombourne
Oaken
Lower Penn
Willenhall
Bilston
Walsall
Maw Green
Sutton Coldfield
Wishaw
Marston
Wylde Green
Walmley
Minworth
Curdworth
Water Orton
Shustoke
Nether Whitacre
Over Whitacre
Ansley
Stockingford
Nuneaton
Attleborough
Hinckley
Aston Flamville
Sapcote
Primethorpe
Sharnford
Burbage
Leire

Halfpenny Green
Bobbington
Swindon
Himley
Sedgley
Coseley
Horseley Heath
Darlaston
Wednesbury
Churchfield
Kingstanding
Perry Barr
Short Heath
Tyburn
Castle Bromwich
Coleshill
Astley
Maxstoke
Fillongley
Corley
Corley Moor
Griff
Bulkington
Wolvey
Wibtoft
Ullesthorpe
Bitteswell
Claybrooke Magna

Six Ashes
Enville
Kingswinford
Tipton
Oldbury
Rowley Regis
West Bromwich
Handsworth
Aston
Washwood Heath
Coleshill
Barnacle
Shilton
Ansty
Withybrook

Potter's Cross
Stourton
Wordsley
Brierley Hill
Amblecote
Smethwick
Warley
WEST MIDLANDS
BIRMINGHAM
Sheldon
Marston Green
Bickenhill
Elmdon
A45
Meriden
Eastern Green
Allesley
Foleshill
Walsgrave on Sowe
Stretton under Fosse
Pailton
Harborough Magna
Rugby

Romsley
Kinver
Stourbridge
Pedmore
Halesowen
Harborne
Edgbaston
Moseley
Olton
Solihull
Balsall Common
Berkswell
Bedworth

Kingsford
Caunsall
Cookley
West Hagley
Hagley
Broome
Blakedown
Holy Cross
Selly Oak
King's Heath
Woodgate
Rubery
Northfield
Longbridge
Shirley
Hall Green
Knowle
Dorridge
Hampton in Arden
Eastcote
Fen End
Meer End
Honiley
Kenilworth
Stoneleigh
Ryton-on-Dunsmore
Wolston
Brandon
Bretford
Long Lawford
Coventry
Cathedral
Stivichall
Brinklow
Wolvey
Shilton

Kidderminster
Habberley
Blakebrook
Franche
Wribbenhall
Stone
Mustow Green
Belbroughton
Fairfield
Bournheath
Lickey
Cofton Hackett
Barnt Green
Wythall
Portway
Hockley Heath
Chadwick End
Wroxall
Rowington
Leek Wootton
Leamington Spa
Cubbington
Princethorpe
Hunningham
Marton
Birdingbury
Hardwick
Bourton on Dunsmore

Bewdley
Ribbesford
Trimpley
Wolverley
Shatterford
Shenstone
Chaddesley Corbett
Dodford
Catshill
Blackwell
Alvechurch
Beoley
Redditch
Crabbs Cross
Studley
Henley-in-Arden
Claverdon
Norton Lindsey
Warwick
Royal Leamington Spa
Radford Semele
Ashow
Offchurch
Napton on the Hill

Habberley
Callow Hill
Bewdley
Areley Kings
Stourport-on-Severn
Astley
Dunley
Hartlebury
Crossway Green
Ombersley
Doverdale
Hampton Lovett
Oldfield
Droitwich
Bromsgrove
WORCESTER AND HEREFORD
Tardebigge
Finstall
Aston Fields
Elmbridge
Webheath
Bentley
Wood End
Ullenhall
Haseley
Hatton
Shrewley
Wasperton
Little Witley
Holt Heath
Sytchampton
Shrawley
Salwarpe
Hadzor
Oddingley
Bradley Green
Feckenham
Astwood Bank
Sambourne
Coughton
Kinwarton
Wixford
Dunchurch
Leamington Hastings
Grandborough
Willoughby
Kites Hardwick
Flecknoe

1:300 000

© Times Books Ltd

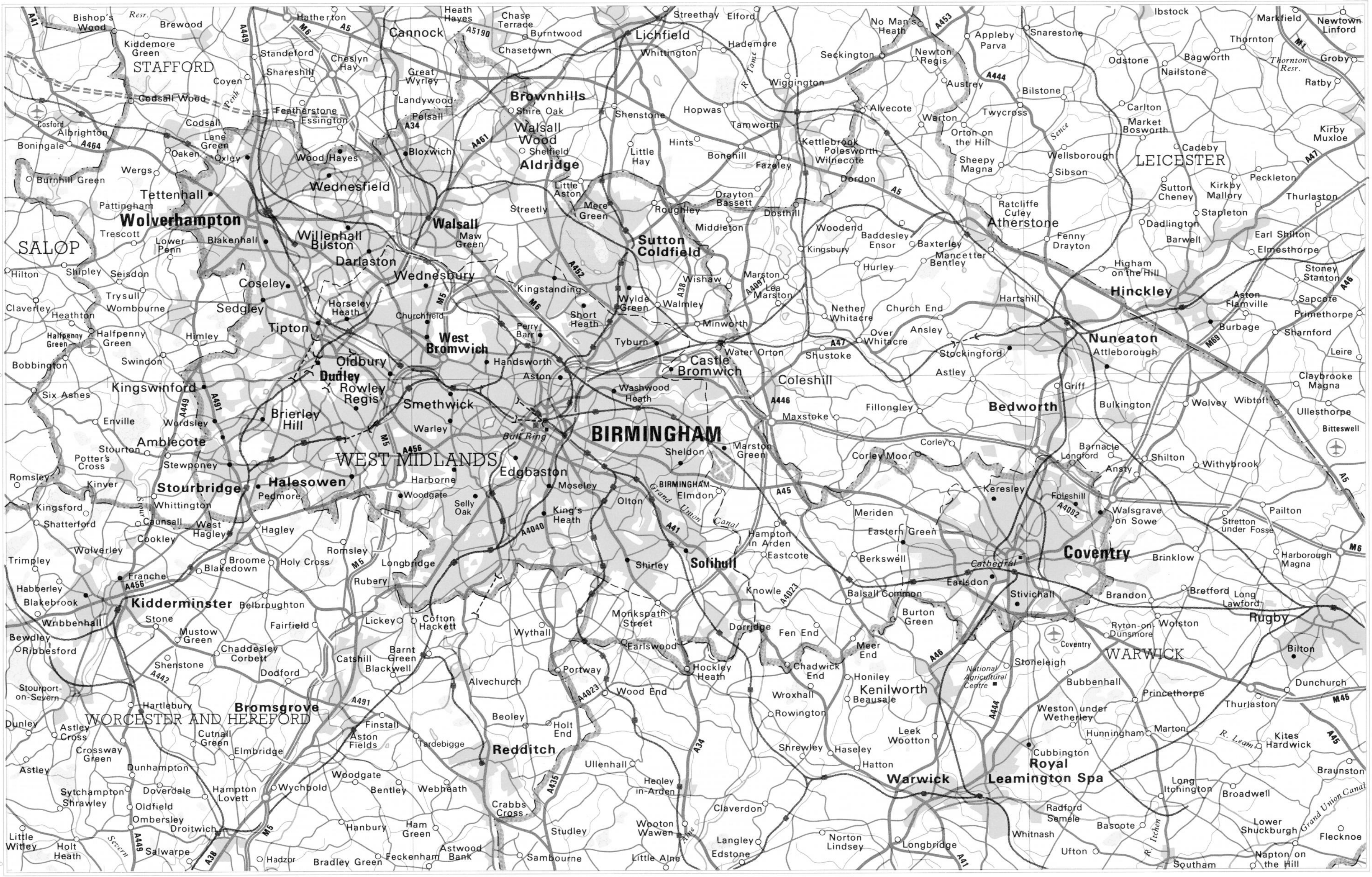

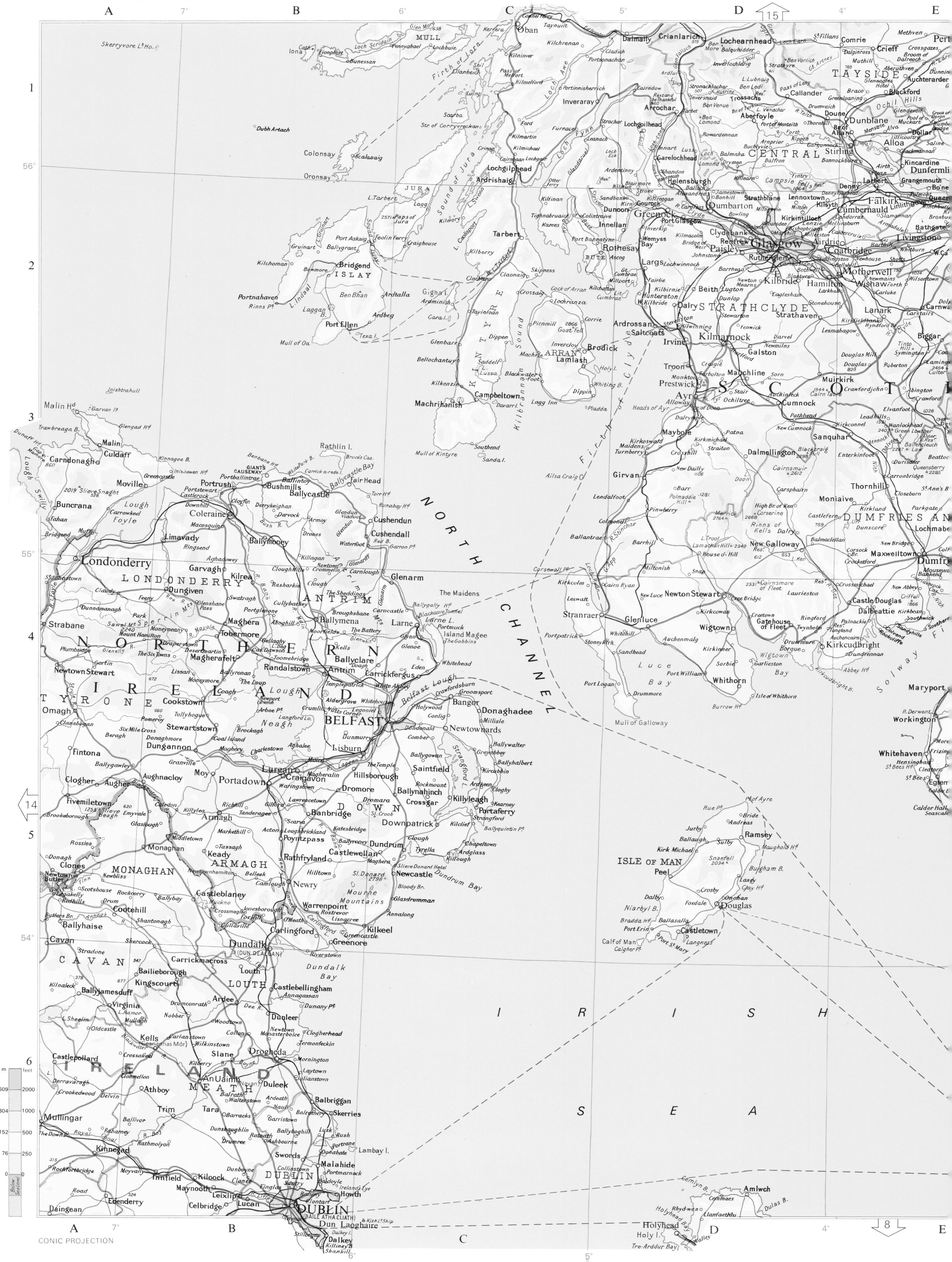

NORTH CHANNEL

IRISH SEA

NORTHERN IRELAND

IRELAND

SCOTLAND

CENTRAL

TAYSIDE

STRATHCLYDE

DUMFRIES AN

Glasgow

BELFAST

DUBLIN (BAILE ATHA CLIATH)

Londonderry

LONDONDERRY

ANTRIM

TYRONE

DOWN

ARMAGH

MONAGHAN

CAVAN

LOUTH

MEATH

ISLE OF MAN

JURA

ISLAY

ARRAN

KINTYRE

MULL

Oban, Inveraray, Arrochar, Helensburgh, Dumbarton, Paisley, Greenock, Gourock, Stirling, Dunblane, Alloa, Falkirk, Livingston, Motherwell, Hamilton, Kilmarnock, Ayr, Prestwick, Troon, Irvine, Saltcoats, Ardrossan, Girvan, Stranraer, Newton Stewart, Wigtown, Whithorn, Kirkcudbright, Castle Douglas, Dalbeattie, Maxwelltown, Maryport, Workington, Whitehaven

Belfast, Lisburn, Bangor, Newtownards, Donaghadee, Portaferry, Downpatrick, Newcastle, Newry, Warrenpoint, Kilkeel, Greenore, Carlingford, Dundalk, Drogheda, Navan, Kells, Trim, Mullingar, Kinnegad, Maynooth, Lucan, Dublin, Dun Laoghaire, Howth, Malahide, Swords, Balbriggan, Skerries

Portadown, Lurgan, Craigavon, Banbridge, Armagh, Dungannon, Cookstown, Magherafelt, Ballymena, Antrim, Randalstown, Carrickfergus, Larne, Ballyclare, Ballymoney, Coleraine, Limavady, Strabane, Omagh, Enniskillen, Clones, Monaghan, Cavan, Castleblaney, Carrickmacross, Kingscourt, Bailieborough, Virginia

Holyhead, Amlwch

CONIC PROJECTION

m feet
609 2000
304 1000
152 500
76 250
0

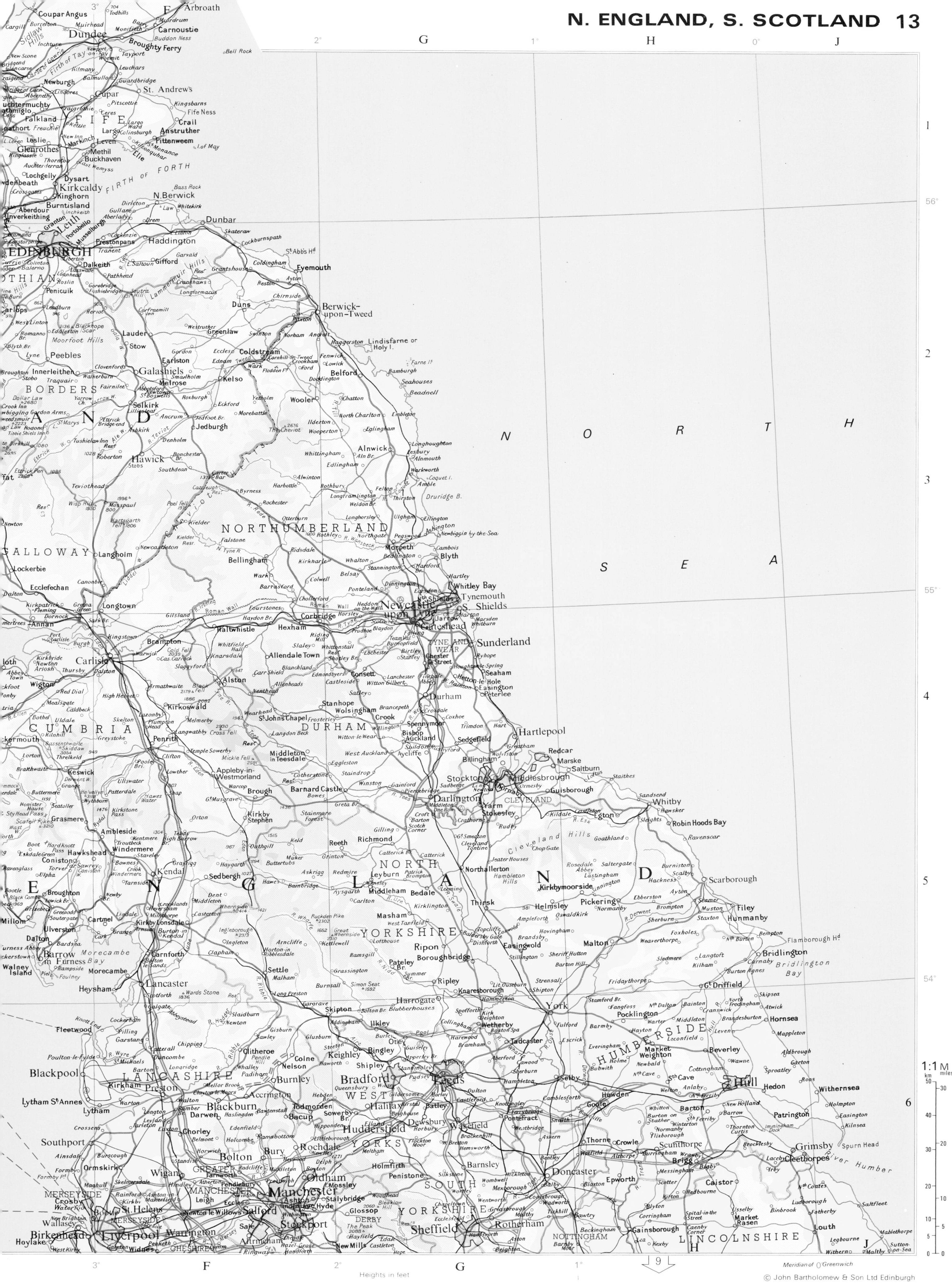

G   H   J

FIFE

FIRTH OF FORTH

EDINBURGH

BORDERS

NORTH

SEA

NORTHUMBERLAND

GALLOWAY

Carlisle

CUMBRIA

DURHAM

TYNE AND WEAR

Newcastle upon Tyne

Sunderland

Hartlepool

Middlesbrough

Darlington

CLEVELAND

Whitby

Scarborough

ENGLAND

NORTH

Kendal

Lancaster

YORKSHIRE

York

Filey

Bridlington

HUMBERSIDE

Blackpool

LANCASHIRE

Preston

Blackburn

Burnley

Bradford

Leeds

WEST

Halifax

Huddersfield

Wakefield

YORKS

Hull

Withernsea

Grimsby

Cleethorpes

Southport

Bolton

Wigan

GREATER

MANCHESTER

MANCHESTER

Salford

Stockport

Oldham

SOUTH

YORKSHIRE

Sheffield

Rotherham

Doncaster

Scunthorpe

LINCOLNSHIRE

MERSEYSIDE

Liverpool

Birkenhead

CHESHIRE

Heights in feet

Meridian of 0° Greenwich

© John Bartholomew & Son Ltd Edinburgh

1:1 M

km   miles

A B C D E F

ATLANTIC OCEAN

NORTH CHANNEL

IRISH SEA

ST GEORGE'S CHANNEL

ULSTER

LONDONDERRY
ANTRIM
TYRONE
DOWN
FERMANAGH
ARMAGH
MONAGHAN
CAVAN
DONEGAL

NORTHERN IRELAND

CONNACHT

SLIGO
LEITRIM
MAYO
ROSCOMMON
GALWAY

LEINSTER

LONGFORD
WESTMEATH
MEATH
LOUTH
OFFALY
KILDARE
DUBLIN
LAOIS
CARLOW
WICKLOW
KILKENNY
WEXFORD

IRELAND (EIRE)

MUNSTER

CLARE
LIMERICK
TIPPERARY
KERRY
CORK
WATERFORD

Dublin
Baile Átha Cliath
Belfast
Cork (Corcaigh)
Limerick (Luimneach)
Galway (Gaillimh)
Waterford (Port Láirge)
Londonderry (Derry)

Heights and Depths in metres

Longitude West of Greenwich

CONIC PROJECTION

1:1.5 M

| m | 200 | 100 | 50 | 0 | 50 | 100 | 200 | 500 | 1000 | m |
| feet | 660 | 330 | 160 | 0 | 160 | 330 | 660 | 1640 | 3280 | feet |

0 10 20 40 60 80 km

0 5 10 20 30 40 50 miles

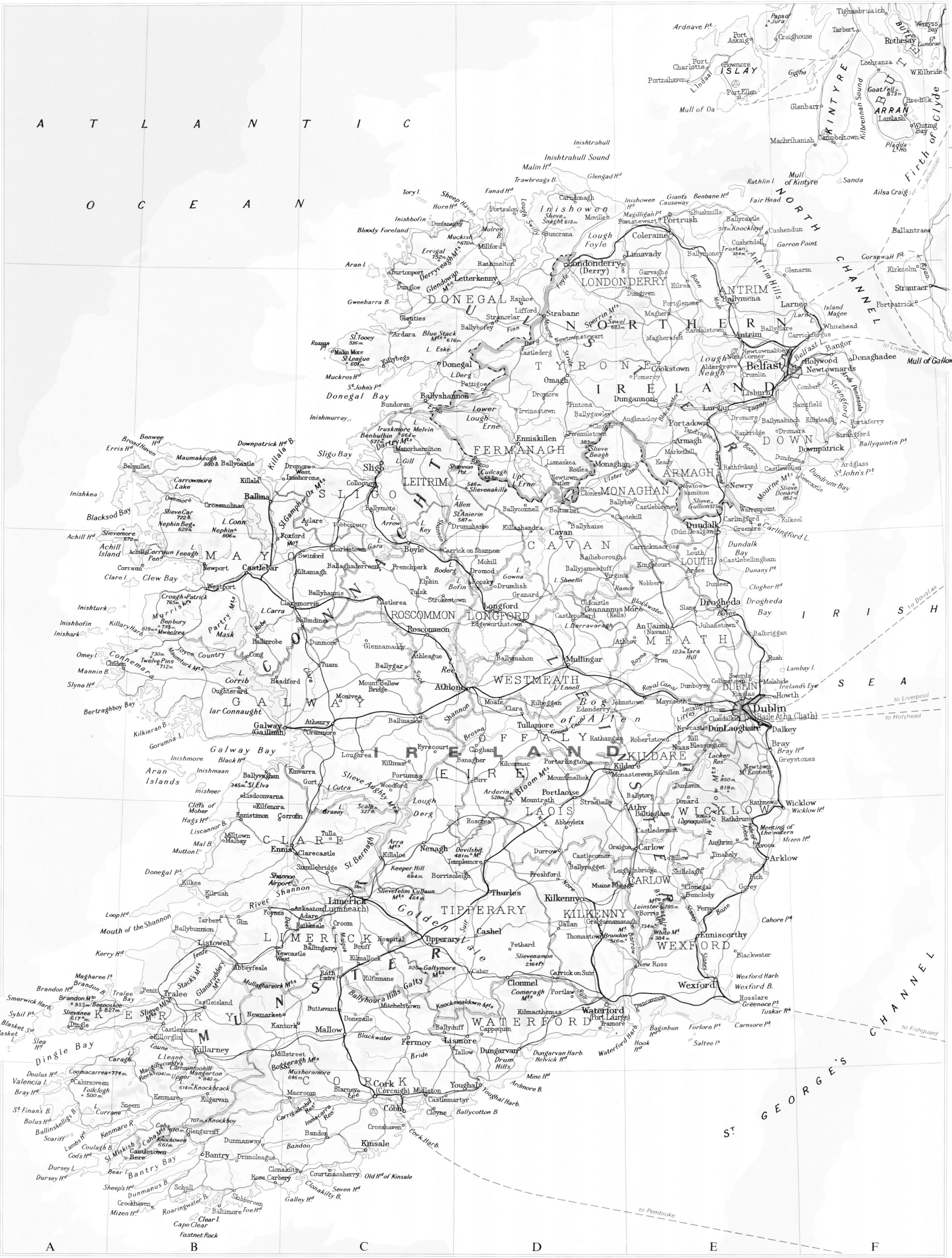

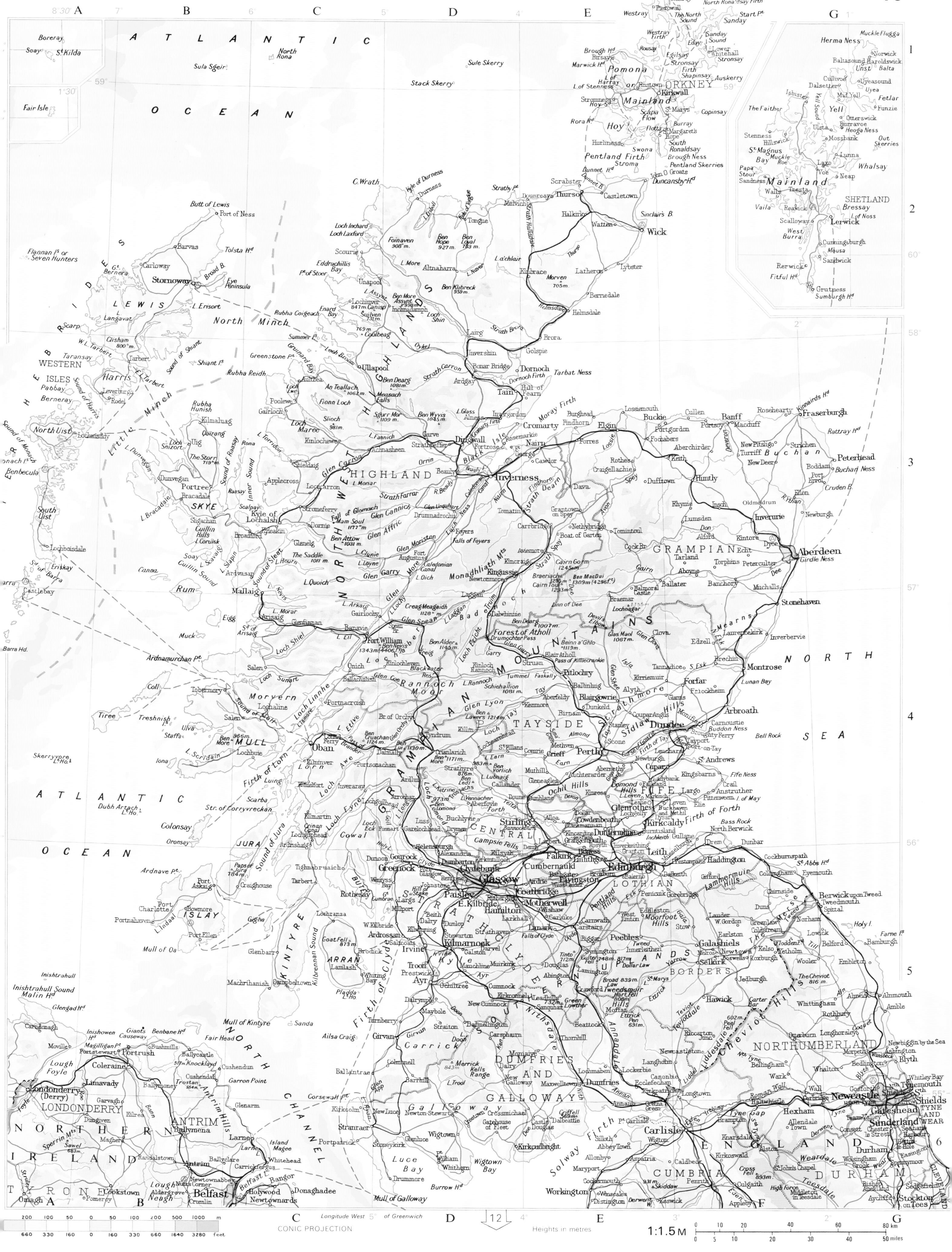
ATLANTIC OCEAN
NORTH SEA
NORTH CHANNEL
ORKNEY
SHETLAND
WESTERN ISLES
HIGHLAND
GRAMPIAN
TAYSIDE
FIFE
LOTHIAN
CENTRAL
STRATHCLYDE
BORDERS
DUMFRIES AND GALLOWAY
NORTHUMBERLAND
CUMBRIA
DURHAM
TYNE AND WEAR
CLEVELAND
ENGLAND
NORTHERN IRELAND
LONDONDERRY
ANTRIM
TYRONE
NORTH WEST HIGHLANDS
GRAMPIAN MOUNTAINS
SOUTHERN UPLANDS
Cheviot Hills
LEWIS
Harris
North Uist
Benbecula
South Uist
SKYE
Rum
Eigg
MULL
JURA
ISLAY
ARRAN
KINTYRE
Hoy
Mainland
Yell
Unst
Fair Isle
St. Kilda
North Minch
Little Minch
Firth of Lorn
Firth of Clyde
Firth of Forth
Moray Firth
Pentland Firth
Solway Firth
Stornoway
Kirkwall
Lerwick
Thurso
Wick
Ullapool
Inverness
Fort William
Oban
Mallaig
Aberdeen
Peterhead
Fraserburgh
Elgin
Dundee
Perth
Stirling
Edinburgh
Leith
Glasgow
Paisley
Greenock
Ayr
Kilmarnock
Dumfries
Carlisle
Newcastle upon Tyne
Sunderland
Berwick upon Tweed
Belfast
Londonderry (Derry)
Ben Nevis 1343m (4406ft.)
Ben Macdui 1309m (4296ft.)
Longitude West of Greenwich
CONIC PROJECTION
Heights in metres
1:1.5M
12

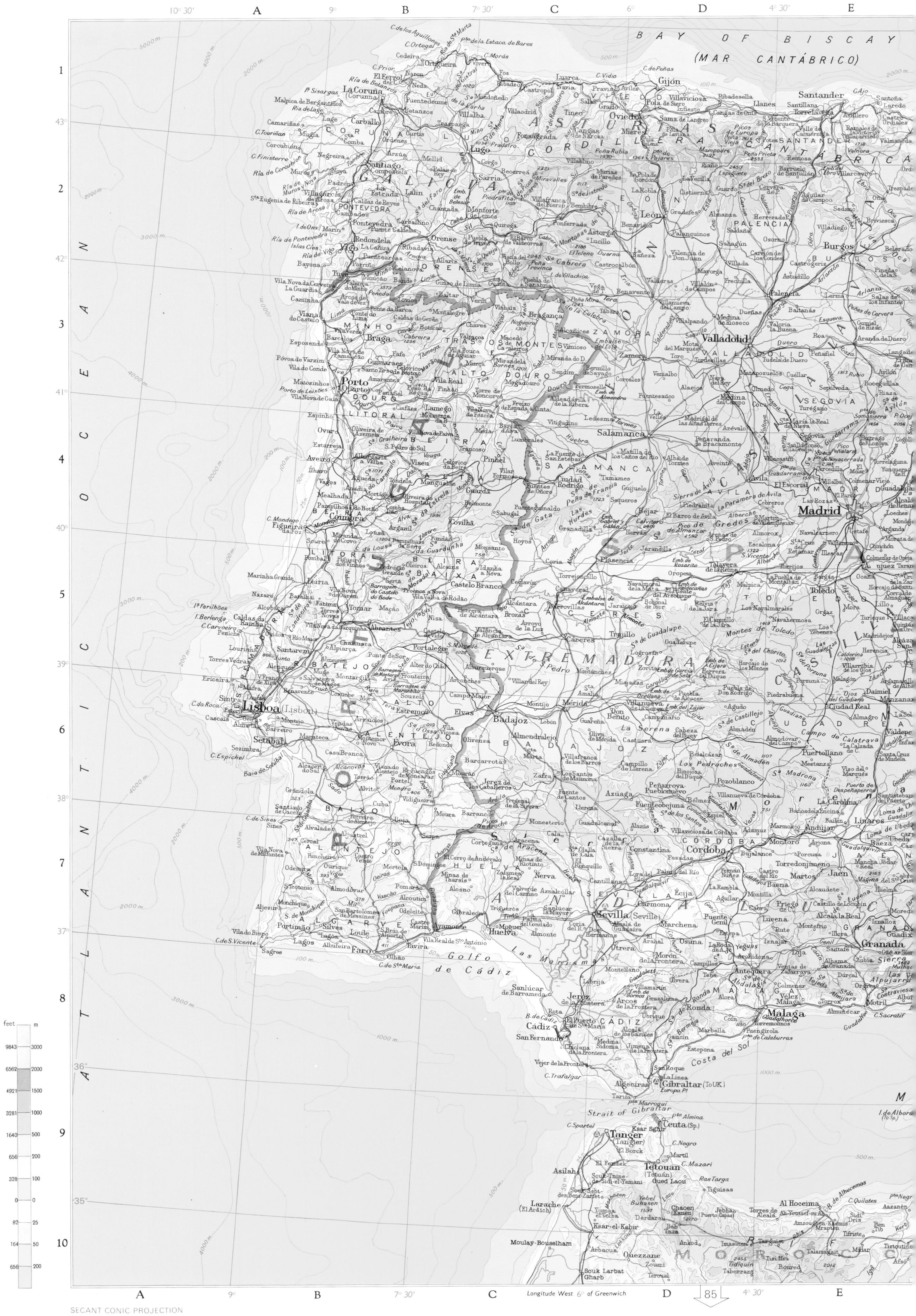
BAY OF BISCAY
(MAR CANTÁBRICO)
ATLANTIC OCEAN
GALICIA
ASTURIAS
CORDILLERA CANTÁBRICA
LEÓN
CASTILLA
EXTREMADURA
ANDALUCÍA
MOROCCO
Strait of Gibraltar
Golfo de Cádiz
Costa del Sol
La Coruña
Santiago
Lugo
Oviedo
Gijón
Santander
Burgos
León
Valladolid
Salamanca
Madrid
Toledo
Porto
Coimbra
Lisboa (Lisbon)
Setúbal
Évora
Faro
Badajoz
Cáceres
Mérida
Sevilla (Seville)
Huelva
Cádiz
Córdoba
Jaén
Granada
Málaga
Gibraltar (To UK)
Ceuta (Sp.)
Tanger (Tangier)
Tetouan
Larache
Ksar-el-Kebir
Al Hoceima
Longitude West 6° of Greenwich
feet
m
9843
3000
6562
2000
4921
1500
3281
1000
1640
500
656
200
328
100
0
0
82
25
164
50
656
200

85

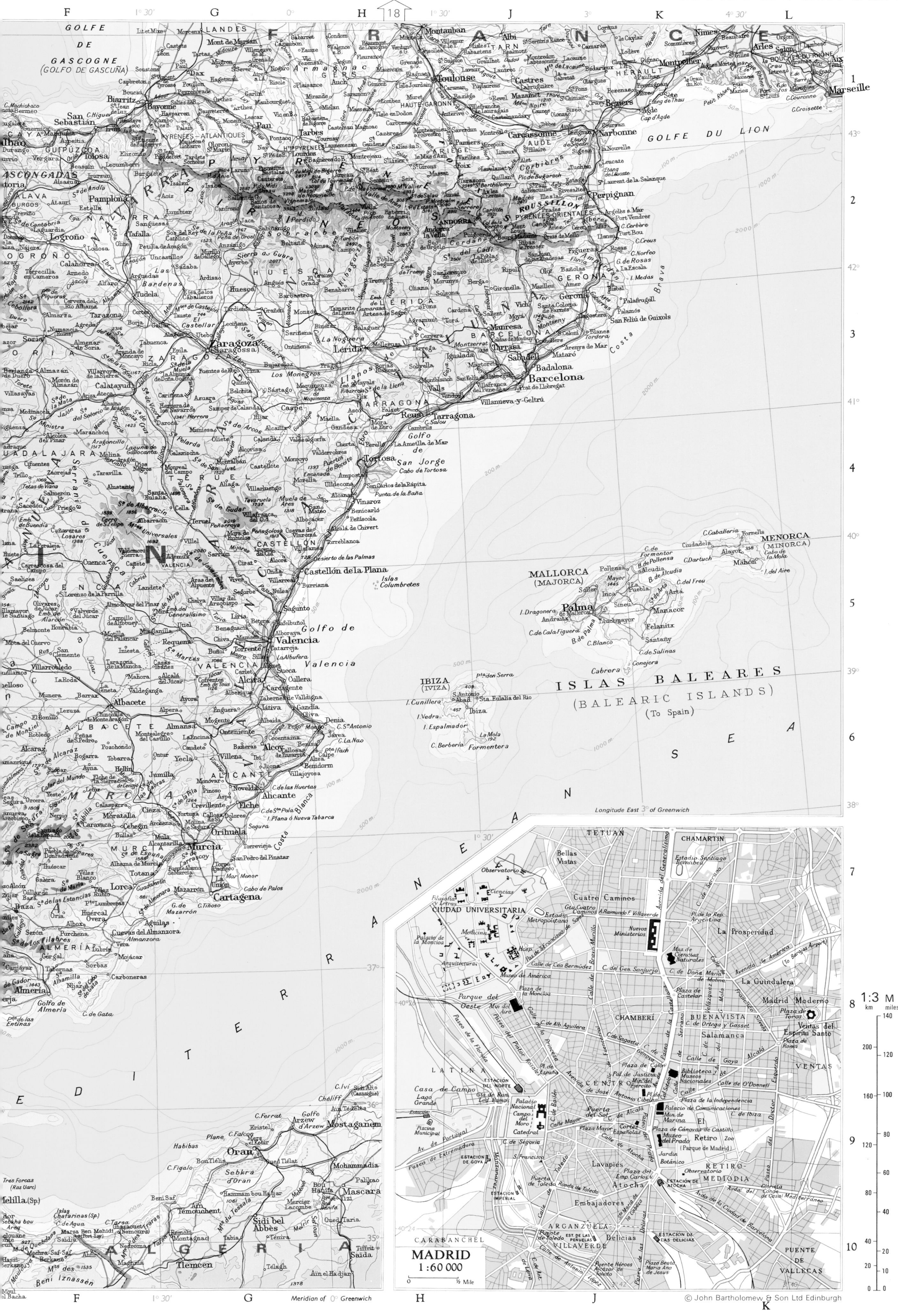

MADRID
1:60 000

© John Bartholomew & Son Ltd Edinburgh

1:3 M

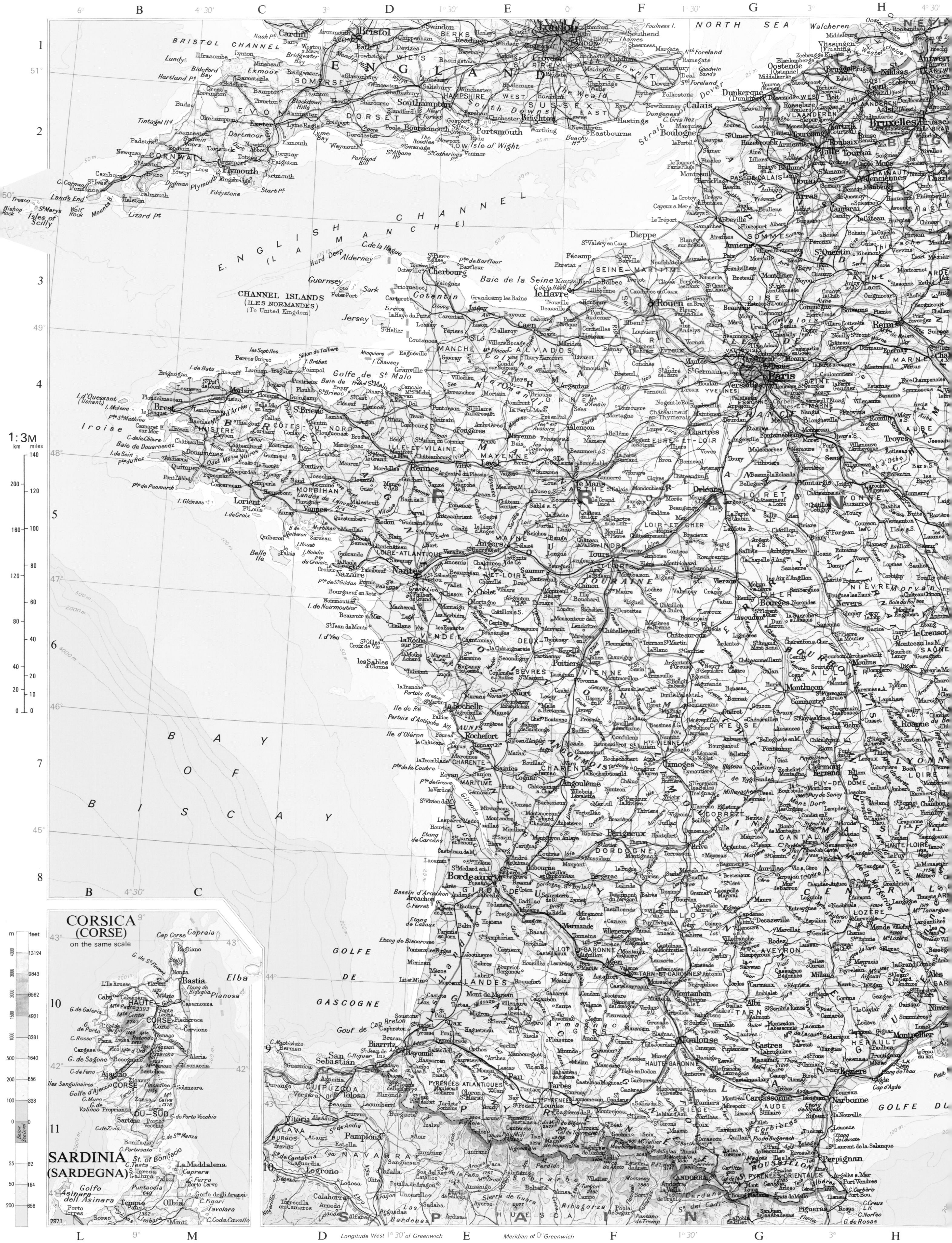

NORTH SEA

ENGLAND

BRISTOL CHANNEL

ENGLISH CHANNEL (LA MANCHE)

CHANNEL ISLANDS
(ILES NORMANDES)
(To United Kingdom)

F R A N C E

BAY OF BISCAY

GOLFE DE GASCOGNE

1:3M

km   miles

CORSICA
(CORSE)
on the same scale

SARDINIA
(SARDEGNA)

CONIC PROJECTION

Longitude West 1°30′ of Greenwich   Meridian of 0° Greenwich

Heights and Depths in metres

RHÔNE VALLEY
1:1 000 000

MEDITERRANEAN SEA

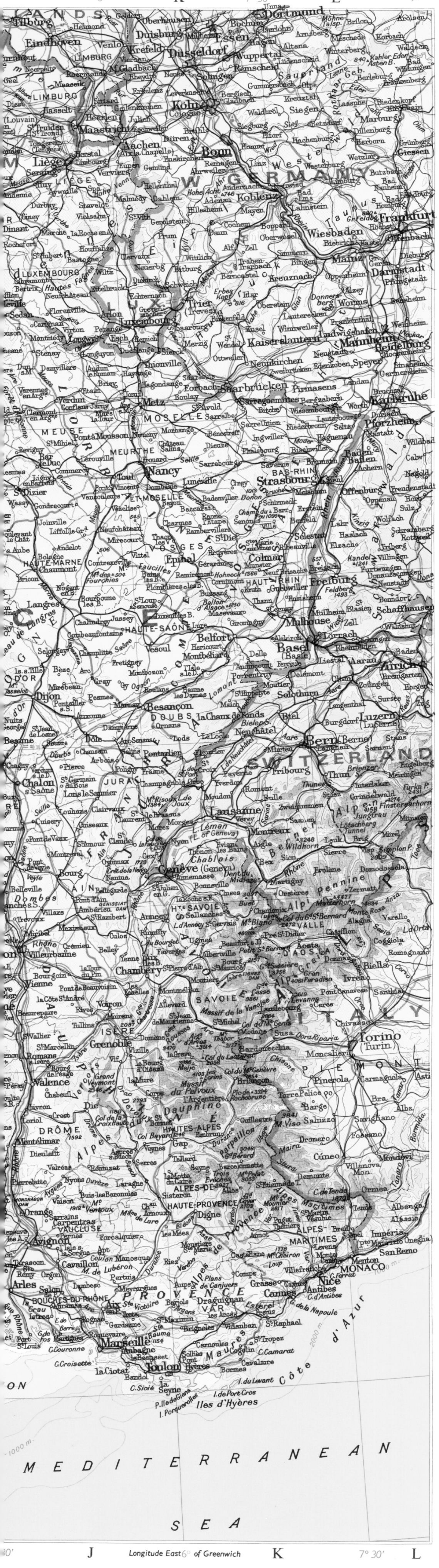

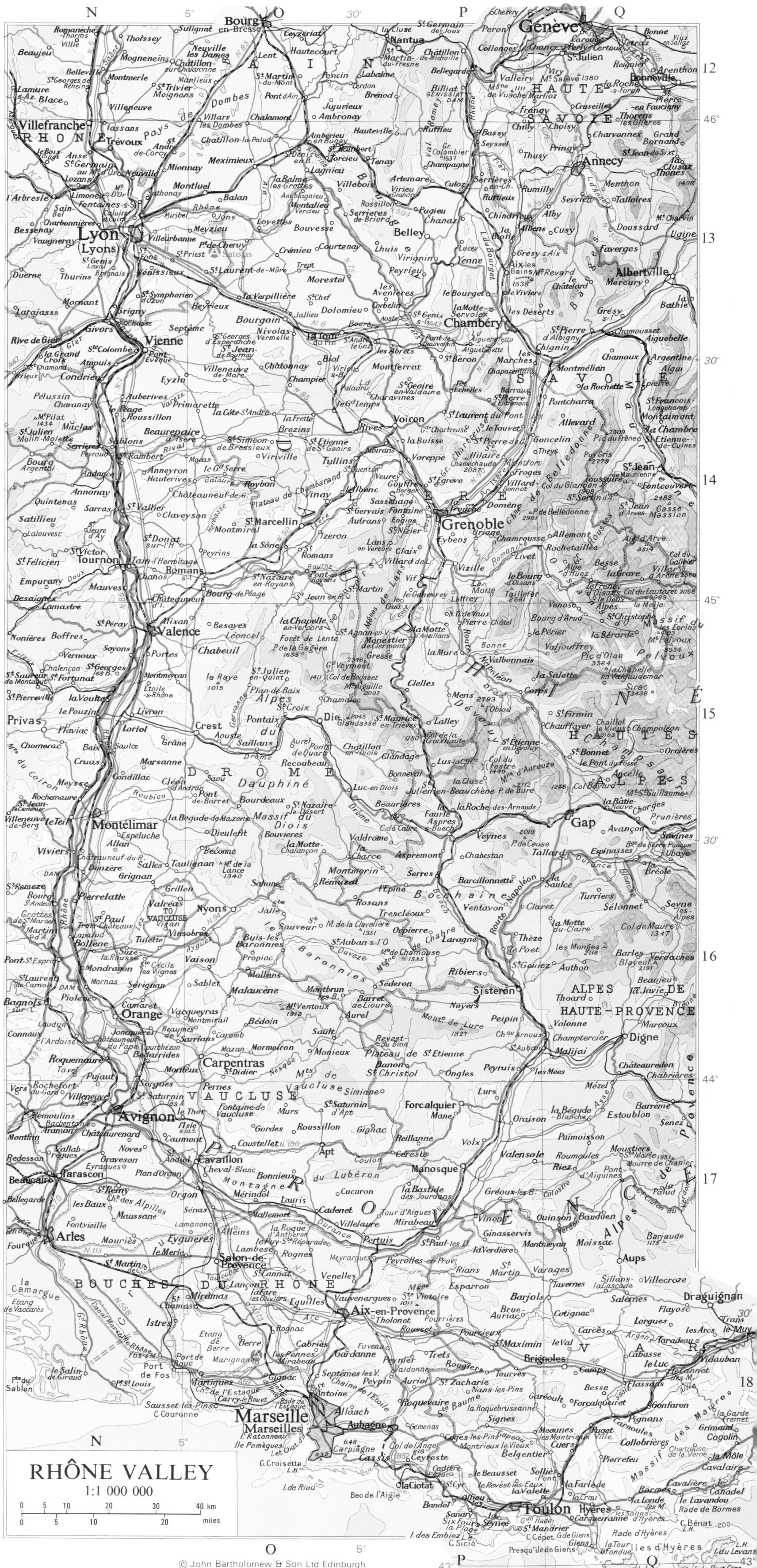

© John Bartholomew & Son Ltd Edinburgh

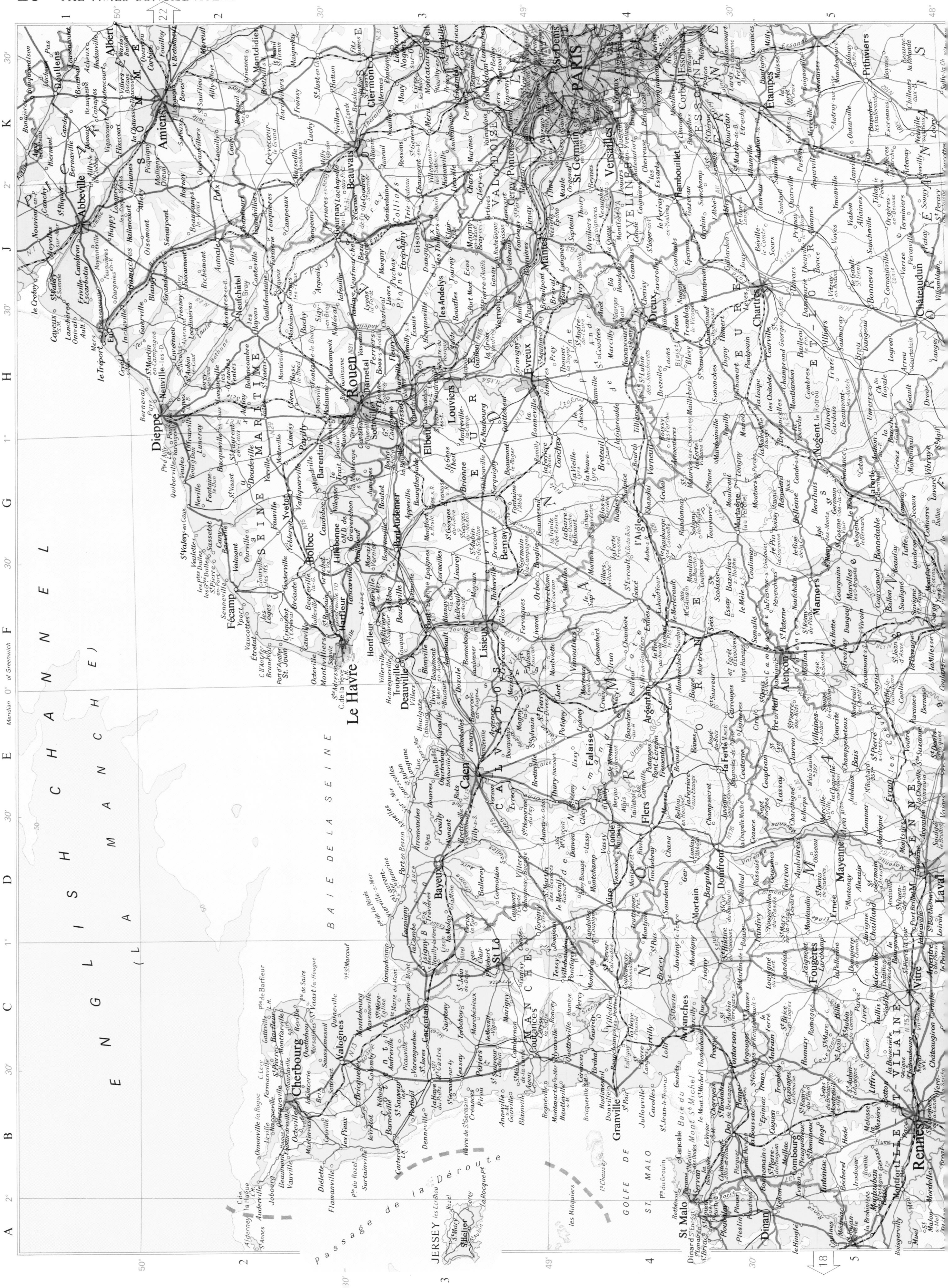
ENGLISH CHANNEL
(LA MANCHE)
BAIE DE LA SEINE
GOLFE DE ST. MALO
PARIS
Rouen
Le Havre
Caen
Cherbourg
Rennes
Amiens
Abbeville
Dieppe
Chartres
Versailles
Beauvais
Evreux
Lisieux
Alençon
Laval
Granville
Bayeux
JERSEY
Meridian 0° of Greenwich

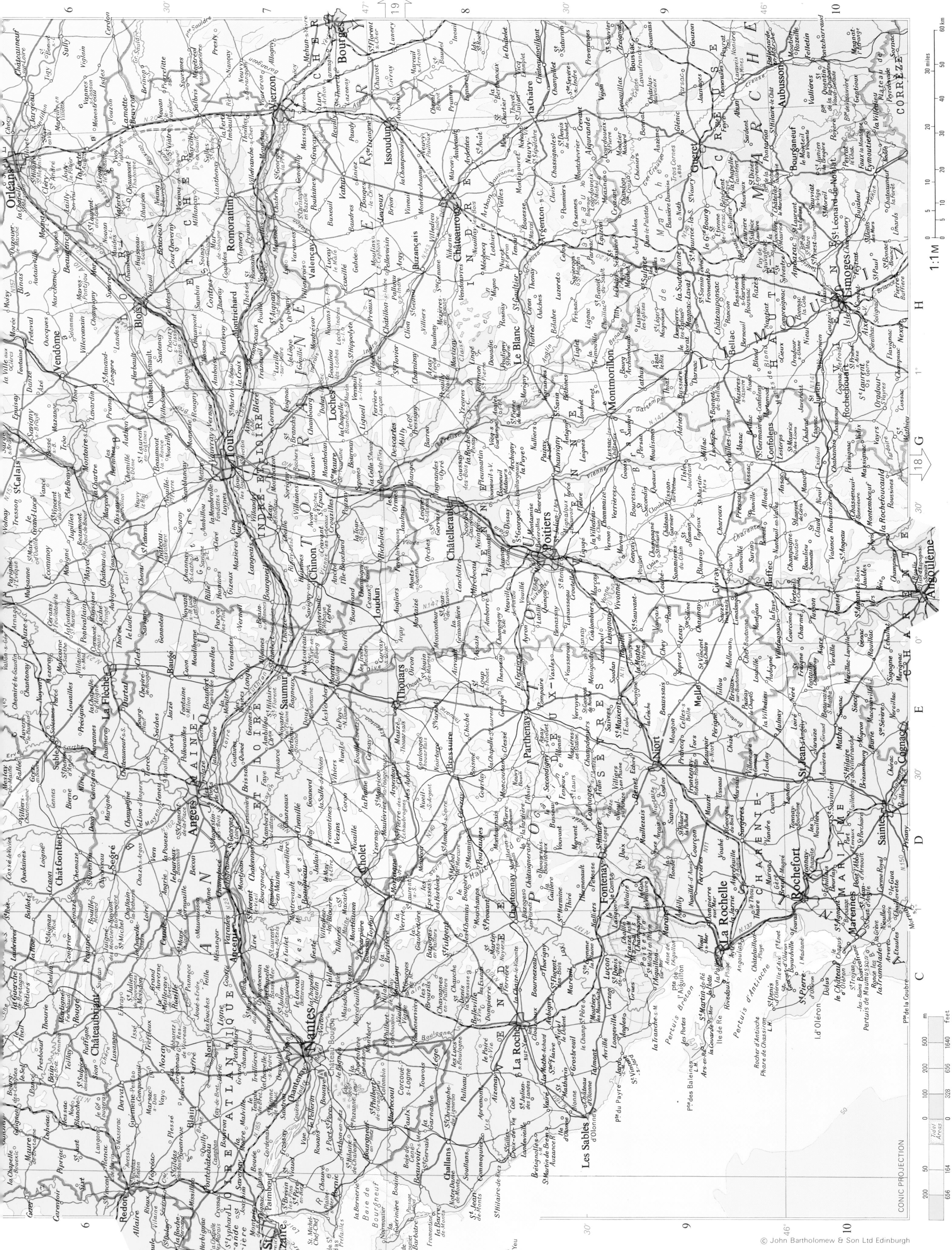
Orléans
Blois
Vendôme
Romorantin
Vierzon
Bourges
Issoudun
Châteauroux
Tours
Loches
Chinon
Saumur
Angers
La Flèche
Châtellerault
Poitiers
Le Blanc
Montmorillon
Guéret
Aubusson
Limoges
Bellac
Confolens
Rochechouart
Angoulême
Cognac
Saintes
Rochefort
La Rochelle
Niort
Parthenay
Bressuire
Thouars
Loudun
Cholet
Fontenay
La Roche-sur-Yon
Les Sables d'Olonne
Nantes
Châteaubriant
Redon
Challans
Ancenis
Segré
Château-Gontier
Ruffec
St Jean-d'Angély
I. d'Oléron
I. de Ré
CONIC PROJECTION
1:1M

© John Bartholomew & Son Ltd Edinburgh

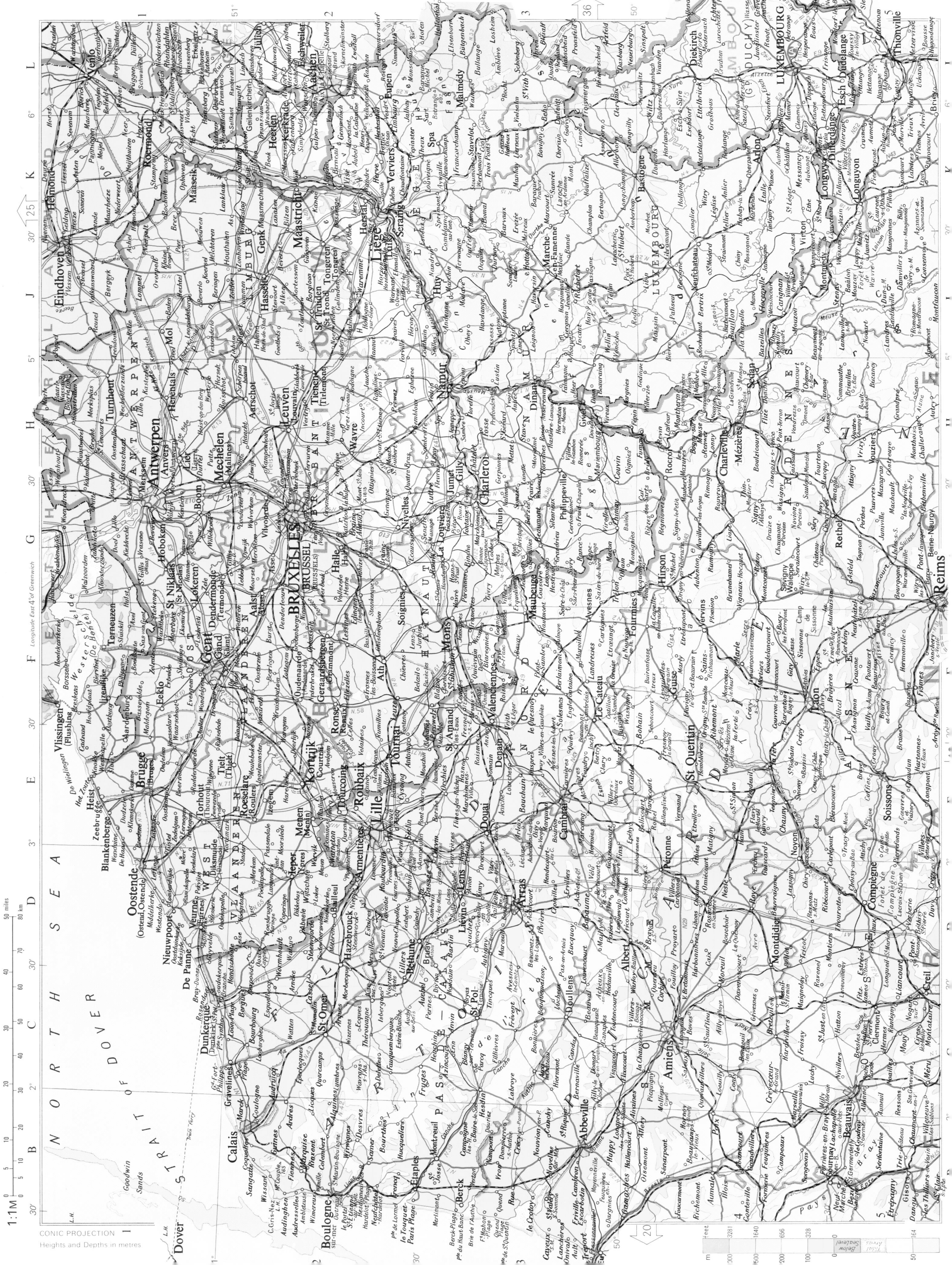
NORTH SEA
STRAIT OF DOVER
BRUXELLES
BRUSSEL
Antwerpen
Gent
Brugge
Liège
Namur
Charleroi
Mons
Lille
Calais
Boulogne
Dunkerque
Arras
Amiens
Abbeville
St Quentin
Reims
Laon
Soissons
Compiègne
Beauvais
Sedan
Charleville-Mézières
LUXEMBOURG
Thionville
Longwy
Maastricht
Aachen
Venlo
Eindhoven
Oostende
Vlissingen
1:1M
CONIC PROJECTION
Heights and Depths in metres

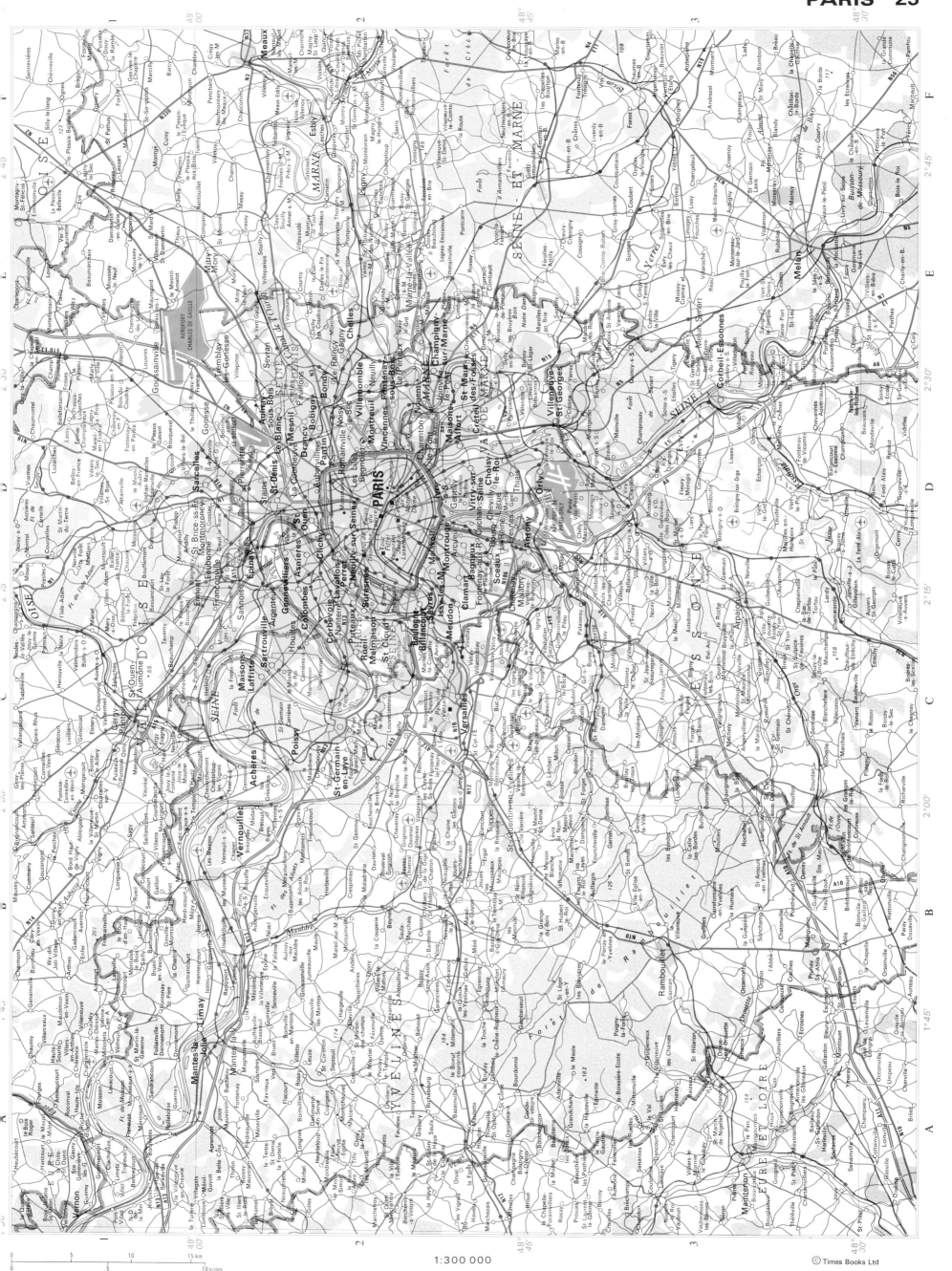
PARIS
Versailles
Meaux
Melun
Corbeil-Essonnes
Rambouillet
Mantes-la-Jolie
Vernon
Maintenon
St-Germain-en-Laye
Pontoise
Cergy
Poissy
SEINE-ET-MARNE
YVELINES
ESSONNE
VAL-D'OISE
OISE
EURE
EURE-ET-LOIR
SEINE
MARNE
AEROPORT CHARLES DE GAULLE
AEROPORT PARIS-ORLY
Orly
Forêt de Rambouillet

0 5 10 15 km
0 5 10 miles

1:300 000

© Times Books Ltd

A 4°15' B 4°30' C 4°45' D 5°00' E 5°15'

Lighthouse
Velsen-Noord
Velsen-Zuid
Ijmuiden
Santpoort-Noord
Santpoort-Zuid
Bloemendaal
Overveen
Haarlem
Zandvoort
Bentveld
Aerdenhout
Heemstede
Vijfhuizen
Manpad
Bennebroek
Vogelenzang
De Zilk
Hillegom
Noord-wijkerhout
Lisse
Noordwijk aan Zee
Noordwijk Binnen
Voorhout
Sassenheim
Katwijk aan Zee
Katwijk aan den Rijn
Rijnsburg
Oegstgeest
Valkenburg
Wassenaar
De Kieviet
Scheveningen
Nieuw–Wassenaar
Voorschoten
Kerkehout
Leiden
Leiderdorp
Maaldrift
Hooge Rijndijk
Achthoven
Koudekerk

DEN HAAG
's-Gravenhage
The Hague
Kijkduin
Vredes-Paleis
Voorburg
Leidschendam
Loosduinen
Zoetermeer
Rijswijk
Den Haag Voorburg Nootdorp
Katwijkerlaan

N O R T H   S E A

NOORDHOLLAND
Velsen-Noord
Koog aan de Zaan
Zaandam
Hembrug
Den Ilp
Monnikendam
Watergang
Landsmeer
Broek in Waterland
Oostzaan
Marken
MARKERWAARD
Kerkbuurt
Gouwzee
Ipendam
Zunderdorp
Ransdorp
Durgerdam
AMSTERDAM
AMSTERDAM (Schiphol) Airport
Badhoevedorp
Sloten
Osdorp
Diemen
Amstelveen
Ouderkerk
Bovenkerk
Duivendrecht
Muiden
Muiderberg
IJMEER
GOOIMEER
Weesp
ZUIDELIJK - FLEVOLAND
Naarden
Bussum
Huizen
Blaricum
Naardermeer
Nederhorst den Berg
's Graveland
Laren
Hilversum
Abcoude
Nigtevecht
Vreeland
Loenersloot
Kortenhoef
Loosdrachtsche Plassen
Oud-Loosdrecht
Nieuw-Loosdrecht
Lage Vuursche
UTRECHT
Maartensdijk
Bilthoven
De Bilt
Zeist
Bunnik
Utrecht
De Meern
Vleuten
Nieuw-Zuilen
Oud-Zuilen
Maarssen
Harmelen
Woerden
Breukelen
Tienhoven

ZUID-HOLLAND
Aalsmeer
Kudelstaart
Uithoorn
Amstelhoek
Waverveen
Mijdrecht
Wilnis
Vinkeveen
Nieuwer-Ter-Aar
Leimuiden
Kalslagen
Oude Wetering
Rijnsaterwoude
Langeraar
Papenveen
Nieuwveen
Zevenhoven
Noorden
Nieuwkoop
Aarlanderveen
Woerdens Verlaat
Kockengen
Portengen
Woerden
Alphen aan den Rijn
Zwammerdam
Bodegraven
Zegveld
Kamerik
Haarzuilens
Hazerswoude
Boskoop
Reeuwijk
Waarder
Linschoten
Montfoort
Benthuizen
Moerkapelle
Waddinxveen
Driebruggen
Jutphaas
Houten

Times Books Ltd

BRUSSELS

A 3°45' B 4°00' C 4°15' D 4°30' E

Sleidinge
Mendonk
Zaffelare
Daknam
Belsele
Steendorp
Rupelmonde
Schelle
Aartselaar
Kontich
Lier
Kessel
Evergem
Lovendegem
Vinderhoute
Wondelgem
Oostakker
Lochristi
Zeveneken
Beervelde
Waasmunster
Tielrode
Hingene
Hamme
Temse
Niel
Boom
Willebroek
ANTWERPEN
Waarloos
Reet
Duffel
Koningshooikt
Gent
Gand
Sint-Amandsberg
Gentbrugge
Ledeberg
Lokeren
Zele
Moerzeke
Mariekerke
Sint-Amands
Liezele
Puurs
Bornem
Ruisbroek
Heindonk
Willebroek
Mechelen
Mechelen
Drongen
Heusden
Kalken
Laarne
Uitbergen
Schellebelle
Wichelen
Dendermonde
Appels
Baasrode
Opdorp
Malderen
Ramsdonk
Kapelle-Op-Den-Bos
Hombeek
Leest
Muizen
Bonheiden
Rijmenam
Merelbeke
Gijzegem
Wetteren
Schoonaarde
Oudegem
Denderbelle
Lebbeke
Heizijde
Londerzeel
Steenhuffel
Nieuwenrode
Westrode
Keerbergen
Haacht
OOST VLAANDEREN
Massemen
Wanzele
Smetlede
Impe
Lede
Erondegem
Hofstade
Herdersem
Opwijk
Merchtem
Kobbegem
Wolvertem
Meise
Grimbergen
Zemst
Hofstade
Weerde
Schiplaken
Elewijt
Aalst
Moorsel
Meldert
Erembodegem
Asse
Wemmel
Jette
Brussegem
Eppegem
Vilvoorde
Vilvoorde
Machelen
Diegem
Zaventem
Steenokkerzeel
Nossegem
Kortenberg
Everberg
Meerbeek
Bertem
BRUSSELS NATIONAAL
Evere
Schaarbeek
Schaerbeek
Molenbeek-St-Jean
Sint-Jans-Molenbeek
Koekelberg
Ganshoren
Anderlecht
Atomium
Grand Place
Manneken Pis
BRUXELLES
BRUSSEL
Ixelles
Elsene
Etterbeek
St-Gilles
St-Gillis
Uccle
Ukkel
Watermaal-Bosvoorde
Watermael-Boitsfort
Tervuren
Overijse
Neerijse
BRABANT
Ninove
Meerbeke
Denderwindeke
Pollare
Okegem
Pamel
Liedekerke
Roosdaal
Schepdaal
Dilbeek
Sint-Ulriks-Kapelle
Groot-Bijgaarden
Strombeek-Bever
HAINAUT
Lessines
Flobecq
Ronse
Muziekberg
Louise-Marie
Pottelberg
Everbeek
Brakel
Nederbrakel
Zarlardinge
Galmaarden
Viane
Bever
Herne
Bois De Haller Bos
Coquiamont
Strihoux
Saintes
Bogaarden
Herfelingen
Bellingen
Beert
Halle
Buizingen
Huizingen
Alsemberg
Sint-Genesius-Rode
Rhode-St-Genèse
Dworp
Huldenberg
Hoeilaart
La Hulpe
Terlanen
Tombeek
Rosières
Genval
Waterloo
Braine-l'Alleud
Wavre
Rixensart
Ohain
Mont-St-Jean
Lasne

1 : 300 000

0 5 10 15 km
0 5 10 miles

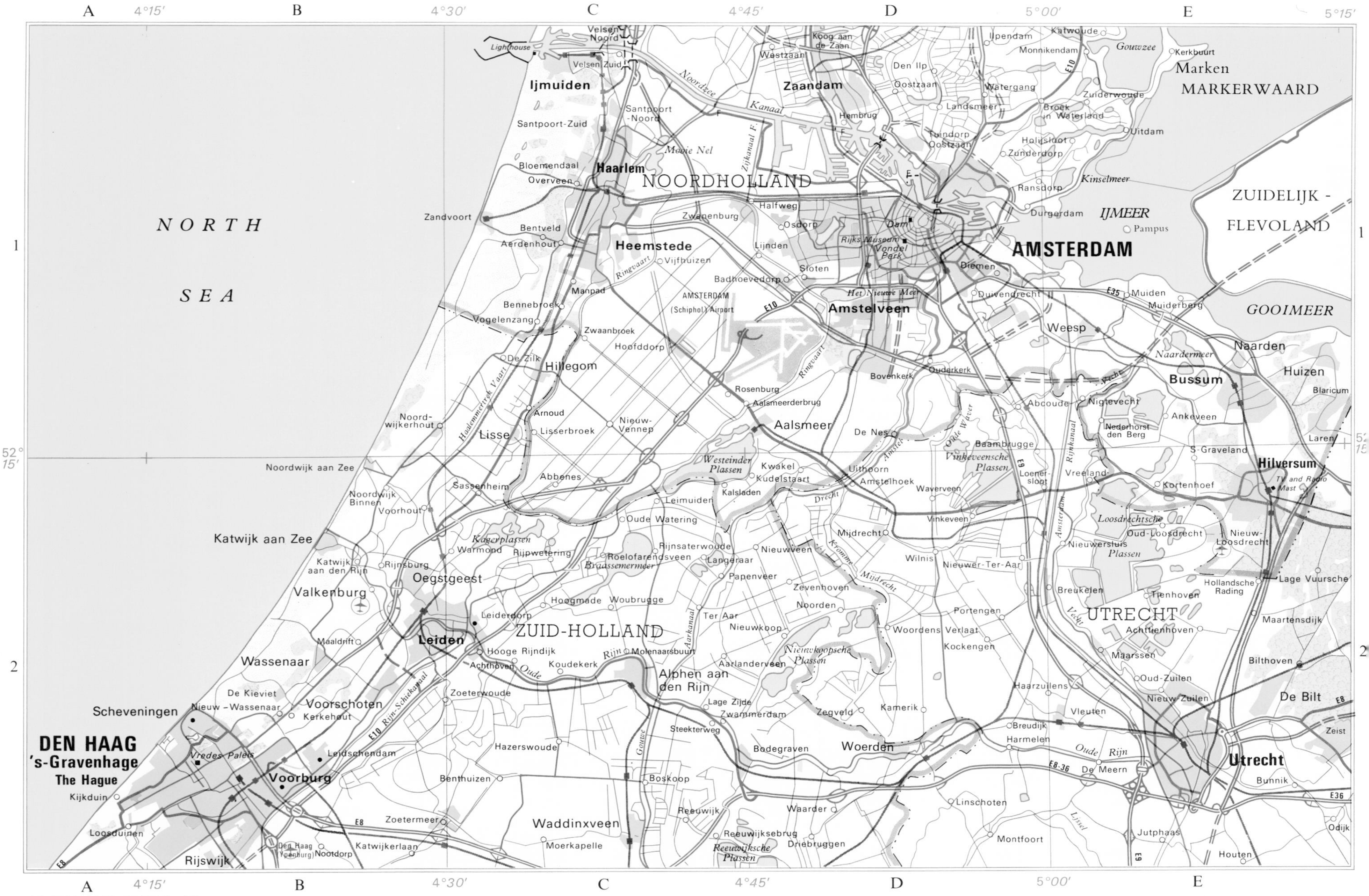

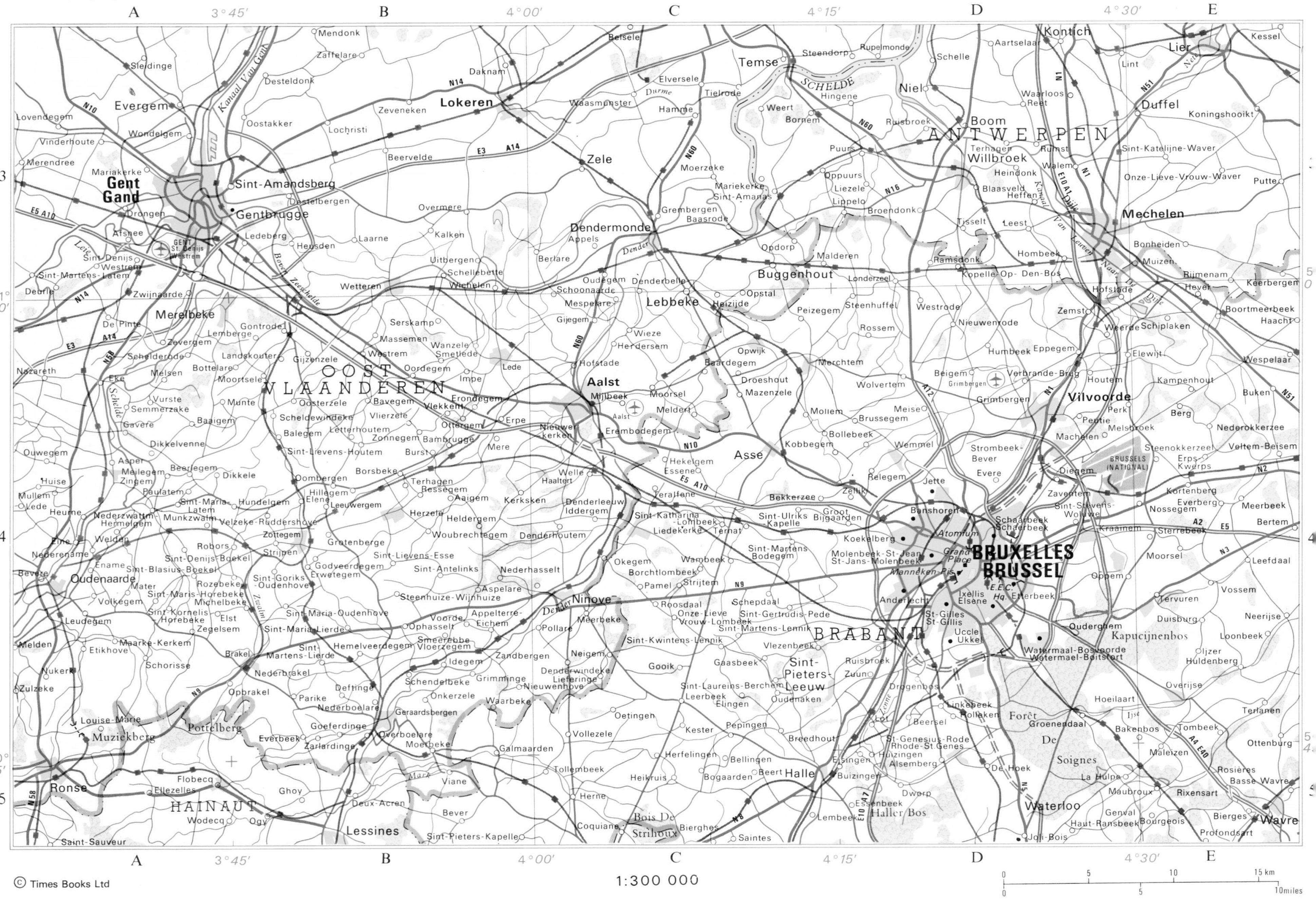

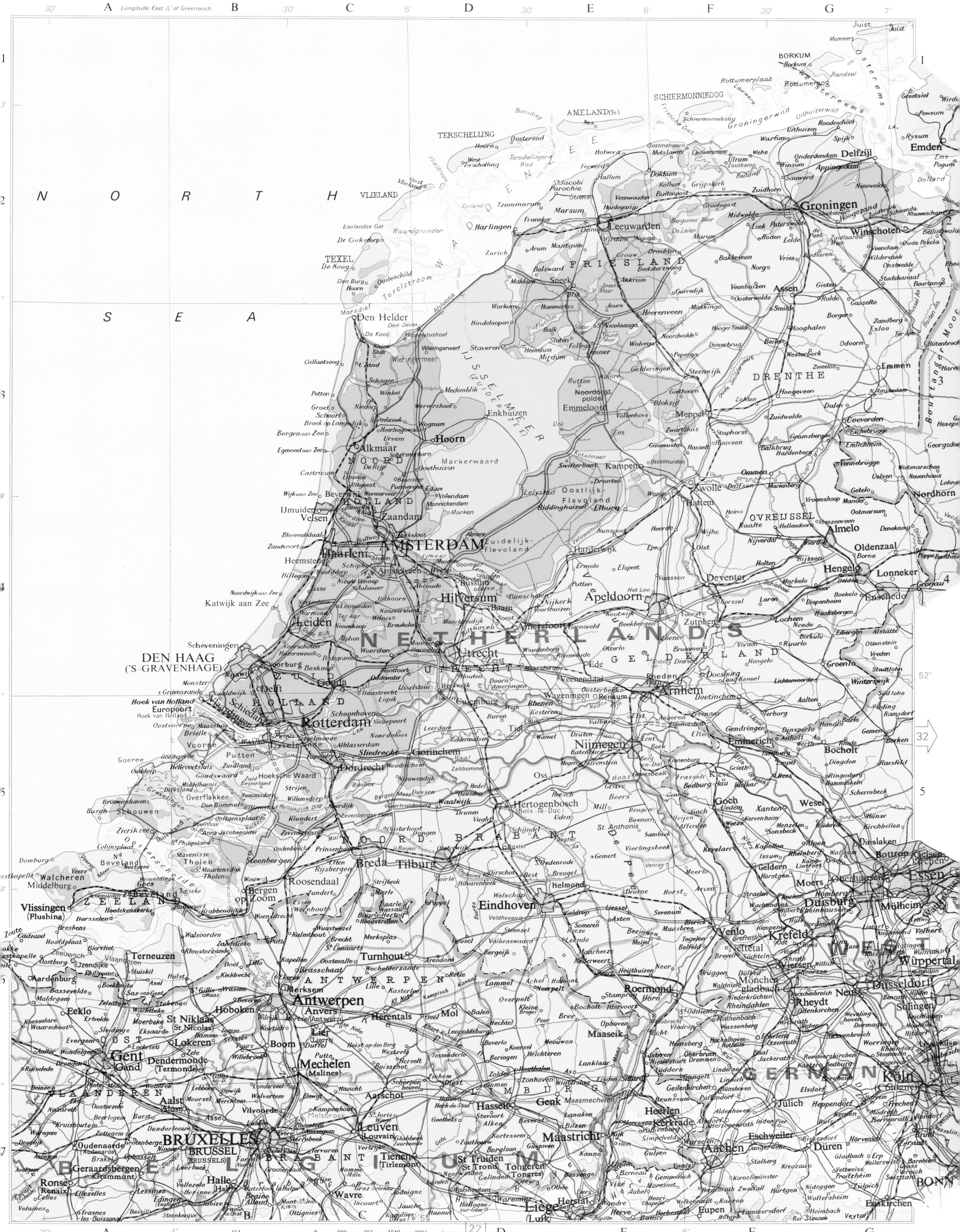

NORTH SEA

NETHERLANDS

NOORD HOLLAND

ZUID HOLLAND

UTRECHT

FRIESLAND

DRENTHE

OVERIJSSEL

GELDERLAND

NOORD BRABANT

ZEELAND

LIMBURG

BELGIUM

GERMANY

WEST

VLAANDEREN

OOST

BRABANT

AMSTERDAM
DEN HAAG ('S-GRAVENHAGE)
Rotterdam
Utrecht
Haarlem
Leiden
Groningen
Leeuwarden
Zwolle
Arnhem
Nijmegen
Apeldoorn
Deventer
Enschede
Hengelo
Almelo
Breda
Tilburg
Eindhoven
Hertogenbosch (Bois-le-Duc)
Roosendaal
Bergen op Zoom
Middelburg
Vlissingen (Flushing)
Terneuzen
Maastricht
Roermond
Venlo
Heerlen
Kerkrade
Hilversum
Amersfoort
Zaandam
Alkmaar
Hoorn
Den Helder
Dordrecht
Gorinchem
Zutphen
Doetinchem
Winterswijk

TEXEL
VLIELAND
TERSCHELLING
AMELAND (Fr)
SCHIERMONNIKOOG
BORKUM
IJSSELMEER (ZUIDERZEE)
Markerwaard
Noordoost polder
Oostelijk-Flevoland
Zuidelijk-Flevoland

Antwerpen (Anvers)
Gent (Gand)
Mechelen (Malines)
Leuven (Louvain)
Bruxelles (Brussel / Brussels) Brabant
Turnhout
Hasselt
Genk
Aachen
Düsseldorf
Krefeld
Mönchengladbach
Neuss
Köln
Wuppertal
Mülheim
Duisburg
Oberhausen
Essen
Wesel
Emmerich
Bocholt
Kleve
Emden
Delfzijl

CONIC PROJECTION

1:1M

164 0 328 656 1640 3281 feet
Tidal Areas Below Sea level
50 0 100 200 500 1000 m

0 5 10 20 30 miles
0 5 10 20 30 40 60 km

© John Bartholomew & Son Ltd Edinburgh

Longitude East 4° of Greenwich

52°

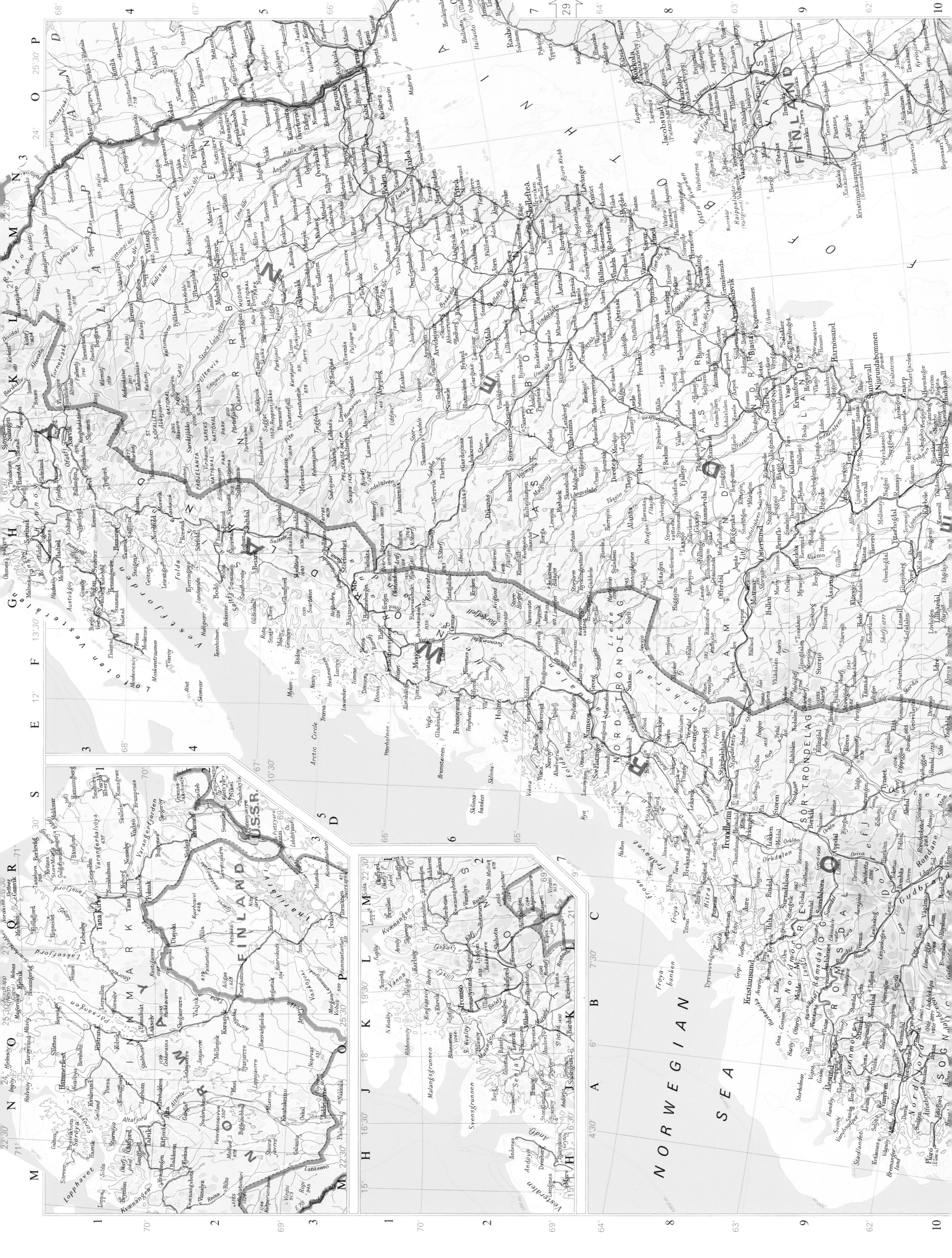
NORWEGIAN SEA
FINLAND
U.S.S.R.
FINNMARK
NORD-TRØNDELAG
SØR-TRØNDELAG
Trondheim
Narvik
Bodø
Tromsø
Hammerfest
Luleå
Oulu
Umeå
Östersund
Kristiansund
Ålesund
Molde
Arctic Circle
Vestfjorden
Lofoten
Skellefteå
Sundsvall
Härnösand
Kokkola
Jakobstad
Vaasa
Raahe
Kemi
Tornio
Kiruna
Gällivare
Boden
Piteå
Mo i Rana
Mosjøen
Namsos
Steinkjer
Vadsø
Kirkenes
Alta
Vardø
Ivalo

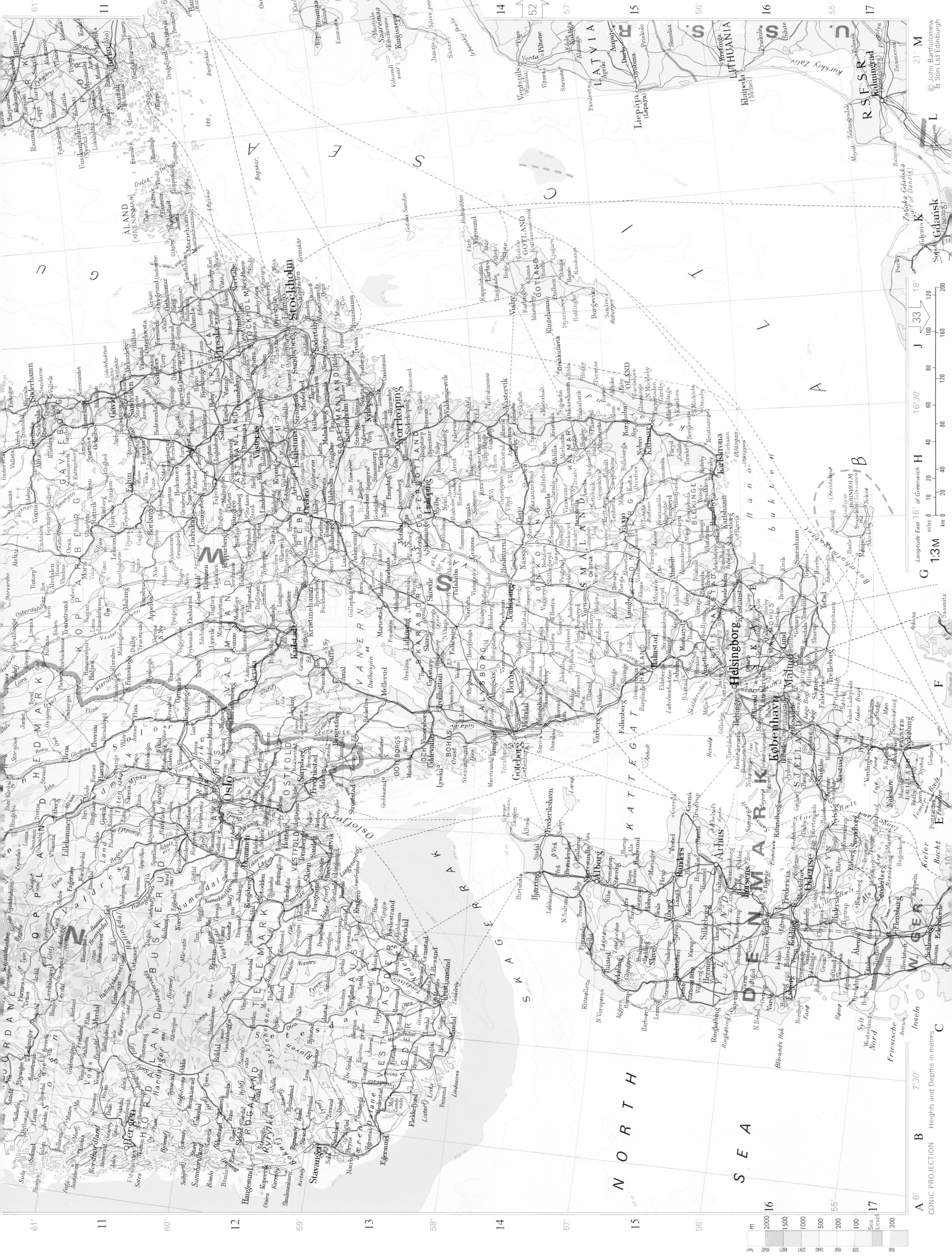
CONIC PROJECTION
Heights and Depths in metres
1:3M
Longitude East 15° of Greenwich
© John Bartholomew & Son Ltd Edinburgh
NORTH SEA
SKAGERRAK
KATTEGAT
DENMARK
LATVIA
LITHUANIA
R.S.F.S.R.
Oslo
Stockholm
Göteborg
København
Malmö
Helsingborg
Bergen
Stavanger
Kristiansand
Norrköping
Linköping
Västerås
Uppsala
Karlstad
Jönköping
Kalmar
Karlskrona
Gävle
Ålborg
Århus
Odense
Esbjerg
Flensburg
Liepāja
Ventspils
Kaliningrad
Gdańsk
GOTLAND
ÖLAND
BORNHOLM
ÅLAND

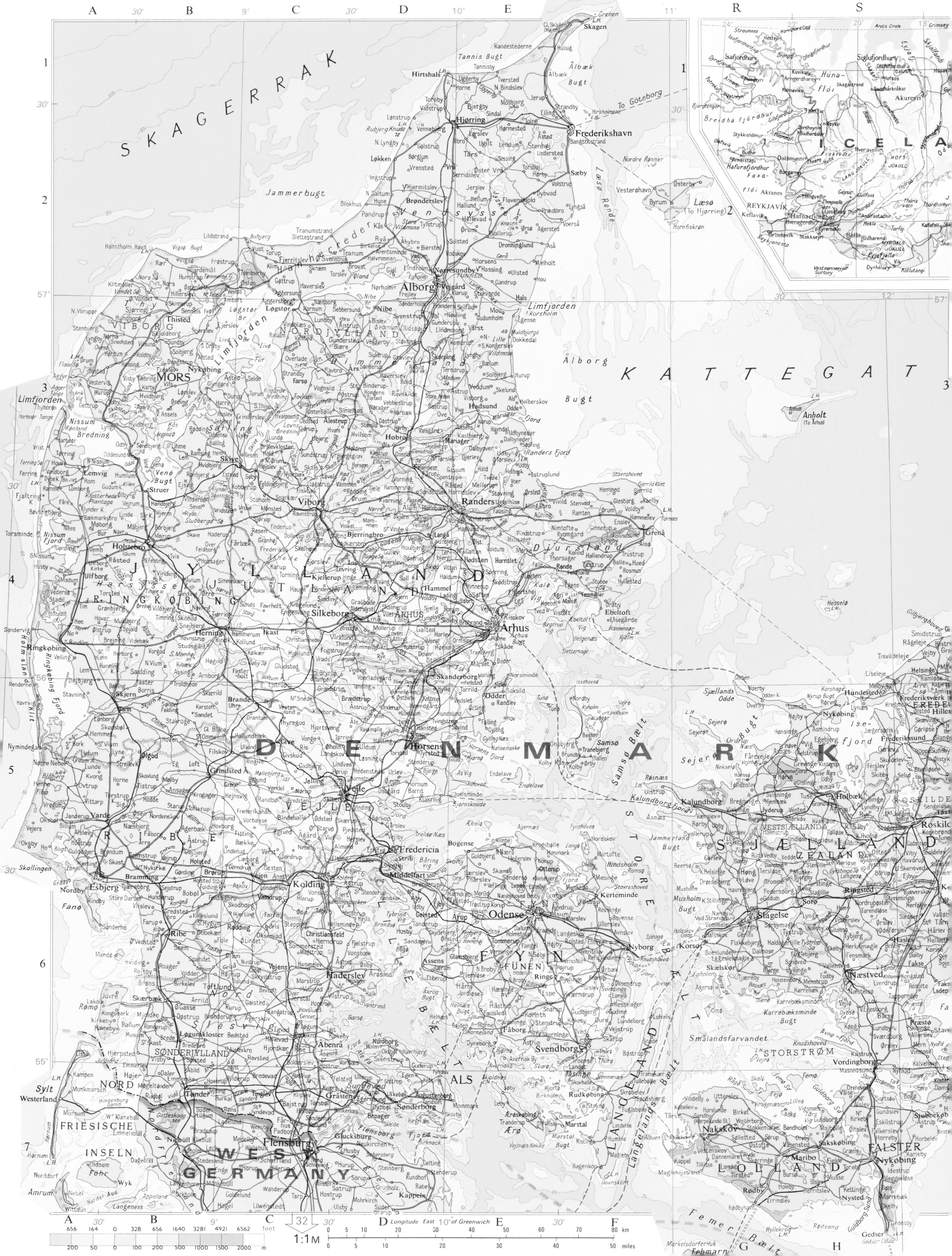
SKAGERRAK
KATTEGAT
DENMARK
JYLLAND
SJÆLLAND
ZEALAND
FYN
FÜNEN
LOLLAND
FALSTER
ICELA
WEST GERMANY
FRIESISCHE INSELN
Skagen
Frederikshavn
Hjørring
Ålborg
Limfjorden
Randers
Viborg
Århus
Silkeborg
Horsens
Vejle
Fredericia
Kolding
Esbjerg
Ribe
Haderslev
Åbenrå
Tønder
Flensburg
Sønderborg
Odense
Nyborg
Svendborg
Kalundborg
Slagelse
Korsør
Næstved
Vordingborg
Nakskov
Nykøbing
Holbæk
Roskilde
Ringkøbing
Holstebro
Herning
Skive
Thisted
Hobro
Grenå
Læsø
Anholt
Samsø
Langeland
Ærø
Als
Rømø
Fanø
Sylt
Store Bælt
Lille Bælt
Jammerbugt
Ålborg Bugt
1:1M

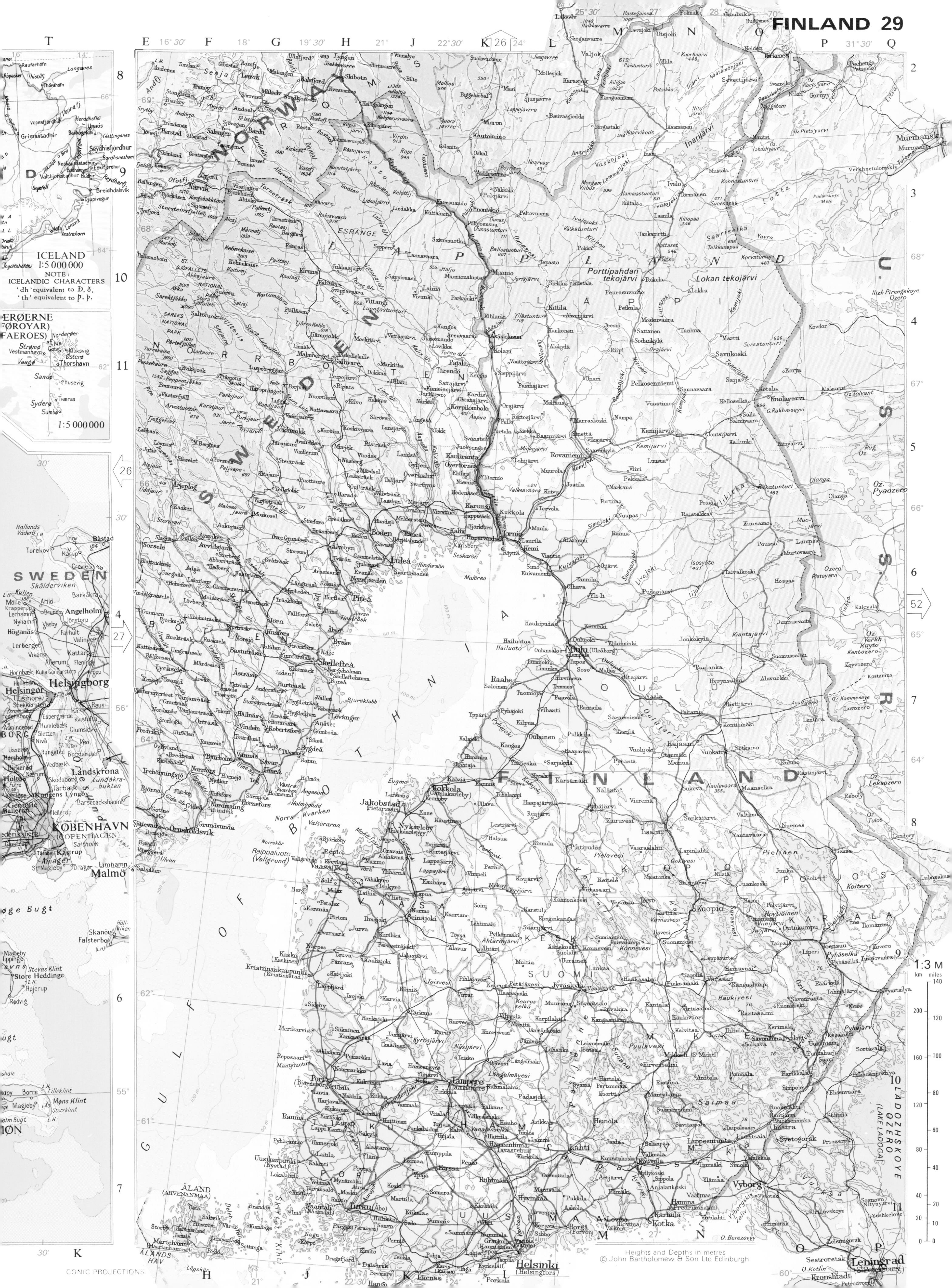
FINLAND
SWEDEN
NORWAY
U. S. S. R.
GULF OF BOTHNIA
LAPPI
OULU
VAASA
KESKI SUOMI
KUOPIO
POHJOIS KARJALA
MIKKELI
HÄME
TURKU-PORI
UUSIMAA
KYMI
ICELAND 1:5 000 000
NOTE: ICELANDIC CHARACTERS 'dh' equivalent to Ð, ð, 'th' equivalent to Þ, þ.
FÆRØERNE (FØROYAR) (FAEROES)
1:5 000 000
Helsinki (Helsingfors)
Leningrad
Murmansk
Oulu (Uleåborg)
Tampere
Turku (Åbo)
Vaasa (Vasa)
Kuopio
Jyväskylä
Rovaniemi
Luleå
Umeå
Narvik
Malmö
København (Copenhagen)
Helsingborg
Vyborg
Lahti
Pori (Björneborg)
Kotka
Kemi
Tornio
Kiruna
Gällivare
Kokkola (Gamlakarleby)
Jakobstad (Pietarsaari)
Skellefteå
Piteå
Örnsköldsvik
Ladozhskoye Ozero (Lake Ladoga)
Åland (Ahvenanmaa)
Saimaa
Päijänne
1:3 M
km
miles
Heights and Depths in metres
© John Bartholomew & Son Ltd Edinburgh
CONIC PROJECTIONS

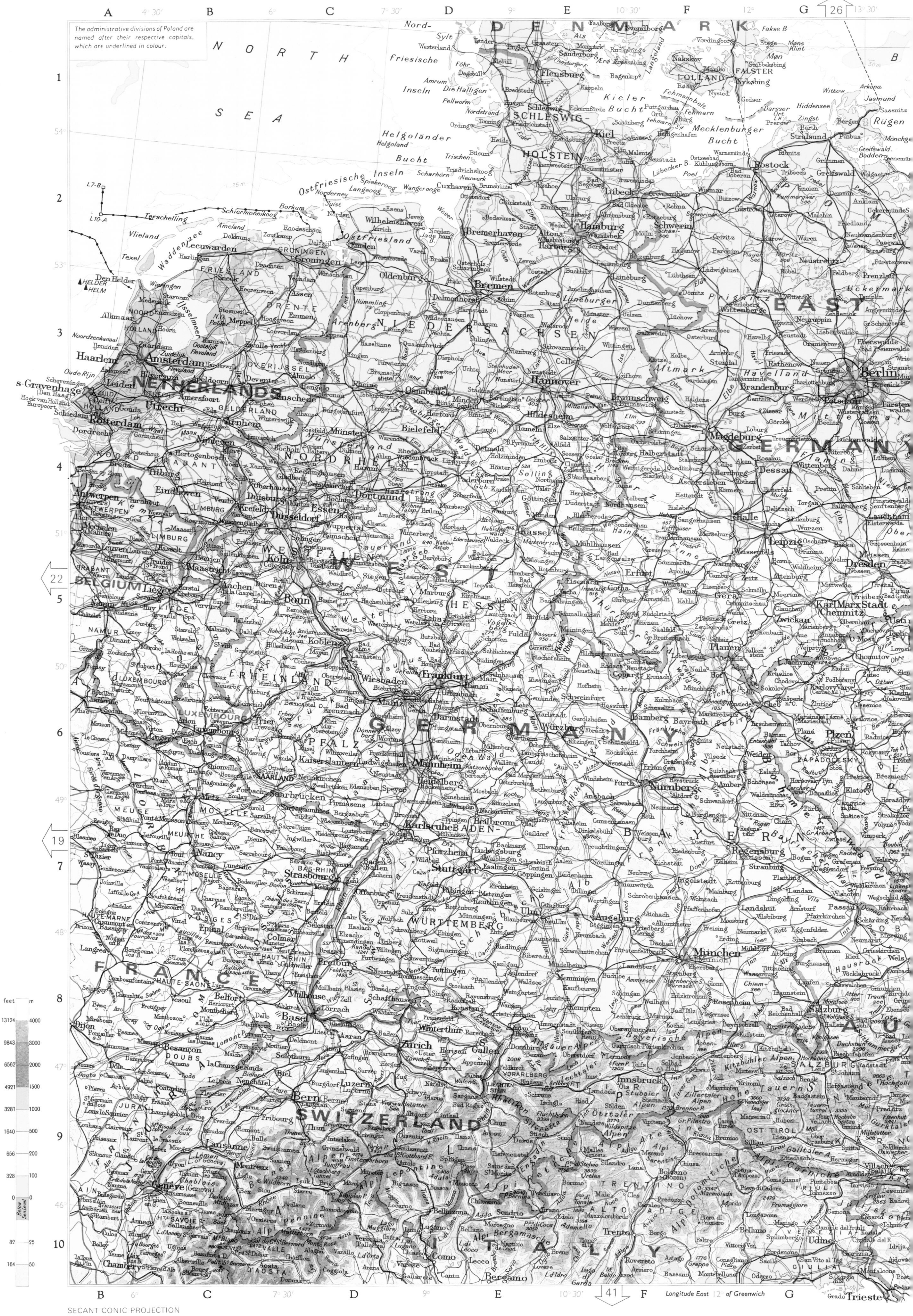

The administrative divisions of Poland are named after their respective capitals, which are underlined in colour.
NORTH SEA
DENMARK
NETHERLANDS
BELGIUM
LUXEMBOURG
GERMANY
EAST GERMANY
WEST GERMANY
FRANCE
SWITZERLAND
ITALY
Amsterdam
Hamburg
Bremen
Hannover
Berlin
Köln
Frankfurt
Stuttgart
München
Nürnberg
Dresden
Leipzig
Strasbourg
Zürich
Bern
Genève
Innsbruck
Longitude East of Greenwich

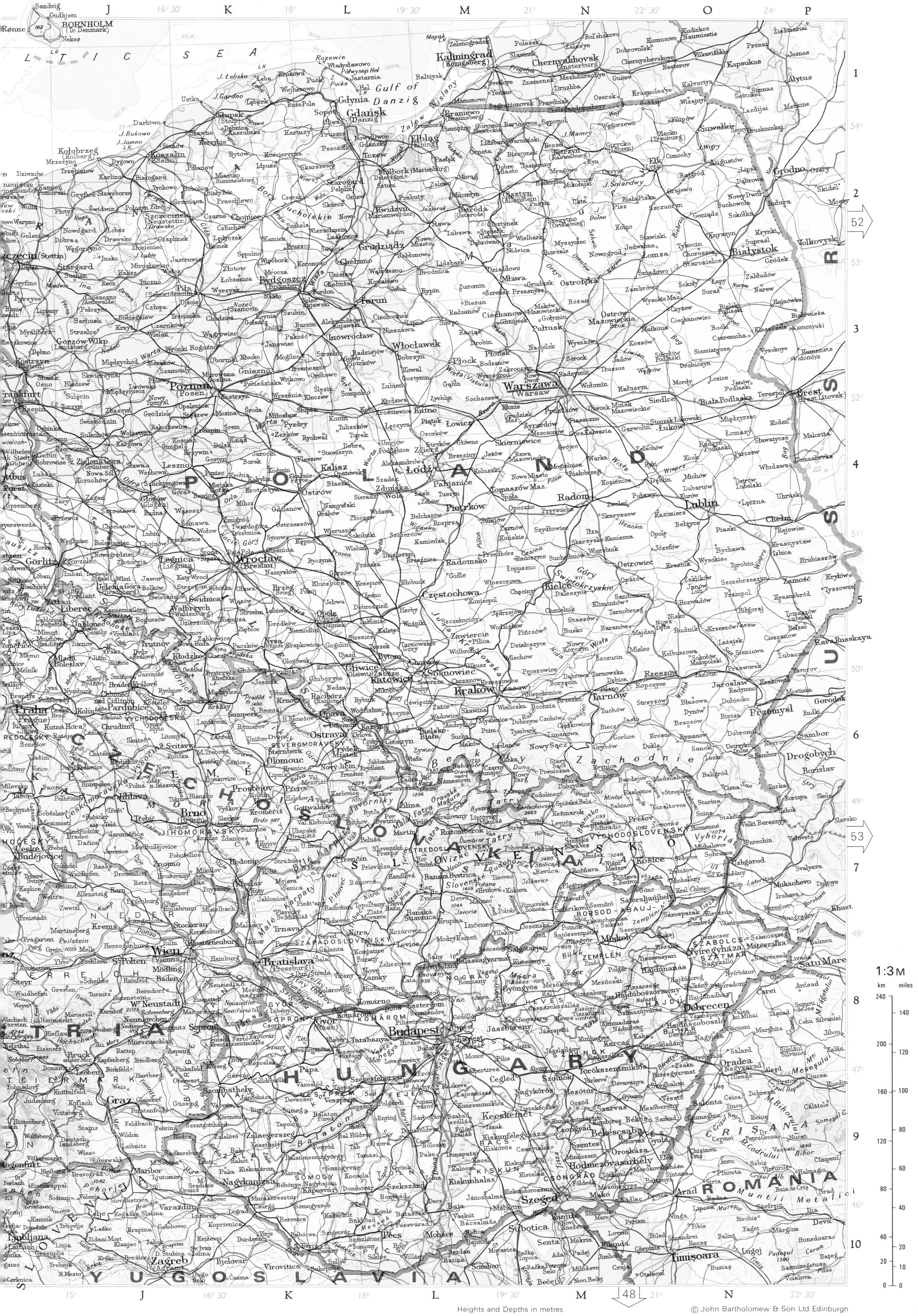

NORTH SEA

HELGOLÄNDER BUCHT

OSTFRIESISCHE INSELN

SCHLESWIG

HOLSTEIN

NIEDERSACHSEN

NETHERLANDS

WESTFALEN

NORDRHEIN

HESSEN

GERMANY

Hamburg

Bremen

Bremerhaven

Cuxhaven

Hannover

Oldenburg

Osnabrück

Münster

Bielefeld

Kassel

Göttingen

Groningen

CONIC PROJECTION

NOTE: 'ß'-German equivalent to 'ss'

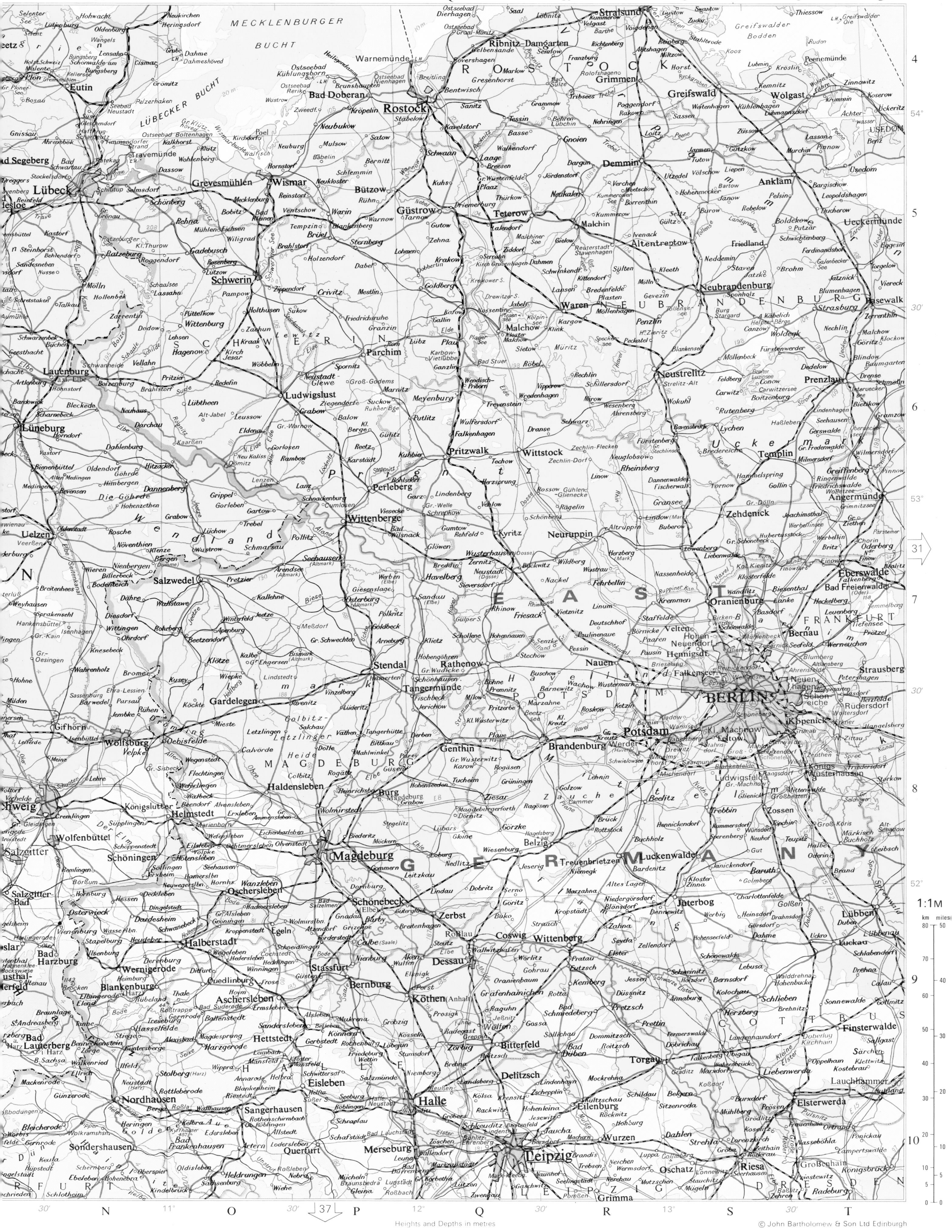
MECKLENBURGER BUCHT
LÜBECKER BUCHT
ROSTOCK
NEUBRANDENBURG
SCHWERIN
EAST GERMANY
POTSDAM
FRANKFURT
MAGDEBURG
HALLE
LEIPZIG
COTTBUS
DRESDEN
ERFURT
Stralsund
Greifswald
Rostock
Lübeck
Wismar
Schwerin
Güstrow
Neubrandenburg
Ueckermünde
Anklam
Demmin
Waren
Neustrelitz
Prenzlau
Pasewalk
Templin
Wittstock
Pritzwalk
Perleberg
Wittenberge
Parchim
Ludwigslust
Lüneburg
Uelzen
Salzwedel
Stendal
Neuruppin
Oranienburg
Eberswalde
BERLIN
Potsdam
Brandenburg
Rathenow
Tangermünde
Gardelegen
Wolfsburg
Haldensleben
Magdeburg
Burg
Schönebeck
Halberstadt
Wernigerode
Quedlinburg
Aschersleben
Bernburg
Dessau
Köthen
Wittenberg
Zerbst
Bitterfeld
Halle
Merseburg
Leipzig
Torgau
Eisleben
Sangerhausen
Nordhausen
Jüterbog
Luckenwalde
Lübben
Finsterwalde
Riesa
Elsterwerda
Oschatz
Grimma
Wurzen
Delitzsch
Eilenburg
Helmstedt
Wolfenbüttel
Salzgitter
Braunschweig
Gifhorn
Dannenberg
Lauenburg
Ratzeburg
Eutin
USEDOM
Heights and Depths in metres
1:1M

31
37

© John Bartholomew & Son Ltd Edinburgh

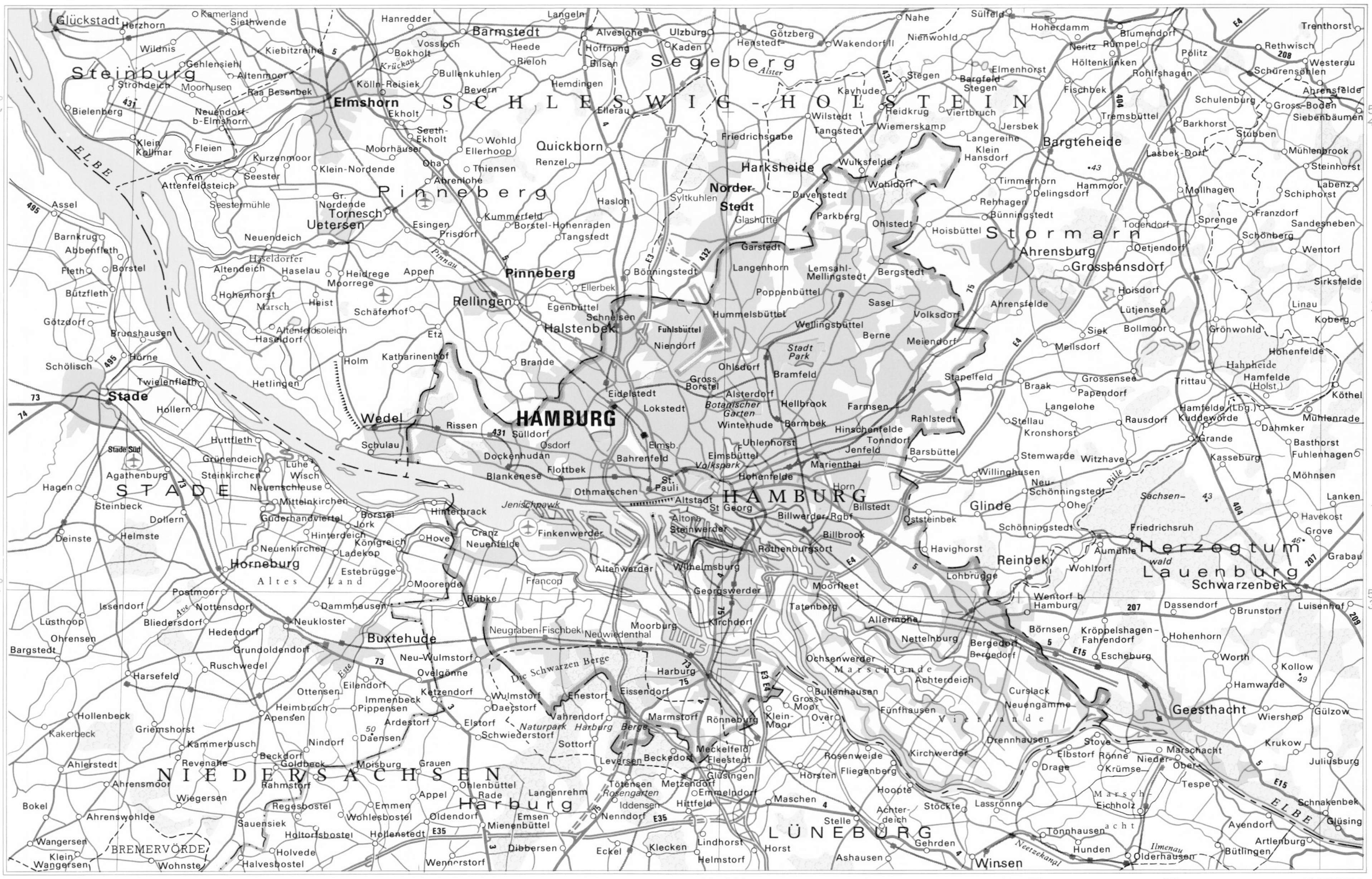

HAMBURG

SCHLESWIG-HOLSTEIN

Elmshorn · **Pinneberg** · **Quickborn** · **Norderstedt** · **Harksheide**

Stade · **Wedel** · **HAMBURG** · **Stormarn** · **Ahrensburg** · **Grosshansdorf** · **Bargteheide**

STADE · **Buxtehude** · **Horneburg** · **Herzogtum Lauenburg** · **Reinbek** · **Schwarzenbek**

NIEDERSACHSEN · **Harburg** · **Geesthacht** · **LÜNEBURG**

ELBE

BERLIN

Hohen-Neudorf · **Bernau** · **Hennigsdorf** · **Wittenau** · **Tegel** · **Pankow** · **Weissensee** · **FRANKFURT**

Falkensee · **Spandau** · **Wedding** · **Prenzlauer Berg** · **BERLIN** · **Mitte** · **EAST-** · **Lichtenberg** · **Marzahn**

POTSDAM · **Charlottenburg** · **Schöneberg** · **WEST-** · **Kreuzberg** · **Friedrichshain** · **Friedrichsfelde** · **Biesdorf** · **Rüdersdorf**

Wilmersdorf · **Tempelhof** · **Karlshorst** · **Oberschöneweide** · **Köpenick** · **Friedrichshagen**

Steglitz · **Zehlendorf** · **Neukölln** · **Britz** · **Buckow** · **Johannisthal**

Potsdam · **Wannsee** · **Lichterfelde** · **Klein-Machnow** · **Mariendorf** · **Marienfelde** · **Lichtenrade**

Teltow · **Ludwigsfelde** · **Zeuthen**

Havel · *Grosser Müggelsee*

1:300 000

0   5   10   15 km
0   5   10 miles

© Times Books Ltd

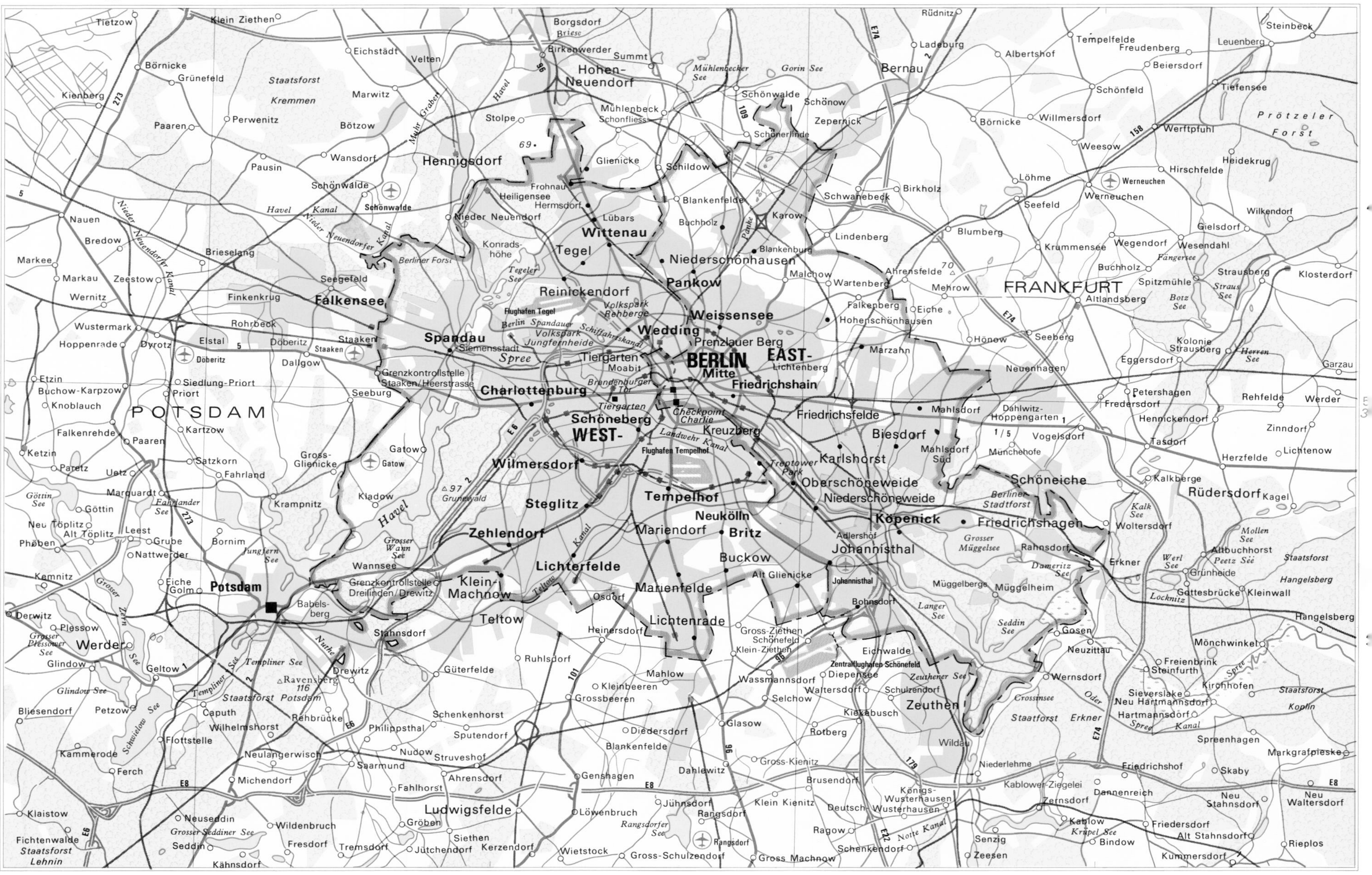

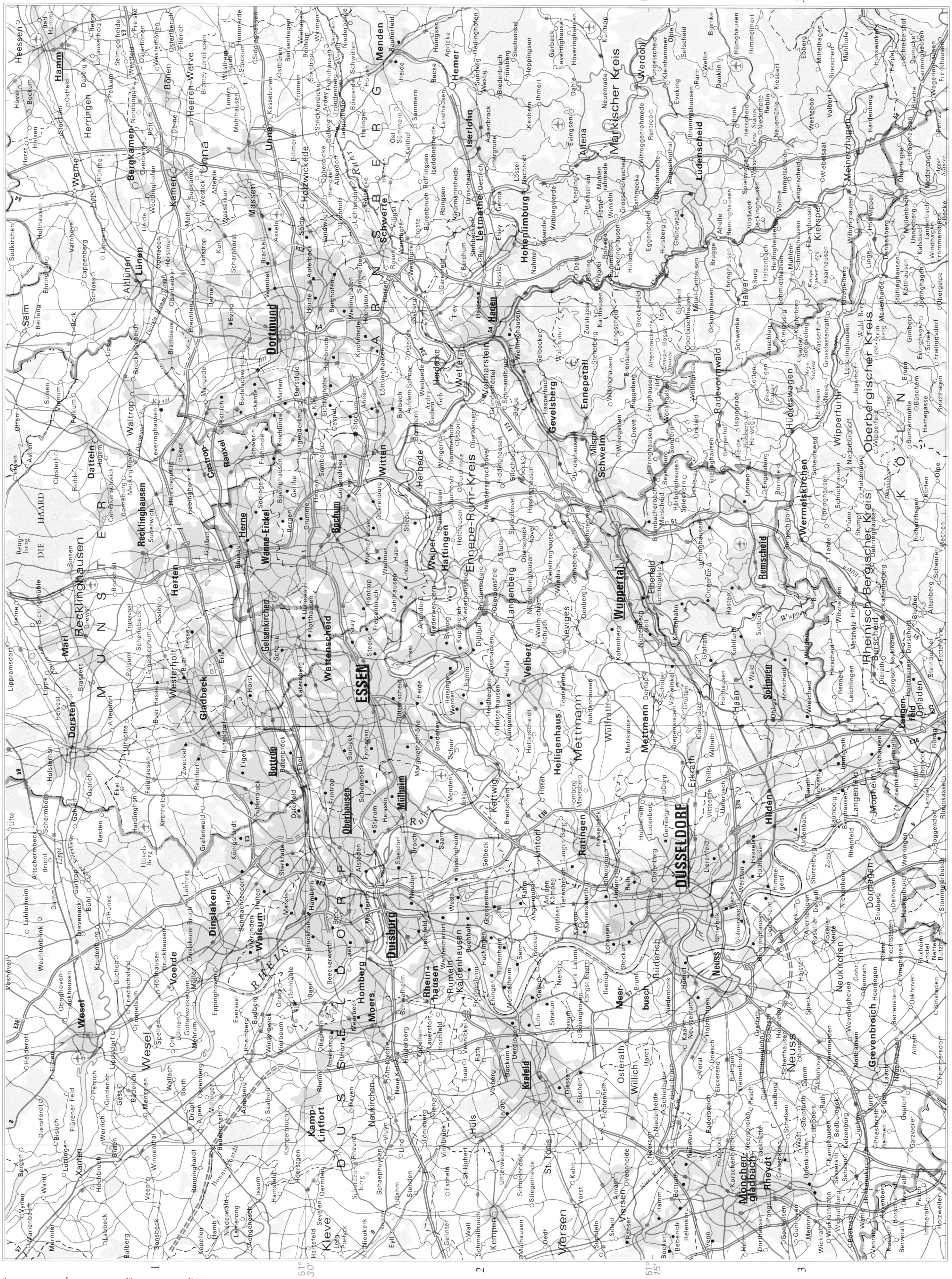
Dortmund
ESSEN
Bochum
Duisburg
DÜSSELDORF
Wuppertal
Gelsenkirchen
Oberhausen
Mülheim
Krefeld
Hagen
Hamm
Recklinghausen
Solingen
Remscheid
Neuss
Mönchengladbach
Herne
Wanne-Eickel
Bottrop
Witten
Wesel
Unna
Iserlohn
Lünen
MÜNSTER
DÜSSELDORF
KÖLN
SAUERLAND
Ennepe-Ruhr-Kreis
Märkischer Kreis
Oberbergischer Kreis
Rheinisch-Bergischer Kreis
Ruhr
RHEIN
Lippe
Wupper
Emscher

0 5 10 15 km
0 5 10 miles

1:300 000

© Times Books Ltd

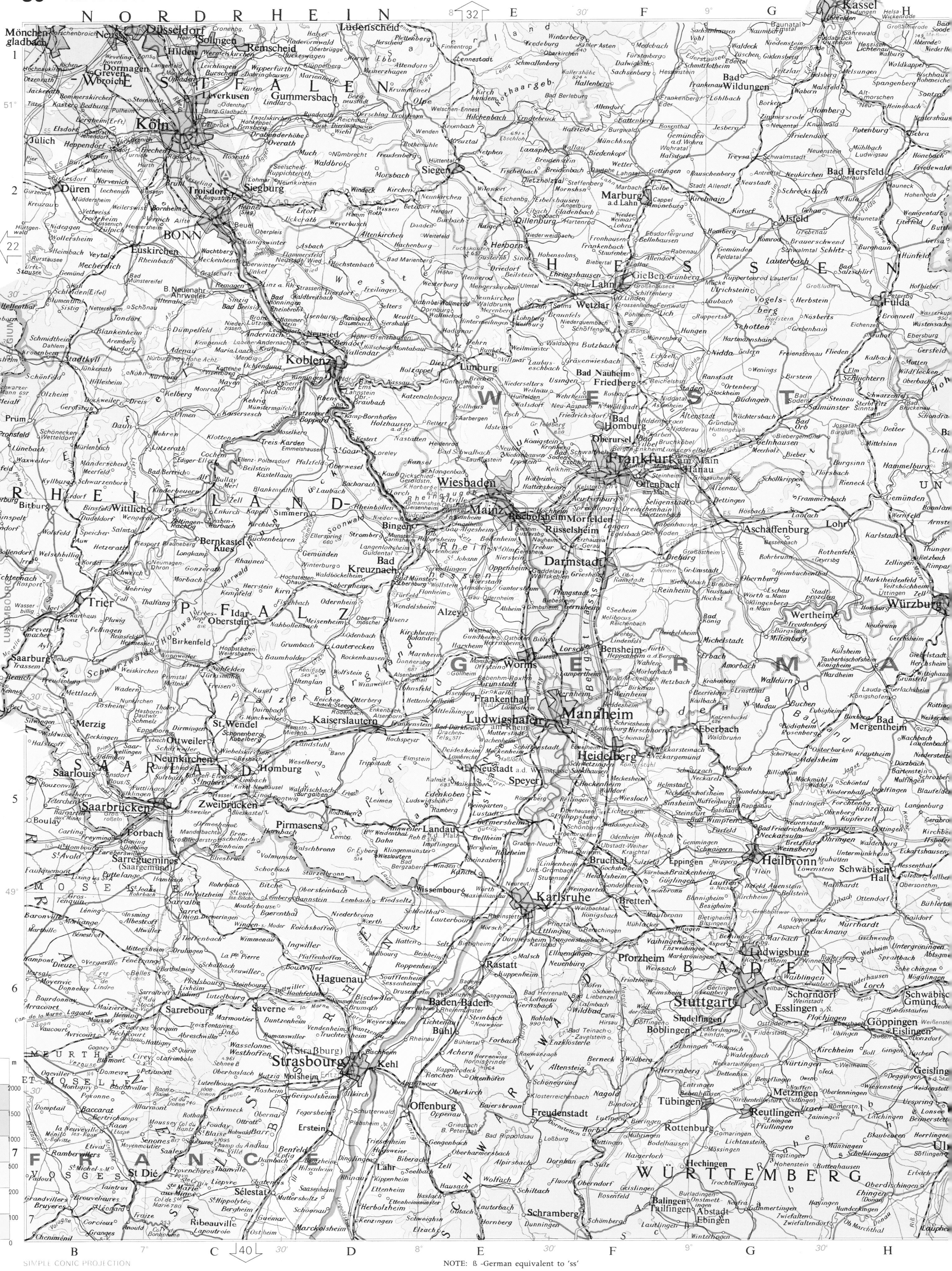

NORDRHEIN

Mönchengladbach · Neuss · Düsseldorf · Solingen · Remscheid · Lüdenscheid

Köln · Leverkusen · Gummersbach

Düren · Troisdorf · Siegburg · Siegen · Marburg a.d.Lahn · Alsfeld · Bad Hersfeld

BONN · Euskirchen · Kassel

HESSEN

Koblenz · Lahn · Gießen · Grünberg · Wetzlar · Fulda · Vogelsberg

Limburg · Bad Nauheim · Friedberg

WEST

Frankfurt am Main · Hanau · Offenbach am Main

RHEINLAND- · Wiesbaden · Mainz · Aschaffenburg

Bingen · Darmstadt

Trier · Bad Kreuznach · Alzey · Würzburg

PFALZ · Idar-Oberstein · Worms · GERMANY

Frankenthal · Mannheim · Bensheim

Ludwigshafen · Heidelberg · Eberbach

SAARLAND · Kaiserslautern · Neustadt a.d. Weinstrasse · Speyer

Saarbrücken · Zweibrücken · Pirmasens · Landau · Bruchsal · Heilbronn

Forbach · Sarreguemines (Saargemünd) · Karlsruhe · Pforzheim · Ludwigsburg

MOSELLE · Haguenau · Rastatt · BADEN- · Stuttgart · Esslingen · Göppingen

Saverne · Baden-Baden · Schorndorf · Sindelfingen · Böblingen

Strasbourg · Kehl · Offenburg · Tübingen · Reutlingen

MEURTHE-ET-MOSELLE

FRANCE · St Dié · Lahr · WÜRTEMBERG

LUXEMBOURG

BELGIUM

SIMPLE CONIC PROJECTION

NOTE: ß -German equivalent to 'ss'

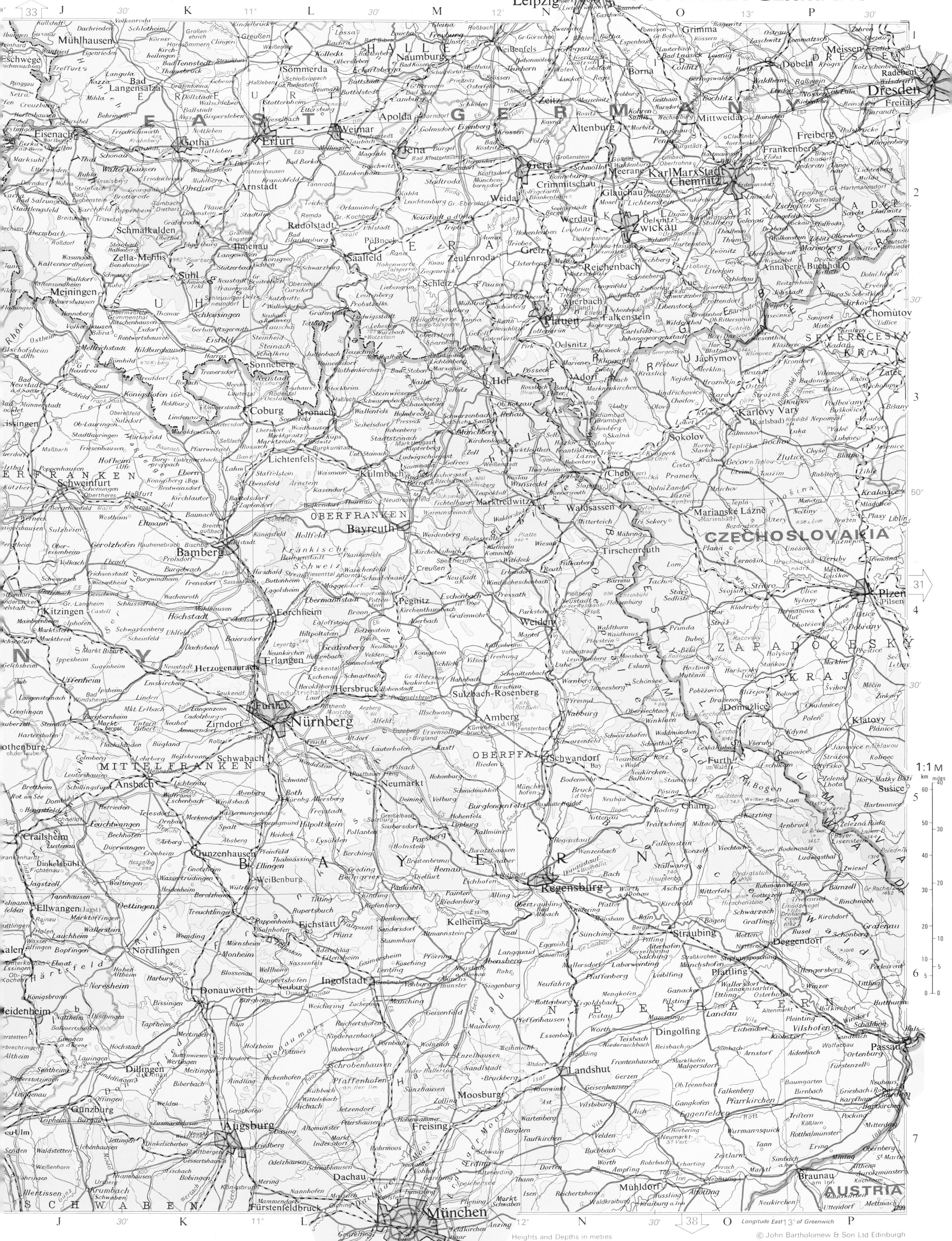

EAST GERMANY

CZECHOSLOVAKIA

AUSTRIA

Dresden
Leipzig
KarlMarxStadt Chemnitz
Zwickau
Plauen
Karlovy Vary
Plzeň Pilsen
Erfurt
Gotha
Jena
Gera
Weimar
Coburg
Bamberg
Bayreuth
Nürnberg
Fürth
Erlangen
Regensburg
Straubing
Deggendorf
Passau
Ingolstadt
Augsburg
München
Schweinfurt
Ansbach
Nördlingen
Donauwörth
Landshut
Braunau

OBERFRANKEN
MITTELFRANKEN
OBERPFALZ
NIEDERBAYERN
BAYERN
SCHWABEN
UNTERFRANKEN

SEVEROČESKÝ KRAJ
ZÁPADOČESKÝ KRAJ

Heights and Depths in metres

© John Bartholomew & Son Ltd Edinburgh

Longitude East 13° of Greenwich

1:1 M

km   miles

Scale

CENTRAL AUSTRIA

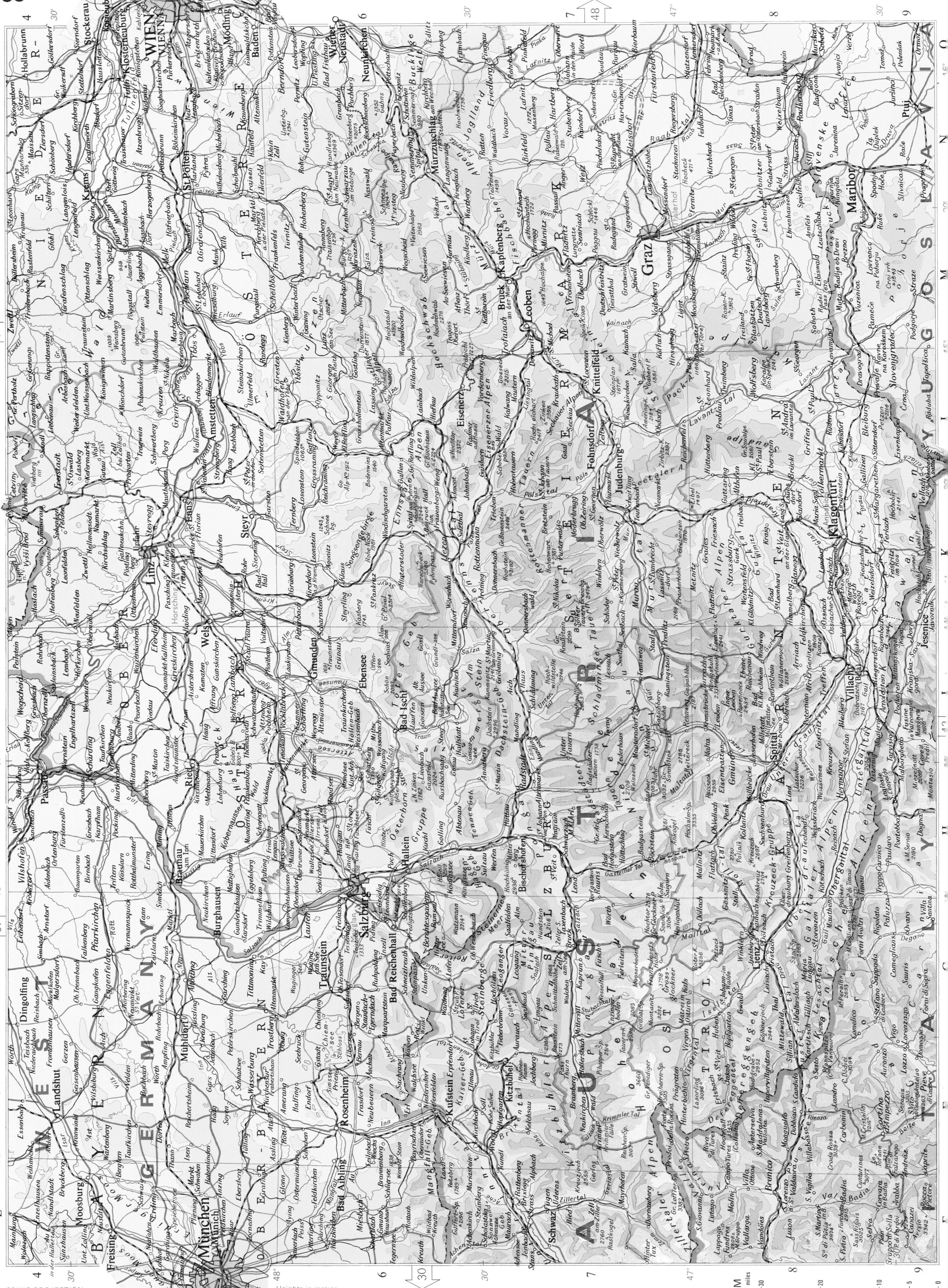

Heights in metres

1:1M

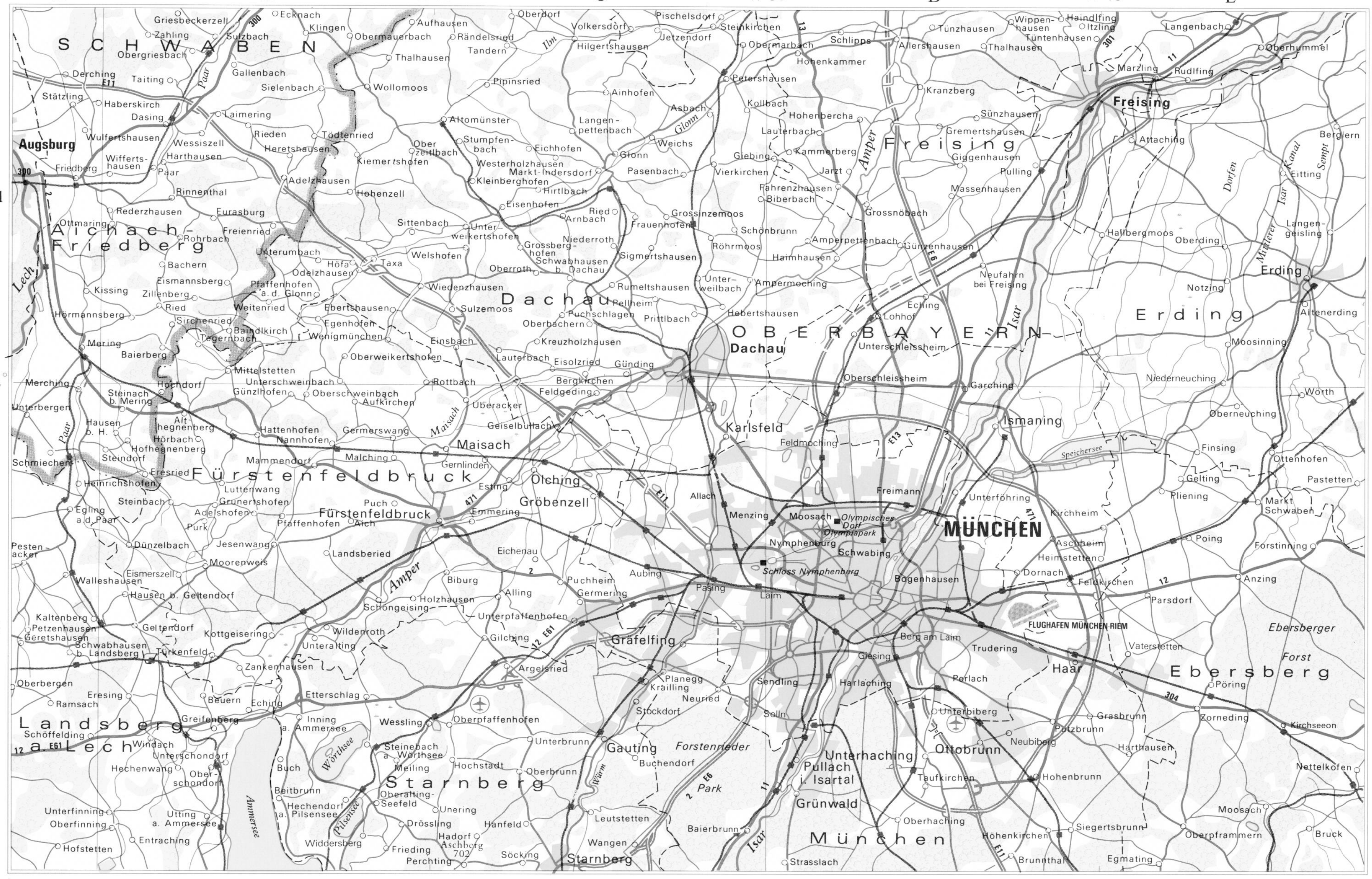

SCHWABEN

Augsburg

Aichach-Friedberg

DACHAU

Dachau

OBERBAYERN

FREISING

Freising

Erding

Erding

MÜNCHEN

Olympisches Dorf
Olympiapark
Nymphenburg
Schwabing
Schloss Nymphenburg
Bogenhausen

FLUGHAFEN MÜNCHEN RIEM

Ismaning

Fürstenfeldbruck

Fürstenfeldbruck

Gröbenzell
Olching

Gräfelfing

Haar

Ebersberg
Forst

Ebersberg

Landsberg
a Lech

Starnberg

Ammersee

Würmsee

München

Grünwald

MILAN

SCHWABEN / LOMBARDIA

Como

Somma
Lombardo
Gallarate

Varese

Busto Arsizio

Legnano

Saronno

Seregno
Cesano
Maderno
Desio
Lissone

Monza

Parabiago

Milano

Dugnano Paderno
Ciniselo
Balsamo
Cusano
Milanino

Sesto
San Giovanni

Cologno
Monzese

Rho

Bollate
Novate
Milanese

Milano

Novara

Galliate

PIEMONTE

Novara

Milano

MILANO
(Malpensa)

Castello
Sforzesco
Duomo
Teatro della Scala
Stazione
Centrale

MILANO (Mailand)

MILANO
(Linate)

Abbiategrasso

LOMBARDIA

Magenta

Vigevano

Pavia

Melegnano

Lodi

Cremona

Pavia

Milano

Mortara

TICINO

1:300 000

0   5   10   15 km
0   5   10 miles

© Times Books Ltd

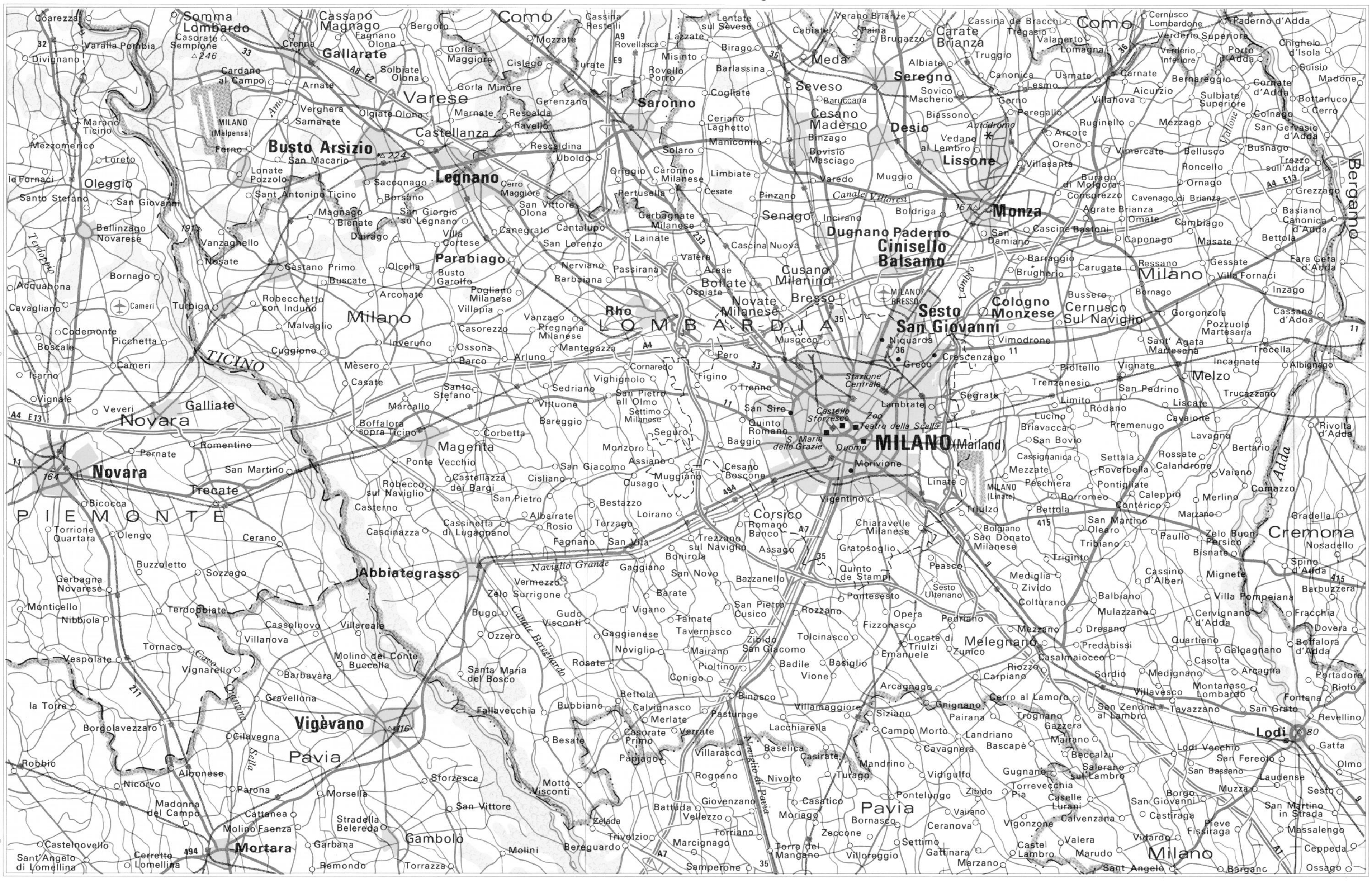

CONIC PROJECTION

Heights and Depths in metres

0	328	656	1640	1381	4921	6562	9843	13124	feet
0	100	200	500	1000	1500	2000	3000	4000	m

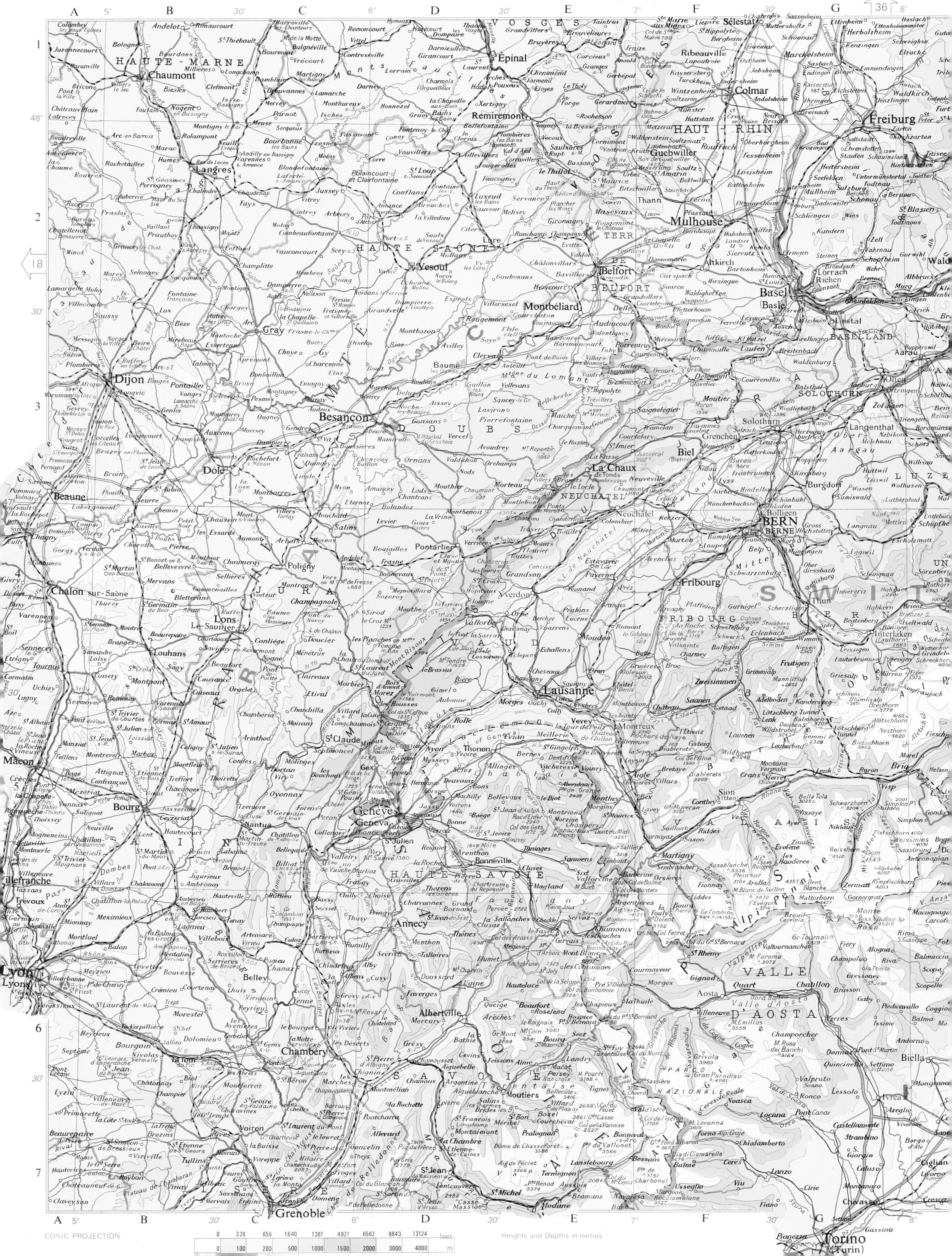

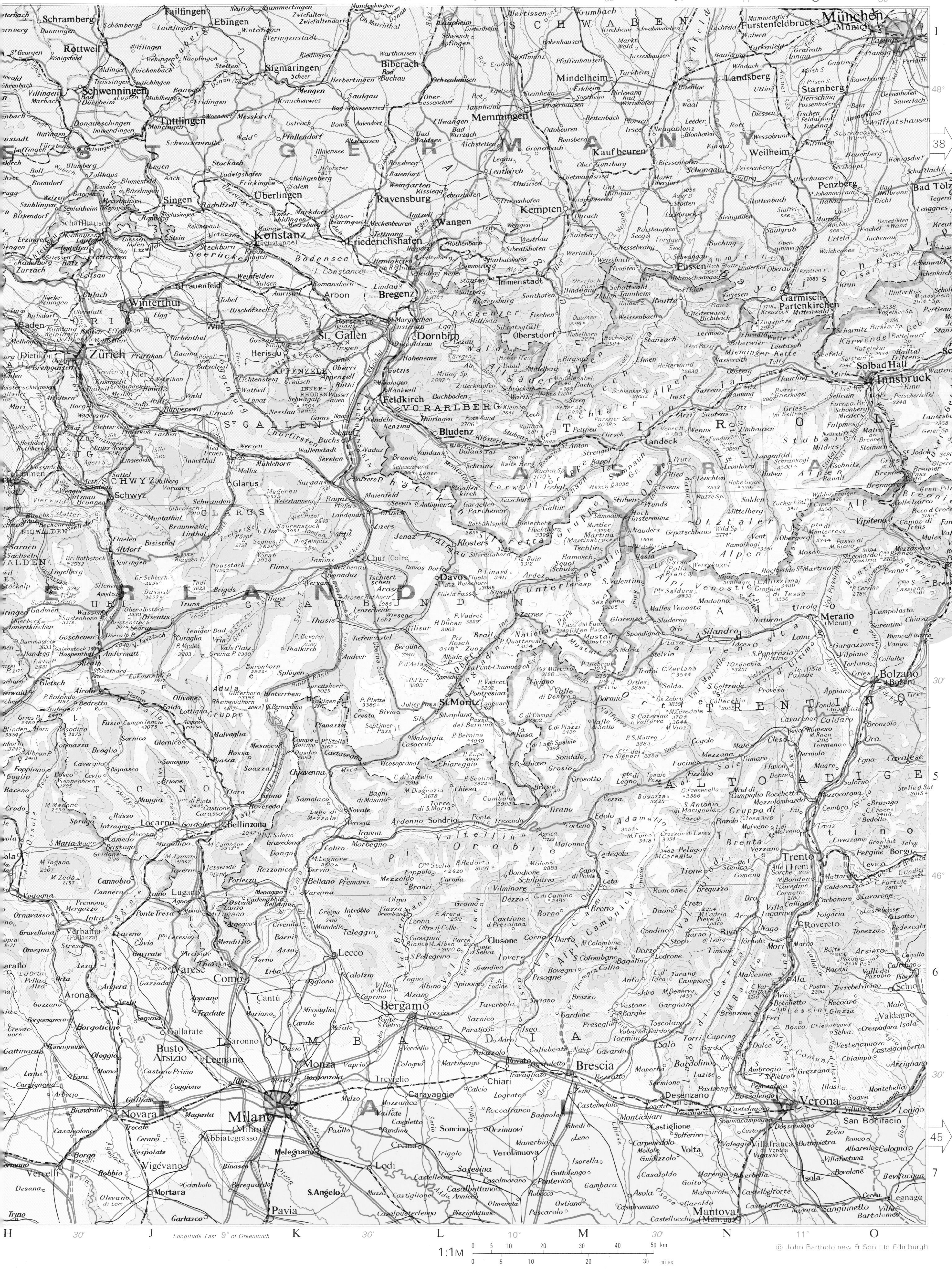

Longitude East 9° of Greenwich

1:1M

0 5 10   20   30   40   50 km
0   10   20   30 miles

© John Bartholomew & Son Ltd Edinburgh

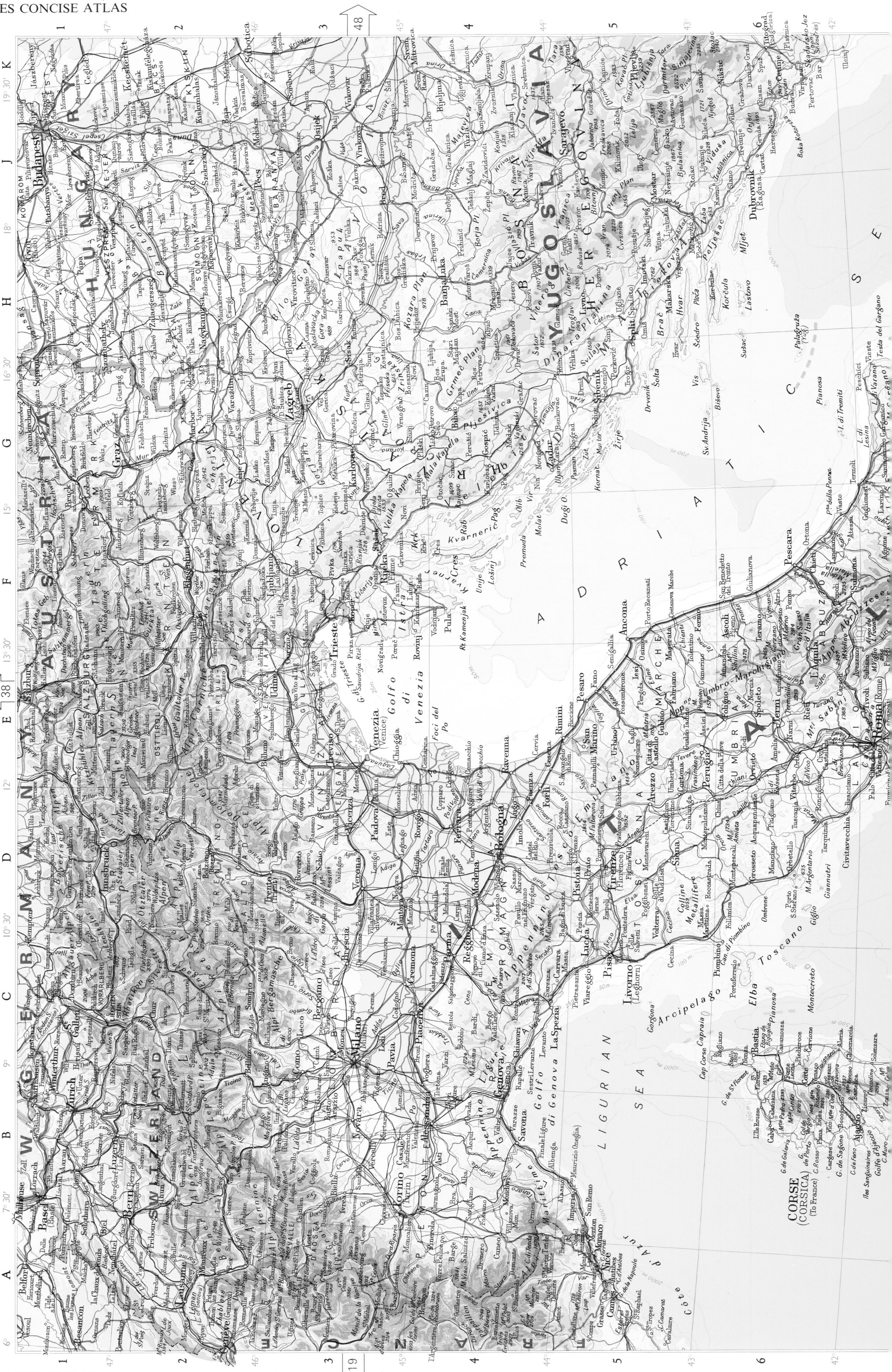
SWITZERLAND
AUSTRIA
HUNGARY
YUGOSLAVIA
LIGURIAN SEA
Golfo di Venezia
Golfo di Genova
CORSE (CORSICA) (To France)
Budapest
Zagreb
Ljubljana
Trieste
Venezia (Venice)
Milano
Torino (Turin)
Genova
Bologna
Firenze (Florence)
Roma (Rome)
Sarajevo
Split (Spalato)
Dubrovnik (Ragusa)
Bern (Berne)
Zürich
Innsbruck
Graz
Ancona
Pescara
Livorno (Leghorn)
Pisa
Perugia
Bastia
Ajaccio
Nice

CONIC PROJECTION

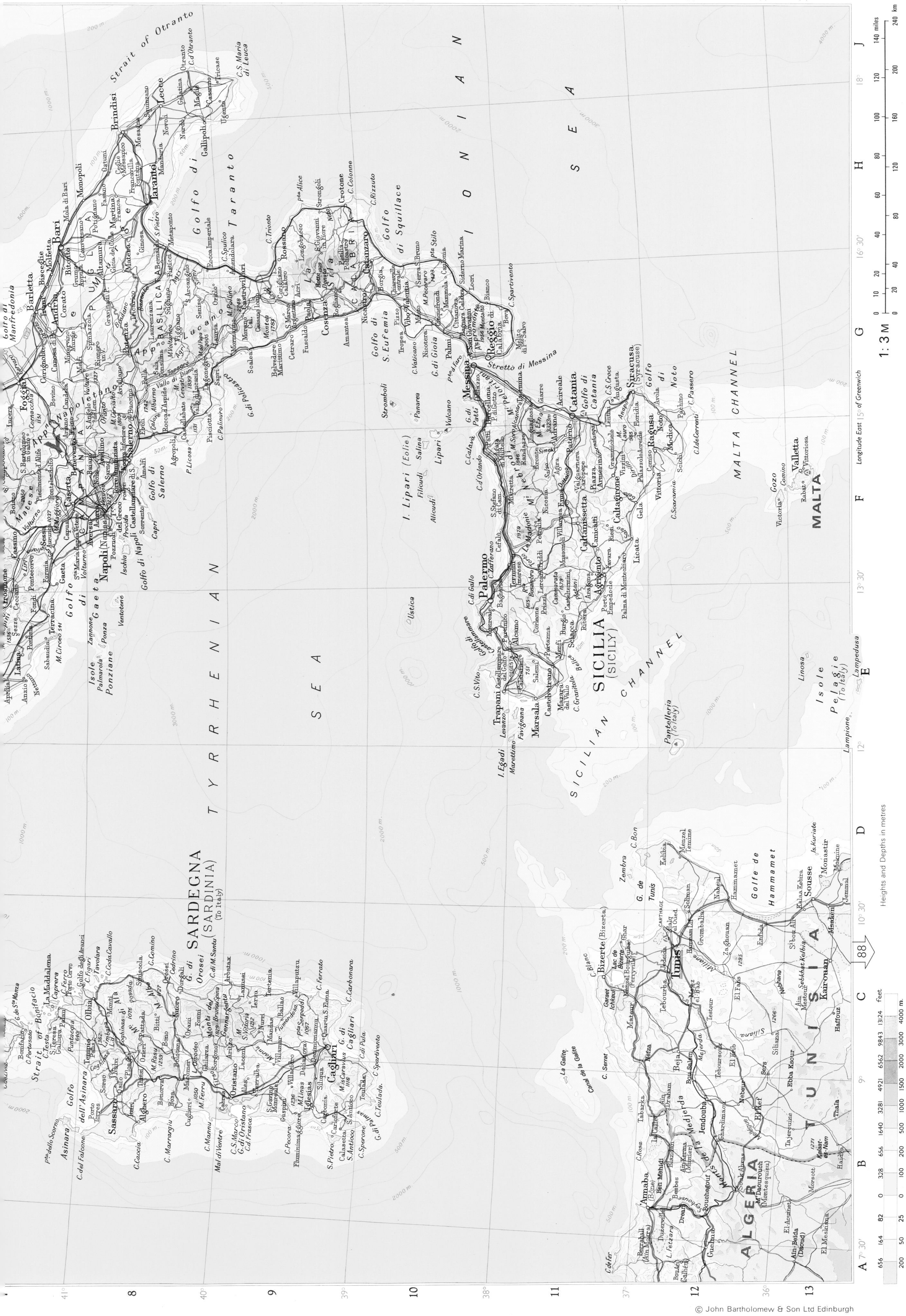
1: 3M
Longitude East 15° of Greenwich
Heights and Depths in metres
IONIAN SEA
TYRRHENIAN SEA
Strait of Otranto
Golfo di Taranto
Golfo di Squillace
Stretto di Messina
MALTA CHANNEL
SICILIAN CHANNEL
Strait of Bonifacio
SICILIA (SICILY)
SARDEGNA (SARDINIA) (To Italy)
MALTA
TUNISIA
ALGERIA
Bari
Brindisi
Lecce
Taranto
Napoli (Naples)
Salerno
Palermo
Messina
Catania
Siracusa (Syracuse)
Cagliari
Sassari
Tunis
Valletta
I. Lipari (Eolie)
Isole Pelagie (To Italy)
Pantelleria (To Italy)

© John Bartholomew & Son Ltd Edinburgh

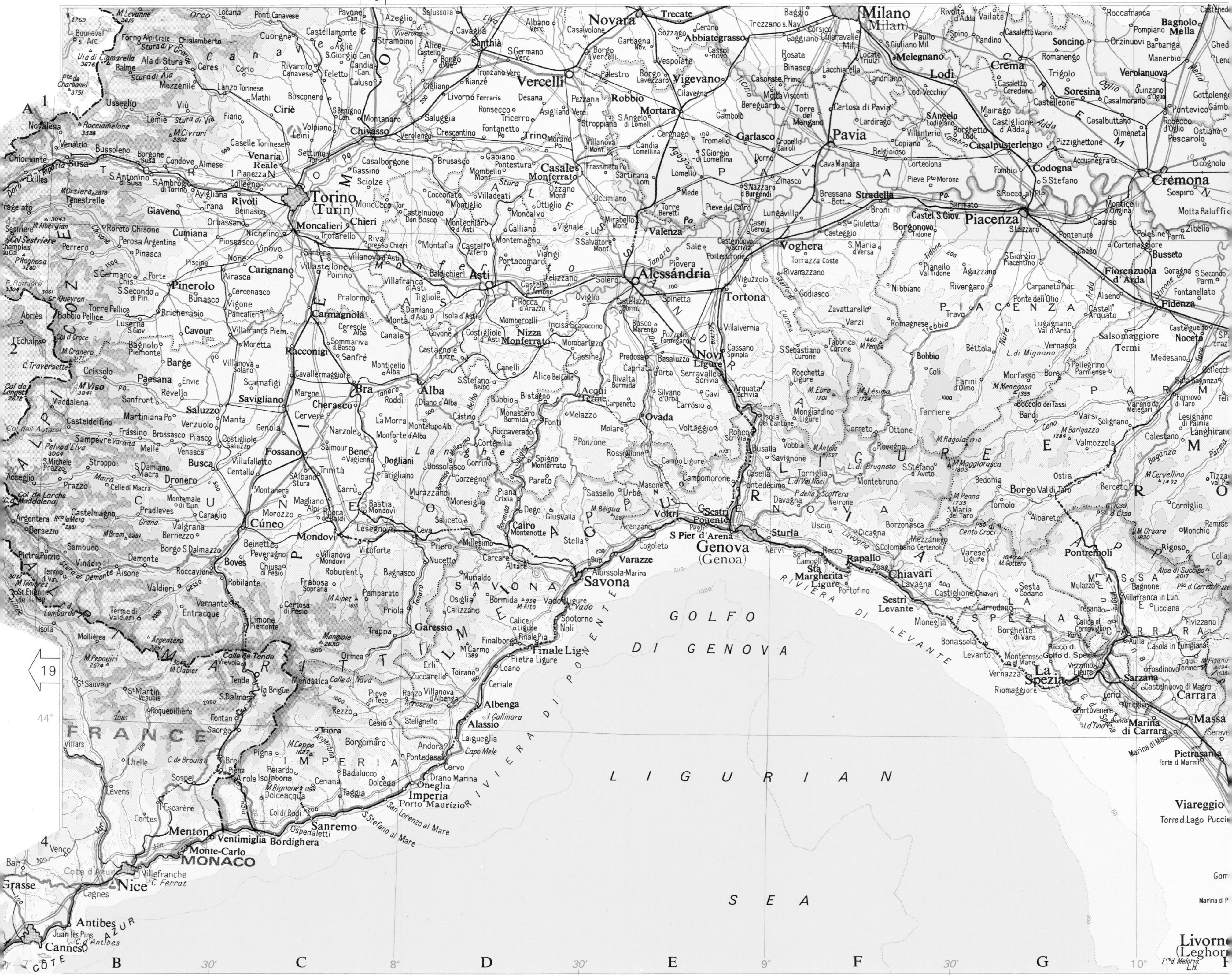

LIGURIAN SEA

GOLFO DI GENOVA

RIVIERA DI PONENTE

RIVIERA DI LEVANTE

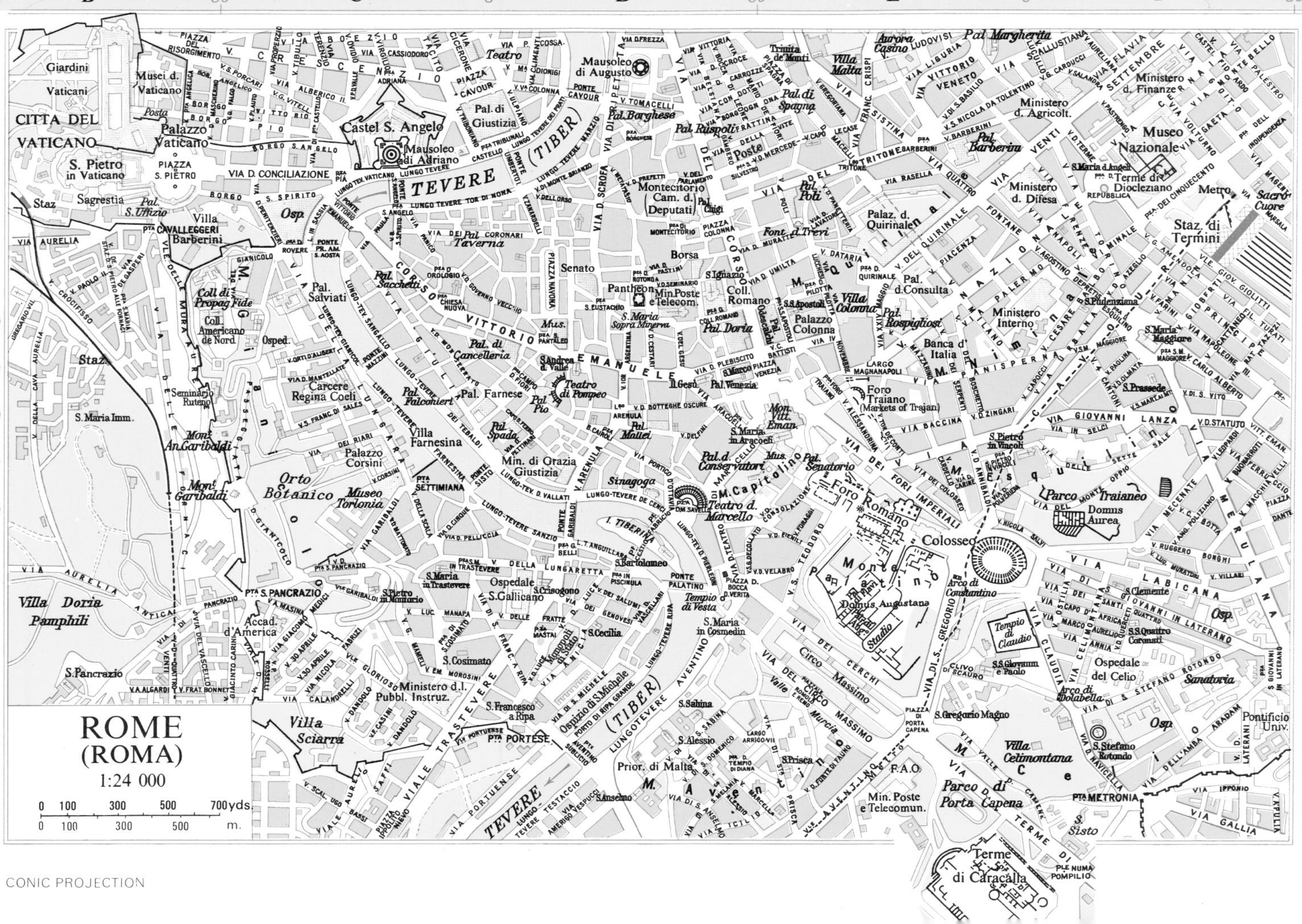

FRANCE

Milano (Milan)

Torino (Turin)

Genova (Genoa)

Pavia

Piacenza

Cremona

Alessandria

Novara

Vercelli

Asti

Cuneo

Savona

La Spezia

Carrara

Massa

Sanremo

Imperia

Monte-Carlo MONACO

Nice

Cannes

Livorno (Leghorn)

ROME (ROMA)
1:24 000

CITTÀ DEL VATICANO

S. Pietro in Vaticano

Castel S. Angelo

TEVERE (TIBER)

Foro Romano

Colosseo

ROME (ROMA)
on the same scale

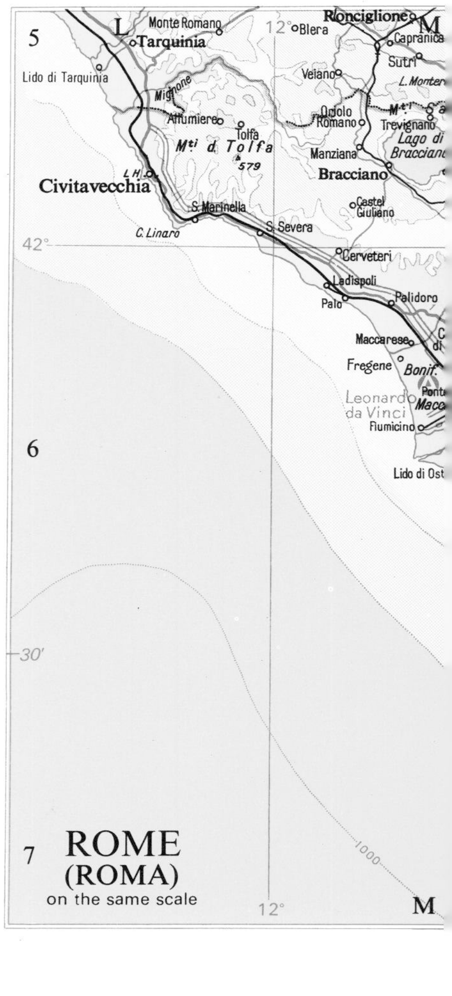

Tarquinia

Civitavecchia

Bracciano

Conic Projection

NAPLES
(NAPOLI)
on the same scale

1:1M

Heights and Depths in metres

© John Bartholomew & Son Ltd Edinburgh

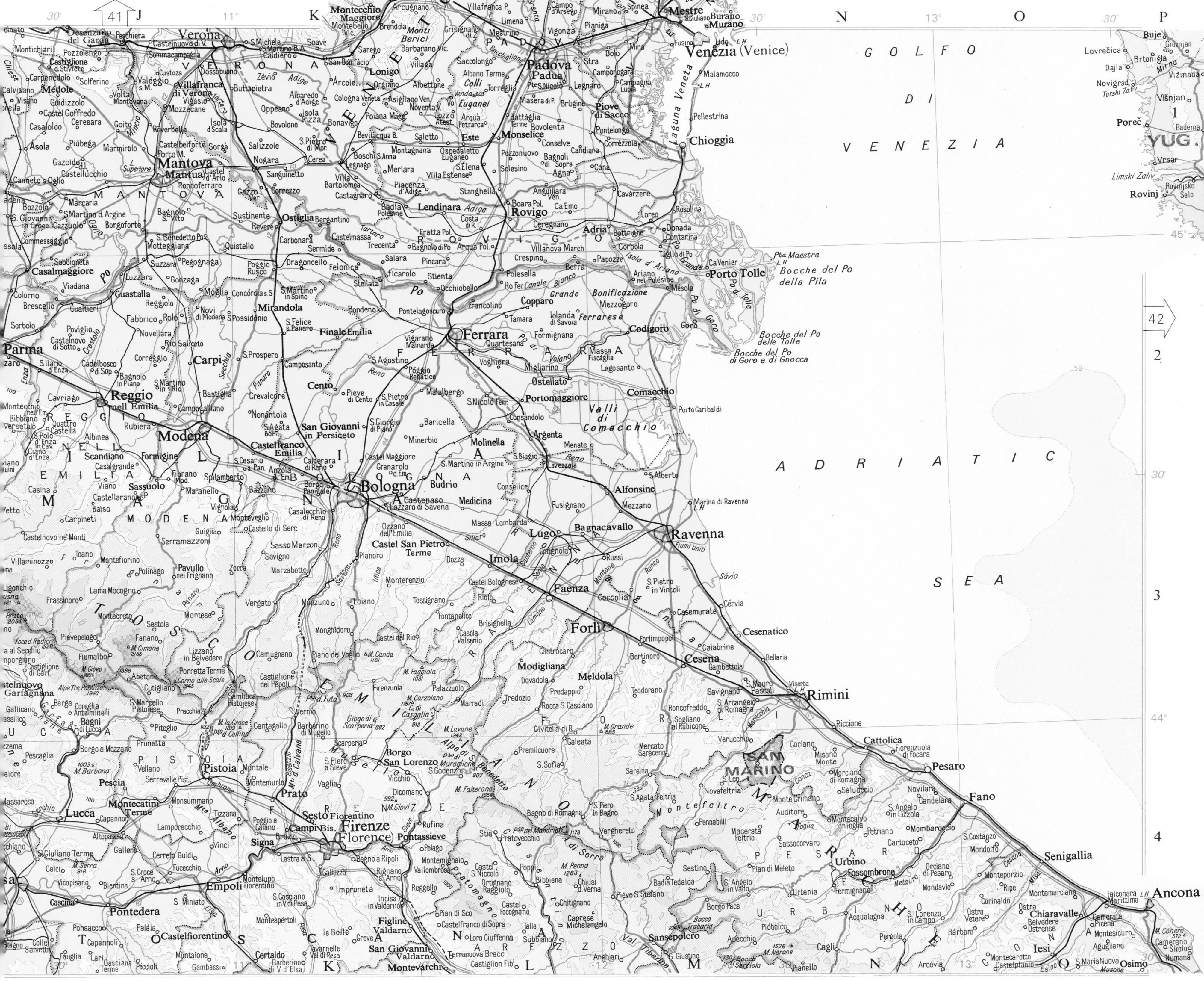

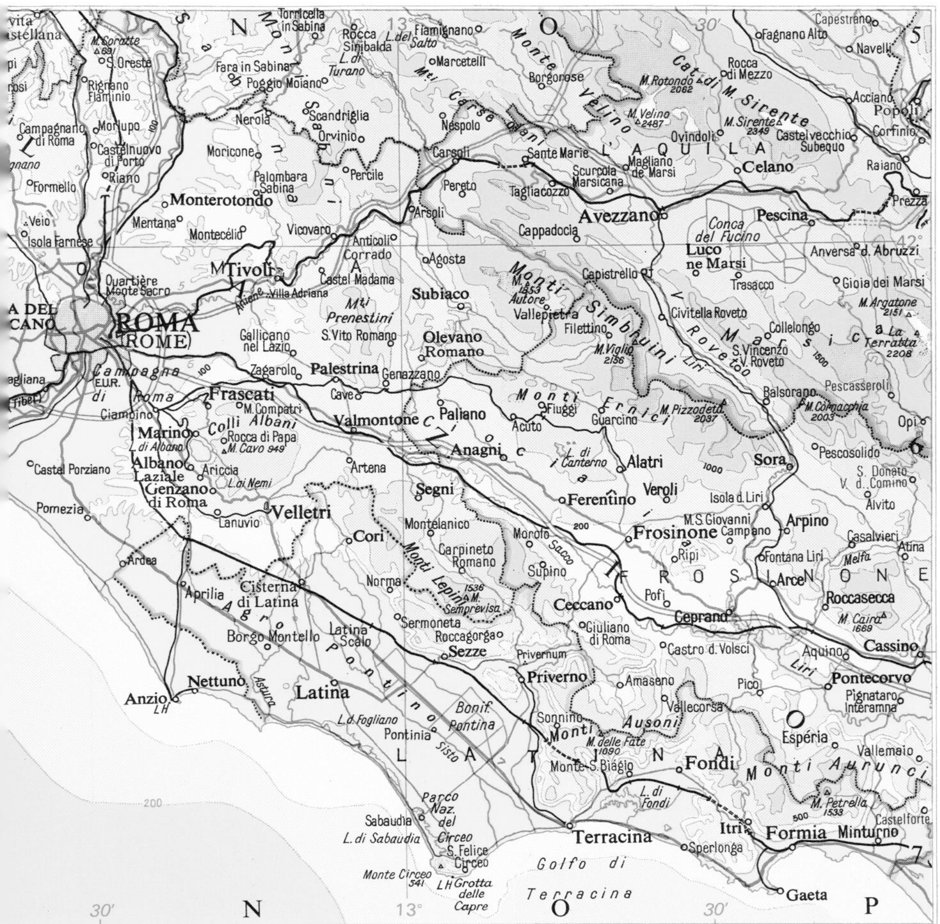

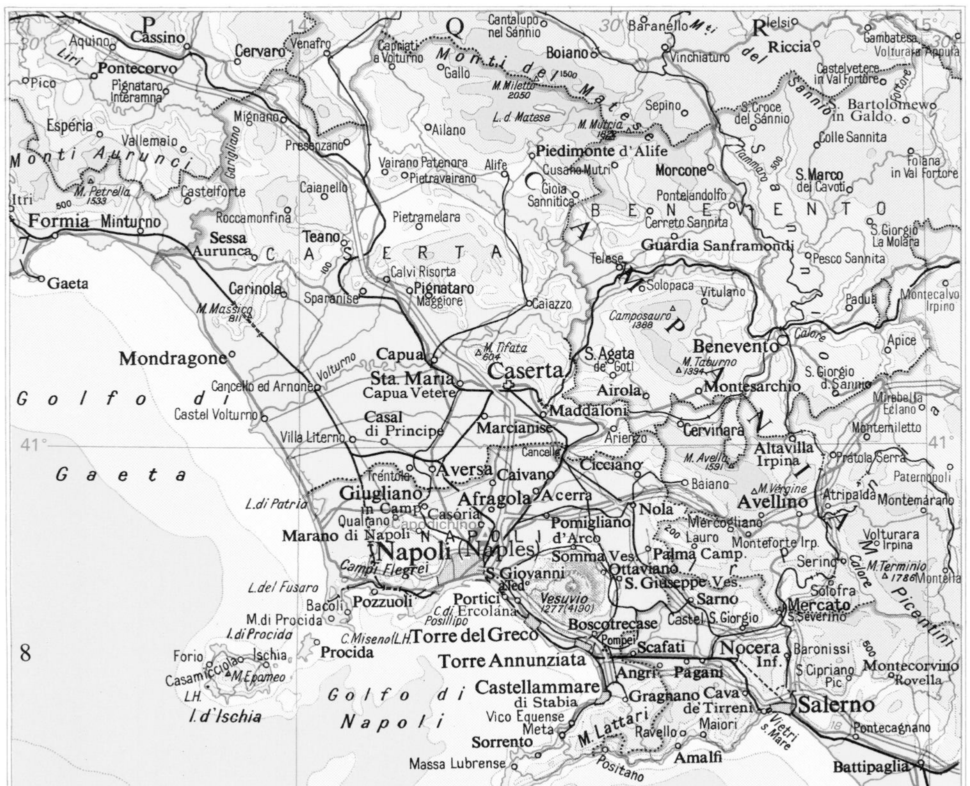

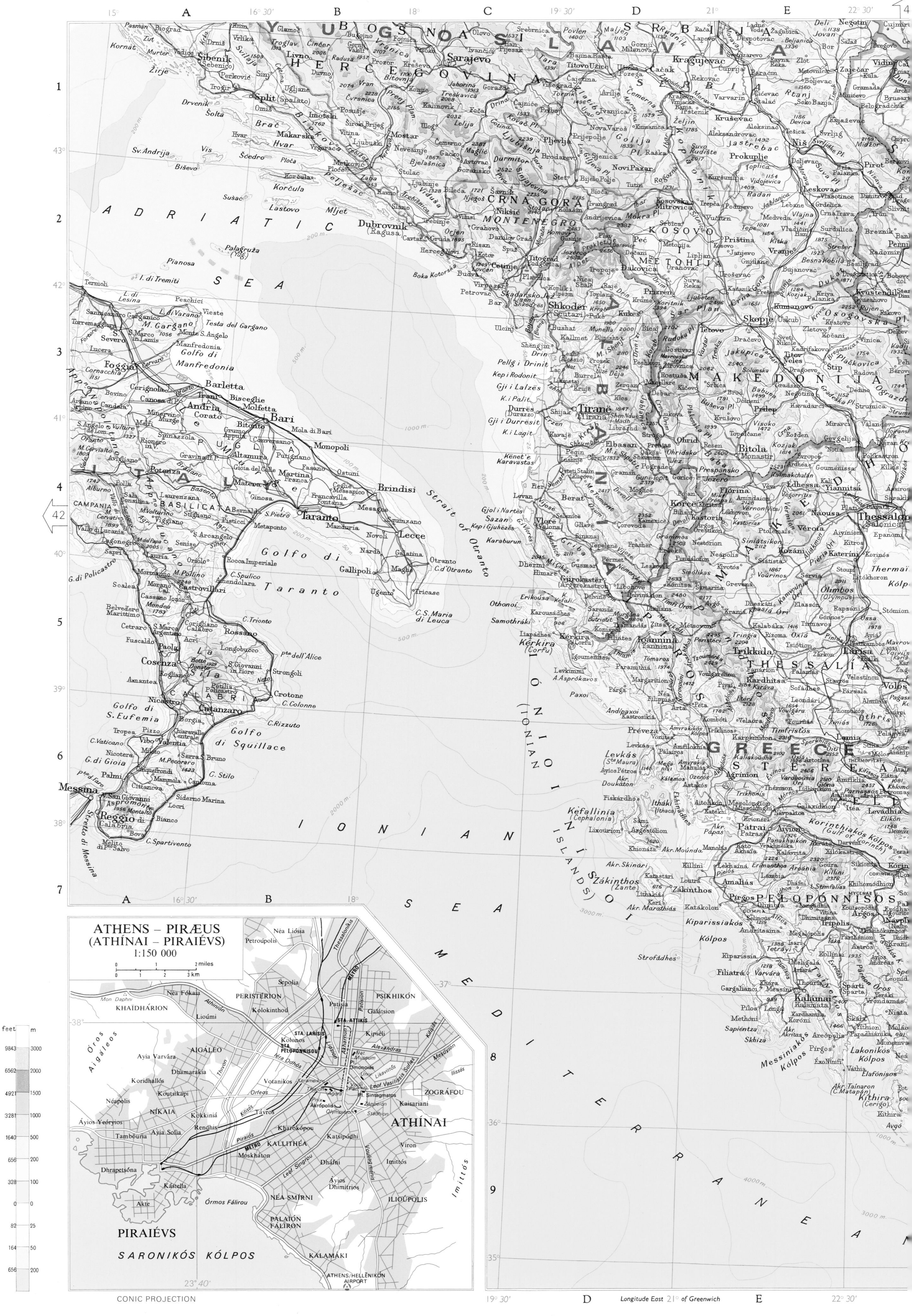

ATHENS – PIRÆUS
(ATHÍNAI – PIRAIÉVS)
1:150 000

PIRAIÉVS

SARONIKÓS KÓLPOS

Longitude East 21° of Greenwich

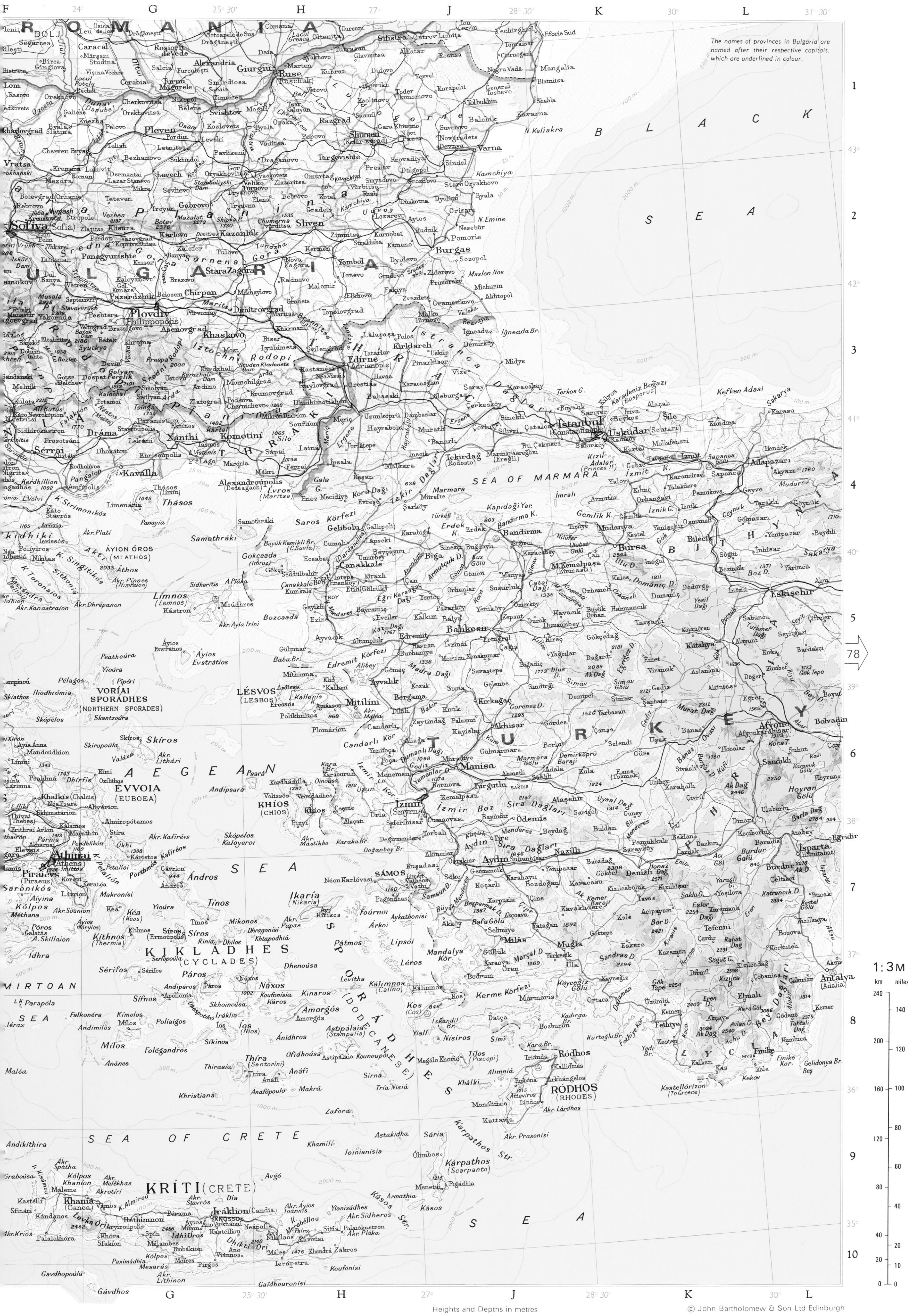
The names of provinces in Bulgaria are named after their respective capitals, which are underlined in colour.
ROMANIA
BULGARIA
BLACK SEA
SEA OF MARMARA
AEGEAN SEA
SEA OF CRETE
MIRTOAN SEA
TURKEY
THRAKI
BITHYNIA
Sofiya (Sofia)
Plovdiv (Philippopolis)
Varna
Burgas
Edirne (Adrianople)
İstanbul (Constantinople)
Üsküdar (Scutari)
Bursa
Eskişehir
İzmir (Smyrna)
Manisa
Aydın
Afyon (Afyonkarahisar)
Isparta (Hamitabat)
Antalya (Adalia)
Athínai (Athens)
Piraiévs (Piraeus)
Thásos
Sporádhes
LÉSVOS (LESBOS)
KHÍOS (CHIOS)
SÁMOS
EVVOIA (EUBOEA)
KIKLÁDHES (CYCLADES)
DODECANESE
RÓDHOS (RHODES)
KRÍTI (CRETE)
Iráklion (Candia)
Khaniá (Canea)
Kárpathos (Scarpanto)
78
1:3M
km
miles

© John Bartholomew & Son Ltd Edinburgh

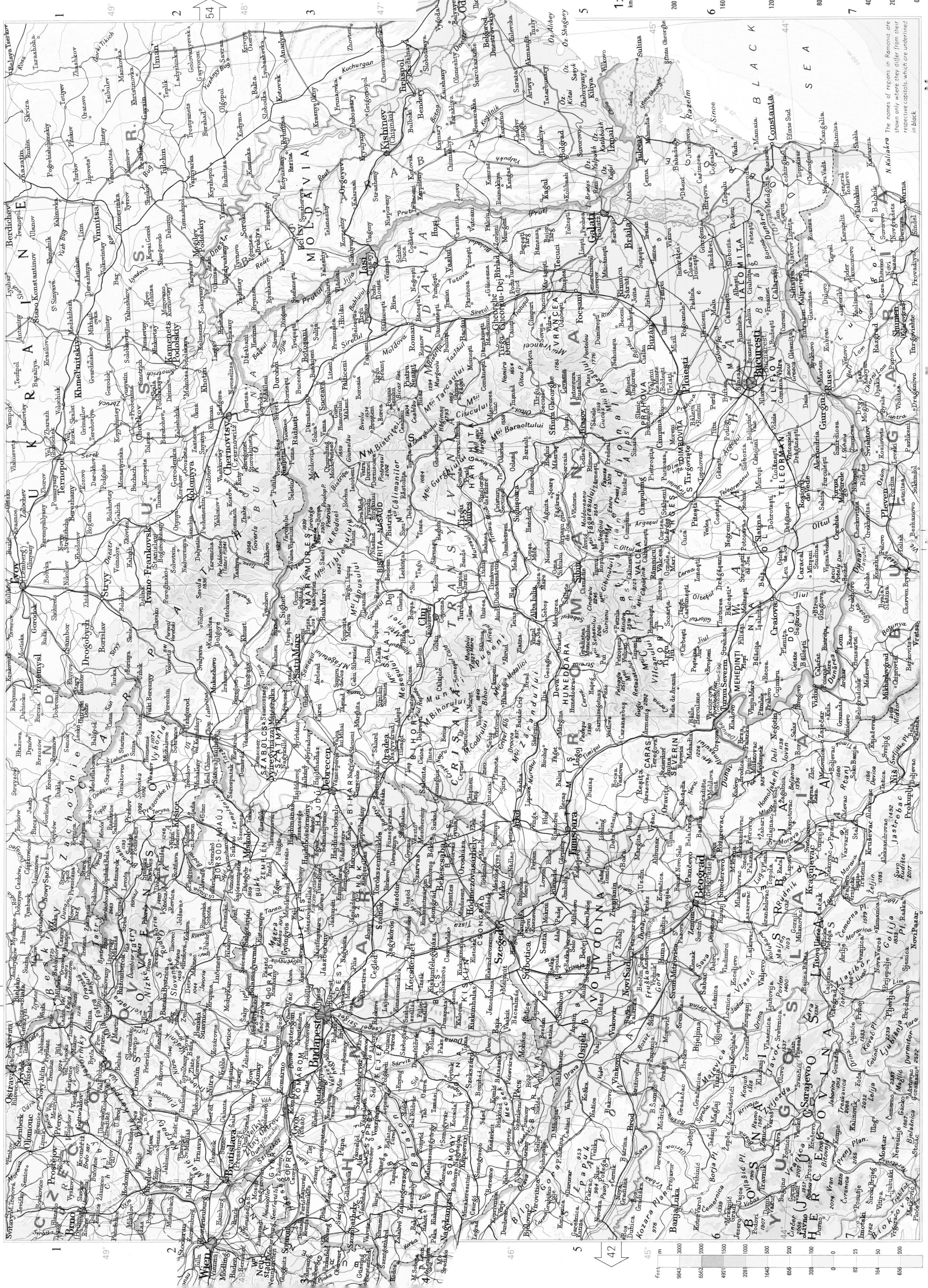
1:3M
The names of regions in Romania are shown only where they differ from their respective capitals, which are underlined in black
BLACK SEA
Budapest
Bucureşti
Beograd
Kishinev
Odessa
Lvov
Cluj
Debrecen
Sarajevo
Bratislava
Wien
Constanţa
Timişoara
Szeged

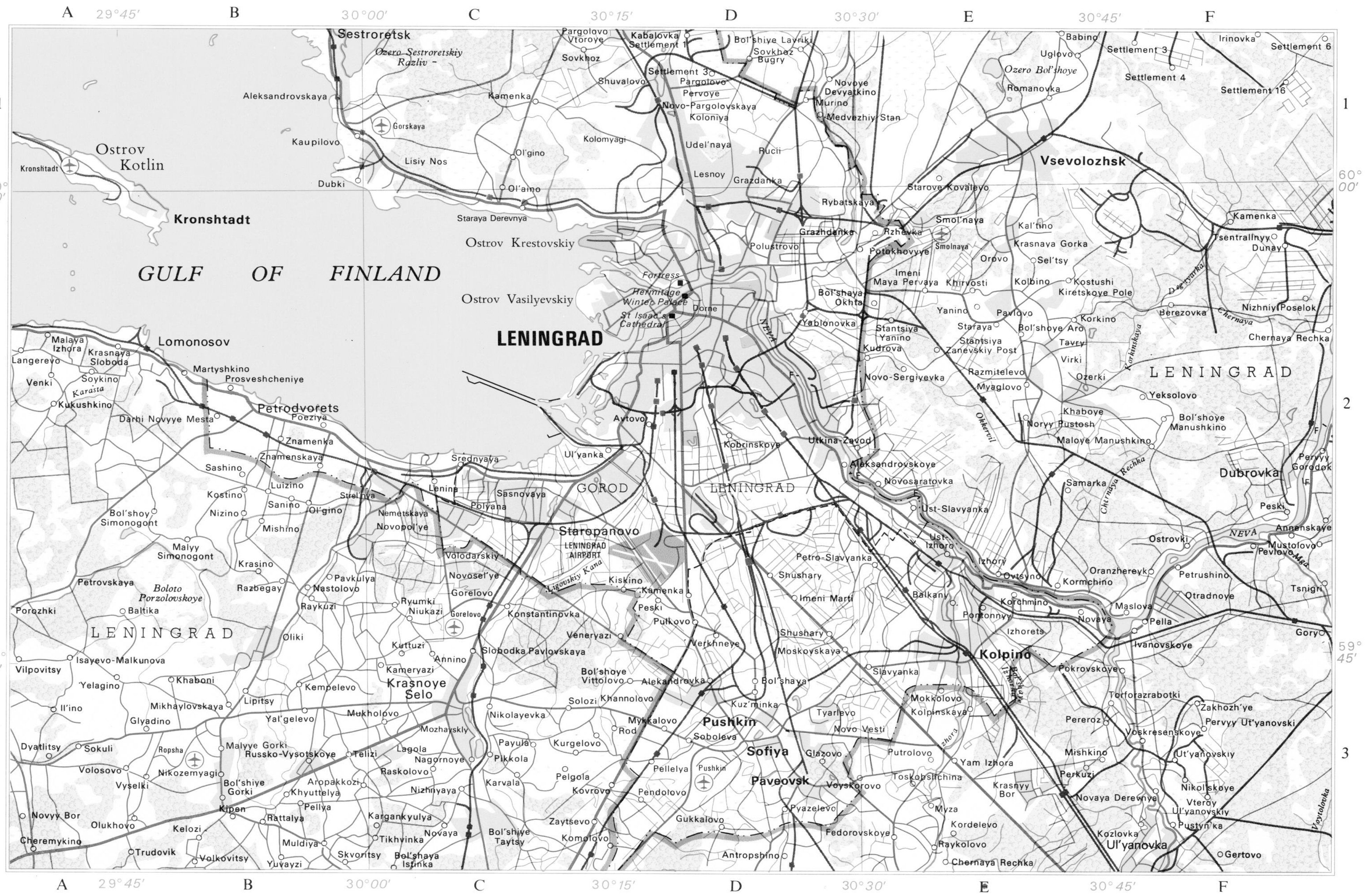

LENINGRAD

GULF OF FINLAND

Ostrov Kotlin

Kronshtadt

Ostrov Krestovskiy
Ostrov Vasilyevskiy

Fortress
Hermitage
Winter Palace
St Isaac Cathedral

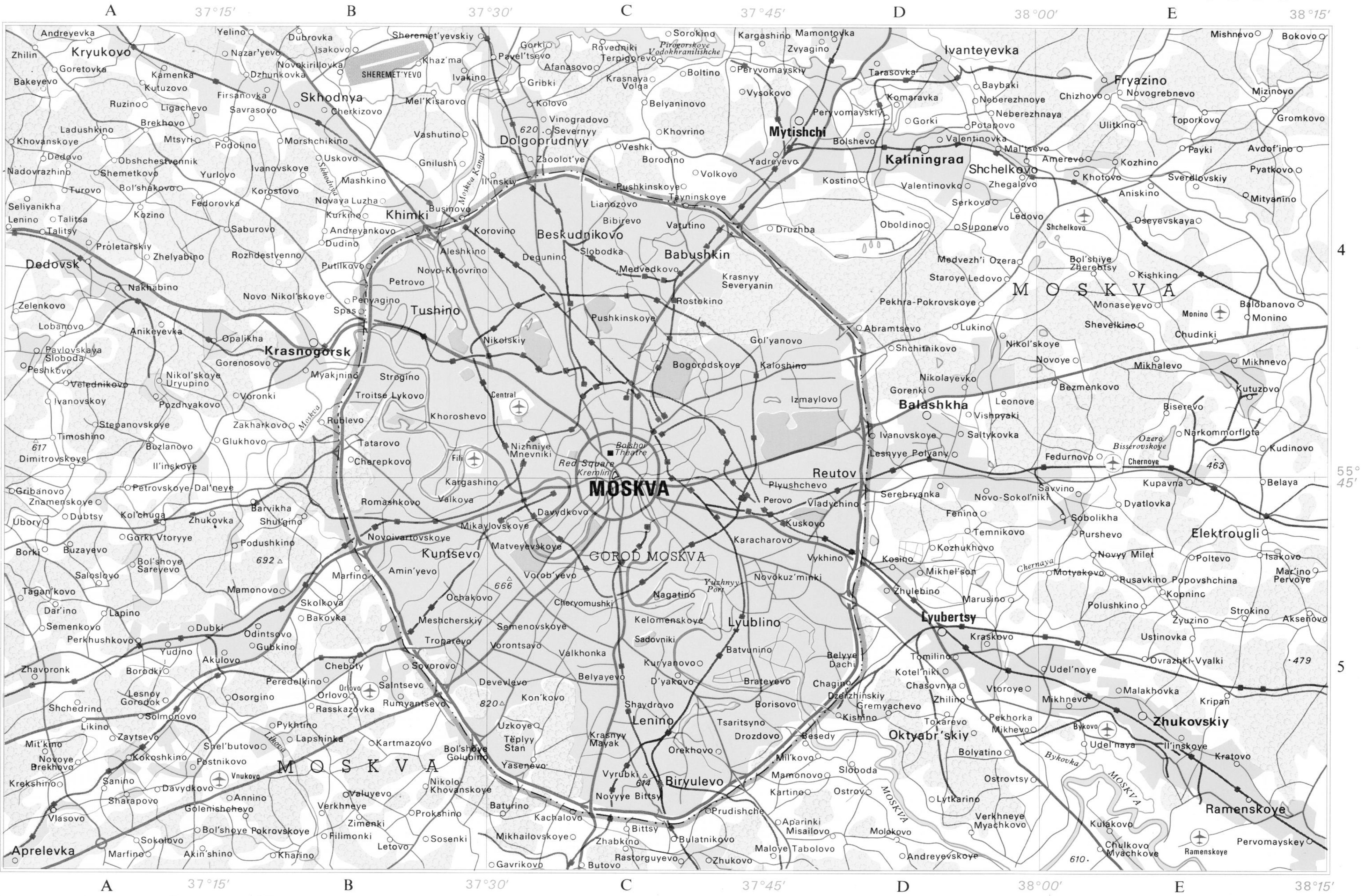

Sestroretsk
Ozero Sestroretskiy Razliv

Vsevolozhsk

LENINGRAD

GOROD
LENINGRAD

LENINGRAD AIRPORT

Lomonosov
Petrodvorets

Krasnoye Selo

Pushkin
Sofiya
Paveovsk

Kolpino

Dubrovka

NEVA

Ul'yanovka

MOSCOW

MOSKVA

GOROD MOSKVA

SHEREMET'YEVO

Kryukovo
Skhodnya
Khimki
Tushino
Krasnogorsk
Dedovsk
Kuntsevo

Mytishchi
Kaliningrad
Shchelkovo

Ivanteyevka
Fryazino

MOSKVA

Balashkha
Reutov
Lyublino
Lyubertsy
Biryulevo
Lenino

Elektrougli
Zhukovskiy

MOSKVA

Red Square
Kremlin
Bolshoi Theatre

1:300 000

© Times Books Ltd

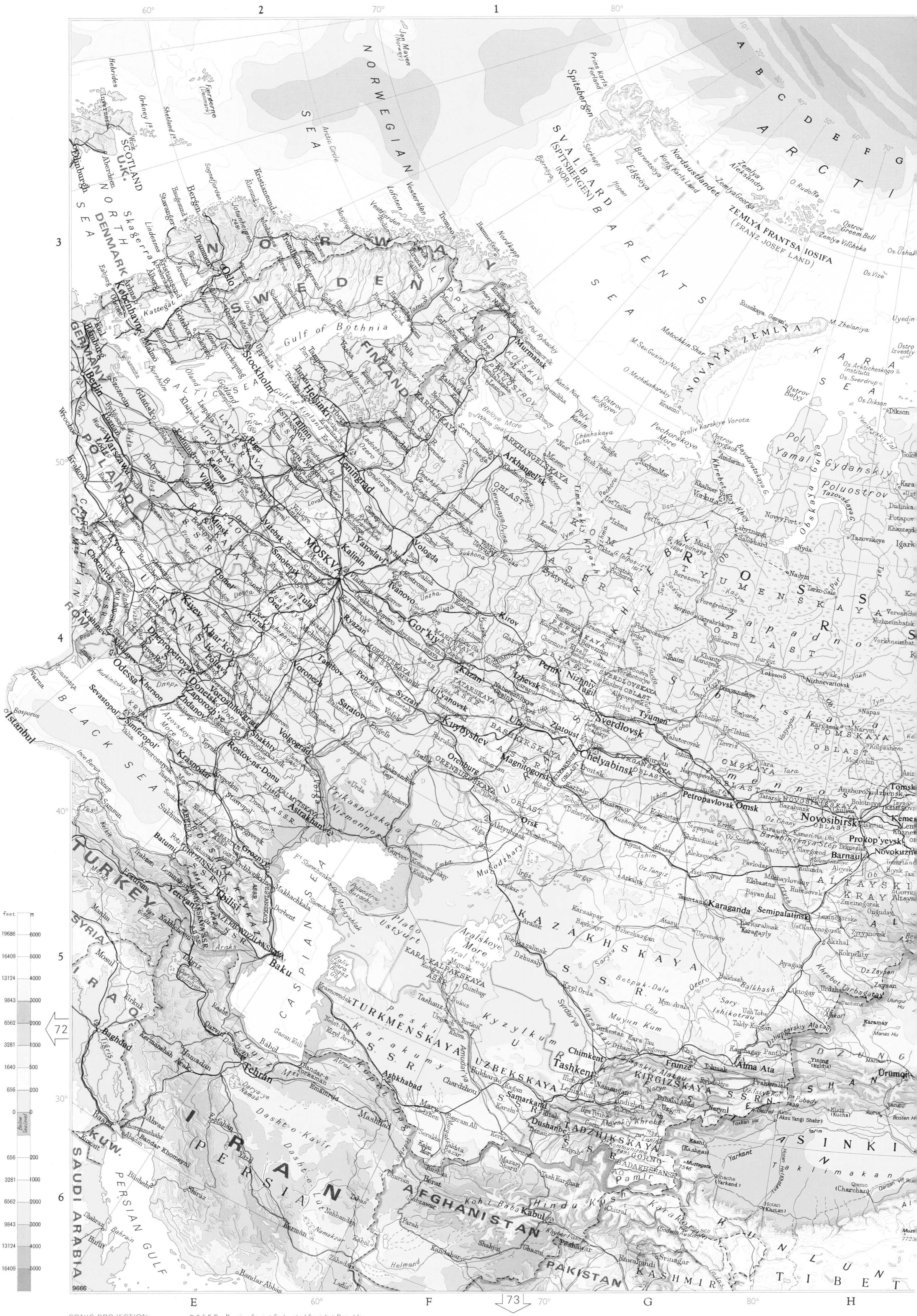

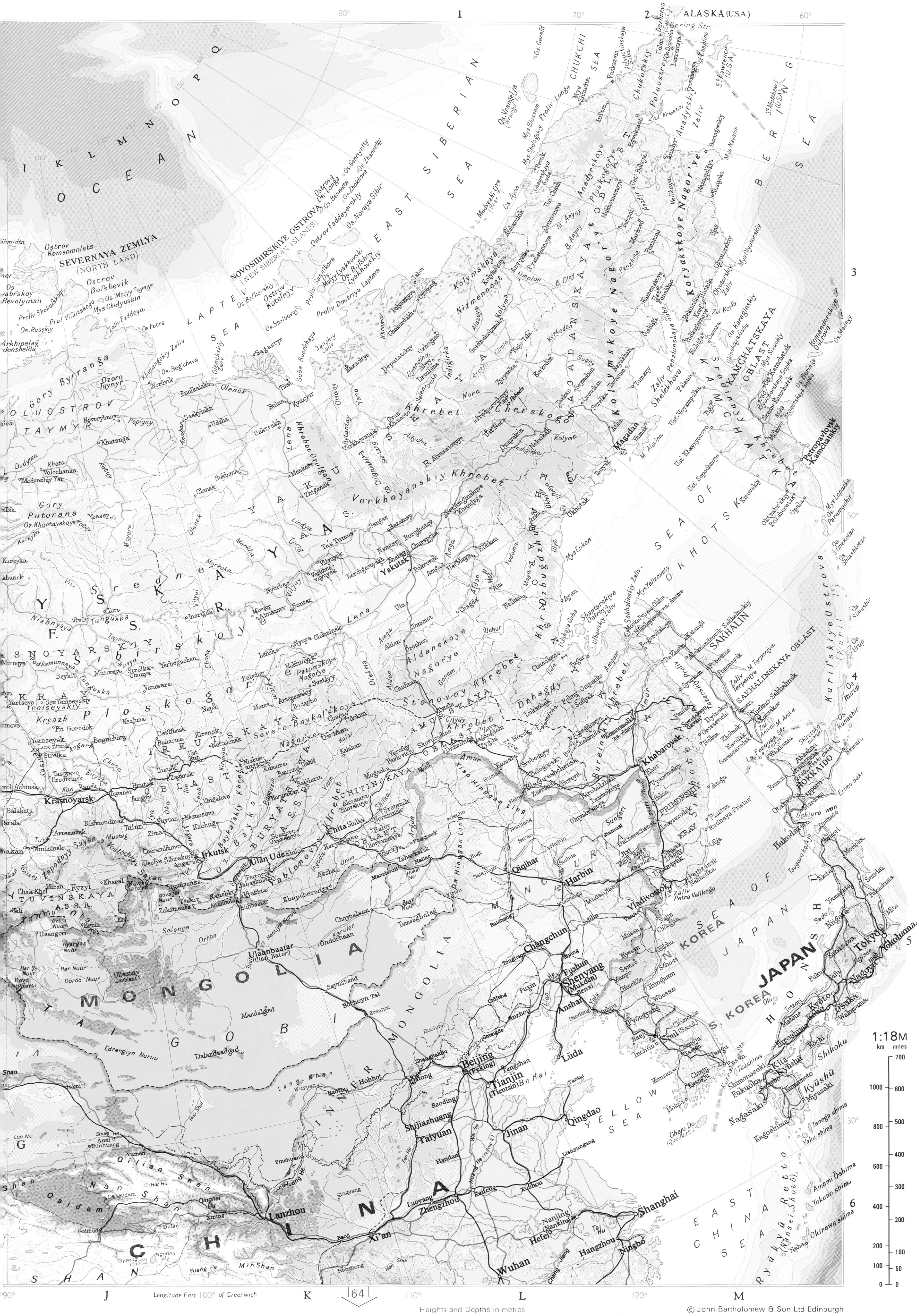

1:18M

km miles

700

1000 — 600

500

800 — 400

300

600 — 200

400 — 100

200 — 50

0 — 0

Heights and Depths in metres

© John Bartholomew & Son Ltd Edinburgh

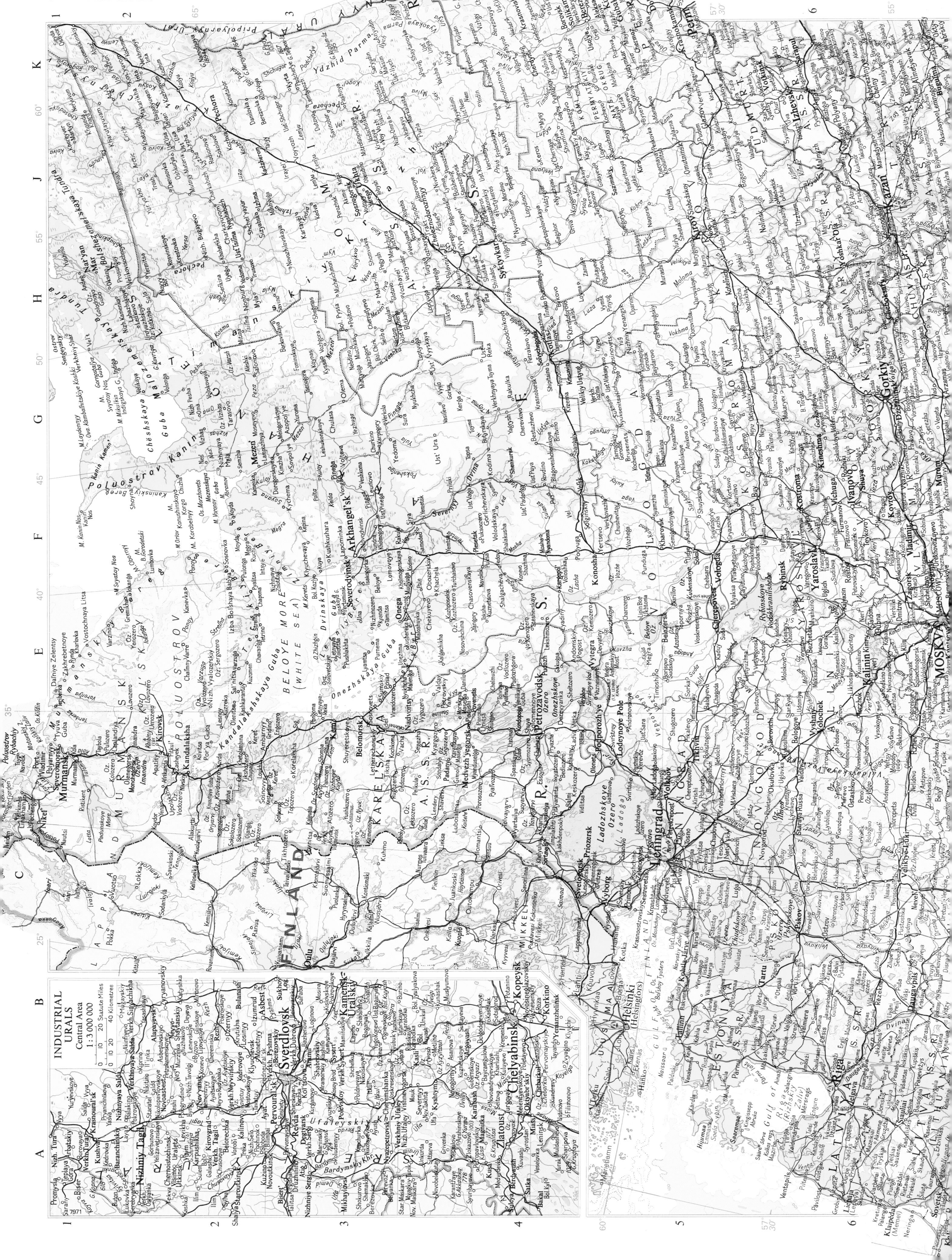

INDUSTRIAL URALS
Central Area
1:3 000 000

0 10 20 40 Statute Miles
0 10 20 40 Kilometres

Nizhniy Tagil

Sverdlovsk

Chelyabinsk

Zlatoust

MOSKVA (MOSCOW)

Leningrad

Gorky

Perm

Kazan

Murmansk

Arkhangel'sk

Kirovsk

Kandalaksha

Belomorsk

Petrozavodsk

Vologda

Yaroslavl'

Rybinsk

Cherepovets

Kalinin

Novgorod

Pskov

Riga

Tallinn

Helsinki (Helsingfors)

FINLAND

ESTONIA S.S.R.

LATVIA S.S.R.

Tartu

Narva

Vyborg

KAREL'SKA A.S.S.R.

MURMANSKAYA

Naryan Mar

Pechora R.

Mezen'

Onega

Severodvinsk

Kirov

Izhevsk

U'D'MURT. A.S.S.R.

KOMI A.S.S.R.

Syktyvkar

BELOYE MORE (WHITE SEA)

Dvinskaya Guba

Onezhskaya Guba

Poluostrov Kanin

Chëshskaya Guba

Kaninskaya Tundra

Bol'shezemel'skaya Tundra

Ladozhskoye Ozero (L. Ladoga)

Onezhskoye Ozero

Beloye Oz.

Rybinskoye Vodokhranilishche

Nikel'

Gulf of Finland

Gulf of Riga

LITHUANIA S.S.R.

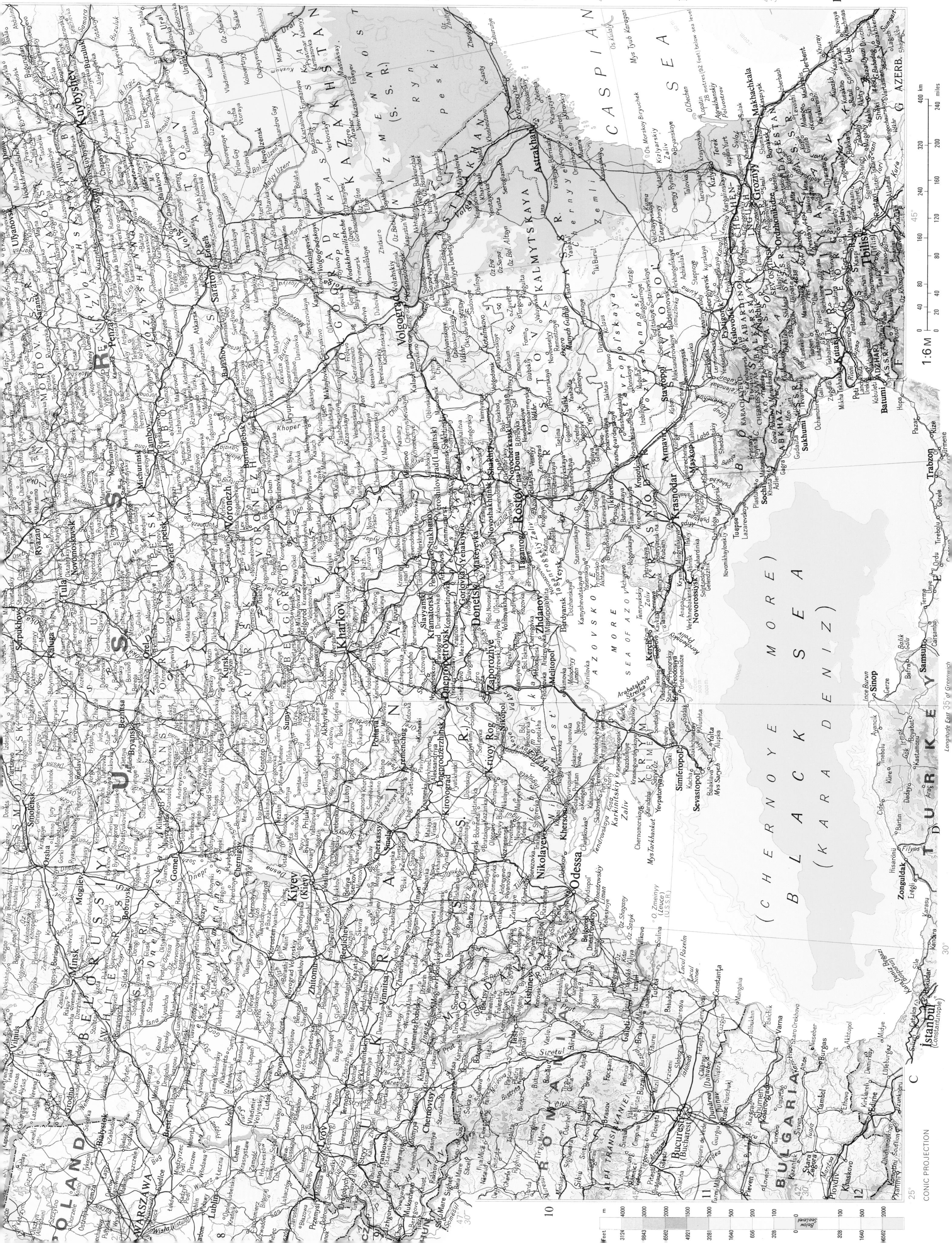
BLACK SEA
(CHERNOYE MORE)
(KARA DENIZ)
CASPIAN SEA
SEA OF AZOV
AZOVSKOYE MORE
TURKEY
ROMANIA
BULGARIA
POLAND
1:6M
CONIC PROJECTION
Longitude East 35° of Greenwich

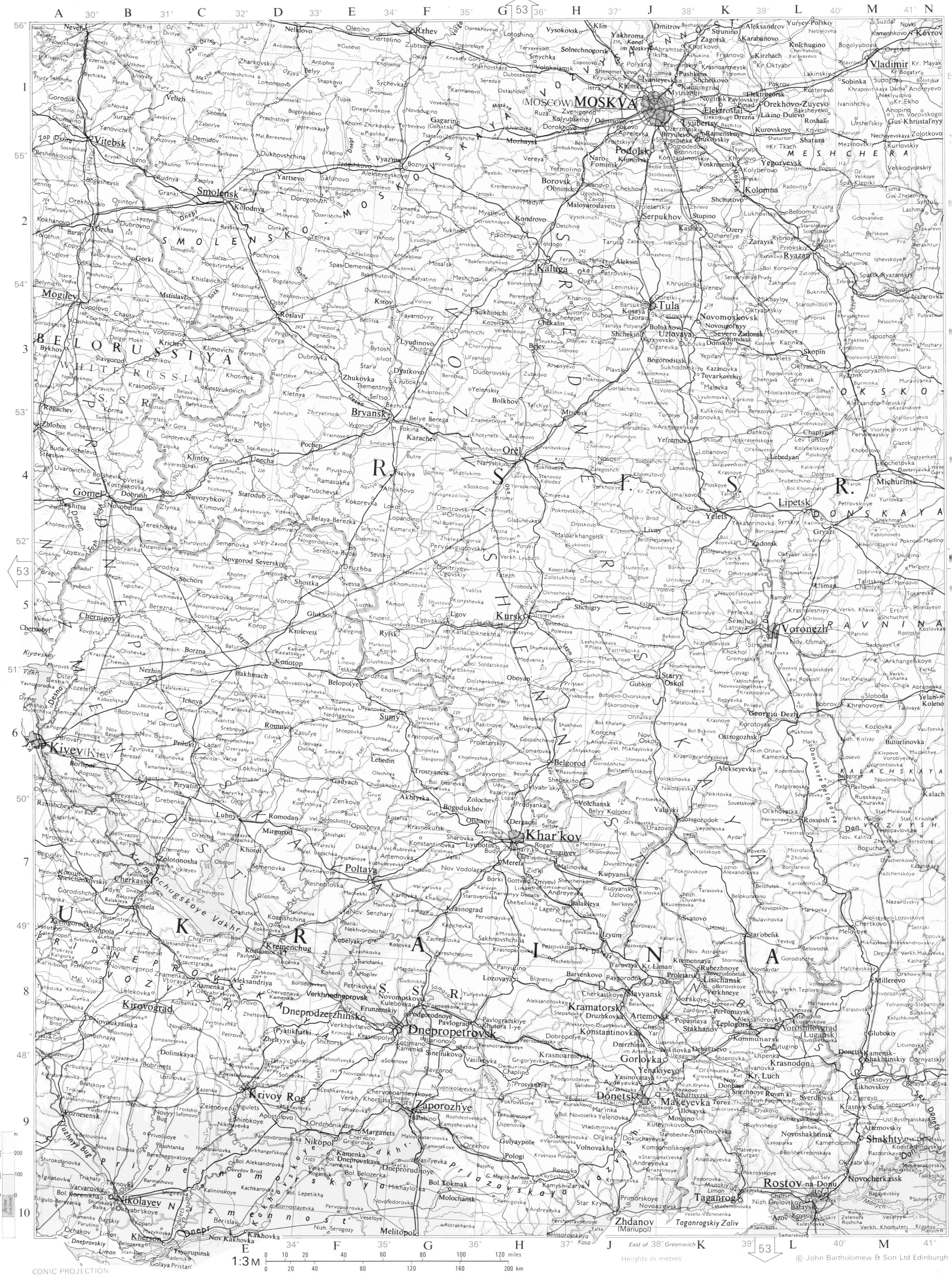

MOSKVA (MOSCOW)

BELORUSSIYA — WHITE RUSSIA — S.S.R.

R.S.F.S.R.

U K R A I N A — S.S.R.

MESHCHERA

DONSKAYA — RAVNINA

KALACHSKAYA

Vitebsk · Smolensk · Mogilev · Gomel · Bryansk · Orel · Kaluga · Tula · Ryazan · Lipetsk · Michurinsk · Voronezh · Kursk · Belgorod · Khar'kov · Sumy · Kiyev (Kiev) · Poltava · Kremenchug · Dnepropetrovsk · Kirovograd · Krivoy Rog · Zaporozh'ye · Donetsk (Stalino) · Makeyevka · Gorlovka · Voroshilovgrad (Lugansk) · Shakhty · Rostov-na-Donu · Taganrog · Zhdanov (Mariupol) · Kherson · Nikolayev · Chernigov · Cherkassy · Vladimir · Kolomna · Serpukhov · Smolensk

Taganrogskiy Zaliv

Kremenchugskoye Vdkhr. · Dneprovskoye Vdkhr.

Vladimir

CONIC PROJECTION

1:3 M

| 10 | 20 | 40 | 60 | 80 | 100 | 120 miles |

| 20 | 40 | 80 | 120 | 160 | 200 km |

East of 38° Greenwich

Heights in metres

feet — 656 — 328

200 — 100 — 0

© John Bartholomew & Son Ltd Edinburgh

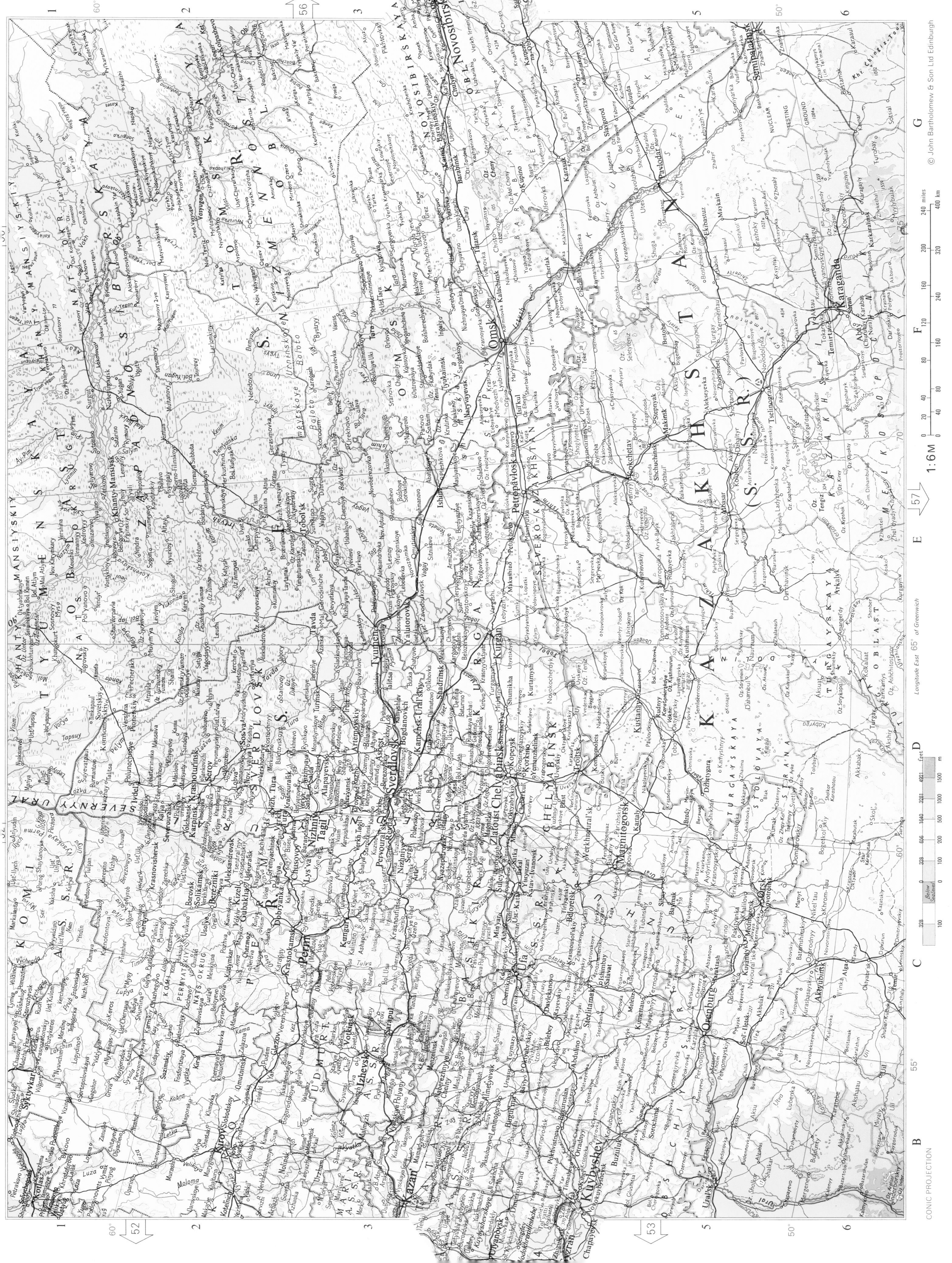
© John Bartholomew & Son Ltd Edinburgh
CONIC PROJECTION
1:6M
Longitude East 65° of Greenwich
Sverdlovsk
Chelyabinsk
Omsk
Novosibirsk
Karaganda
Tselinograd
Semipalatinsk
Kuybyshev
Orenburg
Ufa
Perm
Kazan
Kurgan
Tyumen
Petropavlovsk
Kustanay
Magnitogorsk
Aktyubinsk
Pavlodar
Kokchetav
Uralsk
Izhevsk
Tobol'sk
Khanty-Mansiysk
NUCLEAR TESTING GROUND

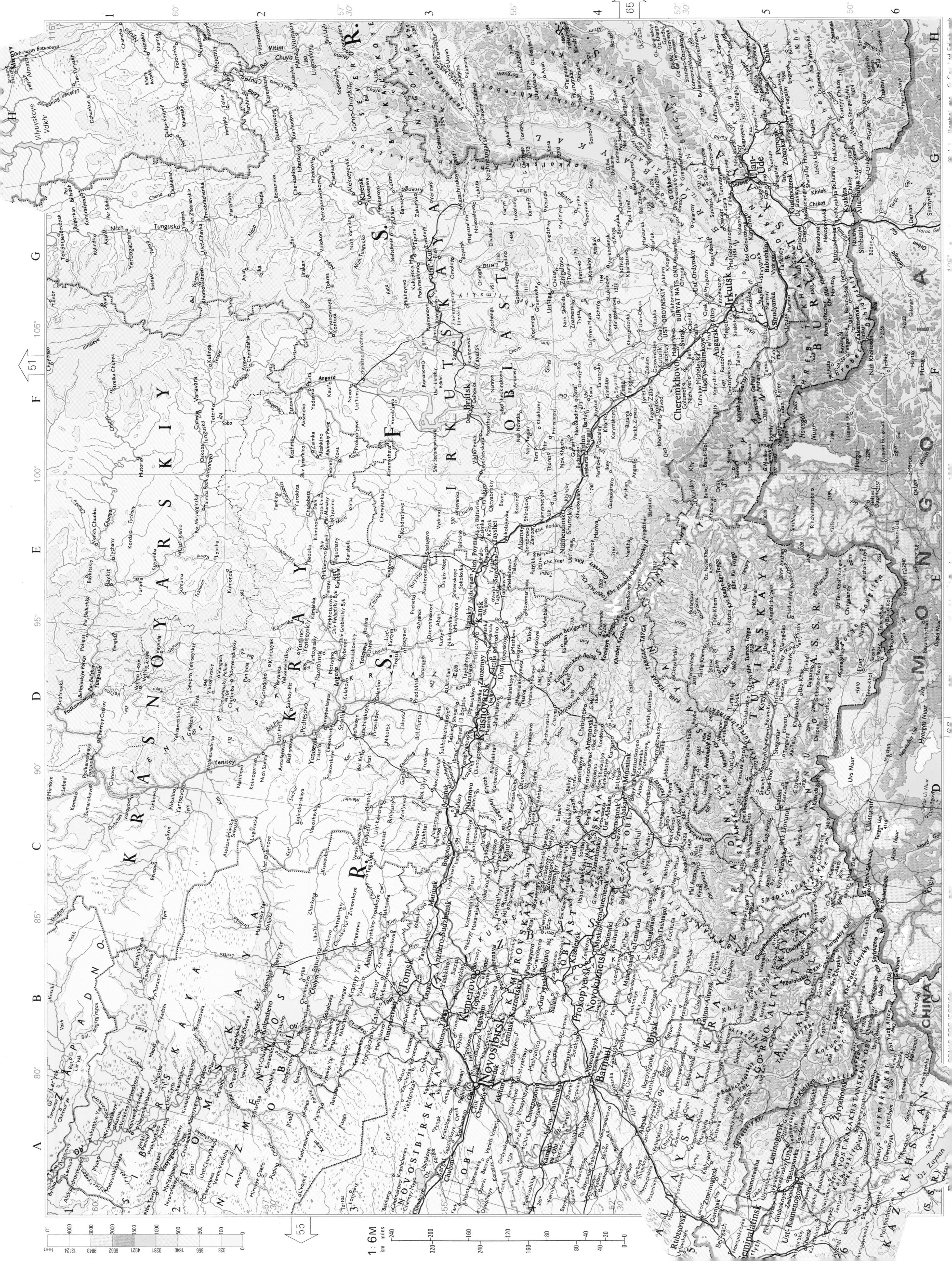
KRASNOYARSKIY KRAY
IRKUTSKAYA OBLAST'
TOMSKAYA OBLAST'
NOVOSIBIRSKAYA OBL.
KEMEROVSKAYA OBLAST'
ALTAYSKIY KRAY
TUVINSKAYA A.S.S.R.
BURYATSKAYA A.S.S.R.
M O N G O L I A
CHINA
KAZAKHSTAN S.S.R.
Novosibirsk
Krasnoyarsk
Irkutsk
Tomsk
Kemerovo
Barnaul
Ulan-Ude
Bratsk
Yenisey
Angara
1:6M

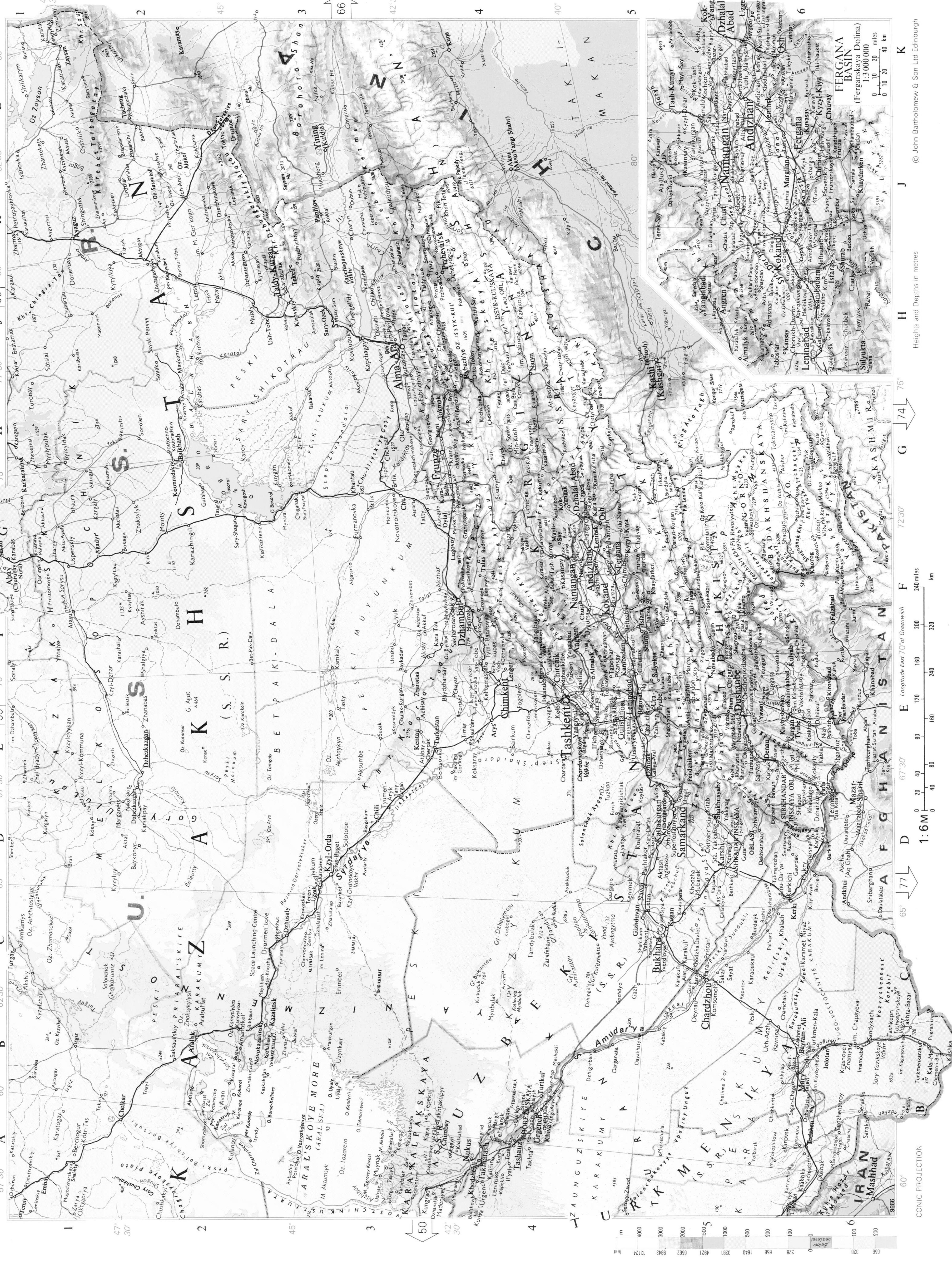

FERGANA
BASIN
(Ferganskaya Dolina)
1:3000000

© John Bartholomew & Son Ltd Edinburgh

Heights and Depths in metres

CONIC PROJECTION

1:6M

Longitude East 70 of Greenwich

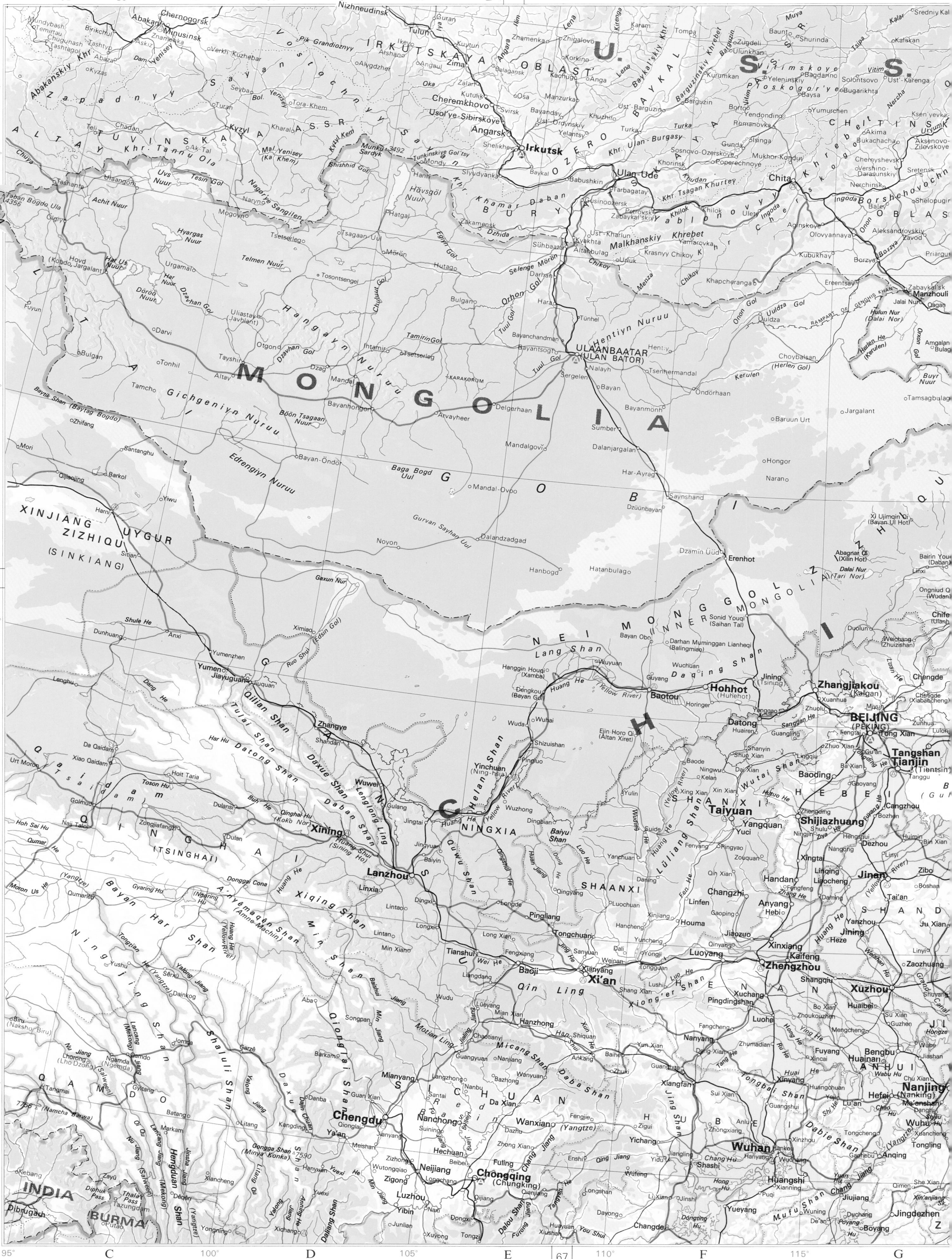

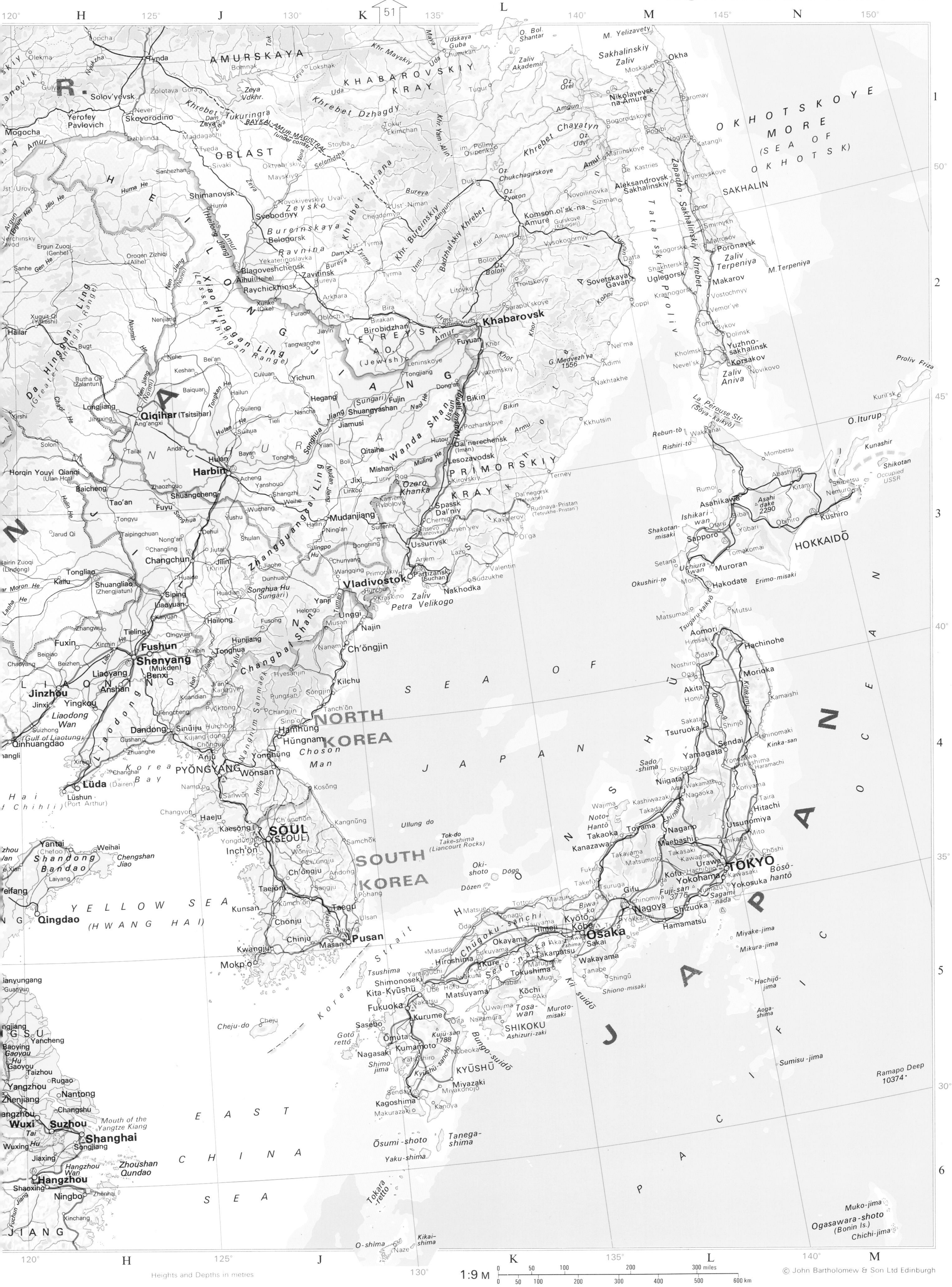
R.
AMURSKAYA
OBLAST
KHABAROVSKIY
KRAY
Khrebet Dzhagdy
Khrebet Tukuringra
BAYKAL-AMUR MAGISTRAL (under constr.)
Tynda
Skovorodino
Yerofey Pavlovich
Mogocha
Zeya
Zeya Vdkhr.
Shimanovsk
Svobodnyy
Belogorsk
Blagoveshchensk
Aihui (Heihe)
Raychikhinsk
Zavitinsk
Khabarovsk
Birobidzhan
YEVREYSKAYA A.O. (Jewish)
Komsomol'sk-na-Amure
Nikolayevsk-na-Amure
Okha
Sakhalinskiy Zaliv
O. Bol. Shantar
Tatarskiy Proliv
SAKHALIN
Aleksandrovsk-Sakhalinskiy
Poronaysk
Zaliv Terpeniya
M. Terpeniya
Uglegorsk
Makarov
Sovetskaya Gavan'
Yuzhno-sakhalinsk
Korsakov
Zaliv Aniva
La Pérouse Str. (Sōya-kaikyō)
OKHOTSKOYE MORE (SEA OF OKHOTSK)
Proliv Friza
Kuril'sk
O. Iturup
Kunashir
Shikotan
Occupied USSR
HEILONGJIANG
Amur (Heilong Jiang)
Xiao Hinggan Ling (Lesser Khingan Range)
Da Hinggan Ling (Greater Khingan Range)
Hailar
Qiqihar (Tsitsihar)
Harbin
Jiamusi
Mudanjiang
Jixi
Ozero Khanka
Bikin
Dal'nerechensk
Lesozavodsk
PRIMORSKIY KRAY
Spassk Dal'niy
Ussuriysk
Vladivostok
Partizansk
Nakhodka
Zaliv Petra Velikogo
JILIN
Changchun
Jilin
Siping
Tonghua
Changbai Shan
LIAONING
Shenyang (Mukden)
Fushun
Anshan
Benxi
Jinzhou
Liaodong Wan
Dandong
Lüda (Dairen)
Lüshun (Port Arthur)
Bo Hai (Gulf of Chihli)
Korea Bay
NORTH KOREA
Chosŏn Man
Ch'ŏngjin
Hamhŭng
Hŭngnam
Wŏnsan
P'YŎNGYANG
Sinŭiju
Kaesŏng
SŎUL (SEOUL)
Inch'ŏn
SOUTH KOREA
Taejŏn
Taegu
Kwangju
Pusan
Mokp'o
Cheju-do
Ullung do
Tok-do Take-shima (Liancourt Rocks)
Korea Strait
Tsushima
SEA OF JAPAN
NIHON-KAI
HOKKAIDŌ
Sapporo
Asahikawa
Asahi dake 2290
Kushiro
Hakodate
Muroran
Erimo-misaki
Tsugaru-kaikyō
Aomori
Hachinohe
Morioka
Akita
Sendai
Yamagata
Niigata
Sado-shima
Noto-hantō
Toyama
Kanazawa
Nagano
Utsunomiya
Maebashi
TOKYO
Yokohama
Yokosuka
Bōsō-hantō
Fuji-san 3776
Shizuoka
Nagoya
Gifu
Kyōto
Kōbe
Ōsaka
Wakayama
Hamamatsu
Okayama
Hiroshima
Kure
Takamatsu
Tokushima
Matsuyama
Kōchi
SHIKOKU
Shimonoseki
Kita-Kyūshū
Fukuoka
Sasebo
Nagasaki
Kumamoto
Kujū-san 1788
Miyazaki
KYŪSHŪ
Kagoshima
Tanega-shima
Yaku-shima
Ōsumi-shoto
Tokara-retto
Miyake-jima
Mikura-jima
Hachijō-jima
Aoga-shima
Sumisu-jima
Ramapo Deep 10374
Muko-jima
Chichi-jima
Ogasawara-shoto (Bonin Is.)
PACIFIC OCEAN
JAPAN
YELLOW SEA (HWANG HAI)
Shandong Bandao
Yantai
Weihai
Qingdao
EAST CHINA SEA
Shanghai
Suzhou
Wuxi
Nantong
Hangzhou
Ningbo
Zhoushan Qundao
Mouth of the Yangtze Kiang
51

© John Bartholomew & Son Ltd Edinburgh

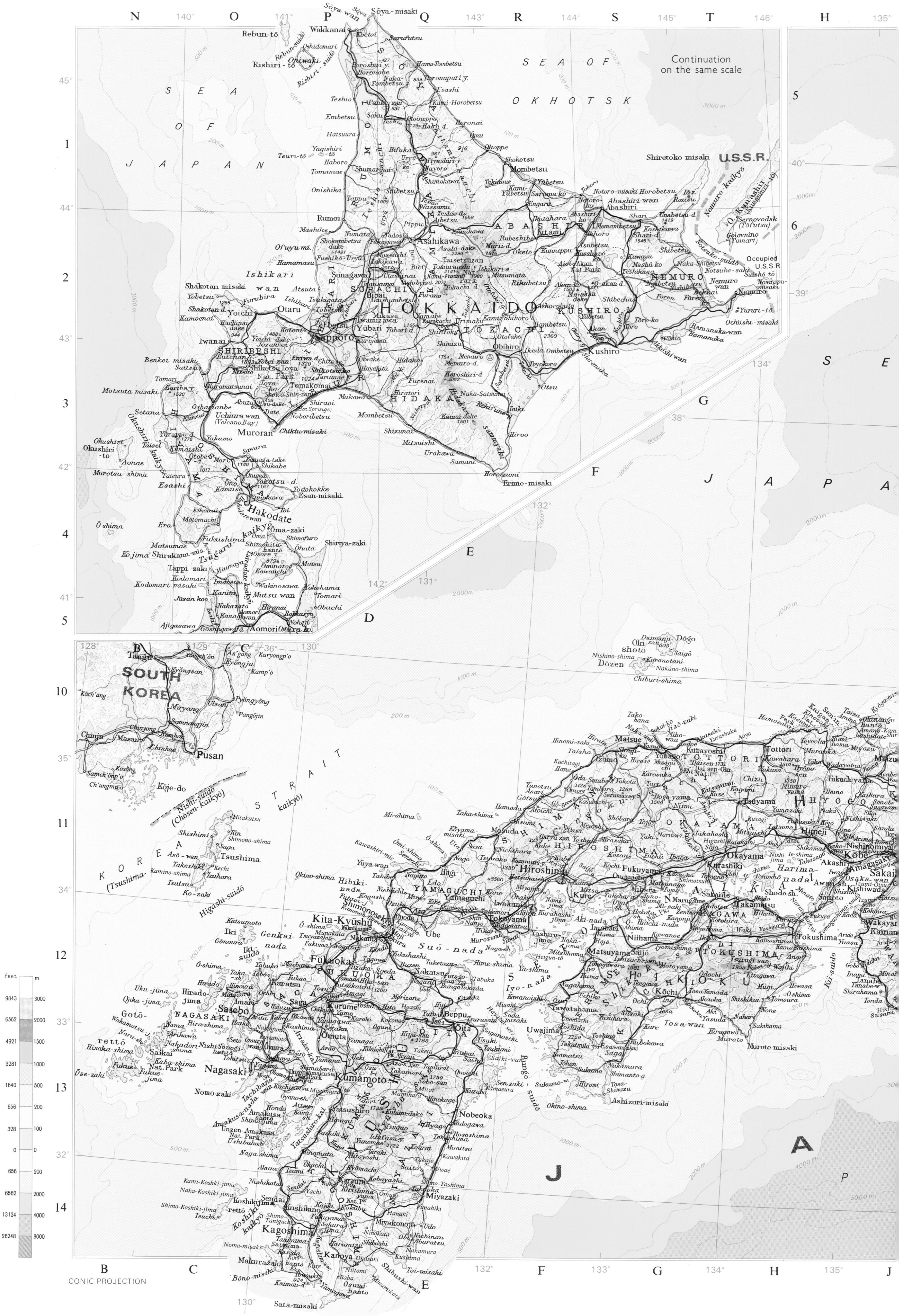
SEA OF JAPAN
SEA OF OKHOTSK
Continuation on the same scale
HOKKAIDO
U.S.S.R.
Occupied U.S.S.R.
SOUTH KOREA
KOREA STRAIT
Sapporo
Asahikawa
Hakodate
Muroran
Otaru
Kushiro
Obihiro
Wakkanai
Abashiri
Nemuro
Aomori
Pusan
Hiroshima
Okayama
Fukuoka
Kita-Kyūshū
Kumamoto
Nagasaki
Kagoshima
Miyazaki
Matsuyama
Kōchi
Tokushima
Takamatsu
Kōbe
Himeji
Tottori
Matsue
Ōita
Beppu
Sasebo
Shimonoseki
Tsushima
Oki-shotō
SHIKOKU
KYŪSHŪ
HONSHŪ
HYŌGO
OKAYAMA
HIROSHIMA
YAMAGUCHI
TOTTORI
SHIMANE
FUKUOKA
SAGA
NAGASAKI
KUMAMOTO
ŌITA
MIYAZAKI
KAGOSHIMA
EHIME
KAGAWA
TOKUSHIMA
KŌCHI
Tsugaru kaikyō
Suō-nada
Iyo-nada
Bungo suidō
Kii-suidō
CONIC PROJECTION
feet
m

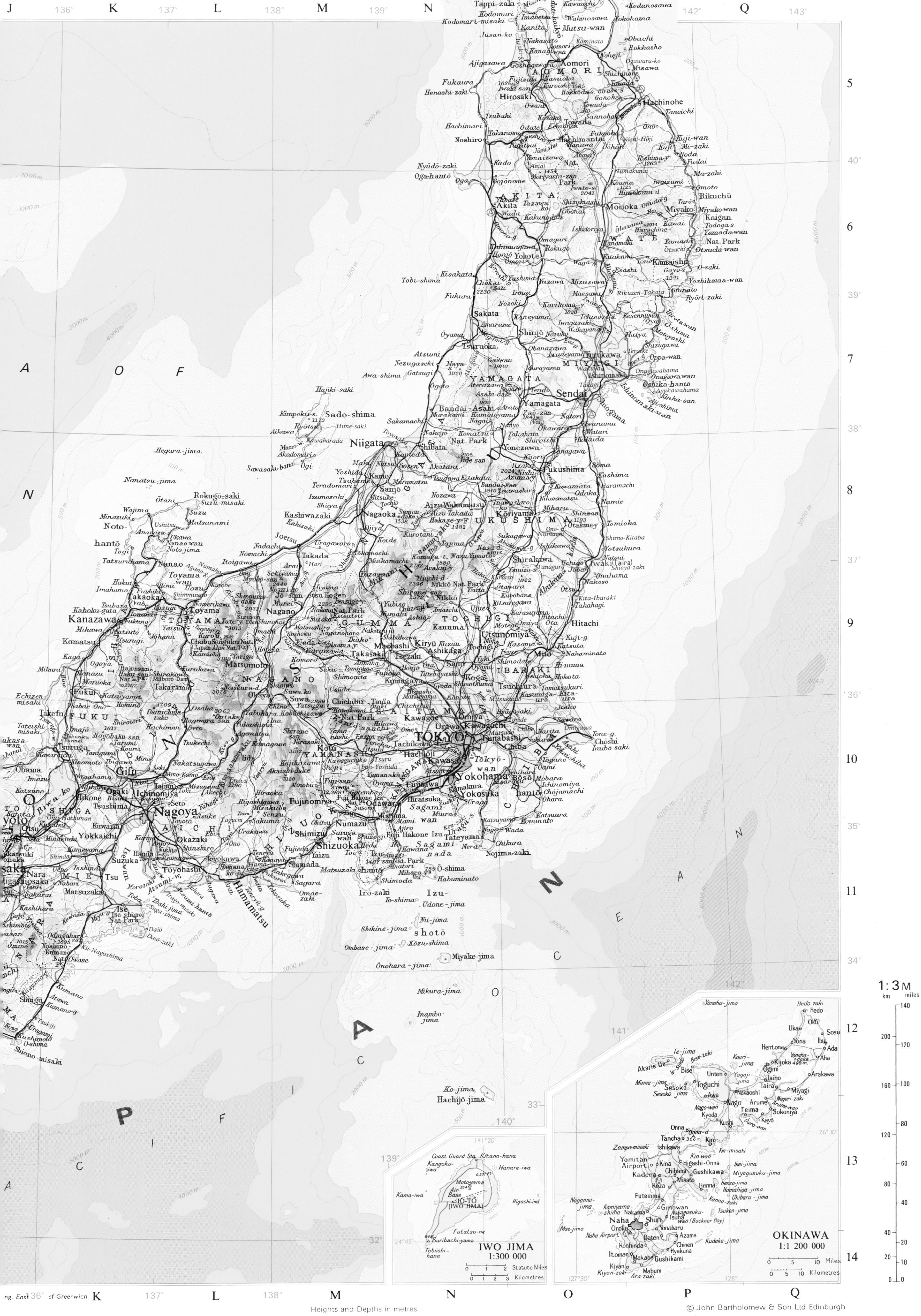

IWO JIMA
1:300 000

OKINAWA
1:1 200 000

1:3 M

Heights and Depths in metres

© John Bartholomew & Son Ltd Edinburgh

TOKYO

A
B
C
D
139°30′
139°45′
140°00′
1
2
3
35° 45′
35° 30′
SAITAMA-KEN
TŌKYŌ-TO
KANAGAWA-KEN
CHIBA-KEN
TŌKYŌ-WAN
TŌKYŌ
YOKOHAMA
Kawasaki
Iruma
Shiki
Asaka
Niiza
Kiyose
Tokorozawa
Higashi-Murayama
Warabi
Hatogaya
Sōka
Toda
Kawaguchi
Yashio
Misato
Wako
Matsudo
Mizuho
Musashi-Murayama
Hōya
Tanashi
Kodaira
Kokubunji
Akishima
Tachikawa
Koganei
Musashino
Mitaka
Kunitachi
Fuchū
Chōfu
Hino
Hachiōji
Tama
Komae
Inagi
Fussa
Nerima
Itabashi
Kita
Adachi
Arakawa
Katsushika
Edogawa
Ichikawa
Funabashi
Narashino
Yachiyo
Kamagaya
Toshima
Bunkyo
Taitō
Sumida
Nakano
Shinjuku
Suginami
Shibuya
Chiyoda
Chūō
Kōtō
Urayasu
Setagaya
Minato
Meguro
Shinagawa
Ōta
Tokyo Tower
Meiji Shrine
Imperial Palace
TOKYO INTERNATIONAL AIRPORT HANEDA
Sagamihara
Machida
Midori
Nakahara
Saiwai
Tsurumi
Kanagawa
Zama
Yamato
Seya
Asahi
Atsugi
Ebina
Hodogaya
Nishi
Naka
Totsuka
Kōnan
Isogo
Minami
Chōgo
Chiba
Ichihara
Kisarazu
Tama-gawa
Arakawa-hosuiro
Edo-gawa
Tsurumi-gawa
Tōkyō-kō

OSAKA

A
B
C
D
135°15′
135°30′
135°45′
See Inset
4
5
34° 45′
HYŌGO-KEN
ŌSAKA-FU
KYŌTO-FU
NARA-KEN
SHIGA-KEN
ŌSAKA-WAN
ŌSAKA
KŌBE
Kōbe-kō
Nishinomiya
Amagasaki
Ashiya
Takarazuka
Kawanishi
Ikeda
Minoo
Itami
Toyonaka
Suita
Senri
Settsu
Ibaraki
Takatsuki
Hirakata
Neyagawa
Moriguchi
Kadoma
Daitō
Higashi-Ōsaka
Yao
Kashiwara
Fujiidera
Matsubara
Habikino
Sakai
Takaishi
Sanda
Inada
Dōjō
Arima
Katano
Shijōnawate
Nagaoka
Uji
Jōyō
Kumiyama
Yawata
Ikoma
Nara
Todaiji Temple
Yamato-Kōriyama
Tanabe
Kamo
Kizu
Kisabe
Sonenji
OSAKA INTERNATIONAL AIRPORT
Ōsaka Castle
Ōsaka-kō
Lighthouse
Nishi-Yodogawa
Fukushima
Higashi-Yodogawa
Higashi-Sumiyoshi
Sumiyoshi
Abeno
Tennōji
Naniwa
Minato
Konohana
Taishō
Nishinari
Ikuno
Higashinari
Jōtō
Asahi
Miyakojima
Kita
Yodogawa
Higashi
Minami
Nishi
Higashi-Nada
Nada
Fukiai
Ikuta
Hyōgo
Nagata
Suma
Nishi-Suma
Ōtori-Minami
Yamato-Takada
KYŌTO
KYŌTO-FU
Kita
Sakyō
Kamigyō
Ukyō
Nakagyō
Higashiyama
Shimogyō
Minami
Fushimi
Mukō
Nagaoka
Nijō Castle
Former Imperial Palace
Ginkakuji Temple
Yodo-gawa

© Times Books Ltd.

1:300 000

0 5 10 15 km
0 5 10 miles

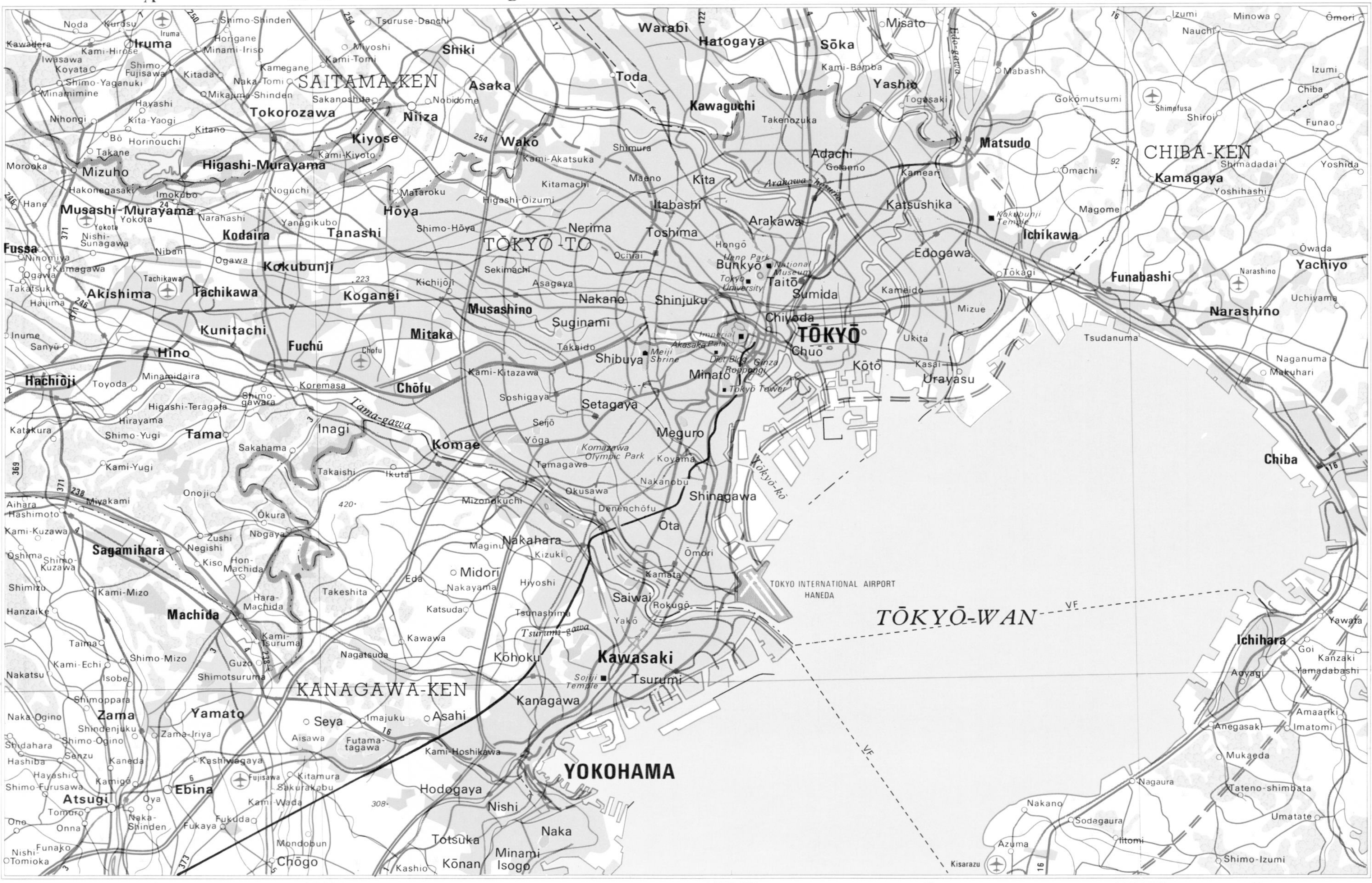

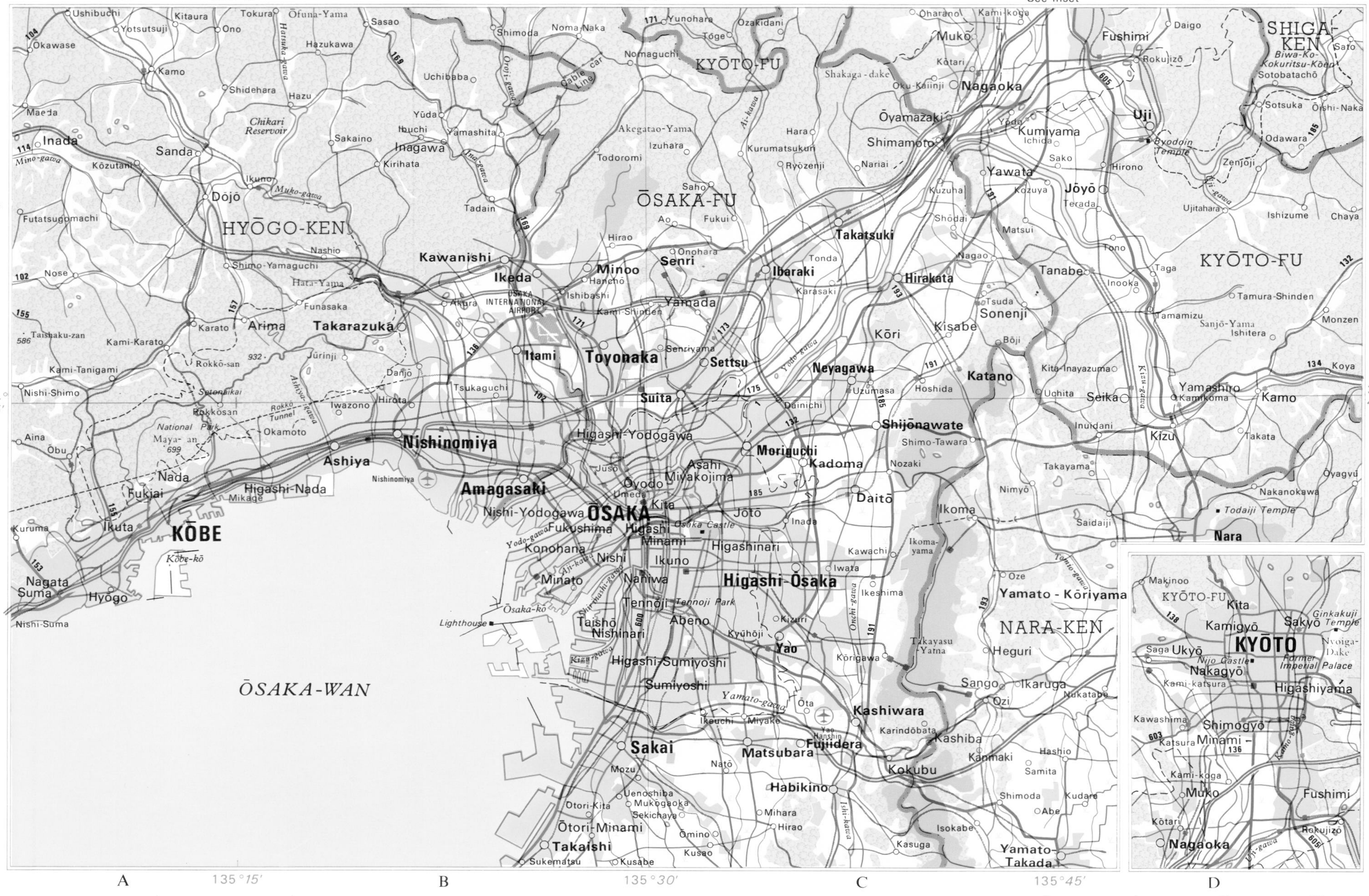

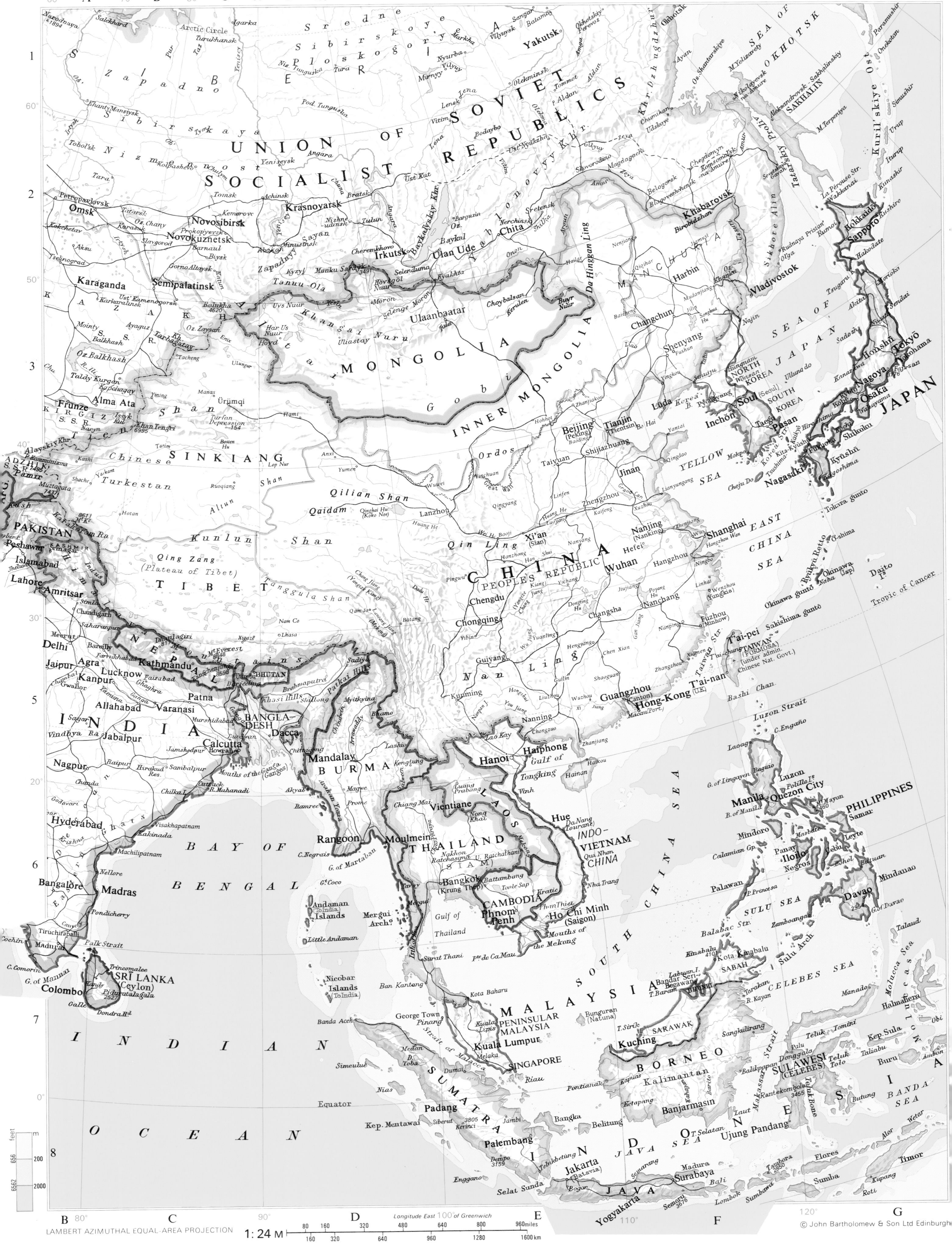

JAPAN

U.S.S.R.

NORTH KOREA

SOUTH KOREA

SEOUL

MONGOLIA

HEILONGJIANG

JILIN (KIRIN)

LIAONING

NEI MONGOL AUTONOMOUS REGION

HEBEI

SHANXI

SHANDONG

BEIJING

SEA OF JAPAN

YELLOW SEA (HUANG HAI)

BO HAI (GULF OF CHIHLI)

KOREA BAY

CONIC PROJECTION

1:6 M

Heights and Depths in metres

© John Bartholomew & Son Ltd Edinburgh

© Times Books Ltd

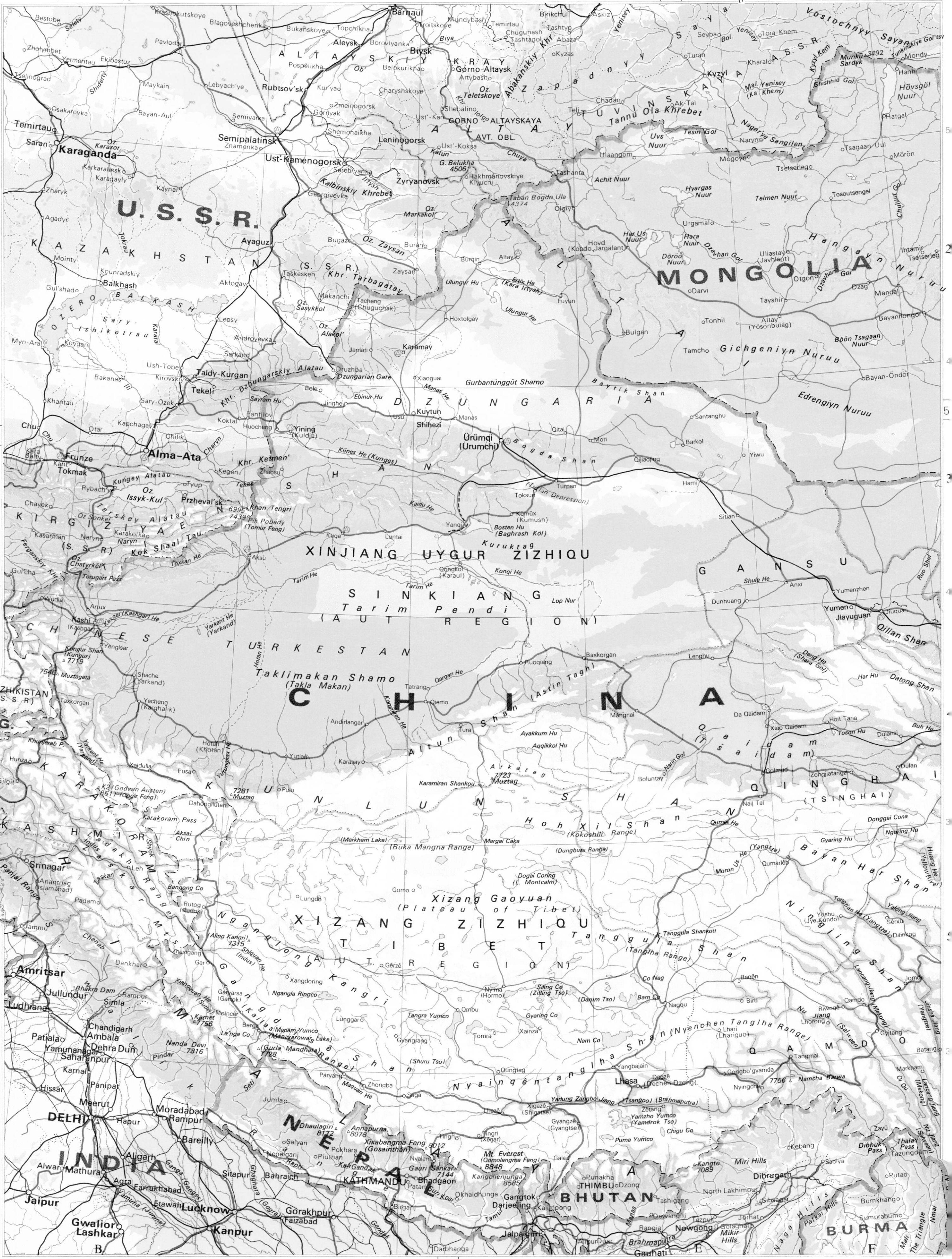

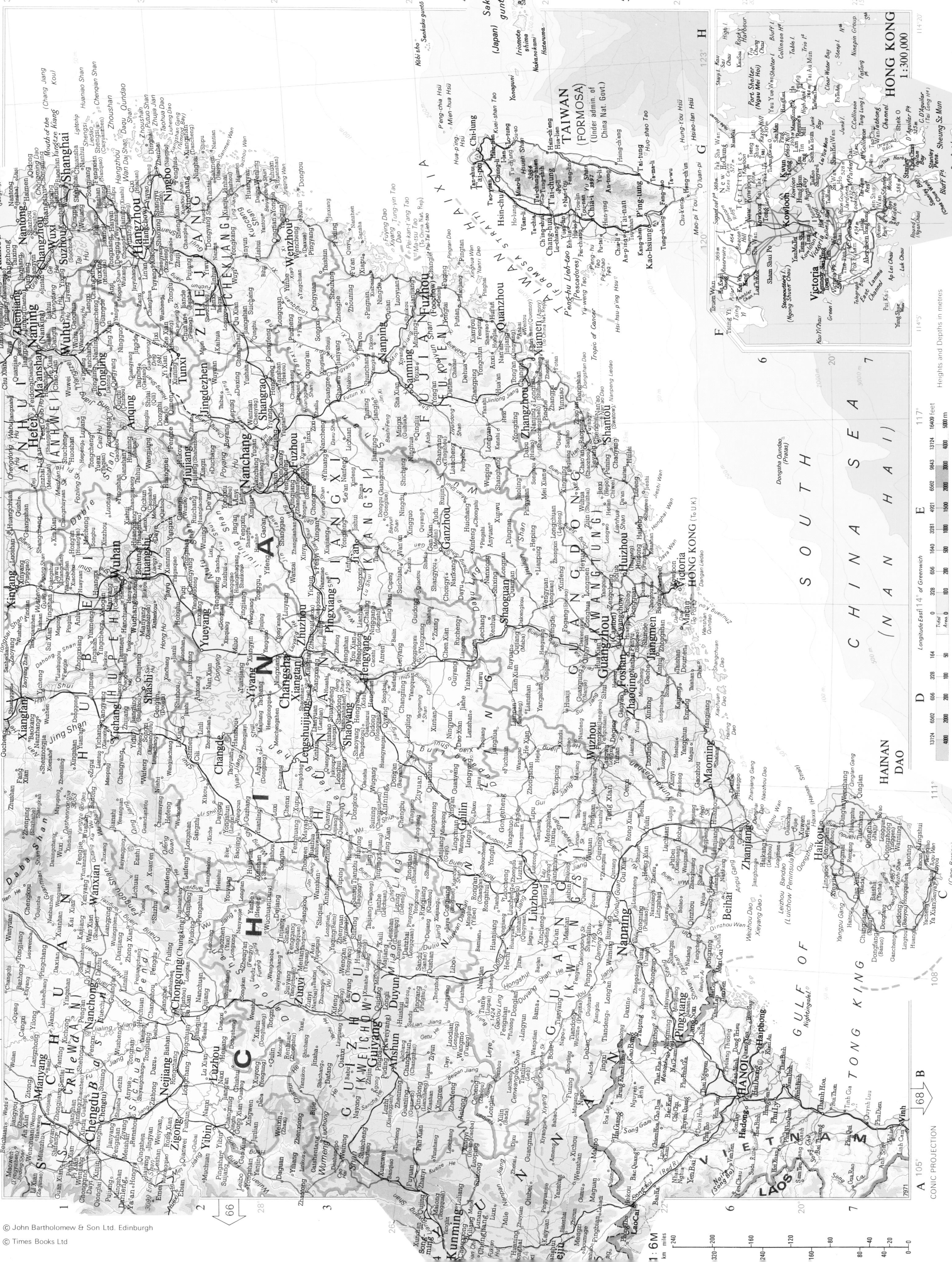

HONG KONG
1:300,000

CONIC PROJECTION

1:6M

© John Bartholomew & Son Ltd. Edinburgh
© Times Books Ltd

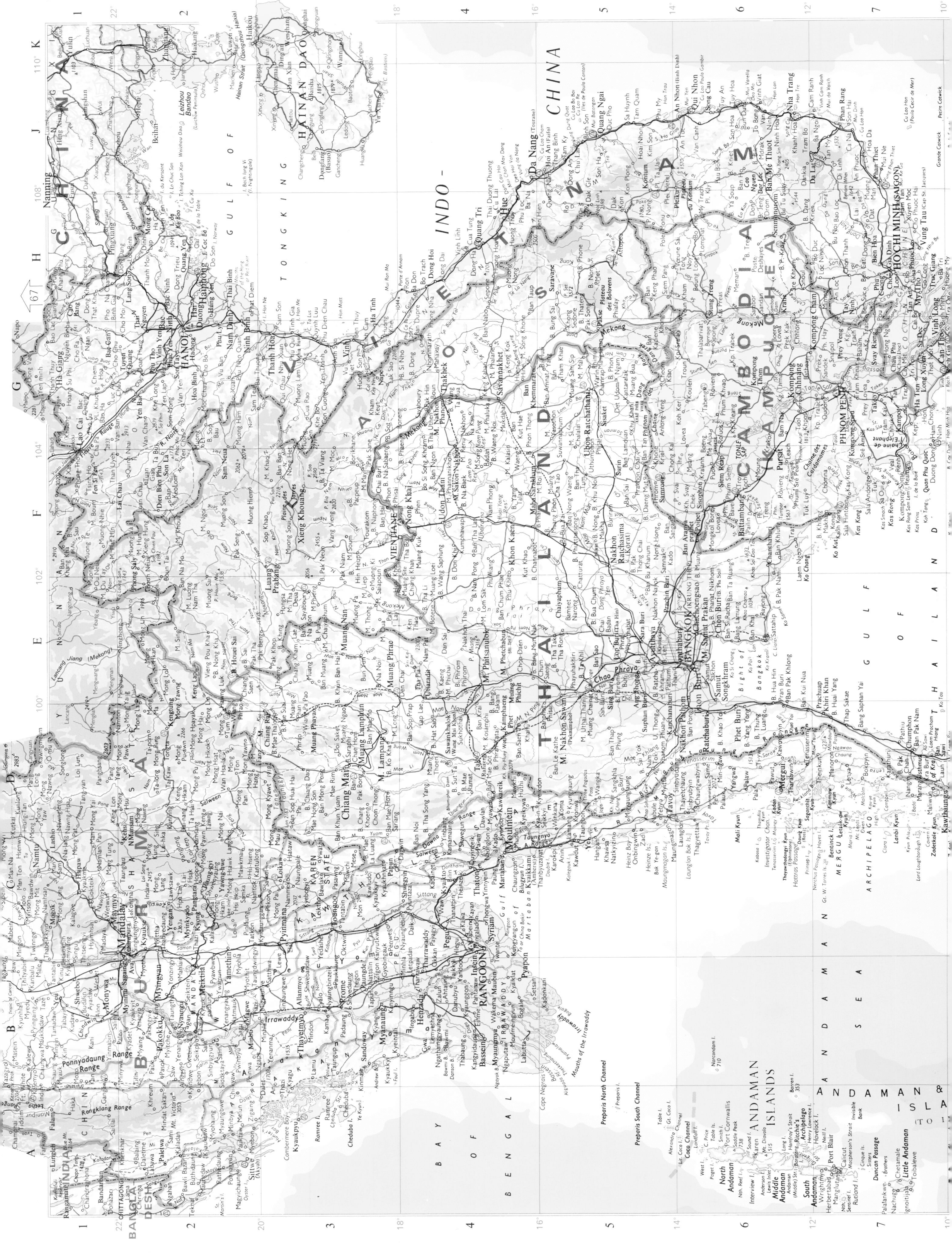

CHINA

INDO-

VIETNAM

LAOS

THAILAND

CAMBODIA · KAMPUCHEA

BURMA

SHAN STATE

KAREN STATE

KAYAH

INDIA

BANGLADESH

HAINAN DAO

GULF OF TONGKING

BAY OF BENGAL

ANDAMAN SEA

GULF OF THAILAND

MERGUI ARCHIPELAGO

ANDAMAN ISLANDS

HANOI

HAIPHONG

Da Nang

Hue

HO CHI MINH SAIGON

PHNOM PENH

BANGKOK

VIENTIANE

Luang Prabang

Mandalay

RANGOON

Moulmein

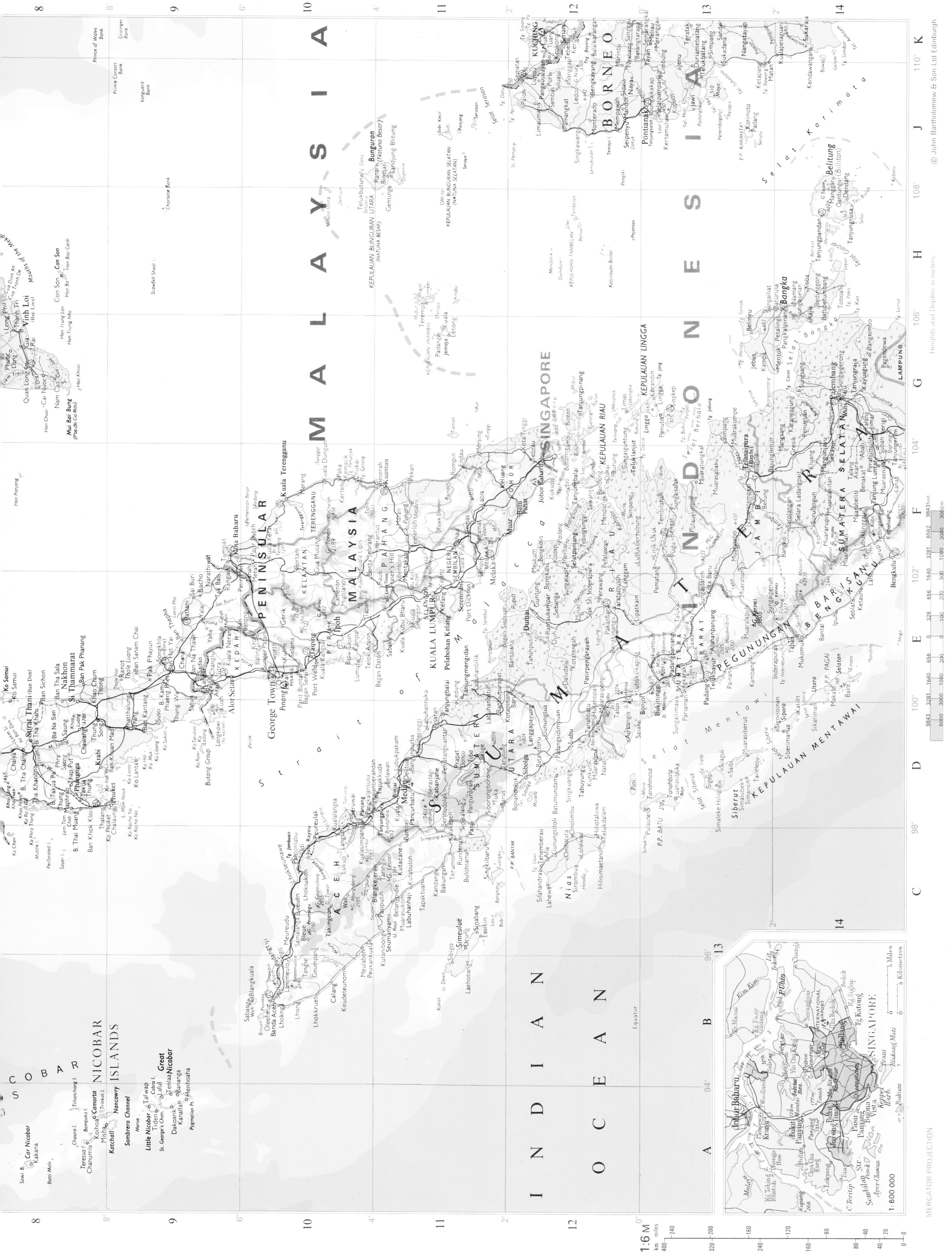

MALAYSIA

INDONESIA

BORNEO

SINGAPORE

KUCHING

PENINSULAR MALAYSIA

SUMATERA

SUMATERA UTARA

SUMATERA BARAT

KEPULAUAN RIAU

KEPULAUAN LINGGA

KEPULAUAN BUNGURAN UTARA (NATUNA BESAR)

KEPULAUAN BUNGURAN SELATAN (NATUNA SELATAN)

KEPULAUAN TAMBELAN

KEPULAUAN ANAMBAS

PEGUNUNGAN BARISAN

KEPULAUAN MENTAWAI

NICOBAR ISLANDS

Great Nicobar

Little Nicobar

Car Nicobar

Nancowry Channel

Sombrero Channel

INDIAN OCEAN

Kuala Lumpur

Kuala Terengganu

George Town

Penang

Ipoh

Taiping

Klang

Pelabohan Keling

Port Dickson

Melaka

Muar

Seremban

Johor Baharu

Pahang

Kelantan

Terengganu

Perak

Kedah

Selangor

Negeri Sembilan

Alor Setar

Kota Bharu

Medan

Padang

Pakanbaru

Jambi

Palembang

Bengkulu

Pontianak

Belitung (Billiton)

Bangka

Lampung

Bunguran (Natuna Besar)

SINGAPORE

Johor Baharu

Woodlands

Bukit Timah

Changi

Keppel Harb.

Str. of Johor

Selat Sinki

1:600 000

0 — 5 Miles

0 — 5 Kilometres

Equator

1:6 M

km 400 320 240 160 80 0

miles 240 200 160 120 80 40 0

MERCATOR PROJECTION

Heights and Depths in metres

9843 5000 3281 1640 656 328 0 328 656 1640 3281 6562 9843 ft

© John Bartholomew & Son Ltd Edinburgh

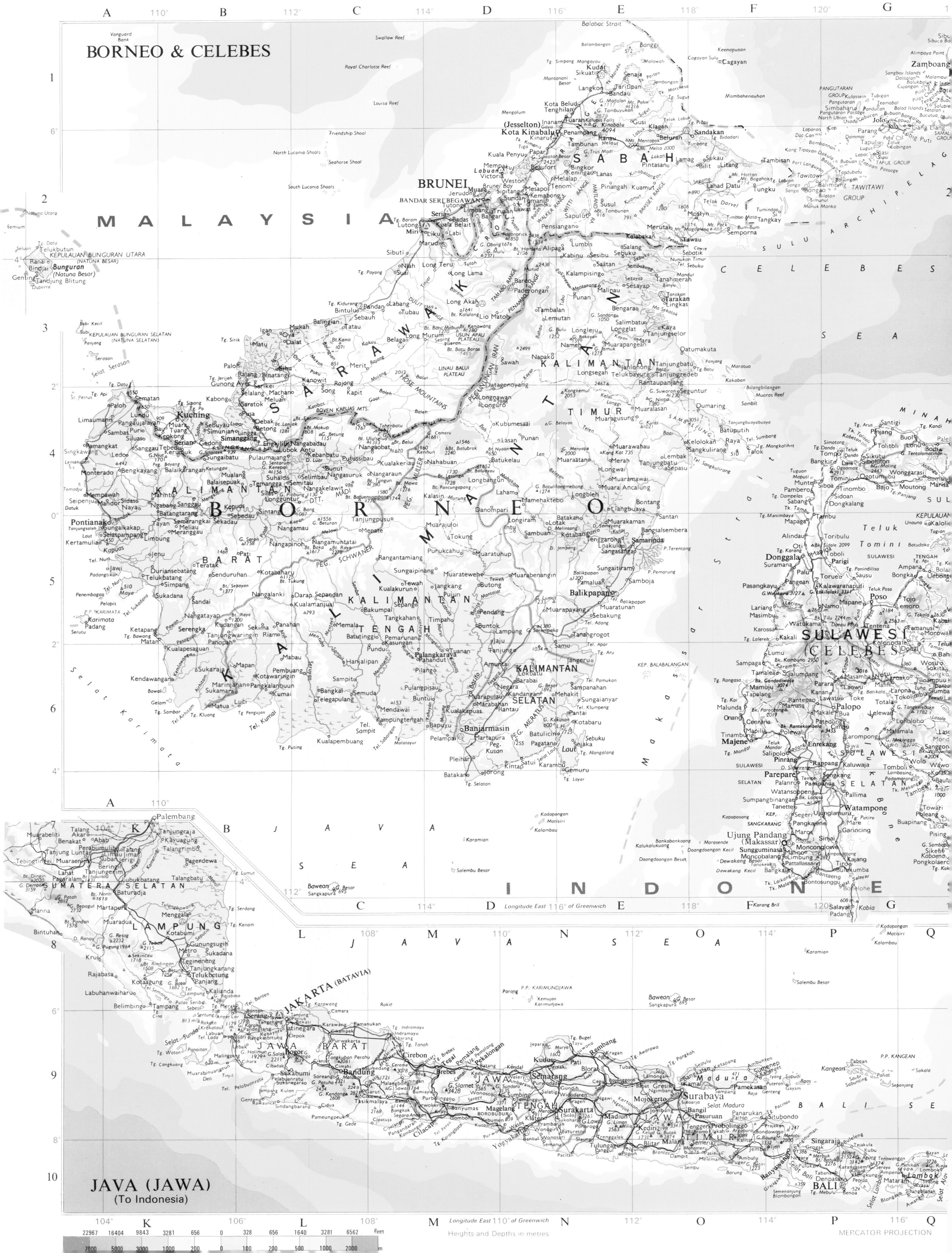

BORNEO & CELEBES

MALAYSIA

BRUNEI
BANDAR SERI BEGAWAN

SABAH

Kota Kinabalu
(Jesselton)

KEPULAUAN BUNGURAN UTARA
(NATUNA BESAR)
Bunguran
(Natuna Besar)

KEPULAUAN BUNGURAN SELATAN
(NATUNA SELATAN)

S A R A W A K

Kuching

Pontianak

KALIMANTAN
BARAT

B O R N E O

KALIMANTAN
TIMUR

Samarinda

Balikpapan

KALIMANTAN
TENGAH

Palangkaraya

KALIMANTAN
SELATAN

Banjarmasin

C E L E B E S   S E A

SULAWESI
CELEBES

Donggala
Palu

Poso

Majene

Parepare

Watampone

Ujung Pandang
(Makassar)

I N D O N E

J A V A   S E A

JAVA (JAWA)
(To Indonesia)

SUMATERA
SELATAN

LAMPUNG

PALEMBANG

JAKARTA (BATAVIA)

Serang

JAWA BARAT

Bogor
Bandung
Cirebon

Semarang

JAWA TENGAH

Surakarta
Yogyakarta

JAWA TIMUR

Surabaya
Madura
Pamekasan

Malang

B A L I   S E

BALI

Heights and Depths in metres

MERCATOR PROJECTION

Feet
22967 16404 9843 3281 656 0 328 656 1640 3281 6562
7000 5000 3000 1000 200 0 100 200 500 1000 2000 m

Longitude East 110° of Greenwich

Longitude East 116° of Greenwich

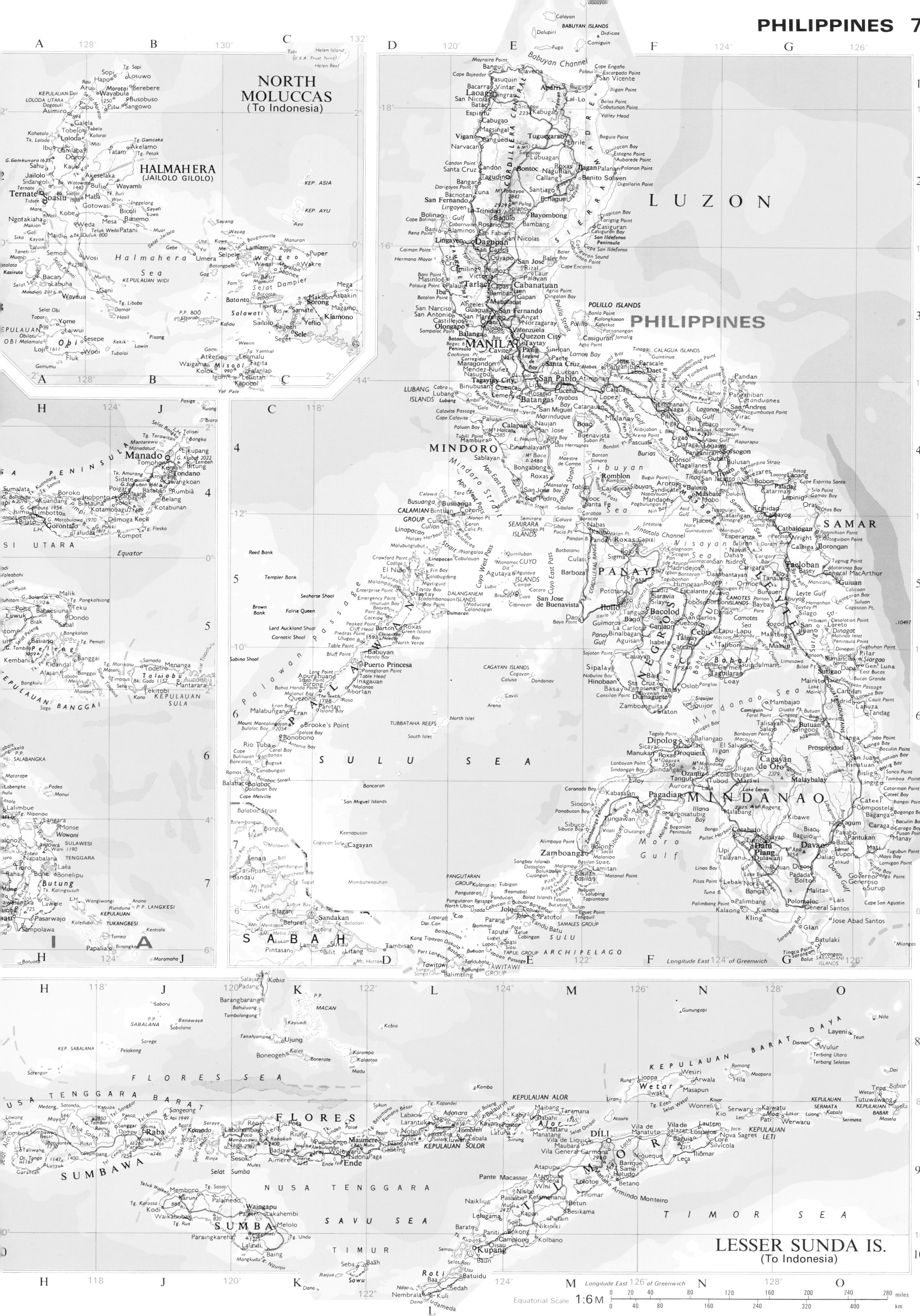
NORTH MOLUCCAS
(To Indonesia)
HALMAHERA
(JAILOLO GILOLO)
Halmahera Sea
Ternate
Sorong
Obi
LUZON
PHILIPPINES
MANILA
Quezon City
Babuyan Channel
BABUYAN ISLANDS
CORDILLERA CENTRAL
SIERRA MADRE
MINDORO
Mindoro Strait
Sibuyan Sea
Visayan Sea
SAMAR
PANAY
NEGROS
CEBU
LEYTE
Bohol
Mindanao Sea
MINDANAO
Moro Gulf
Davao Gulf
Zamboanga
Davao
Cagayan de Oro
Iloilo
Bacolod
Tacloban
Puerto Princesa
PALAWAN
Palawan Passage
SULU SEA
SULU ARCHIPELAGO
SABAH
Sandakan
Manado
Equator
Longitude East 124° of Greenwich
FLORES SEA
FLORES
SUMBAWA
SUMBA
NUSA TENGGARA
SAVU SEA
TIMOR
TIMOR SEA
KEPULAUAN BARAT DAYA
Wetar
DILI
Kupang
LESSER SUNDA IS.
(To Indonesia)
Longitude East 126° of Greenwich
Equatorial Scale 1:6M
miles
km

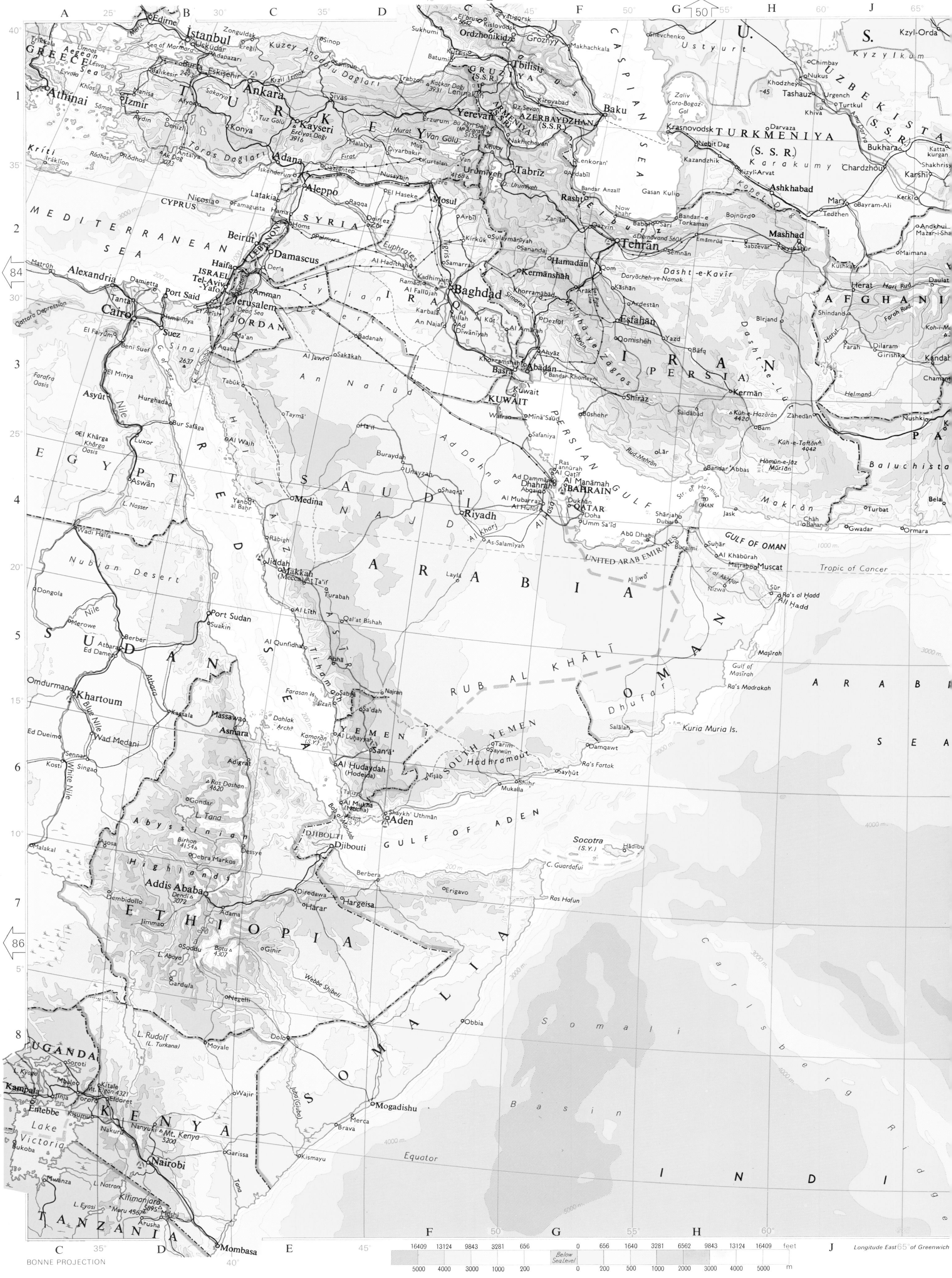

MEDITERRANEAN SEA
CASPIAN SEA
PERSIAN GULF
GULF OF OMAN
GULF OF ADEN
ARABIAN SEA
INDIAN
TURKEY
SYRIA
LEBANON
ISRAEL
JORDAN
IRAQ
KUWAIT
BAHRAIN
QATAR
UNITED ARAB EMIRATES
OMAN
SAUDI ARABIA
YEMEN
SOUTH YEMEN
IRAN (PERSIA)
EGYPT
SUDAN
ETHIOPIA
DJIBOUTI
SOMALIA
KENYA
UGANDA
TANZANIA
CYPRUS
GREECE
AFGHANISTAN
U.S.S.R.
GRUZIYA (S.S.R.)
ARMENIYA (S.S.R.)
AZERBAYDZHAN (S.S.R.)
TURKMENIYA (S.S.R.)
UZBEKISTAN (S.S.R.)
Istanbul
Ankara
Izmir
Adana
Aleppo
Damascus
Beirut
Jerusalem
Amman
Baghdad
Basra
Tehrān
Esfahān
Shīrāz
Kermān
Mashhad
Tabrīz
Baku
Tbilisi
Yerevan
Riyadh
Medina
Makkah (Mecca)
Jiddah
Kuwait
Doha
Muscat
San'ā'
Aden
Cairo
Alexandria
Port Said
Suez
Khartoum
Omdurman
Port Sudan
Asmara
Addis Ababa
Djibouti
Mogadishu
Nairobi
Mombasa
Kampala
Dubai
Abū Dhabī
Hargeisa
An Nafūd
Rub' al Khālī
Syrian Desert
Nubian Desert
Abyssinian Highlands
Dasht-e-Kavīr
Dasht-e-Lūt
Kūhhā-ye Zāgros
Toros Dağlari
Socotra (S.Y.)
Somali Basin
Carlsberg Ridge
Lake Victoria
L. Rudolf (L. Turkana)
L. Tana
Equator
Tropic of Cancer
BONNE PROJECTION
Longitude East of Greenwich
feet
m
Below Sea Level

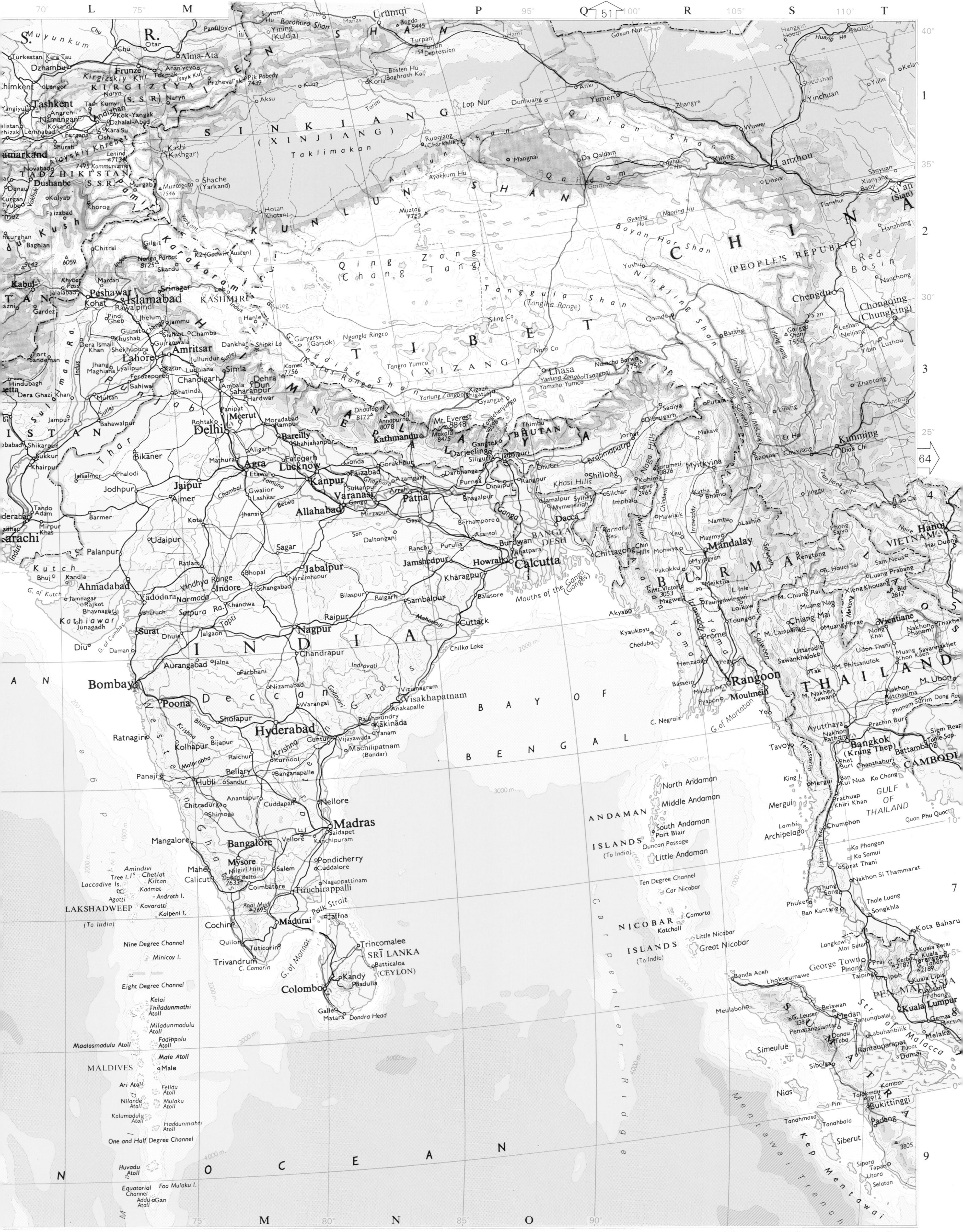

1:15 M

Heights and Depths in metres

© John Bartholomew & Son Ltd Edinburgh

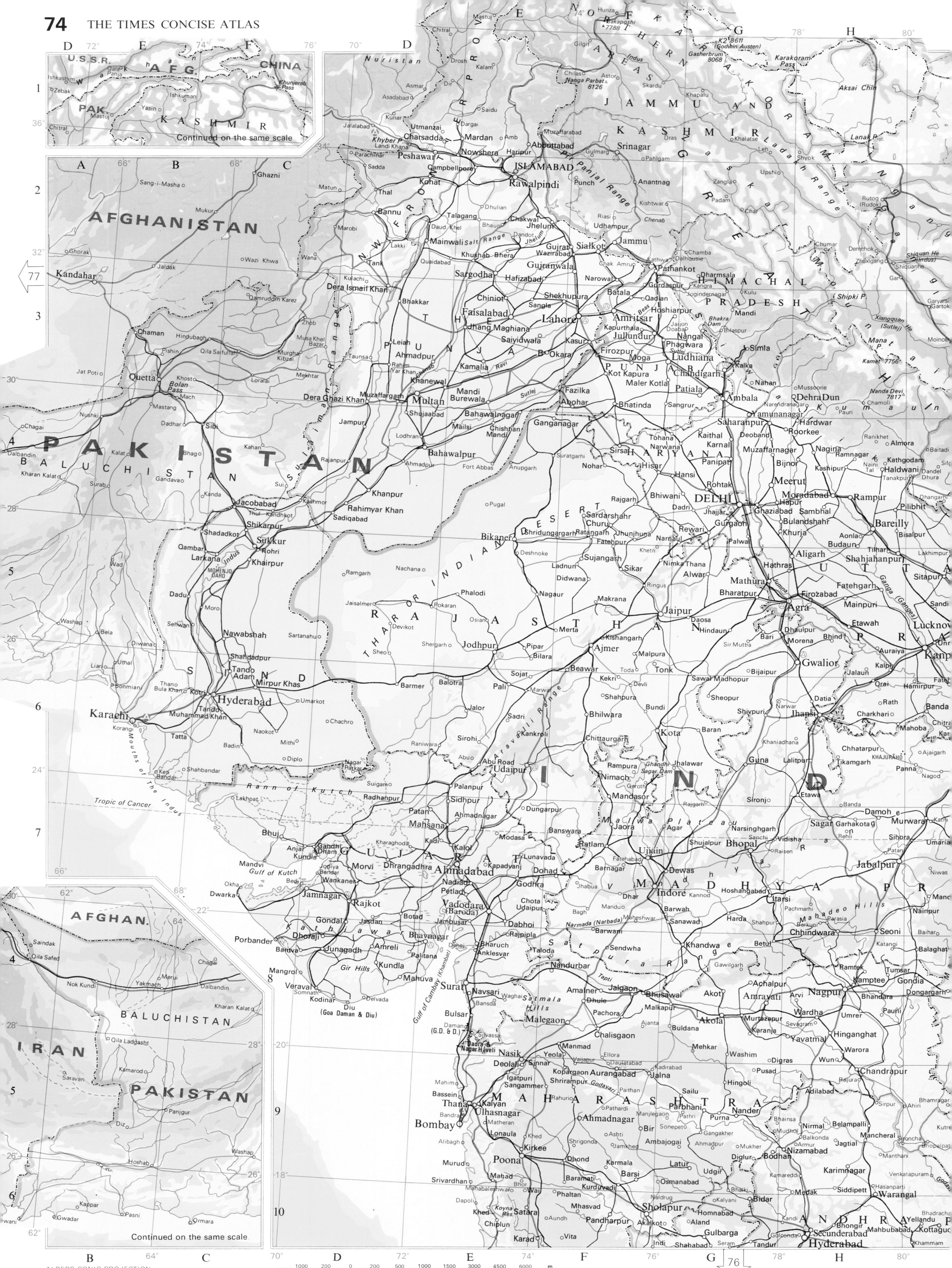

ALBERS CONIC PROJECTION

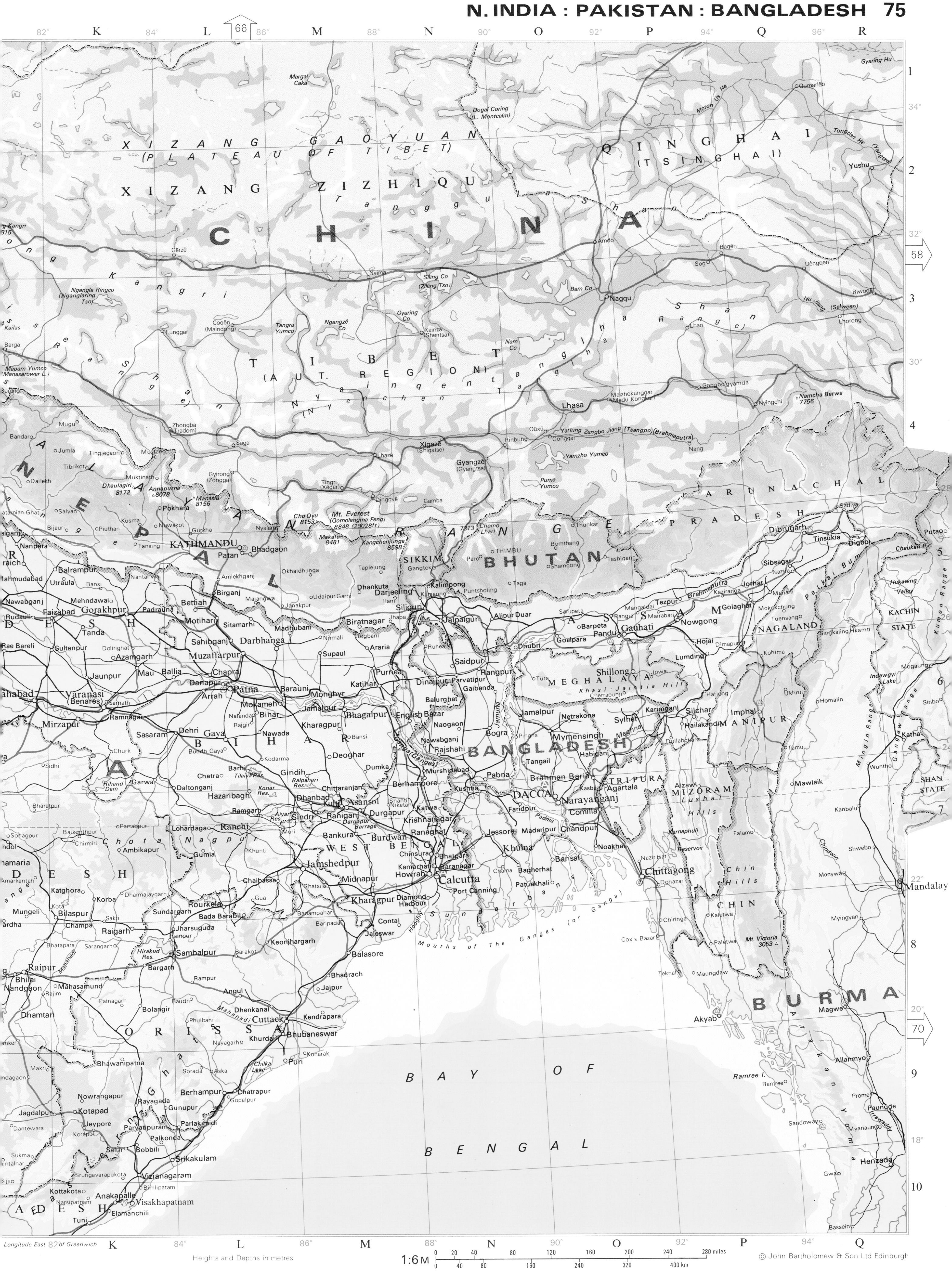

© John Bartholomew & Son Ltd Edinburgh

Longitude East 82° of Greenwich

Heights and Depths in metres

1:6 M

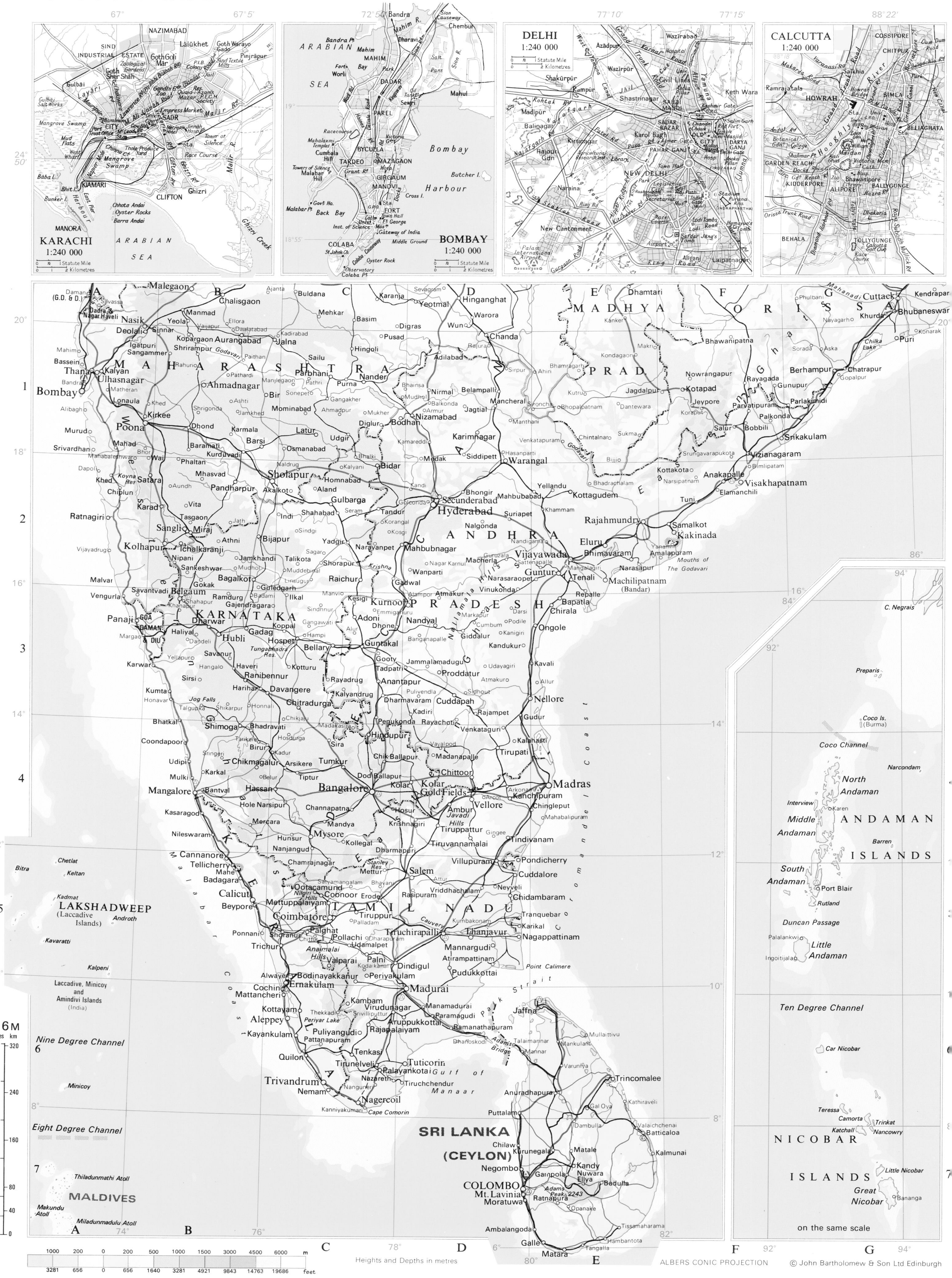

KARACHI
1:240 000

BOMBAY
1:240 000

DELHI
1:240 000

CALCUTTA
1:240 000

MADHYA PRADESH

MAHARASHTRA

KARNATAKA

ANDHRA PRADESH

TAMIL NADU

ORISSA

LAKSHADWEEP
(Laccadive Islands)

Laccadive, Minicoy and Amindivi Islands
(India)

ANDAMAN ISLANDS

NICOBAR ISLANDS

SRI LANKA
(CEYLON)

MALDIVES

Bombay
Poona
Nasik
Ahmadnagar
Sholapur
Gulbarga
Hyderabad
Secunderabad
Warangal
Bangalore
Madras
Mysore
Mangalore
Calicut
Coimbatore
Madurai
Trivandrum
Cochin
Ernakulam
Vijayawada
Guntur
Nellore
Visakhapatnam
Kakinada
Rajahmundry
Cuttack
Bhubaneswar
Puri
Berhampur
Colombo
Kandy
Galle
Jaffna
Trincomalee

Nine Degree Channel
Eight Degree Channel
Ten Degree Channel
Coco Channel
Duncan Passage

North Andaman
Middle Andaman
South Andaman
Little Andaman
Great Nicobar
Car Nicobar
Port Blair

Cape Comorin
Kanniyakumari
Adam's Bridge
Palk Strait
Gulf of Mannar

1:6 M
200 miles km 320

Heights and Depths in metres
ALBERS CONIC PROJECTION
© John Bartholomew & Son Ltd Edinburgh

on the same scale

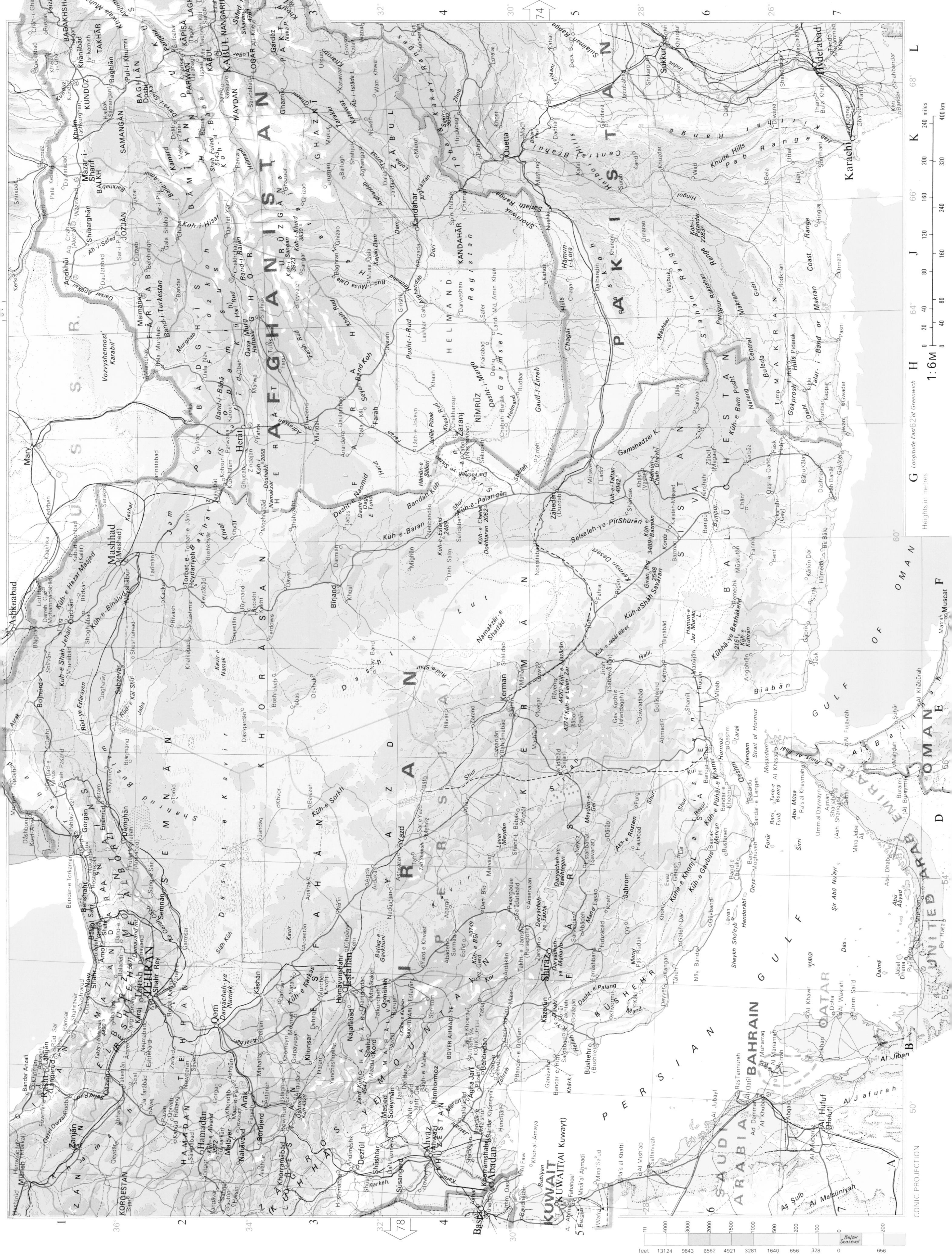
IRAN
AFGHANISTAN
PAKISTAN
PERSIAN GULF
GULF OF OMAN
KUWAIT
BAHRAIN
QATAR
UNITED ARAB EMIRATES
SAUDI ARABIA
OMAN
U. S. S. R.
TEHRAN
Mashhad (Meshed)
Herāt
Kandahar
Kābul
Quetta
Karachi
Hyderabad
Eşfahān
Shīrāz
Kermān
Yazd
Zāhedān
Ahvāz
Ābādān
Baghdad
Muscat
Dasht-e Kavīr
Dasht-e Lut
Hindu Kush
Zagros Mountains
ELBURZ
1:6M
CONIC PROJECTION
Heights in metres
Longitude East 62° of Greenwich
feet 13124 9843 6562 4921 3281 1640 656 328 0 656
m 4000 3000 2000 1500 1000 500 200 100 0 200
Below Sea Level
miles 0 20 40 80 120 160 240
km 0 40 80 160 240 320 400
74
78

TURKEY:SYRIA:IRAQ:JORDAN

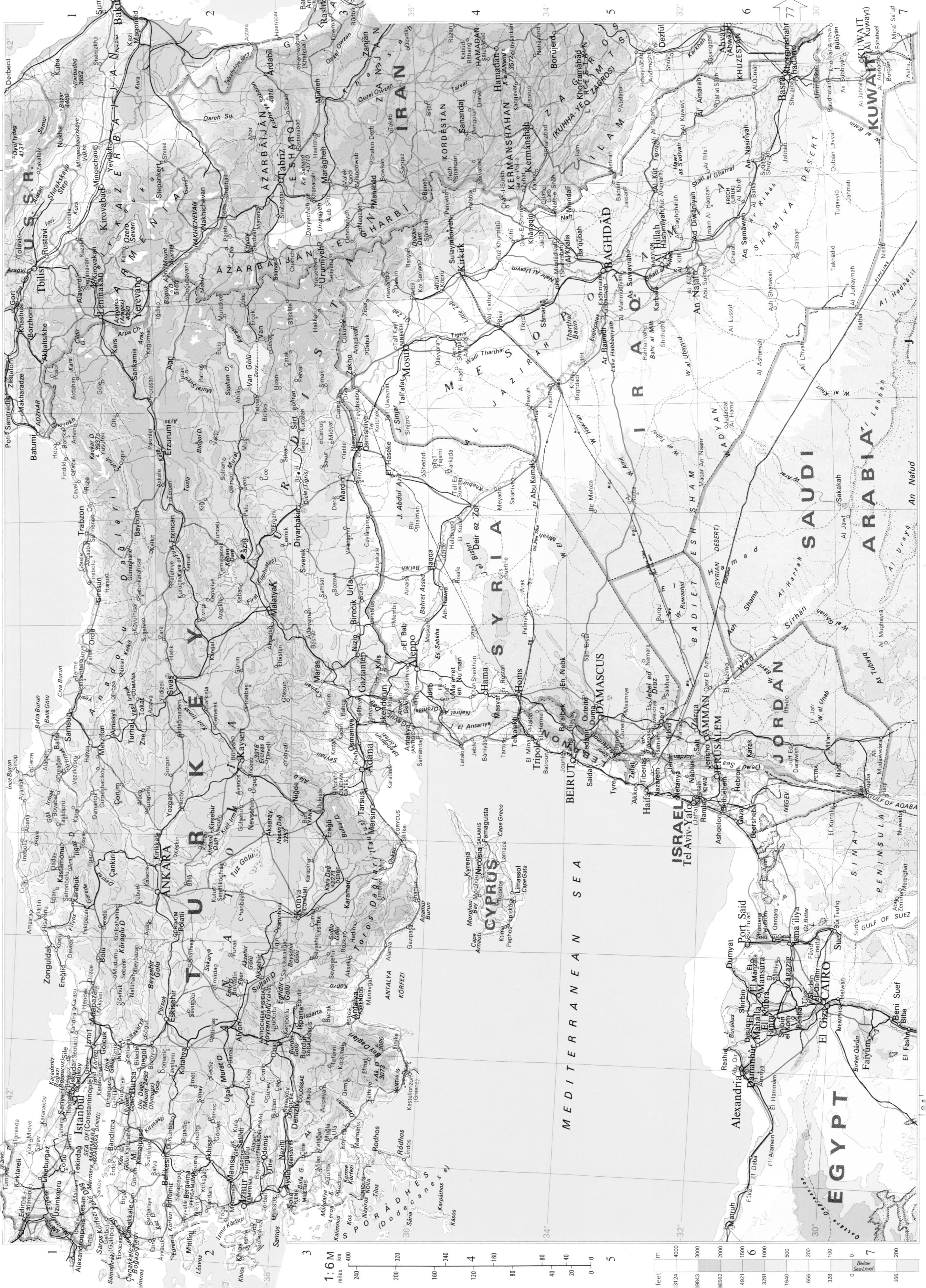
TURKEY
SYRIA
IRAQ
JORDAN
SAUDI ARABIA
IRAN
EGYPT
CYPRUS
ISRAEL
KUWAIT
U.S.S.R.
MEDITERRANEAN SEA
ANKARA
BAGHDAD
DAMASCUS
AMMAN
BEIRUT
JERUSALEM
CAIRO
Istanbul
Aleppo
Homs
Mosul
Kirkuk
Basra
Tabriz
Tbilisi
Yerevan
Baku
Adana
Konya
Izmir
Nicosia
Tel Aviv-Yafo
Alexandria
Port Said
Suez
GULF OF AQABA
GULF OF SUEZ
SINAI PENINSULA
SYRIAN DESERT
1:6M

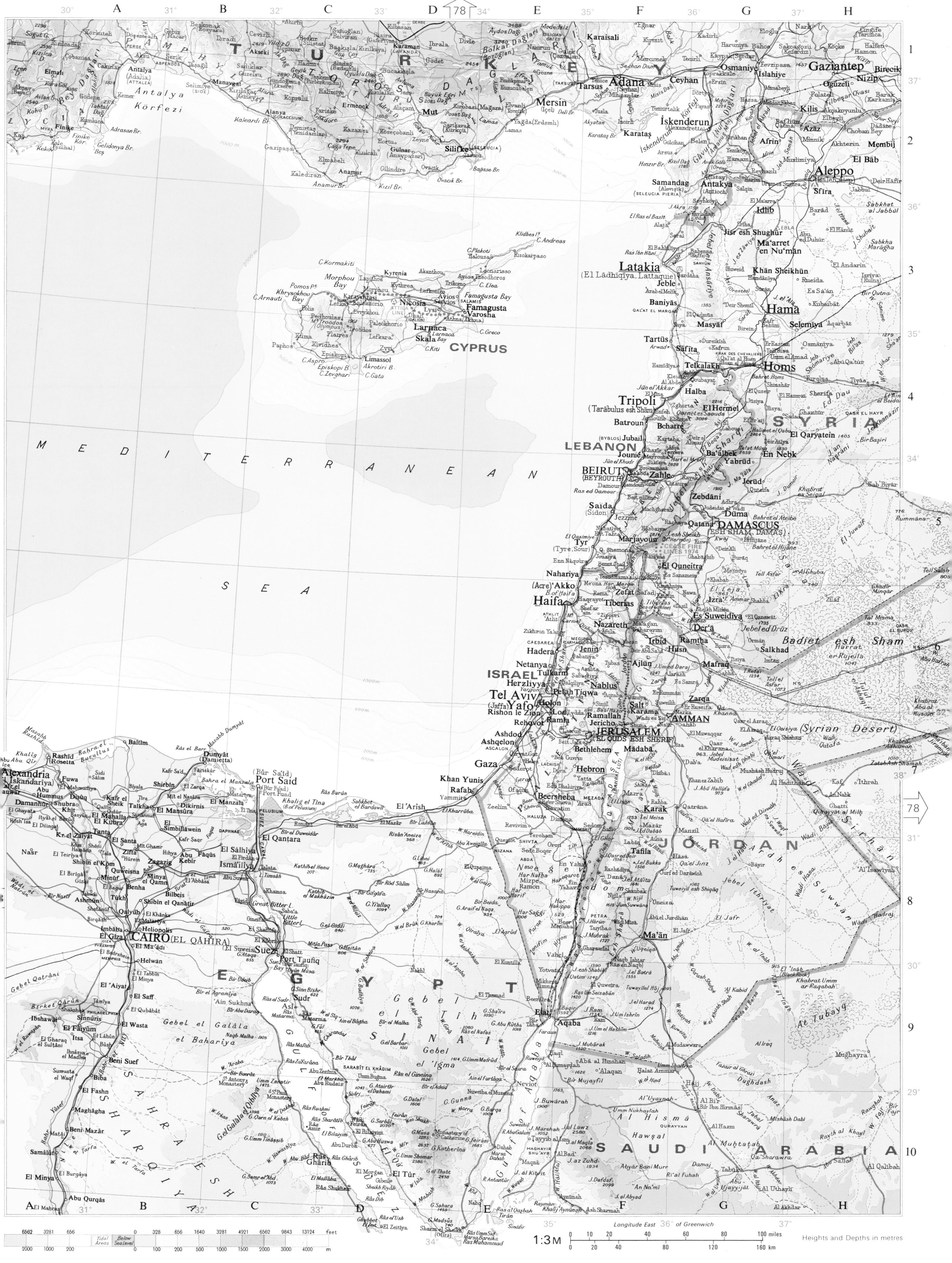

TURKEY
CYPRUS
LEBANON
SYRIA
ISRAEL
JORDAN
EGYPT
SAUDI ARABIA
MEDITERRANEAN SEA
Antalya Körfezi
Gulf of Suez
Gulf of Aqaba
SINAI
Adana
Mersin
Gaziantep
Aleppo
Latakia
Hama
Homs
Tripoli
BEIRUT
DAMASCUS
Haifa
Tel Aviv Yafo
JERUSALEM
AMMAN
Gaza
Port Said
Alexandria
CAIRO (EL QAHIRA)
Suez
Nicosia
Famagusta
Larnaca
Limassol
Aqaba
Elat
Ma'ān
CEASE FIRE LINES 1974
(Syrian Desert)
1:3M
Longitude East 36° of Greenwich
Heights and Depths in metres
Tidal Areas
Below Sea Level
feet
m
100 miles
160 km

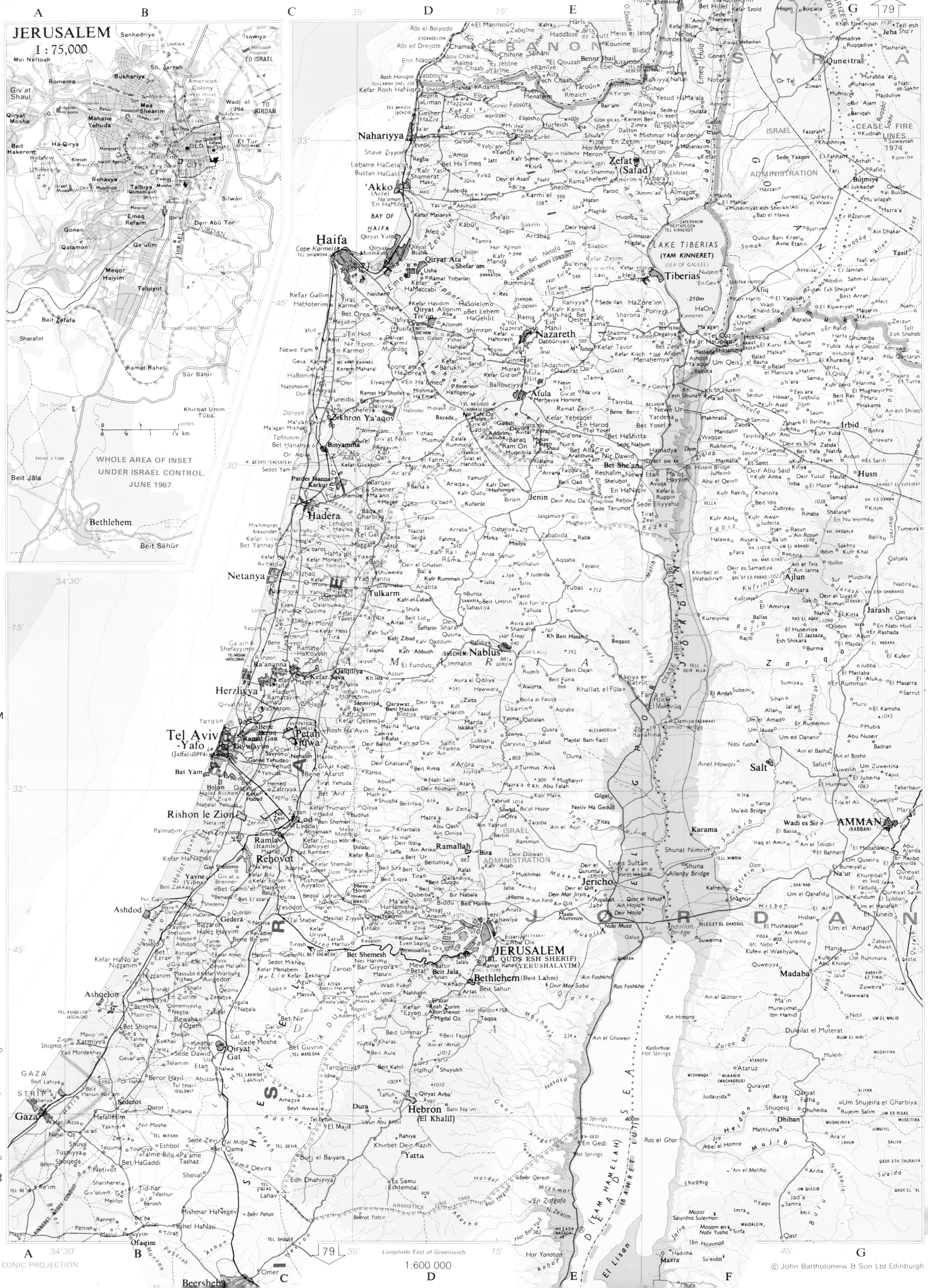

JERUSALEM
1 : 75,000

WHOLE AREA OF INSET
UNDER ISRAEL CONTROL,
JUNE 1967.

1:0.6M

1:600 000

CONIC PROJECTION

Longitude East of Greenwich

© John Bartholomew & Son Ltd Edinburgh

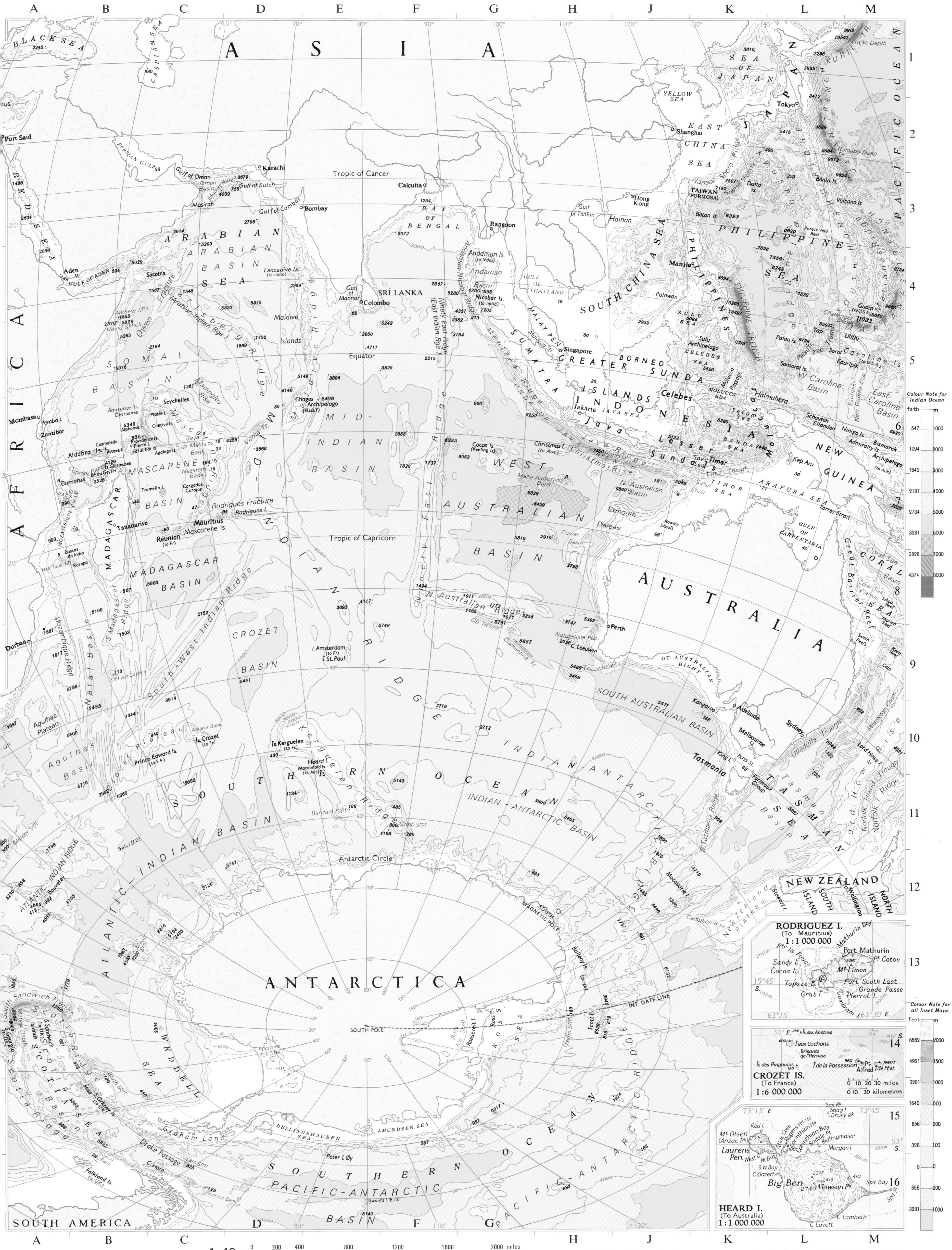

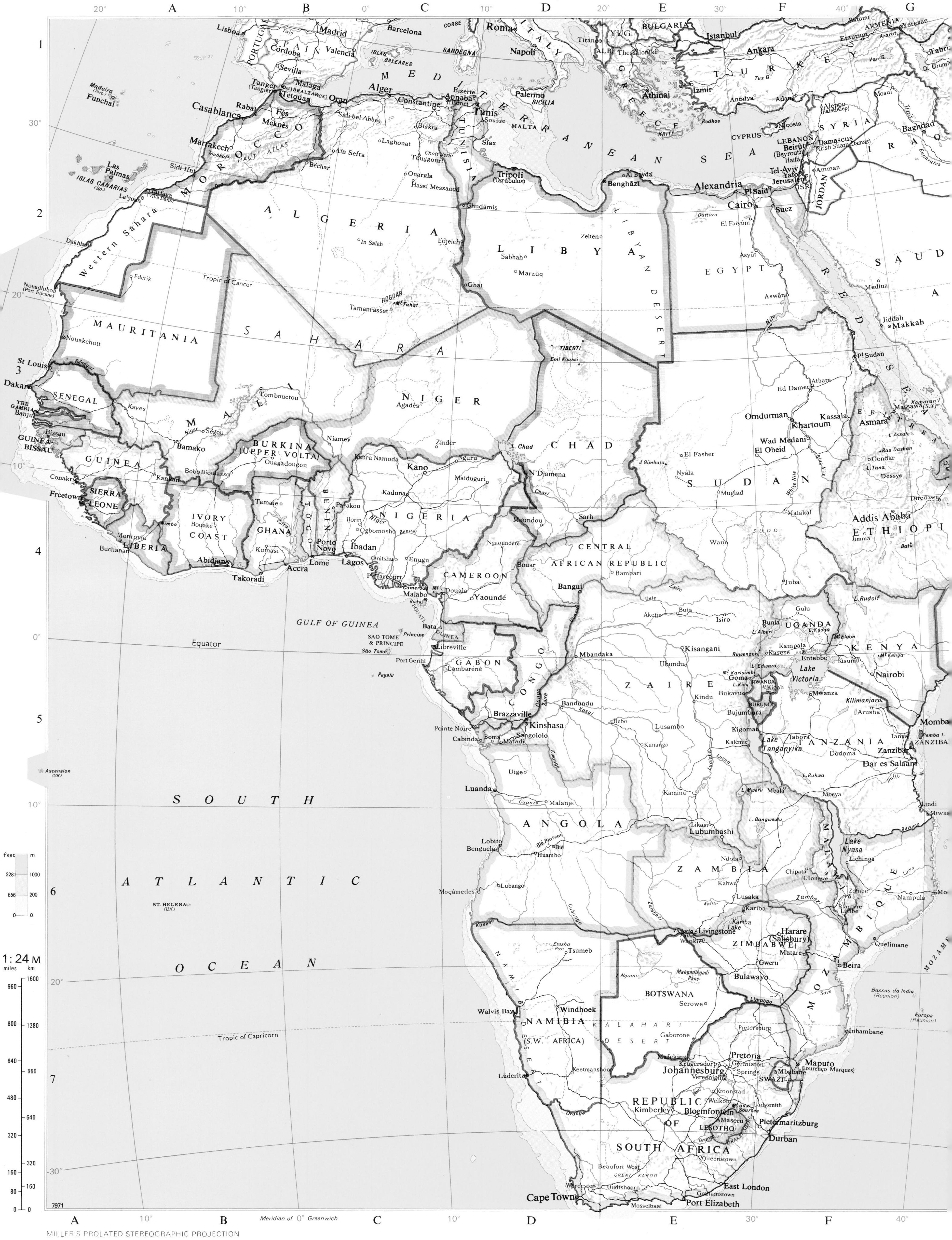

1 : 24 M

feet	m
3281	1000
656	200
0	0

miles km
1600
960
800 1280
640 960
480
640
320
160 320
160
0 0

MILLER'S PROLATED STEREOGRAPHIC PROJECTION

Meridian of 0° Greenwich

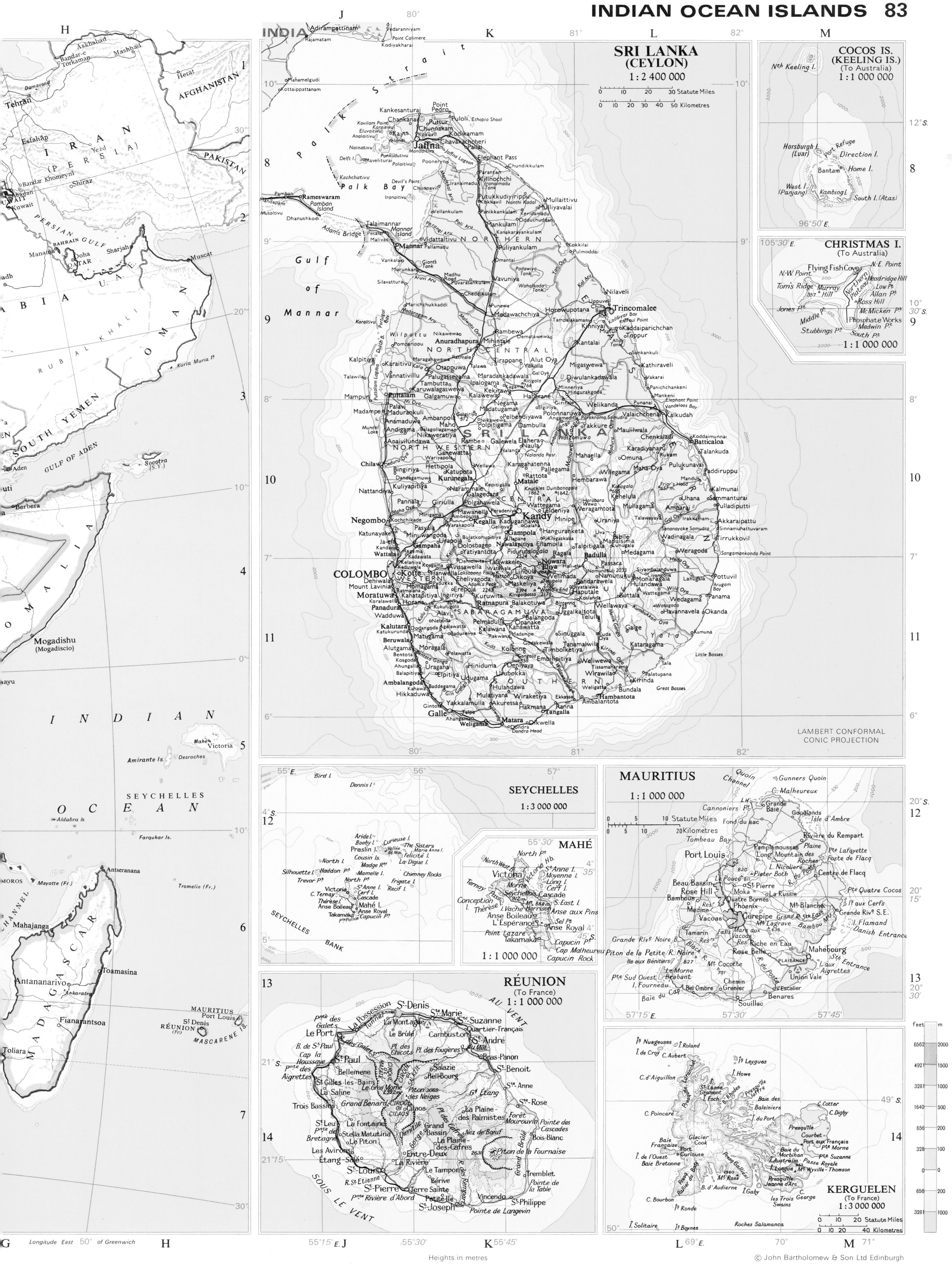
SRI LANKA
(CEYLON)
1: 2 400 000
Statute Miles
Kilometres
LAMBERT CONFORMAL CONIC PROJECTION
COCOS IS.
(KEELING IS.)
(To Australia)
1 : 1 000 000
CHRISTMAS I.
(To Australia)
1 : 1 000 000
SEYCHELLES
1 : 3 000 000
MAHÉ
1 : 1 000 000
MAURITIUS
1 : 1 000 000
RÉUNION
(To France)
1 : 1 000 000
KERGUELEN
(To France)
1 : 3 000 000
Longitude East 50° of Greenwich
INDIAN OCEAN
IRAN (PERSIA)
AFGHANISTAN
PAKISTAN
SAUDI ARABIA
OMAN
SOUTH YEMEN
SOMALIA
MADAGASCAR
Palk Strait
Gulf of Mannar
COLOMBO
Jaffna
Trincomalee
Kandy
Port Louis
St Denis
Victoria

© John Bartholomew & Son Ltd Edinburgh

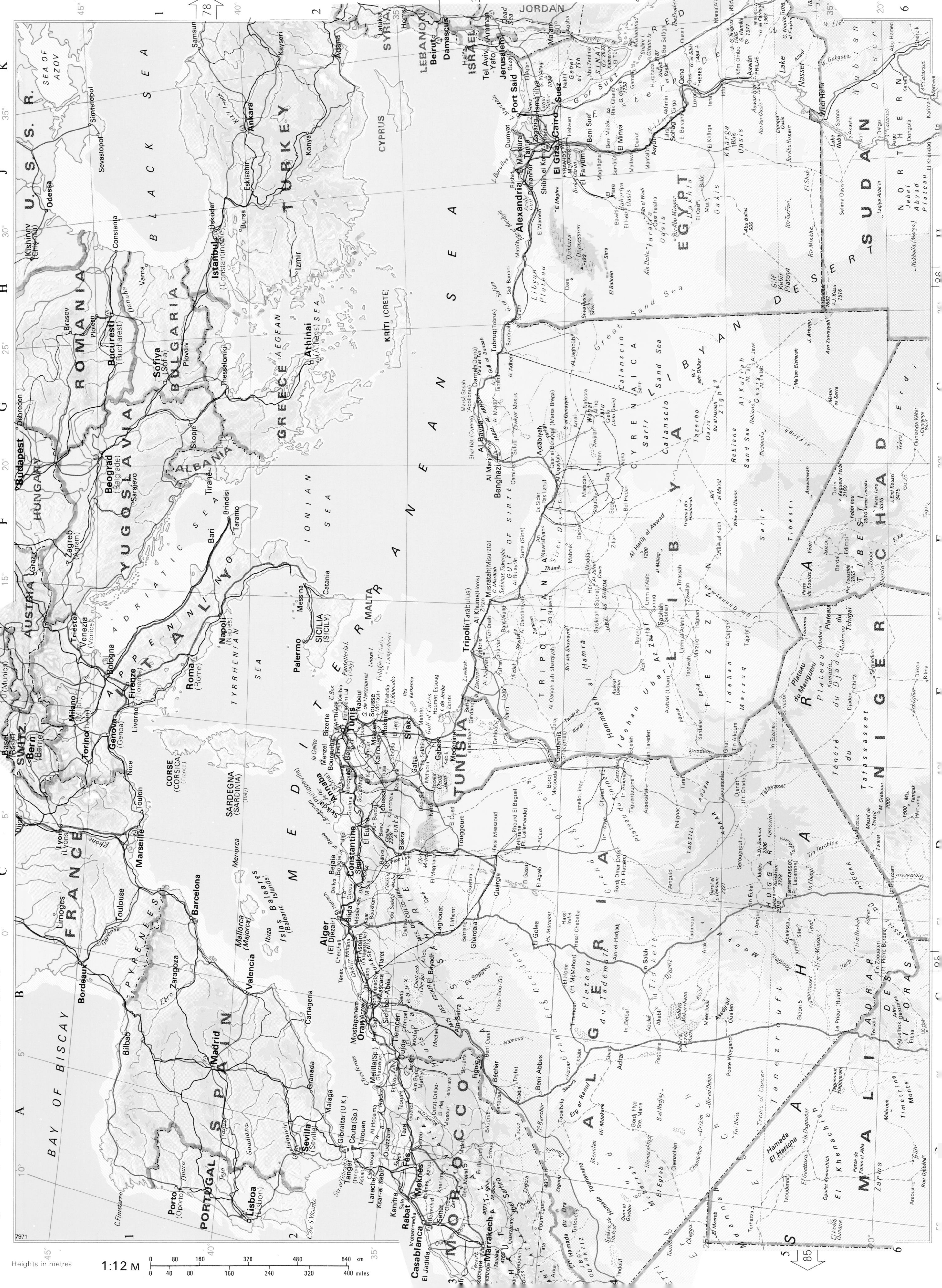

MEDITERRANEAN SEA
BLACK SEA
AEGEAN SEA
IONIAN SEA
ADRIATIC SEA
TYRRHENIAN SEA
SEA OF AZOV
BAY OF BISCAY
RED SEA
U. S. S. R.
TURKEY
ROMANIA
BULGARIA
YUGOSLAVIA
ALBANIA
GREECE
HUNGARY
AUSTRIA
SWITZ.
ITALY
FRANCE
SPAIN
PORTUGAL
MOROCCO
ALGERIA
TUNISIA
LIBYA
EGYPT
SUDAN
CHAD
NIGER
MALI
SYRIA
LEBANON
ISRAEL
JORDAN
CYPRUS
MALTA
CORSE (CORSICA)
SARDEGNA (SARDINIA)
SICILIA (SICILY)
KRITI (CRETE)
Islas Baleares (Balearic Islands)
SAHARA
Istanbul (Constantinople)
Ankara
Athinai (Athens)
Beograd (Belgrade)
Bucuresti (Bucharest)
Sofiya (Sofia)
Budapest
Roma (Rome)
Napoli (Naples)
Madrid
Lisboa (Lisbon)
Alger (El Djezair)
Tunis
Tripoli (Tarabulus)
Al Qahira (Cairo)
Alexandria
Rabat
Casablanca
Marrakech
Marseille
Barcelona
Heights in metres
1:12 M
km 0 80 160 320 480 640
miles 0 40 80 160 240 320 400
7971

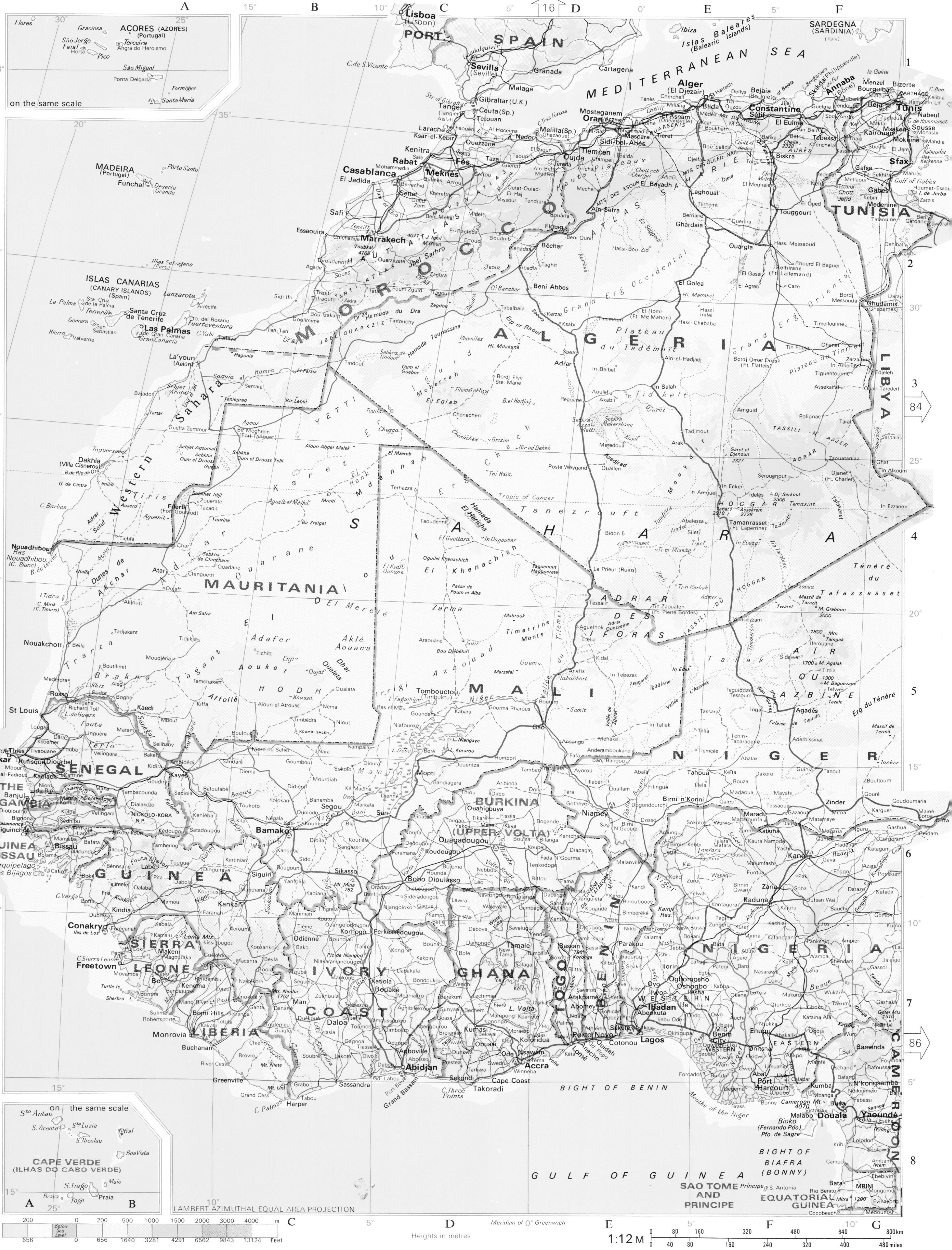

AÇORES (AZORES)
(Portugal)
on the same scale

MADEIRA
(Portugal)

ISLAS CANARIAS
(CANARY ISLANDS)
(Spain)

CAPE VERDE
(ILHAS DO CABO VERDE)
on the same scale

PORTUGAL
SPAIN
MEDITERRANEAN SEA
SARDEGNA
(SARDINIA)
(Italy)

MOROCCO
ALGERIA
TUNISIA
LIBYA

Lisboa
(Lisbon)
Sevilla (Seville)
Granada
Cartagena
Malaga
Gibraltar (U.K.)
Tanger
Ceuta (Sp.)
Tetouan
Melilla (Sp.)
Oran
Alger (El Djezair)
Constantine
Annaba
Tunis
Sfax
Gabes

Rabat
Casablanca
Meknès
Fès
Marrakech
Agadir

WESTERN SAHARA
Dakhla
La'youn (Aaiún)
Nouadhibou

MAURITANIA
Nouakchott
Atar

S A H A R A
MALI
Tombouctou (Timbuktu)
Gao
NIGER

SENEGAL
Dakar
St Louis
THE GAMBIA
Banjul
GUINEA BISSAU
Bissau
GUINEA
Conakry
SIERRA LEONE
Freetown
LIBERIA
Monrovia

BURKINA (UPPER VOLTA)
Ouagadougou
Bobo Dioulasso
Niamey

IVORY COAST
Bamako
Abidjan
GHANA
Accra
Kumasi
TOGO
BENIN
Lomé
Cotonou
Porto Novo
Lagos
NIGERIA
Kaduna
Kano
Ibadan
Enugu
Port Harcourt
CAMEROON
Yaoundé
Douala

BIGHT OF BENIN
GULF OF GUINEA
BIGHT OF BIAFRA (BONNY)
SAO TOME AND PRINCIPE
EQUATORIAL GUINEA

LAMBERT AZIMUTHAL EQUAL AREA PROJECTION
Heights in metres
Meridian of 0° Greenwich
1:12 M

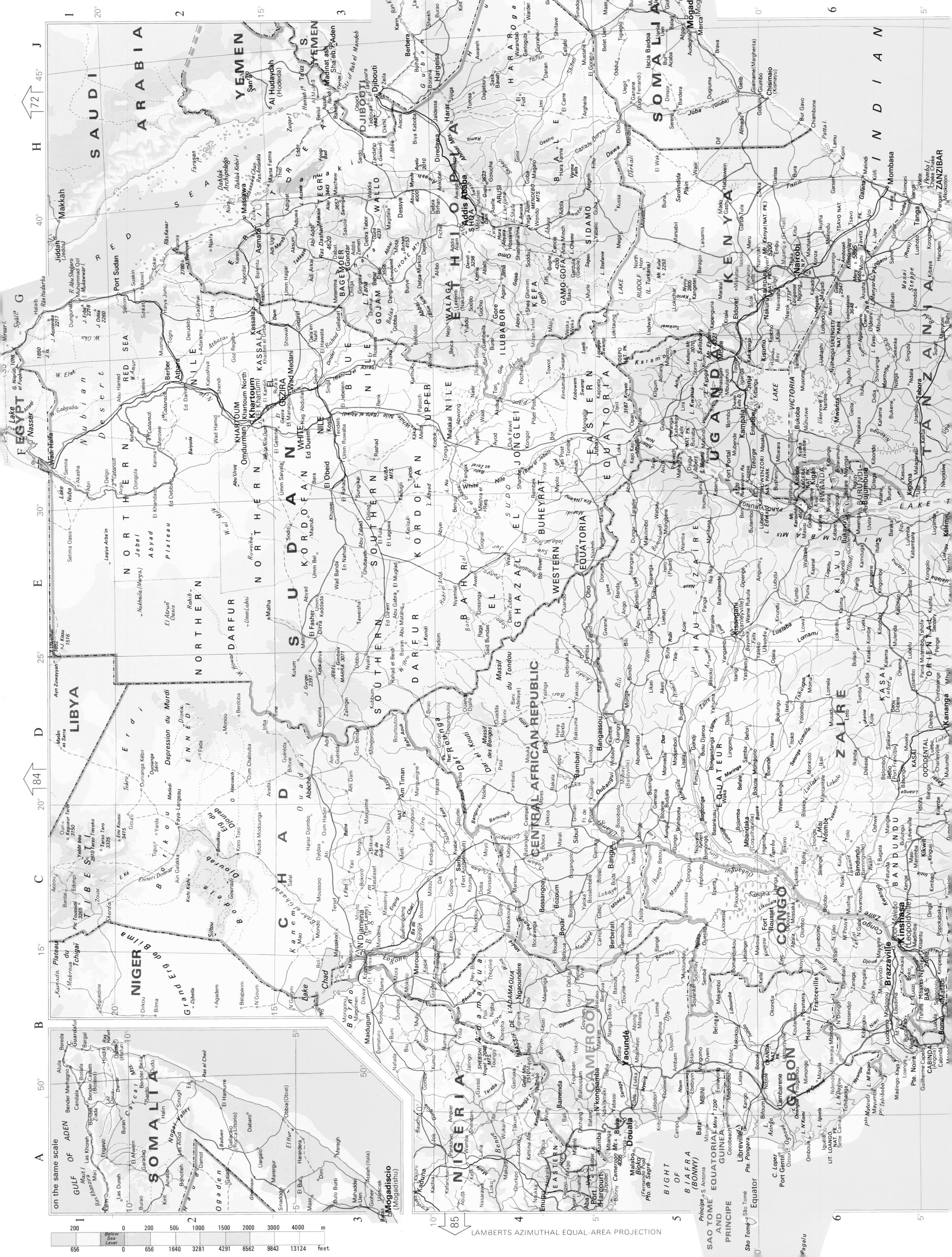
SAUDI ARABIA
YEMEN
DJIBOUTI
ETHIOPIA
SOMALIA
KENYA
UGANDA
TANZANIA
SUDAN
EGYPT
LIBYA
CHAD
NIGER
NIGERIA
CAMEROON
CENTRAL AFRICAN REPUBLIC
ZAIRE
CONGO
GABON
EQUATORIAL GUINEA
SAO TOME AND PRINCIPE
RWANDA
BURUNDI
Khartoum
Addis Ababa
Nairobi
Kampala
Mogadiscio (Mogadishu)
Kinshasa (Léopoldville)
Brazzaville
Bangui
N'Djamena (Fort Lamy)
Yaoundé
Libreville
RED SEA
INDIAN OCEAN
GULF OF ADEN
on the same scale
72
84
85
LAMBERTS AZIMUTHAL EQUAL-AREA PROJECTION
200 Below Sea Level 0 200 500 1000 1500 2000 3000 4000 m
656 0 656 1640 3281 4291 6562 9843 13124 feet

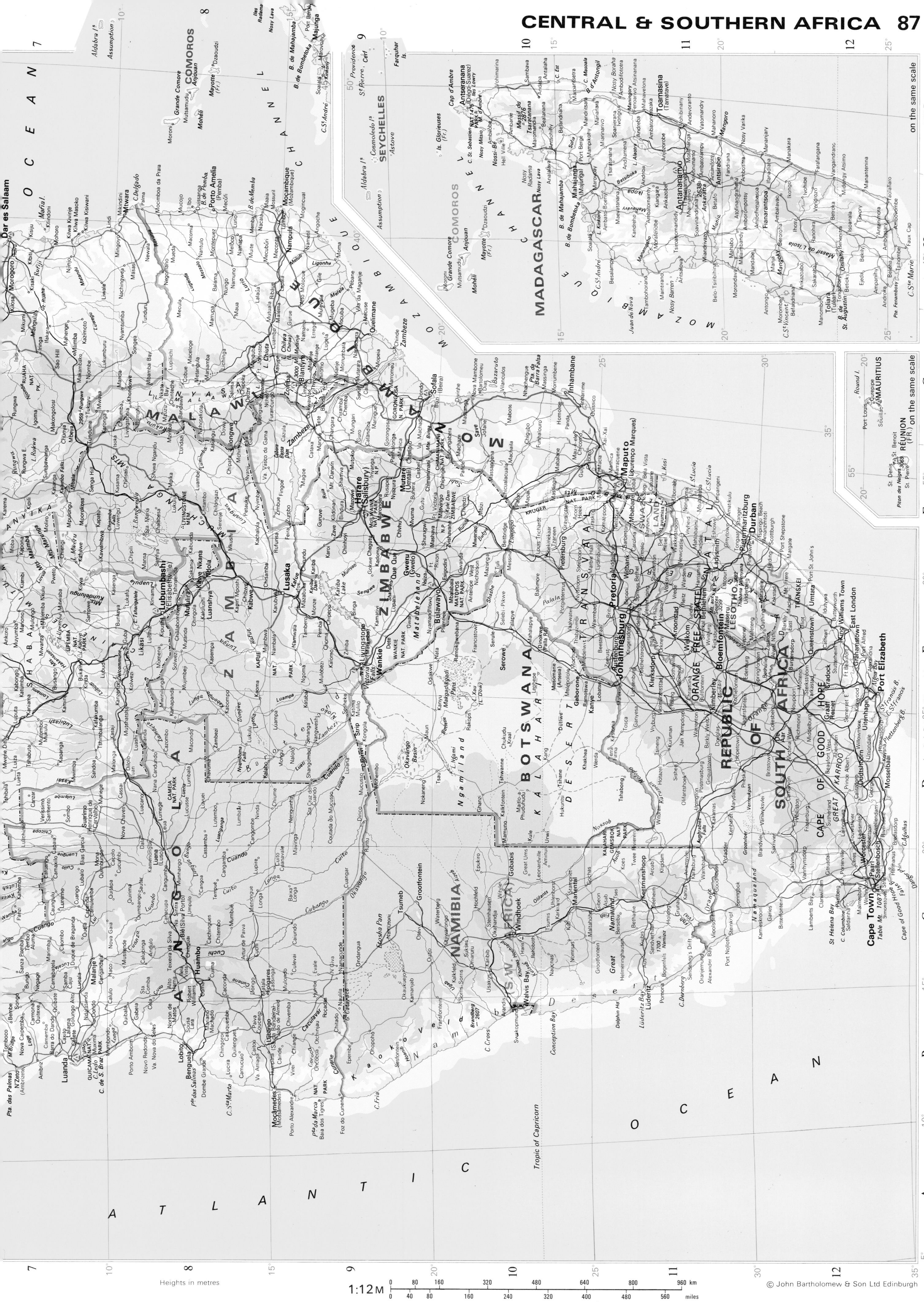

Heights in metres

1:12 M

© John Bartholomew & Son Ltd Edinburgh

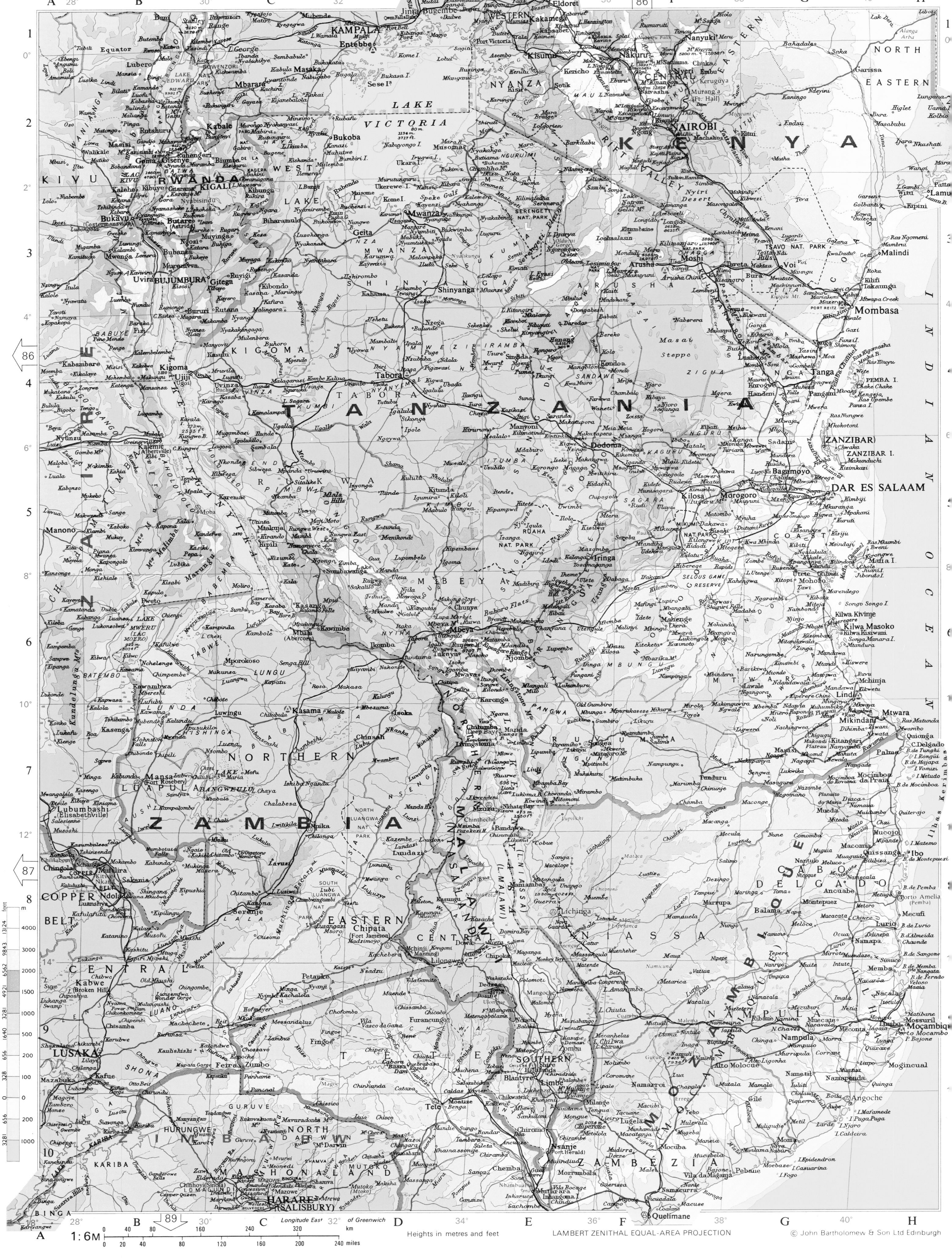

KENYA

TANZANIA

ZAMBIA

MOZAMBIQUE

ZIMBABWE

LAKE VICTORIA

NAIROBI

DAR ES SALAAM

Mombasa

INDIAN OCEAN

1 : 6M

LAMBERT ZENITHAL EQUAL-AREA PROJECTION

Heights in metres and feet

© John Bartholomew & Son Ltd Edinburgh

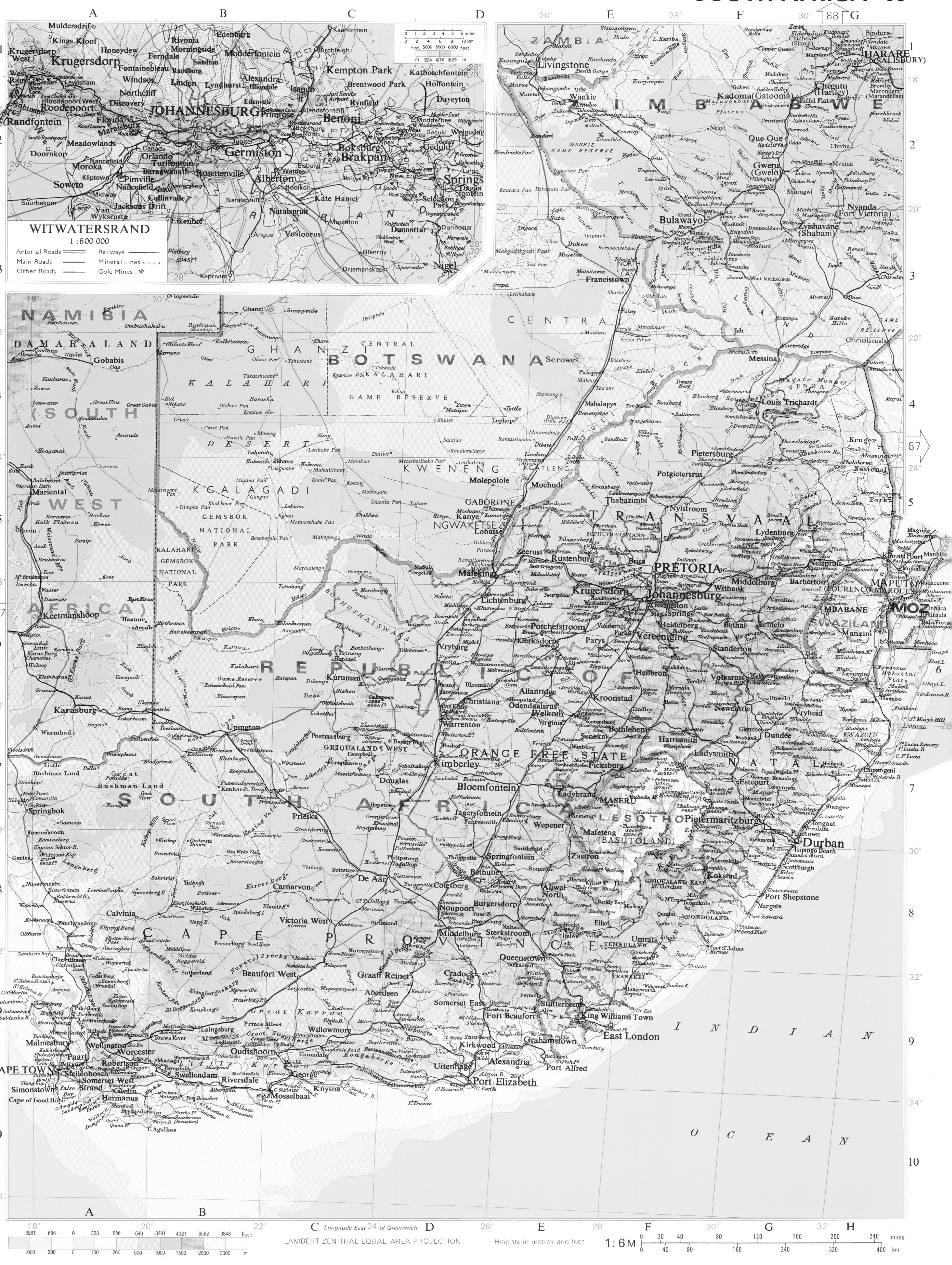

WITWATERSRAND
1:600 000

Arterial Roads — Railways
Main Roads — Mineral Lines
Other Roads — Gold Mines

JOHANNESBURG — Krugersdorp — Kempton Park — Germiston — Benoni — Boksburg — Brakpan — Springs — Randfontein — Roodepoort — Soweto — Nigel

---

ZAMBIA
Livingstone · Wankie

ZIMBABWE
Bulawayo · Gweru (Gwelo) · Que Que (Kadoma/Gatooma) · HARARE (SALISBURY) · Zvishavane (Shabani) · Nyanda (Fort Victoria)

NAMIBIA (SOUTH WEST AFRICA)
DAMARALAND · Gobabis · Mariental · Keetmanshoop · Karasburg · Warmbad · Springbok

BOTSWANA
GHANZI · KALAHARI · CENTRAL · GABORONE · Kanye · Lobatse · Serowe · Molepolole · Mahalapye · Francistown · KALAHARI GEMSBOK NATIONAL PARK · GEMSBOK NATIONAL PARK

REPUBLIC OF SOUTH AFRICA

TRANSVAAL
PRETORIA · Johannesburg · Germiston · Springs · Rustenburg · Pietersburg · Potgietersrus · Nylstroom · Witbank · Middelburg · Nelspruit · Barberton · Messina · Louis Trichardt · Lydenburg · Lichtenburg · Potchefstroom · Klerksdorp · Vereeniging · Heidelberg · Standerton

BOPHUTHATSWANA · Mafeking · Zeerust · Vryburg · Kuruman

ORANGE FREE STATE
Bloemfontein · Kroonstad · Welkom · Virginia · Kimberley · Bethlehem · Harrismith · Ladybrand · Zastron

LESOTHO (BASUTOLAND) · MASERU · Mafeteng

NATAL · KWAZULU
Pietermaritzburg · Durban · Newcastle · Ladysmith · Dundee · Vryheid · Estcourt · Kokstad · Port Shepstone · PONDOLAND

SWAZILAND · MBABANE · Manzini

MOZ · MAPUTO · LOURENÇO MARQUES

CAPE PROVINCE
CAPE TOWN · Paarl · Worcester · Stellenbosch · Beaufort West · Graaff Reinet · De Aar · Cradock · Queenstown · East London · Grahamstown · Port Elizabeth · Uitenhage · Oudtshoorn · George · Knysna · Mosselbaai · Upington · Prieska · Carnarvon · Victoria West · Middelburg · Colesberg · Aliwal North · Burgersdorp · Umtata · TEMBULAND · TRANSKEI · King Williams Town · Somerset East · Malmesbury · Calvinia · Cape of Good Hope · C. Agulhas

INDIAN OCEAN

LAMBERT ZENITHAL EQUAL-AREA PROJECTION · Heights in metres and feet · 1:6 M

Longitude East of Greenwich

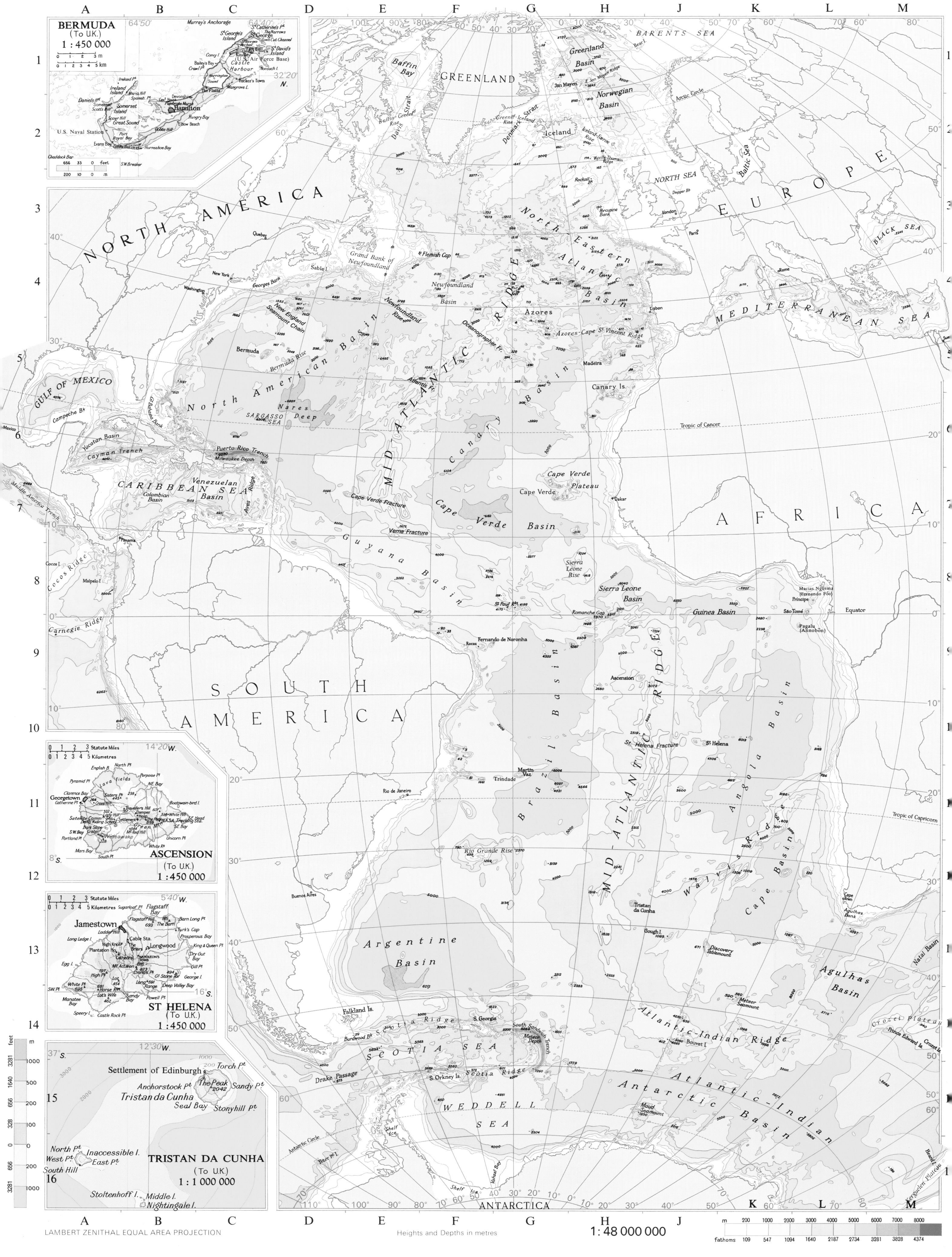
BERMUDA
(To U.K.)
1 : 450 000
St George
Hamilton
Castle Harbour
Great Sound
U.S. Naval Station
NORTH AMERICA
GREENLAND
Baffin Bay
Greenland Basin
Norwegian Basin
Iceland
Jan Mayen
BARENTS SEA
NORTH SEA
Baltic Sea
EUROPE
BLACK SEA
MEDITERRANEAN SEA
Grand Bank of Newfoundland
Flemish Cap
Newfoundland Basin
Newfoundland Rise
New England Seamount Chain
North Eastern Atlantic Basin
MID-ATLANTIC RIDGE
Azores
Azores-Cape St Vincent Ridge
Oceanographer Fr.
Bermuda
Bermuda Rise
North American Basin
Nares Deep
SARGASSO SEA
Atlantis Fr.
Madeira
Canary Is.
Canary Basin
Tropic of Cancer
GULF OF MEXICO
Campeche Bk
Yucatan Basin
Cayman Trench
Puerto Rico Trench
Milwaukee Depth
CARIBBEAN SEA
Venezuelan Basin
Colombian Basin
Aves Ridge
Cape Verde Plateau
Cape Verde
Cape Verde Fracture
Cape Verde Basin
Vema Fracture
Dakar
AFRICA
Guyana Basin
Sierra Leone Rise
Sierra Leone Basin
Romanche Gap
Guinea Basin
St Paul Rks
Equator
São Tomé
Principe
Pagalu (Annobón)
Cocos Ridge
Malpelo I.
Carnegie Ridge
Panama
Fernando de Noronha
Rocas
SOUTH AMERICA
Ascension
St Helena
St Helena Fracture
Angola Basin
Brazil Basin
Trindade
Martin Vaz
Rio de Janeiro
Tropic of Capricorn
Rio Grande Rise
Walvis Ridge
Cape Basin
Buenos Aires
Tristan da Cunha
Gough I.
Discovery Tablemount
Argentine Basin
Agulhas Basin
Agulhas Bank
Natal Basin
Meteor Seamount
Falkland Is.
Burdwood Bk
Scotia Ridge
S. Georgia
South Sandwich Trench
Meteor Depth
SCOTIA SEA
Drake Passage
S. Orkney Is.
Bouvet I.
Atlantic-Indian Ridge
Atlantic-Indian Antarctic Basin
Prince Edward Is.
Crozet Plateau
Maud Seamount
WEDDELL SEA
Antarctic Circle
Peter I
Shelf Ice
ANTARCTICA
Kerguelen Plateau
ASCENSION
(To U.K.)
1 : 450 000
Georgetown
Green Mt
ST HELENA
(To U.K.)
1 : 450 000
Jamestown
Longwood
TRISTAN DA CUNHA
(To U.K.)
1 : 1 000 000
Settlement of Edinburgh
The Peak 2042
Inaccessible I.
Stoltenhoff I.
Middle I.
Nightingale I.
LAMBERT ZENITHAL EQUAL AREA PROJECTION
Heights and Depths in metres
1: 48 000 000
m 200 1000 2000 3000 4000 5000 6000 7000 8000
fathoms 109 547 1094 1640 2187 2734 3281 3828 4374

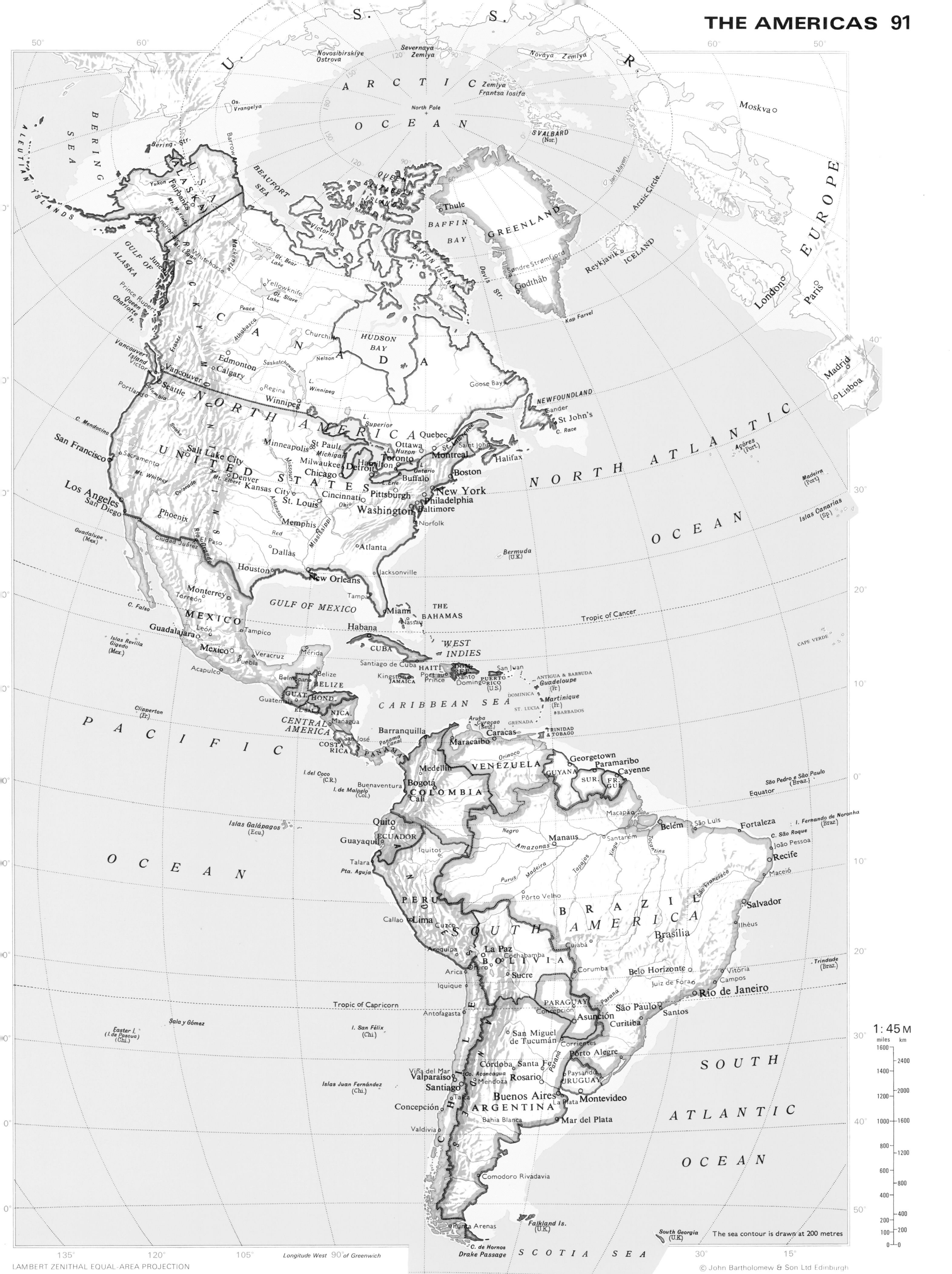

1 : 45 M

The sea contour is drawn at 200 metres

LAMBERT ZENITHAL EQUAL-AREA PROJECTION

© John Bartholomew & Son Ltd Edinburgh

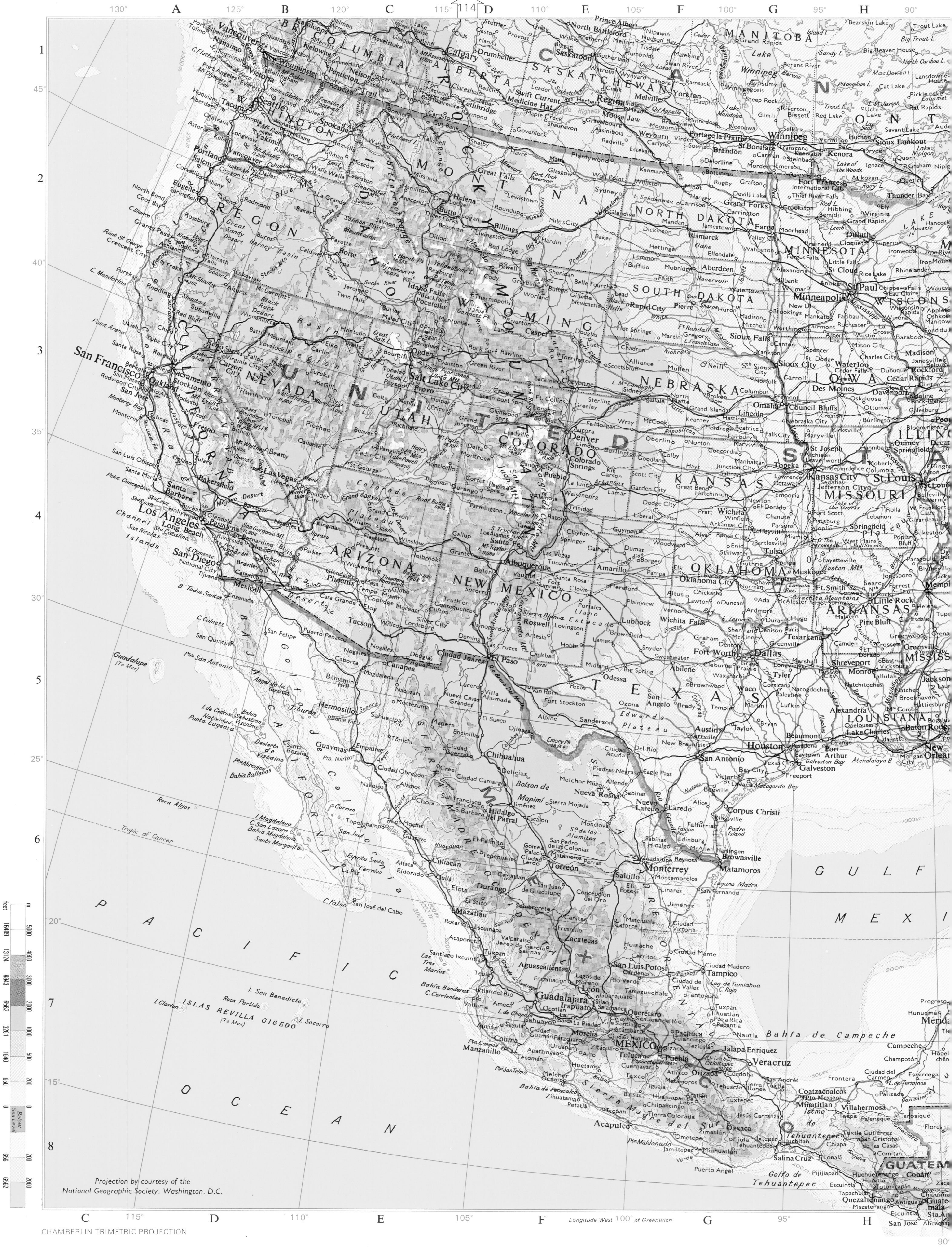

CHAMBERLIN TRIMETRIC PROJECTION

Projection by courtesy of the
National Geographic Society, Washington, D.C.

Longitude West 100° of Greenwich

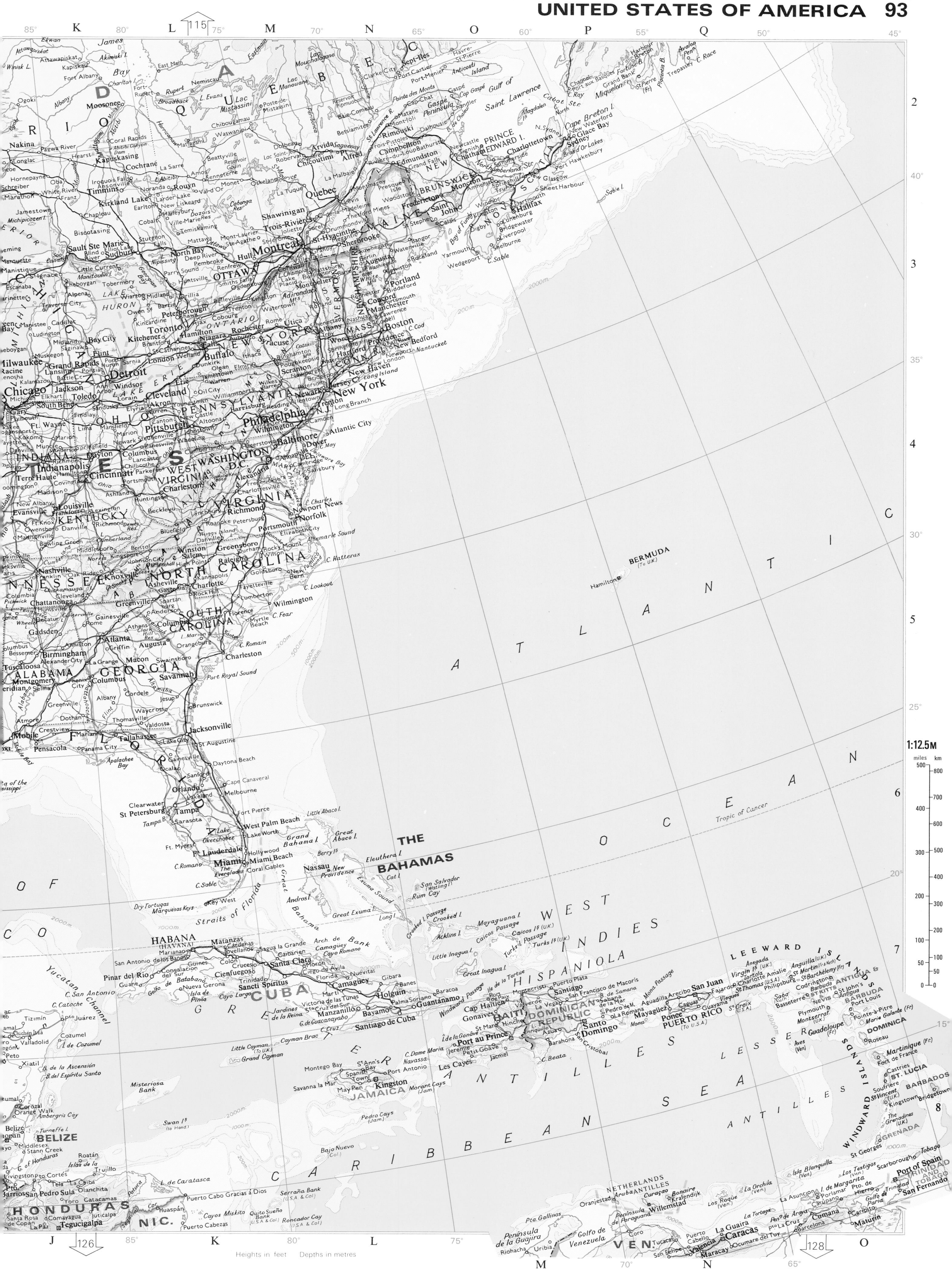

ATLANTIC OCEAN

THE BAHAMAS

WEST INDIES

CUBA

HABANA
HAVANA

HISPANIOLA

HAITI

DOMINICAN REPUBLIC

PUERTO RICO
(To U.S.A)

JAMAICA

CARIBBEAN SEA

GREATER ANTILLES

LESSER ANTILLES

LEEWARD IS.

WINDWARD ISLANDS

BERMUDA
(To U.K.)

Tropic of Cancer

QUEBEC

NEW BRUNSWICK

MAINE

NEW YORK

PENNSYLVANIA

WEST VIRGINIA

VIRGINIA

NORTH CAROLINA

SOUTH CAROLINA

GEORGIA

FLORIDA

ALABAMA

TENNESSEE

KENTUCKY

INDIANA

OHIO

MICHIGAN

ONTARIO

New York
Philadelphia
Washington D.C.
Baltimore
Boston
Montreal
Ottawa
Toronto
Detroit
Chicago
Cleveland
Pittsburgh
Buffalo
Cincinnati
Indianapolis
Nashville
Atlanta
Birmingham
Charlotte
Richmond
Norfolk
Jacksonville
Orlando
Tampa
Miami
Miami Beach
Ft. Lauderdale
Key West
Quebec
Halifax
Charleston
Savannah

HONDURAS
BELIZE
NIC.
VEN.
Caracas
Maracaibo

1:12.5M

miles
500
400
300
200
100
50
0

km
800
700
600
500
400
300
200
100
50
0

Heights in feet   Depths in metres

LAKE MICHIGAN

LAKE HURON

GEORGIAN BAY

LAKE ONTARIO

LAKE ERIE

ONTARIO

MICHIGAN

INDIANA

OHIO

PENNSYLVANIA

WEST VIRGINIA

VIRGINIA

KENTUCKY

TENNESSEE

NORTH CAROLINA

Traverse City
Muskegon
Grand Rapids
Lansing
Kalamazoo
Battle Creek
Detroit
Ann Arbor
Windsor
Toledo
Fort Wayne
South Bend
Elkhart
Indianapolis
Dayton
Cincinnati
Louisville
Lexington
Frankfort
Columbus
Springfield
Newark
Zanesville
Cleveland
Akron
Canton
Youngstown
Mansfield
Marion
Lima
Sandusky
Elyria
Lorain
Erie
Buffalo
Niagara Falls
St. Catharines
Hamilton
Toronto
Kitchener
Guelph
London
Sarnia
Port Huron
Bay City
Saginaw
Flint
Midland
Oshawa
Peterborough
Parry Sound
Pittsburgh
Wheeling
Steubenville
Washington
Altoona
Johnstown
New Castle
Warren
Sharon
Beaver Falls
Aliquippa
McKeesport
Cumberland
Morgantown
Fairmont
Clarksburg
Parkersburg
Charleston
Huntington
Ashland
Portsmouth
Chillicothe
Lancaster
Roanoke
Bluefield
Beckley
Lynchburg
Staunton
Charlottesville
Martinsburg
New Albany

CONFORMAL CONIC PROJECTION

feet
3281 656 0 300 600 1500 3000 6000

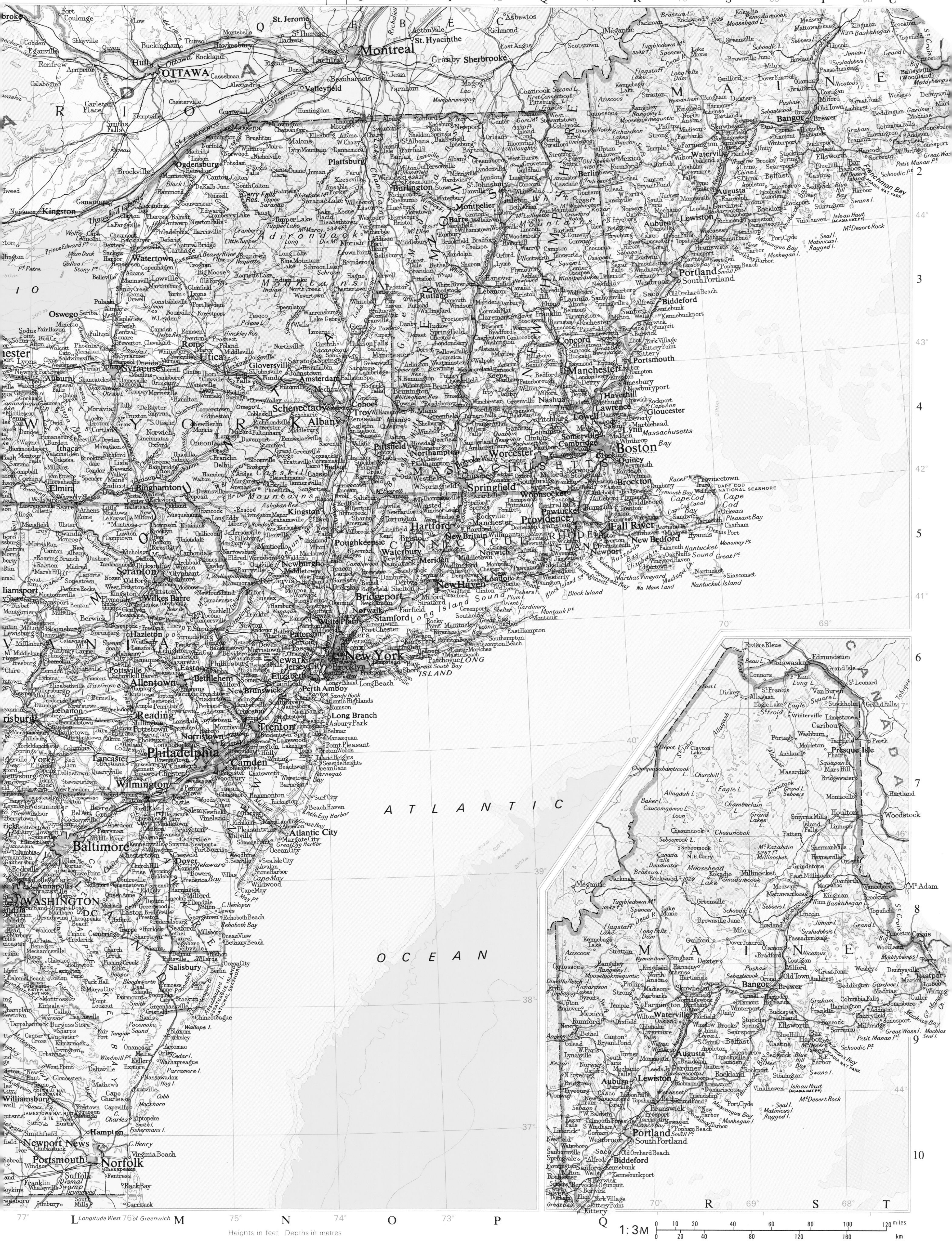

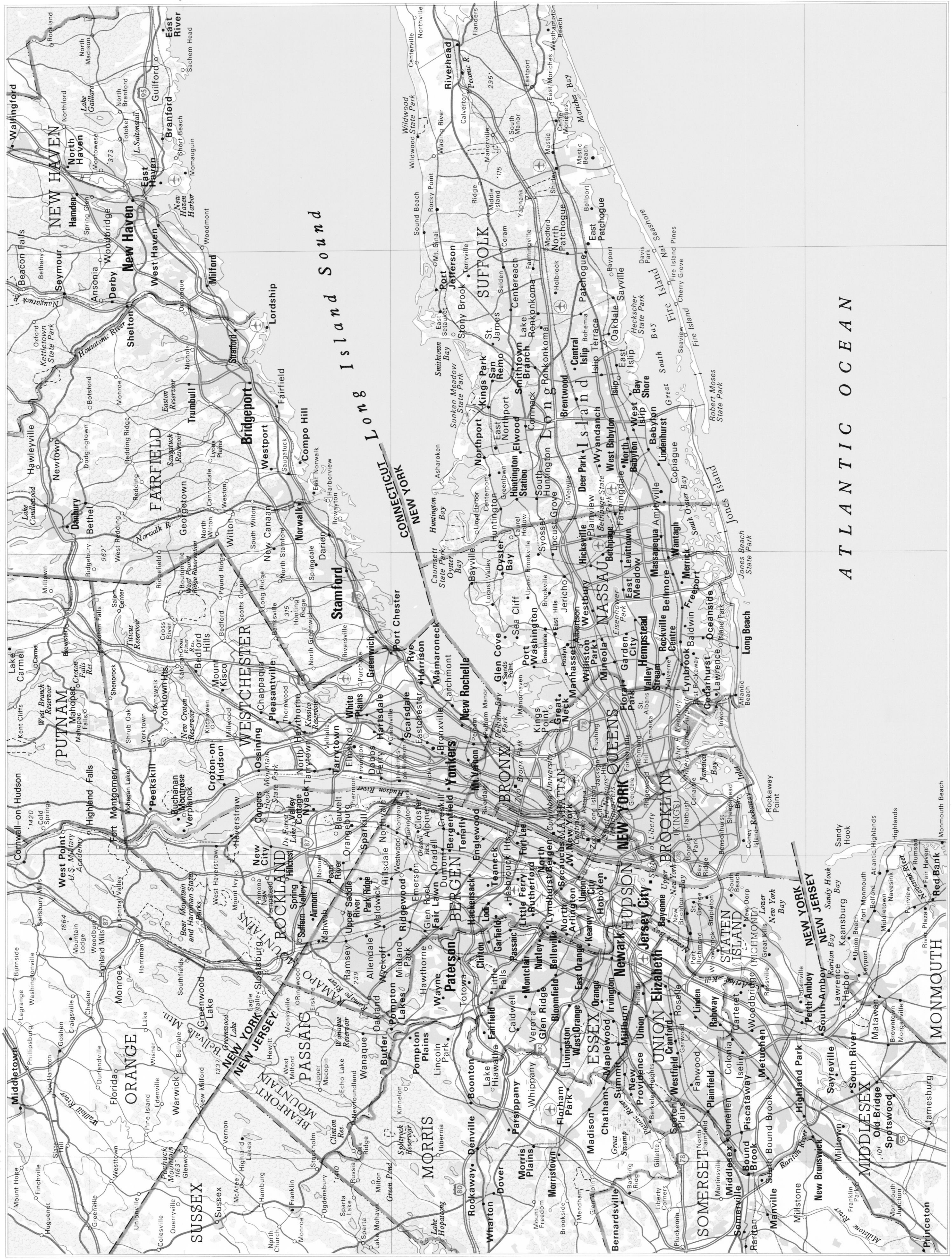

ATLANTIC OCEAN

Long Island Sound

CONNECTICUT
NEW YORK

NEW HAVEN

New Haven

SUFFOLK

NASSAU

Long Island

FAIRFIELD

Bridgeport

Stamford

WESTCHESTER

PUTNAM

ORANGE

SUSSEX

MORRIS

PASSAIC

BERGEN

ROCKLAND

ESSEX

UNION

HUDSON

Paterson

Newark

Elizabeth

Jersey City

NEW YORK

BRONX

MANHATTAN

QUEENS

BROOKLYN (KINGS)

STATEN ISLAND (RICHMOND)

NEW JERSEY

MIDDLESEX

SOMERSET

MONMOUTH

Yonkers

RAMAPO MOUNTAINS

BEARFORT MOUNTAIN

Robert Moses State Park

Jones Beach State Park

Fire Island Nat. Seashore

1:500 000

© Times Books Ltd

PHILADELPHIA

A 75°15' B 75°00' C

Green Lane
Souderton
New Britain
Doylestown
Pineville
1
Harleysville
Hatfield
Chalfont
BUCKS
Schwenksville
Lansdale
Montgomeryville
Wrightstown
Dolington
40°15'
Skippack
Warminster
Jacksonville
Newtown
Yardley
North Wales
Richboro
MONTGOMERY
Center Square
Ambler
Hatboro
Southampton
Langhorne
2
Trooper
Fort Washington
Willow Grove
Feasterville
Levittown
Audubon
Norristown
Abington
Holland
Valley Forge
State Park
Bridgeport
Glenside
Croydon
King of
Prussia
Conshohocken
Elkins Park
Cornwells
Hts.
Bristol
CHESTER
Berwyn
Wayne
Jenkintown
Burlington
Paoli
Bryn Mawr
Fairmount
Park
Germantown
Olney
Riverside
Willingboro
Newton Square
Havertown
Ardmore
Frankford
Palmyra
40°00'
Broomall
Upper
Darby
Drexel Hill
Cinnaminson
BURLINGTON
Ridley Creek
State Park
DELAWARE
Zoo
PHILADELPHIA
Moorestown
Springfield
Lansdowne
Pennsauken
Lima
Collingdale
Darby
Camden
Merchantville
Cherry Hill
Media
Swarthmore
Ridley Park
Gloucester City
Collingswood
Haddonfield
Medford
Village
Green
Brookhaven
Glenolden
Philadelphia
International
Airport
Naval
Shipyard
Audubon
Haddon
Hts.
Ashland
Marlton
3
Boothwyn
Chester
National Park
Magnolia
Gibbsboro
PENNSYLVANIA
Paulsboro
Woodbury
Runnemede
Stratford
Lindenwold
Claymont
NEW JERSEY
Gibbstown
Woodbury Hts.
Blackwood
West Berlin
Bridgeport
Mantua
Wenonah
Pine Hill
Berlin
Swedesboro
Sewell
39°45'
Penns Grove
Mullica Hill
Pitman
CAMDEN
GLOUCESTER
Glassboro
4
Woodstown
Williamstown
SALEM
Clayton
Pole Tavern
Franklinville

A 75°15' B 75°00' C

BOSTON 97

D 71°15' E 71°00' F

NEW HAMPSHIRE
MASSACHUSETTS
Methuen
Lawrence
Georgetown
Rowley
Georgetown
Rowley
State Forest
1
West
Chelmsford
Dracutt
ESSEX
Andover
Boxford
State Forest
Willowdale
State Forest
Ipswich
Palmer
State Park
Lowell
Boston
Hill
Harold Parker
State Forest
South Hamilton
Chelmsford Center
N. Billerica
Wenham
42°30'
Robins Hill
Billerica
Silver Lake
Danvers
Beverly
Littleton Common
Nutting Lake
Wilmington
Reading
South
Lynnfield
Peabody
Salem
Carlisle
Pinehurst
North
Woburn
Wakefield
South
Peabody
Marblehead
Bedford
Burlington
Stoneham
Lynn Woods
Reservation
Lynn
Swampscott
Concord
Woburn
Melrose
Saugus
Nahant
Bay
West Concord
Lexington
Winchester
Malden
Revere
Nahant
Maynard
Minute Man
Natural History Park
Arlington
Medford
Everett
Chelsea
2
MIDDLESEX
Belmont
Somerville
Winthrop
Sudbury
Waltham
Harvard
University
Bunker Hill
Logan
Boston Bay
International Airport
Massachusetts
Bay
Cochituate
Watertown
Cambridge
BOSTON
Weston
Newton
Brookline
Roxbury
Boston
Harbor
Wellesley
Newton
Center
Point Allerton
42°15'
Framingham
Natick
Arnold
Arboretum
Long
Allerton
Needham
Quincy
Bay
Nantasket Beach
Sherborn
Dover
Charles R.
Milton
Quincy
North
Weymouth
Hingham
Dedham
Islington
Blue Hills
Reservation
Braintree
Weymouth
Whitney Woods
Reservation
Holliston
Harding
Westwood
Medfield
Norwood
North Randolph
South Weymouth
Norwell
369
Noon Hill
East Walpole
Canton
Randolph
Medway
NORFOLK
North Abington
Rockland
Hanover
42°00'
Walpole
Avon
Sharon
Stoughton
Abington
3
Franklin
Brockton
PLYMOUTH
Wrentham
North Easton
Whitman
Foxboro
Bryantville
MASS.
R.I.
Mansfield
East Bridgewater
BRISTOL
42°00'

D 71°15' E 71°00' F

WASHINGTON

G 77°15' H 77°00'

Etchison
Glenelg
Ellicott City
Baltimore
39°15'
Clarksburg
Dayton
Elioak
Halethorpe
Neelsville
Laytonsville
Triadelphia
Reservoir
HOWARD
Elkridge
MONTGOMERY
Brookeville
Clarksville
Germantown
Highland
Simpsonville
Friendship
International
Airport
Gaithersburg
Ashton
Fulton
Jessup
Darnestown
Redland
Olney
Ednor
Rocky Gorge Reservoir
Severn
Norbeck
Spencerville
5
Hunting Hill
Rockville
Burtonsville
Laurel
ANNE
ARUNDEL
Travilah
Glenmont
Meadowood
Odenton
Potomac River
Wheaton
Beltsville
Bowie
Great Falls
of the Potomac
Kensington
White
Oak
College
Park
Greenbelt
Springfield
Glenn Dale
Cabin John
Woodside
Silver
Spring
Greenbelt
Park
39°00'
Bethesda
Langley Park
Riverdale
Lanham
Collington
Glen Echo
Chevy
Chase
Takoma
Park
Hyattsville
FAIRFAX
McLean
Rock Creek
Park Zoo
Mt.
Rainier
Bladensburg
Cheverly
Mitchellville
Tysons' Corner
Pimmit Hills
Georgetown
White House
WASHINGTON
Fairmount Hts.
Largo
Vienna
Franklin
Park
The Capitol
Seat
Pleasant
Hall
Oakton
Falls Church
Arlington
Capitol Hts.
Pentagon
Anacostia
District Hts
6
Merrifield
Nat. Cemetery
Suitland
Ritchie
Masonville
Baileys
Crossroads
Hillcrest
Hts.
Morningside
Forestville
Upper
Marlboro
Fairfax
Lincolnia
Hts.
Congress
Hts.
Forest
Hts.
Meadows
Annandale
Camp Springs
Fairfax Station
Alexandria
Phelps Temple
Corner Hills
38°45'
Burke
Grovetop
Belle
Haven
PRINCE GEORGES
Clinton
Springfield
Gum
Springs
Tippett
North
Keys
Nottingham
Devonans
Corner
Mt. Vernon
Piscataway
Brandywine
Pohick
Accotink
Piscataway Creek
Bader
VIRGINIA
MARYLAND
Agnewville
Marshall Hall
Accokeek
Berry
Eagle
Harbor
7
Woodbridge
Bryans Road
Waldorf
Malcolm
Indian
Head
Potomac Hts.
Mason Springs
CHARLES
White Plains
Dumfries
Pomonkey
Pomfret
Triangle
Indian
Head
Rison

G 77°15' H 77°00'

BALTIMORE

J 76°45' K 76°30' L

Greenmount
933
Pretty Boy
Reservoir
Shawsville
Hampstead
Whitehouse
Hereford
Madonna
Jarrettsville
4
Fowblesburg
Butler
Manor
Forest Hill
BALTIMORE
Phoenix
Jacksonville
HARFORD
Churchville
Finksburg
Shawan
Benson
Bel Air
39°30'
Glyndon
Reisterstown
Cronhardt
Baldwin
Abingdon
Liberty
Reservoir
670
Cockeysville
Long Green
Fork
Loch Raven
Reservoir
Kingsville
95
Owings Mills
Lutherville-Timonium
Garrison
Ruxton
Towson
Carney
Perry Hall
Edgewood
Joppatowne
Harrisonville
Pikesville
Parkville
Fullerton
White Marsh
Chase
39°00'
Randallstown
Stoneleigh
Buck River
Rockdale
CITY OF BALTIMORE
Overlea
Middle
River
5
Johns Hopkins
University
Golden Ring
Essex
Patapsco
State Park
Granite
464
Woodlawn
Washington
Monument
Rosedale
Middle River
Pooles
Island
Belmont
BALTIMORE
Hart
Island
Catonsville
Fort McHenry
Nat. Mon.
Dundalk
Ellicott City
Arbutus
Lansdowne
Edgemere
39°15'
Elioak
Columbia
Halethorpe
TUNNEL
HOWARD
Elkridge
Linthicum
Hts.
Curtis
Bay
Sparrows Point
Simpsonville
Stony Run
Fort Howard
Friendship
International
Airport
Orchard Beach
Glen Burnie
Fort Smallwood
6
Jessup
Rivera Beach
Severn
Green Haven
Laurel
Jacobsville
Pinehurst
ANNE ARUNDEL
Odenton
Pasadena
39°00'
Beltsville
Millersville
Magothy River
Crownsville
Arnold
Love Point
Greenbelt
Bowie
Skidmore
Kent
Island
Springfield
Severn
Parole
CHESAPEAKE
BAY
BRIDGE
Stevensville
Glenn Dale
Riva
Lanham
Collington
Annapolis
Eastport
7
PRINCE
GEORGES
Cheverly
Davidsonville
Normans
Brightseat
Mitchellville
Woodland Beach
Arundel
on the Bay
Chester

J 76°45' K 76°30' L

km miles
25
20
15
10

1:500 000

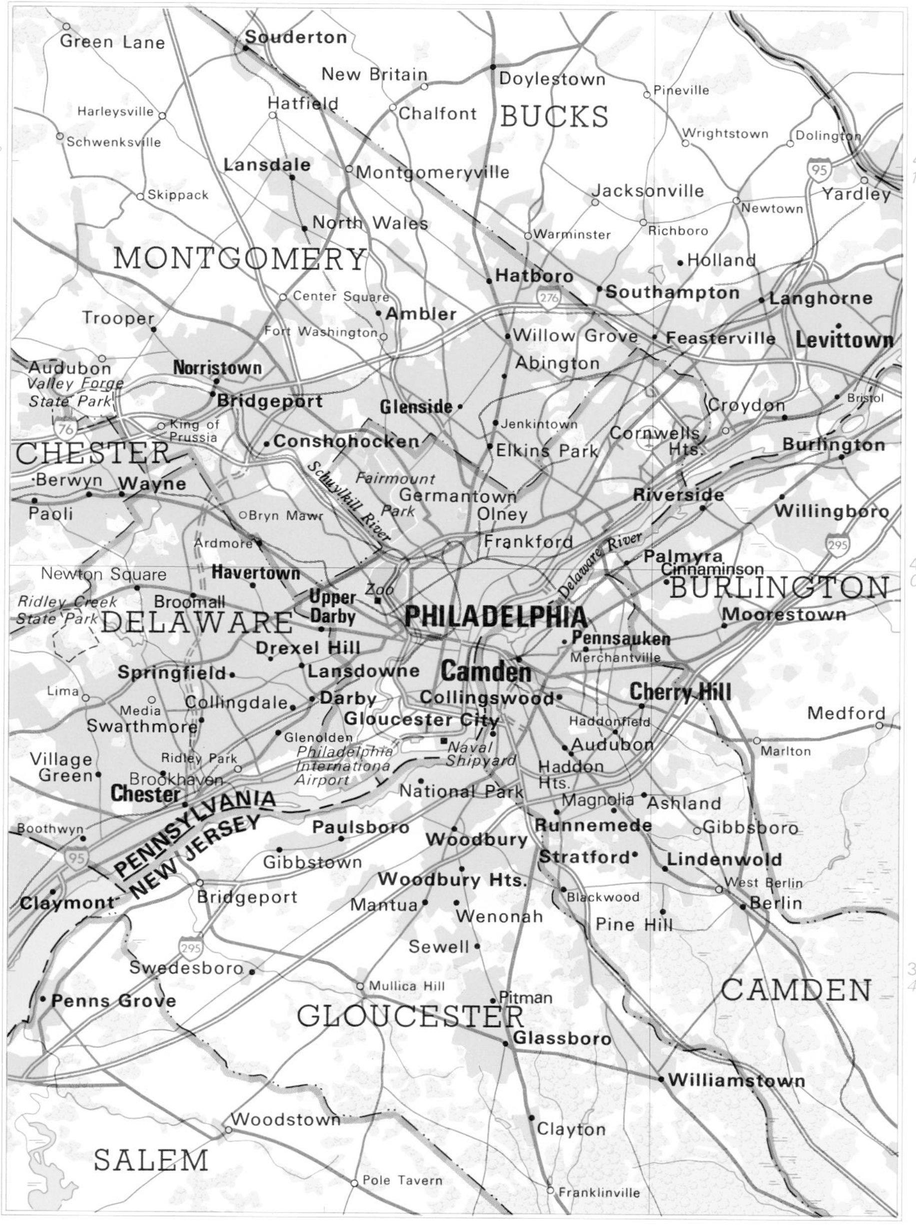

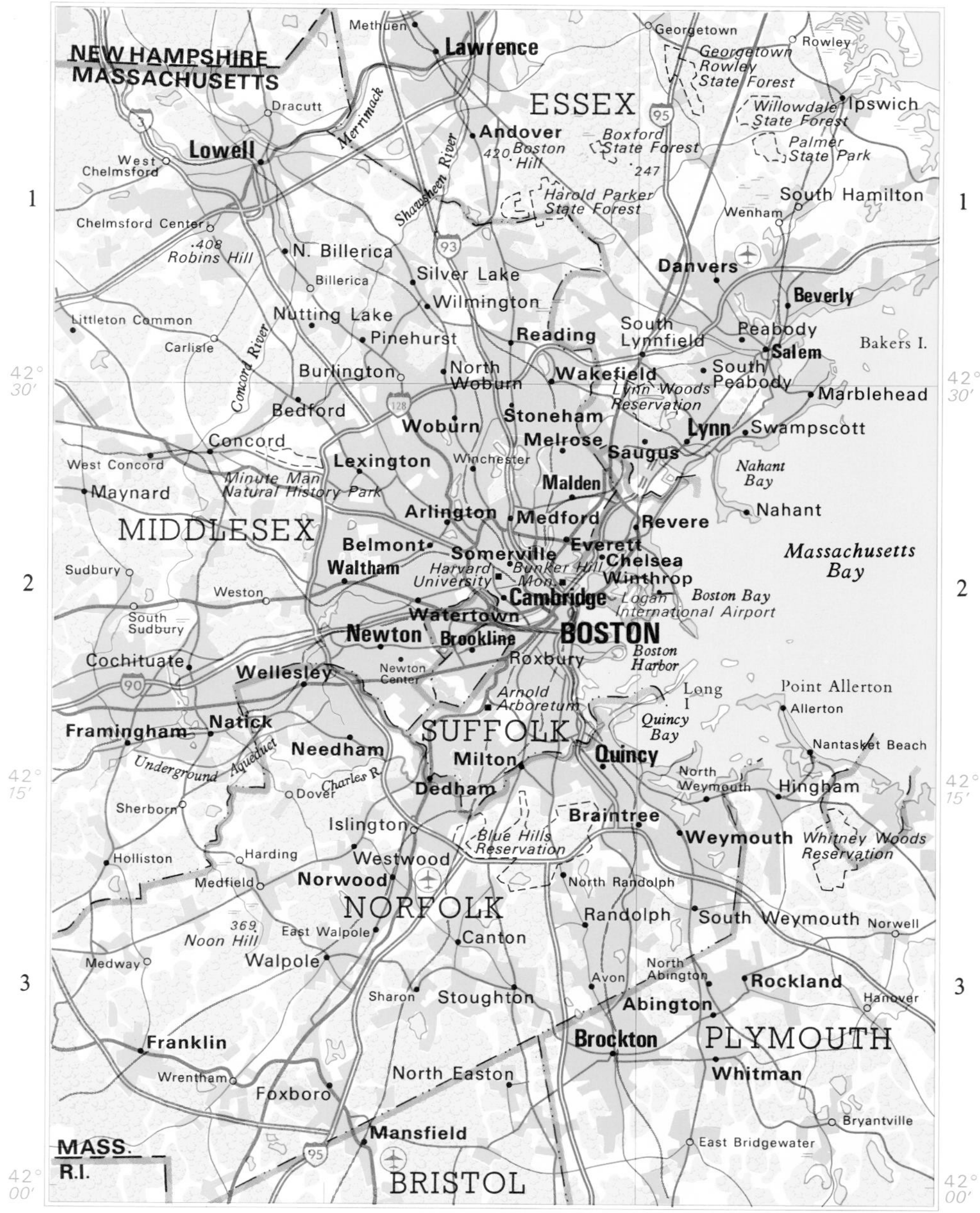

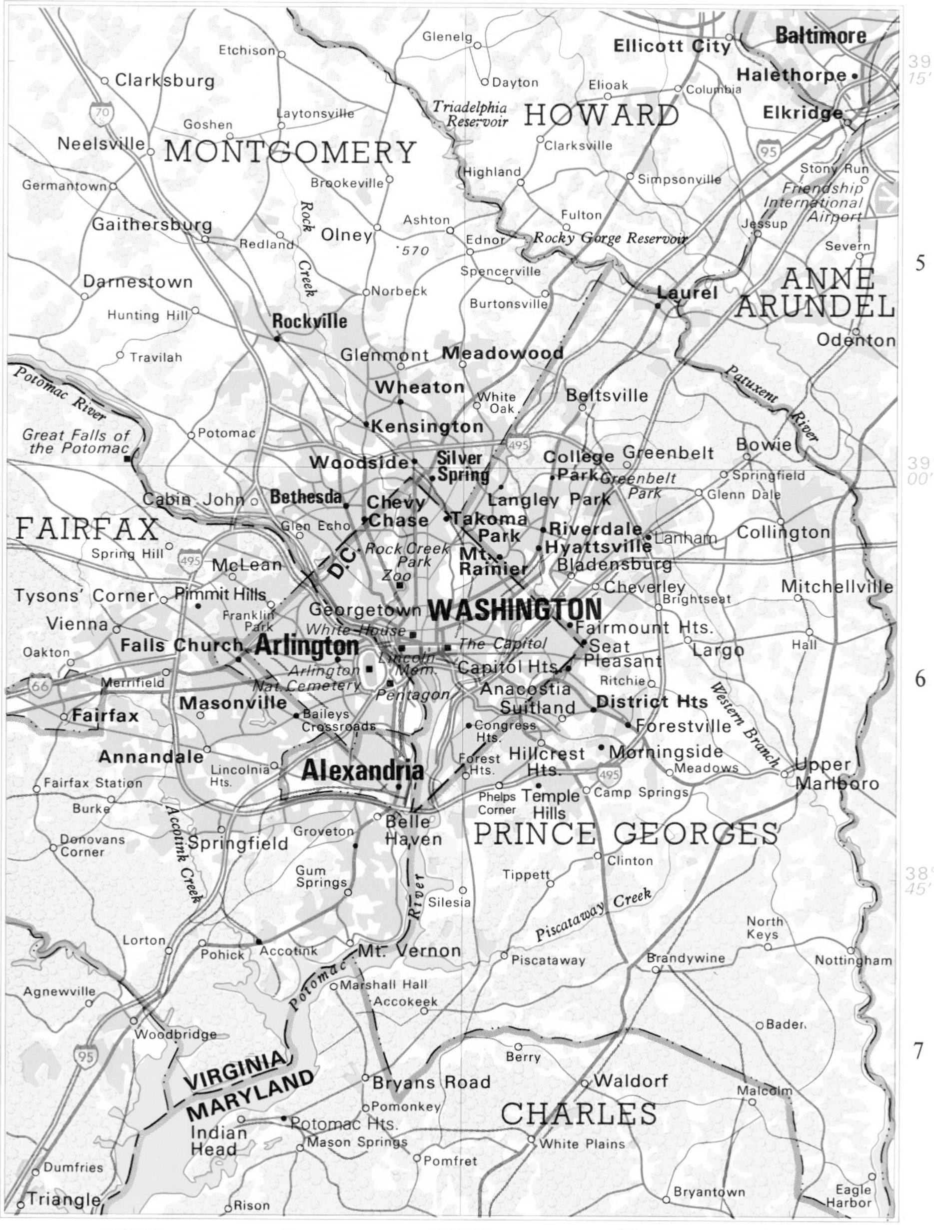

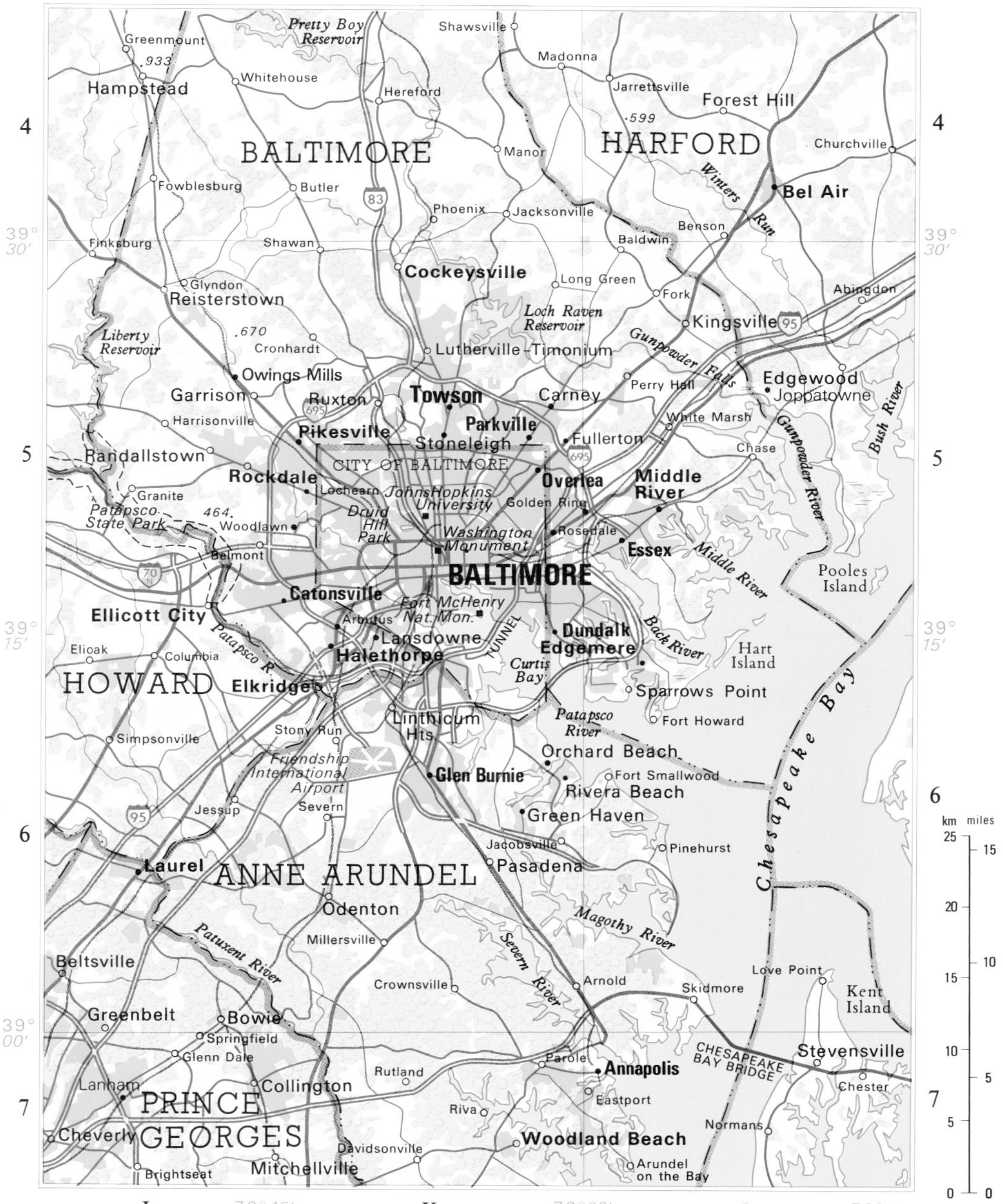

© Times Books Ltd

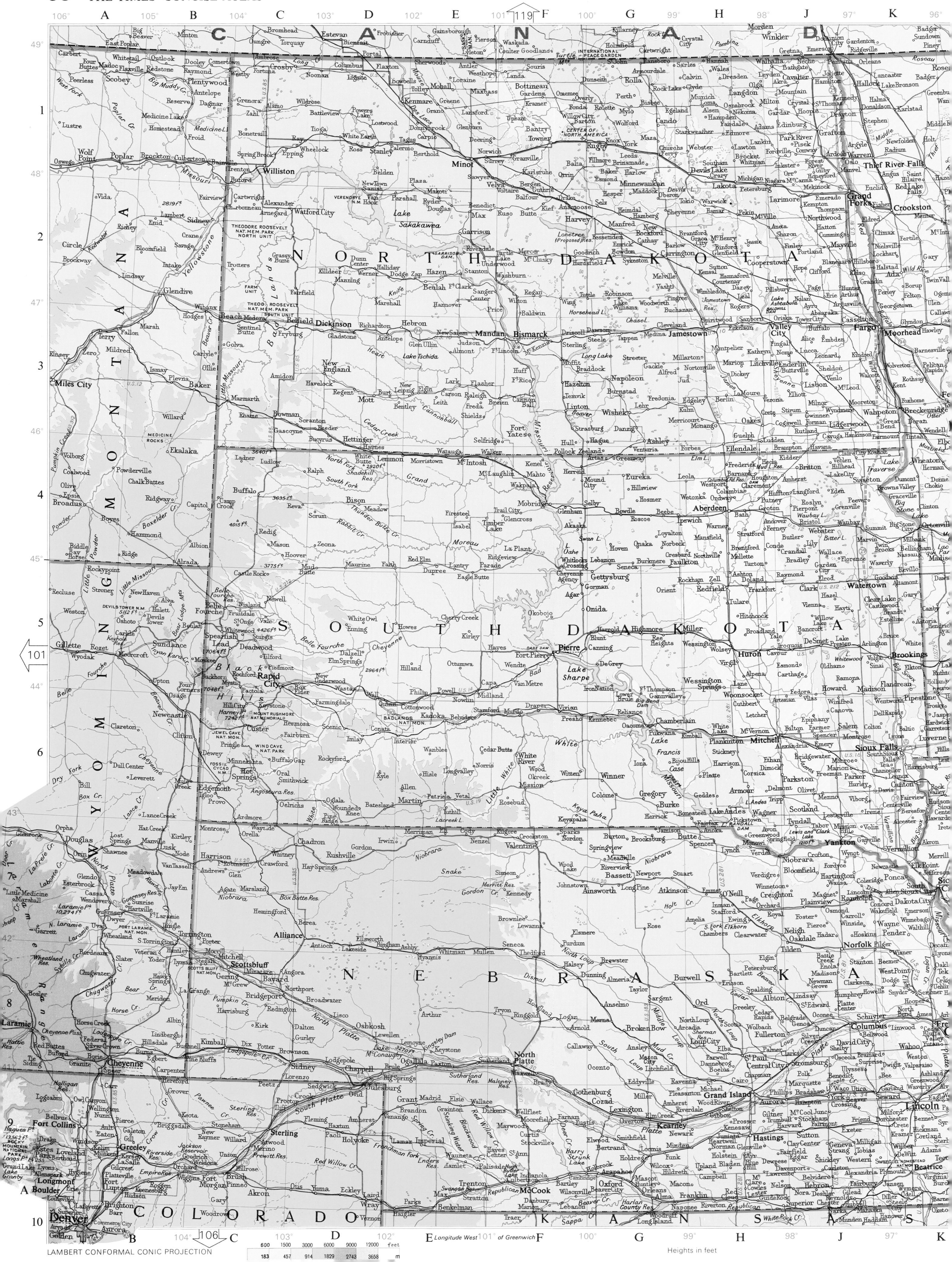

LAMBERT CONFORMAL CONIC PROJECTION

Longitude West of Greenwich

Heights in feet

600	1500	3000	6000	9000	12000	feet
183	457	914	1829	2743	3658	m

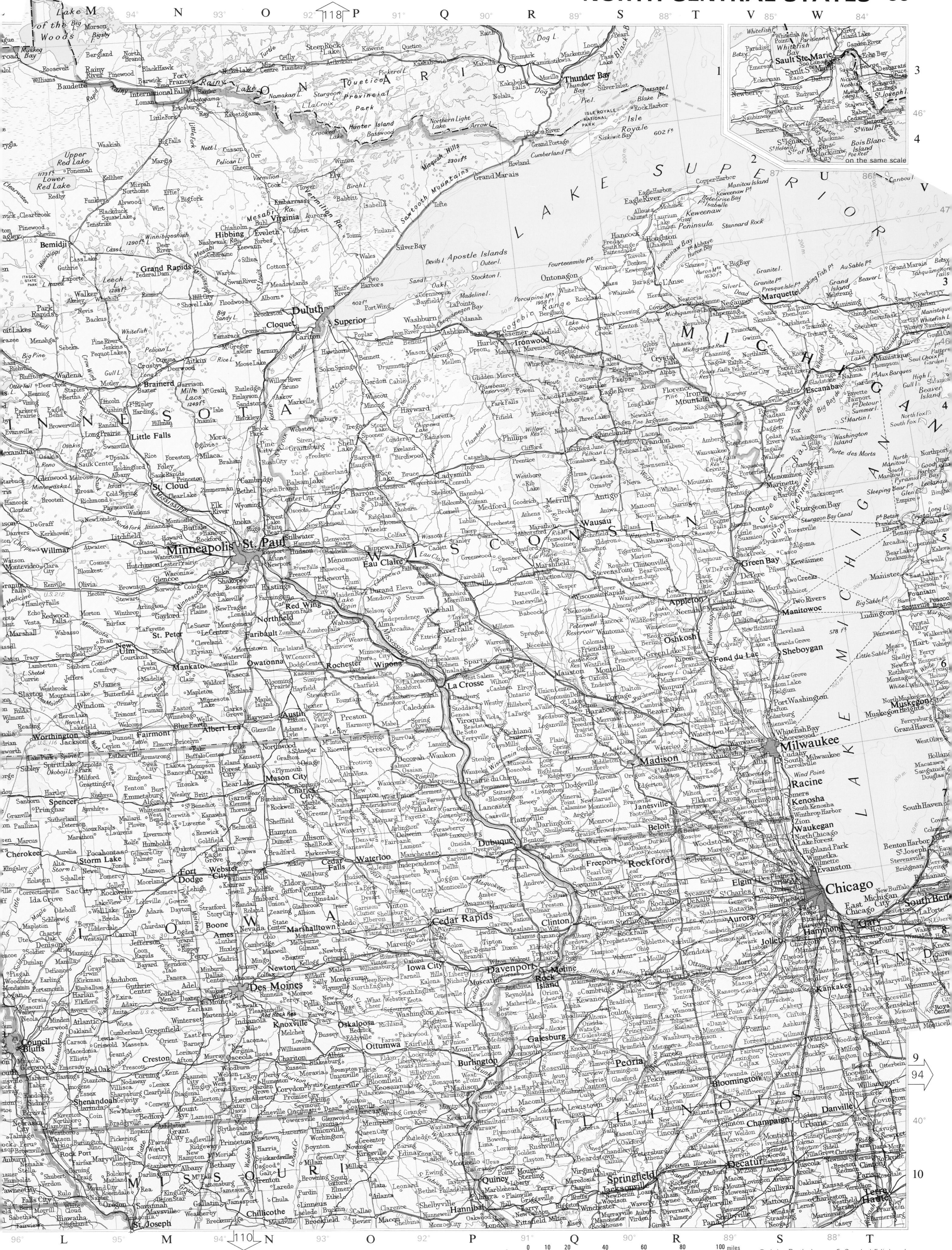

ONTARIO

LAKE SUPERIOR

MINNESOTA

WISCONSIN

MICHIGAN

IOWA

ILLINOIS

MISSOURI

INDIANA

Lake of the Woods

Upper Red Lake
Lower Red Lake

Thunder Bay

Isle Royale National Park

Sault Ste Marie

Bemidji
Grand Rapids
Hibbing
Virginia
Eveleth
Duluth
Superior
Cloquet
Carlton
Ashland
Ironwood
Hurley
Marquette
Escanaba

Brainerd
Little Falls
St Cloud
Minneapolis St Paul
Eau Claire
Wausau
Green Bay
Appleton
Manitowoc

Willmar
Red Wing
Faribault
Owatonna
Rochester
Winona
La Crosse
Oshkosh
Fond du Lac
Sheboygan

Mankato
New Ulm
Albert Lea
Austin
Milwaukee
Madison
Racine
Kenosha
Waukegan

Worthington
Mason City
Charles City
Waterloo
Cedar Falls
Dubuque
Freeport
Rockford
Beloit
Janesville
Monroe
Elgin
Aurora
Chicago
Gary
Hammond
Joliet

Fort Dodge
Webster City
Boone
Ames
Marshalltown
Cedar Rapids
Clinton
Kankakee

Des Moines
Newton
Iowa City
Davenport
Rock Island
Moline
Peoria

Council Bluffs
Ottumwa
Burlington
Galesburg
Bloomington
Danville
Champaign
Urbana

St Joseph
Quincy
Springfield
Jacksonville
Decatur
Terre Haute

1:3M

0 10 20 30 40 50 100 miles
0 20 40 60 80 120 160 km

© John Bartholomew & Son Ltd Edinburgh

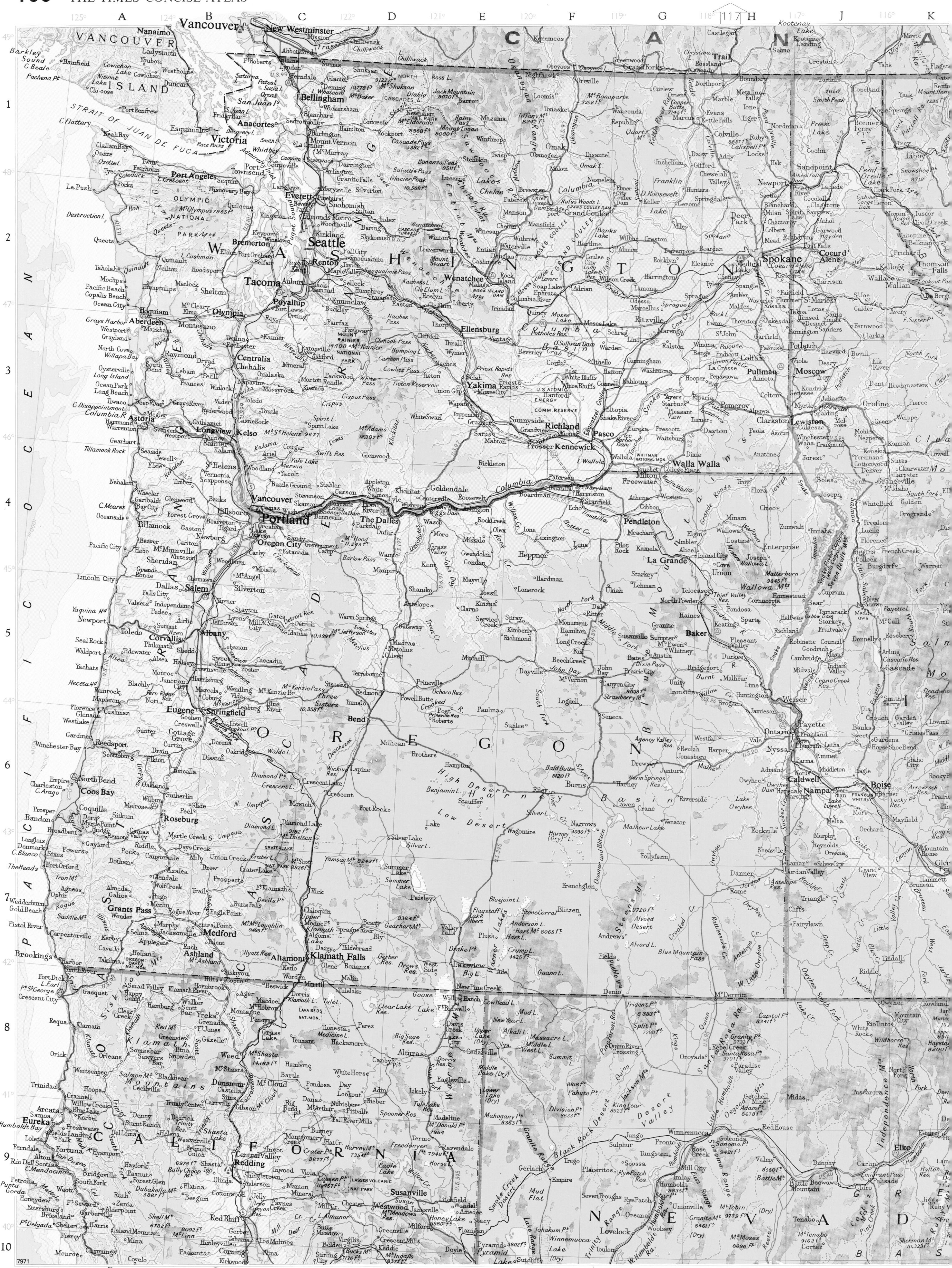
CANADA
VANCOUVER ISLAND
Vancouver
Victoria
STRAIT OF JUAN DE FUCA
WASHINGTON
Seattle
Tacoma
Olympia
Spokane
Yakima
Walla Walla
PACIFIC OCEAN
OREGON
Portland
Salem
Eugene
Bend
Pendleton
La Grande
Baker
Medford
Klamath Falls
IDAHO
Boise
CALIFORNIA
Eureka
Redding
NEVADA
Winnemucca
Elko
Columbia R.
Snake R.
High Desert
Harney Basin
Klamath Mountains
Black Rock Desert
117
102
3281 656 0 300 600 1500 3000 6000 9000 12000 feet
1000 200 0 91 183 457 914 1829 2743 3658 m
LAMBERT CONFORMAL CONIC PROJECTION

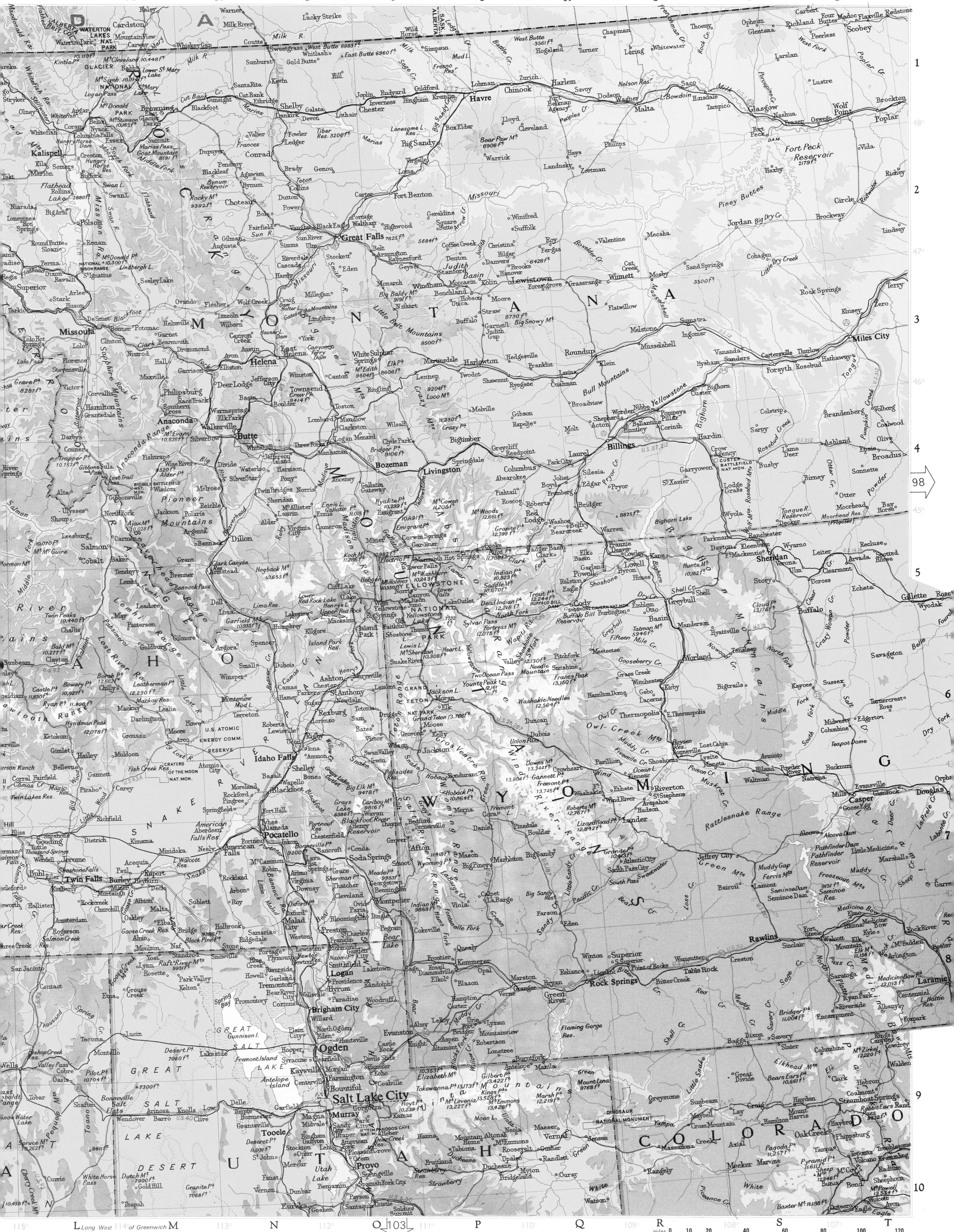

© John Bartholomew & Son Ltd Edinburgh

1:3M

Heights in feet
Depths in metres

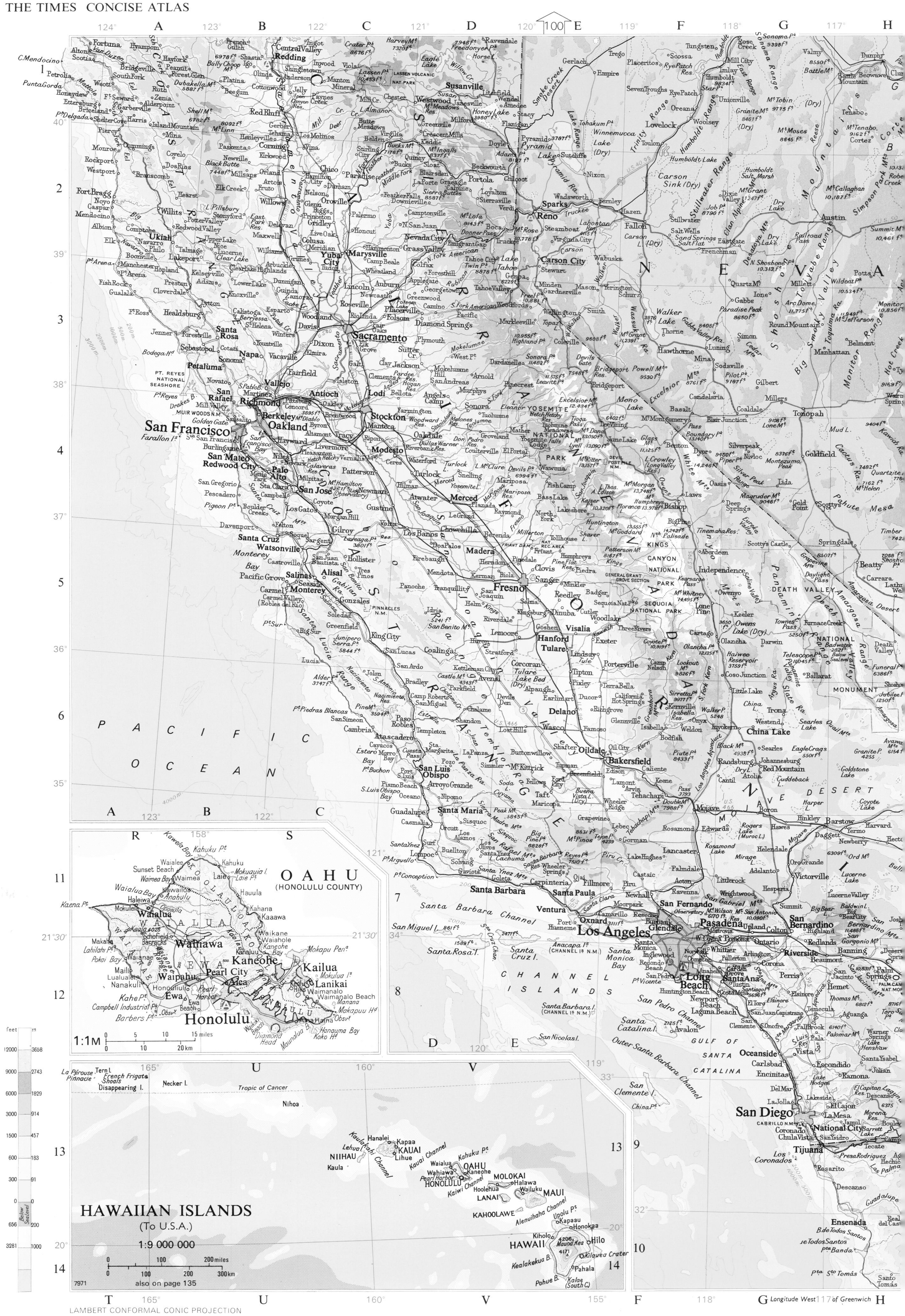

100
PACIFIC OCEAN
NEVADA
San Francisco
Sacramento
Oakland
San Jose
Fresno
Bakersfield
Los Angeles
San Diego
Reno
Carson City
Santa Barbara
Long Beach
Tijuana
Ensenada
CHANNEL ISLANDS
GULF OF SANTA CATALINA
MOJAVE DESERT
DEATH VALLEY
YOSEMITE NATIONAL PARK
SEQUOIA NATIONAL PARK
KINGS CANYON NATIONAL PARK
OAHU
(HONOLULU COUNTY)
Honolulu
1:1M
HAWAIIAN ISLANDS
(To U.S.A.)
1:9 000 000
also on page 135
Tropic of Cancer
NIIHAU
KAUAI
OAHU
MOLOKAI
LANAI
MAUI
KAHOOLAWE
HAWAII
Longitude West 117 of Greenwich
LAMBERT CONFORMAL CONIC PROJECTION

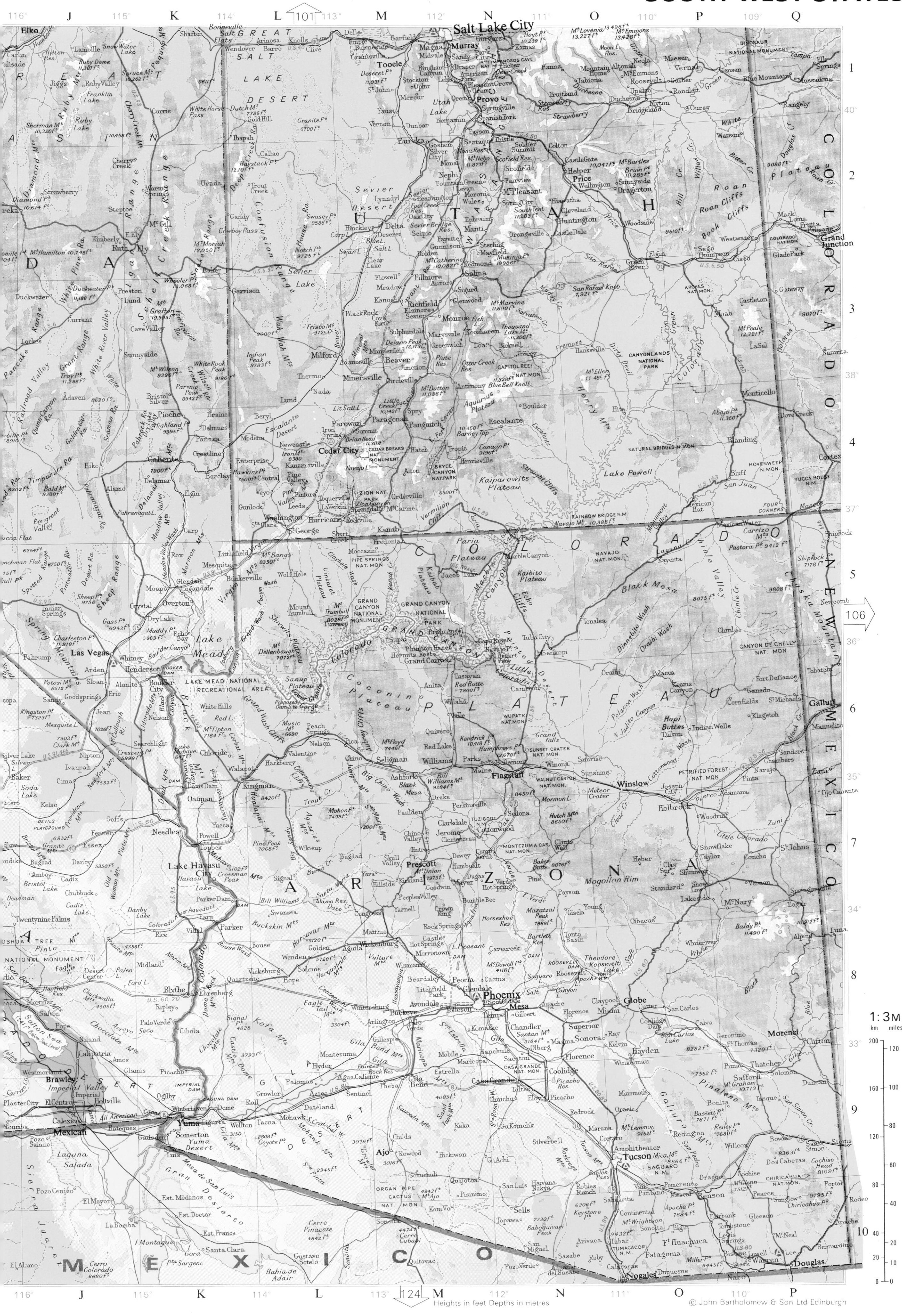

1:3M

km   miles
200 ─ 120

160 ─ 100

─ 80

120 ─

─ 60

80 ─

─ 40

40 ─

─ 20

0 ─ 0

Heights in feet Depths in metres

© John Bartholomew & Son Ltd Edinburgh

PACIFIC
OCEAN
MARIN
CONTRA
COSTA
ALAMEDA
SAN
MATEO
SANTA CLARA
SAN
JOAQUIN
STANISLAUS
SAN FRANCISCO
Kent Lake
San Anselmo
San Rafael
San Pablo
Bay
San Pablo
Ross
Kentfield
Larkspur
San
Quentin
Corte Madera
Mill
Valley
Mt. Tamalpais
2571
Mt. Tamalpais
State Park
Muir Woods
Nat. Monument
Stinson
Beach
Tiburon
Belvedere
Sausalito
GOLDEN GATE BRIDGE
Alcatraz I.
Golden
Gate
Treasure
Island
Richmond
Golden Gate Park
Univ. of San Francisco
Sunset
Mission
Mt. Davidson
929
Lake
Merced
Naval
Shipyard
Daly City
Brisbane
Edgemar
Pacifica
South San Francisco
San Bruno
San Francisco
International
Airport
Millbrae
Shelter Cove
San Pedro Point
Pedro
Valley
San
Andreas
Lake
Burlingame
Hillsborough
San Francisco State
Fish and Game Reserve
San Mateo
Foster City
Montara
Moss Beach
El Granada
Crystal
Springs
Lake
Belmont
San
Carlos
Redwood
City
Pillar Point
Half
Moon Bay
Half Moon Bay
Woodside
Menlo
Park
Stanford
University
Palo Alto
Portola
Valley
Tunitas
San Gregorio
Redwood
Terrace
La Honda
SANTA CRUZ MTS
Mountain
View
Los
Altos
Black
Mountain
2750
Cupertino
Stevens Cr.
Reservoir
Sunnyvale
Santa Clara
San Jose
Campbell
Alviso
Milpitas
Agnew
Berryessa
Alum Rock
Evergreen
Mt. Hamilton
4261
Lick
Observatory
Black Mountain
3951
Calaveras
Reservoir
DIABLO
RANGE
Monument
Peak
2594
Warm
Springs
Mission
San Jose
Irvington
Fremont
Newark
Niles
Sunol
Alameda Cr.
Hetch Hetchy Aqueduct
(Underground)
3817
Union City
Mt. Eden
Hayward
San
Lorenzo
San Francisco Bay
SAN
MATEO
BRIDGE
DUMBARTON
BRIDGE
Castro
Valley
Lake Chabot
San
Leandro
Oakland
International
Airport
Alameda
Redwood
Regional
Park
Upper
San Leandro
Reservoir
Oakland
Piedmont
Moraga
CALDECOTT
TUNNEL
Berkeley
Angel Island
State Park
University of California
Albany
El Cerrito
Richmond
El Sobrante
RICHMOND-
SAN RAFAEL
BRIDGE
McNears
Beach
San Pablo
Ridge
San Pablo
Res.
Charles
Lee Tilden
Regional
Park
Briones Res.
Orinda
Village
Orinda
Lafayette
Lafayette Reservoir
Saranap
Walnut Creek
Pleasant Hill
Concord
Alamo
Danville
San Ramon
San Ramon Village
Dublin
Pleasanton
Livermore
State Game
Refuge
Mt. Diablo
3849
Mt. Diablo
State Park
Black Hills
Cowell
Clayton
Antioch
Oakley
Sand Hill
Knightsen
Brentwood
Byron
Old River
San Joaquin River
Middle River
Union Island
Old River
Tracy
Carbona
Delta Mendota
Canal
Dam
Alameda Cr.

LOS ANGELES

ANGELES
NATIONAL
8020
FOREST
San Gabriel Mountains
Mt. San Antonio
10.064
LOS
ANGELES
SAN
BERNARDINO
VENTURA
RIVERSIDE
ORANGE
PACIFIC
OCEAN
Santa
Monica
Bay
Santa Monica Mts.
Van Norman Lakes
Sylmar
San Fernando
Santa Susana
Simi Valley
Chatsworth
Chatsworth
Reservoir
Northridge
Sepulveda
Winnetka
Canoga Park
San Fernando Valley
Tarzana
Woodland
Hills
Encino
Sherman
Oaks
Sunland
Sun
Valley
Verdugo Mountains
La Crescenta
Montrose
La Canada
Burbank
North
Hollywood
San Rafael Hills
Rose
Bowl
Altadena
San Gabriel Peak
6161
Mt. Wilson
Observatory
Cogswell
Reservoir
San Gabriel
Reservoir
Morris
Reservoir
Sierra Madre
Monrovia
Duarte
Azusa
Glendora
Glendale
Griffith
Park
Eagle Rock
Pasadena
South
Pasadena
Arcadia
San
Marino
Temple City
Hollywood
Bowl
West
Hollywood
Hollywood
Beverly Hills
University
of California
Elysian
Park
Dodgers Stad.
LOS ANGELES
Arroyo
Seco
Park
Alhambra
San
Gabriel
Rosemead
El Monte
Monterey
Park
South
San Gabriel
East Los Angeles
Puddingstone
Reservoir
State Rec. Area
San Dimas
La Verne
Claremont
Upland
Cucamonga
Etiwanda
Baldwin
Park
Covina
West
Covina
Pomona
Ontario
Saddle Peak
2805
Malibu
Beach
Topanga
Beach
Pacific
Palisades
Santa Monica
Venice
Culver City
Boyle
Heights
Montebello
Puente Hills
La Puente
North Whittier
Hts.
Diamond
Bar
Chino
Mira Loma
Marina
del Rey
Los Angeles
International
Airport
Maywood
Florence
Commerce
Pico Rivera
Huntington Park
Bell Gardens
Hacienda
Hts.
Rowland
Heights
Whittier
La Habra
Heights
Los
Serranos
Chino Hills
Inglewood
Lennox
Watts
South
Gate
Downey
Hollydale
La Habra
Brea
El Segundo
Manhattan
Beach
Hawthorne
Lawndale
Willow
Brook
Lynwood
Paramount
Norwalk
South
Whittier
La Mirada
Yorba Linda
Prado Flood
Control Basin
Prado Dam
Pedley
Arlanza
Village
Norco
Corona
Home
Gardens
Gardena
Compton
Bellflower
Buena
Park
Fullerton
Hermosa
Beach
Redondo
Beach
Dominguez
Hills
North
Long Beach
Artesia
Cerritos
Lakewood
La Palma
Cypress
Anaheim
Torrance
Carson
Los
Alamitos
Disneyland
Santa Ana
River
SANTA ANA MTS.
Palos Verdes
Estates
Lomita
Signal Hill
Rossmoor
Stanton
Garden
Grove
Orange
Irvine
Lake
Rocky Point
Wilmington
Long
Beach
Palos Verdes
Hills
Westminster
Santa Ana
Cowan
Heights
Lemon Heights
Tustin
CLEVELAND
NATIONAL
FOREST
4007
Marineland
of the Pacific
San Pedro
San Pedro Bay
Seal
Beach
Sunset
Bay
Sunset Beach
Santiago
Peak
5687
Point
Fermin
Passenger Ferry
to Santa Catalina
Island
San Pedro Channel
Fountain
Valley
Como
Huntington
Beach
Irvine
Costa Mesa
Newport Beach
km
miles

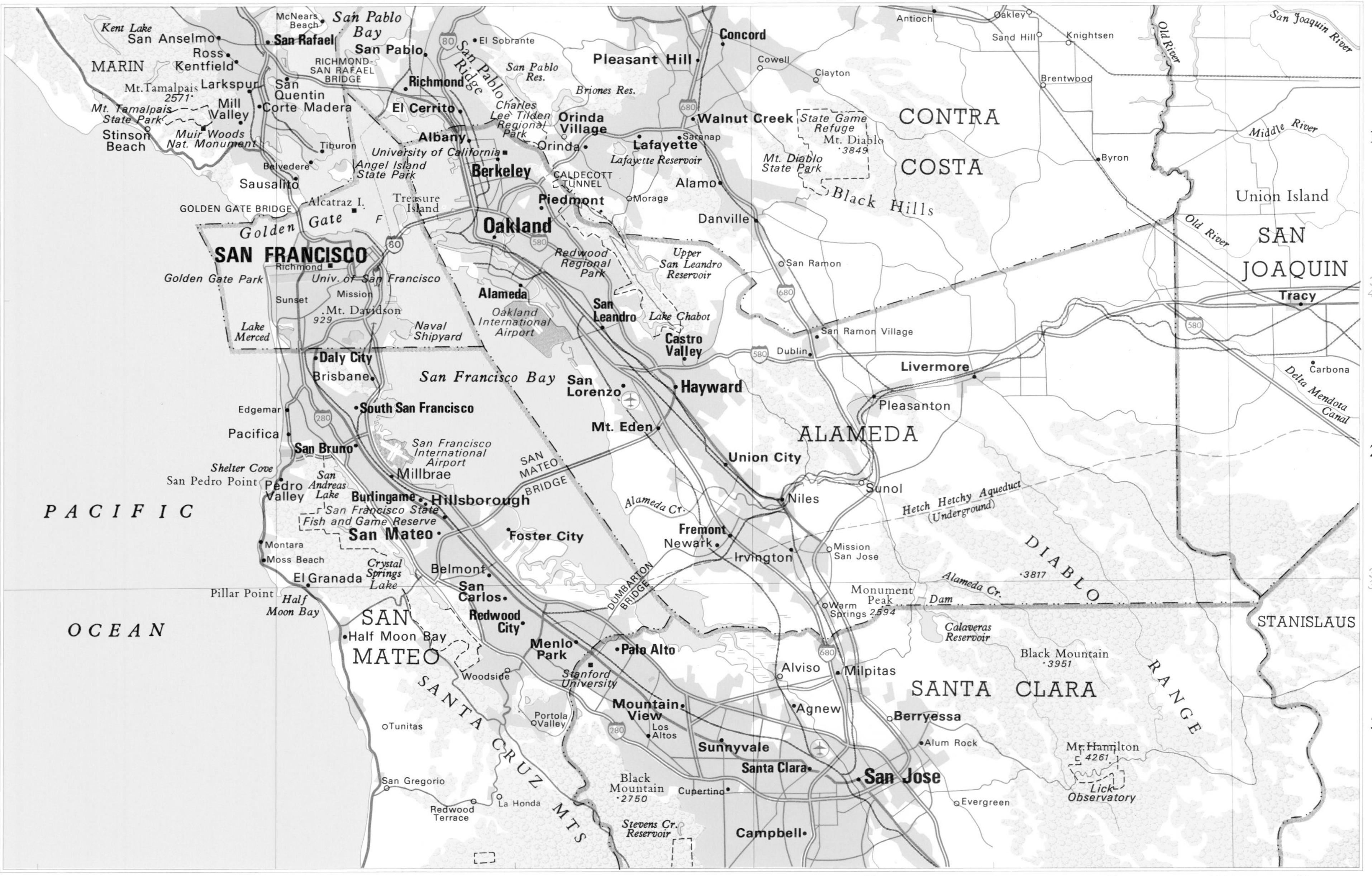

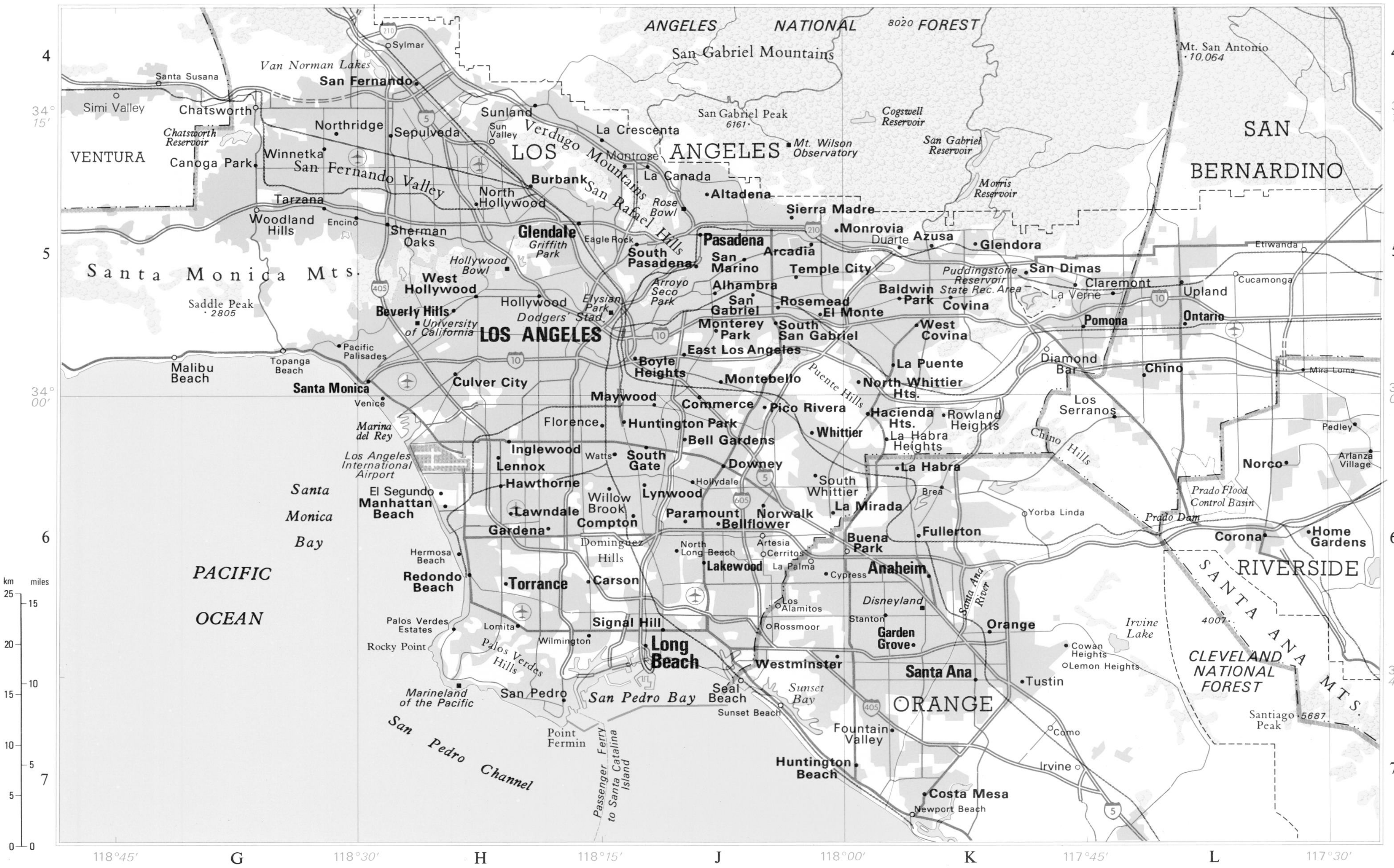

1:500 000

© Times Books Ltd

A
B
C
D
E
LAKE
COOK
DU PAGE
KANE
WILL
KENDALL
LAKE
PORTER
LAKE MICHIGAN
ILLINOIS
MICHIGAN
INDIANA
CHICAGO
Algonquin
Cuba
Barrington
Buffalo Grove
Deerfield
Highland Park
Spring Lake Reserve
Wheeling
Glencoe
Carpentersville
Inverness
Palatine
Northbrook
Sutton
Prospect Hts.
Arlington Hts.
Winnetka
Kenilworth
Wilmette
Rolling Meadows
Mt. Prospect
Elgin
Glenview
Hoffman Estates
Des Plaines
Morton Grove
Skokie
Evanston
Busse Forest
Niles
Schaumburg
Elk Grove Village
Park Ridge
S. Elgin
Lincolnwood
Bartlett
Hanover Park
Keeneyville
O'Hare International Airport
Roselle
Itasca
Valley View
Bensenville
Harwood Hts.
Lincoln Park
Belmont Harbor
Wayne
Bloomingdale
Wood Dale
Franklin Park
St. Charles
Elmwood Park
Geneva
Villa Park
Elmhurst
Melrose Park
Oak Park
W.Chicago
Lombard
Glen Ellyn
Bell Wood
Maywood
Art Institute
Chicago Harbor
Wheaton
Batavia
Broadview
Forest Park
Berwyn
North Aurora
Warrenhurst
Warrenville
Morton Arboretum
Brookfield Zoo
Cicero
Riverside
Stickney
La Grange
Brookfield
Lisle
Hinsdale
Downers Grove
University of Chicago
Jackson Park
Museum of Science and Industry
Naperville
Summit
Aurora
S. Stickney
South Chicago
Bridgeview
Evergreen Park
Oak Lawn
Barbers Corner
Willow Springs
Des Plaines River
Argonne Forest
Calumet Harbor
Michigan City
Oswego
Hastings
Sag Bridge
Worth
Merrionette Park
Calumet Sag
Lemont
Calumet Park
Whiting
Beverly Shores
Palos Park
Palos Hts.
Lake Calumet Harbor
Wolf Lake
East Chicago
Normantown
Romeoville
Blue Island
Riverdale
Dune Acres
Tremont
Plainfield
Goodings Grove
Orland Park
Midlothian
Harvey
Dolton
Burnham
Calumet City
Ogden Dunes
Du Page River
Hammond
Porter
Chesterton
Oak Forest
Crest Hill
Lockport
Markham
S. Holland
Gary
Otis
Tinley Park
Lansing
Homewood
E. Gary
Black Oak
Marley
Munster
Highland
Liverpool
New Chicago
Portage
Woodville
Westville
Shorewood
Joliet
Ridgewood
Mokena
Flossmoor
Glen Park
Hobart
Rockdale
Ingalls Park
Lincoln Estates
Griffith
Chicago Hts.
Lake George
Wheeler
Burlington Beach
Coburg
New Lenox
Frankfort
Matteson
S. Chicago Heights
Lottaville
Sedley
Birds
Schereville
Merrillville
Valparaiso
Independence Hill
Park Forest

ST. LOUIS

F
G
H
Pere Marquette State Park
Grafton
Fosterburg
Brussels
Godfrey
Melville
MADISON
Centerville
Portage des Sioux
ILLINOIS
MISSOURI
Alton
Midway
Bethalto
Orchard Farm
East Alton
Peruque
Black Walnut
West Alton
Wood River
Gard
Kampville
Fort Bellefontaine
Roxana
Boschertown
ST. CHARLES
St. Peters
Spanish Lake
Edwardsville
Florissant
St.Charles
Hazelwood
Larimore
Lewis and Clark State Memorial
Robertson
Mitchell
Harvester
Bridgeton
Ferguson
Bellefontaine Neighbors
Berkeley
Maryland Hts.
St. Ann
Jennings
Pontoon Beach
Overland
Breckenridge Hills
Granite City
Madison
Horseshoe Lake
Pagedale
Olivette
University City
Venice
Collinsville
Creve Coeur
Clayton
Bellefontaine
Ladue
Washington University
Forest Park
ST. LOUIS
Caseyville
Washington Park
Clarkson Valley
Richmond Hts.
Jefferson Nat. Expansion Mem.
East St.Louis
French Village
Ballwin
Manchester
Des Peres
Rock Hill
Glendale
Maplewood
Fairview Hts.
ST. LOUIS
Kirkwood
Brentwood
Webster Groves
Frank Holten State Park
Allorton
Valley Park
Crestwood
Cahokia
Centerville
Affton
Belleville
Sappington
Lemay
Times Beach
Dupo
ST.CLAIR
Murphy
Mehlville
Oakville
High Ridge
Paulina Hills
Millstadt
Byrnes Mill
Arnold
Columbia
Maxville
House Springs
Seckman
Smithton
JEFFERSON
Ottoville
Antonia
MONROE
Sand Ridge
Floraville
Fountain
Barnhart
Mississippi River
Waterloo
Foster Pond
Hecker
Belew Creek
Valmeyer
Harrisonville
Burksville
Madonnaville

ATLANTA

J
K
L
Allatoona Reservoir
CHEROKEE
Arnold Mill
FORSYTH
Big Creek
Woodstock
Acworth
Crabapple
Noonday
Sweat Mountain
Alpharetta
Blackwells
Big Creek
Kennesaw
Roswell
Warsaw
Due West
Kennesaw Mtn. National Battlefield Park
Marietta
Mt. Bethel
GWINNETT
Dunwoody
Sandy Springs
Norcross
Fair Oaks
Mackland
COBB
Chamblee
Doraville
Smyrna
North Atlanta
Vinings
Lilburn
Powder Springs
Oakdale
Tucker
Clarkdale
Harryat
Oak Grove
Stone Mountain Park
Austell
Mableton
Buckhead
Cooks
Emory University
Clarkston
Stone Mountain
Emory
Scottdale
DOUGLAS
Chattahoochee River
Grove Park
ATLANTA
Decatur
Avondale Estates
Glen Haven
Redan
State Capitol
DE KALB
Cascade Heights
Lakewood Heights
Lithonia
Panthersville
Constitution
East Point
Snapfinger
Hapeville
Henrico
College Park
Panola
Klondike
Conley
Red Oak
Hartsfield Atlanta Airport
Forest Park
Camp Smyrna
FULTON
ROCKDALE
Union City
Morrow
Lake City
Fairburn
CLAYTON
Whitehouse
Stockbridge
Palmetto
Jonesboro
FAYETTE
HENRY
Flint River
Stop
Hastings
Fayetteville
McDonough
km
miles

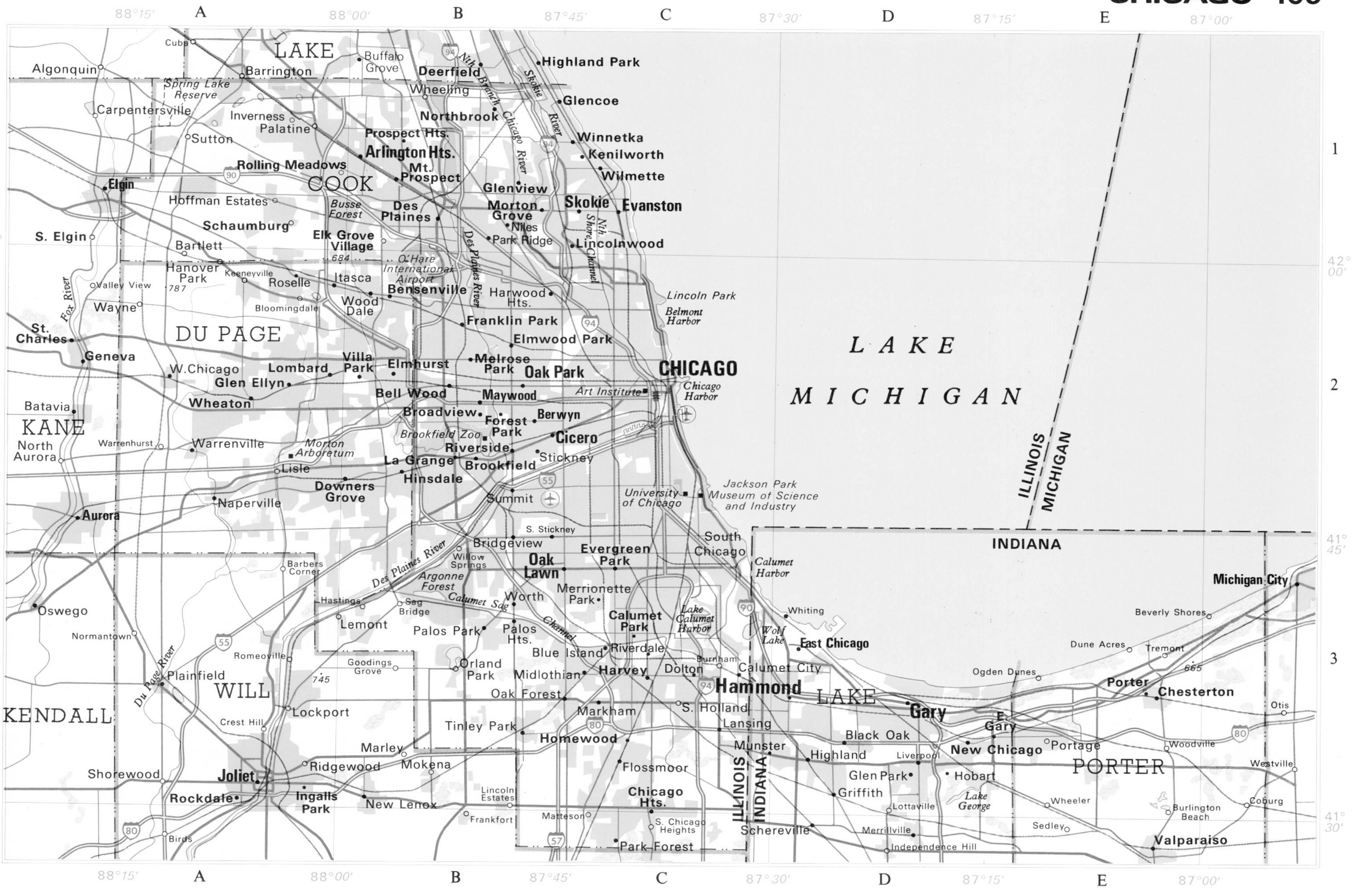

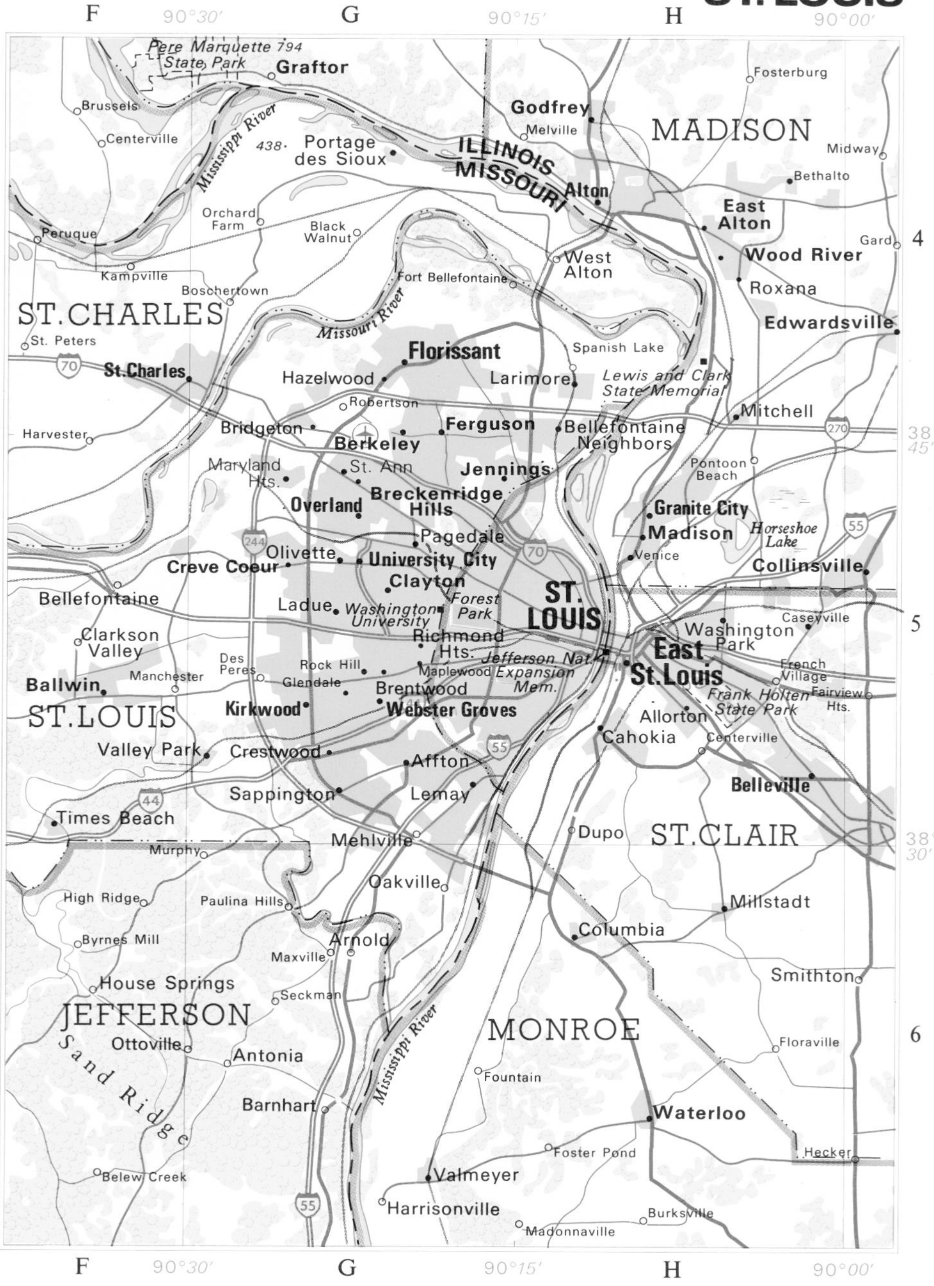

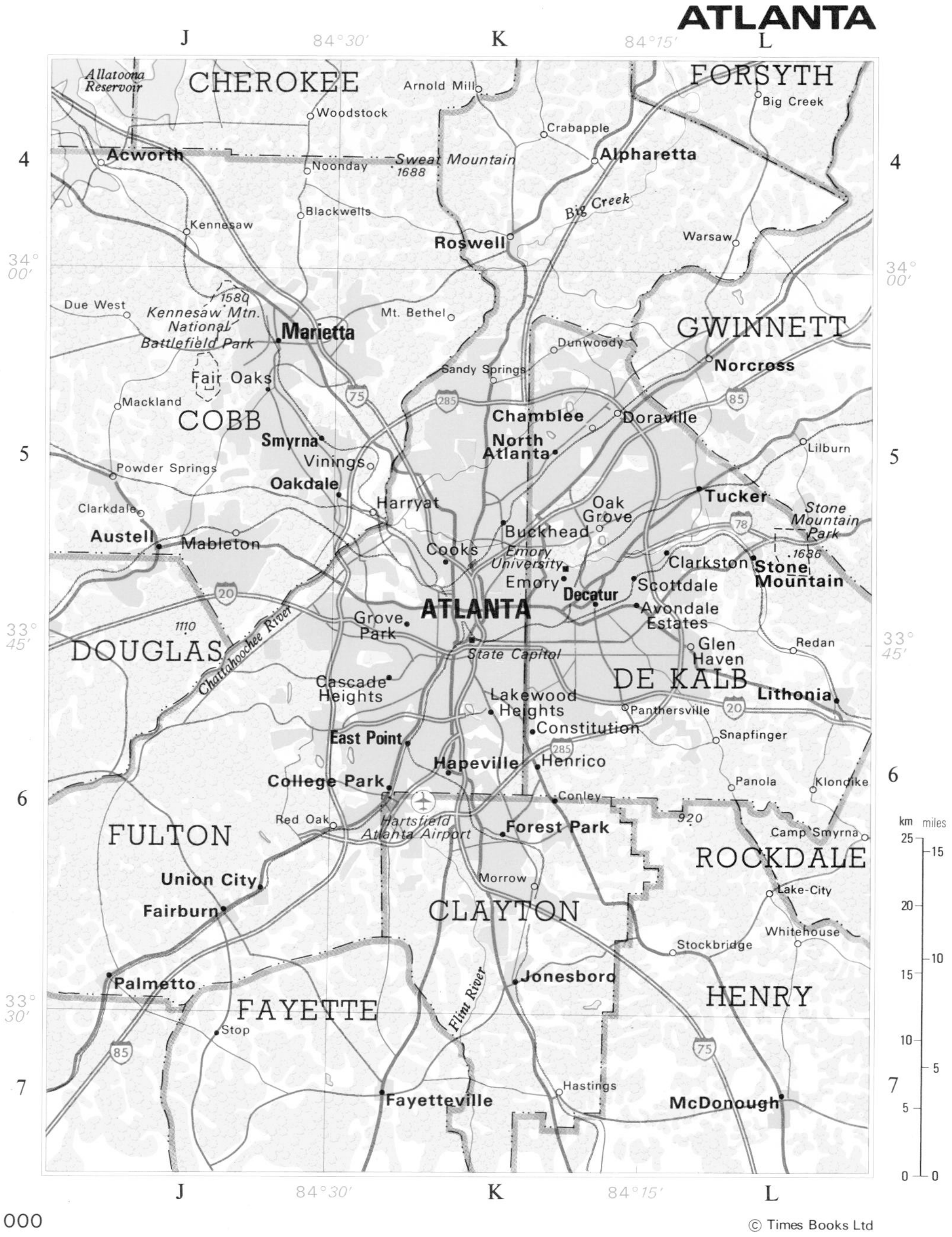

1:500 000

© Times Books Ltd

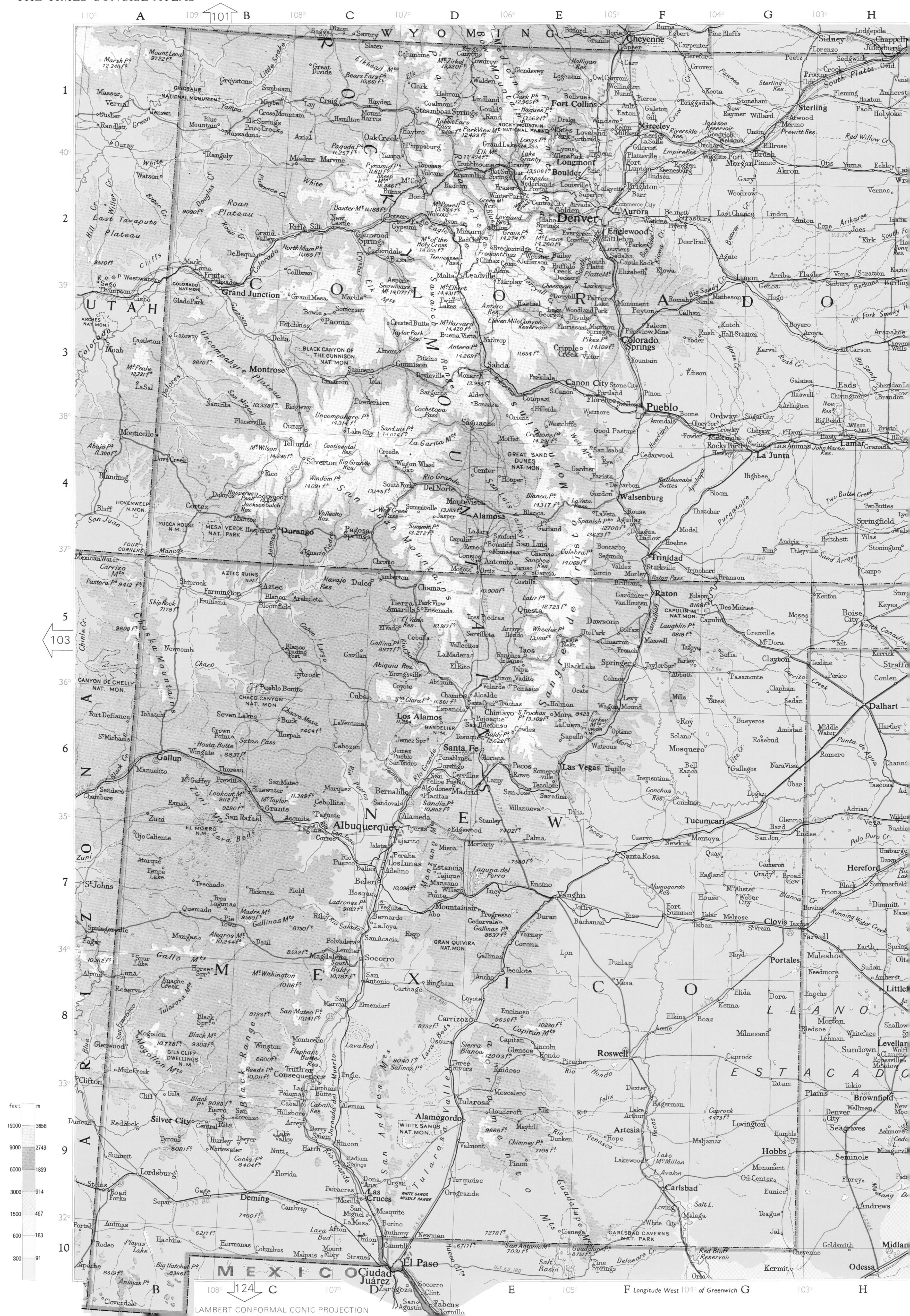
A B C D E F G H
1 2 3 4 5 6 7 8 9 10
101
103
124
WYOMING
UTAH
COLORADO
NEW MEXICO
ARIZONA
MEXICO
ROCKY MOUNTAINS
SAN JUAN MOUNTAINS
SANGRE DE CRISTO MTS
LLANO ESTACADO
Cheyenne
Fort Collins
Greeley
Boulder
Longmont
Denver
Aurora
Englewood
Colorado Springs
Pueblo
Canon City
Grand Junction
Montrose
Gunnison
Salida
Leadville
Durango
Alamosa
Trinidad
Walsenburg
La Junta
Lamar
Sterling
Raton
Taos
Los Alamos
Santa Fe
Las Vegas
Gallup
Grants
Albuquerque
Farmington
Socorro
Tucumcari
Clovis
Portales
Roswell
Alamogordo
Artesia
Carlsbad
Hobbs
Las Cruces
Silver City
Deming
Lordsburg
El Paso
Ciudad Juárez
Dalhart
Hereford
Odessa
Midland
DINOSAUR NATIONAL MONUMENT
ROCKY MOUNTAIN NATIONAL PARK
BLACK CANYON OF THE GUNNISON NAT. MON.
GREAT SAND DUNES NAT. MON.
MESA VERDE NAT. PARK
CHACO CANYON NAT. MON.
WHITE SANDS NAT. MON.
CARLSBAD CAVERNS NAT. PARK
FOUR CORNERS
Mt Elbert 14,431 ft
Pikes Pk 14,109 ft
Longs Pk 14,255
Blanca Pk 14,317 ft
Wheeler Pk 13,160 ft
feet m
12000 3658
9000 2743
6000 1829
3000 914
1500 457
600 183
300 91
Longitude West of Greenwich
LAMBERT CONFORMAL CONIC PROJECTION

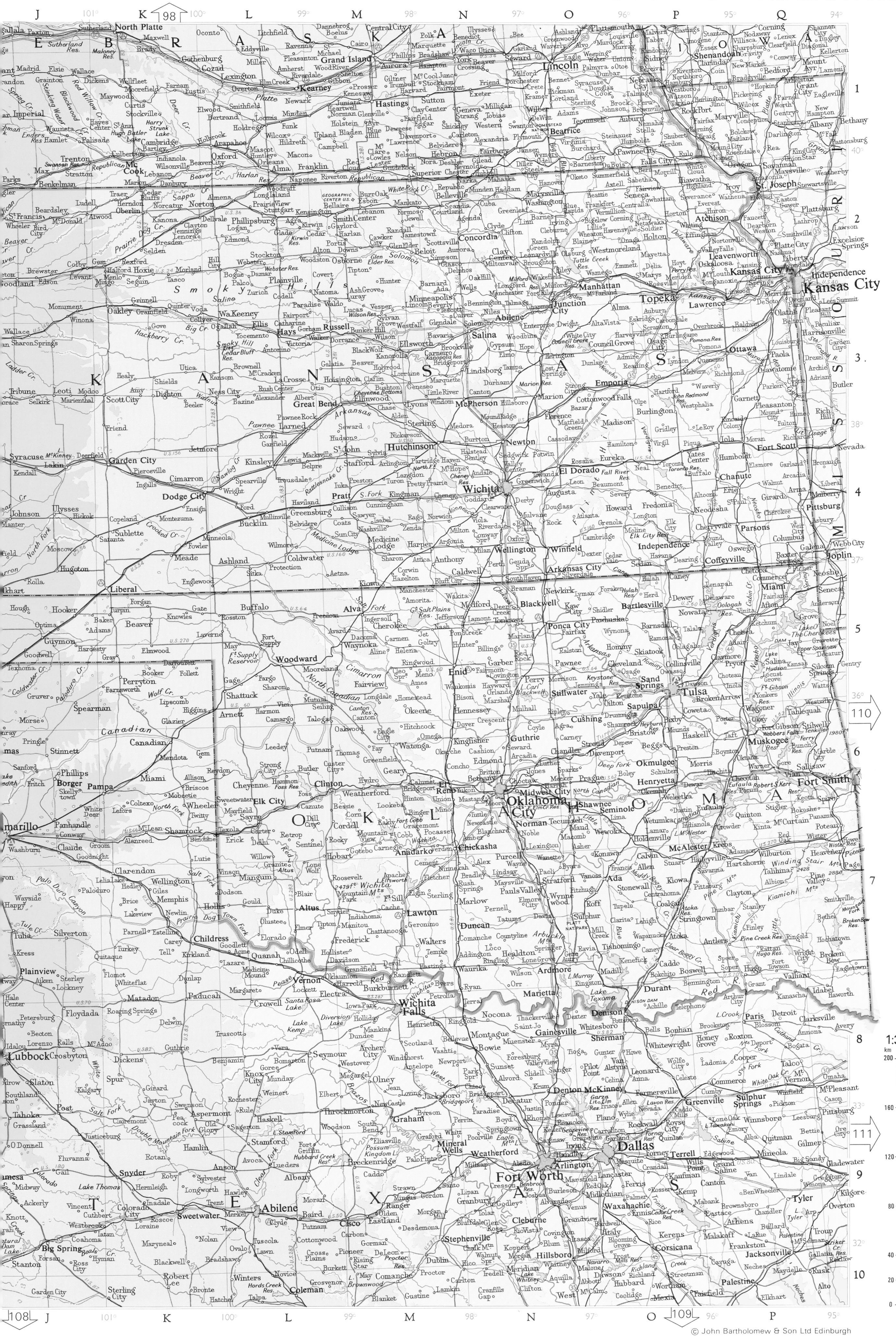
J K L M N O P Q
101° 100° 99° 98° 97° 96° 95° 94°
98
NEBRASKA
IOWA
KANSAS
MISSOURI
OKLAHOMA
TEXAS
North Platte
Grand Island
Kearney
Hastings
Lincoln
Beatrice
St. Joseph
Atchison
Leavenworth
Kansas City
Independence
Topeka
Lawrence
Manhattan
Junction City
Abilene
Salina
Hays
Russell
Great Bend
Dodge City
Garden City
Liberal
Hutchinson
McPherson
Newton
Wichita
Emporia
Ottawa
Fort Scott
Pittsburg
Joplin
Coffeyville
Independence
Arkansas City
Enid
Woodward
Ponca City
Bartlesville
Stillwater
Tulsa
Muskogee
Fort Smith
Oklahoma City
Norman
Shawnee
Lawton
Ada
McAlester
Ardmore
Durant
Amarillo
Lubbock
Wichita Falls
Sherman
Denison
Paris
Denton
McKinney
Dallas
Fort Worth
Waco
Tyler
Abilene
Sweetwater
Big Spring
Corsicana
Palestine
110
111
108
109
1 2 3 4 5 6 7 8 9 10
1:3 M
km
miles
200
160
120
80
40
0
120
100
80
60
40
20
10
0

© John Bartholomew & Son Ltd Edinburgh

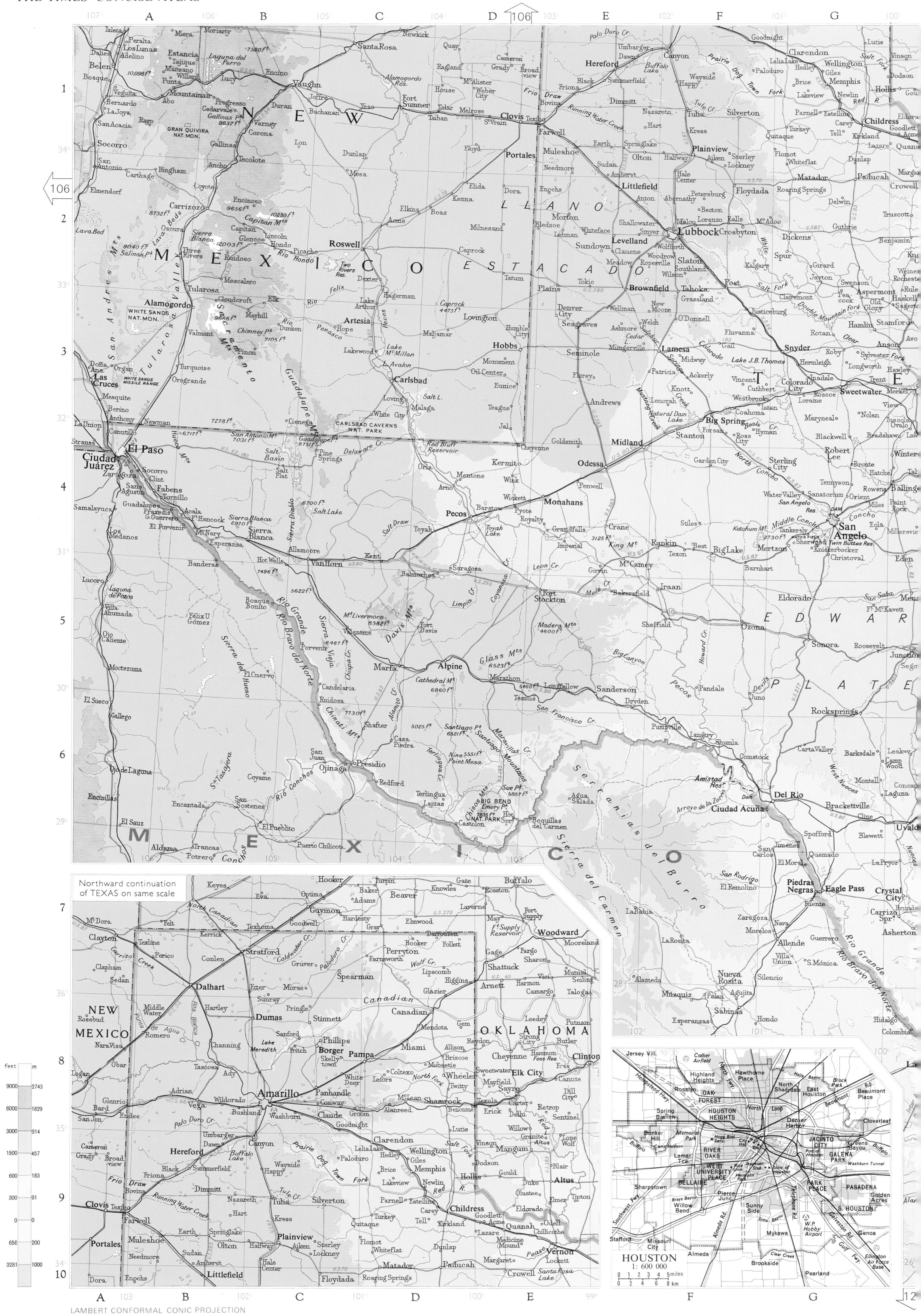
NEW MEXICO
LLANO ESTACADO
EDWARDS PLATEAU
MEXICO
Serranias del Burro
Sierra del Carmen
El Paso
Ciudad Juárez
Roswell
Carlsbad
Lubbock
Midland
Odessa
San Angelo
Del Rio
Ciudad Acuña
Piedras Negras
Eagle Pass
Alpine
Pecos
Big Spring
Hobbs
Clovis
Portales
Rio Grande
Rio Bravo del Norte
CARLSBAD CAVERNS NAT. PARK
BIG BEND NAT. PARK
WHITE SANDS NAT. MON.
GRAN QUIVIRA NAT. MON.
Northward continuation of TEXAS on same scale
NEW MEXICO
OKLAHOMA
Amarillo
Dalhart
Pampa
Borger
Canadian
HOUSTON
1: 600 000
miles
km
feet
m

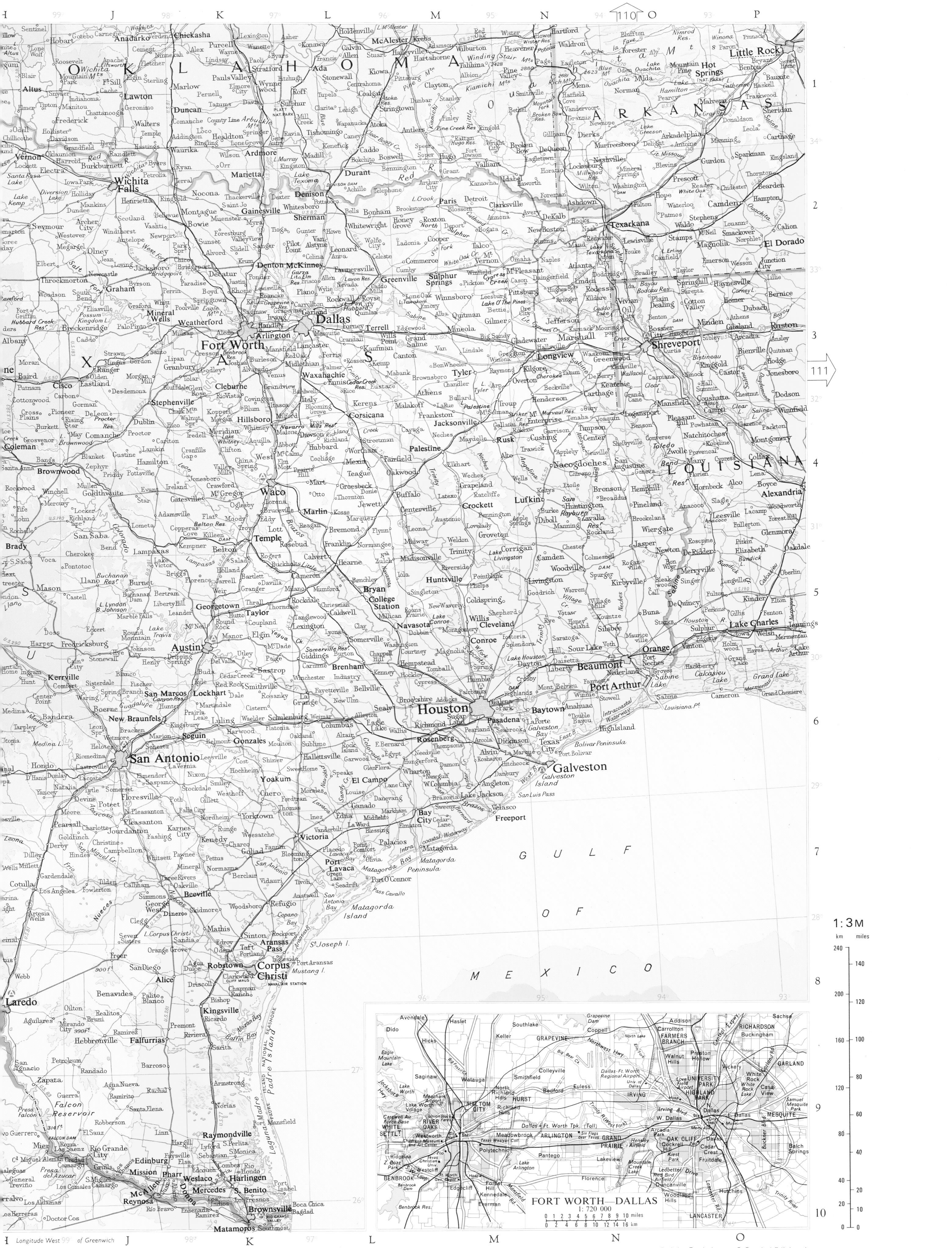

FORT WORTH—DALLAS
1:720 000

© John Bartholomew & Son Ltd Edinburgh

Heights in feet
Depths in metres

Longitude West of Greenwich

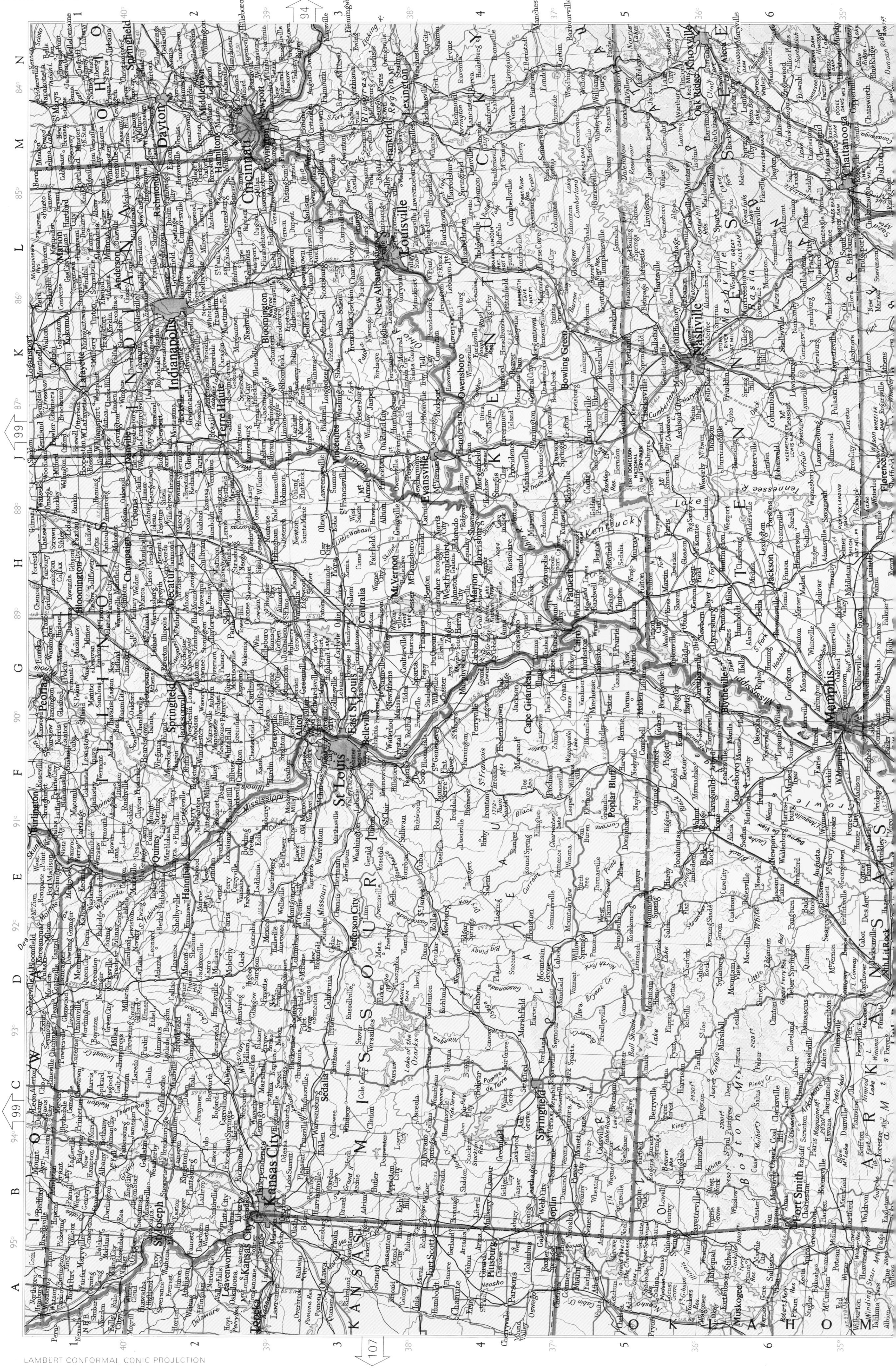

94
99
107
Kansas City
St Louis
East St Louis
Indianapolis
Louisville
Cincinnati
Dayton
Nashville
Memphis
Springfield
Knoxville
Chattanooga
Evansville
Lexington
Peoria
Decatur
Bowling Green
Fort Smith
Joplin
St Joseph
Topeka
Terre Haute
Bloomington
Champaign
Jefferson City
Cape Girardeau
Paducah
Poplar Bluff
Jackson
Hannibal
Quincy
Burlington
Columbia
Sedalia
Owensboro
Frankfort
Richmond
Anderson
Lafayette
Kokomo
Marion
Vincennes
Cairo
Blytheville
Jonesboro
Florence
K A N S A S
M I S S O U R I
I L L I N O I S
I N D I A N A
O H I O
K E N T U C K Y
T E N N E S S E E
A R K A N S A S
O K L A H O M A
Mississippi
Missouri
Lake of the Ozarks
Kentucky Lake
Tennessee
Cumberland
Ohio

LAMBERT CONFORMAL CONIC PROJECTION

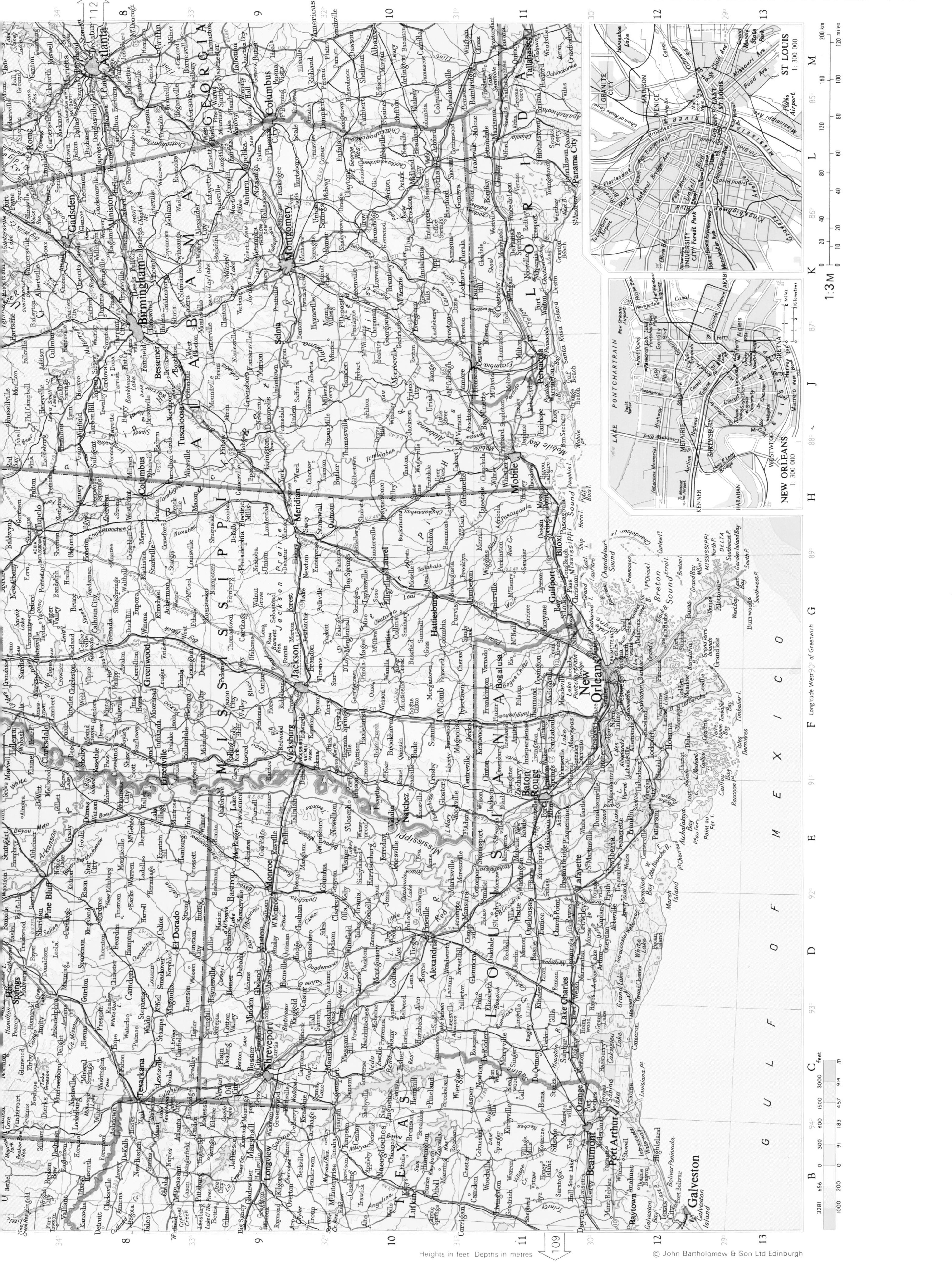

GEORGIA

ALABAMA

MISSISSIPPI

FLORIDA

LOUISIANA

TEXAS

ARKANSAS

ST LOUIS 1: 300 000

NEW ORLEANS 1: 300 000

1:3M

Longitude West 90° of Greenwich

G U L F   O F   M E X I C O

Heights in feet   Depths in metres

© John Bartholomew & Son Ltd Edinburgh

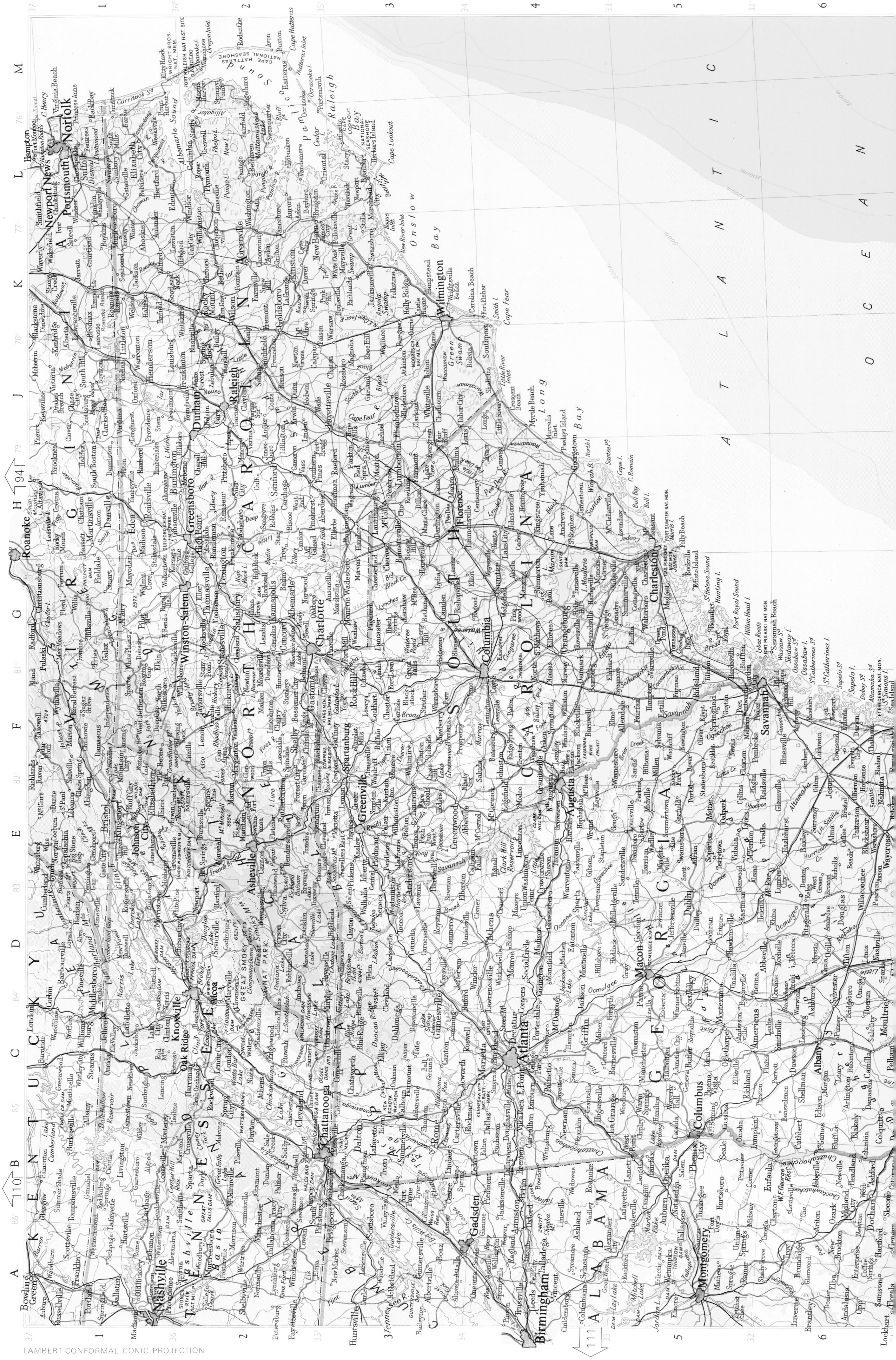
ATLANTIC OCEAN
NORTH CAROLINA
SOUTH CAROLINA
GEORGIA
ALABAMA
TENNESSEE
KENTUCKY
VIRGINIA

LAMBERT CONFORMAL CONIC PROJECTION

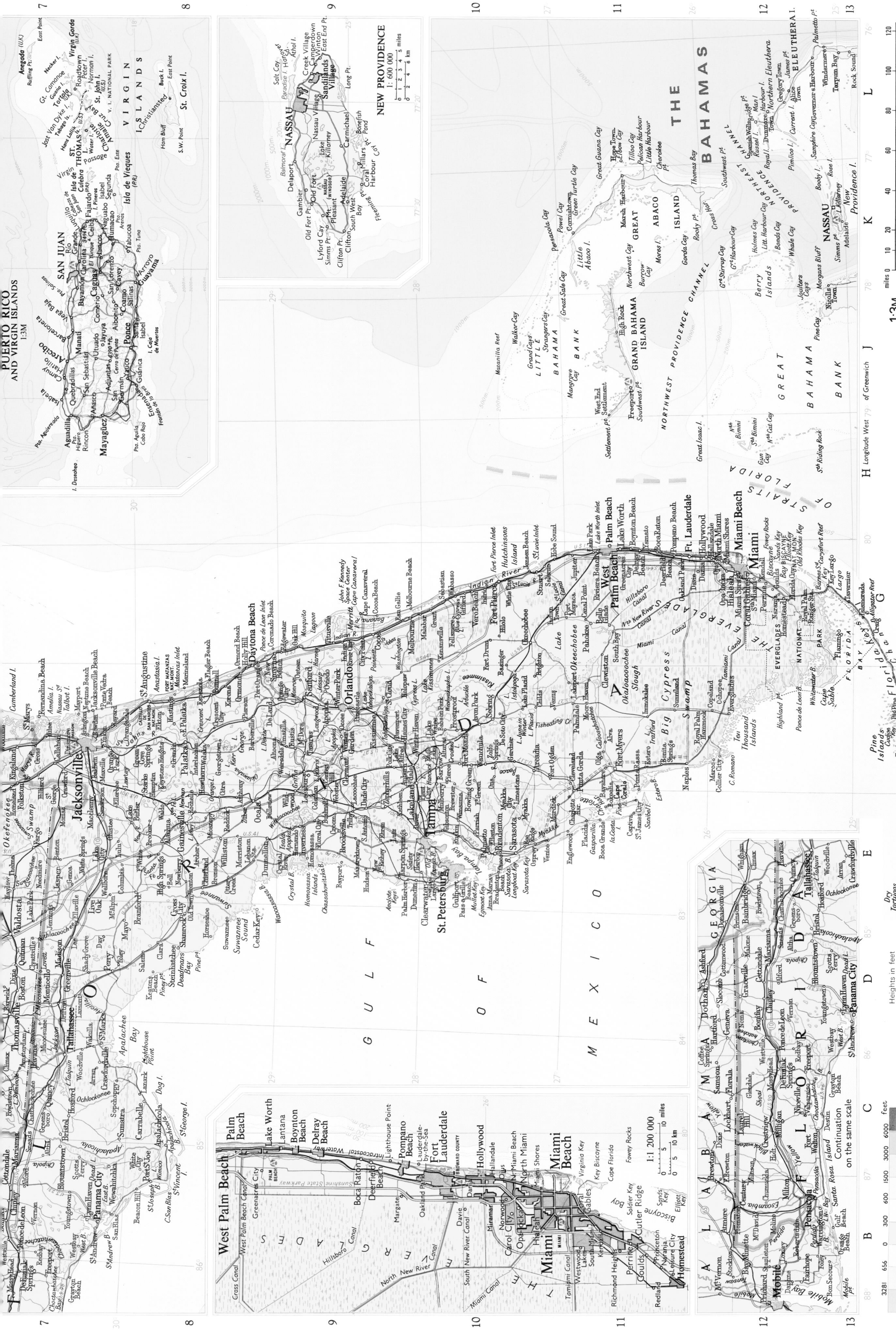
PUERTO RICO AND VIRGIN ISLANDS
1:3M
SAN JUAN
VIRGIN ISLANDS
NASSAU
NEW PROVIDENCE
1: 600 000
THE BAHAMAS
GRAND BAHAMA ISLAND
GREAT ABACO ISLAND
NORTHWEST PROVIDENCE CHANNEL
NORTHEAST PROVIDENCE CHANNEL
ELEUTHERA I.
GREAT BAHAMA BANK
LITTLE BAHAMA BANK
STRAITS OF FLORIDA
1:3M
Longitude West of Greenwich
Jacksonville
St. Augustine
Daytona Beach
Orlando
Tampa
St. Petersburg
Sarasota
Fort Myers
West Palm Beach
Ft. Lauderdale
Miami
Miami Beach
Key West
THE EVERGLADES
EVERGLADES NATIONAL PARK
Lake Okeechobee
GULF OF MEXICO
FLORIDA
GEORGIA
ALABAMA
Tallahassee
Pensacola
Panama City
Mobile
Dry Tortugas
1:1 200 000
Continuation on the same scale
Heights in feet
Depths in metres

© John Bartholomew & Son Ltd Edinburgh

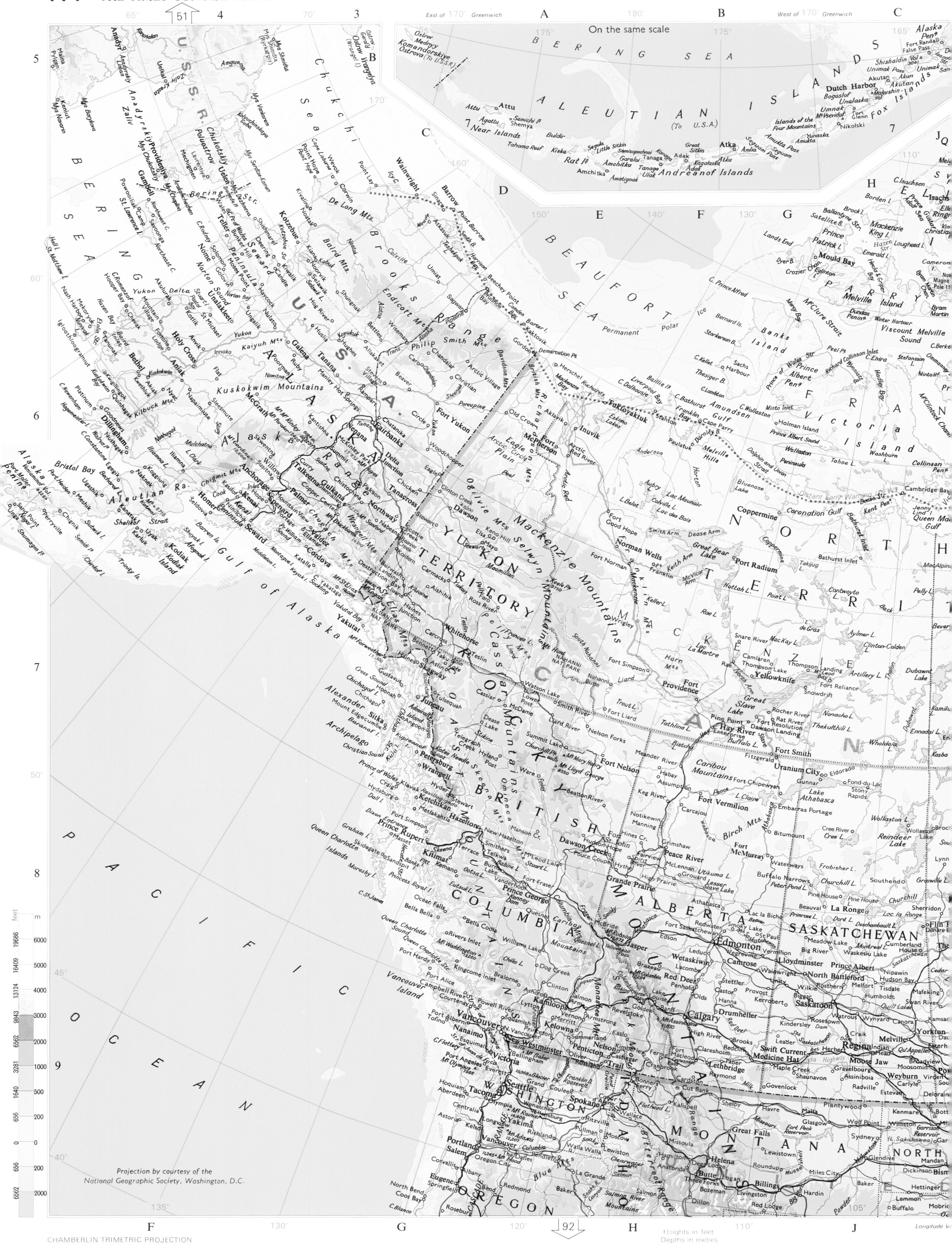

BERING SEA

ALEUTIAN ISLANDS

On the same scale

East of 170° Greenwich   West of 170° Greenwich

Near Islands   Rat Is   Andreanof Islands   Dutch Harbor

Alaska Pen.

Attu   Atka   Nikolski

BEAUFORT SEA

U.S.S.R.

Chukchi Sea

BERING SEA

Wrangel I.

Point Barrow

Barrow

Brooks Range

De Long Mts.   Endicott Mts.

A L A S K A (U.S.A.)

Kotzebue   Fairbanks

Seward Peninsula   Yukon

Nome   Delta Junction

Kuskokwim Mountains

Bethel   Anchorage

Bristol Bay   Kenai

Aleutian Ra.   Kodiak Island

Gulf of Alaska

Alaska Peninsula

PACIFIC OCEAN

YUKON TERRITORY

Dawson   Whitehorse

Mackenzie Mountains

Selwyn Mountains

Inuvik   Tuktoyaktuk

Fort McPherson

Arctic Circle

Great Bear Lake

Fort Good Hope   Norman Wells

NORTH WEST TERRITORIES

MACKENZIE

Yellowknife   Fort Providence

Great Slave Lake

Hay River   Fort Smith

Uranium City

Lake Athabasca

BRITISH COLUMBIA

Prince Rupert   Prince George

Kitimat   Vancouver Island

Queen Charlotte Islands

Juneau   Sitka   Petersburg   Wrangell   Ketchikan

Fort Nelson   Fort St. John

Dawson Creek   Peace River

Grande Prairie

ALBERTA

Edmonton   Calgary   Red Deer   Lethbridge   Medicine Hat

Fort McMurray

SASKATCHEWAN

Saskatoon   Regina   Prince Albert   North Battleford   Moose Jaw   Swift Current   Weyburn

Reindeer Lake

Vancouver   Victoria   Kamloops   Kelowna   Penticton   Nelson   Trail   Nanaimo

New Westminster

Seattle   Tacoma   Olympia   Spokane   Yakima

WASHINGTON

Portland   Salem   Eugene

OREGON

IDAHO

Missoula   Helena   Butte   Great Falls   Billings   Bozeman

MONTANA

NORTH DAKOTA

Projection by courtesy of the National Geographic Society, Washington, D.C.

Heights in feet
Depths in metres

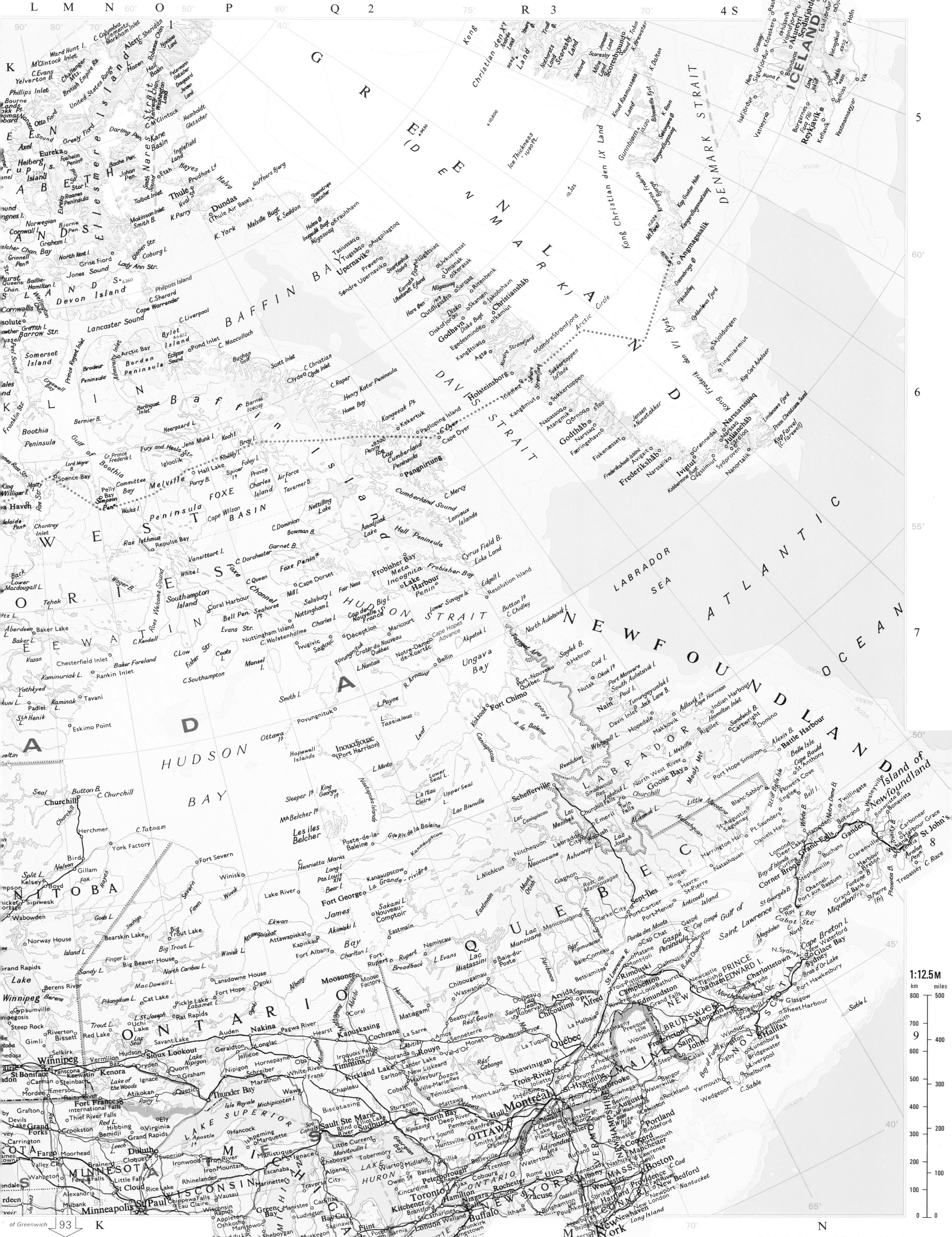
GREENLAND (DENMARK)
ICELAND
Reykjavik
Akureyri
DENMARK STRAIT
BAFFIN BAY
DAVIS STRAIT
Baffin Island
Devon Island
Ellesmere Island
Lancaster Sound
Somerset Island
Boothia Peninsula
Melville Peninsula
FOXE BASIN
Southampton Island
HUDSON STRAIT
Ungava Bay
HUDSON BAY
James Bay
LABRADOR SEA
ATLANTIC OCEAN
NEWFOUNDLAND
Island of Newfoundland
LABRADOR
QUEBEC
ONTARIO
MANITOBA
KEEWATIN
FRANKLIN
NEW BRUNSWICK
NOVA SCOTIA
PRINCE EDWARD I.
Gulf of Saint Lawrence
Cabot Str.
Thule
Godthåb
Frobisher Bay
Fort Chimo
Goose Bay
Schefferville
Churchill
Winnipeg
Thunder Bay
Sault Ste Marie
Sudbury
North Bay
Timmins
Moosonee
OTTAWA
Montréal
Québec
Sept-Îles
Charlottetown
Halifax
Saint John
Fredericton
Gander
St John's
Sydney
Toronto
Hamilton
Buffalo
Detroit
Boston
New York
Minneapolis
St Paul
Duluth
LAKE SUPERIOR
LAKE HURON
LAKE ERIE
LAKE ONTARIO
MICHIGAN
WISCONSIN
MINNESOTA
NEW YORK
MAINE
VERMONT
NEW HAMPSHIRE
MASS.
1:12.5M
km
miles
of Greenwich
93

© John Bartholomew & Son Ltd Edinburgh

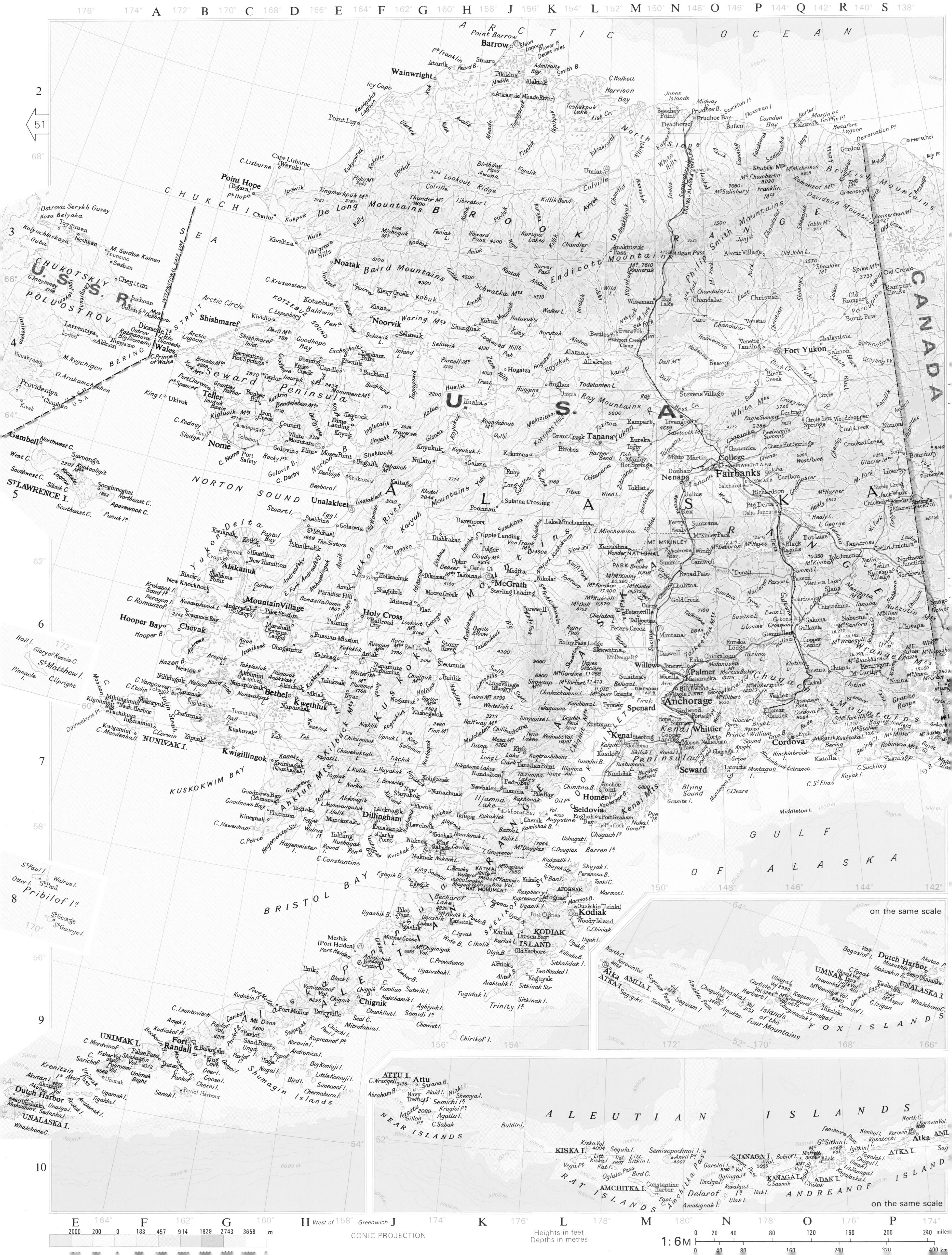

CONIC PROJECTION

Heights in feet
Depths in metres

1 : 6M

on the same scale

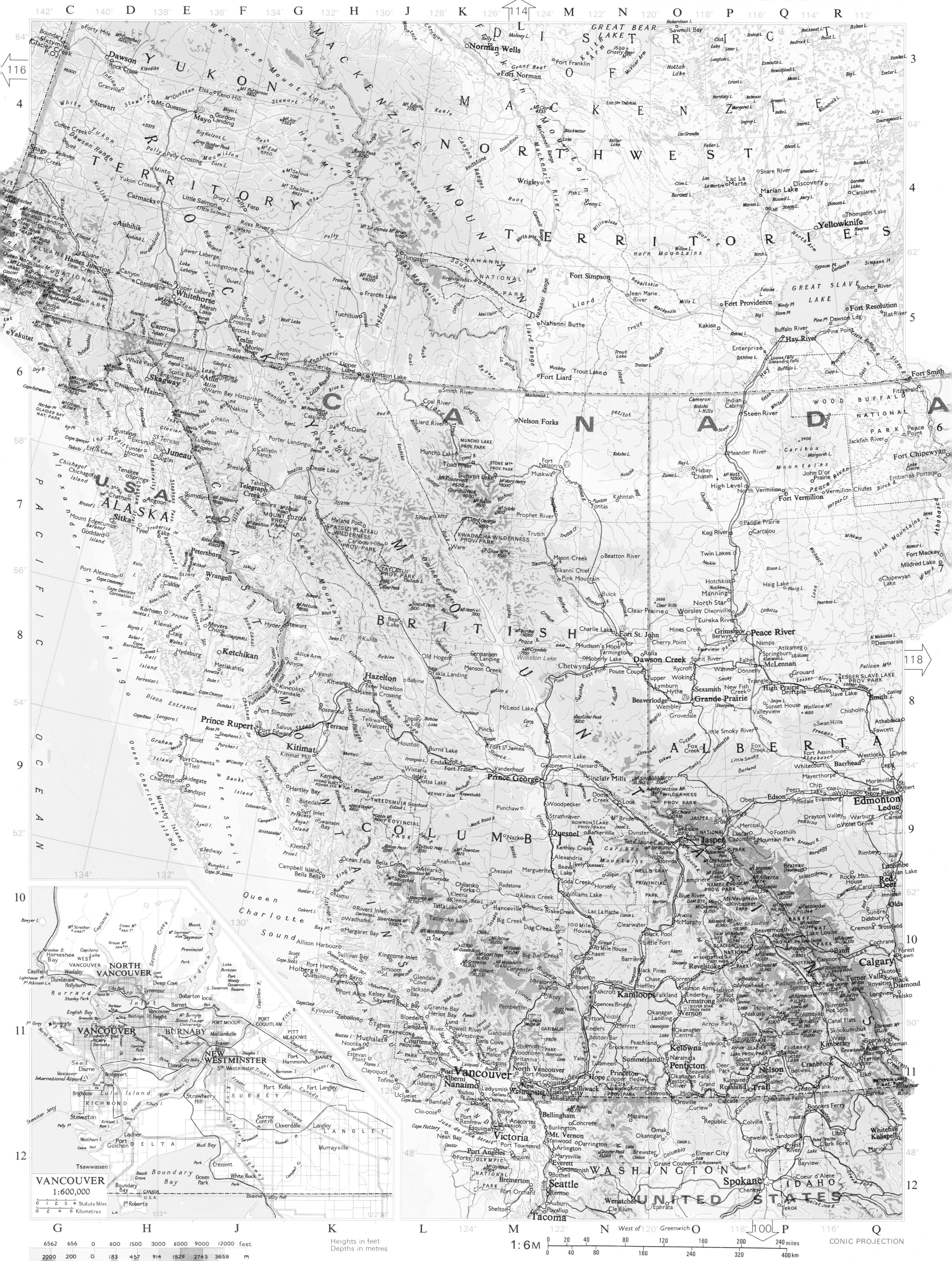

1:6 M

VANCOUVER
1:600,000

Heights in feet
Depths in metres

CONIC PROJECTION

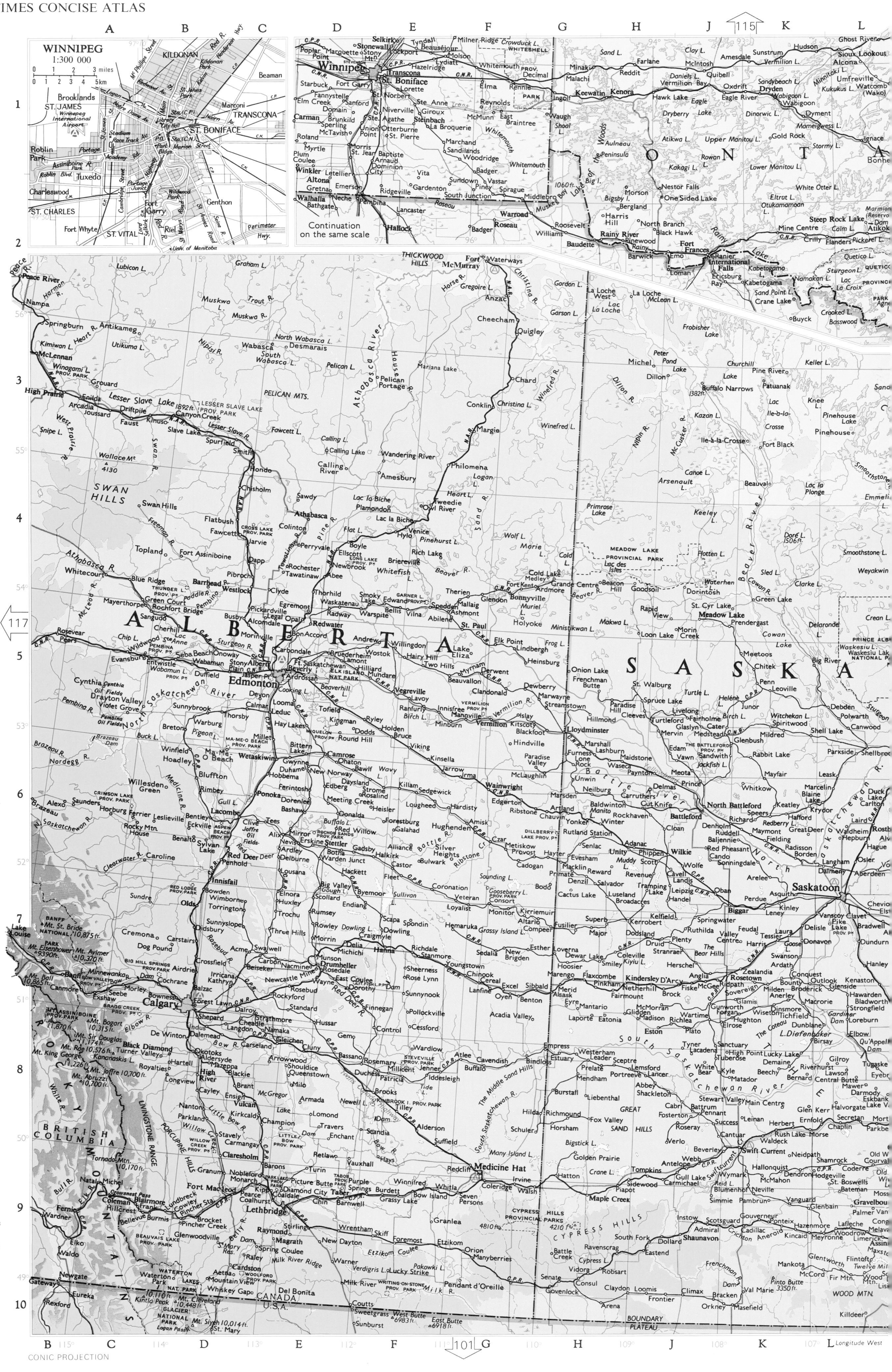
WINNIPEG
1:300 000
Continuation on the same scale
ALBERTA
SASKA
ONTA
ROCKY MOUNTAINS
BRITISH COLUMBIA
SWAN HILLS
Lesser Slave Lake
Athabasca River
North Saskatchewan River
South Saskatchewan River
Edmonton
Calgary
Saskatoon
Lethbridge
Medicine Hat
Red Deer
Swift Current
Winnipeg
Kenora
CANADA
U.S.A.
CYPRESS HILLS
GREAT SAND HILLS
117
115
101
Longitude West
CONIC PROJECTION

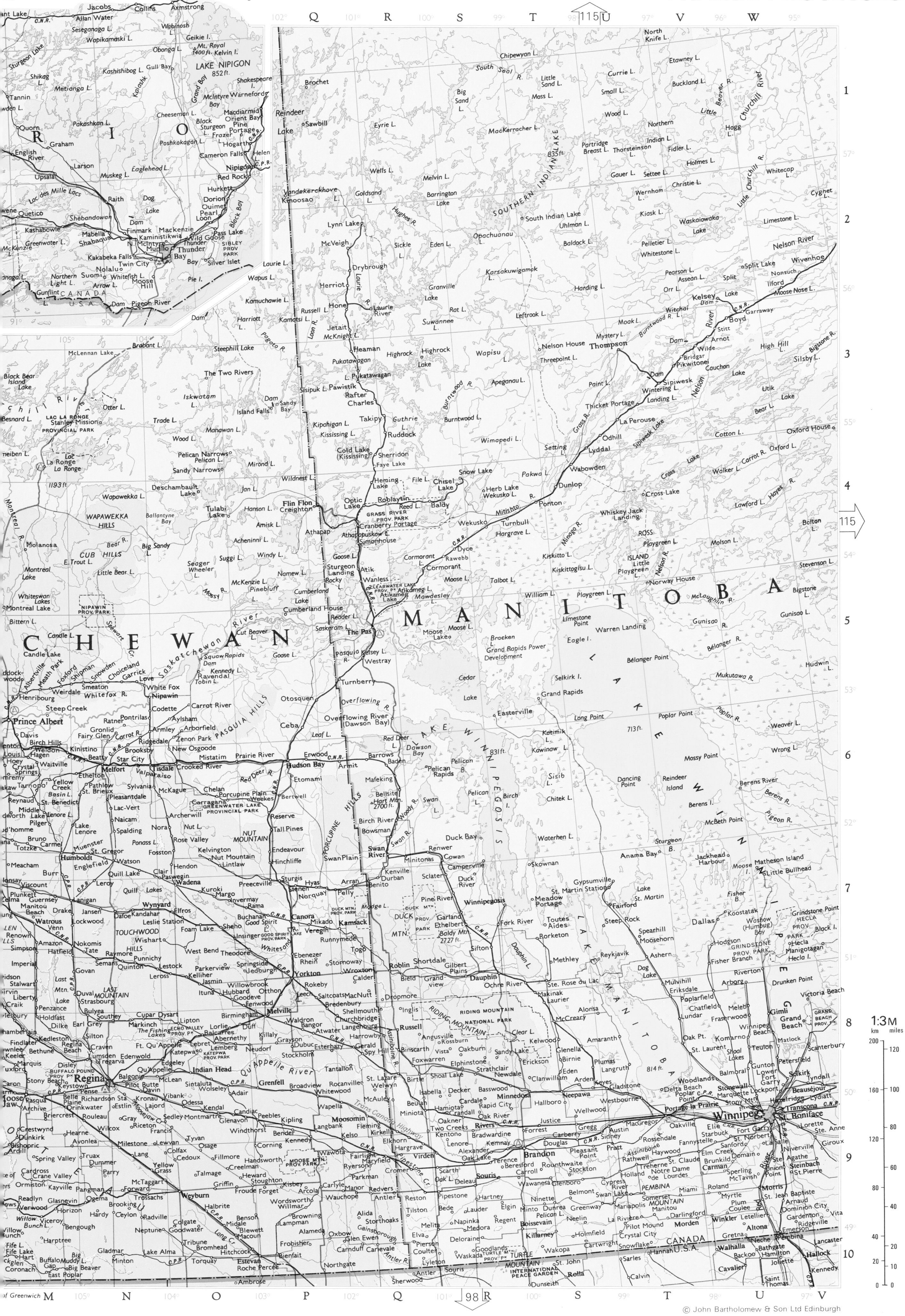

MANITOBA

SASKATCHEWAN

LAKE NIPIGON 852 ft.

LAKE WINNIPEG

LAKE WINNIPEGOSIS

Thompson

Flin Flon
Creighton

The Pas

Prince Albert

Melfort

Hudson Bay

Humboldt

Wynyard

Swan River

Dauphin

Yorkton

Melville

Regina

Indian Head

Moosomin

Brandon

Weyburn

Estevan

Winnipeg

St. Boniface

Transcona

Selkirk

Gimli

Trans Canada Highway

RIDING MOUNTAIN NATIONAL PARK

GRASS RIVER PROV. PARK

DUCK MTN. PROV. PARK

PORCUPINE HILLS

PASQUIA HILLS

TOUCHWOOD HILLS

CANADA
U.S.A.

1:3 M
km   miles

200   120
160   100
120   80
80   60
40   40
       20
0   0

© John Bartholomew & Son Ltd Edinburgh

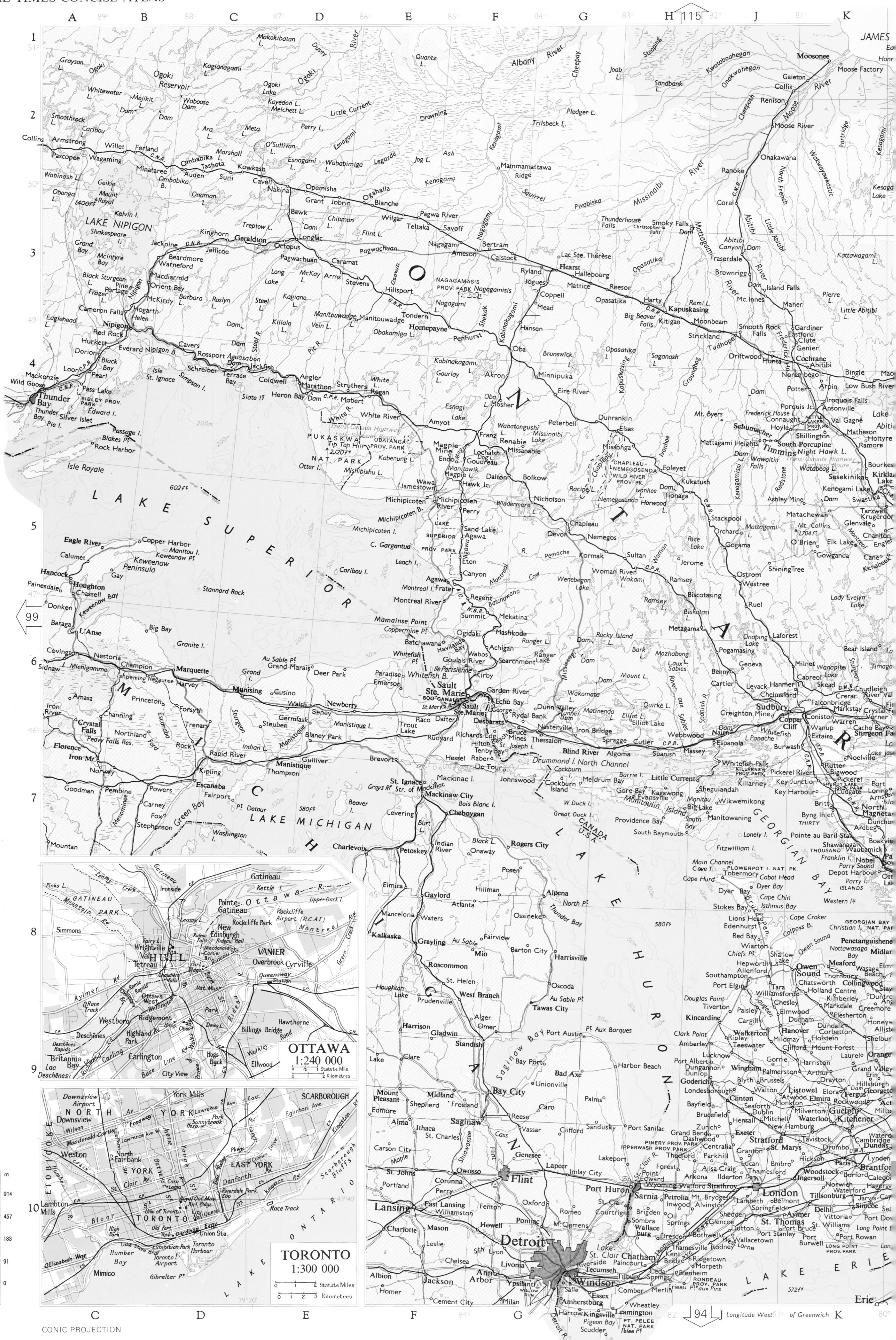
115
99
94
LAKE SUPERIOR
LAKE MICHIGAN
LAKE HURON
LAKE ERIE
GEORGIAN BAY
LAKE NIPIGON
ONTARIO
MICHIGAN
JAMES
Isle Royale
Thunder Bay
Sault Ste. Marie
Sudbury
Detroit
Windsor
Flint
Lansing
Saginaw
Bay City
Sarnia
Port Huron
London
Kitchener
Guelph
Brantford
Timmins
Cochrane
Kapuskasing
Hearst
Moosonee
Nipigon
Marquette
Escanaba
Mackinaw City
Cheboygan
OTTAWA
1:240 000
Statute Mile
Kilometres
HULL
VANIER
TORONTO
1:300 000
Statute Miles
Kilometres
NORTH YORK
EAST YORK
SCARBOROUGH
LAKE ONTARIO
feet
m
3000
914
1500
457
600
183
300
91
0
0
Longitude West of Greenwich

CONIC PROJECTION

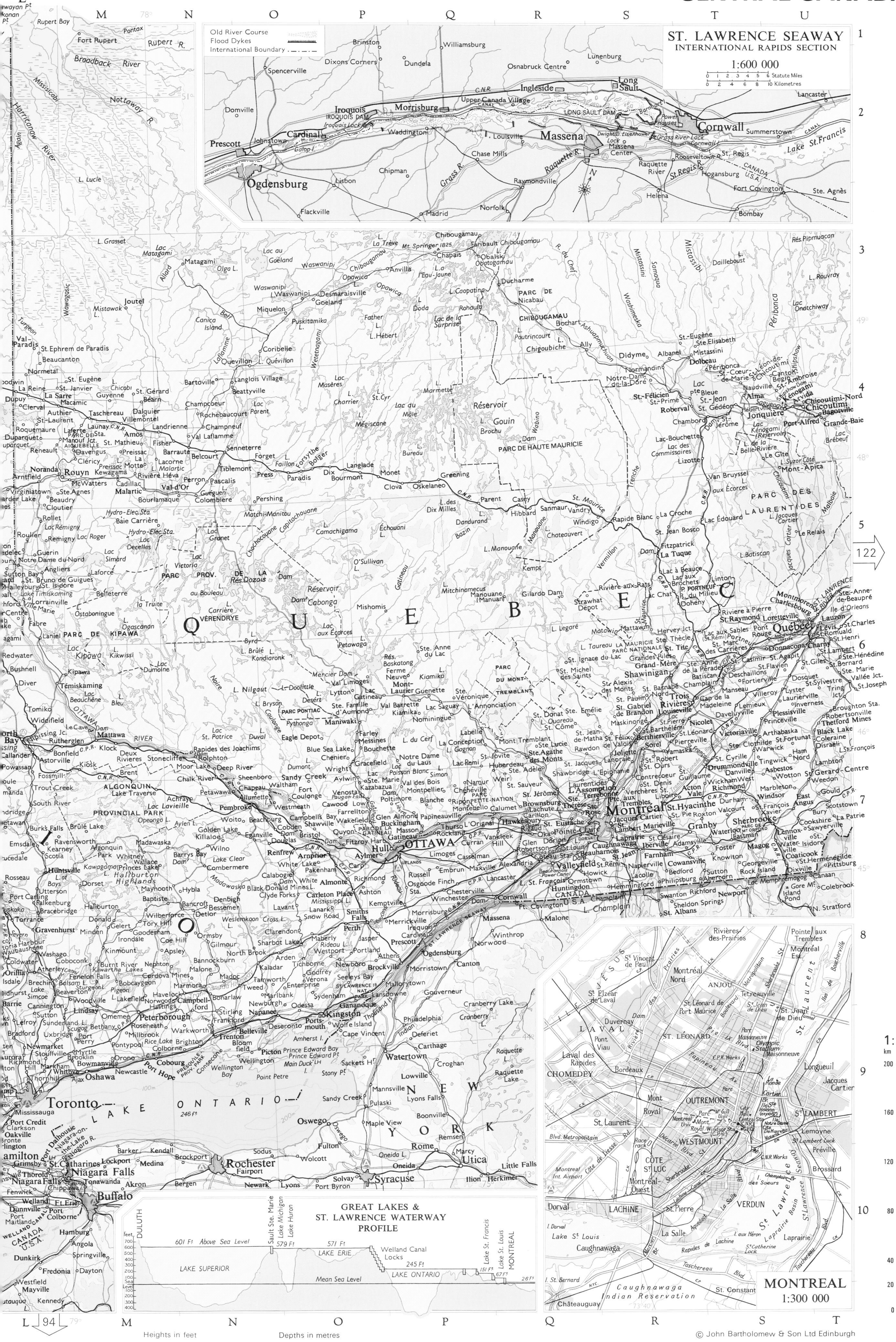

GREAT LAKES &
ST. LAWRENCE WATERWAY
PROFILE

601 Ft Above Sea Level
579 Ft   571 Ft
LAKE ERIE
Welland Canal
Locks
245 Ft
LAKE SUPERIOR
Mean Sea Level
LAKE ONTARIO

QUEBEC

ONTARIO

NEW YORK

MONTREAL
1:300 000

1:3M
km   miles

Heights in feet   Depths in metres

© John Bartholomew & Son Ltd Edinburgh

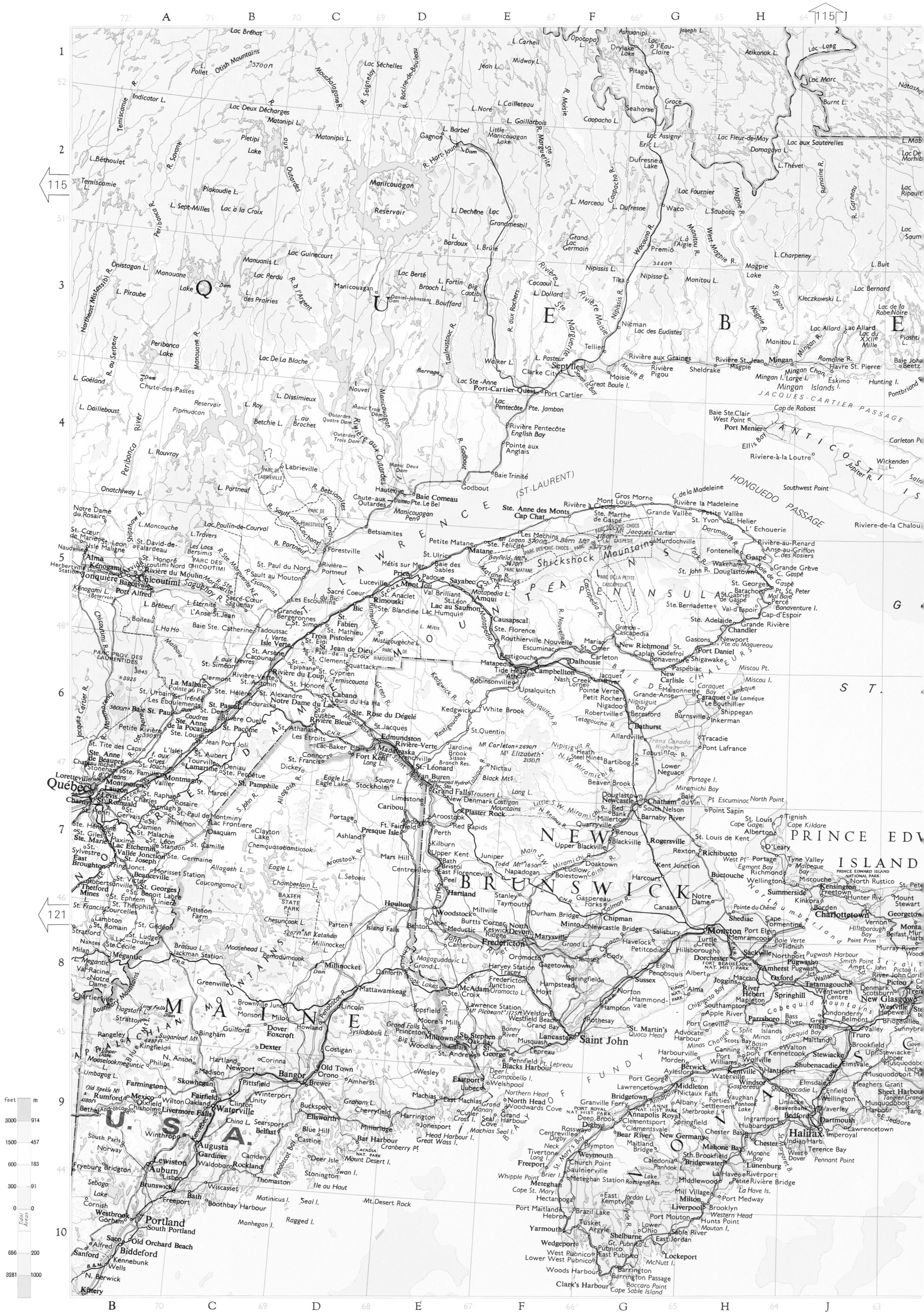

115
121
QUEBEC
NEW BRUNSWICK
MAINE
U.S.A.
NOVA SCOTIA
PRINCE EDWARD ISLAND
GASPÉ PENINSULA
ST. LAWRENCE
HONGUEDO PASSAGE
JACQUES-CARTIER PASSAGE
ANTICOSTI
BAY OF FUNDY
Northumberland Strait
Shickshock Mountains
Manicouagan Reservoir
Québec
Lévis
Chicoutimi
Jonquière
Sept Îles
Baie Comeau
Rimouski
Matane
Gaspé
Campbellton
Bathurst
Edmundston
Chatham
Newcastle
Moncton
Fredericton
Saint John
Charlottetown
Summerside
Amherst
Truro
Halifax
Dartmouth
Yarmouth
Bangor
Augusta
Portland
Lewiston
Waterville
Presque Isle
Houlton
Millinocket
Feet
m
3000
914
1500
457
600
183
300
91
0
0
656
200
3281
1000
Tidal Areas
CONIC PROJECTION

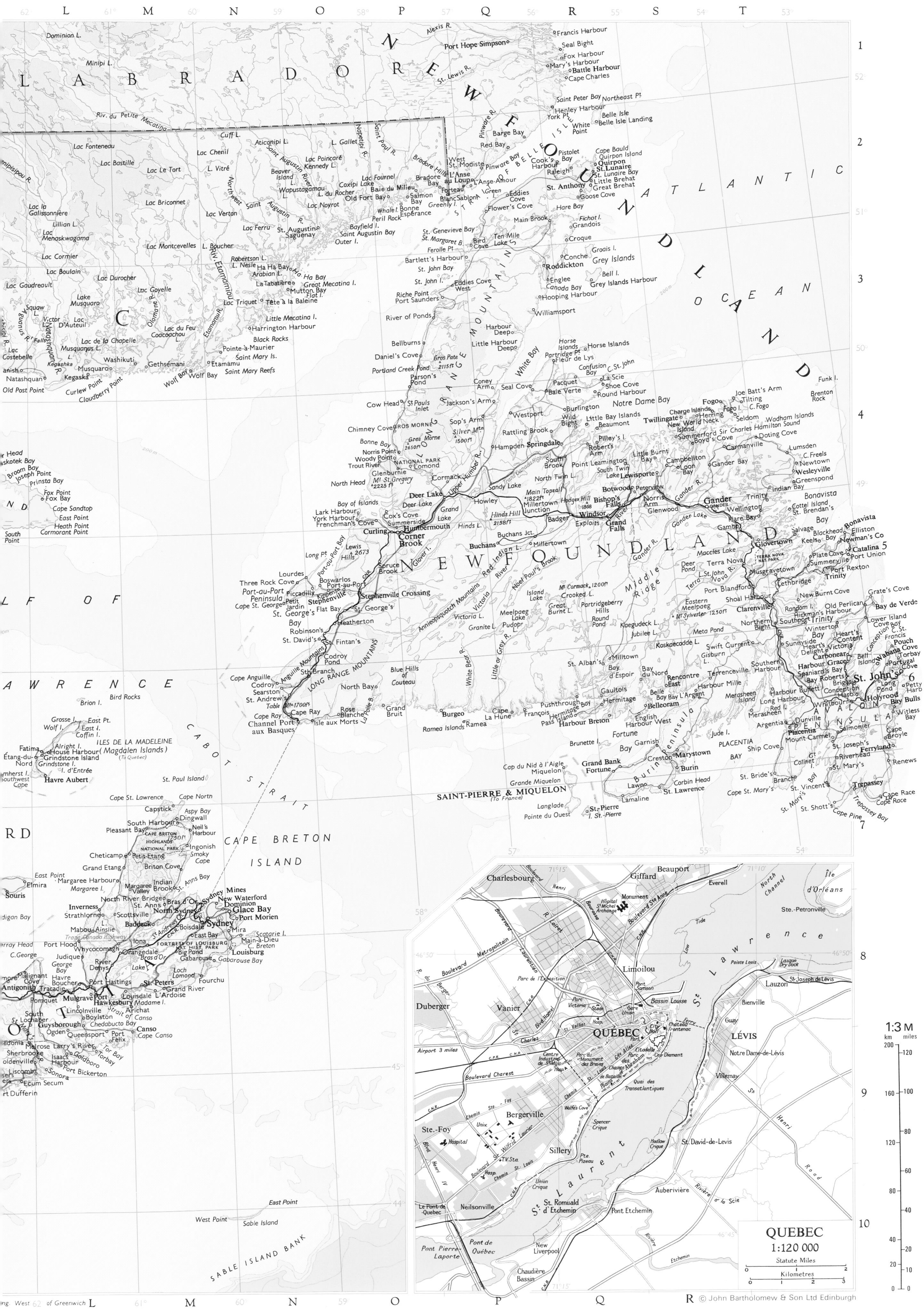

QUEBEC
1:120 000
Statute Miles
Kilometres

1:3 M
km miles

© John Bartholomew & Son Ltd Edinburgh

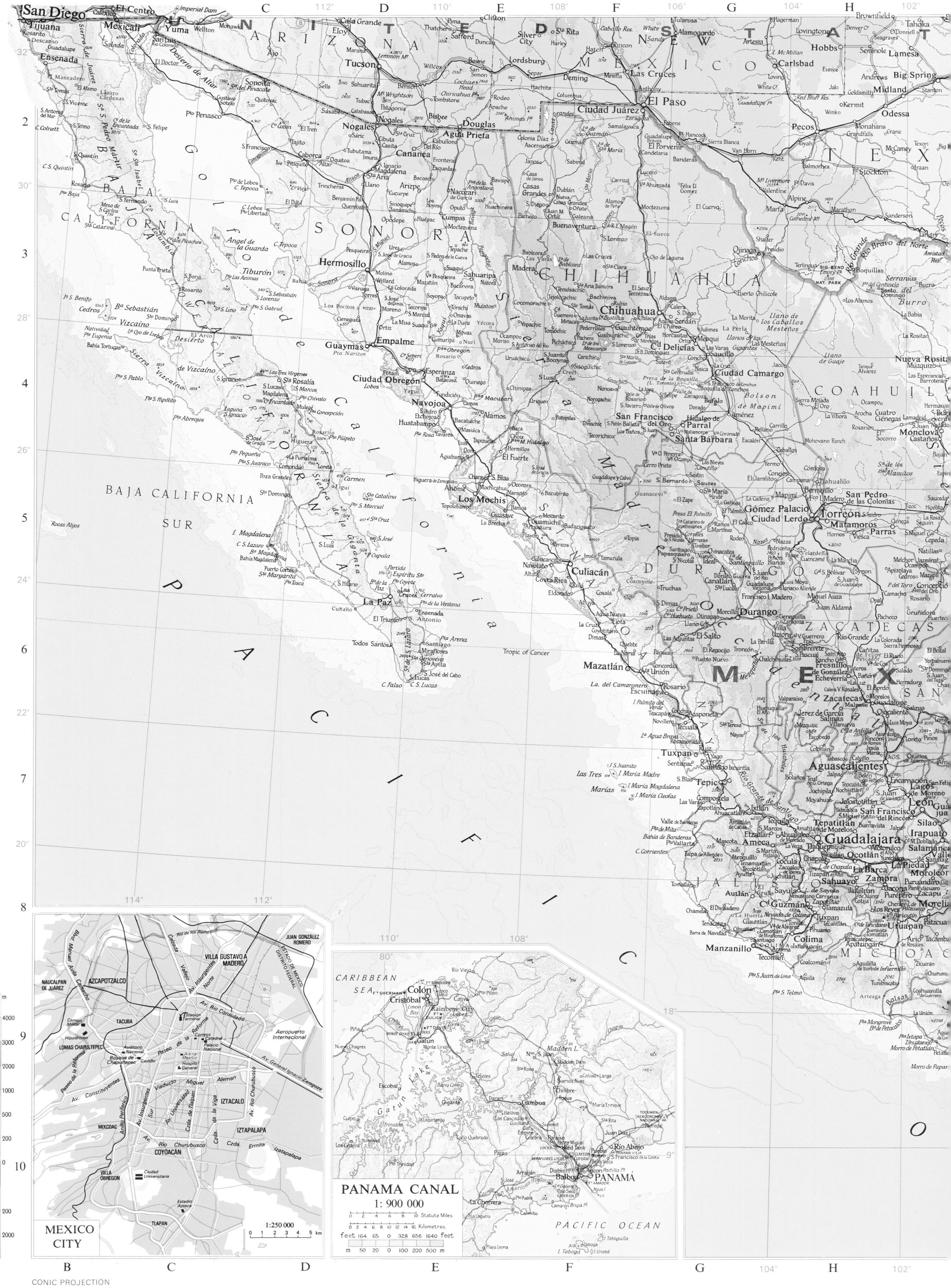

MEXICO CITY
1:250 000

PANAMA CANAL
1: 900 000

CONIC PROJECTION

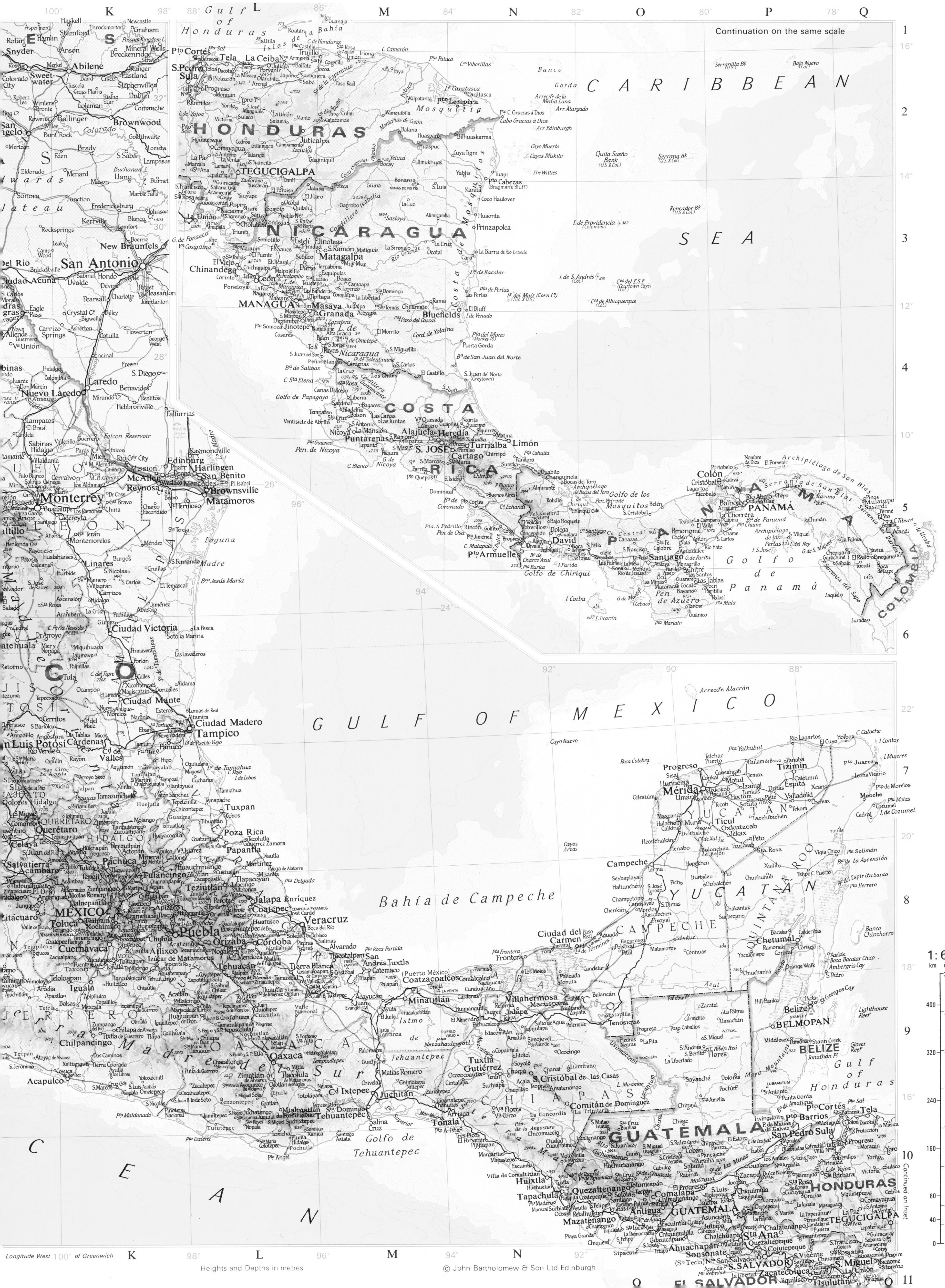

Continuation on the same scale

CARIBBEAN

SEA

HONDURAS

NICARAGUA

TEGUCIGALPA

MANAGUA

Managua

Masaya

Granada

Bluefields

COSTA

RICA

S. JOSE

Cartago

Limón

PANAMA

PANAMÁ

Colón

Cristóbal

Balboa

David

Golfo

de

Panamá

Pen. de Azuero

COLOMBIA

GULF OF MEXICO

Gulf of Honduras

San Antonio

New Braunfels

Laredo

Nuevo Laredo

Monterrey

Matamoros

Brownsville

McAllen

Reynosa

Ciudad Victoria

Tampico

Ciudad Madero

Veracruz

Puebla

MEXICO

Toluca

Cuernavaca

Orizaba

Córdoba

Tehuacán

Oaxaca

Acapulco

Chilpancingo

GUERRERO

OAXACA

CHIAPAS

Tuxtla Gutiérrez

S. Cristóbal de las Casas

Tehuantepec

Juchitán

Golfo de Tehuantepec

Coatzacoalcos

Minatitlán

Villahermosa

TABASCO

Ciudad del Carmen

CAMPECHE

Campeche

Mérida

YUCATÁN

QUINTANA ROO

Chetumal

Progreso

Valladolid

I. de Cozumel

BAHÍA DE CAMPECHE

Bahía de Campeche

GUATEMALA

BELIZE

BELMOPAN

Belize

Quezaltenango

Mazatenango

Tapachula

Huixtla

HONDURAS

San Pedro Sula

Pto Barrios

TEGUCIGALPA

EL SALVADOR

S. SALVADOR

San Miguel

Sta Ana

OCEAN

PACIFIC

1 : 6 M

km   miles

Heights and Depths in metres

© John Bartholomew & Son Ltd Edinburgh

Longitude West of Greenwich

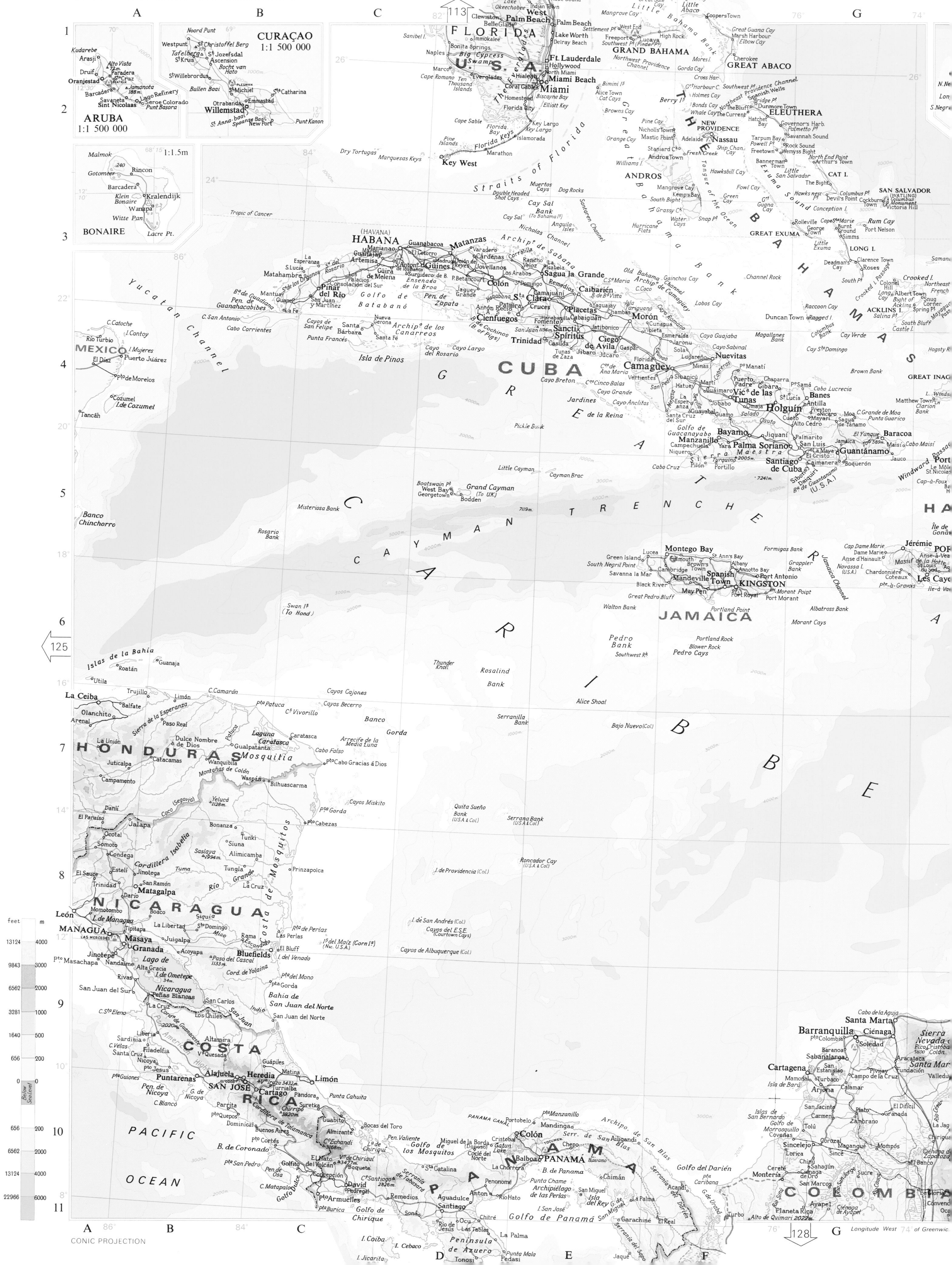
ARUBA
1:1 500 000
CURAÇAO
1:1 500 000
BONAIRE
1:1.5m
Oranjestad
Sint Nicolaas
Willemstad
Kralendijk
FLORIDA
U.S.A.
Miami
Miami Beach
Ft. Lauderdale
West Palm Beach
Key West
Straits of Florida
GRAND BAHAMA
GREAT ABACO
ELEUTHERA
NEW PROVIDENCE
Nassau
ANDROS
THE BAHAMAS
CAT I.
SAN SALVADOR (WATLING)
GREAT EXUMA
LONG I.
ACKLINS I.
GREAT INAGUA
Tropic of Cancer
(HAVANA)
HABANA
Matanzas
Pinar del Río
Cienfuegos
Sta Clara
Sancti Spíritus
Ciego de Avila
Camagüey
Nuevitas
Holguín
Bayamo
Manzanillo
Santiago de Cuba
Guantánamo
Baracoa
CUBA
Isla de Pinos
Golfo de Batabanó
Yucatan Channel
MEXICO
Puerto Juárez
I. de Cozumel
Banco Chinchorro
Little Cayman
Cayman Brac
Grand Cayman
(To U.K.)
Georgetown
CAYMAN TRENCH
GREATER ANTILLES
Montego Bay
Spanish Town
KINGSTON
JAMAICA
Pedro Bank
Jamaica Channel
Windward Passage
Jérémie
HAITI
Swan Is (To Hond.)
CARIBBEAN
Islas de la Bahía
La Ceiba
HONDURAS
Mosquitia
Pto Cabo Gracias á Dios
Serranilla Bank
Bajo Nuevo (Col.)
Alice Shoal
Rosalind Bank
Quita Sueño Bank (U.S.A. & Col.)
Serrana Bank (U.S.A. & Col.)
Roncador Cay (U.S.A. & Col.)
I. de Providencia (Col.)
I. de San Andrés (Col.)
Costa de Mosquitos
NICARAGUA
León
MANAGUA
Masaya
Granada
Matagalpa
Bluefields
Lago de Nicaragua
San Juan del Norte
COSTA RICA
SAN JOSÉ
Alajuela
Heredia
Cartago
Puntarenas
Limón
PACIFIC OCEAN
PANAMA
Colón
PANAMÁ
Golfo de Panamá
Golfo del Darién
Golfo de los Mosquitos
Península de Azuero
Barranquilla
Santa Marta
Cartagena
Montería
COLOMBIA
feet m
13124 4000
9843 3000
6562 2000
3281 1000
1640 500
656 200
0 0
Below Sea Level
656 200
6562 2000
13124 4000
22966 6000
CONIC PROJECTION
Longitude West 74 of Greenwich
113
125
128

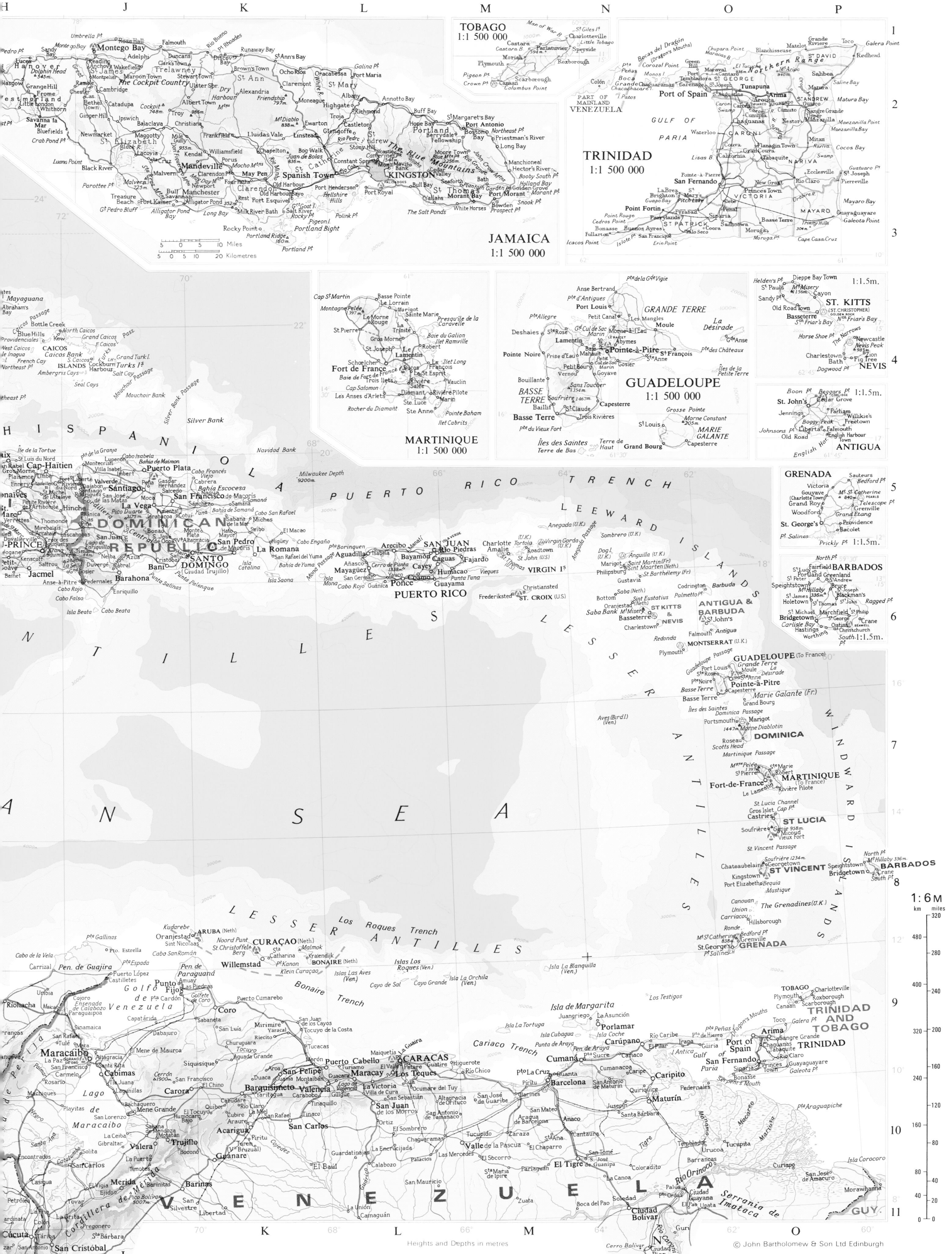

TOBAGO
1:1 500 000

TRINIDAD
1:1 500 000

Port of Spain

San Fernando

JAMAICA
1:1 500 000

Montego Bay

The Cockpit Country

The Blue Mountains

KINGSTON

Spanish Town

May Pen

Mandeville

Morant Bay

HISPANIOLA

DOMINICAN REPUBLIC

SANTO DOMINGO (Ciudad Trujillo)

Santiago

La Vega

San Pedro

La Romana

CAICOS ISLANDS

Turks Is.

Cap-Haitien

PUERTO RICO

SAN JUAN

Ponce

Mayagüez

MARTINIQUE
1:1 500 000

Fort de France

GUADELOUPE
1:1 500 000

Basse Terre

Pointe-à-Pitre

GRANDE TERRE

BASSE TERRE

ST. KITTS (ST. CHRISTOPHER)

Basseterre

NEVIS

ANTIGUA

St. John's

GRENADA

St. George's

BARBADOS

Bridgetown

PUERTO RICO TRENCH

Milwaukee Depth 9200m

L E E W A R D   I S L A N D S

VIRGIN Is

ST. CROIX (U.S.)

ANTIGUA & BARBUDA

ST KITTS & NEVIS

Basseterre

Charlestown

MONTSERRAT (U.K.)

Plymouth

GUADELOUPE (To France)

Basse Terre

Pointe-à-Pitre

Grande Terre

Marie Galante (Fr.)

DOMINICA

Roseau

MARTINIQUE (To France)

Fort-de-France

ST LUCIA

Castries

ST VINCENT

Kingstown

The Grenadines (U.K.)

BARBADOS

Bridgetown

GRENADA

St George's

C A R I B B E A N   S E A

L E S S E R   A N T I L L E S

W I N D W A R D   I S L A N D S

ARUBA (Neth.)
Oranjestad

CURAÇAO (Neth.)
Willemstad

BONAIRE (Neth.)
Kralendijk

Los Roques (Ven.)

Isla de Margarita

Porlamar

TRINIDAD AND TOBAGO

TOBAGO
Scarborough

TRINIDAD

Port of Spain

San Fernando

V E N E Z U E L A

Maracaibo

Lago de Maracaibo

CARACAS

Maracay

Valencia

Barquisimeto

Barcelona

Cumaná

Carúpano

Maturín

Ciudad Bolívar

Rio Orinoco

1:6M

1:1.5m.

Heights and Depths in metres

© John Bartholomew & Son Ltd Edinburgh

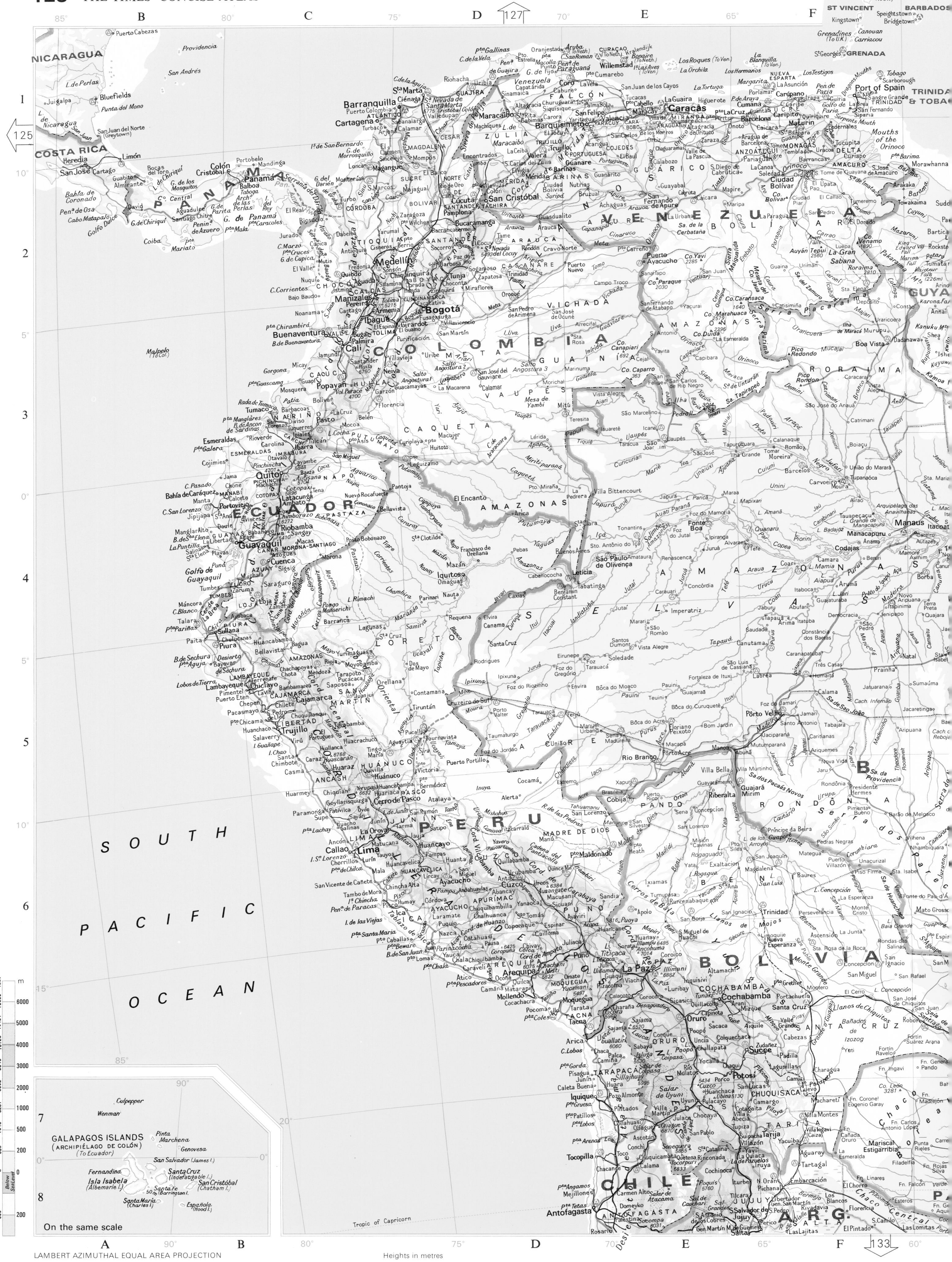

SOUTH

PACIFIC

OCEAN

COLOMBIA

VENEZUELA

ECUADOR

PERU

BOLIVIA

CHILE

ARG.

PANAMÁ

NICARAGUA

COSTA RICA

GUYANA

TRINIDAD & TOBAGO

GRENADA

ST LUCIA

ST VINCENT

BARBADOS

Bogotá

Medellín

Cali

Caracas

Quito

Guayaquil

Lima

Callao

La Paz

Cochabamba

Sucre

Potosí

Antofagasta

Manaus

GALAPAGOS ISLANDS
(ARCHIPIÉLAGO DE COLÓN)
(To Ecuador)

On the same scale

LAMBERT AZIMUTHAL EQUAL AREA PROJECTION

Heights in metres

m	feet
6000	19685
5000	16404
4000	13123
3000	9843
2000	6562
1000	3281
500	1640
200	656
0	Below Sea Level
200	656

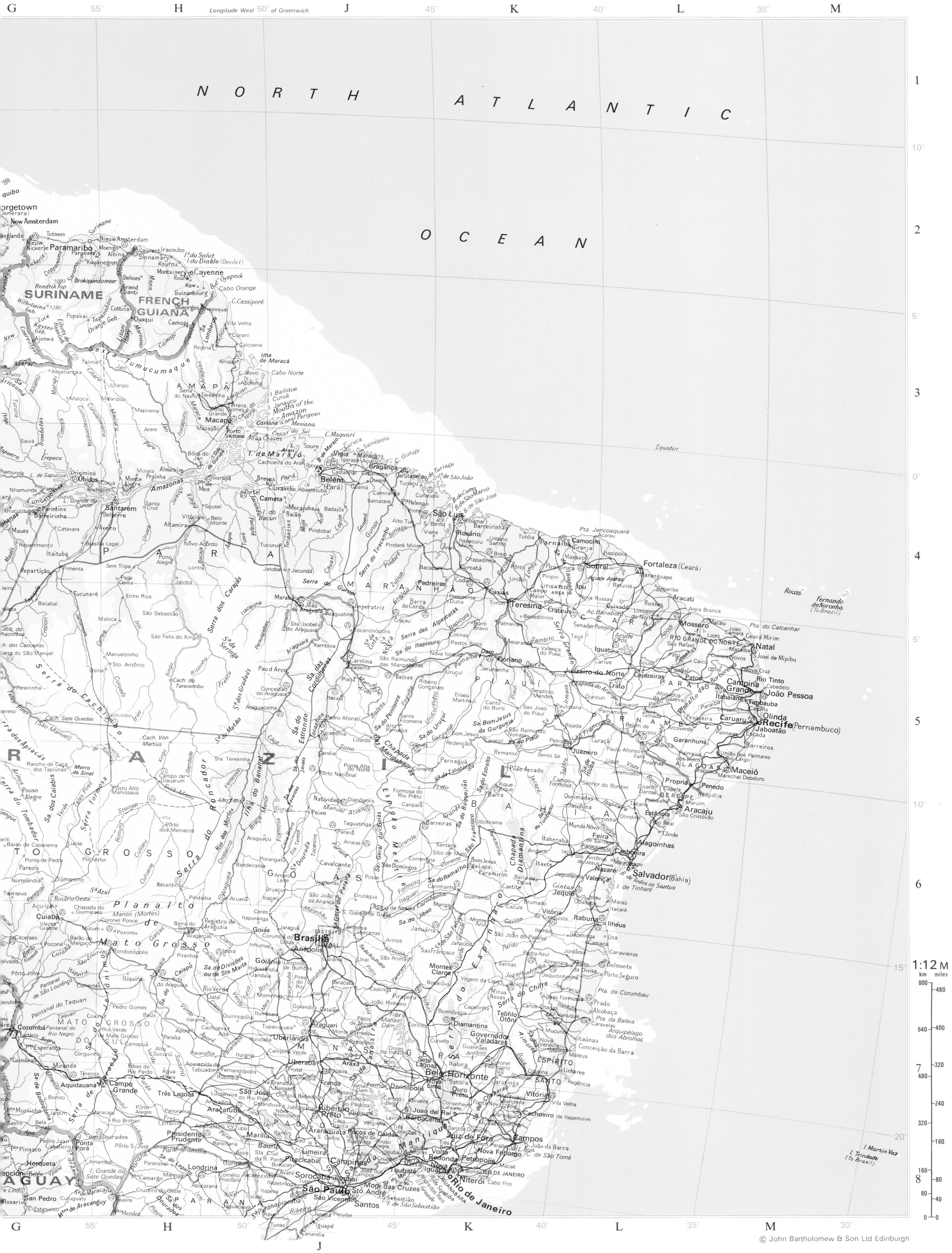
Longitude West 50° of Greenwich
NORTH ATLANTIC OCEAN
SURINAME
FRENCH GUIANA
Paramaribo
Cayenne
Nieuw Amsterdam
Nieuw Nickerie
New Amsterdam
AMAPÁ
Macapá
I. de Marajó
Mouths of the Amazon
Equator
Belém (Pará)
Santarém
Óbidos
Amazonas
São Luís
Serra Tumucumaque
PARÁ
MARANHÃO
PIAUÍ
CEARÁ
RIO GRANDE DO NORTE
PARAÍBA
PERNAMBUCO
ALAGOAS
SERGIPE
BAHIA
GOIÁS
MATO GROSSO
MATO GROSSO DO SUL
MINAS GERAIS
ESPÍRITO SANTO
SÃO PAULO
PARANÁ
BRAZIL
PARAGUAY
Teresina
Fortaleza (Ceará)
Natal
João Pessoa
Campina Grande
Recife (Pernambuco)
Olinda
Jaboatão
Maceió
Aracaju
Salvador (Bahia)
Feira de Santana
Vitória da Conquista
Ilhéus
Itabuna
Brasília
Goiânia
Anápolis
Cuiabá
Corumbá
Campo Grande
Belo Horizonte
Vitória
Rio de Janeiro
Niterói
São Paulo
Santos
Campinas
Sorocaba
Ribeirão Preto
Uberaba
Uberlândia
Juiz de Fora
Montes Claros
Governador Valadares
Londrina
Imperatriz
Marabá
Juazeiro
Juazeiro do Norte
Crato
Caruaru
Mossoró
Sobral
Parnaíba
Caxias
Floriano
Planalto de Mato Grosso
Serra do Espinhaço
Chapada Diamantina
Fernando de Noronha (To Brazil)
Rocas
I. Martin Vaz
I. Trindade (To Brazil)
Abrolhos
1:12 M
km
miles

© John Bartholomew & Son Ltd Edinburgh

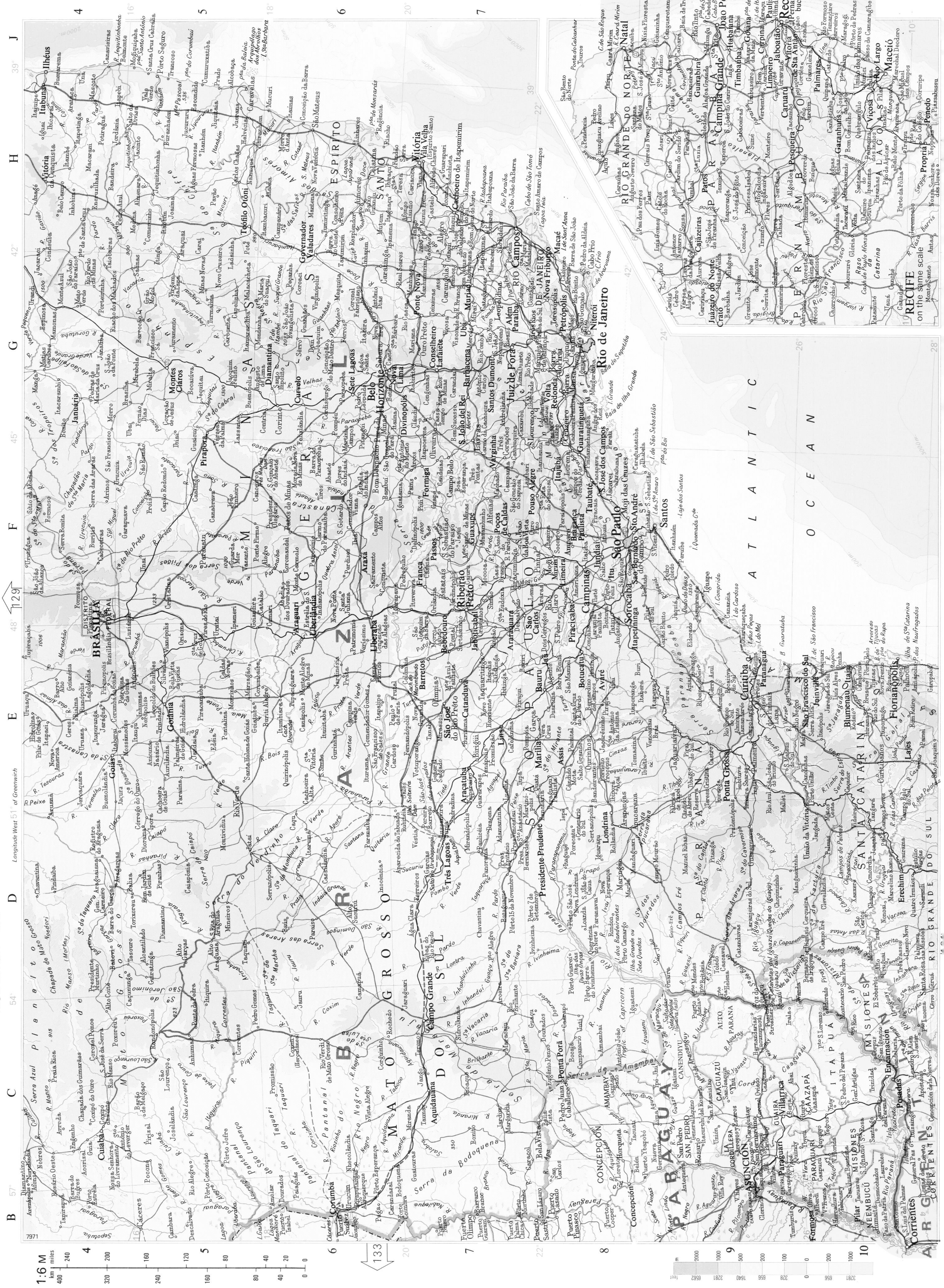

LAMBERT ZENITHAL EQUAL AREA PROJECTION

RECIFE
on the same scale

1·6 M
km miles

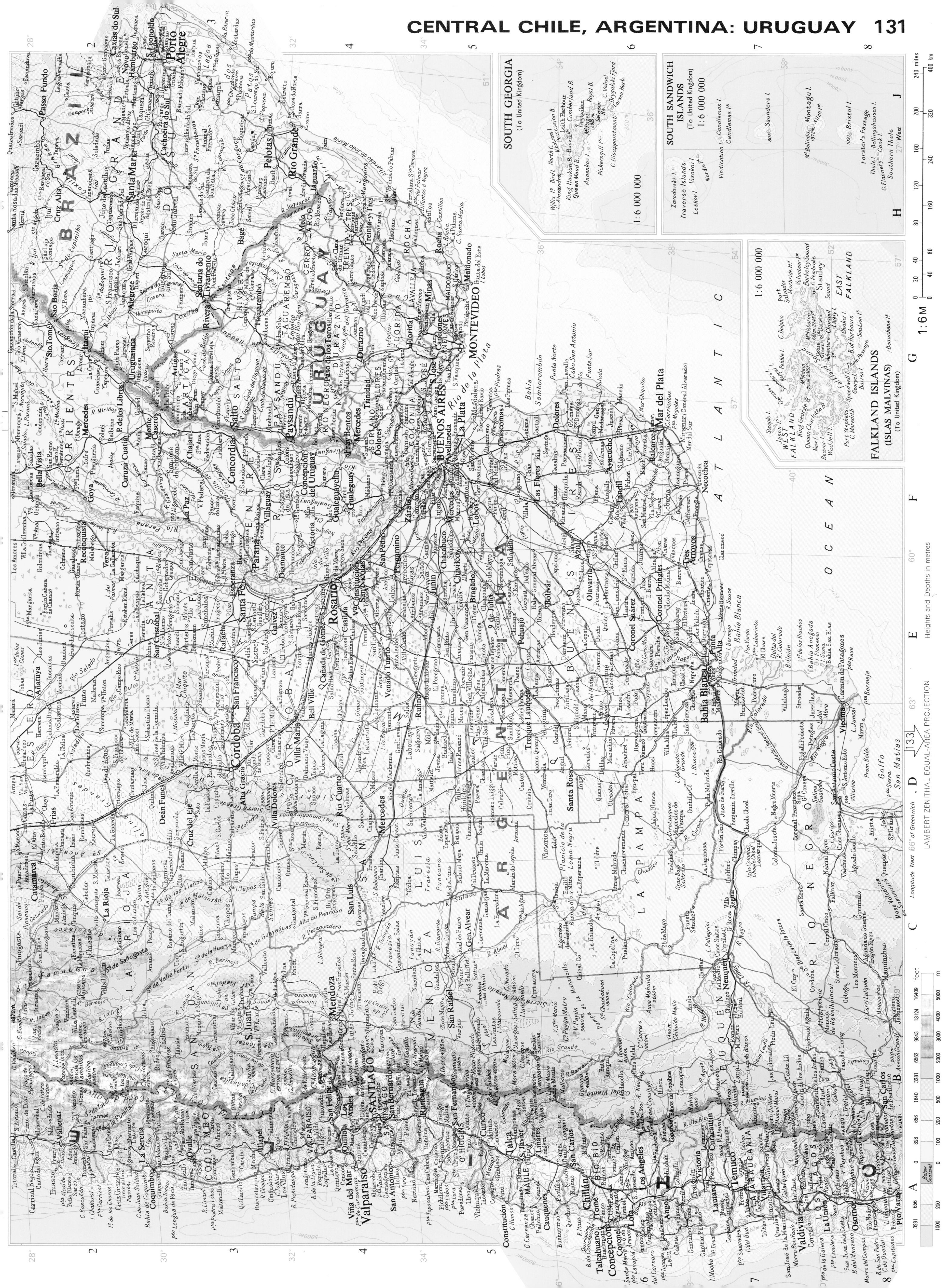

SOUTH GEORGIA
(To United Kingdom)
1:6 000 000

SOUTH SANDWICH
ISLANDS
(To United Kingdom)
1:6 000 000

FALKLAND ISLANDS
(ISLAS MALVINAS)
(To United Kingdom)
1:6 000 000

1:6M

LAMBERT ZENITHAL EQUAL-AREA PROJECTION

Longitude West 66° of Greenwich

Heights and Depths in metres

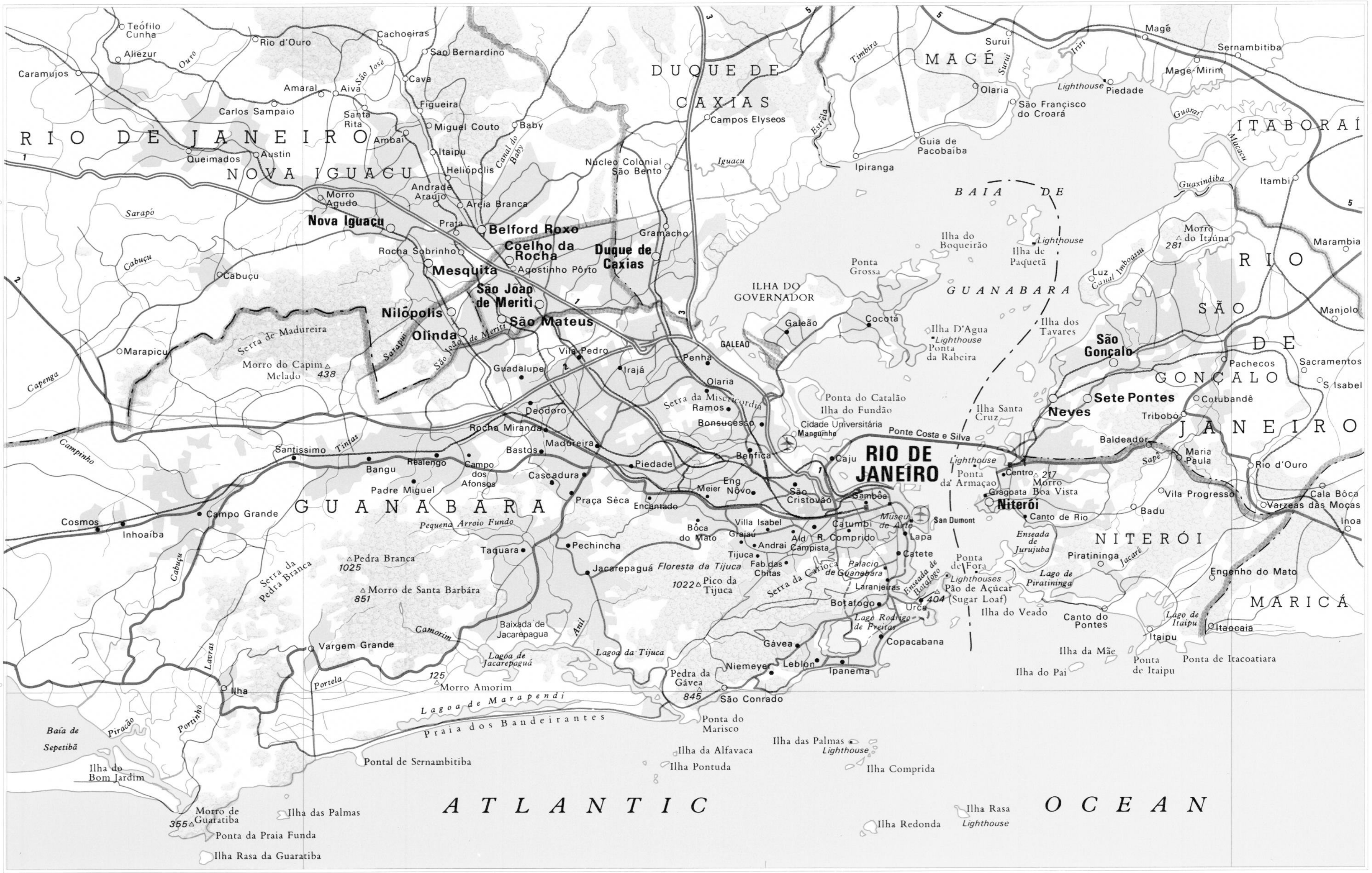

RIO DE JANEIRO map

A 43°30' B 43°15' C 43°00' D

RIO DE JANEIRO
NOVA IGUAÇU
DUQUE DE CAXIAS
MAGÉ
ITABORAÍ
RIO DE SÃO GONÇALO DE JANEIRO
MARICÁ

Teófilo Cunha, Aliezur, Rio d'Ouro, Cachoeiras, São Bernardino, Surui, Piedade, Magé, Sernambitiba, Magé-Mirim
Caramujos, Amaral, Aiva, Cavá, Figueira, Miguel Couto, Baby, Olaria, São Francisco do Croará, Lighthouse
Carlos Sampaio, Santa Rita, Itaipu, Heliópolis, Núcleo Colonial São Bento, Campos Elyseos, Ipiranga, Guia de Pacobaiba, Luz
Queimados, Austin, Andrade Araújo, Prata, Gramacho, Timbra
Nova Iguaçu, Belford Roxo, Coelho da Rocha, Duque de Caxias
Morro Agudo, Rocha Sobrinho, Agostinho Pôrto
Mesquita, São João de Meriti, São Mateus
Nilópolis, Olinda, Vila Pedro, Penha, GALEÃO, Cocotá
Marapicu, Serra de Madureira, Guadalupe, Irajá, Olaria, ILHA DO GOVERNADOR, Galeão, Ilha D'Agua, Ilha dos Tavares, São Gonçalo
Morro do Capim Melado 438, Deodôro, Rocha Miranda, Ramos, Bonsucesso, Cidade Universitária, Ilha do Fundão, Neves, Sete Pontes
Santissimo, Timbó, Bastos, Madureira, Piedade, Meier, Eng Novo, Benfica, Ponte Costa e Silva, Ilha Santa Cruz, Baldeador
Bangu, Realengo, Campo dos Afonsos, Cascadura, São Cristovão, RIO DE JANEIRO, Ponta d'Armação, Centro, 217, Vila Progresso, Rio d'Ouro
Cosmos, Inhoaiba, Campo Grande, Padre Miguel, Praça Sêca, Encantado, Villa Isabel, Grajaú, Andaraí, Lapa, Niterói, Morro Boa Vista, Vila Progresso, Varzeas das Moças
Pechincha, Boca do Mato, Catumbi, Fabricas, Catete, São Dumont, Piratininga, Ihoa
Serra da Pedra Branca 1025, Taquara, Jacarepaguá, Floresta da Tijuca 1022,6, Pico da Tijuca, Palacio de Guanabara, Canto de Rio, Engenho do Mato
Morro de Santa Barbára 851, Botafogo, Urca, Pão de Açucar (Sugar Loaf) 404, Lago de Piratininga
Vargem Grande, Baixada de Jacarepagua, Lagoa Rodrigo de Freitas, Gávea, Leblon, Ipanema, Ilha do Veado, Canto do Pontes, Itaipu
Ilha, Lagoa de Jacarepaguá, Lagoa da Tijuca, Pedra da Gávea 845, São Conrado, Copacabana, Ilha da Mãe, Itaocaia
Baía de Sepetibá, Piração, Portela, 125, Morro Amorim, Niemeyer, Ponta do Marisco, Ponta de Itaipu
Ilha do Bom Jardim, Lagoa de Marapendi, Praia dos Bandeirantes, São Conrado, Ilha das Palmas
Morro de Guaratiba 365, Ilha das Palmas, Pontal de Sernambitiba, Ilha da Alfavaca, Ilha Pontuda, Ilha Comprida, Ilha Rasa
Ponta da Praia Funda, Ilha Rasa da Guaratiba, Ilha Redonda

ATLANTIC OCEAN

BUENOS AIRES map

A 58°45' B 58°30' C 58°15' D

ESCOBAR
PILAR
TIGRE
RÍO DE LA PLATA
BUENOS AIRES
GENERAL RODRIGUEZ
MORENO
MERLO
AIRES
MATANZA
MARCOS PAZ
ESTEBAN ECHEVERRIA
ALMIRANTE BROWN
LOMAS DE ZAMORA
QUILMES
BERAZATEGUI
FLORENCIO VARELA
DISTRITO FEDERAL

Villa Rosa, Benavidez, Tigre, San Fernando
Pilar, Garin, Del Viso, Tortuguitas, General Pacheco, Victoria, San Isidro, Olivos, Vicente López
Presidente Derqui, El Talar, Don Torcuato, Martinez, Juan Anchorena
Manzone, Toro, Villa de Mayo, Boulogne, Florida, Munro
José C Paz, Piñero, SARMIENTO, Villa Adelina, Saavedra, Belgrano, Hippodromo Argentino, Aeroparque
General Sarmiento, Muñiz, Bella Vista, GENERAL SAN MARTIN, Villa Ballester, Nuñez, General Urquiza
Las Berras, TRES DE FEBRERO, Villa Lynch, Palermo
General Rodriguez, Hurlingham, El Palomar, Villa Bosch, Caseros, Villa Santos Lugares, Once, Congreso
Francisco Alvarez, MORON, Ramos Mejia, Villa Sáenz Peña, DISTRITO FEDERAL, Caballito, Constitución, Boca
Moreno, Paso del Rey, Castelar, Ituzaingó, Morón, Mariano J. Haedo, Nueva Chicago, Nueva Pompeya, Barracas, Avellaneda
Merlo, San Antonio de Padua, San Justo, Villa Madero, Parque Almirante Guillermo Brown, Valentin Alsina, Sarandi, Gerli
Mariano Acosta, Libertad, Rafael Castillo, Isidro Casanova, Tablada, Aldo Bonzi, Fiorito, Lanús, Villa Diamante, Don Bosco, Villa Dominico
Elias Romero, Pontevedra, González Catán, San Justo, Ciudad General Belgrano, Ingeniero Budge, Remedios de Escalada, Monte Chingolo, Quilmes
Villars, Marcos Paz, Laferrere, Lomas de Zamora, Temperley, Berazategui
Esteban Echeverria, EZEIZA, Monte Grande, Llavallol, Almirante Brown, Burzaco, Florencio Varela

0 5 10 15 km
0 5 10 miles
1:300 000
© Times Books Ltd

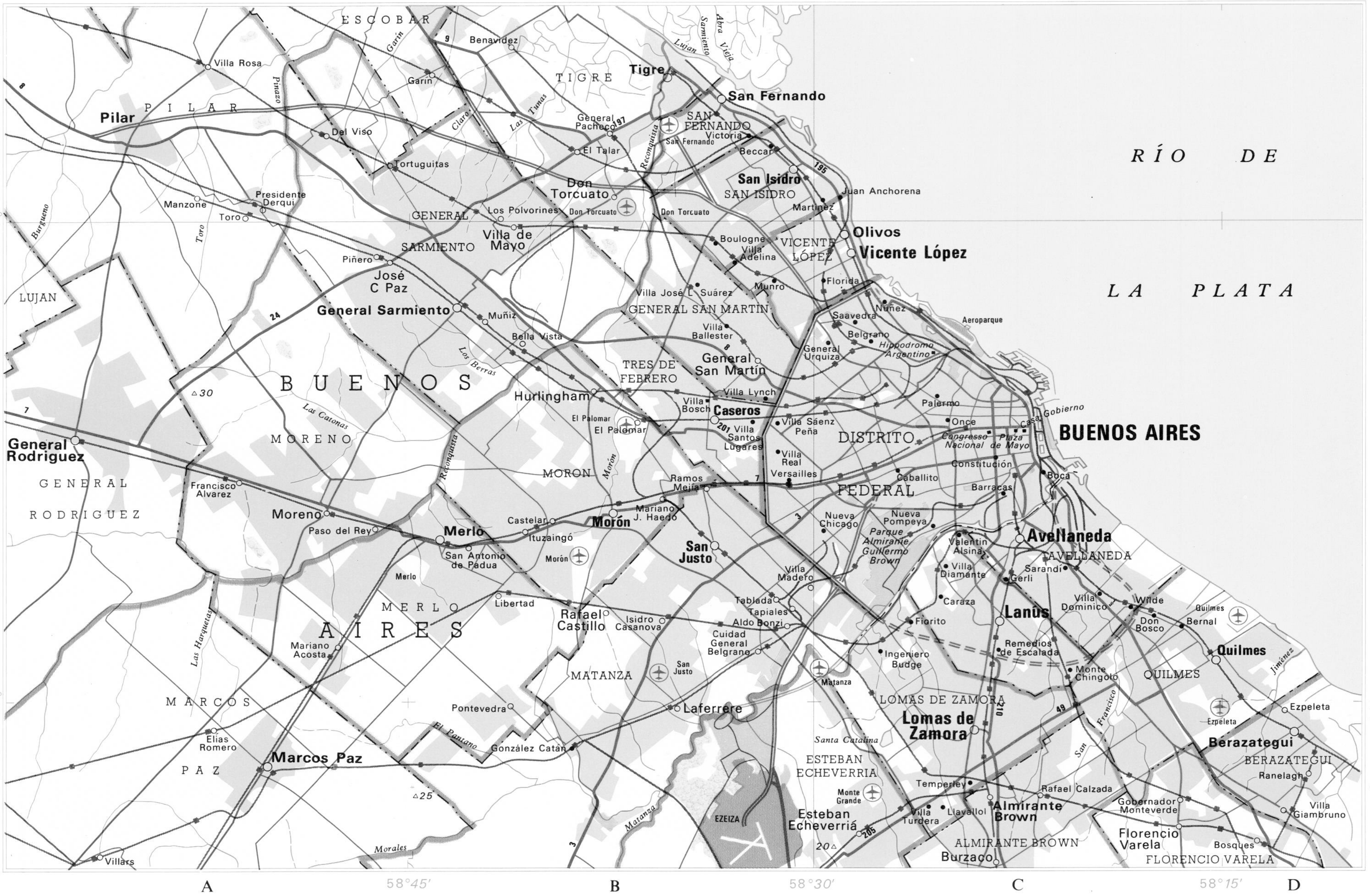

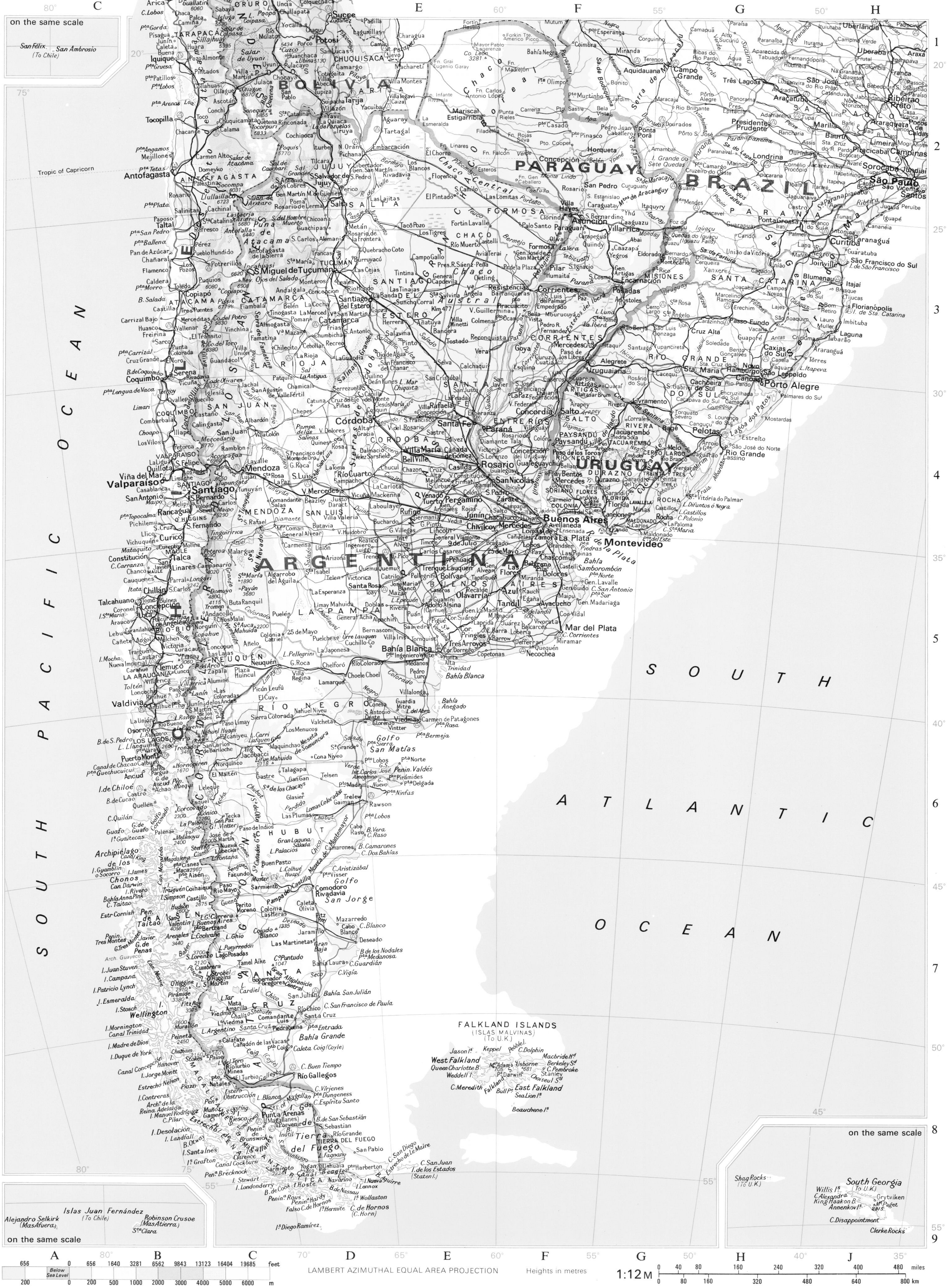
BOLIVIA
PARAGUAY
BRAZIL
URUGUAY
ARGENTINA
CHILE
SOUTH PACIFIC OCEAN
SOUTH ATLANTIC OCEAN
Tropic of Capricorn
FALKLAND ISLANDS
(ISLAS MALVINAS)
(To U.K.)
West Falkland
East Falkland
TIERRA DEL FUEGO
Tierra del Fuego
Golfo San Matías
Golfo San Jorge
Bahía Grande
C. de Hornos (C. Horn)
Buenos Aires
Montevideo
Asunción
Santiago
Valparaíso
Córdoba
Rosario
Mendoza
Bahía Blanca
Mar del Plata
Comodoro Rivadavia
Punta Arenas
Río Gallegos
Porto Alegre
São Paulo
Curitiba
Antofagasta
on the same scale
San Félix
San Ambrosio
(To Chile)
Islas Juan Fernández
(To Chile)
Alejandro Selkirk (Más Afuera)
Robinson Crusoe (Más Atierra)
Sta Clara
Shag Rocks (To U.K.)
South Georgia (To U.K.)
Willis Is
Grytviken
King Haakon B.
C. Disappointment
Clerke Rocks
LAMBERT AZIMUTHAL EQUAL AREA PROJECTION
Heights in metres
1:12 M
feet
m
Below Sea Level
miles
km

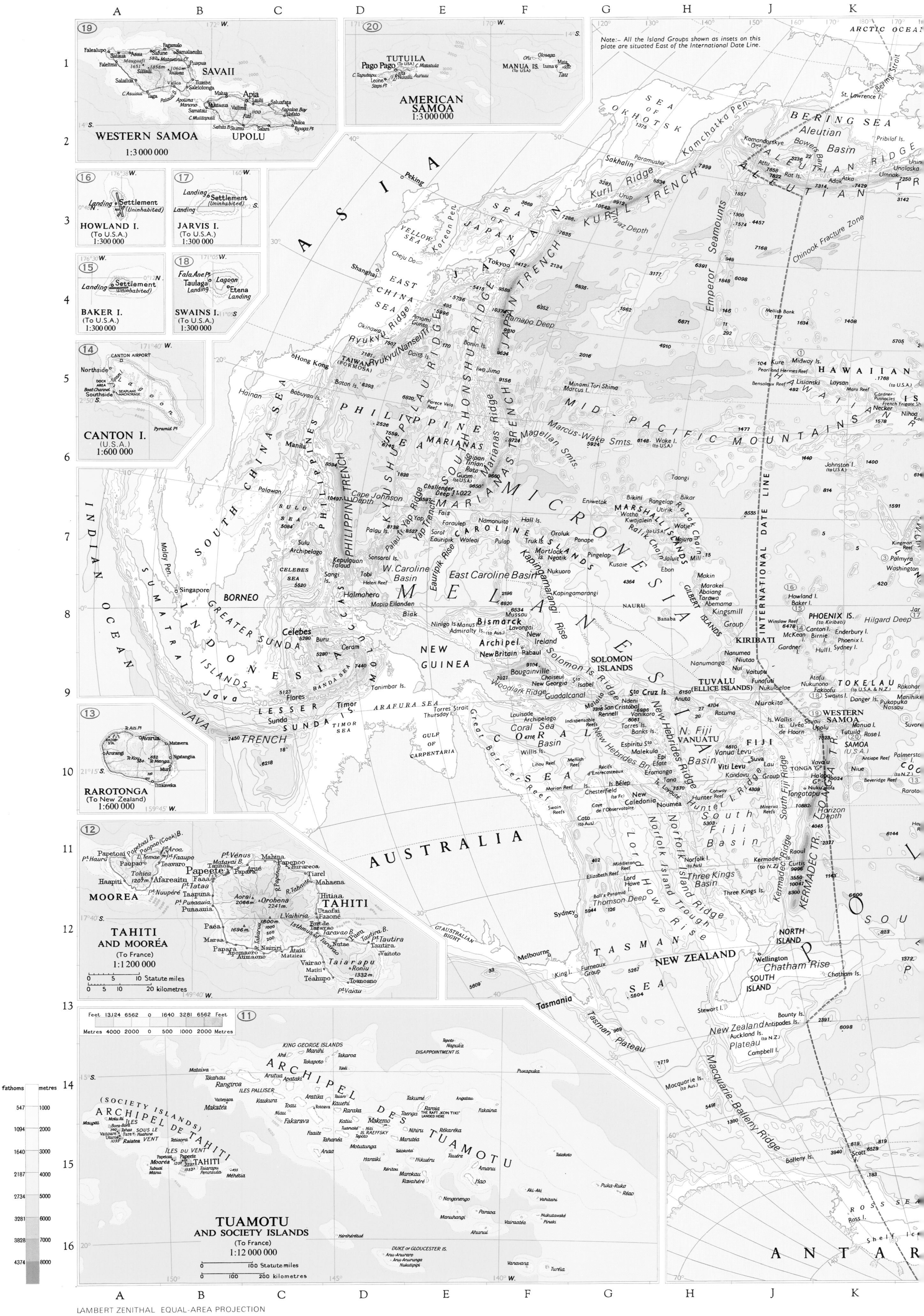

WESTERN SAMOA
1:3 000 000
SAVAII
UPOLU
Apia
AMERICAN SAMOA
1:3 000 000
TUTUILA
Pago Pago
MANUA IS.
(To USA)
HOWLAND I.
(To U.S.A.)
1:300 000
JARVIS I.
(To U.S.A.)
1:300 000
BAKER I.
(To U.S.A.)
1:300 000
SWAINS I.
(To U.S.A.)
1:300 000
CANTON I.
(U.S.A.)
1:600 000
RAROTONGA
(To New Zealand)
1:600 000
TAHITI AND MOORÉA
(To France)
1:1 200 000
MOOREA
TAHITI
Papeete
TUAMOTU AND SOCIETY ISLANDS
(To France)
1:12 000 000
ARCHIPEL DES TUAMOTU
ARCHIPEL DE TAHITI
(SOCIETY ISLANDS)
Note:- All the Island Groups shown as insets on this plate are situated East of the International Date Line.
ASIA
ARCTIC OCEAN
BERING SEA
SEA OF OKHOTSK
SEA OF JAPAN
YELLOW SEA
EAST CHINA SEA
SOUTH CHINA SEA
JAPAN
JAPAN TRENCH
KURIL TRENCH
ALEUTIAN TRENCH
ALEUTIAN RIDGE
Aleutian Basin
Kamchatka Pen.
Sakhalin
Peking
Shanghai
Tokyo
Hong Kong
TAIWAN (FORMOSA)
Manila
PHILIPPINES
PHILIPPINE SEA
PHILIPPINE TRENCH
MARIANAS
Challenger Deep 11 022
MARIANAS TRENCH
HAWAIIAN IS.
MID-PACIFIC MOUNTAINS
MICRONESIA
MELANESIA
CAROLINE ISLANDS
MARSHALL ISLANDS
GILBERT ISLANDS
KIRIBATI
NAURU
TUVALU (ELLICE ISLANDS)
TOKELAU
PHOENIX IS.
INTERNATIONAL DATE LINE
INDIAN OCEAN
BORNEO
Singapore
Celebes
GREATER SUNDA
INDONESIA
LESSER SUNDA IS.
JAVA TRENCH
Timor
ARAFURA SEA
TIMOR SEA
GULF OF CARPENTARIA
NEW GUINEA
Bismarck Archipel
SOLOMON ISLANDS
CORAL SEA
VANUATU
NEW CALEDONIA
FIJI
TONGA
SAMOA
AUSTRALIA
Sydney
Melbourne
Tasmania
TASMAN SEA
NEW ZEALAND
NORTH ISLAND
SOUTH ISLAND
Wellington
Chatham Rise
KERMADEC TR.
TONGA TR.
South Fiji Basin
Lord Howe Rise
Campbell Plateau
Macquarie-Balleny Ridge
ROSS SEA
ANTARCTICA
fathoms metres
547 1000
1094 2000
1640 3000
2187 4000
2734 5000
3281 6000
3828 7000
4374 8000

LAMBERT ZENITHAL EQUAL-AREA PROJECTION

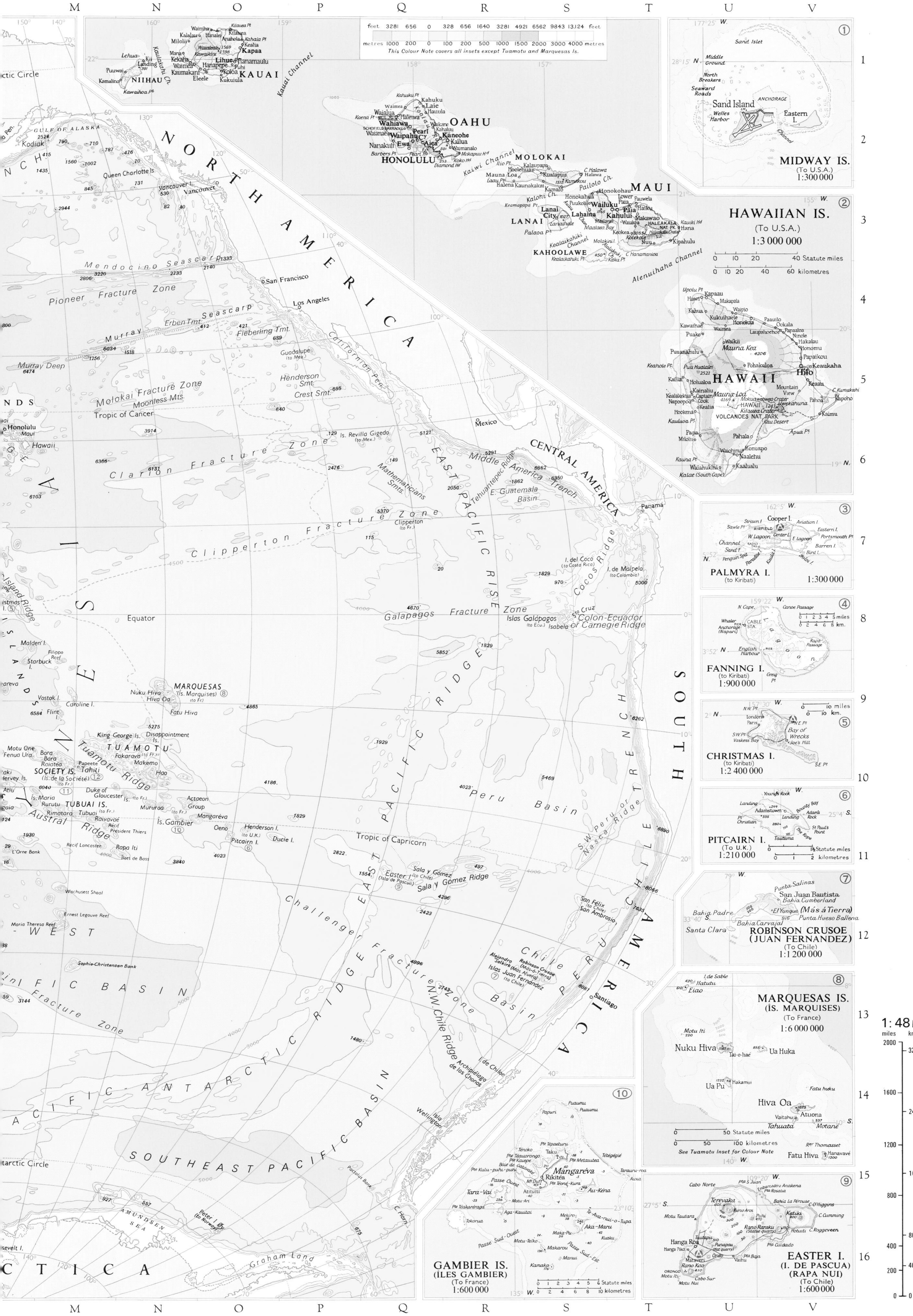

NORTH AMERICA
CENTRAL AMERICA
SOUTH AMERICA
Tropic of Cancer
Equator
Tropic of Capricorn
Clarion Fracture Zone
Clipperton Fracture Zone
Galapagos Fracture Zone
Molokai Fracture Zone
Pioneer Fracture Zone
Murray Seascarp
Mendocino Seascarp
EAST PACIFIC RISE
EAST PACIFIC RIDGE
PACIFIC-ANTARCTIC RIDGE
SOUTHEAST PACIFIC BASIN
Peru Basin
Chile Basin
Challenger Fracture Zone
PERU-CHILE TRENCH
Middle America Trench
MARQUESAS
TUAMOTU
SOCIETY IS.
TUBUAI IS.
Islas Galápagos
San Francisco
Los Angeles
Mexico
Panama
Santiago
1: 48 M
MIDWAY IS. (To U.S.A.) 1:300 000
HAWAIIAN IS. (To U.S.A.) 1:3 000 000
OAHU
MOLOKAI
MAUI
LANAI
KAHOOLAWE
KAUAI
NIIHAU
HONOLULU
HAWAII
PALMYRA I. (to Kiribati) 1:300 000
FANNING I. (to Kiribati) 1:900 000
CHRISTMAS I. (to Kiribati) 1:2 400 000
PITCAIRN I. (To U.K.) 1:210 000
ROBINSON CRUSOE (JUAN FERNANDEZ) (To Chile) 1:1 200 000
MARQUESAS IS. (ÎS. MARQUISES) (To France) 1:6 000 000
See Tuamotu Inset for Colour Note
GAMBIER IS. (ÎLES GAMBIER) (To France) 1:600 000
EASTER I. (I. DE PASCUA) (RAPA NUI) (To Chile) 1:600 000
This Colour Note covers all insets except Tuamotu and Marquesas Is.

© John Bartholomew & Son Ltd Edinburgh.

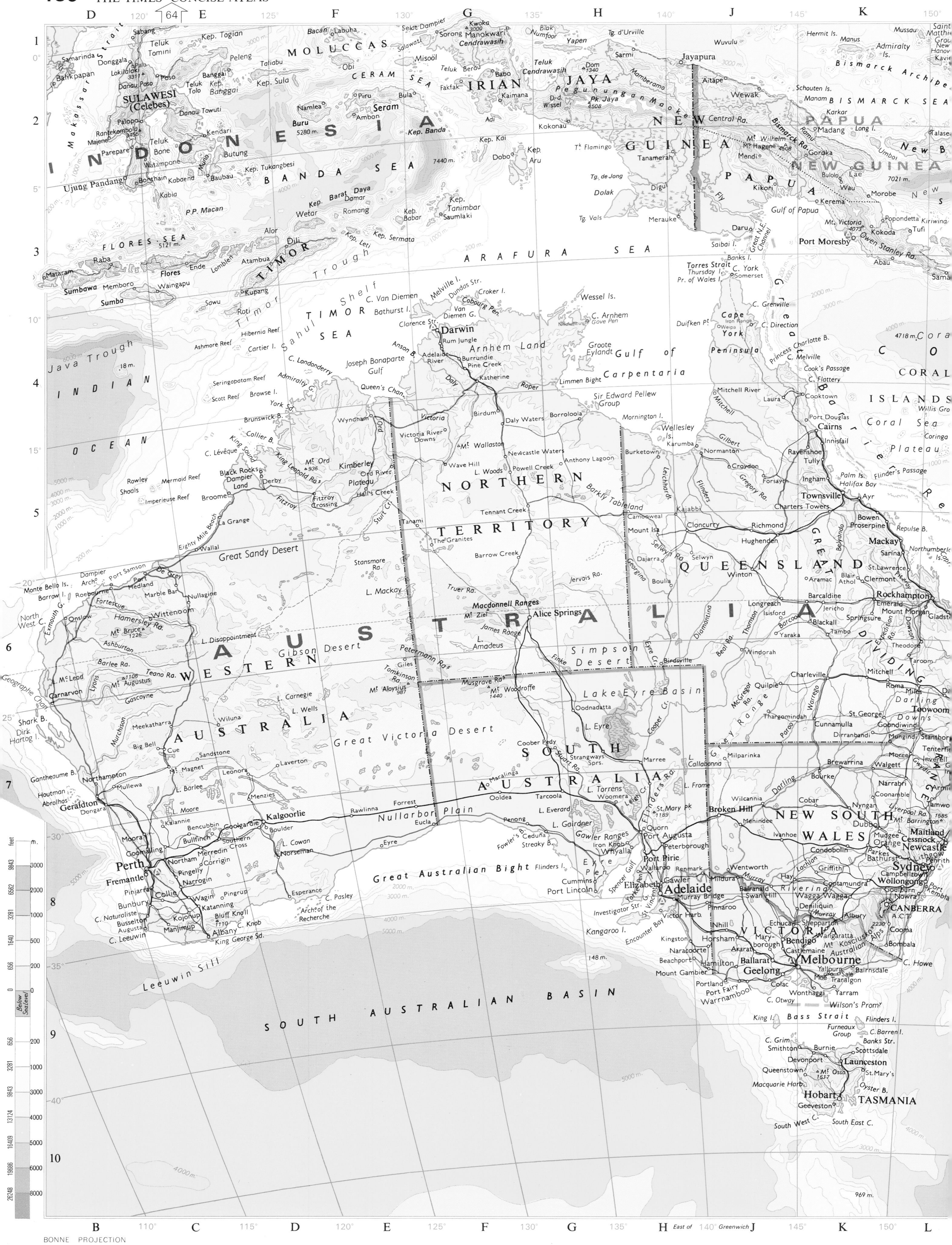

64

D 120° E 125° F 130° G 135° H 140° J 145° K 150°

MOLUCCAS

IRIAN JAYA

NEW GUINEA

PAPUA NEW GUINEA

SULAWESI (Celebes)

INDONESIA

CERAM SEA

BANDA SEA

Pegunungan Maoke
Pk Jaya 4508

PAPUA

Port Moresby

Gulf of Papua

FLORES SEA

TIMOR SEA

ARAFURA SEA

Torres Strait
Thursday I.
Pr. of Wales I.

Cape York Peninsula

TIMOR Trough

INDIAN OCEAN

Java Trough

Darwin

Arnhem Land

Gulf of Carpentaria

CORAL ISLANDS

Coral Sea Plateau

Cairns

Townsville

NORTHERN TERRITORY

QUEENSLAND

Kimberley Plateau

Great Sandy Desert

Tennant Creek

Mount Isa

Broome

AUSTRALIA

WESTERN

Gibson Desert

Alice Springs

Macdonnell Ranges

Simpson Desert

Rockhampton

Hamersley Ra.

AUSTRALIA

Great Victoria Desert

Lake Eyre Basin

L. Eyre

SOUTH AUSTRALIA

Charleville

Toowoomba

Darling

Carnarvon

Geraldton

Kalgoorlie

Nullarbor Plain

L. Torrens

Broken Hill

NEW SOUTH WALES

Newcastle

Perth
Fremantle

Great Australian Bight

Port Augusta
Whyalla

Port Pirie

Adelaide

Sydney
Wollongong

CANBERRA
A.C.T.

Albany
C. Leeuwin

VICTORIA

Ballarat
Geelong

Melbourne

SOUTH AUSTRALIAN BASIN

Bass Strait

Hobart

TASMANIA

BONNE PROJECTION

B 110° C 115° D 120° E 125° F 130° G 135° H East of 140° Greenwich J 145° K 150°

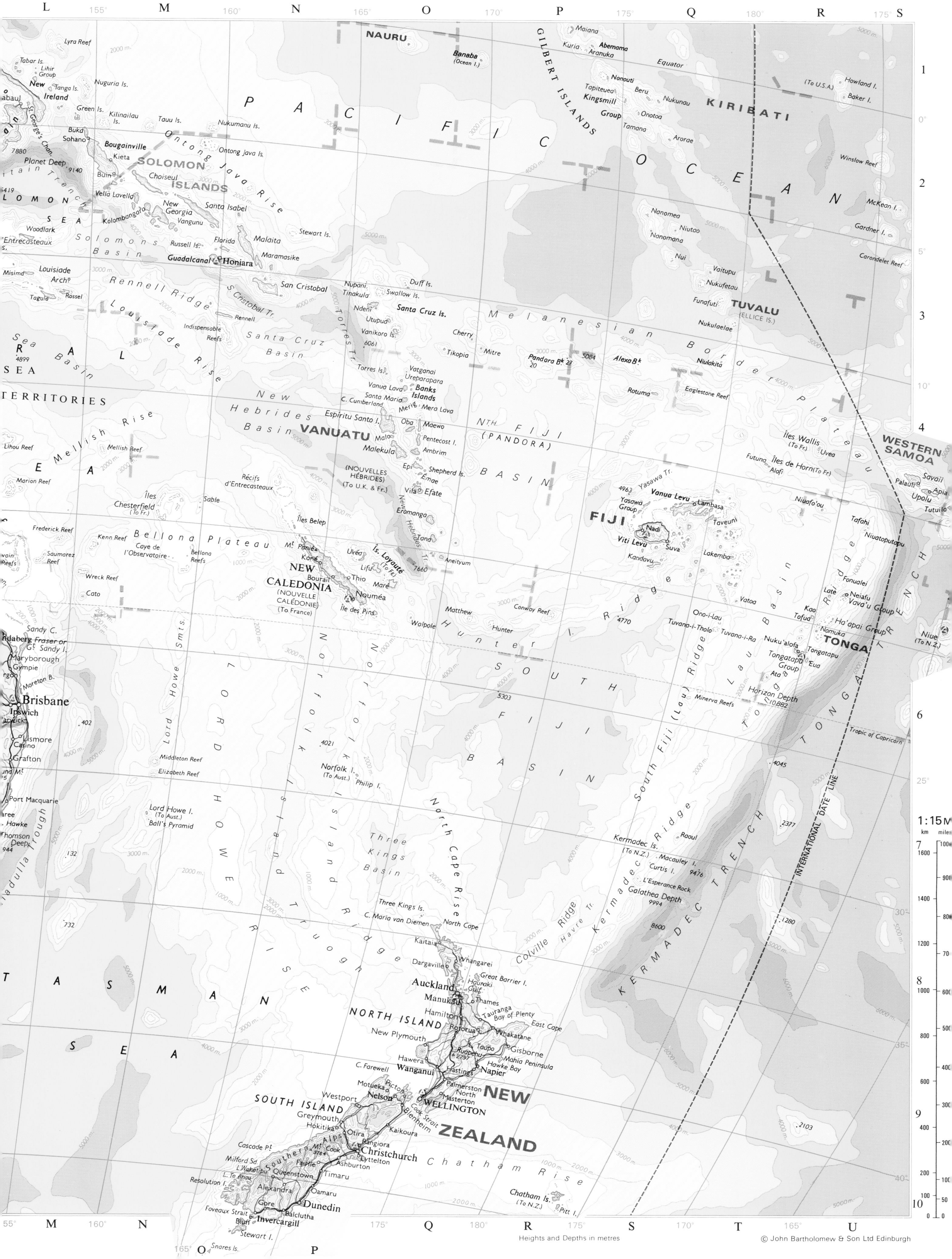

L 155° M 160° N 165° O 170° P 175° Q 180° R 175° S

NAURU

Maiana
Kuria Abemama
Aranuka
GILBERT ISLANDS
Banaba
(Ocean I.)
Nonouti
Tapiteuea Beru Nukunau
Kingsmill Tamana Onotoa
Group Arorae

(To U.S.A.)
Howland I.
Baker I.

KIRIBATI

Lyra Reef
Tabar Is.
Lihir Group
Tanga Is.
New
Ireland
Nuguria Is.
Green Is.
Kilinailau Is.
Tauu Is.
Nukumanu Is.

Winslow Reef

P A C I F I C

Rabaul
Buka
Sohano
Bougainville
Kieta
Planet Deep 9140
Buin

Ontong Java Rise
Ontong Java Is.

McKean I.
Gardner I.

SOLOMON
ISLANDS
Choiseul
Vella Lavella
New Georgia
Vangunu
Santa Isabel
Kolombangara
Russell Is.
Florida
Stewart Is.
Malaita
Maramasike

Carondelet Reef

SEA
Woodlark
Entrecasteaux Is.

Solomons Basin
Guadalcanal Honiara

Nanomea
Niutao
Nanomana
Nui

Misima
Louisiade Arch.
Tagula Rossel

Rennell Ridge
Louisiade Rise

San Cristobal
S. Cristobal Tr.
Rennell
Indispensable Reefs

Nupani Duff Is.
Tinakula Swallow Is.
Ndeni
Utupua Santa Cruz Is.
Vanikoro Is. 6061
Tikopia
Cherry
Mitre
Torres Is.
Vatganai
Ureparapara

Vaitupu
Nukufetau
Funafuti TUVALU
(ELLICE IS.)
Nukulaelae

TERRITORIES

Sea Basin
R 4899

CORAL SEA

Mellish Rise
Lihou Reef
Mellish Reef

Marion Reef

Îles Chesterfield
(To Fr.)

Frederick Reef
Kenn Reef
Saumarez Reef
Wreck Reef
Cato

New
Hebrides
Basin

Santa Cruz Basin

Vanua Lava
Santa Maria
C. Cumberland
Merig Mera Lava
Espiritu Santo I.
Malo Oba Maewo
Malekula Ambrim
Epi
Récifs Shepherd Is.
d'Entrecasteaux Emae
Vila Efate
Tongoa
Eromanga

VANUATU
(NOUVELLES HÉBRIDES)
(To U.K. & Fr.)

Pandora Bk 5084
20

Alexa Bk

NTH. FIJI
(PANDORA)
BASIN

Niulakita

Rotuma
Eaglestone Reef

WESTERN SAMOA

Îles Wallis
(To Fr.)
Uvea
Futuna Îles de Horn (To Fr.)
Alofi

Savaii
Palauli Apia
Upolu
Tutuila

Tafahi
Niuatoputapu

4963 Yasawa Tr.
Yasawa Vanua Levu
Yasawa Group Lambasa
Taveuni

FIJI
Nadi
Viti Levu Suva
Kandavu
Lakemba
Vatoa

Niuafo'ou

Late Neiafu
Kao Vava'u Group
Tofua
Nomuka Ha'apai Group

TONGA

Niue
(To N.Z.)

Bellona Plateau

Caye de l'Observatoire
Bellona Reefs

Îles Belep
Mt. Paniès
Koné
Uvéa
Lifou
Thio
Nouméa
Île des Pins

NEW CALEDONIA
(NOUVELLE CALÉDONIE)
(To France)

Îs. Loyauté
(To Fr.)
Maré
7660
Aneityum

New Hebrides Tr.

Matthew
Hunter
Walpole

Conway Reef

Ono-i-Lau
Tuvana-i-Tholo
Tuvana-i-Ra

Nuku'alofa
Tongatapu Group
Eua
Ata

Minerva Reefs
Horizon Deep 10882

SOUTH
FIJI
BASIN

Hunter Ridge

South Fiji (Lau) Ridge

Lau Basin

Kermadec Trench

Tonga Trench

Tropic of Capricorn

Brisbane
Ipswich
Warwick
Lismore
Casino
Grafton

Norfolk Smts.

Lord Howe Rise

Norfolk Island Ridge

5303
5303

4045

2377

1:15M

km miles
1600 1000

Port Macquarie
Taree
Hawke
Thomson Deep 5944

Middleton Reef
Elizabeth Reef
Lord Howe I.
(To Aust.)
Ball's Pyramid

4021

Norfolk I.
(To Aust.)
Philip I.

Kermadec Ridge
(To N.Z.)
Raoul

Macauley I. 9476
Curtis I.
L'Esperance Rock
Galathea Depth 9994
8600

1280

1400 900
1200 800

Three Kings Basin
Three Kings Is.
C. Maria van Diemen
North Cape

Kaitaia
Dargaville
Whangarei

North Cape Rise

Colville Ridge
Havre Tr.

INTERNATIONAL DATE LINE

2103

1000 700
800 600

T A S M A N
S E A

Great Barrier I.
Auckland Hauraki Gulf
Manukau Thames
Hamilton Tauranga
Bay of Plenty
East Cape
Rotorua
NORTH ISLAND Whakatane
NEW PLYMOUTH
New Plymouth Taupo Gisborne
Ruapehu Mahia Peninsula
Hawera Napier Hawke Bay
Wanganui Hastings
C. Farewell Palmerston North
Motueka Masterton
Nelson Picton
Westport WELLINGTON
Greymouth Blenheim
Hokitika Cook Strait NEW
Kaikoura
ALPS Otira ZEALAND
Mt. Cook Rangiora
Cascade Pt. Christchurch
Milford Sd. Lyttelton
L. Wakatipu Ashburton
Queenstown Timaru
Resolution I. Oamaru
L. Te Anau
Alexandra Balclutha
Foveaux Strait Gore Dunedin
Bluff Invercargill
Stewart I.

Chatham Rise
Chatham Is.
(To N.Z.) Pitt I.

600 400

400 300
200 200

100 100
0 0

O P Q R S T U
155° 160° 165° 175° 180° 175° 170° 165°

Heights and Depths in metres

© John Bartholomew & Son Ltd Edinburgh

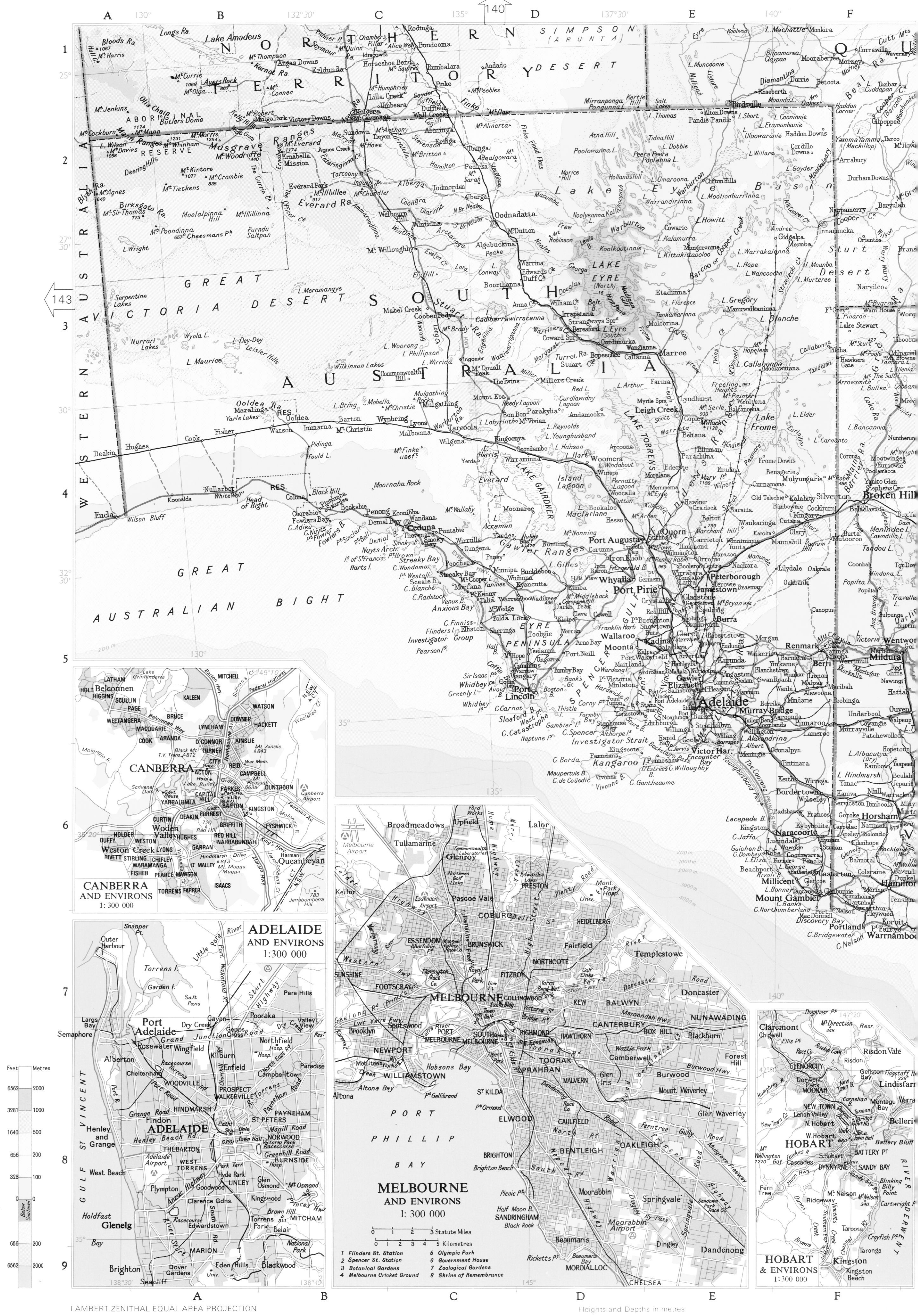

LAMBERT ZENITHAL EQUAL AREA PROJECTION

Heights and Depths in metres

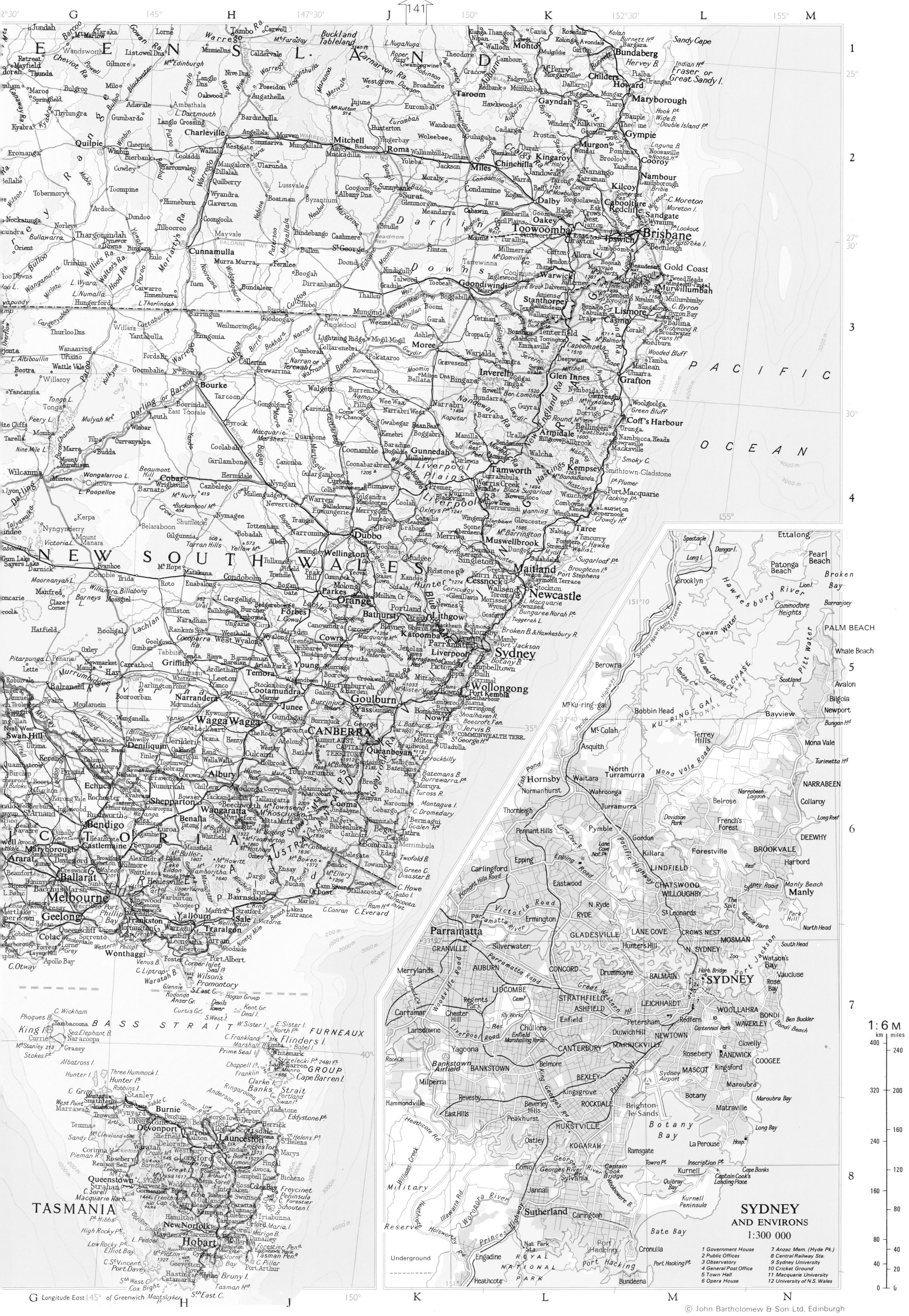

QUEENSLAND

NEW SOUTH WALES

VICTORIA

TASMANIA

PACIFIC OCEAN

BASS STRAIT

FURNEAUX GROUP

SYDNEY AND ENVIRONS
1:300 000

1 Government House
2 Public Offices
3 Observatory
4 General Post Office
5 Town Hall
6 Opera House
7 Anzac Mem. (Hyde Pk.)
8 Central Railway Sta.
9 Sydney University
10 Cricket Ground
11 Macquarie University
12 University of N.S. Wales

1:6 M

© John Bartholomew & Son Ltd, Edinburgh

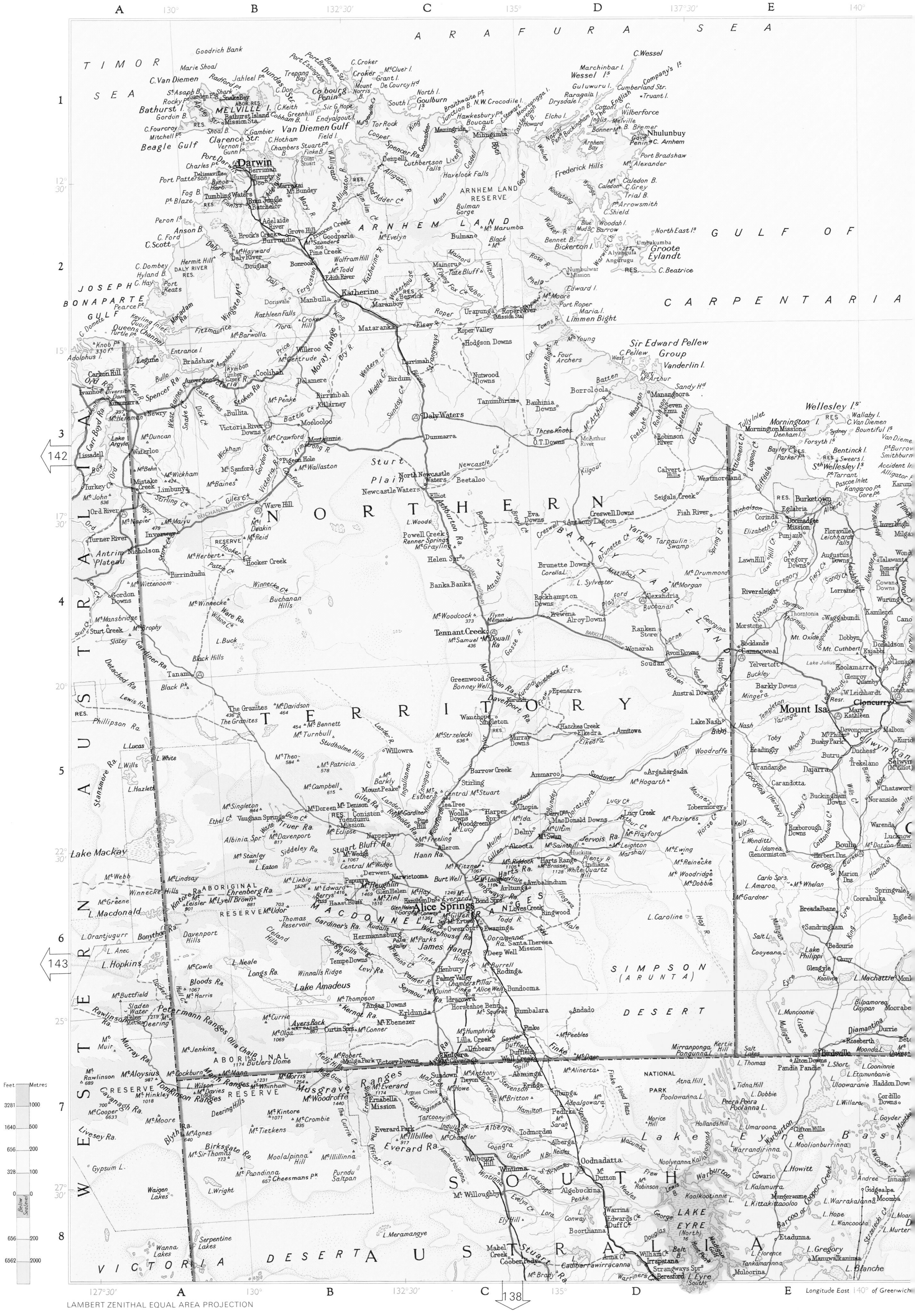

ARAFURA SEA
TIMOR SEA
GULF OF CARPENTARIA
JOSEPH BONAPARTE GULF
NORTHERN TERRITORY
WESTERN AUSTRALIA
SOUTH AUSTRALIA
ARNHEM LAND
ARNHEM LAND RESERVE
BARKLY TABLELAND
SIMPSON (ARUNTA) DESERT
MACDONNELL RANGES
ABORIGINAL RESERVE
Sturt Plain
Darwin
Katherine
Alice Springs
Tennant Creek
Mount Isa
Cloncurry
Burketown
Camooweal
Birdsville
Oodnadatta
Coober Pedy
Daly Waters
Newcastle Waters
Borroloola
Nhulunbuy
Groote Eylandt
Bathurst I.
Melville I.
Wellesley Is.
Sir Edward Pellew Group
Lake Mackay
Lake Amadeus
Ayers Rock
Musgrave Ranges
Petermann Ranges
Lake Eyre (North)
Lake Eyre Basin
Victoria Desert
Feet
Metres
3281
1000
1640
500
656
200
328
100
0
0
656
200
6562
2000
Longitude East 140° of Greenwich
142
143
138

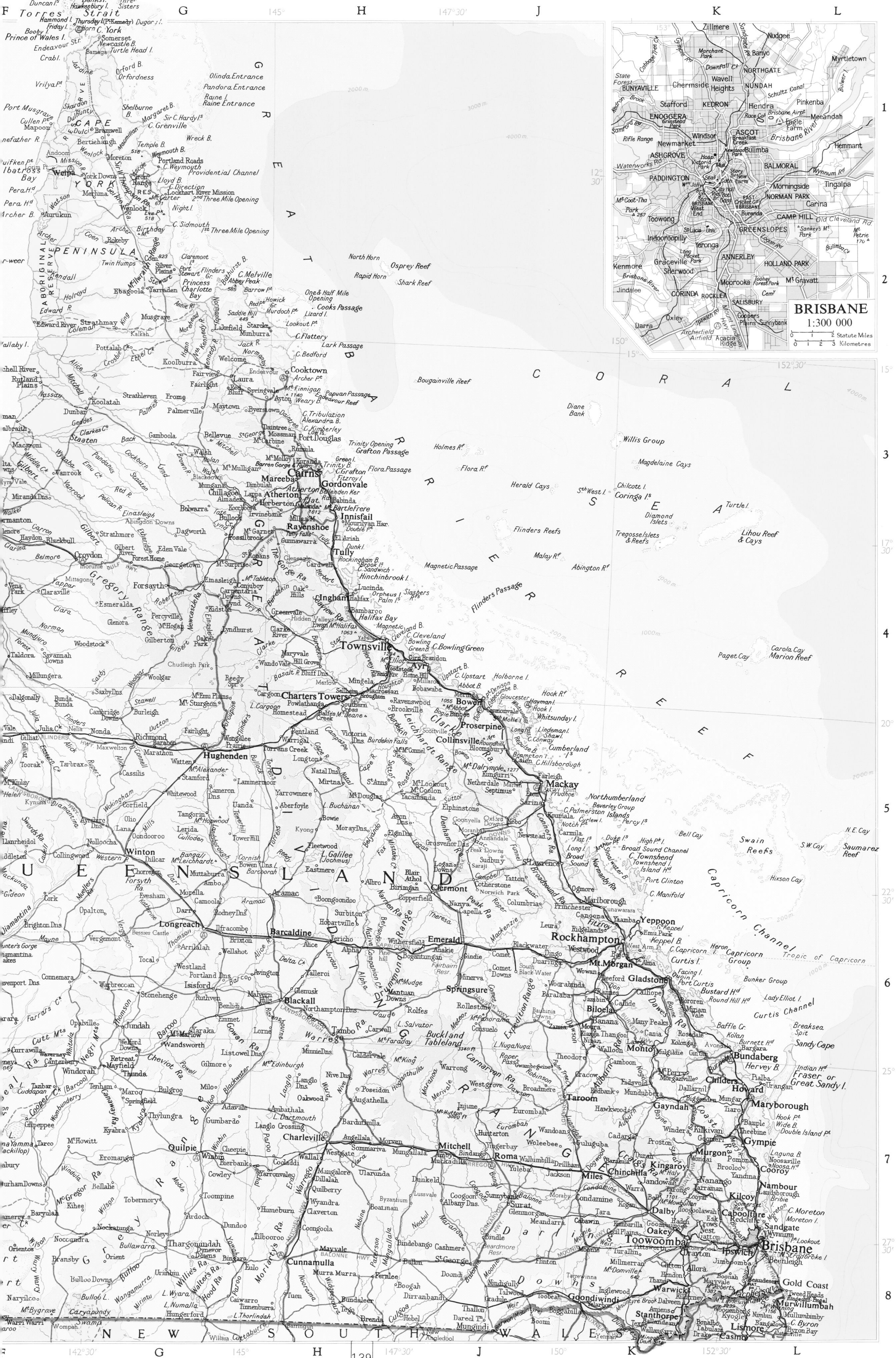

BRISBANE
1:300 000

1:6 M

Heights and Depths in metres

© John Bartholomew & Son Ltd. Edinburgh

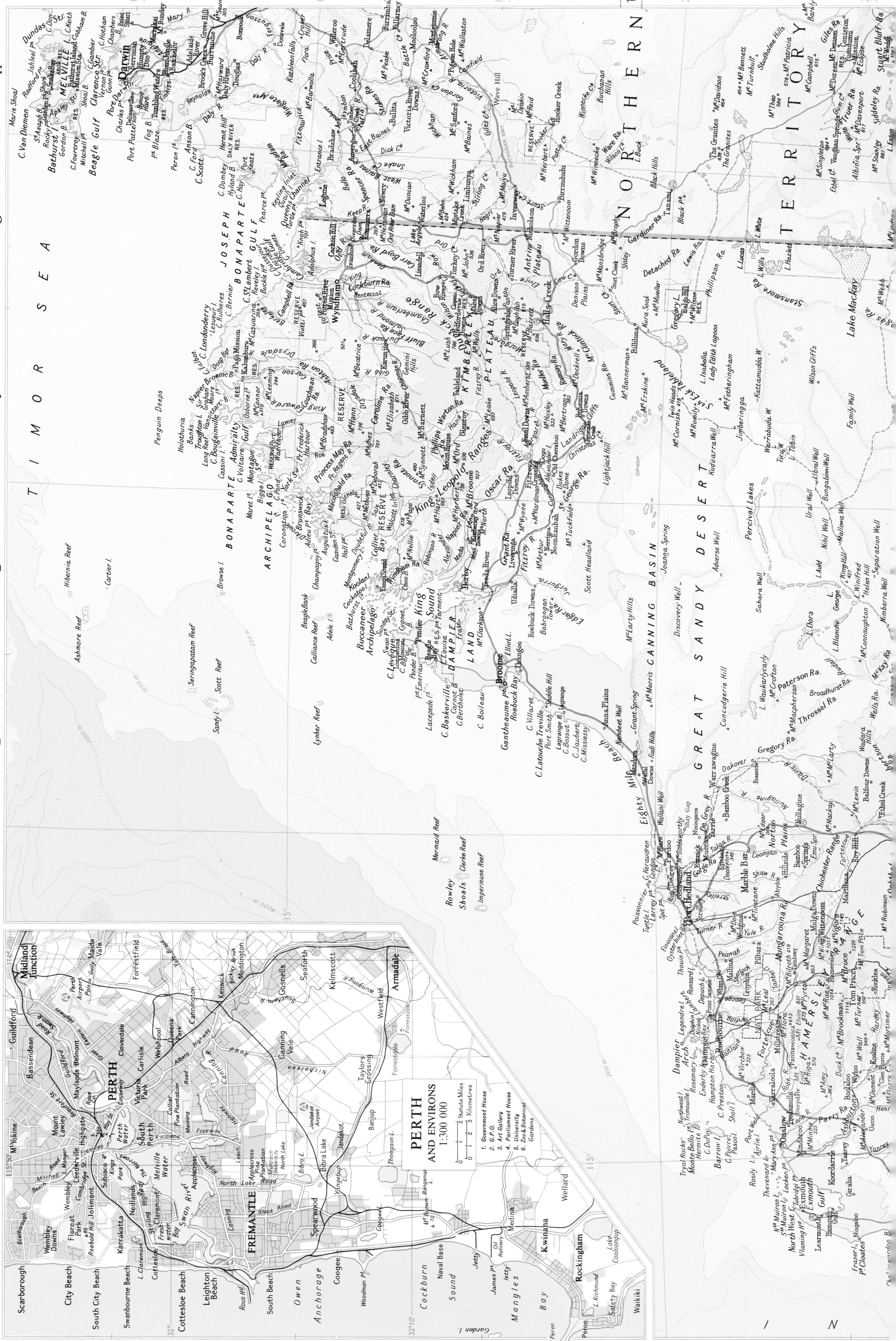

LAMBERT ZENITHAL EQUAL AREA PROJECTION

TIMOR SEA
JOSEPH BONAPARTE GULF
BONAPARTE ARCHIPELAGO
KIMBERLEY PLATEAU
NORTHERN TERRITORY
GREAT SANDY DESERT
CANNING BASIN
DAMPIER LAND
HAMERSLEY RANGE
Eighty Mile Beach
Darwin
Wyndham
Derby
Broome
Port Hedland
PERTH
AND ENVIRONS
1:300 000
1. Government House
2. G.P.O.
3. Art Gallery
4. Parliament House
5. University
6. Zoo & Botanical Gardens
FREMANTLE
Rockingham
Kwinana

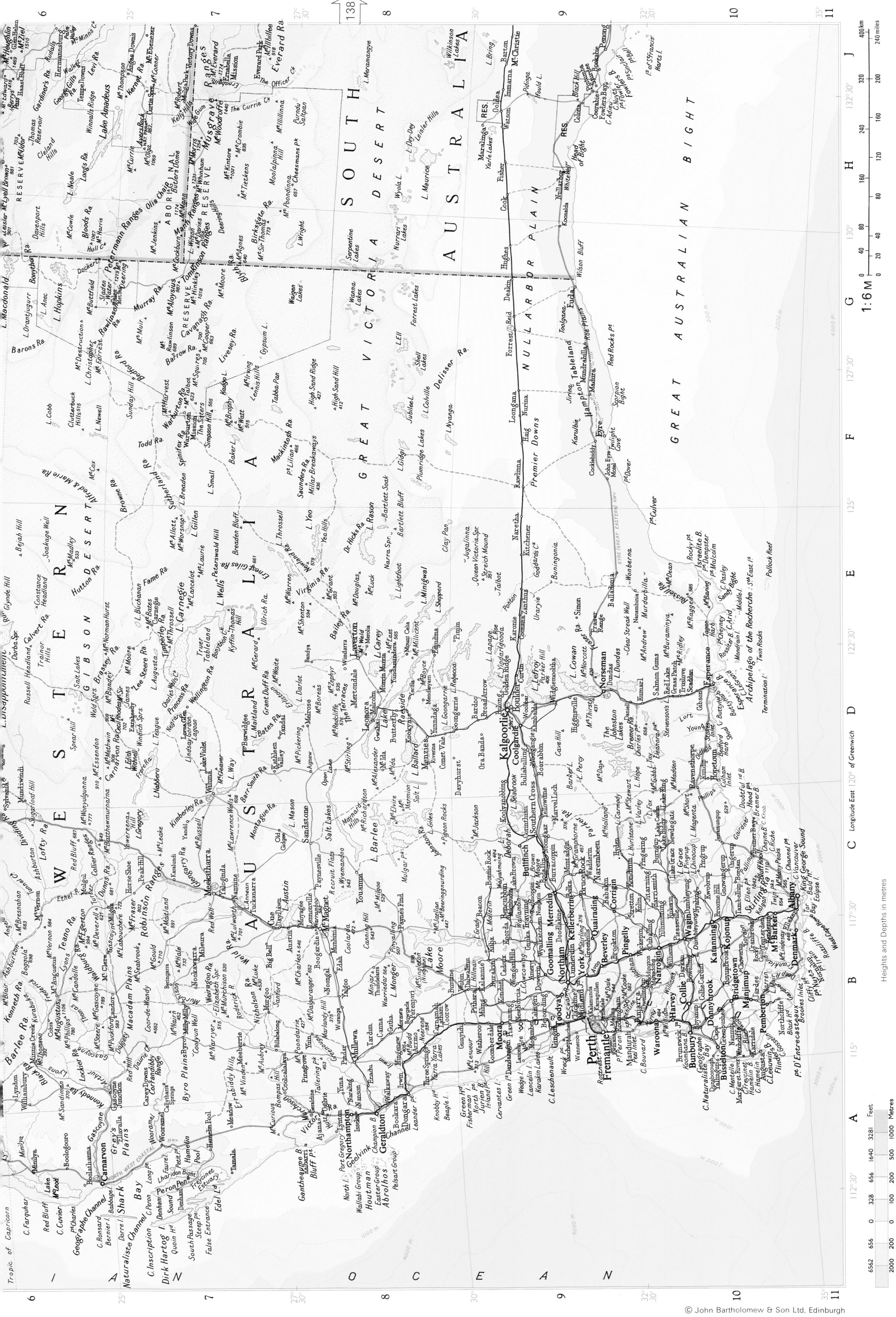

WESTERN AUSTRALIA

S O U T H   A U S T R A L I A

G R E A T   V I C T O R I A   D E S E R T

G I B S O N   D E S E R T

G R E A T   S A N D Y   D E S E R T

NULLARBOR PLAIN

G R E A T   A U S T R A L I A N   B I G H T

I N D I A N   O C E A N

Shark Bay

Naturaliste Channel

Tropic of Capricorn

1:6 M

Heights and Depths in metres

Longitude East 120° of Greenwich

Perth
Fremantle
Kalgoorlie
Coolgardie
Geraldton
Carnarvon
Meekatharra
Norseman
Esperance
Albany
Bunbury
Northam
York

© John Bartholomew & Son Ltd, Edinburgh

Feet	Metres
6562	2000
3281	1000
1640	500
656	200
328	100
0	0

0   40   80   120   160   200   240 miles

0   80   160   240   320   400 km

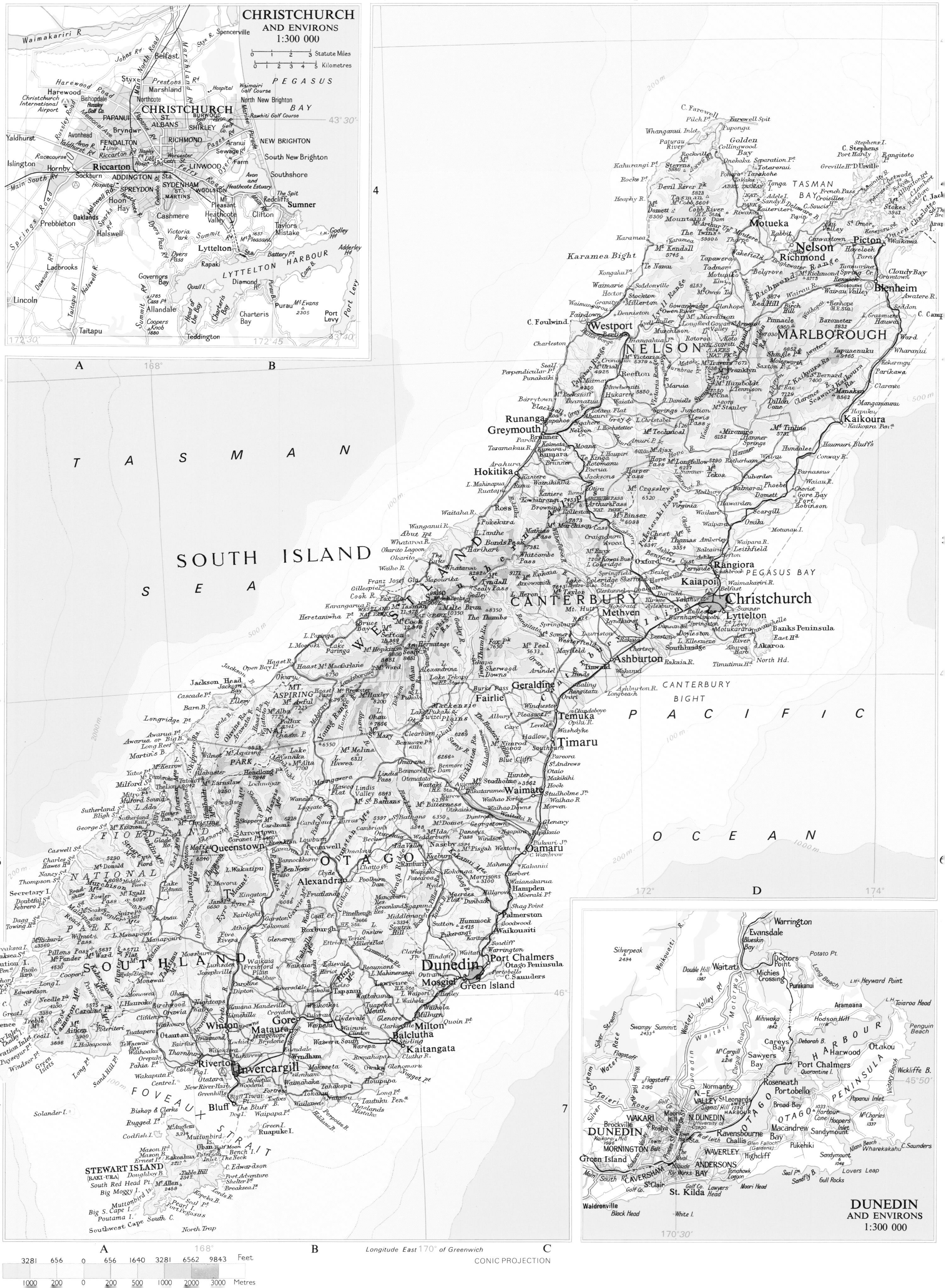

CHRISTCHURCH
AND ENVIRONS
1:300 000

Statute Miles
0 1 2 3 4 5
0 1 2 3 4 5 Kilometres

PEGASUS BAY

TASMAN BAY

TASMAN SEA

SOUTH ISLAND

WESTLAND

NELSON

MARLBOROUGH

CANTERBURY

PACIFIC OCEAN

CANTERBURY BIGHT

OTAGO

SOUTHLAND

FIORDLAND NATIONAL PARK

MT. ASPIRING NATIONAL PARK

FOVEAUX STRAIT

STEWART ISLAND
(RAKI-URA)

DUNEDIN
AND ENVIRONS
1:300 000

OTAGO PENINSULA

Longitude East 170° of Greenwich
CONIC PROJECTION

Feet
3281 656 0 656 1640 3281 6562 9843
1000 200 0 200 500 1000 2000 3000
Metres

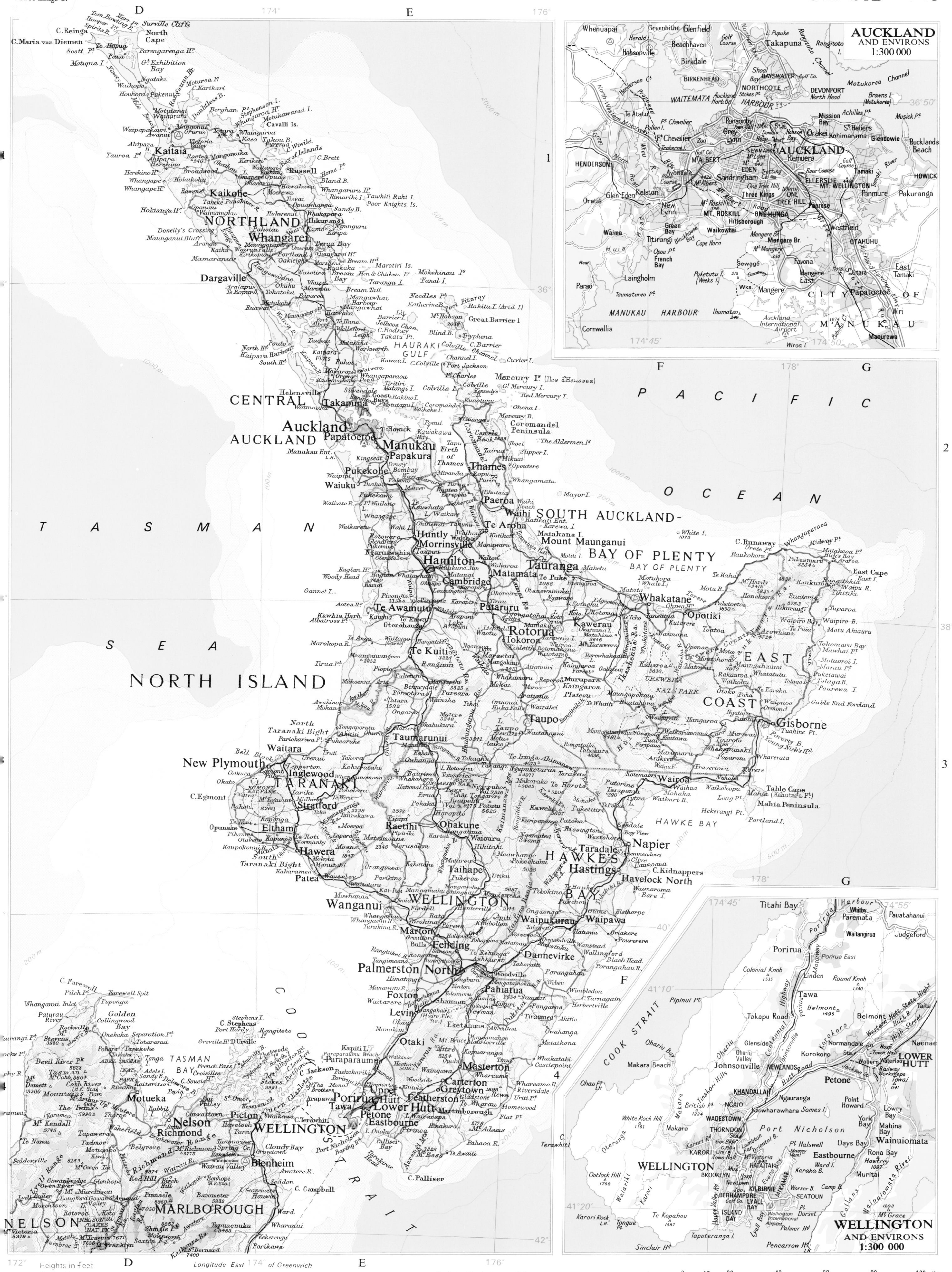

AUCKLAND AND ENVIRONS 1:300 000

WELLINGTON AND ENVIRONS 1:300 000

PACIFIC OCEAN

TASMAN SEA

NORTH ISLAND

COOK STRAIT

Regions and major place names

NORTHLAND

CENTRAL AUCKLAND

SOUTH AUCKLAND–BAY OF PLENTY

EAST COAST

TARANAKI

HAWKE'S BAY

WELLINGTON

MARLBOROUGH

NELSON

UREWERA NAT. PARK

Notable places

North Cape
C. Reinga
C. Maria van Diemen
Kaitaia
Kaikohe
Whangarei
Dargaville
Helensville
Takapuna
Auckland
Papatoetoe
Manukau
Papakura
Pukekohe
Waiuku
Thames
Paeroa
Waihi
Te Aroha
Mount Maunganui
Tauranga
Matamata
Huntly
Morrinsville
Hamilton
Cambridge
Te Awamutu
Te Kuiti
Putaruru
Tokoroa
Rotorua
Kawerau
Whakatane
Opotiki
East Cape
Gisborne
Taupo
Taumarunui
New Plymouth
Inglewood
Stratford
Eltham
Hawera
Patea
Wanganui
Wairoa
Napier
Hastings
Havelock North
Taradale
Raetihi
Ohakune
Taihape
Marton
Feilding
Palmerston North
Foxton
Levin
Otaki
Paraparaumu
Masterton
Carterton
Greytown
Featherston
Dannevirke
Waipukurau
Waipawa
Pahiatua
Porirua
Tawa
Lower Hutt
Petone
Eastbourne
WELLINGTON
Nelson
Richmond
Motueka
Picton
Blenheim

Auckland and Environs inset

Whenuapai
Greenhithe
Glenfield
Takapuna
Rangitoto
Hobsonville
Beachhaven
Birkdale
Birkenhead
Northcote
Devonport
North Head
WAITEMATA HARBOUR
Te Atatu
Henderson
Pt Chevalier
Ponsonby
Grey Lynn
Newmarket
AUCKLAND
Remuera
Orakei
St Heliers
Glendowie
Howick
Pakuranga
New Lynn
Mt Albert
Mt Eden
Mt Roskill
Three Kings
ONE TREE HILL
Mt Wellington
Panmure
Ellerslie
Onehunga
Hillsborough
Mangere
Otahuhu
Westfield
Papatoetoe
MANUKAU HARBOUR
Auckland International Airport
Manurewa
Wiri
Cornwallis

Wellington and Environs inset

Titahi Bay
Porirua
Paremata
Pauatahanui
Judgeford
Tawa
Takapu Road
Johnsonville
Khandallah
Ngaio
Karori
Newlands
Belmont
Lower Hutt
Petone
Woburn
Naenae
Taita
WELLINGTON
Port Nicholson
Eastbourne
Seatoun
Island Bay
Wainuiomata
Pencarrow Hd

Heights in feet
Depths in metres

1:2.5 M
0 10 20 40 60 80 100 miles
0 10 20 40 60 80 100 120 140 160 km

© John Bartholomew & Son Ltd, Edinburgh

Longitude East of Greenwich

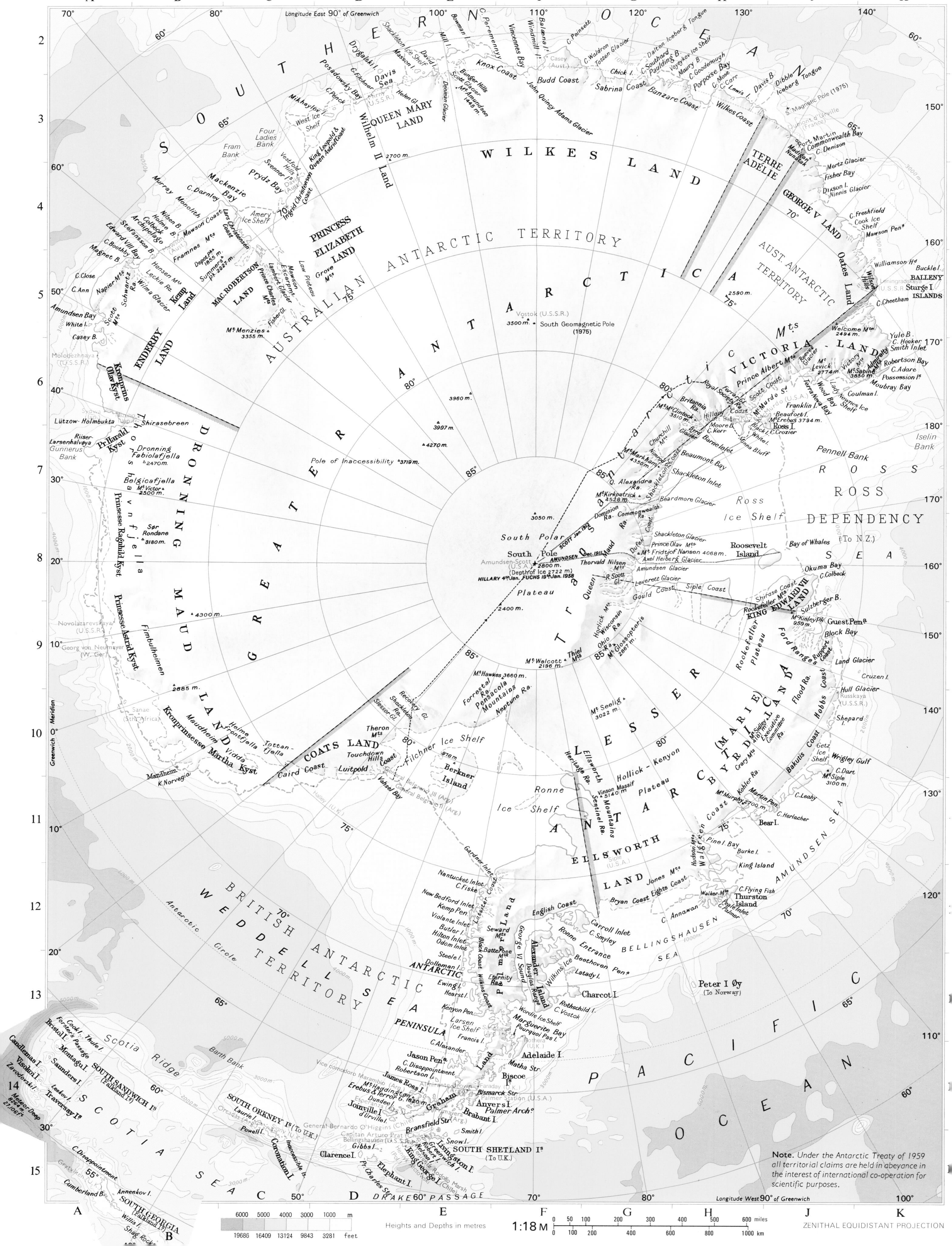

SOUTHERN OCEAN

WILKES LAND

QUEEN MARY LAND

PRINCESS ELIZABETH LAND

AUSTRALIAN ANTARCTIC TERRITORY

ANTARCTICA

MAC·ROBERTSON LAND

KEMP LAND

ENDERBY LAND

DRONNING MAUD LAND

GREATER ANTARCTICA

TERRE ADÉLIE

GEORGE V LAND

AUST. ANTARCTIC TERRITORY

OATES LAND

VICTORIA LAND

Transantarctic Mts

BALLENY ISLANDS

Vostok (U.S.S.R.)
3500 m. • South Geomagnetic Pole (1975)

Pole of Inaccessibility ▲3719 m.

South Polar Plateau

South Pole
Amundsen-Scott (U.S.A.) 2800 m.
(Depth of Ice 2722 m)

AMUNDSEN
SCOTT Jan.1912
Dec. 1911
HILLARY 4th Jan. FUCHS 19 Jan. 1958

ROSS Ice Shelf

ROSS DEPENDENCY (To N.Z.)

ROSS SEA

Roosevelt Island
Bay of Whales
Okuma Bay

KING EDWARD VII LAND

MARIE BYRD LAND

LESSER ANTARCTICA

Rockefeller plateau
Ford Range

ELLSWORTH LAND

AMUNDSEN SEA

Ellsworth Mountains
Vinson Massif 5140 m.
Sentinel Ra.

Hollick - Kenyon Plateau

Thiel Mts

COATS LAND

Filchner Ice Shelf

Berkner Island

Ronne Ice Shelf

Peter I Øy (To Norway)

BELLINGSHAUSEN SEA

WEDDELL SEA

BRITISH ANTARCTIC TERRITORY

ANTARCTIC PENINSULA

Larsen Ice Shelf

Alexander I. Land

Marguerite Bay
Adelaide I.

PACIFIC OCEAN

SCOTIA SEA

SCOTIA Ridge

SOUTH ORKNEY Is (To U.K.)

SOUTH SHETLAND Is (To U.K.)

SOUTH GEORGIA (Falkland Is)

SOUTH SANDWICH Is (Falkland Is)

DRAKE PASSAGE

Amery Ice Shelf

Prydz Bay
Mackenzie Bay

Davis Sea

Knox Coast
Budd Coast
Sabrina Coast
Banzare Coast

S. Magnetic Pole (1975)
Commonwealth Bay

Mt Erebus 3794 m.
Ross I.

Beardmore Glacier

Shackleton Inlet

Mt Kirkpatrick 4528 m.

Queen Maud Mts

Axel Heiberg Glacier

Note. Under the Antarctic Treaty of 1959 all territorial claims are held in abeyance in the interest of international co-operation for scientific purposes.

Longitude East 90° of Greenwich
Longitude West 90° of Greenwich
Greenwich Meridian

Heights and Depths in metres

1:18 M

ZENITHAL EQUIDISTANT PROJECTION

6000 5000 4000 3000 1000 m
19686 16409 13124 9843 3281 feet

0 50 100 200 300 400 500 600 miles
0 100 200 400 600 800 1000 km

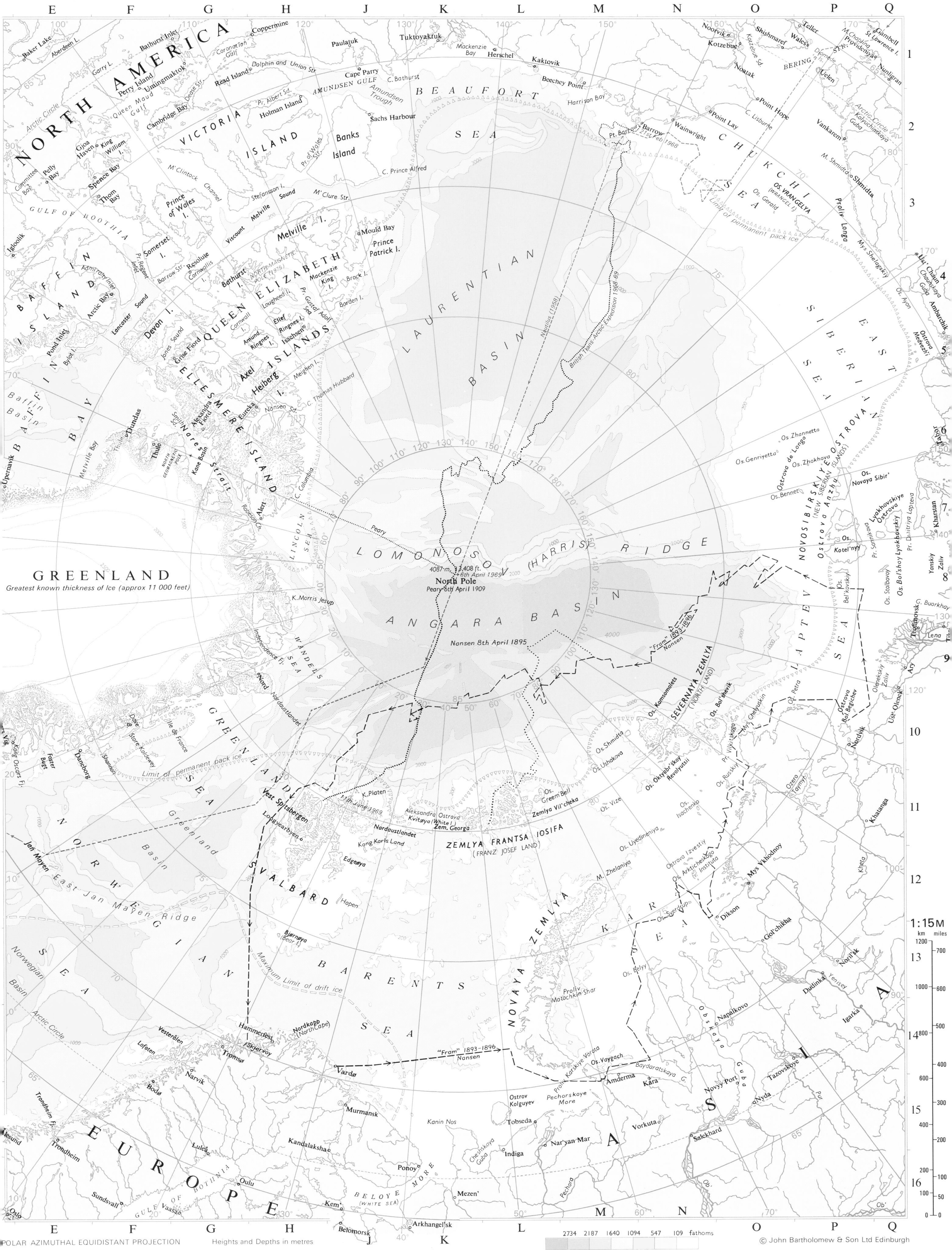

NORTH AMERICA

GREENLAND
Greatest known thickness of Ice (approx 11 000 feet)

BAFFIN
BAY

BAFFIN
ISLAND

VICTORIA
ISLAND

QUEEN ELIZABETH
ISLANDS

ELLESMERE ISLAND

Banks
Island

Melville I.

Prince Patrick I.

BEAUFORT
SEA

CHUKCHI
SEA

BERING

EAST
SIBERIAN
SEA

LAURENTIAN
BASIN

LOMONOSOV (HARRIS) RIDGE

4087 m. 13,408 ft.
16th April 1969
North Pole
Peary 6th April 1909

ANGARA BASIN

Nansen 8th April 1895

NOVOSIBIRSKIYE OSTROVA
(NEW SIBERIAN ISLANDS)

LAPTEV SEA

SEVERNAYA ZEMLYA
(NORTH LAND)

"Fram" 1893-1896
Nansen

WANDELS
SEA

GREENLAND
SEA

NORTH

Limit of permanent pack ice

ZEMLYA FRANTSA IOSIFA
(FRANZ JOSEF LAND)

KARA
SEA

NORWEGIAN
SEA

Greenland
Basin

East Jan Mayen Ridge

SVALBARD

NOVAYA ZEMLYA

BARENTS
SEA

Maximum Limit of drift ice

"Fram" 1893-1896
Nansen

EUROPE

GULF OF
BOTHNIA

BELOYE
(WHITE SEA)

POLAR AZIMUTHAL EQUIDISTANT PROJECTION   Heights and Depths in metres

2734	2187	1640	1094	547	109	fathoms
5000	4000	3000	2000	1000	200	m

1:15 M
km miles

© John Bartholomew & Son Ltd Edinburgh

Geographical comparisons

Populations (estimated) of largest metropolitan areas

New York - N.E. New Jersey	16,678,818
Mexico City Mexico	11,943,050
Tokyo Japan	11,540,283
Shanghai China	11,300,000
Los Angeles - Long Beach Calif., USA	10,350,362
São Paulo Brazil	10,041,132
Paris France	9,878,524
Buenos Aires Argentina	8,925,000
Rio de Janeiro Brazil	8,328,800
Osaka Japan	8,279,000
Beijing (Peking) China	8,000,000
Moscow USSR	7,819,000
Seoul South Korea	7,800,000
Calcutta India	7,700,000
Chicago Illinois - N.W. Indiana, USA	7,658,335
Bombay India	7,450,000
London England, UK	7,110,000
Tianjin (Tientsin) China	7,000,000
Cairo Egypt	6,588,000
Chongqing (Chungking) China	6,000,000
Jakarta Indonesia	5,849,000
Philadelphia, Penn. - New Jersey USA	5,643,223
Guangzhou (Canton) China	5,000,000
Bangkok (Krung Thep) Thailand	4,870,509
Delhi - New Delhi India	4,700,000
Detroit Michigan, USA	4,669,106
San Francisco - Oakland Calif., USA	4,591,928
Hong Kong	4,514,000
Manila Philippines	4,500,000
Tehran Iran	4,498,159
Leningrad USSR	4,425,000
Shenyang (Mukden) China	4,400,000
Madras India	4,100,000
Karachi Pakistan	4,000,000
Santiago Chile	3,899,495
Istanbul Turkey	3,864,493
Boston Massachusetts, USA	3,553,203
Ho Chi Minh (Saigon) Vietnam	3,500,000
Wuhan China	3,500,000
Lima Peru	3,302,000
Madrid Spain	3,206,100
Baghdad Iraq	3,206,000
Washington DC, USA	3,021,801
Rome Italy	2,914,640
Cleveland Ohio, USA	2,902,461
Bogota Colombia	2,855,065
Montreal Canada	2,798,000
Sydney Australia	2,765,040
Toronto Canada	2,741,000
Birmingham England, UK	2,730,000
Manchester England, UK	2,675,000
Ankara Turkey	2,600,000
Athens-Piraeus Greece	2,540,241
Melbourne Australia	2,479,225
St. Louis Missouri - Illinois, USA	2,366,542
Pittsburgh Pennsylvania, USA	2,322,224
Alexandria Egypt	2,320,000
Singapore	2,308,000
Budapest Hungary	2,089,000
Kiev USSR	2,079,000
Bucharest Romania	1,934,025
Berlin W. Germany	1,909,706
Havana Cuba	1,861,442
Barcelona Spain	1,809,722
Casablanca Morocco	1,753,000
Johannesburg S. Africa	1,748,000
Glasgow Scotland, UK	1,727,625
Hamburg W. Germany	1,699,000

Lake Areas

Areas are average and some are subject to seasonal variations

	Sq. Miles	Sq. Km
Caspian USSR – Iran (salt)	143,240	371,000
Superior USA – Canada	32,150	83,270
Victoria Kenya – Uganda – Tanzania	26,560	68,800
Aral USSR (salt)	25,300	65,500
Huron USA – Canada	23,430	60,700
Michigan USA	22,400	58,020
Tanganyika Tanzania – Zambia – Zaire – Burundi	12,700	32,900
Great Bear Canada	12,270	31,790
Baykal USSR	11,800	30,500
Great Slave Canada	10,980	28,440
Erie USA – Canada	9,910	25,680
Winnipeg Canada	9,460	24,510
Nyasa (Malawi) Malawi – Mozambique	8,680	22,490
Ontario USA-Canada	7,430	19,230
Ladoga USSR	7,100	18,390
Balkhash USSR	6,700	17,400
Maracaibo Venezuela	6,300	16,300
Chad Nigeria – Niger – Chad – Cameroon	4-10,000	10-26,000
Onega USSR	3,710	9,600
Eyre Australia	0-3,430	0-8,900
Titicaca Peru – Bolivia	3,220	8,340
Nicaragua Nicaragua	3,190	8,270
Rudolf Kenya-Ethiopia	2,470	6,410
Torrens Australia	2,230	5,780
Vänern Sweden	2,160	5,580
Manitoba Canada	1,820	4,710
Loch Lomond Scotland, UK	27	70
Windermere England, UK	10	26

River Lengths

	Miles	Km
Nile Africa	4,160	6,695
Amazon South America	4,080	6,570
Yangtze Asia	3,964	6,380
Mississippi - Missouri N. America	3,740	6,020
Ob-Irtysh Asia	3,360	5,410
Huang He (Yellow) Asia	3,010	4,840
Zaïre (Congo) Africa	2,880	4,630
Paraná South America	2,796	4,500
Irtysh Asia	2,760	4,440
Amur Asia	2,745	4,416
Lena Asia	2,730	4,400
Mackenzie North America	2,630	4,240
Mekong Asia	2,600	4,180
Niger Africa	2,550	4,100
Yenisey Asia	2,540	4,090
Missouri North America	2,466	3,969
Mississippi North America	2,348	3,779
Murray-Darling Australia	2,330	3,750
Volga Europe	2,292	3,688
Madeira South America	2,013	3,240
Indus Asia	1,980	3,180
St Lawrence North America	1,900	3,058
Rio Grande North America	1,880	3,030
Yukon North America	1,870	3,020
Brahmaputra Asia	1,840	2,960
Danube Europe	1,770	2,850
Salween Asia	1,750	2,820
São Francisco South America	1,730	2,780
Ganges Asia	1,678	2,700
Zambezi Africa	1,650	2,650
Nelson - Saskatchewan North America	1,600	2,570
Euphrates Asia	1,510	2,430
Arkansas North America	1,450	2,330
Colorado North America	1,450	2,330
Dnepr Europe	1,370	2,200
Irrawaddy Asia	1,300	2,090
Orinoco South America	1,280	2,060
Negro South America	1,240	2,000
Don Europe	1,160	1,870
Orange Africa	1,155	1,859
Pechora Europe	1,118	1,799
Marañón South America	1,000	1,609
Dnestr Europe	876	1,410
Rhine Europe	820	1,320
Donets Europe	735	1,183
Elbe Europe	720	1,159
Gambia Africa	680	1,094
Yellowstone North America	671	1,080
Vistula Europe	630	1,014
Tagus Europe	625	1,006
Oder Europe	565	909
Seine Europe	473	761
Thames England, UK	209	336
Liffey Ireland	50	80

Populations - 1982

China	1,031,900,000
India	711,700,000
USSR	270,000,000
USA	232,100,000
Indonesia	156,700,000
Brazil	126,800,000
Japan	118,400,000
Bangladesh	92,600,000
Pakistan	87,100,000
Nigeria	86,100,000
Mexico	73,000,000
West Germany	61,600,000
Italy	56,700,000
United Kingdom	56,200,000
Vietnam	56,100,000
France	54,200,000
Philippines	50,700,000
Thailand	48,500,000
Turkey	46,300,000
Egypt	44,700,000
Iran	40,200,000
South Korea	39,300,000
Spain	37,900,000
Burma	37,100,000
Poland	36,300,000

Mountain Heights

	Feet	Metres
Everest Tibet - Nepal	29,028	8,848
K2 (Godwin Austen) Kashmir - Sinkiang	28,250	8,611
Kangchenjunga Nepal - Sikkim	28,168	8,586
Makalu Tibet - Nepal	27,805	8,475
Dhaulagiri Nepal	26,810	8,172
Nanga Parbat Jammu/Kashmir	26,660	8,126
Annapurna Nepal	26,504	8,078
Gasherbrum Kashmir	26,470	8,068
Gosainthan (Xixabangma Feng) Tibet	26,291	8,013
Nanda Devi India	25,645	7,817
Rakaposhi Jammu/Kashmir	25,550	7,780
Kamet India - Tibet	25,447	7,756
Namcha Barwa Tibet	25,447	7,756
Gurla Mandhata Tibet	25,355	7,728
Ulugh Muztagh Tibet - Sinkiang	25,338	7,723
Kungur (Kongur Shan) Sinkiang	25,325	7,719
Tirich Mir Pakistan	25,230	7,690
Minya Konka (Gongga Shan) China	24,903	7,590
Muztagh Ata Sinkiang	24,757	7,546
Pik Kommunizma USSR	24,590	7,495
Pik Pobedy (Tomur Feng) USSR - Sinkiang	24,407	7,439
Chomo Lhari Bhutan - Tibet	23,993	7,313
Pik Lenina USSR	23,406	7,134
Ojos del Salado Chile - Argentina	23,240	7,084
Ancohuma Bolivia	23,012	7,014
Aconcagua Argentina	22,834	6,960
Bonete Argentina	22,541	6,870
Tupungato Argentina - Chile	22,310	6,800
Mercedario Argentina	22,211	6,770
Huascarán Peru	22,205	6,768
Llullaillaco Argentina - Chile	22,057	6,723
Kailas Tibet	22,028	6,714
Yerupaja Peru	21,765	6,634
Sajama Bolivia	21,463	6,542
Illampu Bolivia	21,276	6,485
Nudo Coropuna Peru	21,079	6,425
Illimani Bolivia	21,004	6,402
Chimborazo Ecuador	20,702	6,310
Mt McKinley USA	20,320	6,194
Logan Canada	19,850	6,050
Kilimanjaro Tanzania	19,340	5,895
Citlaltepetl Mexico	18,700	5,700
El'bruz USSR	18,510	5,642
Popocatepetl Mexico	17,887	5,452
Mt Kenya Kenya	17,058	5,200
Mt Ararat Turkey	16,946	5,165
Vinson Massif Antarctica	16,864	5,140
Stanley Zaire/Uganda	16,763	5,110
Jaya (Carstensz)	16,500	5,030
Mont Blanc France	15,781	4,810
Matterhorn Switzerland - Italy	14,688	4,477
Zugspitze Germany	9,721	2,963
Ben Nevis Scotland	4,406	1,343
Snowdon Wales	3,560	1,085
Carrantuohill Ireland	3,414	1,041
Scafell Pike England, UK	3,210	978

Areas

	Sq. Miles	Sq. Km
USSR	8,600,000	22,271,000
Canada	3,851,809	9,976,185
China	3,691,500	9,560,985
USA	3,615,123	9,363,169
Brazil	3,286,488	8,511,978
Australia	2,967,909	7,686,884
India	1,269,346	3,287,590
Argentina	1,072,067	2,776,654
Sudan	967,491	2,505,802
Algeria	919,591	2,381,741
UK	94,500	244,755

Oceans and Seas
Areas and greatest depths

	Sq. Miles	Sq. Km	Feet	Metres
Pacific Ocean	63,855,000	165,384,000	36,198	11,033
Atlantic Ocean	31,744,000	82,217,000	27,498	8,381
Indian Ocean	28,371,000	73,481,000	26,400	8,047
Arctic Ocean	5,427,000	14,056,000	17,880	5,450
Mediterranean Sea	967,000	2,505,000	15,900	4,846
South China Sea	895,000	2,318,000	18,090	5,514
Bering Sea	876,000	2,269,000	16,800	5,121
Caribbean Sea	750,000	1,943,000	24,580	7,492
Gulf of Mexico	596,000	1,544,000	14,360	4,377
Sea of Okhotsk	590,000	1,528,000	11,400	3,475
East China Sea	482,000	1,248,000	9,840	2,999
Yellow Sea	480,000	1,243,000	300	91
Hudson Bay	476,000	1,233,000	850	259
Sea of Japan	389,000	1,008,000	12,280	3,743
North Sea	222,000	575,000	2,170	661
Black Sea	178,000	461,000	7,360	2,243
Red Sea	169,000	438,000	7,370	2,246
Baltic Sea	163,000	422,000	1,400	439

Countries of the World

Country	Status or title	Capital	Area Sq. km.	Area Sq. miles	Population	Languages	Currency	Page numbers
Afghanistan	Democratic Republic	Kabul	636,266	(245,664)	17,050,000 (1976)*	Pushtu, Dari Persian	Afghani (Afs)	77
Albania	People's Socialist Republic	Tirana	28,748	(11,100)	2,590,600 (1979)	Albanian (Gheg, Tosk)	lek	46
Algeria	Democratic and Popular Republic	Algiers	2,381,745	(919,597)	18,250,000 (1979)*	Arabic, French, Berber	Algerian dinar (DA)	85
Andorra	Co-principality under French/Spanish sovereignty	Andorra la Vella	465	(180)	32,700 (1980)	Catalan, French, Spanish	French franc, Spanish peseta	17
Angola	People's Republic	Luanda	1,246,699	(481,353)	7,000,000 (1979)*	Portuguese, tribal dialects	kwanza	87
Antigua and Barbuda	Independent 1981	St John's	442	(171)	72,000 (1977)*	English	E Caribbean dollar (EC$)	127
Argentina	Republic	Buenos Aires	2,808,602	(1,084,407)	27,860,000 (1980)	Spanish	Arg. new peso	130–3
Australia	Commonwealth Nation	Canberra	7,682,300	(2,966,151)	14,421,900 (1979)*	English	Australian dollar ($A)	136,138–40
Austria	Republic	Vienna	83,853	(32,376)	7,508,400 (1978)*	German	schilling (sch)	38,41
Bahamas	Commonwealth Nation	Nassau	13,864	(5,353)	234,000 (1979)*	English	Bahamian dollar	113,126
Bahrain	State (Sheikhdom)	Manama	661	(255)	350,000 (1980)*	Arabic, English	Bahrain dinar (BD)	77
Bangladesh	People's Republic. Commonwealth Nation *formerly East Pakistan*	Dacca	144,020	(55,606)	88,704,000 (1980)	Bengali, Bihari, Hindi, English	Taka (Tk)	75
Barbados	Commonwealth Nation	Bridgetown	430	(166)	248,983 (1980)	English	Barbados dollar (BD$)	127
Belgium	Kingdom	Brussels	30,519	(11,784)	9,855,110 (1979)	French, Dutch, German	Belgian franc	22
Belize	Commonwealth Nation *formerly British Honduras*	Belmopan	22,963	(8,866)	151,607 (1978)*	English, Spanish, Maya	Belize dollar ($B)	125
Benin	People's Republic *formerly Republic of Dahomey*	Porto Novo	112,622	(43,484)	3,470,000 (1979)	French, Fon, Adja	CFA franc	85
Bhutan	Kingdom	Thimphu	46,600	(17,992)	1,100,000 (1979)*	Dzongkha, Nepali, English	Ngultrum, Indian rupee	75
Bolivia	Republic	La Paz	1,098,579	(424,164)	5,150,000 (1980)*	Spanish, Quechua, Aymará	Bolivian peso ($b)	128,133
Botswana	Republic. Commonwealth Nation	Gaborone	575,000	(222,009)	831,000 (1979)*	Setswana, English	pula (P)	87,89
Brazil	Federative Republic	Brasília	8,511,965	(3,286,487)	123,032,100 (1980)*	Portuguese	Cruzeiro (Cr$)	128–131
Brunei	Due to become fully independent state at end of 1983	Bandar Seri Begawan	5,800	(2,239)	212,840 (1980)*	Malay, English, Chinese	Brunei dollar (B$)	70
Bulgaria	People's Republic	Sofia	110,912	(42,823)	8,880,000 (1980)	Bulgarian	lev	47
Burma	Socialist Republic of the Union of Burma	Rangoon	678,000	(261,777)	33,000,000 (1979)*	Burmese	kyat	68
Burundi	Republic	Bujumbura	27,834	(10,747)	4,280,000 (1978)*	French, Kirundi, Swahili	Burundi franc	88
Cambodia	Democratic Kampuchea *formerly the Khmer Republic*	Phnom Penh	181,036	(69,898)	7,735,279 (1976)	Khmer	riel	68–9
Cameroon	United Republic	Yaoundé	465,054	(179,558)	8,280,000 (1980)*	English, French	CFA franc	86
Canada	Commonwealth Nation	Ottawa	9,220,975	(3,560,237)	23,900,000 (1980)*	English, French	Canadian dollar (C$)	115,117–123
Cape Verde	Republic	Praia	4,033	(1,557)	306,046 (1978)*	Portuguese Creole	escudo Caboverdianos	85
Central African Rep.	Republic (1979) *formerly Empire*	Bangui	624,977	(241,305)	2,088,000 (1980)	French, Sango	CFA franc	86
Chad	Republic	N'Djaména	1,284,000	(495,755)	4,405,000 (1979)*	French, Arabic	CFA franc	86
Chile	Republic	Santiago	751,626	(290,204)	11,100,000 (1980)*	Spanish	Chilean peso	128,131,133
China	People's Republic	Beijing (Peking)	9,597,000	(3,705,421)	970,930,000 (1979)	Mandarin Chinese, regional languages	Renminbi or yuan	65–7
Colombia	Republic	Bogotá	1,138,914	(439,737)	26,400,000 (1979)*	Spanish, Indian languages	Colombian peso	126,128
Comoros	Federal and Islamic Republic	Moroni	1,862	(719)	385,000 (1979)*	Kiswahili, French, Arabic	CFA franc	87
Congo	People's Republic	Brazzaville	342,000	(132,047)	1,434,000 (1978)*	French, Kongo, Teke, Sanga	CFA franc	86
Costa Rica	Republic	San José	50,899	(19,652)	2,192,410 (1979)*	Spanish	colone (₡)	125
Cuba	Republic	Havana	114,525	(44,218)	9,730,000 (1978)*	Spanish	Cuban peso	126
Cyprus	Republic. Commonwealth Nation	Nicosia	9,251	(3,572)	624,600 (1979)*	Greek, Turkish, English	Cyprus pound (£C)	79
Czechoslovakia	Federal Socialist Republic	Prague	127,871	(49,371)	15,184,323 (1979)	Czech, Slovak	koruna (Kčs)	31,37,48
Dahomey	*See Benin*							
Denmark	Kingdom	Copenhagen	43,075	(16,631)	5,122,065 (1980)	Danish	krone	28–9
Djibouti	Republic (1977) *formerly French Territory of Afars and Issas*	Djibouti	23,000	(8,880)	300,000 (1980)*	French, Somali, Dankali, Arabic	Djibouti franc	86
Dominica	Commonwealth Nation	Roseau	728	(281)	83,000 (1978)	English, French patois	E Caribbean dollar (EC$)	127
Dominican Republic	Republic	Santo Domingo	48,441	(18,703)	5,660,000 (1978)	Spanish	Dominican peso	127
Ecuador	Republic	Quito	455,454	(175,852)	7,810,000 (1979)*	Spanish, Quechua, other Indian languages	sucre	128
Egypt	Arab Republic	Cairo	1,000,000	(386,102)	40,980,000 (1979)*	Arabic, Berber, Nubian, English, French	Egyptian pound (£E)	79,84
Eire	*see Irish Republic*							
El Salvador	Republic	San Salvador	21,393	(8,260)	4,364,539 (1979)	Spanish	colón (₡)	125
Equatorial Guinea	Republic	Malabo	28,051	(10,831)	325,000 (1978)*	Spanish, Fang, Bubi, other tribal languages	Ekuele	85–6
Ethiopia	Socialist Republic	Addis Ababa	1,000,000	(386,100)	30,400,000 (1979)*	Amharic, English, Arabic	Birr	86
Fiji	Commonwealth Nation	Suva	18,272	(7,055)	618,979 (1979)*	Fijian, English	Fiji dollar ($F)	137
Finland	Republic	Helsinki	337,032	(130,129)	4,787,784 (1980)	Finnish, Swedish	mark	29
Formosa	*see Taiwan*							
France	Republic	Paris	543,965	(210,026)	53,589,000 (1980)*	French	franc	18–22,40
Gabon	Republic	Libreville	267,667	(103,347)	1,300,200 (1978)*	French, Bantu dialects	CFA franc	86
Gambia, The	Republic. Commonwealth Nation	Banjul	10,689	(4,127)	592,000 (1980)*	English, Madinka	dalasi	85
Germany, East	German Democratic Republic	Berlin (East)	108,177	(41,767)	16,744,700 (1979)	German	Mark of the GDR (M)	30,32–3,36–7
Germany, West	Federal Republic of Germany	Bonn	248,667	(96,011)	61,439,300 (1979)	German	Deutsche Mark (DM)	30,32–9
Ghana	Republic. Commonwealth Nation	Accra	238,305	(92,010)	11,700,000 (1980)*	English, tribal languages	cedi (₵)	85
Gilbert Islands	*see Kiribati*							
Great Britain	*see United Kingdom*							
Greece	The Hellenic Republic	Athens	131,990	(50,962)	9,500,000 (1980)*	Greek	drachma	46–7
Grenada	Commonwealth Nation	St George's	344	(133)	110,394 (1978)*	English	E Caribbean dollar (EC$)	127
Guatemala	Republic	Guatemala City	108,889	(42,042)	7,050,000 (1979)*	Spanish, Indian languages	quetzal (Q)	125
Guinea	Republic	Conakry	245,856	(94,926)	5,130,000 (1978)*	French, Susu, Malinké	syli	85
Guinea-Bissau	Republic	Bissau	36,125	(13,948)	777,214 (1979)	Portuguese, Guinean Créole	peso	85
Guyana	Co-operative Republic. Commonwealth Nation	Georgetown	214,970	(83,000)	824,000 (1978)*	English, Hindu, Urdu, Amerindian dialects	Guyana dollar (G$)	128–9
Haiti	Republic	Port-au-Prince	27,749	(10,714)	5,530,000 (1978)*	French, Créole	gourde	126–7
Honduras	Republic	Tegucigalpa	112,087	(43,277)	3,691,027 (1980)*	Spanish, Indian dialects	lempira or peso	125
Hungary	People's Republic	Budapest	93,030	(35,919)	10,710,000 (1980)*	Hungarian	forint	48
Iceland	Republic	Reykjavík	103,000	(39,769)	226,724 (1978)	Icelandic	króna	115
India	Republic and Union of States. Commonwealth Nation	New Delhi	3,166,828	(1,222,719)	683,000,000 (1981)*	Hindi, English, regional languages	rupee (R)	73–6
Indonesia	Republic	Jakarta	1,903,650	(735,003)	148,500,000 (1979)*	Bahasa Indonesia	rupiah	69–71
Iran	Islamic Republic (1979) *formerly Empire*	Tehrán	1,648,190	(636,370)	34,000,000 (1977)*	Farsi, Kurdish, Arabic, Baluchi	rial	77
Iraq	Republic	Baghdad	438,446	(169,285)	12,171,480 (1977)	Arabic Kurdish	Iraqi dinar (ID)	78
Irish Republic	The Republic of Ireland	Dublin	70,282	(27,136)	3,368,000 (1979)	Irish, English	punt or Irish pound (IR£)	14
Israel	The State of Israel. Republic	Jerusalem	20,702	(7,993)	3,830,000 (1979)*	Hebrew, Arabic	shekel	79–80
Italy	Republic	Rome	301,191	(116,290)	56,999,047 (1980)*	Italian	lira	41–5
Ivory Coast	Republic	Abidjan	322,463	(124,504)	7,920,000 (1979)*	French, tribal languages	CFA franc	85
Jamaica	Commonwealth Nation	Kingston	10,991	(4,244)	2,160,000 (1979)*	English	Jamaican dollar (J$)	127
Japan	Democratic State with Emperor	Tokyo	369,699	(142,742)	116,133,000 (1979)	Japanese	yen	60–1
Jordan	Hashemite Kingdom	Amman	96,000	(37,066)	2,950,000 (1979)*	Arabic	Jordan dinar (JD)	80
Kampuchea	*see Cambodia*							
Kenya	Republic. Commonwealth Nation	Nairobi	582,646	(224,961)	15,320,000 (1979)	Swahili, English, Kikuya, other tribal langs	Kenya Shilling (Sh)	86,88
Khmer Republic	*see Cambodia*							
Kiribati	Republic (1979). Commonwealth Nation *formerly Gilbert Is UK Dependent Territory*	Tarawa	684	(264)	58,518 (1980)	Gilbertese, English	Australian dollar (A$)	137
Korea, North	Democratic People's Republic of Korea	Pyongyang	122,370	(47,247)	17,930,000 (1980)*	Korean	won	65
Korea, South	Republic of Korea	Seoul	98,447	(38,011)	37,019,000 (1978)*	Korean	won	65
Kuwait	Sovereign State	Kuwait	24,280	(9,375)	1,270,000 (1979)*	Arabic, English	Kuwait dinar (KD)	77
Laos	Lao People's Democratic Republic	Vientiane	236,799	(91,429)	3,500,000 (1979)*	Lao, French, tribal langs	kip (K)	68
Lebanon	Republic	Beirut	10,399	(4,015)	2,700,000 (1978)*	Arabic, French, English, Armenian	Lebanese pound (£Leb)	79
Lesotho	Kingdom. Commonwealth Nation	Maseru	30,344	(11,716)	1,279,000 (1978)	Sesotho, English	Loti	89
Liberia	Republic	Monrovia	112,600	(43,475)	1,800,000 (1979)*	English, tribal languages	Liberian dollar (L$)	85
Libya	Socialist People's Libyan Arab Jamahiriyah	Tripoli	1,759,537	(679,361)	2,940,000 (1978)*	Arabic, Italian	Libyan dinar (LD)	84

estimate

Country	Status or title	Capital	Area Sq. km.	Area Sq. miles	Population	Languages	Currency	Page numbers
Liechtenstein	Principality	Vaduz	161	(62)	25,808 (1979)*	Alemannish, German	Swiss franc	41
Luxembourg	Grand Duchy	Luxembourg	2,587	(999)	363,700 (1979)	Luxemburgish, French, German	Luxembourg franc, Belgian franc	22
Madagascar	Democratic Republic	Antananarivo	594,180	(229,414)	8,047,044 (1978)*	Malagasy, French	Malagasy, franc (FMG)	87
Malawi	Republic. Commonwealth Nation	Lilongwe	94,527	(36,497)	5,800,000 (1979)*	Chichewa, English	kwacha (K)	88
Malaysia	Federation of States. Commonwealth Nation (comprising Peninsular Malaysia, Sabah and Sarawak)	Kuala Lumpur	332,318	(128,309)	13,300,000 (1978)*	Malay, English, Chinese, Tamil	Malaysian ringgit (M$)	69–70
Maldives	Republic	Malé	298	(115)	143,046 (1978)	Divehi	Maldivian rupee	73
Mali	Republic	Bamako	1,204,026	(464,877)	6,470,000 (1979)*	French, native languages	Mali franc (MF)	85
Malta	Republic. Commonwealth Nation	Valletta	316	(122)	316,850 (1980)*	Maltese, English	Maltese pound (£M)	43
Mauritania	Islamic Republic	Nouakchott	1,119,367	(432,190)	1,540,000 (1979)*	Arabic, French	ouguiya	85
Mauritius	Commonwealth Nation	Port Louis	1,865	(720)	924,243 (1979)*	English, French, Creole	Mauritius Rupee (R)	83
Mexico	The United Mexican States. Federal Republic	Mexico City	1,972,546	(761,604)	69,400,000 (1979)*	Spanish	peso	125
Monaco	Principality	Monaco	1.5	(0.6)	26,000 (1978)*	French, Monégasque	French franc	44
Mongolia	People's Republic	Ulaanbaatar	1,565,007	(604,252)	1,641,100 (1980)	Mongolian	tugrik	58
Morocco	Kingdom	Rabat	622,014	(240,161)	19,470,000 (1979)*	Arabic, French, Spanish	dirham (DH)	85
Mozambique	People's Republic	Maputo	784,964	(303,076)	19,750,000 (1979)*	Portuguese, tribal langs	metical	87–8
Namibia	United Nations Trust Territory	Windhoek	822,021	(317,384)	908,800 (1977)*	Afrikaans, German, Eng.	South African rand (R)	87,89
Nauru	Republic with special membership of the Commonwealth	Nauru	21	(8)	7,254 (1977)	Nauruan, English	Australian dollar ($A)	137
Nepal	Kingdom	Kathmandu	141,414	(54,600)	13,420,000 (1978)*	Nepali	Nepalese rupee (NR)	75
Netherlands, The	Kingdom	Amsterdam	41,160	(15,892)	14,091,014 (1980)*	Dutch	gulden (guilder, florin)	25
New Hebrides	*see Vanuatu*							
New Zealand	Commonwealth Nation	Wellington	268,676	(103,736)	3,100,000 (1980)*	English, Maori	New Zealand dollar (NZ$)	144–5
Nicaragua	Republic	Managua	148,006	(57,145)	2,568,000 (1980)*	Spanish	córdoba (C$)	125
Niger	Republic	Niamey	1,186,408	(458,075)	5,300,000 (1979)*	French, native languages	CFA franc	85
Nigeria	Federal Republic. Commonwealth Nation	Lagos	923,773	(356,671)	81,039,000 (1978)*	English, Hausa, Yoruba	Naira (₦)	85–6
Norway	Kingdom	Oslo	323,895	(125,057)	4,078,900 (1980)	Norwegian, (Bakmål and Landsmål), Lappish	Norwegian krone	26–7
Oman	Sultanate	Muscat	272,000	(105,020)	820,000 (1980)*	Arabic, English	Rial Omani (RO)	72,77
Pakistan	Islamic Republic	Islamabad	803,944	(310,404)	80,200,000 (1980)*	Punjabi, Sindhi, Urdu, Pushtu	Pakistan rupee (R)	74,77
Panama	Republic	Panama City	78,020	(30,124)	1,890,000 (1980)*	Spanish, English	balboa	125
Papua New Guinea	Commonwealth Nation	Port Moresby	462,840	(178,703)	3,080,000 (1979)*	Pidgin English, native languages	kina (K)	136
Paraguay	Republic	Asunción	406,752	(157,048)	3,000,000 (1980)*	Spanish, Guaraní	guaraní (G)	130
Peru	Republic	Lima	1,285,220	(496,226)	17,293,100 (1979)	Spanish, Quechua, Aymará	sol (S)	128
Philippines	Republic	Manila	299,767	(115,741)	47,914,017 (1980)	Pilipino Tagalog, English, Spanish	Philippine peso (P)	71
Poland	People's Republic	Warsaw	312,683	(120,728)	35,382,000 (1980)	Polish	zlotny	31
Portugal	Republic	Lisbon	91,631	(35,379)	9,862,700 (1979)*	Portuguese	escudo	16
Puerto Rico	Self governing commonwealth associated with the USA	San Juan	8,897	(3,433)	3,187,566 (1980)	English, Spanish	US dollar ($)	127
Qatar	State	Doha	11,000	(4,247)	over 200,000 (1978)*	Arabic, English	Qatar Riyal	77
Rhodesia	*see Zimbabwe*							
Romania	Socialist Republic	Bucharest	237,500	(91,699)	22,050,000 (1979)*	Romanian, Magyar	leu	48
Rwanda	Republic	Kigali	26,338	(10,169)	4,650,000 (1979)*	French, tribal languages,	Rwanda franc	88
St Kitts & Nevis	Commonwealth Nation. Independent 1983	Basseterre	261	(101)	44,404 (1980)	English	E Caribbean dollar (EC$)	127
St Lucia	Commonwealth Nation	Castries	616	(238)	113,000 (1979)	English, French patois	E Caribbean dollar (EC$)	127
St Vincent	Commonwealth Nation	Kingstown	389	(150)	117,646 (1978)	English	E Caribbean dollar (EC$)	127
San Marino	Republic	San Marino	61	(24)	21,000 (1978)	Italian	Italian lira, Papal coinage	45
São Tomé and Principe	Democratic Republic	São Tomé	963	(372)	82,750 (1977)*	Portuguese	dobra	86
Saudi Arabia	Kingdom	Riyadh	2,400,000	(926,645)	7,012,642 (1974)	Arabic	rial	72,86
Senegal	Republic	Dakar	196,722	(75,955)	5,660,000 (1980)*	French, native languages	CFA franc	85
Seychelles	Republic. Commonwealth Nation	Victoria	404	(156)	61,900 (1977)*	English, French	Seychelles rupee (R)	83
Sierra Leone	Republic. Commonwealth Nation	Freetown	73,326	(28,311)	3,470,000 (1978)*	English, (also Krio Temne, Mende)	leone	85
Singapore	Republic. Commonwealth Nation	Singapore	616	(238)	2,390,800 (1980)*	Malay, Chinese (Mandarin), Tamil, English	Singapore dollar (S$)	69
Solomon Islands	Commonwealth Nation	Honiara	29,785	(11,500)	215,000 (1978)*	English, native langs	Solomon Is dollar (SI$)	137
Somalia	The Somali Democratic Republic	Mogadishu	630,000	(243,244)	3,640,000 (1980)*	Somali, Arabic, English, Italian	Somali shilling (Som. Sh.)	86
South Africa	Republic	Pretoria	1,184,831	(457,466)	24,091,000 (1979)*	Afrikaans, English, various African langs	rand (R)	87,89
South West Africa	*see Namibia*							
South Yemen	The People's Democratic Republic of Yemen	Aden	160,300	(61,892)	2,000,000 (1980)*	Arabic	South Yemen dinar	72
Spain	The Spanish State. Kingdom	Madrid	504,879	(194,935)	37,700,000 (1977)*	Spanish, Catalan, Basque	peseta	16–7
Sri Lanka	Democratic Socialist Republic. Commonwealth Nation *formerly Ceylon*	Colombo	65,610	(25,332)	14,470,000 (1979)*	Sinhale, Tamil, English	Sri Lanka rupee (R)	83
Sudan	Democratic Republic	Khartoum	2,505,802	(967,495)	18,400,000 (1980)*	Arabic, tribal languages	Sudanese pound (£S)	86
Suriname	Republic	Paramaribo	163,265	(63,037)	384,900 (1979)*	Dutch, Spanish, Surinamese	Suriname guilder	129
Swaziland	Kingdom. Commonwealth Nation	Mbabane	17,366	(6,705)	563,733 (1979)*	English, SiSwati	emalangeni (E)	89
Sweden	Kingdom	Stockholm	449,792	(173,666)	8,303,010 (1979)*	Swedish, Finnish, Lappish	Swedish krona (kr)	26–7
Switzerland	Republic. Confederation	Bern	41,288	(15,941)	6,356,300 (1979)*	German, French, Italian, Romansch	Swiss franc	40–1
Syria	Arab Republic	Damascus	185,680	(71,691)	8,330,000 (1979)*	Arabic	Syrian pound (£Syr)	78–80
Taiwan	Republic of China	Taipei	35,989	(13,895)	17,480,000 (1979)	Mandarin Chinese	New Taiwan dollar (NT$)	67
Tanzania	United Republic. Commonwealth Nation	Dodoma	939,766	(362,846)	17,600,000 (1979)*	Swahili, English, tribal languages	Tanzanian shilling (Sh)	88
Thailand	Kingdom	Bangkok (Krung Thep)	514,000	(198,456)	45,221,625 (1979)	Thai	baht	68
Togo	Republic	Lomé	56,591	(21,850)	2,470,000 (1979)*	French, tribal languages	CFA franc	85
Tonga	Kingdom. Commonwealth Nation	Nuku'alofa	699	(270)	90,128 (1976)	Tongan, English	pa'anga (T$)	137
Trinidad and Tobago	Republic. Commonwealth Nation	Port of Spain	5,128	(1,980)	1,157,000 (1979)*	English	Trinidad and Tobago dollar (TT$)	127
Tunisia	Republic	Tunis	164,149	(63,378)	6,030,000 (1978)*	Arabic, French	Tunisian dinar	85
Turkey	Republic	Ankara	779,452	(300,948)	45,442,000 (1980)*	Turkish, Arabic, Kurdish	Turkish Lira (TL)	47,78
Tuvalu	Special membership of the Commonwealth *formerly Ellice Islands*	Funafuti	24.5	(9.5)	7,349 (1979)*	Tuvaluan, English	Australian dollar ($A)	134
Uganda	Republic. Commonwealth Nation	Kampala	236,860	(91,452)	13,220,000 (1979)*	English, tribal languages	Uganda shilling	86,88
USSR	Union of Soviet Socialist Republics	Moscow	22,402,200	(8,649,534)	264,500,000 (1980)*	Russian, regional langs	rouble	49–59
United Arab Emirates	Federal union of seven emirates *formerly Trucial States*	Abu Dhabi	92,100	(35,560)	1,040,275 (1980)	Arabic, English	UAE dirham (UD)	77
United Kingdom	United Kingdom of Great Britain and Northern Ireland. Commonwealth Nation	London	244,755	(94,500)	55,945,000 (1981)*	English, Welsh, Gaelic	Pound Sterling (£)	8–15
United States of America	Federal Republic	Washington DC	3,363,168	(3,615,138)	226,504,825 (1980)	English	US dollar ($)	91–116
Upper Volta	Republic. Changed name to Burkina 1984	Ouagadougou	274,123	(105,839)	6,617,000 (1979)*	French, native languages	CFA franc	85
Uruguay	Republic	Montevideo	186,926	(72,173)	2,886,000 (1978)*	Spanish	Nuevo Peso (N$)	131,133
Vanuatu	Republic. Commonwealth Nation. *Formerly Anglo-French Condominium of The New Hebrides*	Vila	14,763	(5,700)	112,596 (1979)	Bislama, English, French, many Melanesian languages	Australian dollar and New Hebrides franc (NH franc)	137
Vatican City	Ecclesiastical State	Vatican City	0.44	(0.17)	about 1,000 (1980)*	Italian, Latin	Italian lira, Papal coinage	44
Venezuela	Republic	Caracas	912,050	(352,144)	14,539,000 (1979)*	Spanish	bolívar (B)	127–8
Vietnam	Socialist Republic	Hanoi	329,566	(127,246)	54,000,000 (1981)	Vietnamese, French, Chinese	dong	65
Western Sahara	Ceded to Morocco and Mauritania (1976) (disputed) *formerly Spanish Sahara*							
Western Samoa	Sovereign State. Commonwealth Nation	Apia	2,831	(1,093)	157,000 (1978)*	English, Samoan	talà dollar ($WS)	137
Yemen	Yemen Arab Republic	San'a	195,000	(75,290)	6,471,893 (1975)	Arabic	riyal	72
Yemen, South	*See South Yemen*							
Yugoslavia	Socialist Federal Republic	Belgrade	255,804	(98,766)	22,300,000 (1980)*	Serbo-Croat, Albanian Macedonian, Slovenian	dinar	42,46,48
Zaire	Republic	Kinshasa	2,345,409	(905,567)	29,270,000 (1979)*	French, Kiswahili Tshiluba, Kikongo	zaïre	86
Zambia	Republic. Commonwealth Nation	Lusaka	752,620	(290,588)	5,600,000 (1979)*	English, African langs	Kwacha (K)	87–8
Zimbabwe	Republic. Commonwealth Nation. Unilaterally independent as Rhodesia 1965 to 1980	Harare (Salisbury)	390,308	(150,699)	7,400,000 (1980)*	English, native languages	Zimbabwe dollar (Z$)	88–9

*estimate**

INDEX

Abbreviations used in the Index

Afghan	Afghanistan	**Conn**	Connecticut	**L**	Lake	**Pen**	Peninsula	**S.S.R.**	Soviet Socialist Republic
Afr	Africa, African	**Czech**	Czechoslovakia	**Lincs**	Lincolnshire	**Penn**	Pennsylvania	**St, Ste**	Saint, Sainte
Ala	Alabama	**Den**	Denmark	**Lt Ho**	Light House	**People's Rep**	People's Republic	**Sta**	Station
Amer	America, American	**Dep**	Département, department	**Madhya Prad**	Madhya Pradesh	**Physical reg**	Physical region	**Stat Area**	Statistical Area
Anc mon	Ancient monument	**Des**	Desert	**Man**	Manitoba	**Pk**	Peak	**Staffs**	Staffordshire
Anc site	Ancient site	**Dist**	District	**Mich**	Michigan	**Port**	Portuguese	**Stony des**	Stony desert
Arch	Archipel, archipelago, archipiélago	**Div**	Division	**Minn**	Minnesota	**Pt, Pta, Pto**	Point	**Str**	Strait
Arg	Argentina	**E**	East	**Miss**	Mississippi	**Prefect**	Prefecture	**Swtz**	Switzerland
Ariz	Arizona	**Equat**	Equatorial	**Mon**	Monument	**Princ**	Principality	**Terr**	Territory
Ark	Arkansas	**Est**	Estuary	**Mont**	Montana	**Prot**	Protectorate	**Tex**	Texas
A.S.S.R.	Autonomous Soviet Socialist Republic	**Fed**	Federal, federation	**Moz**	Mozambique	**Prov**	Province	**Tribal dist**	Tribal district
Aust	Australia	**Fj**	Fjord	**Mt, Mte**	Mountain	**Qnsld**	Queensland	**U.A.E.**	United Arab Emirates
Aut	Autonomous	**Fr**	French	**Mts**	Mountains	**R**	Rio, River	**U.K.**	United Kingdom
B	Bay	**G**	Gulf	**Mt ra**	Mountain range	**Ra**	Range	**Union Terr**	Union Territory
Berks	Berkshire	**Ger**	Germany	**N**	North	**Rdg**	Ridge	**U.S.A.**	United States of America
Br	British	**Gla**	Glacier	**Nether**	Netherlands	**Reg**	Region	**U.S.S.R.**	Union of Soviet Socialist Republics
Br Col	British Columbia	**Gt**	Great	**Nev**	Nevada	**Rep**	Republic	**V**	Valley
C	Cape	**Hbr**	Harbor, harbour	**New Bruns**	New Brunswick	**Res**	Reservoir	**Ven**	Venezuela
Cal	California	**Hd**	Head	**New Hamps**	New Hampshire	**River mth**	River mouth	**Vict**	Victoria
Can	Canal	**H.E.**	Hydro-electricity	**Nex Mex**	New Mexico	**S**	South	**Virg**	Virginia
Cat(s)	Cataract(s)	**Hist reg**	Historical region	**Nfld**	Newfoundland	**Sa**	Serra, Sierra	**Vol**	Volcano
Cent	Central	**I, isld**	Island	**Notts**	Nottinghamshire	**Salt des**	Salt desert	**W**	West
Chan	Channel	**Ind**	Indian	**N Scotia**	Nova Scotia	**Sand des**	Sand desert	**Wash**	Washington
Co	County	**Is, islds**	Islands	**N.S.W.**	New South Wales	**Sask**	Saskatchewan	**Wilts**	Wiltshire
Coastal reg	Coastal region	**Isld king**	Island kingdom	**Oc**	Ocean	**Sd**	Sound		
Colo	Colorado	**Isth**	Isthmus	**Old prov**	Old province	**Sk**	Shuiku (reservoir)		
		Jct, junc, junct	Junction	**Pass**	Passage	**Spr**	Spring		

Aa — Aiguillon

Addenda see page 87

4 Aiguillon,C d' — Altenstadt

83 L13 Aiguillon,C d' Kerguelen Indian Oc
21 I9 Aigurande France
59 J1 Aihui China
61 M7 Aikawa Japan
112 F4 Aiken S Carolina
45 Q7 Ailano Italy
140 C6 Aileron N Terr Aust
22 E5 Ailette R France
29 M2 Ailigas mt Finland
19 Q18 Aille R France
40 D2 Aillevillers France
20 J1 Ailly-le-Haut-Clocher France
20 G2 Ailly,Pte,d' France
20 K2 Ailly-sur-Noye France
120 J9 Ailsa Craig Ontario
12 C3 Ailsa Craig isld Scotland
51 N3 Aim U.S.S.R.
71 K9 Aimere Indonesia
129 K7 Aimores Brazil
129 K7 Aimores,Serra dos mts Brazil
40 B5 Ain dep France
40 B6 Ain R France
86 A2 Ainabo Somalia
78 G3 Ainaisa Syria
52 B5 Ainaži U.S.S.R.
43 A13 Aïn Beïda Algeria
85 F1 Ain Beida Algeria
85 D2 Ain Beni Mathar Morocco
20 J3 Aincourt France
84 H4 'Ain Dalla Egypt
37 K7 Aindling W Germany
43 B12 Aïn Draham Tunisia
80 E1 Aïn Ebel Lebanon
79 H4 'Ain el Beida, El Syria
80 G3 Ain el Ghazal Jordan
80 E7 'Ain el Ghuweir Jordan
85 E3 Aïn-el-Hadjadj Algeria
17 H10 Ain el Hadjar Algeria
84 H4 Aîn el Wadi Egypt
80 G3 Ain esh Shilaq Jordan
86 C2 Aïn Galakka Chad
68 B2 Ainggyi Burma
80 G4 Ain Janna Jordan
43 B12 Aïn-Kerma Algeria
43 C13 Ain Mestour Tunisia
80 E6 Ain Qilt Jordan
17 H2 Ainsa Spain
85 B5 Ain Safra Mauritania
Ain Salah see In Salah
13 E6 Ainsdale England
85 D2 Aïn Sefra Algeria
123 L7 Ainslie,L C Breton I, N Scotia
79 C9 'Ain Sukhna Egypt
98 G7 Ainsworth Nebraska
17 H9 Ain Tédèles Algeria
17 G9 Ain Témouchent Algeria
Aïn Touta see El Homr
60 H11 Aioi Japan
60 R2 Aioi Japan
85 C4 Aïoun Abdel Malek Mauritania
85 C5 Aïoun el Atrouss Mauritania
128 E7 Aiquile Bolivia
69 H11 Airabu isld Indonesia
20 J2 Airaines France
128 F4 Airao Brazil
69 D12 Airbangis Sumatra
118 C7 Airdrie Alberta
12 D2 Airdrie Scotland
22 C2 Aire France
17 K5 Aire,I.del Balearic Is
20 C3 Airel France
13 G6 Aire,R England
18 E9 Airè sur L'Adour France
115 M4 Air Force I N W Terr
65 B3 Airgin Sum China
100 B5 Airlie Oregon
142 B5 Airlie I W Australia
45 R7 Airola Italy
85 F5 Aïr ou Azbine mt reg Niger
12 E1 Airth Scotland
37 K4 Aisch R W Germany
86 H3 Aiscia Ethiopia
133 C7 Aisén prov Chile
114 F5 Aishihik Yukon Terr
22 F5 Aisne dep France
22 H5 Aisne R France
40 D3 Aissey France
80 E1 Aïta ech Chaab Lebanon
136 J2 Aitape Papua New Guinea
37 O6 Aiterhofen W Germany
144 A7 Aitken, Mt New Zealand
99 N3 Aitkin Minnesota
46 E6 Aitolikón Greece
55 B4 Aitova U.S.S.R.
48 H4 Aiud Romania
18 E6 Aix isld France
18 G5 Aix d'Angillon,les France
19 O18 Aix-en-Provence France
21 H10 Aixe-sur-Vienne France
Aix-la-Chapelle see Aachen
117 J8 Aiyansh Br Col
79 B9 'Aiyat,El Egypt
47 F7 Aíyina isld Greece
46 F4 Aiyínion Greece
46 E6 Aíyion Greece
47 G4 Áiyon Óros Greece
46 F7 Áiyos Andréas Greece
47 H9 Áiyos Ioánnis, Akr C Crete Greece
75 P7 Aizawl India
87 C10 Aizeb R Namibia
21 B8 Aizenay France
27 M15 Aizpute U.S.S.R.
61 N8 Aizu-Takada Japan
61 N8 Aizu-Wakamatsu Japan
78 L3 Ajab Shir Iran
18 L11 Ajaccio Corsica
74 J6 Ajaigarh India
128 D3 Ajaju R Colombia
80 G3 'Ajami Syria
143 A8 Ajana W Australia
115 M9 Ajax Ontario
101 M4 Ajax Mt Idaho/Montana
144 D5 Ajax, Mt New Zealand
84 G3 Ajdābiyah Libya
42 F3 Ajdovščina Yugoslavia
61 O5 Ajigasawa Japan
61 N10 Ajiro Japan
61 P7 Aji-shima isld Japan
48 D3 Ajka Hungary
80 G4 Ajlun Jordan
74 F5 Ajmer India
103 M9 Ajo Arizona
16 E1 Ajo,C Spain
129 G3 Ajoewa Suriname
103 M9 Ajo,Mt Arizona
71 C2 Aju isld W Irian
128 E4 Ajuana R Brazil
125 J8 Ajuchitlán Mexico
71 F5 Ajuy Philippines
85 E3 Akabli Algeria
59 L1 Akademii, Zaliv B U.S.S.R.
61 M8 Akadomari Japan
61 M10 Akaishi-dake peak Japan
74 G10 Akalkot India
60 S2 Akan Japan
79 D3 Akanthou Cyprus
60 G12 Akaoka Japan
47 L6 Akar R Turkey
61 P12 Akarie-Ue Okinawa
144 D5 Akaroa New Zealand
27 G15 Åkarp, N Sweden
60 G10 Akasaki Japan
86 F1 Akasha Sudan
60 H11 Akashi Japan
29 K4 Äkäsjoki R Finland
29 K4 Äkäsjokisuu Finland
98 F4 Akaska S Dakota
61 N8 Akatani Japan
26 J4 Akavare mt Sweden
80 F2 'Akbara Israel
57 G1 Akbaur U.S.S.R.
55 F5 Akbent U.S.S.R.
55 C5 Akbulak U.S.S.R.
78 F2 Akçadağ Turkey
78 G3 Akçakale Turkey
47 K8 Akçay Turkey
85 A4 Akchar,Dunes de l' Mauritania
57 G1 Akchatau U.S.S.R.
57 H3 Akchi U.S.S.R.
47 J7 Akçoava Turkey
47 K5 Ak Dağ mt Turkey
47 K6 Ak Dağ mt Turkey
47 K8 Ak Dağ mt Turkey
78 E2 Akdağmadeni Turkey
56 D5 Ak Dovurak U.S.S.R.
61 L10 Akechi Japan
71 B2 Akelamo Halmahera Indonesia
9 F3 Akeley England
99 M2 Akeley Minnesota
27 B13 Åkernes Norway
27 K12 Akersberga Sweden
27 E12 Akershus county Norway
26 G8 Åkersjön Sweden
27 J12 Akers-styckebruk Sweden
71 B2 Akeselaka Halmahera Indonesia
57 B2 Akespe U.S.S.R.
53 F12 Akhalkalaki U.S.S.R.
53 F12 Akhaltsikhe U.S.S.R.
47 F6 Akharnaí Greece
80 F2 'Akhbera Israel
84 G3 Akhdar, Jabal al mts Libya
46 E5 Akhelóös R Greece
116 K8 Akhiok Alaska
78 A2 Akhisar Turkey
84 J4 Akhmim Egypt
Akhna see Athna
79 H2 Akhterin Syria
53 C12 Akhtopol Bulgaria
53 G9 Akhtubinsk U.S.S.R.
53 G12 Akhty U.S.S.R.
53 D8 Akhtyrka U.S.S.R.
60 G12 Aki Japan
116 G6 Akiak Alaska
52 H3 Akim U.S.S.R.
58 G1 Akima U.S.S.R.
115 L7 Akimiski I N W Terr
53 E10 Akimovka U.S.S.R.
60 F11 Aki-nada sea Japan
47 J7 Akıncılar Turkey
27 G16 Akirkeby Denmark
61 O6 Akita Japan
145 F4 Akitio New Zealand
56 G3 Akitkan, Khrebet mts U.S.S.R.
85 B5 Akjoujt Mauritania
80 G4 'Akka Jordan
85 C3 Akka Morocco
55 D6 Akkabak U.S.S.R.
26 J4 Akkajaure L Sweden
57 A3 Akkala, Mys C U.S.S.R.
116 B4 Akkani U.S.S.R.
55 D5 Akkarga U.S.S.R.
80 D2 'Akko Israel
57 H2 Akkol' U.S.S.R.
47 J7 Akköy Turkey
55 B6 Akkozinskiy U.S.S.R.
25 E2 Akkrum Netherlands
46 F7 Akladhókambos Greece
114 F4 Aklavik N W Terr
85 C5 Aklé Aouana reg Mauritania
48 M5 Akmangit U.S.S.R.
52 B6 Akmene U.S.S.R.
52 C6 Akniste U.S.S.R.
86 F4 Akobo R Ethiopia/Sudan
74 G8 Akola India
116 F6 Akolmiut Alaska
74 G8 Akot India
56 C5 Ak-Oyuk, Gora mt U.S.S.R.
115 N5 Akpatok I N W Terr
57 J4 Akqi China
98 J1 Akra N Dakota
27 B12 Åkrafjorden inlet Norway
46 E6 Akráta Greece
46 E8 Akrítas, Akra C Greece
28 D6 Åkrog Bugt B Denmark
111 J9 Akron Alabama
98 C9 Akron Colorado
94 A5 Akron Indiana
98 K7 Akron Iowa
94 D3 Akron Michigan
94 J3 Akron New York
94 F5 Akron Ohio
120 F4 Akron Ontario
95 L6 Akron Pennsylvania
47 G9 Akrotíri Crete Greece
79 D4 Akrotiri B Cyprus
74 H1 Aksai Chin L Kashmir
55 B4 Aksakovo U.S.S.R.
78 E2 Aksaray Turkey
57 F3 Aksay U.S.S.R.
57 H4 Aksay R U.S.S.R.
78 C2 Akşehir Turkey
78 C2 Aksehir Gölü L Turkey
55 B4 Aksenovo U.S.S.R.
58 G1 Aksenovo-Zilovskoye U.S.S.R.
77 D5 Aks-e Rostam R Iran
51 L3 Aksha U.S.S.R.
55 B6 Akshatau U.S.S.R.
57 C1 Akshiy U.S.S.R.
78 K1 Akstafa U.S.S.R.
53 G12 Akstata U.S.S.R.
66 C3 Aksu China
47 L8 Aksu Turkey
47 L7 Aksu R Turkey
57 J2 Aksu R U.S.S.R.
55 D5 Aksuat U.S.S.R.
52 H7 Aksubayevo U.S.S.R.
57 J4 Aksu He R China
86 G3 Aksum Ethiopia
57 E3 Aksumbe U.S.S.R.
Aksu Yangi Shahr see Aksu
52 H6 Aktanysh U.S.S.R.
57 D1 Aktas U.S.S.R.
56 C5 Aktash U.S.S.R.
57 D5 Aktash U.S.S.R.
55 D5 Aktasty U.S.S.R.
55 F5 Aktau U.S.S.R.
47 G4 Akti Greece
57 B1 Aktogay U.S.S.R.
57 J2 Aktogay U.S.S.R.
57 H5 Aktu China
57 A3 Aktumsyk, Mys C U.S.S.R.
55 C5 Aktyubinsk U.S.S.R.
53 D7 Akulichi U.S.S.R.
60 D13 Akune Japan
116 E9 Akun I Aleutian Is
85 F7 Akure Nigeria
115 S4 Akureyri Iceland
116 D9 Akutan I Aleutian Is
116 D9 Akutan Pass Aleutian Is
56 B5 Akutikha U.S.S.R.
Akyab see Sittwe
55 C5 Ak'yar U.S.S.R.
47 L4 Akyazı Turkey
50 H4 Akzhal U.S.S.R.
57 L1 Akzhar U.S.S.R.
57 E3 Akzhaykin, Ozero L U.S.S.R.
27 C11 Ål Norway
41 O6 Ala Italy
111 K8 Alabama state U.S.A.
111 J10 Alabama R Alabama
94 D2 Alabaster Michigan
144 B6 Alabaster, L New Zealand
71 F3 Alabat isld Luzon Philippines
79 F4 Al 'Abde Lebanon
55 E4 Alabota, Oz L U.S.S.R.
78 E1 Alaca Turkey
47 K3 Alaçah Turkey
47 H6 Alaçatı Turkey
113 E8 Alachua Florida
84 G3 Al'Adhem Libya
16 D3 Alaejos Spain
53 F11 Alagir U.S.S.R.
40 G6 Alagna Italy
18 H7 Alagnon R France
130 J9 Alagoa Grande Brazil
130 H10 Alagoas state Brazil
129 L6 Alagoinhas Brazil
17 G3 Alagón Spain
16 C4 Alagón R Spain
71 G7 Alah Mindanao Philippines
69 E13 Alahanpanjang Sumatra
29 K8 Alahärmä Finland
77 A5 Al Ahmadi Kuwait
79 F3 Alaja Syria
29 K8 Alajärvi Finland
79 G3 'Ala,Jebel el mts Syria
86 G3 Alaji mt Ethiopia
125 M4 Alajuela Costa Rica
47 L8 Alakır R Turkey
57 K2 Alakol', Ozero L U.S.S.R.
29 P5 Alakurtti U.S.S.R.
29 L4 Alakylä Finland
80 G3 'Al'al Jordan
135 T3 Alalakeiki Chan Hawaiian Is
128 F4 Alalaú R Brazil
101 N7 Alameda Idaho
124 H3 Alameda Mexico
106 D6 Alameda New Mexico
119 P9 Alameda Sask
71 D2 Alaminos Luzon Philippines
124 D3 Alamito Mexico
108 C6 Alamito Creek Texas
124 H4 Alamítos, Sa. de los ra Mexico
112 E5 Alamo Georgia
98 C1 Alamo N Dakota
103 J4 Alamo Nevada
110 G6 Alamo Tennessee
109 J9 Alamo Texas
103 J9 Alamo R California
106 E9 Alamogordo New Mexico
106 F7 Alamogordo Res New Mexico
43 C8 Ala, Monti di Sardinia
103 L7 Alamo Res Arizona
124 E4 Alamos Mexico
106 E4 Alamosa Colorado
124 F2 Alamos de Peña Mexico
76 D3 Alampor India
26 H7 Alanäs Sweden
74 G10 Aland India
27 J12 Åland Sweden
29 H11 Åland isld Finland
33 P7 Aland R E Germany
26 J9 Ålandsbro Sweden
29 H11 Ålands Hav Finland/Sweden
88 H1 Alanga Bay Kenya
70 E6 Alangalang Tg Kalimantan
69 G13 Alangangtang isld Sumatra
29 L6 Alaniemi Finland
108 D8 Alanreed Texas
87 H11 Alaotra, L Madagascar
112 D6 Alapaha R Georgia
50 F3 Alapayevsk U.S.S.R.
80 G2 'Alaq R Syria
17 F5 Alarcón, Embalse de Spain
71 H5 Alasan Indonesia
78 B2 Alaşehir Turkey
56 C5 Alash R U.S.S.R.
116 Alaska state U.S.A.
116 O7 Alaska,G.of Alaska
135 L2 Alaska Pen Alaska
70 Q10 Alas,Selat Indonesia
44 D3 Alassio Italy
29 K11 Alastaro Finland
57 C5 Alat U.S.S.R.
116 L3 Alatna Alaska
45 O6 Alatri Italy
52 G7 Alatyr' U.S.S.R.
17 F2 Alava prov Spain
78 K1 Alaverdi U.S.S.R.
29 O7 Alavuokki Finland
29 K9 Alavus Finland
138 F5 Alawoona S Australia
17 K5 Alayor Menorca
57 F5 Alayskiy Khrebet mts U.S.S.R.
47 L5 Alayunt Turkey
78 L1 Alazan R U.S.S.R.
109 K8 Alazan Bay Texas
53 G12 Alazani R U.S.S.R.
51 P2 Alazeya R U.S.S.R.
40 H2 Alb R W Germany
44 D2 Alba Italy
94 C2 Alba Michigan
109 M3 Alba Texas
17 F5 Albacete Spain
17 F6 Albacete prov Spain
138 F6 Albacutya,L Victoria
16 D4 Alba de Tormes Spain
28 E1 Albæk Denmark
56 C5 Albagan, Gora mt U.S.S.R.
17 G6 Albaida Spain
48 H4 Alba Iulia Romania
144 B6 Alba, Mt New Zealand
121 S4 Albanel Quebec
46 D2 Albania rep S Europe
42 E7 Albani,Colli hills Italy
45 N6 Albano L Italy
45 N6 Albano Laziale Italy
45 J4 Albano, Mte Italy
111 M10 Albany Georgia
99 Q8 Albany Illinois
110 L1 Albany Indiana
127 L2 Albany Jamaica
110 L5 Albany Kentucky
111 F11 Albany Louisiana
110 B1 Albany Missouri
95 O4 Albany New York
94 E7 Albany Ohio
100 B5 Albany Oregon
109 H3 Albany Texas
95 P2 Albany Vermont
143 C10 Albany W Australia
101 T8 Albany Wyoming
141 J7 Albany Downs Queensland
133 D4 Albardón Argentina
45 K1 Albaredo d'Adige Italy
40 B6 Albarine R France
17 F4 Albarracín, Sa. de mt Spain
141 F2 Albatross B Queensland
126 G6 Albatross Bank Caribbean
141 F1 Albatross Bay Queensland
32 K9 Albaxen W Germany
71 F4 Albay Gulf Luzon Philippines
40 H2 Albbruck W Germany
112 G2 Albemarle N Carolina
112 L1 Albemarle Sound N Carolina
44 D3 Albenga Italy
100 J1 Albeni Falls Dam Idaho
16 E4 Alberche R Spain
130 B10 Alberdi Paraguay
18 G10 Albéres mts France
138 D2 Alberga S Australia
16 B4 Albergaria a Valha Portugal
17 G5 Alberique Spain
117 L11 Alberni Br Col
32 K4 Albersdorf W Germany
22 D3 Albert France
107 L3 Albert Kansas
122 H8 Albert New Brunswick
140 E4 Albert R Queensland
111 J9 Alberta Alabama
118 D5 Alberta Canada
94 K10 Alberta Virginia
114 H7 Alberta prov Canada
117 P9 Alberta,Mt Alberta
48 F3 Albertirsa Hungary
22 J1 Albert Kanaal Belgium
100 E7 Albert, L Oregon
138 E6 Albert, L S Australia
86 F5 Albert, L Uganda/Zaire
86 F5 Albert Nile R Uganda
122 H7 Alberton Pr Edward I
127 K2 Albert Town Jamaica
126 G3 Albert Town Long Cay Bahamas
Albertville see Kalémié
40 D6 Albertville France
119 M5 Albertville Sask
48 L6 Albeşti Romania
36 B6 Albestroff France
45 L1 Albettone Italy
18 G9 Albi France
99 O8 Albia Iowa
98 B8 Albin Wyoming
129 H2 Albina Suriname
45 J2 Albinea Italy
140 B5 Albinia Spring N Terr Aust
102 A2 Albion California
101 M7 Albion Idaho
110 H3 Albion Illinois
94 B5 Albion Indiana
99 O7 Albion Iowa
94 C4 Albion Michigan
98 B4 Albion Montana
98 H8 Albion Nebraska
94 J3 Albion New York
110 A7 Albion Oklahoma
94 G5 Albion Pennsylvania
44 D3 Albissola-Marina Italy
25 C5 Alblasserdam Netherlands
17 H4 Albocácer Spain
27 J15 Alböke Sweden
43 C8 Albo,M Sardinia
17 G5 Alboraya Spain
28 D2 Ålborg Denmark
Ålborg co see Nordjylland
99 O3 Alborn Minnesota
17 F7 Albox Spain
117 O9 Albreda Br Col
8 D2 Albrighton England
141 H6 Albro Queensland
16 B7 Albufeira Portugal
17 G5 Albufera L Spain
41 L4 Albula Pass Switzerland
37 J1 Albungen W Germany
16 E8 Albuñol Spain
130 B6 Albuquerque Brazil
106 D6 Albuquerque New Mexico
95 O2 Alburg Vermont
43 G8 Alburno mt Italy
16 C5 Alburquerque Spain
144 C6 Albury New Zealand
139 H6 Albury Victoria
6 M6 Albuskjell oil rig North Sea
19 Q13 Alby France
26 H9 Alby Sweden
16 B6 Alcacer do Sal Portugal
17 H4 Alcalá de Chivert Spain
16 D7 Alcalá de Guadaira Spain
17 G5 Alcalá del Júcar Spain
16 D8 Alcalá de los Gazules Spain
16 E7 Alcala la Real Spain
131 B2 Alcalde, Pta C Chile
43 E11 Alcamo Sicily
17 G3 Alcanadre R Spain
17 H4 Alcanar Spain
16 C3 Alcañices Spain
17 G3 Alcañiz Spain
16 C5 Alcántara Spain
16 C5 Alcántara, Embalse de res Spain
17 G7 Alcantarilla Spain
130 D5 Alcantilado Brazil
17 F6 Alcaraz Spain
17 F6 Alcaraz, Sa. de mts Spain
16 E7 Alcaudete Spain
16 E5 Alcázar de San Juan Spain
9 E3 Alcester England
98 K6 Alcester S Dakota
17 G5 Alcira Spain
111 C10 Alco Louisiana
112 D2 Alcoa Tennessee
129 L7 Alcobaça Brazil
16 B5 Alcobaca Portugal
17 F3 Alcolea del Pinar Spain
112 G4 Alcolu S Carolina
118 D5 Alcomdale Alberta
118 L1 Alcona Ontario
9 F3 Alconbury Hill England
140 C6 Alcoota N Terr Aust
17 G4 Alcora Spain
17 G4 Alcorisa Spain
101 T7 Alcova Wyoming
17 G6 Alcoy Spain
17 G3 Alcubbiere, Sa. de mt Spain
81 B6 Aldabra I Indian Oc
124 G3 Aldama Mexico
51 M3 Aldan U.S.S.R.
51 M3 Aldanskoye Nagorye U.S.S.R.
9 E5 Aldbourne England
13 H6 Aldbrough England
16 C3 Aldeadávila de la Ribera Spain
9 H3 Aldeburgh England
107 M3 Alden Kansas
94 B2 Alden Michigan
94 J4 Alden New York
25 F7 Aldenhoven W Germany
106 D3 Alder Colorado
9 H3 Alde,R England
101 N4 Alder Montana
14 E2 Aldergrove N Ireland
100 C3 Alder L Washington
9 E5 Aldermaston England
145 F2 Aldermen Is, The New Zealand
20 A2 Alderney isld Channel Is
102 C6 Alder Pk California
101 M4 Alder Pk Montana
102 A1 Alderpoint California
9 F5 Aldershot England
28 D4 Alderslyst Denmark
118 F8 Alderson Alberta
94 G9 Alderson W Virginia
118 D8 Aldersyde Alberta
8 D1 Aldford England
9 E4 Aldsworth England
28 D5 Åle Denmark
99 Q8 Aledo Illinois
109 K3 Aledo Texas
85 B5 Aleg Mauritania
130 B5 Alegra R Brazil
130 F6 Alegre Brazil
133 F3 Alegrete Brazil
106 B7 Alegros Mt New Mexico
133 A9 Alejandro Selkirk isld Juan Fernández Is Pacific Oc
116 H7 Aleknagik Alaska
147 K11 Aleksandra Ostrova U.S.S.R.
54 E8 Aleksandriya U.S.S.R.
54 M3 Aleksandro-Nevskiy U.S.S.R.
52 E6 Aleksandrov U.S.S.R.
48 G6 Aleksandrovac Yugoslavia
53 G8 Aleksandrov Gay U.S.S.R.
52 J5 Aleksandrovsk U.S.S.R.
58 G1 Aleksandrovskiy Zavod U.S.S.R.
53 F11 Aleksandrovskoye U.S.S.R.
59 M1 Aleksandrovsk Sakhalinskiy U.S.S.R.
31 L4 Aleksandrów Poland
31 L3 Aleksandrów Kujawski Poland
50 G3 Alekseyevka U.S.S.R.
56 G2 Alekseyevsk U.S.S.R.
53 F8 Alekseyevskaya U.S.S.R.
54 F1 Alekseyevskoye U.S.S.R.
53 F8 Aleksikovo U.S.S.R.
54 J2 Aleksin U.S.S.R.
46 E1 Aleksinac Yugoslavia
27 F14 Ålekulla Sweden
27 H15 Ålem Sweden
106 C9 Aleman New Mexico
133 D3 Alemania Argentina
129 K8 Alem Paraíba Brazil
20 F5 Alençon France
129 H4 Alenquer Brazil
16 A5 Alenquer Portugal
102 V13 Alenuihaha Chan Hawaiian Is
76 C6 Aleppey India
79 H2 Aleppo Syria
115 N1 Alert N W Terr
128 D6 Alerta Peru
117 K10 Alert Bay Br Col
18 H8 Alès France
43 B9 Ales Sardinia
48 G3 Aleşd Romania
52 G2 Alëshki U.S.S.R.
26 K3 Alesjaure L Sweden
44 E2 Alessándria Italy
44 D1 Alessandria prov Italy
Alessio see Lezhë
28 C3 Ålestrup Denmark
26 B9 Ålesund Norway
18 G10 Alet France
116 L10 Aleutian Is Alaska
116 H8 Aleutian Ra Alaska
107 N7 Alex Oklahoma
137 Q4 Alexa Bank Pacific Oc
20 D5 Alexain France
80 C4 Alexander Israel
107 L3 Alexander Kansas
119 R9 Alexander Manitoba
98 C2 Alexander N Dakota
117 E7 Alexander Archipelago Alaska
87 C11 Alexander B S Africa
111 L9 Alexander City Alabama
146 F12 Alexander I Antarctica
142 F4 Alexander I W Australia
140 D2 Alexander, Mt N Terr Aust
141 G5 Alexander,Mt Queensland
142 B6 Alexander, Mt W Australia
143 D8 Alexander, Mt W Australia
144 B6 Alexandra New Zealand
140 F4 Alexandra R Queensland
133 J8 Alexandra,C S Georgia
117 P5 Alexandra Falls N W Terr
147 G6 Alexandra Fiord N W Terr
146 G7 Alexandra Ra Antarctica
117 M9 Alexandria Br Col
79 A7 Alexandria Egypt
84 H3 Alexandria Egypt
110 L1 Alexandria Indiana
127 K2 Alexandria Jamaica
110 M3 Alexandria Kentucky
111 D10 Alexandria Louisiana
99 L4 Alexandria Minnesota
110 E1 Alexandria Missouri
98 J9 Alexandria Nebraska
140 D4 Alexandria N Terr Australia
121 Q7 Alexandria Ontario
47 G1 Alexandria Romania
89 E9 Alexandria S Africa
12 D2 Alexandria Scotland
98 J6 Alexandria S Dakota
110 K5 Alexandria Tennessee
95 K8 Alexandria Virginia
95 M2 Alexandria Bay New York
144 C5 Alexandrina, L New Zealand
138 E6 Alexandrina, L S Australia
80 E5 Alexandrium Jordan
78 A1 Alexandroúpolis Greece
99 Q8 Alexis Illinois
115 O7 Alexis B Labrador
33 O9 Alexisbad E Germany
117 M9 Alexis Creek Br Col
123 P1 Alexis R Labrador
118 B6 Alexo Alberta
79 F5 'Aley Lebanon
56 B4 Aley R U.S.S.R.
56 B5 Aleysk U.S.S.R.
36 C3 Alf W Germany
36 B3 Alf R W Germany
17 G4 Alfambra R Spain
128 C4 Alfaro Ecuador
17 F2 Alfaro Spain
47 J1 Alfatar Bulgaria
32 L9 Alfeld W Germany
37 M5 Alfeld W Germany
130 F7 Alfenas Brazil
55 G4 Alferovka U.S.S.R.
32 G8 Alfhausen W Germany
45 M3 Alfonsine Italy
9 G1 Alford England
111 L11 Alford Florida
15 F3 Alford Scotland
26 A10 Ålfotbreen gla Norway
95 R3 Alfred Maine
98 G3 Alfred N Dakota
143 F6 Alfred and Marie Ra W Australia
130 H7 Alfredo Chaves Brazil
145 E4 Alfredton New Zealand
9 E1 Alfreton England
9 G6 Alfriston England
27 H10 Alfta Sweden
36 C2 Alfter W Germany
50 E4 Alga U.S.S.R.
27 A13 Algård Norway
133 D5 Algarrobo del Aguila Argentina
16 B7 Algarve prov Portugal
53 F7 Algasovo U.S.S.R.
57 F3 Algatart U.S.S.R.
138 D3 Algebuckina S Australia
16 D8 Algeciras Spain
85 E1 Alger Algeria
94 C2 Alger Michigan
94 D6 Alger Ohio
84 B4 Algeria rep N Africa
43 B8 Alghero Sardinia
27 H14 Älghult Sweden
Algiers see Alger
111 J12 Algiers New Orleans
17 G5 Alginet Spain
89 D9 Algoa B S Africa
130 H10 Algodões Brazil
106 D6 Algodones New Mexico
16 E5 Algodor R Spain
120 H6 Algoma Ontario
100 D7 Algoma Oregon
99 T5 Algoma Wisconsin
99 M6 Algona Iowa
121 M7 Algonquin Park Ontario
110 L5 Algood Tennessee
22 L5 Algrange France
26 J7 Älgsjön Sweden
68 B5 Alguada Reef Burma
17 F2 Alhama R Spain
17 F3 Alhama de Aragón Spain
16 E7 Alhama de Granada Spain
17 F7 Alhama de Murcia Spain
17 F8 Alhamilla, Sa mt Spain
16 E9 Al Hoceima Morocco
86 H3 Al Hudaydah N Yemen
79 E9 Al Ḩumayḑah Egypt
26 B10 Ålhus Norway
17 G4 Aliaga Spain
47 H6 Aliağa Turkey
46 E4 Aliákmon R Greece
74 E9 Alibagh India
48 M5 Alibey,Oz L U.S.S.R.
71 F4 Alibijaban Luzon Philippines
86 G4 Alibo Ethiopia
48 F5 Alibunar Yugoslavia
47 F3 Ali Butús mt Greece
124 F5 Alicama Mexico
17 G6 Alicante Spain
17 G6 Alicante prov Spain
98 J3 Alice N Dakota
141 H6 Alice Queensland
109 J8 Alice Texas
141 F3 Alice R Queensland
117 J8 Alice Arm Br Col
142 G4 Alice Downs W Australia
100 H4 Alicel Oregon
43 H9 Alice,Pta Italy
126 E6 Alice Shoal Caribbean
140 C6 Alice Springs N Terr Aust
126 E2 Alice Town Bimini Is Bahamas
111 H8 Aliceville Alabama
140 C6 Alice Well N Terr Aust
110 E6 Alicia Arkansas
71 F7 Alicia Mindanao Philippines
141 F5 Alick R Queensland
43 F10 Alicudi isld Italy
119 Q9 Alida Sask
45 Q7 Alife Italy
74 H5 Aligarh India
77 A3 Alīgudarz Iran
Alihe see Oroqen Zizhiqi
59 H1 A-li-ho China
77 L3 Ali Khel Afghanistan
52 G6 Alikovo U.S.S.R.
86 B6 Alima R Congo
125 M3 Alimicamba Nicaragua
47 J8 Alimniá isld Greece
71 F5 Alimodian Philippines
71 E7 Alimpaya Pt Mindanao Philippines
86 D4 Alindao Cent Afr Republic
70 F5 Alindau Sulawesi Indonesia
107 M5 Aline Oklahoma
138 D2 Alinerta,Mt S Australia
77 L2 Alingar R Afghanistan
66 C5 Aling Kangri mt China
27 F14 Alingsås Sweden
70 E2 Alipaga Sabah
75 N5 Alipur Duar India
94 G6 Aliquippa Pennsylvania
102 C5 Alisal California
124 D2 Alisos R Mexico
47 F3 Alistáti Greece
116 K8 Alitak B Alaska
47 G6 Alivérion Greece
89 E8 Aliwal North S Africa
118 D6 Alix Alberta
80 G7 Aliyan Jordan
16 E9 Ali-Youssef-ou-Ali Morocco
16 B7 Aljezur Portugal
80 G2 Al Jukhadar Syria
16 B7 Aljustrel Portugal
100 F8 Alkali L Nevada
22 J2 Alken Belgium
25 C3 Alkmaar Netherlands
95 R6 Allagash Maine
95 R7 Allagash L Maine
75 J6 Allahabad India
20 J5 Allaines France
20 J5 Allainville France
21 A6 Allaire France
83 L9 Allai Tank L Sri Lanka
103 J9 All American Can California
108 C4 Allamoore Texas
19 N16 Allan France
118 L7 Allan Sask
80 G2 'Allan R Syria
68 B3 Allanmyo Burma
83 M9 Allan Pt Christmas I Indian Oc
89 E6 Allanridge S Africa
84 J5 Allaqi,Radi Egypt
121 N3 Allard R Quebec
122 G6 Allardville New Brunswick
16 B2 Allariz Spain
36 C7 Allarmont France
112 C3 Allatoona Res Georgia
22 H4 Alle Belgium
94 B4 Allegan Michigan
94 J4 Allegany New York
94 H5 Allegheny R Pennsylvania
94 E10 Allegheny Mts U.S.A.
127 M4 Allegre, Pte Guadeloupe W I
19 O17 Alleins France
111 F12 Allemands Louisiana
89 E7 Allemanskraal Dam res S Africa
19 Q14 Allemont France
94 E9 Allen Kentucky
98 K7 Allen Nebraska
109 L1 Allen Oklahoma
71 G4 Allen Philippines
98 E6 Allen S Dakota
109 L2 Allen Texas
14 D3 Allen, Bog of Irish Rep
112 F4 Allendale S Carolina
13 F4 Allendale Town England
125 J3 Allende Mexico
32 G10 Allendorf W Germany
32 L10 Allendorf W Germany
36 F1 Allendorf W Germany
36 F2 Allendorf W Germany
120 J8 Allenford Ontario
13 F4 Allenheads England
119 M7 Allen Hills Saskatchewan
14 C2 Allen,L Irish Rep
116 Q5 Allen,Mt Alaska
144 A7 Allen, Mt New Zealand
106 E1 Allens Park Colorado
31 J7 Allensteig Austria
Allenstein see Olsztyn
95 Q3 Allenstown New Hampshire
110 J5 Allensville Kentucky
95 M6 Allentown Pennsylvania
33 M7 Aller R W Germany
22 K3 Allerborn Luxembourg
36 E6 Allerheiligen W Germany
37 L5 Allersberg W Germany
28 J6 Allerslev Denmark
110 C1 Allerton Iowa
28 K4 Allerum Sweden
20 J2 Allery France
40 D7 Allevard France
127 K3 Alley,The Jamaica
109 L6 Alleyton Texas
41 M3 Allgäuer Alpen mts W Ger/Austria
8 D1 Allgreave England
9 G5 Allhallows England
118 F6 Alliance Alberta
98 D7 Alliance Nebraska
94 F6 Alliance Ohio
18 H6 Allier dep France
18 H6 Allier R France
145 E4 Alligator Headland New Zealand
127 J3 Alligator Pond Jamaica
112 L2 Alligator R N Carolina
140 C2 Alligator R., E N Terr Aust
113 G13 Alligator Reef Florida
28 D4 Alling Denmark
37 M6 Alling W Germany
28 E4 Alling Å R Denmark
28 E4 Allingåbro Denmark
99 O7 Allison Iowa
117 K10 Allison Harbour Br Col
12 E1 Alloa Scotland
13 E4 Allonby England
80 D3 Allonim Israel
20 K3 Allonne France
20 J5 Allonnes France
21 E7 Allonnes France
80 D7 Allon Shevut Jordan
141 K8 Allora Queensland
143 E7 Allott, Mt W Australia
99 S2 Allouez Michigan
12 D3 Alloway Scotland
33 O10 Allstedt E Germany
121 N7 Allumette I Quebec
121 R4 Ally Quebec
38 G7 Alm Austria
38 J6 Alm R Austria
110 B6 Alma Arkansas
106 D2 Alma Colorado
112 E6 Alma Georgia
107 O2 Alma Kansas
94 C3 Alma Michigan
110 C2 Alma Missouri
98 G9 Alma Nebraska
122 H8 Alma New Brunswick
121 T4 Alma Quebec
99 P5 Alma Wisconsin
57 H3 Alma-Ata U.S.S.R.
16 A6 Almada Portugal
141 G3 Almaden Queensland
16 D6 Almadén Spain
16 D6 Almadén, Sa. de mts Spain
80 F2 Almagor Israel
71 G5 Almagro isld Philippines
57 E4 Almalyk U.S.S.R.
102 C1 Almanor, L California
17 G6 Almansa Spain
16 D2 Almanza Spain
117 K7 Alma Peak Br Col
17 F3 Almarza Spain
130 E4 Almas, R das Brazil
48 H3 Almasul R Romania
48 G6 Almasului Muntii mt Romania
17 F3 Almazán Spain
27 H12 Almby Sweden
32 J9 Alme R W Germany
27 H15 Älmeboda Sweden
100 B7 Almeda Oregon
129 H4 Almeirim Brazil
16 B5 Almeirim Portugal
25 G4 Almelo Netherlands
107 L2 Almena Kansas
129 K7 Almenara Brazil
17 F7 Almenara, Sa. de mt Spain
17 F3 Almenar de Soria Spain
16 C3 Almendra, Embalse de res Spain
16 C6 Almendralejo Spain
20 F4 Alménêches France
55 D4 Al'menevo U.S.S.R.
8 D6 Almer England
98 G8 Almeria Nebraska
17 F8 Almería Spain
17 F7 Almería prov Spain
17 F8 Almería,G.de Spain
52 H7 Al'met'yevsk U.S.S.R.
27 G15 Älmhult Sweden
16 E8 Almijara, Sierra de mts Spain
28 C5 Almind Vejle Denmark
28 C4 Almind Viborg Denmark
100 G2 Almira Washington
130 E9 Almirante Tamandaré Brazil
47 G6 Almiropótamos Greece
46 F5 Almirós Greece
47 G9 Almiroú Kólpos gulf Crete Greece
101 M7 Almo Idaho
16 B7 Almodôvar Portugal
16 E6 Almodóvar del Campo Spain
17 F5 Almodóvar del Pinar Spain
133 D3 Almogasta Argentina
94 K4 Almond New York
99 R5 Almond Wisconsin
15 E4 Almond,R Scotland
8 D4 Almondsbury England
106 D3 Almont Colorado
94 D4 Almont Michigan
98 E3 Almont N Dakota
121 O7 Almonte Ontario
16 C5 Almonte R Spain
74 H4 Almora India
16 E4 Almorox Spain
100 H3 Almota Washington
79 F9 Al Mudawwara Jordan
86 H3 Al Mukhā Yemen
27 G15 Almundsryd Sweden
16 E8 Almuñécar Spain
27 H14 Almvik Sweden
101 P8 Almy Wyoming
111 E7 Almyra Arkansas
13 G3 Aln Br England
15 D3 Alness Scotland
13 G3 Alnmouth England
26 J9 Alnö Sweden
13 G3 Alnwick England
137 R4 Alofi isld Îles de Horn Pacific Oc
94 C1 Aloha Michigan
68 B1 Alon Burma
71 E5 Alonon Pt Philippines
119 T8 Alonsa Manitoba
71 M9 Alor isld Indonesia
16 D8 Alora Spain
71 M8 Alor,Kep isld Indonesia
71 L9 Alor,Selat Indonesia
69 E9 Alor Setar Malaysia
16 C7 Alosno Spain
Alost see Aalst
143 G7 Aloysius, Mt W Australia
52 D2 Alozero U.S.S.R.
133 E5 Alpachiri Argentina
38 E7 Alpbach Austria
19 Q14 Alpe d'Huez mt France
110 C5 Alpena Arkansas
94 D1 Alpena Michigan
98 H5 Alpena S Dakota
94 H8 Alpena W Virginia
17 G6 Alpera Spain
129 J5 Alpercatas, Serra das mts Brazil
19 O15 Alpes du Dauphiné mts France
46 D2 Alpet mt Albania
44 C3 Alpet mt Italy
99 Q8 Alpha Illinois
95 M6 Alpha New Jersey
141 H6 Alpha Queensland
94 J9 Alpha Virginia
25 C4 Alphen Netherlands
81 C6 Alphonse I Indian Oc
16 B5 Alpiarça Portugal
103 P8 Alpine Arizona
108 D5 Alpine Texas
36 E7 Alpirsbach W Germany
16 B7 Alportel,S Braz de Portugal
4 F7 Alps, The mt ra Europe
47 L5 Alpu Turkey
22 B2 Alquines France
9 E5 Alresford England
123 L6 Alright I Madeleine Is, Quebec
28 E5 Alrø isld Denmark
140 D4 Alroy Downs N Terr Aust
28 E3 Als Denmark
28 D7 Als isld Denmark
19 K4 Alsace prov France
118 H7 Alsask Sask
17 F2 Alsasua Spain
25 F7 Alsdorf W Germany
100 B5 Alsea Oregon
117 E6 Alsek R Br Columbia
98 H1 Alsen N Dakota
36 D4 Alsenz W Germany
110 F2 Alsey Illinois
36 G2 Alsfeld W Germany
28 D6 Als Fjord inlet Denmark
36 E4 Alsheim W Germany
26 J5 Alsjaur L Sweden
33 P9 Alsleben E Germany
28 A5 Alslev Denmark
28 C6 Alslevkro Denmark
28 F4 Alsø Denmark
26 F6 Alstahaug Norway
32 E8 Alstätte W Germany
95 P3 Alstead New Hampshire
26 F6 Alsten isld Norway
32 M5 Alster R W Germany
13 F4 Alston England
27 M15 Alsunga U.S.S.R.
101 L4 Alta Montana
26 N2 Alta Norway
26 N2 Altaelv R Norway
26 N1 Altafjord inlet Norway
131 D3 Alta Gracia Argentina
127 J9 Altagracía Venezuela
128 E2 Altagracia de Orituco Venezuela
109 L6 Altair Texas
128 E7 Altamachí Bolivia
112 E6 Altamaha R Georgia
133 E4 Alta Melincué Argentina
129 H4 Altamira Brazil
125 N9 Altamirano Mexico
102 C4 Altamont California
110 H2 Altamont Illinois
100 D7 Altamont Oregon
98 K5 Altamont S Dakota
110 L6 Altamont Tennessee
101 P8 Altamont Wyoming
144 B6 Alta, Mt New Zealand
43 H8 Altamura Italy
65 B2 Altan Bulag China
124 D2 Altar Mexico
118 G7 Altario Alberta
124 F5 Altata Mexico
45 R7 Altavilla Irpina Italy
99 O6 Alta Vista Iowa
107 O3 Alta Vista Kansas
94 H9 Altavista Virginia
66 D2 Altay China
58 C2 Altay Mongolia
56 C5 Altay mts U.S.S.R.
56 B5 Altayskiy Kray terr U.S.S.R.
37 N6 Altdorf Niederbayern W Germany
41 J4 Altdorf Switzerland
37 L5 Altdorf W Germany
17 G6 Altea Spain
33 O6 Alte Elde R E Germany
32 H5 Alte Mellum W Germany
36 B3 Altenahr W Germany
33 M9 Altenau W Germany
32 J9 Altenbeken W Germany
32 F8 Altenberge W Germany
32 J5 Altenbruch W Germany
37 N2 Altenburg E Germany
37 M7 Altenerding W Germany
36 C4 Altenglan W Germany
36 E1 Altenhundem W Germany
36 D2 Altenkirchen W Germany
38 L6 Altenmarkt Ober Österreich Austria
38 H7 Altenmarkt Salzburg Austria
37 P6 Altenmarkt W Germany
33 N6 Alten Medingen W Germany
36 H6 Altenstadt Baden-Württemberg W Germany

Altenstadt — Apgar 5

36 F3 Altenstadt Hessen W Germany
36 F6 Altensteig W Germany
33 S5 Altentreptow E Germany
32 J5 Altenwalde W Germany
16 B5 Alter do Chão Portugal
33 R8 Altes Lager E Germany
26 K3 Altevatn L Norway
111 L11 Altha Florida
37 J6 Altheim W Germany
111 E7 Altheimer Arkansas
38 K8 Althofen Austria
9 G4 Althorne England
13 H6 Althorpe England
138 D6 Althorpe Is S Australia
139 G3 Altiboullin, L New S Wales
45 M1 Altino Italy
47 L5 Altıntaş Turkey
33 O6 Alt-Jabel E Germany
19 K5 Altkirch France
33 T7 Altlandsberg E Germany
36 E5 Altleiningen W Germany
37 M6 Altmannstein W Germany
95 L3 Altmar New York
33 O7 Altmark reg E Germany
36 H1 Altmorschen W Germany
37 K5 Altmühl R W Germany
32 K7 Altmühlen W Germany
15 D2 Altnaharra Scotland
111 A10 Alto Texas
16 B6 Alto Alentejo prov Portugal
130 D5 Alto Araguaia Brazil
126 G4 Alto Cedro Cuba
130 C4 Alto Coité Brazil
130 D5 Alto Garças Brazil
87 C8 Alto Hama Angola
87 G9 Alto Molocue Mozambique
44 D3 Alto,Monte Italy
37 L7 Altomünster W Germany
102 A1 Alton California
9 F5 Alton Hampshire England
110 F3 Alton Illinois
95 L3 Alton New York
103 M4 Alton Utah
99 Q8 Altona Illinois
118 D1 Altona Manitoba
101 P9 Altonah Utah
138 E2 Alton Downs S Australia
111 K7 Altoona Alabama
113 F9 Altoona Florida
107 P4 Altoona Kansas
94 J6 Altoona Pennsylvania
128 G8 Alto Paraguay dep Paraguay
130 C9 Alto Paraná dep Paraguay
129 J5 Alto Parnaiba Brazil
45 J4 Altopascio Italy
129 H7 Alto Sucuriú Brazil
38 G5 Altötting W Germany
129 J4 Alto Turi Brazil
130 C10 Alto Uruguaí Brazil
126 A1 Alto Vista hill Aruba W I
13 F6 Altrincham England
33 R7 Altruppin E Germany
33 T8 Alt-Schadow E Germany
54 F4 Altukhovo U.S.S.R.
78 K4 Altun Köprü Iraq
47 H5 Altunoluk Turkey
66 C4 Altun Shan mts China
99 O5 Altura Minnesota
100 E8 Alturas California
113 F10 Alturas Florida
107 L7 Altus Oklahoma
41 M2 Altusried W Germany
36 B6 Altwiller France
57 C2 Altynasar U.S.S.R.
55 D3 Altynay U.S.S.R.
52 C6 Alūksne U.S.S.R.
86 B1 Alula Somalia
28 D4 Alum Denmark
9 E6 Alum Bay England
133 C5 Aluminé Argentina
26 M6 Ålund Sweden
27 K11 Alunda Sweden
103 K6 Alunite Nevada
76 C3 Alur India
53 D11 Alushta U.S.S.R.
17 F4 Alustante Spain
83 J11 Alutgama Sri Lanka
83 K9 Alut Oya Sri Lanka
113 F11 Alva Florida
94 D10 Alva Kentucky
107 M5 Alva Oklahoma
12 E1 Alva Scotland
98 B5 Alva Wyoming
16 B4 Alva R Portugal
16 B7 Alvalade Portugal
125 M8 Alvarado Mexico
109 K3 Alvarado Texas
128 F4 Alvaraes Brazil
26 E9 Alvdal Norway
118 L6 Alvena Sask
33 O8 Alvensleben E Germany
32 K8 Alverdissen W Germany
117 D5 Alverstone Mt Alaska/Yukon Terr
27 A11 Alversund Norway
27 G15 Alvesta Sweden
8 D4 Alveston England
27 G10 Älvho Sweden
110 J1 Alvin Illinois
109 M6 Alvin Texas
99 S4 Alvin Wisconsin
45 P6 Alvito Italy
16 B6 Alvito Portugal
27 J11 Älvkarleby Sweden
98 K9 Alvo Nebraska
109 K2 Alvord Texas
100 G7 Alvord L Oregon
26 F10 Älvros Sweden
27 F14 Älvsborg reg Sweden
26 M6 Älvsbyn Sweden
27 F14 Älvsered Sweden
99 M2 Alvwood Minnesota
87 E12 Alwal Nth S Africa
74 G5 Alwar India
76 C5 Alwaye India
13 F3 Alwinton England
110 C7 Aly Arkansas
140 D2 Alyangula N Terr Aust
51 N2 Alyaskitovyy U.S.S.R.
55 E2 Alymka R U.S.S.R.
15 E4 Alyth Scotland
31 P1 Alytus U.S.S.R.
38 G5 Alz R W Germany
98 B4 Alzada Montana
36 G3 Alzenau W Germany
22 L4 Alzette R Luxembourg
36 E4 Alzey W Germany
128 F2 Amacuro Delta Venezuela
140 B6 Amadeus,L N Terr Aust
86 F4 Amadi Sudan
115 M4 Amadjuak L N W Terr
60 J11 Amagasaki Japan
28 K5 Amager isld Denmark
60 D12 Amagi Japan
61 N11 Amagi-san mt Japan
22 G5 Amagne France
20 F4 Amain,Mt.d' France
116 F9 Amak I Alaska
60 C13 Amakusa-nada sea Japan
60 D13 Amakusa-shotō islds Japan
84 G4 Amal Libya
27 F12 Åmål Sweden
76 F2 Amalapuram India
43 F8 Amalfi Italy
46 E7 Amaliás Greece
16 C5 Amalia,Sta Spain
74 F8 Amalner India
129 G8 Amambai Brazil
130 C8 Amambaí, Serra de mts Brazil/Paraguay
130 C8 Amambay dep Paraguay
133 F2 Amambay, Sa. de mts Brazil/Paraguay
128 F4 Amaná,L Brazil
40 D2 Amance France
40 D3 Amancey France
94 E7 Amanda Ohio
42 E6 Amandola Italy
55 E6 Amangel'dy U.S.S.R.
55 D4 Amankaragay U.S.S.R.
60 J10 Amano-hashidate inlet Japan
43 G9 Amantea Italy
87 F12 Amanzimtoti S Africa
129 H3 Amapa Brazil
72 F2 Amārah, Al Iraq
88 F9 Amaramba,L Mozambique
129 K5 Amarante Brazil
119 T8 Amaranth Manitoba
68 C2 Amarapura Burma
102 H5 Amargosa Ra California
106 D5 Amarilla New Mexico
108 C8 Amarillo Texas
131 B4 Amarillo,Cerro peak Argentina
75 J7 Amarkantah India
129 J6 Amaro Leite Brazil
140 E6 Amaroo,L Queensland
61 N7 Amarume Japan
99 S3 Amasa Michigan
45 O7 Amaseno Italy
78 D1 Amasra Turkey
78 F1 Amasya Turkey
128 E4 Amataura Brazil
125 N9 Amatenango Mexico
87 F11 Amatikulu S Africa
124 H7 Amatitán Mexico
125 L8 Amatlan Mexico
124 G7 Amatlán de Cañas Mexico
22 J2 Amay Belgium
119 M7 Amazon Sask
Amazon R see Amazonas R
128 C5 Amazonas dep Peru
128 D4 Amazonas div Colombia
129 H4 Amazonas R S America
128 E4 Amazonas state Brazil
128 E3 Amazonas state Venezuela
110 B2 Amazonia Missouri
129 J3 Amazon,Mouths of the Brazil
80 C7 Amazya Israel
74 E1 Amb Pakistan
74 G9 Ambajogai India
74 G3 Ambala India
83 J11 Ambalangodo Sri Lanka
87 H12 Ambalavao Madagascar
140 C6 Ambalindum N Terr Aust
85 G8 Ambam Cameroon
83 K10 Amban Ganga R Sri Lanka
87 H10 Ambanje Madagascar
70 N9 Ambarawa Java
51 Q2 Ambarchik U.S.S.R.
18 E8 Ambarès et Lagrave France
52 D2 Ambarnyy U.S.S.R.
139 H2 Ambathala Queensland
128 C4 Ambato Ecuador
87 H11 Ambato-Boeny Madagascar
87 H11 Ambatolampy Madagascar
131 C2 Ambato,Sa ra Argentina
18 F7 Ambazac France
107 N6 Amber Oklahoma
100 H2 Amber Washington
116 J8 Amber B Alaska
37 M5 Amberg W Germany
99 T4 Amberg Wisconsin
9 E1 Ambergate England
127 H4 Ambergris Cays islds Turks & Caicos Is
19 O13 Ambérieu-en-Bugey France
144 D5 Amberley New Zealand
120 J8 Amberley Ontario
22 K3 Amberloup Belgium
18 H7 Ambert France
18 G9 Ambialet France
85 B6 Ambidédi Mali
75 K7 Ambikapur India
71 E4 Ambil isld Philippines
21 F7 Ambillou France
87 H10 Ambilobe Madagascar
117 H7 Ambition,Mt Br Columbia
20 K3 Amblainville France
13 G3 Amble England
116 J3 Ambler R Alaska
13 F5 Ambleside England
22 B2 Ambleteuse France
22 L3 Amblève Belgium
141 G6 Ambo Queensland
87 H12 Amboasary Madagascar
87 H11 Ambodifototra Madagascar
87 H12 Ambohimahasoa Madagascar
21 H7 Amboise France
136 F2 Ambon Moluccas Indonesia
87 H12 Amborompotsy Madagascar
86 G6 Amboseli, L Kenya
87 H12 Ambositra Madagascar
87 H13 Ambovombe Madagascar
103 J7 Amboy California
99 R8 Amboy Illinois
95 N6 Amboy,S New Jersey
21 I8 Ambrault France
87 H10 Ambre, Cap d' Madagascar
94 G6 Ambridge Pennsylvania
20 D5 Ambrières France
137 O5 Ambrim isld New Hebrides
87 B7 Ambriz Angola
112 D6 Ambrose Georgia
98 C1 Ambrose N Dakota
71 E2 Ambuklao Dam Luzon Philippines
71 K9 Ambulombo Vol Indonesia
70 O10 Ambulu Java
70 O9 Ambunten Java
76 D4 Ambur India
141 J7 Amby Queensland
27 C12 Åmdal Norway
86 D3 Am Dam Chad
85 E4 Amded watercourse Algeria
50 F2 Amderma U.S.S.R.
75 O2 Amdo China
86 G3 Amedamit mt Ethiopia
102 D1 Amedee California
25 E2 Ameland isld Netherlands
42 E6 Amelia Italy
98 H7 Amelia Nebraska
94 K9 Amelia Virginia
113 F7 Amelia I Florida
32 M6 Amelinghausen W Germany
43 H9 Amendolara Italy
67 A5 Ameng China
17 J2 Amer Spain
102 D2 American R California
130 F8 Americana Brazil
101 N7 American Falls Idaho
103 N1 American Fork Utah
134 E1 American Samoa islds Pacific Oc
113 F13 American Shoal lt ho Florida
112 C5 Americus Georgia
25 D4 Amerongen Netherlands
25 D4 Amersfoort Netherlands
9 F4 Amersham England
143 B9 Amery W Australia
99 O4 Amery Wisconsin
146 C4 Amery Ice Shelf Antarctica
99 N7 Ames Iowa
98 K8 Ames Nebraska
107 M5 Ames Oklahoma
118 E3 Amesbury Alberta
9 E5 Amesbury England
95 R4 Amesbury Massachusetts
118 J1 Amesdale Ontario
120 F3 Ameson Ontario
94 F7 Amesville Ohio
122 J8 Amet Sound Nova Scotia
46 F6 Amfíklia Greece
46 E6 Amfilokhía Greece
47 F4 Amfípolis Greece
46 E6 Ámfissa Greece
20 C3 Amfreville France
20 G3 Amfreville-la-Campagne France
51 N2 Amga U.S.S.R.
51 M3 Amga R U.S.S.R.
58 G2 Amgalang Bulag China
51 N3 Amgan R U.S.S.R.
51 N4 Amgu U.S.S.R.
86 D3 Am Guéréda Chad
85 F3 Amguid Algeria
59 K1 Amgun R U.S.S.R.
86 G3 Amhara reg Ethiopia
Amherst see Kyaikkami
106 H1 Amherst Colorado
95 T2 Amherst Maine
95 P4 Amherst Massachusetts
98 G9 Amherst Nebraska
95 Q4 Amherst New Hampshire
115 N8 Amherst Nova Scotia
94 E5 Amherst Ohio
98 J4 Amherst S Dakota
94 H9 Amherst Virginia
120 G10 Amherstburg Ontario
94 F9 Amherstdale W Virginia
123 K6 Amherst I Madeleine Is, Quebec
121 O8 Amherst I Ontario
99 R5 Amherst Junction Wisconsin
142 F4 Amherst, Mt W Australia
42 D6 Amiata,Monte Italy
98 C3 Amidon N Dakota
20 K2 Amiens France
141 K8 Amiens Queensland
78 H5 Amij,Wadi Iraq
46 E4 Amíndaion Greece
73 L6 Amindivi Is Lakshadweep Indian Ocean
60 H10 Amino Japan
87 C10 Aminuis Namibia
79 F4 Amioune Lebanon
80 F1 'Amir Israel
83 H5 Amirante Is Indian Oc
118 F6 Amisk Alberta
119 P4 Amisk L Sask
106 G6 Amistad New Mexico
108 F6 Amistad Res Mexico
111 F11 Amite Louisiana
111 C7 Amity Arkansas
95 O6 Amityville Long I, N Y
75 L5 Amlekhganj Nepal
27 C13 Amli Norway
8 B1 Amlwch Wales
80 G6 'Amman Jordan
8 C4 Ammanford Wales
26 H5 Ammarfjallet mt Sweden
26 H6 Ammarnäs Sweden
140 D5 Ammaroo N Terr Aust
28 E4 Ammelhede Denmark
33 P10 Ammendorf E Germany
32 L9 Ammensen W Germany
41 O2 Ammer R W Germany
41 N2 Ammer Gebirge mt W Germany
41 O2 Ammerland W Germany
32 G6 Ammerland reg W Germany
116 R2 Ammerman Mt Yukon Terr
37 K5 Ammerndorf W Germany
41 O1 Ammer See L W Germany
80 F2 'Ammi 'ad Israel
101 O6 Ammon Idaho
Amne Machin see A'nyêmaqên Shan
77 C1 Āmol Iran
130 B6 Amolar Brazil
109 N9 Amon Carter Airfield Texas
36 F2 Amöneburg W Germany
36 G4 Amorbach W Germany
131 F2 Amores R Argentina
47 H8 Amorgós isld Greece
107 M5 Amorita Oklahoma
111 H8 Amory Mississippi
103 J8 Amos California
115 M8 Amos Quebec
28 G5 Åmose Å R Denmark
27 H11 Åmot Sweden
27 D12 Åmot Akershus Norway
27 C12 Åmotsdal Norway
Amoy see Xiamen
70 G5 Ampana Sulawesi Indonesia
87 G12 Ampanihy Madagascar
130 F8 Amparo Brazil
128 D7 Ampato, Cord. de mts Peru
70 Q10 Ampenan Indonesia
37 M7 Amper R W Germany
37 N7 Ampfing W Germany
103 O9 Amphitheater Arizona
85 F7 Ampier Nigeria
13 G5 Ampleforth England
17 H4 Amposta Spain
9 F3 Ampthill England
19 N14 Ampuis France
17 J2 Ampurdán dist Spain
80 D2 'Amqa Israel
122 E5 Amqui Quebec
74 G8 Amravati India
74 D8 Amreli India
74 F3 Amritsar India
30 D1 Amrum isld W Germany
26 K7 Åmsele Sweden
38 J7 Am Stein mt Austria
25 C4 Amstelveen Netherlands
113 C7 Amsterdam Georgia
101 L7 Amsterdam Idaho
25 C4 Amsterdam Netherlands
95 N4 Amsterdam New York
94 G6 Amsterdam Ohio
24 Amsterdam conurbation Netherlands
81 E9 Amsterdam,I Indian Oc
38 L5 Amstetten Austria
27 F12 Ämtervik, V Sweden
86 D3 Am Timan Chad
28 B2 Amtoft Denmark
41 L2 Amtzell W Germany
127 J9 Amuay Venezuela
57 D5 Amu-Dar'ya U.S.S.R.
57 B4 Amudar'ya R U.S.S.R.
147 H5 Amund Ringness I N W Terr
146 A5 Amundsen B Antarctica
146 G8 Amundsen Glacier Antarctica
147 J1 Amundsen Gulf N W Terr
146 E3 Amundsen, Mt Antarctica
146 J11 Amundsen Sea Antarctica
147 J2 Amundsen Trough Arctic Oc
27 H10 Amungen L Sweden
70 D6 Amuntai Kalimantan
51 N3 Amur R U.S.S.R.
59 J1 Amur reg U.S.S.R.
71 J4 Amurang Sulawesi Indonesia
71 J4 Amurang Teluk B Sulawesi Indonesia
144 D5 Amuri Pass New Zealand
17 F1 Amurrio Spain
59 L1 Amursk U.S.S.R.
51 M3 Amurskaya Oblast' prov U.S.S.R.
55 C4 Amurskiy U.S.S.R.
46 E6 Amvrakía, L Greece
46 D6 Amvrakikós Kólpos gulf Greece
54 K9 Amvrosiyevka U.S.S.R.
107 K3 Amy Kansas
56 D4 Amyl R U.S.S.R.
142 B5 Amy, Mt W Australia
120 F4 Amyot Ontario
16 E9 Amzoughen-Khémis-Mrapten Morocco
68 B3 An Burma
138 F5 Ana Branch R New S Wales
80 D4 Anabta Jordan
102 E7 Anacapa Is California
45 Q8 Anacapri Italy
127 M10 Anaco Venezuela
111 C10 Anacoco Louisiana
114 H8 Anaconda Montana
101 M4 Anaconda Range Montana
100 C1 Anacortes Washington
107 M6 Anadarko Oklahoma
130 H10 Anadia Brazil
16 B4 Anadia Portugal
78 F1 Anadolu Dağlari mt Turkey
51 R2 Anadyr U.S.S.R.
51 R2 Anadyrskoye Ploskogor'ye tableland U.S.S.R.
47 H8 Anáfi isld Greece
26 F9 Anafjället mt Sweden
47 H8 Anafópoulo isld Greece
130 H4 Anagé Brazil
45 O6 Anagni Italy
117 L9 Anahim Lake Br Columbia
135 O1 Anahola Hawaiian Is
125 J4 Anáhuac Mexico
111 B12 Anahuac Texas
102 R11 Anahulu R Hawaiian Is
76 C5 Anaimalai Hills India
75 K10 Anakapalle India
141 J6 Anakie Queensland
116 M2 Anaktuvuk Pass Alaska
87 H10 Analalava Madagascar
128 F4 Anama Brazil
119 T7 Anama Bay Manitoba
126 E4 Ana Maria, Cayos de islds Cuba
69 G11 Anambas, Kep isld Indonesia
61 L8 Anamizu Japan
98 F2 Anamoose N Dakota
129 G3 Anamu R Brazil
78 D3 Anamur Turkey
60 H12 Anan Japan
47 G8 Anánes isld Greece
71 J7 Anano isld Indonesia
76 C3 Anantapur India
74 F2 Anantnag Kashmir
48 M3 Anan'yev U.S.S.R.
53 E11 Anapa U.S.S.R.
43 G11 Anapo R Sicily
129 J7 Anápolis Brazil
129 H4 Anapú R Brazil
77 D4 Anār Iran
77 C3 Anārak Iran
77 G3 Anardarra Afghanistan
26 F8 Anaris Fjällen mt Sweden
26 O3 Anarjokka R Norway/Finland
127 L5 Añasco Puerto Rico
26 M7 Ånäset Sweden
113 F8 Anastasia I Florida
78 D2 Anatolia reg Turkey
100 H3 Anatone Washington
29 O7 Änättijärvi L Finland
131 E2 Añatuya Argentina
128 F3 Anauá R Brazil
69 G8 An Bien Vietnam
128 C5 Ancash dep Peru
9 F2 Ancaster England
101 O4 Anceney Montana
21 C7 Ancenis France
21 F7 Anché France
130 H7 Anchieta Brazil
106 E8 Ancho New Mexico
116 N6 Anchorage Alaska
94 B8 Anchorage Kentucky
94 E4 Anchor Bay Michigan
144 A6 Anchor I New Zealand
116 M7 Anchor Point Alaska
127 J2 Anchovy Jamaica
65 C5 Anci China
121 T6 Ancienne Lorette airport Quebec
113 E9 Anclote Keys islds Florida
128 E7 Ancohuma mt Bolivia
128 C6 Ancón Peru
45 O4 Ancona Italy
128 C3 Ancon de Sardinas B.de Ecuador
95 O4 Ancram New York
22 D4 Ancre R France
13 F2 Ancroft England
13 F3 Ancrum Scotland
88 G8 Ancuabe Mozambique
133 C6 Ancud Chile
59 J2 Anda China
65 F1 Anda China
133 C5 Andacollo Argentina
140 D7 Andado N Terr Aust
128 D6 Andahuaylas Peru
107 N4 Andale Kansas
133 D3 Andalgala Argentina
26 C9 Åndalsnes Norway
16 D7 Andalucia reg Spain
111 K10 Andalusia Alabama
68 A6 Andaman Islands Bay of Bengal
138 D4 Andamooka S Australia
52 G5 Andanga U.S.S.R.
129 K6 Andaria Brazil
67 B5 Ande China
41 K4 Andeer Switzerland
28 N1 Andefjord Faeroes
52 H1 Andeg U.S.S.R.
20 H3 Andelle R France
19 J4 Andelot France
20 H3 Andelys,les France
22 J3 Andenne Belgium
85 E5 Anderamboukane Mali
41 J4 Andermatt Switzerland
36 C3 Andernach W Germany
36 C3 Andernach-Land W Germany
57 F6 Anderov U.S.S.R.
26 L7 Andersfors Sweden
100 C9 Anderson California
94 B6 Anderson Indiana
110 B5 Anderson Missouri
112 E3 Anderson S Carolina
114 G4 Anderson R N W Terr
139 H8 Anderson Bay Tasmania
68 A6 Anderson I Andaman Is
100 F7 Anderson L Oregon
101 K6 Anderson Ranch Res Idaho
112 C5 Andersonville Georgia
110 L2 Andersonville Indiana
27 G14 Anderstorp Sweden
95 N4 Andes New York
133 D3 Andes, Cordillera de los mts S America
98 H6 Andes,L S Dakota
87 H11 Andevoranto Madagascar
26 H2 Andfjord inlet Norway
76 D2 Andhra Pradesh prov India
17 F2 Andía,Sierra de mt Spain
83 J10 Andigama Sri Lanka
47 F9 Andikíthira isld Greece
87 H11 Andilamena Madagascar
47 G8 Andímilos isld Greece
47 G7 Andipáros isld Greece
46 D5 Andípaxoi isld Greece
47 H6 Andípsara isld Greece
78 F3 Andirin Turkey
66 C4 Andirlangar China
47 H5 Ándissa Greece
53 G12 Andiyskoye Koysu R U.S.S.R.
57 F4 Andizhan U.S.S.R.
77 J1 Andkhūi Afghanistan
36 C7 Andlau France
40 F1 Andolsheim France
52 E4 Andomskiy Pogost U.S.S.R.
65 G6 Andong S Korea
65 D7 Andongwei China
141 F1 Andoom Queensland
44 D4 Andora Italy
26 J3 Andörja isld Norway
17 J2 Andorra Pyrenees
17 H2 Andorra la Vella Andorra
20 D5 Andouille France
9 E5 Andover England
95 R2 Andover Maine
122 E7 Andover New Brunswick
95 Q3 Andover New Hampshire
95 N6 Andover New Jersey
94 K4 Andover New York
94 G5 Andover Ohio
98 J4 Andover S Dakota
9 E4 Andoversford England
26 H2 Andöya isld Norway
130 D7 Andradina Brazil
116 F5 Andreafsky Alaska
116 O10 Andreanof Is Aleutian Is
52 D6 Andreapol' U.S.S.R.
12 D5 Andreas I of Man U.K.
79 E3 Andreas,C Cyprus
87 H11 Andreba Madagascar
138 F2 Andree,L S Australia
115 R3 Andrée Land Greenland
130 G7 Andre lándia Brazil
118 E5 Andrew Alberta
99 Q7 Andrew Iowa
68 B3 Andrew B Burma
143 E10 Andrew, Mt W Australia
94 B6 Andrews Indiana
112 D2 Andrews N Carolina
98 C7 Andrews Nebraska
100 G7 Andrews Oregon
112 H4 Andrews S Carolina
108 E3 Andrews Texas
53 H8 Andreyevka U.S.S.R.
54 N1 Andreyevo U.S.S.R.
53 D9 Andreyevo-Ivanovka U.S.S.R.
55 E2 Andreyevskoye, Oz L U.S.S.R.
53 D8 Andreykovichi U.S.S.R.
43 G7 Andria Italy
46 D2 Andrijevica Yugoslavia
46 E7 Andrítsaina Greece
106 G4 Andrix Colorado
87 G12 Androka Madagascar
116 G9 Andronica I Alaska
126 E2 Andros isld Bahamas
47 G7 Ándros isld Greece
95 R2 Androscogg R New Hamps/Maine
53 G7 Androsovka U.S.S.R.
126 F2 Andros Town Andros Bahamas
73 L6 Androth I Lakshadweep Indian Oc
53 C8 Andrushevka U.S.S.R.
31 L6 Andrychów Poland
55 D2 Andryushino U.S.S.R.
26 K2 Andselv Norway
16 E6 Andújar Spain
87 C8 Andulo Angola
18 H8 Anduze France
27 G14 Aneby Sweden
85 E7 Anecho Togo
143 G6 Anec, L W Australia
131 B8 Anecón Grande peak Argentina
85 E5 Anefis Mali
113 L7 Anegada isld Virgin Is
133 E6 Anegado, B Argentina
137 O6 Aneityum isld New Hebrides
118 K7 Anerley Sask
118 K9 Aneroid Sask
20 H4 Anet France
98 J2 Aneta N Dakota
67 E3 Anfu China
140 B3 Angalarri R N Terr Aust
133 C2 Angamos, Pta C Chile
125 J8 Angangue Mexico
59 H2 Ang'angxi China
147 K8 Angara Basin Arctic Oc
56 F4 Angarsk U.S.S.R.
140 B7 Angas Downs N Terr Aust
142 G6 Angas Ra W Australia
138 E5 Angaston S Australia
71 E3 Angat Luzon Philippines
130 E8 Angatuba Brazil
26 H9 Ånge Sweden
26 H10 Ängebo Sweden
124 C3 Angel de la Guarda isld Mexico
71 E3 Angeles Luzon Philippines
128 F2 Angel Falls waterfall Venezuela
27 F15 Ängelholm Sweden
94 J4 Angelica New York
111 B10 Angelina R Texas
141 H7 Angellala Queensland
28 D7 Angeln reg W Germany
43 G8 Angelo de Lom,S Italy
27 H12 Ängelsberg Sweden
102 D3 Angels Camp California
38 N7 Anger Austria
41 J6 Angera Italy
26 K9 Ångermanälven isld Sweden
26 J8 Ångermanälven R Sweden
32 E10 Angermund W Germany
21 D7 Angers France
26 G10 Ängersjö Sweden
20 J5 Angerville France
26 M5 Ängeså Sweden
26 N5 Ängesan R Sweden
26 L8 Ängesön isld Sweden
70 G7 Anggowala, Bk mt Sulawesi Indonesia
45 M4 Anghiari Italy
112 J2 Angier N Carolina
115 K5 Angikuni L N W Terr
8 A4 Angle Wales
144 A7 Anglem, Mt New Zealand
120 D4 Angler Ontario
Anglesey co see Gwynedd
Anglesey isld see Môn
18 D9 Anglet France
109 M6 Angleton Texas
118 J7 Anglia Sask
21 F8 Angliers France
21 H8 Anglin R France
115 Q4 Angmagssalik Greenland
88 G10 Angoche Mozambique
77 E6 Angohrān Iran
131 A6 Angol Chile
87 C8 Angola Africa
94 B5 Angola Indiana
94 H4 Angola New York
90 K11 Angola Basin Atlantic Oc
112 K3 Angola Swamp N Carolina
117 F7 Angoon Alaska
98 C8 Angora Nebraska
124 E5 Angostura Mexico
125 J6 Angostura Mexico
128 D3 Angostura I, Salto cataract Colombia
124 E2 Angostura, Presa de la res Mexico
125 N9 Angostura, Psa. de la res Mexico
98 C6 Angostura Reserve S Dakota
18 F7 Angoulême France
18 F7 Angoumois prov France
129 K8 Angra dos Reis Brazil
45 R8 Angri Italy
21 D6 Angrie France
37 L2 Angstedt-Gräfinau E Germany
68 E5 Ang Thong Thailand
17 G2 Angués Spain
126 E3 Anguila Isles Bahamas
127 N5 Anguilla isld Lesser Antilles
45 L1 Anguillara Ven Italy
123 N6 Anguille, C Newfoundland
75 L8 Angul India
86 E6 Angumu Zaïre
65 C5 Anguo China
140 D2 Angurugu Northern Territory
98 K1 Angus Minnesota
Angus co see Tayside reg
119 Q8 Angusville Manitoba
88 C10 Angwa R Zimbabwe
129 H8 Anhandui R Brazil
28 R3 Anholt Denmark
28 H3 Anholt isld Denmark
68 G3 Anh Son Vietnam
67 D2 Anhua China
58 G5 Anhui prov China
Anhwei prov see Anhui
61 O5 Aniai Japan
116 H6 Aniak Alaska
116 H8 Aniakchak Vol. Crater Alaska
22 E3 Aniche France
130 E5 Anicuns Brazil
47 H8 Ánidhros isld Greece
85 E7 Anié Togo
45 N6 Aniene R Italy
18 E10 Anie, Pic d' mt Spain/France
55 D5 Anikhovka U.S.S.R.
52 F5 Anikovo U.S.S.R.
106 B10 Animas New Mexico
106 C4 Animas R Colorado
124 C3 Animas,Pta Las C Mexico
68 C5 Anin Burma
48 G5 Anina Romania
103 M6 Anita Arizona
99 M8 Anita Iowa
71 G5 Anitaguipan Pt Philippines
130 E10 Anitápolis Brazil
116 J2 Aniuk R Alaska
59 M2 Aniva, Zaliv B U.S.S.R.
99 R4 Aniwa Wisconsin
22 E4 Anizy-le-Chât France
29 M11 Anjalankoski Finland
74 D7 Anjar India
80 G4 'Anjara Jordan
70 K9 Anjer-Lor Java
67 F1 Anji China
65 G2 Anjia China
Anjiang see Qianyang
Anjiangying see Luanping
61 L11 Anjō Japan
21 C7 Anjou prov France
87 G10 Anjouan isld Comoros
87 H11 Anjozorobe Madagascar
59 J4 Anjū N Korea
77 L2 Anjuman reg Afghanistan
58 E5 Ankang China
78 D2 Ankara Turkey
87 H11 Ankaratra mt Madagascar
27 H14 Ankarsrum Sweden
26 J6 Ankarsund Sweden
87 G12 Ankazoabo Madagascar
99 N8 Ankeny Iowa
33 T5 Anklam E Germany
74 E8 Anklesvar India
86 G4 Ankober Ethiopia
16 D10 Ankod Morocco
38 H7 Ankogel mt Austria
87 E7 Ankoro Zaïre
52 E6 An'kovo U.S.S.R.
32 G7 Ankum W Germany
13 H6 Anlaby England
67 E3 Anle China
22 K4 Anlier Belgium
68 H7 An Loc Vietnam
67 B4 Anlong China
68 G5 Anlong Veng Cambodia
58 F5 Anlu China
26 F8 Ånn Sweden
110 G4 Anna Illinois
25 C3 Anna Netherlands
94 C6 Anna Ohio
109 L2 Anna Texas
53 F8 Anna U.S.S.R.
85 F1 Annaba Algeria
38 H7 Annaberg Austria
37 P2 Annaberg-Buchholz E Germany
33 S9 Annaburg E Germany
138 D3 Anna Creek S Australia
128 G3 Annai Guyana
25 B5 Anna Jacobapolder Netherlands
61 M9 Annaka Japan
68 G3 Annam reg Vietnam
113 E10 Anna Maria Florida
13 E4 Annan Scotland
99 M4 Annandale Minnesota
141 J5 Annandale Queensland
15 E5 Annandale Scotland
13 E3 Annan Water Scotland
133 C7 Anna Pink, B Chile
142 D4 Anna Plains W Australia
95 L8 Annapolis Maryland
122 G9 Annapolis R Nova Scotia
75 K4 Annapurna mt Nepal
94 D4 Ann Arbor Michigan
33 O9 Annarode E Germany
78 L7 An Nāsirīyah Iraq
99 R8 Annawan Illinois
146 H12 Annawan,C Antarctica
146 A5 Ann,C Antarctica
143 C7 Annean, L W Australia
20 F3 Annebault France
19 Q13 Annecy France
40 D6 Annecy,L.d' France
146 A15 Annenkov I Antarctica
133 J8 Annenkov Is S Georgia
141 K2 Annerley dist Brisbane, Qnsld
117 H8 Annette I Alaska
20 B3 Anneville-sur-Mer France
19 N14 Anneyron France
68 J6 An Nhon Vietnam
141 G2 Annie R Queensland
123 P5 Annieopsquotch Mts Newfoundland
58 D6 Anning He R China
28 J5 Annisse Denmark
111 L8 Anniston Alabama
140 D5 Annitowa N Terr Aust
40 G5 Anniviers Val d' Switzerland
Annobón isld see Pagalu isld
22 D2 Annœulin France
109 N2 Annona Texas
19 N14 Annonay France
127 L2 Annotto Bay Jamaica
36 D5 Annweiler W Germany
47 G9 Áno Arkhánai Crete Greece
99 N4 Anoka Minnesota
98 H7 Anoka Nebraska
54 M1 Anopino U.S.S.R.
22 G4 Anor France
36 B7 Anould France
47 G9 Áno Viánnos Crete Greece
68 J7 An Phuoc Vietnam
65 C5 Anping China
67 C6 Anpu China
67 C6 Anpu Gang B China
58 G5 Anqing China
65 D6 Anqiu China
25 F6 Anrath W Germany
67 D3 Anren China
32 H9 Anröchte W Germany
22 K2 Ans Belgium
21 G10 Ansac-sur-Vienne France
28 B5 Ansager Denmark
65 A6 Ansai China
79 G3 Ansārīye, Jebel el mts Syria
37 K5 Ansbach W Germany
40 A6 Anse France
127 H5 Anse-à-Galets Haiti
127 J5 Anse-à-Pitre Haiti
122 H5 Anse-au-Griffon Quebec
126 H5 Anse-à-Veau Haiti
127 N4 Anse Bertrand Guadeloupe W I
126 G5 Anse d'Hainault Haiti
98 G8 Anselmo Nebraska
22 H3 Anseremme Belgium
139 H7 Anser Gr islds Tasmania
122 B5 Anse St.Jean,L' Quebec
127 L4 Anses d'Arlets, Les Martinique W I
59 H3 Anshan China
67 B3 Anshun China
131 B3 Ansilta peak Argentina
131 B3 Ansilta, Cord. de ra Argentina
109 P3 Ansley Louisiana
98 G8 Ansley Nebraska
140 B2 Anson B N Terr Aust
85 E5 Ansongo Mali
94 C6 Ansonia Ohio
112 G2 Ansonville N Carolina
115 L8 Ansonville Ontario
28 C6 Anst Denmark
94 F8 Ansted W Virginia
15 F4 Anstruther Scotland
128 D6 Anta Peru
78 C3 Antalya Turkey
87 H11 Antananarivo Madagascar
87 H11 Antanifotsy Madagascar
87 H12 Antanimora Madagascar
90 D16 Antarctic Circle
146 E13 Antarctic Pen Antarctica
81 C10 Antares Bank Indian Oc
130 H11 Antas Brazil
130 D10 Antas,R das Brazil
15 C3 An Teallach mt Scotland
98 B1 Antelope Montana
98 D3 Antelope N Dakota
118 J8 Antelope Sask
109 J2 Antelope Texas
101 Q9 Antelope Utah
100 H7 Antelope Cr Oregon
130 H9 Antenor Navarro Brazil
16 D7 Antequera Spain
130 B9 Antequera,Pto Paraguay
106 D3 Antero Pk Colorado
106 E3 Antero Res Colorado
38 F8 Anterselva Italy
107 N4 Anthony Kansas
106 D9 Anthony New Mexico
108 A3 Anthony New Mex/Tex
136 H5 Anthony Lagoon N Terr Australia
138 C2 Anthony,Mt S Australia
85 C3 Anti Atlas mts Morocco
44 B4 Antibes France
44 B4 Antibes,C.d' France
127 N9 Antica, I Venezuela
45 N5 Anticoli Corrado Italy
122 J4 Anticosti I Quebec
20 F2 Antifer,C.d' France
123 K8 Antigonish Nova Scotia
125 O10 Antigua Guatemala
127 P4 Antigua isld Lesser Antilles
127 N4 Antigues Pte. d' Guadeloupe W I
118 B3 Antikameg Alberta
133 C5 Antilhue Chile
126 G4 Antilla Cuba
103 N3 Antimony Utah
102 C3 Antioch California
99 S7 Antioch Illinois
98 D7 Antioch Nebraska
21 C9 Antioche, Pertuis d' str France
43 B9 Antioco, S Sardinia
43 B9 Antioco,S isld Sardinia
128 C2 Antioquia div Colombia
80 C5 Antipatris Israel
52 D6 Antipovo U.S.S.R.
128 C4 Antisana mt Ecuador
98 E1 Antler N Dakota
119 Q9 Antler Sask
107 P7 Antlers Oklahoma
133 C2 Antofagasta Chile
133 D3 Antofagasta de la Sierra Argentina
133 D3 Antofalla vol Argentina
109 O1 Antoine Arkansas
22 E2 Antoing Belgium
44 F2 Antola,Monte Italy
106 G2 Anton Colorado
108 E2 Anton Texas
87 J11 Antongil, B.d' Madagascar
87 G12 Antongo Madagascar
130 E9 Antonina Brazil
107 L3 Antonino Kansas
48 K1 Antoniny U.S.S.R.
129 K7 Antônio R Brazil
130 G7 Antônio Carlos Brazil
130 G6 Antônio Dias Brazil
Antonio Enes see Angoche
130 C8 Antônio João Brazil
106 D4 Antonito Colorado
126 D3 Antón Recio Cuba
140 D4 Antony Lagoon N Terr Aust
20 C5 Antrain France
52 C4 Antrea U.S.S.R.
36 G5 Antrefftal W Germany
95 P3 Antrim New Hampshire
14 E2 Antrim N Ireland
95 K5 Antrim Pennsylvania
14 E2 Antrim co N Ireland
14 E2 Antrim Hills N Ireland
142 G4 Antrim Plat W Australia
87 G11 Antsalova Madagascar
87 H10 Antseranana Madagascar
52 D5 Antsiferovo U.S.S.R.
87 H11 Antsirabe Madagascar
52 C5 Antsla U.S.S.R.
87 H10 Antsohihy Madagascar
29 N10 Anttola Finland
65 G3 Antu China
68 J6 An Tuc Vietnam
Antwerp see Antwerpen
95 M2 Antwerp New York
94 C5 Antwerp Ohio
22 H1 Antwerpen Belgium
14 E3 An Uaimh Irish Rep
116 F6 Anukslak L Alaska
26 K8 Anundsjö Sweden
74 E4 Anupgarh India
83 K9 Anuradhapura Sri Lanka
Anvers see Antwerpen
45 P6 Anversa degli Abruzzi Italy
146 E14 Anvers I Antarctica
116 G5 Anvik Alaska
121 P3 Anvilla Quebec
22 C3 Anvin France
58 C3 Anxi China
67 F4 Anxi China
67 A1 An Xian China
67 D2 Anxiang China
65 C5 Anxin China
138 C5 Anxious B S Australia
58 F4 Anyang China
58 C5 A'nyêmaqên Shan mts China
65 B7 Anyi China
67 E2 Anyi China
67 D7 Anyou China
117 J8 Anyox Br Col
67 E4 Anyuan China
52 J3 An'yudin U.S.S.R.
67 B1 Anyue China
51 Q2 Anyuy R U.S.S.R.
42 B3 Anza R Italy
118 F2 Anzac Alberta
17 G2 Anzánigo Spain
40 H6 Anzasca, Valle Italy
18 F10 Anzat France
65 B6 Anze China
22 E2 Anzegem Belgium
21 I9 Anzème France
56 C3 Anzhero-Sudzhensk U.S.S.R.
147 P7 Anzhu Os isld U.S.S.R.
22 E3 Anzin France
38 E5 Anzing W Germany
45 N7 Anzio Italy
128 F2 Anzoátegui state Venezuela
45 K2 Anzola dell'Emilia Italy
59 L5 Aoga-shima isld Japan
65 D3 Aohan Qi China
18 E10 Aoiz Spain
61 O5 Aomori Japan
60 N3 Aonae Japan
145 E4 Aorangi Mts New Zealand
145 D4 Aorere R New Zealand
68 D7 Ao Sawi B Thailand
40 F6 Aosta Italy
145 E3 Aotea Harbour New Zealand
85 C5 Aouker reg Mauritania
85 E3 Aoulef Algeria
67 B3 Aoxi China
60 G10 Aoya Japan
86 C1 Aozou Chad
103 P10 Apache Arizona
109 J1 Apache Oklahoma
106 B8 Apache Creek New Mexico
103 N8 Apache Junct Arizona
103 O10 Apache Pk Arizona
113 C7 Apalachee B Florida
112 C2 Apalachia Dam N Carolina
113 C8 Apalachicola Florida
128 D3 Apaporis R Colombia
130 B8 Apa.R Brazil/Paraguay
130 D7 Áparecida do Tabuado Brazil
144 B7 Aparima R New Zealand
71 E1 Aparri Luzon Philippines
70 E6 Apar, Teluk B Kalimantan
48 E5 Apatin Yugoslavia
52 D1 Apatity U.S.S.R.
124 H8 Apatzingán Mexico
116 C5 Apavawook C St. Lawrence I, Alaska
52 C5 Ape U.S.S.R.
45 M4 Apecchio Italy
119 S3 Apeganau L Manitoba
25 E4 Apeldoorn Netherlands
32 G6 Apen W Germany
33 O7 Apenburg E Germany
32 L6 Apensen W Germany
128 E6 Apere R Bolivia
112 J2 Apex N Carolina
41 L1 Apfingen W Germany
101 L1 Apgar Montana

6

Aphek — Ata

80 C5 Aphek Israel
116 E6 Aphrewn R Alaska
86 E5 Api Zaïre
137 S4 Apia W Samoa
129 G5 Apiacás,Serra dos mts Brazil
130 E9 Apiaí Brazil
45 R7 Apice Italy
71 J9 Api,Gunung vol Indonesia
130 B10 Apipe Grande isld Argentina
106 F4 Apishapa R Colorado
70 G5 Api,Tg C Sulawesi Indonesia
145 E3 Apiti New Zealand
125 K8 Apizaco Mexico
124 H5 Apizolaya Mexico
56 F2 Aplinskiy Porog falls U.S.S.R.
129 L5 Apodi R Brazil
71 E4 Apo East Pass Philippines
37 M1 Apolda E Germany
Apollonia see Marsá Sūsah
47 G8 Apollonía Greece
128 E6 Apolo Bolivia
113 F9 Apopka Florida
113 F9 Apopka,L Florida
133 G1 Aporé R Brazil
129 H3 Aporema Brazil
99 Q2 Apostle Is Michigan
133 F3 Apostoles Argentina
54 E9 Apostolovo U.S.S.R.
128 G3 Apoteri Guyana
71 E4 Apo West Pass Philippines
94 E10 Appalachia Virginia
94 F10 Appalachian Mts U.S.A.
27 G11 Äppelbo Sweden
32 F9 Appelhülsen W Germany
28 B7 Appelland isld W Germany
44 D3 Appenino Ligure mt Italy
42 E5 Appennino Umbro-Marchigiano mts Italy
36 D6 Appenweier W Germany
41 K3 Appenzell canton Switzerland
13 G6 Apperley Br England
20 G3 Appeville France
25 G2 Appingedam Netherlands
109 N4 Appleby Texas
13 F4 Appleby-in-Westmorland England
142 A2 Applecross dist Perth, W Aust
8 B5 Appledore England
102 D3 Applegate California
100 B7 Applegate Oregon
122 H8 Apple River Nova Scotia
109 N4 Apple Springs Texas
95 S2 Appleton Maine
100 D4 Appleton Washington
99 S5 Appleton Wisconsin
110 B3 Appleton City Missouri
94 J9 Appomattox Virginia
54 J1 Aprelevka U.S.S.R.
22 J5 Apremont France
27 M15 Apriki U.S.S.R.
43 E7 Aprilia Italy
53 E11 Apsheronsk U.S.S.R.
121 M8 Apsley Ontario
138 F6 Apsley Victoria
140 B1 Apsley Str N Terr Aust
19 O17 Apt France
45 H3 Apuane Italy
135 V6 Apua Pt Hawaiian Is
130 D8 Apucarana Brazil
130 D8 Apucarana, Serra Da mts Brazil
71 D6 Apurauan Philippines
128 E2 Apure state Venezuela
128 D6 Apurímac dep Peru
48 H4 Apuseni Muntii mt Romania
88 D6 Apwa Tanzania
79 F9 'Aqaba Jordan
84 J4 Aqaba,G.of Red Sea
77 J1 Aq Chah Afghanistan
66 D4 Aqqikkol Hu L China
80 G3 'Aqraba Jordan
103 L7 Aquarius Mts Arizona
103 N4 Aquarius Plat Utah
130 B8 Aquidabán,R Paraguay
130 C7 Aquidauana Brazil
130 C6 Aquidauana,R Brazil
124 G3 Aquiles Serdán Mexico
109 K4 Aquilla Texas
126 H5 Aquin Haiti
45 P7 Aquino Italy
17 G2 Ara R Spain
80 F3 Arab R Jordan
53 E10 Arabatskaya Strelka spit U.S.S.R.
38 E8 Arabba Italy
112 D6 Arabi Georgia
111 K12 Arabi New Orleans
123 N3 Arabian L Quebec
84 H3 Arabs Gulf Egypt
78 D1 Araç Turkey
128 F3 Araçá R Brazil
129 L6 Aracaju Brazil
130 C9 Aracanguy, Mt de Paraguay
126 G9 Aracataca Colombia
129 L4 Aracati Brazil
130 E7 Araçatuba Brazil
16 C7 Aracena Spain
16 C7 Aracena, Sa. de mts Spain
130 G5 Araçuaí Brazil
48 G4 Arad Romania
86 D2 Arada Chad
56 D5 Aradanskiy Khrebet mts U.S.S.R.
81 L7 Arafura Sea Aust/New Guinea
129 H7 Aragarças Brazil
78 J1 Aragats mt U.S.S.R.
61 M9 Ara-gawa R Japan
100 A6 Arago,Cape Oregon
17 G2 Aragón R Spain
17 G4 Aragon reg Spain
43 F11 Aragona Sicily
17 F4 Aragoncillo mt Spain
128 E2 Aragua state Venezuela
129 J6 Araguaçu Brazil
128 F2 Aragua de Barcelona Venezuela
129 J7 Araguari Brazil
129 H3 Araguari R Brazil
133 H1 Araguari R Brazil
129 J5 Araguatins Brazil
53 F12 Aragvi R U.S.S.R.
144 C5 Arahura New Zealand
61 M8 Arai Japan
79 E8 Araif el Naqa mt Egypt
80 G8 Ara'ir Jordan
85 E3 Arak Algeria
77 A2 Arāk Iran
78 G4 Arak Syria
61 N8 Arakai-yama mt Japan
128 G2 Arakaka Guyana
116 A4 Arakamchechen, Ostrov isld U.S.S.R.
68 A2 Arakan prov Burma
68 B2 Arakan Yoma ra Burma
46 F6 Arákhova Greece
46 D5 Árakhthos R Greece
120 C2 Ara L Ontario
57 B2 Aral'sk U.S.S.R.
57 A3 Aral'skoye More sea U.S.S.R.
55 B6 Aralsor, Oz L U.S.S.R.
26 A9 Åram Norway
141 H6 Aramac Queensland
141 G6 Aramac R Queensland
125 K5 Aramberri Mexico
19 N17 Aramon France
16 E3 Aranda de Duero Spain
17 F3 Aranda de Moncayo Spain
87 B10 Arandis Namibia
145 D1 Aranga New Zealand
128 E7 Arani Bolivia
14 C1 Aran I Irish Rep
16 E4 Aranjuez Spain
89 A5 Aranos Namibia
109 L7 Aransas B Texas
109 K8 Aransas Pass Texas
130 E6 Arantes,R Brazil
137 P1 Aranuka isld Kiribati
85 D5 Araouane Mali
106 E1 Arapaho mt Colorado
106 H3 Arapahoe Colorado
98 G9 Arapahoe Nebraska
101 R7 Arapahoe Wyoming
128 E7 Arapa,L Peru
145 E4 Arapawa I New Zealand
133 F4 Arapey Uruguay
130 H10 Arapiraca Brazil
78 G2 Arapkir Turkey
130 D8 Arapongas Brazil
145 E3 Arapuni New Zealand
130 E10 Araquari Brazil
80 D4 'Ar'Ara Israel
133 H3 Ararangua Brazil
129 J8 Araraquara Brazil
130 F8 Araras São Paulo Brazil
130 D6 Araras,Serra das Mato Grosso Brazil
130 D9 Araras, Serra das mts Paraná Brazil
139 G6 Ararat Victoria
Ararat,Mt see Bügük Ağri
129 K4 Arari Brazil
75 M5 Araria India
130 G8 Araruama L.de Brazil
78 H6 Arar,Wadi Saudi Arabia
80 D5 A-ras Jordan
78 J1 Aras R Turkey
17 G5 Aras de Alpuente Spain
126 A1 Arasji Aruba W I
145 D2 Aratapu New Zealand
145 F3 Aratiatia New Zealand
61 O7 Arato Japan
128 F5 Araua R Brazil
128 D2 Arauca Colombia
133 C5 Arauco Chile
127 K10 Araure Venezuela
80 E2 'Arav Israel
74 E6 Aravalli Range India
144 B6 Arawata R New Zealand
129 J7 Araxá Brazil
128 F1 Araya,P.de Venezuela
61 P14 Ara-zaki C Okinawa
17 G3 Arba R Spain
86 G4 Arba Minch Ethiopia
43 C9 Arbatax Sardinia
52 G5 Arbazh U.S.S.R.
40 C2 Arbecey France
37 K5 Arberg W Germany
27 H12 Arboga Sweden
27 H12 Arbogaån R Sweden
40 C4 Arbois France
101 N7 Arbon Idaho
41 K2 Arbon Switzerland
119 O5 Arborfield Sask
9 F5 Arborfield Cross England
119 U8 Arborg Manitoba
99 R4 Arbor Vitae Wisconsin
27 H10 Arbrå Sweden
13 F1 Arbroath Scotland
102 B2 Arbuckle California
113 F10 Arbuckle,L Florida
109 K1 Arbuckle Mts Oklahoma
110 F5 Arbyrd Missouri
19 J5 Arc France
19 O18 Arc R France
18 E8 Arcachon France
94 J4 Arcade New York
118 A3 Arcadia Alberta
113 F10 Arcadia Florida
94 A6 Arcadia Indiana
107 Q4 Arcadia Kansas
111 D9 Arcadia Louisiana
99 U5 Arcadia Michigan
110 F4 Arcadia Missouri
98 G8 Arcadia Nebraska
94 D5 Arcadia Ohio
107 N6 Arcadia Oklahoma
99 P5 Arcadia Wisconsin
95 T2 Arcadia Nat. Park Maine
43 G8 Arcangelo,S Italy
94 C7 Arcanum Ohio
102 G3 Arc Dome mt Nevada
45 P6 Arce Italy
125 J8 Arcelia Mexico
25 F6 Arcen Netherlands
45 N4 Arcévia Italy
46 F1 Archar Bulgaria
95 M5 Archbald Pennsylvania
94 C5 Archbold Ohio
112 H2 Archdale N Carolina
113 E8 Archer Florida
141 F2 Archer R Queensland
109 J2 Archer City Texas
141 K2 Archerfield Airfield Brisbane, Qnsld
141 H3 Archer Pt Queensland
119 O6 Archerwill Sask
40 E1 Arches France
103 P3 Arches Nat.Mon Utah
110 B3 Archie Missouri
21 G8 Archigny France
119 M8 Archive Sask
106 C5 Archuleta New Mexico
18 H4 Arcis sur Aube France
138 C2 Arckaringa R S Australia
101 M6 Arco Idaho
98 K5 Arco Minnesota
99 S10 Arcola Illinois
111 F8 Arcola Mississippi
119 P9 Arcola Sask
45 K1 Árcole Italy
18 H6 Arconce R France
138 D4 Arcoona S Australia
131 B7 Arco, Paso de Arg/Chile
130 F7 Arcos Brazil
16 D8 Arcos de la Frontera Spain
16 B3 Arcos de Vale de Vez Portugal
17 G3 Arcos,Sierra de mt Spain
76 D4 Arcot India
130 H10 Arcoverde Brazil
19 J5 Arc-Senans France
147 F4 Arctic Bay N W Terr
90 J2 Arctic Circle
116 D4 Arctic Lagoon Alaska
147 Arctic Ocean
114 F4 Arctic Red River N W Terr
116 P2 Arctic Village Alaska
45 L1 Arcugnano Italy
22 E5 Arcy-Ste. Restitue France
44 G2 Arda R Italy
78 M2 Ardabil Iran
38 L5 Ardagger Austria
78 J1 Ardahan Turkey
77 C3 Ardakan Esfahān Iran
77 C4 Ardakan Fārs Iran
77 B4 Ardal Iran
27 C10 Årdal Opland Norway
27 B12 Årdal Rogaland Norway
14 C2 Ardara Irish Rep
118 K7 Ardath Sask
52 F6 Ardatov U.S.S.R.
120 K7 Ardbeg Ontario
12 B2 Ardbeg Scotland
45 N6 Ardea Italy
48 H3 Ardead Romania
18 H8 Ardèche dep France
14 E3 Ardee Irish Rep
119 S8 Arden Manitoba
103 J5 Arden Nevada
121 O8 Arden Ontario
138 E4 Arden Mt S Australia
22 H4 Ardennes France
21 I8 Ardentes France
12 D1 Ardentinny Scotland
77 C3 Ardestān Iran
15 D3 Ardgay Scotland
14 F2 Ardglass N Ireland
46 E4 Ardhéa Greece
16 C6 Ardila,R Spain
119 M9 Ardill Sask
124 H6 Ardilla, Cerro La peak Mexico
47 G3 Ardino Bulgaria
18 E10 Ardisa Spain
70 P9 Ardjasa Java
70 O9 Ardjuna,G mt Java
145 F3 Ardkeen New Zealand
118 D6 Ardley Alberta
15 D4 Ardlui Scotland
12 C2 Ardminish Scotland
139 H6 Ardmona Victoria
118 G4 Ardmore Alberta
107 N7 Ardmore Oklahoma
98 C6 Ardmore S Dakota
110 K6 Ardmore Tennessee
14 D5 Ardmore B Irish Rep
15 B4 Ardnamurchan Pt Scotland
15 B5 Ardnave Pt Scotland
98 J1 Ardoch N Dakota
141 G7 Ardoch Queensland
22 B2 Ardres France
12 C1 Ardrishaig Scotland
118 D5 Ardrossan Alberta
138 E5 Ardrossan S Australia
15 D5 Ardrossan Scotland
14 F2 Ards Pen N Ireland
12 B2 Ardtalla Scotland
15 C3 Ardvasar Scotland
53 F7 Ardym U.S.S.R.
26 F8 Åre Sweden
26 N4 Areavaara Sweden
127 L5 Arecibo Puerto Rico
131 F5 Areco R Argentina
129 L4 Areia Branca Brazil
45 Q7 Areinzo Italy
118 K6 Arelee Sask
27 E12 Aremark Norway
36 B3 Aremberg W Germany
95 N4 Arena New York
71 E6 Arena Philippines
118 H9 Arena Sask
133 C7 Arenales mt Chile
130 C4 Arenápolis Brazil
71 F4 Arena Pt Luzon Philippines
124 E6 Arena, Pta C Mexico
16 D4 Arenas de S.Pedro Spain
128 D8 Arenas,Pta C Chile
32 F7 Arenberg reg W Germany
27 C13 Arendal Norway
22 J1 Arendonk Belgium
33 O7 Arendsee E Germany
32 L10 Arenshausen E Germany
19 Q12 Arenthon France
28 D2 Arentsminde Denmark
17 J3 Arenys de Mar Spain
46 E8 Areópolis Greece
128 D7 Arequipa Peru
129 H4 Arere Brazil
18 E8 Arés France
16 D3 Arévalo Spain
42 D5 Arezzo Italy
46 E7 Arfará Greece
17 F2 Arga R Spain
140 D5 Argadargada N Terr Aust
16 E5 Argamasilla de Alba Spain
16 E4 Arganda Spain
16 B4 Arganil Portugal
71 F6 Argao Philippines
45 P6 Argatone, M mt Italy
55 D3 Argayash U.S.S.R.
55 D3 Argazi L U.S.S.R.
55 D3 Argazi, Oz U.S.S.R.
18 H10 Argelès sur Mer France
41 L2 Argen R W Germany
20 E3 Argences France
19 Q18 Argens R France
117 P10 Argenta Br Columbia
45 L2 Argenta Italy
101 N4 Argenta Montana
20 E4 Argentan France
42 D6 Argentario,Monte Italy
18 G7 Argentat France
44 B3 Argentera Mt Italy
20 K4 Argenteuil France
123 S6 Argentia Newfoundland
40 E6 Argentières France
44 C4 Argentina R Italy
131 D5 Argentina rep S America
90 E13 Argentine Basin Atlantic Oc
133 C8 Argentino,L Argentina
21 E7 Argenton R France
21 I8 Argenton-sur-Creuse France
122 C3 Argent,R à l' Quebec
20 D5 Argentré France
20 C5 Argentré-du-Plessis France
18 G5 Argent sur Sauldre France
48 J5 Argeş reg Romania
48 J5 Argeşul R Romania
77 J4 Arghandab R Afghanistan
77 K4 Arghastan R Afghanistan
86 H4 Argheile Ethiopia
84 J6 Argo Sudan
46 F7 Argolikós Kólpos B Greece
107 N4 Argonia Kansas
99 S4 Argonne Wisconsin
22 J5 Argonne reg France
70 O9 Argopura G mt Java
101 N5 Argora Idaho
46 F7 Argos Greece
94 A5 Argos Indiana
46 E4 Árgos Orestikón Greece
20 C4 Argouges France
18 D10 Arguedas Spain
20 J2 Argueil France
Argun R China see Ergun He
51 L3 Argun R U.S.S.R.
85 E6 Argungu Nigeria
102 G6 Argus Ra California
98 J2 Argusville N Dakota
112 E6 Argyle Georgia
94 E3 Argyle Michigan
98 K1 Argyle Minnesota
122 G10 Argyle Nova Scotia
99 R7 Argyle Wisconsin
140 A3 Argyle, L W Australia
Argyll co see Strathclyde and Highland regions
6 M6 Argyll oil rig North Sea
Argyrokastron see Gjirokastër
65 E3 Ar Horquin Qi China
28 E4 Århus Denmark
28 D4 Århus co Denmark
145 E3 Aria New Zealand
139 H5 Ariah Pk New S Wales
60 D13 Ariake-kai gulf Japan
87 C11 Ariamsvlei Namibia
43 G7 Ariano Irpino Italy
45 M2 Ariano Nel Polésine Italy
128 D3 Ariari R Colombia
73 L8 Ari Atoll Maldives
85 D6 Aribinda Upper Volta
128 D7 Arica Chile
128 D4 Arica Colombia
45 N6 Ariccia Italy
123 M8 Arichat C Breton I, N Scotia
60 J11 Arida Japan
60 J11 Arida-gawa R Japan
143 E10 Arid, C W Australia
83 J12 Aride I Seychelles
Arid I see Rakitu I
18 G9 Ariège dep France
18 G10 Ariège R France
100 C4 Ariel Washington
48 H4 Arieşul R Romania
80 G8 Ariha Jordan
106 H2 Arikaree R Colorado
60 C13 Arikawa Japan
28 K4 Arild Sweden
48 F7 Arilje Yugoslavia
128 F5 Arima Brazil
60 J11 Arima Japan
127 O2 Arima Trinidad
101 N7 Arimo Idaho
128 G3 Arinda Guyana
129 J7 Arinos Brazil
129 G6 Arinos R Brazil
101 M9 Arinosa Utah
99 L8 Arion Iowa
127 P1 Aripo, Mt Trinidad
128 D2 Ariporo R Colombia
128 F5 Aripuana R Brazil
128 F5 Ariquemes Brazil
130 D5 Ariranha R Brazil
15 C4 Arisaig Scotland
79 D7 'Arîsh, El Egypt
117 J9 Aristazabal I Br Columbia
133 D7 Aristizábal, C Argentina
111 L10 Ariton Alabama
43 C9 Aritzo Sardinia
103 N10 Arivaca Arizona
87 H11 Arivonimamo Madagascar
17 F3 Ariza Spain
18 F9 Arize R France
133 D5 Arizona Argentina
103 M7 Arizona state U.S.A.
124 D2 Arizpe Mexico
27 F12 Årjäng Sweden
26 J5 Arjeplog Sweden
128 D1 Arjona Colombia
16 E7 Arjona Spain
51 O2 Arka U.S.S.R.
53 F8 Arkadak U.S.S.R.
109 O1 Arkadelphia Arkansas
50 F3 Arkalyk U.S.S.R.
110 C6 Arkansas R Arkansas
109 O1 Arkansas state U.S.A.
111 E8 Arkansas City Arkansas
107 O4 Arkansas City Kansas
84 G5 Arkanu Jebel mt Libya
66 D4 Arkatag mts China
117 F5 Arkell,Mt Yukon Terr
27 G15 Arkelstorp Sweden
47 J8 Arkhángelos Rhodes Greece
52 F3 Arkhangel'sk U.S.S.R.
53 F11 Arkhangel'skoye U.S.S.R.
59 K2 Arkhara U.S.S.R.
53 D7 Arkhipovka U.S.S.R.
53 D8 Arkino U.S.S.R.
14 E4 Arklow Irish Rep
47 H7 Árkoi isld Greece
30 H1 Arkona E Germany
120 J9 Arkona Ontario
76 D4 Arkonam India
27 J13 Arkösund Sweden
94 K4 Arkport New York
52 H6 Arkul' U.S.S.R.
95 N4 Arkville New York
27 J12 Ärla Sweden
18 H7 Arlanc France
16 E2 Arlanza R Spain
41 M3 Arlberg pass Austria
101 L2 Arlee Montana
19 N17 Arles Bouches du Rhône France
18 G10 Arles Pyrénées-Orientales France
22 E3 Arleux France
100 J5 Arling Idaho
8 D4 Arlingham England
103 M8 Arlington Arizona
102 G8 Arlington California
106 G3 Arlington Colorado
113 F7 Arlington Florida
112 C6 Arlington Georgia
99 P7 Arlington Iowa
107 M4 Arlington Kansas
110 G5 Arlington Kentucky
99 M5 Arlington Minnesota
98 K8 Arlington Nebraska
94 D6 Arlington Ohio
100 E4 Arlington Oregon
98 J5 Arlington S Dakota
110 G6 Arlington Tennessee
109 N9 Arlington Texas
95 O3 Arlington Vermont
117 M11 Arlington Washington
101 T8 Arlington Wyoming
99 S7 Arlington Heights Illinois
110 E4 Arlington Res Missouri
22 K4 Arlon Belgium
140 C6 Arltunga N Terr Aust
107 Q4 Arma Kansas
118 E8 Armada Alberta
12 E2 Armadale Scotland
143 B9 Armadale W Australia
14 E2 Armagh N Ireland
122 B7 Armagh Quebec
14 E2 Armagh co N Ireland
18 F9 Armagnac reg France
18 H5 Armançon R France
47 H9 Armathia isld Greece
13 F4 Armathwaite England
53 F10 Armavir U.S.S.R.
128 C3 Armenia Colombia
78 K1 Armenia reg U.S.S.R.
48 G5 Armeniş Romania
20 G4 Armentières Eure France
22 D2 Armentières France
101 P2 Armington Montana
101 S6 Arminto Wyoming
119 Q6 Armit Sask
9 E2 Armitage England
55 E3 Armizonskoye U.S.S.R.
119 N5 Armley Sask
98 H6 Armour S Dakota
98 G1 Armourdale N Dakota
120 D3 Arms Ontario
36 E4 Armsheim W Germany
101 N5 Armstead Montana
114 H7 Armstrong Br Columbia
99 T9 Armstrong Illinois
99 M6 Armstrong Iowa
110 D2 Armstrong Missouri
109 K9 Armstrong Texas
140 B3 Armstrong R N Terr Aust
59 L2 Armu R U.S.S.R.
74 H9 Armur India
47 J4 Armutçuk Dağ mt Turkey
47 K4 Armutlu Turkey
53 D10 Armyansk U.S.S.R.
28 B7 Arnå R Denmark
28 M2 Árnafjall mt Faeroes
47 F4 Arnaía Greece
118 D1 Arnaud Manitoba
115 M6 Arnaud,R Quebec
79 C3 Arnauti, C Cyprus
18 J5 Arnay le Duc France
28 B4 Arnborg Denmark
37 P5 Arnbruck W Germany
33 Q7 Arneburg E Germany
18 D10 Arnedo Spain
28 O9 Arnefjord Faeroes
98 C2 Arnegard N Dakota
22 C2 Arneke France
26 M6 Arnemark Sweden
25 A6 Arnemuiden Netherlands
27 E11 Årnes Norway
107 L5 Arnett Oklahoma
94 F9 Arnett W Virginia
25 E5 Arnhem Netherlands
140 D1 Arnhem,C N Terr Aust
140 C2 Arnhem Land reg N Terr Aust
140 C2 Arnhem Land Res N Terr Aust
20 H4 Arnières France
45 H4 Arno R Italy
138 D5 Arno Bay S Australia
102 D3 Arnold California
98 F8 Arnold Nebraska
94 H6 Arnold Pennsylvania
99 L6 Arnolds Park Iowa
38 J8 Arnoldstein Austria
21 J7 Arnon R France
119 V3 Arnot Manitoba
26 L1 Arnöy Norway
16 B2 Arnoya R Spain
12 D1 Arnprior Scotland
32 G10 Arnsberg W Germany
13 F5 Arnside England
37 K2 Arnstadt E Germany
37 L3 Arnstein W Germany
37 O6 Arnstorf W Germany
Arnswalde see Choszczno
121 L4 Arntfield Quebec
28 B6 Arnum Denmark
128 F2 Aro R Venezuela
127 K9 Aroa Venezuela
87 C11 Aroab Namibia
46 E7 Aroánia mt Greece
124 H4 Arocha Mexico
130 C7 Aroeira Brazil
32 K10 Arolsen W Germany
55 E3 Aromashevo U.S.S.R.
20 D5 Aron France
20 D5 Aron R France
42 B3 Arona Italy
122 E7 Aroostook New Brunswick
95 S7 Aroostook R Maine
116 E6 Aropuk L Alaska
137 Q2 Arorae isld Kiribati
71 F4 Aroroy Philippines
28 D6 Arøsund Denmark
127 O2 Arouca Trinidad
145 F3 Arowhana mt New Zealand
106 G3 Aroya Colorado
109 M3 Arp Texas
57 G4 Arpa U.S.S.R.
18 G8 Arpajon France
20 K4 Arpajon France
48 J5 Arpasu de Jos Romania
55 D1 Arpavla U.S.S.R.
120 K4 Arpin Ontario
45 P6 Arpino Italy
45 L1 Arquà Petrarca Italy
45 L1 Arquà Polesine Italy
22 C2 Arques Pas-de-Calais France
20 H2 Arques-la-Bataille France
80 E2 'Arraba Israel
138 F2 Arrabury Queensland
141 F7 Arrabury Queensland
36 B6 Arracourt France
131 D2 Arraga Argentina
16 C4 Arrago R Spain
75 L6 Arrah India
129 J6 Arraias Brazil
16 B6 Arraiolos Portugal
14 C4 Arra Mts Irish Rep
111 M11 Arran Florida
119 Q7 Arran Sask
15 C5 Arran isld Scotland
80 E4 'Arrana Jordan
117 H8 Arrandale Br Col
22 D3 Arras Pas-de-Calais France
18 F9 Arrats R France
28 B5 Arre Denmark
18 F10 Arreau France
128 E3 Arrecifal Colombia
85 B3 Arrecife Canary Is
18 C4 Arrée,Mgnes.d' mts France
28 J5 Arresø L Denmark
106 C9 Arrey New Mexico
45 L4 Arrezzo reg Italy
38 J8 Arriach Austria
125 N9 Arriaga Mexico
106 G2 Arriba Colorado
141 G6 Arrilalah Queensland
28 B6 Arrild Denmark
9 F3 Arrington England
143 B8 Arrino W Australia
12 D1 Arrochar Scotland
133 G4 Arroio Grande Brazil
20 D3 Arromanches France
16 C5 Arronches Portugal
44 M6 Arrone R Italy
18 F9 Arros R France
20 H5 Arrou France
18 H6 Arroux R France
101 Q2 Arrow Cr Montana
117 P10 Arrowhead Br Col
14 C2 Arrow,L Irish Rep
119 O2 Arrow L Ontario
117 O10 Arrow Park Br Col
110 D2 Arrow Rock Missouri
100 K6 Arrowrock Res Idaho
138 F4 Arrowsmith Mt New S Wales
144 C5 Arrowsmith, Mt New Zealand
140 D2 Arrowsmith Pt N Terr Aust
144 B6 Arrowtown New Zealand
118 D8 Arrow Wood Alberta
16 C5 Arroyo de la Luz Spain
108 F6 Arroyo de la Zorra R Mexico
102 D6 Arroyo Grande California
131 F6 Arroyo Grande R Argentina
106 E5 Arroyo Hondo New Mexico
131 F4 Arroyo Negro R Uruguay
103 J8 Arroyo Seco R California
128 F6 Arroyos,L de Los Bolivia
130 B9 Arroyos-y-Esteros Paraguay
130 C4 Arruda Brazil
28 D3 Års Denmark
77 C5 Arsenajan Iran
118 J3 Arsenault L Sask
117 Q3 Arseno L N W Terr
59 K3 Arsen'yev U.S.S.R.
55 C3 Arshinskoye U.S.S.R.
41 O6 Arsiero Italy
76 C4 Arsikere India
52 G6 Arsk U.S.S.R.
26 J9 Årskogen Sweden
45 O5 Arsoli Italy
19 K3 Ars-sur-Moselle France
27 J11 Årsunda Sweden
22 D5 Arsy France
46 D5 Árta Greece
17 K5 Artá Majorca
80 D7 Artas Jordan
98 G4 Artas S Dakota
17 K5 Artá,Sierra de,Mt Majorca
124 H8 Arteaga Mexico
59 K3 Artem U.S.S.R.
126 C3 Artemisa Cuba
51 J3 Artemovak U.S.S.R.
54 G7 Artemovka U.S.S.R.
56 D4 Artemovsk U.S.S.R.
53 F9 Artemovskiy U.S.S.R.
45 N6 Artena Italy
20 J5 Artenay France
33 O10 Artern E Germany
17 H3 Artesa de Segre Spain
Artesia see Mosomane
111 H8 Artesia Mississippi
98 J5 Artesian S Dakota
109 H7 Artesia Wells Texas
26 G6 Artfjallet mt Sweden
121 T6 Arthabaska Quebec
18 E9 Arthez France
110 H2 Arthur Illinois
98 J2 Arthur N Dakota
98 E8 Arthur Nebraska
139 H8 Arthur R Tasmania
109 M2 Arthur City Texas
138 E4 Arthur,L S Australia
139 H8 Arthur,L Tasmania
145 D4 Arthur, Mt New Zealand
142 E4 Arthur, Mt W Australia
141 K5 Arthur Pt Queensland
143 B6 Arthur, R W Australia
144 C5 Arthur's Pass New Zealand
126 G2 Arthur's Town Cat I Bahamas
55 C3 Arti U.S.S.R.
133 F4 Artigas Uruguay
114 J5 Artillery L N W Terr
29 M11 Artjärvi Finland
118 H6 Artland Sask
33 M6 Artlenburg W Germany
102 B2 Artois California
22 C3 Artois prov France
22 D3 Artois Collines d' France
46 E6 Artotína Greece
78 F1 Artova Turkey
Artsakan Nor see Qagan Nur
48 M5 Artsyz U.S.S.R.
87 C8 Artur de Paiva Angola
66 B4 Artux China
71 B1 Aru Halmahera Indonesia
86 F5 Aru Zaïre
129 H6 Aruanã Brazil
126 A2 Aruba isld W Indies
18 E9 Arudy France
80 E8 Arugot R Jordan
136 G3 Aru,Kep islds Moluccas Indonesia
25 D2 Arum Netherlands
128 F4 Arumá Brazil
61 Q12 Arume B Okinawa
75 Q4 Arunachal Pradesh prov India
9 F6 Arundel England
144 C5 Arundel New Zealand
9 F5 Arun,R England
28 E6 Årup Denmark
76 D6 Aruppukkottai India
80 D5 'Arūra Jordan
88 F3 Arusha Tanzania
86 G4 Arusi prov Ethiopia
70 G4 Arus,Tg C Sulawesi Indonesia
70 B5 Arut R Kalimantan
70 E6 Aru,Tg C Kalimantan
83 K9 Aruvi Aru R Sri Lanka
86 D5 Aruwimi R Zaïre
106 E2 Arvada Colorado
101 T5 Arvada Wyoming
26 K7 Arvån Sweden
58 D2 Arvayheer Mongolia
40 D5 Arve R France
26 K5 Arvestuottar mt Sweden
74 H8 Arvi India
115 M8 Arvida Quebec
26 K6 Arvidsjaur Sweden
27 F12 Arvika Sweden
102 F6 Arvin California
94 J9 Arvonia Virginia
65 E1 Arxan China
147 Q9 Ary U.S.S.R.
55 C3 Aryazh U.S.S.R.
47 G9 Aryiroúpolis Crete Greece
55 E4 Aryk-Balyk U.S.S.R.
57 E4 Arys' U.S.S.R.
57 E4 Arys' R U.S.S.R.
57 D2 Arys,Ozero L U.S.S.R.
18 D5 Arz R France
52 F6 Arzamas U.S.S.R.
37 N3 Arzberg W Germany
37 L5 Arzberg mt W Germany
32 K8 Ärzen W Germany
85 D1 Arzew Algeria
36 B3 Arzfeld W Germany
53 F10 Arzgir U.S.S.R.
41 O6 Arzignano Italy
41 N3 Arzl Austria
16 B2 Arzúa Spain
22 K1 As Belgium
37 N3 Aš Czechoslovakia
26 E8 Ås Norway
28 E2 Aså Denmark
27 F14 Åsa Sweden
87 C11 Asab Namibia
74 D1 Asadabad Afghanistan
69 D11 Asahan R Sumatra
61 O10 Asahi Chiba Japan
60 G10 Asahi R Japan
60 Q2 Asahi-dake mt Japan
61 N7 Asahi-dake mt Japan
60 Q2 Asahikawa Japan
61 M9 Asama yama vol Japan
65 G6 Asan Man B S Korea
75 M7 Asansol India
26 G9 Åsarna Sweden
84 F5 Asawanwah Libya
36 C2 Asbach W Germany
71 C3 Asbakin W Irian
55 D3 Asbest U.S.S.R.
121 T7 Asbestos Quebec
89 C7 Asbestos Mts S Africa
107 Q4 Asbury Kansas
110 B4 Asbury Missouri
128 F7 Ascensión Bolivia
124 E2 Ascensión Chihuahua Mexico
126 A1 Ascension Curaçao W I
90 B12 Ascension isld Atlantic Oc
37 O6 Ascha W Germany
38 L5 Aschbach Austria
32 G9 Ascheberg Nordrhein-Westfalen W Germany
33 M4 Ascheberg W Germany
32 F6 Aschendorf W Germany
20 J5 Aschères-le Marche France
33 O9 Aschersleben E Germany
17 H3 Asco Spain
12 C2 Ascog Scotland
42 F6 Ascoli Piceno Italy
9 F5 Ascot England
141 K1 Ascot dist Brisbane, Qnsld
133 D2 Ascotán Chile
27 H14 Åseda Sweden
85 E4 Asedjrad hills Algeria
53 H7 Asekeyevo U.S.S.R.
26 J7 Åsele Sweden
86 G4 Aselle Ethiopia
26 E8 Åsen Norway
27 G10 Åsen Sweden
32 K7 Asendorf W Germany
47 G3 Asenovgrad Bulgaria
27 B13 Åseral Norway
22 G5 Asfeld-la-ville France
27 D12 Asgårdstr Norway
55 C3 Asha U.S.S.R.
52 J5 Ashan U.S.S.R.
80 C8 Ashan R Israel
55 C3 Ashap U.S.S.R.
77 A4 Ashar Iran
9 E1 Ashbourne England
112 D6 Ashburn Georgia
8 C6 Ashburton England
144 C5 Ashburton New Zealand
142 B6 Ashburton R W Australia
143 C6 Ashburton, R W Australia
140 C4 Ashburton Ra N Terr Aust
9 E4 Ashbury England
95 N6 Ashbury Park New Jersey
99 L3 Ashby Minnesota
9 E2 Ashby de la Zouch England
57 D2 Ashchikol', Ozero L U.S.S.R.
57 C1 Ashchitastysor, Ozero L U.S.S.R.
114 G7 Ashcroft Br Columbia
80 B6 Ashdod Israel
109 N2 Ash Down Arkansas
9 G5 Ashdown Forest England
112 H2 Asheboro N Carolina
107 O7 Asher Oklahoma
119 T7 Ashern Manitoba
108 H7 Asherton Texas
112 E2 Asheville N Carolina
110 E5 Ash Flat Arkansas
113 D11 Ashford Alabama
9 G5 Ashford Kent England
100 C3 Ashford Washington
9 E5 Ashford Hill England
103 M6 Ashfork Arizona
107 M2 Ash Grove Kansas
110 C4 Ash Grove Missouri
141 K1 Ashgrove dist Brisbane, Qnsld
145 E4 Ashhurst New Zealand
60 Q2 Ashibetsu Japan
61 N9 Ashikaga Japan
9 F6 Ashington W Sussex England
61 N9 Ashio Japan
52 G6 Ashit R U.S.S.R.
60 J11 Ashiya Japan
60 G13 Ashizuri-misaki C Japan
77 D4 Ashkazar Iran
77 F1 Ashkhabad Iran
50 E5 Ashkhabad U.S.S.R.
13 F3 Ashkirk Scotland
99 T9 Ashkum Illinois
111 L8 Ashland Alabama
110 F2 Ashland Illinois
107 L4 Ashland Kansas
94 E8 Ashland Kentucky
95 S7 Ashland Maine
101 T4 Ashland Montana
98 K8 Ashland Nebraska
95 Q3 Ashland New Hampshire
94 E6 Ashland Ohio
100 C7 Ashland Oregon
95 L6 Ashland Pennsylvania
94 K9 Ashland Virginia
99 Q3 Ashland Wisconsin
110 J5 Ashland City Tennessee
110 G3 Ashley Illinois
94 C3 Ashley Michigan
98 G3 Ashley N Dakota
144 D5 Ashley New Zealand
120 K4 Ashley Mine Ontario
55 E3 Ashlyk R U.S.S.R.
118 F4 Ashmont Alberta
108 E3 Ashmore Texas
142 E1 Ashmore Reef Timor Sea
79 A8 Ashmûn Egypt
80 F1 Ashmura Syria
95 N5 Ashokan Res New York
60 R2 Ashorobuto Japan
80 B7 Ashqelon Israel
78 J4 Ash Sharqat Iraq
94 G5 Ashtabula Ohio
98 J2 Ashtabula,L N Dakota
74 F9 Ashti India
77 A2 Ashtiān Iran
101 O5 Ashton Idaho
99 R8 Ashton Illinois
94 B3 Ashton Michigan
121 O7 Ashton Ontario
98 H5 Ashton S Dakota
142 F3 Ashton Ra W Australia
13 F6 Ashton-under-Lyne England
115 N7 Ashuanipi,L Labrador
121 R3 Ashuapmuchuan R Quebec
78 J4 Ashur Iraq
78 J6 Ashuriyah, Al Iraq
111 K8 Ashville Alabama
79 G3 'Āsi R Syria/Lebanon
42 D3 Asiago Italy
71 C2 Asia Pulau Pulau islds Indonesia
71 F4 Asid Gulf Philippines
124 H6 Asientos Mexico
45 K1 Asigliano Ven Italy
85 C1 Asilah Morocco
71 A1 Asimiro Halmahera Indonesia
43 B7 Asinara isld Sardinia
43 B7 Asinara, Golfo dell' Sardinia
56 C3 Asino U.S.S.R.
75 L9 Aska India
53 D10 Askaniya Nova U.S.S.R.
55 C4 Askarovo U.S.S.R.
14 C4 Askeaton Adare Irish Rep
27 D12 Asker Norway
13 G6 Askern England
27 G13 Askersund Sweden
83 H1 Askhabad Iran
26 J7 Åskilje Sweden
27 E12 Askim Norway
112 K2 Askin N Carolina
55 C3 Askino U.S.S.R.
28 G7 Askø Denmark
29 M11 Askola Finland
65 J3 Askol'd, O isld U.S.S.R.
28 C6 Askov Denmark
99 O3 Askov Minnesota
13 F5 Askrigg England
27 A10 Askvoll Norway
79 C9 Asl Egypt
47 K5 Aslanapa Turkey
74 D1 Asmar Afghanistan
86 G2 Asmara Ethiopia
28 K5 Asminderød Denmark
28 G5 Asnæs Denmark
28 F5 Asnæs pen Denmark
85 E1 Asnam, El Algeria
20 D3 Asnelles France
27 G15 Åsnen Sweden
27 E11 Åsnes Norway
129 G3 Asoenangka Brazil
45 J1 Asola Italy
60 E13 Aso Nat. Park Japan
86 F3 Asosa Ethiopia
86 G1 Asoteriba, Jebel mt Sudan
100 H3 Asotin Washington
85 E3 Asouf watercourse Algeria
60 C11 Asō-wan B Japan
60 E13 Aso zan vol Japan
36 G6 Aspach W Germany
48 C3 Aspang Austria
26 G8 Aspås Sweden
13 E4 Aspatria England
17 G6 Aspe Spain
26 J8 Aspeå Sweden
106 D2 Aspen Colorado
101 P8 Aspen Wyoming
118 D6 Aspen Beach Prov. Park Alberta
36 G6 Asperg W Germany
28 D6 Asperup Denmark
144 B6 Aspiring, Mt New Zealand
19 P16 Aspremont France
46 D5 Asprókavos, Akr C Greece
43 G10 Aspromonte mts Italy
123 M7 Aspy B C Breton I, N Scotia
118 K6 Asquith Sask
86 H3 Assab Ethiopia
74 D1 Assad-Abad Afghanistan
86 H3 Assale, L Ethiopia
75 O5 Assam prov India
95 M8 Assateague I Maryland
22 G2 Asse Belgium
19 Q17 Asse R France
119 V2 Assean L Manitoba
89 G6 Assegai R Swaziland
85 F3 Assekaifaf Algeria
85 F4 Assekreme mt Algeria
32 K5 Assel W Germany
20 E5 Asse-la-Boisne France
22 K3 Asselborn Luxembourg
25 G3 Assen Netherlands
36 F3 Assenheim W Germany
28 E3 Assens Århus Denmark
28 D6 Assens Fyn Denmark
22 J3 Assesse Belgium
122 G2 Assigny,L Quebec
118 L9 Assinboia Sask
28 B4 Assing Denmark
114 J8 Assiniboia Sask
114 H7 Assiniboine,Mt Br Col/Alberta
119 Q8 Assiniboine R Manitoba/Sask
46 F4 Ássiros Greece
129 H8 Assis Brazil
42 E5 Assisi Italy
36 D3 Assmannshausen W Germany
41 K6 Asso Italy
110 G2 Assumption Illinois
87 H9 Assumption isld Seychelles
78 K5 As Suwayrah Iraq
36 C5 Assweiler W Germany
37 N7 Ast W Germany
27 E10 Asta R Norway
18 F8 Astaffort France
47 H9 Astakidha isld Greece
46 E6 Astakós Greece
77 A1 Astaneh Iran
28 E2 Åsted Nordjylland Denmark
28 B3 Åsted Viborg Denmark
25 E6 Asten Netherlands
77 C1 Asterabad Iran
44 D2 Asti Italy
16 E1 Astillero Spain
Astin Tagh mt ra see Altun Shan
47 H8 Astipálaia isld Greece
9 E1 Aston England
8 D3 Aston Cross England
74 F1 Astor Kashmir
16 C2 Astorga Spain
99 Q9 Astoria Illinois
114 G8 Astoria Oregon
98 K5 Astoria S Dakota
27 F15 Åstorp Sweden
121 L6 Astorville Ontario
87 H10 Astove isld Br Indian Oc Terr
53 G10 Astrakhan' U.S.S.R.
55 E5 Astrakhanka U.S.S.R.
26 L7 Åsträsk Sweden
46 F7 Astros Greece
28 E6 Åstrup Fyn Denmark
28 B5 Åstrup Ribe Denmark
28 D6 Åstrup Sønderjylland Denmark
28 D5 Åstrup Vejle Denmark
28 J7 Åstrup isld Storstrøm Denmark
16 E2 Astudillo Spain
45 N7 Astura R Italy
16 C1 Asturias reg Spain
9 F3 Astwood England
28 E6 Åsum Denmark
133 F3 Asunción Paraguay
27 H14 Asunden L Sweden
28 E5 As Vig B Denmark
84 J5 Aswân Egypt
84 J5 Aswan High Dam Egypt
84 J4 Asyût Egypt
48 E3 Aszód Hungary
137 R6 Ata isld Pacific Oc

Barielly — Bela
9

74 H4 Barielly India
44 G2 Barigazzo Monte Italy
85 F1 Barika Algeria
128 F2 Barima,Pta C Venezuela
127 J10 Barinas Venezuela
128 D2 Barinas Venezuela
110 D1 Baring Missouri
100 D2 Baring Washington
143 B6 Baring Downs W Australia
143 E10 Baring, Mt W Australia
28 D5 Båring Vig B Denmark
127 J10 Barinitas Venezuela
75 M8 Baripada India
130 E8 Bariri Brazil
84 J5 Bâris Egypt
22 E4 Barisis France
70 D5 Barito R Kalimantan
19 Q17 Barjaude mt France
19 P17 Barjols France
84 E4 Barjuj watercourse Libya
28 K4 Barkåkra Sweden
58 D5 Barkam China
27 H11 Barken,N L Sweden
94 J3 Barker New York
143 D9 Barker L W Australia
117 N9 Barkerville Br Columbia
94 H5 Barkeyville Pennsylvania
9 G4 Barking England
120 H6 Bark L Ontario
110 J5 Barkley Res Kentucky
100 A1 Barkley Sound Br Columbia
140 E5 Barkly Downs Queensland
140 D4 Barkly Highway rd N Terr Aust
140 B5 Barkly, Mt N Terr Aust
136 H5 Barkly Tableland Qnsld/N Terr
89 D7 Barkly West S Africa
66 E3 Barkol China
99 T4 Bark River Michigan
108 G6 Barksdale Texas
47 L6 Barla Dağ mt Turkey
9 E1 Barlborough England
19 J4 Bar le Duc France
143 C8 Barlee L W Australia
143 B6 Barlee Ra W Australia
8 C5 Barle, R England
19 Q16 Barles France
43 G7 Barletta Italy
22 D3 Barlin France
31 J3 Barlinek Poland
27 K14 Barlingbo isld Gotland Sweden
32 E9 Barlo W Germany
32 L4 Barlohe W Germany
98 G2 Barlow N Dakota
100 D4 Barlow Pass Oregon
57 L2 Barlyk, Khr mts U.S.S.R.
13 H6 Barmby England
139 H5 Barmedman New S Wales
74 D6 Barmer India
138 F5 Barmera S Australia
8 B2 Barmouth Wales
32 L5 Barmstedt W Germany
122 G7 Barnaby River New Brunswick
74 F7 Barnagar India
107 N2 Barnard Kansas
98 H4 Barnard S Dakota
13 G4 Barnard Castle England
117 E6 Barnard,Mt Br Col/Alaska
37 N4 Bärnau W Germany
56 B4 Barnaul U.S.S.R.
56 B4 Barnaulka R U.S.S.R.
139 H8 Barn Bluff mt Tasmania
9 E1 Barnby Moor England
95 N7 Barnegat New Jersey
146 H7 Barne Inlet Antarctica
107 O2 Barnes Kansas
94 J6 Barnesboro Pennsylvania
115 M3 Barnes Icecap N W Terr
113 G12 Barnes Sd Florida
98 K9 Barneston Nebraska
112 C4 Barnesville Georgia
98 K3 Barnesville Minnesota
9 F4 Barnet England
25 E4 Barneveld Netherlands
20 B3 Barneville France
33 R7 Barnewitz E Germany
99 M8 Barney Iowa
103 N4 Barney Top mt Utah
108 F4 Barnhart Texas
33 T7 Barnim reg E Germany
122 F5 Barn Mtn Quebec
107 O5 Barnsdall Oklahoma
13 G6 Barnsley England
95 R5 Barnstable Massachusetts
8 B5 Barnstaple England
8 C6 Barnstaple Cross England
95 Q3 Barnstead New Hampshire
32 H7 Barnstorf W Germany
32 K9 Barntrup W Germany
99 O3 Barnum Minnesota
118 E9 Barnwell Alberta
112 F4 Barnwell S Carolina
37 P6 Bärnzell W Germany
85 F7 Baro Nigeria
86 F4 Baro R Ethiopia
Baroda see Vadodara
145 D4 Barometer mt New Zealand
22 K5 Baroncourt France
45 R8 Baronissi Italy
19 O16 Baronnies, Les reg France
118 D9 Barons Alberta
143 F6 Baron's Ra W Australia
36 B6 Baronville France
87 D8 Barotseland reg Zambia
75 O5 Barpeta India
80 D4 Barqay Israel
99 U4 Barques, Pt. Aux Michigan
127 K9 Barquisimeto Venezuela
98 B10 Barr Colorado
19 K4 Barr France
12 D3 Barr Scotland
129 K6 Barra Brazil
15 A3 Barra isld Scotland
130 E8 Barra Bonita Brazil
130 G5 Barracão Brazil
128 G5 Barracão do Barreto Brazil
89 B10 Barracouta,C S Africa
129 K6 Barra da Estiva Brazil
124 G8 Barra de Navidad Mexico
130 H8 Barra de sã João Brazil
130 B4 Barra do Bugres Brazil
129 J5 Barra do Corda Brazil
130 H6 Barra do Cuieté Brazil
87 B7 Barra do Dande Angola
130 D4 Barra do Garças Brazil
130 F6 Barra do Paraopeba Brazil
130 G8 Barra do Pirai Brazil
129 G5 Barra do São Manuel Brazil
87 G10 Barra Falsa,Pta.da Mozambique
16 B5 Barragem de Maranhão res Portugal
16 B5 Barragem de Montargil Res Portugal
16 B5 Barragem do Castello do Bode Portugal
138 E6 Barrages S Australia
15 A4 Barra Head Scotland
129 K8 Barra Mansa Brazil
128 C4 Barranca Peru
128 D2 Barrancabermeja Colombia
127 H9 Barrancas Colombia
127 N10 Barrancas Venezuela
131 F2 Barrancas R Corrientes Argentina
131 B6 Barrancas,R Mendoza Argentina
130 B7 Barranco Branco Brazil
16 C6 Barrancos Portugal
133 F3 Barranqueras Argentina
126 G9 Barranquilla Colombia
13 F3 Barrasford England
121 N4 Barraute Quebec
19 P14 Barraux France
17 F5 Barrax Spain
95 P4 Barre Massachusetts
95 P2 Barre Vermont
20 G4 Barre-en-Ouche,la France
129 K6 Barreiras Brazil
129 G4 Barreirinha Brazil
129 K4 Barreirinhas Brazil
16 A6 Barreiro Portugal
130 D4 Barreiro R Brazil
130 J10 Barreiros Brazil
110 K5 Barren R Kentucky
68 A6 Barren I Andaman Is
116 L7 Barren Is Alaska
19 P16 Barret de Lioure France
129 J8 Barretos Brazil
102 H9 Barrett L California
142 F4 Barrett, Mt W Australia
118 C4 Barrhead Alberta
12 D2 Barrhead Scotland
15 D5 Barrhill Scotland
8 C5 Barri Wales
115 M9 Barrie Ontario
120 H7 Barrie I Ontario
145 E2 Barrier, C New Zealand
117 N10 Barrière Br Columbia
99 S7 Barrington Illinois
141 H8 Barrington New S Wales
122 G10 Barrington Nova Scotia
119 R1 Barrington L Manitoba
141 H8 Barringun New S Wales
129 L6 Barris R Brazil
28 D5 Barrit Denmark
101 M9 Barro Utah
130 E4 Barro Alto Brazil
100 E1 Barron Washington
99 P4 Barron Wisconsin
99 P4 Barronett Wisconsin
141 H3 Barron Falls & Gorge Queensland
109 J8 Barroso Texas
124 J4 Barroterán Mexico
21 G8 Barrou France
116 J1 Barrow Alaska
133 E5 Barrow Argentina
14 E4 Barrow R Irish Rep
140 D2 Barrow, C N Terr Aust
140 C5 Barrow Creek N Terr Aust
142 B5 Barrow I W Australia
13 E5 Barrow-in-Furness England
147 M2 Barrow,Pt Alaska
141 G2 Barrow Pt Queensland
143 F7 Barrow Ra W Australia
119 Q6 Barrows Manitoba
115 K3 Barrow Str N W Terr
143 D7 Barr Smith Ra W Australia
16 E2 Barruelo de Santullán Spain
110 E2 Barry Illinois
13 F1 Barry Scotland
121 N7 Barrys Bay Ontario
94 B3 Barryton Michigan
144 C5 Barrytown New Zealand
95 N5 Barryville New York
28 H6 Bårse Denmark
28 K5 Barsebäckshamn Sweden
76 B1 Barsi India
32 K8 Barsinghausen W Germany
28 D6 Barsø isld Denmark
32 G6 Barssel W Germany
102 G7 Barstow California
108 D4 Barstow Texas
54 J2 Barsuki U.S.S.R.
19 J4 Bar-sur-Aube France
18 H4 Bar-sur-Seine France
80 D4 Barta'a Jordan
36 H5 Bartenstein W Germany
116 Q1 Barter I Alaska
30 G1 Barth E Germany
146 B14 Barth Bank Antarctica
33 R4 Barthe R E Germany
81 B15 Barth Seamount S Atlantic Oc
122 G6 Bartibog New Brunswick
128 G2 Bartica Guyana
78 D1 Bartin Turkey
100 D8 Bartle California
141 H3 Bartle Frere,Mt Queensland
103 O2 Bartles,Mt Utah
107 P5 Bartlesville Oklahoma
98 H8 Bartlett Nebraska
95 Q2 Bartlett New Hampshire
109 K5 Bartlett Texas
143 E8 Bartlett Bluff W Australia
117 O4 Bartlett L N W Terr
103 N8 Bartlett Res Arizona
123 P3 Bartlett's Harbour Nfld
143 E8 Bartlett Soak L W Australia
98 F9 Bartley Nebraska
117 G8 Bartolome, C Alaska
87 G10 Bartolomeu Dias Mozambique
13 H6 Barton Humberside England
13 F6 Barton Lancs England
98 F1 Barton N Dakota
71 D5 Barton Palawan Philippines
138 C4 Barton S Australia
95 P2 Barton Vermont
94 D2 Barton City Michigan
9 G3 Barton Mills England
31 M1 Bartoszyce Poland
121 N4 Bartoville Quebec
33 S5 Bartow E Germany
113 F10 Bartow Florida
112 E5 Bartow Georgia
126 G9 Barú, I. de Colombia
69 E12 Barumun R Sumatra
70 O10 Barung isld Java
69 D11 Barus Sumatra
33 S8 Baruth E Germany
58 F2 Baruun Urt Mongolia
15 B2 Barvas Scotland
22 J3 Barvaux Belgium
54 J8 Barvenkovo U.S.S.R.
74 G7 Barwah India
74 F7 Barwani India
33 N7 Barwedel W Germany
113 D7 Barwick Georgia
99 N1 Barwick Ontario
143 D7 Barwidgee W Australia
140 B2 Barwolla, Mt N Terr Aust
141 F7 Baryulah Queensland
80 F7 Barza Jordan
77 D6 Basaidu Iran
106 D2 Basalt Colorado
101 N6 Basalt Idaho
102 F3 Basalt Nevada
141 H4 Basalt R Queensland
86 C5 Basankusu Zaïre
48 L6 Basarabi Romania
57 G2 Basaral, Ozero L U.S.S.R.
71 F6 Basay Negros Philippines
71 E8 Basbas Philippines
131 B2 Bascuñán,C Chile
32 K6 Basdahl W Germany
33 S7 Basdorf E Germany
22 F2 Basècles Belgium
40 G2 Basel Switzerland
40 G3 Baselland canton Switzerland
43 G8 Basento R Italy
48 K2 Başeul R Romania
71 G5 Basey Samar Philippines
77 F6 Bashākerd, Kūhhā-ye mts Iran
118 E6 Bashaw Alberta
56 B5 Bashchelakskiy Khrebet mts U.S.S.R.
89 F9 Bashee R S Africa
57 C5 Bashir U.S.S.R.
56 C5 Bashkaus R U.S.S.R.
50 E3 Bashkirskaya ASSR U.S.S.R.
71 F3 Basiad Bay Luzon Philippines
71 H5 Basiano Sulawesi Indonesia
71 F7 Basilan isld Mindanao Philippines
71 F7 Basilan Str Mindanao Philippines
9 G4 Basildon England
111 D11 Basile Louisiana
43 G8 Basilicata prov Italy
101 N3 Basin Montana
101 R5 Basin Wyoming
113 F10 Basinger Florida
9 E5 Basingstoke England
119 M6 Basin L Sask
95 U1 Baskahegan L Maine
78 K2 Båskåle Turkey
121 P6 Baskatong, Rés Quebec
142 D3 Baskerville, C W Australia
Basle see Basel
9 E1 Baslow England
26 G5 Båsmoen Norway
41 H5 Basodino mt Switzerland
86 D5 Basoko Zaïre
86 D6 Basongo Zaïre
126 A2 Basora,Pt Aruba W I
77 A4 Basra Iran
83 G1 Basra Iraq
36 D6 Bas Rhin dep France
118 E8 Bassano Alberta
42 D3 Bassano Italy
85 E7 Bassari Togo
81 A8 Bassas da India isld Mozambique Chan
33 R5 Basse E Germany
22 D3 Bassée, la France
68 B4 Bassein Burma
76 A1 Bassein India
142 B1 Bassendean dist Perth, W Aust
22 K2 Bassenge Belgium
13 E4 Bassenthwaite L England
127 L4 Basse Pointe Martinique W I
127 M4 Basse Terre Guadeloupe W I
127 P4 Basseterre St Kitts W I
127 O3 Basse Terre Trinidad
98 G7 Bassett Nebraska
103 O9 Bassett Pk Arizona
22 F1 Bassevelde Belgium
111 G10 Bassfield Mississippi
85 E7 Bassila Benin
22 F2 Bassilly Belgium
102 E4 Bass Lake California
33 T10 Basslitz E Germany
122 J8 Bass River Nova Scotia
15 F4 Bass Rock Scotland
139 H7 Bass Strait Tasmania
32 J7 Bassum W Germany
119 R8 Basswood Manitoba
99 P1 Basswood L Ontario
19 P13 Bassy France
27 F15 Båstad Sweden
77 D6 Bastak Iran
77 D1 Bastam Iran
18 M10 Bastia Corsica
45 J2 Bastiglia Italy
123 M2 Bastille,L Quebec
22 K3 Bastogne Belgium
112 E4 Bastonville Georgia
111 E9 Bastrop Louisiana
109 K5 Bastrop Texas
26 L7 Bastuträsk Sweden
Basuo see Dongfang
Basutoland see Lesotho
55 D2 Bas'yanovskiy U.S.S.R.
86 B7 Bas Zaïre prov Zaïre
86 A5 Bata Equat Guinea
85 F8 Bata Mbini Eq Guinea
71 E3 Bataan Penin Luzon Philippines
126 C3 Batabanó, G. de Cuba
71 E1 Batac Luzon Philippines
71 G4 Batag isld Philippines
130 D7 Bataguaçu Brazil
47 G3 Batak Bulgaria
70 E5 Batakan Kalimantan
47 G3 Batak Dam Bulgaria
74 F3 Batala India
16 B5 Batalha Portugal
51 M2 Batamay U.S.S.R.
71 G4 Batan isld Philippines
58 C5 Batang China
70 M9 Batang Java
86 C4 Batangafo Cent Afr Republic
71 E4 Batangas Luzon Philippines
71 C3 Batangpele Waigeo Indonesia
69 D12 Batangtoru Sumatra
71 C3 Batanta isld W Irian
48 E4 Bataszék Hungary
130 F7 Batatais Brazil
Batavia see Jakarta
133 D4 Batavia Argentina
99 S8 Batavia Illinois
94 J3 Batavia New York
110 M2 Batavia Ohio
54 L9 Bataysk U.S.S.R.
71 E5 Batbatan Panay Philippines
120 F6 Batchawana Ontario
140 B2 Batchelor N Terr Aust
69 B10 Bateemucica, Gunung mt Sumatra
88 B6 Batembo Zaïre
61 P13 Baten Okinawa
25 E5 Batenburg Netherlands
56 D4 Batenevskiy Kryazh ridge U.S.S.R.
103 J9 Bateques Mexico
101 O6 Bates Idaho
100 G5 Bates Oregon
112 F4 Batesburg S Carolina
98 D6 Batesland S Dakota
143 E7 Bates,Mt W Australia
143 D7 Bates Ra W Australia
110 E6 Batesville Arkansas
110 L2 Batesville Indiana
111 G7 Batesville Mississippi
109 H7 Batesville Texas
52 D5 Batetskiy U.S.S.R.
8 D5 Bath England
110 F1 Bath Illinois
127 M3 Bath Jamaica
95 S3 Bath Maine
112 L2 Bath N Carolina
127 P4 Bath Nevis W I
122 E7 Bath New Brunswick
95 K4 Bath New York
112 F4 Bath S Carolina
98 H4 Bath S Dakota
86 C3 Batha R Chad
68 G6 Batheay Cambodia
98 J1 Bathgate N Dakota
12 E2 Bathgate Scotland
122 G6 Bathurst New Brunswick
139 J5 Bathurst New S Wales
Bathurst The Gambia see Banjul
141 G2 Bathurst Bay Queensland
114 G3 Bathurst,C N W Terr
136 G4 Bathurst I N Terr Australia
115 K2 Bathurst I N W Terr
114 J4 Bathurst Inlet N W Terr
142 E3 Bathurst Is W Australia
140 B1 Bathurst Island Mission Sta N Terr Aust
85 D7 Batié Upper Volta
70 G6 Batikala,Tg B Sulawesi Indonesia
48 E5 Batina Yugoslavia
78 L7 Batin, Wadi al Iraq
121 S6 Batiscan Quebec
121 T5 Batiscan,L Quebec
77 C3 Batlag-e-Gavkhuni Iran
13 G6 Batley England
85 F1 Batna Algeria
71 F4 Bato,L Luzon Philippines
111 E11 Baton Rouge Louisiana
86 B5 Batouri Cameroon
130 D4 Batovi Brazil
68 H7 Ba Tri Vietnam
42 H3 Batrina Yugoslavia
79 F4 Batroun Lebanon
26 R1 Båtsfjord Norway
80 D3 Bat Shelomo Israel
45 L1 Battáglia Terme Italy
68 F6 Battambang Cambodia
140 D3 Batten R N Terr Aust
36 F1 Battenberg W Germany
146 F12 Batterbee Mts Antarctica
143 C6 Batthewmurnarna mt W Aust
83 L10 Batticaloa Sri Lanka
22 K2 Battice Belgium
69 A8 Batti Malv isld Nicobar Is
45 R8 Battipaglia Italy
9 G6 Battle England
100 J7 Battle Cr Idaho
101 Q1 Battle Cr Montana
98 J8 Battle Cr Nebraska
140 B3 Battle Cr N Terr Aust
94 B4 Battle Creek Michigan
118 H9 Battle Creek Sask
118 J6 Battleford Sask
118 J5 Battlefords Prov.Park,The Sask
100 C4 Battle Ground Washington
115 O7 Battle Harbour Labrador
102 G1 Battle Mt Nevada
118 F6 Battle R Alberta
118 H6 Battle R Sask
98 D1 Battleview N Dakota
48 G4 Battonya Hungary
118 J8 Battrum Sask
70 D4 Batuajau, Bt mt Kalimantan
71 H8 Batuata isld Indonesia
69 H14 Batubetumbang Indonesia
70 D3 Batu Bora mt Sarawak
70 D4 Batubrok, Bt mt Kalimantan
70 G5 Batudaka Indonesia
70 C4 Batuensambang mt Kalimantan
69 E10 Batu Gajah Malaysia
71 H5 Batuhitam,Tg C Sulawesi Indonesia
71 L10 Batuidu Roti Indonesia
70 D4 Batuilangmebang, G mt Kalimantan
70 D4 Batukelau Kalimantan
70 P10 Batukou, Bt mt Bali Indonesia
70 D6 Batulitjin Kalimantan
70 D3 Batu Mabun mt Sarawak
78 H1 Batumi U.S.S.R.
69 D12 Batumundam Sumatra
69 F12 Batu Pahat Malaysia
69 C13 Batu,Pulaupulau isld Indonesia
70 F4 Batuputih Kalimantan
70 K8 Baturadja Sumatra Indonesia
70 N9 Baturetno Java
52 D6 Baturino U.S.S.R.
129 L4 Baturité Brazil
69 H14 Baturusa Indonesia
70 F3 Batu Tg B Kalimantan
70 C5 Batutinggi Kalimantan
80 B5 Bat Yam Israel
18 C4 Batz,I.de France
71 H7 Baubau Sulawesi Indonesia
86 A3 Bauchi Nigeria
18 C5 Baud France
75 L8 Baudh India
128 C2 Baudo, Sa. de mts Colombia
21 I7 Baudres France
19 Q17 Bauduen France
21 E6 Baugé France
19 Q13 Bauges dist France
140 D3 Bauhinia Downs N Terr Aust
141 J6 Bauhinia Downs Queensland
70 G7 Baula Sulawesi Indonesia
123 R2 Bauld,C Nfld
18 D5 Baule,la France
21 B6 Baulon France
41 J3 Bauma Switzerland
9 F1 Baumber England
19 K5 Baume les Dames France
33 T6 Baumgarten E Germany
37 O7 Baumgarten W Germany
36 C4 Baumholder W Germany
71 L10 Baun Timor Indonesia
37 K4 Baunach W Germany
37 K3 Baunach R W Germany
58 F1 Baunt U.S.S.R.
141 L7 Bauple Queensland
128 F6 Baures Bolivia
130 E8 Bauru Brazil
130 D6 Baús Brazil
52 B6 Bauska U.S.S.R.
31 H4 Bautzen E Germany
109 P1 Bauxite Arkansas
21 I8 Bauzanne R France
126 E10 Bavano L. Panama
107 N3 Bavaria Kansas
22 F3 Bavay France
89 C9 Baviaanskloofberge mts S Africa
124 E2 Bavispe Mexico
9 H2 Bawdeswell England
9 H3 Bawdsey England
70 O8 Bawean isld Java
32 F7 Bawinkel W Germany
84 H4 Bawîti Egypt
120 D3 Bawk Ontario
85 D6 Bawku Ghana
68 C3 Bawlake Burma
118 E6 Bawlf Alberta
68 A2 Bawli Bazar Burma
68 B4 Bawmi Burma
13 G6 Bawtry England
68 F1 Ba Xat Vietnam
58 G4 Ba Xian China
67 B2 Ba Xian China
66 D4 Baxkorgan China
112 E6 Baxley Georgia
99 N8 Baxter Iowa
99 M3 Baxter Minnesota
101 S10 Baxter Mt Colorado
110 B4 Baxter Springs Kansas
122 C7 Baxter State Park Maine
80 D3 Bayada Israel
126 F4 Bayamo Cuba
127 L5 Bayamón Puerto Rico
59 J2 Bayan China
58 E2 Bayan Mongolia
58 E2 Bayanchandman Mongolia
56 G4 Bayanday U.S.S.R.
Bayan Gol see Dengkou
58 C5 Bayan Har Shan China
58 D2 Bayanhongor Mongolia
65 E1 Bayan Hot China
65 A3 Bayan Hure China
Bayan Huxu see Horqin Youyi Zhongqi
58 E2 Bayanmönh Mongolia
65 C3 Bayan Nur Sum China
58 E3 Bayan Obo China
58 C3 Bayan-Öndör Mongolia
Bayan Qagan see Qahar Youyi Houqi
65 A1 Bayan Qagan China
65 E2 Bayan Qagan China
58 E2 Bayantsogt Mongolia
113 F7 Bayard Florida
99 M8 Bayard Iowa
98 C8 Bayard Nebraska
94 H7 Bayard W Virginia
19 Q15 Bayard, Col pass France
47 L6 Bayat Turkey
71 F6 Bayawan Negros Philippines
71 G5 Baybay Leyte Philippines
112 L2 Bayboro N Carolina
123 U6 Bay Bulls Nfld
78 H1 Bayburt Turkey
69 H8 Bay Canh, Hon isld Vietnam
94 D3 Bay City Michigan
100 B4 Bay City Oregon
109 M7 Bay City Texas
99 O5 Bay City Wisconsin
84 G3 Baydā,Al Libya
50 F2 Baydaratskaya Guba gulf U.S.S.R.
123 U5 Bay de Verde Nfld
123 R6 Bay du Nord Nfld
57 E3 Baydzhansay U.S.S.R.
37 P5 Bayer-Eisenstein W Germany
41 O2 Bayerische Alpen mt W Germany
37 K5 Bayern land W Germany
20 D3 Bayeux France
120 J9 Bayfield Ontario
99 Q3 Bayfield Wisconsin
123 O2 Bayfield I Quebec
122 E5 Bayfield Mtn Quebec
57 D3 Baygakum U.S.S.R.
55 D4 Baygara U.S.S.R.
98 A4 Bay Horse Montana
47 J6 Bayindir Turkey
55 D3 Baykalovo U.S.S.R.
56 G4 Baykal,Ozero L U.S.S.R.
56 G4 Baykal'skiy Khrebet mts U.S.S.R.
57 C2 Bay-Khozha U.S.S.R.
55 C3 Baykibashevo U.S.S.R.
56 E1 Baykit U.S.S.R.
57 D1 Baykonyr U.S.S.R.
71 E3 Bay, Laguna de Luzon Philippines
123 R6 Bay l'Argent Nfld
140 E3 Bayley Pt Queensland
55 C4 Baymak U.S.S.R.
111 J11 Bay Minette Alabama
9 E4 Baynard's Green England
71 E2 Bayombong Luzon Philippines
19 K4 Bayon France
16 B2 Bayona Spain
18 E9 Bayonne France
71 E5 Bayo Pt Panay Philippines
111 E7 Bayou Bartholomew R Arkansas
111 D9 Bayou D'Arbonne Louisiana
110 E6 Bayou de View R Arkansas
111 H11 Bayou La Batre Alabama
111 F12 Bayou Lafourche R Louisiana
111 E9 Bayou Macon R Louisiana
111 E7 Bayou Meto R Arkansas
111 F9 Bayou Pierre R Mississippi
128 B5 Bayovar Peru
113 E9 Bayport Florida
94 D3 Bay Port Michigan
99 O5 Bayport Minnesota
117 K10 Bay Pt Br Col
71 D5 Bay Pt Philippines
47 H5 Bayramiç Turkey
37 M4 Bayreuth W Germany
37 N5 Bayrischer Wald mts W Germany
123 T6 Bay Roberts Nfld
58 F1 Baysa U.S.S.R.
111 G11 Bay St.Louis Mississippi
113 F11 Bayshore Florida
95 O6 Bay Shore Long I, N Y
112 E1 Bays Mt Tennessee
111 G10 Bay Springs Mississippi
Baytag Bogdo see Baytik Shan
9 G3 Baythorn End England
66 E2 Baytik Shan mt ra China/Mongolia
109 N6 Baytown Texas
117 P12 Bayview Idaho
145 F3 Bay View New Zealand
17 F7 Baza Spain
48 K1 Bazaliya U.S.S.R.
22 G5 Bazancourt France
107 O3 Bazar Kansas
87 G10 Bazaruto, I Mozambique
18 E8 Bazas France
17 F7 Baza,Sierra de Spain
22 J4 Bazeilles France
67 B1 Bazhong China
48 G6 Baziaş Romania
18 G9 Baziége France
121 Q5 Bazin R Quebec
107 L3 Bazine Kansas
77 G5 Bazmām, Kūh-e mt Iran
77 F6 Bazman Iran
20 G5 Bazoche-Gouet,la France
22 F5 Bazoches France
20 E4 Bazoches-au-Houlme France
20 K5 Bazoches-les-Gallerandes France
20 F4 Bazoches-sur-Hoëne France
20 F5 Bazoge,la France
21 C8 Bazoges-en-Paillers France
20 D5 Bazougers France
20 B5 Bazouges la Perouse France
45 K3 Bazzano Italy
79 F4 Bcharre Lebanon
112 E6 Beach Georgia
98 C3 Beach N Dakota
95 N7 Beach Haven New Jersey
138 E6 Beachport S Australia
95 N7 Beachwood New Jersey
9 G6 Beachy Head England
95 O5 Beacon New York
143 C9 Beacon W Australia
113 B8 Beacon Hill Florida
118 H4 Beacon Hill Sask
9 F4 Beaconsfield England
139 H8 Beaconsfield Tasmania
13 G2 Beadnell England
142 E3 Beagle Bank W Australia
142 E3 Beagle Bay W Australia
133 D8 Beagle, Canal str Chile/Arg
140 A1 Beagle G N Terr Aust
143 A8 Beagle I W Australia
87 H10 Bealanana Madagascar
117 L11 Beale,C Br Col
94 K8 Bealeton Virginia
141 F7 Beal Ra Queensland
108 F3 Beals Cr Texas
118 C1 Beaman Manitoba
8 D6 Beaminster England
100 J4 Bear Idaho
101 O7 Bear R Idaho etc
111 J7 Bear Cr Alabama
107 J4 Bear Cr Kansas
99 S5 Bear Cr Wisconsin
98 B8 Bear Cr Wyoming
101 Q4 Bearcreek Montana
95 M5 Bear Cr.Res Pennsylvania
111 D8 Bearden Arkansas
120 C3 Beardmore Ontario
146 G7 Beardmore Gl Antarctica
139 J3 Beardmore Res. Queensland
103 M8 Beardsley Arizona
107 J2 Beardsley Kansas
110 F1 Beardstown Illinois
123 K4 Bear Head Anticosti I, Quebec
118 J7 Bear Hills,The Sask
90 H1 Bear I Arctic Oc
14 B5 Bear I Irish Rep
115 L7 Bear I N W Terr
120 K6 Bear Island Ontario
101 O7 Bear L Idaho/Utah
119 V3 Bear L Manitoba
117 K7 Bear Lake Br Col
94 A2 Bear Lake Michigan
98 B5 Bear Lodge Mts Wyoming
101 M3 Bearmouth Montana
121 M4 Béarn Quebec
18 E9 Béarn prov France
101 Q1 Bear Paw Mt Montana
119 N4 Bear R Sask
101 N8 Bear R.City Utah
12 D2 Bearsden Scotland
101 S9 Bears Ears Pk Colorado
115 K7 Bearskin L Ontario
74 F3 Beas R India
18 D9 Beasain Spain
17 F6 Beas de Segura Spain
127 J6 Beata, I Dom Rep
40 G4 Beatenberg Switzerland
117 P10 Beaton Br Col
111 J10 Beatrice Alabama
98 K9 Beatrice Nebraska
6 H4 Beatrice oil rig North Sea
140 D2 Beatrice,C Aust
142 F3 Beatrice,Mt W Australia
107 O2 Beattie Kansas
15 E5 Beattock Scotland
117 N7 Beatton River Br Col
102 H5 Beatty Nevada
100 D7 Beatty Oregon
119 N6 Beatty Sask
94 D9 Beattyville Kentucky
115 M8 Beattyville Quebec
19 N17 Beaucaire France
20 J2 Beaucamps-le-Vieux France
121 L3 Beaucanton Quebec
122 B7 Beauceville Quebec
20 C4 Beauchamps France
133 F8 Beauchene Is Falkland Is
121 M6 Beauchêne, Lac Quebec
141 L8 Beaudesert Queensland
121 L4 Beaudry Quebec
20 F5 Beaufay France
40 E6 Beaufort France
22 L4 Beaufort Luxembourg
112 L3 Beaufort N Carolina
70 D2 Beaufort Sabah
112 G5 Beaufort S Carolina
21 E7 Beaufort-en-Vallée France
146 J6 Beaufort I Antarctica
112 L3 Beaufort Inlet N Carolina
116 R2 Beaufort Lag Alaska
147 K2 Beaufort Sea Arctic Oc
89 B9 Beaufort West S Africa
21 I6 Beaugency France
121 R7 Beauharnois Quebec
121 Q7 Beauharnois Power Canal Quebec
19 N12 Beaujeu France
19 Q16 Beaujeu France
18 H6 Beaujolais, Mts du France
95 S6 Beau L Maine/New Brunswick
9 E6 Beaulieu England
21 H7 Beaulieu-lès-Loches France
15 D3 Beauly Scotland
15 D3 Beauly, R Scotland
8 B1 Beaumaris Wales
22 D3 Beaumetz-les-Loges France
22 G3 Beaumont Belgium
102 H8 Beaumont California
107 O4 Beaumont Kansas
111 H10 Beaumont Mississippi
144 B6 Beaumont New Zealand
123 R4 Beaumont Nfld
111 B11 Beaumont Texas
146 H7 Beaumont B Antarctica
18 F9 Beaumont de Lomogne France
18 F8 Beaumont de Périgord France
22 J4 Beaumont-en-Argonne France
20 F3 Beaumont-en-Auge France
22 E3 Beaumont-en-Cambrésis France
20 B2 Beaumont-Hague France
21 G6 Beaumont la-Ronce France
20 G3 Beaumont-le-Roger France
20 G5 Beaumont-les-Autels France
20 K3 Beaumont-sur-Oise France
20 F5 Beaumont-sur-Sarthe France
19 J5 Beaune France
18 G4 Beaune la Rolande France
21 D7 Beaupréau France
20 K1 Beauquesne France
22 H3 Beauraing Belgium
40 B7 Beaurepaire d'Isère France
19 P15 Beaurières France
22 F5 Beaurieux France
118 E1 Beausejour Manitoba
21 E9 Beaussais France
139 H6 Beauty,Mt Victoria
20 K3 Beauvais France
118 C9 Beauvais Lake Prov. Park Alberta
21 E10 Beauvais sur Matha France
20 K1 Beauval France
118 K3 Beauval Sask
118 F5 Beauvallon Alberta
21 B8 Beauvoir-sur-Mer France
116 O3 Beaver Alaska
107 M3 Beaver Kansas
108 D7 Beaver Oklahoma
100 B4 Beaver Oregon
94 G6 Beaver Pennsylvania
103 M3 Beaver Utah
114 H7 Beaver R Alberta
98 F3 Beaver R N Dakota
103 L3 Beaver R Utah
117 L5 Beaver R Yukon Terr/Br Col
122 J9 Beaverbank Nova Scotia
122 G6 Beaver Brook New Brunswick
98 G9 Beaver City Nebraska
116 O4 Beaver Cr Alaska
106 G2 Beaver Cr Colorado
101 N5 Beaver Cr Idaho
107 J2 Beaver Cr Kansas
110 D5 Beaver Cr Missouri
98 B3 Beaver Cr Montana
98 F9 Beaver Cr Nebraska
98 B6 Beaver Cr Wyoming
114 E5 Beaver Creek Yukon Terr
117 C4 Beaver Creek Yukon Terr
98 J9 Beaver Crossing Nebraska
110 K4 Beaver Dam Kentucky
99 S6 Beaver Dam Wisconsin
117 O11 Beaverdell Falls Br Col
94 G6 Beaver Falls Pennsylvania
101 N4 Beaverhead R Montana
101 M4 Beaverhead Ra Idaho/Montana
118 E5 Beaverhill L Alberta
99 V4 Beaver I Michigan
123 N2 Beaver Island L Quebec
99 U3 Beaver L Michigan
117 N9 Beaver Lake Br Col
117 O8 Beaverlodge Alberta
117 P10 Beavermouth Br Col
116 J5 Beaver Mts Alaska
118 F4 Beaver R Alberta
118 H4 Beaver R Sask
118 K4 Beaver R Sask
110 C5 Beaver Res Arkansas
95 M3 Beaver R.Flow New York
94 C3 Beaverton Michigan
121 L8 Beaverton Ontario
100 C4 Beaverton Oregon
95 K6 Beavertown Pennsylvania
99 T9 Beaverville Illinois
74 F5 Beawar India
133 D4 Beazley Argentina
131 C4 Bebedero, Salina Argentina
129 J8 Bebedouro Brazil
36 G6 Bebenhausen W Germany
129 L4 Beberibe Brazil
36 H2 Bebra W Germany
47 H2 Bebrovo Bulgaria
9 H3 Beccles England
48 F5 Bečej Yugoslavia
48 K5 Beceni Romania
16 C2 Becerreá Spain
126 C7 Becerro,Cayos reefs Caribbean
85 D2 Béchar Algeria
116 J8 Becharof L Alaska
85 D7 Bechem Ghana
144 C5 Beche, Mt de la New Zealand
20 B5 Bécherel France
47 G1 Bechet Romania
116 F9 Bechevin B Alaska
37 K5 Bechhofen W Germany
Bechuanaland Prot see Botswana
31 H6 Bechyně Czechoslovakia
32 M7 Beckedorf W Germany
13 E4 Beckfoot England
9 E5 Beckhampton England
36 B5 Beckingen W Germany
8 D5 Beckington England
94 F9 Beckley W Virginia
144 B6 Becks New Zealand
32 H9 Beckum W Germany
109 N3 Beckville Texas
102 D2 Beckwourth California
48 J3 Beclean Romania
21 D7 Bécon France
19 O16 Béconne France
9 G4 Becontree England
37 O3 Bečov nad Teplou Czechoslovakia
108 F2 Becton Texas
31 K6 Bečva R Czechoslovakia
84 F4 Beda Libya
13 G5 Bedale England
18 H9 Bédarieux France
19 N16 Bedarrides France
36 B1 Bedburg W Germany
8 B1 Beddgelert Wales
9 G6 Beddingham England
119 R9 Bede Manitoba
20 B5 Bédée France
28 E4 Beder Denmark
32 J5 Bederkesa W Germany
55 C3 Bedeyeva Polyana U.S.S.R.
9 F3 Bedford England
110 K3 Bedford Indiana
99 M9 Bedford Iowa
94 B8 Bedford Kentucky
95 Q4 Bedford New Hampshire
122 J9 Bedford Nova Scotia
94 J6 Bedford Pennsylvania
121 S7 Bedford Quebec
94 H9 Bedford Virginia
101 P7 Bedford Wyoming
141 H3 Bedford C Queensland
142 F3 Bedford Downs W Australia
143 D10 Bedford Harb W Australia
127 P5 Bedford Pt Grenada
143 F7 Bedford Ra W Australia
9 F3 Bedfordshire co England
74 D7 Bedi India
69 H14 Bedinggong Indonesia
13 G3 Bedlington England
19 O16 Bédoin France
41 O5 Bedollo Italy
140 E6 Bedourie Queensland
8 A7 Bedruthan Steps England
28 C6 Bedsted Denmark
98 J8 Bee Nebraska
110 E6 Beebe Arkansas
98 G4 Beebe S Dakota
141 H7 Beechal R Queensland
94 K5 Beech Cr Pennsylvania
110 J4 Beech Creek Kentucky
100 F5 Beech Creek Oregon
99 T8 Beecher Illinois
110 H2 Beecher City Illinois
116 N1 Beechey Point Alaska
110 L4 Beech Fork R Kentucky
110 K2 Beech Grove Indiana
99 S3 Beechwood Michigan
139 H6 Beechworth Victoria
118 K8 Beechy Sask
32 M7 Beedenbostel W Germany
100 C9 Beegum California
25 E5 Beek Gelderland Netherlands
25 E4 Beekbergen Netherlands
111 E9 Beekman Louisiana
107 K3 Beeler Kansas
33 R8 Beelitz E Germany
98 K8 Beemer Nebraska
33 O8 Beendorf E Germany
141 L8 Beenleigh Queensland
37 K2 Beerberg mt E Germany
33 S8 Beeren E Germany
36 F4 Beerfelden W Germany
113 E10 Bee Ridge Florida
143 C8 Beeringgnurding, Mt W Aust
22 F2 Beerlegem Belgium
79 F8 Beer Menuha Israel
22 E1 Beernem Belgium
79 E9 Beer Ora Israel
80 C8 Be'er Pehar Israel
25 E5 Beers Netherlands
80 C8 Beersheba Israel
25 D6 Beerze R Netherlands
31 H3 Beeskow E Germany
87 E11 Beestekraal S Africa
9 E2 Beeston England
140 C3 Beetaloo N Terr Aust
146 G13 Beethoven Pen Antarctica
25 F2 Beetsterzwaag Netherlands
33 O7 Beetzendorf E Germany
33 R8 Beetz-see L E Germany
109 K7 Beeville Texas
86 D5 Befale Zaïre
87 H11 Befandriana Madagascar
86 D5 Befori Zaïre
18 C4 Begard France
8 B4 Begelly Wales
127 P4 Beggars Pt Antigua W I
107 O6 Beggs Oklahoma
51 L1 Begicheva, Ostrov isld U.S.S.R.
27 D11 Begna R Norway
57 E4 Begovat U.S.S.R.
28 E4 Begtrup Vig B Denmark
19 N15 Begude-de-Mazenc, la France
77 B4 Behbedān Iran
33 N5 Behlendorf W Germany
117 H8 Behm Can Alaska
140 A3 Behn, Mt N Terr Aust
22 L3 Beho Belgium
33 R4 Behren-Lübchin E Germany
37 L4 Behringersmühle W Germany
77 C1 Behshahr Iran
59 J2 Bei'an China
26 G4 Beiarn Norway
67 B2 Beibei China
86 F4 Beica Ethiopia
67 A1 Beichuan China
65 A6 Beichuan He R China
65 D5 Beidaihehaibin China
32 M10 Beienrode W Germany
37 O2 Beierfeld E Germany
68 J2 Beihai China
36 G6 Beihingen W Germany
67 D4 Bei Jiang R China
63 Beijing conurbation China
85 A5 Beila Mauritania
25 G3 Beilen Netherlands
68 J3 Beili China
68 K1 Beiliu China
37 L5 Beilngries W Germany
36 G5 Beilstein Baden-Württemberg W Germany
36 E2 Beilstein Hessen W Germany
36 C3 Beilstein Rheinland-Pfalz W Germany
86 H3 Beilul Ethiopia
67 B6 Beilun Ai pass China
36 H7 Beimerstetten W Germany
22 G5 Beine France
36 E6 Beinheim France
15 E4 Beinn a' Ghlo mt Scotland
40 H3 Beinwil Switzerland
67 B4 Beipan Jiang R China
65 E4 Beipiao China
Beira see Sofala
16 B4 Beira Alta prov Portugal
16 B5 Beira Baixa prov Portugal
16 B4 Beira Litoral prov Portugal
79 F5 Beirut Lebanon
118 D7 Beiseker Alberta
65 F2 Beitaolaizhao China
87 E10 Beitbridge Zimbabwe
79 F5 Beit ed Dine Lebanon
15 D5 Beith Scotland
80 D6 Beit Haninā Jordan
80 F4 Beit Idis Jordan
80 D7 Beit Jala Jordan
80 D7 Beit Kahil Jordan
80 A7 Beit Lahiya Israel
80 D7 Beit Lahm Jordan
80 G3 Beit Ras Jordan
80 D7 Beit Sahur Jordan
26 E7 Beitstad Norway
26 E8 Beitstadfjord inlet Norway
48 G4 Beius Romania
67 G2 Beiyandang Shan mt China
65 D6 Beizhen China
65 E4 Beizhen China
16 B6 Beja Portugal
43 C12 Beja Tunisia
143 E6 Bejah Hill W Australia
85 E1 Bejaia Algeria
16 D4 Béjar Spain
77 F2 Bejestān Iran
143 B9 Bejoording W Australia
70 L9 Bekasi Java
48 G4 Békés Hungary
48 F4 Békés co Hungary
48 G4 Békéscsaba Hungary
85 D7 Bekwai Ghana
Bela see Villach
74 B5 Bela Pakistan

86 B2 Bélabérim Niger
86 B4 Bélabo Cameroon
48 G6 Bela Crkva Yugoslavia
56 B5 Bel'Agach U.S.S.R.
95 L7 Bel Air Maryland
70 D4 Belajan R Kalimantan
70 D4 Belajan, G mt Kalimantan
16 D6 Belalcázar Spain
74 H9 Belampalli India
37 O4 Belá nad Radbuzou Czechoslovakia
71 J4 Belang Sulawesi Indonesia
119 U5 Bélanger Pt Manitoba
119 U5 Bélanger R Manitoba
69 C11 Belangpidie Sumatra
46 E1 Bela Palanka Yugoslavia
139 H4 Belarabon New S Wales
87 C8 Bela Vista Angola
129 G8 Bela Vista Brazil
133 F2 Bela Vista Brazil
87 F11 Bela Vista Mozambique
130 C8 Bela Vista Paraguay
130 E5 Bela Vista de Goiás Brazil
69 D11 Belawan Sumatra
54 E4 Belaya-Berezka U.S.S.R.
54 M8 Belaya-Kalitva U.S.S.R.
48 N1 Belaya Tserkov U.S.S.R.
44 D2 Belbo R Italy
43 L3 Belceşti Romania
115 K2 Belcher Chan N W Terr
115 M6 Belcher, Îles N W Terr
17 G3 Belchite Spain
14 D2 Belcoo N Ireland
121 N4 Belcourt Quebec
102 C1 Belden California
98 D1 Belden N Dakota
94 B3 Belding Michigan
52 D5 Belebelka U.S.S.R.
54 H5 Belebey U.S.S.R.
129 J4 Belém Brazil
129 L5 Belém de São Francisco Brazil
128 C3 Belén Colombia
108 A1 Belen New Mexico
129 G8 Belén Paraguay
131 G3 Belén, Cuchilla de mt Uruguay
124 H7 Belén del Refugio Mexico
47 G1 Belene Bulgaria
137 N5 Belep, Îles New Caledonia
16 B2 Belesar, Embalse de res Spain
86 J5 Belet Uen Somalia
57 D2 Beleutty R U.S.S.R.
54 H3 Belev U.S.S.R.
86 C5 Bélézé Cent Afr Republic
100 C2 Belfair Washington
95 S2 Belfast Maine
144 B4 Belfast New Zealand
14 F2 Belfast N Ireland
122 K7 Belfast Pr Edward I
25 F6 Belfield N Dakota
98 C3 Belfield N Dakota
86 F3 Belfodío Ethiopia
13 G2 Belford England
19 K5 Belfort France
40 E2 Belfort, Terr De France
101 O4 Belfry Montana
76 B3 Belgaum India
19 P18 Belgentier France
33 S10 Belgern E Germany
146 B7 Belgicafjella Antarctica
22 E2 Belgium
99 T6 Belgium Wisconsin
94 H6 Belgorod U.S.S.R.
48 N4 Belgorod Dnestrovskiy U.S.S.R.
— Belgrade see Beograd
98 H8 Belgrade Montana
133 F5 Belgrade Minnesota
131 E7 Belgrano, Pto Argentina
145 D4 Belgrove New Zealand
112 L2 Belhaven N Carolina
84 F4 Bel Hedam Libya
85 F2 Belhirane Algeria
20 H5 Belhomert France
43 E11 Belice R Sicily
78 G4 Belikh R Syria
47 H1 Beli Lom R Bulgaria
48 E5 Beli Manastir Yugoslavia
70 K8 Belimbing Indonesia
18 E8 Belin France
94 H7 Belington W Virginia
69 G13 Belinyu Indonesia
J14 Belitung isld Indonesia
125 P9 Belize Belize
125 P9 Belize Cent America
48 G6 Beljanica mt Yugoslavia
143 C9 Belka W Australia
99 O9 Belknap Iowa
100 K2 Belknap Montana
147 P8 Bel'kovskiy Os isld U.S.S.R.
113 E8 Bell Florida
141 K7 Bell Queensland
121 N3 Bell R Quebec
114 G7 Bella Bella Br Col
18 F6 Bella France
133 F4 Bellaco Uruguay
117 K9 Bella Coola Br Col
107 M2 Bellaire Kansas
94 B2 Bellaire Michigan
141 G7 Bellaire Queensland
42 C2 Bellano Italy
76 C3 Bellary India
40 G5 Bella Tola mt Switzerland
131 F2 Bella Vista Argentina
128 C4 Bellavista Loreto Peru
128 C5 Bellavista San Martín Peru
139 J8 Bell B Tasmania
145 E3 Bell Block New Zealand
141 K5 Bell Cay isld Gt Barrier Reef Aust
110 E3 Belle Missouri
123 R6 Belle B Nfld
33 P9 Belleben E Germany
40 E7 Bellecôte mt France
19 P14 Belledonne, Pic de mt France
94 D6 Bellefontaine Ohio
94 K6 Bellefonte Pennsylvania
98 C5 Belle Fourche S Dakota
98 J6 Belle Fourche R Wyoming
18 G5 Bellegarde France
19 P12 Bellegarde France
21 J10 Bellegarde en-Marche France
113 G11 Belle Glade Florida
40 E3 Belleherbe France
18 C5 Belle Île isld France
115 O7 Belle Isle Nfld
18 C4 Belle Isle en Terre France
123 R2 Belle Isle Landing Labrador/Nfld
123 Q2 Belle Isle, Strait of Labrador/Nfld
20 G5 Bellême France
95 R3 Belle Meade Tennessee
103 N6 Bellemont Arizona
16 B2 Bellencombre France
141 H3 Bellenden Ker Ra Queensland
22 E4 Belleneuse France
99 Q8 Bellenglise France
107 N4 Belle Plaine Kansas
99 P7 Belle Plaine Minnesota
119 M8 Belle Plaine Sask
94 F7 Belle Plaine Iowa
119 M6 Belle Plaine Sask
121 T4 Belle-Rivière, Lac de la Quebec
121 M5 Belleterre Quebec
22 F2 Belleu France
40 E5 Bel, Val d'Anniviers
40 B4 Bellevaux France
110 G3 Belleville Florida
110 G3 Belleville Illinois
94 K6 Belleville New York
99 K6 Belleville Pennsylvania
99 R7 Belleville Wisconsin
94 F7 Belleville W Virginia

21 C8 Belleville-sur-Vie France
118 C9 Bellevue Alberta
101 L6 Bellevue Idaho
99 Q7 Bellevue Iowa
94 B4 Bellevue Michigan
94 E5 Bellevue Ohio
141 G3 Bellevue Queensland
19 P13 Belley France
109 H1 Bellflower Illinois
110 E2 Bellflower Missouri
36 E5 Bellheim W Germany
123 T6 Bell I Newfoundland
115 O7 Bell I Nfld
86 A1 Bellin Quebec
138 E4 Bellinger R S Australia
139 G6 Bellingen New S Wales
32 K7 Bellingham England
36 D3 Bellingham Minnesota
44 C2 Bellingham Washington
114 G8 Bellingham Washington
146 G12 Bellingshausen Sea Antarctica
25 H2 Bellingwolde Netherlands
41 K5 Bellinzona Switzerland
118 E4 Bellis Alberta
36 F2 Bellnhausen W Germany
12 C2 Bellochantuy Scotland
137 M6 Bellona Plateau Coral Sea
102 C3 Bellota California
95 P3 Bellows Falls Vermont
129 K5 Bello Brazil
87 H12 Benenitra Madagascar
31 H6 Benešov Czechoslovakia
19 K4 Bénestroff France
18 G6 Bénévent-l'Abbaye France
43 F7 Benevento Italy
112 C6 Benevolence Georgia
94 J5 Benezett Pennsylvania
80 C5 Bene Ziyyon Israel
19 L4 Benfeld France
75 N9 Bengal, Bay of S Asia
70 E3 Bengara Kalimantan
85 G2 Ben Gardane Tunisia
58 G5 Bengbu China
84 F3 Benghazi Libya
48 H2 Beng He R China
69 F12 Bengkalis Sumatra
69 J12 Bengkayang Indonesia
119 M9 Bengough Sask
84 J5 Benguela Angola
119 R9 Benha Egypt
28 H5 Ben Hien Vietnam
122 G6 Benhope New Zealand
138 D3 Ben Hope mt Scotland
98 K6 Beniah L N W Terr
16 D4 Beni Bolivia
128 E6 Beni Abbès Algeria
117 R4 Beniah L N W Terr
17 G6 Benicarló Spain
17 G6 Benidorm Spain
85 F4 Beni Mazâr Egypt
85 C2 Beni Mellal Morocco
56 C3 Benin, Bight of W Africa
55 F7 Benin City Nigeria
36 B5 Bening France
9 L1 Benington Belize
85 D2 Benin, Rep. of W Africa
32 N2 Beni Saf Algeria
17 J2 Beni Saf Algeria
22 G15 Beni Suef Egypt
27 H14 Benjamin Utah
78 A2 Benjamin Constant Brazil
42 C3 Benjamin, L Oregon
100 E6 Benjamin L Oregon
60 O3 Benkei Misaki C Japan
98 E9 Benkelman Nebraska
15 D2 Ben Klibreck mt Scotland
42 G4 Benkovac Yugoslavia
15 D4 Ben Lawers mt Scotland
15 D4 Ben Ledi mt Scotland
141 G6 Benlidi Queensland
15 D4 Ben Lomond mt Scotland
15 E3 Ben Loyal mt Scotland
15 E3 Ben Lui mt Scotland
15 E3 Ben Macdhui mt Scotland
43 B12 Ben Mehidi Algeria
25 B6 Ben More mt Central Scotland
15 B4 Ben More mt Highland Scotland
15 D2 Ben More Assynt mt Scotland
144 C6 Benmore Dam New Zealand
144 C6 Benmore Pk mt New Zealand
33 N9 Bennekenstein E Germany
98 K9 Bennet Nebraska
140 D2 Bennet B N Terr Australia
114 F6 Bennett Br Col
99 P8 Bennett Wisconsin
93 P1 Bennett, Ostrov isld U.S.S.R.
117 F6 Bennett L Br Col
140 D5 Bennetts New Zealand
112 H3 Bennettsville S Carolina
144 B6 Ben Nevis mt New Zealand
37 J4 Ben Nevis mt Scotland
145 E3 Bennydale New Zealand
101 O7 Bennington Idaho
107 N2 Bennington Kansas
95 O3 Bennington Vermont
41 L4 Benoa Bali Indonesia
75 L9 Benore Vermont
143 B7 Berici, Monti Italy
36 F5 Beringen Belgium
16 G6 Beringen Netherlands
116 O6 Bering Glacier Alaska
70 D6 Beringin Indonesia
72 A4 Bering Sea
116 C4 Bering Strait U.S.S.R./Alaska

109 L5 Benchley Texas
15 C4 Ben Cruachan mt Scotland
143 C8 Bencubbin W Australia
114 C9 Bend Oregon
109 J4 Bend Texas
15 D3 Ben Dearg mt Scotland
116 F4 Bendeleben Mts Alaska
88 C5 Bende Pimbwe Tanzania
119 P8 Bendel Sask
86 B2 Bender Beila Somalia
86 A1 Bender Cassim Somalia
86 B1 Bender Merhagno Somalia
48 M4 Bendery U.S.S.R.
86 A1 Bender Ziada Somalia
138 G6 Bendigo Victoria
80 C8 Bendosari Israel
32 K7 Bendorf W Germany
36 D3 Bendorf W Germany
44 C2 Bene Italy
80 C5 Bene'Ataqot Israel
80 C5 Bene Beraq Israel
45 L4 Benedetto Alpe di S mt Italy
107 P4 Benedict Kansas
85 P2 Benedict Maryland
98 E2 Benedict N Dakota
98 J8 Benedict Nebraska
36 E1 Benediktenwand mt W Germany
129 K5 Beneditinos Brazil
87 H12 Benenitra Brazil
31 H6 Benešov Czechoslovakia
56 B4 Benguella Angola
20 G5 Benha Egypt
28 H5 Ben Hien Vietnam
122 G6 Benhope New Zealand
138 D3 Ben Hope mt Scotland
98 K6 Beni Zaire
48 L4 Beni Ounif Algeria
48 L1 Beniah L N W Terr
17 G6 Benicarló Spain
17 G6 Benidorm Spain
85 F4 Beni Mazâr Egypt
85 C2 Beni Mellal Morocco
85 E8 Benin, Bight of W Africa
85 F7 Benin City Nigeria
36 B5 Bening France
9 L1 Benington Belize
85 D2 Benin, Rep. of W Africa
32 N2 Beni Saf Algeria
17 J2 Beni Saf Algeria
22 G15 Beni Suef Egypt
27 H14 Benjamin Utah
78 A2 Benjamin Constant Brazil
42 C3 Benjamin L Oregon
100 E6 Benjamin L Oregon
60 O3 Benkei Misaki C Japan
98 E9 Benkelman Nebraska
15 D2 Ben Klibreck mt Scotland

12 D1 Ben Venue mt Scotland
86 M3 Ben Vorlich mt Scotland
109 M3 Benwee Hd Irish Rep
20 D4 Benz E Germany
80 B6 Ben Zakkay Israel
99 U5 Benzonia Michigan
130 D10 Beočin Yugoslavia
130 D10 Beocin Yugoslavia
60 E12 Beppu Japan
80 E5 Beqaot Jordan
20 G3 Beqor Latrun Israel
37 M5 Beratzhausen W Germany
70 E3 Berau R Kalimantan
86 H3 Berber Sudan
86 H3 Berbera Somalia
86 C5 Berberati Cent Afr Republic
16 D2 Berbersaga R Spain
20 H2 Berbezieux France
111 D9 Berbice R Louisiana
110 G5 Berclair Texas
56 B4 Berd' R U.S.S.R.
20 G5 Berd'huis France
51 M2 Berdichev U.S.S.R.
86 C8 Berdoba Chad
56 B4 Berdsk U.S.S.R.
55 C3 Berdyansk U.S.S.R.
94 F5 Berdyuz'ye U.S.S.R.
94 F5 Berea Ohio
71 B1 Berebere Halmahera Indonesia
86 B1 Bereda Somalia
87 H12 Beregomet U.S.S.R.
80 B8 Berosh Israel
86 E6 Béroubouay Benin
30 H6 Berounka R Czechoslovakia
31 G7 Berounka R Czechoslovakia
84 J5 Berovo Yugoslavia
45 L2 Berra Italy
41 H5 Berra mt Switzerland
42 A12 Berrahall Algeria
80 B7 Berre France
15 E2 Berrechid Morocco
80 C8 Berre, Etang de France
87 H12 Berrenrath W Germany
80 B7 Berri Algeria
15 E2 Berriane Algeria
99 U8 Berriedale Scotland
139 H6 Berrien Springs Michigan
140 B1 Berrigan New S Wales
99 U5 Berrima, Pt Michigan
22 G5 Berru France
94 K3 Berry Alabama
75 L5 Berry Kentucky
110 M3 Bertam R prov France
22 F5 Berry-au-Bac France
127 J2 Berrydale Jamaica
102 B3 Berryessa, L California
110 K5 Berry Ford Tennessee
74 G8 Berry Head England
71 M9 Berry Is Bahamas
113 K12 Berrys Pass N Terr Aust
110 C5 Berryville Arkansas
73 D3 Berryville Virginia
73 M3 Berseba Namibia
8 C1 Bersée France
80 C4 Bersenbrück W Germany
48 M2 Bershad U.S.S.R.
32 G7 Bersillies Belgium
37 L4 Bersuat U.S.S.R.
41 G2 Bertam Malaysia
25 E3 Berté, L Quebec
121 R6 Berthierville Quebec
99 V5 Berthoud Colorado
98 A4 Berthoud L Colorado
100 G6 Berthoud Pass Colorado
25 E5 Bertincourt France
98 H3 Bertinoro Italy
45 M3 Bertogne Belgium
22 K3 Bertoua Cameroon
14 B3 Bertraghboy B Irish Rep
109 J5 Bertram Texas
142 F4 Bertram, Mt W Australia
36 B7 Bertrand Nebraska
98 H7 Bertrichamps France
33 N6 Bertry France
106 B7 Berwarth R W Germany
22 G1 Beruri Brazil
128 F4 Beruwala Sri Lanka
137 G2 Berville-sur-Mer France
95 R3 Berwick Maine
118 K8 Berwick Nova Scotia
94 K5 Berwick Pennsylvania
139 H6 Berwick Victoria
141 J5 Berwick or Borders reg
116 H7 Berwyn Alberta
22 J1 Berwyn Alberta
118 D5 Berwyn Alberta
107 M2 Berwyn mts Wales
103 L4 Beryl Utah
98 K1 Berzee Belgium
114 J5 Berzence Hungary
100 C7 Besalampy Madagascar
19 K5 Besançon France

106 D6 Bernalillo New Mexico
99 Q7 Bernard Iowa
118 K8 Bernard Sask
103 P10 Bernardino Arizona
130 E8 Bernardino de Campos Brazil
114 G3 Bernard Is N W Terr
122 J3 Bernard, L Quebec
119 M3 Bernard L Sask
87 C11 Bernathie Namibia
107 N6 Bethany Missouri
95 M8 Bethany Beach Delaware
116 G6 Bethel Alaska
95 O5 Bethel Connecticut
95 M8 Bethel Delaware
99 R2 Bethel Minnesota
99 N4 Bethel Minnesota
99 O10 Bethel Missouri
112 K2 Bethel N Carolina
110 M3 Bethel Ohio
87 E11 Bethel S Africa
95 P3 Bethel Vermont
127 J2 Bethel Town Jamaica
22 G5 Bétheniville France
95 K7 Bethesda Maryland
94 F6 Bethesda Ohio
80 F1 Bet Hillel Israel
22 D5 Béthisy-St.Pierre France
80 D7 Bethlehem Jordan
95 M6 Bethlehem New Hampshire
95 M6 Bethlehem Pennsylvania
89 F7 Bethlehem S Africa
122 A2 Béthoulet, L Quebec
110 K5 Bethpege Tennessee
89 D8 Bethulie S Africa
106 H2 Béthune Colorado
22 D2 Béthune France
119 M8 Béthune Sask
113 G3 Bethune S Carolina
20 H2 Béthune R France
130 G6 Betim Brazil
87 G12 Betioky Madagascar
70 O10 Betiri, G Java
80 D7 Bet Ke'rem Israel
80 D3 Bet Lehem Israel
16 C2 Betley England
80 C7 Bet Nir Israel
70 B4 Betong Sumatra
37 J3 Bibra Suhl E Germany
142 A3 Bibra Lake dist Perth, W Aust
9 E4 Bicester England
122 D5 Bicester England
46 D3 Bicaj Albania
130 G7 Bicas Brazil
48 K4 Bicaz Romania
9 E4 Bicester England
41 H3 Bichelsee Switzerland
41 N3 Bichlbach Austria
115 N8 Bicêtre Quebec
122 C4 Bicknell Indiana
87 H11 Bickerton I N Terr Aust
99 U5 Bickle, Pt Michigan
100 E3 Bickleton Washington
142 B2 Bickley Brook Perth, W Aust
94 F8 Bickmore W Virginia
110 J3 Bicknell Utah
103 N3 Bicske Hungary
85 F7 Bida Nigeria
76 C2 Bidar India
80 B4 Biddeford Maine
95 R5 Biddu Jordan
8 D1 Biddulph England
8 B5 Bideford England

12 C8 Bet 'Arif Israel
122 C4 Bete Grise Bay Michigan
99 T2 Bet Ha'Emeq Israel
80 D2 Bet Ha Gaddi Israel
80 B8 Bethal S Africa
89 F6 Bethal S Africa
80 C3 Bet Hananya Israel
87 C11 Bethanie Namibia
107 N6 Bethany Missouri
95 M8 Bethany Beach Delaware
116 G6 Bethel Alaska
95 O5 Bethel Connecticut
95 M8 Bethel Delaware
99 R2 Bethel Minnesota
99 M8 Bethel Minnesota
99 O10 Bethel Missouri
112 K2 Bethel N Carolina
110 M3 Bethel Ohio
87 E11 Bethel S Africa
95 P3 Bethel Vermont
127 J2 Bethel Town Jamaica
22 G5 Béthéniville France
95 K7 Bethesda Maryland
94 F6 Bethesda Ohio
80 F1 Bet Hillel Israel
22 D5 Béthisy-St.Pierre France

75 K9 Bhawanipatna India
74 E2 Bhera Pakistan
75 J8 Bhilai India
73 M6 Bhima R India
74 H5 Bhind India
74 G4 Bhiwani India
74 H10 Bhopal India
76 E1 Bhopal India
76 F2 Bhopalpatnam India
74 E9 Bhor India
75 L8 Bhubaneswar India
74 C7 Bhuj India
68 D4 Bhumiphol Dam Thailand
74 F8 Bhusawal India
75 N8 Bhutan kingdom S Asia
77 E8 Biaban coastal reg Iran
85 F8 Biafra,Bight of W Africa
71 H5 Biak Sulawesi Indonesia
136 H2 Biak isld Indonesia
31 O3 Biala Piska Poland
31 M4 Biala Podlaska Poland
31 K2 Bialy Bór Poland
31 L2 Bialystok Poland
31 K2 Bianco, R C Italy
43 G10 Bianco Italy
45 L2 Bianco, Canale Italy
65 F4 Bianmen China
— Bianzhuang see Cangshan
71 G7 Biao Mindanao Philippines
73 R5 Biao, mt Laos
77 D1 Biarjmand Iran
71 J4 Biao sld Indonesia
18 D9 Biarritz France
71 H4 Biau Sulawesi Indonesia
55 G3 Biaza U.S.S.R.
79 A10 Bibe Egypt
42 D5 Bibbiena Italy
140 E5 Bibby R N Terr Aust
41 L1 Biberach R W Germany
37 K5 Bibert R W Germany
16 C2 Bibery R England
36 E4 Biblia W Germany
37 J3 Bibra Suhl E Germany
142 A3 Bibra Lake dist Perth, W Aust
9 E4 Bibury England
122 D5 Bic Quebec
46 D3 Bicaj Albania
130 C7 Bicas Brazil
130 G7 Bicas Brazil
48 K4 Bicaz Romania
9 E4 Bicester England
41 H3 Bichelsee Switzerland
41 N3 Bichlbach Austria
115 N8 Bicêtre Quebec
122 C4 Bicknell Indiana
87 H11 Bickerton I N Terr Aust
99 U5 Bickle, Pt Michigan
100 E3 Bickleton Washington
142 B2 Bickley Brook Perth, W Aust
94 F8 Bickmore W Virginia
110 J3 Bicknell Utah
103 N3 Bicske Hungary
85 F7 Bida Nigeria
76 C2 Bidar India
80 B4 Biddeford Maine
95 R5 Biddu Jordan
8 D1 Biddulph England
8 B5 Bideford England

Biggers — Boite 11

110 F5 **Biggers** Arkansas
9 F3 **Biggleswade** England
102 C2 **Biggs** California
100 E4 **Biggs** Oregon
99 Q9 **Biggsville** Illinois
106 B10 **Big Hatchet Pk** New Mexico
118 C7 **Big Hill Sp.Prov.Pk** Alberta
101 N4 **Big Hole** *R* Montana
101 M4 **Big Hole Battlefield Nat. Mon** Montana
114 J8 **Big Horn** *R* Montana
101 S4 **Bighorn** *R* Wyo/Mont
101 S5 **Bighorn Mts** Wyo/Mont
126 G3 **Bight of Acklins** Bahamas
126 G2 **Bight,The** Cat I Bahamas
111 E8 **Big I** Arkansas
115 M5 **Big I** N W Terr
118 H1 **Big I** Ontario
94 H9 **Big Island** Virginia
117 F4 **Big Kalzas L** Yukon Terr
116 H9 **Big Koniuji I** Alaska
95 U1 **Big L** Maine
117 R3 **Big L** N W Terr
100 E7 **Big L** Oregon
116 N3 **Big Lake** Alaska
108 F4 **Big Lake** Texas
95 K7 **Biglerville** Pennsylvania
144 A7 **Big Moggy I** New Zealand
95 N3 **Big Moose** New York
110 G4 **Big Muddy** *R* Illinois
98 B1 **Big Muddy Cr** Montana
119 N9 **Big Muddy L** Sask
44 C4 **Bignone,Monte** Italy
94 H9 **Big Otter** *R* Virginia
102 F4 **Big Pine** California
99 L3 **Big Pine L** Minnesota
102 E7 **Big Pine Peak** California
101 P7 **Big Piney** Wyoming
110 D4 **Big Piney** *R* Missouri
123 M8 **Big Pond** C Breton I, N Scotia
94 B3 **Big Rapids** Michigan
99 Q4 **Big Rib** *R* Wisconsin
114 J7 **Big River** Sask
99 U5 **Big Sable Pt** Michigan
100 E8 **Big Sage Res** California
117 F5 **Big Salmon** *R* Yukon Terr
119 S1 **Big Sand L** Manitoba
101 P1 **Big Sandy** Montana
109 M3 **Big Sandy** Texas
101 Q7 **Big Sandy** Wyoming
103 L7 **Big Sandy** *R* Arizona
106 H3 **Big Sandy Cr** Colorado
99 N3 **Big Sandy L** Minnesota
119 N4 **Big Sandy L** Sask
118 H1 **Bigsby I** Ontario
98 K5 **Big Sioux** *R* S Dakota
102 G3 **Big Smoky Valley** Nevada
101 Q3 **Big Snowy Mt** Montana
144 A7 **Big South Cape I** New Zealand
108 F3 **Big Spring** Texas
101 O5 **Big Springs** Idaho
98 D8 **Big Springs** Nebraska
118 H8 **Bigstick L** Sask
98 K4 **Big Stone City** S Dakota
94 E10 **Big Stone Gap** Virginia
119 W5 **Bigstone L** Manitoba
98 K4 **Big Stone L** Minnesota
119 W3 **Bigstone R** Manitoba
102 C5 **Big Sur** California
109 M5 **Big Thicket L** Texas
101 Q4 **Bigtimber** Montana
101 S6 **Bigtrails** Wyoming
115 L7 **Big Trout Lake** Ontario
130 E10 **Biguacú** Brazil
118 E6 **Big Valley** Alberta
109 H7 **Big Wells** Texas
111 L7 **Big Wills Cr** Alabama
120 K6 **Bigwood** Ontario
101 L6 **Big Wood** *R* Idaho
42 G4 **Bihac** Yugoslavia
75 L6 **Bihar** *prov* India
48 G4 **Bihor** *reg* Romania
48 G4 **Bihorului Muntii** *mts* Romania
67 F2 **Bihu** China
85 A6 **Bijagós, Arquipélago dos** Guinea-Bissau
74 G5 **Bijaipur** India
76 B2 **Bijapur** India
77 A2 **Bijar** Iran
75 K4 **Bijauri** Nepal
42 F3 **Bijela Lasica** *mt* Yugoslavia
48 E6 **Bijeljina** Yugoslavia
46 D1 **Bijelo Polje** Yugoslavia
67 B3 **Bijie** China
76 E1 **Bijji** India
77 F6 **Bijnābād** Iran
74 H4 **Bijnor** India
98 G6 **Bijou Hills** S Dakota
74 E4 **Bikaner** India
79 F5 **Bikfaya** Lebanon
51 N4 **Bikin** U.S.S.R.
65 J1 **Bikin** U.S.S.R.
59 L2 **Bikin** *R* U.S.S.R.
134 G7 **Bikini** *atoll* Marshall Is Pacific Oc
31 L6 **Bílá** Czechoslovakia
71 G6 **Bilaa Pt** Mindanao Philippines
85 E6 **Bilanga** Upper Volta
70 F3 **Bilangbilangen** Kalimantan
74 E5 **Bilara** India
74 G3 **Bilaspur** India
70 F2 **Bilatan** *isld* Philippines
71 H4 **Bilato** Sulawesi Indonesia
68 D5 **Bilauktaung Range** Burma/Thailand
17 F1 **Bilbao** Spain
79 B8 **Bilbeis** Egypt
42 J6 **Bileća** Yugoslavia
78 B1 **Bilecik** Turkey
48 F5 **Biled** Romania
48 D2 **Bilé Karpaty** Czechoslovakia
31 O5 **Biłgoraj** Poland
125 N2 **Bilhuaskarma** Nicaragua
86 E5 **Bili** Zaïre
68 C4 **Bilin** Burma
30 H5 **Bílina** *R* Czechoslovakia
71 D8 **Bilit** Sabah
65 E5 **Biliu He** *R* China
98 A6 **Bill** Wyoming
143 B7 **Billabalong** W Australia
6 D2 **Bill Baileys Bank** N Atlantic Oc
20 C5 **Billé** France
33 M5 **Bille** *R* W Germany
32 F9 **Billerbeck** W Germany
9 G4 **Billericay** England
9 F2 **Billesdon** England
19 P12 **Billiat** France
36 G5 **Billigheim** W Germany
142 G4 **Billiluna** W Australia
9 F2 **Billingborough** England
27 F16 **Billinge** Sweden
9 F1 **Billinghay** England
114 J8 **Billings** Montana
107 N5 **Billings** Oklahoma
9 F5 **Billingshurst** England
8 D3 **Billingsley** England
Billiton *see* **Belitung** *I*
18 H7 **Billom** France
28 A5 **Billum** Denmark
28 C5 **Billund** Denmark
103 M6 **Bill Williams Mt** Arizona
56 G1 **Billyakh Porog** *falls* U.S.S.R.
22 K5 **Billy-sous-Mangiennes** France
86 B2 **Bilma** Niger
141 K6 **Biloela** Queensland
42 H3 **Bilo Gora** *dist* Yugoslavia
111 H11 **Biloxi** Mississippi
140 E7 **Bilpamorea Claypan** Queensland
142 C5 **Bilroth,Mt** W Australia
36 E1 **Bilstein** W Germany
25 D4 **Bilthoven** Netherlands
86 D3 **Biltine** Chad
26 M2 **Bilto** Norway
68 C4 **Bilugyun** *isld* Burma
22 K2 **Bilzen** Belgium
71 J9 **Bima,Teluk** *B* Sumbawa Indonesia
85 E6 **Bimbéréké** Benin
138 F4 **Bimbowrie** S Australia
126 E2 **Bimini Is** Bahamas
75 K10 **Bimlipatam** India
71 F5 **Binalbagan** Negros Philippines
77 F1 **Bīnālūd, Kūh-e-** *mts* Iran
70 B3 **Binatang** Sarawak
141 J5 **Binbee** Queensland
13 H6 **Binbrook** England
22 G3 **Binche** Belgium
141 J7 **Bindango** Queensland
28 C5 **Bindeballe** Denmark
139 H3 **Bindebango** Queensland
28 D3 **Binderup** Denmark
69 J11 **Bindjai** Indonesia
141 J8 **Bindle** Queensland
118 G8 **Bindloss** Alberta
89 G1 **Bindura** Zimbabwe
17 H3 **Binéfar** Spain
98 H2 **Binford** N Dakota
87 E9 **Binga** Zimbabwe
87 F9 **Binga,Mt** Mozambique/Zimbabwe
141 G8 **Bingara** Queensland
36 D4 **Bingen** W Germany
107 M6 **Binger** Oklahoma
9 F2 **Bingham** England
95 S1 **Bingham** Maine
99 V5 **Bingham** Michigan
108 A2 **Bingham** New Mexico
101 N9 **Bingham Canyon** Utah
95 M4 **Binghamton** New York
70 E2 **Bingkor** Sabah
120 K4 **Bingle** Ontario
13 G6 **Bingley** England
Bingmei *see* **Congjiang**
78 H2 **Bingol** Turkey
78 H2 **Bingol D** Turkey
9 G2 **Binham** England
Binh Dinh *see* **An Nhon**
68 G7 **Binh Minh** Vietnam
68 J5 **Binh Son** Vietnam
69 J11 **Binjai** Indonesia
69 D11 **Binjai** Sumatra
71 J7 **Binongka** *isld* Indonesia
119 Q8 **Binscarth** Manitoba
144 C5 **Binser, Mt** New Zealand
36 B4 **Binsfeld** W Germany
69 G12 **Bintan** *isld* Indonesia
71 H4 **Bintauna** Sulawesi Indonesia
71 E4 **Bintuan** Philippines
70 C3 **Bintulu** Sarawak
71 E4 **Binubusan** Philippines
58 G4 **Bin Xian** China
65 G2 **Bin Xian** China
80 C3 **Binyamina** Israel
67 C5 **Binyang** China
Binzhou *see* **Bin Xian**
133 C5 **Bio-Bio** *prov* Chile
46 D2 **Bioča** Yugoslavia
42 G5 **Biograd** Yugoslavia
85 F8 **Bioko** *isld* Eq Guinea
19 O14 **Biol** France
40 E5 **Biot, le** France
32 G7 **Bippen** W Germany
94 B6 **Bippus** Indiana
80 E2 **Biq'at Bet Netofa** Israel
74 F9 **Bir** India
80 D6 **Bira** Jordan
48 L3 **Bîra** Romania
59 K2 **Bira** U.S.S.R.
84 J5 **Bir Abu Husein** Egypt
84 H4 **Bir Abu Minqar** Egypt
71 E2 **Birac** Philippines
59 K2 **Birakan** U.S.S.R.
86 D3 **Birao** Cent Afr Republic
84 E4 **Bi'r Ash Shuwayrif** Libya
75 M5 **Biratnagar** Nepal
77 F7 **Bīr Bālo** Iran
78 G4 **Bir Btaiman** Syria
47 F1 **Bîrca Gîngiova** Romania
116 P3 **Birch Cr** Alaska
116 L4 **Birches** Alaska
145 D4 **Birch Hill** New Zealand
119 M5 **Birch Hills** Sask
119 S6 **Birch I** Manitoba
9 H5 **Birchington** England
48 G5 **Birchiş** Romania
118 F5 **Birch L** Alberta
99 P2 **Birch L** Minnesota
117 P4 **Birch L** N W Terr
118 J5 **Birch L** Sask
114 H6 **Birch Mts** Alberta
117 R6 **Birch R** Alberta
119 Q6 **Birch River** Manitoba
110 E5 **Birch Tree** Missouri
116 N6 **Birchwood** Alaska
144 A6 **Birchwood** New Zealand
99 P4 **Birchwood** Wisconsin
31 N6 **Bircza** Poland
115 K6 **Bird** Manitoba
107 J2 **Bird City** Kansas
116 H9 **Bird I** Alaska
83 J12 **Bird I** Seychelles
89 E9 **Bird I** *lt ho* S Africa
8 D4 **Birdlip** England
123 L6 **Bird Rocks** *lt ho* Madeleine Is, Quebec
110 K3 **Birdseye** Indiana
140 E7 **Birdsville** Queensland
140 C3 **Birdum** N Terr Aust
140 C3 **Birdum** *R* N Terr Aust
85 D3 **Bir ed Deheb** Algeria
79 G3 **Birein** Syria
85 D3 **Bir el Hadjaj** Algeria
69 C10 **Bireuën** Sumatra
79 H10 **Bi'r Fajr** Saudi Arabia
75 L5 **Birganj** Nepal
37 M5 **Birgland** W Germany
27 E11 **Biri** Norway
71 G4 **Biri** *isld* Philippines
89 G1 **Biri** *R* Zimbabwe
130 E7 **Birigüi** Brazil
56 D4 **Birikchul'** U.S.S.R.
141 H6 **Birimgan** Queensland
86 D4 **Birini** Cent Afr Republic
77 F3 **Bīrjand** Iran
28 B6 **Birkelev** Denmark
28 D2 **Birkelse** Denmark
36 F4 **Birkenau** W Germany
41 H2 **Birkendorf** W Germany
27 C13 **Birkenes** Norway
36 C4 **Birkenfeld** W Germany
13 E6 **Birkenhead** England
33 S7 **Birkenwerder** E Germany
28 K5 **Birkerød** Denmark
36 B2 **Birkesdorf** W Germany
28 G7 **Birket** Denmark
79 A9 **Birket Qârûn** *L* Egypt
38 N7 **Birkfeld** Austria
41 O3 **Birkkar Sp** Austria
28 D7 **Birknack** *C* W Germany
138 A2 **Birksgate Ra** S Australia
48 L4 **Bîrlad** Romania
48 L4 **Bîrladul** *R* Romania
79 D7 **Bîr Lahfân** Egypt
85 C3 **Bir Lehlú** Morocco
78 H5 **Bir Meloza** Iraq
111 K8 **Birmingham** Alabama
9 E3 **Birmingham** England
99 P9 **Birmingham** Iowa
94 D4 **Birmingham** Michigan
119 P8 **Birmingham** Sask
11 C5 **Birmingham** *conurbation* England
84 H5 **Bir Misâha** Egypt
85 B3 **Bir Moghrein** Mauritania
15 E4 **Birnam** Scotland
37 P7 **Birnbach** W Germany
101 T4 **Birney** Montana
134 K8 **Birnie I** Phoenix Is Pacific Oc
85 E6 **Birni N'Gaouré** Niger
85 F6 **Birnin Gwari** Nigeria
85 E6 **Birnin-Kebbi** Nigeria
85 F6 **Birni n'Konni** Niger
51 N3 **Birodidzhan** U.S.S.R.
71 D6 **Birong** Palawan Philippines
14 D3 **Birr** Irish Rep
140 B3 **Birrimbah** N Terr Aust
140 A4 **Birrindudu** N Terr Aust
118 K7 **Birsay** Sask
50 E3 **Birsk** U.S.S.R.
13 G6 **Birstal** W Yorks England
36 G3 **Birstein** W Germany
26 L2 **Birtavarre** Norway
141 G2 **Birthday Mt** Queensland
116 J2 **Birthday Pass** Alaska
13 G4 **Birtley** England
66 E5 **Biru** China
56 E3 **Biryusa** *R* U.S.S.R.
52 B6 **Biržai** U.S.S.R.
85 C4 **Bir Zreigat** Mauritania
88 C8 **Bisa** Zambia
61 K10 **Bisai** Japan
74 H4 **Bisalpur** India
103 P10 **Bisbee** Arizona
18 C7 **Biscay,B of** France/Spain
113 G12 **Biscayne Nat. Mon** Florida
43 G7 **Bisceglie** Italy
37 K4 **Bischberg** W Germany
36 H1 **Bischhausen** W Germany
36 D6 **Bischheim** France
37 M3 **Bischofsgrün** W Germany
37 J3 **Bischofsheim** W Germany
38 H7 **Bischofshofen** Austria
31 H4 **Bischofswerda** E Germany
19 L4 **Bischwiller** France
112 H2 **Biscoe** N Carolina
146 F14 **Biscoe I** Antarctica
115 L8 **Biscotasing** Ontario
61 P12 **Bise** Okinawa
45 K4 **Bisenzio** *R* Italy
47 H3 **Biser** Bulgaria
55 C2 **Biser** U.S.S.R.
55 C3 **Bisert'** U.S.S.R.
42 G6 **Biševo** *isld* Yugoslavia
61 P12 **Bise-zaki** *C* Okinawa
67 A5 **Bisezhai** China
67 B2 **Bishan** China
102 F4 **Bishop** California
112 D4 **Bishop** Georgia
95 M8 **Bishop** Maryland
109 K8 **Bishop** Texas
144 A7 **Bishop and Clerks Is** New Zealand
13 G4 **Bishop Auckland** England
12 D2 **Bishopbriggs** Scotland
101 L8 **Bishop Creek Res** Nevada
117 P3 **Bishop L** N W Terr
119 M8 **Bishopric** Sask
9 E7 **Bishop Rock** Isles of Scilly England
8 D3 **Bishops Castle** England
123 R4 **Bishop's Falls** Nfld
8 C5 **Bishop's Lydeard** England
9 G4 **Bishop's Stortford** England
9 E3 **Bishops Tachbrook** England
9 E6 **Bishops Waltham** England
112 G3 **Bishopville** S Carolina
80 G3 **Bishra** Jordan
85 F2 **Biskra** Algeria
31 M2 **Biskupiec** Poland
28 D3 **Bislev** Denmark
9 F5 **Bisley** England
71 G6 **Bislig** Mindanao Philippines
71 G6 **Bislig Bay** Mindanao Philippines
111 C7 **Bismarck** Arkansas
99 T9 **Bismarck** Illinois
110 F4 **Bismarck** Missouri
98 F3 **Bismarck** N Dakota
136 K2 **Bismarck Archipelago** Papua New Guinea
136 J3 **Bismarck Range** Papua New Guinea
136 K2 **Bismarck Sea** Papua New Guinea
146 E14 **Bismarck Str** Antarctica
33 P7 **Bismark** E Germany
78 H3 **Bismil** Turkey
107 N5 **Bison** Oklahoma
98 D4 **Bison** S Dakota
117 P7 **Bison L** Alberta
77 A2 **Bīsotūn** Iran
36 B6 **Bisping** France
32 L6 **Bispingen** W Germany
85 A6 **Bissau** Guinea-Bissau
115 K7 **Bissett** Manitoba
37 K6 **Bissingen** W Germany
114 H6 **Bistcho L** Alberta
47 F1 **Bistretu** Romania
48 J3 **Bistriţa** Romania
48 J3 **Bistrita Năsaud** *reg* Romania
48 K3 **Bistriţei, Muntii** *mt* Romania
71 E5 **Bisucay** *isld* Philippines
31 M1 **Bisztynek** Poland
86 B5 **Bitam** Gabon
36 B4 **Bitburg** W Germany
19 K3 **Bitche** France
80 B8 **Bit'ha** Israel
47 L4 **Bithynia** Turkey
71 B2 **Bitjoli** Halmahera Indonesia
86 C3 **Bitkine** Chad
78 H2 **Bitlis** Turkey
46 E3 **Bitola** Yugoslavia
43 H7 **Bitonto** Italy
42 H5 **Bitovnja** *mt* Yugoslavia
8 B5 **Bittadon** England
103 P2 **Bitter Cr** Utah
101 R8 **Bitter Creek** Wyoming
33 Q9 **Bitterfeld** E Germany
87 C12 **Bitterfontein** S Africa
84 J3 **Bitter L** Egypt
98 J4 **Bitter L** S Dakota
9 E6 **Bitterne** England
144 C6 **Bitterness, Mt** New Zealand
119 M5 **Bittern L** Sask
118 D5 **Bittern Lake** Alberta
101 L3 **Bitterroot** *R* Montana
114 H8 **Bitterroot Ra** Mont/Idaho
43 C8 **Bitti** Sardinia
33 P8 **Bittkau** E Germany
85 D6 **Bittou** Upper Volta
71 J4 **Bitung** Sulawesi Indonesia
86 B3 **Biu** Nigeria
48 L3 **Bivolari** Romania
48 K3 **Bivolu** *mt* Romania
59 L4 **Biwa Ko** *L* Japan
110 E4 **Bixby** Missouri
107 P6 **Bixby** Oklahoma
56 C5 **Biya** *R* U.S.S.R.
86 H3 **Biya Kaboba** Ethiopia
56 C4 **Biysk** U.S.S.R.
18 G9 **Bize** France
85 G1 **Bizerte** Tunisia
43 C11 **Bizerte, Lac de** Tunisia
80 B6 **Bizzaron** Israel
28 J6 **Bjæverskov** Denmark
27 H13 **BJärka-Säby** Sweden
26 J3 **Bjarköy** Norway
26 K8 **Bjästa** Sweden
48 E7 **Bjelašnica** *mt* Yugoslavia
27 C13 **Bjelland** Norway
42 H3 **Bjelovar** Yugoslavia
28 E1 **Bjergby** Denmark
28 G6 **Bjergby** Denmark
28 G5 **Bjerge** Denmark
28 G5 **Bjergsted** Denmark
27 G11 **Björbo** Sweden
27 A10 **Bjordal** Norway
27 B11 **Bjoreia** *R* Norway
26 D9 **Björgan** Norway
27 E12 **Björkelangen** Norway
27 F14 **Björketorp** Sweden
26 H5 **Björkfjall** *mt* Sweden
26 N6 **Björkfors** Sweden
26 K3 **Björkliden** Sweden
27 J11 **Björklinge** Sweden
27 K12 **Björkö** Sweden
29 J8 **Björköby** Finland
26 J8 **Björksele** Sweden
26 K7 **Björksele** Sweden
26 K8 **Björna** Sweden
27 M10 **Björneborg** Finland
27 G12 **Björneborg** Sweden
115 L2 **Bjorne Pen** N W Terr
27 C11 **Bjornesford** *L* Norway
27 J12 **Björnlunda** Sweden
28 E6 **Bjørnø** *isld* Denmark
147 H13 **Björnöya** *isld* Arctic Oc
28 C3 **Bjornsholm Å** *R* Denmark
26 H3 **Björnskinn** Norway
28 E5 **Bjørnsknude** *C* Denmark
27 H13 **Björsäter** Sweden
26 J10 **Bjuråker** Sweden
26 K8 **Bjurholm** Sweden
27 H11 **Bjursås** Sweden
27 G12 **Bjurtjärn** Sweden
26 K7 **Bjurträsk** Sweden
85 C6 **Bla** Mali
28 A5 **Blåbjerg** *hill* Denmark
9 E2 **Blaby** England
19 N12 **Blace** France
122 C3 **Blache,L.de la** Quebec
100 B5 **Blachly** Oregon
111 J8 **Black** *R* Alabama
116 R3 **Black** *R* Alaska/Yukon Terr
103 P8 **Black** *R* Arizona
110 F5 **Black** *R* Arkansas
111 E10 **Black** *R* Louisiana
94 E3 **Black** *R* Michigan
111 H11 **Black** *R* Mississippi
110 F4 **Black** *R* Missouri
112 J3 **Black** *R* N Carolina
112 H4 **Black** *R* S Carolina
99 Q5 **Black** *R* Wisconsin
141 H6 **Blackall** Queensland
144 C5 **Blackball** New Zealand
119 P2 **Black Bay** Ontario
100 B8 **Blackbear** California
119 M3 **Black Bear Island L** Sask
111 H8 **Black Belt** Miss/Ala
8 D2 **Blackbrook** England
141 F4 **Blackbull** Queensland
13 F6 **Blackburn** England
12 E2 **Blackburn** Scotland
116 Q6 **Blackburn,Mt** Alaska
103 K6 **Black Canyon** Nevada
106 C3 **Black Canyon of the Gunnison Nat.Mon** Colorado
146 E12 **Black Coast** Antarctica
103 P6 **Black Creek** Arizona
99 S5 **Black Creek** Wisconsin
118 C8 **Black Diamond** Alberta
100 C2 **Black Diamond** Washington
117 K9 **Black Dome** *mt* Br Col
121 O7 **Black Donald Mines** Ontario
141 G3 **Blackdown** Queensland
8 C6 **Blackdown Hills** England
99 M2 **Blackduck** Minnesota
101 O2 **Black Eagle** Montana
94 E9 **Blackey** Kentucky
13 F4 **Black Fell** England
118 G5 **Blackfoot** Alberta
101 N6 **Blackfoot** Idaho
101 N1 **Blackfoot** Montana
101 O6 **Blackfoot** *R* Idaho
12 E1 **Blackford** Scotland
118 J2 **Black Hawk** Ontario
14 B3 **Black Head** Irish Rep
145 F4 **Black Head** New Zealand
123 T5 **Blackhead B** Nfld
139 K5 **Blackheath** New S Wales
138 B4 **Black Hill** S Australia
140 A4 **Black Hills** N Terr Aust
98 C5 **Black Hills** S Dakota
146 H7 **Black I** Antarctica
119 V7 **Black I** Manitoba
15 D3 **Black I** Scotland
118 D8 **Blackie** Alberta
116 H8 **Black L** Alaska
111 C9 **Black L** Louisiana
94 C1 **Black L** Michigan
112 J3 **Black L** N Carolina
95 M2 **Black L** New York
106 E5 **Black Lake** New Mexico
121 T6 **Black Lake** Quebec
101 N1 **Blackleaf** Montana
127 P6 **Blackman's** Barbados
103 M6 **Black Mesa** *plat* Arizona
112 E2 **Black Mountain** N Carolina
102 G6 **Black Mt** California
106 B8 **Black Mt** New Mexico
140 C2 **Black Mt** N Terr Aust
103 K6 **Black Mts** Arizona
122 E6 **Black Mts** Quebec
8 C3 **Black Mts** Wales/England
101 M7 **Black Pine Pk** Idaho
117 N10 **Black Pines** Br Col
106 B9 **Black Pk** New Mexico
140 A5 **Black Pk** N Terr Aust
117 N10 **Black Pool** Br Col
13 E6 **Blackpool** England
83 L13 **Black R** Mauritius
143 B6 **Black Ra** W Australia
106 C8 **Black Range** New Mexico
94 D2 **Black River** Michigan
99 Q5 **Black River Falls** Wisconsin
110 E5 **Black Rock** Arkansas
103 M3 **Black Rock** Utah
100 F9 **Black Rock Desert** Nevada
112 F2 **Blacksburg** S Carolina
94 G9 **Blacksburg** Virginia
53 D11 **Black Sea** S E Europe
101 P8 **Blacks Fork** *R* Utah/Wyoming
122 F8 **Blacks Hbr** New Brunswick
112 E6 **Blackshear** Georgia
112 D6 **Blackshear, L** Georgia
14 A2 **Blacksod B** Irish Rep
106 B8 **Black Springs** New Mexico
27 H14 **Blackstad** Sweden
14 E4 **Blackstairs Mts** Irish Rep
112 F3 **Blackstock** S Carolina
94 J9 **Blackstone** Virginia
120 B3 **Black Sturgeon L** Ontario
94 G7 **Blacksville** W Virginia
94 H6 **Blackuck** Pennsylvania
122 G7 **Blackville** New Brunswick
112 F4 **Blackville** S Carolina
14 E4 **Blackwater** Irish Rep
110 D3 **Blackwater** Missouri
141 J6 **Blackwater** Queensland
113 C12 **Blackwater** *R* Florida
14 E3 **Blackwater** *R* Irish Rep
110 C3 **Blackwater** *R* Missouri
141 G7 **Blackwater** *R* Queensland
12 C3 **Blackwaterfoot** Scotland
117 M3 **Blackwater L** N W Terr
9 G4 **Blackwater,R** England
15 D4 **Blackwater Reservoir** Scotland
107 N5 **Blackwell** Oklahoma
108 G3 **Blackwell** Texas
107 M3 **Black Wolf** Kansas
98 E9 **Blackwood Cr** Nebraska
143 B10 **Blackwood, R** W Australia
112 F6 **Bladen** Georgia
98 H9 **Bladen** Nebraska
112 J3 **Bladenboro** N Carolina
118 L7 **Bladworth** Sask
8 C2 **Blaenau-Ffestiniog** Wales
8 C4 **Blaenavon** Wales
8 B3 **Blaenporth** Wales
8 C4 **Blaen Rhondda** Wales
28 C3 **Blære** Denmark
8 C6 **Blagdon** England
18 F9 **Blagnac** France
47 F2 **Blagoevgrad** Bulgaria
51 M3 **Blagoveshchensk** U.S.S.R.
28 B5 **Blåhøj** Denmark
21 B7 **Blain** France
94 K6 **Blain** Pennsylvania
107 O2 **Blaine** Kansas
117 M11 **Blaine** Washington
94 H7 **Blaine** W Virginia
118 L6 **Blaine Lake** Sask
20 B3 **Blainville** France
98 K8 **Blair** Nebraska
107 L7 **Blair** Oklahoma
99 P5 **Blair** Wisconsin
94 F9 **Blair** W Virginia
141 H6 **Blair Athol** Queensland
15 E4 **Blair Atholl** Scotland
15 E4 **Blairgowrie** Scotland
102 G3 **Blair Junction** Nevada
12 D1 **Blairmore** Scotland
143 B6 **Blair,Mt** W Australia
102 D2 **Blairsden** California
112 D3 **Blairsville** Georgia
94 H6 **Blairsville** Pennsylvania
20 H4 **Blaise** *R* Eure France
48 H4 **Blaj** Romania
112 C6 **Blakely** Georgia
9 H2 **Blakeney** England
99 S1 **Blake Pt** Michigan
99 O9 **Blakesburg** Iowa
26 K2 **Blåmannen** *mt* Norway
26 H4 **Blåmannsisen** *mt* Norway
36 B6 **Blâmont** France
43 C11 **Blanc** *C* Tunisia
131 E7 **Blanca,B** Argentina
106 G7 **Blanca Cr** New Mex/Tex
131 D7 **Blanca Grande,L** Argentina
133 C8 **Blanca,L** Chile
106 E4 **Blanca Pk** Colorado
106 E8 **Blanca, Sa** *mt* New Mexico
100 J1 **Blanchard** Idaho
94 B3 **Blanchard** Michigan
98 J2 **Blanchard** N Dakota
107 N6 **Blanchard** Oklahoma
120 E2 **Blanche** Ontario
121 P7 **Blanche** Quebec
138 C5 **Blanche,C** S Australia
138 F3 **Blanche,L** S Australia
142 E5 **Blanche, L** W Australia
94 D7 **Blanchester** Ohio
138 E5 **Blanchetown** S Australia
127 O1 **Blanchisseuse** Trinidad
13 F4 **Blanchland** England
106 C5 **Blanco** New Mexico
109 J5 **Blanco** Texas
128 F7 **Blanco** *R* Bolivia
128 D5 **Blanco** *R* Peru
114 G9 **Blanco,C** Oregon
128 B4 **Blanco,C** Peru
115 O7 **Blanc-Sablon** Quebec
94 F9 **Bland** Virginia
43 B12 **Blandan** Algeria
8 D6 **Blandford** England
103 P4 **Blanding** Utah
99 Q9 **Blandinsville** Illinois
17 J3 **Blanes** Spain
112 G3 **Blaney** S Carolina
99 V3 **Blaney Park** Michigan
69 C11 **Blangkejeren** Sumatra
69 B10 **Blangkuala** Sumatra
20 J2 **Blangy** France
20 F3 **Blangy-le-Château** France
22 C3 **Blangy-sur-Ternoise** France
30 H6 **Blanice** *R* Czechoslovakia
33 P5 **Blankenberg** E Germany
22 E1 **Blankenberge** Belgium
33 N9 **Blankenburg** E Germany
37 L2 **Blankenhain** Erfurt E Germany
37 N2 **Blankenhain** Karl-Marx-Stadt E Germany
33 O9 **Blankenheim** E Germany
36 B3 **Blankenheim** W Germany
36 C3 **Blankenrath** W Germany
33 S6 **Blankensee** E Germany
109 J4 **Blanket** Texas
9 F1 **Blankney** England
31 K6 **Blansko** Czechoslovakia
87 G9 **Blantyre** Malawi
12 D2 **Blantyre** Scotland
21 F9 **Blanzay** France
22 F3 **Blaregnies** Belgium
94 J4 **Blasdell** New York
26 G7 **Blåsjön** *L* Sweden
31 L4 **Błaszki** Poland
47 J1 **Blatnitsa** Bulgaria
37 P3 **Blatno** Czechoslovakia
22 F3 **Blaton** Belgium
26 J6 **Blattnicksele** Sweden
36 H7 **Blaubeuren** W Germany
36 H5 **Blaufelden** W Germany
32 J4 **Blauort** *isld* W Germany
18 C5 **Blavet** *R* France
13 H6 **Blaxton** England
13 G4 **Blaydon** England
18 E7 **Blaye** France
142 C5 **Blaze,Mt** W Australia
140 B2 **Blaze Pt** N Terr Aust
31 N6 **Błazowa** Poland
33 N6 **Bleckede** W Germany
42 F2 **Bled** Yugoslavia
8 C3 **Bleddfa** Wales
31 J3 **Bledzew** Poland
27 D12 **Blefjell** *mt* Norway
22 E3 **Bleharies** Belgium
36 B3 **Bleialf** W Germany
38 L8 **Bleiburg** Austria
33 N10 **Bleicherode** E Germany
37 M3 **Bleilochsperre** *res* E Germany
27 H15 **Blekinge** *reg* Sweden
99 L8 **Blencoe** Iowa
145 D4 **Blenheim** New Zealand
120 J10 **Blenheim** Ontario
21 G7 **Bléré** France
25 F6 **Blerick** Netherlands
19 J4 **Blesmes** France
109 L7 **Blessing** Texas
14 E3 **Blessington** Irish Rep
9 E4 **Bletchingdon** England
9 F3 **Bletchley** England
40 B4 **Bletterans** France
69 C10 **Bleuë** Sumatra
121 M6 **Bleu,L** Quebec
111 C8 **Blevins** Arkansas
20 H4 **Blévy** France
119 O9 **Blewett** Sask
108 G6 **Blewett** Texas
112 H2 **Blewett Falls L** N Carolina
32 J5 **Blexen** W Germany
85 E1 **Blida** Algeria
27 K12 **Blidö** Sweden
27 F14 **Blidsberg** Sweden
36 C5 **Blies** *R* W Germany
36 C5 **Blieskastel** W Germany
116 O6 **Bligh I** Alaska
38 L5 **Blindenmarkt** Austria
33 T6 **Blindow** E Germany
115 L8 **Blind River** Ontario
46 D3 **Blinisht** Albania
138 E4 **Blinman** S Australia
101 L7 **Bliss** Idaho
94 D5 **Blissfield** Michigan
9 F3 **Blisworth** England
70 O10 **Blitar** Java
85 E7 **Blitta** Togo
100 F7 **Blitzen** Oregon
37 O5 **Blížejov** Czechoslovakia
146 J9 **Block B** Antarctica
95 Q5 **Block I** Rhode I
117 L10 **Bloedel** Br Col
25 C4 **Bloemehdaal** Netherlands
89 E7 **Bloemfontein** S Africa
87 E11 **Bloemhof** S Africa
21 H6 **Blois** France
28 D2 **Blokhus** Denmark
25 E3 **Blokzijl** Netherlands
32 K9 **Blomberg** W Germany
99 L5 **Blomkest** Minnesota
21 H9 **Blond** France
21 G10 **Blond, Monts de** *mts* France
115 R4 **Blönduos** Iceland
70 Q10 **Blongas** Indonesia
31 M3 **Błonie** Poland
33 R9 **Blönsdorf** E Germany
20 F3 **Blonville** France
140 A6 **Bloods Ra** N Terr Aust
95 L8 **Bloodsworth I** Maryland
14 C1 **Bloody Foreland** Irish Rep
106 G4 **Bloom** Colorado
99 P4 **Bloomer** Wisconsin
110 K2 **Bloomfield** Indiana
110 D1 **Bloomfield** Iowa
94 B9 **Bloomfield** Kentucky
110 G5 **Bloomfield** Missouri
98 B2 **Bloomfield** Montana
98 J7 **Bloomfield** Nebraska
106 C5 **Bloomfield** New Mexico
121 N9 **Bloomfield** Ontario
95 Q2 **Bloomfield** Vermont
109 L3 **Blooming Grove** Texas
99 N6 **Blooming Prairie** Minnesota
101 O7 **Bloomington** Idaho
99 S9 **Bloomington** Illinois
110 K2 **Bloomington** Indiana
109 L7 **Bloomington** Texas
99 Q7 **Bloomington** Wisconsin
95 L5 **Bloomsburg** Pennsylvania
141 J5 **Bloomsbury** Queensland
110 F3 **Bloomsdale** Missouri
95 N4 **Bloomville** New York
94 D5 **Bloomville** Ohio
70 N9 **Blora** Java
37 K6 **Blosenau** W Germany
95 K5 **Blossburg** Pennsylvania
115 R4 **Blosseville Kyst** *coast* Greenland
109 M2 **Blossom** Texas
51 R2 **Blossom Mys** *C* U.S.S.R.
111 L11 **Blountstown** Florida
126 F6 **Blower Rock** Caribbean
112 F1 **Blowing Rock** N Carolina
9 E3 **Bloxham** England
95 M9 **Bloxom** Virginia
13 G6 **Blubberhouses** England
41 L3 **Bludenz** Austria
103 P8 **Blue** *R* Arizona
106 D2 **Blue** *R* Colorado
107 O7 **Blue** *R* Oklahoma
103 N3 **Blue Bell Knoll** *peak* Utah
117 N7 **Blueberry** *R* Br Col
144 C6 **Blue Cliffs** New Zealand
101 N8 **Blue Creek** Utah
113 G10 **Blue Cypress L** Florida
94 D9 **Blue Diamond** Kentucky
99 M6 **Blue Earth** Minnesota
99 M6 **Blue Earth** *R* Minnesota
110 C5 **Blue Eye** Missouri
94 F9 **Bluefield** W Virginia/Virg
125 N3 **Bluefields** Nicaragua
110 M3 **Bluegrass Reg** Kentucky
95 T2 **Blue Hill** Maine
98 H9 **Blue Hill** Nebraska
127 H4 **Blue Hills** Turks & Caicos Is
123 O6 **Blue Hills of Couteau** Nfld
100 F7 **Bluejoint L** Oregon
94 J6 **Blue Knob** *mt* Pennsylvania
103 M2 **Blue L** Utah
100 B9 **Blue Lake** California
99 T8 **Blue Lake** Illinois
94 K7 **Bluemont** Virginia
110 G2 **Blue Mound** Illinois
106 B1 **Blue Mountain** Colorado
110 B7 **Blue Mt** Arkansas
94 K6 **Blue Mt** Pennsylvania
95 L6 **Blue Mt** Pennsylvania
110 C6 **Blue Mt,L** Arkansas
95 N3 **Blue Mt. Lake** New York
100 H7 **Blue Mt. Pass** Oregon
127 M2 **Blue Mt.Pk** Jamaica
144 B6 **Blue Mts** New Zealand
114 H8 **Blue Mts** Oregon/Wash
127 L2 **Blue Mts, The** Jamaica
140 D2 **Blue Mud B** N Terr Aust
86 F3 **Blue Nile** *prov* Sudan
Blue Nile *R see* **Bahr el Azraq**
114 H4 **Bluenose L** N W Terr
117 J6 **Blue R** Br Col
107 O2 **Blue Rapids** Kansas
118 B4 **Blue Ridge** Alberta
112 C3 **Blue Ridge** Georgia
94 G10 **Blue Ridge** *mts* Virginia
112 C3 **Blue Ridge L** Georgia
117 O9 **Blue River** Br Col
100 C5 **Blue River** Oregon
121 O6 **Blue Sea Lake** Quebec
14 C2 **Blue Stack Mt** Irish Rep
106 C6 **Bluewater** New Mexico
144 B7 **Bluff** New Zealand
103 P4 **Bluff** Utah
107 N4 **Bluff City** Kansas
112 E1 **Bluff City** Tennessee
109 J3 **Bluffdale** Texas
141 H4 **Bluff Downs** Queensland
142 F3 **Bluff Face Ra** W Australia
143 C10 **Bluff Knoll** *mt* W Australia
71 D6 **Bluff Pt** Palawan Philippines
143 A8 **Bluff Pt** W Australia
110 F2 **Bluffs** Illinois
126 F2 **Bluff, The** Eleuthera Bahamas
118 C6 **Bluffton** Alberta
110 C7 **Bluffton** Arkansas
112 C6 **Bluffton** Georgia
94 B6 **Bluffton** Indiana
99 L3 **Bluffton** Minnesota
94 D6 **Bluffton** Ohio
112 G5 **Bluffton** S Carolina
109 K3 **Blum** Texas
130 E10 **Blumenau** Brazil
33 O8 **Blumenberg** E Germany
33 T5 **Blumenhagen** E Germany
118 K8 **Blumenhof** Sask
32 J6 **Blumenthal** W Germany
36 B3 **Blumenthal** W Germany
40 G4 **Blümlisalp** *mt* Switzerland
98 G5 **Blunt** S Dakota
100 D7 **Bly** Oregon
89 C9 **Blyde Berg** *mt* S Africa
116 N7 **Blying Sound** Alaska
13 G3 **Blyth** England
120 J9 **Blyth** Ontario
140 C1 **Blyth** *R* N Terr Aust
13 E2 **Blyth Br** Scotland
9 H3 **Blythburgh** England
110 C1 **Blythedale** Missouri
138 A2 **Blythe Ra** W Australia
110 G6 **Blytheville** Arkansas
143 G7 **Blyth Ra** S/W Australia
13 H6 **Blyton** England
55 G3 **Blyudtsy** U.S.S.R.
26 G3 **Bö** Norway
85 B7 **Bo** Sierra Leone
27 H13 **Bo** Sweden
71 E4 **Boac** *isld* Philippines
125 M3 **Boaco** Nicaragua
130 F7 **Bóa Esperança** Brazil
65 B7 **Bo'ai** China
120 K7 **Boakview** Ontario
67 D7 **Bo'ao** China
45 L1 **Boara Polesine** Italy
94 B2 **Boardman** *R* Michigan
141 H7 **Boatman** Queensland
15 E3 **Boat of Garten** Scotland
128 F3 **Boa Vista** Brazil
71 D5 **Boayan** *isld* Palawan Philippines
111 K7 **Boaz** Alabama
106 G8 **Boaz** New Mexico
68 J1 **Bobai** China
141 J4 **Bobawaba** Queensland
75 K9 **Bobbili** India
44 F2 **Bobbio** Italy
121 M8 **Bobcaygeon** Ontario
36 E4 **Bobenheim-Roxheim** W Germany
37 K7 **Bobingen** W Germany
33 O5 **Bobitz** E Germany
36 F6 **Böblingen** W Germany
85 D6 **Bobo Dioulasso** Upper Volta
31 K2 **Bobolice** Poland
71 G4 **Bobon** Philippines
128 C4 **Bobonaza** Ecuador
46 F2 **Bobov Dol** Bulgaria
31 J4 **Bóbr** *R* Poland
54 D8 **Bobrinets** U.S.S.R.
48 J1 **Bobrka** U.S.S.R.
54 M5 **Bobrov** U.S.S.R.
54 C6 **Bobrovitsa** U.S.S.R.
31 H4 **Bobrowice** Poland
94 H7 **Bobtown** Pennsylvania
109 K10 **Boca Chica** Texas
113 F13 **Boca Chica** *isld* Florida
127 M10 **Boca del Pao** Venezuela
128 E5 **Bôca do Acre** Brazil
128 E5 **Bôca do Curuquetê** Brazil
129 H4 **Bôca do Jari** Brazil
128 E5 **Bôca do Moaca** Brazil
21 D6 **Bocages** *reg* France
113 E11 **Boca Grande** Florida
127 N1 **Boca Grande** *chan* Trinidad/Ven
113 F13 **Boca Grande Key** *isld* Florida
129 K7 **Bocaiúva** Brazil
130 E9 **Bocaiúva do Sul** Brazil
130 C8 **Bocajá** Brazil
113 G11 **Boca Raton** Florida
127 N1 **Bocas del Dragon** *chan* Trinidad
125 M2 **Bocay** Nicaragua
45 M2 **Bocche del Po Della Pila** Italy
45 M2 **Bocche del Po Delle Tolle** Italy
45 M2 **Bocche del Po di Goro e di Gnocca** Italy
16 E3 **Boceguillas** Spain
19 P16 **Bochaine** *reg* France
121 R3 **Bochart** Quebec
31 M6 **Bochnia** Poland
22 K1 **Bocholt** Belgium
32 E9 **Bocholt** W Germany
37 P3 **Bochov** Czechoslovakia
32 F10 **Bochum** W Germany
37 O3 **Bockau** E Germany
32 M8 **Bockenem** W Germany
32 H6 **Bockhorn** W Germany
31 O3 **Boćki** Poland
38 H7 **Böckstein** Austria
33 T10 **Bockwitz** E Germany
127 J10 **Boconó** Venezuela
124 F4 **Bocoyna** Mexico
48 G5 **Bocsa Vasiovei** Romania
86 C5 **Boda** Cent Afr Republic
27 H10 **Boda** Sweden
27 J14 **Böda** Sweden
27 G14 **Bodafors** Sweden
143 C9 **Bodallin** W Australia
51 L3 **Bodaybo** U.S.S.R.
15 G3 **Boddam** Scotland
99 M7 **Bode** Iowa
102 A3 **Bodega Head** California
86 C2 **Bodele** *dist* Chad
36 F7 **Bodelhausen** W Germany
26 M6 **Boden** Sweden
32 L8 **Bodenburg** W Germany
36 E4 **Bodenheim** W Germany
37 J3 **Bodenlaube** W Germany
37 P5 **Bodenmais** W Germany
41 K2 **Bodensee** *L* Switzerland
33 N7 **Bodenteich** W Germany
32 L9 **Bodenwerder** W Germany
38 L6 **Bodenwies** *mt* Austria
37 N5 **Bodenwöhr** W Germany
14 C3 **Boderg,L** Irish Rep
102 F6 **Bodfish** California
74 G9 **Bodhan** India
70 G4 **Bodi** Sulawesi Indonesia
36 G5 **Bödigheim** W Germany
76 C5 **Bodinayakkanur** India
8 B7 **Bodinnick** England
70 O9 **Bodjonegoro** Java
8 B7 **Bodmin** England
8 B6 **Bodmin Moor** England
118 G6 **Bodo** Alberta
26 G4 **Bodö** Norway
25 C4 **Bodograven** Netherlands
130 C6 **Bodoquena** Brazil
78 A3 **Bodrum** Turkey
26 G9 **Bodsjö** Sweden
68 H7 **Bo Duc** Vietnam
26 H8 **Bodum** Sweden
48 F2 **Bodva** *R* Hungary
31 M3 **Bodzanów** Poland
40 D5 **Boëge** France
25 G4 **Boekelo** Netherlands
22 F1 **Boekhoute** Belgium
98 H8 **Boelus** Nebraska
18 H7 **Boën** France
86 D6 **Boende** Zaïre
68 G6 **Boeng Lovea** Cambodia
68 G6 **Boeng Me Alpa** Cambodia
109 J6 **Boerne** Texas
25 H2 **Boertange** Netherlands
28 G6 **Boeslunde** Denmark
111 E8 **Boeuf** *R* Arkansas
83 K14 **Bœuf, Nez de** *peak* Réunion
85 B6 **Boffa** Guinea
14 D3 **Bofin,L** Irish Rep
68 B4 **Bogale** Burma
68 B5 **Bogale** *R* Burma
111 F11 **Bogalusa** Louisiana
85 D6 **Bogande** Upper Volta
86 C4 **Bogangolo** Cent Afr Republic
141 H6 **Bogantungan** Queensland
17 F6 **Bogarra** Spain
118 B8 **Bogart,Mt** Alberta
109 M2 **Bogata** Texas
53 H7 **Bogatoye** U.S.S.R.
31 H5 **Bogatynia** Poland
86 C5 **Bogbonga** Zaïre
55 D3 **Bogdanovich** U.S.S.R.
66 D3 **Bogda Shan** *mts* China
27 K14 **Boge** *isld* Gotland Sweden
55 F4 **Bogembay** U.S.S.R.
37 O6 **Bogen** W Germany
87 C11 **Bogenfels** Namibia
28 E5 **Bogense** Denmark
14 C4 **Boggeragh Mts** Irish Rep
143 C6 **Boggola** *mt* W Australia
26 H8 **Boggsjö** Sweden
85 B5 **Boghé** Mauritania
141 J5 **Bogie** *R* Queensland
9 F6 **Bognor Regis** England
22 H4 **Bogny-sur-Meuse** France
71 F5 **Bogo** Cebu Philippines
28 J7 **Bogø** Denmark
54 G6 **Bogodukhov** U.S.S.R.
70 L9 **Bogor** Java
48 J2 **Bogorodchany** U.S.S.R.
51 O3 **Bogorodskoy** U.S.S.R.
128 D3 **Bogotá** Colombia
111 A8 **Bogota** Texas
56 C3 **Bogotol** U.S.S.R.
75 N6 **Bogra** Bangladesh
27 L12 **Bogskär** *lt ho* Finland
56 E2 **Boguchany** U.S.S.R.
54 M7 **Boguchar** U.S.S.R.
55 E4 **Bogudukhovka** U.S.S.R.
107 L2 **Bogue** Kansas
111 F10 **Bogue Chitto** Mississippi
112 K3 **Bogue Inlet** N Carolina
54 B2 **Bogushevsk** U.S.S.R.
54 B7 **Boguslav** U.S.S.R.
31 J5 **Boguszów** Poland
127 L2 **Bog Walk** Jamaica
65 D5 **Bo Hai** *gulf* China
65 E5 **Bohai Haixia** *str* China
22 E4 **Bohain** France
65 D5 **Bohai Wan** *B* China
119 M8 **Boharm** Sask
38 N5 **Böheimkirchen** Austria
30 H6 **Bohemia** *old region* Czech
142 F4 **Bohemia Downs** W Australia
85 E7 **Bohicon** Benin
42 F2 **Bohiniska Bistrica** Yugoslavia
37 N1 **Böhlen** W Germany
32 K7 **Böhme** W Germany
37 N4 **Böhmer Wald** *mts* W Germany
32 H8 **Bohmte** W Germany
33 Q7 **Böhne** E Germany
71 G6 **Bohol** *isld* Philippines
71 F6 **Bohol Str** Philippines
16 D5 **Bohonal de Ibor** Spain
48 D4 **Böhönye** Hungary
86 J4 **Bohotleh** Somalia
80 B8 **Bohu** Israel
128 F4 **Boiaçu** Brazil
43 F7 **Boiano** Italy
122 F7 **Boiestown** New Brunswick
20 K5 **Boigneville** France
122 B5 **Boileau** Quebec
130 C9 **Boi Preto,Serra de** *mts* Brazil
130 F8 **Boi, Pta. do** *C* Brazil
129 J7 **Bois** *R* Brazil
94 C1 **Bois Blanc I** Michigan
123 M7 **Boisdale** C Breton I, N Scotia
40 D4 **Bois d' Amont** France
18 H5 **Bois du Roi** *mt* France
100 J6 **Boise** Idaho
106 H5 **Boise City** Oklahoma
20 A5 **Boisgervilly** France
20 H3 **Bois Guillaume** France
114 G4 **Bois, Lac Des** *L* N W Terr
Bois-le-Duc *see* **'s-Hertogenbosch**
18 H7 **Bois Noirs** *hills* France
22 H1 **Boisschot** Belgium
119 R9 **Boissevain** Manitoba
20 G4 **Boissy-les-Perche** France
20 G5 **Boissy-Maugis** France
38 F9 **Boite** *R* Italy

130 F8 **Boituva** Brazil
33 T6 **Boitzenburg** E Germany
33 N6 **Boize** *R* E Germany
33 N6 **Boizenburg** E Germany
85 B3 **Bojador** Morocco
46 C3 **Bojana** *R* Albania
28 E6 **Bøjden** Denmark
71 E1 **Bojeador,C** Luzon Philippines
77 E1 **Bojnūrd** Iran
69 D13 **Bojo** *isld* Indonesia
48 F5 **Boka** Yugoslavia
42 J6 **Boka Kotorska** *B* Yugoslavia
85 F7 **Bokani** Nigeria
85 B6 **Boké** Guinea
113 E11 **Bokeelia** Florida
32 J6 **Bokel** W Germany
32 K8 **Bokeloh** W Germany
68 H6 **Bo Kheo** Cambodia
89 A8 **Bokkeveld Berg** *mt* S Africa
27 A12 **Boknfjorden** *inlet* Norway
56 B6 **Boko** Kazakhstan U.S.S.R.
86 C3 **Bokoro** Chad
107 Q6 **Bokoshe** Oklahoma
86 D6 **Bokote** Zaïre
59 H2 **Bo-ko-tu** China
68 D7 **Bokpyin** Burma
86 D6 **Bokungu** Zaïre
68 C5 **Bok Ye-gan** *isld* Burma
70 G5 **Bolaäng** Sulawesi Indonesia
71 J4 **Bolaang** Sulawesi Indonesia
86 D6 **Bolaiti** Zaïre
85 A6 **Bolama** Guinea-Bissau
75 K8 **Bolangir** India
124 H7 **Bolaños** Mexico
67 C5 **Bolao** China
20 F2 **Bolbec** France
55 E2 **Bolchary** U.S.S.R.
99 M9 **Bolckow** Missouri
48 E4 **Bölcske** Hungary
33 T5 **Boldekow** E Germany
28 C6 **Bolderslev** Denmark
48 K5 **Boldeşti** Romania
66 C3 **Bole** China
85 D7 **Bole** Ghana
101 N2 **Bole** Montana
48 H1 **Bolekhov** U.S.S.R.
86 D6 **Boleko** Zaïre
71 L9 **Boleng,Selat** Flores Indonesia
100 J4 **Boles** Idaho
31 J4 **Bolesławiec** Poland
107 O6 **Boley** Oklahoma
85 D6 **Bolgatanga** Ghana
121 O4 **Bolger** Quebec
48 M5 **Bolgrad** U.S.S.R.
59 K2 **Boli** China
86 C6 **Bolia** Zaïre
26 L7 **Boliden** Sweden
111 H9 **Boligee** Alabama
71 D2 **Bolinao,C** Luzon Philippines
48 K6 **Bolintin Vale** Romania
71 H4 **Boliohutu,Gunung** *mt* Sulawesi Indonesia
131 E6 **Bolivár** Argentina
128 C3 **Bolivar** Colombia
110 C4 **Bolivar** Missouri
94 J4 **Bolivar** New York
110 H6 **Bolivar** Tennessee
128 D2 **Bolivar** *div* Colombia
128 C4 **Bolivar** *prov* Ecuador
128 E2 **Bolivar** *state* Venezuela
128 F2 **Bolivar,Cerro** *mt* Venezuela
109 N6 **Bolivar Pen** Texas
112 J3 **Bolivia** N Carolina
128 E7 **Bolivia** *rep* S America
46 E1 **Boljevac** Yugoslavia
78 E3 **Bolkar Dağları** *mts* Turkey
27 D12 **Bolkesjö** Norway
120 G4 **Bolkow** Ontario
31 J5 **Bolków** Poland
36 H6 **Boll** W Germany
41 H2 **Boll** W Germany
45 K4 **Bolle,Le** Italy
36 B4 **Bollendorf** W Germany
19 N16 **Bollène** France
40 G4 **Bolligen** Switzerland
28 B5 **Bølling** Denmark
8 D1 **Bollington** England
27 H10 **Bollnäs** Sweden
141 H8 **Bollon** Queensland
27 G15 **Bolmen** *L* Sweden
9 F6 **Bolney** England
71 F5 **Bolo** Panay Philippines
86 C6 **Bolobo** Zaïre
71 E7 **Bolod Islands** Philippines
42 D4 **Bologna** Italy
19 J4 **Bologne** France
52 D6 **Bologovo** U.S.S.R.
54 J2 **Bolokhovo** U.S.S.R.
86 C5 **Bolomba** Zaïre
86 D6 **Bolombo** Zaïre
59 L2 **Bolon** U.S.S.R.
125 P7 **Bolonchén de Rejón** Mexico
71 F7 **Bolong** Mindanao Philippines
59 L2 **Bolon,Oz** *L* U.S.S.R.
71 F1 **Bolos Pt** Luzon Philippines
43 B8 **Bolotana** Sardinia
56 B3 **Bolotnoye** U.S.S.R.
68 H5 **Bolovens, Plateau des** Laos
131 C2 **Bolsa,Cerro** *peak* Argentina
42 D6 **Bolsena,L.di** Italy
31 N1 **Bol'shakovo** U.S.S.R.
54 F9 **Bolshaya Belozerka** U.S.S.R.
55 F3 **Bol'shaya Tava** *R* U.S.S.R.
56 G1 **Bol'shaya Yerema** *R* U.S.S.R.
55 F3 **Bol'sherech'ye** U.S.S.R.
51 P3 **Bol'sheretsk** U.S.S.R.
55 C3 **Bolshe-ustikinskoye** U.S.S.R.
54 B4 **Bol'shevik** U.S.S.R.
51 K1 **Bol'shevik, Ostrov** *isld* U.S.S.R.
55 F3 **Bolshiye Uki** U.S.S.R.
56 B1 **Bolshoi Megtyg'yegan** *R* U.S.S.R.
54 G9 **Bolshoi Tokmak** U.S.S.R.
48 J1 **Bolshovtsy** U.S.S.R.
55 E1 **Bol'shoy Atlym** U.S.S.R.
55 F1 **Bol'shoy Balyk** *R* U.S.S.R.
147 P10 **Bol'shoy Begichev,Os** *isld* U.S.S.R.
56 H2 **Bol'shoy Chuya** *R* U.S.S.R.
55 E3 **Bol'shoye Sorokino** U.S.S.R.
55 G4 **Bol'shoye Topol'noye, Oz** *L* U.S.S.R.
55 G4 **Bol'shoye Yaravoye, Oz** *L* U.S.S.R.
55 E1 **Bol'shoy Kamen** U.S.S.R.
55 F2 **Bol'shoy Kun'yak** U.S.S.R.
55 D3 **Bol'shoy Kuyash** U.S.S.R.
51 O1 **Bolshoy Lyakhovskiy,O** *isld* U.S.S.R.
56 D2 **Bol'shoy Pit** *R* U.S.S.R.
55 F1 **Bolshoy Salym** *R* U.S.S.R.
59 L1 **Bol'shoy Shantar,Oz** *isld* U.S.S.R.
55 E1 **Bol'shoy Tap** *R* U.S.S.R.
52 C5 **Bol'shoy Tyuters, Os.** *isld* U.S.S.R.
55 F3 **Bol'shoy Uvat, Oz** *L* U.S.S.R.
56 D5 **Bolshoy Yenisey** *R* U.S.S.R.
55 F2 **Bol'shoy Yugan** *R* U.S.S.R.
25 E2 **Bolsward** Netherlands
17 H2 **Boltaña** Spain
8 C7 **Bolt Head** England
13 F6 **Bolton** England
112 J3 **Bolton** N Carolina
121 L9 **Bolton** Ontario
13 G6 **Bolton Br** England
119 W4 **Bolton L** Manitoba
13 F5 **Bolton le-Sands** England
78 C1 **Bolu** Turkey
66 E4 **Boluntay** China
14 A5 **Bolus Hd** Irish Rep
54 F3 **Bolva** *R* U.S.S.R.
47 L6 **Bolvadin** Turkey
78 C2 **Bolvadin** Turkey
8 B6 **Bolventor** England
141 G4 **Bolwarra** Queensland
48 E5 **Bóly** Hungary
42 D2 **Bolzano** Italy
86 B7 **Boma** Zaïre
22 K3 **Bomal** Luxembourg/Belgium
86 B5 **Bomandjokou** Congo
109 H2 **Bomarton** Texas
86 C5 **Bomassa** Congo
74 E9 **Bombay** India
145 E2 **Bombay** New Zealand
87 H11 **Bombetoka,B.de** Madagascar
86 F5 **Bombo** Uganda
86 C5 **Bomboma** Zaïre
130 H10 **Bom Conselho** Brazil
129 J7 **Bom Despacho** Brazil
27 J11 **Bomhus** Sweden
85 B7 **Bomi Hills** Liberia
130 J9 **Bom Jardim** Brazil
130 D5 **Bom Jardim de Goiás** Brazil
128 E5 **Bom Jardin** Brazil
129 K5 **Bom Jesus** Brazil
129 K5 **Bom Jesus da Gurgueia, Serra** *mts* Brazil
129 K6 **Bom Jesus da Lapa** Brazil
130 H7 **Bom Jesus do Itabapoana** Brazil
130 H7 **Bom Jesus do Norte** Brazil
27 A12 **Bömlafjorden** *inlet* Norway
27 A12 **Bömlo** Norway
51 M3 **Bomnak** U.S.S.R.
86 E5 **Bomokandi** *R* Zaïre
86 C5 **Bomongo** Zaïre
143 B7 **Bompas Hill** W Australia
130 E10 **Bom Retiro** Brazil
130 G7 **Bom Sucesso** Brazil
118 D5 **Bon Accord** Alberta
94 K9 **Bon Air** Virginia
127 K8 **Bonaire** *isld* Lesser Antilles
127 K9 **Bonaire Trench** Caribbean
116 R6 **Bona,Mt** Alaska
69 D12 **Bonandolok** Sumatra
106 D3 **Bonanza** Colorado
125 M3 **Bonanza** Nicaragua
100 D7 **Bonanza** Oregon
127 J5 **Bonao** Dom Rep
99 P9 **Bonaparte** Iowa
142 E2 **Bonaparte Arch** W Australia
100 F1 **Bonaparte,Mt** Washington
15 D3 **Bonar Bridge** Scotland
121 N8 **Bonarlaw** Ontario
116 G5 **Bonasila Dome** *mt* Alaska
127 N3 **Bonasse** Trinidad
44 G3 **Bonassola** Italy
122 G5 **Bonaventure** Quebec
122 H5 **Bonaventure I** Quebec
115 O8 **Bonavista** Nfld
40 C3 **Bonboillon** France
138 D4 **Bon Bon** S Australia
85 G1 **Bon,C** Tunisia
106 F4 **Boncarbo** Colorado
20 J5 **Bonce** France
13 F3 **Bonchester Br** Scotland
9 E6 **Bonchurch** England
101 T10 **Bond** Colorado
28 C7 **Bonden Au** *R* W Germany
45 K2 **Bondeno** Italy
86 D5 **Bondo** Zaïre
71 F4 **Bondoc Penin** Luzon Philippines
71 F4 **Bondoc Pt** Luzon Philippines
36 F6 **Bondorf** W Germany
85 D7 **Bondoukou** Ivory Coast
70 O9 **Bondowoso** Java
126 F2 **Bonds Cay** *isld* Bahamas
144 C5 **Bonds Peak** *mt* New Zealand
140 C6 **Bond Springs** N Terr Aust
99 S5 **Bonduel** Wisconsin
101 P6 **Bondurant** Wyoming
Bône *see* **Annaba**
101 O6 **Bone** Idaho
113 L9 **Bonefish Pond** New Providence I Bahamas
71 H7 **Bonelipu** Indonesia
70 G7 **Bonelohe** Indonesia
68 G4 **Boneng** Laos
71 K8 **Boneogeh** Indonesia
71 K8 **Bonerate** *isld* Indonesia
26 K3 **Bones** Norway
15 E5 **Boness** Scotland
98 H6 **Bonesteel** S Dakota
131 C2 **Bonete,Cerro** *peak* Argentina
70 G7 **Bone, Teluk** *B* Sulawesi Indonesia
98 C1 **Bonetraill** N Dakota
121 L6 **Bonfield** Ontario
71 E4 **Bongabong** Philippines
86 D5 **Bongandanga** Zaïre
70 F2 **Bongao** Philippines
70 G5 **Bongka** Sulawesi Indonesia
70 M9 **Bongkok** *mt* Java
71 G7 **Bongo** *isld* Mindanao Philippines
86 C3 **Bongor** Chad
109 L2 **Bonham** Texas
118 L1 **Bonheur** Ontario
12 D2 **Bonhill** Scotland
36 C7 **Bonhomme, Col du** *pass* France
43 B7 **Bonifacio,Str.of** Corsica/Sardinia
111 L11 **Bonifay** Florida
Bonin Is *see* **Ogasawara-shoto**
103 P9 **Bonita** Arizona
111 E9 **Bonita** Louisiana
113 F11 **Bonita Springs** Florida
130 C7 **Bonito** Brazil
69 E13 **Bonjol** Sumatra
36 C2 **Bonn** W Germany
18 G6 **Bonnat** France
19 Q12 **Bonne** France
19 P15 **Bonne** *R* France
123 P4 **Bonne Bay** Nfld
20 F3 **Bonnebosq** France
22 G3 **Bonne Esperance** Belgium
123 P2 **Bonne Espérance** Quebec
20 K4 **Bonnelles** France
20 B5 **Bonnemain** France
101 M3 **Bonner** Montana
140 D1 **Bonner Mt** N Terr Aust
114 H8 **Bonners Ferry** Idaho
110 B2 **Bonner Springs** Kansas
28 A3 **Bonnet** Denmark
20 F5 **Bonnétable** France
110 F4 **Bonne Terre** Missouri
20 K2 **Bonneuil-les-Eaux** France
20 H5 **Bonneval** Eure-et-Loir France
40 F7 **Bonneval-sur-Arc** France
40 D4 **Bonnevaux** France
19 Q12 **Bonneville** France
100 D4 **Bonneville** Oregon
101 R6 **Bonneville** Wyoming
20 H3 **Bonneville,la** France
101 N7 **Bonneville Pk** Idaho
101 L9 **Bonneville Salt Flats** Utah/Nev
138 F6 **Bonney,L** S Australia
140 C5 **Bonney Well** N Terr Aust
20 K1 **Bonnières** Pas-de-Calais France
20 J3 **Bonnières** Yvelines France
143 C9 **Bonnie Rock** W Australia
19 O17 **Bonnieux** France
36 G5 **Bönnigheim** W Germany
36 H3 **Bonnland** W Germany
18 G5 **Bonny** France
85 F8 **Bonny** Nigeria
Bonny, Bight Of *see* **Biafra, Bight Of**
106 H2 **Bonny Res** Colorado
122 F8 **Bonny River** New Brunswick
118 G4 **Bonnyville** Alberta
110 F6 **Bono** Arkansas
43 C8 **Bono** Sardinia
71 C6 **Bonobond** Palawan Philippines
60 D14 **Bōno-misaki** *C* Japan
68 H7 **Bonom Mhai** *mt* Vietnam
43 B8 **Bonorva** Sardinia
140 B2 **Bonrook** N Terr Aust
111 J11 **Bon Secour** Alabama
70 E4 **Bontang** Kalimantan
89 A9 **Bonteberg** *mts* S Africa
85 B7 **Bonthe** Sierra Leone
71 E2 **Bontoc** Luzon Philippines
70 G7 **Bontosunggu** Sulawesi
109 O5 **Bon Wier** Texas
48 E4 **Bonyhád** Hungary
143 G6 **Bonython Ra** N Terr/W Aust
113 K12 **Booby I** Bahamas
141 F1 **Booby I** Queensland
127 M3 **Booby South Pt** Jamaica
36 D7 **Boofzheim** France
141 H8 **Boogah** Queensland
143 C8 **Boogardie** W Australia
138 C4 **Bookabie** S Australia
138 D4 **Bookaloo,L** S Australia
143 A8 **Bookara** W Australia
103 P2 **Book Cliffs** Utah
108 D7 **Booker** Texas
85 C7 **Boola** Guinea
142 B6 **Boolaloo** W Australia
143 A6 **Boolathanna** W Australia
138 E5 **Booleroo Centre** S Australia
143 A6 **Boologooro** W Australia
22 G1 **Boom** Belgium
94 B2 **Boon** Michigan
141 L8 **Boonah** Queensland
106 F3 **Boone** Colorado
99 N7 **Boone** Iowa
112 F1 **Boone** N Carolina
94 H9 **Boones Mill** Virginia
110 C6 **Booneville** Arkansas
110 N4 **Booneville** Kentucky
94 D9 **Booneville Res** Kentucky
141 H6 **Boongoondoo** Queensland
127 P4 **Boon Pt** Antigua W I
94 K7 **Boonsboro** Maryland
58 C2 **Bööntsagaan Nuur** *L* Mongolia
102 A2 **Boonville** California
110 J3 **Boonville** Indiana
110 D3 **Boonville** Missouri
95 M3 **Boonville** New York
71 B3 **Boo,Pulau Pulau** *islds* W Irian
143 D9 **Boorabbin** W Australia
138 D3 **Boorthanna** S Australia
20 H3 **Boos-sur-Andelle** France
13 E5 **Boot** England
146 A4 **Boothby,C** Antarctica
147 E3 **Boothia, Gulf of** N W Terr
115 K3 **Boothia Pen** N W Terr
111 J8 **Boothton** Alabama
13 E5 **Bootle** England
13 F6 **Bootle** England
37 J6 **Bopfingen** W Germany
89 C6 **Bophuthatswana** *reg* S Africa
65 C6 **Boping** China
36 D3 **Boppard** W Germany
129 K6 **Boqueirão, Serra do** *mts* Brazil
128 F8 **Boquerón** *dep* Paraguay
124 G4 **Boquilla de Conchos** Mexico
37 O4 **Bor** Czechoslovakia
86 E4 **Bo R** Sudan
78 E3 **Bor** Turkey
48 G6 **Bor** Yugoslavia
135 M10 **Bora-Bora** *isld* Society Is Pac Oc
101 M5 **Borah Pk** Idaho
86 H4 **Borama** Somalia
27 F14 **Borås** Sweden
77 B5 **Borāzjān** Iran
128 G4 **Borba** Brazil
28 B4 **Borbjerg** Denmark
71 G5 **Borbon** Cebu Philippines
130 H9 **Borborema, Planalto da** *plat* Brazil
48 K3 **Borca** Romania
48 L6 **Borcea** *R* Romania
78 H1 **Borçka** Turkey
138 D6 **Borda,C** S Australia
47 K7 **Bor Dağı** *mt* Turkey
18 E8 **Bordeaux** France
98 B8 **Bordeaux** Wyoming
122 J7 **Borden** Pr Edward I
118 K6 **Borden** Sask
143 C10 **Borden** W Australia
114 H2 **Borden I** N W Terr
115 L3 **Borden Pen** N W Terr
95 N6 **Bordentown** New Jersey
15 F5 **Borders** *reg* Scotland
138 F6 **Bordertown** S Australia
32 M4 **Bordesholm** W Germany
44 C4 **Bordighera** Italy
85 D3 **Bordj Flye Ste Marie** Algeria
85 F2 **Bordj Messouda** Algeria
85 F3 **Bordj Omar Driss** Algeria
28 O9 **Bordø** *isld* Faeroes
57 H4 **Bordunskiy** U.S.S.R.
85 D5 **Boré** Mali
143 D8 **Boreas,Mt** W Australia
31 K4 **Borek** Poland
29 M11 **Borgå** Finland
115 R5 **Borgarnes** Iceland
26 G3 **Borge** Norway
26 G6 **Börgefjell** *mt* Norway
32 K9 **Borgentreich** W Germany
25 G3 **Borger** Netherlands
108 C8 **Borger** Texas
32 G7 **Börger** W Germany
32 K9 **Borgholz** W Germany
32 H8 **Borgholzhausen** W Germany
32 F8 **Borghorst** W Germany
43 H10 **Borgia** Italy
28 N3 **Borgin** Faeroes
22 J2 **Borgloon** Belgium
28 D2 **Børglum** Denmark
40 G5 **Borgne** *R* Switzerland
41 O5 **Borgo** Italy
45 J4 **Borgo a Mozzano** Italy
45 J1 **Borgoforte** Italy
45 N6 **Borgo Montello** Italy
44 F1 **Borgonovo Val Tidone** Italy
45 M4 **Borgo Pace** Italy
45 K2 **Borgo Panigale** Italy
45 O5 **Borgorose** Italy
42 D5 **Borgo S. Lorenzo** Italy
41 J6 **Borgoticino** Italy
44 G3 **Borgo Val di Taro** Italy
42 D2 **Borgo Valsugana** Italy
41 H7 **Borgo Vercelli** Italy
26 H9 **Borgsjö** Sweden
27 F14 **Borgstena** Sweden
12 D4 **Borgue** Scotland
26 B9 **Borgund** Norway
27 C10 **Borgund** Norway
26 H8 **Borgvattnet** Sweden
98 B8 **Borie** Wyoming
68 F3 **Borikhane** Laos
31 O6 **Borinya** U.S.S.R.
26 S2 **Boris Gleb** U.S.S.R.
31 O6 **Borislav** U.S.S.R.
57 E3 **Borisovka** U.S.S.R.
55 F4 **Borisovskiy** U.S.S.R.
54 B6 **Borispol** U.S.S.R.
130 C9 **Borja** Paraguay
17 F3 **Borja** Spain
42 H4 **Borja Planina** Yugoslavia
17 H3 **Borjas Blancas** Spain
26 M6 **Börjelslandet** Sweden
32 F9 **Bork** W Germany
32 E9 **Borken** W Germany
36 G1 **Borken** W Germany
54 H7 **Borki** U.S.S.R.
28 D5 **Børkop** Denmark
86 C2 **Borkou** *dist* Chad
52 C6 **Borkovichi** U.S.S.R.
25 G4 **Borkulo** Netherlands
32 E5 **Borkum** W Germany
27 H11 **Borlänge** Sweden
47 J6 **Borlu** Turkey
44 D3 **Bormida di Millésimo** *R* Italy
44 D3 **Bormida di Spigno** *R* Italy
42 C2 **Bormio** Italy
37 O1 **Borna** E Germany
25 E2 **Borndiep** Netherlands
25 G4 **Borne** Netherlands
70 B4 **Borneo** *isld* E Indies
16 C3 **Bornes** *mt* Portugal
36 B2 **Bornheim** W Germany
27 H16 **Bornholm** *isld* Denmark
27 G16 **Bornholmsgattet** *str* Sweden/Denmark
32 M4 **Bornhöved** W Germany
33 R7 **Börnicke** E Germany
33 R8 **Bornim** E Germany
86 B3 **Borno** *prov* Nigeria
16 D8 **Bornos, Embalse de** *res* Spain
86 E4 **Boro** *R* Sudan
48 K3 **Boroaia** Romania
70 M9 **Borobudur** *ruins* Java
71 E5 **Borocay** *isld* Panay Philippines
51 N2 **Borogontsy** U.S.S.R.
57 L3 **Borohoro Shan** *mt ra* China
71 H4 **Boroko** Sulawesi Indonesia
85 D6 **Boromo** Upper Volta
102 G6 **Boron** California
141 K6 **Bororen** Queensland
13 G5 **Boroughbridge** England
56 B5 **Borovlyanka** U.S.S.R.
55 F4 **Borovoye** U.S.S.R.
54 H1 **Borovsk** U.S.S.R.
55 E3 **Borovskiy** U.S.S.R.
55 D4 **Borovskoye** U.S.S.R.
27 G16 **Borrby** Sweden
28 K6 **Borre** Denmark
33 R5 **Borrenthin** E Germany
138 E5 **Borrika** S Australia
28 B5 **Borris** Denmark
14 E4 **Borris** Irish Rep
14 D4 **Borrisoleigh** Irish Rep
140 D3 **Borroloola** N Terr Aust
27 J13 **Börrum** Sweden
48 J3 **Borşa** Romania
58 G1 **Borsch Chovochnyy Khrebet** *mt* U.S.S.R.
33 R10 **Borsdorf** E Germany
26 P1 **Börselv** Norway
48 H2 **Borshava** *R* U.S.S.R.
48 K2 **Borshchev** U.S.S.R.
48 F2 **Borsod-Abaúj Zemplén** Hungary
25 A6 **Borsselen** Netherlands
33 N8 **Börssum** W Germany
28 K5 **Borstahusen** Sweden
32 J7 **Borstel** W Germany
57 K3 **Bortala He** *R* China
8 B3 **Borth** Wales
18 G7 **Bort-les-Orgues** France
26 G9 **Börtnan** Sweden
58 F1 **Borto** U.S.S.R.
77 B4 **Borūjen** Iran
77 A3 **Borūjerd** Iran
28 E4 **Borum** Denmark
28 H5 **Borup** Denmark
98 K2 **Borup** Minnesota
56 D4 **Borus,Khrebet** *mts* U.S.S.R.
31 K2 **Bory Tucholskie** *forest* Poland
31 M5 **Borzęcin** Poland
78 J1 **Borzhomi** U.S.S.R.
54 D5 **Borzna** U.S.S.R.
51 L3 **Borzya** U.S.S.R.
58 G1 **Borzya** *R* U.S.S.R.
57 G1 **Bosaga** U.S.S.R.
Bosaso *see* **Bender Cassim**
33 M4 **Bosau** W Germany
8 B6 **Boscastle** England
95 Q3 **Boscawen** New Hampshire
45 K1 **Boschi Santa Anna** Italy
20 H2 **Bosc-le-Hard** France
99 Q6 **Boscobel** Wisconsin
9 E6 **Boscombe** England
45 Q8 **Boscotrecase** Italy
67 B5 **Bose** China
38 K7 **Bosenstein,Gross** *mt* Austria
65 D6 **Boshan** China
55 F5 **Boshchekul'** U.S.S.R.
89 D7 **Boshof** S Africa
77 E3 **Boshruyeh** Iran
46 E2 **Bosiljgrad** Yugoslavia
68 G4 **Bo Si Song Khram** Thailand
27 G12 **Bosjön** Sweden
25 C4 **Boskoop** Netherlands
98 A8 **Bosler** Wyoming
8 D1 **Bosley** England
42 H4 **Bosna** *R* Yugoslavia
86 C5 **Bosobolo** Zaïre
61 O10 **Bōsō-hantō** *pen* Japan
32 G10 **Bösperde** W Germany
Bosporus Turkey *see* **Karadeniz Boğazı**
106 D7 **Bosque** New Mexico
124 G2 **Bosque Bonito** Mexico
86 C4 **Bossangoa** Cent Afr Republic
86 C4 **Bossèmbélé** Cent Afr Republic
86 C4 **Bossemtele** Cent Afr Republic
111 C9 **Bossier City** Louisiana
86 B3 **Bosso** Niger
66 D3 **Bosten Hu** *L* China
9 F2 **Boston** England
113 D7 **Boston** Georgia
95 Q4 **Boston** Massachusetts
97 **Boston** *conurbation* Massachusetts
138 D5 **Boston B** S Australia
117 N11 **Boston Bar** Br Col
127 M2 **Boston Bay** Jamaica
110 C6 **Boston Mts** Arkansas
13 G6 **Boston Spa** England
28 F6 **Bøstrup** Fyn Denmark
28 D4 **Bøstrup** Viborg Denmark
48 E5 **Bosut** *R* Yugoslavia
123 O5 **Boswarlos** Nfld
117 P11 **Boswell** Br Col
99 T9 **Boswell** Indiana
107 P7 **Boswell** Oklahoma
94 H6 **Boswell** Pennsylvania
110 C2 **Bosworth** Missouri
74 D7 **Botad** India
139 K5 **Botany B** New S Wales
26 J8 **Boteå** Sweden
47 G2 **Botev** *mt* Bulgaria
47 F2 **Botevgrad** Bulgaria
118 E6 **Botha** Alberta
9 F1 **Bothamsall** England
87 E11 **Bothaville** S Africa
13 E4 **Bothel** England
117 M12 **Bothell** Washington
26 L8 **Bothnia,Gulf of** Sweden/Finland
120 J10 **Bothwell** Ontario
12 D2 **Bothwell** Scotland
139 H8 **Bothwell** Tasmania
86 B1 **Botiala** Somalia
16 B3 **Boticas** Portugal
87 D10 **Botletle** *R* Botswana
9 E6 **Botley** England
48 M4 **Botna** *R* U.S.S.R.
28 H7 **Bøtø** Denmark
71 D3 **Botolan Pt** Luzon Philippines
48 K3 **Botoşani** Romania
68 H4 **Bo Trach** Vietnam
22 L3 **Botrange** *mt* Belgium
26 L7 **Botsmark** Sweden
89 C4 **Botswana** *rep* Africa
43 G9 **Botte Donato** *mt* Italy
89 A8 **Botter Kloof Pass** S Africa
9 F2 **Bottesford** England
114 J8 **Bottineau** N Dakota
9 G3 **Bottisham** England
127 N6 **Bottom** Saba W I
9 E1 **Bottom House** England
45 M1 **Bottrighe** Italy
32 E9 **Bottrop** W Germany
47 F1 **Botunya** *R* Bulgaria
115 O8 **Botwood** Nfld
43 A12 **Bou Aci** Algeria
85 C7 **Bouaflé** Ivory Coast
20 H3 **Bouafles** France
85 D7 **Bouaké** Ivory Coast
86 C4 **Bouala** Cent Afr Republic
86 C4 **Bouar** Cent Afr Republic
85 D2 **Bouârfa** Morocco
21 B7 **Bouaye** France
30 H6 **Boubín** *mt* Czechoslovakia
86 C4 **Bouca** Cent Afr Republic
18 D9 **Boucau** France
140 C1 **Boucaut B** N Terr Aust
20 E4 **Boucé** France
22 E3 **Bouchain** France
22 D4 **Bouchavesnes** France
43 B12 **Bouchegouf** Algeria
123 N2 **Boucher,L** Quebec
19 N17 **Bouches-du-Rhône** *dep* France
121 P6 **Bouchette** Quebec
22 D4 **Bouchoir** France
85 D5 **Bou Djébéha** Mali
84 A3 **Boudnib** Morocco
40 A2 **Boudreville** France
40 E4 **Boudry** Switzerland
21 B7 **Bouée** France
122 E3 **Bouffard,L** Quebec
137 M3 **Bougainville** *isld* Solomon Is
142 F2 **Bougainville, C** W Australia
141 H3 **Bougainville Reef** Gt Barrier Reef Aust
71 C2 **Bougainville,Selat** W Irian
85 F1 **Bougaroun,C** Algeria
21 I7 **Bouges-le-Château** France
Bougie *see* **Bejaia**
85 C6 **Bougouni** Mali
43 C11 **Bouhairet Benzart** *gulf* Tunisia
17 G9 **Bou Hanifa** Algeria
17 G9 **Bou Hanifa, Barrage de** Algeria
127 M4 **Bouillante** Guadeloupe W I
20 G3 **Bouille,la** France
21 E7 **Bouillé-Loretz** France
21 D6 **Bouillé-Ménard** France
22 J4 **Bouillon** Belgium
85 C3 **Bou Izakam** Morocco
123 L3 **Boulain,L** Quebec
19 K3 **Boulay** France
98 A9 **Boulder** Colorado
101 N3 **Boulder** Montana
103 N4 **Boulder** Utah
143 D9 **Boulder** W Australia
101 Q7 **Boulder** Wyoming
103 K5 **Boulder Can** Nevada
103 K6 **Boulder City** Nevada
102 B4 **Boulder Cr** California
100 J7 **Boulder Cr** Idaho
121 N5 **Bouleau, L. au** Quebec
102 H9 **Boulevard** California
136 H6 **Boulia** Queensland
140 E6 **Boulia** Queensland
22 B2 **Boulogne** France
21 G6 **Bouloire** France
85 C5 **Boulouli** Mali
85 D6 **Boulsa** Upper Volta
22 H5 **Boult-aux-Bois** France
85 G6 **Boultoum** Niger
22 H4 **Boulzicourt** France
86 C5 **Boumba** *R* Cameroon
85 D7 **Bouna** Ivory Coast
117 C3 **Boundary** Alaska
116 R4 **Boundary** Yukon Terr
102 F4 **Boundary Pk** Nevada
118 J9 **Boundary Plateau** Mont/Sask
114 G7 **Boundary Ranges** Br Col
85 C7 **Boundiali** Ivory Coast
68 H6 **Boung Long** Cambodia
68 E2 **Boun Neua** Laos
106 E4 **Bountiful** Colorado
140 E3 **Bountiful Is** Queensland
118 K7 **Bounty** Sask
20 K1 **Bouquemaison** France
28 M2 **Bøur** Faeroes
110 E3 **Bourbeuse** *R* Missouri
94 A5 **Bourbon** Indiana
110 E3 **Bourbon** Missouri
83 L14 **Bourbon,C** Kerguelen Indian Oc
18 H6 **Bourbon-Lancy** France
18 H6 **Bourbon l'Archambault** France
18 H6 **Bourbonnais** *prov* France
40 C2 **Bourbonne les Bains** France
18 G7 **Bourboule,la** France
19 J5 **Bourboune les Bassigny** France
22 C2 **Bourbourg** France
19 O13 **Bourbre** *R* France
19 O15 **Bourdeaux** France
36 B6 **Bourdonnay** France
16 E10 **Boured** Morocco
85 D5 **Bourem** Mali
18 E7 **Bourg** Gironde France
20 G3 **Bourg-Achard** France
21 I10 **Bourganeuf** France
21 H9 **Bourg Archambault** France
18 H7 **Bourg Argental** France
19 Q15 **Bourg d'Arud** France
19 O14 **Bourg-de-Péage** France
21 B6 **Bourg-des-Comptes** France
20 G2 **Bourg Dun** France
19 O12 **Bourg-en-Bresse** Ain France
18 G5 **Bourges** France
22 F5 **Bourg et Comin** France
40 C6 **Bourget,L.du** France
20 K4 **Bourget,le** France
18 G10 **Bourg-Madame** France
21 D7 **Bourgneuf** Maine-et-Loire France
21 E6 **Bourg-Neuf** Maine-et-Loire France
21 B7 **Bourgneuf-en-Retz** France
20 D5 **Bourgneuf,le** France
22 G5 **Bourgogne** France
19 O13 **Bourgoin** France
40 E6 **Bourg-St-Maurice** France
20 G3 **Bourgtheroulde** France
20 E3 **Bourguébus** France
21 F7 **Bourgueil** France
120 K4 **Bourkes** Ontario
121 N4 **Bourlamaque** Quebec
22 E3 **Bourlon** France
40 C1 **Bourmont** France
121 P4 **Bourmont** Quebec
21 G7 **Bournan** France
21 F7 **Bournand** France
9 F2 **Bourne** England
115 K1 **Bourne,C** N W Terr
9 F4 **Bourne End** England
9 E6 **Bournemouth** England
20 G3 **Bourneville** France
21 C8 **Bournezeau** France
18 E8 **Bourriot Bergonce** France
32 F7 **Bourtanger Moor** W Germany
20 G4 **Bourth** France
22 B2 **Bourthes** France
8 D5 **Bourton** England
86 D3 **Bourtoutou** Chad
22 L4 **Bous** Luxembourg
85 E1 **Bou Saâda** Algeria
43 B12 **Bou Salem** Tunisia
103 K8 **Bouse** Arizona
103 K8 **Bouse Wash** *R* Arizona
36 B5 **Bous/Saar** W Germany
21 J9 **Boussac** France
20 B5 **Boussac, la** France
21 C7 **Boussay** France
22 L5 **Bousse** France
86 C3 **Bousso** Chad
20 K5 **Boutigny** France
85 B5 **Boutilimit** Mauritania
21 E9 **Boutonne** *R* France
143 B10 **Bouvard,C** W Australia
19 O13 **Bouvesse** France
90 J14 **Bouvet** *isld* S Atlantic Oc
81 A12 **Bouvetøy** *isld* S Atlantic Oc
21 B7 **Bouvron** France
36 C6 **Bouxwiller** France
85 F6 **Bouza** Niger
36 B5 **Bouzonville** France
28 C7 **Bov** Denmark
43 G11 **Bova** Italy
32 L9 **Bovenden** W Germany
70 C4 **Boven Kapuas** *mts* Sarawak
28 F6 **Bovense** Denmark
26 C10 **Böverdal** Norway
20 K2 **Boves** France
44 C3 **Boves** Italy
8 C6 **Bovey Tracey** England
22 K3 **Bovigny** Belgium
100 J3 **Bovill** Idaho
43 G7 **Bovino** Italy
28 A4 **Bøvlingbjerg** Denmark
45 L1 **Bovolenta** Italy
45 K1 **Bovolone** Italy
8 C6 **Bow** England
98 D1 **Bowbells** N Dakota
113 F7 **Bowden** Florida
127 M3 **Bowden** Jamaica
98 G4 **Bowdle** S Dakota
101 S1 **Bowdoin,L** Montana
112 B4 **Bowdon** Georgia
98 G2 **Bowdon** N Dakota
143 B10 **Bowelling** W Australia
110 E1 **Bowen** Illinois
141 J5 **Bowen** Queensland
141 J5 **Bowen** *R* Queensland
141 H5 **Bowen Downs** Queensland
117 M11 **Bowen I** Br Col
140 B1 **Bowen Str** N Terr Aust
95 M7 **Bowers** Delaware
94 D7 **Bowersville** Ohio
101 L5 **Bowery Pk** Idaho
13 F5 **Bowes** England
143 B8 **Bowgada** W Australia
103 P9 **Bowie** Arizona
106 C3 **Bowie** Colorado
141 H5 **Bowie** Queensland
109 K2 **Bowie** Texas
118 F9 **Bow Island** Alberta
78 L3 **Bowkan** Iran
12 D2 **Bowling** Scotland
113 F10 **Bowling Green** Florida
110 J2 **Bowling Green** Indiana
110 K4 **Bowling Green** Kentucky
110 E2 **Bowling Green** Missouri
94 D5 **Bowling Green** Ohio
95 K8 **Bowling Green** Virginia
141 H4 **Bowling Green,C** Queensland
112 D3 **Bowman** Georgia
98 C3 **Bowman** N Dakota
121 M9 **Bowmanville** Ontario
15 B5 **Bowmore** Scotland
118 C7 **Bowness** Alberta
13 F5 **Bowness** England
118 C7 **Bow R** Alberta
142 G3 **Bow River** W Australia
117 N9 **Bowron Lake Prov. Park** Br Columbia
117 J7 **Bowser L** Br Columbia
119 Q6 **Bowsman** Manitoba
118 B7 **Bow Valley Prov. Park** Alberta
36 H5 **Boxberg** W Germany
98 C7 **Box Butte Res** Nebraska
98 A6 **Box Cr** Wyoming
101 P1 **Box Elder** Montana
98 C5 **Box Elder** S Dakota
106 F2 **Box Elder Cr** Colorado
98 B4 **Boxelder Cr** Montana
101 R2 **Boxelder Cr** Montana
9 F5 **Box Hill** England
27 H13 **Boxholm** Sweden
58 G5 **Bo Xian** China
65 D6 **Boxing** China
25 E5 **Boxmeer** Netherlands
138 F4 **Box Tank** New S Wales
25 D5 **Boxtel** Netherlands
78 E1 **Boyabat** Turkey
128 D2 **Boyacá** *div* Colombia
86 C4 **Boyali** Cent Afr Republic
47 K3 **Boyalık** Turkey
58 G6 **Boyang** China
143 B10 **Boyanup** W Australia
111 D10 **Boyce** Louisiana
94 J7 **Boyce** Virginia
143 D8 **Boyce,Mt** W Australia
115 K6 **Boyd** Manitoba
101 Q4 **Boyd** Montana
109 K2 **Boyd** Texas
123 S4 **Boyd's Cove** Newfoundland
94 J10 **Boydton** Virginia
65 C5 **Boye** China
99 L7 **Boyer** Iowa
99 L7 **Boyer** *R* Iowa
106 G3 **Boyero** Colorado
95 M6 **Boyertown** Pennsylvania
98 A4 **Boyes** Montana
95 K10 **Boykins** Virginia
118 E4 **Boyle** Alberta
14 C3 **Boyle** Irish Rep
111 F8 **Boyle** Mississippi
123 L8 **Boylston** Nova Scotia
14 E3 **Boyne** *R* Irish Rep
141 K6 **Boyne** *R* Queensland
94 C1 **Boyne City** Michigan
94 C1 **Boyne Falls** Michigan
20 K5 **Boynes** France
110 C1 **Boynton** Missouri
107 P6 **Boynton** Oklahoma
113 G11 **Boynton Beach** Florida
86 E5 **Boyoma Falls** Zaire
101 R6 **Boysen Res** Wyoming
143 B10 **Boyup Brook** W Australia
47 J8 **Bozburun** Turkey
47 H5 **Bozcaada** *isld* Turkey
47 L5 **Boz Dağ** *mt* Turkey
47 J7 **Bozdoğan** Turkey
114 H8 **Bozeman** Montana
Bozen *see* **Bolzano**
86 C5 **Bozene** Zaïre
31 K1 **Boże Pole** Poland
65 C5 **Bozhen** China
37 O3 **Boží Dar** Czechoslovakia
78 D3 **Bozkir** Turkey
54 F1 **Boznya** U.S.S.R.
78 G3 **Bozova** Turkey
48 G6 **Bozovici** Romania
45 J1 **Bozzolo** Italy
44 C2 **Bra** Italy
22 G2 **Brabançonne** *prov* Belgium
22 G2 **Brabant** *prov* Belgium
146 E14 **Brabant I** Antarctica
119 O2 **Brabant L** Sask
28 E4 **Brabrand** Denmark
28 H6 **Bråby** Denmark
42 H5 **Brač** *isld* Yugoslavia
15 B3 **Bracadale** Scotland
129 H6 **Braça Menor** *R* Brazil
44 M5 **Bracciano** Italy
42 E6 **Bracciano,Lago di** Italy
44 M5 **Bracciano, Lago di** Italy
121 L7 **Bracebridge** Ontario
84 E4 **Brach** Libya
21 I6 **Bracieux** France
26 H9 **Bräcke** Sweden
118 J9 **Bracken** Sask
109 J6 **Bracken** Texas
36 G5 **Brackenheim** W Germany
13 G6 **Brackenhill** England
119 S5 **Bracken L** Manitoba
108 G6 **Brackettville** Texas
9 E3 **Brackley** England
9 F5 **Bracknell** England
32 J9 **Brackwede** W Germany
12 E1 **Braco** Scotland
43 G8 **Bradano** *R* Italy
98 F3 **Braddock** N Dakota
94 H6 **Braddock** Pennsylvania
99 L9 **Braddyville** Iowa
113 E10 **Bradenton** Florida
113 E10 **Bradenton Beach** Florida
28 B7 **Braderup** W Germany
110 E6 **Bradford** Arkansas
8 D5 **Bradford** England
13 G6 **Bradford** England
99 R8 **Bradford** Illinois
99 N7 **Bradford** Iowa
95 T1 **Bradford** Maine
95 P3 **Bradford** New Hampshire
94 C6 **Bradford** Ohio
121 L8 **Bradford** Ontario
94 J5 **Bradford** Pennsylvania
95 Q5 **Bradford** Rhode I
94 B9 **Bradfordsville** Kentucky
111 C8 **Bradley** Arkansas
102 D6 **Bradley** California
99 T8 **Bradley** Illinois
107 N7 **Bradley** Oklahoma
110 D5 **Bradleyville** Missouri
94 D5 **Bradner** Ohio
123 P2 **Bradore Bay** Quebec
123 P2 **Bradore Hills** Quebec
98 J9 **Bradshaw** Nebraska
140 B3 **Bradshaw** N Terr Aust
142 F3 **Bradshaw,Mt** W Australia
119 R9 **Bradwardine** Manitoba
9 G4 **Bradwell** England
118 L7 **Bradwell** Sask
98 F8 **Brady** Nebraska
109 H4 **Brady** Texas
117 E6 **Brady Glacier** Alaska
138 C3 **Brady,Mt** S Australia
28 D5 **Brædstrup** Denmark
138 E5 **Braemar** S Australia
15 E3 **Braemar** Scotland
15 E3 **Braeriach** *mt* Scotland
142 D5 **Braeside** W Australia
16 B3 **Braga** Portugal
131 E5 **Bragado** Argentina
129 J4 **Bragança** Brazil
16 C3 **Bragança** Portugal
130 F8 **Bragança Paulista** Brazil
112 E6 **Braganza** Georgia
110 G5 **Bragg City** Missouri
118 C7 **Bragg Creek Prov. Park** Alberta
54 B5 **Bragin** U.S.S.R.
99 N4 **Braham** Minnesota
33 N6 **Brahlstorf** Schwerin E Germany
75 O7 **Brahmanbaria** Bangladesh
75 P5 **Brahmaputra** *R* S Asia
32 L4 **Brahmsee** *L* W Germany
77 K5 **Brahui,Cen** *reg* Pakistan
99 S8 **Braidwood** Illinois
48 L5 **Brăila** Romania
9 E2 **Brailsford** England
98 J8 **Brainard** Nebraska
22 F5 **Braine** France
22 G2 **Braine L'Alleud** Belgium
22 G2 **Braine-le Château** Belgium
22 G2 **Braine-le Comte** Belgium
99 M3 **Brainerd** Minnesota
21 F7 **Brain-sur-Allonnes** France
9 G4 **Braintree** England
13 E4 **Braithwaite** England
111 G12 **Braithwaite** Louisiana
140 C1 **Braithwaite Pt** N Terr Aust
22 J2 **Braives** Belgium
89 F4 **Brak** *R* S Africa
32 H6 **Brake** W Germany
22 F2 **Brakel** Belgium
32 K9 **Brakel** W Germany
85 B5 **Brakna** *reg* Mauritania
57 D1 **Brali** U.S.S.R.
114 G7 **Bralorne** Br Columbia
107 N5 **Braman** Oklahoma
Brambach *see* **Radiumbad-Brambach**
38 F7 **Bramberg** Austria
13 G6 **Bramham** England
32 H6 **Bramloge** W Germany
28 B6 **Bramming** Denmark
44 B3 **Bram,Monte** Italy
26 J9 **Brämö** *isld* Sweden
9 H3 **Brampton** England
98 J3 **Brampton** N Dakota
141 J5 **Brampton I** Queensland
32 G8 **Bramsche** W Germany
141 G1 **Bramwell** Queensland
94 F9 **Bramwell** W Virginia
9 G2 **Brancaster** England
13 G4 **Brancepeth** England
99 U6 **Branch** Michigan
123 T7 **Branch** Nfld
95 K4 **Branchport** New York
112 G4 **Branchville** S Carolina
130 B7 **Branco** *R* Mato Grosso Brazil
128 F3 **Branco** *R* Roraima Brazil
130 J9 **Branco,Cabo** Brazil
131 B2 **Branco,R** Argentina
41 L3 **Brand** Austria
37 O3 **Brand** Czechoslovakia
87 B10 **Brandberg** *mt* Namibia
26 H9 **Brändbo** Sweden
28 C5 **Brande** Denmark
32 L5 **Brande-Hörnerkirchen** W Germany
101 T4 **Brandenberg** Montana
33 R8 **Brandenburg** E Germany
110 K4 **Brandenburg** Kentucky
37 P2 **Brand-Erbisdorf** E Germany
28 C6 **Branderup** Denmark
21 G9 **Brandes** *reg* France
13 H6 **Brandesburton** England
89 E7 **Brandfort** S Africa
33 R10 **Brandis** E Germany
29 J11 **Brändö** Finland
106 H3 **Brandon** Colorado
9 G3 **Brandon** England
119 S9 **Brandon** Manitoba
98 E9 **Brandon** Nebraska
141 H4 **Brandon** Queensland
95 O3 **Brandon** Vermont
99 S6 **Brandon** Wisconsin
14 A4 **Brandon B** Irish Rep
14 A4 **Brandon Hd** Irish Rep
14 A4 **Brandon Mt** Irish Rep
95 N3 **Brandreth** New York
13 G5 **Brandsby** England
133 F5 **Brandsen** Argentina
28 D6 **Brandsø** *isld* Denmark
110 E5 **Brandsville** Missouri
98 K5 **Brandt** S Dakota
27 F11 **Brandval** Norway
87 D12 **Brandvlei** S Africa
94 K8 **Brandy** Virginia
95 L8 **Brandywine** Maryland
48 K6 **Braneşti** Romania
95 P5 **Branford** Connecticut
113 E8 **Branford** Florida
31 M1 **Braniewo** Poland
27 L17 **Braniewo** U.S.S.R.
31 M6 **Branisko** *mts* Czechoslovakia
18 E8 **Branne** France
47 H3 **Brannitsa** Bulgaria
141 F8 **Bransby** Queensland
102 A2 **Branscomb** California
146 E14 **Bransfield Str** Antarctica
106 G4 **Branson** Colorado
110 C5 **Branson** Missouri
9 F1 **Branston** England
118 D8 **Brant** Alberta
70 O9 **Brantas** Java
70 O10 **Brantas** *R* Java
98 H2 **Brantford** N Dakota
115 L9 **Brantford** Ontario
111 K10 **Brantley** Alabama
18 F7 **Brantôme** France
138 F7 **Branxholme** Victoria
115 N8 **Bras d'or L** Nova Scotia
99 O9 **Brashear** Missouri
128 E6 **Brasiléia** Brazil
129 J7 **Brasília** Brazil
129 G4 **Brasilia Legal** Brazil
52 C6 **Braslav** U.S.S.R.
48 K5 **Brasov** Romania
85 F8 **Brass** Nigeria
22 G1 **Brasschaat** Belgium
140 C6 **Brassey Mt** N Terr Aust
143 D6 **Brassey Ra** W Australia
70 E2 **Brassey Ra** *mts* Sabah
139 G5 **Brassi** New S Wales
28 D4 **Brassø** *L* Denmark
95 R1 **Brassua L** Maine
48 H4 **Bratca** Romania
48 L5 **Brates, L** Romania
31 K7 **Bratislava** Czechoslovakia
47 G3 **Bratsigovo** Bulgaria
56 F3 **Bratsk** U.S.S.R.
48 M2 **Bratslav** U.S.S.R.

Brattleboro — Bungay 13

95 P4 Brattleboro Vermont
32 M8 Brau W Germany
36 D3 Braubach W Germany
36 G2 Brauerschwend W Germany
38 H5 Braunau Austria
36 E3 Braunfels W Germany
33 N9 Braunlage W Germany
33 P10 Braunsbedra E Germany
Braunsberg see Braniewo
8 B5 Braunton England
36 B2 Brauweiler W Germany
86 H5 Brava Somalia
131 D4 Brava, L. la Argentina
94 G7 Brave Pennsylvania
27 H13 Bråviken L Sweden
131 D2 Bravo,Sa mt Argentina
14 E3 Bray Irish Rep
22 D1 Bray-Dunes France
22 E5 Braye France
21 G6 Braye R France
20 J3 Bray-et-Lû France
8 C5 Brayford England
14 A5 Bray Hd Irish Rep
115 M4 Bray I N W Terr
110 C2 Braymer Missouri
18 H4 Bray sur Seine France
22 D4 Bray-sur-Somme France
118 A6 Brazeau Alberta
118 B6 Brazeau Dam Alberta
110 J2 Brazil Indiana
128 F6 Brazil rep S America
90 G11 Brazil Basin Atlantic Oc
109 M6 Brazoria Texas
109 L4 Brazos R Texas
86 C6 Brazzaville Congo
48 E6 Brčko Yugoslavia
31 K2 Brda R Poland
48 D1 Brdo mt Czechoslovakia
140 E6 Breadalbane Queensland
143 E7 Breaden Bluff hill W Australia
143 F7 Breaden,L W Australia
141 K1 Breakfast Creek dist Brisbane, Qnsld
144 A6 Breaksea I New Zealand
144 B7 Breaksea Is New Zealand
141 L6 Breaksea Spit Queensland
20 B5 Breal-s-M France
8 D4 Bream England
145 E1 Bream Bay New Zealand
27 F15 Breared Sweden
20 F2 Bréaute France
111 E11 Breaux Bridge Louisiana
70 M9 Brebes Java
70 M9 Brebes,Tg C Java
121 U4 Brébeuf, L Quebec
122 B5 Brébeuf,L Quebec
20 C4 Brécey France
36 E3 Brechen W Germany
121 L8 Brechin Ontario
15 F4 Brechin Scotland
22 H1 Brecht Belgium
106 D2 Breckenridge Colorado
98 K3 Breckenridge Minnesota
110 C2 Breckenridge Missouri
109 J3 Breckenridge Texas
133 C8 Brecknock, Pen Chile
31 K7 Břeclav Czechoslovakia
8 C4 Brecon Wales
8 C4 Brecon Beacons mts Wales
Breconshire co see Powys, Gwent, Mid Glamorgan counties
99 M7 Breda Iowa
25 C5 Breda Netherlands
26 M6 Bredåker Sweden
27 H15 Bredåkra Sweden
27 G14 Bredaryd Sweden
87 D12 Bredasdorp S Africa
33 Q7 Breddin E Germany
32 K6 Breddorf W Germany
28 B6 Brede Denmark
9 G6 Brede England
28 B6 Brede Å R Denmark
28 B6 Bredebro Denmark
32 J10 Bredelar W Germany
22 E1 Bredene Belgium
33 R5 Bredenfelde E Germany
119 P8 Bredenyur Sask
33 S6 Bredereiche E Germany
28 C7 Bredevad Denmark
27 G12 Bredsjö Sweden
30 E1 Bredstedt W Germany
28 C5 Bredsten Denmark
26 K8 Bredträsk Sweden
55 D4 Bredy U.S.S.R.
22 K1 Bree Belgium
89 A9 Breede R S Africa
110 G3 Breese Illinois
33 Q5 Breesen E Germany
46 E3 Bregalnica R Yugoslavia
41 H2 Brege R W Germany
41 L2 Bregenz Austria
41 L3 Bregenzer Ache R Austria
41 L3 Bregenzer Wald mt Austria
28 G5 Bregninge Denmark
48 H6 Bregovo Bulgaria
20 C4 Bréhal France
18 C4 Bréhat, I France
122 B1 Bréhat, L Quebec
33 Q9 Brehna E Germany
33 T9 Brehnitz E Germany
36 E2 Breidenbach W Germany
98 E3 Breien N Dakota
20 G5 Breil-sur-Mérize, le France
26 B10 Breim Norway
40 G1 Breisach W Germany
37 M5 Breitenbrunn W Germany
33 Q10 Breitenfeld E Germany
37 K4 Breitengüssbach W Germany
33 P9 Breitenhagen E Germany
33 M7 Breitenhees W Germany
37 O3 Breitenhof E Germany
33 S6 Breiter Luzinsee L E Germany
40 G5 Breithorn mt Switzerland
33 Q4 Breitling E Germany
37 J2 Breitungen W Germany
26 M1 Breivikbotn Norway
28 A4 Brejning Denmark
129 K4 Brejo Brazil
94 C3 Brekenridge Michigan
26 E9 Brekken Norway
26 D8 Brekstad Norway
26 A10 Bremangerland isld Norway
41 L6 Brembana, Val Italy
41 L6 Brembo R Italy
112 B4 Bremen Georgia
94 A5 Bremen Indiana
94 E7 Bremen Ohio
32 J6 Bremen W Germany
140 D1 Bremer isld N Terr Aust
143 C10 Bremer Bay W Australia
32 J5 Bremerhaven W Germany
143 D10 Bremer Ra W Australia
117 M12 Bremerton Washington
32 K6 Bremervörde W Germany
41 H3 Bremgarten Switzerland
116 Q6 Bremner R Alaska
109 L4 Bremond Texas
26 E6 Bremsteinen lt ho Norway
139 H3 Brenda New S Wales
141 H8 Brenda Queensland
28 D6 Brenderup Denmark
45 K1 Brendola Italy
8 C5 Brendon Hills England
109 L5 Brenham Texas
21 G7 Brenne R France
41 O3 Brenner Austria
101 M5 Brenner Montana
41 O4 Brennero Italy
41 O3 Brenner Pass Austria/Italy
41 M6 Breno Italy
42 C3 Breno Italy
19 P12 Brénod France
36 C5 Brenschelbach W Germany
111 J9 Brent Alabama
121 M6 Brent Ontario
42 D3 Brenta R Italy
41 N5 Brenta, Gruppa di mt Italy
9 F5 Brentford England
98 H4 Brentford S Dakota
123 T4 Brenton Rock Nfld
102 C4 Brentwood California
9 G4 Brentwood England
37 J6 Brenz R W Germany
9 G5 Brenzett England
45 J2 Brescello Italy
41 M6 Brescia Italy
25 A6 Breskens Netherlands
Breslau see Wrocław
20 J2 Bresle R France
20 K3 Bresles France
143 C6 Bresnahan,Mt W Australia
41 P4 Bressanone Italy
21 E8 Bressuire France
18 B4 Brest France
31 O3 Brest U.S.S.R.
18 D5 Brest R France
18 C4 Bretagne prov France
83 J14 Bretagne, Pnte de Réunion Indian Oc
48 K4 Breţcu Romania
18 G8 Bretenoux France
20 G4 Breteuil-sur-Iton France
20 K2 Breteuil-sur-Noye France
20 K4 Bretigny France
118 C5 Breton Alberta
20 G5 Bretoncelles France
111 G12 Breton I Louisiana
20 K2 Bretonneux,V France
21 C9 Breton, Pertuis str France
95 N6 Breton Woods New Jersey
38 K7 Bretstein Austria
145 E1 Brett, C New Zealand
36 F5 Bretten W Germany
20 E3 Bretteville France
20 D3 Bretteville l'Orgueilleuse France
37 J5 Brettheim W Germany
36 G5 Bretzfeld W Germany
36 G4 Breuberg W Germany
69 B10 Breueh isld Sumatra
25 E5 Breugel Netherlands
20 F3 Breuil-en-Auge,le France
20 H4 Breuilpont France
25 D4 Breukelen Netherlands
40 C1 Breuvannes France
20 J4 Bréval France
112 E2 Brevard N Carolina
129 H4 Breves Brazil
27 D12 Brevik Norway
95 T2 Brewer Maine
95 L3 Brewerton New York
113 E10 Brewster Florida
107 J2 Brewster Kansas
98 G8 Brewster Nebraska
95 O5 Brewster New York
94 F6 Brewster Ohio
117 O11 Brewster Washington
144 B6 Brewster, Mt New Zealand
111 J10 Brewton Alabama
25 F6 Breyell W Germany
19 O14 Brezins France
46 F2 Breznik Bulgaria
48 F2 Brezno Czechoslovakia
38 M8 Brezno Yugoslavia
20 H4 Brezolles France
16 D2 Brezo, Sa. del mts Spain
47 G2 Brezovo Bulgaria
86 D4 Bria Cent Afr Republic
103 M4 Brian Head Utah
18 G5 Briare France
141 L7 Bribie I Queensland
108 G1 Brice Texas
99 N6 Bricelyn Minnesota
48 L2 Brichany U.S.S.R.
110 F7 Brickeys Arkansas
19 J4 Bricon France
123 M2 Briconnet,L Quebec
20 B3 Bricquebec France
20 B4 Bricqueville-sur-Mer France
12 D5 Bride I of Man U.K.
14 C4 Bride R Irish Rep
8 B3 Bridell Wales
8 B6 Bridestowe England
119 U3 Bridgar Manitoba
101 M7 Bridge Idaho
117 M10 Bridge R Br Columbia
112 D6 Bridgeboro Georgia
12 B2 Bridgend Islay Scotland
13 E1 Bridgend Tayside Scotland
8 C5 Bridgend Wales
12 E1 Bridge of Allan Scotland
12 D3 Bridge of Doon Scotland
12 D2 Bridge of Weir Scotland
102 E3 Bridgeport California
95 O5 Bridgeport Connecticut
107 N3 Bridgeport Kansas
98 C8 Bridgeport Nebraska
100 H5 Bridgeport Oregon
100 F2 Bridgeport Washington
102 E3 Bridgeport Res California
113 L12 Bridge Pt Bahamas
101 R4 Bridger Montana
101 P4 Bridger Pk Montana
101 S8 Bridger Pk Wyoming
112 K2 Bridgeton N Carolina
95 M7 Bridgeton New Jersey
127 P6 Bridgetown Barbados
122 G9 Bridgetown Nova Scotia
143 B10 Bridgetown W Australia
100 B9 Bridgeville California
122 K8 Bridgeville Nova Scotia
95 S7 Bridgewater Maine
95 R5 Bridgewater Massachusetts
115 N9 Bridgewater Nova Scotia
98 J6 Bridgewater S Dakota
94 J8 Bridgewater Virginia
138 F7 Bridgewater,C Victoria
94 A5 Bridgman Michigan
8 D2 Bridgnorth England
95 R2 Bridgton Maine
8 C5 Bridgwater England
13 H5 Bridlington England
8 D6 Bridport England
139 H8 Bridport Tasmania
18 G4 Brie reg France
Brieg see Brzeg
25 B5 Brielle Netherlands
112 F4 Brier Creek Georgia
119 M8 Briercrest Sask
118 F4 Briereville Alberta
122 F9 Brier I Nova Scotia
22 H5 Brieulles-sur-Bar France
22 K5 Briey France
40 G5 Brig Switzerland
41 H1 Brigarh R W Germany
120 H10 Brigden Ontario
13 H6 Brigg England
109 K5 Briggs Texas
98 B9 Briggsdale Colorado
101 N8 Brigham City Utah
13 G6 Brighouse England
9 E6 Brighstone England
103 M5 Bright Angel Pt Arizona
9 H4 Brightlingsea England
98 B10 Brighton Colorado
9 F6 Brighton England
113 F10 Brighton Florida
110 F2 Brighton Illinois
99 P8 Brighton Iowa
94 D4 Brighton Michigan
121 N8 Brighton Ontario
138 E6 Brighton S Australia
141 F6 Brighton Downs Queensland
145 D4 Brightwater New Zealand
18 C4 Brignogan France
123 T6 Brigus Nfld
17 F4 Brihuega Spain
26 G4 Briksvoer isld Norway
130 C7 Brilhante,R Brazil
21 G9 Brillac France
106 F5 Brilliant New Mexico
99 S5 Brillion Wisconsin
32 J10 Brilon W Germany
99 R9 Brimfield Illinois
43 H8 Brindisi Italy
138 C4 Bring,L S Australia
94 E6 Brinkhaven Ohio
110 E7 Brinkley Arkansas
9 G3 Brinkley England
9 E3 Brinklow England
32 J6 Brinkum W Germany
138 E5 Brinkworth S Australia
21 J6 Brinon-sur-Sauldre France
98 G1 Brinsmade N Dakota
113 C7 Brinson Georgia
123 L6 Brion I Madeleine Is, Quebec
20 G3 Brionne France
18 H7 Brioude France
21 E9 Brioux-sur-Boutonne France
20 E4 Briouze France
141 L8 Brisbane Queensland
141 L7 Brisbane R Queensland
108 D8 Briscoe Texas
45 L3 Brisighella Italy
21 E7 Brissac France
41 J4 Bristenstock mt Switzerland
106 H3 Bristol Colorado
95 P5 Bristol Connecticut
8 D5 Bristol England
113 C7 Bristol Florida
112 E6 Bristol Georgia
94 B5 Bristol Indiana
122 E7 Bristol New Brunswick
95 Q3 Bristol New Hampshire
95 M6 Bristol Pennsylvania
121 O7 Bristol Quebec
95 Q5 Bristol Rhode I
98 J4 Bristol S Dakota
95 O2 Bristol Vermont
94 E10 Bristol Virginia/Tenn
116 G8 Bristol B Alaska
8 C5 Bristol Chan England/Wales
146 A13 Bristol I Antarctica
103 J7 Bristol L California
103 J7 Bristol Mts California
103 K3 Bristol Silver Nevada
107 O6 Bristow Oklahoma
117 M11 Britannia Beach Br Col
146 H6 Britannia Ra Antarctica
146 C12 British Antarctic Territory Antarctica
117 L8 British Columbia prov Canada
115 L1 British Empire Ra N W Terr
British Guiana see Guyana
British Honduras see Belize
83 H5 British Ind.Oc.Terr colony Indian Oc
114 F4 British Mts Alaska/Yukon Terr
British N. Borneo see Sabah
British Solomon Is see Solomon Is.
123 M7 Briton Cove C Breton I, N Scotia
8 C4 Briton Ferry Wales
87 E11 Brits S Africa
87 D12 Britstown S Africa
99 N6 Britt Iowa
120 K7 Britt Ontario
27 G14 Brittatorp Sweden
107 N6 Britton Oklahoma
98 J4 Britton S Dakota
138 C2 Britton,Mt S Australia
33 T7 Britz E Germany
18 G7 Brive France
16 E2 Briviesca Spain
20 B2 Brix France
38 F7 Brixental V Austria
8 C7 Brixham England
141 G6 Brixton Queensland
48 D1 Brno Czechoslovakia
27 F12 Bro Sweden
112 D3 Broad R Georgia
112 F3 Broad R S Carolina
118 J6 Broadacres Sask
95 N3 Broadalbin New York
143 D9 Broad Arrow W Australia
115 M7 Broadback R Quebec
15 B2 Broad Bay Scotland
100 A6 Broadbent Oregon
109 N4 Broaddus Texas
15 C3 Broadford Scotland
14 B2 Broad Haven Irish Rep
8 A4 Broad Haven Wales
9 E5 Broad Hinton England
142 D5 Broadhurst Ra W Australia
98 H5 Broadland S Dakota
15 E5 Broad Law Scotland
141 J7 Broadmere Queensland
116 N5 Broad Pass Alaska
141 J5 Broad Sound Queensland
141 K5 Broad Sound Chan Queensland
141 J6 Broadsound Ra Queensland
9 H5 Broadstairs England
98 A4 Broadus Montana
101 R3 Broadview Montana
108 A9 Broadview New Mexico
119 P8 Broadview Sask
9 F6 Broadwater England
98 D8 Broadwater Nebraska
9 E3 Broadway England
8 D6 Broadwey England
8 D6 Broadwindsor England
145 D1 Broadwood New Zealand
126 C3 Broa, Ensenada de la B Cuba
28 D7 Broager Denmark
28 E6 Broby Denmark
27 G15 Broby Sweden
119 Q1 Brochet Manitoba
122 C4 Brochet,L.au Quebec
32 G8 Brochterbeck W Germany
121 Q4 Brochu,L Quebec
99 L9 Brock Nebraska
118 J7 Brock Sask
32 L6 Brockel W Germany
33 N9 Brocken mt E Germany
9 E6 Brockenhurst England
118 D9 Brocket Alberta
98 H1 Brocket N Dakota
114 H2 Brock I N W Terr
13 H6 Brocklesby England
142 B6 Brockman,Mt W Australia
94 K3 Brockport New York
98 G7 Brocksburg Nebraska
140 B2 Brock's Creek N Terr Aust
95 Q4 Brockton Massachusetts
98 B1 Brockton Montana
121 P8 Brockville Ontario
98 A2 Brockway Montana
94 J5 Brockway Pennsylvania
110 J2 Brocton Illinois
94 H4 Brocton New York
48 E5 Brod Yugoslavia
48 F7 Brodarevo Yugoslavia
118 L7 Broderick Sask
115 L3 Brodeur Pen N W Terr
99 R7 Brodhead Wisconsin
48 G6 Brodica Yugoslavia
12 C2 Brodick Scotland
94 K10 Brodnax Virginia
31 L2 Brodnica Poland
55 D3 Brodokalmak U.S.S.R.
25 C3 Broek op Langedijk Netherlands
100 H5 Brogan Oregon
20 G3 Broglie France
20 A5 Brohinière,la France
36 C3 Brohl-Lützing W Germany
33 T5 Brohm-Cosa E Germany
33 M8 Broistedt W Germany
31 N3 Brok Poland
99 R4 Brokaw Wisconsin
32 K5 Brokdorf W Germany
107 P5 Broken Arrow Oklahoma
139 K5 Broken Bay New S Wales
98 G8 Broken Bow Nebraska
107 Q7 Broken Bow Oklahoma
138 F4 Broken Hill New S Wales
Broken Hill Zambia see Kabwe
129 G3 Brokopondomeer L Suriname
29 K12 Bromarv Finland
Bromberg see Bydgoszcz
33 N7 Brome W Germany
8 D3 Bromfield England
98 C1 Bromhead Sask
9 G5 Bromley England
27 D11 Bromma Norway
28 G5 Bromme Denmark
70 O9 Bromo mt Java
13 H5 Brompton England
99 O9 Brompton Iowa
8 D3 Bromsgrove England
8 D3 Bromyard England
110 B4 Bronaugh Missouri
28 D2 Brønderslev Denmark
28 A5 Brøndum Denmark
8 C3 Bronllys Wales
37 L4 Bronn W Germany
27 G15 Brönnestad Sweden
55 E2 Bronnikovo U.S.S.R.
26 F6 Brönnöysund Norway
36 H2 Bronnzell W Germany
28 B6 Brøns Denmark
113 E8 Bronson Florida
94 B5 Bronson Michigan
109 N4 Bronson Texas
121 L9 Bronte Ontario
43 F11 Bronte Sicily
108 G4 Bronte Texas
139 H8 Bronte Park Tasmania
95 O6 Bronx New York
41 O5 Bronzolo Italy
122 E3 Brooch L Quebec
99 T9 Brook Indiana
94 K8 Brooke Virginia
109 O4 Brookeland Texas
113 E8 Brooker Florida
71 C6 Brooke's Pt Palawan Philippines
110 C2 Brookfield Missouri
122 J8 Brookfield Nova Scotia
111 F10 Brookhaven Mississippi
119 N9 Brooking Sask
100 A7 Brookings Oregon
98 K5 Brookings S Dakota
141 H4 Brook Is.Lt.Ho Queensland
9 G6 Brookland England
94 K5 Brookland Pennsylvania
112 F5 Brooklet Georgia
121 M9 Brooklin Ontario
95 Q4 Brookline Massachusetts
110 K2 Brooklyn Indiana
99 O8 Brooklyn Iowa
94 C4 Brooklyn Michigan
111 G10 Brooklyn Mississippi
95 O6 Brooklyn New York
95 M5 Brooklyn Pennsylvania
117 N11 Brookmere Br Columbia
94 H10 Brookneal Virginia
99 N4 Brook Park Minnesota
110 H4 Brookport Illinois
114 H7 Brooks Alberta
95 S2 Brooks Maine
101 Q2 Brooks Montana
117 G5 Brooks Brook Yukon Terr
119 N5 Brooksby Sask
109 M6 Brookshire Texas
116 D4 Brooks Mt Alaska
116 M5 Brooks,Mt Alaska
116 H2 Brooks Range Alaska
99 O3 Brookston Minnesota
109 M2 Brookston Texas
113 E9 Brooksville Florida
95 U1 Brookton Maine
143 B9 Brookton W Australia
95 L4 Brooktondale New York
110 M2 Brookville Indiana
107 N3 Brookville Kansas
111 H8 Brookville Mississippi
94 H5 Brookville Pennsylvania
141 H5 Brookville Queensland
111 J8 Brookwood Alabama
141 L7 Brooloo Queensland
123 K4 Broom B Anticosti I, Quebec
142 D4 Broome W Australia
143 C10 Broome Hill W Australia
142 F3 Broome, Mt W Australia
18 D4 Broons France
99 L4 Brooten Minnesota
142 G4 Brophy,Mt W Australia
143 F7 Brophy,Mt W Australia
15 E2 Brora Scotland
28 B5 Brørup Denmark
27 G16 Brösarp Sweden
14 D3 Brosna R Irish Rep
48 K3 Brosteni Romania
100 E6 Brothers Oregon
68 A7 Brothers islds Andaman Is
145 E4 Brothers, The New Zealand
84 K4 Brothers,The islds Red Sea
37 J2 Brotterode E Germany
20 H5 Brou France
13 F4 Brough England
15 E1 Brough Hd Orkney Scotland
15 F2 Brough Ness Scotland
13 E5 Broughton Cumbria England
110 H4 Broughton Illinois
107 N2 Broughton Kansas
9 F3 Broughton Northants England
141 H5 Broughton Queensland
13 E2 Broughton Scotland
121 T6 Broughton Station Quebec
15 F4 Broughty Ferry Scotland
86 C2 Broulkou Chad
79 F5 Broummanâ Lebanon
36 B7 Brouvelieures France
25 A5 Brouwershaven Netherlands
40 E4 Brove R Switzerland
85 C7 Brovio Liberia
28 D2 Brovst Denmark
99 L3 Browerville Minnesota
71 C5 Brown Bank Palawan Philippines
94 E3 Brown City Michigan
107 L3 Brownell Kansas
143 E7 Browne Ra W Australia
108 E2 Brownfield Texas
110 C1 Browning Missouri
101 M1 Browning Montana
119 P9 Browning Sask
144 C5 Browning Pass New Zealand
143 C9 Brown,L W Australia
98 F7 Brownlee Nebraska
119 M8 Brownlee Sask
138 E4 Brown,Mt S Australia
138 F3 Brown,Mt S Australia
142 A3 Brown,Mt W Australia
138 C4 Brown Pt S Australia
141 G3 Brown R Queensland
120 J3 Brownrigg Ontario
110 J3 Browns Illinois
144 B7 Browns New Zealand
109 M3 Brownsboro Texas
110 K2 Brownsburg Indiana
121 Q7 Brownsburg Quebec
126 E2 Browns Cay isld Bahamas
145 G1 Browns I New Zealand
98 C8 Brownson Nebraska
94 A8 Brownstown Indiana
127 K2 Brown's Town Jamaica
98 K4 Browns Valley Minnesota
110 L2 Brownsville Indiana
110 K4 Brownsville Kentucky
100 C5 Brownsville Oregon
94 H6 Brownsville Pennsylvania
110 G6 Brownsville Tennessee
109 K10 Brownsville Texas
99 M5 Brownton Minnesota
99 R7 Browntown Wisconsin
111 J8 Brownville Alabama
99 L9 Brownville Nebraska
95 M2 Brownville New York
95 S1 Brownville Junc Maine
109 J4 Brownwood, L Texas
136 E4 Browse I Australia
142 E2 Browse I Indian Ocean
15 E5 Broxburn Scotland
112 E6 Broxton Georgia
16 C5 Brozas Spain
45 K4 Brozzi Italy
45 P1 Brtonigla Yugoslavia
22 D3 Bruay France
22 F3 Bruay-sur-l'Escaut France
118 E5 Bruce Alberta
127 P6 Bruce Barbados
111 G7 Bruce Mississippi
145 E4 Bruce New Zealand
99 P4 Bruce Wisconsin
144 B5 Bruce Bay New Zealand
99 R3 Bruce Crossing Michigan
120 J9 Brucefield Ontario
142 C6 Bruce,Mt W Australia
120 J7 Bruce Pen Ontario
143 C9 Bruce Rock W Australia
110 H5 Bruceton Tennessee
109 K4 Bruceville Texas
19 K4 Bruche R France
32 K7 Bruchhausen-Vilsen W Germany
36 F3 Bruchköbel W Germany
36 F5 Bruchsal W Germany
31 K7 Bruck Austria
37 L4 Bruck Bayern W Germany
33 R8 Brück E Germany
38 M7 Bruck-an-der-Mur Austria
37 M6 Bruckberg W Germany
38 L8 Brückl Austria
20 E3 Brucourt France
19 P18 Brue-Auriac France
118 E5 Bruederheim Alberta
33 P5 Brüel E Germany
14 C4 Bruff Irish Rep
Bruges see Brugge
40 H3 Brugg Switzerland
22 E1 Brugge Belgium
36 D1 Brügge W Germany
25 F6 Brüggen W Germany
45 L1 Brùgine Italy
44 F2 Brugneto, L. di Italy
36 B2 Brühl W Germany
94 H5 Bruin Pennsylvania
103 O2 Bruin Pt Utah
117 P9 Brûlé Alberta
98 E8 Brule Nebraska
99 P3 Brule Wisconsin
121 N6 Brûlé, L Quebec
121 M7 Brûlé Lake Ontario
21 E6 Brûlon France
22 J4 Brûly Belgium
129 K6 Brumado Brazil
25 F4 Brummen Netherlands
43 C8 Bruncu Spina mt Sardinia
108 H7 Brundage Texas
111 L10 Brundidge Alabama
100 K7 Bruneau Idaho
22 G4 Brunehamel France
70 D2 Brunei state Borneo
70 D2 Brunei B Brunei
Brunei Town see Bandar Seri Begawan
140 D4 Brunette Downs N Terr Aust
123 Q6 Brunette I Nfld
20 F2 Bruneval France
26 G8 Brunflo Sweden
109 J8 Bruni Texas
42 D2 Brunico Italy
118 D1 Brunkild Manitoba
Brünn see Brno
37 N2 Brunn E Germany
28 K4 Brunnby Sweden
41 J3 Brunnen Switzerland
144 C5 Brunner New Zealand
99 O3 Bruno Minnesota
119 M6 Bruno Sask
32 K5 Brunsbüttelkoog W Germany
33 M8 Brunschweig W Germany
32 L5 Brunshausen W Germany
25 E7 Brunssum Netherlands
Brunswick see Braunschweig
112 F6 Brunswick Georgia
95 S3 Brunswick Maine
94 K7 Brunswick Maryland
94 F5 Brunswick Ohio
142 E3 Brunswick B W Australia
143 B10 Brunswick Junction W Australia
120 G3 Brunswick L Ontario
133 C8 Brunswick, Pen. de Chile
31 K6 Bruntál Czechoslovakia
139 H9 Bruny I Tasmania
26 G6 Brurskanken mt Norway
46 F1 Brusartsi Bulgaria
106 G1 Brush Colorado
95 N2 Brushton New York
112 F1 Brushy Mts N Carolina
130 E10 Brusque Brazil
Brussels see Bruxelles
120 J9 Brussels Ontario
99 T5 Brussels Wisconsin
8 D5 Bruton England
22 G2 Bruxelles Belgium
24 Bruxelles conurbation Belgium
19 K4 Bruyères France
20 B5 Bruz France
128 E2 Bruzual Venezuela
22 F3 Bry France
94 C5 Bryan Ohio
109 L5 Bryan Texas
101 Q8 Bryan Wyoming
138 E5 Bryan,Mt S Australia
54 F3 Bryansk U.S.S.R.
109 P1 Bryant Arkansas
110 M1 Bryant Indiana
110 D5 Bryant Cr Missouri
95 R2 Bryant Pond Maine
22 C3 Bryas France
103 M4 Bryce Canyon Nat. Park Utah
144 B7 Brydone New Zealand
9 F7 Bryher isld Isles of Scilly England
8 C4 Bryn-amman Wales
8 B2 Bryn-crug Wales
8 C1 Bryneglwys Wales
26 M1 Brynilen Norway
8 C4 Bryn Mawr Wales
48 L2 Brynzen U.S.S.R.
28 C4 Bryrup Denmark
112 D2 Bryson City N Carolina
121 N6 Bryson,L Quebec
48 G6 Brza Palanka Yugoslavia
31 K5 Brzeg Poland
31 M6 Brzesko Poland
31 M4 Brzeziny Poland
31 L4 Brzeźnica Poland
31 N6 Brzozów Poland
20 J4 Bû France
70 G6 Bua Sulawesi Indonesia
88 E8 Bua R Malawi
70 G7 Buapinang Sulawesi Indonesia
84 F3 Bu Ayrāt,Al Libya
33 S7 Buberow E Germany
89 F2 Bubi R Zimbabwe
77 A5 Bubiyan isld Kuwait
71 F7 Bubuan isld Mindanao Philippines
13 H6 Bubwith England
87 F10 Bubye R Zimbabwe
47 L7 Bucak Turkey
128 D2 Bucaramanga Colombia
71 G6 Bucas Grande Philippines
111 H10 Bucatunda Mississippi
142 E3 Buccaneer Arch W Australia
43 G8 Buccino Italy
48 K3 Bucecea Romania
47 K3 Bü Çekmece Turkey
48 J1 Buchach U.S.S.R.
15 F3 Buchan dist Scotland
6 L5 Buchan oil rig North Sea
112 B4 Buchanan Georgia
85 B7 Buchanan Liberia
99 U8 Buchanan Michigan
98 G2 Buchanan N Dakota
106 F7 Buchanan New Mexico
119 P7 Buchanan Sask
94 H9 Buchanan Virginia
140 D4 Buchanan R N Terr Aust
109 J5 Buchanan Dam Texas
140 B4 Buchanan Hills N Terr Aust
141 H5 Buchanan,L Queensland
143 E7 Buchanan,L W Australia
109 J5 Buchanan Res Texas
115 M3 Buchan Gulf N W Terr
15 G3 Buchan Ness Scotland
115 O8 Buchans Nfld
123 Q5 Buchans Jnct Nfld
133 E4 Buchardo Argentina
Bucharest see București
37 N7 Buchbach W Germany
36 G4 Buchen W Germany
36 C4 Büchenbeuren W Germany
37 L1 Buchenwald E Germany
33 R8 Buchholz E Germany
32 L6 Buchholz W Germany
41 N2 Buching W Germany
41 N1 Buchloe W Germany
15 D4 Buchlyvie Scotland
41 K3 Buchs Switzerland
20 H2 Buchy France
106 C6 Buck New Mexico
9 F3 Buckden England
32 K8 Bückeburg W Germany
32 K7 Bücken W Germany
103 M8 Buckeye Arizona
94 E7 Buckeye Lake Ohio
95 K7 Buckeystown Maryland
8 C7 Buckfastleigh England
94 G8 Buckhannon W Virginia
15 E4 Buckhaven & Methil Scotland
98 C5 Buckhorn Wyoming
15 E3 Buckie Scotland
9 E3 Buckingham England
121 P7 Buckingham Quebec
94 J9 Buckingham Virginia
140 D1 Buckingham B N Terr Aust
140 E5 Buckingham Downs Queensland
118 C5 Buck L Alberta
140 B4 Buck,L N Terr Aust
116 G4 Buckland Alaska
119 V1 Buckland L Manitoba
145 G1 Bucklands Beach New Zealand
141 J6 Buckland Tableland Queensland
146 K5 Buckle I Antarctica
110 H1 Buckley Illinois
94 B2 Buckley Michigan
100 C2 Buckley Washington
140 E5 Buckley R Queensland
38 O6 Bucklige Welt reg Austria
107 L4 Bucklin Kansas
110 D2 Bucklin Missouri
Buckner Bay see Nakagusuku-wan
102 C2 Bucks California
103 L7 Buckskin Mts Arizona
102 C2 Bucks Mt California
95 T2 Bucksport Maine
33 Q7 Bückwitz E Germany
31 K6 Bučovice Czechoslovakia
86 B6 Buco Zau Angola
22 D3 Bucquoy France
122 H7 Buctouche New Brunswick
48 K6 București Romania
71 E7 Bucutua isld Philippines
22 F4 Bucy-les-Pierrepont France
98 D3 Bucyrus N Dakota
26 B9 Bud Norway
109 K5 Buda Texas
48 E3 Budafok Hungary
54 B4 Buda-Koshelevo U.S.S.R.
68 B1 Budalin Burma
48 E3 Budapest Hungary
74 H4 Budaun India
9 E1 Budby England
146 F3 Budd Coast Antarctica
53 F10 Buddenovsk U.S.S.R.
143 B8 Budd,Mt W Australia
15 F4 Buddon Ness Scotland
8 B6 Bude England
32 L4 Büdelsdorf W Germany
32 G9 Büderich W Germany
22 K4 Buderscheid Luxembourg
48 K6 Budești Romania
131 A7 Budi,L.del Chile
36 G3 Büdingen W Germany
86 C5 Budjala Zaïre
8 C6 Budleigh Salterton England
45 L2 Budrio Italy
42 J6 Budva Yugoslavia
54 H7 Budy U.S.S.R.
86 A5 Buéa Cameroon
19 P16 Buech R France
20 H4 Buéil France
102 D7 Buellton California
128 C3 Buenaventura Colombia
106 D3 Buena Vista Colorado
112 C5 Buena Vista Georgia
71 G6 Buenavista Mindanao Philippines
71 E4 Buenavista Philippines
94 H9 Buena Vista Virginia
126 E3 Buena Vista, B. de Cuba
17 F4 Buendia, Embalse de Spain
Buene R see Bojana
131 A8 Bueno R Chile
130 E4 Buenolândia Brazil
129 K7 Buenópolis Brazil
128 D4 Buenos Aires Colombia
132 Buenos Aires conurbation Argentina
131 E6 Buenos Aires prov Argentina
133 C7 Buenos Aires,L Chile/Arg
127 N3 Buenos Ayres Trinidad
133 D7 Buen Pasto Argentina
133 D8 Buen Tiempo,C Argentina
130 H4 Buerarema Brazil
40 E5 Buet,Mt France
107 P4 Buffalo Kansas
110 L4 Buffalo Kentucky
99 N4 Buffalo Minnesota
110 C4 Buffalo Missouri
101 Q3 Buffalo Montana
94 J4 Buffalo New York
107 L5 Buffalo Oklahoma
112 F3 Buffalo S Carolina
98 C4 Buffalo S Dakota
101 T5 Buffalo Wyoming
117 Q6 Buffalo R Alberta/N W Terr
110 C5 Buffalo R Arkansas
98 K3 Buffalo R Minnesota
89 G6 Buffalo R S Africa
110 J6 Buffalo R Tennessee
99 P5 Buffalo R Wisconsin
101 Q5 Buffalo Bill Dam Wyoming
101 Q5 Buffalo Bill Res Wyoming
99 N6 Buffalo Center Iowa
106 E2 Buffalo Creek Colorado
119 M9 Buffalo Gap Sask
98 C6 Buffalo Gap S Dakota
118 E6 Buffalo, L Alberta
114 H5 Buffalo L N W Terr
108 E1 Buffalo L Texas
139 H6 Buffalo,Mt Victoria
114 J6 Buffalo Narrows Sask
119 M8 Buffalo Pound Prov Park Sask
127 L2 Buff Bay Jamaica
112 C3 Buford Georgia
98 C1 Buford N Dakota
98 A8 Buford Wyoming
48 K6 Buftea Romania
31 O4 Bug R Poland/U.S.S.R.
128 C3 Buga Colombia
18 G10 Bugarach, Pic de mt France
58 G1 Bugarikhta U.S.S.R.
48 N4 Bugaz U.S.S.R.
47 J4 Buğdaylı Turkey
70 N9 Bugel,Tg Java
40 B6 Bugey dist France
Buggs Island Lake see Kerr Lake
88 D1 Bugiri Uganda
26 R2 Bugöynes Norway
54 C10 Bugskiy Liman lagoon U.S.S.R.
71 C6 Bugsuk isld Palawan Philippines
59 H2 Bugt China
18 F8 Bugue,Le France
71 E1 Buguey Luzon Philippines
78 K2 Bügük Ağri mt Turkey
87 F9 Buhera Zimbabwe
58 C4 Buh He R China
71 F4 Buhi Luzon Philippines
101 L7 Buhl Idaho
99 O2 Buhl Minnesota
36 E6 Bühl W Germany
36 E6 Bühlerhöhe W Germany
36 E6 Bühlertal W Germany
36 H5 Bühlertann W Germany
88 E6 Buhoro Flats Tanzania
78 J3 Bühtan R Turkey
48 K4 Buhuşi Romania
117 N7 Buick British Columbia
25 C4 Buiksloot Netherlands
8 C3 Builth Wells Wales
137 M3 Buin Bougainville I Solomon Is
41 M4 Buin,Piz mt Switz/Austria
130 H10 Buíque Brazil
36 B2 Buir W Germany
22 B3 Buire-le-Sec France
22 F4 Buironfosse France
19 O16 Buis-les-Baronnies France
25 F2 Buitenpost Netherlands
67 B7 Bui Thon Vietnam
122 J2 Buit,L Quebec
16 E7 Bujalance Spain
21 I10 Bujaleuf France
46 E2 Bujanovac Yugoslavia
17 G3 Bujaraloz Spain
42 F3 Buje Yugoslavia
48 L5 Bujor Târg Romania
88 B3 Bujumbura Burundi
48 D3 Bük Hungary
137 L3 Buka isld Solomon Is
88 D2 Bukakata Uganda
87 E7 Bukama Zaïre
66 C5 Buka Mangna Range China
88 D2 Bukasa I Uganda
88 B3 Bukavu Zaïre
88 C2 Bukene Tanzania
57 C5 Bukhara U.S.S.R.
69 E13 Bukittinggi Sumatra
48 F2 Bükk mt Hungary
79 F8 Bukka, J. el mt Jordan
48 D4 Bükkösd Hungary
33 Q9 Buko E Germany
88 C2 Bukoba Tanzania
48 J2 Bukovina old prov U.S.S.R.
31 J1 Bukowo,Jezioro L Poland
136 G2 Bula Moluccas Indonesia
41 J2 Bülach Switzerland
65 D2 Bulag Sum China
71 E5 Bulalacao Calamian Grp Philippines
71 E4 Bulalacao Philippines
71 F4 Bulan Philippines
71 E7 Bulan isld Philippines
55 D3 Bulanash U.S.S.R.
55 C4 Bulanovo U.S.S.R.
89 F3 Bulawayo Zimbabwe
55 F3 Bulayevo U.S.S.R.
28 C2 Bulbjerg hill Denmark
48 M4 Bulboki U.S.S.R.
47 K6 Buldan Turkey
74 G8 Buldana India
77 H6 Buleda reg Pakistan
70 P10 Buleleng Bali Indonesia
9 E5 Bulford England
58 B2 Bulgan Mongolia
58 D2 Bulgan Mongolia
47 F2 Bulgaria
40 C1 Bulgnéville France
141 G7 Bulgroo Queensland
86 H3 Bulhar Somalia
71 B2 Buli Halmahera Indonesia
71 C6 Buliluyan,C Palawan Philippines
141 K1 Bulimba dist Brisbane, Qnsld
141 L2 Bulimba Cr Brisbane, Qnsld
67 B4 Buliu He R China
117 K8 Bulkley R Br Col
143 D9 Bullabulling W Australia
22 L3 Bullange Belgium
16 E5 Bullaque R Spain
109 M3 Bullard Texas
27 E13 Bullaren S L Sweden
17 F6 Bullas Spain
139 G3 Bullawarra,L Queensland
36 C3 Bullay W Germany
127 L3 Bull Bay Jamaica
112 H5 Bull Bay S Carolina
40 F4 Bulle Switzerland
138 F4 Bullea,L New S Wales
116 O1 Bullen Alaska
126 A1 Bullen Baai B Curaçao
145 D4 Buller R New Zealand
143 C9 Bullfinch W Australia
112 H5 Bull I S Carolina
102 H7 Bullion Mts California
140 B3 Bullita N Terr Aust
101 R3 Bull Mts Montana
141 G5 Bullock R Queensland
141 G4 Bullock Creek Queensland
141 G8 Bulloo R Queensland
141 G8 Bulloo Downs Queensland
141 F8 Bulloo, L Queensland
133 F8 Bull Pt Falkland Is
118 B9 Bull R Br Col
145 E4 Bulls New Zealand
127 J3 Bull Savannah Jamaica
110 D5 Bull Shoals Lake Missouri
22 D3 Bully France
100 C9 Bully Choop Mt California
140 C2 Bulman N Terr Australia
140 C2 Bulman Gorge N Terr Aust
86 J5 Bulo Berti Somalia
69 C11 Bulohsama Sumatra
139 G6 Buloke,L Victoria
77 L2 Bulola Afghanistan
136 K3 Bulolo Papua New Guinea
143 D9 Bulong W Australia
138 F5 Bulpunga New S Wales
74 E8 Bulsar India
87 E11 Bultfontein S Africa
71 G7 Buluan Mindanao Philippines
70 E3 Bulu, G mt Kalimantan
51 M1 Bulun U.S.S.R.
86 D7 Bulungu Zaïre
71 G4 Bulusan Luzon Philippines
118 F6 Bulwark Alberta
9 E2 Bulwell England
141 L1 Bulwer I Brisbane, Qnsld
9 F2 Bulwick England
119 N8 Bulyea Sask
86 D5 Bumba Zaïre
48 H5 Bumbeşti Jiu Romania
103 M7 Bumble Bee Arizona
70 G4 Bumbulan Sulawesi Indonesia
70 F2 Bum-Bum Sabah
70 M9 Bumiaju Java
66 F6 Bumkhang Burma
100 D3 Bumping L Washington
40 F4 Bümpliz Switzerland
75 O5 Bumthang Bhutan
109 O5 Buna Texas
71 G7 Bunawan Mindanao Philippines
84 G3 Bunbah,Gulf of Libya
143 B10 Bunbury W Australia
110 B6 Bunch Oklahoma
14 E4 Bunclody Irish Rep
14 D1 Buncrana Irish Rep
141 K6 Bundaberg Queensland
141 F5 Bunda Bunda Queensland
141 H8 Bundaleer Queensland
140 C4 Bundara creek N Terr Aust
32 F6 Bunde W Germany
32 J8 Bünde W Germany
140 D5 Bundey R N Terr Aust
143 D7 Bundey,Mt W Australia
74 F6 Bundi India
111 C11 Bundick L Louisiana
111 C11 Bundicks Cr Louisiana
140 C6 Bundooma N Terr Aust
14 C2 Bundoran Irish Rep
68 J6 Bun Duc Vietnam
12 B1 Bunessan Scotland
71 G7 Bunga R Mindanao Philippines
142 F5 Bungabinni Well W Australia
9 H3 Bungay England

Campagne-lès-Hesdin — Castelfranco Emilia 15

22 B3 **Campagne-lès-Hesdin** France
125 L2 **Campamento** Honduras
133 F4 **Campana** Argentina
124 H4 **Campana** Mexico
133 B7 **Campana, I** Chile
130 C8 **Campanario** Mato Grosso Brazil
130 H6 **Campanário** Minas Gerais Brazil
16 D6 **Campanario** Spain
133 C5 **Campanario** *mt* Chile/Arg
45 Q8 **Campanella, Pta** *C* Italy
130 F7 **Campanha** Brazil
139 H8 **Campania** Tasmania
45 R7 **Campania** *reg* Italy
117 J9 **Campania I** Br Col
141 H5 **Campaspe** *R* Queensland
102 C2 **Camp Beale** California
102 C4 **Campbell** California
110 F5 **Campbell** Missouri
98 H9 **Campbell** Nebraska
95 K4 **Campbell** New York
94 G5 **Campbell** Ohio
141 J6 **Campbell** *R* Queensland
145 E4 **Campbell, C** New Zealand
121 N8 **Campbellford** Ontario
68 D7 **Campbell I** Burma
102 R12 **Campbell Industrial Pk** Hawaiian Is
117 J9 **Campbell Island** Br Col
140 B5 **Campbell, Mt** N Terr Aust
117 D3 **Campbell, Mt** Yukon Terr
74 E2 **Campbellpore** Pakistan
142 G2 **Campbell Ra** W Australia
81 K12 **Campbell Rise** S Pacific Oc
117 L10 **Campbell River** Br Col
121 O7 **Campbell's Bay** Quebec
99 S6 **Campbellsport** Wisconsin
110 L4 **Campbellsville** Kentucky
122 F6 **Campbellton** New Brunswick
123 S4 **Campbellton** Nfld
109 J7 **Campbellton** Texas
139 K5 **Campbelltown** New S Wales
139 J8 **Campbell Town** Tasmania
12 C3 **Campbeltown** Scotland
98 C4 **Camp Crook** S Dakota
99 Q6 **Camp Douglas** Wisconsin
20 J2 **Campeaux** France
125 O8 **Campeche** Mexico
90 A6 **Campeche Bank** Atlantic Oc
125 N8 **Campeche, B.de** Mexico
126 F4 **Campechuela** Cuba
48 H4 **Câmpeni** Romania
113 L9 **Camperdown** New Providence I Bahamas
139 G7 **Camperdown** Victoria
119 R7 **Camperville** Manitoba
111 L9 **Camp Hill** Alabama
141 K2 **Camphill** *dist* Brisbane, Qnsld
45 K4 **Campi Bisenzio** Italy
45 Q8 **Campi Flegrei** Italy
16 D6 **Campillo de Llerena** Spain
16 D7 **Campillos** Spain
130 H9 **Campina Grande** Brazil
130 F8 **Campinas** Brazil
130 E6 **Campina Verde** Brazil
102 F5 **Camp Nelson** California
86 A5 **Campo** Cameroon
106 H4 **Campo** Colorado
18 F10 **Campo** Spain
43 F7 **Campobasso** Italy
122 F9 **Campobello I** New Brunswick
130 F7 **Campo Belo** Brazil
130 E10 **Campo Belo do Sul** Brazil
45 L1 **Campo d'Arsego** Italy
16 E6 **Campo de Calatrava** *physical reg* Spain
16 E5 **Campo de Criptana** Spain
129 H6 **Campo de Diauarum** Brazil
126 G9 **Campo de la Cruz** Colombia
130 D10 **Campo Erê** Brazil
130 E6 **Campo Florido** Brazil
129 K6 **Campo Formoso** Brazil
45 J2 **Campogalliano** Italy
133 E3 **Campo Gallo** Argentina
133 G2 **Campo Grande** Brazil
130 C7 **Campo Grande** Mato Grosso Brazil
130 B9 **Campo Grande** *airport* Paraguay
130 E9 **Campo Largo** Brazil
129 K4 **Campo Maior** Brazil
130 D9 **Campo Mourão** Brazil
130 D10 **Campo Novo** Brazil
45 H3 **Camporgiano** Italy
130 H7 **Campos** Brazil
130 F6 **Campos Altos** Brazil
45 K2 **Camposanto** Italy
45 R7 **Camposauro** *mt* Italy
130 D10 **Campos de Palmas** *plains* Brazil
130 F8 **Campos do Jordão** Brazil
130 D9 **Campos Eré** Brazil
133 G3 **Campos Novos** Brazil
41 J5 **Campo Tencia** *mt* Switzerland
128 E3 **Campo Troco** Colombia
42 D2 **Campo Tures** Italy
99 P9 **Camp Point** Illinois
102 D6 **Camp Roberts** California
109 H5 **Camp San Saba** Texas
12 D1 **Campsie Fells** Scotland
111 C10 **Campti** Louisiana
94 D9 **Campton** Kentucky
95 Q3 **Campton** New Hampshire
102 C2 **Camptonville** California
103 N7 **Camp Verde** Arizona
68 J7 **Cam Ranh** Vietnam
118 E5 **Camrose** Alberta
45 L1 **Camsano Vicentino** Italy
117 M4 **Camsell Range** N W Terr
87 B8 **Camucuio** Angola
45 K3 **Camugnano** Italy
47 J4 **Çan** Turkey
95 O4 **Canaan** Connecticut
122 G7 **Canaan** New Brunswick
127 M2 **Canaan** Tobago
121 T8 **Canaan** Vermont
103 N4 **Canaan Pk** Utah
122 G8 **Canaan R** New Brunswick
130 F5 **Canabrava** Brazil
129 J6 **Cana Brava** *R* Brazil
71 C6 **Canabungan** *isld* Philippines
87 C8 **Canacupa** Angola
115 **Canada**
123 Q3 **Canada B** Nfld
131 E4 **Cañada de Gómez** Argentina
95 R8 **Canada Falls** Maine
95 M5 **Canadensis** Pennsylvania
108 D8 **Canadian** Texas
106 F5 **Canadian** *R* New Mexico
108 D8 **Canadian** *R* Texas etc
133 D8 **Cañadón de las Vacas** Argentina
133 D6 **Cañadón Grande, Sa** *ra* Argentina
112 G4 **Canadys** S Carolina
47 H4 **Canakkale** Turkey
47 H4 **Çanakkale Boğazi** *str* Turkey
43 B11 **Canal de la Galite** *str* Tunisia
127 H5 **Canal de St. Marc** Haiti
129 H3 **Canal do Norte** Brazil
129 J4 **Canal do Sul** Brazil
117 Q10 **Canal Flats** Br Col
110 G5 **Canalou** Missouri
113 G11 **Canal Point** Florida
94 E7 **Canal Winchester** Ohio
128 D5 **Canama** Brazil
95 K4 **Canandaigua L** New York
124 D2 **Cananea** Mexico
130 F9 **Cananéia** Brazil
128 E3 **Canapiari,Co** *mt* Colombia
20 K1 **Canaples** France
130 E6 **Canápolis** Brazil
128 C4 **Cañar** *prov* Ecuador
126 C4 **Canarreos,Arch.de los** Cuba
90 K10 **Canary Basin** Atlantic Oc
85 A3 **Canary Is** Atlantic Oc
94 K4 **Canaseraga** New York
130 E4 **Canastra, Serra da** *mts* Brazil
130 F7 **Canastra,Serra do** *mts* Minas Gerais Brazil
124 G5 **Canatlán** Mexico
44 B1 **Canave** Italy
16 C5 **Cañaveral** Spain
113 G9 **Canaveral, C** Florida
17 F4 **Cañaveras** Spain
129 L7 **Canavieiras** Brazil
141 G7 **Canaway Ra** Queensland
38 E9 **Canazei** Italy
139 H4 **Canbelego** New S Wales
139 J6 **Canberra** Aust Capital Terr
138 A6 **Canberra & Environs** Australia
100 E8 **Canby** California
98 K5 **Canby** Minnesota
100 C4 **Canby** Oregon
20 B4 **Cancale** France
45 Q8 **Cancello** Italy
45 Q7 **Cancello ed Arnone** Italy
22 B3 **Canche** *R* France
20 J1 **Canchy** France
18 F8 **Cancon** France
86 A1 **Candala** Somalia
45 K3 **Canda, M** *mt* Italy
47 H6 **Candarli** Turkey
47 H6 **Candarlı Körfezi** *gulf* Turkey
20 K1 **Candas** France
21 C6 **Candé** France
16 B5 **Candeeiros,Sa.de** Portugal
130 F7 **Candeias** Brazil
128 F5 **Candeias** *R* Brazil
43 G7 **Candela** Italy
45 N4 **Candelara** Italy
130 C10 **Candelaria** Argentina
124 F2 **Candelaria** Mexico
102 F3 **Candelaria** Nevada
108 C5 **Candelaria** Texas
139 J6 **Candelo** New S Wales
Candia Crete *see* **Iráklion**
119 O8 **Candiac** Sask
45 L1 **Candiana** Italy
130 D9 **Cândido de Abreu** Brazil
130 E8 **Cândido Mota** Brazil
116 F4 **Candle** Alaska
119 M5 **Candle L** Sask
146 A14 **Candlemas I** Antarctica
95 O5 **Candlewood,L** Connecticut
98 G1 **Cando** N Dakota
118 J6 **Cando** Sask
133 G3 **Candói** Brazil
143 B6 **Candolle, Mt** W Australia
71 E2 **Candon** Luzon Philippines
112 H2 **Candor** N Carolina
95 L4 **Candor** New York
120 K5 **Cane** Ontario
Canea Crete *see* **Khaniá**
94 J4 **Caneadea** New York
129 J6 **Canéia** Brazil
133 G3 **Canela** Brazil
133 F4 **Canelones** Uruguay
130 C9 **Canendiyu** *dep* Paraguay
133 C5 **Cañete** Chile
17 F4 **Cañete** Spain
128 C6 **Cañete** *R* Peru
107 P4 **Caney** Kansas
107 O7 **Caney** Oklahoma
110 L6 **Caney Fork** *R* Tennessee
110 K4 **Caneyville** Kentucky
111 C8 **Canfield** Arkansas
94 G5 **Canfield** Ohio
18 E10 **Canfranc** Spain
87 C8 **Cangamba** Angola
87 C7 **Cangandala** Angola
16 C1 **Cangas de Narcea** Spain
16 D1 **Cangas de Onís** Spain
21 H7 **Cangey** France
87 C8 **Cangoa** Angola
89 B9 **Cango Caves** S Africa
87 D8 **Cangombe** Angola
65 D7 **Cangshan** China
130 J9 **Canguaretama** Brazil
133 G4 **Canguçu** Brazil
131 H3 **Canguçu,Sa.do** *mt* Brazil
87 C8 **Cangumbe** Angola
67 D5 **Cangwu** China
67 B1 **Cangxi** China
65 C5 **Cang Xian** China
68 D1 **Cangyuan** China
65 C5 **Cangzhou** China
130 H10 **Canhotinho** Brazil
141 K6 **Cania** Queensland
115 N6 **Caniapiscau** *R* Quebec
115 N7 **Caniapiscau,Lac** Quebec
121 N3 **Canica I** Quebec
43 F11 **Canicatti** Sicily
71 G5 **Canigao Ch** Philippines
18 G10 **Canigou** *mt* France
17 F7 **Caniles** Spain
117 N10 **Canim L** Br Col
129 K5 **Caninde** *R* Brazil
71 E5 **Canipo** *isld* Philippines
15 C2 **Canisp Mt** Scotland
94 K4 **Canisteo** New York
95 K4 **Canisteo** *R* New York
20 C3 **Canisy** France
124 H6 **Cañitas** Mexico
17 F7 **Canjáyar** Spain
78 D1 **Çankiri** Turkey
71 E3 **Canlubang** Luzon Philippines
118 B7 **Canmore** Alberta
143 B8 **Canna** W Australia
15 B3 **Canna** *isld* Scotland
76 B5 **Cannanore** India
110 K4 **Cannelton** Indiana
41 J5 **Cannero** Italy
44 B4 **Cannes** France
45 J1 **Canneto s. Oglio** Italy
122 H8 **Canning** Nova Scotia
98 G5 **Canning** S Dakota
116 O2 **Canning** *R* Alaska
142 E4 **Canning Basin** W Australia
143 C8 **Canning Hill** W Australia
142 B2 **Canning River** W Australia
121 L8 **Cannington** Ontario
142 B2 **Cannington** *dist* Perth, W Aust
142 B2 **Canning Vale** W Australia
41 J5 **Cannobio** Italy
99 O5 **Cannon** *R* Minnesota
98 F3 **Cannon Ball** N Dakota
98 E3 **Cannonball** *R* N Dakota
99 O5 **Cannon Falls** Minnesota
141 J5 **Cannonsvale** Queensland
139 J7 **Cann R** Victoria
133 G3 **Canoas** Brazil
130 D10 **Canõas, R. das** Brazil
140 F4 **Canobie** Queensland
130 F6 **Canoeiros** Brazil
118 J3 **Canoe L** Sask
117 O9 **Canoe R** Br Col
130 E10 **Canoinhas** Brazil
139 H4 **Canonba** New S Wales
15 F5 **Canonbie** Scotland
106 E3 **Canon City** Colorado
106 C5 **Cañon Largo** *R* New Mexico
94 G6 **Canonsburg** Pennsylvania
112 F6 **Canoochia** *R* Georgia
141 K6 **Canoona** Queensland
138 F5 **Canopus** S Australia
119 P7 **Canora** Sask
43 G7 **Canosa di Puglia** Italy
127 O8 **Canouan** *isld* Lesser Antilles
98 J6 **Canova** S Dakota
139 J5 **Canowindra** New S Wales
47 K6 **Çanşa** Turkey
71 F6 **Cansilan Pt** Negros Philippines
123 M8 **Canso** Nova Scotia
123 L8 **Canso,Str.of** Nova Scotia
18 D10 **Cantabria,Sierra de** *mts* Spain
45 K3 **Cantagallo** Italy
18 G7 **Cantal** *dep* France
45 Q6 **Cantalupo nel Sánnio** Italy
127 O2 **Cantaro** Trinidad
127 M10 **Cantaura** Venezuela
20 H3 **Canteleu** France
9 H5 **Canterbury** England
122 E8 **Canterbury** New Brunswick
144 C5 **Canterbury** *stat area* New Zealand
144 D6 **Canterbury Bight** New Zealand
144 C6 **Canterbury Plains** New Zealand
45 O6 **Canterna, L. di** Italy
68 G7 **Can Tho** Vietnam
102 G6 **Cantil** California
71 G6 **Cantilan** Mindanao Philippines
16 D7 **Cantillana** Spain
129 K5 **Canto do Buriti** Brazil
Canton China *see* **Guangzhou**
112 C3 **Canton** Georgia
110 F1 **Canton** Illinois
107 N3 **Canton** Kansas
95 R2 **Canton** Maine
111 F9 **Canton** Mississippi
110 E1 **Canton** Missouri
101 O3 **Canton** Montana
112 E2 **Canton** N Carolina
121 P8 **Canton** New York
94 F6 **Canton** Ohio
107 M5 **Canton** Oklahoma
95 L5 **Canton** Pennsylvania
98 K6 **Canton** S Dakota
109 M3 **Canton** Texas
121 T4 **Canton-Bégin** Quebec
134 A5 **Canton I** Pacific Oc
110 D1 **Cantril** Iowa
41 K6 **Cantù** Italy
118 J8 **Cantuar** Sask
130 D9 **Cantú,R** Brazil
130 D9 **Cantú, Serra do** *mt* Brazil
130 G10 **Canudos** Brazil
133 F5 **Cañuelas** Argentina
128 G4 **Canuma** Brazil
128 F5 **Canutama** Brazil
107 L6 **Canute** Oklahoma
124 G4 **Canutillo** Mexico
108 A4 **Canutillo** Texas
145 D4 **Canvastown** New Zealand
9 G5 **Canvey I** England
118 L5 **Canwood** Sask
20 G2 **Cany-Barville** France
120 F5 **Canyon** Ontario
108 F1 **Canyon** Texas
101 P5 **Canyon** Wyoming
117 E5 **Canyon** Yukon Terr
100 G5 **Canyon City** Oregon
100 K6 **Canyon Cr** Idaho
118 C3 **Canyon Creek** Alberta
101 N3 **Canyon Creek** Montana
103 P5 **Canyon de Chelly Nat.Mon** Arizona
101 O3 **Canyon Ferry Dam** Montana
103 N8 **Canyon L** Arizona
103 O3 **Canyonlands Nat. Park** Utah
117 K4 **Canyon Ranges** N W Terr
109 J6 **Canyon Res** Texas
100 B7 **Canyonville** Oregon
87 D7 **Canzar** Angola
33 T6 **Canzow** E Germany
67 B5 **Cao Bang** Vietnam
65 C5 **Caogoubu** China
67 A3 **Cao Hai** *L* China
65 F4 **Cao He** *R* China
65 F4 **Caohekou** China
Caojiahe *see* **Qichun**
12 C2 **Caolisport, L** Scotland
87 C7 **Caombo** Angola
68 J6 **Cao Nguen Dar Lac** *plat* Vietnam
122 F1 **Caopacho L** Quebec
122 F2 **Caopacho R** Quebec
121 Q3 **Caopatina, L** Quebec
65 F3 **Caoshi** China
67 D3 **Caoshi** China
65 C7 **Cao Xian** China
98 F5 **Capa** S Dakota
87 D7 **Capaia** Angola
128 E2 **Capanaparo** *R* Venezuela
129 J4 **Capanema** Brazil
130 D9 **Capanema, R** Brazil
45 J4 **Capannoli** Italy
45 J4 **Capannori** Italy
130 F5 **Capão Redondo** Brazil
130 H7 **Caparaó,Sa do** *mts* Brazil
128 E3 **Caparro, Co** *mt* Colombia
71 E3 **Capas** Luzon Philippines
127 J9 **Capatárida** Venezuela
48 H5 **Căpăţîna, Muntii** *mt* Romania
71 D7 **Capayan Sulu** *isld* Philippines
18 D9 **Capbreton** France
122 F4 **Cap Chat** Quebec
121 S6 **Cap de la Madeleine** Quebec
18 G8 **Capdenac** France
122 H4 **Cap de Rabast** Quebec
122 H5 **Cap-d'Espoir** Quebec
95 R4 **Cape Ann** Massachusetts
139 J8 **Cape Barren I** Tasmania
90 K12 **Cape Basin** Atlantic Oc
67 C7 **Cape Bastion** China
123 M7 **Cape Breton Highlands Nat Pk** C Breton I, N Scotia
123 N7 **Cape Breton I** Nova Scotia
123 U6 **Cape Broyle** Nfld
113 G9 **Cape Canaveral** Florida
123 R1 **Cape Charles** Labrador
95 L9 **Cape Charles** Virginia
85 D7 **Cape Coast** Ghana
95 S5 **Cape Cod** Massachusetts
95 R5 **Cape Cod B** Massachusetts
95 R5 **Cape Cod Canal** Massachusetts
95 R5 **Cape Cod Nat.Seashore** Massachusetts
115 M5 **Cape Dorset** N W Terr
115 N4 **Cape Dyer** N W Terr
112 K4 **Cape Fear** N Carolina
110 G4 **Cape Girardeau** Missouri
112 M2 **Cape Hatteras** N Carolina
115 N5 **Cape Hopes Advance** Quebec
Cape Horn *see* **Hornos, C. de**
112 H4 **Cape I** S Carolina
143 B10 **Capel** W Australia
129 L6 **Capela** Brazil
123 P6 **Cape la Hune** Nfld
8 C1 **Capel Curig** Wales
130 G5 **Capelinha** Brazil
116 E2 **Cape Lisburne** Alaska
141 J6 **Capella** Queensland
22 F4 **Capelle-en-Thierache, la** France
22 K4 **Capellen** Luxembourg
95 N8 **Cape May** New Jersey
87 C7 **Capenda-Camulemba** Angola
89 A10 **Cape of Good Hope** S Africa
114 G3 **Cape Parry** N W Terr
89 B8 **Cape Province** S Africa
89 A10 **Cape Pt** S Africa
141 H5 **Cape R** Queensland
123 T7 **Cape Race** Nfld
123 N6 **Cape Ray** Nfld
80 F2 **Capernaum** Israel
112 H5 **Cape Romain** S Carolina
103 N5 **Cape Royal** Arizona
113 F12 **Cape Sable** *pen* Florida
122 G10 **Cape Sable I** Nova Scotia
122 F9 **Cape St.Mary** Nova Scotia
123 S7 **Cape St. Mary's** *lt ho* Nfld
127 N4 **Capesterre** Guadeloupe W I
127 N5 **Capesterre** Marie Galante W I
45 P5 **Capestrallo** Italy
89 A9 **Cape Town** S Africa
90 G7 **Cape Verde** *islds, rep* Atlantic Oc
90 E7 **Cape Verde Fracture** Atlantic Oc
90 H7 **Cape Verde Plateau** Atlantic Oc
95 M9 **Capeville** Virginia
95 L2 **Cape Vincent** New York
15 C2 **Cape Wrath** Scotland
141 F1 **Cape York Pen** Queensland
127 H5 **Cap-Haïtien** Haiti
130 B9 **Capiatá** Paraguay
128 E3 **Capibara** Venezuela
130 J9 **Capiberibe** *R* Brazil
133 F4 **Capilla** Argentina
133 E4 **Capilla del Monte** Argentina
129 J4 **Capim** *R* Brazil
128 E7 **Capinota** Bolivia
41 H6 **Capio, Monte** Italy
45 O6 **Capistrello** Italy
121 O5 **Capitachouane** *R* Quebec
106 E8 **Capitan** New Mexico
130 C8 **Capitán Bado** Paraguay
131 A8 **Capitanes, Pta** *C* Chile
106 E8 **Capitan Mts** New Mexico
42 E6 **Capitignano** Italy
98 B4 **Capitol** Montana
100 H8 **Capitol Peak** *mt* Nevada
103 N3 **Capitol Reef Nat.Mon** Utah
122 G5 **Caplan** Quebec
71 E5 **Capnoyan** *isld* Philippines
88 D9 **Capoche** *R* Mozambique
129 G5 **Capoeiras, Cachoeira das** *waterfall* Brazil
44 D4 **Capo Mele** Italy
139 K3 **Capoompeta** *mt* New S Wales
45 O5 **Cappadocia** Italy
36 F2 **Cappel** W Germany
14 D4 **Cappoquin** Irish Rep
127 O7 **Cap Pt** St Lucia
120 K6 **Capreol** Ontario
43 C7 **Caprera** *isld* Sardinia
45 L4 **Caprese Michelangelo** Italy
45 Q8 **Capri** Italy
45 Q7 **Capriati a Volturno** Italy
141 K5 **Capricorn Chan** Gt Barrier Reef **Aust**
141 K6 **Capricorn Grp** *islds* Gt Barrier Reef **Aust**
143 B6 **Capricorn Ra** W Australia
42 D3 **Caprino** Italy
87 D9 **Caprivi Strip** Namibia
108 D2 **Caprock** New Mexico
123 M7 **Capstick** C Breton I, N Scotia
135 U5 **Captain Cook** Hawaiian Is
139 J6 **Captain's Flat** New S Wales
18 E8 **Captieux** France
113 E11 **Captiva** Florida
45 Q7 **Capua** Italy
71 E7 **Capual** *isld* Philippines
83 K12 **Capucin Pt** Mahé I Indian Oc
71 G4 **Capul** Philippines
106 D4 **Capulin** Colorado
106 G5 **Capulin** New Mexico
128 D3 **Caqueta** *div* Colombia
128 D4 **Caquetá** *R* Colombia
71 E4 **Carabao** *isld* Philippines
128 D6 **Carabaya, Cord.de** *mts* Peru
128 F4 **Carabinani** *R* Brazil
128 E1 **Carabobo** *state* Venezuela
48 J6 **Caracal** Romania
127 L9 **Caracas** Venezuela
129 K5 **Caracol** Brazil
130 C7 **Caracol** Brazil
125 J8 **Caracuaro** Mexico
71 G7 **Caraga** Mindanao Philippines
14 B4 **Caragh,L** Irish Rep
131 G4 **Caraguatá** *R* Uruguay
130 F8 **Caraguata-tuba** Brazil
130 C9 **Caraĝuatay** Paraguay
133 C5 **Carahue** Chile
130 H5 **Caraí** Brazil
12 C2 **Cara I** Scotland
129 H5 **Carajás, Serra dos** *mts* Brazil
18 G9 **Caraman** France
120 D3 **Caramat** Ontario
71 F4 **Caramoan Pen** Philippines
128 F5 **Caranapatuba** Brazil
130 G7 **Carandaí** Brazil
130 B6 **Carandazal** Brazil
140 E5 **Carandotta** Queensland
129 K8 **Carangola** Brazil
128 F3 **Caransaca,Co** *mt* Venezuela
48 G5 **Caransebeş** Romania
130 B9 **Carapeguá** Paraguay
138 D5 **Carappee Hill** S Australia
122 H6 **Caraquet** New Brunswick
122 H6 **Caraquet Bay** New Brunswick
128 B4 **Caráquez,B.de** Ecuador
48 G5 **Carasova** Romania
48 G5 **Caras-Severin** *reg* Romania
125 N2 **Caratasca** Honduras
130 G6 **Caratinga** Brazil
69 G14 **Carat, Tanjung** *C* Indonesia
128 E4 **Carauari** Brazil
130 H8 **Caraúbas** Brazil
17 F6 **Caravaca** Spain
41 L7 **Caravaggio** Italy
130 H5 **Caravelas** Brazil
128 D7 **Caraveli** Peru
43 B9 **Caravius, M. is** *mt* Sardinia
128 C5 **Caraz** Peru
131 H2 **Carazinho** Brazil
16 B2 **Carballino** Spain
16 B1 **Carballo** Spain
16 B1 **Carba, Sa. de la** *mts* Spain
119 S9 **Carberry** Manitoba
101 U1 **Carbert** Montana
118 D7 **Carbon** Alberta
45 K1 **Carbonara** Italy
43 C9 **Carbonara,C** Sardinia
118 D5 **Carbondale** Alberta
106 C2 **Carbondale** Colorado
107 P3 **Carbondale** Kansas
95 M5 **Carbondale** Pennsylvania
123 T6 **Carbonear** Nfld
17 F8 **Carboneras** Spain
111 J8 **Carbon Hill** Alabama
43 B9 **Carbonia** Sardinia
38 F8 **Carbonin** Italy
130 G5 **Carbonita** Brazil
18 F9 **Carbonne** France
17 G5 **Carcagente** Spain
117 P7 **Carcajou** Alberta
18 E7 **Carcans, Etang de** *L* France
71 F5 **Carcar** Cebu Philippines
131 E4 **Carcaraña** *R* Argentina
86 A2 **Carcar Mts** Somalia
18 G9 **Carcassonne** France
128 C3 **Carchi** *prov* Ecuador
139 J5 **Carcoan** New S Wales
117 F5 **Carcross** Yukon Terr
47 K7 **Cardak** Turkey
119 R8 **Cardale** Manitoba
68 F7 **Cardamomes,Chaine des** *mts* Cambodia
125 K6 **Cárdenas** Mexico
139 G3 **Cardenyabba** *R* New S Wales
133 C7 **Cardiel,L** Argentina
8 C5 **Cardiff** Wales
8 B3 **Cardigan** Wales
Cardigan *co see* **Dyfed**
123 K7 **Cardigan B** Pr Edward I
8 B2 **Cardigan B** Wales
121 P8 **Cardinal** Ontario
94 E6 **Cardington** Ohio
17 J3 **Cardona** Spain
17 J3 **Cardoner,R** Spain
127 J9 **Cardón,Pta** Venezuela
130 E7 **Cardoso** Brazil
130 F9 **Cardoso,I.do** Brazil
144 B6 **Cardrona** New Zealand
144 B6 **Cardrona, Mt** New Zealand
119 M9 **Cardross** Sask
12 D2 **Cardross** Scotland
118 D9 **Cardston** Alberta
141 H4 **Cardwell** Queensland
48 G3 **Carei** Romania
127 O2 **Carenage** Trinidad
22 D3 **Carency** France
20 C3 **Carentan** France
21 A6 **Carentoir** France
8 B4 **Carew** Wales
101 M6 **Carey** Idaho
94 D6 **Carey** Ohio
108 G1 **Carey** Texas
143 B7 **Carey Downs** W Australia
143 D8 **Carey, L** W Australia
81 C7 **Cargados Carajos** *islds* Indian Oc
120 J8 **Cargill** Ontario
13 E1 **Cargill** Scotland
141 G5 **Cargoon** Queensland
18 C4 **Carhaix** France
122 E1 **Carheil,L** Quebec
130 H7 **Cariacica** Brazil
127 N9 **Cariaco** Venezuela
126 F10 **Caribana,Pta** Colombia
93 L7 **Caribbean Sea** Cent America
117 N9 **Cariboo Mts** Br Col
95 S7 **Caribou** Maine
122 K8 **Caribou** Nova Scotia
116 G9 **Caribou** *R* Alaska
117 K5 **Caribou** *R* N W Terr
117 K7 **Caribou Hide** Br Col
122 K8 **Caribou I** Nova Scotia
120 E5 **Caribou I** Ontario
117 R5 **Caribou Is** N W Terr
101 O6 **Caribou Mt** Idaho
117 Q6 **Caribou Mts** Alberta
124 F4 **Carichic** Mexico
119 Q9 **Carievale** Sask
71 G5 **Carigara** Leyte Philippines
22 J4 **Carignan** France
44 C2 **Carignano** Italy
121 Q7 **Carillon** Quebec
139 J4 **Carinda** New S Wales
17 G3 **Cariñena** Spain
129 K6 **Carinhanha** Brazil
45 P7 **Carinola** Italy
129 J6 **Caripare** Brazil
127 N9 **Caripe** Venezuela
127 N9 **Caripito** Venezuela
130 G9 **Caririaçu** Brazil
128 F5 **Caritianas** Brazil
130 G9 **Cariús** Brazil
107 N5 **Carl Blackwell, L** Oklahoma
22 E4 **Carlepont** France
17 G5 **Carlet** Spain
94 D4 **Carleton** Michigan
98 J9 **Carleton** Nebraska
122 F5 **Carleton** Quebec
122 F6 **Carleton,Mt** New Brunswick
121 O7 **Carleton Place** Ontario
122 K4 **Carleton Pt** Quebec
98 B5 **Carlile** Wyoming
103 H1 **Carlin** Nevada
36 B5 **Carling** France
14 E2 **Carlingford** Irish Rep
110 G2 **Carlinville** Illinois
110 E7 **Carlisle** Arkansas
13 F4 **Carlisle** England
110 J3 **Carlisle** Indiana
94 C8 **Carlisle** Kentucky
95 K6 **Carlisle** Pennsylvania
112 F3 **Carlisle** S Carolina
142 B2 **Carlisle** *dist* Perth, W Aust
127 P6 **Carlisle B** Barbados
18 G10 **Carlitte** *mt* France
43 B9 **Carloforte** Sardinia
13 E2 **Carlops** Scotland
133 E6 **Carlos Ameghino, Istmo** Argentina
133 E5 **Carlos Casares** Argentina
130 H5 **Carlos Chagas** Brazil
140 E6 **Carlo Springs** Queensland
131 G4 **Carlos Reyles** Uruguay
14 E4 **Carlow** Irish Rep
14 E4 **Carlow** *co* Irish Rep
15 B2 **Carloway** Scotland
102 G8 **Carlsbad** California
Carlsbad Czechoslovakia *see* **Karlovy Vary**
108 C3 **Carlsbad** New Mexico
108 C3 **Carlsbad Caverns Nat. Park** New Mexico
72 H7 **Carlsberg Ridge** Indian Oc
37 O3 **Carlsfeld** E Germany
99 T3 **Carlshend** Michigan
99 O3 **Carlton** Minnesota
100 B4 **Carlton** Oregon
118 L6 **Carlton** Sask
109 J4 **Carlton** Texas
142 G3 **Carlton Hill** W Australia
9 F1 **Carlton on Trent** England
100 D3 **Carlton Pass** Washington
12 E2 **Carluke** Scotland
110 G3 **Carlyle** Illinois
98 B3 **Carlyle** Montana
119 P9 **Carlyle** Sask
118 D1 **Carman** Manitoba
118 D8 **Carmangay** Alberta
123 S4 **Carmanville** Nfld
8 B4 **Carmarthen** Wales
Carmarthen *co see* **Dyfed**
8 C4 **Carmarthen Van** *mt* Wales
18 G8 **Carmaux** France
102 C5 **Carmel** California
95 O5 **Carmel** New York
119 M6 **Carmel** Sask
95 S2 **Carmell** Maine
80 D3 **Carmel,Mt** Israel
112 E3 **Carmel, Mt** S Carolina
133 F4 **Carmelo** Uruguay
127 J9 **Carmelo** Venezuela
102 C5 **Carmel Valley** California
126 G10 **Carmen** Colombia
101 M4 **Carmen** Idaho
107 M5 **Carmen** Oklahoma
71 G6 **Carmen** Philippines
124 D5 **Carmen** *isld* Mexico
124 F2 **Carmen** *R* Mexico
133 D2 **Carmen Alto** Chile
130 C10 **Carmen del Paraná** Paraguay
133 E6 **Carmen de Patagones** Argentina
131 B2 **Carmen,R.del** Chile
133 D5 **Carmensa** Argentina
108 E7 **Carmen, Sa del** *mts* Mexico
110 H3 **Carmi** Illinois
113 L9 **Carmichael** New Providence I **Bahamas**
118 J8 **Carmichael** Sask
141 J5 **Carmila** Queensland
109 L5 **Carmine** Texas
130 G7 **Carmo** Brazil
44 D3 **Carmo** *mt* Italy
130 F7 **Carmo da Cachoeira** Brazil
130 F6 **Carmo do Paranaiba** Brazil
143 C9 **Carmody, L** W Australia
16 D7 **Carmona** Spain
13 H5 **Carnaby** England
143 B8 **Carnamah** W Australia
138 F4 **Carnanto,L** S Australia
89 C8 **Carnarvon** S Africa
143 A6 **Carnarvon** W Australia
141 J7 **Carnarvon Ra** Queensland
143 D7 **Carnarvon Ra** W Australia
71 C5 **Carnatic Shoal** S China Sea
14 D1 **Carndonagh** Irish Rep
119 Q9 **Carnduff** Sask
8 C1 **Carnedd Llewelyn** *mt* Wales
107 M6 **Carnegie** Oklahoma
94 G6 **Carnegie** Pennsylvania
143 E7 **Carnegie** W Australia
143 E7 **Carnegie, L** W Australia
90 A9 **Carnegie Ridge** Pacific Oc
20 E4 **Carneille,la** France
107 N3 **Carneiro** Kansas
131 A6 **Carnero,B.del** Chile
112 D3 **Carnesville** Georgia
99 T4 **Carney** Michigan
107 O6 **Carney** Oklahoma
13 F5 **Carnforth** England
42 E2 **Carniche, Alpi** *mts* Italy
69 A8 **Car Nicobar** *isld* Nicobar Is
22 E3 **Carnieres** France
86 C5 **Carnot** Cent Afr Republic
138 D5 **Carnot,C** S Australia
19 Q18 **Carnoules** France
13 F1 **Carnoustie** Scotland
14 E4 **Carnsore Pt** Irish Rep
12 E2 **Carnwath** Scotland
116 N3 **Caro** Alaska
94 D3 **Caro** Michigan
141 K4 **Carola Cay** *isld* Gt Barrier Reef **Australia**
112 F2 **Caroleen** N Carolina
129 J5 **Carolina** Brazil
128 C3 **Carolina** Ecuador
87 F11 **Carolina** S Africa
112 K3 **Carolina Beach** N Carolina
118 C6 **Caroline** Alberta
144 B6 **Caroline** New Zealand
135 M9 **Caroline I** Pacific Oc
134 E7 **Caroline Is** Pacific Oc
140 D6 **Caroline, L** N Terr Aust
32 G5 **Carolinensiel** W Germany
144 A6 **Caroline Pk** New Zealand
142 F3 **Caroline Ra** W Australia
20 B4 **Carolles** France
119 M8 **Caron** Sask
137 S3 **Carondelet Reef** Phoenix Is Pacific Oc
127 O2 **Caroni** Trinidad
128 F2 **Caroni** *R* Venezuela
127 O2 **Caroni Swamp** Trinidad
127 J9 **Carora** Venezuela
103 K4 **Carp** Nevada
121 O7 **Carp** Ontario
53 B9 **Carpathian Mts** E Europe
48 H5 **Carpaţii Meridionali** *mts* Romania
41 M7 **Carpenèdolo** Italy
45 J1 **Carpenedolo** Italy
141 G4 **Carpentaria Downs** Queensland
136 H4 **Carpentaria,Gulf of** Australia
98 B8 **Carpenter** Wyoming
100 A7 **Carpenterville** Oregon
19 O16 **Carpentras** France
45 J2 **Carpi** Italy
19 P18 **Carpiâgne** *mt* France
130 J9 **Carpina** Brazil
45 J3 **Carpineti** Italy
45 O6 **Carpineto Romano** Italy
48 F5 **Cărpinis** Romania
102 E7 **Carpinteria** California
98 E1 **Carpio** N Dakota
117 M8 **Carp L** Br Col
103 M2 **Carp L** Utah
94 C1 **Carp Lake** Michigan
138 F6 **Carpolac** Victoria
21 C7 **Carquefou** France
19 Q18 **Carqueiranne** France
106 F1 **Carr** Colorado
113 C8 **Carrabelle** Florida
119 O6 **Carragana** Sask
14 B3 **Carra,L** Irish Rep
16 B4 **Carramulo, Sa. do** *mts* Portugal
131 A5 **Carranza,C** Chile
125 J4 **Carranza, Presa V.** *res* Mexico
128 F2 **Carrao** *R* Venezuela
44 H3 **Carrara** Italy
102 H5 **Carrara** Nevada
17 F4 **Carrascosa del Campo** Spain
17 G7 **Carrascoy,Sierra de** *mts* Spain
139 H5 **Carrathool** New S Wales
14 B5 **Carrauntoohil** *mt* Irish Rep
142 G3 **Carr Boyd Ra** W Australia
15 E3 **Carrbridge** Scotland
146 H3 **Carr,C** Antarctica
133 F2 **Carreria** Paraguay
131 B6 **Carrero,Cerro** *peak* Argentina
127 O8 **Carriacou** *isld* Lesser Antilles
15 D5 **Carrick** Scotland
14 F2 **Carrickfergus** N Ireland
14 E3 **Carrickmacross** Irish Rep
14 C3 **Carrick on Shannon** Irish Rep
14 D4 **Carrick on Suir** Irish Rep
111 G11 **Carriere** Mississippi
121 N5 **Carrière,L** Quebec
110 H4 **Carriers Mills** Illinois
138 E4 **Carrieton** S Australia
131 B8 **Carri Lafquén, L** Argentina
98 G2 **Carrington** N Dakota
16 D2 **Carrion** *R* Spain
16 D2 **Carrión de los Condes** Spain
127 H8 **Carrizal** Colombia
124 F2 **Carrizal** Mexico
133 C3 **Carrizal Bajo** Chile
131 B2 **Carrizal, Pta** *C* Chile
103 H9 **Carrizo Cr** California
106 G5 **Carrizo Cr** New Mex/Tex
103 P5 **Carrizo Mts** Arizona
108 H7 **Carrizo Springs** Texas
106 E8 **Carrizozo** New Mexico
99 M7 **Carroll** Iowa
119 R9 **Carroll** Manitoba
98 J7 **Carroll** Nebraska
146 G12 **Carroll Inlet** Antarctica
111 H8 **Carrollton** Alabama
112 B4 **Carrollton** Georgia
110 F2 **Carrollton** Illinois
94 B8 **Carrollton** Kentucky
111 G8 **Carrollton** Mississippi
110 C2 **Carrollton** Missouri
94 F6 **Carrollton** Ohio
109 O8 **Carrollton** Texas
94 J6 **Carrolltown** Pennsylvania
99 T7 **Carrollville** Wisconsin
141 F4 **Carron** *R* Queensland
12 E3 **Carronbridge** Scotland
119 V4 **Carrot R** Manitoba
119 O5 **Carrot River** Sask
20 E4 **Carrouges** France
14 B2 **Carrowmore L** Irish Rep
118 H6 **Carruthers** Sask
100 C8 **Carrville** California
95 N2 **Carry Falls Res** New York
19 O18 **Carry-le-Rouet** France
78 F1 **Çarşamba** Turkey
118 D8 **Carseland** Alberta
13 E1 **Carse of Gowrie** *dist* Scotland
45 O5 **Carseolani, Mti** Italy
45 O5 **Carsoli** Italy
99 L8 **Carson** Iowa
98 E3 **Carson** N Dakota
100 D4 **Carson** Washington
102 E2 **Carson** *R* Nevada
94 C3 **Carson City** Michigan
102 E2 **Carson City** Nevada
102 F2 **Carson L** Nevada
142 F3 **Carson, R** W Australia
102 F2 **Carson Sink** Nevada
94 E3 **Carsonville** Michigan
12 D3 **Carsphairn** Scotland
118 C7 **Carstairs** Alberta
12 E2 **Carstairs** Scotland
Carstensz, G *see* **Jaya Pk**
128 C1 **Cartagena** Colombia
17 G7 **Cartagena** Spain
102 F5 **Cartago** California
128 C3 **Cartago** Colombia
125 N5 **Cartago** Costa Rica
108 G6 **Carta Valley** Texas
101 P2 **Carter** Montana
107 L6 **Carter** Oklahoma
101 P8 **Carter** Wyoming
13 F3 **Carter Bar** England
20 B3 **Carteret** France
141 G2 **Carter, Mt** Queensland
9 G3 **Carters Bridge** England
111 M7 **Cartersville** Georgia
101 T3 **Cartersville** Montana
145 E4 **Carterton** New Zealand
109 P1 **Carthage** Arkansas
99 P9 **Carthage** Illinois
94 B7 **Carthage** Indiana
111 G9 **Carthage** Mississippi
110 B4 **Carthage** Missouri
112 H2 **Carthage** N Carolina
106 D8 **Carthage** New Mexico
95 M3 **Carthage** New York
98 J5 **Carthage** S Dakota
94 B10 **Carthage** Tennessee
109 N3 **Carthage** Texas
43 C12 **Carthage** Tunisia
85 G1 **Carthage** *ruins* Tunisia
120 J6 **Cartier** Ontario
142 E1 **Cartier I** Timor Sea
22 F3 **Cartignies** France
13 F5 **Cartmel** England
45 N4 **Cartoceto** Italy
48 J6 **Cărtojani** Romania
115 O7 **Cartwright** Labrador
119 S9 **Cartwright** Manitoba
98 C2 **Cartwright** N Dakota
129 L5 **Caruaru** Brazil
130 H10 **Caruarú** Brazil
128 F1 **Carúpano** Venezuela
129 J4 **Carutapera** Brazil
110 G5 **Caruthersville** Missouri
94 D9 **Carver** Kentucky
22 D3 **Carvin** France
16 A5 **Carvoeira,C** Portugal
128 F4 **Carvoeiro** Brazil
101 M1 **Carway** Alberta
141 H6 **Carwell** Queensland
33 S6 **Carwitz** E Germany
111 F9 **Cary** Mississippi
112 J2 **Cary** N Carolina
139 G3 **Caryapundy Swamp** Queensland
113 G12 **Carysfort Reef** Florida
45 K3 **Carzolano,Mt** Italy
133 C4 **Casablanca** Chile
85 C2 **Casablanca** Morocco
130 F7 **Casa Branca** Brazil
16 B6 **Casa Branca** Portugal
42 F7 **Casacalenda** Italy
41 L5 **Casaccia** Switzerland
127 P3 **Casa Cruz, C** Trinidad
124 E2 **Casa de János** Mexico
129 G8 **Casado** Paraguay
103 N9 **Casa Grande** Arizona
103 N9 **Casa Grande Nat. Mon** Arizona
17 G5 **Casa Ibáñez** Spain
41 L7 **Casalbuttano** Italy
45 Q7 **Casal di Principe** Italy
44 D1 **Casale** Italy
45 K3 **Casalecchio di Reno** Italy
45 J2 **Casalgrande** Italy
45 H2 **Casalmaggiore** Italy
45 J1 **Casaloldo** Italy
44 G1 **Casalpusterlengo** Italy
45 P6 **Casalvieri** Italy
45 P8 **Casamicciola** Italy
116 E4 **Casapedaga** Alaska
108 C6 **Casa Piedra** Texas
43 J8 **Casarano** Italy
124 F2 **Casas Grandes** Mexico
109 O9 **Casa View** Texas
100 J5 **Cascade** Idaho
101 O2 **Cascade** Montana
95 Q2 **Cascade** New Hampshire
100 D4 **Cascade Locks** Oregon
117 N11 **Cascade Mts** Br Col/Wash
100 D1 **Cascade Pass** Washington
100 C7 **Cascade Ra** U.S.A.
100 K5 **Cascade Res** Idaho
100 D2 **Cascade Tunnel** Washington
100 C5 **Cascadia** Oregon
16 A6 **Cascais** Portugal
122 G5 **Cascapedia** Quebec
122 F5 **Cascapedia R** Quebec
130 D9 **Cascavel** Brazil
45 J4 **Cascina** Italy
95 R2 **Casco** Maine
99 T5 **Casco** Wisconsin
95 R3 **Casco B** Maine
45 M3 **Casemurate** Italy
45 L4 **Casentina** Italy
133 E5 **Caseros** Argentina
45 Q7 **Caserta** Italy
94 D3 **Caseville** Michigan
99 T10 **Casey** Illinois
121 Q5 **Casey** Quebec
146 A5 **Casey B** Antarctica
14 D4 **Cashel** Irish Rep
87 F9 **Cashel** Zimbabwe
107 N6 **Cashion** Oklahoma
141 J8 **Cashmere** Queensland **Aust**
100 E2 **Cashmere** Washington
99 Q6 **Cashton** Wisconsin
71 F2 **Casiguran** Luzon Philippines
71 F2 **Casiguran B** Luzon Philippines
71 E3 **Casiguran Sound** Luzon Philippines
133 E4 **Casilda** Argentina
48 L6 **Casimcea** Romania
130 G8 **Casimiro de Abreu** Brazil
45 H2 **Casina** Italy
139 L3 **Casino** New S Wales
128 E3 **Casiquiare** *R* Venezuela
124 D2 **Casita** Mexico
31 J6 **Čáslav** Czechoslovakia
128 C5 **Casma** Peru
102 D7 **Casmalia** California
71 G5 **Casogoran B** Philippines
45 L3 **Casola Valsenio** Italy
109 N2 **Cason** Texas
45 Q8 **Casória** Italy
102 A2 **Caspar** California
17 G3 **Caspe** Spain
101 T7 **Casper** Wyoming
111 C9 **Caspiana** Louisiana
53 G10 **Caspian Sea**
110 C6 **Cass** Arkansas
144 C5 **Cass** New Zealand
94 H8 **Cass** W Virginia
94 D3 **Cass** *R* Michigan
144 C5 **Cass** *R* New Zealand
98 B7 **Cassa** Wyoming
18 G8 **Cassagnes-Bégonhès** France
87 D8 **Cassai** Angola
130 F7 **Cássai** Brazil
87 D8 **Cassamba** Angola
43 G9 **Cassano Ionio** Italy
94 D3 **Cass City** Michigan
121 P7 **Casselman** Ontario
98 J3 **Casselton** N Dakota
19 Q14 **Casse Massion** *mt* France
117 J6 **Cassiar** Br Col
117 H6 **Cassiar Mts** Br Col
130 D6 **Cassilândia** Brazil
139 J4 **Cassilis** New S Wales
141 G5 **Cassilis** Queensland
87 C9 **Cassinga** Angola
142 F2 **Cassini I** W Australia
133 G4 **Cassino** Brazil
43 F7 **Cassino** Italy
129 H3 **Cassiporé** *R* Brazil
19 P18 **Cassis** France
99 M2 **Cass L** Minnesota
107 O3 **Cassoday** Kansas
94 B5 **Cassopolis** Michigan
110 C5 **Cassville** Missouri
99 Q7 **Cassville** Wisconsin
45 K1 **Castagnaro** Italy
102 F7 **Castaic** California
129 J4 **Castanhal** Brazil
133 D4 **Castaño** Argentina
131 B3 **Castaño** *R* Argentina
124 J4 **Castaños** Mexico
127 M1 **Castara** Tobago
17 G3 **Castejón,Mt.de** Spain
45 J1 **Castelbelforte** Italy
45 L3 **Castel Bolognese** Italy
45 J1 **Castel d'Ario** Italy
42 D4 **Castel del Rio** Italy
42 F7 **Castel di Sangro** Italy
45 L4 **Castel Focognano** Italy
45 P7 **Castelforte** Italy
42 D3 **Castelfranco** Veneto Italy
45 L4 **Castelfranco di Sopra** Italy
45 K2 **Castelfranco Emilia** Italy

16
Castel Goffredo — Charlestown

45 J1 Castel Goffredo Italy
18 F8 Casteljaloux France
109 J5 Castell Texas
37 J4 Castell W Germany
100 C8 Castella California
43 F8 Castellabate Italy
43 E10 Castellammare del Golfo Sicily
45 Q8 Castellammare di Stabia Italy
40 G7 Castellamònte Italy
45 J2 Castellarano Italy
133 F5 Castelli Argentina
45 K3 Castello di Serravalle Italy
17 G4 Castellón prov Spain
17 G5 Castellón de la Plana Spain
17 G4 Castellote Spain
45 J1 Castellucchio Italy
45 N6 Castel Madama Italy
45 K2 Castel Maggiore Italy
45 K1 Castelmassa Italy
18 G9 Castelnaudary France
18 E7 Castelnau de Médoc France
18 F8 Castelnau de Montratier France
18 F9 Castelnau-Magnoac France
45 J2 Castelnovo di Sotto Italy
45 H3 Castel novo ne'Monti Italy
45 H3 Castelnuovo di Garfagnana Italy
45 N5 Castelnuovo di Porto Italy
45 J1 Castelnuovo di Verona Italy
130 H7 Castelo Brazil
16 C5 Castelo de Vide Portugal
45 O4 Castelplanio Italy
45 M6 Castel Porziano Italy
45 R8 Castel San Giorgio Italy
45 L4 Castel San Niccolo Italy
45 L3 Castel San Pietro Terme Italy
18 F8 Castelsarrasin France
44 F1 Castel S.Giov Italy
43 F11 Casteltermini Sicily
45 P5 Castelvecchio Subequo Italy
43 E11 Castelvetrano Sicily
45 P7 Castel Volturno Italy
45 K3 Castenaso Italy
41 M7 Castenedolo Italy
138 F6 Casterton Victoria
18 E9 Castets France
122 F7 Castigan Mts New Brunswick
45 K3 Castiglione dei Pepoli Italy
45 J1 Castiglione delle Stiviere Italy
45 H3 Castiglione di Garfagnana Italy
45 L4 Castiglion Fibocchi Italy
42 D5 Castiglion Fiorentino Italy
94 K4 Castile New York
133 C3 Castilla Chile
16 D4 Castilla Lavieja reg Spain
71 E3 Castillejos Luzon Philippines
16 D6 Castillejo, Sa. de mts Spain
127 J9 Castilletes Venezuela
133 C7 Castillo mt Chile
131 B4 Castillo,Cerro del peak Argentina
113 F8 Castillo de San Marcos Nat. Mon Florida
124 H3 Castillón Mexico
18 F8 Castillon et Capitourlan France
18 F8 Castillonnés France
133 D7 Castillo,Pampa del plain Argentina
133 G4 Castillos Uruguay
95 T2 Castine Maine
9 G2 Castle Acre England
14 B3 Castlebar Irish Rep
15 A4 Castlebay Scotland
14 E3 Castlebellingham Irish Rep
111 J10 Castleberry Alabama
14 E2 Castleblayney Irish Rep
9 E3 Castle Bromwich England
13 F4 Castle Carrock England
8 D5 Castle Cary England
14 D4 Castlecomer Irish Rep
100 J7 Castle Cr Idaho
103 N2 Castle Dale Utah
14 D2 Castlederg N Ireland
14 E4 Castledermot Irish Rep
103 K8 Castle Dome Mts Arizona
9 E2 Castle Donington England
12 E4 Castle Douglas Scotland
12 E3 Castlefern Scotland
13 G6 Castleford England
101 L7 Castleford Idaho
100 H1 Castlegar Br Col
103 O2 Castle Gate Utah
90 C1 Castle Harbour Bermuda
112 K3 Castle Hayne N Carolina
103 M8 Castle Hot Sp Arizona
126 G3 Castle I Bahamas
14 B4 Castleisland Irish Rep
14 B4 Castlemaine Irish Rep
139 G6 Castlemaine Victoria
14 C5 Castlemartyr Irish Rep
102 D6 Castle Mt California
101 L5 Castle Peak Idaho
145 F4 Castlepoint New Zealand
14 D3 Castlepollard Irish Rep
14 C3 Castlerea Irish Rep
139 J4 Castlereagh R New S Wales
140 D1 Castlereagh B N Terr Aust
9 G2 Castle Rising England
106 F2 Castle Rock Colorado
98 C5 Castle Rock S Dakota
101 O8 Castle Rock Utah
100 C3 Castle Rock Washington
99 R6 Castle Rock Res Wisconsin
13 G4 Castleside England
9 E1 Castleton England
127 L2 Castleton Jamaica
103 P3 Castleton Utah
95 O3 Castleton Vermont
95 O4 Castleton on Hudson New York
12 D5 Castletown I of Man U.K.
14 B5 Castletown Bere Irish Rep
14 F2 Castlewellan N Ireland
98 J5 Castlewood S Dakota
108 D6 Castolon Texas
118 F6 Castor Alberta
111 C9 Castor Louisiana
111 D9 Castor R Louisiana
95 M3 Castorland New York
20 B3 Castre,Mt France
18 G9 Castres France
25 C3 Castricum Netherlands
127 O7 Castries St Lucia
133 C6 Castro Chile
16 D2 Castrocalbón Spain
45 L3 Castrocaro Italy
45 O6 Castro dei Volsci Italy
16 E2 Castrogeriz Spain
16 C1 Castropol Spain
32 F9 Castrop-Rauxel W Germany
16 E1 Castro Urdiales Spain
16 B7 Castro Verde Portugal
43 G9 Castrovillari Italy
102 C5 Castroville California
109 J6 Castroville Texas
16 D6 Castuera Spain
88 G10 Casuarina isld Mozambique
142 G2 Casuarina, Mt W Australia
116 N6 Caswell Alaska
144 A6 Caswell Sd New Zealand
48 E3 Čata Czechoslovakia
127 J2 Catadupa Jamaica
130 G7 Cataguases Brazil
111 D10 Catahoula L Louisiana
71 F4 Catainĝan Philippines
78 J2 Çatak Turkey
130 F6 Catalão Brazil
47 J3 Çatalca Turkey
47 J5 Çatal Daği mt Turkey
127 K5 Catalina, I Dominican Rep
139 H9 Catamaran Tasmania
131 D2 Catamarca Argentina
133 D3 Catamarca prov Argentina
71 F4 Catanauan Philippines
87 F9 Catandica Mozambique
71 G4 Catanduanes isld Philippines
130 E7 Catanduva Brazil
130 D9 Catanduvas Brazil
43 G11 Catania Sicily
43 G11 Catania,Golfo di Sicily
43 H10 Catanzaro Italy
111 F12 Cataouatche,L Louisiana
110 K2 Cataract L Indiana
71 G4 Catarman Philippines
71 G7 Catarman Pt Mindanao Philippines
17 G5 Catarroja Spain
95 M6 Catasauqua Pennsylvania
138 D6 Catastrophe, C S Australia
128 D2 Catatumbo R Venezuela/Colombia
111 M9 Cataula Georgia
129 G4 Catavara Brazil
99 Q4 Catawba Wisconsin
112 F2 Catawba L S Carolina
95 L6 Catawissa Pennsylvania
87 F9 Cataxa Mozambique
71 G5 Catbalogan Samar Philippines
126 E2 Cat Cays islds Bahamas
101 R2 Cat Creek Montana
22 F3 Cateau,Le France
71 G7 Cateel Mindanao Philippines
9 G6 Catel Channel Is
22 E3 Catelet, le France
125 M8 Catemaco Mexico
45 P5 Catena di Monte Sirente Italy
130 J10 Catende Brazil
118 J5 Cater Sask
9 F5 Caterham England
87 B7 Catete Angola
107 L3 Catharine Kansas
98 G2 Cathay N Dakota
139 J6 Cathcart New S Wales
87 E12 Cathcart S Africa
108 D5 Cathedral Mt Texas
109 P1 Catherine,L Arkansas
103 M2 Catherine, Mt Utah
127 L2 Catherine's Peak Jamaica
89 F7 Cathkin Pk mt Lesotho
100 B3 Cathlamet Washington
94 D1 Cathro Michigan
126 G2 Cat I Bahamas
111 G11 Cat I Mississippi
22 F3 Catillon-sur-Sambre France
85 A6 Catio Guinea-Bissau
128 F3 Catisimiña Venezuela
115 K7 Cat Lake Ontario
94 E8 Catlettsburg Kentucky
99 T9 Catlin Illinois
144 B7 Catlins R New Zealand
95 L3 Cato New York
137 M6 Cato isld Coral Sea
94 K7 Catoctin Mt Maryland/Virg
130 H9 Catolé do Rocha Brazil
42 E5 Catria,Monte Italy
133 E5 Catrilo Argentina
128 F3 Catrimani Brazil
95 O4 Catskill New York
95 N4 Catskill Mts New York
94 J4 Cattaraugus New York
22 L5 Cattenom France
13 F6 Catterall England
13 G5 Catterick England
45 N4 Cattolica Italy
87 F11 Catuane Mozambique
133 D4 Catuna Argentina
128 E3 Cauaburi R Brazil
45 M1 Cauárzera Italy
129 J4 Cauaxi R Brazil
71 F6 Cauayan Negros Philippines
128 C3 Cauca div Colombia
126 G10 Cauca,R Colombia
72 E1 Caucasus mt ra U.S.S.R.
119 V3 Cauchon L Manitoba
95 R7 Caucomgomoc L Maine
20 G2 Caudebec France
20 H3 Caudebec-les-Elbeuf France
17 G6 Caudete Spain
22 E3 Caudry France
88 C9 Cauese Mts Mozambique
121 R7 Caughnawaga Quebec
71 G6 Cauit Pt Philippines
20 A5 Caulnes France
43 G10 Caulonia Italy
19 N17 Caumont France
20 D3 Caumont-l'Eventé France
126 E4 Caunao R Cuba
18 G9 Caunes France
87 C7 Caungulu Angola
131 A5 Cauquenes Chile
133 C5 Cauquenes Chile
128 F2 Caura R Venezuela
122 E5 Causapscal Quebec
18 G8 Caussade France
128 F6 Cautário R Brazil
18 E10 Cauterets France
131 A7 Cautin prov Chile
126 F4 Cauto Cuba
76 D5 Cauvery R India
20 F2 Cauville France
45 R8 Cava Italy
16 B3 Cavado R Portugal
40 H7 Cavaglia Italy
19 O17 Cavaillon France
19 Q18 Cavalaire France
129 J6 Cavalcante Brazil
41 O5 Cavalese Italy
98 J1 Cavalier N Dakota
119 U10 Cavalier N Dakota
145 D1 Cavalli Is New Zealand
109 L7 Cavallo, Pass Texas
85 C7 Cavally R Ivory Co/Liberia
14 D3 Cavan Irish Rep
14 D3 Cavan co Irish Rep
143 G7 Cavanagh Ra W Australia
47 K7 Çavdır Turkey
45 N6 Cave Italy
144 C6 Cave New Zealand
110 E6 Cave City Arkansas
94 B9 Cave City Kentucky
103 N8 Cavecreek Arizona
143 D9 Cave Hill W Australia
110 H4 Cave in Rock Illinois
130 E10 Caveiras,R Brazil
100 B7 Cave Junction Oregon
120 C2 Cavell Ontario
118 J6 Cavell Sask
138 C2 Cavenagh,Mt N Terr Australia
118 G8 Cavendish Alberta
9 G3 Cavendish England
138 F6 Cavendish Victoria
45 M2 Ca Venier Italy
131 G3 Cavera R Brazil
131 G3 Cavera, Serra do mts Brazil
68 C7 Cavern I Burma
130 D9 Cavernoso, Serra do mts Brazil
120 C4 Cavers Ontario
9 F5 Caversham England
111 L7 Cave Spring Georgia
103 K3 Cave Valley Nevada
129 H3 Caviana isld Brazil
18 E7 Cavignac France
71 E6 Cavili Philippines
71 E3 Cavite Luzon Philippines
45 N6 Cavo, M mt Italy
44 B2 Cavour Italy
98 H5 Cavour S Dakota
45 J2 Cavriago Italy
42 J6 Cavtat Yugoslavia
15 E3 Cawdor Scotland
107 M2 Cawker City Kansas
138 F4 Cawndilla L New S Wales
Cawnpore see Kanpur
13 G6 Cawood England
121 P7 Cawood Low Quebec
9 H2 Cawston England
130 G7 Caxambu Brazil
128 D4 Caxias Amazonas Brazil
129 K4 Caxias Brazil
131 H2 Caxias do Sul Brazil
87 B7 Caxito Angola
9 F3 Caxton England
9 F3 Caxton Gibbet England
47 L6 Çay Turkey
128 C3 Cayambe vol Ecuador
112 F4 Cayce S Carolina
68 F8 Cay Dua B Vietnam
78 H1 Cayeli Turkey
129 H3 Cayenne Fr Guiana
20 H1 Cayeux-sur-Mer France
127 L5 Cayey Puerto Rico
18 H9 Caylar, le France
118 D8 Cayley Alberta
18 G8 Caylus France
126 E5 Cayman Brac isld W Indies
126 D5 Cayman, Grand isld W Indies
126 D5 Cayman, Little isld W Indies
90 A6 Cayman Trench Caribbean
68 G7 Cay Mit Vietnam
125 P9 Cayo Belize
127 P4 Cayon St Kitts W I
126 D3 Cay Sal Bank Bahamas
102 D6 Cayucos California
99 T10 Cayuga Indiana
98 J3 Cayuga N Dakota
109 M4 Cayuga Texas
95 L4 Cayuga L New York
16 D7 Cazalla de la Sierra Spain
48 L6 Căzăneşti Romania
18 E9 Cazaubon France
18 E8 Cazaux, Etang de L France
85 F2 Caze Algeria
95 M4 Cazenovia New York
18 F9 Cazères France
42 G4 Cazin Yugoslavia
42 H3 Čazma Yugoslavia
87 D8 Cazombo Angola
16 E7 Cazorla Spain
87 F9 Cazula Mozambique
16 D2 Cea R Spain
48 K3 Ceahlau Romania
48 K4 Ceahlău mt Romania
14 E3 Ceanannus Mór Irish Rep
130 J8 Ceará Mirim Brazil
20 D5 Ceauce France
21 F7 Ceaux France
119 P5 Ceba Sask
125 O6 Cebaco,I Panama
124 G4 Ceballos Mexico
106 D5 Cebolla New Mexico
133 D3 Cebollar Argentina
133 G4 Cebollati R Uruguay
17 F3 Cebollera mt Spain
106 C6 Cebollita New Mexico
16 E4 Cebreros Spain
71 F5 Cebu Philippines
71 F7 Cebuano Barracks Mindanao Philippines
43 E7 Ceccano Italy
48 E4 Cece Hungary
94 C5 Cecil Ohio
99 S5 Cecil Wisconsin
141 K8 Cecil Plains Queensland
143 D7 Cecil Rhodes, Mt mt W Australia
95 M7 Cecilton Maryland
100 B8 Cecilville California
42 D5 Cecina Italy
16 C5 Ceclavín Spain
107 M2 Cedar Kansas
99 O7 Cedar R Iowa
94 C2 Cedar R Michigan
98 H8 Cedar R Nebraska
111 H8 Cedarbluff Mississippi
94 F9 Cedar Bluff Virginia
107 L3 Cedar Bluff Res Kansas
107 K2 Cedar Bluffs Kansas
98 K8 Cedar Bluffs Nebraska
103 M4 Cedar Breaks Nat.Mon Utah
99 T6 Cedarburg Wisconsin
98 E6 Cedar Butte S Dakota
110 D3 Cedar City Missouri
103 L4 Cedar City Utah
98 D3 Cedar Cr N Dakota
109 K5 Cedar Creek Texas
109 O9 Cedar Crest Texas
101 L7 Cedar Cr.Res Idaho
109 L3 Cedar Cr.Res Texas
99 O7 Cedar Falls Iowa
127 P4 Cedar Grove Antigua W I
99 T6 Cedar Grove Wisconsin
94 F8 Cedar Grove W Virginia
112 L2 Cedar I N Carolina
95 M9 Cedar I Virginia
113 D8 Cedar Key Florida
119 R5 Cedar L Manitoba
108 E3 Cedar L Texas
99 T8 Cedar Lake Indiana
109 M7 Cedar Lane Texas
102 G3 Cedar Mts Nevada
94 D5 Cedar Pt Ohio
99 P8 Cedar Rapids Iowa
98 H8 Cedar Rapids Nebraska
95 K5 Cedar Run Pennsylvania
94 B3 Cedar Springs Michigan
120 H10 Cedar Springs Ontario
111 L7 Cedartown Georgia
107 O4 Cedar Vale Kansas
106 E7 Cedarvale New Mexico
127 L2 Cedar Valley Jamaica
100 E8 Cedarville California
95 M7 Cedarville New Jersey
110 N2 Cedarville Ohio
106 F4 Cedarwood Colorado
94 K8 Cedon Virginia
119 O9 Cedoux Sask
43 C8 Cedrino R Sardinia
130 G9 Cedro Brazil
124 E4 Cedros Mexico
124 B3 Cedros isld Mexico
127 N3 Cedros Pt Trinidad
138 C4 Ceduna S Australia
43 F10 Cefalù Sicily
16 E3 Cega R Spain
48 F3 Cegléd Hungary
43 H8 Ceglie Messapico Italy
17 F6 Cehegin Spain
67 B4 Ceheng China
48 H3 Cehu Silvaniei Romania
48 G4 Ceica Romania
128 E3 Cejal Colombia
87 C8 Cela Angola
45 P5 Celano Italy
16 B2 Celanova Spain
125 J7 Celaya Mexico
Celebes isld see Sulawesi
70 G3 Celebes Sea Indonesia
109 L2 Celeste Texas
94 C6 Celina Ohio
110 M1 Celina Ohio
94 B10 Celina Tennessee
109 L2 Celina Texas
17 G4 Cella Spain
48 D3 Celldömölk Hungary
32 M7 Celle W Germany
22 E2 Celles Belgium
21 H6 Cellettes France
16 B3 Celorico de Basto Portugal
7 E12 Celtic Sea British Isles/France
47 L7 Çeltikçi Turkey
41 O5 Cembra Italy
107 M7 Cement Oklahoma
94 C4 Cement City Michigan
46 D1 Čemerna Planina mt Yugoslavia
42 H4 Čemernica mt Yugoslavia
48 E7 Čemerno Yugoslavia
8 B1 Cemlyn B Wales
8 B1 Cemmaes Wales
17 F6 Cenajo,Embalso de res Spain
8 B3 Cenarth Wales
86 G4 Cencia Ethiopia
136 G2 Cendrawasih pen W Irian
44 G2 Ceno R Italy
133 C6 Cenoa R Argentina
86 C4 Cent.Afr.Rep Equat Africa
130 D8 Centenario do Sul Brazil
112 H3 Centenary S Carolina
101 T8 Centennial Wyoming
103 L8 Centennial Wash R Arizona
106 D4 Center Colorado
110 E2 Center Missouri
98 E2 Center N Dakota
111 B10 Center Texas
94 E6 Centerburg Ohio
99 O4 Center City Minnesota
95 L9 Center Cross Virginia
113 F9 Center Hill Florida
110 L5 Center Hill Res Tennessee
95 P6 Center Moriches Long I, N Y
95 Q3 Center Ossipee New Hampshire
109 H6 Center Point Texas
111 J9 Centerville Alabama
110 D1 Centerville Iowa
111 E12 Centerville Louisiana
94 H6 Centerville Pennsylvania
98 K6 Centerville S Dakota
110 J6 Centerville Tennessee
109 M4 Centerville Texas
101 O9 Centerville Utah
100 E4 Centerville Washington
124 H3 Centinela, Pico del mt Mexico
42 D4 Cento Italy
44 G3 Cento Croci, Passo di Italy
107 O7 Centrahoma Oklahoma
109 L1 Centrahoma Oklahoma
116 P4 Central Alaska
106 B9 Central New Mexico
112 E3 Central S Carolina
103 L4 Central Utah
130 B9 Central dep Paraguay
89 D3 Central dist Botswana
15 D4 Central reg Scotland
145 E2 Central Auckland stat area New Zealand
118 L8 Central Butt Sask
106 E2 Central City Colorado
99 P7 Central City Iowa
110 J4 Central City Kentucky
98 H8 Central City Nebraska
94 J6 Central City Pennsylvania
95 Q5 Central Falls Rhode I
110 G3 Centralia Illinois
107 O2 Centralia Kansas
110 D2 Centralia Missouri
100 C3 Centralia Washington
94 G8 Centralia W Virginia
94 B1 Central Lake Michigan
140 C5 Central Mt. Stewart N Terr Aust
100 C7 Central Point Oregon
136 J2 Central Ra Papua New Guinea
56 Central Siberia
95 L3 Central Square New York
102 B1 Central Valley California
111 L7 Centre Alabama
144 A7 Centre I New Zealand
95 L7 Centreville Maryland
94 B5 Centreville Michigan
111 E10 Centreville Mississippi
122 E7 Centreville New Brunswick
122 F9 Centreville Nova Scotia
111 J11 Century Florida
94 G7 Century W Virginia
67 B4 Cenwanglao Shan mt China
67 C5 Cenxi China
19 P18 Cépet,C France
Cephalonia isld Greece see Kefallinía I
44 C4 Ceppo Monte mt Italy
45 O6 Ceprano Italy
136 F2 Ceram Sea Indonesia
21 F6 Cérans-Foulletourte France
128 E2 Cerbatana, Sa. de la mts Venezuela
103 K6 Cerbat Mts Arizona
18 H10 Cerbère, C France
16 B7 Cercal Portugal
16 E4 Cercedilla Spain
37 O5 Čerchov mt Czechoslovakia
20 J6 Cercottes France
18 H6 Cercy la Tour France
18 G10 Cerdaña dist Spain
21 J6 Cerdon France
21 H7 Cere France
18 G8 Cère R France
45 K1 Cerea Italy
118 G7 Cereal Alberta
45 L1 Ceregnano Italy
20 C4 Cérences France
130 E4 Ceres Brazil
102 C4 Ceres California
40 F7 Ceres Italy
87 C12 Ceres S Africa
13 F1 Ceres Scotland
45 J1 Ceresara Italy
40 F7 Ceresole Reale Italy
18 G10 Céret France
126 G10 Cereté Colombia
87 J9 Cerf isld Br Indian Oc Terr
83 J12 Cerf I Mahé I Indian Oc
121 P6 Cerf. L du Quebec
22 G3 Cerfontaine Belgium
20 K3 Cergy-Pontoise France
44 D3 Ceriale Italy
43 G7 Cerignola Italy
Cerigo isld Greece see Kíthira I
18 G6 Cerilly France
20 D3 Cerisy-la Forêt France
20 C3 Cerisy-la-Salle France
47 J3 Çerkesköy Turkey
42 F3 Cerknica Yugoslavia
48 G4 Cermei Romania
48 L5 Cerna Romania
48 H5 Cerna R Romania
48 L6 Cernavodă Romania
19 K5 Cernay France
8 D6 Cerne Abbas England
42 H3 Çernik Yugoslavia
37 O4 Černošin Czechoslovakia
109 H9 Cerralvo Mexico
124 E5 Cerralvo isld Mexico
45 J4 Cerreto Guidi Italy
44 H3 Cerreto, Passo di Italy
45 R7 Cerreto Sannita Italy
8 C1 Cerrigydrudion Wales
46 D3 Cerrik Albania
106 D6 Cerrillos New Mexico
125 J6 Cerritos Mexico
130 E9 Cêrro Azul Brazil
128 C6 Cerro de Pasco Peru
127 L5 Cerro de Punta peak Puerto Rico
110 H2 Cerro Gordo Illinois
131 G4 Cerro Largo dep Uruguay
127 J9 Cerrón mt Venezuela
124 F4 Cerro Prieto Mexico
21 E7 Cersay France
45 K4 Certaldo Italy
143 B9 Cervantes I W Australia
45 P7 Cervaro Italy
43 G7 Cervaro R Italy
43 G8 Cervati, M mt Italy
44 H2 Cervellino mt Italy
17 H3 Cervera Spain
17 F2 Cervera del Rio Alhama Spain
16 D2 Cervera de P Spain
42 E4 Cervia Italy
43 G8 Cervialto, M mt Italy
45 R7 Cervinara Italy
44 D4 Cervo Italy
41 H7 Cervo R Italy
128 D2 César div Colombia
126 H10 César,R Colombia
42 E4 Cesena Italy
45 M3 Cesenatico Italy
52 C6 Cēsis U.S.S.R.
37 O5 Česká Kubice Czechoslovakia
31 H5 Česká Lípa Czechoslovakia
31 H7 Ceské Budějovice Czechoslovakia
31 H6 Českézemě reg Czechoslovakia
31 J6 Českomoravská Vysočina mts Czechoslovakia
31 H5 Český Brod Czechoslovakia
31 H7 Český Krumlov Czechoslovakia
37 O4 Český les Sumava mts Czechoslovakia
48 E1 Český Těšin Czechoslovakia
78 A2 Çesme Turkey
47 H6 Çeşnıe Turkey
139 K5 Cessnock New S Wales
48 H6 Cetate Romania
42 H5 Cetina R Yugoslavia
42 J6 Cetinje Yugoslavia
20 G5 Ceton France
43 G9 Cetraro Italy
19 P15 Ceuse, Pic de mt France
16 D9 Ceuta Spain
85 C1 Ceuta Span exclave Morocco
41 N5 Cevedale mt Italy
18 H8 Cevennes mts France
78 G3 Ceylânpinar Turkey
99 M6 Ceylon Minnesota
119 N9 Ceylon Sask
Ceylon rep see Sri Lanka Rep
19 P18 Ceyreste France
57 B6 Chaacha U.S.S.R.
21 G10 Chabanais France
19 P16 Chabestan France
19 O15 Chabeuil France
142 A6 Chabjuwardoo B W Australia
18 H5 Chablis France
19 P16 Chabre, Mt de France
19 Q16 Chabrières France
21 I7 Chabris France
133 C1 Chaca Chile
131 E5 Chacabuco Argentina
127 N1 Chacachacare I Trinidad
133 D2 Chacance Chile
133 C6 Chacao, Canal de Chile
133 D6 Chacays, Sa. de los mts Argentina
131 C6 Chachahuen,Sa mt Argentina
128 D7 Chachani mt Peru
128 C5 Chachapoyas Peru
68 E6 Chachoengsao Thailand
74 D6 Chachro Pakistan
128 F8 Chaco dep Paraguay
133 E3 Chaco prov Argentina
133 E3 Chaco Austral reg Argentina
128 F8 Chaco Boreal plain Paraguay
133 E2 Chaco Boreal reg Paraguay
106 B5 Chaco Canyon Nat. Mon New Mexico
133 E2 Chaco Central reg Argentina
117 H8 Chacon,C Pr of Wales I, Alaska
129 G5 Chacorão, Cachoeira do waterfall Brazil
106 C6 Chacra Mesa mt New Mexico
86 C3 Chad rep Equat Africa
56 D5 Chadan U.S.S.R.
112 J3 Chadbourn N Carolina
131 C6 Chadileo,R Argentina
133 D5 Chadileuvú R Argentina
86 B3 Chad,L Equat Africa
56 F2 Chadobets R U.S.S.R.
98 D7 Chadron Nebraska
99 R7 Chadwick Illinois
48 M4 Chadyr Lunga U.S.S.R.
110 G4 Chaffee Missouri
94 J4 Chaffee New York
74 A4 Chagai Pakistan
77 H5 Chagai Hills Pakistan
53 H8 Chagan R U.S.S.R.
51 N3 Chagda U.S.S.R.
8 C6 Chagford England
55 E4 Chaglinka R U.S.S.R.
40 A4 Chagny France
52 E5 Chagoda U.S.S.R.
52 E5 Chagodoshcha R U.S.S.R.
81 E6 Chagos Arch Indian Oc
57 A2 Chagrayskoye Plato U.S.S.R.
94 F5 Chagrin Falls Ohio
127 O2 Chaguanas Trinidad
127 N1 Chaguaramas Trinidad
127 L10 Chaguaramas Venezuela
77 H4 Chahah Burjak Afghanistan
77 G7 Chāh Bahār Iran
77 G5 Chah Ghevhī, Hamún-e L Iran
77 L1 Chāh-i-Ghab Afghanistan
78 K4 Chah-I-Surkh Iraq
78 K2 Chai Iran
68 E5 Chai Badan Thailand
75 L7 Chaibassa India
68 F3 Chai Buri Thailand
Chaigoubu see Huai'an
20 D5 Chailland France
19 P14 Chaine de Belledonne mts France
85 E6 Chaîne de l'Atakora mts Benin
19 N17 Chaine des Alpilles mts France
18 H7 Chaise Dieu, la France
69 D8 Chaiya Thailand
68 E5 Chaiyaphum Thailand
131 F3 Chajari Argentina
116 L6 Chakachamna L Alaska
74 F2 Chak Amru Pakistan
88 G4 Chake Chake Tanzania
77 H4 Chakhansur Afghanistan
77 J2 Chakhcharan Afghanistan
74 E2 Chakwal Pakistan
128 D7 Chala Peru
87 F8 Chalabesa Zambia
40 C4 Chalain,L.de France
59 H2 Cha-lan-t'un China
128 D7 Chala,Pta Peru
125 P10 Chalatenango Honduras
69 D9 Chalaung Thailand
124 H6 Chalchihuites Mexico
125 P11 Chalchuapa El Salvador
Chalcis Greece see Khalkís
9 E6 Chale England
122 G6 Chaleurs, Baie des Quebec/New Bruns
128 D6 Chalhuanca Peru
133 C7 Chalía R Argentina
88 B7 Chali,L Zambia
19 J5 Chalindrey France
67 D3 Chaling China
74 F8 Chalisgaon India
9 G5 Chalk England
98 B4 Chalk Buttes Montana
109 K3 Chalk Mountain Texas
121 N6 Chalk River Ontario
144 A7 Chalky Inlet New Zealand
116 Q3 Chalkyitsik Alaska
21 C6 Challain-la-Potherie France
21 B8 Challans France
133 D1 Challapata Bolivia
115 M1 Challenger Mts N W Terr
22 H5 Challerange France
101 L5 Challis Idaho
111 G12 Chalmette Nat. Hist. Park Louisiana
52 E2 Chal'mny Varre U.S.S.R.
75 N7 Chalna Bangladesh
52 D4 Chalna U.S.S.R.
21 D7 Chalonnes France
18 H4 Chalons-sur-Marne France
19 J6 Chalon-sur-Saône France
65 J3 Chaluhe China
18 F7 Châlus France
57 B4 Chalysh U.S.S.R.
37 O5 Cham W Germany
37 O5 Cham R W Germany
106 E4 Chama Colorado
106 D5 Chama New Mexico
69 E10 Chamah, Gunung Malaysia
74 B3 Chaman Pakistan
68 E6 Chamao,Khao mt Thailand
106 D5 Chama, R New Mexico
128 C5 Chamaya R Peru
74 G2 Chamba India
73 M3 Chambal Madhya Prad/Rajasthan India
40 B7 Chambaran, Plat. de France
126 E3 Chambas Cuba
119 M8 Chamberlain Sask
98 G6 Chamberlain S Dakota
95 R7 Chamberlain L Maine
142 G3 Chamberlain R W Australia
116 P2 Chamberlin,Mt Alaska
103 P6 Chambers Arizona
98 H7 Chambers Nebraska
140 B1 Chambers B N Terr Aust
94 K7 Chambersburg Pennsylvania
99 T4 Chambers I Wisconsin
138 C1 Chambers Pillar peak N Terr Australia
19 P13 Chambéry France
88 C7 Chambeshi R Zambia
128 C4 Chambira R Peru
20 K3 Chambly France
20 F4 Chambois France
18 H7 Chambon, le Loire France
121 S4 Chambord Quebec
21 G7 Chambourg-sur-Indre France
66 E5 Chamdo prov China
124 G8 Chamela Mexico
77 B4 Cham-e Zeydun Iran
77 B3 Chamgordan Iran
133 D4 Chamical Argentina
106 D5 Chamita New Mexico
110 E3 Chamois Missouri
86 G4 Chamo, L Ethiopia
74 H3 Chamoli India
40 E6 Chamonix France
19 P16 Chamouse,Mt.de France
75 K7 Champa India
21 C9 Champagné Vendée France
89 F7 Champagne Castle mt Lesotho
21 F10 Champagne-Mouton France
40 C4 Champagnole France
142 E3 Champagny Is W Australia
99 S9 Champaign Illinois
131 D3 Champaqui peak Argentina
121 N4 Champcoeur Quebec
21 E9 Champdeniers France
36 C7 Champ du Feu mt France
20 E5 Champgeneteux France
19 O14 Champier France
21 D6 Champigné France
21 H6 Champigny France
21 F7 Champigny-sur-Veude France
21 J8 Champillet France
118 D8 Champion Alberta
22 J3 Champion Belgium
99 T3 Champion Michigan
94 G5 Champion Heights Ohio
95 O2 Champlain New York
121 R8 Champlain New York
121 S6 Champlain Quebec
95 O3 Champlain Canal New York
19 J5 Champlitte France
40 B2 Champlitte France
121 N4 Champneuf Quebec
40 G6 Champorcher Italy
20 H5 Champrond France
20 D4 Champsecret France
21 D7 Champtocé France
21 C7 Champtoceaux France
76 C5 Chamrajnagar India
19 P14 Chamrousse France
16 B5 Chamusca Portugal
69 E9 Chana Thailand
18 H8 Chanac France
133 C3 Chañaral Chile
131 B2 Chañaral R Chile
131 B2 Chañaral, I Chile
98 K6 Chancellor S Dakota
133 C5 Chanco Chile
116 N3 Chandalar Alaska
116 P2 Chandalar R Alaska
111 G11 Chandeleur Sound Louisiana
103 N8 Chandler Arizona
107 O6 Chandler Oklahoma
122 H5 Chandler Quebec
109 M3 Chandler Texas
116 M2 Chandler R Alaska
116 L2 Chandler L Alaska
138 C2 Chandler,Mt S Australia
99 Q9 Chandlerville Illinois
128 D6 Chandless R Peru/Brazil
75 O7 Chandpur Bangladesh
74 H9 Chandrapur India
77 G6 Chānf Iran
Chang'an see Rong'an
65 A7 Chang'an China
87 F9 Changara Mozambique
65 G4 Changbai China
65 G4 Changbai Shan mt ra China
67 B1 Changchi China
65 F3 Changchun China
65 F2 Changchunling China
67 F1 Changdang Hu L China
67 D2 Changde China
123 S4 Change I Nfld
65 B7 Changge China
65 E5 Changhai China
58 F5 Chang Hu L China
67 F1 Changhua China
67 G4 Chang-hua Taiwan
67 C7 Changhua Jiang R China
67 A4 Changjiang China
68 J3 Changjiang China
67 C1 Chang Jiang R China
67 E2 Chang Jiang R Jiangxi China
Chang Jiang Kou see Mouth of the Yangtze Kiang
65 G4 Changjin Res N Korea
68 F6 Chang,Ko isld Thailand
65 D6 Changle China
67 F4 Changle China
67 G2 Changle China
65 D5 Changli China
59 H3 Changling China
69 E9 Changlun Malaysia
67 A2 Changning China
67 D3 Changning China
65 C4 Changping China
Changpuzhen see Suining
65 C6 Changqing China
65 F5 Changsan-got C N Korea
67 D2 Changsha China
67 F2 Changshan China
65 E5 Changshan Qundao islds China
65 D4 Changshanyu China
67 B2 Changshou China
67 G1 Changshu China
67 B3 Changshun China
67 F4 Changtai China
65 G2 Changting China
67 E4 Changting China
65 F3 Changtu China
65 G2 Changwu China
67 F1 Changxing China
65 E5 Changxing Dao isld China
67 D1 Changyang China
65 D6 Changyi China
59 H4 Changyon N Korea
65 C7 Changyuan China
Changzhai see Changshun
65 B6 Changzhi China
67 G1 Changzhou Jiangsu China
67 E1 Changzhuyuan China
83 J8 Chankanai Sri Lanka
116 H8 Chankluit I Alaska
69 C8 Chan,Ko isld Thailand
21 F7 Channay-sur-Lathan France
145 E2 Channel I New Zealand
102 E8 Channel Is California
9 H7 Channel Is English Chan
123 N6 Channel Port aux Basques Nfld
143 C10 Channel Pt W Australia
126 F3 Channel Rock Bahamas
22 B1 Channel Tunnel
76 C4 Channiapatna India
99 S3 Channing Michigan
108 B8 Channing Texas
119 P4 Channing airfield Manitoba
16 B2 Chantada Spain
21 B7 Chantenay Loire-Atlantique France
21 E6 Chantenay Sarthe France
68 F6 Chanthaburi Thailand
18 G3 Chantilly France
21 C8 Chantonnay France
115 K4 Chantrey Inlet N W Terr
20 D4 Chanu France
69 A8 Chanumla Nicobar Is
107 P4 Chanute Kansas
110 A4 Chanute Kansas
55 G3 Chany U.S.S.R.
21 D7 Chanzeaux France
17 G10 Chanzy Algeria
67 E5 Chao'an China
65 C6 Chaocheng China
16 D9 Chaoen Morocco
58 G5 Chao Hu L China
128 C5 Chao, I Peru
68 E5 Chao Phraya Ra Thailand
65 E1 Chaor He R China
58 E5 Chaotianyi China
67 F1 Chao Xian China
Chaoyang see Huinan
59 K2 Ch'ao-Yang China
67 E5 Chaoyang Guangdong China
65 E4 Chaoyang Liaoning China
65 A7 Chaoyi China
Chaozhou see Chao'an
68 F1 Cha Pa Vietnam
129 J5 Chapada das Mangabeiras mts Brazil
129 K6 Chapada Diamantina mts Brazil
129 K5 Chapada do Araripe mts Brazil
130 C4 Chapada dos Guimarães Brazil
129 K4 Chapadinha Brazil
121 Q3 Chapais Quebec
124 H7 Chapala,L.de Mexico
129 K8 Chaparao,Serra do mts Brazil
126 F4 Chaparra Cuba
57 C6 Chapayeva, Imeni U.S.S.R.
53 G7 Chapayevsk U.S.S.R.
121 N7 Chapeau Quebec
130 D10 Chapecó Brazil
130 D10 Chapecózinho R Brazil
9 E1 Chapel en le Frith England
112 H2 Chapel Hill N Carolina
110 K6 Chapel Hill Tennessee
20 E5 Chapelle-au-Riboul,la France
18 G5 Chapelle d' Angillon,la France
22 J4 Chapelle, la France
123 L3 Chapelle,L. de la Quebec
20 E4 Chapelle Moche,la France
20 D5 Chapelle-Rainsouin,la France
20 H5 Chapelle-Royale France
9 G1 Chapel St Leonards England
127 K2 Chapelton Jamaica
13 G6 Chapeltown England
99 Q10 Chapin Illinois
110 F2 Chapin Illinois
115 L8 Chapleau Ontario
120 G4 Chapleau R Ontario
120 H4 Chapleau-Nemecosenda Wild R. Prov. Pk Ontario
118 L8 Chaplin Sask
147 P1 Chaplina,Mys C U.S.S.R.
54 H8 Chaplino U.S.S.R.
54 L3 Chaplygin U.S.S.R.
111 K10 Chapman Alabama
107 N3 Chapman Kansas
101 R1 Chapman Montana
98 H8 Chapman Nebraska
117 O10 Chapman,Mt Br Col
142 F3 Chapman R W Australia
109 K8 Chapman Ranch Texas
94 E9 Chapmanville W Virginia
52 E2 Chapoma U.S.S.R.
98 D8 Chappell Nebraska
109 L5 Chappell Hill Texas
139 J8 Chappell Is Tasmania
75 L6 Chapra India
95 L8 Chaptico Maryland
18 E7 Chapus, le France
120 K4 Chaput Ontario
128 E7 Chaqui Bolivia
133 D1 Chaqui Bolivia
74 G2 Char Kashmir
85 B4 Char Mauritania
51 L3 Chara U.S.S.R.
133 E1 Charagua Bolivia
124 E4 Charay Mexico
98 C2 Charbonneau N Dakota
40 C3 Charcenne France
20 E5 Charchigné France
109 K7 Charco Texas
146 F13 Charcot I Antarctica
118 G3 Chard Alberta
8 D6 Chard England
57 E4 Chardara U.S.S.R.
57 E4 Chardarinskoye Vdkhr res U.S.S.R.
94 F5 Chardon Ohio
126 G5 Chardonnière Haiti
57 C5 Chardzhou U.S.S.R.
21 E10 Charente dep France
21 D10 Charente R France
18 E7 Charente-Maritime dep France
20 G3 Charentonne R France
86 C3 Chari R Chad
77 L2 Charikar Afghanistan
9 G5 Charing England
116 D2 Chariot Alaska
18 H5 Charité, la France
99 N8 Chariton Iowa
99 N9 Chariton R Iowa
110 D2 Chariton R Missouri
128 G2 Charity Guyana
52 H2 Charkayuvom U.S.S.R.
74 H6 Charkhari India
57 F5 Charku U.S.S.R.
9 E4 Charlbury England
22 H3 Charleroi Belgium
94 H6 Charleroi Pennsylvania
119 Q3 Charles Manitoba
121 T6 Charlesbourg Quebec
95 M9 Charles,C Virginia
99 O6 Charles City Iowa
115 M5 Charles I N W Terr
143 B8 Charles,Mt W Australia
143 D10 Charles Pk W Australia
140 B1 Charles Pt N Terr Australia
144 A6 Charles Sd New Zealand
110 B6 Charleston Arkansas
99 S10 Charleston Illinois
111 F7 Charleston Mississippi
110 G5 Charleston Missouri
144 C4 Charleston New Zealand
100 A6 Charleston Oregon
112 H5 Charleston S Carolina
112 C2 Charleston Tennessee
94 F8 Charleston W Virginia
103 J5 Charleston Pk Nevada
94 B8 Charlestown Indiana
14 C3 Charlestown Irish Rep
127 P4 Charlestown Nevis W I
95 P3 Charlestown New Hampshire

95 L7 Columbia Maryland
111 G10 Columbia Mississippi
110 D3 Columbia Missouri
112 L2 Columbia N Carolina
95 L6 Columbia Pennsylvania
112 F3 Columbia S Carolina
98 H4 Columbia S Dakota
110 J6 Columbia Tennessee
94 J9 Columbia Virginia
117 O10 Columbia R Br Col
117 O11 Columbia R Wash/Br Col
100 E4 Columbia R Wash/Oregon
100 F2 Columbia Basin reg Washington
115 N1 Columbia, C N W Terr
94 B5 Columbia City Indiana
95 L8 Columbia, Dist. of (D.C.) U.S.A.
101 L1 Columbia Falls Montana
116 O6 Columbia Glacier Alaska
117 Q10 Columbia Lake Br Columbia
117 P9 Columbia, Mt Br Col/Alberta
114 G7 Columbia Mts R Columbia
111 K8 Columbiana Alabama
94 G6 Columbiana Ohio
100 E2 Columbia River Washington
98 H4 Columbia Road Res S Australia
95 O4 Columbiaville New York
106 D1 Columbine Colorado
101 T6 Columbine Wyoming
89 A9 Columbine, C S Africa
17 H5 Columbretes, I Spain
141 J6 Columbria Queensland
111 M9 Columbus Georgia
110 L2 Columbus Indiana
107 Q4 Columbus Kansas
111 H8 Columbus Mississippi
101 Q4 Columbus Montana
98 D1 Columbus N Dakota
98 J8 Columbus Nebraska
106 C10 Columbus New Mexico
94 D7 Columbus Ohio
109 L6 Columbus Texas
99 R6 Columbus Wisconsin
126 G3 Columbus Bank Bahamas
99 P8 Columbus Junction Iowa
126 G2 Columbus Mon San Salvador Bahamas
126 G2 Columbus Pt Cat I Bahamas
127 M2 Columbus Pt Tobago
102 B2 Colusa California
12 E4 Colvend Scotland
94 J6 Colver Pennsylvania
145 E2 Colville New Zealand
100 H1 Colville Washington
116 L2 Colville R Alaska
114 G4 Colville L N W Terr
143 F8 Colville, Lake W Australia
137 Q8 Colville Ridge sea feature Pacific Oc
13 F3 Colwell England
99 O6 Colwell Iowa
8 C6 Colwyn Bay Wales
8 C6 Colyford England
45 M2 Comacchio Italy
125 O10 Comalapa Guatemala
125 N8 Comalcalco Mexico
131 B8 Comallo R Argentina
48 K6 Comana Romania
107 N7 Comanche Oklahoma
109 J4 Comanche Texas
133 D7 Comandante Luis Piedrabuena Argentina
130 H4 Comandante Salas Argentina
48 K4 Comanesti Romania
125 L2 Comayagua Honduras
16 B4 Comba Dão Portugal
112 G5 Combahee R S Carolina
133 C4 Combarbala Chile
40 C2 Combeaufontaine France
8 B5 Comber Martin England
14 F2 Comber N Ireland
120 H10 Comber Ontario
21 N7 Combermere France
46 A3 Combermere B Burma
109 K9 Combes Texas
22 D3 Combes France
20 B5 Combourg France
139 L4 Comboyne New S Wales
20 H5 Combrée France
94 D9 Combs Kentucky
131 D4 Comechingones, Sa. de ra Argentina
38 G8 Comeglians Italy
38 G8 Comelico Italy
130 L8 Comendador Gomes Brazil
111 L9 Comer Alabama
113 D3 Comer Georgia
14 D4 Comeragh Mts Irish Rep
130 H5 Comercinho Brazil
98 B1 Comertown Montana
141 J6 Comet Queensland
141 J6 Comet R Queensland
141 J6 Comet Downs Queensland
143 D8 Comet Vale W Australia
109 J8 Comfort Texas
99 M5 Comfrey Minnesota
75 O7 Comilla Bangladesh
22 E2 Comines France
43 F12 Comino isld Malta
43 C8 Comino, C Sardinia
43 C2 Cominio Michigan
43 F12 Comiso Sicily
125 N9 Comitán de Dominguez Mexico
25 L7 Commanda Ontario
18 G6 Commentry France
20 D5 Commer France
112 D3 Commerce Georgia
107 Q5 Commerce Oklahoma
109 M2 Commerce Texas
106 F2 Commerce City Colorado
19 J4 Commercy France
45 J1 Commessaggio Italy
121 S4 Commissaires, Lac des Quebec
115 L4 Committee B N W Terr
146 J3 Commonwealth B Antarctica
138 C3 Commonwealth Hill S Australia
146 G7 Commonwealth Ra Antarctica
139 K6 Commonwealth Terr New S Wales
106 E2 Como Colorado
38 F3 Como Italy
111 G7 Como Mississippi
133 D7 Comodoro Rivadavia Argentina
41 K5 Como, Lago di Italy
124 D6 Comondú Mexico
76 C6 Comorin, C India
87 G10 Comoro Ridge Indian Oc
87 G10 Comoro islds, rep Indian Oc
118 D7 Compeer Alberta
22 D5 Compiègne France
20 E4 Compiègne, Forêt de France
124 G7 Compostela Mexico
71 G7 Compostela Mindanao Philippines
21 H10 Comprégnac France
130 F9 Comprida, I São Paulo Brazil
102 A2 Comptche California
102 B2 Compton California
99 R8 Compton Illinois
12 E1 Comrie Scotland
106 F6 Comstock Texas
45 O4 Cona Italy
66 E5 Co Nag L China
85 B7 Conakry Guinea
133 D6 Cona Niyeo Argentina
22 D5 Conara Junct Tasmania
112 C3 Conasauga R Georgia
98 D6 Conata S Dakota

45 N4 Conca R Italy
45 P5 Conca del Fucino Italy
108 H6 Concan Texas
18 C5 Concarneau France
130 H9 Conceição Paraiba Brazil
130 H6 Conceição da Barra Brazil
130 E6 Conceição das Alagoas Brazil
129 J5 Conceição do Araguaia Brazil
130 G6 Conceição do Mato Dentro Brazil
133 D3 Concepción Argentina
128 E6 Concepción Beni Bolivia
131 A6 Concepción Chile
128 F7 Concepción Paraguay
128 F7 Concepción Santa Cruz Bolivia
128 F5 Concepción dep Paraguay
124 C2 Concepción R Mexico
131 A6 Concepción, B. del Chile
133 B8 Concepción, Can str Chile
94 B5 Concepción Harb Nfld
117 C5 Concepción, Mt Mexico
131 F4 Concepción del Oro Mexico
131 F4 Concepción del Uruguay Argentina
128 F7 Conception, L Bolivia
99 M9 Conception Missouri
87 B10 Conception B Namibia
123 U8 Conception B Nfld
123 T6 Conception Harb Nfld
126 G3 Conception I Bahamas
83 K12 Conception I Mahé I Indian Oc
75 M8 Contai India
45 L2 Conchas Mexico
130 E8 Conchas New Mexico
128 F3 Conchas Res New Mexico
131 D4 Conches France
133 C9 Conchi Chile
103 P7 Concho Arizona
124 G4 Concho New Mexico
107 N6 Concho Oklahoma
106 C4 Concho R Texas
95 O3 Conchos, Rio Mexico
102 B4 Concord California
111 M8 Concord Georgia
94 C4 Concord Michigan
121 R7 Concord N Carolina
133 C8 Concord Nebraska
21 H7 Concord New Hampshire
22 H5 Concord Vermont
22 H5 Contres France
40 C1 Contrexéville France
48 J4 Copsa Mica Romania
130 G6 Contria Brazil
118 F7 Control Alberta
36 C5 Contwig W Germany
75 L3 Contwoyto L N W Terr
20 K2 Conty France
126 H10 Convención Colombia
43 H8 Conversano Italy
94 B6 Converse Indiana
111 C10 Converse Louisiana
131 B2 Converse Ohio
101 T7 Convoy Ohio
110 D6 Conway Arkansas
99 M9 Conway Iowa
47 G1 Conway Iowa
130 Q5 Conway Missouri
112 K1 Conway N Carolina
98 J1 Conway N Dakota
112 H4 Conway S Carolina
114 J5 Conway, C Queensland
110 D6 Conway, L Arkansas
138 D3 Conway, L S Australia
140 C6 Conway, N Terr Aust
95 Q2 Conway, N New Hampshire
144 D5 Conway R New Zealand
137 P6 Conway Reef Pacific Oc
107 N4 Conway Springs Kansas
8 B4 Conwil Elvet Wales
8 C1 Conwy Wales
22 K3 Conyers Georgia
22 C3 Coo Belgium
141 L7 Coober Pedy S Australia
42 B4 Cooden England
22 E5 Cooge Belgium
120 K8 Coogan, C Queensland
20 K2 Coogee L W Australia
9 H7 Coogoon Queensland
141 J7 Coogoon Queensland
18 G10 Cooiron reg France
143 D9 Cook I Alabama
94 H5 Cook Michigan
107 M6 Cook Nebraska
123 R7 Cook, B.de Chile
117 K10 Cook, C Br Col
6 D6 Cook Montana
143 B9 Cooke, Mt W Australia
94 B10 Cookeville Tennessee
9 F4 Cookham England
42 A13 Cook I Pacific Oc
146 K4 Cook Ice Shelf Antarctica
19 J3 Cook I Alberta
116 L7 Cook Inlet Alaska
117 D5 Cook, Mt Alaska/Yukon Terr
144 C5 Cook, Mt New Zealand
94 U4 Cook Islands
18 U8 Cook's Hbr Nfld
121 T7 Cookshire Quebec
141 H2 Cook's Passage Queensland
16 D1 Cooks Pk New Mexico
120 C3 Cookstown N Ireland
121 L8 Cookstown Ontario
145 H3 Cook Strait New Zealand
141 H3 Cooktown Queensland
139 J4 Cooladdi Queensland
139 H4 Coolah New S Wales
139 K5 Coolamon New S Wales
143 A2 Coolardie W Australia
141 A7 Coolbellup, L W Australia
112 C5 Coolcalalaya W Australia
127 N4 Coolee N Carolina
99 U4 Coolee Michigan
18 G8 Coolee Georgia
129 J5 Coolgardie W Australia
16 D1 Coolibah N Terr Aust
103 Q3 Coolidge Arizona
112 D6 Coolidge Georgia
109 L4 Coolidge Texas
138 F7 Coolidge Dam Arizona
139 G6 Coolin Idaho
141 K8 Coolmunda Dam Queensland
142 A4 Coolongup, L W Australia
16 D7 Coolville Ohio
143 B7 Coolyie Well W Australia
131 D3 Coolyin New S Wales
139 J6 Coolyie, Mt N Terr Aust
14 A5 Coomacarrea mt Irish Rep
131 D3 Coomandook S Australia
76 B4 Coonabar Queensland
141 J6 Coonamble New S Wales
45 J3 Coonana W Australia
138 F6 Coonbah New S Wales
139 H1 Coonamia S Australia

45 L3 Conselice Italy
45 L1 Conselve Italy
22 J5 Conservoye France
13 G4 Consett England
95 M6 Conshohocken Pennsylvania
141 L7 Cons-la-Grandville France
126 C3 Consolación del Sur Cuba
112 C3 Con Son Vietnam
100 A6 Con Son isld Vietnam
143 E6 Consort Alberta
14 E2 Constableville New York
141 K7 Constance Headland hill W Aust
140 E6 Constance, L see Bodensee
128 F5 Constance, L see Bodensee
100 A6 Constância dos Baetas Brazil
48 M6 Constanta Romania
16 D7 Constantia Spain
100 C8 Constantine Algeria
106 F2 Constantine Michigan
128 F4 Constantine, C Alaska
113 F12 Constantine, Mt Yukon Terr
100 J1 Constantinople Turkey see Istanbul
94 B2 Constant, Morne hill Guadeloupe W I
95 M3 Constant, L New York
127 L2 Constant Spring Jamaica
139 K3 Constitución Chile
13 G4 Constitution B Nfld
14 C5 Consul Sask
15 C3 Contact Nevada
138 E4 Contagalo Brazil
128 D6 Contai India
45 L2 Contamana Peru
128 F3 Contão Brazil
131 D4 Contara R Argentina
95 M6 Contarina Italy
32 L8 Contas R Brazil
129 K6 Contas R Brazil
116 P6 Conteville France
109 K4 Contewille Switzerland
94 E7 Continental Arizona
141 G5 Continental Res Colorado
116 P6 Contoocook New Hampshire
120 J6 Contoy, I Mexico
141 H4 Contraries, Sa mts Spain
120 F6 Contrecoeur Quebec
117 N11 Contreras, I Chile
100 K8 Contres France
117 Q5 Converse France
48 J4 Copsa Mica Romania
121 Q7 Contia Brazil
107 N8 Contwoyto L N W Terr
100 K8 Conty France
13 G3 Conway Indiana
13 G3 Conway, Q England
100 A6 Conway, I Chile
131 B6 Conway Wyoming
76 E5 Cora Corabia Romania
130 Q5 Coração de Jesus Brazil
133 L3 Coraki New S Wales
102 C8 Coral B Palawan Philippines
106 E7 Coral Harbour New Providence I Bahamas
115 L5 Coral Harbour N W Terr
137 K4 Coral Sea Islands Terr Australasia
129 M6 Coral Sea Islands Terr Australasia
113 L9 Coralville Res Iowa
139 G7 Coram Montana
139 G7 Corangamite, L Victoria
129 G3 Corantijn R Suriname
94 G6 Coraopolis Pennsylvania
43 G7 Corato Italy
20 K4 Corbeil-Essonnes France
71 F5 Corbett Chile
131 A6 Corbie France
9 H7 Corbière Channel Is
110 G5 Corbières reg France
130 C4 Corbigny France
131 E6 Corbin Kentucky
123 R7 Corbin Hd Nfld
45 M1 Córbola Italy
13 F4 Corbridge England
128 D7 Corby England
9 F2 Corby Northants England
126 G10 Corcaigh see Cork
127 D1 Corcieux France
130 C10 Corcoran California
102 C4 Corcoran California
133 C6 Corcovado Chile
130 D1 Corcovado, Golfo Chile
16 A2 Corcubion Spain
112 D6 Cordele Georgia
106 M6 Cordell Oklahoma
18 G8 Cordes France
133 F4 Cordilheiras, Serra das mts Brazil
16 D1 Cordillera Cantábrica mts Spain
128 C3 Cordillera Central mts Dom Rep
127 O5 Cordillera Central mts Luzon Philippines
128 C5 Cordillera Central mts Peru
127 J10 Cordillera de Mérida mts Venezuela
21 J10 Cordillera Occidental mts Colombia
18 C3 Cordillera Oriental mts Colombia
71 F5 Cordillera Ra mts Philippines
138 D7 Cordillo Downs S Australia
130 G6 Cordisburgo Brazil
128 G3 Córdoba Argentina
124 H8 Córdoba Mexico
16 D7 Córdoba Spain
130 D7 Córdoba prov Argentina
131 D3 Córdoba, Sierra de ra Argentina
16 D7 Córdoba prov Spain
94 H6 Cordova Alabama
116 P6 Cordova Alaska
94 H5 Cordova Alaska
12 C1 Cordova Peru
145 J3 Coreglia Antelminelli Italy
12 G3 Corella R W Australia
145 G4 Corella L N Terr Aust
18 L0 Corfinio Italy
8 D5 Corfu France
109 L3 Corfu New York
8 D5 Corfu isld Greece see Kérkira I

140 F6 Coorabulka Queensland
143 B7 Coor-de-Wandy mt W Australia
138 E6 Coorong, The L S Australia
143 B8 Coorow W Australia
130 C6 Cooroy Queensland
14 C5 Coosa Alabama
43 E11 Coosawattee R Georgia
14 C5 Coosawhatchie R S Carolina
100 A6 Coos Bay Oregon
123 P4 Cootamundra New S Wales
123 Q5 Cootehill Irish Rep
20 J5 Cooyar Queensland
20 F3 Cooyeena Queensland
133 C5 Copahue mt Chile/Arg
131 B6 Copahue peak Chile
100 A2 Copalis Beach Washington
119 R4 Copano B Texas
123 L4 Cope Colorado
107 M6 Copa, Paraná R Brazil
41 M6 Copeland Florida
45 P6 Copeland Idaho
32 H7 Copeland Kansas
21 E6 Copenhagen Georgia
133 G2 Copenhagen R Brazil
99 S9 Copenhagen L Brazil
99 P4 Copenhagen New York
123 P5 Copenhagen, L New York
139 H7 Copeton Res.
110 K6 Copiago Chile
111 D9 Copiapo, R Chile
103 P6 Copinsay Scotland
13 F2 Copley S Australia
20 C5 Coporaque Peru
40 E2 Copparo R Suriname
102 G5 Coppell Ontario
99 M9 Coppell Texas
94 E7 Copperas R Suriname
94 E7 Copperas Cove Texas
119 P9 Copper Butte mt Washington
141 G5 Copperfield Queensland
94 B7 Copper Hbr Michigan
120 F4 Coppermine N W Terr
142 F5 Coppermine Pt Ontario
113 K11 Coppermine R N W Terr
42 F6 Copper Mt Br Col
100 H4 Copper Mt Nevada
99 P3 Copp L N W Terr
95 P3 Coppull England
45 J10 Copsa Mica Romania
94 K3 Coqualeetza W Australia
133 D5 Coquet R England
129 K9 Coquet I England
87 B9 Coquihatville see Mbandaka
128 E7 Coquille Oregon
130 F6 Coquimbo Chile
101 P7 Cora Wyoming
145 E2 Corabia Romania
13 C9 Coraki New S Wales
102 G8 Coral B Palawan Philippines
106 E7 Coral Harbour New Providence I Bahamas
111 M9 Coral Sea Islands Terr
102 G9 Coral Harbour N W Terr
71 F7 Coral Sea Islands Terr Australasia
48 L3 Coralville Res Iowa
139 P8 Coram Montana
139 G7 Corangamite, L Victoria
139 G3 Corantijn R Suriname
94 G6 Coraopolis Pennsylvania
43 G7 Corato Italy
20 K4 Corbeil-Essonnes France

95 O3 Corinth New York
130 E4 Corinth, Gulf of Greece see Korinthiakós Kólpos
130 E5 Corinth Mississippi
130 H5 Corinth New York
130 D5 Corinto Brazil
128 F6 Corixinha, R Brazil
128 F2 Corumo R Venezuela
16 B1 Coruña prov Spain
16 B1 Coruña, la see La Coruña
94 C4 Corunna Michigan
138 D4 Corunna S Australia
130 H11 Corurripe Brazil
101 L3 Corvallis Montana
100 B5 Corvallis Oregon
38 E8 Corvara in Badia Italy
32 K9 Corvey W Germany
8 C2 Corwen Wales
107 N4 Corwin Kansas
116 E7 Corwin, C Alaska
101 P4 Corwin Springs Montana
22 H2 Cosham England
99 N8 Corydon Iowa
110 J4 Corydon Kentucky
94 J5 Corydon Pennsylvania
9 G5 Coryton England
21 E6 Corzé France
107 M6 Cosala Mexico
125 M8 Cosamaloapan Mexico
43 G9 Cosenza Italy
18 H3 Cosham England
22 J2 Coshocton Ohio
21 E6 Cosmoledo I Indian Oc
99 M5 Cosmos Minnesota
18 G6 Cosne-d'Allier France
102 G5 Coso Junction California
131 A6 Cosquin Argentina
22 I6 Cost Texas
109 K6 Cost Texas
17 K3 Costa Blanca Spain
45 L1 Costa Brava Spain
45 E11 Costa I, La Florida
102 G8 Costa Rica Mexico
124 C2 Costa Rica Mexico
125 M4 Costa Rica rep Cent America
9 E3 Costebelle, L Quebec
123 K3 Costello Pennsylvania
107 M2 Covert Kansas
94 K3 Costello Pennsylvania
94 J9 Costessey England
48 K5 Cosquin Argentina
109 N1 Cove Arkansas
131 A6 Cost Texas
112 K2 Cove City N Carolina
103 M3 Cove Fort Utah
50 B10 Cove California
94 K7 Cove Mt Pennsylvania
126 G10 Covenas Colombia
9 E3 Coventry England
95 L8 Cove Point Maryland
107 M2 Covert Kansas
99 R8 Covina California
94 J6 Covington Georgia
18 G6 Covington Indiana
102 G5 Covington Kentucky
22 J3 Covington Louisiana
94 J9 Covington Michigan
99 S3 Covington Ohio
107 N5 Covington Tennessee
109 L5 Covington Tennessee
109 G3 Covington Virginia
120 G5 Cow R Ontario
14 C4 Cowal Scotland
111 L4 Cowal, L New S Wales
102 C4 Cowan Manitoba
110 K6 Cowan Tennessee
140 E4 Cowan Downs Queensland
138 F6 Cowangie Victoria
143 D9 Cowan, Lake W Australia
141 S7 Cowansville Quebec
138 D3 Coward Springs S Australia
138 E2 Cowarie S Australia
9 F2 Cowbit England
103 L2 Cowboy Pass Utah
8 C5 Cowbridge Wales
20 C4 Cowcowing, L W Australia
100 G2 Cow Cr Washington
18 E1 Cowden Illinois
13 E1 Cowdenbeath Scotland
101 T9 Cowdrey Colorado
9 E6 Cowes England
139 H7 Cowes Victoria
107 P6 Coweta Oklahoma
141 S7 Coweta Queensland
142 A2 Cowichan L Br Col
123 P4 Cow Head L California
100 A1 Cowichan L Br Col
70 F2 Cowie Harb Kalimantan
100 E8 Cowles Nebraska
99 G2 Cowley Alberta
141 H7 Cowley Queensland
101 R5 Cowley Wyoming
106 C3 Cowlitz R Washington
100 D3 Cowra Texas
94 H8 Cowpasture R Virginia
112 F2 Cowpens S Carolina
112 F2 Cowpens Nat.Bat.Site S Carolina
130 G4 Cowra New S Wales
130 G4 Coxa, R Brazil
130 H9 Cox Bight Tasmania
22 F3 Coxheath England
130 C4 Coxilbo do Ouro Brazil
130 C4 Coxim Brazil

21 F10 Courcôme France
21 D9 Courçon France
20 F5 Courgains France
20 F5 Courières France
18 H9 Courtanes France
20 E3 Courseules-sur-Mer France
18 H5 Courtalain France
40 F3 Courtelary Switzerland
114 G8 Court By Columbia
98 H2 Courtenay N Dakota
18 G7 Courtine, la France
107 N2 Courtland Kansas
99 M5 Courtland Minnesota
95 K10 Courtland Virginia
14 C5 Courtmacsherry Irish Rep
109 L5 Courtney Texas
20 F4 Courtomer France
22 H2 Courtrai see Kortrijk
Court Saint-Étienne Belgium
14 C5 Courval Sask
118 L3 Courville France
20 H5 Courville France
109 O3 Coushatta Louisiana
83 J12 Cousin I Seychelles
87 D9 Coutada do Mucusso Angola
20 C3 Coutances France
20 E5 Couterne France
122 J2 Couthuin Belgium
18 E7 Coutras France
101 N1 Coutts Alberta
127 O2 Couva Trinidad
20 B2 Couvin France
22 F4 Couvron-et-Aumencourt France
48 K5 Covasna Romania
109 N1 Cove Arkansas
100 H4 Cove Oregon
100 B10 Cove California
94 K7 Cove Mt Pennsylvania
126 G10 Covenas Colombia
9 E3 Coventry England
95 L8 Cove Point Maryland
107 M2 Covert Kansas
99 R8 Covina California
94 J6 Covington Georgia
18 G6 Covington Indiana
102 G5 Covington Kentucky
22 J3 Covington Louisiana
94 J9 Covington Michigan
99 S3 Covington Ohio
107 N5 Covington Tennessee
109 L5 Covington Tennessee
109 G3 Covington Virginia
120 G5 Cow R Ontario
14 C4 Cowal Scotland
111 L4 Cowal, L New S Wales
102 C4 Cowan Manitoba
110 K6 Cowan Tennessee
140 E4 Cowan Downs Queensland
138 F6 Cowangie Victoria
143 D9 Cowan, Lake W Australia
141 S7 Cowansville Quebec
138 D3 Coward Springs S Australia
138 E2 Cowarie S Australia
9 F2 Cowbit England
103 L2 Cowboy Pass Utah
8 C5 Cowbridge Wales
20 C4 Cowcowing, L W Australia
100 G2 Cow Cr Washington
18 E1 Cowden Illinois
13 E1 Cowdenbeath Scotland
101 T9 Cowdrey Colorado
9 E6 Cowes England
139 H7 Cowes Victoria
107 P6 Coweta Oklahoma
141 S7 Coweta Queensland
142 A2 Cowichan L Br Col
123 P4 Cow Head L California
100 A1 Cowichan L Br Col
70 F2 Cowie Harb Kalimantan
100 E8 Cowles Nebraska
99 G2 Cowley Alberta
141 H7 Cowley Queensland
101 R5 Cowley Wyoming
106 C3 Cowlitz R Washington
100 D3 Cowra Texas
94 H8 Cowpasture R Virginia
112 F2 Cowpens S Carolina
112 F2 Cowpens Nat.Bat.Site S Carolina
130 G4 Cowra New S Wales
130 G4 Coxa, R Brazil
130 H9 Cox Bight Tasmania
22 F3 Coxheath England
130 C4 Coxilbo do Ouro Brazil
130 C4 Coxim Brazil
130 D5 Coxipó da Ponté Brazil
143 F6 Cox,Mt W Australia
130 C4 Cox R N Terr Australia
140 D3 Coxsackie New York
21 C10 Coxs Bazar Bangladesh
95 O4 Cox's Cove Nfld
123 P4 Cox's Cove Nfld
108 B6 Coy Texas
108 D5 Coyanosa Cr Texas
20 K3 Coye-la-Forêt France
20 N6 Coyle France
102 H6 Coyle Wisconsin
99 S6 Coyle New Mexico
103 T6 Coyote L California
102 C4 Coyote Peak California
103 P3 Coyote Pk Arizona
20 G6 Coyreux France
20 H4 Coyto, Pta C Mexico
20 N5 Coyotitán Mexico
99 S8 Cozad Nebraska
44 B2 Cozie Alpi mt Italy
125 Q7 Cozumel, I.de Mexico
103 M3 Crab Cr Washington
99 K8 Crab Orchard Kentucky
110 G4 Crab Orchard Tennessee
110 G4 Crab Orchard L Illinois
127 H2 Crab Pond Pt Jamaica
139 H7 Crackenback R Tasmania
20 E5 Cracklybank England
Cracow see Kraków
141 K7 Cracow Queensland
89 S4 Cradock S Africa
141 K7 Cradle, Mt Tasmania
139 G8 Cradock S Africa
98 L9 Craft Sask
12 E1 Craig Alaska
101 S9 Craig Colorado
13 G13 Craig Florida
13 E2 Craig Missouri
101 S8 Craig Alaska
18 H7 Craighouse Scotland
12 G5 Craigie Scotland
100 B1 Craigieburn New Zealand
99 K6 Craigmyle Alberta
118 E7 Craigmyle Alberta
100 O5 Craigsburn Haven England
141 K7 Crags Ra mts Queensland
94 H3 Craigsville Virginia
118 L5 Craiguanamagh Irish Rep
119 M7 Crail Sask
13 E1 Crail Scotland
37 J5 Craisheim W Germany
48 H6 Craiova Romania

20

Cramond — Damville

13 E2 Cramond Scotland
85 D2 Crampel Algeria
86 C4 Crampel Cent Afr Republic
121 Q8 Cranberry, L New York
119 Q4 Cranberry Portage Manitoba
9 E6 Cranborne England
114 H8 Cranbrook Br Columbia
9 G5 Cranbrook England
143 C10 Cranbrook W Australia
119 R8 Crandall Manitoba
98 J4 Crandall S Dakota
109 L3 Crandall Texas
99 S4 Crandon Wisconsin
127 P6 Crane Barbados
110 C5 Crane Missouri
98 B2 Crane Montana
100 G6 Crane Oregon
108 E4 Crane Texas
100 J5 Crane Cr.Res Idaho
118 H8 Crane L Sask
119 M9 Crane Valley Sask
109 K4 Cranfills Gap Texas
9 F5 Cranleigh England
100 A8 Crannell California
13 F2 Cranshaws Scotland
95 Q5 Cranston Rhode I
13 H6 Cranswick England
21 D6 Craon France
22 F5 Craonne France
139 K2 Craoow Queensland
18 H7 Craponne-sur-Arzon France
98 H1 Crary N Dakota
146 H10 Crary Mts Antarctica
48 L4 Crasna Romania
48 H3 Crasna R Romania
48 H3 Crasnei, Muntii mt Romania
100 C7 Crater L Oregon
100 C7 Crater Lake Nat. Park Oregon
100 D9 Crater Peak mt California
101 M6 Craters of the Moon Nat.Mon Idaho
43 G9 Crati R Italy
130 G9 Crato Brazil
21 F7 Cravant les Coteaux France
119 N8 Craven Sask
130 F7 Cravinhos Brazil
128 D2 Cravo Norte R Colombia
112 D4 Crawford Georgia
111 H8 Crawford Mississippi
98 C7 Crawford Nebraska
12 E3 Crawford Scotland
109 K4 Crawford Texas
12 E3 Crawfordjohn Scotland
140 B3 Crawford,Mt N Terr Australia
95 Q2 Crawford Notch New Hampshire
71 D5 Crawford Pt Philippines
110 K1 Crawfordsville Indiana
111 M11 Crawfordville Florida
112 E4 Crawfordville Georgia
9 F5 Crawley England
8 C4 Cray Wales
9 G5 Crayford England
116 P4 Crazy Mts Alaska
101 P3 Crazy Mts Montana
101 P4 Crazy Pk Montana
101 T5 Crazy Woman Cr Wyoming
15 D4 Creag Meagaidh mt Scotland
20 B3 Créances France
118 L4 Crean L Sask
40 A5 Crêches France
22 B3 Crécy-en-Pontieu France
22 F4 Crécy-sur-Serre France
8 C6 Crediton England
12 D4 Cree Bridge Scotland
106 D4 Creede Colorado
112 J1 Creedmoor N Carolina
101 R9 Creek Colorado
94 H6 Creekside Pennsylvania
113 L9 Creek Village New Providence I Bahamas
124 F4 Creel Mexico
114 J6 Cree L Sask
119 O9 Creelman Sask
120 K8 Creemore Ontario
114 J6 Cree River Saskatchewan
12 D4 Creetown Scotland
37 J5 Creglingen W Germany
98 H7 Creighton Nebraska
119 P4 Creighton Sask
120 J6 Creighton Mine Ontario
44 G1 Crema Italy
19 O13 Crémieu France
118 C7 Cremona Alberta
44 G1 Crémona Italy
111 F7 Crenshaw Mississippi
18 E8 Créon France
48 F5 Crepaja Yugoslavia
129 G5 Crepori R Brazil
22 D5 Crépy-en-Valois France
120 K6 Crerar Ontario
42 F4 Cres Yugoslavia
98 G4 Cresbard S Dakota
107 N6 Crescent Oklahoma
112 J4 Crescent Beach S Carolina
100 A8 Crescent City California
113 F8 Crescent L Florida
100 D6 Crescent L Oregon
100 B1 Crescent, L Washington
100 E9 Crescent Mills California
103 J6 Crescent Pk Nevada
99 O6 Cresco Iowa
45 L2 Crespino Italy
8 B4 Cresselly Wales
109 K3 Cresson Texas
139 H8 Cressy Tasmania
139 G7 Cressy Victoria
19 O15 Crest France
103 K4 Crestline Nevada
94 E6 Crestline Ohio
100 J1 Creston Br Col
99 M8 Creston Iowa
101 L1 Creston Montana
123 R6 Creston Nfld
100 G2 Creston Washington
101 S8 Creston Wyoming
106 E3 Crestone Pk Colorado
111 K11 Crestview Florida
110 J6 Crestview Tennessee
119 M8 Crestwynd Sask
112 L2 Creswell N Carolina
100 B6 Creswell Oregon
115 K3 Creswell B N W Terr
140 D4 Creswell Downs N Terr Australia
139 G7 Creswick Victoria
19 J6 Crêt de la Neige mt France
99 T8 Crete Illinois
98 H3 Crete N Dakota
98 K9 Crete Nebraska
Crete isld Greece see Kríti
47 G9 Crete, Sea of Greece
20 D3 Creully France
17 K2 Creus, C Spain
21 I9 Creuse dep France
18 G6 Creuse R France
37 M4 Creussen W Germany
37 J1 Creuzburg E Germany
45 K2 Crevalcore Italy
20 F3 Crèvecoeur France
20 K2 Crèvecoeur-le-Grand France
17 G6 Crevillente Spain
41 H5 Crevola Italy
8 D1 Crewe England
94 J9 Crewe Virginia
8 D6 Crewkerne England
12 D1 Crianlarich Scotland
8 B2 Criccieth Wales
9 E1 Crich England
118 K9 Crichton Sask
133 H3 Criciuma Brazil
9 E3 Crick England
8 C4 Crickhowell Wales
9 E4 Cricklade England
94 C6 Cridersville Ohio
12 E1 Crieff Scotland
20 H1 Criel-sur-Mer France
15 E6 Criffell mt Scotland
42 F3 Crikvenica Yugoslavia
117 E6 Crillon, Mt Alaska
99 O1 Crilly Ontario
Crimea see Krym
37 N2 Crimmitschau E Germany
12 C1 Crinan Scotland
15 C4 Crinan Canal Scotland
106 E3 Cripple Creek Colorado
116 J5 Cripple Landing Alaska
9 G6 Cripps's Corner England
20 F2 Criquetot-l'Esneval France
48 G4 Crişana Romania
130 F5 Cristalina Brazil
129 H6 Cristalino R Brazil
38 F8 Cristallo mt Italy
126 H10 Cristóbal Colón, Pico mt Colombia
48 J4 Cristuru Secuiesc Romania
48 G4 Crişul Alb R Romania
48 G4 Crişul Negru R Romania
48 H4 Crişul Repede R Romania
94 C8 Crittenden Kentucky
33 P5 Crivitz E Germany
99 S4 Crivitz Wisconsin
38 L9 Črna Yugoslavia
46 E3 Crna R Yugoslavia
46 E2 Crna Gora mt Yugoslavia
46 E2 Crna Trava Yugoslavia
46 D3 Crni Drim R Yugoslavia
38 M9 Crni-vrh mt Yugoslavia
14 B3 Croagh Patrick Mt Irish Rep
Croatia see Hrvatska
41 O5 Croce, C mt Italy
43 G11 Croce, S., C Sicily
110 D4 Crocker Missouri
70 D2 Crocker Ra Borneo
12 E3 Crocketford Scotland
109 M4 Crockett Texas
9 G5 Crockham Hill England
20 E4 Crocy France
38 F8 Croda Rossa mt Italy
110 J4 Crofton Kentucky
98 J7 Crofton Nebraska
142 D5 Crofton,Mt W Australia
95 M3 Croghan New York
19 O18 Croisette, C France
18 D5 Croisic, le France
22 D3 Croisilles France
145 D4 Croisilles Harbour New Zealand
127 H5 Croix des Bouquets Haiti
19 P15 Croix Haute, Col de la pass France
20 C5 Croixille, la France
122 B2 Croix, L.à la Quebec
122 E8 Croix R New Brunswick
20 H3 Croix-St.Leufroy, la France
22 D5 Croix-St.Ouen, la France
120 K8 Croker, Cape Ontario
140 B2 Croker Hill N Terr Australia
140 C1 Croker I N Terr Australia
15 D3 Cromarty Scotland
15 D3 Cromarty Firth Scotland
138 B2 Crombie, Mt S Australia
9 H2 Cromer England
119 Q9 Cromer Manitoba
99 O3 Cromwell Minnesota
144 B6 Cromwell New Zealand
144 C5 Cronadun New Zealand
37 K5 Cronheim W Germany
98 D9 Crook Colorado
13 F5 Crook Cumbria England
13 G4 Crook Durham England
107 K4 Crooked Cr Kansas
100 G7 Crooked Cr Oregon
126 G3 Crooked I Bahamas
126 G3 Crooked I.Passage Bahamas
113 F10 Crooked L Florida
123 Q5 Crooked L Nfld
117 M8 Crooked R Br Columbia
100 E5 Crooked R Oregon
119 O6 Crooked River Sask
13 F2 Crookham England
14 B5 Crookhaven Irish Rep
109 M2 Crook, L Texas
13 F5 Crooklands England
12 E1 Crook of Devon Scotland
98 K2 Crookston Minnesota
98 F7 Crookston Nebraska
94 E7 Crooksville Ohio
139 J5 Crookwell New S Wales
113 E9 Croom Florida
14 C4 Croom Irish Rep
139 K3 Croppa Cr New S Wales
123 R2 Croque Nfld
141 G3 Crosbie R Queensland
99 N3 Crosby Minnesota
111 E10 Crosby Mississippi
98 C1 Crosby N Dakota
109 M6 Crosby Texas
108 F2 Crosbyton Texas
8 D5 Cross England
85 F7 Cross R Nigeria
21 A7 Crossac France
12 C2 Crossaig Scotland
87 B10 Cross, C Namibia
113 D8 Cross City Florida
111 E8 Crossett Arkansas
13 F4 Cross Fell England
118 C7 Crossfield Alberta
13 E1 Crossgates Scotland
8 C3 Cross Gates Wales
8 B4 Cross Hands Wales
113 K12 Cross Harbour Bahamas
14 C5 Crosshaven Irish Rep
112 F3 Cross Hill S Carolina
12 D3 Crosshill Scotland
111 C9 Cross L Louisiana
121 O8 Cross, L Ontario
119 U4 Cross Lake Manitoba
144 D5 Crossley, Mt New Zealand
118 D4 Cross L. Prov. Park Alberta
12 B5 Crossmaglen N Ireland
103 K7 Crossman Pk Arizona
12 E4 Crossmichael Scotland
14 B2 Crossmolina Irish Rep
106 B1 Cross Mountain Colorado
109 H3 Cross Plains Texas
94 B1 Cross Village Michigan
110 L6 Crossville Tennessee
116 P5 Crosswind L Alaska
45 J2 Crostolo R Italy
94 E3 Croswell Michigan
110 L3 Crothersville Indiana
43 H9 Crotone Italy
20 J1 Crotoy, le France
37 O3 Crottendorf E Germany
100 K5 Crouch Idaho
9 G4 Crouch, R England
21 F8 Croutelle France
22 E5 Crouy France
21 F7 Crouzilles France
101 S4 Crow Agency Montana
139 H4 Crowal R New S Wales
9 G5 Crowborough England
8 C5 Crowcombe England
106 F1 Crow Cr Colorado
111 F7 Crowder Mississippi
107 P6 Crowder Oklahoma
118 F1 Crowduck L. Manitoba
139 L4 Crowdy Hd New S Wales
108 H2 Crowell Texas
139 G7 Crowes Victoria
101 Q6 Crowheart Wyoming
139 H4 Crowl R New S Wales
9 F2 Crowland England
13 H6 Crowle England
106 G3 Crowley Colorado
111 D11 Crowley Louisiana
102 F4 Crowley, L California
94 E8 Crown City Ohio
103 M7 Crown King Arizona
106 B6 Crown Point New Mexico
95 O3 Crown Point New York
115 L4 Crown Prince Frederick I N W Terr
99 T8 Crown Pt Indiana
127 M2 Crown Pt Tobago
101 O3 Crow Peak Montana
141 K7 Crow's Nest Queensland
118 C9 Crowsnest Pass Alberta/Br Col
99 M3 Crow Wing R Minnesota
13 G4 Croxdale England
8 B5 Croyde England
9 F5 Croydon England
144 B7 Croydon New Zealand
141 F4 Croydon Queensland
142 C5 Croydon W Australia
83 L13 Croy, Î de Kerguelen Indian Oc
21 I9 Crozant France
94 J8 Crozet Virginia
81 D9 Crozet Basin Indian Oc
81 C10 Crozet, Îs Indian Oc
81 B10 Crozet Plateau Indian Oc
146 J7 Crozier, C Antarctica
114 G2 Crozier Chan N W Terr
18 B4 Crozon France
19 N15 Cruas France
103 H6 Crucero California
126 D3 Cruces Cuba
128 C2 Cruces, Pta point Colombia
22 L4 Cruchten Luxembourg
94 H7 Crucible Pennsylvania
15 G3 Cruden B Scotland
8 D2 Crudgington England
8 D4 Crudwell England
111 F8 Cruger Mississippi
20 G4 Crulai France
14 E2 Crumlin N Ireland
100 F7 Crump L Oregon
22 K5 Crusnes France
133 E4 Cruz Argentina
133 G3 Cruz Alta Brazil
131 D3 Cruz del Eje Argentina
130 G8 Cruzeiro Brazil
133 G2 Cruzeiro do Oeste Brazil
128 D5 Cruzeiro do Sul Brazil
146 K9 Cruzen I Antarctica
133 C3 Cruz Grande Chile
128 C3 Cruz, La Colombia
18 G9 Cruzy France
117 M8 Crysdale, Mt Br Columbia
98 J1 Crystal N Dakota
103 K5 Crystal Nevada
106 C2 Crystal R Colorado
113 E9 Crystal B Florida
138 E5 Crystal Bridge S Australia
119 T9 Crystal City Manitoba
108 H7 Crystal City Texas
99 S3 Crystal Falls Michigan
99 S7 Crystal L Illinois
99 U5 Crystal L Michigan
99 N6 Crystal Lake Iowa
113 E9 Crystal River Florida
111 F9 Crystal Springs Mississippi
119 M6 Crystal Springs Sask
99 U6 Crystal Valley Michigan
48 F4 Csanytelek Hungary
48 E3 Csepel Sziget R Hungary
48 F4 Csongrád Hungary
48 F4 Csongrád co Hungary
48 D3 Csorna Hungary
48 F4 Csorvas Hungary
48 E3 Csóványos mt Hungary
48 D4 Csurgó Hungary
127 L9 Cúa Venezuela
88 F9 Cuambo Mozambique
87 D9 Cuando R Angola
87 C9 Cuangar Angola
87 C7 Cuango Angola
86 C7 Cuango Zaïre
87 B7 Cuanza R Angola
67 A7 Cua Rao Vietnam
133 F4 Cuareim Brazil
131 F3 Cuaro R Uruguay
133 E4 Cuarto R Argentina
124 H4 Cuatro Ciénegas de Carranza Mexico
68 H4 Cua Tung Vietnam
124 F3 Cuauhtémoc Mexico
124 G8 Cuautitlán Mexico
125 K8 Cuautla Mexico
110 F1 Cuba Illinois
107 N2 Cuba Kansas
110 E3 Cuba Missouri
106 D5 Cuba New Mexico
94 J4 Cuba New York
16 B6 Cuba Portugal
126 D4 Cuba rep W Indies
103 M10 Cubabi, Cerro peak Mexico
99 Q7 Cuba City Wisconsin
127 M9 Cubagua, I Venezuela
143 B10 Cuballing W Australia
87 C9 Cubango R Angola
130 F8 Cubatão Brazil
119 N4 Cub Hills Sask
127 K10 Cubiro Venezuela
48 J6 Cuca Romania
133 C6 Cucao, B.de Chile
133 F4 Cuchilla de Haedo hills Uruguay
9 F5 Cuckfield England
9 E1 Cuckney England
94 K9 Cuckoo Virginia
87 C8 Cucumbi Angola
124 D2 Cucurpe Mexico
128 D2 Cúcuta Colombia
99 T7 Cudahy Wisconsin
76 D5 Cuddalore India
76 D3 Cuddapah India
141 F7 Cuddapan,L Queensland
102 G6 Cuddeback L California
113 F13 Cudjoe Key isld Florida
119 M6 Cudworth Sask
143 C7 Cue W Australia
16 E3 Cuéllar Spain
128 C4 Cuenca Ecuador
71 E4 Cuenca Philippines
17 F4 Cuenca Spain
17 F5 Cuenca prov Spain
124 H5 Cuencamé de Ceniceros Mexico
17 F4 Cuenca, Serrania de Spain
125 K8 Cuernavaca Mexico
109 K6 Cuero Texas
19 Q18 Cuers France
106 F6 Cuervo New Mexico
102 D6 Cuesta Pass California
126 G4 Cueto Cuba
17 F7 Cuevas del Almanzora Spain
133 E2 Cuevo Bolivia
22 E5 Cuffies France
123 N2 Cuff L Quebec
19 P18 Cuges-les-Pins France
43 B8 Cuglieri Sardinia
20 B5 Cuguen France
130 C4 Cuiabá Brazil
14 D2 Cuilcagh mt N Ireland
15 B3 Cuillin Hills Scotland
87 C7 Cuilo R Angola
59 J2 Cuiluan China
87 C8 Cuima Angola
22 D2 Cuinchy France
36 B4 Cuint W Germany
22 E5 Cuise-la-Motte France
130 H9 Cuité Brazil
130 H6 Cuité, R Brazil
87 C9 Cuito R Angola
87 C9 Cuito Cuanavale Angola
128 F4 Cuiuni R Brazil
110 E2 Cuivre R Missouri
71 E7 Cujangan isld Philippines
48 H6 Cujmiru Romania
78 J3 Cukurca Turkey
68 H4 Cu Lai Vietnam
18 G6 Culan France
68 J5 Cu Lao Bo Bai isld Vietnam
68 J5 Cu Lao Cham isld Vietnam
68 J7 Cu Lao Hon isld Vietnam
68 J5 Cu Lao Re isld Vietnam
71 F5 Culasi Panay Philippines
98 B1 Culbertson Montana
98 F9 Culbertson Nebraska
139 H6 Culcairn New S Wales
22 G4 Cul-des-Sarts Belgium
106 E4 Culebra Pk Colorado
16 C3 Culebra, Sa de la mts Spain
25 D5 Culemborg Netherlands
87 C9 Culevai Angola
141 H8 Culgoa R N S W/Qnsld
139 H3 Culgoa, R Australia
124 F5 Culiacán Mexico
124 F5 Culiacancito Mexico
71 D5 Culion Philippines
129 H6 Culiseu R Brazil
17 F7 Cúllar de Baza Spain
139 J5 Cullarin Rge New S Wales
15 F3 Cullen Scotland
17 G5 Cullera Spain
107 M4 Cullison Kansas
111 K7 Cullman Alabama
141 G5 Culloden R Queensland
8 C6 Cullompton England
125 M2 Culmi Honduras
8 D3 Culmington England
19 P13 Culoz France
94 J8 Culpeper Virginia
128 A7 Culpepper isld Galapagos Is
15 E5 Culter Fell Scotland
139 G4 Cultowa New S Wales
129 H6 Culuene R Brazil
99 U8 Culver Indiana
107 N3 Culver Kansas
100 D5 Culver Oregon
144 D5 Culverden New Zealand
143 E10 Culver,Pt W Australia
87 C8 Cuma Angola
129 K4 Cuma, B.de Brazil
47 H4 Cumalı Turkey
128 F1 Cumana Venezuela
127 N9 Cumanacoa Venezuela
47 J6 Cumaovası Turkey
130 E6 Cumari Brazil
117 L11 Cumberland Br Columbia
99 M8 Cumberland Iowa
94 D9 Cumberland Kentucky
94 J7 Cumberland Maryland
94 F7 Cumberland Ohio
94 J9 Cumberland Virginia
99 O4 Cumberland Wisconsin
Cumberland co see Cumbria
110 J5 Cumberland R Tennessee
146 A15 Cumberland B Antarctica
137 O4 Cumberland, C New Hebrides
110 J5 Cumberland City Tennessee
94 D10 Cumberland Gap Tenn/Virg
119 P5 Cumberland House Sask
113 F7 Cumberland I Georgia
141 J5 Cumberland Is Queensland
94 B10 Cumberland, L Kentucky
110 L5 Cumberland, L Kentucky
119 P4 Cumberland L Sask
94 D10 Cumberland Mts Tennessee etc
115 N4 Cumberland Pen N W Terr
99 R2 Cumberland Pt Michigan
94 D10 Cumberland R Kentucky
94 J7 Cumberland Res Pennsylvania
115 N4 Cumberland Sound N W Terr
140 D1 Cumberland Str N Terr Australia
12 E2 Cumbernauld Scotland
139 J3 Cumborah New S Wales
133 C7 Cumbrera mt Chile
13 E4 Cumbria co England
76 D3 Cumbum India
109 M2 Cumby Texas
44 B2 Cumiana Italy
129 G4 Cumina R Brazil
129 G3 Cuminapanema R Brazil
13 E4 Cummertrees Scotland
112 C3 Cumming Georgia
102 A2 Cummings California
98 J2 Cummings N Dakota
138 D5 Cummins S Australia
142 F4 Cummins Ra W Australia
139 J5 Cumnock New S Wales
12 D3 Cumnock Scotland
48 J5 Cumpăna Romania
124 E2 Cumpas Mexico
78 D3 Çumra Turkey
124 E3 Cumuripa Mexico
130 H5 Cumuruxatiba Brazil
127 O2 Cumuto Trinidad
126 E3 Cunagua Cuba
129 H3 Cunani Brazil
124 D6 Cuñaño Mexico
131 G3 Cuñapiru R Uruguay
133 C5 Cunco Chile
142 D5 Cuncudgerie Hill W Australia
143 B9 Cunderdin W Australia
128 D3 Cundinamarca div Colombia
87 B9 Cunene R Angola
44 B3 Cúneo Italy
138 C4 Cungena S Australia
17 H6 Cunillera isld Balearic Is
18 H7 Cunlhat France
141 H8 Cunnamulla Queensland
107 M4 Cunningham Kansas
100 G3 Cunningham Washington
127 O2 Cunupia Trinidad
21 E7 Cuon France
119 N8 Cupar Sask
13 E1 Cupar Scotland
128 C2 Cupica, G.de Colombia
46 E1 Ćuprija Yugoslavia
100 J4 Cuprum Idaho
124 D5 Cupula, P Mexico
129 G7 Curabá R Brazil
129 L5 Curaçá Brazil
126 B1 Curaçao isld W Indies
131 B7 Curacáutin Chile
131 D7 Curaco, R Argentina
131 E6 Cura Malal, Cerro peak Argentina
133 C5 Curanilahue Chile
128 C4 Curaray R Peru/Ecuador
131 B4 Curaumilla, Pta de C Chile
139 J4 Curban New S Wales
48 K6 Curcani Romania
21 E7 Curcay-sur-Dive France
138 D3 Curdimurka S Australia
138 D4 Curdlawidny Lagoon S Australia
9 E2 Curdworth England
18 H5 Cure R France
83 M13 Curepipe Mauritius
87 G12 Curepipe Mauritius
133 C5 Curepto Chile
127 O10 Curiapo Venezuela
131 B5 Curico Chile
131 D8 Curico, L Argentina
128 E4 Curicuriari R Brazil
83 J12 Curieuse I Seychelles
130 J9 Curimataú R Brazil
143 A7 Curious,Mt W Australia
128 D3 Curiplaya Colombia
133 H3 Curitiba Brazil
130 E10 Curitibanos Brazil
100 G1 Curlew Washington
141 J5 Curlew I Queensland
111 H12 Curlew Is Louisiana
139 K4 Curlewis New S Wales
116 F5 Curlew L Alaska
123 L3 Curlew Pt Quebec
123 O5 Curling Nfld
138 E4 Curnamona S Australia
44 F2 Curone R Italy
139 K4 Currabubula New S Wales
130 H9 Currais Novas Brazil
138 C2 Curralulla R S Australia
94 D2 Curran Michigan
121 Q7 Curran Ontario
103 J3 Currant Nevada
139 G4 Curranyalpa New S Wales
141 F7 Currawilla Queensland
110 E4 Current R Missouri
113 L12 Current I Bahamas
126 F2 Current, The Eleuthera Bahamas
99 L5 Currie Minnesota
112 J3 Currie N Carolina
103 K1 Currie Nevada
13 E2 Currie Scotland
139 G7 Currie Tasmania
138 B2 Currie Cr., The S Australia
119 U1 Currie L Manitoba
140 B7 Currie,Mt N Terr Australia
112 L1 Currituck N Carolina
112 M1 Currituck Sound N Carolina
139 K6 Currockbilly, Mt New S Wales
110 E2 Curryville Missouri
37 L2 Cursdorf E Germany
45 L1 Curtarolo Italy
48 J5 Curtea de Argeş Romania
100 B6 Curtin Oregon
143 D9 Curtin W Australia
140 B7 Curtin Springs N Terr Aust
111 C9 Curtis Louisiana
99 V3 Curtis Michigan
98 F9 Curtis Nebraska
16 B1 Curtis Spain
141 L6 Curtis Chan Gt Barrier Reef Australia
139 H7 Curtis Group islds Tasmania
137 R8 Curtis I Kermadec Is Pacific Oc
141 K6 Curtis I Queensland
94 D2 Curtisville Michigan
129 G4 Curuá Brazil
129 H5 Curuaés R Brazil
129 H3 Curuá, I Brazil
129 G3 Curuapanema R Brazil
129 J4 Curuca Brazil
128 D5 Curuçá R Brazil
133 F2 Curuguaty Paraguay
129 J4 Cururupu Brazil
131 F2 Curuzú Cuatiá Argentina
129 K7 Curvelo Brazil
94 J6 Curwensville Pennsylvania
14 E1 Cushendall N Ireland
14 E1 Cushendun N Ireland
99 M3 Cushing Minnesota
107 O6 Cushing Oklahoma
111 B10 Cushing Texas
110 E6 Cushman Arkansas
101 Q3 Cushman Montana
100 A6 Cushman Oregon
100 B2 Cushman, L Washington
124 F3 Cusihuiráchic Mexico
45 H3 Cusna, Mt Italy
18 H6 Cusset France
112 C5 Cusseta Georgia
99 O1 Cusson Minnesota
144 D5 Cust New Zealand
101 S3 Custer Montana
98 C6 Custer S Dakota
101 S4 Custer Battlefield Nat.Mon Montana
107 M6 Custer City Oklahoma
45 J1 Custoza Italy
138 F4 Cutana S Australia
101 N1 Cut Bank Montana
117 O8 Cutbank R Alberta
119 P5 Cut Beaver L Sask
111 A8 Cuthand Cr Texas
112 C6 Cuthbert Georgia
98 H6 Cuthbert S Dakota
108 F3 Cuthbert Texas
140 E4 Cuthbert, Mt Queensland
45 J3 Cutigliano Italy
118 H6 Cut Knife Sask
102 E5 Cutler California
95 T9 Cutler Maine
120 H6 Cutler Ontario
116 H3 Cutler R Alaska
14 C3 Cutra, L Irish Rep
22 E4 Cuts France
139 H3 Cuttaburra R New S Wales
75 L8 Cuttack India
103 O8 Cutter Arizona
141 F7 Cutts Mts Queensland
81 H7 Cuvier Basin Indian Oc
143 A6 Cuvier,C W Australia
145 E2 Cuvier I New Zealand
87 C8 Cuvo R Angola
32 J5 Cuxhaven W Germany
68 H2 Cu Xu isld Vietnam
94 F5 Cuyahoga R Ohio
94 F5 Cuyahoga Falls Ohio
102 E6 Cuyama R California
71 E3 Cuyapo Luzon Philippines
71 E5 Cuyo isld Philippines
71 E5 Cuyo East Passage Philippines
71 E5 Cuyo West Passage Philippines
99 N3 Cuyuna Minnesota
128 G2 Cuyuni R Guyana
125 N2 Cuyu Tigni Nicaragua
128 D6 Cuzco Peru
128 E8 Cuzco mt Bolivia
42 H5 Čvrsnica mt Yugoslavia
8 C4 Cwmbran Wales
88 B3 Cyangugu Rwanda
31 H3 Cybinka Poland
Cyclades islds see Kiklädhes Is
139 H9 Cygnet Tasmania
119 W2 Cygnet L Manitoba
118 B5 Cynthia Alberta
110 M3 Cynthiana Kentucky
110 G4 Cypress Illinois
111 C10 Cypress Louisiana
109 M6 Cypress Texas
111 A8 Cypress Cr Texas
109 N3 Cypress Cr., Lit Texas
118 H9 Cypress Hills Sask
118 G9 Cypress Hills Prov. Park Alberta
113 F9 Cypress L Florida
119 S9 Cypress River Manitoba
79 D4 Cyprus rep Mediterranean Sea
84 G4 Cyrenaica reg Libya
Cyrene see Shahhāt
115 N5 Cyrus Field B N W Terr
22 E2 Cysoing France
31 J2 Czaplinek Poland
118 G6 Czar Alberta
31 M4 Czarna R Poland
31 K2 Czarne Poland
31 K3 Czarnków Poland
31 M6 Czarny Dunajec Poland
31 M6 Czchów Poland
31 J6 Czechoslovakia rep Europe
31 K3 Czempin Poland
31 O3 Czeremcha Poland
Czernowitz see Chernovtsy
31 K2 Czersk Poland
31 J3 Czerwiensk Poland
31 L5 Czestochowa Poland
31 J2 Człopa Poland
31 K2 Człuchów Poland
31 N3 Czyżew Poland
36 D2 Daaden W Germany
65 F2 Da'an China
71 F5 Daanbantayan Cebu Philippines
122 B7 Daaquam Quebec
67 B2 Daba China
79 F7 Dabāb, J. Ed mt Jordan
127 J9 Dabajuro Venezuela
85 D7 Dabakala Ivory Coast
58 D4 Daban Shan mt China
86 A2 Dabaro Somalia
67 C1 Daba Shan mts China
86 G3 Dabat Ethiopia
128 C2 Dabeiba Colombia
68 C4 Dabein Burma
33 P5 Dabel E Germany
74 E7 Dabhoi India
31 H2 Dąbie Poland
67 E1 Dabie Shan mts China
36 C6 Dabo France
85 B6 Dabola Guinea
85 D7 Dabou Ivory Coast
85 D7 Daboya Ghana
36 C1 Dabringhausen W Germany
31 O2 Dąbrowa Poland
31 M2 Dąbrówno Poland
65 D7 Dabu China
67 E4 Dabu China
65 F2 Dabusu Pao L China
75 O7 Dacca Bangladesh
65 C5 Dachang China
37 L7 Dachau W Germany
37 L7 Dachauer Moos marshes W Germany
37 K4 Dachsbach W Germany
38 J7 Dachstein mt Austria
38 J7 Dachstein-Gebirge mts Austria
31 J6 Dačice Czechoslovakia
107 M5 Dacoma Oklahoma
128 G3 Dadanawa Guyana
79 H2 Dādāte Syria
78 D1 Daday Turkey
113 E9 Dade City Florida
111 L9 Dadeville Alabama
74 B4 Dadhar Pakistan
65 D7 Dadian China
65 G3 Dadianzi China
71 C3 Dadi, Tg C W Irian
68 J1 Dadong China
18 G9 Dadou R France
27 H11 Dådran Sweden
74 E8 Dadra & Nagar Haveli Union Terr India
74 G4 Dadri India
74 B5 Dadu Pakistan
68 H7 Da Dung R Vietnam
48 L6 Dăeni Romania
65 C4 Da'erhao China
140 D7 Daer,Mt N Terr Australia
71 F3 Daet Philippines
67 B3 Dafang China
80 F1 Dafna Israel
119 N7 Dafoe Sask
68 B4 Daga R Burma
86 H4 Dagabur Ethiopia
27 C11 Dagali Norway
85 A5 Dagana Senegal
47 K5 Dağardı Turkey
71 A1 Dagasuli Indonesia
30 D1 Dagebüll W Germany
9 G4 Dagenham England
53 G11 Dagestan A.S.S.R U.S.S.R.
102 H7 Daggett California
99 T4 Daggett Michigan
78 K5 Daghgharah, Al Iraq
27 G12 Daglösen Sweden
98 B1 Dagmar Montana
65 D5 Dagu China
67 A3 Daguan China
71 E2 Dagupan Luzon Philippines
94 J5 Dagus Mines Pennsylvania
68 C4 Dagwin Burma
141 G4 Dagworth Queensland
66 E6 Dagzê China
79 E10 Dahab Egypt
117 L4 Dahadinni R N W Terr
67 D5 Dahao Dao isld China
65 J1 Dahezhen China
59 H2 Da Hinggan Ling mt ra China
86 H2 Dahlak Arch Ethiopia
86 H2 Dahlak Kebir I Ethiopia
32 G10 Dahle W Germany
36 B3 Dahleim W Germany
33 R10 Dahlen E Germany
33 N6 Dahlenburg W Germany
33 S8 Dahlewitz E Germany
95 K8 Dahlgren Virginia
112 C3 Dahlonega Georgia
33 S9 Dahme E Germany
33 O4 Dahme W Germany
33 T8 Dahme R E Germany
33 R5 Dahmen E Germany
33 O4 Dahmeshöved W Germany
36 D5 Dahn W Germany
72 F3 Dahnā, Ad reg Saudi Arabia
78 J3 Dahok Iraq
Dahomey rep see Benin, Rep. of
66 B4 Dahongliutan China
65 E4 Dahongqi China
67 D1 Dahong Shan mts China
84 F4 Dahra Libya
33 N7 Dähre E Germany
78 J3 Dahuk Iraq
65 E4 Dahushan China
139 G5 Dahwilly New S Wales
71 O8 Dai isld Indonesia
48 K7 Daia Romania
65 C5 Daicheng China
65 B4 Dai Hai L China
68 C4 Daik-U Burma
75 J4 Dailekh Nepal
121 T3 Dailleboust, L Quebec
60 G9 Daimanji-san mt Japan
16 E5 Daimiel Spain
109 N2 Daingerfield Texas
61 K10 Dainichiga-take peak Japan
66 F5 Dainkog China
141 H3 Daintree Queensland
141 H3 Daintree R Queensland
61 K11 Daiō Japan
65 E2 Daiqin Tal China
126 G5 Daiquiri Cuba
Dairen see Lüda
84 J4 Dairût Egypt
100 D7 Dairy Oregon
60 G10 Daisen mt Japan
60 G10 Dai sen-Oki Nat. Park Japan
109 N5 Daisetta Texas
67 G1 Dai Shan isld China
129 K5 Dais Irmaos, Serra mts Brazil
100 G1 Daisy Washington
58 F4 Dai Xian China
Daiyue see Shanyin
67 F4 Daiyun Shan mts China
127 J5 Dajabón Dom Rep
140 E5 Dajarra Queensland
58 D5 Dajin Chuan R China
67 G2 Dajing China
45 P1 Dajla Yugoslavia
70 D5 Daju Kalimantan
85 A6 Dakar Senegal
67 D4 Dakengkou China
67 D5 Dakengkou China
68 H5 Dak Gle Vietnam
85 A4 Dakhla Mauritania
85 A4 Dakhla Western Sahara
84 H4 Dakhla Oasis Egypt
68 H5 Dak Kon Vietnam
69 A9 Dakoank Nicobar Is
85 F6 Dakoro Niger
99 R7 Dakota Illinois
99 P6 Dakota Minnesota
99 M7 Dakota City Iowa
98 K7 Dakota City Nebraska
46 D2 Dakovica Yugoslavia
48 E5 Dakovo Yugoslavia
28 D3 Dal Denmark
27 E11 Dal Norway
87 D8 Dala Angola
27 J11 Dalä L Sweden
41 L3 Dalaas Tal Austria
85 B6 Dalaba Guinea
65 A4 Dalad Qi China
Dalai see Da'an
Dalai Nor L see Hulun Nur
58 G3 Dalai Nur L China
65 C3 Dalai Nur L China
27 G11 Dala-Järna Sweden
78 B3 Dalaman R Turkey
58 D3 Dalandzadgad Mongolia
71 E5 Dalanganem islds Philippines
58 E2 Dalanjargalan Mongolia
27 K12 Dalarö Sweden
70 B3 Dalat Sarawak
68 J7 Da Lat Vietnam
71 C6 Dalawan B Philippines
77 J5 Dalbandin Pakistan
15 E6 Dalbeattie Scotland
27 F13 Dalbosjön L Sweden
28 F5 Dalby Denmark
12 D5 Dalby I of Man U.K.
141 K7 Dalby Queensland
27 F11 Dalby Sweden
28 E3 Dalbyneder Denmark
28 E3 Dalbyover Denmark
110 K3 Dale Indiana
27 A10 Dale Norway
27 A11 Dale Norway
100 G5 Dale Oregon
94 J6 Dale Pennsylvania
109 K6 Dale Texas
8 A4 Dale Wales
118 D8 Dalemead Alberta
143 B9 Dale,Mt W Australia
25 G3 Dalen Netherlands
28 B7 Daler Denmark
31 M5 Daleszyce Poland
68 A3 Dalet Burma
68 A2 Dalet R Burma
68 A2 Daletme Burma
110 L1 Daleville Indiana
27 H10 Dalfors Sweden
25 F4 Dalfsen Netherlands
143 B8 Dalgaranger,Mt W Australia
139 J6 Dalgety New S Wales
12 E1 Dalginross Scotland
141 F5 Dalgonally Queensland
108 B7 Dalhart Texas
114 G3 Dalhousie, C N W Terr
65 A7 Dali China
Dalian see Lüda
58 D6 Daliang Shan China
65 E5 Dalian Wan B China
71 G7 Daliao Philippines
106 D7 Dalies New Mexico
65 A6 Dali He R China
Dalinghe see Jin Xian
80 D3 Daliyat el Karmil Israel
65 G4 Dalizi China
48 E5 Dalj Yugoslavia
15 E5 Dalkeith Scotland
14 E3 Dalkey Irish Rep
141 K7 Dallarnil Queensland
111 M8 Dallas Georgia
119 U7 Dallas Manitoba
100 B5 Dallas Oregon
109 N10 Dallas Texas
99 P4 Dallas Wisconsin
99 N8 Dallas Center Iowa
99 P9 Dallas City Illinois
95 L7 Dallastown Pennsylvania
102 D4 Dallas Warner Res California
100 D4 Dalles, The Oregon
117 G8 Dall I Alaska
116 F6 Dall L Alaska
116 N3 Dall Mt Alaska
85 E6 Dallol Bosso watercourse Niger
77 C7 Dalmā isld U.A.E.
133 E4 Dalmacio Velez Sarsfield Argentina
12 D1 Dalmally Scotland
42 G4 Dalmatia reg Yugoslavia
55 D3 Dalmatovo U.S.S.R.
12 D3 Dalmellington Scotland
118 L6 Dalmeny Sask
28 G6 Dalmose Denmark
12 D2 Dalmuir Scotland
59 L3 Dal'negorsk U.S.S.R.
52 F6 Dal'ne-Konstantinovo U.S.S.R.
59 K2 Dal'nerechensk U.S.S.R.
52 E1 Dal'niye Zelentsy U.S.S.R.
85 C7 Daloa Ivory Coast
67 C5 Dalongdong Shuiku res China
67 B3 Dalou Shan mt ra China
121 M4 Dalquier Quebec
118 D7 Dalroy Alberta
15 D5 Dalry Dumfries & Galloway Scotland
15 D5 Dalry Strathclyde Scotland
141 H4 Dalrymple Queensland
15 D5 Dalrymple Scotland
141 J5 Dalrymple,Mt Queensland
29 K11 Dalsbruk Finland
13 F4 Dalston England
112 C3 Dalton Georgia
95 O4 Dalton Massachusetts
98 D8 Dalton Nebraska
120 F4 Dalton Ontario
95 M5 Dalton Pennsylvania
13 E3 Dalton Scotland
75 L6 Daltonganj India
146 G2 Dalton Iceberg Tongue Antarctica
115 R4 Dalton, Kap C Greenland
69 E12 Daludalu Sumatra
65 F5 Dalu Dao isld China
28 E6 Dalum Denmark
68 E2 Daluo China
65 H2 Daluolemi China
65 G1 Daluozhen China
71 G4 Dalupiri Philippines
71 E1 Dalupiri isld Philippines
141 K8 Dalveen Queensland
12 E3 Dalveen P Scotland
143 B9 Dalwallinu W Australia
15 D4 Dalwhinnie Scotland
36 F1 Dalwigksthal W Germany
136 G4 Daly R N Terr Australia
140 B2 Daly R N Terr Aust
140 B2 Daly River N Terr Aust
140 C3 Daly Waters N Terr Aust
98 D5 Dalzell S Dakota
74 E8 Daman India
79 A7 Damanhûr Egypt
65 C4 Damaqun Shan mt ra China
107 L2 Damar Kansas
71 B3 Damar isld Indonesia
71 O8 Damar isld Indonesia
86 C5 Damara Cent Afr Republic
89 A4 Damaraland reg Namibia
95 S2 Damariscotta L Maine
Damas see Damascus
110 D6 Damascus Arkansas
95 K7 Damascus Maryland
79 G5 Damascus Syria
94 F10 Damascus Virginia
131 B5 Damas, Paso de las Chile/Arg
86 B3 Damaturu Nigeria
77 C2 Damavand Iran
87 C7 Damba Angola
36 C7 Dambach France
83 K10 Dambulla Sri Lanka
68 J4 Dam Cau Hai Vietnam
126 G5 Dame Marie Haiti
77 D1 Dāmghān Iran
28 A4 Damhus Å R Denmark
65 D3 Damiao China
48 L4 Dămieneşti Romania
20 F5 Damigni France
65 C6 Daming China
67 C5 Daming Shan mts China
80 F5 Damiya Jordan
80 F5 Damiya Br Jordan
71 E8 Dammai isld Philippines
77 B6 Dammam, Ad Saudi Arabia
20 J5 Dammarie France
18 G3 Dammartin-en-Goële France
22 E1 Damme Belgium
32 H7 Damme W Germany
74 H7 Damoh India
109 M6 Damon Texas
85 D7 Damongo Ghana
86 A2 Damot Ethiopia
79 F5 Damour Lebanon
70 F4 Dampelas, Tg C Celebes
22 K4 Dampicourt Belgium
142 B5 Dampier W Australia
142 B5 Dampier Arch W Australia
142 E3 Dampier Land pen W Australia
40 C2 Dampierre-sur-Saône France
71 C3 Dampier, Selat str W Irian
70 O10 Dampit Java
28 J7 Damsholte Denmark
19 J3 Damvillars France
20 H4 Damville France

Dâmvillers — Devli 21

22 J5 Dâmvillers France
112 H1 Dan R N Carolina
94 J10 Dan R Virginia
99 S9 Dana Illinois
110 J2 Dana Indiana
79 F8 Danā Jordan
119 M6 Dana Sask
71 K10 Dana isld Indonesia
69 F12 Danai Sumatra
86 H3 Danakil tribal dist Ethiopia
86 H4 Danan Ethiopia
85 C7 Danané Ivory Coast
68 J4 Da Nang Vietnam
75 L6 Danapur India
116 G9 Dana Vol Alaska
58 D5 Danba China
95 O5 Danbury Connecticut
98 F9 Danbury Nebraska
95 Q3 Danbury New Hampshire
109 M6 Danbury Texas
99 O4 Danbury Wisconsin
103 J7 Danby California
103 J7 Danby L California
119 T6 Dancing Point Manitoba
143 B9 Dandaragan W Australia
74 J4 Dandel Dhura Nepal
76 B3 Dandeli India
139 H7 Dandenong Victoria
59 H3 Dandong China
74 E2 Dandot Pakistan
121 Q5 Dandurand, L Quebec
99 R6 Dane Wisconsin
147 E10 Daneborg Greenland
109 L6 Danevang Texas
65 A8 Danfeng China
67 E6 Dangan Liedao isld China
57 E5 Dangara U.S.S.R.
65 J2 Dangbizhen China
Dangcheng see Xiangshan
21 G8 Dangé France
20 H5 Dangeau France
89 A10 Danger Pt S Africa
20 F5 Dangeul France
66 F4 Dang He R China
86 G3 Dangila Ethiopia
68 G5 Dangrek, Chaîne des mts Cambodia
65 C7 Dangshan China
67 F1 Dangtu China
70 J3 Dangu France
67 D1 Dangyang China
68 J7 Da Nhim R Vietnam
113 G11 Dania Florida
101 P7 Daniel Wyoming
42 E2 Daniele del Friuli, S Italy
122 D3 Daniel-Johnston Dam Quebec
143 D10 Daniell W Australia
144 D5 Daniells, L New Zealand
123 P3 Daniel's Cove Nfld
115 O7 Daniels Har Nfld
118 J1 Daniels L Ontario
95 Q5 Danielson Connecticut
112 D3 Danielsville Georgia
52 F5 Danilov U.S.S.R.
42 J6 Danilov Grad Yugoslavia
55 J3 Danilovka U.S.S.R.
55 F4 Danilovka U.S.S.R.
52 E3 Danilovo U.S.S.R.
58 F4 Daning China
67 C1 Daningchang China
Danjiang see Leishan
68 J6 Dankia Vietnam
67 A1 Danleng China
85 F6 Danmarks Har Ø isld
98 H8 Dannebrog Nebraska
115 Q4 Dannebrogs Ø isld Greenland
28 G7 Dannemare Denmark
95 O2 Dannemora New York
27 J11 Dannemora Sweden
33 O6 Dannenberg W Germany
33 S6 Dannenwalde E Germany
100 H7 Danner Oregon
145 F4 Dannevirke New Zealand
70 D4 Danompari Kalimantan
68 E4 Dan Sai Thailand
144 C6 Danseys Pass New Zealand
67 E5 Danshui China
68 B4 Danson B Burma
94 C4 Dansville Michigan
94 K4 Dansville New York
86 B1 Dante Somalia
94 E10 Dante Virginia
76 E1 Dantewara India
Dantu see Zhenjiang
Danube R Bulgaria/Yugoslavia see Dunav R
Danube R Czechoslovakia see Dunaj R
Danube R Hungary see Duna R
Danube R Romania see Dunărea R
Danube R W Germany/Austria see Donau R
68 B4 Danubyu Burma
110 G1 Danvers Illinois
99 L4 Danvers Minnesota
101 Q2 Danvers Montana
110 C5 Danville Arkansas
112 D5 Danville Georgia
99 T9 Danville Illinois
110 K2 Danville Indiana
95 R2 Danville Maine
94 E6 Danville Ohio
95 L6 Danville Pennsylvania
121 S7 Danville Quebec
95 P2 Danville Vermont
94 H10 Danville Virginia
94 F8 Danville W Virginia
20 D4 Danvou France
67 C7 Dan Xian China
67 F1 Danyang China
21 H6 Danzé France
67 B3 Danzhai China
67 C5 Danzhu China
Danzig see Gdańsk
98 G3 Danzig N Dakota
Danzig, G. of see Gdańska, Zatoka
71 E5 Dao Panay Philippines
16 B4 Dão R Portugal
67 B6 Dao Bach Long Vi isld Vietnam
Daokou see Hua Xian
21 D6 Daon France
74 G5 Daosa India
Daoud see Aïn Beïda
18 C4 Daoulas France
85 D3 Daoura watercourse Algeria/Morocco
67 D4 Dao Xian China
67 B2 Daozhen China
71 G6 Dapa Philippines
85 E6 Dapango Togo
111 J11 Daphne Alabama
71 F6 Dapiak, Mt Philippines
65 E4 Dapingfang China
71 F6 Dapitan Philippines
74 E10 Dapoli India
118 D4 Dapp Alberta
66 F4 Da Qaidam China
65 E5 Daqin Dao isld China
65 A4 Daqing Shan mt ra China
65 B4 Daqing Shan mts China
Daqin Tal see Naiman Qi
67 G1 Daqu Shan isld China
85 A5 Dara Senegal
79 D5 Darab Iran
48 K2 Dărăbani Romania
71 F5 Daraga Philippines
85 F2 Daraj Libya
71 G5 Daram isld Philippines
77 B3 Daran Iran
48 D5 Darány Hungary
70 C5 Darap Kalimantan
46 D2 Daravice mt Yugoslavia
85 G6 Darazo Nigeria
52 B6 Darbėnai U.S.S.R.
101 L3 Darby Montana
116 F4 Darby C Alaska
116 F4 Darby Mts Alaska
33 N6 Darchau E Germany
142 E3 D'Arcole Is W Australia
117 M10 D'Arcy Br Col
118 J7 D'Arcy Sask
110 C6 Dardanelle Arkansas
102 E3 Dardanelle California
Dardanelles Turkey see Çanakkale Boğazi
33 N9 Dardesheim E Germany
141 J8 Dareel Town Queensland
Dar el Beida see Casablanca
86 D4 Dar-el-Kouti dist Cent Afr Republic
88 G5 Dar es Salaam Tanzania
144 D5 Darfield New Zealand
Darfur prov Sudan see Northern and Southern Darfur provs
74 D1 Dargai Pakistan
57 B4 Darganata U.S.S.R.
145 D1 Dargaville New Zealand
20 J1 Dargnies France
139 H6 Dargo Victoria
33 R5 Dargun E Germany
58 E2 Darhan Mongolia
59 F3 Darhan Muminggan Lianheqi China
112 F6 Darien Georgia
126 F10 Darién, G.del Colombia/Panama
125 Q5 Darién, Serranía del ra Panama
71 E2 Darigayos Pt Luzon Philippines
125 L3 Darío Nicaragua
66 D6 Darjeeling India
143 B10 Darkan W Australia
138 D5 Darke Peak S Australia
77 A4 Darkhazineh Iran
138 F5 Darling R S Australia
139 J3 Darling Downs Queensland
141 J8 Darling Downs reg Queensland
119 T9 Darlingford Manitoba
115 M1 Darling Pen N W Terr
13 G5 Darlington England
101 M6 Darlington Idaho
99 M9 Darlington Missouri
112 H3 Darlington S Carolina
99 Q7 Darlington Wisconsin
139 H5 Darlington Pt New S Wales
143 D8 Darlot, L W Australia
31 J1 Darłowo Poland
48 K3 Dărmăneşti Romania
77 F3 Darmian Iran
118 L8 Darmody Sask
36 F4 Darmstadt W Germany
84 G3 Darnah Libya
111 E9 Darnell Louisiana
20 H3 Darnétal France
139 G5 Darnick New S Wales
114 G4 Darnley B N W Terr
146 B4 Darnley, C Antarctica
17 G3 Daroda Spain
48 J1 Darokhov U.S.S.R.
52 G5 Darovskoye U.S.S.R.
141 G6 Darr Queensland
141 G6 Darr R Queensland
141 K2 Darra sub Brisbane, Qnsld
77 F1 Darreh Gaz Iran
100 D1 Darrington Washington
86 A1 Darror R Somalia
86 D4 Dar Rounga reg Cent Afr Republic
108 D7 Darrouzett Texas
76 D3 Darsi India
30 G1 Darsser Ort C E Germany
146 J10 Dart, C Antarctica
9 G5 Dartford England
138 F7 Dartmoor Victoria
8 C6 Dartmoor Forest England
8 C7 Dartmouth England
122 J9 Dartmouth Nova Scotia
141 H7 Dartmouth L Queensland
122 H4 Dartmouth R Quebec
8 C4 Dart, R England
14 C2 Dartry Mts Irish Rep
136 J3 Daru Papua New Guinea
66 E5 Darum Tso L China
42 H3 Daruvar Yugoslavia
15 D5 Darvel Scotland
70 F2 Darvel B Sabah
58 B2 Darvi Mongolia
13 F6 Darwen England
77 L4 Darweshan Afghanistan
102 G5 Darwin California
140 B1 Darwin N Terr Aust
88 C10 Darwin Zimbabwe
133 C7 Darwin, Can str Chile
77 G4 Daryacheh L Iran
57 D4 Dar'yegan R U.S.S.R.
77 C7 Das isld U.A.E.
22 L3 Dasburg W Germany
67 C1 Dashennongjia mt China
65 A4 Dashetai China
Dashiqiao see Yingkou
Dashizhai China
65 E1 Dasht Iran
77 H7 Dasht R Pakistan
77 C2 Dasht-e-Kavir Iran
77 G7 Dashtiari Iran
65 C3 Dashui Nur China
120 J9 Dashwood Ontario
37 L7 Dasing W Germany
71 E7 Dassalan isld Philippines
99 M4 Dassel Minnesota
32 L9 Dassel W Germany
33 N5 Dassow E Germany
77 E2 Dastgardān Iran
70 D4 Datagenojang Kalimantan
65 C4 Datan China
66 C4 Datang China
47 J8 Datça Turkey
9 F5 Datchet England
60 J11 Date Japan
103 O7 Date Cr Arizona
103 L9 Dateland Arizona
74 H6 Datia India
67 F4 Datian China
106 C7 Datil New Mexico
67 F1 Datong Anhui China
67 F1 Datong Heilongjiang China
65 B4 Datong Shanxi China
58 C4 Datong Shan mt ra China
140 F6 Datson,Mt Queensland
59 M2 Datta U.S.S.R.
36 D2 Datteln W Germany
70 E3 Datumakuta Kalimantan
65 J2 Dabikhe R U.S.S.R.
74 D2 Daud Khel India
32 K7 Dauelsen W Germany
115 N1 Daugaard Jensen Land Greenland
28 D5 Daugård Denmark
52 C6 Daugav'pils U.S.S.R.
77 K1 Daulatabad Afghanistan
74 F9 Daulatabad India
77 J2 Daulat Yar Afghanistan
128 C4 Daule Ecuador
41 M3 Daumen mt W Germany
21 E6 Daumeray France
36 B3 Daun W Germany
68 C6 Daung Kyun isld Burma
119 R7 Dauphin Manitoba
95 L6 Dauphin Pennsylvania
19 O14 Dauphiné prov France
111 H11 Dauphin I Alabama
119 S7 Dauphin L Manitoba
85 F6 Daura Nigeria
15 E3 Dava Scotland
76 B3 Davangere India
71 G7 Davao Mindanao Philippines
71 G7 Davao Gulf Mindanao Philippines
12 C3 Davarr I Scotland
147 F10 Dave isld Greenland
121 S6 Daveluyville Quebec
22 D4 Davenescourt France
121 M4 Davengus Quebec
116 J5 Davenport Alaska
102 B4 Davenport California
113 F9 Davenport Florida
99 Q8 Davenport Iowa
98 J9 Davenport Nebraska
95 N4 Davenport New York
107 O6 Davenport Oklahoma
100 G2 Davenport Washington
141 F6 Davenport Downs Queensland
140 A6 Davenport Hills N Terr Aust
140 B5 Davenport,Mt N Terr Aust
140 C5 Davenport Ra N Terr Aust
9 E3 Daventry England
80 E3 Daverat Israel
32 K7 Daverden W Germany
125 N5 David Panama
146 E2 David isld Antarctica
116 J8 David City Nebraska
112 G2 Davidson N Carolina
107 L7 Davidson Oklahoma
119 M7 Davidson Sask
140 B5 Davidson,Mt N Terr Aust
116 Q2 Davidson Mts Alaska
8 B6 Davidstow England
113 G11 Davie Florida
138 A2 Davies, Mt S Australia
26 A10 Davik Norway
109 K5 Davilla Texas
119 N8 Davin Sask
102 C3 Davis California
99 R7 Davis Illinois
107 N7 Davis Oklahoma
119 M5 Davis Sask
98 K6 Davis S Dakota
94 H7 Davis W Virginia
146 H3 Davis B Antarctica
112 E5 Davisboro Georgia
99 N9 Davis City Iowa
100 E8 Davis Creek California
103 K6 Davis Dam Arizona
115 N6 Davis Inlet Labrador
94 H7 Davis, Mt Pennsylvania
108 C5 Davis Mts Texas
94 D3 Davison Michigan
146 D3 Davis Sea Antarctica
115 O4 Davis Str Greenland/Canada
110 E4 Davisville Missouri
55 C4 Davlekanovo U.S.S.R.
41 L4 Davos Switzerland
94 F9 Davy W Virginia
143 D9 Davyhurst W Australia
65 E4 Dawa China
67 F3 Dawa China
86 H5 Dawa R Ethiopia
65 C6 Dawenkou China
141 K6 Dawes Ra Queensland
68 D4 Dawlan Burma
8 C6 Dawlish England
110 C2 Dawn Missouri
108 E1 Dawn Texas
68 C4 Dawna Ra Burma
111 M10 Dawson Georgia
98 K5 Dawson Minnesota
98 G3 Dawson N Dakota
106 F5 Dawson New Mexico
107 P5 Dawson Oklahoma
109 L4 Dawson Texas
117 D3 Dawson Yukon Terr
141 J6 Dawson R Queensland
119 R6 Dawson Bay Manitoba
117 N8 Dawson Creek Br Columbia
114 H5 Dawson Landing N W Terr
117 O5 Dawson Lodge N W Terr
117 P10 Dawson, Mt Br Columbia
117 D4 Dawson Range Yukon Terr
110 J4 Dawson Springs Kentucky
111 M7 Dawsonville Georgia
67 E1 Dawu China
18 E9 Dax France
67 B1 Da Xian China
68 H1 Daxin China
65 D6 Daxindian China
65 C5 Daxing China
59 J3 Daxinggou China
36 E5 Daxlanden W Germany
67 A3 Daxu China
67 C5 Daxuan China
Daxue see Wencheng
58 D4 Daxue Shan mt ra China
58 D5 Daxue Shan mt China
67 F3 Daxu Shan pass China
100 D8 Day California
113 D7 Day Florida
57 B4 Dayakhatyn U.S.S.R.
67 E5 Dayang He R China
67 C5 Dayao Shan mts China
67 E8 Daye Wan B China
65 E4 Day Dawn W Australia
67 E1 Daye China
65 E1 Dayi China
67 A1 Dayi China
67 B4 Dayi China
Dayishan see Guanyun
139 G6 Daylesford Victoria
102 G5 Daylight Pass California
99 L3 Dayman R Uruguay
98 F9 Dayman, Cuchilla del mts Uruguay
131 F3 Day, Mt W Australia
143 D9 Dayong China
67 C2 Days Creek Oregon
100 B7 Daysland Alberta
118 E6 Dayton Iowa
99 M7 Dayton New York
94 J4 Dayton Ohio
94 C7 Dayton Pennsylvania
94 H6 Dayton Tennessee
112 B2 Dayton Texas
109 N5 Dayton Washington
100 H3 Dayton Wyoming
101 S5 Daytona Beach Florida
113 F8 Dayu China
67 E4 Dayu Ling mt China
67 E4 Dayville Oregon
100 F5 Dazey N Dakota
98 H2 Dazhang Xi R China
67 F4 Dazhu China
67 B1 Dazu China
67 B2 De Aar S Africa
89 D8 Dead R Michigan
99 T3 Deadhorse Alaska
116 N1 Dead Indian Pk Wyoming
101 O5 Deadman L California
111 L11 Deadmans B Florida
103 H7 Deadman's Cay Long I Bahamas
113 D8 Dead Mts Cal/Nev
126 G3 Dead Sea Israel/Jordan
103 K6 Deadwater L Maine
80 E8 Deadwood S Dakota
95 R8 Deadwood Res Idaho
98 C5 Deaf Adder Cr N Terr Aust
100 K5 Deakin W Australia
140 C2 Deakin,Mt N Terr Aust
143 G9 Deal England
140 B4 Deal I Tasmania
9 H5 Deale Maryland
95 L8 Deal Island Maryland
139 H7 De'an China
95 M8 Dean Iowa
67 E2 Dean Ch Br Columbia
110 D1 Dean, Forest of England
117 K9 Deane,Mt Queensland
141 H5 Deán Funes Argentina
8 D4 Dean,Mt W Australia
131 D3 Dean R Br Columbia
143 E10 Deansboro New York
117 L9 Dearborn Michigan
95 M4 Dearborn Missouri
94 D4 Dearing Kansas
110 B2 Deary Idaho
107 P4 Dease Arm B N W Terr
100 J3 Dease Inlet Alaska
114 G4 Dease Lake Br Col
116 K1 Dease Str N W Terr
116 J6 Death Valley California
102 G5 Deauville France
20 F3 Debak Sarawak
101 R5 Debal'tsevo U.S.S.R.
70 B4 Debao China
54 K8 Debar Yugoslavia
67 B5 Debauch Mt Alaska
46 D3 Debba, El Sudan
116 H4 Debden Sask
84 J6 Debden Sask
118 L5 Debden Sask
127 O3 Débé Trinidad
122 E7 Debec New Brunswick
9 H3 Debenham England
9 H3 Deben, R England
106 B2 De Beque Colorado
109 N3 De Berry Texas
52 H5 Debessy U.S.S.R.
31 N5 Dębica Poland
31 N4 Dęblin Poland
31 K1 Dębnica Kaszubska Poland
31 H3 Dębno Poland
85 D5 Débo, L Mali
143 C9 Deborah,L W Australia
116 O5 Deborah, Mt Alaska
142 F3 Deborah,Mt W Australia
100 K2 De Borgia Montana
86 G4 Debra Birhan Ethiopia
86 G3 Debra Markos Ethiopia
86 G3 Debra Tabor Ethiopia
48 F6 Debrc Yugoslavia
48 G3 Debrecen Hungary
71 E2 Debutunan Pt Luzon Philippines
86 G2 Decamere Ethiopia
46 D2 Dečani Yugoslavia
111 K7 Decatur Alabama
110 B5 Decatur Arkansas
112 C3 Decatur Georgia
111 M8 Decatur Illinois
99 S10 Decatur Illinois
110 H2 Decatur Indiana
94 C6 Decatur Iowa
99 N9 Decatur Michigan
94 B4 Decatur Mississippi
111 G9 Decatur Nebraska
98 K7 Decatur Texas
109 K2 Decaturville Tennessee
110 H6 Decazeville France
18 G8 Deccan plat India
76 C2 Decelles, Lac Quebec
121 M5 Déception Quebec
115 M5 Deception watercourse Botswana
89 C3 Dechen Dzong see Dagzê
122 E2 Dechêne, L Quebec
110 K6 Decherd Tennessee
22 E3 Dechy France
118 F1 Decimal Manitoba
43 B9 Decimomannu Sardinia
31 H5 Děčín Czechoslovakia
117 F7 Decision, C Alaska
18 H6 Decize France
110 J3 Decker Indiana
119 R8 Decker Manitoba
101 T4 Decker Montana
106 E2 Deckers Colorado
25 C2 De Cocksdorp Netherlands
140 C1 De Courcy Hd N Terr Aust
48 E4 Decs Hungary
48 J4 Deda Romania
9 E4 Deddington England
Dedeagach see Alexandroúpolis
33 N8 Dedeleben E Germany
33 T6 Dedelow E Germany
33 M8 Dedham Iowa
46 E3 Dedino Yugoslavia
130 F9 Dedo de Deus mt Brazil
85 D6 Dédougou Upper Volta
52 C6 Dedovichi U.S.S.R.
100 B9 Dedrick California
83 J10 Deduru Oya R Sri Lanka
56 E1 Deduśhka, Porog falls U.S.S.R.
88 E9 Dedza Malawi
15 F3 Dee R Scotland
141 K6 Deeford Queensland
14 C4 Deel R Irish Rep
112 H2 Deep R N Carolina
Deep Bay Malawi see Chilumba
122 G9 Deep Brook Nova Scotia
100 J7 Deep Cr Idaho
94 H7 Deep Creek L Maryland
103 L2 Deep Creek Ra Utah
142 B5 Deepdale Western Australia
107 O6 Deep Fork R Oklahoma
112 F1 Deep Gap N Carolina
95 P5 Deep River Connecticut
99 O8 Deep River Iowa
121 N6 Deep River Ontario
100 B3 Deep River Washington
102 G4 Deep Sp California
110 C3 Deepwater Missouri
139 K3 Deepwater New S Wales Australia
140 C6 Deep Well N Terr Aust
110 C6 Deer Arkansas
8 C1 Dee, R England/Wales
12 E4 Dee, R Scotland
100 D9 Deer Cr California
99 L3 Deer Cr Minnesota
98 F9 Deer Cr Nebraska
98 F9 Deer Cr Wyoming
101 T7 Deer Creek Oklahoma
107 N5 Deer Cr.Res Utah
103 N1 Deerfield Kansas
107 J3 Deerfield Beach Florida
113 G11 Deer I Alaska
116 F9 Deer I Maine
95 T2 Deer I New Brunswick
122 F9 Deering Alaska
116 F3 Deering N Dakota
98 E1 Deering Hills S Australia
138 A2 Deering,Mt W Australia
143 G7 Deer Lake Nfld
123 P4 Deerlijk Belgium
22 E2 Deer Lodge Montana
101 N3 Deer Park Alabama
111 H10 Deer Park Washington
100 H2 Deer Pk Br Columbia
117 O11 Deer Pond Nfld
123 S5 Deer River Minnesota
99 N2 Deerton Michigan
99 T3 Deer Trail Colorado
106 F2 Deerwood Minnesota
99 N3 Deeson Mississippi
111 F7 Deeth Nevada
100 K8 Defeng see Liping
38 F8 Defereggengeb mt Austria
38 F8 Defereggental V Austria
95 M2 Deferiet New York
133 F5 Defferrari Argentina
99 L8 Defiance Iowa
94 C5 Defiance Ohio
95 O5 De Funiak Springs Florida
111 K11 Degebe R Portugal
16 B6 Degema Nigeria
85 F8 Degerfors Sweden
27 G12 Deggendorf W Germany
37 O6 Deggingen W Germany
36 H6 Degimendere Turkey
47 J6 De Graff Minnesota
99 L4 Degraff Ohio
94 D6 De Gray Res Arkansas
111 C7 De Grey S Dakota
98 G5 De Grey W Australia
142 C5 De Grey R W Australia
142 D5 Degtyarsk U.S.S.R.
55 D3 De Haan Belgium
22 E1 Deh Bid Iran
77 C4 Dehej India
74 E8 Dehibat Tunisia
84 E3 Dehra Dun India
74 H3 Dehri India
75 L6 Dehrn W Germany
36 E3 Deh Salm Iran
77 F4 Dehua China
67 F4 Dehui China
59 J3 Deidesheim W Germany
36 E5 Deim Zubeir Sudan
86 E4 Deining W Germany
37 M5 Deinum Netherlands
25 E2 Deinze Belgium
22 F2 Deir el Ahmar Lebanon
79 G4 Deir es Samadiya Jordan
80 G4 Deir Istiya Jordan
80 D5 Deir Mar Jiryis Jordan
80 E7 Deir Sharaf Jordan
80 D4 Deir Shemil Syria
79 G3 Deister hills W Germany
32 K8 Deja Romania
48 G5 Deja mt Albania
46 D3 Deja mt Albania
71 B2 Dejailolo, Selat str Indonesia
28 A5 Dejbjerg Denmark
27 F12 Deje Sweden
86 G3 Dejen Ethiopia
67 C2 Dejiang China
95 S8 De Kalb Illinois
111 H9 De Kalb Mississippi
109 N2 De Kalb Texas
95 M2 De Kalb Junc New York
51 O3 De Kastri U.S.S.R.
59 M1 De Kastries U.S.S.R.
86 D6 Dekese Zaïre
86 C4 Dekoa Cent Afr Republic
25 C2 De Koog Netherlands
25 C3 De Kooij Netherlands
111 G12 Delacroix Louisiana
106 F4 Delagua Colorado
100 J6 Delamar Idaho
103 K4 Delamar Mts Nevada
140 B3 Delamere N Terr Aust
113 F8 De Land Florida
102 E6 Delano California
103 M3 Delano Peak Utah
113 L9 Delaport New Providence I Bahamas
118 K4 Delaronde L Sask
110 G1 Delavan Illinois
99 S7 Delavan Wisconsin
94 D6 Delaware Ohio
107 P5 Delaware Oklahoma
107 P2 Delaware R Kansas
95 N5 Delaware R U.S.A.
95 M7 Delaware state U.S.A.
145 D4 Delaware B New Zealand
95 M7 Delaware B U.S.A.
95 M7 Delaware City Delaware
108 C4 Delaware Cr Texas/New Mex
94 D6 Delaware Res Ohio
118 E9 Del Bonita Alberta
32 J9 Delbrück W Germany
118 D6 Delburne Alberta
111 E12 Delcambre Louisiana
106 F4 Delcarbon Colorado
46 F3 Delčevo Yugoslavia
87 E8 Delcommune, L Zaïre
25 G4 Delden Netherlands
119 R9 Deleau Manitoba
139 J6 Delegate New S Wales
25 F2 De Leien Netherlands
40 F3 Delémont Switzerland
109 J3 De Leon Texas
29 H11 Delet Teili chan Finland
22 C2 Delettes France
102 B2 Delevan California
94 J4 Delevan New York
130 F7 Delfinópolis Brazil
25 B5 Delfshaven Netherlands
25 B4 Delft Netherlands
83 J8 Delft isld Sri Lanka
25 G2 Delfzijl Netherlands
100 A3 Delgada, Pt California
133 E6 Delgada, Pta Argentina
88 H7 Delgado, C Mozambique
58 D2 Delgerhaan Mongolia
86 F1 Delgo Sudan
74 G4 Delhi India
99 P7 Delhi Iowa
111 E9 Delhi Louisiana
107 L6 Delhi Oklahoma
120 K10 Delhi Ontario
70 K9 Deli isld Java
118 E7 Delia Alberta
107 P3 Delia Kansas
129 H3 Delices Fr Guiana
109 O1 Delight Arkansas
77 B3 Delijan Iran
46 E1 Deli Jovan mt Yugoslavia
118 K7 Delisle Sask
140 B2 Delissaville N Terr Aust
143 F8 Delisser Ra W Australia
69 D11 Delitua Sumatra
33 Q9 Delitzsch E Germany
110 F6 Dell Arkansas
101 N5 Dell Montana
36 C2 Dellbrück W Germany
40 E2 Delle France
101 N9 Delle Utah
103 L5 Dellenbaugh, Mt Arizona
26 J10 Dellen, N L Sweden
100 B9 Dell Lona California
98 K6 Dell Rapids S Dakota
107 L2 Dellvale Kansas
102 G9 Del Mar California
99 O7 Delmar Iowa
95 M8 Delmar Maryland
118 J6 Delmas Sask
32 J6 Delmenhorst W Germany
130 H10 Delmiro Gouveia Brazil
98 H6 Delmont S Dakota
103 K6 Delmues Nevada
42 F3 Delnice Yugoslavia
106 D4 Del Norte Colorado
140 C6 Delny N Terr Aust
116 F2 De Long Mts Alaska
119 R9 Deloraine Manitoba
139 H8 Deloraine Tasmania
13 F6 Delph England
46 E6 Delphi Greece
110 K1 Delphi Indiana
107 N2 Delphos Kansas
94 C6 Delphos Ohio
113 G11 Delray Beach Florida
124 D2 Del Rio Mexico
108 G6 Del Rio Texas
26 J10 Delsbo Sweden
106 B3 Delta Colorado
103 M3 Delta Missouri
110 G4 Delta Ohio
94 C5 Delta Pennsylvania
95 L7 Delta Utah
103 M2 Delta Beach Manitoba
119 T8 Delta Downs Queensland
141 F3 Delta Junction Alaska
116 O4 Delta Mendota Canal California
102 C4 Delta Res New York
95 M3 Deltaville Virginia
95 L9 Delton Michigan
94 B4 Delungra New S Wales
139 K3 Delvada India
74 D8 Del Valle Texas
109 K5 Delve W Germany
32 K4 Delvinákion Greece
46 D5 Delvinë Albania
46 D5 Delyatin U.S.S.R.
48 J2 Dema R U.S.S.R.
55 B4 Demanda, S. de la mts Spain
118 K8 Demaine Sask
70 N9 Demak Java
16 E2 Demarcation Pt Alaska
116 R2 Dembia Zaïre
86 D7 Dembia Cent Afr Republic
86 D4 Dembi Dolo Ethiopia
86 F4 Demchok India
74 H2 Demecser Hungary
48 G2 Demer R Belgium
22 J2 Demerara see Georgetown Guyana
54 C1 Demidov U.S.S.R.
55 D3 Demina U.S.S.R.
106 C9 Deming New Mexico
100 C1 Deming Washington
128 F3 Demini R Brazil
47 K5 Demirci Turkey
47 J6 Demirköprü Baraji L Turkey
47 J3 Demirköy Turkey
33 S5 Demmin E Germany
128 F5 Democracia Brazil
111 J9 Demopolis Alabama
143 E10 Dempster, Pt W Australia
50 G3 Dem'yanka R U.S.S.R.
55 F1 Dem'yanskaya U.S.S.R.
50 F3 Dem'yanskoye U.S.S.R.
22 E3 Denain France
116 O5 Denali Alaska
114 J7 Denare Beach Saskatchewan
57 E5 Denau U.S.S.R.
121 N7 Denbigh Ontario
8 C1 Denbigh Wales
Denbigh co see Clwyd and Gwynedd counties
116 G4 Denbigh, C Alaska
25 B5 Den Bommel Netherlands
25 C2 Den Burg Netherlands
68 E4 Den Chai Thailand
69 J14 Dendang Indonesia
22 G2 Dender R Belgium
22 G2 Denderleeuw Belgium
22 G1 Dendermonde Belgium
25 D3 Den Dever Netherlands
86 G4 Dendi mt Ethiopia
118 K8 Dendron Sask
25 H4 Denekamp Netherlands
55 C1 Denezhkin Kamen', G mt U.S.S.R.
65 B7 Dengfeng China
58 E3 Dengkou China
75 Q3 Dêngqên China
58 F5 Deng Xian China
65 C4 Dengyoufang China
65 E6 Dengzhou China
24 A2 Den Haag conurbation Netherlands
9 F4 Denham England
143 A7 Denham W Australia
142 G3 Denham R W Australia
140 E3 Denham I Queensland
141 J5 Denham Ra Queensland
143 A7 Denham Sd W Australia
111 F11 Denham Springs Louisiana
25 C3 Den Helder Netherlands
118 K6 Denholm Sask
13 F3 Denholm Scotland
17 G7 Denia Spain
138 C4 Denial Bay S Australia
122 C6 Deniau Quebec
139 G6 Deniliquin New S Wales
100 G7 Denio Oregon
99 L7 Denison Iowa
109 L2 Denison Texas
146 J3 Denison, C Antarctica
107 O8 Denison Dam Oklahoma
116 K7 Denison, Mt Alaska
142 G4 Denison Plains W Australia
141 J4 Denison Pt Queensland
55 D4 Denisovka Kazakhstan U.S.S.R.
52 J2 Denisovka Komi U.S.S.R.
83 K11 Deniyaya Sri Lanka
47 K7 Denizli Turkey
37 L6 Denkendorf W Germany
139 K4 Denman New S Wales
146 E3 Denman Gl Antarctica
122 J8 Denmark Nova Scotia
100 A7 Denmark Oregon
112 F4 Denmark S Carolina
143 B10 Denmark W Australia
99 T5 Denmark Wisconsin
28 Denmark kingdom N W Europe
115 R4 Denmark Str Greenland/Iceland
20 B3 Denneville France
33 S9 Dennewitz E Germany
83 J12 Dennis I Seychelles
94 F6 Dennison Ohio
95 R5 Dennis Port Massachusetts
144 C4 Denniston New Zealand
94 H10 Denniston Virginia
100 B9 Denny California
12 E1 Denny Scotland
12 E2 Dennyloanhead Scotland
95 U2 Dennysville Maine
70 P10 Denpasar Bali Indonesia
13 F5 Dent England
100 J3 Dent Idaho
48 G5 Denta Romania
40 G5 Dent Blanche mt Switzerland
40 E5 Dent du Midi mt Switzerland
9 H5 Denton England
112 E6 Denton Georgia
110 H4 Denton Kentucky
95 M8 Denton Maryland
109 K2 Denton Texas
137 L3 D'Entrecasteaux Is Papua New Guinea
106 E2 Denver Colorado
100 J6 Denver Idaho
94 A6 Denver Indiana
99 O7 Denver Iowa
95 L6 Denver Pennsylvania
108 E3 Denver City Texas
118 H6 Denzil Sask
86 B4 Deo R Cameroon
74 G4 Deoband India
75 M6 Deogarh India
68 J4 Deo Hai Van Vietnam
74 E9 Deolali India
68 J6 Deo Ma Vietnam
22 D1 De Panne Belgium
25 E6 De Peel Netherlands
99 S5 De Pere Wisconsin
94 J4 Depew New York
107 O6 Depew Oklahoma
65 C6 Deping China
66 C6 Deping China
22 F2 De Pinte Belgium
71 F9 Depok Java
109 K2 Deport Texas
109 M2 Deposit New York
128 F3 Depósito Brazil
95 Q3 Depot New Hampshire
120 K7 Depot Harbour Ontario
146 B5 Depot Pk Antarctica
86 D2 Depression du Murdi Chad
9 E5 Deptford England
142 C5 Depuch I W Australia
99 R8 Depue Illinois
25 E5 De Punt Netherlands
51 Q2 Deputatskiy U.S.S.R.
58 C6 Dêqên China
67 D5 Deqing China
67 G1 Deqing China
111 B7 De Queen Arkansas
111 C11 De Quincy Louisiana
77 L5 Dera Bugti Pakistan
74 D3 Dera Ghazi Khan Pakistan
74 D3 Dera Ismail Khan Pakistan
55 D4 Derazhnya U.S.S.R.
33 Q8 Derben E Germany
78 M1 Derbent U.S.S.R.
48 N1 Derbeshkinskiy U.S.S.R.
86 D4 Derbisaka Cent Afr Republic
95 O5 Derby Connecticut
9 E2 Derby England
99 N9 Derby Iowa
107 N4 Derby Kansas
139 J8 Derby Tasmania
109 H7 Derby Texas
142 E3 Derby W Australia
95 P2 Derby Center Vermont
9 E1 Derbyshire co England
16 D9 Derdara Morocco
48 G3 Derecske Hungary
33 N8 Derenburg E Germany
52 D4 Dereyanka U.S.S.R.
14 D2 Derg R N Ireland
54 H6 Dergachi U.S.S.R.
14 C4 Derg, L Irish Rep
37 J2 Der Hohe Weg sandbank W Germany
111 C11 De Ridder Louisiana
25 C3 De Rijp Netherlands
86 H5 Derkali Kenya
54 K8 Derkul R U.S.S.R.
47 G1 Dermantsi Bulgaria
37 M4 Dermbach E Germany
111 E8 Dermott Arkansas
Derna see Darnah
87 C11 Dernberg, C Namibia
32 M8 Derneburg W Germany
111 F12 Dernieres, Is Louisiana
138 C2 De Rose Hill S Australia
22 B3 Déroute, Passage de la France
14 D3 Derravaragh, L Irish Rep
Derry see Londonderry
95 Q4 Derry New Hampshire
106 C9 Derry New Mexico
94 H6 Derry Pennsylvania
140 D5 Derry Downs N Terr Aust
14 C2 Derryveagh Mts Irish Rep
36 D1 Derschlag W Germany
9 G2 Dersingham England
86 G2 Derudeb Sudan
95 M4 De Ruyter New York
21 B6 Derval France
46 E6 Derveni Greece
42 H4 Derventa Yugoslavia
118 F5 Derwent Alberta
140 B6 Derwent N Terr Aust
139 H8 Derwent R Tasmania
139 H8 Derwent Bridge Tasmania
12 E4 Derwent, R England
13 E4 Derwent Water L England
55 E5 Derzhavinsk U.S.S.R.
133 D4 Desaguadero R Argentina
131 B5 Desague, Cerro peak Argentina
110 E7 Des Arc Arkansas
110 F4 Des Arc Missouri
102 G2 Desatoya Mts Nevada
9 F3 Desborough England
130 B5 Descalvado Mato Grosso Brazil
130 F7 Descalvado São Paulo Brazil
102 H9 Descanso California
124 A1 Descanso Mexico
21 G8 Descartes France
121 S6 Deschaillons Quebec
100 E4 Deschutes R Oregon
109 J3 Desdemona Texas
45 M1 Dese R Italy
133 P7 Deseado Argentina
41 N7 Desenzano del Garda Italy
103 M2 Deseret Utah
101 N9 Deseret Pk Utah
121 N8 Deseronto Ontario
103 J8 Desert Center California
102 H8 Desert Hot Springs California
121 O6 Desért, L Quebec
101 M8 Desert Pk Utah
103 J5 Desert Ra Nevada
103 L7 Desert Valley Nevada
103 N5 Desert View Arizona
127 M4 Deshaies Guadeloupe W I
67 A3 Deshengpo China
98 J9 Deshler Nebraska
94 D5 Deshler Ohio
74 E5 Deshnoke India
77 H4 Deshu Afghanistan
124 B1 Desierto de Altar des Mexico
17 H4 Desierto de las Palmas Spain
98 E1 Des Lacs R N Dakota
118 D3 Desmarais Alberta
100 J2 Desmet Idaho
101 L3 De Smet Montana
98 J5 De Smet S Dakota
130 B10 Desmochados Paraguay
99 N8 Des Moines Iowa
106 G5 Des Moines New Mexico
99 M7 Des Moines R Iowa
99 L6 Des Moines R Minnesota
54 B6 Desna R U.S.S.R.
133 C8 Desolación, I Chile
71 G5 Desolation Pt Philippines
110 E3 De Soto Illinois
107 Q3 De Soto Kansas
110 F3 De Soto Missouri
99 P6 De Soto Wisconsin
113 F10 De Soto City Florida
16 E6 Despeñaperros, Pto. de Spain
99 T7 Des Plaines Illinois
48 G6 Despotovac Yugoslavia
83 H5 Desroches isld Seychelles
33 Q9 Dessau E Germany
40 E3 Dessoubre R France
86 G3 Dessye Ethiopia
111 K11 Destin Florida
106 F5 Deštné mt Poland
138 E6 D'Estrees, B S Australia
117 D5 Destruction Bay Yukon Terr
100 A2 Destruction I Washington
143 G6 Destruction,Mt W Australia
22 B2 Desvres France
48 G5 Deta Romania
142 G4 Detached Ra W Australia
32 G6 Detern W Germany
121 N7 Detlor Ontario
32 J9 Detmold W Germany
94 D1 Detour Michigan
94 D1 Detour Passage Michigan
99 U4 Detour, Pt Michigan
94 D4 Detroit Michigan
109 M2 Detroit Texas
121 H4 Détroit d'Honguedo Quebec
99 L3 Detroit Lakes Minnesota
94 D4 Detroit R Michigan
100 C5 Detroit Res Oregon
87 E9 Dett Zimbabwe
37 J4 Dettelbach W Germany
36 G6 Dettenhausen W Germany
36 H3 Detter W Germany
36 F7 Dettingen Baden-Württemberg W Germany
36 G3 Dettingen Bayern W Germany
36 C6 Dettwiller France
68 G5 Det Udom Thailand
48 E2 Detva Czechoslovakia
25 E6 Deurne Netherlands
37 Q2 Deutsch-Einsiedel E Germany
33 R7 Deutschhof E Germany
48 D3 Deutschkreutz Austria
37 P2 Deutsch-Neudorf E Germany
122 B2 Deux Décharges, L Quebec
121 M6 Deux Rivieres Ontario
21 E9 Deux-Sèvres dep France
48 H5 Deva Romania
16 D1 Deva R Spain
110 E7 De Valls Bluff Arkansas
48 F3 Dévaványa Hungary
48 D3 Devecser Hungary
78 E2 Develi Turkey
25 F4 Deventer Netherlands
143 C6 Deverell,Mt W Australia
112 D4 Devereux Georgia
15 F3 Deveron R Scotland
46 E4 Devica mt Yugoslavia
74 D5 Devikot India
20 H3 Deville France
116 E3 Devil Mt Alaska
102 E4 Devil Post Pile Nat.Mon California
145 D4 Devil River Pk New Zealand
108 F5 Devils R Texas
14 D4 Devilsbit Mt Irish Rep
8 C3 Devils Bridge Wales
102 E6 Devils Den California
12 E3 Devil's Elbow Scotland
116 K5 Devils Elbow V Alaska
102 E3 Devils Gate California
89 E1 Devil's Gorge Zambia
6 L6 Devil's Hole North Sea
99 Q2 Devils I Michigan
110 H4 Devil's Kitchen L Illinois
98 H1 Devils Lake N Dakota
98 H1 Devils L. Res N Dakota
117 G6 Devils Paw mt Br Col/Alaska
100 C7 Devils Peak mt Oregon
102 E4 Devils Pk California
103 J7 Devils Playground des California
126 G2 Devil's Point Cat I Bahamas
101 O8 Devils Slide Utah
98 B5 Devils Tower Wyoming
139 H7 Devils Tower isld Tasmania
47 G3 Devin Bulgaria
109 J6 Devine Texas
80 C8 Devira Israel
9 E5 Devizes England
74 F6 Devli India

116 L3 Endicott Mts Alaska
117 G4 End,Mt Yukon Terr
8 D1 Endon England
80 E3 'En Dor Israel
140 C1 Endyalgout I N Terr Aust
128 D6 Ene R Peru
47 H4 Enez Turkey
78 A1 Enez Turkey
79 F4 Enfeh Lebanon
43 C12 Enfida Tunisia
9 F4 Enfield England
110 H3 Enfield Illinois
112 K1 Enfield N Carolina
95 P3 Enfield New Hampshire
122 J9 Enfield Nova Scotia
127 K5 Engaño, C Dom Rep
71 E1 Engaño,C Luzon Philippines
60 R1 Engaru Japan
28 B7 Enge W Germany
80 E8 En Gedi Israel
41 H4 Engelberg Switzerland
112 M2 Engelhard N Carolina
38 J5 Engelhartszell Austria
53 G8 Engel's U.S.S.R.
36 C2 Engelskirchen W Germany
41 J2 Engen W Germany
130 C4 Engenho Brazil
138 D3 Engenina R S Australia
32 J8 Enger W Germany
26 E10 Engerdal Norway
27 F10 Engeren,L Norway
36 D3 Engers W Germany
89 G3 Engesi R Zimbabwe
28 C4 Engesvang Denmark
80 F2 'En Gev Israel
Enghien see Edingen
20 K4 Enghien France
117 F6 Engineer Br Columbia
22 J2 Engis Belgium
70 B4 Engkilili Sarawak
111 E7 England Arkansas
8 D3 England U.K.
106 C8 Engle New Mexico
123 Q3 Englee Nfld
119 N6 Englefield Sask
117 K10 Englewood Br Columbia
106 F2 Englewood Colorado
113 E11 Englewood Florida
107 L4 Englewood Kansas
112 C2 Englewood Tennessee
110 K3 English Indiana
116 L7 English Bay Alaska
122 E4 English Bay Quebec
75 N6 English Bazar India
20 D1 English Channel France/England
146 F12 English Coast Antarctica
140 D1 English Company's Is N Terr Aust
127 P4 English Harbour Town Antigua W I
123 R6 English Harbour W Nfld
119 N1 English River Ontario
52 D2 Engozero U.S.S.R.
36 G7 Engstingen W Germany
17 G6 Enguera Spain
52 B6 Engure U.S.S.R.
80 D3 'En Ha'Emeq Israel
80 D2 'En HaMifraz Israel
80 E3 'En Harod Israel
80 C3 'En Hod Israel
98 B2 Enid Montana
107 N5 Enid Oklahoma
111 G7 Enid L Mississippi
142 B5 Enid, Mt W Australia
118 A3 Enilda Alberta
36 G7 Eningen W Germany
60 P3 Eniwa dake mt Japan
134 G7 Eniwetok atoll Marshall Is Pacific Oc
85 C5 Enji Mauritania
80 C3 'En Karmel Israel
89 G2 Enkeldoorn Zimbabwe
36 D5 Enkenbach-Alsenborn W Germany
25 D3 Enkhuizen Netherlands
36 C4 Enkirch W Germany
27 J12 Enköping Sweden
128 G8 En Madrejón Paraguay
114 J5 Ennadai N W Terr
86 E3 En Nahud Sudan
79 G4 En Nebk Syria
86 D2 Ennedi plat Chad
14 D3 Ennell,L Irish Rep
32 F10 Ennepetal W Germany
127 H5 Ennery Haiti
139 H3 Enngonia New S Wales
32 H9 Ennigerloh W Germany
98 D5 Enning S Dakota
27 E13 Enningdal Norway
14 C4 Ennis Irish Rep
101 O4 Ennis Montana
109 L3 Ennis Texas
14 E4 Enniscorthy Irish Rep
14 D2 Enniskillen N Ireland
14 B4 Ennistimon Irish Rep
80 D1 Enn Nâqoûra Lebanon
38 K6 Ennstaler Alpen mts Austria
80 G4 En Nu'eiyima Jordan
140 C5 Ennugan Cr N Terr Aust
29 P9 Eno Finland
108 E2 Enochs Texas
141 K1 Enoggera dist Brisbane, Qnsld
98 J8 Enola Nebraska
29 O9 Enonkoski Finland
29 K3 Enontekiö Finland
112 F3 Enoree S Carolina
112 F3 Enoree R S Carolina
95 P2 Enosburg Falls Vermont
67 D5 Enping China
70 F6 Enrekang Sulawesi
71 E2 Enrile Luzon Philippines
127 J5 Enriquillo, Lago de Dom Rep
25 E3 Ens Netherlands
139 J6 Ensay Victoria
25 G4 Enschede Netherlands
36 B5 Ensdorf W Germany
32 H10 Ense W Germany
133 F4 Ensenada Argentina
124 A2 Ensenada Mexico
106 D5 Ensenada New Mexico
36 C5 Ensheim W Germany
80 D4 'En Shemer Israel
67 C1 Enshi China
118 D8 Ensign Alberta
107 K4 Ensign Kansas
99 U4 Ensign Michigan
19 K5 Ensisheim France
28 F4 Enslev Denmark
9 E4 Enstone England
86 F5 Entebbe Uganda
37 N4 Entenbühl mt W Germany
12 E3 Enterkinfoot Scotland
111 L10 Enterprise Alabama
107 N3 Enterprise Kansas
111 H9 Enterprise Mississippi
114 H5 Enterprise N W Terr
121 O8 Enterprise Ontario
100 H4 Enterprise Oregon
103 L4 Enterprise Utah
71 D5 Enterprise Pt Philippines
100 E2 Entiat Mts Washington
70 C4 Entimau, Bt mt Sarawak
17 F8 Entinas,Pta. De Las Spain
133 D8 Entrada,Pta Argentina
18 H5 Entrains France
20 D5 Entrammes France
140 A3 Entrance I N Terr Aust
18 G8 Entraygues France
143 B10 Entrecasteaux, Pt.d' W Australia
137 N5 Entrecasteaux, Récifs D' reefs New Caledonia
83 J14 Entre-Deux Réunion Indian Ocean
123 L6 Entré, I. d' Madeleine Is, Quebec
129 H5 Entre Rios Brazil
130 G7 Entre Rios de Minas Brazil
36 F6 Entringen W Germany
103 M7 Entro Arizona
118 C5 Entwistle Alberta
85 F7 Enugu Nigeria
100 D2 Enumclaw Washington
20 H2 Envermeu France
27 H11 Enviken Sweden
8 D3 Enville England
128 D5 Envira Brazil
79 F8 En Yahav Israel
67 B1 Enyang China
48 E4 Enying Hungary
144 C5 Enys, Mt New Zealand
36 F6 Enz R W Germany
45 H2 Enza R Italy
80 E8 'En Zafzafa Israel
61 M10 Enzan Japan
37 M6 Enzelhausen W Germany
36 E6 Enzklösterle W Germany
80 B7 En Zurim Israel
36 F6 Enzweihingen W Germany
111 D11 Eola Louisiana
110 E2 Eolia Missouri
20 F3 Epaignes France
45 P8 Epameo, M mt Italy
20 E4 Epaney France
46 F4 Epanomí Greece
25 E4 Epe Netherlands
32 F8 Epe W Germany
133 E5 Epecuén,L Argentina
22 E3 Epéhy France
140 D5 Epenarra N Terr Aust
22 C2 Éperlecques France
18 H3 Épernay France
87 B9 Epernbe Namibia
20 J4 Épernon France
111 H9 Epes Alabama
36 C7 Epfig France
103 N2 Ephraim Utah
95 L6 Ephrata Pennsylvania
100 F2 Ephrata Washington
137 O5 Epi isld New Hebrides
88 G10 Epidendron isld Mozambique
46 F7 Epídhavros Greece
20 J5 Epieds France
17 G3 Epila Spain
19 K4 Epinal France
20 B5 Epiniac France
98 J6 Epiphany S Dakota
79 C4 Episkopi Cyprus
20 J4 Epône France
36 B5 Eppelborn W Germany
37 P2 Eppendorf E Germany
22 F4 Eppes France
22 G3 Eppe-Sauvage France
9 G4 Epping England
98 C1 Epping N Dakota
95 Q3 Epping New Hampshire
36 F5 Eppingen W Germany
36 E3 Eppstein W Germany
98 A4 Epsie Montana
9 F5 Epsom England
21 G6 Epuisay France
87 C10 Epukiro Namibia
13 H6 Epworth England
99 Q7 Epworth Iowa
77 C4 Eqlid Iran
110 H4 Equality Illinois
86 D5 Equateur prov Zaïre
86 E4 Equatoria prov Sudan
73 L9 Equatorial Chan Maldives
85 F8 Equatorial Guinea rep W Africa
20 B2 Equeurdreville France
95 M5 Equmunk Pennsylvania
60 O4 Era Japan
86 E4 Era watercourse Sudan
141 H7 Erac R Queensland
143 B8 Eradu W Australia
71 C6 Eran Palawan Philippines
71 C6 Eran Bay Palawan Philippines
111 D12 Erath Louisiana
78 F1 Erbaa Turkey
36 H7 Erbach Baden-Württemberg W Germany
36 G4 Erbach Hessen W Germany
36 D5 Erbach R W Germany
86 G1 Erba, Jebel mt Sudan
37 N4 Erbendorf W Germany
135 N4 Erben Tablemount Pacific Oc
36 C4 Erbes Kopf mt W Germany
22 D4 Ercheu France
78 E2 Erciyas Dag Turkey
48 E3 Ercsi Hungary
48 E3 Erd Hungary
65 H2 Erdaohezi China
65 G3 Erdao Jiang R China
47 J4 Erdek Turkey
47 J4 Erdek Körfezi B Turkey
86 D2 Erdi dist Chad
37 M7 Erding W Germany
37 M7 Erdinger Moos marsh W Germany
9 E2 Erdington England
37 P2 Erdmansdorf E Germany
36 B3 Erdorf W Germany
21 C7 Erdre R France
128 F2 Erebato R Venezuela
146 J6 Erebus,Mt Antarctica
146 D14 Erebus & Terror G Antarctica
78 K6 Erech Iraq
130 D10 Erechim Brazil
58 G2 Ereentsav Mongolia
Ereğli see Marmaraereğlisi
78 C1 Ereğli Turkey
47 L7 Eren R Turkey
47 K8 Eren Dağ mt Turkey
65 D2 Eren Gobi China
65 B3 Erenhot China
Erenköy see İntepe
129 G4 Erepecu, L Brazil
16 D3 Eresma R Spain
47 H5 Eressós Greece
80 B7 Erez Israel
22 K3 Erezée Belgium
32 K4 Erfde W Germany
89 E7 Erfenis Dam res S Africa
65 A4 Erfenzi China
85 D2 Erfoud Morocco
36 B2 Erft R W Germany
36 B2 Erftstadt W Germany
37 L2 Erfurt E Germany
78 G2 Ergani Turkey
85 D4 Erg Chech des reg Mali/Algeria
86 C2 Erg du Djourab dist Chad
47 H3 Ergene R Turkey
85 D3 Erg er Raoul des reg Algeria
85 C3 Erg Iguid sand des Algeria/Mauritania
55 E1 Erginskiy Sor, Oz L U.S.S.R.
52 C6 Ērgli U.S.S.R.
37 N6 Ergolding W Germany
37 N6 Ergoldsbach W Germany
65 G1 Ergu China
86 C3 Erguig R Chad
59 H1 Ergun Zuoqi China
37 O7 Erharting W Germany
16 D2 Eria R Spain
86 G2 Eriba Sudan
16 A6 Ericeira Portugal
32 K7 Erichshagen W Germany
107 L6 Erick Oklahoma
119 S8 Erickson Manitoba
122 G2 Eric L Quebec
99 N1 Ericsburg Minnesota
98 H8 Ericson Nebraska
98 A9 Erie Colorado
99 Q8 Erie Illinois
107 P4 Erie Kansas
94 D5 Erie Michigan
98 J2 Erie N Dakota
103 J6 Erie Nevada
94 G4 Erie Pennsylvania
120 J10 Erieau Ontario
120 K10 Erie, L Ontario/Mich
94 G4 Erie,L U.S.A./Canada
86 A1 Erigavo Somalia
46 D5 Erikoúsa isld Greece
119 T8 Eriksdale Manitoba
46 E7 Erímanthos mt Greece
57 C3 Erimbet U.S.S.R.
60 R4 Erimo-misaki C Japan
22 C3 Erin France
37 P7 Ering W Germany
27 H15 Eringsboda Sweden
127 N3 Erin Pt Trinidad
15 A3 Eriskay isld Scotland
9 G5 Erith England
47 F6 Erithraí Greece
86 G2 Eritrea prov Ethiopia
25 F6 Erkelenz W Germany
27 K12 Erken Sweden
33 T8 Erkner E Germany
86 G2 Erkowit Sudan
38 F6 Erl Austria
Erlangdiang see Dawu
37 L4 Erlangen W Germany
94 C7 Erlanger Kentucky
38 M5 Erlauf R Austria
37 N3 Erlbach E Germany
140 C7 Erldunda N Terr Aust
36 F3 Erlensee W Germany
111 C8 Erling,L Arkansas
65 G3 Erlong Shan mt China
38 F8 Erlsbach Austria
25 E4 Ermelo Netherlands
89 F6 Ermelo S Africa
78 D3 Ermenek Turkey
20 K4 Ermont France
Ermoúpolis see Síros
33 O9 Ermsleben E Germany
138 B2 Ernabella R S Australia
138 B2 Ernabella Mission S Australia
76 C6 Ernakulam India
36 E1 Erndtebrück W Germany
14 C2 Erne R Irish Rep
20 D5 Ernée France
20 D5 Ernée R France
14 D2 Erne,L.Lower N Ireland
14 D2 Erne,L.Upper N Ireland
143 E7 Ernest Giles Ra W Australia
144 A7 Ernest Is New Zealand
135 M12 Ernest Legouve Reef Pacific Oc
117 G8 Ernest Sd Alaska
118 L8 Ernfold Sask
45 O6 Ernici, Monti mt Italy
36 G4 Ernstthal W Germany
76 C5 Erode India
78 J2 Erois Turkey
141 G7 Eromanga Queensland
137 O5 Eromanga isld New Hebrides
111 D9 Eros Louisiana
36 B2 Erp W Germany
22 G3 Erquelinnes Belgium
18 D4 Erquy France
143 B7 Errabiddy Hills W Australia
85 C2 Er-Rachida Morocco
86 F3 Er Rahad Sudan
80 G6 Er Rajib Jordan
79 G4 Er Rastan Syria
88 F10 Errego Mozambique
14 C1 Errigal mt Irish Rep
28 G7 Errindlev Denmark
14 A2 Erris Hd Irish Rep
28 D5 Erritsø Denmark
111 G12 Errol I Louisiana
86 F3 Er Roseires Sudan
46 D4 Ersekë Albania
118 E6 Erskine Alberta
142 F4 Erskine, Mount W Australia
26 M6 Ersnäs Sweden
36 D7 Erstein France
19 L4 Ersteir France
36 H3 Erthal W Germany
54 M5 Ertil' U.S.S.R.
66 D2 Ertix He R China
47 J5 Ertugrul Turkey
22 F1 Ertvelde Belgium
145 E3 Erua New Zealand
138 E4 Erudina S Australia
27 H12 Ervalla Sweden
21 E6 Erve R France
37 Q2 Ervěnice Czechoslovakia
22 D3 Ervillers France
112 J2 Erwin N Carolina
112 E1 Erwin Tennessee
32 H9 Erwitte W Germany
119 P6 Erwood Sask
8 C3 Erwood Wales
33 O8 Erxleben E Germany
46 D3 Erzen R Albania
37 N3 Erzgebirge E Germany
56 E5 Erzin U.S.S.R.
78 G2 Erzincan Turkey
78 H2 Erzurum Turkey
52 B7 Erzvilkas U.S.S.R.
60 P4 Esan-misaki C Japan
20 D3 Esaue R France
28 A6 Esbjerg Denmark
107 M2 Esbon Kansas
17 G2 Esca R Spain
18 E10 Esca R Spain
130 J10 Escada Brazil
103 N4 Escalante Utah
103 N4 Escalante R Utah
103 L4 Escalante Des Utah
131 A8 Escalera,Pta Chile
124 G4 Escalón Mexico
16 E4 Escalona Spain
111 J11 Escambia R Florida
99 T4 Escanaba Michigan
99 T3 Escanaba R Michigan
125 O8 Escárcega Mexico
22 E3 Escaut R France
22 L5 Esch Luxembourg
36 E3 Esch W Germany
36 G4 Eschau W Germany
36 F3 Eschborn W Germany
22 K4 Eschdorf Luxembourg
32 E7 Eschebrügge W Germany
32 M7 Eschede W Germany
37 L4 Eschenau W Germany
37 M4 Eschenbach W Germany
36 E2 Eschenberg W Germany
32 L9 Eschershausen W Germany
40 G4 Escholzmatt Switzerland
116 G3 Eschscholtz B Alaska
22 K4 Esch-sur-la-Sûre Luxembourg
37 J1 Eschwege W Germany
25 F7 Eschweiler W Germany
127 K5 Escocesa, B Dom Rep
130 H5 Escondido Brazil
102 G8 Escondido California
122 C5 Escoumins,R Quebec
20 K5 Escrennes France
13 G6 Escrick England
124 G6 Escuinapa de Hidalgo Mexico
122 F5 Escuminac Quebec
122 H6 Escuminac, Pt New Brunswick
86 B5 Eséka Cameroon
32 G5 Esens W Germany
17 H2 Esera R Spain
77 B3 Eşfahān Iran
80 B8 Eshbol Israel
80 B8 Eshel Ha Nasi Israel
9 F5 Esher England
87 F11 Eshowe S Africa
Esh Sham see Damascus
77 B2 Eshtehard Iran
80 D8 Eshtemoa Jordan
42 E5 Esino R Italy
141 K7 Esk Queensland
139 H8 Esk R Tasmania
116 N6 Eska Alaska
118 L8 Eskbank Sask
145 F3 Eskdale New Zealand
13 E5 Eskdale Green England
14 C2 Eske, L Irish Rep
47 K7 Eskere Turkey
115 S4 Eskifjördhur Iceland
28 H5 Eskildstrup Denmark
28 H7 Eskilstrup Denmark
27 H12 Eskilstuna Sweden
122 J3 Eskimo I Quebec
114 F4 Eskimo Lakes N W Terr
115 K5 Eskimo Point N W Terr
78 D1 Eskipazar Turkey
47 L5 Eskişehir Turkey
13 H5 Esk,R England
15 E5 Esk,R Scotland
107 O3 Eskridge Kansas
16 D2 Esla R Spain
16 D3 Esla, Embalse del res Spain
37 O4 Eslarn W Germany
47 K7 Eşler Daği mt Turkey
32 H10 Eslohe W Germany
27 F16 Eslöv Sweden
121 O3 Oesmaraisville Quebec
47 K6 Esme Turkey
126 E4 Esmeralda Cuba
141 G4 Esmeralda Queensland
133 B7 Esmeralda, I Chile
128 C3 Esmeraldas Ecuador
98 G1 Esmond N Dakota
98 J5 Esmond S Dakota
120 D2 Esnagami L Ontario
120 F4 Esnagi L Ontario
22 J2 Esnaux Belgium
27 E11 Espa Norway
127 J8 Espada,Pta Colombia
18 G8 Espalion France
17 H6 Espalmador isld Balearic Is
113 F8 Espanola Florida
106 D6 Espanola New Mexico
120 J6 Espanola Ontario
128 B8 Española isld Galapagos Is
19 P17 Esparron France
102 B3 Esparto California
125 M5 Esparza Costa Rica
28 E6 Espe Denmark
27 D10 Espedals-vatn L Norway
32 J8 Espelkamp W Germany
116 E3 Espenberg,C Alaska
37 N1 Espenhain E Germany
88 F8 Esperança Mozambique
143 D10 Esperance W Australia
143 D10 Esperance B W Australia
131 E3 Esperanza Argentina
124 E4 Esperanza Mexico
108 B4 Esperanza Texas
108 F8 Esperanzas Mexico
125 M2 Esperanza, Sa. de la ra Honduras
28 K5 Espergærde Denmark
45 P7 Esperia Italy
16 A6 Espichel,C Portugal
16 D6 Espiel Spain
130 E10 Espigão,Serra do mts Brazil
16 D2 Espigüete mt Spain
128 D6 Espinar Peru
19 Q16 Espinasses France
124 J4 Espinazo Mexico
130 G6 Espinhaço,Serra,do mt Brazil
16 B4 Espinho Portugal
131 G2 Espinilho, Serra do ra Brazil
130 G4 Espinosa Brazil
130 H6 Espirito Santo state Brazil
124 D5 Espíritu Santo isld Mexico
125 Q8 Espíritu Santo, B. del Mexico
133 D8 Espíritu Santo,C Chile/Arg
71 G4 Espiritu Santo,C Philippines
137 O5 Espiritu Santo I New Hebrides
125 P7 Espita Mexico
123 R6 Espoir, B. d' Nfld
16 B3 Esposende Portugal
40 D2 Esprels France
87 F10 Espungabera Mozambique
100 F3 Esquatzel Coulee R Washington
124 E2 Esqueda Mexico
133 C6 Esquel Argentina
22 C2 Esquelbecq France
16 E3 Esqueva R Spain
100 B1 Esquimalt Br Columbia
117 M11 Esquimalt Br Columbia
133 F3 Esquina Argentina
28 K4 Esrum Sø L Denmark
55 D1 Ess R U.S.S.R.
80 F3 Es Samt Jordan
80 D8 Es Samu Jordan
85 C2 Essaouira Morocco
80 G3 Es Sarih Jordan
20 J4 Essarts,les France
20 F4 Essay France
29 K8 Esse Finland
85 E2 Es Seggeur watercourse Algeria
85 F1 Es-sekhina Tunisia
32 L7 Essel W Germany
22 G1 Essen Belgium
32 G7 Essen Niedersachsen W Germany
32 E10 Essen Nordrhein-Westfalen W Germany
37 N6 Essenbach W Germany
143 D6 Essendon, Mt W Australia
103 J7 Essex California
95 P5 Essex Connecticut
99 L9 Essex Iowa
101 M1 Essex Montana
95 O2 Essex New York
120 H10 Essex Ontario
9 G4 Essex co England
95 O2 Essex Junct Vermont
87 E10 Essexvale Zimbabwe
94 D3 Essexville Michigan
37 M6 Essing W Germany
37 J6 Essingen W Germany
36 G6 Esslingen W Germany
20 K4 Essonne dep France
20 K5 Essonne R France
52 D4 Essoyla U.S.S.R.
78 G4 Es Sukhne Syria
100 C4 Estacada Oregon
16 B1 Estaca de Bares, Pta. de la Spain
106 G8 Estacado, Llano plain New Mex/Tex
103 K10 Estacion Doctor Mexico
103 K10 Estacion France Mexico
103 K9 Estación Mèdanos Mexico
133 E8 Estados, I. de los Argentina
18 G10 Estagel France
71 F2 Estagno Pt Luzon Philippines
77 D5 Estahbānāt Iran
120 K6 Estaire Ontario
22 D2 Estaires France
129 L6 Estância Brazil
108 A1 Estancia New Mexico
17 F7 Estancias, Sierra de las mts Spain
77 G4 Estand, Kūh-e- mt Iran
125 O9 Estapilla Mexico
16 B4 Estarreja Portugal
18 F10 Estats, Pic d' mt Spain
40 E4 Estavayer le Lac Switzerland
87 J11 Est, C Madagascar
89 F7 Estcourt S Africa
42 D3 Este Italy
32 L6 Este R W Germany
125 L3 Estelí Nicaragua
18 D10 Estella Spain
98 K5 Estelline S Dakota
16 D5 Estena R Spain
16 D7 Estepa Spain
16 D8 Estepona Spain
133 G4 Este, Pta. del Uruguay
116 N4 Ester Alaska
98 A7 Esterbrook Wyoming
119 P8 Esterhazy Sask
18 H4 Esternay France
113 F11 Estero Florida
102 C6 Estero B California
133 C8 Estero Obstrucción Chile
125 K6 Esteros Mexico
133 E2 Esteros Paraguay
133 F3 Esteros del Iberá swamp Argentina
18 F10 Esterri de Aneu Spain
32 G6 Esterwegen W Germany
98 A9 Estes Pk Colorado
119 P9 Estevan Sask
117 J9 Estevan Group islds Br Columbia
117 K11 Estevan Point Br Columbia
118 G7 Esther Alberta
140 C5 Esther Mt N Terr Aust
99 M6 Estherville Iowa
112 F5 Estill S Carolina
18 H4 Estissac France
119 N8 Estlin Sask
118 J7 Eston Sask
52 B5 Estoniya S.S.R. U.S.S.R.
16 A6 Estoril Portugal
19 Q17 Estoublon France
22 C2 Estree Blanche France
22 D5 Estrées St. Denis France
133 G4 Estreito Brazil
130 F6 Estrêla do Indaiá Brazil
130 F6 Estrêla do Sul Brazil
16 B4 Estrela, Sa. da mts Portugal
103 M9 Estrella Arizona
102 D6 Estrella R California
103 M8 Estrella,Sierra mt Arizona
129 K6 Estrelto, Serra do mts Brazil
16 A6 Estremadura prov Portugal
16 B6 Estremoz Portugal
129 J5 Estrondo, Serra do mts Brazil
28 E3 Estruplund Denmark
118 H8 Estuary Sask
28 B3 Estvad Denmark
48 E3 Esztergom Hungary
138 E3 Etadunna S Australia
115 M2 Etah Greenland
19 J3 Etain France
22 K4 Étalle Belgium
123 N3 Etamamiou,R Quebec
123 N3 Etamamu Quebec
123 N3 Etamamu R Quebec
20 K5 Étampes France
138 F2 Etamunbanie,L S Australia
80 B7 Etan Israel
18 H6 Étang France
123 L6 Étang-du-Nord Madeleine Is, Quebec
22 B2 Étaples France
74 H6 Etawa India
119 V1 Etawney L Manitoba
124 E4 Etchojoa Mexico
27 K14 Etelhem Gotland Sweden
85 E5 Etelia Mali
32 K7 Etelsen W Germany
122 B5 Eternité,L Quebec
146 F13 Eternity Ra Antarctica
98 H6 Ethan S Dakota
22 K4 Ethe Belgium
111 E11 Ethel Louisiana
111 G8 Ethel Mississippi
110 D2 Ethel Missouri
94 F9 Ethel W Virginia
119 R7 Ethelbert Manitoba
140 A5 Ethel Cr N Terr Aust
141 G3 Ethel Cr Queensland
142 D6 Ethel Creek W Australia
143 C6 Ethel R W Australia
111 H8 Ethelsville Alabama
119 N6 Ethelton Sask
141 G4 Etheridge R Queensland
101 R6 Ethete Wyoming
86 G4 Ethiopia,Empire of
101 N1 Ethridge Montana
47 H5 Etili Turkey
40 F5 Etivaz, l' L Switzerland
116 J2 Etivluk R Alaska
95 S2 Etna Maine
101 M8 Etna Utah
27 D10 Etna R Norway
43 F11 Etna, M Sicily
27 A12 Etne Norway
27 D11 Etnedal Norway
111 B10 Etoile Texas
116 D6 Etolin,C Alaska
117 G7 Etolin I Alaska
116 E6 Etolin Str Alaska
119 P6 Etomami Sask
9 F5 Eton England
22 K5 Eton France
120 F5 Eton Ontario
141 J5 Eton Queensland
87 C9 Etosha Pan Namibia
112 C2 Etowah Tennessee
112 B3 Etowah R Georgia
22 F4 Etreaupont France
20 K5 Etrechy France
22 E4 Etreillers France
20 J3 Étrépagny France
20 F2 Étretat France
22 F4 Etreux France
22 D3 Éricourt-Manancourt France
40 A4 Etrigny France
22 F3 Etrœungt France
47 F2 Etropole Bulgaria
22 L4 Ettelbrück Luxembourg
25 C5 Etten Netherlands
36 D7 Ettenheim W Germany
100 A9 Ettersburg California
37 L1 Ettersburg E Germany
37 J2 Etterwinden E Germany
9 E3 Ettington England
37 O6 Ettling W Germany
36 E6 Ettlingen W Germany
144 B6 Ettrick New Zealand
142 C5 Ettrick W Australia
99 P5 Ettrick Wisconsin
15 E5 Ettrick Pen mt Scotland
13 E3 Ettrick Water Scotland
80 G6 Et Tuneib Jordan
80 G3 Et Turra Jordan
9 E2 Etwall England
124 G7 Etzatlán Mexico
37 P1 Etzdorf E Germany
118 F9 Etzikom Alberta
118 F9 Etzikom Coulee R Alberta
20 H1 Eu France
137 S6 'Eua isld Tonga
139 H5 Euabalong New S Wales
94 C9 Eubank Kentucky
36 H4 Eubigheim W Germany
Euboea Greece see Évvoia
143 G9 Eucla W Australia
98 K2 Euclid Minnesota
94 F5 Euclid Ohio
139 J6 Eucumbene,L New S Wales
122 G3 Eudites,L.des Quebec
111 E8 Eudora Arkansas
138 E5 Eudunda S Australia
37 J3 Euerdorf W Germany
111 L10 Eufala Alabama
107 P6 Eufaula Oklahoma
107 P6 Eufaula Res Oklahoma
43 G10 Eufemia,S.,Golfo di Italy
45 L1 Euganei, Colli hills Italy
100 B5 Eugene Oregon
124 B4 Eugenia, Pta C Mexico
130 C8 Eugênio Penzo Brazil
29 K8 Eugmo isld Finland
139 J5 Eugowra New S Wales
37 O1 Eula R E Germany
109 N9 Euless Texas
141 H8 Eulo Queensland
112 F6 Eulonia Georgia
139 J4 Eumaungerie New S Wales
16 B1 Eume R Spain
111 D11 Eunice Louisiana
108 D3 Eunice New Mexico
22 L2 Eupen Belgium
78 J5 Euphrates R S W Asia
111 G8 Eupora Mississippi
27 M10 Eura Finland
29 J10 Eurajoki Finland
20 G3 Eure dep France
20 H3 Eure R France
20 H5 Eure-et-Loir dep France
100 A9 Eureka California
99 R9 Eureka Illinois
107 O4 Eureka Kansas
101 L1 Eureka Montana
103 J2 Eureka Nevada
115 L1 Eureka N W Terr
98 G4 Eureka S Dakota
101 N10 Eureka Utah
100 G3 Eureka Washington
116 O6 Eureka Lodge Alaska
117 O7 Eureka River Alberta
115 L2 Eureka Snd N W Terr
110 C5 Eureka Springs Arkansas
102 G4 Eureka Valley California
138 F4 Eurinilla R S Australia
138 F4 Euriowie New S Wales
139 H6 Euroa Victoria
141 J7 Eurombah Queensland
141 J7 Eurombah R Queensland
81 A8 Europa isld Mozambique Chan
25 B5 Europoort Netherlands
61 J11 Eushimi Japan
36 B2 Euskirchen W Germany
109 L3 Eustace Texas
113 F9 Eustis Florida
98 F9 Eustis Nebraska
139 G5 Euston New S Wales
111 J9 Eutaw Alabama
112 G4 Eutawville S Carolina
33 N4 Eutin W Germany
36 F7 Eutingen W Germany
114 G7 Eutsuk L Br Col
33 R9 Eutzsch E Germany
13 F6 Euxton England
111 E10 Eva Louisiana
108 C7 Eva Oklahoma
140 C4 Eva Downs N Terr Aust
87 C9 Evale Angola
99 M5 Evan Minnesota
139 H8 Evandale Tasmania
100 H1 Evans Washington
118 B5 Evansburg Alberta
115 L1 Evans,C N W Terr
94 G6 Evans City Pennsylvania
139 L3 Evans Hd New S Wales
115 M7 Evans,L Quebec
117 O9 Evans,Mt Alberta
106 E2 Evans,Mt Colorado
101 M3 Evans, Mt Montana
115 L5 Evans Str N W Terr
99 T7 Evanston Illinois
101 P8 Evanston Wyoming
116 M3 Evansville Alaska
110 G3 Evansville Illinois
110 J3 Evansville Indiana
99 L3 Evansville Minnesota
120 H7 Evansville Ontario
99 R7 Evansville Wisconsin
101 T7 Evansville Wyoming
109 J4 Evant Texas
94 B3 Evart Michigan
94 D10 Evarts Kentucky
18 G6 Evaux France
47 H5 Evciler Turkey
99 O2 Eveleth Minnesota
138 C3 Evelyn Ck S Australia
140 C2 Evelyn, Mt N Terr Aust
26 J3 Evenes Norway
110 E5 Evening Shade Arkansas
80 E1 Even Menahem Israel
80 C4 Even Yehuda Israel
141 G2 Eve Pk Queensland
22 G3 Evêque Belgium
120 B4 Everard Ontario
139 J7 Everard,C Victoria
138 D4 Everard,L S Australia
140 C6 Everard, Mt N Terr Aust
138 B2 Everard,Mt S Australia
138 C2 Everard Pk S Australia
138 C2 Everard Ra S Australia
28 H6 Everdrup Denmark
22 G2 Evere Belgium
107 P2 Everest Kansas
75 M5 Everest, Mt Xizang Zizhiqu/Nepal
94 J6 Everett Pennsylvania
100 C2 Everett Washington
112 F6 Everett City Georgia
95 O4 Everett, Mt Massachusetts
22 F1 Evergem Belgium
113 F12 Everglades Florida
113 G12 Everglades Nat. Park Florida
111 K10 Evergreen Alabama
106 E2 Evergreen Colorado
112 J3 Evergreen N Carolina
109 M10 Everman Texas
27 G16 Everöd Sweden
32 H10 Eversberg W Germany
32 K6 Eversen W Germany
9 E3 Evesham England
141 G6 Evesham Queensland
118 H6 Evesham Sask
29 K8 Evijärvi Finland
85 G8 Evinayong Mbini Eq Guinea
46 E6 Évinos R Greece
27 C13 Evje Norway
80 D2 Evlayim Israel
40 G5 Evolène Switzerland
16 B6 Évora Portugal
20 B5 Evran France
20 E3 Evrecy France
47 H4 Evreşe Turkey
20 H3 Évreux France
20 E5 Évron France
80 D2 Evron Israel
46 E3 Évropos Greece
47 H4 Évros R Greece
46 E7 Evrótas R Greece
79 C3 Evrykhou Cyprus
47 G6 Évvoia isld Greece
102 R12 Ewa Hawaiian Is
102 R12 Ewa Bch Hawaiian Is
141 H4 Ewan Queensland
100 H2 Ewan Washington
140 C6 Ewaninga N Terr Aust
116 P5 Ewan L Alaska
127 K2 Ewarton Jamaica
86 B6 Ewc Congo
9 F5 Ewell England
36 E2 Ewersbach W Germany
94 D8 Ewing Kentucky
99 P9 Ewing Missouri
98 H7 Ewing Nebraska
146 E13 Ewing I Antarctica
140 D6 Ewing, Mt N Terr Aust
128 E6 Exaltación Bolivia
118 G7 Excel Alberta
110 B2 Excelsior Missouri
102 E3 Excelsior Mt California
102 F3 Excelsior Mts Nevada
117 F6 Excursion Alaska
37 K3 Exdorf E Germany
146 J10 Executive Com.Ra Antarctica
99 P4 Exeland Wisconsin
8 C5 Exe,R England
102 E5 Exeter California
8 C6 Exeter England
110 C5 Exeter Missouri
98 J9 Exeter Nebraska
95 R4 Exeter New Hampshire
120 J9 Exeter Ontario
117 S3 Exeter L N W Terr
8 C5 Exford England
99 M8 Exira Iowa
99 O9 Exline Iowa
25 G3 Exloo Netherlands
20 F4 Exmes France
8 C6 Exminster England
8 C5 Exmoor Forest England
95 M9 Exmore Virginia
8 C6 Exmouth England
142 A5 Exmouth W Australia
142 A5 Exmouth Gulf W Australia
117 Q3 Exmouth L N W Terr
81 J7 Exmouth Plateau Indian Oc
46 E8 Éxo Nímfi Greece
141 J6 Expedition Ra Queensland
123 R5 Exploits R Nfld
118 B7 Exshaw Alberta
32 K8 Extertal W Germany
8 C5 Exton England
16 C5 Extremadura reg Spain
128 D6 Extremo Brazil
126 F2 Exuma Sd Bahamas
116 P6 Eyak Alaska
80 C5 Eyal Israel
88 E3 Eyasi,L Tanzania
19 P14 Eybens France
27 C13 Eydehamn Norway
9 F2 Eye England
9 H3 Eye Suffolk England
118 L8 Eyebrow Sask
13 F2 Eyemouth Scotland
18 G7 Eygurande France
18 F8 Eymet France
18 G7 Eymoutiers France
9 E4 Eynsham England
99 O6 Eyota Minnesota
118 H7 Eyre Sask
143 F9 Eyre W Australia
140 E6 Eyre R Queensland
14 C3 Eyrecourt Irish Rep
136 H7 Eyre Cr R Queensland
138 D3 Eyre,L (N) S Australia
138 D3 Eyre,L (S) S Australia
138 E4 Eyre,Mt S Australia
144 B6 Eyre Mts New Zealand
138 D5 Eyre Pen S Australia
119 R1 Eyrie L Manitoba
37 L5 Eysölden W Germany
28 O9 Eystnes C Faeroes
32 K7 Eystrup W Germany
19 N14 Eyzin France
48 J5 Ezeru mt Romania
47 H5 Ezine Turkey
77 A3 Ezna Iran
134 C12 Faaoné Tahiti I Pac Oc
45 J2 Fabbrico Italy
108 A4 Fabens Texas
27 D10 Fåberg Norway
117 P4 Faber L N W Terr
121 L5 Fabre Quebec
42 E5 Fabriano Italy
130 E9 Fábrica de Papel Brazil
48 L6 Făcăeni Romania
128 D3 Facatativa Colombia
144 A6 Facile Harb New Zealand
141 K6 Facing I Queensland
18 E8 Facture France
133 C7 Facundo Argentina
86 D2 Fada Chad
85 E6 Fada N'Gourma Upper Volta
51 K1 Faddeya,Zaliv gulf U.S.S.R.
51 O1 Faddeyevskiy Ostrov isld U.S.S.R.
73 L7 Fadippolu Atoll Maldives
42 D4 Faenza Italy
115 O5 Færingehavn Greenland
6 E1 Faeroe Bank N Atlantic Oc
28 M2 Færøerne islds N Atlantic Oc
Faeroes, The islds see Færøerne
85 E5 Fafa Mali
86 C4 Fafa R Cent Afr Republic
86 H4 Fafan watercourse Ethiopia
71 C3 Fafanlap W Irian
16 B3 Fafe Portugal
48 J5 Făgăraş Romania
48 J5 Făgarasului, Muntii mts Romania
26 G10 Fågelsjö Sweden
27 H14 Fagerhult Sweden
27 H12 Fagersta Sweden
48 G5 Făget Romania
48 H3 Făgetului, Muntii mts Romania
45 L3 Faggiola, M mt Italy
71 C3 Fagita W Irian
45 P5 Fagnano Alto Italy
133 D8 Fagnano, L Chile/Arg
22 G3 Fagnes Belgium
85 D5 Faguibine,L Mali
77 A5 Fahaheel Kuwait
77 F5 Fahraj Iran
41 J5 Faido Switzerland
Faifo see Hoi An
121 O4 Faillon,L Quebec
106 D9 Fairacres New Mexico
141 J6 Fairbairn Res Queensland
103 O10 Fairbank Arizona
99 O7 Fairbank Iowa
116 O4 Fairbanks Alaska
95 R2 Fairbanks Maine
109 M6 Fairbanks Texas
112 H3 Fair Bluff N Carolina
94 C7 Fairborn Ohio
111 M8 Fairburn Georgia
98 C6 Fairburn S Dakota
99 S9 Fairbury Illinois
98 J9 Fairbury Nebraska
94 H7 Fairchance Pennsylvania
99 Q5 Fairchild Wisconsin
98 H1 Fairdale N Dakota
144 C4 Fairdown New Zealand
111 L9 Fairfax Alabama
99 M5 Fairfax Minnesota
99 L9 Fairfax Missouri
144 B7 Fairfax New Zealand
107 O5 Fairfax Oklahoma
112 F5 Fairfax S Carolina
98 H6 Fairfax S Dakota
95 O2 Fairfax Vermont
100 C2 Fairfax Washington
111 K8 Fairfield Alabama
127 P6 Fairfield Barbados
102 B3 Fairfield California
95 O5 Fairfield Connecticut
101 L6 Fairfield Idaho
110 H3 Fairfield Illinois
99 P8 Fairfield Iowa
95 S2 Fairfield Maine
101 N2 Fairfield Montana
98 C2 Fairfield N Dakota
98 H9 Fairfield Nebraska
95 K7 Fairfield Pennsylvania
109 L4 Fairfield Texas
95 P2 Fairfield Vermont
100 H2 Fairfield Washington
9 E4 Fairford England
119 T7 Fairford Manitoba
110 C4 Fair Grove Missouri
95 R5 Fairhaven Massachusetts
95 L3 Fair Haven New York
95 O3 Fair Haven Vermont
100 B1 Fairholm Washington
118 J5 Fairholme Sask
113 B12 Fairhope Alabama
71 C5 Fairie Queen Philippines
107 Q5 Fairland Oklahoma
144 C6 Fairlie New Zealand
12 D2 Fairlie Scotland
144 B6 Fairlight New Zealand
141 G3 Fairlight Queensland
141 G5 Fairlight Queensland
119 Q9 Fairlight Sask
99 M6 Fairmont Minnesota
112 H3 Fairmont N Carolina
98 J9 Fairmont Nebraska
107 N5 Fairmont Oklahoma
94 G7 Fairmont W Virginia
117 Q10 Fairmont Hot Springs Br Columbia
111 M7 Fair Mount Georgia
94 B6 Fairmount Indiana
95 M8 Fairmount Maryland
98 K3 Fairmount N Dakota
118 H7 Fairmount Sask
115 M5 Fair Ness C N W Terr
13 F2 Fairnilee Scotland
110 E6 Fairoaks Arkansas
102 C3 Fair Oaks California
99 T8 Fair Oaks Indiana
106 E2 Fairplay Colorado
110 C4 Fair Play Missouri
107 L2 Fairport Kansas
99 U4 Fairport Michigan
95 K3 Fairport New York
95 L9 Fair Port Virginia
94 F5 Fairport Harbor Ohio
114 H6 Fairview Alberta
99 Q9 Fairview Illinois
107 P2 Fairview Kansas
94 C2 Fairview Michigan
98 B2 Fairview Montana
107 M5 Fairview Oklahoma
94 G4 Fairview Pennsylvania
141 G3 Fairview Queensland
98 K6 Fairview S Dakota
103 N2 Fairview Utah

Folteşti — Fukuma 27

48 L5 Folteşti Romania
126 E3 Fómento Cuba
52 F6 Fominki U.S.S.R.
52 G2 Fominskaya U.S.S.R.
52 F5 Fominskoye U.S.S.R.
99 M7 Fonda Iowa
98 F1 Fonda N Dakota
95 N4 Fonda New York
114 J6 Fond-du-Lac Sask
99 S6 Fond du Lac Wisconsin
94 D10 Fonde Kentucky
43 E7 Fondi Italy
45 O7 Fondi, L. di Italy
26 E8 Fongen mt Norway
43 C8 Fonni Sardinia
16 C1 Fonsagrada Spain
28 D6 Fønsskov Denmark
22 G3 Fontaine Belgium
21 H6 Fontaine France
18 G4 Fontainebleau France
19 O17 Fontaine-de-Vaucluse France
40 B2 Fontaine-Française France
20 G3 Fontaine-l'Abbé France
20 H2 Fontaine-le-Bourg France
20 G2 Fontaine-le-Dun France
21 E7 Fontaine Milon France
133 C6 Fontana,L Argentina
112 D2 Fontana L N Carolina
45 P6 Fontana Liri Italy
45 L3 Fontanelice Italy
117 N6 Fontas Br Columbia
40 D7 Fontcouvert France
38 F7 Fonte Italy
128 E4 Fonte Boa Brazil
128 G6 Fonte do Pau d'Água Brazil
21 D9 Fontenay-le Comte France
20 J3 Fontenay-St.Père France
123 L2 Fonteneau,L Quebec
122 H5 Fontenelle Quebec
101 P7 Fontenelle Fork R Wyoming
22 E2 Fontenoy Belgium
21 F7 Fontevrault-l'abbaye France
8 D6 Fontmell Magna England
22 L5 Fontoy France
137 S5 Fonualei isld Tonga
48 D4 Fonyód Hungary
Foochow see Fuzhou
103 M2 Fool Cr.Res Utah
117 P9 Foothills Alberta
99 R7 Footville Wisconsin
41 H5 Foppiano Italy
27 J14 Föra Sweden
107 O5 Foraker Oklahoma
116 M5 Foraker,Mt Alaska
19 K3 Forbach France
36 E6 Forbach W Germany
99 O2 Forbes Minnesota
98 H4 Forbes N Dakota
139 J5 Forbes New S Wales
117 P10 Forbes, Mt Alberta
85 F7 Forcados Nigeria
19 Q18 Forcalqueiret France
19 P17 Forcalquier France
38 E8 Forchetta mt Italy
37 L4 Forchheim W Germany
36 H5 Forchtenberg W Germany
13 F2 Ford England
107 L4 Ford Kansas
94 C9 Ford Kentucky
99 T3 Ford R Michigan
140 A2 Ford, C N Terr Aust
102 E6 Ford City California
94 H6 Ford City Pennsylvania
26 A10 Förde Norway
145 E3 Fordell New Zealand
33 P9 Förderstedt E Germany
9 G3 Fordham England
9 E6 Fordingbridge England
103 J8 Ford L California
110 D4 Fordland Missouri
31 L2 Fordon Poland
146 J9 Ford Rge Antarctica
139 H3 Ford's Br New S Wales
110 K4 Fordsville Kentucky
109 K6 Fordtran Texas
98 J1 Fordville N Dakota
111 D8 Fordyce Arkansas
98 J7 Fordyce Nebraska
26 G5 Fore Norway
85 B7 Forécariah Guinea
8 C5 Foreland,The England
115 Q4 Forel, Mt Greenland
109 N2 Foreman Arkansas
118 F9 Foremost Alberta
22 G2 Forest Belgium
100 J3 Forest Idaho
111 G9 Forest Mississippi
94 D6 Forest Ohio
120 H9 Forest Ontario
141 F4 Forest R Queensland
118 E6 Forestburg Alberta
109 K2 Forestburg Texas
110 F6 Forest City Arkansas
99 N6 Forest City Iowa
112 F2 Forest City N Carolina
95 M5 Forest City Pennsylvania
95 O3 Forest Dale Vermont
142 B3 Forestdale dist Perth, W Aust
109 O1 Forester Arkansas
94 E3 Forester Michigan
100 B9 Forest Glen California
101 Q3 Forestgrove Montana
100 B4 Forest Grove Oregon
102 D2 Foresthill California
111 D10 Forest Hill Louisiana
109 M9 Forest Hill Texas
141 G4 Forest Home Queensland
139 J8 Forestier, C Tasmania
139 J9 Forestier Pen Tasmania
99 O4 Forest Lake Minnesota
118 D7 Forest Lawn Alberta
15 D4 Forest of Atholl Scotland
99 N4 Foreston Minnesota
95 M3 Forestport New York
98 J1 Forest River N Dakota
9 G5 Forest Row England
102 B3 Forestville California
94 E3 Forestville Michigan
94 H4 Forestville New York
122 C5 Forestville Quebec
122 C5 Forestville, Parc de Quebec
19 J3 Forêt d'Argonne France
20 K5 Forêt Ste. Croix, la France
18 H7 Forez, Mts du France
15 F4 Forfar Scotland
107 K5 Forgan Oklahoma
118 K7 Forgan Sask
20 J2 Forges-les-Eaux France
121 O4 Forget Quebec
119 P9 Forget Sask
41 N2 Forggen See L W Germany
45 P8 Forio Italy
110 G6 Forked Deer R Tennessee
119 R7 Fork River R Manitoba
100 A2 Forks Washington
144 C5 Forks, The New Zealand
94 J9 Fork Union Virginia
42 E4 Forlì Italy
45 M3 Forlimpopoli Italy
14 E4 Forlorn Pt Irish Rep
98 J3 Forman N Dakota
13 E6 Formby England
138 D6 Formby B S Australia
13 E6 Formby Pt England
45 M5 Formello Italy
17 H6 Formentera isld Balearic Is
20 J2 Formerie France
43 F7 Formia Italy
130 F7 Formiga Brazil
126 G5 Formigas Bank Caribbean
45 J2 Formigine Italy
45 L2 Formignana Italy
20 D3 Formigny France
26 F7 Formofoss Norway
Formosa see Taiwan
133 F3 Formosa Argentina
129 J7 Formosa Brazil
129 J6 Formosa R Brazil
129 J6 Formosa do Rio Prêto Brazil
129 G6 Formosa, Serra mts Brazil
130 F4 Formoso Brazil
107 M2 Formoso Kansas
28 F4 Fornæs C Denmark
17 K4 Fornells Menorca
38 G8 Forni Avoltri Italy
15 E3 Forres Scotland
99 S9 Forrest Illinois
119 S9 Forrest Manitoba
143 G9 Forrest W Australia
146 E10 Forrestal Ra Antarctica
117 G8 Forrester I Alaska
142 C2 Forrestfield dist Perth, W Aust
143 G8 Forrest Lakes W Australia
143 G6 Forrest, Mt W Australia
99 R7 Forreston Illinois
142 G3 Forrest River Mission W Aust
26 J9 Fors Sweden
26 J3 Forsa Norway
26 J10 Forsa Sweden
108 F3 Forsan Texas
27 B13 Forsand Norway
141 G4 Forsayth Queensland
27 J11 Forsbacka Sweden
27 F12 Forshaga Sweden
27 F13 Forshem Sweden
27 F15 Förslöv Sweden
27 K11 Forsmark Sweden
26 J8 Forsmo Sweden
26 K5 Forsnäs Sweden
26 C8 Forsnes Norway
29 K11 Forssa Finland
31 H4 Forst E Germany
139 L4 Forster New S Wales
146 A13 Forster's Passage Antarctica
112 D4 Forsyth Georgia
99 S10 Forsyth Illinois
101 T3 Forsyth Montana
121 O4 Forsythe Quebec
145 E4 Forsyth I New Zealand
140 E3 Forsyth Is Queensland
141 G6 Forsyth Ra Queensland
74 E4 Fort Abbas Pakistan
111 E10 Fort Adams Mississippi
115 L7 Fort Albany Ontario
129 L4 Fortaleza Brazil
128 E5 Fortaleza de Ituxi Brazil
122 G9 Fort Anne Nat. Hist. Park Nova Scotia
Fort Archambault see Sarh
94 J7 Fort Ashby W Virginia
118 C4 Fort Assiniboine Alberta
99 S7 Fort Atkinson Wisconsin
15 D3 Fort Augustus Scotland
87 E12 Fort Beaufort S Africa
122 H8 Fort Beau Sejour Nat. Hist. Park New Brunswick
101 R1 Fort Belknap Agency Montana
111 M9 Fort Benning Georgia
101 P2 Fort Benton Montana
100 E8 Fort Bidwell California
118 K3 Fort Black Sask
102 A2 Fort Bragg California
112 H2 Fort Bragg N Carolina
110 J3 Fort Branch Indiana
101 P8 Fort Bridger Wyoming
99 K8 Fort Calhoun Nebraska
Fort Carnot see Ikongo
Fort Charlet see Djanet
115 N6 Fort Chimo Quebec
114 H6 Fort Chipewyan Alberta
98 E2 Fort Clark N Dakota
107 M6 Fort Cobb Oklahoma
98 A9 Fort Collins Colorado
140 F5 Fort Constantine Queensland
121 O7 Fort Coulonge Quebec
95 N2 Fort Covington New York
Fort Dauphin see Taolañaro
111 L9 Fort Davis Alabama
108 D5 Fort Davis Texas
103 P6 Fort Defiance Arizona
127 L4 Fort de France Martinique W I
111 K10 Fort Deposit Alabama
100 A8 Fort Dick California
99 M7 Fort Dodge Iowa
110 J5 Fort Donelson Nat Mil Park Tennessee
113 G10 Fort Drum Florida
9 E3 Fort Dunlop England
123 P2 Forteau Labrador
130 B6 Forte Coimbra Brazil
44 H4 Forte dei Marmi Italy
121 L10 Fort Erie Ontario
142 B5 Fortescue R W Australia
142 C5 Fortescue, R W Australia
95 L9 Fort Eustis Virginia
95 T7 Fort Fairfield Maine
112 K4 Fort Fisher N Carolina
Fort Flatters see Bordj Omar Driss
99 N1 Fort Frances Ontario
114 G4 Fort Franklin N W Terr
114 G7 Fort Fraser Br Col
112 F6 Fort Frederica Nat. Mon Georgia
111 L10 Fort Gaines Georgia
Fort Garaud see Fdérik
106 E4 Fort Garland Colorado
118 B1 Fort Garry Manitoba
94 E8 Fort Gay W Virginia
115 M7 Fort George Quebec
15 D3 Fort George Scotland
107 P6 Fort Gibson Oklahoma
114 G4 Fort Good Hope N W Terr
113 F10 Fort Green Florida
138 F3 Fort Grey New S Wales
109 H3 Fort Griffin Texas
12 E2 Forth Scotland
Fort Hall see Murango Kenya
101 N6 Fort Hall Idaho
13 F1 Forth, Firth of Scotland
115 L7 Fort Hope Ontario
12 D1 Forth, R Scotland
103 O10 Fort Huachuca Arizona
121 S6 Fortierville Quebec
6 L5 Forties oil rig North Sea
122 H9 Forties Settlement Nova Scotia
103 K3 Fortification Ra Nevada
128 F8 Fortin Carlos Antonio López Paraguay
101 L1 Fortine Montana
128 G8 Fortin Falcón Paraguay
133 F2 Fortin Gen. Caballero Paraguay
128 F8 Fortin General Eugenio Garay Paraguay
128 F8 Fortin Infante Rivarola Paraguay
122 E3 Fortin, L Quebec
133 E3 Fortin Lavalle Argentina
128 F8 Fortin Linares Paraguay
133 F2 Fortín Madrejón Paraguay
128 F7 Fortin Ravelo Bolivia
128 G8 Fortin Rojas Silva Paraguay
128 F7 Fortin Suárez Arana Bolivia
128 G7 Fortin Teniente Américo Picco Paraguay
Fort Jameson Zambia see Chipata
113 E13 Fort Jefferson Nat.Mon Florida
Fort Johnston see Mangoche
100 C8 Fort Jones California
118 G4 Fort Kent Alberta
95 S6 Fort Kent Maine
100 C7 Fort Klamath Oregon
94 B9 Fort Knox Kentucky
Fort Lallemande see Belhirane
Fort Lamy see N'Djamena
Fort Laperrine see Tamanrasset
98 B7 Fort Laramie Wyoming
113 G11 Fort Lauderdale Florida
112 G3 Fort Lawn S Carolina
100 C2 Fort Lewis Washington
114 G5 Fort Liard N W Terr
127 J5 Fort Liberté Haiti
98 F3 Fort Lincoln N Dakota
112 C2 Fort Loudon Lake Tennessee
98 B9 Fort Lupton Colorado
106 G3 Fort Lyon Colorado
108 G5 Fort McKavett Texas
117 S7 Fort MacKay Alberta
101 S5 Fort Mackenzie Wyoming
118 D9 Fort Macleod Alberta
Fort McMahon see El Homr
118 F2 Fort McMurray Alberta
114 F4 Fort McPherson N W Terr
99 P9 Fort Madison Iowa
22 B3 Fort Mahon Plage France
Fort Manning see Mchinji
113 F8 Fort Matanzas Nat.Mon Florida
113 F10 Fort Meade Florida
112 G2 Fort Mill S Carolina
98 C9 Fort Morgan Colorado
106 G1 Fort Morgan Colorado
113 F11 Fort Myers Florida
114 G6 Fort Nelson Br Col
117 M6 Fort Nelson Br Col
114 G5 Fort Norman N W Terr
113 F10 Fort Ogden Florida
43 G7 Fortore R Italy
111 L7 Fort Payne Alabama
114 J8 Fort Peck Res Montana
113 G10 Fort Pierce Florida
98 F5 Fort Pierre S Dakota
Fort Pierre Bordes see Tin Zaouaten
95 N4 Fort Plain New York
86 F5 Fort Portal Uganda
114 H5 Fort Providence N W Terr
112 G5 Fort Pulaski Nat. Mon Georgia
119 O8 Fort Qu' Appelle Sask
112 M2 Fort Raleigh Nat.Hist.Site N Carolina
116 F9 Fort Randall Alaska
98 H6 Fort Randall Dam S Dakota
94 C6 Fort Recovery Ohio
114 J5 Fort Reliance N W Terr
114 H5 Fort Resolution N W Terr
101 Q5 Fortress Mt Wyoming
123 M8 Fortress of Louisburg Nat. Hist. Park C Breton I, N Scotia
98 F3 Fort Rice N Dakota
107 O2 Fort Riley Kansas
99 M3 Fort Ripley Minnesota
87 E10 Fort Rixon Zimbabwe
98 C7 Fort Robinson Nebraska
100 D6 Fort Rock Oregon
144 B7 Fortrose New Zealand
Fort Rosebery Zambia see Mansa
102 A3 Fort Ross California
86 C6 Fort Rousset Congo
121 M1 Fort Rupert Quebec
117 L8 Fort St. James Br Col
114 G6 Fort St. John Br Col
74 C3 Fort Sandeman Pakistan
114 H7 Fort Saskatchewan Alberta
107 Q4 Fort Scott Kansas
115 L6 Fort Severn Ontario
100 B9 Fort Seward California
107 M7 Fort Sill Oklahoma
114 G5 Fort Simpson N W Terr
107 Q6 Fort Smith Arkansas
114 H5 Fort Smith N W Terr
101 T8 Fort Steele Wyoming
108 E5 Fort Stockton Texas
108 C1 Fort Sumner New Mexico
112 H5 Fort Sumter Nat.Mon S Carolina
107 L5 Fort Supply Oklahoma
108 E7 Fort Supply Res Oklahoma
103 P8 Fort Thomas Arizona
98 G5 Fort Thompson S Dakota
107 P7 Fort Towson Oklahoma
27 C10 Fortun Norway
100 A9 Fortuna California
98 C1 Fortuna N Dakota
17 G6 Fortuna Spain
116 F6 Fortuna Lodge Alaska
123 R6 Fortune Nfld
106 E6 Fort Union Nat.Mon New Mexico
112 D5 Fort Valley Georgia
114 H6 Fort Vermilion Alberta
89 G3 Fort Victoria Zimbabwe
94 B7 Fortville Indiana
111 K11 Fort Walton Florida
101 R6 Fort Washakie Wyoming
94 B5 Fort Wayne Indiana
113 E8 Fort White Florida
118 A2 Fort Whyte Manitoba
15 C4 Fort William Scotland
109 M10 Fort Worth Texas
98 F3 Fort Yates N Dakota
116 R5 Fortymile R Alaska
116 P3 Fort Yukon Alaska
77 D6 Forūr isld Iran
22 J2 Forville Belgium
119 N9 Forward Sask
52 H5 Fosforitnaya U.S.S.R.
67 D5 Foshan China
115 L2 Fosheim Pen N W Terr
26 D8 Fosna Norway
26 E7 Fosnes Norway
107 L6 Foss Oklahoma
44 C2 Fossano Italy
22 H3 Fosse Belgium
100 E4 Fossil Oregon
101 P8 Fossil Wyoming
141 G4 Fossilbrook Queensland
98 C6 Fossil Cycad Nat.Mon S Dakota
142 F4 Fossil Downs W Australia
121 L6 Fossmill Ontario
42 E5 Fossombrone Italy
99 L2 Fosston Minnesota
119 O6 Fosston Sask
98 J7 Foster Nebraska
100 C5 Foster Oregon
121 S7 Foster Quebec
139 H7 Foster Victoria
147 E10 Foster Bugt Greenland
99 T4 Foster City Michigan
118 J8 Fosterton Sask
110 K6 Fosterville Tennessee
94 D5 Fostoria Ohio
109 M5 Fostoria Texas
67 F4 Fotan China
142 F5 Fotheringham, Mt W Australia
20 J2 Foucarmont France
36 C7 Fouday France
18 C5 Fouesnant France
86 B6 Fougamou Gabon
20 C5 Fougères France
83 K13 Fougères,Pl.des Réunion Indian Oc
20 D5 Fougerolles-du-Plessis France
20 K2 Fouilloy France
109 O2 Fouke Arkansas
68 B3 Foul isld Burma
84 K5 Foul Bay Egypt
9 G4 Foulness Pt England
13 E5 Foulney isld England
144 C4 Foulwind, C New Zealand
86 B4 Foumban Cameroon
85 C2 Foum Zguid Morocco
106 F3 Fountain Colorado
99 U5 Fountain Michigan
99 O6 Fountain Minnesota
112 K2 Fountain N Carolina
103 N2 Fountain Grn Utah
111 E8 Fountain Hill Arkansas
112 E3 Fountain Inn S Carolina
16 B7 Foupana R Portugal
140 D3 Four Archers mt N Terr Aust
18 E7 Fouras France
101 U1 Four Buttes Montana
20 G5 Fourche, la France
110 B7 Fourche la Fave R Arkansas
19 J4 Fourchies, Mts des France
123 M8 Fourchu C Breton I, N Scotia
103 P4 Four Corners Utah
98 B5 Four Corners Wyoming
140 A1 Fourcroy, C N Terr Aust
146 C3 Four Ladies Bank Antarctica
22 G3 Fourmies France
83 K14 Fournaise, Piton de la vol Réunion Indian Oc
46 E5 Fournás Greece
83 L13 Fourneau isld Mauritius
123 P2 Fournel, L Quebec
22 D2 Fournes-en-Weppes France
122 G2 Fournier, L Quebec
47 H7 Foúrnoi isld Greece
127 K3 Four Paths Jamaica
19 N17 Fourques France
13 F3 Fourstones England
99 R3 Fourteenmile Pt Michigan
85 B6 Fouta Djalon mt reg Guinea
85 B5 Fouta Ferlo reg Senegal
8 D5 Fovant England
144 A7 Foveaux Strait New Zealand
28 C3 Fovlum Denmark
8 B7 Fowey England
113 G12 Fowey Rocks Florida
126 F2 Fowl Cay isld Bahamas
106 F3 Fowler Colorado
99 T9 Fowler Indiana
107 K4 Fowler Kansas
94 C3 Fowler Michigan
101 O1 Fowler Montana
144 A6 Fowler Pass New Zealand
138 B4 Fowler Pt S Australia
138 B4 Fowlers B S Australia
109 J7 Fowlerton Texas
94 C4 Fowlerville Michigan
110 G6 Fowlkes Tennessee
111 M11 Fowlstown Georgia
77 A1 Fowman Iran
99 T4 Fox Michigan
100 F5 Fox Oregon
99 S8 Fox R Illinois
115 K6 Fox R Manitoba
99 U3 Fox R Michigan
99 P9 Fox R Missouri
99 S5 Fox R Wisconsin
123 L4 Fox B Anticosti I, Quebec
94 H5 Foxburg Pennsylvania
117 O8 Fox Creek Alberta
117 P8 Fox Creek Alberta
115 M4 Foxe Basin N W Terr
115 L4 Foxe Chan N W Terr
115 M5 Foxe Pen N W Terr
14 B3 Foxford Irish Rep
119 M5 Foxford Sask
123 R1 Fox Harbour Labrador
13 H5 Foxholes England
98 K3 Foxhome Minnesota
116 P8 Fox Islands isld Aleutian Is
143 C10 Fox, L W Australia
99 S6 Fox Lake Wisconsin
101 T8 Foxpark Wyoming
144 C5 Fox Peak mt New Zealand
123 L4 Fox Pt Anticosti I, Quebec
117 L7 Fox R Br Col
145 E4 Foxton New Zealand
118 H8 Fox Valley Sask
119 Q8 Foxwarren Manitoba
111 G10 Foxworth Mississippi
15 D3 Foyers Scotland
14 D2 Foyle R N Ireland
14 D1 Foyle, L Irish Rep
14 B4 Foynes Irish Rep
16 C1 Foz Spain
87 B9 Foz do Cunene Angola
128 D5 Foz do Gregório Brazil
130 C9 Foz do Iguaçú Brazil
128 F5 Foz do Jamari Brazil
128 D5 Foz do Jordao Brazil
128 E4 Foz do Jutai Brazil
128 E4 Foz do Mamoriá Brazil
128 D5 Foz do Riozinho Brazil
67 E1 Foziling Shuiku res China
128 E5 Foz Tarauacá Brazil
95 L6 Frackville Pennsylvania
8 B7 Fraddon England
17 H3 Fraga Spain
36 B7 Fraize France
146 C3 Fram Bank Antarctica
22 F3 Frameries Belgium
95 Q4 Framingham Massachusetts
9 H3 Framlingham England
36 G3 Frammersbach W Germany
146 B5 Framnes Mts Antarctica
31 O5 Frampol Poland
130 F7 Franca Brazil
43 H8 Francavilla Fontana Italy
18 France rep W Europe
20 K3 France, Île de reg France
147 G10 France, Ile de Greenland
138 F6 Frances S Australia
100 B3 Frances Washington
117 J5 Frances R Yukon Terr
140 B2 Frances Creek N Terr Aust
101 N1 Frances, L Montana
114 G5 Frances L Yukon Terr
127 K5 Francés Viejo, C Dominican Rep
99 U9 Francesville Indiana
86 B6 Franceville Gabon
19 J6 Franche Comté prov France
107 O7 Francis Oklahoma
119 O8 Francis Sask
146 E13 Francis isld Antarctica
98 G6 Francis Case, L S Dakota
128 D4 Francisco de Orellana Peru
124 H5 Francisco I. Madero Coahuila Mexico
124 G5 Francisco I. Madero Durango Mexico
130 C9 Francisco, S R Brazil
130 G5 Francisco Sá Brazil
123 R1 Francis Harbour Labrador
95 Q1 Francis, L New Hampshire
89 E3 Francistown Botswana
123 Q6 François Nfld
117 K8 François L Br Col
127 M4 François, Le Martinique W I
45 L2 Francolino Italy
22 K2 Francorchamps Belgium
101 Q6 Francs Pk Wyoming
21 H7 Francueil France
25 E2 Franeker Netherlands
118 C9 Frank Alberta
36 F1 Frankenau W Germany
36 F2 Frankenbach W Germany
37 P2 Frankenberg E Germany
36 F1 Frankenberg/Eder W Germany
37 J5 Frankenhardt W Germany
37 J5 Frankenhöhe mts W Germany
94 D3 Frankenmuth Michigan
36 D5 Frankenstein W Germany
36 E4 Frankenthal W Germany
37 M3 Frankenwald mts E & W Germany
127 K2 Frankfield Jamaica
110 E2 Frankford Missouri
121 N8 Frankford Ontario
94 G9 Frankford W Virginia
94 A6 Frankfort Indiana
107 O2 Frankfort Kansas
94 C8 Frankfort Kentucky
99 U5 Frankfort Michigan
95 M3 Frankfort New York
94 D7 Frankfort Ohio
98 H5 Frankfort S Dakota
33 T7 Frankfurt E Germany
36 F3 Frankfurt am Main W Germany
31 H3 Frankfurt an der Oder E Germany
37 K6 Fränkische Alb mts W Germany
37 L4 Fränkische Schweiz reg W Germany
139 J7 Frankland, C Tasmania
111 L8 Franklin Georgia
101 O7 Franklin Idaho
94 A7 Franklin Indiana
110 K5 Franklin Kentucky
111 E12 Franklin Louisiana
95 T2 Franklin Maine
95 Q4 Franklin Massachusetts
101 Q3 Franklin Montana
112 D2 Franklin N Carolina
98 H9 Franklin Nebraska
95 Q3 Franklin New Hampshire
95 N5 Franklin New Jersey
95 M4 Franklin New York
94 C7 Franklin Ohio
94 H5 Franklin Pennsylvania
110 K6 Franklin Tennessee
109 L4 Franklin Texas
95 L10 Franklin Virginia
94 H8 Franklin W Virginia
114 G3 Franklin B N W Terr
115 H3 Franklin, Dist.of N W Terr
100 G1 Franklin D. Roosevelt L Washington
99 R8 Franklin Grove Illinois
138 D5 Franklin Harb S Australia
146 J6 Franklin I Antarctica
120 K7 Franklin I Ontario
103 J1 Franklin L Nevada
116 P2 Franklin Mts Alaska
144 A6 Franklin Mts New Zealand
117 L3 Franklin Mts N W Terr
116 H1 Franklin, Pt Alaska
139 J8 Franklin Snd Tasmania
115 K3 Franklin Str N W Terr
111 F11 Franklinton Louisiana
112 J1 Franklinton N Carolina
112 H2 Franklinville N Carolina
94 J4 Franklinville New York
100 J6 Franklin Whitney airport Idaho
144 D5 Franklyn, Mt New Zealand
37 J3 Fränk Saale R W Germany
109 M3 Frankston Texas
139 H7 Frankston Victoria
99 T7 Franksville Wisconsin
144 B6 Frankton New Zealand
101 R5 Frannie Wyoming
87 B10 Fransfontein Namibia
9 G5 Frant England
37 N3 Františkovy Lázně Czechoslovakia
147 L11 Frantsa Iosifa, Zemlya Arctic Oc
115 L8 Franz Ontario
33 R4 Franzburg E Germany
144 C5 Franz Josef Gla New Zealand
Franz Josef Land see Frantsa Iosifa, Zemlya
38 G7 Franz-Josefs Höhe mt Austria
43 B9 Frasca, C. d Sardinia
42 E7 Frascati Italy
106 E2 Fraser Colorado
139 L2 Fraser isld Queensland
100 C1 Fraser R Br Col
87 D12 Fraserburg S Africa
15 F3 Fraserburgh Scotland
120 J3 Fraserdale Ontario
141 L7 Fraser I Queensland
142 A6 Fraser I W Australia
143 C7 Fraser, Mt W Australia
143 E9 Fraser Range W Australia
69 E11 Fraser's Hill Malaysia
145 F3 Frasertown New Zealand
119 U8 Fraserwood Manitoba
46 D4 Frashër Albania
48 K6 Frasinet Romania
19 K6 Frasne France
22 F2 Frasnes-les-Buissenal Belgium
25 F5 Frasselt W Germany
45 J3 Frassinoro Italy
120 F5 Frater Ontario
45 L1 Fratta Polesine Italy
41 J2 Frauenfeld Switzerland
33 S10 Frauenhain E Germany
37 O5 Frauenstein mt W Germany
37 K2 Frauenwald E Germany
28 E6 Fraugde Denmark
131 F4 Fray Bentos Uruguay
20 H5 Frazé France
99 L3 Frazee Minnesota
101 T1 Frazer Montana
120 B3 Frazer L Ontario
36 B2 Frechen W Germany
16 D2 Frechilla Spain
32 G9 Freckenhorst W Germany
99 S2 Freda Michigan
98 E3 Freda N Dakota
36 E1 Fredeburg W Germany
32 L9 Freden W Germany
28 K5 Fredensborg Denmark
94 C2 Frederic Michigan
99 O4 Frederic Wisconsin
95 M7 Frederica Delaware
28 D5 Fredericia Denmark
99 Q9 Frederick Illinois
95 K7 Frederick Maryland
107 L7 Frederick Oklahoma
98 H4 Frederick S Dakota
140 D2 Frederick Hills N Terr Aust
120 J3 Frederick House R Ontario
137 L6 Frederick Reef Coral Sea
99 O7 Fredericksburg Iowa
95 L6 Fredericksburg Pennsylvania
94 K8 Fredericksburg Virginia
117 F7 Frederick Sd Alaska
110 F4 Fredericktown Missouri
94 E6 Fredericktown Ohio
122 F8 Fredericton New Brunswick
122 F8 Fredericton Junct New Brunswick
28 C4 Frederiks Denmark
29 K5 Frederiksberg Denmark
28 C5 Frederikshåb Denmark
115 P5 Frederikshåb Greenland
28 F2 Frederikshavn Denmark
28 H5 Frederikssund Denmark
127 M5 Frederiksted Virgin Is
28 J5 Frederiksværk Denmark
103 M5 Fredonia Arizona
128 C2 Fredonia Colombia
107 P4 Fredonia Kansas
110 H4 Fredonia Kentucky
98 G3 Fredonia N Dakota
94 H4 Fredonia New York
109 J5 Fredricksburg Texas
26 K7 Fredrika Sweden
27 E12 Fredrikstad Norway
110 E3 Freeburg Missouri
95 K6 Freeburg Pennsylvania
100 J4 Freedom Idaho
110 K2 Freedom Indiana
107 L5 Freedom Oklahoma
100 E9 Freedonyer Peak mt California
95 N6 Freehold New Jersey
94 C3 Freeland Michigan
95 M5 Freeland Pennsylvania
138 E4 Freeling Heights mt S Australia
140 C6 Freeling Mt N Terr Aust
102 E3 Freel Peak California
123 T4 Freels, C Nfld
98 J6 Freeman S Dakota
118 B4 Freeman R Alberta
110 K1 Freeman, L Indiana
111 G12 Freemason I Louisiana
111 K11 Freeport Florida
113 J11 Freeport Grand Bahama I
99 R7 Freeport Illinois
95 R3 Freeport Maine
122 F9 Freeport Nova Scotia
94 F6 Freeport Ohio
94 H6 Freeport Pennsylvania
109 M7 Freeport Texas
109 J8 Freer Texas
99 U5 Freesoil Michigan
127 P4 Freetown Antigua W I
126 F2 Freetown Eleuthera Bahamas
94 A8 Freetown Indiana
122 J7 Freetown Pr Edward I
85 B7 Freetown Sierra Leone
95 L4 Freeville New York
100 G4 Freewater Oregon
101 T7 Freezeout Mts Wyoming
16 C6 Fregenal de la Sierra Spain
26 C8 Frei Norway
37 P2 Freiberg E Germany
36 G6 Freiberg W Germany
37 O1 Freiberger Mulde R E Germany
40 G1 Freiburg W Germany
32 K10 Freienhagen W Germany
32 H10 Freienohl W Germany
36 G3 Freiensteinau W Germany
37 M4 Freihung W Germany
36 D2 Freilingen W Germany
133 C3 Freirina Chile
36 C4 Freisen W Germany
37 M7 Freising W Germany
38 L4 Freistadt Austria
16 C3 Freixo de Espada à Cinta Portugal
28 D2 Frejlev Denmark
143 B9 Fremantle W Australia
94 C5 Fremont Indiana
99 V6 Fremont Michigan
112 K2 Fremont N Carolina
98 K8 Fremont Nebraska
94 D5 Fremont Ohio
103 O3 Fremont R Utah
101 N8 Fremont I Utah
101 Q7 Fremont L Wyoming
106 D2 Fremont Pass Colorado
101 Q6 Fremont Pk Wyoming
106 F5 French New Mexico
112 D2 French Broad R Tennessee
94 D9 Frenchburg Kentucky
94 G5 French Cr Pennsylvania
100 J4 French Creek Idaho
102 T13 French Frigate Shoals Hawaiian Is
100 G7 Frenchglen Oregon
129 H3 French Guiana S America
100 C9 French Gulch California
139 H7 French I Victoria
110 K3 French Lick Indiana
102 F2 Frenchman Nevada
95 T2 Frenchman Bay Maine
118 H5 Frenchman Butte Sask
139 H8 Frenchman Cap Tasmania
101 S1 Frenchman Cr Mont/Sask
103 J5 Frenchman Flat dry lake Nevada
98 E9 Frenchman Fork R Nebraska
118 J9 Frenchman R Sask
123 O4 Frenchman's Cove Nfld
14 C3 Frenchpark Irish Rep
145 D4 French Pass New Zealand
French Terr. of the Afars and the Issas (FTAI) see Djibouti rep
95 M6 Frenchtown New Jersey
22 B2 Frencq France
19 Q14 Frêne, Pic du mt France
20 G3 Freneuse-sur-Risle France
37 K4 Frensdorf W Germany
31 L6 Frenštát Czechoslovakia
32 G8 Freren W Germany
143 D7 Frere Ra W Australia
129 H5 Fresco R Brazil
146 K4 Freshfield, C Antarctica
14 D4 Freshford Irish Rep
144 B6 Freshford Plain New Zealand
100 A9 Freshwater California
9 E6 Freshwater England
20 F5 Fresnay France
20 F5 Fresnaye-sur-Chédouet, la France
40 C2 Fresnes France
22 F3 Fresnes-sur-L'Escaut France
124 H6 Fresnillo de González Echeverría Mexico
102 E5 Fresno California
102 E4 Fresno R California
101 P1 Fresno Res Montana
20 H2 Fresnoy-Folny France
22 E4 Fresnoy-le-Grand France
40 C4 Fresse, Mt.de France
20 J1 Fressenneville France
27 B10 Fresvik Norway
21 H6 Fréteval France
27 B11 Fretheim Norway
19 J5 Fretigney France
13 E1 Freuchie Scotland
36 G4 Freudenberg Baden-Württemberg W Germany
36 D2 Freudenberg Nordrhein-Westfalen W Germany
36 E7 Freudenstadt W Germany
22 C3 Frévent France
138 D2 Frew R S Australia
140 D4 Frewena N Terr Aust
94 H4 Frewsburg New York
37 M1 Freyburg E Germany
143 A10 Freycinet, C W Australia
143 A7 Freycinet Estuary inlet W Aust
139 J8 Freycinet Pen Tasmania
33 Q6 Freyenstein E Germany
36 B5 Freyming France
37 L5 Freystadt W Germany
30 H7 Freyung W Germany
85 B6 Fria Guinea
87 B9 Fria, C Namibia
102 E5 Friant California
102 E5 Friant Dam California
111 F7 Friar Port Mississippi
127 P4 Friar's B., North St Kitts W I
83 L10 Friar's Hood mt Sri Lanka
131 D2 Frias Argentina
40 F4 Fribourg Switzerland
36 E3 Frickhofen W Germany
22 D3 Fricourt France
100 B1 Friday Harbour Washington
141 F1 Friday I Queensland
13 H5 Fridaythorpe England
146 G8 Fridtjof Nansen, Mt Antarctica
38 O7 Friedberg Austria
37 K7 Friedberg Bayern W Germany
36 F3 Friedberg Hessen W Germany
33 P9 Friedeburg E Germany
38 M4 Friedersbach Austria
33 T8 Friedersdorf E Germany
33 T5 Friedland E Germany
32 L10 Friedland W Germany
37 K2 Friedrichroda E Germany
36 F3 Friedrichsdorf W Germany
33 T7 Friedrichsfelde E Germany
41 K2 Friedrichshafen W Germany
33 T8 Friedrichshagen E Germany
32 J4 Friedrichskoog W Germany
33 P5 Friedrichsruhe E Germany
30 E1 Friedrichstadt W Germany
33 T6 Friedrichswalde E Germany
37 K2 Friedrichswerth E Germany
36 G2 Frielendorf W Germany
107 K3 Friend Kansas
98 J9 Friend Nebraska
Friendly Is see Tonga
95 S3 Friendship Maine
94 J4 Friendship New York
94 D8 Friendship Ohio
99 R6 Friendship Wisconsin
127 K2 Friendship peak Jamaica
70 C2 Friendship Shoal S China Sea
94 H7 Friendsville Maryland
27 D12 Frierfjord inlet Norway
94 F10 Fries Virginia
38 K8 Friesach Austria
33 R7 Friesack E Germany
25 F2 Friesche Gat Netherlands
36 D7 Friesenheim W Germany
28 A7 Friesische Inseln islds W Germany
25 E2 Friesland Netherlands
32 G6 Friesoythe W Germany
83 J12 Frigate isld Seychelles
45 J3 Frignano Italy
9 H4 Frinton England
124 H6 Frío Mexico
109 J7 Frio R Texas
130 H8 Frio, C Brazil
15 F4 Friockheim Scotland
108 E1 Frio Draw R New Mex/Tex
36 F6 Friolzheim W Germany
22 L4 Frisange Luxembourg
109 L2 Frisco Texas
111 J10 Frisco City Alabama
103 L3 Frisco Mt Utah
108 C8 Fritch Texas
8 B6 Frithelstock Stone England
36 G1 Fritzlar W Germany
42 E2 Friuli-Venezia-Giulia prov Italy
20 J1 Friville-Escarbotin France
12 E5 Frizington England
26 D8 Froan isld Norway
119 P9 Frobisher Sask
115 N5 Frobisher Bay N W Terr
114 J6 Frobisher L Sask
19 P14 Froges France
118 G5 Frog L L.Alberta
26 D8 Frohavet inlet Norway
37 O1 Frohburg E Germany
33 S7 Frohnau E Germany
33 P8 Frohse E Germany
98 B1 Froid Montana
22 G3 Froid-Chapelle Belgium
130 F5 Fróis Brazil
20 K2 Froïssy France
36 B2 Froitzheim W Germany
52 H4 Frolovskaya U.S.S.R.
55 E1 Froly U.S.S.R.
101 R4 Fromberg Montana
31 M1 Frombork Poland
8 D5 Frome England
127 H1 Frome Jamaica
141 G3 Frome Queensland
138 E3 Frome R S Australia
138 E4 Frome Downs S Australia
138 E4 Frome, L S Australia
22 D2 Fromelles France
32 G10 Fröndenberg W Germany
36 F2 Fronhausen W Germany
16 B5 Fronteira Portugal
18 E6 Frontenay France
21 D9 Frontenay-Rohan-Rohan France
37 O6 Frontenhausen W Germany
125 N8 Frontera Mexico
124 E2 Fronteras Mexico
118 J9 Frontier Sask
101 P8 Frontier Wyoming
18 H9 Frontignan France
106 E1 Front Range Colorado
94 J8 Front Royal Virginia
28 F6 Frørup Denmark
33 O9 Frose E Germany
43 E7 Frosinone Italy
28 B3 Frøslev Denmark
21 B7 Frossay France
109 L3 Frost Texas
26 E8 Frosta Norway
94 J7 Frostburg Maryland
113 F10 Frostproof Florida
28 B2 Frøstrup Denmark
26 G7 Frostviken Sweden
37 K2 Fröttstädt E Germany
19 K4 Frouard France
119 O9 Froude Sask
27 H12 Frövi Sweden
9 E5 Froxfield England
26 C8 Fröya isld Norway
26 B8 Fröyabanken Norway
22 C3 Fruges France
106 B2 Fruita Colorado
111 H10 Fruitdale Alabama
98 C5 Fruitdale S Dakota
100 J5 Fruitland Idaho
106 B5 Fruitland New Mexico
101 P9 Fruitland Utah
144 B6 Fruitlands New Zealand
100 J5 Fruitvale Idaho
48 K3 Frumuşica Romania
57 G3 Frunze U.S.S.R.
54 F8 Frunzenskiy U.S.S.R.
48 M3 Frunzovka U.S.S.R.
48 F5 Fruška Gora mt Yugoslavia
130 E7 Frutal Brazil
40 G4 Frutigen Switzerland
102 B2 Fruto California
54 K1 Fryanovo U.S.S.R.
98 C3 Fryburg N Dakota
48 E1 Frýdek Mistek Czechoslovakia
95 R2 Fryeburg Maine
27 F11 Fryksände Sweden
46 E5 Ftéri mt Greece
67 F3 Fu'an China
45 J4 Fucecchio Italy
65 B7 Fucheng China
65 C6 Fucheng China
36 E2 Fuchskauten mt W Germany
60 G11 Fuchū Japan
67 D4 Fuchuan China
59 G6 Fuchun Jiang R China
42 F7 Fucino, Alveo del L Italy
61 P5 Fudai Japan
67 G3 Fuding China
16 D8 Fuengirola Spain
108 G7 Fuente Mexico
17 G7 Fuente Alamo de Murcia Spain
16 C6 Fuente de Cantos Spain
16 C4 Fuenteguinaldo Spain
16 D6 Fuenteobejuna Spain
16 D3 Fuentesaúco Spain
17 G3 Fuentes de Ebro Spain
16 C4 Fuentes de Oñoro Spain
130 B7 Fuerte Olimpo Paraguay
85 B3 Fuerteventura isld Canary Is
71 E1 Fuga isld Luzon Philippines
38 E7 Fügen Austria
28 M2 Fuglebjærge Faeroes
28 H6 Fuglebjerg Denmark
28 O9 Fuglø isld Faeroes
26 L1 Fuglöy isld Norway
28 F7 Fuglsbølle Denmark
65 C7 Fugou China
65 B5 Fugu China
Fuguo see Zhanhua
33 Q9 Fuhne R E Germany
32 L7 Fuhrberg W Germany
77 E7 Fujayrah, Al U.A.E.
67 B1 Fu Jiang R China
67 F3 Fujian prov China
61 M10 Fuji Hakone Izu Nat. Park Japan
61 M10 Fuji-kawa R Japan
59 K2 Fujin China
61 M10 Fujinomiya Japan
61 N9 Fujioka Japan
61 O5 Fujisaki Japan
59 L4 Fuji San mt Japan
61 M10 Fuji-san vol Japan
61 N10 Fujisawa Japan
61 M10 Fujiyoshida Japan
61 N5 Fukaura Japan
Fukien prov see Fujian
60 J10 Fukuchiyama Japan
60 B13 Fukue Japan
60 B13 Fukue-jima isld Japan
61 K9 Fukui Japan
60 D12 Fukuma Japan

28 Fukuno — Georgetown

61 K9 **Fukuno** Japan
60 D12 **Fukuoka** Japan
60 H11 **Fukura** Japan
61 L11 **Fukuroi** Japan
60 O4 **Fukushima** Hokkaido Japan
61 O8 **Fukushima** Honshu Japan
61 L10 **Fukushima** Nagano Japan
61 O8 **Fukushima** *prefect* Japan
60 G11 **Fukuyama** Honshu Japan
60 D14 **Fukuyama** Kyūshū Japan
60 H10 **Fukuzaki** Japan
85 B6 **Fulacunda** Guinea-Bissau
77 C1 **Fulād Mahalleh** Iran
99 L6 **Fulda** Minnesota
36 H2 **Fulda** W Germany
32 L10 **Fulda** *R* W Germany
36 H2 **Fulda** *R* W Germany
36 G1 **Fuldabrück** W Germany
13 G6 **Fulford** England
58 D6 **Fulin** China
67 B2 **Fuling** China
67 F3 **Fuling** China
127 N3 **Fullarton** Trinidad
141 F5 **Fullarton** *R* Queensland
102 G8 **Fullerton** California
94 E8 **Fullerton** Kentucky
109 P4 **Fullerton** Louisiana
98 H8 **Fullerton** Nebraska
65 F2 **Fulongquan** China
48 E4 **Fülöpszállás** Hungary
41 O3 **Fulpmes** Austria
111 J10 **Fulton** Alabama
111 C8 **Fulton** Arkansas
99 Q8 **Fulton** Illinois
94 A6 **Fulton** Indiana
107 O3 **Fulton** Kansas
110 H5 **Fulton** Kentucky
111 C11 **Fulton** Louisiana
111 H7 **Fulton** Mississippi
110 E3 **Fulton** Missouri
95 L3 **Fulton** New York
94 E6 **Fulton** Ohio
98 J6 **Fulton** S Dakota
95 N4 **Fultonham** New York
95 N4 **Fultonville** New York
27 F10 **Fuluälven** *R* Sweden
27 F10 **Fulufj** *mt* Sweden
27 F10 **Fulunäs** Sweden
22 H4 **Fumay** France
18 F8 **Fumel** France
41 N5 **Fumo, Mt** Italy
61 N10 **Funabashi** Japan
137 Q3 **Funafuti** *atoll* Tuvalu
60 E14 **Funahiki** Japan
Funan *see* **Fusui**
65 F4 **Funan** China
26 F9 **Funäsdalen** Sweden
85 A2 **Funchal** Madeira
16 B7 **Funcheira** Portugal
126 G9 **Fundación** Colombia
130 H6 **Fundão** Brazil
124 E4 **Fundición** Mexico
28 N1 **Funding** Faeroes
38 E8 **Fundres** Italy
48 K6 **Fundulea** Romania
41 N3 **Fundus Feiler** *mt* Austria
122 G8 **Fundy, B. of** Nova Scotia/New Bruns
122 G8 **Fundy Nat. Park** New Brunswick
Funen *isld see* **Fyn**
102 H5 **Funeral Peak** California
87 F10 **Funhalouro** Mozambique
65 D5 **Funing** China
67 B5 **Funing** China
98 G9 **Funk** Nebraska
123 T4 **Funk I** Nfld
141 J5 **Funnel** *R* Queensland
117 F6 **Funter** Alaska
85 F6 **Funtua** Nigeria
65 A7 **Fuping** China
65 C5 **Fuping** China
67 F4 **Fuqing** China
112 J2 **Fuquay Springs** N Carolina
88 D9 **Furancungo** Mozambique
60 Q2 **Furano** Japan
59 J2 **Furao** China
47 G1 **Furculeşti** Romania
83 G3 **Fureidis** Israel
60 O3 **Furenai** Japan
60 T2 **Füren ko** *L* Japan
28 K5 **Furesø** *L* Denmark
36 G5 **Fürfeld** Baden-Württemberg W Germany
36 D4 **Fürfeld** Rheinland-Pfalz W Germany
77 D5 **Furg** Iran
112 F5 **Furman** S Carolina
52 F6 **Furmanov** U.S.S.R.
57 G3 **Furmanovka** U.S.S.R.
12 C1 **Furnace** Scotland
130 F7 **Furnas Dam** Brazil
139 J8 **Furneaux Group** *islds* Tasmania
138 F6 **Furner** S Australia
Furnes *see* **Veurne**
27 E11 **Furnes** Norway
118 H5 **Furness** Sask
67 B2 **Furong Jiang** *R* China
67 E3 **Furong Shan** *mt* China
32 G7 **Fürstenau** W Germany
33 S6 **Fürstenberg** E Germany
36 F1 **Fürstenberg** W Germany
38 O7 **Fürstenfeld** Austria
37 L7 **Fürstenfeldbrück** W Germany
30 H3 **Fürstenwalde** E Germany
33 T6 **Fürstenwerder** E Germany
37 P6 **Fürstenzell** W Germany
36 F4 **Fürth** W Germany
37 O5 **Furth im Wald** W Germany
41 H1 **Furtwangen** W Germany
60 O2 **Furubira** Japan
61 L9 **Furukawa** Japan
61 O7 **Furukawa** Japan
115 L4 **Fury & Hecla Str** N W Terr
27 A11 **Fusa** Norway
128 D3 **Fusagasuga** Colombia
45 Q8 **Fusaro** *L* Italy
43 G9 **Fuscaldo** Italy
38 G7 **Fusch** Austria
32 M8 **Fuse** *R* W Germany
65 B6 **Fushan** China
65 E6 **Fushan** China
68 J3 **Fushan** China
13 E2 **Fushiebridge** Scotland
61 K9 **Fushiki** Japan
60 P2 **Fushiko-Uryū** Japan
59 H3 **Fushun** China
67 A2 **Fushun** China
45 L3 **Fusignano** Italy
118 H7 **Fusilier** Sask
Fusin *see* **Fuxin**
45 M1 **Fusina** Italy
41 J5 **Fusio** Switzerland
59 J3 **Fusong** China
41 N2 **Füssen** W Germany
28 D4 **Fussing Sø** *L* Denmark
67 B5 **Fusui** China
61 L11 **Futagawa** Japan
60 E12 **Futago-san** *mt* Japan
60 D11 **Futaoi-jima** *isld* Japan
45 K3 **Futa, Passo di** Italy
61 O5 **Futatsui** Japan
61 N13 **Futatsu-ne** *rocks* Japan
61 P13 **Futemma** Okinawa
137 R4 **Futuna** *isld* Îles de Horn Pacific Oc
67 F3 **Futun Xi** *R* China
79 A7 **Fuwa** Egypt
65 A6 **Fu Xian** China
65 E5 **Fu Xian** China
67 A4 **Fuxian Hu** *L* China
65 E3 **Fuxin** China
Fuxing *see* **Wangmo**
58 G5 **Fuyang** China
67 F1 **Fuyang** China
67 F5 **Fuyang** China
58 G4 **Fuyang He** *R* China
67 G3 **Fuying Dao** *isld* China
59 H2 **Fuyu** China
59 K2 **Fuyuan** China
67 A4 **Fuyuan** China
66 D2 **Fuyun** China
48 F3 **Füzesabony** Hungary
48 G3 **Füzesgyarmat** Hungary
67 F3 **Fuzhou** Fujian China
67 E2 **Fuzhou** Jiangxi China
65 E5 **Fuzhoucheng** China
9 G4 **Fyfield** Essex England
9 E4 **Fyfield** Oxon England
28 E6 **Fyn** *co* Denmark
28 E6 **Fyn** *isld* Denmark
12 C1 **Fyne, L** Scotland
28 D7 **Fynshav** Denmark
28 F5 **Fynshoved** *C* Denmark
27 C12 **Fyresv** *L* Norway
127 O3 **Fyzabad** Trinidad
70 C4 **Gaat** *R* Sarawak
52 D4 **Gabanova** U.S.S.R.
123 M8 **Gabarouse** C Breton I, N Scotia
18 F9 **Gabarret** France
102 G3 **Gabbs** Nevada
102 F3 **Gabbs Valley Ra** Nevada
87 B8 **Gabela** Angola
Gaberones *see* **Gaborone**
85 F2 **Gabès** Tunisia
85 G2 **Gabès, Gulf of** Tunisia
84 J5 **Gabgaba, Wadi** *watercourse* Sudan
102 C5 **Gabilan Ra** California
31 M3 **Gąbin** Poland
145 G3 **Gable End Foreland** New Zealand
117 K9 **Gable Mt** Br Columbia
139 J7 **Gabo** *isld* Victoria
61 C6 **Gabol** Denmark
86 B6 **Gabon** *rep* Equat Africa
89 D5 **Gaborone** Botswana
95 N2 **Gabriels** New York
16 C4 **Gabriel y Galán, Embalse** *res* Spain
77 F7 **Gābrik** Iran
47 G2 **Gabrovo** Bulgaria
83 L14 **Gaby** *isld* Kerguelen Indian Oc
20 F4 **Gacé** France
77 B4 **Gach Sārān** Iran
98 G3 **Gackle** N Dakota
48 E7 **Gacko** Yugoslavia
74 E3 **Gadag** India
86 G2 **Gadamai** Sudan
28 C5 **Gadbjerg** Denmark
26 G7 **Gäddede** Sweden
32 J8 **Gadderbaum** W Germany
33 O5 **Gadebusch** E Germany
80 D3 **Gadish** Israel
17 F8 **Gador, Sierra de** Spain
80 F1 **Gadot** Israel
118 E6 **Gadsby** Alberta
111 L8 **Gadsden** Alabama
103 K9 **Gadsden** Arizona
28 J5 **Gadstrup** Denmark
76 C2 **Gadwal** India
54 F6 **Gadyach** U.S.S.R.
89 G2 **Gadzema** Zimbabwe
86 C6 **Gadzi** Cent Afr Republic
48 J6 **Găeşti** Romania
43 F8 **Gaeta** Italy
45 P8 **Gaeta, Gulf of** Italy
112 F2 **Gaffney** S Carolina
71 A2 **Gafi** *isld* Indonesia
38 L6 **Gaflenz** Austria
85 F2 **Gafsa** Tunisia
57 E4 **Gafurov** U.S.S.R.
71 B3 **Gag** *isld* Indonesia
54 F1 **Gagarin** U.S.S.R.
106 B9 **Gage** New Mexico
107 L5 **Gage** Oklahoma
122 H7 **Gage, C** Pr Edward I
99 R4 **Gagen** Wisconsin
19 O15 **Gagère, P. de la** *mt* France
122 F8 **Gagetown** New Brunswick
36 E6 **Gaggenau** W Germany
52 F6 **Gagino** U.S.S.R.
27 H11 **Gagnef** Sweden
85 C7 **Gagnoa** Ivory Coast
115 N7 **Gagnon** Quebec
121 P6 **Gagnon, L** Quebec
52 H4 **Gagshor** U.S.S.R.
38 N6 **Gahns** *mt* Austria
130 B5 **Gaiab** *watercourse* Namibia
133 E5 **Gaiba** *L* Bolivia/Brazil
75 N6 **Gaibanda** Bangladesh
48 L4 **Găiceana** Romania
47 H10 **Gaïdhouronísi** *isld* Crete Greece
38 J8 **Gail** *R* Austria
36 J6 **Gaildorf** W Germany
18 G9 **Gaillac** France
122 E1 **Gaillarbois, L** Quebec
20 J2 **Gaillefontaine** France
20 H3 **Gaillon** France
38 G8 **Gailtaler Alpen** *mts* Austria
133 D6 **Gaiman** Argentina
37 L6 **Gaimersheim** W Germany
94 B10 **Gainesboro** Tennessee
111 H9 **Gainesville** Alabama
113 F8 **Gainesville** Florida
109 K2 **Gainesville** Texas
13 G4 **Gainford** England
13 H6 **Gainsborough** England
119 Q9 **Gainsborough** Sask
138 D4 **Gairdner L** S Australia
15 C3 **Gairloch** Scotland
15 C4 **Gairlochy** Scotland
15 E3 **Gairn** *R* Scotland
38 L7 **Gaishorn** Austria
95 K7 **Gaithersburg** Maryland
65 C4 **Gai Xian** China
70 P9 **Gajam** Indonesia
76 B3 **Gajendragara** India
89 C6 **Gakarosa** *mt* S Africa
116 P5 **Gakona** Alaska
52 E4 **Gakugsa** U.S.S.R.
86 D6 **Gala** China
15 F5 **Gala** *R* Scotland
77 H2 **Gāl'a, Band-i-** *mts* Afghanistan
86 J4 **Galadi** Ethiopia
83 K10 **Galagedara** Sri Lanka
47 H4 **Gala Gölü** *L* Turkey
118 F6 **Galahad** Alberta
79 B9 **Galâla el Baharîya, G. el** *mts* Egypt
79 C10 **Galâla el Qiblîya, G. el** *mts* Egypt
17 G4 **Galamocha** Spain
88 G3 **Galana** *R* Kenya
69 G12 **Galang** *isld* Indonesia
26 N3 **Galanito** Norway
48 D2 **Galanta** Czechoslovakia
128 A7 **Galapagos Is** Pacific Oc
13 F2 **Galashiels** Scotland
101 O1 **Galata** Montana
47 F7 **Galatás** Greece
106 G3 **Galatea** Colorado
145 F3 **Galatea** New Zealand
137 P8 **Galathea Depth** Pacific Oc
48 L5 **Galati** Romania
110 H4 **Galatia** Illinois
107 M3 **Galatia** Kansas
43 J8 **Galatina** Italy
Galatz *see* **Galati**
19 O14 **Galaure** *R* France
94 G10 **Galax** Virginia
46 E6 **Galaxidhion** Greece
141 F3 **Galbraith** Queensland
124 J5 **Gal. Cepeda** Mexico
26 C10 **Galdhöpiggen** *mt* Norway
124 G2 **Galeana** Mexico
130 G8 **Galeão** Brazil
45 L4 **Galeata** Italy
77 C6 **Galeh Dār** Iran
71 A2 **Galela** Indonesia
116 J4 **Galena** Alaska
99 Q7 **Galena** Illinois
107 Q4 **Galena** Kansas
95 M7 **Galena** Maryland
110 C5 **Galena** Missouri
109 G9 **Galena Park** Texas
33 T5 **Galenbecker See** *L* E Germany
127 P3 **Galeota Pt** Trinidad
17 F7 **Galera** Spain
128 B3 **Galera, Pta** *point* Ecuador
131 A8 **Galera, Pta. de la** Chile
99 Q9 **Galesburg** Illinois
94 B4 **Galesburg** Michigan
99 P5 **Galesville** Wisconsin
98 B9 **Galeton** Colorado
120 K1 **Galeton** Ontario
94 K5 **Galeton** Pennsylvania
83 J13 **Galets, Pte des** Réunion Indian Oc
13 F6 **Galgate** England
83 K10 **Galgiriya** *mt* Sri Lanka
117 M11 **Galiano I** Br Columbia
19 Q14 **Galibier, Col du** *pass* France
100 B7 **Galice** Oregon
48 J1 **Galich** U.S.S.R.
47 F1 **Galiche** Bulgaria
52 F5 **Galichskoye, Oz** *L* U.S.S.R.
16 B2 **Galicia** Spain
99 U8 **Galien** Michigan
145 E2 **Galilee** *L* Queensland
141 H5 **Galilee, Sea of** Israel
80 F2 **Galilee, Sea of** Israel
127 L2 **Galina Pt** Jamaica
94 E6 **Galion** Ohio
127 M4 **Galion, Baie du** Martinique W I
123 O2 **Galissonnière, L.la** Quebec
43 C11 **Galite, La** Tunisia
103 O9 **Galiurov Mts** Arizona
55 D3 **Galkino** U.S.S.R.
86 G3 **Gallabat** Sudan
86 A2 **Gallacaio** Somalia
42 B3 **Gallarate** Italy
20 J4 **Gallardon** France
99 N10 **Gallatin** Missouri
110 K5 **Gallatin** Tennessee
109 M4 **Gallatin** Texas
101 O4 **Gallatin** *R* Montana
101 O4 **Gallatin Gateway** Montana
101 O4 **Gallatin Pk** Montana
101 P4 **Gallatin Ra** Mont/Wyoming
83 K11 **Galle** Sri Lanka
17 G3 **Gállego** *R* Spain
106 G6 **Gallegos** New Mexico
133 C6 **Gallegos** *R* Argentina
45 J4 **Galleno** Italy
123 O2 **Gallet** *L* Quebec
14 C5 **Galley Hd** Irish Rep
45 J3 **Gallicano** Italy
45 N6 **Gallicano nel Lazio** Italy
46 F4 **Gallikós** *R* Greece
33 Q5 **Gallin** E Germany
106 D5 **Gallina Pk** New Mexico
44 D3 **Gallinara** *isld* Italy
108 B1 **Gallinas Peak** New Mexico
128 D1 **Gallinas, Pta** *C* Colombia
43 H8 **Gallipoli** Italy
Gallipoli Turkey *see* **Gelibolu**
94 E8 **Gallipolis** Ohio
94 J6 **Gallitzin** Penn
26 L4 **Gallivare** Sweden
45 Q7 **Gallo** Italy
26 H9 **Gällö** Sweden
17 F4 **Gallo** *R* Spain
17 F4 **Gallocanta, L.de** Spain
43 E10 **Gallo, C.di** Sicily
106 B8 **Gallo Mts** New Mexico
95 L3 **Galloo I** New York
7 M11 **Galloper Lightship** North Sea
15 D6 **Galloway** Scotland
27 F14 **Gällstad** Sweden
106 B6 **Gallup** New Mexico
17 G3 **Gallur** Spain
45 J3 **Galluzzo** Italy
85 F6 **Galmi** Niger
139 J5 **Galong** New S Wales
83 L10 **Gal Oya** *R* Sri Lanka
130 H10 **Galpão** Brazil
28 C6 **Galsted** Denmark
12 D2 **Galston** Scotland
26 J9 **Galström** Sweden
102 C3 **Galt** California
99 N9 **Galt** Missouri
28 D4 **Galten** Denmark
26 N1 **Galten** Norway
124 F3 **Gal. Trías** Mexico
41 M4 **Galtür** Austria
14 C4 **Galtymore** *mt* Irish Rep
72 F6 **Galumpang** Sulawesi
99 R8 **Galva** Illinois
94 A6 **Galveston** Indiana
111 B12 **Galveston** Texas
131 E4 **Galvez** Argentina
14 B3 **Galway** Irish Rep
14 B3 **Galway** *co* Irish Rep
14 B3 **Galway Bay** Irish Rep
71 B3 **Gam** *isld* Indonesia
71 C3 **Gam** *isld* W Irian
20 J2 **Gamaches** France
61 L11 **Gamagōri** Japan
131 E8 **Gamas, l** Argentina
94 B10 **Gamaliel** Kentucky
86 H3 **Gamarri, L** Ethiopia
71 G4 **Gamay Bay** Philippines
75 N4 **Gamba** China
86 B6 **Gamba** Ghana
20 J4 **Gambais** France
45 J4 **Gambassi** Italy
45 R6 **Gambatesa** Italy
86 F4 **Gambela** Ethiopia
116 B5 **Gambell** St Lawrence I, Alaska
45 M3 **Gambettola** Italy
85 A6 **Gambia** *R* The Gambia/Senegal
85 A6 **Gambia, The** *rep* W Africa
113 L9 **Gambier** New Providence I Bahamas
94 E6 **Gambier** Ohio
140 B1 **Gambier, C** N Terr Aust
135 R15 **Gambier Is** Pacific Oc
138 D6 **Gambier Is** S Australia
124 F9 **Gamboa** Panama Canal Zone
86 C6 **Gamboma** Congo
141 G3 **Gamboola** Queensland
86 C5 **Gamboula** Cent Afr Republic
71 H4 **Gamdaha** Sri Lanka
130 J10 **Gameleira** Brazil
71 E7 **Gamkunoro Gunung** *mt* Indonesia
71 A2 **Gamlaba** Indonesia
27 H14 **Gamleby** Sweden
26 M6 **Gammelstad** Sweden
36 G7 **Gammertingen** W Germany
16 D4 **Gamo** *R* Spain
86 G4 **Gamo-Gofa** *prov* Ethiopia
76 E7 **Gampola** Sri Lanka
77 G5 **Gamshadzai K** *mts* Iran
71 E5 **Gamtjaka, Tg** *C* Indonesia
26 Q1 **Gamvik** Norway
18 E9 **Gan** France
73 L9 **Gan** Maldives
107 O6 **Ganacker** W Germany
86 G4 **Ganado** Arizona
109 L6 **Ganado** Texas
86 H4 **Ganale Dorya** *R* Ethiopia
86 H5 **Ganane** Somalia
121 O8 **Gananoque** Ontario
67 C7 **Gancheng** China
Gand *see* **Gent**
70 F6 **Gandadiwata G** *mt* Sulawesi
87 D7 **Gandajika** Zaïre
74 B4 **Gandava** Pakistan
115 O8 **Gander** Nfld
123 S4 **Gander Bay** Nfld
32 J6 **Ganderkesee** W Germany
123 R5 **Gander** *R* Nfld
17 H3 **Gandesa** Spain
17 G6 **Gandia** Spain
28 E2 **Gandrup** Denmark
103 L2 **Gandy** Utah
77 B5 **Ganēveh** Iran
83 K10 **Ganewatta** Sri Lanka
74 H5 **Ganga** *R* India
74 G9 **Gangakher** India
133 D6 **Gan Gan** Argentina
74 E4 **Ganganagar** India
68 B1 **Gangaw** Burma
76 C3 **Gangawati** India
75 R6 **Gangaw Range** Burma
66 C5 **Gangdisê Shan** *mt ra* China
25 F7 **Gangelt** W Germany
18 H9 **Ganges** France
Ganges *R see* **Ganga** *R*
75 N8 **Ganges, Mouths of the** Bangladesh/India
27 F14 **Gånghester** Sweden
37 O7 **Gangkofen** W Germany
65 F4 **Gangou** China
75 N5 **Gangtok** India
65 A6 **Ganguan** China
65 A6 **Gangui** China
71 B3 **Gani** Indonesia
67 E3 **Gan Jiang** *R* China
Ganjig *see* **Horqin Zuoyi Houqi**
139 H5 **Ganmam** New S Wales
18 H6 **Gannat** France
145 E2 **Gannet I** New Zealand
101 L6 **Gannett** Idaho
101 Q6 **Gannett Pk** Wyoming
80 C5 **Ganne Yehuda** Israel
98 G5 **Gannvalley** S Dakota
80 C6 **Gan Shelomo** Israel
58 C3 **Gansu** *prov* China
Gantang *see* **Taiping**
143 A8 **Gantheaume B** W Australia
138 E6 **Gantheaume, C** S Australia
142 D4 **Gantheaume Pt** W Australia
69 J14 **Gantung** Indonesia
67 E4 **Gan Xian** China
80 B6 **Gan Yavne** Israel
87 D11 **Ganyesa** S Africa
65 D7 **Ganyu** China
65 D4 **Ganzhao** China
67 E4 **Ganzhou** China
33 Q6 **Ganzlin** E Germany
85 D5 **Gao** Mali
67 E2 **Gao'an** China
Gaobeidian *see* **Xincheng**
65 C5 **Gaocheng** China
67 F1 **Gaochun** China
Gaocun *see* **Mayang**
65 B5 **Gaocun** China
67 D5 **Gaode** China
67 E1 **Gaohebu** China
65 A5 **Gaojiabu** China
67 D4 **Gaoling** China
67 B4 **Gaolou Ling** *mt* China
65 D6 **Gaomi** China
67 E4 **Gaopi** China
65 B7 **Gaoping** China
65 D6 **Gaoqing** China
67 C3 **Gaosha** China
65 B4 **Gaoshan** China
65 E3 **Gaotaishan** China
65 C6 **Gaotang** China
85 D6 **Gaoua** Upper Volta
85 B6 **Gaoual** Guinea
67 A5 **Gao Xian** China
65 C7 **Gaoxianji** China
65 G4 **Gaoyang** China
67 D5 **Gaoyao** China
65 C6 **Gaoyi** China
59 G5 **Gaoyou** China
59 G5 **Gaoyou Hu** *L* China
67 C6 **Gaozhou** China
19 Q15 **Gap** France
71 E3 **Gapan** Luzon Philippines
19 P18 **Gapeau** *R* France
86 C5 **Gar** China
86 J5 **Garadag** Somalia
43 C11 **Garaet Ichkeul** *L* Tunisia
139 J3 **Garah** New S Wales
47 H1 **Gara Khitrino** Bulgaria
14 C3 **Gara, L** Irish Rep
130 H10 **Garanhuns** Brazil
71 H9 **Garantah** Indonesia
130 F5 **Garapuava** Brazil
86 D4 **Garba** Cent Afr Republic
107 N5 **Garber** Oklahoma
100 B9 **Garberville** California
13 G6 **Garboldisham** England
130 E8 **Garça** Brazil
130 D4 **Garças** *R* Brazil
37 M7 **Garching** W Germany
106 E4 **Garcia** Colorado
16 D5 **García de Sola, Embalse de** Spain
130 D7 **Garcias** Brazil
18 H8 **Gard** *dep* France
18 H9 **Gard** *R* France
41 N6 **Garda, Lago di** Italy
42 D3 **Garda, Lago di** Italy
19 O18 **Gardanne** France
98 J1 **Gardar** N Dakota
27 J15 **Gårdby** Sweden
33 O7 **Gardelegen** E Germany
99 U4 **Garden** Michigan
99 J6 **Garden** Idaho
98 E2 **Garden** N Dakota
111 K7 **Garden City** Alabama
110 B3 **Garden City** Missouri
112 F5 **Garden City** S Carolina
98 H5 **Garden City** S Dakota
108 F4 **Garden City** Texas
103 N1 **Garden City** Utah
109 H7 **Gardendale** Texas
102 G8 **Garden Grove** California
99 N9 **Garden Grove** Iowa
99 U4 **Garden I** Michigan
142 A3 **Garden I** W Australia
143 B9 **Garden I** W Australia
111 G12 **Garden I Bay** Louisiana
140 B1 **Garden Point** N Terr Aust
102 H5 **Gardens Corner** S Carolina
100 H5 **Garden Valley** Idaho
77 L3 **Gardēz** Afghanistan
115 M6 **Gardiner** Maine
101 P4 **Gardiner** Montana
106 F5 **Gardiner** New Mexico
100 A6 **Gardiner** Oregon
118 L7 **Gardiner Dam** Sask
140 C5 **Gardiner, Mt** N Terr Aust
142 G4 **Gardiner Ra** Australia
95 P5 **Gardiners I** New York
140 B6 **Gardiner's Range** N Terr Aust
32 J4 **Garding** W Germany
106 E4 **Gardner** Colorado
113 F10 **Gardner** Florida
99 S8 **Gardner** Illinois
95 Q4 **Gardner** Massachusetts
137 S2 **Gardner I** Phoenix Is Pacific Oc
146 E11 **Gardner Inlet** Antarctica
95 U2 **Gardner L** Maine
140 E6 **Gardner, Mt** N Terr Aust
100 J2 **Gardnerville** Nevada
86 A2 **Gardo** Somalia
27 G13 **Gårdsjö** Sweden
26 H6 **Gardsjönäs** Sweden
27 J15 **Gärdslösa** Sweden
86 H4 **Garduula** Ethiopia
12 D1 **Gare L** Scotland
12 D1 **Garelochhead** Scotland
42 H3 **Garešnica** Yugoslavia
44 D3 **Garessio** Italy
85 F3 **Garet el Djenoun** *mt* Algeria
45 H3 **Garfagnana** *R* Italy
110 C5 **Garfield** Arkansas
106 D3 **Garfield** Colorado
107 L3 **Garfield** Kansas
101 N9 **Garfield** Utah
100 H2 **Garfield** Washington
101 N5 **Garfield Mt** Idaho/Montana
46 E7 **Gargaliánoi** Greece
17 F3 **Gargáligas** *R* Spain
16 D5 **Gargáligas** *R* Spain
42 G7 **Gargano, M** *mt* Italy
120 E5 **Gargantua, C** Ontario
26 N2 **Gargia** Norway
41 N6 **Gargnano** Italy
26 J6 **Gargnäs** Sweden
13 F6 **Gargrave** England
12 D1 **Gargunnock** Scotland
52 B6 **Gargždai** U.S.S.R.
74 H7 **Garhakota** India
55 D2 **Gari** U.S.S.R.
100 B4 **Garibaldi** Oregon
117 M11 **Garibaldi Prov. Park** Br Columbia
43 F7 **Garigliano** *R* Italy
70 G7 **Garintjing** Sulawesi
15 F3 **Garioch** Scotland
88 G2 **Garissa** Kenya
107 Q4 **Garland** Kansas
119 R7 **Garland** Manitoba
112 J3 **Garland** N Carolina
98 K9 **Garland** Nebraska
94 H5 **Garland** Pennsylvania
109 O9 **Garland** Texas
101 N8 **Garland** Utah
101 R5 **Garland** Wyoming
44 E1 **Garlasco** Italy
12 D4 **Garlieston** Scotland
18 E9 **Garlin** France
111 K10 **Garlrand** Alabama
32 M6 **Garlstorf** W Germany
57 F5 **Garm** U.S.S.R.
41 O3 **Garmisch-Partenkirchen** W Germany
77 H4 **Garmsel** *reg* Afghanistan
99 P7 **Garnavillo** Iowa
122 J2 **Garneau, R** Quebec
101 Q3 **Garneill** Montana
99 N6 **Garner** Iowa
112 J2 **Garner** N Carolina
118 E4 **Garner Lake Prov. Park** *peak* Alberta
101 M3 **Garnet** Montana
115 M4 **Garnet Bay** N W Terr
107 P3 **Garnett** Kansas
18 F9 **Garonne** *R* France
130 E11 **Garopaba** Brazil
74 F6 **Garoth** India
86 B4 **Garoua** Cameroon
86 B4 **Garoua Doulai** Cameroon
119 T4 **Garraway** Manitoba
32 H7 **Garrel** W Germany
98 K6 **Garretson** S Dakota
94 B5 **Garrett** Indiana
94 H7 **Garrett** Pennsylvania
101 U7 **Garrett** Wyoming
94 F5 **Garrettsville** Ohio
119 N5 **Garrick** Sask
99 O7 **Garrison** Iowa
94 D8 **Garrison** Kentucky
99 N3 **Garrison** Minnesota
101 N3 **Garrison** Montana
114 J8 **Garrison** N Dakota
95 O5 **Garrison** New York
109 N4 **Garrison** Texas
103 L3 **Garrison** Utah
98 E2 **Garrison Dam** N Dakota
16 C5 **Garrovillas** Spain
15 D4 **Garry, L** Scotland
115 K4 **Garry L** N W Terr
101 S4 **Garryowen** Montana
88 H3 **Garsen** Kenya
28 D5 **Gårslev** Denmark
27 G16 **Gärsnäs** Sweden
118 G2 **Garson L** Alberta
32 M7 **Garssen** W Germany
38 F7 **Garsstein** *mt* Austria
13 F6 **Garstang** England
13 F6 **Garston** England
144 B6 **Garston** New Zealand
21 G9 **Gartempe** *R* France
8 C3 **Garth** Wales
8 C2 **Garthmyl** Wales
Gartok *see* **Garyarsa**
33 O6 **Gartow** W Germany
31 H2 **Gartz** E Germany
70 M9 **Garut** Java
13 F2 **Garvald** Scotland
15 D3 **Garve** Scotland
144 B6 **Garvie Mts** New Zealand
31 N4 **Garwolin** Poland
100 J2 **Garwood** Idaho
109 L6 **Garwood** Texas
98 C9 **Gary** Colorado
99 T8 **Gary** Indiana
98 K2 **Gary** Minnesota
98 K5 **Gary** S Dakota
109 N3 **Gary** Texas
94 F9 **Gary** W Virginia
66 C5 **Garyarsa** China
60 F11 **Garyū zan** *mt* Japan
33 Q6 **Garz** E Germany
109 L2 **Garza Little Elm Res** Texas
108 G3 **Garza** Texas
128 C3 **Garzón** Colombia
50 E5 **Gasan-Kuli** U.S.S.R.
33 Q10 **Gaschwitz** E Germany
45 J4 **Gasciana Terme** Italy
94 B6 **Gas City** Indiana
Gascogne *prov* France
18 E9 **Gascogne, Golfe de** *see* **Biscay, Bay of**
110 E3 **Gasconade** *R* Missouri
122 H5 **Gascons** Quebec
98 C3 **Gascoyne** N Dakota
143 B7 **Gascoyne Junction** W Australia
143 B6 **Gascoyne, Mt** W Australia
143 A6 **Gascoyne, R** W Australia
86 G2 **Gash** *R* Ethiopia
85 G7 **Gashaka** Nigeria
74 G1 **Gasherbrum** *mt* Kashmir
85 G6 **Gashua** Nigeria
Gashuun Nuur *L see* **Gaxu Nur**
26 H4 **Gaskacok** *mt* Norway
126 E4 **Gaspar** Cuba
127 J5 **Gaspar Hernández** Dominican Rep
113 E11 **Gasparilla** *isld* Florida
69 H14 **Gaspar, Selat** *str* Indonesia
115 N8 **Gaspé** Quebec
122 H5 **Gaspé, B. de** Quebec
122 H5 **Gaspé, C** Quebec
122 F5 **Gaspé Pen** Quebec
122 F8 **Gaspereau** *L* Nova Scotia
122 H9 **Gaspereau** *L* Nova Scotia
122 G7 **Gaspereau Forks** New Brunswick
122 F5 **Gaspesie, Parc de la** Quebec
100 B8 **Gasquet** California
61 O7 **Gassan** *mt* Japan
94 G8 **Gassaway** W Virginia
25 G3 **Gasselte** Netherlands
85 F2 **Gassi, El** Algeria
85 G7 **Gassol** Nigeria
103 J5 **Gass Pk** Nevada
85 E3 **Gassum** Denmark
28 H7 **Gasteiner Tal** Austria
100 B4 **Gaston** Oregon
112 F2 **Gaston** N Carolina
94 J10 **Gaston Res** Virginia
133 D6 **Gastre** Argentina
17 G8 **Gata, C.de** Spain
126 F6 **Gatas, C.de** Spain
48 G5 **Gataia** Romania
16 C4 **Gata, Sa. de** *mts* Spain
52 D5 **Gatchina** U.S.S.R.
108 D7 **Gate** Oklahoma
94 E10 **Gate City** Virginia
12 D4 **Gatehouse of Fleet** Scotland
100 C5 **Gates** Oregon
13 G4 **Gateshead** England
101 O3 **Gates of the Mts** *pass* Montana
112 L1 **Gatesville** N Carolina
109 K4 **Gatesville** Texas
106 B3 **Gateway** Colorado
100 K1 **Gateway** Montana
100 D5 **Gateway** Oregon
21 F7 **Gâtine** *reg* France
121 P7 **Gatineau** Quebec
121 P5 **Gatineau** *R* Quebec
112 D2 **Gatlinburg** Tennessee
80 D1 **Ga'ton** Israel
89 F2 **Gatooma** Zimbabwe
33 S8 **Gatow** E Germany
61 N7 **Gatsugi** Japan
20 C2 **Gatteville** France
41 H6 **Gattinara** Italy
141 K8 **Gatton** Queensland
124 E9 **Gatun** Panama Canal Zone
9 F5 **Gatwick Airport** England
36 E4 **Gau-Algesheim** W Germany
16 D8 **Gaucin** Spain
16 D6 **Gaudalmellato** *R* Spain
77 H5 **Gaud-i-Zirreh** *salt des* Afghanistan
123 K3 **Gaudreault, L** Quebec
119 U1 **Gauer** *L* Manitoba
75 O5 **Gauhati** India
26 E9 **Gauldalen** *R* Norway
94 F8 **Gauley Bridge** W Virginia
20 G5 **Gault, le** France
123 R6 **Gaultois** Nfld
20 H5 **Gault-St. Denis, le** France
36 E4 **Gau-Odernheim** W Germany
66 D6 **Gauri Sankar** *mt* Nepal/China
27 D10 **Gausdal, Ö** Norway
27 D10 **Gausdal, V** Norway
27 C12 **Gausta** *mt* Norway
17 J3 **Gavarras** *mt* Spain
77 G7 **Gavāter** Iran
77 C6 **Gāvbandi** Iran
77 C6 **Gavbus Kūh-e** *mt* Iran
47 F10 **Gavdhopoúla** *isld* Crete Greece
47 G10 **Gávdhos** *isld* Crete Greece
18 E9 **Gave de Pau** *R* France
130 H4 **Gavião, R** Brazil
106 C5 **Gavilan** New Mexico
43 B9 **Gavino Monreale, S** Sardinia
102 D7 **Gaviota** California
77 E5 **Gāv Koshi** Iran
27 J11 **Gävle** Sweden
27 J11 **Gävlebukten** *B* Sweden
20 C4 **Gavray** France
52 E6 **Gavrilov Yam** U.S.S.R.
52 F5 **Gavrino** U.S.S.R.
47 G8 **Gavrion** Greece
47 K4 **Gavur Dağları** *mts* Turkey
74 G8 **Gawilgarh** India
138 E5 **Gawler** S Australia
138 D4 **Gawler Ranges** S Australia
26 H8 **Gäxsjö** Sweden
58 D3 **Gaxun Nur** *L* China
99 S2 **Gay** Michigan
75 L6 **Gaya** India
85 E6 **Gaya** Niger
85 F6 **Gaya** Nigeria
17 H3 **Gaya** *R* Spain
65 H3 **Gaya He** *R* China
9 E3 **Gaydon** England
107 M2 **Gaylord** Kansas
94 C1 **Gaylord** Michigan
99 M5 **Gaylord** Minnesota
100 A7 **Gaylord** Oregon
139 K2 **Gayndah** Queensland
141 K7 **Gayndah** Queensland
52 H4 **Gayny** U.S.S.R.
48 M2 **Gaysin** U.S.S.R.
99 Q6 **Gays Mills** Wisconsin
52 E5 **Gayutino** U.S.S.R.
98 J7 **Gayville** S Dakota
48 M2 **Gayvoron** U.S.S.R.
79 E7 **Gaza** Egypt
85 F6 **Gazaoua** Niger
80 A7 **Gaza Strip** Israel
100 C8 **Gazelle** California
20 J4 **Gazeran** France
57 D4 **Gazgan** U.S.S.R.
78 F3 **Gaziantep** Turkey
78 D3 **Gazipaşa** Turkey
57 C4 **Gazli** U.S.S.R.
45 J1 **Gazoldo degli Ippoliti** Italy
45 K1 **Gazzo Veronese** Italy
45 J1 **Gazzuolo** Italy
85 C7 **Gbanga** Liberia
85 F7 **Gboko** Nigeria
31 L1 **Gdańsk** Poland
27 K17 **Gdańska, Zatoka** Poland
52 C5 **Gdov** U.S.S.R.
31 L1 **Gdynia** Poland
80 B7 **Ge'a** Israel
103 N8 **Gearhart** Oregon
100 E7 **Gearhart Mt** Oregon
107 M6 **Geary** Oklahoma
71 C3 **Gebe** *isld* Indonesia
37 K1 **Gebesee** E Germany
47 K4 **Gebze** Turkey
86 G3 **Gedaref** Sudan
98 H6 **Geddes** S Dakota
141 F3 **Geddes** *R* Queensland
13 H6 **Geddington** England
36 G3 **Gedern** W Germany
28 H7 **Gedesby** Denmark
70 G6 **Gede, Tg** *C* Java
28 C4 **Gedhus** Denmark
22 H4 **Gedinne** Belgium
47 K5 **Gediz** Turkey
47 J6 **Gediz** *R* Turkey
Gedong *see* **Fangshan**
70 B4 **Gedong** Sarawak
28 H7 **Gedser** Denmark
28 G7 **Gedser Odde** Denmark
22 H1 **Geel** Belgium
139 G7 **Geelong** Victoria
143 A8 **Geelvink Chan** W Australia
89 A7 **Geel Vloer** S Africa
110 D6 **Geers Ferry Res** Arkansas
25 C5 **Geertruidenberg** Netherlands
32 J5 **Geestekanal** W Germany
32 J5 **Geestensetn** W Germany
33 M6 **Geesthacht** W Germany
22 J2 **Geetbets** Belgium
139 H9 **Geeveston** Tasmania
37 M3 **Gefell** E Germany
80 C7 **Gefen** Israel
37 M3 **Gefrees** W Germany
65 E2 **Gegenmiao** China
65 D5 **Gegu** China
65 G7 **Gehaku** *lt ho* S Korea
36 G2 **Gehau** W Germany
32 K8 **Gehrden** W Germany
67 F1 **Ge Hu** *L* China
85 G6 **Geidam** Nigeria
38 E7 **Geierspitze** *mt* Austria
120 B2 **Geikie I** Ontario
141 G2 **Geikie Ra** Queensland
25 F7 **Geilenkirchen** W Germany
27 C11 **Geilo** Norway
33 R5 **Geilow** E Germany
37 K5 **Geilsheim** W Germany
26 B9 **Geiranger** Norway
37 N6 **Geiselhöring** W Germany
37 J4 **Geiselwind** W Germany
37 M6 **Geisenfeld** W Germany
37 N7 **Geisenhausen** W Germany
36 F3 **Geisenheim** W Germany
37 J4 **Geisingen** W Germany
36 G7 **Geislingen** W Germany
36 H6 **Geislingen an der Steige** W Germany
37 J1 **Geismar** E Germany
36 D6 **Geispolsheim** France
88 D3 **Geita** Tanzania
37 O1 **Geithain** E Germany
27 D12 **Geithus** Norway
67 A5 **Gejiu** China
43 F11 **Gela** Sicily
43 F11 **Gela** *R* Sicily
88 E3 **Gelai** *mt* Tanzania
33 Q4 **Gelbensande** E Germany
37 J4 **Gelchsheim** W Germany
25 F3 **Gelderingen** Netherlands
25 F4 **Gelderland** Netherlands
25 D5 **Geldermalsen** Netherlands
25 F5 **Geldern** W Germany
25 E6 **Geldrop** Netherlands
37 O2 **Gelenau** E Germany
47 J5 **Gelenbe** Turkey
121 M8 **Gelert** Ontario
47 L8 **Gelidonya Burun** *C* Turkey
22 J2 **Gelinden** Belgium
67 F4 **Geling** China
71 L9 **Geliting** Indonesia
36 G3 **Gelnhausen** W Germany
28 C6 **Gelså** *R* Denmark
Gelsdorf *see* **Grafschaft**
32 F9 **Gelsenkirchen** W Germany
28 D6 **Gelsted** Denmark
28 D7 **Gelting** W Germany
118 E8 **Gem** Alberta
107 K2 **Gem** Kansas
69 F11 **Gemas** Malaysia
22 H2 **Gembloux** Belgium
32 E9 **Gemen** W Germany
86 C5 **Gemena** Zaïre
19 P18 **Gémenos** France
78 F2 **Gemerek** Turkey
25 E5 **Gemert** Netherlands
142 F3 **Gemini Hills** W Australia
47 K4 **Gemlik Körfezi** *B* Turkey
22 K2 **Gemmenich** Belgium
36 F5 **Gemmingen** W Germany
42 E2 **Gemona** Italy
18 E7 **Gémozac** France
84 J4 **Gemsa** Egypt
89 B5 **Gemsbok Nat. Park** Botswana
36 B2 **Gemünd** W Germany
36 H3 **Gemünden** Bayern W Germany
36 F2 **Gemünden** Hessen W Germany
36 D4 **Gemünden** Rheinland-Pfalz W Germany
70 E7 **Gemuru** Kalimantan
22 G2 **Genappe** Belgium
27 F16 **Genarp** Sweden
45 N6 **Genazzano** Italy
78 H2 **Genç** Turkey
18 F6 **Gençay** France
25 F5 **Gendringen** Netherlands
107 N7 **Gene Autry** Oklahoma
86 D3 **Geneina** Sudan
25 F3 **Genemuiden** Netherlands
133 E5 **General Acha** Argentina
133 E5 **General Alvear** Argentina
131 C5 **General Alvear** Mendoza Argentina
130 C9 **General Aquvino** Paraguay
133 E4 **General Arenales** Argentina
130 C10 **General Artigas** Paraguay
130 D4 **General Caneiro** Brazil
133 E3 **General Capdevila** Argentina
102 F5 **General Grant Grove Sctn** California
133 F5 **General Guido** Argentina
17 G5 **Generalisimo, Emb. de** Spain
48 L5 **Generalisinnul Suverov** Romania
133 F3 **General José de San Martín** Argentina
133 E5 **General La Madrid** Argentina
133 F5 **General Lavalle** Argentina
71 G6 **General Luna** Philippines
71 G5 **General MacArthur** Philippines
133 F5 **General Madariaga** Argentina
128 E8 **General Martín M. de Güemes** Argentina
130 B10 **General Paz** Argentina
133 C6 **General Paz, L** Argentina
71 G7 **General Santos** Philippines
47 J1 **General Toshevo** Bulgaria
109 H9 **General Treviño** Mexico
133 E5 **General Viamonte** Argentina
100 J3 **Genesee** Idaho
94 D3 **Genesee** Michigan
94 K4 **Genesee** *R* New York
99 Q8 **Geneseo** Illinois
107 M3 **Geneseo** Kansas
94 K4 **Geneseo** New York
20 C4 **Genêts** France
Geneva *see* **Genève**
111 L10 **Geneva** Alabama
111 M9 **Geneva** Georgia
99 S8 **Geneva** Illinois
94 C6 **Geneva** Indiana
98 J9 **Geneva** Nebraska
94 G5 **Geneva** Ohio
109 O4 **Geneva** Texas
Geneva, L *see* **Léman, Lac**
99 S7 **Geneva, L** Wisconsin
120 J8 **Geneva Lake Mine** Ontario
40 D5 **Genève** Switzerland
36 E7 **Gengenbach** W Germany
68 D1 **Gengma** China
Genhe *see* **Ergun Zuoqi**
59 H1 **Gen He** *R* China
120 J3 **Genier** Ontario
16 E7 **Genil** *R* Spain
21 H7 **Génillé** France
22 K2 **Genk** Belgium
60 D12 **Genkai-nada** *sea* Japan
40 B3 **Genlis** France
25 E5 **Gennep** Netherlands
28 C6 **Genner** Denmark
21 E7 **Gennes** France
21 C6 **Gennes-sur-Seiche** France
21 F6 **Gennetail** France
Genoa *see* **Genova**
106 G2 **Genoa** Colorado
113 E7 **Genoa** Florida
99 R7 **Genoa** Illinois
98 J8 **Genoa** Nebraska
102 E2 **Genoa** Nevada
94 D5 **Genoa** Ohio
139 J6 **Genoa** Victoria
99 P6 **Genoa** Wisconsin
99 S7 **Genoa City** Wisconsin
101 O1 **Genou** Montana
21 J9 **Genouillac** France
21 I7 **Genouilly** France
45 J3 **Genova** Italy
128 B7 **Genovesa** *isld* Galapagos Is
51 P1 **Genriyetty, Ostrov** *isld* U.S.S.R.
22 F1 **Gent** Belgium
70 P9 **Genteng** Indonesia
70 L9 **Genteng** Java
33 Q8 **Genthin** E Germany
111 K12 **Gentilly** New Orleans
69 H11 **Genting** *isld* Indonesia
21 J10 **Gentioux** France
118 K1 **Gent Lon** Manitoba
28 B5 **Gentofte** Denmark
110 B5 **Gentry** Arkansas
99 M9 **Gentry** Missouri
45 N6 **Genzano di Roma** Italy
48 H5 **Geoagiu** Romania
143 B10 **Geographe B** W Australia
143 A6 **Geographe Chan** W Australia
107 M2 **Geographic Center of US** Kansas
22 H3 **Geognennes** Belgium
99 L6 **George** Iowa
89 C9 **George** S Africa
83 M14 **George** *C* Kerguelen Indian Oc
116 J5 **George** *R* Alaska
115 N6 **George** *R* Quebec
138 D3 **George** *R* S Australia
123 L8 **George B** Nova Scotia
123 K8 **George, C** Nova Scotia
140 B6 **George Gills Ra** N Terr Aust
116 N6 **George, L** Alaska
113 F8 **George, L** Florida
139 J6 **George, L** New S Wales
99 W3 **George, L** Ontario
138 F6 **George, L** S Australia
88 C1 **George, L** Uganda
142 E5 **George, L** W Australia
37 L5 **Georgensgmünd** W Germany
37 K2 **Georgenthal** E Germany
90 C4 **Georges Bank** Atlantic Oc
144 A6 **George Sd** New Zealand
110 E6 **Georgetown** Arkansas
90 A11 **Georgetown** Ascension I
102 D3 **Georgetown** California
95 M8 **Georgetown** Delaware
113 F8 **Georgetown** Florida

111 L10 Georgetown Georgia
129 G2 Georgetown Guyana
101 O7 Georgetown Idaho
99 T10 Georgetown Illinois
94 C8 Georgetown Kentucky
69 E10 Georgetown Malaysia
111 F10 Georgetown Mississippi
144 C6 Georgetown New Zealand
94 D8 Georgetown Ohio
122 K7 Georgetown Pr Edward I
141 G4 Georgetown Queensland
127 O8 Georgetown St Vincent
138 E5 Georgetown S Australia
112 H4 Georgetown S Carolina
139 H8 George Town Tasmania
109 K5 Georgetown Texas
85 B6 Georgetown The Gambia
121 S7 Georgeville Quebec
146 F12 George VI Snd Antarctica
146 J4 George V Land Antarctica
109 J7 George West Texas
Georgia *S.S.R.* U.S.S.R. *see* Gruziya
112 C5 Georgia *state* U.S.A.
111 K10 Georgiana Alabama
115 L8 Georgian B Ontario
114 G8 Georgia, St. of Br Columbia
140 E5 Georgina *R* N Terr/Queensland
136 H6 Georgina *R* Queensland
140 E4 Georgina Cr N Terr Aust
54 L6 Georgiu-Dezh U.S.S.R.
53 F11 Georgiyevsk U.S.S.R.
32 F7 Georgsdorf W Germany
32 F6 Georgsheil W Germany
32 H8 Georgsmarienhütte W Germany
41 N4 Gepatschhaus Austria
20 D4 Ger France
37 N2 Gera E Germany
28 E2 Gerå *R* Denmark
37 K2 Gera *R* E Germany
22 F2 Geraardsbergen Belgium
36 H5 Gerabronn W Germany
110 E3 Gerald Missouri
119 Q8 Gerald Sask
101 P2 Geraldine Montana
144 C6 Geraldine New Zealand
143 A8 Geraldine W Australia
51 S2 Gerald, Ostrov *islds* U.S.S.R.
115 L8 Geraldton Ontario
120 D3 Geraldton Ontario
143 A8 Geraldton W Australia
130 E10 Geral, Serra *mts* Brazil
80 B8 Gerar *R* Israel
19 K4 Gérardmer France
143 E7 Gerard, Mt W Australia
80 G4 Gerasa Jordan
55 F2 Gerasimovka U.S.S.R.
100 C9 Gerber California
100 D7 Gerber Res Oregon
33 P9 Gerbstedt E Germany
36 H4 Gerchsheim W Germany
78 H3 Gercuş Turkey
116 L6 Gerdine, Mt Alaska
21 D9 Gère *R* France
78 D1 Gerede Turkey
17 F7 Gérgal Spain
40 A4 Gergy France
37 K3 Gerhardtsgereuth E Germany
69 E10 Gerik Malaysia
98 C8 Gering Nebraska
37 O1 Geringswalde E Germany
100 F9 Gerlach Nevada
48 F1 Gerlachovsky *mt* Czechoslovakia
36 H4 Gerlachsheim W Germany
28 G6 Gerlev Denmark
36 G6 Gerlingen W Germany
86 H4 Gerlogubi Ethiopia
38 E7 Gerlostal *R* Austria
133 E4 Germania Argentina
117 L8 Germansen Landing Br Columbia
110 G3 Germantown Illinois
95 K7 Germantown Maryland
95 O4 Germantown New York
94 C7 Germantown Ohio
110 G6 Germantown Tennessee
47 J7 Germencik Turkey
37 L7 Germering W Germany
36 E5 Germersheim W Germany
89 F6 Germiston S Africa
28 C5 Gerndrup Denmark
36 E6 Gernsbach W Germany
36 F4 Gernsheim W Germany
61 L10 Gero Japan
36 B3 Gerolstein W Germany
37 J4 Gerolzhofen W Germany
100 G1 Gerome Washington
17 J3 Gerona Spain
17 J2 Gerona *prov* Spain
103 O8 Geronimo Arizona
107 M7 Geronimo Oklahoma
139 K5 Gerringong New S Wales
18 F9 Gers *R* France
36 H3 Gersfeld W Germany
36 F4 Gersprenz *R* W Germany
37 J6 Gerstetten Herbrechtingen W Germany
37 K7 Gersthofen W Germany
37 J2 Gerstingen E Germany
116 P5 Gerstle *R* Alaska
33 T6 Gerswalde E Germany
140 B3 Gertrude, Mt N Terr Aust
48 K2 Gertsa U.S.S.R.
80 C4 Gerulim Israel
19 O15 Gervanne *R* France
66 C5 Gêrzê China
78 E1 Gerze Turkey
37 N7 Gerzen W Germany
32 E9 Gescher W Germany
32 J9 Geseke W Germany
80 D1 Gesher HaZiv Israel
22 H4 Gespunsart France
37 K7 Gessertshausen W Germany
44 B3 Gesso *R* Italy
21 C7 Gesté France
28 C5 Gesten Denmark
86 H4 Gestro *R* Ethiopia
26 H8 Gesunden *L* Sweden
29 H11 Geta Finland
16 E4 Getafe Spain
100 H8 Getchell Mine Nevada
22 J2 Gete *R* Belgium
123 M3 Gethsémani Quebec
28 A3 Gettrup Denmark
95 K7 Gettysburg Pennsylvania
98 G5 Gettysburg S Dakota
67 B4 Getu He *R* China
130 D10 Getúlio Vargas Brazil
146 J10 Getz Ice Shelf Antarctica
107 N4 Geuda Springs Kansas
69 C10 Geumpang Sumatra
69 C10 Geureudong, Gunung *mt* Sumatra
139 J4 Geurie New S Wales
80 C3 Geva' Karmel Israel
32 F10 Gevelsberg W Germany
80 B7 Gever'am Israel
20 B5 Geveze France
33 S5 Gevezin E Germany
46 E3 Gevgelija Yugoslavia
19 K6 Gex France
Gexianzhuang *see* Qinghe
37 O2 Geyer E Germany
36 G4 Geyersberg *mt* W Germany
47 H5 Geyikli Turkey
101 P2 Geyser Montana
81 B7 Geyser, Banc du Madagascar
47 L4 Geyve Turkey
Ghadames *see* Ghudamis
80 G2 Ghadir al Bustan Syria
77 C1 Ghaem Shahr Iran
73 N3 Ghaghara *R* India
85 D7 Ghana *rep* W Africa
74 D7 Ghandi Dham India
89 B3 Ghanzi Botswana
89 C4 Ghanzi *dist* Botswana
43 C11 Ghar Tunisia
80 E7 Ghar *R* Jordan
78 K6 Gharab Iraq
85 E2 Ghardaia Algeria
43 B12 Ghardimaou Tunisia
84 J4 Gharib, Gebel Egypt
84 E3 Gharyan Libya
85 G4 Ghat Libya
75 M7 Ghatsila India
17 F9 Ghazaouet Algeria
74 G4 Ghaziabad India
77 L3 Ghaznī Afghanistan
77 K3 Ghazoor Afghanistan
99 O2 Gheen Minnesota
86 J4 Ghelinsor Somalia
Ghent *see* Gent
94 B8 Ghent Kentucky
99 L5 Ghent Minnesota
48 K4 Gheorgheni Romania
48 K4 Gherghiului Muntii *mt* Romania
48 H3 Gherla Romania
43 B8 Ghilarza Sardinia
48 H3 Ghilvaci Romania
48 K4 Ghimeş Făget Romania
133 C7 Ghio, L Argentina
22 F2 Ghislenghien Belgium
77 J3 Ghizao Afghanistan
77 J2 Ghor Afghanistan
118 L1 Ghost *R* Ontario
117 Q4 Ghost L N W Terr
117 P9 Ghost Mt Br Columbia
86 E3 Ghubaysh Sudan
85 G2 Ghudamis Libya
77 G2 Ghurian Afghanistan
22 D1 Ghyvelde France
68 H7 Gia Dinh Vietnam
84 G4 Gialo Libya
86 H5 Giamame Somalia
42 D6 Giannutri *isld* Italy
89 F7 Giants Castle *mt* S Africa
14 E1 Giant's Causeway N Ireland
83 K9 Giants Tank *L* Sri Lanka
69 G8 Gia Rai Vietnam
43 G11 Giarre Sicily
18 G7 Giat France
44 B1 Giaveno Italy
126 F4 Gibara Cuba
98 H9 Gibbon Nebraska
100 G4 Gibbon Oregon
101 M4 Gibbons Pass Montana
101 M4 Gibbonsville Idaho
142 F3 Gibb River W Australia
99 S3 Gibbs City Michigan
146 D15 Gibbs I S Shetland Is
143 C10 Gibbs, Mt W Australia
87 C11 Gibeon Namibia
26 K2 Gibostad Norway
16 C7 Gibraleón Spain
16 D8 Gibraltar S W Europe
127 J10 Gibraltar Venezuela
16 D9 Gibraltar, Str of Spain/Africa
111 C9 Gibsland Louisiana
100 C8 Gibson California
112 E4 Gibson Georgia
101 Q3 Gibson Montana
94 D5 Gibsonburg Ohio
99 S9 Gibson City Illinois
143 D6 Gibson Des W Australia
117 M11 Gibsons Br Columbia
143 D10 Gibson Soak W Australia
113 E10 Gibsonton Florida
112 H1 Gibsonville N Carolina
58 B2 Gichgeniyn Nuruu *mt* Mongolia
52 H5 Gidayevo U.S.S.R.
76 D3 Giddalur India
79 D8 Giddi, G el Egypt
109 L5 Giddings Texas
26 K8 Gideå Sweden
26 K8 Gideå *R* Sweden
110 G5 Gideon Missouri
141 F6 Gideon, Mt Queensland
138 F3 Gidgelpa S Australia
143 F8 Gidgi, L W Australia
31 L5 Gidle Poland
Gidole *see* Gardula
36 H4 Giebelstadt W Germany
32 M9 Gieboldehausen W Germany
18 G5 Gien France
37 J6 Giengen W Germany
19 Q18 Giens France
19 N13 Gier *R* France
33 P7 Giesenslage E Germany
36 F2 Giessen W Germany
25 G2 Gieten Netherlands
25 F3 Giethoorn Netherlands
84 J4 Gifatin I Egypt
113 G10 Gifford Florida
99 N7 Gifford Iowa
13 F2 Gifford Scotland
100 G1 Gifford Washington
33 N8 Gifhorn W Germany
61 K10 Gifu Japan
124 D5 Giganta, Sa de la Mexico
124 E9 Gigante Panama Canal Zone
124 G3 Gigantes, Llanos de los Mexico
15 C5 Gigha *isld* Scotland
42 D6 Giglio *isld* Italy
18 H9 Gignac France
19 P17 Gignac France
40 F6 Gignod Italy
17 F5 Giguela *R* Spain
16 D1 Gijón Spain
106 B9 Gila New Mexico
103 P9 Gila *R* Arizona
103 M9 Gila Bend Arizona
103 L8 Gila Bend Mts Arizona
106 B8 Gila Cliff Dwellings Nat.Mon New Mexico
103 K9 Gila Mts Arizona
77 A1 Gilān Iran
78 K4 Gilan Garb Iran
121 R5 Gilardo Dam Quebec
48 H4 Gilău Romania
103 N8 Gilbert Arizona
99 O2 Gilbert Minnesota
102 G3 Gilbert Nevada
94 F9 Gilbert W Virginia
141 F3 Gilbert *R* Queensland
137 P1 Gilbert Is Pacific Oc
116 O6 Gilbert, Mt Alaska
117 L10 Gilbert, Mt Br Columbia
141 G4 Gilberton Queensland
111 H10 Gilbertown Alabama
101 P9 Gilbert Pk Utah
119 R7 Gilbert Plains Manitoba
141 G4 Gilbert River Queensland
28 J4 Gilbjerghoved *C* Denmark
129 J5 Gilbués Brazil
98 J1 Gilby N Dakota
98 B9 Gilcrest Colorado
13 G6 Gildersome England
26 G4 Gildeskal Norway
101 P1 Gildford Montana
88 G10 Gilé Mozambique
95 R2 Gilead Maine
98 J9 Gilead Nebraska
108 G1 Giles Texas
136 F7 Giles W Australia
143 G7 Giles W Australia
143 C8 Giles, L W Australia
140 B5 Giles Ra N Terr Aust
84 H5 Gilf Kebir Plateau Egypt
139 K3 Gilgai New S Wales
139 J4 Gilgandra New S Wales
80 E6 Gilgat Jordan
88 F2 Gilgil Kenya
139 J3 Gil Gil *R* New S Wales
74 F1 Gilgit Kashmir
139 H4 Gilgunnia New S Wales
117 J9 Gil I Br Columbia
70 P10 Gilimanuk Bali Indonesia
46 D1 Giljeva Planina *mt* Yugoslavia
98 B9 Gill Colorado
115 K6 Gillam Manitoba
28 J4 Gilleleje Denmark
143 E7 Gillen, L W Australia
140 C6 Gillen, Mt N Terr Aust
138 D4 Gilles, L S Australia
103 M8 Gillespie Arizona
110 G2 Gillespie Illinois
144 B5 Gillespie Pt New Zealand
111 E7 Gillett Arkansas
95 L5 Gillett Pennsylvania
109 K6 Gillett Texas
99 S5 Gillett Wisconsin
98 A5 Gillette Wyoming
109 N1 Gillham Arkansas
26 G9 Gillhov Sweden
110 C2 Gilliam Missouri
141 F5 Gilliat Queensland
141 F5 Gilliat *R* Queensland
13 G5 Gilling England
8 D5 Gillingham Dorset England
9 G5 Gillingham Kent England
109 O5 Gillis Louisiana
14 C2 Gill, L Irish Rep
99 T4 Gills Rock Wisconsin
22 G3 Gilly Belgium
99 S9 Gilman Illinois
99 O8 Gilman Iowa
101 N2 Gilman Montana
99 Q4 Gilman Wisconsin
110 C1 Gilman City Missouri
109 N3 Gilmer Texas
101 M5 Gilmore Idaho
141 G7 Gilmore Queensland
99 M7 Gilmore City Iowa
121 N8 Gilmour Ontario
86 F4 Gilo *R* Ethiopia
48 H6 Gilortul *R* Romania
141 F7 Gilpeppee Queensland
117 N9 Gilpin Br Columbia
102 C4 Gilroy California
118 L8 Gilroy Sask
13 F3 Gilsland England
98 H9 Giltner Nebraska
8 C4 Gilwern Wales
51 M3 Gilyuy *R* U.S.S.R.
86 D3 Gimbala *mt* Sudan
127 O8 Gimie *mt* St Lucia
101 L6 Gimlet Idaho
115 K7 Gimli Manitoba
27 K11 Gimo Sweden
52 D3 Gimoly U.S.S.R.
18 F9 Gimone *R* France
18 F9 Gimont France
26 G3 Gimsöy Norway
80 C6 Gimzo Israel
19 P17 Ginasservis France
141 J6 Gindie Queensland
76 D4 Gingee India
36 H6 Gingen W Germany
127 J2 Ginger Hill Jamaica
141 K6 Gin Gin Queensland
143 B9 Gingin W Australia
71 G6 Gingoog B Philippines
86 H4 Ginir Ethiopia
80 E3 Ginnegar Israel
28 F4 Ginnerup Denmark
80 F2 Ginnosar Israel
43 H8 Ginosa Italy
61 P13 Ginowan Okinawa
16 B2 Ginzo de Limia Spain
45 K3 Giogo di Casaglia Italy
45 K3 Giogo di Scarperia Italy
86 J5 Gioher Somalia
45 P6 Gioia dei Marsi Italy
43 G10 Gioia,G.di Italy
45 Q7 Gioia Sannitica Italy
46 E6 Gióna *mt* Greece
41 J5 Giornico Switzerland
43 H9 Giovanni in Fiore, S Italy
45 K4 Giovi *mt* Italy
139 H7 Gippsland Victoria
142 A6 Giralia W Australia
31 N6 Giraltovce Czechoslovakia
40 D1 Girancourt France
77 F5 Giran Rig *mt* Iran
99 R10 Girard Illinois
107 Q4 Girard Kansas
94 G5 Girard Ohio
94 G4 Girard Pennsylvania
108 G2 Girard Texas
128 D3 Girardot Colombia
15 F3 Girdle Ness Scotland
78 G1 Giresun Turkey
84 J4 Girga Egypt
74 D8 Gir Hills India
86 C5 Giri *R* Zaïre
75 M6 Giridih India
139 H4 Girilambone New S Wales
77 J4 Girishk Afghanistan
83 K10 Giriulla Sri Lanka
19 K5 Giromagny France
18 E8 Gironde *dep* France
18 E7 Gironde *R* France
17 J2 Gironella Spain
18 G9 Girou *R* France
119 V9 Giroux Manitoba
141 H4 Giru Queensland
130 C11 Giruá Brazil
15 D5 Girvan Scotland
15 D5 Girvan *R* Scotland
119 M7 Girvin Sask
108 E4 Girvin Texas
116 H4 Gisasa *R* Alaska
145 G3 Gisborne New Zealand
13 F6 Gisburn England
123 S6 Gisburn L Nfld
117 M8 Giscome Br Columbia
103 N7 Gisela Arizona
88 B2 Gisenye Rwanda
26 A9 Giske *isld* Norway
28 F6 Gislev Denmark
28 H5 Gislinge Denmark
20 J3 Gisors France
37 K1 Gispersleben E Germany
57 E5 Gissar U.S.S.R.
57 E5 Gissarskiy Khr *mts* U.S.S.R.
22 D1 Gistel Belgium
88 B3 Gitega Burundi
32 M9 Gittelde W Germany
Giuba *R* *see* Juba *R*
41 N6 Giudicarie Val Italy
45 Q8 Giugliano in Campo Italy
45 O6 Giuliano di Roma Italy
42 F6 Giulianova Italy
48 J3 Giumalău *mt* Romania
86 H6 Giumbo Somalia
48 L6 Giurgeni Romania
47 H1 Giurgiu Romania
80 C3 Giv'at 'Ada Israel
80 C5 Giv'atayim Israel
22 D3 Givenchy-en-Gohelle France
22 H3 Givet Belgium
22 G3 Givry Belgium
19 J6 Givry France
40 A4 Givry France
28 C5 Givskud Denmark
79 B8 Gîza, El Egypt
21 F7 Gizeux France
57 C5 Gizhduvan U.S.S.R.
51 Q2 Gizhiga U.S.S.R.
22 F4 Gizy France
31 N1 Gizycko Poland
27 C10 Gjende *L* Norway
27 C10 Gjendesheim Norway
28 E3 Gjerlev Denmark
28 D4 Gjern Denmark
28 F3 Gjerrild Denmark
27 C13 Gjerstad Norway
26 F7 Gjersvik Norway
26 D9 Gjevil-vatn *L* Norway
46 D4 Gjirokastër Albania
115 K4 Gjoa Haven N W Terr
28 N1 Gjógv Faeroes
28 D2 Gjøl Denmark
28 C3 Gjørup Denmark
27 C13 Gjovdal Norway
27 E11 Gjövik Norway
46 C4 Gjuhëzës, Kep I *C* Albania
22 H2 Glabbeek Zuurbemde Belgium
115 O8 Glace B Nova Scotia
20 B2 Glacerie, la France
117 P10 Glacier Br Columbia
117 E6 Glacier B Alaska
117 E6 Glacier Bay Nat. Park Alaska
116 O6 Glacier I Alaska
116 Q4 Glacier Mt Alaska
117 O10 Glacier Nat. Park Br Columbia
101 M1 Glacier Nat. Park Montana
100 D1 Glacier Peak Washington
115 M2 Glacier Str N W Terr
36 B2 Gladbach W Germany
99 O7 Gladbrook Iowa
107 L2 Glade Kansas
36 F2 Gladenbach W Germany
106 B3 Glade Park Colorado
94 F10 Glade Spring Virginia
109 N3 Gladewater Texas
119 N9 Gladmar Sask
26 E6 Gladstad Norway
119 T8 Gladstone Manitoba
99 T4 Gladstone Michigan
98 D3 Gladstone N Dakota
145 E4 Gladstone New Zealand
141 K6 Gladstone Queensland
138 E5 Gladstone S Australia
139 J8 Gladstone Tasmania
94 C3 Gladwin Michigan
94 H8 Glady W Virginia
94 H9 Gladys Virginia
117 G6 Gladys L Br Columbia
28 G6 Glænø *isld* Denmark
27 F12 Glafsfj *L* Sweden
103 J8 Glamis California
118 K7 Glamis Sask
15 F4 Glamis Scotland
42 H4 Glamoe Yugoslavia
Glamorgan *co see* W., Mid & S.Glam. *counties*
28 E6 Glamsbjerg Denmark
71 G8 Glan Mindanao Philippines
27 H13 Glan *L* Sweden
38 K8 Glan *R* Austria
36 D4 Glan *R* W Germany
14 B4 Glanaruddery Mts Irish Rep
19 P15 Glandage France
19 Q14 Glandon, Col du *pass* France
32 G8 Glandorf W Germany
32 G8 Glane *R* W Germany
38 K8 Glanegg Austria
41 J4 Glärnisch *mt* Switzerland
41 K3 Glarus Switzerland
107 N2 Glasco Kansas
95 O4 Glasco New York
99 R9 Glasford Illinois
127 H1 Glasgow Jamaica
94 B10 Glasgow Kentucky
110 D2 Glasgow Missouri
114 J8 Glasgow Montana
12 D2 Glasgow Scotland
94 H9 Glasgow Virginia
38 M8 Glashutten Austria
133 D6 Glasier Argentina
118 J5 Glaslyn Sask
15 E4 Glas Maol *mt* Scotland
119 M9 Glasnevin Sask
95 M7 Glassboro New Jersey
108 D5 Glass Mts Texas
8 D5 Glastonbury England
41 J3 Glatt *R* Switzerland
Glatz *see* Kłodzko
37 N2 Glauchau E Germany
47 H1 Glavinitsa Bulgaria
108 D7 Glazier Texas
52 H5 Glazov U.S.S.R.
31 K2 Gtda *R* Poland
110 H5 Gleason Tennessee
99 R4 Gleason Wisconsin
94 K5 Gleasonton Pennsylvania
103 P10 Gleeson Arizona
37 K3 Gleichberg *mt* E Germany
118 D8 Gleichen Alberta
33 P10 Gleina E Germany
38 L7 Glein Alpe *mts* Austria
38 N7 Gleisdorf Austria
Gleiwitz *see* Gliwice
28 B5 Glejbjerg Denmark
98 C7 Glen Nebraska
95 Q2 Glen New Hampshire
100 A6 Glenada Oregon
15 D3 Glen Affric Scotland
145 E2 Glen Afton New Zealand
121 P7 Glen Almond Quebec
112 F2 Glen Alpine N Carolina
18 C5 Glénans, Iles France
15 D5 Glen App Scotland
144 B6 Glenaray New Zealand
14 F2 Glenarm N Ireland
12 D1 Glen Artney Scotland
119 O8 Glenavon Sask
144 C6 Glenavy New Zealand
118 K9 Glenbain Sask
12 C2 Glenbarr Scotland
139 K4 Glenbawn Reservoir New S Wales
119 S9 Glenboro Manitoba
98 E1 Glenburn N Dakota
95 L7 Glen Burnie Maryland
123 P4 Glenburnie Nfld
138 F6 Glenburnie S Australia
118 K5 Glenbush Sask
15 D3 Glen Cannich Scotland
103 N5 Glen Canyon Arizona
15 C3 Glen Carron *R* Scotland
13 E1 Glencarse Scotland
15 E4 Glen Clova Scotland
111 L8 Glencoe Alabama
99 M5 Glencoe Minnesota
106 E8 Glencoe New Mexico
120 J10 Glencoe Ontario
89 G7 Glencoe S Africa
138 F6 Glencoe S Australia
98 F4 Glencross S Dakota
103 M8 Glendale Arizona
102 F7 Glendale California
111 K11 Glendale Florida
107 N3 Glendale Kansas
103 K5 Glendale Nevada
94 C7 Glendale Ohio
100 B7 Glendale Oregon
94 G7 Glendale W Virginia
117 L10 Glendale Cove Br Columbia
12 C1 Glendaruel Scotland
139 K5 Glen Davis New S Wales
106 E1 Glendevey Colorado
12 E1 Glendevon Scotland
114 J8 Glendive Montana
98 A7 Glendo Wyoming
118 F4 Glendon Alberta
111 F8 Glendora Mississippi
14 C2 Glendowan Mts Irish Rep
141 H4 Gleneagle Queensland
15 E4 Gleneagles Scotland
107 M2 Glen Elder Kansas
138 E5 Glenelg S Australia
15 C3 Glenelg Scotland
138 F6 Glenelg *R* Victoria
119 S8 Glenella Manitoba
119 P9 Glen Ewen Sask
12 D1 Glen Falloch Scotland
13 E1 Glenfarg Scotland
98 H2 Glenfield N Dakota
95 M3 Glenfield New York
15 C4 Glenfinnan Scotland
109 L6 Glen Flora Texas
142 B6 Glen Florrie W Australia
14 D1 Glengad Hd Irish Rep
14 B5 Glengariff Irish Rep
15 D4 Glen Garry Scotland
15 C3 Glen Garry *R* Scotland
143 C7 Glengarry Ra W Australia
127 L2 Glengoffe Jamaica
140 E6 Glengyle Queensland
144 B7 Glenham New Zealand
98 F4 Glenham S Dakota
140 C6 Glen Helen N Terr Aust
140 C6 Glen Helen Gorge N Terr Aust
145 D4 Glenhope New Zealand
139 K3 Glen Innes New S Wales
118 K8 Glen Kerr Sask
99 V5 Glen L Michigan
12 D4 Glenluce Scotland
139 G4 Glen Lyon New S Wales
95 L5 Glen Lyon Pennsylvania
15 D4 Glen Lyon Scotland
145 E2 Glen Massey New Zealand
109 P5 Glenmora Louisiana
15 D3 Glen More Scotland
141 J7 Glenmorgan Queensland
15 D3 Glen Moriston Scotland
102 B2 Glenn California
116 P5 Glennallen Alaska
14 C3 Glennamaddy Irish Rep
94 D2 Glennie Michigan
139 H7 Glennie *isld* Victoria
103 P9 Glenn, Mt Arizona
100 K7 Glenns Ferry Idaho
102 F6 Glennville California
112 F6 Glennville Georgia
12 D1 Glen Ogle Scotland
144 B7 Glenomaru New Zealand
117 H7 Glenora Br Columbia
141 G4 Glenora Queensland
144 B6 Glenorchy New Zealand
15 D4 Glen Orchy Scotland
144 B7 Glenore New Zealand
141 F4 Glenore Queensland
140 E6 Glenormiston Queensland
139 L4 Glenreagh New S Wales
108 A8 Glenrio New Mex/Tex
121 Q7 Glen Robertson Ontario
98 A7 Glenrock Wyoming
109 K3 Glen Rose Texas
13 E1 Glenrothes Scotland
140 E5 Glenroy Queensland
142 F3 Glenroy W Australia
95 O3 Glens Falls New York
15 E4 Glen Shee Scotland
118 L7 Glenside Sask
15 D4 Glen Spean Scotland
28 D3 Glenstrup Sø *L* Denmark
101 T1 Glentana Montana
14 C2 Glenties Irish Rep
144 C5 Glentunnel New Zealand
118 L9 Glentworth Sask
98 E3 Glen Ullin N Dakota
15 D3 Glen Urquhart Scotland
141 H6 Glenusk Queensland
120 K5 Glenvale Ontario
99 T7 Glenview Illinois
99 N6 Glenville Minnesota
98 H9 Glenville Nebraska
94 G8 Glenville W Virginia
112 D2 Glenville L N Carolina
111 K10 Glenwood Alabama
111 C7 Glenwood Arkansas
112 E5 Glenwood Georgia
94 B7 Glenwood Indiana
99 L8 Glenwood Iowa
99 L4 Glenwood Minnesota
99 O9 Glenwood Missouri
112 F2 Glenwood N Carolina
106 B8 Glenwood New Mexico
123 S5 Glenwood Nfld
100 B4 Glenwood Oregon
103 N3 Glenwood Utah
100 D3 Glenwood Washington
99 O4 Glenwood Wisconsin
94 E8 Glenwood W Virginia
106 C2 Glenwood Springs Colorado
118 D9 Glenwoodville Alberta
28 F4 Glesborg Denmark
33 N4 Gleschendorf W Germany
41 H4 Gletsch Switzerland
118 H7 Glidden Sask
99 Q3 Glidden Wisconsin
100 B6 Glide Oregon
33 S8 Glienick E Germany
33 S7 Glienicke E Germany
14 B4 Glin Irish Rep
32 M5 Glinde W Germany
31 M3 Glinojeck Poland
48 J1 Glinyany U.S.S.R.
26 G9 Glissjöberg Sweden
26 C10 Glittertind *mt* Norway
31 L5 Gliwice Poland
46 D4 Gllavë Albania
103 O8 Globe Arizona
Glogau *see* Głogów
48 C3 Gloggnitz Austria
31 J4 Głogów Poland
31 K5 Glogówek Poland
33 Q8 Gloine E Germany
26 G5 Glomfjord Norway
26 E9 Glomma *R* Norway
26 L6 Glommerstrask Sweden
27 J15 Glönminge Sweden
130 H10 Glória Brazil
106 E6 Glorieta New Mexico
87 H10 Glorieuses, Is Indian Oc
116 C6 Glory of Russia C Alaska
20 F3 Glos France
20 G4 Glos-la-Ferrière France
13 G6 Glossop England
146 G9 Glossopteris, Mt Antarctica
20 G3 Glos-sur-Risle France
111 E10 Gloster Mississippi
28 K5 Glostrup Denmark
52 G3 Glotovo U.S.S.R.
8 D4 Gloucester England
95 R4 Gloucester Massachusetts
95 M7 Gloucester New Jersey
139 K4 Gloucester New S Wales
95 L9 Gloucester Virginia
141 J4 Gloucester I Queensland
94 E7 Glouster Ohio
123 P5 Glover I Nfld
95 N3 Gloversville New York
33 Q7 Glöwen E Germany
31 M4 Głowno Poland
31 K5 Głubczyce Poland
54 M8 Glubokiy U.S.S.R.
56 B5 Glubokoye U.S.S.R.
28 D7 Glucksburg W Germany
32 K5 Glückstadt W Germany
28 D5 Glud Denmark
28 C4 Gludsted, L Denmark
28 N3 Gluggarnir *mt* Faeroes
54 E5 Glukhov U.S.S.R.
52 F6 Glukhovo U.S.S.R.
28 K5 Glumslöv Sweden
28 H6 Glumsø Denmark
13 F6 Glusburn England
55 E4 Glyadyanskoye U.S.S.R.
48 K2 Glyboka U.S.S.R.
8 B1 Glyder Fawr *mt* Wales
143 E6 Glynde Hill W Australia
95 L7 Glyndon Maryland
98 K3 Glyndon Minnesota
28 B3 Glyngøre Denmark
8 C4 Glynneath Wales
8 C4 Glyntawe Wales
31 J7 Gmünd Austria
38 J6 Gmunden Austria
33 P9 Gnadau E Germany
94 F6 Gnadenhutten Ohio
26 J9 Gnarp Sweden
32 K6 Gnarrenburg W Germany
38 N8 Gnas Austria
28 G4 Gniben *C* Denmark
31 L2 Gniew Poland
31 K3 Gniezno Poland
33 M4 Gnissau W Germany
46 E2 Gnjilane Yugoslavia
33 R5 Gnoien E Germany
8 D2 Gnosall England
37 K5 Gnotzheim W Germany
143 C10 Gnowangerup W Australia
143 B9 Gnuka W Australia
32 L4 Gnutz W Germany
76 A3 Goa, Daman & Diu *terr* India
139 K6 Goalen Head New S Wales
75 O5 Goalpara India
12 C2 Goat Fell *mt* Scotland
13 H5 Goathland England
101 M1 Goat Mt Montana
87 F11 Goba Mozambique
89 A4 Gobabis Namibia
58 D3 Gobi Desert Mongolia
60 J12 Gobō Japan
8 C2 Gobowen England
86 H6 Gobuin Somalia
25 F5 Goch W Germany
87 C10 Gochas Namibia
86 G4 Gocho Ethiopia
36 F5 Gochsheim W Germany
9 F5 Godalming England
74 J9 Godavari *R* India
76 F2 Godavari, Mouths of the India
122 E4 Godbout Quebec
122 E4 Godbout, R Quebec
117 E7 Goddard Alaska
107 N4 Goddard Kansas
36 F4 Goddelau-Wolfskehlen W Germany
46 F1 Godech Bulgaria
27 H13 Godegård Sweden
32 K9 Godelheim W Germany
47 L8 Gödene Turkey
120 J9 Goderich Ontario
20 F2 Goderville France
22 D2 Godewaersvelde France
110 F3 Godfrey Illinois
121 O8 Godfrey Ontario
115 O4 Godhavn Greenland
74 E7 Godhra India
109 K3 Godley Texas
144 C5 Godley Gl New Zealand
144 C5 Godley R New Zealand
9 F3 Godmanchester England
71 J5 Godo *mt* Indonesia
48 E3 Gödöllö Hungary
9 E6 Godshill England
115 K7 Gods L Manitoba
9 F5 Godstone England
115 O5 Godthåb Greenland
112 J2 Godwin N Carolina
Godwin Austen *see* K2 *Mt*
25 A5 Goedereede Netherlands
121 O3 Goeland Quebec
25 A5 Goeree Netherlands
25 A6 Goes Netherlands
107 P2 Goff Kansas
103 J7 Goffs Carolina
95 Q3 Goffstown New Hampshire
120 J5 Gogama Ontario
60 F10 Gō-gawa *R* Japan
99 R3 Gogebic Michigan
99 R3 Gogebic Range *mts* Michigan
37 K7 Goggingen W Germany
41 H5 Goglio Italy
7 L10 Gog Magog Hills England
36 B6 Gogney France
22 F3 Gognies-Chaussée Belgium
142 F4 Gogo W Australia
31 K5 Gogolin Poland
86 E4 Gogrial Sudan
33 Q9 Gohrau E Germany
33 N6 Göhrde W Germany
130 J9 Goiana Brazil
130 E6 Goiandira Brazil
130 E4 Goianésia Brazil
130 E5 Goiânia Brazil
130 J9 Goianinha *It ho* Brazil
130 E4 Goiás Brazil
130 E6 Goiatuba Brazil
12 D1 Goil, L Scotland
130 D9 Goio Erê Brazil
25 D5 Goirle Netherlands
45 J1 Goito Italy
86 G4 Gojab *R* Ethiopia
86 G3 Gojam *prov* Ethiopia
61 J11 Gojō Japan
61 O6 Gojōme Japan
47 K5 Gök *R* Turkey
76 B2 Gokak India
47 K7 Gökbel *mt* Turkey
47 H4 Gökçe Turkey
47 H4 Gökçeada *isld* Turkey
47 K5 Gökçedağ Turkey
32 K4 Gokels W Germany
77 H7 Gokprosh Hills Pakistan
78 D3 Goksu *R* Turkey
78 F2 Göksun Turkey
68 C1 Gokteik Burma
47 K7 Göktepe Turkey
47 K8 Gök Tepe *mt* Turkey
87 E9 Gokwe Zimbabwe
27 C11 Gol Norway
75 P5 Golaghat India
80 G2 Golan Syria
31 K3 Golańcz Poland
77 E6 Golāshkerd Iran
38 G8 Gölbnerjoch *mt* Austria
50 H1 Gol'chikha U.S.S.R.
110 H4 Golconda Illinois
74 H10 Golconda India
100 H9 Golconda Nevada
Gölcük *see* Etili
94 K5 Gold Pennsylvania
31 N1 Gołdap Poland
100 A7 Gold Beach Oregon
33 P7 Goldbeck E Germany
33 Q5 Goldberg E Germany
123 L8 Goldboro Nova Scotia
101 M5 Goldburg Idaho
101 O1 Gold Butte Montana
141 L8 Gold Coast Queensland Australia
28 C7 Goldelund W Germany
103 L8 Golden Arizona
117 P10 Golden Br Columbia
98 A10 Golden Colorado
100 K4 Golden Idaho
110 E1 Golden Illinois
145 D4 Golden Bay New Zealand
110 B4 Golden City Missouri
100 E4 Goldendale Washington
33 N10 Goldene Aue E Germany
102 B4 Golden Gate California
103 J4 Golden Gate Ra Nevada
127 M3 Golden Grove Jamaica
121 N7 Golden Lake Ontario
111 F12 Golden Meadow Louisiana
110 H5 Golden Pond Kentucky
118 H8 Golden Prairie Sask
143 D9 Golden Ridge W Australia
127 P4 Golden Rock *airport* St Kitts W I
32 H7 Goldenstedt W Germany
14 C4 Golden Vale Irish Rep
123 K8 Goldenville Nova Scotia
99 N7 Goldfield Iowa
102 G4 Goldfield Nevada
109 J7 Goldfinch Texas
101 M9 Gold Hill Utah
102 G4 Gold Point Nevada
118 K1 Gold Rock Ontario
119 R1 Goldsand L Manitoba
95 M7 Goldsboro Maryland
112 K2 Goldsboro N Carolina
108 E4 Goldsmith Texas
102 H6 Goldstone L California
142 C5 Goldsworthy W Australia
142 C5 Goldsworthy, Mt W Australia
109 J4 Goldthwaite Texas
112 F3 Goldville S Carolina
78 J1 Göle Turkey
85 E2 Golea, El Algeria
31 H2 Goleniów Poland
102 E7 Goleta California
56 G5 Golets Davydov, Gora *mt* U.S.S.R.
56 G3 Golets-Inyaptuk, Gora *mt* U.S.S.R.
16 C7 Golfo de Cádiz Spain
43 C7 Golfo degli Aranci Sardinia
43 E10 Golfo di Castellammare Sicily
43 E7 Golfo di Gaeta Italy
44 E3 Golfo di Genova Italy
45 N1 Golfo di Venezia Adriatic Sea
138 F5 Gol Gol New S Wales
109 K7 Goliad Texas
46 D1 Golija Planina *mt* Yugoslavia
65 E2 Golin Baixing China
47 H1 Gol. Kamchiya *R* Bulgaria
47 G2 Gol. Konare Bulgaria
Gollel *see* Lavumisa
33 T6 Gollin E Germany
38 H6 Golling Austria
33 S10 Gollmberg *peak* E Germany
33 T9 Gollmitz E Germany
47 J6 Gölmarmara Turkey
33 S8 Golmberg *peak* E Germany
37 M2 Golmsdorf E Germany
66 E4 Golmud China
71 E4 Golo *isld* Philippines
86 H4 Golocha Ethiopia
52 H1 Golodnaya Guba, Oz *L* U.S.S.R.
57 E4 Golodnaya Step' U.S.S.R.
88 E9 Golomoti Malawi
48 N2 Golovanyevsk U.S.S.R.
116 F4 Golovin Alaska
60 T2 Golovnino Kuril Is U.S.S.R.
77 B3 Golpayegan Iran
47 L4 Gölpazarı Turkey
116 G5 Golsovia Alaska
15 E3 Golspie Scotland
33 T9 Golssen E Germany
28 D2 Gølstrup Denmark
107 M5 Goltry Oklahoma
31 L2 Golub Poland
55 F4 Golubovka U.S.S.R.
89 F3 Golulu Ruins Zimbabwe
87 B7 Golungo Alto Angola
98 C3 Golva N Dakota
47 G3 Golyam Perelik *mt* Bulgaria
31 M3 Gołymin Poland
55 E3 Golyshmanovo U.S.S.R.
33 R8 Golzow E Germany
88 B2 Goma Zaïre
85 G6 Gombe Nigeria
44 H4 Gombo Italy
70 M9 Gombong Java
47 H5 Gömeç Turkey
54 B4 Gomel' U.S.S.R.
85 A3 Gomera *isld* Canary Is
124 H5 Gómez Palacio Mexico
125 K4 Gómez, Presa M.R. *res* Mexico
33 P8 Gommern E Germany
66 C5 Gomo China
71 A3 Gomumu *isld* Indonesia
127 H5 Gonaïves Haiti
51 M3 Gonam *R* U.S.S.R.
126 H5 Gonâve, Île de la Haiti
48 G2 Gönc Hungary
74 D8 Gondal India
86 G3 Gondar Ethiopia
36 F5 Gondelsheim W Germany
74 J8 Gondia India
19 J4 Gondrecourt France
80 F1 Gonen Israel
47 J4 Gönen Turkey
47 J4 Gönen *R* Turkey
20 K4 Gonesse France
19 Q18 Gonfaron France
20 F3 Gonfreville l'Orcher France
83 K11 Gongala *mt* Sri Lanka
67 D1 Gong'an China
66 E5 Gongbo'gyamda China
67 C4 Gongcheng China
75 O4 Gonggar China
58 D6 Gongga Shan *mt* China
57 K3 Gongliu China
Gonglüe *see* Donggu
85 G6 Gongola *R* Nigeria
139 H4 Gongolgon New S Wales
67 D3 Gongpingxu China
67 D2 Gongtian China
65 B7 Gong Xian China
65 D4 Gongyingzi China
Gongzhuling *see* Huaide
31 O2 Goniądz Poland
88 G4 Gonja Tanzania
36 G7 Gönningen W Germany
21 D7 Gonnord France
46 E5 Gónnos Greece
61 P5 Gonohe Japan
60 C12 Gōnoura Japan
40 D3 Gonsans France
99 L2 Gonvick Minnesota
45 J2 Gonzaga Italy
102 C5 Gonzales California
109 K6 Gonzales Texas
36 C4 Gonzerath W Germany
94 K9 Goochland Virginia
146 H2 Goodenough, C Antarctica
121 M8 Gooderham Ontario
119 O7 Goodeve Sask
94 B1 Good Hart Michigan
99 V4 Good Hbr. B Michigan
116 E4 Goodhope *R* Alaska
116 F3 Goodhope B Alaska
87 C12 Good Hope, C. of S Africa
117 L10 Good Hope, Mt Br Columbia
87 C11 Goodhouse S Africa
99 O5 Goodhue Minnesota
101 L7 Gooding Idaho
107 J2 Goodland Kansas
119 R9 Goodlands Manitoba
83 M12 Goodlands Mauritius
110 K5 Goodlettsville Tennessee
99 S4 Goodman Wisconsin
116 F7 Goodnews B Alaska
108 C8 Goodnight Texas
139 H3 Goodooga New S Wales
140 B2 Goodparla N Terr Aust
116 P4 Goodpaster *R* Alaska
106 F3 Good Pasture Colorado
98 B9 Goodrich Colorado
100 J5 Goodrich Idaho
98 F2 Goodrich N Dakota
111 B11 Goodrich Texas
99 Q4 Goodrich Wisconsin
140 B1 Goodrich Bank N Terr Aust
117 P10 Goodsir, Mt Br Columbia
118 H4 Goodsoil Sask
119 P7 Good Spirit L Sask
103 J6 Goodsprings Nevada
111 K8 Good Water Alabama
119 O9 Goodwater Sask
107 J5 Goodwell Oklahoma
8 B3 Goodwick Wales
103 M7 Goodwin Arizona
121 L4 Goodwin Ontario
98 K5 Goodwin S Dakota
7 M11 Goodwin Sands English Chan
144 C6 Goodwood New Zealand
9 F6 Goodwood Park England
13 H6 Goole England
139 H5 Goolgowi New S Wales
139 J4 Goolma New S Wales
139 J5 Gooloogong New S Wales
138 E6 Goolwa S Australia
140 C1 Goomadeer *R* N Terr Aust
143 B9 Goomalling W Australia
139 H3 Goombalie New S Wales
141 K7 Goombungee Queensland
141 K7 Goomeri Queensland
141 K8 Goondiwindi Queensland
143 D9 Goongarrie W Australia
143 D8 Goongarrie, L W Australia
141 J5 Goonyella Queensland
25 G4 Goor Netherlands
117 P8 Goose *R* Alberta
115 N7 Goose Bay Labrador
101 R5 Gooseberry Cr Wyoming
118 G6 Gooseberry L. Prov. Park Alberta
123 R2 Goose Cove Nfld
101 M7 Goose Cr Idaho
101 M8 Goose Cr. Mts Utah
101 T7 Goose Egg Wyoming
116 F9 Goose I Alaska
100 E8 Goose L California
119 Q4 Goose L Manitoba
76 C3 Gooty India
75 L9 Gopalpur India
31 L3 Gopło, Jezioro *L* Poland
36 H6 Göppingen W Germany
31 K4 Góra Poland
103 K10 Gora *isld* Mexico
31 N4 Gora Kalwaria Poland
75 K5 Gorakhpur India
42 J5 Goransko Yugoslavia
48 E7 Goražde Yugoslavia
113 K11 Gorda Cay *isld* Bahamas
128 D7 Gorda, Pta *C* Chile
19 O17 Gordes France
47 J6 Gördes Turkey
86 D4 Gordil Cent Afr Republic
28 B6 Gørding Denmark
111 J8 Gordo Alabama
116 R2 Gordon Alaska
106 F4 Gordon Colorado
112 D5 Gordon Georgia
98 D7 Gordon Nebraska
13 F2 Gordon Scotland
109 J3 Gordon Texas
99 P3 Gordon Wisconsin
139 H8 Gordon *R* Tasmania
13 E3 Gordon Arms Scotland
140 B1 Gordon B N Terr Aust

13 F4 Greystoke England
101 R9 Greystone Colorado
14 E3 Greystones Irish Rep
145 E4 Greytown New Zealand
89 G7 Greytown S Africa
37 P7 Grez-Doiceau Belgium
21 E6 Grez-en-Bouère France
46 D4 Griba mt Albania
81 F11 Gribb Seamount Southern Oc
86 C4 Gribingui R Cent Afr Republic
52 D2 Gridino U.S.S.R.
102 C2 Gridley California
99 S9 Gridley Illinois
107 P3 Gridley Kansas
25 D2 Griend Netherlands
37 F4 Griesbach W Germany
41 O3 Gries im Sellrain Austria
Griessen see Klettgau
25 F5 Grieth W Germany
38 L8 Griffen Austria
111 M8 Griffin Georgia
113 F9 Griffin, L Florida
116 Q1 Griffin Pt Alaska
139 H5 Griffith New S Wales
115 K3 Griffith I N W Terr
110 E6 Griffithville Arkansas
114 H6 Grifton N Carolina
99 Q10 Griggsville Illinois
41 K6 Grigna mt Italy
19 N16 Grignan France
18 E8 Grignols France
48 M3 Grigoriopol U.S.S.R.
25 F2 Grijpskerk Netherlands
48 K1 Grimailov U.S.S.R.
86 C4 Grimari Cent Afr Republic
19 Q18 Grimaud France
139 G8 Grim, C Tasmania
102 C2 Grimes California
100 K5 Grimes Pass Idaho
33 R10 Grimm E Germany
33 S4 Grimmen E Germany
Grimmenthal see Obermassfeld-Grimmenthal
37 J2 Grimmenthal E Germany
33 T7 Grimnitzsee E Germany
13 H6 Grimsby England
121 L9 Grimsby Ontario
41 H4 Grimsel mt Switzerland
115 S4 Grimsey isld Iceland
114 H6 Grimshaw Alberta
27 C13 Grimstad Norway
28 B5 Grimstrup Denmark
40 H4 Grindelwald Switzerland
28 C3 Grinderslev Denmark
28 B5 Grindsted Å R Denmark
95 S8 Grindstone Maine
123 L6 Grindstone Island Quebec
119 U7 Grindstone Prov. Park Manitoba
119 V7 Grindstone Pt Manitoba
99 O8 Grinnell Iowa
107 K2 Grinnell Kansas
115 K2 Grinnell Pen N W Terr
42 F2 Grintavec mt Yugoslavia
13 G5 Grinton England
26 C8 Grip It ho Norway
33 O6 Grippel W Germany
89 F8 Griqualand E reg S Africa
89 F7 Griqualand W reg S Africa
87 D11 Griquatown S Africa
40 F6 Grischuna, Val Italy
115 L2 Grise Fiord N W Terr
45 L1 Grisignano Italy
22 B2 Gris Nez, C France
18 F9 Grisolles France
27 K11 Grisslehamn Sweden
99 L8 Griswold Iowa
52 H4 Griva U.S.S.R.
20 K2 Grivesnes France
40 F6 Grivola mt Italy
39 H3 Grizeline E Germany
85 D3 Grizim Algeria
117 N3 Grizzly Bear Mt N W Terr
26 C9 Grjotli Norway
42 G4 Grmeč Plan Yugoslavia
123 R3 Groais I Nfld
33 S10 Groba E Germany
33 O10 Gröbers E Germany
27 M15 Gröbming U.S.S.R.
9 E2 Gröby Poland
33 P9 Gröbzig E Germany
31 O2 Gródek Poland
33 S10 Gröditz E Germany
31 O2 Grodków U.S.S.R.
31 J3 Grodzisk Poland
31 M3 Grodzisk Mazowiecki Poland
89 C8 Groen watercourse S Africa
22 G2 Groenendaal Belgium
25 G4 Groenlo Netherlands
109 L4 Groesbeck Texas
25 E5 Groesbeek Netherlands
25 C3 Groet Netherlands
70 P10 Grogak Bali Indonesia
32 K8 Grohnde W Germany
22 F3 Groise, la France
37 N1 Groitzsch E Germany
18 C5 Groix l.de France
31 M4 Grojec Poland
34 C12 Grombalia Tunisia
28 C7 Gronau W Germany
32 L8 Gronau Niedersachsen W Germany
32 F8 Gronau Nordrhein-Westfalen W Germany
28 B4 Grønbjerg Denmark
26 F7 Grong Norway
28 C4 Grønhøj Denmark
33 O9 Gröningen E Germany
25 F2 Groningen Netherlands
25 F2 Groningen prov Netherlands
119 N5 Grønli Sask
115 P5 Grønnedal Greenland
26 F5 Grønøy Norway
27 K12 Grönskär It ho Sweden
27 H14 Grönsö Sweden
28 J7 Grønsund chan Denmark
89 D9 Groot R S Africa
89 B7 Groot Aughrabies Falls Orange R S Africa
140 D2 Groote Eylandt isld N Terr Aust
25 F2 Grootegast Netherlands
87 C9 Grootfontein Namibia
89 B3 Groot Laagte watercourse Namibia
89 B9 Groot Swartberge mts S Africa
89 C8 Groot Tafelberg mt S Africa
89 B7 Groot Vloer S Africa
87 D11 Grootvloer L S Africa
89 E9 Groot Winterberg mt S Africa
22 K4 Grosbous Luxembourg
127 O7 Gros Islet St Lucia
27 G14 Grosjö Sweden
127 H5 Gros Morne Haiti
127 L4 Gros Morne Martinique W I
122 G4 Gros Morne peak Nfld
123 P4 Gros Morne Nat. Park Newfoundland
19 J6 Grosne R France
9 H7 Grosnez Pt Channel Is
41 M5 Grosotto Italy
123 P3 Gros Pate peak Nfld
113 F7 Gross Florida
37 M4 Gross Albershof W Germany
40 H4 Gross Aletsch Gl Switzerland
32 L10 Grossenrode W Germany
33 O9 Gross Alsleben E Germany
33 P8 Gross Ammensleben E Germany
37 P5 Gross Arber mt W Germany
33 S8 Grossbeeren E Germany

33 T8 Grossbesten E Germany
33 M10 Grossbodungen E Germany
37 O1 Gross Bothen E Germany
36 G5 Grossbottwar W Germany
37 L2 Gross-Breitenbach E Germany
37 T7 Gross-Dölln E Germany
37 M2 Gross Ebersdorf E Germany
123 L6 Grosse I Madeleine Is. Quebec
36 F2 Grossenbuseck W Germany
37 K1 Grossenehrich E Germany
33 O7 Gross Engersen W Germany
33 T10 Grossenhain E Germany
32 H7 Grossenkneten W Germany
37 N2 Grossenstein E Germany
127 N4 Grosse Pointe Guadeloupe W I
33 S10 Grosse Röder R E Germany
42 D6 Grosseto Italy
51 N4 Grossevichi U.S.S.R.
36 D5 Gross Eyberg mt W Germany
36 E3 Gross Feldberg mt W Germany
33 T6 Gross Fredenwalde E Germany
36 E4 Gross-Gerau W Germany
33 M8 Gross Gleidingen W Germany
38 G7 Gross-Glockner Austria
33 P6 Gross-Godems E Germany
37 N1 Gross Görschen E Germany
33 N5 Gross Gronau W Germany
33 M5 Gross Hansdorf W Germany
37 P2 Gross Hartmannsdorf E Germany
32 F5 Grossheide W Germany
37 M1 Gross Heringen E Germany
33 M7 Gross-Kain W Germany
36 E4 Gross Karlbach W Germany
33 O4 Grosse Klützhöved E Germany
37 L2 Gross Kochberg E Germany
33 Q10 Gross Korbetha E Germany
33 T8 Gross Köris E Germany
33 R8 Gross Kreutz E Germany
37 N6 Gross Laaber R E Germany
37 J4 Gross-Langheim W Germany
36 H2 Gross-Lindow E Germany
33 S8 Gross-Machnow E Germany
37 M6 Grossmehring W Germany
33 M7 Gross-Oesingen W Germany
33 M4 Grosse Plöner See L W Germany
37 P6 Gross Rachel mt W Germany
38 L6 Grossraming Austria
32 M9 Gross Rhüden W Germany
36 B5 Grossrosseln W Germany
37 L1 Gross Rudestedt E Germany
33 T7 Gross Schönebeck E Germany
16 E4 Gross Schwechten E Germany
33 S10 Gross Selchower See L E Germany
33 S6 Gross Stechlinsee L E Germany
36 H6 Gross Süssen W Germany
36 F4 Gross-Umstadt W Germany
37 P2 Gross Waltersdorf E Germany
33 P6 Gross Warnow E Germany
33 Q6 Gross Welle E Germany
33 Q7 Gross Wudicke E Germany
33 R5 Gross Wüstenfelde E Germany
33 Q8 Gross Wusterwitz E Germany
33 T7 Gross Ziethen E Germany
36 F4 Gross-Zimmern W Germany
36 B6 Gros Tenquin France
42 F3 Grouplje Yugoslavia
141 J5 Grosvenor Downs Queensland
116 K7 Grosvenor, L Alaska
101 P6 Gros Ventre Ra Wyoming
32 J9 Grotenberg mt W Germany
22 F2 Grotenbergs Belgium
22 H1 Grote Nete R Belgium
95 Q5 Groton Connecticut
95 Q4 Groton Massachusetts
95 P4 Groton New York
5 D3 Groton S Dakota
95 P2 Groton Vermont
26 G4 Grötøy Norway
45 Q8 Grotta Azzurra Italy
45 O7 Grotta delle Capre Italy
22 J3 Grotte-de-Han Belgium
9 N16 Grottes de St. Marcel France
99 T5 Grottoes Virginia
36 F5 Grotzingen W Germany
114 H6 Grouard Alberta
20 B4 Grouin, Pte. du France
6 E10 Grou Musang Malaysia
101 M8 Grouse Creek Utah
25 E2 Grouw Netherlands
27 C13 Grovane Norway
57 Q6 Grove City Ohio
94 G5 Grove City Pennsylvania
111 O8 Grovedale Alberta
111 J10 Grove Hill Alabama
140 B2 Grove Hill N Terr Aust
28 C4 Grove Kirke Denmark
102 E6 Groveland California
112 A6 Grovetown Georgia
145 D4 Grovetown New Zealand
101 P6 Grover Wyoming
103 L9 Growler Arizona
103 M6 Growler Mts Arizona
53 G11 Groznyy U.S.S.R.
41 H3 Gr. Scheern mt Switzerland
47 J1 Grozd'ovo Bulgaria
45 P1 Groznjan Yugoslavia
58 E5 Grube W Germany
42 H3 Grubišno Polje Yugoslavia
37 P6 Grünbach E Germany
20 F2 Gruchet-le-Valasse France
19 P13 Grude Yugoslavia
4 J2 Gruda Yugoslavia
31 M2 Grudusk Poland
31 L2 Grudziadz Poland
122 D8 Gruesa, Pta C Chile
58 E5 Grues, l. aux Quebec
42 F12 Gruinart, Loch Scotland
15 C3 Gruinard Bay Scotland
33 T8 Grunau E Germany

87 C11 Grunau Namibia
36 G6 Grunbach W Germany
36 F2 Gründberg W Germany
36 G3 Gründau W Germany
Gründelhardt see Frankenhardt
26 K8 Grundsunda Sweden
26 J8 Grundtjärn Sweden
99 O7 Grundy Center Iowa
120 K7 Grundy Lake Prov. Park Ontario
28 D7 Grünholz W Germany
124 J5 Grunidora Mexico
33 Q8 Grünhof E Germany
36 F2 Grünberg E Germany
36 H4 Grünstadt W Germany
38 E8 Gruppo mt Italy
130 H7 Guará Brazil
40 F4 Gruyère, L de la Switzerland
108 C7 Gruver Texas
52 B6 Gruzdžiai U.S.S.R.
53 F12 Gruziya S.S.R. U.S.S.R.
54 L4 Gryazi U.S.S.R.
52 F5 Gryazovets U.S.S.R.
31 M6 Grybów Poland
27 H11 Grycksbo Sweden
31 J12 Gryfice Poland
31 H2 Gryfino Poland
99 L1 Grygla Minnesota
27 G12 Grythyttehed Sweden
26 H3 Grytøy I Norway
26 C9 Grytten Norway
133 J8 Grytviken S Georgia
31 J2 Grzmięca Poland
41 O3 Gschnitz Austria
41 O3 Gschwend W Germany
45 R7 Gstaad Switzerland
16 B4 Gua India
41 O7 Gua R Italy
128 D2 Guacamaya Colombia
126 F4 Guacanayabo, G.de Cuba
127 L9 Guacara Venezuela
128 C3 Guachiria R Colombia
130 C6 Guaçu Brazil
124 J6 Guadalajara Mexico
17 F4 Guadalajara Spain
17 F4 Guadalajara prov Spain
16 D6 Guadalcanal Spain
137 M3 Guadalcanal isld Solomon Is
16 E6 Guadalén R Spain
17 F7 Guadalentín R Spain
16 E2 Guadalete R Spain
131 C3 Guadalfeo R Spain
16 E6 Guadalhorce R Spain
16 E6 Guadalimar R Spain
16 E6 Guadalmena R Spain
16 D6 Guadalmez R Spain
16 D7 Guadalquivir R Spain
131 C5 Guadal, Sa. de Argentina
102 C7 Guadalupe California
71 F5 Guadalupe Cebu Philippines
108 A4 Guadalupe Mexico
124 H6 Guadalupe Mexico
109 J6 Guadalupe R Texas
108 B3 Guadalupe Mts New Mex/Tex
87 E8 Guadalupe Pk Texas
16 D5 Guadalupe, Sa de mts Spain
124 G5 Guadalupe Victoria Durango Mexico
16 E4 Guadalupe y Calvo Mexico
17 F5 Guadarrama, Sa. de mts Spain
127 N4 Guadeloupe islds Lesser Antilles
16 E6 Guadiana R Spain
126 B3 Guadiana, B.de Cuba
16 E7 Guadiana Menor R Spain
17 G4 Guadiato R Spain
17 F4 Guadix Spain
28 C9 Guafo isld Chile
130 G1 Guaico Trinidad
130 E1 Guaicurus Brazil
36 F4 Guaimaca Venezuela
28 D6 Guaina R Colombia
130 C9 Guaira Paraguay
77 J6 Guaira Brazil
26 B8 Guaitecas, Is Chile
130 C7 Guajaba, Cayo isld Cuba
28 E3 Guajará Mirim Brazil
28 F5 Guajarrá Brazil
124 H4 Guaje, Llano de mar Mexico
125 L2 Guajiníguil Honduras
128 D1 Guajira div Colombia
128 D1 Guajira, Pena de pen Colombia
20 J5 Guala California
121 H4 Gualala Italy
42 E5 Gualdo Tadino Italy
131 E7 Gualeguay Argentina
86 C3 Gualeguay R Argentina
85 F1 Gualeguaychu Argentina
141 H3 Gualicho Salina salt pan Argentina
128 E7 Guallatiri mt Morocco
85 D5 Guam Mali
36 C7 Guémar France
21 B6 Guémené France
121 P6 Guenette Canada
133 C7 Gunguel R Argentina
21 E6 Gua R Brazil
133 B6 Gamblin, l Chile
21 A6 Guer France
78 A5 Guera Spain
86 C3 Guéréande France
21 C6 Guéra, Pic de mt Chad
85 E2 Guerche-sur-l'Aubois, la France
86 D3 Guéréda Chad
21 G8 Gueret France
37 J9 Guernica Spain
36 E4 Guernsey isld Channel Is
101 P7 Guernsey Wyoming
130 G5 Guéroulde, la France
21 K8 Guerville France
71 H6 Guest pen Antarctica
21 C6 Guettara, El Mali
21 J7 Gueugnon France
21 D12 Gueydan Louisiana
36 E6 Güferborn mt Switzerland
86 G6 Gughe mt Ethiopia
42 F7 Guglionesi Italy
65 C7 Guguan China
21 J14 Gugu mt Ethiopia
130 C4 Guia Brazil
67 F1 Guichen China
130 G8 Guichi China
67 B1 Guichicovi Mexico
45 J1 Guidizzolo Italy
19 P13 Guidon France
100 B6 Guiding China
86 B5 Guidimaka reg Mauritania
21 G12 Guiers R France
45 J3 Guiglia Italy
33 N9 Guiglio Ivory Coast
21 J9 Guijo de Hizán Spain

65 D7 Guannan China
100 F7 Guannan China
65 G1 Guanosonghen China
Guanxian see Guanling
128 F1 Guanta Venezuela
126 G4 Guantánamo Cuba
126 G5 Guantánamo, B. de Cuba
65 C6 Guantao China
65 C4 Guanting Shuiku res China
67 A1 Guan Xian China
67 D4 Guanxian China
65 D7 Guanyun China
130 F7 Guapé Brazil
128 C3 Guapi Colombia
133 G3 Guaporé Brazil
130 J9 Guarabira Brazil
95 B6 Guaranésia Brazil
130 F8 Guaraná Brazil
130 D10 Guarama Brazil
130 H7 Guarantinguetá Brazil
130 H7 Guarapari Brazil
130 D9 Guarapuava Brazil
130 E9 Guararapes Brazil
130 E7 Guararapes Brazil
130 J10 Guararapes Brazil
17 G2 Guara, Sa. de Spain
18 C4 Guarcino Italy
71 F3 Guardafui, C Somalia
17 F1 Guardal R Spain
130 F5 Guarda Mor Brazil
127 L10 Guardatinajas Venezuela
13 F1 Guardbridge Scotland
133 E6 Guardia Mitre Argentina
133 D7 Guardián, C Argentina
45 R7 Guardia Sanframondi Italy
16 D2 Guardo Spain
16 B4 Guardão Sa.da mts Portugal
128 F5 Guariba R Amazonas Brazil
71 L10 Guárico R Venezuela
128 E2 Guárico state Venezuela
130 D10 Guarita R Brazil
71 G6 Guasave Mexico
128 C3 Guascama, Pta point Colombia
124 E5 Guasima Mexico
130 C9 Guassú, R Brazil
22 B2 Guastalla Italy
125 O10 Guastatoya Guatemala
18 C4 Guatemala rep Cent America
139 J4 Guatemala Guatemala
127 L9 Guatire Venezuela
128 E3 Guaviare R Spain
128 E2 Guayabal Cuba
128 D3 Guayabo R Colombia
131 C3 Guayaguas, Sa. da R Argentina
127 P3 Guayaguayare Trinidad
127 L5 Guayama Puerto Rico
128 E6 Guayaquil Ecuador
128 A10 Guayaquil, Golfo de Ecuador
112 H2 Guayaramerin Bolivia
128 B4 Guayas prov Ecuador
133 B7 Guayco Arch islds Chile
141 G4 Guayi Queensland
124 C2 Guaymas Mexico
117 F6 Guaynabo Puerto Rico
36 P9 Güsten E Germany
33 S4 Güstrow E Germany
16 D5 Gusum Sweden
27 H13 Gusum Sweden
87 C8 Guta Angola
68 F2 Ha Coi Vietnam
21 J11 Gutenfürst E Germany
43 B9 Gutenstein Austria
99 V3 Gutersloh W Germany
99 M3 Gutii Mt Romania
118 J8 Gull Lake Sask
36 K6 Gülklön Sweden
99 J8 Güllspäng Sweden
47 D2 Güllük Turkey
65 E7 Gulong China
55 E7 Gulper Netherlands
33 Q7 Gulpen W Germany
47 H5 Gülpınar Turkey
21 F7 Gulran Afghanistan
78 E2 Gülşehir Turkey
26 J8 Gulsele Sweden
84 G7 Gul'shad U.S.S.R.
33 S5 Gultz E Germany
38 L8 Gütz E Germany
21 W9 Gütting W Germany
21 L8 Guttaring Austria
99 P7 Guttenberg Iowa
38 E3 Gutzkow E Germany
80 C7 Guty U.S.S.R.
80 C6 Guxian China
28 B4 Guyan China
72 G4 Guyana rep S America
140 G6 Gum Cr N Terr Aust
68 C5 Guyang Reg W Virginia
72 G6 Guyang China
72 E2 Guyang China
21 E5 Guyancourt France
9 G4 Guyenne Quebec
121 M4 Guyenne prov France
144 C4 Guyhirn England
139 K4 Guyra New S Wales
28 E4 Guyton Georgia
116 O3 Guzhou see Rongjiang
65 F5 Guzhou China
124 F2 Guzmán, L. de Mexico
48 K1 Gvardeiskoe U.S.S.R.
43 K9 Gvozd Yugoslavia
46 J3 Gwa Burma
48 E2 Gwabegar New S Wales
74 B10 Gwadar Pakistan
115 N2 Gwaii Haanas Canada
37 J9 Gwai R Zimbabwe
13 C4 Gwalchmai Wales
13 J3 Gwalior India
75 F2 Gwanda Zimbabwe
86 F3 Gwanda Zimbabwe
89 F3 Gwane Zaire
38 H7 Gwbert-on-Sea Wales
77 H2 Gwedore Irish Rep
14 C2 Gweebarra B Irish Rep
89 F2 Gwelo R Zimbabwe
112 F5 Gwelo Zimbabwe
142 H5 Gwent co Wales
35 G5 Gweru Zimbabwe
32 H6 Gweru-Gebirge mts Austria
27 J11 Gwinn Michigan
118 D6 Gwynedd Alberta
142 F10 Gwynedd co Wales
28 F5 Gyangze China
28 F5 Gyaring Co L China
66 D3 Gyaring Hu L China
50 G1 Gydanskiy Poluostrov pen U.S.S.R.
65 F2 Gyitang China
65 E1 Gyixong China
65 C7 Gylden China
115 P5 Gyldenløves Fjord Greenland
28 H5 Gylling Denmark
28 G5 Gylling Denmark
48 F5 Gyöma Hungary
48 F3 Gyömrő Hungary
48 F3 Gyöngyös Hungary
48 F3 Gyönk Hungary
48 D3 Györ Hungary

48 D3 Györ-Sopron Hungary
106 D2 Gypsum Colorado
107 N3 Gypsum Kansas
117 L9 Gypsum W Australia
143 F7 Gypsumville Manitoba
119 T7 Gypsum Pt N W Terr
27 J11 Gysinge Sweden
46 F2 Gyueshovo Bulgaria
48 G4 Gyula Hungary
52 D6 Gzhatsk see Gagarin

22 H2 Haacht Belgium
37 M4 Haag W Germany
143 B9 Haaksbergen Netherlands
137 S5 Ha'apai Group islds Tonga
26 M5 Haapajärvi Finland
119 T7 Haapamäki Finland
27 G14 Haapavesi Finland
52 B5 Haapsalu U.S.S.R.
32 G9 Haarlem Netherlands
144 B5 Haast New Zealand
140 B6 Haast Bluff N Terr Aust
25 C5 Haastrecht Netherlands
80 G4 Habaka Jordan
126 C3 Habana Cuba
83 K9 Habarat Sri Lanka
86 G5 Habaswein Kenya
114 H6 Habay Alberta
22 K4 Habay-la-Neuve Belgium
78 J5 Habbamyah Iraq
32 K10 Habichtswald wood W Germany
75 O6 Habiganj Bangladesh
65 C3 Habirag China
78 J9 Habis R Jordan
80 C5 Habla Israel
27 G14 Habo Sweden
59 H4 Habo Israel
60 P1 Haboro Japan
22 L3 Habscheid W Germany
61 N11 Habuminato Japan
61 P13 Gushikawa Okinawa
... Gushikami Okinawa
22 L3 Habscheid W Germany
61 N11 Habuminato Japan
59 L5 Hachijō Jima isld Japan
60 O2 Hachinai dake mt Japan
59 J6 Hachioji Japan
108 B10 Hachita New Mexico
26 G9 Hackås Sweden
103 L6 Hackberry Arizona
107 K3 Hackberry Cr Louisiana
118 E6 Hackett Alberta
110 B6 Hackett Arkansas
95 P4 Hackettstown New Jersey
111 J7 Hackleburg Alabama
138 E4 Hackness England
87 C8 Haco Angola
68 F2 Ha Coi Vietnam
36 E3 Hadamar W Germany
27 D11 Hadejia R Nigeria
32 K2 Hadelner Kanal W Germany
80 E3 Hadera Israel
80 C1 Hadera R Israel
28 C6 Hadersdorf Austria
28 N5 Hadersleben see Sønderjylland
28 B4 Haderup Denmark
77 J3 Hadhramaut reg S Yemen
72 G6 Hadībū Socotra
72 E2 Hadithah, Al Iraq
9 G4 Hadleigh England
9 G4 Hadleigh Suffolk England
114 J3 Hadley B N W Terr
144 C6 Hadlow New Zealand
33 O9 Hadmersleben E Germany
116 E4 Hadnor Norway
22 H3 Hadmersleben E Germany
32 K4 Hadeln W Germany
72 H4 Hadd, Al Oman
107 N2 Haddam Kansas
9 G3 Haddenham England
13 F2 Haddington Scotland
146 D14 Haddington, Mt Antarctica
9 H2 Haddiscoe England
112 D4 Haddock Georgia
141 F7 Haddon Corner Qnsld/S Aust
138 F2 Haddon Downs S Australia
73 L8 Haddummati Atoll Maldives
27 N3 Hadejia R Nigeria
27 D11 Hadeland Norway
32 L7 Hademarschen W Germany
80 C4 Hadera Israel
80 N5 Hadersdorf Austria
28 C6 Hadersleben see Sønderjylland
28 B4 Haderup Denmark
28 B4 Haderslev Denmark
28 E6 Hässleholm Sweden
40 J1 Hafelekar mt Austria
41 H5 Hafez Hayyim Israel
... Haffkrug-Scharbeutz
115 N2 Haffners Bjerg mt Greenland
118 D8 Hafford Sask
14 C2 Hafnir Iceland
34 F4 Hafik Turkey
72 E2 Hafizabad Pakistan
75 H6 Hafnar India
77 H7 Hafner mt Austria
45 R9 Haft Gel Iran
62 B8 Hafun, Ras Somalia
86 F3 Hag Abdullah Sudan
80 A6 Hagan Georgia
13 F6 Hagastrom Sweden
32 G7 Hagen W Germany
... Hagen-Gebirge mts Austria
139 F8 Hagemeister I Alaska
32 G8 Hagen W Germany
28 D6 Hagen W Germany
32 K6 Hagenberg W Germany
32 L10 Hagenow E Germany
6 L10 Hagiwara Japan
61 B9 Hagi Japan
9 F4 Hagley England
48 F2 Hagondange France
5 C9 Hagood S Carolina
32 K6 Hags Hd Irish Rep
14 B4 Hague Netherlands
118 D6 Hague New York
20 B2 Hague, C. de la France

19 L4 Haguenau France
98 A9 Hagues Pk Colorado
Hague, The see Den Haag
18 E9 Haguetmau France
85 B3 Hagunia Morocco
123 O3 Haha Bay Quebec
122 B5 Ha Ha, L Quebec
80 D6 Ha Hamisha Jordan
113 D7 Hahira Georgia
37 M4 Hahnbach W Germany
36 D2 Hahnbei W Germany
33 M9 Hahnenklee-Bockswiese W Germany
80 C3 Ha Hoterim Israel
67 C6 Hai'an China
67 G1 Hai'an China
65 E4 Haicheng China
67 F4 Haicheng China
37 N5 Haidhof W Germany
43 B13 Haïdra Tunisia
37 O5 Haidstein mt W Germany
68 H2 Hai Duong Vietnam
22 J2 Haien Belgium
80 C2 Haifa Israel
80 D2 Haifa, Bay of Israel
67 E5 Haifeng China
143 F9 Haig W Australia
36 E2 Haiger W Germany
36 F7 Haigerloch W Germany
117 P7 Haig Lake Alberta
98 E10 Haigler Nebraska
65 D5 Hai He R China
67 C6 Haikang China
60 C12 Haiki Japan
69 D9 Hai,Ko isld Thailand
68 K2 Haikou China
135 T3 Haiku Hawaiian Is
75 P6 Hailakandi India
59 G2 Hailar China
101 L6 Hailey Idaho
115 M8 Haileybury Ontario
107 P7 Haileyville Oklahoma
59 J3 Hailin China
67 D6 Hailing Dao isld China
65 J3 Hailong China
9 G6 Hailsham England
59 J2 Hailun China
29 L6 Hailuoto isld Finland
32 M8 Haimar W Germany
67 G1 Haimen China
67 G2 Haimen China
67 D7 Hainan Dao isld China
67 D2 Hai-nang Burma
Hainan Strait see Qiongzhou Haixia
22 F2 Hainaut Belgium
22 F3 Hainaut France
31 K7 Hainburg Austria
117 F6 Haines Alaska
100 H5 Haines Oregon
22 G3 Haine-St-Paul Belgium
111 F5 Haines City Florida
117 F5 Haines Junct Yukon Terr
38 N5 Hainfeld Austria
68 B4 Haing R Burma
37 P2 Hainichen E Germany
67 G1 Haining China
33 N10 Hainleite E Germany
37 Q2 Hainsberg E Germany
94 C4 Haintramck Michigan
68 H2 Haiphong Vietnam
118 F5 Hairy Hill Alberta
65 E3 Haisgai China
127 H5 Haiti rep W Indies
68 J3 Haitou China
65 F2 Haituo China
103 N9 Haivana Nakya Arizona
102 G5 Haiwee Res California
65 D5 Haixing China
86 G2 Haiya Junct Sudan
65 E6 Haiyang China
65 F5 Haiyang Dao isld China
Haiyou see Sanmen
67 B5 Haiyuan China
68 H1 Haiyuan China
48 G3 Hajdú-Bihar co Hungary
48 G3 Hajdúböszörmény Hungary
48 G3 Hajdúdorog Hungary
48 G3 Hajdúhadház Hungary
48 G3 Hajdúnánás Hungary
48 G3 Hajdúszoboszló Hungary
61 M7 Hajiki-saki C Japan
79 G9 Hajj Saudi Arabia
31 O3 Hajnówka Poland
65 F7 Hajo isld S Korea
68 A1 Haka Burma
135 V5 Hakalou Hawaiian Is
80 G3 Hakama Jordan
87 E7 Hakansson mts Zaïre
27 F13 Håkantorp Sweden
144 A7 Hakapoua, L New Zealand
61 N8 Hakase-yama mt Japan
144 C6 Hakataramea New Zealand
60 G11 Hakata shima isld Japan
131 B8 Hakelhuincul, Altiplanicie de plat Argentina
78 J3 Hakkari Turkey
26 M5 Hakkas Sweden
61 O5 Hakkōda san Japan
60 Q1 Hako dake mt Japan
59 M3 Hakodate Japan
60 O4 Hakodate wan B Japan
61 P7 Hakui-san mt Japan
61 K9 Hakusan Nat. Park Japan
Hal see Halle
78 K4 Halabja Iraq
65 F2 Halahai China
86 G1 Halaib Sudan
79 D8 Halâl, G mt Egypt
48 G3 Halasto L Hungary
79 G9 Halat 'Ammar Saudi Arabia
48 K3 Hălăucești Romania
135 S2 Halawa Hawaiian Is Pacific Ocean
80 F4 Halawa Jordan
135 S2 Halawa, C Hawaiian Is
79 G4 Halba Lebanon
33 T8 Halbe E Germany
33 O9 Halberstadt E Germany
8 C6 Halberton England
119 O9 Halbrite Sask
145 E4 Halcombe New Zealand
71 E4 Halcon, Mt Philippines
117 P10 Halcyon Hot Springs Br Columbia
28 E3 Hald Århus Denmark
28 C3 Hald Viborg Denmark
28 H6 Haldagerlille Denmark
27 E12 Halden Norway
33 O8 Haldensleben E Germany
28 K1 Haldersvig Faeroes
28 C4 Hald Sø L Denmark
28 E4 Haldum Denmark
74 H4 Haldwani India
106 H2 Hale Colorado
94 D2 Hale Michigan
110 C2 Hale Missouri
140 D6 Hale R N Terr Aust
135 T3 Haleakala Crater Hawaiian Is
86 H3 Haleb I Red Sea
79 G4 Halebiye Syria
108 F1 Hale Center Texas
135 Q2 Haleiwa Hawaiian Is
145 H7 Hale, Mt W Australia
135 R2 Halena Hawaiian Is
112 B2 Hales Bar Dam Tennessee
9 D3 Halesowen England
9 G5 Hale Street England
9 H3 Halesworth England
111 J7 Haleyville Alabama
144 B7 Half Moon B New Zealand
9 E3 Halford England
107 K2 Halford Kansas
94 K7 Halfway Maryland
100 H5 Halfway Oregon
108 F1 Halfway Texas
117 M7 Halfway R Br Columbia
116 K6 Halfway Mt Alaska
25 C4 Halfweg Netherlands
80 B7 Halib Israel
121 M7 Haliburton Ontario
13 G6 Halifax England
112 K1 Halifax N Carolina
115 N9 Halifax Nova Scotia
95 L6 Halifax Pennsylvania
141 H4 Halifax Queensland
94 H10 Halifax Virginia
136 K5 Halifax B Queensland
141 H4 Halifax, Mt Queensland
29 K11 Halikko Finland
77 E6 Halil R Iran
79 G4 Halimet el Qabu mt Lebanon
70 L9 Halimun, G mt Java
86 A2 Halin Somalia
Haliut see Urad Zhonghou Lianheqi
76 B3 Haliyal India
26 N4 Halju mt Sweden
28 D6 Halk Denmark
116 L1 Halkett, C Alaska
118 E6 Halkirk Alberta
15 E2 Halkirk Scotland
20 O2 Halkkavarre mt Norway
101 M3 Hall Montana
26 J8 Hälla Sweden
9 G6 Halland England
27 F8 Halland Sweden
27 F15 Halland county Sweden
113 G12 Hallandale Florida
27 F15 Hallandsås hills Sweden
28 K4 Hallands Väderö isld Sweden
138 D5 Hall B S Australia
115 N1 Hall Basin Canada/Greenland
119 S8 Hallboro Manitoba
22 G2 Halle Belgium
33 P10 Halle E Germany
36 H1 Halle W Germany
33 O9 Halle reg E Germany
27 H15 Hälleberga Sweden
120 G3 Hallebourg Ontario
28 G5 Halleby Å R Denmark
100 K9 Halleck Nevada
27 G12 Hällefors Sweden
38 H6 Hallein Austria
26 G8 Hallen Sweden
36 F1 Hallenberg W Germany
20 J2 Hallencourt France
28 F4 Hallendrup Denmark
26 H9 Hällesjö Sweden
109 L6 Hallettsville Texas
111 E8 Halley Arkansas
116 B6 Hall I Bering Sea
98 D2 Halliday N Dakota
98 A9 Halligan Res Colorado
20 D11 Hallingdalselv R Norway
27 C11 Hallingskarvet mt Norway
27 B11 Hallingskeid Norway
115 L4 Hall Lake L N W Terr
27 J11 Hällnäs Sweden
119 V10 Hallock Minnesota
118 K8 Hallonquist Sask
115 M4 Hall Pen N W Terr
110 G6 Halls Tennessee
8 C7 Hallsands England
27 H12 Hallsberg Sweden
142 G4 Halls Creek W Australia
37 K4 Hallstadt W Germany
27 H12 Hallstahammar Sweden
106 G3 Hall Station Colorado
38 J6 Hallstatt Austria
27 K11 Hallstavik Sweden
95 M5 Hallstead Pennsylvania
111 C9 Hall Summit Louisiana
110 D2 Hallsville Missouri
109 N3 Hallsville Texas
81 A8 Hall Table Mt Indian Oc
41 O3 Halltal Austria
94 J5 Hallton Pennsylvania
22 E2 Halluin France
25 E2 Hallum Netherlands
28 E2 Hallund Denmark
28 C5 Hallundbæk Denmark
26 H8 Hallviken Sweden
98 K1 Halma Minnesota
71 B3 Halmahera isld Indonesia
71 B3 Halmahera sea Indonesia
48 H3 Halmeu Romania
27 F15 Halmstad Sweden
43 C12 Halq el Oued Tunisia
28 E2 Hals Denmark
26 C8 Halsa Norway
37 P2 Halsbrucke E Germany
36 F2 Halsdorf W Germany
98 F8 Halsey Nebraska
100 B5 Halsey Oregon
71 D5 Halsey Harbour Philippines
28 H5 Halsnæs pen Denmark
28 G6 Halsskov Denmark
98 K2 Halstad Minnesota
9 G4 Halstead England
107 N4 Halstead Kansas
36 B5 Halstroff France
29 L8 Halsua Finland
26 E9 Haltdalen Norway
26 D7 Halten Norway
32 F9 Haltern W Germany
29 J2 Halti mt Finland
109 M9 Haltom City Texas
13 F4 Haltwhistle England
77 C7 Ḥālūl isld Qatar
36 C1 Halver W Germany
118 L8 Halvorgate Sask
28 D2 Halvrimmen Denmark
141 K7 Haly, Mt Queensland
22 E4 Ham France
80 G3 Ham Jordan
60 F12 Hama Japan
79 G3 Hama Syria
60 F11 Hamada Japan
85 F3 Hamada de Tinrhert stony des Algeria
85 D4 Hamada El Haricha reg Mali
72 F2 Hamadān Iran
85 C3 Hamada Tounassine stony des Algeria
80 F3 Hamadya Israel
61 P13 Hamahika-jima isld Okinawa
61 L11 Hamakita Japan
60 P2 Hamamasu Japan
59 L5 Hamamatsu Japan
60 T2 Hamanaka Japan
61 L11 Hamana ko L Japan
80 C4 Ha Ma 'Pil Israel
98 G1 Hamar N Dakota
27 E11 Hamar Norway
26 H3 Hamaröy Norway
60 H10 Hamasaka Japan
84 J5 Hamâta, Gebel mt Egypt
80 F3 Hamat Gader Jordan
60 O1 Hama-Tombetsu Japan
36 C5 Hambach France
83 L11 Hambantota Sri Lanka
98 G2 Hamberg N Dakota
32 J6 Hambergen W Germany
117 O9 Hamber Prov. Park Br Columbia
9 F5 Hambledon England
13 G6 Hambleton England
13 G5 Hambleton Hills England
100 D8 Hambone California
32 L7 Hambühren W Germany
111 E8 Hamburg Arkansas
100 B8 Hamburg California
99 L9 Hamburg Iowa
95 N5 Hamburg New Jersey
94 J4 Hamburg New York
95 M6 Hamburg Pennsylvania
34 Hamburg conurbation W Germany
20 C4 Hambye France
79 G3 Hamdāniya Syria
95 M4 Hamden New York
94 E6 Hamden Ohio
29 L10 Hame prov Finland
29 K10 Hämeenkyrö Finland
29 L11 Hämeenlinna Finland
143 A10 Hamelin B W Australia
143 A7 Hamelin Pool W Australia
32 K8 Hameln W Germany
101 N6 Hamer Idaho
33 O8 Hamersleben E Germany
142 C5 Hamersley W Australia
142 B5 Hamersley Ra W Australia
33 P7 Hamerten E Germany
65 G5 Hamhŭng N Korea
66 E3 Hami China
111 J7 Hamilton Alabama
90 B2 Hamilton Bermuda
101 S9 Hamilton Colorado
111 M9 Hamilton Georgia
99 P8 Hamilton Illinois
110 K4 Hamilton Indiana
107 O4 Hamilton Kansas
94 O4 Hamilton Michigan
114 H8 Hamilton Montana
119 U10 Hamilton N Dakota
95 M4 Hamilton New York
145 E2 Hamilton New Zealand
94 C7 Hamilton Ohio
115 M9 Hamilton Ontario
100 F5 Hamilton Oregon
140 F6 Hamilton Queensland
12 D2 Hamilton Scotland
139 H8 Hamilton Tasmania
109 J4 Hamilton Texas
138 F6 Hamilton Victoria
100 D1 Hamilton Washington
140 F6 Hamilton R Queensland
138 C2 Hamilton R S Australia
102 C2 Hamilton City California
101 R6 Hamilton Dome Wyoming
140 C6 Hamilton Downs N Terr Aust
115 O7 Hamilton Inlet Labrador
111 C7 Hamilton,L Arkansas
103 J2 Hamilton, Mt Nevada
29 N11 Hamina Finland
74 J6 Hamirpur India
Hamitabat see Isparta
94 C5 Hamler Ohio
94 A5 Hamlet Indiana
112 H3 Hamlet N Carolina
98 E9 Hamlet Nebraska
142 B6 Hamlet, Mt W Australia
138 E5 Hamley Bridge S Australia
94 K3 Hamlin New York
108 G3 Hamlin Texas
94 E8 Hamlin W Virginia
94 A2 Hamlin L Michigan
32 G9 Hamm W Germany
84 E4 Hammādah Al Ḥamrā plat Libya
17 G9 Hammam Bou Hadjar Algeria
43 D12 Hammamet Tunisia
85 G1 Hammamet, G de Tunisia
85 G1 Hammam Lif Tunisia
29 H11 Hammarland Finland
27 F11 Hammarsbyn Sweden
29 M3 Hammastunturi mt Finland
22 G1 Hamme Belgium
32 J6 Hamme R W Germany
28 D4 Hammel Denmark
36 H3 Hammelburg W Germany
28 C5 Hammelev Denmark
28 F4 Hammelev Denmark
33 S6 Hammelspring E Germany
20 B6 Hamme-Mille Belgium
26 H8 Hammerdal Sweden
147 H14 Hammerfest Norway
28 D3 Hammershøj Denmark
36 C3 Hammerstein W Germany
13 G6 Hammerton England
28 C4 Hammerum Denmark
100 K7 Hammett Idaho
32 E9 Hamminkeln W Germany
107 L6 Hammon Oklahoma
99 T8 Hammond Illinois
110 H2 Hammond Illinois
111 F11 Hammond Louisiana
98 B4 Hammond Montana
95 M2 Hammond New York
100 B3 Hammond Oregon
138 E4 Hammond S Australia
99 O5 Hammond Wisconsin
94 D1 Hammond B Michigan
141 F1 Hammond I Queensland
95 K4 Hammondsport New York
122 G8 Hammond Vale New Brunswick
102 C2 Hammonton California
95 N7 Hammonton New Jersey
26 O1 Hamnbukt Norway
26 L2 Hamneidet Norway
26 S1 Hamningberg Norway
68 G7 Ham Ninh Vietnam
121 T7 Ham Nord Quebec
26 L4 Håmojokk Sweden
22 K1 Hamont Belgium
86 G2 Hamoyet, Jebel mt Sudan
98 H1 Hampden N Dakota
144 C6 Hampden New Zealand
115 O8 Hampden Nfld
95 T2 Hampden Highlands Maine
28 C4 Hampen Denmark
36 B6 Hampont France
9 E5 Hampshire co England
95 K7 Hampstead Maryland
112 K3 Hampstead N Carolina
122 F8 Hampstead New Brunswick
111 D8 Hampton Arkansas
9 F5 Hampton England
113 E8 Hampton Florida
111 M8 Hampton Georgia
99 N7 Hampton Iowa
98 J9 Hampton Nebraska
122 G8 Hampton New Brunswick
95 R4 Hampton New Hampshire
100 E6 Hampton Oregon
112 F5 Hampton S Carolina
95 L9 Hampton Virginia
101 P8 Hampton Wyoming
95 P6 Hampton Bays Long I, N Y
142 B5 Hampton Harb W Australia
143 F8 Hampton Tableland W Australia
27 H10 Hamra Sweden
27 J11 Hamrånge Sweden
101 P7 Hams Fork R Wyoming
9 G5 Ham Street England
68 H7 Ham Tan Vietnam
135 T3 Hana Hawaiian Is
126 D3 Hanábana R Cuba
135 O1 Hanalei Hawaiian Is
135 T3 Hanamanioa, C Hawaiian Is
135 O1 Hanamaulu Hawaiian Is
135 U5 Hanapepe Hawaiian Is
61 N13 Hanare-iwa islds Japan
36 F3 Hanau W Germany
135 U4 Hanauma B Hawaiian Is
121 L5 Hanbury Ontario
111 K7 Hanceville Alabama
117 M10 Hanceville Br Col
58 F4 Hancheng China
67 C1 Hanchuan China
95 T2 Hancock Maine
94 J7 Hancock Maryland
99 S2 Hancock Michigan
99 L3 Hancock Minnesota
95 P4 Hancock New Hampshire
95 M5 Hancock New York
99 O6 Hancock Wisconsin
113 F10 Hancock, L Florida
61 K11 Handa Japan
58 F4 Handan China
28 B4 Handbjerg Denmark
9 F5 Handcross England
118 J6 Handel Sask
87 G7 Handeni Tanzania
28 D3 Handest Denmark
70 C6 Handjalipan Kalimantan
109 K3 Handley Texas
119 P9 Handsworth Sask
32 K4 Hanerau W Germany
102 E5 Hanford California
100 E3 Hanford Washington
76 B3 Hangal India
65 B1 Hangan Burma
66 G5 Hangang R S Korea
145 F3 Hangaroa New Zealand
27 C11 Hangastöl Norway
145 E3 Hangatiki New Zealand
58 C2 Hangayn Nuruu mt Mongolia
Hangchow see Hangzhou
33 T8 Hangelsberg E Germany
27 G14 Hånger Sweden
58 E3 Hanggin Houqi China
94 E8 Hanging Rock Ohio
89 A10 Hangklip, C S Africa
100 H2 Hangman Cr Washington
29 K12 Hango Finland
65 D5 Hangu China
67 D4 Hanguang China
59 H5 Hangzhou China
59 H5 Hangzhou Wan B China
32 M7 Hänigsen W Germany
86 H3 Hanish I Red Sea
80 D1 Ḥanita Israel
Hanjiang see Yangzhou
67 F4 Hanjiang China
29 M9 Hankasalmi Finland
85 C4 Hank, El Mauritania
98 J3 Hankinson N Dakota
58 F5 Hankou China
103 O3 Hanksville Utah
8 D1 Hanley England
118 L7 Hanley Sask
99 L5 Hanley Falls Minnesota
144 D5 Hanmer Springs New Zealand
118 F7 Hanna Alberta
101 P9 Hanna Utah
101 T8 Hanna Wyoming
98 H2 Hannaford N Dakota
119 T10 Hannah N Dakota
120 K1 Hannah B Ontario
99 P10 Hannibal Missouri
99 Q4 Hannibal Wisconsin
28 A4 Hanning Kirke Denmark
142 F3 Hann, Mt W Australia
98 E2 Hannover N Dakota
32 L8 Hannover W Germany
140 C6 Hann Ra N Terr Aust
22 J2 Hannut Belgium
27 H16 Hanöbukten B Sweden
68 G2 Hanoi Vietnam
48 D4 Hanót Hungary
107 O2 Hanover Kansas
99 N4 Hanover Minnesota
101 O2 Hanover Montana
95 P3 Hanover New Hampshire
120 J8 Hanover Ontario
89 D8 Hanover S Africa
127 H1 Hanover parish Jamaica
133 C8 Hanover, I Chile
48 E6 Han Pijesak Yugoslavia
98 G1 Hansboro N Dakota
120 F3 Hansen Ontario
146 B5 Hansen Mt Antarctica
67 F1 Hanshan China
67 E1 Hanshou China
58 E5 Han Shui R China
67 D1 Han Shui R China
74 F4 Hansi India
27 G10 Hansjö Sweden
140 C5 Hanson R N Terr Aust
119 P4 Hanson L Sask
138 D4 Hanson, L S Australia
28 D5 Hansted Vejle Denmark
28 B2 Hanstholm Havn C Denmark
65 D2 Han Sum China
22 J3 Han-sur-Lesse Belgium
25 B6 Hansweert Netherlands
Hantan see Handan
Hanting see Wei Xian
Hants co see Hampshire
122 H8 Hantsport Nova Scotia
36 C7 Hantz, Col du pass France
65 D2 Han Ul China
67 A1 Hanwang China
83 K11 Hanwella Sri Lanka
58 F5 Hanyang China
58 D6 Hanyuan China
58 E5 Hanzhong China
65 D7 Hanzhuang China
135 N10 Hao atoll Tuamotu Arch Pacific Oc
65 H1 Haolianghe China
80 F3 Ha Or Israel
26 N6 Haparanda Sweden
71 B1 Hapo Halmahera Indonesia
9 H2 Happisburgh England
100 B8 Happy Camp California
140 E5 Happy Cr N Terr Aust
144 D4 Hapuku New Zealand
83 L11 Haputale Sri Lanka
79 E9 Ḥaql Saudi Arabia
58 E2 Hara Mongolia
26 M5 Harads Sweden
86 H4 Hara Fanna Ethiopia
111 H12 Harahan New Orleans
26 B9 Haram Norway
59 M4 Haramachi Japan
86 H4 Harar Ethiopia
86 A3 Harardera Somalia
Harare see Salisbury Zimbabwe
58 E2 Har-ayrag Mongolia
86 C3 Haraz Djombo Chad
86 D3 Haraze Chad
80 E8 Har Ben Yai'r Israel
65 G2 Harbin China
27 J11 Harbo Sweden
77 K5 Harboi Hills Pakistan
28 J7 Harbølle Denmark
22 D4 Harbonnières France
28 A3 Harboør Denmark
28 A3 Harboør Tange pen Denmark
100 A7 Harbor Oregon
94 E3 Harbor Beach Michigan
117 E6 Harbor Pt Alaska
94 B1 Harbor Springs Michigan
13 E3 Harbottle England
123 S6 Harbour Breton Nfld
123 S6 Harbour Buffett Nfld
113 K12 Harbour Cay, Little isld Bahamas
123 Q3 Harbour Deep Nfld
115 O8 Harbour Grace Nfld
126 F2 Harbour I Bahamas
123 S6 Harbour Mille Nfld
122 H8 Harbourville Nova Scotia
37 K6 Harburg Bayern W Germany
32 L6 Harburg Niedersachsen W Germany
28 E6 Hårby Denmark
122 G7 Harcourt New Brunswick
103 L7 Harcuvar Mts Arizona
74 G7 Harda India
27 B11 Hardanger Norway
27 B11 Hardanger-fjorden inlet Norway
27 C11 Hardangervidda plat Norway
89 A5 Hardap Dam Namibia
111 F9 Hardee Mississippi
112 F5 Hardeeville S Carolina
25 E2 Hardegarijp Netherlands
32 G9 Hardegsen W Germany
22 E2 Hardelot-Plage France
25 G3 Hardenberg Netherlands
70 D2 Harden, Bt mt Kalimantan
25 E4 Harderwijk Netherlands
107 O5 Hardesty Oklahoma
142 B6 Hardey, R W Australia
36 H4 Hardheim W Germany
110 F4 Hardin Illinois
110 C2 Hardin Missouri
114 J8 Hardin Montana
99 M3 Harding Minnesota
87 E12 Harding S Africa
116 M6 Harding Icefield Alaska
111 L9 Harding, L Georgia
119 T2 Harding L Manitoba
110 K4 Hardinsburg Kentucky
118 F6 Hardisty Alberta
117 P3 Hardisty L N W Terr
20 K2 Hardivillers France
102 C4 Hardman Oregon
140 A2 Hardman, Mt W Australia
80 D2 Hardof R Jordan
74 H4 Hardwar India
98 K6 Hardwick Minnesota
95 P2 Hardwick Vermont
138 D5 Hardwicke B S Australia
110 E5 Hardy Arkansas
101 O2 Hardy Montana
119 N9 Hardy Sask
145 F2 Hardy, Mt New Zealand
133 D9 Hardy, Pen Chile
94 B3 Hardy Res Michigan
123 S5 Hare B Nfld
80 E4 Hare Gilboa Israel
26 B9 Hareid Norway
22 E2 Harelbeke Belgium
32 F6 Haren W Germany
115 O3 Hare Øen isld Greenland
9 F1 Hare Park England
13 G6 Harewood England
79 F5 Harf el Mreffi mt Lebanon
20 F3 Harfleur France
27 K11 Harg Sweden
36 B5 Hargarten aux Mines France
86 H4 Hargeisa Somalia
48 K4 Harghitei Muntii mt Romania
22 E4 Hargicourt France
109 J9 Hargill Texas
22 J3 Hargimont Belgium
22 H3 Hargnies France
119 Q9 Hargrave Manitoba
119 S4 Hargrave L Manitoba
79 E8 Har Hakippa mt Israel
79 E8 Har Harif Israel
80 D8 Har Hezron Israel
66 F4 Har Hu L China
61 M9 Hari Japan
76 B3 Harihar India
144 C5 Harihari New Zealand
60 H11 Harima-nada sea Japan
25 B5 Haringvliet Netherlands
74 E1 Haripur Pakistan
77 J2 Hari Rud R Afghanistan/Iran
79 G6 Harir, Wādī watercourse Syria
87 C10 Haris Namibia
26 G10 Härjån R Sweden
29 J10 Harjavalta Finland
26 F10 Härjehågna mt Sweden
80 F2 Har Kena'an peak Israel
112 L3 Harkers I N Carolina
99 L8 Harlan Iowa
107 M2 Harlan Kansas
94 D10 Harlan Kentucky
98 G9 Harlan Co. Res Nebraska
22 K4 Harlange Luxembourg
32 G5 Harle W Germany
8 B2 Harlech Wales
112 E4 Harlem Georgia
101 R1 Harlem Montana
32 L5 Harlesiel W Germany
9 H3 Harleston England
28 D4 Harlev Denmark
28 J6 Hårlev Denmark
112 G4 Harleyville S Carolina
25 D2 Harlingen Netherlands
109 K9 Harlingen Texas
32 G5 Harlinger Land W Germany
33 M9 Harlingerode W Germany
9 G4 Harlow England
98 G1 Harlow N Dakota
101 O3 Harlowton Montana
94 H8 Harman W Virginia
47 K5 Harmancık Turkey
26 J10 Harmånger Sweden
25 C4 Harmelen Netherlands
79 F4 Har Meron peak Israel
107 L5 Harmon Oklahoma
118 A2 Harmon R Alberta
95 S2 Harmony Maine
99 O6 Harmony Minnesota
79 E8 Har Natha mt Israel
100 G6 Harney Oregon
100 F6 Harney Basin reg Oregon
113 F9 Harney, L Florida
100 F6 Harney L Oregon
98 C6 Harney Pk S Dakota
28 E6 Harnorup Denmark
26 J9 Härnösand Sweden
65 E7 Har Nur China
58 B2 Har Nuur L Mongolia
80 E3 Harod R Israel
26 B9 Haröy isld Norway
9 F4 Harpenden England
107 M4 Harper Kansas
85 C8 Harper Liberia
100 H6 Harper Oregon
109 H5 Harper Texas
116 L4 Harper Bend Alaska
117 G6 Harper Cr Alberta
102 G6 Harper L California
116 Q4 Harper, Mt Alaska
144 C5 Harper Pass New Zealand
94 K7 Harpers Ferry W Virginia
140 C5 Harper Springs N Terr Aust
110 J5 Harpeth R Tennessee
8 C6 Harpford England
9 G2 Harpley England
27 F15 Harplinge Sweden
32 H8 Harpstedt W Germany
119 M9 Harptree Sask
65 D4 Harqin China
65 D4 Harqin Qi China
103 L8 Harquahala Mts Arizona
85 E1 Harrach, El Algeria
107 N6 Harrah Oklahoma
26 F7 Harran Norway
37 K3 Harras E Germany
28 B3 Harre Denmark
111 D8 Harrell Arkansas
144 D5 Harrelville New Zealand
115 M7 Harricana R Quebec
28 E3 Harridslev Denmark
94 B2 Harrietta Michigan
112 C2 Harriman Tennessee
95 M8 Harrington Delaware
95 U2 Harrington Maine
100 G2 Harrington Washington
115 O7 Harrington Harbour Quebec
119 P2 Harriot L Sask
100 B9 Harris California
99 N9 Harris Missouri
118 K7 Harris Sask
15 B3 Harris div Scotland
110 F6 Harrisburg Arkansas
110 H4 Harrisburg Illinois
98 C8 Harrisburg Nebraska
94 D7 Harrisburg Ohio
100 B5 Harrisburg Oregon
95 L6 Harrisburg Pennsylvania
98 K6 Harrisburg S Dakota
118 H2 Harris Hill Ontario
110 F9 Harris, L Florida
138 D4 Harris, L S Australia
143 C10 Harrismith W Australia
140 A6 Harris, Mt N Terr Aust
144 B6 Harris Mts New Zealand
110 C5 Harrison Arkansas
112 E5 Harrison Georgia
100 J2 Harrison Idaho
94 C2 Harrison Michigan
101 O4 Harrison Montana
98 C7 Harrison Nebraska
98 H6 Harrison S Dakota
116 L1 Harrison B Alaska
94 J8 Harrisonburg Virginia
115 O7 Harrison, C Labrador
117 M11 Harrison L Br Columbia
83 K12 Harrison, Mt Mahé I Ind Oc
110 B3 Harrisonville Missouri
94 D2 Harrisville Michigan
95 M2 Harrisville New York
94 F7 Harrisville W Virginia
110 K2 Harrodsburg Indiana
94 C9 Harrodsburg Kentucky
13 G6 Harrogate England
98 G5 Harrold S Dakota
109 H1 Harrold Texas
120 H10 Harrow Ontario
119 O8 Harrowby Manitoba
27 F14 Härryda Sweden
98 F9 Harry Strunk L Nebraska
79 E8 Har Saggi mt Israel
32 K6 Harsefeld W Germany
32 H9 Harsewinkel W Germany
78 G1 Harsit Turkey
26 L5 Harsprånget Sweden
26 J3 Harstad Norway
32 L8 Harsum W Germany
28 A4 Harsyssel reg Denmark
13 G4 Hart England
99 U6 Hart Michigan
119 M9 Hart Sask
65 E3 Hartao China
89 B7 Hartbees watercourse S Africa
38 N7 Hartberg Austria
89 E5 Hartebeespoort Dam S Africa
27 B11 Hårteigen mt Norway
118 C8 Hartell Alberta
22 E5 Hartennes-et-Taux France
36 E2 Hartenrod W Germany
37 O2 Hartenstein E Germany
37 J5 Hartershofen W Germany
15 E5 Hart Fell Scotland
9 G5 Hartfield England
111 L10 Hartford Alabama
109 N1 Hartford Arkansas
95 P5 Hartford Connecticut
107 P3 Hartford Kansas
110 K4 Hartford Kentucky
94 A4 Hartford Michigan
94 E6 Hartford Ohio
112 D2 Hartford Tennessee
99 S6 Hartford Wisconsin
94 B6 Hartford City Indiana
95 P5 Hartford, E Connecticut
37 O1 Hartha E Germany
37 O2 Harthau E Germany
12 E2 Harthill Scotland
9 E1 Hartington England
98 J7 Hartington Nebraska
80 E2 Har Tir'an Israel
122 D2 Hart-jaune, R Quebec
138 D4 Hart, L S Australia
8 B6 Hartland England
95 S2 Hartland Maine
122 E7 Hartland New Brunswick
8 B5 Hartland Pt England
8 D3 Hartlebury England
13 G4 Hartlepool England
13 G3 Hartley England
99 L6 Hartley Iowa
108 B8 Hartley Texas
89 G2 Hartley Zimbabwe
117 J9 Hartley Bay Br Columbia
9 F5 Hartley Wintney England
100 F2 Hartline Washington
106 H3 Hartman Colorado
37 P5 Hartmanice Czechoslovakia
37 O2 Hartmannsdorf E Germany
36 G3 Hartmannshain W Germany
119 Q6 Hart Mt Manitoba
100 F7 Hart Mt Oregon
142 F3 Hart, Mt W Australia
119 R9 Hartney Manitoba
29 M10 Hartola Finland
13 G4 Harton England
106 E2 Hartsel Colorado
111 K7 Hartselle Alabama
37 J6 Härtsfeld mts W Germany
107 P7 Hartshorne Oklahoma
138 C4 Harts I S Australia
140 C6 Harts Range N Terr Aust
112 G3 Hartsville S Carolina
110 K5 Hartsville Tennessee
89 D6 Hartswater S Africa
80 C6 Hartuv Israel
110 D4 Hartville Missouri
98 B7 Hartville Wyoming
112 E3 Hartwell Georgia
112 D3 Hartwell Res S Carolina
120 H3 Harty Ontario
89 D6 Hartz R S Africa
84 F4 Harūj al Aswad, Al Libya
58 B2 Har Us Nuur L Mongolia
80 C7 Haruvit Israel
102 H7 Harvard California
100 J3 Harvard Idaho
99 S7 Harvard Illinois
98 H9 Harvard Nebraska
116 O6 Harvard Gl Alaska
106 D3 Harvard, Mt Colorado
143 F7 Harvest, Mt W Australia
99 T8 Harvey Illinois
99 O8 Harvey Iowa
98 F2 Harvey N Dakota
111 J13 Harvey New Orleans
143 B10 Harvey W Australia
102 C1 Harvey Mt California
122 F8 Harvey Stn New Brunswick
107 P3 Harveyville Kansas
9 E4 Harwell England
9 H4 Harwich England
109 K6 Harwood Texas
36 E4 Harxheim W Germany
74 F4 Haryana prov India
80 E8 Har Yeroham Israel
33 N9 Harz mts Germany
33 O9 Harzgerode E Germany
79 F8 Hasā Jordan
72 F4 Hasā, Al reg Saudi Arabia
74 F9 Hasanparti India
80 E7 Hasa R Jordan
79 F5 Hāsbaiya Lebanon
32 G8 Hasbergen W Germany
36 B5 Hasborn-Dautweiler W Germany
32 G7 Hase R W Germany
78 H3 Haseke, El Syria
32 K2 Hasel R E Germany
32 K2 Haseldorf W Germany
32 F7 Haselünne W Germany
80 D4 Hashimiye Jordan
61 J11 Hashimoto Japan
78 M2 Hashtpar Iran
77 A1 Hashtrūd Iran
71 B3 Hasil Indonesia
26 H8 Hasjö Sweden
111 C7 Haskell Arkansas
107 P6 Haskell Oklahoma
108 H2 Haskell Texas
38 K4 Haslach Austria
36 E7 Haslach W Germany
27 G16 Hasle Denmark
109 M9 Haslet Texas
28 H6 Haslev Denmark
13 F6 Haslingden England
41 H4 Hasli Tal Switzerland
28 E4 Haslund Denmark
28 E5 Hasmark Denmark
22 E3 Hasnon France
18 E9 Hasparren France
32 F10 Haspe W Germany
22 E3 Haspres France
76 C4 Hassan India
103 M8 Hassayampa R Arizona
37 K3 Hassberge mts W Germany
26 J9 Hassela Sweden
33 N9 Hasselfelde E Germany
115 K2 Hassel Sd N W Terr
22 J2 Hasselt Belgium
25 F3 Hasselt Netherlands
28 F4 Hasselø Denmark
33 N8 Hasserode E Germany
37 K3 Hassfurt W Germany
85 E2 Hassi-Bou-Zid Algeria
85 E3 Hassi Chebaba Algeria
28 E3 Hassing Denmark
79 H3 Hass, Jebel el mts Syria
37 L3 Hasslach W Germany
33 T6 Hassleben E Germany
37 K1 Hassleben Erfurt E Germany
27 G15 Hässleholm Sweden
27 G13 Hässleby Sweden
36 E5 Hassloch W Germany
22 H3 Hastière-Lavaux Belgium
127 P6 Hastings Barbados
9 G6 Hastings England
113 F8 Hastings Florida
99 L9 Hastings Iowa
94 B4 Hastings Michigan
99 O5 Hastings Minnesota
98 H9 Hastings Nebraska
145 F3 Hastings New Zealand
107 M7 Hastings Oklahoma
121 N8 Hastings Ontario
94 J6 Hastings Pennsylvania
139 H9 Hastings Tasmania
139 L4 Hastings R New S Wales
139 K4 Hastings Ra mts New S Wales
28 E6 Håstrup Denmark
27 G15 Hästveda Sweden
106 H3 Hasty Colorado
26 M1 Hasvik Norway
106 G3 Haswell Colorado
58 E3 Hatanbulag Mongolia
95 M6 Hatboro Pennsylvania
106 C9 Hatch New Mexico
103 M4 Hatch Utah
140 D5 Hatches Cr N Terr Aust
126 F2 Hatchet Bay Eleuthera Bahamas
110 G6 Hatchie R Tennessee
98 B7 Hat Cr Wyoming
100 D9 Hat Creek California
48 H5 Haţeg Romania
67 H4 Haterumashima Japan
111 B7 Hatfield Arkansas
9 F4 Hatfield Herts England
98 K6 Hatfield Minnesota
139 G5 Hatfield New S Wales
119 M7 Hatfield Sask
9 G4 Hatfield Peverel England
101 T3 Hathaway Montana
8 B6 Hatherleigh England
138 F6 Hatherleigh S Australia
9 E1 Hathersage England
74 H5 Hathras India
68 G7 Ha Tien Vietnam
80 G3 Hatim Jordan
68 G3 Ha Tinh Vietnam
127 K5 Hato Mayor Dominican Rep
56 C3 Hatskiy U.S.S.R.
60 F11 Hatsukaichi Japan
138 F5 Hattah Victoria
70 F2 Hattan, Mt Sabah
25 F4 Hattem Netherlands
36 D6 Hatten France
112 M2 Hatteras N Carolina
112 M2 Hatteras Inlet N Carolina
36 E3 Hattersheim W Germany
28 O9 Hattervig Faeroes
26 G6 Hattfjelldal Norway
111 G10 Hattiesburg Mississippi
36 B6 Hattigny France
28 D5 Hatting Denmark
32 F10 Hattingen W Germany
20 K3 Hatton France
98 J2 Hatton N Dakota
118 H8 Hatton Sask
100 G3 Hatton Washington
68 C6 Hattras Passage Burma
40 F1 Hattstatt France
29 L10 Hattula Finland
126 F4 Hatuey Cuba
145 F4 Hatuma New Zealand
48 F3 Hatvan Hungary
38 O8 Hatzendorf Austria
36 C3 Hatzenport W Germany
36 F2 Hatzfeld W Germany
68 J6 Hau Bon Vietnam
22 D2 Haubourdin France
86 A2 Haud reg Ethiopia
80 G4 Haufa Jordan
28 C4 Hauge Denmark
27 C10 Hauge Norway
99 P4 Haugen Wisconsin
27 A12 Haugesund Norway
111 C9 Haughton Louisiana
31 J7 Haugsdorf Austria
29 L10 Hauho Finland
145 E3 Hauhungaroa Ra New Zealand
27 B12 Haukeliseter Norway
29 L6 Haukipudas Finland
29 N9 Haukivesi L Finland
29 N9 Haukivuori Finland
145 F3 Haumoana New Zealand
36 H2 Haune R W Germany
36 H2 Hauneck W Germany
36 H2 Haunetal Hessen W Germany
37 K7 Haunstetten W Germany
144 C5 Haupiri, L New Zealand
37 O5 Hauptenberg mt W Germany
145 E2 Hauraki Gulf New Zealand
144 A6 Hauroko, L New Zealand
27 A11 Haus Norway
36 E7 Hausach W Germany
32 J8 Hausberge W Germany
101 O3 Hauser L. Dam Montana
38 H5 Hausruck mts Austria
Haussez Iles d' see Mercury Is
41 K4 Hausstock mt Switzerland
22 B3 Haut Banc, Pte du France
40 B2 Haut du Sec mt France
18 L10 Haute-Corse dep Corsica
18 F7 Hautefort France
18 F9 Haute-Garonne dep France
18 H7 Haute-Loire dep France
40 E6 Hauteluce France
19 J4 Haute-Marne dep France
121 Q4 Haute Mauricie, Parc de Quebec
122 D4 Hauterive Quebec
19 Q15 Hautes Alpes dep France
19 J5 Haute-Saône dep France
40 D6 Haute-Savoie dep France
22 L2 Hautes Fagnes Belgium
22 H4 Hautes Rivières France
21 D8 Hauteurs de Gâtine hills France
21 H9 Haute-Vienne dep France
36 B5 Haut-Hombourg France
95 T2 Haut, I. au Maine
22 F3 Hautmont France
19 K5 Haut-Rhin dep France
85 D2 Hauts Plateaux Morocco/Algeria
20 B4 Hautteville-sur-Mer France
86 E5 Haut-Zaïre prov Zaire
135 Q2 Hauula Hawaiian Is
145 E4 Hauwai New Zealand
110 C6 Havana Arkansas
Havana Cuba see Habana
111 M11 Havana Florida
99 R9 Havana Illinois
107 P4 Havana Kansas
98 J4 Havana N Dakota
9 F6 Havant England
103 K7 Havasu L Cal/Ariz
28 C3 Havbro Denmark
28 J5 Havdrup Denmark
33 R6 Havel E Germany
22 J3 Havelange Belgium
33 Q7 Havelberg E Germany
33 R7 Havelland reg E Germany
33 R7 Havelland Grosse Haupt-kanal E Germany
112 L3 Havelock N Carolina
98 J1 Havelock N Dakota
122 G8 Havelock New Brunswick
144 D4 Havelock New Zealand
121 N8 Havelock Ontario
140 C2 Havelock Falls N Terr Aust
68 A7 Havelock I Andaman Is
145 F3 Havelock North New Zealand
107 N2 Haven Kansas
107 O4 Havensville Kansas
8 B4 Haverfordwest Wales
9 G3 Haverhill England
95 Q4 Haverhill Massachusetts
95 Q3 Haverhill New Hampshire
76 B3 Haveri India
26 H9 Haverö Sweden
22 J3 Haversin Belgium
28 D3 Haverslev Nordjylland Denmark
95 N5 Haverstraw New York
107 L4 Haviland Kansas
94 C5 Haviland Ohio
120 F6 Haviland Bay Ontario

Havirna — Hindenburg 33

48 K2 Havirna Romania
31 J6 Havlíčkův Brod Czechoslovakia
28 D6 Havnbjerg Denmark
28 E3 Havndal Denmark
28 B6 Havneby Denmark
28 G5 Havnsø Denmark
28 B4 Havnstrup Denmark
26 O1 Havoysund Norway
47 J5 Havran Turkey
22 G3 Havre Belgium
114 J8 Havre Montana
123 L6 Havre Aubert Madeleine Is, Quebec
28 G6 Havrebjerg Denmark
123 L8 Havre Boucher Nova Scotia
95 L7 Havre de Grace Maryland
20 F3 Havre, Le France
115 N7 Havre-St-Pierre Quebec
137 Q8 Havre Trench *sea feature* Pacific Oc
28 A5 Havrvig Denmark
26 H7 Havsnäs Sweden
78 E1 Havza Turkey
135 U5 Hawaii *isld* Hawaiian Is
135 Hawaiian Is Pacific Oc
86 B3 Hawal *R* Nigeria
98 K6 Hawarden Iowa
144 D5 Hawarden New Zealand
118 L7 Hawarden Sask
8 C1 Hawarden Wales
138 F6 Hawdon, L S Australia
144 B6 Hawea Flat New Zealand
145 E3 Hawera New Zealand
102 G7 Hawes California
110 K4 Hawesville Kentucky
13 F5 Hawes Water England
135 U4 Hawi Hawaiian Is
13 F3 Hawick Scotland
144 B6 Hawkdun Range New Zealand
145 F3 Hawke Bay New Zealand
139 L4 Hawke, C New S Wales
138 E4 Hawker S Australia
138 F3 Hawker Gate New S Wales
145 F3 Hawke's Bay *stat area* New Zealand
141 F1 Hawkesbury I Queensland
140 C1 Hawkesbury Pt N Terr Aust
139 K5 Hawkesbury R New S Wales
146 F9 Hawkes, Mt Antarctica
9 G5 Hawkhurst England
103 L4 Hawkins Pk Utah
112 D5 Hawkinsville Georgia
120 F4 Hawk Junct Ontario
118 J1 Hawk Lake Ontario
110 E3 Hawk Point Missouri
94 D1 Hawks Michigan
126 F2 Hawksbill Cay *isld* Bahamas
13 E5 Hawkshead England
126 G2 Hawks Nest Pt Cat I Bahamas
98 B8 Hawk Springs Wyoming
141 K7 Hawkwood Queensland
106 G4 Hawley Colorado
98 K3 Hawley Minnesota
95 M5 Hawley Pennsylvania
108 H3 Hawley Texas
68 D2 Hawng Luk Burma
13 G6 Haworth England
107 Q8 Haworth Oklahoma
112 H2 Haw R N Carolina
78 H5 Hawran, Wadi Iraq
78 L5 Hawr as S'adiyah *L* Iraq
13 H5 Hawsker England
113 E8 Hawthorn Florida
102 F3 Hawthorne Nevada
99 P3 Hawthorne Wisconsin
80 D5 Hawwara Jordan
65 F2 Haxat China
65 B2 Haxat Hudag China
101 T2 Haxby Montana
98 D9 Haxtun Colorado
139 G5 Hay New S Wales
100 H3 Hay Washington
117 N6 Hay *R* Br Columbia
99 P4 Hay *R* Wisconsin
61 P6 Hayachine-san *mt* Japan
60 P3 Hayakita Japan
19 K3 Hayange France
60 E12 Hayasui-seto *str* Japan
101 T9 Haybro Colorado
103 O8 Hayden Arizona
101 S9 Hayden Colorado
100 J2 Hayden L Idaho
141 F4 Haydon Queensland
13 F4 Haydon Br England
20 B3 Haye-du-Puits, la France
20 H3 Haye, la France
20 C4 Haye-Pesnel, la France
111 D11 Hayes Louisiana
98 E5 Hayes S Dakota
115 K6 Hayes *R* Manitoba
20 G4 Haye St. Sylvestre, la France
98 E9 Hayes Center Nebraska
116 L6 Hayes Glaciers Alaska
115 N2 Hayes Halvø *pen* Greenland
68 C7 Hayes I Burma
116 O5 Hayes, Mt Alaska
112 D2 Hayesville N Carolina
13 G6 Hayfield England
99 O6 Hayfield Minnesota
103 J8 Hayfield Res Carolina
102 A1 Hayfork California
13 F5 Haygarth England
36 G7 Hayingen W Germany
117 O6 Hay L Alberta
118 D5 Hay Lakes Alberta
8 A7 Hayle England
9 F6 Hayling England
113 E7 Haylow Georgia
141 J5 Hayman I Queensland
94 K8 Haymarket Virginia
140 C6 Hay, Mt N Terr Aust
109 O3 Haynesville Louisiana
95 T8 Haynesville Maine
111 K9 Hayneville Alabama
20 H2 Hayons, les France
8 C3 Hay-on-Wye England
141 J5 Hay Point Queensland
140 D6 Hay R N Terr Aust
47 J3 Hayrabolu Turkey
47 J3 Hayrabolu *R* Turkey
114 H5 Hay River N W Terr
118 F8 Hays Alberta
107 L3 Hays Kansas
101 R1 Hays Montana
98 D7 Hay Springs Nebraska
100 K8 Haystack Mt Nevada
103 L2 Haystack Pk Utah
118 G6 Hayter Alberta
110 G5 Hayti Missouri
98 J5 Hayti S Dakota
13 H6 Hayton England
102 B4 Hayward California
99 N6 Hayward Minnesota
107 N5 Hayward Oklahoma
99 P4 Hayward Wisconsin
140 B2 Hayward, Mt N Terr Aust
9 F6 Haywards Heath England
119 T9 Haywood Manitoba
80 E2 Hazan Israel
57 F6 Hazara Afghanistan
77 J3 Hazarajat *reg* Afghanistan
94 D9 Hazard Kentucky
95 P4 Hazardville Connecticut
75 L7 Hazaribagh India
77 F1 Hazar Masjed, Kūh-e *mts* Iran
22 D2 Hazebrouck France
98 K1 Hazel Minnesota
98 J5 Hazel S Dakota
119 V9 Hazelridge Manitoba
117 K8 Hazelton Br Col
107 M4 Hazelton Kansas
98 F3 Hazelton N Dakota
110 E7 Hazen Arkansas
98 E2 Hazen N Dakota
102 E2 Hazen Nevada
116 E6 Hazen B Alaska
115 N1 Hazen, L N W Terr
118 K9 Hazenmore Sask
114 H2 Hazen Str N W Terr
80 B8 Hazerim Israel
25 C4 Hazerswoude Netherlands
79 F8 Hazeva Israel
112 E2 Hazewood N Carolina
112 E6 Hazlehurst Georgia
111 F10 Hazlehurst Mississippi
95 M6 Hazleton Pennsylvania
142 G5 Hazlett, L W Australia
37 N3 Hazlov Czechoslovakia
80 F2 Hazor Israel
80 F3 HaZore'im Israel
80 C7 He Israel
9 G2 Heacham England
9 G5 Headcorn England
14 B3 Headford Irish Rep
140 E5 Headingly Queensland
111 L10 Headland Alabama
144 B6 Headlong Pk New Zealand
138 B4 Head of Bight *B* S Australia
100 K3 Headquarters Idaho
83 M9 Headridge Hill Christmas I Indian Oc
100 A7 Heads, The *C* Oregon
99 R4 Heafford Junct Wisconsin
102 B3 Healdsburg California
109 K1 Healdton Oklahoma
139 H7 Healesville Victoria
116 N5 Healy Alaska
107 K3 Healy Kansas
116 P4 Healy *R* Alaska
116 P5 Healy L Alaska
119 Q3 Heaman Manitoba
9 E1 Heanor England
90 M16 Heard I Southern Oc
119 M8 Hearne Sask
109 L5 Hearne Texas
117 R4 Hearne L N W Terr
102 A2 Hearst California
115 L8 Hearst Ontario
146 E13 Hearst I Antarctica
98 D3 Heart *R* N Dakota
118 F3 Heart L Alberta
101 P5 Heart L Wyoming
118 A3 Heart R Alberta
123 T6 Heart's Content Nfld
123 T6 Heart's Delight Nfld
98 H9 Heartwell Nebraska
128 E6 Heath *R* Bolivia/Peru
139 G6 Heathcote Victoria
6 L2 Heather *oil rig* North Sea
123 O5 Heatherton Nfld
9 G6 Heathfield England
123 L4 Heath Pt Anticosti I, Quebec
9 F5 Heathrow Airport England
112 G3 Heath Springs S Carolina
122 F6 Heath Steel Mines New Brunswick
95 L9 Heathsville Virginia
107 Q7 Heavener Oklahoma
109 J8 Hebbronville Texas
13 F6 Hebden Br England
65 C5 Hebei *prov* China
103 O7 Heber Arizona
101 O9 Heber Utah
32 L6 Heber W Germany
110 D6 Heber Springs Arkansas
121 P3 Hébert, L Quebec
20 C3 Hébert, Pt France
121 T4 Hébertville Station Quebec
101 O5 Hebgen L Montana
65 C7 Hebi China
100 B4 Hebo Oregon
101 T9 Hebron Colorado
99 S7 Hebron Illinois
99 T8 Hebron Indiana
80 D7 Hebron Jordan
115 N6 Hebron Labrador
98 E3 Hebron N Dakota
98 J9 Hebron Nebraska
122 F10 Hebron Nova Scotia
94 E7 Hebron Ohio
27 J12 Heby Sweden
114 F7 Hecate Str Br Columbia
100 A5 Heceta Head Oregon
117 G8 Heceta I Alaska
67 C4 Hechi China
36 F7 Hechingen W Germany
22 J1 Hechtel Belgium
32 K5 Hechthausen W Germany
36 E4 Hechtsheim W Germany
67 B1 Hechuan China
33 T7 Heckelberg E Germany
9 F2 Heckington England
33 P9 Hecklingen E Germany
98 H4 Hecla S Dakota
114 H2 Hecla & Griper B N W Terr
119 V7 Hecla I Manitoba
119 V7 Hecla Prov. Park Manitoba
122 F9 Hectanooga Nova Scotia
102 H7 Hector California
99 M5 Hector Minnesota
144 C4 Hector New Zealand
145 E4 Hector *mt* New Zealand
117 P10 Hector, Mt Alberta
127 M2 Hector's River Jamaica
27 H12 Hed Sweden
61 M11 Heda Japan
27 D11 Hedal Norway
20 K1 Hedauville France
26 K6 Hedberg Sweden
27 D12 Heddal Norway
36 F4 Heddesheim W Germany
13 G3 Heddon on-the-Wall England
20 B5 Hédé France
26 G9 Hede Sweden
25 D5 Hedel Netherlands
27 H11 Hedemora Sweden
32 L10 Hedemunden W Germany
28 E6 Heden Denmark
26 M6 Heden Sweden
26 N5 Hedenäset Sweden
28 D5 Hedensted Denmark
33 O9 Hedersleben E Germany
27 J11 Hedesunda Sweden
26 G9 Hedeviken Sweden
144 B7 Hedgehope New Zealand
101 Q3 Hedgesville Montana
94 J7 Hedgesville W Virginia
67 C6 Hedi Shuiku *res* China
117 N11 Hedley Br Columbia
27 E11 Hedmark Norway
27 E10 Hedmark *county* Norway
61 Q12 Hedo Okinawa
13 H6 Hedon England
83 L11 Hedo Oya *R* Sri Lanka
61 Q12 Hedo-zaki *C* Okinawa
99 O8 Hedrick Iowa
28 A4 Hee Denmark
32 F7 Heede W Germany
33 T7 Heegermühle E Germany
32 F8 Heek W Germany
25 C4 Heemstede Netherlands
32 J8 Heepen W Germany
22 H3 Heer Belgium
25 E7 Heer Netherlands
25 F4 Heerde Netherlands
25 E3 Heerenveen Netherlands
25 C3 Heerhugo-waard Netherlands
25 E7 Heerlen Netherlands
25 E5 Heesch Netherlands
25 E6 Heeze Netherlands
67 F1 Hefei China
67 C2 Hefeng China
117 N10 Heffley Br Columbia
111 L8 Heflin Alabama
59 K2 Hegang China
65 H1 Hegang China
61 K8 Hegura-jima *isld* Japan
88 E5 Hehe Tanzania
26 D10 Heidal Norway
80 F8 Heidan *R* Jordan
32 K4 Heide W Germany
37 L5 Heideck W Germany
111 H10 Heidelberg Mississippi
87 E11 Heidelberg S Africa
36 F5 Heidelberg W Germany
110 N4 Heidelburg Kentucky
36 F5 Heidelsheim W Germany
37 M4 Heide Naab *R* W Germany
37 J6 Heidenheim W Germany
36 D3 Heidenrod W Germany
94 B2 Heights, The Michigan
60 F12 Heigun-tō *isld* Japan
Heihe *see* Aihui
59 J1 Hei-ho China
25 E6 Heijthuizsen Netherlands
87 E11 Heilbron S Africa
36 G5 Heilbronn W Germany
38 G7 Heiligenblut Austria
33 P4 Heiligendamm E Germany
30 F1 Heiligenhafen W Germany
32 M10 Heiligenstadt E Germany
37 L4 Heiligenstadt W Germany
65 D7 Heilin China
59 H1 Heilongjiang *prov* China
59 J1 Heilong Jiang *R* China
37 K5 Heilsbronn W Germany
Heilungkiang *prov see* Heilongjiang
36 B2 Heimbach W Germany
36 G4 Heimbuchenthal W Germany
33 N9 Heimburg E Germany
98 G2 Heimdal N Dakota
26 D8 Heimdal Norway
146 C10 Heimefrontfjella *ra* Antarctica
36 F6 Heimsheim W Germany
29 O9 Heinävesi Finland
36 H1 Heinebach W Germany
22 L3 Heinerscheid Luxembourg
37 L3 Heinersdorf E Germany
36 C5 Heinitz W Germany
25 F4 Heino Netherlands
29 M10 Heinola Finland
33 P8 Heinrichsburg E Germany
25 F6 Heinsberg W Germany
118 G5 Heinsburg Alberta
33 S9 Heinsdorf E Germany
68 C5 Heinz B Burma
68 C5 Heinze I Burma
65 E4 Heishan China
65 C3 Heishantou China
67 C2 Heishui China
118 E6 Heisler Alberta
22 E1 Heist Belgium
22 H1 Heist-op-den-Berg Belgium
80 G3 Heit Syria
80 G2 Heital Syria
79 D8 Heitân, G *mt* Egypt
40 G2 Heitersheim W Germany
65 F2 Heiyupao China
84 H4 Heiz, El Egypt
65 A5 Hejialiang China
67 B2 Hejiang China
67 C6 Hejiang China
67 D5 He Jiang *R* China
67 D4 Hejie China
65 A7 Hejin China
28 D6 Hejls Denmark
28 C6 Hejlsminde Denmark
28 B5 Hejnsvig Denmark
28 D6 Hejsager Denmark
145 F3 Hekerangi Pt New Zealand
115 S5 Hekla *vol* Iceland
Hekou *see* Yanshan
65 B4 Hekou China
67 D5 Hekou Guangdong China
67 A5 Hekou Yunnan China
31 L1 Hel Poland
80 E2 Hela Israel
26 F9 Helagsfjället *mt* Sweden
58 E4 Helan Shan *mt ra* China
37 K1 Helbe *R* E Germany
28 E3 Helberskov Denmark
33 O9 Helbra E Germany
22 J1 Helchteren Belgium
37 K3 Heldburg E Germany
36 F3 Heldenbergen W Germany
127 P3 Helden's Pt St Kitts W I
33 O10 Heldrungen E Germany
112 D3 Helen Georgia
111 K8 Helena Alabama
111 F7 Helena Arkansas
100 B9 Helena California
112 E5 Helena Georgia
114 H8 Helena Montana
107 M5 Helena Oklahoma
102 G7 Helendale California
118 J5 Helénè L Sask
146 D3 Helen Gl Antarctica
142 E6 Helen Hill W Australia
71 C1 Helen I Pacific Oc
119 P1 Helen L Ontario
141 F5 Helen, Mt Queensland
15 D4 Helensburgh Scotland
140 C4 Helen Springs N Terr Aust
145 E2 Helensville New Zealand
33 P10 Helfta E Germany
26 F6 Helgeland *reg* Norway
27 D12 Helgen Norway
32 G4 Helgoländ *isld* W Germany
32 H4 Helgoländer Bucht W Germany
26 K1 Helgöy Norway
65 H1 Heli China
79 B8 Heliopolis Egypt
26 E8 Hell Norway
33 O7 Hellberg *hills* E Germany
28 K4 Hellebæk Denmark
77 B5 Helleh *R* Iran
26 J4 Hellemobotn Norway
25 F4 Hellendoorn Netherlands
36 B3 Hellenthal W Germany
28 K5 Hellerup Denmark
28 J6 Hellested Denmark
26 B9 Hellesylt Norway
28 E2 Hellevad Nordjylland Denmark
28 C6 Hellevad Sønderjylland Denmark
26 L2 Helligskogen Norway
26 G4 Helligvoer *isld* Norway
17 F6 Hellin Spain
Hell's Canyon *see* Snake River Canyon
127 L3 Hellshire Hills Jamaica
28 E2 Hellum Denmark
87 H10 Hell-Ville Madagascar
32 K6 Hellwege W Germany
102 D5 Helm California
72 J2 Helmand *R* Afghanistan
32 K9 Helmarshausen W Germany
37 M3 Helmbrechts W Germany
33 N10 Helme *R* E Germany
87 C11 Helmeringhausen Namibia
37 J2 Helmershausen E Germany
9 H3 Helmingham England
25 E6 Helmond Netherlands
32 J4 Helmsand *sandbank* W Germany
15 E2 Helmsdale Scotland
15 E2 Helmsdale *R* Scotland
13 G5 Helmsley England
36 F5 Helmstadt W Germany
33 O8 Helmstedt W Germany
101 N3 Helmville Montana
28 D6 Helnæs Denmark
28 E6 Helnæs Bugt *B* Denmark
26 P1 Helnes Norway
59 J3 Helong China
65 F2 Helong China
109 J6 Helotes Texas
103 O2 Helper Utah
33 T6 Helpter Berge *peak* E Germany
32 L10 Helsa-Wickenrode W Germany
29 K4 Helsingborg Sweden
28 J4 Helsinge Denmark
Helsingfors *see* Helsinki
28 K4 Helsingør Denmark
29 L11 Helsinki Finland
9 G6 Helston England
32 L7 Helstorf W Germany
28 O9 Heltnin Faeroes
110 K3 Heltonville Indiana
130 H5 Helvécia Brazil
14 D4 Helvick Hd Irish Rep
84 J4 Helwan Egypt
28 D4 Hem Vejle Denmark
28 B3 Hem Viborg Denmark
118 F7 Hemaruka Alberta
37 M5 Hemau W Germany
32 E9 Hemden W Germany
9 F4 Hemel Hempstead England
25 D3 Hemelum Netherlands
32 G10 Hemer W Germany
102 H8 Hemet California
36 B6 Héming France
98 C7 Hemingford Nebraska
119 Q4 Heming Lake Manitoba
112 H4 Hemingway S Carolina
141 L1 Hemmant *dist* Brisbane, Qnsld
32 J4 Hemme W Germany
28 F3 Hemmed Denmark
32 L8 Hemmendorf W Germany
28 A5 Hemmet Denmark
32 L8 Hemmingen W Germany
121 R7 Hemmingford Quebec
32 K5 Hemmoor W Germany
26 G5 Hemnesberget Norway
111 C10 Hemphill Texas
95 O6 Hempstead Long I, N Y
109 L5 Hempstead Texas
9 H2 Hemsby England
27 K14 Hemse *isld* Gotland Sweden
27 C11 Hemsedal Norway
27 C11 Hemsil *R* Norway
27 G15 Hemsjö Sweden
32 L6 Hemslingen W Germany
26 K9 Hemsö Sweden
13 G6 Hemsworth England
65 B7 Henan *prov* China
145 E1 Hen and Chicken Is New Zealand
16 E4 Henares *R* Spain
61 N5 Henashi-zaki *C* Japan
140 C6 Henbury N Terr Aust
18 D9 Hendaye France
22 D3 Hendecourt-lès Cagnicourt France
47 L4 Hendek Turkey
112 J1 Henderson N Carolina
103 K5 Henderson Nevada
95 L3 Henderson New York
110 H6 Henderson Tennessee
109 N3 Henderson Texas
94 E8 Henderson W Virginia
135 O11 Henderson I Pacific Oc
112 E2 Hendersonville N Carolina
77 A4 Hendījān Iran
9 F4 Hendon England
141 K8 Hendon Queensland
119 O6 Hendon Sask
77 C6 Hendorābī *isld* Iran
48 J4 Hendorf Romania
141 K1 Hendra *dist* Brisbane, Qnsld
98 K5 Hendricks Minnesota
94 H7 Hendricks W Virginia
129 G3 Hendrik Top *mt* Suriname
89 D8 Hendrik Verwoerd Dam S Africa
8 B4 Hendy Wales
101 O8 Henefer Utah
65 H2 Hengdaohezi China
65 G3 Hengdaozi China
67 D3 Hengdong China
58 C6 Hengduan Shan *mts* China
25 G4 Hengelo Netherlands
37 P6 Hengersberg W Germany
67 F2 Hengfeng China
67 A2 Heng Jiang *R* China
67 D2 Henglongqiao China
67 D3 Hengnan China
67 D3 Hengshan China
67 D3 Heng Shan *mt* China
58 G4 Hengshui China
37 J5 Hengstfeld W Germany
67 C5 Heng Xian China
69 A9 Henhoaha Nicobar Is
22 D3 Henin Lietard France
144 C6 Henley New Zealand
123 R2 Henley Hbr Labrador
9 E3 Henley in Arden England
9 F4 Henley-on-Thames England
100 C10 Henleyville California
9 F3 Henlow England
109 J5 Henly Texas
27 E12 Henmes Norway
61 P13 Henna Okinawa
26 H9 Hennan Sweden
28 A5 Henne Denmark
37 J3 Henneberg E Germany
18 C5 Hennebont France
36 C2 Hennef W Germany
37 K5 Hennenbach W Germany
99 R8 Hennepin Illinois
20 F3 Hennequeville France
107 N5 Hennessey Oklahoma
33 S8 Hennickendorf E Germany
33 S7 Hennigsdorf E Germany
95 Q3 Henniker New Hampshire
110 J1 Henning Illinois
99 L3 Henning Minnesota
110 G6 Henning Tennessee
26 G3 Henningsvaer Norway
32 K4 Hennstedt W Germany
20 K3 Hénonville France
77 D6 Henqam *isld* Iran
119 M5 Henribourg Sask
22 K2 Henri-Chapelle Belgium
109 J2 Henrietta Texas
115 L6 Henrietta Maria, C Ontario
103 N4 Henrieville Utah
117 L7 Henri, Mt Br Col
Henrique de Carvalho *see* Suarimo
101 O7 Henry Idaho
99 R8 Henry Illinois
95 M10 Henry, C Virginia
146 E15 Henryk Arckowski Poland
115 N4 Henry Kater Pen N W Terr
111 K8 Henry L Alabama
68 A6 Henry Lawrence I Andaman Is
100 K1 Henry, Mt Montana
103 O4 Henry Mts Utah
142 B6 Henry, R W Australia
101 O5 Henrys Fork *R* Idaho
110 L3 Henryville Indiana
120 J9 Hensall Ontario
110 H4 Henshaw Kentucky
102 H8 Henshaw, L California
12 E5 Hensingham England
142 G3 Hensman, Mt W Australia
32 L5 Henstedt-Ulzburg W Germany
8 D6 Henstridge England
58 E2 Hentiy Mongolia
58 E2 Hentiyn Nuruu *mt* Mongolia
139 H6 Henty New S Wales
68 B4 Henzada Burma
61 P13 Henza-jima *isld* Okinawa
118 L6 Hepburn Sask
67 E1 Hepeng China
112 E4 Hephzibah Georgia
Heping *see* Yanhe
67 E4 Heping China
Hepo *see* Jiexi
36 B2 Heppendorf W Germany
36 F4 Heppenheim W Germany
100 F4 Heppner Oregon
80 F2 Heptapegon Israel
68 J2 Hepu China
120 J8 Hepworth Ontario
65 B5 Hequ China
27 E11 Heradsbygd Norway
141 J3 Herald Cays *islds* Gt Barrier Reef Aust
72 J2 Herat Afghanistan
18 H9 Hérault *R* France
19 O14 Herbasse *R* France
21 H6 Herbault France
32 F10 Herbede W Germany
36 D3 Herberge, K *mt* W Germany
32 G9 Herbern W Germany
144 C6 Herbert New Zealand
114 J7 Herbert Sask
140 E5 Herbert *R* N Terr Aust
141 H4 Herbert *R* Queensland
68 A7 Herbertabad Andaman Is
140 E6 Herbert Downs Queensland
140 B4 Herbert, Mt N Terr Aust
142 F3 Herbert, Mt W Australia
141 H3 Herberton Queensland
145 F4 Herbertville New Zealand
22 K2 Herbesthal Belgium
22 J4 Herbeumont Belgium
21 A7 Herbignac France
36 C5 Herbitzheim France
119 S4 Herb L Manitoba
36 D7 Herbolzheim W Germany
36 E2 Herborn W Germany
36 G2 Herbstein W Germany
31 L5 Herby Poland
42 J6 Herceg Novi Yugoslavia
42 H5 Hercegovina *reg* Yugoslavia
115 K6 Herchmer Manitoba
36 H4 Herchsheim W Germany
107 O5 Herd Oklahoma
32 F10 Herdecke W Germany
125 M4 Heredia Costa Rica
98 B9 Hereford Colorado
8 D3 Hereford England
108 E1 Hereford Texas
Hereford *co see* Hereford and Worcester *co*
8 D3 Hereford and Worcester *co* England
145 D1 Herekino New Zealand
16 E5 Herencia Spain
40 F5 Herens, Val. d' Switzerland
22 H1 Herentals Belgium
144 B5 Heretaniwha Pt New Zealand
28 J6 Herfølge Denmark
32 J8 Herford W Germany
22 L2 Hergenrath Belgium
19 K5 Hericourt France
33 N10 Heringen E Germany
107 O3 Herington Kansas
22 G2 Herinnes Belgium
144 B6 Heriot New Zealand
13 F2 Heriot Scotland
117 L10 Heriot Bay Br Col
41 K3 Herisau Switzerland
146 F10 Heritage Rge Antarctica
22 J2 Herk-de-Stad Belgium
95 N3 Herkimer New York
121 Q9 Herkimer New York
146 J11 Herlacher, C Antarctica
37 N2 Herlasgrün E Germany
58 F2 Herlen Gol *R* Mongolia
58 G2 Herlen He *R* China
37 J1 Herleshausen W Germany
28 K5 Herlev Denmark
28 H6 Herlufmagle Denmark
9 H6 Herm *isld* Channel Is
38 H8 Hermagor Austria
99 S3 Herman Michigan
98 K4 Herman Minnesota
98 K8 Herman Nebraska
71 D3 Hermana Mayor *isld* Philippines
124 J4 Hermanas Mexico
106 C10 Hermanas New Mexico
110 E3 Hermann Missouri
32 M7 Hermannsberg W Germany
140 C6 Hermannsburg N Terr Aust
37 P4 Heřmanova Hut' Czechoslovakia
99 T4 Hermansville Michigan
89 A10 Hermanus S Africa
111 F10 Hermanville Mississippi
79 G4 Hermel, El Lebanon
20 K3 Hermes France
36 B4 Hermeskeil W Germany
22 H3 Hermeton-sur-Meuse Belgium
139 H4 Hermidale New S Wales
22 E3 Hermies France
100 F4 Hermiston Oregon
111 D8 Hermitage Arkansas
144 C5 Hermitage New Zealand
123 R6 Hermitage Nfld
123 Q3 Hermitage B Nfld
142 B5 Hermite I W Australia
133 D9 Hermite, Is Chile
140 B2 Hermit Hill N Terr Aust
136 K2 Hermit Is Bismarck Arch
103 M5 Hermits Rest Arizona
108 G3 Hermleigh Texas
Hermôn, Mt *see* Sheikh, J. esh
22 F5 Hermonville France
98 C6 Hermosa S Dakota
124 D3 Hermosillo Mexico
Hermsdorf *see* Ottendorf-Okrilla
130 C9 Hernandarias Paraguay
113 E9 Hernando Florida
102 E5 Herndon California
99 M8 Herndon Iowa
107 K2 Herndon Kansas
110 J5 Herndon Kentucky
95 L6 Herndon Pennsylvania
94 K8 Herndon Virginia
94 F9 Herndon W Virginia
32 F9 Herne W Germany
9 H5 Herne Bay England
28 B4 Herning Denmark
124 C2 Heroica Caborca Mexico
37 L4 Heroldsberg W Germany
22 J2 Héron Belgium
100 K1 Heron Montana
120 D4 Heron Bay Ontario
25 F6 Herongen W Germany
141 K6 Heron I Gt Barrier Reef Aust
99 L6 Heron L Minnesota
144 C5 Heron, L New Zealand
26 A9 Heroy Norway
42 F3 Herpelje Kozina Yugoslavia
130 B10 Herradura Argentina
16 D5 Herrara del Duque Spain
98 F4 Herreid S Dakota
36 F6 Herrenberg W Germany
36 E6 Herrenwies W Germany
133 E3 Herrera Argentina
17 G3 Herrera *mt* Spain
16 C5 Herrera de Alcántara Spain
17 G3 Herrera de los Navarros Spain
124 G5 Herreras Mexico
28 F6 Herrested Denmark
98 G6 Herrick S Dakota
139 J8 Herrick Tasmania
110 G4 Herrin Illinois
123 S4 Herring Neck Nfld
94 C9 Herrington L Kentucky
119 Q2 Herriot Manitoba
28 H7 Herritslev Denmark
36 H7 Herrlingen W Germany
27 F13 Herrljunga Sweden
36 E4 Herrnsheim W Germany
36 C4 Herrstein W Germany
18 G9 Hers *R* France
37 L5 Hersbruck W Germany
36 D1 Herscheid W Germany
118 J7 Herschel Sask
116 S2 Herschel Yukon Terr
99 S8 Herscher Illinois
37 J3 Herschfeld W Germany
22 H1 Herselt Belgium
94 B3 Hersey Michigan
95 L6 Hershey Pennsylvania
28 D5 Herslev Denmark
28 D3 Hersom Denmark
22 K2 Herstal Belgium
9 G6 Herstmonceux England
22 E2 Hertain Belgium
32 F9 Herten W Germany
9 F4 Hertford England
112 L1 Hertford N Carolina
9 F4 Hertfordshire *co* England
80 C5 Herut Israel
16 D4 Hervas Spain
22 K2 Herve Belgium
141 L7 Hervey B Queensland
121 S6 Hervey Junction Quebec
141 H4 Hervey Ra Queensland
36 E5 Herxheim W Germany
33 S9 Herzberg E Germany
33 M9 Herzberg W Germany
33 T8 Herzfelde E Germany
32 G7 Herzlake W Germany
80 C5 Herzliyya Israel
37 K4 Herzogenaurach W Germany
38 N5 Herzogenburg Austria
25 F7 Herzogenrath W Germany
33 Q6 Herzsprung E Germany
22 B2 Hesdigneul-lès-Boulogne France
22 C3 Hesdin France
32 G6 Hesel W Germany
67 D5 Heshui China
65 B6 Heshun China
27 B13 Heskestad Norway
98 G2 Hesper N Dakota
22 L4 Hesperange Luxembourg
102 G7 Hesperia California
94 A3 Hesperia Michigan
106 B4 Hesperus Colorado
106 B4 Hesperus Pk Colorado
117 G4 Hess *R* Yukon Terr
116 N4 Hess Cr Alaska
28 F6 Hesselager Denmark
37 K5 Hesselberg *mt* W Germany
28 H4 Hesselø *isld* Denmark
33 N8 Hessen E Germany
36 F2 Hessen *land* W Germany
36 F1 Hessenstein W Germany
36 H5 Hessenthal W Germany
36 H1 Hessisch Lichtenau W Germany
117 H4 Hess Mts Yukon Terr
138 D4 Hesso S Australia
107 N3 Hesston Kansas
28 J7 Hestehoved *C* Denmark
26 F5 Hestmannen *isld* Norway
28 N2 Hestø *isld* Faeroes
27 G14 Hestra, N Sweden
22 G3 Hestrud France
102 C4 Hetch Hetchy California
94 C2 Hetherton Michigan
25 E4 Het Loo Netherlands
68 J2 Hetou China
22 L5 Hettange Gde France
Hettenhausen *see* Ebersburg
36 E4 Hettenleidelheim W Germany
114 J8 Hettinger N Dakota
13 G4 Hetton-le-Hole England
33 P9 Hettstedt E Germany
36 F4 Hetzbach W Germany
36 B4 Hetzerath W Germany
22 E1 Het Zoute Belgium
36 H6 Heubach W Germany
41 J1 Heuberg *dist* W Germany
22 C3 Heuchin France
33 N9 Heudeber E Germany
140 B6 Heughlin, Mt N Terr Aust
36 C2 Heumar W Germany
20 H3 Heuqueville France
25 D5 Heusden Netherlands
37 J3 Heustreu W Germany
95 M2 Heuvelton New York
20 F3 Hève, C. de la France
80 E8 Hever *R* Jordan
13 F5 Heversham England
48 F3 Heves Hungary
28 E3 Hevring Å *R* Denmark
80 C8 Hevron *R* Israel
119 O9 Heward Sask
7 M9 Hewett *sea rig* North Sea
13 F4 Hexham England
67 F4 Hexi China
67 D4 He Xian China
67 F1 He Xian China
65 D3 Hexigten Qi China
109 H5 Hext Texas
65 A7 Heyang China
101 M7 Heyburn Idaho
107 O6 Heyburn Res Oklahoma
13 F5 Heysham England
8 D5 Heytesbury England
67 E5 Heyuan China
13 F6 Heywood England
138 F7 Heywood Victoria
65 C7 Heze China
113 G12 Hialeah Florida
112 D3 Hiawassee Georgia
107 P2 Hiawatha Kansas
103 O2 Hiawatha Utah
121 Q5 Hibbard Quebec
99 O2 Hibbing Minnesota
142 E1 Hibernia Reef Timor Sea
60 D11 Hibiki-nada *sea* Japan
71 G5 Hibuson *isld* Philippines
103 M9 Hickiwan Arizona
13 G6 Hickleton England
110 G5 Hickman Kentucky
98 K9 Hickman Nebraska
106 C7 Hickman New Mexico
123 T5 Hickman's Hbr Nfld
107 J4 Hickok Kansas
111 G9 Hickory Mississippi
112 F2 Hickory N Carolina
112 F2 Hickory, L N Carolina
110 G6 Hickory Valley Tennessee
109 M8 Hicks Texas
145 G2 Hick's Bay New Zealand
125 P9 Hicks Cays *islds* Belize
94 C5 Hicksville Ohio
109 J4 Hico Texas
48 H3 Hida Romania
60 Q3 Hidaka Japan
60 J12 Hidaka *R* Japan
60 R3 Hidaka-sammyaku *mts* Japan
124 G4 Hidalgo de Parral Mexico
32 J8 Hiddenhausen W Germany
30 G1 Hiddensee *isld* E Germany
141 H4 Hidden Valley Queensland
32 J9 Hiddesen W Germany
130 E5 Hidrolândia Brazil
130 E4 Hidrolina Brazil
20 K1 Hiermont France
85 A3 Hierro *isld* Canary Is
127 N9 Hierro, Pto. de Venezuela
61 O13 Higashi-iwa *islds* Japan
61 N9 Higashi-Matsuyama Japan
61 P13 Higashi-Onna Okinawa
61 J11 Higashiosaka Japan
60 C12 Higashi-suidō *str* Japan
110 D2 Higbee Missouri
94 C2 Higgins L Michigan
110 C2 Higginsville Missouri
143 D9 Higginsville W Australia
9 E1 Higham England
9 F3 Higham Ferrers England
8 B6 Highampton England
106 G4 Highbee Colorado
8 D5 Highbridge England
95 N6 High Bridge New Jersey
12 D3 High Br. of Ken Scotland
9 E5 Highclere England
99 S5 High Cliff Wisconsin
100 E6 High Desert Oregon
99 S4 High Falls Reservoir Wisconsin
9 G5 Highgate England
127 L2 Highgate Jamaica
142 B1 Highgate *dist* Perth, W Aust
13 F4 High Hesket England
119 W3 High Hill L Manitoba
99 V4 High I Michigan
109 N6 High Island Texas
102 G7 Highland California
110 G3 Highland Illinois
107 P2 Highland Kansas
99 Q6 Highland Wisconsin
15 C3 Highland *reg* Scotland
99 T7 Highland Park Illinois
94 D4 Highland Park Michigan
109 O9 Highland Park Texas
102 E3 Highland Peak California
103 K4 Highland Pk Nevada
112 D2 Highlands N Carolina
109 M6 Highlands Texas
95 K9 Highland Springs Virginia
117 P6 High Level Alberta
98 G5 Highmore S Dakota
141 K5 High Peak I Queensland
112 H2 High Point N Carolina
118 K8 High Point Sask
114 H6 High Prairie Alberta
114 H7 High River Alberta
113 J11 High Rock Grand Bahama I
119 R3 Highrock Manitoba
112 G2 High Rock L N Carolina
139 H9 High Rocky Pt Tasmania
143 F8 High Sand Hill W Australia
143 F8 High Sand Ridge W Australia
113 E8 High Springs Florida
95 N6 Hightstown New Jersey
99 S7 Highwood Illinois
101 P2 Highwood Montana
9 E4 Highworth England
9 F4 High Wycombe England
124 E5 Higuera de Zaragoza Mexico
17 F1 Higuer, C Spain
127 L9 Higuerote Venezuela
127 K5 Higüey Dom Rep
145 E3 Hihitahi New Zealand
27 N13 Hiiumaa *isld* U.S.S.R.
79 G5 Hijāne, Bahret el *L* Syria
17 G3 Hijar Spain
69 F14 Hijau, Gunung *mt* Sumatra
60 E12 Hiji Japan
71 G7 Hijo Philippines
60 E12 Hikari Japan
60 H11 Hiketa Japan
60 J12 Hiki *R* Japan
83 J11 Hikkaduwa Sri Lanka
103 J4 Hiko Nevada
61 K10 Hikone Japan
60 D12 Hiko-san *mt* Japan
145 E2 Hikuai New Zealand
145 E1 Hikurangi New Zealand
145 G2 Hikurangi *mt* New Zealand
145 E2 Hikutaia New Zealand
71 N8 Hila Indonesia
101 S6 Hiland Wyoming
36 E1 Hilchenbach W Germany
118 G8 Hilda Alberta
37 K3 Hildburghausen E Germany
100 D7 Hildebrand Oregon
36 B1 Hilden W Germany
37 J2 Hilders W Germany
32 L8 Hildesheim W Germany
98 G9 Hildreth Nebraska
101 Q2 Hilger Montana
69 C12 Hiliotaluwa Indonesia
69 C12 Hilisimaetano Indonesia
101 O1 Hill Montana
127 P6 Hillaby, Mt Barbados
78 K5 Hillah, Al Iraq
98 E5 Hilland S Dakota
27 F14 Hillared Sweden
146 H6 Hillary Coast Antarctica
125 P9 Hill Bank Belize
101 K6 Hill City Idaho
107 L2 Hill City Kansas
99 N3 Hill City Minnesota
98 C6 Hill City S Dakota
103 P2 Hill Cr Utah
118 C9 Hillcrest Alberta
117 Q11 Hillcrest Creek Alberta
25 C4 Hillegom Netherlands
32 J8 Hillegossen W Germany
28 J5 Hillerød Denmark
28 B2 Hillerslev Denmark
28 E6 Hillerslev Denmark
28 C7 Hillerup W Germany
36 B3 Hillesheim W Germany
26 K2 Hillesöy Norway
139 K4 Hillgrove New S Wales
144 C6 Hillgrove New Zealand
141 H4 Hill Grove Queensland
98 J4 Hillhead S Dakota
118 E5 Hilliard Alberta
113 F7 Hilliard Florida
9 G2 Hillington England
94 D1 Hillman Michigan
99 N3 Hillman Minnesota
143 B9 Hillman, L W Australia
118 H5 Hillmond Sask
15 E3 Hill of Fearn Scotland
15 D5 Hill of Stake *mt* Scotland
98 C9 Hillrose Colorado
99 P8 Hills Iowa
98 K6 Hills Minnesota
112 D4 Hillsboro Georgia
110 G2 Hillsboro Illinois
99 P9 Hillsboro Iowa
107 N3 Hillsboro Kansas
110 F3 Hillsboro Missouri
112 H1 Hillsboro N Carolina
98 J2 Hillsboro N Dakota
95 Q3 Hillsboro New Hampshire
106 C9 Hillsboro New Mexico
110 N2 Hillsboro Ohio
100 C4 Hillsboro Oregon
109 K3 Hillsboro Texas
94 G8 Hillsboro W Virginia
113 G11 Hillsboro Can Florida
122 H8 Hillsborough New Brunswick
122 J7 Hillsborough B Pr Edward I
141 J5 Hillsborough, C Queensland
36 D3 Hillscheid W Germany
94 C5 Hillsdale Michigan
121 L8 Hillsdale Ontario
98 B8 Hillsdale Wyoming
103 M7 Hillside Arizona
106 E3 Hillside Colorado
142 C5 Hillside W Australia
120 E3 Hillsport Ontario
139 H5 Hillston New S Wales
138 D5 Hills View Queensland
98 G4 Hillsview S Dakota
94 G10 Hillsville Virginia
112 F5 Hilltonia Georgia
110 F2 Hillview Illinois
102 D4 Hilmar California
102 V14 Hilo Hawaiian Is
113 G10 Hilolo Florida
37 L5 Hilpoltstein W Germany
36 F5 Hilsbach W Germany
8 B7 Hilsea Pt England
36 D7 Hilsenheim France
94 K3 Hilton New York
112 G5 Hilton Head I S Carolina
146 E12 Hilton Inlet Antarctica
37 L4 Hiltpoltstein W Germany
32 G9 Hiltrup W Germany
100 C8 Hilts California
29 N10 Hiltula Finland
25 D6 Hilvarenbeck Netherlands
25 D4 Hilversum Netherlands
74 G2 Himachal Pradesh *prov* India
74 F1 Himalayan Mt.Ra.,Great Asia
29 K7 Himanka Finland
46 D4 Himarë Albania
145 E4 Himatangi New Zealand
33 N6 Himbergen W Germany
60 H11 Himeji Japan
61 P6 Himekami dake *mt* Japan
101 R5 Himes Wyoming
60 E12 Hime-shima *isld* Japan
61 K9 Himi Japan
32 K5 Himmelpforten W Germany
32 K9 Himmighausen W Germany
71 F5 Himugaan Philippines
60 D13 Hinagu Japan
69 C12 Hinako *isld* Indonesia
145 E4 Hinakura New Zealand
71 G6 Hinatuan Philippines
127 J5 Hinche Haiti
116 O6 Hinchinbrook Entrance *str* Alaska
116 O6 Hinchinbrook I Alaska
141 H4 Hinchinbrook I Queensland
119 P6 Hinchliffe Sask
9 E2 Hinckley England
99 O3 Hinckley Minnesota
103 M2 Hinckley Utah
95 N3 Hinckley Res New York
74 G5 Hindaun India
41 M2 Hindelang W Germany
25 D3 Hindeloopen Netherlands
Hindenburg *see* Lindenhagen

34
Hindenburg Damm — Huairen

28 A7 Hindenburg Damm causeway W Germany
26 N6 Hindersön isld Sweden
109 J7 Hindes Texas
9 F5 Hindhead England
13 F6 Hindley England
138 F6 Hindmarsh, L Victoria
8 D5 Hindon England
144 C6 Hindon New Zealand
144 C6 Hinds New Zealand
123 Q4 Hinds Hill peak Nfld
28 F5 Hindsholm Denmark
123 P5 Hinds L Nfld
74 B3 Hindubagh Pakistan
72 K1 Hindu Kush mts Afghanistan
76 C4 Hindupur India
118 G5 Hindville Alberta
68 G4 Hine Laos
95 O2 Hinesburg Vermont
117 O7 Hines Creek Alberta
112 F6 Hinesville Georgia
74 H8 Hinganghat India
28 D4 Hinge Denmark
101 P1 Hingham Montana
77 J7 Hinglaj Pakistan
20 A5 Hinglé, le France
77 K6 Hingol R Pakistan
74 G9 Hingoli India
102 G7 Hinkley California
143 G7 Hinkley, Mt W Australia
29 J11 Hinnerjoki Finland
28 E4 Hinnerup Denmark
26 H3 Hinnöy isld Norway
61 K9 Hino R Japan
71 F6 Hinoba-an Philippines
16 D6 Hinojosa del Duque Spain
60 E13 Hinokage Japan
60 F10 Hinomi saki C Japan
99 S8 Hinsdale Illinois
95 O4 Hinsdale Massachusetts
101 S1 Hinsdale Montana
94 J4 Hinsdale New York
8 D2 Hinstock England
38 F7 Hinterbichl Austria
36 E3 Hintermeilingen W Germany
41 K4 Hinterrhein Switzerland
41 O3 Hinter Riss Austria
38 K6 Hinterstoder Austria
41 P3 Hinter Tux Austria
36 D5 Hinter Weidenthal W Germany
9 H3 Hintlesham England
117 P9 Hinton Alberta
107 M6 Hinton Oklahoma
61 O9 Hi-numa Japan
129 J7 Hiocolândia Brazil
135 R2 Hio Pt Hawaiian Is
124 J5 Hipólito Mexico
25 C3 Hippolytushoef Netherlands
80 F2 Hippos Syria
60 C12 Hirado Japan
60 C12 Hirado-jima isld Japan
75 K8 Hirakud Res India
95 R3 Hiram Maine
60 C12 Hira shima isld Japan
60 F10 Hirata Japan
61 N10 Hiratsuka Japan
124 D5 Hiray Mexico
78 D2 Hirfanli Dam Turkey
48 K3 Hîrlău Romania
61 O8 Hirono Japan
60 R3 Hiroo Japan
61 O5 Hirosaki Japan
60 G10 Hirose Japan
60 F11 Hiroshima Japan
61 P7 Hirota-wan B Japan
36 F6 Hirsau W Germany
37 M4 Hirschau W Germany
Hirschberg see Jelenia Góra
37 M3 Hirschberg E Germany
38 L7 Hirschegg Austria
37 O6 Hirschenstein mt W Germany
36 F5 Hirschhorn W Germany
28 F2 Hirsholmene isld Denmark
22 G4 Hirson France
48 L6 Hîrşova Romania
28 D1 Hirtshals Denmark
29 M10 Hirvensalmi Finland
29 L7 Hirvineva Finland
8 C4 Hirwaun Wales
60 B13 Hisaka-shima isld Japan
74 F4 Hisar India
77 J2 Hisar, Koh-i- mts Afghanistan
80 F6 Hisban R Jordan
27 F15 Hishult Sweden
98 E6 Hisle S Dakota
80 E6 Hisma Jordan
127 J5 Hispaniola isld W Indies
80 G1 Hispin Syria
79 G4 Hisya Syria
78 J5 Hit Iraq
60 D12 Hita Japan
61 O9 Hitachi Japan
61 O9 Hitachi-Ōta Japan
60 C11 Hitakatsu Japan
9 G3 Hitcham England
107 M6 Hitchcock Oklahoma
119 O9 Hitchcock Sask
98 H5 Hitchcock S Dakota
109 M6 Hitchcock Texas
9 F4 Hitchin England
107 P6 Hitchita Oklahoma
103 O4 Hite Utah
60 D13 Hitoyoshi Japan
26 C8 Hitra Norway
32 L6 Hittfeld W Germany
33 O6 Hitzacker W Germany
61 N9 Hiuchi dake mt Japan
60 G11 Hiuchi-nada sea Japan
135 N9 Hiva Oa isld Pacific Oc
60 H12 Hiwasa Japan
112 C2 Hiwassee R N Carolina/Tenn
112 C2 Hiwassee Lake N Carolina
141 L5 Hixson Cay isld Gt Barrier Reef Aust
60 O3 Hiyama prefect Japan
78 J2 Hizan Turkey
28 E2 Hjallerup Denmark
27 H12 Hjälmaren L Sweden
28 C3 Hjarbæk Denmark
28 B2 Hjardemål Denmark
26 G6 Hjarfjell mt Norway
28 E5 Hjarnø isld Denmark
27 C12 Hjartdal Norway
28 C6 Hjarup Denmark
26 B10 Hjelle Norway
28 F4 Hjelm isld Denmark
28 K7 Hjelm Bugt B Denmark
27 B12 Hjelmeland Norway
26 O1 Hjelmsöy isld Norway
28 G5 Hjembæk Denmark
26 D9 Hjerkinn Norway
28 B4 Hjerm Denmark
28 C6 Hjerndrup Denmark
28 B6 Hjerpsted Denmark
28 A5 Hjerting Denmark
27 G13 Hjo Sweden
28 C4 Hjøllund Denmark
28 C6 Hjordkær Denmark
28 D2 Hjørring Denmark
Hjørring co see Nordjylland
28 E7 Hjortø Denmark
28 E4 Hjortshøj Denmark
28 C5 Hjortsvang Denmark
26 B9 Hjörundfjord Norway
27 D12 Hjuksebö Norway
68 D2 Hka R Burma
68 D2 Hkok R Burma
68 C4 Hlegu Burma
37 P3 Hlinec R Czechoslovakia
31 K7 Hlohovec Czechoslovakia
28 A5 Ho Denmark
85 E7 Ho Ghana
67 B6 Hoa Binh Vietnam
68 J7 Hoa Da Vietnam
118 C6 Hoadley Alberta
98 F8 Hoagland Nebraska
68 J5 Hoai Nhon Vietnam
68 G1 Hoang Su Phi Vietnam
87 B9 Hoanib R Namibia
60 E12 Hoashi Japan
101 P6 Hoback R Wyoming
101 P6 Hoback Pk Wyoming
99 T8 Hobart Indiana
107 L6 Hobart Oklahoma
138 F8 Hobart Tasmania
141 H6 Hobartville Queensland
108 D3 Hobbs New Mexico
146 J10 Hobbs Coast Antarctica
111 K7 Hobbs Island Alabama
113 G10 Hobe Sound Florida
112 K1 Hobgood N Carolina
22 G1 Hoboken Belgium
112 E6 Hoboken Georgia
Hobot Xar see Xianghuang Qi
28 D3 Hobro Denmark
101 Q3 Hobson Montana
145 E2 Hobson, Mt New Zealand
112 L2 Hobucken N Carolina
28 A5 Ho Bugt B Denmark
27 K15 Hoburgen lt ho Sweden
71 D5 Hoc isld Philippines
47 K6 Hocalar Turkey
111 B7 Hochatown Oklahoma
38 N8 Hocheck mt Austria
87 C10 Hochfeld Namibia
36 D6 Hochfelden France
38 G7 Hochfilzen Austria
38 F8 Hochgall mt Italy
37 K2 Hochheim E Germany
109 K6 Hochheim Texas
36 E3 Hochheim W Germany
68 H7 Ho Chi Minh Vietnam
38 K8 Hochobir mt Austria
41 N2 Hoch Platte mt W Germany
38 M6 Hochschwab mt Austria
36 D5 Hochspeyer W Germany
37 K4 Höchstadt W Germany
37 K6 Höchstädt W Germany
36 D2 Höchstenbach W Germany
144 C5 Hochstetter, L New Zealand
38 K9 Hochstuhl mt Yugoslavia
36 F5 Hockenheim W Germany
94 E7 Hocking R Ohio
94 F7 Hockingport Ohio
109 M5 Hockley Texas
9 E3 Hockley Heath England
9 F4 Hockliffe England
28 B5 Hodde Denmark
13 F6 Hodder, R England
9 F4 Hoddesdon England
Hodeida see Hudaydah, Al
111 D9 Hodge Louisiana
110 L4 Hodgenville Kentucky
98 B3 Hodges Montana
112 E3 Hodges S Carolina
123 Q4 Hodges Hill peak Nfld
102 G8 Hodges, L California
118 L8 Hodgeville Sask
119 U7 Hodgson Manitoba
140 C3 Hodgson Downs N Terr Aust
85 C5 Hodh reg Mauritania
80 B7 Hodiyya Israel
48 F4 Hódmezövásárhely Hungary
85 E1 Hodna, Mts. du Algeria
31 K7 Hodonín Czechoslovakia
48 C4 Hodos Yugoslavia
28 B4 Hodsager Denmark
116 N3 Hodzana, R Alaska
28 F4 Hoed Denmark
25 A6 Hoedekenskerke Netherlands
18 D5 Hoëdic, I France
106 F4 Hoehne Colorado
25 B5 Hoeksche Waard Netherlands
25 B5 Hoek van Holland Netherlands
119 M6 Hoey Sask
37 M3 Hof W Germany
36 H2 Hofbieber W Germany
Hofei see Hefei
36 F6 Höfen W Germany
37 J6 Hofen W Germany
98 L4 Hoffman Minnesota
112 H2 Hoffman N Carolina
32 K10 Hofgeismar W Germany
36 E3 Hofheim W Germany
37 K3 Hofheim W Germany
37 P6 Hofkirchen W Germany
115 S5 Höfn Iceland
60 E11 Hōfu Japan
28 K4 Höganäs Sweden
139 H7 Hogan Group islds Tasmania Australia
102 D3 Hogan Res California
111 M8 Hogansville Georgia
141 H7 Hoganthulla R Queensland
119 P1 Hogarth Ontario
140 D5 Hogarth, Mt N Terr Aust
116 K3 Hogatza Alaska
116 K3 Hogatza R R Alaska
101 N5 Hogback Mt Montana
27 F12 Hogboda Sweden
27 J14 Högby Sweden
28 C7 Högel W Germany
101 R1 Hogeland Montana
27 H12 Högfors Sweden
85 F4 Hoggar mt reg Algeria
119 V1 Hogg L Manitoba
48 J5 Hoghiz Romania
94 B1 Hog I Michigan
95 M9 Hog I Virginia
28 B4 Høgild Denmark
80 C4 Hogla Israel
27 H14 Högsby Sweden
26 J9 Högsjö Sweden
126 H4 Hogsty Reef Bahamas
26 G5 Högtuvbre mt Norway
100 A2 Hoh R Washington
33 R10 Hohburg E Germany
36 C3 Hohe Acht mt W Germany
41 N3 Hohe Geige mt Austria
37 K6 Hohen-Altheim W Germany
38 N6 Hohenberg Austria
37 M3 Hohenberg W Germany
33 S9 Hohenbucke E Germany
37 M5 Hohenburg W Germany
33 N10 Hohenebra E Germany
32 M8 Hoheneggelsen W Germany
36 H1 Hoheneiche W Germany
41 L3 Hohenems Austria
37 M5 Hohenfels W Germany
33 Q7 Hohengöhren E Germany
36 G6 Hohenheim W Germany
37 M7 Hohenkammer W Germany
33 Q10 Hohenleina E Germany
37 N2 Hohenleuben E Germany
32 G10 Hohenlimburg W Germany
32 L5 Hohenlockstedt W Germany
33 S5 Hohenmocker E Germany
37 N1 Hohenmölsen E Germany
33 Q7 Hohennauen E Germany
36 H2 Hohenroda W Germany
33 Q8 Hohenseeden E Germany
33 S9 Hohenseefeld E Germany
36 E2 Hohensolms W Germany
36 H6 Hohenstaufen W Germany
36 G7 Hohenstein W Germany
37 O2 Hohenstein-Ernstthal E Germany
110 J6 Hohenwald Tennessee
37 L6 Hohenwart W Germany
32 K9 Hohenwepel W Germany
32 L4 Hohenwestedt W Germany
33 N6 Hohenzethen W Germany
36 F7 Hohenzollern W Germany
41 M3 Hoher Ifen mt Austria
41 M3 Hohes Licht mt Austria
37 J5 Hohe Steig mt W Germany
38 F7 Hohe Tauern Austria
58 F3 Hohhot China
36 E6 Hohloh mt W Germany
33 M7 Hohne W Germany
19 K4 Hohneck mt France
33 N6 Hohnstorf W Germany
116 J6 Hoholitna R Alaska
32 K4 Hohrr W Germany
66 E4 Hoh Sai Hu L China
33 N4 Hohwacht W Germany
36 C7 Hohwald France
66 D4 Hoh Xil Shan ra China
68 J5 Hoi An Vietnam
107 M3 Hoisington Kansas
66 F4 Hoit Taria China
67 B6 Hoi-Xuan Vietnam
75 P6 Hojai India
28 E6 Højby Denmark
28 C5 Højen Denmark
28 B7 Højer Denmark
28 K6 Højerup Denmark
60 F12 Hōjō Japan
28 B6 Højrup Denmark
28 C3 Højslev Denmark
68 D2 Hok R Burma
99 P6 Hokah Minnesota
Hokang see Hegang
27 K11 Hökhuvud Sweden
61 N9 Hōki R Japan
145 D1 Hokianga Harbour New Zealand
144 C5 Hokitika New Zealand
60 Q2 Hokkaido isld Japan
27 D12 Hokksund Norway
61 O9 Hokota Japan
61 K10 Hokunō Japan
61 K10 Hokuriku Tunnel Japan
27 C11 Hol Norway
27 E12 Höland Norway
28 E3 Holbæk Denmark
28 H5 Holbæk Denmark
Holbæk co see Vestjælland
9 G2 Holbeach England
117 K10 Holberg Br Col
28 C7 Holbøl Denmark
141 J4 Holborne I Queensland
103 O7 Holbrook Arizona
101 N7 Holbrook Idaho
98 F9 Holbrook Nebraska
139 H6 Holbrook New S Wales
13 F6 Holcombe England
99 P4 Holcombe Wisconsin
118 E5 Holden Alberta
95 Q4 Holden Massachusetts
110 C3 Holden Missouri
103 M2 Holden Utah
94 E9 Holden W Virginia
107 O6 Holdenville Oklahoma
119 M8 Holdfast Sask
99 M4 Holdingford Minnesota
32 H7 Holdorf W Germany
98 G9 Holdrege Nebraska
28 G7 Holeby Denmark
27 E12 Hölen Norway
76 C4 Hole Narsipur India
31 K6 Holešov Czechoslovakia
127 P6 Holetown Barbados
94 C5 Holgate Ohio
126 F4 Holguín Cuba
48 D2 Holič Czechoslovakia
116 H5 Holikachuk Alaska
116 J6 Holitna R Alaska
27 F11 Höljes Sweden
119 T9 Holland Manitoba
99 U7 Holland Michigan
98 K5 Holland Minnesota
94 J4 Holland New York
100 B7 Holland Oregon
109 K5 Holland Texas
9 F2 Holland div England
111 F8 Hollandale Mississippi
127 M3 Holland B Jamaica
120 K8 Holland Centre Ontario
143 C9 Holland,Mt W Australia
141 K2 Holland Park dist Brisbane, Qnsld
25 C5 Hollandsch Diep Netherlands
138 E2 Hollands Hill S Australia
22 K4 Hollange Belgium
32 M8 Holle W Germany
33 N5 Hollenbek W Germany
32 L6 Hollenstedt W Germany
38 N6 Hollen-Tal V Austria
38 F7 Hollersbach Austria
9 H3 Hollesley B England
94 J3 Holley New York
37 L4 Hollfeld W Germany
146 G10 Hollick-Kenyon Pl Antarctica
109 J2 Holliday Texas
94 J6 Hollidaysburg Pennsylvania
107 L7 Hollis Oklahoma
102 C5 Hollister California
101 L7 Hollister Idaho
110 C5 Hollister Missouri
107 M7 Hollister Oklahoma
22 J2 Hollogne-sur-Geer Belgium
111 D10 Holloway Louisiana
28 K6 Höllviken C Sweden
106 H3 Holly Colorado
94 D4 Holly Michigan
111 F9 Holly Bluff Mississippi
144 B6 Hollyford R New Zealand
111 E7 Holly Grove Arkansas
113 F8 Holly Hill Florida
112 G4 Holly Hill S Carolina
112 K3 Holly Ridge N Carolina
113 G11 Hollywood Florida
95 L8 Hollywood Maryland
28 D6 Holm Denmark
26 F6 Holm Norway
26 J9 Holm Sweden
106 E5 Holman New Mexico
114 H3 Holman Island N W Terr
28 B5 Holme Å R Denmark
146 B4 Holme B Antarctica
99 P6 Holmen Wisconsin
113 K12 Holmes Cay isld Bahamas
8 D1 Holmes Chapel England
119 V1 Holmes L Manitoba
101 P5 Holmes, Mt Wyoming
141 J3 Holmes Reef Great Barrier Reef Aust
27 D12 Holmestr Norway
119 S9 Holmfield Manitoba
13 G6 Holmfirth England
26 K6 Holmfors Sweden
26 L8 Holmögadd lt ho Sweden
26 L8 Holmön Sweden
13 J6 Holmpton England
27 D12 Holmsbu Norway
26 J8 Holmsjö Sweden
26 H9 Holmsjön L Sweden
28 A4 Holmsland Klit sand spit Denmark
115 O3 Holms Ø isld Greenland
28 E6 Holmstrup Fyn Denmark
28 G5 Holmstrup Vestjælland Denmark
26 L8 Holmsund Sweden
27 K14 Holmudden lt ho Gotland Sweden
111 C11 Holmwood Louisiana
37 M5 Holnstein W Germany
27 J12 Hölö Sweden
88 C5 Holoholo Tanzania
80 C5 Holon Israel
87 C11 Holoog Namibia
113 F9 Holopaw Florida
80 B6 Holot Ashdod Israel
142 F2 Holothuria Banks W Australia
80 B6 Holot Yavne Israel
26 E9 Holöydal Norway
141 F2 Holroyd R Queensland
28 B4 Holstebro Denmark
28 B5 Holsted Denmark
99 L7 Holstein Iowa
98 H9 Holstein Nebraska
120 K8 Holstein Ontario
28 G6 Holsteinborg Denmark
115 O4 Holsteinsborg Greenland
112 E1 Holston R Tennessee
94 F10 Holston R Virginia
33 N4 Holst Schweiz W Germany
8 B6 Holsworthy England
111 J8 Holt Alabama
9 H2 Holt England
111 K11 Holt Florida
94 C4 Holt Michigan
98 K1 Holt Minnesota
8 D1 Holt Wales
98 G7 Holt Cr Nebraska
28 K5 Holte Denmark
33 O9 Holtemme R E Germany
25 F4 Holten Netherlands
101 O3 Holter L. Dam Montana
33 O5 Holthusen E Germany
94 B7 Holton Indiana
107 P2 Holton Kansas
94 B3 Holton Michigan
65 D2 Holt Sum China
28 C4 Holtum Å R Denmark
103 J9 Holtville California
120 K4 Holtyre Ontario
135 U5 Holualoa Hawaiian Is
27 C13 Holum Norway
25 E2 Holwerd Netherlands
116 H5 Holy Cross Alaska
Holyhead see Caergybi
Holy I see Lindisfarne
12 C3 Holy I Scotland
8 B1 Holy I Wales
118 G4 Holyoke Alberta
106 H1 Holyoke Colorado
95 P4 Holyoke Massachusetts
107 M3 Holyrood Kansas
123 T6 Holyrood Nfld
37 P4 Holýšov Czechoslovakia
8 D6 Holywell England
8 C1 Holywell Wales
14 F2 Holywood N Ireland
36 D3 Holzappel W Germany
33 S9 Holzdorf E Germany
33 P5 Holzendorf E Germany
32 H8 Holzhausen W Germany
36 D3 Holzhausen W Germany
37 K6 Holzheim W Germany
32 K9 Holzminden W Germany
32 G10 Holzwickede W Germany
28 H6 Høm Denmark
86 G6 Homa Bay Kenya
75 Q6 Homalin Burma
36 G1 Homberg W Germany
60 R2 Hombetsu Japan
22 E4 Homblières France
85 D5 Hombori Mali
Homburg see Nümbrecht
36 H4 Homburg Bayern W Germany
36 C5 Homburg Rheinland-Pfalz W Germany
115 N4 Home B N W Terr
100 J6 Homedale Idaho
141 H4 Home Hill Queensland
83 M8 Home I Cocos Is Indian Oc
116 M7 Homer Alaska
99 T9 Homer Illinois
111 C9 Homer Louisiana
94 C4 Homer Michigan
94 H6 Homer City Pennsylvania
9 H3 Homersfield England
144 A6 Homer Tun New Zealand
112 E6 Homerville Georgia
113 G12 Homestead Florida
99 P8 Homestead Iowa
98 B1 Homestead Montana
107 M5 Homestead Oklahoma
100 J4 Homestead Oregon
141 H5 Homestead Queensland
98 K9 Homestead Nat Mon Nebraska
111 K8 Homewood Alabama
145 E4 Homewood New Zealand
68 A6 Homfray's Str Andaman Is
107 O5 Hominy Oklahoma
26 E9 Hommelfjell mt Norway
26 E8 Hommelvik Norway
25 E3 Hommerts Netherlands
21 F7 Hommes France
74 G10 Homnabad India
89 H5 Homoine Mozambique
48 G6 Homoljske Planina mt Yugoslavia
71 G5 Homonhon Philippines
48 J4 Homorod Romania
113 E9 Homosassa Florida
Homs Libya see Khums, Al
79 G4 Homs Syria
60 F12 Honai Japan
Honan prov see Henan
76 B3 Honavar India
47 K7 Honaz Dağ mt Turkey
68 G7 Hon Chong Vietnam
102 C2 Honcut California
128 D2 Honda Colombia
71 D6 Honda B Palawan Philippines
118 D3 Hondo Alberta
60 D13 Hondo Japan
106 E8 Hondo New Mexico
109 H6 Hondo Texas
125 P8 Hondo R Belize
22 D2 Hondschoote France
125 L2 Honduras rep Cent America
119 Q2 Hone Manitoba
112 E3 Honea Path S Carolina
36 H2 Hönebach W Germany
27 D11 Hönefoss Norway
95 M5 Honesdale Pennsylvania
102 A1 Honeydew California
98 J1 Honeyford N Dakota
109 M2 Honey Grove Texas
109 N5 Honey Island Texas
100 E9 Honey L California
120 K8 Honeywood Ontario
20 F3 Honfleur France
28 G5 Høng Denmark
65 G2 Hongai China
68 H2 Hon Gai Vietnam
67 B6 Hon Gay Vietnam
67 E5 Honghai Wan B China
58 F5 Hong He R China
67 D2 Honghu China
67 C3 Hongjiang China
67 G6 Hong Kong colony E Asia
67 F4 Honglai China
68 G7 Hong Ngu Vietnam
Hongning see Wulian
58 F2 Hongor Mongolia
Hongqiao see Qidong
67 D7 Hongqizhen China
68 E3 Hongsa Laos
67 B4 Hongshui He R China
65 B6 Hongtong China
61 J12 Hongū Japan
122 H4 Honguedo Passage Canada
67 A2 Hongya China
58 G5 Hongze Hu L China
137 N3 Honiara Guadalcanal I Solomon Is
9 H2 Honingham England
8 C6 Honiton England
61 O6 Honjō Japan
29 J10 Honkajoki Finland
68 H3 Hon Matt isld Vietnam
68 G3 Hon Me isld Vietnam
76 B3 Honnali India
26 P1 Honningsvåg Norway
102 V13 Honokaa Hawaiian Is
135 S3 Honokahua Hawaiian Is
145 F2 Honokawa New Zealand
135 S3 Honokohau Hawaiian Is
102 S12 Honolulu Hawaiian Is
135 V5 Honomu Hawaiian Is
102 R12 Honouliuli Hawaiian Is
17 F5 Honrubia Spain
59 K4 Honshū isld Japan
28 H5 Hønsinge Denmark
135 U6 Honuapo Hawaiian Is
100 D4 Hood, Mt Oregon
143 C10 Hood Pt W Australia
141 G8 Hood Ra Queensland
100 D4 Hood River Oregon
100 B2 Hoodsport Washington
32 K10 Hoof W Germany
25 C4 Hoofddorp Netherlands
25 A6 Hoofdplaat Netherlands
25 F3 Hooger Smilde Netherlands
25 G3 Hoogeveen Netherlands
25 G2 Hoogezand Netherlands
25 G3 Hooghalen Netherlands
75 M8 Hooghly R India
22 D2 Hoogstade Belgium
22 H1 Hoogstraten Belgium
41 K2 Höohster mt W Germany
9 F5 Hook England
144 C6 Hook New Zealand
135 U5 Hookena Hawaiian Is
107 J5 Hooker Oklahoma
146 K6 Hooker, C Antarctica
140 B4 Hooker Creek N Terr Aust
14 E4 Hook Hd Irish Rep
141 J5 Hook I Queensland
141 L7 Hook Pt Queensland
141 J4 Hook Reef Gt Barrier Reef Aust
109 N2 Hooks Texas
95 Q3 Hooksett New Hampshire
32 H5 Hooksiel W Germany
102 V13 Hoolehua Hawaiian Is
117 F6 Hoonah Alaska
100 B8 Hoopa California
106 E4 Hooper Colorado
98 K8 Hooper Nebraska
101 N8 Hooper Utah
100 G3 Hooper Washington
116 D6 Hooper Bay Alaska
95 L8 Hooper I Maryland
99 T9 Hoopeston Illinois
123 Q3 Hooping Hbr Nfld
98 J1 Hoople N Dakota
89 D6 Hoopstad S Africa
27 G16 Höör Sweden
25 D3 Hoorn Noord Netherlands
25 C2 Hoorn Texel Netherlands
95 O4 Hoosick Falls New York
118 H7 Hoosier Sask
98 C4 Hoover S Dakota
103 K5 Hoover Dam Arizona
94 E6 Hoover Res Ohio
94 J6 Hooversville Pennsylvania
78 H1 Hopa Turkey
95 M5 Hop Bottom Pennsylvania
9 E4 Hopcrofts Holt England
103 L8 Hope Arizona
111 C8 Hope Arkansas
117 N11 Hope Br Col
94 B7 Hope Indiana
107 N3 Hope Kansas
98 J2 Hope N Dakota
127 M2 Hope Bay Jamaica
115 N6 Hopedale Labrador
Hopeh prov see Hebei
138 E3 Hope, L S Australia
138 E3 Hopeless, Mt S Australia
112 J3 Hope Mills N Carolina
138 D5 Hope, Mt S Australia
147 J12 Hopen isld Arctic Oc
144 D5 Hope Pass New Zealand
116 D2 Hope, Pt Alaska
138 F6 Hopetoun Victoria
143 D10 Hopetoun W Australia
113 L11 Hope Town Bahamas
89 D7 Hopetown S Africa
122 K8 Hopewell Nova Scotia
94 J6 Hopewell Pennsylvania
95 K9 Hopewell Virginia
115 M6 Hopewell Is N W Terr
103 O6 Hopi Buttes mt Arizona
67 E4 Ho-p'ing China
94 B4 Hopkins Michigan
99 M9 Hopkins Missouri
139 G7 Hopkins R Victoria
143 G6 Hopkins,L W Australia
144 B5 Hopkins, Mt New Zealand
110 J5 Hopkinsville Kentucky
102 A3 Hopland California
68 C2 Hopong Burma
33 T7 Hoppegarten E Germany
26 Q1 Hopseidet Norway
32 G8 Hopsten W Germany
9 H2 Hopton England
28 C6 Hoptrup Denmark
94 H7 Hopwood Pennsylvania
141 G5 Hopwood,Mt Queensland
114 G8 Hoquiam Washington
86 G4 Hora Abyata dist Ethiopia
107 J3 Horace Kansas
37 P2 Hora Svatého Šebastiána Czechoslovakia
37 P2 Hora Svaté Katering Czechoslovakia
111 B8 Horatio Arkansas
30 H6 Horaždovice Czechoslovakia
36 F7 Horb W Germany
28 J7 Horbelev Denmark
37 O7 Horbering W Germany
118 B6 Horburg Alberta
13 G6 Horbury England
28 D3 Hørby Nordjylland Denmark
28 E2 Hørby Nordjylland Denmark
27 G16 Hörby Sweden
16 D5 Horcajo de los Montes Spain
16 E5 Horcajo de Santiago Spain
124 G3 Horcasitas Mexico
36 E4 Horchheim W Germany
27 A11 Hordaland reg Norway
86 B1 Hordio Somalia
109 H4 Hords Cr. Res Texas
28 A3 Hørdum Denmark
8 B3 Horeb Wales
88 C6 Hore B Zambia
48 H5 Horezu Romania
48 F4 Horgos Yugoslavia
31 J5 Hořice Czechoslovakia
99 S6 Horicon Wisconsin
58 F3 Horinger China
22 J2 Horion Hozémont Belgium
119 M9 Horizon Sask
137 S6 Horizon Depth Pacific Oc
31 H4 Horka E Germany
9 F5 Horley England
146 G9 Horlick Mts Antarctica
28 E2 Hørmested Denmark
Hormo see Nyima
77 E6 Hormoz isld Iran
77 E6 Hormuz, Strait of Iran
31 J7 Horn Austria
25 E6 Horn Netherlands
27 H14 Horn Sweden
48 F2 Hornad R Czechoslovakia
26 J5 Hornavan L Sweden
36 C5 Hornbach W Germany
32 J9 Horn-Bad Meinog W Germany
28 K4 Hornbæk Denmark
111 C10 Hornbeck Louisiana
36 E7 Hornberg W Germany
27 G13 Hornborgasjön L Sweden
100 C8 Hornbrook California
33 N8 Hornburg W Germany
9 F1 Horncastle England
27 H11 Horndal Sweden
33 N6 Horndorf W Germany
28 D1 Horne Denmark
28 B5 Horne Ribe Denmark
32 L5 Horneburg W Germany
26 L8 Hörnefors Sweden
28 E6 Horneland Denmark
94 K4 Hornell New York
115 L8 Hornepayne Ontario
110 F5 Hornersville Missouri
27 C13 Hornesund Norway
28 G2 Hornfiskrøn isld Denmark
14 C1 Horn Hd Irish Rep
33 O8 Hornhsleben E Germany
111 H11 Horn I Mississippi
141 F1 Horn I Queensland
31 K6 Horni Benešov Czechoslovakia
137 R4 Horn, Îles de Îles Wallis Pacific Oc
124 E4 Hornillos Mexico
26 B10 Hornindal Norway
26 B10 Hornindalsvatn L Norway
36 E6 Hornisgrinde mt W Germany
37 O3 Horní Slavkov Czechoslovakia
41 J3 Hörnli mt Switzerland
116 H6 Horn Mts Alaska
114 G5 Horn Mts N W Terr
27 C13 Hornnes Norway
133 C6 Hornopiren mt Chile
124 H5 Hornos Mexico
133 D9 Hornos, C. de Chile
20 J2 Hornoy France
117 O4 Horn R N W Terr
139 K5 Hornsby New S Wales
110 H6 Hornsby Tennessee
8 B6 Horns Cross England
13 H6 Hornsea England
26 L8 Hörnsjö Sweden
28 E4 Hornslet Denmark
80 E2 Horns of Hittin Israel
37 K1 Hornsömmern E Germany
33 P5 Hornstorf E Germany
28 D5 Hornstrup Denmark
28 D5 Hornum Vejle Denmark
28 A7 Hørnum W Germany
33 S6 Horn Zieritz E Germany
60 T1 Horobetsu Japan
60 R3 Horoizumi Japan
60 Q1 Horonai Japan
145 E3 Horopito New Zealand
144 C5 Hororata New Zealand
60 Q3 Horoshiri-dake mt Japan
65 A5 Horo Sum China
30 H6 Hořovice Czechoslovakia
145 E4 Horowhenua Plain New Zealand
83 K9 Horowupotana Sri Lanka
20 E5 Horps, le France
59 H2 Horqin Youyi Qianqi China
65 E2 Horqin Youyi Zhongqi China
65 F2 Horqin Zouyi Zhongqi China
65 E3 Horqin Zuoyi Houqi China
129 G8 Horqueta Paraguay
133 F2 Horqueta Paraguay
28 H7 Horreby Denmark
27 F14 Horred Sweden
36 B2 Horrem W Germany
83 M8 Horsburgh I Cocos Is Indian Oc
37 J1 Hörschel E Germany
110 K4 Horse Branch Kentucky
9 G6 Horsebridge E Sussex England
94 B9 Horse Cave Kentucky
106 G3 Horse Cr Colorado
110 B4 Horse Cr Missouri
140 D6 Horse Cr N Terr Aust
98 A8 Horse Cr Wyoming
117 N9 Horsefly Br Col
98 F2 Horsehead L N Dakota
95 L4 Horseheads New York
123 R3 Horse Is Nfld
102 D1 Horse L California
37 J2 Hörsel R E Germany
37 J2 Hörsel Berge mt E Germany
28 D5 Horsens Vejle Denmark
28 E5 Horsens Fjord inlet Denmark
118 F2 Horse, R Alberta
113 D8 Horseshoe Florida
143 C7 Horse Shoe W Australia
100 J6 Horse Shoe Bend Idaho
140 C7 Horseshoe Bend N Terr Aust
138 C2 Horseshoe Bend N Terr Australia
127 P4 Horse Shoe Pt St Kitts W I
103 N7 Horseshoe Res Arizona
106 B8 Horse Springs New Mexico
9 F5 Horsham England
118 H8 Horsham Sask
138 F6 Horsham Victoria
28 K5 Hørsholm Denmark
13 G4 Horsley England
28 G7 Horslunde Denmark
37 O4 Horšovský Týn Czechoslovakia
33 S4 Horst E Germany
25 F6 Horst Netherlands
32 L5 Horst W Germany
32 G8 Hörstel W Germany
25 F6 Hörstgen W Germany
32 F8 Horstmar W Germany
48 E2 Hor Stubňa Czechoslovakia
27 D12 Horten Norway
112 F6 Hortense Georgia
26 M6 Hortlax Sweden
107 P2 Horton Kansas
114 G4 Horton R N W Terr
27 C10 Horungane Norway
28 C7 Hörup W Germany
28 G5 Hørve Denmark
27 G15 Hörvik Sweden
13 F6 Horwich England
120 H5 Horwood L Ontario
37 P5 Hory Matky Boží Czechoslovakia
31 J5 Hory Orlické mts Czechoslovakia
47 K7 Horzom R Turkey
36 G3 Hösbach W Germany
76 C4 Hosdurga India
70 C3 Hose Mts Sarawak
84 G5 Hosenofu Libya
77 A3 Hoseynābād Iran
111 M11 Hosford Florida
74 C10 Hoshab Pakistan
74 G7 Hoshangabad India
74 F3 Hoshiarpur India
98 J7 Hoskins Nebraska
98 G4 Hosmer S Dakota
60 E13 Hososhima Japan
106 C6 Hospah New Mexico
76 C3 Hospet India
14 C4 Hospital Irish Rep
131 G3 Hospital, Cuchilla del mt Uruguay
29 O6 Hossa Finland
86 G4 Hosseina Ethiopia
106 B6 Hosta Butte mt New Mexico
133 D9 Hoste, I Chile
18 E8 Hostens France
27 G13 Höstholmen Sweden
37 O4 Hostouň Czechoslovakia
28 A5 Hostrup Ribe Denmark
28 B7 Hostrup Sønderjylland Denmark
28 D7 Hostrup W Germany
28 C7 Hostrup Sø L Denmark
76 C4 Hosur India
26 G8 Hotagen Sweden
61 L9 Hotaka Japan
66 B4 Hotan China
66 C4 Hotan He R China
87 D11 Hotazel S Africa
117 P7 Hotchkiss Alberta
106 C3 Hotchkiss Colorado
102 H3 Hot Creek Ra Nevada
33 O8 Hötensleben E Germany
140 B1 Hotham,C N Terr Aust
116 F3 Hotham Inlet Alaska
139 H6 Hotham, Mt Victoria
26 H7 Hoting Sweden
111 C7 Hot Springs Arkansas
80 E8 Hot Springs Israel
101 L2 Hot Springs Montana
112 E2 Hot Springs N Carolina
98 C6 Hot Springs S Dakota
108 D6 Hot Springs Texas
94 H9 Hot Springs Virginia
109 O1 Hot Springs nat park Arkansas
106 D1 Hot Sulphur Springs Colorado
114 H4 Hottah L N W Terr
22 J3 Hotton Belgium
108 B5 Hot Wells Texas
32 L6 Hötzingen W Germany
28 E2 Hou Denmark
18 D5 Houat, I France
22 D3 Houdain France
20 J4 Houdan France
22 G3 Houdeng Belgium
18 E8 Houeillès France
22 K3 Houffalize Belgium
107 J5 Hough Oklahoma
99 S2 Houghton Michigan
94 J4 Houghton New York
98 H4 Houghton S Dakota
141 H4 Houghton R Queensland
94 C2 Houghton L Michigan
13 G4 Houghton-le-Spring England
145 D1 Houhora New Zealand
20 K4 Houilles France
144 B7 Houipapa New Zealand
20 E3 Houlgate France
111 G7 Houlka Mississippi
20 H3 Houlme, le France
95 T7 Houlton Maine
65 B7 Houma China
111 F12 Houma Louisiana
85 G2 Houmet Essoug Tunisia
85 D6 Houndé Upper Volta
9 F5 Hounslow England
18 E7 Hourtin France
95 O5 Housatonic R Connecticut
108 D1 House New Mexico
123 L6 House Hbr Madeleine Is, Quebec
12 D3 House o'-Hill Scotland
118 E3 House R Alberta
103 L2 House Ra Utah
117 K8 Houston Br Col
99 P6 Houston Minnesota
111 H8 Houston Mississippi
110 E4 Houston Missouri
109 F9 Houston Texas
110 C3 Houstonia Missouri
109 M5 Houston, L Texas
111 C11 Houston R Louisiana
89 F4 Hout R S Africa
89 A10 Hout B S Africa
25 D4 Houten Netherlands
22 J1 Houthalen Belgium
143 A8 Houtman Abrolhos arch W Aust
94 J6 Houtzdale Pennsylvania
22 J3 Houyet Belgium
28 E5 Hov Denmark
28 N3 Hov Faeroes
28 K4 Hov Sweden
27 G13 Hova Sweden
28 B5 Hovborg Denmark
58 B2 Hovd Mongolia
27 B12 Hovden Norway
26 H9 Hovdsjö Sweden
28 A3 Hove Denmark
9 F6 Hove England
28 G5 Høve Vestjælland Denmark
28 D5 Hovedgård Denmark
32 J9 Hövelhof W Germany
28 B5 Hoven Denmark
98 G4 Hoven S Dakota
103 P4 Hovenweep Nat. Mon Utah
28 A4 Hover Denmark
28 A4 Hover Å R Denmark
77 A4 Hoveyzeh Iran
99 R2 Hovland Minnesota
53 F9 Hovlya U.S.S.R.
28 C6 Hovslund Denmark
107 O4 Howard Kansas
94 E6 Howard Ohio
94 K5 Howard Pennsylvania
141 L7 Howard Queensland
98 J5 Howard S Dakota
94 B3 Howard City Michigan
108 F5 Howard Cr Texas
140 D1 Howard I N Terr Aust
99 M4 Howard L Minnesota
116 J2 Howard Pass Alaska
99 T6 Howards Grove Wisconsin
86 D2 Howar, Wadi watercourse Sudan
13 H6 Howden England
101 M6 Howe Idaho
94 B5 Howe Indiana
109 N1 Howe Oklahoma
109 L2 Howe Texas
139 J6 Howe, C New S Wales
83 L13 Howe, Î Indian Oc
94 D4 Howell Michigan
139 K3 Howell New S Wales
101 N8 Howell Utah
98 J8 Howells Nebraska
138 C2 Howe, Mt S Australia
15 F4 Howe of Mearns Scotland
98 D5 Howes S Dakota
117 M11 Howe Sound Br Col
145 E2 Howick New Zealand
121 R7 Howick Quebec
141 H2 Howick Group islds Gt Barrier Reef Aust
138 E2 Howitt, L S Australia
139 H6 Howitt, Mt Victoria
95 T1 Howland Maine
137 R1 Howland I Pacific Oc
123 P4 Howley Nfld
75 N7 Howrah India
117 P10 Howser Br Col
14 E3 Howth Irish Rep
110 F5 Hoxie Arkansas
107 K2 Hoxie Kansas
32 K9 Höxter W Germany
66 D2 Hoxtolgay China
15 E2 Hoy Scotland
32 K7 Hoya W Germany
31 H4 Hoyerswerda E Germany
8 C1 Hoylake England
26 F7 Höylandet Norway
120 J4 Hoyle Ontario
110 G3 Hoyleton Illinois
33 O9 Hoym E Germany
16 C4 Hoyos Spain
47 L6 Hoyran Turkey
15 E2 Hoy Snd Scotland
107 P2 Hoyt Kansas
122 F8 Hoyt New Brunswick
29 O9 Höytiäinen L Finland
101 O9 Hoyt Pk Utah
68 C2 Hpa Lai Burma
37 P4 Hracholuská Nádrž res Czechoslovakia
31 J5 Hradec Králové Czechoslovakia
37 P3 Hradiště mt Czechoslovakia
Hranice Czechoslovakia see Rossbach
31 K6 Hranice Czechoslovakia
48 F2 Hriňová Czechoslovakia
31 L7 Hron R Czechoslovakia
37 O3 Hroznetín Czechoslovakia
31 O5 Hrubieszów Poland
31 J7 Hrušovany Czechoslovakia
42 G4 Hrvatska reg Yugoslavia
68 C2 Hsa Mong Hkam Burma
68 C3 Hsataw Burma
66 D5 Hsia-ju Ts'o L China
67 G6 Hsiao-lan Hsü isld Taiwan
68 C2 Hsi Hkip Burma
68 C2 Hsi-hseng Burma
58 F4 Hsin-ch'iang China
67 G4 Hsin-chu Taiwan
59 H3 Hsin-min China
68 C1 Hsipaw Burma
66 D5 Hsi-tsang Kao-yüan reg China
68 C1 Hsumhsai Burma
67 F4 Hua'an China
128 C6 Huacho Peru
65 H1 Huachuan China
128 C5 Huacrachuco Peru
65 C4 Huade China
59 J3 Huadian China
67 G2 Huading Shan mt China
68 F5 Huai R Thailand
65 C4 Huai'an China
58 G5 Huaibei China
65 F3 Huaide China
65 F3 Huaidezhen China
58 F5 Huai He R China
67 C3 Huaihua China
67 D5 Huaiji China
65 C4 Huailai China
68 F4 Huai Luang R Thailand
58 G5 Huainan China
67 E1 Huaining China
58 F4 Huairen China

36 Inerie — Jarmen

71 K9 **Inerie** *mt* Flores Indonesia
109 L7 **Inez** Texas
85 G4 **In Ezzane** Algeria
89 B10 **Infanta, C** S Africa
16 E6 **Infantes** Spain
128 F5 **Infernão, Cach** *rapids* Brazil
124 H8 **Infiernillo, L** Mexico
16 D1 **Infiesto** Spain
130 J9 **Ingá** Brazil
29 L11 **Inga** Finland
85 F5 **Inga** Niger
68 B4 **Ingabu** Burma
140 C5 **Ingallanna** *R* N Terr Aust
94 B7 **Ingalls** Indiana
107 K4 **Ingalls** Kansas
99 T4 **Ingalls** Michigan
100 E10 **Ingalls, Mt** California
55 F3 **Ingaly** U.S.S.R.
9 G4 **Ingatestone** England
36 H5 **Ingelfingen** W Germany
36 E4 **Ingelheim** W Germany
22 E2 **Ingelmunster** Belgium
86 C6 **Ingende** Zaïre
133 E5 **Ingeniero Luiggi** Argentina
131 E7 **Ingeniero, Pto** Argentina
117 L7 **Ingenika** *R* Br Col
116 E7 **Ingeramuit** Alaska
107 M5 **Ingersoll** Oklahoma
71 B2 **Inggelang** *isld* Halmahera Indonesia
141 H4 **Ingham** Queensland
83 K11 **Ingiriya** Sri Lanka
13 F5 **Ingleborough** *mt* England
140 F6 **Ingledoon** Queensland
115 N2 **Inglefield Land** Greenland
109 K8 **Ingleside** Texas
13 F5 **Ingleton** England
102 F8 **Inglewood** California
145 E3 **Inglewood** New Zealand
141 K8 **Inglewood** Queensland
139 G6 **Inglewood** Victoria
119 Q8 **Inglis** Manitoba
140 D1 **Inglis** *isld* N Terr Aust
116 G4 **Inglutalik** *R* Alaska
51 L3 **Ingoda** *R* U.S.S.R.
76 G5 **Ingoitijala** Andaman Is
118 F1 **Ingolf** Ontario
86 C7 **Ingololo** Zaïre
37 L6 **Ingolstadt** W Germany
101 S3 **Ingomar** Montana
138 C3 **Ingomar** S Australia
123 M7 **Ingonish** C Breton I, N Scotia
102 B1 **Ingot** California
26 N1 **Ingöy** Norway
109 H5 **Ingram** Texas
99 Q4 **Ingram** Wisconsin
122 J9 **Ingramport** Nova Scotia
21 D7 **Ingrandes** France
21 G8 **Ingrandes** France
117 P3 **Ingray L** N W Terr
146 C4 **Ingrid Christensen Coast** Antarctica
28 D2 **Ingstrup** Denmark
85 F5 **In Guezzam** Algeria
54 D9 **Ingul** *R* U.S.S.R.
54 E9 **Ingulets** U.S.S.R.
54 D10 **Ingulets** *R* U.S.S.R.
55 F1 **Inguyagun** *R* U.S.S.R.
19 K4 **Ingwiller** France
89 H6 **Inhaca Pen** Mozambique
87 G10 **Inhambane** Mozambique
130 C7 **Inhandui, R** Brazil
130 C7 **Inhanduizinho, R** Brazil
88 E10 **Inhangoma I** Mozambique
130 C10 **Inhanhora** *R* Brazil
130 G6 **Inhapim** Brazil
87 G10 **Inharrime** Mozambique
47 L4 **İnhisar** Turkey
130 H4 **Inhobim** Brazil
129 J7 **Inhumas** Brazil
116 L3 **Iniakuk** *R* Alaska
71 K9 **Inielika** *mt* Flores Indonesia
17 F5 **Iniesta** Spain
85 E3 **Inifel, Hassi** Algeria
27 M11 **Iniö** Finland
128 E3 **Inírida** *R* Colombia
14 A3 **Inishark** *isld* Irish Rep
14 A3 **Inishbofin** *isld* Irish Rep
14 C1 **Inishbofin** *isld* Irish Rep
14 B2 **Inishcrone** Irish Rep
14 B3 **Inisheer** *isld* Irish Rep
14 A2 **Inishkea** *isld* Irish Rep
14 B3 **Inishmaan** *isld* Irish Rep
14 B3 **Inishmore** *isld* Irish Rep
14 C2 **Inishmurray** *isld* Irish Rep
14 D1 **Inishowen** *dist* Irish Rep
14 E1 **Inishowen Hd** Irish Rep
14 D1 **Inishtrahull** *isld* Irish Rep
14 A3 **Inishturk** *isld* Irish Rep
65 D2 **Injgan Sum** China
141 J7 **Injune** Queensland
122 H6 **Inkerman** New Brunswick
141 F3 **Inkerman** Queensland
86 C7 **Inkis** *R* Zaïre
117 G6 **Inklin** Br Col
101 N7 **Inkom** Idaho
52 F5 **Inkovo** U.S.S.R.
98 J1 **Inkster** N Dakota
68 C2 **Inle, L** Burma
98 H7 **Inman** Nebraska
95 N2 **Inman** New York
112 E2 **Inman** S Carolina
41 O3 **Inn** *R* Austria
38 F6 **Inn** *R* W Germany
138 F2 **Innamincka** S Australia
15 E5 **Innerleithen** Scotland
Inner Mongolia *see* **Nei Monggol Zizhiqu**
Inner Mongolia *aut reg see* **Nei Monggol Zizhiqu**
41 K3 **Inner-Rhoden** *dist* Switzerland
15 C3 **Inner Sound** Scotland
32 M8 **Innerste** *R* W Germany
41 H4 **Innertkirchen** Switzerland
38 F8 **Innervillgraten** Austria
Innien *see* **Aukrug**
14 C5 **Inniscarra Res** Irish Rep
118 D6 **Innisfail** Alberta
141 H3 **Innisfail** Queensland
118 F5 **Innisfree** Alberta
116 J5 **Innoko** *R* Alaska
60 G11 **Inno-shima** Japan
41 O3 **Innsbruck** Austria
26 K3 **Innset** Norway
26 B10 **Innvik** Norway
116 A3 **Innymney, Gora** *mt* U.S.S.R.
71 H4 **Inobonto** Sulawesi
130 D6 **Inocência** Brazil
107 P5 **Inola** Oklahoma
47 L5 **İnönü** Turkey
141 G4 **Inorunie** Queensland
31 L3 **Inowrocław** Poland
128 E7 **Inquisivi** Bolivia
40 F3 **Ins** Switzerland
85 E3 **In Salah** Algeria
15 F3 **Insch** Scotland
143 A7 **Inscription, C** W Australia
68 B4 **Insein** Burma
37 J2 **Inselsberg** *mt* E Germany
119 O7 **Insinger** Sask
87 E9 **Insiza** Zimbabwe
89 F2 **Insiza** *R* Zimbabwe
31 J2 **Insko** Poland
36 B6 **Insming** France
Insterburg *see* **Chernyakhovsk**
8 B5 **Instow** England
118 J9 **Instow** Sask
48 L6 **Insurăţei** Romania
52 K2 **Inta** U.S.S.R.
98 B2 **Intake** Montana
85 E5 **In Tebezas** Mali
47 H4 **İntepe** Turkey
98 E6 **Interior** S Dakota
113 F8 **Interlachen** Florida
40 G4 **Interlaken** Switzerland
139 H8 **Interlaken** Tasmania
99 N1 **International Falls** Minnesota
119 R10 **International Peace Gdn** Canada/U.S.A.
117 O9 **Intersection Mt** Alberta/Br Col
68 A6 **Interview I** Andaman Is
48 K5 **Intorsura Buzăului** Romania
41 J5 **Intragna** Switzerland
32 G8 **Intrup** W Germany
52 F2 **Intsy** U.S.S.R.
70 D5 **Intu** Kalimantan
61 O10 **Inubō saki** Japan
115 O3 **Inugsulik Bugt** *B* Greenland
133 C8 **Inútil, B** Chile
114 F4 **Inuvik** N W Terr
128 D6 **Inuya** *R* Peru
52 J5 **In'va** *R* U.S.S.R.
15 C4 **Inveraray** Scotland
15 F4 **Inverbervie** Scotland
144 B7 **Invercargill** New Zealand
12 C2 **Invercloy** Scotland
139 K3 **Inverell** New S Wales
15 D3 **Invergordon** Scotland
15 E4 **Inverkeithing** Scotland
12 D2 **Inverkip** Scotland
140 F4 **Inverleigh** Queensland
12 D1 **Inverlochlarig** Scotland
119 O7 **Invermay** Sask
117 P10 **Invermere** Br Col
123 L7 **Inverness** C Breton I, N Scotia
113 E9 **Inverness** Florida
101 P1 **Inverness** Montana
121 T6 **Inverness** Quebec
15 D3 **Inverness** Scotland
Inverness *co see* **Highland** *reg*
15 D3 **Invershin** Scotland
15 F3 **Inverurie** Scotland
140 A4 **Inverway** N Terr Aust
68 C6 **Investigator Chan** Burma
138 C5 **Investigator Group** *islds* S Australia
138 D6 **Investigator Str** S Australia
68 A7 **Invisible Bank** Andaman Is
102 C1 **Inwood** California
120 J10 **Inwood** Ontario
56 B3 **Inya** *R* U.S.S.R.
98 B5 **Inyan Kara Cr** Wyoming
87 F9 **Inyazura** Zimbabwe
102 G6 **Inyokern** California
55 C4 **Inzer** U.S.S.R.
86 C7 **Inzia** *R* Zaïre
46 D5 **Ioánnina** Greece
47 H9 **Ioinianísia** *isld* Greece
52 E1 **Iokanga** U.S.S.R.
106 C3 **Iola** Colorado
107 P4 **Iola** Kansas
109 L5 **Iola** Texas
45 L2 **Iolanda di Savoia** Italy
57 B6 **Iolotan'** U.S.S.R.
123 M8 **Iona** C Breton I, N Scotia
101 O6 **Iona** Idaho
99 L6 **Iona** Minnesota
98 G6 **Iona** S Dakota
12 B1 **Iona** *isld* Scotland
47 J1 **Ion Corvin** Romania
102 G3 **Ione** Nevada
100 F4 **Ione** Oregon
100 H1 **Ione** Washington
48 J6 **Ioneşti** Romania
99 O6 **Ionia** Iowa
94 B3 **Ionia** Michigan
110 C3 **Ionia** Missouri
Ionian Is *see* **Iónioi Nísoi**
43 H10 **Ionian Sea** S Europe
46 D5 **Iónioi Nísoi** *islds* Greece
116 A4 **Ioniveen** *R* U.S.S.R.
78 K1 **Iori** *R* U.S.S.R.
47 G8 **Íos** *isld* Greece
52 H3 **Iosser** U.S.S.R.
61 N13 **Iō tō** *isld* Japan
111 C11 **Iowa** Louisiana
99 N7 **Iowa** *R* Iowa
99 N7 **Iowa** *state* U.S.A.
99 P8 **Iowa City** Iowa
99 N7 **Iowa Falls** Iowa
109 J2 **Iowa Park** Texas
124 G7 **Ipala** Mexico
83 K9 **Ipalogama** Sri Lanka
130 E5 **Ipameri** Brazil
130 H6 **Ipanema** Brazil
130 H10 **Ipanema** *R* Brazil
130 H8 **Ipanguacu** Brazil
99 Q9 **Ipava** Illinois
48 E2 **Ipel'** *R* Czechoslovakia
116 E2 **Ipewik** *R* Alaska
37 J4 **Iphofen** W Germany
128 C3 **Ipiales** Colombia
129 L6 **Ipiau** Brazil
Ipin *see* **Yibin**
128 E4 **Ipiranga** Amazonas Brazil
130 E9 **Ipiranga** Paraná Brazil
128 D5 **Ipixuna** Amazonas Brazil
128 F5 **Ipixuna** *R* Amazonas Brazil
69 E10 **Ipoh** Malaysia
130 J10 **Ipojuca** *R* Brazil
71 C6 **Ipolote B** Palawan Philippines
129 H7 **Iporá** Brazil
130 E9 **Iporanga** Brazil
120 J9 **Ipperwash Prov. Park** Ontario
37 J4 **Ippesheim** W Germany
86 D4 **Ippy** Cent Afr Republic
78 A1 **Ipsala** Turkey
9 H3 **Ipswich** England
127 J2 **Ipswich** Jamaica
95 R4 **Ipswich** Massachusetts
141 L8 **Ipswich** Queensland
98 G4 **Ipswich** S Dakota
129 K4 **Ipu** Brazil
54 C4 **Iput'** *R* U.S.S.R.
78 K2 **Iğdir** Turkey
128 D8 **Iquique** Chile
128 D4 **Iquitos** Peru
80 F6 **'Ira** Jordan
108 F5 **Iraan** Texas
61 L11 **Irago-misaki** Japan
130 D10 **Irai** Brazil
47 G8 **Iráklia** *isld* Greece
47 G9 **Iráklion** Crete
130 C9 **Irala** Paraguay
77 C4 **Iran** *empire* S W Asia
130 D10 **Irani** *R* Brazil
77 G6 **Irānshahr** Iran
128 F1 **Irapa** Venezuela
124 J7 **Irapuato** Mexico
78 H5 **Iraq** *rep* S W Asia
95 P2 **Irasburg** Vermont
129 H3 **Iratapuru** *R* Brazil
130 E9 **Iratí** Brazil
133 G3 **Irati** Brazil
17 G2 **Irati** *R* Spain
84 E4 **Irāwan** Libya
52 J3 **Irayel'** U.S.S.R.
27 M14 **Irbenskiy Proliv** *str* U.S.S.R.
80 G3 **Irbid** Jordan
50 F3 **Irbit** U.S.S.R.
55 D2 **Irbit** *R* U.S.S.R.
9 G1 **Irby** England
38 K7 **Irdning** Austria
54 C7 **Irdyn'** U.S.S.R.
109 K4 **Iredell** Texas
109 K4 **Ireland** Texas
90 A1 **Ireland I** Bermuda
14 **Ireland, Rep of**
14 E3 **Ireland's Eye** *isld* Irish Rep
55 C3 **Iren** *R* U.S.S.R.
98 J6 **Irene** S Dakota
98 K7 **Ireton** Iowa
57 B1 **Irgiz** *R* U.S.S.R.
85 F5 **Irhazer Wan Agadez** *V* Niger
86 D2 **Iriba** Chad
129 G3 **Iricoumé, Serra** *mts* Brazil
71 F4 **Iriga** Philippines
55 C5 **Iriklinskiy** U.S.S.R.
87 G7 **Iringa** Tanzania
67 H4 **Iriomote-shima** *isld* Japan
125 M2 **Iriona** Honduras
129 H5 **Iriri** *R* Brazil
14 C3 **Irish Republic**
139 H8 **Irishtown** Tasmania
47 K3 **İriva** Turkey
56 E2 **Irkineyeva** *R* U.S.S.R.
56 F5 **Irkutsk** U.S.S.R.
56 F3 **Irkutskaya Oblast'** U.S.S.R.
118 F6 **Irma** Alberta
99 R4 **Irma** Wisconsin
36 E2 **Irmgarteichen** W Germany
112 F3 **Irmo** S Carolina
20 B5 **Irodouer** France
18 B4 **Iroise** *gulf* France
86 C3 **Iro, L** Chad
138 D4 **Iron Baron** S Australia
8 D2 **Ironbridge** England
120 G6 **Iron Bridge** Ontario
100 C9 **Iron Canyon Res** California
110 J6 **Iron City** Tennessee
110 F4 **Irondale** Missouri
94 G6 **Irondale** Ohio
121 M8 **Irondale** Ontario
138 D4 **Iron Knob** S Australia
99 S4 **Iron Mountain** Michigan
100 A7 **Iron Mt** Oregon
103 L4 **Iron Mt** Utah
98 G5 **Iron Nation** S Dakota
141 G2 **Iron Range** Queensland
99 S6 **Iron Ridge** Wisconsin
99 S3 **Iron River** Michigan
99 P3 **Iron River** Wisconsin
94 B2 **Irons** Michigan
100 H5 **Ironside** Oregon
103 L4 **Iron Sp** Utah
94 B1 **Ironton** Michigan
110 F4 **Ironton** Missouri
94 E8 **Ironton** Ohio
99 Q3 **Ironwood** Michigan
98 J5 **Iroquois** S Dakota
99 T9 **Iroquois** *R* Illinois
120 K4 **Iroquois Falls** Ontario
71 G4 **Irosin** Philippines
61 M11 **Irō zaki** *C* Japan
45 R8 **Irpinia** Italy
138 D3 **Irrapatana** S Australia
68 B4 **Irrawaddy** *prov* Burma
68 B5 **Irrawaddy** *R* Burma
68 B5 **Irrawaddy, Mouths of** Burma
36 B4 **Irrel** W Germany
118 D7 **Irricana** Alberta
85 D5 **Irrigi** *reg* Mali/Mauritania
56 D3 **Irsha** U.S.S.R.
48 H2 **Irshava** U.S.S.R.
52 G4 **Irta** U.S.S.R.
13 F3 **Irthing, R** England
55 D3 **Irtyash, Oz** *L* U.S.S.R.
55 F4 **Irtysh** U.S.S.R.
55 E2 **Irtysh** *R* U.S.S.R.
55 F4 **Irtyshsk** U.S.S.R.
86 E5 **Irumu** Zaïre
18 D9 **Irun** Spain
17 F2 **Irurzun** Spain
18 D10 **Irurzun** Spain
128 E8 **Iruya** Argentina
52 G3 **Irva** *R* U.S.S.R.
118 G9 **Irvine** Alberta
110 N4 **Irvine** Kentucky
15 D5 **Irvine** Scotland
15 D5 **Irvine** *R* Scotland
141 H3 **Irvinebank** Queensland
14 D2 **Irvinestown** N Ireland
107 O2 **Irving** Kansas
109 N9 **Irving** Texas
143 F7 **Irving, Mt** W Australia
110 K4 **Irvington** Kentucky
95 L9 **Irvington** Virginia
94 J6 **Irvona** Pennsylvania
13 F6 **Irwell, R** England
101 O6 **Irwin** Idaho
99 L8 **Irwin** Iowa
98 D7 **Irwin** Nebraska
143 B8 **Irwin** W Australia
143 B11 **Irwin, Pt** W Australia
112 D5 **Irwinton** Georgia
141 J6 **Isaac** *R* Queensland
117 N9 **Isaac L** Br Col
123 L8 **Isaacs Hbr** Nova Scotia
17 G2 **Isaba** Spain
107 M4 **Isabel** Kansas
98 E4 **Isabel** S Dakota
71 F5 **Isabela** Negros Philippines
71 E7 **Isabela** Philippines
127 L5 **Isabela** Puerto Rico
128 A8 **Isabela, Isla** Galapagos Is
125 M3 **Isabelia, Cord** *ra* Nicaragua
102 F6 **Isabella** California
119 Q8 **Isabella** Manitoba
99 P2 **Isabella** Minnesota
142 F5 **Isabella, L** W Australia
147 N11 **Isachenko, Ostrov** *isld* U.S.S.R.
114 J2 **Isachsen** N W Terr
60 D13 **Isahaya** Japan
52 F3 **Isakogorka** U.S.S.R.
48 H6 **Işalniţat** Romania
86 D5 **Isangi** Zaïre
37 N7 **Isar** *R* W Germany
42 D2 **Isarco** *R* Italy
46 E7 **Isari** Greece
41 O2 **Isar Tal** W Germany
111 J7 **Isbell** Alabama
22 C2 **Isbergues** France
15 G1 **Isbister** Scotland
40 C1 **Isches** France
41 M3 **Ischgl** Austria
45 P8 **Ischia** Italy
86 H5 **Iscia Baidoa** Somalia
142 F3 **Isdell, R** W Australia
21 J6 **Isdes** France
59 L5 **Ise** Japan
28 H5 **Isefjord** *inlet* Denmark
41 O3 **Isel Berg** *mt* Austria
146 K7 **Iselin Bank** Antarctica
81 H14 **Iselin Seamount** Southern Oc
52 H6 **Isenbayevo** U.S.S.R.
36 D3 **Isenburg** W Germany
33 N8 **Isenbüttel** W Germany
33 N7 **Isenhagen** W Germany
28 C4 **Isenvad** Denmark
42 C3 **Iseo** Italy
42 C3 **Iseo, L. d'** Italy
19 P14 **Isère** *dep* France
19 O14 **Isère** *R* France
32 G10 **Iserlohn** W Germany
43 F7 **Isernia** Italy
61 K11 **Ise shima Nat. Park** Japan
55 E3 **Isetskoye** U.S.S.R.
61 K11 **Ise-wan** *B* Japan
85 E7 **Iseyin** Nigeria
61 N9 **Isezaki** Japan
Isfahan *see* **Eşfahān**
57 E5 **Isfana** U.S.S.R.
57 F4 **Isfara** U.S.S.R.
80 D3 **Isfiya** Israel
52 J4 **Isherim, Gora** *mt* U.S.S.R.
128 G3 **Isherton** Guyana
88 C7 **Ishiba Ngandu** Zambia
67 H4 **Ishigaki** Japan
67 H4 **Ishigaki-shima** *isld* Japan
61 K9 **Ishika** *prefect* Japan
60 P2 **Ishikari** Japan
60 R2 **Ishikari dake** *mt* Japan
59 M3 **Ishikari-wan** *B* Japan
50 F3 **Ishim** U.S.S.R.
55 C4 **Ishimbay** U.S.S.R.
55 F5 **Ishimo** *R* U.S.S.R.
55 F3 **Ishimskaya Step** *steppe* U.S.S.R.
55 E5 **Ishimskoye** U.S.S.R.
59 M4 **Ishinomaki** Japan
60 G12 **Ishizuchi-san** *mt* Japan
86 G6 **Isiolo** Kenya
87 F11 **Isipingo Bch** S Africa
86 E5 **Isiro** Zaire
141 G6 **Isisford** Queensland
86 G1 **Is, Jebel** *mt* Sudan
55 E3 **Iska** *R* U.S.S.R.
80 D5 **Iskāka** Jordan
57 E4 **Iskander** U.S.S.R.
47 J8 **İskandil Burun** *C* Turkey
78 F3 **Iskenderun** Turkey
57 G4 **Iski-Naukat** U.S.S.R.
56 B4 **Iskitim** U.S.S.R.
47 G1 **Iskür** *R* Bulgaria
117 J7 **Iskut** Br Columbia
117 H7 **Iskut** *R* Br Col
119 O3 **Iskwatam L** Sask
15 E4 **Isla** *R* Scotland
78 F3 **Islâhiye** Turkey
74 E2 **Islamabad** Pakistan
113 G13 **Islamorada** Florida
110 J4 **Island** Kentucky
117 N5 **Island** *R* N W Terr
71 D6 **Island B** Palawan Philippines
100 H4 **Island City** Oregon
95 S7 **Island Falls** Maine
120 J3 **Island Falls** Ontario
119 P3 **Island Falls** Sask
141 K5 **Island Hd** Queensland
95 N7 **Island Heights** New Jersey
115 K7 **Island L** Manitoba
123 Q5 **Island L** Nfld
120 K7 **Island L** Ontario
138 D4 **Island Lagoon** S Australia
99 W3 **Island Lake** Ontario
100 B9 **Island Mountain** California
101 O5 **Island Park** Idaho
95 Q2 **Island Pond** Vermont
143 B9 **Island Pt** W Australia
145 E1 **Islands, Bay of** New Zealand
115 O8 **Islands, Bay of** Nfld
17 J5 **Islas Baleares** Spain
16 B2 **Islas Cíes** Spain
127 M5 **Isla Verde** *airport* Puerto Rico
118 G5 **Islay** Alberta
15 B5 **Islay** *isld* Scotland
21 H10 **Isle** France
99 N3 **Isle** Minnesota
18 F7 **Isle** *R* France
20 K3 **Isle Adam, l'** France
123 O6 **Isle aux Morts** Nfld
95 T2 **Isleboro** Maine
18 F9 **Isle en Dodon, L'** France
18 F9 **Isle Jourdain, L'** Gers France
18 F6 **Isle Jourdain, L'** Vienne France
118 H4 **Isle, Lac des** Sask
122 A5 **Isle Maligne** Quebec
112 F6 **Isle of Hope** Georgia
15 G2 **Isle of Noss** Scotland
12 D4 **Isle of Whithorn** Scotland
99 S1 **Isle Royale** Michigan
22 G5 **Isles-sur-Suippes** France
18 H5 **Isle-sur-Serein, L'** France
106 D7 **Isleta** New Mexico
102 C3 **Isleton** California
122 C5 **Isle Verte** Quebec
9 E4 **Islip** England
127 N3 **Islote Pt** Trinidad
133 D1 **Isluga** *mt* Chile
128 E7 **Isluga** *vol* Chile
131 F4 **Ismael Cortinas** Uruguay
84 J3 **Ismâ'ilîya** Egypt
37 M7 **Ismaning** W Germany
98 B3 **Ismay** Montana
78 A2 **Ismir Körfezi** Turkey
84 J4 **Isna** Egypt
87 H12 **Isoanala** Madagascar
29 J9 **Isojoki** Finland
87 F8 **Isoka** Zambia
29 J8 **Isokyrö** Finland
41 O7 **Isola** Italy
111 F8 **Isola** Mississippi
45 P6 **Isola d. Liri** Italy
45 M5 **Isola Farnese** Italy
87 H12 **Isola, Massif de L'** *mts* Madagascar
45 K1 **Isola Rizza** Italy
110 L5 **Isoline** Tennessee
45 J1 **Isorella** Italy
29 N6 **Isosyöte** *mt* Finland
78 C3 **Isparta** Turkey
47 H1 **Isperikh** Bulgaria
78 H1 **Ispir** Turkey
80 **Israel** *rep* S W Asia
143 E10 **Israelite B** W Australia
28 F4 **Issehoved** *C* Denmark
143 A8 **Isseka** W Australia
25 F5 **Isselburg** W Germany
85 C7 **Issia** Ivory Coast
18 H7 **Issoire** France
21 I8 **Issoudun** France
25 F5 **Issum** W Germany
57 H4 **Issyk-Kul, Ozero** *L* U.S.S.R.
57 J4 **Issyk-Kul'skaya** *oblast* U.S.S.R.
77 L2 **Istalif** Afghanistan
47 K3 **İstanbul** Turkey
120 J7 **Isthmus Bay** Ontario
46 F6 **Istiaía** Greece
78 H3 **Istilil** Turkey
128 C2 **Istmina** Colombia
54 H1 **Istra** U.S.S.R.
42 F3 **Istra** *pen* Yugoslavia
47 J3 **Istranca Dağları** *mts* Turkey
19 N18 **Istres** France
61 M11 **Isu hantō** *pen* Japan
55 C5 **Isyangulovo** U.S.S.R.
130 B9 **Itá** Paraguay
129 L6 **Itabaiana** Brazil
130 H7 **Itabapoana** Brazil
130 E8 **Itaberá** Brazil
130 E5 **Itaberaí** Brazil
129 K7 **Itabira** Brazil
130 G7 **Itabirito** Brazil
128 F4 **Itaboca** Brazil
129 L6 **Itabuna** Brazil
129 J5 **Itacajá** Brazil
129 H5 **Itacajuna** *R* Brazil
130 G4 **Itacarambi** Brazil
129 L6 **Itacaré** Brazil
128 G4 **Itacoatiara** Brazil
128 D5 **Itacuai** *R* Brazil
130 C9 **Itacurubí del Rosario** Paraguay
130 H6 **Itaguaçu** Brazil
130 D8 **Itaguaje** Brazil
129 J6 **Itaguari** *R* Brazil
130 E8 **Itaí** Brazil
130 E10 **Itaiópolis** Brazil
129 G4 **Itaituba** Brazil
130 E10 **Itajai Acú, R** Brazil
129 J8 **Itajuba** Brazil
130 H4 **Itajuipe** Brazil
61 O10 **Itako** Japan
Itala *see* **Ataleh**
109 L3 **Italy** Texas
42 **Italy** *rep* S Europe
130 G5 **Itamarandiba** Brazil
129 J4 **Itamatare** Brazil
130 H6 **Itambacuri** Brazil
129 K7 **Itambé** Brazil
130 G6 **Itambe, P. de** *mt* Brazil
60 J11 **Itami** Japan
130 F9 **Itanhaém** Brazil
129 K7 **Itanhém** *R* Brazil
129 H3 **Itany** *R* Suriname
130 H5 **Itaobim** Brazil
129 J6 **Itapaci** Brazil
130 E6 **Itapajipe** Brazil
130 H4 **Itapebi** Brazil
130 F7 **Itapecerica** Brazil
129 K4 **Itapecuru Mirim** Brazil
130 H7 **Itapemirim** Brazil
129 K8 **Itaperuna** Brazil
129 K7 **Itapetinga** Brazil
129 J8 **Itapetininga** Brazil
129 J8 **Itapeva** Brazil
129 G3 **Itapi** *R* Brazil
129 K5 **Itapicura** *R* Brazil
129 J5 **Itapicuru, Serra do** *mts* Brazil
128 F5 **Itapinima** Brazil
129 L4 **Itapipoca** Brazil
128 G4 **Itapira** Brazil
130 E10 **Itapocu, R** Brazil
130 E7 **Itápolis** Brazil
130 H9 **Itaporanga** Brazil
130 C10 **Itapuá** *reg* Paraguay
129 H7 **Itapuranga** Brazil
131 G2 **Itaqui** Brazil
133 F2 **Itaquyry** Paraguay
129 J8 **Itararé** Brazil
74 G7 **Itarsi** India
130 D6 **Itarumá** Brazil
109 K3 **Itasca** Texas
99 L2 **Itasca State Park** Minnesota
131 A6 **Itata, R** Chile
130 F8 **Itatiba** Brazil
131 F2 **Itati, L** Argentina
130 E8 **Itatinga** Brazil
128 F5 **Itatuba** Brazil
130 E5 **Itauçu** Brazil
130 G7 **Itaúna** Brazil
129 L7 **Itaúnas** Brazil
130 H6 **Itaúnas** Brazil
9 E5 **Itchin, R** England
55 F4 **Itemgen, Oz** *L* U.S.S.R.
94 C3 **Ithaca** Michigan
95 L4 **Ithaca** New York
Ithaca *isld* Greece *see* **Itháki**
46 D6 **Itháki** *isld* Greece
8 C3 **Ithon, R** Wales
86 D5 **Itimbiri** *R* Zaïre
130 H5 **Itinga** Brazil
129 H7 **Itiquira** Brazil
129 K6 **Itiúba, Serra de** *mts* Brazil
115 O4 **Itivdleq** Greenland
116 M2 **Itkillik** *R* Alaska
61 N11 **Itō** Japan
61 L8 **Itoigawa** Japan
86 D6 **Itoko** Zaïre
61 P14 **Itoman** Okinawa
20 H4 **Iton** *R* France
45 P7 **Itri** Italy
79 A9 **Itsa** Egypt
111 F8 **Itta Bena** Mississippi
25 E6 **Ittervoort** Netherlands
43 B8 **Ittiri** Sardinia
130 F8 **Itu** Brazil
131 G2 **Itú** *R* Brazil
129 J7 **Ituiutaba** Brazil
88 A3 **Itula** Zaïre
88 E5 **Itumba** Tanzania
129 J7 **Itumbiara** Brazil
119 O7 **Ituna** Sask
128 G2 **Ituni** Guyana
130 E10 **Ituporanga** Brazil
128 E8 **Iturbe** Argentina
130 C10 **Iturbe** Paraguay
59 N3 **Iturup, Ostrov** *isld* U.S.S.R.
130 F7 **Ituverava** Brazil
130 C10 **Ituzaingo** Argentina
37 K3 **Itz** *R* W Germany
32 L5 **Itzehoe** W Germany
32 K5 **Itzwärden** W Germany
88 D6 **Iufira** *R* Malawi
110 H3 **Iuka** Illinois
107 M4 **Iuka** Kansas
130 H7 **Iúna** Brazil
112 E3 **Iva** S Carolina
129 H8 **Ivaí** *R* Brazil
29 N3 **Ivalo** Finland
29 N3 **Ivalojoki** *R* Finland
48 E7 **Ivančići** Yugoslavia
46 D2 **Ivangrad** Yugoslavia
98 K5 **Ivanhoe** Minnesota
139 G5 **Ivanhoe** New S Wales
94 G10 **Ivanhoe** Virginia
142 G3 **Ivanhoe** W Australia
120 H4 **Ivanhoe** *R* Ontario
54 M1 **Ivanishchi** U.S.S.R.
48 F7 **Ivanjica** Yugoslavia
53 B9 **Ivano-Frankovsk** U.S.S.R.
48 L1 **Ivanopol** U.S.S.R.
55 G3 **Ivanovka** Omsk U.S.S.R.
55 B4 **Ivanovka** U.S.S.R.
52 F6 **Ivanovo** U.S.S.R.
103 J6 **Ivanpah** California
54 J1 **Ivanteyvka** U.S.S.R.
47 H3 **Ivaylovgrad** Bulgaria
55 D1 **Ivdel'** U.S.S.R.
33 R5 **Ivenack** E Germany
99 S10 **Ivesdale** Illinois
17 H8 **Ivi, C** Algeria
115 P5 **Ivigtut** Greenland
86 B5 **Ivindo** *R* Gabon
9 F4 **Ivinghoe** England
129 H8 **Ivinheima** *R* Brazil
116 N2 **Ivishak** *R* Alaska
Iviza *see* **Ibiza**
95 L10 **Ivor** Virginia
85 C7 **Ivory Coast** *rep* W Africa
27 G15 **Ivösjön** Sweden
54 F3 **Ivot** U.S.S.R.
42 B3 **Ivrea** Italy
47 J5 **İvrindi** Turkey
20 J4 **Ivry-la-Bataille** France
115 M5 **Ivugivik** Quebec
8 C7 **Ivybridge** England
94 F8 **Ivydale** W Virginia
61 O7 **Iwadeyama** Japan
61 O7 **Iwai-gawa** *R* Japan
61 P6 **Iwaizumi** Japan
61 O9 **Iwaki** Japan
61 O5 **Iwaki** *R* Japan
61 O5 **Iwaki-san** *mt* Japan
59 K5 **Iwakuni** Japan
60 P2 **Iwamizawa** Japan
70 D3 **Iwan** *R* Kalimantan
60 O3 **Iwanai** Japan
61 O7 **Iwanuma** Japan
61 O9 **Iwase** Japan
61 M9 **Iwasuge-yama** *mt* Japan
61 L11 **Iwata** Japan
61 P6 **Iwate** Japan
60 H11 **Iwaya** Japan
85 E7 **Iwo** Nigeria
Iwo Jima *see* **Iō-tō**
61 N13 **Iwo Jima** *isld* Japan
22 E3 **Iwuy** France
128 E6 **Ixiamas** Bolivia
125 M9 **Ixtepec, Ciudad** Mexico
124 H8 **Ixtlahuacán** Mexico
124 G7 **Ixtlán del Río** Mexico
9 G3 **Ixworth** England
56 F4 **Iya** *R* U.S.S.R.
55 E3 **Iyevlevo** U.S.S.R.
60 G12 **Iyomishima** Japan
60 F12 **Iyo-nada** *sea* Japan
48 J3 **Iza** *R* Romania
125 P10 **Izabal, L. de** Guatemala
17 G2 **Izalzu** Spain
116 F6 **Izaviknek** *R* Alaska
31 O5 **Izbica** Poland
54 E1 **Izdeshkovo** U.S.S.R.
22 E2 **Izegem** Belgium
19 O14 **Izeron** France
52 H6 **Izhevsk** U.S.S.R.
52 H2 **Izhma** U.S.S.R.
53 C10 **Izmail** U.S.S.R.
78 A2 **Izmir** Turkey
47 J6 **İzmir Boz Sira Dağları** *mts* Turkey
78 C1 **Izmit** Turkey
47 K4 **İzmit Körfezi** *B* Turkey
16 E7 **Iznajar** Spain
16 E7 **Iznalloz** Spain
78 B1 **Iznik** Turkey
78 B1 **Iznik Gölü** Turkey
128 F7 **Izozog, Bañados de** Bolivia
79 G6 **Izra'** Syria
48 E4 **Izsák** Hungary
47 G3 **Iztochni Rodopi** Bulgaria
60 C11 **Izuhara** Japan
60 D13 **Izumi** Japan
60 J11 **Izumi-ōtsu** Japan
60 F10 **Izumo** Japan
61 M8 **Izumozaki** Japan
55 D3 **Izumrud** U.S.S.R.
61 N11 **Izu-shotō** *islds* Japan
147 N12 **Izvestiy, Os** *isld* U.S.S.R.
50 H1 **Izvestiy Tsik, Ostrova** *isld* U.S.S.R.
48 K4 **Izvorul Oltului** Romania
57 A2 **Izyndy** U.S.S.R.
54 J7 **Izyum** U.S.S.R.
29 M10 **Jaala** Finland
29 L5 **Jaatila** Finland
77 E2 **Jaba** *R* Iran
84 G3 **Jabal al Akhdar** *mts* Libya
77 C7 **Jabal Dhana** U.A.E.
16 E6 **Jabalón** *R* Spain
74 H7 **Jabalpur** India
22 E1 **Jabbeke** Belgium
33 R5 **Jabel** E Germany
46 D3 **Jablanica** Albania
46 E2 **Jablanica** *R* Yugoslavia
31 J5 **Jablonec nad Nisou** Czechoslovakia
31 K7 **Jablonica** Czechoslovakia
31 L2 **Jabłonowo** Poland
31 L6 **Jablunkov** Czechoslovakia
129 M5 **Jaboatão** Brazil
129 J8 **Jaboticabal** Brazil
69 G13 **Jabung, Tanjung** *C* Sumatra
128 F5 **Jaburu** Brazil
17 G2 **Jaca** Spain
130 B6 **Jacadigo** *L* Brazil
130 G4 **Jacaraci** Brazil
129 K6 **Jacaré** *R* Brazil
130 F8 **Jacareí** Brazil
128 G5 **Jacaretinga** Brazil
130 E8 **Jacarezinho** Brazil
133 D4 **Jachal** Argentina
37 O3 **Jáchymov** Czechoslovakia
130 H5 **Jacinto** Brazil
109 M5 **Jacinto, S** *R* Texas
128 F5 **Jaciparaná** Brazil
120 D4 **Jackfish** Ontario
118 J5 **Jackfish L** Sask
117 R6 **Jackfish River** Alberta
119 U7 **Jackhead Harbour** Manitoba
115 N6 **Jack Lane B** Labrador
95 R1 **Jackman** Maine
100 E1 **Jack Mt** Washington
120 C3 **Jackpine** Ontario
141 G3 **Jack R** Queensland
112 C1 **Jacksboro** Tennessee
109 J2 **Jacksboro** Texas
94 K6 **Jacks Mt** Pennsylvania
111 J10 **Jackson** Alabama
102 D3 **Jackson** California
112 D4 **Jackson** Georgia
94 D9 **Jackson** Kentucky
111 E11 **Jackson** Louisiana
111 F9 **Jackson** Mississippi
110 G4 **Jackson** Missouri
101 M4 **Jackson** Montana
112 K1 **Jackson** N Carolina
94 E7 **Jackson** Ohio
141 J7 **Jackson** Queensland
112 F4 **Jackson** S Carolina
110 H6 **Jackson** Tennessee
101 P6 **Jackson** Wyoming
94 H8 **Jackson** *R* Virginia
117 L10 **Jackson Bay** Br Col
144 B5 **Jackson Bay** New Zealand
145 E4 **Jackson, C** New Zealand
110 M1 **Jackson Cen** Ohio
106 B4 **Jackson Gulch Res** Colorado
113 C7 **Jackson, L** Florida
112 D4 **Jackson L** Georgia
101 P6 **Jackson L** Wyoming
143 C9 **Jackson, Mt** W Australia
100 G8 **Jackson Mts** Nevada
99 T5 **Jacksonport** Wisconsin
111 G9 **Jackson Prairie** Mississippi
106 F1 **Jackson Res** Colorado
144 C5 **Jacksons** New Zealand
123 Q4 **Jackson's Arm** Nfld
111 L8 **Jacksonville** Alabama
110 D7 **Jacksonville** Arkansas
113 F7 **Jacksonville** Florida
99 Q10 **Jacksonville** Illinois
110 D2 **Jacksonville** Missouri
112 K3 **Jacksonville** N Carolina
100 C7 **Jacksonville** Oregon
109 M4 **Jacksonville** Texas
113 F7 **Jacksonville Beach** Florida
127 H5 **Jacmel** Haiti
124 G4 **Jaco** Mexico
71 N9 **Jaco** *isld* Timor
74 C4 **Jacobabad** Pakistan
129 K6 **Jacobina** Brazil
103 M5 **Jacob L** Arizona
80 E5 **Jacob's Well** Jordan
124 H8 **Jacona** Mexico
121 T9 **Jacques Cartier** Quebec
121 T5 **Jacques Cartier, L** Quebec
122 G4 **Jacques Cartier, Mt** Quebec
122 F6 **Jacquet R** New Brunswick
130 J9 **Jacú** *R* Brazil
130 F7 **Jacuí** Minas Gerais Brazil
131 H2 **Jacui** Rio Grande do Sul Brazil
131 H2 **Jacui** *R* Rio Grande do Sul Brazil
129 L6 **Jacuípe** *R* Brazil
103 H9 **Jacumba** California
129 J4 **Jacundá** Brazil
129 H4 **Jacunda** *R* Brazil
130 F9 **Jacupiranga** Brazil
129 E4 **Jaçura** Brazil
80 G8 **Jad'a** Jordan
48 E6 **Jadar** *R* Yugoslavia
32 H6 **Jade** W Germany
32 H6 **Jade** *R* W Germany
85 C2 **Jadida, El** Morocco
87 E8 **Jadotville** Zaïre
31 N3 **Jadów** Poland
17 F4 **Jadraque** Spain
84 E3 **Jādū** Libya
28 H5 **Jægerspris** Denmark
22 F3 **Jaeibise** Belgium
143 C8 **Jaellan, Mt** W Australia
71 E3 **Jaen** Luzon Philippines
16 E7 **Jaén** Spain
16 E7 **Jaén** *prov* Spain
27 A13 **Jaeren** *R* Norway
26 F7 **Jaevsjo** Norway
77 A2 **Ja'farābād** Iran
80 C5 **Jaffa** Israel
138 E6 **Jaffa, C** S Australia
83 K8 **Jaffna** Sri Lanka
75 K9 **Jagdalpur** India
87 E11 **Jagersfontein** S Africa
84 G4 **Jaghbūb, Al** Libya
116 Q2 **Jago** *R* Alaska
36 H5 **Jagst** *R* W Germany
37 J5 **Jagstzell** W Germany
74 H9 **Jagtial** India
129 K6 **Jaguaquara** Brazil
131 H4 **Jaguarão** Brazil
131 G2 **Jaguari** *R* Brazil
129 H8 **Jaguariaiva** Brazil
129 L5 **Jaguaribe** *R* Brazil
131 C2 **Jagüe, R** Argentina
126 D3 **Jaguey Grande** Cuba
140 B1 **Jahleel Pt** N Terr Aust
78 K7 **Jahmah** Iraq
48 E7 **Jahorina** *mt* Yugoslavia
77 C5 **Jahrom** Iran
74 G3 **Jaijon Doaba** India
74 F5 **Jaipur** India
74 D5 **Jaisalmer** India
42 H4 **Jajce** Yugoslavia
75 M8 **Jajpur** India
70 L9 **Jakarta** Java
63 **Jakarta** *conurbation* Indonesia
26 J5 **Jäkkvik** Sweden
26 S2 **Jakobselv** *R* Norway/U.S.S.R.
29 K8 **Jakobstad** Finland
46 E3 **Jakupica** Yugoslavia
106 G9 **Jal** New Mexico
77 H6 **Jāla** Iran
58 G2 **Jalai Nur** China
77 L2 **Jalalabad** Afghanistan
125 L3 **Jalapa** Nicaragua
125 L8 **Jalapa Enríquez** Mexico
29 K9 **Jalasjärvi** Finland
74 H5 **Jalaun** India
140 C2 **Jalboi** *R* N Terr Aust
86 H4 **Jaldessa** Ethiopia
130 E7 **Jales** Brazil
75 M8 **Jaleswar** India
74 F8 **Jalgaon** India
22 K2 **Jalhay** Belgium
78 L6 **Jalibah** Iraq
86 B4 **Jalingo** Nigeria
124 G8 **Jalisco** *state* Mexico
21 D7 **Jallais** France
74 F9 **Jalna** India
17 F3 **Jalón** *R* Spain
Jalo Oasis *see* **Gialo**
74 E6 **Jalor** India
124 H7 **Jalostotitlán** Mexico
124 H7 **Jalpa** Mexico
75 N5 **Jalpaiguri** India
124 K7 **Jalpan** Mexico
77 L2 **Jalrez** Afghanistan
84 G4 **Jalu** Libya
78 K4 **Jalūlā** Iraq
77 G2 **Jam** *reg* Iran
128 B4 **Jama** Ecuador
126 G4 **Jamaica** Cuba
95 P3 **Jamaica** Vermont
127 K2 **Jamaica** W I
126 G5 **Jamaica Chan** Caribbean
27 M13 **Jämaja** U.S.S.R.
75 N6 **Jamalpur** Bangladesh
75 M6 **Jamalpur** India
126 A2 **Jamanota** *hill* Aruba W I
129 G5 **Jamanxim** *R* Brazil
128 F5 **Jamari** Brazil
66 C2 **Jamati** China
139 K5 **Jamberoo** New S Wales
Jambi *see* **Telanaipura**
69 F13 **Jambi** *dist* Sumatra
141 K6 **Jambin** Queensland
69 C10 **Jamboaye** *R* Sumatra
122 F4 **Jambon, Pte** Quebec
69 C10 **Jambuair, Tanjung** *C* Sumatra
110 C5 **James** *R* Missouri
98 H3 **James** *R* N Dakota
98 J6 **James** *R* S Dakota
115 L7 **James B** Canada
95 N6 **Jamesburg** New Jersey
112 K2 **James City** N Carolina
94 J5 **James City** Pennsylvania
112 F2 **James, L** N Carolina
99 N9 **Jameson** Missouri
115 R3 **Jameson Land** Greenland
99 N10 **Jamesport** Missouri
113 L12 **James Pt** Bahamas
140 D5 **James R** N Terr Aust
95 L9 **James R** Virginia
140 C6 **James Ra** N Terr Aust
146 D14 **James Ross I** Antarctica
115 K4 **James Ross Str** N W Terr
110 K2 **Jamestown** Indiana
107 N2 **Jamestown** Kansas
94 B4 **Jamestown** Michigan
98 H3 **Jamestown** N Dakota
94 H4 **Jamestown** New York
94 D7 **Jamestown** Ohio
94 G5 **Jamestown** Pennsylvania
95 Q5 **Jamestown** Rhode I
90 A13 **Jamestown** St Helena
138 E5 **Jamestown** S Australia
112 H4 **Jamestown** S Carolina
94 C10 **Jamestown** Tennessee
95 L9 **Jamestown Nat. Hist. Site** Virginia
112 L2 **Jamesville** N Carolina
95 L4 **Jamesville** New York
22 J5 **Jametz** France
100 H5 **Jamieson** Oregon
29 K10 **Jämijärvi** Finland
125 L9 **Jamilzepec** Mexico
98 G7 **Jamison** Nebraska
76 B2 **Jamkhandi** India
74 F9 **Jamkhed** India
76 D3 **Jammalamadugu** India
28 C2 **Jammerbugt** *B* Denmark
28 F5 **Jammerland Bugt** *B* Denmark
74 F2 **Jammu** Kashmir
Jammu and Kashmir *see* **Kashmir**
74 G1 **Jammu and Kashmir** India
74 D7 **Jamnagar** India
31 J1 **Jamno, Jezioro** *L* Poland
22 J4 **Jamoigne** Belgium
74 D4 **Jampur** Pakistan
29 L10 **Jämsä** Finland
29 L10 **Jämsänkoski** Finland
75 M7 **Jamshedpur** India
26 F8 **Jämtland** Sweden
26 H8 **Jämtl Sikås** Sweden
71 C3 **Jamtup, Tg** *C* W Irian
70 E3 **Jamuk, G** *mt* Kalimantan
102 H9 **Jamul** California
75 N6 **Jamuna** *R* Bangladesh
128 C3 **Jamundí** Colombia
75 M5 **Janakpur** Nepal
129 K7 **Janaúba** Brazil
129 H3 **Janaucu, I** Brazil
130 E5 **Jandaia** Brazil
142 B3 **Jandakot** *dist* Perth, W Aust
142 B3 **Jandakot, L** W Australia
77 D2 **Jandaq** Iran
28 A5 **Janderup** Denmark
128 E5 **Jandiatuba** *R* Brazil
141 K7 **Jandowae** Queensland
94 G7 **Jane Lew** W Virginia
144 B6 **Jane Pk** New Zealand
100 E9 **Janesville** California
99 O7 **Janesville** Iowa
99 N5 **Janesville** Minnesota
99 R7 **Janesville** Wisconsin
130 D10 **Jangada** Brazil
130 C7 **Jango** Brazil
69 G13 **Jang, Tanjung** *C* Indonesia
33 S8 **Jänickendorf** E Germany
46 E2 **Janjevo** Yugoslavia
89 D6 **Jan Kemp** S Africa
119 P4 **Jan L** Sask
90 H1 **Jan Mayen** *isld* Arctic Oc
90 H1 **Jan Mayen Ridge, E** Arctic Oc
77 G2 **Jannatabad** Iran
124 E2 **Janos** Mexico
48 E4 **Jánoshalma** Hungary
48 D3 **Jánosháza** Hungary
37 P5 **Janovice nad Uhlavou** Czechoslovakia
33 S5 **Janow** E Germany
31 K3 **Janowiec** Poland
31 N5 **Janów Lubelski** Poland
31 O3 **Janów Podlaski** Poland
98 K9 **Jansen** Nebraska
119 N7 **Jansen** Sask
130 G4 **Januária** Brazil
20 J5 **Janville** France
21 C6 **Janzé** France
130 G5 **Jaoquim Felício** Brazil
74 F7 **Jaora** India
61 **Japan** *empire* E Asia
59 K3 **Japan, Sea of** E Asia
29 N9 **Jäppilä** Finland
128 E4 **Japurá** Brazil
127 J5 **Jarabacoa** Dom Rep
129 J7 **Jaraguá** Brazil
130 E10 **Jaraguá do Sul** Brazil
130 C7 **Jaraguari** Brazil
130 E10 **Jaraguá Serra** *mts* Brazil
16 D5 **Jaraicejo** Spain
16 E4 **Jarama** *R* Spain
133 D7 **Jaramillo** Argentina
16 D4 **Jarandilla** Spain
129 H4 **Jarauçu** *R* Brazil
100 K8 **Jarbidge** Nevada
100 K7 **Jarbidge** *R* Idaho
27 J11 **Järbo** Sweden
143 B10 **Jardee** W Australia
130 G9 **Jardim** Ceará Brazil
130 C7 **Jardim** Mato Grosso Brazil
130 H9 **Jardim do Seridó** Brazil
141 F1 **Jardine** *R* Queensland
122 E6 **Jardine Brook** New Brunswick
126 E4 **Jardines de la Reina** *islds* Cuba
130 E6 **Jardinésia** Brazil
130 F7 **Jardinópolis** Brazil
21 B9 **Jard-sur-Mer** France
27 H14 **Järeda** Sweden
27 E11 **Jaren** Norway
38 N8 **Jarenina** Yugoslavia
58 G2 **Jargalant** Mongolia
21 J6 **Jargeau** France
129 H3 **Jari** *R* Brazil
128 F4 **Jari, L** Brazil
33 S5 **Jarmen** E Germany

Järna — Kahemba 37

27 J12 Järna Sweden
18 E7 Jarnac France
27 H13 Järnlunden *L* Sweden
71 F5 Jaro Panay Philippines
31 K4 Jarocin Poland
31 J5 Jaroměř Czechoslovakia
31 J6 Jaroměřice Czechoslovakia
126 F4 Jaronu Cuba
31 O5 Jaroslaw Poland
106 E4 Jaroso Colorado
26 F8 Järpen Sweden
80 F8 Jarra *R* Jordan
94 K10 Jarratt Virginia
26 K5 Jarre *mt* Sweden
109 K5 Jarrell Texas
68 F3 Jarres, Plaine des Laos
118 F6 Jarrow Alberta
13 G4 Jarrow England
128 F6 Jaru Brazil
65 E2 Jarud Qi China
52 C5 Järva-Jaani U.S.S.R.
118 D4 Jarvie Alberta
134 B3 Jarvis I Pacific Oc
26 H10 Järvsö Sweden
21 E6 Jarzé France
48 F5 Jaša Tomic Yugoslavia
74 D7 Jasdan India
33 T8 Jasdorf E Germany
85 E7 Jasikan Ghana
77 E7 Jäsk Iran
31 N6 Jasło Poland
119 O7 Jasmin Sask
30 H1 Jasmund *pen* E Germany
133 E8 Jason Is Falkland Is
146 E14 Jason Pen Antarctica
110 J2 Jasonville Indiana
111 J8 Jasper Alabama
114 H7 Jasper Alberta
110 C5 Jasper Arkansas
106 D4 Jasper Colorado
113 E7 Jasper Florida
111 M7 Jasper Georgia
110 K3 Jasper Indiana
94 C5 Jasper Michigan
98 K6 Jasper Minnesota
110 B4 Jasper Missouri
94 K4 Jasper New York
121 P8 Jasper Ontario
112 B2 Jasper Tennessee
111 C11 Jasper Texas
117 O9 Jasper Nat. Park Alberta
118 D5 Jasper Place Alberta
78 K5 Jassan Iraq
Jassy *see* Iasi
31 L1 Jastarnia Poland
48 E1 Jastrebac *mt* Yugoslavia
31 K2 Jastrowie Poland
48 F3 Jászapáti Hungary
48 F3 Jászarokszállás Hungary
48 F3 Jászberény Hungary
48 F3 Jászfényszaru Hungary
48 F3 Jászladány Hungary
129 H7 Jataí Brazil
129 G4 Jatapu *R* Brazil
76 B2 Jath India
126 E4 Jatibonico Cuba
17 G6 Játiva Spain
129 H4 Jatobá Brazil
129 J4 Jatobal Brazil
80 D4 Jatt Israel
128 F5 Jatuarana Brazil
33 T5 Jatzke E Germany
33 T5 Jatznick E Germany
129 J8 Jaú Brazil
128 F4 Jaú *R* Brazil
128 F3 Jauaperi *R* Brazil
22 H2 Jauche Belgium
126 G4 Jauco Cuba
128 C6 Jauja Peru
21 F10 Jauldes France
128 G5 Jauna *R* Brazil
21 F8 Jaunay-Clan France
52 B6 Jaunjelgava U.S.S.R.
52 C6 Jaunpiebalga U.S.S.R.
75 K6 Jaunpur India
38 L8 Jauntal *V* Austria
129 G7 Jauru *R* Brazil
130 D6 Jauru, R Brazil
22 D5 Jaux France
Java *isld* Indonesia *see* Jawa
76 D4 Javadi Hills India
129 J6 Javaés, Serra dos *mts* Brazil
17 G4 Javalambre, Sierra de *mts* Spain
128 D4 Javari *R* Brazil/Peru
70 M8 Java Sea Indonesia
136 D4 Java Trough Indian Oc
17 H6 Jávea Spain
Javhlant *see* Uliastay
133 C7 Javier *B* Chile
48 E6 Javor *mts* Yugoslavia
48 E2 Javoria *mt* Czechoslovakia
38 K9 Javornik Yugoslavia
48 E1 Javorniky *mt* Czechoslovakia
26 M6 Jävre Sweden
20 E5 Javron France
80 G6 Jawa Jordan
70 Jawa *isld* Indonesia
74 G5 Jawf, Al Libya
69 J13 Jawi Indonesia
31 J4 Jawor Poland
31 L5 Jaworzno Poland
107 Q5 Jay Oklahoma
136 H2 Jaya Pk *mt* W Irian
136 J2 Jayapura W Irian
98 B7 Jay Em Wyoming
33 P7 Jayenitz E Germany
9 H4 Jaywick Sands England
78 H4 Jazirah, Al Iraq
124 J5 Jazminal Mexico
77 F6 Jaz Murian, Hamun-e *L* Iran
78 G4 Jdaide Syria
103 J6 Jean Nevada
109 J2 Jean Texas
111 E12 Jeanerette Louisiana
122 E1 Jean L Quebec
117 N5 Jean Marie River N W Terr
94 H6 Jeannette Pennsylvania
127 H5 Jean Rabel Haiti
13 G5 Jeater Houses England
80 G1 Jeba Syria
77 F5 Jebāl Bārez, Kūh-e *mts* Iran
85 E7 Jebba Nigeria
86 E2 Jebel Abyad Plateau Sudan
16 D9 Jebha Morocco
28 B3 Jebjerg Denmark
79 F3 Jeble Syria
88 E8 Jeci *mt* Mozambique
119 P7 Jedburgh Sask
13 F2 Jedburgh Scotland
Jedda *see* Jiddah
94 E3 Jeddo Michigan
43 C12 Jedeida Tunisia
13 F3 Jedfoot Br Scotland
31 M5 Jedrzejów Poland
31 M2 Jedwabne Poland
117 H9 Jedway Br Col
29 M4 Jeesiö Finland
33 O7 Jeetze E Germany
33 O6 Jeetze *R* W Germany
99 L5 Jeffers Minnesota
106 E2 Jefferson Colorado
112 D3 Jefferson Georgia
94 K7 Jefferson Maryland
94 G5 Jefferson Ohio
107 N5 Jefferson Oklahoma
100 C5 Jefferson Oregon
98 K7 Jefferson S Dakota
111 B9 Jefferson Texas
99 S6 Jefferson Wisconsin
110 D3 Jefferson City Missouri
101 N3 Jefferson City Montana
112 D1 Jefferson City Tennessee
102 H4 Jefferson Island Montana
100 D5 Jefferson, Mt Oregon
94 B8 Jeffersontown Kentucky
110 L3 Jeffersontown Kentucky
112 D5 Jeffersonville Georgia
94 B8 Jeffersonville Indiana
95 N5 Jeffersonville New York
94 D7 Jeffersonville Ohio
95 P2 Jeffersonville Vermont
101 S7 Jeffrey City Wyoming
71 C3 Jef Lio W Irian
85 E6 Jega Nigeria
28 B3 Jegindø *isld* Denmark
18 F9 Jegun France
77 G4 Jehīle Pūzak *L* Iran
28 B7 Jejsing Denmark
130 C9 Jejui Guazú, R Paraguay
52 C6 Jēkabpils U.S.S.R.
112 F6 Jekyll I Georgia
31 J5 Jelenia Góra Poland
52 B6 Jelgava U.S.S.R.
115 L8 Jellicoe Ontario
28 C5 Jelling Denmark
102 B1 Jelly California
31 L5 Jełowa Poland
27 E12 Jelöy *isld* Norway
28 C6 Jels Denmark
27 B12 Jelsa Norway
48 F2 Jelšava Czechoslovakia
69 G11 Jemaja Indonesia
22 F3 Jemappes Belgium
33 N8 Jembke W Germany
70 E1 Jembongan *isld* Sabah
85 G1 Jem, El Tunisia
22 J3 Jemelle Belgium
106 D6 Jemez *R* New Mexico
106 D6 Jemez Pueblo New Mexico
106 D6 Jemez Springs New Mexico
32 F6 Jemgum W Germany
43 D13 Jemmal Tunisia
31 J6 Jemnice Czechoslovakia
122 F8 Jemseg New Brunswick
37 M2 Jena E Germany
111 D10 Jena Louisiana
38 E7 Jenbach Austria
80 E4 Jenin Jordan
94 F9 Jenkinjones W Virginia
94 E9 Jenkins Kentucky
99 M3 Jenkins Minnesota
140 A7 Jenkins,Mt N Terr Aust
118 F8 Jenner Alberta
102 A3 Jenner California
127 O4 Jennings Antigua W I
113 D7 Jennings Florida
107 K2 Jennings Kansas
111 D11 Jennings Louisiana
107 O5 Jennings Oklahoma
117 H6 Jennings *R* Br Col
114 J4 Jenny Lind I N W Terr
139 K5 Jenolan Caves New S Wales
101 Q9 Jensen Utah
113 G10 Jensen Beach Florida
115 P5 Jensen Nunatakker *peak* Greenland
115 L4 Jens Munk I N W Terr
69 J13 Jenu Indonesia
138 F6 Jeparit Victoria
29 K8 Jeppo Finland
129 K6 Jequie Brazil
130 G5 Jequitai Brazil
129 K7 Jequitinhonha Brazil
85 D2 Jerada Morocco
69 F11 Jerantut Malaysia
85 G2 Jerba, I de Tunisia
126 G5 Jérémie Haiti
129 L6 Jeremoabo Brazil
124 H6 Jerez de García Salinas Mexico
16 C8 Jerez de la Frontera Spain
16 C6 Jerez de los Caballeros Spain
80 E6 Jericho Jordan
141 H6 Jericho Queensland
33 Q8 Jerichow E Germany
129 K4 Jericoaquara, Pta *C* Brazil
69 G14 Jerigi Sumatra
26 N5 Jerijärvi Sweden
70 B3 Jerijeh, Tg *C* Sarawak
139 H6 Jerilderie New S Wales
29 L4 Jerisjärvi *L* Finland
130 E4 Jeroaquara Brazil
103 M7 Jerome Arizona
101 L7 Jerome Idaho
120 H5 Jerome Ontario
129 H7 Jerônimo, Serra do *mts* Brazil
143 C10 Jerraymungup W Australia
9 H7 Jersey *isld* Channel Is
95 N6 Jersey City New Jersey
95 K5 Jersey Shore Pennsylvania
110 F2 Jerseyville Illinois
28 E2 Jerslev Denmark
28 C6 Jerstal Denmark
16 D4 Jerte *R* Spain
79 G5 Jerūd Syria
70 D2 Jerudong Brunei
129 K5 Jerumenha Brazil
28 E1 Jerup Denmark
80 D6 Jerusalem Israel
145 E3 Jerusalem New Zealand
136 H6 Jervais Ra N Terr Australia
139 K6 Jervis Bay New S Wales
138 E6 Jervis, C S Australia
117 M10 Jervis Inlet Br Col
140 D6 Jervois Ra N Terr Aust
33 N8 Jerxheim W Germany
36 G2 Jesberg W Germany
37 P3 Jesenice Czechoslovakia
42 F2 Jesenice Yugoslavia
31 K5 Jeseník Czechoslovakia
48 F2 Jesenské Czechoslovakia
33 Q8 Jeserig E Germany
33 R10 Jesewitz E Germany
Jesselton Sabah *see* Kota Kinabalu
27 E11 Jessheim Norway
98 H2 Jessie N Dakota
33 Q9 Jessnitz E Germany
113 F9 Jessup, L Florida
32 L6 Jesteburg W Germany
112 F6 Jesup Georgia
99 O7 Jesup Iowa
133 E4 Jesús María Argentina
124 H7 Jesús María Mexico
107 M5 Jet Oklahoma
119 Q2 Jetait Manitoba
94 J9 Jetersville Virginia
107 L3 Jetmore Kansas
37 J7 Jettingen W Germany
37 L7 Jetzendorf W Germany
22 G3 Jeumont France
32 L4 Jevenau *R* W Germany
32 L4 Jevenstedt W Germany
32 G5 Jever W Germany
48 D1 Jevíčko Czechoslovakia
27 D11 Jevnaker Norway
98 C6 Jewel Cave Nat. Mon S Dakota
99 N7 Jewell Iowa
107 M2 Jewell Kansas
100 B4 Jewell Oregon
110 H2 Jewett Illinois
94 G6 Jewett Ohio
109 L4 Jewett Texas
95 Q5 Jewett City Connecticut
75 K9 Jeypore India
46 D2 Jezerce *mt* Albania
37 P5 Jezerni *mt* Czechoslovakia
42 H4 Jezero Yugoslavia
31 M2 Jeziorak, Jezioro *L* Poland
31 M2 Jeziorany Poland
31 P1 Jeznas U.S.S.R.
31 M4 Jeżów Poland
79 F5 Jezzine Lebanon
74 F7 Jhabua India
74 G4 Jhajjar India
74 G6 Jhalawar India
74 E3 Jhang Maghiana Pakistan
74 H6 Jhansi India
75 M5 Jhapa Nepal
74 E2 Jhelum India
74 E2 Jhelum *R* Pakistan
74 F4 Jhunjhuna India
65 E3 Jiade He *R* China
67 G1 Jiading China
67 C4 Jiagui China
67 D4 Jiahe China
Jiaji *see* Qionghai
67 A2 Jiajiang China
58 E5 Jialing Jiang *R* China
65 G4 Ji'an China
67 E3 Ji'an China
65 D4 Jianchang China
65 F4 Jianchang China
67 F2 Jiande China
67 C2 Jiang'an China
67 B2 Jiangbei China
68 E1 Jiangcheng China
67 C3 Jiangdong China
67 F1 Jiangdu China
67 C6 Jianghong China
67 D4 Jianghua China
67 B2 Jiangjin China
Jiangkou *see* Fengkai
67 C3 Jiangkou China
67 D1 Jiangkou China
67 F3 Jiangle China
67 D1 Jiangling China
67 D5 Jiangmen China
58 G5 Jiangsu *prov* China
67 E3 Jiangxi *prov* China
65 B7 Jiang Xian China
67 F1 Jiangxiang China
67 G1 Jiangyin China
67 D4 Jiangyong China
67 A1 Jiangyou China
67 E4 Jianhe China
Jianjun *see* Yongshou
67 D2 Jianli China
67 E4 Jianning China
67 F3 Jian'ou China
65 D4 Jianping China
65 D5 Jianping China
67 C1 Jianshi China
67 A5 Jianshui China
58 D5 Jianyang China
67 F3 Jianyang China
65 B6 Jiaocheng China
59 J3 Jiaohe China
65 C5 Jiaohe China
65 B6 Jiaokou China
67 E4 Jiaoling China
65 E7 Jiaonan China
65 D6 Jiao Xian China
58 F4 Jiaozuo China
65 G3 Jiapigou China
58 G5 Jiashan China
67 G1 Jiashan China
57 H5 Jiashi China
65 D7 Jiawang China
65 A5 Jia Xian China
65 B7 Jia Xian China
59 H5 Jiaxing China
67 C4 Jiaya China
59 K2 Jiayin China
67 D2 Jiayu China
58 C4 Jiayuguan China
65 E6 Jiazhou Wan *B* China
77 B7 Jiban, Al Saudi Arabia
129 J7 Jibao, Serra do *mts* Brazil
126 E4 Jibaro Cuba
88 G6 Jibondo *isld* Tanzania
48 H3 Jibou Romania
67 B3 Jichang China
31 J5 Jičín Czechoslovakia
86 G1 Jiddah Saudi Arabia
65 H2 Jidong China
Jiehu *see* Yinan
26 L2 Jiekkevarre *mt* Norway
67 E5 Jieshi China
67 E5 Jieshi Wan *B* China
26 O2 Jiesjavrre *L* Norway
67 E5 Jiexi China
65 B6 Jiexiu China
143 D6 Jiggalong W Australia
100 K9 Jiggs Nevada
67 E1 Jigong Shan *mt* China
79 H4 Jihār, Wādi el *watercourse* Syria
31 J6 Jihlava Czechoslovakia
31 H6 Jihočesky *reg* Czechoslovakia
31 J6 Jihomoravský *reg* Czechoslovakia
85 F1 Jijel Algeria
48 L3 Jijia *R* Romania
86 H4 Jijiga Ethiopia
80 G3 Jijjin Jordan
17 G6 Jijona Spain
59 H2 Jilin *prov* China
65 G3 Jilin China
65 F3 Jilin Hada Ling *mt ra* China
59 H1 Jiliu He *R* China
17 G4 Jiloca *R* Spain
116 M3 Jim *R* Alaska
86 G4 Jimā Ethiopia
69 G14 Jimar Sumatra
142 F5 Jimberingga W Australia
48 F5 Jimbolia Romania
141 L8 Jimboomba Queensland
16 D8 Jimena de la Frontera Spain
124 G4 Jiménez Mexico
140 C2 Jim Jim Cr N Terr Aust
65 E6 Jimo China
65 C6 Jinan China
65 B7 Jincheng China
139 J6 Jindabyne New S Wales
37 O3 Jindřichovice Czechoslovakia
31 J6 Jindřichův Hradec Czechoslovakia
67 E2 Jing'an China
67 F1 Jingde China
67 F2 Jingdezhen China
Jingfeng *see* Hexigten Qi
65 D5 Jinghai China
65 E6 Jinghaiwei China
66 C3 Jinghe China
58 E5 Jing He *R* China
68 E2 Jinghong China
67 G1 Jingjiang China
65 B5 Jingle China
67 D1 Jingmen China
Jingping *see* Pinglu
65 G2 Jingpo Hu *L* China
65 G3 Jingshan China
67 D1 Jingshan China
58 F5 Jing Shan *mt ra* China
58 D4 Jingtai China
65 C6 Jing Xian China
67 C3 Jing Xian China
67 F1 Jing Xian China
59 H2 Jingxin China
67 A2 Jingyan China
65 A7 Jingyang China
65 G3 Jingyu China
58 D4 Jingyuan China
Jingzhou *see* Jiangling
67 F2 Jinhua China
65 C7 Jining China
65 B4 Jining Nei Monggol Zizhiqu China
88 D1 Jinja-Bugembe Uganda
67 F4 Jinjiang China
67 C3 Jinjiang China
67 E2 Jin Jiang *R* China
67 D2 Jin Jiang *R* China
65 E6 Jinjing China
67 E1 Jinkou China
67 F4 Jinlong Jiang *R* China
125 M4 Jinotega Nicaragua
125 L4 Jinotepe Nicaragua
67 C3 Jinping China
68 F1 Jinping China
Jinsha *see* Nantong
67 B3 Jinsha China
58 C6 Jinsha Jiang *R* China
Jinshan *see* Harqin Qi
67 G1 Jinshan China
67 D2 Jinshi China
67 F1 Jintan China
67 A1 Jintang China
67 C5 Jintian Shuiku *res* China
71 F5 Jintotolo *isld* Philippines
71 F5 Jintotolo Ch Philippines
59 H3 Jinxi China
67 B5 Jinxi China
67 E3 Jinxi China
67 F3 Jin Xi China
65 C5 Jin Xian China
65 E4 Jin Xian China
65 E5 Jin Xian China
67 E2 Jinxian China
65 C7 Jinxiang China
67 G3 Jinxiang China
67 C4 Jinxiu China
67 G2 Jinyun China
67 E1 Jinzhai China
65 E4 Jinzhou China
65 E5 Jinzhou Wan *B* China
128 B4 Jipijapa Ecuador
126 F4 Jiquaní Cuba
130 H5 Jiquitaia Brazil
143 F9 Jirina W Australia
65 D2 Jirin Gol China
37 P3 Jirkov Czechoslovakia
48 L5 Jirlău Romania
65 A7 Jishan China
67 C2 Jishou China
67 E3 Jishui China
79 G3 Jisr esh Shughūr Syria
16 C2 Jistredo, Sa. de *mts* Spain
143 C10 Jitarning W Australia
69 E9 Jitra Malaysia
Jiucheng *see* Wucheng
67 A1 Jiuding Shan *mt* China
58 G6 Jiujiang China
67 E2 Jiujiang China
67 D1 Jiukou China
48 H6 Jiul *R* Romania
67 E4 Jiulian Shan *mts* China
67 E2 Jiuling Shan *mt ra* China
58 C4 Jiuquan China
65 E6 Jiurongcheng China
59 J3 Jiutai China
67 C4 Jiuwan Dashan *mts* China
65 C5 Jiuwuqing China
65 C5 Jiuxincheng China
67 B4 Jiuxu China
67 F1 Jiuyuhang China
67 B4 Jiuzhou China
72 G4 Jiwā', Al *oasis* U.A.E.
77 G7 Jiwani Iran
74 B10 Jiwani Pakistan
65 H2 Jixi China
67 F1 Jixi China
65 A6 Ji Xian China
65 C6 Ji Xian China
65 C7 Ji Xian China
65 D4 Ji Xian China
65 D6 Jiyang China
65 B7 Jiyuan China
65 D5 Jiyun He *R* China
80 G7 Jiza Jordan
65 C6 Jize China
31 H5 Jizera *R* Czechoslovakia
60 G10 Jizō zaki *C* Japan
86 E1 J. Kissu *mt* Sudan
120 G1 Joab L Ontario
130 D10 Joaçaba Brazil
33 T7 Joachimsthal E Germany
130 H5 Joaíma Brazil
85 A6 Joal-Fadiout Senegal
142 E5 Joanna Spring W Australia
129 L5 Joao Camara Brazil
129 J4 João Coelho Brazil
87 B9 João de Almeid Angola
131 H4 João Maria, Albardão do Brazil
130 E10 João Paulo *R* Brazil
129 M5 João Pessoa Brazil
130 J9 João Pessoa Brazil
130 F5 João Pinheiro Brazil
111 B10 Joaquin Texas
126 F4 Jobabo Cuba
61 O9 Jōban Japan
71 G6 Jobo Pt Mindanao Philippines
20 B2 Jobourg France
102 F2 Job Pk Nevada
120 D2 Jobrin Ontario
38 F7 Jochberg Austria
16 E7 Jódar Spain
74 E5 Jodhpur India
74 D7 Jodiya Bandar India
22 H2 Jodoigne Belgium
123 S4 Joe Batt's Arm Nfld
29 O9 Joensuu Finland
106 H2 Joes Colorado
26 G6 Joeström Sweden
19 K3 Jœuf France
87 F10 Jofane Mozambique
106 E7 Joffre New Mexico
117 Q10 Joffre, Mt Br Col
61 L9 Joganji *R* Japan
75 M5 Jogbani India
65 C3 Jogdor China
52 C5 Jõgeva U.S.S.R.
122 H8 Joggins Nova Scotia
74 G3 Jogindernagar India
120 E2 Jog L Ontario
38 N7 Joglland Austria
61 K9 Jōhana Japan
32 J9 Johannaberg W Germany
102 G6 Johannesburg California
89 A1 Johannesburg S Africa
37 O3 Johanngeorgenstadt E Germany
115 M2 Johan Pen N W Terr
60 F13 Jōhen Japan
116 L3 John *R* Alaska
122 J8 John, C Nova Scotia
127 M2 John Crow Mts Jamaica
100 G5 John Day Oregon
100 E4 John Day *R* Oregon
117 Q6 John d'Or Prairie Alberta
143 F9 John Eyre Motel W Australia
113 G9 John F. Kennedy Space Center Florida
106 H3 John Martin Res Colorado
142 G3 John,Mt W Australia
15 E2 John O'Groats Scotland
146 F3 John Quincey Adams Gl Antarctica
107 P3 John Redmond Res Kansas
107 J4 Johnson Kansas
99 K9 Johnson Nebraska
94 J5 Johnsonburg Pennsylvania
95 M4 Johnson City New York
94 E10 Johnson City Tennessee
109 J5 Johnson City Texas
99 S6 Johnson Cr Wisconsin
117 G5 Johnsons Crossing Yukon Terr
127 P4 Johnsons Pt Antigua W I
112 H4 Johnsonville S Carolina
112 F4 Johnston S Carolina
8 A4 Johnston Wales
110 H4 Johnston City Illinois
15 D5 Johnstone Scotland
117 K10 Johnstone Str Br Col
88 B7 Johnston Falls Zambia
143 D9 Johnston Ls.,The W Australia
143 C8 Johnston Ra W Australia
14 E3 Johnstown Irish Rep
98 F7 Johnstown Nebraska
95 N4 Johnstown New York
94 E6 Johnstown Ohio
94 J6 Johnstown Pennsylvania
94 E9 John W Flannagan Res Virginia
61 P5 Jōhōji Japan
69 F12 Johor Malaysia
69 F12 Johor Baharo Malaysia
37 P2 Jöhstadt E Germany
52 C5 Jõhvi U.S.S.R.
18 H5 Joigny France
110 F6 Joiner Arkansas
130 E10 Joinville Brazil
19 J4 Joinville France
146 D14 Joinville I Antarctica
48 L5 Joita Romania
125 K8 Jojutla Mexico
26 N5 Jokk Sweden
26 L5 Jokkmokk Sweden
27 C10 Jokuleggi *mt* Norway
78 K2 Jolfa Iran
99 S8 Joliet Illinois
101 Q4 Joliet Montana
119 U10 Joliette N Dakota
115 M8 Joliette Quebec
142 A1 Jolimont *dist* Perth, W Aust
99 M7 Jolley Iowa
117 S3 Jolly L N W Terr
71 E7 Jolo Philippines
102 C6 Jolon California
26 B10 Jölstervatn *L* Norway
26 G7 Joma *mt* Norway
29 H11 Jomala Finland
71 F3 Jomalig *isld* Luzon Philippines
69 F12 Jombol *isld* Indonesia
66 F5 Jomda China
71 A3 Jome Indonesia
27 D13 Jomfruland *isld* Norway
52 B6 Jonava U.S.S.R.
22 F5 Jonchery-sur-Vesle France
7 E13 Jones Bank Atlantic Oc
110 F6 Jonesboro Arkansas
111 M8 Jonesboro Georgia
110 G4 Jonesboro Illinois
109 P3 Jonesboro Louisiana
95 U2 Jonesboro Maine
112 H2 Jonesboro N Carolina
100 H6 Jonesboro Oregon
112 E1 Jonesboro Tennessee
109 K4 Jonesboro Texas
116 N1 Jones Is Alaska
146 G12 Jones Mts Antarctica
95 U2 Jonesport Maine
83 M9 Jones Pt Christmas I Indian Oc
115 L2 Jones Sound N W Terr
111 F7 Jonestown Mississippi
94 B7 Jonesville Indiana
111 E10 Jonesville Louisiana
94 C5 Jonesville Michigan
112 F3 Jonesville S Carolina
94 D10 Jonesville Virginia
86 F4 Jonglei *prov* Sudan
52 B6 Joniskis U.S.S.R.
27 G14 Jönköping Sweden
27 G14 Jönköping *county* Sweden
115 M8 Jonquière Quebec
28 K4 Jönstorp Sweden
18 E7 Jonzac France
110 B4 Joplin Missouri
101 P1 Joplin Montana
110 H4 Joppa Illinois
80 B5 Joppa Israel
99 N5 Jordan Minnesota
101 T2 Jordan Montana
95 L3 Jordan New York
80 Jordan *kingdom* S W Asia
80 F1 Jordan *R* Israel/Jordan
100 H7 Jordan *R* Oregon
141 H6 Jordan *R* Queensland
129 K7 Jordânia Brazil
111 K9 Jordan L Alabama
122 G9 Jordan L Nova Scotia
48 F1 Jordanow Poland
100 H7 Jordan Valley Oregon
130 D9 Jordão, R Brazil
28 C3 Jordbro Å *R* Denmark
33 R5 Jördenstorf E Germany
27 F10 Jordet Norway
28 E6 Jordløse Denmark
28 C5 Jordrup Denmark
28 B6 Jordsand *isld* Denmark
26 P2 Jorgastak Norway
133 B8 Jorge Montt, I Chile
75 Q5 Jorhat India
32 L5 Jork W Germany
26 L6 Jörn Sweden
106 C9 Jornada del Muerto *reg* New Mexico
27 B12 Jörpeland Norway
20 E4 Jort France
85 F7 Jos Nigeria
71 G8 Jose Abad Santos Mindanao Philippines
133 C6 José de San Martín Argentina
129 J8 José dos Campos Brazil
130 C5 Joselândia Brazil
133 E5 José Maria Blanco Argentina
27 B12 Josenfjord *inlet* Norway
71 F3 Jose Pañganiban Philippines
100 J4 Joseph Idaho
100 H4 Joseph Oregon
142 G2 Joseph Bonaparte G Australia
136 F4 Joseph Bonaparte Gulf Australia
103 O7 Joseph City Arizona
115 N7 Joseph L Labrador
123 K4 Joseph Pt Anticosti I, Quebec
144 B6 Josephville New Zealand
61 M9 Jōshin-etsu Kogen Nat. Park Japan
109 K3 Joshua Texas
102 H7 Joshua Tree California
21 I6 Josnes France
36 H3 Jossatal W Germany
18 D5 Josselin France
26 E7 Jössund Nord-Tröndelag Norway
26 D8 Jössund Sör-Tröndelag Norway
26 B10 Jostedal Norway
26 B10 Jostedalsbreen *gla* Norway
48 F2 Josvafö Hungary
26 N2 Jotkajavrre Norway
27 C10 Jotunheimen *mt* Norway
79 F5 Jouaiya Lebanon
20 J4 Jouars France
20 E4 Joué-du-Bois France
21 G7 Joué les Tours France
21 C7 Joué sur Erdre France
29 N6 Joukokylä Finland
113 J12 Joulters Cays *islds* Bahamas
79 F5 Jounié Lebanon
109 J7 Jourdanton Texas
25 E3 Joure Netherlands
118 B3 Joussard Alberta
121 M3 Joutel Quebec
29 M10 Joutsa Finland
29 N5 Joutsijärvi Finland
40 D4 Joux, L.de Switzerland
20 J5 Jouy France
21 I6 Jouy-le Potier France
126 D3 Jovellanos Cuba
75 P6 Jowai India
14 B3 Joyce Country Irish Rep
117 G4 Joy, Mt Yukon Terr
60 O3 Jōzankei Japan
31 N4 Józefów Poland
77 J1 Jozjān Afghanistan
71 B3 Ju *isld* Indonesia
124 H5 Juan Aldama Mexico
65 C7 Juancheng China
141 J7 Juandah *R* Queensland
127 K2 Juan de Bolas *peak* Jamaica
114 G8 Juan de Fuca, Str. of Canada/U.S.A.
87 G11 Juan de Nova *isld* Madagascar
133 A9 Juan Fernández, Is Pacific Oc
127 N9 Juangriego Venezuela
88 G6 Juani *isld* Tanzania
128 C5 Juanjui Peru
29 N8 Juankoski Finland
44 B4 Juan les Pins France
124 E2 Juan M. Ortíz Mexico
131 B2 Juan Soldado, C.de Chile
133 B7 Juan Stuven, I Chile
133 F5 Juárez Argentina
103 J9 Juárez, Sa *ra* Mexico
129 K5 Juazeiro Brazil
130 G9 Juàzeiro do Norte Brazil
86 F5 Juba Sudan
86 H5 Juba *R* Somalia
79 F4 Jubail Lebanon
77 A6 Jubayl, Al Saudi Arabia
80 G5 Jubba Jordan
123 R5 Jubilee L Nfld
143 F8 Jubilee Lake W Australia
102 H6 Jubilee Peak California
20 E5 Jublains France
17 F5 Júcar *R* Spain
36 B1 Jüchen W Germany
124 H7 Juchipila Mexico
125 M9 Juchitán Mexico
124 H7 Juchitlán Mexico
129 K7 Jucurucú *R* Brazil
98 H3 Jud N Dakota
99 R7 Juda Wisconsin
80 B7 Judaea Israel
123 S6 Jude I Nfld
80 D2 Judeida Israel
37 L3 Judenbach E Germany
38 L7 Judenburg Austria
123 L8 Judique C Breton I, N S
101 Q2 Judith *R* Montana
101 Q2 Judith Basin *reg* Montana
101 Q3 Judith Gap Montana
98 E3 Judson N Dakota
Juegang *see* Rudong
28 E5 Juelsminde Denmark
130 H5 Juerana Brazil
128 F4 Jufari *R* Brazil
84 F4 Jufrah Oasis, Al Libya
143 E9 Jugalinna W Australia
18 D4 Jugon France
65 E4 Juhua Dao *isld* China
18 F7 Juillac France
32 F5 Juist W Germany
32 E5 Juist *isld* W Germany
129 K8 Juiz de Fora Brazil
65 D3 Jujinchang China
69 E13 Jujuhan *R* Sumatra
128 E8 Jujuy *prov* Argentina
26 L7 Juken Sweden
26 L4 Jukkasjärvi Sweden
67 D3 Jukoupu China
26 H6 Juktån *R* Sweden
128 E8 Julaca Bolivia
98 D9 Julesburg Colorado
128 E7 Julí Peru
141 F5 Julia *R* Queensland
128 D7 Juliaca Peru
141 F5 Julia Creek Queensland
100 J3 Juliaetta Idaho
102 H8 Julian California
115 P5 Julianehåb Greenland
14 E3 Julianstown Irish Rep
36 B2 Jülich W Germany
42 E2 Julijske A *mts* Yugoslavia
124 G3 Julimes Mexico
80 D2 Jūlis Israel
27 H12 Julita Sweden
140 E5 Julius L. Queensland
20 B4 Jullouville France
28 D4 Julsø *L* Denmark
65 C6 Julu China
69 C10 Julu Rayeu Sumatra
80 G8 Jumaiyil Jordan
117 P10 Jumbo Mt Br Col
21 E7 Jumelles France
22 G3 Jumet Belgium
20 G3 Jumièges France
17 G6 Jumilla Spain
75 K4 Jumla Nepal
74 G5 Jumna *R* India
74 D8 Junagadh India
65 D7 Junan China
65 D2 Jun Bulen China
124 D5 Juncal Mexico
131 D8 Juncal, L Argentina
108 H5 Junction Texas
103 M3 Junction Utah
140 C1 Junction B N Terr Australia
111 D8 Junction City Arkansas
111 M9 Junction City Georgia
107 O2 Junction City Kansas
94 C9 Junction City Kentucky
110 M4 Junction City Kentucky
100 B5 Junction City Oregon
99 R5 Junction City Wisconsin
141 G8 Jundah Queensland
65 C4 Jundu Shan *mt ra* China
117 F6 Juneau Alaska
99 S6 Juneau Wisconsin
139 J5 Junee New S Wales
113 F10 June in Winter, L Florida
102 E4 June Lake California
79 F4 Jūn el 'Akkar Lebanon
65 A5 Jungar Qi China
40 G4 Jungfrau *mt* Switzerland
40 G4 Jungfraujoch Switzerland
22 L4 Junglinster Luxembourg
100 G9 Jungo Nevada
98 H9 Juniata Nebraska
95 K6 Juniata *R* Pennsylvania
131 E5 Junin Argentina
128 D7 Junín Chile
128 C6 Junin Peru
133 C5 Junín de los Andes Argentina
94 H8 Junior W Virginia
95 T1 Junior L Maine
122 E7 Juniper New Brunswick
103 L6 Juniper Mts Arizona
102 C5 Junipero Sierra Pk California
61 O5 Jūni sho Japan
22 G5 Juniville France
116 O2 Junjik *R* Alaska
36 B3 Jünkerath W Germany
26 H5 Junkerdal Norway
67 A2 Junlian China
108 F5 Juno Texas
118 K5 Junor Sask
26 M4 Junosuando Sweden
26 J8 Junsele Sweden
67 E2 Junshan Hu *L* China
16 A5 Junto *mt* Portugal
65 A5 Juntuliang China
100 G6 Juntura Oregon
29 O6 Juntusranta Finland
29 O9 Juojärvi *L* Finland
26 N5 Juoksengi Sweden
130 H6 Juparaña, Lagoa *L* Brazil
130 D7 Jupia Brazil
130 D7 Jupia Dam Brazil
22 K2 Jupille Belgium
21 F6 Jupilles France
113 G11 Jupiter Florida
122 J4 Jupiter R Quebec
129 J8 Juquiá Brazil
86 E4 Jur *R* Sudan
15 C4 Jura Scotland
40 F3 Jura *canton* Switzerland
40 C4 Jura *dep* France
128 C2 Jurado Colombia
31 L5 Jura Krakowska *reg* Poland
130 G5 Juramento Brazil
52 B6 Jurbarkas U.S.S.R.
12 D5 Jurby I of Man U.K.
79 F8 Jurf ed Darāwīsh Jordan
142 E4 Jurgurra,R W Australia
65 E2 Jurh China
143 B9 Jurien B W Australia
48 M6 Jurilovca Romania
57 F6 Jurm Afghanistan
52 B6 Jurmala U.S.S.R.
67 F1 Jurong China
38 N9 Juršinci Yugoslavia
128 E4 Juruá Brazil
128 D5 Juruá *R* Brazil
128 G6 Juruena Brazil
129 G4 Juruti Brazil
29 J9 Jurva Finland
61 O5 Jūsan-ko *L* Japan
127 N10 Jusepín Venezuela
79 G4 Jūsiya Syria
19 J5 Jussey France
119 S8 Justice Manitoba
108 F2 Justiceburg Texas
109 K2 Justin Texas
133 D4 Justo Daract Argentina
128 E5 Jutaí Brazil
33 S9 Jüterbog E Germany
130 C8 Juti Brazil
125 L2 Juticalpa Honduras
26 J5 Jutis Sweden
Jutland *see* Jylland
26 E10 Jutulhugget *pass* Norway
29 O8 Juuka Finland
29 N10 Juva Finland
20 C5 Juvigné France
20 C4 Juvigny-le-Tertre France
20 E4 Juvigny-sous-Andaine France
20 K4 Juvisy France
28 B6 Juvre Denmark
79 H5 Juwaīf, El Syria
65 D7 Ju Xian China
65 C7 Juye China
77 F2 Jūymand Iran
40 A1 Juzennecourt France
Jye Kundo *see* Yushu
28 B4 Jylland *reg* Denmark
29 M9 Jyväskylä Finland
66 B4 K2 *mt* Kashmir/China
85 E6 Ka *R* Nigeria
102 S11 Kaaawa Hawaiian Is
89 B7 Kaaing Veld *plat* S Africa
57 A5 Kaakhka U.S.S.R.
102 R11 Kaala *peak* Hawaiian Is
26 L4 Kaalasjarvi *L* Sweden
135 U6 Kaalualu Hawaiian Is
29 N2 Kaamanen Finland
89 C7 Kaap Plato S Africa
33 O6 Kaarssen E Germany
29 N9 Kaavi Finland
48 G3 Kaba Hungary
70 G7 Kabaena *isld* Sulawesi
85 B7 Kabala Sierra Leone
86 F5 Kabalega Falls Uganda
70 G5 Kabali Sulawesi
86 E7 Kabalo Zaïre
88 A4 Kabambare Zaïre
69 D11 Kabanjahe Sumatra
85 D5 Kabara Mali
53 F11 Kabardino Balkarskaya U.S.S.R.
88 B3 Kabare Zaïre
71 F7 Kabasalang Philippines
60 C13 Kaba shima *isld* Japan
68 C3 Kabaung *R* Burma
85 F7 Kabba Nigeria
26 G3 Kabelvåg *lt ho* Norway
120 E4 Kabenung L Ontario
70 G4 Kabetan. I Sulawesi
99 O1 Kabetogama Minnesota
99 N1 Kabetogama L Minnesota
71 L8 Kabia *isld* Indonesia
120 F3 Kabinakagami *R* Ontario
86 D7 Kabinda Zaïre
70 E2 Kabinu Kalimantan
71 M9 Kabir Indonesia
57 E5 Kabla U.S.S.R.
86 C4 Kabo Cent Afr Republic
87 D8 Kabompo *R* Zambia
70 B4 Kabong Sarawak
87 E7 Kabongo Zaïre
68 C6 Kabosa I. Burma
80 D1 Kabri Israel
77 F1 Kabūd Gonbad Iran
71 E2 Kabugao Philippines
77 L2 Kābul Afghanistan
80 D2 Kābūl Israel
88 C2 Kabula Uganda
88 B7 Kabunda Zambia
87 E8 Kabunda Zaïre
86 F2 Kabushiya Sudan
88 B9 Kabwe Zambia
55 F3 Kabyrdak U.S.S.R.
55 D5 Kabyrga *R* U.S.S.R.
46 E2 Kačanik Yugoslavia
87 F8 Kachalola Zambia
116 M7 Kachemak B Alaska
100 D2 Kachess L Washington
85 F7 Kachia Nigeria
75 R5 Kachin State *prov* Burma
55 G4 Kachiry U.S.S.R.
55 C2 Kachkanar U.S.S.R.
56 G4 Kachug U.S.S.R.
78 H1 Kackar D Turkey
60 J11 Kada Japan
68 C4 Kadaingti Burma
86 F5 Kadam Mt Uganda
37 P3 Kadaň Czechoslovakia
68 D6 Kadan Kyun *isld* Burma
70 D7 Kadapongan *isld* Indonesia
48 D4 Kadarkút Hungary
71 H7 Kadatuang *isld* Indonesia
41 H2 Kadelburg W Germany
61 P13 Kadena Okinawa
143 F7 Kadgo L W Australia
72 E2 Kadhimain Iraq
74 E7 Kadi India
85 C6 Kadiana Mali
46 F3 Kadijica *mt* Yugoslavia
47 K4 Kadıköy Turkey
138 E5 Kadina S Australia
74 F9 Kadirabad India
47 J8 Kadírga Burun *C* Turkey
76 D3 Kadiri India
78 F3 Kadirli Turkey
70 G7 Kadjang Sulawesi
77 F2 Kadkan Iran
73 L6 Kadmat *isld* Lakshadweep Indian Oc
52 F5 Kadnikov U.S.S.R.
68 C4 Kado Burma
60 E13 Kadogawa Japan
98 E6 Kadoka S Dakota
68 B5 Kadonkani Burma
46 E3 Kadrifakovo Yugoslavia
86 E3 Kadugli Sudan
86 A3 Kaduna Nigeria
76 C4 Kadur India
52 E5 Kaduy U.S.S.R.
56 E5 Kadyr-Egi-Tayga, Khrebet *mts* U.S.S.R.
52 F5 Kadyy U.S.S.R.
57 H4 Kadzhi-Say U.S.S.R.
85 B5 Kaedi Mauritania
123 R5 Kaegudeck L Nfld
86 B3 Kaélé Cameroon
145 D1 Kaeo New Zealand
28 D6 Kærum Denmark
65 G5 Kaesŏng N Korea
87 D7 Käfakumba Zaïre
85 F7 Kafanchan Nigeria
85 A6 Kaffrine Senegal
47 G7 Kafiréos, Porthmós *str* Greece
47 G6 Kafirévs, Akr *C* Greece
26 N2 Kåfjord Norway
26 L2 Kåfjord *inlet* Norway
80 D5 Kafr 'Abbush Jordan
80 D5 Kafr 'Ain Jordan
79 G3 Kafr Behūm Syria
80 F6 Kafrein *R* Jordan
79 A7 Kafr el Dauwâr Egypt
80 D4 Kafr-el-Labad Jordan
79 A7 Kafr el Sheik Egypt
79 A8 Kafr el Zaiyât Egypt
80 D2 Kafr Mandā Israel
80 D4 Kafr Qud Jordan
80 D4 Kafr Ra'i Jordan
80 D4 Kafr Rumman Jordan
79 G4 Kafrun Syria
80 D5 Kafr Zibad Jordan
88 B9 Kafue Zambia
87 E8 Kafue Nat. Park Zambia
87 E7 Kafulwe Zambia
55 C4 Kaga U.S.S.R.
60 G10 Kagami Japan
57 C5 Kagan U.S.S.R.
116 G7 Kagati L Alaska
60 G11 Kagawa *prefect* Japan
120 H7 Kagawong Ontario
26 M7 Kåge Sweden
88 C2 Kagera National Park Rwanda
28 J5 Kagerup Denmark
120 C2 Kagianagami L Ontario
120 D3 Kagiano L Ontario
78 J1 Kagizman Turkey
60 D14 Kagoshima Japan
48 L5 Kagul Moldavia U.S.S.R.
48 L5 Kagul, Ozero *L* U.S.S.R.
116 L8 Kaguyak Alaska
70 D6 Kahajan *R* Kalimantan
135 O1 Kahala Pt Hawaiian Is
102 S12 Kahaluu Hawaiian Is
88 D3 Kahama Tanzania
74 C4 Kahan Pakistan
102 S11 Kahana Hawaiian Is
145 F3 Kaharoa *mt* New Zealand
71 A2 Kahatola *isld* Halmahera Indonesia
87 C7 Kahemba Zaire

102 R12 **Kahe Pt** Hawaiian Is
144 A6 **Kaherekoau Mts** New Zealand
116 M5 **Kahiltna Gl** Alaska
36 G3 **Kahl** *R* W Germany
37 M2 **Kahla** E Germany
36 F1 **Kahler-Asten** *mt* W Germany
100 G3 **Kahlotus** Washington
117 N6 **Kahntah** Br Columbia
77 E6 **Kahnuj** Iran
110 E1 **Kahoka** Missouri
61 K9 **Kahoku-gata** *L* Japan
102 V13 **Kahoolawe** *isld* Hawaiian Is
29 J2 **Kahperusvaara** *mt* Finland
135 U4 **Kahua** Hawaiian Is
135 Q1 **Kahuku** Hawaiian Is
102 S11 **Kahuku Pt** Hawaiian Is
135 T3 **Kahului** Hawaiian Is
Kahutara Pt *see* **Table Cape**
85 E7 **Kaiama** Nigeria
144 D5 **Kaiapoi** New Zealand
119 O1 **Kaiashk** *R* Ontario
103 M5 **Kaibab Plat** Arizona
60 J10 **Kaibara** Japan
103 N5 **Kaibito Plat** Arizona
66 D3 **Kaidu He** *R* China
128 G2 **Kaieteur Falls** Guyana
65 C7 **Kaifeng** China
145 D1 **Kaihu** New Zealand
67 F2 **Kaihua** China
145 E3 **Kai-Iwi** New Zealand
67 B1 **Kaijiang** China
136 G3 **Kai, Kep** *islds* Moluccas Indonesia
145 D1 **Kaikohe** New Zealand
67 B3 **Kaikou** China
144 D5 **Kaikoura** New Zealand
144 D5 **Kaikoura Range** New Zealand
75 J3 **Kailas** *mt* Xizang Zizhiqu
Kailas Range *see* **Gangdisê Shan**
36 G4 **Kailbach** W Germany
67 B3 **Kaili** China
65 E3 **Kailu** China
102 S12 **Kailua** Hawaiian Is
135 R2 **Kailua** Hawaiian Is
135 T5 **Kailua** Hawaiian Is
145 E2 **Kaimai Ra** New Zealand
46 E4 **Kaïmakchalán** *mt* Greece
136 G2 **Kaimana** W Irian
145 E3 **Kaimanawa Mts** New Zealand
144 C5 **Kaimata** New Zealand
60 D14 **Kaimon-dake** *peak* Japan
135 V5 **Kaimu** Hawaiian Is
27 N13 **Käina** U.S.S.R.
38 M7 **Kainach** *R* Austria
135 U5 **Kainaliu** Hawaiian Is
60 J11 **Kainan** Japan
47 G3 **Kainchal** *mt* Greece
57 G3 **Kainda** U.S.S.R.
68 B2 **Kaing** Burma
145 F3 **Kaingaroa Forest** New Zealand
145 F3 **Kaingaroa Plat.** New Zealand
38 J6 **Kainisch** Austria
85 E6 **Kainji Res** Nigeria
55 G3 **Kainsk-Barabinskiy** U.S.S.R.
71 H7 **Kaioba** Indonesia
145 E2 **Kaipara Flats** New Zealand
103 N4 **Kaiparowits Plat** Utah
65 D5 **Kaiping** China
67 D5 **Kaiping** China
43 C13 **Kairouan** Tunisia
38 F6 **Kaiser-Gebirge** *mts* Austria
102 E4 **Kaiser Pk** California
36 C3 **Kaisersesch** W Germany
36 D5 **Kaiserslautern** W Germany
40 G1 **Kaiserstuhl** *mt* W Germany
32 E10 **Kaiserswerth** W Germany
60 F11 **Kaita** Japan
145 D1 **Kaitaia** New Zealand
144 B7 **Kaitangata** New Zealand
70 F6 **Kai, Tanjung** *C* Sulawesi
145 F3 **Kaitawa** New Zealand
145 D4 **Kaiteriteri** New Zealand
74 G4 **Kaithal** India
145 E4 **Kaitoki** New Zealand
Kaitong *see* **Tongyu**
26 K4 **Kaitumälven** *R* Sweden
26 K4 **Kaitumj** Sweden
26 L3 **Kaivare** *mt* Sweden
145 E2 **Kaiwaka** New Zealand
71 N9 **Kaiwatu** Indonesia
102 V13 **Kaiwi Ch** Hawaiian Is
67 C1 **Kai Xian** China
67 B3 **Kaiyang** China
59 H3 **Kaiyuan** China
67 A5 **Kaiyuan** China
116 H5 **Kaiyuh Mts** Alaska
60 J11 **Kaizuka** Japan
70 E3 **Kaja** Kalimantan
29 N7 **Kajaani** Finland
141 F5 **Kajabbi** Queensland
77 J3 **Kajaki Dam** Afghanistan
71 L9 **Kajan** *isld* Indonesia
69 E11 **Kajang** Malaysia
88 F2 **Kajiado** Kenya
61 M10 **Kajikazawa** Japan
60 D14 **Kajiki** Japan
71 A2 **Kajoa** *isld* Halmahera Indonesia
86 F5 **Kajo Kaji** Sudan
71 K8 **Kajuadi** *isld* Indonesia
85 F6 **Kajuru** Nigeria
103 M9 **Kaka** Arizona
86 F3 **Kaka** Sudan
70 F3 **Kakaban** *isld* Kalimantan
119 O2 **Kakabeka Falls** Ontario
118 J1 **Kakagi L** Ontario
145 E3 **Kakahi** New Zealand
71 G7 **Kakal** *R* Mindanao Philippines
70 F5 **Kakali** Sulawesi
87 D11 **Kakamas** S Africa
88 E1 **Kakamega** Kenya
69 A8 **Kakana** Nicobar Is
144 C6 **Kakanui** New Zealand
135 T3 **Kaka Pt** Hawaiian Is
145 E3 **Kakaramea** New Zealand
85 B7 **Kakata** Liberia
145 E3 **Kakatahi** New Zealand
117 G7 **Kake** Alaska
60 F11 **Kake** Japan
42 F3 **Kake** Yugoslavia
61 M11 **Kakegawa** Japan
56 E5 **Ka-Khem** *R* U.S.S.R.
116 K7 **Kakhonak** Alaska
54 E10 **Kakhovka** U.S.S.R.
54 E10 **Kakhovskoye Vdkhr** *res* U.S.S.R.
77 F2 **Kakht** Iran
77 B5 **Kākī** Iran
76 F2 **Kakinada** India
117 P5 **Kakisa L** N W Terr
61 M8 **Kakizaki** Japan
60 H11 **Kakogawa** Japan
55 E4 **Kak, Oz** *L* U.S.S.R.
85 D7 **Kakpin** Ivory Coast
116 Q1 **Kaktovik** Alaska
61 O8 **Kakuda** Japan
61 O6 **Kakumagawa** Japan
61 O6 **Kakunodate** Japan
70 C3 **Kakus** *R* Sarawak
86 E7 **Kakuyu** Zaïre
117 O8 **Kakwa** *R* Alberta
48 F3 **Kál** Hungary
43 D13 **Kalaa Kebira** Tunisia
43 B13 **Kalaat-es-Nam** *mt* Tunisia
71 M9 **Kalabahi** Indonesia
46 E5 **Kalabáka** Greece
70 E2 **Kalaban** Sabah
138 F4 **Kalabity** S Australia
87 D8 **Kalabo** Zambia
54 N6 **Kalach** U.S.S.R.
55 F3 **Kalachinsk** U.S.S.R.
53 F9 **Kalach-na-donu** U.S.S.R.
54 N6 **Kalachskaya Vozvyshennost'** *uplands* U.S.S.R.
68 A2 **Kaladan** Burma
121 N8 **Kaladar** Ontario
70 G6 **Kaladu** *R* Sulawesi
102 V14 **Kalae** Hawaiian Is
70 G6 **Kalaena** *R* Sulawesi
68 C1 **Kalagwe** Burma
89 B4 **Kalahari Desert** Botswana
89 B6 **Kalahari Game Res** S Africa
89 B5 **Kalahari Gemsbok Nat. Park** S Africa
76 D4 **Kalahasti** India
57 F5 **Kalai-Khumb** U.S.S.R.
57 B6 **Kalai-Mor** U.S.S.R.
29 K7 **Kalajoki** Finland
29 L8 **Kalajoki** *R* Finland
58 G1 **Kalakan** U.S.S.R.
69 C11 **Kalakepen** Sumatra
135 O1 **Kalalau** Hawaiian Is
74 E1 **Kalam** Pakistan
100 C3 **Kalama** Washington
46 E7 **Kalámai** Greece
Kalamata Greece *see* **Kalámai**
94 B4 **Kalamazoo** Michigan
70 D7 **Kalambau** *isld* Indonesia
87 F7 **Kalambo Falls** Tanzania
47 F6 **Kálamos** Greece
46 D6 **Kálamos** *isld* Greece
70 E3 **Kalampising** Kalimantan
143 B9 **Kalamunda** W Australia
138 E3 **Kalamurra, L** S Australia
143 B9 **Kalannie** W Australia
29 J11 **Kalanti** Finland
71 K8 **Kalao** *isld* Indonesia
71 G7 **Kalaong** Mindanao Philippines
71 K8 **Kalaotoa** *isld* Indonesia
83 K9 **Kala Oya** *R* Sri Lanka
58 G1 **Kalar** *R* U.S.S.R.
48 L3 **Kalarash** U.S.S.R.
26 H9 **Kälarne** Sweden
83 L9 **Kal Aru** *R* Sri Lanka
70 D4 **Kalasin** Kalimantan
74 B4 **Kalat** Pakistan
77 G6 **Kalateh-Masjed** Iran
135 S2 **Kalaupapa** Hawaiian Is
53 F10 **Kalaus** *R* U.S.S.R.
46 E6 **Kalávrita** Greece
68 C2 **Kalaw** Burma
70 F5 **Kalawaranaputi** Sulawesi
83 K9 **Kalawewa** Sri Lanka
36 H3 **Kalbach** W Germany
28 N2 **Kalbak** Faeroes
143 A8 **Kalbarri** W Australia
33 O7 **Kalbe** E Germany
56 B6 **Kalbinskiy Khrebet** *mts* U.S.S.R.
55 B5 **Kaldygayty** *R* U.S.S.R.
47 K7 **Kale** Turkey
78 D1 **Kalecik** Turkey
71 H7 **Kaledupa** *isld* Indonesia
68 C5 **Kalegauk I** Burma
52 H6 **Kalegino** U.S.S.R.
88 E6 **Kalehe** Zaïre
68 B3 **Kaleindaung** *inlet* Burma
86 D6 **Kalema** Zaïre
88 B4 **Kalémié** Zaïre
32 K7 **Kalenberg** *reg* W Germany
31 L5 **Kalety** Poland
94 B2 **Kaleva** Michigan
29 P6 **Kalevala** U.S.S.R.
52 E3 **Kalgachikha** U.S.S.R.
Kalgan *see* **Zhangjiakou**
58 G3 **Kalgan** China
143 C10 **Kalgan,R** W Australia
108 F2 **Kalgary** Texas
116 M6 **Kalgin I** Alaska
143 D9 **Kalgoorlie** W Australia
46 E4 **Kalí** Greece
47 L6 **Kalı** *R* Turkey
46 E6 **Kaliakoúdha** *mt* Greece
47 J1 **Kaliakra, N** Bulgaria
70 K8 **Kalianda** Sumatra
70 O9 **Kalianget** Indonesia
55 F4 **Kalibek, Oz** *L* U.S.S.R.
71 F5 **Kalibo** Philippines
94 C6 **Kalida** Ohio
86 E6 **Kalima** Zaïre
70 **Kalimantan** Borneo
70 B4 **Kalimantan Barat** Borneo
70 D6 **Kalimantan Selatan** Kalimantan
70 C5 **Kalimantan Tengah** Kalimantan
70 E3 **Kalimantan Timur** Kalimantan
47 H8 **Kálimnos** *isld* Greece
75 N5 **Kalimpong** India
71 H7 **Kalingsusuh Tk** *B* Indonesia
52 E6 **Kalinin** U.S.S.R.
57 E5 **Kalininabad** U.S.S.R.
27 L17 **Kaliningrad** U.S.S.R.
55 C3 **Kalinino** U.S.S.R.
53 F8 **Kalininsk** U.S.S.R.
48 E7 **Kalinovik** Yugoslavia
48 M1 **Kalinovka** U.S.S.R.
55 C6 **Kalinovka** U.S.S.R.
55 D3 **Kalinovo** U.S.S.R.
70 O10 **Kalisat** Java
101 L1 **Kalispell** Montana
31 L4 **Kalisz** Poland
53 F9 **Kalitva** *R* U.S.S.R.
88 C4 **Kaliua** Tanzania
26 N6 **Kalix** Sweden
26 N5 **Kalix älv** *R* Sweden
26 L4 **Kalixfors** Sweden
74 G3 **Kalka** India
141 G2 **Kalkah** Queensland
47 K8 **Kalkan** Turkey
25 F5 **Kalkar** W Germany
94 B2 **Kalkaska** Michigan
33 T8 **Kalkberge** E Germany
87 C10 **Kalkfeld** Namibia
87 D10 **Kalkfontein** Botswana
33 O5 **Kalkhorst** E Germany
47 J5 **Kalkım** Turkey
89 A5 **Kalk Plateau** Namibia
83 L10 **Kalkudah** Sri Lanka
138 D2 **Kallakoopah** *R* S Australia
52 C5 **Kallaste** U.S.S.R.
29 N9 **Kallavesi** *L* Finland
33 O7 **Kallehne** E Germany
32 H10 **Kallenhardt** W Germany
32 J8 **Kalletal** W Germany
37 P2 **Kallich** Czechoslovakia
47 J8 **Kallidhiés** Rhodes Greece
80 F7 **Kallirhoe Hot Sp** Jordan
46 D3 **Kallmet** Albania
37 M5 **Kallmünz** W Germany
47 H5 **Kalloní** Greece
47 H5 **Kallonís Kólpos** Greece
26 F8 **Kallsjön** Sweden
29 O5 **Kallunki** Finland
28 N1 **Kallur** Faeroes
27 H15 **Kalmar** Sweden
27 H14 **Kalmar** *county* Sweden
27 H15 **Kalmarsund** *chan* Sweden
36 E5 **Kalmit** *mt* W Germany
53 E10 **Kal'mius** U.S.S.R.
22 H1 **Kalmthout** Belgium
76 E7 **Kalmunai** Sri Lanka
55 B6 **Kalmykovo** U.S.S.R.
53 G9 **Kalmytskaya A.S.S.R** U.S.S.R.
48 E4 **Kalocsa** Hungary
47 G2 **Kalofer** Bulgaria
135 S3 **Kalohi Ch** Hawaiian Is
79 C3 **Kalokhorio** Cyprus
74 E7 **Kalol** India
70 G5 **Kalolio** Sulawesi
87 E9 **Kalomo** Zambia
47 F4 **Kalón** Greece
99 P8 **Kalona** Iowa
117 K9 **Kalone Peak** Br Col
71 F3 **Kalongkooan** *isld* Luzon Philippines
71 F3 **Kalotkot** *isld* Luzon Philippines
28 E4 **Kalø Vig** *B* Denmark
47 G2 **Kaloyanovc** Bulgaria
73 L6 **Kalpeni I** Lakshadweep Indian Oc
74 H5 **Kalpi** India
57 J4 **Kalpin** China
83 J9 **Kalpitiya** Sri Lanka
28 E5 **Kalsenakke** Denmark
77 E1 **Kāl-Shūr, Rūd-e** *R* Iran
28 N1 **Kalsø** *isld* Faeroes
116 H4 **Kaltag** Alaska
56 C4 **Kaltan** U.S.S.R.
41 M3 **Kalte Berg** *mt* Austria
37 M4 **Kaltenbrunn** W Germany
32 L5 **Kaltenkirchen** W Germany
37 J2 **Kaltennordheim** E Germany
37 J2 **Kaltensundheim** E Germany
54 H2 **Kaluga** U.S.S.R.
83 K11 **Kalu Ganga** *R* Sri Lanka
70 E7 **Kalukalukuang** *isld* Indonesia
70 D3 **Kalulong, Bt** *mt* Sarawak
87 E8 **Kalulushi** Zambia
142 F2 **Kalumburu** W Australia
28 G5 **Kalundborg** Denmark
28 F5 **Kalundborg Fjord** *inlet* Denmark
88 D6 **Kalungu** *R* Zambia
88 B6 **Kalungwishi** *R* Zambia
70 E1 **Kalupis Falls** Sabah
48 J1 **Kalush** U.S.S.R.
31 N3 **Kałuszyn** Poland
83 J11 **Kalutara** Sri Lanka
70 G6 **Kaluwadja** Sulawesi
31 O1 **Kalvariya** U.S.S.R.
28 J6 **Kalvehave** Denmark
29 K8 **Kälviä** Finland
29 N10 **Kalvitsa** Finland
29 L10 **Kalvola** Finland
28 B6 **Kalvslund** Denmark
38 L7 **Kalwang** Austria
55 C1 **Kal'ya** U.S.S.R.
74 E9 **Kalyan** India
76 C3 **Kalyandrug** India
74 G10 **Kalyani** India
68 B3 **Kama** Burma
55 G3 **Kama** Novosibirsk U.S.S.R.
55 D1 **Kama** Sverdlovsk U.S.S.R.
52 H5 **Kama** *R* U.S.S.R.
86 B1 **Kamada** Niger
60 E13 **Kamae** Japan
61 P6 **Kamaishi** Japan
61 N13 **Kama iwa** *islds* Iwo Jima Japan
135 S2 **Kamakou** *peak* Hawaiian Is
61 N10 **Kamakura** Japan
70 O9 **Kamal** Indonesia
74 E3 **Kamalia** Pakistan
135 S3 **Kamalo** Hawaiian Is
85 B7 **Kamalu** Sierra Leone
68 C4 **Kamamaung** Burma
78 D2 **Kaman** Turkey
56 F2 **Kamanga** *R* U.S.S.R.
87 D8 **Kamapanda** Zambia
72 E5 **Kamarān** *isld* S Yemen
77 K2 **Kamard** *reg* Afghanistan
74 H9 **Kamareddi** India
75 N7 **Kamarhati** India
74 B9 **Kamarod** Pakistan
101 O9 **Kamas** Utah
87 E9 **Kamativi** Zimbabwe
119 P2 **Kamatsi L** Sask
60 H11 **Kamatsushima** Japan
143 D9 **Kambalda** W Australia
52 G1 **Kambal'nitskiye Koshki, Ova** *islds* U.S.S.R.
76 C6 **Kambam** India
69 E13 **Kambang** Sumatra
70 M9 **Kambangan** *isld* Java
52 H6 **Kambarka** U.S.S.R.
85 B7 **Kambia** Sierra Leone
83 M8 **Kambing** *isld* Cocos Is Indian Oc
65 H4 **Kambo Ho** *mt* N Korea
70 F6 **Kambuno** *mt* Sulawesi
51 Q3 **Kamchatka Pen** U.S.S.R.
51 Q3 **Kamchatskaya Oblast'** *prov* U.S.S.R.
47 J1 **Kamchiya** *R* Bulgaria
52 F4 **Kamchuga** U.S.S.R.
61 N8 **Kameda** Japan
100 G4 **Kamela** Oregon
32 G9 **Kamen** W Germany
52 D6 **Kamenets** U.S.S.R.
48 K2 **Kamenets Podolskiy** U.S.S.R.
46 D4 **Kamenicë** Albania
42 F4 **Kamenjak. Rt** *C* Yugoslavia
52 F2 **Kamenka** U.S.S.R.
56 E2 **Kamenka** *R* U.S.S.R.
54 F9 **Kamenka-Dneprovskaya** U.S.S.R.
56 B4 **Kamen'na-Obi** U.S.S.R.
52 D3 **Kamennoye, Oz** *L* U.S.S.R.
47 J2 **Kameno** Bulgaria
54 M9 **Kamenolomni** U.S.S.R.
87 D8 **Kamenongue** Angola
59 K3 **Kamen Rybolov** U.S.S.R.
56 G5 **Kamensk** U.S.S.R.
55 E3 **Kamenskoye** U.S.S.R.
53 F9 **Kamensk-Shakhtinskiy** U.S.S.R.
55 D3 **Kamensk-Ural'skiy** U.S.S.R.
31 O3 **Kamenyuki** U.S.S.R.
30 H4 **Kamenz** E Germany
61 J10 **Kameoko** Japan
12 C2 **Kames** Scotland
54 N1 **Kameshkovo** U.S.S.R.
74 H3 **Kamet** *mt* India/Xizang Zizhiqu
61 K11 **Kameyama** Japan
100 J3 **Kamiah** Idaho
31 K2 **Kamien** Poland
31 J5 **Kamienna Góra** Poland
31 H2 **Kamień Pomorski** Poland
31 L4 **Kamieńsk** Poland
87 C12 **Kamieskroon** S Africa
89 A8 **Kamies Sektor Berg** *mt* S Africa
60 Q2 **Kami-Furano** Japan
60 Q2 **Kamikawa** *prefect* Japan
60 C14 **Kami koshiki jima** *isld* Japan
140 F4 **Kamileroi** Queensland
114 J5 **Kamilukuak L** N W Terr
87 D7 **Kamina** Zaïre
115 K5 **Kaminak L** N W Terr
99 R1 **Kaministikwia** Ontario
60 C11 **Kami no-shima** *isld* Japan
115 K5 **Kaminuriak L** N W Terr
61 L9 **Kamioka** Japan
116 L7 **Kamishak B** Alaska
60 R2 **Kami-Shihoro** Japan
88 B3 **Kamituga** Zaïre
61 O13 **Kamiyama jima** *isld* Okinawa
60 R1 **Kami-Yūbetsu** Japan
57 F3 **Kamkaly** U.S.S.R.
117 N10 **Kamloops** Br Col
29 P7 **Kammenoye, Oz** *L* U.S.S.R.
60 E12 **Kammon Kaikyō** *str* Japan
60 D12 **Kammon Tunnels** Japan
60 J10 **Kammuri shima** *isld* Japan
60 F11 **Kammuri-yama** *mt* Japan
42 F2 **Kamnik** Yugoslavia
61 M8 **Kamo** Japan
145 E1 **Kamo** New Zealand
78 K1 **Kamo** U.S.S.R.
56 E1 **Kamo** *R* U.S.S.R.
128 G3 **Kamoa Mts** Guyana
60 O2 **Kamoenai** Japan
60 H11 **Kamojima** Japan
122 C6 **Kamouraska** Quebec
38 N4 **Kamp** *R* Austria
69 G13 **Kampa** Indonesia
86 F5 **Kampala** Uganda
69 E12 **Kampar** *R* Sumatra
36 D3 **Kamp-Bornhofen** W Germany
25 E3 **Kampen** Netherlands
28 A7 **Kampen** W Germany
86 E6 **Kampene** Zaïre
22 H2 **Kampenhout** Belgium
38 M5 **Kamp, Gr** *R* Austria
68 D4 **Kamphaeng Phet** Thailand
88 B6 **Kampinda** Zambia
88 B7 **Kampolombo, L** Zambia
68 G7 **Kampot** Cambodia
74 H8 **Kamptee** India
85 D6 **Kampti** Upper Volta
Kampuchea *see* **Cambodia**
Kampuchea *rep see* **Cambodia**
70 C6 **Kampungtengah** Kalimantan
99 N7 **Kamrar** Iowa
119 Q7 **Kamsack** Sask
52 G6 **Kamskoye Ust'ye** U.S.S.R.
119 P2 **Kamuchawie L** Sask
60 Q3 **Kamui-dake** *mt* Japan
46 E4 **Kamvoúnia, Óri** *mts* Greece
53 G8 **Kamyshin** U.S.S.R.
55 D3 **Kamyshlov** U.S.S.R.
55 D5 **Kamyshnyy** U.S.S.R.
54 H9 **Kamysh-Zarya** U.S.S.R.
68 B1 **Kan** Burma
85 G6 **Kan** Nigeria
56 D3 **Kan** *R* U.S.S.R.
89 E2 **Kana** *R* Zimbabwe
115 M7 **Kanaaupscow** Quebec
103 M4 **Kanab** Utah
103 M5 **Kanab Cr** Arizona
70 C3 **Kana, Bt** *mt* Sarawak
61 O5 **Kanagi** Japan
42 F2 **Kanal** Yugoslavia
46 F5 **Kanália** Greece
69 A9 **Kanalla** Nicobar Is
70 G6 **Kanan** Sulawesi
118 C8 **Kananaskis L** Alberta
86 D7 **Kananga** Zaïre
55 C4 **Kananikol'skoye** U.S.S.R.
103 L4 **Kanarraville** Utah
52 G6 **Kanash** U.S.S.R.
47 F5 **Kanastraion, Ákr** *C* Greece
116 K8 **Kanatak** Alaska
52 H4 **Kanava** U.S.S.R.
99 N7 **Kanawha** Iowa
109 M2 **Kanawha** Texas
94 E8 **Kanawha** *R* W Virginia
94 F7 **Kanawha, Little** *R* W Virginia
61 M11 **Kanaya** Japan
61 K9 **Kanazawa** Japan
61 K9 **Kanazu** Japan
75 Q7 **Kanbalu** Burma
68 D5 **Kanchanaburi** Thailand
76 D4 **Kanchipuram** India
60 D12 **Kanda** Japan
74 B4 **Kanda** Pakistan
77 J4 **Kandahar** Afghanistan
119 N7 **Kandahar** Sask
52 D2 **Kandalaksha** U.S.S.R.
52 D2 **Kandalakshskaya Guba** *B* U.S.S.R.
69 C11 **Kandang** Sumatra
70 D6 **Kandangan** Kalimantan
47 F9 **Kándanos** Crete **Greece**
52 B6 **Kandava** U.S.S.R.
137 Q5 **Kandavu** *isld* Fiji
85 E6 **Kandé** Togo
36 E5 **Kandel** W Germany
40 G2 **Kandern** W Germany
28 E1 **Kandestederne** Denmark
74 C4 **Kandhkot** Pakistan
85 E6 **Kandi** Benin
76 D2 **Kandi** India
77 K5 **Kandi** Pakistan
116 R4 **Kandik** *R* Alaska
47 L3 **Kandıra** Turkey
70 G4 **Kandi, Tg** *C* Sulawesi
139 J5 **Kandos** New S Wales
87 H11 **Kandreho** Madagascar
55 B4 **Kandry** U.S.S.R.
76 D3 **Kandukur** India
83 K10 **Kandy** Sri Lanka
110 F2 **Kane** Illinois
94 J5 **Kane** Pennsylvania
101 R5 **Kane** Wyoming
115 M2 **Kane Basin** Canada/Greenland
116 G7 **Kanektok** *R* Alaska
86 C3 **Kanem** *dist* Chad
102 S12 **Kaneohe** Hawaiian Is
102 S12 **Kaneohe Bay** Hawaiian Is
54 C7 **Kanev** U.S.S.R.
52 E2 **Kanevka** U.S.S.R.
61 O7 **Kaneyama** Japan
42 F3 **Kanfanar** Yugoslavia
87 D10 **Kang** Botswana
85 C6 **Kangaba** Mali
78 F2 **Kangal** Turkey
115 O4 **Kangâmiut** Greenland
77 C6 **Kangan** Iran
69 E9 **Kangar** Malaysia
138 D6 **Kangaroo I** S Australia
140 E4 **Kangaroo Pt** Queensland
29 L7 **Kangas** Finland
29 N9 **Kangaslampi** Finland
29 M9 **Kangasniemi** Finland
115 O4 **Kangâtsiaq** Greenland
77 A2 **Kangāvar** Iran
48 M4 **Kangaz** U.S.S.R.
65 C4 **Kangbao** China
75 N5 **Kangchenjunga** *mt* Nepal/India
58 D5 **Kangding** China
70 P9 **Kangean** *isld* Indonesia
115 N4 **Kangeeak Pt** N W Terr
115 Q4 **Kangerdlugssuaq** *inlet* Greenland
115 Q4 **Kangerdlugssvatsiaq** *inlet* Greenland
86 G5 **Kangetet** Kenya
59 J3 **Kanggye** N Korea
65 B5 **Kangjiahui** China
65 G1 **Kangjinjing** China
59 J4 **Kangnŭng** S Korea
86 B5 **Kango** Gabon
61 N13 **Kangoku-iwa** *islds* Iwo Jima Japan
26 N4 **Kangos** Sweden
65 F3 **Kangping** China
71 E8 **Kang Tipayan Dakula** *isld* Philippines
57 E5 **Kangurt** U.S.S.R.
Kan-hsien *see* **Ganzhou**
68 B1 **Kani** Burma
87 D7 **Kaniama** Zaïre
57 F4 **Kanibadam** U.S.S.R.
144 C5 **Kaniere** New Zealand
144 C5 **Kaniere, L** New Zealand
76 D3 **Kanigiri** India
52 F1 **Kanin Nos, Mys** *C* U.S.S.R.
52 F1 **Kanin, Poluostrov** *pen* U.S.S.R.
52 F1 **Kaninskiy Bereg** *coast* U.S.S.R.
61 O5 **Kanita** Japan
26 N5 **Kaniulasjärvi** Sweden
138 F6 **Kaniva** Victoria
48 F4 **Kanjiža** Yugoslavia
29 J10 **Kankaanpää** Finland
99 S8 **Kankakee** *R* Illinois
85 C6 **Kankan** Guinea
75 J8 **Kanker** India
83 J8 **Kankesanturai** Sri Lanka
29 L4 **Kankonen** Finland
74 E6 **Kankroli** India
68 D7 **Kanmaw Kyun** *isld* Burma
56 D5 **Kanmegirskiy Khrebet** *mts* U.S.S.R.
27 G15 **Kånna** Sweden
112 G2 **Kannapolis** N Carolina
61 P13 **Kanna-zaki** *C* Okinawa
22 K2 **Kanne** Belgium
74 G7 **Kannod** India
29 L9 **Kannonkoski** Finland
29 K8 **Kannus** Finland
60 E11 **Kano** Japan
85 F6 **Kano** Nigeria
71 J6 **Kano** *isld* Indonesia
107 K2 **Kanona** Kansas
55 G5 **Kanonerka** U.S.S.R.
60 G11 **Kanonji** Japan
126 B2 **Kanon, Pt** Curaçao
107 M3 **Kanopolis** Kansas
103 M3 **Kanosh** Utah
70 C3 **Kanowit** Sarawak
60 D14 **Kanoya** Japan
74 J5 **Kanpur** India
99 T10 **Kansas** Illinois
107 Q5 **Kansas** Oklahoma
107 P2 **Kansas** *R* Kansas
107 K3 **Kansas** *state* U.S.A.
107 Q2 **Kansas City** Kansas
110 B2 **Kansas City** Missouri
67 E4 **Kanshi** China
56 E3 **Kansk** U.S.S.R.
56 E4 **Kanskoye Belogor'ye** *mts* U.S.S.R.
88 A5 **Kansonge** Zaïre
Kansu *prov see* **Gansu**
57 G3 **Kant** U.S.S.R.
29 N9 **Kantala** Finland
68 G5 **Kantaralak** Thailand
85 E6 **Kantchari** Upper Volta
116 M4 **Kantishna** *R* Alaska
61 M10 **Kanto sanchi** *mts* Japan
68 C2 **Kantulong** Burma
14 C4 **Kanturk** Irish Rep
77 J5 **Kanuk** Afghanistan
102 S11 **Kanuku** Hawaiian Is
128 G3 **Kanuku Mts** Guyana
61 N9 **Kanuma** Japan
87 C11 **Kanus** Namibia
116 M3 **Kanuti** *R* Alaska
89 D5 **Kanye** Botswana
68 B3 **Kanyinngu** Burma
68 C3 **Kanyutkwin** Burma
38 J8 **Kanzel** *mt* Austria
87 E8 **Kanzenze** Zaïre
137 R5 **Kao** *isld* Tonga
87 B9 **Kaoko Veld** *reg* Namibia
85 A6 **Kaolack** Senegal
47 J1 **Kaolinovo** Bulgaria
87 D8 **Kaoma** Zambia
65 F2 **Kaoshan** China
102 V13 **Kapaa** Hawaiian Is
102 V13 **Kapaau** Hawaiian Is
74 E7 **Kapadvanj** India
57 J2 **Kapal** U.S.S.R.
71 O9 **Kapala** *isld* Indonesia
71 M9 **Kapan** Timor Indonesia
87 D7 **Kapanga** Zaïre
145 E3 **Kapara** New Zealand
87 F7 **Kapatu** Zambia
66 B3 **Kapchagay** U.S.S.R.
57 H3 **Kapchagayskoye Vdkhr.** *res* U.S.S.R.
22 G1 **Kapellen** Belgium
25 F5 **Kapellen** W Germany
86 G5 **Kapenguria** Kenya
38 M7 **Kapfenberg** Austria
47 J4 **Kapıdaği Yar** *pen* Turkey
70 G5 **Kapinju, Tg** *C* Sulawesi
87 E8 **Kapiri Mposhi** Zambia
77 L2 **Kāpīsā** Afghanistan
115 L7 **Kapiskau** Ontario
70 C4 **Kapit** Sarawak
145 E4 **Kapiti I** New Zealand
111 D11 **Kaplan** Louisiana
31 H7 **Kaplice** Czechoslovakia
69 D8 **Kapoe** Thailand
86 F5 **Kapoeta** Sudan
135 V5 **Kapoho** Hawaiian Is
145 E3 **Kaponga** New Zealand
70 F7 **Kapoposang** *isld* Indonesia
48 E4 **Kapos** *R* Hungary
48 D4 **Kaposvár** Hungary
71 C3 **Kapotjol** W Irian
74 B10 **Kappar** Pakistan
28 G7 **Kappel** Denmark
36 C3 **Kappel** W Germany
28 D7 **Kappeln** W Germany
36 E6 **Kappelrodeck** W Germany
27 K14 **Kappelshamn** *isld* Gotland Sweden
41 M3 **Kappl** Austria
38 G7 **Kaprun** Austria
31 O1 **Kapsukas** U.S.S.R.
88 C9 **Kapsuku** *mt* Zimbabwe
70 B4 **Kapuas** *R* Kalimantan
70 D5 **Kapuas** *R* Kalimantan
70 C4 **Kapuas Hulu, Peg** Kalimantan
138 E5 **Kapunda** S Australia
145 E3 **Kapuni** New Zealand
74 F3 **Kapurthala** India
120 H3 **Kapuskasing** Ontario
120 H4 **Kapuskasing** *R* Ontario
139 K4 **Kaputar** *mt* New S Wales
48 D3 **Kapuvár** Hungary
56 H4 **Kapylyushi, Oz** *L* U.S.S.R.
78 G2 **Kara** *R* Turkey
57 J1 **Karaaul** U.S.S.R.
57 G3 **Kara-Balty** U.S.S.R.
54 K1 **Karabanovo** U.S.S.R.
57 H2 **Karabas** U.S.S.R.
57 C5 **Karabekaul** U.S.S.R.
47 J4 **Karabiga** Turkey
57 C6 **Karabil', Vozvyshennost'** *uplands* U.S.S.R.
78 D1 **Karabuk** Turkey
46 C4 **Karaburun** Albania
47 H6 **Karaburun** Turkey
47 H6 **Kara Burun** *C* Turkey
55 D6 **Karabutak** U.S.S.R.
47 J4 **Karacabey** Turkey
47 J3 **Karacaköy** Turkey
47 J3 **Karacaoğlan** Turkey
47 K7 **Karacasu** Turkey
53 F11 **Karachayevo-Cherkesskaya Aut. Obl.** U.S.S.R.
54 F3 **Karachev** U.S.S.R.
74 B6 **Karachi** Pakistan
76 B2 **Karad** India
47 K3 **Karadeniz Boğazı** *str* Turkey
55 F2 **Karagach** U.S.S.R.
50 G3 **Karaganda** U.S.S.R.
50 G4 **Karagayly** U.S.S.R.
51 Q4 **Karaginskiy, Ostrova** *islds* U.S.S.R.
47 K8 **Kara Göl** *L* Turkey
47 K6 **Karahalh** Turkey
47 J7 **Karahayıt** Turkey
55 C3 **Karaidel'** U.S.S.R.
Kara Irtysh *R see* **Ertix He**
83 J9 **Karaitivu** Sri Lanka
77 B2 **Karaj** Iran
79 F7 **Karak** Jordan
47 H6 **Karaka Burun** *C* Turkey
57 A3 **Karakalpakskaya A.S.S.R** *prov* U.S.S.R.
57 C2 **Karaketken** U.S.S.R.
143 B9 **Karakin Ls** W Australia
57 E2 **Karakoin, Ozero** *L* U.S.S.R.
57 H4 **Karakolka** U.S.S.R.
74 F1 **Karakoram** *ra* Kashmir
74 G1 **Karakoram Pass** Kashmir
85 B5 **Karakoro** *R* Mauritania/Mali
58 D2 **Karakorum** Mongolia
55 G5 **Karakuduk** U.S.S.R.
55 F4 **Kara-Kuga** U.S.S.R.
57 C5 **Karakul'** U.S.S.R.
57 G4 **Kara-Kul'dzha** U.S.S.R.
52 H6 **Karakulino** U.S.S.R.
57 G5 **Kara-Kul', Ozero** *L* U.S.S.R.
55 D4 **Karakul'skoye** U.S.S.R.
57 C5 **Karakumskiy Kanal** U.S.S.R.
57 A5 **Karakumy, Peski** *des* U.S.S.R.
38 M8 **Karalpe** *mts* Austria
143 C7 **Karalundi** W Australia
70 F6 **Karam** *R* Sulawesi
80 F6 **Karama** Jordan
47 K7 **Karaman** Turkey
47 K7 **Karamanlı** Turkey
66 C2 **Karamay** China
70 E6 **Karambu** Kalimantan
145 D4 **Karamea** New Zealand
70 D7 **Karamian** *isld* Indonesia
47 L6 **Karamık Gölü** *L* Turkey
66 C4 **Karamiran He** *R* China
66 D4 **Karamiran Shankou** *pass* China
86 F5 **Karamoja** *dist* Uganda
47 K4 **Karamürsel** Turkey
78 L4 **Karand** Iran
69 G14 **Karangagung** Sumatra
144 B5 **Karangarua R** New Zealand
70 P10 **Karangasem** Indonesia
70 M9 **Karangboto Tg** *C* Java
70 F7 **Karang Bril** Indonesia
70 F5 **Karang, Tg** *C* Sulawesi
74 G8 **Karanja** India
47 J7 **Karaova** Turkey
57 D3 **Karaozek** U.S.S.R.
47 J1 **Karapelit** Bulgaria
78 D3 **Karapinar** Turkey
145 E2 **Karapiro** New Zealand
66 C4 **Karasay** China
57 J4 **Karasay** U.S.S.R.
89 A7 **Karasburg** Namibia
147 N12 **Kara Sea** Arctic Oc
55 G5 **Karashoky** U.S.S.R.
26 O2 **Karasjok** Norway
26 O2 **Karasjokka** *R* Norway
55 G5 **Karasor** U.S.S.R.
55 D5 **Karasu** Kustanay U.S.S.R.
55 F4 **Karasu** Makinsk U.S.S.R.
47 L3 **Karasu** Turkey
55 G4 **Karasuk** U.S.S.R.
56 B4 **Karasuk** *R* U.S.S.R.
61 O9 **Karasuyama** Japan
55 E2 **Karas'ye, Oz** *L* U.S.S.R.
57 H2 **Karatal** *R* U.S.S.R.
78 E3 **Karatas** Turkey
57 F3 **Kara Tau** U.S.S.R.
68 D7 **Karathuri** Burma
26 K5 **Karatjaur** *L* Sweden
55 B6 **Karatobe** U.S.S.R.
57 B2 **Karatobe, Mys** *C* U.S.S.R.
55 D5 **Karatomarskoye Vodokhranilishche** *res* U.S.S.R.
60 C12 **Karatsu** Japan
55 E6 **Karaturgay** *R* U.S.S.R.
57 A2 **Karatyup, Poluostrov** *pen* U.S.S.R.
Karaul *see* **Qongkol**
50 H1 **Karaul** U.S.S.R.
57 H4 **Karaultëbë** U.S.S.R.
60 D14 **Karauni** Japan
57 A3 **Kara-uzyak** U.S.S.R.
46 E5 **Karáva** *mt* Greece
57 F4 **Karavan** U.S.S.R.
46 C4 **Karavastas, Kënet'e** Albania
79 C4 **Karavostasi** Cyprus
70 L9 **Karawang** Java
70 L8 **Karawang Tg.** *cape* Java
38 K8 **Karawanken** *mt* Austria
57 F1 **Karazhal** U.S.S.R.
57 G2 **Karazhingil** U.S.S.R.
78 J5 **Karbala** Iraq
36 F3 **Karben** W Germany
26 H10 **Kårböle** Sweden
33 Q6 **Karbow-Vietlübbe** E Germany
28 B3 **Karby** Denmark
48 F3 **Karcag** Hungary
46 E8 **Kardhamíla** Greece
47 H6 **Kardhámila** Greece
46 E5 **Kardhítsa** Greece
26 N5 **Kardis** Sweden
52 B5 **Kärdla** U.S.S.R.
138 B2 **Karee** N Terr Australia
52 D3 **Karelskaya** *A.S.S.R.* U.S.S.R.
52 D3 **Karel'skaya Masel'ga** U.S.S.R.
87 F7 **Karema** Tanzania
76 G4 **Karen** Andaman Is
68 C3 **Karen State** Burma
52 J4 **Karepino** U.S.S.R.
85 C4 **Karet** Mauritania
145 F2 **Karewa I** New Zealand
57 G1 **Kargaly** U.S.S.R.
55 D3 **Kargapolye** U.S.S.R.
56 B3 **Kargat** *R* U.S.S.R.
Karghalik *see* **Yecheng**
52 E4 **Kargopol'** U.S.S.R.
33 R6 **Kargow** E Germany
31 J3 **Kargowa** Poland
85 G6 **Kargueri** Niger
117 G8 **Karheen** Alaska
29 M11 **Karhula** Finland
88 B10 **Kariba** Zimbabwe
88 B10 **Kariba Dam** Zimbabwe/Zambia
88 B10 **Kariba,L** Zimbabwe/Zambia
60 N3 **Kariba yama** *mt* Japan
87 C10 **Karibib** Namibia
89 C9 **Kariega** *watercourse* S Africa
29 M2 **Karigasniemi** Finland
29 J9 **Karijoki** Finland
76 D5 **Karikal** India
145 D1 **Karikari, C** New Zealand
86 F2 **Karima** Sudan
75 P6 **Karimganj** India
74 H9 **Karimnagar** India
70 N8 **Karimundjawa** *isld* Indonesia
70 N8 **Karimundjawa, Pulau** **Pulau** *islds* Indonesia
86 A1 **Karin** Somalia
145 E3 **Karioi** New Zealand
145 E2 **Karioi** *mt* New Zealand
29 K11 **Karis** Finland
28 J6 **Karise** Denmark
88 E6 **Karisimbi. Mt** Zaïre
47 G6 **Káristos** Greece
144 C6 **Karitane** New Zealand
76 B4 **Karkal** India
136 K2 **Karkar** *isld* Papua New Guinea
57 H1 **Karkaralinsk** U.S.S.R.
77 F7 **Kārkīn Dar** Iran
29 L11 **Karkkila** Finland
29 L11 **Kärkölä** Finland
Karlá *L see* **Voïvi'ïs** *L*
54 G5 **Karla Libknekhta** U.S.S.R.
57 G6 **Karla Marksa, Pik** *mt* U.S.S.R.
28 F4 **Karlby** Denmark
26 R1 **Karlebotn** Norway
28 J7 **Karleby** Denmark
31 J1 **Karlino** Poland
37 O2 **Karl-Marx-Stadt** E Germany
42 G4 **Karlobag** Yugoslavia
54 G7 **Karlovka** U.S.S.R.
47 G2 **Karlovo** Bulgaria
37 O3 **Karlovy Vary** Czechoslovakia
26 K8 **Karlsbäck** Sweden
36 E6 **Karlsbad** W Germany
29 K6 **Karlsberg** Sweden
27 G13 **Karlsborg** Sweden
37 L7 **Karlsfeld** W Germany
32 K9 **Karlshafen** W Germany
27 G15 **Karlshamn** Sweden
27 G12 **Karlskoga** Sweden
27 H15 **Karlskrona** Sweden
26 L1 **Karlsöy** Norway
98 F1 **Karlsruhe** N Dakota
36 E5 **Karlsruhe** W Germany
98 K1 **Karlstad** Minnesota
27 F12 **Karlstad** Sweden
36 H4 **Karlstadt** W Germany
116 K8 **Karluk L** Alaska
57 D5 **Karlyuk** U.S.S.R.
76 B1 **Karmala** India
52 E6 **Karmanovo** U.S.S.R.
80 C2 **Karmel, Cape** Israel
80 E2 **Karmi'el** Israel
80 B7 **Karmiyya** Israel
27 A12 **Karmöy** *isld* Norway
109 N3 **Karnack** Texas
110 H4 **Karnak** Illinois
74 G4 **Karnal** India
76 B3 **Karnataka** *prov* India
109 K7 **Karnes City** Texas
38 G8 **Karnische Alpen** *mts* Austria
47 H2 **Karnobat** Bulgaria
27 E13 **Kärnsj** *L* Sweden
38 H8 **Kärnten** Austria
87 E9 **Karoi** Zimbabwe
77 H2 **Karokh** Afghanistan
68 C5 **Karokpi** Burma
138 E4 **Karolta** S Australia
71 K8 **Karompa** *isld* Indonesia
128 G3 **Karona Fall** Guyana
88 D6 **Karonga** Malawi
143 D9 **Karonie** W Australia
138 E6 **Karoonda** S Australia
47 H8 **Káros** *isld* Greece
70 F5 **Karossa** Sulawesi Indonesia
71 J9 **Karossa, Tg** *C* Indonesia
46 D5 **Karousádhes** Greece
33 Q5 **Karow** E Germany
57 G2 **Karoy** U.S.S.R.
47 J9 **Kárpathos** *isld* Greece
47 J9 **Karpathos Str** Greece
46 E6 **Karpenision** Greece
41 K4 **Kärpf** *mt* Switzerland
37 P7 **Karpfham** W Germany
55 C2 **Karpinsk** U.S.S.R.
52 F3 **Karpogory** U.S.S.R.
55 C2 **Karpushikha** U.S.S.R.
47 J7 **Karpuzlu** Turkey
143 B9 **Karragullen** W Australia
142 A1 **Karrakatta** *dist* Perth, W Aust
115 O3 **Karrats Fjord** Greenland
28 H6 **Karrebæk** Denmark
28 H6 **Karrebæksminde** Denmark
28 G6 **Karrebæksminde Bugt** *B* Denmark
89 B8 **Karree Berge** *mts* S Africa
143 B10 **Karridale** W Australia
78 J1 **Kars** Turkey
57 D1 **Karsakpay** U.S.S.R.
119 S2 **Karsakuwigamak L** Manitoba
29 M8 **Kärsämäki** Finland
52 C6 **Kārsava** U.S.S.R.
57 D5 **Karshi** U.S.S.R.
57 D5 **Karshinskaya Step'** U.S.S.R.
50 E1 **Karskiye Vorota, Proliv** *str* U.S.S.R.
33 P6 **Karstädt** E Germany
28 B5 **Karstoft** Denmark
29 L9 **Karstula** Finland
26 H10 **Karsvall** Sweden
79 F4 **Kartaba** Lebanon
47 K4 **Kartal** Turkey
47 G3 **Kartál** *mt* Greece
50 F3 **Kartaly** U.S.S.R.
52 H3 **Kartayël** U.S.S.R.
94 J5 **Karthaus** Pennsylvania
36 B4 **Karthaus** W Germany
29 N9 **Karttula** Finland
31 L1 **Kartuzy** Poland
87 E9 **Karubwe** Zambia
61 M9 **Karuizawa** Japan
143 F9 **Karulbie** W Australia
140 F3 **Karumba** Queensland
77 A4 **Karun** *R* Iran
26 N5 **Karungi** Sweden
71 J9 **Karuni** Indonesia
142 G3 **Karunjie** W Australia
106 G3 **Karval** Colorado
29 K9 **Karvia** Finland
26 K2 **Kårvik** Norway
31 L6 **Karviná** Czechoslovakia
48 E1 **Karvina** Czechoslovakia
76 B3 **Karwar** India
41 O3 **Karwendel Geb** *mts* Austria
55 E1 **Karym** U.S.S.R.
55 C4 **Karzala** U.S.S.R.
28 D2 **Kås** Denmark
47 K8 **Kas** Turkey
56 C2 **Kas** *R* U.S.S.R.
88 C6 **Kasaba B** Zambia
86 D6 **Kasai** *prov* Zaïre
87 D7 **Kasai** *R* Zaïre
87 D8 **Kasaji** Zaïre
61 O9 **Kasama** Japan
88 C7 **Kasama** Zambia
88 C6 **Kasanga** Tanzania
57 F4 **Kasansay** U.S.S.R.
76 B4 **Kasaragod** India
75 O7 **Kasba** Bangladesh
114 J5 **Kasba L** N W Terr
27 G16 **Kåseberga** Sweden
60 D14 **Kaseda** Japan
116 F1 **Kasegaluk Lag** Alaska
87 E8 **Kasempa** Zambia
37 L3 **Kasendorf** W Germany
88 B7 **Kasenga** Zaïre
86 F5 **Kasenyi** Zaïre
77 B5 **Kāserūn** Iran
88 C1 **Kasese** Uganda
86 E6 **Kasese** Zaïre
119 N2 **Kashabowie** Ontario
77 B2 **Kāshān** Iran
Kashgar *see* **Kashi**
66 B4 **Kashi** China
61 J11 **Kashihara** Japan
60 D12 **Kashima** Japan
52 E6 **Kashin** U.S.S.R.
74 H4 **Kashipur** India
54 K2 **Kashira** U.S.S.R.
119 O1 **Kashishibog L** Ontario
61 M8 **Kashiwazaki** Japan
57 D5 **Kashkadar'in-skaya Oblast** U.S.S.R.
57 G2 **Kashkanteniz** U.S.S.R.
52 D4 **Kashkany** U.S.S.R.
52 E2 **Kashkarantsy** U.S.S.R.
57 H4 **Kashkasu** U.S.S.R.
77 F2 **Kāshmar** Iran
66 B5 **Kashmir** India/Pakistan
74 C4 **Kashmor** Pakistan
88 G3 **Kasigao Mt** Kenya
71 A3 **Kasiruta** *isld* Indonesia
110 G2 **Kaskaskia** *R* Illinois
26 K6 **Kasker** Sweden
29 J9 **Kaskö** Finland
68 F7 **Kas Kong** Cambodia
55 D3 **Kasli** U.S.S.R.
117 P11 **Kaslo** Br Col
86 E6 **Kasongo** Zaïre
87 C7 **Kasongo-Lunda** Zaïre
47 H9 **Kásos** *isld* Greece
47 H9 **Kásos Str** Greece
54 C1 **Kasplya** *R* U.S.S.R.
68 H6 **Kas Preas** Cambodia
68 F7 **Kas Prins** *isld* Cambodia
68 F7 **Kas Rong** *isld* Cambodia
68 F7 **Kas Rong Sam Lem** *isld* Cambodia
86 G2 **Kassala** Sudan
47 F4 **Kassándra** Greece
32 L10 **Kassel** W Germany
85 F1 **Kasserine** Tunisia
68 F7 **Kas Smach** *isld* Cambodia
99 O5 **Kasson** Minnesota
78 D1 **Kastamonu** Turkey
47 H3 **Kastanéai** Greece
28 E3 **Kastbjerg** Denmark
36 E3 **Kastel** W Germany
36 C3 **Kastellaun** W Germany
47 F9 **Kastélli** Crete **Greece**
47 G9 **Kastéllion** Crete **Greece**
47 K8 **Kastellórizon** *isld* Greece
36 B1 **Kaster** W Germany
22 H1 **Kasterlee** Belgium
37 M5 **Kastl** W Germany
27 H15 **Kastlösa** Sweden
33 N5 **Kastorf** W Germany
46 E4 **Kastoría** Greece
46 E4 **Kastorías, L** Greece
47 G5 **Kástron** Límnos I **Greece**
47 F4 **Kástron Nigrita** Greece
46 D5 **Kastrosikiá** Greece
28 K5 **Kastrup** Denmark
60 F10 **Kasubuchi** Japan
61 K10 **Kasugai** Japan
61 O9 **Kasumiga-ura** *L* Japan
70 C6 **Kasungan** Kalimantan
87 F8 **Kasungu** Malawi
88 E9 **Kasupe** Malawi
74 F3 **Kasur** Pakistan
71 H7 **Katabu** Indonesia
85 G6 **Katagum** Nigeria
95 S8 **Katahdin, Mt** Maine
86 D6 **Katako-Kombe** Zaïre
46 E7 **Katákolon** Greece
116 P2 **Katakturuk** *R* Alaska
116 P6 **Katalla** Alaska
86 D7 **Katanda** Zaïre
74 H8 **Katangi** India
59 M1 **Katangli** U.S.S.R.
143 C10 **Katanning** W Australia
75 J4 **Katarnian Ghat** India
46 D7 **Katastári** Greece

61 J10	Katata Japan
77 L3	Katawāz-Urgan Afghanistan
55 D3	Katayak U.S.S.R.
69 A9	Katchall isld Nicobar Is
38 J7	Katchberg Austria
116 H4	Kateel R Alaska
119 O8	Katepwa Sask
46 F4	Katerini Greece
25 F4	Katerveer Netherlands
114 F6	Kates Needle mt Br Col
75 K7	Katghora India
75 R6	Katha Burma
84 J4	Katherina, Gebel hill Egypt
140 B2	Katherine N Terr Aust
140 C2	Katherine R N Terr Aust
74 H4	Kathgodam India
74 D8	Kathiawar reg India
76 E6	Kathiraveli Sri Lanka
113 E9	Kathleen Florida
140 B2	Kathleen Falls N Terr Aust
143 D7	Kathleen Valley W Australia
75 L5	Kathmandu Nepal
118 D7	Kathryn Alberta
98 H3	Kathryn N Dakota
74 F2	Kathua Kashmir
64	Kati Mali
70 C4	Katibas R Sarawak
69 D14	Katiet Indonesia
75 M6	Katihar India
145 E2	Katikati New Zealand
87 D9	Katima Mulilo Namibia
8 L	Katimik L Manitoba
85 C7	Katiola Ivory Coast
29 L3	Kätkäsuntturi mt Finland
89 A8	Katkop Hills S Africa
48 M5	Katlabukh, Oz L U.S.S.R.
32 M9	Katlehong W Germany
116 K8	Katmai B Alaska
116 K7	Katmai Nat. Monument Alaska
116 K7	Katmai Vol., Mt Alaska
74 J7	Katni India
46 E6	Káto Akhaïa Greece
46 E6	Katokhi Greece
88 C9	Katondwe Zambia
47 F3	Káto Nevrokópion Greece
139 K5	Katoomba New S Wales
47 F4	Káto Stavrós Greece
31 L5	Katowice Poland
27 H10	Katrancik Dağ mt Turkey
27 H13	Katrineholm Sweden
12 D1	Katrine, L Scotland
85 F6	Katsina Nigeria
61 O9	Katsuta Japan
61 O10	Katsuura Japan
61 K9	Katsuyama Fukui Japan
61 N10	Katsuyama Japan
60 G10	Katsuyama Okayama Japan
57 D5	Kattakurgan U.S.S.R.
142 F5	Kattamudda Well W Australia
28 K4	Kattarp Sweden
47 J9	Kattavia Rhodes Greece
120 K3	Kattegat str Denmark
28 E3	Kattegat str Denmark
32 G8	Kattenvenne W Germany
27 K14	Katthammarsvik isld Gotland Sweden
28 D5	Kattrup Denmark
88 A8	Katua R Zambia
87 E7	Katumba Zaïre
88 B4	Katumbi Malawi
56 C5	Katun' R U.S.S.R.
56 C6	Katunakiy Khr mts U.S.S.R.
71 J9	Katupa Sumbawa Indonesia
75 N7	Katwa India
88 B2	Katwe Uganda
25 B4	Katwijk aan Zee Netherlands
31 K4	Katy Wrocł Poland
36 G5	Katzenbuckel mt W Germany
36 D3	Katzenelnbogen W Germany
37 L2	Katzhütte E Germany
71 A2	Kau Halmahera Indonesia
102 V13	Kauai isld Hawaiian Is
102 U13	Kauai Ch Hawaiian Is
144 B7	Kauana New Zealand
36 D3	Kaub W Germany
135 U6	Kau Desert Hawaiian Is
41 N2	Kaufbeuren W Germany
41 N1	Kaufering W Germany
102	Kaufman Texas
32 L10	Kaufungen W Germany
29 K8	Kauhava Finland
135 T3	Kauiki Hd Hawaiian Is
145 E2	Kaukapakapa New Zealand
99 S5	Kaukauna Wisconsin
102 U13	Kaula isld Hawaiian Is
102 U13	Kaulakahi Ch Hawaiian Is
135 O1	Kaumakani Hawaiian Is
135 R2	Kaunakakai Hawaiian Is
135 U8	Kauna Pt Hawaiian Is
53 B7	Kaunas U.S.S.R.
85 F6	Kaura Namoda Nigeria
84 M4	Kaushany U.S.S.R.
29 K8	Kaustinen Finland
22 L4	Kautenbach Luxembourg
71 A2	Kau, Tk B Halmahera Indonesia
26 N3	Kautokeino Norway
68 D7	Kau-ye Kyun isld Burma
97 K5	Kavacik Turkey
46 E3	Kavadarci Yugoslavia
46 D3	Kavajë Albania
47 J7	Kavaklidere Turkey
59 K3	Kavalerovo U.S.S.R.
76 E3	Kavali India
47 G4	Kavala Greece
73 L6	Kavaratti isld Lakshadweep Indian Oc
47 J1	Kavarna Bulgaria
33 O4	Kavelstorf E Germany
136 L2	Kaviong New Ireland
116 O2	Kavik R Alaska
27 F16	Kävlinge Sweden
47 H9	Kavousi Crete Greece
88 C5	Kavula R Tanzania
88 D2	Kavul Israel
129 H3	Kaw Fr Guiana
121 M7	Kawa R Ontario
61 N10	Kawagoe Japan
61 N10	Kawaguchi Japan
60 H10	Kawahara Japan
61 M7	Kawaharada Japan
135 U4	Kawaihae Hawaiian Is
135 T3	Kawaihoa Pt Hawaiian Is
135 O1	Kawaikini peak Hawaiian Is
102 R11	Kawailoa Bch Hawaiian Is
61 M10	Kawajiri Japan
145 E1	Kawakawa New Zealand
145 E2	Kawakawa B New Zealand
88 C6	Kawambwa Zambia
61 N11	Kawanehon Japan
71 J10	Kawangkoan Sulawesi
144 B6	Kawarau R New Zealand
75 J7	Kawardha India
121 M8	Kawartha Lakes Ontario
61 N10	Kawasaki Japan
60 D11	Kawasaki-miisaki C Japan
60 O4	Kawauchi Japan
145 E2	Kawau I New Zealand
107 O5	Kaw City Oklahoma
71 C2	Kawe isld Indonesia
102 E5	Kaweah R California
145 E3	Kaweka mt New Zealand
102 R11	Kawela B Hawaiian Is
145 E3	Kawerau New Zealand
102 H4	Kawhia New Zealand
88 C6	Kawimbe Zambia
61 N11	Kawinaw L Manitoba

68 D4	Kawkareik Burma
68 C3	Kawludo Burma
68 D6	Kawmapyin Burma
68 D4	Kawthaung Burma
68 C3	Kawthoolei prov Burma
66 B4	Kaxgar He R China
52 H4	Kay U.S.S.R.
85 D6	Kaya Upper Volta
116 P7	Kayak I Alaska
117 M3	Keith Arm B N W Terr
117 N9	Keithley Creek Br Col
11 G5	Keith S Australia
85 B7	Kenema Sierra Leone
70 B4	Kenepai mt Kalimantan
135 D4	Kenepuru Sound New Zealand
98 H9	Kenesaw Nebraska
56 B3	Kenga U.S.S.R.
86 C6	Kenge Zaïre
57 A3	Kenge U.S.S.R.
26 N4	Kengis Sweden
68 G4	Keng Kabao Laos
68 G4	Keng Kok Laos
68 D1	Keng Lap Burma
68 D2	Keng Tawng Burma
68 D2	Kengtung Burma
68 G4	Kenhardt S Africa
116 L6	Kenibuna L Alaska
85 B6	Keniéba Mali
112 G1	Kenilworth N Carolina
140 B7	Keninagau Sabah
102 F6	Kenitra Morocco
12 D3	Ken, L Scotland
65 D6	Kenli China
112 J2	Kenly N Carolina
14 B5	Kenmare Irish Rep
98 E1	Kenmare N Dakota
14 A5	Kenmare, R Irish Rep
15 E4	Kenmore Scotland
141 K2	Kenmore dist Brisbane, Qnsld
108 D2	Kenna New Mexico
94 F8	Kenna W Virginia
95 R1	Kennebago Lake Maine
98 G6	Kennebec S Dakota
95 S2	Kennebec R Maine
109 M10	Kennedale Texas
98 J1	Kennedy Minnesota
98 F7	Kennedy Nebraska
94 J4	Kennedy New York
119 P8	Kennedy Sask
115 N1	Kennedy Channel Canada/Greenland
119 P5	Kennedy L Sask
117 D5	Kennedy, Mt Yukon Terr
141 G3	Kennedy R Queensland
36 H2	Kenzell W Germany
95 M7	Kennedyville Maryland
111 F11	Kenner Louisiana
122 H12	Kennet R England
109 P7	Kenneth Missouri
59 J2	Keshan China
99 S5	Keshena Wisconsin
76 C4	Keshod India
55 K4	Keslerovo U.S.S.R.
52 F5	Kesova Gora U.S.S.R.
147 Q7	Kessel W Germany
25 E8	Kessel Netherlands
56 C2	Kestenga U.S.S.R.

13 G6	Keighley England
100 J3	Kendrick Idaho
103 N6	Kendrick Pk Arizona
57 B3	Kendyrli, Ozero L U.S.S.R.
139 J4	Kenebri New S Wales
109 K7	Kenedy Texas
107 O7	Kenefick Oklahoma
85 G2	Kenena, Is Tunisia
99 L4	Kenki U.S.S.R.
75 J7	Kenkini U.S.S.R.
47 F3	Kenkintis, L U.S.S.R.
14 A5	Kenmare, R Irish Rep
54 F9	Kenmore U.S.S.R.
94 J10	Kerr L N Carolina/Virg
118 H7	Kerrobert Sask
145 D1	Kerr Pt New Zealand
94 H9	Kerrs L Sask
109 K5	Kerrville Tennessee
109 H5	Kerrville Texas
8 C3	Kerry Wales
14 A4	Kerry co Irish Rep
36 F3	Kerry Hd Irish Rep
121 P7	Kersaint, I, du Vietnam
108 F1	Kersey Colorado
112 G3	Kershaw S Carolina
69 F10	Kerteh Malaysia
28 F6	Kerteminde Denmark
140 E7	Kertie Hill N Terr Aust
70 O9	Keroa U.S.S.R.
75 M6	Kerulen R see Herlen He
25 E5	Kervenheim W Germany
78 A1	Kerzaz Australia
54 J4	Kerzhenets R U.S.S.R.
72 H4	Kesan Turkey
78 B5	Kesariya Kashmir
141 K6	Kesch, Piz mt Switzerland
59 J2	Keshan China

75 M8	Kendrapara Indiana
100 J3	Kendrick Idaho
103 N6	Kendrick Pk Arizona
69 E13	Kendyrlik U.S.S.R.
139 J4	Kenebri New S Wales
109 K7	Kenedy Texas
107 O7	Kenefick Oklahoma
85 G2	Kenena, Is Tunisia
99 L4	Kenki U.S.S.R.
52 D5	Kenki China
47 F3	Kerkira isld Greece
25 F7	Kerkrade Netherlands
139 R8	Kermadec Is Pacific Oc
102 D5	Kerman California
79 H4	Kerman Iran
77 F5	Kerman Desert Iran
78 L4	Kermānshāh Iran
78 A3	Kerme Körfezi Turkey
76 B3	Kermen Bulgaria
108 D4	Kermit Texas
94 F9	Kermit W Virginia
102 F6	Kern R California
36 B2	Kernen W Germany
112 G1	Kernersville N Carolina
140 B7	Kernot Ra N Terr Aust
74 D3	Kernowa India
55 D1	Kenanwal Pakistan
85 C7	Kérouané Guinea
139 G4	Kerpa New S Wales
47 G9	Kerpen W Germany
42 H3	Kerr, C Scotland
54 F9	Kerr L N Carolina/Virg

145 D1	Kerikeri New Zealand
29 O10	Kerimäki Finland
69 E13	Kerinci, Danau L Sumatra
69 E13	Kerinci, Gunung mt Sumatra
25 F6	Kerken W Germany
85 G2	Kerkenna, Is Tunisia
99 L4	Kerkhoven Minnesota
25 J7	Kerki U.S.S.R.
57 D5	Kerkini U.S.S.R.
47 F3	Kerkinitis, L U.S.S.R.
25 F7	Kerkrade Netherlands
77 A4	Khalafābād Iran
74 G1	Khalatse Kashmir
55 C5	Khalilovo U.S.S.R.
78 K5	Khālis, Al Iraq
47 F5	Khálki isld Greece
52 G5	Khalkidhón Greece
78 J7	Khamaria India
89 F2	Khambat R Zimbabwe
47 H9	Khamili isld Greece
68 G3	Kham Keut Laos
47 H7	Khammam India
68 G3	Khampho R Laos
72 F7	Khamsara R U.S.S.R.
77 A1	Khamseh Iran
57 F4	Khamza U.S.S.R.

54 K1	Khot'kovo U.S.S.R.
116 H4	Khotol mt Alaska
53 F12	Khotin U.S.S.R.
54 M5	Khrapovitskaya U.S.S.R.
68 A2	Khraum Burma
47 G4	Khrisoúpolis Greece
47 G8	Khristianá isld Greece
52 G4	Khristoforovo U.S.S.R.
47 G3	Khrony, Bulgaria
55 C5	Khroni-Tau U.S.S.R.
79 C3	Khrysokhou B Cyprus
47 H7	Khtapodhiá isld Greece
77 B6	Khubar, Al Saudi Arabia
77 K6	Khude Hills Pakistan
56 G5	Khuduknakiy Khr mts U.S.S.R.
68 G5	Khu Khan Thailand
77 K1	Khulm U.S.S.R.
75 N7	Khulna Bangladesh
84 E3	Khums, Al Libya
77 B3	Khunsar Iran
75 L7	Khunti India
75 L8	Khurda India
77 J3	Khurd, Koh-i- mt Afghanistan
74 G4	Khurja India
74 E2	Khushab Pakistan
48 H2	Khust U.S.S.R.
86 E3	Khuwei Sudan
77 A4	Khuzestan Iran
77 G3	Khuzhir U.S.S.R.
77 D3	Khvor Iran
78 K2	Khvor Iran
52 D5	Khvoynaya U.S.S.R.
77 L1	Khwaja-Ghar Afghanistan
77 L1	Khwaja Muhammad Range Afghanistan
74 D1	Khyber Pass Pakistan/Afghan
48 H1	Khyrov U.S.S.R.
139 K5	Kiama New S Wales
71 G7	Kiamba Mindanao Philippines
88 D2	Kiambu Kenya
55 J3	Kiangsu prov see Jiangsu
141 K6	Kiangsi prov see Jiangxi
29 O6	Kiantajärvi L Finland
119 U2	Kiask L Manitoba
28 B4	Kiask Denmark
29 S9	Kiato Greece
29 E10	Kiboha Tanzania
88 E10	Kiberit, J, al Saudi Arabia
53 J5	Kibungu Rwanda
71 G2	Kibungu Indonesia
43 M3	Kichi Kichi Chad
52 G5	Kichmengsky Gorodok U.S.S.R.
99 Q6	Kickapoo R Wisconsin
117 P10	Kicking Horse Pass Br Col
85 B5	Kidal Mali
8 E3	Kidderminster England
85 F5	Kidepo Nat. Park Kenya
9 E4	Kidlington England
145 F3	Kidnappers, C New Zealand
141 G4	Kidston Queensland
70 C3	Kidurong, Tg C Sarawak
98 B4	Kiekie New Zealand
98 G4	Kiel N Dakota
54 W Germany
99 Q6	Kiel Wisconsin
31 M5	Kielce Poland
13 F3	Kielder England
13 F3	Kielder Res England
22 G1	Kieldrecht Belgium
30 E1	Kieler Bucht B W Germany
93 Kielpa S Australia
54 W An Vietnam
69 G8	Kien Hung Vietnam
36 D1	Kienberg W Germany
109 N9	Kiest Park Texas
52 E9	Kiev = Kiyev U.S.S.R.
139 K6	Kiewa R Victoria
85 F8	Kiffa Mauritania
47 G3	Kifissós R Greece
78 L3	Kifri, Al Iraq
88 D2	Kigali Rwanda
116 F4	Kigalik R Alaska
88 B4	Kigoma Tanzania
88 B4	Kigoma dist Tanzania
141 F7	Kikaau Qld
145 E3	Kikhchik U.S.S.R.
145 M13	Kikaiwara N Zealand
29 K4	Kihlanki Finland
102 V13	Kiholo Hawaiian Is
29 K11	Kiikala Finland
135 N1	Kii Landing Hawaiian Is
29 M6	Kiiminki Finland
61 K12	Kii Peninsula Japan
60 H12	Kii suidō str Japan
116 K6	Kijik Alaska
71 G7	Kijoka Okinawa
59 J6	Kikai-shima isld Japan
116 L3	Kikiakrorak R Alaska
46 A3	Kikinda Yugoslavia
47 J5	Kiklades isld Greece
57 F4	Kikonai Japan
136 D2	Kikori Papua New Guinea
60 D13	Kikuchi Japan
59 G2	Kikvoras Berg S Africa
121 M6	Kikwissi, L Quebec
101 L1	Kila Montana
27 J10	Kilafors Sweden
13 C10	Kilarney, L New Zealand / Bahamas
135 U6	Kilauea Crater mt Hawaiian Is
14 G3	Kilbeggan Irish Rep
12 F4	Kilbirnie Scotland
122 E2	Kilbuck Mts New Brunswick
15 D3	Kilchoman Scotland
12 C1	Kilchrenan Scotland
14 B4	Kilcommon Irish Rep
71 J6	Kilchu N Korea
11 G4	Kilcoy Queensland
14 H3	Kilcormac Irish Rep
141 J7	Kilcoy Queensland
14 J3	Kilcullen Irish Rep
117 K5	Kildala Arm R Br Columbia
14 K3	Kildare Irish Rep
14 J3	Kildare co Irish Rep
109 N3	Kildare Texas
119 P6	Kildonan Sask
117 K5	Kildonan Br Col
118 M1	Kildonan Manitoba
87 B1	Kildonan Zimbabwe
86 C7	Kilembe Zaïre

40 Kilen — Konda

28 A3 Kilen L Denmark
14 B4 Kilfenora Irish Rep
12 C2 Kilfinan Scotland
14 C4 Kilfinnane Irish Rep
14 B5 Kilgarvan Irish Rep
101 O5 Kilgore Idaho
98 F7 Kilgore Nebraska
111 B9 Kilgore Texas
13 H5 Kilham England
85 E7 Kilibo Benin
88 G3 Kilifi Kenya
88 F3 Kilimanjaro mt Tanzania
137 M2 Kilinailau Is Solomon Is
47 K4 Kılınç Turkey
15 C4 Kilinelfort Scotland
52 B5 Kilingi-Nõmme U.S.S.R.
83 K8 Kilinochchi Sri Lanka
78 F3 Kilis Turkey
116 L8 Kiliuda B Alaska
48 M5 Kiliya U.S.S.R.
14 B4 Kilkee Irish Rep
14 F2 Kilkeel N Ireland
14 D4 Kilkenny Irish Rep
14 D4 Kilkenny co Irish Rep
12 C3 Kilkenzie Scotland
8 B6 Kilkhampton England
14 B3 Kilkieran B Irish Rep
46 F4 Kilkís Greece
141 K7 Kilkivan Queensland
14 E3 Kill Irish Rep
14 B2 Killala Irish Rep
14 B2 Killala B Irish Rep
120 D3 Killala L Ontario
14 C4 Killaloe Irish Rep
121 N7 Killaloe Ontario
119 P8 Killaly Sask
118 F6 Killam Alberta
14 B4 Killarney Irish Rep
119 S9 Killarney Manitoba
140 B3 Killarney N Terr Aust
120 J7 Killarney Ontario
141 K8 Killarney Queensland
120 J6 Killarney Prov. Park Ontario
14 A3 Killary Hbr Irish Rep
14 D2 Killashandra Irish Rep
98 D2 Killdeer N Dakota
118 L9 Killdeer Sask
99 O8 Killduff Iowa
12 D1 Killearn Scotland
109 K4 Killeen Texas
47 J5 Kıller R Turkey
15 E4 Killiecrankie, Pass of Scotland
116 K2 Killik Bend Alaska
14 C3 Killimor Irish Rep
15 D4 Killin Scotland
26 E9 Killingdal Norway
46 E7 Killíni Greece
46 E7 Killini mt Greece
14 B4 Killorglin Irish Rep
14 C2 Killybegs Irish Rep
14 F2 Killyleagh N Ireland
14 C4 Kilmallock Irish Rep
15 B3 Kilmaluag Scotland
13 F1 Kilmany Scotland
12 D2 Kilmarnock Scotland
95 L9 Kilmarnock Virginia
12 C1 Kilmartin Scotland
52 H6 Kil'mez U.S.S.R.
111 G8 Kilmichael Mississippi
139 G6 Kilmore Victoria
12 C2 Kilmory Scotland
12 D1 Kilmun Scotland
13 E4 Kilnhill England
12 C1 Kilninver Scotland
13 J6 Kilnsea England
88 F6 Kilombero R Tanzania
88 F5 Kilosa Tanzania
29 H2 Kilpisjärvi Finland
29 L7 Kilpua Finland
29 Q2 Kilp'yavr U.S.S.R.
14 E2 Kilrea N Ireland
14 B4 Kilrush Irish Rep
9 E3 Kilsby England
12 D2 Kilsyth Scotland
14 C3 Kiltamagh Irish Rep
73 L6 Kiltan isld Lakshadweep Indian Oc
26 M5 Kilvo Sweden
87 E7 Kilwa Zaïre
88 B6 Kilwa isld Zambia
88 G6 Kilwa Kisiwani Tanzania
88 G6 Kilwa Kivinje Tanzania
88 G6 Kilwa Masoko Tanzania
12 D2 Kilwinning Scotland
47 K3 Kilyos Turkey
106 G4 Kim Colorado
101 M7 Kimama Idaho
70 D2 Kimanis B Sabah
138 D5 Kimba S Australia
98 C8 Kimball Nebraska
98 H6 Kimball S Dakota
94 F9 Kimball W Virginia
116 P5 Kimball, Mt Alaska
99 L8 Kimballton Iowa
86 C7 Kimbao Zaïre
117 Q11 Kimberley Br Col
120 K8 Kimberley Ontario
89 D7 Kimberley S Africa
141 H3 Kimberley,C Queensland
142 E3 Kimberley Downs W Australia
142 F3 Kimberley Plateau W Australia
143 C7 Kimberley Ra W Australia
101 L7 Kimberly Idaho
103 J2 Kimberly Nevada
99 S5 Kimberly Wisconsin
9 F3 Kimbolton England
145 E4 Kimbolton New Zealand
88 D5 Kimbu Tanzania
47 G6 Kími Greece
29 K11 Kimito Finland
118 A3 Kimiwan Lake Alberta
110 F3 Kimmswick Missouri
47 G8 Kímolos isld Greece
61 M7 Kimpoku-san mt Japan
52 E6 Kimry U.S.S.R.
68 J5 Kim Son Vietnam
27 H13 Kimstad Sweden
52 F2 Kimzha U.S.S.R.
68 B1 Kin Burma
61 P13 Kin Okinawa
61 P13 Kina Okinawa
70 E1 Kinabalu mt Sabah
70 E2 Kinabatangan R Sabah
88 F2 Kinangop, Mt Kenya
47 H8 Kínaros isld Greece
70 D2 Kinarut Sabah
117 O10 Kinbasket Br Col
118 F8 Kinbrook I. Prov. Pk Alberta
107 P3 Kincaid Kansas
118 K9 Kincaid Sask
120 J8 Kincardine Ontario
12 E1 Kincardine Scotland
Kincardine co see Grampian reg
117 J8 Kincolith Br Col
15 E3 Kincraig Scotland
87 E7 Kinda Zaïre
94 E3 Kinde Michigan
33 O10 Kindelbrück E Germany
109 P5 Kinder Louisiana
36 C3 Kinderbeuern W Germany
118 J7 Kindersley Sask
85 B6 Kindia Guinea
98 J3 Kindred N Dakota
86 E6 Kindu Zaïre
116 G7 Kinegnak Alaska
53 H7 Kinelyu R U.S.S.R.
52 F6 Kineshma U.S.S.R.
140 C1 King R N Terr Aust
140 E6 King R Queensland
141 G2 King R Queensland
141 K7 Kingaroy Queensland
133 C6 King, Canal str Chile
114 J2 King Christian I N W Terr
102 C5 King City California
99 M9 King City Missouri
117 K10 Kingcome Inlet Br Col
116 F9 King Cove Alaska
142 F3 King Edward R W Australia
146 J8 King Edward V11 Land Antarctica
95 R2 Kingfield Maine
107 N6 Kingfisher Oklahoma
146 E15 King George 1 S Shetland Is
115 M6 King George Is N W Terr
135 N10 King George Is Tuamotu Arch Pacific Oc
118 B8 King George, Mt Br Col
117 D5 King George, Mt Yukon Terr
143 C11 King George Sd W Australia
133 J8 King Haakon B S Georgia
142 E6 King Hill W Australia
120 C3 Kinghorn Ontario
13 E1 Kinghorn Scotland
146 H11 King I Antarctica
117 K9 King I Br Col
73 Q6 King I Burma
139 G7 King I Tasmania
52 C5 Kingisepp U.S.S.R.
52 B5 Kingissepp U.S.S.R.
100 G8 King Lear mt Nevada
146 D3 King Leopold & Queen Astrid Coast Antarctica
142 E3 King Leopold Ra W Australia
118 E5 Kingman Alberta
103 K6 Kingman Arizona
107 M4 Kingman Kansas
95 T1 Kingman Maine
141 H7 King, Mt Queensland
108 E4 King Mt Texas
142 C5 King, Mt W Australia
86 E6 Kingombe Zaïre
138 D4 Kingoonya S Australia
139 H8 King, R Tasmania
142 G3 King, R W Australia
102 D5 Kings R California
100 G8 Kings R Nevada
116 J7 King Salmon Alaska
13 F1 Kingsbarns Scotland
8 C7 Kingsbridge England
102 E5 Kingsburg California
109 K6 Kingsbury Texas
106 D1 Kings Canyon Colorado
102 F4 Kings Canyon Nat Park California
9 E5 Kingsclere England
139 L3 Kingscliff-Fingal New S Wales
138 D6 Kingscote S Australia
14 E3 Kingscourt Irish Rep
145 E2 Kingseat New Zealand
9 G5 Kingsferry Bridge England
9 F5 Kingsfold England
109 P2 Kingsland Arkansas
113 F7 Kingsland Georgia
9 F4 Kings Langley England
99 L7 Kingsley Iowa
94 B2 Kingsley Michigan
98 E8 Kingsley Dam Nebraska
9 G2 King's Lynn England
137 P2 Kingsmill Group islds Kiribati
112 F2 Kings Mt N Carolina
95 O6 Kings Park Long I, N Y
101 P9 Kings Pks Utah
122 H8 Kingsport Nova Scotia
94 E10 Kingsport Tennessee
142 E3 Kings Sd W Australia
8 C6 Kingsteignton England
110 C5 Kingston Arkansas
9 F5 Kingston England
127 L3 Kingston Jamaica
110 B2 Kingston Missouri
95 R4 Kingston New Hampshire
95 N5 Kingston New York
144 B6 Kingston New Zealand
94 E7 Kingston Ohio
107 O7 Kingston Oklahoma
121 O8 Kingston Ontario
95 M5 Kingston Pennsylvania
138 E6 Kingston S Australia
139 H9 Kingston Tasmania
100 C2 Kingston Washington
94 F9 Kingston W Virginia
9 E4 Kingston Lisle England
103 J6 Kingston Pk California
13 F4 Kingstown England
127 O8 Kingstown St Vincent
112 H4 Kingstree S Carolina
94 G5 Kingsville Ohio
120 H10 Kingsville Ontario
109 K8 Kingsville Texas
8 C7 Kingswear England
8 C3 Kington England
86 C7 Kinguji Zaïre
15 D3 Kingussie Scotland
115 K4 King William I N W Terr
89 E9 King William's Town S Africa
94 H7 Kingwood W Virginia
87 E8 Kiniama Zaïre
47 J5 Kınık Turkey
119 M6 Kinistino Sask
61 P7 Kinka-san C Japan
87 H11 Kinkony, L Madagascar
122 J7 Kinkora Pr Edward I
145 E3 Kinleith New Zealand
118 K6 Kinley Sask
144 B6 Kinloch New Zealand
15 C3 Kinlochewe Scotland
15 D4 Kinlochleven Scotland
15 D4 Kinloch Rannoch Scotland
68 B3 Kinmaw Burma
61 P13 Kin-misaki C Okinawa
121 M8 Kinmount Ontario
110 H3 Kinmundy Illinois
27 F14 Kinna Sweden
117 P11 Kinnaird Br Col
15 F3 Kinnairds Hd Scotland
101 R6 Kinnear Wyoming
80 F3 Kinneret Israel
80 B8 Kinneret-Negev-Conduit Israel
83 L9 Kinniyai Sri Lanka
29 L8 Kinnula Finland
60 J11 Kino R Japan
61 K10 Kinomoto Japan
119 Q1 Kinoosa Manitoba
60 H10 Kinosaki Japan
13 E1 Kinqlassie Scotland
13 E1 Kinross Scotland
Kinross co see Tayside reg
14 C5 Kinsale Irish Rep
95 L8 Kinsale Virginia
7 E11 Kinsale oil rig Celtic Sea
14 C5 Kinsale, Old Hd of C Irish Rep
118 F5 Kinsella Alberta
101 U3 Kinsey Montana
86 C6 Kinshasa Zaïre
60 C11 Kin Shimo no-shima Japan
107 L4 Kinsley Kansas
94 G5 Kinsman Ohio
112 K2 Kinston N Carolina
107 P6 Kinta Oklahoma
70 P10 Kintamani, G mt Indonesia
70 D6 Kintap Kalimantan
85 C6 Kintinian Guinea
101 L1 Kintla Pk Montana
71 H5 Kintom Sulawesi
15 F3 Kintore Scotland
138 B2 Kintore, Mt S Australia
140 A6 Kintore Ra N Terr Aust
55 F1 Kintus U.S.S.R.
12 C2 Kintyre pen Scotland
68 B1 Kinu Burma
61 N9 Kinu R Japan
118 B3 Kinuso Alberta
14 C3 Kinvarra Irish Rep
61 P13 Kin wan B Okinawa
86 F5 Kinyeti mt Sudan
55 C6 Kinzhaly U.S.S.R.
36 D7 Kinzig R Baden-Württemberg W Germany
36 G3 Kinzig R Hessen W Germany
100 E5 Kinzua Oregon
94 J5 Kinzua Pennsylvania
71 N9 Kio Indonesia
100 F3 Kiona Washington
121 M6 Kiosk Ontario
106 F2 Kiowa Colorado
107 M4 Kiowa Kansas
107 P7 Kiowa Oklahoma
119 Q3 Kipahigan L Manitoba
135 T3 Kipahulu Hawaiian Is
46 E7 Kiparissia Greece
46 E7 Kiparissiakós Kolpos B Greece
121 M6 Kipawa Quebec
88 C5 Kipili Tanzania
86 H6 Kipini Kenya
119 P8 Kipling Sask
116 E7 Kipnuk Alaska
118 E9 Kipp Alberta
12 D1 Kippen Scotland
36 D7 Kippenheim W Germany
123 O5 Kippens Nfld
95 M9 Kiptopeke Virginia
87 E8 Kipushi Zaïre
60 H12 Kiragawa Japan
47 H4 Kirazh Turkey
Kirberg see Hünfelden
111 C7 Kirby Arkansas
9 H4 Kirby England
120 F6 Kirby Ontario
101 R6 Kirby Wyoming
111 C11 Kirbyville Texas
38 N8 Kirchbach Austria
38 M5 Kirchberg Austria
36 H5 Kirchberg Baden-Württemberg W Germany
37 O2 Kirchberg E Germany
36 C4 Kirchberg Rheinland-Pfalz W Germany
33 O5 Kirchdorf E Germany
37 P6 Kirchdorf W Germany
37 M4 Kirchenlaibach W Germany
37 M3 Kirchenlamitz W Germany
36 D2 Kirchen-Sieg W Germany
36 G6 Kirchentellinsfurt W Germany
37 M4 Kirchenthumbach W Germany
33 T9 Kirchhain E Germany
36 F2 Kirchhain W Germany
37 K1 Kirchheilingen E Germany
36 G5 Kirchheim W Germany
36 D4 Kirchheim Bolanden W Germany
32 E9 Kirchhellen W Germany
36 E1 Kirchhundem W Germany
33 O6 Kirch Jesar E Germany
32 H6 Kirchkimmen W Germany
37 K3 Kirchlauter W Germany
32 J8 Kirchlengern W Germany
32 K7 Kirchlinteln W Germany
38 K5 Kirchschlag Austria
32 J7 Kirchweyhe W Germany
32 J6 Kirchwistedt W Germany
47 J5 Kireç Turkey
33 Q5 Kireh Grubenhagen E Germany
56 G3 Kirenga R U.S.S.R.
47 K7 Kirenis R Turkey
56 G2 Kirensk U.S.S.R.
55 E6 Kirey R U.S.S.R.
54 J3 Kireyevsk U.S.S.R.
83 K11 Kirgalpotta mt Sri Lanka
55 G6 Kirgiziya U.S.S.R.
57 F4 Kirgiziya S.S.R rep U.S.S.R.
55 B4 Kirgiz-Miyaki U.S.S.R.
86 C6 Kiri Zaïre
78 F3 Kirikhan Turkey
78 D2 Kirikkale Turkey
145 E1 Kirikopuni New Zealand
29 O11 Kirillovskoye U.S.S.R.
Kirin see Jilin
Kirin prov see Jilin
83 L11 Kirindi Oya R Sri Lanka
145 E1 Kiripa New Zealand
52 D5 Kirishi U.S.S.R.
60 D14 Kirishima-yama mt Japan
86 A2 Kirit Somalia
136 L3 Kiriwina Is Papua New Guinea
106 H2 Kirk Colorado
98 C8 Kirk Nebraska
100 D7 Kirk Oregon
47 L5 Kırka Turkey
47 J5 Kırkağaç Turkey
12 E4 Kirkbean Scotland
13 E4 Kirkbride England
13 F5 Kirkby Lonsdale England
13 H5 Kirkbymoorside England
13 F5 Kirkby Stephen England
118 D8 Kirkcaldy Alberta
13 E1 Kirkcaldy Scotland
12 C4 Kirkcolm Scotland
12 D4 Kirkcowan Scotland
12 D4 Kirkcudbright Scotland
Kirkcudbright co see Dumfries and Galloway reg
12 D4 Kirkcudbright B Scotland
13 G6 Kirk Deighton England
28 N2 Kirkebø Faeroes
28 F6 Kirkeby Fyn Denmark
28 B6 Kirkeby Sønderjylland Denmark
28 G5 Kirke Helsinge Denmark
28 H5 Kirke Hvalsø Denmark
28 H5 Kirke Hyllinge Denmark
119 Q8 Kirkella Manitoba
36 C5 Kirkel-Neuhausel W Germany
26 R2 Kirkenes Norway
28 H5 Kirke Såby Denmark
28 G6 Kirke Stillinge Denmark
26 K3 Kirkestind mt Norway
12 E2 Kirkfieldbank Scotland
13 F6 Kirkham England
12 D4 Kirkinner Scotland
12 D2 Kirkintilloch Scotland
28 N2 Kirkjubønes Faeroes
103 M7 Kirkland Arizona
99 S7 Kirkland Illinois
12 E3 Kirkland Scotland
100 C2 Kirkland Washington
120 K4 Kirkland Lake Ontario
47 J3 Kirklareli Turkey
94 A6 Kirklin Indiana
9 F1 Kirklington Notts England
13 G5 Kirklington N Yorks England
12 E2 Kirkliston Scotland
144 C6 Kirkliston Range New Zealand
99 L8 Kirkman Iowa
12 D3 Kirkmichael Scotland
13 F4 Kirkoswald England
12 D3 Kirkoswald Scotland
13 E3 Kirkpatrick-Fleming Scotland
146 G7 Kirkpatrick, Mt Antarctica
13 F5 Kirkstone Pass England
110 D1 Kirksville Missouri
78 K4 Kirkūk Iraq
15 F2 Kirkwall Scotland
102 B2 Kirkwood California
95 M4 Kirkwood New York
89 D9 Kirkwood S Africa
98 E5 Kirley S Dakota
47 K5 Kirmasti R Turkey
12 D2 Kirn Scotland
36 C4 Kirn W Germany
54 F2 Kirov Kaluga U.S.S.R.
52 G5 Kirov Kirov U.S.S.R.
78 L1 Kirovabad Azerbaydzhan U.S.S.R.
57 E6 Kirovabad Tadzhik U.S.S.R.
78 K1 Kirovakan U.S.S.R.
55 D3 Kirovo U.S.S.R.
54 D8 Kirovograd U.S.S.R.
52 D1 Kirovsk U.S.S.R.
118 G7 Kirriemuir Alberta
15 E4 Kirriemuir Scotland
52 H5 Kirs U.S.S.R.
78 E2 Kirşehir Turkey
87 D11 Kirstonia S Africa
98 B7 Kirtley Wyoming
13 H6 Kirton England
9 F2 Kirton Holme England
36 G2 Kirtorf W Germany
26 L4 Kiruna Sweden
86 E6 Kirundu Zaïre
144 D5 Kirwee New Zealand
107 M2 Kirwin Kansas
61 N9 Kiryū Japan
54 K1 Kirzhach U.S.S.R.
27 H14 Kisa Sweden
61 N6 Kisakata Japan
87 G7 Kisaki Tanzania
47 F9 Kisámou, K B Crete Greece
86 E5 Kisangani Zaïre
71 N9 Kisar isld Indonesia
116 G6 Kisaralik R Alaska
69 D11 Kisaran Sumatra
61 N10 Kisarazu Japan
48 D3 Kisbér Hungary
119 P9 Kisbey Sask
56 C4 Kiselevsk U.S.S.R.
74 F5 Kishangarh India
85 E7 Kishi Nigeria
55 F4 Kishikaroy, Oz L U.S.S.R.
48 M3 Kishinev U.S.S.R.
60 J11 Kishiwada Japan
74 F2 Kishtwar Kashmir
Kisi see Jixi
88 G3 Kisigau Mt Kenya
88 E5 Kisigo R Tanzania
88 E2 Kisii Kenya
119 T4 Kiskittogisu L Manitoba
119 T4 Kiskitto L Manitoba
48 D4 Kiskomárom Hungary
48 E4 Kiskörei-viztárole L Hungary
48 F3 Kisköreiviztároló L Hungary
48 F4 Kiskundorozsma Hungary
48 F4 Kiskunfélegyháza Hungary
48 E4 Kiskunhalas Hungary
48 F4 Kiskunmajsa Hungary
53 F11 Kislovodsk U.S.S.R.
Kismayu see Chisimaio
61 L10 Kiso Japan
61 L10 Kiso-sammyaku mts Japan
48 E3 Kispest Hungary
117 J8 Kispiox R Br Col
28 H5 Kisserup Denmark
85 B7 Kissidougou Guinea
113 F9 Kissimmee Florida
113 F10 Kissimmee R Florida
119 Q3 Kississing L Manitoba
41 L2 Kisslegg W Germany
84 H5 Kissu, Jebel mt Sudan
26 L3 Kistefjell mt Norway
48 F4 Kistelek Hungary
48 F2 Kisterenye Hungary
26 O1 Kistrand Norway
48 F3 Kisújszállás Hungary
88 E2 Kisumu Kenya
48 G2 Kisvárda Hungary
50 E5 Kisyl Arvat U.S.S.R.
85 C6 Kita Mali
57 D5 Kitab U.S.S.R.
60 H12 Kitagawa Japan
61 O9 Kita-Ibaraki Japan
48 M5 Kitai, Ozero L U.S.S.R.
26 L5 Kitajaur Sweden
61 P6 Kitakami Japan
61 N8 Kitakata Japan
60 D12 Kita-Kyūshū Japan
86 G5 Kitale Kenya
60 R2 Kitami Japan
60 Q1 Kitami-sanchi mts Japan
88 G7 Kitangari Tanzania
61 N13 Kitano-hana C Japan
61 O9 Kita-ura L Japan
61 J12 Kitayama R Japan
106 H3 Kit Carson Colorado
115 L9 Kitchener Ontario
143 E9 Kitchener W Australia
112 E5 Kite Georgia
29 P9 Kitee Finland
86 F5 Kitgum Uganda
47 F6 Kithairón mt Greece
46 F8 Kíthira isld Greece
47 G7 Kíthnos isld Greece
120 H3 Kitigan Ontario
80 G4 Kitim Jordan
117 J8 Kitimat Br Col
117 J9 Kitimat Mill Alberta
29 M4 Kitinen R Finland
52 C1 Kitinen R Finland
46 E2 Kitka mt Yugoslavia
46 F4 Kítros Greece
118 G5 Kitscoty Alberta
48 K2 Kitsman U.S.S.R.
60 E12 Kitsuki Japan
61 O9 Kitsuregawa Japan
138 E3 Kittakittaooloo, L S Australia
94 H6 Kittanning Pennsylvania
95 N5 Kittatinny Mts New Jersey
33 R5 Kittendorf E Germany
95 R3 Kittery Maine
29 L4 Kittilä Finland
112 M1 Kitty Hawk N Carolina
88 G2 Kitui Kenya
88 D5 Kitunda Tanzania
117 J8 Kitwanga Br Col
88 B8 Kitwe-Nkana Zambia
38 F7 Kitzbühler Alpen mts Austria
37 J4 Kitzingen W Germany
27 M10 Kiukainen Finland
116 L7 Kiukpalik I Alaska
86 E7 Kiumbi Zaïre
29 M8 Kiuruvesi Finland
116 A4 Kivak U.S.S.R.
116 E3 Kivalina Alaska
116 E3 Kividlo Alaska
29 L8 Kivijärvi Finland
27 G17 Kivik Sweden
52 C5 Kiviõli U.S.S.R.
46 E4 Kivotós Greece
88 B2 Kivu, Lac Zaire/Rwanda
145 D4 Kiwi New Zealand
56 C3 Kiya R U.S.S.R.
55 E6 Kiyakty, Oz L U.S.S.R.
61 O14 Kiyan Okinawa
61 O14 Kiyan-zaki C Okinawa
54 B6 Kiyev U.S.S.R.
55 F5 Kiyevka U.S.S.R.
54 B5 Kiyevskoy Vdkr res U.S.S.R.
47 L5 Kıyır R Turkey
118 H7 Kiyiu L Sask
55 E5 Kiyma U.S.S.R.
52 J5 Kizel U.S.S.R.
52 F4 Kizema U.S.S.R.
47 K4 Kızıl Adalar islds Turkey
47 K7 Kızılcabölük Turkey
47 K7 Kızılcadağ Turkey
47 K8 Kızılca Dağ mt Turkey
78 D1 Kizilcahamam Turkey
47 K7 Kızılhişar Turkey
78 E2 Kizil Irmak R Turkey
77 G2 Kizil Islam Afghanistan
47 L7 Kızılkaya Turkey
55 C5 Kizil'skoye U.S.S.R.
56 D4 Kizir R U.S.S.R.
53 G11 Kizlyar U.S.S.R.
26 M2 Kjaekan Norway
28 C4 Kjellerup Denmark
26 P1 Kjelvik Norway
26 G4 Kjerringöy Norway
26 Q1 Kjöllefjord Norway
71 J4 Klabat mt Sulawesi
48 E6 Kladanj Yugoslavia
30 H5 Kladno Czechoslovakia
48 H6 Kladovo Yugoslavia
37 O4 Kladruby Czechoslovakia
70 E2 Klagan Sabah
38 K8 Klagenfurt Austria
103 P6 Klagetoh Arizona
27 M16 Klaipeda U.S.S.R.
52 B6 Klaipėda U.S.S.R.
28 D5 Klakring Denmark
28 O9 Klaksvig Faeroes
100 A8 Klamath California
100 B8 Klamath R California
100 D7 Klamath Falls Oregon
100 B8 Klamath Mts California
100 C8 Klamath River California
71 C3 Klamono W Irian
117 J7 Klappan R Br Col
27 F12 Klarä R Sweden
27 F11 Klarabro Sweden
27 F11 Klarälven R Sweden
37 P3 Klášterec Czechoslovakia
70 N9 Klaten Java
37 P5 Klatovy Czechoslovakia
38 O5 Klausen-Leopoldsdorf Austria
41 J4 Klausen P mt Switzerland
117 G8 Klawak Alaska
31 K3 Kłecko Poland
31 L3 Kleczew Poland
122 J3 Kleczkowski L Quebec
117 L10 Kleena Kleene Br Col
101 S5 Kleenburn Wyoming
33 S5 Kleeth E Germany
25 F5 Klefe W Germany
79 F4 Kleiat Lebanon
101 R3 Klein Montana
33 P6 Kleinberge E Germany
22 J1 Kleine-Brogel Belgium
33 S9 Kleine Elster R E Germany
32 J9 Kleinenberg W Germany
22 H1 Kleine Nete R Belgium
33 R8 Klein Kreutz E Germany
37 N6 Klein Laaber R W Germany
36 F2 Klein Linden W Germany
89 B9 Klein Roggeveld Berge mts S Africa
89 B9 Klein Swartberge mts S Africa
33 N5 Klein Thurow E Germany
33 Q8 Klein Wusterwitz E Germany
38 N6 Klein Zell Austria
28 D3 Klejtrup Denmark
42 H4 Klekovača mt Yugoslavia
99 N6 Klemme Iowa
22 E1 Klemskerke Belgium
117 J9 Klemtu Br Col
48 F6 Klenak Yugoslavia
33 N7 Klenze W Germany
89 E6 Klerksdorp S Africa
116 G3 Klery Creek Alaska
54 E3 Kletnya U.S.S.R.
53 F9 Kletskiy U.S.S.R.
41 H2 Klettgau R W Germany
33 T9 Klettwitz E Germany
100 D3 Klickitat R Washington
79 E3 Klidhes Is Cyprus
33 Q7 Klietz E Germany
28 C2 Klim Denmark
31 N5 Klimontów Poland
54 C3 Klimovichi U.S.S.R.
52 H5 Klimovka U.S.S.R.
54 D4 Klimovo U.S.S.R.
54 J1 Klimovsk U.S.S.R.
26 G6 Klimpfjäll Sweden
54 H1 Klin U.S.S.R.
117 L10 Klinaklini R Br Col
112 F4 Kline S Carolina
71 G8 Kling Mindanao Philippines
37 Q2 Klingenberg E Germany
36 G4 Klingenberg W Germany
36 D5 Klingenmünster W Germany
37 N3 Klingenthal E Germany
70 B4 Klingkang Ra Sarawak
41 H2 Klingnau W Germany
33 R6 Klink E Germany
37 O3 Klínovec mt Czechoslovakia
28 E5 Klinte Denmark
27 K14 Klintehamn Sweden
54 D4 Klintsy U.S.S.R.
47 H5 Klió Greece
27 F15 Klippan Sweden
89 A8 Kliprug Berg mt S Africa
47 G2 Klisura Bulgaria
28 B2 Klitmøller Denmark
28 B7 Klixbüll W Germany
42 H4 Ključ Yugoslavia
31 L5 Kłobuck Poland
121 M6 Klock Ontario
33 U6 Klockow E Germany
31 L3 Kłodawa Poland
31 K5 Kłodzko Poland
27 E11 Klöfta Norway
103 H7 Klondike California
25 B6 Kloosterzande Netherlands
46 D3 Klos Albania
41 L3 Kloster R Austria
33 S7 Klosterfelde E Germany
28 A4 Klosterhede Plantage Denmark
41 M3 Klösterle Austria
33 Q6 Kloster Malchow E Germany
33 O9 Kloster Mansfeld E Germany
31 J7 Klosterneuburg Austria
36 E6 Klosterreichenbach W Germany
41 L4 Klosters Switzerland
33 S8 Kloster Zinna E Germany
27 H12 Kloten Sweden
36 C3 Klotten W Germany
33 O7 Klötze E Germany
28 C5 Klovborg Denmark
26 G9 Klövsjö Sweden
117 D5 Kluane Yukon Terr
117 D5 Kluane Nat. Park Yukon Terr
69 F14 Kluang Sumatra
31 L5 Kluczbork Poland
70 E6 Klumpeng, Teluk B Kalimantan
25 C5 Klundert Netherlands
70 P10 Klungkung Indonesia
36 C1 Kluppelberg W Germany
116 P6 Klutina L Alaska
26 L7 Klutmark Sweden
33 O5 Klütz E Germany
71 L9 Kluwang Indonesia
52 H7 Klyavlino U.S.S.R.
52 F6 Klyazma R U.S.S.R.
52 F2 Klyuchevaya U.S.S.R.
55 D2 Klyuchi U.S.S.R.
55 G4 Klyuchi U.S.S.R.
27 B13 Knabengruber Norway
38 J7 Knallstein, Gross mt Austria
99 O5 Knapp Wisconsin
13 G5 Knaresborough England
13 F4 Knarsdale England
37 M2 Knau E Germany
9 F4 Knebworth England
32 H5 Knechtsand sandbank W Germany
118 K3 Knee L Sask
33 N7 Knesebeck W Germany
22 E1 Knesselare Belgium
37 K4 Knetsgau W Germany
117 L9 Knewstubb L Br Col
47 G1 Knezha Bulgaria
98 D2 Knife R N Dakota
116 K7 Knife Pk Alaska
99 P3 Knife River Minnesota
101 P8 Knight Wyoming
116 O6 Knight I Alaska
117 K10 Knight Inlet Br Col
8 C3 Knighton Wales
94 B7 Knightstown Indiana
110 J2 Knightsville Indiana
42 G4 Knin Yugoslavia
32 H5 Kniphausen W Germany
109 H6 Knippa Texas
38 L7 Knittelfeld Austria
27 J12 Knivsta Sweden
46 E1 Knjaževac Yugoslavia
110 F5 Knobel Arkansas
142 G2 Knob Pk W Australia
14 B5 Knockboy mt Irish Rep
14 B5 Knockbrack mt Irish Rep
14 E1 Knocklayd mt N Ireland
14 D4 Knockmealdown Mts Irish Rep
14 B5 Knockowen mt Irish Rep
22 E1 Knokke Belgium
29 O5 Knolayarvi U.S.S.R.
101 M9 Knolls Utah
29 L10 Knorevesi Finland
28 E2 Knøsen hill Denmark
47 G9 Knossos Crete Greece
108 F3 Knott Texas
9 E3 Knowle England
107 K5 Knowles Oklahoma
121 S7 Knowlton Quebec
99 R5 Knowlton Wisconsin
99 U8 Knox Indiana
98 G1 Knox N Dakota
94 H5 Knox Pennsylvania
117 G8 Knox, C Graham I, Br Col
110 E1 Knox City Missouri
108 H2 Knox City Texas
146 F2 Knox Coast Antarctica
102 B3 Knoxville California
99 Q9 Knoxville Illinois
99 N8 Knoxville Iowa
111 E10 Knoxville Mississippi
94 K5 Knoxville Pennsylvania
112 C1 Knoxville Tennessee
83 K10 Knuckles mt Sri Lanka
115 R4 Knud Rasmussens Land Greenland
28 H6 Knudshoved C Denmark
36 G2 Knüllwald W Germany
8 D1 Knutsford England
52 D2 Knyazhaya Guba U.S.S.R.
52 F5 Knyazhevo U.S.S.R.
87 D12 Knysna S Africa
31 O2 Knyszyn Poland
29 M2 Koarvikods mt Finland
69 H14 Koba Indonesia
60 D14 Koba Japan
28 H6 Kobanke hill Denmark
42 F2 Kobarid Yugoslavia
60 D13 Kobayashi Japan
115 P5 Kobbermine Bugt B Greenland
28 C3 Kobberup Denmark
Kobdo Jargalant see Hovd
71 A2 Kobe Halmahera Indonesia
60 J11 Kōbe Japan
28 G7 Købelev Denmark
54 F7 Kobelyaki U.S.S.R.
89 A8 Kobe Mts S Africa
28 K5 København Denmark
38 H5 Kobernausser Wald reg Austria
36 C3 Kobern-Gondorf W Germany
67 H4 Kōbi-sho isld Japan
36 D3 Koblenz W Germany
86 F4 Kobowem Swamp Sudan
52 E5 Kobozha R U.S.S.R.
52 H5 Kobra R U.S.S.R.
61 M10 Kobuchizawa Japan
116 J3 Kobuk Alaska
116 H3 Kobuk R Alaska
31 K4 Kobylin Poland
47 K8 Koca R Turkey
47 J4 Kocabaş R Turkey
46 E3 Kočani Yugoslavia
47 J7 Koçarlı Turkey
47 L6 Koca Tepe mt Turkey
48 F6 Koceljevo Yugoslavia
42 F3 Kočevje Yugoslavia
73 R6 Ko Chang isld Thailand
52 F4 Kochen'ga U.S.S.R.
36 H5 Kocher R W Germany
54 M4 Kochetovka U.S.S.R.
52 H5 Kochevo U.S.S.R.
60 F11 Kōchi Japan
60 G12 Kōchi Japan
115 M4 Koch I N W Terr
60 G12 Kōchi prefect Japan
61 P14 Kochinda Okinawa
52 D3 Kochkoma U.S.S.R.
57 H4 Kochkorka U.S.S.R.
52 K2 Kochmes U.S.S.R.
101 O4 Koch Mt Montana
31 K4 Kocie Góry mts Poland
31 N4 Kock Poland
33 O7 Köckte E Germany
48 E4 Kocsola Hungary
52 J3 Kodachdikost U.S.S.R.
76 C5 Kodaikanal India
60 O4 Kodamari misaki C Japan
75 L6 Kodarma India
83 L9 Koddiyar B Sri Lanka
31 O4 Kodeń Poland
116 L8 Kodiak Alaska
116 L8 Kodiak I Alaska
83 K8 Kodikamam Sri Lanka
52 F4 Kodima U.S.S.R.
74 D8 Kodinar India
52 E3 Kodino U.S.S.R.
86 F4 Kodok Sudan
60 O4 Kodomari Japan
48 M2 Kodyma U.S.S.R.
22 D1 Koekelare Belgium
22 J1 Koersel Belgium
87 C11 Koes Namibia
60 P1 Koetoi Japan
103 L8 Kofa Mts Arizona
37 N6 Köfering W Germany
87 E11 Koffiefontein S Africa
71 C3 Kofiau isld W Irian
85 D7 Koforidua Ghana
61 M10 Kōfu Japan
61 N9 Koga Japan
141 K7 Kogan Queensland
28 J6 Køge Denmark
28 K6 Køge Bugt B Denmark
52 J3 Kogel' R U.S.S.R.
48 M4 Kogilnik R U.S.S.R.
116 H6 Kogrukluk R Alaska
60 D11 Kogushi Japan
74 D2 Kohat Pakistan
52 B5 Kohila U.S.S.R.
75 Q6 Kohima India
68 G6 Koh Ker Cambodia
146 H11 Kohler Ra Antarctica
37 O1 Kohren Sahlis E Germany
77 G2 Kohsun Afghanistan
68 F7 Koh Tang isld Cambodia
52 C5 Kohtla-Järve U.S.S.R.
47 K8 Kohu Dağ mt Turkey
145 E3 Kohuratahi New Zealand
61 M8 Koide Japan
114 E5 Koidern Yukon Terr
69 A8 Koihoa Nicobar Is
52 H3 Koin R U.S.S.R.
78 K3 Koi Sanjaq Iraq
29 P8 Koitere L Finland
29 L5 Koivu Finland
65 G7 Kōje isld S Korea
31 K6 Kojetín Czechoslovakia
60 N4 Ko jima isld Japan
143 B10 Kojonup W Australia
86 G4 Koka Dam Ethiopia
95 S1 Kokadjo Maine
83 L10 Kokagala mt Sri Lanka
55 D6 Kokalaat U.S.S.R.
57 F4 Kokand U.S.S.R.
117 P11 Kokanee Glacier Nat. Park Br Col
57 B2 Kokaral U.S.S.R.
48 F2 Kokava Czechoslovakia
60 J11 Kokawa Japan
57 D5 Kokayty U.S.S.R.
57 F6 Kokcha R Afghanistan
55 E4 Kokchetav U.S.S.R.
29 K10 Kokemäenjoki R Finland
29 J10 Kokemäki Finland
54 A2 Kokhanovo U.S.S.R.
80 B7 Kokhav Israel
29 K8 Kokkola Finland
85 E6 Koko Nigeria
136 K3 Kokoda Papua New Guinea
102 S12 Koko Head Hawaiian Is
116 F2 Kokolik R Alaska
94 A6 Kokomo Indiana
136 H2 Kokonau W Irian
144 C6 Kokonga New Zealand
Koko Nor see Qinghai Hu
52 C4 Kokonselka L Finland
54 F4 Kokorevka U.S.S.R.
69 B11 Kokos isld Indonesia
116 K4 Kokrines Hills Alaska
57 E4 Koksaray U.S.S.R.
66 B3 Kok Shaal Tau mts U.S.S.R.
52 G6 Kokshaga R U.S.S.R.
52 F4 Kokshen'ga R U.S.S.R.
22 D1 Koksijde Belgium
115 N6 Koksoak R Quebec
54 M8 Koksovyy U.S.S.R.
89 F8 Kokstad S Africa
60 D14 Kokubu Japan
60 D12 Kokura Japan
70 G7 Koku, Tg C Sulawesi
116 H7 Kokwok R Alaska
57 G4 Kok-Yangak U.S.S.R.
52 D1 Kola U.S.S.R.
70 G7 Kolaka Sulawesi
71 F6 Kolambugan Mindanao Philippines
139 K1 Kolan Queensland
141 K6 Kolan R Queensland
76 D4 Kolar India
76 D4 Kolar Gold Fields India
29 K4 Kolari Finland
Kolarovgrad Bulgaria see Shumen
48 D3 Kolárovo Czechoslovakia
26 F8 Kolåsen Sweden
46 D2 Kolašin Yugoslavia
27 H12 Kolbäck Sweden
71 M10 Kolbano Timor
Kolberg see Kołobrzeg
38 H8 Kölbnitz Austria
26 D9 Kolbotn Norway
31 N5 Kolbuszowa Poland
28 F5 Kolby Denmark
52 E6 Kol'chugino U.S.S.R.
85 A6 Kolda Senegal
28 B3 Koldby Denmark
28 C6 Kolding Denmark
86 E5 Kole Zaïre
135 T3 Kolekole peak Hawaiian Is
37 P5 Koleveč Czechoslovakia
52 B5 Kolga laht G U.S.S.R.
50 D2 Kolguyev Ostrov isld U.S.S.R.
76 B2 Kolhapur India
29 O8 Koli Finland
48 L5 Kolibash U.S.S.R.
116 J7 Koliganek Alaska
31 J5 Kolín Czechoslovakia
101 Q2 Kolin Montana
28 F4 Kolind Denmark
37 P5 Kolinec Czechoslovakia
28 C4 Kølkær Denmark
33 T7 Kol Kienitz E Germany
121 N7 Kol. Kienitz Ontario
37 L1 Kölleda E Germany
28 N2 Kollefjord Faeroes
76 C4 Kollegal India
46 E7 Kollínai Greece
25 F2 Kollum Netherlands
28 C4 Kollund Ringkøbing Denmark
28 C7 Kollund Sønderjylland Denmark
36 B2 Köln W Germany
31 N2 Kolno Poland
31 L3 Koło Poland
135 O1 Koloa Hawaiian Is
31 J1 Kołobrzeg Poland
33 S9 Kolochau E Germany
54 D2 Kolodnya U.S.S.R.
52 F5 Kologriv U.S.S.R.
71 B3 Kolok Indonesia
85 C6 Kolokani Mali
137 M3 Kolombangara isld Solomon Is
54 K1 Kolomna U.S.S.R.
48 J2 Kolomyya U.S.S.R.
141 K6 Kolonga Queensland
70 G6 Kolono Sulawesi
70 G6 Kolonodale Sulawesi
71 B2 Kolorai isld Halmahera Indonesia
55 F3 Kolosovka U.S.S.R.
Kolozsvar see Cluj
52 E5 Kolp' R U.S.S.R.
56 B2 Kolpashevo U.S.S.R.
33 R6 Kölpin-See L E Germany
33 Q10 Kölsa E Germany
26 G9 Kolsätt Sweden
52 D1 Kol'skiy Poluostrov pen U.S.S.R.
52 D1 Kol'skiy Zaliv gulf U.S.S.R.
28 F6 Kølstrup Denmark
27 H12 Kolsva Sweden
28 N2 Kolter Faeroes
52 A3 Kol'tsovo U.S.S.R.
48 F6 Kolubara R Yugoslavia
145 D1 Koluikohu New Zealand
73 L8 Kolumadulu Atoll Maldives
31 M4 Koluszki Poland
55 E5 Koluton U.S.S.R.
52 J1 Kolva R Komi U.S.S.R.
52 J4 Kolva R Perm U.S.S.R.
26 E7 Kolvereid Norway
26 O1 Kolvik Norway
52 D2 Kolvitsa U.S.S.R.
87 E8 Kolwezi Zaïre
54 K1 Kolyberovo U.S.S.R.
54 H1 Kolyubakino U.S.S.R.
147 P2 Kolyuchinskaya U.S.S.R.
116 A3 Kolyuchinskaya Guba gulf U.S.S.R.
56 B5 Kolyvan' U.S.S.R.
27 G14 Kölzby Sweden
46 F1 Kom mt Bulgaria
68 D5 Koma Burma
86 G4 Koma Ethiopia
61 P6 Kōma Japan
85 G6 Komadugu Gana R Nigeria
61 L10 Komagane Japan
60 O3 Komaga-take mt Hokkaido Japan
61 N8 Komaga-take mt Honshu Japan
26 N1 Komagfjord Norway
26 S1 Komagvaer Norway
48 E3 Komárno Czechoslovakia
119 U8 Komarno Manitoba
48 E3 Komárom Hungary
48 E3 Komárom co Hungary
89 G6 Komati R Swaziland
89 G5 Komati Poort S Africa
103 M8 Komatke Arizona
61 K9 Komatsu Ishikawa Japan
61 O7 Komatsu Yamagata Japan
71 L8 Komba isld Indonesia
46 E5 Kombóti Greece
28 E3 Komdrup Denmark
88 D2 Kome I Uganda
61 O5 Kominato Japan
48 E2 Komjatice Czechoslovakia
48 E4 Komló Hungary
53 E9 Kommunarsk U.S.S.R.
57 F5 Kommunizma, Pik mt U.S.S.R.
71 J9 Komodo isld Indonesia
85 D7 Komoé R Ivory Coast
84 J5 Kôm Ombo Egypt
61 M9 Komoro Japan
47 G3 Komotiní Greece
46 D2 Komovi mt Yugoslavia
89 D8 Kompas Berg mt S Africa
68 G7 Kompong Cham Cambodia
68 G6 Kompong Chhnang Cambodia
68 G6 Kompong Kleang Cambodia
68 F7 Kompong Som Cambodia
68 G7 Kompong Speu Cambodia
68 G6 Kompong Sralao Cambodia
68 G6 Kompong Thom Cambodia
68 G6 Kompong Trabek Cambodia
68 G7 Kompong Trach Cambodia
68 G7 Kompong Tralach Cambodia
71 J4 Kompot Sulawesi
48 M4 Komrat U.S.S.R.
89 B9 Komsbergeskarp mts S Africa
55 D4 Komsomolets U.S.S.R.
51 J1 Komsomolets, Ostrov isld U.S.S.R.
54 E8 Komsomol'sk Ukraine U.S.S.R.
52 F6 Komsomol'sk U.S.S.R.
55 D1 Komsomol'skiy U.S.S.R.
54 K9 Komsomol'skoye U.S.S.R.
59 L1 Komsomol'skoye-na-Amure U.S.S.R.
103 M10 Kom Vo Arizona
52 E6 Konakovo U.S.S.R.
77 B5 Konār Takhteh Iran
109 L1 Konawa Oklahoma
42 H3 Končanica Yugoslavia
71 C3 Konda W Irian

55 E2	Konda R U.S.S.R.
76 E1	Kondagaon India
121 O6	Kondiaronk, L Quebec
143 C10	Kondinin W Australia
88 E4	Kondoa Tanzania
52 D4	Kondopoga U.S.S.R.
48 F4	Kondoros Hungary
54 G2	Kondrovo U.S.S.R.
86 B3	Konduga Nigeria
143 B9	Kondut W Australia
56 D2	Konduyak U.S.S.R.
52 J3	Konetsbor U.S.S.R.
52 E4	Konevo U.S.S.R.
28 H6	Kong Denmark
85 D7	Kong Ivory Coast
116 R2	Kongakut R Alaska
115 Q4	Kong Christian den IX Land Greenland
115 R3	Kong Christian den X Land Greenland
28 B6	Kongeå R Denmark
28 K5	Kongens Lyngby Denmark
115 P5	Kong Frederik den VI Kyst coast Greenland
29 M9	Konginkangas Finland
68 F7	Kong Kaôh Kong Cambodia
50 B1	Kong Karls Land isld Spitzbergen
70 E4	Kong Kat mt Kalimantan
70 E4	Kongkemul mt Kalimantan
70 G6	Kongkong R Sulawesi
87 D9	Kongola Namibia
86 E7	Kongolo Zaïre
86 F4	Kongor Sudan
147 E10	Kong Oscars Fj Greenland
26 J3	Kongsbekktind mt Norway
27 D12	Kongsberg Norway
26 R1	Kongsfjord Norway
22 J2	Kongsfjord inlet Norway
28 B6	Kongsmark Denmark
26 F7	Kongsmoen Norway
28 J6	Kongsted Denmark
27 E11	Kongsvinger Norway
66 B4	Kongur Shan mt China
88 F5	Kongwa Tanzania
31 M5	Koniecpol Poland
36 H4	Konigheim W Germany
36 F6	Königsberg W Germany
	Königsberg see Kaliningrad
36 D6	Königstein mt W Germany
37 J6	Königsbronn W Germany
33 T10	Königsbrück E Germany
37 K7	Königsbrunn W Germany
41 O2	Königsdorf W Germany
37 L2	Königsee E Germany
37 L4	Königsfeld W Germany
	Königshofen see Lauda-Königshofen
36 H4	Königshofen W Germany
33 N8	Königslutter W Germany
36 F5	Königsstuhl mt W Germany
36 E3	Königstein W Germany
38 L5	Königswiesen Austria
36 C2	Königswinter W Germany
33 T8	Königs Wusterhausen E Germany
31 L3	Konin Poland
145 E4	Konini New Zealand
48 D5	Konispol Albania
42 H5	Konitsa Yugoslavia
48 E6	Konjuh mt Yugoslavia
26 M3	Konkämä Älv R Sweden/Finland
88 A8	Konkola Zambia
85 B6	Konkoure R Guinea
33 P9	Konnern E Germany
37 N3	Konnersreuth W Germany
29 M9	Konnevesi Finland
85 D7	Konongo Ghana
88 C5	Konongo Tanzania
61 N9	Konosu Japan
54 E5	Konotop U.S.S.R.
66 D3	Konqi He R China
85 C7	Konsankoro Guinea
31 M4	Końskie Poland
53 F10	Konstantinovsk U.S.S.R.
41 K2	Konstanz W Germany
85 F6	Kontagora Nigeria
86 B4	Kontcha Cameroon
22 G1	Kontich Belgium
29 N7	Kontiomäki Finland
116 L6	Kontrashibuna L Alaska
68 J6	Kontum, Plat. du Vietnam
52 F2	Konushinskaya Korga C U.S.S.R.
78 D3	Konya Turkey
36 B4	Konz W Germany
88 F2	Konza Kenya
37 O5	Konzell W Germany
55 C2	Konzhakovskiy Kamen', G U.S.S.R.
25 C4	Koog Netherlands
116 C5	Kookooligit Mts St Lawrence I, Alaska
143 D8	Kookynie W Australia
140 F5	Koolamarra Queensland
141 F3	Koolatah Queensland
142 E4	Koolatong R N Terr Australia
102 S11	Koolaulos Hawaiian Is
102 S12	Koolaupoko Hawaiian Is
141 G3	Koolburra Queensland
142 B6	Kooline W Australia
143 C9	Koolivoo, L Queensland
143 G3	Koolyanobbing W Australia
141 G3	Koonalda S Australia
143 B9	Koorda W Australia
142 E4	Koordarrie W Australia
144 A7	Kopeka B New Zealand
33 T8	Köpenick E Germany
26 K8	Kopparberg county Sweden
145 E2	Kopu New Zealand
145 E4	Kopuaranga New Zealand
77 C4	Kor R Iran
75 K7	Korba India
32 J10	Korbach W Germany
100 B9	Korbel California
69 E10	Korbu, G. mt Malaysia
46 D4	Korçë Albania
42 H6	Korčula Yugoslavia
36 B4	Kordel W Germany
77 A2	Kordent Iran
77 D1	Kord Kuy Iran
	Kordofan prov Sudan see Northern and Southern Kordofan provs
77 G6	Kords reg Iran
64 H4	Korea Bay China/Korea
65 G4	Korea, North rep E Asia
65 H6	Korea, South rep E Asia
52 D2	Korelaksha U.S.S.R.
54 E5	Korenevo U.S.S.R.
53 F9	Korenovsk U.S.S.R.
60 D14	Kori Japan
46 F4	Koritnik mt Yugoslavia
28 E6	Kori Denmark
48 E6	Korita Yugoslavia
61 N9	Köriyama Japan
55 D4	Korkino U.S.S.R.
47 L7	Korkuteli Turkey
54 B3	Korma U.S.S.R.
120 G5	Kormakiti, C Cyprus
04 D3	Körmend Hungary
55 F3	Kormilovka U.S.S.R.
42 G5	Kornat isld Yugoslavia
37 L5	Kornburg W Germany
39 N6	Kornelimünster W Germany
27 K1	Körner W Germany
48 L3	Korneuburg Austria
55 F5	Korneyevka U.S.S.R.
27 E13	Kornsjö Norway
28 C3	Kornum Denmark

36 G6	Kornwestheim W Germany
70 G5	Koro R Sulawesi
55 G6	Korobovskiy U.S.S.R.
54 J8	Korocha U.S.S.R.
78 C1	Köroglu D Turkey
88 G4	Korogwe Tanzania
138 F7	Koroit Victoria
113 P8	Korona Florida
85 E7	Koropa mt Togo
139 G6	Korong Vale Victoria
46 E8	Koróni Greece
47 F4	Korónia, L Greece
31 K2	Koronowo Poland
54 D5	Korop U.S.S.R.
48 C1	Koropets U.S.S.R.
47 F7	Koropi Greece
48 F4	Körös R Hungary
53 C8	Korosten U.S.S.R.
86 C2	Koro Toro Chad
54 L6	Korotoyak U.S.S.R.
61 Q12	Kouri-jima isld Okinawa
29 M9	Korpilahti Finland
26 N5	Korpilombolo Sweden
29 J11	Korpo Finland
59 M2	Korsakov U.S.S.R.
27 H14	Korsberga Sweden
36 B1	Korschenbroich W Germany
28 H5	Korsør R C Denmark
48 J2	Korshev U.S.S.R.
28 E3	Korsholm isld Denmark
27 H11	Korsnäs Sweden
26 H3	Korsnes Norway
28 G6	Korsør Denmark
54 C7	Korsun' Shevchenkovskiy U.S.S.R.
22 E1	Kortemark Belgium
29 K8	Kortesjärvi Finland
22 J2	Kortessem Belgium
27 G12	Kortfors Sweden
25 A5	Kortgene Netherlands
52 H4	Kortkoros U.S.S.R.
22 E2	Kortrijk Belgium
47 J5	Kortsovo U.S.S.R.
47 N4	Koru Dağı mt Turkey
144 C5	Korumburra Victoria
29 O3	Korvatunturi mt Finland
29 O4	Korya U.S.S.R.
52 G4	Koryazhma U.S.S.R.
54 D5	Koryukovka U.S.S.R.
47 J8	Kos isld Greece
52 H5	Kosa U.S.S.R.
56 A3	Kosaga Japan
61 O5	Kosaka Japan
73 R7	Ko Samui isld Thailand
57 D1	Kosa Gora U.S.S.R.
54 J2	Kosaya Gora U.S.S.R.
52 G3	Kosbogat U.S.S.R.
37 M6	Kösching W Germany
31 K3	Kościan Poland
31 K1	Kościerzyna Poland
111 G8	Kosciusko Mississippi
117 G7	Kosciusko I Alaska
139 J6	Kosciusko, Mt Victoria
33 S10	Koselitz E Germany
33 U4	Koserow E Germany
56 B1	Koses R U.S.S.R.
76 C2	Kosgi India
47 J5	Kosh Agach U.S.S.R.
55 D2	Koshay U.S.S.R.
60 S2	Koshikawa Japan
60 C14	Koshiki-kaikyö str Japan
60 C14	Koshiki-rettö islds Japan
110 E5	Koshkonong Missouri
57 B4	Kosh-Kupyr U.S.S.R.
61 M9	Koshoku Japan
48 G2	Košice Czechoslovakia
89 H6	Kosi L S Africa
55 C5	Kos-Istek U.S.S.R.
48 E5	Koška Yugoslavia
52 J2	Kožim U.S.S.R.
52 J3	Kozhim-Iz, Gora mt U.S.S.R.
38 L5	Kosk R U.S.S.R.
26 M5	Koskivaara Sweden
57 D1	Koskol' U.S.S.R.
57 H3	Koskuduk U.S.S.R.
26 L4	Koskullskulle Sweden
52 G3	Koslan U.S.S.R.
	Köslin see Koszalin
52 G2	Kosma R U.S.S.R.
48 J2	Kosmach U.S.S.R.
100 C3	Kosmos Washington
59 J4	Kosong N Korea
54 M6	Kosovo Yugoslavia
48 C1	Kosovka U.S.S.R.
72 H4	Kosovska Mitrovica Yugoslavia
33 S10	Kossdorf E Germany
109 L4	Kosse Texas
36 E1	Kösseln E Germany
37 O1	Kössern E Germany
37 P7	Kössern E Germany
31 N3	Kossów Poland
27 H15	Kosta Sweden
33 T9	Kostebrau E Germany
28 J7	Koster Denmark
54 L1	Kosterevo U.S.S.R.
86 F3	Kosti Sudan
52 F5	Kostroma U.S.S.R.
54 B4	Kostyukovichi U.S.S.R.
61 L9	Kosugi Japan
50 H2	Kos'yu U.S.S.R.
52 J2	Kos'yuvom U.S.S.R.
31 J1	Koszalin Poland
48 D3	Kőszeg Hungary
75 K7	Kota India
64 B2	Kota Cambodia
69 F9	Kota Baharu Malaysia
69 E13	Kota Baru Sumatra
70 E4	Kota Belud Sabah
70 K8	Kotabumi Sumatra
71 J4	Kotabunan Sulawesi
70 E2	Kota Kinabalu Sabah
29 O4	Kotala Finland
70 F1	Kotamobagu Sulawesi
69 E12	Kotapinang Baru Sumatra
69 F11	Kota Tinggi Malaysia
70 B6	Kotawaringin Kalimantan
117 N6	Kotcho R Br Col
26 S1	Kotelnes Norway
25 F5	Kotel Bulgaria
54 E5	Koteltsy U.S.S.R.
52 E5	Kotelnich U.S.S.R.
53 F8	Kotelnikovo U.S.S.R.
51 N1	Kotel'nyy, Ostrov isld U.S.S.R.
145 E3	Kotemaori New Zealand
33 P9	Köthen E Germany
37 F3	Kot Kapura India
29 J9	Kotka Finland
55 G2	Kotkino U.S.S.R.
54 G4	Kotlas U.S.S.R.
52 H5	Kotlin, O isld U.S.S.R.
61 N8	Kotohira Japan
60 P2	Kotor Japan
42 H4	Kotor Varoš Yugoslavia
53 C10	Kotovsk U.S.S.R.
54 A1	Kotri Pakistan
74 A7	Kotr-Tas U.S.S.R.
54 J8	Kotsenarmeysk U.S.S.R.
54 A1	Kotsenarmeysk U.S.S.R.
39 N7	Kronwinkl W Germany
86 C4	Kotto R Cent Afr Republic
31 O5	Kotuń Poland
76 C3	Kottayam India
51 M1	Kotuy R U.S.S.R.
116 F3	Kotzebue Alaska
116 F3	Kotzebue Sd Alaska
116 E3	Kotzenbroda E Germany
37 O5	Kötzting W Germany
85 E8	Kouandé Benin
86 B4	Kouango Cent Afr Republic
86 C2	Kóuba Modéounga Chad
85 D6	Koudougou Upper Volta

89 A9	Koue Bokkeveld reg S Africa
89 D8	Koueveld Berge mts S Africa
47 H10	Koufonisi isld Crete Greece
47 H8	Koufonisia isld Greece
89 C9	Kougaberge mts S Africa
7 L9	Kough oil rig North Sea
86 B6	Koulamoutou Gabon
68 G6	Koulen Cambodia
85 C6	Koulikoro Mali
141 J5	Koumala Queensland
86 C4	Koumra Chad
86 C4	Koungouri Chad
86 F3	Kounoupo isld Greece
57 G2	Kounradskiy U.S.S.R.
111 B11	Kountze Texas
85 D6	Koupela Upper Volta
	Kouqian see Yongji
61 Q12	Kouri-jima isld Okinawa
84 F5	Kourionisi isld Crete Greece
84 H2	Kourou, Passe de Chad
129 H2	Kourou Fr Guiana
85 C6	Kouroussa Guinea
89 B9	Kousberg mt S Africa
86 B3	Koussa Mauritania
85 C6	Kousséri Cameroon
85 C7	Koutiala Mali
46 F7	Koutsopódhi Greece
54 K8	Kouyou R Congo
54 N1	Kouvola Finland
86 C6	Kova R Congo
56 F2	Kova U.S.S.R.
48 F5	Kovačica Yugoslavia
46 C1	Kovač Planina mt Yugoslavia
52 D2	Kovda U.S.S.R.
55 E1	Kovdozero, Oz L U.S.S.R.
52 F6	Kovernino U.S.S.R.
29 P9	Kovero Finland
48 F6	Kovin Yugoslavia
52 G1	Kovriga, Gora mt U.S.S.R.
54 N1	Kovrov U.S.S.R.
52 E5	Kovzha R U.S.S.R.
54 C2	Kovzhskoye, Oz L U.S.S.R.
52 G6	Kovrov U.S.S.R.
52 E5	Kovzha R U.S.S.R.
52 D2	Kovzhskoye, Oz L U.S.S.R.
144 C5	Kowai Bush New Zealand
31 L3	Kowal Poland
14 L2	Kowalewo Poland
115 O3	Kowhitirangi New Zealand
120 C2	Kowkash Ontario
67 G6	Kowloon Hong Kong
32 K5	Koyasan Japan
107 P7	Krebs Oklahoma
28 G6	Krefeld W Germany
28 J5	Kregme Denmark
47 K8	Köyceğiz Turkey
47 J8	Köyceğiz Gölü L Turkey
52 F2	Koyda U.S.S.R.
52 H4	Koygorodok U.S.S.R.
52 G3	Koyp, Gora mt U.S.S.R.
54 L9	Koysug U.S.S.R.
57 D4	Koytash U.S.S.R.
116 G4	Koyuk Alaska
116 L3	Koyuk R Alaska
116 J4	Koyukuk I Alaska
78 E1	Koyulhisar Turkey
52 Q4	Koyva R U.S.S.R.
32 K5	Koyvozero U.S.S.R.
61 P13	Koza Okinawa
61 J12	Koza R Japan
47 J5	Kozak Turkey
60 C11	Ko-zaki C Japan
60 O11	Kōzan Japan
78 E3	Kozan Turkey
46 E6	Kozáni Greece
42 H3	Kozara Plan Yugoslavia
48 E2	Kozárovce Czechoslovakia
54 C6	Kozelets U.S.S.R.
54 E7	Kozel'sk U.S.S.R.
54 G2	Kozel'sk U.S.S.R.
52 J2	Kozhim U.S.S.R.
52 J3	Kozhim-Iz, Gora mt U.S.S.R.
52 J2	Kozhmozero, Oz L U.S.S.R.
52 E3	Kozhposelok U.S.S.R.
55 G3	Kozhurla U.S.S.R.
52 J2	Kozhva R U.S.S.R.
31 N4	Kozienice Poland
46 E3	Kozjak mt Yugoslavia
48 F7	Kozloduy Bulgaria
54 M6	Kozlovac Yugoslavia
78 C1	Kozlu Turkey
31 K4	Koźmin Poland
48 J1	Kozova U.S.S.R.
54 L6	Kozuchow Poland
76 C2	Krishna R India
81 N11	Kōzu-shima isld Japan
75 N7	Krishnanagar India
85 D8	Kpandu Ghana
17 G9	Kristel Algeria
27 H15	Kristianopel Sweden
27 C13	Kristiansand Norway
27 F15	Kristianstad county Sweden
26 D13	Kristiansund Norway
29 J9	Kristiinankaupunki Finland
28 E4	Kristrup Denmark
46 E2	Kriva R Yugoslavia
46 E2	Krivaja R Yugoslavia
46 F5	Krivelj Yugoslavia
47 N4	Krivi Rog U.S.S.R.
54 G5	Krivoy Rog U.S.S.R.
31 O1	Krivoye Ozero U.S.S.R.
42 K6	Križevci Yugoslavia
31 J5	Krk Yugoslavia
	Krkonose mts Czechoslovakia
80 G1	Krnjeuša Yugoslavia
116 G8	Krnov Czechoslovakia
142 F3	Krobia Poland
28 B5	Kröderen Norway
70 N9	Krogager Denmark
27 P1	Kroghville Denmark
28 B5	Krokmagle Denmark
47 K6	Kroja Java
47 H13	Krokek Sweden
89 E5	Krokodil R S Africa
80 F4	Krokom Sweden
26 J9	Krokow Sweden
26 S1	Kroksjø Sweden
54 E5	Krolevets U.S.S.R.
36 E4	Krombach W Germany
28 C6	Kroměrž Czechoslovakia
25 D5	Kromme Rijn R Netherlands
37 L3	Kronach W Germany
119 N8	Kronau Sask
116 F4	Krondorf Czechoslovakia
116 N3	Kronenberg W Germany
77 Q6	Krong Poko R Vietnam
77 B3	Kronoby Finland
77 B3	Kronprins Frederiks Bjerge mts Greenland
29 O7	Kronprins Martha Antarctica
146 A6	Kronprins Olav Kyst Antarctica
37 L5	Kronsdorf Austria
54 J8	Kronshtadt U.S.S.R.
89 B9	Kroonstad S Africa
37 N7	Kronwinkl W Germany
117 P2	Kronstad S Africa
29 L6	Kropachevo U.S.S.R.
33 P4	Kröpelin E Germany
29 L6	Kropotkin U.S.S.R.
33 S9	Kroppenstedt E Germany
33 Q7	Kröslin E Germany
33 T4	Krościenko Poland
54 C2	Krośniewice Poland
53 C6	Krosno Poland
31 J3	Krosno Odrzańskie Poland
54 K8	Krotoszyn Poland
31 K4	Krotten Kopf mt W Germany
111 E11	Krotz Springs Louisiana
46 F3	Kroússa mt Greece
52 H6	Krrab mt Albania
46 D2	Krrabë mt Albania

54 G6	Krasnokutsk U.S.S.R.
55 G4	Krasnokutskoye Pavlodar U.S.S.R.
89 G4	Krasnolesniyy U.S.S.R.
31 N1	Krasnoles'ye U.S.S.R.
52 C4	Krasnoostrovskiy U.S.S.R.
53 F9	Krasnoslobodsk U.S.S.R.
55 D2	Krasnotur'insk U.S.S.R.
55 D2	Krasnoufimsk U.S.S.R.
52 J4	Krasnoural'skiy U.S.S.R.
50 E4	Krasnovishersk U.S.S.R.
55 F3	Krasnoyarka U.S.S.R.
55 D2	Krasnoyarka Omsk U.S.S.R.
55 D2	Krasnoyarka Sverdlovsk U.S.S.R.
56 D3	Krasnoyarsk U.S.S.R.
54 M1	Krasnoye Ekho U.S.S.R.
57 B6	Krasnoye Znamya U.S.S.R.
52 H4	Krasnozatonskiy U.S.S.R.
116 F3	Krasnozaterskiy U.S.S.R.
46 E1	Kruševac Yugoslavia
55 C4	Krasnoznamenskiy Bashkirskaya U.S.S.R.
52 C6	Krasny Bor U.S.S.R.
52 H3	Krasny Okny U.S.S.R.
54 J7	Krasny Liman U.S.S.R.
54 K8	Krasny Luch U.S.S.R.
54 N1	Krasny Mayak U.S.S.R.
54 L1	Krasny Tkach U.S.S.R.
52 G6	Krasnyye-Baki U.S.S.R.
52 E5	Krasnyye Tkachi U.S.S.R.
55 B5	Krasnyy Kholm Kalinin U.S.S.R.
54 E4	Krasnyy Kholm Orenburg U.S.S.R.
55 D3	Krasny-Klyuch U.S.S.R.
55 D3	Krasnyy Oktyabr U.S.S.R.
52 E5	Krasnyy Pereval U.S.S.R.
54 D7	Krasnyy Yar Omsk U.S.S.R.
55 D2	Krasnyy Yar Sverdlovsk U.S.S.R.
52 H6	Kratie Cambodia
38 L7	Kraubath Austria
41 K1	Krauchenwies W Germany
115 O3	Kraulshavn Greenland
36 H5	Krautheim W Germany
16 D9	Ksar el Boukhari Algeria
52 J4	Ksenofontova U.S.S.R.
36 H4	Külsheim W Germany
79 C4	Ktima Cyprus
69 D9	Kuah Malaysia
69 F10	Krehberg mt W Germany
69 G11	Kreiensen W Germany
47 F1	Krekatok I Alaska
46 E4	Kremena Bulgaria
54 D7	Kremenchug U.S.S.R.
54 E5	Kremenchugskoye Vdkhr res U.S.S.R.
54 K7	Kremennaya U.S.S.R.
47 F2	Kremikovtsi Bulgaria
38 M5	Kremlin Russia
33 N8	Kremlingen W Germany
37 M8	Kremmen E Germany
105 F4	Kremmling Colorado
37 O6	Kremmling W Germany
70 B6	Kualabatim W Germany
55 D5	Kumak U.S.S.R.
37 N8	Krempe W Germany
33 R5	Krems Austria
116 D9	Krenitzin Is Aleutian Is
33 Q10	Krenitz E Germany
48 F7	Kreševo Yugoslavia
108 F1	Kress Texas
52 D6	Kresti U.S.S.R.
70 E2	Krešuvard ? Sabah
51 H1	Kresty U.S.S.R.
27 M16	Kretinga U.S.S.R.
38 L5	Kreuth W Germany
48 J7	Kreuzeck-Gruppe mts Austria
38 L5	Kreuzen Austria
41 K2	Kreuzlingen Switzerland
52 E3	Kreuzlingen, Oz L U.S.S.R.
36 E4	Kreuztal W Germany
36 A5	Kreuzwald, Oz L U.S.S.R.
28 A3	Krik Denmark
38 F7	Krik Vig B Denmark
52 G6	Krik U.S.S.R.
28 A3	Krik Denmark
28 D10	Kringen Norway
75 N7	Krionéri Greece
70 P10	Kriós, Akr C Crete Greece
58 F1	Krishna R India
76 C2	Krishna India
75 N7	Krishnagiri India
48 G6	Krivaševsky U.S.S.R.
52 F4	Krivel' Yugoslavia
55 F2	Krita Kyustendil U.S.S.R.
47 L6	Kriti isld Greece
70 P14	Kriva R Yugoslavia
42 K6	Krivaja R Yugoslavia
70 E1	Kuda R Sri Lanka
48 N3	Kuda Burma
54 G3	Kudap Sumatra
54 G5	Krivongo R U.S.S.R.
31 O1	Kudat Malaysia
74 D1	Kudiakof Is Alaska
55 D4	Kudymkar U.S.S.R.
141 K6	Kunashir O U.S.S.R.
55 D5	Kuduarra Well W Australia
70 N9	Kuduk U.S.S.R.
80 C3	Kudus Java
143 D10	Kudus Java
47 K6	Kühe, Küh-e mt Iran
84 F4	Kufrah Oasis, Al Libya
80 F4	Kufr Abil Jordan
80 G4	Kufr Jayiz Jordan
80 F4	Kufr Khal Jordan
80 F5	Kufr Kifiya Jordan
80 F5	Kufr Rakib Jordan
80 F5	Kufr Saum Jordan
38 M4	Kufstein Austria
60 D13	Kuga Japan
56 C2	Kugitangtau, Khr mts U.S.S.R.
116 J4	Kiva R U.S.S.R.
116 L7	Kiva U.S.S.R.
37 N6	Kronwinkl W Germany
116 L7	Kronstad S Africa

36 C3	Kruft-Mendig W Germany
89 G4	Kruger Nat. Park S Africa
89 E6	Krugersdorp S Africa
70 K8	Krui Sumatra
22 F2	Kruishoutem Belgium
46 D3	Kruje Albania
109 K2	Krum Texas
38 O6	Krumbach Austria
46 D2	Krume Albania
32 F6	Krummennerl W Germany
33 T4	Krummin E Germany
41 O2	Krün W Germany
	Krungkao see Ayutthaya
68 E6	Krung Thep cap Thailand
46 E6	Krupanj Yugoslavia
55 F6	Krupina U.S.S.R.
71 F7	Krusenstern, C Alaska
47 F3	Krušné Hory mts Czechoslovakia
27 M15	Kruševo Yugoslavia
52 C6	Kruspils U.S.S.R.
52 H6	Krutaya U.S.S.R.
52 H3	Kruth France
42 G4	Krutoyarskiy U.S.S.R.
55 D4	Kulevcha U.S.S.R.
140 C7	Kulgera N Terr Aust
69 E10	Krylbo Sweden
52 H5	Krylov Poland
48 J1	Kromy U.S.S.R.
69 E10	Krynica Poland
143 C10	Krylov U.S.S.R.
143 B9	Kryukovo U.S.S.R.
54 J1	Krylovskaya U.S.S.R.
56 E4	Kryzhina, Khr mts U.S.S.R.
31 L5	Krzepice Poland
32 M10	Krzeszowice Poland
98 H3	Krzywin Poland
31 J3	Krzyz Poland
85 C4	Ksabi Algeria
85 C4	Ksaib Ounane, El Mali
16 D9	Ksar el Boukhari Algeria
16 D9	Ksar-el-Kebir Morocco
16 D9	Ksar Sghir Morocco
52 J4	Ksenofontova U.S.S.R.
85 C4	Ksour, Mts. des Algeria
79 C4	Ktima Cyprus
69 D9	Kuah Malaysia
26 H7	Kuaize R China
26 G6	Kuala Indonesia
69 D11	Kuala Sumatra
69 E10	Kuala Dungun Malaysia
69 E10	Kuala Kangsar Malaysia
70 C5	Kuala Kerai Malaysia
70 C5	Kualakurun Kalimantan
69 E10	Kualalangsa Sumatra
69 F10	Kuala Lipis Malaysia
69 E11	Kuala Lumpur Malaysia
70 C5	Kuala Kapuas Kalimantan
70 C6	Kuala Nerang Malaysia
70 B6	Kualapembuang Kalimantan
70 B6	Kuala Penyu Sabah
69 E10	Kuala Pilah Malaysia
69 D13	Kualasimpang Indonesia
48 F7	Kuala Selangor Malaysia
61 K12	Kuala Terengganu Malaysia
46 E2	Kuamut R Sabah
70 E2	Kuamut Sabah
70 E2	Kuancheng China
71 H4	Kuandang, Tk B Sulawesi Indonesia
59 H3	Kuandian China
69 F11	Kuantan Malaysia
145 E2	Kuaotunu New Zealand
87 C10	Kub Namibia
53 G12	Kuba U.S.S.R.
53 F11	Kuban' R U.S.S.R.
78 G4	Kubar, el Syria
80 F5	Kubbum Sudan
80 F5	Kubena R U.S.S.R.
52 E4	Kubena U.S.S.R.
52 E4	Kubenskoye, Oz L U.S.S.R.
52 E3	Kubnya R U.S.S.R.
89 H7	Kubokawa Japan
79 A4	Kubra, El Egypt
47 H5	Kubrat Bulgaria
29 H11	Kubu Indonesia
116 J8	Kubukhay U.S.S.R.
52 E5	Kubumesaäi Kalimantan
55 D4	Kubsevskiy U.S.S.R.
48 G6	Kučevo Yugoslavia
48 G6	Kuchen W Germany
70 B4	Kuchen Spitze mt Austria
55 F4	Kuching Sarawak
70 B4	Kuchinotsu Japan
55 D4	Kuchurgan R U.S.S.R.
47 K5	Küçnitz W Germany
52 D6	Kückurgan R U.S.S.R.
70 B5	Kuda R Sri Lanka
83 K11	Kudat Malaysia
135 V5	Kudamatsu Japan
80 F1	Kudangan Kalimantan
80 F1	Kudap Sumatra
69 F12	Kudat Malaysia
116 J2	Kudap Sumatra
48 N3	Kudaw Burma
143 B6	Kudow R U.S.S.R.
74 D1	Kunar Afghanistan
53 B5	Kunashak U.S.S.R.
31 O1	Kunashir O U.S.S.R.
55 T1	Kunashir O U.S.S.R.
80 B5	Kunaysah, Al Jordan
55 C2	Kugitangtau, Khr mts U.S.S.R.

116 F2	Kukpowruk R Alaska
116 E2	Kukpuk R Alaska
135 U4	Kukuihaele Hawaiian Is
118 K1	Kukukus L Ontario
69 F12	Kukulugala mt Sri Lanka
70 D6	Kukup, G mt Kalimantan
89 B4	Kul Botswana
46 F1	Kula Bulgaria
47 K6	Kula Turkey
48 F5	Kula Yugoslavia
69 D12	Kulabu, Gunung mt Sumatra
117 Q7	Kupreanof I Alaska
116 H9	Kupreanof Pt Alaska
116 L7	Kupreanof St Alaska
37 L3	Kups W Germany
54 J7	Kupyansk U.S.S.R.
66 C3	Kuqa China
59 L1	Kur R U.S.S.R.
57 G3	Kuragaty U.S.S.R.
52 J2	Kurahashi-jima isld Japan
53 G12	Kurakh R U.S.S.R.
57 E4	Kuramins'kiy Khr mts U.S.S.R.
60 C12	Kuramoto Japan
141 H3	Kuranda Queensland
52 J4	Kurashasayskiy U.S.S.R.
60 G11	Kurashiki Japan
142 G4	Kura Soak W Australia
60 G10	Kurayoshi Japan
56 C5	Kurazhskiy Khr mts U.S.S.R.
47 G3	Kurazhali Dam Bulgaria
55 D4	Kurchum U.S.S.R.
57 H3	Kurdai U.S.S.R.
	Kürdistan reg Turkey/Iraq/Iran
74 F9	Kurduvadi India
47 G3	Kürdzhali Bulgaria
60 F11	Kure Japan
51 H2	Kureyka U.S.S.R.
51 J2	Kureyka R U.S.S.R.
55 F5	Kurgal'dzhino U.S.S.R.
52 F4	Kuloy U.S.S.R.
50 F3	Kurganskaya Oblast' prov U.S.S.R.
57 E5	Kurgan-Tyube U.S.S.R.
57 D1	Kurgasyn U.S.S.R.
137 P1	Kuria Muria isld Arabian Sea
83 H3	Kuria Muria islds Arabian Sea
43 D13	Kuriate Is. Tunisia
140 F5	Kuridala Queensland
29 J9	Kurikka Finland
61 O7	Kurikoma-yama mt Japan
	Kuril Is see Kuril'skiye Ostrova
52 F5	Kurilovo U.S.S.R.
59 N2	Kuril'sk U.S.S.R.
51 O4	Kuril'skiye Ostrova islds U.S.S.R.
145 F3	Kuripapango New Zealand
60 P2	Kuriyama Japan
29 O10	Kurikäki U.S.S.R.
84 J5	Kurkur Oasis Egypt
52 F6	Kurlovskiy U.S.S.R.
86 F3	Kurmuk Sudan
76 B6	Kurnool India
61 O9	Kurobane Japan
61 L9	Kurobe Japan
61 O5	Kuroiso Japan
119 O7	Kuroki Sask
60 O3	Kuromatsunai Japan
60 G10	Kurowaka Japan
54 K1	Kurovskoye U.S.S.R.
144 C6	Kurow New Zealand
31 N4	Kurow Poland
139 K5	Kurri Kurri New S Wales
27 M16	Kuršiu Zaliv U.S.S.R.
46 E1	Kuršumlija Yugoslavia
57 A4	Kurt U.S.S.R.
47 K8	Kürten W Germany
38 C1	Kürten W Germany
47 K8	Kurtalan Turkey
56 D5	Kurtoğlu Burun C Turkey
56 D5	Kurtushibinskiy, Khr mts U.S.S.R.
29 K10	Kuru Finland
78 E2	Kuruçay Turkey
89 C5	Kuruman S Africa
60 D12	Kurume Japan
140 C5	Kurumkan U.S.S.R.
69 F1	Kurun' R Aust
83 K10	Kurunegala Sri Lanka
146 H2	Kururi Japan
52 J10	Kuskhan Burma
61 J12	Kusa R China
60 O3	Kushalino U.S.S.R.
60 F2	Kushima Japan
61 P4	Kushimoto Japan
60 O3	Kushiro Japan
61 S2	Kushiro Japan
75 K9	Kushkhaaza Afghanistan
57 S4	Kushka U.S.S.R.
54 H2	Kushmurun U.S.S.R.
116 K2	Kushrabat U.S.S.R.
116 N6	Kushtaka L Alaska
75 N5	Kushtia Bangladesh
55 T1	Kushuk Afghanistan
116 G6	Kuskokwim R Alaska
116 K6	Kuskokwim Mts Alaska
116 H6	Kuskokwim Bay Alaska
116 K5	Kusma Nepal
86 G5	Kussa Ethiopia
80 S2	Kussharo L Japan
52 L4	Küstanai U.S.S.R.
54 J11	Kustanaraksa mt Sweden
33 Q7	Kusel E Germany
86 F7	Kuta Nigeria
59 C11	Kutabuloh Sumatra
54 L5	Kutacane Sumatra
53 F12	Kutaisi U.S.S.R.
54 K5	Kut al Imam Ali Iraq
74 K5	Kut, al Iraq
59 C11	Kutanibong Sumatra
70 B6	Kutawaringin Sumatra
70 M1	Kutina Yugoslavia
42 H5	Kutina Yugoslavia
29 J11	Kutno Poland
76 M1	Kutch India
56 N3	Kuttanen Sweden
54 K4	Kuttura Kentucky
52 H6	Kuty U.S.S.R.
48 J2	Kuty U.S.S.R.
106 G3	Kutch Colorado
60 O3	Kutch, Gulf of India
42 H3	Kutina Yugoslavia
29 J11	Kutno Poland
80 C3	Kuta Java
70 B6	Kutu Zaïre
28 H2	Kutum Sudan
53 F7	Kutno Poland
73 K5	Kut, Ko isld Thailand
56 D4	Kuturchinskoye Belog mt U.S.S.R.

42
Kuty — Langesundsfjord

48 J2 **Kuty** U.S.S.R.
37 J3 **Kützberg** W Germany
95 M6 **Kutztown** Pennsylvania
29 O6 **Kuusamo** Finland
29 M11 **Kuusankoski** Finland
52 H5 **Kuva** U.S.S.R.
55 C5 **Kuvandyk** U.S.S.R.
52 D6 **Kuvshinovo** U.S.S.R.
77 A5 **Kuwait** Kuwait
77 A5 **Kuwait** *sheikhdom* The Gulf
61 K10 **Kuwana** Japan
Kuwayt, Al *see* **Kuwait**
78 L5 **Kuwayt, Al** Iraq
52 F2 **Kuya** U.S.S.R.
53 H7 **Kuybyshev** U.S.S.R.
57 E5 **Kuybyshevskiy** U.S.S.R.
53 G7 **Kuybyshev-skoye** U.S.S.R.
55 C3 **Kuyeda** U.S.S.R.
65 A5 **Kuye He** *R* China
66 D3 **Kuytun** China
55 D5 **Kuyukkol', Oz** *L* U.S.S.R.
128 G3 **Kuyuwini** *R* Guyana
56 C3 **Kuzbass** *basin* U.S.S.R.
116 E4 **Kuzitrin** *R* Alaska
53 G7 **Kuznetsk** U.S.S.R.
56 C3 **Kuznetskiy Alatau** *mt* U.S.S.R.
55 D2 **Kuznetsovo** U.S.S.R.
52 E2 **Kuzomen** U.S.S.R.
26 H3 **Kvaefjord** Norway
26 M2 **Kvaenangen** Norway
26 M1 **Kvaenangen** *inlet* Norway
26 M2 **Kvaenangsbotn** Norway
28 H6 **Kværkeby** Denmark
28 F6 **Kværndrup** Denmark
28 C7 **Kværs** Denmark
28 N3 **Kvalbø** Faeroes
26 N1 **Kvalöya** *isld* Norway
26 K1 **Kvalöy, N** *isld* Norway
26 K2 **Kvalöy, S** *isld* Norway
26 N1 **Kvalsund** Norway
28 M2 **Kvalvig** Faeroes
26 D10 **Kvam** Norway
28 O9 **Kvannesund** Faeroes
55 C5 **Kvarkeno** U.S.S.R.
27 G15 **Kvarnamåla** Sweden
26 G7 **Kvarnbergsvattnet** *L* Sweden
42 F4 **Kvarner** *chan* Yugoslavia
42 F4 **Kvarnerić** *chan* Yugoslavia
27 J13 **Kvarsebo** Sweden
27 C11 **Kvenna** *R* Norway
26 C8 **Kvernes** Norway
26 L2 **Kvesmenes** Norway
29 J8 **Kvevlax** Finland
116 J7 **Kvichak** Alaska
26 G6 **Kvigtind** *mt* Norway
26 J5 **Kvikkjock** Sweden
26 D9 **Kvikne** Norway
27 B13 **Kvina** *R* Norway
27 B13 **Kvinesdal** Norway
27 B12 **Kvinnherad** Norway
27 G12 **Kvistbro** Sweden
28 K5 **Kvistofta** Sweden
26 C8 **Kvisvik** Norway
27 C12 **Kviteseid** Norway
26 R1 **Kvitnes** Norway
147 K11 **Kvitöya** *isld* Spitzbergen
27 A12 **Kvitsöy** *isld* Norway
28 M2 **Kvivig** Faeroes
28 A5 **Kvong** Denmark
28 D4 **Kvorning** Denmark
117 L7 **Kwadacha Wilderness Prov. Park** Br Columbia
134 G7 **Kwajalein** *atoll* Marshall Is Pacific Oc
129 G2 **Kwakoegron** Suriname
88 G4 **Kwale** Kenya
85 F7 **Kwale** Nigeria
86 C6 **Kwamouth** Zaïre
Kwangchow *see* **Guangzhou**
65 G7 **Kwangju** S Korea
86 C6 **Kwango** *R* Zaïre
Kwangsi *aut reg see* **Guangxi**
Kwangtung *prov see* **Guangdong**
86 F5 **Kwania, L** Uganda
120 H1 **Kwataboahegan** *R* Ontario
89 G7 **Kwazulu** *reg* S Africa
Kweichow *prov see* **Guizhou**
Kweilin *see* **Guilin**
89 D5 **Kweneng** *dist* Botswana
87 C7 **Kwenge** *R* Zaïre
116 G6 **Kwethluk** Alaska
31 L2 **Kwidzyn** Poland
116 D7 **Kwigamiuk** Alaska
116 F7 **Kwigillingok** Alaska
116 E5 **Kwiguk** Alaska
116 E5 **Kwikpak** Alaska
87 C7 **Kwilu** *R* Zaïre
142 A4 **Kwinana** W Australia
31 J4 **Kwisa** *R* Poland
128 G3 **Kwitaro** *R* Guyana
143 C10 **Kwobrup** W Australia
136 G2 **Kwoka** *mt* W Irian
26 D7 **Kya** *isld* Norway
86 C4 **Kyabé** Chad
141 G7 **Kyabra** Queensland
139 H6 **Kyabram** Victoria
68 B2 **Kyadet** Burma
68 B3 **Kyagu** Burma
68 C4 **Kyaikkami** Burma
68 B4 **Kyaiklat** Burma
68 C4 **Kyaikto** Burma
68 D5 **Kya-in Seikkyi** Burma
88 C2 **Kyaka** Tanzania
56 G5 **Kyakhta** U.S.S.R.
139 G5 **Kyalite** New S Wales
138 D5 **Kyancutta** S Australia
52 E3 **Kyanda** U.S.S.R.
52 D3 **Kyargozero** U.S.S.R.
68 C3 **Kyaukhnyat** Burma
68 B3 **Kyaukkyi** Burma
68 C1 **Kyaukme** Burma
68 B1 **Kyaukmyaung** Burma
68 A3 **Kyaukpyu** Burma
68 C2 **Kyaukse** Burma
68 A2 **Kyauktaw** Burma
68 B2 **Kyaukyit** Burma
68 B4 **Kyaunggon** Burma
138 F6 **Kybybolite** S Australia
52 F2 **Kychema** U.S.S.R.
26 G7 **Kycklingvattnet** Sweden
68 C3 **Kyebogyi** Burma
144 C6 **Kyeburn** New Zealand
68 D5 **Kyeikdon** Burma
68 D4 **Kyeikywa** Burma
68 B3 **Kyeintali** Burma
33 O10 **Kyffhäuser** *mt* E Germany
143 E7 **Kyffin-Thomas Hill** W Australia
28 F5 **Kyholm** *isld* Denmark
68 C3 **Kyidaunggan** Burma
68 A2 **Kyindwe** Burma
31 K6 **Kyjov** Czechoslovakia
118 J8 **Kyle** Sask
98 D6 **Kyle** S Dakota
109 K6 **Kyle** Texas
101 T8 **Kyle** Wyoming
15 C3 **Kyleakin** Scotland
87 F10 **Kyle Dam** Zimbabwe
15 D2 **Kyle of Durness** Scotland
15 C3 **Kyle of Lochalsh** Scotland
15 D2 **Kyle of Tongue** Scotland
12 C2 **Kyles of Bute** *chan* Scotland
36 B3 **Kyll** *R* W Germany
36 B3 **Kyllburg** W Germany
29 N10 **Kymi** *prov* Finland
29 M11 **Kymijoki** *R* Finland
55 C2 **Kyn** U.S.S.R.
139 G6 **Kyneton** Victoria
37 O3 **Kynšperk nad Ohři** Czechoslovakia
141 F5 **Kynuna** Queensland
61 P12 **Kyoda** Okinawa
86 F5 **Kyoga, L** Uganda
60 J10 **Kyōga-misaki** *C* Japan
139 L3 **Kyogle** New S Wales
65 F5 **Kyŏmip'o** N Korea
68 D4 **Kyondo** Burma
68 C2 **Kyong** Burma
141 H5 **Kyong** Queensland
62 **Kyōto** *conurbation* Japan
60 J10 **Kyōto** *prefect* Japan
55 E6 **Kypshak, Oz** *L* U.S.S.R.
79 D3 **Kyrenia** Cyprus
33 Q7 **Kyritz** E Germany
29 L11 **Kyrkslätt** Finland
29 J8 **Kyröjoki** *R* Finland
29 K10 **Kyrösjärvi** *L* Finland
52 J3 **Kyrta** U.S.S.R.
55 D2 **Kyrtym'ya** U.S.S.R.
55 C2 **Kyr'ya** U.S.S.R.
55 G3 **Kyshtovka** U.S.S.R.
55 D3 **Kyshtym** U.S.S.R.
52 G3 **Kyssa** U.S.S.R.
79 D3 **Kythrea** Cyprus
55 C2 **Kytlym** U.S.S.R.
68 D5 **Kyungyaung** Burma
68 C7 **Kyun Pila** *islds* Burma
117 K10 **Kyuquot** Br Col
60 D13 **Kyūshū** *isld* Japan
60 E13 **Kyūshū-sanchi** *mts* Japan
46 F2 **Kyustendil** Bulgaria
51 M1 **Kyusyur** U.S.S.R.
139 H6 **Kywong** New S Wales
29 L8 **Kyyjärvi** Finland
56 D5 **Kyzyl** U.S.S.R.
57 E1 **Kyzyldyykan** U.S.S.R.
56 E5 **Kyzyl-Khem** *R* U.S.S.R.
57 F4 **Kyzyl-Kiya** U.S.S.R.
57 J2 **Kyzylkiya** U.S.S.R.
57 E1 **Kyzyl-Kommuna** U.S.S.R.
57 C4 **Kyzylkum, Peski** *des* U.S.S.R.
55 F5 **Kyzyltas** U.S.S.R.
57 H1 **Kyzyltu** U.S.S.R.
57 D1 **Kyzyluy** U.S.S.R.
57 C1 **Kyzylzhar** U.S.S.R.
57 J3 **Kyzylzhide** U.S.S.R.
57 E1 **Kzyl-Dzhar** U.S.S.R.
57 D3 **Kzyl-Orda** U.S.S.R.
55 F4 **Kzyltu** U.S.S.R.
31 J7 **Laa** Austria
37 M5 **Laaber** W Germany
36 C3 **Laacher See** *L* W Germany
33 Q5 **Laage** E Germany
25 F4 **Laag Keppel** Netherlands
124 C4 **La Angostura** Mexico
29 N3 **Laanila** Finland
36 E2 **Laasphe** W Germany
127 N9 **La Asunción** Venezuela
135 R2 **Laau Pt** Hawaiian Is
108 E7 **La Babia** Mexico
110 F3 **Labadie** Missouri
7 E12 **Labadie Bank** Atlantic Oc
111 F12 **Labadieville** Louisiana
71 L9 **Labala** Indonesia
79 F8 **Labān** Jordan
16 D2 **La Baneza** Spain
71 L9 **Labao** Flores Indonesia
124 H7 **La Barca** Mexico
101 P7 **La Barge** Wyoming
21 A8 **La Barre-de-Monts** France
19 P17 **La Bastide-des-Jourdans** France
18 G8 **Labastide Murat** France
19 Q13 **La Bathie** France
19 Q15 **La Bâtie-Neuve** France
68 A2 **Labawa** Burma
52 H2 **Labazhskoye** U.S.S.R.
26 J5 **Labbas** Sweden
80 D1 **Labbouna** Lebanon
26 R3 **Labdshy'aur, Oz** *L* U.S.S.R.
85 B6 **Labé** Guinea
31 J5 **Labe** *R* Czechoslovakia
19 Q17 **La Bégude Blanche** France
99 P9 **La Belle** Missouri
121 Q6 **Labelle** Quebec
71 H6 **Labengke** *isld* Sulawesi
19 Q15 **La Bérarde** France
117 F5 **Laberge, L** Yukon Terr
131 E7 **Laberinto, Pta** Argentina
21 A7 **La Bernerie** France
21 J8 **La Berthenoux** France
37 N6 **Laberweinting** W Germany
70 D2 **Labi** Brunei
117 L5 **La Biche** *R* Yukon Terr/Br Col
42 F3 **Labin** Yugoslavia
69 F11 **Labis** Malaysia
127 M9 **La Blanquilla, I** Venezuela
71 F3 **Labo** Philippines
71 H5 **Labobo** *isld* Indonesia
103 J10 **La Bomba** Mexico
101 U7 **Labonte Cr** Wyoming
31 N6 **Laborec** *R* Czechoslovakia
48 G1 **Laborec** *R* Czechoslovakia
70 G6 **Labota** Sulawesi
143 C7 **Labouchere, Mt** W Australia
18 E8 **Labouheyre** France
133 E4 **Laboulaye** Argentina
115 N7 **Labrador City** Labrador
115 O6 **Labrador Sea** Nfld/Greenland
128 F5 **Labrea** Brazil
128 B4 **La Brea, Cer. de** *hill* Peru
124 E5 **La Brecha** Mexico
18 E8 **Labrède** France
122 C4 **Labrieville** Quebec
122 C4 **Labrieville, Parc de** Quebec
18 E8 **Labrit** France
118 E1 **La Broquerie** Manitoba
22 B3 **Labroye** France
21 C7 **La Bruffière** France
18 G9 **Labruguière** France
136 F2 **Labuha** Moluccas Indonesia
71 J9 **Labuhanbadjo** Sumba Indonesia
69 E11 **Labuhanbatu** Sumatra
69 E11 **Labuhanbilik** Sumatra
69 C11 **Labuhanhaji** Sumatra
69 D11 **Labuhanruku** Sumatra
70 K8 **Labuhanwaiharu** Sumatra
19 P14 **La Buisse** France
70 E2 **Labuk** *R* Sabah
70 E1 **Labuk B** Sabah
68 B4 **Labutta** Burma
138 D4 **Labyrinth, L** S Australia
50 F2 **Labytnangi** U.S.S.R.
46 D3 **Laç** Albania
124 G5 **La Cadena** Mexico
118 J8 **Lacadena** Sask
122 J3 **Lac Allard** Quebec
111 D10 **Lacamp** Louisiana
18 E8 **Lacanau** France
128 F2 **La Canoa** Venezuela
125 O9 **Lacantum** *R* Mexico
18 G8 **Lacapelle-Marival** France
131 B8 **Lacar, L** Argentina
133 E4 **La Carlota** Argentina
71 F5 **La Carlota** Negros Philippines
16 E6 **La Carolina** Spain
18 G9 **Lacaune** France
Laccadive Is *see* **Lakshadweep**
122 B8 **Lac-Drolet** Quebec
99 R4 **Lac du Flambeau** Wisconsin
13 H6 **Laceby** England
125 L2 **La Ceiba** Honduras
128 D2 **La Ceiba** Venezuela
21 G7 **La Celle St Avant** France
138 E6 **Lacepede B** S Australia
142 D3 **Lacepede Is** W Australia
21 C8 **La Chaize-le-Vicomte** France
19 Q14 **La Chambre** France
52 E4 **Lacha, Oz** *L* U.S.S.R.
20 J3 **Lachapelle-aux-Pots** France
21 C7 **La Chapelle Basse Mer** France
21 G7 **La Chapelle-Blanche-St. Martin** France
21 B6 **La Chapelle-Bouexic** France
21 E6 **La Chapelle-d'Aligné** France
19 O15 **La Chapelle-en-Vercors** France
21 C6 **La Chapelle-Glain** France
21 I6 **La Chapelle St. Mesmin** France
21 I9 **La Chapelle-Taillefert** France
21 G6 **La Chartre** France
21 J8 **La Châtre** France
128 C6 **Lachay, Pta** *point* Peru
41 J3 **Lachen** Switzerland
36 E5 **Lachen** W Germany
21 B7 **La Chevroliere** France
94 D1 **Lachine** Michigan
139 H5 **Lachlan** *R* New S Wales
125 P5 **La Chorrera** Panama
33 M7 **Lachte** *R* W Germany
121 Q7 **Lachute** Quebec
19 P18 **La Ciotat** France
94 J4 **Lackawanna** New York
14 E3 **Lacken Res** Irish Rep
71 M9 **Lacla** *R* Timor
114 H7 **Lac la Biche** Alberta
117 N10 **Lac La Hache** Br Columbia
119 M3 **Lac la Ronge** Sask
100 J1 **Laclede** Idaho
99 N10 **Laclede** Missouri
19 Q13 **La Clusaz** France
133 D3 **La Cocha** Argentina
8 D5 **Lacock** England
121 R7 **Lacolle** Quebec
124 D3 **La Colorada** Mexico
118 D6 **Lacombe** Alberta
111 G11 **Lacombe** Louisiana
99 R8 **Lacon** Illinois
99 N8 **Lacona** Iowa
95 L3 **Lacona** New York
43 C9 **Laconi** Sardinia
95 Q3 **Laconia** New Hampshire
113 E9 **Lacoochee** Florida
130 B9 **La Cordillera** *dep* Paraguay
121 N4 **Lacorne** Quebec
21 D7 **La Cornuaille** France
16 B1 **Lá Coruña** Spain
109 J6 **Lacoste** Texas
19 O14 **La Côte St. André** France
127 J2 **Lacovia** Jamaica
98 K4 **Lac Qui Parle** Minnesota
98 E6 **Lacreek L** S Dakota
126 A3 **Lacre Pt** Bonaire **W Indies**
99 P6 **La Crescent** Minnesota
21 H7 **La Croix** France
99 O1 **La Croix,L** Ontario
99 U8 **La Crosse** Indiana
107 L3 **La Crosse** Kansas
94 J10 **La Crosse** Virginia
99 P6 **La Crosse** Wisconsin
133 F3 **La Cruz** Argentina
125 M4 **La Cruz** Costa Rica
124 F6 **La Cruz** Mexico
124 G4 **La Cruz** Mexico
120 G3 **Lac Ste. Thérèse** Ontario
133 C5 **La Cueva** Chile
106 E6 **La Cueva** New Mexico
119 N6 **Lac Vert** Sask
107 Q3 **La Cygne** Kansas
21 E7 **La Daguenière** France
130 H5 **Ladainha** Brazil
74 G1 **Ladakh Range** Kashmir
54 D6 **Ladan'** U.S.S.R.
69 D9 **Ladang, Ko** *isld* Thailand
129 G7 **Ladário** Brazil
70 K9 **Lada, Teluk** *B* Java
9 E3 **Ladbroke** England
99 R8 **Ladd** Illinois
107 J3 **Ladder Cr** Kansas
110 E2 **Laddonia** Missouri
111 E8 **Ladelle** Arkansas
28 C7 **Ladelund** W Germany
36 F5 **Ladenburg** W Germany
127 O4 **La Désirade** *isld* Guadeloupe W I
Lādhiqīya, El *see* **Latakia**
46 E7 **Ládhon** *R* Greece
83 J12 **La Digue** *isld* Seychelles
28 D4 **Lading** Denmark
89 B9 **Ladismith** S Africa
77 G5 **Ladīz** Iran
98 C4 **Ladner** S Dakota
48 G6 **Ladne Vode** Yugoslavia
74 F5 **Ladnun** India
8 B7 **Ladock** England
110 K2 **Ladoga** Indiana
Ladoga *L see* **Ladozhskoye Oz**
109 M2 **Ladonia** Texas
128 D2 **La Dorada** Colombia
52 D4 **Ladozhskoye Oz** *L* U.S.S.R.
106 C7 **Ladrones Pk** New Mexico
116 R5 **Ladue** *R* Alaska/Yukon Terr
124 E3 **La Dura** Mexico
52 D4 **Ladva Vetka** U.S.S.R.
115 L2 **Lady Ann Str** N W Terr
15 E4 **Ladybank** Scotland
139 J8 **Lady Barron** Tasmania
89 E7 **Ladybrand** S Africa
142 F5 **Lady Edith L** W Australia
141 L6 **Lady Elliot I** Gt Barrier Reef Aust
120 K5 **Lady Evelyn L** Ontario
146 J6 **Lady Newnes Ice Shelf** Antarctica
100 B1 **Ladysmith** Br Columbia
89 F7 **Ladysmith** S Africa
99 P4 **Ladysmith** Wisconsin
55 E5 **Ladyzhenka** U.S.S.R.
136 K3 **Lae** Papua New Guinea
68 E3 **Lae** Thailand
71 H7 **Laëa** Indonesia
28 C5 **Læborg** Denmark
69 B11 **Laehobang** Indonesia
22 G2 **Laeken** Belgium
68 F6 **Laem Ngop** Thailand
17 G6 **La Encina** Spain
127 L10 **La Encrucijada** Venezuela
27 B10 **Laerdalsöyri** Norway
128 F8 **La Esmeralda** Paraguay
28 G2 **Læsø** *isld* Denmark
28 F2 **Læsø Rende** *str* Denmark
133 D5 **La Esperanza** Argentina
126 F4 **La Esperanza** Cuba
16 B2 **La Estrada** Spain
26 P2 **Laevajoki** Norway
131 D3 **La Falda** Argentina
95 M2 **La Fargeville** New York
19 Q18 **La Farlède** France
111 L9 **Lafayette** Alabama
106 E2 **Lafayette** Colorado
112 B3 **Lafayette** Georgia
110 K1 **Lafayette** Indiana
111 E11 **Lafayette** Louisiana
99 M5 **Lafayette** Minnesota
94 B10 **Lafayette** Tennessee
95 Q2 **Lafayette, Mt** New Hampshire
126 B3 **La Fe** Cuba
109 K9 **La Feria** Texas
21 E8 **La Ferrière-en-Parthenay** France
121 M4 **Laferte** Quebec
21 I7 **La Ferte Imbault** France
21 I6 **La Ferté-St. Aubin** France
21 I6 **La Ferté St. Cyr** France
85 F7 **Lafia** Nigeria
85 F7 **Lafiagi** Nigeria
121 N3 **Laflamme** *R* Quebec
21 E6 **La Flèche** France
118 L9 **Lafleche** Sask
38 O7 **Lafnitz** *R* Austria
94 C10 **La Follette** Tennessee
21 F6 **La Fontaine-St. Martin** France
121 M5 **Laforce** Quebec
120 J5 **Laforest** Ontario
18 F8 **Lafrançaise** France
112 E3 **La France** S Carolina
36 C6 **Lafrimbole** France
16 C4 **La Fuente de San Esteban** Spain
69 A9 **Laful** Nicobar Is
124 G5 **La Gallega** Mexico
14 E2 **Lagan** *R* N Ireland
27 G15 **Lagan** *R* Sweden
16 B2 **La Gañiza** Spain
36 B6 **Lagarde** France
41 N6 **Lagarina, Val** Italy
106 D4 **La Garita Mts** Colorado
21 B8 **La Garnache** France
129 H8 **Lagarto, Serra do** *mts* Brazil
21 C8 **La Gaubretière** France
32 J8 **Lage** W Germany
26 D10 **Lågen** *R* Norway
32 L5 **Lägerdorf** W Germany
54 H7 **Lagery** U.S.S.R.
12 C2 **Lagg** Scotland
15 D3 **Laggan** Scotland
12 B2 **Laggan B** Scotland
77 L2 **Laghmān** Afghanistan
85 E2 **Laghouat** Algeria
40 B6 **Lagnieu** France
16 B7 **Lagôa** Portugal
130 G6 **Lagoa Santa** Brazil
130 E4 **Lagolândia** Brazil
43 G8 **Lagonegro** Italy
71 F4 **Lagonoy Gulf** Philippines
133 C7 **Lago Posadas** Argentina
85 E7 **Lagos** Nigeria
16 B7 **Lagos** Portugal
45 M2 **Lagosanto** Italy
100 G4 **La Grande** Oregon
115 M7 **La Grande-Rivière** *R* Quebec
111 L8 **La Grange** Georgia
94 B5 **Lagrange** Indiana
94 B8 **La Grange** Kentucky
99 P9 **La Grange** Missouri
112 K2 **La Grange** N Carolina
94 E5 **Lagrange** Ohio
109 L6 **La Grange** Texas
142 D4 **Lagrange** W Australia
98 B8 **La Grange** Wyoming
128 F2 **La Gran Sabana** *reg* Venezuela
19 Q14 **La Grave** France
83 M13 **Lagrave** *mt* Mauritius
127 J10 **La Grita** Venezuela
27 L12 **Lågskär** Finland
29 H11 **Lågskär** *lt ho* Finland
127 L9 **La Guaira** Venezuela
133 D3 **La Guardia** Argentina
16 B3 **La Guardia** Portugal
17 F2 **Laguardia** Spain
16 C2 **La Gudiña** Spain
21 C6 **La Guerche de Bretagne** France
21 A8 **La Guérinière** France
18 G8 **Laguiole** France
133 H3 **Laguna** Brazil
42 E3 **Laguna** Italy
106 C6 **Laguna** New Mexico
141 L7 **Laguna B** Queensland
102 G8 **Laguna Beach** California
103 O5 **Laguna Cr** Arizona
103 K9 **Laguna Dam** Cal/Ariz
102 H9 **Laguna Mts** California
128 C5 **Lagunas** Peru
133 E1 **Lagunillas** Bolivia
127 J9 **Lagunillas** Venezuela
65 F4 **Lagushao** China
70 F2 **Lahad Datu** Sabah
68 F1 **Lahadi** China
135 S3 **Lahaina** Hawaiian Is
70 D4 **Laham** Kalimantan
99 Q9 **La Harpe** Illinois
70 K7 **Lahat** Sumatra
80 C8 **Lahav** Israel
122 H9 **La Have** Nova Scotia
80 F1 **Lahavot HaBashan** Israel
32 J8 **Lahde** W Germany
124 D4 **La Higuera** Mexico
77 B1 **Lāhījān** Iran
102 R12 **Lahilahi Pt** Hawaiian Is
37 K3 **Lahm** W Germany
30 D5 **Lahn** W Germany
36 E2 **Lahn** *R* W Germany
36 F2 **Lahntal** W Germany
27 F15 **Laholm** Sweden
27 F15 **Laholmsbukten** Sweden
71 F4 **Lahong** Philippines
102 E2 **Lahontan Res** Nevada
74 F3 **Lahore** Pakistan
36 D7 **Lahr** W Germany
73 L6 **Lahshadweep** *islds* Indian Oc
32 M8 **Lahstedt** W Germany
29 M11 **Lahti** Finland
124 G8 **La Huerta** Mexico
80 G8 **Lahun** Jordan
71 F4 **Lahuy** *isld* Philippines
86 C4 **Lai** Chad
67 F1 **Lai'an** China
133 F3 **La Iberá** *L* Argentina
67 C5 **Laibin** China
68 F2 **Lai Chau** Vietnam
36 H7 **Laichingen** W Germany
139 K3 **Laidley** Queensland
141 K8 **Laidley** Queensland
102 S11 **Laie** Hawaiian Is
67 C2 **Laifeng** China
22 H4 **Laifour** France
20 C5 **Laignelet** France
18 H5 **Laignes** France
44 D4 **Laigueglia** Italy
21 C9 **L'Aiguillon-sur-Mer** France
29 J9 **Laihia** Finland
68 C2 **Lai-Hka** Burma
68 C2 **Lai-Hsak** Burma
70 F7 **Laikang, Tk** *B* Sulawesi
21 I6 **Lailly-en-Val** France
71 E1 **Lai-Lo** Luzon Philippines
47 H3 **Lainá** Greece
38 L6 **Lainbach** Austria
94 C4 **Laingsburg** Michigan
89 B9 **Laingsburg** S Africa
26 K6 **Lainijaur** Sweden
26 M4 **Lainio** Sweden
26 M3 **Lainio älv** *R* Sweden
98 D9 **Laird** Colorado
118 L6 **Laird** Sask
15 D2 **Lairg** Scotland
71 G7 **Lais** Mindanao Philippines
70 G4 **Lais** Sulawesi
126 D3 **La Isabela** Cuba
86 G5 **Laisamis** Kenya
52 G6 **Laishevo** U.S.S.R.
65 C5 **Laishui** China
20 E3 **Laison** *R* France
18 G8 **Laissac** France
26 J5 **Laisvall** Sweden
26 K4 **Laitaure** *L* Sweden
29 J11 **Laitila** Finland
65 D6 **Laiwu** China
65 E6 **Laixi** China
71 E4 **Laiya** Philippines
59 H4 **Laiyang** China
65 C5 **Laiyuan** China
20 E3 **Laize** *R* France
65 D6 **Laizhou Wan** *B* China
133 C5 **Laja, L** Chile
131 B6 **Laja, L. de** Chile
133 D5 **La Japonesa** Argentina
131 A6 **Laja, R** Chile
106 E4 **La Jara** Colorado
70 E7 **Lajar, Tg** *C* Kalimantan
19 Q16 **La Javie** France
130 F9 **Laje dos Santos** *isld* Brazil
71 O8 **Lajeni** Indonesia
130 E10 **Lajes** Brazil
108 D6 **Lajitas** Texas
133 E2 **Lajitas, Las** Argentina
48 F6 **Lajkovac** Yugoslavia
102 G9 **La Jolla** California
119 N8 **Lajord** Sask
48 F3 **Lajosmizse** Hungary
124 F4 **La Joya** Mexico
106 D7 **La Joya** New Mexico
21 D7 **La Jumellière** France
128 F7 **La Junta** Bolivia
106 G4 **La Junta** Colorado
124 F3 **La Junta** Mexico
71 K9 **Lakahembi** Sumba Indonesia
26 J8 **Lakasjö** Sweden
26 M5 **Lakaträsk** Sweden
101 O5 **Lake** Idaho
94 B3 **Lake** Michigan
100 E6 **Lake** Oregon
113 F9 **Lake Alfred** Florida
119 N9 **Lake Alma** Sask
109 P5 **Lake Arthur** Louisiana
106 F8 **Lake Arthur** New Mexico
98 K5 **Lake Benton** Minnesota
143 C10 **Lake Biddy** W Australia
98 K1 **Lake Bronson** Minnesota
143 C9 **Lake Brown** W Australia
113 E7 **Lake Butler** Florida
143 C10 **Lake Camm** W Australia
109 O5 **Lake Charles** Louisiana
110 F6 **Lake City** Arkansas
100 E8 **Lake City** California
106 C3 **Lake City** Colorado
113 E7 **Lake City** Florida
99 M7 **Lake City** Iowa
94 B2 **Lake City** Michigan
99 O5 **Lake City** Minnesota
94 G4 **Lake City** Pennsylvania
112 H4 **Lake City** S Carolina
98 J4 **Lake City** S Dakota
94 C10 **Lake City** Tennessee
144 C5 **Lake Coleridge** New Zealand
100 J8 **Lake Cr** Nevada
99 M5 **Lake Crystal** Minnesota
99 R6 **Lake Delton** Wisconsin
118 F5 **Lake Eliza** Alberta
138 D2 **Lake Eyre Basin** S Australia
99 L6 **Lakefield** Minnesota
121 M8 **Lakefield** Ontario
141 G2 **Lakefield** Queensland
99 T7 **Lake Forest** Illinois
99 S7 **Lake Geneva** Wisconsin
106 E3 **Lake George** Colorado
95 O3 **Lake George** New York
115 N5 **Lake Harbour** N W Terr
101 U8 **Lake Hattie Res** Wyoming
103 K7 **Lake Havasu City** Arizona
102 F7 **Lake Hughes** California
95 N6 **Lakehurst** New Jersey
109 M6 **Lake Jackson** Texas
142 C10 **Lake King** W Australia
143 C10 **Lake King** W Australia
112 D6 **Lakeland** Georgia
119 N6 **Lake Lenore** Sask
99 S2 **Lake Linden** Michigan
117 P10 **Lake Louise** Alberta
137 R5 **Lakemba** *isld* Fiji
99 N6 **Lake Mills** Iowa
94 G5 **Lake Milton** Ohio
116 L5 **Lake Minchumina** Alaska
95 S1 **Lake Moxie** Maine
140 E5 **Lake Nash** N Terr Aust
37 P5 **Laken Berg** *mt* W Germany/Czech
9 G3 **Lakenheath** England
94 B4 **Lake Odessa** Michigan
99 M1 **Lake of the Woods** *L* Ontario
94 D4 **Lake Orion** Michigan
100 C4 **Lake Oswego** Oregon
107 Q5 **Lake O' The Cherokees** *L* Oklahoma
109 N3 **Lake O'The Pines** *L* Texas
101 P5 **Lake Outlet** Wyoming
144 B5 **Lake Paringa** New Zealand
113 G11 **Lake Park** Florida
113 D7 **Lake Park** Georgia
99 L6 **Lake Park** Iowa
113 F10 **Lake Placid** Florida
95 O2 **Lake Placid** New York
102 B2 **Lakeport** California
113 F11 **Lakeport** Florida
94 E3 **Lakeport** Michigan
98 J5 **Lake Preston** S Dakota
111 E9 **Lake Providence** Louisiana
144 C6 **Lake Pukaki** New Zealand
100 F9 **Lake Range** *mts* Nevada
115 L7 **Lake River** Ontario
139 J7 **Lakes Entrance** Victoria
102 E4 **Lakeshore** California
103 P7 **Lakeside** Arizona
102 H9 **Lakeside** California
98 D7 **Lakeside** Nebraska
101 N8 **Lakeside** Utah
120 F5 **Lake Superior Prov. Park** Ontario
144 C5 **Lake Tekapo** New Zealand
101 O8 **Laketown** Utah
121 M7 **Lake Traverse** Ontario
106 C9 **Lake Valley** New Mexico
118 L8 **Lake Valley** Sask
109 J5 **Lake Victor** Texas
99 L7 **Lake View** Iowa
94 B3 **Lakeview** Michigan
101 O5 **Lakeview** Montana
100 E7 **Lakeview** Oregon
112 H3 **Lake View** S Carolina
109 N9 **Lakeview** Texas
111 E8 **Lake Village** Arkansas
95 O5 **Lakeville** Connecticut
94 A5 **Lakeville** Indiana
99 N5 **Lakeville** Minnesota
94 K4 **Lakeville** New York
143 D7 **Lake Violet** W Australia
113 F10 **Lake Wales** Florida
98 G2 **Lake Williams** N Dakota
95 N6 **Lakewood** New Jersey
106 F9 **Lakewood** New Mexico
94 H4 **Lakewood** New York
94 F5 **Lakewood** Ohio
113 G11 **Lake Worth** Florida
52 D4 **Lakhdenpokh'ya** U.S.S.R.
74 J5 **Lakhimpur** India
80 B6 **Lakhish** Israel
80 C7 **Lakhish** Israel
80 C7 **Lakhish** *R* Israel
74 C7 **Lakhpat** India
107 J4 **Lakin** Kansas
54 L1 **Lakinskiy** U.S.S.R.
74 D2 **Lakki** Pakistan
28 A6 **Lakoik** Denmark
46 F8 **Lakonikós Kólpos** *B* Greece
71 O9 **Lakor** *isld* Indonesia
99 M6 **Lakota** Iowa
85 C7 **Lakota** Ivory Coast
98 H1 **Lakota** N Dakota
68 G3 **Lak Sao** Laos
26 P1 **Lakse Fjord** *inlet* Norway
26 O1 **Lakselv** Norway
26 F6 **Laksfors** Norway
76 A5 **Lakshadweep** *islds terr* India
71 F7 **Lala** Mindanao Philippines
88 C8 **Lala** Zambia
87 B7 **Lalama** Angola
47 H3 **Lâlapaşa** Turkey
86 B5 **Lalare** Gabon
87 G8 **Lalaúa** Mozambique
18 G8 **Lalbenque** France
77 E5 **Lāleh Zar, Kūh-e** *mt* Iran
33 Q5 **Lalendorf** E Germany
70 F5 **Lalereh, Tg** *C* Sulawesi
77 A3 **Lāli** Iran
128 B4 **La Libertad** Ecuador
125 O9 **La Libertad** Guatemala
133 C4 **La Ligua** Chile
71 H6 **Lalimbuë** Sulawesi
65 G2 **Lalin** China
16 B2 **Lalin** Spain
18 F8 **Lalinde** France
71 K10 **Lalindi** Sumba Indonesia
70 G6 **Lalindu** *R* Sulawesi
65 G2 **Lalin He** *R* China
74 H6 **Lalitpur** India
19 P15 **Lalley** France
70 G7 **Laloa** Sulawesi
118 H2 **La Loche West** Sask
71 A2 **Laloda** Halmahera Indonesia
52 G4 **Lal'sk** U.S.S.R.
124 H6 **La Luz** Mexico
46 C3 **Lalzës, Gji i** *B* Albania
37 P5 **Lam** W Germany
52 E6 **Lama** *R* U.S.S.R.
128 D3 **La Macarena** Colombia
43 C7 **La Maddalena** Sardinia
106 D5 **La Madera** New Mexico
65 D4 **Lamadong** China
124 J4 **Lamadrid** Mexico
70 E2 **Lamag** Sabah
68 C5 **Lamaing** Burma
85 E7 **Lama-Kara** Togo
71 L9 **Lamakera** Indonesia
115 M8 **La Malbaie** Quebec
123 R7 **Lamaline** Nfld
45 J3 **Lama Mocogno** Italy
124 H5 **La Mancha** Mexico
17 F5 **La Mancha** *reg* Spain
125 M4 **La Mansión** Costa Rica
110 C6 **Lamar** Arkansas
106 H3 **Lamar** Colorado
110 B4 **Lamar** Missouri
98 E9 **Lamar** Nebraska
107 O6 **Lamar** Oklahoma
112 G3 **Lamar** S Carolina
101 P5 **Lamar** *R* Wyoming
40 C1 **Lamarche** France
40 A2 **Lamargelle** France
133 D5 **Lamarque** Argentina
109 N6 **La Marque** Texas
122 B6 **Lamartine** Quebec
125 L2 **La Masica** Honduras
19 N15 **Lamastre** France
126 G4 **La Maya** Cuba
18 D4 **Lamballe** France
86 B6 **Lambarene** Gabon
130 F7 **Lambari** Brazil
137 Q5 **Lambasa** Vanua Levu **Fiji**
70 G7 **Lambasina** *isld* Sulawesi
28 O9 **Lamba Vig** *inlet* Faeroes
128 B5 **Lambayeque** *dep* Peru
14 E3 **Lambay I** Irish Rep
9 G5 **Lamberhurst** England
112 F6 **Lambert** Georgia
111 F7 **Lambert** Mississippi
98 B2 **Lambert** Montana
142 B5 **Lambert, C** W Australia
146 C5 **Lambert Gl** Antarctica
99 L5 **Lamberton** Minnesota
87 C12 **Lamberts B** S Africa
95 N6 **Lambertville** New Jersey
19 O17 **Lambesc** France
120 J10 **Lambeth** Ontario
73 Q6 **Lambi** *isld* Burma
46 E7 **Lámbia** Greece
9 E5 **Lambourn** England
36 E5 **Lambrecht** W Germany
41 K7 **Lambro** *R* Italy
94 G10 **Lambsburg** Virginia
14 A5 **Lambs Hd** Irish Rep
36 E4 **Lambsheim** W Germany
121 T7 **Lambton** Quebec
114 G3 **Lambton, C** N W Terr
68 F5 **Lam Chi** *R* Thailand
68 G5 **Lam Dom Noi** *R* Thailand
101 T4 **Lame Deer** Montana
16 B3 **Lamego** Portugal
21 C6 **La Meilleraye-de-Bret** France
21 G7 **La Membrolle** France
21 E7 **La Ménitre** France
127 N4 **Lamentin** Guadeloupe **W I**
122 H6 **Lameque** New Brunswick
122 H6 **Lamèque, Ile** New Brunswick
133 D3 **La Merced** Argentina
138 F6 **Lameroo** S Australia
102 G9 **La Mesa** California
106 D9 **La Mesa** New Mexico
108 F3 **Lamesa** Texas
43 F7 **La Meta** *mt* Italy
46 E6 **Lamia** Greece
127 K10 **La Miel** Venezuela
71 G7 **Lamigan Pt** Mindanao Philippines
15 E5 **Lamington** Scotland
124 D3 **La Misa** Mexico
71 F7 **Lamitan** Philippines
109 J4 **Lamkin** Texas
71 C3 **Lamlam** Indonesia
15 C5 **Lamlash** Scotland
144 B6 **Lammerlaw Range** New Zealand
141 G5 **Lammermoor** Queensland
15 F5 **Lammermuir Hills** Scotland
25 F7 **Lammersdorf** W Germany
69 B10 **Lammeulo** Sumatra
27 G14 **Lammhult** Sweden
29 L10 **Lammi** Finland
20 G5 **Lamnay** France
21 B7 **La Moëre** France
99 R8 **La Moille** Illinois
103 J1 **Lamoille** Nevada
95 P2 **Lamoille** *R* Vermont
110 F1 **La Moine** *R* Illinois
100 G2 **Lamona** Washington
71 E3 **Lamon B** Luzon Philippines
42 D4 **Lamone** *R* Italy
70 O9 **Lamongan** Java
110 C1 **Lamoni** Iowa
118 E5 **Lamont** Alberta
102 F6 **Lamont** California
113 D7 **Lamont** Florida
101 O6 **Lamont** Idaho
99 P7 **Lamont** Iowa
107 N5 **Lamont** Oklahoma
101 S7 **Lamont** Wyoming
124 G3 **La Morita** Mexico
19 P14 **La Morte** France
22 J4 **Lamorteau** Belgium
21 E9 **La Mothe St. Héraye** France
121 M4 **La Motte** Quebec
21 J6 **Lamotte-Beuvron** France
19 P15 **La Motte d'Aveillans** France
19 P13 **La Motte-Servolex** France
98 H3 **La Moure** N Dakota
68 F4 **Lam Pao Res** Thailand
109 J4 **Lampasas** Texas
109 K5 **Lampasas** *R* Texas
125 K4 **Lampazos** Mexico
36 E4 **Lampertheim** W Germany
33 T10 **Lampërtswalde** E Germany
8 B3 **Lampeter** Wales
8 B4 **Lamphey** Wales
47 F5 **Lampinoú** Greece
43 E13 **Lampione** *isld* Italy
68 F5 **Lam Plai** *R* Thailand
119 P9 **Lampman** Sask
45 J4 **Lamporecchio** Italy
9 F3 **Lamport** England
52 F2 **Lampozhnya** U.S.S.R.
29 O6 **Lämpsä** Finland
70 D5 **Lampung** Kalimantan
70 K8 **Lampung Teluk** *B* Sumatra
68 G5 **Lam Si Bai** *R* Thailand
32 M9 **Lamspringe** W Germany
32 K5 **Lamstedt** W Germany
68 B3 **Lamu** Burma
86 H6 **Lamu** Kenya
19 P15 **La Mure** France
19 N12 **Lamure-sur-Azergues** France
106 E6 **Lamy** New Mexico
42 D2 **Lana** Italy
141 G5 **Lana** Queensland
135 S3 **Lanai** *isld* Hawaiian Is
135 S3 **Lanai City** Hawaiian Is
135 S3 **Lanaihale** *peak* Hawaiian Is
22 K2 **Lanaken** Belgium
74 H1 **Lanak Pass** Kashmir/Xizang Zizhiqu
71 G7 **Lanao** *L* Mindanao Philippines
113 C8 **Lanark** Florida
99 R7 **Lanark** Illinois
121 O7 **Lanark** Ontario
12 E2 **Lanark** Scotland
Lanark *co see* **Strathclyde** *reg*
70 E2 **Lanas** Sabah
68 C7 **Lanbi Kyun** *isld* Burma
71 F6 **Lanboyan Pt** Mindanao Philippines
68 D1 **Lancang** China
Lancang Jiang *R see* **Mekong**
13 F6 **Lancashire** *co* England
102 F7 **Lancaster** California
13 F5 **Lancaster** England
110 M4 **Lancaster** Kentucky
98 K1 **Lancaster** Minnesota
110 D1 **Lancaster** Missouri
122 F8 **Lancaster** New Brunswick
95 Q2 **Lancaster** New Hampshire
94 J4 **Lancaster** New York
94 E7 **Lancaster** Ohio
121 Q7 **Lancaster** Ontario
95 L6 **Lancaster** Pennsylvania
112 G3 **Lancaster** S Carolina
109 L3 **Lancaster** Texas
95 L9 **Lancaster** Virginia
99 Q7 **Lancaster** Wisconsin
115 L3 **Lancaster Sd** N W Terr
98 B6 **Lance Cr** Wyoming
143 B9 **Lancelin** W Australia
143 B9 **Lancelin I** W Australia
143 E7 **Lancelot, Mt** W Australia
19 O16 **Lance, Mt. de la** France
118 J8 **Lancer** Sask
20 H1 **Lanchères** France
13 G4 **Lanchester** England
66 C5 **Lan-chia Ts'o** *L* China
48 J2 **Lanchin** U.S.S.R.
Lanchow *see* **Lanzhou**
42 F6 **Lanciano** Italy
94 C10 **Lancing** Tennessee
19 O17 **Lançon** France
31 N5 **Łańcut** Poland
27 D11 **Land** *reg* Norway
98 F1 **Landa** N Dakota
32 K10 **Landau** Hessen W Germany
36 E5 **Landau** Rheinland-Pfalz W Germany
20 C5 **Landéan** France
41 N3 **Landeck** Austria
26 G4 **Landegode** *isld* Norway
20 C4 **Landelles-et-Coupigny** France
22 J2 **Landen** Belgium
101 R7 **Lander** Wyoming
140 C5 **Lander** *R* N Terr Aust
18 C4 **Landerneau** France
140 B5 **Lander R** N Terr Aust
27 F14 **Landeryd** Sweden
94 H8 **Landes** W Virginia
18 D5 **Landes de Lanvaux** *reg* France
18 E8 **Landes, Les** *reg* France
28 G7 **Landet** Denmark
17 G5 **Landete** Spain
68 A6 **Landfall I** Andaman Is
133 C8 **Landfall, I** Chile
9 E6 **Landford** England
146 J9 **Land Glacier** Antarctica
33 S5 **Landgraben** *R* E Germany
32 J5 **Land Hadeln** W Germany
74 D1 **Landi Khana** Pakistan
77 H4 **Landi Md. Amin Khan** Afghanistan
119 U3 **Landing L** Manitoba
112 G2 **Landis** N Carolina
118 J6 **Landis** Sask
18 C4 **Landivisiau** France
20 C5 **Landivy** France
112 F3 **Lando** S Carolina
99 R3 **Land O Lakes** Wisconsin
143 B7 **Landor** W Australia
26 G8 **Landösjön** *L* Sweden
22 F3 **Landrecies** France
22 J5 **Landres** Ardennes France
22 K5 **Landres** Meurthe-et-Moselle France
121 N4 **Landrienne** Quebec
142 F4 **Landrigan Cliffs** W Australia
38 F8 **Landro** Italy
112 E2 **Landrum** S Carolina
40 E6 **Landry** France
26 M5 **Landså** Sweden
Landsberg *see* **Gorzów Wielkopolski**
33 Q9 **Landsberg** E Germany
41 N1 **Landsberg** W Germany
141 L7 **Landsborough** Queensland
144 B5 **Landsborough** *R* New Zealand
141 G5 **Landsborough** *R* Queensland
9 F7 **Land's End** England
114 G2 **Lands End** *C* N W Terr
37 N6 **Landshut** W Germany
28 K5 **Landskrona** Sweden
36 D5 **Landstuhl** W Germany
101 R2 **Landusky** Montana
32 L10 **Landwehrhagen** W Germany
37 N3 **Landwüst** E Germany
112 H4 **Lane** S Carolina
98 H5 **Lane** S Dakota
109 L6 **Lane City** Texas
22 G3 **Laneffe** Belgium
99 P6 **Lanesboro** Minnesota
111 L9 **Lanett** Alabama
22 D5 **Laneuville-Roy** France
22 J5 **Laneuville-sur-Meuse** France
Lanfeng *see* **Lankao**
118 G7 **Lanfine** Alberta
119 N9 **Lang** Sask
28 F6 **Langå** Denmark
66 C5 **La'nga Co** *L* China
16 E3 **Langa de Duero** Spain
47 F4 **Langadhás** Greece
46 E7 **Langádhia** Greece
86 G4 **Langana, L** Ethiopia
71 H7 **Langara** Sulawesi
117 G8 **Langara I** Br Columbia
77 A1 **Langarūd** Iran
119 P8 **Langbank** Sask
67 B6 **Lang Chanh** Vietnam
Lang-ch'u Ho *see* **Sutlej**
111 L9 **Langdale** Alabama
118 D8 **Langdon** Alberta
107 M4 **Langdon** Kansas
98 H1 **Langdon** N Dakota
13 F4 **Langdon Beck** England
18 H7 **Langeac** France
21 F7 **Langeais** France
89 A9 **Langeberg** *mts* S Africa
89 C7 **Langebergen** *mts* S Africa
19 P18 **L'Ange, Col de** France
28 F7 **Langeland** *isld* Denmark
29 L10 **Längelmäki** Finland
29 L10 **Längelmävesi** *L* Finland
33 M9 **Langelsheim** W Germany
22 D2 **Langemark** Belgium
36 F4 **Langen** Hessen W Germany
32 J5 **Langen** W Germany
37 P2 **Langenau** E Germany
37 J7 **Langenau** W Germany
37 N2 **Langenberg** Gera W Germany
32 F10 **Langenberg** W Germany
37 M4 **Langenbruck** W Germany
119 Q8 **Langenburg** Sask
36 H5 **Langenburg** W Germany
26 H2 **Langenes** *lt ho* Norway
28 B7 **Langeness** *isld* W Germany
32 L8 **Langenhagen** W Germany
28 B7 **Langenhorn** W Germany
37 O6 **Langenisarhofen** W Germany
38 N5 **Langenlois** Austria
36 D4 **Langenlonsheim** W Germany
33 S9 **Langennaundorf** E Germany
36 G3 **Langenselbold** W Germany
37 J5 **Langensteinach** W Germany
36 F6 **Langensteinbach** W Germany
40 G3 **Langenthal** Switzerland
38 N6 **Langenwang** Austria
37 K5 **Langenzenn** W Germany
32 F5 **Langeoog** W Germany
28 E2 **Lange-Rak** *inlet* Denmark
28 F6 **Langeskov** Denmark
28 H5 **Langesø** *L* Denmark
27 D12 **Langesund** Norway
27 D13 **Langesundsfjord** *inlet* Norway

26 B9 Langevag Norway
37 K2 Langewiesen E Germany
20 H5 Langey France
Langfang see Anci
26 M1 Langfjord Norway
26 Q1 Langfjord inlet Finnmark Norway
26 C9 Langfjord inlet More og Romsdal Norway
98 J4 Langford S Dakota
32 H7 Langförden W Germany
69 E12 Langgam Sumatra
69 D12 Langgapayung Sumatra
118 L6 Langham Sask
44 D2 Langhe Italy
44 H2 Langhirano Italy
68 C2 Langhko Burma
15 F5 Langholm Scotland
115 R5 Langjökull ice cap Iceland
69 D9 Langkawi isld Malaysia
69 D8 Lang Kha Toek, Khao mt Thailand
70 E1 Langkon Sabah
121 P4 Langlade Quebec
123 Q7 Langlade isld Atlantic Oc
100 C1 Langley Washington
28 A5 Langli isld Denmark
139 H2 Langlo R Queensland
139 H2 Langlo Crossing Queensland
141 H7 Langlo Downs Queensland
100 A7 Langlois Oregon
121 N4 Langlois Village Quebec
32 H5 Langlütjensand sandbank W Germany
36 D4 Langmeil W Germany
29 J9 Langnau Switzerland
28 J7 Lango isld Denmark
18 H8 Langogne France
28 F5 Langør Denmark
28 G2 Langøy isld Norway
8 D5 Langport England
37 N6 Langquaid W Germany
40 B2 Langres France
44 D2 Langres, Plat. de France
20 E3 Langrune France
119 T8 Langruth Manitoba
69 C10 Langsa Sumatra
69 C10 Langsa, Teluk B Sumatra
28 J8 Långsele Sweden
26 J7 Långselen R Sweden
58 E3 Lang Shan mt China
27 H11 Långshyttan Sweden
28 D5 Langskov Denmark
67 B6 Lang Son Vietnam
13 H5 Langtoft England
26 L8 Långträsk Sweden
108 F6 Langtry Texas
18 H8 Languedoc prov France
110 F6 L'Anguille R Arkansas
37 J1 Langula E Germany
32 H5 Langwarden W Germany
32 K7 Langwedel W Germany
9 F1 Langworth England
67 F1 Langxi China
67 F2 Langxi China
58 E5 Langzhong China
67 G5 Lan Hsü isld Taiwan
121 L5 Laniel Quebec
119 N7 Lanigan Sask
102 S12 Lanikai Hawaiian Is
133 C5 Lanin mt Argentina
131 B7 Lanin, Vol Arg/Chile
8 B4 Lanjak, Bt mt Sarawak
32 E10 Lank W Germany
65 C7 Lankao China
33 T7 Lanke E Germany
98 J1 Lankin N Dakota
22 K1 Lanklaer Belgium
26 M3 Lannavaara Sweden
18 H9 Lannemezan France
18 C4 Lannion France
22 K2 Lannoy France
17 H3 La Noguera dist Spain
121 R7 Lanoraie Quebec
124 F6 La Noria New Mexico
48 K1 Lanovtsy U.S.S.R.
95 M6 Lansdale Pennsylvania
121 P8 Lansdowne Ontario
115 L7 Lansdowne House Ontario
99 S3 L'Anse Michigan
123 Q2 L'Anse-Amour Labrador
123 P2 L'Anse au Loup Quebec
83 R5 Lansen E Germany
19 P14 Lans en Vercors France
98 E1 Lansford N Dakota
95 M6 Lansford Pennsylvania
99 D6 Lanshan China
70 F5 Lansing Iowa
107 Q2 Lansing Kansas
94 C4 Lansing Michigan
112 F1 Lansing N Carolina
31 K6 Länskroun Czechoslovakia
40 E7 Lanslebourg France
19 P14 Lans, Mts de France
69 D9 Lanta Ko Thailand
69 D9 Lanta, Ko isld Thailand
21 I7 Lanthenay France
Lantian see Lianyuan
123 Q4 Lantian China
98 E4 Lantry S Dakota
43 C9 Lanusei Sardinia
71 G6 Lanuza Mindanao Philippines
65 G1 Lanxi China
65 E1 Lanxi China
65 B5 Lan Xian China
33 P6 Lanz E Germany
85 B3 Lanzarote isld Canary Is
85 B3 Lanzarote isld Canary Is
64 C2 Lanzhou China
71 E1 Lanzijing China
71 G4 Laoag Luzon Philippines
67 A5 Lao Cai Vietnam
67 A4 Laochang China
66 D4 Laogou China
66 D4 Laoha He R China
53 H3 Lao-ho-k'ou China
14 D4 Laois co Irish Rep
65 G4 Laoling China
Laolong see Longchuan
22 F4 Laon France
99 S4 Laona Wisconsin
20 H4 Laona France
127 L9 La Orchila, I Venezuela
128 C6 La Oroya Peru
68 F3 Laos S E Asia
16 E9 Laotie Shan C China
16 E9 Laou il Morocco
65 G2 Laowu Sulawesi
65 H3 Laoye Ling mts China
65 H3 Laoye Ling mts China
71 E8 Lapac isld Philippines
143 D9 Lapage, U W Australia
97 G8 La Palisse France
18 H6 Lapalisse France
85 A3 La Palma isld Canary Is
16 C7 La Palma del Concado Spain
131 C8 La Pampa prov Argentina
102 D6 La Panza California
102 D6 La Panza Ra California
17 F4 La Paragila L Spain
16 D4 La Paramera de Avila Spain
71 D7 Laparan isld Sulu Arch Philippines
124 A5 La Parilla Mexico
133 D4 La Paz Argentina
128 E7 La Paz Bolivia
131 E7 La Paz Entre Rios Argentina
24 A5 La Paz Mexico
124 H3 La Paz Mexico
128 E7 La Paz Bolivia
124 C3 La Paz Mexico
127 H9 La Paz Venezuela
128 E4 La Pedrera Colombia
94 B6 Lapeer Indiana
124 G3 La Perla Mexico
119 U3 La Perouse Manitoba

102 T13 La Pérouse Pinnacle Hawaiian Is
59 M2 La Pérouse Strait Japan/U.S.S.R.
124 H7 La Piedad Mexico
100 D8 Lapine Oregon
71 G5 Lapinin Bohol Philippines
29 N8 Lapinlahti Finland
79 D3 Lapithos Cyprus
111 F11 Laplace Louisiana
21 D7 La Plaine France
52 D1 Laplandiya U.S.S.R.
131 F5 La Plata Argentina
95 L8 La Plata Maryland
99 O9 La Plata Missouri
123 O6 La Poile B Nfld
99 O3 La Pola de Gordón Spain
16 D2 La Pola de Gordón Spain
102 D2 La Porte California
21 D6 La Pouèze France
36 C7 Lapoutroie France
48 G6 Lapovo Yugoslavia
29 K8 Lappajärvi Finland
141 G3 Lappa Junction Queensland
29 N10 Lappeenranta Finland
29 J8 Lappfjärd Finland
27 M10 Lappi Finland
29 J10 Lappi Kauttua Finland
26 L3 Lappland Sweden/Finland
26 N5 Lappträsk Sweden
121 R7 Laprairie Quebec
101 U7 La Prele Cr Wyoming
133 E5 Laprida Argentina
108 H7 La Pryor Texas
47 H4 Lápseki Turkey
54 J2 Laptevo U.S.S.R.
51 M1 Laptev Sea U.S.S.R.
29 K9 Lapua Finland
29 K8 Lapuanjoki R Finland
16 E5 La Puebla de Montalbán Spain
127 J10 La Puerta Venezuela
128 B4 La Puntilla point Ecuador
124 C4 La Purisima Mexico
100 A2 La Push Washington
48 H3 Lāpusului, Muntii mts Romania
21 G8 La Puye France
31 O3 Łapy Poland
84 H5 Laqiya Arba'in Sudan
128 E8 La Quiaca Argentina
42 E6 L'Aquila Italy
77 D6 Lār Iran
16 C9 Laracha Morocco
19 P16 Laragne France
77 E6 Larak isld Iran
128 D6 Laramate Peru
16 D7 La Rambla Spain
98 A8 Laramie Wyoming
98 A7 Laramie R Wyoming
98 A7 Laramie Mts Wyoming
130 F8 Laramie Pk mt Wyoming
130 E8 Laranjeiras do Sul Brazil
130 D9 Laranjinha, R Brazil
71 L9 Larantuka Flores Indonesia
32 G5 Larrelt W Germany
32 L9 Lärbro Sweden
77 D6 Lār Iran
19 O15 La Raye mt France
15 G4 Larbert Scotland
127 H5 L'Arbresle France
124 C3 L'Arcahaie Haiti
20 D5 Larchamp France
121 L4 Larder Lake Ontario
47 J8 Lárdhos, Akr Rhodes Greece
123 M8 L'Ardoise C Breton I, N Scotia
20 K5 Lardy s Ferte-Alais France
99 N9 Laredo Missouri
16 E1 Laredo Spain
109 H8 Laredo Texas
48 K2 Larga U.S.S.R.
122 J3 Larga I Quebec
32 H8 Largentière France
113 E10 Largo Florida
15 F4 Largo Scotland
126 D4 Largo, Cayo isld Cuba
13 F1 Largo Ward Scotland
15 D5 Largs Scotland
94 J4 Lari Italy
70 F5 Lariang Sulawesi
70 F5 Lariang R Sulawesi
47 F6 Lárimna Greece
98 J2 Larino Italy
42 F7 Larino Italy
131 C2 La Rioja Argentina
46 E5 Lérisa Greece
77 D6 Laristan Iran
119 T9 La Rivière Manitoba
98 E3 Lark N Dakota
12 E2 Larkana Pakistan
12 E2 Larkhall Scotland
123 O4 Lark Harb Nfld
141 H3 Lark Pass Gt Barrier Reef Aust
9 G3 Lark, R England
106 F2 Larkspur Colorado
13 E9 Larling England
55 F2 Lárnaka Cyprus
121 S5 Larne N Ireland
14 F2 Larne N Ireland
107 L3 Larned Kansas
85 G2 La Roble Spain
36 D3 Laroche Rheinland-Pfalz W Germany
21 F10 La Rochefoucauld France
21 C8 La Rochelle France
21 C8 Laroche-Migennes France
21 C8 La Roche-Posay France
21 C8 La Roche-sur-Yon France
19 Q14 La Rochette France
22 L4 Larochette Luxembourg
17 F5 La Rocque Pt Channel Is
37 J6 Lauchhammer E Germany
36 H4 Lauda-Königshofen W Germany
27 C13 Lauder Scotland
36 H5 Laudenbach W Germany
119 R9 Lauder Manitoba
13 F2 Lauder Scotland
88 C8 Lauenen mt Zambia
21 D9 La Ronge Sask
119 M3 La Ronge Sask
124 J3 La Ronge Mexico
111 F12 La Rose Louisiana
124 J3 La Rosita Mexico
85 J7 Larrey Pt W Australia
140 C3 Larrimah N Terr Aust
123 L8 Larrislée France
146 C4 Lars Christensen Coast Antarctica
146 E13 Larsen Ice Shelf Antarctica
101 N1 Larslan Montana
29 K8 Larsmo Finland
119 N1 Larson Ontario
109 M3 La Rue Texas
13 E1 Larvik Norway
50 G2 Laryak U.S.S.R.
56 B1 Lar'yak U.S.S.R.
124 G6 La Adjuntas Mexico
103 P3 La Sal Utah
99 R8 La Salle Colorado
72 B3 La Salle Illinois
118 L6 La Salle Manitoba
119 U9 La Salle Manitoba
70 D4 Lasan Kalimantan
131 B7 La Sangre Mexico
124 H3 La Santa Mexico
133 H1 Las Animas Colorado
106 G3 Las Anod Somalia
121 L10 Las Aves, Is Venezuela
38 L5 Lasberg Austria

28 D4 Lásby Denmark
127 J5 Lascahobas Haiti
133 E3 Las Cejas Argentina
123 R4 La Scie Nfld
133 C5 Las Coloradas Neuquén Argentina
124 F3 Las Cruces Mexico
106 D9 Las Cruces New Mexico
86 J3 Las Dureh Somalia
21 F8 La Selle mt Haiti
131 B2 La Serena Chile
16 D6 La Serena reg Spain
124 J4 Las Esperancas Mexico
19 P18 La Seyne France
131 F6 Las Flores Argentina
16 E5 Las Guadalerzas reg Spain
118 H5 Lashburn Sask
77 G4 Lash-è Joveyn Afghanistan
68 C1 Lashio Burma
77 A4 Lashkar Gah Afghanistan
54 N2 Lashma U.S.S.R.
13 H4 Las Hurdes Spain
69 C11 Lasikin Indonesia
69 C11 La Sila dist Italy
31 L2 Lasin Poland
31 L4 Lask Poland
88 A1 Las Khoreh Somalia
31 L2 Laskowice Poland
133 C5 Las Lajas Argentina
128 F8 Las Lajitas Argentina
128 F8 Las Lomitas Argentina
16 C7 Las Marismas dist Spain
133 D7 Las Mercedes Venezuela
127 L10 Las Mercedes Venezuela
124 G4 Las Mestenas Mexico
16 E6 Las Nieves Mexico
16 E6 La Solana Spain
70 G6 Lasolo Sulawesi
71 H6 Lasolo R Sulawesi
19 J14 Las Sóns France
38 F8 Lasorling mt Austria
21 H9 La Souterraine France
85 A3 Las Palmas de Gran Canaria Canary Is
106 C8 Las Palmas New Mexico
44 G3 La Spezia Italy
117 L11 Lasqueti I Br Col
16 E4 Las Rozas Spain
33 N5 Lassan E Germany
33 T5 Lassan E Germany
130 G5 Lassance Brazil
20 E5 Lassay France
100 D9 Lassen Peak mt California
100 D9 Lassen Vol. Nat. Park California
22 D4 Lassigny France
38 L6 Lassing Austria
146 E12 Lassiter Coast Antarctica
38 K7 Lassnitz-Dorf Austria
38 N7 Lassnitzhöhe Austria
121 R7 L'Assomption Quebec
13 E2 Lastarria mt Chile/Arg
20 D4 Lassy France
133 D3 Lasterria mt Chile/Arg
106 G2 Last Chance Colorado
13 H5 Lastingham England
119 N7 Last Mountain Sask
119 M7 Last Mountain L Sask
88 B6 Lastoursville Gabon
42 H6 Lastovo isld Yugoslavia
124 F7 Las Tres Marias islds Mexico
32 G2 Lastrup W Germany
21 H6 La Suze-sur-Sarthe France
124 E3 Las Varas Mexico
124 G3 Las Varas Mexico
103 J5 Las Vegas Nevada
106 E6 Las Vegas New Mexico
19 P18 La Vallette France
72 B3 La Valle Wisconsin
101 M5 Lavalleja dep Uruguay
122 C5 Laval, R Quebec
38 L8 Lavamünd Austria
77 C6 Lavan isld Iran
45 L3 Lavane, M mt Italy
31 K1 Lavanggruppen Norway
9 F6 Lavant England
107 P2 Lavant Ontario
38 L8 Lavant R England
71 G7 Lavant W Germany
38 L8 Lavanttal V Austria
131 A6 Lavapié, Pta C Chile
18 F8 Lavardac France
44 F7 Lavagna France
44 F7 Lavagna R Italy
101 O7 Lavaur France
20 D5 Laval France
19 P18 La Valette France
72 B3 La Valle Wisconsin
38 L6 La Vallée France
94 E10 Laventie France
130 B10 La Verá L Paraguay
133 F3 La Verá L Paraguay
103 L4 La Verkin Utah
107 L5 Laverne Oklahoma
109 J6 La Vernia Texas
143 D8 Laverton W Australia
54 L3 Lavezzola Italy
71 G4 Lavezares Philippines
26 U1 Lavrentiya Norway
21 H8 Le Blanc France
107 P3 Lebo Kansas
89 G4 Lebombo Mts Mozambique
68 A2 Lebon Poland
141 H5 Leichhardt R Queensland
21 H6 La Villedieu France
21 H9 La Voulte France
21 F9 La Villedieu-du-Clain France
110 P13 Le Bourget France
122 H6 Le Bouthillier New Brunswick
101 R3 La Viña Montana
128 C5 La Viña Peru
119 O8 Lebret Sask
16 E8 Lebrija Spain
31 K1 Lebsko, Jeziero L Poland
128 E2 Lebu Chile
37 S9 Lebus E Germany
28 F7 Leby Denmark
52 G5 Lebyazh'ye Kazakhstan
52 E3 Lebyazh'ye Kirov U.S.S.R.
52 E6 Lebyazh'ye Kurgan U.S.S.R.
71 N9 Leça Turo
19 Q18 Le Canadel France
68 C8 Leck W Germany
41 L5 Lecco Italy
41 L5 Lecco, Lago di Italy
16 E8 Lécera Spain
99 M9 Le Center Minnesota
37 K7 Lech R W Germany
67 D4 Lechang China

71 E3 Laur Luzon Philippines
141 G3 Laura Queensland
118 K7 Laura Sask
138 E5 Laura S Australia
128 E2 La Urbana Venezuela
95 M8 Lurbjerg Denmark
94 B7 Laurel Delaware
95 L7 Laurel Indiana
111 G10 Laurel Maryland
94 B7 Laurel Mississippi
107 M7 Laurel Montana
27 G12 Laxá Sweden
94 H6 Laurel New York
9 H3 Laurel Hill Florida
15 G2 Laurel Hill Pennsylvania
26 G8 Laxo Scotland
101 S9 Laxsjö Sweden
21 C8 Lay Colorado
52 J2 Lay R France
52 G1 Laye R U.S.S.R.
20 K5 Laye R France
139 G7 Layers Hill Victoria
111 K9 Lay L Alabama
146 C14 Lazarevac Yugoslavia
57 A3 Lazarevo, Oz isld U.S.S.R.
124 B2 Lázaro Cárdenas Mexico
47 G1 Lazar Stanevo Bulgaria
86 A1 Laz Daua Somalia
31 O1 Lazdijai U.S.S.R.
21 J7 Lazenay France
42 E6 Lazio prov Italy
37 O3 Lazonby England
59 K3 Lazo U.S.S.R.
94 D7 Leaburg Oregon
110 B3 Leach Cambodia
110 F6 Leachville Arkansas
98 C5 Lead S Dakota
13 E2 Leadburn Scotland
9 F1 Leadenham England
110 E8 Leadenham England
94 H9 Leadgate England
94 H6 Leadhills Scotland
106 D2 Leadville Colorado
139 J4 Leadville N S Wales
146 M6 Leaf R Illinois
146 J11 Leahy,C Antarctica
142 F4 Leake, Mt W Australia
143 C7 Leake, Mt W Australia
111 H10 Leaksville Mississippi
108 F5 Leakey Texas
111 D4 Leal N Dakota
111 D4 Leal R Mississippi
133 C3 Leales Argentina
142 B5 Leal, Mt W Australia
145 B2 Leamington New Zealand
119 T2 Leamington L Manitoba
21 C7 Le Fullet France
118 D5 Legal Alberta
120 E2 Legarde R Ontario
121 R6 Legaré, L Quebec
8 G1 Legbourne England
21 B7 Le Gavre France
21 B5 Legbourne England
37 O9 Legden W Germany
21 B7 Lège France
21 J5 Legazpi Philippines
19 P14 Le Genevrey France
111 M10 Leghorn see Livorno
7 L4 LegGeorgia
121 T4 Le Gîte Quebec
21 C8 L'Église France
45 K1 Legnago Italy
41 L5 Legnano Italy
31 K4 Legnica Poland
41 K5 Legnone mt Italy
118 D5 Legrade it France
120 E2 Legraré, L Quebec
21 R6 Legrand Philippines
53 G4 Legume N S Wales
100 G4 Leh Kashmir
74 G1 Lehi Utah
101 U7 Lehi Utah
109 M5 Lehighton Pennsylvania
109 I5 Lehman Oregon
33 R6 Lehnin E Germany
20 A5 Lehon France
79 D4 Lehrberg W Germany
33 M8 Lehre W Germany
33 G6 Lehrte W Germany
94 E10 Lehsen W Germany
29 K9 Lehtimäki Finland
67 E2 Lehua Hawaiian Is
84 G2 Lehua I Hawaiian Is
8 E3 Lehua, E Germany
111 F8 Leiah Pakistan
87 B7 Leibnitzer Austria
36 L8 Leibo China
37 T8 Leibsch E Germany
91 H8 Leibstadt Austria
28 P8 Leidschendam Neth
108 B4 Leif Belgium
33 M8 Leiferde W Germany
127 H15 Lenhovda Sweden
94 B4 Leigh England
8 E5 Leigh England
138 G4 Leigh Creek S Australia
14 E4 Leighlinbridge Irish Rep
9 G5 Leighton Buzzard England
94 C4 Leighton, Mt N Terr Aust
7 C8 Leighton Buzzard England
140 D6 Leignon Belgium
55 C4 Leintwardine England
65 B4 Leipsic Ohio
33 O8 Leinster prov Irish Rep
14 D3 Leipzig E Germany

94 K10 Lawrenceville Virginia
143 D7 Lawrence Wells, Mt W Australia
41 N6 Ledro,L di Italy
102 F4 Laws California
110 B2 Lawson Missouri
31 K2 Ledyczek Poland
99 N4 Lawton Michigan
28 D4 Lee Denmark
107 M7 Lawton Oklahoma
99 S8 Lee Illinois
95 O4 Lee Massachusetts
121 P9 Leech Pennsylvania
41 N2 Leeder W Germany
142 B1 Leederville dist Perth, W Aust
108 E8 Leedey Oklahoma
111 K8 Leeds Alabama
13 G6 Leeds England
98 G1 Leeds N Dakota
103 L4 Leeds Utah
121 L4 Le Lamentin Martinique W I
99 N6 Leland Iowa
94 D4 Leland Michigan
111 F8 Leland Mississippi
27 E12 Lelången l Sweden
133 C6 Leleque Argentina
42 F5 Leeton New S Wales
99 L4 Leeton Ohio
120 E8 Leeuwarden Netherlands
142 N5 Leeuwin,C W Australia
32 M5 Leezen W Germany
21 D7 Leffinge Belgium
11 H10 Lefini R Congo
108 D6 Leakey Texas
79 C3 Lefka Cyprus
79 D3 Lefkoniko Cyprus
3 M9 Leman Bank see rig North Sea
9 R7 Leaf River Illinois
146 J11 Leeuwen,C W Australia
102 K4 Lee Vining California
127 N5 Leeward Is W Indies
21 F7 Le Fullet France
68 J3 Ledong China
21 H9 Le Dorat France
118 D5 Leduc Alberta
69 D11 Leduna Sumatra
41 N6 Ledro,L di Italy
103 P10 Lee Arizona
28 D4 Lee Denmark
113 D7 Lee Florida
99 S8 Lee Illinois
95 O4 Lee Massachusetts
25 C6 Lek R Netherlands
28 E6 Leka isld Norway
4 G3 Lekáni Greece
86 G4 Lekemti Ethiopia
46 E4 Lékhovon Greece
16 D10 Lékkous R Morocco
28 J4 Leksand Sweden
29 P8 Leksozero, Ozero L U.S.S.R.
26 K5 Leksvik Norway
127 L4 Le Lamentin Martinique W I

68 J3 Ledong China
21 H9 Le Dorat France
118 D5 Leduc Alberta
69 D11 Leduna Sumatra
31 K2 Ledyczek Poland
103 P10 Lee Arizona
28 D4 Lee Denmark
113 D7 Lee Florida
99 S8 Lee Illinois
95 O4 Lee Massachusetts
25 C6 Leka R Netherlands
28 E6 Leka isld Norway
4 G3 Lekáni Greece
86 G4 Lekemti Ethiopia
46 E4 Lékhovon Greece
16 D10 Lékkous R Morocco
28 J4 Leksand Sweden
29 P8 Leksozero, Ozero L U.S.S.R.
26 K5 Leksvik Norway
127 L4 Le Lamentin Martinique W I
99 N6 Leland Iowa
94 D4 Leland Michigan
111 F8 Leland Mississippi
27 E12 Lelången l Sweden
133 C6 Leleque Argentina
48 E7 Lelija mt Yugoslavia
113 D6 Leling China
71 C3 Lelintah W Irian
21 D6 Le Lion-d'Angers France
28 J6 Lellinge Denmark
71 L9 Lelogama Timor Indonesia
21 D7 Le Louroux-Botterau France
127 L4 Le Lorrain Martinique W I
21 D7 Le Louroux-Beconnais France
19 Q18 Le Luc France
21 F6 Le Lude France
25 D3 Lelystad Netherlands
14 E1 Lenmore Ireland
12 A4 Le Madonie mts Sicily
133 E8 Le Maire, Estrecho de str Argentina
7 M9 Leman Bank see rig North Sea
32 P5 Leeuwarden Netherlands
48 E7 Leeuwarden Netherlands
102 K4 Lee Vining California
127 N5 Leeward Is W Indies
21 F7 Le Mans France
21 F7 Le Mans France
108 G1 Le Mars Iowa
21 H7 Le Liège France
21 E7 Lembach W Germany
48 E7 Lelija mt Yugoslavia

144 D5 Leithfield New Zealand
9 F5 Leith Hill England
14 C2 Leitrim co Irish Rep
33 P8 Leitzkau E Germany
29 M10 Leivonmäki Finland
14 E3 Leixlip Irish Rep
67 D3 Leizhou China
67 C6 Leizhou Bandao pen China
67 C6 Leizhou Wan inlet China
28 M2 Lejnum Faeroes
25 C5 Lek R Netherlands
26 E6 Leka isld Norway
119 P7 Leech R Minnesota
43 G3 Lékani Greece
86 G4 Lekemti Ethiopia
46 E4 Lékhovon Greece
16 D10 Lékkous R Morocco
28 J4 Leksand Sweden
29 P8 Leksozero Ozero L U.S.S.R.
26 K5 Leksvik Norway
127 L4 Le Lamentin Martinique W I
99 N6 Leland Iowa
94 D4 Leland Michigan
111 F8 Leland Mississippi
27 E12 Lelången l Sweden
133 C6 Leleque Argentina
48 E7 Lelija mt Yugoslavia
113 D6 Leling China
71 C3 Lelintah W Irian
21 D6 Le Lion-d'Angers France
28 J6 Lellinge Denmark
71 L9 Lelogama Timor Indonesia
21 D7 Le Louroux-Botterau France
127 L4 Le Lorrain Martinique W I
21 D7 Le Louroux-Beconnais France
19 Q18 Le Luc France
21 F6 Le Lude France
25 D3 Lelystad Netherlands
14 E1 Lenmore Ireland
12 A4 Le Madonie mts Sicily
133 E8 Le Maire, Estrecho de str Argentina
7 M9 Leman Bank see rig North Sea
102 K4 Lee Vining California
108 G1 Le Mars Iowa
21 H7 Le Liège France
21 E7 Lembach W Germany
36 D5 Lembach W Germany
36 C5 Lembang Sulawesi
21 C5 Lemberg Sask
47 G3 Lemberg see L'vov
36 D5 Lemberg W Germany
32 H1 Lembeek Belgium
36 M1 Lembeye France
70 E4 Lembu, Gunung mt Sumatra
130 E8 Leme São Paulo Brazil
32 H8 Lemförde W Germany
32 H8 Lemgo W Germany
101 M5 Lemhi Idaho
101 M5 Lemhi Ra Idaho
95 O4 Lemieux Quebec
115 N5 Lemieux Is N W Terr
121 J8 Lemitar New Mexico
19 P14 Lemmenjoki R Finland
32 M3 Lemmenjärvi R Finland
25 E4 Lemmer Netherlands
28 D4 Lemming Denmark
114 J8 Lemmon S Dakota
103 O9 Lemnos isld Greece see Limnos I
26 H5 Le Môle St. Nicolas Haiti
111 G9 Lemoore California
102 C5 Lemoore California
70 G6 Lemoro Sulawesi
98 E8 Lemoyne Nebraska
125 P11 Lempa R El Salvador
29 K10 Lempäälä Finland
21 H7 Lempdes France
21 J7 Lempriere Br Columbia
118 H8 Lemsford Sask
70 D3 Lemutan Kalimantan
28 G7 Lemvig Denmark
33 O8 Lenartovce Czechoslovakia
32 H5 Lemwerder W Germany
70 B4 Lemyethna Burma
70 B4 Len R Kalimantan
70 C4 Lena Illinois
109 J6 Lena Mississippi
94 J5 Lena Oregon
27 J11 Lena Sweden
99 S5 Lena Wisconsin
21 C7 Lena R U.S.S.R.
101 Q5 Lenah Nevada
43 D8 Lendery Scotland
21 G9 Lennox Sask
36 J7 Lennep W Germany
33 P2 Lengefeld E Germany
37 P2 Lengerich W Germany
32 H6 Lenggries W Germany
66 E4 Lenghu China
131 B3 Lengua de Vaca,Pta Chile
65 E4 Lengpui China
36 B4 Lenham England
27 H15 Lenhovda Sweden
70 G5 Lenina, Pik mt U.S.S.R.
21 C6 Lénine France
49 Leningrad conurbation U.S.S.R.
146 K5 Leninград Beach dist Perth, W Aust
50 F3 Leningradskaya U.S.S.R. in I.V. Kanal see Volgo Sea
140 D6 Leignon Belgium
55 C4 Lengnau Romania
33 T8 Lehnin E Germany
29 P8 Leningradskaya U.S.S.R.
57 A4 Leninsk U.S.S.R.
57 A4 Leninsk Turkmenia U.S.S.R.
57 A4 Leninsk Mariy U.S.S.R.
54 H5 Leninsk Tula U.S.S.R.
56 B4 Leninsk-Kuznetskiy U.S.S.R.
52 G4 Leninskiy Kirgiziya U.S.S.R.
52 G5 Leninskoye Kirov U.S.S.R.
52 G9 Lenin Zambia
71 C3 Len-k'i U.S.S.R.
71 C3 Lenmalu W Irian
142 E12 Lennards Pt W Australia
27 E12 Lennartsfors Sweden
143 C7 Lennonville W Australia
99 K6 Lennox Iowa
112 J3 Lennox S Dakota
102 D5 Lennox Head N S Wales
127 J5 Lennox, I Chile/Arg
13 G1 Lennoxtown Scotland
112 F2 Lenoir N Carolina
107 K2 Lenoir City Tennessee
99 R8 Lenora Colorado
99 R9 Lenora Kansas
107 L2 Lenore Sask
1 C6 Lenore, L Washington
22 C6 Lenox Georgia
70 E8 Lenox Iowa
99 M9 Lenox Iowa
95 O4 Lenox Massachusetts
22 D4 Lens France
38 L5 Lensahn W Germany
26 D8 Lensvik Norway
25 E5 Lent Netherlands

26 M7 Lövånger Sweden
48 E3 Lovasberény Hungary
48 D3 Lovászpatona Hungary
54 B1 Lovat' R U.S.S.R.
26 K6 Lövberg Sweden
26 H8 Lövberga Sweden
42 J6 Lovćen mt Yugoslavia
28 G5 Løve Denmark
119 N5 Love Sask
68 F6 Lovea Cambodia
47 G1 Lovech Bulgaria
109 O9 Love Field Airport Texas
28 C3 Løvel Denmark
109 M4 Lovelady Texas
98 A9 Loveland Colorado
110 M2 Loveland Ohio
106 E2 Loveland Pass Colorado
101 R5 Lovell Wyoming
94 C2 Lovells Michigan
100 G9 Lovelock Nevada
103 O1 Lovenia, Mt Utah
95 L7 Love Point Maryland
42 C3 Lovere Italy
118 H7 Loverna Sask
140 C6 Loves Creek N Terr Aust
113 D7 Lovett Florida
26 F10 Lövhögen Sweden
26 N4 Lovikka Sweden
106 F9 Loving New Mexico
109 J2 Loving Texas
94 J9 Lovingston Virginia
99 S10 Lovington Illinois
106 G9 Lovington New Mexico
16 B3 Lovíos Spain
29 M11 Lovisa Finland
26 J5 Lövnäs Sweden
28 C3 Lovns Bredning B Denmark
30 H5 Lovosice Czechoslovakia
52 E1 Lovozero U.S.S.R.
45 P1 Lovre čica Yugoslavia
48 F5 Lovrin Romania
26 H7 Lövsjön Sweden
26 F5 Lovunden isld Norway
103 L1 Low Utah
86 E6 Lowa Zaïre
144 B6 Lowburn New Zealand
120 K4 Low Bush River Ontario
115 L5 Low, C N W Terr
99 P8 Lowden Iowa
100 E6 Low Desert Oregon
9 F1 Lowdham England
103 P10 Lowell Arizona
110 B5 Lowell Arkansas
100 K3 Lowell Idaho
99 T8 Lowell Indiana
95 Q4 Lowell Massachusetts
94 B4 Lowell Michigan
94 F7 Lowell Ohio
100 C6 Lowell Oregon
100 J6 Lowell, L Idaho
33 S7 Löwenberg E Germany
28 C7 Löwenstedt W Germany
36 G5 Löwenstein W Germany
117 P11 Lower Arrow L Br Col
98 G5 Lower Brule S Dakota
101 P5 Lower Falls Wyoming
119 V8 Lower Ft.Garry Manitoba
103 L6 Lower Granite Gorge Arizona
145 G4 Lower Hutt New Zealand
123 U6 Lower Island Cove Nfld
100 D8 Lower Klamath L California
102 B3 Lower L California
117 F5 Lower Laberge Yukon Terr
115 K4 Lower Macdougall L N W Terr
122 G6 Lower Neguac New Brunswick
122 G10 Lower Ohio Nova Scotia
135 T3 Lower Paia Hawaiian Is
117 J6 Lower Post Br Columbia
99 L2 Lower Red L Minnesota
101 O5 Lower Red Rock L Montana
115 N5 Lower Savage Is N W Terr
122 G10 Lower West Pubnico Nova Scotia
15 F1 Lower Whitehall Scotland
110 H5 Lowes Kentucky
9 H3 Lowestoft England
139 H8 Low Head Tasmania
13 G2 Lowick England
13 E5 Lowick Br England
31 M3 Łowicz Poland
141 H3 Low Is Queensland
100 K5 Lowman Idaho
111 K9 Lowndesboro Alabama
83 M9 Low Pt Christmas I Indian Oc
139 H9 Low Rocky Pt Tasmania
110 C3 Lowry City Missouri
87 H10 Lowry, Iles Madagascar
112 F3 Lowrys S Carolina
13 F4 Lowther England
115 K3 Lowther I N W Terr
121 P9 Lowville New York
125 L9 Loxicha Mexico
111 J11 Loxley Alabama
138 F5 Loxton S Australia
99 Q5 Loyal Wisconsin
118 F7 Loyalist Alberta
94 D10 Loyall Kentucky
95 L5 Loyalsock Cr Pennsylvania
102 D2 Loyalton California
98 G4 Loyalton S Dakota
Loyang see Luoyang
137 O6 Loyauté, Is Pacific Oc
54 B5 Loyev U.S.S.R.
52 G4 Loyma U.S.S.R.
52 H5 Loyno U.S.S.R.
47 H2 Lozarevo Bulgaria
18 H8 Lozère dep France
18 H8 Lozère, Mt France
48 E6 Loznica Yugoslavia
54 H8 Lozovaya U.S.S.R.
50 F2 Lozva R U.S.S.R.
86 C5 Lua R Zaïre
87 D8 Luacano Angola
87 D7 Luachimo Angola
69 D13 Luahasibuka Indonesia
88 F10 Luala R Mozambique
86 E6 Lualaba R Zaïre
86 E6 Luama R Zaïre
87 F8 Luambe Zambia
87 D9 Luampa Zambia
87 D8 Luan Angola
58 G5 Lu'an China
127 J2 Luana Pt Jamaica
68 F2 Luan Chau Vietnam
65 C6 Luancheng China
67 C5 Luancheng China
65 B8 Luanchuan China
87 B7 Luanda Angola
87 C8 Luando R Angola
71 O9 Luang isld Indonesia
87 D8 Luanganga R Angola
69 D8 Luang, Khao mt Thailand
68 F3 Luang Prabang Laos
69 E9 Luang, Thale L Thailand
87 C7 Luangue R Angola
88 C8 Luangwa R Zambia
65 D4 Luan He R China
65 D5 Luannan China
88 B9 Luano Zambia
65 D4 Luanping China
88 B8 Luanshya Zambia
65 D5 Luan Xian China
88 B7 Luapula Zambia
88 B8 Luapula R Zaïre
16 C1 Luarca Spain
70 C4 Luar, D L Kalimantan
87 D8 Luashi Zaïre
88 F8 Luatize R Mozambique
125 P9 Lubaantum Belize
31 O5 Lubaczów Poland
87 C7 Lubalo Angola
31 J4 Lubań Poland
52 C6 Lubāna U.S.S.R.
52 C6 Lubānasezers L U.S.S.R.
71 E4 Lubang Philippines
82 D6 Lubango Angola
88 C7 Lubansenshi R Zambia
33 Q8 Lübars E Germany
31 O4 Lubartów Poland
31 M2 Lubawa Poland
32 J8 Lübbecke W Germany
33 T9 Lübben E Germany
33 T9 Lübbenau E Germany
108 F2 Lubbock Texas
139 G6 Lubeck Victoria
33 N5 Lübeck W Germany
33 O4 Lübecker Bucht W Germany
86 D6 Lubefu Zaïre
37 P3 Lubenec Czechoslovakia
55 B5 Lubenka U.S.S.R.
88 B2 Lubero Zaïre
19 O17 Lubéron, Montagne du mts France
88 C8 Lubi R Zambia
71 E5 Lubic isld Philippines
118 B2 Lubicon L Alberta
31 J2 Lubie, Jezioro L Poland
31 L3 Lubień Poland
87 D7 Lubilash R Zaïre
31 J4 Lubiń Poland
31 O4 Lublin Poland
99 Q4 Lublin Wisconsin
31 L5 Lubliniec Poland
33 T4 Lubmin E Germany
15 D4 Lubnaig, L Scotland
54 D6 Lubny U.S.S.R.
70 B4 Lubok Anto Sarawak
29 P8 Lubosalma U.S.S.R.
17 F7 Lubrín Spain
31 H4 Lubsko Poland
33 O6 Lübtheen E Germany
71 E2 Lubuagan Luzon Philippines
87 E7 Lubudi Zaïre
87 D7 Lubudi R Zaïre
70 K8 Lubukbatang Sumatra
69 F12 Lubukbertubung Sumatra
69 F14 Lubuklinggau Sumatra
69 D11 Lubukpakam Sumatra
69 E12 Lubuksikaping Sumatra
88 B6 Lubule R Zaïre
87 E8 Lubumbashi Zaïre
86 E6 Lubutu Zaïre
37 N3 Luby Czechoslovakia
33 Q6 Lübz E Germany
20 E3 Luc France
87 C7 Lucala Angola
14 E3 Lucan Irish Rep
120 J9 Lucan Ontario
68 G1 Luc An Chau Vietnam
116 R6 Lucania, Mt Yukon Terr
43 G8 Lucano, Appennino mts Italy
129 G6 Lucas Brazil
99 N8 Lucas Iowa
107 M2 Lucas Kansas
94 E6 Lucas Ohio
142 G5 Lucas, L W Australia
126 E1 Lucaya Grand Bahama I
21 H7 Luçay le Mâle France
71 E3 Lucban Luzon Philippines
45 J4 Lucca Italy
98 J3 Lucca N Dakota
129 G3 Luce R Suriname
127 H1 Lucea Jamaica
15 D6 Luce B Scotland
111 H11 Lucedale Mississippi
130 E7 Lucélia Brazil
71 E4 Lucena Philippines
17 G4 Lucena del Cid Spain
16 E7 Lucena, Sa. de mts Spain
48 F2 Lučenec Czechoslovakia
43 G7 Lucera Italy
Lucerne see Luzern
102 B2 Lucerne California
99 N9 Lucerne Missouri
100 E1 Lucerne Washington
101 R6 Lucerne Wyoming
102 H7 Lucerne L California
102 H7 Lucerne Valley California
124 F2 Lucero Mexico
122 D5 Luceville Quebec
65 B6 Lucheng China
67 B4 Lucheng China
88 E9 Luchenza Malawi
21 F6 Luché-Pringé France
111 F11 Lucher Louisiana
54 B2 Luchesa R U.S.S.R.
20 K1 Lucheux France
33 O7 Lüchow W Germany
68 K1 Luchuan China
20 K2 Luchy France
102 C5 Lucia California
121 M2 Lucie, L Quebec
100 J4 Lucile Idaho
16 C2 Lucillo Spain
101 M8 Lucin Utah
94 H5 Lucinda Pennsylvania
141 H4 Lucinda Queensland
138 F6 Lucindale S Australia
87 B8 Lucira Angola
99 O4 Luck Wisconsin
37 N1 Lucka E Germany
33 T9 Luckau E Germany
33 S8 Luckenwalde E Germany
143 E8 Luck, Mt W Australia
74 J5 Lucknow India
120 J9 Lucknow Ontario
140 F6 Lucknow Queensland
118 K8 Lucky Lake Sask
100 K6 Lucky Peak Res Idaho
118 F9 Lucky Strike Alberta
21 C9 Luçon France
45 O6 Luco ne Marsi Italy
108 A5 Lucoro Mexico
22 G4 Lucquy France
126 G4 Lucrecia, C Cuba
87 D8 Lucusse Angola
106 E7 Lucy New Mexico
140 D5 Lucy Creek N Terr Aust
140 C6 Lucy, Mt N Terr Aust
59 H4 Lüda China
13 H6 Ludborough England
98 H3 Ludden N Dakota
107 K2 Ludell Kansas
32 G10 Lüdenscheid W Germany
33 P7 Lüderitz E Germany
87 C11 Lüderitz Namibia
120 K7 Ludgate Ontario
9 E5 Ludgershall England
74 F3 Ludhiana India
32 F9 Lüdinghausen W Germany
99 U6 Ludington Michigan
103 H7 Ludlow California
106 F4 Ludlow Colorado
8 D3 Ludlow England
99 S9 Ludlow Illinois
122 F7 Ludlow New Brunswick
94 J5 Ludlow Pennsylvania
98 C4 Ludlow S Dakota
95 P3 Ludlow Vermont
47 H1 Ludogorie Bulgaria
52 C5 Ludoni U.S.S.R.
112 F6 Ludowici Georgia
36 E5 Ludswigshöhe W Germany
48 J4 Luduş Romania
27 H11 Ludvika Sweden
36 H2 Ludwigsau W Germany
36 G6 Ludwigsburg W Germany
37 M3 Ludwigschorgast W Germany
36 E5 Ludwigshafen W Germany
37 L5 Ludwigs Kanal canal W Germany
33 O6 Ludwigslust E Germany
37 L3 Ludwigsstadt W Germany
52 C6 Ludza U.S.S.R.
86 D7 Luebo Zaïre
109 H3 Lueders Texas
86 E6 Lueki Zaïre
87 C8 Luena Angola
87 D8 Luena R Angola
87 D8 Luena R Zambia
88 D10 Luenha R Mozambique
128 F2 Luepa Venezuela
87 D7 Lueta Zaïre
87 D9 Lueti R Zambia
58 E5 Lüeyang China
67 E5 Lufeng China
111 B10 Lufkin Texas
88 C6 Lufubu R Zambia
88 B10 Lufya R Zambia
48 F6 Lug R Yugoslavia
52 C5 Luga U.S.S.R.
52 C5 Luga R U.S.S.R.
88 B4 Lugamba Zaïre
41 J5 Lugano Switzerland
42 B3 Lugano, L. di Italy
Lugansk see Voroshilovgrad
126 F4 Lugareño Cuba
32 K9 Lügde W Germany
88 F10 Lugela Mozambique
88 F10 Lugela R Mozambique
88 F8 Lugenda R Mozambique
144 B6 Luggate New Zealand
8 D3 Lugg, R England
Lugh Ferrandi see Ganane
14 E4 Lugnaquilla mt Irish Rep
41 K4 Lugnezer Tal Switzerland
45 L3 Lugo Italy
16 B1 Lugo Spain
16 B1 Lugo prov Spain
48 G5 Lugoj Romania
55 E1 Lugovoy U.S.S.R.
12 D2 Lugton Scotland
86 E6 Lugulu R Zaïre
71 E8 Lugus isld Philippines
70 G6 Luha isld Celebes
29 M10 Luhanka Finland
72 E5 Luḩayyah, Al N Yemen
67 F1 Luhe China
37 N4 Luhe W Germany
32 M6 Luhe R W Germany
65 D1 Luhin Sum China
33 T4 Lühmannsdorf E Germany
87 C7 Lui R Angola
88 D10 Luia R Mozambique
87 D9 Luiana Angola
Luichow Pen see Leizhou Bandao
Luik see Liège
86 D6 Luilaka R Zaïre
20 K4 Luine R France
15 C4 Luing isld Scotland
42 B2 Luino Italy
29 N4 Luira R Finland
124 E4 Luis Mexico
130 E10 Luís Alves Brazil
130 H9 Luís Gomes Brazil
87 E8 Luishia Zaïre
124 H5 Luis Moya Mexico
146 D10 Luitpold Coast Antarctica
87 D7 Luiza Zaïre
88 A5 Luizi R Zaïre
133 D4 Lujan Argentina
131 F5 Lujan R Argentina
67 F1 Lujiang China
67 C5 Lujing China
37 P3 Luka Czechoslovakia
87 E8 Lukafu Zaïre
88 A8 Lukanga R Zambia
88 A9 Lukanga Sw Zambia
143 B7 Luke, Mt W Australia
86 C6 Lukenie R Zaïre
52 F6 Lukh U.S.S.R.
54 L2 Lukhovitsy U.S.S.R.
41 J4 Lukmanier Pass Switzerland
86 C6 Lukolela Zaïre
67 D3 Lukou China
46 D3 Lukova Yugoslavia
47 G1 Lukovit Bulgaria
31 N4 Łuków Poland
52 F6 Lukoyanov U.S.S.R.
86 B7 Lukula Zaïre
88 G7 Lukuledi R Tanzania
87 D8 Lukulu Zambia
88 C8 Lukulu R Zambia
87 G7 Lukumburu Tanzania
69 C10 Lukup Sumatra
88 D8 Lukuzye R Zambia
112 D3 Lula Georgia
111 F7 Lula Mississippi
26 M6 Luleå Sweden
26 M6 Lule älv R Sweden
47 J3 Lüleburgaz Turkey
87 D7 Lulembe R Angola
67 A4 Luliang China
65 B6 Lüliang Shan ra China
111 F12 Luling Louisiana
109 K6 Luling Texas
65 D5 Lulong China
86 C5 Lulonga R Zaïre
113 E7 Lulu Florida
86 D7 Lulua R Zaïre
Luluabourg see Kananga
8 D6 Lulworth Cove England
143 C7 Lulworth, Mt W Australia
70 O10 Lumadjang Java
70 D2 Lumaku mt Sabah
87 D8 Lumbala Angola
112 H3 Lumber R N Carolina
112 E6 Lumber City Georgia
94 J6 Lumber City Pennsylvania
94 G7 Lumberport W Virginia
111 G10 Lumberton Mississippi
112 H3 Lumberton N Carolina
106 D5 Lumberton New Mexico
18 E10 Lumbier Spain
70 E2 Lumbis Kalimantan
88 H9 Lumbo Mozambique
52 F1 Lumbovka U.S.S.R.
16 C4 Lumbrales Spain
22 C2 Lumbres France
28 E6 Lumby Denmark
75 P6 Lumding India
29 L7 Lumijoki Finland
88 D8 Lumimba R Zambia
22 J2 Lummen Belgium
29 H11 Lumparland Finland
111 M9 Lumpkin Georgia
28 H5 Lumsås Denmark
144 B6 Lumsden New Zealand
123 T4 Lumsden Nfld
119 N8 Lumsden Sask
15 F3 Lumsden Scotland
70 F6 Lumu Sulawesi
69 E10 Lumut Malaysia
70 D5 Lumut, Bt mt Kalimantan
71 E2 Luna Luzon Philippines
106 B8 Luna New Mexico
131 G2 Luna, L Argentina
67 A4 Lunan China
15 F4 Lunan B Scotland
74 E7 Lunavada India
117 L10 Lund Br Columbia
28 D5 Lund Denmark
103 J3 Lund Nevada
27 F16 Lund Sweden
103 L3 Lund Utah
27 J13 Lunda Sweden
88 B7 Lunda Chishinga Zambia
28 K5 Lundåkrabukten B Sweden
119 T8 Lundar Manitoba
87 F8 Lundazi Zambia
88 D8 Lundazi R Zambia
118 C9 Lundbreck Alberta
28 H6 Lundby Denmark
28 A5 Lunde Denmark
28 F6 Lundeborg Denmark
28 C6 Lunderskov Denmark
27 B13 Lunde-Vatn L Norway
89 G3 Lundi R Zimbabwe
28 C3 Lundø Denmark
28 D5 Lundum Denmark
8 B5 Lundy isld England
33 M6 Lüne W Germany
32 J6 Lüne R W Germany
36 B3 Lünebach W Germany
33 M6 Lüneburg W Germany
32 M6 Lüneburger Heide reg W Germany
18 H9 Lunel France
32 G9 Lünen W Germany
122 H9 Lunenburg Nova Scotia
95 Q2 Lunenburg Vermont
20 G2 Luneray France
41 L3 Lüner See L Austria
19 K4 Lunéville France
87 D8 Lunga R Zambia
68 H1 Lung-chou China
66 C5 Lungdo China
66 C5 Lunggar China
44 G3 Lungiana Italy
26 H8 Lungsjön Sweden
27 G12 Lungsund Sweden
88 C6 Lungu Zambia
87 C8 Lungue Bungo R Angola
102 F3 Luning Nevada
71 H9 Lunjuk Sumbawa Indonesia
15 G2 Lunna Scotland
32 F8 Lünne W Germany
85 B7 Lunsar Sierra Leone
88 B8 Lunsemfwa R Zambia
66 C3 Luntai China
38 M6 Lunz am See Austria
37 O2 Lunzenau E Germany
88 D7 Lunzi R Zambia
86 B6 Luobomo Congo
67 C4 Luocheng China
58 E4 Luochuan China
67 B4 Luodian China
67 D5 Luoding China
65 A7 Luo He R China
65 B7 Luo He R China
67 A1 Luojiang China
67 D5 Luojing China
67 B2 Luolong China
65 A7 Luonan China
26 M4 Luongastunturi mt Sweden
88 B7 Luongo R Zambia
65 B7 Luoning China
67 A4 Luoping China
67 C4 Luoqing Jiang R China
67 C4 Luorong China
67 D2 Luoshan China
67 E1 Luoshan China
67 E1 Luotian China
65 E1 Luotuobozi China
67 B1 Luowenba China
65 B7 Luoyang China
67 F3 Luoyuan China
86 B6 Luozi Zaïre
88 D6 Lupa R Tanzania
88 D8 Lupachi R Malawi
89 F2 Lupani R Zimbabwe
70 B4 Lupar R Sarawak
31 K1 Łupawa R Poland
37 M5 Lupburg W Germany
48 H5 Lupeni Romania
127 J5 Luperón Dom Rep
41 J1 Lupfen mt W Germany
87 G8 Lupilichi Mozambique
67 B3 Luping China
87 C8 Lupire Angola
54 B3 Lupolovo U.S.S.R.
71 G7 Lupon Mindanao Philippines
33 R10 Luppa E Germany
110 D3 Lupus Missouri
87 D7 Luputa Zaïre
52 H4 Lup'ya R U.S.S.R.
130 B9 Luque Paraguay
107 M2 Luray Kansas
94 J8 Luray Virginia
112 E2 Lure, L N Carolina
19 P16 Lure, Mt de France
14 E2 Lurgan N Ireland
128 E7 Luribay Bolivia
128 C6 Lurín Peru
87 H8 Lurio Mozambique
26 F5 Luröy Norway
19 P17 Lurs France
110 C6 Lurton Arkansas
21 J7 Lury-sur-Arnon France
88 B9 Lusaka Zambia
86 D6 Lusambo Zaïre
88 C8 Lusangazi Zambia
21 B6 Lusanger France
117 P9 Luscar Alberta
118 H6 Luseland Sask
75 P7 Lushai Hills India
65 D6 Lu Shan mt China
58 F5 Lushi China
142 F3 Lush, Mt W Australia
88 G4 Lushoto Tanzania
67 E3 Lu Shui R China
65 E5 Lüshun China
67 G1 Lüsi China
70 N9 Lusi R Java
21 F9 Lusignan France
98 B7 Lusk Wyoming
19 P15 Lus-la-Croix Haute France
38 E8 Luson Italy
26 L4 Luspebryggan Sweden
15 D4 Luss Scotland
18 F6 Lussac les Châteaux France
21 H9 Lussac-les-Eglises France
12 C3 Lussa, L Scotland
129 H8 Lussanvira Brazil
78 J6 Lussuf, Al Iraq
141 J7 Lussvale Queensland
36 E5 Lustadt W Germany
41 L3 Lustenau Austria
37 J5 Lustenau W Germany
27 B10 Luster Norway
22 H3 Lustin Belgium
101 U1 Lustre Montana
Lutai see Ninghe
77 E3 Lut, Dasht-e des Iran
87 D8 Lutembo Angola
110 G4 Lutesville Missouri
99 N8 Luther Iowa
107 N6 Luther Oklahoma
108 G1 Lutie Texas
33 N4 Lütjenburg W Germany
9 F4 Luton England
40 E4 Lutry Switzerland
87 C7 Lutshima R Zaïre
32 M9 Lutter am Barenberge W Germany
32 M7 Lutterloh W Germany
9 E3 Lutterworth England
22 G3 Luttre Belgium
112 D1 Luttrell Tennessee
36 C1 Lüttringhausen W Germany
113 E9 Lutz Florida
36 C6 Lutzelbourg France
36 C6 Lutzelhouse France
33 Q10 Lützen E Germany
36 B3 Lutzerath W Germany
33 O5 Lützow E Germany
146 A6 Lützow-Holmbukta Antarctica
29 N11 Luumäki Finland
29 N5 Luusua Finland
111 K10 Luverne Alabama
99 M7 Luverne Iowa
98 K6 Luverne Minnesota
98 J2 Luverne N Dakota
29 J10 Luvia Finland
26 K5 Luvos Sweden
29 P7 Luvozero U.S.S.R.
87 E7 Luvua R Zaïre
87 D8 Luvuei Angola
88 F6 Luwegu R Tanzania
87 F8 Luwingu Zambia
71 B2 Luwo isld Halmahera Indonesia
68 J1 Luwu China
71 H5 Luwuk Sulawesi
88 D7 Luwumbu R Zambia
111 J8 Luxapalila R Alabama
22 L4 Luxembourg Luxembourg
22 L4 Luxembourg, Gd. Duchy of Europe
99 P7 Luxemburg Iowa
40 D2 Luxeuil-les-Bains France
67 A4 Luxi China
67 C2 Luxi China
67 B2 Lu Xian China
84 J4 Luxor Egypt
18 E9 Luy R France
21 G7 Luynes France
18 E10 Luz France
52 G4 Luza U.S.S.R.
52 J2 Luza R Komi U.S.S.R.
20 K3 Luzarches France
18 F8 Luzech France
21 H8 Luzeret France
41 H3 Luzern Switzerland
94 C2 Luzerne Michigan
95 O3 Luzerne New York
67 C4 Luzhai China
67 B3 Luzhi China
67 B2 Luzhou China
130 F5 Luziânia Brazil
21 H7 Luzille-sur-Indre France
31 H6 Lužnice R Czechoslovakia
71 E2 Luzon Philippines
18 H6 Luzy France
45 J2 Luzzara Italy
48 J1 L'vov U.S.S.R.
88 B7 Lwela R Zambia
88 C7 Lwitikila R Zambia
31 J3 Lwówek Poland
31 J4 Lwówek Sląski Poland
52 E4 Lyadiny U.S.S.R.
48 L2 Lyadova R U.S.S.R.
147 Q7 Lyakhovskiye Os isld U.S.S.R.
144 A6 Lyall, Mt New Zealand
Lyallpur see Faisalabad
57 E5 Lyal'-Mikar U.S.S.R.
55 D2 Lyalya R U.S.S.R.
55 F1 Lyamin R U.S.S.R.
57 D4 Lyangar U.S.S.R.
52 D4 Lyaskelya U.S.S.R.
47 H1 Lyaskovets Bulgaria
106 C5 Lybrook New Mexico
15 E2 Lybster Scotland
28 C3 Lyby Denmark
106 H4 Lycan Colorado
33 S6 Lychen E Germany
52 D5 Lychkovo U.S.S.R.
47 K8 Lycia Turkey
Lyck see Ełk
26 K7 Lycksele Sweden
9 G6 Lydd England
Lydda see Lod
119 T3 Lyddal Manitoba
89 G5 Lydenburg S Africa
8 B6 Lydford England
8 D3 Lydham England
112 G3 Lydia S Carolina
119 V8 Lydiatt Manitoba
8 D4 Lydney England
8 B6 Lyd, R England
28 A5 Lydum Denmark
21 H7 Lye France
145 D4 Lyell New Zealand
140 B6 Lyell Brown, Mt N Terr Aust
117 H9 Lyell I Br Col
139 H8 Lyell, Mt Tasmania
111 L7 Lyerly Georgia
26 K2 Lyfjord Norway
109 K9 Lyford Texas
113 K9 Lyford Cay isld New Providence I Bahamas
27 B13 Lygna R Norway
95 L6 Lykens Pennsylvania
52 D5 Lykoshino U.S.S.R.
99 O6 Lyle Minnesota
100 D4 Lyle Washington
110 J6 Lyles Tennessee
119 Q9 Lyleton Manitoba
111 G11 Lyman Mississippi
107 O5 Lyman Oklahoma
112 E3 Lyman S Carolina
101 P8 Lyman Wyoming
117 O8 Lymburn Alberta
95 P3 Lyme New Hampshire
8 D6 Lyme B England
8 D6 Lyme Regis England
9 H5 Lyminge England
9 E6 Lymington England
31 M1 Łyna R Poland
28 H5 Lynæs Denmark
98 H7 Lynch Nebraska
94 D7 Lynchburg Ohio
110 K6 Lynchburg Tennessee
94 H9 Lynchburg Virginia
112 G3 Lynches R S Carolina
95 R2 Lynchville Maine
141 G4 Lynd Queensland
141 G3 Lynd R Queensland
28 H5 Lyndby Denmark
100 C1 Lynden Washington
9 E6 Lyndhurst England
144 C5 Lyndhurst New Zealand
141 G4 Lyndhurst Queensland
138 E4 Lyndhurst S Australia
107 P3 Lyndon Kansas
95 P2 Lyndon Vermont
143 B6 Lyndon W Australia
109 J5 Lyndon B. Johnson, L Texas
143 A6 Lyndon, R W Australia
94 J3 Lyndonville New York
95 P2 Lyndonville Vermont
28 A5 Lyne Denmark
13 E2 Lyne Scotland
28 F4 Lyngby Denmark
28 D4 Lyngbygd Å R Denmark
27 B13 Lyngdal Norway
28 H6 Lynge Denmark
26 L2 Lyngen Norway
27 D13 Lyngör Norway
28 A3 Lyngs Denmark
28 F2 Lyngså Denmark
26 L2 Lyngseidet Norway
26 L2 Lyngsfjord inlet Norway
142 D3 Lynher Reef W Australia
8 C5 Lynmouth England
111 J7 Lynn Alabama
94 C6 Lynn Indiana
95 R4 Lynn Massachusetts
101 M8 Lynn Utah
117 F6 Lynn Canal Alaska
103 M2 Lynndyl Utah
111 L11 Lynn Haven Florida
119 Q2 Lynn Lake Manitoba
99 O8 Lynnville Iowa
110 J6 Lynnville Tennessee
8 C5 Lynton England
143 A8 Lynton W Australia
28 E6 Lyø Denmark
40 A6 Lyon France
94 C2 Lyon Manor Michigan
95 O2 Lyon Mountain New York
18 H7 Lyonnais, Mts.du France
Lyons see Lyon
98 A9 Lyons Colorado
112 E5 Lyons Georgia
110 J3 Lyons Indiana
107 M3 Lyons Kansas
94 C4 Lyons Michigan
98 K8 Lyons Nebraska
95 L3 Lyons New York
94 C5 Lyons Ohio
100 C5 Lyons Oregon
138 C4 Lyons S Australia
98 K6 Lyons S Dakota
109 L5 Lyons Texas
99 S7 Lyons Wisconsin
95 M3 Lyons Falls New York
20 H3 Lyons-la-Forêt France
143 B6 Lyons, R W Australia
137 L2 Lyra Reef Bismarck Arch
22 D2 Lys R France
42 B3 Lys R Italy
31 H5 Lysá Czechoslovakia
27 B12 Lyse Norway
27 B13 Lysefjorden inlet Norway
27 E13 Lysekil Sweden
79 D3 Lysi Cyprus
101 S6 Lysite Wyoming
40 F3 Lyss Switzerland
121 T6 Lyster Quebec
55 C2 Lys'va U.S.S.R.
27 F11 Lysvik Sweden
8 D6 Lytchett England
13 E6 Lytham St.Annes England
109 J6 Lytle Texas
144 B4 Lyttleton New Zealand
117 N10 Lytton Br Columbia
102 B3 Lytton California
121 O6 Lytton Quebec
52 D5 Lyuban' U.S.S.R.
48 N3 Lyubashevka U.S.S.R.
52 E6 Lyubertsu U.S.S.R.
54 J1 Lyubertsy U.S.S.R.
52 F5 Lyubim U.S.S.R.
47 H3 Lyubimets Bulgaria
55 C2 Lyubimova U.S.S.R.
55 F3 Lyubinskiy U.S.S.R.
52 D5 Lyublino U.S.S.R.
54 F3 Lyubokhna U.S.S.R.
54 G7 Lyubotin U.S.S.R.
54 F3 Lyudinovo U.S.S.R.
52 H6 Lyuk U.S.S.R.
52 G6 Lyunda R U.S.S.R.
52 J2 Lyzha R U.S.S.R.
68 D1 Ma R Burma
80 F3 Ma'ad Jordan
79 B9 Ma'âdi Egypt
80 F3 Ma'agan Israel
80 C3 Ma'agan Mikha'el Israel
87 H8 Maaia Mozambique
135 T3 Maalaea Hawaiian Is
80 E6 Maale Alummin Jordan
73 L7 Maalosmadulu Atoll Maldives
79 F8 Ma'ān Jordan
29 N8 Maaninka Finland
29 O8 Maanselkä Finland
58 G5 Ma'anshan China
71 F5 Ma-ao Negros Philippines
25 E6 Maarheeze Netherlands
79 G3 Ma'arret en Nu'mān Syria
25 D4 Maarsbergen Netherlands
25 D5 Maarsser Netherlands
25 D4 Maartensdijk Netherlands
86 A3 Maas Somalia
25 D5 Maas R Netherlands
25 E6 Maasbracht Netherlands
22 K1 Maaseik Belgium
22 K2 Maasmechelen Belgium
25 B5 Maassluis Netherlands
22 K2 Maastricht Belgium
25 E7 Maastricht Netherlands
139 H9 Maatsuyker Is Tasmania
Maba see Qujiang
71 B2 Maba Halmahera Indonesia
87 F10 Mabalane Mozambique
109 L3 Mabank Texas
80 C4 Ma'barot Israel
71 F4 Mabatobato Philippines
70 B6 Mabau Kalimantan
99 P6 Mabel Minnesota
138 C3 Mabel Creek S Australia
142 G3 Mabel Downs W Australia
119 O2 Mabella Ontario
94 F9 Maben W Virginia
121 O8 Maberly Ontario
122 K2 Mabille, L Quebec
28 B4 Måbjerg Denmark
9 G1 Mablethorpe England
123 L7 Mabou C Breton I, N Scotia
85 D5 Mabrouk Mali
84 E5 Mabrous Niger
84 F4 Mabruk Libya
100 E3 Mabton Washington
61 P14 Mabuni Okinawa
133 C7 Maca mt Chile
122 E8 McAdam New Brunswick
143 B7 Macadam Plains W Australia
140 A2 Macadam Ra N Terr Aust
130 H8 Macaé Brazil
130 J8 Macaiba Brazil
71 G6 Macajalar B Philippines
109 M1 McAlester Oklahoma
139 J5 McAlister, Mt New S Wales
109 J9 McAllen Texas
101 O4 McAllister Montana
113 E7 McAlpin Florida
114 J4 MacAlpine L N W Terr
121 L4 Macamic Quebec
71 K8 Macan, Pulau Pulau islds Indonesia
Macao see Macau
16 B5 Macão Portugal
128 E5 Macapá Amazonas Brazil
130 H4 Macarani Brazil
127 O10 Macareo R Venezuela
141 F3 Macaroni Queensland
100 D8 McArthur California
94 E7 McArthur Ohio
138 F7 Macarthur Victoria
140 D3 McArthur R N Terr Aust
140 D3 McArthur River N Terr Aust
94 A4 Macatawa Michigan
129 L5 Macau Brazil
67 D5 Macau prov E Asia
119 Q8 McAuley Manitoba
137 R8 Macauley I Kermadec Is Pacific Oc
94 B2 McBain Michigan
110 D3 McBaine Missouri
112 F4 McBean Georgia
112 G3 McBee S Carolina
119 U6 McBeth Pt Manitoba
117 N9 McBride Br Col
133 F8 Macbride Hd Falkland Is
100 J5 McCall Idaho
108 E4 McCamey Texas
101 N7 McCammon Idaho
122 H8 Maccan Nova Scotia
98 J1 McCanna N Dakota
44 M6 Maccarese Italy
117 H9 McCauley I Br Col
100 B2 McCleary Washington
112 H4 McClellanville S Carolina
113 E7 Macclenny Florida
8 D1 Macclesfield England
123 S5 Maccles L Newfoundland
114 J3 McClintock Ch N W Terr
146 H6 McClintock, Mt Antarctica
142 F4 McClintock Ra W Australia
100 C8 McCloud California
140 C1 McCluer I N Terr Aust
94 D5 McClure Ohio
95 K6 McClure Pennsylvania
102 D4 McClure, L California
114 H3 McClure Str N W Terr
118 H3 McClusker R Sask
98 F2 McClusky N Dakota
111 F10 McComb Mississippi
94 D5 McComb Ohio
98 D8 McConaughy, L Nebraska
117 M3 McConnell Range N W Terr
94 J7 McConnellsburg Pennsylvania
98 F9 McCook Nebraska
111 G8 McCool Mississippi
98 J9 McCool Junct Nebraska
118 L9 McCord Sask
112 E4 McCormick S Carolina
106 D2 McCoy Colorado
107 L3 McCracken Kansas
119 S8 McCreary Manitoba
110 E3 McCredie Missouri
110 E6 McCrory Arkansas
115 M3 Macculloch, C N W Terr
103 J6 McCullough Ridge Nevada
110 B6 McCurtain Oklahoma
109 K5 McDade Texas
117 J6 McDame Br Col
100 H8 McDermitt Nevada
94 D8 McDermott Ohio
120 B3 Macdiarmid Ontario
100 C8 Macdoel California
107 J2 McDonald Kansas
140 D5 MacDonald Downs N Terr Aust
81 E10 Macdonald Is Indian Oc
101 M1 McDonald, L Montana
143 G6 Macdonald, L W Australia
100 E9 McDonald Peak mt California
101 M2 McDonald Pk Montana
142 E3 Macdonald Ra W Australia
101 L1 Macdonald Range Br Col
138 E3 McDonnell R S Australia
136 G6 MacDonnell Ranges N Terr Australia
112 C4 McDonough Georgia
138 D3 McDouall Peak S Australia
140 C4 McDouall Ra N Terr Aust
115 K7 MacDowell L Ontario
103 N8 McDowell Pk Arizona
15 F3 MacDuff Scotland
16 C3 Macedo de Chavaleiros Portugal
95 K3 Macedon New York
Macedonia see Makedhonia
99 L8 Macedonia Iowa
139 G7 Macedon, Mt Victoria
130 J10 Maceió Alagoas Brazil
87 G8 Maceloge Mozambique
85 C7 Macenta Guinea
42 E5 Macerata Italy
100 G5 McEwen Oregon
110 J5 McEwen Tennessee
101 T8 McFadden Wyoming
99 M9 McFall Missouri
107 O2 McFarland Kansas
138 D4 Macfarlane, L S Australia
144 B5 Macfarlane, Mt New Zealand
106 B6 McGaffey New Mexico
118 J7 McGee Sask
111 E8 McGehee Arkansas
103 K2 McGill Nevada
100 K1 McGillvray Range mts Br Col
14 B5 Macgillycuddy's Reeks mts Irish Rep
116 K5 McGrath Alaska
95 L4 McGraw New York
119 T9 MacGregor Manitoba
94 E3 McGregor Michigan
99 N3 McGregor Minnesota
109 K4 McGregor Texas
118 E8 McGregor L Alberta
117 N8 McGregor R Br Col
141 F7 McGregor Ra Queensland
138 F2 McGregor Rge Queensland
98 C8 McGrew Nebraska
101 L4 McGuire, Mt Idaho
77 K5 Mach Pakistan
89 F7 Machache Mt Lesotho
128 C4 Machachi Ecuador
130 F7 Maçhado Brazil
80 F7 Machaerus Jordan
87 F10 Machaila Mozambique
88 F2 Machakos Kenya
128 C4 Machala Ecuador
70 C4 Machan Sarawak
67 B3 Machangping China
133 E2 Macharetí Bolivia
140 E6 Machattie L Queensland
22 G5 Machault France
87 F10 Machaze Mozambique
21 B8 Machecoul France
112 D4 Machen Georgia
67 E1 Macheng China
99 S7 McHenry Illinois
111 G11 McHenry Mississippi
76 D2 Macherla India
33 R10 Machern E Germany
79 F5 Machgharah Lebanon
95 U2 Machias Maine
95 S7 Machias R Maine
17 F1 Machichaco, C Spain
76 E2 Machilipatnam India
127 H9 Machiques Venezuela
12 C2 Machrie Scotland
12 C3 Machrihanish Scotland
8 C2 Machynlleth Wales
87 F10 Macia Mozambique
Macias Nguema Biyogo see Bioko
87 F9 McIlwaine Nat. Park Zimbabwe
141 G2 McIlwraith Ra Queensland
48 L5 Măcin Romania
85 C6 Macina reg Mali
120 J3 Mc. Innes Ontario
99 O6 McIntire Iowa
118 J1 McIntosh Ontario
98 E4 McIntosh S Dakota
120 B3 McIntyre B Ontario
141 K8 Macintyre Brook Queensland
139 K3 MacIntyre, R Queensland
106 B2 Mack Colorado
119 O6 McKague Sask
101 M6 Mackay Idaho
141 J5 Mackay Queensland
142 G6 Mackay, L N Terr/W Aust
114 H5 MacKay L N W Terr
120 D3 McKay L Ontario
142 D5 Mackay, Mt W Australia
117 R7 McKay R Alberta
143 D6 McKay Ra W Australia
137 S2 McKean I Phoenix Is Pacific Oc
94 H6 McKeesport Pennsylvania
94 G6 McKees Rocks Pennsylvania
33 T10 Mäckenberg E Germany
133 E4 Mackenna Argentina
33 N9 Mackenrode E Germany
111 K10 McKenzie Alabama
98 F3 McKenzie N Dakota
110 H5 McKenzie Tennessee
114 G5 Mackenzie R N W Terr
141 J6 Mackenzie R Queensland
146 C4 Mackenzie B Antarctica
114 F4 Mackenzie B Yukon Terr
100 C5 McKenzie Bridge Oregon
114 H5 Mackenzie, Dist.of N W Terr
114 H2 Mackenzie King I N W Terr
119 N2 McKenzie L Ontario
119 P4 McKenzie L Sask
117 H3 Mackenzie Mts Yukon Terr/N W Terr
100 D5 McKenzie Pass Oregon
144 C6 Mackenzie Plains New Zealand
119 S1 MacKerracher L Manitoba
144 B6 McKerrow, L New Zealand
94 C1 Mackinac Michigan
94 C1 Mackinac, Str. of Michigan
99 R9 Mackinaw Illinois
99 R9 Mackinaw R Illinois
94 C1 Mackinaw City Michigan
141 F5 McKinlay Queensland
141 F5 McKinlay R Queensland
116 M5 McKinley, Mt Alaska
146 J9 McKinley Pk Antarctica
110 M4 McKinney Kentucky
109 L2 McKinney Texas
107 J3 McKinney, L Kansas
144 A6 McKinnon Pass New Zealand
139 H8 Mackintosh L. Tasmania
143 F7 Mackintosh Ra W Australia
120 B3 McKirdy Ontario
102 E6 McKittrick California
118 H6 Macklin Sask
119 Q2 McKnight L Manitoba
94 F7 Macksburg Ohio
101 O5 Macks Inn Idaho
107 M4 Macksville Kansas
139 L4 Macksville New S Wales
141 F6 Mackunda R Queensland
111 H10 McLain Mississippi
116 O5 Maclaren R Alaska
142 E4 McLarty Hills W Australia
142 D5 McLarty, Mt W Australia
118 G6 McLaughlin Alberta
98 F4 McLaughlin S Dakota
119 U5 McLaughlin R Manitoba
99 R9 McLean Illinois
139 L3 Maclean New S Wales
119 N8 McLean Sask
118 H2 McLean L Sask
110 H3 McLeansboro Illinois
87 E12 Maclear S Africa
88 E8 Maclear, C Malawi
139 L4 Macleay R New S Wales
118 A3 McLennan Alberta
119 N3 McLennan Lake Saskatchewan
98 J3 McLeod N Dakota
114 J5 McLeod B N W Terr
142 A6 McLeod, L W Australia
117 M8 McLeod Lake Br Col
118 B5 McLeod R Alberta
68 C7 McLeods I Burma
110 A2 McLouth Kansas
118 K8 McMahon Sask
94 G7 McMechen W Virginia
83 M9 McMicken Pt Christmas I Indian Oc
99 V3 McMillan Michigan
141 G1 Macmillan R Queensland
117 F4 Macmillan R Yukon Terr
106 F9 McMillan, L New Mexico
140 C6 McMinns Cr N Terr Aust
100 B4 McMinnville Oregon
110 L6 McMinnville Tennessee
118 J7 McMorran Sask
118 F1 McMunn Manitoba

McMurdo Sound — Manito 47

146 H6 McMurdo Sound Antarctica
117 O10 McMurphy Br Col
100 C1 McMurray Washington
111 E10 McNair Mississippi
103 P7 McNary Arizona
108 B4 McNary Texas
100 F4 McNary Dam Oregon
117 O9 McNaughton, L Canada
103 P10 McNeal Arizona
111 C8 McNeil Arkansas
109 K5 McNeil Texas
111 G11 McNeill Mississippi
119 Q7 MacNutt Sask
122 G10 McNutt I Nova Scotia
128 D1 Macollo, Pta C Venezuela
110 F1 Macomb Illinois
107 O6 Macomb Oklahoma
43 B8 Macomer Sardinia
88 H8 Macomia Mozambique
22 G3 Maçon Belgium
19 J6 Mâcon France
112 D5 Macon Georgia
99 S10 Macon Illinois
111 H8 Macon Mississippi
99 O10 Macon Missouri
98 G9 Macon Nebraska
87 D8 Macondo Angola
119 O9 Macoun Sask
107 N3 McPherson Kansas
142 D5 Macpherson, Mt W Australia
141 L8 Macpherson Ra N S W/Qnsld
68 A7 Macpherson's Str Andaman Is
139 J4 MacQuarie R New S Wales
139 H8 Macquarie R Tasmania
139 H8 Macquarie Harbour Tasmania
81 J12 Macquarie I S Pacific Oc
139 K5 Macquarie, L New S Wales
139 J4 Macquarie Marshes New S Wales
139 J5 Macquarie, Mt New S Wales
22 G4 Macquenoise Belgium
117 E4 McQuesten Yukon Terr
117 E4 McQuesten R Yukon Terr
112 E5 McRae Georgia
144 D5 McRae, L New Zealand
142 C5 McRae, Mt W Australia
144 C6 Macraes Flat New Zealand
94 E9 McRoberts Kentucky
146 C5 MacRobertson Land Antarctica
14 C5 Macroom Irish Rep
118 K7 Macrorie Sask
141 H4 Macrossan Queensland
119 N9 McTaggart Sask
71 G5 Mactan isld Philippines
118 D1 McTavish Manitoba
128 D3 Macujer Colombia
71 G4 Maculiv Philippines
138 D2 Macumba R S Australia
95 M6 Macungie Pennsylvania
128 D6 Macusani Peru
87 G9 Macuse Mozambique
125 N9 Macuspana Mexico
124 E4 Macuzari, Presa res Mexico
94 E9 McVeigh Kentucky
119 Q2 McVeigh Manitoba
117 N3 McVicar Arm inlet N W Terr
98 H2 McVille N Dakota
121 M4 McWatters Quebec
111 J10 McWilliams Alabama
86 A4 Mada R Nigeria
80 G7 Madaba Jordan
86 D2 Madadi Chad
87 H11 Madagascar Indian Oc
81 C8 Madagascar Basin Indian Oc
76 C4 Madakasira India
70 E1 Madalon mt Sabah
84 E5 Madama Niger
76 D4 Madanapalle India
136 K3 Madang Papua New Guinea
85 F6 Madaoua Niger
75 O7 Madaripur Bangladesh
85 F6 Madarounfa Niger
95 S6 Madawaska Maine
121 M7 Madawaska Ontario
121 N7 Madawaska R Ontario
122 D6 Madawaska R Quebec
68 C1 Madaya Burma
45 Q7 Maddaloni Italy
143 C10 Madden, Mt W Australia
142 C2 Maddington dist Perth, W Aust
98 G2 Maddock N Dakota
85 A2 Madeira Atlantic Oc
128 F5 Madeira R Brazil
128 F5 Madeirinho R Brazil
41 M3 Madelegabel mt Austria
20 G5 Madeleine Bouvet, la France
123 L6 Madeleine, Iles de la Quebec
18 H6 Madeleine, Mts.de la France
99 M5 Madelia Minnesota
100 E8 Madeline California
99 Q3 Madeline I Wisconsin
57 J1 Madeniyet U.S.S.R.
102 D5 Madera California
124 E3 Madera Mexico
94 J6 Madera Pennsylvania
108 E5 Madera Mt Texas
32 J10 Madfeld W Germany
119 Q7 Madge L Sask
83 J12 Madge Rocks Seychelles
75 M5 Madhubani India
74 G7 Madhya Pradesh prov India
65 H3 Madida China
128 E6 Madidi R Bolivia
70 C4 Madi, Dtt Kalimantan
138 E3 Madigan Gulf S Australia
146 J3 Madigan Nunatak Antarctica
109 L1 Madill Oklahoma
86 C6 Madimba Zaïre
86 H3 Madinat ash Sha'ab S Yemen
81 C5 Madingley Rise Indian Oc
86 B6 Madingo-Kayes Congo
86 B6 Madingou Congo
110 F6 Madison Arkansas
113 D7 Madison Florida
112 D4 Madison Georgia
107 O3 Madison Kansas
98 K4 Madison Minnesota
110 D2 Madison Missouri
112 H1 Madison N Carolina
98 J8 Madison Nebraska
94 F5 Madison Ohio
111 M12 Madison St Louis
118 J7 Madison Sask
98 J5 Madison S Dakota
110 K5 Madison Tennessee
94 J8 Madison Virginia
99 R6 Madison Wisconsin
94 F8 Madison W Virginia
101 O4 Madison R Montana
94 H9 Madison Heights Virginia
101 P5 Madison Junct Wyoming
101 O4 Madison Ra Montana
110 J4 Madisonville Kentucky
111 F11 Madisonville Louisiana
112 C2 Madisonville Tennessee
109 M5 Madisonville Texas
70 N9 Madiun Java
8 D3 Madley England
143 E6 Madley, Mt W Australia
98 A1 Madoc Montana
121 N8 Madoc Ontario
86 G5 Mado Gashi Kenya
52 C6 Madona U.S.S.R.
100 B9 Mad R California
47 J5 Madra Dağı mt Turkey
76 E4 Madras India
100 D5 Madras Oregon
128 D6 Madre de Dios dep Peru
128 E6 Madre de Dios R Bolivia/Peru
133 B8 Madre de Dios, I Chile
125 L5 Madre. Laguna Mexico
109 K9 Madre, Laguna Texas
124 F4 Madre Occidental, Sierra mts Mexico
18 G10 Madrès mt France
71 F2 Madre, Sierra mts Luzon Philippines
99 N8 Madrid Iowa
71 G6 Madrid Mindanao Philippines
98 E9 Madrid Nebraska
106 D6 Madrid New Mexico
95 M2 Madrid New York
16 E4 Madrid Spain
16 E4 Madrid prov Spain
71 F5 Madridejos Philippines
16 E5 Madridejos Spain
16 D3 Madrigal de las Atlas Torres Spain
16 E6 Madrona, Sa mts Spain
128 G4 Madruba, L Brazil
126 D3 Madruga Cuba
79 E11 Madsûs, G mt Egypt
71 K8 Madu isld Indonesia
71 E5 Maducang isld Philippines
28 A4 Madum Denmark
28 D3 Madum Sø Denmark
143 F9 Madura W Australia
70 O9 Madura isld Indonesia
76 D6 Madurai India
70 O9 Madura, Selat str Java
83 L10 Maduru Oya R Sri Lanka
52 H4 Madzha U.S.S.R.
60 D12 Maebaru Japan
61 N9 Maebashi Japan
68 C3 Mae Hong Son Thailand
61 O13 Mae-jima isld Okinawa
68 D5 Mae Khlong R Thailand
69 D8 Mae Kirirath R Thailand
27 C12 Mael Norway
68 D3 Mae Lao R Thailand
68 D3 Mae Li R Thailand
17 H3 Maella Spain
69 D8 Mae Luang R Thailand
68 F4 Mae Nam R Thailand
68 E3 Mae Nam Ing R Thailand
68 F5 Mae Nam Mun R Thailand
68 E3 Mae Nam Nan R Thailand
68 D3 Mae Nam Ping R Thailand
68 E3 Mae Nam Yom R Thailand
68 D3 Mae Rim Thailand
48 K5 Măeruş Romania
103 P1 Maeser Utah
8 C4 Maesteg Wales
45 M2 Maestra, Pta Italy
126 F4 Maestra, Sierra mts Cuba
71 E4 Maestre de Campo isld Philippines
137 O5 Maewo isld New Hebrides
88 H10 Mafameda isld Mozambique
114 J7 Mafeking Manitoba
89 D5 Mafeking S Africa
89 E7 Mafeteng Lesotho
139 H7 Maffra Victoria
88 G5 Mafia Channel Tanzania
88 G5 Mafia,I Tanzania
88 E8 Mafinto Mozambique
67 E1 Ma-fou China
130 E10 Mafra Brazil
16 A6 Mafra Portugal
89 F2 Mafungabusi Plateau Zimbabwe
51 P3 Magadan U.S.S.R.
51 P2 Magadanskaya Oblast' U.S.S.R.
88 F2 Magadi Kenya
88 F2 Magadi L Kenya
122 E8 Magaguadavic L New Brunswick
71 F4 Magallanes Philippines
133 C8 Magallanes prov Chile
133 C8 Magallanes, Estrecho de chan Chile
71 F5 Magallon Negros Philippines
86 H4 Magalo Ethiopia
71 C3 Magamo W Irian
126 G10 Magangué Colombia
128 C2 Magangue Colombia
85 F6 Magaria Niger
61 Q12 Magari-zaki C Okinawa
71 E2 Magat R Luzon Philippines
89 G4 Magato Mts S Africa
110 C6 Magazine Mt Arkansas
85 B7 Magburaka Sierra Leone
59 J1 Magdagachi U.S.S.R.
37 L2 Magdala E Germany
86 G3 Magdala Ethiopia
128 F6 Magdalena Bolivia
106 C7 Magdalena New Mexico
124 D2 Magdalena Sonora Mexico
128 D2 Magdalena div Colombia
128 C3 Magdalena R Colombia
133 C6 Magdalena, I Chile
124 C5 Magdalena, I Mexico
70 E2 Magdalena, Mt Sabah
115 N8 Magdalen Is Quebec
33 P8 Magdeburg E Germany
33 P8 Magdeburg reg E Germany
33 Q8 Magdeburgerforth E Germany
141 K3 Magdelaine Cays islds Gt Barrier Reef Aust
33 O9 Mägdesprung E Germany
80 C5 Magdi'el Israel
111 G10 Magee Mississippi
14 F2 Magee, I N Ireland
116 K7 Mageik Vol Alaska
70 N9 Magelang Java
133 D8 Magellan, Str. of Chile
80 E3 Magen Shaul Israel
41 J7 Magenta Italy
143 C10 Magenta, L W Australia
41 K3 Magereu mt Switzerland
26 P1 Mageröya isld Norway
80 D4 Maggal Israel
41 J5 Maggia, Val Switzerland
44 F2 Maggiorasca mt Italy
41 J6 Maggiore, Lago Italy
43 F7 Maggiore, M mt Italy
127 J2 Maggotty Jamaica
79 A10 Maghâgha Egypt
79 D8 Maghâra, G mt Egypt
14 A4 Magharee Is Irish Rep
14 E2 Maghera N Ireland
14 E2 Magherafelt N Ireland
17 F10 Maghnia Algeria
84 H3 Maghra, El Egypt
13 F6 Maghull England
101 L6 Magic Res Idaho
14 E1 Magilligan Pt N Ireland
16 E7 Mágina mt Spain
56 G3 Magistral'niy U.S.S.R.
48 E6 Maglaj Yugoslavia
40 E5 Magland France
28 K6 Magleby Denmark
28 K7 Magleby isld Denmark
28 G7 Maglehöjstrand Denmark
45 M6 Magliana Italy
45 O5 Magliano de Marsi Italy
48 E7 Maglić mt Yugoslavia
43 J8 Maglie Italy
103 N8 Magma Arizona
21 H9 Magnac-Laval France
21 J10 Magnat-l'Etange France
98 J7 Magnet Nebraska
121 L7 Magnetawan Ontario
146 A5 Magnet B Antarctica
141 H4 Magnetic I Queensland
55 C3 Magnitka U.S.S.R.
55 C4 Magnitogorsk U.S.S.R.
109 O2 Magnolia Arkansas
111 F10 Magnolia Mississippi
112 J3 Magnolia N Carolina
109 M5 Magnolia Texas
27 F12 Magnor Norway
6 L1 Magnus oil rig North Sea
20 J3 Magny-en-Vexin France
20 E3 Magny-la-Campagne France
88 C9 Magoe Mozambique
121 S7 Magog Quebec
8 D4 Magor Wales
120 F4 Magpie Ontario
122 H3 Magpie Quebec
122 H2 Magpie L Quebec
120 F4 Magpie Mine Ontario
122 H2 Magpie R Quebec
44 G3 Magra, R Italy
118 E9 Magrath Alberta
17 G5 Magro R Spain
102 G4 Magruder Mt Nevada
71 E2 Magsingal Luzon Philippines
28 C6 Magstrup Denmark
67 A5 Maguan China
129 J4 Maguari, C Brazil
89 H5 Magude Mozambique
67 D5 Magui China
86 B3 Magumeri Nigeria
68 B2 Magwe Burma
68 A2 Magyichaung Burma
78 K3 Mahābād Iran
74 E10 Mahabaleshwar India
87 G12 Mahabo Madagascar
74 E9 Mahad India
86 A3 Mahaddei Uen Somalia
74 H7 Mahadeo Hills India
94 J6 Mahaffey Penn
86 F5 Mahagi Zaïre
87 H11 Mahajamba, B.de Madagascar
87 H11 Mahajanga Madagascar
70 D4 Mahakam R Kalimantan
89 E4 Mahalapye Botswana
46 E6 Mahalás Greece
79 B8 Mahalla, El Egypt
77 B3 Maḩallat Iran
77 E4 Mahān Iran
75 K8 Mahanadi R India
71 G5 Mahanay isld Philippines
95 L6 Mahanoy City Pennsylvania
65 G3 Mahao China
83 J10 Maha Oya R Sri Lanka
74 E9 Maharashtra prov India
75 K8 Mahasamund India
68 F4 Maha Sarakham Thailand
98 J10 Mahaska Kansas
87 H11 Mahavavy R Madagascar
87 H11 Mahavelona Madagascar
83 K10 Mahaweli Ganga R Sri Lanka
68 G4 Mahaxay Laos
74 H10 Mahbubabad India
76 C2 Mahbubnagar India
77 D7 Maḩḑah Oman
85 G1 Mahdia Tunisia
76 B5 Mahe India
83 J12 Mahé isld Seychelles
83 M13 Mahebourg Mauritius
88 F6 Mahenge Tanzania
144 C6 Maheno New Zealand
120 J3 Maher Ontario
74 F7 Maheshwar India
145 F3 Mahia New Zealand
74 E9 Mahim India
144 C5 Mahinapua, L New Zealand
144 B6 Mahinerangi, L New Zealand
80 G6 Mahis Jordan
87 F11 Mahlabatini S Africa
68 B2 Mahlaing Burma
33 S8 Mahlow E Germany
33 P8 Mahlwinkel E Germany
75 J5 Mahmudabad India
48 M5 Mahmudia Romania
83 K10 Maho Sri Lanka
74 H6 Mahoba India
145 E3 Mahoenui New Zealand
100 F8 Mahogany Peak mt Nevada
99 S9 Mahomet Illinois
17 K5 Mahón Menorca
122 H9 Mahone Bay Nova Scotia
117 L3 Mahony L N W Terr
17 F5 Mahora Spain
85 G2 Mahrès Tunisia
74 E7 Mahsana India
98 F4 Mahto S Dakota
145 E4 Mahuri New Zealand
74 D8 Mahuva India
137 P1 Maiana atoll Kiribati
71 M9 Maibang Indonesia
61 K10 Maibara Japan
48 L5 Măicăneşti Romania
19 K5 Maich France
40 E3 Maiche France
68 J2 Maichen China
86 G3 Maichew Ethiopia
68 J2 Mai-ch'u China
129 H3 Maicuru R Brazil
142 C1 Maida Vale W Australia
112 F2 Maiden N Carolina
8 D5 Maiden Bradley England
9 F4 Maidenhead England
8 D6 Maiden Newton England
99 O5 Maiden Rock Wisconsin
12 D3 Maidens Scotland
71 A2 Maidi Halmahera Indonesia
9 G5 Maidstone England
118 H5 Maidstone Sask
86 B3 Maidugun Nigeria
42 F6 Maiella, M.della Italy
41 L3 Maienfeld Switzerland
20 K2 Maignelay France
128 E2 Maigualida, Sierra mts Venezuela
14 C4 Maigue R Irish Rep
74 J8 Maikala Range India
36 E5 Maikammer W Germany
102 R12 Maili Hawaiian Is
20 H4 Maillebois France
20 G3 Mailleraye-sur-Seine, la France
21 D9 Maillezais France
22 D3 Mailly Maillet France
74 E4 Mailsi Pakistan
144 C5 Maimai New Zealand
77 J2 Maimaña Afghanistan
127 J5 Maimon, B.de Dom Rep
80 F7 Ma'in Jordan
14 E2 Main R N Ireland
37 K3 Main R W Germany
123 N8 Main-à-Dieu C Breton I, N Scotia
37 J4 Mainbernheim W Germany
123 Q2 Main Brook Nfld
37 M6 Mainburg W Germany
118 K8 Main Centre Sask
120 J7 Main Channel Cave I Ontario
86 C6 Mai Ndombe, L Zaïre
Maindong see Coqên
121 O9 Main Duck I Ontario
103 N6 Maine Arizona
95 L4 Maine New York
21 C7 Maine R France
20 F5 Maine reg France
95 R1 Maine state U.S.A.
21 D7 Maine-et-Loire dep France
85 G6 Mainé-Soroa Niger
110 M2 Maineville Ohio
68 D6 Maingy isld Burma
36 H5 Mainhardt W Germany
71 G6 Mainit, L Mindanao Philippines
15 G2 Mainland Shetland Scotland
140 C2 Mainoru N Terr Aust
74 H5 Mainpuri India
138 F4 Main Range Barrier New S Wales
122 F7 Main S.W. Miramichi R New Brunswick
36 F3 Maintal W Germany
20 J4 Maintenon France
87 G11 Maintirano Madagascar
123 Q4 Main Topsail peak Newfoundland
29 N7 Mainua Finland
74 D2 Mainwali Pakistan
36 E3 Mainz W Germany
45 R8 Maiori Italy
133 D4 Maipo mt Chile/Arg
133 C4 Maipo R Chile
131 B5 Maipo, Vol peak Arg/Chile
133 F5 Maipu Argentina
127 L9 Maiquetia Venezuela
44 B3 Maira R Italy
75 P5 Mairabari India
37 L7 Maisach W Germany
21 C7 Maisdon France
126 G4 Maisí Cuba
122 G6 Maisonnette New Brunswick
20 K4 Maisons-Laffitte France
38 N4 Maissau Austria
20 K5 Maisse France
22 J4 Maissin Belgium
86 J3 Mait Somalia
99 L9 Maitland Missouri
139 K5 Maitland New S Wales
122 J8 Maitland Nova Scotia
138 D5 Maitland S Australia
122 G9 Maitland Br Nova Scotia
143 D7 Maitland, L W Australia
143 C7 Maitland, Mt W Australia
142 B5 Maitland, R W Australia
70 E2 Maitland Ra Sabah
140 C2 Maiwok R N Terr Aust
61 P7 Maiya Japan
140 A4 Maiyu, Mt N Terr Aust
75 O4 Maizhokunggar China
36 B6 Maizières-les-Vic France
60 J10 Maizuru Japan
128 D2 Majagual Colombia
128 F3 Majari R Brazil
26 F6 Majavatn L Norway
28 H7 Majbølle Denmark
80 E5 Majdal Bani Fadil Jordan
80 F8 Majdalein Jordan
31 N5 Majdan Poland
48 G6 Majdanpek Yugoslavia
80 D2 Majd el Kurum Israel
130 G8 Majé Brazil
70 F6 Majene Sulawesi
48 E6 Majevica mts Yugoslavia
86 G4 Maji Ethiopia
67 B3 Majiang China
67 D5 Majiang China
67 A4 Majie China
67 F2 Majin China
67 D2 Majitang China
118 H7 Major Sask
Majorca isld see Mallorca
89 F6 Majuba Hill S Africa
Majunga see Mahajanga
85 B6 Maka Senegal
61 P14 Makabe Okinawa
102 R12 Makaha Hawaiian Is
86 G3 Makale Ethiopia
70 F6 Makale Sulawesi
69 E14 Makalo Indonesia
75 M5 Makalu mt Xizang Zizhiqu/Nepal
87 F7 Makambako Tanzania
135 U4 Makapala Hawaiian Is
102 S12 Makapuu Hd Hawaiian Is
145 E2 Makarau New Zealand
144 B7 Makarewa New Zealand
52 G3 Makar-Ib U.S.S.R.
52 J2 Makarikha U.S.S.R.
144 B6 Makarora R New Zealand
59 M2 Makarov U.S.S.R.
42 H5 Makarska Yugoslavia
52 G5 Makar'ye U.S.S.R.
Makassar see Ujung Pandang
70 F5 Makassar Str Indonesia
89 H6 Makatini Flats reg S Africa
135 T3 Makawao Hawaiian Is
71 C3 Makbon W Irian
46 E4 Makedhonia Greece
46 E3 Makedonija Yugoslavia
135 N10 Makemo atoll Pac Oc
85 B7 Makeni Sierra Leone
145 F2 Maketu New Zealand
54 K8 Makeyevka U.S.S.R.
89 D3 Makgadikgadi Pans salt pans Botswana
78 J1 Makharadze U.S.S.R.
16 D9 Makhazen R Morocco
55 D2 Makhnevo U.S.S.R.
55 E4 Makhorovka U.S.S.R.
80 F3 Makhraba Jordan
61 M8 Maki Japan
71 A2 Makian Halmahera Indonesia
144 C6 Makikihi New Zealand
84 G3 Makilī Al Libya
119 S8 Makinak Manitoba
55 F4 Makinsk U.S.S.R.
115 M2 Makinson Inlet N W Terr
26 S1 Makkaur Norway
25 F3 Makkinga Netherlands
115 O6 Makkovik Labrador
25 D2 Makkum Netherlands
48 F4 Makó Hungary
120 C1 Makokibatan L Ontario
87 F7 Makongolosi Tanzania
145 F3 Makorako mt New Zealand
98 E2 Makoti N Dakota
145 F4 Makotuku New Zealand
86 C5 Makoua Congo
31 L6 Makov Czechoslovakia
31 M6 Maków Poland
31 N3 Maków Mazowiecki Poland
80 D2 Makr Israel
47 H8 Makrá isld Greece
74 F5 Makrana India
77 J7 Makran Coast Range Pakistan
47 H4 Mákri Greece
76 E1 Makri India
47 G7 Makronísi isld Greece
52 J3 Maksim U.S.S.R.
85 F1 Maktar Tunisia
78 K2 Maku Iran
70 C4 Makup, Bt mt Kalimantan
60 D14 Makurazaki Japan
86 A4 Makurdi Nigeria
55 E3 Makushino U.S.S.R.
116 D10 Makushin Vol Aleutian Is
88 D7 Makutu Mts Zambia
118 H4 Makwa L Sask
89 G1 Makwiro Zimbabwe
128 C6 Mala Peru
71 G7 Malabang Mindanao Philippines
113 G9 Malabar Florida
76 B5 Malabar Coast India
70 L9 Malabar, G mt Java
85 F8 Malabo Bioko Equat Guinea
85 F8 Malabo Fernando Póo Eq Guinea
71 C6 Malabuñgan Palawan Philippines
69 E11 Malacca, Str. of Malaysia
118 H1 Malachi Ontario
31 K7 Malacky Czechoslovakia
101 N7 Malad City Idaho
17 H2 Maladeta Spain
31 L6 Malá Fatra mts Czechoslovakia
16 E8 Málaga Spain
100 E2 Malaga Washington
16 D8 Málaga prov Spain
88 C4 Malagarasi Tanzania
Malagasy Rep see Madagascar
16 E5 Malagón Spain
14 E3 Malahide Irish Rep
87 G12 Malaimbandy Madagascar
137 N3 Malaita isld Solomon Is
71 J9 Malaka mt Sumbawa Indonesia
86 F4 Malakal Sudan
42 G4 Mala Kapela Yugoslavia
109 L3 Malakoff Texas
71 B2 Malaku islds Indonesia
45 L2 Malalbergo Italy
70 G6 Malamala Sulawesi
71 A3 Malamala isld Indonesia
71 E7 Malamaui isld Philippines
45 M1 Malamocco Italy
71 D5 Malampaya Snd Philippines
141 H3 Malanda Queensland
70 O10 Malang Java
88 E6 Malangali Tanzania
70 M9 Malangbong Java
26 K2 Malangen Norway
26 K2 Malangen inlet Norway
26 J2 Malangsgrunnen shoal Norway
75 L5 Malangwa Nepal
48 K3 Mălani Romania
71 F7 Malanipa isld Philippines
87 C7 Malanje Angola
71 D6 Malanut B Philippines
85 E6 Malanville Benin
65 D4 Malanyu China
131 C3 Malanzaán, Sa. de mts Argentina
27 J12 Mälaren L Sweden
133 D5 Malargue Argentina
131 B5 Malargue R Argentina
129 H3 Malaripo Brazil
121 M4 Malartic Quebec
70 F7 Malasoro, Tk B Sulawesi
117 C6 Malaspina Gl Alaska
144 A6 Malaspina Reach New Zealand
117 L11 Malaspina Str Br Col
26 K6 Malåtrask Sweden
78 G2 Malatya Turkey
19 O16 Malaucène France
20 H2 Malaunay France
70 E1 Malawali isld Sabah
88 D8 Malawi rep Africa
Malawi, L see Nyasa, L
29 J9 Malax Finland
55 D1 Malaya Sos'va R U.S.S.R.
52 D5 Malaya Vishera U.S.S.R.
77 A2 Malāyer Iran
141 J4 Malay Reef Gt Barrier Reef Aust
69 Malaysia S E Asia
69 E10 Malaysia, Peninsular S E Asia
14 B4 Mal B Irish Rep
122 H5 Mal Baie Quebec
122 B6 Malbaie R Quebec
131 B6 Malbarco, L Argentina
140 F5 Malbon Queensland
138 C4 Malbooma S Australia
38 J9 Malborghetto Italy
31 L1 Malbork Poland
41 N6 Malcesine Italy
33 R5 Malchin E Germany
33 Q6 Malchow E Germany
143 D8 Malcolm W Australia
116 R2 Malcolm R Yukon Terr
68 D7 Malcolm I Burma
143 E10 Malcolm,Pt W Australia
99 O8 Malcom Iowa
22 E1 Maldegem Belgium
95 Q4 Malden Massachusetts
110 G5 Malden Missouri
100 H2 Malden Washington
94 F8 Malden W Virginia
135 M8 Malden I Pacific Oc
73 L8 Maldive Is rep Indian Oc
43 B9 Mal di Ventre isld Sardinia
73 L9 Maldive Ridge Indian Oc
9 G4 Maldon England
131 G5 Maldonado Uruguay
131 G5 Maldonado dep Uruguay
41 N5 Male Italy
73 L8 Male Maldives
47 H5 Maléa, Akr Turkey
47 F8 Maléa, Akr C Greece
74 F8 Malegaon India
48 D2 Malé Karpaty Czechoslovakia
137 O5 Malekula isld New Hebrides
121 P4 Mâle, L.du Quebec
88 F9 Malema Mozambique
87 E7 Malemba Nkulu Zaïre
47 F9 Máleme Crete
52 E3 Malen'ga U.S.S.R.
33 N4 Malente W Germany
74 F3 Maler Kotla India
47 H9 Máles Crete Greece
18 G4 Malesherbes France
54 K3 Malevka U.S.S.R.
37 O6 Malgersdorf W Germany
86 E2 Malha Sudan
13 F5 Malham England
100 H5 Malheur Oregon
100 H6 Malheur R Oregon
83 K12 Malheureu, Cap Mahé I Indian Oc
100 G6 Malheur L Oregon
66 F6 Mali R Burma
85 D5 Mali rep W Africa
21 E6 Malicorne-sur-Sarthe France
71 F7 Maligoy B Mindanao Philippines
80 F4 Malih R Jordan
19 Q16 Malijai France
71 H5 Malik Sulawesi
68 D6 Mali Kyun isld Burma
70 G6 Malili Sulawesi
27 H14 Målilla Sweden
88 B5 Malimba mts Zaïre
100 D7 Malin Oregon
71 G5 Malinao Inlet Philippines
70 E3 Malinau Kalimantan
71 F6 Malindang, Mt Mindanao Philippines
88 H3 Malindi Kenya
48 F2 Malinec Czechoslovakia
Malines see Mechelen
70 G4 Maling, G mt Sulawesi
70 L9 Malingping Java
27 H12 Malingsbo Sweden
14 D1 Malin Hd Irish Rep
14 C2 Malin More Irish Rep
70 F7 Malino Sulawesi
54 H7 Malinovka U.S.S.R.
55 G5 Malinovoye Ozero U.S.S.R.
28 M2 Malinstindur mt Faeroes
68 G1 Malipo China
71 G7 Malita Mindanao Philippines
71 G5 Malitbog Leyte Philippines
68 D7 Maliwun Burma
106 G9 Maljamar New Mexico
48 F6 Maljen mt Yugoslavia
80 F3 Malka Jordan
53 F11 Malka R U.S.S.R.
74 G8 Malkapur India
47 H4 Malkara Turkey
56 G5 Malkhanskiy Khr mts U.S.S.R.
31 N3 Małkinia Poland
80 F1 Malkiyya Israel
47 J2 Malko Türnovo Bulgaria
139 J7 Mallacoota Victoria
118 F4 Mallaig Alberta
15 C3 Mallaig Highland Scotland
99 M7 Mallard Iowa
84 J4 Mallawi Egypt
131 A7 Malleco prov Chile
19 O17 Mallemort France
37 N6 Mallersdorf W Germany
41 N4 Malles Venosta Italy
130 E9 Mallét Brazil
142 C5 Mallina W Australia
28 E4 Malling Denmark
38 H8 Mallnitz Austria
17 J5 Mallorca isld Balearic Is
94 F9 Mallory W Virginia
121 P8 Mallorytown Ontario
14 C4 Mallow Irish Rep
142 E5 Mallowa Well W Australia
8 B1 Malltraeth B Môn Wales
22 F5 Malmaison, la France
27 G14 Malmbäck Sweden
26 L4 Malmberget Sweden
22 L3 Malmédy Belgium
8 D4 Malmesbury England
89 A9 Malmesbury S Africa
26 K6 Malmesjaure L Sweden
27 J12 Malmköping Sweden
28 K5 Malmö Sweden
27 F16 Malmöhus county Sweden
126 A2 Malmok pt Bonaire W Indies
52 H6 Malmyzh U.S.S.R.
26 G3 Malnes Norway
137 O5 Malo isld New Hebrides
129 G3 Maloca Amapá Brazil
129 H5 Maloca Pará Brazil
41 L5 Maloggia Switzerland
71 E3 Malolos Luzon Philippines
55 C2 Malomal'sk U.S.S.R.
88 E9 Malombe,L Malawi
47 H2 Malomir Bulgaria
113 B7 Malone Florida
95 N2 Malone New York
121 N8 Malone Ontario
109 L4 Malone Texas
98 F8 Maloney Res Nebraska
67 A4 Malong China
87 D8 Malonga Zaïre
26 N6 Malören Sweden
31 P4 Malorita U.S.S.R.
52 E3 Maloshuyka U.S.S.R.
89 F7 Maloti Mts Lesotho
100 F1 Malott Washington
55 C4 Malouchalinskiy U.S.S.R.
26 A10 Målöy Norway
54 H1 Maloyaroslavets U.S.S.R.
55 E2 Maloye Gorodishche U.S.S.R.
52 H1 Malozemel'skaya Tundra plain U.S.S.R.
106 C10 Malpais New Mexico
8 D1 Malpas England
138 F5 Malpas S Australia
124 H6 Malpaso Mexico
90 A8 Malpelo I Pacific Oc
122 J7 Malpeque B Pr Edward I
16 D5 Malpica Spain
16 B1 Malpica de Bergantiños Spain
131 B4 Malpo R Chile
73 L5 Malprabha R India
74 F5 Malpura India
36 E6 Malsch W Germany
31 H7 Malše R Czechoslovakia
26 K2 Målselv Norway
26 K2 Målselv R Norway
36 H1 Malsfeld W Germany
77 A7 Malsūnīyah, Al Saudi Arabia
38 J8 Malta Austria
106 D2 Malta Colorado
101 M7 Malta Idaho
101 S1 Malta Montana
94 F7 Malta Ohio
43 F13 Malta rep Mediterranean Sea
43 F12 Malta Ch Med Sea
87 C10 Maltahöhe Namibia
38 H7 Maltatel V Austria
9 G1 Maltby Lincs England
13 G6 Maltby S Yorks England
144 C5 Malte Brun mt New Zealand
13 H5 Malton England
121 L9 Malton airport Ontario
48 K6 Malu Romania
71 D5 Malubutglubut isld Philippines
85 F6 Malumfashi Nigeria
70 F6 Malunda Sulawesi
27 G11 Malung Sweden
41 K5 Malvaglia Switzerland
76 A2 Malvan India
109 P1 Malvern Arkansas
99 L9 Malvern Iowa
127 J2 Malvern Jamaica
94 F6 Malvern Ohio
127 J3 Malvern peak Jamaica
141 H6 Malvern Hills Queensland
8 D3 Malvern Wells England
21 B7 Malville France
Malvinas, Is see Falkland Is.
74 F7 Malwa Plateau India
83 K9 Malwatu Oya R Sri Lanka
78 K1 Maly Kavkaz mt U.S.S.R.
55 E1 Malyy Atlym U.S.S.R.
55 F1 Malyy Balyk R U.S.S.R.
55 G4 Malyye Chany, Oz L U.S.S.R.
52 G6 Malyy Kundysh R U.S.S.R.
51 O1 Malyy Lyakhovski,Ostrov isld U.S.S.R.
51 K1 Malyy Taymyr, Ostrov isld U.S.S.R.
55 G2 Malyy Yugan R U.S.S.R.
56 H2 Mama U.S.S.R.
56 H2 Mama R U.S.S.R.
52 H6 Mamadysh U.S.S.R.
48 M6 Mamaia Romania
120 F5 Mamainse Point Ontario
145 F3 Mamaku New Zealand
145 D1 Mamaranui New Zealand
70 F6 Mamasa Sulawesi
71 D7 Mambahenauhan isld Philippines
71 G6 Mambajao Philippines
89 F3 Mambala Cave Zimbabwe
86 E5 Mambasa Zaïre
136 H2 Mamberamo R W Irian
86 C4 Mambéré R Cent Afr Republic
71 E4 Mamburao Philippines
70 D4 Mamehaktebo Kalimantan
118 K1 Mameigwess L Ontario
83 J12 Mamelle isld Seychelles
118 D6 Ma-Me-O Beach Alberta
118 D5 Ma-Me-O Beach Prov. Park Alberta
22 K4 Mamer Luxembourg
20 F5 Mamers France
86 A4 Mamfé Cameroon
128 F4 Mamia, L Brazil
40 D3 Mamirolle France
55 E4 Mamlyutka U.S.S.R.
120 F2 Mammamattawa Ontario
28 D4 Mammen Denmark
37 L7 Mammendorf W Germany
37 O6 Mamming W Germany
43 G10 Mammola Italy
94 F8 Mammoth W Virginia
110 K4 Mammoth Cave Kentucky
101 P5 Mammoth Hot Springs Wyoming
110 E5 Mammoth Spring Arkansas
126 G9 Mamonal Colombia
130 G4 Mamonas Brazil
31 M1 Mamo-novo U.S.S.R.
128 E6 Mamore R Bolivia/Brazil
128 F4 Mamoré, L Brazil
85 B6 Mamou Guinea
111 D11 Mamou Louisiana
87 H11 Mampikohy Madagascar
16 D1 Mampodre mt Spain
85 D7 Mampong Ghana
83 J9 Mampuri Sri Lanka
31 N1 Mamry,Jezioro L Poland
15 C3 Mam Soul mt Scotland
70 F6 Mamudju Sulawesi
Mamuji see Yucheng
87 D10 Mamuno Botswana
55 C5 Mamyt U.S.S.R.
85 C7 Man Ivory Coast
94 F9 Man W Virginia
135 N1 Mana Hawaiian Is
129 H3 Mana R Fr Guiana
56 D3 Mana R U.S.S.R.
128 B4 Manabi Ecuador
128 F4 Manacapuru Brazil
128 F4 Manacapuru,L.Grande de Brazil
17 K5 Manacor Majorca
71 J4 Manado Sulawesi
71 J4 Manadotua isld Sulawesi
22 G3 Manage Belgium
140 D3 Managoora N Terr Aust
125 L3 Managua Nicaragua
145 E4 Mana I New Zealand
145 E3 Manaia New Zealand
87 H12 Manakara Madagascar
145 E4 Manakau New Zealand
144 D5 Manakau mt New Zealand
136 K2 Manam isld Papua New Guinea
76 D6 Manamadurai India
77 B6 Manamah,Al Bahrain
87 G11 Manambaho R Madagascar
127 N10 Mánamo R Venezuela
71 E5 Manamoc isld Philippines
102 S12 Manana Hawaiian Is
87 H11 Mananara Madagascar
139 G6 Manangatang Victoria
87 H12 Mananjary Madagascar
128 F2 Manano,Caño creek Venezuela
87 H12 Manantenina Madagascar
144 A6 Manapouri New Zealand
66 D3 Manas China
Manasarowar Lake see Mapam Yumco
66 D3 Manas He R China
75 L4 Manaslu mt Nepal
95 N6 Manasquan New Jersey
106 E4 Manassa Colorado
94 K8 Manassas Virginia
71 M9 Manatang Indonesia
127 L5 Manatí Puerto Rico
128 G4 Manaus Brazil
78 C3 Manavgat Turkey
99 S5 Manawa Wisconsin
119 P3 Manawan L Sask
145 E2 Manawaru New Zealand
145 E4 Manawatu R New Zealand
71 G7 Manay Mindanao Philippines
140 B2 Manbulla N Terr Aust
94 C2 Mancelona Michigan
16 E7 Mancha Real Spain
20 C3 Manche dep France
20 K5 Manchecourt France
Manche,la see English Channel
74 H9 Mancheral India
102 A3 Manchester California
95 P5 Manchester Connecticut
112 C5 Manchester Georgia
110 F2 Manchester Illinois
99 P7 Manchester Iowa
107 N2 Manchester Kansas
110 N4 Manchester Kentucky
94 C4 Manchester Michigan
95 Q4 Manchester New Hampshire
95 K4 Manchester New York
94 D8 Manchester Ohio
107 M5 Manchester Oklahoma
95 L6 Manchester Pennsylvania
110 K6 Manchester Tennessee
95 O3 Manchester Vermont
11 E2 Manchester conurbation England
127 K3 Manchester parish Jamaica
37 M6 Manching W Germany
127 M2 Manchioneal Jamaica
65 E1 Manchuria reg China
42 D6 Manciano Italy
128 B4 Máncora Peru
106 B4 Mancos Colorado
77 B5 Mand R Iran
87 F8 Manda Tanzania
130 D8 Mandaguari Brazil
80 F3 Mandah Jordan
88 D7 Manda Hd Zambia
77 G3 Mandal Afghanistan
58 D2 Mandal Mongolia
27 B13 Mandal Norway
68 C2 Mandalay Burma
78 A3 Mandalaya isld Turkey
58 E2 Mandalgovi Mongolia
78 K5 Mandalī Iraq
58 D3 Mandal-Ovoo Mongolia
27 B13 Mandalsåni R Norway
Mandalt see Sonid Zuoqi
47 J7 Mandalya Körfezi B Turkey
98 F3 Mandan N Dakota
36 C5 Mandelbachtal W Germany
127 K2 Mandeville Jamaica
111 F11 Mandeville Louisiana
144 B7 Mandeville New Zealand
146 B10 Mandheim Antarctica
130 B6 Mandioré, Lagoa L Bolivia/Brazil
74 J7 Mandla India
142 D4 Mandora W Australia
47 F6 Mandoúdhion Greece
143 B10 Mandurah W Australia
145 E4 Mangahao New Zealand
145 E3 Mangakino New Zealand
76 E2 Mangalagiri India
76 B4 Mangalore India
141 H7 Mangalore Queensland
145 E4 Mangamahoe New Zealand
145 E3 Mangamahu New Zealand
144 D5 Mangamaunu New Zealand
145 D1 Mangamuka New Zealand
145 E3 Mangapehi New Zealand
145 E4 Mangatainoka New Zealand
145 E3 Mangaweka New Zealand
145 E2 Mangawhai New Zealand
142 A4 Mangles B W Australia
66 E4 Mangnai China
88 E9 Mangoche Malawi
87 G12 Mangoky R Madagascar
145 D1 Mangonui New Zealand
87 H12 Mangoro Madagascar
74 D8 Mangrol India
126 F2 Mangrove Cay Andros Bahamas
113 J11 Mangrove Cay isld Bahamas
71 E4 Mangsoagui Pt Philippines
130 H10 Manguaba,L Brazil
16 B4 Mangualde Portugal
86 D3 Mangueigne Chad
131 H4 Mangueira, L Brazil
130 D9 Mangueirinha Brazil
84 E5 Mangueni,Pl.du Niger
87 G7 Mangula Tanzania
108 E9 Mangum Oklahoma
69 F14 Mangunjaya Sumatra
67 A5 Manhao China
99 T8 Manhattan Illinois
107 O2 Manhattan Kansas
101 O4 Manhattan Montana
102 G3 Manhattan Nevada
22 K3 Manhay Belgium
130 H7 Manhuaçu Brazil
130 H6 Manhuaçu,R Brazil
113 L12 Man I Bahamas
87 E7 Mani Zaïre
87 H11 Mania R Madagascar
42 E2 Maniago Italy
88 E8 Maniamba Mozambique
87 F9 Manica Mozambique
71 G5 Manicani isld Philippines
122 D4 Manic Deux Dam Quebec
128 F5 Manicoré R Brazil
122 D3 Manicouagan Quebec
122 D4 Manicouagan Pen Quebec
122 D4 Manicouagan R Quebec
122 D2 Manicouagan Res. Quebec
141 K6 Manifold, C Queensland
119 V7 Manigotagan Manitoba
110 F6 Manila Arkansas
71 E3 Manila Luzon Philippines
101 Q9 Manila Utah
71 E3 Manila B Luzon Philippines
139 J5 Manildra New S Wales
99 L8 Manilla Iowa
139 K4 Manilla New S Wales
70 F5 Manimbaja,Tg C Sulawesi
69 E13 Manindjan,Danau L Sumatra
87 H11 Maningory Madagascar
140 C1 Maningrida N Terr Aust
85 C6 Maninian Ivory Coast
69 E13 Maninjau Danau L Sumatra
75 P6 Manipur prov India
73 P4 Manipur R Burma
47 J6 Manisa Turkey
17 G5 Manises Spain
12 D5 Man,Isle of U.K.
99 U5 Manistee Michigan
94 B2 Manistee R Michigan
99 U4 Manistique Michigan
99 U3 Manistique R Michigan
99 V3 Manistique L Michigan
99 R9 Manito Illinois

48 Manitoba — Massif du Tondou

119 Manitoba Canada
119 S7 Manitoba, L Manitoba
118 H6 Manito L Sask
119 T9 Manitou Manitoba
109 J1 Manitou Oklahoma
119 M7 Manitou Bch Sask
99 T2 Manitou I Michigan
120 J7 Manitou L Ontario
122 G3 Manitou,L Quebec
120 H7 Manitoulin I Ontario
122 G2 Manitou R Quebec
106 F3 Manitou Springs Colorado
120 E3 Manitouwadge Ontario
120 J7 Manitowaning Ontario
120 F4 Manitowik L Ontario
99 T5 Manitowoc Wisconsin
121 P6 Maniwaki Quebec
128 C2 Manizales Colombia
80 G6 Manja Jordan
87 G12 Manja Madagascar
143 B10 Manjimup W Australia
74 G9 Manjlegaon India
38 M5 Mank Austria
107 M2 Mankato Kansas
99 N5 Mankato Minnesota
86 B5 Mankim Cameroon
109 J2 Mankins Texas
85 C7 Mankono Ivory Coast
118 K9 Mankota Sask
48 N2 Mankovka U.S.S.R.
76 E6 Mankulam Sri Lanka
95 M3 Manlius New York
17 J2 Manlleu Spain
99 N6 Manly Iowa
139 K5 Manly New S Wales
74 F8 Manmad India
140 C2 Mann R N Terr Aust
138 F4 Mannahill S Australia
83 J9 Mannar Sri Lanka
73 M7 Mannar,G.of India/Sri Lanka
76 D5 Mannargudi India
83 J8 Mannar I Sri Lanka
36 F5 Mannheim W Germany
14 A3 Mannin B Irish Rep
117 P7 Manning Alberta
109 P1 Manning Arkansas
99 L8 Manning Iowa
98 D2 Manning N Dakota
112 G4 Manning S Carolina
109 N4 Manning Texas
139 K4 Manning R New S Wales
117 N11 Manning Prov. Park Br Col
94 G7 Mannington W Virginia
9 H4 Manningtree England
140 A7 Mann, Mt N Terr Aust
140 A7 Mann Ranges N Terr/S Aust
112 M2 Manns Harbor N Carolina
95 L3 Mannsville New York
43 C9 Mannu R Sardinia
43 B8 Mannu,C Sardinia
138 E5 Mannum S Australia
118 F5 Mannville Alberta
85 B7 Mano Sierra Leone
128 E5 Manoa Bolivia
80 B8 Manoah R Israel
127 N1 Man of War B Tobago
116 H7 Manokotak Alaska
136 G2 Manokwari W Irian
46 E6 Manolás Greece
87 G12 Manombo Madagascar
88 A5 Manono Zaïre
112 E6 Manor Georgia
119 Q9 Manor Sask
109 K5 Manor Texas
8 B4 Manorbier Wales
144 B6 Manorburn Res New Zealand
14 C2 Manorhamilton Irish Rep
85 B7 Mano River Liberia
68 D7 Manoron Burma
19 P17 Manosque France
21 G10 Manot France
20 G5 Manou France
121 Q5 Manouane Quebec
122 B3 Manouane L Quebec
61 M8 Mano-wan B Japan
68 C1 Man Pan Burma
17 J3 Manresa Spain
88 B7 Mansa Zambia
85 A6 Mansaba Guinea-Bissau
85 A6 Mansa Konko The Gambia
71 E4 Mansalay B Philippines
68 C1 Man Sam Burma
142 G4 Mansbridge, Mt W Australia
115 L5 Mansel I N W Terr
33 O9 Mansfeld E Germany
110 B6 Mansfield Arkansas
9 E1 Mansfield England
112 D4 Mansfield Georgia
99 S9 Mansfield Illinois
109 O3 Mansfield Louisiana
95 Q4 Mansfield Massachusetts
110 D4 Mansfield Missouri
94 E6 Mansfield Ohio
98 H4 Mansfield S Dakota
109 K3 Mansfield Texas
139 H6 Mansfield Victoria
100 F2 Mansfield Washington
95 P2 Mansfield,Mt Vermont
56 D4 Manskoye Belogor'ye mts U.S.S.R.
21 F10 Mansle France
99 M7 Manson Iowa
100 E2 Manson Washington
117 L8 Manson Creek Br Col
130 C4 Manso,R Brazil
8 D6 Manston England
71 C3 Mansuar isld W Irian
111 D10 Mansura Louisiana
79 B7 Mansûra,El Egypt
128 B4 Manta Ecuador
71 C6 Mantalingajan, Mt Palawan Philippines
70 E1 Mantanani Besar isld Sabah
86 D6 Mantantale Zaïre
65 H4 Mantap-san mt N Korea
71 J5 Mantarara Indonesia
118 H7 Mantario Sask
128 C6 Mantaro R Peru
102 C4 Manteca California
111 G8 Mantee Mississippi
37 N4 Mantel W Germany
130 H6 Mantena Brazil
99 T8 Manteno Illinois
112 M2 Manteo N Carolina
107 J4 Manter Kansas
71 J4 Manterawo isld Sulawesi
20 J4 Mantes France
25 E2 Mantgum Netherlands
74 H9 Manthani India
21 G7 Manthelan France
103 N2 Manti Utah
130 F8 Mantiqueira,Serra da mts Brazil
100 D9 Manton California
94 B2 Manton Michigan
65 B5 Mantou Shan mt ra China
45 J1 Mantova Italy
29 L11 Mäntsälä Finland
29 L10 Mänttä Finland
126 B3 Mantua Cuba
Mantua Italy see Mantova
94 F5 Mantua Ohio
141 H6 Mantuan Downs Queensland
52 F5 Manturovo U.S.S.R.
29 J10 Mäntyluoto Finland
128 D6 Manú Peru
Manuan see Manouane
122 B3 Manuanis,L Quebec
71 F6 Manucan Mindanao Philippines
129 J5 Manuel Alves R Brazil
106 B6 Manuelito New Mexico
130 D9 Manuel Ribas Brazil
133 C8 Manuel Rodriguez, I Chile
128 E5 Manuel Urbano Brazil
129 H5 Manuelzinho Brazil
71 H6 Manui isld Indonesia
77 E6 Manūjān Iran
145 G2 Manukau New Zealand
70 F2 Manuk Manka Philippines
138 E4 Manunda R S Australia
145 E3 Manunui New Zealand
71 C3 Manuran isld W Irian
128 E6 Manuripe R Bolivia/Peru
136 K2 Manus isld Bismarck Arch
145 E3 Manutahi New Zealand
138 E3 Manuwalkaninna S Australia
98 J1 Manvel N Dakota
76 C3 Manvi India
98 B7 Manville Wyoming
109 O4 Many Louisiana
52 K4 Man'ya U.S.S.R.
88 B10 Manyangau mt Zimbabwe
88 G3 Manyara,L Tanzania
47 J4 Manyas Turkey
118 G9 Manyberries Alberta
54 M9 Manych R U.S.S.R.
118 G8 Many Island I Alberta
88 E4 Manyoni Tanzania
141 K6 Many Peaks Queensland
143 C10 Many Peaks, Mt W Australia
79 B7 Manzala,El Egypt
84 J3 Manzala, L Egypt
89 E2 Manzamnyama R Zimbabwe
16 E5 Manzanares Spain
127 P2 Manzanilla B Trinidad
126 F4 Manzanillo Cuba
124 G8 Manzanillo Mexico
106 D7 Manzano New Mexico
131 A8 Manzano,B del Chile
106 G3 Manzanola Colorado
106 D7 Manzano Mts New Mexico
58 G2 Manzhouli China
79 G7 Manzil Jordan
89 G6 Manzini Swaziland
Manzovka see Sibirtsevo
86 C3 Mao Chad
65 G2 Mao'ershan China
136 H2 Maoke, Pegunungan ra W Irian
65 F4 Maokui Shan mt China
65 G3 Maolin China
67 C6 Maoming China
67 C1 Maoping China
67 G6 Mao-pi T'ou C Taiwan
67 B3 Maotai China
67 A1 Maowen China
65 F2 Maoxing China
80 F4 Ma'oz Israel
70 F5 Mapaga Sulawesi
87 F10 Mapai Mozambique
66 C5 Mapam Yumco L China
70 B6 Mapan Kalimantan
70 G5 Mapane Sulawesi
70 F5 Mapida Sulawesi
70 F6 Mapili Sulawesi
124 G4 Mapimí, Bolson de dist Mexico
67 D1 Maping China
128 F2 Mapire Venezuela
129 H3 Mapireme Brazil
128 E7 Mapiri R La Paz Bolivia
128 F4 Mapixari, L Brazil
99 L7 Maple R Iowa
94 C3 Maple R Michigan
118 H9 Maple Creek Sask
99 N6 Maple Island Minnesota
111 K9 Maplesville Alabama
99 L7 Mapleton Iowa
95 S7 Mapleton Maine
99 N6 Mapleton Minnesota
122 H8 Mapleton Nova Scotia
100 B5 Mapleton Oregon
100 C2 Maple Valley Washington
95 L3 Maple View New York
141 F1 Mapoon Queensland
144 C5 Mapourika, L New Zealand
13 H6 Mappleton England
129 G4 Mapuera R Brazil
69 G12 Mapur isld Indonesia
89 H5 Maputo Mozambique
89 H6 Maputo R Mozambique
80 F8 Maqam en Nabi Yusha Jordan
78 H6 Maqar an Naam Iraq
46 D3 Maqellarë Albania
65 H2 Maqiaohe China
79 E10 Maqnā Saudi Arabia
66 C6 Maquan He R China
71 G4 Maqueda Chan Philippines
122 H5 Maquereau Pte.au Quebec
133 D6 Maquinchao Argentina
131 B8 Maquinchao, R Argentina
99 Q7 Maquoketa Iowa
99 Q9 Maquon Illinois
70 E3 Mara Kalimantan
127 J9 Mara Venezuela
128 E4 Maraa Brazil
129 J5 Marabá Brazil
70 D6 Marabahan Kalimantan
40 B2 Marac France
127 J9 Maracaibo Venezuela
127 J9 Maracaibo, L. de Venezuela
129 H3 Maracá, Ilha de Amapá Brazil
128 F3 Maracá, Ilha de Roraima Brazil
133 F2 Maracaju Brazil
130 C7 Maracaju,Serra de mts Brazil
129 J4 Maracana Brazil
127 O2 Maracas B Trinidad
127 L9 Maracay Venezuela
84 F4 Maradah Libya
85 F6 Maradi Niger
145 E3 Maraetai New Zealand
78 L3 Marāgheh Iran
130 J10 Maragogi Brazil
128 E3 Marahuaca,Co mt Venezuela
65 E2 Marain Sum China
110 A3 Marais des Cygnes R Kansas/Missouri
20 F3 Marais-Vernier France
129 J4 Marajó,I.de Brazil
86 G5 Maralal Kenya
55 G4 Maraldy U.S.S.R.
86 C4 Marali Cent Afr Republic
137 N3 Maramasike isld Solomon Is
Maramba see Livingstone Zambia
48 H3 Maramures old prov Romania
69 F11 Maran Malaysia
103 N9 Marana Arizona
140 C2 Maranboy N Terr Aust
17 F3 Maranchón Spain
78 K2 Marand Iran
89 G2 Marandellas Zimbabwe
45 J2 Maranello Italy
68 D7 Marang Burma
69 F10 Marang Malaysia
129 L4 Maranguape Brazil
130 E4 Maranhão R Brazil
129 J4 Maranhão state Brazil
141 J7 Maranoa R Queensland
45 Q8 Marano di Napoli Italy
128 D4 Marañón R Peru
21 C9 Marans France
40 A1 Maranville France
16 B3 Marão, Sa do mts Portugal
129 G3 Marapi R Brazil
128 E5 Marari Brazil
144 B6 Mararoa R New Zealand
78 F3 Maras Turkey
70 F7 Marasende isld Indonesia
48 L5 Mărăşeşti Romania
71 C6 Marasi B Palawan Philippines
16 B6 Marateca Portugal
46 D7 Marathiás,Akr C Greece
113 F13 Marathon Florida
47 F6 Marathón Greece
95 L4 Marathon New York
120 D4 Marathon Ontario
141 G5 Marathon Queensland
108 D5 Marathon Texas
99 R5 Marathon Wisconsin
70 F3 Maratua isld Indonesia
129 L6 Maraú Brazil
128 E3 Marauaí R Brazil
127 O2 Maraval Trinidad
108 E6 Maravillas Cr Texas
71 G7 Marawi Mindanao Philippines
38 M5 Marbach Austria
36 F2 Marbach W Germany
22 K4 Marbehan Belgium
106 C2 Marble Colorado
100 H1 Marble Washington
142 C5 Marble Bar W Australia
103 N5 Marble Canyon Arizona
110 B6 Marble City Oklahoma
109 J5 Marble Falls Texas
87 E10 Marble Hall S Africa
99 P10 Marblehead Illinois
95 R4 Marblehead Massachusetts
94 E5 Marblehead Ohio
99 O7 Marble Rock Iowa
121 T7 Marbleton Quebec
101 P7 Marbleton Wyoming
36 F2 Marburg W Germany
95 K8 Marbury Maryland
26 G8 Marby Sweden
48 D3 Marcal R Hungary
47 J7 Marçal Dağ mt Turkey
48 D4 Marcali Hungary
45 J1 Marcaria Italy
21 F9 Marçay France
122 F2 Marceau,L Quebec
118 L6 Marcelin Sask
110 D2 Marceline Missouri
133 G3 Marcelino Ramos Brazil
110 E6 Marcella Arkansas
94 B4 Marcellus Michigan
100 G2 Marcellus Washington
45 O5 Marcetelli Italy
9 G2 March England
20 G4 Marchainville France
118 E2 Marchand Manitoba
138 E4 Marchant Hill S Australia
40 D3 Marchaux France
21 I9 Marche reg France
45 N4 Marche reg Italy
22 J3 Marche-en-Famenne Belgium
16 D7 Marchena Spain
128 A7 Marchena isld Galapagos Is
21 H6 Marchenoir France
70 E1 Marchesa B Sabah
20 C3 Marchésieux France
127 P6 Marchfield Barbados
22 E3 Marchiennes-Ville France
22 J3 Marchin Belgium
140 D1 Marchinbar I N Terr Aust
131 E3 Mar Chiquita, L Córdoba Argentina
45 Q7 Marcianise Italy
18 H6 Marcigny France
18 G8 Marcillac France
20 D5 Marcille-la-Ville France
20 H4 Marcilly France
21 I7 Marcilly-en Gault France
21 J6 Marcilly-en Villette France
40 G1 Marckolsheim France
122 J1 Marc,L Labrador
113 F12 Marco Florida
110 J3 Marco Indiana
43 G9 Marco Argentano, S Italy
22 E3 Marcoing France
100 C5 Marcola Oregon
21 G6 Marçon France
118 C1 Marconi Manitoba
22 K3 Marcourt Belgium
99 L7 Marcus Iowa
100 G1 Marcus Washington
116 O6 Marcus Baker,Mt Alaska
134 G5 Marcus I Pacific Oc
95 M3 Marcy New York
95 O2 Marcy, Mt New York
80 D5 Marda Jordan
74 E1 Mardan Pakistan
131 F6 Mar del Plata Argentina
9 G5 Marden England
142 B5 Mardie W Australia
78 H3 Mardin Turkey
26 M5 Mårdsel Sweden
26 K7 Mårdsele Sweden
26 J7 Mardsjö Sweden
26 H8 Mårdsjön Sweden
70 G7 Mare Sulawesi
71 A2 Mare isld Halmahera Indonesia
137 O6 Maré isld Îles Loyauté Pac Oc
86 G3 Mareb R Ethiopia
45 M3 Marecchia R Italy
130 J10 Marechal Deodoro Brazil
141 H3 Mareeba Queensland
110 K3 Marengo Indiana
99 P8 Marengo Iowa
41 N7 Marengo Italy
94 E6 Marengo Ohio
118 H7 Marengo Sask
100 G2 Marengo Washington
99 Q3 Marengo Wisconsin
99 R3 Marenisco Michigan
21 C10 Marennes France
145 E2 Mareretu New Zealand
86 A2 Marergur Somalia
9 G6 Maresfield England
43 E11 Marettimo isld Sicily
22 E3 Maretz France
21 C8 Mareuil France
21 J8 Mareuil-sur-Arnon France
108 C5 Marfa Texas
66 D4 Margai Caka L China
75 M1 Margai Caka L China
8 C4 Margam Wales
57 D1 Marganets U.S.S.R.
76 A3 Margao India
123 L7 Margaree Harbour C Breton I, N Scotia
123 L7 Margaree I Nova Scotia
123 M7 Margaree Valley C Breton I, N Scotia
108 H1 Margaret Texas
138 D3 Margaret R S Australia
117 K10 Margaret Bay Br Col
141 G1 Margaret Bay Queensland
117 Q6 Margaret L Alberta
117 P3 Margaret L N W Terr
142 C5 Margaret, Mt W Australia
143 B10 Margaret R W Australia
95 N4 Margaretville New York
130 C7 Margarida Brazil
127 N9 Margarita I. de Venezuela
46 D5 Margarítion Greece
9 H5 Margate England
89 G8 Margate S Africa
139 H9 Margate Tasmania
95 N7 Margate City New Jersey
18 H8 Margeride, Mts de la France
Margherita see Giamame Somalia
48 G3 Mărghita Romania
118 F3 Margie Alberta
99 N1 Margie Minnesota
57 F4 Margilan U.S.S.R.
48 G5 Mărgina Romania
48 G5 Margita Yugoslavia
119 O7 Margo Sask
77 H4 Margo, Dasht-i- des Afghanistan
71 F7 Margosatubig Mindanao Philippines
94 C2 Margrethe, L Michigan
117 M9 Marguerite Br Columbia
146 F13 Marguerite B Antarctica
22 J4 Margut France
80 F3 Marhaba Jordan
122 F5 Maria Quebec
124 F7 María Cleofas, I Mexico
28 D3 Mariager Denmark
32 M7 Mariaglück W Germany
68 C7 Maria I Burma
140 D2 Maria I N Terr Aust
139 J8 Maria I Tasmania
36 C3 Maria Laach W Germany
38 G8 Maria Luggau Austria
124 F7 María Madre, I Mexico
124 F7 María Magdalena, I Mexico
103 K8 Maria Mts California
141 J5 Marian Queensland
130 G7 Mariana Brazil
118 E3 Mariana Lake Alberta
126 C3 Marianao Cuba
134 E6 Marianas islds Pacific Oc
75 Q5 Mariani India
117 P4 Marian L N W Terr
110 F7 Marianna Arkansas
113 B7 Marianna Florida
27 H14 Mariannelund Sweden
87 B8 Mariano Machado Angola
37 O4 Marianské Lázně Czechoslovakia
119 T9 Mariapolis Manitoba
101 N1 Marias R Montana
17 F7 Maria,Sierra de mts Spain
101 M1 Marias Pass Montana
38 F6 Mariastein Austria
135 M12 Maria Theresa Reef Pacific Oc
145 D1 Maria van Diemen, C New Zealand
38 M6 Mariazell Austria
99 T5 Maribel Wisconsin
28 G7 Maribo Denmark
Maribo co see Storstrøm
38 N8 Maribor Yugoslavia
71 E4 Maricaban isld Philippines
89 E5 Marico R Botswana
103 M8 Maricopa Arizona
102 E6 Maricopa California
103 M8 Maricopa Mts Arizona
115 M5 Maricourt Quebec
86 E5 Maridi Sudan
128 E4 Marié R Brazil
83 K12 Marie Anne I Seychelles
146 H10 Marie Byrd Land Antarctica
27 H13 Mariedam Sweden
27 J12 Mariefred Sweden
127 N5 Marie Galante isld Guadeloupe W Indies
27 L11 Mariehamn Finland
118 G4 Marie L Alberta
126 C3 Mariel Cuba
Marienbad see Marianské Lázně
37 P2 Marienberg E Germany
25 G3 Marienberg Netherlands
32 L8 Marienberg W Germany
22 H3 Marienbourg Belgium
Marienburg see Malbork
36 C2 Marienburg Nordrhein-Westfalen W Germany
37 N3 Marieney E Germany
32 F5 Marienhafe W Germany
36 C1 Marienheide W Germany
28 G7 Marienleuchte C W Germany
89 A5 Mariental Namibia
107 J3 Marienthal Kansas
94 H5 Marienville Pennsylvania
Marienwerder see Kwidzyn
140 B1 Marie Shoal N Terr Aust
27 G13 Mariestad Sweden
112 C4 Marietta Georgia
94 F7 Marietta Ohio
109 K2 Marietta Oklahoma
112 E2 Marietta S Carolina
121 R7 Marieville Quebec
19 O18 Marignane France
21 F6 Marigné France
20 C3 Marigny France
127 N5 Marigot Saint Martin W I
56 C3 Mariinsk U.S.S.R.
55 D4 Mariinskoye U.S.S.R.
52 G6 Mariinsky Posad U.S.S.R.
71 J5 Marikasu,Tg C Indonesia
130 D8 Marila Brazil
133 H2 Marilia Brazil
142 C6 Marillana W Australia
130 E7 Marimbondo Cachoeira rapids Brazil
127 M4 Marin Martinique W I
16 B2 Marín Spain
44 H3 Marina di Carrara Italy
44 H3 Marina di Massa Italy
44 H4 Marina di Pisa Italy
45 M3 Marina di Ravenna Italy
128 G2 Marina Fall Guyana
70 B6 Marindjahan Kalimantan
71 E4 Marinduque isld Philippines
110 G3 Marine Illinois
113 F8 Marineland Florida
20 K3 Marines France
99 T4 Marinette Wisconsin
129 H8 Maringá Brazil
86 D5 Maringa R Zaïre
111 E11 Maringouin Louisiana
87 F9 Maringue Mozambique
16 B5 Marinha Grande Portugal
54 J9 Mar'inka U.S.S.R.
42 E7 Marino Italy
128 E3 Marinuma Colombia
111 J9 Marion Alabama
110 F6 Marion Arkansas
117 Q11 Marion Idaho
110 H4 Marion Illinois
94 B6 Marion Indiana
99 P7 Marion Iowa
107 O3 Marion Kansas
110 H4 Marion Kentucky
111 D9 Marion Louisiana
95 U2 Marion Maine
94 B2 Marion Michigan
111 H9 Marion Mississippi
101 L1 Marion Montana
112 E2 Marion N Carolina
98 H3 Marion N Dakota
98 F9 Marion Nebraska
94 D6 Marion Ohio
112 H3 Marion S Carolina
98 J6 Marion S Dakota
109 J6 Marion Texas
94 F10 Marion Virginia
99 S5 Marion Wisconsin
139 J8 Marion B Tasmania
140 E6 Marion Downs Queensland
111 J9 Marion Junction Alabama
137 L5 Marion Reef Coral Sea
141 K4 Marion Reef Gt Barrier Reef Aust
110 C4 Marionville Missouri
128 E2 Maripa Venezuela
71 G5 Maripipi isld Philippines
102 E4 Mariposa California
102 D4 Mariposa R California
70 G4 Marisa Sulawesi
133 E2 Mariscal Estigarribia Paraguay
110 G3 Marissa Illinois
47 H2 Maritsa Bulgaria
Maritsa R see Évros R
47 G2 Maritsa R Bulgaria
44 B3 Marittime, Alpi mts Italy/France
52 G6 Mari Turek U.S.S.R.
Mariupol see Zhdanov
127 O10 Mariusa R Venezuela
77 J4 Marja Afghanistan
84 G3 Marj, Al Libya
26 N5 Marjärv Sweden
79 F5 Marjayoûn Lebanon
25 C5 Mark R Netherlands
80 G6 Marka Jordan
26 E8 Markabygd Norway
78 H4 Markada Syria
56 C6 Markakal', Oz L U.S.S.R.
52 J4 Markalasta U.S.S.R.
58 C6 Markam China
76 D3 Markapur India
120 K8 Markdale Ontario
41 K2 Markdorf W Germany
110 F6 Marked Tree Arkansas
25 G4 Markelo Netherlands
28 G7 Markelsdorfe Huk C W Germany
25 D4 Marken Netherlands
25 D3 Markerwaard Netherlands
99 S6 Markesan Wisconsin
9 F2 Market Deeping England
8 D2 Market Drayton England
9 F3 Market Harborough England
14 E2 Markethill N Ireland
13 H6 Market Rasen England
9 E1 Market Warsop England
13 H6 Market Weighton England
36 G6 Markgröningen W Germany
121 L9 Markham Ontario
109 L7 Markham Texas
100 B3 Markham Washington
66 C4 Markham Lake China
9 F1 Markham Moor England
146 G7 Markham,Mt Antarctica
119 N8 Markinch Sask
15 E4 Markinch Scotland
33 T8 Märkisch Buchholz E Germany
26 M4 Markitta Sweden
102 E3 Markleeville California
37 O6 Marklkofen W Germany
37 N3 Markneukirchen E Germany
26 J4 Markotjàkko mt Sweden
33 Q10 Markrapstädt E Germany
111 F7 Marks Mississippi
8 D5 Marksbury England
120 K6 Markstay Ontario
9 G4 Marks Tey England
37 J2 Marksuhl E Germany
111 D10 Marksville Louisiana
37 J5 Marktbergel W Germany
37 J4 Markt Bibart W Germany
37 J4 Marktbreit W Germany
37 L3 Marktgraitz W Germany
36 H4 Marktheidenfeld W Germany
37 L7 Markt Indersdorf W Germany
37 O7 Marktl W Germany
37 M3 Marktleugast W Germany
37 J6 Marktoffingen W Germany
37 N3 Marktredwitz W Germany
37 M3 Marktschorgast W Germany
37 J4 Marktsteft W Germany
41 N1 Markt Wald W Germany
37 L3 Marktzeuln W Germany
99 O3 Markville Minnesota
32 F9 Marl W Germany
107 N5 Marland Oklahoma
143 B8 Marlandy Hill W Australia
121 N8 Marlbank Ontario
95 Q4 Marlboro Massachusetts
95 P4 Marlboro New Hampshire
9 E5 Marlborough England
128 G2 Marlborough Guyana
141 J6 Marlborough Queensland
145 D4 Marlborough stat area New Zealand
22 F4 Marle France
33 S8 Marlendorf E Germany
33 S8 Marlenfelde E Germany
94 D3 Marlette Michigan
109 L4 Marlin Texas
94 G8 Marlinton W Virginia
139 J7 Marlo Victoria
22 J3 Marloie Belgium
33 R4 Marlow E Germany
9 F4 Marlow England
95 P3 Marlow New Hampshire
109 K1 Marlow Oklahoma
141 H5 Marlow Queensland
22 F4 Marly France
20 K4 Marly-le-Roi France
27 J10 Marma Sweden
110 F5 Marmaduke Arkansas
18 F8 Marmande France
47 J4 Marmara Turkey
47 J4 Marmaraereğlisi Turkey
47 J6 Marmara Gölü L Turkey
47 J4 Marmara,Sea of Turkey
47 J8 Marmaris Turkey
98 C3 Marmarth N Dakota
26 K3 Mårmatj mt Sweden
94 E4 Marme City Michigan
16 B2 Marmed,Sa des S mts Spain
128 F5 Marmelos R Brazil
94 F8 Marmet W Virginia
121 P4 Marmette,L Quebec
118 L1 Marmion L res Ontario
143 C8 Marmion, Mt W Australia
45 J1 Marmirolo Italy
42 D2 Marmolada mt Italy
16 E6 Marmolejo Spain
116 L7 Marmot B Alaska
125 M9 Mar Muerto B Mexico
19 J5 Marnay France
32 K5 Marne W Germany
18 H4 Marne dep France
40 B1 Marne R France
36 B6 Marne, Canal de la France
36 D4 Marnheim W Germany
33 P6 Marnitz E Germany
139 G6 Marnoo Victoria
99 S9 Maroa Illinois
145 F3 Maroa New Zealand
87 H11 Maroantsetra Madagascar
74 C2 Marobi Pakistan
22 D3 Marœuil France
22 F3 Maroilles France
37 K3 Maroldsweisach W Germany
20 F5 Marolles-les-Braults France
87 H10 Maromandia Madagascar
20 H3 Maromme France
47 H4 Marónia Greece
18 G7 Maronne R France
141 G7 Maroo Queensland
143 B6 Maroonah W Australia
127 J2 Maroon Town Jamaica
70 F7 Maros Sulawesi
70 F7 Maros R Sulawesi
145 E1 Marotiri Is New Zealand
86 B3 Maroua Cameroon
121 L4 Marouf Jct Quebec
129 H3 Marouini R Fr Guiana
87 H11 Marovoay Madagascar
110 F4 Marquano Missouri
135 U13 Marquesas Is Pacific Oc
113 E13 Marquesas Keys islds Florida
130 G8 Marquês de Valença Brazil
99 P6 Marquette Iowa
107 N3 Marquette Kansas
118 D1 Marquette Manitoba
99 T3 Marquette Michigan
98 H8 Marquette Nebraska
99 U6 Marquette R Michigan
106 C6 Marquez New Mexico
109 L4 Marquez Texas
17 F1 Marquina Spain
22 E3 Marquion France
119 M8 Marquis Sask
22 B2 Marquise France
139 G4 Marra New S Wales
139 H4 Marra R New S Wales
89 H5 Marracuene Mozambique
45 L3 Marradi Italy
143 B10 Marradong W Australia
86 D3 Marra, Jebel mts Sudan
140 B2 Marrakai N Terr Aust
85 C2 Marrakech Morocco
85 E2 Marraket, Hassi Algeria
139 H5 Marrar New S Wales
43 B8 Marrargiu, C Sardinia
139 G8 Marrawah Tasmania
28 H7 Marrebæk Denmark
138 E3 Marree S Australia
111 J13 Marrero New Orleans
87 G9 Marromeu Mozambique
16 D8 Marroqui,Pta Spain
88 F8 Marrupa Mozambique
138 C2 Marryat R S Australia
94 G6 Mars Pennsylvania
84 K4 Marsá Alam Egypt
17 F9 Marsa Ben Mehidi Algeria
86 G5 Marsabit Kenya
Marsa Brega see Qasr al Burayqal
21 B6 Marsac-sur-Don France
130 F8 Mar,Sa.do mts Brazil
86 H3 Marsa Fatma Ethiopia
36 B6 Marsal France
43 E11 Marsala Sicily
19 N15 Marsanne France
84 G3 Marsá Sūsah Libya
13 G4 Marsden England
139 J5 Marsden New S Wales
118 H6 Marsden Sask
19 O18 Marseille France
20 J2 Marseille-en-Beauvaisis France
19 N18 Marseille-Rhône, Canal France
Marseilles France see Marseille
99 S8 Marseilles Illinois
94 D6 Marseilles Ohio
98 B3 Marsh Montana
79 E10 Marshah, J mt Saudi Arabia
110 D6 Marshall Arkansas
99 T10 Marshall Illinois
94 C4 Marshall Michigan
99 L5 Marshall Minnesota
110 C2 Marshall Missouri
112 E2 Marshall N Carolina
98 D2 Marshall N Dakota
107 N5 Marshall Oklahoma
118 H5 Marshall Sask
109 N3 Marshall Texas
94 K8 Marshall Virginia
101 U7 Marshall Wyoming
140 D6 Marshall R N Terr Aust
139 J7 Marshall B Tasmania
134 G7 Marshall Is Pacific Oc
120 C2 Marshall L Ontario
99 O7 Marshalltown Iowa
8 D3 Marshbrook England
8 D5 Marshfield England
110 D4 Marshfield Missouri
99 Q5 Marshfield Wisconsin
113 K11 Marsh Harbour Great Abaco I Bahamas
95 L5 Marsh Hill Pennsylvania
95 T7 Mars Hill Maine
111 D12 Marsh Island Louisiana
117 F5 Marsh L Yukon Terr
98 K4 Marsh Lake Minnesota
101 Q9 Marsh Pk Utah
112 G3 Marshville N Carolina
100 J6 Marsing Idaho
98 C7 Marsland Nebraska
19 J3 Mars la Tour France
28 E4 Mårslet Denmark
28 F6 Marslev Denmark
27 J12 Märsta Sweden
28 F7 Marstal Denmark
28 E7 Marstal Bugt B Denmark
101 Q8 Marston Wyoming
27 E14 Marstrand Sweden
28 C6 Marstrup Denmark
25 E2 Marsum Netherlands
55 D1 Marsyaty U.S.S.R.
109 L4 Mart Texas
42 D6 Marta R Italy
68 C4 Martaban Burma
73 Q5 Martaban,G.of Burma
21 F8 Martaizé France
70 D6 Martapura Kalimantan
70 K8 Martapura Sumatra
18 G8 Martel France
22 K4 Martelange Belgium
41 N4 Martello, Val Italy
47 H1 Marten Bulgaria
99 N8 Martensdale Iowa
17 G5 Martés,Sierra mts Spain
139 J4 Marthaguy R New S Wales
110 E3 Marthasville Missouri
95 R5 Marthas Vineyard Massachusetts
36 B6 Marthille France
126 F4 Martí Cuba
45 M5 Martignano,L.di Italy
20 D5 Martigné France
21 E7 Martigné-Briand France
21 C6 Martigné-Ferchaud France
40 F5 Martigny Switzerland
40 C1 Martigny-les-Bains France
19 O18 Martigues France
16 D9 Martil Morocco
116 N4 Martin Alaska
31 L6 Martin Czechoslovakia
94 E9 Martin Kentucky
94 B4 Martin Michigan
98 E6 Martin S Dakota
110 H5 Martin Tennessee
17 G4 Martin R Spain
41 M4 Martina Switzerland
43 H8 Martina Franca Italy
145 E4 Martinborough New Zealand
109 K6 Martindale Texas
102 B3 Martinez California
125 L7 Martínez Mexico
32 M10 Martinfeld E Germany
130 F6 Martinho Campos Brazil
127 L4 Martinique isld Lesser Antilles
111 L9 Martin L Alabama
130 D8 Martinópolis Brazil
146 H11 Martin Pen Antarctica
116 Q1 Martin Pt Alaska
144 A6 Martin's B New Zealand
38 M5 Martinsberg Austria
Martinsbrück see Martina
110 E2 Martinsburg Missouri
95 M3 Martinsburg New York
94 E6 Martinsburg Ohio
94 J6 Martinsburg Pennsylvania
94 K7 Martinsburg W Virginia
101 P3 Martinsdale Montana
94 G6 Martins Ferry Ohio
99 T10 Martinsville Illinois
94 A7 Martinsville Indiana
94 H10 Martinsville Virginia
20 B2 Martinvast France
21 H8 Martizay France
9 H3 Martlesham England
8 D6 Martock England
28 F5 Martofte Denmark
9 F1 Marton England
145 E4 Marton New Zealand
17 J3 Martorell Spain
16 E7 Martos Spain
117 O4 Martre, Lac La N W Terr
29 N4 Martti Finland
29 K11 Marttila Finland
55 C5 Martuk U.S.S.R.
52 J2 Martyn U.S.S.R.
80 G3 Maru Jordan
77 H2 Maruchak Afghanistan
70 D2 Marudi Sarawak
70 E1 Marudu Bay Sabah
77 K4 Maruf Afghanistan
60 G11 Marugame Japan
144 D5 Maruia New Zealand
129 L6 Maruim Brazil
28 J4 Mårum Denmark
25 F2 Marum Netherlands
145 F3 Marumaru New Zealand
140 C2 Marumba Mt N Terr Aust
88 B5 Marungu mts Zaïre
61 K9 Maruoka Japan
77 D4 Marvast Iran
27 C11 Mår-vatn L Norway
18 H8 Marvejols France
111 F7 Marvell Arkansas
143 C9 Marvel Loch W Australia
22 J5 Marville France
98 K4 Marvin S Dakota
106 C1 Marvine Colorado
103 N3 Marvine,Mt Utah
77 H2 Marwa Afghanistan
74 E6 Marwar India
118 G5 Marwayne Alberta
15 E1 Marwick Hd Orkney Scotland
32 G6 Marx W Germany
33 S9 Marxdorf E Germany
37 M3 Marxgrün W Germany
77 G1 Mary U.S.S.R.
142 B5 Mary Ann Pt W Australia
55 F3 Mar'yanovka U.S.S.R.
139 G6 Maryborough New S Wales
141 L7 Maryborough Queensland
87 D11 Marydale S Africa
55 E4 Mar'yevka U.S.S.R.
119 Q9 Maryfield Sask
117 L6 Mary Henry,Mt Br Col
12 D2 Maryhill Scotland
140 F5 Mary Kathleen Queensland
111 E10 Mary,L Mississippi
89 G1 Maryland Zimbabwe
95 K7 Maryland state U.S.A.
108 G3 Maryneal Texas
12 E4 Maryport England
141 K7 Mary R Queensland
123 R1 Mary's Hbr Labrador
100 K8 Marys R Nevada
123 R6 Marystown Newfoundland
103 M3 Marysvale Utah
101 O5 Marysville Idaho
107 O2 Marysville Kansas
94 E4 Marysville Michigan
122 F8 Marysville New Brunswick
94 D6 Marysville Ohio
100 C1 Marysville Washington
141 H4 Maryvale Queensland
141 K8 Maryvale Queensland
99 M9 Maryville Missouri
112 D2 Maryville Tennessee
45 K3 Marzabotto Italy
85 D5 Marzafal Mali
130 E5 Marzagão Brazil
33 R8 Marzahna E Germany
33 R7 Marzahne E Germany
128 C2 Marzo,C Colombia
84 E4 Marzūq Libya
70 O9 Mas R Java
69 D13 Masa isld Indonesia
Masada see Mezada
80 F1 Mas'ada Syria
88 F4 Masai Steppe Tanzania
88 C2 Masaka Uganda
86 C3 Masalasef Chad
70 G6 Masamba Sulawesi
65 G7 Masan S Korea
71 N8 Masapun Indonesia
95 S7 Masardis Maine
113 E9 Masaryktown Florida
88 G7 Masasi Tanzania
Mas Atierra isld see Robinson Crusoe I
71 F4 Masbate isld Philippines
32 F9 Masbeck W Germany
17 H9 Mascara Algeria
81 C7 Mascarene Basin Indian Oc
81 C7 Mascarene I Indian Oc
81 C7 Mascarene Rge Indian Oc
98 G9 Mascot Nebraska
112 D1 Mascot Tennessee
130 H4 Mascote Brazil
110 G3 Mascoutah Illinois
18 F9 Mas d'Azil, le France
118 K9 Masefield Sask
70 E3 Ma Sekatok Kalimantan
71 O9 Masela isld Indonesia
38 N7 Masenberg mt Austria
45 L1 Masera di P Italy
121 P4 Masères,L Quebec
89 E7 Maseru Lesotho
40 E2 Masevaux France
87 F9 Mashabe Zimbabwe
13 G5 Masham England
65 H2 Mashan China
67 C5 Mashan China
80 G1 Masharah Syria
80 E7 Mashash R Jordan
80 F2 Mashfa Syria
77 F1 Mashhad Iran
85 E7 Mashi R Nigeria
60 P2 Mashike Japan
77 E5 Mashīz Iran
77 H6 Mashkel R Pakistan
120 F5 Mashkode Ontario
89 C6 Mashowing watercourse S Africa
95 R5 Mashpee Massachusetts
60 S2 Mashū-ko L Japan
26 N2 Masi Norway
124 E4 Masiáca Mexico
86 C6 Masi-Manimba Zaïre
70 F5 Masimbu Sulawesi
86 F5 Masindi Uganda
71 D3 Masinloc Luzon Philippines
72 H4 Maşīrah isld Oman
77 B4 Masiri Iran
89 G5 Masitonto R S Africa
77 A4 Masjed Soleymān Iran
125 P9 Maskall Belize
121 R6 Maskinongé Quebec
14 B3 Mask,L Irish Rep
29 J11 Masku Finland
47 J2 Maslen Nos Bulgaria
55 D1 Maslovo U.S.S.R.
56 B4 Maslyanino U.S.S.R.
55 F3 Maslyanskoye U.S.S.R.
28 H7 Masnedssund Denmark
22 E3 Masnieres France
87 I11 Masoala, C Madagascar
110 H3 Mason Illinois
94 C4 Mason Michigan
102 E3 Mason Nevada
110 M2 Mason Ohio
98 C4 Mason S Dakota
110 G6 Mason Tennessee
109 H5 Mason Texas
99 P3 Mason Wisconsin
101 P7 Mason Wyoming
144 A7 Mason Bay New Zealand
99 R9 Mason City Illinois
99 N6 Mason City Iowa
98 G8 Mason City Nebraska
117 M7 Mason Creek Br Columbia
88 F3 Masongaleni Kenya
71 J5 Masoni isld Indonesia
143 C8 Mason, L W Australia
94 H7 Masontown Pennsylvania
94 H7 Masontown W Virginia
26 O1 Måsöy isld Norway
99 R3 Mass Michigan
44 H3 Massa Italy
95 P4 Massachusetts state U.S.A.
95 R4 Massachusetts B U.S.A.
45 H4 Massaciuccoli,L.di Italy
100 F8 Massacre L Nevada
80 F3 Massada Israel
106 B1 Massadona Colorado
45 M2 Massa Fiscáglia Italy
86 C3 Massaguet Chad
86 C3 Massakoti Chad
45 L3 Massa Lombarda Italy
45 Q8 Massa Lubrense Italy
42 D5 Massa Marittima Italy
87 F10 Massanga Mozambique
87 F10 Massangena Mozambique
94 J8 Massanutten Mt Virginia
129 K4 Massape Brazil
94 K8 Massaponax Virginia
45 H4 Massarosa Italy
18 F10 Massat France
55 D1 Massava U.S.S.R.
86 G2 Massawa Ethiopia
86 H2 Massawa Chan Ethiopia
21 I7 Massay France
37 J3 Massbach W Germany
99 M8 Massena Iowa
95 N2 Massena New York
86 C3 Massénya Chad
117 G9 Masset Br Col
18 F9 Masseube France
120 H6 Massey Ontario
18 H7 Massiac France
45 P7 Massico, M mt Italy
94 H9 Massies Mill Virginia
18 H7 Massif Central plat France
86 B4 Massif de l'Adamaoua mt Cameroon
18 F10 Massif de Néouvieille mt France
86 D4 Massif des Bongos mts Cent Afr Republic
19 Q18 Massif des Maures mts France
85 F4 Massif de Tarazit mts Niger
85 G5 Massif de Termit mts Niger
19 O15 Massif du Diois mts France
19 Q15 Massif du Pelvoux mts France
86 D4 Massif du Tondou mts Cent Afr Republic

Massillon — Merid 49

94 F6 **Massillon** Ohio
87 G10 **Massinga** Mozambique
89 G4 **Massingir** Mozambique
121 P7 **Masson** Quebec
80 C7 **Massu'a** Israel
74 B4 **Mastang** Pakistan
27 K14 **Mästerby** Sweden
145 E4 **Masterton** New Zealand
95 P6 **Mastic Beach** Long I, N Y
126 E2 **Mastic Point** Andros Bahamas
47 H6 **Mástikho,Akr** *C* Greece
37 P3 **Maštov** Czechoslovakia
74 E1 **Mastuj** Pakistan
60 E11 **Masuda** Japan
79 G3 **Masyáf** Syria
46 D3 **Mat** *R* Albania
68 F5 **Mat** *R* Thailand
133 C7 **Mata Amarilla** Argentina
89 E2 **Matabeleland** *reg* Zimbabwe
71 H4 **Matabulawa** *mt* Sulawesi
88 F8 **Mataca** Mozambique
120 K5 **Matachewan** Ontario
86 B7 **Matadi** Zaïre
118 K8 **Matador** Sask
108 G1 **Matador** Texas
125 M3 **Matagalpa** Nicaragua
115 M8 **Matagami** Quebec
109 M7 **Matagorda** Texas
109 L7 **Matagorda I** Texas
130 H10 **Mata Grande** Brazil
126 C3 **Matahambre** Cuba
145 F3 **Matahina** New Zealand
134 C12 **Mataiea** Tahiti I Pac Oc
145 F4 **Mataikona** New Zealand
145 E3 **Mataimoana** *mt* New Zealand
69 H11 **Matak** *isld* Indonesia
139 H5 **Matakana** New S Wales
145 E2 **Matakana** New Zealand
145 F2 **Matakana I** New Zealand
145 G2 **Matakaoa Pt** New Zealand
144 D5 **Matakitaki** *R* New Zealand
145 E2 **Matakohe** New Zealand
87 C8 **Matala** Angola
85 B5 **Matam** Senegal
145 E2 **Matamata** New Zealand
145 F4 **Matamau** New Zealand
85 F6 **Matameye** Niger
95 N5 **Matamoras** Pennsylvania
124 H5 **Matamoros** Coahuila Mexico
125 L5 **Matamoros** Tamaulipas Mexico
71 F7 **Matanal Pt** Philippines
86 D1 **Matan as Sarra** Libya
84 G5 **Ma'tan Bisharah** Libya
88 G6 **Matandu** *R* Tanzania
115 N8 **Matane** Quebec
122 F5 **Matane,Parc** Quebec
122 E5 **Matane R** Quebec
145 E2 **Matangi** New Zealand
145 E2 **Matangi I** New Zealand
113 J10 **Matanilla Reef** Bahamas
116 O6 **Matanuska** *mt* Alaska
126 D3 **Matanzas** Cuba
113 F8 **Matanzas Inlet** Florida
131 C6 **Matanzilla, Pampa de la** *plain* Argentina
129 H5 **Matão, Serra do** *mts* Brazil
Matapán, C Greece *see* **Taínaron, Akr**
122 F6 **Matapedia** Quebec
122 E5 **Matapedia L** Quebec
122 E5 **Matapedia R** Quebec
16 D3 **Matapozuelos** Spain
131 B5 **Mataquito** *R* Chile
83 K12 **Matara** Sri Lanka
70 Q10 **Mataram** Indonesia
128 D7 **Matarani** Peru
140 C2 **Mataranka** N Terr Aust
71 H6 **Matarape,Tk** *B* Sulawesi
17 J3 **Mataró** Spain
145 E3 **Mataroa** New Zealand
71 M9 **Mataru** Indonesia
17 F3 **Mata,Sierra de la** *mts* Spain
145 F2 **Matata** New Zealand
87 E12 **Matatiele** S Africa
144 B7 **Mataura** New Zealand
145 F3 **Matawai** New Zealand
121 R6 **Matawin** *R* Quebec
57 J2 **Matay** U.S.S.R.
57 E5 **Matcha** U.S.S.R.
121 N5 **Matchi-Manitou, L** Quebec
128 F6 **Mategua** Bolivia
125 J6 **Matehuala** Mexico
89 G3 **Mateke Hills** Zimbabwe
127 P1 **Matelot** Trinidad
145 E3 **Matemateaonga Ra** New Zealand
88 H8 **Matemo** *isld* Mozambique
43 H8 **Matera** Italy
45 Q7 **Matese** *L* Italy
45 Q7 **Matese, Monti del** *mts* Italy
48 G3 **Mátészalka** Hungary
43 C11 **Mateur** Tunisia
129 L7 **Mateus** Brazil
129 K7 **Mateus** *R* Brazil
94 E9 **Matewan** W Virginia
107 O3 **Matfield Green** Kansas
26 J9 **Matfors** Sweden
21 E10 **Matha** France
146 F14 **Matha Strait** Antarctica
102 E4 **Mather** California
94 G7 **Mather** Pennsylvania
74 E9 **Matheran** India
99 Q8 **Matherville** Illinois
106 G2 **Matheson** Colorado
120 K4 **Matheson** Ontario
119 V7 **Matheson Island** Manitoba
111 K9 **Mathews** Alabama
95 L9 **Mathews** Virginia
144 C5 **Mathias Pass** New Zealand
109 K7 **Mathis** Texas
108 G4 **Mathis Field** *airport* Texas
111 G8 **Mathiston** Mississippi
80 F8 **Mathlutha** Jordan
20 H2 **Mathonville** France
139 G6 **Mathoura** New S Wales
8 A4 **Mathry** Wales
74 G5 **Mathura** India
71 G7 **Mati** Mindanao Philippines
125 M9 **Matías Romero** Mexico
145 E3 **Matiere** New Zealand
22 E4 **Matigny** France
16 D4 **Matilla de los Caños del Rio** Spain
120 H6 **Matinenda L** Ontario
70 D7 **Matisiri** *isld* Indonesia
134 C13 **Matiti** Tahiti I Pac Oc
89 E5 **Matlabas** *R* S Africa
119 V8 **Matlock** Manitoba
100 B2 **Matlock** Washington
9 E1 **Matlock Bath** England
94 F9 **Matoaka** W Virginia
50 E1 **Matochkin Shar** U.S.S.R.
129 G6 **Mato Grosso** *reg* Brazil
130 D4 **Mato Grosso,Chapada de** *hills* Brazil
130 C7 **Mato Grosso do Sul** *state* Brazil
130 C4 **Mato Grosso,Planalto de** *plat* Brazil
122 C2 **Matonipi L** Quebec
122 C2 **Matonipis L** Quebec
89 F3 **Matopo Hills Nat. Park** Zimbabwe
87 E10 **Matopos Nat. Park** Zimbabwe
130 D10 **Matos Costa** Brazil
16 B3 **Matosinhos** Portugal
Matou *see* **Qiu Xian**
86 B6 **Matouti, Pto** Gabon
130 G4 **Mato Verde** Minas Gerais Brazil
48 F3 **Mátra** *mts* Hungary
72 H4 **Maṭraḥ** Oman
27 F11 **Matrand** Norway
83 K13 **Mât, R. du** Réunion Indian Ocean
27 A11 **Matre** Norway
41 O3 **Matrei am Brenner** Austria
89 A9 **Matroos Berg** *mt* S Africa
59 M2 **Matrosov** U.S.S.R.
84 H3 **Matrûh** Egypt
61 N10 **Matsudo** Japan
59 K4 **Matsue** Japan
60 O4 **Matsumae** Japan
61 L9 **Matsumoto** Japan
60 G11 **Matsunaga** Japan
61 M9 **Matsushiro** Japan
67 G3 **Ma-tsu Tao** *isld* Taiwan
61 K9 **Matsuto** Japan
60 C12 **Matsuura** Japan
61 P7 **Matsuyama** Honshu Japan
60 F12 **Matsuyama** Shikoku Japan
61 K11 **Matsuzaka** Japan
61 M11 **Matsuzaki** Japan
120 J4 **Mattagami Heights** Ontario
120 J5 **Mattagami L** Ontario
120 H2 **Mattagami R** Ontario
112 L2 **Mattamuskeet L** N Carolina
76 C6 **Mattancheri** India
95 K9 **Mattaponi** *R* Virginia
115 M8 **Mattawa** Ontario
95 T1 **Mattawamkeag** Maine
89 E3 **Mattengwe** *R* Botswana
100 H4 **Matterhorn** *mt* Oregon
40 G6 **Matterhorn** *mt* Switzerland
48 C3 **Mattersburg** Austria
137 P6 **Matthew** *isld* Pacific Oc
126 H4 **Matthew Town** Great Inagua I Bahamas
103 M7 **Matthie** Arizona
120 G3 **Mattice** Ontario
38 H5 **Mattig** *R* Austria
95 P6 **Mattituck** Long I, N Y
26 G8 **Mattmar** Sweden
102 A1 **Mattole** *R* California
99 S10 **Mattoon** Illinois
110 H4 **Mattoon** Kentucky
99 R4 **Mattoon** Wisconsin
113 E7 **Mattox** Georgia
115 K4 **Matty I** N W Terr
70 B3 **Matu** Sarawak
70 B6 **Matua** Kalimantan
128 C6 **Matucana** Peru
144 B6 **Matukituki** *R* New Zealand
77 L3 **Matūn** Afghanistan
145 D1 **Matupia I** New Zealand
127 P2 **Matura** Trinidad
127 N10 **Maturín** Venezuela
55 B4 **Matveyevka** U.S.S.R.
75 K6 **Mau** India
87 G8 **Maua** Mozambique
71 M9 **Maubara** Timor
18 F10 **Mauberme, Pic de** *mt* France/Spain
22 G4 **Maubert-Fontaine** France
22 F3 **Maubeuge** France
68 B4 **Maubin** Burma
18 E9 **Maubourguet** France
12 D3 **Mauchline** Scotland
94 A8 **Mauckport** Indiana
107 O6 **Maud** Oklahoma
109 N2 **Maud** Texas
146 B10 **Maudheim Vidda** Antarctica
101 O3 **Maudlow** Montana
90 J15 **Maud Seamount** S Atlantic Oc
87 F10 **Mau-é-ele** Mozambique
129 G4 **Maués** Brazil
134 A1 **Maugaafi** Western Samoa
94 K7 **Maugansville** Maryland
12 D5 **Maughold Hd** I of Man U.K.
135 T3 **Maui** *isld* Hawaiian Is
36 F6 **Maulbronn** W Germany
22 E3 **Maulde** France
20 J4 **Maule** France
131 A5 **Maule** *prov* Chile
131 B5 **Maule** *R* Chile
18 E9 **Mauléon Licharre** France
21 D7 **Maulévrier** France
14 B2 **Maumakeogh** *mt* Irish Rep
94 D5 **Maumee** Ohio
94 D5 **Maumee Bay** Michigan/Ohio
110 D7 **Maumelle, L** Arkansas
71 L9 **Maumere** Flores Indonesia
14 B3 **Maumturk Mts** Irish Rep
21 C7 **Maumusson** France
21 C10 **Maumusson, Pertuis de** *str* France
87 D9 **Maun** Botswana
135 U5 **Mauna Kea** *peak* Hawaiian Is
135 R2 **Mauna Loa** Hawaiian Is
135 U5 **Mauna Loa** *vol* Hawaiian Is
102 S12 **Maunalua Bay** Hawaiian Is
116 K3 **Mauneluk** *R* Alaska
145 F3 **Maungahaumi** *mt* New Zealand
145 E3 **Maungamangero** *mt* New Zealand
145 F3 **Maungapohatu** New Zealand
145 F3 **Maungataniwha** *mt* New Zealand
145 E1 **Maungatapere** New Zealand
145 E2 **Maungaturoto** New Zealand
144 B6 **Maungawera** New Zealand
68 A2 **Maungdaw** Burma
68 C5 **Maungmagan** *islds* Burma
114 G4 **Maunoir,L** N W Terr
138 D6 **Maupertuis B** S Australia
100 D4 **Maupin** Oregon
38 E7 **Maurach** Austria
19 Q16 **Maure,Col de** *pass* France
21 B6 **Maure de-Bretagne** France
111 F11 **Maurepas,L** Louisiana
18 G7 **Mauriac** France
145 E4 **Mauriceville** New Zealand
111 C11 **Mauriceville** Texas
19 Q14 **Maurienne** *dist* France
40 D7 **Maurienne** *V* France
98 D4 **Maurine** S Dakota
85 B4 **Mauritania** *rep* W Africa
83 L12 **Mauritius** Indian Oc
18 D4 **Mauron** France
18 G8 **Maurs** France
19 N17 **Maussane** France
99 Q6 **Mauston** Wisconsin
38 N5 **Mautern** Austria
38 J7 **Mauterndorf** Austria
38 L5 **Mauthausen** Austria
40 B2 **Maûtz** France
19 N14 **Mauves** France
18 F9 **Mauvezin** France
21 D9 **Mauzé** France
21 E8 **Mauzé-Thouarsais** France
128 E3 **Mavaca** *R* Venezuela
21 H6 **Maves-Pontijou** France
87 D9 **Mavinga** Angola
127 L2 **Mavis Bank** Jamaica
144 B6 **Mavora L, N** New Zealand
46 F5 **Mavrovqúni** *mt* Greece
88 D9 **Mavudzi** *R* Mozambique
88 C10 **Mavuradonha Mts** Zimbabwe
70 C4 **Mawa, Bt** *mt* Kalimantan
71 H7 **Mawasangka** Indonesia
68 C3 **Mawchi** Burma
68 D7 **Mawdaung** *pass* Burma/Thailand
119 R4 **Mawdesley L** Manitoba
118 L8 **Mawer** Sask
144 C5 **Mawheraiti** New Zealand
68 D4 **Mawkhi** Burma
68 C2 **Mawkmai** Burma
75 Q7 **Mawlaik** Burma
146 B4 **Mawson Coast** Antarctica
146 C5 **Mawson Escarpment** Antarctica
146 K4 **Mawson Pen** Antarctica
70 L9 **Mawuk** Java
98 E2 **Max** N Dakota
98 E9 **Max** Nebraska
98 E1 **Maxbass** N Dakota
21 A6 **Maxent** France
112 D4 **Maxeys** Georgia
117 M6 **Maxhamish L** Br Col
37 N5 **Maxhütte-Haidof** W Germany
36 E5 **Maximiliansau** W Germany
94 G10 **Max Meadows** Virginia
29 J8 **Maxmo** Finland
118 L9 **Maxstone** Sask
112 H3 **Maxton** N Carolina
113 E7 **Maxville** Florida
101 M3 **Maxville** Montana
121 Q7 **Maxville** Ontario
102 B2 **Maxwell** California
99 N8 **Maxwell** Iowa
98 F8 **Maxwell** Nebraska
106 F5 **Maxwell** New Mexico
12 E3 **Maxwelltown** Scotland
141 G5 **Maxwelton** Queensland
101 M5 **May** Idaho
108 E7 **May** Oklahoma
109 J4 **May** Texas
59 K1 **Maya** *R* U.S.S.R.
55 C4 **Mayachnyy** U.S.S.R.
126 H3 **Mayaguana Passage** Bahamas
127 L5 **Mayagüez** Puerto Rico
85 F6 **Mayahi** Niger
55 C5 **Mayak** U.S.S.R.
31 M1 **Mayak** *lt ho* U.S.S.R.
17 H3 **Mayals** Spain
77 D1 **Mayamey** Iran
80 D3 **May 'Ami** Israel
125 P9 **Maya Mts** Belize
67 C3 **Mayang** China
126 G4 **Mayari** Cuba
127 P3 **Mayaro** *co* Trinidad
94 D4 **Maybee** Michigan
106 B1 **Maybell** Colorado
12 D3 **Maybole** Scotland
77 L2 **Maydan** Afghanistan
127 K3 **May Day Mts** Jamaica
109 M4 **Maydelle** Texas
139 H9 **Maydena** Tasmania
36 C3 **Mayen** W Germany
20 D5 **Mayenne** France
20 D5 **Mayenne** *dep* France
103 M7 **Mayer** Arizona
118 B5 **Mayerthorpe** Alberta
112 G4 **Mayesville** S Carolina
21 F6 **Mayet** France
107 P2 **Mayetta** Kansas
118 K5 **Mayfair** Sask
9 G5 **Mayfield** E Sussex England
100 K6 **Mayfield** Idaho
110 H5 **Mayfield** Kentucky
144 C5 **Mayfield** New Zealand
107 L6 **Mayfield** Oklahoma
95 M5 **Mayfield** Pennsylvania
141 G7 **Mayfield** Queensland
9 E1 **Mayfield** Staffs England
103 N2 **Mayfield** Utah
110 D7 **Mayflower** Arkansas
111 H8 **Mayhew** Mississippi
106 E9 **Mayhill** New Mexico
65 G2 **Mayi He** *R* China
13 F1 **May, I. of** Scotland
55 G5 **Maykain** U.S.S.R.
57 H2 **Maykamys** U.S.S.R.
53 F11 **Maykop** U.S.S.R.
52 J5 **Maykor** U.S.S.R.
110 L5 **Mayland** Tennessee
142 B1 **Maylands** *dist* Perth, W Aust
57 C2 **Maylibash** U.S.S.R.
57 L2 **Mayli, Khrebet** *mts* U.S.S.R.
57 D2 **Maylykum** U.S.S.R.
57 F3 **Maymak** U.S.S.R.
118 K6 **Maymont** Sask
68 C1 **Maymyo** Burma
99 P7 **Maynard** Iowa
143 C8 **Maynard Hills** W Australia
141 F6 **Mayne** *R* Queensland
14 E3 **Maynooth** Irish Rep
121 N7 **Maynooth** Ontario
51 R2 **Maynopilgyn** U.S.S.R.
113 D7 **Mayo** Florida
95 L8 **Mayo** Maryland
117 F4 **Mayo** Yukon Terr
14 B3 **Mayo** *co* Irish Rep
128 C5 **Mayo** *R* Peru
71 G7 **Mayo B** Mindanao Philippines
86 B4 **Mayo Daga** Nigeria
94 G10 **Mayodan** N Carolina
71 F4 **Mayon** *mt* Philippines
17 F4 **Mayor** *R* Spain
16 D2 **Mayorga** Spain
145 F2 **Mayor I** New Zealand
133 E2 **Mayor Pablo Lagerenza** Paraguay
87 H10 **Mayotte** *isld* Comoros
127 K3 **May Pen** Jamaica
113 F7 **Mayport** Florida
142 E3 **May R** W Australia
71 E1 **Mayraira Pt** Luzon Philippines
38 E7 **Mayrhofen** Austria
79 F5 **Mayrouba** Lebanon
55 G2 **Maysk** U.S.S.R.
59 J1 **Mayskiy** U.S.S.R.
55 G5 **Mayskoye** U.S.S.R.
95 N7 **Mays Landing** New Jersey
112 D3 **Maysville** Georgia
94 D8 **Maysville** Kentucky
99 M10 **Maysville** Missouri
112 K3 **Maysville** N Carolina
107 N7 **Maysville** Oklahoma
71 D5 **Maytiguid** Philippines
141 G3 **Maytown** Queensland
68 A2 **Mayu** *R* Burma
86 B6 **Mayumba** Gabon
94 D3 **Mayville** Michigan
98 J2 **Mayville** N Dakota
94 H4 **Mayville** New York
100 E4 **Mayville** Oregon
99 S6 **Mayville** Wisconsin
98 F9 **Maywood** Nebraska
133 E5 **Maza** Argentina
98 G1 **Maza** N Dakota
88 A9 **Mazabuka** Zambia
129 H4 **Mazagão** Brazil
22 H5 **Mazagram** France
47 G2 **Mazalat** *mt* Bulgaria
100 E1 **Mazama** Washington
18 G9 **Mazamet** France
77 B1 **Mazandaran** Iran
124 J5 **Mazapil** Mexico
79 F7 **Mazār** Jordan
43 E11 **Mazara del Vallo** Sicily
16 D9 **Mazari,C** Morocco
77 K1 **Mazar-i-Sharif** Afghanistan
133 D7 **Mazarredo** Argentina
17 G7 **Mazarrón** Spain
80 F8 **Mazar Saiyidna Suleiman** Jordan
128 F2 **Mazaruni** *R* Guyana
124 D3 **Mazatán** Mexico
125 O10 **Mazatenango** Guatemala
124 F6 **Mazatlán** Mexico
103 N7 **Mazatzal Pk** Arizona
77 B3 **Mazdaj** Iran
52 B6 **Mazeikiai** U.S.S.R.
118 D8 **Mazeppa** Alberta
21 F7 **Mazières** France
21 E8 **Mazieres-en-Gatine** France
52 B5 **Mazirbe** U.S.S.R.
80 C6 **Mazliaḥ** Israel
89 G1 **Mazoe** Zimbabwe
88 C10 **Mazoe** *R* Zimbabwe
99 R6 **Mazomanie** Wisconsin
99 S8 **Mazon** Illinois
80 F8 **Mazra'** Jordan
86 E3 **Mazrub** Sudan
87 E10 **Mazunga** Zimbabwe
22 H4 **Mazures, les** France
31 M2 **Mazury** *reg* Poland
89 G6 **Mbabane** Swaziland
86 C5 **Mbaéré** *R* Cent Afr Republic
85 D7 **Mbahiakro** Ivory Coast
86 C5 **Mbaïki** Cent Afr Republic
88 C6 **Mbala** Zambia
86 F5 **Mbale** Uganda
86 B5 **Mbalmayo** Cameroon
86 B4 **Mbam** *R* Cameroon
87 F8 **Mbamba B** Tanzania
86 C5 **Mbandaka** Zaïre
85 F8 **Mbanga** Cameroon
86 B6 **M'Banio, L** Gabon
86 B7 **Mbanza-Ngungu** Zaïre
88 C2 **Mbarara** Uganda
88 F6 **Mbarika** *mt* Tanzania
88 G6 **Mbemkuru** *R* Tanzania
88 D6 **Mbeya** Tanzania
88 D6 **Mbeya** *mt* Tanzania
85 G8 **Mbini** *prov* Eq Guinea
87 F10 **Mbizi** Zimbabwe
86 C4 **Mbo** Cent Afr Republic
85 A6 **Mbour** Senegal
85 B5 **Mbout** Mauritania
87 B7 **M'Bridge** *R* Angola
86 D7 **Mbuji Mayi** Zaïre
86 F5 **Mbulamuti** Uganda
88 E3 **Mbulu** Tanzania
88 F6 **Mbungu** Tanzania
133 F3 **Mburucuyá** Argentina
88 G6 **Mchinja** Tanzania
88 D8 **Mchinji** Malawi
117 F5 **M'Clintock** Yukon Terr
115 M1 **M'Clintock, C** N W Terr
115 L1 **M'Clintock Inlet** N W Terr
85 C3 **Mdakane, Hassi** Algeria
43 B12 **M'Daourouch** Algeria
85 C4 **Mdennah** Mali/Mauritania
68 J6 **Mdrak** Vietnam
71 C3 **Me** *isld* Indonesia
100 G4 **Meacham** Oregon
119 M6 **Meacham** Sask
120 G3 **Mead** Ontario
100 H2 **Mead** Washington
107 K4 **Meade** Kansas
116 K1 **Meade** *R* Alaska
101 O7 **Meade Pk** Idaho
103 K5 **Mead,L** Nev/Ariz
103 K6 **Mead, L. National Recreational Area** Arizona
98 D4 **Meadow** S Dakota
108 E2 **Meadow** Texas
143 A7 **Meadow** W Australia
94 G9 **Meadow Bridge** W Virginia
109 M9 **Meadowbrook** Texas
94 G9 **Meadow Creek** W Virginia
98 B7 **Meadowdale** Wyoming
118 J4 **Meadow Lake** Sask
99 O2 **Meadowlands** Minnesota
118 H4 **Meadow L. Prov. Park** Sask
119 S7 **Meadow Portage** Manitoba
100 J5 **Meadows** Idaho
103 K4 **Meadow Val.Mts** Nevada
103 K5 **Meadow Val.Wash** *R* Nevada
110 C2 **Meadville** Missouri
98 G7 **Meadville** Nebraska
94 G5 **Meadville** Pennsylvania
120 K8 **Meaford** Ontario
122 J9 **Meaghers Grant** Nova Scotia
60 R2 **Me-akan dake** *mt* Japan
16 B4 **Mealhada** Portugal
13 E4 **Mealsgate** England
115 N7 **Mealy Mts** Labrador
141 J7 **Meandarra** Queensland
117 P6 **Meander River** Alberta
100 B4 **Meares,Cape** Oregon
80 C3 **Me 'Arot Karmel** Israel
99 U6 **Mears** Michigan
15 C3 **Measach Falls** Scotland
9 E2 **Measham** England
14 E3 **Meath** *co* Irish Rep
119 M5 **Meath Park** Sask
18 G4 **Meaux** France
112 H1 **Mebane** N Carolina
17 G9 **Mebtoub** *R* Algeria
70 P10 **Mebulu,Tg** *C* Bali Indonesia
101 S2 **Mecaha** Montana
123 O3 **Mecatina I.,Gt** Quebec
123 N3 **Mecatina I.,Little** Quebec
123 M1 **Mecatina,Riv.du Petite** Quebec
103 H8 **Mecca** California
86 G1 **Mecca** Saudi Arabia
95 R2 **Mechanic Falls** Maine
94 D6 **Mechanicsburg** Ohio
95 K6 **Mechanicsburg** Pennsylvania
95 L8 **Mechanicsville** Maryland
95 O4 **Mechanicville** New York
111 F12 **Mechant,L** Louisiana
22 G1 **Mechelen** Belgium
85 D2 **Mecheria** Algeria
36 B2 **Mechernich** W Germany
122 F5 **Méchins,Les** Quebec
37 Q3 **Mecholupy** Czechoslovakia
33 M6 **Mechtersen** W Germany
47 H4 **Mecidiye** Turkey
37 P5 **Měčin** Czechoslovakia
41 L2 **Meckenbeuren** W Germany
36 C2 **Meckenheim** W Germany
36 E5 **Meckenheim** W Germany
36 F5 **Meckesheim** W Germany
33 O5 **Mecklenburg** E Germany
30 F1 **Mecklenburger Bucht** *B* W Germany
88 G9 **Meconta** Mozambique
94 B3 **Mecosta** Michigan
48 E4 **Mecsek** *mts* Hungary
88 G9 **Mecuburi** *R* Mozambique
88 H8 **Mecufi** Mozambique
87 G8 **Mecula** Mozambique
16 C4 **Meda** Portugal
74 H9 **Medak** India
42 G4 **Medak** Yugoslavia
69 D11 **Medan** Sumatra
71 H9 **Medang** *isld* Indonesia
124 D4 **Médano** Mexico
133 E5 **Médanos** Argentina
133 D7 **Medanosa,Pta** Argentina
99 U8 **Medaryville** Indiana
17 K2 **Medas** *isld* Spain
83 K9 **Medawachchiya** Sri Lanka
144 D5 **Medbury** New Zealand
95 U1 **Meddybemps L** Maine
85 E1 **Médéa** Algeria
36 F1 **Medebach** W Germany
41 J4 **Medel** *mt* Switzerland
28 C7 **Medelby** W Germany
128 C2 **Medellín** Colombia
32 J5 **Medem** *R* W Germany
25 D3 **Medemblik** Netherlands
85 G2 **Medenine** Tunisia
85 A5 **Mederdra** Mauritania
22 L4 **Medernach** Luxembourg
95 Q4 **Medford** Massachusetts
107 N5 **Medford** Oklahoma
100 C7 **Medford** Oregon
99 Q4 **Medford** Wisconsin
116 K5 **Medfra** Alaska
48 L6 **Medgidia** Romania
99 P8 **Mediapolis** Iowa
48 J4 **Mediaş** Romania
100 H2 **Medical Lake** Washington
45 L3 **Medicina** Italy
101 T8 **Medicine Bow** Wyoming
101 T8 **Medicine Bow** *R* Wyoming
106 D1 **Medicine Bow Mts** Wyo/Colo
101 T8 **Medicine Bow Pk** Wyoming
118 G8 **Medicine Hat** Alberta
100 D8 **Medicine L** California
98 B1 **Medicine L** Montana
107 M4 **Medicine Lodge** Kansas
109 H1 **Medicine Mound** Texas
118 C6 **Medicine R** Alberta
98 B3 **Medicine Rocks** Montana
130 H5 **Medina** Brazil
98 G3 **Medina** N Dakota
94 J3 **Medina** New York
94 F5 **Medina** Ohio
72 D4 **Medina** Saudi Arabia
110 H6 **Medina** Tennessee
109 H6 **Medina** Texas
143 B9 **Medina** W Australia
17 F3 **Medinaceli** Spain
16 D3 **Medina de Campo** Spain
16 D3 **Medina de Rioseco** Spain
131 F2 **Medina,L** Argentina
16 D8 **Medina Sidonia** Spain
33 N6 **Medingen** W Germany
84 F2 **Mediterranean Sea** Europe/Africa
85 F1 **Medjerda** *R* Tunisia
43 B12 **Medjerda, Monts de la** Algeria/Tunisia
118 G4 **Medley** Alberta
55 C5 **Mednogorsk** U.S.S.R.
18 E7 **Medoc** *reg* France
45 J1 **Médole** Italy
110 H6 **Medon** Tennessee
110 F2 **Medora** Illinois
107 N3 **Medora** Kansas
119 R9 **Medora** Manitoba
98 C3 **Medora** N Dakota
86 B5 **Medounou** Gabon
20 A5 **Médréac** France
118 J5 **Medstead** Sask
122 E8 **Meductic** New Brunswick
Medu Kongkar *see* **Maizhokunggar**
46 E2 **Medveda** Yugoslavia
55 E2 **Medvedchikovo** U.S.S.R.
52 H6 **Medvedok** U.S.S.R.
51 J1 **Medvezhiy Yar** U.S.S.R.
59 L2 **Medvezh'ya, Gora** *mt* U.S.S.R.
55 F3 **Medvezh'ye** U.S.S.R.
52 D3 **Medvezh'yegorsk** U.S.S.R.
52 E6 **Medvyeditsa** *R* U.S.S.R.
95 T1 **Medway** Maine
9 G5 **Medway,R** England
83 M9 **Medwin Pt** Christmas I Indian Oc
54 G2 **Medyn** U.S.S.R.
48 L1 **Medzhibozh** U.S.S.R.
31 N6 **Medzilaborce** Czechoslovakia
141 L1 **Meeandah** *dist* Brisbane, Qnsld
143 B7 **Meeberrie** W Australia
37 K3 **Meeder** W Germany
143 C7 **Meekatharra** W Australia
106 C1 **Meeker** Colorado
107 O6 **Meeker** Oklahoma
123 Q5 **Meelpaeg L** Newfoundland
37 N2 **Meerane** E Germany
36 B3 **Meerfeld** W Germany
25 F5 **Meerlo** Netherlands
25 E7 **Meerssen** Netherlands
74 G4 **Meerut** India
101 R5 **Meeteetse** Wyoming
118 E6 **Meeting Cr** Alberta
14 E4 **Meeting of the Waters** Irish Rep
118 K5 **Meetoos** Sask
33 R5 **Meetschow** E Germany
22 K1 **Meeuwen** Belgium
80 B7 **Mefallesim** Israel
86 G5 **Mega** Ethiopia
71 C3 **Mega** W Irian
69 E14 **Mega** *isld* Indonesia
80 C3 **Megadim** Israel
18 H7 **Megal** *mt* France
47 J8 **Megálo Khorió** Tílos I Greece
46 E7 **Megalópolis** Greece
46 D6 **Meganisi** *mt* Greece
122 B8 **Mégantic** Quebec
122 B8 **Megantic,L** Quebec
47 F6 **Mégara** Greece
109 J2 **Megargel** Texas
46 E5 **Mégdhova** *R* Greece
25 E5 **Megen** Netherlands
40 E6 **Megève** France
36 E1 **Meggen** W Germany
112 G5 **Meggett** S Carolina
85 F2 **Meghaiër, El** Algeria
75 O6 **Meghalaya** *prov* India
75 O6 **Meghna** *R* Bangladesh
121 P4 **Mégiscane, L** Quebec
100 B3 **Megler** Washington
52 F2 **Megra** Arkhangelsk U.S.S.R.
52 E4 **Megra** Vologda U.S.S.R.
48 G6 **Mehadia** Romania
70 D6 **Mehakit** Kalimantan
26 Q1 **Mehamn** Norway
48 H6 **Mehedinti** *reg* Romania
94 J9 **Meherrin** Virginia
94 J10 **Meherrin** *R* Virginia
37 N2 **Mehitheuer** E Germany
74 G8 **Mehkar** India
75 K5 **Mehndawal** India
78 L5 **Mehran** Iran
36 B3 **Mehren** W Germany
36 B4 **Mehring** W Germany
77 D4 **Mehriz** Iran
21 J7 **Mehun sur Yèvre** France
130 E5 **Meia Ponte,R** Brazil
67 D2 **Meichengzhen** China
67 E1 **Meichuan** China
8 C2 **Meifod** Wales
86 B4 **Meiganga** Cameroon
114 K1 **Meighen I** N W Terr
112 C6 **Meigs** Georgia
25 E6 **Meijel** Netherlands
67 E5 **Mei Jiang** *R* China
117 O7 **Meikle** *R* Alberta
68 B2 **Meiktila** Burma
Meilin *see* **Gan Xian**
20 B5 **Meillac** France
117 L5 **Meilleur Cr** N W Terr
33 N8 **Meine** W Germany
33 M8 **Meinersen** W Germany
36 D1 **Meinerzhagen** W Germany
37 J2 **Meiningen** E Germany
16 C1 **Meira, Sa. de** *mts* Spain
41 H4 **Meiringen** Switzerland
80 C3 **Me'ir Shefeya** Israel
36 D4 **Meisenheim** W Germany
67 A1 **Meisham** China
Meishan *see* **Jinzhai**
67 E1 **Meishan Shuiku** *res* China
37 P1 **Meissen** E Germany
32 L7 **Meissendorf** W Germany
36 H1 **Meissner** *mt* W Germany
67 B3 **Meitan** China
37 K6 **Meitingen** W Germany
67 E4 **Mei Xian** China
65 E2 **Meiyao** China
43 C12 **Mejerda** *R* Tunisia
43 C12 **Mejez el-Bab** Tunisia
133 C2 **Mejillones** Chile
28 B4 **Mejrup** Denmark
86 B5 **Mekambo** Gabon
120 F5 **Mekatina** Ontario
55 D3 **Mekhonskoye** U.S.S.R.
74 C3 **Mekhtar** Pakistan
98 J1 **Mekinock** N Dakota
85 C2 **Meknès** Morocco
68 G6 **Mekong** *R* S E Asia
70 G6 **Mekongga, G** *mt* Sulawesi
70 G7 **Mekongga, Tk** *B* Sulawesi
69 H8 **Mekong, Mouths of the** Vietnam
116 D6 **Mekoryuk** Alaska
85 E6 **Mekrou** *R* Benin/Niger
69 F11 **Melaka** Malaysia
47 G9 **Mélambes** Crete Greece
134 E8 **Melanesia** Pac Oc
137 P4 **Melanesian Border Plat** Pacific Oc
70 D2 **Melapap** Sabah
70 E2 **Melaut** *mt* Sabah
118 L9 **Melaval** Sask
70 C5 **Melawi** *R* Kalimantan
21 D7 **Melay** France
100 J6 **Melba** Idaho
33 M6 **Melbeck** W Germany
9 G3 **Melbourn** England
9 E2 **Melbourne** England
113 G9 **Melbourne** Florida
99 N8 **Melbourne** Iowa
138 C7 **Melbourne** Victoria
113 G9 **Melbourne Beach** Florida
26 G3 **Melbu** Norway
28 H5 **Melby** Denmark
99 N8 **Melcher** Iowa
120 D2 **Melchett L** Ontario
124 J5 **Melchor Ocampo** Coahuila Mexico
124 H8 **Melchor Ocampo** Michigan Mexico
26 D8 **Meldal** Norway
26 M6 **Melderstein** Sweden
45 M3 **Meldola** Italy
32 K4 **Meldorf** W Germany
112 F5 **Meldrim** Georgia
120 G7 **Meldrum Bay** Ontario
80 D3 **Melea** Israel
119 U8 **Meleb** Manitoba
44 F1 **Melegnano** Italy
47 G9 **Melékhas, Akr** *C* Crete Greece
52 J5 **Melekhina** U.S.S.R.
87 G9 **Melela** *R* Mozambique
70 O10 **Meleman** Java
52 F6 **Melenki** U.S.S.R.
55 D3 **Melent'yevskoye** U.S.S.R.
20 B5 **Melesse** France
20 F5 **Mêle-sur-Sarthe, le** France
55 C4 **Meleuz** U.S.S.R.
95 M9 **Melfa** Virginia
45 P6 **Melfa** *R* Italy
86 C3 **Melfi** Chad
43 G8 **Melfi** Italy
114 J7 **Melfort** Sask
28 E2 **Melholt** Denmark
26 D8 **Melhus** Norway
36 F4 **Melibocus** *mt* W Germany
20 G4 **Melicourt** France
130 E9 **Mel, I. do** Brazil
46 E7 **Meligalá** Greece
71 H5 **Melilis** *isld* Indonesia
85 D1 **Melilla** *Span exclave* Morocco
133 C6 **Melimoyu** *mt* Chile
144 B6 **Melina, Mt** New Zealand
48 H6 **Melineşti** Romania
70 E5 **Melintang, D** *L* Kalimantan
133 C4 **Melipilla** Chile
119 R9 **Melita** Manitoba
43 G11 **Melito di Porto Salvo** Italy
54 G10 **Melitopol'** U.S.S.R.
38 M5 **Melk** Austria
8 D5 **Melksham** England
44 H1 **Mella** *R* Italy
26 H9 **Mellansjö** Sweden
22 F2 **Melle** Belgium
21 E9 **Melle** France
32 H8 **Melle** W Germany
43 B12 **Mellégue** *R* Tunisia
99 Q3 **Mellen** Wisconsin
32 L7 **Mellendorf** W Germany
27 F13 **Mellerud** Sweden
18 E6 **Melle S. Bretonne** France
98 H4 **Mellette** S Dakota
16 B2 **Mellid** Spain
22 K4 **Mellier** Belgium
37 L2 **Mellingen** E Germany
137 M5 **Mellish Rise** Coral Sea
86 E3 **Mellit** Sudan
13 F6 **Mellor Brook** England
32 H5 **Mellun** *isld* W Germany
111 E7 **Mellwood** Arkansas
13 F4 **Melmerby** England
47 F3 **Melnik** Bulgaria
31 H5 **Mělník** Czechoslovakia
48 K2 **Melnitsa Podolskaya** U.S.S.R.
131 G4 **Melo** Uruguay
52 G2 **Melogorskoye** U.S.S.R.
71 K9 **Melolo** Sumba Indonesia
102 D4 **Melones Res** California
54 M7 **Melovoye** U.S.S.R.
26 F5 **Melöy** Norway
116 K4 **Melozitna** *R* Alaska
22 J3 **Melreux** Belgium
17 G9 **Melrir** *R* Algeria
100 J3 **Melrose** Idaho
99 M4 **Melrose** Minnesota
101 N4 **Melrose** Montana
106 G7 **Melrose** New Mexico
123 K8 **Melrose** Nova Scotia
100 B6 **Melrose** Oregon
13 F2 **Melrose** Scotland
143 D8 **Melrose** W Australia
99 P5 **Melrose** Wisconsin
87 F9 **Melsetter** Zimbabwe
101 S3 **Melstone** Montana
99 U3 **Melstrand** Michigan
36 H1 **Melsungen** W Germany
70 E2 **Melta, Mt** Sabah
29 L5 **Meltaus** Finland
13 G6 **Meltham** England
9 F2 **Melton Mowbray** England
88 G10 **Meluli** *R* Mozambique
68 A2 **Melun** Burma
18 G4 **Melun** France
86 F3 **Melut** Sudan
107 P3 **Melvern** Kansas
15 E2 **Melvich** Scotland
111 E11 **Melville** Louisiana
101 Q3 **Melville** Montana
98 G2 **Melville** N Dakota
119 P8 **Melville** Sask
140 D1 **Melville B** N Terr Aust
115 N2 **Melville Bugt** *B* Greenland
141 G2 **Melville, C** Queensland
71 C6 **Melville, Cape** Philippines
114 G4 **Melville Hills** N W Terr
140 B1 **Melville I** N Terr Aust
114 H2 **Melville I** N W Terr
115 O7 **Melville, L** Labrador
115 L4 **Melville Pen** N W Terr
142 A1 **Melville Water** *B* Perth, W Aust
109 H4 **Melvin** Texas
14 C2 **Melvin, L** Irish Rep
119 R1 **Melvin L** Manitoba
48 E4 **Mélykút** Hungary
70 C5 **Memala** Kalimantan
68 H6 **Meman** Cambodia
88 H9 **Memba** Mozambique
79 H2 **Membij** Syria
71 J9 **Memboro** Sumba Indonesia
22 H4 **Membre** France
Memel *see* **Klaipeda**
32 E5 **Memmert** *isld* W Germany
41 M2 **Memmingen** W Germany
70 D2 **Mempakul** Sabah
99 O9 **Memphis** Missouri
110 G6 **Memphis** Tennessee
108 G1 **Memphis** Texas
84 J4 **Memphis** *ruins* Egypt
121 S8 **Memphremagog, L** Vermont
122 H7 **Memramcook** New Brunswick
60 R3 **Memuro** Japan
110 B7 **Mena** Arkansas
71 M9 **Ména** Timor Indonesia
54 D5 **Mena** U.S.S.R.
80 F3 **Menaḥemya** Israel
99 L3 **Menahga** Minnesota
8 B1 **Menai Str** Wales
85 E5 **Menaka** Mali
101 O4 **Menard** Montana
108 H5 **Menard** Texas
99 S5 **Menasha** Wisconsin
123 L2 **Menaskwagama, L** Quebec
45 M2 **Menate** Italy
70 C5 **Menate** Kalimantan
69 H14 **Mendanau** *isld* Indonesia
130 G6 **Mendanha** Brazil
69 H12 **Mendarik** Indonesia
70 C6 **Mendawai** Kalimantan
18 H8 **Mende** France
86 G4 **Mendebo Mts** Ethiopia
56 D3 **Mendel'** *R* U.S.S.R.
32 G10 **Menden** W Germany
111 G10 **Mendenhall** Mississippi
116 D7 **Mendenhall, C** Alaska
47 K6 **Menderes** *R* Turkey
55 E5 **Mendesh** U.S.S.R.
71 E3 **Mendez-Nuñez** Luzon Philippines
118 H8 **Mendham** Sask
136 J3 **Mendi** Papua New Guinea
8 D5 **Mendip Hills** England
143 D8 **Mendleyarri** W Australia
100 A9 **Mendocino, C** California
135 N4 **Mendocino Seascarp** Pacific Oc
94 B4 **Mendon** Michigan
110 M1 **Mendon** Ohio
139 J4 **Mendooran** New S Wales
102 D5 **Mendota** California
99 R8 **Mendota** Illinois
108 D8 **Mendota** Texas
99 R6 **Mendota, L** Wisconsin
131 C4 **Mendoza** Argentina
128 C5 **Mendoza** Peru
131 C5 **Mendoza** *prov* Argentina
16 B6 **Mendro** *mt* Portugal
69 F12 **Mendung** Sumatra
44 G2 **Menegosa** *mt* Italy
127 J10 **Mene Grande** Venezuela
47 J6 **Menemen** Turkey
22 E2 **Menen** Belgium
47 J9 **Menetai** Kárpathos I Greece
21 J7 **Ménétréol-sous-Sancerre** France
43 E11 **Menfi** Sicily
70 D1 **Mengalum** *isld* S China Sea
58 G5 **Mengcheng** China
65 D5 **Mengcun** China
41 K1 **Mengen** W Germany
32 J10 **Mengeringhausen** W Germany
36 E2 **Mengerskirchen** W Germany
70 K8 **Menggala** Sumatra
68 E2 **Menghai** China
65 H1 **Mengjiagang** China
67 C5 **Mengjiang** China
65 A5 **Mengjiawan** China
65 B7 **Mengjin** China
70 B4 **Mengkiang** *R* Kalimantan
37 N6 **Mengkofen** W Germany
68 E2 **Mengla** China
68 D1 **Menglian** China
68 E1 **Meng man** China
67 C4 **Mengshan** China
68 E1 **Mengwang** China
65 B7 **Meng Xian** China
65 D7 **Mengyin** China
68 E2 **Mengyuan** China
67 A5 **Mengzi** China
21 E9 **Ménigoute** France
115 N7 **Menihek, Lac** Labrador
83 L11 **Menik Ganga** *R* Sri Lanka
20 H3 **Menilles** France
36 B7 **Ménil-sur-Bélvitte** France
Menin *see* **Menen**
139 G4 **Menindee** New S Wales
138 E6 **Meningie** S Australia
70 E4 **Menjapa, Gt** *mt* Kalimantan
51 M2 **Menkere** U.S.S.R.
112 B3 **Menlo** Georgia
99 M8 **Menlo** Iowa
107 K2 **Menlo** Kansas
102 B4 **Menlo Pk** California
20 K4 **Mennecy** France
21 I7 **Mennetou-sur-Cher** France
98 J6 **Menno** S Dakota
12 E3 **Mennock P** Scotland
99 T4 **Menominee** *R* Michigan
99 S6 **Menomonee Falls** Wisconsin
99 P5 **Menomonie** Wisconsin
17 K4 **Menorca** *isld* Balearic Is
55 G3 **Men'shchikovo** U.S.S.R.
66 C5 **Men-shih** China
32 G7 **Menslage** W Germany
12 E1 **Menstrie** Scotland
28 H6 **Menstrup** Denmark
70 C5 **Mentaja** *R* Kalimantan
69 F11 **Mentakab** Malaysia
45 N5 **Mentana** Italy
70 E2 **Mentapok** Sabah
70 E3 **Mentarang** *R* Kalimantan
116 Q5 **Mentasta Mts** Alaska
73 Q9 **Mentawai, Kep** *islds* Indonesia
69 G14 **Mentok** Sumatra
44 B4 **Menton** France
94 A5 **Mentone** Indiana
108 D4 **Mentone** Texas
98 K2 **Mentor** Minnesota
94 F5 **Mentor** Ohio
70 C5 **Mentubar** *R* Kalimantan
89 D9 **Mentz, L** S Africa
58 E2 **Menza** *R* Mongolia
56 G5 **Menza** *R* U.S.S.R.
43 C11 **Menzel Bourguiba** Tunisia
52 H6 **Menzelinsk** U.S.S.R.
43 D12 **Menzel Temime** Tunisia
143 D8 **Menzies** W Australia
146 C5 **Menzies, Mt** Antarctica
Menzingen *see* **Kraichtal**
9 G5 **Meopham** England
124 G3 **Meoqui** Mexico
118 J5 **Meota** Sask
25 F3 **Meppel** Netherlands
32 F7 **Meppen** W Germany
17 H3 **Mequinenza** Spain
21 I6 **Mer** France
52 F5 **Mera** *R* U.S.S.R.
47 H9 **Merabéllou, Kólpos** *B* Crete Greece
70 E4 **Merah** Kalimantan
70 K8 **Merak** Java
26 E8 **Meråker** Norway
137 O4 **Mera Lava** *isld* New Hebrides
138 B3 **Meramangye, L** S Australia
110 F3 **Meramec Park** Missouri
Meran *see* **Merano**
41 O4 **Merano** Italy
70 P9 **Merapi, G** *mt* Java
123 S6 **Merasheen** Newfoundland
70 D6 **Meratus, Peg** *mts* Kalimantan
136 J3 **Merauke** W Irian
69 F12 **Merbau** Sumatra
138 F5 **Merbein** Victoria
22 G3 **Merbes-le-Château** Belgium
70 P10 **Merbuk** *mt* Indonesia
86 H5 **Merca** Somalia
76 B4 **Mercara** India
45 M4 **Mercato Saraceno** Italy
102 D4 **Merced** California
102 D4 **Merced** *R* California
131 B3 **Mercedario, Cerro** *mt* Chile/Arg
131 D4 **Mercedes** Argentina
131 F5 **Mercedes** Buenos Aires Argentina
131 F2 **Mercedes** Corrientes Argentina
109 K9 **Mercedes** Texas
131 F4 **Mercedes** Uruguay
133 C3 **Merceditas** Chile
99 N9 **Mercer** Missouri
98 F2 **Mercer** N Dakota
145 E2 **Mercer** New Zealand
94 G5 **Mercer** Pennsylvania
110 H6 **Mercer** Tennessee
99 Q3 **Mercer** Wisconsin
94 J7 **Mercersburg** Pennsylvania
22 G2 **Merchtem** Belgium
121 O6 **Mercier Dam** Quebec
117 P9 **Mercoal** Alberta
45 R8 **Mercogliano** Italy
103 M1 **Mercur** Utah
48 H5 **Mercurea** Romania
109 H4 **Mercury** Texas
19 Q13 **Mercury-Gemilly** France
145 E2 **Mercury Is** New Zealand
114 H3 **Mercy B** N W Terr
115 N5 **Mercy, C** N W Terr
20 C3 **Merderet** *R* France
18 D4 **Merdrignac** France
8 D5 **Mere** England
133 E8 **Meredith, C** Falkland Is
95 Q3 **Meredith Hill** New Hampshire
108 C8 **Meredith, L** Texas
99 Q10 **Meredosia** Illinois
85 E3 **Meredoua** Algeria
54 H7 **Merefa** U.S.S.R.
86 A3 **Meregh** Somalia
85 C5 **Mereié, El** *reg* Mauritania/Mali
36 E3 **Merenberg** W Germany
20 K5 **Méréville** France
9 G5 **Mereworth** England
Merga *see* **Nukheila**
68 D6 **Mergui** Burma
73 Q6 **Mergui Arch** Burma
138 F5 **Meribah** S Australia
47 H3 **Meriç** Turkey
47 H3 **Meriç** *R* Greece
118 H7 **Merid** Sask

50

Mérida — Misiones

125 P7 **Mérida** Mexico
16 C6 **Mérida** Spain
128 D2 **Mérida** Venezuela
95 O5 **Meriden** Connecticut
107 P2 **Meriden** Kansas
95 P3 **Meriden** New Hampshire
98 B8 **Meriden** Wyoming
102 C2 **Meridian** California
100 J6 **Meridian** Idaho
111 H9 **Meridian** Mississippi
95 L3 **Meridian** New York
109 K4 **Meridian** Texas
137 O4 **Merig** *isld* New Hebrides
29 J10 **Merikarvia** Finland
141 J4 **Merinda** Queensland
19 O17 **Mérindol** France
37 L7 **Mering** W Germany
138 F5 **Meringur** Victoria
106 G1 **Merino** Colorado
138 F6 **Merino** Victoria
Merioneth *co see* **Gwynedd**
70 C3 **Merit** Sarawak
139 J2 **Merivale** *R* Queensland
57 G3 **Merke** U.S.S.R.
22 D2 **Merkem** Belgium
37 K5 **Merkendorf** W Germany
26 H5 **Merkenes** Sweden
31 P1 **Merkine** U.S.S.R.
37 O3 **Merklín** Czechoslovakia
37 P4 **Merklín** Czechoslovakia
22 G1 **Merksem** Belgium
22 H1 **Merksplas** Belgium
55 D2 **Merkushino** Sverdlovsk U.S.S.R.
55 E2 **Merkushino** Tyumen U.S.S.R.
36 C3 **Merl** W Germany
45 K1 **Merlara** Italy
20 F4 **Merlerault, le** France
22 B3 **Merlimont** France
120 H10 **Merlin** Ontario
100 B7 **Merlin** Oregon
141 F2 **Merluna** Queensland
142 C3 **Mermaid Reef** Indian Oc
111 C12 **Mermentau** *R* Louisiana
28 J6 **Mern** Denmark
98 G8 **Merna** Nebraska
101 P7 **Merna** Wyoming
138 E4 **Mernemerna** S Australia
69 A9 **Meroe** *isld* Nicobar Is
143 D8 **Merolia** W Australia
80 E2 **Meron** Israel
86 F2 **Merowe** Sudan
143 C9 **Merredin** W Australia
110 B2 **Merriam** Kansas
15 D5 **Merrick Mt** Scotland
121 P8 **Merrickville** Ontario
98 H3 **Merricourt** N Dakota
98 K7 **Merrill** Iowa
94 C3 **Merrill** Michigan
111 H11 **Merrill** Mississippi
100 D7 **Merrill** Oregon
99 R4 **Merrill** Wisconsin
99 Q5 **Merrillan** Wisconsin
99 R6 **Merrimac** Wisconsin
95 Q3 **Merrimack** *R* New Hamps/Mass
98 E7 **Merriman** Nebraska
139 J6 **Merrimbula** New S Wales
117 N10 **Merritt** Br Col
98 F7 **Merritt Res** Nebraska
139 K4 **Merriwa** New S Wales
111 E9 **Mer Rouge** Louisiana
9 F5 **Merrow** England
139 J4 **Merrygoen** New S Wales
109 O5 **Merryville** Louisiana
20 H1 **Mers** France
22 L4 **Mersch** Luxembourg
9 G4 **Mersea I** England
33 P10 **Merseburg** E Germany
17 G9 **Mers el Kebir** Algeria
8 D1 **Mersey, R** England
13 F6 **Merseyside** *co* England
69 F11 **Mersing** Malaysia
52 B6 **Mērsrags** U.S.S.R.
74 F5 **Merta** India
8 C4 **Merthyr Tydfil** Wales
37 K6 **Mertingen** W Germany
16 B7 **Mértola** Portugal
8 B6 **Merton** England
143 D8 **Mertondale** W Australia
146 J4 **Mertz Gl** Antarctica
108 G4 **Mertzon** Texas
20 K3 **Méru** France
88 F1 **Meru** Kenya
88 F3 **Meru** *mt* Tanzania
74 C8 **Merui** Pakistan
70 E2 **Merutai** Sabah
22 D2 **Merville** France
118 J5 **Mervin** Sask
100 C4 **Merwin, L** Washington
18 H4 **Méry-sur-Seine** France
78 E1 **Merzifon** Turkey
36 B5 **Merzig** W Germany
103 N8 **Mesa** Arizona
71 B2 **Mesa** Halmahera Indonesia
100 J5 **Mesa** Idaho
106 F8 **Mesa** New Mexico
17 F3 **Mesa** *R* Spain
99 N2 **Mesabi Ra** *mts* Minnesota
43 H8 **Mesagne** Italy
117 Q3 **Mesa L** N W Terr
116 K6 **Mesa Mt** Alaska
69 G12 **Mesanak** *isld* Indonesia
21 C7 **Mésanger** France
70 D2 **Mesapo** Sabah
47 G10 **Mesarás, Kólpos** *B* Crete Greece
106 B4 **Mesa Verde Nat. Park** Colorado
103 O10 **Mescal** Arizona
106 E8 **Mescalero** New Mexico
32 H10 **Meschede** W Germany
68 C3 **Mese** Burma
26 J7 **Meselefors** Sweden
48 H3 **Meseşului, Muntii** *mts* Romania
128 F2 **Meseta del Cerro Jaua** *mts* Venezuela
52 G6 **Mesha** *R* U.S.S.R.
54 L1 **Meshchera** *lowland* U.S.S.R.
54 G2 **Meshchovsk** U.S.S.R.
52 H3 **Meshchura** U.S.S.R.
Meshed *see* **Mashhad**
57 B4 **Meshekli** U.S.S.R.
116 H8 **Meshik** Alaska
86 E4 **Meshra er Req** Sudan
94 B2 **Mesick** Michigan
117 L7 **Mesilinka** *R* Br Col
106 D9 **Mesilla** New Mexico
80 C6 **Mesillat Ziyyon** Israel
28 F5 **Mesinge** Denmark
69 F12 **Meskum** Sumatra
21 D6 **Meslay-du-Maine** France
27 E10 **Mesna** *L* Norway
20 H2 **Mesnières-en-Bêthune** France
20 D4 **Mesnil Auzouf, le** France
20 K2 **Mesnil St. Firmin, le** France
20 C3 **Mesnil-Vigot, le** France
20 E4 **Mesnil-Villement, le** France
41 K5 **Mesocco** Switzerland
45 M2 **Mésola** Italy
41 K5 **Mesolcina, Valle** Switzerland
46 E6 **Mesolóngion** Greece
78 J4 **Mesopotamia** Iraq
130 G6 **Mesquita** Brazil
103 K5 **Mesquite** Nevada
106 D9 **Mesquite** New Mexico
109 O9 **Mesquite** Texas
103 J6 **Mesquite L** California
21 B6 **Messac** France
Messalo *R see* **Mualo** *R*
87 G8 **Messalo** *R* Mozambique
22 K4 **Messancy** Belgium
85 F2 **Messaoud, Hassi** Algeria
33 P7 **Messdorf** E Germany
20 D4 **Messei** France
Messick *see* **Poquoson**
133 C7 **Messie, Can** *str* Chile
89 F4 **Messina** S Africa
43 G10 **Messina** Sicily
22 J4 **Messincourt** France
121 O6 **Messines** Quebec
13 H6 **Messingham** England
46 E7 **Messini** Greece
46 E8 **Messiniakós Kólpos** *B* Greece
41 K2 **Messkirch** W Germany
Mesta *R see* **Néstos** *R*
47 F3 **Mesta** *R* Bulgaria
16 E6 **Mestanza** Spain
33 P5 **Mestlin** E Germany
42 G3 **Mesto, N** Yugoslavia
37 P4 **Město-Touškov** Czechoslovakia
42 E3 **Mestre** Italy
45 L1 **Mestrino** Italy
45 Q8 **Meta** Italy
110 D3 **Meta** Missouri
128 D3 **Meta** *div* Colombia
128 E2 **Meta** *R* Venezuela/Colombia
115 N5 **Meta Incognita Pen** N W Terr
111 H12 **Metairie** New Orleans
120 C2 **Meta L** Ontario
48 H4 **Metalici, Muntii** *mts* Romania
117 P11 **Metaline Falls** Washington
42 D5 **Metallifere, Colline** *hills* Italy
99 R9 **Metamora** Illinois
133 E3 **Metán** Argentina
87 F8 **Metangula** Mozambique
43 H8 **Metaponto** Italy
42 E5 **Metauro** *R* Italy
80 E3 **Metav** Israel
122 F9 **Meteghan** Nova Scotia
32 F8 **Metelen** W Germany
86 G3 **Metemma** Ethiopia
141 J6 **Meteor** *R* Queensland
90 G14 **Meteor Depth** S Atlantic Oc
90 K14 **Meteor Seamount** S Atlantic Oc
22 D2 **Méteren** France
47 F7 **Méthana** Greece
119 S7 **Methley** Manitoba
46 E8 **Methóni** Greece
100 E1 **Methow** *R* Washington
95 Q4 **Methuen** Massachusetts
142 E3 **Methuen,Mt** W Australia
144 C5 **Methven** New Zealand
12 E1 **Methven** Scotland
143 D7 **Methwin,Mt** W Australia
9 G2 **Methwold** England
119 N1 **Metionga L** Ontario
118 G6 **Metiskow** Alberta
122 E5 **Metis L** Quebec
42 H5 **Metković** Yugoslavia
117 H8 **Metlakahtla** Alaska
85 F2 **Metlaoui** Tunisia
38 K8 **Metnitz** Austria
46 D2 **Metohija** Yugoslavia
100 D5 **Metolius** Oregon
46 E1 **Metovnica** Yugoslavia
70 K8 **Metro** Sumatra
110 H4 **Metropolis** Illinois
25 F2 **Metslawier** Netherlands
46 E5 **Métsovon** Greece
37 O6 **Metten** W Germany
36 B4 **Mettendorf** W Germany
112 E5 **Metter** Georgia
22 H3 **Mettet** Belgium
32 G8 **Mettingen** W Germany
36 B4 **Mettlach** W Germany
32 E10 **Mettmann** W Germany
36 B4 **Mettnich** W Germany
76 C5 **Mettuppalaiyam** India
76 C5 **Mettur** India
88 H7 **Metudo** *isld* Mozambique
79 F5 **Metulla** Israel
19 K3 **Metz** France
40 F1 **Metzeral** France
22 L5 **Metzervisse** France
36 G6 **Metzingen** W Germany
20 A5 **Meu** *R* France
88 G9 **Meucate** Mozambique
36 D3 **Meudt** W Germany
69 C10 **Meulaboh** Sumatra
20 J3 **Meulan** France
22 E2 **Meulebeke** Belgium
20 F4 **Meulles** France
21 I6 **Meung sur-Loire** France
69 C10 **Meureudu** Sumatra
40 A4 **Meursault** France
19 K4 **Meurthe** *R* France
36 B6 **Meurthe et Moselle** *dep* France
19 J4 **Meuse** *dep* France
22 H3 **Meuse** *R* Belgium
19 J3 **Meuse** *R* France
37 N1 **Meuselwitz** E Germany
21 I7 **Meusnes** France
8 B7 **Mevagissey** England
80 D6 **Meva Horon** Jordan
80 C6 **Meva Modiin** Jordan
13 G6 **Mexborough** England
109 L4 **Mexia** Texas
129 J3 **Mexiana** *isld* Brazil
103 J9 **Mexicali** Mexico
103 P4 **Mexican Hat** Utah
124 F3 **Mexicanos, Lago de los** Mexico
103 P5 **Mexican Water** Arizona
94 A6 **Mexico** Indiana
95 R2 **Mexico** Maine
110 E2 **Mexico** Missouri
95 L3 **Mexico** New York
124 G6 **Mexico** *rep* N America
125 K8 **Mexico City** Mexico
125 M6 **Mexico, G. of** Mexico etc
40 B6 **Meximieux** France
71 E3 **Meycawayan** Luzon Philippines
77 D5 **Meydān-e-Gel** *salt lake* Iran
33 Q6 **Meyenburg** E Germany
117 G8 **Meyers Chuck** Alaska
94 H7 **Meyersdale** Pennsylvania
18 G7 **Meymac** France
77 B3 **Meymeh** Iran
118 L8 **Meyronne** Sask
18 H8 **Meyrueis** France
18 G7 **Meyssac** France
80 E8 **Mezada** Israel
125 N9 **Mezcalapa** *R* Mexico
47 F1 **Mezdra** Bulgaria
18 H9 **Mèze** France
19 Q17 **Mézel** France
52 F2 **Mezen'** Arkhangelsk U.S.S.R.
52 G3 **Mezen'** *R* U.S.S.R.
52 F2 **Mezenskaya Guba** *B* U.S.S.R.
80 D4 **Mezer** Israel
54 C1 **Mezha** *R* U.S.S.R.
56 C4 **Mezhdurechensk** U.S.S.R.
31 N1 **Mezhdurech'ye** U.S.S.R.
50 D1 **Mezhdusharskiy Ostrov** *isld* U.S.S.R.
42 F2 **Mežica** Yugoslavia
20 E3 **Mézidon** France
20 B5 **Meziére, la** France
20 J4 **Mézières** Yvelines France
21 H8 **Mézières-en-Brenne** France
31 H6 **Mezimostí** Czechoslovakia
18 F8 **Mézin** France
54 M1 **Mezinovskiy** U.S.S.R.
48 G4 **Mezöberény** Hungary
48 F3 **Mezöcsát** Hungary
48 F4 **Mezöhegyes** Hungary
48 F4 **Mezökovacsháza** Hungary
48 F3 **Mezökövesd** Hungary
18 E8 **Mézos** France
48 F3 **Mezötúr** Hungary
124 G6 **Mezquital** Mexico
124 G6 **Mezquital** *R* Mexico
124 H6 **Mezquitic** Mexico
41 N5 **Mezzana** Italy
45 M3 **Mezzano** Italy
41 O4 **Mezzaselva** Italy
45 M2 **Mezzogoro** Italy
41 K5 **Mezzola, Lago di** Italy
41 L5 **Mezzoldo** Italy
42 D2 **Mezzolombardo** Italy
52 D5 **Mga** U.S.S.R.
74 F10 **Mhasvad** India
125 L9 **Miahuatián de Porfirio Diaz** Mexico
16 D5 **Miajadas** Spain
103 O8 **Miami** Arizona
113 G12 **Miami** Florida
119 T9 **Miami** Manitoba
107 Q5 **Miami** Oklahoma
108 D8 **Miami** Texas
94 C7 **Miami** *R* Ohio
113 G12 **Miami Beach** Florida
113 G11 **Miami Canal** Florida
94 C6 **Miami, Great** *R* Ohio
94 C7 **Miami, Little** *R* Ohio
94 C7 **Miamisburg** Ohio
113 G12 **Miami Shores** Florida
113 G12 **Miami Springs** Florida
65 B7 **Mianchi** China
78 L3 **Miandowab** Iran
87 H11 **Miandrivazo** Madagascar
77 A1 **Mianeh** Iran
67 E4 **Mian Shui** *R* China
58 E5 **Mian Xian** China
58 D5 **Mianyang** China
67 D1 **Mianyang** China
67 A1 **Mianzhu** China
65 E6 **Miao Dao** *isld* China
65 E5 **Miaodao Qundao** *islds* China
65 H3 **Miaoling** China
67 B3 **Miao Ling** *mt ra* China
67 C4 **Miaoping** China
87 H11 **Miarinarivo** Madagascar
55 D3 **Miass** *R* U.S.S.R.
31 K1 **Miastko** Poland
103 O9 **Mica Mt** Arizona
58 E5 **Micang Shan** *mt ra* China
113 E8 **Micanopy** Florida
128 C3 **Micay** Colombia
113 C7 **Miccosukee** Florida
52 H3 **Michaichmon'** U.S.S.R.
48 G2 **Michal'any** Czechoslovakia
48 G2 **Michalovce** Czechoslovakia
118 C9 **Michel** Br Col
118 H3 **Michel** Sask
38 N5 **Michelbach** Austria
36 E3 **Michelbach** W Germany
116 Q2 **Michelson, Mt** Alaska
36 G4 **Michelstadt** W Germany
33 S8 **Michendorf** E Germany
127 K5 **Miches** Dominican Rep
118 E7 **Michichi** Alberta
112 J1 **Michie, L** N Carolina
99 S3 **Michigamme** Michigan
99 S3 **Michigamme L** Michigan
99 S3 **Michigamme Res** Michigan
98 H1 **Michigan** N Dakota
94 A1 **Michigan** *state* U.S.A.
94 C4 **Michigan Center** Michigan
99 U8 **Michigan City** Indiana
94 A4 **Michigan, L** U.S.A.
110 K1 **Michigantown** Indiana
120 F5 **Michipicoten** Ontario
31 N4 **Michów** Poland
47 J2 **Michurin** Bulgaria
54 M4 **Michurinsk** U.S.S.R.
13 F4 **Mickle Fell** *mt* England
9 E3 **Mickleton** Gloucs England
127 O8 **Micoud** St Lucia
134 F7 **Micronesia** Pac Oc
69 H11 **Midai** *isld* Indonesia
119 O9 **Midale** Sask
100 J8 **Midas** Nevada
90 E6 **Mid-Atlantic Ridge** Atlantic Oc
12 E2 **Mid Calder** Scotland
89 D8 **Middelburg** Cape Prov S Africa
25 A6 **Middelburg** Netherlands
87 D12 **Middelburg** S Africa
89 F5 **Middelburg** Transvaal S Africa
25 B5 **Middelharnis** Netherlands
22 D1 **Middelkerke** Belgium
89 B9 **Middel Roggeveld** *reg* S Africa
87 E10 **Middelwit** S Africa
90 A7 **Middle America Trench** Pacific Oc
68 A6 **Middle Andaman** *isld* Andaman Is
138 D5 **Middleback, Mt** S Australia
95 R5 **Middleboro** Massachusetts
94 G7 **Middlebourne** W Virginia
118 F1 **Middlebro** Manitoba
95 N4 **Middleburg** New York
95 K6 **Middleburg** Pennsylvania
94 K8 **Middleburg** Virginia
94 B5 **Middlebury** Indiana
95 O2 **Middlebury** Vermont
108 G4 **Middle Concho** *R* Texas
28 D5 **Middlefart** Denmark
144 A6 **Middle Fiord** New Zealand
13 G5 **Middleham** England
94 D1 **Middle I** Michigan
69 C8 **Middle I** Thailand
90 B16 **Middle I** Tristan da Cunha
143 E10 **Middle I** W Australia
100 F8 **Middle L** Nevada
119 M6 **Middle Lake** Sask
98 G8 **Middle Loup** *R* Nebraska
144 C6 **Middlemarch** New Zealand
8 D6 **Middlemarsh** England
94 J3 **Middleport** New York
94 E8 **Middleport** Ohio
83 M9 **Middle Pt** Christmas I Indian Oc
94 C6 **Middle Pt** Ohio
98 K1 **Middle R** Minnesota
123 R5 **Middle Rge** Newfoundland
95 L7 **Middle River** Maryland
118 G8 **Middle Sand Hills, The** Alberta
94 D10 **Middlesboro** Kentucky
13 G4 **Middlesbrough** England
125 P9 **Middlesex** Belize
95 K4 **Middlesex** New York
13 F5 **Middleton** Cumbria England
13 F6 **Middleton** Greater Manchester England
13 H6 **Middleton** Humberside England
100 J6 **Middleton** Idaho
94 C3 **Middleton** Michigan
122 G9 **Middleton** Nova Scotia
141 F5 **Middleton** Queensland
110 H6 **Middleton** Tennessee
99 R6 **Middleton** Wisconsin
116 P7 **Middleton I** Alaska
13 F4 **Middleton in Teesdale** England
95 P5 **Middletown** Connecticut
95 M7 **Middletown** Delaware
94 B6 **Middletown** Indiana
94 K7 **Middletown** Maryland
95 N5 **Middletown** New York
110 M2 **Middletown** Ohio
95 L6 **Middletown** Pennsylvania
8 D2 **Middletown** Wales
94 B4 **Middleville** Michigan
95 N3 **Middleville** New York
108 B8 **Middle Water** Texas
8 D1 **Middlewich** England
122 H9 **Middlewood** Nova Scotia
85 D2 **Midelt** Morocco
109 L7 **Midfield** Texas
8 C4 **Mid Glamorgan** *co* Wales
145 E3 **Midhirst** New Zealand
9 F6 **Midhurst** England
121 L8 **Midhurst** Ontario
18 G9 **Midi, Canal du** France
18 E10 **Midi d'Ossau, Pic du** *mt* France
18 F10 **Midi du Bigorre, Pic du** *mt* France
110 B6 **Midland** Arkansas
103 K8 **Midland** California
94 J7 **Midland** Maryland
94 C3 **Midland** Michigan
98 E5 **Midland** S Dakota
108 E4 **Midland** Texas
111 L10 **Midland City** Alabama
143 B9 **Midland Junc** W Australia
14 C5 **Midleton** Irish Rep
109 K3 **Midlothian** Texas
94 K9 **Midlothian** Virginia
Midlothian *co see* **Lothian and Borders** *regions*
32 J5 **Midlum** W Germany
75 M7 **Midnapur** India
111 F8 **Midnight** Mississippi
87 H12 **Midongy Atsimo** Madagascar
60 D13 **Midori-kawa** *R* Japan
18 E9 **Midouze** *R* France
134 G5 **Mid-Pacific Mountains** Pac Oc
71 G7 **Midsayap** Philippines
100 J5 **Midvale** Idaho
101 O9 **Midvale** Utah
112 E5 **Midville** Georgia
111 L9 **Midway** Alabama
117 O11 **Midway** Br Col
112 F6 **Midway** Georgia
94 C8 **Midway** Kentucky
109 M4 **Midway** Texas
116 O1 **Midway Is** Alaska
135 U2 **Midway Is** *atoll* Hawaiian Is
122 E1 **Midway L** Quebec
143 E6 **Midway Well** W Australia
101 T6 **Midwest** Wyoming
107 N6 **Midwest City** Oklahoma
25 F2 **Midwolde** Netherlands
78 H3 **Midyat** Turkey
47 J3 **Midye** Turkey
15 G1 **Mid Yell** Scotland
46 F1 **Midžor** *mt* Yugoslavia
61 K11 **Mie** *prefect* Japan
31 M5 **Miechów** Poland
40 F3 **Miécourt** Switzerland
31 J3 **Międzychód** Poland
31 K5 **Międzylesie** Poland
31 O4 **Międzyrzec** Poland
31 J3 **Międzyrzecz** Poland
31 K4 **Miejska Gorka** Poland
29 L5 **Miekojärvi** *L* Finland
18 F9 **Miélan** France
31 N5 **Mielec** Poland
41 N3 **Mieminger Kette** *mt* Austria
27 G15 **Mien** *L* Sweden
139 H8 **Miena** Tasmania
67 G4 **Mien-hua Hsü** *isld* Taiwan
109 H9 **Mier** Mexico
106 D7 **Miera** New Mexico
48 K4 **Miercurea Cinc** Romania
16 D1 **Mieres** Spain
26 N2 **Mieron** Norway
38 E6 **Miesbach** W Germany
86 H4 **Miesso** Ethiopia
33 O8 **Mieste** E Germany
31 H3 **Mieszkowice** Poland
94 K6 **Mifflin** Pennsylvania
95 K6 **Mifflinburg** Pennsylvania
95 K6 **Mifflintown** Pennsylvania
83 L9 **Migaswewa** Sri Lanka
80 F2 **Migdal** Israel
80 D7 **Migdal Oz** Jordan
77 F4 **Mighān** Iran
45 L2 **Migliarino** Italy
45 P7 **Mignano** Italy
44 G2 **Mignano, L. di** Italy
44 L5 **Mignone** *R* Italy
124 H5 **Miguel Auza** Mexico
88 H2 **Migwani** Kenya
68 B3 **Migyaunye** Burma
48 K3 **Mihăileni** Romania
60 G11 **Mihara** Japan
61 N11 **Mihara-yama** *vol* Japan
61 O8 **Miharu** Japan
37 J1 **Mihla** E Germany
60 G10 **Miho wan** *B* Japan
40 D5 **Mijoux** France
94 D2 **Mikado** Michigan
119 P7 **Mikado** Sask
60 P2 **Mikasa** Japan
61 K9 **Mikawa** Japan
48 L1 **Mikhailovka** U.S.S.R.
54 L2 **Mikhaylov** U.S.S.R.
47 F1 **Mikhaylovgrad** Bulgaria
146 D3 **Mikhaylov I** Antarctica
55 G4 **Mikhaylovka** Altay U.S.S.R.
47 H2 **Mikhaylovo** Bulgaria
55 C3 **Mikhaylovsk** U.S.S.R.
80 C4 **Mikhmoret** Israel
79 E9 **Mikhrot Timna** Israel
88 H7 **Mikindani** Tanzania
100 E4 **Mikkalo** Oregon
29 N10 **Mikkeli** Finland
117 Q7 **Mikkwa** *R* Alberta
31 N2 **Mikołajki** Poland
31 L5 **Mikołow** Poland
47 G1 **Mikre** Bulgaria
46 E4 **Mikrí Préspa L** Greece
47 H3 **Mikrón Dhérion** Greece
52 G1 **Mikulkin, Mys** *C* U.S.S.R.
48 D2 **Mikulov** Czechoslovakia
87 G7 **Mikumi** Tanzania
88 F5 **Mikumi Nat. Park** Tanzania
61 N8 **Mikuni sammyaku** *mts* Japan
61 N12 **Mikura-jima** *isld* Japan
99 N4 **Milaca** Minnesota
73 L7 **Miladunmadulu Atoll** Maldives
130 H9 **Milagres** Brazil
Milan *see* **Milano**
94 B7 **Milan** Indiana
107 N4 **Milan** Kansas
94 D4 **Milan** Michigan
99 L4 **Milan** Minnesota
99 N9 **Milan** Missouri
94 E5 **Milan** Ohio
122 A8 **Milan** Quebec
110 H6 **Milan** Tennessee
100 H2 **Milan** Washington
138 E6 **Milang** S Australia
88 E10 **Milange** Mozambique
70 G4 **Milango** *R* Sulawesi
109 L5 **Milano** Texas
39 **Milano** *conurbation* Italy
17 G4 **Milares** *R* Spain
47 J7 **Milâs** Turkey
43 G10 **Milazzo** Sicily
98 K4 **Milbank** S Dakota
94 A4 **Milburg** Michigan
144 B7 **Milburn** New Zealand
9 G3 **Mildenhall** England
120 J8 **Mildmay** Ontario
98 A3 **Mildred** Montana
95 L5 **Mildred** Pennsylvania
118 K5 **Mildred** Sask
117 R7 **Mildred Lake** Alberta
138 F5 **Mildura** Victoria
67 A4 **Mile** China
46 F5 **Miléai** Greece
127 J2 **Mile Gully** Jamaica
141 K7 **Miles** Queensland
100 G2 **Miles** Washington
101 U3 **Miles City** Montana
119 N9 **Milestone** Sask
43 G10 **Mileto** Italy
45 Q7 **Miletto, M** *mt* Italy
143 B7 **Mileura** W Australia
31 H6 **Milevsko** Czechoslovakia
102 D1 **Milford** California
95 O5 **Milford** Connecticut
95 M8 **Milford** Delaware
9 E6 **Milford** Hampshire England
99 T9 **Milford** Illinois
94 B5 **Milford** Indiana
99 L6 **Milford** Iowa
107 O2 **Milford** Kansas
95 T2 **Milford** Maine
95 Q4 **Milford** Massachusetts
94 D4 **Milford** Michigan
98 J9 **Milford** Nebraska
95 Q4 **Milford** New Hampshire
95 N4 **Milford** New York
9 F5 **Milford** Surrey England
109 L3 **Milford** Texas
103 L3 **Milford** Utah
94 K8 **Milford** Virginia
94 D6 **Milford Center** Ohio
8 A4 **Milford Haven** Wales
144 A6 **Milford Sound** New Zealand
140 F4 **Milgarra** Queensland
143 C8 **Milgoo, Mt** W Australia
143 C7 **Milgun** W Australia
85 E1 **Miliana** Algeria
43 C12 **Miliane** *R* Tunisia
31 K4 **Milicz** Poland
143 B9 **Miling** W Australia
140 C1 **Milingimbi** N Terr Aust
51 P3 **Milkovo** U.S.S.R.
118 F9 **Milk R** Alberta/Montana
127 K3 **Milk River Bath** Jamaica
86 E2 **Milk, Wadi el** *watercourse* Sudan
25 E5 **Mill** Netherlands
141 H4 **Millaa Millaa** Queensland
21 G9 **Millac** France
21 I7 **Millançay** France
143 F8 **Millar Breakaways** W Australia
99 O9 **Millard** Missouri
141 H4 **Millaroo** Queensland
98 H3 **Millarton** N Dakota
94 H9 **Millboro** Virginia
95 U2 **Millbridge** Maine
95 O5 **Millbrook** New York
121 M8 **Millbrook** Ontario
102 F1 **Mill City** Nevada
100 C5 **Mill City** Oregon
102 C1 **Mill Creek** California
109 L1 **Mill Creek** Oklahoma
94 H8 **Mill Creek** W Virginia
112 D4 **Milledgeville** Georgia
99 R8 **Milledgeville** Illinois
101 O2 **Millegan** Montana
99 N3 **Mille Lacs** *L* Minnesota
119 N2 **Mille Lacs, Lac des** Ontario
112 F5 **Millen** Georgia
110 C4 **Miller** Missouri
98 G9 **Miller** Nebraska
98 H5 **Miller** S Dakota
138 D3 **Miller** *R* S Australia
124 B3 **Miller, Desembarcadero de** Mexico
116 Q6 **Miller, Mt** Alaska
54 M8 **Millerovo** U.S.S.R.
103 O10 **Miller Pk** Arizona
102 G3 **Millers** Nevada
94 B5 **Millersburg** Indiana
110 M3 **Millersburg** Kentucky
94 D1 **Millersburg** Michigan
94 F6 **Millersburg** Ohio
95 L6 **Millersburg** Pennsylvania
138 D4 **Millers Creek** S Australia
95 P4 **Millers Falls** Massachusetts
111 J9 **Millers Ferry** Alabama
144 B6 **Miller's Flat** New Zealand
12 D2 **Millerston** Scotland
94 H6 **Millerstown** Pennsylvania
108 H4 **Millersview** Texas
122 G7 **Millerton** New Brunswick
95 O5 **Millerton** New York
144 C4 **Millerton** New Zealand
102 E4 **Millerton L** California
123 Q5 **Millertown** Newfoundland
123 Q4 **Millertown Junct** Newfoundland
118 D5 **Millet** Alberta
94 E9 **Millet** W Virginia
102 G2 **Millett** Nevada
109 H7 **Millett** Texas
18 G7 **Millevaches, Plateau de** France
14 D1 **Millford** Irish Rep
94 K5 **Mill Hall** Penn
146 E2 **Mill I** Antarctica
115 M5 **Mill I** N W Terr
100 E6 **Millican** Oregon
109 L5 **Millican** Texas
118 F8 **Millicent** Alberta
138 F6 **Millicent** S Australia
143 D8 **Millicent,Mt** W Australia
111 K11 **Milligan** Florida
98 J9 **Milligan** Nebraska
106 F1 **Milliken** Colorado
95 M7 **Millington** Maryland
94 D3 **Millington** Michigan
95 S8 **Millinocket** Maine
141 K8 **Millmerran** Queensland
13 E5 **Millom** England
111 H8 **Millport** Alabama
95 L4 **Millport** New York
12 D2 **Millport** Scotland
111 H10 **Millry** Alabama
106 F5 **Mills** New Mexico
101 T7 **Mills** Wyoming
141 G5 **Mills** *R* Queensland
109 J3 **Millsap** Texas
102 B2 **Millsaps** California
95 M8 **Millsboro** Delaware
94 G7 **Millsboro** Penn
117 O5 **Mills L** N W Terr
99 Q5 **Millston** Wisconsin
142 B5 **Millstream** W Australia
14 B4 **Millstreet** Irish Rep
8 C2 **Milltir Cerig** *mt* Wales
122 E8 **Milltown** New Brunswick
123 R6 **Milltown** Newfoundland
14 B4 **Milltown Malbay** Irish Rep
141 F4 **Millungera** Queensland
102 B4 **Mill Valley** California
122 H9 **Mill Village** Nova Scotia
122 E7 **Millville** New Brunswick
94 C7 **Millville** Ohio
95 L5 **Millville** Pennsylvania
109 N2 **Millwood Res** Arkansas
20 K5 **Milly** France
143 B7 **Milly Milly** W Australia
20 K3 **Milly sur-Therain** France
33 T6 **Milmersdorf** E Germany
13 E1 **Milnathort** Scotland
115 R3 **Milne Land** Greenland
112 C4 **Milner** Georgia
101 L7 **Milner** Idaho
118 E1 **Milner Ridge** Manitoba
120 K6 **Milnet** Ontario
12 D2 **Milngavie** Scotland
98 J3 **Milnor** N Dakota
13 F5 **Milnthorpe** England
118 E8 **Milo** Alberta
99 N8 **Milo** Iowa
95 S1 **Milo** Maine
100 B7 **Milo** Oregon
141 G7 **Milo** Queensland
88 E6 **Milo** Tanzania
135 U6 **Milolii** Hawaiian Is
31 M2 **Miłomłyn** Poland
47 G8 **Mílos** *isld* Greece
48 F5 **Miloševo** Yugoslavia
31 K3 **Miłosław** Poland
33 Q7 **Milow** E Germany
31 L6 **Milówka** Poland
138 F3 **Milparinka** New S Wales
102 C4 **Milpitas** California
110 L2 **Milroy** Indiana
94 K6 **Milroy** Pennsylvania
37 O5 **Miltach** W Germany
36 G4 **Miltenberg** W Germany
95 M8 **Milton** Delaware
111 J11 **Milton** Florida
99 Q10 **Milton** Illinois
110 D1 **Milton** Iowa
107 N4 **Milton** Kansas
95 R3 **Milton** Maine
94 H10 **Milton** N Carolina
98 J1 **Milton** N Dakota
139 K6 **Milton** New S Wales
144 B7 **Milton** New Zealand
122 H9 **Milton** Nova Scotia
100 G4 **Milton** Oregon
95 L5 **Milton** Pennsylvania
12 D2 **Milton** Scotland
95 O2 **Milton** Vermont
99 S7 **Milton** Wisconsin
94 E8 **Milton** W Virginia
8 B6 **Milton Abbot** England
139 J3 **Milton Downs** New S Wales
12 D3 **Miltonish** Scotland
9 F3 **Milton Keynes** England
107 N2 **Miltonvale** Kansas
86 C3 **Miltou** Chad
33 S4 **Miltzow** E Germany
67 D2 **Miluo** China
8 C5 **Milverton** England
99 T6 **Milwaukee** Wisconsin
127 K5 **Milwaukee Depth** Caribbean
60 E13 **Mimitsu** Japan
18 E8 **Mimizan** France
31 H5 **Mimoň** Czechoslovakia
86 B6 **Mimongo** Gabon
60 H10 **Mimuro yama** *mt* Japan
102 A2 **Mina** California
102 F3 **Mina** Nevada
77 A5 **Mina' al Ahmadi** Iran
77 E6 **Mināb** Iran
60 J12 **Minabe** Japan
124 F3 **Miñaca** Mexico
119 T4 **Minago R** Manitoba
71 H4 **Minahassa Peninsula** Sulawesi Indonesia
77 D7 **Mina Jebel Ali** United Arab Emirates
118 H1 **Minaki** Ontario
100 H4 **Minam** Oregon
60 D13 **Minamata** Japan
85 C6 **Mina, Mt** Mali
126 F4 **Minas** Cuba
69 E12 **Minas** Sumatra
131 G5 **Minas** Uruguay
77 A5 **Mina' Sa'ud** Kuwait
122 H8 **Minas Basin** Nova Scotia
16 C7 **Minas de Riotinto** Spain
16 C7 **Minas de Tharsis** Spain
130 F5 **Minas Gerais** *state* Brazil
129 K7 **Minas Novas** Brazil
130 G5 **Minas Novas** Brazil
125 P10 **Minas, Sa. de las** *mts* Guatemala
98 C8 **Minatare** Nebraska
120 B2 **Minataree** Ontario
125 M9 **Minatitlán** Mexico
68 B2 **Minbu** Burma
118 F5 **Minburn** Alberta
99 M8 **Minburn** Iowa
68 A2 **Minbya** Burma
116 M5 **Minchumina, L** Alaska
45 J1 **Mincio** *R* Italy
107 N6 **Minco** Oklahoma
31 M6 **Minčol** *mt* Czechoslovakia
71 G7 **Mindanao** Philippines
71 G6 **Mindanao Sea** Philippines
138 F5 **Mindarie** S Australia
68 A2 **Mindat Sakan** Burma
37 J7 **Mindel** *R* W Germany
41 M1 **Mindelheim** W Germany
111 C9 **Minden** Louisiana
98 G9 **Minden** Nebraska
102 E3 **Minden** Nevada
121 M8 **Minden** Ontario
32 J8 **Minden** W Germany
94 F9 **Minden** W Virginia
94 E3 **Minden City** Michigan
142 B5 **Minderoo** W Australia
68 B3 **Mindon** Burma
138 F5 **Mindona L** New S Wales
71 E4 **Mindoro** *isld* Philippines
71 E4 **Mindoro Str** Philippines
48 F4 **Mindszent** Hungary
55 C4 **Mindyak** U.S.S.R.
60 E11 **Mine** Japan
99 O1 **Mine Centre** Ontario
48 K5 **Mîneci-Ungureni** Romania
14 D5 **Mine Hd** Irish Rep
8 C5 **Minehead** England
130 D5 **Mineiros** Brazil
20 D3 **Mine, la** France
99 L8 **Mineola** Iowa
109 M3 **Mineola** Texas
101 P4 **Miner** Montana
102 C1 **Mineral** California
109 K7 **Mineral** Texas
94 K8 **Mineral** Virginia
100 C3 **Mineral** Washington
125 K7 **Mineral del Monte** Mexico
103 M3 **Mineral Mts** Utah
99 Q7 **Mineral Pt** Wisconsin
109 O2 **Mineral Springs** Arkansas
109 J3 **Mineral Wells** Texas
45 K2 **Minerbio** Italy
103 M3 **Minersville** Utah
94 F6 **Minerva** Ohio
141 J6 **Minerva** Queensland
137 R6 **Minerva Rfs** Pacific Oc
43 G7 **Minervino Murge** Italy
95 L3 **Minetto** New York
94 E8 **Minford** Ohio
68 C4 **Mingaladon** Burma
122 H3 **Mingan** Quebec
122 J3 **Mingan Chan** Quebec
122 J3 **Mingan Is** Quebec
138 F4 **Mingary** S Australia
67 D5 **Mingcheng** China
78 L1 **Mingechaur** U.S.S.R.
78 L1 **Mingechaurskoye Vdkhr** *res* U.S.S.R.
141 H4 **Mingela** Queensland
143 B8 **Mingenew** W Australia
140 E5 **Mingera** *R* Queensland
68 B1 **Mingin** Burma
75 Q6 **Mingin Range** Burma
67 B5 **Mingjiang** China
58 G5 **Ming-kuang** China
17 G5 **Minglanilla** Spain
67 C4 **Minglun** China
99 N8 **Mingo** Iowa
107 K2 **Mingo** Kansas
94 G6 **Mingo Junct** Ohio
Mingolsheim *see* **Bad Schönborn**
87 G8 **Mingoyo** Tanzania
67 A1 **Mingshan** China
Mingshui *see* **Zhangqiu**
65 F1 **Mingshui** China
109 J3 **Mingus** Texas
67 F3 **Mingxi** China
68 G8 **Minh Hoa, Hon** *isld* Vietnam
68 B4 **Minhla** Burma
16 B3 **Minho** *prov* Portugal
16 B2 **Minho** *R* Spain/Portugal
127 K2 **Minho, R** Jamaica
20 B4 **Miniac Morvan** France
46 E1 **Minićevo** Yugoslavia
73 L7 **Minicoy I** Lakshadweep Indian Oc
101 M7 **Minidoka** Idaho
99 R9 **Minier** Illinois
143 E8 **Minigwal,L** W Australia
143 A6 **Minilya** W Australia
143 A6 **Minilya R** W Australia
110 K4 **Mining City Res** Kentucky
119 Q8 **Miniota** Manitoba
83 K10 **Minipe** Sri Lanka
123 L1 **Minipi L** Labrador
118 H4 **Ministikwan L** Sask
17 F3 **Ministra, Sierra** Spain
119 Q6 **Minitonas** Manitoba
143 B8 **Minjar** *hill* W Australia
58 D5 **Min Jiang** *R* China
67 F3 **Min Jiang** *R* China
102 E5 **Minkler** California
48 L2 **Minkovtsy** U.S.S.R.
57 G4 **Min-Kush** U.S.S.R.
138 D5 **Minlaton** S Australia
85 F7 **Minna** Nigeria
146 H7 **Minna Bluff** Antarctica
61 P12 **Minna-jima** *isld* Okinawa
107 N2 **Minneapolis** Kansas
99 N4 **Minneapolis** Minnesota
119 S8 **Minnedosa** Manitoba
98 C6 **Minnekahta** S Dakota
107 L4 **Minneola** Kansas
99 M5 **Minnesota** *R* Minnesota
99 N3 **Minnesota** *state* U.S.A.
99 P5 **Minnesota City** Minnesota
99 N6 **Minnesota Lake** Minnesota
27 E11 **Minnesund** Norway
118 B7 **Minnewanka, L** Alberta
99 L4 **Minnewaska L** Minnesota
98 G1 **Minnewaukan** N Dakota
68 D6 **Min-Ngaw** Burma
143 B6 **Minnie Creek** W Australia
141 H7 **Minnie Downs** Queensland
142 B5 **Minnie,Mt** W Australia
79 H2 **Minnik** Syria
138 D5 **Minnipa** S Australia
120 G4 **Minnipuka** Ontario
118 K1 **Minnitaki L** Ontario
61 K10 **Mino** Japan
16 B2 **Miño** *R* Spain
61 M10 **Minobu** Japan
99 R4 **Minocqua** Wisconsin
61 K10 **Minokamo** Japan
61 K11 **Minokuchi** Japan
99 P3 **Minong** Wisconsin
99 R9 **Minonk** Illinois
99 S8 **Minooka** Illinois
Minorca *see* **Menorca**
40 A2 **Minot** France
98 E1 **Minot** N Dakota
67 F3 **Minqing** China
65 C7 **Minquan** China
20 A4 **Minquiers, les** English Chan
32 G5 **Minsen** W Germany
65 A4 **Minsheng Canal** China
53 C7 **Minsk** U.S.S.R.
31 N3 **Mińsk Mazowieckie** Poland
9 H5 **Minster** England
94 C6 **Minster** Ohio
111 J9 **Minter** Alabama
111 F8 **Minter City** Mississippi
119 S9 **Minto** Manitoba
122 F7 **Minto** New Brunswick
117 E4 **Minto** Yukon Terr
114 J3 **Minto Hd** N W Terr
114 H3 **Minto Inlet** N W Terr
115 M6 **Minto, L** Quebec
98 B1 **Minton** Sask
106 D2 **Minturn** Colorado
45 P7 **Minturno** Italy
79 A8 **Minûf** Egypt
56 D4 **Minusinsk** U.S.S.R.
58 D5 **Min Xian** China
79 A10 **Minya, El** Egypt
79 B8 **Minya el Qamn** Egypt
Minya Konka *mt see* **Gongga Shan**
55 C3 **Min'yar** U.S.S.R.
138 F6 **Minyip** Victoria
68 B1 **Minywa** Burma
94 C2 **Mio** Michigan
83 J10 **Mi Oya** *R* Sri Lanka
78 K5 **Miqdādiyah** Iraq
121 O3 **Miquelon** Quebec
123 Q6 **Miquelon, Grande, I** Atlantic Oc
118 E5 **Miquelon Prov. Park** Alberta
123 N7 **Mira** C Breton I, N Scotia
45 M1 **Mira** Italy
17 G5 **Mira** Spain
16 B7 **Mira** *R* Portugal
19 P17 **Mirabeau** France
130 G5 **Mirabela** Brazil
45 R7 **Mirabella Eclano** Italy
130 G7 **Miracema** Brazil
128 D2 **Miraflores** Boyaca Colombia
124 E6 **Miraflores** Mexico
102 G7 **Mirage L** California
130 G7 **Miraí** Brazil
76 B2 **Miraj** India
130 G5 **Miralta** Brazil
19 O17 **Miràmas** France
18 E7 **Mirambeau** France
122 G6 **Miramichi B** New Brunswick
18 F8 **Miramont de Guyenne** France
133 F5 **Miranda** Argentina
145 E2 **Miranda** New Zealand
128 E1 **Miranda** *state* Venezuela
17 F2 **Miranda de E.Haro** Spain
16 C3 **Miranda do D** Portugal
141 F3 **Miranda Downs** Queensland
130 C6 **Miranda, R** Brazil
18 F9 **Mirande** France
16 C3 **Mirandela** Portugal
109 J8 **Mirando City** Texas
45 K2 **Mirandola** Italy
130 D7 **Mirandópolis** Brazil
45 M1 **Mirano** Italy
130 E8 **Mirante Serra do** *mts* Brazil
60 F11 **Mirasaka** Japan
17 G5 **Mira, Sierra de** *mts* Spain
130 E7 **Mirassol** Brazil
16 C2 **Miravalles** *mt* Spain
46 E3 **Miravci** Yugoslavia
77 L2 **Mir Bachech Kūt** Afghanistan
25 E3 **Mirdum** Netherlands
21 D6 **Miré** France
86 G1 **Mirear I** Egypt
127 H5 **Mirebalais** Haiti
19 J5 **Mirebeau** Côte-d'Or France
21 F8 **Mirebeau** Vienne France
18 G9 **Mirepoix** France
54 E7 **Mirgorod** U.S.S.R.
70 D2 **Miri** Sarawak
141 K6 **Miriam Vale** Queensland
85 A5 **Mirik, C** Mauritania
127 K9 **Mirimire** Venezuela
131 H4 **Mirim, L** Brazil/Uruguay
131 F2 **Miriñay, R** Argentina
141 G8 **Mirintu** *R* Queensland
128 D4 **Miriti-Paraná** *R* Colombia
77 G5 **Mīrjāveh** Iran
80 D4 **Mirka** Jordan
45 P1 **Mirna** *R* Yugoslavia
56 H1 **Mirnyy** U.S.S.R.
40 E3 **Miroir, Mt** France
144 D5 **Miromiro** *mt* New Zealand
119 P3 **Mirond L** Sask
54 B7 **Mironovka** U.S.S.R.
48 J6 **Miroşi** Romania
31 J2 **Mirosławiec** Poland
33 R6 **Mirow** E Germany
77 L7 **Mirpur Khas** Pakistan
140 D7 **Mirranponga Pongunna L** N Terr Aust
85 F6 **Mirria** Niger
118 D6 **Mirror** Alberta
48 J6 **Mîrşani** Romania
56 D5 **Mirskoy Khrebet** *mts* U.S.S.R.
141 H5 **Mirtna** Queensland
47 F7 **Mirtoan Sea** Greece
59 J4 **Miryang** S Korea
56 E1 **Miryuyginski Porog** *falls* U.S.S.R.
57 B5 **Mirzachiria** U.S.S.R.
75 K6 **Mirzapur** India
45 O4 **Misa** *R* Italy
60 F12 **Misaki** Japan
60 G11 **Mi-saki** *C* Japan
61 L10 **Misakubo** Japan
45 N4 **Misano Monte** Italy
61 P13 **Misato** Okinawa
61 P5 **Misawa** Japan
32 L8 **Misburg** W Germany
40 G5 **Mischabel** *mt* Switzerland
122 J7 **Miscouche** Pr Edward I
122 H6 **Miscou I** New Brunswick
122 H5 **Miscou, Pt** New Brunswick
127 P4 **Misery, Mt** St Kitts W I
80 F1 **Misgav 'Am** Israel
69 A9 **Misha** Nicobar Is
77 A5 **Mish'ab, Al** U.A.E.
128 D6 **Mishahua** *R* Peru
65 H2 **Mishan** China
94 A5 **Mishawaka** Indiana
116 G2 **Misheguk Mt** Alaska
56 F4 **Mishelevka** U.S.S.R.
120 E4 **Mishibishu L** Ontario
99 T5 **Mishicot** Wisconsin
61 M10 **Mishima** Japan
60 E11 **Mi shima** *isld* Japan
55 C3 **Mishkino** Bashkirskaya U.S.S.R.
55 D3 **Mishkino** Sverdlovsk U.S.S.R.
80 F7 **Mishmaqa** Jordan
80 C6 **Mishmar 'Ayyalon** Israel
80 B8 **Mishmar Ha Negev** Israel
121 P5 **Mishomis** Quebec
52 J2 **Mishvan'** U.S.S.R.
80 E4 **Misilya** Jordan
137 L4 **Misima** *isld* Louisiade Arch
128 E6 **Misión Cavinas** Bolivia
130 B10 **Misiones** *dep* Paraguay
130 C10 **Misiones** *prov* Argentina

Column 1

139 G4 Mulyah,Mt New S Wales
55 D1 Mulym'ya U.S.S.R.
55 E1 Mulym'ya R U.S.S.R.
138 F4 Mulyunparie S Australia
8 C4 Mumbles Wales
87 B8 Mumbondo Angola
87 C8 Mumbué Angola
87 E8 Mumbwa Zambia
87 E8 Mumena Zaïre
109 L5 Mumford Texas
69 D9 Mum Nauk,Laem C Thailand
125 P7 Muna Mexico
71 H7 Muna isld Indonesia
67 B5 Munankwan Lin pass Vietnam/China
143 B8 Munbinia Queensland
141 G2 Munburra Queensland
37 M3 Müncheberg W Germany
30 H3 Müncheberg E Germany
39 München conurbation W Germany
37 M2 Münchernbernsdorf E Germany
36 F2 Münchhausen W Germany
117 L6 Muncho Lake Br Col
37 N5 Münchshofen W Germany
37 O6 Münchshofen W Germany
37 M6 Münchsmünster W Germany
110 L1 Muncie Indiana
140 E7 Muncoonie, L Queensland
95 L5 Muncy Pennsylvania
118 E5 Mundare Alberta
109 H2 Munday Texas
99 S7 Mundelein Illinois
83 J10 Mundel L Sri Lanka
98 J10 Munden Kansas
36 H7 Munderkingen W Germany
9 H2 Mundesley England
9 G2 Mundford England
143 D6 Mundiwindi W Australia
141 F4 Mundjura R Queensland
17 F6 Mundo R Spain
129 K6 Mundo Nôvo Brazil
143 G9 Mundrabilla W Australia
141 K7 Mundubbera Queensland
56 C4 Mundybash U.S.S.R.
46 D3 Munella mt Albania
17 F5 Munera Spain
110 L4 Munfordville Kentucky
141 G8 Mungallala Queensland
141 H8 Mungallala R Queensland
141 G3 Mungana Queensland
141 L7 Mungar Queensland
87 F9 Mungari Mozambique
142 C5 Mungaroona Ra W Australia
56 D5 Mungash-Kul', Gora mt U.S.S.R.
86 E5 Mungbere Zaïre
75 J7 Munger India
94 D3 Munger Michigan
138 E3 Mungeranie S Australia
141 J8 Mungindi Queensland
87 C6 Munhango Angola
98 H1 Munich N Dakota
Munich W Germany see München
88 B8 Muniengashi R Zaïre
17 G3 Muniesa Spain
130 H7 Muniz Freire Brazil
28 H5 Munke Bjergby Denmark
6 D8 Munkebo Denmark
27 E13 Munkedal Sweden
26 G8 Munkflohögen Sweden
27 G12 Munkfors Sweden
28 A7 Munkmarsch W Germany
26 M6 Munksund Sweden
56 G1 Munku-Sardyk,Gora mt Mongolia/U.S.S.R.
37 J3 Münnerstadt W Germany
22 J4 Muno Belgium
71 E3 Muñoz Luzon Philippines
133 C8 Muñoz Gamero, Pen Chile
141 H8 Munro,Mt Tasmania
36 H7 Münsingen W Germany
118 E7 Munson Alberta
111 K11 Munson Florida
40 F1 Münster France
32 M7 Münster Niedersachsen W Germany
32 G9 Münster Nordrhein-Westfalen W Germany
41 H5 Münster Switzerland
14 B4 Munster prov Irish Rep
36 C3 Münstermaifeld W Germany
143 C9 Muntadgin W Australia
70 F4 Munte Sulawesi
48 H4 Muntelui Mare mt Romania
70 P10 Muntjer Java
36 F3 Münzenberg W Germany
29 O6 Muojärvi L Finland
68 F1 Muong Boum Vietnam
68 F2 Muong Hiem Laos
68 F3 Muong Hin Xieng Hung Laos
68 F3 Muong Khao Laos
68 G1 Muong Khoua Laos
68 F3 Muong Khuong Vietnam
68 G3 Muong Ki Laos
68 G3 Muong Lam Vietnam
68 E3 Muong Liep Laos
68 E2 Muong Luong Nam Tha Laos
68 H7 Muong Mai Vietnam
68 F3 Muong May Laos
68 F3 Muong Mo Laos
68 E1 Muong Ngoi Laos
68 H4 Muong Nhie Vietnam
68 F1 Muong Nong Laos
68 E1 Muong ou Neua Laos
68 E1 Muong ou Tay Laos
68 E3 Muong Pa Laos
68 E3 Muong Phalane Laos
68 E3 Muong Phieng Laos
68 E3 Muong Sai Laos
68 E3 Muong Saiapoun Laos
68 G3 Muong Sen Vietnam
68 E3 Muong Sing Laos
68 F2 Muong Son Laos
68 G4 Muong Song Khone Laos
68 E3 Muong Soui Laos
68 F3 Muong Soum Laos
68 F1 Muong Te Vietnam
68 E3 Muong Thong Laos
68 F2 Muong Va Laos
29 K6 Muonio Finland
26 N3 Muonio älv R Sweden/Finland
26 N4 Muonioalusta Sweden
29 N4 Muonionjoki R Finland
41 J4 Muotathal Switzerland
88 B9 Mupata Gorge Zambia
65 E8 Muping China
80 G4 Muqdib Jordan
130 H7 Muqui Brazil
38 J7 Mur R Austria
54 F3 Mura R U.S.S.R.
55 D6 Mura R Yugoslavia
47 J6 Muradiye Turkey
61 N7 Muraglione,Pso.di pass Italy
61 N7 Murakami Japan
44 H3 Murakeresztúr Hungary
133 C7 Murallón mt Chile/Arg
61 N8 Muramatsu Japan
88 E7 Murang'a Kenya
54 M1 Murano Italy
52 G5 Murashi U.S.S.R.
18 G7 Murat France
47 K6 Murat Turkey
47 K8 Murat R Turkey
78 J2 Murat Suyu R Turkey
38 K7 Murau Austria

Column 2

77 C7 Mur'ban U.A.E.
16 C3 Murça Portugal
77 B3 Murcheh Khvort Iran
33 T5 Murchin E Germany
145 D4 Murchison New Zealand
139 H6 Murchison Victoria
6 M1 Murchison oil rig North Sea
144 C5 Murchison, Mt New Zealand
145 D4 Murchison, Mt New Zealand
143 B7 Murchison, Mt W Australia
144 A6 Murchison Mts New Zealand
143 A8 Murchison, R W Australia
140 C5 Murchison R N Terr Aust
89 G4 Murchison Ra S Africa
88 E9 Murchison Rapids Malawi
17 G7 Murcia Spain
17 G7 Murcia prov Spain
71 F6 Murcielagos B Mindanao Philippines
143 E10 Murdarbilla W Australia
18 G8 Mur-de-Barrez France
21 I7 Mur de-Sologne France
98 F6 Murdo S Dakota
141 G2 Murdoch Pt Queensland
122 G5 Murdochville Quebec
113 E10 Murdock Florida
38 N8 Mureck Austria
47 J4 Mürefte Turkey
61 N6 Murei Japan
48 J4 Muresul R Romania
18 F9 Muret France
111 C7 Murfreesboro Arkansas
95 K10 Murfreesboro N Carolina
110 K6 Murfreesboro Tennessee
36 G6 Murg R W Germany
57 G5 Murgab U.S.S.R.
57 G5 Murgab R U.S.S.R.
46 D5 Murgás mt Greece
47 F2 Murgash mt Bulgaria
52 H1 Murgenella Cr N Terr Aust
48 L4 Murgeni Romania
77 H2 Murghab R Afghanistan
74 C3 Murgha Kibzai Pakistan
48 K4 Murgociu mt Romania
72 F6 Murgon Queensland
55 G3 Murgoo W Australia
75 L7 Muri India
130 G7 Muriaé Brazil
16 C2 Murias de Paredes Spain
87 D7 Muriege Angola
118 G4 Muriel L Alberta
60 R2 Muriri-dake mt Japan
119 G2 Murillo Ontario
17 G2 Murillo de Gállego Spain
33 R8 Müritz L E Germany
145 F3 Muriwai New Zealand
26 L5 Murjek Sweden
70 N9 Murjo, G mt Java
86 G4 Murle Ethiopia
36 B3 Mürlenbach W Germany
52 D1 Murmansk U.S.S.R.
54 M2 Murmashi U.S.S.R.
41 O2 Murnau W Germany
102 G7 Muroc L California
52 F6 Murom U.S.S.R.
55 G3 Muromtsevo U.S.S.R.
21 D9 Muron France
60 O3 Muroran Japan
48 L2 Murovano Kurilovtsy U.S.S.R.
31 K3 Murowana Goslina Poland
100 J8 Murphy Idaho
112 C2 Murphy N Carolina
100 B7 Murphy Oregon
65 D3 Murphys California
65 D3 Murphysboro Illinois
141 H8 Murra Warra Queensland
99 R8 Murray Iowa
110 H5 Murray Kentucky
99 K9 Murray Utah
103 N1 Murray New S Wales
139 G6 Murray R New S Wales
138 E6 Murray Bridge S Australia
94 E7 Murray City Ohio
135 M5 Murray Deep Pacific Oc
140 C5 Murray Downs N Terr Aust
14 A4 Murray Hbr Pr Edward I
123 K8 Murray Hd Pr Edward I
83 M9 Murray Hill peak Christmas I Indian Oc
107 N7 Murray,L Oklahoma
112 F3 Murray,L S Carolina
146 B4 Murray Monolith Antarctica
117 N8 Murray R Br Col
143 B10 Murray, R W Australia
122 K7 Murray Ra W Australia
89 C8 Murray River Pr Edward I
135 M5 Murray Seascarp Pacific Oc
99 Q10 Murrayville Illinois
138 F6 Murrayville Victoria
74 E1 Murree Pakistan
75 L3 Murren Inlet S Carolina
40 H4 Murren Switzerland
36 H6 Murrhardt W Germany
139 J5 Murringo New S Wales
143 D8 Murrin Murrin W Australia
14 B3 Murrisk mts Irish Rep
139 G5 Murrumbidgee R New S Wales
139 J5 Murrumburrah & Harden New S Wales
139 K4 Murrurundi New S Wales
19 017 Murs France
139 K4 Murska Sobota Yugoslavia
38 O8 Murska Sobota Yugoslavia
38 K7 Mur Tal V Austria
41 M4 Murtaroli,Piz mt Italy
101 L7 Murtaugh Idaho
74 G8 Murtazapur India
139 G4 Murtee New S Wales
9 M8 Murten See L Switzerland
138 F3 Murtensee L Switzerland
110 G4 Murto L Br Col
138 F6 Murtoa Victoria
29 O6 Murtovaara Finland
74 E9 Murud India
74 D3 Murud R Kalimantan
70 D3 Murud, G mt Kalimantan
145 F3 Murupara New Zealand
70 D4 Murui,R Kalimantan
87 D7 Murung,R Kalimantan
139 L3 Murwillumbah New S Wales
138 E4 Muryo,G mt Java

Column 3

123 S5 Musgravetown Newfoundland
89 G3 Mushandike Dam Zimbabwe
80 G8 Mushasirfa Jordan
14 C5 Mushayrib mt Irish Rep
86 C6 Mushie Zaïre
28 G6 Musholm isld Denmark
103 L6 Music Mt Arizona
103 N2 Musinia Pk Utah
71 M5 Musing R N W Terr
95 R5 Musket Chan Massachusetts
119 O1 Muskeg L Ontario
94 A3 Muskegon Michigan
94 A3 Muskegon R Michigan
94 A3 Muskegon Heights Michigan
26 H4 Musken Norway
94 F7 Muskingum R Ohio
110 A6 Muskö Sweden
121 L7 Muskoka,L Ontario
101 S6 Muskrat Cr Wyoming
77 F6 Müskütän Iran
118 C2 Muskwa R Alberta
52 H1 Muslyumovo U.S.S.R.
80 B3 Musmus Israel
88 D2 Musoma Tanzania
45 O4 Musone Italy
45 M1 Musone R Italy
123 L3 Musquanus L Quebec
122 J7 Musquaro Quebec
122 F8 Musquash New Brunswick
122 J8 Musquodoboit Nova Scotia
122 J9 Musquodoboit Hbr Nova Scotia
28 H7 Musse Denmark
25 H3 Musselburgh Scotland
13 E2 Musselshell Montana
101 S3 Musselshell Montana
101 R3 Musselshell R Montana
87 C8 Mussende Angola
80 H4 Mussidan France
43 F11 Mussomeli Sicily
47 K4 Mustafa Kemalpaşa Turkey
86 H4 Mustahil Ethiopia
75 K4 Mustang Nepal
107 N6 Mustang Oklahoma
108 E3 Mustang Cr Texas
109 K8 Mustang I Texas
55 B5 Mustayevo U.S.S.R.
133 D7 Muster,L Argentina
98 K4 Mustinka R Minnesota
127 O8 Mustique isld Lesser Antilles
27 M13 Mustjala Estonia U.S.S.R.
52 C5 Mustla U.S.S.R.
29 N3 Mustola Finland
13 H5 Muston England
52 C5 Mustvee U.S.S.R.
139 K4 Muswellbrook New S Wales
48 H1 Muszyna Poland
84 H4 Mut Egypt
78 D3 Mut Turkey
38 M8 Muta,H Yugoslavia
88 C1 Mutai Uganda
89 G4 Mutale R S Africa
87 E8 Mutanda Zambia
141 G6 Mutarara Mozambique
37 O4 Mutdorin Czechoslovakia
12 E1 Muthill Scotland
52 J2 Mutis mt Timor Indonesia
37 N5 Mütlangen W Germany
65 D4 Mutomba Mukulu Zaïre
130 B7 Mutoroco S Australia
65 D3 Mutoúgou China
45 R7 Mutrá, M mt Italy
87 G10 Mutsamudu Comoros
60 P4 Mutsu Japan
61 O5 Mutsu-wan B Japan
141 G6 Mutterham Queensland
40 G1 Muttersholtz France
125 L3 Mutton I Irish Rep
87 B5 Mutton Bay Quebec
144 B7 Muttonbird Is New Zealand
14 A4 Mutton Oklahoma
107 L5 Mutual Oklahoma
143 B8 Mutuáis Mozambique
103 E4 Mutum Mato Grosso Brazil
130 H6 Mutum Minas Gerais Brazil
138 E4 Mutumparaná Brazil
83 L9 Mutur Sri Lanka
36 C6 Mutzig France
111 B10 Mutscommon E Germany
29 M9 Muurame Finland
29 L5 Muurola Finland
88 C3 Muya Burundi
125 M3 Muy Muy Nicaragua
57 A3 Muyinga Burundi
74 E1 Muyumba Zaïre
74 D3 Muzaffarabad Kashmir
74 D3 Muzaffargarh Pakistan
75 L5 Muzaffarnagar India
130 F7 Muzaffarpur India
57 K4 Muzat He R China
50 F2 Muzhi U.S.S.R.
18 D5 Muzillac France
77 C3 Müzquiz Mexico
52 F4 Muzon,C Alaska
62 J2 Muztag mt China
50 G2 Muztag R China
27 A13 Muztagata mt China
26 B7 Mvaérøy Norway
26 K5 Mvolo Sudan
28 N10 Mvomero Tanzania
28 C5 Mvouni R Tanzania
28 E6 Mvuma Zimbabwe
87 D9 Mwadui Tanzania
103 M7 Mwali isld Zaïre
89 B8 Mweelrea mts Irish Rep
28 H5 Mwene Ditu Zaïre
89 F3 Mwenga Zaïre
88 A6 Mweru, L Zaïre/Zambia
89 B8 Mwenezi R Zimbabwe
89 F3 Mwewe R Zimbabwe
29 D7 Mwinilunga Zambia
29 L7 Myanaung Burma
120 F3 Myaungmya Burma
60 F12 Myebon Burma
120 H3 Myeik Burma
76 D5 Myers,Mt Burma
76 D5 Myerstown Pennsylvania
29 L1 Myggenaes Faeroes
79 H6 Myingyan Burma
68 B2 Myinkado Burma
68 D2 Myint Burma
68 C2 Myittha Burma
68 B2 Myittha R Burma
68 B3 Mylau E Germany
29 H3 Myall L New S Wales
139 K4 Myall L New S Wales
28 G7 Mylińborz Poland

Column 4

75 O6 Mymensingh Bangladesh
29 J11 Mynämäki Finland
57 G2 Mynaral U.S.S.R.
57 C4 Mynbulak U.S.S.R.
80 G8 Mynddd Bach hills Wales
14 C5 Mynydd Eppynt mts Wales
68 A2 Myohaung Burma
68 B2 Myohla Burma
68 B2 Myothit Burma
47 K8 Myra Turkey
141 F3 Myra Vale Queensland
27 B11 Myrdal Norway
26 H3 Myre Norway
27 G14 Myresjö Sweden
26 L6 Myrheden Sweden
118 F5 Myrnam Alberta
100 J3 Myrtle Idaho
119 U9 Myrtle Ontario
111 G7 Myrtle Mississippi
121 N8 Myrtle Ontario
100 B6 Myrtle Cr Oregon
139 H6 Myrtleford Victoria
100 A6 Myrtle Point Oregon
138 E4 Myrtle Springs S Australia
141 L1 Myrtletown Queensland
80 D1 Mysaki Israel
77 A2 Myski U.S.S.R.
36 C4 Myślenice Poland
36 C4 Nahbóllenbach W Germany
21 I7 Myslowice Poland
80 C3 Mysore India
131 B8 Mystery L Manitoba
133 D6 Mystic Connecticut
71 E3 Mystic Iowa
94 C1 Mystic S Dakota
119 N6 Myszków Poland
66 E4 My Tho Vietnam
71 L9 Mytishchi U.S.S.R.
37 M3 My Trach Vietnam
65 D4 Mže R Czechoslovakia
77 C3 Mzreb,El Mali
115 N6 Mzimba Malawi
88 D7 Mzuzu Malawi
88 E7

Column 5

37 M5 Naab R W Germany
25 B5 Naaldwijk Netherlands
135 U6 Naalehu Hawaiian Is
80 O6 Na'an Israel
86 E4 Naandi Sudan
29 J11 Naantali Finland
25 D4 Naarden Netherlands
14 E3 Naas Irish Rep
29 N2 Näätämönjoki R Finland
16 B5 Nabã R Portugal
61 K11 Nabari Japan
71 F5 Nabas Panay Philippines
79 F5 Nabatiyet Ett Tahta Lebanon
88 E10 Nabire Mozambique
37 O4 Nabburg Luzon Philippines
37 N5 Nabburg W Germany
52 H6 Naberezhnye Chelny U.S.S.R.
116 Q5 Nabesna R U S Wales
43 D12 Nabeul Tunisia
130 B7 Nabiabwe,R Brazil
123 K3 Nabisipi R Quebec
80 E5 Nablus Jordan
79 E10 Nabq Egypt
71 F6 Nabua Negros Philippines
68 D5 Nabule Burma
88 H9 Nacala Mozambique
125 L3 Nacaome Honduras
60 T2 Nabatiya Japan
55 D2 Nakatay U.S.S.R.
61 L10 Naka-Tombetsu Japan
60 G10 Naka-umi Japan
118 J8 Nachkamik I Alaska
100 D2 Naches Washington
100 D2 Naches Pass Washington
87 G8 Nachingwea Tanzania
34 Ch'u R India
86 G2 Nakfa Ethiopia
78 K2 Nachichevan U.S.S.R.
84 J4 Nakhl Egypt
61 F9 Nakhodka U.S.S.R.
68 D4 Nakhon Nayok Thailand
68 F5 Nakhon Pathom Thailand
68 F5 Nakhon Ratchasima Thailand
69 E8 Nakhon Si Thammarat Thailand
68 E4 Nakhon Thai Thailand
59 L2 Nakhtakhe U.S.S.R.
61 P12 Nakijin Japan
60 B2 Nakina Br Col
119 K3 Nakina Ontario
29 J10 Nakkila Finland
28 O10 Nakkur Fjord inlet Faeroes
31 K2 Nakło Poland
116 J7 Naknek Alaska
61 O9 Nakoso Japan
18 G4 Nakou China
65 G5 Naksho Biru see Biru
28 G7 Nakskov Denmark
26 G9 Näkten I Sweden
57 K3 Naktong R S Korea
88 E2 Nakuru Kenya
14 L Nakuru, L Kenya
117 P10 Nakusp Br Col
68 C1 Na-lang Burma
71 L9 Nalayh Mongolia
53 L5 Naldrug India
76 D2 Nalgonda India
22 D3 Nalinnes Belgium
67 F2 Nallamala Hills India
94 G8 Nallen W Virginia
48 H1 Naltuhin Turkey
67 F4 Namaacha Mozambique
118 D8 Namak Alberta
24 C8 Namakan L Minn/Ontario
119 H4 Namakan L Minn/Ontario
37 L7 Namakzár-e Shadád salt lake Iran
143 C7 Namak, Kavir-e salt waste Iran
69 H14 Namang Indonesia
137 Q3 Namanga Tanzania
57 E6 Namangan U.S.S.R.
69 E6 Namapa Mozambique
88 H8 Namaponda Mozambique
115 P5 Namarrói Mozambique
75 J5 Namasagali Uganda
88 E6 Namatanai New Ireland
67 C5 Nambé Well W Australia
65 H3 Namber Indonesia
141 L7 Nambour Queensland
139 L4 Nambucca Heads New S Wales
28 G6 Nam Ca Dinh R Laos
69 E6 Nam Can Vietnam
141 G4 Namcha Barwa mt China
51 J5 Nam Co L China
26 G8 Namdalen V Norway
26 H7 Nam Dinh Vietnam
26 H6 Namecala Mozambique
70 E5 Nameh Kalimantan
60 C4 Namen see Namur
45 K2 Nametil Mozambique
141 J6 Namew L Sask

Column 6

61 K10 Nagoya Japan
74 H8 Nagpur India
66 E5 Nagqu China
29 J11 Nagu Finland
127 K5 Nagua Dom Rep
71 E2 Naguilian Luzon Philippines
71 G4 Nagumbuaya Pt Philippines
48 D4 Nagyatád Hungary
44 H4 Nagybajom Hungary
48 D4 Nagyecsed Hungary
48 E4 Nagykálló Hungary
44 G3 Nagykanizsa Hungary
48 F3 Nagykáta Hungary
48 F3 Nagykörös Hungary
48 G3 Nagyléta Hungary
61 P13 Nagyvárad see Oradea
70 A4 Naha Okinawa
80 D3 Nahal Israel
80 C7 Nahalal Israel
74 G3 Nahan India
114 G5 Nahanni Butte N W Terr
117 M5 Nahanni N W Terr
117 L5 Nahanni Nat. Park N W Terr
80 D1 Nahariyya Israel
77 A2 Nahávand Iran
100 A8 Nahby W Germany
85 C5 Nahuala Mali
68 E1 Nam Pa Sak R Thailand
68 D1 Nam Phang Thailand
68 F4 Nam Phong Thailand
22 B3 Nampont France
88 G9 Nampula Mozambique
68 G4 Nam Pung Res Thailand
68 F2 Namrole Norway
26 F1 Namsen R Norway
26 E2 Namsos Norway
68 E1 Nam Suong R Laos
26 G7 Namsvatn L Norway
68 F1 Nam Teng Burma
68 E2 Namtha R Laos
68 G4 Nam Theun R Laos
68 C2 Namtok Burma
68 D5 Nam Tok Thailand
68 D1 Namton Burma
51 M2 Namtsy U.S.S.R.
89 S3 Namuli mt Mozambique
83 L11 Namunukula mt Sri Lanka
88 E8 Namutoni Mozambique
22 H3 Namur Belgium
22 H3 Namur prov Belgium
117 R7 Namur L Alberta
57 C9 Namutoni Namibia
87 E9 Namwala Zambia
68 D4 Nam Wang R Thailand
89 E4 Namwera Malawi
31 L4 Namysláki Poland
31 K4 Namyslow Poland
100 B1 Nanaimo Br Col
102 R12 Nanakuli Hawaiian Is
65 H4 Nanam N Korea
143 E10 Nanambinia W Australia
67 B6 Nanan China
67 F4 Nan'an China
141 K7 Nanango Queensland
67 F5 Nan'ao China
61 K8 Nanao Japan
61 K8 Nanao-wan B Japan
67 B3 Nanbai China
67 B1 Nanbu China
21 H7 Nançay France
59 J2 Nancha China
67 E2 Nanchang China
67 E6 Nanchangshan Dao isld China
67 B1 Nanchong China
140 A5 Nancowry isld Nicobar Is
19 K4 Nancy France
144 E8 Nancy Sd New Zealand
74 H3 Nanda Devi mt India
67 C9 Nandan China
61 J11 Nandan Japan
85 C5 Nane Mali
37 M6 Nanderstadt W Germany
139 H5 Nandewar Ra mts New S Wales
74 F8 Nandurbar India
117 O11 Nandyal India
65 C2 Nanfen China
69 E2 Nanfeng China
75 P4 Nanga Parbat mt Kashmir
70 C4 Nangapinoh Kalimantan
77 C2 Nangarhar Afghanistan
31 O3 Nangar India
65 G3 Narong China
69 E3 Narachit Thailand
19 H7 Nara New Mexico
106 G6 Nara Victoria
75 O7 Narayanganj Bangladesh
57 D7 Narayangaon India
71 L9 Narbada R see Narmada R
18 H9 Narbonne France
9 G2 Narborough England
65 H1 Narcea R Spain
9 H3 Nard Italy
60 C2 Nare Head England
143 C9 Narembeen W Australia
90 D6 Narendranagar India
31 O3 Nares Deep Atlantic Oc
115 M2 Nares Str Greenland/Canada
48 D1 Nares Poland
31 O3 Naretha Poland
65 G3 Narhong China
69 E2 Nari R Gol'r China
146 L Narino dif'r Colombia
127 O2 Narita Japan
60 G11 Nariva co Trinidad
60 G11 Nariva Swamp Trinidad
107 N2 Nariva Kansas
70 K3 Narken Sweden
8 C4 Narmada R India

Column 7

68 F2 Nam Het R Laos
68 D2 Nam Hsin R Burma
87 B10 Namib Des Namibia
87 C10 Namibia terr Africa
88 F9 Namicunde Mozambique
61 O8 Namie Japan
61 K8 Namioka Japan
87 C11 Namiziz mt Namibia
68 F3 Nam Khan R Laos
68 D2 Nam Kok R Thailand
68 C1 Namlan Burma
61 O9 Namling R Burma
8 D1 Namlwich England
146 M2 Namnetum England
88 G8 Namtu Mozambique
8 D1 Nantwich England
118 M2 Nanuque Brazil
87 N Nanushuk R Alaska
67 A4 Nanxi China
67 D1 Nanxian China
141 J6 Nanxiang China
58 F5 Nanyang Kenya
67 C2 Nanyi China
67 F1 Nanyo Japan
65 C5 Nanyuan China
88 F1 Nanyuki Kenya
65 F4 Nanzamu China
67 D1 Nanzheng China
67 G3 Nanzhou China
54 H1 Nao,C.de la Spain
115 M7 Naococcan,L Quebec
61 M8 Naogaon Bangladesh
75 N6 Naokot Pakistan
74 C6 Naol He R China
59 K2 Naomi Pk Utah
103 O8 Naomid, Dasht-e des Iran
46 E4 Náousa Greece
65 C6 Naozhou Dao isld China
102 B3 Napa California
71 H7 Napabalana Indonesia
122 K4 Napadogan New Brunswick
70 D3 Napaku Kalimantan
121 O8 Napanee Ontario
115 O4 Napassoq Greenland
100 C3 Napavine Washington
71 F4 Napayauan Philippines
103 L8 Naperville Illinois
123 O2 Napetipi R Quebec
40 G4 Napf mt Switzerland
99 L9 Napier Missouri
143 E8 Napier New Zealand
142 F2 Napier Broome B W Australia
140 A4 Napier, Mt N Terr Aust
146 A5 Napier Mts Antarctica
146 E10 Napier Pen N Terr Aust
143 E9 Napier Ra W Australia
121 R9 Naperville Quebec
113 F11 Naples Florida
95 K4 Naples New York
109 N2 Naples Texas
61 G1 Napo China
128 C4 Napo R Peru/Ecuador
94 B7 Napoleon Indiana
98 G3 Napoleon N Dakota
94 C5 Napoleon Ohio
111 E12 Napoleonville Louisiana
43 G7 Napoleono, Appennino mts Italy
45 Q8 Nápoli Italy
98 Q9 Naponee Nebraska
131 H2 Napoora R Argentina
141 H8 Nappanee Indiana
140 C6 Napperby N Terr Aust
110 C2 Napton Missouri
79 F8 Naqadeh Iran
79 F8 Naqb Istrar Jordan
79 C9 Naqb Malba mt Egypt
61 J11 Nara Japan
85 C5 Nara Mali
75 M3 Naracoorte S Australia
139 H5 Naradhan New S Wales
143 A8 Naraling W Australia
117 O11 Naramata Br Col
65 C2 Naran Bulag China
125 O6 Naranjo Mexico
69 E2 Narathiwat Thailand
106 G6 Nara View New Mexico

Column 8

18 F6 Nantiat France
95 L5 Nanticoke Pennsylvania
95 M8 Nanticoke R Delaware/Maryland
8 C4 Nant Moel Wales
118 D8 Nanton Alberta
67 G1 Nantong China
8 F4 Nantua France
146 E12 Nantucket I Massachusetts
146 E12 Nantucket Inlet Antarctica
88 G8 Nantulo Mozambique
8 D1 Nantwich England
94 J6 Nantyglo Pennsylvania
130 H3 Nanuque Brazil
116 M4 Nanushuk R Alaska
67 A2 Nanxi China
67 C2 Nanxian China
67 C2 Nanxiang China
58 F5 Nanyang China
141 J6 Nanxiong China
67 F1 Nanyang China
65 E6 Nanyo Japan
67 C2 Nanyuan China
65 C5 Nanyuki Kenya
88 F1 Nanzamu China
67 F7 Nanzheng China
67 G2 Nanzhou China
142 B1 Naqadeh Iran
143 B7 Narrard, Mt W Australia
74 O1 Narsinghgarh India
74 H7 Narsinghpur India
115 O5 Narsaq Greenland
115 O5 Narsaq Greenland
65 C3 Narssarssuaq Greenland
65 C3 Nart China
60 I3 Nartës,Gjol i isld Albania
131 F2 Naru-shima isld Japan
60 D13 Naru-shima isld Japan
61 J11 Naruto Japan
60 H11 Naruto-kaikyō str Japan
52 C5 Narva U.S.S.R.
52 C5 Narva-Jõesuu U.S.S.R.
26 J3 Narvik Norway

54 Narvskiy Zaliv — Newton Stewart

52 C5 **Narvskiy Zaliv** *gulf* U.S.S.R.
74 G4 **Narwana** India
74 G6 **Narwar** India
140 C6 **Narwietooma** N Terr Aust
52 H1 **Nar'yan Mar** U.S.S.R.
141 F8 **Naryilco** Queensland
56 B6 **Narymskiy Khrebet** *mts* U.S.S.R.
57 H4 **Naryn** U.S.S.R.
57 G4 **Naryn Ugyut** *R* U.S.S.R.
54 G4 **Naryshkino** U.S.S.R.
27 G11 **Nås** Sweden
85 F7 **Nasarawa** Nigeria
48 J3 **Năsăud** Romania
26 M5 **Näsberg** Sweden
18 H8 **Nasbinals** France
144 C6 **Naseby** New Zealand
107 M5 **Nash** Oklahoma
8 C5 **Nash** Wales
122 F6 **Nash Cr** New Brunswick
116 D6 **Nash Harbor** Alaska
140 E5 **Nash, L** Queensland
8 C5 **Nash Pt** Wales
99 O7 **Nashua** Iowa
101 T1 **Nashua** Montana
95 Q4 **Nashua** New Hampshire
111 C8 **Nashville** Arkansas
112 D6 **Nashville** Georgia
110 G3 **Nashville** Illinois
94 A7 **Nashville** Indiana
107 M4 **Nashville** Kansas
94 B4 **Nashville** Michigan
112 J2 **Nashville** N Carolina
94 E6 **Nashville** Ohio
110 K5 **Nashville** Tennessee
99 N2 **Nashwauk** Minnesota
48 E5 **Našice** Yugoslavia
29 K10 **Näsijärvi** *L* Finland
74 E8 **Nasik** India
86 F4 **Nasir** Sudan
79 A8 **Nasr** Egypt
79 H4 **Naşrānī, Jebel an** *mts* Syria
117 J8 **Nass** *R* Br Col
98 K4 **Nassau** Minnesota
113 L9 **Nassau** New Providence I Bahamas
95 O4 **Nassau** New York
36 D3 **Nassau** W Germany
141 F3 **Nassau** *R* Queensland
133 D9 **Nassau,B.de** Chile
113 F7 **Nassau Sd** Florida
95 M9 **Nassawadox** Virginia
33 T10 **Nasseböhla** E Germany
37 L6 **Nassenfels** W Germany
33 S7 **Nassenheide** E Germany
84 J5 **Nasser, L** Egypt
27 G14 **Nässjö** Sweden
22 J3 **Nassogne** Belgium
38 N6 **Nasswald** Austria
115 M6 **Nastapoka Is** N W Terr
36 D3 **Nastätten** W Germany
71 E3 **Nasugbu** Luzon Philippines
61 N8 **Nasu-Yumoto** Japan
52 D6 **Nasva** U.S.S.R.
26 J10 **Näsviken** Sweden
87 E10 **Nata** Botswana
89 E3 **Nata** *R* Botswana
128 F5 **Natal** Brazil
118 C9 **Natal** Br Col
69 D12 **Natal** Sumatra
89 F7 **Natal** *prov* S Africa
141 H5 **Natal** *R* Queensland
90 M13 **Natal Basin** Indian Oc
141 H5 **Natal Downs** Queensland
109 J6 **Natalia** Texas
55 C3 **Natalinsk** U.S.S.R.
77 B3 **Natanz** Iran
123 L3 **Natashquan** Quebec
123 L3 **Natashquan R** Quebec/Labrador
116 K3 **Natavukti L** Alaska
116 R6 **Natazhat Mt** Alaska
111 E10 **Natchez** Mississippi
111 C10 **Natchitoches** Louisiana
139 H6 **Nathalia** Victoria
115 R3 **Nathorsts Land** Greenland
106 D3 **Nathrop** Colorado
124 J5 **Natillas** Mexico
138 F6 **Natimuk** Victoria
116 R4 **Nation** Alaska
101 L2 **National Bison Ra** Montana
102 G9 **National City** California
86 C3 **National Park** Chad
117 L8 **Nation R** Br Col
123 K4 **Natiskotek B** Anticosti I, Quebec
141 H6 **Native Companion Cr** Queensland
124 B4 **Natividad** *isld* Mexico
129 J6 **Natividade** Brazil
68 C5 **Natkyizin** Burma
107 M2 **Natoma** Kansas
124 E3 **Nátora** Mexico
61 O7 **Natori** Japan
22 J3 **Natoye** Belgium
101 T6 **Natrona** Wyoming
88 F3 **Natron L** Tanzania
68 B3 **Nattalin** Burma
83 J10 **Nattandiya** Sri Lanka
29 N3 **Nattaset** *mt* Finland
68 C3 **Nattaung** *mt* Burma
26 L5 **Nattavaara** Sweden
37 O6 **Natternberg** W Germany
37 J6 **Nattheim** W Germany
27 H15 **Nättraby** Sweden
Natuna Besar *see* **Bunguran Utara, Kep.** *I*
Natuna Selatan *see* **Bunguran Selatan Kep** *I*
69 H10 **Natuna Utara** Indonesia
95 M2 **Natural Bridge** New York
94 H9 **Natural Bridge** Virginia
103 O4 **Natural Br.Nat.Mon** Utah
108 F3 **Natural Dam L** Texas
143 B10 **Naturaliste, C** W Australia
143 A7 **Naturaliste Chan** W Australia
81 H9 **Naturaliste Plateau** Indian Oc
106 B3 **Naturita** Colorado
99 V3 **Naubinway** Michigan
87 C10 **Nauchas** Namibia
121 T4 **Naudville** Quebec
33 R7 **Nauen** E Germany
130 E10 **Naufragados, Pta Dos** *C* Brazil
95 O5 **Naugatuck** Connecticut
71 E4 **Naujan** Philippines
29 N8 **Naulavaara** *mt* Finland
87 B9 **Naulila** Angola
37 M1 **Naumburg** E Germany
36 G1 **Naumburg** W Germany
68 C4 **Naunglon** Burma
68 C3 **Naungpale** Burma
33 R10 **Naunhof** E Germany
80 G6 **Na'ur** Jordan
36 D2 **Nauroth** W Germany
137 O2 **Nauru** *rep* Pacific Oc
55 D5 **Naurzum** U.S.S.R.
26 A10 **Naustdal** Norway
26 C9 **Nauste** Norway
128 D4 **Nauta** Peru
26 R3 **Nautsi** U.S.S.R.
111 J8 **Nauvoo** Alabama
99 P9 **Nauvoo** Illinois
108 G7 **Nava** Mexico
16 D3 **Nava de Rey** Spain
16 E5 **Navahermosa** Spain
103 P6 **Navajo** Arizona
103 M4 **Navajo L** Utah
103 O4 **Navajo Mt** Utah
103 O5 **Navajo Nat.Mon** Arizona
103 N5 **Navajo Pt** Arizona
106 C5 **Navajo Res** Colo/New Mex
16 E4 **Navalcarnero** Spain
16 D5 **Navalmoral de la Mata** Spain
86 E5 **Nava R** Zaïre
133 D9 **Navarino, I** Chile
17 F2 **Navarra** *prov* Spain
94 F6 **Navarre** Ohio
139 G6 **Navarre** Victoria
102 A2 **Navarro** California
102 A2 **Navarro** *R* California
109 L4 **Navarro Mills Res** Texas
109 L5 **Navasota** Texas
126 G5 **Navassa I** Caribbean
45 P5 **Navelli** Italy
9 F1 **Navenby** England
16 C1 **Navia** Spain
16 C1 **Navia** *R* Spain
109 L6 **Navidad** *R* Texas
127 K4 **Navidad Bank** Caribbean
130 H10 **Navio** *R* Brazil
54 F4 **Navlya** U.S.S.R.
54 F4 **Navlya** *R* U.S.S.R.
57 D4 **Navoi** U.S.S.R.
124 E4 **Navojoa** Mexico
124 F5 **Navolato** Mexico
52 E3 **Navolok** U.S.S.R.
52 F5 **Navoloki** U.S.S.R.
46 E6 **Návpaktos** Greece
46 F7 **Návplion** Greece
28 B4 **Navr** Denmark
85 D6 **Navrongo** Ghana
74 E8 **Navsari** India
75 N6 **Nawabganj** Bangladesh
75 J5 **Nawabganj** India
74 C5 **Nawabshah** Pakistan
75 L6 **Nawada** India
77 K3 **Nāwah** Afghanistan
83 K10 **Nawalapitiya** Sri Lanka
84 F3 **Nawfalīyah,an** Libya
138 F5 **Nawingi** Victoria
68 D1 **Nawng-Hpa** Burma
68 C1 **Nawngkio** Burma
68 D1 **Nawngleng** Burma
67 B2 **Naxi** China
47 G7 **Náxos** Greece
47 H7 **Náxos** *isld* Greece
18 E9 **Nay** France
69 J12 **Naya** Indonesia
16 E4 **Nayacerrada, Pto. de** *peak* Spain
75 L8 **Nayagarh** India
124 G6 **Nayar** Mexico
124 G7 **Nayarit** *state* Mexico
77 E3 **Nay Band** Iran
9 G4 **Nayland** England
113 D7 **Naylor** Georgia
110 F5 **Naylor** Missouri
67 B3 **Nayong** China
59 M3 **Nayoro** Japan
129 L6 **Nazaré** Brazil
16 A5 **Nazaré** Portugal
130 J9 **Nazaré da Mata** Brazil
22 F2 **Nazareth** Belgium
Nazareth Ethiopia *see* **Adama**
76 C6 **Nazareth** India
80 E3 **Nazareth** Israel
95 M6 **Nazareth** Pennsylvania
130 E5 **Nazário** Brazil
54 N2 **Nazarovka** U.S.S.R.
56 D3 **Nazarovo** Krasnoyarskiy Kray U.S.S.R.
55 F3 **Nazarovo** Tyumenskaya U.S.S.R.
124 G5 **Nazas** Mexico
128 D6 **Nazca** Peru
59 J6 **Naze** Japan
9 H4 **Naze,The** *C* England
47 J7 **Nazilli** Turkey
56 A1 **Nazinskaya** *R* U.S.S.R.
75 Q5 **Nazira** India
75 O7 **Nazir Hat** Bangladesh
117 M9 **Nazko** Br Col
80 A7 **Nazla** Israel
80 D4 **Nazlat** Jordan
86 G4 **Nazret** Ethiopia
67 B4 **Nazuo** China
55 E1 **Nazym** *R* U.S.S.R.
55 F3 **Nazyvayevsk** U.S.S.R.
37 J1 **Nazza** E Germany
89 F3 **Ncema Dam** Zimbabwe
88 A8 **Nchanga** Zambia
88 E9 **Ncheu** Malawi
87 B7 **Ndalakanda** Angola
85 E6 **Ndali** Benin
71 L10 **Ndao** *isld* Indonesia
86 D4 **Ndele** Cent Afr Republic
86 B6 **Ndendé** Gabon
137 O4 **Ndeni** *isld* Santa Cruz Is
86 B5 **Ndikiniméki** Cameroon
86 B6 **Ndindi** Gabon
86 C3 **N'Djamena** Chad
86 B6 **Ndjolé** Gabon
86 B6 **N'Dogou, L** Gabon
88 B8 **Ndola** Zambia
71 K9 **Ndona** Flores Indonesia
86 B6 **N'Dongo** Congo
26 E8 **Nea** Norway
139 J3 **Neabul** *R* Queensland
46 D5 **Néa Filippías** Greece
14 E2 **Neagh,L** N Ireland
107 O4 **Neal** Kansas
140 B6 **Neale,L** N Terr Aust
138 D3 **Neales** *R* S Australia
47 F4 **Neá Moudhaniá** Greece
21 I6 **Néant** *R* France
15 G2 **Neap** Shetland Scotland
47 H9 **Néapolis** Crete Greece
46 E4 **Neápolis** Makedhonia Greece
46 F8 **Neápolis** Pelopónnisos Greece
47 F6 **Néa Psará** Greece
116 J9 **Near Is** Aleutian Is
8 C4 **Neath** Wales
20 J4 **Neauphle-le-Château** France
47 H3 **Néa Víssi** Greece
85 D6 **Nebbou** Upper Volta
52 G3 **Nebdino** U.S.S.R.
28 A7 **Nebel** W Germany
33 Q5 **Nebel** *R* E Germany
41 M3 **Nebelhorn** *mt* W Germany
43 B12 **Nebeur** Tunisia
43 C12 **Nebhana** *R* Tunisia
141 H8 **Nebine** *R* Queensland
50 E5 **Nebit-Dag** U.S.S.R.
141 J5 **Nebo** Queensland
52 D5 **Nebolchi** U.S.S.R.
80 F6 **Nebo, Mt** Jordan
103 N2 **Nebo,Mt** Utah
33 P10 **Nebra** E Germany
98 G8 **Nebraska** *state* U.S.A.
99 L9 **Nebraska City** Nebraska
43 F11 **Nebrodi,Monti** Sicily
99 Q5 **Necedah** Wisconsin
117 L9 **Nechako R** Br Col
98 J1 **Neche** N Dakota
109 M4 **Neches** *R* Texas
128 D2 **Nechi** *R* Colombia
33 T6 **Nechlin** E Germany
36 F7 **Neckar** *R* W Germany
36 F5 **Neckarbischofsheim** W Germany
36 G5 **Neckarelz** W Germany
36 F5 **Neckargemünd** W Germany
36 F5 **Neckarsteinach** W Germany
36 G5 **Neckarsulm** W Germany
102 U13 **Necker I** Hawaiian Is
144 B7 **Neck, The** New Zealand
131 F7 **Necochea** Argentina
37 P4 **Nečtiny** Czechoslovakia
86 B6 **Necuto** Angola
20 E4 **Nécy** France
16 B1 **Neda** Spain
33 S5 **Neddemin** E Germany
121 L5 **Nedelec** Quebec
106 E2 **Nederland** Colorado
109 N6 **Nederland** Texas
25 E5 **Neder Rijn** *R* Netherlands
25 E6 **Nederweert** Netherlands
142 A2 **Nedlands** *dist* Perth, W Aust
33 Q8 **Nedlitz** E Germany
17 F9 **Nedroma** Algeria
31 L5 **Nedza** Poland
25 G4 **Neede** Netherlands
9 H3 **Needham Market** England
101 Q5 **Needle Mt** Wyoming
144 A6 **Needle Pk** New Zealand
103 K7 **Needles** California
145 E2 **Needles Pt** New Zealand
9 E6 **Needles, The** *rocks* England
109 M6 **Needville** Texas
119 S9 **Neelin** Manitoba
101 N7 **Neely** Idaho
110 F5 **Neelyville** Missouri
130 B10 **Neembucú** *dep* Paraguay
99 S5 **Neenah** Wisconsin
119 S8 **Neepawa** Manitoba
25 E6 **Neer** Netherlands
143 B8 **Neereno** *hill* W Australia
106 H3 **Nee Res** Colorado
115 M3 **Neergaard L** N W Terr
22 J1 **Neerpelt** Belgium
22 J2 **Neerwinden** Belgium
28 A4 **Nees** Denmark
112 F4 **Neeses** S Carolina
55 F2 **Nefedovo** U.S.S.R.
85 F2 **Nefta** Tunisia
57 F4 **Nefteabad** U.S.S.R.
8 B2 **Nefyn** Wales
43 C12 **Nefza** Tunisia
87 C7 **Negage** Angola
85 C6 **Negala** Mali
83 K10 **Negama** Sri Lanka
70 P10 **Negara** Bali Indonesia
70 D6 **Negara** Kalimantan
70 D6 **Negara** *R* Kalimantan
99 T3 **Negaunee** Michigan
80 B7 **Negba** Israel
86 G4 **Negelli** Ethiopia
69 F11 **Negeri Sembilan** Malaysia
79 E8 **Negev** *mt reg* Israel
130 C8 **Negla** *R* Paraguay
48 J5 **Negoiu** *mt* Romania
87 G8 **Negomano** Mozambique
83 J10 **Negombo** Sri Lanka
48 H6 **Negotin** Yugoslavia
46 E3 **Negotino** Yugoslavia
73 P5 **Negrais,C** Burma
143 D7 **Negrara,R** W Australia
130 G6 **Negra,Serra** *mts* Brazil
16 B2 **Negreira** Spain
48 J6 **Negreni** Romania
18 G8 **Nègrepelisse** France
48 L4 **Negreşti** Romania
127 H1 **Negril Pt.N** Jamaica
141 F7 **Negri Mts** Queensland
16 E9 **Negri,Pta** Morocco
128 F4 **Negro** *R* Brazil
16 D9 **Negro,C** Morocco
94 H7 **Negro Mt** Penn/Maryland
131 C7 **Negro,R** Argentina
130 B9 **Negro,R** Paraguay
131 F4 **Negro,R** Uruguay
71 F5 **Negros** *isld* Philippines
47 J1 **Negru Vadă** Romania
100 B4 **Nehalem** Oregon
80 C5 **Nehalim** Israel
77 G4 **Nehbandān** Iran
59 H2 **Nehe** China
32 G10 **Neheim-Hüsten** W Germany
48 K5 **Nehoiaşu** Romania
20 B3 **Néhou** France
33 R4 **Nehringen** E Germany
137 S5 **Neiafu** Tonga
127 J5 **Neiba** Dom Rep
33 R10 **Neichen** E Germany
52 C1 **Neiden** Norway
118 K8 **Neidpath** Sask
101 P3 **Neihart** Montana
65 C7 **Neihuang** China
67 B2 **Neijiang** China
Neikiang *see* **Neijiang**
16 E2 **Neila,Sa.de** *mts* Spain
118 H6 **Neilburg** Sask
68 A7 **Neill I** Andaman Is
99 Q5 **Neillsville** Wisconsin
123 M7 **Neil's Harbour** C Breton I, N Scotia
100 B2 **Neilton** Washington
58 E3 **Nei Monggol Zizhiqu** *aut reg* China
33 N8 **Neindorf** W Germany
36 G5 **Neipperg** W Germany
65 C6 **Neiqiu** China
Neisse *see* **Nysa**
31 H4 **Neisse** *R* E Ger/Poland
128 C3 **Neiva** Colombia
37 O3 **Nejdek** Czechoslovakia
86 G4 **Nejo** Ethiopia
98 H1 **Nekoma** N Dakota
99 R5 **Nekoosa** Wisconsin
28 G5 **Nekselø** *isld* Denmark
51 O2 **Neksikan** U.S.S.R.
27 H16 **Neksø** Denmark
27 C13 **Nelaug** Norway
141 F5 **Nelia** Queensland
52 D6 **Nelidovo** U.S.S.R.
54 D1 **Nelidovo** U.S.S.R.
98 J7 **Neligh** Nebraska
142 E3 **Nellie,Mt** W Australia
139 K6 **Nelligen** New S Wales
76 D3 **Nellore** India
59 L2 **Nel'ma** U.S.S.R.
52 F5 **Nel'sha** U.S.S.R.
103 L6 **Nelson** Arizona
117 P11 **Nelson** Br Col
102 C2 **Nelson** California
13 F6 **Nelson** England
112 J2 **Nelson** N Carolina
98 H9 **Nelson** Nebraska
103 K6 **Nelson** Nevada
145 D4 **Nelson** New Zealand
95 K5 **Nelson** Pennsylvania
138 F7 **Nelson** Victoria
8 C4 **Nelson** Wales
99 P5 **Nelson** Wisconsin
144 C4 **Nelson** *stat area* New Zealand
138 F7 **Nelson,C** Victoria
144 C5 **Nelson Cr** New Zealand
133 C8 **Nelson,Estrecho** *chan* Chile
117 M6 **Nelson Forks** Br Col
119 T3 **Nelson House** Manitoba
116 E6 **Nelson I** Alaska
146 E15 **Nelson I** S Shetland Is
145 D4 **Nelson Lakes Nat. Park** New Zealand
119 V3 **Nelson R** Manitoba
101 S1 **Nelson Res** Montana
94 E7 **Nelsonville** Ohio
89 G5 **Nelspruit** S Africa
52 J4 **Nem** *R* U.S.S.R.
85 C5 **Néma** Mauritania
52 H5 **Nema** U.S.S.R.
99 O3 **Nemadji** *R* Minnesota
99 L9 **Nemaha** Nebraska
76 C6 **Nemam** India
31 O2 **Neman** *R* U.S.S.R.
71 L10 **Nembrala** Indonesia
52 F5 **Nemda** *R* U.S.S.R.
52 H3 **Nemed** U.S.S.R.
120 G5 **Nemegos** Ontario
120 G4 **Nemegosenda L** Ontario
119 M3 **Nemeiban** Sask
46 D4 **Nëmerçkë** Albania
45 N6 **Nemi** *L* Italy
48 K4 **Nemira** *mt* Romania
48 M2 **Nemirov** U.S.S.R.
115 M7 **Nemiscau** Quebec
18 G4 **Nemours** France
60 T2 **Nemuro** Japan
60 S2 **Nemuro** *prefect* Japan
60 T1 **Nemuro-kaikyō** *str* Japan/Kuril Is
14 C4 **Nenagh** Irish Rep
116 N4 **Nenana** Alaska
41 L3 **Nendeln** Liechtenstein
9 F2 **Nene, R** England
59 J2 **Nenjiang** China
59 H2 **Nen Jiang** *R* China
36 B4 **Nennig** W Germany
36 H1 **Nentershausen** W Germany
13 F4 **Nenthead** England
98 E7 **Nenzel** Nebraska
41 L3 **Nenzing** Austria
107 P4 **Neodesha** Kansas
99 S10 **Neoga** Illinois
99 L8 **Neola** Iowa
103 O1 **Neola** Utah
47 H7 **Néon Karlóvasi** Greece
99 S5 **Neopit** Wisconsin
130 H11 **Neópolis** Brazil
99 S6 **Neosho** Wisconsin
107 P4 **Neosho** *R* Kansas/Okla
80 D3 **Neot Golan** Israel
80 F1 **Ne'ot Mordekhay** Israel
56 G2 **Nepa** *R* U.S.S.R.
75 K4 **Nepal** *kingdom* S Asia
75 J5 **Nepalganj** India
103 N2 **Nephi** Utah
14 B2 **Nephin** *mt* Irish Rep
14 B2 **Nephin Beg** *mt* Irish Rep
121 N8 **Nephton** Ontario
45 M5 **Nepi** Italy
37 P3 **Nepomyšl** Czechoslovakia
119 N9 **Neptune** Sask
113 F7 **Neptune Beach** Florida
138 D6 **Neptune Is** S Australia
146 F10 **Neptune Rge** Antarctica
52 F6 **Ner'** U.S.S.R.
31 L4 **Ner** *R* Poland
42 E6 **Nera** *R* Italy
48 G6 **Nera** *R* Romania
18 F8 **Nérac** France
116 D6 **Neragon I** Alaska
58 G1 **Nercha** *R* U.S.S.R.
33 R10 **Nerchau** E Germany
58 G1 **Nerchinsk** U.S.S.R.
59 G1 **Nerchinsky Zavod** U.S.S.R.
68 C7 **Nerchus Passage** Burma
52 J5 **Nerdva** U.S.S.R.
21 E10 **Néré** France
52 F5 **Nerekhta** U.S.S.R.
37 J6 **Neresheim** W Germany
42 H5 **Neretva** *R* Yugoslavia
87 D9 **Neriquinha** Angola
116 H7 **Nerka,L** Alaska
52 E6 **Nerl'** U.S.S.R.
45 N5 **Nerola** Italy
18 G5 **Nerondes** France
45 N4 **Nerone, M** *mt* Italy
130 E5 **Nerópolis** Brazil
52 J3 **Neroyka, Gora** *mt* U.S.S.R.
17 F6 **Nerpio** Spain
139 K6 **Nerriga** New S Wales
142 E4 **Nerrima** W Australia
54 E4 **Nerussa** *R* U.S.S.R.
16 C7 **Nerva** Spain
44 F3 **Nervi** Italy
52 K2 **Ner'yuvom** U.S.S.R.
25 E2 **Nes** Netherlands
27 D11 **Nesbyen** Norway
95 L5 **Nescopeck** Pennsylvania
47 J2 **Nesebūr** Bulgaria
52 C6 **Neshcherdo Oz** *L* U.S.S.R.
80 D2 **Nesher** Israel
116 A3 **Neshkan** Alaska
99 R6 **Neshkoro** Wisconsin
111 G9 **Neshoba** Mississippi
27 D13 **Neslandsvatn** Norway
22 D4 **Nesle** France
123 N3 **Nesle,L** Quebec
26 F5 **Nesna** Norway
26 F5 **Nesöy** *isld* Norway
100 G1 **Nespelem** Washington
45 O5 **Nespolo** Italy
19 O16 **Nesque** *R* France
107 L3 **Ness City** Kansas
37 K1 **Nesse** *R* E Germany
26 R1 **Nesseby** Norway
117 F6 **Nesselrode,Mt** Br Col/Alaska
18 F10 **Neste** *R* France
31 O1 **Nesterov** U.S.S.R.
120 G6 **Nesterville** Ontario
52 G6 **Nestiary** U.S.S.R.
127 P2 **Nestor** Trinidad
118 J1 **Nestor Falls** Ontario
99 S3 **Nestoria** Michigan
46 E4 **Nestórion** Greece
47 G3 **Néstos** *R* Greece
27 A11 **Nesttun** Norway
80 C6 **Nes Ziyyona** Israel
80 C4 **Netanya** Israel
107 P2 **Netawaka** Kansas
95 N6 **Netcong** New Jersey
32 K9 **Nethe** *R* W Germany
141 J5 **Netherdale** Queensland
118 H7 **Netherhill** Sask
25 **Netherlands** *kingdom* Europe
8 C5 **Nether Stowey** England
145 E2 **Netherton** New Zealand
15 E3 **Nethy Bridge** Scotland
80 C6 **Netiva** Israel
80 C7 **Netiv HaLamed** Israel
80 B8 **Netivot** Israel
43 H9 **Neto** *R* Italy
36 E2 **Netphen** W Germany
37 J1 **Netra** W Germany
75 O6 **Netrakona** Bangladesh
36 C3 **Nette** *R* W Germany
36 B3 **Nettersheim** W Germany
25 F6 **Nettetal** W Germany
115 M4 **Nettilling L** N W Terr
99 N1 **Nett L** Minnesota
9 F4 **Nettlebed** England
120 K4 **Nettle Lakes Prov. Park** Ontario
110 F6 **Nettleton** Arkansas
111 H7 **Nettleton** Mississippi
45 N7 **Nettuno** Italy
125 N9 **Netzahaulcoyotl, Presa** *res* Mexico
37 N2 **Netzschkau** E Germany
36 H1 **Neu** W Germany
32 G7 **Neu Arenberg** W Germany
37 N5 **Neubäu** W Germany
32 H9 **Neubeckum** W Germany
20 G3 **Neubourg,le** France
33 S5 **Neubrandenburg** E Germany
33 R5 **Neubrandenburg** *reg* E Germany
32 J7 **Neubruchhausen** W Germany
36 H4 **Neubrunn** W Germany
33 P4 **Neubukow** E Germany
33 P5 **Neuburg** E Germany
37 L6 **Neuburg** W Germany
40 E3 **Neuchâtel** *canton* Switzerland
40 E4 **Neuchâtel, Lac de** Switzerland
32 M9 **Neuckrug** W Germany
119 P8 **Neudorf** Sask
37 M3 **Neudrossenfeld** W Germany
32 L10 **Neu-Eichenberg** W Germany
36 F6 **Neuenburg** Baden-Württemberg W Germany
32 G6 **Neuenburg** Niedersachsen W Germany
32 E7 **Neuenhaus** W Germany
32 J6 **Neuenkirchen** Niedersachsen W Germany
32 F8 **Neuenkirchen** Nordrhein-Westfalen W Germany
32 G10 **Neuenrade** W Germany
36 G5 **Neuenstadt** W Germany
36 H5 **Neuenstein** W Germany
36 G2 **Neuental** W Germany
32 J5 **Neuenwalde** W Germany
37 M7 **Neufahrn** W Germany
40 G1 **Neuf Brisach** France
22 J4 **Neufchateau** Belgium
19 J4 **Neufchâteau** France
20 F5 **Neufchâtel** France
20 H2 **Neufchâtel-en-Bray** France
22 B2 **Neufchâtel-Hardelot** France
22 F5 **Neufchâtel-sur-Aisne** France
38 K5 **Neufelden** Austria
36 G6 **Neuffen** W Germany
20 J3 **Neufmarche** France
36 G7 **Neufra** W Germany
41 N2 **Neugablonz** W Germany
33 S6 **Neuglobsow** E Germany
32 G5 **Neuharlingersiel** W Germany
37 M4 **Neuhaus** Bayern W Germany
33 N6 **Neuhaus** E Germany
32 K5 **Neuhaus** Niedersachsen W Germany
37 P2 **Neuhausen** E Germany
36 G6 **Neuhausen** W Germany
33 S8 **Neuhof** E Germany
38 K5 **Neuhofen** Austria
36 G5 **Neuhütten** W Germany
21 G6 **Neuillé-Pt. Pierre** France
20 G4 **Neuilly** France
20 K3 **Neuilly-en-Thelle** France
20 C3 **Neuilly-la-Fôret** France
36 F3 **Neu-Isenburg** W Germany
33 R5 **Neukalen** E Germany
33 O6 **Neu Kaliss** E Germany
38 F7 **Neukirchen** Austria
37 O2 **Neukirchen** E Germany
33 O4 **Neukirchen** Schleswig-Holstein W Germany
37 N5 **Neukirchen Balbini** W Germany
33 P5 **Neukloster** E Germany
32 L6 **Neukloster** W Germany
37 N2 **Neumark** E Germany
38 H6 **Neumarkt** Salzburg Austria
38 K7 **Neumarkt** Steiermark Austria
37 L5 **Neumarkt** W Germany
37 O7 **Neumarkt-St Veit** W Germany
32 L4 **Neumünster** W Germany
37 N5 **Neunburg** W Germany
21 I6 **Neung sur-Beuvron** France
38 O6 **Neunkirchen** Austria
36 D2 **Neunkirchen** Nordrhein-Westfalen W Germany
36 E2 **Neunkirchen** Rheinland-Pfalz W Germany
36 C5 **Neunkirchen** Saarland W Germany
36 C2 **Neunkirchen** W Germany
37 O7 **Neuötting** W Germany
131 C7 **Neuquén** Argentina
131 B7 **Neuquén** *terr* Argentina
131 B7 **Neuquén, R** Argentina
33 R7 **Neuruppin** E Germany
37 K7 **Neusäss** W Germany
112 L3 **Neuse R** N Carolina
48 D3 **Neusiedla** Austria
48 D3 **Neusiedler See** Austria
36 B1 **Neuss** W Germany
18 H7 **Neussargues** France
48 C3 **Neustadt** Austria
37 M2 **Neustadt** Gera E Germany
36 G2 **Neustadt** Hessen W Germany
36 G4 **Neustadt** Hessen W Germany
36 H3 **Neustadt** Hessen W Germany
33 Q7 **Neustadt** Potsdam E Germany
36 E5 **Neustadt** Rheinland-Pfalz W Germany
37 K2 **Neustadt** Suhl E Germany
37 K4 **Neustadt an der Aisch** W Germany
37 N4 **Neustadt an der Waldnaab** W Germany
37 L3 **Neustadt bei Coburg** W Germany
33 P6 **Neustadt-Glewe** E Germany
32 G6 **Neustadt-gödens** W Germany
Neustettin *see* **Szczecinek**
37 M7 **Neustift** W Germany
33 S6 **Neustrelitz** E Germany
37 J7 **Neu Ulm** W Germany
22 D2 **Neuve Chapelle** France
20 G4 **Neuve-Lyre, la** France
40 F3 **Neuveville** Switzerland
18 G7 **Neuvic** France
109 N4 **Neuville** Texas
20 K5 **Neuville-aux-Bois** France
21 F8 **Neuville-de-Poitou** France
22 G5 **Neuville-en-Tourne-à-Fuy** France
19 O12 **Neuville-les-Dames** France
20 H2 **Neuville-lès-Dieppe** France
21 I8 **Neuvy-St. Sépulchre** France
21 J7 **Neuvy sur Barangeon** France
33 O8 **Neuwegersleben** E Germany
36 E6 **Neuweier** W Germany
32 H5 **Neuwerk** *isld* W Germany
36 C3 **Neuwied** W Germany
36 C6 **Neuwiller** France
32 L6 **Neu-Wulmstorf** W Germany
27 G11 **Neva** Sweden
99 R4 **Neva** Wisconsin
52 D5 **Neva** *R* U.S.S.R.
99 N7 **Nevada** Iowa
110 B4 **Nevada** Missouri
109 L2 **Nevada** Texas
92 C3 **Nevada** *state* U.S.A.
102 C2 **Nevada City** California
128 D2 **Nevada de Cocuy,Sa** *mts* Colombia
124 H8 **Nevada de Colima** Mexico
16 E7 **Nevada, Sierra** *mts* Spain
131 C5 **Nevado, Cerro** *peak* Argentina
131 B6 **Nevados Chillán** *mt* Chile
131 C5 **Nevado, Sierra del** *ra* Argentina
54 A1 **Nevel'** U.S.S.R.
59 M2 **Nevel'sk** U.S.S.R.
59 H1 **Never** U.S.S.R.
8 B3 **Nevern** Wales
26 F6 **Nevernes** Norway
18 H5 **Nevers** France
139 J4 **Nevertire** New S Wales
48 E7 **Nevesinje** Yugoslavia
45 H2 **Neviano d'Arduini** Italy
32 F10 **Neviges** W Germany
20 G2 **Neville** France
118 K9 **Neville** Sask
112 F5 **Nevils** Georgia
53 F11 **Nevinnomyssk** U.S.S.R.
79 E9 **Neviot** Egypt
118 D6 **Nevis** Alberta
99 M3 **Nevis** Minnesota
127 P4 **Nevis** *isld* Lesser Antilles
127 P4 **Nevis Pk** Nevis W I
80 E6 **Nevit HaGedud** Jordan
78 E2 **Nevşehir** Turkey
65 J2 **Nevskoye** U.S.S.R.
55 D2 **Nev'yansk** U.S.S.R.
103 J9 **New** *R* California
112 F1 **New** *R* N Carolina
94 F9 **New** *R* Virginia/W Virginia
12 E4 **New Abbey** Scotland
95 S3 **Newagen** Maine
87 G8 **Newala** Tanzania
94 B8 **New Albany** Indiana
111 G7 **New Albany** Mississippi
95 L5 **New Albany** Pennsylvania
99 P6 **New Albin** Iowa
99 S4 **Newald** Wisconsin
141 J8 **New Angledool** New S Wales
110 E6 **Newark** Arkansas
102 B4 **Newark** California
95 M7 **Newark** Delaware
9 F1 **Newark** England
99 S8 **Newark** Illinois
98 G9 **Newark** Nebraska
95 N6 **Newark** New Jersey
95 K3 **Newark** New York
94 E6 **Newark** Ohio
95 L4 **Newark Valley** New York
110 G3 **New Athens** Illinois
99 P4 **New Auburn** Wisconsin
111 G10 **New Augusta** Mississippi
94 E4 **New Baltimore** Michigan
94 J7 **New Baltimore** Pennsylvania
95 R5 **New Bedford** Massachusetts
146 E12 **New Bedford Inlet** Antarctica
100 C4 **Newberg** Oregon
99 Q10 **New Berlin** Illinois
95 M4 **New Berlin** New York
111 J9 **Newbern** Alabama
112 K2 **New Bern** N Carolina
110 G5 **Newbern** Tennessee
102 H7 **Newberry** California
113 E8 **Newberry** Florida
110 J3 **Newberry** Indiana
99 V3 **Newberry** Michigan
112 F3 **Newberry** S Carolina
94 H5 **New Bethlehem** Pennsylvania
13 G3 **Newbiggin by-the-Sea** England
13 E3 **Newbigging** Scotland
110 D3 **New Bloomfield** Missouri
99 R4 **Newbold** Wisconsin
121 O8 **Newboro** Ontario
8 B1 **Newborough** Môn Wales
99 Q8 **New Boston** Illinois
109 N2 **New Boston** Texas
109 J6 **New Braunfels** Texas
94 C6 **New Bremen** Ohio
12 E3 **New Bridge** Scotland
8 C3 **Newbridge** Wales
118 G7 **New Brigden** Alberta
95 P5 **New Britain** Connecticut
111 L10 **New Brockton** Alabama
95 N6 **New Brunswick** New Jersey
115 N8 **New Brunswick** *prov* Canada
9 H3 **New Buckenham** England
99 U8 **New Buffalo** Michigan
99 O8 **Newburg** Iowa
110 E4 **Newburg** Missouri
94 K6 **Newburg** Pennsylvania
94 H7 **Newburg** W Virginia
15 E4 **Newburgh** Fife Scotland
15 F3 **Newburgh** Grampian Scotland
110 J4 **Newburgh** Indiana
95 N5 **Newburgh** New York
121 O8 **Newburgh** Ontario
123 T5 **New Burnt Cove** Nfld
9 E5 **Newbury** England
95 R4 **Newburyport** Massachusetts
85 E6 **New Bussa** Nigeria
137 N6 **New Caledonia** *isld* Pacific Oc
95 O5 **New Canaan** Connecticut
99 P10 **New Canton** Illinois
94 C7 **New Carlisle** Ohio
122 G5 **New Carlisle** Quebec
102 C3 **Newcastle** California
106 C2 **New Castle** Colorado
94 B7 **New Castle** Indiana
14 E3 **Newcastle** Irish Rep
127 L2 **Newcastle** Jamaica
110 L3 **New Castle** Kentucky
98 K7 **Newcastle** Nebraska
127 P4 **Newcastle** Nevis W I
122 G6 **Newcastle** New Brunswick
95 M7 **New Castle** New Jersey
139 K5 **Newcastle** New S Wales
14 F2 **Newcastle** N Ireland
107 N6 **Newcastle** Oklahoma
121 M9 **Newcastle** Ontario
94 G6 **New Castle** Pennsylvania
89 F6 **Newcastle** S Africa
109 J2 **Newcastle** Texas
103 L4 **Newcastle** Utah
94 G9 **New Castle** Virginia
98 B6 **Newcastle** Wyoming
141 G1 **Newcastle B** Queensland
122 F7 **Newcastle Br** New Brunswick
8 B3 **Newcastle Emlyn** Wales
118 E7 **Newcastle Mine** Alberta
141 G4 **Newcastle Ra** Queensland
15 F5 **Newcastleton** Scotland
8 D1 **Newcastle Under Lyme** England
13 G4 **Newcastle-upon-Tyne** England
140 C3 **Newcastle Waters** N Terr Aust
14 B4 **Newcastle West** Irish Rep
9 F5 **New Chapel** England
106 B5 **Newcomb** New Mexico
94 F6 **Newcomerstown** Ohio
94 F7 **New Concord** Ohio
12 D3 **New Cumnock** Scotland
12 D3 **New Dailly** Scotland
101 O6 **Newdale** Idaho
119 R8 **Newdale** Manitoba
118 E9 **New Dayton** Alberta
15 F3 **New Deer** Scotland
143 C10 **Newdegate** W Australia
76 **New Delhi** India
117 P11 **New Denver** Br Col
111 M7 **New Echota Nat.Mon** Georgia
111 D8 **New Edinburg** Arkansas
113 E7 **Newell** Georgia
99 L7 **Newell** Iowa
112 G2 **Newell** N Carolina
98 C5 **Newell** S Dakota
112 F4 **New Ellenton** S Carolina
118 E8 **Newell L** Alberta
143 F6 **Newell,L** W Australia
111 E9 **Newellton** Louisiana
98 D3 **New England** N Dakota
139 K4 **New England Ra** *mts* New S Wales
90 D4 **New England Seamount Chain** Atlantic Oc
116 F7 **Newenham,C** Alaska
8 D4 **Newent** England
94 A3 **New Era** Michigan
80 F3 **Newe Ur** Israel
80 C3 **Newe Yam** Israel
94 J3 **Newfane** New York
95 P3 **Newfane** Vermont
141 K1 **New Farm** *dist* Brisbane, Qnsld
95 R3 **Newfield** Maine
95 M7 **Newfield** New Jersey
117 P8 **New Fish Creek** Alberta
110 E3 **New Florence** Missouri
98 K1 **Newfolden** Minnesota
9 E6 **New Forest** England
95 Q3 **Newfound L** New Hampshire
95 M5 **Newfoundland** Pennsylvania
123 P1 **Newfoundland** *prov* Canada
90 F5 **Newfoundland Basin** Atlantic Oc
90 E4 **Newfoundland Rise** Atlantic Oc
110 D2 **New Franklin** Missouri
95 L7 **New Freedom** Pennsylvania
8 A4 **Newgale** Wales
12 D3 **New Galloway** Scotland
118 B9 **Newgate** Br Col
137 M3 **New Georgia** *isld* Solomon Is
122 H9 **New Germany** Nova Scotia
99 R7 **New Glarus** Wisconsin
122 K8 **New Glasgow** Nova Scotia
95 R3 **New Gloucester** Maine
127 O3 **New Grant** Trinidad
136 J3 **New Guinea** *isld* S E Asia
109 M6 **Newgulf** Texas
100 D1 **Newhalem** Washington
116 K7 **Newhalen** Alaska
102 F7 **Newhall** California
116 F5 **New Hamilton** Alaska
95 Q4 **New Hampshire** *state* U.S.A.
99 O6 **New Hampton** Iowa
99 M9 **New Hampton** Missouri
95 S3 **New Harbor** Maine
110 J3 **New Harmony** Indiana
95 O5 **New Hartford** Connecticut
95 P5 **New Haven** Connecticut
9 G6 **Newhaven** England
94 B5 **New Haven** Indiana
110 E3 **New Haven** Missouri
94 F8 **New Haven** W Virginia
98 B5 **New Haven** Wyoming
117 K8 **New Hazelton** Br Col
137 O5 **New Hebrides** *islds* Pacific Oc
13 F6 **New Hey** England
13 H6 **New Holland** England
99 R9 **New Holland** Illinois
99 S6 **New Holstein** Wisconsin
109 O1 **Newhope** Arkansas
12 E2 **Newhouse** Scotland
111 E12 **New Iberia** Louisiana
9 H5 **Newington** England
112 F5 **Newington** Georgia
137 L2 **New Ireland** *isld* Bismarck Arch
95 N7 **New Jersey** *state* U.S.A.
94 H6 **New Kensington** Pennsylvania
95 L9 **New Kent** Virginia
106 F6 **Newkirk** New Mexico
107 N5 **Newkirk** Oklahoma
143 E8 **Newland Ra** W Australia
98 E3 **New Leipzig** N Dakota
94 E7 **New Lexington** Ohio
99 Q6 **New Lisbon** Wisconsin
121 L5 **New Liskeard** Ontario
99 P9 **New London** Iowa
99 M4 **New London** Minnesota
99 P10 **New London** Missouri
94 E5 **New London** Ohio
99 S5 **New London** Wisconsin
12 D4 **New Luce** Scotland
110 G5 **New Madrid** Missouri
12 E2 **Newmains** Scotland
102 C4 **Newman** California
99 T10 **Newman** Illinois
106 D9 **Newman** New Mexico
145 E4 **Newman** New Zealand
143 C6 **Newman** W Australia
98 J8 **Newman Gr** Nebraska
142 C6 **Newman,Mt** W Australia
123 T5 **Newman's Cove** Nfld
9 G3 **Newmarket** England
99 M9 **New Market** Iowa
14 B4 **Newmarket** Irish Rep
127 J2 **Newmarket** Jamaica
95 Q3 **Newmarket** New Hampshire
139 G5 **Newmarket** New S Wales
121 L8 **Newmarket** Ontario
94 J8 **New Market** Virginia
141 K1 **Newmarket** *dist* Brisbane, Qnsld
94 E7 **New Marshfield** Ohio
94 G7 **New Martinsville** W Virginia
94 F7 **New Matamoras** Ohio
100 J5 **New Meadows** Idaho
106 D6 **New Mexico** *state* U.S.A.
94 C7 **New Miami** Ohio
95 O5 **New Milford** Connecticut
95 M5 **New Milford** Pennsylvania
12 D2 **Newmilns** Scotland
108 E2 **New Moore** Texas
111 M8 **Newnan** Georgia
113 E8 **Newnan L** Florida
139 K5 **Newnes** New S Wales
8 D4 **Newnham** England
143 B9 **New Norcia** W Australia
139 H8 **New Norfolk** Tasmania
118 E6 **New Norway** Alberta
111 F11 **New Orleans** Louisiana
119 O6 **New Osgoode** Sask
95 K7 **New Oxford** Pennsylvania
95 N5 **New Paltz** New York
94 C7 **New Paris** Ohio
94 A8 **New Pekin** Indiana
94 F6 **New Philadelphia** Ohio
100 E7 **New Pine Creek** Oregon
15 F3 **New Pitsligo** Scotland
100 J6 **New Plymouth** Idaho
145 E3 **New Plymouth** New Zealand
110 E6 **Newport** Arkansas
126 B2 **New Port** Curaçao
8 B3 **Newport** Dyfed Wales
9 G4 **Newport** Essex England
8 D4 **Newport** Gwent Wales
99 T10 **Newport** Indiana
9 E6 **Newport** I of Wight England
14 B3 **Newport** Irish Rep
127 K3 **Newport** Jamaica
110 M2 **Newport** Kentucky
94 D5 **Newport** Michigan
99 O5 **Newport** Minnesota
112 L3 **Newport** N Carolina
98 G7 **Newport** Nebraska
95 P3 **Newport** New Hampshire
95 M7 **Newport** New Jersey
100 A5 **Newport** Oregon
95 K6 **Newport** Pennsylvania
122 H5 **Newport** Quebec
95 Q5 **Newport** Rhode I
8 D2 **Newport** Salop England
112 D2 **Newport** Tennessee
109 J2 **Newport** Texas
95 P2 **Newport** Vermont
100 H1 **Newport** Washington
102 G8 **Newport Beach** California
95 L10 **Newport News** Virginia
13 F1 **Newport-on-Tay** Scotland
9 F3 **Newport Pagnell** England
113 E9 **New Port Richey** Florida
112 D1 **New Powell** Tennessee
99 N5 **New Prague** Minnesota
113 L9 **New Providence** *isld* Bahamas
8 A7 **Newquay** England
8 B3 **New Quay** Wales
113 E8 **New R** Florida
8 C3 **New Radnor** Wales
106 G1 **New Raymer** Colorado
99 N6 **New Richland** Minnesota
94 C8 **New Richmond** Ohio
122 G5 **New Richmond** Quebec
99 O4 **New Richmond** Wisconsin
110 M5 **New River** Tennessee
112 K3 **New River Inlet** N Carolina
111 E11 **New Roads** Louisiana
98 G2 **New Rockford** N Dakota
9 G6 **New Romney** England
110 K2 **New Ross** Indiana
14 E4 **New Ross** Irish Rep
95 R2 **Newry** Maine
14 E2 **Newry** N Ireland
140 A3 **Newry** N Terr Aust
94 J6 **Newry** Pennsylvania
14 E2 **Newry Canal** N Ireland
98 E3 **New Salem** N Dakota
94 H7 **New Salem** Pennsylvania
13 E1 **New Scone** Scotland
99 O8 **New Sharon** Iowa
New Siberian Is *see* **Novosibirskiye Os**
113 G8 **New Smyrna Beach** Florida
139 **New South Wales** *state* Australia
141 J5 **Newstead** Queensland
94 E7 **New Straitsville** Ohio
85 D7 **New Tamale** Ghana
94 D10 **New Tazewell** Tennessee
116 E6 **Newtok** Alaska
111 L10 **Newton** Alabama
9 G2 **Newton** England
110 H3 **Newton** Illinois
99 N8 **Newton** Iowa
107 N3 **Newton** Kansas
95 Q4 **Newton** Massachusetts
111 G9 **Newton** Mississippi
112 F2 **Newton** N Carolina
13 E3 **Newton** Scotland
109 O5 **Newton** Texas
8 C6 **Newton Abbot** England
13 E4 **Newton Arlosh** England
95 M2 **Newton Falls** New York
94 G5 **Newton Falls** Ohio
8 B7 **Newton Ferrers** England
112 J2 **Newton Grove** N Carolina
94 K6 **Newton Hamilton** Pennsylvania
13 F6 **Newton-le-Willows** England
12 D2 **Newton Mearns** Scotland
15 D3 **Newtonmore** Scotland
101 O8 **Newton Res** Utah
12 D4 **Newton Stewart** Scotland

Newtown — North Uist 55

110 C1 Newtown Missouri
123 T4 Newtown Nfld
95 K9 Newtown Virginia
8 C3 Newtown Wales
14 E2 Newtownabbey N Ireland
14 F2 Newtownards N Ireland
14 D2 Newtown Butler N Ireland
14 E2 Newtownhamilton N Ireland
14 E3 Newtown Mt.Kennedy Irish Rep
98 D2 New Town Sanish N Dakota
14 D2 Newtown Stewart N Ireland
99 M5 New Ulm Minnesota
109 L6 New Ulm Texas
98 D5 New Underwood S Dakota
111 L10 Newville Alabama
102 B2 Newville California
94 K6 Newville Pennsylvania
99 N8 New Virginia Iowa
94 E6 New Washington Ohio
123 M7 New Waterford C Breton I, N S
109 M5 New Waverly Texas
117 J11 New Westminster Br Col
95 K7 New Windsor Maryland
123 S4 New World I Nfld
100 F8 New Year L Nevada
96 New York conurbation
95 K4 New York state U.S.A.
103 J6 New York Mts California
144 New Zealand state S W Pacific
21 H10 Nexon France
94 C5 Ney Ohio
52 F5 Neya U.S.S.R.
8 B4 Neyland Wales
77 D5 Neyrīz Iran
77 F1 Neyshābūr Iran
55 D2 Neyvo Shaytanskiy U.S.S.R.
31 H6 Nežárka R Czechoslovakia
54 C5 Nezhin U.S.S.R.
100 J3 Nezperce Idaho
61 N7 Nezugaseki Japan
86 C6 N'Gabé Congo
68 D5 Nga Chong,Khao mt Burma/Thailand
68 H5 Ngac Linh mt Vietnam
68 A2 Ngahan Burma
144 C5 Ngahere New Zealand
145 F3 Ngamatea Swamp New Zealand
66 F5 Ngamda China
87 D10 Ngami, L Botswana
70 N9 Ngandjuk Java
66 C5 Ngangla Ringco L China
Nganglaring Tso see Ngangla Ringco
66 C5 Nganglong Kangri China
74 J2 Nganglong Kangri mt ra China
75 M3 Ngangzê Co L China
68 G3 Ngan Pha R Vietnam
68 G3 Ngan Sau R Vietnam
68 G1 Ngan Son Vietnam
86 C6 N'Gao Congo
86 B4 Ngaoundéré Cameroon
144 C6 Ngapara New Zealand
68 B2 Ngape Burma
145 F3 Ngapuketurua mt New Zealand
144 C6 Ngapuna New Zealand
145 E3 Ngaroma New Zealand
145 E2 Ngaruawahia New Zealand
145 F3 Ngaruroro R New Zealand
145 D1 Ngataki New Zealand
145 F3 Ngatapo New Zealand
145 E2 Ngatea New Zealand
68 B4 Ngathainggyaung Burma
145 E3 Ngatira New Zealand
145 E3 Ngauruhoe vol New Zealand
68 D7 Ngawan Chaung R Burma
145 F2 Ngawaro New Zealand
70 N9 Ngawi Java
68 B4 Ngayok B Burma
Ngemda see Ngamda
89 G2 Ngezi R Zimbabwe
89 G2 Ngezi Dam Zimbabwe
Nghia Hung see Phu Qui
70 O9 Ngimbang Java
88 F6 Ngindo Tanzania
87 C9 N'Giva Angola
86 C5 Ngoko R Congo
87 E9 Ngoma Zambia
88 F2 Ngong Kenya
145 F3 Ngongotaha New Zealand
88 D7 Ngoni Malawi
66 F5 Ngoring Hu L China
88 E3 Ngorongoro Crater Tanzania
71 A2 Ngotakiaha Halmahera Indonesia
86 B6 N'Gounié R Gabon
86 B2 N'Gourti Niger
88 B3 Ngozi Burundi
86 B3 N'Guigmi Niger
68 F3 Ngum R Laos
71 K10 Ngundju,Tg C Sumba Indonesia
145 E1 Ngunguru New Zealand
88 E7 Nguni Tanzania
70 O10 Ngunut Java
85 G6 Nguru Nigeria
67 B5 Nguyen Binh Vietnam
89 D5 Ngwaketse dist Botswana
87 G10 Nhachengue Mozambique
128 G6 Nhambiquara Brazil
129 G4 Nhamunda Brazil
67 A6 Nhan Nghia Vietnam
68 J6 Nha Trang Vietnam
130 C6 Nhecolândia Brazil
68 F3 Nhiep R Laos
138 F6 Nhill Victoria
68 G4 Nhommarath Laos
140 D1 Nhulunbuy N Terr Aust
68 G3 Nhu Xuan Vietnam
98 H1 Niagara N Dakota
144 B7 Niagara New Zealand
99 S4 Niagara Wisconsin
94 J3 Niagara Falls New York
121 L9 Niagara Falls Ontario
121 L9 Niagara-on-the-Lake Ontario
70 C3 Niah Sarawak
85 C7 Niakaramandougou Ivory Coast
85 E6 Niamey Niger
86 E5 Niangara Zaïre
85 D5 Niangaye,L Mali
85 C7 Niangbo,Pic de mt Ivory Coast
85 D6 Niangoloko Upper Volta
110 D4 Niangua R Missouri
Niangxi see Xinshao
86 E5 Nia Nia Zaïre
95 P5 Niantic Connecticut
65 E1 Nianzishan China
70 E4 Niapa, G mt Kalimantan
101 L2 Niarada Montana
86 B6 Niari R Congo
69 C12 Nias isld Indonesia
88 F8 Niassa Mozambique
46 F8 Niata Greece
101 R4 Nibbe Montana
28 D3 Nibe Denmark
28 D2 Nibe Bredning B Denmark
142 E5 Nibil Well W Australia
121 R3 Nicabau Quebec
125 L3 Nicaragua rep Cent America
95 T1 Nicatous L
102 B2 Nice California
44 B4 Nice France
111 K11 Niceville Florida
115 M7 Nichicun, L Quebec
60 E11 Nichihara Japan
112 E6 Nicholls Georgia
99 P8 Nichols Iowa
95 L4 Nichols New York
142 G4 Nicholson W Australia
140 E4 Nicholson R Queensland
143 B7 Nicholson Ra W Australia
95 N2 Nicholville New York
99 O1 Nickel L Ontario
129 G2 Nickerie R Suriname
107 M3 Nickerson Kansas
142 B5 Nickol B W Australia
122 F3 Nicman Quebec
69 A8 Nicobar Is Bay of Bengal
117 N10 Nicola Br Col
121 S6 Nicolet Quebec
99 M5 Nicollet Minnesota
78 D4 Nicosia Cyprus
43 F11 Nicosia Sicily
43 G10 Nicotera Italy
125 M4 Nicoya Costa Rica
125 M5 Nicoya,Pen.de Costa Rica
122 E6 Nictau New Brunswick
31 M5 Nida R Poland
123 Q6 Nid á L'Aigle,C.du Miquelon I Atlantic Oc
40 F3 Nidau Switzerland
36 G3 Nidda W Germany
36 F3 Nidda R W Germany
36 F3 Niddatal W Germany
36 B2 Nideggen W Germany
27 C13 Nidelv R Norway
41 H4 Nidwalden canton Switzerland
31 M2 Nidzica Poland
30 D1 Niebüll W Germany
36 G1 Niedenstein W Germany
37 N6 Niederaichbach W Germany
37 L6 Niederarnbach W Germany
36 H2 Nieder Aula W Germany
37 N6 Niederbayern dist W Germany
36 C3 Niederbieber Germany
19 L4 Niederbronn France
33 O6 Nieder Elde R E Germany
36 G2 Nieder Gemünden W Germany
33 R9 Niedergörsdorf E Germany
25 F6 Niederkrüchten W Germany
36 D3 Nieder Lahnstein W Germany
32 J10 Nieder Marsberg W Germany
33 M6 Nieder Marschacht W Germany
36 H5 Niedernhall W Germany
36 E3 Niedernhausen W Germany
36 E4 Nieder Olm W Germany
36 E3 Nieder Ouembach W Germany
32 J7 Niedersachsen land W Germany
36 D2 Nieder Schelden W Germany
36 E3 Niederselters W Germany
32 J10 Niedersfeld W Germany
36 H5 Niederstetten W Germany
37 J6 Niederstotzingen W Germany
36 D4 Niederwald W Germany
36 E2 Nieder Weidbach W Germany
36 F2 Nieder Weimar W Germany
37 P2 Niederwiesa E Germany
36 F3 Nieder Wöllstadt W Germany
36 C3 Nieder Zissen W Germany
33 T8 Nieder Zittau E Germany
32 K9 Nieheim W Germany
98 K2 Nielsville Minnesota
88 B4 Niemba Zaïre
88 B5 Niemba R Zaïre
33 Q9 Niemberg E Germany
31 K5 Niemcza Poland
33 R8 Niemegk E Germany
26 N5 Niemis Sweden
31 K5 Niemodlin Poland
33 N7 Nienbergen W Germany
32 F8 Nienborg W Germany
33 P9 Nienburg E Germany
32 K7 Nienburg W Germany
33 N5 Niendorf W Germany
31 M5 Niepołomice Poland
22 D2 Nieppe France
25 F5 Niers R W Germany
36 E4 Nierstein W Germany
31 L3 Nieszawa Poland
85 C7 Niete, Mt Liberia
33 P10 Nietleben E Germany
21 H10 Nieul France
129 G2 Nieuw Amsterdam Suriname
25 B5 Nieuwe Maas Netherlands
25 C5 Nieuwendijk Netherlands
25 D4 Nieuwersluis Netherlands
25 H2 Nieuweschans Netherlands
32 F6 Nieuweschans W Germany
22 D2 Nieuwkerke Belgium
25 C4 Nieuwkoop Netherlands
129 G2 Nieuw Nickerie Suriname
25 G2 Nieuwolda Netherlands
22 D1 Nieuwpoort Belgium
25 C5 Nieuwpoort Netherlands
25 E6 Nieuwstadt Netherlands
25 C4 Nieuw-Vennep Netherlands
18 H5 Nièvre dep France
122 G6 Nigadoo New Brunswick
78 E3 Niğde Turkey
85 B6 Niger R W Africa
85 F5 Niger rep W Africa
85 F7 Nigeria rep W Africa
85 F8 Niger,Mouths of the Nigeria
144 B6 Nightcaps New Zealand
100 F1 Nighthawk Washington
141 G2 Night I Great Barrier Reef Aust
Nightingale I see Dao Bach Long Vi
90 B16 Nightingale I Atlantic Oc
116 K2 Nigu R Alaska
102 U13 Nihoa Hawaiian Is
131 C5 Nihuili, Embalse del res Argentina
61 N8 Niigata Japan
60 G12 Niihama Japan
135 N1 Niihau isld Hawaiian Is
61 N11 Nii-jima isld Japan
60 Q3 Niikappu R Japan
60 G10 Niimi Japan
60 D4 Niitomi Japan
61 N8 Niitsu Japan
17 F8 Níjar Spain
25 F2 Nijega Netherlands
60 S2 Nijibetsu Japan
79 F8 Nijil Jordan
25 D4 Nijkerk Netherlands
25 E5 Nijmegen Netherlands
25 F4 Nijverdal Netherlands
116 K6 Nikabuna Lakes Alaska
Nikaria isld see Ikaría I Greece
26 S2 Nikel U.S.S.R.
55 C5 Nikel'tau U.S.S.R.
71 M9 Nikiniki Timor Indonesia
47 F4 Nikitas Greece
52 D6 Nikitinka U.S.S.R.
54 K8 Nikitovka U.S.S.R.
85 E7 Nikki Benin
61 N9 Nikkō Japan
61 N9 Nikkō Nat. Park Japan
40 G5 Niklaus Switzerland
48 H1 Nikolaev U.S.S.R.
116 K5 Nikolai Alaska
54 D10 Nikolayev U.S.S.R.
55 E4 Nikolayevka U.S.S.R.
53 G8 Nikolayevsk U.S.S.R.
55 D4 Nikolayevskiy U.S.S.R.
59 M1 Nikolayevsk-na-Amure U.S.S.R.
52 G5 Nikol'sk U.S.S.R.
52 F5 Nikolskoye U.S.S.R.
55 C5 Nikol'skoye U.S.S.R.
88 C3 Nikonga R Tanzania
47 G1 Nikopol Bulgaria
54 F9 Nikopol U.S.S.R.
77 G6 Nīkshahr Iran
42 J6 Nikšić Yugoslavia
78 F1 Niksir Turkey
71 O8 Nila isld Indonesia
103 J8 Niland California
73 L8 Nilande Atoll Maldives
83 L9 Nilaveli Sri Lanka
86 F2 Nile prov Sudan
84 J4 Nile R N E Africa
102 B4 Niles California
107 N3 Niles Kansas
94 A5 Niles Michigan
94 G5 Niles Ohio
121 N6 Nilgaut, L Quebec
76 C5 Nilgiri Hills India
116 E6 Nilikluguk Alaska
57 K3 Nilka China
146 B4 Nilsen B Antarctica
29 N8 Nilsiä Finland
47 K4 Nilüfer R Turkey
83 K11 Nilwala R Sri Lanka
28 D5 Nim Denmark
74 F6 Nimach India
85 C7 Nimba, Mts Guinea/Liberia/Ivory Co
142 E6 Nimberra Well W Australia
139 L3 Nimbin New S Wales
18 H9 Nîmes France
74 F5 Nimka Thana India
139 J6 Nimmitabel New S Wales
101 M3 Nimrod Montana
Nimrod Bay see Xiangshan Gang
146 G7 Nimrod Gl Antarctica
110 C7 Nimrod L Arkansas
144 C6 Nimrod, Mt New Zealand
109 O1 Nimrod Res Arkansas
77 H4 Nīmrūz reg Afghanistan
28 F4 Nimtofte Denmark
42 G4 Nin Yugoslavia
71 F4 Nin Bay Philippines
87 D8 Ninda Angola
139 J3 Nindigully Queensland
141 J8 Nindigully Queensland
73 L7 Nine Degree Chan Lakshadweep Indian Ocean
13 E2 Nine Mile Burn Scotland
139 G4 Nine Mile L New S Wales
103 H2 Ninemile Pk Nevada
108 D6 Nine Point Mesa mt Texas
119 S9 Ninette Manitoba
145 D1 Ninety Mile Beach New Zealand
139 J7 Ninety Mile Beach Victoria
112 E3 Ninety Six S Carolina
94 G7 Ninevah Pennsylvania
133 E6 Ninfas,Pta Argentina
9 G6 Ninfield England
143 A6 Ningaloo W Australia
59 J3 Ning'an China
67 G2 Ningbo China
65 D4 Ningcheng China
67 F3 Ningde China
67 E3 Ningdu China
67 D3 Ninggang China
67 F1 Ningguo China
67 G2 Ninghai China
Ninghan mt see Singleton,Mt
65 D5 Ninghe China
Ning-hsia see Yinchuan
67 E3 Ninghua China
58 F4 Ningjin China
65 C6 Ningjin China
66 F5 Ningjing Shan ra China
65 C7 Ningling China
67 B5 Ningming China
Ningpo see Ningpo
Ningsia aut reg see Ningxia
58 E4 Ningxia Hui Aut Reg China
58 D4 Ningxia aut reg China
67 D2 Ningxiang China
65 C7 Ningyang China
67 D4 Ningyuan China
67 B6 Ninh Binh Vietnam
68 J6 Ninh Hoa Vietnam
116 M6 Ninilchik Alaska
142 C5 Niningarra W Australia
107 N7 Ninnekah Oklahoma
107 N4 Ninnescah R Kansas
146 J4 Ninnis Gl Antarctica
111 C9 Ninock Louisiana
60 E14 Ninokata Japan
22 G2 Ninove Belgium
130 C7 Nioaque Brazil
94 H4 Niobe New York
98 J7 Niobrara Nebraska
98 E7 Niobrara R Nebraska
86 C6 Nioki Zaïre
85 B6 Niokolo-koba,Parc Nat.du Senegal
85 A6 Nioro du Rip Senegal
85 C5 Nioro du Sahel Mali
18 E6 Niort France
21 D9 Niortaise R France
21 E9 Niort St.Florent France
Nios isld see Íos I Greece
99 P9 Niota Illinois
112 C2 Niota Tennessee
85 C5 Niout Mauritania
139 K1 Nipan Queensland
76 B2 Nipani India
71 H6 Nipanipa,Tg C Sulawesi
119 N5 Nipawin Sask
119 N4 Nipawin Prov.Park Sask
120 B3 Nipigon Ontario
120 C4 Nipigon B Ontario
120 B3 Nipigon, Lake Ontario
118 H3 Nipin R Sask
118 C3 Nipisi R Alberta
122 G6 Nipisquit,B New Brunswick
121 L6 Nipissing Junc Ontario
115 L8 Nipissing,L Ontario
122 F3 Nipissis L Quebec
122 F3 Nipissis R Quebec
122 G3 Nipisso L Quebec
102 D6 Nipomo California
103 J6 Nipton California
84 J5 Niqrûb el Fuqâni, Gebel mt Egypt
126 F4 Niquero Cuba
61 M10 Nirasaki Japan
80 C3 Nir 'Ezyon Israel
80 B6 Nir Gallim Israel
80 B7 Nir Hen Israel
74 H9 Nirmal India
75 M5 Nirmali India
80 B8 Nir Moshe Israel
94 B3 Nirvana Michigan
80 C6 Nir Zevi Israel
46 E1 Niš Yugoslavia
16 B5 Nisa Portugal
72 F6 Nişāb S Yemen
46 F1 Nisava R Yugoslavia
95 K5 Nisbet Pennsylvania
60 O3 Niseko Japan
67 C2 Nishi China
61 P5 Nishi-Hōji Japan
60 J11 Nishinomiya Japan
60 F9 Nishino-shima isld Japan
61 L11 Nishio Japan
60 C13 Nishi-Sonogi-hantō pen Japan
60 C11 Nishi-suidō str Japan
60 H10 Nishiwaki Japan
116 H6 Nishlik L Alaska
99 L8 Nishnabotna, E R Iowa
99 L8 Nishnabotna, W R Iowa
130 J9 Nísia Floresta Brazil
48 J3 Nisipitul Romania
47 J8 Nísíros isld Greece
31 N5 Nisko Poland
98 C5 Nisland S Dakota
117 D4 Nisling R Yukon Terr
48 L3 Nisporeny U.S.S.R.
100 C3 Nisqually R Washington
27 F15 Nissan R Sweden
27 C12 Nissedal Norway
27 C12 Nisserv L Norway
28 A3 Nissum Bredning B Denmark
28 A4 Nissum Fjord inlet Denmark
117 G5 Nisutlin R Yukon Terr
115 M7 Nitchequon Quebec
130 G8 Niterói Brazil
15 E5 Nith,R Scotland
15 E5 Nithsdale* Scotland
71 M9 Nitibe Timor
80 G7 Nitil Jordan
100 A1 Nitinat L Br Col
9 E6 Niton England
48 E2 Nitra Czechoslovakia
31 L7 Nitra R Czechoslovakia
94 F8 Nitro W Virginia
55 D2 Nitsa R U.S.S.R.
29 N2 Nitsjärvi L Finland
37 N5 Nittenau W Germany
37 M5 Nittendorf W Germany
29 P11 Nityuyarvi U.S.S.R.
137 R5 Niuafo'ou isld Pacific Oc
137 S5 Niuatoputapu isld Pacific Oc
137 T5 Niue isld Pacific Oc
137 Q4 Niulakita isld Tuvalu
65 F4 Niumaowu China
Niushan see Donghai
137 Q3 Niutao isld Tuvalu
65 E4 Niuzhuang China
28 K5 Nivå Denmark
29 L8 Nivala Finland
18 E9 Nive R France
139 H2 Nive R Queensland
139 H2 Nive Downs Queensland
141 H7 Nive Downs Queensland
22 G2 Nivelles Belgium
18 H5 Nivernais prov France
118 D1 Niverville Manitoba
20 K3 Nivillers France
102 G4 Nivloc Nevada
40 B6 Nivolas-Vermelle France
52 D2 Nivskiy U.S.S.R.
74 J7 Niwas India
102 E2 Nixon Nevada
109 K6 Nixon Texas
74 H9 Nizamabad India
52 E3 Nizhmozero U.S.S.R.
56 G3 Nizhneangarsk U.S.S.R.
52 H2 Nizhne Bugayevo U.S.S.R.
54 L9 Nizhne Gnilovskoy U.S.S.R.
50 H2 Nizhneimbatskoye U.S.S.R.
52 H1 Nizhne Kamenka U.S.S.R.
55 B4 Nizhne-troitskiy U.S.S.R.
56 E4 Nizhneudinsk U.S.S.R.
50 G2 Nizhnevartovsk U.S.S.R.
55 B4 Nizhneye Il'yasovo U.S.S.R.
52 D2 Nizhneye Kuyto, Oz L U.S.S.R.
55 C3 Nizhni Irginski U.S.S.R.
Nizhniy Novgorod see Gor'kiy
55 C2 Nizhniy Tagil U.S.S.R.
52 E2 Nizhniy Vyalozerskiy U.S.S.R.
52 G4 Nizhniy Yenangsk U.S.S.R.
55 E2 Nizhnyaya Aremzyan U.S.S.R.
55 F3 Nizhnyaya Omka U.S.S.R.
52 J3 Nizhnyaya-Omra U.S.S.R.
52 G2 Nizhnyaya Pesha U.S.S.R.
56 E3 Nizhnyaya Pomya U.S.S.R.
55 D2 Nizhnyaya Salda U.S.S.R.
55 G4 Nizhnyaya Suyetka U.S.S.R.
55 E2 Nizhnyaya Tavda U.S.S.R.
52 F3 Nizhnyaya Toyma R U.S.S.R.
56 G1 Nizhnyaya Tunguska R U.S.S.R.
55 C2 Nizhnyaya Tura U.S.S.R.
52 H4 Nizhnyaya Voch' U.S.S.R.
52 F2 Nizhnyaya Zolotitsa U.S.S.R.
29 Q4 Nizh Pirengskoye Ozero L U.S.S.R.
56 G2 Nizh Tunguska R U.S.S.R.
116 Q6 Nizina Alaska
78 F3 Nizip Turkey
31 L7 Nízké Tatry mts Czechoslovakia
48 F2 Nižm Medzev Czechoslovakia
72 H4 Nizwa Oman
22 G4 Nizy-le-Comte France
44 D2 Nizza Italy
80 C4 Nizzane 'Oz Israel
80 B7 Nizzanim Israel
70 D4 Njaän mt Kalimantan
42 J6 Njegoš mt Yugoslavia
87 G7 Njinjo Tanzania
87 D9 Njoko R Zambia
88 E6 Njombe Tanzania
88 E5 Njombe R Tanzania
88 G10 Njoro isld Mozambique
26 J9 Njurundabommen Sweden
27 J10 Njutånger Sweden
88 D7 Nkanka R Zambia
88 E7 Nkhata B Malawi
88 E8 Nkhotakota Malawi
86 A6 N'komi L Gabon
86 B5 N'kongsamba Cameroon
88 D5 Nkululu R Tanzania
28 A4 No Denmark
20 K3 Noailles France
75 O7 Noakhali Bangladesh
45 M1 Noale Italy
128 C3 Noanama Colombia
95 Q5 Noank Connecticut
26 O3 Noarvas mt Norway
40 F7 Noasca Italy
116 F3 Noatak Alaska
14 E3 Nobber Irish Rep
120 K7 Nobel Ontario
60 E13 Nobeoka Japan
110 H3 Noble Illinois
107 N6 Noble Oklahoma
118 D9 Nobleford Alberta
111 E7 Noble Lake Arkansas
94 A6 Noblesville Indiana
71 L9 Nobo Flores Indonesia
60 P3 Noboribetsu Japan
130 C4 Nobres Brazil
141 G8 Noccundra Queensland
20 G5 Noce France
41 O5 Noce R Italy
45 R8 Nocera Inferiore Italy
44 H2 Noceto Italy
124 H7 Nochistlán Mexico
141 G8 Nockatunga Queensland
109 K2 Nocona Texas
48 J5 Nocrich Romania
61 P5 Noda Japan
133 D7 Nodales,B.de los Argentina
99 M9 Nodaway Iowa
99 M8 Nodaway R Iowa
98 B7 Node Wyoming
21 B6 Noé Blanche France
130 D4 Noedori R Brazil
110 B5 Noel Missouri
123 Q5 Noel Paul's Brook Nfld
120 K6 Noelville Ontario
22 D3 Noeux les Mines France
103 O10 Nogales Arizona
124 D2 Nogales Sonora Mexico
125 L8 Nogales Vera Cruz Mexico
86 A2 Nogal Valley Somalia
116 J6 Nogamut Alaska
45 K1 Nogara Italy
18 E9 Nogaro France
31 L1 Nogat R Poland
60 D12 Nōgata Japan
40 B1 Nogent en Bassigny France
20 F5 Nogent-le-Bernard France
20 J4 Nogent-le-Roi France
20 G5 Nogent le Rotrou France
20 K3 Nogent-sur-Oise France
18 H4 Nogent-sur-Seine France
54 K1 Noginsk U.S.S.R.
59 M1 Nogliki U.S.S.R.
40 C4 Nogno France
141 K7 Nogo R Queensland
141 J6 Nogoa R Queensland
61 K10 Nōgōhaku san mt Japan
131 F4 Nogoya R Argentina
48 E3 Nograd co Hungary
16 C3 Nogueira mt Portugal
17 H2 Noguera Pallarésa R Spain
17 H2 Noguera Ribagorzana R Spain
74 F4 Nohar India
61 P5 Noheji Japan
36 C4 Nohfelden W Germany
36 B3 Nohn W Germany
121 N6 Noire R Quebec
67 A6 Noire R Vietnam
86 B6 Noire,Pte Congo
18 C4 Noires, Mgnes mts France
18 D6 Noirmoutier Île de France
17 H9 Noisy les Bains Algeria
61 N11 Nojima-zaki C Japan
61 M9 Nojiri-ko L Japan
87 D9 Nokaneng Botswana
29 K10 Nokia Finland
74 B8 Nok Kundi Pakistan
144 B6 Nokomai New Zealand
110 G2 Nokomis Illinois
119 N7 Nokomis Sask
86 C5 Nola Cent Afr Republic
45 R8 Nola Italy
119 O2 Nolalu Ontario
98 J2 Nolan N Dakota
108 G3 Nolan Texas
28 E5 Nølev Denmark
44 D3 Noli Italy
112 E1 Nolichucky R Tennessee
112 E1 Nolichucky Dam Tennessee
52 G5 Nolinsk U.S.S.R.
20 H3 Nolléval France
28 O10 Nølsø isld Faeroes
69 E9 Nol,Thale L Thailand
111 L11 Noma Florida
60 D14 Noma-misaki C Japan
95 R5 No Mans Land isld Massachusetts
116 E4 Nome Alaska
98 J3 Nome N Dakota
116 E4 Nome C Alaska
19 K4 Nomeny France
121 P6 Nominingue Quebec
60 C13 Nomo-zaki C Japan
87 C10 Nomtsas Namibia
137 S6 Nomuka isld Tonga
114 J5 Nonacho L N W Terr
20 H4 Nonancourt France
20 D3 Nonant France
20 F4 Nonant-le-Pin France
45 K2 Nonantola Italy
52 H2 Nonburg U.S.S.R.
65 F2 Nong'an China
68 F3 Nong Het Laos
68 F5 Nong Hong Thailand
68 F4 Nong Khai Thailand
87 F11 Nongoma S Africa
19 N15 Nonières France
Nonni R see Nen Jiang R
138 D4 Nonning S Australia
138 D4 Nonning,Mt S Australia
36 B4 Nonnweiler W Germany
130 D10 Nonoaí Brazil
124 F4 Nonoava Mexico
71 G6 Nonoc isld Philippines
137 P2 Nonouti atoll Kiribati
119 W2 Nonsuch Manitoba
68 E6 Nonthaburi Thailand
18 F7 Nontron France
116 K7 Nonvianuk L Alaska
139 H7 Noojee Victoria
143 B7 Nookawarra W Australia
138 D2 Noolyeanna,L S Australia
98 C1 Noonan N Dakota
143 C9 Noongaar W Australia
143 B8 Noongal W Australia
142 E4 Noonkanbah W Australia
139 H3 Noorama R Queensland
25 A5 Noord-Beveland Netherlands
25 D5 Noord Brabant Netherlands
25 C5 Noordeloos Netherlands
25 C3 Noord-Holland Netherlands
25 E3 Noordoost Polder Netherlands
126 A1 Noord Pt Curaçao
25 B4 Noordwijk aan zee Netherlands
7 N9 Noordwinning oil rig North Sea
25 F3 Noordwolde Netherlands
25 C4 Noordzee-Kanaal Netherlands
29 J10 Noormarkku Finland
116 G3 Noorvik Alaska
139 L2 Noosa Head Queensland
141 L7 Noosaville Queensland
117 K11 Nootka Br Col
117 K11 Nootka I Br Col
103 H5 Nopah Ra California
99 T4 Noquebay,L Wisconsin
98 J9 Nora Nebraska
119 O6 Nora Sask
27 H12 Nora Sweden
27 J11 Nora Sweden
59 J1 Nora R U.S.S.R.
28 D3 Nørager Denmark
86 G2 Nora I Ethiopia
71 G7 Norala Mindanao Philippines
121 L4 Noranda Quebec
140 F5 Noranside Queensland
99 O6 Nora Springs Iowa
98 G4 Norbeck S Dakota
27 H11 Norberg Sweden
110 C2 Norborne Missouri
107 K2 Norcatur Kansas
42 E6 Norcia Italy
143 D9 Norcott,Mt W Australia
111 M8 Norcross Georgia
27 D12 Nordaguta Norway
26 K7 Nordanås Sweden
27 D11 Nord-Aurdal Norway
50 B1 Nordaustlandet isld Spitzbergen
28 D6 Nordborg Denmark
28 A6 Nordby Denmark
26 B9 Norddal Norway
28 O9 Norddeble Faeroes
32 F5 Norddeich W Germany
28 A7 Norddorf W Germany
32 L7 Norddrebber W Germany
118 B6 Nordegg R Alberta
9 G2 Nordelph England
32 F5 Norden W Germany
37 K6 Nordendorf W Germany
32 H5 Nordenham W Germany
51 J1 Nordenshel'da Arkhipelag U.S.S.R.
117 E5 Nordenskiold R Yukon Terr
28 A7 Norder Aue chan W Germany
32 J5 Nordergründe sandbank W Germany
32 F5 Norderney W Germany
32 F5 Norderney isld W Germany
26 A10 Nordfjord inlet Norway
26 A10 Nordfjord reg Norway
26 B10 Nordfjordeid Norway
26 H4 Nordfold Norway
28 B7 Nordfriesand reg W Germany
30 D1 Nord-friesische Inseln islds W Germany
37 M3 Nordhalben W Germany
33 N10 Nordhausen E Germany
109 K7 Nordheim Texas
32 J5 Nordholz W Germany
27 A11 Nordhordland reg Norway
32 F8 Nordhorn W Germany
26 K9 Nordingrå Sweden
80 C4 Nordiyya Israel
28 C3 Nordjylland co Denmark
26 P1 Nordkapp C Norway
26 Q1 Nordkinn Norway
26 L2 Nordkjosbotn Norway
26 F6 Nordland Fylker Norway
26 G7 Nordli Norway
37 K6 Nördlingen W Germany
26 K8 Nordmaling Sweden
100 J1 Nordman Idaho
27 G12 Nordmark Sweden
27 D11 Nordmarka reg Norway
26 B9 Nordmöre reg Norway
98 F7 Nordon Nebraska
28 O9 Nordöre Faeroes
32 K4 Nord-Ostsee Kanal W Germany
28 F2 Nordre Rønner isld Denmark
115 O4 Nordre Strömfjord inlet Greenland
32 E9 Nordrhein Westfalen land W Germany
28 C7 Nord Schleswig W Germany
28 B6 Nord Slesvig reg Denmark
32 L8 Nord-Stemmen W Germany
30 D1 Nordstrand isld W Germany
26 E7 Nord-Tröndelag Fylker Norway
51 L1 Nordvik U.S.S.R.
32 F8 Nordwalde W Germany
27 C11 Nore Norway
14 D4 Nore R Irish Rep
27 D11 Norefjell mt Norway
122 E1 Nore,L Quebec
120 K4 Norembego Ontario
17 K2 Norfeo,C Spain
110 D5 Norfolk Arkansas
95 O5 Norfolk Connecticut
98 J7 Norfolk Nebraska
95 L10 Norfolk Virginia
9 H2 Norfolk co England
137 O7 Norfolk I Pacific Oc
110 D5 Norfolk L Arkansas
25 F2 Norg Netherlands
13 F2 Norham England
109 K9 Norias Texas
61 L9 Norikura-dake mt Japan
51 H2 Noril'sk U.S.S.R.
141 G8 Norley Queensland
112 J1 Norlina N Carolina
45 N6 Norma Italy
111 C7 Norman Arkansas
98 H9 Norman Nebraska
107 N6 Norman Oklahoma
141 F4 Norman R Queensland
13 H5 Normanby England
145 E3 Normanby New Zealand
141 G2 Normanby R Queensland
141 K5 Normanby Ra Queensland
20 F4 Normandie reg France
121 S4 Normandin Quebec
110 K6 Normandy Tennessee
109 L4 Normangee Texas
143 E7 Norman Hurst,Mt W Australia
112 F2 Norman, L N Carolina
109 K7 Normanna Texas
141 K2 Norman Park dist Brisbane, Qnsld
141 F4 Normanton Queensland
114 G4 Norman Wells N W Terr
121 L4 Normetal Quebec
143 B10 Nornalup W Australia
124 F4 Norogachic Mexico
111 D8 Norphlet Arkansas
119 Q7 Norquay Sask
133 C5 Norquin Argentina
133 C6 Norquinco Argentina
29 J8 Norra Kvarken chan Finland/Sweden
27 J10 Norrala Sweden
27 G15 Norraryd Sweden
26 J4 Norrbotten reg Sweden
28 D4 Nørreå R Denmark
28 C5 Nørre Bramdrup Denmark
28 A5 Nørre Nebel Denmark
22 C2 Norrent-Fontès France
28 D2 Nørre Saltum Denmark
28 D2 Nørresundby Denmark
26 M6 Norrfjärden Sweden
26 K8 Norrfors Sweden
26 J9 Norrhassel Sweden
95 S2 Norridgewock Maine
99 Q9 Norris Illinois
101 O4 Norris Montana
98 E6 Norris S Dakota
112 C1 Norris Tennessee
101 P5 Norris Wyoming
123 R4 Norris Arm Nfld
110 H4 Norris City Illinois
112 C1 Norris Dam Tennessee
112 D1 Norris Lake Tennessee
123 P4 Norris Point Newfoundland
95 M6 Norristown Pennsylvania
27 H13 Norrköping Sweden
29 H8 Norrskär lt ho Finland
27 J11 Norrsundet Sweden
27 K12 Norrtälje Sweden
26 H6 Norrvik Sweden
28 B2 Nors Denmark
27 F12 Norsä R Sweden
143 D9 Norseman W Australia
145 F4 Norsewood New Zealand
27 H13 Norsholm Sweden
26 K7 Norsjö Sweden
27 D12 Norsjö L Norway
26 Q1 Norskholmen Norway
21 B7 Nort France
129 H3 Norte,C Brazil
128 D2 Norte de Santander div Colombia
32 L9 Nörten Hardenburg W Germany
133 E6 Norte,Pta Argentina
131 D3 Norte,Sa de ra Argentina
128 G6 Norte,Serra do mts Brazil
112 F4 North S Carolina
111 J8 North R Alabama
94 C5 North Adams Michigan
13 G5 Northallerton England
143 B9 Northam W Australia
98 F1 North America, Center of N Dakota
90 C6 North American Basin Atlantic Oc
9 F3 Northampton England
95 P4 Northampton Massachusetts
143 A8 Northampton W Australia
141 H6 Northampton Downs Queensland
9 F3 Northamptonshire co England
68 A6 North Andaman isld Andaman Is
94 K8 North Anna R Virginia
95 S2 North Anson Maine
Northants co see Northamptonshire co
117 Q4 North Arm inlet N W Terr
112 E4 North Augusta Georgia
115 N6 North Aulatsivik I Labrador
94 D5 North Baltimore Ohio
118 J6 North Battleford Sask
123 O6 North Bay Nfld
121 L6 North Bay Ontario
98 K8 North Bend Nebraska
100 A6 North Bend Oregon
13 F1 North Berwick Scotland
99 L9 Northboro Iowa
139 H4 North Bourke New S Wales
94 D3 North Branch Michigan
99 O4 North Branch Minnesota
118 H2 North Branch Ontario
121 N8 North Brook Ontario
13 H5 North Burton England
123 M6 North,C C Breton I, N Scotia
108 B7 North Canadian R Oklahoma etc
145 D1 North Cape New Zealand
137 P8 North Cape Rise sea feature Pacific Oc
115 L7 North Caribou L Ontario
112 E2 North Carolina state U.S.A.
100 D1 North Cascades Nat. Park Washington
113 H12 North Cat Cay isld Bahamas
14 F1 North Chan N Ireland/Scotland
120 G6 North Channel Ontario
112 H5 North Charleston S Carolina
13 G2 North Charlton England
99 T7 North Chicago Illinois
143 B10 Northcliffe W Australia
108 F4 North Concho R Texas
100 A3 North Cove Washington
95 N3 North Creek New York
98 F2 North Dakota state U.S.A.
122 F8 North Devon New Brunswick
9 F5 North Downs England
94 H4 North East Pennsylvania
95 R8 North East Carry Maine
141 L5 North-East Cay isld Gt Barrier Reef Aust
90 G3 North Eastern Atlantic Basin Atlantic Oc
122 A3 Northeast Mistassibi R Quebec
126 F2 Northeast Providence Chan Bahamas
123 R1 Northeast Pt Belle Isle, Nfld
83 M9 North East Pt C Christmas I Indian Oc
32 L9 Northeim W Germany
99 O8 North English Iowa
123 T5 Northern Bight Nfld
86 E2 Northern Darfur prov Sudan
113 L12 Northern Eleuthera dist Bahamas
122 F9 Northern Hd New Brunswick
119 U1 Northern Indian L Manitoba
12 A4 Northern Ireland U.K.
86 E2 Northern Kordofan prov Sudan
99 Q1 Northern Light L Ontario
83 M9 Northern Plateau Christmas I Indian Oc
127 O2 Northern Range Trinidad
Northern Sporades islds see Voríai Sporádhes Is
138 B1 Northern Territory Australia
139 H8 North Esk R Tasmania
9 E3 Northfield England
95 P4 Northfield Massachusetts
99 N5 Northfield Minnesota
95 P2 Northfield Vermont
144 A6 North Fiord New Zealand
99 S6 North Fond du Lac Wisconsin
9 H5 North Foreland head England
102 E4 North Fork California
101 M4 North Fork Idaho
100 K8 North Fork Nevada
94 B1 North Fox I Michigan
99 R6 North Freedom Wisconsin
120 J2 North French R Ontario
13 H6 North Frodingham England
13 G3 Northgate England
119 P9 Northgate Sask
141 K1 Northgate dist Brisbane, Qnsld
North Girard see Lake City
95 P5 North Haven Connecticut
144 D5 North Hd. New Zealand
122 F9 North Head New Brunswick
123 O4 North Head Nfld
141 H2 North Horn C Gt Barrier Reef Aust
86 G5 North Horr Kenya
112 H4 North I S Carolina
83 J12 North I Seychelles
9 G6 Northiam England
145 E3 North Island New Zealand
71 E6 North Islet Philippines
103 O6 North Jadito Canyon R Arizona
83 M8 North Keeling I Cocos Is Indian Oc
115 L2 North Kent I N W Terr
94 G5 North Kingsville Ohio
119 V1 North Knife L Manitoba
59 J3 North Korea People's Rep E Asia
North Land see Severnaya Zemlya
99 T3 Northland Michigan
145 D1 Northland stat area New Zealand
9 E4 Northleach England
99 U8 North Liberty Indiana
110 D7 North Little Rock Arkansas
98 H8 North Loup Nebraska
98 H8 North Loup R Nebraska
88 D7 North Luangwa Nat. Park Zambia
70 C2 North Luconia Shoals S China Sea
106 C2 North Mam Pk Colorado
94 B5 North Manchester Indiana
99 U4 North Manitou I Michigan
88 C10 North Mashonaland Zimbabwe
113 G12 North Miami Florida
15 B2 North Minch Scotland
142 E4 North, Mt W Australia
94 A3 North Muskegon Michigan
117 L4 North Nahanni R N W Terr
113 G11 North New River Can Florida
99 M2 Northome Minnesota
8 C1 Northop Wales
102 F4 North Palisade peak California
98 F8 North Platte Nebraska
98 D8 North Platte R Nebraska
101 T8 North Platte R Wyoming
111 J8 Northport Alabama
99 V4 Northport Michigan
98 C8 Northport Nebraska
122 J8 Northport Nova Scotia
100 H1 Northport Washington
100 H4 North Powder Oregon
99 S7 North Prairie Wisconsin
139 J7 North Pt Flinders I, Tasmania
83 J12 North Pt Mahé I Indian Oc
94 D1 North Pt Michigan
122 H6 North Pt Pr Edward I
100 B3 North R Washington
68 A6 North Reef I Andaman Is
109 M9 North Richland Hills Texas
123 M7 North River Bridge C Breton I, N Scotia
15 C1 North Rona Scotland
15 F1 North Ronaldsay Orkney Scotland
15 F1 North Ronaldsay Firth Orkney Scotland
122 J7 North Rustico Pr Edward I
102 C2 North San Juan California
100 C5 North Santiam R Oregon
118 B6 North Sask R Alberta
90 J3 North Sea W Europe
68 A7 North Sentinel I Andaman Is
13 G3 North Shields England
102 G2 North Shoshone Pk Nevada
99 O8 North Skunk R Iowa
116 M1 North Slope Alaska
117 P7 North Star Alberta
110 M1 North Star Ohio
141 L8 North Stradbroke I Queensland
109 M2 North Sulphur R Texas
123 M7 North Sydney C Breton I, N Scotia
8 C6 North Tawton England
144 A7 North Trap islds New Zealand
71 E7 North Ubian isld Philippines
15 A3 North Uist isld Scotland

Oil City — Ostend
57

111 C9 Oil City Louisiana
94 H5 Oil City Pennsylvania
120 H10 Oil Springs Ontario
107 O5 Oilton Oklahoma
109 J8 Oilton Texas
94 K9 Oilville Virginia
47 H6 Oinoúsa isld Greece
58 C6 Oi Qu R China
61 P5 Oirase-gawa R Japan
21 E8 Oiron France
25 D5 Oirschot Netherlands
19 Q14 Oisans dist France
71 L10 Oisau Timor Indonesia
20 K3 Oise dep France
20 K3 Oise R France
20 J2 Oisemont France
20 D5 Oisseau France
20 H3 Oissel France
25 D5 Oisterwijk Netherlands
127 P6 Oistins Barbados
22 E3 Oisy-le-Verger France
60 E12 Ōita Japan
46 E6 Oíti mt Greece
48 K4 Oituz pass Romania
60 P3 Oiwake Japan
102 E7 Ojai California
27 G11 Öje Sweden
61 J11 Ōji Japan
60 B12 Ojika-jima isld Japan
124 G3 Ojinaga Mexico
61 M8 Ojiya Japan
124 H6 Ojocaliente Mexico
106 B7 Ojo Caliente New Mexico
133 E3 Ojo de Agua Argentina
124 F3 Ojo de Laguna Mexico
124 C4 Ojo de Liebre Mexico
16 E5 Ojos del Guadiana mt Spain
133 D3 Ojos del Salado, Nev mt Chile/Arg
17 F4 Ojos Negros Spain
113 G12 Ojus Florida
27 F10 Öjvallberget Sweden
121 Q7 Oka Quebec
54 G4 Oka R U.S.S.R.
56 F4 Oka R U.S.S.R.
87 C10 Okahandja Namibia
145 E1 Okahu New Zealand
145 E3 Okahukura New Zealand
145 E3 Okaiawa R New Zealand
145 D1 Okaihau New Zealand
115 N6 Okak Is Labrador
113 F11 Okaloacoochee Slough swamp Florida
117 O10 Okanagan Centre Br Col
117 O11 Okanagan Falls Br Col
86 B6 Okanda Nat. Park Gabon
100 F1 Okanogan Washington
100 F1 Okanogan Range Wash/Br Col
74 E3 Okara Pakistan
107 N6 Okarche Oklahoma
144 C5 Okarito New Zealand
60 D14 Okasaki Japan
145 F3 Okataina L New Zealand
145 D3 Okato New Zealand
111 G10 Okatoma R Mississippi
87 C9 Okaukuejo Namibia
87 C9 Okavango R Namibia
87 D9 Okavango Basin Botswana
60 D12 Ōkawa Japan
61 N8 Ō-kawa R Japan
61 O7 Okawara Japan
110 G3 Okawville Illinois
107 P6 Okay Oklahoma
61 L9 Okaya Japan
60 G11 Okayama Japan
60 G11 Okayama prefect Japan
61 L11 Okazaki Japan
113 G10 Okeechobee Florida
113 G11 Okeechobee,L Florida
107 M5 Okeene Oklahoma
113 E7 Okefenokee Swamp Georgia
8 B6 Okehampton England
107 O6 Okemah Oklahoma
85 F7 Okene Nigeria
33 M9 Oker W Germany
33 N8 Oker R W Germany
60 R2 Oketo Japan
98 K10 Oketo Kansas
74 C7 Okha India
59 M1 Okha U.S.S.R.
75 M5 Okhaldhunga Nepal
47 G6 Ókhi mt Greece
51 O3 Okhotsk U.S.S.R.
59 N1 Okhotskoye More sea E Asia
Okhotsk,Sea of see Okhotskoye More
85 F7 Okigwi Nigeria
61 P13 Okinawa isld Japan
60 F13 Okino-shima Japan
60 D11 Okino-shima isld Japan
56 E4 Okinskiy Khrebet mts U.S.S.R.
60 G9 Oki shotō islds Japan
85 E7 Okitipupa Nigeria
68 B4 Okkan Burma
107 N6 Oklahoma state U.S.A.
107 N6 Oklahoma City Oklahoma
109 H1 Oklaunion Texas
113 F8 Oklawaha R Florida
107 P6 Okmulgee Oklahoma
48 K2 Okna U.S.S.R.
48 L2 Oknitsa U.S.S.R.
99 L6 Okoboji L Iowa
98 F5 Okobojo S Dakota
145 E3 Okoia New Zealand
111 H7 Okolona Mississippi
86 B6 Okondja Gabon
31 K2 Okonek Poland
60 R1 Okoppe Japan
145 E2 Okoroire New Zealand
118 D8 Okotoks Alberta
86 B6 Okoyo Congo
85 E7 Okpara R Benin/Nigeria
98 F6 Okreek S Dakota
26 C9 Oksendal Norway
26 M1 Öksfjord Norway
26 M1 Öksfjord-jökel mt Norway
52 H1 Oksino U.S.S.R.
54 M3 Oksko-Donskaya Ravnina plain U.S.S.R.
26 G3 Öksnes Norway
26 G5 Okstinderne mt Norway
107 P6 Oktaha Oklahoma
68 C3 Oktwin Burma
55 C6 Oktyabr'sk U.S.S.R.
55 D3 Oktyabr'skiy Chelyabinsk U.S.S.R.
52 F5 Oktyabr'skiy Kostroma U.S.S.R.
55 E5 Oktyabr'skiy Kushmurun U.S.S.R.
55 D4 Oktyabr'skiy Kustanay U.S.S.R.
55 E2 Oktyabr'skiy Tobol'sk U.S.S.R.
55 D4 Oktyabr'skoye Chelyabinsk U.S.S.R.
55 E1 Oktyabr'skoye Khanty-Mansiysk U.S.S.R.
55 C4 Oktyabr'skoye Orenburg U.S.S.R.
54 D10 Oktyabr'skoye Ukraine U.S.S.R.
51 J1 Oktyabr'skoy Rovolyutsii, Os isld U.S.S.R.
61 Q12 Oku Okinawa
60 D13 Ōkuchi Japan
144 D5 Okuku R New Zealand
52 D5 Okulovka U.S.S.R.
146 J8 Okuma Bay Antarctica
144 B5 Okuru New Zealand
60 N3 Okushiri-kaikyō str Japan
60 N3 Okushiri-tō isld Japan
60 J10 Okutango-hantō pen Japan
89 B4 Okwa watercourse Botswana
110 C6 Ola Arkansas
100 J5 Ola Idaho
16 C7 Olalla de Cala, Sta Spain
95 T1 Olamon Maine
27 J15 Öland isld Sweden
28 D2 Øland reg Denmark
52 D2 Olanga U.S.S.R.
29 P5 Olanga R U.S.S.R.
112 H4 Olanta S Carolina
18 G9 Olargues France
138 C2 Olarinna R S Australia
138 F4 Olary S Australia
107 Q3 Olathe Kansas
131 E6 Olavarria Argentina
31 K5 Oława Poland
103 N8 Olberg Arizona
37 P2 Olbernhau E Germany
37 L1 Olbersleben E Germany
43 C8 Olbia Sardinia
37 L7 Olching W Germany
94 J3 Olcott New York
126 E3 Old Bahama Chan Caribbean
14 D3 Oldcastle Irish Rep
142 F4 Old Cherrabun W Australia
141 F6 Old Cork Queensland
114 F4 Old Crow Yukon Terr
116 R2 Old Crow R Alaska/Yukon Terr
88 E3 Oldeani Tanzania
109 J3 Olden Texas
32 H6 Oldenbrok W Germany
33 N4 Oldenburg W Germany
33 N6 Oldendorf W Germany
33 N7 Oldenstadt W Germany
25 G4 Oldenzaal Netherlands
32 F6 Oldersum W Germany
26 B10 Oldevatn L Norway
101 P5 Old Faithful Wyoming
95 M3 Old Forge New York
95 M5 Old Forge Pennsylvania
112 E2 Old Fort N Carolina
123 O2 Old Fort Bay Quebec
143 C8 Old Gidgee W Australia
108 G2 Old Glory Texas
13 F6 Oldham England
98 J5 Oldham S Dakota
116 L8 Old Harbor Alaska
127 K3 Old Harbour Jamaica
110 K5 Old Hickory Tennessee
117 L8 Old Hogem Br Columbia
9 F3 Old Hurst England
33 O10 Oldisleben E Germany
116 P2 Old John L Alaska
95 P5 Old Lyme Connecticut
15 F3 Oldmeldrum Scotland
110 F3 Old Monroe Missouri
95 R3 Old Orchard Beach Maine
123 T5 Old Perlican Newfoundland
123 L3 Old Post Pt Quebec
116 R3 Old Rampart Alaska
113 G12 Old Rhodes Key isld Florida
127 O5 Old Road Antigua W I
127 P4 Old Road Town St Kitts W I
118 C7 Olds Alberta
95 R2 Old Spekle Mt Maine
9 F3 Old Stratford England
28 A7 Oldsum W Germany
113 E10 Old Tampa B Florida
138 E4 Old Telichie S Australia
113 D8 Old Town Florida
95 T2 Old Town Maine
88 E3 Olduvai Gorge Tanzania
Old Viking Bank see Bergen Bank
118 L8 Old Wives L Sask
116 H5 Old Woman R Alaska
103 J7 Old Woman Mts California
94 J4 Olean New York
122 H7 O'Leary Pr Edward I
31 N1 Olecko Poland
69 B10 Oleehoue Sumatra
16 B5 Oleiros Portugal
59 G1 Olekminski Stanovik mt ra U.S.S.R.
52 G3 Olema U.S.S.R.
27 A12 Ölen Norway
100 D7 Olene Oregon
52 D1 Olenegorsk U.S.S.R.
51 L2 Olenek R U.S.S.R.
52 D6 Olenino U.S.S.R.
52 E2 Olenitsa U.S.S.R.
55 B5 Olenty R U.S.S.R.
18 E7 Oléron,Ile d' France
48 J1 Olesko U.S.S.R.
31 K4 Oleśnica Poland
31 L5 Olesno Poland
45 O6 Olevano Romano Italy
100 E4 Olex Oregon
32 F9 Olfen W Germany
113 F11 Olga Florida
98 H1 Olga N Dakota
59 L3 Ol'ga U.S.S.R.
116 K8 Olga B Alaska
121 N3 Olga,L Quebec
140 B7 Olga, Mt N Terr Aust
54 J9 Ol'ginka U.S.S.R.
55 F3 Ol'gino U.S.S.R.
66 D2 Ölgiy Mongolia
28 B5 Ølgod Denmark
48 M2 Olgopol U.S.S.R.
16 B7 Olhão Portugal
29 L6 Olhava Finland
85 E7 Oli R Benin/Nigeria
140 A7 Olia Chain mts N Terr Aust
138 A2 Olia Chain mts N Terr Australia
17 H2 Oliana Spain
42 F4 Olib isld Yugoslavia
17 G4 Oliete Spain
89 A8 Olifants S Africa
87 C10 Olifants R Namibia
89 G5 Olifants R S Africa
89 A5 Olifants watercourse Namibia
87 D11 Olifantshoek S Africa
89 A9 Olifants R. Berge mts S Africa
131 G4 Olimar R Uruguay
46 E7 Olimbía Greece
46 E4 Ólimbos mt Greece
133 F2 Olimpo Paraguay
99 P7 Olin Iowa
100 C9 Olinda California
141 G1 Olinda Ent Gt Barrier Reef Aust
129 L6 Olindina Brazil
141 G5 Olio Queensland
17 F2 Olite Spain
17 G6 Oliva Spain
131 B2 Oliva, Cord. de mt ra Arg/Chile
16 C6 Oliva de Mérida Spain
131 B3 Olivares,Cerro del peak Arg/Chile
17 F5 Olivares de Júcar Spain
98 A4 Olive Montana
94 D8 Olive Hill Kentucky
130 G7 Oliveira Brazil
16 B4 Oliveira de Azemeis Portugal
16 B4 Oliveira do Hospital Portugal
112 J2 Olive, Mt N Carolina
Olivenca see Lupilichi
16 C6 Olivenza Spain
117 O11 Oliver Br Col
112 F5 Oliver Georgia
21 I6 Olivet France
94 C4 Olivet Michigan
98 J6 Olivet S Dakota
99 M5 Olivia Minnesota
109 L7 Olivia Texas
144 B6 Olivine Range New Zealand
41 J5 Olivone Switzerland
31 L1 Oliwa Poland
65 D3 Olji Moron He R China
54 L6 Ol'khovatka U.S.S.R.
55 D3 Ol'khovka U.S.S.R.
31 M5 Olkusz Poland
111 D10 Olla Louisiana
133 D2 Ollague vol Bolivia/Chile
9 E1 Ollerton England
98 B3 Ollie Montana
29 N2 Ollila Finland
131 B3 Ollita, Cord. de ra Arg/Chile
131 B3 Ollitas peak Argentina
27 G12 Ölme Sweden
16 D3 Olmeda Spain
131 D4 Olmos,L Argentina
9 F3 Olney England
110 H3 Olney Illinois
101 L1 Olney Montana
109 J2 Olney Texas
106 G3 Olney Springs Colorado
26 K8 Olofsfors Sweden
27 G15 Olofström Sweden
123 M3 Olomane R Quebec
86 C6 Olombo Congo
48 D1 Olomouc Czechoslovakia
41 K7 Olona R Italy
48 M4 Oloneshty U.S.S.R.
52 D4 Olonets U.S.S.R.
71 E3 Olongapo Luzon Philippines
18 G9 Olonzac France
18 E9 Oloron-St.Marie France
17 J2 Olot Spain
37 O3 Olovi Czechoslovakia
48 E6 Olovo Yugoslavia
58 G1 Olovyannaya U.S.S.R.
107 O3 Olpe Kansas
36 D1 Olpe W Germany
41 P3 Olperer mt Austria
107 O2 Olsburg Kansas
31 L6 Olše R Czechoslovakia
54 G6 Ol'shany U.S.S.R.
25 F4 Olst Netherlands
31 M2 Olsztyn Poland
31 M2 Olsztynek Poland
40 G3 Olten Switzerland
48 K6 Oltenița Romania
133 D6 Olte,Sa.de mts Argentina
48 H6 Oltețul R Romania
108 E1 Olton Texas
78 H1 Oltu Turkey
48 K4 Oltul R Romania
67 G6 O-luan-pi C Taiwan
113 E7 Olustee Florida
107 L7 Olustee Oklahoma
71 F7 Olutanga isld Philippines
33 P8 Olvenstedt E Germany
16 D8 Olvera Spain
46 E7 Olympia Greece
100 C2 Olympia Washington
100 B2 Olympic Mts Washington
100 B2 Olympic Nat. Park Washington
Olympus mt Cyprus see Troödos Mt
Olympus mt Greece see Ólimbos Mt
100 B2 Olympus,Mt Washington
95 M5 Olyphant Pennsylvania
51 R2 Olyutorskiy U.S.S.R.
36 B3 Olzheim W Germany
56 B3 Om' R U.S.S.R.
60 O4 Ōma Japan
111 F10 Oma Mississippi
52 G2 Oma U.S.S.R.
61 L9 Ōmachi Japan
61 M11 Omae zaki C Japan
14 D2 Omagh N Ireland
128 D4 Omaguas Peru
110 C5 Omaha Arkansas
99 L8 Omaha Nebraska
109 N2 Omaha Texas
126 F4 Omaja Cuba
100 F1 Omak Washington
144 B6 Omakau New Zealand
145 F4 Omakere New Zealand
72 H5 Oman sultanate Arabian Pen
77 F7 Oman, Gulf of Iran/Oman
145 D1 Omapere, L New Zealand
94 E9 Omar W Virginia
144 B6 Omarama New Zealand
87 C10 Omaruru Namibia
128 D7 Omate Peru
60 O4 Ōma-zaki C Japan
120 C2 Ombabika Ontario
120 B2 Ombabika B Ontario
71 M9 Ombai,Selat str Indonesia
69 C12 Ombalata Indonesia
61 N11 Ombase-jima isld Japan
8 D3 Ombersley England
86 A6 Omboue Gabon
45 J4 Ombrone R Italy
66 D5 Ombu China
86 F2 Omdurman Sudan
61 N10 Ome Japan
111 L10 Omega Alabama
112 D6 Omega Georgia
107 M6 Omega Oklahoma
98 F1 Omemee N Dakota
121 M8 Omemee Ontario
94 B1 Omena Michigan
80 C8 'Omer Israel
94 D2 Omer Michigan
47 J5 Ömerköy Turkey
14 A3 Omey I Irish Rep
61 L8 Ōmi Japan
22 D4 Omiecourt France
144 D5 Omihi New Zealand
57 L2 O-min U.S.S.R.
60 P4 Ōminato Japan
117 L8 Omineca R Br Col
114 G6 Omineca Mts Br Col
117 K7 Omineca Mts Br Col
61 J11 Ōmine San mt Japan
42 H5 Omis Yugoslavia
60 E11 Ōmi-shima isld Japan
60 F11 Ōmi-shima isld Japan
61 N10 Ōmiya Japan
117 F7 Ommaney,C Alaska
114 J3 Ommanney B N W Terr
28 B5 Omme Å R Denmark
25 F3 Ommen Netherlands
28 G6 Omø Denmark
86 G4 Omo R Ethiopia
51 P2 Omolon R U.S.S.R.
51 N2 Omolov R U.S.S.R.
61 O6 Omono-gawa R Japan
22 H4 Omont France
20 B2 Omonville-la Rogue France
61 O6 Ōmori Japan
61 P6 Omoto Japan
61 P6 Omoto-gawa R Japan
99 S5 Omro Wisconsin
55 F3 Omsk U.S.S.R.
50 G3 Omskaya Oblast' prov U.S.S.R.
68 D1 O-mu Burma
60 Q1 Ōmu Japan
31 N2 Omulew R Poland
83 L10 Omuna Sri Lanka
60 C13 Ōmura Japan
60 C13 Ōmura wan B Japan
47 H1 Omurtag Bulgaria
60 D12 Ōmuta Japan
55 E3 Omutinskiy U.S.S.R.
52 H5 Omutninsk U.S.S.R.
113 F10 Ona Florida
26 B9 Ona Norway
16 E2 Oña Spain
56 C5 Ona R U.S.S.R.
107 O2 Onaga Kansas
61 P7 Onagawahama Japan
61 P7 Onagawa-wan B Japan
61 O9 Onahama Japan
98 G4 Onaka S Dakota
120 J2 Onakawana Ontario
120 J1 Onakwehegan R Ontario
100 C3 Onalaska Washington
99 P6 Onalaska Wisconsin
120 C2 Onaman L Ontario
99 N3 Onamia Minnesota
70 F6 Onan Sulawesi
95 M9 Onancock Virginia
86 B6 Onangue, L Gabon
120 J5 Onaping L Ontario
110 H1 Onarga Illinois
121 U3 Onatchiway,L Quebec
124 F2 Oñate Mexico
124 E3 Onavas Mexico
98 K7 Onawa Iowa
94 C1 Onaway Michigan
68 C5 Onbingwin Burma
87 B9 Oncocua Angola
17 G5 Onda Spain
87 C9 Ondangua Namibia
31 N6 Ondava R Czechoslovakia
25 G2 Onderdendam Netherlands
85 E7 Ondo Nigeria
58 F2 Öndörhaan Mongolia
65 E2 Ondor Had China
73 L8 One and Half Degree Chan Indian Ocean
113 E10 Oneco Florida
52 E3 Onega U.S.S.R.
Onega L see Onezhskoye, Oz
52 E4 Onega R U.S.S.R.
44 D4 Oneglia Italy
141 H2 One & Half Mile Opening str Gt Barrier Reef Aust
99 Q8 Oneida Illinois
99 P7 Oneida Iowa
94 D9 Oneida Kentucky
95 M3 Oneida New York
110 M5 Oneida Tennessee
95 L3 Oneida L New York
98 H7 O'Neill Nebraska
145 D4 Onekaka New Zealand
94 A2 Onekama Michigan
86 D6 Onema Zaïre
111 K8 Oneonta Alabama
95 M4 Oneonta New York
145 F3 Onepoto New Zealand
145 E1 Onerahi New Zealand
118 J1 One Sided Lake Ontario
52 E4 Onezhskoye,Oz L U.S.S.R.
145 F3 Ongaonga New Zealand
9 G4 Ongar England
145 E3 Ongarue New Zealand
89 C8 Ongers watercourse S Africa
143 C10 Ongerup W Australia
65 B3 Onggon Ul China
19 P16 Ongles France
65 D3 Ongniud Qi China
76 E3 Ongole India
15 C4 Onich Scotland
98 G5 Onida S Dakota
87 G12 Onilahy R Madagascar
118 H5 Onion Lake Sask
60 P1 Onishika Japan
122 A3 Onistagan L Quebec
85 F7 Onitsha Nigeria
20 H1 Onival France
29 N8 Onkivesi L Finland
95 M9 Onley Virginia
61 P13 Onna Okinawa
61 P13 Onna-dake mt Okinawa
22 F3 Onnaing France
60 O4 Ōno Japan
60 E11 Onoda Japan
61 N11 Ōnohara-jima isld Japan
137 R6 Ono-i-lau isld Pacific Oc
145 E4 Onoke, L New Zealand
69 C12 Onolimbu Indonesia
60 G11 Onomichi Japan
58 G1 Onon R U.S.S.R.
94 C4 Onondaga Michigan
58 F2 Onon Gol R Mongolia
61 O8 Ono-Niimachi Japan
59 M1 Onor U.S.S.R.
128 E2 Onoto Venezuela
137 Q2 Onotoa atoll Kiribati
118 C5 Onoway Alberta
28 F5 Onsbjerg Denmark
16 B2 Ons., I.de Spain
28 H7 Ønslev Denmark
142 B5 Onslow W Australia
112 K3 Onslow B N Carolina
144 B6 Onslow, L New Zealand
94 C4 Onsted Michigan
36 G7 Onstmettingen W Germany
25 H2 Onstwedde Netherlands
61 L10 Ontake-san mt Japan
102 G7 Ontario California
100 J5 Ontario Oregon
99 Q6 Ontario Wisconsin
120 E3 Ontario prov Canada
94 J3 Ontario,L U.S.A./Canada
17 G6 Onteniente Spain
99 R3 Ontonagon Michigan
137 M3 Ontong Java Is Solomon Is
17 G6 Ontur Spain
60 O4 Onuma Japan
111 F9 Onward Mississippi
102 F6 Onyx California
21 H7 Onzain France
138 D2 Oodnadatta S Australia
135 V4 Ookala Hawaiian Is
107 P5 Oolagah Oklahoma
138 B4 Ooldea S Australia
138 B4 Ooldea Ra S Australia
110 K3 Oolitic Indiana
107 P5 Oologah Res Oklahoma
25 B5 Ooltgensplaat Netherlands
141 G5 Oondooroo Queensland
140 C6 Ooraminna Ra N Terr Aust
140 D5 Ooratippra R N Terr Aust
141 F5 Oorindi Queensland
111 L7 Oostanaula R Georgia
25 A6 Oostburg Netherlands
22 D2 Oost Cappel France
22 D1 Oostduinkerke Belgium
22 D1 Oostende Belgium
25 E5 Oosterbeër Netherlands
25 D2 Oosterend Netherlands
25 C5 Oosterhout Netherlands
25 A5 Oosterschelde Netherlands
25 F3 Oosterwolde Netherlands
22 F2 Oosterzele Belgium
25 D3 Oosthuizen Netherlands
25 E4 Oostlijk-Flevoland Netherlands
25 F2 Oostmahoorn Netherlands
22 H1 Oostmalle Belgium
22 F1 Oost Vlaanderen Belgium
25 D2 Oost Vlieland Netherlands
25 B5 Oostvoorne Netherlands
76 C5 Ootacamund India
25 G4 Ootmarsum Netherlands
117 L9 Ootsa Lake Br Col
119 S2 Opachuanau L Manitoba
102 R11 Opaeula R Hawaiian Is
47 H1 Opaka Bulgaria
145 E4 Opaki New Zealand
118 D5 Opal Alberta
124 H5 Opal Mexico
101 P8 Opal Wyoming
51 P3 Opala U.S.S.R.
86 D6 Opala Zaïre
31 J3 Opalenica Poland
113 G12 Opa-Locka Florida
141 G6 Opalton Queensland
141 G6 Opalville Queensland
76 E7 Opanake Sri Lanka
86 F5 Opari Sudan
52 G5 Oparino U.S.S.R.
120 H3 Opasatika Ontario
120 G3 Opasatika L Ontario
42 F3 Opatija Yugoslavia
31 N5 Opatów Poland
31 L4 Opatówek Poland
31 K6 Opava Czechoslovakia
31 K5 Opava R Czechoslovakia
121 P3 Opawica, L Quebec
111 L9 Opelika Alabama
111 D11 Opelousas Louisiana
120 D2 Opemisha Ontario
144 B5 Open Bay Is New Zealand
143 D8 Open L W Australia
121 M7 Opeongo L Ontario
22 F2 Ophasselt Belgium
101 T1 Opheim Montana
100 A7 Ophir Oregon
101 N9 Ophir Utah
22 K1 Ophoven Belgium
142 C6 Ophthalmia Ra W Australia
45 P6 Opi Italy
86 E5 Opienge Zaïre
144 C6 Opihi R New Zealand
36 B1 Opladen W Germany
85 F8 Opobo Nigeria
52 C6 Opochka U.S.S.R.
122 F1 Opocopa L Quebec
31 M4 Opoczno Poland
124 D3 Opodepe Mexico
31 K5 Opole Poland
145 F3 Oponae New Zealand
145 D1 Opononi New Zealand
Oporto see Porto
54 F7 Oposhnya U.S.S.R.
145 F3 Opotiki New Zealand
145 E2 Opoutere New Zealand
111 K10 Opp Alabama
61 P7 Oppa-gawa R Japan
61 P7 Oppa-wan B Japan
26 D9 Oppdal Norway
45 K1 Oppeano Italy
33 T9 Oppelhaun E Germany
Oppeln see Opole
36 E7 Oppenau W Germany
36 E4 Oppenheim W Germany
36 G6 Oppenweiler W Germany
28 J5 Oppe Sundby Denmark
27 D10 Oppland county Norway
119 Q4 Optic Lake Manitoba
107 J5 Optima Oklahoma
106 F6 Optimo New Mexico
145 E1 Opua New Zealand
145 E1 Opuawhanga New Zealand
145 D3 Opunake New Zealand
124 E2 Oputo Mexico
22 G2 Opwijk Belgium
99 Q9 Oquawka Illinois
124 D2 Oquitoa Mexico
95 R2 Oquossoc Maine
27 G15 Ör Sweden
55 C5 Or' R U.S.S.R.
41 O5 Ora Italy
84 F4 Ora Libya
143 D9 Ora Banda W Australia
127 L2 Oracabessa Jamaica
103 O9 Oracle Arizona
48 G3 Oradea Romania
74 H6 Orai India
103 O6 Oraibi Arizona
103 O5 Oraibi Wash creek Arizona
29 L5 Orajärvi Finland
29 M4 Orajärvi L Finland
98 C6 Oral S Dakota
85 D1 Oran Algeria
110 G4 Oran Missouri
19 N16 Orange France
95 P4 Orange Massachusetts
139 J5 Orange New S Wales
109 O5 Orange Texas
94 J8 Orange Virginia
87 C11 Orange R S Africa/Namibia
111 J11 Orange Beach Alabama
112 G4 Orangeburg S Carolina
129 H3 Orange,C Brazil
126 E2 Orange Cay isld Bahamas
113 F9 Orange City Florida
116 Q3 Orange Cr Alaska
123 L8 Orangedale C Breton I, N Scotia
113 F7 Orangedale Florida
95 N6 Orange, E New Jersey
89 D7 Orange Free State prov S Africa
129 G3 Orange Gebergte mts Suriname
109 K8 Orange Grove Texas
113 E8 Orange L Florida
113 F7 Orange Park Florida
99 R7 Orangeville Illinois
103 N2 Orangeville Utah
145 E3 Orangimea New Zealand
71 E3 Orani Luzon Philippines
43 C8 Orani Sardinia
33 Q9 Oranienbaum E Germany
33 S7 Oranienburg E Germany
80 D3 Oranim Israel
87 C11 Oranjemund Namibia
126 A1 Oranjestad Aruba W I
127 N6 Oranjestad St Eustatius W I
14 C3 Oranmore Irish Rep
133 E2 Orán, N Argentina
Orantes R see 'Āsi R
143 G6 Orantjugurr,L W Australia
80 C3 Or'Aqiva Israel
144 C6 Orari New Zealand
71 G4 Oras Philippines
71 G4 Oras B Philippines
48 E5 Orašje Yugoslavia
48 H5 Orăștie Romania
48 H3 Orașu Nou Romania
124 H5 Oratario Mexico
48 M1 Oratovo U.S.S.R.
31 L6 Orava R Czechoslovakia
29 J8 Oravais Finland
48 G5 Oravița Romania
31 L6 Oravská Magura mts Czechoslovakia
144 A7 Orawia New Zealand
18 H9 Orb R France
44 E2 Orba R Italy
20 F3 Orbec France
42 D6 Orbetello Italy
21 H7 Orbigny France
16 D2 Orbigo R Spain
94 K6 Orbisonia Pennsylvania
139 J7 Orbost Victoria
27 F14 Örby Sweden
27 J11 Örbyhus Sweden
116 O6 Orca B Alaska
128 E1 Orchila, La isld Venezuela
16 B1 Ordenes Spain
103 M4 Orderville Utah
28 B3 Ørding Denmark
102 H7 Ord Mt California
142 F3 Ord,Mt W Australia
52 D3 Ordozero U.S.S.R.
142 G3 Ord River W Australia
78 F1 Ordu Turkey
78 K2 Ordubail U.S.S.R.
16 E2 Orduña Spain
106 G3 Ordway Colorado
98 H4 Ordway S Dakota
53 F11 Ordzhonikidze U.S.S.R.
56 C4 Ordzhonikidzevskiy U.S.S.R.
28 E5 Ore Denmark
26 C9 Öre Norway
26 K7 Oreälv R Sweden
100 J6 Oreana Idaho
102 F1 Oreana Nevada
27 H12 Örebro Sweden
27 G12 Örebro county Sweden
109 N3 Ore City Texas
99 R7 Oregon Illinois
110 A2 Oregon Missouri
99 R7 Oregon Wisconsin
100 E6 Oregon state U.S.A.
100 B7 Oregon Caves Nat. Mon Oregon
100 C4 Oregon City Oregon
112 M2 Oregon Inlet N Carolina
27 K11 Öregrund Sweden
54 G9 Orekhov U.S.S.R.
47 G1 Orekhovitsa Bulgaria
47 F1 Orekhovo Bulgaria
52 E6 Orekhovo Zuyevo U.S.S.R.
54 B2 Orekhovsk U.S.S.R.
54 H4 Orël Orlov U.S.S.R.
52 J5 Orël Perm U.S.S.R.
54 F8 Orel' R U.S.S.R.
98 C7 Orella Nebraska
128 C5 Orellana Peru
16 D5 Orellana, Embalse de res Spain
59 L1 Orel, Oz L U.S.S.R.
103 N1 Orem Utah
47 J7 Ören Turkey
55 C5 Orenburg U.S.S.R.
50 E3 Orenburgskaya Oblast' prov U.S.S.R.
16 B2 Orense Spain
16 B2 Orense prov Spain
46 F6 Oreoí Greece
144 A7 Orepuki New Zealand
47 H3 Orestiás Greece
28 K5 Öresund str Sweden/Denmark
144 B7 Oreti R New Zealand
145 E2 Orewa New Zealand
22 J2 Oreye Belgium
9 H3 Orford England
95 P3 Orford New Hampshire
139 J8 Orford Tasmania
9 H3 Orford Ness England
141 G1 Orfordness Queensland
106 D9 Organ New Mexico
126 C3 Organos, Sa. de los hills Cuba
103 M9 Organ Pipe Cactus Nat. Mon Arizona
16 E5 Orgaz Spain
20 K4 Orge R France
40 C4 Orgelet France
20 J5 Orgères-en-Beauce France
20 J4 Orgeval France
48 M3 Orgeyev U.S.S.R.
45 K1 Orgiano Italy
16 E8 Orgiva Spain
65 B3 Orgon Tal China
52 F6 Orgtrud U.S.S.R.
47 K5 Orhaneli Turkey
47 K5 Orhaneli R Turkey
47 K4 Orhangazi Turkey
Orhanie see Botevgrad
47 J5 Orhanlar Turkey
58 D2 Orhon Gol R Mongolia
17 F7 Oria Spain
17 F1 Oria R Spain
52 G5 Orichi U.S.S.R.
100 A8 Orick California
106 E3 Orient Colorado
99 M8 Orient Iowa
141 G8 Orient Queensland
98 G5 Orient S Dakota
108 G4 Orient Texas
100 G1 Orient Washington
112 L2 Oriental N Carolina
120 B3 Orient Bay Ontario
95 P5 Orient I New York
138 F3 Orientos New S Wales
141 F8 Orientos Queensland
22 G4 Origny-en-Thiérache France
22 E4 Origny-St.-Benoîte France
17 G6 Orihuela Spain
121 L8 Orillia Ontario
29 M11 Orimattila Finland
98 A7 Orin Wyoming
128 F2 Orinoco R Venezuela
128 F2 Orinoco, Mouths of the Venezuela
43 G8 Oriolo Italy
118 G9 Orion Alberta
99 Q8 Orion Illinois
98 J3 Oriska N Dakota
95 M4 Oriskany Falls New York
75 K8 Orissa prov India
43 B9 Oristano Sardinia
43 B9 Oristano, G. di Sardinia
128 E2 Orituco R Venezuela
29 O9 Orivesi L Finland
129 G4 Oriximiná Brazil
52 D2 Oriyarvi, Oz L U.S.S.R.
125 L8 Orizaba Mexico
47 J2 Orizare Bulgaria
42 J6 Orjen mt Yugoslavia
26 D8 Orkdalen V Norway
27 F15 Örkelljunga Sweden
27 G15 Örkened Sweden
26 D9 Orkla R Norway
87 E11 Orkney S Africa
118 K9 Orkney Sask
15 F1 Orkney isld Scotland
108 D4 Orla Texas
37 M2 Orla R E Germany
31 K4 Orla R Poland
37 M2 Orlamünde E Germany
102 B2 Orland California
94 B5 Orland Indiana
95 T2 Orland Maine
113 F9 Orlando Florida
107 N5 Orlando Oklahoma
43 F10 Orlando, C.d' Sicily
20 J5 Orleanais reg France
100 B8 Orleans California
21 I6 Orleans France
110 K3 Orleans Indiana
95 S5 Orleans Massachusetts
98 K1 Orleans Minnesota
98 G9 Orleans Nebraska
95 P2 Orleans Vermont
121 U6 Orleans, Île d' Quebec
Orléansville see Asnam, El
31 J5 Orlice R Czechoslovakia
56 E5 Orlik U.S.S.R.
31 L6 Orlová Czechoslovakia
56 C2 Orlovka R U.S.S.R.
52 F2 Orlov, Mys C U.S.S.R.
55 F3 Orlovo U.S.S.R.
74 C10 Ormara Pakistan
13 G4 Ormesby England
36 C5 Ormesheim W Germany
119 M9 Ormiston Sask
71 G5 Ormoc Philippines
113 F8 Ormond Florida
145 F3 Ormond New Zealand
113 F8 Ormond Beach Florida
145 F4 Ormondville New Zealand
38 O9 Ormoz Yugoslavia
99 M6 Ormsby Minnesota
99 R4 Ormsby Wisconsin
26 H7 Ormsjö Sweden
13 F6 Ormskirk England
121 R7 Ormstown Quebec
19 J4 Ornain R France
19 K5 Ornans France
41 H6 Ornavasso Italy
37 K5 Ornbau W Germany
20 F4 Orne dep France
20 F5 Orne R France
31 M1 Orneta Poland
27 K12 Orno Sweden
26 K8 Örnsköldsvik Sweden
28 H5 Orø Denmark
41 L5 Orobie, Alpi mt Italy
51 M3 Orochen U.S.S.R.
128 D3 Orocué Colombia
85 D6 Orodara Upper Volta
100 J3 Orofino Idaho
102 G7 Oro Grande California
100 K4 Orogrande Idaho
106 D9 Orogrande New Mexico
61 P13 Oroku Okinawa
122 F8 Oromocto New Brunswick
122 F8 Oromocto L New Brunswick
79 F8 Oron Israel
95 T2 Orono Maine
121 M9 Orono Ontario
110 B4 Oronogo Missouri
12 B1 Oronsay isld Scotland
16 D5 Oropesa Spain
89 H6 Oro Pt S Africa
127 P2 Oropuche R Trinidad
59 H1 Oroqen Zizhiqi China
71 F6 Oroquieta Mindanao
129 L5 Orós, Açude res Brazil
43 C8 Orosei Sardinia
43 C8 Orosei, G.di Sardinia
48 F4 Orosháza Hungary
48 E3 Oroszlany Hungary
51 P2 Orotukan U.S.S.R.
145 E4 Oroua R New Zealand
100 H8 Orovada Nevada
102 C2 Oroville California
100 F1 Oroville Washington
101 U7 Orpha Wyoming
141 H4 Orpheus I Queensland
20 J4 Orphin France
19 P16 Orpierre France
98 J1 Orr N Dakota
107 N7 Orr Oklahoma
27 H15 Orrefors Sweden
98 F1 Orrin N Dakota
15 D3 Orrin R Scotland
119 U2 Orr L Manitoba
26 G10 Orrmosjön L Sweden
138 E4 Orroroo S Australia
27 J11 Orrskog Sweden
94 K6 Orrstown Pennsylvania
94 F6 Orrville Ohio
27 G10 Orsa Sweden
44 H3 Orsaro mt Italy
9 G5 Orsett England
54 B2 Orsha U.S.S.R.
52 G6 Orshanka U.S.S.R.
27 H15 Örsjö Sweden
55 C5 Orsk U.S.S.R.
27 F13 Örslösa Sweden
28 E2 Ørsø Denmark
48 G6 Orșova Romania
32 E9 Orsoy W Germany
26 B9 Örsta Norway
27 J12 Örsundsbro Sweden
47 K8 Ortaca Turkey
47 J7 Ortaklar Turkey
80 G1 Or Tal Syria
41 H6 Orta, L. d' Italy
26 K7 Örtäsk Sweden
42 E6 Orte Italy
16 B1 Ortegal, C Spain
Ortelsburg see Szczytno
36 G3 Ortenberg W Germany
37 P6 Ortenburg W Germany
30 F1 Orth W Germany
18 E9 Orthez France
45 L4 Ortignano Raggiolo Italy
16 B1 Ortigueira Spain
100 C2 Orting Washington
106 D4 Ortiz Colorado
124 D3 Ortiz Mexico
128 E2 Ortiz Venezuela
41 N4 Ortles mt Italy
37 O2 Ortmannsdorf E Germany
127 P3 Ortoire R Trinidad
13 F5 Orton England
128 E6 Orton R Bolivia
42 F6 Ortona Italy
98 K4 Ortonville Minnesota
57 H4 Orto-Tokoy U.S.S.R.
33 T10 Ortrand E Germany
32 M7 Ortze R W Germany
145 F3 Oruanui New Zealand
51 M2 Orulgan, Khrebet mt U.S.S.R.
28 D4 Ørum Denmark
28 E2 Ørum Denmark
133 D1 Oruro Bolivia
145 D1 Oruru New Zealand
27 E13 Orust isld Sweden
21 B7 Orvault France
42 E6 Orvieto Italy
20 J4 Orvilliers France
45 N5 Orvinio Italy
94 K5 Orviston Pennsylvania
95 L3 Orwell New York
94 G5 Orwell Ohio
95 O3 Orwell Vermont
58 G2 Orxon Gol R China
41 L7 Orzinuovi Italy
31 M2 Orzyc R Poland
31 N2 Orzysz Poland
26 E9 Os Norway
27 E10 Osa R Norway
99 O6 Osage Iowa
107 O5 Osage Oklahoma
119 O9 Osage Sask
98 B6 Osage Wyoming
107 P3 Osage City Kansas
110 D4 Osage Fork R Missouri
62 Ōsaka conurbation Japan
55 F5 Osakarovka U.S.S.R.
99 L4 Osakis Minnesota
99 L4 Osakis L Minnesota
107 Q3 Osawatomie Kansas
120 E3 Osawin R Ontario
142 F2 Osborne Is W Australia
27 G14 Os bruk Sweden
27 G15 Osby Sweden
142 F4 Oscar Ra W Australia
110 G6 Osceola Arkansas
99 N8 Osceola Iowa
110 C3 Osceola Missouri
98 J8 Osceola Nebraska
94 J6 Osceola Pennsylvania
99 O4 Osceola Wisconsin
33 S10 Oschatz E Germany
33 O8 Oschersleben E Germany
94 D2 Oscoda Michigan
106 D8 Oscura New Mexico
26 E7 Osen Norway
54 K2 Osetr R U.S.S.R.
60 B13 Ōse-zaki C Japan
94 B7 Osgood Indiana
110 C1 Osgood Missouri
121 P7 Osgoode Station Ontario
100 H8 Osgood Mts Nevada
57 G4 Osh U.S.S.R.
55 F3 Osha R U.S.S.R.
60 O3 Oshamanbe Japan
121 M9 Oshawa Ontario
60 P1 Oshidomari Japan
61 P7 Oshika-Hantō pen Japan
59 J6 O-shima isld Japan
61 N11 Ō-shima isld Japan
98 D8 Oshkosh Nebraska
99 S6 Oshkosh Wisconsin
52 J2 Oshkur'ya U.S.S.R.
55 D1 Oshmar'ye U.S.S.R.
78 K3 Oshnoviyeh Iran
85 E7 Oshogbo Nigeria
98 B5 Oshoto Wyoming
77 A3 Oshtorān Kūh mt Iran
52 K2 Oshvor U.S.S.R.
86 C6 Oshwe Zaïre
74 E5 Osian India
47 G1 Osica Romania
48 J6 Osica de Jos Romania
48 E5 Osijek Yugoslavia
45 O4 Osimo Italy
56 C4 Osinniki U.S.S.R.
54 B2 Osintorf U.S.S.R.
26 N3 Oskal Norway
99 O8 Oskaloosa Iowa
107 P2 Oskaloosa Kansas
27 H14 Oskarshamn Sweden
27 F15 Oskarström Sweden
121 P4 Oskelaneo Quebec
54 J7 Oskol R U.S.S.R.
31 J6 Oslava R Czechoslovakia
118 L6 Osler Sask
98 J1 Oslo Minnesota
27 E12 Oslo Norway
71 F6 Oslob Cebu Philippines
27 E13 Oslofjord inlet Norway
28 C2 Øsløs Denmark
54 E2 Os'ma R U.S.S.R.
74 G9 Osmanabad India
78 E1 Osmancik Turkey
47 K4 Osmaneli Turkey
52 C5 Osmino U.S.S.R.
27 J13 Ösmo Sweden
98 J7 Osmond Nebraska
98 H1 Osnabrock N Dakota
32 H8 Osnabrück W Germany
31 H3 Ośno Poland
46 E2 Osogovska Planina mt Yugoslavia
41 N7 Osone R Italy
60 O4 Osore yama mt Japan
131 A8 Osorno Chile
16 E2 Osorno Spain
131 A8 Osorno prov Chile
131 A8 Osorno, Vol peak Chile
133 C6 Osorro mt Chile
100 F1 Osoyoos Br Col
44 C4 Ospedaletti Italy
117 M7 Ospika R Br Col
113 E10 Osprey Florida
141 H2 Osprey Reef Gt Barrier Reef Aust
9 G5 Ospringe England
25 E5 Oss Netherlands
46 F5 Óssa mt Greece
112 F6 Ossabaw I Georgia
139 H8 Ossa, Mt Tasmania
16 B6 Ossa, Sa. d' mts Portugal
85 F7 Osse R Nigeria
27 K12 Össeby-Garn Sweden
99 P5 Osseo Wisconsin
38 J8 Ossiach Austria
99 P6 Ossian Iowa
94 D2 Ossineke Michigan
95 O5 Ossining New York
95 Q3 Ossipee L New Hampshire
27 E10 Os-sjöen L Norway
32 J8 Ossning hills W Germany
41 H5 Ossola, Val d' Italy
51 Q3 Ossora U.S.S.R.
121 M5 Ostaboningue, L Quebec
77 A2 Ostan-e Markazi Iran
52 E6 Ostashevo U.S.S.R.
52 D6 Ostashkov U.S.S.R.
26 H9 Östavell Sweden
32 G8 Ostbevern W Germany
32 K5 Oste R W Germany
113 F9 Osteen Florida
45 L2 Ostellato Italy
32 K5 Osten W Germany
Ostend see Oostende

58 Ostenholz — Paoli

32 L7 **Ostenholz** W Germany
41 K6 **Osteno** Italy
54 D3 **Oster** *R* U.S.S.R.
33 P7 **Osterburg** E Germany
94 J6 **Osterburg** Pennsylvania
36 G5 **Osterburken** W Germany
27 J11 **Österby** Sweden
27 H14 **Österbymo** Sweden
32 H8 **Ostercappeln** W Germany
27 G10 **Österdalälven** *R* Sweden
32 E5 **Osterems** *est* W Germany
27 H13 **Östergotland** *county* Sweden
37 P6 **Osterhofen** W Germany
32 J6 **Osterholz-Scharmbeck** W Germany
38 H6 **Osterhorn Gruppe** *mts* Austria
28 D3 **Øster Hornum** Nordjylland Denmark
27 J11 **Österlövsta** Sweden
26 J7 **Östernoret** Sweden
28 N2 **Østerø** *isld* Faeroes
Osterode Poland *see* **Ostróda**
32 M9 **Osterode** W Germany
27 A11 **Osteröy** *isld* Norway
38 H5 **Osterreich** *dist* Austria
26 G8 **Östersund** Sweden
28 H7 **Øster Ulslev** Denmark
27 J11 **Östervåla** Sweden
33 N9 **Osterwieck** E Germany
36 G6 **Ostfildern** W Germany
27 E12 **Östfold** *reg* Norway
32 F5 **Ostfriesische Inseln** *islds* W Germany
32 F6 **Ostfriesland** *reg* W Germany
32 G6 **Ostgrossefehn** W Germany
27 K11 **Östhammar** Sweden
36 C7 **Ostheim** France
37 J3 **Ostheim** W Germany
45 M6 **Ostia** Italy
45 K1 **Ostiglia** Italy
27 F11 **Östmark** Sweden
33 R5 **Ost Peene** *R* E Germany
45 O4 **Ostra** Italy
94 D6 **Ostrander** Ohio
37 P1 **Ostrau** E Germany
31 L6 **Ostrava** Czechoslovakia
45 O4 **Ostra Vetere** Italy
31 M2 **Ostróda** Poland
31 N2 **Ostrołęka** Poland
120 J5 **Ostrom** Ontario
37 O3 **Ostrov** Czechoslovakia
48 L6 **Ostrov** Romania
52 C6 **Ostrov** U.S.S.R.
55 F3 **Ostrovnaya** U.S.S.R.
51 Q2 **Ostrovnoye** U.S.S.R.
65 J3 **Ostrov Russkiy** *isld* U.S.S.R.
31 K4 **Ostrów** Poland
31 N5 **Ostrowiec** Poland
31 O4 **Ostrów Lubelski** Poland
31 N3 **Ostrów Mazowieckia** Poland
28 C3 **Østrup** Denmark
37 P5 **Ostrý** *mt* Czechoslovakia
31 K4 **Ostrzeszów** Poland
33 O5 **Ostseebad Boltenhagen** E Germany
33 Q4 **Ostseebad Graal-Müritz** E Germany
33 P4 **Ostseebad Kühlungsborn** E Germany
33 P4 **Ostseebad Nienhagen** E Germany
33 P4 **Ostseebad Rerik** E Germany
43 H8 **Ostuni** Italy
52 D6 **Osuga** *R* U.S.S.R.
100 F3 **O'Sullivan Dam** Washington
120 D2 **O'Sullivan, L** Ontario
121 P5 **O'Sullivan, L** Quebec
46 D4 **Osum** *R* Albania
47 G1 **Osŭm** *R* Bulgaria
60 D14 **Ōsumi-hantō** *pen* Japan
16 D7 **Osuna** Spain
52 J2 **Os'van'** U.S.S.R.
52 C6 **Osveya** U.S.S.R.
13 G5 **Oswaldkirk** England
94 J5 **Oswayo** Pennsylvania
95 M2 **Oswegalchie** *R* New York
99 S8 **Oswego** Illinois
107 P4 **Oswego** Kansas
101 U1 **Oswego** Montana
95 L3 **Oswego** New York
8 C2 **Oswestry** England
31 L5 **Oświęcim** Poland
111 F10 **Osyka** Mississippi
61 N9 **Ōta** Japan
60 F11 **Ōta** *R* Japan
144 B6 **Otago** *stat area* New Zealand
144 D7 **Otago Peninsula** New Zealand
144 C6 **Otaio** New Zealand
60 F11 **Ōtake** Japan
145 E3 **Otakeho** New Zealand
61 M10 **Ōtaki** Japan
145 E4 **Otaki** New Zealand
61 O8 **Ōtakine-yama** *mt* Japan
145 F3 **Otane** New Zealand
145 F2 **Otanewainuku** New Zealand
29 N7 **Otanmäki** Finland
83 K9 **Otappuwa** Sri Lanka
57 H3 **Otar** U.S.S.R.
60 O2 **Otaru** Japan
144 B7 **Otatara** New Zealand
144 B7 **Otautau** New Zealand
30 H6 **Otava** *R* Czechoslovakia
128 C3 **Otavalo** Ecuador
87 C9 **Otavi** Namibia
87 B9 **Otchinjau** Angola
95 M4 **Otego** New York
144 C6 **Otekaieke** New Zealand
48 F5 **Otelec** Romania
144 C6 **Otematata** New Zealand
52 C5 **Otepää** U.S.S.R.
58 C2 **Otgon** Mongolia
22 K5 **Othain** *R* France
22 J2 **Othée** Belgium
18 H4 **Othe, Forêt d'** France
100 F3 **Othello** Washington
27 K14 **Othem** Sweden
8 D5 **Othery** England
46 C5 **Othonoí** *isld* Greece
46 F5 **Óthris** *mt* Greece
70 F5 **Oti** Sulawesi
85 E7 **Oti** *R* W Africa
124 G5 **Otinapa** Mexico
144 C5 **Otira** New Zealand
106 H1 **Otis** Colorado
107 L3 **Otis** Kansas
95 O4 **Otis** Massachusetts
95 L4 **Otisco L** New York
122 B1 **Otish Mts** Quebec
95 N5 **Otisville** New York
87 C10 **Otjiwarongo** Namibia
60 O3 **Otobe-dake** *mt* Japan
42 G4 **Otočac** Yugoslavia
99 K9 **Otoe** Nebraska
60 R2 **Otofuke** Japan
60 Q1 **Otoineppu** Japan
145 F3 **Otoko** New Zealand
145 E3 **Otorohanga** New Zealand
119 P5 **Otosquen** Sask
27 C13 **Otra** *R* Norway
126 B1 **Otrabanda** Curaçao
43 J8 **Otranto** Italy
43 J8 **Otranto, C.d'** Italy
46 C4 **Otranto, Str of** Adriatic Sea
94 C2 **Otsego** Michigan
95 N4 **Otsego I** New York
94 C2 **Otsego Lake** Michigan
95 M4 **Otselic, South** New York
60 R3 **Ōtsu** Hokkaido Japan
61 J10 **Ōtsu** Honshu Japan
61 P6 **Ōtsuchi-wan** *B* Japan
61 M10 **Ōtsuki** Japan
26 D10 **Otta** Norway
26 C10 **Otta** *R* Norway
22 L5 **Ottange** France
27 F16 **Ottarp** Sweden
45 Q8 **Ottaviano** Italy
99 S8 **Ottawa** Illinois
107 P3 **Ottawa** Kansas
94 C5 **Ottawa** Ohio
120 D9 **Ottawa** Ontario
115 L6 **Ottawa Is** N W Terr
121 M6 **Ottawa, R** Quebec
32 K9 **Ottbergen** W Germany
27 H15 **Ottenby** Sweden
36 H5 **Ottendorf** W Germany
37 M2 **Ottendorf-Okrilla** E Germany
36 E6 **Ottenhöfen** W Germany
38 M5 **Ottenshlag** Austria
32 K9 **Ottenstein** Niedersachsen W Germany
32 E8 **Ottenstein** Nordrhein-Westfalen W Germany
101 T4 **Otter** Montana
110 J1 **Otterbein** Indiana
36 D4 **Otterberg** W Germany
13 F3 **Otterburn** England
118 D1 **Otterburne** Manitoba
113 E8 **Otter Creek** Florida
103 N3 **Otter Cr Res** Utah
38 E6 **Otterfing** W Germany
120 D4 **Otter I** Ontario
116 D8 **Otter I** Pribilof Is Bering Sea
119 N3 **Otter L** Sask
94 D3 **Otter Lake** Michigan
25 E4 **Otterlo** Netherlands
32 J5 **Otterndorf** W Germany
26 E7 **Otteröy** Norway
26 B9 **Otteröy** *isld* Norway
32 K6 **Ottersberg** W Germany
9 F5 **Ottershaw** England
33 P8 **Ottersleben** E Germany
15 G1 **Otterswick** Scotland
98 K3 **Otter Tail** *R* Minnesota
99 L3 **Otter Tail L** Minnesota
28 E5 **Otterup** Denmark
8 B6 **Ottery, R** England
8 C6 **Ottery St. Mary** England
119 P7 **Otthon** Sask
22 H2 **Ottignies** Belgium
109 L4 **Otto** Texas
101 R5 **Otto** Wyoming
37 M7 **Ottobrunn** W Germany
115 L1 **Otto Fiord** N W Terr
94 C6 **Ottoville** Ohio
36 C7 **Ottrott** France
99 O8 **Ottumwa** Iowa
98 E5 **Ottumwa** S Dakota
36 C5 **Ottweiler** W Germany
118 K2 **Otukamanoan L** Ontario
144 B6 **Oturehua** New Zealand
85 F7 **Oturkpo** Nigeria
94 D8 **Otway** Ohio
133 C8 **Otway, B** Chile
139 G7 **Otway, C** Victoria
31 N3 **Otwock** Poland
48 J2 **Otynya** U.S.S.R.
41 N3 **Ötz** Austria
36 B1 **Otzenrath** W Germany
41 N3 **Ötztal** Austria
41 N4 **Ötztaler Alpen** *mt* Austria
111 D8 **Ouachita** *R* Arkansas
110 C7 **Ouachita, L** Arkansas
109 N1 **Ouachita Mts** Ark/Okla
86 D3 **Ouadai** *dist* Chad
85 B4 **Ouadane** Mauritania
86 D4 **Ouadda** Cent Afr Republic
85 D6 **Ouagadougou** Upper Volta
85 D6 **Ouahigouya** Upper Volta
86 D4 **Ouaka** *R* Cent Afr Republic
85 C5 **Oualata** Mauritania
85 E4 **Ouallen** Algeria
86 D5 **Ouango** Cent Afr Republic
85 C7 **Ouangolodougou** Ivory Coast
18 H5 **Ouanne** *R* France
85 F3 **Ouan Taredert** Algeria
129 H3 **Ouaqui** Fr Guiana
85 C4 **Ouarane** *reg* Mauritania
121 Q6 **Ouareau, L** Quebec
85 F2 **Ouargla** Algeria
85 C3 **Ouarkziz, Jbel** *mt reg* Morocco/Algeria
20 J5 **Ouarville** France
85 C2 **Ouarzazate** Morocco
86 D5 **Oubangui** *R* Cent Afr Republic/Zaire
40 B3 **Ouche** *R* France
21 H6 **Oucques** France
25 A5 **Ouddorp** Netherlands
25 B5 **Oude** *R* Netherlands
25 F5 **Oude Ijssel** *R* Netherlands
22 D1 **Oudekapelle** Belgium
22 F2 **Oudenaarde** Belgium
25 C5 **Oudenbosch** Netherlands
25 H2 **Oude Pekela** Netherlands
25 C4 **Oude Rijn** Netherlands
25 C2 **Oudeschild** Netherlands
25 F3 **Oude Smildervaart** *R* Netherlands
25 C4 **Oudewater** Netherlands
22 L3 **Oudler** Belgium
21 C7 **Oudon** France
21 D6 **Oudon** *R* France
68 G7 **Oudong** Cambodia
89 C9 **Oudtshoorn** S Africa
85 F2 **Oued, El** Algeria
16 D9 **Oued Laou** Morocco
17 H9 **Oued Taria** Algeria
85 C2 **Oued Zem** Morocco
85 E7 **Ouémé** *R* Benin
18 B4 **Ouessant, I. d'** France
86 C5 **Ouesso** Congo
83 L14 **Ouest, î de l'** Kerguelen Indian Oc
123 Q7 **Ouest, Pte du** Miquelon I Atlantic Oc
71 F5 **Ouezon** Negros Philippines
85 C2 **Ouezzane** Morocco
22 J3 **Ouffet** Belgium
14 B3 **Oughterard** Irish Rep
40 C3 **Ougney** France
86 C4 **Ouham** *R* Cent Afr Republic
85 E7 **Ouidah** Benin
119 P2 **Ouimet** Ontario
124 E4 **Ouiriego** Mexico
18 H9 **Ouissac** France
20 E3 **Ouistreham** France
85 C5 **Oujaf** Mauritania
85 D2 **Oujda** Morocco
29 L7 **Oulainen** Finland
85 E2 **Ouled-Nail, Mts. des** Algeria
85 C2 **Oulmès** Morocco
13 G6 **Oulton** England
29 L6 **Oulu** Finland
29 M7 **Oulujoki** *R* Finland
86 D2 **Oum Chalouba** Chad
85 C3 **Oum el Guebor** Algeria
85 C2 **Oum er Rbia** *R* Morocco
86 C3 **Oum Hadjer** Chad
29 K3 **Ounasjärvi** *L* Finland
29 L4 **Ounasjoki** *R* Finland
29 K3 **Ounastunturi** *mt* Finland
9 F3 **Oundle** England
98 C1 **Oungre** Sask
84 G6 **Ounianga Kébir** Chad
84 G6 **Ounianga Sérir** Chad
85 C6 **Ouolodo** Mali
61 Q12 **Ōura-wan** *B* Okinawa
106 C3 **Ouray** Colorado
103 P1 **Ouray** Utah
28 F6 **Oure** Denmark
84 F5 **Ouri** Chad
129 K5 **Ouricuri** Brazil
130 H9 **Ouricuri, R** Brazil
130 E8 **Ourinhos** Brazil
16 B7 **Ourique** Portugal
130 F8 **Ouro Fino** Brazil
130 G7 **Ouro Prêto** Brazil
22 K3 **Ourthe** *R* Belgium
20 G2 **Ourville** France
139 H8 **Ouse** Tasmania
9 G2 **Ouse, R** Norfolk England
13 G6 **Ouse, R** N Yorks England
18 D5 **Oust** *R* France
122 D4 **Outardes, R. aux** Quebec
122 D4 **Outardes Trois Dam** Quebec
20 K5 **Outarville** France
85 D2 **Outat-Oulad-El-Haj** Morocco
6 B2 **Outer Bailey** N Atlantic Oc
15 A3 **Outer Hebrides** Scotland
102 F8 **Outer Santa Barbara Chan** California
13 F5 **Outhgill** England
87 C10 **Outjo** Namibia
101 V1 **Outlook** Montana
118 K7 **Outlook** Sask
29 O9 **Outokumpu** Finland
144 C6 **Outram** New Zealand
22 B2 **Outreau** France
15 G2 **Out Skerries** *isld* Scotland
19 O16 **Ouveze** *R* France
138 F6 **Ouyen** New S Wales
21 I6 **Ouzouer-le-Marché** France
44 E2 **Ovada** Italy
131 B3 **Ovalle** Chile
108 H3 **Ovalo** Texas
101 M2 **Ovando** Montana
16 B4 **Ovar** Portugal
38 G9 **Ovaro** Italy
32 H6 **Ovelgönne** W Germany
139 H6 **Ovens** *R* Victoria
36 C2 **Overath** W Germany
107 P3 **Overbrook** Kansas
25 B5 **Overflakkee** Netherlands
119 Q5 **Overflowing R** Manitoba
26 G9 **Överhogdal** Sweden
22 H2 **Overijse** Belgium
26 N5 **Överkalix** Sweden
107 Q3 **Overland Park** Kansas
98 F1 **Overly** N Dakota
29 J9 **Övermark** Finland
131 B5 **Overo, Vol** Argentina
22 J1 **Overpelt** Belgium
9 E5 **Overton** England
98 G9 **Overton** Nebraska
103 K5 **Overton** Nevada
109 N3 **Overton** Texas
8 D2 **Overton** Wales
26 N5 **Övertorneå** Sweden
27 H14 **Överum** Sweden
26 G5 **Över-uman** *L* Sweden
111 G10 **Ovett** Mississippi
106 H1 **Ovid** Colorado
101 O7 **Ovid** Idaho
94 C3 **Ovid** Michigan
95 L4 **Ovid** New York
113 F9 **Oviedo** Florida
16 D1 **Oviedo** Spain
16 C1 **Oviedo** *prov* Spain
26 G9 **Oviken** Sweden
45 P5 **Ovindoli** Italy
52 E5 **Ov'nishche** U.S.S.R.
26 K8 **Öv Nyland** Sweden
27 B13 **Övrebygd** Norway
26 L6 **Övre Grundsel** Sweden
25 F4 **Ovreijssel** *prov* Netherlands
27 B13 **Öv-Sirdal** Norway
26 H8 **Övsjö** Sweden
145 F4 **Owahanga** New Zealand
144 B7 **Owaka** New Zealand
61 O5 **Ōwani** Japan
95 L4 **Owasco L** New York
61 K11 **Owase** Japan
107 P5 **Owasso** Oklahoma
99 N5 **Owatonna** Minnesota
95 L4 **Owego** New York
14 B2 **Owemore** *R* Irish Rep
36 G6 **Owen** W Germany
99 Q5 **Owen** Wisconsin
142 A3 **Owen Anchorage** W Australia
86 F5 **Owen Falls D** Uganda
68 C7 **Owen I** Burma
145 D4 **Owen, Mt** New Zealand
145 D4 **Owen River** New Zealand
94 F8 **Owens** W Virginia
102 F4 **Owens** *R* California
110 J4 **Owensboro** Kentucky
102 G5 **Owens L** California
120 K8 **Owen Sound** Ontario
140 C6 **Owen Springs** N Terr Aust
136 K3 **Owen Stanley Ra** Papua New Guinea
110 J3 **Owensville** Indiana
110 E3 **Owensville** Missouri
110 M3 **Owenton** Kentucky
102 F5 **Owenyo** California
9 E6 **Ower** England
85 F7 **Owerri** Nigeria
145 E3 **Owhango** New Zealand
117 K10 **Owikeno L** Br Col
94 D8 **Owingsville** Kentucky
36 F5 **Öwisheim** W Germany
106 E1 **Owl Canyon** Colorado
101 R6 **Owl Cr** Wyoming
101 R6 **Owl-Creek Mts** Wyoming
118 F4 **Owl R** Alberta
85 F7 **Owo** Nigeria
94 C3 **Owosso** Michigan
100 J8 **Owyhee** Nevada
100 H6 **Owyhee** Oregon
27 G10 **Oxberg** Sweden
119 P9 **Oxbow** Sask
100 J5 **Oxbow Dam** Oregon
111 F7 **Oxbow L** Mississippi
118 K1 **Oxdrift** Ontario
27 J13 **Oxelösund** Sweden
111 L8 **Oxford** Alabama
9 E4 **Oxford** England
101 N7 **Oxford** Idaho
110 J1 **Oxford** Indiana
99 P8 **Oxford** Iowa
107 N4 **Oxford** Kansas
95 R2 **Oxford** Maine
95 L8 **Oxford** Maryland
95 Q4 **Oxford** Massachusetts
94 D4 **Oxford** Michigan
111 G7 **Oxford** Mississippi
112 J1 **Oxford** N Carolina
98 G9 **Oxford** Nebraska
95 M4 **Oxford** New York
144 D5 **Oxford** New Zealand
122 J8 **Oxford** Nova Scotia
94 C7 **Oxford** Ohio
99 R6 **Oxford** Wisconsin
141 J5 **Oxford Downs** Queensland
119 W4 **Oxford House** Manitoba
101 N7 **Oxford Pk** Idaho
9 E4 **Oxfordshire** *co* England
46 E5 **Oxiá** *mt* Greece
140 E4 **Oxide, Mt** Queensland
47 G6 **Oxílithos** Greece
125 P7 **Oxkutzcab** Mexico
139 G5 **Oxley** New S Wales
141 K2 **Oxley** *sub* Brisbane, Qnsld
139 K4 **Oxleys Pk** New S Wales
14 C2 **Ox Mts** Irish Rep
102 E7 **Oxnard** California
Oxon *co see* **Oxfordshire**
9 E1 **Oxton** England
8 B4 **Oxwich** Wales
70 B3 **Oya** Sarawak
70 C3 **Oya** *R* Sarawak
56 D4 **Oya** *R* U.S.S.R.
61 K9 **Oyabe** Japan
61 M10 **Oyama** Shizuoka Japan
61 N9 **Oyama** Tochigi Japan
61 N7 **Ōyama** Yamagata Japan
60 D13 **Ōyano shima** *isld* Japan
129 H3 **Oyapock, B. d'** Fr Guiana
86 B5 **Oyem** Gabon
118 G7 **Oyen** Alberta
22 C2 **Oye Plage** France
27 E12 **Oyeren** *L* Norway
56 B3 **Oyesh** *R* U.S.S.R.
26 J3 **Öyjord** Norway
15 D3 **Oykel** *R* Scotland
51 O2 **Oymyakon** U.S.S.R.
85 E7 **Oyo** Nigeria
128 C6 **Oyón** Peru
40 C5 **Oyonnax** France
21 G8 **Oyré** France
109 M6 **Oyster Cr** Texas
68 A2 **Oyster I** Burma
142 C5 **Oyster Inlet** W Australia
100 A3 **Oysterville** Washington
57 G3 **Oytal** U.S.S.R.
32 K6 **Oyten** W Germany
51 N2 **Oyun Khomoto** U.S.S.R.
71 F6 **Ozamiz** Mindanao Philippines
111 L10 **Ozark** Alabama
110 C6 **Ozark** Arkansas
110 C4 **Ozark** Missouri
110 C5 **Ozark Plateau** Missouri
110 C3 **Ozarks, L. of the** Missouri
48 F2 **Ozd** Hungary
80 B7 **Ozem** Israel
55 F3 **Ozernoye** U.S.S.R.
55 D4 **Ozernyy** Kustanay U.S.S.R.
54 D1 **Ozernyy** Smolensk U.S.S.R.
55 D3 **Ozernyy** Sverdlovsk U.S.S.R.
55 G3 **Ozero Karachi** U.S.S.R.
65 J2 **Ozero Khanka** *L* China/U.S.S.R.
46 E6 **Ozerós, L** Greece
31 N1 **Ozersk** U.S.S.R.
54 K2 **Ozery** U.S.S.R.
100 A1 **Ozette L** Washington
54 K2 **Ozherel'ye** U.S.S.R.
51 O2 **Ozhogino** U.S.S.R.
43 C8 **Ozieri** Sardinia
31 L5 **Ozimek** Poland
108 F5 **Ozona** Texas
48 E4 **Ozora** Hungary
31 L4 **Ozorków** Poland
55 C5 **Ozorodnyy** U.S.S.R.
86 A6 **Ozouri** Gabon
60 F12 **Ōzu** Japan
60 D13 **Ōzu** *R* Japan
60 E11 **Ozuki** Japan
48 K5 **Ozun** Romania
45 K3 **Ozzano dell'Emilia** Italy
80 B8 **Pa'ame Tashaz** Israel
68 C4 **Pa-an** Burma
37 L6 **Paar** *R* W Germany
33 R7 **Paaren** E Germany
89 A9 **Paarl** S Africa
29 O3 **Paatsjoki** *R* Finland
135 U4 **Paauilo** Hawaiian Is
29 L7 **Paavola** Finland
15 A3 **Pabbay** *isld* Outer Hebrides Scotland
70 P9 **Pabean** Indonesia
31 L4 **Pabjanice** Poland
77 K6 **Pab Range** Pakistan
128 F6 **Pacaás Novos, Sa. dos** *mts* Brazil
129 H4 **Pacajá** *R* Brazil
128 F3 **Pacaraima, Sa** *mts* Brazil/Venezuela
128 C5 **Pacasmayo** Peru
111 F8 **Pace** Mississippi
67 F5 **Pa'-chao Hsü** *isld* Taiwan
124 E2 **Pacheco** Chihuahua Mexico
124 H5 **Pacheco** Zacatecas Mexico
100 A1 **Pachena Pt** Br Col
124 F3 **Pachera** Mexico
43 G12 **Pachino** Sicily
128 D5 **Pachitea** *R* Peru
125 K7 **Pachuca** Mexico
111 H9 **Pachuta** Mississippi
102 D3 **Pacific** California
110 F3 **Pacific** Missouri
135 L14 **Pacific Antarctic Ridge** Pac Oc
100 A2 **Pacific Beach** Washington
100 B4 **Pacific City** Oregon
101 Q7 **Pacific Cr** Wyoming
102 C5 **Pacific Grove** California
135 **Pacific Ocean**
71 G5 **Pacijan** *isld* Philippines
145 E4 **Packakariki** New Zealand
38 L7 **Pack Alpe** *mts* Austria
111 D10 **Packton** Louisiana
99 O8 **Packwood** Iowa
100 D3 **Packwood** Washington
112 E2 **Pacolet** *R* S Carolina
112 F3 **Pacolet Mills** S Carolina
31 J6 **Pacov** Czechoslovakia
123 R4 **Pacquet** Newfoundland
98 C5 **Pactola** S Dakota
135 Q15 **Pactolus Bank** Pacific Oc
130 G5 **Pacui** *R* Brazil
20 H3 **Pacy** France
31 K5 **Paczków** Poland
71 H6 **Padabale** *isld* Sulawesi
71 G7 **Padada** Mindanao Philippines
70 G7 **Padamarang** *isld* Sulawesi
69 G11 **Padang** Indonesia
69 F12 **Padang** Riau Arch Indonesia
69 E13 **Padang** Sumatra
69 E13 **Padangpanjang** Sumatra
69 D12 **Padangsidimpuan** Sumatra
69 B10 **Padangtiji** Sumatra
52 D3 **Padany** U.S.S.R.
70 D2 **Padas** *R* Sabah
29 L10 **Padasjoki** Finland
128 F3 **Padauiri** *R* Brazil
68 B3 **Padaung** Burma
83 K9 **Padawiya Tank** Sri Lanka
141 K1 **Paddington** *dist* Brisbane, Qnsld
117 P7 **Paddle Prairie** Alberta
119 M5 **Paddockwood** Sask
71 H6 **Padea** *isld* Indonesia
94 G7 **Paden City** W Virginia
32 J9 **Paderborn** W Germany
70 D3 **Paderongan** Kalimantan
48 G5 **Padeşu** *mt* Romania
13 F6 **Padiham** England
128 F7 **Padilla** Bolivia
48 L6 **Padina** Romania
26 J4 **Padjelanta Nat. Park** Sweden
115 K5 **Padlei** N W Terr
115 N4 **Padloping Island** N W Terr
122 E5 **Padoue** Quebec
36 B7 **Padoux** France
45 L1 **Padova** Italy
109 K9 **Padre I** Texas
16 B2 **Padrón** Spain
8 B6 **Padstow** England
138 F6 **Padthaway** S Australia
Padua *see* **Padova**
110 H4 **Paducah** Kentucky
108 G1 **Paducah** Texas
45 R7 **Paduli** Italy
52 D1 **Padunskoye More** *L* U.S.S.R.
145 F2 **Paengaroa** New Zealand
65 F6 **Paengnyŏng-do** *isld* S Korea
145 E2 **Paeroa** New Zealand
44 B2 **Paesana** Italy
45 R8 **Paestum** Italy
71 E3 **Paete** Luzon Philippines
87 F10 **Pafuri** Mozambique
42 G4 **Pag** Yugoslavia
42 F4 **Pag** *isld* Yugoslavia
71 L9 **Paga** Flores Indonesia
129 H4 **Paga Centa** Brazil
71 F7 **Pagadian** Mindanao Philippines
69 E14 **Pagai, Pulau** *isld* Indonesia
90 L9 **Pagalu** *isld* Equat Guinea
68 B2 **Pagan** Burma
45 R8 **Pagani** Italy
70 K7 **Pagaralam** Sumatra
46 F5 **Pagasitikós, Kólpos** *B* Greece
70 D6 **Pagatan** Kalimantan
119 P2 **Pagato R** Sask
71 F4 **Pagbulungan Pt** Philippines
103 N5 **Page** Arizona
98 J2 **Page** N Dakota
98 H7 **Page** Nebraska
107 Q7 **Page** Oklahoma
52 B6 **Pagėgiai** U.S.S.R.
112 G3 **Pageland** S Carolina
142 E3 **Page, Mt** W Australia
69 G14 **Pagerdewa** Sumatra
141 K4 **Paget Cay** *isld* Gt Barrier Reef Australia
68 A6 **Paget I** Andaman Is
133 J8 **Paget, Mt** S Georgia
77 L2 **Paghman** Afghanistan
42 D6 **Paglia** *R* Italy
101 S9 **Pagoda Pk** Colorado
142 F2 **Pago Mission** W Australia
47 H7 **Pagóndhas** Greece
70 D2 **Pagonprick, G** *mt* Sarawak
137 S4 **Pago Pago** Amer Samoa
106 C4 **Pagosa Springs** Colorado
106 C6 **Paguate** New Mexico
71 H4 **Pagujaman** *R* Sulawesi
120 D3 **Pagwachuan** Ontario
120 E3 **Pagwachuan** *R* Ontario
120 E2 **Pagwa River** Ontario
116 K3 **Pah** *R* Alaska
102 V14 **Pahala** Hawaiian Is
70 C6 **Pahandut** Kalimantan
73 R8 **Pahang** *R* Malaysia
69 F11 **Pahang, S** *R* Malaysia
145 E4 **Pahaoa R** New Zealand
144 A7 **Pahia Pt** New Zealand
145 E4 **Pahiatua** New Zealand
135 V5 **Pahoa** Hawaiian Is
77 G2 **Pahra** Afghanistan
103 J4 **Pahranagat L** Nevada
103 J4 **Pahranagat Ra** Nevada
103 K4 **Pahrock Ra** Nevada
103 J5 **Pahrump** Nevada
101 M5 **Pahsimeroi** *R* Idaho
102 H4 **Pahute Mesa** Nevada
100 F8 **Pahute Peak** *mt* Nevada
135 T3 **Paia** Hawaiian Is
130 B6 **Paiaguás** Brazil
52 C5 **Paide** U.S.S.R.
109 K5 **Paige** Texas
8 C7 **Paignton** England
145 E1 **Paihia** New Zealand
29 M10 **Päijänne** *reg* Finland
68 F6 **Pailin** Cambodia
Pailing *see* **Chun'an**
135 S3 **Pailolo Ch** Hawaiian Is
9 E3 **Pailton** England
21 A7 **Paimboeuf** France
116 G5 **Paimiut** Alaska
18 C4 **Paimpol** France
69 E13 **Painan** Sumatra
120 H10 **Paincourt** Ontario
133 C8 **Paine** *mt* Chile
99 S2 **Painesdale** Michigan
94 F5 **Painesville** Ohio
103 N5 **Painted Des** Arizona
103 L8 **Painted Rock Res** Arizona
37 M6 **Painten** W Germany
138 E4 **Painter, Mt** S Australia
119 T3 **Paint L** Manitoba
120 J8 **Paisley** Ontario
100 E7 **Paisley** Oregon
12 D2 **Paisley** Scotland
29 M2 **Paistunturit** *mt* Finland
128 B5 **Paita** Peru
67 G4 **Pai-tai Lieh-tao** *islds* Taiwan
70 E1 **Paitan B** Sabah
70 O9 **Paiton** Java
26 K4 **Paittasjärbi** *L* Sweden
16 B4 **Paiva** *R* Portugal
87 B8 **Paiva Couceiro** Angola
21 G8 **Paizay le-Sec** France
69 E13 **Pajakumbuh** Sumatra
26 N4 **Pajala** Sweden
16 D1 **Pajares, Pto. de** Spain
106 D7 **Pajarito** New Mexico
131 B2 **Pajaros** *isld* Chile
71 K9 **Pajeti** Sumba Indonesia
129 L5 **Pajeu** Brazil
130 H10 **Pajeú, R** Brazil
48 D4 **Páka** Hungary
69 F10 **Paka** Malaysia
69 E12 **Pakanbaru** Sumatra
68 B2 **Pakangyi** Burma
128 F2 **Pakaraima Mts** Guyana
119 N1 **Pakashkhan L** *isld* Ontario
68 E3 **Pak Beng** Laos
121 O7 **Pakenham** Ontario
145 D1 **Pakenui** New Zealand
70 E3 **Pakerajan** *R* Kalimantan
68 G4 **Pak Hin Boun** Laos
57 D4 **Pakhtakor** U.S.S.R.
85 F6 **Paki** Nigeria
74 A4 **Pakistan** *rep* Asia
68 E3 **Pak Khop** Laos
68 E3 **Pak Lay** Laos
Paknampho *see* **Muang Nakhon Sawan**
68 E3 **Pak Niam** Laos
68 B2 **Pakokku** Burma
145 D1 **Pakotai** New Zealand
69 E9 **Pak Phayun** Thailand
42 H3 **Pakrac** Yugoslavia
48 E4 **Paks** Hungary
68 F3 **Pak Sane** Laos
68 G5 **Pakse** Laos
68 E2 **Pak Tha** Laos
77 L3 **Paktiā** Afghanistan
70 C3 **Paku** *R* Sarawak
119 T4 **Pakwa L** Manitoba
89 F4 **Pakwe** *R* Botswana
86 F5 **Pakwich** Uganda
68 D6 **Pala** Burma
102 G8 **Pala** California
86 C4 **Pala** Chad
109 L7 **Palacios** Texas
127 L10 **Palacios** Venezuela
133 D6 **Palacios, L** Argentina
17 K3 **Palafrugell** Spain
42 G6 **Palagruža** *isld* Yugoslavia
46 F7 **Palaiá** Greece
45 J4 **Paláia** Italy
47 H9 **Palaiókastron** Crete Greece
47 F9 **Palaiokhóra** Crete Greece
46 D6 **Pálairos** Greece
20 K4 **Palaiseau** France
18 C5 **Palais, le** France
89 F4 **Palala** *R* S Africa
68 A7 **Palalankwe** Andaman Is
46 E5 **Palamás** Greece
71 J9 **Palamedo** Sumba Indonesia
17 K3 **Palamós** Spain
47 J6 **Palamut** Turkey
71 F2 **Palanan** Luzon Philippines
17 G5 **Palancia** *R* Spain
52 B6 **Palanga** U.S.S.R.
77 G4 **Palangān, Kūh-e-** *mts* Iran
70 C6 **Palangka Raya** Kalimantan
16 D2 **Palanquinos** Spain
70 F7 **Palanro** Sulawesi
135 S3 **Palaoa Pt** Hawaiian Is
71 G4 **Palapag** Philippines
89 E4 **Palapye** Botswana
16 B2 **Palas de Rey** Spain
113 F8 **Palatka** Florida
56 B6 **Palattsy** U.S.S.R.
108 F8 **Palau** Mexico
43 C7 **Palau** Sardinia
71 F1 **Palaui** *isld* Luzon Philippines
71 D3 **Palauig** Luzon Philippines
68 D6 **Palauk** Burma
83 J10 **Palavi** Sri Lanka
68 D6 **Palaw** Burma
71 D6 **Palawan** *isld* Philippines
71 C6 **Palawan Passage** Philippines
41 L6 **Palazzolo** Italy
43 F11 **Palazzolo Acreide** Sicily
45 L3 **Palazzuolo** Italy
133 D1 **Palca** Chile
52 B5 **Paldiski** U.S.S.R.
68 B2 **Pale** Burma
70 G4 **Paleleh** Sulawesi
69 G14 **Palembang** Sumatra
38 K6 **Palen** *R* Austria
16 D2 **Palencia** *prov* Spain
103 J8 **Palen L** California
79 D4 **Paleokhorio** Cyprus
102 C2 **Palermo** California
98 D1 **Palermo** N Dakota
43 E10 **Palermo** Sicily
128 E8 **Palestina** Chile
110 J3 **Palestine** Illinois
109 M4 **Palestine** Texas
110 M1 **Palestine Hill** Ohio
109 M3 **Palestine, L** Texas
45 N6 **Palestrina** Italy
68 A2 **Paletwa** Burma
143 B6 **Palgrave, Mt** W Australia
45 O6 **Paliano** Italy
83 K8 **Pali Aru** *R* Sri Lanka
70 P9 **Paliat** *isld* Indonesia
71 G7 **Palimbang** Mindanao Philippines
85 E7 **Palime** Togo
70 E1 **Palin, Mt** Sabah
43 G8 **Palinuro, C** Italy
106 B2 **Palisade** Colorado
98 E9 **Palisade** Nebraska
103 H1 **Palisade** Nevada
101 O6 **Palisades Res** Idaho
127 L3 **Palisadoes** *airport* Jamaica
22 J4 **Paliseul** Belgium
109 J8 **Palito Blanco** Texas
26 K5 **Paljaape** *mt* Sweden
29 L10 **Pälkäne** Finland
83 J8 **Palk Bay** Sri Lanka
52 F5 **Palkino** U.S.S.R.
83 J8 **Palk Str** India/Sri Lanka
83 K8 **Pallai** Sri Lanka
Pallanza *see* **Verbania**
Palla Rd *see* **Dinokwe** Botswana
18 F10 **Pallaresa** *R* Spain
29 L3 **Pallastunturi** *mt* Finland
83 K10 **Pallegama** Sri Lanka
26 K3 **Pallemtjåkko** *mt* Sweden
18 E6 **Pallice, la** France
36 B4 **Pallien** W Germany
70 G7 **Pallima** Sulawesi
9 H2 **Palling** England
Pallíni Greece *see* **Kassándra**
143 C10 **Pallinup, R** W Australia
145 E4 **Palliser Bay** New Zealand
21 H8 **Palluau-sur-Indre** France
88 H7 **Palma** Mozambique
106 E6 **Palma** New Mexico
17 J5 **Palma, B. de** Majorca
45 R8 **Palma Camp** Italy
17 J5 **Palma de Mallorca** Majorca
43 F11 **Palma di Montechiaro** Sicily
80 B6 **Palmahim** Israel
127 H9 **Palmar** *R* Venezuela
133 G4 **Palmares do Sul** Brazil
126 G4 **Palmarito** Cuba
43 E8 **Palmarola** *isld* Italy
85 C8 **Palmas, C** Liberia
43 B10 **Palmas, G. di** Sardinia
128 E1 **Palma Sola** Venezuela
126 G4 **Palma Soriano** Cuba
87 B7 **Palmas, Pta. das** Angola
113 G11 **Palm Beach** Florida
142 A4 **Palm Beach** W Australia
102 H8 **Palm Canyon Nat. Mon** California
102 F7 **Palmdale** California
113 F11 **Palmdale** Florida
133 G3 **Palmeira** Brazil
116 N6 **Palmer** Alaska
99 R10 **Palmer** Illinois
99 M7 **Palmer** Iowa
99 T3 **Palmer** Michigan
98 H8 **Palmer** Nebraska
118 L9 **Palmer** Sask
110 L6 **Palmer** Tennessee
109 L3 **Palmer** Texas
141 G3 **Palmer** *R* Queensland
146 F14 **Palmer Arch** Antarctica
146 H12 **Palmer, C** Antarctica
140 C6 **Palmer R** N Terr Aust
144 C6 **Palmerston** New Zealand
141 J5 **Palmerston, C** Queensland
145 E4 **Palmerston North** New Zealand
95 M6 **Palmerton** Pennsylvania
140 C6 **Palmer Valley** N Terr Aust
141 G3 **Palmerville** Queensland
113 E10 **Palmetto** Florida
112 C4 **Palmetto** Georgia
127 N6 **Palmetto Pt** Barbuda W I
126 F2 **Palmetto Pt** Eleuthera Bahamas
113 E9 **Palm Harbor** Florida
43 G10 **Palmi** Italy
128 C3 **Palmira** Colombia
126 D3 **Palmira** Cuba
141 H4 **Palm Is** Queensland
124 G6 **Palmito del Verde, I** Mexico
94 E3 **Palms** Michigan
102 H8 **Palm Springs** California
141 J7 **Palm Tree Cr** Queensland
140 C6 **Palm Valley** N Terr Aust
110 G2 **Palmyra** Illinois
99 P10 **Palmyra** Missouri
98 K9 **Palmyra** Nebraska
95 N7 **Palmyra** New Jersey
95 K3 **Palmyra** New York
95 L6 **Palmyra** Pennsylvania
72 D2 **Palmyra** Syria
110 J5 **Palmyra** Tennessee
94 J9 **Palmyra** Virginia
99 S7 **Palmyra** Wisconsin
135 U7 **Palmyra I** *atoll* Pacific Oc
12 E4 **Palnackie** Scotland
52 J4 **Pal'niki** U.S.S.R.
99 P7 **Palo** Iowa
42 E7 **Palo** Italy
71 G5 **Palo** Leyte Philippines
70 F5 **Palo** Sulawesi
102 B4 **Palo Alto** California
108 B8 **Palo Duro Cr** Texas
108 C7 **Paloduro Cr** Texas/Okla
71 K9 **Paloe** *isld* Flores Indonesia
70 B3 **Paloh** Sarawak
86 F3 **Paloich** Sudan
29 K3 **Palojärvi** Finland
29 K3 **Palojoensuu** Finland
29 K3 **Palojoki** *R* Finland
102 H8 **Palomar Mt** California
103 L9 **Palomas** Arizona
45 N5 **Palombara Sabina** Italy
17 G4 **Palomera, Sa** *mts* Spain
109 J3 **Palo Pinto** Texas
70 G6 **Palopo** Sulawesi
133 F3 **Palo Santo** Argentina
17 G7 **Palos, C. de** Spain
127 O3 **Palo Seco** Trinidad
100 H3 **Palouse** Washington
103 M8 **Palo Verde** Arizona
103 K8 **Palo Verde** California
141 F6 **Palparara** Queensland
27 H12 **Pålsboda** Sweden
29 N7 **Paltamo** Finland
38 H5 **Palting** Austria
70 F5 **Palu** *R* Sulawesi
127 N10 **Palúa** Venezuela
71 E4 **Paluan** Philippines
83 K9 **Palugassegama** Sri Lanka
57 C5 **Pal'vart** U.S.S.R.
85 E6 **Pama** Upper Volta
70 E5 **Pamaluan** Kalimantan
70 L9 **Pamanukan** Java
83 J8 **Pamban** *isld* India
70 F4 **Pambero** Sulawesi
118 K9 **Pambrun** Sask
139 J6 **Pambula** New S Wales
38 M8 **Pameče** Yugoslavia
70 O9 **Pamekasan** Java
70 L9 **Pameungpeuk** Java
18 G9 **Pamiers** France
46 E7 **Pámisos** *R* Greece
112 L2 **Pamlico R** N Carolina
68 E4 **Pamong D.Site** Thailand
133 D4 **Pampa de las Salinas** Argentina
70 G7 **Pampanua** Sulawesi
128 D6 **Pampas** Peru
133 E5 **Pampas, Plains** Argentina
16 B4 **Pampilhosa da Serra** Portugal
16 B4 **Pampilhosa do Botão** Portugal
94 J9 **Pamplin City** Virginia
128 D2 **Pamplona** Colombia
71 F6 **Pamplona** Negros Philippines
17 F2 **Pamplona** Spain
33 O5 **Pampow** E Germany
70 E6 **Pamukan, Teluk** *B* Kalimantan
47 K7 **Pamukkale** Turkey
47 L4 **Pamukova** Turkey
95 K9 **Pamunkey** *R* Virginia
99 R10 **Pana** Illinois
71 F7 **Panabutan B** Mindanao Philippines
103 K4 **Panaca** Nevada
120 J6 **Panache, L** Ontario
83 J11 **Panadura** Sri Lanka
71 D6 **Panagtaran** *point* Palawan Philippines
47 G2 **Panagyurishte** Bulgaria
70 B5 **Panahan** Kalimantan
70 K9 **Panaitan** *isld* Java
76 A3 **Panaji** India
46 E6 **Panakhaikón** *mt* Greece
94 H4 **Panama** New York
107 Q6 **Panama** Oklahoma
125 P5 **Panamá** Panama
125 O5 **Panama** *rep* Cent America
124 E10 **Panama Canal** Cent America
124 E9 **Panama Canal Zone** Central America
113 B7 **Panama City** Florida
125 P5 **Panamá, Golfo de** Panama
102 G5 **Panamint V** California
71 G6 **Panaon** *isld* Philippines
43 G10 **Panarea** *isld* Italy
45 K2 **Panaro** *R* Italy
70 O9 **Panarukan** Java
71 G4 **Panay** Philippines
71 F5 **Panay** *isld* Philippines
71 F5 **Panay Gulf** Philippines
47 G4 **Panayía** Greece
103 J3 **Pancake Ra** Nevada
21 B6 **Pancé** France
48 F6 **Pančevo** Yugoslavia
48 L5 **Panciu** Romania
69 D11 **Pancurbatu** Sumatra
87 F10 **Panda** Mozambique
108 F5 **Pandale** Texas
71 G3 **Pandan** Catanduanes Philippines
71 F5 **Pandan** Panay Philippines
70 C3 **Pandan** Sarawak
71 C6 **Pandanan** *isld* Palawan Philippines
71 F5 **Pandan Bay** Panay Philippines
70 K8 **Pandan, Bt** *mt* Sumatra
141 F3 **Pandanus** *R* Queensland
87 F10 **Pande** Mozambique
133 C3 **Pan de Azúcar** Chile
71 F5 **Pan de Azucar** Philippines
70 L9 **Pandeglang** Java
130 G4 **Pandeiros** *R* Brazil
138 E2 **Pandie Pandie** S Australia
70 F3 **Pandjang** *isld* Kalimantan
70 G4 **Pandjang, Tg** *C* Sulawesi
133 F4 **Pando** Uruguay
128 E6 **Pando** *dep* Bolivia
125 N5 **Pandora** Costa Rica
141 G1 **Pandora Ent** Gt Barrier Reef Aust
71 E7 **Panducan** *isld* Philippines
8 D4 **Pandy** Wales
52 B6 **Panevėžys** U.S.S.R.
138 D4 **Paney** S Australia
66 C3 **Panfilov** U.S.S.R.
57 H3 **Panfilova, Imeni** U.S.S.R.
86 E5 **Panga** Zaïre
47 F4 **Pangaion** *mt* Greece
70 M9 **Pangandaran** Java
88 G4 **Pangani** Tanzania
88 F4 **Pangani** *R* Tanzania
71 F4 **Panganiran** Philippines
69 J12 **Pangaujalayan** Indonesia
9 E5 **Pangbourne** England
110 E6 **Pangburn** Arkansas
70 F5 **Pangean** Sulawesi
70 N10 **Panggul** Java
68 D1 **Panghsang** Burma
86 E6 **Pangi** Zaïre
70 F7 **Pangkadjene** Sulawesi
70 O9 **Pangkah, Tg** *C* Java
70 B6 **Pangkalanbuun** Kalimantan
69 D10 **Pangkalansusu** Sumatra
69 H14 **Pangkalpinang** Sumatra
71 H5 **Pangkalsiang, Tg** *C* Sulawesi
71 F6 **Panglao** *isld* Philippines
68 C2 **Panglong** Burma
119 N9 **Pangman** Sask
115 N4 **Pangnirtung** N W Terr
70 L9 **Pangrongo, G** *mt* Java
68 C2 **Pangtara** Burma
133 C5 **Panguipulli** *mt* Chile
131 A7 **Panguipulli, L** Chile
103 M4 **Panguitch** Utah
71 E7 **Pangutaran** *isld* Philippines
71 E7 **Pangutaran Group** *islds* Philippines
88 E7 **Pangwa** Tanzania
68 D1 **Pang Yang** Burma
87 F9 **Panhalonga** Zimbabwe
108 C8 **Panhandle** Texas
65 A7 **Panhe** China
86 D7 **Pania Mutembo** Zaïre
137 N6 **Panié, Mt** New Caledonia
71 G5 **Paninihian Pt** Samar Philippines
71 D6 **Panitan** Palawan Philippines
69 D10 **Panjang** Sumatra
Panjang *isld* Cocos Is *see* **West I**
69 J11 **Panjang** *isld* Indonesia
69 F8 **Panjang, Hon** *isld* G of Thailand
77 H6 **Panjgur** *reg* Pakistan
69 C11 **Panji** Sumatra
77 L2 **Panjshir** *reg* Afghanistan
60 Q1 **Panke-zan** *mt* Japan
116 F9 **Pankof, C** Aleutian Is
33 S7 **Pankow** E Germany
85 F7 **Pankshin** Nigeria
65 H3 **Pan Ling** *mts* China
25 F5 **Pannerden** Netherlands
102 D5 **Panoche** California
70 B5 **Panopah** Kalimantan
99 M8 **Panora** Iowa
133 G2 **Panorama** Brazil
141 J6 **Panorama, Mt** Queensland
55 F3 **Panovo** U.S.S.R.
52 D2 **Panozero** U.S.S.R.
65 E4 **Panshan** China
65 G3 **Panshi** China
70 E6 **Pantai** Kalimantan
129 G7 **Pantanal de São Lourénço** *swamp* Brazil
68 B4 **Pantanaw** Burma
103 O9 **Pantano** Arizona
18 F10 **Pantano de Tremp** *L* Spain
71 M9 **Pantar** *isld* Indonesia
112 L2 **Pantego** N Carolina
109 M9 **Pantego** Texas
43 E12 **Pantelleria** *isld* Italy
41 N6 **Pantena, Val** Italy
110 J4 **Panther** *R* Kentucky
71 J9 **Pantjo** Sumbawa Indonesia
70 D4 **Pantjungapang, Bt** *mt* Kalimantan
128 C4 **Pantoja** Peru
69 C10 **Pantonlabu** Sumatra
125 K6 **Pánuco** Mexico
67 A4 **Pan Xian** China
67 D5 **Panyu** China
54 H8 **Panyutino** U.S.S.R.
87 C7 **Panzi** Zaïre
Paoki *see* **Baoji**
43 G9 **Paola** Italy
107 Q3 **Paola** Kansas
98 D9 **Paoli** Colorado
110 K3 **Paoli** Indiana
107 N7 **Paoli** Oklahoma

60
Perforated I — Plainview

69 C8 Perforated I Thailand
131 E4 Pergamino Argentina
Pergamum see Bergama
45 N4 Pergola Italy
52 E4 Perguba U.S.S.R.
99 L3 Perham Minnesota
69 F10 Perhentian Besar isld Malaysia
29 L8 Perho Finland
29 L8 Perhojoki R Finland
48 F4 Periam Romania
121 S4 Péribonca Quebec
121 T3 Péribonca R Quebec
122 A3 Peribonca L Quebec
133 D2 Perico Argentina
124 F5 Pericos Mexico
20 C3 Périers France
21 E9 Périgne France
129 J3 Perigoso, Can Brazil
18 F7 Périgueux France
127 H9 Perijá, Sa. de mts Colombia/Venezuela
123 P2 Peril Rock Quebec
117 F7 Peril Str Alaska
72 E6 Perim isld S Yemen
118 C2 Perimeter Highway Manitoba
130 H10 Periquito, Sa do mts Brazil
48 K6 Periş Romania
46 E5 Peristéri mt Greece
133 C7 Perito Moreno Argentina
76 C5 Periyakulam India
95 M6 Perkasie Pennsylvania
112 F5 Perkins Georgia
111 C11 Perkins Louisiana
99 T4 Perkins Michigan
111 G11 Perkinston Mississippi
103 M7 Perkinsville Arizona
22 L5 Perl W Germany
41 P1 Perlach W Germany
125 P5 Perlas, Arch. de las islds Panama
33 P6 Perleberg E Germany
37 P6 Perlesreut W Germany
54 K5 Perlevka U.S.S.R.
98 K2 Perley Minnesota
48 F5 Perlez Yugoslavia
69 E9 Perlis prov Malaysia
52 J5 Perm' U.S.S.R.
101 L2 Perma Montana
52 G5 Permas U.S.S.R.
46 D4 Përmet Albania
Pernambuco see Recife
130 H9 Pernambuco state Brazil
138 D4 Pernatty Lagoon S Australia
107 N7 Pernell Oklahoma
46 F2 Pernik Bulgaria
29 K11 Perniö Finland
25 B5 Pernis Netherlands
40 C5 Peron France
143 A7 Peron, C W Australia
140 B2 Peron Is N Terr Aust
22 D4 Péronne France
22 G3 Peronnes Belgium
143 A7 Peron Pen W Australia
143 B9 Peron, Pt W Australia
20 J5 Péronville France
18 G10 Perpignan France
112 L1 Perquimans R N Carolina
8 A7 Perranporth England
20 J4 Perray-en-Yvelines, le France
109 J2 Perrin Texas
113 G12 Perrine Florida
102 G8 Perris California
40 B2 Perrogney France
108 B1 Perro, Laguna del New Mexico
121 N4 Perron Quebec
18 C4 Perros Guirec France
110 D6 Perry Arkansas
113 D7 Perry Florida
112 D5 Perry Georgia
110 F2 Perry Illinois
99 M8 Perry Iowa
94 C4 Perry Michigan
110 E2 Perry Missouri
94 K4 Perry New York
107 N5 Perry Oklahoma
120 F5 Perry Ontario
116 O6 Perry I Alaska
120 D2 Perry L Ontario
95 L7 Perryman Maryland
110 A2 Perry Res Kansas
94 D5 Perrysburg Ohio
108 D7 Perryton Texas
118 D4 Perryvale Alberta
110 D6 Perryville Arkansas
110 G4 Perryville Missouri
20 K3 Persan France
Persepolis see Takht-e Jamshid
128 F6 Perseverancia Bolivia
121 O4 Pershing Quebec
8 D3 Pershore England
Persia see Iran
99 L8 Persia Iowa
Persian Gulf see Gulf, The
27 J14 Persnäs Sweden
107 N4 Perth Kansas
98 G1 Perth N Dakota
122 E7 Perth New Brunswick
121 O8 Perth Ontario
12 E1 Perth Scotland
139 H8 Perth Tasmania
143 B9 Perth W Australia
Perth co see Central and Tayside regions
95 N6 Perth Amboy New Jersey
38 L4 Pertholz Austria
41 P3 Pertisau Austria
52 E3 Pertominsk U.S.S.R.
42 J6 Pertovac Yugoslavia
20 C5 Pertre, le France
29 M10 Pertunmaa Finland
52 G5 Pertyugskiy U.S.S.R.
99 R8 Peru Illinois
94 A6 Peru Indiana
99 L9 Peru Nebraska
95 O2 Peru New York
128 D6 Peru rep S America
135 S12 Peru-Chile Trench Pacific Oc
42 E5 Perugia Italy
129 J8 Peruibe Brazil
42 G4 Perušić Yugoslavia
22 F3 Peruwelz Belgium
78 J3 Pervari Turkey
20 F5 Pervencheres France
54 G4 Pervoavgustovskiy U.S.S.R.
55 F5 Pervomayka U.S.S.R.
54 K8 Pervomaysk U.S.S.R.
52 H4 Pervomayskaya U.S.S.R.
55 B5 Pervomayskiy Orenburg U.S.S.R.
55 D2 Pervomayskiy Serov U.S.S.R.
55 C4 Pervomayskiy Ufa U.S.S.R.
55 C3 Pervoural'sk U.S.S.R.
22 H2 Perwez Belgium
52 D5 Pes' R U.S.S.R.
45 K4 Pesa R Italy
45 N4 Pesaro Italy
102 B4 Pescadero California
Pescadores islds see P'eng-hu Lieh-tao
128 D7 Pescadores, Pta C Peru
45 H4 Pescaglia Italy
42 F6 Pescara Italy
42 F6 Pescara R Italy
45 P6 Pescasseroli Italy
42 G7 Peschici Italy
45 J1 Peschiera Italy
45 J4 Pescia Italy
45 P5 Pescina Italy
45 R7 Pesco Sannita Italy
45 P6 Pescosolido Italy
52 G2 Pesha R U.S.S.R.
74 D1 Peshawar Pakistan
46 D3 Peshkopi Albania
47 G2 Peshtera Bulgaria
99 T4 Peshtigo Wisconsin
99 S4 Peshtigo R Wisconsin
26 J5 Peskehaure Sweden
50 E5 Peski Karakumy U.S.S.R.
57 B2 Peski Priaral'skiye Karkumy U.S.S.R.
57 C5 Peski Sundukli U.S.S.R.
52 H5 Peskovka U.S.S.R.
38 N8 Pesnica R Yugoslavia
16 B3 Péso de Regua Portugal
110 H2 Pesotum Illinois
129 L5 Pesqueira Brazil
18 E8 Pessac France
33 R7 Pessin E Germany
48 E3 Pest co Hungary
48 H6 Peşteana Jiu Romania
52 E5 Pestovo U.S.S.R.
52 F6 Pestyaki U.S.S.R.
46 E5 Péta Greece
80 C5 Petah Tiqwa Israel
29 L9 Petäjävesi Finland
71 B2 Petak, Tg C Halmahera Indonesia
111 G10 Petal Mississippi
29 J9 Petalax Finland
69 G14 Petaling Sumatra
47 G7 Petalioí isld Greece
47 G7 Petalión Kólpos gulf Greece
102 B3 Petaluma California
22 K4 Petange Luxembourg
127 L9 Petare Venezuela
88 C9 Petauke Zambia
121 P6 Petawaga, L Quebec
121 N7 Petawawa Ontario
125 P9 Petén Itzá, L Guatemala
99 R5 Petenwell Res Wisconsin
120 G4 Peterbell Ontario
9 F2 Peterborough England
95 Q4 Peterborough New Hampshire
121 M8 Peterborough Ontario
138 E5 Peterborough S Australia
15 F3 Peterculter Scotland
15 G3 Peterhead Scotland
135 O16 Peter I. Øy Antarctica
13 G4 Peterlee England
115 O1 Petermann Gletscher gla Greenland
143 G6 Petermann Ra N Terr/W Aust
131 B5 Peteroa, Vol peak Arg/Chile
118 H2 Peter Pond L Sask
36 H2 Petersberg W Germany
117 G7 Petersburg Alaska
110 G1 Petersburg Illinois
110 J3 Petersburg Indiana
94 D5 Petersburg Michigan
98 H1 Petersburg N Dakota
98 H8 Petersburg Nebraska
94 J6 Petersburg Pennsylvania
110 K6 Petersburg Tennessee
108 F2 Petersburg Texas
94 K9 Petersburg Virginia
94 H7 Petersburg W Virginia
116 M5 Peters Creek Alaska
9 F5 Petersfield England
119 V8 Petersfield Manitoba
33 T7 Petershagen E Germany
32 J8 Petershagen W Germany
37 L7 Petershausen W Germany
99 L7 Peterson Iowa
90 D16 Peter 1st I Antarctica
116 M5 Petersville Alaska
143 E7 Peterswald Hill W Australia
123 R4 Peterview Nfld
43 H9 Petilia Policastro Italy
17 G2 Petilla de Aragón Spain
111 H11 Petit Bois I Mississippi
127 N4 Petit Bourg Guadeloupe W I
127 N4 Petit Canal Guadeloupe W I
122 G8 Petitcodiac New Brunswick
127 N4 Petit Cul de Sac Marin B Guadeloupe W I
122 G5 Petite Cascapedia, Parc de la Quebec
122 E5 Petite Matane Quebec
121 Q7 Petite-Nation, Parc Quebec
122 B6 Petite Rivière Quebec
122 H9 Petite Rivière Bridge Nova Scotia
127 H5 Petite Rivière de l'Artibonite Haiti
21 J7 Petite Sauldre R France
20 G2 Petites Dalles, les France
123 M7 Petit Etang C Breton I, N Scotia
127 O4 Petite Terre, Îles de la Guadeloupe W I
122 G4 Petite Vallèe Quebec
127 H5 Petit Goâve Haiti
123 N5 Petit Jardin Nfld
110 C6 Petit Jean R Arkansas
95 U2 Petit Manan Pt Maine
36 B6 Petitmont France
117 N6 Petitot R Br Col
122 G6 Petit Rocher New Brunswick
29 M4 Petkula Finland
74 E7 Petlad India
125 P7 Peto Mexico
145 G4 Petone New Zealand
133 C4 Petorca Chile
94 C1 Petoskey Michigan
52 G4 Petrakovo U.S.S.R.
43 F11 Petralia Sicily
51 L1 Petra, Ostrov isld U.S.S.R.
65 H3 Petra Velikogo, Zaliv B U.S.S.R.
45 P7 Petrella, M mt Italy
121 N9 Petre, Pt Ontario
52 J4 Petretsovo U.S.S.R.
45 N4 Petriano Italy
47 F3 Petricn Bulgaria
141 L2 Petrie, Mt Brisbane, Qnsld
103 O6 Petrified Forest Nat Mon Arizona
54 F8 Petrikovka U.S.S.R.
48 H5 Petrila Romania
8 B6 Petrockstow England
52 C5 Petrodvorets U.S.S.R.
47 F1 Petrokhanski P Bulgaria
52 D5 Petrokrepost' U.S.S.R.
129 L5 Petrolândia Brazil
109 J8 Petroleum Texas
100 A9 Petrolia California
120 H10 Petrolia Ontario
109 J2 Petrolia Texas
129 K5 Petrolina Brazil
46 F6 Petromagoúla Greece
55 E3 Petropavlosk U.S.S.R.
56 G5 Petropavlovka U.S.S.R.
51 P3 Petropavlovsk-Kamchatskiy U.S.S.R.
129 K8 Petrópolis Brazil
112 C1 Petros Tennessee
48 H5 Petroseni Romania
48 G6 Petrovac Yugoslavia
48 F5 Petrovaradin Yugoslavia
55 E4 Petrovka U.S.S.R.
52 E3 Petrovskiy Yam U.S.S.R.
55 C4 Petrovskoye Bashkirskaya U.S.S.R.
52 E6 Petrovskoye Yaroslavl' U.S.S.R.
56 G5 Petrovsk-Zabaykal'skiy U.S.S.R.
52 D4 Petrozavodsk U.S.S.R.
52 K2 Petrun' U.S.S.R.
Petsamo see Pechenga
29 N2 Petsikko mt Finland
25 C3 Petten Netherlands
38 K6 Pettenbach Austria
14 D2 Pettigoe Irish Rep
110 C6 Pettigrew Arkansas
109 K7 Pettus Texas
123 U6 Petty Hbr Nfld
55 E3 Petukhovo U.S.S.R.
9 F6 Petworth England
38 L8 Petzen mt Austria
38 J5 Peuerbach Austria
69 C10 Peuetsagu, Gunung mt Sumatra
69 C10 Peukankuala Sumatra
116 J8 Peulik, Mt Alaska
69 B10 Peunasu isld Sumatra
29 M4 Peurasuvanto Finland
26 J5 Peuraure Sweden
69 C10 Peureulak Sumatra
9 G6 Pevensey England
94 C3 Pewamo Michigan
99 S6 Pewaukee Wisconsin
9 E5 Pewsey England
32 F6 Pewsum W Germany
36 B7 Pexonne France
19 P18 Peynier France
19 P18 Peypin France
21 I10 Peyrat-le Chateau France
18 E9 Peyrehorade France
18 H8 Peyreleau France
19 P17 Peyrolles-en-Provence France
19 P16 Peyruis France
106 F2 Peyton Colorado
52 G2 Peza R U.S.S.R.
18 H9 Pézenas France
31 K7 Pezinok Czechoslovakia
52 H4 Pezmog U.S.S.R.
37 N6 Pfaffenberg W Germany
37 L6 Pfaffenhofen an der Ilm W Germany
36 D6 Pfaffenhoffen France
41 J3 Pfäffikon Switzerland
37 P2 Pfaffroda E Germany
36 C4 Pfälzer Bergland reg W Germany
36 D5 Pfalzer Wald mts W Germany
36 D3 Pfalzfeld W Germany
36 F6 Pfalzgrafenweiler W Germany
37 L6 Pfalzpaint W Germany
37 O7 Pfarrkirchen W Germany
37 K3 Pfarrweisach W Germany
37 N6 Pfatter W Germany
36 E4 Pfeddersheim W Germany
37 M6 Pfeffenhausen W Germany
36 F6 Pfinztal W Germany
140 C6 Pfitzner, Mt N Terr Aust
41 N2 Pflach Austria
37 M6 Pförring W Germany
36 F6 Pforzheim W Germany
37 N5 Pfreimd W Germany
36 D4 Pfrimm R W Germany
41 K2 Pfullendorf W Germany
36 G7 Pfullingen W Germany
41 N4 Pfunds Austria
36 F4 Pfungstadt W Germany
37 L6 Pfünz W Germany
74 F3 Phagwara India
95 T7 Phair Maine
74 E5 Phalodi India
88 E9 Phalombe Malawi
36 C6 Phalsbourg France
76 B2 Phaltan India
69 D8 Pha Luai, Ko isld Thailand
69 E8 Phangan, Ko isld Thailand
69 D8 Phangnga Thailand
68 G5 Phanom Dang Raek mt Thailand
68 D5 Phanom Thuan Thailand
68 J7 Phan Rang Vietnam
68 J7 Phan Thiet Vietnam
103 M5 Phantom Ranch Arizona
109 J9 Pharr Texas
68 H2 Phat Diem Vietnam
69 D9 Phatthalung Thailand
69 D8 Phayam, Ko isld Thailand
68 E5 Phayuhakhiri Thailand
140 D2 Phelp R N Terr Aust
94 E9 Phelps Kentucky
95 K4 Phelps New York
109 M5 Phelps Texas
99 R3 Phelps Wisconsin
112 L2 Phelps L N Carolina
68 F4 Phen Thailand
94 J9 Phenix Virginia
111 L9 Phenix City Alabama
68 D6 Phet Buri Thailand
68 H5 Phiafay Laos
111 G9 Philadelphia Mississippi
99 P10 Philadelphia Missouri
95 M2 Philadelphia New York
97 Philadelphia conurbation Pennsylvania
84 J5 Philae ruins Egypt
111 J7 Phil Campbell Alabama
98 E5 Philip S Dakota
137 O7 Philip I Pacific Oc
111 F8 Philipp Mississippi
Philippeville see Skikda
22 G3 Philippeville Belgium
94 G7 Philippi W Virginia
140 E6 Philippi, L Queensland
25 A6 Philippine Netherlands
71 Philippines rep E Indies
89 D8 Philippolis S Africa
Philippopolis Bulgaria see Plovdiv
36 E5 Philippsburg W Germany
101 M3 Philipsburg Montana
94 J6 Philipsburg Pennsylvania
121 R7 Philipsburg Quebec
116 O2 Philip Smith Mts Alaska
139 H7 Phillip I Victoria
95 R2 Phillips Maine
101 R1 Phillips Montana
98 H9 Phillips Nebraska
108 C8 Phillips Texas
99 Q4 Phillips Wisconsin
107 L2 Phillipsburg Kansas
115 L1 Phillips Inlet N W Terr
143 B6 Phillips, Mt W Australia
138 C3 Phillipson, L S Australia
142 G5 Phillipson Ra W Australia
142 F3 Phillips Ra W Australia
95 O4 Philmont New York
102 A2 Philo California
100 B5 Philomath Oregon
118 F3 Philomena Alberta
115 M3 Philpots Island N W Terr
94 G10 Philpott Dam Virginia
68 G5 Phimun Mangsahan Thailand
118 J6 Phippen Sask
106 D1 Phippsburg Colorado
68 G7 Phnom Penh Cambodia
67 B6 Pho Binh Gia Vietnam
144 D5 Phoebe New Zealand
95 N4 Phoenicia New York
103 M8 Phoenix Arizona
111 G12 Phoenix Louisiana
95 L3 Phoenix New York
134 K8 Phoenix Is Pacific Oc
95 M6 Phoenixville Pennsylvania
68 G1 Pho Lu Vietnam
68 H4 Phong Nha Vietnam
68 F2 Phong Saly Laos
73 R4 Phong Saly Thailand
68 F1 Phong Tho Vietnam
68 F3 Phon Phisai Thailand
139 G7 Phoques B Tasmania
68 H7 Phouc Le Vietnam
68 D3 Phrao Thailand
68 E5 Phra Phutthabat Thailand
69 D8 Phra Saeng Thailand
69 C8 Phra Thong, Ko isld Thailand
68 E5 Phrom Buri Thailand
47 L6 Phrygia Turkey
68 H7 Phu Cuong Vietnam
68 G2 Phuc Yen Vietnam
67 B7 Phu Dien Vietnam
68 G3 Phu Dien Chau Vietnam
69 D9 Phuket, Ko isld Thailand
68 F4 Phu Khieo Thailand
67 B6 Phulang Thuong Vietnam
75 L8 Phulbani India
68 H4 Phu Loc Vietnam
68 G2 Phu Ly Vietnam
68 F6 Phum Bavel Cambodia
68 G7 Phum Hay Cambodia
68 G6 Phum Khvao Cambodia
68 F6 Phum Siem Cambodia
68 F6 Phum Svai Cambodia
68 F6 Phum Treng Cambodia
68 F6 Phum Troy Toch Cambodia
68 J5 Phu My Vietnam
68 G2 Phu Nho Quan Vietnam
75 N5 Phuntsholing Bhutan
69 G8 Phuoc Long Vietnam
68 G3 Phu Qui Vietnam
68 G2 Phu Tho Vietnam
129 J5 Piaca Brazil
44 G1 Piacenza Italy
44 F2 Piacenza prov Italy
45 L1 Piacenza d'Adige Italy
45 J1 Piadena Italy
122 B2 Piakoudie L Quebec
141 L7 Pialba Queensland
139 J4 Pian R New S Wales
41 K5 Pianazzo Italy
130 H9 Piancó R Brazil
45 L4 Pian de Sco Italy
45 M4 Pian di Meleto Italy
45 N4 Pianello Italy
139 G6 Piangil Victoria
45 M1 Pianiga Italy
45 K3 Piano del Voglio Italy
42 G6 Pianosa isld Adriatic Sea
42 C6 Pianosa isld Italy
65 B5 Pianquan China
118 H9 Piapot Sask
127 O2 Piarco airport Trinidad
31 M3 Piaseczno Poland
122 K3 Piashti, L Quebec
31 O4 Piaski Poland
31 L3 Piątek Poland
48 K4 Piatra Neamt Romania
129 K5 Piauí state Brazil
129 K5 Piaui, Sa. do mts Brazil
42 E2 Piave R Italy
143 B9 Piawaning W Australia
45 H3 Piazza al Serchio Italy
43 F11 Piazza Armerina Sicily
133 C8 Piazzi isld Chile
45 L1 Piazzolas B Italy
86 F4 Pibor Post Sudan
118 D4 Pibroch Alberta
103 L6 Pica Arizona
101 L6 Picabo Idaho
103 N9 Picacho Arizona
103 K8 Picacho California
106 E8 Picacho New Mexico
103 N9 Picacho Res Arizona
124 B3 Picachos, Cerro dos mt Mexico
22 D4 Picardie France
20 K1 Picardie reg
20 C3 Picauville France
111 G11 Picayune Mississippi
123 O5 Piccadilly Nfld
106 B2 Piceance Cr Colorado
45 R8 Picentini, Mti mt Italy
124 F3 Picháchic Mexico
133 E2 Pichanal Argentina
131 B4 Pichidangul, B Chile
133 C4 Pichilemu Chile
128 C4 Pichincha prov Ecuador
52 G6 Pichkasy U.S.S.R.
118 D4 Pickardville Alberta
111 F9 Pickens Mississippi
112 E3 Pickens S Carolina
94 G8 Pickens W Virginia
120 K7 Pickerel Ontario
99 P1 Pickerel L Ontario
13 H5 Pickering England
110 B1 Pickering Missouri
143 D8 Pickering, Mt W Australia
126 D4 Pickle Bank Caribbean
115 K7 Pickle Lake Ontario
98 H6 Pickstown S Dakota
109 M2 Pickton Texas
110 H6 Pickwick L Tennessee
45 P7 Pico Italy
16 D4 Pico de Almanzor mt Spain
16 E4 Pico Penalara mt Spain
129 K5 Picos Brazil
16 C2 Picos de Ancares, Sa. de mts Spain
16 C6 Picos de Aroche mt Spain
20 K2 Picquigny France
120 D4 Pic R Ontario
139 K5 Picton New S Wales
145 E4 Picton New Zealand
121 N8 Picton Ontario
139 H9 Picton, Mt Tasmania
122 K8 Pictou Nova Scotia
122 K8 Pictou I Nova Scotia
118 E9 Picture Butte Alberta
95 L5 Picture Rocks Pennsylvania
130 H9 Picuí Brazil
131 B7 Picún Leufú Argentina
138 B4 Pidinga S Australia
45 Q7 Piedimonte d'Alife Italy
111 L8 Piedmont Alabama
110 F4 Piedmont Missouri
112 E3 Piedmont S Carolina
98 C5 Piedmont S Dakota
94 F6 Piedmont Res Ohio
102 E5 Piedra California
106 C4 Piedra R Colorado
17 F3 Piedra R Spain
16 E5 Piedrabuena Spain
16 C2 Piedrafita, Pto. de pass Spain
16 D4 Piedrahita Spain
131 B3 Piedra Lobos, Pta Chile
125 J3 Piedras Negras Mexico
71 D5 Piedras Point Philippines
133 F5 Piedras, Pta Argentina
128 D6 Piedras, R.de las R Peru
99 R1 Pie I Ontario
29 N9 Pieksämäki Finland
38 M5 Pielach R Austria
29 M8 Pielavesi L Finland
29 O8 Pielinen L Finland
29 O9 Pielisjoki R Finland
139 H8 Pieman R Tasmania
31 M1 Pieniężno Poland
22 K5 Piennes France
36 B2 Pier W Germany
106 F1 Pierce Colorado
113 F10 Pierce Florida
100 K3 Pierce Idaho
98 J7 Pierce Nebraska
13 G4 Piercebridge England
110 B5 Pierce City Missouri
94 B5 Pierceton Indiana
107 K4 Pierceville Kansas
102 A2 Piercy California
46 E4 Piéria Óri Greece
15 F1 Pierowall Orkney Scotland
98 J4 Pierpont S Dakota
19 J6 Pierre France
98 F5 Pierre S Dakota
21 H10 Pierre-Buffiere France
19 P15 Pierre-Châtel France
22 D5 Pierrefonds France
120 K3 Pierre L Ontario
19 N16 Pierrelatte France
22 K5 Pierrepont France
121 S6 Pierreville Quebec
127 P3 Pierreville Trinidad
113 F8 Pierson Florida
119 Q9 Pierson Manitoba
36 B4 Piesport W Germany
143 B10 Piesseville W Australia
31 K7 Piešťany Czechoslovakia
Pietarsaari see Jakobstad
89 G7 Pietermaritzburg S Africa
89 F4 Pietersburg S Africa
22 G3 Piéton Belgium
106 B7 Pie Town New Mexico
44 D3 Pietra Ligure Italy
45 Q7 Pietramelara Italy
44 H4 Pietrasanta Italy
45 Q7 Pietravairano Italy
87 F11 Piet Retief S Africa
43 B9 Pietro, S isld Sardinia
48 J5 Pietroşiţa Romania
48 J3 Pietrosu mt Romania
48 J3 Pietrosul mt Romania
29 P2 Piets'yarvi, Oz L U.S.S.R.
20 B2 Pieux, les France
38 F9 Pieve Italy
42 E2 Pieve di Cadore Italy
45 K2 Pieve di Cento Italy
45 J3 Pievepelago Italy
45 M4 Pieve S. Stefano Italy
47 J9 Pigádhia Kárpathos I Greece
94 D3 Pigeon Michigan
94 C1 Pigeon R Michigan
120 H10 Pigeon B Ontario
111 K10 Pigeon Cr Alabama
140 B3 Pigeon Hole N Terr Aust
127 K3 Pigeon I Jamaica
118 C5 Pigeon L Alberta
121 M8 Pigeon L Ontario
102 B4 Pigeon Pt California
127 M2 Pigeon Pt Tobago
119 V6 Pigeon R Manitoba
119 O2 Pigeon River Ontario
143 C8 Pigeon Rocks W Australia
94 H10 Pigg R Virginia
110 F5 Piggott Arkansas
89 G8 Pigg's Peak Swaziland
19 Q18 Pignans France
45 P7 Pignataro Interamna Italy
45 Q7 Pignatoro Maggiore Italy
133 E5 Pigüe Argentina
145 D3 Pihaina New Zealand
67 E1 Pi He R China
29 L9 Pihlajavesi Finland
56 E4 Pik Grandioznyy mt U.S.S.R.
31 K2 Piła Poland
129 K6 Pilao Arcado Brazil
19 N14 Pilat, Mt France
142 C5 Pilbara W Australia
48 F3 Pilis Hungary
48 E3 Pilisvörösvár Hungary
144 A6 Pillans Pass New Zealand
98 J2 Pillsbury N Dakota
102 B2 Pillsbury, L California
52 G6 Pil'na U.S.S.R.
8 D4 Pilning England
130 F5 Pilões, Sa. dos mts Brazil
46 E8 Pílos Greece
119 N8 Pilot Butte Sask
110 D3 Pilot Grove Missouri
119 T9 Pilot Mound Manitoba
112 G1 Pilot Mountain N Carolina
102 G3 Pilot Pk Nevada
101 Q5 Pilot Pk Wyoming
116 J8 Pilot Point Alaska
109 L2 Pilot Point Texas
100 G4 Pilot Rock Oregon
116 F5 Pilot Station Alaska
139 J6 Pilot, The mt New S Wales
133 E2 Piloya R Bolivia
37 M5 Pilsach W Germany
Pilsen see Plzeň
99 T5 Pilsen Wisconsin
41 O1 Pilsen See L W Germany
37 O6 Pilsting W Germany
55 F1 Pil'tan-Lor, Oz L U.S.S.R.
27 M14 Piltene U.S.S.R.
8 D5 Pilton England
52 J4 Pil'va R U.S.S.R.
31 N6 Pilzno Poland
55 F1 Pim U.S.S.R.
103 P9 Pima Arizona
129 G4 Pimenta Brazil
128 F6 Pimenta Bueno Brazil
127 J5 Pimental Dom Rep
128 C5 Pimentel Peru
113 L12 Pimlico I Bahamas
71 H4 Pimpi Sulawesi
86 D5 Pimu Zaïre
17 G3 Pina Spain
103 L10 Pinacate, Cerro peak Mexico
124 C2 Pinacate, Sa. del mt Mexico
103 O9 Pinaleno Mts Arizona
71 E4 Pinamalayan Philippines
69 E10 Pinang isld Malaysia
70 E2 Pinangah Sabah
78 F2 Pinarbaşi Turkey
126 C3 Pinar del Río Cuba
47 J3 Pinarhisar Turkey
138 F3 Pinaroo, L New S Wales
133 D4 Piñas Argentina
45 L2 Pincara Italy
9 F2 Pinchbeck England
118 D9 Pincher Creek Alberta
117 L8 Pinchi Br Col
128 C4 Pinchincha mt Ecuador
94 D4 Pinckney Michigan
110 G3 Pinckneyville Illinois
20 D4 Pinçon, Mt France
94 C3 Pinconning Michigan
48 G4 Pîncota Romania
31 M5 Pińczów Poland
129 H6 Pindaiba Brazil
110 D5 Pindall Arkansas
143 B8 Pindar W Australia
129 J4 Pindaré R Brazil
70 G4 Pindjang Sulawesi
28 E4 Pindstrup Denmark
103 N7 Pine Arizona
100 K6 Pine Idaho
94 B2 Pine R Michigan
138 F4 Pine R New S Wales
99 Q6 Pine R Wisconsin
111 K10 Pine Apple Alabama
111 D7 Pine Bluff Arkansas
119 P4 Pinebluff L Sask
98 B8 Pine Bluffs Wyoming
123 T7 Pine, C Nfld
113 F9 Pinecastle Florida
126 E2 Pine Cay isld Bahamas
111 E7 Pine City Arkansas
99 O4 Pine City Minnesota
103 H1 Pine Cr Nevada
94 K5 Pine Cr Pennsylvania
140 B2 Pine Creek N Terr Aust
102 E3 Pinecrest California
107 P7 Pine Cr. Res Oklahoma
16 E2 Pineda de la S Spain
117 P9 Pinedale Alberta
102 E5 Pinedale California
101 Q7 Pinedale Wyoming
102 E5 Pine Flat Res California
100 G8 Pine Forest Range Nevada
52 F3 Pinega U.S.S.R.
52 G3 Pinega R U.S.S.R.
95 L6 Pine Grove Pennsylvania
143 B8 Pinegrove W Australia
140 C5 Pine Hill N Terr Aust
141 H6 Pinehill Queensland
114 J6 Pine House Saskatchewan
118 L3 Pine House L Sask
112 H2 Pinehurst N Carolina
100 C2 Pinehurst Washington
118 F4 Pinehurst L Alberta
113 E11 Pine I Florida
99 O5 Pine Island Minnesota
99 S4 Pine L Wisconsin
109 O4 Pineland Texas
146 H11 Pinel B Antarctica
144 B6 Pinelheugh mt New Zealand
113 E10 Pinellas airport Florida
102 C6 Pine Mt California
107 P7 Pine Mt Oklahoma
103 L7 Pine Pk Arizona
117 Q5 Pine Point N W Terr
119 P1 Pine Portage Ontario
113 D8 Pine Pt Florida
114 H5 Pine Pt N W Terr
118 D4 Pine R Alberta
117 M8 Pine R Br Col
98 D6 Pine Ridge S Dakota
119 R7 Pine River Manitoba
99 M3 Pine River Minnesota
118 K3 Pine River Sask
44 B2 Pinerolo Italy
120 J9 Pinery Prov. Park Ontario
111 B9 Pines, L. O'The Texas
108 C4 Pine Springs Texas
89 G7 Pinetown S Africa
110 B7 Pine Valley Oklahoma
103 L4 Pine Valley Utah
103 L4 Pine Valley Mts Utah
94 D10 Pineville Kentucky
111 D10 Pineville Louisiana
110 B5 Pineville Missouri
112 G2 Pineville N Carolina
94 F9 Pineville W Virginia
99 L2 Pinewood Minnesota
99 M1 Pinewood Ontario
112 G4 Pinewood S Carolina
98 K1 Piney Manitoba
101 T2 Piney Buttes hills Montana
110 C6 Piney Cr Arkansas
113 D8 Piney Pt Florida
65 F2 Ping'an China
143 C10 Pingaring W Australia
67 A5 Pingbian China
67 B1 Pingchang China
65 D7 Ping Dao isld China
67 C3 Pingdeng China
65 B6 Pingding China
Pingdingbu see Guyan
58 F5 Pingdingshan China
65 F4 Pingdingshan China
65 G1 Pingding Shan mt China
65 D6 Pingdu China
143 B10 Pingelly W Australia
65 C7 Pinggang China
65 F3 Pinggang China
65 D4 Pinggu China
67 B5 Pingguo China
67 F4 Pinghai China
67 F4 Pinghe China
Pinghu see Pingtang
67 G1 Pinghu China
67 D2 Pingjiang China
67 C4 Pingle China
58 E4 Pingliang China
67 D1 Pinglin China
65 B5 Pinglu China
65 B7 Pinglu China
58 E4 Pingluo China
Pingma see Tiandong
75 N6 Pingna Bangladesh
67 C5 Pingnan China
67 F3 Pingnan China
Pingqiao see Xinyang
65 D4 Pingquan China
101 N6 Pingree Idaho
98 G2 Pingree N Dakota
143 C10 Pingrup W Australia
65 C5 Pingshan China
67 A2 Pingshan China
65 D7 Pingshang China
67 D4 Pingshi China
67 E4 Pingshi China
65 B6 Pingshun China
67 F4 Pingtan China
67 F4 Pingtan Dao isld China
67 B4 Pingtang China
67 G5 P'ing-tung Taiwan
67 B5 Pingxiang China
67 D3 Pingxiang China
65 F1 Pingyang China
67 G3 Pingyang China
65 B6 Pingyao China
65 D7 Pingyi China
65 C6 Pingyin China
67 C3 Pingyong China
65 C6 Pingyuan China
67 E4 Pingyuan China
67 A5 Pingyuanjie China
130 F8 Pinhal Brazil
16 B3 Pinhão Portugal
129 J4 Pinheiro Brazil
16 C4 Pinhel Portugal
69 D12 Pini isld Indonesia
46 E5 Piniós R Greece
46 E7 Piniós R Greece
143 B10 Pinjarra W Australia
143 E9 Pinjin W Australia
38 O7 Pinka R Austria
38 O7 Pinkafeld Austria
141 K1 Pinkenba dist Brisbane, Qnsld
118 H7 Pinkham Sask
112 K2 Pink Hill N Carolina
117 M7 Pink Mountain Br Col
20 G5 Pin la Garenne, le France
68 C2 Pinlaung Burma
145 D4 Pinnacle mt New Zealand
116 C6 Pinnacle I Bering Sea
102 C5 Pinnacles Nat. Mon California
138 F6 Pinnaroo S Australia
32 L5 Pinn Au R W Germany
32 L5 Pinneberg W Germany
106 G1 Pinneo Colorado
9 F4 Pinner England
33 T5 Pinnow E Germany
70 B5 Pinoh R Kalimantan
111 F10 Pinola Mississippi
106 F3 Pinon Colorado
106 E9 Pinon New Mexico
112 H4 Pinopolis Dam S Carolina
126 C4 Pinos, I. de Cuba
102 E7 Pinos, Mt California
17 G6 Pinoso Spain
125 K9 Pinotepa Nacional Mexico
70 F6 Pinrang Sulawesi
137 O6 Pins, Île Des New Caledonia
53 C8 Pinsk U.S.S.R.
111 K8 Pinson Alabama
110 H6 Pinson Tennessee
120 J10 Pins, Pte. aux Ontario
103 P6 Pinta Arizona
128 A7 Pinta isld Galapagos Is
133 D2 Pintados Chile
103 L9 Pinta, Sa Arizona
70 E2 Pintasan Sabah
133 E3 Pinto Argentina
118 K9 Pinto Butte peak Sask
103 J8 Pinto Mts California
138 B4 Pintumba S Australia
103 L4 Pintura Utah
103 J5 Pintwater Ra Nevada
123 Q2 Pinware R Labrador
12 D3 Pinwherry Scotland
143 B8 Pinyalling mt W Australia
52 G4 Pinyug U.S.S.R.
41 N5 Pinzolo Italy
45 M4 Pióbbico Italy
103 K4 Pioche Nevada
19 N16 Piolenc France
42 D6 Piombino Italy
94 C5 Pioneer Ohio
109 H3 Pioneer Texas
101 M4 Pioneer Mts Montana
56 C3 Pioner U.S.S.R.
51 J1 Pioner, Ostrova islds U.S.S.R.
55 D1 Pionerskiy U.S.S.R.
145 E3 Piopio New Zealand
128 F4 Piorini L Brazil
31 L3 Piotrków Bydgoszcz Poland
31 M4 Piotrków Trybunalski Łódź Poland
45 M1 Piove di Sacco Italy
65 G3 Pipa Dingzi mt China
74 E5 Pipar India
102 G4 Piper Pk Nevada
103 M5 Pipe Sp. Nat. Mon Arizona
119 R9 Pipestone Manitoba
98 K6 Pipestone Minnesota
119 Q9 Pipestone Cr Manitoba
98 K5 Pipestone Nat. Mon Minnesota
145 E3 Pipipi mt New Zealand
145 E3 Pipiriki New Zealand
121 U3 Pipmuacan, Rés Quebec
122 B4 Pipmuacan, Res Quebec
60 Q2 Pippu Japan
21 B6 Pipriac France
107 P4 Piqua Kansas
110 M1 Piqua Ohio
17 F2 Piqueras, Pto. de Spain
130 C5 Piquiri, R Mato Grosso Brazil
130 D9 Piquiri, R Paraná Brazil
85 E7 Pira Benin
130 E5 Piracanjuba Brazil
129 J7 Piracanjuba R Brazil
129 J8 Piracicaba Brazil
130 G6 Piracicaba R Brazil
133 F3 Piracuacito Argentina
130 F7 Piraçununga Brazil
129 K4 Piraeuruca Brazil
47 F7 Piraiévs Greece
56 E4 Piramida, G mt U.S.S.R.
42 F3 Piran Yugoslavia
129 L5 Piranhas Alagoas Brazil
129 H7 Piranhas Goiás Brazil
130 D5 Piranhas Goiás Brazil
130 D8 Pirapó, R Brazil
129 K7 Pirapora Brazil
122 A3 Piraube, L Quebec
130 C10 Piray R Argentina
128 F7 Piray R Bolivia
9 F5 Pirbright England
47 G2 Pirdop Bulgaria
20 C5 Piré France
129 J7 Pires do Rio Brazil
47 G9 Pírgos Crete Greece
46 E7 Pírgos Greece
130 B9 Piribebuy Paraguay
17 G2 Pirineos mt Spain
145 E4 Pirinoa New Zealand
145 F3 Piripaua New Zealand
129 K4 Piripiri Brazil
127 M9 Píritu Anzoátegui Venezuela
127 K10 Piritu Miranda Venezuela
37 N3 Pirk E Germany
29 K10 Pirkkala Finland
36 D5 Pirmasens W Germany
30 H5 Pirna E Germany
12 C2 Pirnmill Scotland
145 E2 Pirongia New Zealand
46 F1 Pirot Yugoslavia
20 B3 Pirou France
74 F2 Pir Panjal Rge Kashmir
102 F7 Piru California
136 F2 Piru Moluccas Indonesia
54 D6 Piryatin U.S.S.R.
47 H6 Piryí Greece
77 J4 Pirzada Afghanistan
45 H4 Pisa Italy
133 C1 Pisagua Chile
71 B3 Pisang isld Indonesia
44 H3 Pisanino mt Italy
21 D10 Pisany France
144 B6 Pisa Range New Zealand
70 F1 Pisau, Tg C Sabah
43 G8 Pisciotta Italy
128 C6 Pisco Peru
Piscopi isld see Tílos
95 N3 Piseco New York
30 H6 Písek Czechoslovakia
98 J1 Pisek N Dakota
80 F6 Pisga Jordan
99 L8 Pisgah Iowa
112 E2 Pisgah, Mt N Carolina
144 C6 Pisgah, Mt New Zealand
77 G6 Pishin Iran
74 B3 Pishin Pakistan
29 P6 Pishta R U.S.S.R.
70 G7 Pising Sulawesi
103 M9 Pisinimo Arizona
102 D6 Pismo Bch California
128 F6 Piso Firme Bolivia
41 M6 Pisogne Italy
85 D6 Pissila Upper Volta
29 P6 Pistayarvi L U.S.S.R.
43 H8 Pisticci Italy
45 J4 Pistoia Italy
123 R2 Pistolet B Nfld
100 A7 Pistol River Oregon
52 F6 Pistsovo U.S.S.R.
8 C2 Pistyll Rhaeadr mt Wales
16 E3 Pisuerga R Spain
31 N2 Pisz Poland
100 D8 Pit R California
85 B6 Pita Guinea
122 G1 Pitaga Labrador
70 D6 Pitap, R Kalimantan
139 G5 Pitarpunga L New S Wales
71 G7 Pitas Pt Mindanao Philippines
135 U11 Pitcairn I Pacific Oc
101 Q5 Pitchfork Wyoming
127 O3 Pitch L Trinidad
26 M6 Piteå Sweden
26 L6 Piteälv R Sweden
45 J3 Piteglio Italy
48 J6 Piteşti Romania
143 B9 Pithara W Australia
20 K5 Pithiviers France
42 D6 Pitigliano Italy
124 C2 Pitiquito Mexico
106 D3 Pitkin Colorado
111 D11 Pitkin Louisiana
52 D1 Pitkul' U.S.S.R.
52 D4 Pitkyaranta U.S.S.R.
15 E4 Pitlochry Scotland
95 M7 Pitman New Jersey
87 G12 Piton des Neiges mt Réunion
111 G11 Pitre, I. au Louisiana
13 F1 Pitscottie Scotland
9 G4 Pitsea England
13 F1 Pittenweem Scotland
117 J9 Pitt I Br Col
137 R10 Pitt I Chatham Is Pacific Oc
112 H2 Pittsboro N Carolina
102 C3 Pittsburg California
110 B4 Pittsburg Kansas
110 M4 Pittsburg Kentucky
121 T7 Pittsburg New Hampshire
107 P7 Pittsburg Oklahoma
109 N3 Pittsburg Texas
94 H6 Pittsburgh Pennsylvania
110 E2 Pittsfield Illinois
95 S2 Pittsfield Maine
95 O4 Pittsfield Massachusetts
95 Q3 Pittsfield New Hampshire
94 C5 Pittsford Michigan
94 K3 Pittsford New York
95 O3 Pittsford Vermont
95 M5 Pittston Pennsylvania
111 L9 Pittsview Alabama
95 M8 Pittsville Maryland
110 C3 Pittsville Missouri
99 Q5 Pittsville Wisconsin
141 K8 Pittsworth Queensland
100 D8 Pittville California
71 B1 Pitu Halmahera Indonesia
88 E6 Pitu R Tanzania
140 E6 Pituri R Queensland
41 N3 Pitz Tal Austria
45 J1 Piú bega Italy
19 Q17 Piumoisson France
128 B5 Piura Peru
128 B4 Piura dep Peru
103 J7 Piute Mts California
102 F6 Piute Pk California
103 M3 Piute Res Utah
75 K4 Piuthan Nepal
42 J5 Piva R Yugoslavia
120 G2 Pivabiska R Ontario
126 G9 Pivijay Colombia
31 M6 Piwniczna Poland
102 E6 Pixley California
46 E5 Piyaí Greece
60 Q1 Piyashiri yama mt Japan
128 E7 Pizacoma Peru
52 G5 Pizhanka U.S.S.R.
52 G5 Pizhma U.S.S.R.
41 K4 Pizol mt Switzerland
43 G10 Pizzo Italy
45 O6 Pizzodeta, M mt Italy
33 Q5 Plaaz E Germany
109 L7 Placedo Texas
123 T6 Placentia Nfld
71 G6 Placer Mindanao Philippines
102 F1 Placeritos Nevada
102 D3 Placerville California
106 B3 Placerville Colorado
126 E3 Placetas Cuba
113 E11 Placida Florida
113 F10 Placid, L Florida
106 D6 Placitas New Mexico
46 E3 Plačkovica mt Yugoslavia
12 C3 Pladda I Scotland
15 C5 Pladda Lt. Ho Scotland
40 F4 Plaffeien Switzerland
99 Q6 Plain Wisconsin
94 D6 Plain City Ohio
101 N8 Plain City Utah
111 C9 Plain Dealing Louisiana
20 J3 Plaine et Collines reg France
94 A7 Plainfield Indiana
99 O7 Plainfield Iowa
95 N6 Plainfield New Jersey
99 R5 Plainfield Wisconsin
112 C5 Plains Georgia
101 L2 Plains Montana
108 E2 Plains Texas
94 K8 Plains, The Virginia
110 C6 Plainview Arkansas
99 O5 Plainview Minnesota
98 J7 Plainview Nebraska
108 F1 Plainview Texas

Plainville — Portree 61

95 P5 Plainville Connecticut
110 E2 Plainville Illinois
107 L2 Plainville Kansas
94 B4 Plainwell Michigan
18 F9 Plaisance France
127 H5 Plaisance Haiti
69 G14 Plaju Sumatra
47 G4 Pláka, Akr C Greece
47 H9 Pláka, Akra C Crete Greece
46 D3 Plakenska Pl mt Yugoslavia
118 E4 Plamondon Alberta
71 H9 Plampang Indonesia
37 O4 Planá Czechoslovakia
102 D4 Planada California
129 L5 Planalto da Borborema plat Brazil
129 H7 Planalto de Mato Grosso plat Brazil
17 G6 Plana Ó Nueva Tabarca isld Spain
40 E2 Plancher les Mines France
40 D4 Planches-en-Montagne, Les France
131 B5 Planchon, Paso de Chile/Arg
18 D4 Plancoët France
19 O15 Plan-de-Baix France
19 N17 Plan d'Orgon France
17 G9 Plane isld Algeria
33 R8 Plane, R E Germany
126 G10 Planeta Rica Colombia
137 L3 Planet Deep Solomon Sea
37 P5 Plánice Czechoslovakia
37 L4 Plankenfels W Germany
98 H6 Plankinton S Dakota
109 L2 Plano Texas
127 M3 Plantain Garden R Jamaica
113 E9 Plant City Florida
111 K9 Plantersville Alabama
111 E11 Plaquemine Louisiana
16 C4 Plasencia Spain
27 F10 Plassen Norway
55 D4 Plast U.S.S.R.
33 R5 Plasten E Germany
103 J9 Plaster City California
37 P4 Plasy Czechoslovakia
43 E11 Platani R Sicily
133 C2 Plata, Puerta Chile
131 G5 Plata, Rio de la Arg/Uruguay
19 O14 Plateau de Chambarand France
19 J15 Plateau de Langres France
21 K10 Plateau de Peyrelevade France
19 P16 Plateau de St. Etienne France
86 B1 Plateau du Tchigaï Niger
85 C3 Plateau du Tinrhert stony des Algeria
Plateau of Tibet see Xizang Gaoyuan
21 H9 Plateaux de la Marche France
123 T5 Plate Cove Nfld
124 H6 Plateros Mexico
46 F4 Platí Greece
47 G4 Platí Ákra C Greece
46 F5 Platíkambos Greece
102 B1 Platina California
116 G7 Platinum Alaska
126 G10 Plato Colombia
110 D4 Plato Missouri
118 J7 Plato Sask
56 D5 Plato Alash U.S.S.R.
79 C4 Platres Cyprus
98 H6 Platte S Dakota
37 N4 Platte mt W Germany
99 M9 Platte R Missouri
98 G9 Platte R Nebraska
98 J8 Platte Center Nebraska
110 B2 Platte City Missouri
106 E2 Platte Mt Colorado
98 B9 Platteville Colorado
99 Q7 Platteville Wisconsin
36 E6 Plättig W Germany
37 O6 Plattling W Germany
107 O7 Platt Nat. Park Oklahoma
110 B2 Plattsburg Missouri
95 O2 Plattsburg New York
99 K8 Plattsmouth Nebraska
33 Q6 Plau E Germany
33 Q8 Plaue E Germany
37 K2 Plaue Erfurt E Germany
37 N3 Plauen E Germany
46 D2 Plav Yugoslavia
52 C6 Pļaviņas U.S.S.R.
42 J6 Plavnica Yugoslavia
54 J3 Plavsk U.S.S.R.
128 B4 Playas Ecuador
106 B10 Playas L New Mexico
140 D4 Playford R N Terr Aust
140 D6 Playford Mt N Terr Aust
119 U4 Playgreen L Manitoba
124 E5 Playón Mexico
98 E1 Plaza N Dakota
133 D5 Plaza Huincul Argentina
12 E1 Plean Scotland
110 M1 Pleasant Ohio
95 S5 Pleasant B Massachusetts
123 M7 Pleasant Bay C Breton I, N S
94 F7 Pleasant City Ohio
119 N6 Pleasantdale Sask
94 K6 Pleasant Gap Pennsylvania
101 O9 Pleasant Grove Utah
110 F2 Pleasant Hill Illinois
111 C10 Pleasant Hill Louisiana
110 B3 Pleasant Hill Missouri
94 E6 Pleasant Hill Res Ohio
103 M8 Pleasant, L Arizona
122 F8 Pleasant, Mt New Brunswick
112 H5 Pleasant, Mt S Carolina
102 C4 Pleasanton California
110 B3 Pleasanton Kansas
98 G9 Pleasanton Nebraska
109 J7 Pleasanton Texas
110 E6 Pleasant Plains Arkansas
119 S9 Pleasant Pt Manitoba
144 C6 Pleasant Pt New Zealand
100 H5 Pleasant Valley Oregon
100 G3 Pleasant View Washington
99 N8 Pleasantville Iowa
95 N7 Pleasantville New Jersey
94 H5 Pleasantville Pennsylvania
9 E1 Pleasley England
110 L3 Pleasureville Kentucky
18 G7 Pleaux France
37 L4 Plech W Germany
120 G2 Pledger L Ontario
133 F4 Piedra Sola Uruguay
70 D3 Pleieran R Sarawak
70 D6 Pleihari Kalimantan
68 J5 Plei Herel Vietnam
68 J6 Plei Kly Vietnam
68 J6 Pleiku Vietnam
20 B4 Pleine Fougères France
37 L5 Pleinfeld W Germany
9 G6 Pleinmont Pt Channel Is
37 P6 Pleinting W Germany
37 N1 Pleisse R E Germany
68 H5 Plei Ta Uan Vietnam
20 A5 Plélan-le-Grand France
17 F1 Plencia Spain
18 D4 Pléneuf France
48 H6 Plentiţa Romania
118 J7 Plenty Sask
145 F2 Plenty, Bay of New Zealand
140 D6 Plenty R N Terr Aust
98 B1 Plentywood Montana
20 B4 Plerguer France
52 F3 Plesetsk U.S.S.R.
55 E3 Pleshkova U.S.S.R.
48 F2 Plešivec Czechoslovakia
20 A4 Pleslin France
21 B6 Plessé France
121 T6 Plessisville Quebec
122 B2 Pletipi L Quebec
36 D1 Plettenberg W Germany
89 C10 Plettenberg B S Africa
20 B4 Pleudihen France
20 B5 Pleugueneuc France
20 A4 Pleurtuit France
47 G1 Pleven Bulgaria
98 B3 Plevna Montana
18 C4 Pleyben France
37 N4 Pleystein W Germany
145 E4 Plimmerton New Zealand
48 M1 Pliskov U.S.S.R.
42 G4 Pljesivica dist Yugoslavia
48 E7 Pljevlja Yugoslavia
43 B8 Ploaghe Sardinia
36 D7 Plobsheim France
42 H5 Ploča lt ho Yugoslavia
42 H5 Ploče Yugoslavia
36 G6 Plochingen W Germany
31 M3 Płock Poland
30 H7 Plöckenstein mt Czechoslovakia
22 D2 Ploegsteert Belgium
18 D5 Ploërmel France
48 K6 Ploieşti Romania
47 H6 Plomárion Greece
18 G7 Plomb du Cantal mt France
40 A3 Plombières France
19 K5 Plombières-les-Bains France
22 G4 Plomion France
33 M4 Plön W Germany
31 J2 Płona R Poland
31 M3 Płońsk Poland
48 H6 Plopi Romania
52 D6 Ploskosh' U.S.S.R.
37 N4 Plössberg W Germany
31 J2 Płoty Poland
18 C4 Plouaret France
18 C5 Plouay France
20 A4 Ploubalay France
31 H5 Ploučnice R Czechoslovakia
18 B4 Ploudalmezeau France
20 B4 Plouer France
18 D4 Plouguenast France
18 D4 Plouha France
47 G2 Plovdiv Bulgaria
99 M7 Plover Iowa
99 R5 Plover Wisconsin
99 R5 Plover R Wisconsin
116 K1 Plover Is Alaska
36 H6 Plüderhausen W Germany
119 S8 Plumas Manitoba
99 O5 Plum City Wisconsin
118 D1 Plum Coulee Manitoba
139 L4 Plumer, Pt New S Wales
95 P5 Plum I New York
100 J2 Plummer Idaho
116 H6 Plummer, Mt Alaska
110 D6 Plummerville Arkansas
13 F4 Plumpton Hd England
143 F8 Plumridge Lakes W Australia
87 E10 Plumtree Zimbabwe
52 B6 Plunge U.S.S.R.
119 M7 Plunkett Sask
100 F7 Plush Oregon
18 D5 Pluvigner France
36 B4 Pluwig W Germany
102 D3 Plymouth California
8 B7 Plymouth England
94 A5 Plymouth Indiana
99 N6 Plymouth Iowa
95 R5 Plymouth Massachusetts
127 O6 Plymouth Montserrat W Indies
98 K9 Plymouth Nebraska
95 Q3 Plymouth New Hampshire
94 E6 Plymouth Ohio
95 M5 Plymouth Pennsylvania
127 M2 Plymouth Tobago
101 N8 Plymouth Utah
95 P3 Plymouth Vermont
99 T6 Plymouth Wisconsin
8 B7 Plympton England
122 G9 Plympton Nova Scotia
8 C3 Plynlimon Fawr mt Wales
52 C5 Plyusa U.S.S.R.
52 C5 Plyussa R U.S.S.R.
37 P4 Plzeň Czechoslovakia
31 J3 Pniewy Poland
85 D6 Po Upper Volta
44 C1 Po R Italy
45 J2 Po R Italy
139 H8 Poatina Tasmania
85 E7 Pobé Benin
66 C3 Pobedy, Pik mt U.S.S.R./China
37 O5 Poběžovice Czechoslovakia
31 K3 Pobiedziska Poland
17 J2 Pobla de Lilleta, L Spain
17 H2 Pobla de Segur Spain
110 F5 Pocahontas Arkansas
99 M7 Pocahontas Iowa
94 F9 Pocahontas Virginia
107 N6 Pocasse Oklahoma
94 F8 Pocatalico R W Virginia
101 N7 Pocatello Idaho
31 J6 Počátky Czechoslovakia
131 D3 Pocha, Sa. de mts Argentina
54 E4 Pochep U.S.S.R.
54 D2 Pochinok U.S.S.R.
38 M5 Pochlarn Austria
125 L10 Pochutla Mexico
37 P5 Pocinovice Czechoslovakia
37 P2 Pockau E Germany
37 P7 Pocking W Germany
13 H6 Pocklington England
70 F2 Pock, Mt Sabah
128 D7 Pocoma Peru
95 M8 Pocomoke City Maryland
95 M9 Pocomoke Sd Virginia
129 G7 Poconé Brazil
95 M6 Pocono Mts Pennsylvania
95 M5 Pocono Pines Pennsylvania
129 J8 Pocos de Caldas Brazil
125 O6 Pocrí Panama
125 P9 Poctún Guatemala
103 L5 Pocum Wash creek Arizona
138 F4 Podamacca New S Wales
37 P3 Podbořany Czechoslovakia
52 J3 Podcher'ye U.S.S.R.
31 L4 Poddębice Poland
118 C4 Poddle R Alberta
52 D5 Poddor'ye U.S.S.R.
31 J5 Poděbrady Czechoslovakia
45 M2 Po delle Tolle R Italy
18 E8 Podensac France
48 J1 Podgaits U.S.S.R.
Podgorica see Titograd
54 G8 Podgorodnoye U.S.S.R.
45 M2 Po di Goro R Italy
76 D3 Podile India
45 L2 Po di Volano R Italy
51 Q2 Podkagernoye U.S.S.R.
56 D1 Podkamennay R U.S.S.R.
38 J9 Podkoren Yugoslavia
47 G3 Podkova Bulgaria
55 C5 Podnikovskiy U.S.S.R.
48 F1 Podolinec Czechoslovakia
54 J1 Podolsk U.S.S.R.
85 B5 Podor Senegal
52 G4 Podosinovets U.S.S.R.
42 H4 Podovi Yugoslavia
52 D4 Podporozh'ye U.S.S.R.
55 E2 Podrezovo U.S.S.R.
56 D2 Podtesovo U.S.S.R.
48 L3 Podu Iloaiei Romania
46 E2 Podujevo Yugoslavia
48 L4 Podu Turcului Romania
52 F4 Podyuga U.S.S.R.
33 O4 Poel isld E Germany
22 D2 Poelkapelle Belgium
94 C1 Poe Reef Lt. Ho Michigan
144 C5 Poerua New Zealand
87 C11 Pofadder S Africa
45 O6 Pofi Italy
120 J6 Pogamasing Ontario
54 E4 Pogar U.S.S.R.
33 S4 Poggendorf E Germany
42 D5 Poggibonsi Italy
45 K4 Poggio a Caiano Italy
45 N5 Poggio Moiano Italy
45 K2 Pòggio Renatico Italy
45 K2 Póggio Rusco Italy
59 M1 Pogibi U.S.S.R.
48 L6 Pogoanele Romania
46 D4 Pogradec Albania
45 M2 Po Grande R Italy
59 K3 Pogranichnyy U.S.S.R.
48 M1 Pogrebishchenskiy U.S.S.R.
116 E9 Pogromni Vol Aleutian Is
32 F6 Pogum W Germany
71 H5 Poh Sulawesi
135 U5 Pohakuloa Hawaiian Is
59 J4 Pohang S Korea
145 E4 Pohangina New Zealand
145 D4 Pohara New Zealand
29 K11 Pohja Finland
29 O8 Pohjois-Karjala prov Finland
36 F3 Pohl-Göns W Germany
36 F2 Pohlheim W Germany
145 E3 Pohokura New Zealand
145 F3 Pohokura mt New Zealand
48 F2 Pohorelá Czechoslovakia
31 K7 Pohořelice Czechoslovakia
38 M9 Pohorje mt Yugoslavia
102 V14 Pohue B Hawaiian Is
45 K1 Poiana Magg Italy
46 F1 Poiana Mare Romania
48 K3 Poiana Teiului Romania
71 J4 Poigar Sulawesi
29 M4 Poikela Finland
123 O2 Poincaré, L Quebec
146 F2 Poinsett, C Antarctica
113 G9 Poinsett, L Florida
102 D7 Point Arguello California
109 M5 Pointblank Texas
138 E5 Point Broughton S Australia
102 D6 Point Buchon California
139 G7 Point Campbell Victoria
109 L7 Point Comfort Texas
102 D7 Point Conception California
123 N3 Pointe-à Maurier Quebec
127 O3 Pointe-á-Pierre Trinidad
127 N4 Pointe-á-Pitre Guadeloupe W I
120 K7 Pointe au Baril Station Ontario
122 E4 Pointe aux Anglais Quebec
121 R7 Pointe aux Trembles Quebec
121 S4 Pointe Bleue Quebec
122 H7 Pointe du Chêne New Brunswick
120 H9 Point Edward Ontario
122 D4 Pointe le Bel Quebec
127 M4 Pointe Noire Guadeloupe W I
22 C1 Pointe Synthe France
122 G6 Pointe Verte New Brunswick
138 F7 Point Fairy S Australia
127 N3 Point Fortin Trinidad
112 M1 Point Harbor N Carolina
139 H8 Point Hills Tasmania
116 D2 Point Hope Alaska
117 R3 Point L N W Terr
116 F2 Point Lay Alaska
95 L8 Point Lookout Maryland
139 L4 Point Lookout mt New S Wales
94 H7 Point Marion Pennsylvania
94 K7 Point of Rocks Maryland
101 R8 Point of Rocks Wyoming
120 H10 Point Pelee Nat Park Ontario
102 C6 Point Piedras Blancas California
95 N6 Point Pleasant New Jersey
94 E8 Point Pleasant W Virginia
142 B5 Point Samson W Australia
140 B1 Point Stuart N Terr Aust
102 C5 Point Sur California
138 D5 Point Turton S Australia
145 E2 Point Waikato New Zealand
68 F6 Poipet Cambodia
52 H6 Poisevo U.S.S.R.
101 S6 Poison Cr Wyoming
142 B1 Poison Gully R Perth, W Aust
121 P6 Poisson Blanc, L Quebec
142 C5 Poissonnier Pt W Australia
20 K4 Poissy France
21 F8 Poitiers France
21 D8 Poitou reg France
142 B5 Poivre, C W Australia
20 J2 Poix France
22 J3 Poix St. Hubert Belgium
22 H4 Poix-Terron France
46 D4 Pojan Albania
106 D6 Pojoaque New Mexico
102 R12 Pokai Bay Hawaiian Is
145 E3 Pokaka New Zealand
74 D5 Pokaran India
139 J3 Pokataroo New S Wales
52 J3 Pokcha U.S.S.R.
145 E2 Pokeno New Zealand
75 L4 Pokhara Nepal
29 M3 Pokka Finland
86 E5 Poko Zaïre
31 K5 Pokój Poland
116 F2 Poko Mt Alaska
54 L1 Pokrov U.S.S.R.
55 E5 Pokrovka Atbasar U.S.S.R.
55 G3 Pokrovka Novosibirsk U.S.S.R.
55 B5 Pokrovka Orenburg U.S.S.R.
55 E3 Pokrovskoye U.S.S.R.
52 F3 Pokshen'ga R U.S.S.R.
71 E4 Pola Philippines
71 E4 Pola B Philippines
103 O6 Polacca Arizona
103 O6 Polacca Wasa R Arizona
16 D1 Pola de Laviana Spain
16 D1 Pola de Lena Spain
16 D1 Pola de Siero Spain
95 M3 Poland New York
31 K4 Poland rep Europe
31 K1 Polanow Poland
99 S4 Polar Wisconsin
101 M4 Polaris Montana
78 D2 Polatli Turkey
8 B7 Polbathick England
36 C3 Polch W Germany
133 C5 Polcura Chile
31 J2 Połczyn Zdrój Poland
138 D5 Polda S Australia
52 E3 Pole U.S.S.R.
70 G7 Poleang Sulawesi
37 P5 Poledník mt Czechoslovakia
80 C5 Poleg R Israel
9 G6 Polegate England
68 H5 Polei Monu Vietnam
37 P5 Poleň Czechoslovakia
146 D7 Pole of Inaccessibility Antarctica
45 L2 Polesella Italy
31 N1 Polessk U.S.S.R.
53 C8 Polesye marsh U.S.S.R.
55 D3 Polevskoy U.S.S.R.
70 F6 Polewali Sulawesi
48 G3 Polgár Hungary
48 E3 Polgárdi Hungary
55 E3 Polgovskoye U.S.S.R.
86 B4 Poli Cameroon
47 G8 Políaigos isld Greece
43 G8 Policastro, G. di Italy
31 H2 Police Poland
31 J6 Polička Czechoslovakia
85 F3 Polignac Algeria
19 J6 Poligny France
46 F3 Políkastron Greece
47 H5 Políkhnitos Greece
71 E3 Polillo isld Luzon Philippines
45 J3 Polinago Italy
38 H8 Polinik mt Austria
127 L3 Polink Pt Jamaica
79 C3 Polis Cyprus
52 D5 Polist' R U.S.S.R.
52 G3 Politovo U.S.S.R.
98 J8 Polk Nebraska
94 H5 Polk Pennsylvania
56 D1 Polkan, Gora mt U.S.S.R.
113 F9 Polk City Florida
33 P7 Polkritz E Germany
76 C5 Pollachi India
37 L5 Pollanten W Germany
110 F5 Pollard Arkansas
38 N7 Pöllau Austria
32 K9 Polle W Germany
122 A1 Pollet, L Quebec
43 G9 Pollino, M mt Italy
33 P7 Pollitz E Germany
100 J4 Pollock Idaho
111 D10 Pollock Louisiana
98 F4 Pollock S Dakota
143 E10 Pollock Reef W Australia
112 K3 Pollocksville N Carolina
118 F7 Pollockville Alberta
144 B6 Pollux mt New Zealand
29 N2 Polmak Finland
26 Q1 Polmak Norway
12 E2 Polmont Scotland
31 J6 Polná Czechoslovakia
52 C5 Polna U.S.S.R.
99 R8 Polo Illinois
110 B2 Polo Missouri
54 H9 Pologi U.S.S.R.
71 G7 Polomoloc Mindanao Philippines
47 J3 Polos Turkey
54 G2 Polotnanyy U.S.S.R.
52 C6 Polotsk U.S.S.R.
55 E4 Polovinnoye U.S.S.R.
52 H3 Polovniki U.S.S.R.
8 B7 Polperro England
83 K10 Polpitigama Sri Lanka
38 L7 Pöls R Austria
101 L2 Polson Montana
38 K7 Pöls-Tal V Austria
52 F2 Polta R U.S.S.R.
48 F2 Poltár Czechoslovakia
54 F7 Poltava U.S.S.R.
55 F4 Poltavka U.S.S.R.
121 P7 Poltimore Quebec
52 C5 Põltsamaa U.S.S.R.
55 E4 Poludino U.S.S.R.
55 D1 Polunochnoye U.S.S.R.
50 E4 Poluostrov Buzachi pen U.S.S.R.
106 D7 Polvadera New Mexico
29 O9 Polvijärvi Finland
118 L5 Polwarth Sask
31 L1 Półwysep Hel pen Poland
55 E1 Pol'yanovo U.S.S.R.
52 D1 Polyarnyy U.S.S.R.
116 N5 Polychrome Pass Alaska
47 F4 Políyiros Greece
56 C4 Polysayevo U.S.S.R.
37 N2 Pölzig E Germany
133 D2 Poma Argentina
144 B6 Pomahaka R New Zealand
133 D3 Poman Argentina
71 L9 Pomana Besar isld Flores Indonesia
16 B7 Pomarão Portugal
112 F3 Pomaria S Carolina
29 J10 Pomarkku Finland
130 G7 Pomba R Brazil
129 L5 Pombal Brazil
16 B5 Pombal Portugal
130 D7 Pombo, R Brazil
19 O18 Pomègues, Île France
31 G2 Pomerania reg E Germany/Poland
99 M7 Pomercy Iowa
103 O9 Pomerene Arizona
14 E2 Pomeroy N Ireland
94 E7 Pomeroy Ohio
100 H3 Pomeroy Washington
45 M6 Pomezia Italy
95 P5 Pomfret Connecticut
45 Q8 Pomigliano d'Arco Italy
110 C4 Pomme de Terre R Missouri
37 M5 Pommelsbrunn W Germany
107 P3 Pomoma Kansas
125 P9 Pomona Belize
102 G7 Pomona California
110 E5 Pomona Missouri
87 C11 Pomona Namibia
141 L7 Pomona Queensland
47 J2 Pomorie Bulgaria
52 E3 Pomorskiy Bereg coast U.S.S.R.
48 J1 Pomoryany U.S.S.R.
54 C8 Pomoshnaya U.S.S.R.
21 E8 Pompaire France
113 G11 Pompano Beach Florida
45 Q8 Pompei Italy
95 L4 Pompey New York
101 S4 Pompeys Pillar Montana
95 N5 Pompton Lakes New Jersey
88 D10 Pompué R Mozambique
123 L8 Pomquet Nova Scotia
33 R10 Pomssen E Germany
119 N6 Ponass L Sask
98 K7 Ponca Nebraska
107 N5 Ponca City Oklahoma
127 L5 Ponce Puerto Rico
111 L11 Ponce de Leon Florida
113 F12 Ponce de Leon B Florida
113 F8 Ponce de Leon Inlet Florida
111 F11 Ponchatoula Louisiana
124 H7 Poncitlán Mexico
107 N5 Pond Creek Oklahoma
109 K2 Ponder Texas
76 D5 Pondicherry India
115 M3 Pond Inlet N W Terr
89 F8 Pondoland reg S Africa
100 D8 Pondosa California
100 H4 Pondosa Oregon
99 M1 Ponemah Minnesota
44 E3 Ponente Italy
94 B6 Poneto Indiana
16 C2 Ponferrada Spain
86 A5 Pongara, Pte Gabon
145 F4 Pongaroa New Zealand
38 H7 Pongau reg Austria
70 G7 Pongkolaero Sulawesi
52 D2 Pon'goma U.S.S.R.
122 H9 Ponhook L Nova Scotia
33 T10 Ponickau E Germany
31 K4 Poniec Poland
71 H4 Poniki, Mt Sulawesi
70 G5 Ponindilisa, Tg C Sulawesi
68 A2 Ponnagyun Burma
68 B1 Ponnyadaung ra Burma
118 D6 Ponoka Alberta
55 B4 Ponomarevka U.S.S.R.
70 N9 Ponorogo Java
52 F2 Ponoy U.S.S.R.
52 E2 Ponoy R U.S.S.R.
18 E7 Pons France
17 H3 Pons Spain
45 J4 Ponsacco Italy
71 G5 Ponson isld Philippines
18 E9 Pontacq France
130 E9 Ponta Grossa Brazil
40 B3 Pontailler France
19 J5 Pontailler-sur-Saône France
19 O15 Pontaix France
22 E3 Pont-à-Marcq France
19 J4 Pont à Mousson France
129 G8 Ponta Porá Brazil
8 C4 Pontardawe Wales
8 B4 Pontarddulais Wales
19 K6 Pontarlier France
45 K4 Pontassieve Italy
20 C4 Pontaubault France
20 G3 Pont Audemer France
18 G7 Pontaumur France
22 F5 Pontavert France
121 M1 Pontax R Quebec
122 K3 Pontbriand B Quebec
40 G7 Pont-Canav Italy
19 Q14 Pontcharra France
21 J10 Pontcharraud France
111 F11 Pontchartrain, L Louisiana
21 A7 Pontchâteau France
19 O12 Pont d'Ain France
19 O15 Pont-de-Barret France
40 C4 Pont-de-Poitte France
19 J6 Pont de Vaux France
19 J6 Pont de Veyle France
20 E4 Pont d'Ouilly France
129 J6 Ponte Alta do Norte Brazil
42 E2 Pontebba Italy
45 R8 Pontecagnano Italy
45 P7 Pontecorvo Italy
20 E4 Pont-Ecrepin Fromentel France
16 B3 Ponte da Barca Portugal
129 G6 Ponte de Pedra Brazil
45 J4 Pontedera Italy
16 B5 Ponte de Sor Portugal
16 B3 Ponte do Lima Portugal
13 G6 Pontefract England
118 K9 Ponteix Sask
45 L2 Pontelagoscuro Italy
13 G3 Ponteland England
45 R7 Pontelandolfo Italy
45 M1 Pontelongo Italy
130 G7 Ponte Nova Brazil
18 E8 Pontenx les Forges France
16 B2 Pontevedra Spain
16 B2 Pontevedra prov Spain
113 F7 Ponte Vedra Beach Florida
41 M7 Pontevico Italy
20 C4 Pontfarcy France
22 G5 Pont Faverger France
20 H5 Pontgouin France
99 S9 Pontiac Illinois
94 D4 Pontiac Michigan
70 A5 Pontianak Kalimantan
43 E7 Pontinia Italy
18 D4 Pontivy France
18 C5 Pont l'Abbé France
122 H6 Pont Lafrance New Brunswick
40 A1 Pont la Ville France
20 F3 Pont-l'Evêque France
21 H7 Pontlevoy France
60 S2 Pōnto Japan
119 S4 Ponton Manitoba
20 B4 Pontorson France
111 G7 Pontotoc Mississippi
109 J5 Pontotoc Texas
44 G3 Pontremoli Italy
41 L4 Pontresina Switzerland
8 C3 Pontrhydfendigaid Wales
18 C4 Pontrieux France
8 D4 Pontrilas England
119 N5 Pontrilas Sask
121 T6 Pont Rouge Quebec
19 N16 Pont-St. Esprit France
22 D5 Pont-Ste. Maxence France
22 F3 Pont-sur-Sambre France
18 H4 Pont-sur-Yonne France
21 F6 Pontvallain France
121 M8 Pontypool Ontario
8 C4 Pontypool Wales
8 C4 Pontypridd Wales
145 E2 Ponui I New Zealand
101 O4 Pony Montana
43 E8 Ponza lt ho Italy
43 E8 Ponziane, Isole isld Italy
138 C4 Poochera S Australia
13 G6 Pool England
138 D2 Poolawanna L S Australia
144 B6 Poolburn Dam New Zealand
9 E6 Poole England
138 F3 Poole, Mt New S Wales
112 F5 Pooler Georgia
95 K7 Poolesville Maryland
15 C3 Poolewe Scotland
12 E1 Pool of Muckart Scotland
109 K3 Poolville Texas
76 A1 Poona India
139 G5 Pooncarie New S Wales
143 B8 Poondarrie,Mt W Australia
139 G4 Poopelloe, L New S Wales
128 E7 Poopó Bolivia
145 E1 Poor Knights Is New Zealand
116 K4 Poorman Alaska
86 C7 Popakabaka Zaïre
129 G3 Popakai Suriname
54 K8 Popasnaya U.S.S.R.
128 C3 Popayan Colombia
103 J8 Pope California
111 G7 Pope Mississippi
27 M14 Pope U.S.S.R.
99 N7 Popejoy Iowa
58 F1 Poperechnoye U.S.S.R.
22 D2 Poperinge Belgium
95 L8 Popes Creek Maryland
95 S3 Popham Beach Maine
51 K1 Popigay R U.S.S.R.
138 F5 Popiltah New S Wales
98 A1 Poplar Montana
99 P3 Poplar Wisconsin
110 F5 Poplar Bluff Missouri
101 U1 Poplar Cr Montana
119 U6 Poplar Pt Manitoba
111 G11 Poplarville Mississippi
125 K8 Popocatepetl vol Mexico
116 G9 Popof I Alaska
70 N10 Popoh Java
45 P5 Popoli Italy
136 K3 Popondetta Papua New Guinea
47 H1 Popovo Bulgaria
37 M5 Poppberg mt W Germany
25 H4 Poppe Netherlands
22 J1 Poppel Belgium
37 J3 Poppenhausen W Germany
45 L4 Poppi Italy
31 M6 Poprad Czechoslovakia
48 F1 Poprad R Czechoslovakia
128 E8 Poquis mt Chile/Arg
95 L9 Poquoson Virginia
145 F4 Porangahau New Zealand
74 C8 Porbander India
117 H9 Porcher I Br Col
133 D1 Porco Bolivia
16 E7 Porcuna Spain
116 R3 Porcupine R Alaska/Yukon Terr
141 G5 Porcupine R Queensland
90 H3 Porcupine Bank Atlantic Oc
101 T1 Porcupine Cr Montana
118 C8 Porcupine Hills Alberta
119 Q6 Porcupine Hills Man/Sask
99 R3 Porcupine Mts Michigan
119 O6 Porcupine Plain Sask
42 E3 Pordenoné Italy
47 G1 Pordim Bulgaria
42 F3 Poreč Yugoslavia
130 D8 Porecatu Brazil
55 D2 Porech'ye U.S.S.R.
52 G6 Poretskoye U.S.S.R.
145 E4 Porewa New Zealand
85 E6 Porga Benin
29 J10 Pori Finland
145 F4 Porirua New Zealand
80 F3 Poriyya Israel
26 L5 Porjus Sweden
29 L12 Porkala Finland
28 N3 Porkere Faeroes
52 C5 Porkhov U.S.S.R.
128 F1 Porlamar Venezuela
41 K5 Porlezza Italy
8 C5 Porlock England
37 L6 Pörnbach W Germany
21 A7 Pornic France
71 G5 Poro isld Philippines
52 E3 Porog Arkhangelsk U.S.S.R.
52 J4 Porog Komi U.S.S.R.
59 M2 Poronaysk U.S.S.R.
68 G6 Porong R Cambodia
60 Q1 Poronupuri yama mt Japan
145 E3 Porootarao New Zealand
47 F7 Póros isld Greece
60 Q1 Poroshiri yama mt Japan
52 D3 Porosozero U.S.S.R.
52 H3 Porozhsk U.S.S.R.
56 F3 Porozhskiy U.S.S.R.
146 H3 Porpoise B Antarctica
19 Q18 Porquerolles, I. de France
120 K4 Porquis Junct Ontario
40 F3 Pörrentruy Switzerland
45 J3 Porretta Terme Italy
16 B2 Porriño Spain
26 N1 Porsa Norway
26 O1 Pórsangen inlet Norway
27 D12 Porsgrunn Norway
33 Q9 Porst E Germany
47 L5 Porsük R Turkey
78 C2 Porsuk R Turkey
128 F7 Portachuelo Bolivia
138 E5 Port Adelaide S Australia
14 E2 Portadown N Ireland
144 B7 Port Adventure New Zealand
14 F2 Portaferry N Ireland
116 N6 Portage Alaska
95 S7 Portage Maine
101 O2 Portage Montana
94 J6 Portage Pennsylvania
122 H7 Portage Pr Edward I
101 N8 Portage Utah
94 D5 Portage R Ohio
110 F3 Portage des Sioux Missouri
122 G6 Portage I New Brunswick
119 T9 Portage la Prairie Manitoba
110 G5 Portageville Missouri
94 J4 Portageville New York
103 P10 Portal Arizona
112 F5 Portal Georgia
98 D1 Portal N Dakota
14 D3 Portalaoise Irish Rep
117 L11 Port Alberni Br Col
145 E2 Port Albert New Zealand
120 J9 Port Albert Ontario
139 H7 Port Albert Victoria
16 C5 Portalegre Portugal
106 G7 Portales New Mexico
117 F7 Port Alexander Alaska
121 U4 Port Alfred Quebec
89 E9 Port Alfred S Africa
117 K10 Port Alice Br Col
94 J5 Port Allegany Pennsylvania
111 E11 Port Allen Louisiana
141 K6 Port Alma Queensland
117 M11 Port Angeles Washington
109 K8 Port Aransas Texas
102 A3 Port Arena California
14 D3 Portarlington Irish Rep
Port Arthur see Lüshun
139 J9 Port Arthur Tasmania
109 N6 Port Arthur Texas
12 B2 Port Askaig Scotland
138 D4 Port Augusta S Australia
123 O5 Port-au-Port Nfld
123 N5 Port-au-Port pen Nfld
127 H5 Port-au-Prince Haiti
94 D2 Port Austin Michigan
32 J8 Porta Westfalica W Germany
20 B3 Portbail France
12 C2 Port Bannatyne Scotland
111 E11 Port Barre Louisiana
71 D5 Port Barton Palawan Philippines
87 H11 Port Bergé Madagascar
123 L8 Port Bickerton Nova Scotia
68 A7 Port Blair Andaman Is
109 N6 Port Bolivar Texas
17 K2 Port Bou Spain/France
85 D8 Port Bouet Ivory Coast
140 D2 Port Bradshaw inlet N Terr Aust
140 B1 Port Bremer inlet N Terr Aust
20 D5 Port Brillet France
120 J10 Port Bruce Ontario
120 K10 Port Burwell Ontario
99 Q8 Port Byron Illinois
95 L3 Port Byron New York
75 N7 Port Canning India
121 L7 Port Carling Ontario
13 E4 Port Carlisle England
122 F3 Port Cartier Quebec
144 D7 Port Chalmers New Zealand
145 E2 Port Charles New Zealand
15 B5 Port Charlotte Scotland
95 O6 Port Chester New York
111 G12 Port Chicot I Louisiana
116 D4 Port Clarence hbr Alaska
117 G9 Port Clements Br Col
94 E5 Port Clinton Ohio
141 K5 Port Clinton inlet Queensland
95 S3 Port Clyde Maine
121 L10 Port Colborne Ontario
117 M11 Port Coquitlam Br Col
68 A6 Port Cornwallis Andaman Is
121 L9 Port Credit Ontario
19 Q18 Port Cros, I. de France
141 K6 Port Curtis inlet Queensland
121 L9 Port Dalhousie Ontario
122 H5 Port Daniel Quebec
133 F8 Port Darwin Falkland Is
139 H9 Port Davey Tasmania
19 N18 Port de Bouc France
102 A1 Port Delgada California
127 H5 Port-de-Paix Haiti
21 G7 Port-de-Piles France
69 E11 Port Dickson Malaysia
141 H3 Port Douglas Queensland
120 K10 Port Dover Ontario
123 K9 Port Dufferin Nova Scotia
111 G12 Porte a la Hache Louisiana
99 U4 Porte des Morts Wisconsin
117 H8 Port Edward Br Col
89 G8 Port Edward S Africa
130 G4 Porteirinha Brazil
129 H4 Portel Brazil
16 B6 Portel Portugal
130 H7 Portela Brazil
122 H7 Port Elgin New Brunswick
120 J8 Port Elgin Ontario
127 O8 Port Elizabeth Lesser Antilles
89 D9 Port Elizabeth S Africa
22 B2 Portel, le France
12 B2 Port Ellen Scotland
130 B9 Porteña R Argentina
20 D3 Port-en-Bessin France
98 K5 Porter Minnesota
98 C7 Porter Nebraska
107 P6 Porter Oklahoma
112 D4 Porterdale Georgia
99 T4 Porterfield Wisconsin
12 D5 Port Erin I of Man U.K.
117 H6 Porter Landing Br Col
15 G3 Port Errol Scotland
102 E5 Porterville California
87 C12 Porterville S Africa
127 K3 Port Esquivel Jamaica
140 B1 Port Essington inlet N Terr Aust
8 B4 Port Eynon Wales
123 L8 Port Felix Nova Scotia
145 E2 Port Fitzroy New Zealand
Port Francqui see Ilebo
86 A6 Port Gentil Gabon
122 G9 Port George Nova Scotia
111 E10 Port Gibson Mississippi
12 D2 Port Glasgow Scotland
14 E2 Portglenone N Ireland
15 E3 Portgordon Grampian Scotland
145 E4 Port Gore New Zealand
116 M7 Port Graham Alaska
143 A8 Port Gregory B W Australia
122 H8 Port Greville Nova Scotia
8 C4 Porth Wales
85 F8 Port Harcourt Nigeria
117 K10 Port Hardy Br Col
145 D4 Port Hardy New Zealand
123 L8 Port Hastings C Breton I, N Scotia
123 L8 Port Hawkesbury C Breton I, N Scotia
8 C5 Porthcawl Wales
142 C5 Port Hedland W Australia
127 L3 Port Henderson Jamaica
95 O3 Port Henry New York
Port Herald see Nsanje
100 J1 Porthill Idaho
8 B2 Porth Neigwl Wales
123 L8 Port Hood C Breton I, N Scotia
94 E3 Port Hope Michigan
121 M9 Port Hope Ontario
123 Q1 Port Hope Simpson Labrador
102 E7 Port Hueneme California
94 E4 Port Huron Michigan
120 H10 Port Huron Ontario
45 Q8 Portici Italy
16 B7 Portimão Portugal
29 M5 Portimo Finland
12 C1 Portinnisherrich Scotland
107 M2 Portis Kansas
8 B6 Port Isaac England
109 K9 Port Isabel Texas
99 T2 Port Isabelle Michigan
8 D5 Portishead England
139 K5 Port Jackson New S Wales
145 E2 Port Jackson New Zealand
95 O6 Port Jefferson Long I, N Y
95 N5 Port Jervis New York
127 J3 Port Kaiser Jamaica
140 A2 Port Keats N Terr Aust
139 K5 Port Kembla New S Wales
127 P6 Portland Barbados
106 E3 Portland Colorado
94 C6 Portland Indiana
95 R3 Portland Maine
94 C4 Portland Michigan
98 J2 Portland N Dakota
139 J5 Portland New S Wales
145 E1 Portland New Zealand
121 O8 Portland Ontario
100 C4 Portland Oregon
110 K5 Portland Tennessee
109 K8 Portland Texas
138 F7 Portland Victoria
127 M2 Portland parish Jamaica
127 K3 Portland Bight Jamaica
8 D7 Portland, Bill of head England
139 J8 Portland, C Tasmania
117 H8 Portland Canal Br Col/Alaska
123 P3 Portland Cr. Pond Nfld
141 G6 Portland Downs Queensland
8 D6 Portland Hbr England
145 F3 Portland I New Zealand
117 H8 Portland Inlet Br Col
127 K3 Portland Ridge Jamaica
141 G2 Portland Roads Queensland
126 F6 Portland Rock Caribbean
71 E8 Port Languyan Philippines
139 H8 Port Latta Tasmania
109 L7 Port Lavaca Texas
14 D4 Portlaw Irish Rep
144 B4 Port Levy New Zealand
95 M3 Port Leyden New York
138 D5 Port Lincoln S Australia
12 D4 Port Logan Scotland
120 K7 Port Loring Ontario
18 C5 Port Louis France
127 N4 Port Louis Guadeloupe W I
83 L14 Port Louis Kerguelen
83 L12 Port Louis Mauritius
140 D3 Port McArthur B N Terr Aust
138 F7 Port MacDonnell S Australia
121 L8 Port McNicoll Ontario
139 L4 Port Macquarie New S Wales
8 B2 Portmadog Wales
122 F10 Port Maitland Nova Scotia
121 L10 Port Maitland Ontario
109 K9 Port Mansfield Texas
115 N6 Port Manvers Labrador
127 L2 Port Maria Jamaica
146 J3 Port Martin Antarctica
94 J6 Port Matilda Pennsylvania
113 G11 Port Mayaca Florida
122 H9 Port Medway Nova Scotia
117 M11 Port Mellon Br Col
122 H4 Port Menier Quebec
116 G8 Port Moller Alaska
117 M11 Port Moody Br Col
127 M3 Port Morant Jamaica
136 K3 Port Moresby Papua New Guinea
123 N7 Port Morien C Breton I, N Scotia
20 H3 Port Mort France
122 H10 Port Mouton Nova Scotia
141 F1 Port Musgrave inlet Queensland
15 C4 Portnacroish Scotland
12 B2 Portnahaven Scotland
109 O6 Port Neches Texas
138 D5 Port Neill S Australia
126 G3 Port Nelson Bahamas
101 N7 Portneuf Idaho
121 S5 Portneuf, Parc Quebec
122 C5 Portneuf, R Quebec
145 G4 Port Nicholson New Zealand
138 E6 Port Noarlunga S Australia
87 C11 Port Nolloth S Africa
95 M7 Port Norris New Jersey
115 N6 Port-Nouveau Québec Quebec
129 K4 Pôrto Brazil
16 B3 Porto Portugal
128 E5 Pôrto Acre Brazil
130 D7 Pôrto Alegre Mato Grosso Brazil
131 H3 Pôrto Alegre Rio Grande do Sul Brazil
87 B9 Porto Alexandre Angola
87 B8 Porto Amboim Angola
Porto Amelia see Pemba Mozambique
129 G6 Porto Artur Brazil
144 D7 Portobello New Zealand
13 E2 Portobello Scotland
130 E10 Pôrto Belo Brazil
116 L8 Port O'Brian Alaska
130 C9 Pôrto Britânia Brazil
43 C7 Porto Cervo Sardinia
109 L7 Port O'Connor Texas
16 B3 Porto de Leixões Portugal
129 H4 Pôrto de Mos Brazil
129 H6 Pôrto dos Meinacos Brazil
43 F11 Porto Empedocle Sicily
128 G7 Pôrto Espiridião Brazil
42 C6 Portoferraio Elba Italy
44 F3 Portofino Italy
12 D1 Port of Menteith Scotland
15 B2 Port of Ness Scotland
127 O2 Port of Spain Trinidad
45 M2 Porto Garibaldi Italy
129 H3 Pôrto Grande Brazil
42 E3 Portogruaro Italy
129 G7 Pôrto Jofre Brazil
102 D2 Portola California
29 J9 Pörtom Finland
45 L2 Portomaggiore Italy
44 D4 Porto Maurizio Italy
88 H9 Porto Mocambo Mozambique
129 G8 Pôrto Murtinho Brazil
129 J6 Pôrto Nacional Brazil
85 E7 Porto Novo Benin
113 G8 Port Orange Florida
117 M12 Port Orchard Washington
42 F5 Porto Recanati Italy
100 A7 Port Orford Oregon
133 G2 Pôrto San José Brazil
42 D6 Porto San Stefano Italy
85 A2 Pôrto Santo isld Madeira
129 H8 Pôrto São José Brazil
130 H5 Pôrto Seguro Brazil
45 M2 Porto Tolle Italy
43 B8 Porto Torres Sardinia
133 G3 Pôrto União Brazil
128 F5 Pôrto Velho Brazil
44 G3 Portovenere Italy
128 B4 Portoviejo Ecuador
12 C4 Portpatrick Scotland
140 B2 Port Patterson inlet N Terr Aust
144 A7 Port Pegasus New Zealand
121 M8 Port Perry Ontario
139 G7 Port Phillip B Victoria
138 E5 Port Pirie S Australia
114 H4 Port Radium N W Terr
8 A7 Portreath England
15 B3 Portree Scotland

62 Portreeve — Pyaozero, Oz

118 J8 Portreeve Sask
83 M8 Port Refuge Cocos Is Indian Oc
100 A1 Port Renfrew Br Col
123 T5 Port Rexton Nfld
102 A4 Port Reyes California
100 B1 Port Roberts Washington
144 D5 Port Robinson New Zealand
140 D2 Port Roper *inlet* N Terr Aust
120 K10 Port Rowan Ontario
127 L3 Port Royal Jamaica
112 G5 Port Royal S Carolina
95 K8 Port Royal Virginia
122 G9 Port Royal Nat. Hist. Park Ontario
14 E1 Portrush N Ireland
79 C7 Port Said Egypt
113 B8 Port St. Joe Florida
89 F8 Port St Johns S Africa
19 N18 Port St. Louis France
18 F8 Port St. Marie France
21 B7 Port St. Père France
14 D1 Portsalon Irish Rep
94 E3 Port Sanilac Michigan
102 D6 Port San Luis California
123 P3 Port Saunders Nfld
38 K8 Pörtschach Austria
89 G8 Port Shepstone S Africa
117 H8 Port Simpson Br Col
142 D4 Port Smith *B* W Australia
127 O7 Portsmouth Dominica
9 E6 Portsmouth England
99 L8 Portsmouth Iowa
112 L2 Portsmouth N Carolina
95 R3 Portsmouth New Hampshire
94 E8 Portsmouth Ohio
121 O8 Portsmouth Ontario
95 Q5 Portsmouth Rhode I
95 L10 Portsmouth Virginia
12 C1 Portsonachan Scotland
15 F3 Portsoy Scotland
120 J10 Port Stanley Ontario
139 K5 Port Stephens New S Wales
14 E1 Port Stewart N Ireland
141 G2 Port Stewart *inlet* Queensland
86 G2 Port Sudan Sudan
8 C4 Port Talbot Wales
71 F4 Port Tambang Philippines
79 C9 Port Taufiq Egypt
127 O2 Port Tembladora Trinidad
29 M3 Porttipahdan tekojärvi *L* Finland
114 G8 Port Tofino Br Col
117 M11 Port Townsend Washington
16 B7 Portugal *rep*
83 J9 Portugal B Sri Lanka
123 U6 Portugal Cove Nfld
17 F1 Portugalete Spain
128 E2 Portuguesa *state* Venezuela
Portuguese Guinea *see* Guinea-Bissau *rep*
14 C3 Portumna Irish Rep
123 T5 Port Union Nfld
18 H10 Port Vendres France
102 F8 Port Vicente California
88 D1 Port Victoria Kenya
94 J4 Portville New York
138 E5 Port Vincent S Australia
52 D1 Port Vladimir U.S.S.R.
138 E5 Port Wakefield S Australia
142 F2 Port Warrender *inlet* W Australia
99 T6 Port Washington Wisconsin
142 B5 Port Weld *B* W Australia
116 N6 Port Wells *inlet* Alaska
112 F5 Port Wentworth Georgia
12 D4 Port William Scotland
122 H8 Port Williams Nova Scotia
99 P3 Port Wing Wisconsin
107 P6 Porum Oklahoma
127 K2 Porus Jamaica
133 C8 Porvenir Chile
108 C5 Porvenir Texas
52 D2 Por'ya Guba U.S.S.R.
36 C2 Porz W Germany
16 E5 Porzuna Spain
16 E5 Porzuna, Sa. de *mts* Spain
43 C8 Posada *R* Sardinia
133 F3 Posadas Argentina
16 D7 Posadas Spain
41 M5 Poschiavo Switzerland
141 H7 Poseidon Queensland
94 D1 Posen Michigan
110 J3 Poseyville Indiana
52 E5 Poshekhonye U.S.S.R.
119 O1 Poshkokagan L Ontario
47 F5 Posídhion, Ákr *C* Greece
41 O6 Posina *R* Italy
37 O5 Pösing W Germany
29 N5 Posio Finland
45 Q8 Positano Italy
70 G5 Poso Sulawesi
78 J1 Posof Turkey
129 J6 Posse Brazil
37 N3 Posseck E Germany
146 K6 Possession I Antarctica
37 M2 Pössneck E Germany
38 M8 Possruck Yugoslavia
109 J3 Possum Kingdom L Texas
100 E5 Post Oregon
37 N6 Postau W Germany
37 L5 Postbauer-Heng W Germany
8 C6 Postbridge England
115 M6 Poste-de-la-Baleine Quebec
68 H6 Poste Deshayes Cambodia
83 M12 Poste, R du Mauritius
85 E4 Poste Weygand Algeria
100 J2 Post Falls Idaho
114 J7 Posthern Sask
71 J8 Postiljon Pulau *isld* Indonesia
89 C7 Postmasburg S Africa
129 H6 Pôsto Alto Manissaua Brazil
128 C4 Posto Bobonazo Peru
42 F3 Postojna Yugoslavia
99 P6 Postville Iowa
42 H5 Posušje Yugoslavia
71 K9 Pota Indonesia
124 D4 Pótam Mexico
47 G3 Potamoí Greece
46 F8 Potamós Greece
50 H2 Potapovo U.S.S.R.
128 G2 Potaro *R* Guyana
89 E6 Potchefstroom S Africa
48 J6 Potcoava Romania
130 H5 Poté Brazil
107 Q6 Poteau Oklahoma
107 Q7 Poteau *R* Okla/Ark
109 J6 Poteet Texas
47 G1 Potelu Lacul *L* Romania
130 J8 Potengi *R* Brazil
43 G8 Potenza Italy
144 A7 Poteriteri, L New Zealand
16 D1 Potes Spain
89 F5 Potgietersrus S Africa
109 J6 Poth Texas
100 F2 Potholes Res Washington
129 K5 Poti *R* Brazil
20 E4 Potigny France
85 G6 Potiskum Nigeria
71 K9 Potjo Mandasawu *mt* Indonesia
100 J3 Potlatch Idaho
89 B8 Potloer *mt* S Africa
48 K6 Potlogi Romania
101 M3 Potomac Montana
94 J7 Potomac S. Branch *R* W Virginia
133 D1 Potosí Bolivia
110 F4 Potosi Missouri
133 D2 Potosí *dep* Bolivia
103 J6 Potosi Mt Nevada
71 F5 Pototan Panay Philippines
133 D3 Potrerillos Chile
131 B2 Potro, Cerro de *peak* Chile
33 S8 Potsdam E Germany
95 N2 Potsdam New York
33 R7 Potsdam *reg* E Germany
141 G3 Pottalah Cr Queensland
37 L4 Pottenstein W Germany
98 C8 Potter Nebraska
120 K4 Potter Ontario
9 E5 Potterne England
9 F4 Potter's Bar England
102 A2 Potter Valley California
94 C4 Potterville Michigan
37 L6 Pottmes W Germany
9 F3 Potton England
109 L2 Pottsboro Texas
111 G7 Potts Camp Mississippi
95 M6 Pottstown Pennsylvania
95 L6 Pottsville Pennsylvania
109 J4 Pottsville Texas
83 L11 Pottuvil Sri Lanka
107 N4 Potwin Kansas
21 C6 Pouancé France
68 F3 Pou Bia *mt* Laos
117 N8 Pouce Coupé Br Col
123 U6 Pouch Cove Nfld
95 O5 Poughkeepsie New York
18 H5 Pougues les Eaux France
21 H7 Pouillé France
18 E9 Pouillon France
18 J5 Pouilly en Auxois France
21 I7 Poulaines France
122 B5 Poulin de Courval, L Quebec
68 J5 Poulo Canton, Is de Vietnam
69 G8 Poulo Dama, Iles Vietnam
68 J6 Poulo Gambir, Cu Lao *isld* Vietnam
95 O3 Poultney Vermont
13 E6 Poulton-le-Fylde England
68 E4 Pou Miang *mt* Thailand
99 S4 Pound Wisconsin
9 F5 Pound Hill England
19 P18 Pourcieux France
145 F4 Pourerere New Zealand
145 G3 Pourewa I New Zealand
146 F13 Pourquoi Pas I Antarctica
40 E6 Pourri, Mont France
20 G2 Pourville France
68 F3 Pou San *mt* Laos
68 F3 Pou Sao *mt* Laos
68 H5 Pou Set *mt* Laos
129 G6 Pouso Alegre Mato Grosso Brazil
130 F8 Pouso Alegre Minas Gerais Brazil
29 O6 Poussu Finland
144 A7 Poutama I New Zealand
145 E2 Pouto New Zealand
121 Q3 Poutrincourt, L Quebec
40 D1 Pouxeux France
21 D8 Pouzauges France
48 E1 Pov Bystrica Czechoslovakia
52 D3 Povenets U.S.S.R.
145 F3 Poverty Bay New Zealand
9 F5 Povey Cross England
45 J2 Poviglio Italy
48 F6 Povlen *mt* Yugoslavia
16 B3 Póvoa de Varzim Portugal
65 J3 Povorotnyy, Mys *C* U.S.S.R.
115 M5 Povungnituk Quebec
121 L6 Powassan Ontario
101 T5 Powder *R* Wyo/Mont
106 C3 Powderhorn Colorado
100 H5 Powder R Oregon
98 A4 Powderville Montana
113 K11 Powel Cay *isld* Bahamas
103 K7 Powell Arizona
98 E5 Powell S Dakota
99 R3 Powell Wisconsin
101 R5 Powell Wyoming
139 G2 Powell *R* Queensland
94 D10 Powell *R* Tenn/Virg
100 D5 Powell Butte Oregon
140 C4 Powell Creek N Terr Aust
146 C14 Powell I S Orkney Is
103 O4 Powell, L Ariz/Utah
106 D2 Powell, Mt Colorado
102 F3 Powell Mt Nevada
126 F2 Powell Pt Eleuthera Bahamas
117 L10 Powell River Br Col
94 F8 Powellton W Virginia
101 O2 Power Montana
99 T4 Powers Michigan
100 A7 Powers Oregon
98 D1 Powers L N Dakota
110 C1 Powersville Missouri
111 C10 Powhatan Louisiana
94 K9 Powhatan Virginia
107 P2 Powhattan Kansas
8 D3 Powick England
141 H5 Powlathanga Queensland
95 O4 Pownal Vermont
8 C3 Powys *co* Wales
130 C5 Poxoreu *R* Brazil
67 E2 Poyang Hu *L* China
111 D7 Poyen Arkansas
99 S5 Poygan, L Wisconsin
31 K7 Poysdorf Austria
124 C5 Poza Grande Mexico
78 E3 Pozanti Turkey
48 G6 Požarevac Yugoslavia
125 L7 Poza Rica Mexico
59 K2 Pozharskoye U.S.S.R.
52 J5 Pozhva U.S.S.R.
22 D3 Pozières France
140 D5 Pozieres,Mt N Terr Aust
31 K3 Poznań Poland
102 D6 Pozo California
17 F7 Pozo Alcón Spain
133 D2 Pozo Almonte Chile
16 D6 Pozoblanco Spain
103 J9 Pozo Cenizo Mexico
17 F6 Pozohondo Spain
103 J9 Pozo Salado Mexico
103 N10 Pozo Verde Mexico
52 H4 Poztykeros U.S.S.R.
133 D2 Pozuelos, L. de Argentina
45 J1 Pozzolengo Italy
45 L1 Pozzonuovo Italy
45 Q8 Pozzuoli Italy
68 F2 P. Phac Mo *mt* Vietnam
85 D7 Pra *R* Ghana
31 L2 Prabuty Poland
45 J3 Pracchia Italy
68 D7 Pracham Hiang, Laem Thailand
30 H7 Prachatice Czechoslovakia
68 E5 Prachin Buri Thailand
68 D7 Prachuap Khiri Khan Thailand
16 C1 Pradairo Spain
31 K5 Praděd *mt* Czechoslovakia
18 G10 Prades France
70 P9 Pradjekan Java
28 E2 Præstbro Denmark
28 J6 Præsto Denmark
Præstø *co see* Storstrøm and Roskilde *counties*
38 N9 Pragersk Yugoslavia
38 F7 Prägraten Austria
Prague *see* Praha
107 O6 Prague Oklahoma
31 H5 Praha Czechoslovakia
21 E9 Prahecq France
48 K5 Prahova Romania
48 H6 Prahova Yugoslavia
48 K6 Prahova *R* Romania
133 G4 Praia Albardão *beach* Brazil
48 J4 Praid Romania
129 H4 Prainha Brazil
122 B3 Praires, L. des Quebec
109 K6 Prairia Lea Texas
100 K6 Prairie Idaho
141 G5 Prairie Queensland
110 F1 Prairie City Illinois
100 G5 Prairie City Oregon
107 K2 Prairie Dog Cr Kansas
108 F1 Prairie Dog Town Fork *R* Texas
99 P6 Prairie du Chien Wisconsin
99 R6 Prairie du Sac Wisconsin
110 B6 Prairie Grove Arkansas
109 L4 Prairie Hill Texas
119 P6 Prairie River Sask
110 J2 Prairieton Indiana
107 L2 Prairie View Kansas
111 F11 Prairieville Louisiana
94 E9 Praise Kentucky
70 Q10 Praja Indonesia
68 F5 Prakhon Chai Thailand
40 E7 Pralognan France
42 E2 Pramaggiore *mt* Italy
70 N9 Prambanan Java
37 O3 Prameny Czechoslovakia
69 D8 Pram, Khao *mt* Thailand
68 D6 Pran *R* Thailand
68 D6 Pran Buri Thailand
38 K7 Prankerhöhe *mt* Austria
69 D11 Prapat Sumatra
40 B2 Praslay France
83 J12 Praslin *isld* Seychelles
47 J9 Prasonísi, Akr *C* Rhodes Greece
31 L4 Praszka Poland
129 J7 Prata *R* Brazil
Pratas *isld see* Dongsha Qundao
33 R9 Pratau E Germany
17 J3 Prat de Llobregat Spain
41 L4 Prätigau *V* Switzerland
45 K4 Prato Italy
45 R8 Prátola Serra Italy
45 L4 Pratomagno Italy
42 D5 Pratomagno *mt* Italy
45 H3 Prato, Mt Italy
45 L4 Pratovecchio Italy
18 G10 Prats-de-Mollo France
107 M4 Pratt Kansas
119 T9 Pratt Manitoba
95 N4 Prattsville New York
111 K9 Prattville Alabama
40 B2 Prauthoy France
31 N1 Pravdinsk U.S.S.R.
54 J1 Pravdinskiy U.S.S.R.
70 M9 Prav, G *mt* Java
16 C1 Pravia Spain
8 C7 Prawle Pt England
21 H7 Préaux France
37 O3 Přebuz Czechoslovakia
20 C4 Precey France
52 D6 Prechistoye U.S.S.R.
20 K3 Précy-sur-Oise France
45 L3 Predappio Italy
42 D2 Predazzo Italy
37 O5 Predigtstuhl *mt* W Germany
38 M8 Preding Austria
38 J7 Predlitz Austria
38 F7 Predoi Italy
44 E2 Predosa Italy
51 O2 Predporozhnyy U.S.S.R.
119 P7 Preeceville Sask
20 E5 Pré-en-Pail France
33 M4 Preetz W Germany
31 M1 Pregolya *R* U.S.S.R.
127 J10 Pregonero Venezuela
18 E8 Preignac France
52 C6 Preiļi U.S.S.R.
121 M4 Preissac Quebec
68 G6 Prek Kak Cambodia
68 H6 Prek Preas *R* Cambodia
68 G7 Prek Sandek Cambodia
68 F7 Prek Taley *R* Cambodia
143 F9 Premier Downs W Australia
8 B3 Pren-gwyn Wales
46 D4 Prenjas Albania
33 T6 Prenzlau E Germany
144 A7 Preservation Inlet New Zealand
130 D8 Presidente Prudente Brazil
108 C6 Presidio Texas
13 F6 Preston England
101 O7 Preston Idaho
95 M8 Preston Maryland
99 O6 Preston Minnesota
110 C4 Preston Missouri
103 J3 Preston Nevada
107 P6 Preston Oklahoma
9 E5 Preston Candover England
109 O9 Preston Hollow Texas
13 F2 Prestonpans Scotland
94 E9 Prestonsburg Kentucky
13 F6 Prestwich England
12 D3 Prestwick Scotland
129 K6 Preto *R* Bahia Brazil
129 J7 Prêto *R* Minas Gerais Brazil
128 F4 Prêto do Igapó Açu *R* Brazil
89 F5 Pretoria S Africa
33 R9 Prettin E Germany
95 L7 Prettyboy Res Maryland
107 M4 Pretty Prairie Kansas
33 O7 Pretzier E Germany
33 R9 Pretzsch E Germany
21 G8 Preuilly-sur-Claise France
38 L8 Prevalje Yugoslavia
46 D6 Préveza Greece
106 B6 Prewitt New Mexico
106 G1 Prewitt Res Colorado
20 H4 Prey France
68 G7 Prey Lovea Cambodia
68 G7 Prey Veng Cambodia
45 P5 Prezza Italy
54 H9 Priazovskaya Vozvyshenost' *uplands* U.S.S.R.
116 D8 Pribilof Is Bering Sea
30 H6 Příbram Czechoslovakia
95 M7 Price Maryland
98 F2 Price N Dakota
122 D5 Price Quebec
103 O2 Price Utah
103 O2 Price *R* Utah
68 A6 Price, C Andaman Is
106 B1 Price Creek Colorado
117 J9 Price I Br Col
111 H11 Prichard Alabama
100 K2 Prichard Idaho
54 E9 Prichernomorskaya Nizmennost' *lowland* U.S.S.R.
37 J4 Prichsenstadt W Germany
127 P5 Prickly Pt Grenada
109 J4 Priddy Texas
54 D7 Pridneprovskaya Nizmennost' *lowland* U.S.S.R.
54 C8 Pridneprovskaya Vozvyshennost' *uplands* U.S.S.R.
17 F4 Priego Spain
16 E7 Priego de C Spain
27 M15 Priekule Latvia U.S.S.R.
27 M16 Priekulė Lithuania U.S.S.R.
33 Q5 Priemerburg E Germany
89 C7 Prieska S Africa
37 M1 Priessnitz E Germany
33 T10 Priestewitz E Germany
100 J1 Priest L Idaho
127 M2 Priestman's River Jamaica
100 F3 Priest Rapids Washington
100 J1 Priest River Idaho
117 P11 Priest River Idaho
31 L7 Prievidza Czechoslovakia
33 Q6 Prignitz *reg* E Germany
56 C4 Priiskovyy U.S.S.R.
42 H4 Prijedor Yugoslavia
53 G9 Prikaspiyskaya Nizmennost *lowlands* U.S.S.R.
46 E3 Prilep Yugoslavia
54 D6 Priluki U.S.S.R.
40 B7 Primarette France
118 H6 Primate Sask
37 O4 Přimda Czechoslovakia
131 D3 Primero, R Argentina
139 J8 Prime Seal I Tasmania
99 L6 Primghar Iowa
52 C4 Primorsk U.S.S.R.
59 K3 Primorskiy U.S.S.R.
56 F5 Primorskiy Khrebet *mts* U.S.S.R.
59 K2 Primorskiy Kray *reg* U.S.S.R.
47 J2 Primorsko Bulgaria
54 J9 Primorskoye U.S.S.R.
122 J7 Prim, Pt Pr Edward I
117 F5 Primrose *R* Br Col/Yukon Terr
118 H4 Primrose L Sask
36 B5 Prims *R* W Germany
36 C4 Primstal W Germany
118 J6 Prince Sask
89 C9 Prince Albert S Africa
119 M5 Prince Albert Sask
118 L5 Prince Albert Nat. Park Sask
114 H3 Prince Albert Pen N W Terr
114 G3 Prince Alfred, C N W Terr
115 M4 Prince Charles I N W Terr
146 C5 Prince Charles Mts Antarctica
146 D15 Prince Charles Str S Shetland Is
121 O9 Prince Edward B Ontario
90 M14 Prince Edward I Indian Oc
115 N8 Prince Edward I *prov* Canada
122 J7 Prince Edward I. Nat. Park Canada
95 L8 Prince Frederick Maryland
142 F3 Prince Frederick Harb W Australia
117 M9 Prince George Br Col
114 J2 Prince Gustaf Adolf Sea N W Terr
116 C4 Prince of Wales, C Alaska
117 G8 Prince of Wales I Alaska
115 J3 Prince of Wales I N W Terr
141 F1 Prince of Wales I Queensland
114 H3 Prince of Wales Str N W Terr
146 G8 Prince Olav Mts Antarctica
114 H2 Prince Patrick I N W Terr
115 K3 Prince Regent Inlet N W Terr
142 F3 Prince Regent R W Australia
117 H8 Prince Rupert Br Col
130 H9 Princesa Isabel Brazil
Princes Is *see* Kızıl Adalar
Princes Lake Ontario *see* Wallace
9 F4 Princes Risborough England
95 M8 Princess Anne Maryland
141 G2 Princess Charlotte B Queensland
146 D4 Princess Elizabeth Land Antarctica
142 F3 Princess May Ra W Australia
144 A6 Princess Mts New Zealand
143 D7 Princess Ra W Australia
117 J9 Princess Royal I Br Col
127 O3 Prince's Town Trinidad
9 E3 Princethorpe England
117 N11 Princeton Br Col
102 B2 Princeton California
99 R8 Princeton Illinois
110 J3 Princeton Indiana
110 J4 Princeton Kentucky
95 U1 Princeton Maine
99 T3 Princeton Michigan
99 N4 Princeton Minnesota
99 N9 Princeton Missouri
112 J2 Princeton N Carolina
95 N6 Princeton New Jersey
99 R6 Princeton Wisconsin
94 F9 Princeton W Virginia
8 C6 Princetown England
99 R9 Princeville Illinois
121 T6 Princeville Quebec
116 O6 Prince William Sound Alaska
141 J6 Princhester Queensland
86 A5 Príncipe *isld* G of Guinea
128 F6 Principe da Beira Brazil
100 E5 Prineville Oregon
98 C6 Pringle S Dakota
108 C8 Pringle Texas
19 Q13 Pringy France
115 P5 Prins Christians Sund Greenland
25 C5 Prinsenhage Netherlands
68 C6 Prinsep I Burma
146 A9 Prinsesse Astrid Kyst Antarctica
146 A8 Prinsesse Ragnhild Kyst Antarctica
146 A7 Prins Harald Kyst Antarctica
50 A1 Prins Karls Forland Spitzbergen
123 L4 Prinsta B Anticosti I, Quebec
125 N3 Prinzapolca Nicaragua
54 L2 Priokskiy U.S.S.R.
16 B1 Prior, C Spain
52 D4 Priozersk U.S.S.R.
52 K3 Pripolyarnyy Ural *mts* U.S.S.R.
53 C8 Pripyat *R* U.S.S.R.
29 P3 Prirechnyy U.S.S.R.
37 P3 Přísečnice Czechoslovakia
48 J3 Prislop Pass Romania
46 E2 Priština Yugoslavia
106 H4 Pritchett Colorado
33 Q8 Pritzerbe E Germany
33 O6 Pritzier E Germany
33 Q6 Pritzwalk E Germany
19 N15 Privas France
45 O7 Priverno Italy
45 O6 Privernum Italy
42 F3 Privka Yugoslavia
52 F6 Privolzhsk U.S.S.R.
53 G7 Privolzhskaya Vozvyshennost *uplands* U.S.S.R.
46 D2 Prizren Yugoslavia
43 E11 Prizzi Sicily
70 O9 Probolinnggo Java
37 L2 Probstzella E Germany
8 B7 Probus England
31 J4 Prochowice Poland
45 Q8 Procida Italy
43 F8 Procida *isld* Italy
106 H1 Proctor Colorado
109 J4 Proctor Texas
95 O3 Proctor Vermont
109 J3 Proctor Res Texas
95 P3 Proctorsville Vermont
16 B5 Proènca a Nova Portugal
37 N1 Profen E Germany
22 H3 Profondeville Belgium
125 L2 Progreso Honduras
125 P7 Progreso Mexico
106 E7 Progresso New Mexico
56 B6 Prokhladnoye U.S.S.R.
46 D2 Prokletije Yugoslavia
56 C4 Prokop'yevsk U.S.S.R.
46 E1 Prokuplje Yugoslavia
52 D5 Proletariy U.S.S.R.
54 K8 Proletarsk U.S.S.R.
54 G6 Proletarskiy U.S.S.R.
54 J1 Proletarskiy U.S.S.R.
59 N2 Proliv Frizi *str* U.S.S.R.
37 K4 Prolsdorf W Germany
68 B3 Prome Burma
99 N9 Promise City Iowa
101 N8 Promontory Utah
56 C3 Promyshlennaya U.S.S.R.
52 F5 Pronino U.S.S.R.
100 G9 Pronto Nevada
54 M2 Pronya *R* U.S.S.R.
117 M6 Prophet River Br Col
99 R8 Prophetstown Illinois
130 H11 Propriá Brazil
46 D3 Prosek Albania
33 S10 Prösen E Germany
141 J5 Proserpine Queensland
33 Q9 Prosigk E Germany
31 K3 Prosna *R* Poland
52 H5 Prosnitsa U.S.S.R.
47 F3 Prosotsáni Greece
95 M3 Prospect New York
94 D6 Prospect Ohio
100 C7 Prospect Oregon
94 G6 Prospect Pennsylvania
127 M3 Prospect Pt Jamaica
100 A6 Prosper Oregon
112 F3 Prosperity S Carolina
98 H9 Prosser Nebraska
100 F3 Prosser Washington
48 D1 Prostějov Czechoslovakia
141 K7 Proston Queensland
52 H2 Prosunduy U.S.S.R.
54 H8 Prosyanaya U.S.S.R.
31 M5 Proszowice Poland
107 L4 Protection Kansas
99 O6 Protivin Iowa
54 J2 Protva *R* U.S.S.R.
33 T7 Prötzel E Germany
47 J1 Provadiya Bulgaria
115 O3 Prøven Greenland
111 C10 Provencal Louisiana
19 O17 Provence *prov* France
36 C7 Provenchères-sur-Fave France
127 P5 Providence Grenada
110 J4 Providence Kentucky
112 J1 Providence N Carolina
95 Q5 Providence Rhode I
101 O8 Providence Utah
120 H7 Providence Bay Ontario
116 J8 Providence, C Alaska
144 A7 Providence, C New Zealand
87 J9 Providence I Br Indian Oc Terr
103 J7 Providence Mts California
127 H4 Providenciales *isld* Turks & Caicos Is
128 F6 Providencia, Sa. da *mts* Brazil
116 A4 Provideniya U.S.S.R.
141 G2 Providential Chan Gt Barrier Reef Aust
95 R4 Provincetown Massachusetts
18 H4 Provins France
98 C6 Provo S Dakota
103 N1 Provo Utah
118 G6 Provost Alberta
22 D4 Proyart France
42 H5 Prozor Yugoslavia
52 H4 Prub *R* U.S.S.R.
130 E9 Prudentópolis Brazil
94 C2 Prudenville Michigan
13 G4 Prudhoe England
116 O1 Prudhoe Bay Alaska
141 J5 Prudhoe I Queensland
115 N2 Prudhoe Land Greenland
119 M6 Prud'homme Sask
31 K5 Prudnik Poland
54 H6 Prudyanka U.S.S.R.
36 B3 Prüm W Germany
21 G6 Prunay France
45 J3 Prunetta Italy
19 Q15 Prunières France
21 I7 Pruniers Cher France
21 J8 Pruniers Indre France
31 K2 Pruszcz Poland
31 M3 Pruszków Poland
48 L4 Prut *R* U.S.S.R.
48 L3 Prutul *R* Romania
41 N3 Prutz Austria
52 D4 Pryazha U.S.S.R.
31 L6 Prýdek Mistek Czechoslovakia
146 C4 Prydz B Antarctica
101 R4 Pryor Montana
107 P5 Pryor Oklahoma
31 M2 Przasnysz Poland
31 K2 Przechlewo Poland
31 M4 Przedbórz Poland
31 O6 Przemyśl Poland
31 N5 Przeworsk Poland
31 H4 Przewóz Poland
57 J4 Przheval'sk U.S.S.R.
31 M4 Przysucha Poland
47 F6 Psakhná Greece
47 H6 Psará *isld* Greece
31 K4 Psie Pole Poland
47 H9 Psíra *isld* Greece
52 C5 Pskov U.S.S.R.
52 C5 Pskovskoye, Ozero *L* U.S.S.R.
42 H3 Psunj *mt* Yugoslavia
31 L1 Pszczółki Poland
31 L6 Pszczyna Poland
53 C7 Ptich' *R* U.S.S.R.
46 E4 Ptolemaïs Greece
38 N9 Ptuj Yugoslavia
71 H5 Puah *isld* Sulawesi
135 U4 Puako Hawaiian Is
116 K8 Puale B Alaska
133 E5 Puán Argentina
67 C5 Pubei China
122 G10 Pubnico Nova Scotia
128 C5 Pucacaca Peru
128 D5 Pucallpa Peru
20 J3 Puchay France
38 N6 Puchberg Austria
65 A7 Pucheng China
65 C7 Pucheng China
67 F3 Pucheng China
52 F6 Puchezh U.S.S.R.
31 L6 Puchov Czechoslovakia
71 E5 Pucio Pt Panay Philippines
31 L1 Puck Poland
99 R6 Puckaway L Wisconsin
9 G4 Puckeridge England
111 G9 Puckett Mississippi
143 B7 Puckford,Mt W Australia
29 M6 Pudasjärvi Finland
8 D6 Puddletown England
52 H5 Pudem U.S.S.R.
67 B3 Puding China
123 Q5 Pudops L Nfld
52 E4 Pudozh U.S.S.R.
52 E4 Pudozhgora U.S.S.R.
13 G6 Pudsey England
125 K8 Puebla Mexico
16 D5 Puebla de Alcocer Spain
17 F7 Puebla de Don Fadrique Spain
16 D5 Puebla de Don Rodrigo Spain
16 C2 Puebla de Sanabria Spain
16 C2 Puebla de Trives Spain
106 F3 Pueblo Colorado
106 C5 Pueblo Bonito New Mexico
133 C3 Pueblo Hundido Chile
100 G7 Pueblo Mts Oregon
124 G6 Pueblo Nuevo Mexico
125 N9 Pueblo Viejo Mexico
125 L6 Pueblo Viejo, L. de Mexico
133 D5 Puelches Argentina
133 D5 Puelén Argentina
16 B2 Puenteareas Spain
16 B2 Puente Caldelas Spain
16 D7 Puente Genil Spain
103 P7 Puerco *R* Arizona
106 C6 Puerco, R New Mexico
128 C2 Puerta Mutis Colombia
133 C7 Puerto Aisén Chile
125 N5 Puerto Armuelles Panama
128 C3 Puerto Asis Colombia
128 E2 Puerto Ayacucho Venezuela
125 P10 Puerto Barrios Guatemala
128 D6 Puerto Bermúdez Peru
128 D2 Puerto Berrio Colombia
133 C7 Puerto Bertrand Chile
128 C6 Puerto Caballas Peru
128 E1 Puerto Cabello Venezuela
125 N2 Puerto Cabezas Nicaragua
Puerto Capaz Morocco *see* El Jebha
128 E2 Puerto Carreño Colombia
130 B8 Puerto Casado Paraguay
128 C5 Puerto Chicama Peru
124 G3 Puerto Chilicote Mexico
133 C6 Puerto Cisnes Chile
133 D8 Puerto Coig Argentina
128 D1 Puerto Colombia Colombia
125 Q10 Puerto Cortés Honduras
128 E1 Puerto Cumarebo Venezuela
127 J8 Puerto Estrella Colombia
128 C5 Puerto Eten Peru
133 C5 Puerto Fuy Chile
128 F7 Puerto Grether Bolivia
133 D8 Puerto Harberton Argentina
128 E6 Puerto Heath Bolivia
128 D3 Puerto Huitoto Colombia
133 E5 Puerto Ingeniero White Argentina
127 M9 Puerto La Cruz Venezuela
128 D4 Puerto Leguizamo Colombia
125 N2 Puerto Lempira Honduras
16 E6 Puertollano Spain
128 D7 Puerto Lomas Peru
127 J9 Puerto López Colombia
17 F7 Puerto Lumbreras Spain
133 D6 Puerto Madryn Argentina
128 E6 Puerto Maldonado Peru
126 F4 Puerto Manatí Cuba
128 D4 Puerto Miraña Colombia
133 C6 Puerto Montt Chile
133 C8 Puerto Natales Chile
128 E2 Puerto Nuevo Colombia
133 F3 Puerto Ocampo Argentina
128 F2 Puerto Ordaz Venezuela
126 F4 Puerto Padre Cuba
133 C2 Puerto Patillos Chile
124 C2 Puerto Penasco Mexico
133 F2 Puerto Pinasco Paraguay
133 E6 Puerto Pirámides Argentina
128 F1 Puerto Piritu Venezuela
127 J5 Puerto Plata Dom Rep
128 D5 Puerto Portillo Peru
71 D6 Puerto Princesa Palawan Philippines
125 M5 Puerto Quepos Costa Rica
128 E6 Puerto Rico Bolivia
113 J7 Puerto Rico *terr* Caribbean
127 L5 Puerto Rico Trench Caribbean
126 G4 Puerto Samá Cuba
130 B8 Puerto Sastre Paraguay
128 E6 Puerto Siles Bolivia
130 C9 Puerto Strossner Paraguay
130 B6 Puerto Suárez Bolivia
124 G7 Puerto Vallarta Mexico
133 C6 Puerto Varas Chile
128 F7 Puerto Velarde Bolivia
128 D5 Puerto Victoria Peru
128 D2 Puerto Villamizar Colombia
133 D7 Puerto Visser Argentina
128 D2 Puerto Wilches Colombia
133 C7 Pueyrredón, L Chile/Arg
25 F7 Puffendorf W Germany
124 G7 Puga Mexico
52 H6 Pugachevo U.S.S.R.
74 E4 Pugal India
88 G10 Puga Puga *isld* Mozambique
70 O10 Puger Java
100 C2 Puget Sound Washington
19 P13 Pugieu France
43 G8 Puglia *prov* Italy
71 K9 Pugubengo Flores Indonesia
70 K8 Pugung, G *mt* Sumatra
122 J8 Pugwash Nova Scotia
145 F3 Puha New Zealand
135 O1 Puhi Hawaiian Is
145 E2 Puhoi New Zealand
48 H5 Pui Romania
48 L4 Puieşti Romania
17 J2 Puigcerda Spain
71 G7 Pujada B Mindanao Philippines
65 G4 Pujan Res N Korea
19 N16 Pujaut France
67 A1 Pujiang China
67 F2 Pujiang China
119 Q3 Pukatawagan Manitoba
46 D2 Pukë Albania
145 G2 Pukeamaru *mt* New Zealand
145 E3 Pukearuhe New Zealand
145 F3 Pukehou New Zealand
145 E2 Pukekawa New Zealand
145 E2 Pukekohe New Zealand
144 C5 Pukekura New Zealand
145 E2 Pukemiro New Zealand
145 D1 Pukenui New Zealand
145 F3 Pukeokahu New Zealand
144 C6 Pukerangi New Zealand
144 B7 Pukerau New Zealand
145 E3 Pukeroa New Zealand
145 G3 Puketawai New Zealand
144 D5 Puketeraki Range New Zealand
145 F3 Puketitiri New Zealand
145 F2 Puketoetoe *mt* New Zealand
145 F4 Puketoi Range New Zealand
145 E3 Puketutu New Zealand
145 F2 Puketutu I New Zealand
144 C6 Pukeuri Junction New Zealand
29 M11 Pukkila Finland
67 F1 Pukou China
52 F3 Puksa U.S.S.R.
52 F3 Puksoozero U.S.S.R.
52 H5 Puksub U.S.S.R.
98 G6 Pukwana S Dakota
42 F4 Pula Yugoslavia
128 E8 Pulacayo Bolivia
43 C9 Pula, C. di Sardinia
Pulandian *see* Xinjin
71 G6 Pulangi *R* Mindanao Philippines
70 D6 Pulangpisau Kalimantan
70 K8 Pulao Seribu *isld* Sumatra
70 K9 Pulasari *mt* Java
99 O9 Pulaski Iowa
95 L3 Pulaski New York
110 J6 Pulaski Tennessee
94 G9 Pulaski Virginia
99 S5 Pulaski Wisconsin
69 F13 Pulaukidjang Sumatra
70 B4 Pulaumadjang Kalimantan
69 D13 Pulautelo Indonesia
31 N4 Puławy Poland
9 F6 Pulborough England
77 L2 Pul-i-Khumri Afghanistan
76 D3 Pulivendla India
76 C6 Puliyangudi India
83 K9 Puliyankulam Sri Lanka
29 M7 Pulkkila Finland
100 H3 Pullman Washington
71 E2 Pulog, Mt Luzon Philippines
83 K8 Puloli Sri Lanka
52 F2 Pulonga U.S.S.R.
52 D1 Pulozero U.S.S.R.
124 D4 Púlpito, Pta *C* Mexico
33 T10 Pulsnitz *R* E Germany
31 M3 Pułtusk Poland
66 C4 Pulu China
70 P10 Pulukan Bali Indonesia
66 E6 Puma Yumco *L* China
Pumiao *see* Yongning
98 A4 Pumpkin Cr Montana
98 C8 Pumpkin Cr Nebraska
108 F6 Pumpville Texas
8 C3 Pumsaint Wales
128 B4 Puná *isld* Ecuador
70 G5 Puna *R* Sulawesi
144 C5 Punakaiki New Zealand
145 D1 Punakitere R New Zealand
70 D4 Punan Kalimantan
74 F2 Punch Kashmir
117 M9 Punchaw Br Col
70 C6 Pundu Kalimantan
52 F4 Punduga U.S.S.R.
55 D1 Punga *R* U.S.S.R.
112 L2 Pungo N Carolina
59 J3 Pungsan N Korea
86 E6 Punia Zaïre
70 Q10 Punikan, G *mt* Indonesia
131 B2 Punilla, Sa. de la *mts* Chile
74 F3 Punjab *prov* India
74 D3 Punjab, The *prov* Pakistan
140 E4 Punjaub Queensland
29 O10 Punkaharju Finland
29 K10 Punkalaidun Finland
119 N7 Punnichy Sask
128 D7 Puno Peru
128 D6 Puno *dep* Peru
106 D7 Punta New Mexico
131 E7 Punta Alta Argentina
133 C8 Punta Arenas Chile
43 C7 Puntaccia *mt* Sardinia
133 C3 Punta Colorada Chile
108 B8 Punta de Agua Cr. *R* Texas/New Mex
17 H4 Punta de la Baña Spain
125 P9 Punta Gorda Belize
100 A9 Punta Gorda California
113 E11 Punta Gorda Florida
125 N4 Punta Gorda Nicaragua
131 G6 Punta Norte Argentina
127 J5 Punta Palenque Dom Rep
124 B3 Punta Prieta Mexico
125 M5 Puntarenas Costa Rica
128 G8 Punta Rieles Paraguay
125 N5 Punta San Pedrillo Costa Rica
127 M5 Punta Tuna Puerto Rico
128 D1 Punto Fijo Venezuela
47 G4 Punto Lágo Greece
133 D7 Puntudo, Cerro *mt* Argentina
116 C5 Punuk Is Bering Sea
94 J6 Punxsutawney Pennsylvania
68 F6 Puok Cambodia
29 N7 Puolanka Finland
26 L5 Puottaure Sweden
128 E6 Puoya *mt* Bolivia
145 D4 Puponga New Zealand
58 F6 Puqi China
128 D6 Puquio Peru
133 D3 Puquios Chile
50 G2 Pur *R* U.S.S.R.
128 C3 Puracé *vol* Colombia
70 M9 Purbolinggo Java
107 N7 Purcell Oklahoma
116 J3 Purcell Mt Alaska
117 P10 Purcell Mts Br Col
100 K1 Purcell Range Montana
94 K7 Purcellville Virginia
17 F7 Purchena Spain
99 N10 Purdin Missouri
98 F7 Purdum Nebraska
110 C5 Purdy Missouri
145 E3 Pureora *mt* New Zealand
124 H8 Purépero Mexico
145 E1 Purerua New Zealand
9 E6 Purewell England
106 G4 Purgatoire *R* Colorado
116 N3 Purgatory Alaska
38 M5 Purgstall Austria
75 L9 Puri India
128 D3 Purificación Colombia
145 E2 Puriri New Zealand
9 F5 Purley England
25 C3 Purmerend Netherlands
74 G9 Purna India
138 B2 Purndu Saltpan S Australia
75 M6 Purnea India
52 E3 Purnema U.S.S.R.
118 F9 Purple Springs Alberta
68 F6 Pursat Cambodia
128 E4 Purué *R* Brazil
70 D5 Puruktjahu Kalimantan
128 F4 Purus *R* Brazil
29 O10 Puruvesi *L* Finland
111 G10 Purvis Mississippi
47 G2 Pŭrvomay Bulgaria
70 N9 Purwodadi Java
70 M9 Purwokerto Java
70 M9 Purworedjo Java
110 H5 Puryear Tennessee
66 B4 Pusa China
70 B4 Pusa Sarawak
52 C6 Puša U.S.S.R.
74 G9 Pusad India
52 B6 Pušalotas U.S.S.R.
65 H7 Pusan S Korea
71 G7 Pusan Pt Mindanao Philippines
65 D6 Pushang China
95 T2 Pushaw L Maine
52 D5 Pushkin U.S.S.R.
54 J1 Pushkino U.S.S.R.
52 E3 Pushlakhta U.S.S.R.
123 Q6 Pushthrough Nfld
77 H4 Pusht-i-Rud *reg* Afghanistan
120 E4 Puskaskwa Nat. Park Ontario
121 O3 Puskitamika L Quebec
48 G3 Püspökladány Hungary
20 J5 Pussay France
22 H4 Pussemange Belgium
38 K7 Pusterwald Austria
52 C6 Pustoshka U.S.S.R.
102 B3 Putah Cr California
67 G5 Pu-tai Taiwan
71 M9 Putain Timor Indonesia
20 E4 Putanges France
75 R5 Putao Burma
145 E3 Putaruru New Zealand
30 G1 Putbus E Germany
70 P9 Puteran *isld* Indonesia
67 F4 Putian China
43 H8 Putignano Italy
48 J3 Putila U.S.S.R.
52 F5 Putilovo U.S.S.R.
70 B6 Puting Tg *C* Kalimantan
54 E5 Putivl' U.S.S.R.
33 Q6 Putlitz E Germany
48 K3 Putna Romania
95 Q5 Putnam Connecticut
108 E8 Putnam Oklahoma
109 H3 Putnam Texas
112 C6 Putney Georgia
98 H4 Putney S Dakota
95 P4 Putney Vermont
51 J2 Putorana, Gory *mt* U.S.S.R.
145 F3 Putorino New Zealand
83 J9 Puttalam Sri Lanka
83 J9 Puttalam Lag Sri Lanka
22 G1 Putte Belgium
36 B5 Puttelange France
33 O5 Püttelkow E Germany
25 E4 Putten Netherlands
28 G7 Puttgarden W Germany
36 B5 Püttlingen W Germany
54 L8 Putugino U.S.S.R.
83 K8 Putukkudiyirippu Sri Lanka
128 C3 Putumayo *div* Colombia
128 D4 Putumayo *R* Peru/Colombia
67 G1 Putuo Shan *isld* China
70 C4 Putussibau Kalimantan
33 T5 Putzar E Germany
135 U5 Puuanahulu Hawaiian Is
135 U5 Puu Hualalei *crater* Hawaiian Is
135 S3 Puukoli Hawaiian Is
29 M10 Puulavesi *L* Finland
29 N10 Puumala Finland
22 G1 Puurs Belgium
135 N1 Puuwai Hawaiian Is
Puxian *see* Pucheng
65 A6 Pu Xian China
117 M12 Puyallup Washington
65 C7 Puyang China
18 G7 Puy de Dôme *dep* France
18 G7 Puy-de-Sancy *mt* France
131 A8 Puyehue, L de Chile
131 B8 Puyehue, P. de Argentina
131 A8 Puyehue, V Chile
19 Q14 Puy Gris *mt* France
18 G9 Puylaurens France
18 H7 Puy, le France
18 F8 Puy l'Evêque France
18 G7 Puy Mary *mt* France
20 H2 Puys France
52 H4 Puzla U.S.S.R.
88 B6 Pweto Zaïre
68 B2 Pwinbyu Burma
8 B2 Pwllheli Wales
52 E2 Pyalitsa U.S.S.R.
52 E4 Pyal'ma U.S.S.R.
68 B3 Pyalo Burma
68 B5 Pyamalaw *R* Burma
52 F6 Pyana *R* U.S.S.R.
57 E6 Pyandzh *R* U.S.S.R./Afghanistan
52 J4 Pyanteg U.S.S.R.
52 D2 Pyaozero, Oz *L* U.S.S.R.

76 C3	Pyapalli India
68 B4	Pyapon Burma
51 H1	Pyasina R U.S.S.R.
53 F11	Pyatigorsk U.S.S.R.
54 E8	Pyatikhatki U.S.S.R.
52 H4	Pyatigory U.S.S.R.
110 D5	Pyatt Arkansas
52 H6	Pychas U.S.S.R.
116 M7	Pye Is Alaska
29 M8	Pyhäjärvi Finland
27 M11	Pyhäjärvi L Finland
29 L7	Pyhäjoki Finland
29 J11	Pyhäranta Finland
29 O9	Pyhäselkä Finland
38 N5	Pyhra Austria
68 C3	Pyinmana Burma
8 C4	Pyle Wales
29 L9	Pylkönmäki Finland
94 G5	Pymatuning Res Ohio/Penn
69 A9	Pymgalion Pt Nicobar Is
59 J3	Pyŏktong N Korea
65 F5	Pyŏngyang N Korea
100 F9	Pyramid Nevada
67 G1	Pyramid Canyon Ariz/Nev
103 K6	Pyramid Pk Colorado
139 G6	Pyramid Hill Victoria
106 C1	Pyramid Pk Colorado
94 A2	Pyramid Pt Michigan
102 E2	Pyramid Rge Nevada
18 F9	Pyrénées mts France/Spain
18 E9	Pyrénées Atlantiques dep France
18 G10	Pyrénées-Orientales dep France
142 B5	Pyrton,Mt W Australia
31 H2	Przyzoe Poland
52 G5	Pyshchug U.S.S.R.
55 D3	Pyshma U.S.S.R.
52 C6	Pytalovo U.S.S.R.
121 G6	Pythonga, L Quebec
68 C3	Pyu Burma
68 C3	Pyu R Burma
68 C4	Pyuntaza Burma
31 K3	Pyzdry Poland
84 E3	Qaddáhiyah, Al Libya
74 F3	Qadian India
80 G4	Qafqafa Jordan
58 G2	Qagan China
	Qagan Nur see Zhengxiangbai Qi
65 B3	Qagan Nur China
65 H1	Qagan Nur L China
65 C3	Qagan Nur L China
65 F2	Qagan Nur L China
65 D1	Qagan Qulut China
65 D3	Qagan Us China
115 P5	Qagssimiut Greenland
65 B4	Qahar Youyi Houqi China
65 B4	Qahar Youyi Qianqi China
65 B4	Qahar Youyi Zhongqi China
	Qâhira, El see Cairo
66 E4	Qaidam Pendi reg China
74 J4	Qala Bist Afghanistan
86 G3	Qala'en Nahl Sudan
77 J3	Qala-i-Ghor Afghanistan
77 H3	Qala-i-Kâl Afghanistan
77 K3	Qalât Afghanistan
79 F3	Qal'at el Marqab Syria
80 F4	Qal'at er Rabad Jordan
81 L6	Qal'at Salih Iraq
80 C5	Qalqilya Israel
80 E6	Qalya Jordan
79 B8	Qalyûb Egypt
80 G3	Qam Jordan
74 C5	Qamdo China
66 F3	Qaminis Libya
74 H3	Qamishliye, El Syria
74 C3	Qamruddin Karez Pakistan
80 D5	Qana Israel
65 C3	Qangdin Gol China
65 D3	Qangdin Sum China
79 C8	Qantara, El Egypt
84 H4	Qara Egypt
80 D5	Qarawat Bani Hassan Jordan
79 G3	Qardaha Syria
78 L2	Qareh Su R Iran
79 C10	Qarn el Kabsh, G mt Egypt
66 D4	Qarqan He China
84 E3	Qaryahash Sharqiyah Libya
79 H4	Qaryatein, El Syria
80 G7	Qaryat Falha Jordan
77 H2	Qasa Murg Afghanistan
80 F8	Qasr Jordan
84 G3	Qasr al Burayqat Libya
79 F8	Qasr ed Deir, J mt Jordan
79 H4	Qasr el Hayr Syria
78 K4	Qasr-e-Shirin Iran
80 G8	Qasr eth Thuraiyat Jordan
84 H4	Qasr Farâfra Egypt
79 G5	Qatana Syria
79 F7	Qatar sheikhdom The Gulf
77 B6	Qatif, Al Saudi Arabia
79 G7	Qatrana Jordan
84 H4	Qattara Depression Egypt
77 F3	Qâyen Iran
77 H3	Qayyarah Iraq
77 A1	Qazvin Iran
84 J4	Qena Egypt
77 E6	Qeshm Iran
77 A1	Qeydar Iran
77 C6	Qeys isld Iran
84 J4	Qezel Owzan R Iran
65 D4	Qian'an China
65 F2	Qian'an China
67 C3	Qiancheng China
65 F2	Qian Gorlos China
67 C3	Qiangu'ao China
	Qianguozhen see Qian Gorlos
65 D7	Qiangwei He R China
67 D1	Qianjiang China
67 C2	Qianjiang R China
67 E1	Qianshan China
65 E4	Qianwei China
65 D4	Qianxi China
67 D3	Qianyang China
67 D3	Qiaotou China
67 E1	Qiaotou China
65 D7	Qidong China
67 G1	Qidong China
66 C2	Qiemo China
66 C2	Qijiang China
65 C6	Qijiaojing China
66 E3	Qiktim China
65 D7	Qikou China
74 H3	Qila Abdullah Pakistan
74 A8	Qila Ladgasht Pakistan
64 C3	Qila Shan mt ra China
74 A8	Qila Safed Pakistan
74 C3	Qila Saifullah Pakistan
	Qili see Shitai
65 F4	Qilian China
67 F11	Qimen China
67 E1	Qimen She mt ra China
67 E11	Qimen China
65 E2	Qin'an China
65 E5	Qingdao China
58 C5	Qingduizi China
67 A2	Qingfu China
65 G1	Qinggang China

58 D4	Qinghai prov China
58 D4	Qinghai Hu L China
65 C6	Qinghe China
65 H1	Qinghe China
65 H1	Qinghecheng China
65 E4	Qinghemen China
65 F3	Qinghe Shuiku res China
67 F2	Qinghu China
65 A6	Qingjian China
59 G5	Qingjiang China
65 E3	Qingjiang China
67 C1	Qing Jiang R China
65 A6	Qingjian He R China
13 E2	Qingkou see Ganyu
67 C7	Qinglan China
65 D7	Qinglong China
67 B4	Qinglong China
65 C6	Qinglong He R China
67 D4	Qingliu China
65 D4	Qinglong China
67 B4	Qinglong China
65 C6	Qingping China
68 J2	Qingping China
65 A5	Qingpu China
58 E4	Qingshuihe China
67 C3	Qingshui Jiang R China
67 G2	Qingtian China
65 C5	Qing Xian China
65 B6	Qingyang China
58 E4	Qingyang see Jinjiang
67 F1	Qingyang China
59 J3	Qingyuan China
67 D5	Qingyuan China
67 F3	Qingyuan China
65 D6	Qingyuan China
58 F4	Qingyuan see Yishan
67 C6	Qinyang China
58 F4	Qinyang China
67 G3	Qinyu China
65 C6	Qinyuan China
65 C6	Qinzhou China
68 J2	Qinzhou Wan B China
68 K3	Qionghai China
58 D5	Qionglai China
58 D5	Qionglai Shan mt ra China
68 K3	Qiongshan China
67 C7	Qiongzhong China
	Qiongzhou see Qiongshan
68 J2	Qiongzhou Haixia China
67 B1	Qiping China
59 H2	Qiqihar China
77 C5	Qir Iran
80 D7	Qiryat Arba' Jordan
80 D2	Qiryat Ata Israel
80 C7	Qiryat Bialik Israel
80 D2	Qiryat Gat Israel
80 D3	Qiryat Motmkin Israel
80 D2	Qiryat Tiv'on Israel
80 D7	Qiryat Yam Israel
80 D8	Qiryat Yeroham Israel
67 C6	Qisha China
80 D3	Qishon 'Eneq Yizre'el Israel
68 J2	Qishui China
65 H2	Qitai China
67 A4	Qiubei China
65 C6	Qiu Xian China
65 E6	Qixia China
65 B6	Qi Xian China
65 A5	Qi Xian China
58 B4	Qixianing China
65 J1	Qixing He R China
67 D3	Qiyang China
67 E1	Qizhou China
65 C2	Qog Ul China
	Qogir Feng mt see K2
87 B8	Qoiba Angola
87 B7	Qoibate Angola
128 C2	Quibdó Colombia
118 J1	Quibell Ontario
18 F9	Quibervon France
20 G2	Quiberon France
127 K10	Quibor Venezuela
87 B7	Quicama Nat. Park Angola
68 G3	Qui Chau Vietnam
32 L5	Quickborn W Germany
36 C5	Quierschied W Germany
117 G5	Quiet L Yukon Terr
22 F3	Quievrain Belgium
22 E3	Quiévy France
22 F2	Quigley Alaska
70 F7	Quiindy Paraguay
124 F5	Quilá Mexico
133 C6	Quilán, C Chile
133 C6	Quilates, C Morocco
141 H7	Quilberry Queensland
128 D7	Quilcas Peru
100 C2	Quilcene Washington
87 B8	Quilengues Angola
133 E4	Quilino Argentina
128 D6	Quillabamba Peru
68 H4	Quillan France
18 G10	Quillan France
128 C5	Quillacollo Bolivia
20 G3	Quillan France
119 N6	Quillebeuf France
18 G10	Quillén, L Argentina
119 N6	Quill Lake Sask
119 N7	Quill Lakes L Sask
21 B7	Quilly France
141 G7	Quilpie Queensland
87 C8	Quimbango Angola
18 C5	Quimper France
18 C5	Quimperlé France
71 F3	Quinabucasan Pt Philippines
71 F4	Quinalasag isld Philippines
100 B3	Quinault Washington
100 A2	Quinault R Washington
122 D1	Quince-de-Bouleau, R Quebec
120 G4	Quincemil Peru
120 G3	Quincy California
111 M11	Quincy Florida
99 P10	Quincy Illinois
95 R4	Quincy Massachusetts
48 E1	Quincy Michigan
100 B3	Quincy Oregon
100 F2	Quincy Washington
20 C2	Quinéville France
68 F2	Quinh Nhai Vietnam
68 J6	Qui Nhon Vietnam
30 H4	Quinquaïs, Cerro mts Venezuela
71 E5	Quinluban isld Philippines
109 L3	Quinlan Texas
98 D6	Quinn S Dakota
103 J4	Quinn Canyon Ra Nevada
141 N7	Quinn, Mt N Terr Aust
100 D3	Quinn River Crossing Nevada
19 Q17	Quinson France
16 E5	Quintanar de la Orden Spain
125 P8	Quintana Roo terr Mexico
107 K2	Quinter Kansas
119 N9	Quinton Sask
33 O9	Quintin France
13 G3	Quinto R Argentina
109 N7	Quinton Oklahoma
119 N7	Quinton Sask
45 L1	Quintrell Downs England
106 D9	Quinwood W Virginia
70 B9	Quionga Mozambique
15 B3	Quirang Scotland
87 C8	Quirima Angola
70 B9	Quirimbas isld Mozambique
131 K4	Quirindi New S Wales
131 A6	Quirinópolis Brazil
127 N10	Quiriquire Venezuela
38 L6	Quirke L Ontario
120 C5	Quiroga Mexico
16 C5	Quiroga Spain
47 H2	Quirquina isld Chile
140 B1	Quiros, Pt N Terr Aust

146 D3	Queen Mary Land Antarctica
117 D5	Queen Mary, Mt Yukon Terr
114 J4	Queen Maud Gulf N W Terr
146 G8	Queen Maud Ra Antarctica
13 G6	Queensbury England
140 A2	Queens Chan N Terr Australia
115 K2	Queens Chan N W Terr
139 G7	Queenscliff Victoria
13 E2	Queensferry Scotland
139	Queensland state Australia
142 B2	Queens Park dist Perth, W Aust
123 L8	Queenston Nova Scotia
118 E8	Queenstown Alberta
95 L8	Queenstown Maryland
144 B6	Queenstown New Zealand
89 E8	Queenstown S Africa
139 H8	Queenstown Tasmania
100 A2	Queenstown W Australia
131 F4	Queets Washington
72 E5	Queguay Grande R Uruguay
36 E5	Queich R W Germany
16 C2	Queija, S. de mts Spain
129 L6	Queimadas Brazil
87 C7	Quela Angola
21 D6	Quelaines France
87 B7	Quela Angola
88 F10	Quelimane Mozambique
124 F6	Quelite Mexico
133 C6	Quellen Chile
106 B7	Quemado New Mexico
108 G7	Quemado Texas
	Quemoy see Chin-men
133 E5	Quemu Quemu Argentina
22 B3	Quend France
9 G4	Quendon England
70 P3	Quenemo Kansas
111 F10	Quentin Mississippi
89 F2	Que Que Zimbabwe
133 F5	Quequén Argentina
22 C2	Quercamps France
130 D8	Querência do Norte Brazil
125 J7	Querétaro Mexico
33 P10	Querfurt E Germany
124 D2	Querobabi Mexico
33 R6	Querqueville France
20 K2	Querrieu France
117 M9	Quesnel Br Columbia
117 N9	Quesnel L Br Columbia
22 D4	Quesnoy France
44 F2	Quesnoy, le France
22 E2	Quesnoy-sur-Deule, le France
106 E5	Questa New Mexico
18 D2	Questembert France
133 D2	Quetena Bolivia
99 Q1	Quetico Ontario
118 L2	Quetico L Ontario
99 P1	Quetico Provincial Park Ontario
74 A5	Quetta Pakistan
20 C2	Quettehou France
20 F3	Quetteville France
22 D4	Quettreville France
111 D11	Queue de Tortue R Louisiana
20 J4	Queue-lez-Yvelines, la France
20 K2	Queuille France
121 O3	Quévillon Quebec
78 E8	Qeziot Israel
71 C6	Quezon Palawan Philippines
71 E3	Quezon City Luzon Philippines
65 D7	Qufu China
87 B8	Quibala Angola
87 B7	Quibaxe Angola
128 C2	Quibdó Colombia
118 J1	Quibell Ontario
18 F9	Quibervon France
20 G2	Quiberon France
127 K10	Quibor Venezuela
87 B7	Quicama Nat. Park Angola

45 J1	Quistello Italy
87 C8	Quitapa Angola
126 D7	Quita Sueño Bank Caribbean
130 D6	Quitéria R Brazil
87 B7	Quitexe Angola
110 D6	Quitman Arkansas
113 D7	Quitman Georgia
109 P3	Quitman Louisiana
111 G6	Quitman Mississippi
109 M3	Quitman Texas
128 C4	Quito Ecuador
103 M10	Quitovac Mexico
20 H3	Quittebeuf France
103 M6	Quivera Arizona
128 C5	Quivilla Peru
67 B1	Qu Jiang China
67 B1	Qu Jiang R China
31 N3	Qujie China
67 A4	Qujie China
67 A4	Qujing China
46 D3	Qukës-Skhumbin Albania
80 G8	Quleib R Jordan
64 H4	Qumar He R China
58 C5	Qumarlêb China
64 G4	Qumar R China
80 G1	Qumeitra Syria
34 L2	Qunayyin, S. al Libya
80 G1	Quneitra Syria
77 D4	Qunfidhah, Al Saudi Arabia
66 D5	Qungtag China
83 M12	Quoin Chan Mauritius
140 A2	Quoin I N Terr Aust
141 K6	Quoin I Queensland
89 A10	Quoin Pt S Africa
80 D5	Quorn S Australia
129 J4	Qurem Brazil
84 J4	Qus Egypt
101 M7	Quseir Egypt
65 E4	Qusr-e-Qand Iran
71 G7	Qutang Xia Wu Xia China
26 H3	Quthing Lesotho
84 E4	Quweiq R Syria
71 G7	Quweisna Egypt
79 B8	Quwo China
72 E9	Quwu Shan mt ra China
32 J4	Quxi China
67 B1	Qu Xian China
67 F2	Qu Xian China
75 O4	Qüxü China
66 C5	Quyang China
67 B7	Quyang China
67 B1	Quynh Luu Vietnam
121 O7	Quyon Quebec
65 C6	Quzhou China
28 K5	Rá Sweden
27 F16	Råå Sweden
	Raab see Györ
31 J7	Raab R Austria
38 N7	Raab Tal V Austria
29 L7	Raahe Finland
25 F4	Raalte Netherlands
115 L2	Raanes Pen N W Terr
29 L5	Raanujärvi Finland
70 P9	Raas isld Indonesia
77 A5	Ra'as Al Khafti Saudi Arabia
15 B3	Raasay, Sd of Scotland
42 F4	Rab isld Yugoslavia
80 E4	Raba Jordan
71 J9	Raba Sumbawa Indonesia
43 O3	Raba R Hungary
48 F1	Raba R Poland
16 C3	Rabaçal R Portugal
19 F9	Rabastens de Bigorre Hautes-Pyrénées France
37 J6	Rabaté W Germany
86 G7	Rabaul New Britain
103 O4	Rabbah see 'Amman
117 K6	Rabbit R Br Columbia
98 D4	Rabbit Cr S Dakota
106 D1	Rabbit Ears Pass Colorado
145 D4	Rabbit I New Zealand
118 K5	Rabbit Lake Sask
117 N5	Rabbitskin R N W Terr
28 D7	Rabel W Germany
77 E5	Rabenau W Germany
37 F6	Rabenstein W Germany
52 E6	Rabotki U.S.S.R.
99 M1	Rabun L Georgia
118 J2	Rabun, L Georgia
112 D3	Rabupura India
46 D1	Rača Yugoslavia
44 C2	Racconigi Italy
126 J3	Raccoon Cay Bahamas
94 E8	Raccoon Cr Ohio
75 J8	Race, C Nfld
106 D8	Race Track New Mexico
122 A5	Race, C Nfld
100 B1	Race Rocks Br Columbia
101 N3	Race Track Montana
119 O2	Rachal Texas
76 D4	Racha Noi, Ko isld Thailand
70 B5	Racha, Bt mt Kalimantan
76 E2	Racha Yai, Ko isld Thailand
94 E8	Rach Gia Vietnam
31 L5	Raciborz Poland
37 P3	Racic Czechoslovakia
94 F8	Racine Ohio
99 T7	Racine Wisconsin
46 C11	Raja, Ujung C Sumatra
46 D2	Racine-de-Bouleau, R Quebec
120 G4	Racine L Ontario
37 O4	Rackwitz E Germany
	Racovský mt Czechoslovakia
69 G14	Radack Is isld Pacific Oc
112 D3	Radan mt Yugoslavia
48 E1	Rădăuti Romania
90 B3	Radbuza R Czechoslovakia
13 F6	Radcliffe England
9 N7	Radcliffe England
28 H2	Råde Norway
37 H7	Radeberg E Germany
9 P6	Radebeul E Germany
33 G7	Radegast E Germany
38 T10	Radegast E Germany
19 Q18	Rade d'Hyères B France
33 O9	Radegast E Germany
38 M8	Radel Pass Austria
36 C1	Radevormwald W Germany
106 C6	Radford Virginia
140 B1	Radford Pt N Terr Aust
112 E2	Radhanpur India
80 H5	Radi India
142 F4	Radi Hills W Australia
119 K6	Radisson Quebec
119 K6	Radisson Sask
99 R3	Radisson Wisconsin
140 B1	Radium Hill peak S Australia
117 P10	Radium Hot Springs Br Columbia
106 D9	Radium Springs New Mexico
15 B3	Radja, I Indonesia
70 P9	Radja, I Indonesia
112 C3	Radja, I Indonesia
91 J10	Radkov Czechoslovakia
31 M4	Radom Poland

86 D4	Radom Sudan
46 F2	Radomir Bulgaria
31 L4	Radomsko Poland
37 P3	Radonice Czechoslovakia
31 K7	Radošina Czechoslovakia
31 M4	Radosyce Poland
46 E3	Radovis Yugoslavia
42 F2	Radovljica Yugoslavia
38 H7	Radstadt Austria
8 D5	Radstock England
16 E1	Raduha mt Yugoslavia
38 L9	Raduha mt Yugoslavia
42 H5	Radusa mt Yugoslavia
52 B6	Radviliškis U.S.S.R.
119 N9	Radville Sask
118 E4	Radway Alberta
31 M3	Radzanow Poland
31 N3	Radziejow Poland
31 O6	Radzymin Poland
31 N3	Radzymin Poland
31 M3	Radzyn Podlaski Poland
117 P4	Rae N W Terr
112 H3	Rae Bareli India
115 L4	Rae Isthmus N W Terr
114 H5	Rae L N W Terr
118 B8	Rae, Mt Br Columbia
22 L2	Raeren Belgium
32 E9	Raesfeld W Germany
83 K9	Rafaela Sri Lanka
127 J2	Ramble Jamaica
133 D4	Rambon Argentina
20 J4	Rambouillet France
36 B7	Rambow E Germany
15 A4	Rannoch Moor Scotland
87 H12	Ranohira Madagascar
120 J2	Ranoke Ontario
76 B3	Ranong Thailand
1 H5	Ranot Thailand
29 N9	Ransaren I Sweden
31 N7	Rantauprapat Sumatra
70 F6	Rantekombola, Bk mt Sulawesi
70 F6	Rantepao Sulawesi
20 K3	Rantigny France
110 H1	Rantoul Illinois
102 H1	Rant Pass Nevada
29 M7	Rantsila Finland
16 D9	Ranua Finland
28 C3	Ranum Denmark
78 K3	Ranya Iraq
68 G3	Rao Go mt Laos
67 E5	Raohe China
36 C6	Raon-l'Etape France
36 C6	Raon-sur-Plaine France
67 E5	Raoping China
41 O6	Raossi Italy
137 R7	Raoul isld Kermadec Is Pacific Oc
65 C5	Raoyang China
144 C5	Raoparoa New Zealand
131 B4	Rapel R Chile
101 O4	Rapel R Chile
115 N9	Raper, C N W Terr
106 C1	Raphine Virginia
14 D2	Rapid I Irish Rep
116 R3	Rapid R Alaska
99 M1	Rapid R Minnesota
32 H10	Rapid R W Australia
94 A8	Rapidan Virginia
138 E6	Rapid B S Australia
119 R8	Rapid City Manitoba
98 C5	Rapid City S Dakota
121 R5	Rapide Blanc Quebec
121 N6	Rapides des Joachims Quebec
141 H2	Rapid Horn C Queensland
	Gt Barrier Reef Aust
99 U4	Rapid River Michigan
118 H4	Rapid View Sask
52 B3	Rápina U.S.S.R.
70 F6	Rappahannock R Virginia
41 J3	Rapperswil Switzerland
46 F5	Rapsáni Greece
126 E6	Rapulo R Bolivia
71 G4	Rapu Rapu Philippines
72 G4	Raquel Syria
95 N2	Raquette Lake New York
71 K9	Rarakan mt Flores
95 N6	Raritan B New Jersey
40 G5	Raron Switzerland
134 A10	Rarotonga isld Pacific Oc
42 F3	Rasa Yugoslavia
71 D6	Rasa isld Palawan Philippines
77 D7	Ra's al Khaymah U.A.E.
86 H2	Ras Andadda C Ethiopia
133 E6	Rasa, Pta Argentina
131 F8	Rasa, Pta C Argentina
86 G3	Ras Dashen mt Ethiopia
86 J3	Raseiniai U.S.S.R.
80 A2	Ras el Aqra Jordan
86 C4	Ras el Cheil Somalia
80 F8	Ras el Ghor Jordan
86 A3	Ras-e Kenés C Egypt
86 M6	Ras Gar Somalia
72 G5	Ras Gharib C Egypt
86 G1	Ras Hadarba C Egypt
108 F4	Ras Hafun Somalia
79 A7	Rashd Egypt
79 D10	Rashid Egypt
75 D6	Rashipuram India
77 G6	Rask Iran
46 D1	Raška Yugoslavia
86 C3	Ras Kasar C Sudan
86 A3	Ras Khanzira Somalia
28 C5	Raskmølle Denmark
77 H3	Raso el Pakistan
52 L5	Raslavice Czechoslovakia
77 J5	Ras Madrakah C Oman
84 J4	Ras Muhammad C Egypt
85 A4	Ras Nouadhibou C Western Sahara
133 D6	Raso, C Argentina
130 H10	Raso de Catarina Brazil
143 E8	Raso I Madagascar
46 D1	Raška Yugoslavia
116 L7	Raspberry I Alaska
30 K7	Raso Bulgaria
86 B3	Ras Targa Morocco
28 A4	Rasted Denmark
28 C3	Råsted Denmark
36 C6	Rastede W Germany
	Rastenberg see Ketrzyn
36 E1	Rastenfeld Austria
36 M3	Rastorkino U.S.S.R.
35 P1	Rastolita Romania
28 M5	Rastu, R New Zealand
145 E3	Rastatt New Zealand
31 J4	Rataje Czechoslovakia
26 L1	Ratalovka U.S.S.R.
28 B5	Rateje Sweden
26 L6	Rateje Sweden
133 G6	Ratak Is isld Pacific Oc
76 F3	Ratangarh India
76 C4	Ratchaburi Thailand
94 J6	Ratcliff Arkansas
110 C6	Ratcliff Arkansas
109 M4	Ratcliff Texas
33 N5	Ratekau W Germany
74 H6	Rath India

Rio Vista — Rovno
65

109 K3 Rio Vista Texas
130 C6 Riozinho, R Brazil
48 F6 Ripanj Yugoslavia
44 B1 Riparia Italy
100 G3 Riparia Washington
26 L5 Ripats Sweden
122 K2 Ripault, L Quebec
45 O4 Ripe Italy
45 O6 Ripi Italy
103 K8 Ripley California
9 E1 Ripley Derby England
94 H4 Ripley New York
13 G5 Ripley N Yorks England
110 N3 Ripley Ohio
107 O5 Ripley Oklahoma
120 J8 Ripley Ontario
9 F5 Ripley Surrey England
110 G6 Ripley Tennessee
94 F8 Ripley W Virginia
17 J2 Ripoll Spain
102 C4 Ripon California
13 G5 Ripon England
121 P7 Ripon Quebec
99 S6 Ripon Wisconsin
99 M8 Rippey Iowa
13 G6 Ripponden England
100 J4 Riqgins Idaho
45 N5 Riqnano Flaminio Italy
28 C5 Ris Denmark
78 G4 Risafe Syria
42 J6 Risan Yugoslavia
79 D8 Risân 'Aneiza mt Egypt
26 H7 Risbäck Sweden
18 E9 Riscle France
131 B5 Risco Plateado peak Argentina
139 H9 Risdon V Tasmania
28 C6 Rise Denmark
26 H7 Risede Sweden
28 C3 Risgårde Bredning B Denmark
47 H2 Rish Bulgaria
60 P1 Rishiri-suidō str Japan
60 P1 Rishiri-tō isld Japan
80 C6 Rishon le Zion Israel
112 B3 Rising Fawn Georgia
109 J3 Rising Star Texas
95 L7 Rising Sun Maryland
94 D5 Rising Sun Ohio
110 M3 Risinq Sun Indiana
117 M10 Riske Creek Br Columbia
20 G4 Risle R France
42 F3 Risnjak mt Yugoslavia
48 J5 Rîsnov Romania
111 D8 Rison Arkansas
27 D13 Risör Norway
20 K4 Ris-Orandis France
40 D4 Risoux, Mont France
19 K6 Risoux, Mt France
36 H7 Riss R W Germany
26 D8 Rissa Norway
145 F3 Rissington New Zealand
52 B5 Rist U.S.S.R.
29 N10 Ristiina Finland
29 N7 Ristijärvi Finland
52 D1 Ristikent U.S.S.R.
28 F7 Ristinge Denmark
26 M5 Risträsk Sweden
108 B8 Rita Blanca Cr R Texas
142 B5 Ritchie Reef W Australia
68 A6 Ritchie's Arch Andaman Is
115 O4 Ritenbenk Greenland
83 K9 Ritigala mt Sri Lanka
37 J3 Ritschenhausen E Germany
100 F5 Ritter Oregon
32 J6 Ritterhude W Germany
102 E4 Ritter, Mt California
94 F6 Rittman Ohio
32 M10 Rittmarshausen W Germany
100 G2 Ritzville Washington
68 D7 Riu, Laem Thailand
71 K9 Riung Flores Indonesia
41 N6 Riva Italy
20 E3 Riva Bella France
133 E2 Rivadavia Argentina
133 C3 Rivadavia Chile
38 F8 Riva di Tures Italy
22 K3 Rivage Belgium
19 N14 Rival R France
125 M4 Rivas Nicaragua
21 C9 Rivedoux-Plage France
133 E5 Rivera Argentina
131 G3 Rivera Uruguay
102 D4 Riverbank California
85 C7 River Cess Liberia
102 E5 Riverdale California
107 N4 Riverdale Kansas
101 O2 Riverdale Montana
98 E2 Riverdale N Dakota
98 G9 Riverdale Nebraska
123 L8 River Denys C Breton I, N S
111 K10 River Falls Alabama
99 O5 River Falls Wisconsin
95 P6 Riverhead Long I, N Y
123 T7 Riverhead Nfld
122 H8 River Hébert Nova Scotia
118 L8 Riverhurst Sask
143 D8 Riverina W Australia
139 H5 Riverina reg New S Wales
122 J8 River John Nova Scotia
109 L9 River Oaks Texas
123 P3 River of Ponds Nfld
133 C7 Rivero, I Chile
122 H9 Riverport Nova Scotia
119 R8 Rivers Manitoba
144 B6 Riversdale New Zealand
145 F4 Riversdale New Zealand
89 B10 Riversdale S Africa
102 G8 Riverside California
95 K8 Riverside Maryland
120 H10 Riverside Ontario
100 G6 Riverside Oregon
109 M5 Riverside Texas
101 N8 Riverside Utah
101 T8 Riverside Wyoming
98 B9 Riverside Res Colorado
117 K10 Rivers Inlet Br Columbia
140 E4 Riversleigh Queensland
119 M9 Rivers, L. of the Sask
110 G2 Riverton Illinois
99 L9 Riverton Iowa
119 U8 Riverton Manitoba
98 H9 Riverton Nebraska
144 B7 Riverton New Zealand
138 E5 Riverton S Australia
94 J8 Riverton Virginia
101 R6 Riverton Wyoming
110 F6 Rivervale Arkansas
98 G7 Riverview Nebraska
19 P14 Rives France
110 G5 Rives Tennessee
94 C4 Rives Junc Michigan
94 G7 Rivesville W Virginia
109 K8 Riviera Texas
113 G11 Riviera Beach Florida
44 F3 Riviera di Levante Italy
44 D4 Riviera di Ponente Italy
20 D4 Rivière Orne France
22 D3 Rivière Pas-de-Calais France
122 G4 Rivière à Claude Quebec
122 J4 Rivière-à-la-Loutre Quebec
121 S6 Rivière à Pierre Quebec
122 H5 Rivière-au-Renard Quebec
122 G3 Rivière aux Graines Quebec
121 S5 Rivière-aux-Rats Quebec
122 D6 Rivière Bleue Quebec
122 K4 Rivière-de-la-Chaloupe Quebec
122 C6 Rivière du Loup Quebec
121 S5 Rivière du Milieu Quebec
122 B5 Rivière du Moulin Quebec
121 M4 Rivière Héva Quebec
122 G4 Rivière La Madeleine Quebec
122 B6 Rivière Ouelle Quebec
122 E4 Rivière Pentecôte Quebec
122 G3 Rivière Pigou Quebec
127 M4 Rivière Pilote Martinique W I
122 C5 Rivière-Portneuf Quebec
122 H3 Rivière St. Jean Quebec
20 F3 Rivière-St. Sauveur, la France
127 L4 Rivière Salée Martinique W I
122 D6 Rivière-Verte New Brunswick
122 C6 Rivière Verte Quebec
44 C1 Rivoli Italy
138 E6 Rivoli B S Australia
28 N1 Rivtangi C Faeroes
145 D4 Riwaka New Zealand
72 F4 Riyadh Saudi Arabia
71 E3 Rizal Luzon Philippines
78 H1 Rize Turkey
65 D7 Rizhao China
Rizhskiy Zaliv see Riga, Gulf of
79 E3 Rizokarpaso Cyprus
46 E5 Rízoma Greece
43 H10 Rizzuto, C Italy
27 C12 Rjukan Norway
27 B12 Rjuven Norway
85 A5 Rkiz, L Mauritania
80 E1 Rmaïch Lebanon
68 H5 Ro Vietnam
144 C5 Roa New Zealand
27 E11 Roa Norway
16 E3 Roa Spain
110 K2 Roachdale Indiana
9 F3 Roade England
106 B9 Road Forks New Mexico
127 M5 Roadtown Virgin Is
28 B6 Roager Denmark
103 P2 Roan Cliffs Utah
106 B2 Roan Cr Colorado
112 E1 Roan Mt N Carolina
18 H6 Roanne France
111 L8 Roanoke Alabama
99 R9 Roanoke Illinois
94 B6 Roanoke Indiana
109 K3 Roanoke Texas
94 H9 Roanoke Virginia
112 M2 Roanoke I N Carolina
112 K1 Roanoke Rapids N Carolina
106 B2 Roan Plateau Colorado
103 P2 Roan Plateau Utah
109 M5 Roans Prairie Texas
95 L5 Roaring Branch Pennsylvania
112 F1 Roaring Gap N Carolina
108 G2 Roaring Springs Texas
14 B5 Roaringwater B Irish Rep
77 D4 Robāt Iran
77 B2 Robąt Karim Iran
109 J9 Robberson Texas
112 H2 Robbins N Carolina
139 G8 Robbins I Tasmania
112 D2 Robbinsville N Carolina
44 E1 Robbio Italy
138 E6 Robe S Australia
14 B3 Robe R Irish Rep
33 R6 Röbel E Germany
109 O4 Robeline Louisiana
138 F4 Robe, Mt New S Wales
122 K3 Robe Noir, L. de la Quebec
142 B5 Robe R W Australia
112 K2 Robersonville N Carolina
127 L4 Robert Martinique W I
146 E15 Robert I S Shetland Is
108 G4 Robert Lee Texas
140 B7 Robert, Mt N Terr Aust
13 F3 Roberton Scotland
101 N6 Roberts Idaho
101 Q4 Roberts Montana
100 E5 Roberts Oregon
123 R4 Robert's Arm Nfld
9 G6 Robertsbridge England
102 H2 Roberts Cr. Mt Nevada
111 J11 Robertsdale Alabama
26 L7 Robertsfors Sweden
110 A6 Robert S. Kerr Res Oklahoma
141 K8 Roberts, Mt Queensland
101 Q7 Roberts Mt Wyoming
89 A9 Robertson S Africa
101 P8 Robertson Wyoming
141 G4 Robertson R Queensland
146 K6 Robertson B Antarctica
146 E14 Robertson L Antarctica
142 D6 Robertson Ra W Australia
121 T6 Robertsonville Quebec
85 B7 Robertsport Liberia
14 E3 Robertstown Irish Rep
138 E5 Robertstown S Australia
122 G6 Robertville New Brunswick
87 C8 Robert Williams Angola
121 S4 Roberval Quebec
115 N1 Robeson Chan Canada/Greenland
8 B4 Robeston Wathen Wales
101 N7 Robin Idaho
100 J5 Robinette Oregon
13 H5 Robin Hoods Bay England
110 J2 Robinson Illinois
98 G2 Robinson N Dakota
141 J7 Robinson R Queensland
133 B9 Robinson Crusoe isld Juan Fernández Is Pac Oc
138 D2 Robinson, Mt S Australia
142 C6 Robinson, Mt W Australia
116 Q6 Robinson Mts Alaska
143 C7 Robinson Ras W Australia
140 D3 Robinson River N Terr Aust
122 F6 Robinsonville New Brunswick
139 G5 Robinvale New S Wales
17 F6 Robledo Spain
103 N9 Robles Pass Arizona
103 N9 Robles Ranch Arizona
118 A1 Roblin Park Manitoba
128 G7 Robore Bolivia
118 H9 Robsart Sask
114 H7 Robson, Mt Alberta/Br Col
117 O9 Robson, Mt Br Columbia
109 K8 Robstown Texas
16 A6 Roca, C. da Portugal
87 B9 Rocadas Angola
119 Q8 Rocanville Sask
129 M4 Rocas isld Brazil
124 B5 Rocas Alijos isld Mexico
43 G8 Rocca d'Aspide Italy
45 P5 Rocca di Mezzo Italy
45 N6 Rocca di Papa Italy
45 O6 Roccagorga Italy
43 H8 Rocca Imperiale Italy
Rocca Littorio see Gallacaio
45 P7 Roccamonfina Italy
38 E9 Rocca Pietore Italy
45 L3 Rocca San Casciano Italy
45 P6 Roccasecca Italy
45 N5 Rocca Sinibalda Italy
42 D5 Roccastrada Italy
44 B1 Rocciamelone mt Italy
40 E5 Roc d'Enfer mt France
131 G5 Rocha Uruguay
131 G4 Rocha dep Uruguay
20 E5 Rochard, Mt France
13 F6 Rochdale England
121 N4 Rochebaucourt Quebec
18 D5 Roche-Bernard, la France
21 G10 Rochechouart France
22 K3 Roche-en-Ardenne, La Belgium
22 J3 Rochefort Belgium
21 D10 Rochefort France
19 N17 Rochefort-du-Gard France
18 G7 Rochefort-Montagne France
18 F7 Rochefoucauld, la France
20 J3 Roche Guyon, la France
22 J4 Rochehaut Belgium
113 E8 Rochelle Florida
112 D6 Rochelle Georgia
99 R8 Rochelle Illinois
111 D10 Rochelle Louisiana
109 H4 Rochelle Texas
119 P9 Roche Percee Sask
110 D3 Rocheport Missouri
21 C9 Rocher d'Antioche France
127 L4 Rocher du Diamant Martinique W I
123 O2 Rocher, L. du Quebec
117 R5 Rocher River N W Terr
122 E3 Rochers, R. aux Quebec
83 M12 Roches, Plaine des Mauritius
40 E1 Rochesson France
118 D4 Rochester Alberta
110 G2 Rochester Illinois
94 A5 Rochester Indiana
9 G5 Rochester Kent England
94 D4 Rochester Michigan
99 O5 Rochester Minnesota
95 Q3 Rochester New Hampshire
95 K3 Rochester New York
121 N9 Rochester New York
13 F3 Rochester Northumberland England
94 E5 Rochester Ohio
94 G6 Rochester Pennsylvania
108 H2 Rochester Texas
139 G6 Rochester Victoria
100 B3 Rochester Washington
9 G4 Rochford England
98 C5 Rochford S Dakota
118 B5 Rochfort Br Alberta
37 O1 Rochlitz E Germany
118 E6 Rochon Sands Prov. Park Alberta
20 K3 Rochy Conde France
107 O4 Rock Kansas
99 T3 Rock Michigan
98 K6 Rock R Iowa/Minnesota
99 S6 Rock R Wisconsin
117 K5 Rock R Yukon Terr
6 B5 Rockall N Atlantic Oc
90 H3 Rockall Bank Atlantic Oc
144 C6 Rock and Pillar Range New Zealand
117 L10 Rock Bay Br Columbia
12 E4 Rockcliffe Scotland
101 M3 Rock Cr Montana
101 S1 Rock Cr Montana
94 G5 Rock Cr Ohio
100 E4 Rock Cr Oregon
101 T8 Rock Cr Wyoming
101 L7 Rockcreek Idaho
117 D3 Rock Creek Yukon Terr
109 K5 Rockdale Texas
36 D4 Rockenhausen W Germany
146 H9 Rockerfeller Mts Antarctica
99 R8 Rock Falls Illinois
94 J9 Rockfish Virginia
111 K9 Rockford Alabama
101 N6 Rockford Idaho
99 R7 Rockford Illinois
94 B3 Rockford Michigan
99 N4 Rockford Minnesota
94 C6 Rockford Ohio
100 H2 Rockford Washington
119 M9 Rockglen Sask
98 H5 Rockham S Dakota
141 K6 Rockhampton Queensland
140 D4 Rockhampton Downs N Terr Aust
99 S1 Rock Harbor Michigan
118 J6 Rockhaven Sask
112 F3 Rock Hill S Carolina
99 Q8 Rock I Illinois
112 H3 Rockingham N Carolina
143 B9 Rockingham W Australia
141 H4 Rockingham B Queensland
121 S7 Rock Island Quebec
109 L6 Rock Island Texas
98 G1 Rock L N Dakota
100 H2 Rock L Washington
101 N7 Rockland Idaho
95 S2 Rockland Maine
99 R3 Rockland Michigan
121 P7 Rockland Ontario
109 N4 Rockland Texas
140 E4 Rocklands Queensland
138 F6 Rocklands Res Victoria
142 B6 Rocklea W Australia
141 K2 Rocklea dist Brisbane, Qnsld
100 G2 Rocklyn Washington
112 B3 Rockmart Georgia
117 Q3 Rocknest L N W Terr
33 R10 Röcknitz E Germany
95 L8 Rock Point Maryland
102 A2 Rockport California
110 E2 Rockport Illinois
110 J4 Rockport Indiana
95 S2 Rockport Maine
95 R4 Rockport Massachusetts
110 A1 Rock Port Missouri
109 K7 Rockport Texas
100 D1 Rockport Washington
101 U8 Rock River Wyoming
113 L13 Rock Sound Bahamas
126 F2 Rock Sound Eleuthera Bahamas
103 M7 Rock Springs Arizona
101 T3 Rock Springs Montana
108 G5 Rocksprings Texas
101 Q8 Rock Springs Wyoming
144 D4 Rocks Pt. New Zealand
128 G2 Rockstone Guyana
99 R7 Rockton Illinois
98 K6 Rock Valley Iowa
95 P5 Rockville Connecticut
110 J2 Rockville Indiana
95 K7 Rockville Maryland
145 D4 Rockville New Zealand
100 H6 Rockville Oregon
112 G5 Rockville S Carolina
103 L4 Rockville Utah
109 L3 Rockwall Texas
99 N7 Rockwell Iowa
112 G2 Rockwell N Carolina
99 M7 Rockwell City Iowa
106 C4 Rockwood Colorado
95 S1 Rockwood Maine
94 H7 Rockwood Pennsylvania
112 C2 Rockwood Tennessee
109 H4 Rockwood Texas
107 L6 Rocky Oklahoma
112 G2 Rocky R N Carolina
112 E3 Rocky R S Carolina
100 K6 Rocky Bar Idaho
118 D7 Rockyford Alberta
106 G3 Rocky Ford Colorado
112 F5 Rocky Ford Georgia
98 D6 Rockyford S Dakota
94 D7 Rocky Fork Res Ohio
94 H5 Rocky Grove Pennsylvania
143 B10 Rocky Gully W Australia
120 H5 Rocky Island L Ontario
119 Q4 Rocky L Manitoba
112 K2 Rocky Mount N Carolina
94 H10 Rocky Mount Virginia
118 C6 Rocky Mountain House Alberta
101 N2 Rocky Mt Montana
98 A9 Rocky Mt Nat. Park Colorado
118 B8 Rocky Mts Br Columbia
106 C1 Rocky Mts N America
127 K3 Rocky Point Jamaica
95 P6 Rocky Point Long I, N Y
98 A5 Rockypoint Wyoming
116 F4 Rocky Pt Alaska
113 K11 Rocky Pt Bahamas
94 F5 Rocky River Ohio
131 D7 Ró Colorado Argentina
20 A3 Rocque Pt., La Jersey, Channel Is
22 H4 Rocroi France
37 M2 Roda R E Germany
36 D5 Rodalben W Germany
27 C11 Rödberg Norway
28 G7 Rødby Denmark
28 G7 Rødbyhavn Denmark
123 Q3 Roddickton Nfld
28 B3 Rødding Denmark
28 C6 Rødding Sønderjylland Denmark
27 H15 Rödeby Sweden
25 F2 Roden Netherlands
32 K8 Rodenberg W Germany
27 E12 Rödenes Norway
32 H6 Rodenkirchen W Germany
37 L3 Rödental W Germany
124 G5 Rodeo Mexico
106 B10 Rodeo New Mexico
33 S10 Röderau E Germany
109 O3 Rodessa Louisiana
32 K7 Rodewald W Germany
37 N2 Rodewisch E Germany
18 G8 Rodez France
36 F2 Rodheim-Bieber W Germany
47 F4 Rodholívos Greece
47 J8 Ródhos Greece
37 O5 Roding W Germany
140 C6 Rodinga N Terr Aust
52 J2 Rodionovo U.S.S.R.
28 C4 Rødkærsbro Denmark
77 J6 Rodkhan Pakistan
48 J3 Rodnei, Muntii Romania
94 B3 Rodney Michigan
120 J10 Rodney Ontario
116 D4 Rodney, C Alaska
141 G6 Rodney Downs Queensland
52 F6 Rodniki U.S.S.R.
139 H7 Rodondo isld Victoria
13 E3 Rodono Scotland
47 G3 Rodopi Planina Bulgaria
Rodosto see Tekirdağ
26 F5 Rödöy Norway
128 D5 Rodrigues Brazil
81 D7 Rodrigues I Indian Oc
28 H7 Rødsand sandbank Denmark
28 D3 Rød Sø Denmark
28 K6 Rødvig Denmark
111 E7 Roe Arkansas
14 E2 Roe R N Ireland
142 B5 Roebourne W Australia
142 D4 Roebuck B W Australia
142 E4 Roebuck Downs W Australia
143 E9 Roe, L W Australia
143 G9 Roe Plains W Australia
25 E6 Roermond Netherlands
22 D2 Roesbrugge-Haringe Belgium
22 E2 Roeselare Belgium
115 L5 Roes Welcome Sound N W Terr
22 G3 Rœulx Belgium
45 L2 Ro Ferrarese Italy
109 L1 Roff Oklahoma
54 B3 Rogachev U.S.S.R.
128 E7 Rogaguado, L Bolivia
128 E6 Rogagua, L Bolivia
27 A12 Rogaland county Norway
54 H7 Rogan' U.S.S.R.
109 O5 Roganville Texas
48 J1 Rogatin U.S.S.R.
33 P8 Rogatz E Germany
26 F9 Rogen L Sweden
121 M5 Roger, Lac Quebec
110 B5 Rogers Arkansas
98 H2 Rogers N Dakota
109 K5 Rogers Texas
94 D1 Rogers City Michigan
102 G7 Rogers L. California
117 P10 Rogers, Mt Br Columbia
101 L7 Rogerson Idaho
110 C4 Rogersville Missouri
122 G7 Rogersville New Brunswick
112 D1 Rogersville Tennessee
98 B9 Roggen Colorado
33 O5 Roggendorf E Germany
89 A8 Roggeveld Berge mts S Africa
8 D4 Rogiet Wales
43 G9 Rogliano Italy
19 O18 Rognac France
26 H4 Rognan Norway
19 O17 Rognes France
33 O6 Rögnitz R E Germany
44 B2 Rognosa, Punta mt Italy
46 D1 Rogozna mt Yugoslavia
31 K3 Rogoźno Poland
100 A7 Rogue R Oregon
18 E6 Rohan France
121 Q3 Rohault, L Quebec
33 P6 Rohlsdorf E Germany
28 J6 Roholte Denmark
37 M6 Rohr W Germany
38 J4 Rohrbach Austria
36 C5 Rohrbach France
37 O7 Rohrbach W Germany
33 O7 Rohrberg E Germany
36 G4 Rohrbrunn W Germany
74 C5 Rohri Pakistan
37 L7 Röhrmoos W Germany
74 G4 Rohtak India
111 E8 Rohwer Arkansas
22 E4 Roisel France
22 F3 Roisin Belgium
33 Q9 Roitzsch Halle E Germany
33 R9 Roitzsch Leipzig E Germany
52 B6 Roja U.S.S.R.
26 G9 Röjan Sweden
133 E4 Rojas Argentina
127 L5 Rojo, C Puerto Rico
141 G2 Rokeby Queensland
119 P7 Rokeby Sask
52 C6 Rokiškis U.S.S.R.
61 P5 Rokkasho Japan
26 M6 Roknäs Sweden
61 O6 Rokugō Japan
61 L8 Rokugō-saki C Japan
30 H6 Rokycany Czechoslovakia
44 C4 Rola R Italy
40 B2 Rolampont France
110 D7 Roland Arkansas
99 N7 Roland Iowa
118 D1 Roland Manitoba
83 L13 Roland isld Kerguelen Indian Oc
130 D8 Rolândia Brazil
27 B12 Röldal Norway
25 G3 Rolde Netherlands
98 G1 Rolette N Dakota
99 M7 Rolfe Iowa
94 J5 Rolfe Pennsylvania
141 H6 Rolfes Queensland
103 L9 Roll Arizona
117 N8 Rolla Br Columbia
107 J4 Rolla Kansas
110 E4 Rolla Missouri
98 G1 Rolla N Dakota
27 D11 Rollag Norway
144 D5 Rolleston New Zealand
141 J6 Rolleston Queensland
144 C5 Rolleston, Mt New Zealand
121 L5 Rollet Quebec
20 F2 Rolleville France
111 F9 Rolling Fork Mississippi
110 L4 Rolling Fork R Kentucky
101 L2 Rollins Montana
45 J2 Rolo Italy
33 R4 Rolofshagen E Germany
68 G6 Rolous Cambodia
121 N6 Rolphton Ontario
28 F6 Rolsted Denmark
26 N1 Rolvsöy isld Norway
28 A3 Rom Denmark
44 M6 Roma Italy
141 J7 Roma Queensland
27 K14 Roma Sweden
45 M3 Romagna reg Italy
42 B3 Romagnano Italy
20 C5 Romagné France
22 J5 Romagne-sous-Montfaucon France
144 B7 Romahapa New Zealand
122 J3 Romaine, R Quebec
109 H9 Roma Los Saenz Texas
47 F1 Roman Bulgaria
48 K4 Roman Romania
126 F3 Romana, Cayo isld Cuba
19 P14 Romanche R France
90 H8 Romanche Gap Atlantic Oc
19 N12 Romanèche-Thorins France
71 N8 Romang isld Indonesia
48 G5 Romania rep E Europe
113 F12 Romano, C Florida
58 F1 Romanovka U.S.S.R.
55 D2 Romanovo U.S.S.R.
36 C6 Romanswiller France
116 D6 Romanzof, C Alaska
116 Q2 Romanzof Mts Alaska
128 F4 Romão Brazil
20 B5 Romazy France
71 F4 Romblon Philippines
Rome see Roma
111 L7 Rome Georgia
95 M3 Rome New York
95 L5 Rome Pennsylvania
110 K5 Rome Tennessee
106 E4 Romeo Colorado
94 D4 Romeo Michigan
36 E5 Römerberg W Germany
22 H3 Romerée Belgium
27 E11 Romerike reg Norway
125 K8 Romero Mexico
106 E6 Romeroville New Mexico
36 H7 Römerstein W Germany
40 C6 Romey, Val France
9 G4 Romford England
37 K3 Römhild E Germany
20 B5 Romille France
18 H4 Romilly France
20 H3 Romilly-sur-Andelle France
142 F5 Romily, Mt W Australia
36 B1 Rommerskirchen W Germany
94 J7 Romney W Virginia
54 E6 Romny U.S.S.R.
28 A6 Rømo isld Denmark
54 E6 Romodan U.S.S.R.
21 I7 Romorantin France
69 F11 Rompin Malaysia
36 G2 Romrod W Germany
26 C9 Romsdal V Norway
26 B9 Romsdalsfjord inlet Norway
9 E6 Romsey England
28 F5 Romsø isld Denmark
94 D4 Romulus Michigan
68 H4 Ron Vietnam
15 C3 Rona isld Scotland
101 L2 Ronan Montana
28 B3 Rønbjerg Denmark
129 H6 Roncador, Sa. do mts Brazil
94 G9 Ronceverte W Virginia
20 C4 Roncey France
40 E2 Ronchamp France
44 M5 Ronciglione Italy
45 M3 Ronco R Italy
45 J1 Roncoferraro Italy
45 M3 Roncofreddo Italy
22 E2 Roncq France
16 D8 Ronda Spain
26 D10 Rondane Norway
16 D8 Ronda, Sa. de mts Spain
128 F7 Rondas-das-Salinas Brazil
28 E4 Rønde Denmark
120 J10 Rondeau Prov. Park Ontario
83 L14 Ronde I Kerguelen Indian Oc
26 D10 Rondeslottet mt Norway
128 D2 Rondón Colombia
128 F6 Rondônia Brazil
130 C5 Rondonópolis Brazil
128 F3 Rondon, Pico mt Brazil
88 G7 Rondo Plat Tanzania
36 B2 Rondorf W Germany
95 N5 Rondout Res New York
27 K14 Ronehamn Sweden
67 C4 Rong'an China
67 B2 Rongchang China
65 C5 Rongcheng China
65 E6 Rongcheng China
67 C4 Rongjiang China
67 C4 Rong Jiang R China
68 A1 Rongklang Ra Burma
145 E4 Rongotea New Zealand
67 C4 Rongshui China
88 H7 Rongüi isld Mozambique
67 A2 Rong Xian China
67 C5 Rong Xian China
27 G16 Rønne Denmark
27 F15 Rönnea R Sweden
37 N2 Ronneburg E Germany
27 H15 Ronneby Sweden
146 F12 Ronne Entrance Antarctica
146 F11 Ronne Ice Shelf Antarctica
32 L8 Ronnenberg W Germany
26 G8 Rönnöfors Sweden
142 C5 Ronsard I W Australia
22 F2 Ronse Belgium
129 H6 Ronuro R Brazil
25 G2 Roodeschool Netherlands
110 F2 Roodhouse Illinois
22 L4 Roodt Luxembourg
89 F4 Rooiberg mt S Africa
25 B5 Roosendaal Netherlands
103 N8 Roosevelt Arizona
99 L1 Roosevelt Minnesota
109 H1 Roosevelt Oklahoma
108 G5 Roosevelt Texas
101 P9 Roosevelt Utah
100 E4 Roosevelt Washington
103 N8 Roosevelt Dam Arizona
117 O12 Roosevelt, F.D., L Washington
135 L16 Roosevelt I Antarctica
117 L6 Roosevelt, Mt Br Columbia
14 D3 Roosky Irish Rep
89 F5 Roossenekal mt S Africa
99 P6 Root R Minnesota
117 L4 Root R N W Terr
116 E9 Rootok I Aleutian Is
52 B6 Ropaži U.S.S.R.
52 H3 Ropcha U.S.S.R.
31 N5 Ropczyce Poland
112 L2 Roper N Carolina
140 D2 Roper R N Terr Aust
141 J7 Roper Pass Queensland
140 C2 Roper River N Terr Aust
29 J3 Ropi mt Finland
36 D6 Roppenheim France
18 E8 Roquefort France
19 N16 Roquemaure France
121 L4 Roquemaure Quebec
19 P18 Roquevaire France
15 E2 Rora Head Scotland
128 F2 Roraima mt Guyana
128 F3 Roraima state Brazil
27 F10 Rörbäcksnäs Sweden
28 D3 Rørbæk Denmark
28 G5 Rørby Denmark
119 S7 Rorketon Manitoba
26 E9 Röros Norway
41 L3 Rorschach Switzerland
26 H4 Rörstad Norway
28 H5 Rørvig Denmark
26 E7 Rörvik Norway
26 G6 Röså R Norway
43 B12 Rosa, C Algeria
122 B7 Rosaire Quebec
107 O4 Rosalia Kansas
100 H2 Rosalia Washington
118 E6 Rosalind Alberta
126 D6 Rosalind Bank Caribbean
102 F7 Rosamond California
102 F7 Rosamond L California
40 G6 Rosa, Monte mt Italy
124 G6 Rosamorada Mexico
109 K6 Rosanky Texas
41 M3 Rosanna R Austria
124 E4 Rosa, Pta C Mexico
131 E4 Rosario Argentina
124 B2 Rosario Baja California Mexico
129 K4 Rosário Brazil
128 E8 Rosario Chile
124 H4 Rosario Coahuila Mexico
124 E4 Rosario Mexico
130 B9 Rosario Paraguay
71 E4 Rosario Philippines
127 H9 Rosario Venezuela
126 B5 Rosario Bank Caribbean
126 D4 Rosario, Cayo del Cuba
133 E3 Rosario de la Frontera Argentina
133 D2 Rosario de Lerma Argentina
133 F4 Rosario del Tala Argentina
126 C3 Rosario, Sa. del hills Cuba
124 B3 Rosarito Mexico
124 D4 Rosarito Mexico
16 D4 Rosarito Embalse de res Spain
18 H10 Rosas Spain
33 N7 Rosche W Germany
99 S7 Roscoe Illinois
101 Q4 Roscoe Montana
95 N5 Roscoe New York
98 G4 Roscoe S Dakota
108 G3 Roscoe Texas
18 C4 Roscoff France
14 C3 Roscommon Irish Rep
94 C2 Roscommon Michigan
14 C3 Roscommon co Irish Rep
14 D4 Roscrea Irish Rep
98 G7 Rose Nebraska
127 O7 Roseau Dominica
98 K1 Roseau R Minnesota
100 J5 Roseberry Idaho
139 H8 Roseberry Tasmania
140 E7 Roseberth Queensland Aust
123 O6 Rose Blanche Nfld
112 J3 Roseboro N Carolina
118 D7 Rosebud Alberta
110 E3 Rosebud Missouri
101 T3 Rosebud Montana
108 A8 Rosebud New Mexico
98 F6 Rosebud S Dakota
109 L4 Rosebud Texas
101 T4 Rosebud Cr Montana
101 S4 Rosebud Mts Montana
100 B6 Roseburg Oregon
94 C3 Rosebush Michigan
94 C2 Rose City Michigan
102 G1 Rose Creek Nevada
118 E7 Rosedale Alberta
110 J2 Rosedale Indiana
111 F8 Rosedale Mississippi
141 K6 Rosedale Queensland
13 H5 Rosedale Abbey England
22 H3 Rosée Belgium
38 K8 Rosegg Austria
127 J1 Rose Hall Jamaica
99 O8 Rose Hill Iowa
83 L12 Rose Hill Mauritius
112 J3 Rose Hill N Carolina
113 K12 Rose I Bahamas
111 F11 Roseland Louisiana
118 F7 Rose Lynn Alberta
118 E8 Rosemary Alberta
6 D3 Rosemary Bank N Atlantic Oc
142 B5 Rosemary I W Australia
99 N5 Rosemount Minnesota
102 E2 Rose, Mt Nevada
38 J8 Rosenbach mt Austria
33 O5 Rosenberg E Germany
109 M6 Rosenberg Texas
36 G5 Rosenberg W Germany
22 C1 Rosendaël France
32 F8 Rosendahl W Germany
110 B1 Rosendale Missouri
121 M8 Roseneath Ontario
12 D1 Roseneath Scotland
36 F7 Rosenfeld W Germany
32 L6 Rosengarten W Germany
38 F6 Rosenheim W Germany
38 M8 Rosenkopf mt Austria
38 J8 Rosennock mt Austria
38 K8 Rosental V Austria
36 F2 Rosenthal W Germany
109 O5 Rosepine Louisiana
117 H8 Rose Pt Br Columbia
140 D2 Rose R N Terr Aust
118 J8 Roseray Sask
126 G3 Roses Long I Bahamas
118 K7 Rosetown Sask
Rosetta Egypt see Rashîd
141 H5 Rosetta R Queensland
101 M8 Rosette Utah
119 O6 Rose Valley Sask
110 F1 Roseville Illinois
94 E7 Roseville Ohio
118 A5 Rosewear Alberta
141 K8 Rosewood Queensland
101 L7 Roseworth Idaho
52 E6 Roshal' U.S.S.R.
109 M6 Rosharon Texas
52 C4 Roshchino U.S.S.R.
36 C6 Rosheim France
80 C5 Rosh Ha 'Ayin Israel
77 F2 Roshkhvār Iran
98 K4 Rosholt S Dakota
99 R5 Rosholt Wisconsin
80 F2 Rosh Pinna Israel
57 F6 Roshtkala U.S.S.R.
80 D7 Rosh Zurim Jordan
31 J6 Rosice Czechoslovakia
110 H4 Rosiclare Illinois
22 D4 Rosières-en-Santerre France
122 H5 Rosiers, C.des Quebec
142 A5 Rosily I W Australia
47 G1 Roşiorii de Vede Romania
47 J1 Rositsa Bulgaria
47 G1 Rositsa R Bulgaria
37 N1 Rositz E Germany
28 J5 Roskilde Denmark
28 J5 Roskilde co Denmark
33 R8 Roskow E Germany
103 N9 Roskruge Mts Arizona
54 D3 Roslavl' U.S.S.R.
14 D2 Roslea N Ireland
28 B3 Roslev Denmark
52 F5 Roslyatino U.S.S.R.
98 J4 Roslyn S Dakota
100 D2 Roslyn Washington
120 C3 Roslyn L Ontario
28 F4 Rosmus Denmark
28 F5 Røsnæs C Denmark
21 H8 Rosnay France
45 M1 Rosolina Italy
18 C5 Rosporden France
22 L4 Rosport Luxembourg
36 C2 Rosrath W Germany
98 D1 Ross N Dakota
144 C5 Ross New Zealand
139 J8 Ross Tasmania
101 U6 Ross Wyoming
83 L14 Ross mt Kerguelen Indian Oc
48 N1 Ross R U.S.S.R.
41 K5 Rossa Switzerland
37 K3 Rossach W Germany
Ross and Cromarty co see Highland reg
43 H9 Rossano Italy
14 C2 Rossan Pt Irish Rep
37 N3 Rossbach Czechoslovakia
33 P10 Rossbach E Germany
111 G9 Ross Barnett Res Mississippi
119 R8 Rossburn Manitoba
14 B5 Ross Carbery Irish Rep
108 F3 Ross City Texas
146 J7 Ross Dependency Antarctica
37 J2 Rossdorf E Germany
121 L7 Rosseau Ontario
137 L4 Rossel isld Louisiade Arch
119 T9 Rossendale Manitoba
109 L3 Rosser Texas
8 D1 Rossett Wales
26 K2 Rossfjord Norway
83 M9 Ross Hill mt Christmas I Indian Oc
146 J6 Ross I Antarctica
119 U4 Ross I Manitoba
146 H7 Ross Ice Shelf Antarctica
22 J4 Rossignal Belgium
122 G9 Rossignol Res Nova Scotia
94 J6 Rossiter Pennsylvania
143 E10 Rossiter B W Australia
52 Rossiyskaya SFSR U.S.S.R.
100 D1 Ross L Washington
33 O10 Rossla E Germany
100 H1 Rossland Br Columbia
14 E4 Rosslare Irish Rep
33 Q9 Rosslau E Germany
33 O10 Rossleben E Germany
145 E4 Ross, Mt New Zealand
85 A5 Rosso Mauritania
8 D4 Ross-on-Wye England
54 L6 Rossosh' U.S.S.R.
33 R6 Rossow E Germany
120 C4 Rossport Ontario
117 G4 Ross River Yukon Terr
146 J7 Ross Sea Antarctica
37 K5 Rosstal W Germany
108 E7 Rosston Oklahoma
33 O9 Rosstrappe E Germany
26 G6 Rössvassbukt Norway
26 G6 Rössvatn L Norway
110 J5 Rossview Res Tennessee
112 B3 Rossville Georgia
110 J1 Rossville Illinois
107 P2 Rossville Kansas
37 P1 Rosswein E Germany
117 J8 Rosswood Br Columbia
26 F4 Röst isld Norway
26 L3 Rosta Norway
26 L3 Rostaelv R Norway
26 L2 Rostafjord mt Norway
27 F16 Röstånga Sweden
118 L6 Rosthern Sask
36 C2 Rostingen W Germany
33 Q4 Rostock E Germany
33 Q4 Rostock reg E Germany
52 E6 Rostov U.S.S.R.
53 E10 Rostov-na-Donu U.S.S.R.
18 C4 Rostrenen France
28 D3 Rostrup Denmark
46 D3 Rostuša Yugoslavia
26 D9 Röstvangen Norway
52 H2 Rosvinskoye U.S.S.R.
112 C3 Roswell Georgia
108 C2 Roswell New Mexico
27 G10 Rot Sweden
41 M1 Rot R W Germany
16 C8 Rota Spain
26 F5 Rota C Norway
37 J5 Rot am See W Germany
108 G3 Rotan Texas
37 N5 Rot Buhl mt W Germany
36 H2 Rotenburg Hessen W Germany
32 K6 Rotenburg/Wümme Niedersachsen W Germany
38 G8 Roter Kopf mt Austria
37 L3 Roter Main R W Germany
32 H5 Roter Sand W Germany
41 L3 Rote Wand mt Austria
25 F7 Rotgen W Germany
36 D2 Roth W Germany
37 N1 Rötha E Germany
36 E1 Rothaargebirge mts W Germany
36 C7 Rothau France
13 G3 Rothbury England
99 U6 Rothbury Michigan
36 D2 Rothe Mühle W Germany
37 L5 Röthenbach W Germany
41 L2 Röthenbach W Germany
33 P9 Rothenburg E Germany
37 J5 Rothenburg ober der Tauber W Germany
20 B4 Rothéneuf France
36 E6 Rothenfels Baden-Württemberg W Germany
36 H4 Rothenfels W Germany
37 L3 Rothenkirchen W Germany
33 O10 Rothenschirmbach E Germany
13 G6 Rotherham England
144 D5 Rotherham New Zealand
9 G5 Rother, R England
15 E3 Rothes Scotland
122 G8 Rothesay New Brunswick
12 C2 Rothesay Scotland
40 H4 Rothorn mt Switzerland
98 K3 Rothsay Minnesota
146 F13 Rothschild I Antarctica
71 L10 Roti, Selat Indonesia
139 H5 Roto New S Wales
145 E3 Rotoaira, L New Zealand
145 F2 Rotoehu, L New Zealand
145 D4 Rotoiti, L New Zealand
145 F3 Rotoiti, L New Zealand
145 F3 Rotomahana New Zealand
145 F3 Rotoma, L New Zealand
144 C5 Rotomanu New Zealand
45 O5 Rotondo, M mt Italy
145 D4 Rotoroa, L New Zealand
145 F3 Rotorua New Zealand
145 E2 Rotowaro New Zealand
20 E3 Rots France
41 N2 Rott W Germany
37 O7 Rott R W Germany
33 R9 Rotta E Germany
36 F7 Rottenburg W Germany
37 J4 Rottendorf W Germany
38 K6 Rottenmann Austria
38 K7 Rottenmanner Tauern mts Austria
25 C5 Rotterdam Netherlands
37 P7 Rotthalmünster W Germany
9 F6 Rottingdean England
36 H4 Rottingen W Germany
33 N9 Rottleberode E Germany
143 B9 Rottnest I W Australia
33 R8 Rottstock E Germany
25 G1 Rottumeroog isld Netherlands
25 F2 Rottumerplaat Netherlands
41 J1 Rottweil W Germany
137 Q4 Rotuma isld Pacific Oc
37 O5 Rötz W Germany
21 B7 Rouans France
22 E2 Roubaix France
19 N15 Roubion R France
31 H5 Roudnice Czechoslovakia
20 H3 Rouen France
40 F2 Rouffach France
21 C6 Rougé France
40 D3 Rougemont France
8 D2 Roughclose England
144 B6 Rough Ridge New Zealand
110 K4 Rough R. Res Kentucky
19 P18 Rougiers France
21 E10 Rouillac France
119 N8 Rouleau Sask
Roulers see Roeselare
94 J5 Roulette Pennsylvania
121 L5 Roulier Quebec
18 F7 Roumazières France
116 J4 Roundabout Mt Alaska
101 L2 Round Butte Montana
123 R4 Round Harbour Nfld
118 E5 Round Hill Alberta
141 K6 Round Hill Hd Queensland
141 J5 Roundhill, Mt Queensland
116 H7 Round I Alaska
87 G12 Round I Mauritius
109 J5 Round Mountain Texas
102 G3 Round Mt Nevada
139 K4 Round Mt New S Wales
95 S3 Round Pond Maine
123 R5 Round Pond Nfld
109 K5 Round Rock Texas
117 R3 Roundrock L N W Terr
110 E4 Round Spring Missouri
101 R3 Roundup Montana
119 S9 Rounthwaite Manitoba
129 H3 Roura Fr Guiana
75 L7 Rourkela India
15 F1 Rousay Orkney Scotland
106 F4 Rouse Colorado
94 H5 Rouseville Pennsylvania
142 A2 Rous Hd Perth, W Aust
133 D9 Rous, Pen Chile
19 O17 Roussillon France
21 G10 Roussines France
22 L5 Roussy-le-Village France
19 P15 Route Napoléon France
20 G3 Routot France
25 F3 Rouveen Netherlands
121 U3 Rouvray, L Quebec
40 A2 Rouvres France
22 H4 Rouvroy-sur-Audry France
22 G3 Roux Belgium
89 E8 Rouxville S Africa
121 M4 Rouyn Quebec
48 L1 Rov R U.S.S.R.
41 M6 Rovato Italy
26 A9 Rovde Norway
52 F4 Rovdino U.S.S.R.
54 L8 Roven'ki U.S.S.R.
45 J1 Roverbella Italy
41 O6 Rovereto Italy
68 F6 Rovieng Cambodia
45 L1 Rovigo Italy
45 P1 Rovinj Yugoslavia
45 P1 Rovinjsko Selo Yugoslavia
53 C8 Rovno U.S.S.R.

66
Rovuma — St. Germain au Mt D'Or

87 G8 Rovuma R Mozambique
99 N7 Rowan Iowa
118 J1 Rowan L Ontario
106 E6 Rowe New Mexico
139 J3 Rowena New S Wales
108 G4 Rowena Texas
112 G4 Rowesville S Carolina
100 K8 Rowland Nevada
94 H7 Rowlesburg W Virginia
118 E7 Rowley Alberta
115 M4 Rowley I N W Terr
142 C3 Rowley Shoals W Australia
103 M9 Rowood Arizona
9 E1 Rowsley England
103 K5 Rox Nevada
71 E2 Roxas Luzon Philippines
71 E4 Roxas Mindoro Philippines
71 D5 Roxas Palawan Philippines
71 F5 Roxas Panay Philippines
112 H1 Roxboro N Carolina
127 N2 Roxborough Tobago
140 E6 Roxborough Downs Queensland
144 B6 Roxburgh New Zealand
Roxburgh co see Borders reg
95 N4 Roxbury New York
95 P2 Roxbury Vermont
27 H13 Roxen L Sweden
111 E10 Roxie Mississippi
121 S7 Roxton Quebec
109 M2 Roxton Texas
101 N7 Roy Idaho
101 R2 Roy Montana
106 F6 Roy New Mexico
100 C2 Roy Washington
98 H7 Royal Nebraska
14 E3 Royal Canal Irish Rep
99 U9 Royal Center Indiana
70 C1 Royal Charlotte Reef S China Sea
113 L12 Royal I Bahamas
120 B3 Royal, Mount Ontario
119 P1 Royal, Mt Ontario
89 F7 Royal Natal Nat. Park S Africa
94 D4 Royal Oak Michigan
113 F12 Royal Palm Hammock Florida
113 G12 Royal Palm Ranger Sta Florida
146 H6 Royal Society Rge Antarctica
118 C8 Royalties Alberta
18 E7 Royan France
19 O14 Roybon France
22 D4 Roye France
95 M6 Royersford Pennsylvania
142 C6 Roy Hill W Australia
27 D11 Röykenvik Norway
122 C4 Roy, L Quebec
26 G7 Röyrvik Norway
109 L3 Royse City Texas
26 C10 Röysheim Norway
9 F3 Royston England
112 D3 Royston Georgia
29 L6 Röytta Finland
31 N3 Różan Poland
46 E3 Rožden Yugoslavia
20 A3 Rozel Jersey, Channel Is
107 L3 Rozel Kansas
20 B3 Rozel, Pte.du France
98 A5 Rozet Wyoming
31 L1 Rozewie C Poland
55 F5 Rozhdestvenka U.S.S.R.
52 G5 Rozhdestvenskoye U.S.S.R.
22 G4 Rozoy France
31 M4 Rozprza Poland
31 N5 Rozwadów Poland
46 E1 Rtanj mt Yugoslavia
87 G7 Ruaha, Gt R Tanzania
88 E5 Ruaha Nat. Park Tanzania
145 F4 Ruahine Range New Zealand
145 E1 Ruakaka New Zealand
145 E2 Ruakura Jun New Zealand
71 J4 Ruang isld Indonesia
145 E3 Ruapehu vol New Zealand
144 B7 Ruapuke I New Zealand
145 F3 Ruatahuna New Zealand
144 C5 Ruatapu New Zealand
71 J9 Rua, Tg C Sumba Indonesia
145 F3 Ruatoki New Zealand
145 G2 Ruatoria New Zealand
145 E2 Ruawai New Zealand
77 C7 Ru'ays U.A.E.
83 G3 Rub al Khali des Saudi Arabia
33 N9 Rübeland E Germany
60 R2 Rubeshibe Japan
54 K7 Rubezhnoye U.S.S.R.
15 C2 Rubha Coigeach Scotland
15 B3 Rubha Hunish Scotland
15 C3 Rubha Reidh Scotland
86 E5 Rubi R Zaïre
102 D3 Rubicon R California
45 J2 Rubiera Italy
133 G2 Rubinéia Brazil
124 F3 Rubio Mexico
16 E3 Rubio mt Spain
28 D2 Rubjerg Knude hill Denmark
56 B5 Rubtsovsk U.S.S.R.
116 K4 Ruby Alaska
103 N10 Ruby Arizona
100 H1 Ruby Washington
101 N4 Ruby R Montana
103 J1 Ruby Dome peak Nevada
103 J1 Ruby L Nevada
103 J1 Ruby Mts Nevada
103 J1 Ruby Valley Nevada
100 B7 Ruch Oregon
52 H4 Ruch' U.S.S.R.
67 D4 Rucheng China
52 F2 Ruch'i U.S.S.R.
Ruchugi see Uvinza
27 H14 Ruda Sweden
143 E6 Rudall, R W Australia
140 B6 Rudalls R N Terr Aust
77 E6 Rudan Iran
75 J5 Rudauli India
77 H4 Rudbar Afghanistan
77 A1 Rudbār Iran
28 B7 Rudbøl Denmark
118 K6 Ruddell Sask
22 E1 Ruddervoorde Belgium
119 R3 Ruddock Manitoba
116 P6 Rude R Alaska
38 L8 Ruden Austria
33 T4 Ruden isld E Germany
36 H6 Rudersberg W Germany
33 T8 Rudersdorf E Germany
36 D4 Rüdesheim W Germany
31 O6 Rudki U.S.S.R.
28 F7 Rudkøbing Denmark
31 J4 Rudna Poland
59 L3 Rudnaya Pristan' U.S.S.R.
52 H5 Rudnichnyy U.S.S.R.
47 J2 Rudnik Bulgaria
31 N5 Rudnik Poland
54 C2 Rudnya U.S.S.R.
55 D4 Rudnyy U.S.S.R.
Rudok see Rutog
46 D3 Rudoka Planina mt Yugoslavia
50 E1 Rudol'fa, O isld U.S.S.R.
86 G5 Rudolf, L Kenya
37 L2 Rudolstadt E Germany
67 G1 Rudong China
77 B1 Rūd Sar Iran
28 G5 Ruds Vedby Denmark
101 P1 Rudyard Montana
22 B3 Rue France
120 J5 Ruel Ontario
20 K3 Rue St. Pierre, la France
86 F3 Rufa'a Sudan
21 F9 Ruffec Charente France
21 H8 Ruffec Indre France
21 C6 Ruffigne France
112 G4 Ruffin S Carolina
88 F6 Rufiji R Tanzania
45 K4 Rufina Italy
131 E5 Rufino Argentina
85 A6 Rufisque Senegal
88 C9 Rufunsa R Zambia
100 F1 Rufus Woods L Washington
67 G1 Rugao China
9 E3 Rugby England
98 G1 Rugby N Dakota
9 E2 Rugeley England
30 H1 Rügen isld E Germany
144 A7 Rugged Is New Zealand
37 K5 Rügland W Germany
20 G4 Rugles France
29 P5 Rug Oz L U.S.S.R.
52 D3 Rugozero U.S.S.R.
80 B7 Ruhama Israel
75 N5 Ruhea Bangladesh
33 N7 Rühen W Germany
29 L11 Rühimäki Finland
37 J2 Ruhla E Germany
33 T10 Ruhland E Germany
33 S7 Ruhleben E Germany
37 O6 Ruhmannsfelden W Germany
33 P5 Rühn E Germany
33 P6 Ruhner Bge mt E Germany
32 F10 Ruhr R W Germany
35 Ruhr, The reg W Germany
88 E6 Ruhudji R Tanzania
88 E7 Ruhuhu R Tanzania
88 C10 Ruia R Zimbabwe
67 G3 Rui'an China
67 E2 Ruichang China
65 A7 Ruicheng China
108 C6 Ruidosa Texas
106 E8 Ruidoso New Mexico
108 B2 Ruidoso New Mexico
67 E4 Ruijin China
80 G7 Ruim el Hiri Jordan
22 E1 Ruiselede Belgium
9 F4 Ruislip England
25 H3 Ruiten Aa R Netherlands
124 G7 Ruiz Mexico
80 G7 Rujeim Salim Jordan
46 E2 Rujen mt Yugoslavia
52 C5 Rūjiena U.S.S.R.
29 O5 Rukatunturi mt U.S.S.R.
88 C10 Rukovakuona Mts Zimbabwe
88 D7 Rukuru R Malawi
88 C5 Rukwa reg Tanzania
88 D5 Rukwa, L Tanzania
107 J2 Ruleton Kansas
111 F8 Ruleville Mississippi
26 G10 Rullbo Sweden
99 L9 Rulo Nebraska
36 E5 Rülzheim W Germany
15 B3 Rum isld Scotland
48 F5 Ruma Yugoslavia
Rumania see Romania
140 C7 Rumbalara N Terr Aust
86 E4 Rumbek Sudan
71 J4 Rumbiä Sulawesi
31 H5 Rumburk Czechoslovakia
126 G3 Rum Cay isld Bahamas
22 E3 Rumegies France
22 L5 Rumelange Luxembourg
95 R2 Rumford Maine
22 G4 Rumigny France
22 E2 Rumillies Belgium
140 B2 Rum Jungle N Terr Aust
80 E2 Rummāna Israel
Rummelsburg see Miastko
60 P2 Rumoi Japan
88 D7 Rumphi Malawi
118 E7 Rumsey Alberta
95 N6 Rumson New Jersey
144 C5 Rumu New Zealand
141 H3 Rumula Queensland
144 C5 Runanga New Zealand
127 K1 Runaway Bay Jamaica
8 D1 Runcorn England
69 C11 Rundeng Sumatra
36 C1 Ründeroth W Germany
28 D7 Rundhof W Germany
26 A9 Rundöy Norway
71 J7 Runduma isld Indonesia
29 G8 Rundvik Sweden
71 M8 Rung isld Indonesia
70 C6 Rungan R Kalimantan
109 K7 Runge Texas
28 K5 Rungsted Denmark
88 D5 Rungwa R Tanzania
88 D6 Rungwe peak Tanzania
27 J11 Runhällen Sweden
36 E3 Runkel W Germany
27 H11 Runn L Sweden
99 N8 Runnells Iowa
108 E1 Running Water Cr Texas/Okla
119 Q7 Runnymede Sask
143 E6 Runton Ra W Australia
87 C9 Runtu Namibia
29 O10 Ruokolahti Finland
66 D4 Ruoqiang China
58 D3 Ruo Shui R China
29 L10 Ruovesi Finland
131 A8 Rupanco, L Chile
139 G6 Rupanyup Victoria
69 E12 Rupat isld Sumatra
101 M7 Rupert Idaho
95 O3 Rupert Vermont
94 G9 Rupert W Virginia
141 F5 Rupert R Queensland
121 L1 Rupert B Quebec
121 N1 Rupert, R Quebec
37 L6 Rupertsbuch W Germany
146 J9 Ruppert Coast Antarctica
36 G2 Ruppertenrod W Germany
36 F2 Ruppertsberg W Germany
36 C2 Ruppichteroth W Germany
33 S7 Ruppiner Kanal E Germany
128 G3 Rupununi R Guyana
80 G2 Ruqqād R Syria
80 G1 Ruqqād Sakhr Syria
25 F6 Rur R W Germany
112 G1 Rural Hall N Carolina
94 F10 Rural Retreat Virginia
128 E6 Rurrenabaque Bolivia
28 C6 Rurup Denmark
17 F5 Rus R Spain
87 F9 Rusape Zimbabwe
Ruschuk see Ruse Bulgaria
47 H1 Ruse Bulgaria
38 M8 Ruše Yugoslavia
37 P6 Rusel W Germany
106 F3 Rush Colorado
14 E3 Rush Irish Rep
9 E5 Rushall England
65 E6 Rushan China
57 F5 Rushanskiy Khrebet mts U.S.S.R.
107 L3 Rush Center Kansas
99 O4 Rush City Minnesota
106 G3 Rush Cr Colorado
9 F3 Rushden England
99 P6 Rushford Minnesota
94 J4 Rushford New York
118 K8 Rush Lake Sask
107 N7 Rush Springs Oklahoma
110 F1 Rushville Illinois
110 L2 Rushville Indiana
98 D7 Rushville Nebraska
139 H6 Rushworth Victoria
109 M4 Rusk Texas
113 E10 Ruskin Florida
26 K7 Rusksele Sweden
26 K7 Ruskträsk Sweden
98 F2 Ruso N Dakota
129 L4 Russas Brazil
38 H6 Russbachsaag Austria
113 L12 Russel I Bahamas
99 N9 Russell Iowa
107 M3 Russell Kansas
94 E8 Russell Kentucky
119 Q8 Russell Manitoba
99 L5 Russell Minnesota
95 M2 Russell New York
145 E1 Russell New Zealand
121 P7 Russell Ontario
94 H5 Russell Pennsylvania
143 E6 Russell Headland mt W Aust
115 K3 Russell I N W Terr
137 M3 Russell Is Solomon Is
119 Q2 Russell L Manitoba
117 Q4 Russell L N W Terr
116 M5 Russell, Mt Alaska
143 C7 Russell,Mt W Australia
143 E10 Russell Ra W Australia
110 L4 Russell Springs Kentucky
110 N1 Russells Pt Ohio
111 J7 Russellville Alabama
110 D6 Russellville Arkansas
110 K5 Russellville Kentucky
110 D3 Russellville Missouri
94 D8 Russellville Ohio
45 M3 Russi Italy
116 G6 Russian Mission Alaska
116 H6 Russian Mts Alaska
Russian Soviet Federated Socialist Republic see Rossiyskaya SFSR
50 F1 Russkaya Gavan' U.S.S.R.
55 F4 Russkaya-Polyana U.S.S.R.
55 D3 Russkaya-Techa U.S.S.R.
54 M6 Russkaya-Zhuravka U.S.S.R.
51 J1 Russkiy, Ostrova islds U.S.S.R.
77 L1 Rustak Afghanistan
78 K1 Rustavi U.S.S.R.
94 H9 Rustburg Virginia
89 E5 Rustenburg S Africa
32 H5 Rustersiel W Germany
109 P3 Ruston Louisiana
88 C3 Rutana Burundi
16 E7 Rute Spain
27 K14 Rute Sweden
33 S6 Rutenberg E Germany
32 F7 Rütenbrock W Germany
71 K9 Ruteng Flores Indonesia
102 A1 Ruth California
103 K2 Ruth Nevada
32 H10 Rüthen W Germany
112 F2 Rutherfordton N Carolina
121 L6 Rutherglen Ontario
12 D2 Rutherglen Scotland
94 K9 Ruther Glen Virginia
116 M5 Ruth Glacier Alaska
118 J7 Ruthilda Sask
8 C1 Ruthin Wales
98 K5 Ruthton Minnesota
99 M6 Ruthven Iowa
141 G6 Ruthven Queensland
88 E7 Rutikira R Tanzania
52 G6 Rutka R U.S.S.R.
99 R9 Rutland Illinois
98 J3 Rutland N Dakota
94 E7 Rutland Ohio
95 P3 Rutland Vermont
Rutland co see Leicestershire
68 A7 Rutland I Andaman Is
141 F3 Rutland Plains Queensland
118 H6 Rutland Station Sask
9 F2 Rutland Water L England
99 O3 Rutledge Minnesota
110 D1 Rutledge Missouri
66 B5 Rutog China
25 E3 Rutten Netherlands
120 K6 Rutter Ontario
25 F4 Ruurlo Netherlands
87 G7 Ruvu Tanzania
88 G5 Ruvu R Tanzania
88 E7 Ruvuma Tanzania
88 G7 Ruvuma R Tanzania
86 E2 Ruweiba Sudan
88 C1 Ruwenzori Rge mts Uganda
36 B4 Ruwer W Germany
65 B7 Ruyang China
67 D4 Ruyuan China
55 E4 Ruzayevka U.S.S.R.
48 M1 Ruzhin U.S.S.R.
48 E1 Ružomberok Czechoslovakia
88 B2 Rwanda rep Cent Africa
28 D4 Ry Denmark
28 D2 Ryå Denmark
47 H1 Ryakhovo Bulgaria
99 P7 Ryan Iowa
109 K1 Ryan Oklahoma
12 C4 Ryan, Loch Scotland
101 T8 Ryan Park Wyoming
101 L6 Ryan Pk Idaho
53 E7 Ryazan' U.S.S.R.
54 M3 Ryazhsk U.S.S.R.
57 H4 Rybach'ye U.S.S.R.
37 O3 Rybáře Czechoslovakia
52 E5 Rybinsk U.S.S.R.
52 E5 Rybinskoye Vdkhr res U.S.S.R.
31 L5 Rybnik Poland
48 M3 Rybnitsa U.S.S.R.
54 L2 Rybnoye U.S.S.R.
55 D2 Rychkovo U.S.S.R.
31 J5 Rychnov Czechoslovakia
31 L3 Rychwał Poland
33 S4 Ryckgraben R E Germany
117 O8 Rycroft Alberta
120 G6 Rydal Bank Ontario
28 B4 Ryde Denmark
28 G7 Ryde Denmark
9 E6 Ryde England
98 E2 Ryder N Dakota
100 B3 Ryderwood Washington
27 H14 Ryd, V Sweden
106 F4 Rye Colorado
28 D4 Rye Denmark
28 H5 Rye Denmark
9 G6 Rye England
95 R3 Rye New Hampshire
109 N5 Rye Texas
77 B5 R-ye Dalaki R Iran
101 Q3 Ryegate Montana
100 G9 Rye Patch Nevada
102 F1 Rye Patch Res Nevada
119 Q9 Ryerson Sask
20 D3 Ryes France
27 A12 Ryfylke Norway
13 G4 Ryhope England
31 N4 Ryki Poland
120 G3 Ryland Ontario
118 E5 Ryley Alberta
54 F5 Ryl'sk U.S.S.R.
139 J5 Rylstone New S Wales
31 N6 Rymanow Poland
31 K6 Rýmařov Czechoslovakia
55 F1 Rymovy U.S.S.R.
31 N2 Ryn Poland
52 E1 Rynda U.S.S.R.
53 G9 Ryn Peski des U.S.S.R.
28 F4 Ryomgard Denmark
61 P7 Ryōri-zaki C Japan
61 M7 Ryōtsu Japan
31 L2 Rypin Poland
48 L3 Ryshkany U.S.S.R.
28 F6 Ryslinge Denmark
32 F6 Rysum W Germany
61 O10 Ryūgasaki Japan
134 D4 Ryukyu Ridge Pac Oc
134 D5 Ryukyu Tr Pac Oc
31 H3 Rzepin Poland
31 N5 Rzeszów Poland
52 D6 Rzhev U.S.S.R.
77 C4 Sa'ādatābād Iran
33 R4 Saal E Germany
37 J3 Saal W Germany
36 F5 Saal R W Germany
38 G7 Saalach R Austria
37 M3 Saalburg E Germany
36 F3 Saalburg W Germany
33 P9 Saale R E Germany
37 M3 Saale R W Germany
36 C7 Saales France
37 L2 Saalfeld E Germany
40 F5 Saanen Switzerland
117 M11 Saanich Br Col
36 B5 Saar R W Germany
19 K3 Saarbrücken France
36 B5 Saarbrücken W Germany
36 B4 Saarburg W Germany
27 M14 Sääre U.S.S.R.
27 M13 Saaremaa U.S.S.R.
29 M5 Saarenkylä Finland
29 O10 Saari Finland
29 L9 Saarijärvi Finland
29 N3 Saariselkä mts Finland
36 B5 Saarland land W Germany
36 B5 Saarlouis W Germany
33 S8 Saarmund E Germany
36 B5 Saar-Wellingen W Germany
36 D7 Saasenheim France
40 G5 Saas Tal Switzerland
70 E3 Saätan Kalimantan
133 E5 Saavedra Argentina
131 A7 Saavedra, Pto Chile
125 L2 Sabá Honduras
127 N6 Saba isld Lesser Antilles
32 L9 Sababurg W Germany
48 F6 Sabac Yugoslavia
17 J3 Sabadell Spain
70 E2 Sabah state Borneo
69 E11 Sabak Malaysia
71 H5 Sabal Sulawesi
71 J8 Sabalana isld Indonesia
44 M5 Saba, Mt Italy
126 D3 Sabana, Arch. de islds Cuba
127 K5 Sabana de la Mar Dominican Rep
127 J10 Sabana de Mendoza Venezuela
128 D1 Sabanalarga Colombia
127 K9 Sabaneta Venezuela
70 F4 Sabang Sulawesi
69 B10 Sabang Sumatra
70 C6 Sabangan Teluk B Kalimantan
83 K11 Sabaragamuwa reg Sri Lanka
71 J8 Sabaru isld Indonesia
80 D4 Sabastiya Jordan
45 O7 Sabaudia Italy
128 E7 Sabaya Bolivia
41 M6 Sabbia, V Italy
45 H2 Sabbioneta Italy
77 G4 şāberi, Hāmūn-e L Iran
107 P2 Sabetha Kansas
84 E4 Sabhah Libya
87 F10 Sabi R Zimbabwe
89 G5 Sabie R S Africa
52 B6 Sabile U.S.S.R.
45 N5 Sabina Italy
94 D7 Sabina Ohio
124 F2 Sabinal Mexico
109 H6 Sabinal Texas
17 G2 Sabiñánigo Spain
108 F8 Sabinas Mexico
125 J4 Sabinas Hidalgo Mexico
111 C11 Sabine R Louisiana/Texas
146 K6 Sabine, Mt Antarctica
42 E6 Sabini, Monti Italy
79 H2 Sabkhat al Jabbūl Syria
79 D7 Sabkhet el Bardawîl Egypt
71 E4 Sablayan Philippines
137 M5 Sable isld Coral Sea
115 N9 Sable, C Nova Scotia
123 N10 Sable I Nova Scotia
122 G10 Sable River Nova Scotia
120 H6 Sables, L. aux Ontario
120 H6 Sables, River Aux Ontario
19 O16 Sablet France
19 N18 Sablon, Pte. du France
19 N14 Sablons France
16 C3 Sabor R Portugal
131 G2 Sā Borja Brazil
94 H7 Sabraton W Virginia
18 E8 Sabres France
146 G3 Sabrina Coast Antarctica
28 E4 Sabro Denmark
16 C4 Sabugal Portugal
99 Q7 Sabula Iowa
47 L5 Sabuncu Turkey
70 P9 Sabunting isld Indonesia
77 E1 Sabzevār Iran
110 C4 Sac R Missouri
128 E7 Sacaca Bolivia
95 N3 Sacandaga Res New York
103 N8 Sacaton Arizona
99 L7 Sac City Iowa
43 E7 Sacco R Italy
45 L1 Saccolongo Italy
17 F4 Sacedón Spain
115 K7 Sachigo R Ontario
109 O8 Sachse Texas
36 F1 Sachsenberg W Germany
38 H8 Sachsenburg Austria
33 O10 Sachsenburg E Germany
32 K8 Sachsenhagen W Germany
32 K10 Sachsenhausen W Germany
114 G3 Sachs Harbour N W Terr
42 E3 Sacile Italy
95 L3 Sackets Harbor New York
122 H8 Sackville New Brunswick
110 B3 Sac, L Missouri
20 K5 Saclas France
95 R3 Saco Maine
101 S1 Saco Montana
71 F7 Sacol isld Philippines
40 B2 Sacquenay France
102 C3 Sacramento California
102 B2 Sacramento R California
108 B3 Sacramento Mts New Mexico
102 B1 Sacramento V California
103 K6 Sacramento Wash R Arizona
16 E8 Sacratif, C Spain
122 D5 Sacré Coeur Quebec
122 C5 Sacré-Coeur Saguenay Quebec
130 F6 Sacremento Brazil
48 G3 Săcueni Romania
18 E10 Sadaba Spain
77 B5 Sa'dabad Iran
72 E5 Şa'dah N Yemen
60 F12 Sada-misaki Japan
69 E9 Sadao Thailand
13 G4 Sadberge England
74 D2 Sadda Pakistan
141 G2 Saddle Hill Queensland
142 D4 Saddle Hill W Australia
100 A7 Saddle Mt Oregon
101 Q5 Saddle Mt Wyoming
68 A6 Saddle Pk Andaman Is
68 G7 Sa Dec Vietnam
48 K2 Sadgora U.S.S.R.
127 O3 Sadhoowa Trinidad
94 C8 Sadieville Kentucky
85 B6 Sadiola Mali
74 D4 Sadiqabad Pakistan
16 B6 Sado R Portugal
61 M7 Sado-shima isld Japan
74 E6 Sadri India
26 H5 Sadvajaur L Sweden
28 F2 Sæby Nordjylland Denmark
28 G5 Sæby Vestjælland Denmark
28 J6 Sædder Denmark
28 B4 Sædding Denmark
60 E13 Saeki Japan
60 E13 Saeki-wan B Japan
17 F5 Saelices Spain
32 G8 Saerbeck W Germany
28 E5 Særslev Denmark
22 K4 Saeul Luxembourg
Safad see Zefat
55 D4 Safakulevo U.S.S.R.
48 F2 Sáfárikovo Czechoslovakia
57 F5 Safed Khirs reg Afghanistan
77 L2 Safed Koh mt Afghanistan
38 O7 Safen R Austria
77 J4 Safer Afghanistan
142 A4 Safety Bay dist W Aust
80 D5 Saffārin Jordan
79 B9 Şaff, El Egypt
27 F12 Säffle Sweden
111 J9 Safford Alabama
103 P9 Safford Arizona
21 B7 Saffré France
9 G3 Saffron Walden England
85 C2 Safi Morocco
77 G4 Safidabeh Iran
77 A1 Safid Rud R Iran
41 K4 Safier Tal Switzerland
130 H6 Safiras, Sa. das mts Brazil
79 G4 Sāfīta Syria
54 K3 Safonovka U.S.S.R.
52 G2 Safonovo U.S.S.R.
78 D1 Safronbolu Turkey
27 G11 Säfsnäs Sweden
80 G5 Safut Jordan
66 D6 Saga China
60 D12 Saga Kyūshū Japan
60 G12 Saga Shikoku Japan
60 C11 Saga Tsushima Japan
57 C1 Saga U.S.S.R.
60 D12 Saga prefect Japan
61 O7 Sagae Japan
68 B2 Sagaing Burma
59 L5 Sagami-nada B Japan
61 N10 Sagami-wan B Japan
94 H6 Sagamore Pennsylvania
86 G4 Sagan watercourse Ethiopia
119 N2 Saganaga L Ontario
120 H3 Saganash L Ontario
60 E12 Saganoseki Japan
68 D6 Saganthit Kyun isld Burma
76 C2 Sagar India
61 M11 Sagara Japan
88 F5 Sagara Tanzania
57 B5 Sagar-Chaga U.S.S.R.
116 N2 Sagavanirkok R Alaska
32 H7 Sage W Germany
101 P8 Sage Wyoming
101 P1 Sage Cr Montana
101 S8 Sage Cr Wyoming
27 G11 Sågen Sweden
26 H4 Sagfjord Norway
26 J5 Saggat L Sweden
95 P6 Sag Harbor Long I, N Y
94 D3 Saginaw Michigan
109 L9 Saginaw Texas
94 D3 Saginaw Bay Michigan
88 D2 Sagitu isld Uganda
115 N6 Saglek B Labrador
71 H6 Sago isld Indonesia
99 S3 Sagola Michigan
17 F7 Sagra, La mt Spain
85 F8 Sagre, Pto.de Bioko Eq Guinea
16 B7 Sagres Portugal
71 L9 Sagu Indonesia
106 D3 Saguache Colorado
126 G4 Sagua de Tánamo Cuba
126 D3 Sagua la Grande Cuba
103 N8 Saguaro L Arizona
103 O9 Saguaro Nat.Mon Arizona
115 M8 Saguenay R Quebec
85 B3 Saguia el Hamra terr Morocco
17 G5 Sagunto Spain
114 E4 Sagwan Alaska
80 G3 Saham Jordan
85 C4 Sahara des N Africa
79 E10 Sahara, G mt Egypt
74 G4 Saharanpur India
142 E5 Sahara Well W Australia
75 L5 Sahibganj India
28 D4 Sahl Denmark
71 A2 Sahu Halmahera Indonesia
124 E3 Sahuaripa Mexico
103 O10 Sahuarita Arizona
124 H7 Sahuayo Mexico
136 F4 Sahul Shelf Timor Sea
19 O16 Sahune France
68 J5 Sa Huynh Vietnam
61 L9 Sai R Japan
136 J3 Saibai I Papua New Guinea
69 D13 Saibi Indonesia
69 E9 Sai Buri Thailand
69 E9 Sai Buri R Thailand
85 E2 Saïda Algeria
79 F5 Saïda Lebanon
77 D5 Sa'īdābād Iran
68 F6 Sai Dao Tai, Khao mt Thailand
86 D4 Said Bundas Sudan
75 N6 Saidpur Bangladesh
74 E1 Saidu Pakistan
40 E3 Saignelégier Switzerland
60 G9 Saigō Japan
Saigon see Ho Chi Minh
68 H7 Saigon R Vietnam
29 O4 Saija Finland
60 G12 Saijō Japan
60 C13 Saikai Nat. Park Japan
71 C3 Saileen W Irian
19 O15 Saillans France
71 C3 Sailolof W Irian
100 K7 Sailor Cr Idaho
76 C1 Sailu India
65 F4 Saima China
29 N10 Saimaa L Finland
29 N11 Saimaa Canal Finland/U.S.S.R.
124 H6 Sain Alto Mexico
74 A8 Saindak Pakistan
22 D2 Sainghin-en-Weppes France
22 G3 Sains-du-Nord France
22 F4 Sains-Richaumont France
15 F5 St. Abb's Head Scotland
122 H5 Ste. Adelaide Quebec
121 Q7 Ste.Adèle Quebec
20 F3 Ste.Adresse France
38 N6 St.Aegyd Austria
18 G9 St.Affrique France
121 T6 St.Agapit Quebec
119 U9 Ste.Agathe Manitoba
121 Q6 Ste.Agathe des Monts Quebec
20 G5 St.Agil France
8 A7 St.Agnes England
121 L4 Ste.Agnes Quebec
9 F7 St.Agnes isld Isles of Scilly England
21 H7 St.Aignan-la-Ronde France
21 C6 St. Aignan sur Roë France
28 D3 Ste. Ajstrup Denmark
9 F4 St.Albans England
123 R6 St.Alban's Nfld
95 P2 St.Albans Vermont
94 F8 St.Albans W Virginia
118 D5 St.Albert Alberta
122 C6 St.Alexandre Quebec
121 R6 St.Alexis des Monts Quebec
22 E3 St.Amand-les-Eaux France
21 H6 St.Amand-Longpre France
18 G6 St. Amand Mont Rond France
21 D8 St.Amand-sur-Sevre France
21 F10 St. Amant de Boixe France
40 F2 St.Amarin France
121 T4 St.-Ambroise Quebec
21 J8 St.Ambroix France
122 D5 St.Anaclet Quebec
38 L8 St. Andra-im-Lavanttal Austria
83 K13 St.André Réunion Indian Oc
33 M9 St. Andreasberg W Germany
87 G11 St.André, C Madagascar
19 N13 St.Andre-de-Corcy France
18 E8 St.André-de-Cubzac France
20 H4 St.André-de-l'Eure France
20 H4 St.André, Plaine de France
111 L11 St.Andrew Florida
127 P2 St.Andrew co Trinidad
127 L2 St.Andrew parish Jamaica
144 C6 St. Andrews New Zealand
123 N6 St.Andrew's Nfld
13 F1 St.Andrews Scotland
123 M7 St.Andrew's Chan Nova Scotia
113 F7 St.Andrew Sd Georgia
21 F10 St.Angeau France
98 F9 St.Ann Nebraska
127 K2 St.Ann parish Jamaica
126 B2 St. Anna-Baai B Curaçao
9 H6 St.Anne Channel Is
20 G4 Ste.Anne France
127 N4 Ste.Anne Guadeloupe W Indies
99 T8 St.Anne Illinois
119 V9 Ste.Anne Manitoba
127 L4 Ste.Anne Martinique W Indies
121 U5 Ste.-Anne-de-Beaupré Quebec
121 S6 Ste. Anne de la Pérade Quebec
122 B6 Ste.Anne de la Pocatière Quebec
122 F4 Ste.Anne des Monts Quebec
121 P6 Ste.Anne du Lac Quebec
122 E3 Ste.Anne, L Quebec
118 C5 Ste. Anne, Lac Alberta
122 B6 Ste.Anne, R Quebec
20 A2 St.Annes Alderney, Channel Is
117 Q9 St.Ann, L Alberta
123 M7 St. Anns Nova Scotia
141 H5 St.Anns Queensland
127 K2 St. Ann's Bay Jamaica
12 E3 St Ann's Bridge Scotland
99 O6 St.Ansgar Iowa
25 E5 St.Anthonis Netherlands
101 O6 St.Anthony Idaho
115 O7 St.Anthony Nfld
19 O18 St.Antoine France
41 M3 St.Anton Austria
18 G8 St.Antonin France
122 C6 St.Antonin Quebec
21 I8 St.Août France
20 H3 St.Aquilin-de-Pacy France
145 D4 St. Arnaud New Zealand
139 G6 St.Arnaud Victoria
20 J4 St.Arnoux France
122 C6 St.Arsène Quebec
140 B1 St.Asaph B N Terr Aust
18 F7 St.Astier France
122 C6 St.Athanase Quebec
122 B6 St.Aubert Quebec
20 E3 St.Aubin France
20 A3 St.Aubin Jersey, Channel Is
20 B5 St. Aubin-d'Aubigné France
20 C4 St.Aubin-de-Terregatte France
20 C5 St.Aubin-du-Cormier France
20 H2 St.Aubin-le-Cauf France
123 O2 St.Augustin Quebec
36 C2 St. Augustin W Germany
123 O2 St.Augustin B Quebec
87 G12 St.Augustin, B.de Madagascar
21 D7 St.Augustin-des-Bois France
113 F8 St.Augustine Florida
127 O2 St.Augustine Trinidad
123 N2 St.Augustin R Quebec
18 F7 St.Aulaye France
8 B7 St. Austell England
19 K3 St.Avold France
121 S6 St.Barnabé Nord Quebec
121 R6 St.Barthélémi Quebec
18 G10 St.Barthélemy France
127 N5 St. Barthélemy isld Lesser Antilles
144 B6 St. Bathans New Zealand
19 P18 Ste.Baume France
18 F10 St. Béat France
12 E5 St.Bees England
99 M6 St.Benedict Iowa
119 M6 St.Benedict Sask
21 H9 St.Benoit-du-Sault France
122 B7 St.Benoit Labre Quebec
122 H5 Ste.Bernadette Quebec
121 T6 St.Bernard Quebec
144 D5 St. Bernard mt New Zealand
40 F6 St. Bernard, Col du Gd. Switz/Italy
42 A3 St. Bernard, Petit pass Italy/France
110 J2 St.Bernice Indiana
19 P13 St.Beron France
20 D5 St.Berthevin France
36 C7 St.Blaise France
122 D5 Ste.Blandine Quebec
8 B7 St.Blazey England
118 D1 St.Boniface Manitoba
21 H10 St. Bonnet-Briance France
118 L8 St.Boswells Sask
13 F2 St. Boswells Scotland
21 G7 St.Branchs France
123 T5 St.Brendan's Nfld
21 A7 St. Brévin les Pins France
20 A4 St.Briac France
20 C5 St.Brice-en-Cogles France
118 B7 St.Bride, Mt Alberta
123 S7 St.Bride's Nfld
8 A4 St. Bride's Wales
18 D4 St. Brieuc France
119 N6 St.Brieux Sask
20 B4 St.Broladre France
121 L5 St. Bruno de Guiques Quebec
21 G6 St.Calais France
119 T9 St.Calude Manitoba
122 B7 St.Camille Quebec
121 S6 St.Casimir Quebec
18 D4 St.Cast France
115 M9 St. Catharines Ontario
127 K2 St. Catherine parish Jamaica
127 P5 St.Catherine, Mt Grenada
112 F6 St.Catherines I Georgia
9 E6 St.Catherines Pt England
122 B8 Ste.Cécile Quebec
18 G8 St. Céré France
18 G7 St.Cernin France
121 R7 St.Césaire Quebec
18 H7 St.Chamond France
101 O7 St.Charles Idaho
99 S8 St.Charles Illinois
118 A1 St.Charles Manitoba
94 C3 St.Charles Michigan
99 O6 St.Charles Minnesota
110 F3 St.Charles Missouri
18 H8 St. Chély l'Apcher France
20 K4 St.Chéron France
18 G9 St.Chinian France
126 A1 St.Christoffel Berg mt Curaçao
19 Q15 St.Christophe d'Oisans France
St. Christopher isld see St Kitts
121 T4 St.-Cîour-de-Marie Quebec
20 C3 St. Clair France
94 E4 St.Clair Michigan
99 N5 St.Clair Minnesota
110 F3 St.Clair Missouri
94 E4 St. Clair, L U.S.A./Canada
120 H9 St.Clair R Ontario/Mich
20 J3 St.Clair-sur-Epte France
19 J6 St.Claude France
127 N4 St.Claude Guadeloupe W I
8 B4 St.Clears Wales
122 C6 St.Clement Quebec
21 D7 St. Clement-de-la-Place France
121 S7 Ste.Clothilde Quebec
113 F9 St.Cloud Florida
20 K4 St.Cloud France
99 M4 St.Cloud Minnesota
8 B7 St.Columb England
121 R6 St.Côme Quebec
20 C3 St.Côme-du-Mont France
20 F5 St.Cosme-de-Vair France
122 E8 Ste.Croix New Brunswick
40 D4 Ste.Croix Switzerland
95 T8 St. Croix R Maine/New Brunswick
99 O4 St. Croix R Wisconsin
36 C7 Ste.Croix aux Mines France
113 L8 St.Croix I Virgin Is
18 E7 St. Cybard Chalais France
18 F8 St.Cyprien France
122 C6 St.Cyprien Quebec
19 P18 St.Cyr France
20 D4 St.Cyr-du-Bailleul France
21 I6 St. Cyr-en Val France
121 S7 St.Cyrille Quebec
121 P4 St.Cyr, L Quebec
118 J4 St. Cyr Lake Sask
122 B7 St.Damien Quebec
110 F1 St.David Illinois
127 P1 St.David co Trinidad
122 A5 St.David-de-Falardeau Quebec
123 O5 St. David's Nfld
8 A4 St. David's Wales
90 D1 St.Davids I Bermuda
22 G3 St.Denis Belgium
20 K4 St. Denis France
121 R7 St.Denis Quebec
83 J13 St.Denis Réunion Indian Oc
21 E6 St.Denis d'Anjou France
20 D5 St.Denis-de-Gastines France
21 C9 St.Denis-d'Oléron France
20 E5 St. Denis-d'Orques France
20 E5 St.Denis-sur-Sarthon France
19 O16 St.Didier France
36 B7 St. Dié France
19 J4 St.Dizier France
20 B5 St. Domineuc France
19 N14 St.Donat sur l'Herbasse France
98 J8 St.Edward Nebraska
116 P7 St.Elias, C Alaska
117 D5 St. Elias Mts Alaska/Yukon Terr
121 S4 Ste.Elisabeth Quebec
127 J2 St.Elizabeth parish Jamaica
110 H2 St.Elmo Illinois
122 C5 St.Eloi Quebec
18 G6 St Éloy-les-Mines France
121 R6 Ste.Emélie Quebec
18 H8 Ste.Enimie France
20 C3 Sainteny France
21 G7 St.Epain France
122 B7 St.Ephrem Quebec
121 L3 St.Ephrem de Paradis Quebec
122 C6 St.-Epiphane Quebec
20 B5 St.Erblon France
22 F5 St.Erme-Outre-et-Ramecourt France
21 D10 Saintes France
127 L4 St. Ésprit, Le Martinique W Indies
22 B2 St.Étienne-au-Mont France
18 E9 St. Étienne de Baïgorry France
19 O14 St.Étienne de St.Geoirs France
20 H3 St.Étienne-du-Rouvray France
121 M4 St. Eugène Quebec
121 S4 St.-Eugène Quebec
122 D6 St.Eusèbe Quebec
121 R7 St.Eustache Quebec
20 F4 St.Evroult Notre Dame-du-Bois France
122 D5 St.Fabien Quebec
122 B7 Ste.Familie Quebec
121 P6 Ste.Famille d'Aumond Quebec
18 H5 St.Fargeau France
121 S4 St.Félicien Quebec
122 E5 Ste.Félicité Quebec
121 R6 St. Félix de Valois Quebec
12 D1 St.Fillans Scotland
14 A5 St. Finan's B Irish Rep
123 O5 St.Fintan's Nfld
121 T6 St.Flavien Quebec
122 E5 Ste.Florence Quebec
21 C8 St.Florent-des-Bois France
18 H4 St.Florentin France
18 G6 St.Florent-sur-Cher France
18 H7 St.Flour France
21 H8 St.Flovier France
19 N15 St.Fortunat France
121 T7 St.Fortunat Quebec
18 F8 Ste.Foy-la-Grande France
107 J2 St.Francis Kansas
95 R6 St. Francis R Maine/New Brunswick
110 F5 St. Francis R Missouri/Ark
89 D10 St. Francis B S Africa
123 U6 St.Francis, C Nfld
89 D10 St. Francis C S Africa
138 C4 St.Francis, I.of S Australia
110 J3 St. Francisville Illinois
111 E11 St.Francisville Louisiana
127 N4 St.François Guadeloupe W Indies
121 S7 St. François R Quebec
121 T7 St. François, L Quebec
110 F4 St. Francois Mts Missouri
121 S7 St.François Xavier Quebec
95 S7 St.Froid L Maine
21 C8 St.Fulgent France
111 E11 St.Gabriel Louisiana
121 R6 St.Gabriel de Brandon Quebec
122 H5 St.Gabriel de Gaspé Quebec
41 K3 St. Gallen Switzerland
20 F4 Ste.Gauburge-Ste. Colombe France
18 F9 St.Gaudens France
21 H8 St.Gaultier France
122 B8 St.Gédéon Quebec
20 K3 St. Genevieve France
110 F4 Ste.Genevieve Missouri
123 P2 St.Genevieve B Quebec
18 G8 St.Geniez France
19 P14 St Geoire-en-Valdaine France
90 C1 St.George Bermuda
113 E7 St.George Georgia
122 F8 St.George New Brunswick
141 J8 St.George Queensland
112 G4 St.George S Carolina
103 L4 St.George Utah
127 O2 St.George co Trinidad
127 P6 St.George parish Barbados
141 G3 St. George R Queensland
123 N5 St.George, C Nfld
139 K6 St.George Hd New S Wales
113 C8 St.George I Florida
116 D8 St. George I Pribilof Is Bering Sea
41 H1 St.Georgen W Germany
100 A8 St.George, Pt California
142 E4 St.George Ra W Australia
36 B6 St.Georges France
129 H3 St.Georges Fr Guiana
127 P5 St.George's Grenada
123 O5 St.George's Nfld
122 B7 St.Georges Quebec
123 N5 St.George's B Nfld
125 P9 St. Georges Cay isld Belize
7 F11 St Georges Chan U.K.
137 L2 St.George's Channel Bismarck Arch
14 E5 St. Georges Channel Ireland/U.K.
69 A9 St.George's Channel Nicobar Is
20 C5 St. Georges-de-Reintembault France
21 C10 St. Georges-d'Oléron France
20 G3 St.Georges-du-Mesnil France
20 G3 St.Georges-du-Vièvre France
90 C1 St.George's, I Bermuda
21 F8 St. Georges-les-Baillargeaux France
20 H4 St.Georges Motel France
20 H5 St.Georges-sur-Eure France
21 I7 St. Georges-sur-la Prée France
21 D7 St.Georges-sur-Loire France
22 H3 St.Gérard Belgium
121 M4 St. Gerard-Centre Quebec
19 N13 St. Germain au Mt D'Or France

St.Germain d'Anxure — Sambapolulu, G 67

20 D5 St.Germain d'Anxure France
20 G5 St. Germain-de-la-Coudre France
18 H6 St.Germain-des-Fosses France
19 J6 St.Germain du Bois France
122 B7 Ste.Germaine Quebec
20 K4 St.Germain-en-Laye France
20 B3 St.Germain, Hâvre de France
20 F3 St. Germain-la Campagne France
18 G7 St.Germain-les-Belles France
20 B3 St.Germain-sur-Ay France
8 B7 St.Germans England
20 J3 St.Germer-de-Fly France
22 F3 St.Ghislain Belgium
21 B6 St.Gildas des Bois France
18 D5 St.Gildas, Pte.de C France
121 T6 St.Giles Quebec
127 N1 St. Giles Is Tobago
22 G1 St. Gillis-bij-Dendermonde Belgium
22 G1 St.Gillis-Waas Belgium
18 F10 St.Girons France
27 F12 St.Gla L Sweden
36 D3 St.Goar W Germany
22 E4 St.Gobain France
122 G5 St.Godefroi Quebec
41 J4 St.Gotthard P Switzerland
8 B4 St.Govan's Hd Wales
119 N6 St.Gregor Sask
123 O4 St.Gregory, Mt Nfld
121 S7 St. Guillaume Quebec
19 Q15 St. Guillaume, Mt France
94 C2 St.Helen Michigan
102 B3 St.Helena California
90 B14 St. Helena isld Atlantic Oc
89 A9 St.Helena B S Africa
90 J10 St Helena Fracture Atlantic Oc
94 B1 St.Helena I Michigan
112 G5 St.Helena Sd S Carolina
18 E8 Ste.Hélène France
122 B6 Ste.Hélène Quebec
13 F6 St.Helens England
100 C4 St.Helens Oregon
139 J8 St.Helens Tasmania
100 C3 St.Helens, Mt Washington
139 J8 St.Helens Pt Tasmania
20 A3 St.Hélier Jersey, Channel Is
122 H4 St.Helier Quebec
121 U6 Ste.Hénédine Quebec
121 T6 St.Henri Quebec
121 T7 St.Herménégilde Quebec
18 G9 St.Hilaire France
98 K1 St.Hilaire Minnesota
21 B7 St. Hilaire-de-Chaleons France
21 C7 St.Hilaire de Loulay France
21 D9 St.Hilaire-des-Loges France
20 C4 St. Hilaire du-Harcouet France
21 I10 St. Hilaire-le Château France
21 E7 St. Hilaire-St. Florent France
140 D6 Sainthill,Mt N Terr Aust
19 K5 St.Hippolyte Doubs France
21 H7 St.Hippolyte Indre-et-Loire France
18 H9 St.Hippolyte du Fort France
122 A5 St.Honoré Quebec
122 C6 St.Honoré Quebec
20 D3 Ste.Honorine France
20 E3 Ste.Honorine-du-Fay France
22 J3 St.Hubert Belgium
25 F6 St.Hubert W Germany
115 M8 St-Hyacinthe Quebec
28 K5 St Ibb Sweden
94 C1 St.Ignace Michigan
121 R6 St.Ignace du Lac Quebec
120 C4 St. Ignace, Isle Ontario
101 L2 St.Ignatius Montana
40 E3 St.Imier Switzerland
36 C5 St.Ingbert W Germany
122 B6 St.Irénée Quebec
121 L5 St.Isidore Quebec
121 T7 St.Isidore Quebec
26 K3 St.Istind mt Norway
9 F3 St.Ives Cambridge England
8 A7 St.Ives Cornwall England
25 E2 St.Jacobi Parochie Netherlands
122 D6 St.Jacques New Brunswick
20 B5 St.Jacques-de-la-Lande France
38 F8 St.Jakob Austria
20 C4 St.James France
118 A1 St.James Manitoba
99 V4 St.James Michigan
99 M5 St.James Minnesota
110 E3 St.James Missouri
127 J2 St.James parish Jamaica
117 H10 St.James, C Br Columbia
113 E11 St.James City Florida
121 L4 St.Janvier Quebec
20 E5 St.Jean France
121 R7 St.Jean Quebec
119 U9 St.Jean Baptiste Manitoba
121 S5 St.Jean Bosco Quebec
21 E10 St. Jean d'Angély France
21 D10 St. Jean-d'Angle France
20 F5 St.Jean-d'Asse France
19 O13 St.Jean-de-Bournay France
20 C3 St.Jean-de-Daye France
122 C5 St.Jean de Dieu Quebec
19 J5 St.Jean de Losne France
18 D9 St.Jean-de-Luz France
121 R6 St. Jean-de-Matha Quebec
19 Q14 St.Jean-de-Maurienne France
21 A8 St.Jean-de-Monts France
21 F8 St.Jean-de-Sauves France
18 H8 St.Jean du Gard France
19 O14 St.Jean-en-Royans France
115 M8 Saint-Jean, Lac Quebec
20 B4 St.Jean-le-Thomas France
18 E9 St.Jean Pied de Port France
122 B6 St.Jean Port Joli Quebec
122 H3 St.Jean, R Quebec
36 B5 St.Jean Rohrbach France
20 C5 St.Jean-sur-Couesnon France
121 Q7 St.Jérôme Quebec
19 N14 St. Jeure D'Ay France
109 K2 St.Jo Texas
21 A7 St.Joachim France
122 B6 St.Joachim Quebec
41 O3 St.Jodok Austria
110 D5 St.Joe Arkansas
100 J2 St.Joe Idaho
94 C5 St.Joe Indiana
36 E4 St.Johann W Germany
38 G8 St. Johann-im-Walde Austria
107 M3 St.John Kansas
119 S10 St.John N Dakota
115 N8 St.John New Brunswick
103 M1 St.John Utah
100 H2 St.John Washington
127 P6 St.John parish Barbados
95 R7 St. John R Maine
123 P3 St John B Nfld
123 R3 St.John, C Nfld
113 L7 St.John I Virgin Is
123 S5 St.John, L Nfld
122 E7 St. John R New Brunswick
122 G5 St. John R Quebec
127 P4 St.John's Antigua W Indies
103 P7 St.Johns Arizona
94 C3 St.Johns Michigan
115 O8 St. John's Nfld
95 P2 St.Johnsbury Vermont
13 F4 St.John's Chapel England
14 C2 St.John's Pt Irish Rep
113 F7 St.Johns R Florida
95 N3 St.Johnsville New York
20 C3 St.Jores France
22 H2 St.Joris-Winge Belgium
111 E10 St.Joseph Louisiana
127 L4 St.Joseph Martinique W Indies
127 P2 St.Joseph Mayoro Trinidad
99 U7 St.Joseph Michigan
99 M10 St.Joseph Missouri
121 U6 St.Joseph Quebec
83 K14 St.Joseph Réunion Indian Oc
127 O2 St.Joseph St George Trinidad
127 P6 St.Joseph parish Barbados
94 A5 St. Joseph R Michigan
113 B8 St. Joseph Bay Florida
120 G6 St. Joseph I Ontario
109 L8 St. Joseph I Texas
115 K7 St. Joseph, L Ontario
123 T6 St.Joseph's Nfld
22 B3 St.Josse France
20 A5 St. Jouan-de-l'Isle France
20 A4 St. Jouan des-Guerets France
20 F2 St.Jouin France
121 Q6 St. Jovite Quebec
126 A1 St. Jozefsdal Curaçao
19 N14 St.Julian Molin-Molette France
40 D5 St.Julien France
21 C7 St. Julien-de-Concelles France
21 C6 St. Julien de-Vouvantes France
19 O15 St.Julien en Quint France
20 F3 St. Julien-le-Faucon France
18 F7 St.Junien France
9 F7 St.Just England
20 K2 St.Just-en-Chausée France
18 H7 St.Just-en-Chevalet France
38 M7 St.Katherein Austria
127 P3 St.Kitts isld Lesser Antilles
126 A1 St.Kruis Curaçao
121 R7 St.Lambert Quebec
121 T6 St.Lambert Quebec
142 G2 St.Lambert,C W Australia
21 E7 St. Lambert-des-Levées France
21 D7 St. Lambert-du-Lattay France
111 D11 St.Landry Louisiana
19 J6 St. Laurent France
129 H2 St.Laurent Fr Guiana
119 U8 St.Laurent Manitoba
121 L4 Saint-Laurent Quebec
18 G10 St.Laurent de la Salanque France
19 O13 St.Laurent-de-Mûre France
21 I6 St. Laurent-des Eaux France
19 P14 St.Laurent-du-Pont France
20 G2 St.Laurent-en-Caux France
21 G6 St. Laurent-en-Gâtines France
18 E7 St.Laurent-et-Benon France
121 U5 St.Laurent, R Quebec
21 G10 St.Laurent-sur-Gorre France
20 D3 St.Laurent-sur-Mer France
22 K5 St.Laurent-sur-Othain France
123 R7 St.Lawrence Nfld
141 J5 St.Lawrence Queensland
95 M2 St. Lawrence R Canada/U.S.A.
115 N8 St.Lawrence, G.of Canada
116 B5 St.Lawrence I Bering Sea
121 O8 St. Lawrence I Nat. Park Ontario
121 P8 St.Lawrence Seaway Canada/U.S.A.
119 Q8 St.Lazare Manitoba
22 K4 St.Léger Belgium
20 J4 St. Léger-en-Yvelines France
22 H1 St.Lenaarts Belgium
122 E5 St.Léon Quebec
36 B7 St. Léonard France
122 E6 St.-Léonard New Brunswick
121 S6 St.Léonard Quebec
21 I10 St. Léonard-de-Noblat France
9 G6 St.Leonards England
121 T4 St.-Léon-de-Chicoutimi Quebec
122 B7 St.Léon de Standon Quebec
38 L8 St.Leonhard Kärnten Austria
38 N4 St.Leonhard Nieder Österreich Austria
20 K3 St.Leu-la-Forêt France
123 Q1 St.Lewis R Labrador
121 S7 St.Liboire Quebec
18 F8 Ste. Livrade France
18 F9 St.Lizier France
20 C3 St.Lô France
127 N4 St.Louis Marie Galante W Indies
85 A5 St.Louis Mauritania
94 C3 St.Louis Michigan
122 H7 St.Louis Pr Edward I
83 J14 St.Louis Réunion Indian Oc
119 M6 St.Louis Sask
105 St.Louis conurbation Missouri
99 O2 St. Louis R Minnesota
122 H7 St.Louis de Kent New Brunswick
122 D6 St.Louis du Ha Ha Quebec
126 H5 St.Louis du Sud Haiti
122 B6 Ste.Louise Quebec
121 R7 St.Louis, L Quebec
36 C5 St. Louis-lès-Bitche France
94 E6 St.Louisville Ohio
40 D2 St. Loup-sur-Semoise France
19 K5 St.Loup-sur-Semouse France
20 H4 St.Lubin-des-Joncherets France
127 L4 Ste.Luce Martinique W Indies
141 K2 St.Lucia dist Brisbane, Qnsld
127 O8 St. Lucia isld Lesser Antilles
87 F11 St. Lucia, C S Africa
121 Q6 Ste.Lucie Quebec
113 G10 St. Lucie Canal Florida
127 P6 St.Lucy parish Barbados
122 B8 St.Ludger Quebec
127 H5 St.Luis du Nord Haiti
20 A4 St.Lunaire France
123 R2 St Lunaire Nfld
21 A7 St. Lyphard France
25 B5 St.Maartens-dijk Netherlands
18 E8 St. Macaire Gironde France
21 D7 St.Macaire Maine-et-Loire France
15 G2 St.Magnus B Scotland
21 E9 St.Maixent-l'Ecole France
122 B7 St.Malachie Quebec
20 A4 St.Malo France
20 B3 St. Mâlo-de-la-Lande France
20 B4 St.Malo, G.de France
20 A5 St.Malon-sur-Mel France
19 P18 St.Mandrier France
127 H5 St.Marc Haiti
121 S6 St.Marc des Carrières Quebec
122 B7 St.Marcel Quebec
19 O14 St.Marcellin France
20 C3 St. Marcouf, I France
20 C5 St.Marc-sur-Couesnon France
22 K4 St.Mard Belgium
123 P2 St.Margaret B Nfld
122 J9 St.Margaret B Nova Scotia
38 K8 St.Margarethen Austria
32 K5 St.Margarethen W Germany
15 F2 St.Margarets Hope Scotland
122 B5 Ste.Marguerite, R Quebec
122 F3 Ste.Marguerite, R Quebec
110 H3 Ste.Marie Illinois
127 L4 Ste.Marie Martinique W Indies
121 T6 Ste.Marie Quebec
83 K13 Ste.Marie Réunion Indian Oc
19 K4 Ste.Marie aux Mines France
36 C7 Ste. Marie, Col de pass France
20 C3 Ste.Marie-du-Mont France
19 Q17 St Marie Mourre de Chanier mt France
100 J2 St.Maries Idaho
113 C7 St.Marks Florida
21 F6 St. Mars-d'Outillé France
21 C7 St. Mars-du-Désert France
20 F5 St.Mars-la-Brière France
21 C7 St.Mars la Jaille France
20 C5 St.Mars-sur-la-Futaie France
122 F4 Ste.Marthe de Gaspé Quebec
18 E6 St.Martin France
127 N5 St.Martin isld Lesser Antilles
22 B2 St.Martin-Boulogne France
127 L4 St. Martin, C Martinique W Indies
89 A9 St.Martin, C S Africa
20 J5 St.Martin-de-Bretencourt France
19 N17 St.Martin-de-Crau France
20 C4 St.Martin-de-Landelle France
21 C9 St.Martin-de-Ré France
20 D3 St.Martin-des-Besaces France
16 E4 St.Martin de Valdeiglesias Spain
19 P12 St.Martin-du-Fresne France
19 O12 St.Martin-du-Mont France
40 B4 St.Martin en Bresse France
20 H2 St.Martin-en-Campagne France
99 U4 St.Martin I Michigan
119 T7 St. Martin, L Manitoba
122 G8 St. Martin's New Brunswick
9 F7 St. Martin's isld Isles of Scilly England
68 A2 St.Martin's I Burma
119 T7 St. Martin Station Manitoba
111 E11 St.Martinville Louisiana
9 H7 St.Mary Channel Is
127 L2 St.Mary parish Jamaica
101 M1 St. Mary R Mont/Alberta
123 N3 St. Mary Is Quebec
101 M1 St.Mary L Montana
117 P11 St. Mary, Mt Br Columbia
144 B6 St. Mary, Mt New Zealand
123 N3 St.Mary Reefs Quebec
118 D9 St.Mary Res Alberta
113 F7 St. Marys Georgia
107 O2 St Marys Kansas
110 G4 St.Marys Missouri
123 T7 St.Marys Nfld
94 C6 St.Marys Ohio
94 J5 St.Marys Pennsylvania
15 F2 St. Marys Scotland
139 J8 St.Marys Tasmania
127 O3 St. Mary's Trinidad
94 F7 St.Marys W Virginia
9 F7 St.Mary's isld Isles of Scilly England
94 B6 St. Marys R Indiana
123 T7 St.Mary's B Nfld
122 F9 St.Mary's B Nova Scotia
95 L8 St. Marys City Maryland
89 H6 St.Mary's Hill S Africa
15 E5 St. Marys Loch Scotland
113 F7 St.Marys R Florida/Georgia
123 K8 St.Mary's, R Nova Scotia
112 G4 St. Mathews S Carolina
21 G10 St.Mathieu France
121 M4 St.Mathieu Quebec
18 B4 St. Mathieu, Pte France
116 C6 St.Matthew I Bering Sea
136 K2 St. Matthias Group islds Bismarck Arch
21 G7 Ste. Maure de-Touraine France
40 E2 St.Maurice France
21 D7 St.Maurice-la-Fougereuse France
20 G4 St. Maurice-les-Charencey France
121 R5 St-Maurice, Parc Quebec
8 A7 St. Mawes England
122 B7 St. Maxime Quebec
19 P18 St.Maximin France
22 J4 St. Médard Belgium
18 E8 St Medard en Jalles France
110 K3 St.Meinrad Indiana
8 C4 St.Mellons Wales
20 B4 St. Meloir-des-Ondes France
19 J3 St. Menehould France
22 H4 St.Menges France
20 C3 Ste. Mère-Eglise France
98 H8 St.Michael Nebraska
127 P6 St.Michael parish Barbados
32 K5 St.Michaelisdonn W Germany
103 P6 St.Michaels Arizona
95 L8 St.Michaels Maryland
22 G4 St.Michel Aisne France
21 C6 St.Michel Maine-et-Loire France
127 H5 St.Michel de L'Atalaye Haiti
121 R6 St.Michel des Saints Quebec
36 B7 St.Michel-sur-Meurthe France
126 B1 St.Michiel Curaçao
19 J4 St Mihiel France
22 C2 St.Momelin France
13 F1 St.Monance Scotland
41 L5 St.Moritz Switzerland
21 A7 St.Nazaire France
19 O14 St.Nazaire-en-Royans France
9 F3 St.Neots England
St.Nicolas see St.Niklaas
20 H2 St.Nicolas-d'Aliermont France
22 G1 St.Niklaas Belgium
119 U9 St.Norbert Manitoba
25 F6 St.Odilienberg Netherlands
25 D5 St.Oedenrode Netherlands
22 C2 St.Omer France
145 D4 St. Omer New Zealand
122 F5 St.Omer Quebec
98 C5 St.Onge S Dakota
18 E7 Saintonge prov France
20 C4 St.Osvin France
20 D5 St.Ouen-des-Toits France
20 K3 St.Ouen-l'Aumône France
121 R7 St.Ours Quebec
122 C6 St.Pacôme Quebec
20 B4 St.Pair France
18 E9 St.Palais France
122 C7 St.Pamphile Quebec
18 F7 St.Pardoux la Rivière France
94 D6 St.Paris Ohio
122 C6 St.Pascal Quebec
20 F5 St.Paterne France
121 N6 St.Patrice, L Quebec
127 O3 St.Patrick co Trinidad
114 H7 St.Paul Alberta
110 C6 St.Paul Arkansas
38 L8 St.Paul Austria
18 E9 St.Paul France
94 B7 St.Paul Indiana
107 P4 St.Paul Kansas
99 N4 St.Paul Minnesota
98 H8 St.Paul Nebraska
83 J13 St.Paul Réunion Indian Oc
112 G4 St.Paul S Carolina
94 E10 St.Paul Virginia
85 C7 St. Paul R Guinea/Liberia
18 G10 St. Paul de Fenouillet France
122 C6 St.-Paul-de-la-Croix Quebec
122 B7 St.Paul de Montriny Quebec
122 C5 St.Paul du Nord Quebec
123 M6 St.Paul I C Breton I, N S
81 E9 St. Paul, Î Indian Oc
116 D8 St. Paul I Pribilof Is Bering Sea
18 H7 St.Paulien France
121 R6 St.Paulin Quebec
19 P17 St.Paul-les-Durance France
123 P2 St.Paul R Quebec
90 G8 St.Paul Rocks Atlantic Oc
112 H3 St.Pauls N Carolina
127 P4 St.Pauls St Kitts W Indies
123 P4 St.Paul's Inlet Nfld
19 N16 St Paul-Trois-Châteaux France
18 E9 St.Pé de B France
20 J5 St. Peravy-la-Colombe France
21 A7 St. Père-en-Retz France
122 C6 Ste.Perpétue Quebec
110 H3 St.Peter Illinois
38 K7 St.Peter-am-Kammersberg Austria
123 R1 St.Peter B Labrador
32 J4 St Peter-Ording W Germany
9 G6 St.Peter Port Channel Is
122 H5 St.Peter, Pt Quebec
123 M8 St.Peters C Breton I, N S
122 K7 St.Peters Pr Edward I
St.Petersburg see Leningrad
113 E10 St.Petersburg Florida
69 J12 St.Petrus isld Indonesia
21 B7 St.Philbert de Grandlieu France
122 B7 St.Philémon Quebec
127 P6 St. Philip parish Barbados
25 B5 St.Philipsland Netherlands
121 S7 St.Pie Quebec
123 Q7 St. Pierre Atlantic Oc
119 V9 St.Pierre Manitoba
127 L4 St.Pierre Martinique W Indies
83 J14 St.Pierre Réunion Indian Oc
19 Q13 St Pierre d'Albigny France
20 H3 St.Pierre-d'Autils France
20 B5 St.Pierre-de-Plesguen France
21 D8 St.Pierre-des-Echaubrognes France
20 E5 St. Pierre-des-Nids France
21 C10 St. Pierre-d'Oléron France
20 H3 St.Pierre-du-Vauvray France
20 C2 St. Pierre Eglise France
20 F2 St.Pierre-en-Port France
81 C6 St.Pierre I Indian Oc
121 S6 St.Pierre, L Quebec
20 C5 St.Pierre-la-Cour France
20 B4 St.Pierre-Langers France
18 H6 St. Pierre le Môutier France
20 H3 St. Pierre-les-Elbeuf France
20 E3 St.Pierre-sur-Dives France
20 E5 St.Pierre-sur-Orthe France
20 C4 St.Pois France
21 C6 St.Poix France
22 C1 St.Pol France
22 C3 St.Pol France
18 C4 St.Pol-de-Léon France
38 N5 St.Pölten Austria
19 K6 St.Pon, L.de France
18 G9 St Pons France
18 H6 St.Pourcain-sur-Sioule France
121 S4 St.-Prime Quebec
22 E4 St.Quentin Aisne France
21 D6 St.Quentin Maine-et-Loire France
122 E6 St.Quentin New Brunswick
20 K4 St. Quentin-en-Yvelines France
22 B3 St.Quentin, Pte.de France
36 C6 St.Quirin France
18 H7 St.Rambert France
122 B7 St.Raphaël Quebec
121 T6 St.Raymond Quebec
101 L2 St.Regis Montana
95 N2 St. Regis Falls New York
121 R7 St.Rémi Quebec
19 N17 St. Rémy Bouches du Rhône France
20 E4 St.Rémy Calvados France
20 F5 St.Rémy-des-Monts France
20 F5 St.Rémy-du-Plain France
20 B5 St. Remy-du-Plein France
20 H4 St. Remy-sur-Avre France
18 H7 St. Rémy-sur-Durolle France
40 F6 St.Rhémy Italy
20 J1 St.Riquier France
121 R7 St.Robert Quebec
122 A8 St.Romain Quebec
20 F2 St.Romain-de-Colbosc France
21 H7 St.Romain-sur-Cher France
121 T6 St.Romuald Quebec
141 G4 St. Ronans Queensland
127 N4 Ste.Rose Guadeloupe W Indies
121 R7 Ste.Rose Quebec
119 S7 Ste.Rose de Lac Manitoba
122 D6 Ste.Rose du Dégelé Quebec
38 N7 St.Ruprecht-an-der-Raab Austria
20 H2 St.Saëns France
31 O6 St.Sambor U.S.S.R.
9 G6 St.Sampson Channel Is
19 O17 St.Saturnin d'Apt France
19 N17 St Saturnin-lès-Avig-non France
20 K2 St.Saufleu France
20 E4 St.Sauveur France
121 Q7 St.Sauveur Quebec
20 C3 St. Sauveur Lendelin France
20 B3 St.Sauveur-le-Vicomte France
18 E7 St.Savin France
21 D10 St.Savinien France
20 F4 Ste.Scolasse France
87 H10 St.Sebastien, C Madagascar
18 G9 St.Sernin-sur-Rance France
20 A4 St.Servan France
18 E9 St.Sever France
20 C4 St.Sever-Calyados France
21 E10 Ste Sévère France
123 T7 St.Shott's Nfld
22 E4 St.Simon France
122 C5 St.Simon Quebec
112 F6 St. Simons Georgia
26 J4 St. Sjöfallets Nat. Park Sweden
115 N8 St.Stephen New Brunswick
112 H4 St.Stephen S Carolina
101 R7 St.Stephens Wyoming
18 G9 St.Sulpice France
20 G4 St.Sulpice France
21 B6 St.Sulpice des Landes France
18 G6 St. Sulpice Laurière France
21 H9 St.Sulpice les Feuilles France
20 E5 Ste.Suzanne France
83 K13 Ste.Suzanne Réunion Indian Oc
20 E3 St.Sylvain France
121 T6 St.-Sylvestre Quebec
18 E8 St.Symphorien France
117 F6 St. Terese Alaska
122 E5 St.Tharsicius Quebec
121 S6 Ste.Thècle Quebec
122 B8 St. Théophile Quebec
121 R7 Ste.Thérèse Quebec
117 N3 Ste. Thérèse, Lac N W Terr
40 C1 St.Thiébault France
98 J1 St.Thomas N Dakota
120 J10 St.Thomas Ontario
127 P6 St.Thomas parish Barbados
127 M3 St.Thomas parish Jamaica
113 K7 St.Thomas I Virgin Is
121 S6 St.Tite Quebec
122 B6 St.Tite des Caps Quebec
40 B5 St.Trivier de Courtes France
19 N12 St. Trivier-Moignans France
St.Trond see St.Truiden
22 J2 St.Truiden Belgium
8 B2 St. Tudwal's Is Wales
27 H11 St.Tuna Sweden
122 E5 St.Ulric Quebec
122 B6 St.Urbain Quebec
20 G2 St.Vaast France
20 C2 St.Vaast-la-Hougue France
20 G2 St.Valery-en-Caux France
20 J1 St. Valéry-sur-Somme France
122 B7 St.Vallier Quebec
38 H7 St.Veit Austria
38 K8 St.Veit-an-der-Glan Austria
22 D2 St.Venant France
121 Q6 Ste.Véronique Quebec
21 I6 St. Viâtre France
19 P17 Ste Victoire, Mt France
21 A6 St.Vincent France
127 O8 St. Vincent isld Lesser Antilles
87 G12 St.Vincent, C Madagascar
139 H9 St.Vincent, C Tasmania
18 E9 St.Vincent-de-Tyrosse France
138 E5 St.Vincent, G S Australia
113 B8 St. Vincent I Florida
123 T7 St.Vincent's Nfld
21 B9 St.Vincent-sur-Jard France
118 A2 St.Vital Manitoba
94 C1 St. Vital Pt Michigan
22 L3 St.Vith Belgium
18 E7 St.Vivien-de-Médoc France
106 G7 St.Vrain New Mexico
118 H5 St.Walburg Sask
20 G2 St.Wandrille France
36 C5 St.Wendel W Germany
126 A1 St. Willebrordus Curaçao
120 K10 St.Williams Ontario
101 S4 St.Xavier Montana
18 F7 St. Yrieix France
122 H4 St.Yvon Quebec
19 P18 St.Zacharie France
20 J5 Sainville France
134 E6 Saipan isld Mariana Is Pacific Oc
20 C2 Saire R France
20 C2 Saire, Pte. de France
18 E9 Saison R France
61 M10 Saitama prefect Japan
68 A1 Saitlai Burma
60 E13 Saito Japan
26 N3 Saivomuotka Sweden
21 E9 Saivres France
77 L2 Saiydabad Afghanistan
77 L1 Saiyid Afghanistan
74 E3 Saiyidwala Pakistan
71 B2 Sajafi isld Indonesia
128 E7 Sajama Bolivia
71 B2 Sajang isld Indonesia
48 F2 Sajó R Hungary
89 B7 Sak watercourse S Africa
88 G2 Saka Kenya
Saka Dzong see Saga
59 L5 Sakai Japan
60 G11 Sakaide Japan
60 G10 Sakai Minato Japan
72 E2 Sakākah Saudi Arabia
78 H7 Sakakah Saudi Arabia
98 E2 Sakakawea, L N Dakota
70 Q9 Sakala isld Indonesia
61 N7 Sakamachi Japan
115 M7 Sakami L Quebec
88 B8 Sakania Zaïre
Sakar see Brannitsa Bulgaria
57 C5 Sakar U.S.S.R.
87 G12 Sakaraha Madagascar
78 C1 Sakarya R Turkey
78 C2 Sakarya R Turkey
59 L4 Sakata Japan
111 H8 Sakatonchee R Mississippi
85 E7 Sakete Benin
51 O3 Sakhalin isld U.S.S.R.
51 O4 Sakhalinskaya Oblast' U.S.S.R.
51 O3 Sakhalinskiy Zaliv B U.S.S.R.
54 G7 Sakhnovshchina U.S.S.R.
52 B7 Šakiai U.S.S.R.
80 G4 Sakib Jordan
60 H12 Sakihama Japan
67 H4 Sakishima-guntō islds Japan
55 C5 Sakmara U.S.S.R.
68 C3 Sa-koi Burma
95 Q5 Sakonnet R Rhode I
86 G3 Sakota Ethiopia
87 D12 Sakrivier S Africa
28 E5 Saksild Denmark
28 H7 Sakskøbing Denmark
75 K7 Sakti India
51 M1 Saktyakh U.S.S.R.
61 M9 Saku Japan
61 L10 Sakuma Japan
61 J11 Sakurai Japan
60 D14 Sakura jima isld Japan
27 M10 Säkylä Finland
80 G3 Sal Jordan
53 F9 Sal R U.S.S.R.
48 D2 Šala Czechoslovakia
27 J12 Sala Sweden
68 F7 Sala Andong Tuk Cambodia
71 H6 Salabangka isld Sulawesi
52 B5 Salacgriva U.S.S.R.
43 G8 Sala Consilina Italy
109 K5 Salad Texas
133 C3 Salada, B Chile
131 G6 Salada, L Buenos Aires Argentina
131 F2 Salada, L Corrientes Argentina
124 B1 Salada, L Mexico
103 J9 Salada, Laguna L Mexico
131 E4 Saladillo R Argentina
131 B2 Salado R La Rioja Argentina
106 C7 Salado, R New Mexico
131 E2 Salado, R Santa Fé Argentina
85 D7 Salaga Ghana
68 F7 Sala Hintoun Cambodia
78 H4 Salahiye Syria
56 C4 Salair U.S.S.R.
56 C4 Salairskiy Kryazh ridge U.S.S.R.
48 H3 Šalaj prov Romania
71 K8 Salajar Indonesia
70 G7 Salajar, Selat str Sulawesi
70 L9 Salak, G mt Java
86 C3 Salal Chad
72 G5 Salālah Oman
125 O10 Salamá Guatemala
94 J4 Salamanca New York
16 D4 Salamanca Spain
16 C4 Salamanca prov Spain
86 C4 Salamat R Chad
128 C2 Salamina Colombia
79 D3 Salamis Cyprus
47 F7 Salamís Greece
94 B6 Salamonie R Indiana
70 E2 Salang Kalimantan
26 J3 Salangen Norway
52 B6 Salantai U.S.S.R.
45 K2 Salara Italy
48 G3 Sălard Romania
133 D2 Salar de Arizaro salt pan Argentina
133 D2 Salar de Atacama salt pan Chile
133 D2 Salar de Cauchari salt pan Argentina
133 D1 Salar de Coipasa salt pan Bolivia
133 D3 Salar del Hombre Muerto salt pan Argentina
133 D2 Salar de Uyuni salt pan Bolivia
16 C1 Salas Spain
46 E1 Salaš Yugoslavia
16 E2 Salas de los Infantes Spain
18 F9 Salat R France
70 N9 Salatiga Java
18 F10 Salau, Pont de pass France/Spain
52 H6 Salaushi U.S.S.R.
55 C4 Salavat U.S.S.R.
128 C5 Salaverry Peru
133 E3 Salavina Argentina
71 C3 Salawati isld W Irian
71 G6 Salay Mindanao Philippines
135 Q11 Sala y Gómez isld Pacific Oc
Salazar see Ndalatanda
21 J7 Salbris France
126 D3 Sal, Cay isld Bahamas
127 J5 Salcedo Dominican Rep
116 P4 Salcha R Alaska
116 O4 Salchaket Alaska
33 P8 Salchau E Germany
37 O6 Salching W Germany
47 G1 Salcia Romania
8 C7 Salcombe England
47 K7 Salda Gölü L Turkey
16 D2 Saldaña Spain
87 C12 Saldanha S Africa
41 N4 Saldura, Pta mt Italy
52 B6 Saldus U.S.S.R.
68 B2 Sale Burma
8 D1 Sale England
85 C2 Sale Morocco
139 H7 Sale Victoria
112 C6 Sale City Georgia
112 B2 Sale Creek Tennessee
77 A2 Sālehābad Iran
71 H9 Saleh, Teluk B Indonesia
147 N15 Salekhard U.S.S.R.
111 L9 Salem Alabama
110 E5 Salem Arkansas
113 D8 Salem Florida
110 H3 Salem Illinois
76 D5 Salem India
110 K3 Salem Indiana
95 R4 Salem Massachusetts
110 E4 Salem Missouri
95 Q4 Salem New Hampshire
95 M7 Salem New Jersey
106 C9 Salem New Mexico
95 O3 Salem New York
94 G6 Salem Ohio
100 B5 Salem Oregon
112 E3 Salem S Carolina
98 J6 Salem S Dakota
94 G9 Salem Virginia
99 S7 Salem Wisconsin
70 D7 Salembu Besar isld Indonesia
43 E11 Salemi Sicily
15 C4 Salen Scotland
27 F10 Sälen Sweden
142 E3 Sale, R W Australia
19 Q17 Salernes France
113 G10 Salerno Florida
43 F8 Salerno Italy
43 F8 Salerno, Golfo di Italy
45 L1 Saletto Italy
20 K2 Saleux France
19 Q12 Salève, Mt France
13 F6 Salford England
130 H9 Salgado R Brazil
131 H2 Salgado Filho airport Brazil
48 F2 Salgótarján Hungary
130 G10 Salgueiro Brazil
79 C8 Sâlhîya, El Egypt
127 P2 Salibea Trinidad
106 D3 Salida Colorado
18 E9 Salies de Béarn France
18 F9 Salies du Salat France
47 J6 Salihli Turkey
87 F8 Salima Malawi
70 E3 Salimbatu Kalimantan
68 B2 Salin Burma
68 B2 Salin R Burma
107 N3 Salina Kansas
110 A5 Salina Oklahoma
103 N3 Salina Utah
43 F10 Salina isld Italy
125 M9 Salina Cruz Mexico
133 D4 Salina La Antigua salt pan Argentina
126 G3 Salina Pt Acklins I Bahamas
129 K7 Salinas Brazil
102 C5 Salinas California
128 B4 Salinas Ecuador
128 C6 Salinas Peru
102 C5 Salinas R California
133 D4 Salinas Grandes Argentina
131 C3 Salinas, Pampa de la Argentina
106 D8 Salinas Pk New Mexico
87 B8 Salinas, Pte. das Angola
94 D4 Saline Michigan
12 E1 Saline Scotland
111 D8 Saline R Arkansas
110 H4 Saline R Illinois
107 L2 Saline R Kansas
127 P2 Saline B Trinidad
109 P3 Saline Bayou R Louisiana
109 P4 Saline L Louisiana
127 P5 Salines, Pt Grenada
102 G5 Saline V California
94 G6 Salineville Ohio
68 B1 Salingyi Burma
133 C3 Salinitas Chile
129 J4 Salinópolis Brazil
70 F6 Salipolo Sulawesi
95 O4 Salisbury Connecticut
9 E5 Salisbury England
95 M8 Salisbury Maryland
110 D2 Salisbury Missouri
112 G2 Salisbury N Carolina
122 G7 Salisbury New Brunswick
94 H7 Salisbury Pennsylvania
138 E5 Salisbury S Australia
95 O3 Salisbury Vermont
88 C10 Salisbury Zimbabwe
141 K2 Salisbury dist Brisbane, Qnsld
115 M5 Salisbury I N W Terr
86 F5 Salisbury, L Uganda
116 O2 Salisbury, Mt Alaska
9 E5 Salisbury Plain England
48 H5 Săliste Romania
129 K6 Salitre R Brazil
80 G8 Saliya Jordan
45 K1 Salizzole Italy
112 F4 Salkehatchie R S Carolina
79 G6 Salkhad Syria
28 D4 Sall Denmark
38 L7 Salla Austria
29 O5 Salla Finland
17 G2 Sallent de G Spain
19 N16 Salles France
18 G8 Salles-Curan France
112 F4 Salley S Carolina
33 T9 Sallgast E Germany
28 B3 Salling reg Denmark
107 Q6 Sallisaw Oklahoma
86 G2 Sallom Sudan
78 K6 Salman, As Iraq
78 K2 Salmas Iran
17 F4 Salmerón Spain
29 N5 Salmivaara Finland
100 H1 Salmo Br Columbia
116 Q3 Salmon Alaska
101 M4 Salmon Idaho
117 M8 Salmon R Br Columbia
114 H7 Salmon Arm Br Columbia
123 P2 Salmon Bay Quebec
101 L7 Salmon Cr.Res Idaho
142 F3 Salmond R W Australia
101 L7 Salmon Falls Idaho
116 R4 Salmon Fork R Alaska
143 D10 Salmon Gums W Australia
123 T6 Salmonier Nfld
100 B8 Salmon Mt California
122 G7 Salmon R New Brunswick
122 K4 Salmon, R Quebec
95 M3 Salmon Res New York
114 H9 Salmon River Mts Idaho
36 G3 Salmünster W Germany
52 E2 Sal'nitsa U.S.S.R.
42 D3 Salò Italy
52 G6 Salobelyak U.S.S.R.
130 C7 Salobra, R Brazil
29 L7 Saloinen Finland
99 L1 Salol Minnesota
103 L8 Salome Arizona
127 L4 Salomon, C Martinique W Indies
40 C2 Salon R France
19 O17 Salon-de-Provence France
Salonica see Thessaloníki
48 G4 Salonta Romania
8 D2 Salop co England
17 H3 Salou, C Spain
29 M11 Salpausselkä reg Finland
26 K9 Salsåker Sweden
53 F10 Sal'sk U.S.S.R.
43 F11 Salso R Sicily
44 G2 Salsomaggiore Terme Italy
80 F5 Salt Jordan
103 N8 Salt R Arizona
110 L3 Salt R Kentucky
110 E2 Salt R Missouri
133 D2 Salta Argentina
55 F3 Saltaim, Oz L U.S.S.R.
8 B7 Saltash England
28 G5 Saltbæk Vig lagoon Denmark
108 B4 Salt Basin Texas
13 H4 Saltburn England
119 P7 Saltcoats Sask
12 D2 Saltcoats Scotland
110 G1 Salt Cr Illinois
94 E7 Salt Cr Ohio
101 T6 Salt Cr Wyoming
99 R9 Salt Cr R Illinois
26 H4 Saltdal Norway
108 C4 Salt Draw R Texas
14 E4 Saltee Is Irish Rep
26 H5 Saltelv R Norway
26 G4 Salten reg Norway
28 D4 Salten Langsø L Denmark
26 G4 Saltfjord inlet Norway
108 B4 Salt Flat Texas
13 J6 Saltfleet England
107 M5 Salt Fork R Oklahoma
108 F2 Salt Fork R Texas
109 H4 Salt Gap Texas
28 K5 Saltholm isld Denmark
125 J5 Saltillo Mexico
94 J6 Saltillo Pennsylvania
110 H6 Saltillo Tennessee
106 G9 Salt L New Mexico
108 C4 Salt L Texas
140 E6 Salt Lake Queensland
101 O9 Salt Lake City Utah
143 C8 Salt Lakes W Australia
94 D8 Salt Lick Kentucky
143 D6 Salt Ls W Australia
133 E4 Salto Argentina
130 F8 Salto Brazil
131 F3 Salto Uruguay
131 F3 Salto dep Uruguay
42 E6 Salto R Italy
130 C9 Salto das Sete Quedas falls Paraguay
130 D7 Salto do Urubupungá falls Brazil
45 O5 Salto, L. del Italy
26 K4 Saltoluokta Sweden
103 J8 Salton California
103 J8 Salton Sea California
127 L3 Salt Ponds, The Jamaica
74 E2 Salt Range Pakistan
127 K3 Salt River Jamaica
127 H5 Saltrou Haiti
101 P7 Salt R. Ra Wyoming
27 K12 Saltsjöbaden Sweden
27 L11 Saltvik Finland
94 F10 Saltville Virginia
102 F2 Salt Wells Nevada
112 F3 Saluda S Carolina
112 E3 Saluda R S Carolina
71 H5 Salue isld Indonesia
71 H5 Salue Timpaus, Selat str Indonesia
84 H3 Salûm Egypt
45 N4 Saluoecio Italy
71 F7 Saluping isld Philippines
76 F1 Salur India
110 C6 Salus Arkansas
129 H2 Salut, I.du Fr Guiana
44 B2 Saluzzo Italy
129 L6 Salvador Brazil
84 E5 Salvador Niger
118 H6 Salvador Sask
111 F12 Salvador, L Louisiana
123 T5 Salvage Nfld
16 B5 Salvaterra de Magos Portugal
125 J7 Salvatierra Mexico
103 N3 Salvation Cr Utah
141 H6 Salvator, L Queensland
18 G8 Salvetat, la Aveyron France
18 G9 Salvetat, la Hérault France
117 J8 Salvus Br Columbia
73 Q5 Salween R Burma/Thailand
75 K4 Salyan Nepal
94 D9 Salyersville Kentucky
38 L6 Salza R Austria
32 F8 Salzbergen W Germany
38 H6 Salzburg Austria
38 H7 Salzburg prov Austria
32 L9 Salzderhelden W Germany
33 M8 Salzgitter W Germany
33 M8 Salzgitter-Bad W Germany
38 J6 Salzkammer-gut res Austria
32 J9 Salzkotten W Germany
33 P9 Salzmünde E Germany
33 O7 Salzwedel E Germany
101 O6 Sam Idaho
80 G3 Sama Jordan
80 G4 Samad Jordan
71 J5 Samada isld Indonesia
16 D1 Sama de Langreo Spain
56 E5 Samagaltay U.S.S.R.
80 F2 Samak Syria
71 G7 Samal isld Mindanao Philippines
69 C10 Samalanga Sumatra
108 A4 Samalayuca Mexico
71 E7 Samales Group islds Philippines
76 F2 Samalkot India
84 J4 Samâlût Egypt
127 K5 Samaná Dominican Rep
126 H3 Samana Cay isld Bahamas
78 E3 Samandag Turkey
60 Q3 Samani Japan
121 S3 Samaqua R Quebec
80 G3 Samar Jordan
71 G5 Samar isld Philippines
53 H7 Samara R U.S.S.R.
136 L4 Samarai Papua New Guinea
101 N7 Samaria Idaho
80 D4 Samaria Jordan
46 E4 Samarína Greece
70 E5 Samarinda Kalimantan
57 D5 Samarkand U.S.S.R.
78 J4 Sāmarrā' Iraq
71 G5 Samar Sea Philippines
71 C3 Samate W Irian
78 K6 Samāwah, Aq Iraq
86 D5 Samba Equateur Zaïre
86 E6 Samba Kasai Oriental Zaïre
70 C5 Samba R Kalimantan
87 C7 Samba Caju Angola
71 A3 Sambaki, Selat Indonesia
70 F4 Sambaliung mts Kalimantan
75 L8 Sambalpur India
70 G7 Sambapolulu, G mt Sulawesi

68 Sambava — Santo Antonio do Zaire

87 J10 **Sambava** Madagascar
25 E5 **Sambeek** Netherlands
74 H4 **Sambhal** India
21 H7 **Sambin** France
70 F4 **Sambit** *isld* Kalimantan
129 K5 **Sambito** *R* Brazil
70 E5 **Sambodja** Kalimantan
68 H6 **Sambor** Cambodia
48 H1 **Sambor** U.S.S.R.
131 G6 **Samborombón, B** Argentina
22 H3 **Sambre** *R* Belgium
69 F12 **Sambu** Indonesia
70 D5 **Sambuan** Kalimantan
45 J3 **Sambuca Pistojese** Italy
59 J4 **Samchŏk** S Korea
68 D6 **Same** Burma
88 F4 **Same** Tanzania
22 B2 **Samer** France
68 E6 **Samet, Ko** *isld* Thailand
87 E8 **Samfya** Zambia
68 A2 **Sami** Burma
46 D6 **Sámi** Greece
71 H4 **Samia, Tg** *C* Sulawesi Indonesia
128 D5 **Samiria** *R* Peru
85 E5 **Samit** Mali
68 C2 **Samka** Burma
29 K11 **Sammatti** Finland
80 F3 **Sammu'** Jordan
68 F5 **Samnak Kado** Thailand
41 M3 **Samnaun Gruppe** *mt* Austria
68 F2 **Sam Neua** Laos
80 E6 **Samniya Auja** *R* Jordan
84 F4 **Samnū** Libya
100 A9 **Samoa** California
Samoa i Sisifo *islds see* **Western Samoa**
52 F3 **Samoded** U.S.S.R.
40 E5 **Samoëns** France
47 F2 **Samokov** Bulgaria
68 C2 **Samon** *R* Burma
92 C4 **Samora Desert** Cal/Ariz
47 H7 **Sámos** *isld* Greece
46 D5 **Samothráki** *isld* Ionian Is Greece
47 H4 **Samothráki** *isld* Thraki Greece
133 E4 **Sampacho** Argentina
70 F6 **Sampaga** Sulawesi
71 E3 **Sampaloc Pt** Luzon Philippines
70 O9 **Sampang** Indonesia
17 G3 **Samper de Calanda** Spain
113 L12 **Samphire Cay** *isld* Bahamas
70 C6 **Sampit** Kalimantan
70 C6 **Sampit, Teluk** *B* Kalimantan
71 H7 **Sampolawa** Indonesia
87 E7 **Sampwe** Zaïre
80 F8 **Samra** Jordan
111 B10 **Sam Rayburn Res** Texas
22 K3 **Samrée** Belgium
68 F6 **Samrong** *R* Cambodia
78 G3 **Samsat** Turkey
28 F5 **Samsø** *isld* Denmark
111 K10 **Samson** Alabama
68 G3 **Sam Son** Vietnam
78 F1 **Samsun** Turkey
47 J7 **Samsun Dağ** *mt* Turkey
67 A6 **Sam Teu** Laos
140 C4 **Samuel, Mt** N Terr Aust
47 H1 **Samuil** Bulgaria
56 B3 **Samus'** U.S.S.R.
68 E6 **Samut Sakhon** Thailand
68 E6 **Samut Songkhram** Thailand
85 D6 **San** Mali
31 N6 **San** *R* Poland
72 E5 **San'ā'** N Yemen
42 H4 **Sana** *R* Yugoslavia
106 D7 **San Acacia** New Mexico
86 B5 **Sanaga** *R* Cameroon
106 D10 **San Agustin** Mexico
71 G7 **San Agustin, C** Mindanao Philippines
133 D4 **San Agustín de Valle Fértil** Argentina
116 F9 **Sanak I** Aleutian Is
45 M2 **San Alberto** Italy
135 S12 **San Ambrosio** *isld* Pacific Oc
102 D3 **San Andreas** California
125 P9 **San Andrés** Guatemala
106 D9 **San Andres Mts** New Mexico
125 M8 **San Andrés Tuxtla** Mexico
41 K7 **San Angelo** Italy
108 G4 **San Angelo** Texas
126 C3 **San Anton de los Baños** Cuba
125 P9 **San Antonio** Belize
131 B4 **San Antonio** Chile
113 E9 **San Antonio** Florida
125 L2 **San Antonio** Honduras
71 E2 **San Antonio** Luzon Philippines
124 E6 **San Antonio** Mexico
106 D8 **San Antonio** New Mexico
109 J6 **San Antonio** Texas
128 E3 **San Antonio** Venezuela
109 K7 **San Antonio** *R* Texas
17 H6 **San Antonio Abad** Ibiza
71 C6 **San Antonio B** Palawan Philippines
109 L7 **San Antonio B** Texas
133 F5 **San Antonio, C** Argentina
126 B4 **San Antonio, C** Cuba
17 H6 **San Antonio, C** Spain
133 D2 **San Antonio de los Cobres** Argentina
124 E3 **San Antonio del Rio** Mexico
127 N9 **San Antonio de Maturín** Venezuela
127 L10 **San Antonio de Tamanaco** Venezuela
102 G7 **San Antonio, Mt** California
108 B4 **San Antonio Mt** Texas
133 E6 **San Antonio Oeste** Argentina
130 J9 **San Antonio, Pta. de** *C* Brazil
128 E2 **Sanariapo** Venezuela
19 P18 **Sanary** France
111 B10 **San Augustine** Texas
74 G7 **Sanawad** India
16 B7 **San Bartolómeu de Messines** Portugal
45 R7 **San Bartolomew in Galdo** Italy
42 F6 **San Benedetto del Tronto** Italy
45 J1 **San Benedetto Po** Italy
125 P9 **San Benito** Guatemala
109 K9 **San Benito** Texas
102 C5 **San Benito** *R* California
102 D5 **San Benito Mt** California
71 G4 **San Bernadino Str** Philippines
109 M6 **San Bernard** *R* Texas
102 G7 **San Bernardino** California
130 B9 **San Bernardino** Paraguay
103 J8 **San Bernardino Mts** California
41 K5 **San Bernardino P** Switzerland
131 B4 **San Bernardo** Chile
124 G4 **San Bernardo** Mexico
128 C2 **San Bernardo, I.de** Colombia
60 F10 **Sanbe-san** *mt* Japan
45 L2 **San Biagio** Italy
113 B7 **San Blas** Florida
124 G7 **San Blas** Nayarit Mexico
124 E4 **San Blas** Sonora Mexico
125 P5 **San Blas, Archipélago de** *islds* Panama
113 B8 **San Blas, C** Florida
125 P5 **San Blas, Serrania de** *mts* Panama
41 O7 **San Bonifacio** Italy
128 E6 **San Borja** Bolivia
124 C3 **San Borja** Mexico
99 L6 **Sanborn** Iowa
99 L5 **Sanborn** Minnesota
98 H3 **Sanborn** N Dakota
95 Q3 **Sanbornville** New Hampshire
124 J4 **San Buenaventura** Mexico
68 E5 **San Buri** Thailand
128 F8 **San Camilo** Argentina
133 D4 **San Carlos** Argentina
103 O8 **San Carlos** Arizona
124 C4 **San Carlos** Baja Calif Sur Mexico
131 B6 **San Carlos** Chile
124 H5 **San Carlos** Coahuila Mexico
71 E3 **San Carlos** Luzon Philippines
71 F5 **San Carlos** Negros Philippines
133 G4 **San Carlos** Uruguay
127 K10 **San Carlos** Venezuela
131 B8 **San Carlos de Bariloche** Argentina
17 H4 **San Carlos de la Rápita** Spain
128 D2 **San Carlos del Zulia** Venezuela
128 E3 **San Carlos de Rio Negro** Venezuela
103 O8 **San Carlos L** Arizona
124 B3 **San Carlos, Mesa de** *mt* Mexico
45 K4 **San Casciano in Valdi Pesa** Italy
17 J3 **San Celoní** Spain
18 G5 **Sancergues** France
18 G5 **Sancerre** France
45 K2 **San Cesario sul Panaro** Italy
20 J5 **Sancheville** France
127 K5 **Sánchez** Dominican Rep
106 E4 **Sanchez Res** Colorado
52 G6 **Sanchursk** U.S.S.R.
125 K7 **San Ciro de Acosta** Mexico
102 G8 **San Clemente** California
17 F5 **San Clemente** Spain
102 F9 **San Clemente** *isld* California
18 G6 **Sancoins** France
71 G6 **Sanco Pt** Mindanao Philippines
130 B10 **San Cosme** Argentina
133 F3 **San Cosme** Paraguay
45 O4 **San Costanzo** Italy
131 E3 **San Cristóbal** Argentina
127 J5 **San Cristóbal** Dom Rep
137 N4 **San Cristobal** Solomon Is
128 D2 **San Cristóbal** Venezuela
128 B8 **San Cristóbal** *isld* Galapagos Is
125 N9 **San Cristóbal de las Casas** Mexico
103 L9 **San Cristobal Wash** *R* Arizona
45 J4 **San Croce sulee Arno** Italy
133 C4 **San Cruz** Chile
126 E4 **Sancti Spíritus** Cuba
118 J7 **Sanctuary** Sask
22 K5 **Sancy** France
28 N2 **Sand** Faeroes
27 B12 **Sand** Norway
89 E7 **Sand** *R* Orange Free State S Africa
89 F4 **Sand** *R* Transvaal S Africa
60 J11 **Sanda** Japan
15 C5 **Sanda** *isld* Scotland
28 D6 **Sandager** Denmark
70 F2 **Sandakan** Sabah
68 H6 **Sandan** Cambodia
26 B10 **Sandane** Norway
47 F3 **Sandanski** Bulgaria
65 H2 **Sandaotong** China
65 G1 **Sandaozhen** China
85 B6 **Sandare** Mali
27 J10 **Sandarne** Sweden
106 H4 **Sand Arroyo** *R* Colo/Kansas
33 Q7 **Sandau** E Germany
15 F1 **Sanday** Scotland
8 D1 **Sandbach** England
37 P6 **Sandbach** W Germany
27 G15 **Sandbäck** Sweden
12 D2 **Sandbank** Scotland
120 H1 **Sandbank L** Ontario
28 G7 **Sandby** Denmark
26 F7 **Sanddöla** *R* Norway
26 A9 **Sande** Norway
27 A10 **Sande** Norway
32 H5 **Sande** W Germany
27 D12 **Sandefj** Norway
103 P6 **Sanders** Arizona
100 J2 **Sanders** Idaho
37 M6 **Sandersdorf** W Germany
33 P9 **Sandersleben** E Germany
113 E7 **Sanderson** Florida
108 E5 **Sanderson** Texas
112 E5 **Sandersville** Georgia
111 H10 **Sandersville** Mississippi
33 M5 **Sandesneben** W Germany
28 B5 **Sandet** Denmark
28 M2 **Sandevåg** Faeroes
118 L3 **Sandfly L** Sask
94 G8 **Sand Fork** W Virginia
9 H5 **Sandgate** England
141 L7 **Sandgate** Queensland
36 F5 **Sandhausen** W Germany
12 D4 **Sandhead** Scotland
26 G4 **Sandhornöy** *isld* Norway
99 Q3 **Sand I** Wisconsin
109 K7 **Sandia** Texas
106 D6 **Sandia Pk** New Mexico
102 G9 **San Diego** California
124 G3 **San Diego** Mexico
109 J8 **San Diego** Texas
102 G8 **San Diego Aqueduct** California
133 D8 **San Diego, C** Argentina
128 F2 **San Diego de Cabrutica** Venezuela
47 L6 **Sandıklı** Turkey
74 J5 **Sandila** India
118 E1 **Sandilands** Manitoba
113 M9 **Sandilands Village** New Providence I Bahamas
143 B6 **Sandiman, Mt** W Australia
124 G5 **San Dimas** Mexico
69 E14 **Sanding** *isld* Indonesia
116 D5 **Sand Is** Alaska
52 J2 **Sandivey** *R* U.S.S.R.
32 H6 **Sandkrug** W Germany
38 L4 **Sandl** Austria
120 F5 **Sand Lake** Ontario
27 C13 **Sandnes** Aust Agder Norway
27 A13 **Sandnes** Rogaland Norway
15 G2 **Sandness** Scotland
26 F5 **Sandnessjöen** Norway
28 N2 **Sandø** *isld* Faeroes
87 D7 **Sandoa** Zaïre
31 N5 **Sandomierz** Poland
45 P6 **San Donato Val di Comino** Italy
110 G3 **Sandoval** Illinois
106 D6 **Sandoval** New Mexico
140 D5 **Sandover** *R* N Terr Aust
52 E5 **Sandovo** U.S.S.R.
68 B3 **Sandoway** Burma
9 E6 **Sandown** England
89 A10 **Sandown B** S Africa
Sandoy *isld see* **Sandø**
116 G9 **Sand Point** Alaska
117 P11 **Sandpoint** Idaho
118 F4 **Sand R** Alberta
47 K7 **Sandras Dağı** *mt* Turkey
9 G2 **Sandringham** England
140 E6 **Sandringham** Queensland
99 T3 **Sands** Michigan
27 G14 **Sandsjö, N** Sweden
113 G12 **Sands Key** *isld* Florida
117 H9 **Sandspit** Br Columbia
38 G8 **Sandspitze** *mt* Austria
101 S2 **Sand Springs** Montana
107 O5 **Sand Springs** Oklahoma
102 F2 **Sand Springs Salt Flat** Nevada
26 D8 **Sandstad** Norway
32 J6 **Sandstedt** W Germany
95 K9 **Sandston** Virginia
99 O3 **Sandstone** Minnesota
143 C8 **Sandstone** W Australia
103 M9 **Sand Tanks Mts** Arizona
123 L4 **Sandtop, C** Anticosti I, Quebec
67 B3 **Sandu** China
67 B4 **Sandu** Guizhou China
67 E2 **Sandu** Jiangxi China
94 E3 **Sandusky** Michigan
94 E5 **Sandusky** Ohio
94 D5 **Sandusky** *R* Ohio
28 H6 **Sandved** Denmark
87 C11 **Sandverhaar** Namibia
27 G16 **Sandvig** Denmark
27 D12 **Sandvika** Norway
27 J11 **Sandviken** Sweden
9 H5 **Sandwich** England
99 S8 **Sandwich** Illinois
95 R5 **Sandwich** Massachusetts
115 O7 **Sandwich B** Labrador
141 H4 **Sandwich, C** Queensland
15 G2 **Sandwick** Scotland
118 J5 **Sandwith** Sask
103 J6 **Sandy** Nevada
100 C4 **Sandy** Oregon
103 N1 **Sandy** Utah
95 R2 **Sandy** *R* Maine
127 H1 **Sandy Bay** Jamaica
119 P3 **Sandy Bay** Saskatchewan
118 K1 **Sandybeach L** Ontario
141 L6 **Sandy C** Queensland
139 G8 **Sandy C** Tasmania
101 O9 **Sandy City** Utah
109 L6 **Sandy Cr** Texas
101 Q7 **Sandy Cr** Wyoming
95 L3 **Sandy Creek** New York
121 O7 **Sandy Creek** Quebec
95 O5 **Sandy Hook** Connecticut
94 D8 **Sandy Hook** Kentucky
111 G10 **Sandy Hook** Mississippi
95 N6 **Sandy Hook** *point* New Jersey
57 C6 **Sandykachi** U.S.S.R.
123 Q4 **Sandy L** Nfld
115 K7 **Sandy L** Ontario
119 R8 **Sandy Lake** Manitoba
119 O3 **Sandy Narrows** Sask
112 L2 **Sandy Pt** N Carolina
127 P4 **Sandy Pt** St Kitts W Indies
126 G9 **San Estanislao** Colombia
129 G8 **San Estanislao** Paraguay
71 E2 **San Fabian** Luzon Philippines
45 O7 **San Felice Circeo** Italy
45 K2 **San Felice sul Panaro** Italy
124 B2 **San Felipe** Baja California Mexico
124 F4 **San Felipe** Chihuahua Mexico
131 B4 **San Felipe** Chile
128 E3 **San Felipe** Colombia
127 K9 **San Felipe** Venezuela
126 C4 **San Felipe, Cayos de** *islds* Cuba
17 F4 **San Felipe, Cerro de** *peak* Spain
103 H8 **San Felipe Cr** California
106 D6 **San Felipe Pueblo** New Mexico
17 K3 **San Feliú de Guixols** Spain
17 J3 **San Felíu de Llobregat** Spain
135 S12 **San Félix** *isld* Pacific Oc
102 F7 **San Fernando** California
131 B5 **San Fernando** Chile
71 E2 **San Fernando** Luzon Philippines
124 B3 **San Fernando** Mexico
16 C8 **San Fernando** Spain
127 O3 **San Fernando** Trinidad
128 E2 **San Fernando de Apure** Venezuela
128 E3 **San Fernando de Atabape** Venezuela
26 G9 **Sånfjället** *mt* Sweden
106 E4 **Sanford** Colorado
113 F9 **Sanford** Florida
95 R3 **Sanford** Maine
118 D1 **Sanford** Manitoba
112 H2 **Sanford** N Carolina
108 C8 **Sanford** Texas
94 C3 **Sanford L** Michigan
116 Q5 **Sanford, Mt** Alaska
143 B7 **Sanford, R** W Australia
127 N3 **San Francique** Trinidad
131 E3 **San Francisco** Argentina
127 J9 **San Francisco** Venezuela
104 **San Francisco** *conurbation* California
106 B8 **San Francisco** *R* Ariz/New Mex
102 B4 **San Francisco Bay** California
108 E6 **San Francisco Cr** Texas
124 G4 **San Francisco de Conchos** Mexico
133 E3 **San Francisco del Chanar** Argentina
133 D4 **San Francisco del Monte de Oro** Argentina
124 G4 **San Francisco del Oro** Mexico
124 H7 **San Francisco del Rincón** Mexico
127 J5 **San Francisco de Macoris** Dominican Rep
133 D7 **San Francisco de Paula, C** Argentina
133 G4 **San Gabriel** Brazil
102 G7 **San Gabriel Mts** California
124 C3 **San Gabriel, Pta** *C* Mexico
76 B1 **Sangammer** India
99 R10 **Sangamon** *R* Illinois
77 J3 **Sangan, Koh-i** *mt* Afghanistan
51 M2 **Sangar** U.S.S.R.
70 E5 **Sangasanga** Kalimantan
70 F2 **Sanga Sanga** *isld* Philippines
85 C6 **Sangasso** Mali
22 B2 **Sangatte** France
128 C4 **Sangay** *vol* Ecuador
71 E7 **Sangboy Island** Philippines
71 J9 **Sangeang** *isld* Indonesia
102 E5 **Sanger** California
98 E2 **Sanger** N Dakota
109 K2 **Sanger** Texas
33 O10 **Sangerhausen** E Germany
127 L5 **San Germán** Puerto Rico
65 C4 **Sanggan He** *R* China
71 J9 **Sanggar** Sumbawa Indonesia
71 J9 **Sanggar, Teluk** *B* Indonesia
70 G6 **Sanggona** Sulawesi
65 E6 **Sanggou Wan** *B* China
86 C5 **Sangha** *R* Congo
56 B1 **Sangil'ka** *R* U.S.S.R.
45 R7 **San Giorgio del Sannio** Italy
42 E3 **San Giorgio di N** Italy
45 K2 **San Giorgio di Piano** Italy
45 R7 **San Giorgio la Molara** Italy
38 E8 **San Giovanni** Italy
45 Q8 **San Giovanni a Teducio** Italy
45 J1 **San Giovanni in Croce** Italy
45 K2 **San Giovanni in Persiceto** Italy
43 G10 **San Giovanni, V** Italy
45 L4 **San Giovanni Valdarno** Italy
71 E3 **Sangitan** Luzon Philippines
45 M1 **San Giuliano** Italy
45 H4 **San Giuliano Terme** Italy
45 R8 **San Giuseppe Vesuviano** Italy
45 M4 **San Giustino** Italy
65 G6 **Sangju** S Korea
70 C7 **Sangkadura** Indonesia
70 F7 **Sangkarang, Kep** *isld* Sulawesi
68 D5 **Sangkhla Buri** Thailand
70 E4 **Sangkulirang** Kalimantan
70 F4 **Sangkulirang, Teluk** *B* Kalimantan
74 E3 **Sangla** Pakistan
76 B2 **Sangli** India
86 B5 **Sangmélima** Cameroon
45 L4 **San Godenzo** Italy
17 G7 **Sangonera** *R* Spain
102 H7 **San Gorgonio Mt** California
71 B1 **Sangowo** Halmahera Indonesia
106 E5 **Sangre de Cristo Mts** New Mex/Colo
102 B4 **San Gregorio** California
127 P2 **Sangre Grande** Trinidad
42 F6 **Sangro** *R* Italy
74 F3 **Sangrur** India
88 E5 **Sangu** Tanzania
118 C5 **Sangudo** Alberta
129 G6 **Sangue** *R* Brazil
18 E10 **Sangüesa** Spain
41 O7 **Sanguinetto** Italy
Sangyuan *see* **Wuqiao**
67 C2 **Sangzhi** China
Sanhe *see* **Sandu**
59 H1 **Sanhe** China
65 D4 **Sanhe** China
67 D1 **Sanhedian** China
59 J1 **Sanhezhan** China
124 D5 **San Hilario** Mexico
59 H1 **San he** China
67 D1 **San Hu** *L* China
67 B1 **Sanhuizhen** China
113 E11 **Sanibel I** Florida
130 C10 **San Ignacio** Argentina
128 E6 **San Ignacio** Beni Bolivia
124 D2 **San Ignacio** Mexico
128 F7 **San Ignacio** Santa Cruz Bolivia
124 C4 **San Ignacio, Laguna** Mexico
106 D6 **San Ildefonso** New Mexico
16 E4 **San Ildefonso** Spain
71 F2 **San Ildefonso, C** Luzon Philippines
79 H3 **Sanime, Wādī** *watercourse* Syria
60 H10 **San'in** Japan
106 E4 **San Isabel** Colorado
133 F4 **San Isidro** Argentina
71 G5 **San Isidro** Leyte Philippines
124 H5 **San Isidro** Mexico
33 Q4 **Sanitz** E Germany
102 H8 **San Jacinto** California
126 G10 **San Jacinto** Colombia
101 L8 **San Jacinto** Nevada
71 F4 **San Jacinto** Philippines
102 H8 **San Jacinto Mts** California
133 F4 **San Javier** Argentina
124 F4 **San Javier** Mexico
131 F2 **San Javier, R** Argentina
125 J9 **San Jerónimo** Mexico
Sanjiang *see* **Liannan**
67 C4 **Sanjiang** China
65 F3 **Sanjiangkou** China
65 F3 **Sanjiazi** China
61 M8 **Sanjō** Japan
128 F6 **San Joaquin** Bolivia
102 D5 **San Joaquin** California
130 C9 **San Joaquin** Paraguay
102 D4 **San Joaquin** *R* California
102 D5 **San Joaquin Valley** California
108 A8 **San Jon** New Mexico
128 C2 **San Jorge** *R* Colombia
133 D7 **San Jorge, G** Argentina
17 H4 **San Jorge, G.de** Spain
102 C4 **San Jose** California
125 M5 **San José** Costa Rica
99 R9 **San Jose** Illinois
106 E6 **San Jose** New Mexico
71 E4 **San Jose** Philippines
131 G5 **San José** Uruguay
131 G5 **San José** *dep* Uruguay
124 D5 **San José** *isld* Mexico
131 B4 **San Jose** *vol* Chile
131 F3 **San José, Cuchilla de** *mts* Uruguay
128 F2 **San José de Amacuro** Venezuela
128 F7 **San José de Chiquitos** Bolivia
124 D3 **San José de Dimas** Mexico
133 F4 **San José de Feliciano** Argentina
124 F4 **San José de Gracia** Sinaloa Mexico
127 M10 **San José de Guaribe** Venezuela
127 J5 **San José de las Matas** Dominican Rep
124 E6 **San José del Cabo** Mexico
128 D3 **San José del Gauviare** Colombia
127 J5 **San José de Ocoa** Dominican Rep
128 D3 **San José de Ocuné** Colombia
106 C6 **San Jose, R** New Mexico
131 C3 **San Juan** Argentina
128 F7 **San Juan** Bolivia
124 F4 **San Juan** Chihuahua Mexico
124 J4 **San Juan** Coahuila Mexico
127 J5 **San Juan** Dominican Rep
71 G6 **San Juan** Mindanao Philippines
128 D7 **San Juan** Peru
127 L5 **San Juan** Puerto Rico
109 J9 **San Juan** Texas
128 E2 **San Juan** Venezuela
126 D4 **San Juan** *mt* Cuba
131 B3 **San Juan** *prov* Argentina
102 D6 **San Juan** *R* California
128 C3 **San Juan** *R* Colombia
125 M4 **San Juan** *R* Costa Rica
103 P4 **San Juan** *R* Utah
102 C5 **San Juan Bautista** California
128 C7 **San Juan, B. de** *B* Peru
133 E8 **San Juan, C** Argentina
102 G8 **San Juan Capistrano** California
124 H5 **San Juan de Guadalupe** Mexico
18 G10 **San Juan de las Abadesas** Spain
124 H8 **San Juan de Lima, Pta** *C* Mexico
125 N4 **San Juan del Norte** Nicaragua
127 K9 **San Juan de los Cayos** Venezuela
124 H7 **San Juan de los Lagos** Mexico
127 L10 **San Juan de los Morros** Venezuela
125 J7 **San Juan del Río** Mexico
100 C1 **San Juan Is** Washington
124 F7 **San Juanito, I** Mexico
106 C4 **San Juan Mts** Colo/New Mex
125 L9 **San Juan Quiotepec** Mexico
131 C3 **San Juan, R** Argentina
126 C3 **San Juan y Martínez** Cuba
133 D7 **San Julián** Argentina
133 E4 **San Justo** Argentina
17 G4 **San Just, Sa. de** *mts* Spain
85 C6 **Sankarani** *R* Guinea/Mali
76 B2 **Sankeshwar** India
32 J4 **Sankt Peter** W Germany
86 D6 **Sankuru** *R* Zaïre
45 H2 **San Lazzaro** Italy
45 M4 **San Leo** Italy
124 C3 **San Lino, Sa** *mt* Mexico
133 E4 **San Lorenzo** Argentina
128 E6 **San Lorenzo** Bolivia
128 C3 **San Lorenzo** Ecuador
125 P9 **San Lorenzo** Guatemala
124 F3 **San Lorenzo** Mexico
106 C9 **San Lorenzo** New Mexico
128 E6 **San Lorenzo** Peru
127 J10 **San Lorenzo** Venezuela
124 C3 **San Lorenzo** *isld* Mexico
133 C7 **San Lorenzo** *mt* Chile/Arg
44 C4 **San Lorenzo al Mare** Italy
128 B4 **San Lorenzo, C** Ecuador
17 F5 **San Lorenzo de la Parrilla** Spain
17 J2 **San Lorenzo de Morunys** Spain
128 C6 **San Lorenzo, I** Peru
45 N4 **San Lorenzo in Campo** Italy
16 C8 **Sanlúcar de Barrameda** Spain
16 C7 **Sanlúcar la Mayor** Spain
128 E8 **San Lucas** Bolivia
102 C5 **San Lucas** California
124 E6 **San Lucas** Mexico
131 C4 **San Luis** Argentina
103 K9 **San Luis** Arizona
124 F4 **San Luis** Chihuahua Mexico
106 E4 **San Luis** Colorado
126 G4 **San Luis** Cuba
125 P9 **San Luís** Guatemala
71 E2 **San Luis** Luzon Philippines
125 J9 **San Luis** Mexico
124 D3 **San Luís** Sonora Mexico
127 K9 **San Luis** Venezuela
131 C4 **San Luis** *prov* Argentina
124 E4 **San Luis Babarocos** Mexico
125 J7 **San Luis de la Paz** Mexico
128 F6 **San Luis, L** Bolivia
103 K9 **San Luis, Mesa de** Mexico
102 D6 **San Luis Obispo** California
109 M6 **San Luis Pass** Texas
106 D3 **San Luis Pk** Colorado
125 J6 **San Luis Potosí** Mexico
102 G8 **San Luis Rey** *R* California
124 B1 **San Luis Rio Colorado** Mexico
131 C4 **San Luis, Sa. de** *mts* Argentina
71 E3 **San Marcelino** Luzon Philippines
124 D3 **San Marcial** Mexico
106 C8 **San Marcial** New Mexico
124 D5 **San Marcial, Pta** *C* Mexico
43 B9 **San Marco, C** Sardinia
126 G10 **San Marcos** Colombia
124 G7 **San Marcos** Mexico
109 K6 **San Marcos** Texas
124 C4 **San Marcos** *isld* Mexico
42 E5 **San Marino** *rep* S Europe
128 D3 **San Martín** Colombia
128 C5 **San Martin** *dep* Peru
128 F6 **San Martin** *R* Bolivia
133 C6 **San Martín de los Andes** Argentina
133 C7 **San Martin, L** Chile/Arg
45 L2 **San Martino in Argine** Italy
38 E8 **San Martino in Badia** Italy
45 J2 **San Martino in Rio** Italy
45 K2 **San Martino in Spino** Italy
102 B4 **San Mateo** California
125 M5 **San Mateo** Costa Rica
106 C6 **San Mateo** New Mexico
17 H4 **San Mateo** Spain
127 M10 **San Mateo** Venezuela
106 C8 **San Mateo Pk** New Mexico
128 G7 **San Matías** Bolivia
131 D8 **San Matias, G** Argentina
121 R5 **Sanmaur** Quebec
127 L10 **San Mauricio** Venezuela
67 G2 **Sanmen** China
67 G2 **Sanmen Wan** *B* China
65 B7 **Sanmenxia** China
103 N10 **San Miguel** Arizona
102 D6 **San Miguel** California
125 Q11 **San Miguel** Honduras
124 J5 **San Miguel** Mexico
128 D6 **San Miguel** Peru
71 D6 **San Miguel** *islds* Philippines
106 B3 **San Miguel** *R* Colorado
128 C3 **San Miguel** *R* Ecuador
124 D3 **San Miguel** *R* Mexico
71 F4 **San Miguel B** Philippines
109 J9 **San Miguel Camargo** Mexico
109 J7 **San Miguel Cr** Texas
125 J7 **San Miguel de Allende** Mexico
128 E7 **San Miguel de Huachi** Bolivia
133 D3 **San Miguel de Tucumán** Argentina
102 D7 **San Miguel I** California
67 F3 **Sanming** China
45 J4 **San Miniato** Italy
71 E3 **San Narciso** Luzon Philippines
42 G7 **Sannicandro Garganico** Italy
131 E4 **San Nicolas** Argentina
71 E1 **San Nicolas** Luzon Philippines
71 E2 **San Nicolas** Luzon Philippines
124 G5 **San Nicolás** Mexico
102 E8 **San Nicolas I** California
45 L2 **San Nicolo Ferrarese** Italy
27 D13 **Sannidal** Norway
51 O1 **Sannikoya, Proliv** *str* U.S.S.R.
45 R7 **Sannio** *mts* Italy
61 N9 **Sano** Japan
31 N6 **Sanok** Poland
102 G8 **San Onofre** California
133 D8 **San Pablo** Argentina
128 F7 **San Pablo** Bolivia
133 D2 **San Pablo** Bolivia
71 E3 **San Pablo** Luzon Philippines
124 F4 **San Pablo Balleza** Mexico
124 B4 **San Pablo, Pta** *C* Mexico
124 H6 **San Pascual** Mexico
131 F4 **San Pedro** Buenos Aires Argentina
102 F8 **San Pedro** California
128 F8 **San Pedro** Jujuy Argentina
124 E4 **San Pedro** Mexico
130 C10 **San Pedro** Misiones Argentina
130 B9 **San Pedro** Paraguay
128 F2 **San Pedro** Venezuela
103 O9 **San Pedro** *R* Arizona
71 G5 **San Pedro B** Philippines
131 A8 **San Pedro, B.de** Chile
102 F8 **San Pedro Chan** California
128 D3 **San Pedro de Arimena** Colombia
124 E3 **San Pedro de la Cueva** Mexico
124 H5 **San Pedro de las Colonias** Mexico
128 C5 **San Pedro de Lloc** Peru
17 G7 **San Pedro del Pinatar** Spain
127 K5 **San Pedro de Macoris** Dominican Rep
133 C3 **San Pedro, Pta** *C* Chile
16 C5 **San Pedro, Sa. de** *mts* Spain
125 P10 **San Pedro Sula** Honduras
44 E3 **San Pier d'Arena** Italy
45 K4 **San Piero a Sieve** Italy
99 U8 **San Pierre** Indiana
45 K1 **San Pietro di Morubio** Italy
45 K2 **San Pietro di Piano** Italy
43 H8 **San Pietro, I** Italy
42 C3 **San Pietro, Pte** Italy
100 G1 **Sanpoil** *R* Washington
45 H2 **San Polo d'Enza in Caviano** Italy
45 J2 **San Possidónio** Italy
45 K2 **San Prospero** Italy
15 E5 **Sanquhar** Scotland
124 A2 **San Quintín** Mexico
131 C5 **San Rafael** Argentina
128 F7 **San Rafael** Bolivia
102 B4 **San Rafael** California
106 C6 **San Rafael** New Mexico
127 K10 **San Rafael** Venezuela
103 O2 **San Rafael** *R* Utah
127 K5 **San Rafael, C** Dominican Rep
127 K5 **San Rafael del Yuma** Dominican Rep
103 O3 **San Rafael Knob** *mt* Utah
102 E7 **San Rafael Mts** California
125 M3 **San Ramón** Nicaragua
128 C6 **San Ramón** Peru
67 E5 **Sanrao** China
44 C4 **Sanremo** Italy
108 F7 **San Rodrigo** *R* Mexico
127 J8 **San Román, C** Venezuela
16 D8 **San Roque** Spain
109 J4 **San Saba** Texas
108 G5 **San Saba** *R* Texas
21 D9 **Sansais** France
125 P11 **San Salvador** El Salvador
126 A3 **San Salvador** *isld* Bahamas
128 A8 **San Salvador** *isld* Galapagos Is
131 F4 **San Salvador** *R* Uruguay
133 D2 **San Salvador de Jujuy** Argentina
85 E6 **Sansanne-Mango** Togo
133 D8 **San Sebastián** Argentina
85 A3 **San Sebastian** Canary Is
17 F1 **San Sebastian** Spain
127 L10 **San Sebastián** Venezuela
124 C3 **San Sebastián** *isld* Mexico
129 J8 **San Sebastião** Brazil
42 E5 **Sansepolcro** Italy
42 G7 **San Severo** Italy
67 G3 **Sansha** China
128 E6 **San Silvestre** Bolivia
127 J10 **San Silvestre** Venezuela
102 C6 **San Simeon** California
103 P9 **San Simon** Arizona
103 P9 **San Simon Cr** Arizona
42 H4 **Sanski Most** Yugoslavia
145 E4 **Sanson** New Zealand
108 B6 **San Sostenes** Mexico
44 C4 **San Stefano al Mare** Italy
127 N4 **Sans Toucher** *mt* Guadeloupe W Indies
67 C3 **Sansui** China
128 C5 **Santa** Peru
125 O9 **Santa Amelia** Guatemala
128 E6 **Santa Ana** Bolivia
102 G8 **Santa Ana** California
128 B4 **Santa Ana** Ecuador
125 P11 **Santa Ana** El Salvador
124 D2 **Santa Ana** Mexico
127 M10 **Santa Ana** Venezuela
102 G8 **Santa Ana** *R* California
124 F3 **Santa Ana Babicora** Mexico
102 G8 **Santa Ana Mts** California
44 F1 **Santa Angelo** Italy
109 H4 **Santa Anna** Texas
130 G6 **Santa Bárbara** Brazil
102 E7 **Santa Barbara** California
126 C4 **Santa Bárbara** Cuba
124 G4 **Santa Bárbara** Mexico
127 N10 **Santa Bárbara** Venezuela
102 D7 **Santa Barbara Ch** California
102 E8 **Santa Barbara I** California
102 E7 **Santa Barbara Res** California
130 D7 **Santa Barbara, Sa de** *mts* Brazil
128 E8 **Santa Catalina** Argentina
133 D3 **Santa Catalina** Chile
124 D5 **Santa Catalina** *isld* Mexico
102 G8 **Santa Catalina, G.of** California
102 F8 **Santa Catalina, I** California
124 B3 **Santa Catarina** Mexico
133 G3 **Santa Catarina** *state* Brazil
124 G5 **Santa Catarina de Tepehuanes** Mexico
126 B1 **Santa Catharina** Curaçao
102 B4 **Santa Clara** California
128 E4 **Santa Clara** Colombia
126 E3 **Santa Clara** Cuba
103 K10 **Santa Clara** Mexico
95 N2 **Santa Clara** New York
103 L4 **Santa Clara** Utah
133 B9 **Santa Clara** *isld* Juan Fernández Is Pacific Oc
102 E7 **Santa Clara** *R* California
110 K3 **Santa Claus** Indiana
17 J3 **Santa Coloma de Farnés** Spain
87 C8 **Santa Comba** Angola
16 B1 **Santa Comba** Spain
128 D5 **Santa Cruz** Amazonas Brazil
126 A1 **Santa Cruz** Aruba W I
128 F7 **Santa Cruz** Bolivia
102 B5 **Santa Cruz** California
71 D3 **Santa Cruz** Luzon Philippines
71 E2 **Santa Cruz** Luzon Philippines
71 E3 **Santa Cruz** Luzon Philippines
71 F6 **Santa Cruz** Negros Philippines
106 D6 **Santa Cruz** New Mexico
128 C5 **Santa Cruz** Peru
130 J9 **Santa Cruz** Rio Grande do Norte Brazil
128 A8 **Santa Cruz** *isld* Galapagos Is
124 D5 **Santa Cruz** *isld* Mexico
133 C7 **Santa Cruz** *prov* Argentina
130 H5 **Santa Cruz Cabralia** Brazil
85 A3 **Santa Cruz de la Palma** Canary Is
16 E5 **Santa Cruz de la Zarza** Spain
126 F4 **Santa Cruz del Sur** Cuba
16 E6 **Santa Cruz de Mudela** Spain
85 A3 **Santa Cruz de Tenerife** Canary Is
133 G3 **Santa Cruz do Sul** Brazil
137 O4 **Santa Cruz Is** Solomon Is
102 B4 **Santa Cruz Mts** California
127 J2 **Santa Cruz Mts** Jamaica
17 F3 **Santa Cruz, Sa. de** *mts* Spain
79 B8 **Santa, El** Egypt
128 B4 **Santa Elena** Ecuador
109 J9 **Santa Elena** Texas
128 F3 **Santa Elena** Venezuela
128 B4 **Santa Elena, B. de** Ecuador
125 M4 **Santa Elena, C** Costa Rica
100 J2 **Santa Emida** Idaho
16 A2 **Santa Eugenia de Ribeira** Spain
17 G4 **Santa Eulalia** Spain
17 J6 **Santa Eulalia del Rio** Ibiza
131 E3 **Santa Fe** Argentina
126 C4 **Santa Fé** Cuba
106 E6 **Santa Fe** New Mexico
71 F4 **Santa Fe** Philippines
16 E7 **Santafé** Spain
128 A8 **Santa Fe** *isld* Galapagos Is
133 E4 **Santa Fe** *prov* Argentina
113 E8 **Santa Fe** *R* Florida
129 J5 **Santa Filomena** Brazil
124 E6 **Santa Genovéva** *mt* Mexico
124 G4 **Santa Gertrudis** Mexico
129 J4 **Santa Helena** Brazil
58 E5 **Santai** China
133 C8 **Santa Ines, I** Chile
133 D5 **Santa Isabel** Argentina
128 G5 **Santa Isabel** Brazil
Santa Isabel Fernando Póo *see* **Malabo** Macias Nguema Biyogo
137 M3 **Santa Isabel** *isld* Solomon Is
124 B2 **Santa Isabel, Sa** *mts* Mexico
129 J5 **Santa Isobel do Araguaia** Brazil
129 G5 **Santa Julia** Brazil
130 F6 **Santa Juliana** Brazil
126 B3 **Santa Lucia** Cuba
124 G5 **Santa Lucía** Mexico
131 F2 **Santa Lucia, R** Argentina
131 G5 **Santa Lucia, R** Uruguay
102 C5 **Santa Lucia Rge** California
130 C6 **Santa Luisa, Sa. de** *mts* Brazil
130 H9 **Santa Luzia** Brazil
102 D6 **Santa Margarita** California
124 D5 **Santa Margarita** *isld* Mexico
102 G8 **Santa Margarita** *R* California
44 F3 **Santa Margherita** Italy
128 G4 **Santa Maria** Amazonas Brazil
133 D3 **Santa María** Argentina
102 D7 **Santa Maria** California
131 H2 **Santa Maria** Rio Grande do Sul Brazil
87 E8 **Santa Maria** Zambia
128 A8 **Santa Maria** *isld* Galapagos Is
137 O4 **Santa Maria** *isld* New Hebrides
133 D5 **Santa María** *mt* Argentina
103 L7 **Santa Maria** *R* Arizona
131 G3 **Santa Maria** *R* Brazil
124 F2 **Santa María** *R* Mexico
131 G5 **Santa Maria, C** Uruguay
43 F7 **Santa Maria Capua Vetere** Italy
16 B7 **Santa Maria, C. de** Portugal
130 F4 **Santa Maria, Chapadão de** *hills* Brazil
124 F4 **Santa María de Cuevas** Mexico
127 M10 **Santa Maria de Ipire** Venezuela
124 G5 **Santa María del Oro** Mexico
43 J9 **Santa Maria di Leuca, C** Italy
131 A6 **Santa Maria, I** Chile
103 M7 **Santa Maria Mts** Arizona
128 C6 **Santa Maria, Pta** *C* Peru
130 C7 **Santa Maria, R** Brazil
130 F4 **Santa Maria, Sa. de** *mts* Brazil
131 B6 **Santa Mariá, Vol** Argentina
126 G3 **Santa Marie, C** Long I Bahamas
126 G9 **Santa Marta** Colombia
87 B8 **Santa Marta, C** Angola
126 H9 **Santa Marta, Sa. Nevada de** *mts* Colombia
130 D6 **Santa Martha, Sa. de** *mts* Brazil
Santa Maura *isld see* **Levkás** Greece
102 F7 **Santa Monica** California
108 G7 **Santa Mónica** Mexico
109 K9 **Santa Monica** Texas
102 F8 **Santa Monica B** California
102 H8 **Santa Mts** California
70 E5 **Santan** Kalimantan
129 K6 **Santana** Brazil
131 G3 **Santana, Coxilha de** *mt* Brazil/Uruguay
131 G3 **Santana do Livramento** Brazil
128 C3 **Santander** Colombia
16 E1 **Santander** Spain
16 E1 **Santander** *prov* Spain
66 E3 **Santanghu** China
71 G5 **Santa Niño** Samar Philippines
103 N8 **Santan Mt** Arizona
102 E7 **Santa Paula** California
109 K9 **Santa Perlita** Texas
17 G6 **Santa Pola, C. de** Spain
101 O10 **Santaquin** Utah
16 B5 **Santarem** Portugal
130 J9 **Santa Rita** Brazil
101 N1 **Santa Rita** Montana
127 J9 **Santa Rita** Venezuela
131 D6 **Santa Rosa** Argentina
102 B3 **Santa Rosa** California
128 E3 **Santa Rosa** Colombia
108 C1 **Santa Rosa** New Mexico
130 C10 **Santa Rosa** Paraguay
125 M2 **Santa Rosa de Aguán** Honduras
128 F7 **Santa Rosa de la Roca** Bolivia
125 L3 **Santa Rosa de Lima** El Salvador
111 J11 **Santa Rosa I** Florida
109 H2 **Santa Rosa L** Texas
124 C4 **Santa Rosalía** Mexico
130 C10 **Santa Rosa, R** Brazil
100 H8 **Santa Rosa Range** Nevada
103 N9 **Santa Rosa Wash** *R* Arizona
133 E3 **Santa Sylvina** Argentina
124 G6 **Santa Teresa** Mexico
129 J6 **Santa Teresa** *R* Brazil
43 C7 **Santa Teresa Gallura** Sardinia
129 H6 **Santa Teresinha** Brazil
140 C6 **Santa Theresa Mission** N Terr Aust
133 G4 **Santa Vitória do Palmar** Brazil
102 D7 **Santa Ynez** California
102 D7 **Santa Ynez Mts** California
102 H8 **Santa Ysabel** California
112 H4 **Santee** *R* S Carolina
112 H4 **Santee Pt** S Carolina
112 D2 **Santeetlah, L** N Carolina
124 A2 **San Telmo** Mexico
124 H8 **San Telmo, Pta** *C* Mexico
45 O5 **Sante Marie** Italy
21 H6 **Santenay** France
42 D4 **Santerno** *R* Italy
20 J5 **Santeuil** France
44 D1 **Santhià** Italy
124 D6 **Santiago** Baja California Mexico
131 B4 **Santiago** Chile
133 C4 **Santiago** Chile
124 G8 **Santiago** Colima Mexico
127 J5 **Santiago** Dominican Rep
125 O5 **Santiago** Panama
130 C10 **Santiago** Paraguay
131 B4 **Santiago** *prov* Chile
128 C4 **Santiago** *R* Peru
16 B2 **Santiago de Compastela** Spain
126 G4 **Santiago de Cuba** Cuba
17 F6 **Santiago de la Espana** Spain
133 E3 **Santiago del Estero** *prov* Argentina
16 B6 **Santiago do Cacem** Portugal
124 G7 **Santiago Ixcuintla** Mexico
108 D6 **Santiago Mts** Texas
124 G5 **Santiago Papasquiaro** Mexico
102 G8 **Santiago Pk** California
124 H7 **Santiago, Rio Grande de** Mexico
128 G7 **Santiago, Serranía de** *mts* Bolivia
124 G5 **Santiaguillo, L. de** Mexico
70 G4 **Santigi** Sulawesi
16 E1 **Santillana** Spain
16 E6 **Santisteban del Puerto** Spain
109 J3 **Santo** Texas
130 F8 **Santo Amaro, I. de** Brazil
130 G6 **Santo Antônia** *R* Brazil
128 F5 **Santo Antonio** Brazil
129 K6 **Santo Antônio de Jesus** Brazil
128 E4 **Santo Antônio do Iça** Brazil
86 B7 **Santo Antonio do Zaire** Angola

Santo Cristo — Sebkhet Idjil 69

130 C10 Santo Cristo *R* Brazil
87 D9 Santo Cruz do Cuando Angola
124 B3 Santo Domingo Baja California Mexico
124 H3 Santo Domingo Coahuila Mexico
126 D3 Santo Domingo Cuba
127 K5 Santo Domingo Dominican Rep
126 G4 Santo Domingo, Cay *isld* Bahamas
17 F2 Santo Domingo de la Calza Spain
124 C5 Santo Domingo del Pacifico Mexico
130 G6 Santo Maria do Suaçuí Brazil
127 M10 San Tomé Venezuela
128 F2 San Tome de Guayana Venezuela
16 E1 Santoña Spain
65 G3 Santong He *R* China
Santoríni *isld see* Thíra *I* Greece
130 F8 Santos Brazil
128 E5 Santos Dumont Amazonas Brazil
130 G7 Santos Dumont Minas Gerais Brazil
16 D6 Santos, Sa. de los *mts* Spain
16 B3 Santo Tirso Portugal
124 F3 Santo Tomás Mexico
128 D6 Santo Tomás Peru
133 F3 Santo Tomé Argentina
43 C8 Santu, C. di M *mt* Sardinia
65 D4 Santunying China
103 L6 Sanup Plat Arizona
133 C7 San Valentin *mt* Chile
20 F3 Sanvic France
71 F1 San Vicente Luzon Philippines
124 A2 San Vicente Mexico
128 C6 San Vicente de Cañete Peru
16 E1 San Vicente de la Barquera Spain
45 P6 San Vicenze Falle Roveto Italy
42 E3 San Vito al Tag Italy
43 E10 San Vito, C Sicily
38 F9 San Vito di Cadore-Antelao Italy
45 N6 San Vito Romano Italy
Sanya *see* Ya Xian
109 H8 San Ygnacio Texas
102 G9 San Ysidro California
106 D6 San Ysidro New Mexico
58 E5 Sanyuan China
65 F3 Sanyuanpu China
87 C7 Sanza Pomba Angola
65 F2 Sanzhan China
130 F8 São Bernardo do Campo Brazil
130 F8 São Carlos Brazil
129 L6 São Cristóvão Brazil
129 J6 São Domingos Brazil
130 D6 São Domingos, R Brazil
129 K7 São Felippe, Serra de *mts* Brazil
129 H5 São Felix do Xingu Brazil
129 K7 São Francisco Brazil
130 F6 São Francisco *R* Brazil
130 E10 São Francisco do Sul Brazil
130 E10 Sao Francisco, I.de Brazil
129 J7 São Gabriel de Goias Brazil
87 G7 Sao Hill Tanzania
130 D8 São João *R* Brazil
129 J6 São João da Alianca Brazil
130 F7 São João da Boa Vista Brazil
130 G7 São João del Rei Brazil
129 K5 São João do Piauí Brazil
129 J5 São João du Araguaia Brazil
129 K4 São João, I. de Brazil
128 F5 São João, Sa. de *mts* Brazil
128 E4 São Joaquim Brazil
128 E4 São José Brazil
128 F3 São José do Anauá Brazil
133 G4 São José do Norte Brazil
130 E7 São José do Rio Prêto Brazil
130 F8 São José dos Campos Brazil
130 E9 São José dos Pinhais Brazil
71 A2 Saolat, Bukit *mt* Halmahera Indonesia
133 G3 São Leopoldo Brazil
130 C5 São Lourenço Brazil
133 G4 São Lourenço do Sul Brazil
130 C5 São Lourenço, Pantanal de *swamp* Brazil
129 J4 São Luís Brazil
128 F5 São Luis de Cassianá Brazil
133 G3 São Luis Gonzaga Brazil
128 E3 São Marcelino Brazil
129 K4 São Marco, B. de Brazil
130 F5 São Marcos, R Brazil
130 H6 São Mateus Brazil
130 F4 São Miguel *R* Brazil
127 K5 Saona, I Dominican Rep
19 N12 Saône *R* France
71 C3 Saonek W Irian
130 F8 São Paulo Brazil
128 E4 São Paulo de Olivença Brazil
128 F5 São Pedro Brazil
129 L5 São Rafael Brazil
129 J5 São Raimundo das Mangabeiras Brazil
129 K5 São Raimundo Nonato Brazil
128 E5 São Romáo Brazil
129 H5 São Sebastião Brazil
130 F7 São Sebastião do Paraíso Brazil
130 F8 São Sebastião, I. de Brazil
128 F6 São Simão *R* Brazil
86 A5 Sao Tome and Principe *islds, rep* West Africa
130 H7 São Tomé, C. de Brazil
68 F7 Sa Oui Cambodia
85 D3 Saoura *watercourse* Algeria
129 J8 Sao Vicente Brazil
47 H3 Sápai Greece
47 L4 Sapanca Turkey
71 E3 Sapangbato Luzon Philippines
85 F7 Sapele Nigeria
106 E6 Sapello New Mexico
112 F6 Sapelo I Georgia
16 C4 Sa. Peña de Francia *mt* Spain
71 J9 Sape Selat Indonesia
71 J9 Sape Teluk *B* Indonesia
47 K5 Şaphane Turkey
68 G2 Sa Phin, Pou *mt* Vietnam
46 E8 Sapiéntza *isld* Greece
106 C3 Sapinero Colorado
20 F4 Sap, le France
71 E2 Sapocoy, Mt Luzon Philippines
125 P6 Sapo, Serranía del *ra* Panama
128 C5 Saposoa Peru
54 M3 Sapozhok U.S.S.R.
98 F10 Sappa Cr Kansas
38 G8 Sappada Italy
101 M3 Sapphire Mts Montana
26 M4 Sappisaasi Sweden
59 M3 Sapporo Japan
43 G8 Sapri Italy
129 G4 Sapucua, L. de Brazil
70 P9 Sapudi *isld* Indonesia
70 E2 Sapulot Sabah
107 O5 Sapulpa Oklahoma
78 L3 Saqqez Iran
78 L3 Sarab Iran
68 F5 Sara Buri Thailand
106 E6 Sarafina New Mexico
108 D4 Saragosa Texas
Saragossa *see* Zaragoza
128 C4 Saraguro Ecuador
29 M7 Säräisniemi Finland
48 E7 Sarajevo Yugoslavia
140 J5 Saraji Queensland
77 G1 Sarakhs Iran
46 F4 Saraklí Greece
55 C5 Saraktash U.S.S.R.
129 G2 Saramacca R Suriname
18 F9 Saramon France
138 D2 Sara, Mt S Australia
57 G1 Saran' U.S.S.R.
94 B4 Saranac Michigan
95 N2 Saranac Lake New York
46 D5 Sarandë Albania
130 D10 Sarandi Brazil
133 F4 Sarandi del Yi Uruguay
70 B5 Saran, G *mt* Kalimantan
71 G8 Sarangani *isld* Mindanao Philippines
75 K8 Sarangarh India
53 G7 Saransk U.S.S.R.
59 L2 Sarapul'skoye U.S.S.R.
113 E10 Sarasota Florida
113 E10 Sarasota Key *isld* Florida
111 B11 Saratoga Texas
101 T8 Saratoga Wyoming
95 O3 Saratoga Springs New York
70 B4 Saratok Sarawak
53 G8 Saratov U.S.S.R.
77 H6 Saravan Iran
68 H5 Saravane Laos
68 D6 Sarawa *R* Burma
70 Sarawak *state* Malaysia
47 J3 Saray Turkey
47 K7 Sarayköy Turkey
77 G6 Sarbāz Iran
42 D3 Sarca *R* Italy
33 T9 Särchen E Germany
133 C3 Sarco Chile
110 B4 Sarcoxie Missouri
85 G3 Sardalas Libya
74 F4 Sardarshahr India
86 G5 Sardindida Plain Kenya
Sardinia *see* Sardegna
94 D7 Sardinia Ohio
43 B8 Sardinia *isld* Italy
112 F5 Sardis Georgia
111 G7 Sardis Mississippi
110 H6 Sardis Tennessee
47 J6 Sardis Turkey
115 P5 Sårdloq Greenland
86 H3 Sardo Ethiopia
71 J8 Sarege *isld* Indonesia
45 K1 Sarego Italy
26 J4 Sarektjåkko *mt* Sweden
70 D5 Sarempaka *mt* Kalimantan
86 G3 Sarenga *mt* Ethiopia
41 O4 Sarentina, V Italy
42 D2 Sarentine, Alpi *mts* Italy
41 O4 Sarentino Italy
111 C9 Sarepta Louisiana
77 D4 Sar e Yazd Iran
41 K3 Sargans Switzerland
90 C6 Sargasso Sea Atlantic Oc
55 F3 Sargatskoye U.S.S.R.
20 F5 Sargé France
102 C5 Sargent California
98 G8 Sargent Nebraska
116 N6 Sargent Icefield Alaska
106 D3 Sargents Colorado
21 G6 Sargé-sur-Braye France
74 E2 Sargodha Pakistan
86 C4 Sarh Chad
85 C2 Sarhro, Jbel *mts* Morocco
77 C1 Sari Iran
47 J9 Sária *isld* Greece
124 D2 Sáric Mexico
116 E9 Sarichef, C Aleutian Is
80 D3 Sarid Israel
47 K6 Sarigöl Turkey
78 J1 Sarikamis Turkey
70 B3 Sarikei Sarawak
141 J5 Sarina Queensland
17 G3 Sariñena Spain
77 J1 Sar-i-Pul Afghanistan
77 K2 Sar-i-Pul Afghanistan
84 G4 Sarīr Libya
109 K8 Sarita Texas
59 J4 Sariwŏn N Korea
47 K3 Sarıyer Turkey
29 L7 Sarjakylä Finland
9 H6 Sark *isld* Channel Is
57 J2 Sarkand U.S.S.R.
78 F2 Sarkisla Turkey
47 J4 Şarköy Turkey
18 F8 Sarlat France
77 K4 Sarlath Range Afghanistan/Pakistan
98 H1 Sarles N Dakota
119 T10 Sarles N Dakota
52 H6 Sarmany U.S.S.R.
48 J4 Sărmaşu Romania
136 H2 Sarmi W Irian
133 D7 Sarmiento Argentina
133 C8 Sarmiento *mt* Chile
27 F10 Särna Sweden
27 M14 Särnate U.S.S.R.
41 H4 Sarnen Switzerland
115 L9 Sarnia Ontario
41 L6 Sarnico Italy
43 F8 Sarno Italy
27 E14 Särö Sweden
70 G6 Saroako Sulawesi
77 L2 Sarobi Afghanistan
69 F14 Sarolangun Sumatra
60 R1 Saroma-ko *L* Japan
47 F7 Saronikós Kólpos *B* Greece
42 C3 Saronno Italy
47 H4 Saros Körfezi *B* Turkey
46 D2 Šar Planina *mt* Yugoslavia
27 E12 Sarpsborg Norway
101 T4 Sarpy Montana
115 O3 Sarqaq Greenland
36 C6 Sarralbe France
36 C6 Sarraltroff France
19 N14 Sarras France
36 C6 Sarrebourg France
19 K3 Sarreguemines France
16 C2 Sarria Spain
19 N16 Sarrians France
17 G4 Sarrión Spain
80 G5 Sarrut Jordan
55 C3 Sars U.S.S.R.
52 H6 Sarsak Omga U.S.S.R.
45 M4 Sarsina Italy
22 D3 Sars, le France
22 G3 Sars-Poteries France
81 C16 Sars Seamount S Pacific Oc
32 L8 Sarstedt W Germany
22 K2 Sart Belgium
74 D5 Sartanahu Pakistan
51 N2 Sartang *R* U.S.S.R.
21 F6 Sarthe *dep* France
20 E5 Sarthe *R* France
20 C4 Sartilly France
Sartu *see* Anda
60 R3 Sarubetsu *R* Japan
60 F10 Sarumasay Japan
75 O5 Sarupeta India
79 G3 Sarūt *R* Syria
78 L4 Sarvabad Iran
48 E4 Sarviz *R* Hungary
26 F9 Särvsjö Sweden
57 B2 Sarychoganak, Zaliv *gulf* U.S.S.R.
57 H2 Saryishikotrau, Peski *des* U.S.S.R.
57 G2 Sarykomey U.S.S.R.
55 D5 Sarykopa, Oz *L* U.S.S.R.
55 D5 Sarymoin, Oz *L* U.S.S.R.
57 J3 Sary-Ozek U.S.S.R.
57 G2 Sary-Shagan U.S.S.R.
57 E2 Sarysu *R* U.S.S.R.
57 G5 Sary-Tash U.S.S.R.
52 J3 Sar'yudin U.S.S.R.
57 B6 Sary-Yazikskoye Vdkhr *res* U.S.S.R.
44 G3 Sarzana Italy
18 D5 Sarzeau France
86 H4 Sasa Baneh Ethiopia
103 N10 Sasabe Arizona
124 D2 Sásabe Mexico
69 D12 Sasak Sumatra
75 L6 Sasaram India
71 J9 Sasar Tg *C* Sumba Indonesia
60 J10 Sasayama Japan
40 G1 Sasbach W Germany
60 C12 Sasebo Japan
118 H5 Saskatchewan *prov* Canada
118 L6 Saskatoon Sask
119 Q5 Saskeram L Manitoba
51 L1 Saskylakh U.S.S.R.
125 M3 Saslaya *mt* Nicaragua
109 J6 Saspamco Texas
112 E2 Sassafras Mt S Carolina
85 C8 Sassandra Ivory Coast
85 C7 Sassandra *R* Ivory Coast
37 K4 Sassanfahr W Germany
43 B8 Sassari Sardinia
33 S4 Sassen E Germany
19 P14 Sassenage France
32 H9 Sassenberg W Germany
33 N7 Sassenburg W Germany
25 C4 Sassenheim Netherlands
20 G2 Sassetot France
30 H1 Sassnitz E Germany
45 N4 Sassocorvaro Italy
45 K3 Sasso Marconi Italy
38 E8 Sass Rigais *mt* Italy
45 J2 Sassuolo Italy
17 G3 Sástago Spain
133 E4 Sastre Argentina
60 C11 Sasuna Japan
25 A6 Sas-van Gent Netherlands
57 K2 Sasykkol', Ozero *L* U.S.S.R.
48 M5 Sasyk, Oz *L* U.S.S.R.
85 B6 Satadougou Mali
60 D14 Sata-misaki *C* Japan
106 B6 Satan Pass New Mexico
107 K4 Satanta Kansas
76 A2 Satara India
114 H2 Satellite B N W Terr
71 H8 Satengar *isld* Indonesia
27 H11 Säter Sweden
32 G6 Saterland *reg* W Germany
112 E6 Satilla *R* Georgia
19 N14 Satillieu France
128 D6 Satipo Peru
26 K4 Satisjaure *L* Sweden
55 C4 Satka U.S.S.R.
13 G4 Satley England
74 F8 Satmala Hills India
71 H9 Satonda *isld* Indonesia
86 D6 Şatonga *R* Zaïre
42 H4 Šator *mt* Yugoslavia
48 G2 Sátoraljaújhely Hungary
33 P5 Satow E Germany
74 F8 Satpura Range India
28 D7 Satrup W Germany
60 D14 Satsuma-hantō *pen* Japan
26 N4 Sattajärvi Sweden
29 M4 Sattanen Finland
41 J3 Sattel Switzerland
76 E2 Sattenapalle India
68 B3 Satthwa Burma
26 J9 Sättna Sweden
38 K8 Sattnitz *reg* Austria
70 D6 Satui Kalimantan
48 H3 Satu Mare Romania
69 D9 Satun Thailand
100 B1 Saturna I Br Col
100 E3 Satus Washington
76 C5 Satyamangalam India
55 D2 Satyga U.S.S.R.
38 L8 Saualpe *mts* Austria
70 P9 Saubi *isld* Indonesia
20 F3 S.Aubin-de-Scellon France
122 H2 Saubosq, L Quebec
124 J5 Sauceda Mexico
103 M9 Sauceda Mts Arizona
131 E7 Sauce, R Argentina
124 G4 Sauces Mexico
111 G11 Saucier Mississippi
124 G3 Saucillo Mexico
27 B12 Sauda Norway
128 F5 Saudade Brazil
72 E4 Saudi Arabia *kingdom*
36 D1 Sauerland *reg* W Germany
129 G6 Saueruina *R* Brazil
71 G7 Saug *R* Mindanao Philippines
99 U7 Saugatuck Michigan
120 J8 Saugeen *R* Ontario
117 K9 Saugstad, Mt Br Col
18 H8 Saugues France
129 G4 Sauiá Brazil
18 E7 Saujon France
99 M4 Sauk *R* Minnesota
100 D1 Sauk *R* Washington
99 M4 Sauk Center Minnesota
99 R6 Sauk City Wisconsin
52 B6 Šaukenai U.S.S.R.
22 G4 Saulces-Monclin France
18 G5 Sauldre *R* France
20 E5 Saule, Mt.du France
41 L1 Saulgau W Germany
41 O2 Saulgrub W Germany
18 H5 Saulieu France
52 B6 Saulkrasti U.S.S.R.
122 F9 Saulnierville Nova Scotia
19 O16 Sault France
122 C5 Sault au Mouton Quebec
122 C5 Sault-aux-Cochons, R Quebec
115 L8 Sault Ste. Marie Ontario
36 C7 Saulxures France
80 G3 Saum Jordan
141 L5 Saumarez Reef Gt Barrier Reef Aust
127 J5 Saumâtre, Etang *L* Haiti
20 H5 Saumeray France
136 G3 Saumlaki Moluccas Indonesia
21 E7 Saumur France
122 K2 Saumur, L Quebec
29 N4 Saunavaara Finland
118 B6 Saunders Alberta
8 B4 Saundersfoot Wales
146 A14 Saunders I Falkland Is
140 B2 Saunders, Mt N Terr Aust
143 F8 Saunders Ra W Australia
8 B5 Saunton England
57 L2 Saur, Khrebet *mts* U.S.S.R.
41 K4 Sauronstock *mt* Switzerland
38 M8 Sausal *reg* Austria
102 B4 Sausalito California
71 C3 Sausapor W Irian
20 C2 Saussemesnil France
19 O18 Sausset-les-Pins France
40 A3 Saussy France
70 G5 Sausu Sulawesi
87 C8 Sautar Angola
122 H2 Sauterelles, Lac aux Quebec
127 P5 Sauteurs Grenada
21 B7 Sautron France
18 E9 Sauveterre France
18 F8 Sauveterre-de-Guyenne France
21 I10 Sauviat-sur-Vige France
29 K11 Sauvo Finland
25 G2 Sauwerd Netherlands
42 H3 Sava *R* Yugoslavia
95 L7 Savage Maryland
111 F7 Savage Mississippi
98 B2 Savage Montana
101 U6 Savageton Wyoming
137 S4 Savaii *isld* W Samoa
85 E7 Savalou Benin
122 A2 Savan'e, R Quebec
126 A2 Savaneta Aruba W I
99 Q7 Savanna Illinois
107 P7 Savanna Oklahoma
112 F5 Savannah Georgia
110 B2 Savannah Missouri
94 E6 Savannah Ohio
110 H6 Savannah Tennessee
112 E3 Savannah *R* S Carolina
112 F6 Savannah Beach Georgia
141 F4 Savannah Downs Queensland
126 F2 Savannah Sound Eleuthera Bahamas
68 G4 Savannakhet Laos
127 H2 Savanna la Mar Jamaica
76 A3 Savantvadi India
76 B3 Savanur India
26 L8 Sävar Sweden
26 L7 Sävarån *R* Sweden
40 F6 Savaranche, V Italy
26 M6 Sävast Sweden
47 J5 Savaştepe Turkey
85 E7 Savé Benin
18 F9 Save *R* France
87 F10 Save *R* Mozambique
77 B2 Sāveh Iran
85 D7 Savelugu Ghana
45 K3 Savena *R* Italy
21 B7 Savenay France
18 G9 Saverdun France
36 C6 Saverne France
101 S8 Savery Wyoming
44 C2 Savigliano Italy
45 M3 Savignano Italy
21 F6 Savigne France
20 F5 Savigné-l'Evêque France
45 K3 Savigno Italy
21 F7 Savigny-en-Véron France
21 G6 Savigny-sur-Braye France
19 Q15 Savines France
42 F2 Savinja *R* Yugoslavia
52 H2 Savino U.S.S.R.
52 J3 Savinobor U.S.S.R.
45 M3 Savio Italy
45 M4 Såvio *R* Italy
29 N10 Savitaipale Finland
42 J6 Šavnik Yugoslavia
120 F3 Savoff Ontario
117 N10 Savona Br Columbia
44 D3 Savona Italy
95 K4 Savona New York
29 O10 Savonlinna Finland
29 O9 Savonranta Finland
116 B5 Savoonga St Lawrence I, Alaska
111 H9 Savoy Mississippi
101 R1 Savoy Montana
27 G14 Sävsjö Sweden
27 H15 Sävsjöström Sweden
42 F3 Savudrija Rtič *C* Yugoslavia
29 N4 Savukoski Finland
78 H3 Savur Turkey
71 K9 Savu Sea Indonesia
80 C5 Savyon Israel
68 B2 Saw Burma
70 D3 Sawah Kalimantan
69 E13 Sawahlunto Sumatra
74 G6 Sawai Madhopur India
70 M9 Sawall, G *mt* Java
69 F12 Sawang Indonesia
68 D4 Sawankhalok Thailand
60 O3 Sawara Hokkaido Japan
61 O10 Sawara Honshu Japan
61 M8 Sawasaki-bana *C* Japan
106 D2 Sawatch Ra Colorado
121 L1 Sawayan Pt Quebec
119 Q1 Sawbill Manitoba
84 E4 Sawda, Jabal as Libya
118 D4 Sawdy Alberta
14 D2 Sawel *mt* N Ireland
84 E3 Sawfajiin Libya
69 A8 Sawi B Nicobar Is
84 E4 Sawknah Libya
107 L4 Sawlog Cr Kansas
117 O3 Sawmill Bay N W Terr
9 G3 Sawston England
116 N4 Sawtooth Mt Alaska
99 P2 Sawtooth Mts Minnesota
101 L6 Sawtooth Range Idaho
100 E1 Sawtooth Range Washington
71 K10 Sawu *isld* Indonesia
107 M4 Sawyer Kansas
98 E1 Sawyer N Dakota
99 T5 Sawyer Wisconsin
100 B8 Sawyers Bar California
121 T7 Sawyerville Quebec
141 F4 Saxby *R* Queensland
141 G5 Saxby Downs Queensland
9 F1 Saxilby England
9 H3 Saxmundham England
26 H7 Saxnäs Sweden
99 Q3 Saxon Wisconsin
94 J6 Saxton Pennsylvania
144 D5 Saxton Pass New Zealand
85 E6 Say Niger
79 F3 Saya Syria
68 E3 Sayaboury Laos
81 C7 Saya de Malha Bank Indian Oc
57 H2 Sayak Pervyy U.S.S.R.
128 C6 Sayán Peru
56 D5 Sayanskiy Khrebet *mt* U.S.S.R.
57 C5 Sayat U.S.S.R.
125 O9 Sayaxché Guatemala
37 P2 Sayda E Germany
69 C8 Sayer I Thailand
139 G5 Sayers Lake New S Wales
72 G5 Sayḩūt S Yemen
56 C6 Saylyugem, Khrebet *mts* U.S.S.R.
29 M9 Säynätsalo Finland
58 F3 Saynshand Mongolia
108 E8 Sayre Oklahoma
95 L5 Sayre Pennsylvania
124 H8 Sayula Mexico
117 L10 Sayward Br Col
72 F5 Saywūn S Yemen
46 C4 Sazan *isld* Albania
31 J6 Sázava *R* Czechoslovakia
55 C3 Sazhino U.S.S.R.
85 D3 Sbaa Algeria
85 F1 Sbeitla Tunisia
143 D10 Scaddan W Australia
18 C4 Scaër France
45 R8 Scafati Italy
13 E5 Scafell Pikes *mt* England
13 H5 Scalby England
43 G9 Scalea Italy
99 Q7 Scales Mound Illinois
15 G2 Scalloway Shetland Scotland
15 C3 Scalpay *isld* Scotland
116 E6 Scammon Bay Alaska
9 F1 Scampton England
118 F8 Scandia Alberta
107 N2 Scandia Kansas
45 J2 Scandiano Italy
45 N5 Scandriglia Italy
119 V8 Scanterbury Manitoba
118 F7 Scapa Alberta
15 E2 Scapa Flow Orkney Scotland
100 C4 Scappoose Oregon
43 F12 Scaramia, C Sicily
15 C4 Scarba *isld* Scotland
13 H5 Scarborough England
127 M2 Scarborough Tobago
142 A1 Scarborough *dist* Perth, W Aust
144 D5 Scargill New Zealand
14 A5 Scariff *isld* Irish Rep
15 A2 Scarp *isld* Lewis Scotland
Scarpanto *isld see* Karpathos Greece
22 D3 Scarpe *R* France
45 K4 Scarperia Italy
119 R9 Scarth Manitoba
123 N7 Scaterie I C Breton I, N Scotia
15 B3 Scavaig, L Scotland
138 C5 Sceale B S Australia
20 K4 Sceaux Paris France
20 G5 Sceaux Sarthe France
42 G5 Šćedro *isld* Yugoslavia
98 D6 Scenic S Dakota
118 H8 Sceptre Sask
33 N6 Schaale *R* E Germany
33 N5 Schaalsee *L* Germany
38 H6 Schafberg *mt* Austria
99 T4 Schaffer Michigan
41 J2 Schaffhausen Switzerland
28 C7 Schaffland W Germany
33 P10 Schafstädt E Germany
25 C3 Schagen Netherlands
36 C6 Schalbach France
37 P6 Schalding W Germany
32 G8 Schale W Germany
37 L3 Schalkau E Germany
32 G10 Schalksmühle W Germany
99 L7 Schaller Iowa
41 K4 Schams *R* Switzerland
32 G8 Schapen W Germany
38 H5 Schärding Austria
32 H5 Scharhörn *isld* W Germany
33 M6 Scharnebeck W Germany
41 O3 Scharnitz Austria
32 G6 Scharrel W Germany
36 G1 Schauenburg W Germany
37 M3 Schauenstein W Germany
32 K8 Schaumburg W Germany
36 H6 Schechingen W Germany
25 G2 Scheemda Netherlands
41 K1 Scheer W Germany
32 K6 Scheessel W Germany
115 N7 Schefferville Quebec
38 M6 Scheibbs Austria
37 K4 Scheinfeld W Germany
22 G1 Schelde *R* Belgium
36 H7 Schelklingen W Germany
103 K2 Schell Creek Ra Nevada
95 O4 Schenectady New York
32 K4 Schenefeld W Germany
32 L5 Schenefeld W Germany
36 H2 Schenklengsfeld W Germany
32 K9 Scherfede W Germany
32 E9 Schermbeck W Germany
25 C3 Schermerhorn Netherlands
33 N10 Schernberg E Germany
22 H2 Scherpen Heuvel Belgium
28 D7 Schersberg *hill* W Germany
109 J6 Schertz Texas
41 L3 Schesaplana *mt* Austria
37 L4 Schesslitz W Germany
25 B4 Scheveningen Netherlands
38 J7 Schiadming Austria
25 B5 Schiedam Netherlands
32 K9 Schieder W Germany
15 D4 Schiehallion *mt* Scotland
33 N6 Schierling W Germany
25 F2 Schiermonnikoog Netherlands
25 F2 Schiermonnokoog *isld* Netherlands
33 S8 Schiessplatz E Germany
36 F2 Schiffenberg W Germany
36 E5 Schifferstadt W Germany
36 C5 Schiffweiler W Germany
25 D5 Schijndel Netherlands
33 R10 Schildau E Germany
33 N6 Schilde *R* E Germany
33 R6 Schillersdorf E Germany
32 L8 Schillerslage W Germany
32 H5 Schillighörn *point* W Germany
37 J5 Schillingsfürst W Germany
41 M5 Schilpario Italy
36 E7 Schiltach W Germany
38 N4 Schiltern Austria
41 O6 Schio Italy
25 F4 Schipbeek *R* Netherlands
25 C4 Schiphol Netherlands
19 K4 Schirmeck France
33 Q10 Schkeuditz E Germany
37 M1 Schkölen E Germany
33 T9 Schlabendorf E Germany
38 J7 Schladminger Tauern *mts* Austria
36 E3 Schlangenbad W Germany
36 C1 Schlebusch W Germany
30 E1 Schlei *R* W Germany
36 B2 Schleiden W Germany
36 E6 Schleithal France
37 M2 Schleiz E Germany
33 P5 Schlemmin E Germany
99 L7 Schleswig Iowa
30 E1 Schleswig W Germany
32 K4 Schleswig Holstein *land* W Germany
37 O2 Schlettau E Germany
37 K2 Schleusinger-Neundorf E Germany
37 M4 Schlicht W Germany
33 S9 Schlieben E Germany
40 G2 Schliengen W Germany
36 H3 Schliichtern W Germany
36 H2 Schlitz W Germany
32 J9 Schloss-Holte W Germany
37 L1 Schlossvippach E Germany
37 K1 Schlotheim E Germany
40 H2 Schluchsee W Germany
40 F1 Schlucht, Col de la *pass* France
32 K8 Schlüsselburg W Germany
33 N5 Schlutup W Germany
36 E1 Schmallenberg W Germany
33 O7 Schmarsau W Germany
36 B5 Schmelz W Germany
37 M5 Schmidmühlen W Germany
36 B3 Schmidthein W Germany
37 K2 Schmiedefeld E Germany
36 F1 Schmittlotheim W Germany
81 A10 Schmitt-Ott Seamount Atlantic Oc
37 N2 Schmölln E Germany
37 K7 Schmutter *R* W Germany
37 M4 Schnabelwaid W Germany
33 P6 Schnackenburg W Germany
37 N4 Schnaittenbach W Germany
37 O2 Schneeberg E Germany
36 C6 Schnee Berg *mt* France
37 M3 Schneeburg *mt* W Germany
32 K7 Schneeren W Germany
Schneidemühl *see* Piła
33 O9 Schneidlingen E Germany
37 J5 Schnelldorf W Germany
32 L6 Schneverdingen W Germany
38 K7 Schöder Austria
127 L4 Schœlcher Martinique W I
40 G1 Schöenau France
99 R5 Schofield Wisconsin
135 Q2 Schofield Barracks Hawaiian Is
95 N4 Schoharie New York
41 P3 Scholastika Austria
33 Q7 Schollene E Germany
36 G3 Schöllkrippen W Germany
89 D7 Scholtzkop *mt* S Africa
36 F7 Schömberg W Germany
38 J6 Schön *mt* Austria
36 G6 Schönaich W Germany
37 J2 Schönau E Germany
36 B3 Schönau Nordrhein-Westfalen W Germany
36 F5 Schönau W Germany
22 L3 Schonberg Belgium
33 R7 Schönberg E Germany
30 E1 Schönberg W Germany
36 H3 Schondra W Germany
33 P8 Schönebeck E Germany
33 S8 Schöneberg E Germany
37 N3 Schöneck E Germany
36 B3 Schönecken-Wetteldorf W Germany
33 S8 Schönefeld *airport* E Germany
36 C5 Schönenberg-Kubelberg W Germany
33 S9 Schönewalde E Germany
36 B3 Schönfeld W Germany
41 N2 Schongau W Germany
32 L9 Schönhagen W Germany
33 Q7 Schönhausen E Germany
37 O3 Schönheide E Germany
33 N8 Schöningen W Germany
37 O4 Schönsee W Germany
36 H5 Schöntal W Germany
37 O5 Schönthal W Germany
37 J3 Schonungen W Germany
33 S7 Schönwalde E Germany
33 N4 Schönwalde am Bungsberg W Germany
95 S1 Schoodic L Maine
94 B4 Schoolcraft Michigan
25 C5 Schoonhoven Netherlands
25 C3 Schoorl Netherlands
40 G2 Schopfheim W Germany
33 T7 Schopfurch E Germany
33 N8 Schöppenstedt W Germany
32 F8 Schöppingen W Germany
36 C5 Schorbach France
36 H6 Schorndorf W Germany
32 G5 Schortens W Germany
36 G3 Schotten W Germany
139 J8 Schouten I Tasmania
25 A5 Schouwen Netherlands
100 G2 Schrag Washington
36 E7 Schramberg W Germany
33 P10 Schraplau E Germany
40 H4 Schreckhorn *mt* Switzerland
36 G2 Schrecksbach W Germany
115 L8 Schreiber Ontario
33 Q6 Schrepkow E Germany
33 N5 Schretstaken W Germany
36 F5 Schriesheim W Germany
37 L6 Schrobenhausen W Germany
95 O3 Schroon Lake New York
36 H5 Schrozberg W Germany
41 L3 Schruns Austria
103 M9 Schuchuli Arizona
109 L6 Schulenburg Texas
32 L8 Schulenburg W Germany
118 G8 Schuler Alberta
14 B5 Schull Irish Rep
37 M1 Schulpforta E Germany
107 P6 Schulter Oklahoma
141 K1 Schultz Can Brisbane, Qnsld
115 K5 Schultz L N W Terr
33 T8 Schulzendorf E Germany
120 J4 Schumacher Ontario
33 N8 Schunter *R* W Germany
40 H4 Schüpfheim Switzerland
102 F3 Schurz Nevada
41 L2 Schussen *R* W Germany
36 D7 Schutterwald W Germany
32 F8 Schüttorf W Germany
98 J8 Schuyler Nebraska
94 J9 Schuyler Virginia
95 L6 Schuylkill Haven Pennsylvania
33 Q5 Schwaan E Germany
37 L5 Schwabach W Germany
37 J7 Schwaben *reg* W Germany
37 L7 Schwabhausen W Germany
36 G7 Schwäbische Alb *mts* W Germany
36 H6 Schwäbisch Gmünd W Germany
36 H5 Schwäbisch Hall W Germany
41 K3 Schwägalp Switzerland
37 M7 Schwaig W Germany
36 G5 Schwaigern W Germany
32 K9 Schwalenberg W Germany
36 G2 Schwalm *R* W Germany
38 M8 Schwanberg Austria
37 L5 Schwand W Germany
41 K3 Schwanden Switzerland
37 N5 Schwandorf W Germany
33 O9 Schwanebeck E Germany
70 C5 Schwaner Peg *mts* Kalimantan
32 J6 Schwanewede W Germany
32 L7 Schwarmstedt W Germany
146 A5 Schwartz Rge Antarctica
33 R6 Schwarz E Germany
37 L2 Schwarza E Germany
38 H7 Schwarzach Austria
37 N5 Schwarzach *R* W Germany
37 L2 Schwarzburg E Germany
33 S9 Schwarze Elster *R* E Germany
37 M3 Schwarzenbach W Germany
33 M6 Schwarzenbek W Germany
37 K4 Schwarzenberg W Germany
36 G2 Schwarzenborn Hessen W Germany
36 B3 Schwarzenborn Rheinland-Pfalz W Germany
40 F4 Schwarzenburg Switzerland
37 N5 Schwarzenfeld W Germany
36 H3 Schwarzenfels W Germany
36 B3 Schwarzer Mann *mt* W Germany
37 O5 Schwarzer Regen *R* W Germany
37 N5 Schwarzhofen W Germany
40 G5 Schwarzhorn *mt* Switzerland
36 E7 Schwarzwald *mts* W Germany
36 B4 Schwarzwälder Hochwald *mts* W Germany
116 J3 Schwatka Mts Alaska
41 P3 Schwaz Austria
31 H2 Schwedt E Germany
40 F4 Schwefelberg Switzerland
36 B4 Schweich W Germany
36 D7 Schweighausen W Germany
37 J2 Schweina E Germany
33 M7 Schweinau W Germany
37 J3 Schweinfurt W Germany
33 S9 Schweinitz E Germany
32 F10 Schwelm W Germany
Schwenningen *see* Villingen-Schwenningen
33 O5 Schwerin E Germany
33 O6 Schwerin *reg* E Germany
33 O5 Schweriner See *L* E Germany
32 G10 Schwerte W Germany
36 F5 Schwetzingen W Germany
33 T5 Schwichtenberg E Germany
31 H3 Schwielochsee *L* E Germany
33 R8 Schwielowsee *L* E Germany
32 K5 Schwinge *R* W Germany
33 R5 Schwinkendorf E Germany
33 P9 Schwittersaf E Germany
41 J3 Schwyz Switzerland
43 E11 Sciacca Sicily
43 F12 Scicli Sicily
20 H2 Scie *R* France
9 F7 Scilly, Isles of England
31 J4 Ścinawa Poland
94 K4 Scio New York
94 F6 Scio Ohio
94 D8 Scioto *R* Ohio
94 E8 Sciotoville Ohio
103 M2 Scipio Utah
119 R7 Sclater Manitoba
8 B4 Scleddau Wales
48 H5 Scoarţa Romania
98 A1 Scobey Montana
103 N2 Scofield Res Utah
118 E7 Scollard Alberta
139 K4 Scone New S Wales
15 E4 Scone Scotland
111 H9 Scooba Mississippi
115 R3 Scoresby Land Greenland
115 R3 Scoresbysund Greenland
100 G9 Scossa Nevada
102 A1 Scotia California
98 H8 Scotia Nebraska
121 L7 Scotia Ontario
100 H1 Scotia Washington
117 G6 Scotia Bay Br Col
81 A14 Scotia Ridge Antarctica
81 A15 Scotia Sea Antarctica
98 J6 Scotland S Dakota
109 J2 Scotland Texas
15 Scotland U.K.
112 K1 Scotland Neck N Carolina
111 E11 Scotlandville Louisiana
122 H8 Scots B Nova Scotia
122 K8 Scotsburn Nova Scotia
118 J9 Scotsguard Sask
121 T7 Scotstown Quebec
112 E5 Scott Georgia
111 E8 Scott Mississippi
94 C6 Scott Ohio
118 J6 Scott Sask
100 C8 Scott *R* California
138 E4 Scott *R* S Australia
100 C8 Scott Bar California
89 G8 Scottburgh S Africa
117 J10 Scott, C Vancouver I, Br Col
140 A2 Scott, Cape N Terr Aust
107 K3 Scott City Kansas
146 H6 Scott Coast Antarctica
94 H6 Scottdale Pennsylvania
146 E3 Scott Gl Antarctica
142 E4 Scott Headland *mt* W Australia
115 M3 Scott Inlet N W Terr
117 J10 Scott, Is Br Col
100 C7 Scott, Mt Oregon
146 A5 Scott Mts Antarctica
142 D2 Scott Reef Indian Oc
94 B4 Scotts Michigan
98 C8 Scottsbluff Nebraska
98 C8 Scotts Bluff Nat. Mon Nebraska
94 B8 Scottsburg Indiana
100 B6 Scottsburg Oregon
94 J10 Scottsburg Virginia
103 N8 Scottsdale Arizona
139 J8 Scottsdale Tasmania
111 L11 Scotts Ferry Florida
127 O7 Scotts Head Dominica
123 L7 Scottsville C Breton I, N Scotia
107 N2 Scottsville Kansas
110 K5 Scottsville Kentucky
94 J9 Scottsville Virginia
94 A3 Scottville Michigan
141 J5 Scottville Queensland
102 G4 Scottys Castle California
102 G4 Scottys Junct Nevada
15 C2 Scourie Scotland
118 L9 Scout Lake Sask
15 E2 Scrabster Scotland
110 C6 Scranton Arkansas
107 P3 Scranton Kansas
98 C3 Scranton N Dakota
95 M5 Scranton Pennsylvania
95 L3 Scriba New York
98 K8 Scribner Nebraska
15 B4 Scridain, Loch Scotland
44 E2 Scrivia R Italy
120 H10 Scudder Ontario
121 M8 Scugog, L Ontario
13 H6 Scunthorpe England
45 O5 Scurcola Marsicana Italy
Scutari Albania *see* Shkodër
Scutari Turkey *see* Üsküdar
112 K1 Seaboard N Carolina
109 M6 Seabrook Texas
143 C9 Seabrook, L W Australia
143 C7 Seabrook, Mt W Australia
144 C6 Seacliff New Zealand
89 D8 Seacow *R* S Africa
109 L7 Seadrift Texas
139 G7 Sea Elephant B Tasmania
95 M8 Seaford Delaware
9 G6 Seaford England
127 M3 Seaforth Jamaica
120 J9 Seaforth Ontario
142 C3 Seaforth W Australia
119 O4 Seager Wheeler L Sask
108 E3 Seagraves Texas
112 H2 Seagrove N Carolina
13 G4 Seaham England
122 G1 Seahorse Labrador
115 L5 Seahorse Pt N W Terr
70 C2 Seahorse Shoal S China Sea
13 G2 Seahouses England
112 F6 Sea Island Georgia
95 N7 Sea Isle City New Jersey
115 K6 Seal *R* Manitoba
139 G6 Sea Lake Victoria
123 R1 Seal Bight Labrador
116 H9 Seal C Alaska
89 C10 Seal C S Africa
127 J4 Seal Cays *islds* Turks & Caicos Is
122 F9 Seal Cove New Brunswick
123 Q4 Seal Cove Nfld
111 L9 Seale Alabama
144 C5 Seal I New Zealand
133 F8 Sea Lion Is Falkland Is
139 H7 Seal Is Victoria
115 M6 Seal Lakes Quebec
144 A7 Seal Pt New Zealand
100 A5 Seal Rock Oregon
109 L6 Sealy Texas
144 C5 Sealy, Mt New Zealand
144 C5 Sealy Pass New Zealand
103 J4 Seaman Ra Nevada
13 H5 Seamer England
103 K6 Searchlight Nevada
120 F6 Searchmont Ontario
110 E6 Searcy Arkansas
102 G6 Searles California
102 G6 Searles Lake California
95 T2 Searsport Maine
123 N6 Searston Nfld
12 E5 Seascale England
102 C5 Seaside California
100 B4 Seaside Oregon
95 N7 Seaside Heights New Jersey
8 C6 Seaton England
100 C2 Seattle Washington
117 D5 Seattle, Mt Alaska/Yukon Terr
141 H4 Seaview Ra Queensland
95 N7 Seaville, S New Jersey
144 D5 Seaward Kaikoura Range New Zealand
127 P6 Seawell *airport* Barbados
71 K10 Seba Indonesia
118 C5 Seba Beach Alberta
95 R3 Sebago L Maine
70 B5 Sebajan *mt* Kalimantan
70 E5 Sebakung Kalimantan
89 G2 Sebakwe *R* Zimbabwe
69 E12 Sebanga Sumatra
68 G4 Se Bang Fai *R* Laos
69 G12 Sebangka *isld* Indonesia
113 G10 Sebastian Florida
109 K9 Sebastian Texas
124 B3 Sebastián Vizcaíno, B Mexico
95 S2 Sebasticook L Maine
102 B3 Sebastopol California
111 G9 Sebastopol Mississippi
70 E2 Sebatik *isld* Borneo
70 C3 Sebauh Sarawak
28 D3 Sebbersund Denmark
99 L3 Sebeka Minnesota
78 C1 Seben Turkey
124 D4 Seberi, Cerro *mt* Mexico
70 K8 Sebesi *isld* Sumatra
48 H5 Sebesul *R* Romania
48 H5 Sebesului Muntii *mts* Romania
94 D3 Sebewaing Michigan
52 C6 Sebezh U.S.S.R.
78 G1 Şebinkarahisar Turkey
48 G4 Şebis Romania
85 B4 Sebjet Agsumal Morocco
85 B4 Sebkha de Chinchane Mauritania
85 B4 Sebkha Oum el Drouss Guebli Morocco
85 B4 Sebkha Oum el Drouss Telli Mauritania
43 C13 Sebkhat Kelbia *L* Tunisia
84 F3 Sebkhat Taworgha Libya
85 B4 Sebkhet Idjil Mauritania

85 E3 Sebkra Azzel Matti salt flats Algeria
85 C3 Sebkra de Tindouf salt flats Algeria
17 G9 Sebkra d'Oran Algeria
85 E3 Sebkra Mekerrhane salt flats Algeria
69 E14 Seblat Sumatra
31 H5 Sebnitz E Germany
95 T1 Seboeis L Maine
95 R8 Seboomook L Maine
85 C2 Sebou R Morocco
110 J4 Sebree Kentucky
95 K10 Sebrell Virginia
113 F10 Sebring Florida
94 F6 Sebring Ohio
70 E2 Sebuku Kalimantan
70 E6 Sebuku isld Kalimantan
70 B4 Sebuyau Sarawak
37 Q4 Seč Czechoslovakia
42 C4 Secchia R Italy
112 E3 Secession L S Carolina
68 G4 Se Cham R Laos
122 C1 Séchelles, L Quebec
128 B5 Sechura, B. de Peru
128 B5 Sechura, Des. de des Peru
38 L7 Seckau Austria
38 L7 Seckauer Alpen mts Austria
22 E2 Seclin France
133 D7 Seco R Argentina
17 H4 Seco R Spain
21 E8 Secondigny France
118 L8 Secretan Sask
144 A6 Secretary I New Zealand
76 D2 Secunderabad India
128 E7 Sécure R Bolivia
48 E3 Séd R Hungary
52 B6 Seda U.S.S.R.
16 B5 Seda R Portugal
71 L10 Sedah Indonesia
118 G7 Sedalia Alberta
106 F2 Sedalia Colorado
94 D7 Sedalia Ohio
19 J3 Sedan France
107 O4 Sedan Kansas
106 G5 Sedan New Mexico
138 E5 Sedan S Australia
56 F3 Sedannavskaya, Shiver falls U.S.S.R.
16 E2 Sedano Spain
13 F5 Sedbergh England
145 E4 Seddon New Zealand
115 O2 Seddon, Kap C Greenland
144 C4 Seddonville New Zealand
47 H4 Seddülbahir Turkey
79 E8 Sede Boqer Israel
80 B7 Sede Dawid Israel
80 F1 Sede Eli'ezer Israel
80 F4 Sede Eliyyahu Israel
55 G3 Sedel'nikovo U.S.S.R.
80 C7 Sede Moshe Israel
80 F1 Sede Neemya Israel
19 P16 Séderon France
80 B7 Sederot Israel
80 G2 Sede Yaaqov Syria
80 B8 Sede Zevi Israel
9 E3 Sedgeberrow England
13 G4 Sedgefield England
8 D2 Sedgley England
106 H1 Sedgwick Colorado
107 N4 Sedgwick Kansas
95 T2 Sedgwick Maine
70 E6 Sedjaka Kalimantan
31 H6 Sedlčany Czechoslovakia
9 G6 Sedlescombe England
119 O8 Sedley Sask
79 F7 Sedom Israel
103 N7 Sedona Arizona
68 G5 Se Done R Laos
80 C7 Sedot Mikha Israel
80 C4 Sedot Yam Israel
100 C1 Sedro Woolley Washington
52 B6 Šeduva U.S.S.R.
20 C4 See R France
33 O4 Seebad Heringsdorf W Germany
118 C7 Seebe Alberta
37 K2 Seebergen E Germany
33 P10 Seeburg E Germany
41 O3 Seefeld Austria
33 T7 Seefeld E Germany
40 G2 Seefelden W Germany
33 O8 Seehausen E Germany
87 C11 Seeheim Namibia
36 F4 Seeheim W Germany
36 D7 Seelbach W Germany
101 M2 Seeley Lake Montana
121 O8 Seeleys Bay Ontario
146 G10 Seelig, Mt Antarctica
33 R10 Seelingstädt E Germany
36 C2 Seelscheid W Germany
70 P10 Seemanandjung Java
33 S10 Seerhausen E Germany
41 J2 Seerücken mt Switzerland
20 F4 Sées France
32 M9 Seesen W Germany
41 O2 Seeshaupt W Germany
38 L7 Seetaler Alpen mts Austria
41 K3 Seez R Switzerland
47 H6 Seferihisar Turkey
17 G9 Sefioun R Algeria
85 D2 Sefrou Morocco
144 D5 Sefton New Zealand
144 C5 Sefton, Mt New Zealand
70 F2 Segama R Sabah
69 F11 Segamat Malaysia
70 M9 Segara Anakan Java
47 F1 Segarcea Romania
70 F7 Segeri Sulawesi
43 E11 Segesta Sicily
71 C3 Seget W Irian
52 D3 Segezha U.S.S.R.
57 D3 Segiz, Ozero L U.S.S.R.
41 K4 Segnes Pass Switzerland
45 O6 Segni Italy
103 P2 Sego Utah
17 G5 Segorbe Spain
85 C6 Segou Mali
16 E4 Segovia Spain
108 H5 Segovia Texas
16 E3 Segovia prov Spain
52 D3 Segozero, Oz L U.S.S.R.
21 D6 Segré France
17 H2 Segre R Spain
84 E5 Séguedine Niger
85 C7 Séguéla Ivory Coast
107 K2 Seguin Kansas
124 J5 Seguín Mexico
109 K6 Seguin Texas
106 F4 Segundo Colorado
133 E4 Segundo R Argentina
70 E4 Seguntur Kalimantan
17 F6 Segura R Spain
17 F6 Segura, Sa de mts Spain
32 L8 Sehnde W Germany
71 J5 Seho isld Indonesia
74 B5 Sehwan Pakistan
100 B8 Seiad Valley California
37 L3 Seibelsdorf W Germany
106 H2 Seibert Colorado
127 K5 Seibo Dom Rep
21 C6 Seiche R France
21 E6 Seiches France
80 D4 Seidā Jordan
80 F3 Seidur Jordan
140 E4 Seigals Creek N Terr Aust
122 C1 Seignelay, R Quebec
68 B2 Seikpyu Burma
68 B2 Seiktein Burma
12 C1 Seil isld Scotland
26 N1 Seiland isld Norway
18 G7 Seilhac France
107 M5 Seiling Oklahoma
19 K4 Seille R France
29 K9 Seinäjoki Finland
20 H3 Seine R France
20 D2 Seine, B. de la France
18 H4 Seine-et-Marne dep France
20 G2 Seine-Maritime dep France
18 B4 Sein, I. de France
69 J12 Seipenyu Indonesia
38 L5 Seitenstetten Austria
18 F10 Seix France
28 G5 Sejerø isld Denmark
28 B3 Sejerslev Denmark
28 E3 Sejflod Denmark
31 O1 Sejny Poland
28 D4 Sejs Denmark
28 B6 Sejstrup Denmark
70 B5 Sekadau Kalimantan
69 G13 Sekanak, Teluk B Sumatra
69 F14 Sekayu Sumatra
88 E4 Sekenke Tanzania
61 K10 Seki Japan
70 B5 Sekima Kalimantan
70 K8 Sekintjau mt Sumatra
85 D7 Sekondi Ghana
68 H6 Se Kong R Laos/Cambodia
77 G4 Sekuheh Iran
69 E14 Selagan R Sumatra
100 E3 Selah Washington
70 B4 Selalang Sarawak
69 E10 Selama Malaysia
69 E11 Selangor Malaysia
68 H4 Se La Nong R Laos
29 M10 Selänpää Finland
69 F14 Selara Ladangpait Sumatra
70 D7 Selatan, Tg C Kalimantan
69 F12 Selatpanjang Sumatra
69 F12 Selat Panjang R Sumatra
69 D13 Selat Siberut str Sumatra
69 D14 Selat Sipora str Indonesia
116 H3 Selawik Alaska
116 G3 Selawik L Alaska
37 N3 Selb W Germany
37 M3 Selbitz W Germany
27 A12 Selbjörnfj inlet Norway
26 E8 Selbusjö L Norway
13 G6 Selby England
98 F4 Selby S Dakota
116 K3 Selby, L Alaska
95 M8 Selbyville Delaware
28 C3 Selde Denmark
107 K2 Selden Kansas
123 S4 Seldom Nfld
116 M7 Seldovia Alaska
71 C3 Sele W Irian
43 G8 Sele R Italy
87 E10 Selebi-Pikwe Botswana
59 K1 Selemdzha R U.S.S.R.
79 H3 Selemiya Syria
47 K6 Selendi Turkey
56 G5 Selenga R U.S.S.R.
86 C6 Selenge Zaïre
58 E2 Selenge Mörön R Mongolia
46 D4 Selenicë Albania
51 O2 Selennyakh R U.S.S.R.
33 M4 Selent W Germany
33 M4 Selenter See L W Germany
71 C3 Sele, Selat str W Irian
40 F1 Sélestat France
55 F4 Selety R U.S.S.R.
50 G3 Seletyteniz, Ozero L U.S.S.R.
115 R5 Selfoss Iceland
98 F3 Selfridge N Dakota
52 G3 Selib U.S.S.R.
85 B5 Selibaby Mauritania
36 F3 Seligenstadt W Germany
52 D6 Seliger, Oz L U.S.S.R.
103 M6 Seligman Arizona
110 C5 Seligman Missouri
84 H5 Selima Oasis Sudan
70 C4 Selimbau Kalimantan
47 J7 Selimiye Turkey
46 E7 Selinoús Greece
95 L6 Selinsgrove Pennsylvania
55 F1 Seliyarovo U.S.S.R.
52 D6 Selizharovo U.S.S.R.
33 O9 Selke R E Germany
107 J3 Selkirk Kansas
115 K7 Selkirk Manitoba
94 C2 Selkirk Michigan
13 F2 Selkirk Scotland
Selkirk co see Borders reg
114 H7 Selkirk Mts Br Col/Idaho
119 S5 Selkirk T Manitoba
20 K2 Selle R France
100 D2 Selleck Washington
94 B8 Sellersburg Indiana
21 I7 Selles-St Denis France
21 I7 Selles-sur-Cher France
141 H5 Sellheim R Queensland
40 C4 Sellières France
9 G5 Sellindge England
41 O3 Sellrain Austria
103 N10 Sells Arizona
32 F9 Selm W Germany
111 J9 Selma Alabama
111 D10 Selma Louisiana
112 J2 Selma N Carolina
100 B7 Selma Oregon
110 H6 Selmer Tennessee
33 N5 Selmsdorf E Germany
21 H6 Selommes France
70 Q10 Selong Indonesia
40 B2 Selongey France
88 F6 Selous Game Res Tanzania
117 G4 Selous, Mt Yukon Terr
71 C3 Selpele Indonesia
83 K12 Sel Pt Mahé I Indian Ocean
9 F6 Selsey England
32 K6 Selsingen W Germany
36 D2 Selters W Germany
54 F3 Sel'tso U.S.S.R.
52 H6 Selty U.S.S.R.
33 S5 Seltz E Germany
36 E6 Seltz France
69 H10 Seluan isld Indonesia
87 E9 Selukwe Zimbabwe
20 C4 Selune R France
133 E3 Selva Argentina
38 E8 Selva Italy
128 D5 Selvas forests Brazil
140 F5 Selwyn Queensland
117 H4 Selwyn Mts Yukon Terr
140 F5 Selwyn Ra Queensland
98 G2 Selz N Dakota
36 E4 Selz R W Germany
40 F3 Selzach Switzerland
38 K6 Selzthal Austria
70 E5 Semajang, D L Kalimantan
20 F5 Semallé France
46 D4 Seman R Albania
70 K8 Semang Ka, Teluk B Sumatra
79 G2 Semân, Jebel mts Syria
119 N7 Semans Sask
70 N10 Semanu Java
85 B3 Semara Morocco
70 N9 Semarang Java
71 L10 Semau isld Timor Indonesia
88 C2 Sembabule Uganda
70 E3 Sembakung R Kalimantan
86 B5 Sembé Congo
21 G7 Semblancay France
52 F6 Semenov U.S.S.R.
54 D4 Semenovka Chernigov U.S.S.R.
54 E7 Semenovka Poltava U.S.S.R.
52 G6 Semenovo U.S.S.R.
52 F5 Semenovskoye Kostroma U.S.S.R.
52 F5 Sementsovo U.S.S.R.
70 O10 Semeru Java
116 J8 Semidi Is Alaska
52 F5 Semigorodnyaya U.S.S.R.
31 J5 Semily Czechoslovakia
111 G10 Seminary Mississippi
101 T7 Seminoe Dam Wyoming
101 T7 Seminoe Res Wyoming
107 O6 Seminole Oklahoma
108 E3 Seminole Texas
111 M11 Seminole, L Georgia
56 C5 Seminsky Khrebet mts U.S.S.R.
55 D4 Semiozernoye U.S.S.R.
56 B5 Semipalatinsk U.S.S.R.
55 E4 Semipolka U.S.S.R.
71 E5 Semirara isld Philippines
77 B4 Semirom Iran
70 C4 Semitau Kalimantan
69 H10 Semium isld Indonesia
55 G5 Semiyarka U.S.S.R.
55 F5 Semiz-Bugu U.S.S.R.
33 R4 Semlow E Germany
33 T7 Semmelberg mt E Germany
38 N6 Semmering Austria
84 J5 Semna Sudan
86 F1 Semna Sudan
77 C2 Semnān Iran
71 A3 Semo Indonesia
22 J4 Semois R Belgium
89 F3 Semokwe R Zimbabwe
70 E1 Sempang Mangayau, Tg C Sabah
70 F2 Semporna Sabah
45 O6 Semprevisa mt Italy
70 O10 Sempu isld Java
26 H5 Semskefjell mt Norway
129 H4 Sem Tripa Brazil
88 E3 Semu R Tanzania
70 C6 Semuda Kalimantan
18 H5 Semur-en-Auxois France
89 F2 Semwe R Zimbabwe
52 F2 Semzha U.S.S.R.
128 E6 Sena Bolivia
88 E10 Sena Mozambique
129 L5 Senador Pompeu Brazil
70 E1 Senaja Sabah
128 E5 Sena Madureira Brazil
87 D9 Senango Zambia
20 J2 Sénarpont France
19 O17 Sénas France
118 H9 Senate Sask
110 F5 Senath Missouri
111 G7 Senatobia Mississippi
61 O7 Sendai Honshu Japan
60 D14 Sendai Kyūshū Japan
87 C11 Sendeling's Drift Namibia
37 J7 Senden W Germany
32 G9 Sendenhorst W Germany
16 C3 Sendim Portugal
70 B5 Senduruhan Kalimantan
74 F8 Sendwha India
69 E11 Senebui, Tg C Sumatra
99 S8 Seneca Illinois
107 O2 Seneca Kansas
110 B5 Seneca Missouri
98 F7 Seneca Nebraska
100 G5 Seneca Oregon
112 E3 Seneca S Carolina
98 G4 Seneca S Dakota
95 L4 Seneca L New York
94 F7 Seneca Lake Ohio
94 F7 Senecaville Ohio
22 G2 Seneffe Belgium
85 B5 Sénégal R W Africa
85 B6 Senegal rep W Africa
87 E11 Senekal S Africa
99 V3 Seney Michigan
30 H4 Senftenberg E Germany
87 F7 Senga Hill Zambia
52 H1 Sengeyskiy, Ostrov isld U.S.S.R.
70 G7 Sengkang Sulawesi
38 K6 Sengsengebirge mts Austria
133 C7 Senguerr R Argentina
88 B10 Sengwa R Zimbabwe
32 H5 Sengwärden W Germany
87 E9 Sengwe R Zimbabwe
129 K6 Senhor do Bonfim Brazil
45 O4 Senigallia Italy
45 L3 Senio R Italy
80 F1 Senir Israel
43 G8 Senise Italy
42 F4 Senj Yugoslavia
26 J2 Senja isld Norway
67 H4 Senkaku-shotö isld Japan
52 H2 Sen'kina U.S.S.R.
118 H6 Senlac Sask
65 H3 Senlin Shan mt China
68 H6 Senmonorom Cambodia
86 F3 Sennar Sudan
32 J9 Senne reg W Germany
40 A4 Sennecey le Grand France
32 J9 Sennelager W Germany
28 B3 Sennels Denmark
115 M8 Senneterre Quebec
20 F2 Senneville France
54 A2 Senno U.S.S.R.
8 C4 Sennybridge Wales
133 C8 Seno Almirantazgo gulf Chile
68 G4 Se Noi R Laos
111 M8 Senoia Georgia
20 H4 Senonches France
19 K4 Senones France
133 C8 Seno Otway gulf Chile
133 C8 Seno Skyring gulf Chile
18 H4 Sens France
20 B5 Sens-de-Bretagne France
40 F4 Sense R Switzerland
48 F5 Senta Yugoslavia
70 B4 Sentarum L Kalimantan
18 F10 Sentem France
86 E7 Sentery Zaïre
103 L9 Sentinel Arizona
109 H1 Sentinel Oklahoma
98 C3 Sentinel Butte N Dakota
117 N8 Sentinel Pk Br Columbia
146 G11 Sentinel Rge Antarctica
124 G7 Sentispac Mexico
129 K5 Sento Sé Brazil
22 H5 Senuc France
78 H3 Şenyurt Turkey
33 R7 Senzke E Germany
74 H7 Seoni India
Seoul see Sŏul
70 C5 Sepandan Kalimantan
70 P9 Sepandjang Indonesia
70 C5 Sepang Kalimantan
106 B9 Separ New Mexico
142 E6 Separation Well W Australia
70 E4 Sepasu Kalimantan
130 G8 Sepetiba, B. de Brazil
70 D3 Seping R Sarawak
45 R7 Sepino Italy
21 G7 Sepmes France
31 K2 Sępolno Poland
68 H4 Sepone Laos
31 N1 Sępopol Poland
130 B4 Sepotuba R Brazil
32 F9 Seppenrade W Germany
19 O18 Septêmes les Valdonne France
47 G2 Septemvri Bulgaria
20 J4 Septeuil France
20 D5 Sept Forges France
122 F3 Sept Îles Quebec
18 C4 Sept Iles, les France
141 J5 Septimus Queensland
122 B2 Sept-Milles, L Quebec
70 O9 Sepulu Java
16 E3 Sepúlveda Spain
70 K8 Seputih R Sumatra
112 B2 Sequatchie R Tennessee
16 D3 Sequillo R Spain
100 B1 Sequim Washington
102 F5 Sequoia Nat. Park California
79 F3 Serai Syria
22 G4 Seraincourt France
22 K2 Seraing Belgium
71 J9 Seraja isld Indonesia
70 P10 Seraja, G mt Indonesia
70 M9 Seraju R Java
57 B6 Serakhs U.S.S.R.
76 C2 Seram India
136 F2 Seram isld Moluccas Indonesia
70 L9 Serang Java
69 J11 Serasan isld Indonesia
69 J11 Seraya Indonesia
46 D1 Serbia hist reg Yugoslavia
45 H4 Serchio R Italy
70 K8 Serdang, Tg C Sumatra
53 F7 Serdobsk U.S.S.R.
55 F3 Serebryanoye U.S.S.R.
56 B6 Serebryansk U.S.S.R.
88 F5 Serebu mt Tanzania
52 F5 Sereda U.S.S.R.
52 C5 Seredka U.S.S.R.
78 D2 Şereflikoçhisar Turkey
18 H5 Serein R France
69 E11 Seremban Malaysia
71 C3 Seremuk R W Irian
88 E3 Serengeti Nat. Park Tanzania
88 C8 Serenje Zambia
86 H5 Serenli Somalia
48 K1 Seret R U.S.S.R.
52 F6 Serezha R U.S.S.R.
47 G7 Serfopoúla isld Greece
52 G6 Sergach U.S.S.R.
98 K7 Sergeant Bluff Iowa
58 E2 Sergelen Mongolia
87 E7 Serge Tshimbo Zaïre
55 E4 Sergeyevka Kokchetav U.S.S.R.
55 G3 Sergeyevka Novosibirsk U.S.S.R.
50 F2 Sergino U.S.S.R.
129 L6 Sergipe state Brazil
52 E2 Sergozero, Oz L U.S.S.R.
70 D2 Seria Brunei
41 L6 Seriana, Val Italy
69 D11 Seribudolok Sumatra
130 H9 Seridó R Brazil
20 J3 Sérifontaine France
47 G7 Sérifos isld Greece
19 N16 Sérignan France
68 D5 Serim Burma
142 D2 Seringapatam Reef Indian Oc
129 H5 Seringa, Serra da mts Brazil
45 R8 Serino Italy
41 L7 Serio R Italy
85 F4 Serkout, Dj mt Algeria
138 E4 Serle, Mt S Australia
20 K5 Sermaises France
71 O9 Sermata isld Indonesia
45 K1 Sermide Italy
45 N6 Sermoneta Italy
38 H9 Sernio mt Italy
33 U6 Sernitz R E Germany
33 Q8 Serno E Germany
60 T2 Sernovodsk U.S.S.R.
57 A5 Sernyy-Zavod U.S.S.R.
31 N3 Serock Poland
126 A2 Seroe Colorado Aruba W I
17 F7 Serón Spain
85 F4 Serouenout Algeria
55 D2 Serov U.S.S.R.
89 E4 Serowe Botswana
16 B7 Serpa Portugal
87 C8 Serpa Pinto Angola
43 C9 Serpeddi, Pta mt Sardinia
116 E4 Serpentine Hot Springs Alaska
138 A3 Serpentine Lakes S Australia
143 B9 Serpentine, R W Australia
122 A3 Serpent, R. au Quebec
128 F1 Serpents Mouth str Venezuela
17 G6 Serpis R Spain
54 J2 Serpukhov U.S.S.R.
20 J2 Serqueux France
20 G3 Serquigny France
130 H7 Serra Brazil
45 L4 Serra, Alpe di mts Italy
130 E10 Serra Alta Brazil
130 F4 Serra Bonita Brazil
130 F4 Serra das Araras Brazil
129 H3 Serra do Navio Brazil
33 Q5 Serrahn E Germany
47 F3 Sérrai Greece
45 J3 Serramazzoni Italy
125 O2 Serrana Bank Caribbean
125 P2 Serranilla Bank Caribbean
43 G10 Serra San Bruno Italy
43 C11 Serrat, Cape C Tunisia
45 J4 Serravalle Pistojese Italy
22 F4 Serre R France
18 G10 Serrére, Pic de mt France
19 P16 Serres France
133 D4 Serrezuela Argentina
129 L6 Serrinha Brazil
45 M4 Serriola, Bocca pass Italy
43 B12 Sers Tunisia
16 B5 Sertã Portugal
130 F7 Sertãozinho Brazil
70 K9 Sertung isld Sumatra
70 C6 Serujan R Kalimantan
89 E3 Serule Botswana
69 D10 Seruwai Sumatra
40 E2 Servance France
46 E4 Sérvia Greece
100 E5 Service Creek Oregon
138 F6 Serviceton Victoria
106 E5 Servilleta New Mexico
71 N9 Serwaro Indonesia
66 F5 Sêrxü China
22 G4 Séry France
22 E4 Séry-les-Mezières France
68 G4 Se Sang Soi R Laos
70 E3 Sesatap Kalimantan
88 D2 Sese Is Uganda
120 K4 Sesekinika Ontario
71 A3 Sesepe Indonesia
87 B9 Sesfontein Namibia
87 D9 Sesheka Zambia
41 H7 Sesia R Italy
70 E2 Sesibu Kalimantan
26 N6 Seskarön isld Sweden
61 P12 Sesoko-jima isld Okinawa
43 F7 Sessa Aurunca Italy
36 D6 Sessenheim France
110 G3 Sesser Illinois
37 K3 Sesslach W Germany
71 K9 Sessok Flores Indonesia
45 M4 Sestino Italy
45 K4 Sesto Fiorentino Italy
31 O1 Seštokai U.S.S.R.
45 J3 Sestola Italy
52 E6 Sestra R U.S.S.R.
44 E3 Sestri Italy
44 F3 Sestri Levante Italy
29 O11 Sestroretsk U.S.S.R.
60 D12 Setaka Japan
60 N3 Setana Japan
9 G2 Setchey England
18 H9 Sète France
130 G6 Sete Lagoas Brazil
130 D8 Sete Quedas, Ilha Grande ou isld Brazil
27 B12 Setesdal Norway
94 F8 Seth W Virginia
85 F1 Sétif Algeria
60 C13 Seto Japan
59 K5 Seto-naika sea Japan
60 G11 Seto Naikai str Japan
68 B4 Setsan Burma
85 C2 Settat Morocco
86 A6 Sette Cama Gabon
119 U1 Settee L Manitoba
119 T3 Setting L Manitoba
13 F5 Settle England
140 E3 Settlement Cr Queensland
90 C15 Settlement of Edinburgh Tristan da Cunha
113 H11 Settlement Pt Bahamas
16 B6 Setúbal Portugal
37 M5 Seubersdorf W Germany
37 K5 Seukendorf W Germany
55 E1 Seul' R U.S.S.R.
99 V4 Seul Choix Pt Michigan
69 B10 Seulimeum Sumatra
115 K7 Seul, Lac Ontario
20 D3 Seulles R France
69 C11 Seumanyam Sumatra
40 B3 Seurre France
78 K1 Sevan, Ozero U.S.S.R.
53 D11 Sevastopol' U.S.S.R.
54 H6 Sev Donets R U.S.S.R.
28 B4 Sevel Denmark
100 J4 Seven Devils Mts Idaho
140 D3 Seven Emu N Terr Aust
14 C5 Seven Hd Irish Rep
122 F3 Seven Is. Bay Quebec
106 C6 Seven Lakes New Mexico
9 G5 Sevenoaks England
118 G9 Seven Persons Alberta
109 J7 Seven Sisters Texas
112 K2 Seven Springs N Carolina
102 F1 Seven Troughs Nevada
117 N10 Seventy Mile House Br Columbia
25 F6 Sevenum Netherlands
18 H8 Séverac-le-Château France
107 P2 Severance Kansas
139 K3 Severn R New S Wales
121 L8 Severn R Ontario
52 J4 Severnaya Mylva R U.S.S.R.
51 K1 Severnaya Zemlya arch Arctic Oc
55 G3 Severnoye U.S.S.R.
8 D4 Severn, R England
55 D3 Severnyy U.S.S.R.
52 J3 Severnyy Ural mts U.S.S.R.
51 L3 Severo-Baykal'skoye Nagor'ye uplands U.S.S.R.
37 P3 Severocesky Kraj reg Czechoslovakia
52 E3 Severodvinsk U.S.S.R.
31 K6 Severomoravský reg Czechoslovakia
52 D1 Severomorsk U.S.S.R.
55 C1 Severouralsk U.S.S.R.
54 K2 Severo Zadonsk U.S.S.R.
107 O4 Severy Kansas
29 O2 Sevettijarvi Finland
103 M3 Sevier Utah
103 M2 Sevier R Utah
103 M2 Sevier Bridge Res Utah
103 M2 Sevier Des Utah
112 D2 Sevierville Tennessee
22 G4 Sevigny France
16 D7 Sevilla Spain
16 D7 Sevilla prov Spain
126 F4 Sevilla R Cuba
Seville see Sevilla
47 G2 Sevlievo Bulgaria
48 J2 Sevola mt U.S.S.R.
53 F11 Sev. Osetinsk. A.S.S.R U.S.S.R.
18 E6 Sèvre-Niortaise R France
20 K4 Sevres France
40 B5 Sevron R France
54 F4 Sevsk U.S.S.R.
85 B7 Sewa R Sierra Leone
110 L6 Sewanee Tennessee
116 N6 Seward Alaska
107 M3 Seward Kansas
98 J9 Seward Nebraska
107 N6 Seward Oklahoma
94 H6 Seward Pennsylvania
116 R6 Seward Glacier Yukon Terr/Alaska
146 F12 Seward Mts Antarctica
116 E4 Seward Pen Alaska
133 C4 Sewell Chile
40 E2 Sewen France
94 G6 Sewickley Pennsylvania
117 O8 Sexsmith Alberta
124 G4 Sextín Mexico
77 H3 Seyah Band Koh mts Afghanistan
43 B12 Seybouse R Algeria
83 J12 Seychelles islds, rep Indian Oc
33 R9 Seyda E Germany
52 K2 Seyda U.S.S.R.
115 S4 Seydhisfjördhur Iceland
28 O9 Seydhtorva C Faeroes
78 C3 Seydişehir Turkey
20 B3 Seye R France
78 E3 Seyhan R Turkey
47 L5 Seyit R Turkey
47 L5 Seyitgazi Turkey
54 D5 Seym R U.S.S.R.
95 O5 Seymour Connecticut
94 B8 Seymour Indiana
110 C1 Seymour Iowa
110 D4 Seymour Missouri
109 H2 Seymour Texas
139 H6 Seymour Victoria
99 S5 Seymour Wisconsin
140 C6 Seymour Ra N Terr Aust
19 Q16 Seyne-les-Alpes France
42 F3 Sežana Yugoslavia
18 H4 Sezanne France
52 D6 Sezha R U.S.S.R.
16 A6 Sezimbra Portugal
45 O6 Sezze Italy
85 G2 Sfax Tunisia
47 F9 Sfinári Crete Greece
48 K5 Sfîntu Gheorghe Romania
48 M6 Sfîntu Gheorghe R Romania
79 H2 Sfira Syria
's-Gravenhage see Den Haag
25 B5 's-Gravenzande Netherlands
15 D3 Sgurr Mor mt Scotland
58 Shaanxi prov China
80 F3 Sha'ar Israel
79 H4 Sha'ar, Jebel mts Syria
Sha'av see Sha'ab
87 E7 Shaba reg Zaïre
89 G3 Shabani Zimbabwe
119 O2 Shabaqua Ontario
99 S8 Shabbona Illinois
84 H5 Shab, El Egypt
78 K2 Shabestar Iran
79 F9 Shabibī, J. esh mt Jordan
47 J1 Shabla Bulgaria
86 E6 Shabunda Zaïre
55 D2 Shaburovo U.S.S.R.
67 B3 Shachang China
66 B4 Shache China
118 J8 Shackleton Sask
146 G7 Shackleton Coast Antarctica
146 G8 Shackleton Glacier Antarctica
146 D2 Shackleton Ice Shelf Antarctica
146 H7 Shackleton Inlet Antarctica
146 D10 Shackleton Rge Antarctica
74 B5 Shadadkot Pakistan
98 D4 Shadehill Res S Dakota
67 E3 Shadi China
55 D3 Shadrinsk U.S.S.R.
111 K10 Shady Grove Alabama
113 D7 Shady Grove Florida
55 C4 Shafranovo U.S.S.R.
102 E6 Shafter California
101 L9 Shafter Nevada
108 C6 Shafter Texas
8 D5 Shaftesbury England
55 G5 Shagan R U.S.S.R.
65 E4 Shagang China
48 M5 Shagany, Oz L U.S.S.R.
Shagedu see Jungar Qi
55 F4 Shaglyteniz, Oz L U.S.S.R.
56 D5 Shagonar U.S.S.R.
144 C6 Shag R New Zealand
133 H8 Shag Rocks S Georgia
76 C2 Shahabad India
78 L4 Shahabad Iran
76 B3 Shahapur India
80 B7 Shaḥar Israel
74 C6 Shahbadpur Pakistan
74 B6 Shahbandar Pakistan
75 J7 Shahdol India
65 C6 Shahe China
65 D6 Shahe China
67 E2 Shahezhen China
Shahezi see Wan Xian
77 K2 Shah Fuladi mt Afghanistan
84 G3 Shahhāt Libya
78 L3 Shahin Dezh Iran
74 H5 Shahjahanpur India
77 E1 Shāh Jehān, Kuh-e mts Iran
77 K3 Shahjui Afghanistan
65 E4 Shahousuo China
74 G7 Shahpur India
74 F6 Shahpura India
77 J2 Shahrak Afghanistan
77 G3 Shāhrakht Iran
77 D4 Shahr-e Bābak Iran
77 B3 Shahr Kord Iran
77 B2 Shahr Rey Iran
77 D2 Shahrud Bustam Iran
77 B1 Shahsavār Iran
77 F5 Shāh Savāran, Kūh-e mts Iran
50 F2 Shaim U.S.S.R.
80 G3 Shajara Jordan
65 F4 Shajianzi China
52 E6 Shakhovskaya U.S.S.R.
59 M2 Shakhtersk U.S.S.R.
54 M9 Shakhty U.S.S.R.
52 G5 Shakhun'ya U.S.S.R.
85 E7 Shaki Nigeria
84 J4 Shâkir isld Egypt
99 N5 Shakopee Minnesota
60 O2 Shakotan dake mt Japan
59 L3 Shakotan misaki C Japan
55 C4 Shaksha U.S.S.R.
116 G4 Shaktolik Alaska
52 F4 Shalakusha U.S.S.R.
86 G4 Shala, L Ethiopia
117 M10 Shalalth Br Columbia
65 G2 Shalan China
67 D6 Shalang China
55 G4 Shalday U.S.S.R.
52 F6 Shaldezh U.S.S.R.
9 F5 Shalford England
52 E4 Shalgachëva U.S.S.R.
57 F2 Shalgiya U.S.S.R.
77 E4 Shalidab Iran
55 D5 Shalkar Karashatau L U.S.S.R.
55 D5 Shalkar-Yega-Kara L U.S.S.R.
80 G3 Shallala Jordan
112 J4 Shallotte N Carolina
108 E2 Shallowater Texas
120 J8 Shallow Lake Ontario
80 C7 Shalwa Israel
55 C3 Shalya U.S.S.R.
56 C4 Shalym U.S.S.R.
88 D5 Shama R Tanzania
56 G5 Shaman, Khrebet mts U.S.S.R.
55 C3 Shamary U.S.S.R.
86 F4 Shambe Sudan
80 D2 Shamerat Israel
75 O5 Shamgong Bhutan
77 E6 Shamil Iran
80 F1 Shamir Israel
78 K6 Shamiya Des Iraq
95 L6 Shamokin Pennsylvania
113 D8 Shamrock Florida
107 O6 Shamrock Oklahoma
118 L8 Shamrock Sask
108 D8 Shamrock Texas
88 C10 Shamva Zimbabwe
68 C2 Shan prov Burma
80 G6 Sha'nab Jordan
Shanchengzhen see Nanjing
77 G5 Shāndak Iran
58 D4 Shandan China
65 C3 Shandian He R China
102 D6 Shandon California
12 D1 Shandon Scotland
65 C6 Shandong prov China
67 E6 Shandong Bandao pen China
52 F4 Shangaly U.S.S.R.
87 E9 Shangani R Zimbabwe
65 D4 Shangbancheng China
67 E1 Shangcheng China
65 F3 Shangchengzhen China
67 D6 Shangchuan Dao isld China
65 B4 Shangdu China
Shangdundu see Linchuan
67 E2 Shangfu China
67 E2 Shanggao China
67 G1 Shanghai China
63 Shanghai conurbation China
67 E4 Shanghang China
65 D6 Shanghe
65 C4 Shanghuangqi China
67 C1 Shangkan China
67 C5 Shanglin China
87 D9 Shangombo Zambia
Shangpaihe see Feixi
58 G5 Shangqiu China
67 F2 Shangrao China
67 B5 Shangsi China
58 E5 Shang Xian China
65 B5 Shangyangwu China
65 C4 Shangyi China
67 E4 Shangyou China
67 G1 Shangyu China
59 J2 Shangzhi China
65 D5 Shanhaiguan China
65 G2 Shanhetun China
100 E4 Shaniko Oregon
9 E6 Shanklin England
67 E2 Shankou China
94 J6 Shanksville Penn
112 B3 Shannon Georgia
99 R7 Shannon Illinois
111 H7 Shannon Mississippi
145 E4 Shannon New Zealand
14 C4 Shannon Airport Irish Rep
99 M9 Shannon City Iowa
14 D2 Shannon Pot Irish Rep
14 C2 Shannon R Irish Rep
Shansi prov see Shanxi
65 G3 Shansonggang China
80 G4 Shantana Jordan
51 N3 Shantarskiye, Ostrova islds U.S.S.R.
67 E5 Shantou China
Shantung prov see Shandong
Shantung Peninsula see Shandong Bandao
58 F4 Shanxi prov China
65 C7 Shan Xian China
67 F4 Shanyao China
58 F4 Shanyin China
67 F1 Shaobo China
67 D3 Shaodong China
67 D3 Shaoshan China
67 F3 Shaowu China
59 H5 Shaoxing China
67 D3 Shaoyang China
15 F1 Shapinsay Scotland
52 H2 Shapkina R U.S.S.R.
56 C5 Shapshal'skiy Khrebet mts U.S.S.R.
Shara Gol see Dang He
52 H7 Sharan U.S.S.R.
52 G6 Sharanga U.S.S.R.
121 O8 Sharbot Lake Ontario
48 L2 Shargorodo U.S.S.R.
60 S2 Shari Japan
77 D7 Sharjah U.A.E.
52 H6 Sharkan U.S.S.R.
71 D5 Shark Fin B Philippines
52 C6 Sharkovshchina U.S.S.R.
141 H2 Shark Reef Gt Barrier Reef Aust
55 B4 Sharlyk U.S.S.R.
95 O5 Sharon Connecticut
112 E4 Sharon Georgia
107 M4 Sharon Kansas
94 B2 Sharon Michigan
98 J2 Sharon N Dakota
108 E7 Sharon Oklahoma
110 H5 Sharon Tennessee
95 P3 Sharon Vermont
99 S7 Sharon Wisconsin
80 C5 Sharon, Plain of Israel
107 J3 Sharon Springs Kansas
54 G6 Sharovka U.S.S.R.
98 F5 Sharpe, L S Dakota
95 L9 Sharps Virginia
99 M9 Sharpsburg Iowa
94 K7 Sharpsburg Maryland
94 A6 Sharpsville Indiana
79 F5 Sharqi, Jebel esh mts Lebanon
52 G5 Shar'ya U.S.S.R.
86 G4 Shashamanna Ethiopia
89 F3 Shashani R Zimbabwe
89 E3 Shashe Botswana
89 G2 Shashe R Zimbabwe
87 E10 Shashe R Zimbabwe/Botswana
67 D1 Shashi China
100 C9 Shasta L California
100 C8 Shasta, Mt California
67 D4 Shatian China
52 F6 Shatki U.S.S.R.
55 D3 Shatrovo U.S.S.R.
108 E7 Shattuck Oklahoma
54 L1 Shatura U.S.S.R.
79 F8 Shaubak Jordan
80 G3 Shaumar Jordan
118 J9 Shaunavon Sask
52 D3 Shaverki U.S.S.R.
102 E4 Shaver L California
94 H8 Shavers Fork R W Virginia
80 D2 Shave Ẕiyyon Israel
111 F8 Shaw Mississippi
120 K7 Shawanaga Ontario
95 N5 Shawangunk Mts New York
99 S5 Shawano Wisconsin
99 S5 Shawano L Wisconsin
121 R7 Shawbridge Quebec
8 D2 Shawbury England
141 J5 Shaw I Queensland
115 M8 Shawinigan Quebec
101 Q3 Shawmut Montana
94 E7 Shawnee Ohio
107 O6 Shawnee Oklahoma
98 A7 Shawnee Wyoming
110 H4 Shawneetown Illinois
121 O7 Shawville Quebec
67 F3 Sha Xi R China
67 F3 Sha Xian China
67 D1 Shayang China
84 J4 Shayib el Banât, Gebel mt Egypt
72 F6 Shaykh' Uthmān S Yemen
52 J4 Shaytanovka U.S.S.R.
67 G1 Shazhou China
54 J3 Shchekino U.S.S.R.
54 K1 Shchelkovo U.S.S.R.
52 H2 Shchel'yayur U.S.S.R.
55 G4 Shcherbakty U.S.S.R.
54 J1 Shcherbinka U.S.S.R.
54 H5 Shchigry U.S.S.R.
54 C5 Shchors U.S.S.R.
54 F8 Shchorsk U.S.S.R.
50 G3 Shchuchinsk U.S.S.R.
55 D3 Shchuch'ye U.S.S.R.
55 C3 Shchuch'ye Ozero U.S.S.R.
54 K1 Shchurovo U.S.S.R.
128 G3 Shea Guyana
86 G4 Shea Ghimirri Ethiopia
100 H6 Sheaville Oregon
119 O2 Shebandowan L Ontario
54 H6 Shebekino U.S.S.R.
99 T6 Sheboygan Wisconsin
86 B4 Shebshi Mts Nigeria
80 E5 Shechem Jordan
78 H3 Shedadi Syria
100 B5 Shedd Oregon
120 J10 Shedden Ontario
122 H7 Shediac New Brunswick
14 D3 Sheelin, L Irish Rep
121 N7 Sheenboro Quebec
116 Q2 Sheenjek R Alaska
117 O9 Sheep Cr Alberta
101 U7 Sheep Cr Wyoming
14 D1 Sheep Haven Irish Rep
101 T10 Sheephorn Colorado
106 C2 Sheep Mt Colorado
103 J5 Sheep Pk Nevada
103 J5 Sheep Ra Nevada
14 B5 Sheep's Hd Irish Rep
118 F7 Sheerness Alberta
9 G5 Sheerness England
115 N9 Sheet Harbour Nova Scotia
80 D2 Shefar'am Israel
80 C7 Shefela Israel
13 G6 Sheffield England
99 R8 Sheffield Illinois
99 N7 Sheffield Iowa
95 O4 Sheffield Massachusetts
144 D5 Sheffield New Zealand
94 H5 Sheffield Pennsylvania
139 H8 Sheffield Tasmania
108 F5 Sheffield Texas
94 E5 Sheffield Lake Ohio
56 B3 Shegarka R U.S.S.R.
52 G3 Shegmas U.S.S.R.
120 J7 Sheguiandah Ontario
119 O7 Sheho Sask
67 B1 Shehong China
133 C7 Shehuén R Argentina
86 J4 Sheikh Somalia
79 F5 Sheikh, J. esh mt Lebanon/Syria
120 F3 Shekak R Ontario
Shekar Dzong see Tingri
74 F3 Shekhupura Pakistan
53 G12 Sheki U.S.S.R.
52 E5 Sheksna R U.S.S.R.
94 E9 Shelbiana Kentucky
110 D2 Shelbina Missouri
110 J2 Shelburn Indiana
115 N9 Shelburne Nova Scotia
120 K8 Shelburne Ontario
95 O2 Shelburne Vermont
141 G1 Shelburne B Queensland
95 P4 Shelburne Falls Massachusetts
99 T8 Shelby Indiana
99 L8 Shelby Iowa
99 U6 Shelby Michigan
111 F8 Shelby Mississippi
101 O1 Shelby Montana
112 F2 Shelby N Carolina
98 J8 Shelby Nebraska
94 E6 Shelby Ohio
110 H2 Shelbyville Illinois
110 L2 Shelbyville Indiana
110 L3 Shelbyville Kentucky
110 E2 Shelbyville Missouri
110 K6 Shelbyville Tennessee
109 N4 Shelbyville Texas
99 T9 Sheldon Illinois
99 L6 Sheldon Iowa
110 B4 Sheldon Missouri
98 J3 Sheldon N Dakota
117 H4 Sheldon, Mt Yukon Terr
95 P2 Sheldon Springs Vermont
122 H3 Sheldrake Quebec
56 F5 Shelekhov U.S.S.R.
90 F16 Shelf Ice Antarctica
116 K8 Shelikof Str Alaska
101 S5 Shell Wyoming
99 L3 Shell R Minnesota
111 G12 Shell Beach Louisiana
118 L5 Shellbrook Sask
101 R8 Shell Cr Wyoming
101 N6 Shelley Idaho
139 K5 Shellharbour New S Wales
99 P4 Shell L Wisconsin
118 K5 Shell Lake Sask
143 F8 Shell Lakes W Australia
111 M10 Shellman Georgia
119 Q8 Shellmouth Manitoba
102 A1 Shell Mt California
99 O7 Shell Rock Iowa
99 O7 Shellrock R Iowa
99 P7 Shellsburg Iowa
80 D1 Shelomi Israel
58 G1 Shelopugino U.S.S.R.
102 A1 Shelter Cove California
95 P5 Shelter I Long I, New York
144 B7 Shelter Pt New Zealand
95 O5 Shelton Connecticut
98 H9 Shelton Nebraska
117 M12 Shelton Washington
52 E4 Sheltozero U.S.S.R.
78 M1 Shemakha U.S.S.R.
56 B5 Shemonaikha U.S.S.R.
52 H6 Shemordan U.S.S.R.
52 G6 Shemursha U.S.S.R.
99 L9 Shenandoah Iowa
95 L6 Shenandoah Pennsylvania
94 J8 Shenandoah Virginia
94 K7 Shenandoah Junc W Virginia
94 H8 Shenandoah Mts W Virginia/Virginia
94 J8 Shenandoah Nat. Park Virginia
94 G5 Shenango Res Ohio/Penn
57 D1 Shenber U.S.S.R.
65 B5 Shenchi China
86 A4 Shendam Nigeria
86 F2 Shendi Sudan
65 J1 Shending Shan mt China
46 D3 Shëngjin Albania
65 F1 Shengping China
67 G1 Shengsi China
67 G1 Shengsi Liedao islds China
67 G2 Sheng Xian China
52 F4 Shenkursk U.S.S.R.
65 A5 Shenmu China

67 C1 Shennongjia China
Shensi prov see Shaanxi
58 E4 Shensi prov China
52 H7 Shentala U.S.S.R.
143 E8 Shenton, Mt W Australia
Shentza Dzong see Xainza
65 C5 Shen Xian China
65 C6 Shen Xian China
59 H3 Shenyang China
65 C5 Shenze China
Shenzhen see Bao'an
74 D5 Sheo India
74 G6 Sheopur India
118 D7 Shepard Alberta
146 J10 Shepard I Antarctica
94 C3 Shepherd Michigan
101 R4 Shepherd Montana
109 M5 Shepherd Texas
137 O5 Shepherd Is New Hebrides
94 K7 Shepherdstown W Virginia
94 B9 Shepherdsville Kentucky
117 G9 Sheppard, Mt Br Columbia
139 H6 Shepparton Victoria
9 G5 Sheppey isld England
66 B5 Shepton Mallet England
115 M3 Sherard, C N W Terr
55 F4 Sherbakul' U.S.S.R.
8 D6 Sherborne England
85 B7 Sherbro I Sierra Leone
115 M8 Sherbrooke Quebec
122 H9 Sherbrooke L Nova Scotia
13 G6 Sherburn England
13 H5 Sherburn England
99 M6 Sherburn Minnesota
95 M4 Sherburne New York
80 C1 Sherda Chad
9 F5 Shere England
84 J6 Shereik Sudan
54 J1 Sheremet'yevo airport U.S.S.R.
74 E5 Shergarh India
111 D7 Sheridan Arkansas
94 A6 Sheridan Indiana
94 B3 Sheridan Michigan
101 N4 Sheridan Montana
100 B4 Sheridan Oregon
101 T5 Sheridan Wyoming
115 N1 Sheridan, C N W Terr
106 H3 Sheridan L Colorado
101 P5 Sheridan, Mt Wyoming
138 D5 Sheringa S Australia
9 H2 Sheringham England
111 H7 Sherman Mississippi
94 H4 Sherman New York
109 L2 Sherman Texas
95 S8 Sherman Mills Maine
103 J1 Sherman Mt Nevada
101 O7 Sherman Pk Idaho
98 H8 Sherman Res Nebraska
77 L2 Sherpur Afghanistan
119 O3 Sherridon Manitoba
95 M3 Sherrill New York
25 D5 's-Hertogenbosch Netherlands
98 E1 Sherwood N Dakota
108 G4 Sherwood Texas
141 K2 Sherwood dist Brisbane, Qnsld
144 C5 Sherwood Downs New Zealand
9 E1 Sherwood Forest England
52 H6 Sheshma R U.S.S.R.
77 E1 Sheshtamad Iran
67 E1 She Shui R China
117 H6 Sheslay Br Columbia
52 H5 Shestaki U.S.S.R.
99 L5 Shetek, L Minnesota
15 G2 Shetland reg Scotland
50 E4 Shevchenko U.S.S.R.
99 L2 Shevlin Minnesota
58 G6 She Xian China
55 M5 She Xian China
67 F2 She Xian China
98 G2 Sheyenne N Dakota
98 J3 Sheyenne R N Dakota
77 C6 Sheykh Sho'eyb isld Iran
80 E2 Shezor Israel
15 B3 Shiant Scotland
94 C3 Shiawassee R Michigan
77 J1 Shiberghan Afghanistan
61 N8 Shibata Japan
65 B4 Shibati China
60 S2 Shibecha Japan
86 H4 Shibeli R Ethiopia
60 T2 Shibetsu Japan
84 J3 Shibin el Kom Egypt
79 B8 Shibin el Qanatir Egypt
67 C3 Shibing China
61 M9 Shibukawa Japan
60 E14 Shibushi Japan
60 S6 Shibushi-wan Japan
67 B3 Shicheng China
67 E3 Shicheng China
61 P5 Shichinohe Japan
98 J9 Shickley Nebraska
95 L5 Shickshinny Pennsylvania
122 F5 Shickshock Mts Quebec
65 E6 Shidao China
55 F5 Shiderty R U.S.S.R.
107 O5 Shidler Oklahoma
60 H11 Shido Japan
15 C3 Shieldaig Scotland
140 D2 Shield, C N Terr Aust
107 K3 Shields Kansas
98 E3 Shields N Dakota
67 A1 Shifang China
8 D2 Shifnal England
61 K10 Shiga prefect Japan
Shigatse see Xigazê
122 G8 Shigawake Quebec
67 F1 Shih-chiu Hu L China
58 G5 Shi He R China
68 D3 Shezi China
Shihkiachwang see Shijiazhuang
72 F6 Shihr S Yemen
61 M8 Shiiya Japan
46 D3 Shijak Albania
67 E3 Shijiaba China
65 A6 Shijiazi China
Shijiao see Fogang
65 B5 Shijiazhuang China
65 C5 Shijiazhuang China
65 C5 Shijingshan China
67 C5 Shiju Hu China
67 D3 Shijiusuo China
60 O3 Shikabe Japan
119 N1 Shikag L Ontario
61 N1 Shikama Japan
68 J2 Shikang China
77 L2 Shikar, Darya-i- R Afghanistan
76 B3 Shikarpur India
74 C5 Shikarpur Pakistan
61 N11 Shikine-jima Japan
60 G12 Shikoku isld Japan
61 G12 Shikoku-sanchi mts Japan
59 N3 Shikotan isld U.S.S.R.
60 P3 Shikotsu Toya Nat. Park Japan
52 G4 Shilador U.S.S.R.
80 D6 Shilat Jordan
Shilin see Changjiang
59 G1 Shilka R U.S.S.R.
86 H4 Shillave Ethiopia
14 E4 Shillelagh Irish Rep
13 G4 Shillingford England
120 K4 Shillington Ontario
95 M6 Shillington Pennsylvania
75 O6 Shillong India
110 H6 Shiloh Nat. Mil. Park Tennessee
67 C5 Shilong China
67 D3 Shilong China
65 A6 Shilou China
54 M2 Shilovo U.S.S.R.
Shima see Longhai
67 E3 Shima China
60 D13 Shimabara Japan
61 M11 Shimada Japan
60 F13 Shimane prefect Japan
59 J1 Shimanovsk U.S.S.R.
60 F13 Shimanto Japan

67 D2 Shimen China
61 M11 Shimenzhai China
61 M11 Shimizu Japan
61 L9 Shimminato Japan
60 P4 Shimofuro Japan
76 B4 Shimoga India
61 O8 Shimogo Japan
60 E11 Shimogo Japan
60 D13 Shimo-jima isld Japan
60 Q1 Shimokawa Japan
61 O8 Shimo-kitaba Japan
60 O4 Shimokita-hantō pen Japan
60 C14 Shimo koshiki jima isld Japan
61 M9 Shimonita Japan
59 K5 Shimonoseki Japan
60 D14 Shimo-Taniguchi Japan
60 E13 Shimo-Tashima Japan
61 N9 Shimotsuma Japan
80 D3 Shimron Israel
52 D5 Shimsk U.S.S.R.
67 C5 Shinan China
59 L4 Shinano R Japan
77 H3 Shindand Afghanistan
61 K11 Shindo Japan
109 K6 Shiner Texas
67 F2 Shinglehouse Pennsylvania
94 J5 Shingle Pk New Zealand
145 D4 Shingle Pk New Zealand
59 U3 Shingleton Michigan
118 E8 Shingletown California
60 Q7 Shingu Japan
101 L4 Shining Tree Ontario
61 O7 Shinjo Japan
60 E11 Shin-Nanyo Japan
94 G7 Shinnston W Virginia
61 M9 Shinonoi Japan
79 G4 Shinshar Syria
61 L11 Shinshiro Japan
60 Q2 Shintoku Japan
88 D3 Shinyanga Tanzania
61 P7 Shiogama Japan
61 L9 Shiojiri Japan
59 L5 Shiono-misaki C Japan
61 J12 Shiono-misaki C Japan
Shipai see Huaining
126 F2 Ship Chan. Cay isld Bahamas
123 S6 Ship Cove Nfld
9 G2 Shipdham England
111 H11 Ship I Mississippi
52 G4 Shipitsino U.S.S.R.
47 G2 Shipka R Bulgaria
74 H3 Shipki Pass India/Xizang Zizhiqu
13 G6 Shipley England
119 N5 Shipman Sask
94 K6 Shippensburg Pennsylvania
106 B5 Shiprock New Mexico
121 T4 Shippegan Quebec
111 E13 Ship Shoal Lt. Hse Louisiana
13 G5 Shipton N Yorks England
9 E4 Shipton under Wychwood Gloucs England
67 G2 Shipu China
67 C3 Shipu China
67 C3 Shiqian China
80 A7 Shiqiao China
80 C8 Shiqma Israel
80 C8 Shiqma R Israel
59 E6 Shiquan China
74 H2 Shiquan China
66 C5 Shiquan He R China
77 K1 Shirabad U.S.S.R.
60 J12 Shirahama Japan
60 O4 Shirakami-misaki C Japan
80 D4 Shirako Jordan
59 K6 Shirakawa Fukushima, Honshu Japan
61 K9 Shirakawa Toyama, Honshu Japan
78 L1 Shirakskaya Step' U.S.S.R.
57 F5 Shiranuka Japan
60 S3 Shiraoi Japan
90 P3 Shirai Japan
67 A3 Shirasbreen Antarctica
146 J8 Shirase Coast Antarctica
77 C5 Shiraz Iran
79 B7 Shirbin Egypt
88 E9 Shire R Malawi
88 E9 Shire Highlands Malawi
67 F3 Shiretoko-misaki C Japan
60 T1 Shiribeshi prefect Japan
57 C3 Shirikrabat U.S.S.R.
60 O4 Shiriuchi Japan
60 P4 Shiriya-zaki C Japan
110 D6 Shirley Arkansas
59 J3 Shirley England
9 E3 Shirley Hampshire England
9 E3 Shirley W Midlands England
99 Q7 Shiroishi Japan
116 G9 Shirokoye U.S.S.R.
61 K10 Shirotori Japan
77 E1 Shirouma-dake mt Japan
60 Q1 Shirvan Japan
77 E1 Shirvan Iran
116 E9 Shishaldin Vol Aleutian Is
60 H12 Shishikui Japan
55 D5 Shishmaref Alaska
115 D3 Shishmaref Inlet Alaska
67 D2 Shishou China
67 F1 Shishou China
54 A1 Shishui China
52 H4 Shishui China
108 F6 Shiskine Texas
65 E1 Shiukwanu China
74 B4 Shiukou Jordan
67 T1 Shiveluch volc Japan
55 G4 Shujaabad Pakistan
74 H7 Shujalpur India
55 D1 Shukhtungort U.S.S.R.
100 D1 Shuksan, Mt Washington
59 J3 Shulan China
57 H5 Shule China
58 C2 Shule He R China
Shulinzhao see Dalad Qi
99 Q7 Shullsburg Wisconsin
116 G9 Shulu China
116 G9 Shuman Is Alaska
60 Q1 Shumarinai Japan
55 D5 Shumekt U.S.S.R.
54 H11 Shumen Bulgaria
91 G6 Shumerlya U.S.S.R.
59 U6 Shumikha U.S.S.R.
54 A1 Shumilino U.S.S.R.
52 H4 Shumskiy U.S.S.R.
108 F6 Shumla Texas
68 H5 Shun Pang Cambodia
68 H5 Shumgou China
30 O7 Shumway Arizona
67 F3 Shunchang China
67 D5 Shunde China
67 D3 Shunga U.S.S.R.
65 C4 Shuna China
22 L5 Shuolong China
80 F8 Shuo Xian China
9 R7 Shuqeiq R Jordan
111 H9 Shuqualak Mississippi
77 G4 Shur R Iran
77 G4 Shur R Iran
65 A6 Shuranji China
61 P13 Shuri Okinawa
52 H4 Shurma U.S.S.R.
52 H6 Shuryshkary U.S.S.R.
78 L2 Shusha U.S.S.R.
77 A3 Shush Iran
77 C5 Shushica R Albania
77 A3 Shushtar Iran
117 O10 Shuswap L Br Columbia
139 H4 Shuttleton New S Wales
52 D4 Shuya Ivanovo U.S.S.R.
52 D4 Shuya Karelskaya A.S.S.R. U.S.S.R.
116 L7 Shuyak I Alaska
60 N6 Shuyang China
55 D3 Shuyeretskiy U.S.S.R.
55 G4 Shuykovo Oz L U.S.S.R.
61 M11 Shuzenji Japan
68 B8 Shwebandaw Burma
68 B3 Shwebo Burma
68 B3 Shwebu Burma
68 B4 Shwegun Burma
74 H1 Shwegyin Burma
68 C3 Shwegyin Burma
123 R4 Shwenyaung Burma
145 E2 Shoe Cove Nfld
77 F1 Shoghlabad Iran
55 K1 Shokal'skogo, Proliv str U.S.S.R.
Shokambetsu dake mt Japan
60 R1 Shokotsu Japan
59 R1 Shola China
55 D5 Sholaksay U.S.S.R.
31 J1 Sholakshalkar, Oz L U.S.S.R.
69 H11 Sholinur India
76 B2 Sholapur India
142 B5 Sholl I W Australia
52 D4 Sholom Israel
88 D3 Shomera Israel
80 E1 Shomvukva U.S.S.R.
57 A2 Shomyshkol' U.S.S.R.

88 B9 Shona Zambia
55 G5 Shoptykul' U.S.S.R.
52 G6 Shora R U.S.S.R.
76 C5 Shoranur India
76 C2 Shorapur India
77 J5 Shorawak reg Afghanistan
9 F6 Shoreham-by-Sea England
99 T6 Shorewood Wisconsin
55 F5 Shortandy U.S.S.R.
103 M5 Short Cr Arizona
119 Q7 Shortdale Manitoba
111 L9 Shorter Alabama
138 E2 Short, L S Australia
143 C10 Short, Mt W Australia
95 K4 Shortsville New York
102 H6 Shoshone California
101 L7 Shoshone Idaho
86 B6 Shoshone R Wyoming
101 R5 Shoshone Cavern Nat. Mon Wyoming
101 P5 Shoshone L Wyoming
102 J3 Shoshone Mts Nevada
102 H5 Shoshone Pk Nevada
101 R6 Shoshoni Wyoming
54 E5 Shostka U.S.S.R.
71 F7 Shotley Turkey
144 B6 Shotover R New Zealand
67 F2 Shouchang China
67 C4 Shoucheng China
65 D6 Shouguang China
65 D6 Shouguang China
91 G1 Shoulder Mt Alaska
93 U3 Shoulder Mt Alaska
118 Q8 Shouning China
101 L4 Shoup Idaho
85 B6 Shouyang China
80 B8 Shoval Israel
101 L7 Shoval L Minnesota
86 G3 Showak Sudan
71 F4 Showa-Shinzan mt Japan
103 O7 Show Low Arizona
52 F1 Shoyna U.S.S.R.
52 F4 Shozhma U.S.S.R.
94 F6 Shpola U.S.S.R.
94 F6 Shreve Ohio
111 C9 Shreveport Louisiana
8 D2 Shrewsbury England
111 H12 Shrewsbury New Orleans
9 E5 Shrewton England
67 B1 Shrewton England
74 F4 Shrigonda India
43 D11 Shrigonda India
111 E10 Shrirampur India
9 E4 Shrivenham England
Shropshire co see Salop
65 K8 Shterovka U.S.S.R.
65 F2 Shuang-ch'eng China
65 F2 Shuangchengpu China
67 O3 Shuangfeng China
65 E2 Shuanggang China
65 G3 Shuanggou China
65 G3 Shuanghezhen China
59 H3 Shuanghuyu see Zizhou
65 A1 Shuangjiang China
65 F3 Shuangliu China
65 F3 Shuangshan China
59 K2 Shuangyang China
59 S6 Shuangyashan China
79 H3 Shuaybit, Jebel mts Syria
122 J8 Shubenacadie Nova Scotia
122 J9 Shubenacadie L Nova Scotia
99 L9 Shubert Nebraska
116 P2 Shuiberg Mt Alaska
79 A7 Shubra Khit Egypt
111 H10 Shubuta Mississippi
67 E1 Shucheng China
47 F3 Sidhirokastron Greece
17 H8 Sidi Ali Algeria
84 H3 Sidi Barrani Egypt
85 D1 Sidi-bel-Abbes Algeria
63 C13 Sidi bu Ali Tunisia
16 E9 Sidi Dris Morocco
85 B3 Sidi Ifni Morocco
69 D11 Sidikalang Sumatra
13 E1 Sidlaw Hills Scotland
146 H10 Sidley, Mt Antarctica
8 C6 Sidmouth England
141 G2 Sidmouth C Queensland
18 C4 Sillon-de-Talbert C France
47 H3 Sidnaw Michigan
117 M11 Sidney R Columbia
99 S3 Sidney Illinois
99 L9 Sidney Iowa
119 W3 Sidney Manitoba
106 C2 Sidney Montana
119 N8 Sidney Nebraska
86 Q10 Sidney New York
111 K8 Sidney Ohio
52 B8 Sidoardjo Java
16 B7 Sido Mali
29 L5 Sidoktaya Burma
130 E5 Sidolo, Mt mt Sulawesi
Sidon see Saida
36 C2 Sidrolândia Brazil
37 P1 Siebengebirge mt W Germany
21 E10 Siebenlehn E Germany
32 J7 Siedenburg W Germany
31 N3 Sieg R W Germany
36 G2 Siegbach W Germany
31 N3 Siegburg W Germany
Siegelsdorf see Seukendorf
37 M6 Siegen W Germany
31 O3 Siegenburg W Germany
26 H4 Siegen W Germany
54 H3 Siemiatycze Poland
68 H5 Siem Pang Cambodia
68 H5 Siem Reap Cambodia
31 O5 Siena Italy
20 C4 Siene France
29 K4 Sieniawa Poland
40 F2 Sieradz Poland
31 J3 Sierakow Poland
22 L5 Sierck France
40 F2 Sierentz France
31 M3 Sierpc Poland
108 B4 Sierra Blanca Texas
102 D2 Sierra Buttes peak California
133 D6 Sierra Colorada Argentina
133 D6 Sierra Grande Argentina
124 H6 Sierra Hermosa Mexico
85 B7 Sierra Leone rep W Africa
100 D1 Sierra Leone Basin Atlantic Oc.
90 H4 Sierra Leone Rise Atlantic Oc.
125 J9 Sierra Madre del Sur mts Mexico
102 D2 Sierra Madre Mts California
124 H4 Sierra Madre Oriental mts Mexico
124 H4 Sierra Mojada Mexico
102 D2 Sierraville California
86 G4 Siershahn W Germany
69 D11 Sierra Puntas, R Paraguay
43 B8 Sietow E Germany
52 R3 Sieu Romania
71 F5 Sieve R Italy
47 F6 Sieversdorf W Germany
48 J1 Sifang Ling China
80 E1 Sifangtai China
77 F5 Sifnos isld Greece
78 K2 Sifton Br Columbia
29 B8 Simberlik, El Egypt
117 O9 Sig Algeria

71 E8 Siasi Philippines
71 F6 Siaton Negros Philippines
52 B6 Siauliai U.S.S.R.
84 J4 Sîbâi, Gebel mt Egypt
126 F4 Sibanicú Cuba
55 C4 Sibay U.S.S.R.
71 E5 Sibay isld Philippines
89 H6 Sibayi L S Africa
118 D7 Sibbald Alberta
29 L11 Sibbo Finland
69 D14 Siberimanua Indonesia
69 D13 Siberut isld Indonesia
42 E6 Sibillini, Monti Italy
59 K3 Sibirtsevo U.S.S.R.
87 C4 Sibiti Congo
52 F2 Sibiu Romania
9 H3 Sible Hedingham England
99 S9 Sibley Illinois
99 L6 Sibley Iowa
109 O3 Sibley Louisiana
120 B4 Sibley Prov. Park Ontario
70 G4 Siboa Sulawesi
69 D11 Sibolangborong Sumatra
41 M3 Sibratsgfall Austria
75 Q5 Sibsagar India
9 G1 Sibsey England
70 B3 Sibu Sarawak
71 F7 Sibuco Mindanao Philippines
71 F7 Sibuguey Bay Mindanao Philippines
86 C4 Sibut Cent Afr Republic
70 C2 Sibuti Sarawak
71 F4 Sibuyan isld Philippines
48 H4 Sic Romania
71 E1 Sicapoo mt Luzon Philippines
128 E7 Sicasica Bolivia
71 F6 Siccayap Mindanao Philippines
138 E4 Siccus R S Australia
67 A1 Sichuan prov China
43 E11 Sichuan Pendi China
43 D11 Sicilia isld Italy
111 E10 Sicilian Chan S Europe
Sicily see Sicilia
119 R2 Sickle L Manitoba
128 D6 Sicuani Peru
48 E5 Sid Yugoslavia
71 A2 Sidangoli Halmahera Indonesia
71 J4 Sidate Sulawesi
85 F5 Sidawet Niger
9 G5 Sidcot England
9 G5 Sidcup England
140 B6 Siddeley Ra N Terr Aust
8 D1 Siddington England
76 D1 Siddipett India
29 J9 Sidell Illinois
99 T10 Sidell Illinois
112 H2 Siler City N Carolina
101 R4 Silesia Montana
45 K4 Silesia reg Poland/Czech
85 D6 Sidéradougou Upper Volta
84 F3 Sider, Es Libya
43 H10 Siderno Marina Italy
67 C4 Sidewood Sask
47 H8 Sidheri India

69 G13 Sigli Sumatra
115 S4 Siglufjördhur Iceland
71 F5 Sigma Panay Philippines
41 K1 Sigmaringen W Germany
45 K4 Sigma Italy
103 L7 Signal Arizona
18 G7 Signal du Luguet mt France
112 B2 Signal Mt Tennessee
103 K8 Signal Pk Arizona
19 P18 Signes France
22 G4 Signy-l'Abbaye France
22 G4 Signy-le-petit France
21 E10 Sigogne France
69 D14 Sigoinsan Indonesia
99 O8 Sigourney Iowa
128 C4 Sigsig Ecuador
27 J12 Sigtuna Sweden
85 C6 Siguiri Guinea
47 F3 Sigüenza Spain
103 N3 Siguri Utah
20 H2 Sigy-en-Bray France
68 B1 Sihaung Myauk Burma
65 D4 Siheyong China
29 J10 Siikainen Finland
52 C3 Siikajoki R Finland
59 G1 Siilinjärvi Finland
78 H3 Siirt Turkey
117 M7 Sikanni Chief Br Columbia
74 F5 Sikar India
77 L2 Sikaram mt Afghanistan
69 D14 Sikariman Indonesia
85 D6 Sikasso Mali
58 G1 Sikeli Sulawesi
110 G5 Sikeston Missouri
51 N4 Sikhote Alin' mts U.S.S.R.
47 G3 Sikinos isld Greece
46 F6 Sikionia Greece
75 N5 Sikkim prot India
116 B5 Siknik C Alaska
71 A2 Siko isld Halmahera Indonesia
70 E1 Sikuati Sabah
70 G4 Sikuka Indonesia
16 C2 Sil F Spain
69 D13 Silagi Indonesia
59 D11 Silahung mt Sumatra
52 B6 Silalā U.S.S.R.
41 N4 Silandro Italy
86 J3 Sila Pt Philippines
111 H10 Silas Alabama
70 B4 Silat Kalimantan
69 B10 Silawaih Agam vol Sumatra
71 F5 Silay Negros Philippines
26 M1 Silda isld Norway
47 K3 Sile Turkey
68 B1 Silchar India
26 M1 Silda isld Norway
47 K3 Siddingston England
22 G3 Silenrieux Belgium
27 F12 Silen, V L Sweden
112 H2 Siler City N Carolina
101 R4 Silesia Montana
99 T10 Sidell Illinois
68 D1 Silgarhi India
41 N4 Siliguri India
66 D5 Siling Co L China
43 B9 Siliqua Sardinia
70 B4 Silistra Bulgaria
71 J7 Silivri Turkey
27 D11 Siljan L Sweden
27 C13 Siljansnäs Sweden
52 D1 Silkeborg Denmark
13 G6 Silksworth England
70 L9 Sillamae U.S.S.R.
71 K9 Sillé-le-Guillaume France
32 F8 Sillian Austria
20 F4 Silli-en-Gouffern France
18 C4 Sillon-de-Talbert C France
47 J1 Silo mt Greece
101 P3 Siloam Springs Arkansas
109 L9 Siloam Springs Arkansas
75 M7 Silom India
32 G3 Silsbee Texas
106 C2 Silt Colorado
119 N8 Silton Sask
86 C2 Silu China
111 K8 Silungbinak Indonesia
89 J5 Siluria Alabama
52 B8 Silute U.S.S.R.
78 J2 Silvan Turkey
130 E5 Silvânia Brazil
129 J8 Silva Porto see Bié
74 E8 Silvassa India
127 K4 Silver Bank Caribbean
99 P2 Silver Bay Minnesota
103 N5 Silverbell Arizona
101 N3 Silver Bow Montana
69 F12 Silver City Ontario
100 J6 Silver City Idaho
111 F8 Silver City Mississippi
106 B8 Silver City New Mexico
103 M2 Silver City Utah
111 C11 Silver City Louisiana
94 A8 Silver Creek Kentucky
99 A8 Silver Creek New York
101 K4 Silver Crown Wyoming
107 O8 Silverdale Kansas
118 N7 Silverdale New Zealand
104 F6 Silver Heights Alberta
119 D14 Silver Islet Ontario
103 P4 Silver L California
99 T3 Silver L Michigan
123 P4 Silver Mt Nfld
102 G2 Silver peak Nevada
141 G2 Singora Plains Queensland
144 J4 Silver Springs New Zealand
101 M4 Silver Star Montana
117 O10 Silver Star Prov. Park Br Columbia
117 K10 Silverthrone Mt Br Columbia
106 C4 Silverton Colorado
100 C5 Silverton Oregon
108 F1 Silverton Washington
100 D1 Silverton Washington
128 K5 Silves Brazil
16 B8 Silves Portugal
52 B8 Silveys R U.S.S.R.
86 G4 Silvicola Timor
40 F6 Silvretta Gruppe mt Switzerland
102 H4 Silvretta Gruppe mt Switz/Austria
86 G8 Silwad Jordan
36 B5 Silwingen W Germany
55 D3 Sim U.S.S.R.
69 D13 Simalake Hilir Indonesia
70 B3 Simanggang Sarawak
33 J6 Simão Egypt
68 E1 Simard, Lac Quebec
76 B1 Simav Turkey
43 H8 Simat Sulawesi
47 J4 Simav Gölü L Turkey
48 J1 Simav Turkey
71 E5 Simbahan Philippines
71 E7 Simbah Philippines
28 H8 Simbirlawein, El Egypt
41 N8 Simbruini, Monti mt Italy
139 H8 Simbu prov Papua N Guinea
119 U5 Simcoe Ontario
120 K8 Simcoe, L Ontario
78 H2 Simdega India
27 F1 Simeto R Sicily
52 A1 Simeto R Sicily
69 C11 Simeuluë isld Indonesia
50 E4 Simferopol' U.S.S.R.
47 H4 Simi isld Greece
29 S11 Simiaatene Finland
52 K9 Simizu Japan
79 B10 Sigli Sumatra

36 C4 Simmer R W Germany
22 L2 Simmerath W Germany
36 D4 Simmern W Germany
111 E11 Simmesport Louisiana
118 J9 Simmie Sask
102 E6 Simmler California
29 L5 Simms Montana
126 G3 Simms Long I Bahamas
101 O2 Simms Montana
111 B8 Simms Texas
113 K9 Simms Pt New Providence I Bahamas
31 O1 Simo Finland
29 L6 Simo Finland
27 D12 Simo R Norway
29 N11 Simola Finland
102 G3 Simon Nevada
143 E9 Simon W Australia
115 L7 Simonette R Alberta
119 O4 Simonhouse Manitoba
121 P7 Simon, L Quebec
13 G5 Simon Seat mt England
27 H13 Simonstorp Sweden
118 B3 Simonson R Alberta
117 K10 Simoom Sd Br Columbia
69 G13 Simpang Sumatra
29 O10 Simple Finland
25 E7 Simpelveld Netherlands
129 K5 Simplicio Mendes Brazil
40 H5 Simplon Tunnel Italy/Switz
99 Q6 Simpson Kansas
107 N2 Simpson Minnesota
101 P1 Simpson Montana
119 M7 Simpson Sask
140 D6 Simpson Des N Terr Aust
143 F7 Simpson Hill W Australia
133 C7 Simpson, I Chile
117 N9 Simpson, I Chile
115 N9 Simpson Pen N W Terr
115 L4 Simpson Pen N W Terr
102 H2 Simpson Pk Mts Nevada
112 E3 Simpsonville S Carolina
21 G16 Simrishamn Sweden
59 M5 Simushir isld U.S.S.R.
69 C13 Sinabang Indonesia
69 D11 Sinabung mt Sumatra
86 G4 Sinac Yugoslavia
86 F8 Sinadogo Somalia
98 J3 Sinai S Dakota
84 J4 Sinai pen Egypt
124 F5 Sinaloa state Mexico
42 D5 Sinalunga Italy
127 J9 Sinamaica Venezuela
67 C3 Sinan China
46 D4 Sinanaj Albania
68 B3 Sinara R U.S.S.R.
75 B6 Sinbo Burma
68 B2 Sinbyubyin Burma
68 B2 Sinbyudaing Burma
68 B2 Sinbyugyaun Burma
126 G10 Sincelejo Colombia
22 E4 Sincény France
101 S8 Sinclair Wyoming
112 D4 Sinclair L Georgia
117 N9 Sinclair Mills Br Columbia
138 C4 Sinclair, Pt S Australia
29 L5 Sindal Denmark
71 B7 Sindangbarang Java
71 K9 Sind, Tk R Flores Indonesia
47 J1 Sindel Bulgaria
36 G6 Sindelfingen W Germany
55 D1 Sindeya U.S.S.R.
76 C3 Sindhnur India
52 B5 Sindi U.S.S.R.
47 J5 Sindirği Turkey
70 G4 Sindjai Sulawesi
75 M7 Sindri India
32 G3 Sindringen W Germany
54 M3 Sinegorskiy U.S.S.R.
52 H5 Sinekçi Turkey
47 J4 Sinekli Turkey
54 G8 Sinel'nikovo U.S.S.R.
16 B7 Sines Portugal
29 L5 Sinetta Finland
Sinfu see Jianping
69 D12 Singa Burma
127 K4 Singa Sudan
85 D6 Singaingmyo Burma
69 G12 Singapore city Singapore
69 G12 Singapore state S E Asia
69 G12 Singapore, Str. of S E Asia
69 G13 Singaradja Indonesia
69 E13 Singkep Indonesia
69 G13 Singkepe Indonesia
69 C11 Singkawang Kalimantan
69 F10 Singkuang Sumatra
139 K4 Singleton New S Wales
140 C5 Singleton N Terr Aust
109 M5 Singleton Texas
140 B7 Singleton, Mt N Terr Aust
143 B8 Singleton, Mt W Australia
80 F8 Singora see Songkhla
46 E4 Siniatsikon mt Greece
71 E3 Siniloan Luzon Philippines
66 B5 Sining see Xining
Sining see Xining
65 C4 Siniscola Sardinia
55 D5 Siniy-Shikhan U.S.S.R.
86 G2 Sinkat Sudan
Sinkiang see Xinjiang Uygur Zizhiqu
Sinkiang-Uighur aut reg see Xinjiang Uygur Zizhiqu
94 D7 Sinking Spring Ohio
80 B7 Sinmak N Korea
36 H3 Sinn W Germany
129 J2 Sinnamary Fr Guiana
76 B1 Sinnar India
43 H8 Sinni R Italy
48 H2 Sinoe, L Romania
78 F2 Sinop Turkey
80 E1 Sinp'o N Korea
80 B8 Sinsheim W Germany
36 G5 Sinspelt W Germany
119 U3 Sintang Kalimantan
127 N6 Sint Eustatius isld Lesser Antilles
22 D2 Sint Jan Belgium
127 N5 Sint Maarten isld Lesser Antilles
16 B8 Sintra Portugal
80 B7 Sinŭiju N Korea
59 J1 Sinŭiju N Korea
101 M1 Siyeh, Mt Montana

52 C6 Sinyaya R U.S.S.R.
36 E6 Sinzheim W Germany
36 C2 Sinzig W Germany
28 F7 Sio isld Denmark
48 E4 Sió R Hungary
71 F7 Siocon Mindanao Philippines
40 F5 Sion Switzerland
18 G6 Sioule R France
98 K6 Sioux Center Iowa
98 X7 Sioux City Iowa
98 K6 Sioux Falls S Dakota
118 L1 Sioux Lookout Ontario
71 F6 Sipaley Negros Philippines
127 O3 Siparia Trinidad
Siping see Huangpin
59 H3 Siping China
70 D2 Sipitang Sabah
115 J3 Sipiwesk Manitoba
119 L1 Sipiwesk L Manitoba
146 H8 Siple Coast Antarctica
146 J10 Siple, Mt Antarctica
87 F9 Sipolilo Zimbabwe
69 D14 Sipora isld Indonesia
29 N11 Sippola Finland
111 J7 Sipsey Alabama
111 J8 Sipsey R Alabama
71 F6 Siquijor Philippines
128 L1 Siquisique Venezuela
80 G6 Sir R Jordan
102 E6 Sira California
128 D5 Sira mt Peru
27 B13 Sira R Norway
77 D7 Sīr Abu Nu'ayr isld U.A.E.
47 H7 Sirac mt France
43 G11 Siracusa Sicily
17 N9 Sir Alexander, Mt Br Columbia
85 E6 Sirba watercourse Niger/Upper Volta
123 S4 Sir Charles Hamilton Sd Nfld
141 G1 Sir Charles Hardy Is Barrier Reef Aust
B13 Sirdalsvatn L Norway
118 B8 Sir Douglas, Mt Alberta
140 D3 Sir Edward Pellew Group islds N Terr Aust
99 O4 Siren Wisconsin
45 M6 Siret mt Italy
48 K3 Siretul R Romania
80 F8 Sirfa Jordan
140 B1 Sir George Hope Is N Terr Aust
142 F2 Sir Graham Moore Is W Aust
79 H7 Sirhan, Wadi watercourse Saudi Arabia
68 E4 Siri Kit Dam Thailand
70 B3 Sirik, Tg C Sarawak
138 D5 Sir Isaac Pt S Australia
117 J4 Sir James McBrien, Mt N W Terr
143 D7 Sir James, Mt W Australia
29 L4 Sirkka Finland
74 G5 Sir Muttra India
70 E1 Sirna isld Greece
47 H8 Sirna isld Greece
72 F4 Sirmak Turkey
47 H6 Sirohi India
42 H5 Siroki Brijeg Yugoslavia
45 O4 Sirolo Italy
69 C12 Sirombu Indonesia
76 E1 Sironcha India
69 G13 Sironj India
47 G7 Siros Greece
76 D1 Sirpur India
102 F6 Sirretta Pk California
74 F4 Sirsa India
76 D1 Sirsa India
76 B3 Sirsi India
28 K6 Si Tangkay Philippines
70 F2 Si Tangkay Philippines
139 J3 Sisajpore Sweden
47 G4 Sisdone Greece
129 L8 Sishmone Greece
130 F4 Sitia Crete Greece
52 B5 Sitian China
130 H4 Sitio da Abadia Brazil
124 G3 Sitio de Mato Brazil
117 F7 Sitka Alaska
102 F4 Sitka Kansas
107 L8 Sitkalidak I Alaska
116 L8 Sitkinak I Alaska
100 B8 Sitkum Oregon
69 D14 Sitkwin R Yugoslavia
48 K4 Sitojaure L Sweden
86 H4 Sitra oasis Egypt
77 B6 Sitrah Bahrain
68 B7 Sittang R Burma
25 E7 Sitten see Sion
36 B6 Sittensen W Germany
9 G5 Sittingbourne England
68 A2 Sittwe Burma
70 P9 Situbondo Java
69 A8 Siuna Nicaragua
29 L6 Siuntio Finland
77 H7 Siuruanjoki R Finland
59 J1 Sivaki U.S.S.R.
78 G2 Sivas Turkey
47 K5 Sivash Turkey
55 D5 Siverskiy U.S.S.R.
68 K2 Sivomaskinskiy U.S.S.R.
52 D5 Sivrihisar Turkey
47 J5 Sivry France
47 J5 Sivry-sur-Meuse France
29 J5 Siwa oasis Egypt
65 A4 Siyitang China

South Brisbane — Stone Mt. Prov. Park 73

141 K1 South Brisbane dist Brisbane, Qnsld
144 D5 Southbrook New Zealand
123 Q4 South Brook Nfld
122 H9 South Brookfield Nova Scotia
144 C6 Southburn New Zealand
112 F3 South Carolina state U.S.A.
13 H6 South Cave England
94 C1 South Chan Michigan
94 D7 South Charleston Ohio
94 F8 South Charleston W Virginia
67 E6 South China Sea
95 N2 South Colton New York
98 F5 South Dakota state U.S.A.
94 H4 South Dayton New York
13 F3 Southdean Scotland
95 P4 South Deerfield Massachusetts
9 F6 South Downs England
139 H9 South East C Tasmania
139 H7 South East C Victoria
83 K12 South East I Mahé I Indian Oc
135 N15 Southeast Pacific Basin Pac Oc
9 G4 Southend England
114 J6 Southend Sask
12 C3 Southend Scotland
99 O8 South English Iowa
144 C5 Southern Alps mts New Zealand
101 M3 Southern Cross Montana
141 H5 Southern Cross Queensland
143 C9 Southern Cross W Australia
86 D3 Southern Darfur prov Sudan
8 C5 Southerndown Wales
123 T6 Southern Harbour Nfld
119 S2 Southern Indian L Manitoba
86 E3 Southern Kordofan prov Sudan
81 Southern Ocean
111 G10 Southern Pine Hills Miss/Ala
112 H2 Southern Pines N Carolina
142 B2 Southern R Perth, W Aust
142 F5 South Esk Tableland W Australia
119 N8 Southey Sask
110 E2 South Fabius R Missouri
13 H6 South Ferriby England
144 A6 South Fiord New Zealand
100 B9 South Fork California
106 D4 South Fork Colorado
94 J6 South Fork Pennsylvania
118 J9 South Fork Sask
112 F1 South Fork R N Carolina
110 G6 South Fork R Tennessee
98 D4 South Fork R S Dakota
99 V4 South Fox I Michigan
110 H5 South Fulton Tennessee
146 F5 South Geomagnetic Pole (1975) Antarctica
131 H5 South Georgia S Atlantic Oc
99 O9 South Gifford Missouri
8 C4 South Glamorgan co Wales
110 B3 South Grand R Missouri
123 M7 South Harbour Nova Scotia
107 N4 South Haven Kansas
99 U7 South Haven Michigan
115 K5 South Henik L N W Terr
94 J10 South Hill Virginia
94 F10 South Holston L Tenn/Virg
83 M8 South I Cocos Is Indian Oc
140 C1 South I N Terr Aust
119 T2 South Indian L Manitoba
95 P5 Southington Connecticut
144 B5 South Island New Zealand
71 D6 South Islet Sulu Sea
118 F1 South Junc Manitoba
99 T7 South Kenosha Wisconsin
59 J4 South Korea rep Asia
109 M8 Southlake Texas
144 A6 Southland stat area New Zealand
123 K9 South Lochaber Nova Scotia
98 G8 South Loup R Nebraska
88 C8 South Luangwa Nat. Park Zambia
70 C2 South Luconia Shoals S China Sea
94 D4 South Lyon Michigan
120 K7 Southmag Ontario
146 J3 South Magnetic Pole (1975) Antarctica
99 U4 South Manitou I Michigan
95 L10 South Mills N Carolina
99 T7 South Milwaukee Wisconsin
9 G4 Southminster England
141 J5 South Molle I Queensland
8 C5 South Molton England
109 K10 Southmost Texas
95 K6 South Mt Pennsylvania
116 J7 South Naknek Alaska
122 G7 South Nelson New Brunswick
112 F6 South Newport Georgia
95 P5 Southold Long I, New York
90 F15 South Orkney isld S Atlantic Oc
102 B3 South Pablo B California
95 R2 South Paris Maine
94 F7 South Parkersburg W Virginia
101 R7 South Pass Wyoming
101 R7 South Pass City Wyoming
99 R9 South Pekin Illinois
110 L6 South Pittsburg Tennessee
106 E2 South Platte Colorado
146 F8 South Polar Plat Antarctica
146 F8 South Pole Antarctica
120 J4 South Porcupine Ontario
13 E6 Southport England
94 A7 Southport Indiana
112 J4 Southport N Carolina
123 T5 Southport Nfld
139 H9 Southport Tasmania
123 K4 South Pt Anticosti I, Quebec
83 M9 South Pt Christmas I Indian Oc
112 J3 South R N Carolina
99 S2 South Range Michigan
144 A7 South Red Head Pt. New Zealand
113 H12 South Riding Rock Bahamas
95 N6 South River New Jersey
121 L7 South River Ontario
15 F2 South Ronaldsay Scotland
131 J7 South Sandwich Is S Atlantic Oc
102 B4 South San Francisco California
118 J8 South Sask R Sask
9 E6 Southsea England
119 S1 South Seal R Manitoba
146 E15 South Shetland Is Antarctica
13 G3 South Shields England
98 K7 South Sioux City Nebraska
98 K6 South Sioux Falls S Dakota
117 P11 South Slocan Br Columbia
103 N2 South Tent peak Utah
15 A3 South Uist Scotland
9 F1 Southwell England
South West Africa terr see Namibia
113 K9 South West B New Providence I Bahamas
123 K6 Southwest C Madeleine Is, Quebec
139 H9 South West C Tasmania
144 A7 Southwest Cape New Zealand
139 H7 South West I Tasmania
81 C9 South-West Indian Ridge Indian Oc
135 M12 South-West Pacific Basin Pac Oc
113 K12 Southwest Pt Bahamas
122 J4 Southwest Pt Quebec
126 E6 Southwest Rock Caribbean
99 S8 South Wilmington Illinois
9 H3 Southwold England
9 G2 South Wootton England
72 F5 South Yemen rep Arabia
13 G6 South Yorkshire co England
89 F4 Soutpansberg mts S Africa
144 B6 Soutra Hill New Zealand
18 H6 Souvigny France
16 B6 Souzel Portugal
48 J4 Sovata Romania
118 K7 Sovereign Sask
52 B6 Sovetsk U.S.S.R.
52 G5 Sovetsk U.S.S.R.
51 N4 Sovetskaya Gavan U.S.S.R.
52 C4 Sovetskiy Leningrad U.S.S.R.
55 D1 Sovetskiy Tyumenskaya U.S.S.R.
28 E5 Søvind Denmark
52 F2 Sovpol'ye U.S.S.R.
119 N1 Sowden L Ontario
13 G6 Sowerby Br England
60 P1 Sōya Japan
60 P1 Sōya-misaki C Japan
52 F2 Soyana R U.S.S.R.
60 P1 Sōya wan B Japan
38 F5 Soyen W Germany
19 N15 Soyons France
124 E3 Soyopa Mexico
54 B4 Sozh R U.S.S.R.
52 H5 Sozimskiy U.S.S.R.
47 J2 Sozopol Bulgaria
22 K3 Spa Belgium
126 B2 Spaanse Baai B Curaçao
16 Spain rep W Europe
31 M4 Spała Poland
Spalato see Split
9 F2 Spalding England
100 J3 Spalding Idaho
98 H8 Spalding Nebraska
119 N6 Spalding Sask
138 E5 Spalding S Australia
37 K5 Spalt W Germany
25 C3 Spanbroek Netherlands
33 S7 Spandau W Berlin
28 B6 Spandet Denmark
27 H14 Spångenäs Sweden
36 H1 Spangenberg W Germany
100 H2 Spangle Washington
94 J6 Spangler Pennsylvania
123 T6 Spaniard's B Nfld
120 H6 Spanish Ontario
101 O9 Spanish Fork City Utah
106 F4 Spanish Pks Colorado
127 L3 Spanish Town Jamaica
113 L12 Spanish Wells Eleuthera Bahamas
45 Q7 Sparanise Italy
26 E8 Sparbu Norway
28 C4 Sparkær Denmark
111 D8 Sparkman Arkansas
112 D6 Sparks Georgia
98 F7 Sparks Nebraska
102 E2 Sparks Nevada
107 O6 Sparks Oklahoma
99 R8 Sparland Illinois
37 M3 Sparneberg E Germany
94 C1 Sparr Michigan
112 E4 Sparta Georgia
110 G3 Sparta Illinois
94 B3 Sparta Michigan
110 C4 Sparta Missouri
94 F10 Sparta N Carolina
100 H5 Sparta Oregon
110 L6 Sparta Tennessee
99 Q6 Sparta Wisconsin
112 F3 Spartanburg S Carolina
94 H5 Spartansburg Pennsylvania
16 D9 Spartel, C Morocco
43 G11 Spartivento, C Italy
43 B10 Spartivento, C Sardinia
54 M1 Spas-Klepiki U.S.S.R.
56 C4 Spassk U.S.S.R.
52 D4 Spasskaya Guba U.S.S.R.
59 K3 Spassk Dal'niy U.S.S.R.
55 E5 Spasskoye U.S.S.R.
54 M2 Spassk-Ryazanskiy U.S.S.R.
47 F9 Spátha, Akr C Crete Greece
117 J7 Spatsizi Plat. Wilderness Prov. Pk Br Columbia
110 A5 Spavinaw, L Oklahoma
36 D3 Spay W Germany
109 L6 Speaks Texas
15 D4 Spean Bridge Scotland
98 C5 Spearfish S Dakota
119 T7 Spearhill Manitoba
143 D6 Spear Hill W Australia
108 C7 Spearman Texas
107 L4 Spearville Kansas
142 A3 Spearwood dist Perth, W Aust
33 R6 Specker-See L E Germany
95 N3 Speculator New York
118 F4 Spedden Alberta
109 M1 Speer Oklahoma
98 B8 Speer Wyoming
118 K6 Speers Sask
36 B4 Speicher W Germany
37 M4 Speichersdorf W Germany
37 M7 Speichersee L W Germany
127 P6 Speightstown Barbados
116 M6 Spenard Alaska
115 K4 Spence Bay N W Terr
101 N5 Spencer Idaho
110 K2 Spencer Indiana
99 L6 Spencer Iowa
95 P4 Spencer Massachusetts
98 H7 Spencer Nebraska
95 L4 Spencer New York
98 J6 Spencer S Dakota
99 Q5 Spencer Wisconsin
94 F8 Spencer W Virginia
117 E6 Spencer, C Alaska
138 D6 Spencer, C S Australia
138 D5 Spencer Gulf S Australia
95 R1 Spencer L Maine
94 K3 Spencerport New York
116 D4 Spencer, Pt Alaska
140 A3 Spencer Ra N Terr Aust
140 C1 Spencer Ra N Terr Aust
94 C6 Spencerville Ohio
117 N10 Spences Bridge Br Columbia
32 H8 Spenge W Germany
13 G4 Spennymoor England
144 D5 Spenser Mts New Zealand
33 S8 Sperenberg E Germany
27 D11 Sperillen Norway
46 E6 Sperkhiós R Greece
118 D1 Sperling Manitoba
45 O7 Sperlonga Italy
43 B10 Sperone, C Sardinia
14 D2 Sperrin Mts N Ireland
94 J8 Sperryville Virginia
36 G3 Spessart mts W Germany
46 F7 Spétsai isld Greece
15 E3 Spey R Scotland
36 E5 Speyer W Germany
127 N1 Speyside Tobago
44 G3 Spezia, La Italy
115 M4 Spicer Is N W Terr
99 N9 Spickardsville Missouri
32 G5 Spiekeroog W Germany
38 N8 Spielfeld Austria
36 C5 Spiesen-Elversberg W Germany
44 D2 Spigno R Italy
25 G2 Spijk Netherlands
110 C1 Spikard Missouri
116 R3 Spike Mt Alaska
45 K2 Spilamberto Italy
47 G9 Spíli Crete Greece
42 E2 Spilimbergo Italy
9 G1 Spilsby England
28 N3 Spinarnir mt Faeroes
43 G8 Spinazzola Italy
77 K4 Spin Būldak Afghanistan
22 K5 Spincourt France
112 F2 Spindale N Carolina
45 M1 Spinea Italy
143 F7 Spinifex Ra W Australia
89 B8 Spioenberg I mt S Africa
89 A8 Spioenberg II mt S Africa
89 F7 Spioen Kop mt S Africa
144 A6 Spire Pk New Zealand
99 L6 Spirit L Iowa
100 J2 Spirit Lake Idaho
100 C3 Spirit Lake Washington
117 O8 Spirit River Alberta
145 D1 Spirits B New Zealand
98 H3 Spiritwood N Dakota
118 K5 Spiritwood Sask
107 Q6 Spiro Oklahoma
52 D6 Spirovo U.S.S.R.
48 F1 Spišská Belá Czechoslovakia
48 F2 Spišská Nová Ves Czechoslovakia
31 M6 Spišské Podhradie Czechoslovakia
50 A1 Spitsbergen arch Arctic Oc
38 H8 Spittal-an-der-Drau Austria
38 M5 Spitz Austria
28 A4 Spjald Denmark
109 M5 Splendora Texas
42 H5 Split Yugoslavia
122 H8 Split, C Nova Scotia
119 V2 Split L Manitoba
100 G8 Split Pk mt Nevada
38 N9 Spodnje Hoče Yugoslavia
28 F7 Spodsbjerg Denmark
108 G6 Spofford Texas
13 G6 Spofforth England
100 H2 Spokane Washington
41 M4 Spöl R Italy
42 E6 Spoleto Italy
118 F7 Spondin Alberta
68 G6 Spong Cambodia
33 S5 Sponholz E Germany
22 J3 Spontin Belgium
99 Q9 Spoon R Illinois
99 P4 Spooner Wisconsin
100 E8 Spooner Res California
47 H8 Sporádhes islds Greece
33 P6 Spornitz E Germany
28 E4 Spørring Denmark
44 D3 Spotorno Italy
101 U5 Spotted Horse Wyoming
103 J5 Spotted Ra Nevada
111 K9 Sprague Alabama
118 F1 Sprague Manitoba
100 H2 Sprague Washington
99 Q5 Sprague Wisconsin
100 D7 Sprague River Oregon
36 H6 Spraitbach W Germany
33 M7 Sprakensehl W Germany
100 F5 Spray Oregon
48 E6 Spreča R Yugoslavia
54 J4 Spredne Russkaya Vozvyshennost' uplands U.S.S.R.
31 H4 Spree R E Germany
33 T9 Spreewald E Germany
31 H4 Spremberg E Germany
36 F3 Sprendlingen Hessen W Germany
36 E4 Sprendlingen Rheinland-Pfalz W Germany
22 K3 Sprimont Belgium
109 M5 Spring Texas
110 E5 Spring R Arkansas
110 B5 Spring R Oklahoma
101 N8 Spring B Utah
89 A7 Springbok S Africa
94 G5 Springboro Pennsylvania
109 J6 Spring Branch Texas
98 C1 Spring Brook N Dakota
118 A3 Springburn Alberta
144 C5 Springburn New Zealand
95 M6 Spring City Pennsylvania
112 C2 Spring City Tennessee
103 N2 Spring City Utah
118 D9 Spring Coulee Alberta
98 E9 Spring Cr Nebraska
101 L8 Spring Cr Nevada
145 D4 Spring Cr New Zealand
140 E4 Spring Cr N Terr Aust
140 F6 Spring Cr Queensland
110 B5 Springdale Arkansas
101 P4 Springdale Montana
102 H4 Springdale Nevada
123 Q4 Springdale Nfld
103 M4 Springdale Utah
100 H1 Springdale Washington
32 L8 Springe W Germany
106 F5 Springer New Mexico
109 K1 Springer Oklahoma
121 Q3 Springer, Mt Quebec
103 P7 Springerville Arizona
106 H4 Springfield Colorado
112 F5 Springfield Georgia
101 N6 Springfield Idaho
110 G2 Springfield Illinois
94 B9 Springfield Kentucky
95 P4 Springfield Massachusetts
110 C4 Springfield Missouri
122 G8 Springfield New Brunswick
144 C5 Springfield New Zealand
122 H9 Springfield Nova Scotia
94 D7 Springfield Ohio
114 G9 Springfield Oregon
141 G7 Springfield Queensland
112 F4 Springfield S Carolina
98 J7 Springfield S Dakota
110 K5 Springfield Tennessee
95 P3 Springfield Vermont
89 D8 Springfontein S Africa
99 Q6 Spring Green Wisconsin
99 P6 Spring Grove Minnesota
95 L7 Spring Grove Pennsylvania
111 C9 Springhill Louisiana
122 H8 Springhill Nova Scotia
110 K6 Spring Hill Tennessee
112 J2 Spring Hope N Carolina
99 U6 Spring Lake Michigan
95 N6 Spring Lake New Jersey
108 E1 Springlake Texas
103 J5 Spring Mts Nevada
126 H3 Spring Point Acklins I Bahamas
95 K6 Springs Pennsylvania
89 F6 Springs S Africa
119 P7 Springside Sask
144 D5 Springs Junction New Zealand
144 D5 Springston New Zealand
141 J6 Springsure Queensland
109 K3 Springtown Texas
95 R3 Springvale Maine
140 F6 Springvale Queensland
141 G3 Springvale Queensland
142 G4 Springvale W Australia
99 O6 Spring Valley Minnesota
119 M9 Spring Valley Sask
98 G7 Springview Nebraska
111 K8 Springville Alabama
94 J4 Springville New York
101 O9 Springville Utah
118 J7 Springwater Sask
13 H6 Sproatley England
28 F6 Sprogø isld Denmark
32 L6 Sprötze W Germany
94 D2 Spruce Michigan
123 O5 Spruce Brook Nfld
121 L7 Sprucedale Ontario
94 H8 Spruce Knob mt W Virginia
118 H5 Spruce Lake Sask
101 L9 Spruce Mt Nevada
112 E2 Spruce Pine N Carolina
103 M4 Spry Utah
25 B5 Spui R Netherlands
43 H9 Spulico, C Italy
108 G2 Spur Texas
118 C3 Spurfield Alberta
111 B11 Spurger Texas
106 B8 Spur Lake New Mexico
116 L6 Spurr, Mt Alaska
46 C2 Spuž Yugoslavia
22 H3 Spy Belgium
119 Q8 Spy Hill Sask
117 M11 Squamish Br Columbia
95 Q3 Squam L New Hampshire
95 S7 Squapan L Maine
101 P2 Square Butte Montana
95 S6 Square L Maine
122 D6 Squattack Quebec
99 M2 Squaw L Minnesota
123 L3 Squaw L Quebec
119 O5 Squaw Rapids Sask
43 H10 Squillace, Golfo di Italy
43 J8 Squinzano Italy
138 C2 Squires, Mt N Terr Australia
143 G7 Squires,Mt W Australia
116 G3 Squirrel R Alaska
120 F2 Squirrel R Ontario
70 N9 Sragen Java
46 D2 Srbica Yugoslavia
46 D1 Srbija Yugoslavia
48 F5 Srbobran Yugoslavia
68 F7 Srê Âmbêl Cambodia
46 C1 Srebrnica Yugoslavia
47 J2 Sredetska R Bulgaria
47 G2 Sredna Gora Bulgaria
51 K2 Sredne-Sibirskoye Ploskogor'ye tableland U.S.S.R.
52 D2 Sredneye Kuyto, Oz L U.S.S.R.
47 G3 Sredni Rodopi Bulgaria
58 G1 Sredniy Kalar U.S.S.R.
55 C3 Sredniy Ural ra U.S.S.R.
68 H6 Sre Khtum Cambodia
31 K3 Śrem Poland
48 F6 Srem Mitrovica Yugoslavia
48 E6 Srem Raca Yugoslavia
48 F5 Sremski Karlovci Yugoslavia
58 G1 Sretensk U.S.S.R.
76 F1 Srikakulam India
83 Sri Lanka rep S Asia
74 F1 Srinagar Kashmir
76 B4 Sringeri India
76 C6 Srivilliputtur India
42 H4 Srnetica Yugoslavia
31 K3 Środa Poland
31 K4 Środa Śląska Poland
76 F1 Srungavarapukota India
141 F3 Staaten R Queensland
26 O1 Stabburselv R Norway
33 Q4 Stäbelow E Germany
100 D4 Stabler Washington
28 A4 Staby Denmark
120 J5 Stackpool Ontario
15 D1 Stack Skerry isld Scotland
14 B4 Stack's Mts Irish Rep
16 E4 Sta. Cruz del Retamar Spain
100 E9 Stacy California
112 L3 Stacy N Carolina
32 K5 Stade W Germany
22 E2 Staden Belgium
36 F3 Staden W Germany
9 E4 Stadhampton England
28 A4 Stadil Denmark
28 A4 Stadil Fjord inlet Denmark
26 A9 Stadlandet Norway
25 G2 Stadskanaal Netherlands
36 F2 Stadt Allendorf W Germany
37 N5 Stadtamhof W Germany
37 K7 Stadtbergen W Germany
32 K8 Stadthagen W Germany
37 L2 Stadtilm E Germany
36 B3 Stadtkyll W Germany
32 H6 Stadtland W Germany
37 J3 Stadtlauringen W Germany
37 J2 Stadtlengsfeld E Germany
32 E8 Stadtlohn W Germany
32 L9 Stadtoldendorf W Germany
36 G4 Stadtprozelten W Germany
37 M2 Stadtroda E Germany
37 J4 Stadt Schwarzach W Germany
37 M3 Stadtsteinach W Germany
15 B4 Staffa isld Scotland
33 R7 Staffelde E Germany
37 L3 Staffelstein W Germany
44 F2 Staffora R Italy
8 D2 Stafford England
107 M4 Stafford Kansas
98 H7 Stafford Nebraska
94 K8 Stafford Virginia
141 K1 Stafford dist Brisbane, Qnsld
8 D2 Staffordshire co England
95 P5 Stafford Springs Connecticut
117 Q4 Stagg L N W Terr
45 H4 Stagno Italy
9 F3 Stagsden England
33 S4 Stahlbrode E Germany
33 S8 Stahnsdorf E Germany
52 B5 Staicele U.S.S.R.
38 K6 Stainach Austria
9 F5 Staines England
12 D3 Stair Scotland
13 H4 Staithes England
48 G2 Stakčín Czechoslovakia
53 E9 Stakhanov U.S.S.R.
28 B5 Stakroge Denmark
46 E1 Stalać Yugoslavia
27 J12 Stålboga Sweden
8 D6 Stalbridge England
9 H2 Stalham England
27 B11 Stalheim Norway
52 D3 Stalina Kanal U.S.S.R.
Stalingrad see Volgograd
117 L6 Stalin, Mt Br Columbia
Stalino see Donetsk
38 H8 Stall Austria
37 O5 Stallwang W Germany
48 J5 Stâlpeni Romania
119 M7 Stalwart Sask
13 F6 Stalybridge England
47 G1 Stamboliyski Dam Bulgaria
95 O5 Stamford Connecticut
9 F2 Stamford England
95 N4 Stamford New York
141 G5 Stamford Queensland
98 E6 Stamford S Dakota
108 H3 Stamford Texas
37 L6 Stammham W Germany
27 A11 Stamnes Norway
Stampalia isld see Astipálaia / Greece
100 D2 Stampede Washington
94 C8 Stamping Ground Kentucky
87 C10 Stampriet Namibia
25 E6 Stamproij Netherlands
109 O2 Stamps Arkansas
37 O5 Stamsried W Germany
26 G3 Stamsund Norway
94 J8 Stanadsville Virginia
99 M9 Stanberry Missouri
147 Q6 Stanchik U.S.S.R.
118 E7 Standard Alberta
103 O7 Standard Arizona
87 E11 Standerton S Africa
94 D3 Standish Michigan
101 M8 Standrod Utah
100 F4 Stanfield Oregon
110 K2 Stanford Indiana
110 M4 Stanford Kentucky
101 P2 Stanford Montana
9 G4 Stanford-le-Hope England
8 D3 Stanford on Teme England
27 K14 Stånga Sweden
27 E11 Stange Norway
87 F11 Stanger S Africa
45 L1 Stanghella Italy
26 C9 Stangvik Norway
126 F2 Staniard Cr Andros Bahamas
102 D4 Stanislaus R California
Stanislav see Ivano-Frankovsk
46 F2 Stanke Dimitrov Bulgaria
37 P4 Staňkov Czechoslovakia
131 G8 Stanley Falkland Is
101 L5 Stanley Idaho
112 F2 Stanley N Carolina
98 D1 Stanley N Dakota
122 F7 Stanley New Brunswick
106 E6 Stanley New Mexico
109 M1 Stanley Oklahoma
15 E4 Stanley Scotland
139 H8 Stanley Tasmania
94 J8 Stanley Virginia
99 Q5 Stanley Wisconsin
119 M3 Stanley Mission Sask
144 D5 Stanley, Mt New Zealand
140 B6 Stanley,Mt N Terr Aust
139 G8 Stanley, Mt Tasmania
86 C6 Stanley Pool Zaïre
Stanleyville see Kisangani
118 F7 Stanmore Alberta
99 T2 Stannard Rock Michigan
125 P9 Stann Creek Belize
13 G3 Stannington England
55 F3 Stanovka U.S.S.R.
55 D2 Stanovoy U.S.S.R.
51 M3 Stanovoy Khrebet mts U.S.S.R.
41 P3 Stans Austria
138 E5 Stansbury S Australia
136 F6 Stansmore Ra W Australia
142 G5 Stansmore Ra W Australia
9 G4 Stansted England
141 K8 Stanthorpe Queensland
99 L9 Stanton Iowa
94 D9 Stanton Kentucky
94 B3 Stanton Michigan
98 E2 Stanton N Dakota
98 J8 Stanton Nebraska
147 J1 Stanton N W Terr
110 G6 Stanton Tennessee
108 F3 Stanton Texas
6 E6 Stanton Banks Atlantic Oc
94 B3 Stanwood Michigan
117 M11 Stanwood Washington
41 N3 Stanzach Austria
33 N9 Stapelburg E Germany
25 F3 Staphorst Netherlands
9 E5 Stapleford England
111 J11 Stapleton Alabama
112 E4 Stapleton Georgia
111 F9 Star Mississippi
112 H2 Star N Carolina
109 J4 Star Texas
54 F3 Star' U.S.S.R.
48 F1 Stara L'ubovňa Czechoslovakia
37 O3 Stará-Role Czechoslovakia
52 D5 Staraya Russa U.S.S.R.
55 E1 Staraya Vorpavla U.S.S.R.
47 H2 Stara Zagora Bulgaria
119 U9 Starbuck Manitoba
99 L4 Starbuck Minnesota
100 G3 Starbuck Washington
135 L9 Starbuck I Pacific Oc
111 E8 Star City Arkansas
94 A6 Star City Indiana
119 N6 Star City Sask
94 H7 Star City W Virginia
141 G2 Starcke Queensland
8 C6 Starcross England
37 O4 Staré Sedliště Czechoslovakia
31 J2 Stargard Poland
42 H4 Stari Majdan Yugoslavia
31 N6 Starina Czechoslovakia
52 D6 Staritsa U.S.S.R.
103 O10 Stark Arizona
101 L2 Stark Montana
95 Q2 Stark New Hampshire
55 C6 Star Karabutak U.S.S.R.
113 E8 Starke Florida
100 J5 Starkey Idaho
100 G4 Starkey Oregon
109 O5 Starks Louisiana
106 F4 Starkville Colorado
111 H8 Starkville Mississippi
98 H1 Starkweather N Dakota
99 R3 Starlake Wisconsin
41 O1 Starnberg W Germany
54 K7 Star'obel'sk U.S.S.R.
54 D4 Starodub U.S.S.R.
31 L2 Starogard Poland
48 M4 Starokazache U.S.S.R.
48 L1 Staro Konstantinov U.S.S.R.
47 J2 Staro Oryakhovo Bulgaria
31 O2 Starosielce Poland
55 F3 Starosoldatskoye U.S.S.R.
55 C4 Starosubkhangulovo U.S.S.R.
55 C3 Staroutkinsk U.S.S.R.
52 G5 Starovercheskaya U.S.S.R.
52 H6 Staroye Baysarovo U.S.S.R.
102 F1 Star Pk Nevada
8 C7 Start Pt England
15 F1 Start Pt Scotland
48 F1 Stary Sącz Poland
48 H1 Stary Sambor U.S.S.R.
52 H6 Staryye Zyattsy U.S.S.R.
52 H6 Staryy Menzelyabash U.S.S.R.
54 J5 Staryy Oskol U.S.S.R.
52 D5 Staryy Ryad U.S.S.R.
33 P9 Stassfurt E Germany
31 N5 Staszów Poland
99 N7 State Center Iowa
94 K6 State College Pennsylvania
111 H10 State Line Mississippi
Staten I Argentina see Estados, I de los
95 N6 Staten I New York
112 F5 Statesboro Georgia
112 G2 Statesville N Carolina
27 D12 Stathelle Norway
33 S10 Stauchitz E Germany
36 F2 Staufenberg W Germany
100 E6 Stauffer Oregon
8 D4 Staunton England
110 G2 Staunton Illinois
94 H8 Staunton Virginia
27 A13 Stavanger Norway
22 H3 Stave Belgium
117 M11 Stave L Br Columbia
13 F5 Staveley Cumbria England
9 E1 Staveley Derby England
22 K3 Stavelot Belgium
118 D8 Stavely Alberta
33 S5 Staven E Germany
25 B5 Stavenisse Netherlands
25 D3 Staveren Netherlands
28 A5 Stavning Denmark
28 F3 Stavnshoved C Denmark
28 J6 Stavreby Denmark
28 F6 Stavreshoved C Denmark
53 F10 Stavropol' U.S.S.R.
55 E4 Stavropolka U.S.S.R.
53 F10 Stavropol'skaya Vozvyshennost' uplands U.S.S.R.
46 E5 Stavrós Greece
47 G9 Stavrós, Akra C Crete Greece
47 G3 Stavroúpolis Greece
139 G6 Stawell Victoria
31 N2 Stawiski Poland
31 L4 Stawiszyn Poland
120 K8 Stayner Ontario
100 C5 Stayton Oregon
45 H4 Stazzema Italy
102 E2 Steamboat Nevada
106 D1 Steamboat Springs Colorado
94 C10 Stearns Kentucky
31 M2 Stębark Poland
116 F5 Stebbins Alaska
33 Q7 Stechow E Germany
41 J2 Steckborn Switzerland
28 B7 Stedesand W Germany
116 R4 Steel Creek Alaska
111 K8 Steele Alabama
110 G5 Steele Missouri
98 G3 Steele N Dakota
98 K9 Steele City Nebraska
146 E13 Steele I Antarctica
117 C5 Steele,Mt Yukon Terr
110 G3 Steeleville Illinois
120 D4 Steel R Ontario
95 L6 Steelton Pennsylvania
110 E4 Steelville Missouri
25 B5 Steenbergen Netherlands
89 G5 Steenkamps Berg mts S Africa
22 G2 Steenkerque Belgium
117 P6 Steen River Alberta
25 D6 Steensel Netherlands
100 G7 Steens Mt Oregon
115 O2 Steenstrups Gletscher gla Greenland
22 D2 Steenvoorde France
22 D2 Steenwerck France
25 F3 Steenwijk Netherlands
119 M5 Steep Cr Sask
119 O3 Steephill L Sask
71 D6 Steep Pt Philippines
115 K7 Steep Rock Manitoba
118 K2 Steep Rock Ontario
143 B6 Steere, Mt W Australia
13 G6 Steeton England
48 L3 Ştefaneşti Romania
86 G5 Stefanie, L Ethiopia
43 F10 Stefano di Cam., S Sicily
146 A4 Stefansson B Antarctica
147 H3 Stefansson I N W Terr
133 C6 Steffen mt Chile/Arg
36 F2 Steffenberg W Germany
98 C8 Stegall Nebraska
28 J7 Stege Denmark
28 J6 Stege Bugt B Denmark
33 P8 Stegelitz E Germany
99 T8 Steger Illinois
87 F11 Stegi Swaziland
33 S8 Steglitz W Berlin
100 E1 Stehekin Washington
38 L7 Steiermark prov Austria
37 J4 Steigerwald hills W Germany
37 L5 Stein W Germany
37 L3 Steinach E Germany
37 J5 Steinach W Germany
36 H3 Steinau W Germany
99 K9 Steinauer Nebraska
37 J2 Steinbach E Germany
118 E1 Steinbach Manitoba
36 E6 Steinbach W Germany
37 K2 Steinbach Hallenberg E Germany
28 D7 Steinberg W Germany
38 G6 Steinberge Austria
36 C6 Steinbourg France
129 H6 Steinen R Brazil
38 G7 Steinernes Meer mts Austria
32 H7 Steinfeld W Germany
22 K4 Steinfort Luxembourg
32 H8 Steinhagen W Germany
113 D8 Steinhatchee Florida
87 C10 Steinhausen Namibia
37 L3 Steinheid E Germany
36 F3 Steinheim W Germany
33 M5 Steinhorst W Germany
32 K8 Steinhuder Meer L W Germany
32 L5 Steinkirchen W Germany
26 E8 Steinkjer Norway
87 C11 Steinkopf S Africa
38 L7 Steinplan mt Austria
106 B9 Steins New Mexico
36 F5 Steinsfurt W Germany
37 L3 Steinwiesen W Germany
22 G1 Stekene Belgium
112 K3 Stella N Carolina
99 L9 Stella Nebraska
122 K8 Stellarton Nova Scotia
45 K2 Stellata Italy
32 M6 Stelle W Germany
87 C12 Stellenbosch S Africa
116 Q6 Steller, Mt Alaska
42 D2 Stelvio, Passo di Italy
112 J1 Stem N Carolina
32 K7 Stemmen W Germany
26 C8 Stemshaug Norway
32 H8 Stemwede W Germany
22 J5 Stenay France
28 A3 Stenbjerg Denmark
33 P7 Stendal E Germany
52 B6 Stende U.S.S.R.
28 D5 Stenderup Denmark
28 D7 Stenderup W Germany
119 P7 Stenen Sask
28 E2 Stenhöj Denmark
138 D6 Stenhouse B S Australia
28 D3 Stenild Denmark
28 H5 Stenlille Denmark
28 J5 Stenløse Denmark
15 G2 Stenness Shetland Scotland
15 E1 Stenness,L.of Orkney Scotland
26 J6 Stensele Sweden
27 G14 Stensjön Sweden
27 G13 Stenstorp Sweden
28 E6 Stenstrup Denmark
26 L5 Stenträsk Sweden
27 E13 Stenungsund Sweden
28 F4 Stenvad Denmark
78 K1 Stepanavan U.S.S.R.
78 L2 Stepankert U.S.S.R.
55 C5 Stepanovka U.S.S.R.
33 O5 Stepenitz R E Germany
33 P6 Stepenitz R E Germany
37 O6 Stephansposching W Germany
98 K1 Stephen Minnesota
109 O2 Stephens Arkansas
94 J7 Stephens City Virginia
138 F4 Stephens Creek New S Wales
117 H8 Stephens I Br Col
99 T4 Stephenson Michigan
145 D1 Stephenson I New Zealand
117 G7 Stephens Pass Alaska
115 O8 Stephenville Nfld
109 J3 Stephenville Texas
123 O5 Stephenville Crossing Nfld
57 D5 Step' Karnabchul' U.S.S.R.
55 F5 Stepnogorsk U.S.S.R.
57 G3 Stepnoye U.S.S.R.
55 F4 Stepnyak U.S.S.R.
116 G9 Stepovak B Alaska
28 C6 Stepping Denmark
103 K2 Steptoe Nevada
36 H3 Sterbfritz W Germany
87 E12 Sterkstroom S Africa
108 F1 Sterley Texas
55 C4 Sterlibashevo U.S.S.R.
106 G1 Sterling Colorado
99 R8 Sterling Illinois
107 M3 Sterling Kansas
94 C2 Sterling Michigan
98 F3 Sterling N Dakota
98 K9 Sterling Nebraska
109 J1 Sterling Oklahoma
103 N2 Sterling Utah
108 G4 Sterling City Texas
55 C4 Sterlitamak U.S.S.R.
33 P5 Sternberg E Germany
31 K6 Šternberk Czechoslovakia
22 H2 Sterrebeek Belgium
52 E4 Steshevskaya U.S.S.R.
31 K3 Stęszew Poland
46 D1 Stet Yugoslavia
41 K1 Stetten W Germany
Stettin see Szczecin
33 U5 Stettiner Haff E Germany
118 E6 Stettler Alberta
99 U3 Steuben Michigan
99 Q6 Steuben Wisconsin
94 G6 Steubenville Ohio
33 Q9 Steutz E Germany
9 F4 Stevenage England
120 E3 Stevens Ontario
145 D4 Stevens, Mt New Zealand
119 U9 Stevenson Manitoba
100 D4 Stevenson Washington
138 C2 Stevenson R S Australia
119 W5 Stevenson L Manitoba
143 D10 Stevenson's L W Australia
99 R5 Stevens Pt Wisconsin
12 D2 Stevenston Scotland
116 N4 Stevens Village Alaska
94 A4 Stevensville Michigan
32 F9 Stever R W Germany
118 F8 Steveville Prov.Pk Alberta
28 K6 Stevns isld Denmark
22 J2 Stevoort Belgium
99 S8 Steward Illinois
110 H2 Stewardson Illinois
117 H8 Stewart Br Col
99 M5 Stewart Minnesota
102 E2 Stewart Nevada
117 D4 Stewart Yukon Terr
141 G2 Stewart R Queensland
140 C1 Stewart, C N Terr Aust
144 A7 Stewart I New Zealand
137 N3 Stewart Is Pacific Oc
143 C10 Stewart, Mt W Australia
15 D5 Stewarton Scotland
95 L7 Stewartstown Pennsylvania
110 B2 Stewartsville Missouri
127 K2 Stewart Town Jamaica
118 K8 Stewart Valley Sask
99 O6 Stewartville Minnesota
122 J8 Stewiacke Nova Scotia
32 K7 Steyerberg W Germany
9 F6 Steyning England
8 A4 Steynton Wales
38 K5 Steyr Austria
45 L4 Stia Italy
8 B6 Stibb Cross England
100 K5 Stibnite Idaho
9 G1 Stickford England
32 G6 Stickhausen W Germany
9 G1 Stickney England
98 H6 Stickney S Dakota
33 N9 Stiege E Germany
25 E2 Stiens Netherlands
45 L2 Stienta Italy
107 P6 Stigler Oklahoma
43 G8 Stigliano Italy
26 J9 Stigsjö Sweden
114 G6 Stikine R Alaska/Br Col
117 H6 Stikine Ranges Br Col
117 G7 Stikine Str Alaska
108 F4 Stiles Texas
110 K2 Stilesville Indiana
46 F6 Stilís Greece
28 D4 Stilling Denmark
13 G5 Stillington England
99 R7 Stillman Valley Illinois
99 O4 Stillwater Minnesota
102 F2 Stillwater Nevada
107 N5 Stillwater Oklahoma
101 L1 Stillwater R Montana
102 F2 Stillwater Ra Nevada
43 H10 Stilo, Pta Italy
110 B6 Stilwell Oklahoma
46 E7 Stimfalías, L Greece
101 M1 Stimson,Mt Montana
12 D3 Stinchar,R Scotland
98 E9 Stinking Water Cr Nebraska
46 E3 Štip Yugoslavia
47 G6 Stíra Greece
118 E9 Stirling Alberta
144 B7 Stirling New Zealand
140 C5 Stirling N Terr Aust
121 N8 Stirling Ontario
138 E5 Stirling S Australia
12 E1 Stirling Scotland
Stirling co see Strathclyde and Central regions
100 D10 Stirling City California
143 C9 Stirling, Mt W Australia
143 D8 Stirling, Mt W Australia
143 C10 Stirling Ra W Australia
44 H2 Stirone R Italy
98 J3 Stirum N Dakota
100 K3 Stites Idaho
119 V3 Stitt Manitoba
99 Q7 Stitzer Wisconsin
27 K14 Stjärnarve Sweden
26 N1 Stjernöya isld Norway
26 E8 Stjördalselv R Norway
26 E8 Stjördalshalsen Norway
13 E2 Stobo Scotland
41 K2 Stockach W Germany
27 G14 Stockaryd Sweden
9 E5 Stockbridge England
95 O4 Stockbridge Massachusetts
94 C4 Stockbridge Michigan
94 E8 Stockdale Ohio
109 K6 Stockdale Texas
33 N5 Stockelsdorf W Germany
48 C2 Stockerau Austria
36 B6 Stock,Etang du L France
101 O2 Stockett Montana
98 J9 Stockham Nebraska
37 L3 Stockheim W Germany
95 S6 Stockholm Maine
119 P8 Stockholm Sask
27 K12 Stockholm Sweden
27 J12 Stockholm county Sweden
40 G4 Stockhorn mt Switzerland
139 J5 Stockinbingal New S Wales
13 F6 Stockport England
94 F7 Stockport Ohio
111 J10 Stockton Alabama
102 C4 Stockton California
99 Q7 Stockton Illinois
107 L2 Stockton Kansas
119 S9 Stockton Manitoba
95 M8 Stockton Maryland
110 C4 Stockton Missouri
139 K5 Stockton New S Wales
144 C4 Stockton New Zealand
101 N9 Stockton Utah
99 Q3 Stockton I Wisconsin
116 O1 Stockton Is Alaska
13 G4 Stockton-on-Tees England
95 T2 Stockton Springs Maine
98 F9 Stockville Nebraska
31 N4 Stoczek Łukowski Poland
37 P4 Stod Czechoslovakia
26 E7 Stod Norway
99 P6 Stoddard Wisconsin
26 J9 Stöde Sweden
15 C2 Stoer,Pt of Scotland
28 C4 Stoholm Denmark
145 D4 Stoke New Zealand
9 G2 Stoke Ferry England
8 C7 Stoke Fleming England
9 F4 Stokenchurch England
8 D1 Stoke-on-Trent England
120 J7 Stokes Bay Ontario
112 H1 Stokesdale N Carolina
143 D10 Stokes Inlet W Australia
145 E4 Stokes, Mt New Zealand
139 G8 Stokes Pt Tasmania
140 B3 Stokes Ra N Terr Aust
53 C8 Stokhod R U.S.S.R.
28 G7 Stokkemarke Denmark
26 D7 Stokksund Norway
26 G3 Stokmarknes Norway
42 H5 Stolac Yugoslavia
33 N9 Stolberg E Germany
25 F7 Stolberg W Germany
147 Q8 Stolbovoy,Ostrov U.S.S.R.
48 F2 Stolica mt Czechoslovakia
37 O2 Stollberg E Germany
32 H5 Stollhamm W Germany
Stolp see Słupsk
90 A16 Stoltenhoff I Tristan da Cunha
32 K7 Stolzenau W Germany
36 D3 Stolzenfels W Germany
46 F5 Stómion Greece
36 B1 Stommeln W Germany
8 D2 Stone England
94 G5 Stoneboro Pennsylvania
9 E3 Stonebridge England
106 F3 Stone City Colorado
121 N6 Stonecliffe Ontario
100 F7 Stone Corral L Oregon
98 C9 Stoneham Colorado
122 A7 Stoneham Quebec
95 N7 Stone Harbor New Jersey
15 F4 Stonehaven Scotland
141 G6 Stonehenge Queensland
9 E5 Stonehenge anc mon England
8 D4 Stonehouse England
99 P4 Stone L Wisconsin
112 C4 Stone Mt Georgia
117 L6 Stone Mt. Prov. Park Br Col

74
Stonewall — Svir'

118 D1 **Stonewall** Manitoba
111 H9 **Stonewall** Mississippi
109 L1 **Stonewall** Oklahoma
109 J5 **Stonewall** Texas
121 L9 **Stoney Creek** Ontario
12 D4 **Stoneykirk** Scotland
26 J2 **Stonglandet** Norway
106 H4 **Stonington** Colorado
95 Q5 **Stonington** Connecticut
99 R10 **Stonington** Illinois
95 T2 **Stonington** Maine
119 M8 **Stony Beach** Sask
94 K10 **Stony Creek** Virginia
102 B2 **Stonyford** California
127 L2 **Stony Hill** Jamaica
118 D1 **Stony Mountain** Manitoba
118 D5 **Stony Plain** Alberta
112 F2 **Stony Point** N Carolina
95 N5 **Stony Point** New York
144 C6 **Stony R** New Zealand
114 J6 **Stony Rapids** Sask
116 J6 **Stony River** Alaska
9 F3 **Stony Stratford** England
120 H1 **Stooping** *R* Ontario
32 L4 **Stör** *R* W Germany
27 H12 **Storå** Sweden
28 C4 **Storå** *R* Denmark
26 G8 **Storåbränna** Sweden
28 O10 **Stórafjall** *mt* Faeroes
27 E12 **Stora Le** *L* Sweden
26 L5 **Stora Lule älv** *R* Sweden
26 K4 **Stora Lulevatten** *L* Sweden
26 F9 **Storån** *R* Sweden
26 J4 **Stora Sjoffallet** *L* Sweden
26 K6 **Storavan** *L* Sweden
26 K6 **Storberg** Sweden
27 L11 **Storby** Finland
27 A12 **Stord** Norway
26 B9 **Stordal** Möre og Romsdal Norway
26 E8 **Stordal** Sör-Tröndelag Norway
28 D3 **Store Arden** Denmark
28 F5 **Store Bælt** *chan* Denmark
26 G6 **Store Börgefjeld** *mt* Norway
27 H14 **Storebro** Sweden
28 B6 **Store Darum** Denmark
28 N3 **Store Dimon** *isld* Faeroes
28 G5 **Store Fuglede** Denmark
28 K6 **Store Heddinge** Denmark
28 C7 **Store Jyndevad** Denmark
28 K7 **Storeklint** *cliffs* Denmark
147 F10 **Store Koldewey** *isld* Greenland
26 P1 **Storelv** *R* Norway
27 E10 **Stor-Elvdal** Norway
28 K5 **Store Magleby** Denmark
28 H5 **Store Merløse** Denmark
26 R1 **Store Molvik** Norway
26 D8 **Stören** Norway
28 E7 **Store Rise** Denmark
28 J6 **Store Spjellerup** Denmark
28 J6 **Store Tårnby** Denmark
28 D2 **Store Vildmose** Denmark
26 H6 **Storfjellet,N** *mt* Sweden
26 G6 **Storfjellet,S** *mt* Sweden
26 B9 **Storfjord** *inlet* Norway
26 L6 **Storfors** Sweden
26 G5 **Storfosshei** Norway
26 H8 **Storhögen** Sweden
26 A9 **Storholmen** Norway
26 G7 **Storjorm** *L* Sweden
33 P5 **Störkanal** E Germany
114 G3 **Storkerson B** N W Terr
26 F8 **Storlien** Sweden
26 K7 **Storlögda** Sweden
32 L5 **Stormarn** *reg* W Germany
139 J9 **Storm B** Tasmania
89 E8 **Stormberge** *mts* S Africa
99 L7 **Storm L** Iowa
118 K1 **Stormy L** Ontario
119 P7 **Stornoway** Sask
15 B2 **Stornoway** Scotland
52 H4 **Storozhevsk** U.S.S.R.
48 K2 **Storozhinets** U.S.S.R.
26 F8 **Storrensjön** *L* Sweden
9 F6 **Storrington** England
15 B3 **Storr,The** *mt* Scotland
27 E11 **Stor-s** *L* Norway
26 L7 **Storsävarträsk** Sweden
26 F9 **Storsjö** Sweden
27 E10 **Stor-sjöen** *L* Norway
27 J11 **Storsjön** *L* Gävleborg Sweden
26 F9 **Storsjön** *L* Jämtland Sweden
28 H6 **Storstrøm** *co* Denmark
28 H7 **Storstrømmen** *chan* Denmark
119 Q9 **Storthoaks** Sask
26 J6 **Storuman** Sweden
27 G10 **Storvarden** *mt* Sweden
26 F9 **Storvigelen** *mt* Norway
27 J11 **Storvik** Sweden
26 J6 **Stor-vindein** *L* Sweden
28 E2 **Storvorde** Denmark
101 T5 **Story** Wyoming
99 N7 **Story City** Iowa
133 B7 **Stosch, I** Chile
37 M1 **Stössen** E Germany
26 F5 **Stött** Norway
41 N2 **Stotten** W Germany
37 L1 **Stotternheim** E Germany
28 D5 **Stouby** Denmark
121 L9 **Stouffville** Ontario
95 Q4 **Stoughton** Massachusetts
119 O9 **Stoughton** Sask
99 R7 **Stoughton** Wisconsin
22 K3 **Stoumont** Belgium
46 E4 **Stoupí** Greece
8 D3 **Stourbridge** England
8 D3 **Stourport** England
9 H5 **Stour,R** England
8 D3 **Stourton** England
94 E7 **Stoutsville** Ohio
28 D3 **Støvring** Denmark
28 E3 **Støvring** Denmark
13 F2 **Stow** Scotland
95 P2 **Stowe** Vermont
109 N6 **Stowell** Texas
9 G3 **Stowmarket** England
9 E4 **Stow on the Wold** England
28 E6 **Stoy** Denmark
59 K1 **Stoyba** U.S.S.R.
46 C2 **Stožac** *mt* Yugoslavia
45 M1 **Stra** Italy
33 R9 **Straach** E Germany
14 D2 **Strabane** N Ireland
12 C1 **Strachur** Scotland
14 D3 **Stradbally** Irish Rep
139 L3 **Stradbroke,I** Queensland Australia
44 F1 **Stradella** Italy
38 N8 **Straden** Austria
9 G2 **Stradsett** England
25 F6 **Straelen** W Germany
110 C4 **Strafford** Missouri
139 H8 **Strahan** Tasmania
103 N4 **Straight Cliffs** Utah
22 J4 **Straimont** Belgium
12 D3 **Straiton** Scotland
30 H6 **Strakonice** Czechoslovakia
47 H2 **Straldzha** Bulgaria
33 S4 **Stralsund** E Germany
27 E10 **Strand** Hedmark Norway
27 A12 **Strand** Rogaland Norway
89 A10 **Strand** S Africa
26 B9 **Stranda** Norway
28 C3 **Strandby** Nordjylland Denmark
28 F2 **Strandby** Vendsyssel Denmark
98 J9 **Strang** Nebraska
113 J10 **Strangers Cay** *isld* Bahamas
14 F2 **Strangford** N Ireland
14 F2 **Strangford L** N Ireland
27 J12 **Strängnäs** Sweden
27 H13 **Strångsjö** Sweden
140 C3 **Strangways** *R* N Terr Aust
140 C6 **Strangways Ra** N Terr Aust
138 D3 **Strangways Spr** S Australia
14 D2 **Stranorlar** Irish Rep
118 J7 **Stranraer** Sask
12 C4 **Stranraer** Scotland
36 D6 **Strasbourg** France
119 N7 **Strasbourg** Sask
106 F2 **Strasburg** Colorado
33 T5 **Strasburg** E Germany
110 H2 **Strasburg** Illinois
98 F3 **Strasburg** N Dakota
94 F6 **Strasburg** Ohio
94 J8 **Strasburg** Virginia
48 M3 **Strasheny** U.S.S.R.
38 N8 **Strass** Steiermark Austria
38 E7 **Strass** Tirol Austria
27 H12 **Stråssa** Sweden
38 K8 **Strassburg** Austria
36 C2 **Strassenhaus** W Germany
38 M7 **Strassgang** Austria
37 O6 **Strasskirchen** W Germany
38 H6 **Strasswalchen** Austria
95 O5 **Stratford** Connecticut
99 N7 **Stratford** Iowa
95 Q2 **Stratford** New Hampshire
145 E3 **Stratford** New Zealand
109 L1 **Stratford** Oklahoma
122 A8 **Stratford** Quebec
98 H4 **Stratford** S Dakota
108 B7 **Stratford** Texas
139 H7 **Stratford** Victoria
99 Q5 **Stratford** Wisconsin
9 H4 **Stratford St. Mary** England
9 E3 **Stratford upon Avon** England
138 E6 **Strathalbyn** S Australia
15 D5 **Strathaven** Scotland
12 D2 **Strathblane** Scotland
15 D2 **Strath Brora** Scotland
15 D3 **Strath Carron** Scotland
119 R8 **Strathclair** Manitoba
15 D5 **Strathclyde** *reg* Scotland
117 L11 **Strathcona Prov. Park** Br Columbia
15 E3 **Strath Dearn** Scotland
15 D3 **Strath Farrar** Scotland
15 E2 **Strath Halladale** Scotland
141 G3 **Strathleven** Queensland
123 L7 **Strathlorne** Nova Scotia
13 E1 **Strathmiglo** Scotland
118 D7 **Strathmore** Alberta
141 G4 **Strathmore** Queensland
15 E4 **Strathmore** *dist* Scotland
117 M9 **Strathnaver** Br Columbia
15 D3 **Strathpeffer** Scotland
120 J10 **Strathroy** Ontario
15 D2 **Strathy Pt** Scotland
12 D1 **Strathyre** Scotland
106 H2 **Stratton** Colorado
8 B6 **Stratton** England
95 R1 **Stratton** Maine
98 E9 **Stratton** Nebraska
37 O6 **Straubing** W Germany
26 G4 **Straumen** Norway
30 H3 **Strausberg** E Germany
108 A3 **Strauss** New Mexico
37 K1 **Straussfurt** E Germany
101 Q3 **Straw** Montana
103 J2 **Strawberry** Nevada
110 E5 **Strawberry** *R* Arkansas
100 G5 **Strawberry Mt** Oregon
99 P7 **Strawberry Pt** Iowa
101 P9 **Strawberry Res** Utah
121 R5 **Strawhat Depot** Quebec
99 S9 **Strawn** Illinois
109 J3 **Strawn** Texas
37 O4 **Stráž** Czechoslovakia
38 M9 **Straze** Yugoslavia
31 K7 **Strážnice** Czechoslovakia
31 M6 **Štrba** Czechoslovakia
138 C5 **Streaky B** S Australia
118 G5 **Streamstown** Alberta
9 F5 **Streatham** England
9 E4 **Streatley** England
99 S8 **Streator** Illinois
31 H6 **Středočeský** *reg* Czechoslovakia
31 L7 **Strědoslovenský** *reg* Czechoslovakia
8 D5 **Street** England
98 G3 **Streeter** N Dakota
109 H5 **Streeter** Texas
109 L4 **Streetman** Texas
48 H6 **Strehaia** Romania
33 S10 **Strehla** E Germany
143 E9 **Streich Mound** W Australia
37 L4 **Streitberg** W Germany
48 H5 **Streiul** *R* Romania
48 J6 **Strejeştii de Jos** Romania
37 P4 **Střela** *R* Czechoslovakia
54 K5 **Strelitsa** U.S.S.R.
33 S6 **Strelitz-Alt** E Germany
56 D2 **Strelka** U.S.S.R.
28 B5 **Strellev Kirke** Denmark
142 C5 **Strelley** W Australia
142 C5 **Strelley R** W Australia
52 E2 **Strel'na** U.S.S.R.
52 E2 **Strel'na** *R* U.S.S.R.
52 C5 **Strenči** U.S.S.R.
41 M3 **Strengen** Austria
27 C12 **Strengen** Norway
13 G5 **Strensall** England
46 E2 **Strešer** *mt* Yugoslavia
54 B4 **Streshin** U.S.S.R.
9 G3 **Stretham** England
43 G10 **Stretto di Messina** Sicily
9 E1 **Stretton** Derby England
8 D1 **Stretton** England
9 F2 **Stretton** Leicester England
143 C10 **Stretton** W Australia
37 J3 **Streu** *R* W Germany
37 K3 **Streufdorf** E Germany
28 D5 **Strib** Denmark
37 P4 **Stříbro** Czechoslovakia
15 F3 **Strichen** Scotland
120 J3 **Strickland** Ontario
25 C5 **Strijen** Netherlands
109 N4 **Striker Cr.Res** Texas
26 G5 **Strimasund** Sweden
47 F3 **Strimón** *R* Greece
47 F4 **Strimonikós,Kólpos** *gulf* Greece
109 L1 **Stringtown** Oklahoma
12 C2 **Striven,L** Scotland
55 F3 **Strizhovo** U.S.S.R.
48 E5 **Striživojna** Yugoslavia
38 H6 **Strobl** Austria
46 D7 **Strofádhes** *isld* Greece
32 J7 **Ströhen** W Germany
14 C3 **Strokestown** Irish Rep
26 J10 **Ström** Sweden
33 T6 **Strom** *R* E Germany
15 E2 **Stroma** *isld* Orkney Scotland
32 H9 **Stromberg** Nordrhein-Westfalen W Germany
36 D4 **Stromberg** Rheinland-Pfalz W Germany
43 G10 **Stromboli** *isld* Italy
118 E6 **Strome** Alberta
15 C3 **Stromeferry** Scotland
26 L7 **Strömfors** Sweden
15 E2 **Stromness** Orkney Scotland
28 M2 **Strømø** *isld* Faeroes
98 J8 **Stromsburg** Nebraska
27 E13 **Stromstad** Sweden
26 H8 **Strömsund** Sweden
26 H8 **Stromsvattudal** *L* Sweden
12 D1 **Stronachlachar** Scotland
98 A5 **Stroner** Wyoming
111 D8 **Strong** Arkansas
95 R2 **Strong** Maine
111 H8 **Strong** Mississippi
107 O3 **Strong City** Kansas
107 L6 **Strong City** Oklahoma
118 L7 **Strongfield** Sask
99 Q9 **Stronghurst** Illinois
43 H9 **Strongoli** Italy
94 F5 **Strongsville** Ohio
15 F1 **Stronsay** Scotland
15 F1 **Stronsay Firth** Scotland
9 G5 **Strood** England
31 N6 **Stropkov** Czechoslovakia
112 F3 **Strother** S Carolina
8 D4 **Stroud** England
107 O6 **Stroud** Oklahoma
139 K4 **Stroud Road** New S Wales
95 M6 **Stroudsburg** Pennsylvania
138 F6 **Struan** S Australia
15 E4 **Struan** Scotland
32 G6 **Strücklingen** W Germany
38 L5 **Strudengau** *V* Austria
28 B3 **Struer** Denmark
46 D3 **Struga** Yugoslavia
52 C5 **Strugi Krasnye** U.S.S.R.
14 D2 **Strule** *R* N Ireland
99 P5 **Strum** Wisconsin
47 F3 **Struma** *R* Bulgaria
8 A3 **Strumble Head** Wales
46 F3 **Strumica** Yugoslavia
46 F3 **Strumitsa** *R* Yugoslavia
54 K1 **Strunino** U.S.S.R.
94 G5 **Struthers** Ohio
120 E4 **Struthers** Ontario
89 B10 **Struys B** S Africa
37 P3 **Stružná** Czechoslovakia
47 G2 **Stryama** *R* Bulgaria
101 L1 **Stryker** Montana
94 C5 **Stryker** Ohio
31 M4 **Stryków** Poland
28 F7 **Strynø** Denmark
26 B10 **Strynvatn** *L* Norway
48 H1 **Stryy** U.S.S.R.
31 J5 **Strzegom** Poland
31 L5 **Strzeice** Poland
31 J3 **Strzelce** Poland
138 F3 **Strzelecki Cr** S Australia
140 C5 **Strzelecki, Mt** N Terr Aust
139 J8 **Strzelecki Pk** Tasmania
31 K5 **Strzelin** Poland
31 L3 **Strzelno** Poland
31 N6 **Strzyżów** Poland
113 G10 **Stuart** Florida
99 M8 **Stuart** Iowa
98 G7 **Stuart** Nebraska
109 L1 **Stuart** Oklahoma
94 G10 **Stuart** Virginia
141 K7 **Stuart** *R* Queensland
140 B6 **Stuart Bluff Ra** N Terr Aust
138 D3 **Stuart Creek** S Australia
116 F5 **Stuart I** Alaska
117 L8 **Stuart L** Br Col
100 E2 **Stuart, Mt** Washington
144 A6 **Stuart Mts** New Zealand
140 B1 **Stuart Pt** N Terr Aust
138 C3 **Stuart Rge** S Australia
139 J5 **Stuart Town** New S Wales
41 O3 **Stubaier Alpen** *mt* Austria
41 O3 **Stubai Tal** Austria
38 L7 **Stub Alpe** *mts* Austria
28 J7 **Stubbekøbing** Denmark
32 J6 **Stubben** W Germany
28 B4 **Stubbergd Sø** *L* Denmark
28 F4 **Stubbe Sø** *L* Denmark
83 M9 **Stubbings Pt** Christmas I Indian Oc
41 M3 **Stuben** Austria
38 N7 **Stubenberg** Austria
38 M6 **Stübming** *R* Austria
47 H3 **Studen Kladenets Dam** Bulgaria
38 N7 **Studenzen** Austria
140 B5 **Studholme Hills** N Terr Aust
144 C6 **Studholme Junction** New Zealand
144 C6 **Studholme, Mt** New Zealand
47 G1 **Studina** Romania
9 E6 **Studland** England
28 B4 **Studsgård** Denmark
26 H8 **Stugun** Sweden
32 J9 **Stukenbrock** W Germany
9 G3 **Stump Cross** England
112 M2 **Stumpy Point** N Carolina
33 Q9 **Stumsdorf** E Germany
68 G6 **Stung Chinle** *R* Cambodia
68 G6 **Stung Sen** *R* Cambodia
68 H6 **Stung Treng** Cambodia
26 N2 **Stuorajavrre** *L* Norway
117 L9 **Stupendous Mt** Br Columbia
54 K2 **Stupino** U.S.S.R.
40 G7 **Stura** *R* Italy
44 B1 **Stura di Ala** *R* Italy
44 B3 **Stura di Demonte** *R* Italy
44 B1 **Stura di V,Grande** *R* Italy
44 B1 **Stura di Viu** *R* Italy
138 B4 **Sturdee** S Australia
146 K5 **Sturge I** Antarctica
110 D2 **Sturgeon** Missouri
94 C1 **Sturgeon** *R* Michigan
120 K6 **Sturgeon** *R* Ontario
119 U6 **Sturgeon B** Manitoba
94 B1 **Sturgeon B** Michigan
99 T5 **Sturgeon Bay** Wisconsin
99 T5 **Sturgeon Bay Canal** Wisconsin
115 M8 **Sturgeon Falls** Ontario
117 P8 **Sturgeon L** Alberta
121 M8 **Sturgeon L** Ontario
119 Q4 **Sturgeon Landing** Manitoba
118 C5 **Sturgeon R** Alberta
118 L5 **Sturgeon R** Sask
110 J4 **Sturgis** Kentucky
94 B5 **Sturgis** Michigan
111 G8 **Sturgis** Mississippi
106 H5 **Sturgis** Oklahoma
119 P7 **Sturgis** Sask
98 C5 **Sturgis** S Dakota
44 E3 **Sturla** Italy
8 D6 **Sturminster Newton** England
48 E3 **Štúrovo** Czechoslovakia
9 H5 **Sturry** England
138 D6 **Sturt B** S Australia
140 A4 **Sturt Cr** N Terr Aust
136 F5 **Sturt Cr** *R* W Australia
142 G4 **Sturt Creek** W Australia
141 F8 **Sturt Des** Qnsld/S Aust
99 T7 **Sturtevant** Wisconsin
138 F3 **Sturt, Mt** New S Wales
140 C3 **Sturt Plain** N Terr Aust
36 D5 **Stürzelbronn** France
36 E5 **Stutensee** W Germany
89 E9 **Stutterheim** S Africa
111 E7 **Stuttgart** Arkansas
107 L2 **Stuttgart** Kansas
36 G6 **Stuttgart** W Germany
37 K2 **Stützerbach** E Germany
26 H9 **Styggberg** Sweden
130 G6 **Suaçuí Grande, R** Brazil
70 C3 **Suai** Sarawak
86 G2 **Suakin** Sudan
99 T5 **Suamico** Wisconsin
124 E3 **Suaqui** Mexico
128 D2 **Suárez** *R* Colombia
87 D7 **Suarimo** Angola
71 F4 **Suban Pt** Philippines
52 C6 **Subate** U.S.S.R.
45 L4 **Subbiano** Italy
80 F5 **Subeihi** Jordan
69 J11 **Subi** *isld* Indonesia
42 E7 **Subiaco** Italy
142 A1 **Subiaco** *dist* Perth, W Aust
69 J1 **Subi Kecil** *isld* Indonesia
101 M7 **Sublett** Idaho
99 R8 **Sublette** Illinois
107 K4 **Sublette** Kansas
109 L6 **Sublime** Texas
48 F4 **Subotica** Yugoslavia
65 D2 **Subrag** China
110 D4 **Success** Missouri
118 J8 **Success** Sask
44 H3 **Succiso,Alpe di** *mt* Italy
48 F1 **Sucha** Poland
Suchan *see* **Partizansk**
31 J2 **Suchan** Poland
31 H7 **Suchdol** Czechoslovakia
31 M4 **Suchedniów** Poland
Süchow *see* **Xuzhou**
31 O2 **Suchowola** Poland
25 F6 **Süchteln** W Germany
100 C1 **Sucia I** Washington
14 C3 **Suck** *R* Irish Rep
100 H6 **Sucker Cr** Oregon
116 Q7 **Suckling,C** Alaska
33 P6 **Suckow** E Germany
128 E7 **Sucre** Bolivia
126 G10 **Sucre** Colombia
128 G5 **Sucunduri** *R* Brazil
130 D7 **Sucuriu** *R* Brazil
52 E5 **Suda** U.S.S.R.
108 E1 **Sudan** Texas
86 E3 **Sudan** *rep* Africa
52 F5 **Suday** U.S.S.R.
55 B5 **Sud'bodarovka** U.S.S.R.
9 G3 **Sudbury** England
120 J6 **Sudbury** Ontario
141 J5 **Sudbury** Queensland
86 E4 **Sudd** *dist* Sudan
128 G2 **Suddie** Guyana
33 O6 **Sude** *R* E Germany
28 D7 **Süderbrarup** W Germany
33 M7 **Suderburg** W Germany
32 K4 **Süderhastedt** W Germany
32 J4 **Süderhöft** W Germany
28 B7 **Süder Lügum** W Germany
52 E6 **Sudilova** U.S.S.R.
52 F5 **Sudislavl'** U.S.S.R.
32 E9 **Südlohn** W Germany
52 F6 **Sudogda** U.S.S.R.
54 E4 **Sudost'** *R* U.S.S.R.
83 L13 **Sud Ouest, Pte** Mauritius
79 C9 **Sudr** Egypt
54 G5 **Sudzha** U.S.S.R.
59 K3 **Sudzukhe** U.S.S.R.
17 G5 **Sueca** Spain
80 G8 **Su'eida** *R* Jordan
80 F8 **Su'eidat** Jordan
117 G8 **Suemez I** Alaska
108 D6 **Sue Pk** Texas
55 E3 **Suer'** *R* U.S.S.R.
21 H6 **Suèvres** France
84 J3 **Suez** Egypt
79 C8 **Suez Canal** Egypt
84 J4 **Suez,G.of** Egypt
80 G4 **Suf** Jordan
118 F8 **Suffield** Alberta
101 Q2 **Suffolk** Montana
95 L10 **Suffolk** Virginia
9 H3 **Suffolk** *co* England
61 K11 **Suga-jima** *isld* Japan
101 O6 **Sugar** Idaho
99 R7 **Sugar** *R* Wisconsin
106 G3 **Sugar City** Colorado
94 H5 **Sugar Grove** Pennsylvania
94 F10 **Sugar Grove** Virginia
109 M6 **Sugar Land** Texas
132 C2 **Sugarloaf** *mt* Brazil
143 C6 **Sugarloaf Hill** W Australia
113 F13 **Sugarloaf Key** *isld* Florida
139 L4 **Sugarloaf Pt** New S Wales
90 A13 **Sugar Loaf Pt** St Helena
71 G5 **Sugbuhan Pt** Philippines
37 J4 **Sugenheim** W Germany
119 P4 **Suggi L** Sask
69 F12 **Sugi** Indonesia
60 J10 **Sugi** Japan
78 D3 **Suğla Gölü** *L* Turkey
51 P2 **Sugoy** *R* U.S.S.R.
70 E1 **Sugut** *R* Sabah
47 G1 **Suhaia, L** Romania
70 B4 **Suhaid** Kalimantan
77 E7 **Şuḩār** Oman
37 K2 **Suhl** E Germany
42 H3 **Suhopolje** Yugoslavia
40 H3 **Suhr** *R* Switzerland
47 L6 **Suhut** Turkey
74 C4 **Sui** Pakistan
129 H6 **Suiá-Missu** *R* Brazil
100 E1 **Suiattle Pass** Washington
67 F2 **Suichang** China
67 E3 **Suichuan** China
58 F4 **Suide** China
65 H2 **Suifenhe** China
65 H3 **Suifen He** China
74 D6 **Suigam** India
65 G1 **Suihua** China
67 A2 **Suijang** China
67 D5 **Sui Jiang** *R* China
59 J2 **Suileng** China
58 E5 **Suining** China
67 C3 **Suining** China
128 E8 **Suipacha** Bolivia
22 G5 **Suippe** *R* France
14 D4 **Suir** *R* Irish Rep
60 T2 **Suishō tō** *isld* U.S.S.R.
95 L8 **Suitland** Maryland
68 K2 **Suixi** China
65 C7 **Sui Xian** China
67 D1 **Sui Xian** China
67 B2 **Suiyanchang** China
67 B3 **Suiyang** China
40 B2 **Suize** *R* France
59 H3 **Suizhong** China
74 F5 **Sujangarh** India
Suji *see* **Haixing**
70 L9 **Sukabumi** Java
70 K8 **Sukadana** Sumatra
61 O8 **Sukagawa** Japan
70 B6 **Sukamara** Kalimantan
70 L9 **Sukanegara** Java
69 K14 **Sukaraja** Indonesia
70 F2 **Sukau** Sabah
29 N8 **Sukeva** Finland
51 L2 **Sukhana** U.S.S.R.
65 J1 **Sukhanovka** U.S.S.R.
47 G1 **Sukhindol** Bulgaria
54 G2 **Sukhinichi** U.S.S.R.
54 K3 **Sukhodol'skiy** U.S.S.R.
52 F5 **Sukhona** *R* U.S.S.R.
68 D4 **Sukhothai** Thailand
55 D3 **Sukhoy Log** U.S.S.R.
53 F11 **Sukhumi** U.S.S.R.
115 O4 **Sukkertoppen Isflade** Greenland
74 C5 **Sukkur** Pakistan
76 E1 **Sukma** India
70 N9 **Sukohardjo** Java
69 D9 **Sukon,Ko** *isld* Thailand
33 P5 **Sukow** E Germany
87 C10 **Sukses** Namibia
55 C3 **Suksun** U.S.S.R.
60 F13 **Sukumo** Japan
60 F13 **Sukumo-wan** *B* Japan
71 L9 **Sukun** *isld* Indonesia
117 N8 **Sukunka** *R* Br Col
26 F8 **Sul** Norway
101 M4 **Sula** Montana
27 A10 **Sula** *isld* Norway
54 D7 **Sula** *R* U.S.S.R.
125 L2 **Sulaco** Honduras
74 C4 **Sulaiman Range** Pakistan
53 G11 **Sulak** U.S.S.R.
71 J6 **Sula,Kep** *isld* Indonesia
52 F4 **Sulanda** *R* U.S.S.R.
15 B1 **Sular Sgeir** *isld* Scotland
71 G5 **Sulat** Samar Philippines
70 Q10 **Sulat** *isld* Indonesia
116 K4 **Sulatna** Alaska
116 K4 **Sulatna** *R* Alaska
70 **Sulawesi** *isld* Indonesia
70 G7 **Sulawesi Selatan** Sulawesi
71 H4 **Sulawesi Utara** Sulawesi
78 K4 **Sulaymānīyah** Iraq
77 A7 **Şulb, Aş** *plain* Saudi Arabia
27 B12 **Suldal** Norway
27 B12 **Suldalsvatn** Norway
28 D3 **Suldrup** Denmark
31 J3 **Sulechów** Poland
31 J3 **Sulęcin** Poland
77 C1 **Suledeh** Iran
31 M4 **Sulejów** Poland
27 B12 **Suleskar** Norway
15 D1 **Sule Skerry** *isld* Scotland
32 M5 **Sülfeld** W Germany
69 E13 **Suliki** Sumatra
85 B7 **Sulima** Sierra Leone
48 M5 **Sulina** Romania
48 M5 **Sulina** *R* Romania
32 J7 **Sulingen** W Germany
48 K3 **Suliţa** Romania
26 H4 **Sulitjelma** Norway
29 N10 **Sulkava** Finland
128 B4 **Sullana** Peru
111 H8 **Sulligent** Alabama
99 S10 **Sullivan** Illinois
110 E3 **Sullivan** Missouri
117 K10 **Sullivan Bay** Br Columbia
118 F6 **Sullivan L** Alberta
21 J6 **Sully** France
99 O8 **Sully** Iowa
20 K6 **Sully-la-Chapelle** France
18 G5 **Sully-sur-Loire** France
38 N8 **Sulm** *R* Austria
42 F6 **Sulmona** Italy
109 O5 **Sulphur** Louisiana
100 G9 **Sulphur** Nevada
109 L1 **Sulphur** Oklahoma
109 N2 **Sulphur** *R* Texas/Louisiana
103 M3 **Sulphurdale** Utah
109 M2 **Sulphur Springs** Texas
108 E3 **Sulphur Springs Cr** Texas
28 D2 **Sulsted** Denmark
120 H5 **Sultan** Ontario
78 C2 **Sultan Dağları** *mts* Turkey
47 J7 **Sultanhisar** Turkey
75 K5 **Sultanpur** India
33 R5 **Sülten** E Germany
71 G5 **Suluan** *isld* Philippines
70 G1 **Sulu Arch** *islds* Philippines
116 K5 **Sulukna** *R* Alaska
84 G3 **Suluq** Libya
55 E4 **Suly** U.S.S.R.
57 E5 **Sulyukta** U.S.S.R.
36 F7 **Sulz** W Germany
38 H7 **Sulzau** Austria
36 H5 **Sulzbach** Baden-Württemberg W Germany
36 C5 **Sulzbach** Saarland W Germany
37 M5 **Sulzbach-Rosenberg** W Germany
41 L2 **Sulzberg** Austria
41 M2 **Sulzberg** W Germany
146 J9 **Sulzberger B** Antarctica
37 L5 **Sulzbürg** W Germany
37 K3 **Sulzdorf** W Germany
32 M7 **Sülze** W Germany
117 C5 **Sulzer, Mt** Alaska
36 F5 **Sulzfeld** W Germany
37 J4 **Sulzheim** W Germany
37 J3 **Sulzthal** W Germany
71 H4 **Sumalata** Sulawesi Indonesia
100 C1 **Sumas** Washington
69 E13 **Sumatera Barat** *prov* Sumatra
69 F14 **Sumatera Selatan** *prov* Sumatra
69 D11 **Sumatera Utara** *prov* Sumatra
113 C7 **Sumatra** Florida
101 S3 **Sumatra** Montana
64 E8 **Sumatra** *isld* Indonesia
128 G5 **Sumaúma** Brazil
71 J9 **Sumba** *isld* Indonesia
70 F4 **Sumbang Teluk** *B* Kalimantan
71 J9 **Sumba,Selat** *str* Indonesia
71 H9 **Sumbawa** *isld* Indonesia
71 H9 **Sumbawa Besar** Indonesia
88 C5 **Sumbawanga** Tanzania
58 E2 **Sümber** Mongolia
70 N9 **Sumbing, G** *mt* Java
69 E13 **Sumbing Gunung** *mt* Sumatra
28 N3 **Sumbø** Faeroes
15 G2 **Sumburgh Hd** Scotland
117 G7 **Sumdum** Alaska
130 H9 **Sumé** Brazil
70 L9 **Sumedang** Java
48 D4 **Sümeg** Hungary
70 O9 **Sumenep** Indonesia
78 M1 **Sumgait** U.S.S.R.
29 M9 **Sumiainen** Finland
40 G3 **Sumiswald** Switzerland
111 J8 **Sumiton** Alabama
55 E3 **Sumki** U.S.S.R.
55 E2 **Sumkino** U.S.S.R.
98 K10 **Summerfield** Kansas
94 F7 **Summerfield** Ohio
108 E1 **Summerfield** Texas
123 S4 **Summerford** Nfld
99 U4 **Summer I** Michigan
15 C2 **Summer I** Scotland
100 E7 **Summer L** Oregon
114 H8 **Summerland** Br Columbia
94 B10 **Summer Shade** Kentucky
123 P4 **Summerside** Nfld
122 J7 **Summerside** Pr Edward I
146 B5 **Summers Pk** Antarctica
110 E4 **Summersville** Missouri
94 G8 **Summersville** W Virginia
112 G4 **Summerton** S Carolina
112 E5 **Summertown** Georgia
112 B3 **Summerville** Georgia
123 T5 **Summerville** Nfld
94 H5 **Summerville** Pennsylvania
112 G4 **Summerville** S Carolina
116 N5 **Summit** Alaska
102 G7 **Summit** California
101 M1 **Summit** Montana
106 B9 **Summit** New Mexico
120 F5 **Summit** Ontario
100 B5 **Summit** Oregon
98 J4 **Summit** S Dakota
103 M4 **Summit** Utah
145 F4 **Summit** *mt* New Zealand
94 B2 **Summit City** Michigan
116 P5 **Summit L** Alaska
100 F8 **Summit L** Nevada
114 G6 **Summit Lake** Br Columbia
102 H2 **Summit Mt** Nevada
106 D4 **Summit Pk** Colorado
106 D4 **Summitville** Colorado
94 B6 **Summitville** Indiana
110 L6 **Summitville** Tennessee
110 J3 **Sumner** Illinois
99 O7 **Sumner** Iowa
110 C2 **Sumner** Missouri
144 B4 **Sumner** New Zealand
144 D5 **Sumner, L** New Zealand
117 G7 **Sumner Str** Alaska
61 N8 **Sumon-dake** *mt* Japan
48 D5 **Sumony** Hungary
60 H11 **Sumoto** Japan
70 F7 **Sumpangbinangae** Sulawesi
31 K6 **Šumperk** Czechoslovakia
100 G5 **Sumpter** Oregon
111 G10 **Sumrall** Mississippi
52 E3 **Sumskiy Posad** U.S.S.R.
112 G4 **Sumter** S Carolina
54 F6 **Sumy** U.S.S.R.
88 C4 **Suna** Tanzania
52 H5 **Suna** U.S.S.R.
60 P2 **Sunagawa** Japan
101 R9 **Sunbeam** Colorado
101 L5 **Sunbeam** Idaho
94 C10 **Sunbright** Tennessee
101 O1 **Sunburst** Montana
95 L10 **Sunbury** N Carolina
94 E6 **Sunbury** Ohio
95 L6 **Sunbury** Pennsylvania
139 G7 **Sunbury** Victoria
37 N6 **Sünching** W Germany
133 E3 **Suncho Corral** Argentina
107 M4 **Sun City** Kansas
95 Q3 **Suncook** New Hampshire
28 N2 **Sund** Faeroes
98 B5 **Sundance** Wyoming
70 D2 **Sundar** Sarawak
75 N8 **Sundarbans** *tidal forest* India/Bangladesh
70 K9 **Sunda,Selat** *str* Sumatra
140 C3 **Sunday Cr** N Terr Aust
143 F7 **Sunday Hill** W Australia
89 D9 **Sundays** *R* S Africa
142 E3 **Sunday Str** W Australia
28 B3 **Sundby** Denmark
27 J12 **Sundbyberg** Sweden
28 M1 **Sundene** *inlet* Faeroes
13 G4 **Sunderland** England
121 L8 **Sunderland** Ontario
32 H10 **Sundern** W Germany
28 D7 **Sundeved** *reg* Denmark
40 F2 **Sundgau** *reg* France
70 N9 **Sundoro, G** *mt* Java
118 E1 **Sundown** Manitoba
138 C2 **Sundown** S Australia
108 E2 **Sundown** Texas
118 C7 **Sundre** Alberta
27 K15 **Sundre** Sweden
121 L7 **Sundridge** Ontario
28 C4 **Sunds** Denmark
26 H8 **Sundsjö** Sweden
27 C12 **Sundsli** Norway
28 C3 **Sundstrup** Denmark
26 J9 **Sundsvall** Sweden
32 G10 **Sundwig** W Germany
94 B4 **Sunfield** Michigan
111 F8 **Sunflower** Mississippi
70 E6 **Sungaianjar** Kalimantan
69 E12 **Sungaiapit** Sumatra
70 B4 **Sungaibatu** Kalimantan
69 E13 **Sungaidareh** Sumatra
69 G14 **Sungaigerong** Sumatra
69 F12 **Sungaiguntung** Sumatra
69 E13 **Sungailimau** Sumatra
70 D5 **Sungaipinang** Kalimantan
69 F13 **Sungaisalak** Sumatra
69 G14 **Sungaiselan** Indonesia
70 E5 **Sungaitiram** Kalimantan
Sungari *R see* **Songhua Jiang**
69 E10 **Sungei Patani** Malaysia
70 F7 **Sungguminasa** Sulawesi
86 E3 **Sungikai** Sudan
103 P10 **Sunglow** Arizona
67 D3 **Sung-pai** China
69 G14 **Sungsang** Sumatra
78 E1 **Sungurlu** Turkey
120 C2 **Suni** Ontario
70 E2 **Suniatan Besar, G** *mt* Sabah
65 C5 **Suning** China
37 P3 **Suniperk** Czechoslovakia
42 H3 **Sunja** Yugoslavia
94 B7 **Sunman** Indiana
26 C9 **Sunndal** *R* Norway
26 C9 **Sunndalsöra** Norway
27 F12 **Sunne** Sweden
27 A10 **Sunnfjord** Norway
27 A12 **Sunnhordland** *reg* Norway
113 F11 **Sunniland** Florida
26 B9 **Sunnmöre** Norway
141 J7 **Sunnybank** Queensland
141 K2 **Sunnybank** *dist* Brisbane, Qnsld
122 K8 **Sunnybrae** Nova Scotia
118 C5 **Sunnybrook** Alberta
26 B9 **Sunnylven** Norway
118 F7 **Sunnynook** Alberta
103 J3 **Sunnyside** Nevada
123 T6 **Sunnyside** Nfld
103 O2 **Sunnyside** Utah
100 E3 **Sunnyside** Washington
99 R6 **Sun Prairie** Wisconsin
108 C7 **Sunray** Texas
116 N6 **Sunrise** Alaska
103 O6 **Sunrise** Arizona
98 B7 **Sunrise** Wyoming
101 O2 **Sun River** Montana
111 D11 **Sunset** Louisiana
109 K2 **Sunset** Texas
102 R11 **Sunset Beach** Hawaiian Is
103 N6 **Sunset Crater Nat.Mon** Arizona
117 P8 **Sunset House** Alberta
103 N6 **Sunshine** Arizona
101 Q5 **Sunshine** Wyoming
118 K1 **Sunstrum** Ontario
51 L2 **Suntar** U.S.S.R.
32 K8 **Süntel** *hills* W Germany
85 D7 **Sunyani** Ghana
37 M7 **Sünzhausen** W Germany
67 B6 **Suoi Rut** Vietnam
29 M9 **Suolahti** Finland
26 N2 **Suolovuobme** Norway
29 N10 **Suomenniemi** Finland
119 O2 **Suomi** Ontario
29 O7 **Suomussalmi** Finland
60 E12 **Suō-nada** *sea* Japan
29 N9 **Suonenjoki** Finland
29 M10 **Suonne** *L* Finland
29 N3 **Suorsapää** *mt* Finland
26 K4 **Suorva** Sweden
52 D4 **Suoyarvi** U.S.S.R.
Suozhen *see* **Huantai**
103 M5 **Supai** Arizona
75 M5 **Supaul** India
128 C6 **Supe** Peru
118 H7 **Superb** Sask
57 D5 **Superfosfatnyy** U.S.S.R.
103 N8 **Superior** Arizona
106 E2 **Superior** Colorado
101 L2 **Superior** Montana
98 J9 **Superior** Nebraska
99 O3 **Superior** Wisconsin
101 R8 **Superior** Wyoming
45 J1 **Superiore,L** Italy
115 L8 **Superior,L** U.S.A./Canada
68 E5 **Suphan Buri** Thailand
78 J2 **Süphan D** *mt* Turkey
45 O6 **Supino** Italy
100 F5 **Suplee** Oregon
54 C7 **Supoy** *R* U.S.S.R.
33 N8 **Süpplingen** W Germany
31 O2 **Supraśl** Poland
71 A1 **Supu** Halmahera Indonesia
48 H3 **Supuru de Jos** Romania
27 H12 **Sura** Sweden
52 G3 **Sura** U.S.S.R.
52 G6 **Sura** *R* U.S.S.R.
74 B4 **Surab** Pakistan
70 O9 **Surabaja** Java
77 F7 **Sūrak** Iran
70 N9 **Surakarta** Java
70 F5 **Suramana** Sulawesi
79 G3 **Sūrān** Syria
40 B5 **Şuran** *R* France
48 E2 **Šurany** Czechoslovakia
74 E8 **Surat** India
141 J7 **Surat** Queensland
74 E4 **Suratgarhi** India
69 D8 **Surat Thani** Thailand
31 O3 **Suraż** Poland
52 D6 **Surazh** U.S.S.R.
54 D4 **Surazh** U.S.S.R.
9 F5 **Surbiton** England
141 H6 **Surbiton** Queensland
48 F6 **Surčin** Yugoslavia
78 K4 **Sūrdāsh** Iraq
20 F4 **Surdon** France
48 H3 **Surduc** Romania
46 E2 **Surdulica** Yugoslavia
22 L4 **Sure** *R* Luxembourg
41 K4 **Surettahorn** *mt* Switzerland
102 D7 **Surf** California
95 N7 **Surf City** New Jersey
117 J9 **Surf Inlet** Br Col
18 E6 **Surgères** France
126 C3 **Surgidero de Batabanó** Cuba
50 G2 **Surgut** U.S.S.R.
76 D2 **Suriapet** India
61 N13 **Suribachi-yama** *mt* Japan
71 G6 **Surigao** Mindanao Philippines
71 G5 **Surigao Str** Philippines
21 F9 **Surin** France
68 F5 **Surin** Thailand
129 G2 **Suriname** Suriname
129 G3 **Suriname** *state* S America
99 S4 **Suring** Wisconsin
128 D2 **Suripá** *R* Venezuela
57 D5 **Surkhandar'inskaya Oblast** *prov* U.S.S.R.
77 C4 **Surmāq** Iran
26 C9 **Surnadalsöra** Norway
47 G2 **Sŭrnena Gora** Bulgaria
117 G6 **Surprise** Br Columbia
98 J8 **Surprise** Nebraska
121 Q3 **Surprise,L.de la** Quebec
133 F5 **Sur,Pta** Argentina
112 E6 **Surrency** Georgia
98 E1 **Surrey** N Dakota
9 F5 **Surrey** *co* England
95 L9 **Surry** Virginia
40 H3 **Sursee** Switzerland
20 B3 **Surtainville** France
84 F3 **Surte** Libya
71 N9 **Surubec,Danau** *L* Timor
78 G3 **Suruç** Turkey
61 M11 **Suruga-wan** *B* Japan
69 F14 **Surulangun** Sumatra
71 G7 **Surup** Mindanao Philippines
44 B1 **Susa** Italy
60 E11 **Susa** Japan
28 H6 **Susă** *R* Denmark
42 G6 **Sušac** *isld* Yugoslavia
42 F3 **Sušak** Yugoslavia
60 G12 **Susaki** Japan
60 J12 **Susami** Japan
57 G4 **Susamyr** U.S.S.R.
102 D1 **Susan** *R* California
77 A4 **Sūsangerd** Iran
52 F5 **Susanino** U.S.S.R.
102 D1 **Susanville** California
100 G5 **Susanville** Oregon
78 F1 **Suşehri** Turkey
33 N4 **Süsel** W Germany
37 Q5 **Sušice** Czechoslovakia
80 F2 **Susitha** Syria
116 M6 **Susitna** Alaska
116 O5 **Susitna L** Alaska
69 D9 **Suso** Thailand
61 M10 **Susono** Japan
95 M5 **Susquehanna** Pennsylvania
95 L5 **Susquehanna** *R* Pennsylvania
33 P10 **Süsser See** *L* E Germany
122 G8 **Sussex** New Brunswick
95 N5 **Sussex** New Jersey
101 T6 **Sussex** Wyoming
Sussex *co see* **West and East Sussex** *counties*
25 E6 **Susteren** Netherlands
45 K1 **Sustinente** Italy
117 K7 **Sustut Pk** Br Columbia
70 E2 **Susul** Sabah
116 K5 **Susulatna** *R* Alaska
47 J5 **Susurluk** Turkey
69 D12 **Sut** *mt* Sumatra
100 F10 **Sutcliffe** Nevada
48 L5 **Suţeşti** Romania
99 L7 **Sutherland** Iowa
98 E8 **Sutherland** Nebraska
87 D12 **Sutherland** S Africa
Sutherland *co see* **Highland** *reg*
143 F7 **Sutherland Ra** W Australia
98 E8 **Sutherland Res** Nebraska
144 A6 **Sutherland Sd** New Zealand
100 B6 **Sutherlin** Oregon
74 E3 **Sutlej** *R* Pakistan
102 D3 **Sutter Cr** California
9 F2 **Sutterton** England
9 G3 **Sutton** Cambridge England
9 F5 **Sutton** Greater London England
98 H2 **Sutton** N Dakota
98 J9 **Sutton** Nebraska
144 C6 **Sutton** New Zealand
121 L8 **Sutton** Ontario
121 S7 **Sutton** Quebec
94 G8 **Sutton** W Virginia
121 L5 **Sutton Bay** Ontario
9 E2 **Sutton Coldfield** England
9 E1 **Sutton-in-Ashfield** England
94 G8 **Sutton Res** W Virginia
9 E5 **Sutton Scotney** England
141 H5 **Suttor** *R* Queensland
116 J8 **Sutwik I** Alaska
89 D9 **Suurberge** *mts* S Africa
52 C5 **Suure-Jaani** U.S.S.R.
137 Q5 **Suva** Viti Levu Fiji
46 E1 **Suva Pl** *mt* Yugoslavia
46 D2 **Suva Reka** Yugoslavia
29 N9 **Suvasvesi** *L* Finland
Suvla, C *see* **Büyük Kemikli Br.**
54 H2 **Suvorov** U.S.S.R.
47 J1 **Suvorovo** Bulgaria
48 M5 **Suvorovo** U.S.S.R.
46 D1 **Suvo Rudište** *mt* Yugoslavia
61 M9 **Suwa** Japan
61 M9 **Suwa ko** *L* Japan
31 O1 **Suwałki** Poland
68 F5 **Suwannaphum** Thailand
113 D8 **Suwannee** Florida
119 R2 **Suwannee L** Manitoba
113 E7 **Suwanoochee Cr** Georgia
70 E4 **Suwaran, G** *mt* Kalimantan
80 G2 **Suwaysah** Syria
79 G6 **Suweidīya, Es** Syria
80 F6 **Suweima** Jordan
Suweis,El *see* **Suez**
58 G5 **Su Xian** China
88 A9 **Suye,L** Zambia
55 D1 **Suyevatpaul** U.S.S.R.
57 E3 **Suzak** U.S.S.R.
83 M14 **Suzanne,Pte** Kerguelen Indian Oc
52 F6 **Suzdal'** U.S.S.R.
19 N16 **Suze la Rousse** France
59 H5 **Suzhou** China
40 B3 **Suzon** *R* France
121 T4 **Suzor Côté** Quebec
61 L8 **Suzu** Japan
61 K11 **Suzuka** Japan
61 L8 **Suzu-misaki** *C* Japan
56 B4 **Suzun** U.S.S.R.
45 J2 **Suzzara** Italy
27 H10 **Svabensverk** Sweden
28 H6 **Særdborg** Denmark
26 P1 **Svaerholtklubben** *C* Norway
26 H9 **Svågan** *R* Sweden
26 H5 **Svaipa** *mt* Sweden
147 H12 **Svalbard** Arctic Oc
28 G5 **Svallerup** Denmark
48 H2 **Svalyava** U.S.S.R.
27 H16 **Svaneke** Denmark
28 E6 **Svanninge** Denmark
27 F12 **Svanskog** Sweden
26 N5 **Svanstein** Sweden
26 R2 **Svanvik** Norway
54 F5 **Svapa** *R* U.S.S.R.
26 M4 **Svappavaara** Sweden
29 K11 **Svartå** Finland
27 G12 **Svartå** Sweden
26 N5 **Svartbyn** Sweden
115 O3 **Svartenhuk Halvö** *pen* Greenland
28 N1 **Svarthakstindur** *mt* Faeroes
26 G5 **Svartisen** *mt* Norway
26 M6 **Svartlå** Sweden
27 H11 **Svartnäs** Sweden
26 M6 **Svartöstaden** Sweden
54 K7 **Svatovo** U.S.S.R.
27 D10 **Svatsum** Norway
68 G7 **Svay Rieng** Cambodia
52 G5 **Svecha** U.S.S.R.
27 F16 **Svedala** Sweden
26 L7 **Svedun** Sweden
26 G9 **Sveg** Sweden
26 A10 **Svelgen** Norway
27 D12 **Svelvik** Norway
52 C6 **Švenčionėliai** U.S.S.R.
28 F6 **Svendborg** Denmark
Svendborg *co see* **Fyn**
27 F14 **Svenljunga** Sweden
146 C4 **Svenner I** Antarctica
27 H12 **Svennevad** Sweden
26 F6 **Svenningdal** Norway
100 B3 **Svensen** Oregon
26 J2 **Svensgrunnen** *shoal* Norway
28 D6 **Svenstrup** Sønderjylland Denmark
50 F3 **Sverdlovsk** U.S.S.R.
50 F3 **Sverdlovskaya Oblast'** *prov* U.S.S.R.
115 K1 **Sverdrup Chan** N W Terr
50 G1 **Sverdrup, Ostrov** *isld* U.S.S.R.
42 G5 **Sveti Andrija** *isld* Yugoslavia
46 E3 **Sveti Nikole** Yugoslavia
31 M1 **Svetloye** U.S.S.R.
51 L3 **Svetlyy** U.S.S.R.
52 C4 **Svetogorsk** U.S.S.R.
46 E1 **Svetozarevo** Yugoslavia
37 P5 **Švihov** Czechoslovakia
48 G6 **Svilajnac** Yugoslavia
47 H3 **Svilengrad** Bulgaria
28 F6 **Svindinge** Denmark
28 G5 **Svinninge** Denmark
28 O9 **Svinø** Faeroes
Svinoy *isld see* **Svinø**
52 D4 **Svir'** *R* U.S.S.R.

52 D4 Sviritsa U.S.S.R.	15 E5 Symington Scotland	37 O4 Tachov Czechoslovakia	67 G5 Taiwan rep E Asia	139 H6 Tallangatta Victoria
56 F4 Svirak U.S.S.R.	124 H5 Symon Mexico	139 L4 Tacking Pt New S Wales	67 G1 Tai Xian China	111 L8 Tallapoosa Georgia
52 D4 Svir'stroy U.S.S.R.	8 D4 Symonds Yat England	71 G5 Tacloban Philippines	67 G1 Taixing China	111 K9 Tallapoosa R Alabama
47 G1 Svishtov Bulgaria	71 F4 Syndicate Philippines	103 K9 Tacna Arizona	46 E7 Ta'iyetos mt Greece	9 Q16 Tallard France
53 C7 Svisloch' R U.S.S.R.	142 F3 Synnott Ra W Australia	133 C1 Tacna Peru	80 D4 Taiyiba Israel	26 H10 Tållåsen Sweden
31 J6 Svitavy Czechoslovakia	56 H3 Synnyr, Khrebet mts U.S.S.R.	20 J4 Tacoignières France	80 E3 Taiyiba Israel	70 M9 Tanah,Tg C Java
52 G6 Sviyaga R U.S.S.R.		117 M12 Tacoma Washington	79 F7 Taiyiba R Jordan	70 F7 Tanakeke isld Sulawesi
51 M3 Svobodnyy U.S.S.R.	54 N2 Syntul U.S.S.R.	133 E3 Tacó Pozo Argentina	86 B6 Taiyuan China	34 G11 Tananarive see
28 J5 Svogerslev Denmark	55 E1 Syn'yakha R U.S.S.R.	128 E7 Tacora mt Chile	65 B6 Taiyue Shan mt China	8 C4 Antananarivo
37 O4 Svojàin Czechoslovakia	56 C4 Synzas U.S.S.R.	130 E7 Tacarembo Uruguay	Taizhou see Linhai	86 G3 Tana, L Ethiopia
28 G3 Svolvær Norway	48 L3 Synzhereya U.S.S.R.	130 B10 Tacuaras Paraguay	26 M5 Taizhou China	136 J3 Tanamerah W Irian
31 J6 Svratka R Czechoslovakia	94 B5 Syracuse Indiana	131 G3 Tacuarembó Uruguay	40 D6 Taizhou China	140 A4 Tanami N Terr Aust
46 E1 Svrljig Yugoslavia	Syracuse Italy see Siracusa	131 H4 Tacuari,R Uruguay	65 F4 Tai'izz R Yemen	68 H7 Tan An Vietnam
46 E1 Svrljiške Pl mt Yugoslavia	107 J3 Syracuse Kansas	130 C8 Tacuati Paraguay	72 E6 Ta'izz N Yemen	116 L4 Tanana Alaska
52 F5 Svyatogor'ye U.S.S.R.	98 K9 Syracuse Nebraska	124 E3 Tacupeto Mexico	86 H3 Ta'izz Yemen	116 N4 Tanana R Alaska
52 E1 Svyatoy Nos, Mys C U.S.S.R.	121 O9 Syracuse New York	61 N8 Tadami R Japan	110 G2 Tajohli Illinois	Tananarive see
68 C3 Swa R Burma	101 N8 Syracuse Utah	13 G6 Tadcaster England	111 E9 Tallulah Louisiana	140 C3 Antananarivo
9 G2 Swaffham England	57 E4 Syrdarinsk, Obl U.S.S.R.	85 F4 Taddart watercourse Algeria	102 A2 Talmage California	116 E5 Tanunak Alaska
141 K5 Swain Reefs Gt Barrier Reef Aust	57 E3 Syrdar'ya R U.S.S.R.	85 B3 Tadémaït,Pl.du Algeria	107 N2 Talmage Nebraska	5 A Tanzania rep Africa
112 E5 Swainsboro Georgia	57 D3 Syrdar'ya R U.S.S.R.	85 B5 Tadjakant Mauritania	99 J9 Talmage Nebraska	88 C4 Tao'an China
134 B4 Swains I Pacific Oc	57 D4 Syr Dar'ya Oblast' prov U.S.S.R.	85 E3 Tadjmout Algeria	40 B3 Talmont France	67 G2 Taohua Dao isld China
81 E16 Swain's I S Pacific Oc		86 H3 Tadjoura Djibouti	56 B4 Tal'menka U.S.S.R.	
87 B10 Swakopmund S Africa	79 G4 Syriam Burma	9 E3 Tadmarton England	80 B7 Talmey Yafe Israel	67 D2 Taojiang China
9 G5 Swale,R England	68 C4 Syrian Desert see Badiet esh Sham	145 D4 Tadmor New Zealand	18 D6 Talmont France	68 D7 Tao,Ko isld Thailand
137 O4 Swallow Is Santa Cruz Is		60 Q2 Tadoshi Japan	124 H8 Talnoye U.S.S.R.	87 H13 Taolañaro Madagascar
70 C1 Swallow Reef S China Sea	55 E1 Syrkovoye, Oz L U.S.S.R.	61 M8 Tadotsu Japan	107 M5 Taloga Oklahoma	67 D2 Taoluo China
106 F3 Swallows Colorado	28 G2 Syr Odde C Denmark	122 C5 Tadoussec Quebec	70 F4 Talok Kalimantan	125 K7 Tancuayalab Mexico
118 D7 Swalwell Alberta	54 L4 Syrskiy U.S.S.R.	76 D3 Tadpatri India	75 K5 Tanda India	Tsonan see Tao'an
9 E6 Swanage England	55 D3 Syssert' U.S.S.R.	57 E5 Tadzhikistan S.S.R U.S.S.R.	71 G6 Tadag Mindanao	99 O6 Taopi Minnesota
142 A2 Swanbourne Beach dist Perth, W Aust	9 E2 Syston England	65 F6 Taech'ŏngdo isld S Korea	Philippines	43 G11 Taormina Sicily
139 G6 Swan Hill Victoria	52 D6 Syt'kovo U.S.S.R.	65 G5 Taedong R N Korea	106 E5 Tandah Ethiopia	106 E5 Taos New Mexico
118 B4 Swan Hills Alberta	55 F1 Sytomino U.S.S.R.	65 G7 Taehŭksan isld S Korea	48 L6 Tandárel Romania	106 D4 Taoudenni Mali
139 J8 Swan Is Tasmania	52 H4 Syumsi R U.S.S.R.	65 G6 Taejŏn S Korea	28 D6 Tanderup Denmark	85 D2 Taourirt Morocco
126 C6 Swan Is W Indies	52 H6 Syumsi U.S.S.R.	28 J7 Tærø isld Denmark	131 F6 Tandil Argentina	67 D2 Taouz Morocco
117 J8 Swan, L Br Columbia	52 H6 Syun' R U.S.S.R.	137 S5 Tafahi isld Pacific Oc	131 F6 Tandil, Sa del ra Argentina	67 D2 Taoyuan China
98 G4 Swan L S Dakota	47 F3 Syzran' U.S.S.R.	17 F2 Tafalla Spain	52 E6 Tandil R U.S.S.R.	55 E3 Tap R U.S.S.R.
103 M2 Swan L Utah	53 G7 Syzran' U.S.S.R.	85 F4 Tafassaset watercourse Algeria	70 F4 Tandjung Kalimantan	71 E8 Tapaan Passage
119 T9 Swan Lake Manitoba	48 E4 Szabadszállás Hungary	126 A1 Tafelberg mt Curaçao	70 F3 Tandjungbatu Kalimantan	Philippines
101 M2 Swan Lake Montana	48 G2 Szabolcsszatmár co Hungary	79 F8 Taff,R Wales	70 K4 Tandjungbuajabuaja isld	125 N10 Tapachula Mexico
112 E2 Swannanoa N Carolina	31 L4 Szadek Poland	79 F8 Tafila Jordan	Kalimantan	125 E10 Tapah Malaysia
119 Q6 Swan Plain Sask	31 K2 Szamocin Poland	85 C7 Tafiré Ivory Coast	70 C5 Tandjungkarang Sumatra	129 G5 Tapajós P Brazil
142 E3 Swan Pt W Australia	48 G2 Szamosszeg Hungary	26 B9 Tafjord Norway	69 C11 Tandjungpasir Java	129 G1 Tapanahoni R Suriname
31 K2 Swanquarter N Carolina	31 K3 Szamotuly Poland	17 F9 Tafna R Algeria	70 D3 Tandjungpriok Java	145 M9 Tapanatep Mexico
118 B3 Swan R Alberta	48 D3 Szany Hungary	106 F5 Tafoya New Mexico	70 F6 Tandjungredeb Kalimantan	144 B6 Tapanui New Zealand
143 B9 Swan R W Australia	48 F4 Szarvas Hungary	85 C3 Tafraoute Morocco	70 B5 Tandjungselor Kalimantan	128 E5 Tapauá Brazil
138 E5 Swan Reach S Australia	31 O5 Szczebrzeszyn Poland	102 E6 Taft California		128 E5 Tapauá R Brazil
114 J7 Swan River Manitoba	31 H2 Szczecin Poland	107 P6 Taft Oklahoma	74 C6 Tando Adam Pakistan	129 G3 Tapauá R Brazil
99 N2 Swan River Minnesota	31 K2 Szczecinek Poland	109 N8 Taft Texas	74 C6 Tando Muhammad Khan Pakistan	145 M9 Tapanatepec Mexico
103 L7 Swansboro N Carolina	31 M5 Szczerców Poland	95 P5 Taftville Connecticut	138 F4 Tandou L New S Wales	141 J6 Tapeau Brazil
139 K5 Swansea New S Wales	31 L4 Szczucin Poland	75 N5 Tafwap Nicobar Is	14 E2 Tandragee N Ireland	130 H9 Taperoá Brazil
112 F4 Swansea S Carolina	31 N5 Szczuczyn Poland	77 L2 Taga Bhutan	27 G10 Tandsjöborg Sweden	131 H3 Tapes, Pta. de C Brazil
139 J8 Swansea Tasmania	31 N2 Szczytno Poland	116 H4 Tagagawaik R Alaska	28 D7 Tandslet Denmark	32 H7 Tapfheim W Germany
8 C4 Swansea Wales	31 M2 Szecseny Hungary	143 A7 Tagan Harb W Australia	71 E8 Tandubas isld Philippines	71 F7 Tapiantana isld Philippines
95 T2 Swans I Maine	Szechwan prov see Sichuan	53 E10 Taganrog U.S.S.R.	76 C2 Tandur India	128 D5 Tapiche R Peru
118 K7 Swanson Sask	48 F2 Szécsény Hungary	54 K9 Taganrogskiy Zaliv gulf U.S.S.R.	83 L2 Taneatua New Zealand	27 L9 Tapiola Finland
117 J9 Swanson Bay Br Col	48 F4 Szeged Hungary	71 E3 Tagaytay City Philippines	145 F3 Taneatua New Zealand	
98 E9 Swanson Res Nebraska	48 G3 Szeghalom Hungary	71 F6 Tagbilaran Philippines	85 D4 Tanezrouft Algeria	139 K7 Tapirapecó, Serra mts Venezuela/Brazil
98 J9 Swanton Nebraska	48 E3 Székesfehérvár Hungary	85 D2 Taghit Algeria	85 D4 Tanezrouft reg Algeria	128 D3 Tapirapuã Brazil
94 D5 Swanton Ohio	48 E3 Szendrő Hungary	71 F9 Taghma N Terr Algeria	85 D5 Tanezzuft watercourse	71 A3 Tapis mt Malaysia
121 R8 Swanton Vermont	48 E3 Szentendre Hungary	106 F5 Tagliacozzo Italy	Libya/Algeria	124 E4 Tapisuelas Mexico
33 S4 Swanton E Germany	48 C4 Szentes Hungary	42 E2 Tagliamento R Italy	98 G4 Tanga Tanzania	75 M5 Tapljung Nepal
139 K3 Swan Vale New S Wales	48 D4 Szentgotthárd Hungary	45 O5 Táglio di Po Italy	75 N6 Tangail Bangladesh	28 J6 Tappe Denmark
101 O6 Swan Valley Idaho	48 G3 Szentlőrinc Hungary	22 G5 Tagnon France	31 K4 Tangakili C Japan	89 N6 Tappen N Dakota
99 M4 Swanville Minnesota	48 G2 Szerencs Hungary	71 F6 Tagolo Pt Philippines	28 D7 Tanat R Wales	94 C6 Tappan R Ohio
89 A10 Swartberg mt S Africa	48 D3 Szigetvár dist Hungary	26 J8 Tagsjöberg Sweden	88 B5 Tanganyika,L E Africa	74 F8 Tapti R India
120 K4 Swastika Ontario	48 J4 Szigetvár Hungary	48 J4 Tagu Romania	130 D10 Tangará Brazil	145 D4 Tapu New Zealand
81 H9 S. W. Australian Ridge Indian Oc	129 J6 Szikszó Hungary	129 J6 Taguatinga Brazil	28 D4 Tange R Denmark	
	31 N2 Szkwa R Poland	71 F5 Taguban isld Philippines	63 D9 Tanger Morocco	New Zealand
89 G6 Swaziland kingdom Africa	31 J4 Szlichtyngowa Poland	61 L11 Taguchi Japan	71 E8 Tangerang Java	68 C3 Tapun Burma
99 M6 Swea City Iowa	48 F3 Szob Hungary	71 L2 Tagudin Philippines	33 P7 Tangermünde E Germany	71 F7 Tapul Philippines
26 Sweden kingdom W Europe	71 E2 Szokolca Hungary	85 A4 Tagoun007 Morocco	28 J3 Tange Sø L Denmark	128 B3 Tapurucuara Brazil
	48 D3 Szombathely Hungary	137 L4 Tagula isld Louisiade Arch	67 G3 Tanggu China	131 G3 Taquara Brazil
95 M7 Swedesboro New Jersey	31 J4 Szprotawa Poland	98 E1 Tagus N Dakota	124 H8 Tanggula Shan ra China	130 D7 Taquaraçu R Brazil
85 D7 Swedru Ghana	31 M2 Szreńsk Poland	Tagus R Portugal see Tejo R	66 D5 Tanggu China	131 F3 Taquari Brazil
12 C2 Sween, L Scotland	31 L2 Sztum Poland	Tagus R Spain see Tajo R	66 E5 Tanggula Shankou pass China	130 D4 Taquara,Sa.da mts Brazil
109 M6 Sweeny Texas	31 K2 Szubin Poland	144 B3 Tahakopa New Zealand		130 C6 Taquari,Pantanal do swamp Brazil
9 G4 Sweers I Queensland	31 M4 Szydłowiec Poland	73 R8 Tahan, Gunung Malaysia	65 C5 Tang He China	
100 J6 Sweet Idaho		61 L11 Tahara Japan	65 C5 Tang He R China	112 K2 Tar R N Carolina
101 O1 Sweetgrass Montana		85 F4 Tahat mt Algeria	Tangier see Tanger	120 J8 Tara Ontario
111 D7 Sweet Home Arkansas		85 F4 Tahat mt Algeria	130 D10 Tangara Brazil	55 K7 Tara U.S.S.R.
100 C5 Sweet Home Oregon	71 E3 Taal,L Luzon Philippines	145 F4 Taheke New Zealand	122 K9 Tangier Nova Scotia	50 E3 Tara R U.S.S.R.
109 L6 Sweet Home Texas	48 E4 Tab Hungary	77 C6 Taheri Iran	Tangier Grand L	71 F4 Tara isld Philippines
107 L8 Sweetwater Oklahoma	71 F4 Tabaco Philippines	117 G6 Tahiti isld Pacific Oc	Nova Scotia	50 E3 Tara R U.S.S.R.
112 C2 Sweet Water Tennessee	128 E7 Tabajara Brazil	135 M10 Tahiti isld Pacific Oc	48 F2 Tangier I Virginia	55 K7 Tara U.S.S.R.
108 G3 Sweetwater Texas	70 P16 Tabalas Indonesia	110 H6 Tahlequah Oklahoma	111 F11 Tangipahoa R Louisiana	128 E2 Taraba R Nigeria
101 R7 Sweetwater R Wyoming	89 F8 Tabankulu S Africa	117 H6 Tahlkee R Alaska	95 M9 Tangimoana New Zealand	84 C5 Tarabulus see Tripoli Libya
87 D12 Swellendam S Africa	127 O2 Tabaquite Trinidad	102 D2 Tahoe L California	145 E4 Tangier I Virginia	128 E2 Taradale New Zealand
108 G2 Swenson Texas	137 L2 Tabar Is Bismarck Arch	114 J4 Tahoe L N W Terr	70 E3 Tangipahoa R Louisiana	139 J6 Tarago New S Wales
31 J5 Świdnica Poland	85 B12 Tabarka Tunisia	102 D3 Tahoe Valley California	70 G6 Tangkelenbeko, G mt	14 E3 Tara Hill Irish Rep
31 M3 Świdwin Poland	77 E3 Tabas Iran	108 F2 Tahoka Texas	Sulawesi	145 E4 Taranaki reg New Zealand
31 J3 Świebodzin Poland	77 F3 Tabas Iran	100 A2 Taholah Washington	70 L9 Tangkuban Perahu mt	New Zealand
31 L2 Świecie Poland	124 H7 Tabasco state Mexico	145 E3 Tahora New Zealand	Java	71 M9 Tarakan Indonesia
116 K8 Swift R Alaska	125 N8 Tabasco state Mexico	145 F4 Tahoraiti New Zealand		139 J5 Taramana New S Wales
95 R2 Swift R Maine	52 G6 Tabashino U.S.S.R.	85 F6 Tahoua Niger	14 E3 Taranaki stst see	71 M9 Tarakan isld Indonesia
123 S6 Swift Current Nfld	123 N3 Tabatière,La Quebec	99 V3 Tahquamenon Falls	109 L5 Taranaki reg New Zealand	New Zealand
118 K8 Swiftcurrent Sask	128 E4 Tabatinga Brazil	Michigan	66 F5 Tangpeng China	16 E4 Tarancón Spain
116 L5 Swift Fork R Alaska	88 B1 Tabayin Burma	74 E2 Talagang Pakistan	67 D5 Tangpu China	129 O4 Tarancón Spain
110 E6 Swifton Arkansas	71 F2 Tabayoc, Mt Philippines	133 D6 Talagapa Argentina	125 G9 Tangshan China	15 A3 Taransay isld Scotland
100 C3 Swift Res Washington	143 F7 Tabba Pen W Australia	13 L4 Tai Lai Vietnam	67 G1 Tangshan China	43 G4 Taranto Italy
117 H5 Swift River Yukon Terr	85 D7 Taberbla India	83 J8 Talaimannar Sri Lanka	67 D1 Tangsu China	43 G4 Taranto, Golfo di g Italy
100 A1 Swiftsure Bank Lightship Br Col	65 E4 Tabena India	85 B5 Talak reg Niger	145 B2 Tangtang China	128 B5 Tarapacá Brazil
14 D1 Swilly,L Irish Rep	67 F2 Taberg Sweden	73 R8 Talakmau mt Sumatra	145 F3 Tangtang China	128 C6 Tarapoto Peru
8 C5 Swimbridge England	106 F7 Tabernas Spain	107 P5 Talala Oklahoma	16 E4 Tangtou China	129 G1 Tararoto Peru
9 E4 Swindon England	17 F6 Tabernes de Valldigna Spain	71 G6 Talalora Philippines	70 G3 Tangyuan China	22 E3 Tarare France
Swinemünde see Świnoujście		67 G1 Taicang China	85 H4 Tangmarg Sri Lanka	22 E5 Taras France
9 F2 Swineshead England	14 E3 Swords Irish Rep	67 G4 Taichung Taiwan	79 H4 Tangmarg Sri Lanka	
14 C3 Swinford Irish Rep	141 F5 Swords Ra Queensland	144 C6 Taieri airport New Zealand	16 D3 Tangwanghe China	
108 G3 Swink Colorado	52 D4 Syamozero, Oz L U.S.S.R.	85 B5 Taïeri R New Zealand	145 D1 Tangowahine New Zealand	
31 H2 Świnoujście Poland	52 D5 Syamzha U.S.S.R.	61 J9 Taigu China	New Zealand	71 M9 Tarama Indonesia
31 J8 Świnton Scotland	98 A8 Sybille Cr Wyoming	65 B6 Taigu China	70 C6 Tangpeng China	145 F3 Tarana New S Wales
40 F4 Switzerland rep Europe	14 D4 Sybil Pt Irish Rep	130 C10 Talavera,I Paraguay	69 G14 Tangse Sumatra	139 K5 Taranaki steet see
15 E2 Swona isld Orkney Scotland	111 K8 Sycamore Alabama	140 F4 Talawanta Queensland	69 C10 Tanimeg R Sumatra	New Zealand
14 E3 Swords Irish Rep	99 S8 Sycamore Illinois	71 G2 Talayan Philippines	76 C5 Tamil Nadu prov India	16 E4 Tarancón Spain
141 F5 Swords Ra Queensland	94 D6 Sycamore Ohio	65 G3 Talbehat India	71 M9 Tani Cambodia	15 A3 Taransay isld Scotland
52 D4 Syamozero, Oz L U.S.S.R.	112 F4 Sycamore S Carolina	143 B9 Talbingo Sumatra	74 C1 Tanin Switzerland	17 F4 Taravilla Spain
52 D5 Syamzha U.S.S.R.	31 K4 Sycow Poland	70 J1 Talbutta Sri Lanka	40 E5 Tanimbar Is	145 F3 Tararua, Mt
98 A8 Sybille Cr Wyoming	56 D4 Syda R U.S.S.R.	89 B4 Tamchuyukon, G mt Sabah	60 D14 Taniyama Japan	New Zealand
14 D4 Sybil Pt Irish Rep	28 E3 Sydenham Ontario	77 H7 Talai-Band mts Pakistan	71 F6 Tanjay Philippines	
111 K8 Sycamore Alabama	28 N3 Syderø isld Faeroes	113 F7 Talbot C W Australia	70 L9 Tanjerang Java	17 F3 Tarazona Spain
99 S8 Sycamore Illinois	28 O9 Syderstone England	115 M2 Talbot Inlet N W Terr	52 E3 Tamitsa U.S.S.R.	17 E3 Tarazona de la Mancha
94 D6 Sycamore Ohio	9 G2 Sydney Montana	57 C1 Tamkamys U.S.S.R.	69 D11 Tanjungbalai Sumatra	Spain
112 F4 Sycamore S Carolina	72 H5 Sydney New S Wales	139 J4 Talbragar New S Wales	70 K7 Tanjungblitung Sumatra	28 K5 Tårbæk Denmark
31 K4 Sycow Poland	85 M4 Sydney Nova Scotia	131 B5 Talca Chile	70 K7 Tanjungenim Sumatra	57 K2 Tarbagatay, Khrebet mts U.S.S.R.
56 D4 Syda R U.S.S.R.	134 K9 Sydney I Phoenix Is Pacific Oc	131 B5 Talca prov Chile	45 R7 Tammaro R Italy	
28 E3 Sydenham Ontario	130 C6 Sydney I Phoenix Is Pacific Oc	131 A4 Talcahuano Chile	27 J7 Tammerfors see Tampere	15 F3 Tarbert Harris Scotland
28 N3 Syderø isld Faeroes	140 E3 Sydney I Queensland	131 A6 Talca,Pta Chile	109 M2 Tampa Florida	14 B4 Tarbert Irish Rep
28 O9 Syderstone England	86 G3 Sydney Mines Nova Scotia	26 G7 Tällberg Sweden	113 D10 Tampa Florida	12 C2 Tarbert Strathclyde
9 G2 Sydney Montana	115 P5 Sydproven Greenland	84 G9 Talguppa Israel	70 N3 Tampa Kansas	Scotland
72 H5 Sydney New S Wales	32 J7 Syke W Germany	52 E6 Talcott W Virginia	109 G4 Tampere Finland	15 B2 Tarbert,L Scotland
85 M4 Sydney Nova Scotia	98 G3 Sykeston N Dakota	141 F4 Taldora Queensland	29 K10 Tampere Finland	22 D5 Tarbes France
123 M7 Sydney Mines Is Pacific Oc	52 H4 Syktyvkar U.S.S.R.	57 F2 Taldy-Kurgan U.S.S.R.	125 L7 Tampico Illinois	18 F3 Tarbes France
134 K9 Sydney I Phoenix Is Pacific Oc	111 K8 Sylacauga Alabama	77 H7 Taldy-Kurgan U.S.S.R.	109 L8 Tampico Mexico	26 E7 Tärendö Sweden
140 E3 Sydney I Queensland	110 D6 Sylamore Arkansas	77 H7 Talesh, Kuh-e mt Iran	69 J13 Tampines Singapore	15 D3 Tarves Scotland
86 G3 Sydney Mines Nova Scotia	26 F8 Sylene mt Norway	55 M4 Taldom U.S.S.R.	111 T1 Tampines Singapore	141 F5 Tarbrax Queensland
115 P5 Sydproven Greenland	28 A7 Sylt isld W Germany	69 O5 Talfourd, Mt Australia	109 J5 Tampin Malaysia	15 D2 Tarbet Scotland
32 J7 Syke W Germany	28 E3 Sylte Norway	54 E3 Tali India	69 H14 Tamra Israel	54 E3 Tarbolton Scotland
98 G3 Sykeston N Dakota	26 E3 Sylterfjord inlet Norway	65 B6 Taliabu isld Indonesia	80 C2 Tam Quan Vietnam	141 F7 Tarcoola Queensland
52 H4 Syktyvkar U.S.S.R.	112 D2 Sylva N Carolina	61 J11 Tamra Israel	29 N3 Tamra Israel	138 C4 Tarcoola S Australia
111 K8 Sylacauga Alabama	112 C3 Sylva U.S.S.R.	69 G14 Talaikudah Sumatra	80 C2 Tamsagbulag Mongolia	142 E5 Tarcutta New S Wales
110 D6 Sylamore Arkansas	94 J7 Sylvan Pennsylvania	70 G5 Taliku India	58 G2 Tamsaghulag Mongolia	139 J6 Tarcutta New S Wales
26 F8 Sylene mt Norway	107 M2 Sylvan Grove Kansas	65 C5 Talikota India	80 C2 Tamshiyacu Peru	139 J6 Tarcutta New S Wales
28 A7 Sylt isld W Germany	112 F5 Sylvania Georgia	9 E2 Talikhan Afghanistan	86 B7 Tamsweg Austria	
28 E3 Sylte Norway	112 D6 Sylvania Ohio	76 E2 Talikon India	33 N3 Tamtutuk B Japan	99 Q3 Taramakau New Zealand
26 E3 Sylterfjord inlet Norway	113 N6 Sylvania S Australia	70 F10 Talikud isld Mindanao	37 J2 Tamworth England	145 C5 Taramakau New Zealand
112 D2 Sylva N Carolina	143 D6 Sylvania W Australia	Philippines	139 K4 Tamworth New S Wales	
112 C3 Sylva U.S.S.R.	112 E5 Sylvan Lake Alberta	71 G6 Talisayan Mindanao	145 F5 Tamworth New S Wales	
94 J7 Sylvan Pennsylvania	101 P5 Sylvan Pass Wyoming	Philippines	137 H7 Tana R Norway	
107 M2 Sylvan Grove Kansas	112 E5 Sylvester Georgia	111 K11 Talladega Alabama	121 G5 Tan R Norway	
112 F5 Sylvania Georgia	140 D4 Sylvester, L N Terr Aust	67 F5 Ta Hsü isld Taiwan	27 P16 Tana R Norway	
112 D6 Sylvania Ohio	123 R5 Sylvester,Mt Nfld	84 A4 Tahta Egypt	27 K10 Tana R Finland	
113 N6 Sylvania S Australia	117 L6 Sylvia Kansas	67 E14 Tahtali Dag mt Turkey	52 E2 Tana R Finland	
143 D6 Sylvania W Australia	56 C1 Sym R U.S.S.R.	117 L8 Tahtan Br Col	33 M1 Tana R Alaska	
112 E5 Sylvan Lake Alberta		128 D8 Tahuamanu R Peru	52 E2 Tana,R Alaska	
101 P5 Sylvan Pass Wyoming		85 F7 Tahoua Ivory Coast	26 E3 Tanafjord inlet Norway	
112 E5 Sylvester Georgia		145 G4 Tahuna New Zealand	70 F7 Tana,L Sulawesi	
140 D4 Sylvester, L N Terr Aust		65 E4 Tai'an China	33 M4 Tanaku W Germany	
123 R5 Sylvester,Mt Nfld		67 F2 Taibai China	116 H4 Tanaku Alaska	
117 L6 Sylvia Kansas		67 G1 Taibai China	79 B7 Talkha Egypt	
56 C1 Sym R U.S.S.R.		136 L3 Taibai New S Wales	52 H4 Tanafjord inlet Norway	

76
Tarikere — Thompson

76 B4 Tarikere India
145 E3 Tariki New Zealand
72 F5 Tarīm S Yemen
Tarim Basin see Tarim Pendi
88 F6 Tarime Tanzania
66 D3 Tarim He R China
66 C3 Tarim Pendi basin China
69 C11 Taring Sumatra
Tari Nor see Dalai Nur
70 E1 Taritipan Sabah
89 D9 Tarka R S Africa
87 E12 Tarkastad S Africa
110 A1 Tarkio Missouri
101 L2 Tarkio Montana
50 G2 Tarko-Sale U.S.S.R.
85 D7 Tarkwa Ghana
133 C7 Tar,L Argentina
71 E3 Tarlac Philippines
15 F3 Tarland Scotland
13 F6 Tarleton England
28 B5 Tarm Denmark
128 C6 Tarma Peru
32 K6 Tarmstedt W Germany
18 G9 Tarn dep France
18 F9 Tarn R France
48 F3 Tarna R Hungary
26 H6 Tärnaby Sweden
77 K3 Tarnak R Afghanistan
18 F8 Tarn-et-Garonne dep France
18 H8 Tarn,Gorges du France
31 N5 Tarnobrzeg Poland
52 F4 Tarnogskiy Gorodok U.S.S.R.
119 M6 Tarnopo Sask
33 Q5 Tarnow E Germany
31 M5 Tarnow Poland
31 L5 Tarnowskie Gory Poland
44 H2 Taro R Italy
141 K7 Tarong Queensland
141 J7 Taroom Queensland
85 C2 Taroudannt Morocco
28 C7 Tarp W Germany
140 D4 Tarpaulin Swamp N Terr Aust
109 H6 Tarpley Texas
113 E9 Tarpon Springs Florida
113 L12 Tarpum Bay Eleuthera Bahamas
44 L5 Tarquinia Italy
80 D7 Tarqumiya Jordan
17 H3 Tarragona Spain
17 H3 Tarragona prov Spain
139 H8 Tarraleah Tasmania
139 H4 Tarran Hills New S Wales
111 K8 Tarrant City Alabama
8 D6 Tarrant Hinton England
140 E3 Tarrant,Pt Queensland
144 B6 Tarras New Zealand
17 J3 Tarrasa Spain
26 J4 Tarrekaise mt Sweden
41 N3 Tarrenz Austria
141 K8 Tarrewinna Queensland
106 E2 Tarryall Colorado
112 E5 Tarrytown Georgia
95 O5 Tarrytown New York
17 F9 Tarsa,C Algeria
45 P1 Tarski Zaliv B Yugoslavia
84 F5 Tarso Taro mt Chad
86 C1 Tarso Tieroko mt Chad
78 E3 Tarsus Turkey
133 E2 Tartagal Argentina
6 L4 Tartan oil rig North Sea
45 J1 Tártaro R Italy
18 E9 Tartas France
56 A3 Tartas R U.S.S.R.
52 C5 Tartu U.S.S.R.
79 F4 Tartūs Syria
80 C6 Tarum Israel
60 P3 Tarumae yama mt Japan
130 H6 Tarumirim Brazil
60 D14 Tarumizu Japan
54 J2 Tarusa U.S.S.R.
69 D9 Tarutao,Ko isld Thailand
48 M4 Tarutino U.S.S.R.
69 D11 Tarutung Sumatra
26 D8 Tarva isld Norway
38 J9 Tarvisio Italy
120 K5 Tarzwell Ontario
108 B6 Tasajera, Sa mts Mexico
57 G2 Tasaral U.S.S.R.
84 E4 Tasāwah Libya
57 D3 Tas Buget U.S.S.R.
121 M4 Taschereau Quebec
107 K2 Tasco Kansas
69 F11 Tasek Dampar Malaysia
117 M10 Taseko, Mt Br Col
56 D2 Taseyeva R U.S.S.R.
76 B2 Tasgaon India
58 A2 Tashanta U.S.S.R.
57 A4 Tashauz U.S.S.R.
75 O5 Tashigang Bhutan
57 E4 Tashkent U.S.S.R.
57 C6 Tashkepri U.S.S.R.
57 F4 Tash-Kumyr U.S.S.R.
55 B5 Tashla U.S.S.R.
120 C2 Tashota Ontario
56 C4 Tashtagol U.S.S.R.
56 C4 Tashtyp U.S.S.R.
70 M9 Tasikmalaja Java
80 G2 Tasil Syria
28 F7 Tåsinge isld Denmark
115 O3 Tasiussaq Greenland
26 H7 Tåsjö Sweden
26 H7 Tåsjön L Sweden
85 G5 Tasker Niger
56 E5 Taskyl,Khrebet mts U.S.S.R.
145 D4 Tasman Bay New Zealand
139 H9 Tasman Hd Tasmania
139 H8 Tasmania state Australia
145 D4 Tasman Mountains New Zealand
144 C5 Tasman, Mt New Zealand
139 J9 Tasman Pen Tasmania
134 G13 Tasman Plateau Pac Oc
137 M9 Tasman Sea Pacific Oc
48 H3 Tăşnad Romania
85 F5 Tassara Niger
19 J5 Tasselot, Mt France
115 M6 Tassialouc,L Quebec
85 E5 Tassili du Hoggar plat Algeria
85 F3 Tassili-n'-Ajjer plat Algeria
28 J5 Tåstrup Denmark
51 M2 Tas Tumus U.S.S.R.
57 E3 Tasty U.S.S.R.
85 C3 Tata Morocco
48 E3 Tatabanya Hungary
71 E7 Tatalan isld Philippines
71 B2 Tatam Halmahera Indonesia
122 J8 Tatamagouche Nova Scotia
85 G2 Tataouine Tunisia
145 E3 Tatara mt New Zealand
48 M5 Tatarbunary U.S.S.R.
47 H3 Tatarlar Turkey
55 G3 Tatarsk U.S.S.R.
59 M1 Tatarskiy Proliv str U.S.S.R.
70 C3 Tatau Sarawak
112 C3 Tate Georgia
119 N7 Tate Sask
89 E3 Tate R Botswana
141 G3 Tate R Queensland
61 O6 Tateai Japan
140 C2 Tate Bluff hill N Terr Aust
60 O4 Tateura Japan
61 N11 Tateyama Japan
61 L9 Tate yama mt Japan
117 P5 Tathlina L N W Terr
139 K6 Tathra New S Wales
116 O6 Tatitlek Alaska
117 L10 Tatla Lake Br Col
117 K7 Tatlatui Prov. Park Br Columbia
116 K5 Tatlawiksuk R Alaska
117 L10 Tatlayoko Lake Br Col
117 M10 Tatlow, Mt Br Col
101 R5 Tatman Mt Wyoming
116 K6 Tatna L Alaska
115 K6 Tatnam,C Manitoba
139 H6 Tatong Victoria
66 D4 Tatrang China
31 M6 Tatry mts Czech/Poland
117 E6 Tatshenshini R Br Col
61 K8 Tatsuruhama Japan
77 K7 Tatta Pakistan
9 F1 Tattershall England
57 G3 Tatty U.S.S.R.
130 F8 Tatuí Brazil
131 B2 Tatul,Sa de mts Chile
108 D2 Tatum New Mexico
109 N3 Tatum Texas
107 N7 Tatums Oklahoma
Tatung see Datong
139 H6 Tatura Victoria
129 K5 Tauá Brazil
128 F4 Tauapeçaçu Brazil
37 L2 Taubach E Germany
130 F8 Taubaté Brazil
36 H5 Tauber R W Germany
33 R10 Taucha E Germany
38 H7 Tauerin Tunnel Austria
37 N7 Taufkirchen W Germany
36 G2 Taufstein mt W Germany
128 G3 Tauini R Brazil
145 E2 Taukoa New Zealand
19 N16 Taulignan France
28 D5 Taulov Denmark
145 E3 Taumarunui New Zealand
128 D5 Taumaturgo Brazil
110 F4 Taum Sauk Mt Missouri
130 C7 Taunay Brazil
89 D6 Taung S Africa
68 C5 Taungbon Burma
68 B2 Taungdwingyi Burma
68 C2 Taung-Gyi Burma
68 D3 Taunggyi mt Burma/Thailand
68 C2 Taunglau Burma
68 C4 Taungnyo A ra Burma
68 B2 Taungtha Burma
68 B3 Taungup Burma
74 D3 Taunsa Pakistan
8 C5 Taunton England
95 Q5 Taunton Massachusetts
95 R5 Taunton,E Massachusetts
36 E3 Taunus mts W Germany
145 E2 Taupiri New Zealand
145 F3 Taupo New Zealand
52 B6 Tauragė U.S.S.R.
145 E3 Taurakawa mt New Zealand
145 F2 Tauranga New Zealand
121 R6 Taureau, L Quebec
21 H10 Taurion R France
145 D1 Tauroa Pt New Zealand
55 F2 Taurovy U.S.S.R.
Taurus Mts see Toros Dağlari
17 G3 Tauste Spain
144 B7 Tautuku Peninsula New Zealand
137 M2 Tauu Is Solomon Is
115 K5 Tavani N W Terr
40 F3 Tavannes Switzerland
113 F9 Tavares Florida
45 K4 Tavarnelles Val di Pesa Italy
47 K7 Tavas Turkey
26 L3 Tavätno R Sweden
22 F4 Tavaux France
55 E2 Tavda U.S.S.R.
50 F3 Tavda R U.S.S.R.
26 L7 Tavelsjö Sweden
41 J5 Taverne Switzerland
45 K1 Tavernelle Italy
115 M4 Taverner B N W Terr
19 Q17 Tavernes France
113 G12 Tavernier Florida
20 K3 Taverny France
88 F3 Taveta Kenya
137 R5 Taveuni isld Fiji
16 B7 Tavira Portugal
8 B6 Tavistock England
43 C8 Tavolara isld Sardinia
55 G4 Tavolzhan U.S.S.R.
16 B4 Távora R Portugal
68 D5 Tavoy Burma
68 D6 Tavoy Pt Burma
65 H3 Tavrichanka U.S.S.R.
55 F4 Tavricheskoye U.S.S.R.
47 K4 Tavşancıl Turkey
47 K5 Tavşanlı Turkey
145 G4 Tawa New Zealand
109 M3 Tawakoni, L Texas
69 C10 Tawar,Danau L Sumatra
94 D2 Tawas City Michigan
118 D4 Tawatinaw Alberta
70 E2 Tawau Sabah
86 E3 Taweisha Sudan
8 C4 Tawe,R Wales
145 E1 Tawhiti Rahi I New Zealand
70 F2 Tawitawi Philippines
8 B5 Taw,R England
67 G5 Ta-wu Taiwan
38 G7 Taxenbach Austria
27 J12 Taxinge Sweden
66 B4 Taxkorgan China
128 C5 Tayabamba Peru
71 E4 Tayabas B Philippines
69 K13 Tayan Indonesia
52 D1 Taybola U.S.S.R.
13 E1 Tay,Firth of Scotland
56 C3 Tayga U.S.S.R.
12 C2 Tayinloan Scotland
143 D10 Tay,L W Australia
103 O7 Taylor Arizona
109 O2 Taylor Arkansas
117 N7 Taylor Br Col
111 G7 Taylor Mississippi
110 E2 Taylor Missouri
98 G8 Taylor Nebraska
109 K5 Taylor Texas
100 D2 Taylor Washington
99 P5 Taylor Wisconsin
140 C5 Taylor R N Terr Aust
106 C6 Taylor, Mt New Mexico
144 C5 Taylor, Mt New Zealand
116 J6 Taylor Mts Alaska
106 D3 Taylor Park Res Colorado
112 B3 Taylor Ridge Georgia
112 E3 Taylors S Carolina
142 B3 Taylors Crossing W Australia
106 F5 Taylor Springs New Mexico
94 B8 Taylorsville Kentucky
111 G10 Taylorsville Mississippi
112 F2 Taylorsville N Carolina
94 F7 Taylorsville Ohio
110 G2 Taylorville Illinois
122 F7 Taymouth New Brunswick
51 K2 Taymura R U.S.S.R.
51 K1 Taymyr,Ozero L U.S.S.R.
51 J1 Taymyr,Poluostrov pen U.S.S.R.
55 E4 Tayncha U.S.S.R.
68 H7 Tay Ninh Vietnam
12 C1 Taynuilt Scotland
71 G6 Tayoloan R Mindanao Philippines
13 F1 Tayport Scotland
15 E4 Tay,R Scotland
56 E3 Tayshet U.S.S.R.
58 C2 Tayshir Mongolia
15 E4 Tayside reg Scotland
71 E3 Taytay Luzon Philippines
71 D5 Taytay Palawan Philippines
71 G5 Taytay Pt Philippines
77 G2 Tayyebāt Iran
79 E10 Ţayyib al Ism Saudi Arabia
50 H2 Taz R U.S.S.R.
85 D2 Taza Morocco
85 F5 Tazalc Niger
61 O6 Tazawa ko L Japan
84 G4 Tazerbo Oasis Libya
112 D1 Tazewell Tennessee
94 F9 Tazewell Virginia
48 K4 Taziăul R Romania
65 F1 Tazicheng China
116 K7 Tazimina Lakes Alaska
116 O6 Tazlina L Alaska
50 G2 Tazovskaya Guba gulf U.S.S.R.
50 G2 Tazovskoye U.S.S.R.
66 F6 Tazungdam Burma
78 K1 Tbilisi U.S.S.R.
85 E7 Tchaourou Benin
86 B6 Tchibanga Gabon
84 E5 Tchigaï, Plat. du Chad/Niger
68 J2 Tching Lan Xan isld Vietnam
85 F5 Tchin-Tabaradene Niger
86 B4 Tcholliré Cameroon
111 F8 Tchula Mississippi
31 L1 Tczew Poland
98 K6 Tea S Dakota
128 E4 Tea R Brazil
48 J4 Teaca Romania
124 G6 Teacapán Mexico
108 D3 Teague New Mexico
109 L4 Teague Texas
143 D7 Teague,L W Australia
13 G4 Team Valley England
144 A6 Te Anau New Zealand
145 E3 Te Anga New Zealand
45 Q7 Teano Italy
143 C6 Teano Ra W Australia
101 T6 Teapot Dome hill Wyoming
145 G2 Te Araroa New Zealand
145 E2 Te Aroha New Zealand
140 C5 Tea Tree N Terr Aust
145 E4 Te Awaiti New Zealand
145 E3 Te Awamutu New Zealand
16 D8 Teba Spain
70 K8 Tebak, G mt Sumatra
85 F1 Tebessa Algeria
130 B10 Tebicuary Paraguay
69 D11 Tebingtinggi Sumatra
69 F12 Tebingtinggi isld Sumatra
69 E13 Tebo R Sumatra
43 C12 Tebourba Tunisia
43 C12 Teboursouk Tunisia
69 F12 Tebrau Malaysia
18 G10 Tech R France
55 D3 Techa R U.S.S.R.
85 D7 Techiman Ghana
47 J1 Techirghiol Romania
144 D5 Technical, Mt New Zealand
33 Q6 Techow E Germany
36 G6 Teck W Germany
133 C6 Tecka Argentina
32 G8 Tecklenburg W Germany
27 F16 Teckomatorp Sweden
106 E7 Tecolote New Mexico
124 G7 Tecolotlán Mexico
101 L8 Tecoma Nevada
124 H8 Tecomán Mexico
103 H6 Tecopa California
124 F4 Tecorichic Mexico
124 E3 Tecoripa Mexico
125 J9 Tecpan Mexico
124 G6 Tecuala Mexico
48 L5 Tecuci Romania
94 D4 Tecumseh Michigan
110 D5 Tecumseh Missouri
98 K9 Tecumseh Nebraska
107 O6 Tecumseh Oklahoma
120 H10 Tecumseh Ontario
8 C6 Tedburn St Mary England
70 P16 Tedjakula Indonesia
57 B5 Tedzhen U.S.S.R.
77 G1 Tedzhen U.S.S.R.
118 D6 Tees Alberta
13 G5 Tees,R England
120 J9 Teeswater Ontario
71 D6 Teeth,The mt Palawan Philippines
128 F4 Tefe Brazil
47 K7 Tefenni Turkey
26 L8 Teg Sweden
70 M9 Tegal Java
33 S7 Tegel E Germany
25 F6 Tegelen Netherlands
41 P2 Tegernsee L W Germany
85 F6 Tegina Nigeria
70 K8 Tegineneng Sumatra
139 H3 Tego Queensland
86 H3 Tegre prov Ethiopia
125 L2 Tegucigalpa Honduras
85 F5 Teguiddan Tessoum Niger
89 E3 Tegwani R Zimbabwe
102 F6 Tehachapi California
102 F7 Tehachapi Mts California
102 B1 Tehama California
145 E2 Te Hana New Zealand
145 D1 Te Hapua New Zealand
145 F3 Te Haroto New Zealand
145 F3 Te Hauke New Zealand
115 K4 Tehek L N W Terr
69 C12 Tehemberau Indonesia
77 B2 Tehrān Iran
125 L8 Tehuacán Mexico
125 M9 Tehuantepec Mexico
37 L2 Teichel E Germany
8 C3 Teifi R Wales
8 C6 Teignmouth England
8 C6 Teign,R England
21 B6 Teillay France
21 C7 Teille France
61 Q12 Teima Okinawa
Teinach see Bad Teinach-Zavelstein
36 F6 Teinach W Germany
145 F3 Te Iringa Ahimanawa Range New Zealand
37 N6 Teisbach W Germany
29 K10 Teisko Finland
88 G3 Teita Hills Kenya
12 D1 Teith,R Scotland
48 H4 Teius Romania
130 H9 Teixeira Brazil
87 C8 Teixeira da Silva Angola
Teixeira de Sousa see Luan
130 G7 Teixeiras Brazil
130 E9 Teixeira Soares Brazil
16 E8 Tejeda,Sa mts Spain
16 B5 Tejo R Portugal
124 F3 Tejolocachic Mexico
102 F7 Tejon Pk California
130 E6 Tejuco,R Brazil
125 J8 Tejupilco Mexico
145 F2 Te Kaha New Zealand
98 K8 Tekamah Nebraska
145 F3 Te Karaka New Zealand
145 E2 Te Kauwhata New Zealand
145 E3 Te Kawa New Zealand
57 J3 Tekeli U.S.S.R.
55 F4 Teke, Oz L U.S.S.R.
57 K3 Tekes China
66 C3 Tekes R U.S.S.R.
57 K3 Tekes He R China
144 C5 Te Kinga New Zealand
47 J4 Tekirdağ Turkey
47 J4 Tekir Dağları mts Turkey
145 D3 Te Kiri New Zealand
68 A2 Teknaf Burma
100 H2 Tekoa Washington
144 D5 Tekoa, Mt New Zealand
94 C4 Tekonsha Michigan
145 D2 Te Kopuru New Zealand
86 D2 Tekro Chad
71 H5 Teku Sulawesi
145 E3 Te Kuiti New Zealand
125 Q10 Tela Honduras
80 E3 Tel 'Adashim Israel
69 H11 Telaga isld Indonesia
17 G10 Télagh Algeria
80 B7 Telamim Israel
69 G12 Telan isld Indonesia
69 F13 Telanaipura Sumatra
116 L6 Telaquana,L Alaska
80 B6 Tel Ashdod Israel
80 B7 Tel Ashqelon Israel
53 G12 Telavi U.S.S.R.
80 C5 Tel Aviv Israel
80 C7 Tel Azeqa Israel
56 C4 Tel'bes U.S.S.R.
80 F3 Tel Bet She'an Israel
80 C7 Tel Bet Shemesh Israel
80 F3 Tel Bet Yerah Israel
31 J6 Telč Czechoslovakia
48 J3 Telciu Romania
80 C8 Tel Devir Israel
70 C6 Telegapulang Kalimantan
117 H7 Telegraph Creek Br Col
80 F6 Teleilet el Ghassul Jordan
27 C12 Telemark prov Norway
70 E4 Telen R Kalimantan
48 L3 Teleneshty U.S.S.R.
48 J6 Teleormanul R Romania
109 L2 Telephone Texas
102 G5 Telescope Pk California
127 P5 Telescope Pt Grenada
129 G5 Teles Pires R Brazil
56 C5 Teletskoye, Oz L U.S.S.R.
80 C8 Tel Eyton Israel
80 D4 Tel Gat Israel
32 G9 Telgte W Germany
85 B6 Telimele Guinea
80 F2 Tel Kinnerot Israel
78 J3 Tel Kotchek Syria
117 K8 Telkwa Br Col
108 G1 Tell Texas
80 C7 Tel Lakhish Israel
22 K5 Tellancourt Villers France
79 G4 Tell Bisa Syria
110 K4 Tell City Indiana
80 F5 Tell Deir'Alla Jordan
26 L5 Tellejokk Sweden
116 D4 Teller Alaska
76 B5 Tellicherry India
112 C2 Tellico Plains Tennessee
122 F3 Tellier Quebec
22 J3 Tellin Belgium
32 K4 Tellingstedt W Germany
80 C5 Tel Litwinsky Israel
80 F6 Tell Nimrin Jordan
106 C4 Telluride Colorado
57 B4 Tel'mansk U.S.S.R.
80 C7 Tel Maresha Israel
58 C2 Telmen Nuur L Mongolia
80 B8 Tel Mifsah Israel
80 C4 Tel Mond Israel
100 H4 Telocaset Oregon
69 E10 Telok Anson Malaysia
125 K8 Teloloapán Mexico
52 J3 Tel'pos-Iz, Gora mt U.S.S.R.
80 F1 Tel Qedesh Israel
133 D6 Telsen Argentina
80 C2 Tel Shiqmona Israel
80 C8 Tel Shoqet Israel
52 B6 Telšiai U.S.S.R.
120 E3 Teltaka Ontario
33 S8 Teltow E Germany
70 E3 Telukbajur Kalimantan
69 E13 Telukbayur Sumatra
70 K8 Telukbetung Sumatra
69 J10 Telukbutun Indonesia
69 C12 Telukdalam Indonesia
69 F12 Teluklanjut Sumatra
85 F5 Telwes Niger
80 C8 Tel Ziqlag Israel
85 E7 Tema Ghana
69 J12 Temaju isld Indonesia
94 K9 Teman Virginia
70 B4 Temangga Kalimantan
70 N9 Temanggung Java
85 F4 Temasint Algeria
69 E14 Tembesi R Sumatra
69 F13 Tembilahan Sumatra
102 D6 Temblor Rge California
87 C7 Tembo Aluma Angola
89 E8 Tembuland dist S Africa
102 G8 Temecula California
56 E5 Temenchulu,Gora mt U.S.S.R.
8 D3 Teme,R England
48 F5 Temerin Yugoslavia
69 F11 Temerloh Malaysia
69 G12 Temiang isld Indonesia
71 C3 Teminabuan W Irian
57 A1 Temir U.S.S.R.
56 C4 Temirtau U.S.S.R.
122 A2 Temiscamie L Quebec
122 A2 Temiscamie R Quebec
115 M8 Témiscaming Quebec
122 D6 Temiscouata L Quebec
121 L6 Témiskaming Quebec
139 G8 Temma Tasmania
56 F5 Temnik R U.S.S.R.
139 J5 Temora New S Wales
124 F3 Temósachic Mexico
103 N8 Tempe Arizona
70 F7 Tempe, L isld Sulawesi
33 S8 Tempelhof E Germany
94 D5 Temperance Michigan
69 F13 Temping Sumatra
43 C8 Tempio Paus Sardinia
95 R2 Temple Maine
94 C2 Temple Michigan
109 J1 Temple Oklahoma
95 M6 Temple Pennsylvania
109 K4 Temple Texas
141 G1 Temple B Queensland
8 B3 Temple Bar Wales
140 B6 Temple Downs N Terr Aust
9 H5 Temple Ewell England
14 D4 Templemore Irish Rep
13 F4 Temple Sowerby England
102 D6 Templeton California
94 H6 Templeton Pennsylvania
8 B4 Templeton Wales
140 E5 Templeton R Queensland
22 E2 Templeuve Belgium
33 T6 Templin E Germany
87 C8 Tempué Angola
33 P5 Tempzin E Germany
55 E2 Temryak, Oz L U.S.S.R.
22 G1 Temse Belgium
131 A7 Temuco Chile
144 C6 Temuka New Zealand
98 F3 Temvik N Dakota
55 C4 Temyasovo U.S.S.R.
128 C4 Tena Ecuador
102 H1 Tenabo Nevada
124 G8 Tenacatita Mexico
109 N4 Tenaha Texas
117 F7 Tenakee Springs Alaska
29 K11 Tenala Finland
76 E2 Tenali India
124 G7 Tenamaxtlán Mexico
145 D4 Te Namu New Zealand
68 D6 Tenasserim Burma
73 Q6 Tenasserim R Burma
68 C6 Tenasserim I Burma
19 P13 Tenay France
8 D3 Tenbury Wells England
8 B4 Tenby Wales
120 G6 Tenby Bay Ontario
18 H7 Tence France
73 P7 Ten Degree Ch Andaman/Nicobar Is
86 F3 Tendelti Sudan
61 O7 Tendō Japan
101 M5 Tendoy Idaho
85 D2 Tendrara Morocco
40 D4 Tendre, Mt Switzerland
9 H4 Tendring England
85 G4 Ténéré du Tafassasset reg Niger
85 A3 Tenerife isld Canary Is
85 E1 Ténès Algeria
47 H2 Tenevo Bulgaria
70 N9 Tengah, Jawa prov Java
Tengchow see Penglai
70 E5 Tenggarong Kalimantan
70 O9 Tengger Java
69 F10 Tenggol isld Malaysia
70 E1 Tenghilan Sabah
55 E5 Tengiz, Oz L U.S.S.R.
71 E7 Tengolan isld Philippines
67 C7 Tengqiao China
65 D7 Teng Xian China
67 C5 Teng Xian China
141 G7 Tenham Queensland
27 G14 Tenhult Sweden
44 B3 Tenibres mt Italy/France
85 B3 Teniegrad Morocco
100 C3 Tenino Washington
55 F3 Tenis, Oz L U.S.S.R.
55 D4 Teniz, Oz L U.S.S.R.
76 C6 Tenkasi India
52 G6 Ten'ki U.S.S.R.
110 B6 Tenkiller Ferry Res Oklahoma
85 D6 Tenkodogo Upper Volta
69 A9 Tenlaa Nicobar Is
123 Q2 Ten Mile L Nfld
42 F5 Tenna R Italy
100 D8 Tennant California
140 C4 Tennant Creek N Terr Aust
38 H6 Tennen-Geb mts Austria
110 H6 Tennessee state U.S.A.
106 D2 Tennessee Pass Colorado
110 J6 Tennessee R Tennessee
26 F4 Tennholmen Norway
112 E5 Tennille Georgia
29 O4 Tenniöjoki R Finland
144 D5 Tennyson, L New Zealand
131 B5 Teno R Chile
29 M2 Tenojoki R Finland
70 D2 Tenom Sabah
125 O9 Tenosique Mexico
61 J11 Tenri Japan
61 L11 Tenryū Japan
111 E9 Tensas R Louisiana
111 J11 Tensaw R Alabama
100 J2 Tensed Idaho
85 C2 Tensift R Morocco
99 M2 Tenstrike Minnesota
70 G5 Tentena Sulawesi
9 G5 Tenterden England
143 B10 Tenterden W Australia
139 K3 Tenterfield New S Wales
113 F12 Ten Thousand Is Florida
70 G4 Tentolomatinan mt Sulawesi
124 H7 Teocalitche Mexico
45 M3 Teodorano Italy
130 H5 Teófilo Otôni Brazil
48 K1 Teofipol U.S.S.R.
71 E7 Teomabal isld Philippines
125 L8 Teotitlan Mexico
71 O8 Tepa Indonesia
124 E3 Tepache Mexico
124 H7 Tepatitlán de Morelos Mexico
46 E2 Tepe mt Yugoslavia
125 K8 Tepeji Mexico
57 B3 Tepekul' U.S.S.R.
46 D4 Tepelenë Albania
37 O4 Tepelská Plošina mts Czechoslovakia
124 G7 Tepic Mexico
37 O4 Teplá Czechoslovakia
30 H5 Teplice Czechoslovakia
37 O3 Teplička Czechoslovakia
48 M2 Teplik U.S.S.R.
52 H4 Teplogorka U.S.S.R.
54 K8 Teplogorsk U.S.S.R.
124 C2 Tepoca, C Mexico
145 F3 Te Pohue New Zealand
145 G3 Te Puia New Zealand
145 F2 Te Puke New Zealand
80 D7 Teqoa Jordan
124 H7 Tequila Mexico
17 J3 Ter R Spain
85 E6 Téra Niger
16 B6 Tera R Portugal
16 C3 Tera R Spain
25 C4 Ter Aar Netherlands
61 M8 Teradomari Japan
61 P7 Teraike Japan
42 F6 Teramo Italy
139 G7 Terang Victoria
25 H3 Ter Ape Netherlands
77 L5 Teratani R Pakistan
70 P10 Terawangan Indonesia
71 O8 Terbang Selatan Indonesia
71 O8 Terbang Utara isld Indonesia
25 F5 Terborg Netherlands
78 H2 Tercan Turkey
133 E4 Tercero R Argentina
106 E4 Tercio Colorado
48 K1 Terebovlya U.S.S.R.
48 G5 Teregova Romania
53 G11 Terek R U.S.S.R.
56 E5 Tere-Khol',Oz L U.S.S.R.
54 C4 Terekhovka U.S.S.R.
56 C5 Terektinskiy Khrebet mts U.S.S.R.
69 H11 Terempa Indonesia
122 J9 Terence B Nova Scotia
69 F10 Terengganu R Malaysia
69 F10 Terengganu state Malaysia
130 C7 Terenos Brazil
55 C5 Terensay U.S.S.R.
70 E5 Terentang,P Kalimantan
57 C2 Teren Uzyak U.S.S.R.
130 D9 Teresa Cristina Brazil
53 G8 Tereshka R Penza U.S.S.R.
48 H2 Tereshva R Ukraine U.S.S.R.
129 K5 Teresina Brazil
129 H3 Teresinha Brazil
128 E3 Teresita Colombia
130 G8 Teresópolis Brazil
31 O3 Terespol Poland
69 A8 Teressa I Nicobar Is
139 J3 Terewah I New S Wales
16 B7 Terge R Portugal
22 E4 Tergnier France
85 C4 Terhazza Mali
52 E1 Teriberka U.S.S.R.
69 C10 Teripa R Sumatra
47 K3 Terkos Gölü L Turkey
108 D6 Terlingua Texas
78 F1 Terme Turkey
77 K1 Termez U.S.S.R.
40 E7 Termignon France
143 D10 Termination I W Australia
20 J5 Terminiers France
43 F11 Termini Imerese Sicily
42 E6 Terminillo mt Italy
45 R8 Terminio, M mt Italy
125 O8 Términos,L.de Mexico
100 E9 Termo California
42 F7 Termoli Italy
Termonde see Dendermonde
71 A2 Ternate Halmahera Indonesia
83 J12 Ternay,C Mahé I Indian Oc
83 K12 Ternay Pass Mahé I Indian Oc
38 K6 Ternberg Austria
28 E3 Terndrup Denmark
25 A6 Terneuzen Netherlands
59 L2 Terney U.S.S.R.
102 T13 Tern I Hawaiian Is
42 E6 Terni Italy
48 K1 Ternopol U.S.S.R.
54 D9 Ternovka U.S.S.R.
145 E3 Te Roti New Zealand
16 D10 Teroual Morocco
138 E5 Terowie S Australia
59 M2 Terpeniya,Mys C U.S.S.R.
55 E3 Terpugovo U.S.S.R.
94 H7 Terra Alta W Virginia
102 E6 Terra Bella California
117 J8 Terrace Br Col
120 C4 Terrace Bay Ontario
143 D8 Terraces, The hills W Australia
45 O7 Terracina Italy
87 D11 Terra Firma S Africa
109 K2 Terral Oklahoma
43 B9 Terralba Sardinia
123 S5 Terra Nova Nfld
146 J6 Terra Nova B Antarctica
45 L4 Terranuova Bracc Italy
18 F7 Terrasson France
124 F3 Terrazas Mexico
146 H3 Terre Adélie Antarctica
100 D5 Terrebonne Oregon
111 F12 Terrebonne B Louisiana
127 N5 Terre de Bas isld Guadeloupe W Indies
127 N5 Terre de Haut isld Guadeloupe W I
110 J2 Terre Haute Indiana
109 L3 Terrell Texas
123 S6 Terrenceville Nfld
101 N6 Terreton Idaho
20 C3 Terrette R France
40 F3 Terri, Mt Switzerland
111 F9 Terry Mississippi
101 U3 Terry Montana
55 E6 Tersakkan R U.S.S.R.
25 D2 Terschelling isld Netherlands
25 D2 Terschellinger Wad Netherlands
86 C3 Tersef Chad
57 H4 Terskey Alatau, Khrebet mts U.S.S.R.
52 E2 Terskiy Bereg coast U.S.S.R.
43 C9 Tertenia Sardinia
17 G4 Teruel prov Spain
47 J1 Tervel Bulgaria
29 M9 Tervo Finland
29 L5 Tervola Finland
22 H2 Tervuren Belgium
42 H4 Tešanj Yugoslavia
107 N2 Tescott Kansas
52 F6 Tesha R U.S.S.R.
116 L1 Teshekpuk L Alaska
60 S2 Teshikaga Japan
60 H11 Te-shima isld Japan
60 Q1 Teshio R Japan
60 Q2 Teshio dake mt Japan
60 P1 Teshio-sanchi mts Japan
46 E1 Tešica Yugoslavia
117 F5 Teslin R Yukon Terr
117 G5 Teslin L Br Col/Yukon Terr
130 E4 Tesouras, R Brazil
130 D5 Tesouro Brazil
52 D5 Tesovo Netyl'skiy U.S.S.R.
17 G9 Tessala, Mt.du Algeria
85 E4 Tessalit Mali
85 F6 Tessaoua Niger
86 G2 Tessenei Ethiopia
118 K7 Tessier Sask
33 Q4 Tessin E Germany
20 C4 Tessy France
43 C7 Testa, C Sardinia
42 G7 Testa del Gargano Italy
18 E8 Teste-de-Buch, la France
32 L6 Testedt W Germany
43 C12 Testour Tunisia
9 E5 Test, R England
106 E6 Tesuque New Mexico
48 D3 Tét Hungary
18 G10 Tet R France
117 L9 Tetachuck L Br Col
122 F6 Tetagouche R New Brunswick
125 J9 Tetala Mexico
17 F4 Tetas de Viana mt Spain
133 C2 Tetas, Pta Chile
8 D4 Tetbury England
88 D10 Tete Mozambique
123 N3 Tete à la Baleine Quebec
117 O9 Tete Jaune Cache Br Col
145 F3 Te Teko New Zealand
36 B5 Téterchen France
56 F1 Tetere R U.S.S.R.
33 R5 Teterow E Germany
47 G2 Teteven Bulgaria
48 M1 Tetiyev U.S.S.R.
116 Q5 Tetlin Alaska
101 O2 Teton R Montana
101 O6 Tetonia Idaho
101 P6 Teton Ra Wyoming
16 D9 Tetouan Morocco
46 E7 Tetráyi mt Greece
37 L3 Tettau W Germany
32 G5 Tettens W Germany
Tetyukhe see Dal'negorsk
Tetyukhe Pristan' see Rudnaya Pristan'
52 G7 Tetyushi U.S.S.R.
37 N1 Teuchern E Germany
133 E3 Teuco R Argentina
38 N7 Teufelstein mt Austria
128 E5 Teuini Brazil
43 B10 Teulada Sardinia
124 H7 Teul de G. Ortega Mexico
119 U8 Teulon Manitoba
71 O8 Teun isld Indonesia
69 B10 Teunom R Sumatra
33 T8 Teupitz E Germany
60 P1 Teuri-tō isld Japan
37 L3 Teuschnitz W Germany
32 H8 Teutoburger Wald W Germany
29 J9 Teuva Finland
26 H9 Tevansjö Sweden
45 M6 Tevere R Italy
144 B6 Teviot New Zealand
15 F5 Teviotdale V Scotland
13 F3 Teviot, R Scotland
50 G3 Tevriz U.S.S.R.
144 A7 Te Waewae Bay New Zealand
70 C5 Tewah Kalimantan
70 D5 Teweh R Kalimantan
145 E3 Te Wera New Zealand
145 F3 Te Whaiti New Zealand
145 E4 Te Wharau New Zealand
8 D4 Tewkesbury England
117 L11 Texada I Br Col
12 B2 Texa I Scotland
109 O2 Texarkana Texas/Ark
109 N2 Texarkana, L Texas
141 K8 Texas Queensland
109 Texas state U.S.A.
109 N6 Texas City Texas
25 C2 Texel isld Netherlands
25 C2 Texelstroom Netherlands
108 C7 Texhoma Texas/Okla
108 D1 Texico New Mexico
108 B7 Texline Texas
125 K8 Texmelucan Mexico
109 L2 Texoma, L Oklahoma
108 F4 Texon Texas
67 A1 Te-yang China
52 F6 Teykovo U.S.S.R.
77 J3 Teyvareh Afghanistan
52 F6 Teza R U.S.S.R.
125 L8 Teziutlán Mexico
75 P5 Tezpur India
87 E11 Thabana Ntlenyana mt Lesotho
89 E7 Thaba Putsoa mt Lesotho
68 B4 Thabaung Burma
87 E10 Thabazimbi S Africa
68 C1 Thabeikkyin Burma
79 E10 Thabt, G. el mt Egypt
68 C2 Thabyedaung Burma
109 K2 Thackerville Oklahoma
68 D6 Thagyettaw Burma
Tha Hin see Lop Buri
67 B6 Thai Binh Vietnam
68 H4 Thai Duong Thung Vietnam
68 E5 Thailand kingdom S E Asia
73 R6 Thailand, G. of Thailand
67 B6 Thai Nguyen Vietnam
69 D8 Tha Khanon Thailand
68 G4 Thakhek Laos
38 G8 Thal Austria
37 J2 Thal E Germany
74 D2 Thal Pakistan
85 F1 Thala Tunisia
69 D8 Thalang Thailand
66 F6 Thala Pass China/Burma
33 O9 Thale E Germany
73 R7 Thale Luang Thailand
36 B4 Thalfang W Germany
38 H6 Thalgau Austria
37 O2 Thalheim E Germany
41 K4 Thalkirch Switzerland
141 J8 Thallon Queensland
112 F6 Thalmann Georgia
37 L5 Thalmässing W Germany
84 F4 Thamad Bu, Hashīshah Libya
9 F4 Thame England
145 E2 Thames New Zealand
120 H10 Thames R Ontario
120 J9 Thamesford Ontario
9 G4 Thames, R England
120 J10 Thamesville Ontario
68 D6 Thamihla Kyun isld Burma
84 F3 Thāmit, Wadi Libya
37 K1 Thamsbrück E Germany
26 D8 Thamshamn Norway
76 A1 Thana India
68 C4 Thanatpin Burma
68 C5 Thanbyuzayat Burma
141 K8 Thane Queensland
68 J5 Thang Binh Vietnam
142 D4 Thangoo W Australia
141 K6 Thangool Queensland
68 G3 Thanh Hoa Vietnam
68 H2 Thanh Moi Vietnam
68 G1 Thanh Thuy Vietnam
76 D5 Thanjavur India
40 F2 Thann France
38 F5 Thann W Germany
37 J7 Thannhausen W Germany
77 K7 Thano Bula Khan Pakistan
36 C7 Thanville France
40 D1 Thaon France
19 K4 Thaon les Vosages France
68 E4 Tha Pla Thailand
69 D8 Thap Put Thailand
68 D7 Thap Sakae Thailand
73 L3 Thar des India
68 D6 Tharabwin Burma
37 Q2 Tharandt E Germany
74 D5 Thar Desert India
141 G8 Thargomindah Queensland
68 B4 Tharrawaddy Burma
68 B4 Tharrawaw Burma
78 J5 Tharthar Basin Iraq
47 G4 Thásos isld Greece
9 E5 Thatcham England
103 P9 Thatcher Arizona
106 F4 Thatcher Colorado
101 O7 Thatcher Idaho
67 B5 That Khe Vietnam
68 C4 Thaton Burma
18 H9 Thau, Étang de L France
68 D4 Thaungyin R Thailand
68 C6 Thayawthadang-yi Kyun isld Burma
110 E5 Thayer Missouri
68 D6 Thayetchaung Burma
68 B3 Thayetmyo Burma
101 P7 Thayne Wyoming
68 A3 Thazi Arakan Burma
68 B2 Thazi Magwe Burma
68 C2 Thazi Mandalay Burma
9 E5 Theale England
103 M9 Theba Arizona
Thebes see Thívai
110 G4 Thebes Illinois
84 J4 Thebes ruins Egypt
98 F7 Thedford Nebraska
120 J9 Thedford Ontario
32 K7 Thedinghausen W Germany
141 L7 Theebine Queensland
68 B3 Thegon Burma
98 K1 Theif River Falls Minnesota
20 G5 Theil, le France
20 G3 Theil, le Gros France
68 D7 Theinkun Burma
68 C4 Theinzeik Burma
37 N1 Theissen E Germany
114 J5 Thekulthili L N W Terr
8 C6 Thelbridge England
113 E7 Thelma Georgia
114 J5 Thelon R N W Terr
28 D4 Them Denmark
37 K3 Themar E Germany
21 H7 Thenay France
18 F7 Thenon France
111 H11 Theodore Alabama
141 K7 Theodore Queensland
119 P7 Theodore Sask
128 F6 Theodore Roosevelt R Brazil
103 N8 Theodore Roosevelt L Arizona
98 C2 Theodore Roosevelt Nat. Mem. Park N Dakota
140 B5 Theo, Mt N Terr Aust
20 K3 Therain R France
95 M2 Theresa New York
99 S6 Theresa Wisconsin
141 J6 Theresa R Queensland
83 K12 Thérèse isld Mahé I Indian Oc
118 F4 Therien Alberta
111 F12 Theriot Louisiana
46 F4 Thermaïkós, Kólpos B Greece
103 L3 Thermo Utah
46 E6 Thérmon Greece
101 R6 Thermopolis Wyoming
46 F6 Thermopylai Greece
139 H6 The Rock New S Wales
146 D10 Theron Mts Antarctica
22 C2 Thérouanne France
21 H7 Thésée France
114 G3 Thesiger B N W Terr
46 E5 Thessalía Greece
120 G6 Thessalon Ontario
46 F4 Thessaloníki Greece
9 G3 Thetford England
121 T6 Thetford Mines Quebec
68 B5 Thetkethaung R Burma
119 P3 The Two Rivers Sask
20 J5 Theuville France
22 K2 Theux Belgium
138 C4 Thevenard S Australia
142 A5 Thevenard I W Australia
19 P16 Thèze France
46 D5 Thiamis R Greece
111 F12 Thibodaux Louisiana
20 G3 Thibouville France
119 T3 Thicket Portage Manitoba
8 D6 Thickthorn England
118 E2 Thickwood Hills Alberta
100 H4 Thief V.Res Oregon
146 F9 Thiel Mts Antarctica
100 C6 Thielsen, Mt Oregon
Thielt see Tielt
99 T6 Thiensville Wisconsin
22 F4 Thiérache France
18 H7 Thiers France
37 N3 Thiersheim W Germany
85 A6 Thies Senegal
43 B8 Thiesi Sardinia
33 T4 Thiessow E Germany
88 F2 Thika Kenya
73 L7 Thiladunmathi Atoll Maldives
20 J3 Thilliers-en-Vexin, les France
40 E2 Thillot, le France
75 N5 Thimbu Bhutan
20 H4 Thimert France
22 H4 Thin le-Moutier France
86 H3 Thio Ethiopia
137 O6 Thio New Caledonia
19 K3 Thionville France
85 D6 Thiou Upper Volta
47 G8 Thíra isld Greece
47 G8 Thirasía isld Greece
20 H5 Thiron-Gardais France
13 G5 Thirsk England
13 G3 Thirston England
143 D9 Thirsty, Mt W Australia
120 K7 Thirty Thousand Is Ontario
28 B3 Thisted Denmark
Thisted co see Viborg
101 O10 Thistle Utah
138 D5 Thistle I S Australia
68 B1 Thitseingyi Burma
47 F6 Thívai Greece
20 H5 Thivars France
18 F7 Thiviers France
18 H6 Thizy France
115 S5 Thjorsá R Iceland
19 Q16 Thoard France
68 E3 Thoeng Thailand
20 J4 Thoiry France
25 B5 Tholen Netherlands
36 C5 Tholey W Germany
19 P18 Tholonet France
107 M6 Thomas Oklahoma
94 H7 Thomas W Virginia
102 E4 Thomas A Edison, L California
113 K11 Thomas B Bahamas
115 K1 Thomas Hubbard, C N W Terr
108 F3 Thomas, J.B., L Texas
138 E2 Thomas, L S Australia
102 H8 Thomas Mt California
144 D5 Thomas, Mt New Zealand
140 B6 Thomas Res N Terr Aust
111 J9 Thomaston Alabama
112 C5 Thomaston Georgia
95 S2 Thomaston Maine
109 K7 Thomaston Texas
14 D4 Thomastown Irish Rep
111 G9 Thomastown Mississippi
111 J10 Thomasville Alabama
113 D7 Thomasville Georgia
110 E5 Thomasville Missouri
112 G2 Thomasville N Carolina
20 H4 Thomer-la-Sogne France
127 J5 Thomonde Haiti
95 Q5 Thompson Connecticut

78

Tornillo — Tuolumne

108 A4 **Tornillo** Texas
28 C4 **Torning** Denmark
29 L6 **Tornio** Finland
29 L6 **Tornionjoki** *R* Finland
33 S6 **Tornow** E Germany
133 E5 **Tornquist** Argentina
60 S2 **Tōro** Japan
16 D3 **Toro** Spain
28 D6 **Torø** *isld* Denmark
131 B2 **Toro, Cerro de** *peak* Arg/Chile
48 J3 **Toroiaga** *mt* Romania
48 F3 **Törökszentmiklós** Hungary
47 F4 **Toronaíos Kólpos** *gulf* Greece
107 P4 **Toronto** Kansas
139 K5 **Toronto** New S Wales
94 G6 **Toronto** Ohio
121 D9 **Toronto** Ontario
52 D6 **Toropets** U.S.S.R.
124 H5 **Toro, Pico del** *mt* Mexico
102 H8 **Toro Pk** California
131 B4 **Toro, Pta** Chile
88 E1 **Tororo** Uganda
78 D3 **Toros Dağlari** *mts* Turkey
26 H9 **Torp** Sweden
15 F3 **Torphins** Scotland
52 F6 **Torpino** U.S.S.R.
8 B7 **Torpoint** England
26 H9 **Torpshammar** Sweden
133 G4 **Torquato Severo** Brazil
8 C7 **Torquay** England
98 C1 **Torquay** Sask
121 L8 **Torrance** Ontario
16 B6 **Torrão** Portugal
45 Q8 **Torre Annunziata** Italy
41 O6 **Torrebelvicino** Italy
17 H4 **Torreblanca** Spain
17 F2 **Torrecilla en Cameros** Spain
45 Q8 **Torre del Greco** Italy
44 F1 **Torre del Mangano** Italy
16 C3 **Torre de Moncorvo** Portugal
44 H4 **Torre di Lago Puccini** Italy
16 E7 **Torredonjimeno** Spain
45 L1 **Torréglia** Italy
16 C5 **Torrejoncillo** Spain
16 E1 **Torrelavega** Spain
42 G7 **Torremaggiore** Italy
16 E8 **Torremolinos** Spain
141 H5 **Torrens** *R* Queensland
141 H5 **Torrens Cr** Queensland
138 E4 **Torrens, L** S Australia
17 G5 **Torrente** Spain
124 H5 **Torreón** Mexico
17 G7 **Torre Pacheco** Spain
133 H3 **Tôrres** Brazil
124 D3 **Torres** Mexico
16 E9 **Torres de Alealá** Morocco
137 O4 **Torres Is** New Hebrides
16 B5 **Torres Novas** Portugal
141 F1 **Torres Strait** Queensland
16 A5 **Torres Vedras** Portugal
17 G7 **Torrevieja** Spain
103 N3 **Torrey** Utah
45 N5 **Torricella in Sabina** Italy
8 B6 **Torridge, R** England
28 E5 **Torrild** Denmark
28 C5 **Tørring** Denmark
118 D7 **Torrington** Alberta
95 O5 **Torrington** Connecticut
139 K3 **Torrington** New S Wales
98 B7 **Torrington** Wyoming
98 B7 **Torrington, S** Wyoming
140 C1 **Tor Rock** *mt* N Terr Aust
26 F8 **Torröjen** *L* Sweden
16 E8 **Torrox** Spain
27 H11 **Torsåker** Sweden
27 H15 **Torsås** Sweden
27 G15 **Torsås, V** Sweden
26 F9 **Torsborg** Sweden
27 F11 **Torsby** Sweden
27 H12 **Torshälla** Sweden
26 J2 **Torsken** Norway
26 L1 **Torsvåg** Norway
57 E3 **Tortkol'** U.S.S.R.
55 F5 **Tortkuduk** U.S.S.R.
43 F11 **Torto** *R* Sicily
113 L7 **Tortola** *isld* Virgin Is
131 B2 **Tortolas, Cerro las** *peak* Arg/Chile
44 E2 **Tortona** Italy
17 H4 **Tortosa** Spain
127 H4 **Tortue, Île de la** Haiti
77 D2 **Ţorūd** Iran
70 G5 **Torue** Sulawesi
66 B3 **Torugart Pass** *pass* U.S.S.R.
31 L2 **Toruń** Poland
27 F15 **Torup** Sweden
52 C5 **Tõrva** U.S.S.R.
27 G13 **Torved** Sweden
13 E5 **Torver** England
26 J7 **Torvsjö** Sweden
121 M8 **Tory Hill** Ontario
14 C1 **Tory I** Irish Rep
48 G2 **Torysa** *R* Czechoslovakia
31 J3 **Torzym** Poland
60 G12 **Tosa** Japan
60 F13 **Tosa-Shimizu** Japan
60 G12 **Tosa-wan** *B* Japan
60 G12 **Tosa-Yamada** Japan
87 D11 **Tosca** S Africa
45 K4 **Toscana** *reg* Italy
42 C5 **Toscano, Arch** *islds* Italy
124 D5 **Tosca, Pta** *C* Mexico
26 F6 **Tosen** Norway
26 F6 **Tosenfjord** *inlet* Norway
41 N3 **Tösens** Austria
61 K11 **Tōshi-jima** *isld* Japan
61 N11 **To-shima** *isld* Japan
61 P5 **Tōshima-yama** *mt* Japan
52 D5 **Tosno** U.S.S.R.
58 C4 **Toson Hu** *L* China
58 C2 **Tosontsengel** Mongolia
26 F9 **Tossåsen** Sweden
45 L3 **Tossignano** Italy
133 E3 **Tostado** Argentina
101 O3 **Toston** Montana
60 D12 **Tosu** Japan
78 D1 **Tosya** Turkey
31 L5 **Toszek** Poland
70 G6 **Totala** Sulawesi
17 F7 **Totana** Spain
144 C5 **Totara Flat** New Zealand
145 D1 **Totara North** New Zealand
145 D4 **Totaranui** New Zealand
27 E11 **Toten** *reg* Norway
32 L6 **Tötensen** W Germany
20 H2 **Tôtes** France
38 J6 **Totes Gebirge** *mts* Austria
48 F4 **Tótkomlós** Hungary
9 E1 **Totley** England
8 C7 **Totnes** England
129 G2 **Totness** Suriname
89 C6 **Toto** *mt* S Africa
144 B6 **Totoko Pk** New Zealand
125 L9 **Totolápam** Mexico
131 B2 **Totoralillo** Chile
85 C7 **Totota** Liberia
146 C10 **Tottanfjella** *ra* Antarctica
146 G2 **Totten Gl** Antarctica
139 H4 **Tottenham** New S Wales
121 L8 **Tottenham** Ontario
9 E6 **Totton** England
59 K4 **Tottori** Japan
60 G10 **Tottori** *prefect* Japan
83 K11 **Totupola** *mt* Sri Lanka
119 M6 **Totzke** Sask
85 C7 **Touba** Ivory Coast
85 C2 **Toubkal** *mt* Morocco
146 D10 **Touchdown Hills** Antarctica
100 G3 **Touchet** Washington
119 N7 **Touchwood Hills** Sask
18 H5 **Toucy** France
65 G3 **Toudao Jiang** *R* China
65 D3 **Toufendi** China
85 D6 **Tougan** Upper Volta
85 F2 **Touggourt** Algeria
85 B6 **Tougue** Guinea
85 C3 **Touila** Mauritania
19 J4 **Toul** France
85 C7 **Toulépleu** Ivory Coast
122 E3 **Toulnustouc R** Quebec
19 P18 **Toulon** France
99 R8 **Toulon** Illinois
102 F1 **Toulon** Nevada
19 O17 **Touloubre** *R* France
18 F9 **Toulouse** France
84 E5 **Toumma** Niger
85 C7 **Toumodi** Ivory Coast
68 C3 **Toungoo** Burma
20 F3 **Touques** France
22 B2 **Touquet-Paris Plage, le** France
21 F7 **Touraine** *prov* France
68 F3 **Tourakom** Laos
Tourane *see* **Da Nang**
22 E2 **Tourcoing** France
16 A1 **Touriñan, C** Spain
85 B4 **Tourine** Mauritania
20 B2 **Tourlaville** France
18 F10 **Tourmalet, Col du** France
22 E2 **Tournai** Belgium
18 G4 **Tournan St Brie** France
128 D5 **Tournavista** Peru
18 F9 **Tournay** France
19 N14 **Tournon** France
40 A4 **Tournus** France
20 J3 **Tourny** France
130 J8 **Touros** Brazil
20 G4 **Tourouvre** France
21 G7 **Tours** France
40 E5 **Tour Sallière** *mt* Switzerland
22 H4 **Tourteron** France
19 P18 **Tourves** France
20 H3 **Tourville-sur-Andelle** France
20 J5 **Toury** France
86 C1 **Toussidé Pic** *mt* Chad
20 K1 **Toutencourt** France
119 S7 **Toutes Aides** Manitoba
100 C3 **Toutle** Washington
89 B9 **Touws River** S Africa
37 O3 **Toužím** Czechoslovakia
127 J10 **Tovar** Venezuela
54 K3 **Tovarkovskiy** U.S.S.R.
27 C13 **Tovdal** Norway
27 C13 **Tovdalselv** *R* Norway
9 F3 **Tove, R** England
61 O5 **Towada-Hachimantai Nat. Park** Japan
61 O5 **Towada ko** *L* Japan
145 E1 **Towai** New Zealand
128 G2 **Towakaima** Guyana
139 J6 **Towamba** New S Wales
110 H1 **Towanda** Illinois
107 O4 **Towanda** Kansas
95 L5 **Towanda** Pennsylvania
70 G7 **Towari** Sulawesi
9 F3 **Towcester** England
99 O2 **Tower** Minnesota
98 J3 **Tower City** N Dakota
95 L6 **Tower City** Pennsylvania
101 P5 **Tower Falls** Wyoming
110 H2 **Tower Hill** Illinois
141 G5 **Tower Hill** Queensland
144 A6 **Towing Head** New Zealand
106 H3 **Towner** Colorado
98 F1 **Towner** N Dakota
102 G5 **Townes Pass** California
111 J8 **Townley** Alabama
95 M7 **Townsend** Delaware
112 F6 **Townsend** Georgia
101 O3 **Townsend** Montana
112 D2 **Townsend** Tennessee
99 S4 **Townsend** Wisconsin
139 J6 **Townsend, Mt** Victoria
141 K5 **Townshend I** Queensland
141 H4 **Townsville** Queensland
94 H5 **Townville** Pennsylvania
86 F4 **Towot** Sudan
95 L7 **Towson** Maryland
70 G6 **Towuti** *L* Sulawesi
8 C3 **Towy, R** Wales
112 D2 **Toxaway, L** N Carolina
66 B3 **Toxkan He** *R* China
108 D4 **Toyah L** Texas
60 O3 **Tōya-ko** *L* Japan
61 L9 **Toyama** Japan
61 L8 **Toyama wan** *B* Japan
116 A3 **Toygunen** U.S.S.R.
61 L10 **Toyo** Japan
60 G11 **Toyohama** Japan
61 L11 **Toyohashi** Japan
61 L11 **Toyokawa** Japan
60 R3 **Toyokoro** Japan
61 J11 **Toyonaka** Japan
60 H10 **Toyooka** Japan
61 N8 **Toyosaka** Japan
61 L10 **Toyota** Japan
29 K9 **Töysä** Finland
85 F2 **Tozeur** Tunisia
116 M4 **Tozitna** *R* Alaska
36 C4 **Traben-Trarbach** W Germany
78 G1 **Trabzon** Turkey
122 H6 **Tracadie** New Brunswick
123 L8 **Tracadie** Nova Scotia
122 F8 **Tracey** New Brunswick
69 H8 **Tra Cu** Vietnam
102 C4 **Tracy** California
99 O8 **Tracy** Iowa
99 L5 **Tracy** Minnesota
110 L6 **Tracy City** Tennessee
22 E5 **Tracy-le-Mont** France
41 J6 **Tradate** Italy
119 O3 **Trade L** Sask
110 J4 **Tradewater** *R* Kentucky
Tradom *see* **Zhongba**
99 O7 **Traer** Iowa
98 F10 **Traer** Kansas
16 C8 **Trafalgar, C** Spain
111 K8 **Trafford** Alabama
113 F11 **Trafford, L** Florida
131 B8 **Traful** *R* Argentina
131 B8 **Traful, L** Argentina
84 E4 **Trāghan** Libya
38 L5 **Tragwein** Austria
48 L5 **Traian** Romania
130 J9 **Traição, B. de** Brazil
133 C5 **Traiguén** Chile
133 C7 **Traiguén, I** Chile
100 H1 **Trail** Br Col
100 C7 **Trail** Oregon
98 F4 **Trail City** S Dakota
115 R3 **Traill Ø** *isld* Greenland
143 D6 **Trainor Hills** W Australia
117 N5 **Trainor L** N W Terr
20 K6 **Trainou** France
130 H10 **Traipu** Brazil
130 J9 **Trairi** *R* Brazil
38 N5 **Traismauer** Austria
20 G3 **Trait, le** France
52 H3 **Trakt** U.S.S.R.
111 F8 **Tralake** Mississippi
14 B4 **Tralee** Irish Rep
68 J6 **Tram Bo** Vietnam
40 F3 **Tramelan** Switzerland
68 G7 **Tram Kak** Cambodia
68 G7 **Tram Khnan** Cambodia
14 D4 **Tramore** Irish Rep
118 J6 **Tramping** Sask
27 H13 **Tranås** Sweden
28 E4 **Tranbjerg** Denmark
133 D3 **Trancas** Argentina
124 G3 **Trancas** Mexico
18 E6 **Tranche, la** France
130 H5 **Trancoso** Brazil
16 C4 **Trancoso** Portugal
27 F14 **Tranemo** Sweden
13 F2 **Tranent** Scotland
69 D9 **Trang** Thailand
139 J4 **Trangie** New S Wales
28 N3 **Trangisvåg** Faeroes
69 H8 **Tranh De, Cua** *R* Vietnam
43 G7 **Trani** Italy
26 J2 **Tranöy** Norway
76 D5 **Tranquebar** India
102 D5 **Tranquillity** California
19 Q18 **Trans** France
118 C1 **Transcona** Manitoba
89 F8 **Transkei** *dist* S Africa
27 F11 **Transtrand** Sweden
89 E5 **Transvaal** *prov* S Africa
48 J4 **Transylvania** *reg* Romania
Transylvanian Alps *see* **Carpaţii Meridionali** *Mts*
68 G8 **Tra On** Vietnam
41 L5 **Traona** Italy
43 E10 **Trapani** Sicily
101 L4 **Trapper Pk** Montana
131 H3 **Trapua** *R* Brazil
13 E2 **Traquair** Scotland
139 H7 **Traralgon** Victoria
17 F9 **Traras, Mt.des** Algeria
27 G15 **Traryd** Sweden
85 A5 **Trarza** *reg* Mauritania
45 P6 **Trasacco** Italy
42 E5 **Trasimeno, L** Italy
26 L6 **Träskholm** Sweden
109 P1 **Traskwood** Arkansas
16 C3 **Tras os Montes e Alto Douro** *prov* Portugal
16 B1 **Trasparga** Spain
36 B4 **Trassem** W Germany
45 H3 **Trassilico** Italy
68 F6 **Trat** Thailand
38 K5 **Traun** Austria
99 U3 **Traunik** Michigan
38 J6 **Traunsee** *L* Austria
38 G6 **Traunstein** W Germany
38 J6 **Traunstein** *mt* Austria
33 M5 **Trave** *R* W Germany
138 F5 **Travellers L** New S Wales
112 E3 **Travellers Rest** S Carolina
33 N5 **Travemünde** W Germany
33 M5 **Travenberg** W Germany
118 E8 **Travers** Alberta
146 A14 **Traversay I** Antarctica
94 B1 **Traverse B.Grand** Michigan
94 B1 **Traverse B.Little** Michigan
94 B2 **Traverse City** Michigan
98 K4 **Traverse, L** S Dakota
116 H4 **Traverse Pk** Alaska
45 H2 **Traversetolo** Italy
122 B5 **Travers, L** Quebec
144 D5 **Travers, Mt** New Zealand
131 C5 **Travesia Puntana** *reg* Argentina
131 C4 **Travesia Tunuyán** *reg* Argentina
109 J5 **Travis, L** Texas
42 H4 **Travnik** Yugoslavia
55 G4 **Travnoye** U.S.S.R.
44 F2 **Travo** Italy
14 D1 **Trawbreaga B** Irish Rep
109 N4 **Trawick** Texas
143 C9 **Trayning** W Australia
42 G2 **Trbovlje** Yugoslavia
8 B1 **Tre-Arddur B** Wales
127 J3 **Treasure Beach** Jamaica
116 J3 **Treat I** Alaska
44 F2 **Trebbia** *R* Italy
33 S8 **Trebbin** E Germany
33 O7 **Trebel** W Germany
33 R4 **Trebel** *R* E Germany
18 G9 **Trèbes** France
31 J6 **Třebíč** Czechoslovakia
42 J6 **Trebinje** Yugoslavia
42 J6 **Trebišnica** *R* Yugoslavia
48 G2 **Trebišov** Czechoslovakia
42 H5 **Trebižat** *R* Yugoslavia
144 A7 **Treble Mt** New Zealand
42 G3 **Trebnje** Yugoslavia
31 H6 **Třeboň** Czechoslovakia
48 D1 **Třebová** Czechoslovakia
33 R10 **Trebsen** E Germany
36 E4 **Trebur** W Germany
8 C4 **Trecastle** Wales
44 E1 **Trecate** Italy
45 K1 **Trecenta** Italy
106 B7 **Trechado** New Mexico
8 C4 **Tredegar** Wales
41 N6 **Tredici Comuni** *reg* Italy
9 E3 **Tredington** England
45 L3 **Tredozio** Italy
73 L6 **Tree I** Lakshadweep Indian Ocean
21 C6 **Treffieux** France
40 B5 **Treffort** France
8 C1 **Trefnant** Wales
8 C1 **Trefriw** Wales
8 C3 **Tregaron** Wales
119 N8 **Tregarva** Sask
101 L1 **Trego** Montana
102 E1 **Trego** Nevada
99 P4 **Trego** Wisconsin
8 B7 **Tregony** England
141 K4 **Tregosse Islets & Reefs** Gt Barrier Reef Aust
18 C4 **Treguier** France
119 T9 **Treherne** Manitoba
68 G8 **Tre, Hon** *isld* Vietnam
26 K8 **Trehörningsjö** Sweden
15 D4 **Treig, L** Scotland
18 G7 **Treignac** France
131 G4 **Treinta y Tres** Uruguay
36 C3 **Treis-Karden** W Germany
140 E5 **Trekelano** Queensland
89 G1 **Trelawney** Zimbabwe
127 J2 **Trelawney** *parish* Jamaica
21 E7 **Trélazé** France
32 L6 **Trelde** W Germany
28 D5 **Trelde Næs** *C* Denmark
133 D6 **Trelew** Argentina
27 F16 **Trelleborg** Sweden
8 D4 **Trelleck** Wales
22 G3 **Trélon** France
8 B2 **Tremadoc** Wales
18 E7 **Tremblade, la** France
20 H4 **Tremblay-le-Vicomte** France
117 L8 **Trembleur L** Br Col
106 F6 **Trementina** New Mexico
21 D7 **Trementines** France
37 K3 **Tremersdorf** W Germany
42 G6 **Tremiti, I.di** Italy
110 G1 **Tremont** Illinois
111 H7 **Tremont** Mississippi
95 L6 **Tremont** Pennsylvania
101 N8 **Tremonton** Utah
37 P4 **Třemošná** Czechoslovakia
17 H2 **Tremp** Spain
99 P5 **Trempealeau** Wisconsin
33 M5 **Tremsbüttel** W Germany
69 G8 **Trem Trem** *R* Vietnam
99 U3 **Trenary** Michigan
121 S5 **Trenche** *R* Quebec
48 E2 **Trenčin** Czechoslovakia
28 C3 **Trend Å** *R* Denmark
32 K9 **Trendelburg** W Germany
133 E5 **Trenel** Argentina
27 A11 **Trengereid** Norway
70 N10 **Trenggalek** Java
131 E5 **Trenque Lauquen** Argentina
Trent *see* **Trento**
108 G3 **Trent** Texas
112 K2 **Trent** *R* N Carolina
121 L8 **Trent Canal** Ontario
41 N5 **Trentino-Alto Adige** *reg* Italy
41 O5 **Trento** Italy
45 Q8 **Tréntola** Italy
113 E8 **Trenton** Florida
94 D4 **Trenton** Michigan
110 C1 **Trenton** Missouri
98 C1 **Trenton** N Dakota
98 E9 **Trenton** Nebraska
95 N6 **Trenton** New Jersey
95 M3 **Trenton** New York
122 K8 **Trenton** Nova Scotia
110 M2 **Trenton** Ohio
121 N8 **Trenton** Ontario
112 F4 **Trenton** S Carolina
110 H6 **Trenton** Tennessee
13 H6 **Trent, R** England
20 H4 **Tréon** France
46 D2 **Trepča** Yugoslavia
20 H1 **Tréport, le** France
38 H8 **Treppo Carnico** Italy
120 C3 **Treptow L** Ontario
133 F4 **Tres Arboles** Uruguay
131 E7 **Tres Arroyos** Argentina
21 B6 **Tresboeuf** France
128 F5 **Três Casas** Brazil
19 P16 **Trescléoux** France
9 F7 **Tresco** *isld* Isles of Scilly England
130 F7 **Três Corações** Brazil
33 N9 **Treseburg** E Germany
85 D1 **Tres Forcas, C** Morocco
15 B4 **Treshnish I** Scotland
48 E7 **Treskavica** *mt* Yugoslavia
130 D7 **Três Lagoas** Brazil
130 F6 **Três Marias** *dam* Brazil
133 B7 **Tres Montes, Pen** Chile
16 E2 **Trespaderne** Spain
130 D10 **Tres Passos** Brazil
131 E7 **Tres Picos, Cerro** *peak* Argentina
106 E5 **Tres Piedras** New Mexico
102 C5 **Tres Pinos** California
130 F7 **Três Pontas** Brazil
133 C3 **Tres Puentes** Chile
130 G8 **Três Rios** Brazil
21 G6 **Tresson** France
31 J6 **Třešť** Czechoslovakia
15 G2 **Tresta** Shetland Scotland
125 M8 **Tres Zapotes** Mexico
8 C4 **Tretower** Wales
19 P18 **Trets** France
27 D10 **Trettin** Norway
Treuburg *see* **Olecko**
37 K6 **Treuchtlingen** W Germany
33 N2 **Treuen** W Germany
33 R8 **Treuenbrietzen** E Germany
27 C12 **Treungen** Norway
Treves *see* **Trier**
20 D3 **Trévières** France
41 L6 **Treviglio** Italy
17 F2 **Treviño** Spain
42 E3 **Treviso** Italy
8 A6 **Trevose Head** England
40 A6 **Trévoux** France
36 G2 **Treysa** W Germany
31 H7 **Trhové Sviny** Czechoslovakia
27 H14 **Triabo** Sweden
139 J8 **Triabunna** Tasmania
21 C9 **Triaize** France
140 D2 **Trial B** N Terr Aust
47 J8 **Trianda** Rhodes Greece
117 P8 **Triangle** Alberta
100 J7 **Triangle** Idaho
47 H8 **Tría Nisiá** *isld* Greece
48 E2 **Tribeč** *R* Czechoslovakia
20 C3 **Tribehou** France
40 H1 **Triberg** W Germany
33 R4 **Tribsees** E Germany
141 H3 **Tribulation, C** Queensland
107 J3 **Tribune** Kansas
119 O9 **Tribune** Sask
43 G8 **Tricarico** Italy
43 J9 **Tricase** Italy
76 C5 **Trichur** India
9 E6 **Trickett's Cross** England
22 D4 **Tricot** France
139 H5 **Trida** New S Wales
100 G8 **Trident Pk** Nevada
38 K7 **Trieben** Austria
37 N2 **Triebes** E Germany
20 J3 **Trie-Chateau** France
37 P6 **Triefenried** W Germany
20 K4 **Triel-sur-Seine** France
131 G4 **Trienta-y-Tres** Uruguay
36 B4 **Trier** W Germany
37 K5 **Triesdorf** W Germany
42 F3 **Trieste** Italy
42 E3 **Trieste, G.di** Italy
22 K5 **Trieux** France
18 C4 **Trieux** *R* France
37 P7 **Triftern** W Germany
42 F2 **Triglav** *mt* Yugoslavia
42 F7 **Trigno** *R* Italy
16 C7 **Triguerós** Spain
47 F5 **Tríkeri** Greece
46 E6 **Trikhonís, L** Greece
46 E5 **Tríkkala** Greece
46 E6 **Tríklinos** Greece
79 D3 **Trikomo** Cyprus
113 E9 **Trilby** Florida
17 F4 **Trillo** Spain
120 G2 **Trilsbeck L** Ontario
14 E3 **Trim** Irish Rep
13 G4 **Trimdon** England
9 H4 **Trimley** England
99 M6 **Trimont** Minnesota
142 B5 **Trimouille I** W Australia
124 D2 **Trincheras** Mexico
106 F4 **Trinchere** Colorado
83 L9 **Trincomalee** Sri Lanka
90 G11 **Trindade** *isld* Atlantic Oc
9 F4 **Tring** England
46 E5 **Tringía** *mt* Greece
121 T6 **Tring Junction** Quebec
128 F6 **Trinidad** Bolivia
100 A8 **Trinidad** California
128 D2 **Trinidad** Colombia
106 F4 **Trinidad** Colorado
126 D4 **Trinidad** Cuba
130 C10 **Trinidad** Paraguay
71 G4 **Trinidad** Philippines
131 G4 **Trinidad** Uruguay
100 E2 **Trinidad** Washington
127 O2 **Trinidad** *isld* W Indies
133 B7 **Trinidad, Canal** Chile
131 E7 **Trinidad, I** Argentina
20 G4 **Trinite de-Reville, la** France
123 T5 **Trinity** Nfld
109 M5 **Trinity** Texas
109 L3 **Trinity** *R* Texas
141 H3 **Trinity B** Queensland
100 C8 **Trinity Center** California
127 P3 **Trinity Hills** Trinidad
116 K8 **Trinity Is** Alaska
102 F1 **Trinity Ra** Nevada
100 C9 **Trinity Res** California
69 A8 **Trinkat I** Nicobar Is
44 D1 **Trino** Italy
Trinquet, Fort *see* **Bir Moghreim**
112 B3 **Trion** Georgia
43 H9 **Trionto, C** Italy
99 O7 **Tripoli** Iowa
79 F4 **Tripoli** Lebanon
84 E3 **Tripoli** Libya
46 E7 **Trípolis** Greece
84 E3 **Tripolitania** *reg* Libya
98 H6 **Tripp** S Dakota
36 D5 **Trippstadt** W Germany
37 M2 **Triptis** E Germany
75 O7 **Tripura** *prov* India
123 N3 **Triquet, L** Quebec
32 J4 **Trischen** *isld* W Germany
37 O4 **Tři Sekery** Czechoslovakia
90 H12 **Tristan da Cunha** Atlantic Oc
68 G7 **Tri Ton** Vietnam
33 M5 **Trittau** W Germany
130 H9 **Triunfo** Brazil
76 C6 **Trivandrum** India
48 D2 **Trnava** Czechoslovakia
20 E3 **Troarn** France
36 G7 **Trochtelfingen** W Germany
26 F5 **Troena** *isld* Norway
28 F6 **Troense** Denmark
38 M7 **Trofaiach** Austria
147 Q9 **Trofimovsk** U.S.S.R.
42 H5 **Troglav** *mt* Yugoslavia
21 I9 **Trois Cornes** *hill* France
36 C2 **Troisdorf** W Germany
36 C6 **Troisfontaines** France
127 L4 **Trois Ilets** Martinique W Indies
122 C5 **Trois Pistoles** Quebec
22 K3 **Trois Ponts** Belgium
127 N5 **Trois Rivières** Guadeloupe W I
121 S6 **Trois Rivières** Quebec
83 M14 **Trois Swains, Les** *islds* Kerguelen Indian Ocean
22 K3 **Trois Vierges** Luxembourg
54 M2 **Troitsa** U.S.S.R.
55 D4 **Troitsk** U.S.S.R.
55 D3 **Troitskiy** U.S.S.R.
52 J3 **Troitsko-Pechorsk** U.S.S.R.
55 C4 **Troitskoye** Bashkirskaya U.S.S.R.
55 E1 **Troitskoye** Tyumenskaya U.S.S.R.
127 L2 **Troja** Jamaica
28 N1 **Troldenæs** Faeroes
28 B5 **Troldhede** Denmark
28 N2 **Troldhoved** *isld* Faeroes
27 F13 **Trollhättan** Sweden
26 D9 **Trollheimen** *mt* Norway
26 C9 **Trolltindane** *mt* Norway
129 G4 **Trombetas** *R* Brazil
133 C5 **Tromen** *mt* Argentina
131 B6 **Tromen, V** Argentina
41 M6 **Trompia, V** Italy
26 K2 **Tromsö** Norway
26 K2 **Tromsöysund** Norway
55 F1 **Trom'yegan** *R* U.S.S.R.
102 G6 **Trona** California
131 B8 **Tronador** *peak* Arg/Chile
124 G6 **Troncón** Mexico
26 J3 **Trondenes** Norway
26 D8 **Trondheim** Norway
26 D8 **Trondheimsfjord** *inlet* Norway
26 E9 **Tronfjell** *mt* Norway
27 J10 **Trönödal** Sweden
42 F6 **Tronto** *R* Italy
21 G6 **Trôo** France
79 C4 **Troödos, Mt** Cyprus
12 D3 **Trool, L** Scotland
12 D2 **Troon** Scotland
43 G10 **Tropea** Italy
130 G4 **Tropeiros, Sa.dos** *mts* Brazil
103 M4 **Tropic** Utah
46 D2 **Tropojë** Albania
27 J13 **Trosa** Sweden
52 J2 **Trosh** U.S.S.R.
98 K6 **Trosky** Minnesota
119 N9 **Trossachs** Sask
12 D1 **Trossachs** Scotland
14 E1 **Trostan** *mt* N Ireland
28 E6 **Trøstrup Korup** Denmark
48 M2 **Trostyanets** U.S.S.R.
33 P9 **Trotha** E Germany
98 C2 **Trotters** N Dakota
48 K4 **Trotusul** *R* Romania
101 T9 **Troublesome** Colorado
142 F2 **Troughton I** W Australia
68 G6 **Troun** Cambodia
109 M3 **Troup** Texas
107 L4 **Trousdale** Kansas
122 F6 **Trousers, L** New Brunswick
111 D10 **Trout** Louisiana
117 L6 **Trout** *R* Br Col
13 F5 **Troutbeck** England
103 L6 **Trout Cr** Arizona
100 E5 **Trout Cr** Oregon
99 R3 **Trout Creek** Michigan
100 K2 **Trout Creek** Montana
121 L7 **Trout Creek** Ontario
103 L2 **Trout Creek** Utah
117 P10 **Trout L** Br Col
99 R3 **Trout L** Wisconsin
117 N5 **Trout Lake** N W Terr
101 Q5 **Trout Pk** Wyoming
118 C2 **Trout R** Alberta
123 O4 **Trout River** Nfld
95 K5 **Trout Run** Pennsylvania
94 J5 **Troutville** Pennsylvania
94 H9 **Troutville** Virginia
20 F3 **Trouville** France
8 D5 **Trowbridge** England
139 H8 **Trowutta** Tasmania
111 L10 **Troy** Alabama
100 J3 **Troy** Idaho
110 K3 **Troy** Indiana
127 J2 **Troy** Jamaica
110 F3 **Troy** Missouri
100 K1 **Troy** Montana
112 H2 **Troy** N Carolina
95 P4 **Troy** New Hampshire
95 O4 **Troy** New York
110 M1 **Troy** Ohio
100 H4 **Troy** Oregon
95 L5 **Troy** Pennsylvania
109 K4 **Troy** Texas
47 H5 **Troy** Turkey
94 G7 **Troy** W Virginia
47 G2 **Troyan** Bulgaria
18 H4 **Troyes** France
95 P2 **Troy, N** Vermont
103 J3 **Troy Pk** Nevada
37 N3 **Tršnice** Czechoslovakia
48 F1 **Trstená** Czechoslovakia
46 D1 **Trstenik** Yugoslavia
140 D1 **Truant I** N Terr Aust
119 N9 **Truax** Sask
54 E4 **Trubchevsk** U.S.S.R.
54 C6 **Trubezh** *R* U.S.S.R.
68 H7 **Truc Giang** Vietnam
124 G5 **Truchas** Mexico
106 E5 **Truchas** New Mexico
36 D6 **Truchtersheim** France
Trucial States *see* **United Arab Emirates**
102 D2 **Truckee** California
102 E2 **Truckee** *R* Nevada
140 B5 **Truer Ra** N Terr Aust
143 E7 **Truer Tableland** W Australia
15 D4 **Truim** *R* Scotland
121 M5 **Truite, L. la** Quebec
125 L2 **Trujillo** Honduras
106 F6 **Trujillo** New Mexico
128 C5 **Trujillo** Peru
16 D5 **Trujillo** Spain
127 J10 **Trujillo** Venezuela
134 F7 **Truk Is** Caroline Is Pacific Oc
99 M6 **Truman** Minnesota
110 F6 **Trumann** Arkansas
95 L4 **Trumansburg** New York
98 H9 **Trumbull** Nebraska
103 L5 **Trumbull, Mt** Arizona
9 G3 **Trumpington** England
20 F4 **Trun** France
139 J5 **Trundle** New S Wales
67 B5 **Trung Khanh Phu** Vietnam
69 G8 **Trung Lon,Hon** *isld* Vietnam
69 G8 **Trung Nho,Hon** *isld* Vietnam
8 A7 **Truro** England
99 N8 **Truro** Iowa
95 R4 **Truro** Massachusetts
122 J8 **Truro** Nova Scotia
138 E5 **Truro** S Australia
70 D2 **Trusan** Sarawak
108 H2 **Truscott** Texas
48 K3 **Truşeşti** Romania
37 J2 **Trusetal** E Germany
14 C2 **Truskmore** *mt* Irish Rep
143 D10 **Truslove** W Australia
70 E2 **Trus Madi, G** *mt* Sabah
52 H2 **Trusovo** U.S.S.R.
111 K8 **Trussville** Alabama
28 F4 **Trustrup** Denmark
117 M7 **Trutch** Br Col
106 C8 **Truth or Consequences** New Mexico
31 J5 **Trutnov** Czechoslovakia
20 D4 **Truttemer-le-Petit** France
95 L4 **Truxton** New York
18 G8 **Truyère** *R* France
47 G2 **Tryavna** Bulgaria
98 F8 **Tryon** Nebraska
145 E2 **Tryphena** New Zealand
27 F10 **Trysil** Norway
27 E10 **Trysilelv** *R* Norway
52 B6 **Tryškiai** U.S.S.R.
31 J2 **Trzcianka** Poland
31 H2 **Trzebiez** Poland
31 K4 **Trzebnica** Poland
31 K3 **Trzemeszno** Poland
42 F2 **Tržič** Yugoslavia
58 C2 **Tsagaain-uul** Mongolia
Tsaidam *see* **Ch'ai-ta-mu P'en-ti** *reg* China
Tsaidam *basin see* **Qaidam**
46 D5 **Tsamandás** Greece
Tsamkong *see* **Zhanjiang**
Tsangpo *see* **Yarlung Zangbo Jiang**
Tsaochwang *see* **Zaozhuang**
87 H11 **Tsaratanana** Madagascar
87 H10 **Tsaratanana, Massif du** *mt* Madagascar
87 D10 **Tsau** Botswana
88 G3 **Tsavo** Kenya
88 G3 **Tsavo Nat. Park** Kenya
41 M4 **Tschlin** Switzerland
55 D5 **Tselinnyy** U.S.S.R.
55 F5 **Tselinograd** U.S.S.R.
54 F3 **Tsementnyy** U.S.S.R.
58 E2 **Tsenhermandal** Mongolia
52 G3 **Tsenogora** U.S.S.R.
56 C3 **Tsentral'nyy** U.S.S.R.
87 C11 **Tses** Namibia
58 C2 **Tsetserleg** Mongolia
58 D2 **Tsetserleg** Mongolia
85 E7 **Tsevié** Togo
87 D11 **Tshabong** Botswana
87 D7 **Tshabuta** Zaïre
87 D10 **Tshane** Botswana
87 E8 **Tshangalele, L** Zaïre
86 B7 **Tshela** Zaïre
87 D7 **Tshibala** Zaïre
86 B6 **Tshibobo, Pte** Gabon
86 D7 **Tshikapa** Zaïre
87 D7 **Tshimbalanga** Zaïre
87 E8 **Tshinsenda** Zaïre
89 C4 **Tshkudu** Botswana
86 E7 **Tshofa** Zaïre
86 D6 **Tshuapa** *R* Zaïre
87 D10 **Tshwanne** Botswana
48 M1 **Tsibulev** U.S.S.R.
87 H13 **Tsihombe** Madagascar
52 G2 **Tsil'ma** *R* U.S.S.R.
53 F10 **Tsimlyansk** U.S.S.R.
65 D6 **Tsinan** China
87 D11 **Tsineng** S Africa
47 G3 **Tsínga** *mt* Greece

Tsingtao *see* **Qingdao**
68 F1 **Tsinh Ho** Vietnam
Tsining *see* **Jining** Nei Monggol Zizhiqu
Tsin Ling *mt ra see* **Qin Ling**
46 E5 **Tsiótion** Greece
58 G1 **Tsipa** *R* U.S.S.R.
87 H11 **Tsiroanomandidy** Madagascar
Tsitsihar *see* **Qiqihar**
89 C9 **Tsitsikamaberge** *mts* S Africa
52 G6 **Tsivilsk** U.S.S.R.
87 H12 **Tsivory** Madagascar
52 D6 **Tsna** *R* U.S.S.R.

61 K11 **Tsu** Japan
61 M8 **Tsubame** Japan
61 K9 **Tsubata** Japan
61 O9 **Tsuchiura** Japan
60 O4 **Tsugaru-kaikyō** *str* Japan
61 N8 **Tsugawa** Japan
61 P13 **Tsuha** Okinawa
61 L10 **Tsukechi** Japan
61 P13 **Tsuken-jima** *isld* Okinawa
60 P2 **Tsukigata** Japan
61 J12 **Tsukiji** Japan
60 E12 **Tsukumi** Japan
87 C9 **Tsumeb** Namibia
87 C10 **Tsumis** Namibia
61 M10 **Tsuru** Japan
61 K10 **Tsuruga** Japan
61 K10 **Tsuruga-wan** *B* Japan
61 K9 **Tsurugi** Japan
60 H12 **Tsurugi-san** *mt* Japan
61 N7 **Tsuruoka** Japan
59 L4 **Tsururga** Japan
60 E12 **Tsurusaki** Japan
61 K10 **Tsushima** Japan
59 J5 **Tsushima** *isld* Japan
60 C11 **Tsushima-kaikyō** *str* Japan
60 C11 **Tsutsu** Japan
60 E11 **Tsuwano** Japan
60 H10 **Tsuyama** Japan
60 D12 **Tsuyazaki** Japan
55 E1 **Tsyngaly** U.S.S.R.
52 D1 **Tsyp Navolok** U.S.S.R.
54 K1 **Tsyurupi, Im** U.S.S.R.
16 C3 **Tua** *R* Portugal
145 G3 **Tuahine Pt.** New Zealand
145 F3 **Tuai** New Zealand
145 E2 **Tuakau** New Zealand
14 C3 **Tuam** Irish Rep
145 D4 **Tuamarina** New Zealand
135 N10 **Tuamotu** *arch* Pacific Oc
135 M10 **Tuamotu Ridge** Pacific Oc
70 D6 **Tuanan** Kalimantan
68 F2 **Tuan Giao** Vietnam
69 C11 **Tuangku** *isld* Sumatra
67 B3 **Tuanxi** China
144 B7 **Tuapeka Mouth** New Zealand
125 N2 **Tuapi** Nicaragua
53 E11 **Tuapse** U.S.S.R.
70 E1 **Tuaran** Sabah
144 A7 **Tuatapere** New Zealand
70 K8 **Tua, Tg** *C* Sumatra
56 D4 **Tuba** *R* U.S.S.R.
103 N10 **Tubac** Arizona
103 N5 **Tuba City** Arizona
71 B3 **Tubalai** *isld* Indonesia
78 H5 **Tubal, Wadi** Iraq
70 O9 **Tuban** Java
133 H3 **Tubarão** Brazil
80 E4 **Tubas** Jordan
70 C3 **Tubau** Sarawak
71 D6 **Tubbataha Reefs** Sulu Sea
118 J8 **Tuberose** Sask
71 E7 **Tubigan** *isld* Philippines
71 E8 **Tubig Puti** Philippines
71 E4 **Tubile Pt** Philippines
36 G7 **Tübingen** W Germany
55 C4 **Tubinskiy** U.S.S.R.
22 G2 **Tubize** Belgium
71 F6 **Tubod** Mindanao Philippines
142 A5 **Tubridgi Pt** W Australia
84 G3 **Tubruq** Libya
70 E3 **Tubu** *R* Kalimantan
135 M10 **Tubuai Is** Pacific Oc
124 D2 **Tubutama** Mexico
127 K9 **Tucacas** Venezuela
100 H3 **Tucannon** *R* Washington
129 L6 **Tucano** Brazil
128 G7 **Tucavaca** Bolivia
18 G10 **Tuchan** France
67 A3 **Tucheng** China
117 J5 **Tuchitua** Yukon Terr
117 L6 **Tuchodi** *R* Br Col
31 K2 **Tuchola** Poland
48 G1 **Tuchów** Poland
143 C7 **Tuckanarra** W Australia
142 E4 **Tuckfield, Mt** W Australia
103 O9 **Tucson** Arizona
103 N9 **Tucson Mts** Arizona
133 D3 **Tucumán** *prov* Argentina
106 G6 **Tucumcari** New Mexico
129 G5 **Tucunaré** Brazil
127 M10 **Tucupido** Venezuela
127 N10 **Tucupita** Venezuela
129 J4 **Tucurui** Brazil
31 J2 **Tuczno** Poland
71 L10 **Tudameda** Indonesia
25 E6 **Tüddern** W Germany
28 G6 **Tudeå** *R* Denmark
17 F2 **Tudela** Spain
16 D3 **Tudela de Duero** Spain
120 J3 **Tudhope** Ontario
102 C2 **Tudor** California
16 C3 **Tuela** *R* Portugal
28 H5 **Tuelsø** Denmark
141 H8 **Tuen** Queensland
129 H4 **Tueré** *R* Brazil
20 G5 **Tuffe** France
136 K3 **Tufi** Papua New Guinea
8 B4 **Tufton** Wales
112 D3 **Tugaloo L** S Carolina
118 L8 **Tugaske** Sask
89 G7 **Tugela** *R* S Africa
94 E9 **Tug Fork** *R* Kentucky
139 K5 **Tuggerah L** New S Wales
116 K8 **Tugidak I** Alaska
71 G5 **Tugnug Pt** Samar Philippines
55 D1 **Tugrovskiy** U.S.S.R.
115 O3 **Tugssâq** Greenland
70 F4 **Tuguan Maputi** *isld* Indonesia
71 G7 **Tugubun Pt** Philippines
71 E2 **Tuguegarao** Philippines
55 D3 **Tugulym** U.S.S.R.
59 L1 **Tugur** U.S.S.R.
145 D4 **Tui** New Zealand
125 P10 **Tuila** Guatemala
65 A4 **Tui Lamin Sum** China
56 C4 **Tuim** U.S.S.R.
Tujiabu *see* **Yongxiu**
69 D11 **Tuka** Sumatra
55 C4 **Tukan** U.S.S.R.
79 B8 **Tûkh** Egypt
145 F3 **Tukituki R** New Zealand
68 F6 **Tuk Luy** Cambodia
114 F4 **Tuktoyaktuk** N W Terr
52 B6 **Tukums** U.S.S.R.
70 B5 **Tukung, Bt** *mt* Kalimantan
87 F7 **Tukuyu** Tanzania
77 K2 **Tukzar** Afghanistan
125 K6 **Tula** Mexico
54 J2 **Tula** U.S.S.R.
119 O4 **Tulabi Lake** Sask
58 C4 **Tulai Shan** China
117 N11 **Tulameen** Br Col
125 K7 **Tulancingo** Mexico
70 K8 **Tulangbawang** *R* Sumatra
102 E5 **Tulare** California
98 H5 **Tulare** S Dakota
102 E6 **Tulare L.Bed** California
108 A2 **Tularosa** New Mexico
106 B8 **Tularosa Mts** New Mexico
106 D9 **Tularosa V** New Mexico
89 B8 **Tulbagh** *mt* S Africa
128 C3 **Tulcán** Ecuador
48 M5 **Tulcea** Romania
48 M2 **Tulchin** U.S.S.R.
127 H9 **Tulé** Venezuela
102 E5 **Tule** *R* California
Tuléar *see* **Toliara**
108 F1 **Tule Cr** Texas
100 D8 **Tule L** California
100 E8 **Tule L.Res** California
19 N16 **Tulette** France
89 F3 **Tuli** Zimbabwe
31 L3 **Tuliszków** Poland
52 D3 **Tulivaara** Finland
80 D4 **Tulkarm** Jordan
14 C4 **Tulla** Irish Rep
110 K6 **Tullahoma** Tennessee
14 D3 **Tullamore** Irish Rep
139 J5 **Tullamore** New S Wales
18 G7 **Tulle** France
28 F7 **Tullebølle** Denmark
139 H5 **Tullibigeal** New S Wales
40 B7 **Tullins** France
48 C2 **Tulln** Austria
38 N5 **Tullnerfeld** *reg* Austria
111 D10 **Tullos** Louisiana
14 E4 **Tullow** Irish Rep
95 L4 **Tully** New York
141 H4 **Tully** Queensland
141 H4 **Tully Falls** Queensland
140 E3 **Tully Inlet** Queensland
52 D1 **Tuloma** *R* U.S.S.R.
65 H1 **Tulongshan** China
29 P8 **Tulos, Oz** *L* U.S.S.R.
52 D3 **Tulos, Oz** *L* U.S.S.R.
47 H2 **Tulovo** Bulgaria
52 J4 **Tulpan** U.S.S.R.
107 P5 **Tulsa** Oklahoma
117 G6 **Tulsequah** Br Col
14 C3 **Tulsk** Irish Rep
28 D4 **Tulstrup** Denmark
128 C3 **Tuluá** Colombia
125 Q7 **Tulum** Mexico
131 C4 **Tulumaya** *R* Argentina
55 C2 **Tulumbasy** U.S.S.R.
131 C3 **Tulum, V.de** Argentina
56 F4 **Tulun** U.S.S.R.
70 N10 **Tulungagung** Java
71 D5 **Tuluran** Philippines
55 C3 **Tulva** *R* U.S.S.R.
54 M1 **Tuma** U.S.S.R.
103 N10 **Tumacacori Nat.Mon** Arizona
128 C3 **Tumaco** Colombia
71 G7 **Tumadgo Pt** Mindanao Philippines
100 D5 **Tumalo** Oregon
52 D6 **Tumanovo** U.S.S.R.
55 E2 **Tuman, Oz** *L* U.S.S.R.
51 P2 **Tumany** U.S.S.R.
56 E5 **Tumat-Tayga, Khrebet** *mts* U.S.S.R.
128 G2 **Tumatumari** Guyana
86 D6 **Tumba** Zaïre
71 G7 **Tumbao** Philippines
139 J6 **Tumbarumba** New S Wales
128 B4 **Tumbes** Peru
124 H8 **Tumbiscatio** Mexico
95 R1 **Tumbledown Mt** Maine
140 B2 **Tumbling Waters** N Terr Aust
130 B9 **Tumburús** Argentina
9 F1 **Tumby** England
138 D5 **Tumby Bay** S Australia
65 A4 **Tumd Youqi** China
65 B4 **Tumd Zuoqi** China
80 G4 **Tumeira** Jordan
65 H3 **Tumen** China
59 J3 **Tumen** *R* China/Korea
128 F2 **Tumeremo** Venezuela
70 F2 **Tumindao** *isld* Philippines
130 H6 **Tumiritinga** Brazil
76 C4 **Tumkur** India
15 D4 **Tummel** *R* Scotland
59 M2 **Tumnin** *R* U.S.S.R.
77 H6 **Tump** Pakistan
69 F9 **Tumpat** Malaysia
74 H8 **Tumsar** India
85 D6 **Tumu** Ghana
129 G3 **Tumucamaque, Sa** *mts* Brazil
139 J6 **Tumut** New S Wales
52 H6 **Tumutuk** U.S.S.R.
27 F13 **Tun** Sweden
26 J9 **Tuna** Sweden
71 G7 **Tuna Bay** Mindanao Philippines
127 O2 **Tunapuna** Trinidad
128 E7 **Tunari** *mt* Bolivia
126 E4 **Tunas de Zaza** Cuba
131 E5 **Tunas, L** Argentina
77 D6 **Tunb Buzurg** *isld* Iran
139 H8 **Tunbridge** Tasmania
9 G5 **Tunbridge Wells, Royal** England
78 G2 **Tunceli** Turkey
67 C7 **Tunchang** China
139 L4 **Tuncurry** New S Wales
52 F3 **Tundra** U.S.S.R.
87 F7 **Tunduma** Zambia
88 F7 **Tunduru** Tanzania
28 J5 **Tune** Denmark
70 F2 **Tungku** Sabah
29 P6 **Tungozero** U.S.S.R.
67 G5 **Tung Shan** Taiwan
102 F1 **Tungsten** Nevada
117 J5 **Tungsten** N W Terr
Tungting Lake *see* **Dongting Ho**
70 C4 **Tungun, Bt** *mt* Kalimantan
56 F1 **Tunguska** *R* U.S.S.R.

58 E2 **Tünhel** Mongolia
27 C11 **Tunhovdfjord** *L* Norway
76 F2 **Tuni** India
43 C12 **Tunis** Tunisia
43 D11 **Tunis, G. de** Tunisia
84 D3 **Tunisia** *rep* N Africa
128 D2 **Tunja** Colombia
56 F5 **Tunkinskiye Gol'tsy** *mts* U.S.S.R.
65 B6 **Tunliu** China
26 E9 **Tunna** *R* Norway
139 H8 **Tunnack** Tasmania
120 G6 **Tunnel Dam** Ontario
19 O18 **Tunnel du Rove** France
94 H7 **Tunnelton** W Virginia
26 F7 **Tunnsjö** *L* Norway
28 E5 **Tunø** Denmark
8 D1 **Tunstall** Stafford England
9 H3 **Tunstall** Suffolk England
115 N6 **Tunungayualok I** Labrador
131 C4 **Tunuyán, R** Argentina
131 C4 **Tunuyán, Sa. de** *mts* Argentina
67 F2 **Tunxi** China
67 D4 **Tuojiang** China
67 A1 **Tuo Jiang** *R* China
65 E5 **Tuoji Dao** *isld* China
68 G6 **Tuol Khpos** Cambodia
102 D4 **Tuolumne** California

102 E4 Tuolumne Meadows California
29 L7 Tuomioja Finland
51 L2 Tuoy U.S.S.R.
130 E7 Tupã Brazil
130 E6 Tupaciguara Brazil
128 F4 Tupanaoca Brazil
145 G2 Tuparoa New Zealand
111 H7 Tupelo Mississippi
109 L1 Tupelo Oklahoma
52 D6 Tupik U.S.S.R.
128 G4 Tupinambaranas, I Brazil
130 E4 Tupiraçaba Brazil
133 D2 Tupiza Bolivia
102 E6 Tupman California
29 L7 Tupos Finland
117 N8 Tupper Br Col
95 N2 Tupper Lake New York
133 D4 Tupungato mt Arg/Chile
65 E2 Tuquan China
128 C3 Tuquerres Colombia
67 D7 Tuqu Wan B China
66 H4 Tura China
75 O6 Tura India
55 D2 Tura R U.S.S.R.
145 E4 Turakina New Zealand
145 E4 Turakirae Head New Zealand
141 K8 Turallin Queensland
56 D5 Turan U.S.S.R.
59 K1 Turana, Khrebet mt U.S.S.R.
145 E3 Turangi New Zealand
42 E6 Turano R Italy
45 N5 Turano, L di Italy
126 G9 Turbaco Colombia
52 H4 Turbanovo U.S.S.R.
77 H7 Turbat Pakistan
41 J3 Turbenthal Switzerland
126 F10 Turbo Colombia
17 H2 Turbón mt Spain
48 M1 Turburea Romania
48 H6 Turceni Romania
52 E3 Turchasovo U.S.S.R.
48 H4 Turda Romania
143 C6 Turee Cr W Australia
16 E3 Turegano Spain
31 L3 Turek Poland
79 D10 Tûr, Et Egypt
127 K10 Turen Venezuela
66 D3 Turfan Depression China
57 C1 Turgay U.S.S.R.
57 B1 Turgay R U.S.S.R.
55 D5 Turgayskaya Stolovaya Strana dist U.S.S.R.
121 L3 Turgeon R Quebec
47 H1 Türgovishte Bulgaria
47 G3 Turgoyak U.S.S.R.
47 J6 Turgutlu Turkey
78 F1 Turhal Turkey
52 C5 Turi U.S.S.R.
17 G5 Turia R Spain
129 J4 Turiaçu Brazil
127 L9 Turiamo Venezuela
31 L7 Turiec R Czechoslovakia
126 E3 Turimiquire, I Cuba
125 N9 Turin see Torino
118 E9 Turin Alberta
95 M3 Turin New York
55 D2 Turinsk U.S.S.R.
55 D3 Turinskaya-Sloboda U.S.S.R.
59 K2 Turiy Rog U.S.S.R.
48 D3 Türje Hungary
48 H1 Turka U.S.S.R.
56 G4 Turkana, L see Rudolf, L
47 J4 Turkeli isld Turkey
41 O1 Turkenfeld W Germany
57 E1 Turkestan U.S.S.R.
57 E5 Turkestanskiy Khr mts U.S.S.R.
48 F3 Türkeve Hungary
108 L1 Turkey Texas
99 P7 Turkey R Iowa
78 D2 Turkey rep W Asia
142 G3 Turkey Cr W Australia
106 F6 Turkey Mts New Mexico
41 N1 Türkheim W Germany
36 C4 Türkismühle W Germany
47 L5 Turkmen Dagi mt Turkey
57 B5 Turkmen-Kala U.S.S.R.
57 A4 Turkmenkarakul' U.S.S.R.
50 E4 Turkmenskaya S.S.R U.S.S.R.
127 H4 Turks Is W Indies
29 J11 Turku Finland
27 M10 Turku Pori reg Finland
86 G5 Turkwel R Kenya
16 E5 Turleque Spain
102 D4 Turlock California
130 G5 Turmalina Brazil
117 J6 Turnagain R Br Col
145 F4 Turnagain, C New Zealand
38 M6 Turnau Austria
119 Q5 Turnberry Manitoba
31 E3 Turnberry Scotland
119 S4 Turnbull Manitoba
140 B5 Turnbull, Mt N Terr Aust
95 R2 Turner Maine
94 D2 Turner Michigan
101 R1 Turner Montana
100 C5 Turner Oregon
100 H3 Turner Washington
101 U6 Turnercrest Wyoming
142 B6 Turner, Mt W Australia
142 G4 Turner River W Australia
95 P4 Turners Falls Massachusetts
118 C8 Turner Valley Alberta
101 P7 Turnerville Wyoming
22 H1 Turnhout Belgium
38 M6 Turnitz Austria
31 N3 Turnu Czechoslovakia
47 G1 Turnu Măgurele Romania
48 J5 Turnu Roşu Romania
48 H6 Turnu Severin Romania
57 H1 Turobay U.S.S.R.
31 O5 Turobin Poland
107 M4 Turon Kansas
139 J5 Turon R New S Wales
139 J5 Tuross R New S Wales
66 D3 Turpan China
108 D7 Turpin Oklahoma
106 D9 Turquoise New Mexico
116 K6 Turquoise L Alaska
38 J8 Turrach Austria
110 F6 Turrell Arkansas
126 N5 Turrialba Costa Rica
19 Q16 Turriers France
15 F3 Turriff Scotland
55 D1 Turuntskiy Tuman, Oz U.S.S.R.
57 E6 Tursunzade U.S.S.R.
55 E2 Turtas R U.S.S.R.
57 K1 Turtkul' U.S.S.R.
99 O1 Turtle R Ontario
122 H8 Turtle Cr New Brunswick
118 J5 Turtleford Sask
141 G1 Turtlehead L Queensland
141 K1 Turtle I Gt Barrier Reef Aust
142 C5 Turtle I W Australia
85 B7 Turtle Is Sierra Leone
59 F2 Turtle L N Dakota
118 J5 Turtle L Sask
99 O4 Turtle L Wisconsin
98 F1 Turtle Mts Manitoba/N Dakota
92 K5 Turtola Finland
98 H4 Turton S Dakota
145 E2 Turua New Zealand
51 E1 Turukhansk U.S.S.R.
55 E1 Turuna R U.S.S.R.
28 D6 Turup Denmark
28 E9 Turvey England
130 D10 Turvo R Brazil
53 B8 Tur'ya R U.S.S.R.
111 J8 Turzovka Czechoslovakia
111 J8 Tuscaloosa Alabama
115 H6 Tuscany Italy
94 K6 Tuscarora Nevada
110 H2 Tuscola Illinois

100 K2 Tuscor Montana
110 D3 Tuscumbia Missouri
28 H5 Tuse Denmark
14 E4 Tuskar Rock Irish Rep
111 L9 Tuskegee Alabama
122 G10 Tusket Nova Scotia
54 H5 Tuskor' R U.S.S.R.
48 K4 Tusnad Romania
21 F10 Tusson France
102 G8 Tustin California
94 B2 Tustin Michigan
26 C8 Tustna isld Norway
116 M6 Tustumena L Alaska
31 M4 Tuszyn Poland
145 D1 Tutamoe Range New Zealand
52 E5 Tutayev U.S.S.R.
9 E2 Tutbury England
98 E6 Tuthill S Dakota
76 D1 Tutin India
46 D1 Tutin Yugoslavia
145 F3 Tutira L New Zealand
29 O5 Tutiyaryi U.S.S.R.
70 D3 Tutoh R Sarawak
129 K4 Tutóia Brazil
70 D2 Tutong Brunei
48 L4 Tutova R Romania
33 S5 Tutow E Germany
48 K6 Tutrakan Bulgaria
117 F5 Tutshi L Yukon Terr
101 L7 Tuttle Idaho
98 F2 Tuttle N Dakota
107 N6 Tuttle Oklahoma
37 K2 Tuttlingen W Germany
99 M6 Tuttle L Minnesota
41 J2 Tuttwil Switzerland
137 S4 Tutuala isld Amer Samoa
125 L8 Tututepec Mexico
71 G8 Tutuvawang Indonesia
111 F7 Tutwiler Mississippi
41 O2 Tutzing W Germany
58 D2 Tuul Gol R Mongolia
29 L10 Tuulos Finland
29 P9 Tuupovaara Finland
29 O9 Tuusniemi Finland
29 N8 Tuusula Finland
137 Q3 Tuvalu islds Pacific Oc
137 R6 Tuvana-i-Ra isld Pacific Oc
137 R6 Tuvana-i-Tholo isld Pacific Oc
56 E5 Tuvinskaya Aut.Obl U.S.S.R.
103 L5 Tuweep Arizona
65 A5 Tuwei He R China
116 L6 Tuxedni B Alaska
118 A1 Tuxedo Manitoba
112 E2 Tuxedo N Carolina
41 F3 Tuxer Gebirge mt Austria
119 M8 Tuxford Sask
67 C1 Tuxiang China
124 H8 Tuxpan Jalisco Mexico
125 L7 Tuxpan Mexico
125 N9 Tuxtla Gutiérrez Mexico
52 F2 Tuy Spain
55 F2 Tuy R U.S.S.R.
52 D1 Tuya Guba U.S.S.R.
119 O8 Tuya L Br Col
48 M1 Tuy An Vietnam
8 B2 Tuywyn Wales
25 C3 tZand Netherlands
87 F10 Tzaneen S Africa
37 L2 Tzepo isld Zibo
28 C5 Tzoumérka mt Greece
67 G4 Tz'u-kao Shan peak Taiwan
25 E2 Tzummarum Netherlands

31 L5 Tychy Poland
26 E8 Tydal Norway
59 J1 Tyeda U.S.S.R.
117 F7 Tyee Washington
100 A1 Tyee Washington
39 J7 Tyee River Virginia
94 H8 Tygart V W Virginia
101 N7 Tygee Idaho
27 C10 Tyin L Norway
31 O2 Tykocin Poland
98 K5 Tyler Minnesota
109 M3 Tyler Pennsylvania
93 B2 Tyler Texas
100 H2 Tyler Washington
111 A9 Tyler, L Texas
111 F10 Tylertown Mississippi
28 D2 Tylstrup Denmark
52 C1 Tynda U.S.S.R.
48 F1 Tymbark Poland
59 M1 Tymovskoye U.S.S.R.
59 M2 Tynay U.S.S.R.
59 H1 Tynda U.S.S.R.
118 E1 Tyndall Manitoba
98 J3 Tyndall S Dakota
144 C5 Tyndall, Mt New Zealand
26 J9 Tyndorö Sweden
13 G4 Tyne and Wear co England
13 G3 Tynemouth England
118 J7 Tyner Sask
32 E7 Tyne Valley Pr Edward I
27 G11 Tyngsjö Sweden
31 H6 Týn nad Vltava Czechoslovakia
26 E9 Tynset Norway
8 O5 Tyn-y-Groes Wales
79 F5 Tyr Lebanon
37 J4 Tyr see Tyr
55 C3 Tyrifjorden L Norway
27 G15 Tyringe Sweden
59 K1 Tyrma U.S.S.R.
48 L2 Tyrnovo U.S.S.R.
112 E2 Tyron N Carolina
106 B9 Tyrone New Mexico
94 J6 Tyrone Pennsylvania
28 C5 Tyrone co N Ireland
139 G6 Tyrrell R Victoria
116 J8 Tyrrell L Alaska
13 J8 Tyrrhenian Sea S Europe
28 D5 Tyrsted Denmark
26 H3 Tysfjord Norway
27 A12 Tysnesøy isld Norway
27 B11 Tyssedal Norway
28 E1 Tysberga Sweden
31 O5 Tystrup Denmark
31 J13 Tyszowce Poland
57 H4 Tyukalinsk U.S.S.R.
59 M2 Tyulek U.S.S.R.
52 J5 Tyul'kino U.S.S.R.
55 D3 Tyumen U.S.S.R.
57 D3 Tyumen'-Aryk U.S.S.R.
50 F2 Tyumenskaya Oblast' prov U.S.S.R.
55 G4 Tyuntyugur U.S.S.R.
52 C1 Tyuratam U.S.S.R.
52 D1 Tyuva Guba U.S.S.R.
48 M1 Tyvrov U.S.S.R.
25 E2 Tzummarum Netherlands

76 C1 Udgir India
74 F2 Udhampur Kashmir
142 E4 Udialla W Australia
42 E2 Udine Italy
56 E4 Udinskiy Khrebet mts U.S.S.R.
76 B4 Udipi India
71 K8 Udjung Indonesia
70 F7 Udjungpandang Sulawesi
37 P3 Udlice Czechoslovakia
51 K4 Udokan Mongolia
52 E5 Udomlya U.S.S.R.
6 N11 Udone-jima isld Japan
68 F4 Udon Thani Thailand
140 D6 Udor, Mt N Terr Aust
59 L1 Udskaya Guba B U.S.S.R.
47 N2 Udovo U.S.S.R.
59 L1 Udyl, Oz L U.S.S.R.
51 L1 Udzha U.S.S.R.
70 G5 Uebster Sulawesi
33 U5 Uecker R E Germany
33 T6 Ueckermark reg E Germany
33 U5 Ueckermünde E Germany
25 F5 Ueda Japan
32 G8 Uelfeln W Germany
86 H5 Uegit Somalia
98 K8 Uehling Nebraska
60 D13 Ueki Japan
25 D7 Uele R E Germany
15 G1 Uelsta Shetland Scotland
33 N7 Uelsen W Germany
61 K11 Ueno Japan
61 N10 Uenohara Japan
86 E5 Uere R Zaire
32 L5 Uess R W Germany
47 K6 Ufa U.S.S.R.
55 C4 Ufa R U.S.S.R.
37 J4 Uffenheim W Germany
55 C3 Ufimka U.S.S.R.
71 D5 Ugab R Namibia
88 F5 Ugashik I Alaska
69 E11 Ugashik Lakes Alaska
70 E3 Ugashik Bay Alaska
70 C4 Ugento Italy
66 D2 Ugglehuse Denmark
66 D2 Uggerby Denmark
28 E4 Uggelhuse Denmark
28 E1 Uggerby Denmark
28 E5 Uggersley Denmark
16 E8 Ugijar Spain
28 E2 Ugilt Denmark
19 Q13 Ugine France
59 M2 Uglegorsk U.S.S.R.
26 M10 Uglovka U.S.S.R.
52 E6 Uglich U.S.S.R.
52 J5 Uglovka U.S.S.R.
55 E3 Ugljane Yugoslavia
57 D3 Ugljevik Yugoslavia
52 D5 Uglovka U.S.S.R.
54 G2 Ugra R U.S.S.R.
55 F1 Ugut U.S.S.R.
83 L10 Uhak Sri Lanka
31 K6 Uherské Hradiště Czechoslovakia
36 H6 Uhingen W Germany
87 C10 Uhlenhorst Namibia
119 T2 Uhldorf W Germany
37 L2 Uhlstädt E Germany
28 C5 Uhre Denmark
94 F6 Uhrichsville Ohio
31 O4 Uhrusk Poland
15 B3 Uig Skye Scotland
85 G8 Uíge Zaire
113 F9 Uintah Florida
100 F4 Uinta Mts Utah
71 G6 Uinta Mts Utah
95 Q2 Uinskoye U.S.S.R.
101 P9 Uinta Mts Utah
89 D9 Uitenhage S Africa
25 C3 Uitgeest Netherlands
25 C4 Uithoorn Netherlands
25 G2 Uithuizen Netherlands
136 K3 Uithuizerwad Netherlands
31 L5 Ujazd Poland
74 J7 Ujjain India
61 N9 Ujjie Japan
88 B4 Ujiji Tanzania
48 E3 Ujpest Hungary
31 O6 Ujście Poland
61 L8 Uka U.S.S.R.
26 K7 Ukawa Japan
88 D3 Ukerewe isld Tanzania
75 Q6 Ukhrul India
110 U.S.S.R.
71 B3 Ukiah Oregon
80 G7 Ukibaru-jima isld Okinawa
116 D4 Ukivok Alaska
52 D6 Ukkel see Uccle
118 L1 Ukmerge U.S.S.R.
88 B10 Ukraine S.S.R rep U.S.S.R.
54 C7 Ukrainka Omsk U.S.S.R.
41 N3 Ukrina R Yugoslavia
88 B10 Uksyanskoye U.S.S.R.
60 B12 Uku-jima isld Japan
60 B12 Uku-shima isld Japan
47 J7 Ula Turkey
84 F4 Ulaanbaatar Mongolia
80 E3 Ulan Bator Mongolia
65 C2 Ulan Hobor China
46 G6 Ulan Hot see Horqin Youyi Qianqi
48 L1 Ula Hua China
65 A4 Ulanov U.S.S.R.
55 G6 Ulan-Ude U.S.S.R.
131 C3 Ulapes, Sa mts Argentina
55 B5 Ul'ba U.S.S.R.
51 N3 Ulbanskiy Zaliv B U.S.S.R.
28 C3 Ulbjerg Denmark
100 B6 Ulceby Cross England
9 G1 Ulceby England
13 E4 Uldale England
28 D5 Uleåborg see Oulu
27 D12 Ulefoss Norway
59 Minnesota
13 E5 Ulenia Victoria
138 F3 Ulenia, L New S Wales
89 G2 Ulety U.S.S.R.
89 F8 Ulfborg Denmark
28 E10 Ulfborg Kirke Denmark
89 G2 Umtali S Africa
139 U4 Umtata S Africa

13 F4 Ullswater L England
59 K4 Ullung Do isld S Korea
111 E7 Ulm Arkansas
36 H7 Ulm W Germany
101 T5 Ulm Wyoming
139 L3 Ulmarra New S Wales
28 D5 Ulmen W Germany
48 K5 Ulmeni Romania
38 L5 Ulmerfeld Austria
125 M2 Ulmukhuas Nicaragua
48 E7 Ulog Yugoslavia
88 E9 Ulongue Mozambique
139 E2 Uloowaranie, L S Australia
13 E5 Ulpha England
56 H1 Ulqkhan Botuobuya R U.S.S.R.
27 F14 Ulricehamn Sweden
143 E17 Ulrich Ra W Australia
36 G2 Ulrichstein W Germany
26 H8 Ulriksfors Sweden
25 F2 Ulrum Netherlands
59 J4 Ulsan S Korea
28 D7 Ulsby W Germany
15 G1 Ulsta Shetland Scotland
115 M6 Ulster Pennsylvania
139 G6 Ultima Victoria
140 D6 Ultim, Mt N Terr Aust
41 O4 Ultimo.V.d' Italy
51 M2 Ulu U.S.S.R.
85 C8 Uun, Mt Liberia
128 F4 União Brazil
130 D10 União da Vitória Brazil
130 J10 União dos Palmares Brazil
112 E1 Unicoi Tennessee
48 D1 Uničov Czechoslovakia
31 L4 Uniejów Poland
42 F4 Unije isld Yugoslavia
116 E9 Unimak I Aleutian Is
116 E9 Unimak I Aleutian Is
58 F1 Unini R Brazil
95 P10 Union Argentina
133 D5 Union Argentina
47 K6 Union Colorado
99 N7 Union Iowa
111 F11 Union Louisiana
95 S2 Union Maine
111 G9 Union Mississippi
110 E3 Union Missouri
99 L9 Union Nebraska
107 O8 Union Oregon
100 H4 Union Oregon
130 C9 Union Paraguay
53 C9 Union S Carolina
94 B9 Union W Virginia
94 D5 Union Washington
110 G5 Union City Indiana
94 M1 Union City Michigan
65 A4 Union City Ohio/Indiana
94 M5 Union City Pennsylvania
110 G5 Union City Tennessee
100 C7 Union Creek Oregon
95 M5 Uniondale Pennsylvania
126 D3 Unión de Reyes Cuba
100 E3 Union Flat Cr Washington
100 G3 Union Gap Washington
17 G7 Union, La Spain
112 F2 Union Mills N Carolina
103 M7 Union, Mt Arizona
50 Union of Soviet Socialist Republics
101 Q6 Union Pass Wyoming
112 D4 Union Point Georgia
118 D1 Union Pt Manitoba
111 L9 Union Springs Alabama
100 G4 Union Springs New York
94 M10 Union Star Missouri
109 M9 Union Stock Yards Texas
111 J9 Uniontown Alabama
110 J4 Uniontown Kentucky
94 H7 Uniontown Pennsylvania
99 O9 Unionville Michigan
99 N9 Unionville Virginia
102 F1 Unionville Nevada
94 K8 Unionville Virginia
54 K6 Unirea Romania
71 J9 Unisan Philippines
99 N9 Unity Maine
100 G5 Unity Oregon
118 H6 Unity Sask
17 H3 Universales mt Spain
110 D5 University City Missouri
111 K13 University City St Louis
109 O9 University Park Texas
31 M4 Unkei W Germany
38 G6 Unken Austria
38 L5 Unnao India
55 C3 Unna W Germany
74 G4 Unnao India
26 H8 Unni Finland
15 G1 Unst Shetland Scotland
33 O2 Unstrut R E Germany
61 P12 Unten Okinawa
147 G1 Uninngmakkok U.S.A.
38 N6 Untermünkheim W Germany
39 C2 Untereisesheim W Germany
61 P12 Unter der Fels Austria
77 J1 Untergaital V Austria
86 F3 Untergruppenbach W Germany
37 H2 Unterwalden canton Switzerland
36 F3 Unterschwarzach W Germany
87 D9 Uolevi, Cross England
87 C9 Unulapo Angola
80 Q4 Um Qantara Jordan
80 H4 Um Qeis Jordan
80 G8 Um Quleib Jordan
80 G8 Um Quseir Jordan
74 H8 Umrer India
80 H7 Um Rummana Jordan
89 G2 Umuahia Nigeria
117 H7 Unye Turkey
20 H5 Unzen-Amakusa Nat Park Japan
60 D13 Unzen dake mt Japan
38 K7 Unzmarkt Austria
84 C5 Upa R U.S.S.R.

27 G13 Undenäs Sweden
138 F6 Underbool Victoria
28 E2 Understed Denmark
27 K11 Understen It ho Sweden
27 H10 Undersvik Sweden
28 D5 Underup Denmark
98 L8 Underwood Iowa
99 P6 Underwood N Dakota
28 H5 Underwood Washington
71 K10 Undu,Tg C Sumba Indonesia
54 D4 Unecha U.S.S.R.
54 J7 Unéixi R Brazil
79 F8 Uneiza Jordan
37 P4 Unenbo Czechoslovakia
52 E3 Unezhma U.S.S.R.
116 G9 Unga I Alaska
116 G4 Ungalik Alaska
138 D5 Ungarie New S Wales
115 M6 Ungarra S Australia
48 L3 Ungava B Quebec
48 L3 Ungeny U.S.S.R.
41 M1 Ungerhausen W Germany
59 K3 Unggi N Korea
48 L3 Ungwana B S Korea
41 J4 Uni U.S.S.R.
11 J1 Unini R Brazil
133 D5 Unión Argentina
116 C6 Unión Colorado
99 N7 Union Iowa
111 F11 Union Louisiana
95 S2 Union Maine
111 G9 Union Mississippi
110 E3 Union Missouri
99 L9 Union Nebraska
107 O8 Union Oregon
100 H4 Union Oregon
130 C9 Union Paraguay
71 H5 Unión, county Sweden
116 C6 Upright,C St Matthew I Bering Sea
99 M4 Upsala Minnesota
119 N1 Upsala Ontario
122 F6 Upsalquitch New Brunswick
74 G2 Upshi Kashmir
99 Q3 Upshi Wisconsin
141 J4 Upstart, C Queensland
9 H5 Upstreet England
8 D3 Upton England
94 B9 Upton Kentucky
99 Q3 Upton Wyoming
141 J4 Upton Wyoming
84 F2 Upton Cheyney England
85 N2 Upolu Pt Hawaiian Is
101 O5 Urach W Germany
36 G7 Urach W Germany
128 F2 Uracoa Venezuela
65 A4 Urad Qianqi China
54 D7 Urad Zhonghou Lianheqi China
61 N10 Uraga Japan
60 D3 Urakawa Japan
100 K1 Ural Montana
139 H5 Ural mt New S Wales
139 K4 Uralla New S Wales
5 R4 Ural Mts U.S.S.R.
142 F3 Ural Well W Australia
88 D4 Urambo Tanzania
139 H4 Urana New S Wales
139 H4 Urandangie Queensland
130 G4 Urandi Brazil
141 L7 Urangan Queensland
111 D10 Urania Louisiana
114 J6 Uranium City Sask
13 B10 Uraniya Sri Lanka
142 C2 Urapunga N Terr Aust
128 F3 Uraricoera Brazil
143 E9 Uraryie W Australia
61 N10 Ura-Tyube U.S.S.R.
60 P2 Urausai Japan
61 N10 Urawa Japan
99 O9 Urazavo U.S.S.R.
55 G6 Urazovka U.S.S.R.
54 K6 Urazovo U.S.S.R.
99 S5 Urbana Illinois
99 N8 Urbana Indiana
99 P8 Urbana Iowa
99 P8 Urbana Missouri
94 D6 Urbana Ohio
45 L9 Urbania Italy
95 L9 Urbana Virginia
129 K4 Urbano Santos Brazil
16 E2 Urbao Spain
17 F2 Urbión, Se. de mts Spain
22 F5 Urcel France
128 D6 Urcos Peru
52 J4 Urdarhar U.S.S.R.
55 F3 Urekhovo U.S.S.R.
122 E1 Uren U.S.S.R.
145 E3 Urenui New Zealand
137 O4 Urepas ra is'd New Hebrides
124 C3 Ures Mexico
145 F3 Urewera Country New Zealand
55 G2 Urfa Turkey
38 K5 Urfahr Austria
41 O2 Urfeld W Germany
53 A9 Urga R U.S.S.R.
38 D7 Urgel Mongolia
77 J3 Urgun Afghanistan
41 J4 Uri canton Switzerland
79 E11 Uriah Alabama
126 C3 Uribe Colombia
127 H9 Uribia Colombia
101 P8 Urie Wyoming
127 B7 Urimán Venezuela
128 F4 Urimbo Guyana
122 F4 Urique Mexico
87 H4 Uri Rothstock mt Switzerland
139 G3 Urisino New S Wales
99 G3 Uritskoye U.S.S.R.
29 L6 Urjala Finland
25 E6 Urk Netherlands
47 H6 Urla Turkey
26 D5 Urlev Denmark
54 K6 Urman W Germany
51 J7 Urmannay U.S.S.R.
59 K2 Urnäsch Switzerland
5 O9 Urmia, L Iran
55 E2 Urninskoye Boloto U.S.S.R.
52 J5 Uroševac Yugoslavia
131 D7 Urre Lauquen, L Argentina
12 G3 Urr,L Scotland
99 P9 Urrao Illinois
37 J4 Urrat'yevskaya U.S.S.R.
55 D4 Urshel'skiy U.S.S.R.
55 C4 Ursel Netherlands
37 M5 Ursensollen W Germany
37 M5 Urshult Sweden
119 J6 Ursk U.S.S.R.
119 Nevada
84 C5 Ursprung W Germany
55 C4 Urt Moron China

117 P10 Upper Arrow L Br Col
122 G7 Upper Blackville New Brunswick
9 F2 Upper Broughton England
8 C3 Upper Chapel Wales
123 P4 Upper Humber R Nfld
145 E4 Upper Hutt New Zealand
99 P6 Upper Iowa R Iowa
122 E7 Upper Kent New Brunswick
100 D7 Upper Klamath L Oregon
102 B2 Upper L California
14 B5 Upper L Irish Rep
117 F5 Upper Laberge Yukon Terr
117 J8 Upper Liard Yukon Terr
118 J11 Upper Manitou L Ontario
127 P2 Upper Manzanilla Trinidad
95 L8 Upper Marlboro Maryland
145 D4 Upper Moutere New Zealand
122 K8 Upper Musquodoboit Nova Scotia
86 F4 Upper Nile prov Sudan
99 M1 Upper Red L Minnesota
101 O5 Upper Red Rock L Montana
94 D6 Upper Saranac L New York
95 N2 Upper Saranac L New York
122 J8 Upper Stewiacke Nova Scotia
86 F4 Upper Tract W Virginia
94 K7 Upperville Virginia
85 G6 Upper Volta rep W Africa
139 H7 Upper Yarra Dam Victoria
9 F2 Uppingham England
37 J12 Upplands Väsby Sweden
27 J12 Uppsala Sweden
116 C6 Uppsala county Sweden
99 M4 Upsala Minnesota
119 N1 Upsala Ontario
122 F6 Upsalquitch New Brunswick
74 G2 Upshi Kashmir
9 H5 Upstreet England
8 D3 Upton England
94 B9 Upton Kentucky
99 Q3 Upton Wyoming
141 J4 Upstart, C Queensland
36 G7 Urach W Germany
128 F2 Uracoa Venezuela
65 A4 Urad Qianqi China
61 N10 Uraga Japan
60 D3 Urakawa Japan
100 K1 Ural Montana
139 H5 Ural mt New S Wales
139 K4 Uralla New S Wales
5 R4 Ural Mts U.S.S.R.
142 F3 Ural Well W Australia
88 D4 Urambo Tanzania
139 H4 Urana New S Wales
139 H4 Urandangie Queensland
130 G4 Urandi Brazil
141 L7 Urangan Queensland
111 D10 Urania Louisiana
114 J6 Uranium City Sask
13 B10 Uraniya Sri Lanka
142 C2 Urapunga N Terr Aust
128 F3 Uraricoera Brazil
143 E9 Uraryie W Australia
61 N10 Ura-Tyube U.S.S.R.
60 P2 Urausai Japan
61 N10 Urawa Japan
99 O9 Urazavo U.S.S.R.
55 G6 Urazovka U.S.S.R.
54 K6 Urazovo U.S.S.R.
99 S5 Urbana Illinois
99 N8 Urbana Indiana
99 P8 Urbana Iowa
99 P8 Urbana Missouri
94 D6 Urbana Ohio
45 L9 Urbania Italy
95 L9 Urbanna Virginia
129 K4 Urbano Santos Brazil
16 E2 Urbasa Spain
17 F2 Urbión, Se. de mts Spain
22 F5 Urcel France
128 D6 Urcos Peru
52 J4 Urdos France
55 F3 Urdzhar U.S.S.R.
122 E1 Urekhovo U.S.S.R.
145 E3 Uren U.S.S.R.
137 O4 Urenui New Zealand
124 D3 Ures Mexico
145 F3 Urewera Country New Zealand
55 G2 Urfa Turkey
38 K5 Urfahr Austria
41 O2 Urfeld W Germany
53 A9 Urga R U.S.S.R.
58 D7 Urgel Mongolia
47 H6 Urgun Afghanistan
41 J4 Uri canton Switzerland
79 E11 Uriah Alabama
126 C3 Uribe Colombia
127 H9 Uribia Colombia
101 P8 Urie Wyoming
127 B7 Urimán Venezuela
128 F4 Urimbo Guyana
122 F4 Urique Mexico
87 H4 Uri Rothstock mt Switzerland
139 G3 Urisino New S Wales
99 G3 Uritskoye U.S.S.R.
29 L6 Urjala Finland
25 E6 Urk Netherlands
47 H6 Urla Turkey
26 D5 Urlev Denmark
54 K6 Urman W Germany
51 J7 Urmannay U.S.S.R.
59 K2 Urnäsch Switzerland
5 O9 Urmia, L Iran
55 E2 Urninskoye Boloto U.S.S.R.
52 J5 Uroševac Yugoslavia
131 D7 Urre Lauquen, L Argentina
12 G3 Urr,L Scotland
99 P9 Urrao Illinois
37 J4 Urrat'yevskaya U.S.S.R.
55 D4 Urshel'skiy U.S.S.R.
55 C4 Ursel Netherlands
37 M5 Ursensollen W Germany
37 M5 Urshult Sweden
119 J6 Ursk U.S.S.R.
124 E3 Uruáchic Mexico
130 F2 Uruana Brazil
128 E6 Uruapan del Progreso Mexico
128 D6 Urubamba Peru
128 F4 Urubu R Brazil
128 G4 Urucará Brazil
129 K4 Uruçuca Brazil
126 D3 Urucu R Venezuela
116 C6 Urucuia R Brazil
129 J5 Urucuruituba Brazil
130 C6 Uruçuí Brazil
145 K6 Urucurituba Brazil
137 O4 Ure,R England
124 D3 Ures Mexico
145 F3 Urewera New Zealand
93 G3 Uruguaiana Brazil
130 E7 Uruguai R Brazil
131 F4 Uruguay rep S America
131 F4 Uruguay, R Argentina

80 Urumchi — Verkhneye Kuyto, Oz

Urumchi see Ürümqi
79 G2 Urum es Sughra Syria
66 D3 Ürümqi China
69 C11 Urung Indonesia
139 L4 Urunga New S Wales
88 B10 Urungwe Zimbabwe
128 F6 Urupa R Brazil
52 H6 Urussu U.S.S.R.
130 F4 Urutágua Brazil
130 E5 Urutaí Brazil
145 E3 Uruti New Zealand
77 K3 Uruzgan Afghanistan
77 J3 Urūzgān reg Afghanistan
20 B2 Urville France
136 H2 Urville, Tg. D' C W Irian
89 B4 Urwi Botswana
60 Q2 Uryū R Japan
60 Q1 Uryū-ko L Japan
58 G1 Uryum R U.S.S.R.
56 C3 Uryup R U.S.S.R.
53 F8 Uryupinsk U.S.S.R.
52 G6 Urzhum U.S.S.R.
48 K6 Urziceni Romania
36 B4 Urzig W Germany
60 E12 Usa Japan
71 E7 Usada isld Philippines
47 K6 Uşak Turkey
87 C10 Usakos Namibia
80 E5 Üsarin Jordan
133 F8 Usborne hill Falkland Is
33 T5 Usedom E Germany
80 D2 Usha Israel
116 L7 Ushagat I Alaska
50 G1 Ushakova, Ostrova islds U.S.S.R.
55 E3 Ushakovo U.S.S.R.
Ushant see Ouessant, I. d'
60 D13 Ushibuka Japan
61 L8 Ushitsu Japan
60 D12 Ushizu Japan
57 J2 Ush-Tobe U.S.S.R.
133 D8 Ushuaia airport Argentina
129 H5 Usina Brazil
36 F3 Usingen W Germany
8 D4 Usk Wales
27 A12 Uskedal Norway
8 C4 Usk,R Wales
Üskub see Skopje
47 K3 Üsküdar Turkey
47 J3 Üsküp Turkey
32 L9 Uslar W Germany
54 L4 Usman U.S.S.R.
56 D3 Usolka R U.S.S.R.
52 J5 Usol'ye U.S.S.R.
55 G4 Uspenka U.S.S.R.
57 G1 Uspenskiy U.S.S.R.
40 F7 Usseglio Italy
18 G7 Ussel France
13 H6 Usselby England
32 J10 Usseln W Germany
28 K5 Usserød Denmark
18 F6 Usson du Poitou France
59 K2 Ussuri R U.S.S.R.
59 K3 Ussuriysk U.S.S.R.
20 E4 Ussy France
52 G6 Usta R U.S.S.R.
56 D5 Ust'-Abakan U.S.S.R.
52 G4 Ust' Alekseyevo U.S.S.R.
27 C11 Ustaoset Norway
55 D3 Ust-Bagaryak U.S.S.R.
52 H4 Ust' Chernaya U.S.S.R.
48 H2 Ustchorna U.S.S.R.
52 J5 Ust' Dolgaya U.S.S.R.
41 J3 Uster Switzerland
43 E10 Ustica isld Italy
56 F3 Ust'-Ilimskiy Vdkhr U.S.S.R.
52 J3 Ust'-Ilych U.S.S.R.
30 H5 Usti'nad Czechoslovakia
55 F2 Ust'Ishim U.S.S.R.
55 G3 Ust'Izes U.S.S.R.
31 K1 Ustka Poland
56 B6 Ust'-Kamenogorsk U.S.S.R.
58 G1 Ust'Karenga U.S.S.R.
55 C4 Ust'Katav U.S.S.R.
55 C3 Ust Kishert U.S.S.R.
52 H3 Ust'Koin U.S.S.R.
52 H4 Ust'Kulom U.S.S.R.
56 G3 Ust'-Kut U.S.S.R.
55 D2 Ust' Loz'va U.S.S.R.
52 C5 Ust' Luga U.S.S.R.
52 J2 Ust' Lyzha U.S.S.R.
51 N2 Ust'Maya U.S.S.R.
51 L3 Ust'-Muya U.S.S.R.
52 H4 Ust'Nem U.S.S.R.
59 K1 Ust'Niman U.S.S.R.
56 F4 Ust'-Ordynskiy U.S.S.R.
56 F4 Ust'Ordynskiy Buryat Nats Okr dist U.S.S.R.
47 G3 Ustovo Bulgaria
52 F4 Ust' Paden'ga U.S.S.R.
52 F3 Ust' Pinega U.S.S.R.
50 H2 Ust'-Port U.S.S.R.
52 F4 Ust' Puya U.S.S.R.
52 G4 Ust' Reka U.S.S.R.
31 O6 Ustrzyki Dolne Poland
52 D4 Ust'Sara U.S.S.R.
52 J3 Ust'-Shchugor U.S.S.R.
55 D1 Ust'-Tapsuy U.S.S.R.
55 F3 Ust'Tara U.S.S.R.
55 G3 Ust'Tarka U.S.S.R.
55 F3 Ust' Tava U.S.S.R.
52 H2 Ust' Tsil'ma U.S.S.R.
59 K1 Ust'Tyrma U.S.S.R.
52 J4 Ust' Un'ya U.S.S.R.
52 F3 Ust'ura U.S.S.R.
59 H1 Ust'urov U.S.S.R.
52 J2 Ust' Usa U.S.S.R.
55 D4 Ust'-Uyskoye U.S.S.R.
52 G3 Ust' Vacherga U.S.S.R.
52 J3 Ust'-Voya U.S.S.R.
52 G3 Ust' Vyyskaya U.S.S.R.
52 F4 Ust'ya R U.S.S.R.
52 E5 Ust'ye U.S.S.R.
52 E6 Ust'ye R U.S.S.R.
50 E4 Ustyurt,Plato U.S.S.R.
52 E5 Ustyuzhna U.S.S.R.
66 C3 Usu China
71 L10 Usu isld Indonesia
60 E12 Usuki Japan
125 P11 Usulután El Salvador
125 O9 Usumacinta R Mexico
70 D3 Usun Apau Plateau Sarawak
89 G6 Usutu R Swaziland
52 D6 Usvyaty U.S.S.R.
71 B2 Uta isld Indonesia
103 N2 Utah state U.S.A.
103 N1 Utah L Utah
29 M7 Utajärvi Finland
60 Q2 Utashinai Japan
99 L7 Ute Iowa
17 G3 Utebo Spain
106 G6 Ute Cr New Mexico
88 G6 Utenge,L Tanzania
106 E5 Ute Park New Mexico
37 P4 Uterý Czechoslovakia
55 G4 Utes U.S.S.R.
88 G6 Utete Tanzania
77 K7 Uthal Pakistan
32 J6 Uthlede W Germany
68 G5 Uthumphon Phisai Thailand
129 G6 Utiariti Brazil
107 K3 Utica Kansas
94 D4 Utica Michigan
99 P6 Utica Minnesota
111 F9 Utica Mississippi
110 C2 Utica Missouri
101 P3 Utica Montana
98 J9 Utica Nebraska
95 M3 Utica New York
94 E6 Utica Ohio
17 G5 Utiel Spain
26 K7 Utifällan Sweden
119 W3 Utik L Manitoba
145 E3 Utiku New Zealand
118 B3 Utikuma L Alberta
27 H16 Utklippan isld Sweden
27 C10 Utla R Norway
27 H15 Utlängan isld Sweden
109 K5 Utley Texas
106 G4 Utleyville Colorado
74 D1 Utmanzai Pakistan
27 K13 Utö Sweden
27 M12 Utö lt ho Finland
140 C5 Utopia N Terr Aust
109 H6 Utopia Texas
75 K5 Utraula India
25 D4 Utrecht Netherlands
89 G6 Utrecht S Africa
16 D7 Utrera Spain
27 A12 Utsira lt ho Norway
29 N2 Utsjoki Finland
61 N9 Utsunomiya Japan
53 G10 Utta U.S.S.R.
68 E4 Uttaradit Thailand
74 H4 Uttar Pradesh prov India
27 H12 Uttersberg Sweden
28 G7 Utterslev Denmark
36 H4 Üttingen W Germany
9 E2 Uttoxeter England
116 G2 Utukok R Alaska
137 O4 Utupua isld Santa Cruz Is
55 B5 Utva R U.S.S.R.
37 O3 Útvina Czechoslovakia
52 H6 Utyashkino U.S.S.R.
32 M8 Utze W Germany
33 S5 Utzedel E Germany
17 G3 uuadalope R Spain
29 O10 Uukuniem Finland
58 F2 Uuldza R Mongolia
29 L9 Uurainen Finland
Uusikaarlepyy see Nykarleby
29 J11 Uusikaupunki Finland
29 L11 Uusimaa prov Finland
52 H6 Uva U.S.S.R.
48 F7 Uvac R Yugoslavia
103 K2 Uvada Nevada
128 D3 Uva, L Colombia
112 E5 Uvalda Georgia
108 H6 Uvalde Texas
54 B4 Uvarovichi U.S.S.R.
52 E6 Uvarovka U.S.S.R.
55 E2 Uvat U.S.S.R.
137 O6 Uvéa isld Îles Loyauté Pacific Oc
137 R4 Uvea isld Îles Wallis Pacific Oc
55 D4 Uvel'skiy U.S.S.R.
55 D3 Uvil'dy, Oz L U.S.S.R.
88 C4 Uvinza Tanzania
88 B3 Uvira Zaïre
115 O3 Uvkusigssat Greenland
60 E13 Uwae Japan
60 F12 Uwajima Japan
84 H5 Uweinat,Jebel mt Sudan
135 V5 Uwekahuna Hawaiian Is
69 H12 Uwi isld Indonesia
9 F4 Uxbridge England
121 L8 Uxbridge Ontario
65 A5 Uxin Ju China
125 P7 Uxmal Mexico
55 D4 Uy R U.S.S.R.
116 K8 Uyak B Alaska
57 B3 Uyaly, Ozero L U.S.S.R.
51 O2 Uyandina R U.S.S.R.
56 D3 Uyar U.S.S.R.
15 G1 Uyea isld Scotland
15 G1 Uyeasound Scotland
50 H1 Uyedineniya,Ostrov isld U.S.S.R.
52 H2 Uyeg U.S.S.R.
85 F7 Uyo Nigeria
47 K6 Uysal Dağ mt Turkey
55 D4 Uyskoye U.S.S.R.
57 F3 Uyuk U.S.S.R.
133 D2 Uyuni Bolivia
48 G2 Uz R Czechoslovakia
57 B3 Uzbekistan S.S.R rep U.S.S.R.
48 F5 Uzdin Yugoslavia
53 G8 Uzen', Malyy R U.S.S.R.
57 G4 Uzgen U.S.S.R.
48 G2 Uzhgorod U.S.S.R.
48 H2 Uzhok U.S.S.R.
56 C3 Uzhur U.S.S.R.
48 F7 Užicka Požega Yugoslavia
41 J3 Uznach Switzerland
52 F6 Uzola R U.S.S.R.
47 K8 Üzümlü Turkey
47 H6 Uzun isld Turkey
88 E6 Uzungwa Tanzania
47 H3 Uzunköprü Turkey
57 B3 Uzynkair U.S.S.R.
29 M9 Vaajakoski Finland
89 E6 Vaal R S Africa
29 M7 Vaala Finland
89 F6 Vaal Dam S Africa
29 N11 Vaalimaa Finland
87 E10 Vaalwater S Africa
29 M8 Vaaraslahti Finland
21 F6 Vaas France
29 J8 Vaasa Finland
25 E4 Vaassen Netherlands
29 L4 Vaattojärvi Finland
28 H7 Våbensted Denmark
57 C5 Vabkent U.S.S.R.
130 C7 Vacaria,R Brazil
130 C7 Vacaria,Sa mts Brazil
131 B4 Vacas,Pta De Argentina
102 B3 Vacaville California
19 N17 Vaccarès, Etang de L France
52 F6 Vacha U.S.S.R.
126 H5 Vache, Île-à- Haiti
40 E5 Vacheresse France
19 N16 Vacqueyras France
52 F6 Vad U.S.S.R.
100 C3 Vader Washington
27 A10 Vadheim Norway
106 E5 Vadito New Mexico
27 B12 Vadla Norway
44 D3 Vado Italy
74 E7 Vadodara India
124 F2 Vado de Santa María Mexico
52 D1 Vadozero, Oz L U.S.S.R.
26 R1 Vadsö Norway
27 G13 Vadstenna Sweden
48 M6 Vadu Romania
28 D2 Vadum Denmark
41 L3 Vaduz Liechtenstein
28 H7 Væggerløse Denmark
28 K5 Værløsa Denmark
26 F4 Vaeröy Norway
28 G5 Værslev Denmark
28 N3 Våg Faeroes
26 J9 Vaga Sweden
52 F4 Vaga R U.S.S.R.
26 D10 Vågåmo Norway
26 G3 Vagan Norway
42 G4 Vaganski mt Yugoslavia
55 E2 Vagay U.S.S.R.
29 O2 Vaggetem U.S.S.R.
26 R2 Vaggetem-javrre L Norway
45 K4 Vaglia Italy
27 J13 Vagnahärad Sweden
28 M2 Vågø isld Faeroes
16 B4 Vagos Portugal
27 F11 Vägsjöfors Sweden
26 A10 Vågsöy isld Norway
31 L6 Váh R Czechoslovakia
29 J8 Vähäkyrö Finland
79 F8 Vahal Israel
146 D11 Vahsel B Antarctica
111 G8 Vaiden Mississippi
20 E5 Vaiges France
36 F6 Vaihingen W Germany
76 B1 Vaijapur India
52 C5 Väike-Maarja U.S.S.R.
26 L5 Vaikijaur Sweden
103 O9 Vail Arizona
15 G2 Vaila isld Scotland
22 F5 Vailly-sur-Aisne France
134 B1 Vailoa W Samoa
29 N11 Vainikkala Finland
45 Q7 Vairano Patenora Italy
21 B8 Vairé France
137 Q3 Vaitupu isld Tuvalu
47 F2 Vakarel Bulgaria
27 G11 Vakern Sweden
56 B1 Vakh R U.S.S.R.
57 F6 Vakhanskiy Khrebet mts U.S.S.R.
73 K1 Vakhsh R U.S.S.R.
57 E5 Vakhshstroy U.S.S.R.
52 G5 Vakhtan U.S.S.R.
52 D3 Vaknavolok U.S.S.R.
27 A11 Vaksdal Norway
26 F8 Vålådalen Sweden
76 E7 Valaichchenai Sri Lanka
40 F5 Valais canton Switzerland
52 H5 Valamaz U.S.S.R.
46 F3 Valandovo Yugoslavia
27 G12 Valåsen Sweden
95 O4 Valatie New York
47 G6 Valáxa isld Greece
38 E8 Val Badia Italy
121 P6 Val Barrette Quebec
26 G3 Valberg Norway
19 P15 Valbonnais France
122 E5 Val Brilliant Quebec
25 E5 Valburg Netherlands
133 D6 Valcheta Argentina
121 S7 Valcourt Quebec
41 O6 Valdagno Italy
16 D2 Valdavia R Spain
52 D5 Valday U.S.S.R.
52 D6 Valdayskaya Vozvyshennost' uplands U.S.S.R.
17 G4 Valde Algorfa Spain
16 D5 Valdecañas, Embalse de res Spain
17 F5 Valdeganga Spain
52 B6 Valdemārpils U.S.S.R.
27 J13 Valdemarsvik Sweden
16 E4 Valdemoro Spain
17 F4 Valdemoro-Sierra Spain
16 E6 Valdepeñas Spain
16 D3 Valderaduey R Spain
17 H4 Valderrobres Spain
99 T5 Valders Wisconsin
121 P7 Val des Bois Quebec
112 F2 Valdese N Carolina
133 E6 Valdés, Pen Argentina
116 O6 Valdez Alaska
106 F4 Valdez Colorado
131 A7 Valdivia Chile
131 A8 Valdivia prov Chile
20 C5 Val d'Izé France
20 K3 Val-d'Oise dep France
121 N4 Val-d'Or Quebec
113 D7 Valdosta Georgia
27 D11 Valdres plat Norway
19 P16 Valdrome France
9 G6 Vale Channel Is
100 H6 Vale Oregon
98 C5 Vale S Dakota
48 G3 Valea Lui Mihai Romania
48 J3 Valea Vişeului Romania
37 P3 Valeč Czechoslovakia
45 J1 Valéggio Italy
129 L6 Valença Brazil
21 I7 Valençay France
19 N15 Valence France
18 F8 Valence d'Agen France
18 F9 Valence-sur-Baïse France
17 G5 Valencia Spain
127 K9 Valencia Venezuela
17 G5 Valencia prov Spain
16 C5 Valência de Alcantara Spain
16 D2 Valencia de Don Juan Spain
16 B3 Valençia do Minho Portugal
17 H5 Valencia,G de Spain
14 A5 Valencia I Irish Rep
127 L9 Valencia,L.de Venezuela
22 F3 Valenciennes France
48 K5 Vălenii de Munte Romania
19 P17 Valensole France
59 K3 Valentin U.S.S.R.
103 L6 Valentine Arizona
111 F12 Valentine Louisiana
101 R2 Valentine Montana
98 F7 Valentine Nebraska
108 C5 Valentine Texas
44 E1 Valenza Italy
27 E11 Våler Norway
109 H4 Valera Texas
127 J10 Valera Venezuela
27 A12 Valestrand Norway
130 H5 Vale Verde Brazil
41 M4 Valfurva R Italy
52 C5 Valga U.S.S.R.
120 K4 Val Gagné Ontario
43 F11 Valguarnera Caropepe Sicily
101 N1 Valier Montana
28 K4 Vålinge Sweden
48 F6 Valjevo Yugoslavia
26 P2 Valjok Norway
19 Q15 Valjouffrey France
29 L10 Valkeakoski Finland
29 M11 Valkeala Finland
29 L5 Valkeavaara mt Finland
25 E7 Valkenburg Netherlands
25 D6 Valkenswaard Netherlands
54 G7 Valki U.S.S.R.
29 M11 Valkom Finland
19 N17 Vallabrègues France
16 D3 Valladolid Spain
16 D3 Valladolid prov Spain
121 N4 Val Laflamme Quebec
41 P4 Vallarga Italy
41 O6 Vallarsa R Italy
103 M6 Valle Arizona
27 C12 Valle Norway
38 E7 Valle Aurina Italy
106 C4 Vallecito Res Colorado
106 D5 Vallecitos New Mexico
45 O7 Vallecorsa Italy
131 B2 Valle Cura,Rio Del Argentina
42 A3 Valle d'Aosta Italy
40 G6 Valle d'Aosta aut reg Italy
124 G7 Valle de Banderas Mexico
16 E1 Valle de Cabuérniga Spain
127 M10 Valle de la Pascua Venezuela
128 C3 Valle del Cauca div Colombia
124 F4 Valle de Olivos Mexico
124 F4 Valle de Rosario Mexico
124 G4 Valle de Zaragoza Mexico
126 H9 Valledupar Colombia
85 E5 Vallée de Zgarat Mali
122 B7 Vallée Jonction Quebec
85 E5 Vallée L'Azawak Mali/Niger
131 C3 Valle Fértil, Sa. de mts Argentina
128 F7 Valle Grande Bolivia
40 C5 Valleiry France
102 B3 Vallejo California
45 P7 Vallemaio Italy
26 M7 Vallen Västerbotten Sweden
26 J8 Vallen Väster Norrland Sweden
131 B2 Vallenar Chile
36 D3 Vallendar W Germany
28 H6 Vallensved Denmark
45 O6 Vallepretra Italy
133 E2 Valle,R.del Argentina
21 C7 Vallet France
43 F13 Valletta Malta
111 F9 Valley Mississippi
98 K8 Valley Nebraska
122 J8 Valley Nova Scotia
8 B1 Valley Wales
100 H1 Valley Washington
101 Q5 Valley Wyoming
107 N4 Valley Center Kansas
118 K7 Valley Centre Sask
98 J3 Valley City N Dakota
107 P2 Valley Falls Kansas
100 E7 Valley Falls Oregon
121 Q7 Valleyfield Quebec
111 L7 Valley Head Alabama
94 G8 Valley Head W Virginia
109 K4 Valley Mills Texas
116 K7 Valley of Ten Thousand Smokes Alaska
110 F3 Valley Park Missouri
101 L8 Valley Pass Nevada
94 B8 Valley Sta Kentucky
117 P8 Valleyview Alberta
109 K2 Valley View Texas
Vallgrund isld see Rappaluolo
109 M2 Valliant Oklahoma
45 M2 Valli di Comacchio reg Italy
21 J10 Vallières France
18 F10 Vallier, Mt France
121 P6 Val Limoges Quebec
20 G2 Valliquerville France
28 J6 Valløby Denmark
43 G8 Vallo di Diano Italy
43 G8 Vallo di Lucania Italy
45 L4 Vallombrosa Italy
94 A8 Vallonia Indiana
21 E6 Vallon-sur-Gée France
40 D4 Vallorbe Switzerland
27 D12 Vallöy Norway
17 H3 Valls Spain
27 H10 Vallsta Sweden
41 M3 Valluga mt Austria
27 J10 Vallvik Sweden
118 K9 Val Marie Sask
16 E1 Valmaseda Spain
31 K6 Val. Meziříčí Czechoslovakia
52 C5 Valmiera U.S.S.R.
20 K3 Valmondois France
20 G2 Valmont France
106 E9 Valmont New Mexico
45 N6 Valmontone Italy
100 H9 Valmy Nevada
16 E1 Valnera mt Spain
20 C3 Valognes France
Valona see Vlorë
16 D3 Valoria la Buena Spain
16 C3 Valpaços Portugal
76 C5 Valparai India
131 B4 Valparaíso Chile
111 K11 Valparaiso Florida
99 T8 Valparaiso Indiana
124 H6 Valparaíso Mexico
98 K8 Valparaiso Nebraska
119 N6 Valparaiso Sask
131 B4 Valparaiso prov Chile
40 F6 Valpelline V Italy
48 E5 Valpovo Yugoslavia
40 G7 Valprato Soana Italy
122 A8 Val-Racine Quebec
19 N16 Valréas France
89 E6 Vals R S Africa
28 H7 Vålse Denmark
100 B5 Valsetz Oregon
28 D3 Valsgård Denmark
26 G7 Valsjö Sweden
27 H12 Valskog Sweden
29 J8 Valsörarna lt ho Finland
41 L5 Valtellina V Italy
45 M4 Val Tiberina Italy
29 O8 Valtimo Finland
54 K6 Valuyki U.S.S.R.
85 A3 Valverde Canary Is
127 J5 Valverde Dom Rep
17 F5 Valverde de Júcar Spain
16 C7 Valverde del Camino Spain
26 M5 Valvträsk Sweden
48 K3 Vama Romania
28 C6 Vamdrup Denmark
27 G10 Våmhus Sweden
88 H7 Vamizi isld Mozambique
27 E12 Vamma Norway
29 K10 Vammala Finland
47 G9 Vámos Crete Greece
48 G3 Vámospéros Hungary
109 M3 Van Texas
78 J2 Van Turkey
29 L10 Vanajanselka L Finland
109 L2 Van Alstyne Texas
101 S3 Vananda Montana
56 F1 Vanavara U.S.S.R.
68 G1 Van-Ban Vietnam
121 S5 Van Bruyssel Quebec
110 B6 Van Buren Arkansas
94 B6 Van Buren Indiana
95 T6 Van Buren Maine
110 F5 Van Buren Missouri
68 J6 Van Canh Vietnam
22 K4 Vance Belgium
21 G6 Vancé France
112 K2 Vanceboro N Carolina
94 D8 Vanceburg Kentucky
68 G2 Van Chan Vietnam
57 F5 Vanchskiy Khrebet mts U.S.S.R.
117 G11 Vancouver Br Col
100 C4 Vancouver Washington
116 E6 Vancouver, C Alaska
143 C10 Vancouver,C W Australia
117 K10 Vancouver I Br Col
117 D5 Vancouver, Mt Alaska/Yukon Terr
110 G3 Vandalia Illinois
110 E2 Vandalia Missouri
41 L3 Vandans Austria
28 A3 Vandborg Denmark
119 Q1 Vandekerckhove Sask
28 C5 Vandel Denmark
112 L2 Vandemere N Carolina
89 E6 Vanderbijl Pk S Africa
94 C1 Vanderbilt Michigan
109 L7 Vanderbilt Texas
94 H6 Vandergrift Pennsylvania
117 M8 Vanderhoof Br Columbia
140 D3 Vanderlin I N Terr Aust
109 N1 Vandervoort Arkansas
28 B2 Vandet Sø Denmark
136 G4 Van Diemen N Terr Australia
140 E3 Van Diemen,C Queensland
140 B1 Van Diemen G N Terr Aust
140 F3 Van Diemen R Queensland
55 E1 Vandmtor, Oz L U.S.S.R.
121 R5 Vandry Quebec
110 G5 Vanduser Missouri
100 A9 Van Duzen R California
27 F13 Vänern L Sweden
27 F13 Vänersborg Sweden
95 L4 Van Etten New York
27 C10 Vang Norway
88 G4 Vanga Tanzania
87 H12 Vangaindrano Madagascar
27 F13 Vanga,N Sweden
78 J2 Van Gölü L Turkey
27 C10 Vangsmjösa Norway
118 K9 Vanguard Sask
70 A1 Vanguard Bank S China Sea
137 M3 Vangunu isld Solomon Is
68 F3 Vang Vieng Laos
26 S2 Vanhakylä U.S.S.R.
98 D2 Van Hook N Dakota
108 C4 Van Horn Texas
106 F5 Van Houten New Mexico
137 O4 Vanikoro Is Santa Cruz Is
26 K7 Vänjaurbäck Sweden
26 K7 Vänjaurträsk Sweden
51 S2 Vankarem U.S.S.R.
121 Q7 Vankleek Hill Ontario
98 F5 Van Metre S Dakota
26 L1 Vanna isld Norway
26 L8 Vännäs Sweden
83 J9 Vannativillu Sri Lanka
18 D5 Vannes France
21 J6 Vannes sur-Cosson France
68 J6 Van Ninh Vietnam
107 O7 Vanoss Oklahoma
87 C12 Vanrhynsdorp S Africa
141 F3 Vanrook Queensland
94 E9 Vansant Virginia
27 G11 Vansbro Sweden
118 L6 Vanscoy Sask
142 F2 Vansittart B W Australia
115 L4 Vansittart I N W Terr
18 H8 Vans, les France
29 L11 Vantaa Finland
29 L11 Vantaa R Finland
118 L9 Vantage Sask
100 F3 Vantage Washington
98 B7 Van Tassell Wyoming
137 O3 Vanua Lava isld New Hebrides
137 Q5 Vanua Levu isld Fiji
99 N9 Van Wert Iowa
94 C6 Van Wert Ohio
87 D12 Vanwyksvlei S Africa
67 A6 Van Yen Vietnam
26 A9 Vanylven Norway
26 A9 Vanylvsgapet B Norway
110 D5 Vanzant Missouri
48 M2 Vapnyarka U.S.S.R.
19 Q18 Var dep France
44 B4 Var R France
27 F13 Vara Sweden
44 G3 Vara R Italy
126 D3 Varadero Cuba
21 C7 Varades France
19 P17 Varages France
44 B2 Varaita R Italy
41 H6 Varallo Italy
42 B3 Varallo Italy
77 B2 Varamin Iran
75 K6 Varanasi India
26 R1 Varangerfjorden inlet Norway
26 R1 Varangerhalvöya mt Norway
42 G7 Varano, L. di Italy
131 A8 Varas,Pto Chile
16 D6 Varas,R Spain
20 E3 Varaville France
44 E3 Varazze Italy
27 F14 Varberg Sweden
111 G8 Vardaman Mississippi
46 E6 Vardhoúsia Óri mt Greece
27 L11 Vårdö Finland
26 S1 Vardö Norway
52 E5 Varegovo U.S.S.R.
32 H6 Varel W Germany
20 G2 Varengeville France
20 B3 Varenguebec France
20 D5 Varenne R France
21 I7 Varennes France
19 J3 Varennes en Argonne France
40 B5 Varennes St.Sauveur France
48 E6 Vareš Yugoslavia
41 J6 Varese Italy
40 A7 Vareze R France
27 F13 Vårgårda Sweden
55 E3 Vargashi U.S.S.R.
130 G10 Vargem R Brazil
130 F7 Varginha Brazil
18 G9 Varilhes France
112 J2 Varina N Carolina
27 G13 Väring Sweden
20 J5 Varize France
26 K5 Varjisträsk Sweden
29 N9 Varkaus Finland
143 C10 Varley,L W Australia
27 F12 Varmland reg Sweden
47 J1 Varna Bulgaria
55 D4 Varna U.S.S.R.
111 G11 Varnado Louisiana
28 D6 Varnæs Denmark
27 G14 Värnamo Sweden
27 F11 Värnäs Sweden
52 F5 Varnavino U.S.S.R.
108 B1 Varney New Mexico
31 H5 Varnsdorf Czechoslovakia
27 F14 Varnum Sweden
112 F5 Varnville S Carolina
79 D3 Varosha Cyprus
48 D3 Városlöd Hungary
48 E3 Várpalota Hungary
18 F7 Vars France
52 G2 Varsh, Oz L U.S.S.R.
28 E3 Vårst Denmark
78 H2 Varto Turkey
27 G13 Vartofta Sweden
76 E6 Varuniya Sri Lanka
46 E7 Varvára mt Greece
46 E1 Varvarin Yugoslavia
54 C10 Varvarovka U.S.S.R.
130 G9 Várzea Alegre Brazil
130 G5 Várzea da Palma Brazil
129 G7 Várzea Grande Brazil
130 E9 Várzea,R Brazil
52 E1 Varzino U.S.S.R.
52 E2 Varzuga U.S.S.R.
52 E2 Varzuga R U.S.S.R.
18 H5 Varzy France
48 D3 Vas co Hungary
130 H11 Vasa Barris,R Brazil
52 B5 Vasalemma U.S.S.R.
48 G2 Vásárosnamény Hungary
28 K4 Väsby Sweden
16 B7 Vascão R Portugal
48 G4 Vaşcau Romania
20 H3 Vascoeuil France
17 F2 Vascongadas reg Spain
52 G3 Vashka R U.S.S.R.
48 K2 Vashkovtsy U.S.S.R.
100 C2 Vashon I Washington
98 G2 Vashti N Dakota
109 J2 Vashti Texas
52 G3 Vasil'evo U.S.S.R.
54 H8 Vasil'kovka U.S.S.R.
55 F2 Vasiss U.S.S.R.
52 C5 Vasknarva U.S.S.R.
29 M3 Vaskojoki R Finland
48 E4 Vaskút Hungary
21 E8 Vasles France
48 L4 Vaslui Romania
112 H2 Vass N Carolina
118 F1 Vassar Manitoba
94 D3 Vassar Michigan
27 B12 Vassdalseggja mt Norway
26 K3 Vassijuare Sweden
20 D4 Vassy France
26 J4 Vastenjaure L Sweden
27 J12 Västerås Sweden
26 H7 Västerbotten reg Sweden
27 F11 Vasterdalälven R Sweden
26 J5 Västerfjäll Sweden
27 K12 Västerhaninge Sweden
27 H12 Västermo Sweden
26 J7 Vastermyrriset Sweden
26 J8 Väster Norr Land Sweden
27 J14 Västervik Sweden
27 J11 Västland Sweden
27 H12 Västmanland reg Sweden
42 F6 Vasto Italy
33 N6 Vastorf W Germany
26 L8 Vastra Kvarken chan Sweden
48 D3 Vasvár Hungary
55 G2 Vasyugan R U.S.S.R.
21 I7 Vatan France
137 O4 Vatganai isld New Hebrides
33 P8 Väthen E Germany
47 H7 Vathí Greece
46 E8 Váthia Greece
45 M6 Vaticano, Citta del Italy
115 S5 Vatnajökull ice cap Iceland
26 B9 Vatne Norway
115 R4 Vatneyri Iceland
27 K12 Vätö Sweden
137 R5 Vatoa isld Fiji
87 H11 Vatomandry Madagascar
48 J3 Vatra Dornei Romania
27 G13 Vättern L Sweden
41 K4 Vättis Switzerland
26 J10 Vattrång Sweden
40 C5 Vauche Marlioz,Mt.De France
127 M4 Vauclin Martinique W Indies
112 F4 Vaucluse S Carolina
19 O17 Vaucluse dep France
40 C2 Vauconcourt France
20 F2 Vaucottes France
19 J4 Vaucouleurs France
36 B6 Vaucourt France
40 D4 Vaud canton Switzerland
20 H3 Vaudreuil, Le France
122 H9 Vaughan Nova Scotia
140 B5 Vaughan Springs N Terr Aust
101 O2 Vaughn Montana
108 B1 Vaughn New Mexico
128 D3 Vaupés div Colombia
18 H9 Vauvert France
20 B2 Vauville France
40 D2 Vauvillers France
118 E8 Vauxhall Alberta
87 J11 Vavatenina Madagascar
137 S5 Vava'u Group islds Tonga
52 H6 Vavozh U.S.S.R.
83 K9 Vavuniya Sri Lanka
118 J5 Vawn Sask
27 K12 Vaxholm Sweden
27 G15 Växjö Sweden
76 D4 Vayalpod India
50 F1 Vaygach, Ostrov isld U.S.S.R.
52 F3 Vaymuga R U.S.S.R.
129 L5 Vaza R Brazil
130 F5 Vazante Brazil
52 G3 Vazhgort U.S.S.R.
47 G2 Vazovgrad Bulgaria
129 J6 Veadeiras Brazil
68 F7 Veal Renh Cambodia
28 D3 Vebbestrup Denmark
98 J4 Veblen S Dakota
26 M7 Vebomark Sweden
33 M8 Vechelde W Germany
25 F3 Vecht R Netherlands
32 H7 Vechta W Germany
32 H7 Vechta R W Germany
32 L10 Veckerhagen W Germany
27 J12 Veckholm Sweden
28 K5 Vedbæk Denmark
27 F14 Veddige Sweden
28 E3 Veddum Denmark
48 J6 Vedea Romania
28 A4 Vedersø Denmark
27 H12 Vedevåg Sweden
133 E4 Vedia Argentina
17 H6 Vedra isld Balearic Is
22 H3 Vedrin Belgium
28 E5 Vedslet Denmark
28 C6 Vedsted Denmark
28 G6 Ved Stranden Denmark
27 F13 Vedum Sweden
110 J1 Veedersburg Indiana
25 G2 Veendam Netherlands
25 E4 Veenendaal Netherlands
25 F2 Veenhuizen Netherlands
25 E2 Veenwouden Netherlands
25 A5 Veere Netherlands
25 A5 Veerse Meer Netherlands
33 N7 Veerssen W Germany
28 E6 Veflinge Denmark
26 E6 Vega isld Norway
16 C2 Vega de Tera Spain
27 D13 Vegårs Vatn L Norway
28 K4 Vegeån R Sweden
32 J6 Vegesack W Germany
28 D3 Veggerby Denmark
27 D11 Veggli Norway
46 E4 Vegorrítis, L Greece
118 F5 Vegreville Alberta
108 A1 Veguita New Mexico
33 Q6 Vehlow E Germany
27 M11 Vehmaa Finland
52 E4 Veilikaya Guba U.S.S.R.
26 P1 Veines Norway
27 F15 Veinge Sweden
120 D3 Vein L Ontario
133 D5 Veinticinco de Mayo Argentina
45 M5 Veio Italy
36 H4 Veitshöchheim W Germany
28 J4 Vejby Denmark
28 C6 Vejen Denmark
28 A5 Vejers Denmark
28 D4 Vejerslev Denmark
28 E2 Vejgård Denmark
28 E4 Vejlby Århus Denmark
28 D5 Vejlby Vejle Denmark
28 D5 Vejle Denmark
28 C5 Vejle co Denmark
28 D5 Vejle Fjord inlet Denmark
28 H6 Vejlø Denmark
28 E7 Vejnæs Nokke C Denmark
37 P3 Vejprty Czechoslovakia
28 G5 Vejrhøj hill Denmark
28 F5 Vejrø isld Århus Denmark
28 G6 Vejrø isld Storstrøm Denmark
28 B5 Vejrup Denmark
28 F6 Vejstrup Denmark
28 J5 Veksø Denmark
52 F4 Vel R U.S.S.R.
127 H8 Vela, C. de la Colombia
22 E2 Velaines Belgium
46 E5 Velaóra Greece
106 E5 Velarde New Mexico
124 H5 Velardeña Mexico
16 C7 Vela Real de Sto António Portugal
109 M7 Velasco Texas
18 H7 Velay, Mts du France
32 F10 Velbert W Germany
37 M5 Velburg W Germany
37 M4 Velden W Germany
25 D6 Veldhoven Netherlands
47 J2 Veleka R Bulgaria
32 E9 Velen W Germany
48 E3 Velencei Tó L Hungary
46 F5 Velestínon Greece
17 F7 Vélez Bianco Spain
16 E8 Vélez Málaga Spain
17 F7 Vélez Rubio Spain
26 F6 Velfjord Norway
33 R4 Velgast E Germany
130 G6 Velhas,R Brazil
42 H3 Velika Yugoslavia
48 G6 Velika Gradište Yugoslavia
42 F3 Velika Kapela dist Yugoslavia
48 G6 Velika Plana Yugoslavia
52 G2 Velikaya U.S.S.R.
52 C6 Velikaya R U.S.S.R.
52 G5 Velikaya R U.S.S.R.
48 K1 Veliki Borki U.S.S.R.
48 K1 Veliki Glubochek U.S.S.R.
52 D6 Velikiye-Luki U.S.S.R.
52 G4 Velikiy Ustyug U.S.S.R.
54 M1 Velikodvorskiy U.S.S.R.
47 H1 Veliko Turnovo Bulgaria
52 H2 Velikovisochnoye U.S.S.R.
52 F5 Velikovo U.S.S.R.
54 M1 Velikoye, Oz L U.S.S.R.
85 B6 Velingara Senegal
47 F2 Velingrad Bulgaria
42 E6 Velino R Italy
42 E6 Velino, M mt Italy
54 C1 Velizh U.S.S.R.
48 E2 Velká Fatra mt Czechoslovakia
48 E1 Vel Karlovice Czechoslovakia
48 G2 Vel'ké Kapušány Czechoslovakia
31 L6 Velké Karlovice Czechoslovakia
48 G2 Velki Berezny U.S.S.R.
48 D3 Velký ŽitnÝ Ostrov' reg Czechoslovakia
38 L8 Vellach Austria
33 N6 Vellahn E Germany
137 M3 Vella Lavella isld Solomon Is
45 J4 Vellano Italy
36 H5 Vellberg W Germany
45 N6 Velletri Italy
28 D4 Vellev Denmark
28 A4 Velling Denmark
27 F16 Vellinge Sweden
45 O5 Vellino, M mt Italy
76 D4 Vellore India
56 D1 Vel'mo R U.S.S.R.
22 J5 Velosnes France
25 E4 Velp Netherlands
25 C4 Velsen Netherlands
52 F4 Vel'sk U.S.S.R.
52 H1 Vel't U.S.S.R.
33 S7 Velten E Germany
25 E4 Veluwe Netherlands
25 E4 Veluwemeer Netherlands
98 F1 Velva N Dakota
90 E7 Vema Fracture Atlantic Oc
28 A4 Vemb Denmark
26 G9 Vemdalen Sweden
28 G6 Vemmelev Denmark
28 F7 Vemmenæs Denmark
59 M2 Vemor'Ye U.S.S.R.
28 K5 Ven isld Sweden
27 H14 Vena Sweden
27 D10 Venabygd Norway
12 D1 Venachar,L Scotland
131 E4 Venado Tuerto Argentina
45 Q7 Venafro Italy
128 F2 Venamo,Cerro mt Venezuela/Guyana
98 E9 Venango Nebraska
141 F4 Vena Park Queensland
44 C1 Venaria Italy
100 G6 Venator Oregon
130 E8 Venceslau Bráz Brazil
Venda see Vantaa
45 L1 Venda mt Italy
16 B6 Vendas Novas Portugal
21 C8 Vendée dep France
36 D6 Vendenheim France
22 D3 Vendin-le-Viel France
21 H6 Vendôme France
17 H3 Vendrell Spain
22 H4 Vendresse France
28 D2 Vendsyssel reg Denmark
45 M1 Veneta, Laguna Italy
116 P3 Venetie Landing Alaska
45 K1 Veneto reg Italy
52 F6 Venets U.S.S.R.
54 K2 Venev U.S.S.R.
45 M1 Venezia Italy
42 D3 Venezia-Euganea prov Italy
42 E3 Venezia,G.di Italy
128 E2 Venezuela rep S America
127 J9 Venezuela,G.de Venezuela
28 D4 Veng Denmark
55 G3 Vengerovo U.S.S.R.
76 A3 Vengurla India
16 D3 Venialbo Spain
116 H8 Veniaminof Vol Alaska
118 E4 Venice Alberta
113 E10 Venice Florida
Venice Italy see Venezia
111 G12 Venice Louisiana
111 M12 Venice St Louis
19 N13 Vénissieux France
27 G11 Venjan Sweden
76 D4 Venkataguri India
76 E1 Venkatapuram India
98 J3 Venlo N Dakota
25 F6 Venlo Netherlands
119 M7 Venn Sask
28 D2 Vennebjerg Denmark
32 E7 Vennebrügge W Germany
27 C13 Vennesla Norway
28 B3 Venø Denmark
28 B3 Venø Bugt B Denmark
19 Q15 Venosc France
121 O7 Venosta Quebec
41 N4 Venosta, Val Italy
41 N4 Venostie, Alpi Italy
25 E5 Venray Netherlands
27 M14 Venta R U.S.S.R.
124 E5 Ventana,Pta de la C Mexico
133 E5 Ventana,Sa ra Argentina
16 E8 Ventas de Zafarraya Spain
28 H5 Vented Denmark
44 C4 Ventimiglia Italy
9 E6 Ventnor England
43 E8 Ventotene isld Italy
19 O16 Ventoux, Mt France
33 P5 Ventschow E Germany
27 M14 Ventspils U.S.S.R.
128 E3 Ventuari R Venezuela
102 E7 Ventura California
98 G3 Venturia N Dakota
113 F10 Venus Florida
109 K3 Venus Texas
138 C5 Venus B S Australia
124 H8 Venustiano Carranza Mexico
52 D4 Vepsovskaya Vozvyshennost' uplands U.S.S.R.
133 E3 Vera Argentina
17 F7 Vera Spain
109 H2 Vera Texas
133 D6 Vera, B Argentina
130 E8 Vera Cruz Brazil
125 L8 Veracruz Mexico
74 D8 Veraval India
42 B3 Verbania Italy
111 K9 Verbena Alabama
22 D5 Verberie France
52 E6 Verbilki U.S.S.R.
41 H7 Vercelli Italy
33 R5 Verchen E Germany
19 O15 Vercors reg France
19 Q16 Verdaches France
26 E8 Verdal Norway
26 E8 Verdalsöra Norway
71 E4 Verde isld Philippines
133 D6 Verde R Argentina
103 N7 Verde R Arizona
130 E4 Verde R Brazil
133 F2 Verde R Paraguay
85 A6 Verde, C Senegal
126 G3 Verde, Cay isld Bahamas
130 G4 Verde Grande R Brazil
98 H7 Verdel Nebraska
109 J1 Verden Oklahoma
32 K7 Verden W Germany
131 E7 Verde,Pen Argentina
130 G4 Verde Pequeno, R Brazil
130 D7 Verde,R Brazil
21 H6 Verdes France
98 H7 Verdigre Nebraska
107 O3 Verdigris R Okla/Kansas
118 F9 Verdigris L Alberta
130 D5 Verdinho,Sa.do mts Brazil
99 L9 Verdon Nebraska
19 Q17 Verdon R France
18 E7 Verdon, le France
19 J3 Verdun France
18 F9 Verdun-sur-Garonne France
19 J6 Verdun-sur-le-Doubs France
124 E5 Verdura Mexico
52 D6 Vereche U.S.S.R.
89 E6 Vereeniging S Africa
119 P7 Veregin Sask
98 D2 Verendrye Nat.Mon N Dakota
121 N5 Vérendrye, Parc Prov. de la Quebec
52 H5 Vereshchagino U.S.S.R.
52 E5 Verestovo, Oz L U.S.S.R.
54 H1 Vereya U.S.S.R.
85 B6 Verga,C Guinea
17 F1 Vergara Spain
133 G4 Vergara Uruguay
45 K3 Vergato Italy
36 B6 Vergaville France
141 G6 Vergemont Queensland
141 G6 Vergemont R Queensland
95 O2 Vergennes Vermont
45 L4 Verghereto Italy
45 R8 Vérgine, M mt Italy
16 C3 Verín Spain
41 K1 Veringenstadt W Germany
87 D7 Verissimo Sarmento Angola
56 H3 Verkh Angara R U.S.S.R.
55 C3 Verkhiye Kigi U.S.S.R.
52 J5 Verkhnaya Yarva U.S.S.R.
56 H3 Verkhneangarskiy Khrebet mts U.S.S.R.
55 C4 Verkhnearshinskiy U.S.S.R.
55 C4 Verkhne-Avzyan U.S.S.R.
54 F8 Verkhnedneprovsk U.S.S.R.
54 E2 Verkhnedneprovskiy U.S.S.R.
55 D4 Verkhnesanarskiy U.S.S.R.
52 E4 Verkhne Svirskoye Vod res U.S.S.R.
29 Q3 Verkhnetulomskiy U.S.S.R.
55 C4 Verkhneural'sk U.S.S.R.
52 H6 Verkhne Yarkeyevo U.S.S.R.
54 K8 Verkhneye U.S.S.R.
55 G3 Verkhneye Krasnoyarka U.S.S.R.
52 D2 Verkhneye Kuyto, Oz L U.S.S.R.

82 Volta — Washington

130 H10 **Volta** Brazil
41 N7 **Volta** Italy
85 E7 **Volta** *R* Ghana
85 D6 **Volta Blanche** *R* Upper Volta/Ghana
98 F1 **Voltaire** N Dakota
142 F2 **Voltaire, C** W Australia
85 D7 **Volta,L** Ghana
85 D6 **Volta Noire** *R* Upper Volta
130 G8 **Volta Redonda** Brazil
85 D6 **Volta Rouge** *R* Upper Volta/Ghana
42 D5 **Volterra** Italy
52 F3 **Volteva** U.S.S.R.
44 E3 **Voltri** Italy
45 R8 **Volturara Irpina** Italy
45 Q7 **Volturno** *R* Italy
47 F4 **Vólvi, L** Greece
19 P17 **Volx** France
52 G6 **Volzhsk** U.S.S.R.
53 F9 **Volzhskiy** U.S.S.R.
42 F6 **Vomano** *R* Italy
106 H2 **Vona** Colorado
118 L6 **Vonda** Sask
87 H12 **Vondrozo** Madagascar
22 J3 **Vonêche** Belgium
116 K5 **Von Frank Mt** Alaska
52 F3 **Vonga** U.S.S.R.
28 C5 **Vonge** Denmark
40 B3 **Vonges** France
46 D6 **Vónitsa** Greece
129 H5 **Von Martius,Cachoeira** *rapids* Brazil
21 F9 **Vonne** *R* France
28 D6 **Vonsbæk** Denmark
28 C6 **Vonsild** Denmark
25 B4 **Voorburg** Netherlands
25 B5 **Voorne** Netherlands
25 B4 **Voorschoten** Netherlands
25 F4 **Voorst** Netherlands
25 E4 **Voorthuizen** Netherlands
115 S4 **Vopnafjördhur** Iceland
25 F6 **Vopst** W Germany
29 J8 **Vörå** Finland
41 K4 **Vorab** *mt* Switzerland
41 L3 **Vorarlberg** *prov* Austria
38 N7 **Vorau** Austria
28 C5 **Vorbasse** Denmark
25 F4 **Vorden** Netherlands
32 H8 **Vörden** W Germany
38 L7 **Vordernberg** Austria
41 J4 **Vorder Rhein** *R* Switzerland
28 H6 **Vordingborg** Denmark
19 P14 **Voreppe** France
54 D3 **Vorga** U.S.S.R.
28 B4 **Vorgod** Denmark
47 G5 **Voríai Sporádhes** *islds* Greece
50 F2 **Vorkuta** U.S.S.R.
27 E11 **Vorma** *R* Norway
28 D3 **Vorning** Denmark
55 G3 **Vorob'yevo** U.S.S.R.
53 F8 **Vorona** *R* U.S.S.R.
54 C3 **Voronevo** U.S.S.R.
54 E5 **Voronezh** Ukraine U.S.S.R.
54 L5 **Voronezh** Voronezh U.S.S.R.
54 L4 **Voronezh** *R* U.S.S.R.
48 M1 **Voronovitsa** U.S.S.R.
52 F2 **Voronov, Mys** *C* U.S.S.R.
55 D2 **Vorontsovka** U.S.S.R.
52 C6 **Vorontsovo** U.S.S.R.
52 E1 **Voron'ya** *R* U.S.S.R.
52 F5 **Voron'ye** U.S.S.R.
54 L8 **Voroshilovgrad** U.S.S.R.
52 G5 **Voroshno** U.S.S.R.
54 N1 **Vorovskogo, im** U.S.S.R.
54 F5 **Vorozhba** U.S.S.R.
33 S5 **Vorpommern** *reg* E Germany
33 N8 **Vorsfelde** W Germany
54 G6 **Vorskala** *R* U.S.S.R.
52 F6 **Vorsma** U.S.S.R.
52 C5 **Võrtsjärv** U.S.S.R.
52 C5 **Võru** U.S.S.R.
28 E4 **Vorup** Denmark
55 D1 **Vor'ya** *R* U.S.S.R.
55 D1 **Vor'yapaul'** U.S.S.R.
52 H3 **Vorykva** *R* U.S.S.R.
36 B7 **Vosges** *dep* France
40 E2 **Vosges** *mt* France
55 C4 **Voskresenskoye** Bashkirskaya U.S.S.R.
52 G6 **Voskresenskoye** Gor'ki U.S.S.R.
52 E5 **Voskresenskoye** Vologda U.S.S.R.
55 F4 **Vosnesenka** U.S.S.R.
27 B11 **Voss** Norway
56 B6 **Vost Kazakhstanskaya Oblast'** *prov* U.S.S.R.
52 E1 **Vostochnaya Litsa** U.S.S.R.
57 H2 **Vostochno-Kounradskiy** U.S.S.R.
56 E4 **Vostochnyy Sayan** *mts* U.S.S.R.
146 F13 **Vostok,C** Antarctica
135 M9 **Vostok I** Pacific Oc
55 E1 **Vostykhoy** U.S.S.R.
109 N5 **Votaw** Texas
109 N5 **Voth** Texas
31 H6 **Votice** Czechoslovakia
52 H6 **Votkinsk** U.S.S.R.
130 E7 **Votuporanga** Brazil
16 B4 **Vouga** *R* Portugal
46 E5 **Voulgára** *mt* Greece
46 E5 **Voulgarélion** Greece
19 N15 **Voulte, la** France
46 E4 **Voúrinos** *mt* Greece
20 E5 **Voutré** France
21 G7 **Vouvray** France
21 J7 **Vouzeron** France
22 G5 **Vouziers** France
21 J6 **Vouzon** France
20 J5 **Voves** France
27 H10 **Voxna** Sweden
27 H10 **Voxnan** Sweden
27 G14 **Voxtorp** Sweden
52 H5 **Voya** *R* U.S.S.R.
146 G2 **Voyeykov Ice Shelf** Antarctica
52 D2 **Voynitsa** U.S.S.R.
52 H3 **Voy Vozh** U.S.S.R.
52 J3 **Voyvozh** U.S.S.R.
52 G3 **Vozhayel'** U.S.S.R.
52 F4 **Vozhega** U.S.S.R.
52 E4 **Vozhe, Oz** *L* U.S.S.R.
52 H5 **Vozhgaly** U.S.S.R.
52 G3 **Vozhgora** U.S.S.R.
54 C9 **Voznesensk** U.S.S.R.
52 E4 **Voznesenye** U.S.S.R.
55 F4 **Vozvyshenskiy** U.S.S.R.
28 D2 **Vrå** Denmark
48 E2 **Vráble** Czechoslovakia
27 C12 **Vrådalsv** *L* Norway
28 C4 **Vrads** Denmark
46 E6 **Vrakhnéïka** Greece
42 H5 **Vran** *mt* Yugoslavia
48 K5 **Vrancea** *reg* Romania
48 K5 **Vrancei, Muntii** *mts* Romania
147 P3 **Vrangelya, Os** *isld* U.S.S.R.
42 H5 **Vranica** *mt* Yugoslavia
46 E2 **Vranje** Yugoslavia
48 G2 **Vranov** Czechoslovakia
22 G1 **Vrasene** Belgium
47 F1 **Vratsa** Bulgaria
42 H4 **Vrbas** *R* Yugoslavia
31 K5 **Vrbno** Czechoslovakia
31 J5 **Vrchlabí** Czechoslovakia
48 F5 **Vrdnik** Yugoslavia
89 F6 **Vrede** S Africa
32 E8 **Vreden** W Germany
32 G7 **Vrees** W Germany
25 D4 **Vreeswijk** Netherlands
28 D2 **Vrensted** Denmark
28 F6 **Vresen** *isld* Denmark
22 H4 **Vress** France
20 B3 **Vrétot, le** France
27 G12 **Vretstorp** Sweden
42 H5 **Vrgorac** Yugoslavia
76 D5 **Vriddhachalam** India
28 C4 **Vridsted** Denmark
25 G2 **Vries** Netherlands
25 G4 **Vriezenveen** Netherlands
27 G14 **Vrigstad** Sweden
41 K4 **Vrin** Switzerland
22 H4 **Vringe-aux-Bois** France
28 A3 **Vrist** Denmark
22 F3 **Vrith-St.Léger** France
22 H5 **Vrizy** France
28 A5 **Vrøgum** Denmark
22 B3 **Vron** France
47 H6 **Vrondádhes** Greece
46 F8 **Vrondamás** Greece
25 G4 **Vroomshoop** Netherlands
28 C4 **Vroue** Denmark
48 G5 **Vršac** Yugoslavia
45 P1 **Vrsar** Yugoslavia
48 E1 **Vrútky** Czechoslovakia
89 D6 **Vryburg** S Africa
89 G6 **Vryheid** S Africa
37 O5 **Všeruby** Czechoslovakia
37 P4 **Všeruby** Czechoslovakia
31 K6 **Vsetín** Czechoslovakia
55 C1 **Vsevolodo Blagodatskiy** U.S.S.R.
48 E2 **Vtáčnik** *mt* Czechoslovakia
19 P12 **Vuache, Mt de** France
68 G2 **Vu Ban** Vietnam
47 G3 **Vŭcha** *R* Bulgaria
46 D2 **Vučitrn** Yugoslavia
21 B7 **Vue** France
25 D5 **Vught** Netherlands
48 E5 **Vuka** *R* Yugoslavia
48 E5 **Vukovar** Yugoslavia
118 D8 **Vulcan** Alberta
48 H5 **Vulcan** Romania
43 F10 **Vulcano** *isld* Italy
67 B7 **Vu Liet** Vietnam
43 G8 **Vulture** *mt* Italy
103 M8 **Vulture Mts** Arizona
68 J4 **Vung Da Nang** *B* Vietnam
68 J7 **Vung Phan Thiet** *B* Vietnam
68 H7 **Vung Tau** Vietnam
89 F2 **Vungu** *R* Zimbabwe
26 M5 **Vuodas** Sweden
29 N7 **Vuokatti** Finland
29 O11 **Vuoksa** *L* U.S.S.R.
29 O10 **Vuoksenniska** Finland
29 N7 **Vuolijoki** Finland
26 L5 **Vuollerim** Sweden
29 N5 **Vuostimo** Finland
29 N3 **Vuotso** Finland
26 N2 **Vuovdasoaivve** *mt* Norway
47 H2 **Vŭrbitsa** Bulgaria
28 C2 **Vust** Denmark
48 L4 **Vutcani** Romania
55 D4 **Vvedenka** U.S.S.R.
100 F8 **Vya** Nevada
52 E2 **Vyalozero, Oz** *L* U.S.S.R.
52 F5 **Vyaltsevo** U.S.S.R.
29 P9 **Vyartsilya** U.S.S.R.
52 G5 **Vyatka** *R* U.S.S.R.
52 H6 **Vyatskiye Polyany** U.S.S.R.
59 K2 **Vyazemskiy** U.S.S.R.
54 F1 **Vyaz'ma** U.S.S.R.
54 E1 **Vyazma** *R* U.S.S.R.
52 F6 **Vyazniki** U.S.S.R.
52 C6 **Vybor** U.S.S.R.
29 O11 **Vyborg** U.S.S.R.
29 N11 **Vyborgskiy Zaliv** *gulf* U.S.S.R.
52 H4 **Vychegda** *R* U.S.S.R.
31 J5 **Vychodočeský** *reg* Czechoslovakia
52 E3 **Vyg** *R* U.S.S.R.
48 N4 **Vygoda** U.S.S.R.
52 D3 **Vygozero, Oz** *L* U.S.S.R.
48 G2 **Vyhorlát** *mt* Czechoslovakia
52 F6 **Vyksa** U.S.S.R.
52 H3 **Vym'** *R* U.S.S.R.
52 G4 **Vymsk** U.S.S.R.
52 C5 **Vyra** U.S.S.R.
52 D5 **Vyritsa** U.S.S.R.
8 C2 **Vyrnwy, L** Wales
31 K6 **Vyškov** Czechoslovakia
31 L6 **Vysoká** *mt* Czechoslovakia
52 G6 **Vysokaya Gora** U.S.S.R.
52 J4 **Vysokaya Parma** *plat* U.S.S.R.
31 J6 **Vysoké Mýto** Czechoslovakia
59 L1 **Vysokogornyy** U.S.S.R.
52 E6 **Vysokovsk** U.S.S.R.
31 O3 **Vysokoye** U.S.S.R.
29 O11 **Vysotsk** U.S.S.R.
38 K4 **Vyšší Brod** Czechoslovakia
52 E4 **Vytegra** U.S.S.R.
52 G3 **Vyya** *R* U.S.S.R.
85 D6 **Wa** Ghana
25 D5 **Waal** *R* Netherlands
25 B5 **Waalhaven** Netherlands
25 D5 **Waalwijk** Netherlands
25 D2 **Waardgronden** Netherlands
22 E1 **Waarschoot** Belgium
120 D2 **Wababimiga L** Ontario
118 C5 **Wabamun** Alberta
123 U6 **Wabana** Nfld
118 D3 **Wabasca** Alberta
117 Q7 **Wabasca** *R* Alberta
111 F7 **Wabash** Arkansas
94 B6 **Wabash** Indiana
110 J3 **Wabash** *R* U.S.A.
99 O5 **Wabasha** Minnesota
113 G10 **Wabasso** Florida
99 L5 **Wabasso** Minnesota
120 F4 **Wabatongushi L** Ontario
99 S4 **Wabeno** Wisconsin
Wabern *see* **Egling**
118 K1 **Wabigoon** Ontario
121 R4 **Wabino** *R* Quebec
120 A2 **Wabinosh L** Ontario
120 C2 **Waboose Dam** Ontario
120 F6 **Wabos** Ontario
119 T4 **Wabowden** Manitoba
31 L2 **Wąbrzezno** Poland
58 G5 **Wabu Hu** *L* China
115 N7 **Wabush** Labrador
102 E2 **Wabuska** Nevada
112 H4 **Waccamaw** *R* S Carolina
112 J3 **Waccamaw, L** N Carolina
113 D8 **Waccasassa B** Florida
95 M9 **Wachapreague** Virginia
36 H5 **Wachbach** W Germany
36 E5 **Wachenheim** W Germany
37 K4 **Wachenroth** W Germany
33 R7 **Wachow** E Germany
22 F1 **Wachtbeke** Belgium
25 F6 **Wachtendonk** W Germany
36 G3 **Wächtersbach** W Germany
32 G7 **Wachtum** W Germany
95 Q4 **Wachusett Res** Massachusetts
135 M11 **Wachusett Shoal** Pacific Oc
32 K4 **Wacken** W Germany
98 J9 **Waco** Nebraska
122 G2 **Waco** Quebec
109 K4 **Waco** Texas
99 N5 **Waconia** Minnesota
122 G2 **Wacouno R** Quebec
77 K6 **Wad** Pakistan
142 D6 **Wadara Hills** W Australia
60 H10 **Wadayama** Japan
86 E3 **Wad Banda** Sudan
139 H8 **Waddamana** Tasmania
84 F4 **Waddān** Libya
25 D2 **Waddenzee** Netherlands
143 C9 **Wadderin** W Australia
9 F4 **Waddesdon** England
9 F1 **Waddington** England
95 M2 **Waddington** New York
117 L10 **Waddington, Mt** Br Col
94 B8 **Waddy** Kentucky
112 J2 **Wade** N Carolina
8 B7 **Wadebridge** England
99 L3 **Wadena** Minnesota
119 O7 **Wadena** Sask
36 B4 **Wadern** W Germany
32 H9 **Wadersloh** W Germany
112 G3 **Wadesboro** N Carolina
123 T4 **Wadham Is** Nfld
117 K10 **Wadhams** Br Columbia
9 G5 **Wadhurst** England
80 G6 **Wadi es Sir** Jordan
84 K5 **Wâdi Gimâl I** Egypt
86 F1 **Wadi Halfa** Sudan
138 D5 **Wadikee** S Australia
79 F8 **Wādi Mūsā** Jordan
111 L8 **Wadley** Alabama
112 E5 **Wadley** Georgia
86 F3 **Wad Medani** Sudan
31 L6 **Wadowice** Poland
102 E2 **Wadsworth** Nevada
94 F5 **Wadsworth** Ohio
13 G6 **Wadworth** England
65 G7 **Waegwan** S Korea
109 K6 **Waelder** Texas
68 F4 **Waeng** Thailand
65 E2 **Wafang** China
Wafangdian *see* **Fu Xian**
77 A5 **Wafra** Iran
61 O6 **Waga-gawa** *R* Japan
120 B2 **Wagaming** Ontario
111 H10 **Wagarville** Alabama
32 J7 **Wagenfeld** W Germany
25 E5 **Wageningen** Netherlands
140 E4 **Waggabundi** Queensland
139 H6 **Wagga Wagga** New S Wales
74 E8 **Waghai** India
36 F5 **Waghäusel** W Germany
143 B10 **Wagin** W Australia
101 R1 **Wagner** Montana
98 H6 **Wagner** S Dakota
107 P6 **Wagoner** Oklahoma
106 F5 **Wagon Mound** New Mexico
100 F6 **Wagontire** Oregon
106 D4 **Wagon Wheel Gap** Colorado
112 H3 **Wagram** N Carolina
31 K3 **Wągrowiec** Poland
100 J3 **Waha** Idaho
84 G4 **Waha** Libya
83 K9 **Wahalkada Tank** Sri Lanka
145 E2 **Waharoa** New Zealand
84 G4 **Waḥat Jālu** Libya
102 R12 **Wahiawa** Hawaiian Is
145 E2 **Wahi L** New Zealand
36 F4 **Wahlen** W Germany
36 C2 **Wahn** W Germany
32 K7 **Wahnebergen** W Germany
98 K8 **Wahoo** Nebraska
98 K3 **Wahpeton** N Dakota
33 S9 **Wahrenbrück** E Germany
33 N7 **Wahrenholz** W Germany
103 L3 **Wah Wah Mts** Utah
76 A2 **Wai** India
135 U6 **Waiahukini** Hawaiian Is
135 T3 **Waiakoa** Hawaiian Is
135 O1 **Waialeale** *peak* Hawaiian Is
102 R11 **Waialee** Hawaiian Is
102 R11 **Waialua** Hawaiian Is
102 R12 **Waianae** Hawaiian Is
102 R12 **Waianae Ra** Hawaiian Is
144 C6 **Waianakarua** New Zealand
144 B7 **Waianiwa** New Zealand
144 B6 **Waiatoto R** New Zealand
144 D5 **Waiau** New Zealand
144 A6 **Waiau** *R* New Zealand
145 F3 **Waiau R** New Zealand
36 G6 **Waiblingen** W Germany
37 N4 **Waidhaus** W Germany
31 J7 **Waidhofen** Austria
38 L6 **Waidhofen an der Ybbs** Austria
71 B3 **Waigama** Indonesia
143 G8 **Waigen Lakes** W Australia
71 C3 **Waigeo** *isld* W Irian
37 J4 **Waigolshausen** W Germany
144 C6 **Waihao Forks** New Zealand
145 D1 **Waiharara** New Zealand
145 E2 **Waiheke I** New Zealand
145 E2 **Waihi** New Zealand
144 A7 **Waihoaka** New Zealand
144 C7 **Waihola** New Zealand
145 D4 **Waihopai** *R* New Zealand
145 D1 **Waihopo** New Zealand
144 C5 **Waiho R** New Zealand
145 E2 **Waihou** New Zealand
145 E2 **Waihou R** New Zealand
145 F3 **Waihua** New Zealand
71 J9 **Waikabubak** Sumba Indonesia
144 B6 **Waikaia** New Zealand
144 B6 **Waikaia Plain** New Zealand
144 B6 **Waikaka** New Zealand
145 E4 **Waikanae** New Zealand
102 S12 **Waikane** Hawaiian Is
145 F3 **Waikareiti, L** New Zealand
145 E2 **Waikare, L** New Zealand
145 F3 **Waikaremoana, L** New Zealand
145 E2 **Waikaretu** New Zealand
144 D5 **Waikari** New Zealand
145 E3 **Waikato** New Zealand
144 B7 **Waikawa** New Zealand
145 E4 **Waikawa** New Zealand
71 J9 **Waikelo Teluk** *B* Sumba Indonesia
138 E5 **Waikerie** S Australia
135 U5 **Waikii** Hawaiian Is
142 A4 **Waikiki** W Aust
102 S12 **Waikiki Beach** Hawaiian Is
145 F3 **Waikohu** New Zealand
145 F3 **Waikokopu** New Zealand
144 B7 **Waikotkoi** New Zealand
144 C6 **Waikouaiti** New Zealand
144 A7 **Waikouro** New Zealand
102 V13 **Wailuku** Hawaiian Is
144 B7 **Waimahaka** New Zealand
144 A4 **Waimakariri R** New Zealand
145 D1 **Waimamaka** New Zealand
145 F3 **Waimana** New Zealand
102 S12 **Waimanalo** Hawaiian Is
144 C4 **Waimangaroa** New Zealand
145 F3 **Waimarama** New Zealand
144 C4 **Waimarie** New Zealand
144 C6 **Waimate** New Zealand
145 E2 **Waimauku** New Zealand
135 U4 **Waimea** Hawaiian Is
135 Q2 **Waimea** Hawaiin Is Pac Oc
102 R11 **Waimea B** Hawaiian Is
22 L3 **Waimes** Belgium
145 E3 **Waimiha** New Zealand
9 G1 **Wainfleet** England
71 K9 **Waingapu** Sumba Indonesia
145 E4 **Waingawa** New Zealand
135 O1 **Wainiha** Hawaiian Is
144 C5 **Wainihinihi** New Zealand
99 S3 **Wainola** Michigan
116 G1 **Wainwright** Alaska
118 G6 **Wainwright** Alberta
145 F3 **Waioeka R** New Zealand
135 U6 **Waiohinu** Hawaiian Is
145 E1 **Waiolira** New Zealand
145 F3 **Waiotapu** New Zealand
145 E3 **Waiouru** New Zealand
144 B7 **Waipahi** New Zealand
102 R12 **Waipahu** Hawaiian Is
145 F3 **Waipaoa** New Zealand
145 D1 **Waipapakauri** New Zealand
145 E2 **Waipa R** New Zealand
144 D5 **Waipara** New Zealand
145 F3 **Waipawa** New Zealand
144 C6 **Waipiata** New Zealand
135 U4 **Waipio** Hawaiian Is
145 E2 **Waipipi** New Zealand
145 G3 **Waipiro Bay** New Zealand
144 C6 **Waipori, L** New Zealand
145 E1 **Waipu** New Zealand
145 F3 **Waipukurau** New Zealand
145 G2 **Waipu R** New Zealand
145 F3 **Wairakei** New Zealand
145 E4 **Wairarapa, L** New Zealand
145 D4 **Wairau Valley** New Zealand
144 B7 **Wairio** New Zealand
145 F3 **Wairoa** New Zealand
145 E2 **Wairoa R** New Zealand
145 E1 **Wairua** *R* New Zealand
144 B7 **Wairuna** New Zealand
71 C3 **Waisai** W Irian
37 L4 **Waischenfeld** W Germany
145 F3 **Waitahanui** New Zealand
144 C5 **Waitaha R** New Zealand
144 B6 **Waitahuna** New Zealand
145 E2 **Waitakaruru** New Zealand
144 C6 **Waitaki L** New Zealand
145 E1 **Waitangi** New Zealand
145 E3 **Waitara** New Zealand
145 E4 **Waitarere** New Zealand
144 D6 **Waitati** New Zealand
140 B5 **Waite** *R* N Terr Aust
145 F1 **Waitemata Harb** New Zealand
143 D8 **Waite, Mt** W Australia
145 E2 **Waitoa** New Zealand
145 E3 **Waitomo** New Zealand
145 E3 **Waitotara** New Zealand
145 E3 **Waitotara** *R* New Zealand
100 G3 **Waitsburg** Washington
119 M6 **Waitville** Sask
145 E2 **Waiuku** New Zealand
144 C5 **Waiuta** New Zealand
145 E2 **Waiwera** New Zealand
144 B7 **Waiwera South** New Zealand
71 B1 **Wajabula** Halmahera Indonesia
71 C2 **Wajag** *isld* Indonesia
71 B2 **Wajamli** Indonesia
60 H12 **Wajiki** Japan
61 K8 **Wajima** Japan
86 H5 **Wajir** Kenya
69 C10 **Wak** Sumatra
86 D5 **Waka** Zaïre
60 D12 **Wakamatsu** Japan
60 B12 **Wakamatsu-jima** *isld* Japan
120 H5 **Wakami L** Ontario
144 C5 **Wakanui** New Zealand
145 F3 **Wakarara Range** New Zealand
94 A5 **Wakarusa** Indiana
61 J10 **Wakasa-wan** *B* Japan
144 B6 **Wakatipu, L** New Zealand
119 M6 **Wakaw** Sask
60 J11 **Wakayama** Japan
60 J12 **Wakayama** *prefect* Japan
61 P7 **Wakayanagi** Japan
107 L2 **Wa Keeney** Kansas
13 G6 **Wakefield** England
127 J2 **Wakefield** Jamaica
107 O2 **Wakefield** Kansas
99 R3 **Wakefield** Michigan
98 K7 **Wakefield** Nebraska
145 D4 **Wakefield** New Zealand
121 P7 **Wakefield** Quebec
95 Q5 **Wakefield** Rhode I
95 K10 **Wakefield** Virginia
112 J2 **Wake Forest** N Carolina
134 H6 **Wake Island** Pacific Oc
68 B4 **Wakema** Burma
122 H5 **Wakenam** Quebec
94 A5 **Wakerton** Indiana
74 E1 **Wakhan** *reg* Afghanistan
60 H11 **Waki** Japan
60 O4 **Wakinosawa** Japan
107 N5 **Wakita** Oklahoma
60 P1 **Wakkanai** Japan
87 F11 **Wakkerstroom** S Africa
Wako *see* **Watcomb**
120 G6 **Wakomata L** Ontario
139 G6 **Wakool** New S Wales
119 S9 **Wakopa** Manitoba
98 F4 **Wakpala** S Dakota
71 C3 **Wakre** W Irian
113 C7 **Wakulla** Florida
120 K2 **Wakwayowkastic** *R* Ontario
86 G4 **Walaga** *prov* Ethiopia
103 L6 **Walapai** Arizona
83 K11 **Walawe Ganga** *R* Sri Lanka
33 O8 **Walbeck** E Germany
36 D6 **Walbourg** France
94 D5 **Walbridge** Ohio
31 J5 **Wałbrzych** Poland
36 H1 **Walburg** W Germany
139 K4 **Walcha** New S Wales
38 G7 **Walchen** Austria
41 O2 **Walchensee** *L* W Germany
25 A5 **Walcheren** Netherlands
38 F6 **Walchsee** Austria
117 K8 **Walcott** Br Columbia
98 K3 **Walcott** N Dakota
101 T8 **Walcott** Wyoming
142 E3 **Walcott Inlet** W Australia
101 M7 **Walcott, L., Res** Idaho
146 F9 **Walcott,Mt** Antarctica
22 G3 **Walcourt** Belgium
31 J2 **Wałcz** Poland
38 L5 **Wald Aist** *R* Austria
36 F5 **Waldangeloch** W Germany
36 D4 **Waldböckelheim** W Germany
36 C2 **Waldbreitbach** W Germany
36 D2 **Waldbröl** W Germany
36 G5 **Waldbrunn** Baden-Württemberg W Germany
36 G5 **Waldbrunn** Hessen W Germany
143 B6 **Waldburg Ra** W Australia
33 T9 **Walddrehna** E Germany
118 K8 **Waldeck** Sask
36 G1 **Waldeck** W Germany
101 T9 **Walden** Colorado
95 N5 **Walden** New York
37 O2 **Waldenberg** E Germany
36 G6 **Waldenbuch** W Germany
Waldenburg *see* **Wałbrzych**
110 F6 **Waldenburg** Arkansas
36 H5 **Waldenburg** W Germany
37 N4 **Waldershof** W Germany
36 D5 **Waldfischbach** W Germany
37 P1 **Waldheim** E Germany
118 L6 **Waldheim** Sask
86 G3 **Waldia** Ethiopia
36 H1 **Waldkappel** W Germany
40 G1 **Waldkirch** W Germany
30 H7 **Waldkirchen** W Germany
36 F4 **Waldmichelbach** W Germany
37 O5 **Waldmünchen** W Germany
37 N4 **Wald Naab** *R* W Germany
25 F6 **Waldniel** W Germany
109 O2 **Waldo** Arkansas
118 B9 **Waldo** Br Columbia
113 E8 **Waldo** Florida
107 M2 **Waldo** Kansas
94 D6 **Waldo** Ohio
99 T6 **Waldo** Wisconsin
100 C6 **Waldo L** Oregon
95 L8 **Waldorf** Maryland
99 N6 **Waldorf** Minnesota
100 A5 **Waldport** Oregon
109 N1 **Waldron** Arkansas
119 P8 **Waldron** Sask
146 G2 **Waldron,C** Antarctica
37 N3 **Waldsassen** W Germany
41 H2 **Waldshut** W Germany
37 J7 **Waldstetten** W Germany
37 N4 **Waldthurn** W Germany
36 B5 **Waldwisse** France
71 H5 **Waleabahi** *isld* Sulawesi
71 H5 **Waleakodi** *isld* Sulawesi
71 H5 **Walea,Selat** *str* Sulawesi
116 C4 **Wales** Alaska
99 P2 **Wales** Minnesota
98 H1 **Wales** N Dakota
103 N2 **Wales** Utah
8 C3 **Wales** *princ* U.K.
115 L4 **Wales I** N W Terr
85 D6 **Walewale** Ghana
33 O5 **Walfisch** E Germany
139 J4 **Walgett** New S Wales
146 H11 **Walgreen Coast** Antarctica
98 J1 **Walhalla** N Dakota
112 D3 **Walhalla** S Carolina
37 N5 **Walhalla** *mt* W Germany
70 N9 **Walikukun** Java
143 A8 **Walkaway** W Australia
33 R5 **Walkendorf** E Germany
33 N9 **Walkenried** W Germany
100 C8 **Walker** California
99 P7 **Walker** Iowa
107 L3 **Walker** Kansas
111 F11 **Walker** Louisiana
99 M2 **Walker** Minnesota
110 B4 **Walker** Missouri
98 E4 **Walker** S Dakota
102 E2 **Walker** *R* Nevada
140 B6 **Walker** *R* N Terr Aust
141 F3 **Walker** *R* Queensland
89 A10 **Walker B** S Africa
13 E2 **Walkerburn** Scotland
113 J10 **Walker Cay** *isld* Bahamas
116 K3 **Walker L** Alaska
119 V4 **Walker L** Manitoba
102 F3 **Walker L** Nevada
122 E3 **Walker L** Quebec
146 H12 **Walker Mts** Antarctica
102 G6 **Walker Pk** California
140 D2 **Walker R** N Terr Aust
70 D2 **Walker Ra** Sabah
94 G8 **Walkersville** W Virginia
120 J8 **Walkerton** Ontario
112 G1 **Walkertown** N Carolina
99 U6 **Walkerville** Michigan
101 N3 **Walkerville** Montana
98 D5 **Wall** S Dakota
143 A8 **Wallabi Group** *islds* W Australia
140 E3 **Wallaby I** Queensland
141 F3 **Wallaby I** Queensland
138 C4 **Wallaby,Mt** S Australia
114 H8 **Wallace** Idaho
107 J3 **Wallace** Kansas
99 T4 **Wallace** Michigan
112 J3 **Wallace** N Carolina
98 E9 **Wallace** Nebraska
122 J8 **Wallace** Nova Scotia
121 M7 **Wallace** Ontario
98 J4 **Wallace** S Dakota
94 G7 **Wallace** W Virginia
120 H10 **Wallaceburg** Ontario
109 O3 **Wallace L** Louisiana
118 B3 **Wallace Mt** Alberta
120 J10 **Wallacetown** Ontario
141 H7 **Wallal** Queensland
142 D4 **Wallal Downs** W Australia
143 C9 **Wallambin, L** W Australia
141 K8 **Wallangarra** Queensland
142 D5 **Wallani Well** W Australia
141 H8 **Wallan, R** Queensland
138 D5 **Wallaroo** S Australia
8 C1 **Wallasey** England
140 B3 **Wallaston, Mt** N Terr Aust
36 E2 **Wallau** W Germany
139 H6 **Walla Walla** New S Wales
114 H8 **Walla Walla** Washington
100 G4 **Walla Walla** *R* Oregon
138 C2 **Wall Cr** N Terr Australia
140 C7 **Wall Creek** N Terr Aust
37 J2 **Walldorf** E Germany
36 F5 **Walldorf** W Germany
37 L2 **Wallendorf** E Germany
37 L3 **Wallenfels** W Germany
32 H8 **Wallenhorst** W Germany
95 M5 **Wallenpaupack, L** Pennsylvania
41 K3 **Wallen See** *L* Switzerland
32 L8 **Wallensen** W Germany
37 O6 **Wallersdorf** W Germany
36 F1 **Wallershöhe** *mt* W Germany
37 J6 **Wallerstein** W Germany
33 O10 **Wallhausen** E Germany
142 B3 **Walliabup** W Australia
95 P5 **Wallingford** Connecticut
9 E4 **Wallingford** England
145 F4 **Wallingford** New Zealand
95 P3 **Wallingford** Vermont
109 L6 **Wallis** Texas
137 R4 **Wallis, Îles** Pacific Oc
139 L4 **Wallis L** New S Wales
99 L7 **Wall L** Iowa
36 D3 **Wallmerod** W Germany
142 B6 **Wall, Mt** W Australia
86 G3 **Wallo** *prov* Ethiopia
141 K6 **Walloon** Queensland
94 C1 **Walloon L** Michigan
95 M9 **Wallops I** Virginia
100 H4 **Wallowa** Oregon
100 H4 **Wallowa Mts** Oregon
15 G2 **Walls** Scotland
28 C7 **Wallsbüll** W Germany
139 K5 **Wallsend** New S Wales
33 O7 **Wallstawe** E Germany
32 J8 **Wallucke** W Germany
100 G3 **Wallula** Washington
141 J7 **Wallumbilla** Queensland
33 Q9 **Wallwitzhafen** E Germany
9 H5 **Walmer** England
13 E5 **Walney I** England
99 R8 **Walnut** Illinois
107 P4 **Walnut** Kansas
107 K3 **Walnut** *R* Kansas
103 N6 **Walnut Canyon Nat.Mon** Arizona
112 G1 **Walnut Cove** N Carolina
111 G9 **Walnut Grove** Mississippi
110 C4 **Walnut Grove** Missouri
109 O9 **Walnut Hills** Texas
110 F5 **Walnut Ridge** Arkansas
109 K3 **Walnut Springs** Texas
125 M2 **Walpatanta** Honduras
138 F6 **Walpeup** Victoria
95 P3 **Walpole** New Hampshire
137 O6 **Walpole** *isld* Pacific Oc
116 D8 **Walrus I** Pribilof Is Bering Sea
116 G7 **Walrus Is** Alaska
9 E2 **Walsall** England
37 K1 **Walschleben** E Germany
36 E3 **Walsdorf** W Germany
106 F4 **Walsenburg** Colorado
118 G9 **Walsh** Alberta
106 H4 **Walsh** Colorado
141 G3 **Walsh** Queensland
141 G3 **Walsh** *R* Queensland
117 D5 **Walsh, Mt** Yukon Terr
22 J2 **Walshoutem** Belgium
25 B6 **Walsoorden** Netherlands
32 L7 **Walsrode** W Germany
32 E9 **Walsum** W Germany
112 G5 **Walterboro** S Carolina
109 J1 **Walters** Oklahoma
37 K2 **Waltershausen** E Germany
141 G8 **Walter's Ra** Queensland
111 G8 **Walthall** Mississippi
9 F2 **Waltham** England
101 P2 **Waltham** Montana
121 O7 **Waltham** Quebec
9 G4 **Waltham Abbey** England
9 F4 **Waltham Cross** England
98 K7 **Walthill** Nebraska
101 S6 **Waltman** Wyoming
9 F5 **Walton** England
94 A6 **Walton** Indiana
94 C8 **Walton** Kentucky
95 M4 **Walton** New York
145 E2 **Walton** New Zealand
122 J8 **Walton** Nova Scotia
120 J9 **Walton** Ontario
94 F8 **Walton** W Virginia
126 E6 **Walton Bank** Caribbean
94 B2 **Walton Junc** Michigan
9 H4 **Walton on the Naze** England
110 G3 **Waltonville** Illinois
32 F9 **Waltrop** W Germany
87 B10 **Walvis Bay** S Africa
90 J12 **Walvis Ridge** Atlantic Oc
99 S7 **Walworth** Wisconsin
143 C9 **Walyahmoing** *hill* W Australia
36 F5 **Walzbuchtal** W Germany
86 A4 **Wamba** Nigeria
86 E5 **Wamba** Zaïre
87 C7 **Wamba** *R* Zaïre
139 H5 **Wamboyne** New S Wales
107 O2 **Wamego** Kansas
25 D5 **Wamel** Netherlands
100 D4 **Wamic** Oregon
94 G6 **Wampum** Pennsylvania
101 R8 **Wamsutter** Wyoming
77 L3 **Wana** Pakistan
139 G3 **Wanaaring** New S Wales
144 B6 **Wanaka** New Zealand
67 E3 **Wan'an** China
126 A2 **Wanapa** Bonaire W Indies
120 K6 **Wanapitei L** Ontario
95 N5 **Wanaque Res** New Jersey
99 U8 **Wanatah** Indiana
138 F5 **Wanbi** S Australia
98 E6 **Wanblee** S Dakota
112 M2 **Wanchese** N Carolina
138 E3 **Wancoocha, L** S Australia
130 C10 **Wanda** Argentina
138 C4 **Wandana** S Australia
59 K2 **Wanda Shan** *mt ra* China
118 E3 **Wandering River** Alberta
37 K2 **Wandersleben** E Germany
28 C7 **Wanderup** W Germany
33 S7 **Wandlitz** E Germany
141 J7 **Wandoan** Queensland
141 G4 **Wando Vale** Queensland
22 K2 **Wandre** Belgium
109 K1 **Wanette** Oklahoma
65 E4 **Wanfu** China
65 C7 **Wanfu He** *R* China
141 G8 **Wangamurra** *R* Queensland
145 E3 **Wanganui** New Zealand
144 C5 **Wanganui R** New Zealand
139 G6 **Wangaratta** Victoria
138 D5 **Wangary** S Australia
67 B2 **Wangcaoba** China
65 B5 **Wangcun** China
67 C2 **Wangcun** China
67 B4 **Wangdian** China
65 C5 **Wangdu** China
33 N4 **Wangels** W Germany
41 L2 **Wangen** W Germany
32 G5 **Wangerland** *reg* W Germany
32 G5 **Wangerooge** W Germany
9 H3 **Wangford** England
71 K10 **Wanggameti** *mt* Sumba Indonesia
67 D4 **Wanggao** China
Wanggezhuang *see* **Jiaonan**
138 E3 **Wangianna** S Australia
71 H7 **Wangiwangi** *isld* Indonesia
67 D2 **Wangjiachang** China
67 E1 **Wangjiadian** China
67 E1 **Wangjiang** China
68 D5 **Wangka** Thailand
65 G1 **Wangkui** China
Wang Mai Khon *see* **Sawankhalok**
67 C5 **Wangmao** China
67 B4 **Wangmo** China
65 H3 **Wangqing** China
68 D2 **Wan hsa-la** Burma
71 H7 **Wani** *mt* Indonesia
86 E5 **Wanie Rukula** Zaïre
111 F10 **Wanilla** Mississippi
65 E5 **Wanjialing** China
74 D7 **Wankaner** India
32 M4 **Wankendorf** W Germany
89 E2 **Wankie** Zimbabwe
87 E9 **Wankie Nat. Park** Zimbabwe
119 Q4 **Wanless** Manitoba
12 E3 **Wanlockhead** Scotland
143 G8 **Wanna Lakes** W Australia
32 F9 **Wanne-Eickel** W Germany
143 B9 **Wanneroo** W Australia
67 F2 **Wannian** China
68 K3 **Wanning** China
33 S8 **Wannsee** E Germany
76 D2 **Wanparti** India
65 C4 **Wanquan** China
125 M2 **Wanquibila** Honduras
65 A7 **Wanrong** China
13 G3 **Wansbeck, R** England
9 F2 **Wansford** England
67 C3 **Wanshan** China
67 D6 **Wanshan Qundao** *islds* China
145 F4 **Wanstead** New Zealand
9 E4 **Wantage** England
36 D6 **Wantzenau** France
120 K6 **Wanup** Ontario
67 C1 **Wanxian** China
58 E5 **Wanyuan** China
67 E2 **Wanzai** China
Wanzhi *see* **Wuhu**
33 O8 **Wanzleben** E Germany
145 E3 **Waotu** New Zealand
94 C6 **Wapakoneta** Ohio
109 L1 **Wapanucka** Oklahoma
100 E3 **Wapato** Washington
119 N4 **Wapawekka Hills** Sask
119 Q8 **Wapella** Sask
101 N6 **Wapello** Idaho
99 P8 **Wapello** Iowa
119 S3 **Wapisu L** Manitoba
117 O8 **Wapiti** *R* Alberta
101 Q5 **Wapiti Ra** Wyoming
110 F4 **Wappapello Res** Missouri
95 O5 **Wappingers Falls** New York
99 O7 **Wapsipinicon** *R* Iowa
119 P2 **Wapus L** Sask
123 N2 **Wapustagamau L** Quebec
94 F9 **War** W Virginia
86 H4 **Warandab** Ethiopia
76 D1 **Warangal** India
139 H6 **Waranga Res** Victoria
139 H8 **Waratah** Tasmania
139 H7 **Waratah B** Victoria
99 N2 **Warba** Minnesota
9 F3 **Warboys** England
141 G6 **Warbreccan** Queensland
118 C5 **Warburg** Alberta
32 K10 **Warburg** W Germany
139 H7 **Warburton** Victoria
138 E2 **Warburton** *R* S Australia
143 F7 **Warburton Mission** W Australia
143 F7 **Warburton Ra** W Australia
138 C4 **Warburton Rge** S Australia
111 H9 **Ward** Alabama
145 E4 **Ward** New Zealand
141 H7 **Ward** *R* Queensland
138 D5 **Wardang I** S Australia
87 E11 **Warden** S Africa
100 F3 **Warden** Washington
32 H6 **Wardenburg** W Germany
118 E6 **Warden Junc** Alberta
94 J7 **Wardensville** W Virginia
74 H8 **Wardha** India
115 M1 **Ward Hunt I** N W Terr
118 F8 **Wardlow** Alberta
144 A6 **Ward, Mt** New Zealand
144 B5 **Ward, Mt** New Zealand
118 B9 **Wardner** Br Col
13 F5 **Wards Stone** *mt* England
117 L7 **Ware** Br Col
9 F4 **Ware** England
95 P4 **Ware** Massachusetts
145 D3 **Warea** New Zealand
22 E2 **Waregem** Belgium
8 D6 **Wareham** England
22 J2 **Waremme** Belgium
33 R5 **Waren** E Germany
140 F6 **Warenda** Queensland
32 G9 **Warendorf** W Germany
144 B7 **Warepa** New Zealand
140 B4 **Ware Ra** N Terr Aust
112 E6 **Waresboro** Georgia
112 E3 **Ware Shoals** S Carolina
95 N7 **Waretown** New Jersey
25 G2 **Warfum** Netherlands
9 F5 **Wargrave** England
139 K3 **Warialda** New S Wales
33 P5 **Warin** E Germany
68 G5 **Warin Chamrap** Thailand
109 J6 **Waring** Texas
116 H3 **Waring Mts** Alaska
13 F2 **Wark** England
31 N4 **Warka** Poland
13 G3 **Warkworth** England
145 E2 **Warkworth** New Zealand
121 N8 **Warkworth** Ontario
8 D3 **Warley** England
9 F5 **Warlingham** England
20 K2 **Warloy Baillon** France
89 A7 **Warmbad** Namibia
117 G6 **Warm Bay Hotsprings** Br Columbia
32 L8 **Warmbüchen** W Germany
37 M4 **Warmensteinach** W Germany
22 G5 **Warmeriville** France
9 E3 **Warmington** England
8 D5 **Warminster** England
25 C4 **Warmond** Netherlands
32 J8 **Warmsen** W Germany
112 C5 **Warm Springs** Georgia
101 N3 **Warmsprings** Montana
102 H3 **Warm Springs** Nevada
100 D5 **Warm Springs** Oregon
94 H8 **Warm Springs** Virginia
100 G6 **Warm Springs Res** Oregon
89 B9 **Warmwaters Berg** *mt* S Africa
8 D6 **Warmwell** England
22 J2 **Warnant-Dreye** Belgium
120 B3 **Warneford** Ontario
33 Q4 **Warnemünde** E Germany
101 N1 **Warner** Alberta
95 Q3 **Warner** New Hampshire
107 P6 **Warner** Oklahoma
98 H4 **Warner** S Dakota
100 F7 **Warner Lakes** Oregon
100 E8 **Warner Mts** California
112 D5 **Warner Robins** Georgia
102 H8 **Warner Springs** California
22 D2 **Warneton** Belgium
139 L3 **Warning,Mt** New S Wales
33 Q5 **Warnow** *R* E Germany
143 B10 **Waroona** W Australia
74 H8 **Warora** India
141 K7 **Warra** Queensland
142 F5 **Warrabuda Well** W Australia
138 F6 **Warracknabeal** Victoria
139 K5 **Warragamba Res** New S Wales
139 H7 **Warragul** Victoria
138 E3 **Warrakalanna,L** S Australia
138 D5 **Warramboo** S Australia
143 C8 **Warramboo** *mt* W Australia
139 J3 **Warrambool** *R* New S Wales
80 G4 **Warran** *R* Jordan
138 E2 **Warrandininna,L** S Australia
142 D5 **Warrawagine** W Australia
139 H2 **Warrego** *R* Queensland
141 H6 **Warrego Ra** Queensland
103 P10 **Warren** Arizona
111 D8 **Warren** Arkansas
100 K4 **Warren** Idaho
99 R7 **Warren** Illinois
94 B6 **Warren** Indiana
98 K1 **Warren** Minnesota
101 R4 **Warren** Montana
95 Q3 **Warren** New Hampshire
139 J4 **Warren** New S Wales
94 G5 **Warren** Ohio
120 K6 **Warren** Ontario
94 H5 **Warren** Pennsylvania
95 Q5 **Warren** Rhode I
109 N5 **Warren** Texas
94 J9 **Warren** Virginia
115 L3 **Warrender,C** N W Terr
119 U5 **Warren Landing** Manitoba
143 E8 **Warren, Mt** W Australia
14 E2 **Warrenpoint** N Ireland
99 Q5 **Warrens** Wisconsin
99 R10 **Warrensburg** Illinois
110 C3 **Warrensburg** Missouri
95 O3 **Warrensburg** New York
112 E4 **Warrenton** Georgia
110 E3 **Warrenton** Missouri
112 J1 **Warrenton** N Carolina
100 B3 **Warrenton** Oregon
89 D7 **Warrenton** S Africa
94 K8 **Warrenton** Virginia
101 Q1 **Warrick** Montana
143 B8 **Warriedar** *mt* W Australia
141 H5 **Warrigal** Queensland
138 F3 **Warri House** New S Wales
138 D3 **Warrina** S Australia
138 D3 **Warriners Cr** S Australia
13 F6 **Warrington** England
111 J11 **Warrington** Florida
144 D6 **Warrington** New Zealand
111 K8 **Warrior** Alabama
138 E4 **Warriota** *R* S Australia
138 F7 **Warrnambool** Victoria
99 L1 **Warroad** Minnesota
139 J2 **Warrong** Queensland
138 D5 **Warrow** S Australia
139 J4 **Warrumbungle Ra** New S Wales
141 F8 **Warry Warry** *R* Queensland
Warsaw *see* **Warszawa**
99 P9 **Warsaw** Illinois
94 B5 **Warsaw** Indiana
94 C8 **Warsaw** Kentucky
110 C3 **Warsaw** Missouri
112 J2 **Warsaw** N Carolina
94 J4 **Warsaw** New York
95 L9 **Warsaw** Virginia
38 K6 **Warscheneck** *mt* Austria
118 E4 **Warspite** Alberta
32 H10 **Warstein** W Germany
31 M3 **Warszawa** Poland
31 H2 **Warszów** Poland
31 J3 **Warta** *R* Poland
38 N6 **Wartberg** Austria
37 J2 **Wartburg** E Germany
37 M7 **Wartenberg** W Germany
13 H6 **Warter** England
41 M3 **Warth** Austria
118 J7 **Wartime** Sask
13 F6 **Warton** England
142 F3 **Warton Ra** W Australia
110 K6 **Wartrace** Tennessee
13 F4 **Warwick** Cumbria England
112 D6 **Warwick** Georgia
98 H2 **Warwick** N Dakota
95 N5 **Warwick** New York
121 T7 **Warwick** Quebec
141 K8 **Warwick** Queensland
95 Q5 **Warwick** Rhode I
9 E3 **Warwick** Warwicks England
140 D2 **Warwick Chan** N Terr Aust
9 E3 **Warwickshire** England
117 Q11 **Wasa** Br Col
120 K8 **Wasaga Beach** Ontario
85 F6 **Wasagu** Nigeria
103 N2 **Wasatch Ra** Utah
102 E6 **Wasco** California
100 E4 **Wasco** Oregon
99 P3 **Wascott** Wisconsin
99 N5 **Waseca** Minnesota
118 H5 **Waseca** Sask
121 L8 **Washago** Ontario
101 Q6 **Washakie Needles** *mts* Wyoming
9 H3 **Washbrook** England
99 R9 **Washburn** Illinois
95 S7 **Washburn** Maine
98 E2 **Washburn** N Dakota
108 C8 **Washburn** Texas
114 J3 **Washburn L** N W Terr
101 P5 **Washburn,Mt** Wyoming
144 C6 **Washdyke** New Zealand
8 C5 **Washford** England
123 M3 **Washikuti** Quebec
74 G8 **Washim** India
121 S3 **Washimeska** *R* Quebec
109 O2 **Washington** Arkansas
112 E4 **Washington** Georgia
99 R9 **Washington** Illinois
110 J3 **Washington** Indiana
99 P8 **Washington** Iowa

Washington — White L 83

107 N2 Washington Kansas
111 D11 Washington Louisiana
110 E3 Washington Missouri
112 K2 Washington N Carolina
95 P3 Washington New Hampshire
95 N6 Washington New Jersey
94 G6 Washington Penn
109 L5 Washington Texas
103 L4 Washington Utah
94 J8 Washington Virginia
100 F2 Washington state U.S.A.
94 D7 Washington Court Ho Ohio
97 Washington D.C conurbation
99 U4 Washington I Wisconsin
113 G9 Washington,L Florida
115 N1 Washington Land Greenland
95 Q2 Washington, Mt New Hampshire
109 J1 Washita R Oklahoma
101 Q4 Washoe Montana
100 C4 Washougal Washington
119 V7 Washow B Manitoba
9 Q2 Wash, The gulf England
100 G3 Washtucna Washington
22 G4 Wasigny France
79 E9 Wasit Egypt
98 F1 Waskada Manitoba
119 V2 Waskaiowaka L Manitoba
118 L5 Waskesiu L Sask
114 J7 Waskesiu Lake Sask
118 E4 Wasketenau Alberta
99 M1 Waskish Minnesota
109 N3 Waskom Texas
22 F3 Wasmes Belgium
31 K4 Wąsosz Poland
60 Q1 Wassamu Japan
112 F6 Wassaw Sd Georgia
36 C6 Wasselonne France
25 F6 Wassenberg W Germany
37 J6 Wasseralfingen W Germany
22 L4 Wasserbillig Luxembourg
37 K5 Wassermungenau W Germany
37 K5 Wassertrüdingen W Germany
22 F3 Wassigny France
102 F3 Wassuk Ra Nevada
19 J4 Wassy France
98 D5 Wasta S Dakota
79 B9 Wasta,El Egypt
13 E5 Wast Water L England
37 J2 Wasungen E Germany
121 O3 Waswanipi Quebec
120 K4 Watabeag L Ontario
99 Q8 Watago Illinois
83 L11 Watagoda mt Sri Lanka
120 F7 Watampone Sulawesi
70 F7 Watansoppeng Sulawesi
98 E4 Watauga S Dakota
109 M9 Watauga Texas
8 C5 Watchet England
118 L1 Watcomb Ontario
13 G3 Waterbeach England
87 C10 Waterberg Namibia
95 R3 Waterboro Maine
95 O5 Waterbury Connecticut
95 P2 Waterbury Vermont
126 F3 Water Cays islds Bahamas
112 G3 Wateree Pond L S Carolina
102 D4 Waterford California
14 D4 Waterford Irish Rep
120 K10 Waterford Ontario
94 H5 Waterford Pennsylvania
14 D4 Waterford co Irish Rep
14 E4 Waterford Hbr Irish Rep
8 A7 Watergate B England
119 S6 Waterhen L Manitoba
118 J4 Waterhen L Sask
140 C2 Waterhouse R N Terr Aust
140 C6 Waterhouse Ra N Terr Aust
109 O2 Waterloo Arkansas
22 G2 Waterloo Belgium
110 F3 Waterloo Illinois
94 B5 Waterloo Indiana
99 O7 Waterloo Iowa
101 N4 Waterloo Montana
95 L4 Waterloo New York
140 A3 Waterloo N Terr Aust
121 S7 Waterloo Quebec
127 O2 Waterloo Trinidad
8 C6 Waterloo Cross England
99 S8 Waterman Illinois
111 E10 Waterproof Louisiana
94 C2 Waters Michigan
99 R3 Watersmeet Michigan
118 D9 Waterton Pk Alberta
99 N5 Watertown Minnesota
95 M3 Watertown New York
98 J5 Watertown S Dakota
110 K5 Watertown Tennessee
99 S6 Watertown Wisconsin
138 E5 Watervale S Australia
111 G7 Water Valley Mississippi
108 G4 Water Valley Texas
95 O4 Watervliet New York
95 S2 Waterville Maine
99 L4 Waterville Minnesota
95 M4 Waterville New York
122 H8 Waterville Nova Scotia
121 T7 Waterville Quebec
100 E2 Waterville Washington
118 F2 Waterways Alberta
70 N9 Wates Java
9 F4 Watford England
120 J10 Watford Ontario
98 C2 Watford City N Dakota
107 P2 Wathena Kansas
143 B9 Watheroo W Australia
117 P8 Watino Alberta
106 F2 Watkins Colorado
99 M4 Watkins Minnesota
115 R4 Watkins Bjerge mts Greenland
95 L4 Watkins Glen New York
112 D4 Watkinsville Georgia
107 M6 Watonga Oklahoma
70 K9 Waton,Tg C Java
22 D2 Watou Belgium
71 B2 Watowato,Bk mt Halmahera Indonesia
106 F6 Watrous New Mexico
119 M7 Watrous Sask
86 E5 Watsa Zaïre
99 T9 Watseka Illinois
86 D6 Watsi-Kengo Zaïre
111 E8 Watson Arkansas
99 L4 Watson Minnesota
99 L9 Watson Missouri
119 N6 Watson Sask
138 B4 Watson S Australia
101 Q10 Watson Utah
141 F2 Watson R Queensland
117 J5 Watson Lake Yukon Terr
95 L5 Watsontown Pennsylvania
83 J10 Wattala Sri Lanka
22 C2 Watten France
141 G5 Watten Queensland
15 E2 Watten Scotland
32 F10 Wattenscheid W Germany
138 D3 Wattiwarriganna R S Australia
139 G3 Wattle Vale New S Wales
117 P6 Watt,Mt Alberta
143 F7 Watt, Mt W Australia
9 F4 Watton England
13 G2 Watton England
107 Q5 Watts Oklahoma
112 C2 Watts Bar Lake Tennessee
94 H4 Wattsburg Pennsylvania
70 G5 Watukama Sulawesi
70 G5 Watukantjoa Sulawesi
70 G6 Watuwila,Bk mt Sulawesi
38 G8 Watzmann mt W Germany
136 K3 Wau Papua New Guinea
86 E4 Wau Sudan
120 K7 Waubamick Ontario
121 L8 Waubaushene Ontario
98 J4 Waubay S Dakota
98 J4 Waubay L S Dakota
139 L4 Wauchope New S Wales
140 C5 Wauchope N Terr Aust
119 Q9 Wauchope Sask
113 F10 Wauchula Florida
99 O6 Waucoma Iowa
100 G1 Wauconda Washington
118 F1 Waugh Manitoba
138 E4 Waukaringa S Australia
142 D5 Waukarlycarly, L W Australia
70 F5 Waukata, G mt Sulawesi
99 N8 Waukee Iowa
99 T7 Waukegan Illinois
99 S6 Waukesha Wisconsin
107 N5 Waukomis Oklahoma
99 P6 Waukon Iowa
98 E9 Wauneta Nebraska
99 R5 Waupaca Wisconsin
99 S6 Waupun Wisconsin
109 K1 Waurika Oklahoma
98 J7 Wausa Nebraska
99 R5 Wausau Wisconsin
99 T4 Wausaukee Wisconsin
94 C5 Wauseon Ohio
81 G8 W Australian Ridge Indian Oc
99 R5 Wautoma Wisconsin
99 S6 Wauwatosa Wisconsin
140 B3 Wave Hill N Terr Aust
110 J2 Waveland Indiana
141 K1 Wavell Heights dist Brisbane, Qnsld
9 H3 Waveney,R England
145 E3 Waverley New Zealand
122 J9 Waverley Nova Scotia
100 H2 Waverley Washington
112 F6 Waverly Georgia
110 G2 Waverly Illinois
99 O7 Waverly Iowa
107 P3 Waverly Kansas
110 C2 Waverly Missouri
98 K9 Waverly Nebraska
95 L4 Waverly New York
98 K4 Waverly S Dakota
110 J5 Waverly Tennessee
95 K9 Waverly Virginia
111 M9 Waverly Hall Georgia
141 F7 Waverney Queensland
22 C2 Wavrans-sur-l'Aa France
22 H2 Wavre Belgium
22 D2 Wavrin France
118 E6 Wavy L Alberta
68 C4 Waw Burma
120 F4 Wawa Ontario
121 M3 Wawagosic R Quebec
120 J4 Wawaitin Falls Ontario
119 S9 Wawanesa Manitoba
84 F5 Waw an Nāmūs Libya
94 B5 Wawasee,L Indiana
70 G6 Wawo Sulawesi
102 E4 Wawona California
119 Q9 Wawota Sask
70 G6 Wawotobi Sulawesi
109 L3 Waxahachie Texas
112 G3 Waxhaw N Carolina
111 F9 Way Mississippi
101 O7 Wayan Idaho
Wayaobu see Zichang
112 E6 Waycross Georgia
68 F8 Way,Ko isld G of Thailand
143 D7 Way, L W Australia
99 P8 Wayland Iowa
94 E9 Wayland Kentucky
94 B4 Wayland Michigan
99 P9 Wayland Missouri
94 K4 Wayland New York
118 E7 Wayne Alberta
95 R2 Wayne Maine
94 D4 Wayne Michigan
110 C5 Wayne Missouri
98 J7 Wayne Nebraska
107 N7 Wayne Oklahoma
94 E8 Wayne W Virginia
110 H3 Wayne City Illinois
112 F4 Waynesboro Georgia
111 H10 Waynesboro Mississippi
94 K7 Waynesboro Pennsylvania
110 J6 Waynesboro Tennessee
94 J8 Waynesboro Virginia
94 F6 Waynesburg Ohio
94 G7 Waynesburg Pennsylvania
99 R9 Waynesville Illinois
110 D4 Waynesville Missouri
112 E2 Waynesville N Carolina
94 C7 Waynesville Ohio
107 M5 Waynoka Oklahoma
98 C7 Wayside Nebraska
108 F1 Wayside Texas
77 L3 Wazi Khwa Afghanistan
77 K1 Wazirabad Afghanistan
74 F2 Wazirabad Pakistan
31 L2 Wda R Poland
7 L11 Weald, The reg England
13 F4 Wearhead England
140 D3 Wearyan R N Terr Aust
141 H3 Weary B Queensland
99 M10 Weatherby Missouri
107 M6 Weatherford Oklahoma
109 K3 Weatherford Texas
95 M6 Weatherly Pennsylvania
110 C4 Weaubleau Missouri
111 L8 Weaver Alabama
8 D1 Weaverham England
119 V6 Weaver L Manitoba
100 C9 Weaverville California
111 L10 Webb Alabama
111 F8 Webb Mississippi
118 J8 Webb Sask
109 H8 Webb Texas
110 B4 Webb City Missouri
107 Q6 Webbers Falls Oklahoma
142 G6 Webb, Mt W Australia
145 F4 Weber New Zealand
106 G7 Weber City New Mexico
106 E2 Webster Colorado
113 E9 Webster Florida
99 O8 Webster Iowa
107 L2 Webster Kansas
95 Q4 Webster Massachusetts
98 H1 Webster N Dakota
95 K3 Webster New York
98 J4 Webster S Dakota
99 O4 Webster Wisconsin
99 N7 Webster City Iowa
110 F3 Webster Groves Missouri
109 M4 Weches Texas
37 O2 Wechselburg E Germany
71 A2 Weda Halmahera Indonesia
83 L11 Wedagama Sri Lanka
71 B2 Weda,Teluk B Halmahera Indonesia
133 E8 Weddell I Falkland Is
146 D11 Weddell Sea Antarctica
32 L7 Weddemark W Germany
144 C6 Wedderburn New Zealand
100 A7 Wedderburn Oregon
32 K4 Weddinghusen W Germany
32 K4 Weddingstedt W Germany
32 L5 Wedel W Germany
140 B6 Wedge, Central Mt N Terr Aust
112 G4 Wedgefield S Carolina
117 M10 Wedge Mt Br Columbia
140 B6 Wedge, Mt N Terr Aust
122 G10 Wedgeport Nova Scotia
8 D5 Wedmore England
9 D3 Wednesbury England
111 L8 Wedowee Alabama
100 C8 Weed California
9 E3 Weedon England
121 T7 Weedon Quebec
95 L3 Weedsport New York
94 J5 Weedville Pennsylvania
71 C3 Weeim isld W Irian
119 P6 Weekes Sask
111 E12 Weeks Louisiana
94 E9 Weeksbury Kentucky
Weeks I see Puketutu I
112 L1 Weeksville N Carolina
9 H4 Weeley England
139 J3 Weemelah New S Wales
32 F6 Weener W Germany
98 K9 Weeping Water Nebraska
25 E6 Weert Netherlands
109 K7 Weesatche Texas
28 C7 Weesby W Germany
41 K3 Weesen Switzerland
25 D4 Weesp Netherlands
25 G1 Weestereems Netherlands
139 H5 Weethalle New S Wales
9 G3 Weeting England
32 L8 Weetzen W Germany
139 J4 Wee Waa New S Wales
25 F5 Weeze W Germany
33 O8 Wefensleben E Germany
33 O8 Weferlingen E Germany
33 O9 Wegeleben E Germany
33 O8 Wegenstedt E Germany
41 H3 Weggis Switzerland
32 J8 Wegholm W Germany
31 J4 Węgliniec Poland
31 N1 Wegorapa R Poland
31 N1 Węgorzewo Poland
31 J2 Węgorzyno Poland
31 N3 Węgrów Poland
38 M6 Wegscheid Austria
38 J4 Wegscheid W Germany
69 B10 Weh isld Sumatra
25 F2 Wehe Netherlands
40 G2 Wehr W Germany
32 K9 Wehrden W Germany
36 F3 Wehrheim W Germany
65 D4 Weichang China
37 L6 Weichering W Germany
38 M6 Weichselboden Austria
65 C7 Weichuan China
37 N2 Weida E Germany
37 N4 Weiden W Germany
36 E2 Weidenau W Germany
37 M4 Weidenberg W Germany
36 H6 Weidenstetten W Germany
37 L3 Weidhausen W Germany
94 C3 Weidman Michigan
65 D6 Weifang China
65 E6 Weihai China
65 G2 Weihe China
58 E5 Wei He R China
37 N6 Weihmichl W Germany
36 E3 Weilburg W Germany
36 F6 Weil-der-Stadt W Germany
36 B2 Weilerswist W Germany
36 H6 Weilheim W Germany
36 E3 Weilmünster W Germany
36 E3 Weilnau W Germany
37 J5 Weiltingen W Germany
65 B4 Weilu China
37 L2 Weimar E Germany
109 L6 Weimar Texas
58 E5 Weinan China
110 F6 Weiner Arkansas
41 K2 Weinfelden Switzerland
36 E5 Weingarten W Germany
36 F5 Weingarten W Germany
36 F4 Weinheim W Germany
67 A3 Weining China
36 G5 Weinsberg W Germany
36 G6 Weinstadt W Germany
141 F2 Weipa Queensland
100 K3 Weippe Idaho
110 B4 Weir Kansas
111 G8 Weir Mississippi
121 Q7 Weir Quebec
109 K5 Weir Texas
141 J8 Weir R Queensland
143 B7 Weiragoo Ra W Australia
107 Q4 Weir City Kansas
119 M5 Weirdale Sask
113 F9 Weirsdale Florida
94 G6 Weirton W Virginia
37 N3 Weischlitz E Germany
100 J5 Weiser Idaho
65 C7 Weishan Hu L China
65 C7 Weishi China
Weishui see Jingxing
36 B4 Weiskirchen W Germany
37 L3 Weismain W Germany
36 F6 Weissach W Germany
37 K5 Weissenburg W Germany
37 M1 Weissenfels E Germany
37 J7 Weissenhorn W Germany
33 T7 Weissensee E Berlin E Germany
37 L1 Weissensee Erfurt E Germany
37 M3 Weissenstadt W Germany
36 H6 Weissenstein W Germany
37 M3 Weisser Main R W Germany
37 O5 Weisser Regen R W Germany
40 G5 Weisshorn mt Switzerland
38 L7 Weisskirchen Austria
41 N4 Weisskugel mt Austria
89 A5 Weissrand Mts Namibia
41 K3 Weisstannen Switzerland
33 S4 Weitenhagen E Germany
41 M2 Weitnau W Germany
67 F4 Weitou China
31 H7 Weitra Austria
38 N8 Weixelbaum Austria
38 K8 Weixelsdorf Austria
65 C6 Wei Xian China
65 D6 Wei Xian China
67 A3 Weixin China
67 A2 Weiyuan China
38 N7 Weiz Austria
41 H2 Weizen W Germany
Weizhou see Wenchuan
68 J2 Weizhou Dao isld China
31 L1 Wejherowo Poland
119 S4 Wekusko Manitoba
113 F8 Welaka Florida
138 C2 Welbourn Hill S Australia
94 F9 Welch W Virginia
99 M6 Welcome Minnesota
141 G3 Welcome Queensland
89 A8 Welcome Kop mt S Africa
146 J5 Welcome Mt Antarctica
37 K7 Welden W Germany
143 D8 Weld, Mt W Australia
102 F6 Weldon California
99 S9 Weldon Illinois
99 N9 Weldon Iowa
112 L1 Weldon N Carolina
119 M6 Weldon Sask
109 M4 Weldon Texas
99 N9 Weldon R Missouri
106 G1 Weldona Colorado
13 G3 Weldon Br England
143 B7 Weld Ra W Australia
143 D6 Weld Spring W Australia
107 O6 Weleetka Oklahoma
70 N9 Weleri Java
141 G7 Welford Queensland
141 G7 Welford Downs Queensland
83 K12 Weligama Sri Lanka
83 L11 Weliwewa Sri Lanka
22 K2 Welkenraedt Belgium
89 E6 Welkom S Africa
121 L10 Welland Canal Ontario
9 F2 Welland, R England
142 A4 Wellard dist Perth, W Aust
83 L11 Wellawaya Sri Lanka
113 E7 Wellborn Florida
36 H1 Wellerode Wald W Germany
9 E3 Wellesbourne England
140 E3 Wellesley Is Queensland
117 D4 Wellesley L Yukon Terr
98 F9 Wellfleet Nebraska
37 L6 Wellheim W Germany
22 J3 Wellin Belgium
9 F3 Wellingborough England
111 L8 Wellington Alabama
106 E1 Wellington Colorado
99 T9 Wellington Illinois
107 N4 Wellington Kansas
102 E3 Wellington Nevada
139 J4 Wellington New S Wales
145 F4 Wellington New Zealand
123 S5 Wellington Nfld
122 J9 Wellington Nova Scotia
94 E5 Wellington Ohio
121 N9 Wellington Ontario
122 H7 Wellington Pr Edward I
89 A9 Wellington S Africa
8 D2 Wellington Salop England
138 E6 Wellington S Australia
8 C6 Wellington Somerset England
108 G1 Wellington Texas
103 O2 Wellington Utah
145 E3 Wellington stat area New Zealand
115 K2 Wellington Chan N W Terr
133 C7 Wellington, I Chile
139 H7 Wellington, L Victoria
143 D7 Wellington Ra W Australia
108 E2 Wellman Texas
9 F1 Wellow England
107 N2 Wells Kansas
99 N6 Wells Minnesota
101 L8 Wells Nevada
95 N3 Wells New York
9 G2 Wells Norfolk England
8 D5 Wells Somerset England
109 N4 Wells Texas
95 K5 Wellsboro Pennsylvania
99 O7 Wellsburg Iowa
95 L4 Wellsburg New York
94 G6 Wellsburg W Virginia
145 E2 Wellsford New Zealand
117 N9 Wells Gray Prov. Park Br Col
141 G6 Wellshot Queensland
119 R1 Wells L Manitoba
143 E7 Wells, L W Australia
142 F3 Wells, Mt W Australia
142 D6 Wells Ra W Australia
95 P2 Wells River Vermont
94 E7 Wellston Ohio
110 E2 Wellsville Missouri
94 K4 Wellsville New York
101 O8 Wellsville Utah
103 K9 Wellton Arizona
119 S8 Wellwood Manitoba
38 K5 Wels Austria
25 D6 Welschap Netherlands
36 B4 Welschbillig W Germany
36 E1 Welschenennest W Germany
122 F8 Welsford New Brunswick
109 P5 Welsh Louisiana
8 D2 Welshampton England
122 F9 Welshpool New Brunswick
8 C2 Welshpool Wales
142 B2 Welshpool dist Perth, W Aust
13 H6 Welton England
32 G9 Welver W Germany
119 Q8 Welwyn Sask
9 F4 Welwyn Garden City England
36 H6 Welzheim W Germany
8 D2 Wem England
86 D6 Wema Zaïre
117 O8 Wembley Alberta
142 A1 Wembley dist Perth, W Aust
142 A1 Wembley Downs dist Perth, W Aust
8 B7 Wembury England
37 K6 Wemding W Germany
25 A5 Wemeldinge Netherlands
12 D2 Wemyss B Scotland
126 F2 Wemyss Bight Eleuthera Bahamas
65 C5 Wen'an China
100 E2 Wenatchee Washington
67 C7 Wenchang China
67 G3 Wencheng China
85 D7 Wenchi Ghana
67 A1 Wenchuan China
102 D1 Wendel California
101 L7 Wendell Idaho
98 K3 Wendell Minnesota
112 J2 Wendell N Carolina
36 D4 Wendelsheim W Germany
37 L5 Wendelstein W Germany
103 L8 Wenden Arizona
9 G3 Wenden England
36 D2 Wenden W Germany
65 E6 Wendeng China
33 Q6 Wendisch Priborn E Germany
33 O7 Wendland reg W Germany
9 G2 Wendling England
100 C5 Wendling Oregon
33 O5 Wendorf E Germany
9 F4 Wendover England
101 M9 Wendover Utah
98 B7 Wendover Wyoming
98 F5 Wendte S Dakota
22 E1 Wenduine Belgium
120 G5 Wenebegon L Ontario
67 B3 Weng'an China
36 B4 Wengerohr W Germany
67 D2 Wengjiang China
67 E4 Wengyuan China
65 D7 Wen He R China
36 G3 Wenings W Germany
67 A1 Wenjiang China
68 K1 Wenli China
67 G2 Wenling China
141 G2 Wenlock Queensland
141 F1 Wenlock R Queensland
128 A7 Wenman isld Galapagos Is
32 L8 Wennigsen W Germany
41 N3 Wenns Austria
99 R8 Wenona Illinois
67 C1 Wenquan China
67 A5 Wenshan China
65 C7 Wenshang China
65 B6 Wenshui China
67 B2 Wenshui China
139 G7 Wensleydale Victoria
57 K4 Wensu China
13 G6 Wentbridge England
13 G6 Wentworth England
95 Q3 Wentworth New Hampshire
138 F5 Wentworth New S Wales
98 K6 Wentworth S Dakota
122 J8 Wentworth Centre Nova Scotia
110 F3 Wentzville Missouri
65 B7 Wenxi China
65 B7 Wen Xian China
37 N5 Wenzenbach W Germany
67 G3 Wenzhou China
113 F10 Weohyakapka L Florida
100 B9 Weott California
89 E7 Wepener S Africa
22 H3 Wepion Belgium
33 T7 Werbellin E Germany
33 T7 Werbellinsee L E Germany
33 P7 Werben E Germany
33 S9 Werbig E Germany
22 K3 Werbomont Belgium
87 D11 Werda Botswana
37 N2 Werdau E Germany
33 R8 Werder E Germany
32 G10 Werdohl W Germany
32 G9 Werl W Germany
32 G7 Werlte W Germany
36 C1 Wermelskirchen W Germany
33 R10 Wermsdorf E Germany
36 H4 Wern R W Germany
37 N4 Wernberg W Germany
32 G9 Werne W Germany
37 J4 Werneck W Germany
117 F3 Wernecke Mts Yukon Terr
98 D2 Werner N Dakota
33 T7 Werneuchen E Germany
36 H3 Wernfeld W Germany
119 U2 Wernham L Manitoba
25 C6 Wernhout Netherlands
33 N9 Wernigerode E Germany
37 J1 Werra R E & W Germany
139 G7 Werribee Victoria
138 F5 Werrimull Victoria
139 K4 Werris Cr New S Wales
32 G9 Werse R W Germany
37 K7 Wertach R W Germany
36 H4 Wertheim W Germany
37 K6 Wertingen W Germany
25 D3 Wervershoof Netherlands
71 O9 Werwaru Indonesia
32 E9 Wesel W Germany
36 D5 Weselberg W Germany
33 R6 Wesenberg E Germany
32 H5 Weser est W Germany
32 L9 Weser R W Germany
71 N8 Wesiri Indonesia
107 J3 Weskan Kansas
86 G4 Weska Weka Ethiopia
109 K9 Weslaco Texas
121 N8 Weslemkoon L Ontario
95 U2 Wesley Maine
123 T4 Wesleyville Nfld
94 G4 Wesleyville Pennsylvania
32 F5 Wesse W Germany
32 J4 Wesselburen W Germany
36 B2 Wesseling W Germany
140 D1 Wessel Is N Terr Aust
98 H5 Wessington S Dakota
98 H5 Wessington Springs S Dakota
111 D8 Wesson Arkansas
111 F10 Wesson Mississippi
111 G8 West Mississippi
109 K4 West Texas
139 G6 West Victoria
32 G8 West W Germany
94 C7 West Alexandria Ohio
140 B1 West Alligator R N Terr Aust
99 S7 West Allis Wisconsin
138 C5 Westall,Pt S Australia
141 K6 West Arm Pt Queensland
13 G4 West Auckland England
113 B7 West B Florida
111 G12 West B Louisiana
109 N6 West B Texas
140 A3 West Baines R N Terr Aust
8 D6 West Bay England
111 L11 Westbay Florida
99 M7 West Bend Iowa
119 O7 West Bend Sask
99 S6 West Bend Wisconsin
75 M7 West Bengal prov India
111 J8 West Blocton Alabama
99 L9 Westboro Missouri
99 Q4 Westboro Wisconsin
119 T8 Westbourne Manitoba
99 P8 West Branch Iowa
94 C2 West Branch Michigan
13 G6 West Bretton England
117 O11 Westbridge Br Columbia
9 E2 West Bridgford England
9 E2 West Bromwich England
95 R3 Westbrook Maine
99 L5 Westbrook Minnesota
108 F3 Westbrook Texas
95 Q2 West Burke Vermont
15 G2 West Burra Shetland Scotland
8 D5 Westbury England
139 H8 Westbury Tasmania
101 O1 West Butte mt Montana
98 C1 Westby N Dakota
139 H6 Westby New S Wales
99 Q6 Westby Wisconsin
144 A6 West C New Zealand
127 H4 West Caicos isld Turks & Caicos Is
12 E2 West Calder Scotland
85 F7 West Cameroon prov Cameroon
143 C11 West Cape Howe W Australia
99 S8 West Chicago Illinois
106 E3 Westcliffe Colorado
109 M6 West Columbia Texas
99 O5 West Concord Minnesota
102 G7 West Covina California
9 G6 Westdean England
99 S5 West De Pere Wisconsin
99 N8 West Des Moines Iowa
122 J9 West Dover Nova Scotia
102 G6 Westend California
126 E1 West End Grand Bahama I
112 H2 West End N Carolina
141 K2 West End dist Brisbane, Qnsld
22 D1 Westende Belgium
113 J11 West End Settlement Grand Bahama I
32 L4 Westensee L W Germany
25 G3 Westerbork Netherlands
144 C5 Westerfield New Zealand
9 G5 Westerham England
98 J9 Western Nebraska
86 E4 Western Equatoria prov Sudan
76 A1 Western Ghats mts India
122 H10 Western Hd Nova Scotia
120 K7 Western Is Ontario
15 A3 Western Isles reg Scotland
94 H7 Westernport Maryland
139 H7 Western Port Victoria
141 G5 Western R Queensland
85 B4 Western Sahara reg Africa
137 S4 Western Samoa islds Pacific Oc
32 M9 Westerode W Germany
32 G6 Westerstede W Germany
36 D2 Westerwald reg W Germany
107 M3 Westfall Kansas
100 H6 Westfall Oregon
8 D2 West Felton England
99 T10 Westfield Illinois
95 P4 Westfield Massachusetts
94 H4 Westfield New York
94 K5 Westfield Pennsylvania
99 R6 Westfield Wisconsin
142 B3 Westfield dist Perth, W Aust
122 F8 Westfield Beach New Brunswick
110 B6 West Fork Arkansas
99 M6 West Fork R Minnesota
98 A1 West Fork R Montana
110 H4 West Frankfort Illinois
9 H5 Westgate England
141 H7 Westgate Queensland
30 West Germany
8 C4 West Glamorgan co Wales
112 E6 West Green Georgia
9 F6 West Grinstead England
141 J7 Westgrove Queensland
9 E3 West Haddon England
9 G5 West Ham England
94 E8 West Hamlin W Virginia
95 P6 Westhampton Beach Long I, N Y
37 K7 Westheim W Germany
36 E4 West Hofen W Germany
109 K6 Westhoff Texas
36 C6 Westhoffen France
100 B1 Westholme Br Col
98 E1 Westhope N Dakota
68 A6 West I Andaman Is
83 M8 West I Cocos Is Indian Oc
146 C3 West Ice Shelf Antarctica
32 G10 Westig W Germany
93 West Indies Caribbean
94 F10 West Jefferson N Carolina
94 D7 West Jefferson Ohio
22 E1 Westkapelle Belgium
25 A6 Westkapelle Netherlands
15 D5 West Kilbride Scotland
100 F8 West L Nevada
110 J1 West Lafayette Indiana
94 F6 West Lafayette Ohio
100 A6 Westlake Oregon
141 G6 Westland Queensland
144 B5 Westland stat area New Zealand
140 E5 West Leichhardt Queensland
9 H3 Westleton England
99 P8 West Liberty Iowa
94 D9 West Liberty Kentucky
94 D6 West Liberty Ohio
13 E2 West Linton Scotland
118 D4 Westlock Alberta
120 J10 West Lorne Ontario
West Lothian co see Lothian and Central regions
122 H2 West Magpie R Quebec
9 G5 West Malling England
94 C7 West Manchester Ohio
121 O7 Westmeath Ontario
14 D3 Westmeath co Irish Rep
110 F6 West Memphis Arkansas
9 G4 West Mersea England
94 G5 West Middlesex Pennsylvania
9 E2 West Midlands co England
94 C7 West Milton Ohio
95 L7 Westminster Maryland
112 D3 Westminster S Carolina
95 P3 Westminster Vermont
107 O2 Westmoreland Kansas
95 P4 Westmoreland New Hampshire
140 E3 Westmoreland Queensland
110 K5 Westmoreland Tennessee
103 J8 Westmorland California
Westmorland co see Cumbria
127 H2 Westmorland parish Jamaica
87 E10 West Nicholson Zimbabwe
108 G6 West Nueces R Texas
8 D2 Weston England
101 O7 Weston Idaho
94 C5 Weston Michigan
110 B2 Weston Missouri
98 K8 Weston Nebraska
144 C6 Weston New Zealand
94 D5 Weston Ohio
100 G4 Weston Oregon
70 D2 Weston Sabah
94 G7 Weston W Virginia
98 A5 Weston Wyoming
89 E6 Westonaria S Africa
8 D5 Weston-super-Mare England
109 H2 Westover Texas
32 F6 Westoverledingen W Germany
113 G11 West Palm Beach Florida
95 R2 West Paris Maine
110 J3 Westphalia Indiana
107 P3 Westphalia Kansas
94 K5 West Pike Pennsylvania
110 E5 West Plains Missouri
102 D3 West Point California
112 B5 West Point Georgia
110 J1 Westpoint Indiana
99 P9 West Point Iowa
94 B9 West Point Kentucky
111 H8 West Point Mississippi
95 N5 West Point New York
122 H4 West Point Quebec
139 G8 West Point Tasmania
95 L9 West Point Virginia
116 P4 West Point mt Alaska
West Polder see Markerwaard
102 A2 Westport California
94 B7 Westport Indiana
14 B3 Westport Irish Rep
95 O2 Westport New York
144 C4 Westport New Zealand
123 Q4 Westport Nfld
100 B3 Westport Oregon
98 H4 Westport S Dakota
110 H6 Westport Tennessee
100 A3 Westport Washington
118 A3 West Prairie R Alberta
98 K8 West Pt Nebraska
123 M10 West Pt Nova Scotia
122 H7 West Pt Pr Edward I
122 G10 West Pubnico Nova Scotia
126 A1 Westpunt Curaçao
13 G4 West Rainton England
119 Q5 Westray Manitoba
15 F1 Westray Firth Orkney Scotland
120 J5 Westree Ontario
36 C5 Westrich reg W Germany
117 L9 West Road R Br Col
13 F2 Westruther Scotland
123 P2 West St. Modiste Quebec
110 H3 West Salem Illinois
94 E6 West Salem Ohio
99 P6 West Salem Wisconsin
9 E5 West Shefford England
145 F3 Westshore New Zealand
99 L7 Westside Iowa
100 E7 West Side Oregon
139 J7 West Sister I Tasmania
7 L9 West Sole sea rig North Sea
95 Q2 West Stewartstown New Hampshire
9 F6 West Sussex co England
13 G5 West Tanfield England
25 D2 West Terschelling Netherlands
110 J2 West Union Illinois
99 P7 West Union Iowa
94 D8 West Union Ohio
94 G7 West Union W Virginia
94 C5 West Unity Ohio
117 L11 Westview Br Col
111 L11 Westville Florida
99 T9 Westville Illinois
99 U8 Westville Indiana
122 K8 Westville Nova Scotia
107 Q6 Westville Oklahoma
94 G8 West Virginia state U.S.A.
22 D1 West Vlaanderen Belgium
8 B5 Westward Ho England
103 P2 Westwater Utah
111 F12 Westwego Louisiana
95 M4 West Winfield New York
102 D1 Westwood California
141 K6 Westwood Queensland
109 L9 Westworth Texas
139 H5 West Wyalong New S Wales
101 O5 West Yellowstone Montana
13 G6 West Yorkshire co England
71 O8 Wetan isld Indonesia
71 N8 Wetar isld Indonesia
71 N9 Wetar, Selat str Indonesia
118 D6 Wetaskiwin Alberta
88 G4 Wete Tanzania
121 O3 Wetetnagami R Quebec
37 M1 Wethau E Germany
13 G6 Wetherby England
68 B1 Wetlet Burma
106 E3 Wetmore Colorado
109 J6 Wetmore Texas
106 E3 Wet Mts Colorado
98 H4 Wetonka S Dakota
36 F2 Wetter W Germany
36 F3 Wetter R W Germany
36 F3 Wetterau reg W Germany
22 F1 Wetteren Belgium
41 M3 Wetter Spitze mt Austria
41 O3 Wetterstein Geb mt Austria
33 P9 Wettin E Germany
32 F8 Wettringen W Germany
107 O6 Wetumka Oklahoma
111 K9 Wetumpka Alabama
68 C1 Wetwun Burma
36 F2 Wetzlar W Germany
37 L3 Wetzstein mt E Germany
36 B1 Wevelinghoven W Germany
110 E1 Wever Iowa
113 B7 Wewahitchka Florida
136 J2 Wewak Papua New Guinea
107 O6 Wewoka Oklahoma
14 E4 Wexford Irish Rep
14 E4 Wexford co Irish Rep
14 E4 Wexford B Irish Rep
14 E4 Wexford Harb Irish Rep
118 L4 Weyakwin L Sask
99 S5 Weyauwega Wisconsin
9 H2 Weybourne England
9 F5 Weybridge England
119 O9 Weyburn Sask
38 L6 Weyer Austria
36 D2 Weyerbusch W Germany
99 P4 Weyerhauser Wisconsin
36 D6 Weyersheim France
33 M7 Weyhausen W Germany
9 E5 Weyhill England
8 D6 Weymouth England
95 R4 Weymouth Massachusetts
122 G9 Weymouth Nova Scotia
141 G1 Weymouth B Queensland
141 G2 Weymouth,C Queensland
9 F5 Wey, R England
25 F4 Wezep Netherlands
145 E3 Whakahora New Zealand
145 E3 Whakamaru New Zealand
145 E1 Whakapara New Zealand
145 F3 Whakapunaki New Zealand
145 F4 Whakataki New Zealand
145 F2 Whakatane New Zealand
145 F3 Whakatane R New Zealand
68 D7 Whale B Burma
143 C6 Whaleback,Mt W Australia
116 D10 Whalebone C Aleutian Is
113 K12 Whale Cay isld Bahamas
Whale I see Motuhora I
123 P2 Whale I Quebec
146 J8 Whales, B. of Antarctica
9 E1 Whaley Bridge England
95 L10 Whaleyville Virginia
139 J3 Whallan R New S Wales
13 F6 Whalley England
15 G2 Whalsay isld Shetland Scotland
13 G3 Whalton England
145 E4 Whangaehu New Zealand
145 E2 Whangamata New Zealand
145 E3 Whangamomona New Zealand
145 D4 Whanganui Inlet New Zealand
145 E2 Whangaparaoa Pen New Zealand
145 D1 Whangape New Zealand
145 E2 Whangape, L New Zealand
145 G2 Whangapuraoa New Zealand
145 E1 Whangarei New Zealand
145 D1 Whangaroa New Zealand
145 E1 Whangaruru Harbour New Zealand
145 E4 Wharanui New Zealand
145 F4 Whareama New Zealand
145 F3 Wharerata New Zealand
13 G6 Wharfe, R England
95 N6 Wharton New Jersey
94 J5 Wharton Pennsylvania
109 L6 Wharton Texas
144 C5 Whataroa New Zealand
145 F3 Whatatutu New Zealand
145 E2 Whatawhata New Zealand
99 O8 What Cheer Iowa
100 C1 Whatcom, L Washington
111 J10 Whatley Alabama
102 C2 Wheatland California
98 B7 Wheatland Wyoming
98 A8 Wheatland Res Wyoming
110 E7 Wheatley Arkansas
9 E4 Wheatley England
120 H10 Wheatley Ontario
99 S8 Wheaton Illinois
107 O2 Wheaton Kansas
98 K4 Wheaton Minnesota
110 B5 Wheaton Missouri
8 C5 Wheddon Cross England
107 J2 Wheeler Kansas
100 B4 Wheeler Oregon
108 D8 Wheeler Texas
117 Q4 Wheeler L N W Terr
103 K3 Wheeler Pk Nevada
106 E5 Wheeler Pk New Mexico
102 F6 Wheeler Ridge California
94 E8 Wheelersburg Ohio
102 E7 Wheeler Springs California
94 G6 Wheeling W Virginia
98 C1 Wheelock N Dakota
94 E9 Wheelwright Kentucky
140 E6 Whelan,Mt Queensland
13 F5 Whernside mt England
9 E5 Wherwell England
138 C5 Whidbey I S Australia
100 C1 Whidbey I Washington
111 M11 Whigham Georgia
142 C5 Whim Creek W Australia
138 B2 Whinham, Mt S Australia
99 M2 Whipholt Minnesota
122 F9 Whipple Pt Nova Scotia
9 F4 Whipsnade England
101 N1 Whiskey Gap Alberta
119 T4 Whiskey Jack Landing Manitoba
140 D5 Whistleduck Creek N Terr Aust
111 H11 Whistler Alabama
9 E2 Whitacre England
112 K1 Whitakers N Carolina
13 E5 Whitbeck England
123 T6 Whitbourne Nfld
13 G4 Whitburn England
12 E2 Whitburn Scotland
13 H5 Whitby England
121 M9 Whitby Ontario
9 F4 Whitchurch Bucks England
9 E5 Whitchurch Hampshire England
8 D2 Whitchurch Salop England
8 C4 Whitchurch Wales
144 C5 Whitcombe Pass New Zealand
98 K5 White S Dakota
111 E7 White R Arkansas
101 S10 White R Colorado
99 U6 White R Michigan
103 J3 White R Nevada
98 F6 White R S Dakota
108 F2 White R Texas
103 P2 White R Utah
100 D2 White R Washington
99 Q3 White R Wisconsin
123 Q3 White B Nfld
118 J8 White Bear Sask
99 O4 White Bear L Minnesota
123 P6 White Bear R Nfld
100 J4 White Bird Idaho
110 J5 White Bluff Tennessee
100 F3 White Bluffs Washington
122 E6 White Brook New Brunswick
98 D4 White Butte S Dakota
119 W2 Whitecap L Manitoba
111 E11 White Castle Louisiana
113 G10 White City Florida
107 O3 White City Kansas
106 F9 White City New Mexico
139 G4 White Cliffs New S Wales
99 L10 White Cloud Kansas
94 B3 White Cloud Michigan
118 B4 White Court Alberta
98 D1 White Earth N Dakota
108 E2 Whiteface Texas
95 O2 Whiteface Mt New York
117 Q11 Whitefish Idaho
101 L1 Whitefish Montana
120 J6 Whitefish Ontario
99 U4 Whitefish R Michigan
99 T6 Whitefish Bay Wisconsin
116 K6 Whitefish L Alaska
118 E4 Whitefish L Alberta
99 V3 Whitefish L Michigan
99 M3 Whitefish L Minnesota
101 L1 Whitefish L Montana
119 O2 Whitefish L Ontario
119 N5 White Fox Sask
115 N6 Whitegull L Quebec
110 F2 White Hall Illinois
99 U6 Whitehall Michigan
101 N4 Whitehall Montana
99 P5 Whitehall Wisconsin
12 E5 Whitehaven England
95 M5 White Haven Pennsylvania
14 F2 Whitehead N Ireland
12 D4 Whitehill Scotland
116 N2 White Hills Alaska
103 K6 White Hills Arizona
100 D8 White Horse California
117 F5 Whitehorse Yukon Terr
101 L9 White Horse Pass Nevada
127 M3 White Horses Jamaica
White I see Kvitöya
146 H7 White I Antarctica
145 F2 White I New Zealand
115 L4 White I N W Terr
13 F1 Whitekirk Scotland
111 D12 White L Louisiana
99 U6 White L Michigan
140 A5 White L N Terr/W Aust
98 H6 White L S Dakota

84
White, L — Wörth

142 G5 White, L W Australia
99 S4 White Lake Wisconsin
94 A7 Whiteland Indiana
139 J8 Whitemark Tasmania
116 F4 White Mountain Alaska
14 E4 White Mt Irish Rep
116 O4 White Mts Alaska
102 F4 White Mts California
95 Q2 White Mts New Hampshire
117 P7 Whitemud R Alberta
86 F3 White Nile prov Sudan
86 F3 White Nile R Sudan
86 F2 White Nile Dam Sudan
112 K3 White Oak N Carolina
109 M2 White Oak Cr Texas
109 O2 White Oak L Arkansas
118 K1 White Otter L Ontario
98 D5 White Owl S Dakota
9 E5 Whiteparish England
117 F6 White Pass Br Col/Alaska
100 D3 White Pass Washington
94 B5 White Pigeon Michigan
99 R3 White Pine Michigan
100 K2 Whitepine Montana
112 D1 White Pine Tennessee
103 J2 White Pine Ra Nevada
112 G1 White Plains N Carolina
95 N5 White Plains New York
123 R2 White Pt Belle I, Nfld
140 D6 White Quartz Hill mt N Terr Aust
118 B8 White R Br Col
94 B8 White R Indiana
127 L2 White R Jamaica
98 F6 White R S Dakota
120 E4 White River Ontario
95 P3 White River Junc Vermont
103 J3 White River Valley Nevada
100 J8 White Rock Nevada
109 O9 White Rock Texas
107 M2 White Rock Cr Kansas
103 K3 White Rock Peak Nevada
White Russia see Belorussiya S.S.R.
117 K9 Whitesail L Br Col
100 D4 White Salmon Washington
117 P6 Whitesand R Alberta
8 B7 Whitesand B England
119 P7 Whitesand R Sask
108 A3 White Sands Missile Ra New Mexico
108 A3 White Sands Nat. Mon New Mexico
95 M3 Whitesboro New York
109 L2 Whitesboro Texas
112 C4 Whitesburg Georgia
94 E9 Whitesburg Kentucky
White Sea see Beloye More
109 L9 White Settlement Texas
118 F1 Whiteshell Manitoba
100 B4 Whiteson Oregon
119 U2 Whitestone L Manitoba
101 P3 White Sulphur Springs Montana
110 K4 Whitesville Kentucky
94 K4 Whitesville New York
94 F9 Whitesville W Virginia
100 E3 White Swan Washington
119 M4 Whiteswan L Sask
98 A1 Whitetail Montana
112 J3 Whiteville N Carolina
110 G6 Whiteville Tennessee
85 D7 White Volta R Ghana
101 S1 Whitewater Montana
106 B9 Whitewater New Mexico
99 S7 Whitewater Wisconsin
94 B7 Whitewater R Indiana
113 F12 Whitewater B Florida
120 A2 Whitewater L Ontario
138 B4 White Well S Australia
141 G5 Whitewood Queensland
119 P8 Whitewood Sask
98 C5 Whitewood S Dakota
98 J5 Whitewood, L S Dakota
109 L2 Whitewright Texas
139 H6 Whitfield Victoria
13 F4 Whitfield Hall England
127 H2 Whithorn Jamaica
12 D4 Whithorn Scotland
145 E2 Whitianga New Zealand
107 P2 Whiting Kansas
95 N7 Whiting New Jersey
117 G6 Whiting R Br Col/Alaska
12 C3 Whiting B Scotland
95 P4 Whitingham Res Vermont
118 K6 Whitkow Sask
118 F9 Whitla Alberta
8 B4 Whitland Wales
101 O1 Whitlash Montana
13 G3 Whitley Bay England
94 C10 Whitley City Kentucky
98 F4 Whitlocks Crossing S Dakota
95 R4 Whitman Massachusetts
98 H1 Whitman N Dakota
98 E7 Whitman Nebraska
100 G3 Whitman Nat. Mon Washington
112 F3 Whitmire S Carolina
8 C3 Whitney England
98 C7 Whitney Nebraska
103 J5 Whitney Nevada
121 M7 Whitney Ontario
100 G5 Whitney Oregon
109 K4 Whitney, L Texas
102 F5 Whitney, Mt California
109 J7 Whitsett Texas
9 H5 Whitstable England
141 J5 Whitsunday I Queensland
109 J3 Whitt Texas
94 G7 Whittaker W Virginia
99 M6 Whittemore Iowa
94 D2 Whittemore Michigan
116 N6 Whittier Alaska
102 F8 Whittier California
13 G3 Whittingham England
139 H7 Whittlesea Victoria
9 F2 Whittlesey England
139 H5 Whitton New S Wales
8 C3 Whitton Wales
13 G4 Whittonstall England
141 F7 Whitula R Queensland
9 E1 Whitwell England
112 B2 Whitwell Tennessee
114 J5 Wholdaia L N W Terr
138 D5 Whyalla S Australia
123 L8 Whycocomagh Nova Scotia
139 G3 Whyjonta New S Wales
68 D3 Wiang Pa Pao Thailand
68 D2 Wiang Phrao Thailand
120 J8 Wiarton Ontario
31 K5 Wiązów Poland
98 B2 Wibaux Montana
13 G6 Wibsey England
107 N4 Wichita Kansas
109 J1 Wichita R Texas
109 J2 Wichita Falls Texas
109 J1 Wichita Mts Oklahoma
15 E2 Wick Scotland
32 G10 Wickede W Germany
103 M8 Wickenburg Arizona
122 J4 Wickenden L Quebec
143 C10 Wickepin W Australia
100 C1 Wickersham Washington
108 D4 Wickett Texas
9 G4 Wickford England
95 Q5 Wickford Rhode I
9 E6 Wickham England
139 G7 Wickham, C Tasmania
140 A3 Wickham Mt N Terr Aust
121 S7 Wickham West Quebec
100 D6 Wickiup Res Oregon
110 G5 Wickliffe Kentucky
14 E4 Wicklow Irish Rep
14 E4 Wicklow co Irish Rep
8 D4 Wickwar England
31 L4 Widawka R Poland
36 G5 Widdern W Germany
121 L6 Widdifield Ontario
90 A11 Wideawake Ascension I
116 J8 Wide B Alaska
141 L7 Wide B Queensland
8 C6 Widecombe-in-the-Moor England
138 B2 Wide Gum R S Australia
94 G8 Widen W Virginia
141 H8 Widgeegoara R Queensland
143 D9 Widgiemooltha W Australia
71 B3 Widi, Pulau Pulau islds Indonesia
36 F4 Wiebelsbach W Germany
36 C5 Wiebelskirchen W Germany
31 K2 Więcbork Poland
36 C2 Wied W Germany
Wiedenbrück see Rheda-Wiedenbrück
32 H6 Wiefelstede W Germany
33 O10 Wiehe E Germany
32 J8 Wiehengebirge hills W Germany
36 D2 Wiehl W Germany
31 M2 Wielbark Poland
31 J3 Wieleń Poland
31 M6 Wieliczka Poland
31 L4 Wieluń Poland
38 O5 Wien Austria
38 O6 Wiener Neustadt Austria
32 M7 Wienhausen W Germany
116 M4 Wien L Alaska
33 O7 Wiepke E Germany
31 O5 Wieprz R Poland
33 N7 Wieren W Germany
109 O4 Wiergate Texas
25 D3 Wieringen Netherlands
25 C3 Wieringermeer Netherlands
31 L4 Wieruszów Poland
31 N4 Wierzbnik Poland
31 L2 Wierzchucin Poland
31 L2 Wierzyca R Poland
38 N8 Wies Austria
37 N4 Wiesau W Germany
36 E3 Wiesbaden W Germany
40 G2 Wiese R W Germany
33 Q8 Wiesenburg E Germany
36 H6 Wiesensteig W Germany
37 L4 Wiesent R W Germany
37 J4 Wiesentheid W Germany
37 L4 Wiesenttal W Germany
36 F5 Wiesloch W Germany
32 G6 Wiesmoor W Germany
32 F7 Wietmarschen W Germany
32 L7 Wietze W Germany
32 L7 Wietzen W Germany
32 L7 Wietzendorf W Germany
13 F6 Wigan England
98 B9 Wiggins Colorado
111 G11 Wiggins Mississippi
9 E6 Wight, I. of England
8 D3 Wigmore England
31 O2 Wigry, Jezioro L Poland
9 E2 Wigston England
13 E4 Wigton England
12 D4 Wigtown Scotland
Wigtown co see Dumfries and Galloway reg
25 F4 Wijhe Netherlands
25 E7 Wijk Netherlands
25 C5 Wijk aan Zee Netherlands
103 L7 Wikieup Arizona
120 J7 Wikwemikong Ontario
41 K3 Wil Switzerland
83 L11 Wila Oya R Sri Lanka
98 K9 Wilber Nebraska
121 M7 Wilberforce Ontario
140 D1 Wilberforce,C N Terr Aust
144 C5 Wilberforce R New Zealand
101 N3 Wilborn Montana
100 B6 Wilbur Oregon
100 G2 Wilbur Washington
94 E10 Wilbur Dam Tennessee
110 A7 Wilburton Oklahoma
9 F3 Wilby England
139 G4 Wilcannia New S Wales
99 M9 Wilcox Missouri
98 G9 Wilcox Nebraska
94 J5 Wilcox Pennsylvania
119 N8 Wilcox Sask
33 T8 Wildau E Germany
36 F6 Wildbad W Germany
33 R7 Wildberg E Germany
36 F6 Wildberg W Germany
123 Q4 Wild Bight Nfld
102 H2 Wildcat Pk Nevada
119 V3 Wilde Manitoba
37 J2 Wildeck W Germany
37 O2 Wildenfels E Germany
94 B10 Wilder Tennessee
41 O4 Wilder Freiger mt Austria
117 O9 Wilderness Prov. Park Alberta
110 H6 Wildersville Tennessee
25 G2 Wildervank Netherlands
32 H7 Wildeshausen W Germany
36 H3 Wildflecken W Germany
120 A4 Wild Goose Ontario
40 F5 Wildhorn mt Switzerland
101 P1 Wild Horse Alberta
100 K8 Wildhorse Res Nevada
119 P4 Wildnest L Sask
108 B8 Wildorado Texas
33 R8 Wildpark E Germany
98 K2 Wild Rice R Minnesota
98 K3 Wild Rice R N Dakota
98 C1 Wildrose N Dakota
99 R5 Wild Rose Wisconsin
40 G5 Wildstrubel mt Switzerland
118 B5 Wildwood Alberta
113 E9 Wildwood Florida
95 N8 Wildwood New Jersey
118 B1 Wildwood Pk Manitoba
106 H3 Wiley Colorado
36 F6 Wilferdingen W Germany
120 E2 Wilgar Ontario
89 F6 Wilge R S Africa
138 C4 Wilgena S Australia
146 D3 Wilhelm II Land Antarctica
129 G3 Wilhelmina Geb mts Suriname
25 D5 Wilhelmina Kanal Netherlands
136 J3 Wilhelm, Mt Papua New Guinea
31 H4 Wilhelm-Pieck-Stadt East Germany
31 H4 Wilhelm Pieck Stadt E Germany
32 H5 Wilhelmshaven W Germany
36 F2 Wilhelmshütte W Germany
33 O5 Wiligrad E Germany
70 N9 Wilis mt Java
95 M5 Wilkes Barre Pennsylvania
112 F1 Wilkesboro N Carolina
146 H3 Wilkes Coast Antarctica
146 F3 Wilkes Land Antarctica
37 N2 Wilkhau Hasslau E Germany
118 J6 Wilkie Sask
146 E13 Wilkins Coast Antarctica
146 F13 Wilkins Ice Antarctica
138 C3 Wilkinson L S Australia
112 D6 Willacoochee Georgia
103 M6 Willaha Arizona
100 B4 Willamette R Oregon
139 G5 Willangra Billabong R New S Wales
100 B3 Willapa R Washington
139 G3 Willara New S Wales
138 E2 Willara, L S Australia
98 C9 Willard Colorado
124 D3 Willard Mexico
98 B3 Willard Montana
106 D7 Willard New Mexico
94 E5 Willard Ohio
101 N8 Willard Utah
95 M8 Willards Maryland
139 G4 Willaroy New S Wales
103 P9 Willcox Arizona
32 K9 Willebadessen W Germany
22 G1 Willebroek Belgium
22 E2 Willems France
25 C5 Willemsdorp Netherlands
126 B1 Willemstad Curaçao
25 B5 Willemstad Netherlands
140 B3 Willeroo N Terr Aust
8 D3 Willersley England
22 H4 Willerzie Belgium
9 F4 Willesden England
118 C6 Willesden Green Alberta
120 B2 Willet Ontario
143 B6 Williambury W Australia
138 D3 William Creek S Australia
119 S5 William L Manitoba
138 F6 William, Mt Victoria
143 B10 William,Mt W Australia
103 M6 Williams Arizona
102 B2 Williams California
110 K3 Williams Indiana
99 N7 Williams Iowa
99 L1 Williams Minnesota
143 B10 Williams W Australia
140 F5 Williams R Queensland
99 S7 Williams Bay Wisconsin
99 O8 Williamsburg Iowa
94 C10 Williamsburg Kentucky
95 P4 Williamsburg Massachusetts
94 C7 Williamsburg Ohio
94 J6 Williamsburg Pennsylvania
95 L9 Williamsburg Virginia
127 K2 Williamsfield Jamaica
120 K8 Williamsford Ontario
126 E2 Williams I Bahamas
117 M9 Williams Lake Br Columbia
99 N8 Williamson Iowa
95 K3 Williamson New York
94 E9 Williamson W Virginia
146 K3 Williamson Hd Antarctica
99 T9 Williamsport Indiana
94 K7 Williamsport Maryland
123 Q3 Williamsport Nfld
95 K5 Williamsport Pennsylvania
94 C4 Williamston Michigan
112 K2 Williamston N Carolina
112 E3 Williamston S Carolina
94 C8 Williamstown Kentucky
95 O4 Williamstown Massachusetts
95 P2 Williamstown Vermont
94 F7 Williamstown W Virginia
110 F5 Williamsville Missouri
141 G8 Willie's Ra Queensland
127 P4 Willikie's Antigua W Indies
95 P5 Willimantic Connecticut
118 E5 Willingdon Alberta
117 P10 Willingdon, Mt Alberta
32 J10 Willingen W Germany
9 G3 Willingham England
13 G4 Willington England
109 M5 Willis Texas
94 G10 Willis Virginia
40 G3 Willisau Switzerland
141 K3 Willis Grp islds Gt Barrier Reef Aust
146 B15 Willis I S Georgia
113 E8 Williston Florida
98 C1 Williston N Dakota
87 D12 Williston S Africa
112 F4 Williston S Carolina
117 M8 Williston L Br Col
110 G4 Willisville Illinois
8 C5 Williton England
102 A2 Willits California
99 L4 Willmar Minnesota
119 P9 Willmar Sask
94 F5 Willoughby Ohio
138 E6 Willoughby, C S Australia
116 M6 Willow Alaska
108 E8 Willow Oklahoma
117 M9 Willow R Br Col
119 P7 Willowbrook Sask
119 M9 Willow Bunch L Sask
98 F1 Willow City N Dakota
100 E9 Willow Cr California
100 H5 Willow Cr Oregon
118 D8 Willow Cr. Prov. Park Alberta
117 O4 Willow L N W Terr
98 J5 Willow L S Dakota
117 N4 Willowlake R N W Terr
89 C9 Willowmore S Africa
140 C5 Willowra N Terr Aust
100 E8 Willow Ranch California
99 R4 Willow Res Wisconsin
99 O3 Willow River Minnesota
94 D4 Willow Run Michigan
102 B2 Willows California
119 M9 Willows Sask
110 E5 Willow Springs Missouri
139 K4 Willow Tree New S Wales
95 O2 Willsboro New York
142 G5 Wills,L W Australia
109 L3 Wills Point Texas
138 E6 Willunga S Australia
146 B5 Wilma Gl Antarctica
111 H11 Wilmer Alabama
33 T6 Wilmersdorf E Germany
99 T7 Wilmette Illinois
95 M7 Wilmington Delaware
99 S8 Wilmington Illinois
112 K3 Wilmington N Carolina
94 D7 Wilmington Ohio
138 E4 Wilmington S Australia
95 O4 Wilmington Vermont
99 L6 Wilmont Minnesota
107 L4 Wilmore Kansas
94 C9 Wilmore Kentucky
111 E8 Wilmot Arkansas
94 F6 Wilmot Ohio
144 B6 Wilmot, L New Zealand
144 A6 Wilmot Pass New Zealand
25 C4 Wilnis Netherlands
121 N7 Wilno Ontario
36 E2 Wilnsdorf W Germany
83 J9 Wilpattu game reserve Sri Lanka
138 E4 Wilpena R S Australia
22 G1 Wilrijk Belgium
101 P3 Wilsall Montana
37 Q1 Wilsdruff E Germany
32 L6 Wilseder Berg hill W Germany
110 F6 Wilson Arkansas
107 M3 Wilson Kansas
111 E11 Wilson Louisiana
112 K2 Wilson N Carolina
94 J3 Wilson New York
109 K1 Wilson Oklahoma
108 F2 Wilson Texas
101 P6 Wilson Wyoming
139 G3 Wilson R Queensland
138 A4 Wilson Bluff S Australia
115 L4 Wilson, C N W Terr
142 F5 Wilson Cliffs hill W Australia
100 F2 Wilson Creek Washington
103 K3 Wilson Cr. Ra Nevada
106 H3 Wilson Junc Colorado
138 A2 Wilson, L S Australia
102 G7 Wilson, Mt California
106 C4 Wilson, Mt Colorado
103 K3 Wilson, Mt Nevada
142 G5 Wilson,Mt W Australia
107 M3 Wilson Res Kansas
139 H7 Wilson's Promontory Victoria
12 E2 Wilsontown Scotland
98 F9 Wilsonville Nebraska
32 K6 Wilstedt W Germany
32 K5 Wilster W Germany
109 N2 Wilton Arkansas
9 E5 Wilton England
99 P8 Wilton Iowa
98 F2 Wilton N Dakota
95 Q4 Wilton New Hampshire
99 Q6 Wilton Wisconsin
140 C2 Wilton R N Terr Aust
9 E5 Wiltshire co England
22 K4 Wiltz Luxembourg
143 D7 Wiluna W Australia
22 L4 Wilwerwiltz Luxembourg
119 S3 Wimapedi L Manitoba
113 E10 Wimauma Florida
9 F5 Wimbledon England
98 H2 Wimbledon N Dakota
145 F4 Wimbledon New Zealand
118 D7 Wimborne Alberta
9 E6 Wimborne England
22 B2 Wimereux France
113 B8 Wimico, L Florida
22 B2 Wimille France
38 K8 Wimitz R Austria
36 C6 Wimmenau France
138 F6 Wimmera R Victoria
118 A3 Winagami L Alberta
94 A5 Winamac Indiana
88 E2 Winam Gulf Kenya
139 G4 Winbar New S Wales
141 G7 Winbin Queensland
87 E11 Winburg S Africa
8 D5 Wincanton England
12 E2 Winchburgh Scotland
9 E4 Winchcomb England
109 H4 Winchell Texas
9 G6 Winchelsea England
95 P4 Winchendon Massachusetts
9 E5 Winchester England
100 J3 Winchester Idaho
99 Q10 Winchester Illinois
94 C6 Winchester Indiana
94 C9 Winchester Kentucky
95 P4 Winchester New Hampshire
144 C6 Winchester New Zealand
94 D8 Winchester Ohio
121 P7 Winchester Ontario
110 K6 Winchester Tennessee
109 K5 Winchester Texas
101 R6 Winchester Wyoming
100 A6 Winchester Bay Oregon
101 R6 Wind R Wyoming
138 D4 Windabout, L S Australia
101 P2 Windam Montana
143 D8 Windarra W Australia
Windau see Ventspils
94 J6 Windber Pennsylvania
98 C6 Wind Cave Nat. Park S Dakota
36 F3 Windecken W Germany
36 E5 Winden W Germany
112 D4 Winder Georgia
141 K7 Windera Queensland
113 L12 Windermere Bahamas
13 F5 Windermere England
120 G5 Windermere L Ontario
94 B6 Windfall Indiana
95 M6 Wind Gap Pennsylvania
95 R3 Windham, S Maine
32 K8 Windheim W Germany
87 C10 Windhoek Namibia
143 D7 Windich Springs W Australia
121 R5 Windigo Quebec
107 P7 Winding Stair Mts Oklahoma
37 N4 Windischeschenbach W Germany
38 K6 Windischgarsten Austria
146 F2 Windmill I Antarctica
95 M9 Windmill Pt Virginia
107 N3 Windom Kansas
99 L6 Windom Minnesota
106 C4 Windom Pk Colorado
141 G7 Windorah Queensland
37 P6 Windorf W Germany
99 T7 Wind Point Wisconsin
101 Q7 Wind R. Ra Wyoming
37 K5 Windsbach W Germany
106 F1 Windsor Colorado
95 P5 Windsor Connecticut
9 F5 Windsor England
99 S10 Windsor Illinois
95 P4 Windsor Massachusetts
110 C3 Windsor Missouri
112 L2 Windsor N Carolina
139 K5 Windsor New S Wales
95 M4 Windsor New York
144 C6 Windsor New Zealand
123 R5 Windsor Nfld
122 H9 Windsor Nova Scotia
120 H10 Windsor Ontario
121 T7 Windsor Quebec
112 F4 Windsor S Carolina
95 L10 Windsor Virginia
141 K1 Windsor dist Brisbane, Qnsld
94 G6 Windsor Heights W Virginia
126 H4 Windsor L. Great Inagua I Bahamas
95 P5 Windsor Locks Connecticut
109 J2 Windthorst Texas
141 F7 Windula R Queensland
127 O7 Windward Is W Indies
126 H5 Windward Passage Cuba/Haiti
116 N5 Windy Alaska
116 K5 Windy Fork R Alaska
119 P4 Windy L Sask
117 Q5 Windy Pt N W Terr
118 G3 Winefred L Alberta
99 R3 Winegar Wisconsin
94 C3 Winegars Michigan
100 E2 Winesap Washington
111 J8 Winfield Alabama
118 C6 Winfield Alberta
107 O4 Winfield Kansas
109 M2 Winfield Texas
8 D6 Winfrith England
98 F2 Wing N Dakota
110 J1 Wingate Indiana
106 B6 Wingate New Mexico
140 B2 Wingate Mts N Terr Aust
139 K4 Wingen New S Wales
22 E1 Wingene Belgium
36 C6 Wingen-sur-Moder France
9 H5 Wingham England
139 L4 Wingham New S Wales
120 J9 Wingham Ontario
110 H5 Wingo Kentucky
32 K5 Wingst W Germany
71 M9 Wini Timor Indonesia
101 Q2 Winifred Montana
98 J6 Winifred S Dakota
142 E6 Winifred,L W Australia
115 L6 Winisk Ontario
68 D5 Winkana Burma
25 C3 Winkel Netherlands
103 O9 Winkelman Arizona
9 F5 Winkfield England
37 O5 Winklarn W Germany
8 C6 Winkleigh England
119 U9 Winkler Manitoba
38 G8 Winklern Austria
100 C3 Winlock Washington
95 T1 Winn Maine
94 C3 Winn Michigan
140 B6 Winnalls Ridge N Terr Aust
85 D7 Winneba Ghana
99 M6 Winnebago Minnesota
98 K7 Winnebago Nebraska
99 S5 Winnebago, L Wisconsin
142 G6 Winnecke Hills N Terr/W Aust
140 B4 Winnecke,Mt N Terr Aust
142 E6 Winnecke Rock hill W Australia
99 S5 Winneconne Wisconsin
100 H9 Winnemucca Nevada
102 E1 Winnemucca L Nevada
36 G6 Winnenden W Germany
98 G6 Winner S Dakota
99 T7 Winnetka Illinois
98 H7 Winnetoon Nebraska
101 R2 Winnett Montana
109 P4 Winnfield Louisiana
99 M2 Winnibigoshish L Minnesota
109 N6 Winnie Texas
118 F9 Winnifred Alberta
33 O9 Winnigen E Germany
142 A6 Winning W Australia
36 D3 Winningen W Germany
138 E4 Winnininnie S Australia
118 A1 Winnipeg Manitoba
119 V8 Winnipeg Beach Manitoba
119 T5 Winnipeg, L Manitoba
119 S7 Winnipegosis Manitoba
119 R6 Winnipegosis, L Manitoba
95 Q3 Winnipesaukee, L New Hampshire
111 E9 Winnsboro Louisiana
112 F3 Winnsboro S Carolina
109 M3 Winnsboro Texas
112 E6 Winokur Georgia
103 N6 Winona Arizona
107 J2 Winona Kansas
99 S3 Winona Michigan
99 P5 Winona Minnesota
110 E4 Winona Missouri
109 M3 Winona Texas
100 H3 Winona Washington
109 P1 Winona, L Arkansas
95 O2 Winooski Vermont
95 P2 Winooski R Vermont
25 H2 Winschoten Netherlands
32 L7 Winsen W Germany
32 M6 Winsen W Germany
8 D1 Winsford England
98 J7 Winside Nebraska
103 O6 Winslow Arizona
110 B6 Winslow Arkansas
9 F4 Winslow England
110 J3 Winslow Indiana
95 S2 Winslow Maine
100 C2 Winslow Washington
137 R2 Winslow Reef Phoenix Is Pacific Oc
101 N5 Winsper Idaho
95 O5 Winsted Connecticut
9 E1 Winster England
13 G4 Winston England
101 O3 Winston Montana
106 C8 Winston New Mexico
112 G1 Winston Salem N Carolina
25 G2 Winsum Netherlands
118 H6 Winter Sask
38 M6 Winterbach Austria
36 D4 Winterberg W Germany
36 F1 Winterberg W Germany
8 D6 Winterbourne Abbas England
9 E5 Winterbourne Stoke England
33 O7 Winterfeld E Germany
113 F9 Winter Garden Florida
114 J3 Winter Harb N W Terr
103 K9 Winterhaven California
113 F9 Winter Haven Florida
119 U3 Wintering L Manitoba
36 G7 Winterlingen W Germany
106 E2 Winter Park Colorado
113 F9 Winter Park Florida
95 T2 Winterport Maine
102 C3 Winters California
108 H4 Winters Texas
103 M8 Wintersburg Arizona
99 M8 Winterset Iowa
22 K2 Winterslag Belgium
25 G5 Winterswijk Netherlands
41 J3 Winterthur Switzerland
13 H6 Winterton England
123 T6 Winterton Nfld
95 S7 Winterville Maine
95 R4 Winthrop Massachusetts
99 M5 Winthrop Minnesota
95 N2 Winthrop New York
100 E1 Winthrop Washington
99 T7 Winthrop Harbor Illinois
138 C2 Wintinna S Australia
99 P2 Winton Minnesota
112 K1 Winton N Carolina
113 M9 Winton New Providence I Bahamas
144 B7 Winton New Zealand
95 M5 Winton Pennsylvania
141 G5 Winton Queensland
100 E2 Winton Washington
101 Q8 Winton Wyoming
40 F1 Wintzenheim France
112 H4 Winyah B S Carolina
37 P6 Winzer W Germany
99 M8 Wiota Iowa
33 N10 Wipper R E Germany
36 C1 Wipperfürth W Germany
33 O9 Wippra E Germany
41 O3 Wipp Tal Austria
83 K11 Wiraketiya Sri Lanka
25 E2 Wirdum Netherlands
32 F6 Wirdum W Germany
9 E1 Wirksworth England
145 F2 Wiroa I New Zealand
138 E5 Wirrabara S Australia
138 D4 Wirraminna S Australia
138 D4 Wirrapa S Australia
138 F6 Wirrega S Australia
138 C3 Wirrida, L S Australia
138 C4 Wirrulla S Australia
99 N2 Wirt Minnesota
22 B2 Wirwignes France
9 G2 Wisbech England
9 F5 Wisborough Green England
95 S2 Wiscasset Maine
32 K5 Wischhafen W Germany
99 R4 Wisconsin R Wisconsin
99 R5 Wisconsin state U.S.A.
99 R6 Wisconsin Dells Wisconsin
99 R6 Wisconsin, L Wisconsin
146 G9 Wisconsin Ra Antarctica
99 R5 Wisconsin Rapids Wisconsin
101 M4 Wisdom Montana
94 E9 Wise Virginia
116 M3 Wiseman Alaska
101 N4 Wise River Montana
118 K7 Wiseton Sask
119 O7 Wishart Sask
12 E2 Wishaw Scotland
98 G3 Wishek N Dakota
100 E4 Wishram Washington
48 E1 Wisla Poland
31 L2 Wisła R Poland
31 N6 Wisłok R Poland
33 O5 Wismar E Germany
33 O5 Wismarbucht E Germany
111 E10 Wisner Louisiana
98 K8 Wisner Nebraska
22 B2 Wissant France
136 H2 Wissel, Danau D L W Irian
36 D5 Wissembourg France
36 D2 Wissen W Germany
9 G2 Wissey, R England
32 H8 Wissingen W Germany
99 P5 Wissota L Wisconsin
31 N4 Wista R Poland
117 K9 Wistaria Br Columbia
109 N1 Wister Oklahoma
89 F5 Witbank S Africa
89 E8 Witberge mts S Africa
119 U3 Witchai L Manitoba
143 B10 Witchcliffe W Australia
118 K5 Witchekan L Sask
87 D11 Witdrail S Africa
9 G4 Witham England
9 F1 Witham, R England
8 C6 Witheridge England
9 G1 Withern England
13 J6 Withernsea England
141 J6 Withersfield Queensland
106 C8 Withington, Mt New Mexico
113 E9 Withlacoochee R Florida
100 F2 Withrow Washington
31 K3 Witkowo Poland
123 U6 Witless B Nfld
9 E4 Witney England
22 K4 Witry Belgium
22 G5 Witry-les-Reims France
22 D2 Witschate Belgium
110 G2 Witt Illinois
28 A7 Wittdün W Germany
37 L7 Wittelsbach W Germany
98 F6 Witten S Dakota
32 F10 Witten W Germany
33 S7 Wittenau E Germany
33 R9 Wittenberg E Germany
99 R5 Wittenberg Wisconsin
33 P7 Wittenberge E Germany
33 O5 Wittenburg E Germany
142 C5 Wittenoom W Australia
142 G4 Wittenoom,Mt W Australia
37 O2 Wittgensdorf E Germany
125 N2 Witties, The islds Nicaragua
36 H4 Wittighausen W Germany
33 N7 Wittingen W Germany
70 E2 Witti Ra Sabah
32 H8 Wittlage W Germany
36 B4 Wittlich W Germany
32 K7 Wittlohe W Germany
103 M8 Wittmann Arizona
32 G5 Wittmund W Germany
13 G4 Witton Gilbert England
13 G4 Witton-le-Wear England
30 G1 Wittow pen E Germany
33 Q6 Wittstock E Germany
87 C10 Witvlei Namibia
89 E5 Witwatersberg ridge S Africa
89 C2 Witwatersrand S Africa
32 L10 Witzenhausen W Germany
8 C5 Wiveliscombe England
119 W2 Wivenhoe Manitoba
118 L8 Wives Sask
9 H4 Wix England
31 O1 Wizajny Poland
22 C2 Wizernes France
31 M3 Wkra R Poland
31 L1 Władysławowo Poland
31 J4 Wleń Poland
31 L3 Włocławek Poland
31 O4 Włodawa Poland
31 M5 Włoszczowa Poland
33 O6 Wöbbelin E Germany
9 F4 Woburn England
142 C5 Wodgina W Australia
139 H6 Wodonga Victoria
31 L5 Wodzisław Poland
25 B6 Woensdrecht Netherlands
25 C4 Woerden Netherlands
36 D6 Wœrth France
22 J5 Wœvre, Forêt de France
94 C10 Wofford Kentucky
25 D3 Wognum Netherlands
41 H3 Wohlen Switzerland
33 O5 Wohlenberg E Germany
40 F4 Wohlen See L Switzerland
36 F2 Wohratal W Germany
32 J4 Wöhrden W Germany
121 N7 Woito Ontario
143 A8 Wokarina W Australia
65 H1 Woken China
65 H1 Woken He R China
117 O8 Woking Alberta
9 F5 Woking England
9 F5 Wokingham England
141 G5 Wokingham R Queensland
33 S6 Wokuhl E Germany
31 L4 Wola Poland
98 H8 Wolbach Nebraska
32 G9 Wolbeck W Germany
101 T10 Wolcott Colorado
95 L3 Wolcott New York
32 E2 Woldbrunn W Germany
33 T6 Woldegk E Germany
141 J7 Woleebee Queensland
111 G11 Wolf R Mississippi
110 G6 Wolf R Tennessee
99 S4 Wolf R Wisconsin
117 G5 Wolf R Yukon Terr
36 E7 Wolfach W Germany
37 P6 Wolfachau W Germany
123 M3 Wolf Bay Quebec
108 D7 Wolf Cr Texas/Okla
94 B10 Wolf Cr. Dam Kentucky
101 N2 Wolf Creek Montana
100 B7 Wolf Creek Oregon
106 D4 Wolf Cr. Pass Colorado
118 J6 Wolfe Sask
95 Q3 Wolfeboro New Hampshire
109 L2 Wolfe City Texas
121 O8 Wolfe Island Ontario
118 G4 Wolfe L Alberta
33 Q9 Wolfen E Germany
33 N8 Wolfenbüttel W Germany
9 G2 Wolferton England
32 K10 Wolfhagen W Germany
103 L5 Wolf Hole Arizona
123 L6 Wolf I Madeleine Is, Quebec
117 H5 Wolf L Yukon Terr
101 S4 Wolf Mts Wyo/Mont
98 G1 Wolford N Dakota
98 A1 Wolf Pt Montana
140 B2 Wolfram Hill N Terr Aust
37 K5 Wolframs-Eschenbach W Germany
41 O2 Wolfratshausen W Germany
38 L8 Wolfsberg Austria
33 N8 Wolfsburg W Germany
37 N2 Wolfsgefärth E Germany
36 E4 Wolfskehlen W Germany
36 D4 Wolfstein W Germany
122 H8 Wolfville Nova Scotia
33 T4 Wolgast E Germany
33 T4 Wolgaster Fähre E Germany
31 H2 Wolin Poland
37 L3 Wölkendorf W Germany
37 P2 Wolkenstein E Germany
33 N10 Wolkramsh E Germany
114 H3 Wollaston, C N W Terr
133 D9 Wollaston, Is Chile
114 J6 Wollaston Lake Post Sask
114 H4 Wollaston Pen N W Terr
36 B2 Wollersheim W Germany
139 K5 Wollongong New S Wales
36 D4 Wöllstein W Germany
87 E11 Wolmaransstad S Africa
33 O9 Wolmirsleben E Germany
33 P8 Wolmirstedt E Germany
37 M6 Wolnzach W Germany
70 G6 Wolo Sulawesi
31 N3 Wołomin Poland
31 K4 Wołow Poland
71 K9 Wolowaru Flores Indonesia
119 O8 Wolseley Sask
138 F6 Wolseley S Australia
98 H5 Wolsey S Dakota
36 B4 Wolsfeld W Germany
13 G4 Wolsingham England
115 M5 Wolstenholme, C Quebec
31 J3 Wolsztyn Poland
32 L7 Wolthausen W Germany
33 M8 Woltorf W Germany
25 F3 Wolvega Netherlands
8 D2 Wolverhampton England
94 C1 Wolverine Michigan
22 G2 Wolvertem Belgium
9 E5 Wolverton England
98 K3 Wolverton Minnesota
9 E3 Wolvey England
120 H5 Woman River Ontario
141 F7 Wombunderry R Queensland
13 G6 Wombwell England
95 L6 Womelsdorf Pennsylvania
138 F3 Wompah New S Wales
140 D4 Wonarah N Terr Aust
143 E10 Wonberna W Australia
141 K7 Wondai Queensland
22 F1 Wondelgem Belgium
100 B7 Wonder Oregon
116 M5 Wonder L Alaska
140 E6 Wonditti,L Queensland
86 G4 Wondo Ethiopia
138 C4 Wondoma, C S Australia
140 F4 Wondoola Queensland
139 G4 Wongalarroo L New S Wales
141 G5 Wongalee Queensland
143 B9 Wongan Hills W Australia
70 G4 Wonggarasi Sulawesi
59 J4 Wŏnju S Korea
70 N9 Wonogiri Java
70 O9 Wonokromo Java
138 F4 Wonominta R N S Wales
70 N9 Wonosari Java
70 M9 Wonosobo Java
71 N9 Wonreli Indonesia
59 J4 Wŏnsan N Korea
139 H7 Wonthaggi Victoria
143 C6 Wonyulgunna,Mt W Australia
138 D4 Woocalla S Australia
94 J6 Wood Pennsylvania
98 F6 Wood S Dakota
116 O4 Wood R Alaska
140 D2 Woodah I N Terr Aust
146 J6 Wood B Antarctica
113 F7 Woodbine Georgia
99 L8 Woodbine Iowa
107 N3 Woodbine Kansas
94 C10 Woodbine Kentucky
95 N7 Woodbine New Jersey
9 H3 Woodbridge England
121 L9 Woodbridge Ontario
95 K8 Woodbridge Virginia
117 R6 Wood Buffalo Nat. Park Alberta
99 N8 Woodburn Iowa
110 K5 Woodburn Kentucky
139 L3 Woodburn New S Wales
100 C4 Woodburn Oregon
112 C5 Woodbury Georgia
95 M7 Woodbury New Jersey
110 K6 Woodbury Tennessee
112 F5 Woodcliff Georgia
140 C4 Woodcock,Mt N Terr Aust
139 L3 Wooded Bluff New S Wales
139 L3 Woodenbong New S Wales
144 B7 Woodend New Zealand
117 M11 Woodfibre Br Columbia
9 G4 Woodford England
127 P5 Woodford Grenada
14 C3 Woodford Irish Rep
140 C5 Woodforde R N Terr Aust
102 E3 Woodfords California
9 F4 Wood Green England
140 C5 Woodgreen N Terr Aust
9 F1 Woodhall Spa England
13 G6 Woodhead England
99 Q8 Woodhull Illinois
95 K4 Woodhull New York
100 C2 Woodinville Washington
122 K8 Wood Is Pr Edward I
119 U1 Wood L Manitoba
98 F7 Wood L Nebraska
119 O3 Wood L Sask
102 E5 Woodlake California
102 C3 Woodland California
110 J1 Woodland Illinois
94 J6 Woodland Pennsylvania
100 C4 Woodland Washington
109 N10 Woodland Hills Texas
106 E3 Woodland Park Colorado
119 U8 Woodlands Manitoba
137 L3 Woodlark isld Papua New Guinea
110 G3 Woodlawn Illinois
142 A3 Woodman Pt W Australia
101 Q4 Wood, Mt Montana
118 L9 Wood Mt Sask
117 C5 Wood, Mt Yukon Terr
117 M9 Woodpecker Br Columbia
118 E1 Woodridge Manitoba
140 E6 Woodridge,Mt N Terr Aust
110 F3 Wood River Illinois
98 H9 Wood River Nebraska
140 E5 Woodroffe R N Terr/Queensland
138 B2 Woodroffe, Mt S Australia
106 G2 Woodrow Colorado
118 L9 Woodrow Sask
103 O7 Woodruff Arizona
107 L2 Woodruff Kansas
101 O8 Woodruff Utah
101 Q4 Woods mt Montana
109 K7 Woodsboro Texas
94 F7 Woodsfield Ohio
122 G10 Woods Harbour Nova Scotia
145 E4 Woodside New Zealand
103 O2 Woodside Utah
139 H7 Woodside Victoria
140 C4 Woods,L N Terr Aust
118 H1 Woods, Lake of the Minn/Ontario
111 D7 Woodson Arkansas
99 Q10 Woodson Illinois
109 H2 Woodson Texas
139 H7 Woods Pt Victoria
9 E4 Woodstock England
99 S7 Woodstock Illinois
122 E7 Woodstock New Brunswick
141 G4 Woodstock Queensland
141 H4 Woodstock Queensland
95 P3 Woodstock Vermont
95 Q2 Woodstock, N New Hampshire
107 M2 Woodston Kansas
95 M7 Woodstown New Jersey
95 Q2 Woodsville New Hampshire
111 M11 Woodville Florida
111 E10 Woodville Mississippi
145 E4 Woodville New Zealand
94 D5 Woodville Ohio
121 M8 Woodville Ontario
109 N5 Woodville Texas
107 L5 Woodward Oklahoma
102 D4 Woodward Res California
122 F9 Woodwards Cove New Brunswick
109 P4 Woodworth Louisiana
98 G2 Woodworth N Dakota
8 C5 Woody B England
116 L8 Woody Island Alaska
123 P4 Woody Point Newfoundland
119 Q6 Woody R Manitoba
8 D3 Woofferton England
71 A3 Wooi Indonesia
8 D6 Wool England
8 B5 Woolacombe England
110 D3 Wooldridge Missouri
13 F3 Wooler England
118 D9 Woolford Prov. Park Alberta
143 D9 Woolgangie W Australia
141 G4 Woolgar Queensland
143 C6 Woolgathara W Australia
139 L4 Woolgoolga New S Wales
143 D9 Woolibar W Australia
140 C5 Woolla Downs N Terr Aust
9 G3 Woolpit England
102 F1 Woolsey Nevada
138 E4 Wooltana S Australia
8 D5 Woolverton England
9 G5 Woolwich England
138 D4 Woomera S Australia
95 Q5 Woonsocket Rhode I
98 H5 Woonsocket S Dakota
13 G3 Wooperton England
141 J6 Woorabinda Queensland
143 A7 Wooramel W Australia
143 A7 Wooramel R W Australia
8 D2 Woore England
138 C3 Woorong, L S Australia
94 F6 Wooster Ohio
9 E4 Wootton Bassett England
38 O6 Wopfing Austria
117 O7 Wor Alberta
71 B2 Wor isld Halmahera Indonesia
33 M10 Worbis E Germany
8 D3 Worcester England
95 Q4 Worcester Massachusetts
95 N4 Worcester New York
89 A9 Worcester S Africa
Worcester co see Hereford and Worcester co
110 G3 Worden Illinois
101 R4 Worden Montana
100 D7 Worden Oregon
146 F13 Wordie Ice Shelf Antarctica
119 P9 Wordsworth Sask
38 F7 Wörgl Austria
12 E4 Workington England
9 E1 Worksop England
25 D3 Workum Netherlands
101 S5 Worland Wyoming
8 D5 Worle England
33 Q9 Wörlitz E Germany
8 D4 Wormbridge England
25 C4 Wormerveer Netherlands
22 C2 Wormhoudt France
13 F1 Wormit Scotland
33 P10 Wormlitz E Germany
36 E4 Worms W Germany
8 B4 Worms Head Wales
37 K6 Wörnitz R W Germany
32 J6 Worpswede W Germany
36 B1 Worringen W Germany
36 E4 Wörrstadt W Germany
143 E7 Worsnop,Mt W Australia
38 G7 Wörth Austria

86 Yihuang — Zuidbroek

67 E3 Yihuang China
65 A7 Yijun China
65 H1 Yilan China
78 F2 Yildizeli Turkey
67 A3 Yiliang China
67 A4 Yiliang China
143 B10 Yilliminning W Australia
67 B1 Yilong China
65 G2 Yimianpo China
68 B2 Yin R Burma
65 D7 Yinan China
68 C4 Yinbaing Burma
65 B7 Yincheng China
58 E4 Yinchuan China
143 D9 Yindarlgooda, L W Australia
67 D1 Yindian China
67 D1 Yingcheng China
67 F3 Yingchuan China
65 J1 Yingchun China
67 D4 Yingde China
65 F4 Ying'ebu China
141 J7 Yingerbay Queensland
Yinggen see Qiongzhong
65 B7 Ying He R China
59 H3 Yingkou China
65 E4 Yingkou China
67 B1 Yingshan China
67 D1 Yingshan China
67 E2 Yingtan China
65 B5 Ying Xian China
65 D3 Yin He R China
66 C3 Yining China
67 C2 Yinjiang China
138 F5 Yinkame S Australia
68 B1 Yinmabin Burma
65 F2 Yinma He R China
68 C4 Yinnyein Burma
65 A4 Yin Shan mts China
47 G5 Yioúra isld Greece
Yiquan see Meitan
131 G4 Yi, R Uruguay
86 G4 Yirga Alem Ethiopia
80 D2 Yirka Israel
86 F4 Yirol Sudan
80 E1 Yir'on Israel
59 G2 Yirshi China
67 C4 Yishan China
65 D6 Yi Shan mts China
65 D7 Yishui China
80 E6 Yitav Jordan
46 F8 Yíthion Greece
65 F3 Yitong China
65 F2 Yitong He R China
66 E3 Yiwu China
67 G2 Yiwu China
68 E2 Yiwu China
Yixian see Yicheng
65 C5 Yi Xian China
65 E4 Yi Xian China
67 F2 Yi Xian China
67 F1 Yixing China
65 D4 Yixun He R China
65 B7 Yiyang China
67 D2 Yiyang Hunan China
67 F2 Yiyang Jiangxi China
65 D6 Yiyuan China
67 D4 Yizhang China
67 F1 Yizheng China
31 K6 Yizovice Czechoslovakia
29 N11 Ylämaa Finland
29 J11 Yläne Finland
29 K8 Ylihärmä Finland
29 M6 Ylikiiminki Finland
52 C2 Ylikitka L Finland
29 M6 Yli-li Finland
29 K9 Ylistaro Finland
29 K5 Ylitornio Finland
29 L7 Ylivieska Finland
29 L4 Yliästunturi mt Finland
29 K10 Ylöjärvi Finland
115 R3 Ymers Ø isld Greenland
20 J5 Ymonville France
52 J4 Yndin U.S.S.R.
27 J13 Yngaren L Sweden
57 F1 Yntaly U.S.S.R.
86 B3 Yo Nigeria
109 K6 Yoakum Texas
60 O2 Yobetsu Japan
60 C12 Yobuko Japan
128 E7 Yocalla Bolivia
107 L3 Yocemento Kansas
111 G7 Yocono R Mississippi
106 F3 Yoder Colorado
98 B8 Yoder Wyoming
60 J11 Yodo Japan
60 G10 Yodoe Japan
133 D8 Yogan mt Chile
70 N9 Yogyakarta Java
117 P10 Yoho Nat. Park Br Columbia
60 O2 Yoichi Japan
60 O2 Yoichi dake mt Japan
125 L2 Yojoa, L. de Honduras
60 H10 Yōka Japan
86 C5 Yokadouma Cameroon
61 O10 Yōkaichiba Japan
111 F9 Yokena Mississippi
61 K11 Yokkaichi Japan
86 B4 Yoko Cameroon
60 F12 Yokogawara Japan
62 Yokohama conurbation Japan
61 N10 Yokosuka Japan
61 O6 Yokote Japan
60 O4 Yokotsu-dake mt Japan
86 B4 Yola Nigeria
125 M4 Yolaina, Cord. de Nicaragua
57 B5 Yolbarsli U.S.S.R.
65 E2 Yolin Mod China
86 D6 Yolombo Zaïre
61 P13 Yomitan Airport Okinawa
61 Q12 Yona Okinawa
61 P13 Yonabaru Okinawa
60 G10 Yonago Japan
67 G4 Yonagunijima Japan
61 Q12 Yonaha-dake mt Okinawa
100 B6 Yoncalla Oregon
61 O5 Yoneshiro-gawa R Japan
61 O8 Yonezawa Japan
67 F4 Yong'an China
67 D2 Yong'anshi China
67 B2 Yongchuan China
67 F4 Yongchun China
67 C3 Yongcong China
67 E4 Yongding China
65 C5 Yongding He R China
59 J4 Yongdüngpo S Korea
67 E3 Yongfeng China
67 C4 Yongfu China
65 A6 Yonghe China
59 J4 Yonghüng N Korea
65 G5 Yŏnghŭng-man B N Korea
58 F5 Yongji China
65 G3 Yongji China
67 G2 Yongjia China
Yongjing see Xifeng
67 G2 Yongkang China
65 C6 Yongnian China
Yongning see Xuyong
58 D6 Yongning China
67 C5 Yongning China
65 C5 Yongqing China
67 A2 Yongshan China
65 A7 Yongshou China
67 C2 Yongshun China
67 E3 Yongtai China
67 F4 Yongtai China
67 E3 Yongxin China
67 D3 Yongxing China
67 E2 Yongxiu China
Yongyang see Weng'an
118 H6 Yonker Sask
95 O6 Yonkers New York
107 P5 Yonkers Oklahoma
18 H5 Yonne dep France
18 H5 Yonne R France
68 B2 Yonzingyi Burma
57 H5 Yopurga China
111 H9 York Alabama
13 G6 York England
101 O3 York Montana
98 G1 York N Dakota
98 J9 York Nebraska
95 L7 York Pennsylvania
112 F3 York S Carolina
143 B9 York W Australia
141 G1 York, C Queensland
141 F2 York Downs Queensland
138 D5 Yorke Pen S Australia
138 D6 Yorketown S Australia
115 K6 York Factory Manitoba
123 O4 York Harb Nfld
115 N2 York, Kap C Greenland
116 D4 York Mts Alaska
123 R2 York Pt Labrador
122 G5 York R Quebec
142 F2 York Sd W Australia
Yorkshire co see N., W. & S.Yorks, Cleveland, Humberside counties
136 F4 York Sound W Australia
119 P7 Yorkton Sask
109 K7 Yorktown Texas
95 L9 Yorktown Virginia
95 R3 York Village Maine
99 S8 Yorkville Illinois
95 M3 Yorkville New York
125 L2 Yoro Honduras
102 D4 Yosemite L California
102 E4 Yosemite Lodge California
102 E3 Yosemite National Park California
61 M8 Yoshida Japan
61 P6 Yoshihama-wan B Japan
60 F12 Yoshino Japan
60 H11 Yoshino R Japan
61 K11 Yoshino-Kumano Nat. Park Japan
52 G6 Yoshkar Ola U.S.S.R.
60 D12 Yoshu Japan
Yösönbulag see Altay
101 M8 Yost Utah
61 O8 Yotsukura Japan
79 F9 Yotvata Israel
143 C8 Youanmi W Australia
117 L11 Youbou Br Columbia
14 D5 Youghal Irish Rep
67 B5 You Jiang R China
85 B6 Youkounkoun Guinea
9 E1 Youlgreave England
103 O7 Young Arizona
139 J5 Young New S Wales
119 M7 Young Sask
138 D4 Younghusband, L S Australia
138 E6 Younghusband Pen S Australia
140 D3 Young, Mt N Terr Aust
144 B6 Young Range New Zealand
88 E7 Youngs B Malawi
118 F7 Youngstown Alberta
111 L11 Youngstown Florida
94 J3 Youngstown New York
94 G5 Youngstown Ohio
111 D11 Youngsville Louisiana
112 J1 Youngsville N Carolina
106 D5 Youngsville New Mexico
94 H5 Youngsville Pennsylvania
101 Q6 Younts Pk Wyoming
102 B3 Yountville California
67 C2 You Shui R China
67 F3 Youxi China
67 D3 You Xian China
67 C2 Youyang China
65 H1 Youyi China
65 B4 Youyu China
139 G3 Yowah R Queensland
143 C7 Yowereena Hill W Australia
78 E2 Yozgat Turkey
130 B9 Ypacarai, L Paraguay
29 K11 Ypäjä Finland
130 C8 Ypané, R Paraguay
130 C8 Ypé-jhú Paraguay
130 B9 Ypoá L Paraguay
20 F2 Yport France
29 L7 Yppäri Finland
Ypres see Ieper
94 D4 Ypsilanti Michigan
100 C8 Yreka California
8 C3 Yrfon R Wales
8 C3 Yspytty Ystwyth Wales
18 H7 Yssingeaux France
27 G16 Ystad Sweden
8 C4 Ystalyfera Wales
8 B3 Ystrad Wales
8 C3 Ystrad-ffin Wales
8 C3 Ystwyth, R Wales
15 F3 Ythan, R Scotland
26 G9 Ytterhogdal Sweden
27 J12 Ytterjärna Sweden
26 J8 Ytterlännäs Sweden
26 E8 Ytteröy Norway
26 L7 Yttersjön Sweden
67 D1 Yuan'an China
67 C4 Yuanbao Shan mt China
67 E1 Yüan Hu China
67 D2 Yuanjiang China
67 C2 Yuan Jiang R China
68 F1 Yuan Jiang R China
67 C2 Yuanling China
65 B5 Yuanping China
65 B7 Yuanqu China
65 C6 Yuanshi China
67 E3 Yuan Shui R China
65 B7 Yuanyang China
67 D3 Yuanyue China
60 J11 Yuasa Japan
102 C2 Yuba R California
102 C2 Yuba City California
60 P2 Yūbari Japan
60 Q2 Yūbari dake mt Japan
86 G4 Yubdo Ethiopia
60 R1 Yūbetsu Japan
60 S2 Yūbetsu Japan
85 B3 Yubi, C Morocco
61 M9 Yubiso Japan
80 G3 Yubla Jordan
128 D7 Yucamani mt Peru
125 P7 Yucatan state Mexico
90 A6 Yucatan Basin Atlantic Oc
126 A3 Yucatan Chan Caribbean
103 K7 Yucca Arizona
103 H4 Yucca Flat Nevada
106 B4 Yucca House Nat. Mon Colorado
65 C6 Yucheng China
65 C7 Yucheng China
65 B6 Yuci China
65 C3 Yudaokou China
52 G6 Yudino U.S.S.R.
51 N3 Yudoma R U.S.S.R.
67 E4 Yudu China
67 B1 Yuechi China
67 D1 Yuekou China
Yuelai see Huachuan
67 C1 Yuelai China
65 F2 Yueliang Pao L China
140 B5 Yuendumu Mission N Terr Aust
67 G2 Yueqing China
67 G2 Yueqing Wan B China
58 D6 Yuexi China
67 E1 Yuexi China
58 D6 Yuexi He R China
67 A2 Yuexi He R China
Yueyang see Gu Xian
67 D2 Yueyang China
60 E12 Yufu-dake mt Japan
52 G5 Yug R U.S.S.R.
52 G4 Yuga R U.S.S.R.
67 E2 Yugan China
55 F1 Yugan U.S.S.R.
42 H4 Yugoslavia rep S Europe
67 G1 Yuhang China
65 B4 Yu He R China
65 A5 Yuhebu China
67 B4 Yuhong China
67 G2 Yuhuan China
143 B8 Yuin W Australia
67 E2 Yujiang China
67 C2 Yu Jiang R China
67 C5 Yu Jiang R China
52 H5 Yukamenskoye U.S.S.R.
54 G2 Yukhnov U.S.S.R.
61 N9 Yūki Japan
116 J4 Yuki R Alaska
113 F7 Yukon Florida
107 N6 Yukon Oklahoma
117 E4 Yukon Crossing Yukon Terr
55 E1 Yukonda R U.S.S.R.
116 E5 Yukon Delta Alaska
116 M4 Yukon R Alaska/Yukon Terr
114 F5 Yukon Territory Canada
60 E12 Yukuhashi Japan
52 F3 Yula R U.S.S.R.
55 C4 Yuldybayevo U.S.S.R.
146 K5 Yule B Antarctica
141 J7 Yuleba Queensland
142 B2 Yule Brook Perth, W Aust
113 F7 Yulee Florida
142 C5 Yule R W Australia
65 A5 Yulin China
67 C5 Yulin China
67 C7 Yulin China
65 A6 Yulinqiao China
103 K9 Yuma Arizona
98 D9 Yuma Colorado
52 D2 Yuma U.S.S.R.
16 D9 Yumaa el Tolba Morocco
127 K5 Yuma, B. de Dom Rep
103 K9 Yuma Desert Arizona
55 C4 Yumaguzino U.S.S.R.
86 E6 Yumbi Zaïre
58 C3 Yumen China
58 C3 Yü-men-chen China
58 C3 Yumenzhen China
58 F1 Yumurchen U.S.S.R.
143 A8 Yuna W Australia
127 K5 Yuna R Dom Rep
78 C2 Yunak Turkey
67 D5 Yunan China
67 C1 Yun'anzhen China
65 B7 Yuncheng China
65 C7 Yuncheng China
143 D8 Yundamindera W Australia
67 D5 Yunfu China
128 E7 Yungas, Las mts Bolivia
139 G5 Yungera Victoria
Yunhe see Pei Xian
67 F2 Yunhe China
67 C5 Yunkai Dashan mts China
67 D1 Yunmeng China
67 A4 Yunnan prov China
143 D8 Yunndaga W Australia
60 O4 Yunokawa Japan
60 D13 Yunomae Japan
60 F10 Yunotsu Japan
16 E4 Yunquera de H Spain
67 A4 Yunshang China
138 E4 Yunta S Australia
58 F5 Yun Xian China
67 F5 Yunxiao China
67 C1 Yunyang China
65 B5 Yunzhong Shan mts China
67 C3 Yuping China
67 B3 Yuqing China
Yuqingsi see Aoxi
60 O3 Yūrappu-dake mt Japan
124 H7 Yurécharo Mexico
56 B3 Yurga U.S.S.R.
55 D3 Yurgamysh U.S.S.R.
55 E3 Yurginskoye U.S.S.R.
128 C5 Yurimaguas Peru
52 G6 Yurino U.S.S.R.
52 H5 Yurla U.S.S.R.
55 C3 Yurma mt U.S.S.R.
52 G2 Yuroma U.S.S.R.
55 E2 Yurovskoye U.S.S.R.
66 B4 Yurungkax He R China
60 T2 Yururi-tō isld Japan
52 G5 Yur'ya U.S.S.R.
52 J2 Yur'yakha R U.S.S.R.
52 F6 Yur'yevets U.S.S.R.
52 E6 Yur'yev Pol'skiy U.S.S.R.
55 C3 Yuryuzan' Katav-Ivanovsk U.S.S.R.
125 L3 Yuscarán Honduras
67 F2 Yushan China
67 C2 Yushanzhen China
65 B6 Yushe China
52 H1 Yushino U.S.S.R.
29 P11 Yushkelovo U.S.S.R.
52 D3 Yushkozero U.S.S.R.
59 J3 Yushu China
66 F5 Yushu China
65 G2 Yushugou China
Yushuwan see Huaihua
78 H1 Yusufeli Turkey
60 F12 Yusuhara Japan
52 H5 Yus'va U.S.S.R.
65 C7 Yutai China
98 K8 Yutan Nebraska
52 H6 Yutaza U.S.S.R.
128 F7 Yuti Bolivia
65 D5 Yutian Hebei China
66 C4 Yutian Xinjiang Uygur Zizhiqu China
130 C10 Yuty Paraguay
67 F5 Yü-weng Tao Taiwan
Yuxi see Daozhen
65 B5 Yu Xian China
65 B7 Yu Xian China
65 C5 Yu Xian China
67 G1 Yuyao China
60 D11 Yuya-wan B Japan
52 F5 Yuza R U.S.S.R.
61 M9 Yuzawa Japan
52 F6 Yuzha U.S.S.R.
57 G5 Yuzh Alichurskiy, Khrebet mts U.S.S.R.
55 D4 Yuzhno-Ural'sk U.S.S.R.
55 D4 Yuzhnoural'skiy U.S.S.R.
56 C6 Yuzhnyy Altay, Khrebet mts U.S.S.R.
48 M2 Yuzhnyy Bug R U.S.S.R.
55 C4 Yuzhnyy Ural reg U.S.S.R.
Yuzhov see Chongqing
55 G4 Yuzno Podol'skoye U.S.S.R.
20 J4 Yvelines dep France
40 E4 Yverdon Switzerland
20 G2 Yvetot France
22 H3 Yvoir Anhee Belgium
40 E4 Yvonand Switzerland
21 I6 Yvoy-le Marron France
20 F5 Yvre-l'Evêque France
68 B2 Ywamun Burma
68 C3 Ywathit Burma
27 H13 Yxviken Sweden
21 D7 Yzernay France
21 G8 Yzeures-sur-Creuse France
25 C4 Zaandam Netherlands
25 C4 Zaandijk Netherlands
42 H6 Zaba mt Yugoslavia
80 E4 Zababida Jordan
48 F5 Žabalj Yugoslavia
48 G6 Žabari Yugoslavia
58 G2 Zabaykal'sk U.S.S.R.
80 F3 Zabda Jordan
56 F4 Zabituy U.S.S.R.
31 K5 Ząbkowice Poland
31 O3 Zabłudów Poland
77 G4 Zabol Iran
77 G6 Zāboli Iran
48 J2 Zabolotov U.S.S.R.
31 K6 Zábřeh Czechoslovakia
31 L5 Zabrze Poland
77 K3 Zābul reg Afghanistan
125 P9 Zacatal Guatemala
125 N8 Zacatali Mexico
124 H6 Zacatecas Mexico
124 H6 Zacatecas state Mexico
125 P11 Zacatecoluca El Salvador
125 L9 Zacatepec Mexico
111 E11 Zachary Louisiana
33 O6 Zachun E Germany
125 L2 Zacualpa Honduras
42 G4 Zadar Yugoslavia
68 C7 Zadetkale Kyun isld Burma
68 C8 Zadetkyi Burma
68 C5 Zadi Burma
54 K4 Zadonsk U.S.S.R.
80 C5 Zafriyya Israel
31 J4 Żagań Poland
52 B6 Zagare U.S.S.R.
45 N6 Zagarolo Italy
79 B8 Zagazig Egypt
43 C12 Zaghouan Tunisia
46 F5 Zagorá Greece
85 C2 Zagora Morocco
54 K1 Zagorsk U.S.S.R.
42 G3 Zagreb Yugoslavia
77 A3 Zāgros Mountains Iran
48 G6 Zagubica Yugoslavia
Zagunao see Li Xian
77 G5 Zāhedān Iran
98 C1 Zahl N Dakota
79 F5 Zahle Lebanon
33 R9 Zahna E Germany
57 H3 Zailiyskiy Alatau, Khr mts U.S.S.R.
36 H7 Zainingen W Germany
86 D5 Zaïre R W Africa
86 B7 Zaïre Central Zaire
86 D6 Zaire, Rep. of Africa
80 D5 Zaita Jordan
46 E1 Zaječar Yugoslavia
56 F5 Zakamensk U.S.S.R.
78 L1 Zakataly U.S.S.R.
78 J3 Zakho Iraq
46 D7 Zákinthos isld Greece
31 N5 Zaklików Poland
48 F1 Zakopane Poland
31 M3 Zakroczym Poland
47 H9 Zákros Crete Greece
48 D4 Zala R Hungary
48 D4 Zalaegerszeg Hungary
16 C7 Zalamea la Real Spain
Zalantun see Butha Qi
48 D4 Zalaövo Hungary
48 H3 Zalău Romania
48 K2 Zaleshchiki U.S.S.R.
94 E7 Zaleski Ohio
31 N1 Zales'ye U.S.S.R.
31 M2 Zalewo Poland
31 H2 Zalew Szczecinski lagoon Poland/E Germany
86 D3 Zalingei Sudan
50 E4 Zaliv Kara Bogaz Gol B Turkmenia U.S.S.R.
59 K3 Zaliv Petra Velikogo B U.S.S.R.
110 F4 Zalma Missouri
37 O3 Zalmanov Czechoslovakia
25 D5 Zaltbommel Netherlands
52 D5 Zaluch'ye U.S.S.R.
68 B4 Zalun Burma
117 O6 Zama L Alberta
71 E3 Zambales Mts Luzon Philippines
31 J5 Žamberk Czechoslovakia
87 G9 Zambeze R E Africa
87 D8 Zambezi Zambia
88 F10 Zambézia Mozambique
88 C7 Zambia rep Cent Africa
71 F7 Zamboanga Mindanao Philippines
71 F6 Zamboanguita Negros Philippines
126 G10 Zambrano Colombia
31 N3 Zambrów Poland
85 F6 Zamfara R Nigeria
102 C3 Zamora California
128 C4 Zamora Ecuador
124 H8 Zamora Mexico
16 D3 Zamora Spain
16 C3 Zamora prov Spain
125 L3 Zamorano Honduras
31 O5 Zamość Poland
61 P13 Zampa-misaki C Okinawa
128 F3 Zamuro, Sa. del mts Venezuela
84 E3 Zamzam Libya
86 B6 Zanaga Congo
17 F5 Záncara R Spain
25 H3 Zandberg Netherlands
22 G1 Zandvliet Belgium
25 C4 Zandvoort Netherlands
116 J3 Zane Hills Alaska
94 E7 Zanesville Ohio
74 G2 Zangla Kashmir
65 C6 Zanhuang China
41 L6 Zanica Italy
77 A1 Zanjān Iran
131 C3 Zanjón, R Argentina
43 E8 Zannone isld Italy
Zante see Zákinthos
143 E9 Zanthus W Australia
88 G5 Zanzibar Tanzania
88 G5 Zanzibar Chan Tanzania
88 G5 Zanzibar, I Tanzania
67 E3 Zaolin China
65 C6 Zaoqiang China
17 F4 Zaorejas Spain
85 F3 Zaouatanlaz Algeria
67 F1 Zaoxi China
67 D1 Zaoyang China
67 D1 Zaoyang Zhan China
61 O7 Zaō-zan vol Japan
56 D3 Zaozernyy U.S.S.R.
65 D7 Zaozhuang China
98 E2 Zap N Dakota
46 D1 Zapadna Morava R Yugoslavia
54 A1 Zapadnaya Dvina R U.S.S.R.
59 M1 Zapadno Sakhalinskiy Khrebet mt U.S.S.R.
56 B2 Zapadnosibirskaya Nizmennost' lowland U.S.S.R.
56 C5 Zapadnyy Sayan U.S.S.R.
37 O4 Zapadočeský Kraj reg Czechoslovakia
133 C5 Zapala Argentina
109 H9 Zapata Texas
126 D3 Zapata, Pen. de Cuba
125 M4 Zapatera, I Nicaragua
128 D2 Zapatosa Colombia
126 H10 Zapatoza, Ciénaga de Colombia
37 K3 Zapfendorf W Germany
26 S2 Zapoliarno U.S.S.R.
29 P2 Zapolyarnyy U.S.S.R.
54 G9 Zaporozh'ye U.S.S.R.
124 H8 Zapotiltic Mexico
124 G7 Zapotlán Mexico
Zara see Zadar
78 F2 Zara Turkey
57 C4 Zarafshan U.S.S.R.
108 A4 Zaragoza Chihuahua Mexico
108 G7 Zaragoza Coahuila Mexico
71 D2 Zaragoza Luzon Philippines
17 G3 Zaragoza Spain
17 G3 Zaragoza prov Spain
124 H4 Zaragoza, Tiahualilo de Mexico
88 G5 Zaramu Tanzania
77 E4 Zarand Kerman Iran
77 B2 Zarand Ostan-e Markazi Iran
48 G4 Zărandului, Muntii mts Romania
77 G4 Zaranj Afghanistan
52 C6 Zarasai U.S.S.R.
131 F5 Zárate Argentina
54 K2 Zaraysk U.S.S.R.
127 M10 Zaraza Venezuela
57 F5 Zardaly U.S.S.R.
77 B3 Zard Kuh mt Iran
117 G7 Zarembo I Alaska
85 F6 Zaria Nigeria
46 E5 Zárkon Greece
85 D5 Zarma reg Mali
48 J5 Zarneşti Romania
31 M4 Żarnów Poland
33 T5 Zarow R E Germany
80 F7 Zarqa R Jordan
77 C5 Zarqān Iran
33 N5 Zarrentin E Germany
128 C4 Zaruma Ecuador
31 J4 Żary Poland
85 F3 Zarzaïtine Algeria
85 G2 Zarzis Tunisia
37 P1 Zaschwitz E Germany
52 D2 Zasheyek U.S.S.R.
31 H4 Zasieki Poland
48 K2 Zastavna U.S.S.R.
89 E8 Zastron S Africa
54 E6 Zasul'ye U.S.S.R.
79 H7 Zatab ash Shamah Saudi Arabia
37 Q3 Žatec Czechoslovakia
31 L6 Zator Poland
33 R8 Zauche reg E Germany
57 A4 Zaunguzskiye Karakumy U.S.S.R.
109 N4 Zavalla Texas
Zavelstein see Bad Teinach-Zavelstein
22 G2 Zaventem Belgium
48 E6 Zavidovići Yugoslavia
59 J1 Zavitinsk U.S.S.R.
146 A14 Zavodovskil I Antarctica
56 B4 Zavodskoy U.S.S.R.
68 C2 Zawgyi R Burma
89 G1 Zawi Zimbabwe
31 L5 Zawiercie Poland
84 F4 Zawīlah Libya
80 D5 Zawiya Jordan
84 E3 Zāwiyah, Az Libya
84 G3 Zawīyat Masus Libya
79 G3 Zāwiye, Jebel ez mts Syria
56 F3 Zayarsk U.S.S.R.
56 B6 Zaysan, Oz res U.S.S.R.
57 L1 Zaysan, Ozero L U.S.S.R.
48 K1 Zbarazh U.S.S.R.
31 J3 Zbaszyń Poland
48 J1 Zborov U.S.S.R.
48 K1 Zbruch R U.S.S.R.
48 G2 Zdaňa Czechoslovakia
48 D1 Ždanice Czechoslovakia
30 H6 Zdice Czechoslovakia
31 L4 Zduńska Poland
Zealand isld see Sjælland
118 K7 Zealandia Sask
99 N7 Zearing Iowa
57 F6 Zebak Afghanistan
117 K11 Zeballos Br Columbia
79 G5 Zebdāni Syria
112 J2 Zebulon N Carolina
33 R6 Zechlin E Germany
41 H5 Zeda, Monte Italy
22 E1 Zedelgem Belgium
22 E1 Zeebrugge Belgium
139 H8 Zeehan Tasmania
94 A4 Zeeland Michigan
98 G4 Zeeland N Dakota
25 A6 Zeeland Netherlands
79 E7 Zeelim Israel
80 E8 Ze'elim, N R Israel
89 E5 Zeerust S Africa
80 E2 Zefat Israel
85 C3 Zegdou Algeria
85 E5 Zeggeren watercourse Mali
33 S7 Zehdenick E Germany
33 S8 Zehlendorf W Berlin
33 Q5 Zehna E Germany
37 P1 Zehren E Germany
110 G4 Zeigler Illinois
37 K3 Zeil W Germany
86 H3 Zeila Somalia
25 D4 Zeist Netherlands
33 S10 Zeithain E Germany
37 O7 Zeitlarn W Germany
37 N1 Zeitz E Germany
80 G3 Zeizun Syria
22 G1 Zele Belgium
31 N4 Zelechów Poland
37 P5 Zelená Lhota Czechoslovakia
29 O11 Zelenogorsk U.S.S.R.
31 M1 Zelenogradsk U.S.S.R.
54 E9 Zelenoye U.S.S.R.
53 F11 Zelenshuk R U.S.S.R.
94 G6 Zelienople Pennsylvania
48 E2 Želiezovce Czechoslovakia
46 D1 Željin mt Yugoslavia
36 E7 Zell Baden-Württemberg W Germany
36 H4 Zell Bayern W Germany
36 C3 Zell Rheinland-Pfalz W Germany
98 H5 Zell S Dakota
37 K2 Zella-Mehlis E Germany
38 H6 Zell-a-moos Austria
38 G7 Zell-am-see Austria
38 E7 Zell-am-Ziller Austria
38 L5 Zell-bei-zellhof Austria
33 S9 Zellendorf E Germany
36 H4 Zellingen W Germany
119 M7 Zelma Sask
31 L4 Zelów Poland
84 G4 Zelten Libya
36 C4 Zeltingen-Rachtig W Germany
22 F1 Zelzate Belgium
43 D11 Zembra isld Tunisia
50 D1 Zemlya Frantsa Iosifa U.S.S.R.
50 D1 Zemlya Georga isld Franz Josef Land U.S.S.R.
50 F1 Zemlya Vil'cheka Franz Josef Land U.S.S.R.
38 E7 Zemm R Austria
48 G2 Zempléni-Hory mt Hungary
48 F6 Zemun Yugoslavia
107 M4 Zenda Kansas
67 D5 Zengcheng China
100 B9 Zenia California
42 H4 Zenica Yugoslavia
54 F6 Zen'kov U.S.S.R.
56 C4 Zen'kovo U.S.S.R.
37 K5 Zenn R W Germany
22 G1 Zenne R Belgium
119 O5 Zenon Park Sask
60 G11 Zentsūji Japan
125 L9 Zenzontepec Mexico
98 D4 Zeona S Dakota
109 J4 Zephyr Texas
113 E9 Zephyrhills Florida
143 D8 Zephyr,Mt W Australia
57 E5 Zerav'shanskiy Khr mts U.S.S.R.
33 Q9 Zerbst E Germany
36 B4 Zerf W Germany
31 K3 Zerków Poland
40 G5 Zermatt Switzerland
101 U3 Zero Montana
46 D3 Zerqan Albania
33 U6 Zerrenthin E Germany
80 C3 Zerufa Israel
66 E6 Zêtang China
32 G6 Zetel W Germany
Zetland co see Shetland reg
6 K2 Zetland isld Scotland
65 E6 Zetouji China
37 M2 Zeulenroda E Germany
33 T8 Zeuthen E Germany
32 K6 Zeven W Germany
25 C5 Zevenbergen Netherlands
25 C5 Zevenbergse Hoek Netherlands
45 K1 Zevio Italy
59 J1 Zeya U.S.S.R.
59 J1 Zeya Vdkhr U.S.S.R.
25 F5 Zeyenaar Netherlands
59 J1 Zeysko Bureinskaya Ravnina U.S.S.R.
47 J6 Zeytindağ Turkey
16 B4 Zêzere R Portugal
79 F4 Zghorta Lebanon
31 L4 Zgierz Poland
38 N8 Zgornja Kungota Yugoslavia
31 J4 Zgorzelec Poland
48 L2 Zguritsa U.S.S.R.
48 J2 Zhabe U.S.S.R.
67 F3 Zhaili China
67 C5 Zhaixu China
57 E1 Zhaksykon R U.S.S.R.
57 G2 Zhaksylyk U.S.S.R.
57 F1 Zhaksy Sarysu R U.S.S.R.
57 J3 Zhalanash U.S.S.R.
57 C1 Zhamanakkol', Ozero L U.S.S.R.
57 E1 Zhanabas U.S.S.R.
57 B2 Zhanakentkala U.S.S.R.
57 B2 Zhanakurylys U.S.S.R.
57 C3 Zhanala U.S.S.R.
57 C3 Zhanatalap U.S.S.R.
57 E3 Zhanatas U.S.S.R.
65 C4 Zhangbei China
Zhangde see Anyang
Zhangdian see Zibo
65 G3 Zhangguangcai Ling mt ra China
65 E3 Zhanggutai China
65 C6 Zhang He R China
67 C6 Zhanghuang China
65 C4 Zhangjiakou China
67 E1 Zhangjiapang China
67 E2 Zhangjiashan China
67 C5 Zhangmu China
67 F4 Zhangping China
67 F4 Zhangpu China
65 D6 Zhangqiu China
65 D4 Zhangsanying China
67 E4 Zhang Shui R China
Zhangshuzhen see Qingjiang
59 H3 Zhangwu China
58 D4 Zhangye China
67 F4 Zhangzhou Fujian China
65 B6 Zhangzi China
65 E5 Zhangzi Dao isld China
65 D6 Zhanhua China
67 C6 Zhanjiang China
67 C6 Zhanjiang Gang B China
51 P1 Zhannetty, Ostrov isld U.S.S.R.
57 E1 Zhanteli U.S.S.R.
67 A4 Zhanyi China
65 E2 Zhanyu China
67 F5 Zhao'an China
65 B6 Zhaocheng China
65 F1 Zhaodong China
Zhaoge see Qi Xian
67 C4 Zhaoping China
67 D5 Zhaoqing China
66 C3 Zhaosu China
67 A3 Zhaotong China
65 C6 Zhao Xian China
65 E6 Zhaoyuan China
65 F2 Zhaoyuan China
Zhaozhen see Jintang
59 J2 Zhaozhou China
67 G1 Zhapu China
52 D6 Zhari U.S.S.R.
54 D1 Zharkovskiy U.S.S.R.
57 K1 Zharma U.S.S.R.
57 G1 Zharyk U.S.S.R.
48 N1 Zhashkov U.S.S.R.
51 M2 Zhatay U.S.S.R.
Zhaxi see Weixin
66 B5 Zhaxigang China
54 J9 Zhdanov U.S.S.R.
48 M5 Zhebriyany U.S.S.R.
65 C7 Zhecheng China
67 F2 Zhejiang prov China
57 E1 Zhel'dyadyr U.S.S.R.
56 F3 Zheleznodorozhnyy Irkutskaya Oblast U.S.S.R.
31 N1 Zheleznodorozhnyy U.S.S.R.
56 F3 Zheleznogorsk-Ilimsky U.S.S.R.
Zhelou see Ceheng
54 E8 Zheltyye Vody U.S.S.R.
67 B4 Zhenfeng China
67 B2 Zheng'an China
58 F4 Zhengding China
67 F3 Zhenghe China
Zhengjiakou see Gucheng
67 D2 Zhengjiayi China
65 C3 Zhengxiangbai Qi China
65 B7 Zhengzhou China
67 F4 Zhenhai China
67 G2 Zhenhai China
67 F1 Zhenjiang China
65 F2 Zhenlai China
65 C3 Zhenlan Qi China
67 C5 Zhenlong China
67 B3 Zhenning China
67 C1 Zhenping China
Zhenwudong see Ansai
65 F1 Zhenxiang China
67 A3 Zhenxiong China
67 C3 Zhenyuan China
67 C1 Zhenziling China
67 A4 Zhetai China
67 D1 Zhicheng China
67 A5 Zhicun China
48 J1 Zhidachov U.S.S.R.
Zhifang see Wuchang
58 B3 Zhifang China
56 G4 Zhigalovo U.S.S.R.
51 M2 Zhigansk U.S.S.R.
57 E1 Zhigerli U.S.S.R.
67 C3 Zhijiang China
67 D1 Zhijiang China
67 B3 Zhijin China
54 H7 Zhikhar' U.S.S.R.
67 B6 Zhilang China
67 F2 Zhitan China
53 C8 Zhitomir U.S.S.R.
54 F3 Zhizdra U.S.S.R.
54 G2 Zhizdra R U.S.S.R.
54 B4 Zhlobin U.S.S.R.
48 L1 Zhmerinka U.S.S.R.
77 L4 Zhob R Pakistan
51 P1 Zhokhova, Ostrov isld U.S.S.R.
Zhongba see Jiangyou
66 C6 Zhongba China
67 B5 Zhongdong China
67 C4 Zhongdu China
65 F1 Zhonghe China
67 A1 Zhongjiang China
65 B7 Zhongmou China
67 D4 Zhongshan China
67 D5 Zhongshan China
Zhongshu see Renhuai
65 B7 Zhongtiao Shan ra China
67 B1 Zhong Xian China
58 F5 Zhongxiang China
67 E4 Zhongxin China
65 B6 Zhongyang China
68 K3 Zhongyuan China
67 D2 Zhoujiadian China
58 F5 Zhoukouzhen China
67 F3 Zhouning China
67 G1 Zhoushan Dao isld China
59 H5 Zhoushan Qundao China
48 N3 Zhovten U.S.S.R.
59 H4 Zhuanghe China
67 B3 Zhucang China
65 D6 Zhucheng China
Zhuji see Shangqiu
67 G2 Zhuji China
67 G2 Zhujia Jian isld China
67 D6 Zhujiang Kou B China
Zhujing see Jinshan
54 E3 Zhukovka U.S.S.R.
65 C5 Zhulong He R China
65 D4 Zhuluke China
58 F5 Zhumadian China
58 G3 Zhuolu China
58 G4 Zhuo Xian China
65 B4 Zhuozi China
65 E6 Zhuqiao China
57 G3 Zhusandala, Step' U.S.S.R.
67 C1 Zhushan China
67 D3 Zhuting China
58 E5 Zhuxi China
65 A7 Zhuyangzhen China
67 A4 Zhuyuan China
57 J2 Zhuzagashskiy U.S.S.R.
67 D3 Zhuzhou China
78 J3 Zibar Iraq
65 D6 Zibo China
65 A6 Zichang China
22 H2 Zichem Belgium
47 J2 Zidarovo Bulgaria
33 R5 Ziddorf E Germany
54 H7 Zid'ki U.S.S.R.
31 K5 Ziębice Poland
33 P6 Ziegendorf E Germany
36 G2 Ziegenhain W Germany
37 M2 Ziegenrück E Germany
140 B6 Ziel,Mt N Terr Aust
31 J4 Zielona Góra Poland
32 K10 Zierenberg W Germany
25 A5 Zierikzee Netherlands
38 N4 Ziersdorf Austria
33 Q8 Ziesar E Germany
31 P1 Žiežmariai U.S.S.R.
79 B8 Zifta Egypt
68 A2 Zigaing Burma
84 G4 Zighan Libya
68 B3 Zigon Burma
67 A2 Zigong China
58 F5 Zigui China
85 A6 Ziguinchor Senegal
52 C6 Zigure U.S.S.R.
65 D6 Zi He R China
37 P3 Žihle Czechoslovakia
65 C5 Zijingguan China
80 C3 Zikhron Ya'aqov Israel
78 E1 Zile Turkey
48 E1 Žilina Czechoslovakia
84 F4 Zillah Libya
38 E7 Zillertal R Austria
38 E7 Zillertaler Alpen mts Austria
Zilling Tso L see Siling Co
141 K1 Zillmere dist Brisbane, Qnsld
52 C6 Zilupe U.S.S.R.
56 F4 Zima U.S.S.R.
125 K7 Zimapán Mexico
125 L9 Zimatlán de Alvarez Mexico
87 E9 Zimba Zambia
89 G3 Zimbabwe Zimbabwe
87 E9 Zimbabwe rep Africa
87 F9 Zimbue Mozambique
99 N4 Zimmerman Minnesota
36 G1 Zimmersrode W Germany
47 H2 Zimnitsa Bulgaria
47 G1 Zimricea Romania
77 G2 Zindajan Afghanistan
85 F6 Zinder Niger
30 G1 Zingst pen E Germany
38 L7 Zinken mt Austria
37 Q5 Žinkovy Czechoslovakia
33 T4 Zinnowitz E Germany
99 T7 Zion Illinois
127 P4 Zion Nevis W I
103 M4 Zion Can Utah
103 M4 Zion Nat. Park Utah
94 A7 Zionsville Indiana
33 O5 Zippendorf E Germany
80 E3 Zippori Israel
80 D2 Zippori R Israel
80 F3 Ziqlab R Jordan
128 D2 Ziraquirá Colombia
38 L7 Zirbitz Kogel mt Austria
42 G5 Žirje isld Yugoslavia
101 T9 Zirkel, Mt Colorado
37 K5 Zirndorf W Germany
46 D3 Žirovnica Yugoslavia
67 D2 Zi Shui R China
125 J8 Zitácuaro Mexico
67 B1 Zitong China
46 D5 Zítsa Greece
31 H5 Zittau E Germany
41 L3 Zitterklapfen mt Austria
116 M4 Zitziana R Alaska
67 F3 Zixi China
67 D4 Zixing China
65 C5 Ziya He R China
67 A1 Ziyang China
67 C3 Ziyuan China
67 B4 Ziyun China
67 F4 Ziyundong Shan mt China
41 L4 Zizers Switzerland
58 D6 Zizhong China
65 A6 Zizhou China
47 H1 Zlataritsa Bulgaria
31 L7 Zlaté Moravce Czechoslovakia
46 D1 Zlatibor mt Yugoslavia
47 G2 Zlatitsa Bulgaria
48 H4 Zlatna Romania
47 G3 Zlatograd Bulgaria
54 C8 Zlatopol' U.S.S.R.
50 E3 Zlatoust U.S.S.R.
46 E3 Zletovo Yugoslavia
84 E3 Zlitan Libya
31 J2 Złocieniec Poland
31 L4 Złoczew Poland
30 H5 Zloniee Czechoslovakia
48 G6 Zlot Yugoslavia
31 J4 Złotoryja Poland
31 K2 Złotów Poland
37 P3 Žlutice Czechoslovakia
54 C4 Zlynka U.S.S.R.
56 B5 Zmeinogorsk U.S.S.R.
53 D10 Zmeinyy, Ostrov isld U.S.S.R.
31 K4 Żmigród Poland
Zmiyev see Gottvald
56 C4 Znamenityy U.S.S.R.
54 D8 Znamenka U.S.S.R.
54 D8 Znamenka Vtoraya U.S.S.R.
31 K3 Żnin Poland
31 J7 Znojmo Czechoslovakia
37 P2 Zöblitz E Germany
45 J3 Zocca Italy
40 G3 Zofingen Switzerland
80 C5 Zofit Israel
41 L6 Zogno Italy
31 K7 Zohor Czechoslovakia
77 B4 Zohreh Iran
22 J1 Zolder Belgium
113 F10 Zolfo Springs Florida
36 E3 Zollhaus W Germany
48 J1 Zolochev U.S.S.R.
59 J1 Zolotaya Goro U.S.S.R.
54 N1 Zolotkovo U.S.S.R.
56 C4 Zolotogorskiy U.S.S.R.
54 D7 Zolotonosha U.S.S.R.
88 E9 Zomba Malawi
Zongga see Gyirong
66 F4 Zongjiafangzi China
86 C5 Zongo Zaïre
78 C1 Zonguldak Turkey
67 F1 Zongyang China
22 J2 Zonhoven Belgium
33 P10 Zorbau E Germany
33 Q9 Zörbig E Germany
80 F5 Zör el Hanāhina Jordan
33 N9 Zorge W Germany
33 N10 Zörge R E Germany
16 D5 Zorita Spain
48 L4 Zorleni Romania
36 D6 Zorn R France
101 R2 Zortman Montana
31 L5 Zory Poland
85 C7 Zorzor Liberia
33 Q10 Zöschen E Germany
33 S8 Zossen E Germany
22 F2 Zottegem Belgium
86 C1 Zouar Chad
85 B4 Zouerate Mauritania
16 D10 Zoumi Morocco
65 D6 Zouping China
58 F4 Zouquan China
25 F2 Zoutkamp Netherlands
22 J2 Zoutleeuw Belgium
65 D7 Zou Xian China
67 C5 Zouxu China
48 F5 Zrenjanin Yugoslavia
42 G4 Zrmanja R Yugoslavia
31 J6 Zruč Czechoslovakia
48 G3 Zsáka Hungary
33 R10 Zschepplin E Germany
37 P2 Zschopau E Germany
37 O1 Zschopau R E Germany
37 O2 Zschorlau E Germany
127 M10 Zuata Venezuela
128 E2 Zuata R Venezuela
113 E8 Zuber Florida
16 E7 Zubia Spain
54 F1 Zubtsov U.S.S.R.
80 D3 Zububa Israel
37 L6 Zuchering W Germany
41 O4 Zucherkütl mt Austria
133 E1 Zudañez Bolivia
33 S4 Zudar E Germany
85 C7 Zuénoula Ivory Coast
41 H3 Zug canton Switzerland
58 F1 Zugdeli U.S.S.R.
41 H3 Zuger See L Switzerland
41 O3 Zugspitze mt W Germany
25 B5 Zuid Beijerland Netherlands
25 G2 Zuidbroek Netherlands

INDEX ADDENDA

The Index went to press before the maps and the following corrections should be noted for the Index. The maps are correct.

1. For *New Hebrides* read *Vanuatu.*
2. *Panama* has now assumed sovereignty over the *Panama Canal Zone.*
3. *Antigua and Barbuda* became independent on 1 November 1981.
4. *Salisbury* became *Harare* on 18 April 1982. Other names in Zimbabwe have been changed on the maps but the old names appear in brackets.
5. *St Kitts & Nevis* became independent on 19 September 1983.
6. For *Upper Volta* read *Burkina.*

THE TRANSCRIPTION OF CHINESE PLACE-NAMES

Chinese is written in Han characters, a system of writing which has remained in use for more than 3,000 years. Its most conspicuous features are the large number of characters and the complexity of most of them. All told, there cannot be fewer than 50,000, of which perhaps 11,000 may be encountered in bibliographic or similar research. Up to 3,000 characters are used in everyday written communication.

Han characters are ideographs but since the language is a spoken language and not just written, each character can be represented by a syllable – a vowel or a vowel with one or more consonants. Because the spoken language evolves with time and pronunciation varies with dialect many different readings of a character are possible.

Compared with English and other European languages, Chinese has few syllables, in Modern Standard Chinese hardly more than 400. With thousands of characters in use, many are equated with the same syllable. The syllable **sên** is represented by only one character. In contrast **yi** can be expressed by over 215. Tone (the modulation of the voice) helps to distinguish meaning, but generally context alone determines what is meant.

So complex a system of writing is not well suited to a modern industrial society but rather to a peasant community where the literate few have unlimited time to study. Printing is a formidable matter compared with European languages. Learning to read and write involves mastery of a large number of characters, imposing a great demand on memory and requiring a considerable amount of time.

There are many romanization systems for Chinese. Four are widely used in English. Of these the Wade-Giles system is most familiar. All British and American official maps have used the system exclusively since 1942, and millions of references exist in Wade-Giles romanizations. The system was first published in 1859 by Sir Thomas Wade and it was the basis, slightly modified, for the Chinese-English Dictionary of H. A. Giles published in 1912.

Of all the dialects of China, Northern Chinese (formerly called Mandarin Chinese) is most widespread. Wade-Giles and all systems since have used the educated Peking dialect of Northern Chinese as the standard language and the preferred readings of characters are given in that dialect which has become the model for Modern Standard Chinese.

Chinese, as distinct from European, interest in romanization was stimulated by the desire to promote a national language as well as to assist in learning to read the characters. Romanization would also serve as a means of writing the non-Chinese languages spoken within China and to help to write them in Chinese. A further aim was to encourage foreigners to learn Chinese.

As a first step towards these goals the most commonly used characters were simplified. Much discussion has centred around the replacement of Han characters by an alphabet, but this can only happen in the very remote future. Romanized Chinese may increasingly exist side-by-side with the characters but that does not mean that the Han characters are about to be dropped from use.

In 1958, the Chinese government approved the system called **Pinyin zimu** (phonetic alphabet) for the romanization of Chinese. Teachers of Chinese prefer Pinyin to Wade-Giles. It is a better source for up-to-date idiom and vocabulary but a great amount of material is not yet available in Pinyin. Students of Chinese, therefore, have to deal with other systems of romanization. For geographical names almost nothing existed in Pinyin for many years. Everything worth considering was in Wade-Giles. Yet in spite of the fact that the letters **c**, **q** and **x** were used in a way totally alien to English usage, Pinyin was neater than Wade-Giles which, for example, produces **Wu-lu-mu-chi** for English conventional **Urumchi** where Pinyin gives **Urumqi**. **Harbin** is so spelled in Pinyin but becomes **Ha-erh-pin** in Wade-Giles.

Ever since Pinyin was launched in 1958, the publishers of *The Times Atlas* have contemplated but, until now, rejected, the adoption of Pinyin for the map plates covering China. Among the factors considered were the availability of sources for Pinyin names, the extent to which Pinyin was used in China and the acceptance and use of Pinyin outside China, particularly for geographical names. In spite of a State Council directive of 1975 that Pinyin would be used as the standard and sole romanization system for geographical and personal names, little was done in China to follow the directive until 1977. Early in 1979 Pinyin was accepted by most nations of the world as the system to be employed officially for romanized Chinese names. Times Books of London, the publishers of the Atlas, therefore decided to adopt Pinyin in place of Wade-Giles for the names of Mainland China and the map plates in this atlas now contain Pinyin names in place of Wade-Giles.

By way of example Peking in conventional English is **Beijing** in Pinyin and appears in that form in this atlas as opposed to **Pei-ching** in Wade-Giles. **Guangzhou** (Canton) in Pinyin was **Kuang-chou** in Wade-Giles. Further examples are: **Chongqing** (Chungking), **Ch'ung-ch'ing**; **Fuzhou** (Foochow), **Fu-chou**; **Jilin** (Kirin), **Chi-lin**; **Xian** (Sian), **Hsi-an**.

In Taiwan, where Pinyin is not used, Wade-Giles has been retained to conform to local practice. In Hong Kong a romanization based on Cantonese is used. Pinyin would be in conflict with official practice in Hong Kong.

In order to facilitate reference to Wade-Giles names, the relationship of consonants and vowels in the two systems is shown on this page.

No attempt has been made in this atlas to fabricate Pinyin names by conversion from Wade-Giles or by other methods: all Pinyin names have been taken from official Chinese sources. There are several reasons why fabrication would be inadmissible. The name itself may have changed; the administrative status of the place may not be known; there may be errors in the Wade-Giles transcription; the reading of the Han character may have changed. In areas where the people are not Chinese, e.g. Sinkiang, Tibet, Inner Mongolia, guessing at the Pinyin spelling could produce nonsensical names. For example, the character **shen** in Chinese is used to produce **xain** in **xainza** but **sên** in **Sêndo**. Likewise, to convert **Pa-yen-wu-la** from Wade-Giles would give **Bayan Wula** for the place in Inner Mongolia which is shown on Plate 23 as **Xi Ujimqin Qi (Bayan Ul Hot)**.

COMPARATIVE TABLES OF PINYIN AND WADE-GILES

VOWELS

Wade-Giles	Pinyin	Approximate pronunciation	Pinyin	Wade-Giles
eh	e	e as in met	e (after h, g, k)	o
erh	er	er as in her	e (after i, u, y)	eh
i (when initial or standing alone)	yi	yea as in yeast	er	erh
		ie as in fiesta	i (after j, q, r, sh)	ih
ieh	ie		ian	ien
ien	ian	ean as in meander	ie	ieh
ih	i	e as in her	ong	ung
o (standing alone or after h, k, k')	e	e as in her	ou (after y)	u
			u (after j, q, x, y)	ü
o (after f, m, p, p', w)	o	o as in corn	ü (after l, n)	ü
o (after other consonants)	uo	uo as in duo	ui (after g, k')	uei
			uo (after g, h, k, sh)	uo
u (after y)	ou	ou as in you	uo (otherwise)	o
ü (after l, n)	ü	u as in tu (French) or ü as in dünn (German)	yan	yen
			yi	i
ü (after ch, ch', hs, y)	u	o as in do		
uei (occurs only after k, k')	ui	uai as in quaint	Certain syllables eg Wade-Giles **yai** cannot be converted mechanically from system to system
ung	ong	ung as in jung (German)		

Note
In both panels the first column gives the Wade-Giles in alphabetical order; the second gives the Pinyin equivalent; the third, the pronunciation. The fourth and fifth columns give the same information as the first and second, but in Pinyin alphabetical order, to enable the reader to refer back from Pinyin. Unless otherwise stated, consonants are pronounced as in English and vowels as in Italian.

CONSONANTS

Wade-Giles	Pinyin	Approximate pronunciation	Pinyin	Wade-Giles
ch (except when followed by i or ü)	zh	j as in jump	b	p
			c	ts'
ch' (except when followed by i or ü)	ch	ch as in church	ci	tz'u
			chi	ch'ih
chi; chü	ji; ju	j as in jam	ch	ch'
ch'i; ch'ü	qi; qu	ch as in church	d	t
chih	zhi		g	k
ch'ih	chi		j	ch (when followed by i or u)
hs	x	sh as in shoe		
j	r	r as in red or z as in azure	k	k'
k	g	g as in good	p	p
k'	k	k as in kin	q	ch' (when followed by i or u)
p	b	b as in bat	r	j
p'	p	p as in pat	si	ssu (sze)
ssu (sze)	si	si as in sierra	t	t'
t	d	d as in dog	x	hs
t'	t	t as in tot	yi	i
ts	z	z as in zulu	you	yu
ts'	c	ts as in sits	z	ts
tzu	zi	ze as in zero	zi	tzu
tz'u	ci	tsy as in Betsy	zh	ch
yai	ya or ai	yea as in yea	zhi	chih

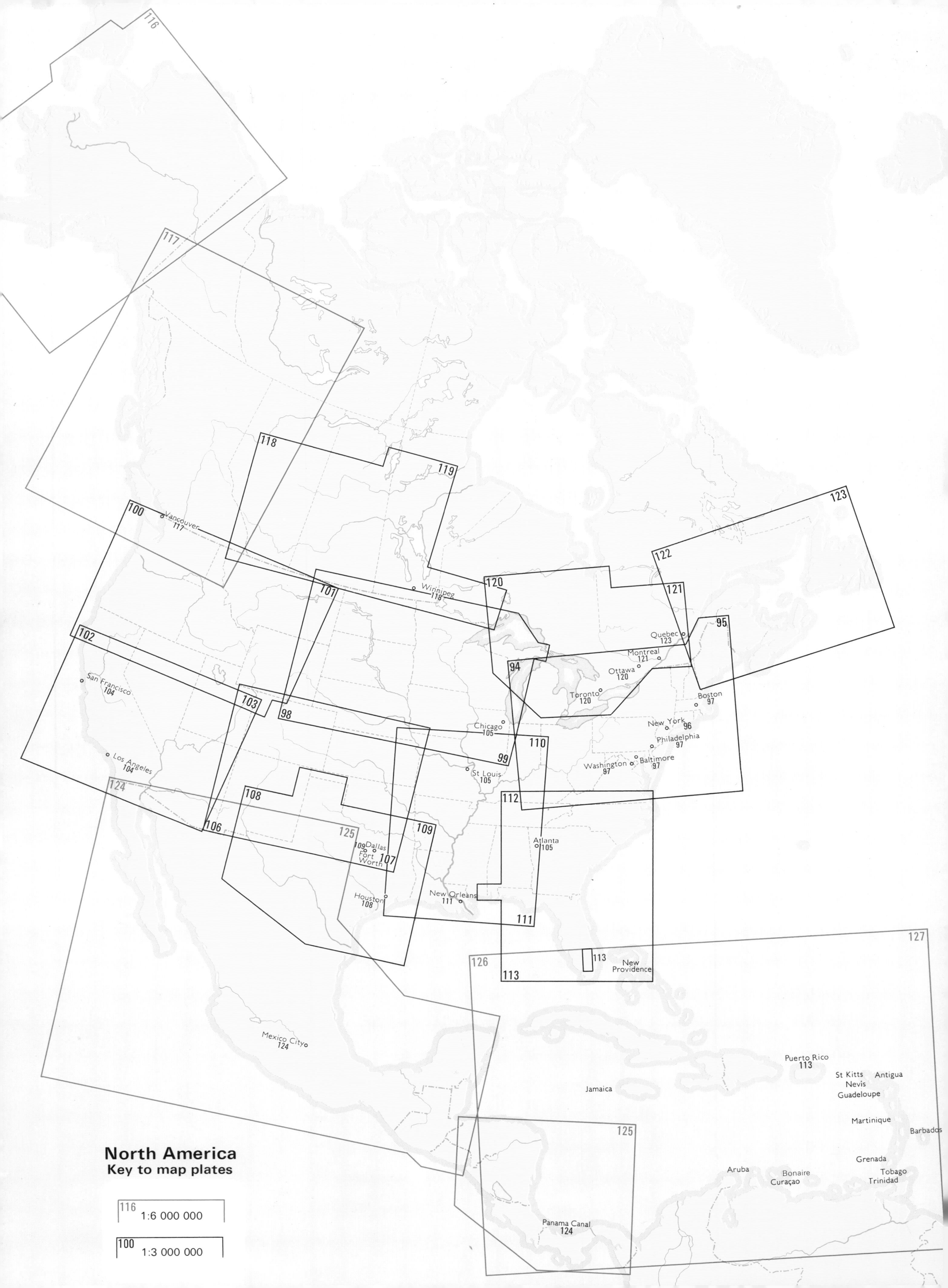

North America
Key to map plates

116 1:6 000 000

100 1:3 000 000

116

117

118

119

123

122

121

95

100 Vancouver 117

101 Winnipeg 118

120

102

San Francisco 104

103

98

94

Quebec 123

Montreal 121

Ottawa 120

Toronto 120

Boston 97

New York 96

Philadelphia 97

Chicago 105

99

110

Los Angeles 104

St Louis 105

Washington 97

Baltimore 97

124

112

108

106

125

Atlanta 105

109

107

Dallas Fort Worth 109

Houston 108

New Orleans 111

111

126

113

113 New Providence

127

Mexico City 124

Puerto Rico 113

St Kitts   Antigua

Nevis

Guadeloupe

Jamaica

Martinique

Barbados

125

Grenada

Aruba

Bonaire

Curaçao

Tobago

Trinidad

Panama Canal 124